WORD
BIBLICAL
COMMENTARY

WORD
BIBLICAL
COMMENTARY

VOLUME 17

Job 1-20

DAVID J. A. CLINES

WORD BOOKS, PUBLISHER • DALLAS, TEXAS

Word Biblical Commentary
Job 1–20
Copyright © 1989 by Word, Incorporated

Library of Congress Cataloging-in-Publication Data
Main entry under title:

Word biblical commentary.

  Includes bibliographies.
  1. Bible—Commentaries   Collected Works.
BS491.2.W67   220.7′7   81–71768
ISBN 0–8499–0216–9 (vol. 17) AACR2

Printed in the United States of America

The author's own translation of the text appears in italic type under the heading "Translation."

8 9 9   QBP   9 8 7 6 5 4 3

To my son
Jeremy
veritate et virtute

Contents

Editorial Preface

The launching of the *Word Biblical Commentary* brings to fulfillment an enterprise of several years' planning. The publishers and the members of the editorial board met in 1977 to explore the possibility of a new commentary on the books of the Bible that would incorporate several distinctive features. Prospective readers of these volumes are entitled to know what such features were intended to be; whether the aims of the commentary have been fully achieved time alone will tell.

First, we have tried to cast a wide net to include as contributors a number of scholars from around the world who not only share our aims, but are in the main engaged in the ministry of teaching in university, college, and seminary. They represent a rich diversity of denominational allegiance. The broad stance of our contributors can rightly be called evangelical, and this term is to be understood in its positive, historic sense of a commitment to Scripture as divine revelation, and to the truth and power of the Christian gospel.

Then, the commentaries in our series are all commissioned and written for the purpose of inclusion in the *Word Biblical Commentary.* Unlike several of our distinguished counterparts in the field of commentary writing, there are no translated works, originally written in a non-English language. Also, our commentators were asked to prepare their own rendering of the original biblical text and to use those languages as the basis of their own comments and exegesis. What may be claimed as distinctive with this series is that it is based on the biblical languages, yet it seeks to make the technical and scholarly approach to a theological understanding of Scripture understandable by—and useful to—the fledgling student, the working minister, and colleagues in the guild of professional scholars and teachers as well.

Finally, a word must be said about the format of the series. The layout, in clearly defined sections, has been consciously devised to assist readers at different levels. Those wishing to learn about the textual witnesses on which the translation is offered are invited to consult the section headed *Notes.* If the readers' concern is with the state of modern scholarship on any given portion of Scripture, they should turn to the sections on *Bibliography* and *Form and Structure.* For a clear exposition of the passage's meaning and its relevance to the ongoing biblical revelation, the *Comment* and concluding *Explanation* are designed expressly to meet that need. There is therefore something for everyone who may pick up and use these volumes.

If these aims come anywhere near realization, the intention of the editors will have been met, and the labor of our team of contributors rewarded.

General Editors: *David A. Hubbard*
Glenn W. Barker†
Old Testament: *John D. W. Watts*
New Testament: *Ralph P. Martin*

Testimonia

The Book of Job is a fireball. It destroys the neat arrangement devised by some adherents of the religion of Israel to reject painful questions. It disturbs the harmony of biblical teaching about God's plan; it makes room for chance, for the irrational. It refuses to soften what everyone seeks to control, suffering, and misfortune. It opposes the clarity of a moral order as the law of history.

C. Duquoc and C. Floristán, *Job and the Silence of God*

> Where Job squats awkwardly upon his ashpit,
> Alone on his denuded battlefield,
> Scraping himself with blunted Occam Razors
> He sharpened once to shave the Absolute . . .
> Eliphaz, Zophar, Bildad rise together,
> Begin to creak a wooden sarabande;
> "Glory to God," they cry, and praise his Name
> In epigrams that trail off in a stammer.
> Suave Death comes, final as a Händel cadence,
> And snaps their limbs like twigs across his knees,
> Silenus nods, his finger to his nose.

W. H. Auden, *Thomas Epilogises*

Some comforters have but one song to sing, and they have no regard to whom they sing it.

John Calvin

The author of the Book of Job knows what people think, what people say in whispers—and not just in Israel.

Christian Duquoc, "Demonism and the Unexpectedness of God"

De tous les livres de l'Ancien Testament, JOB est le plus sublime, le plus poignant, le plus hardi . . . , le plus énigmatique, le plus decevant et . . . le plus rebutant.

Paul Claudel

> [*God to Job, in the afterlife*]
> You realize by now the part you played
> To stultify the Deuteronomist
> And change the tenor of religious thought.

Robert Frost, *A Masque of Reason*

The Book of Job is the Song of Songs of scepticism, and in it terrifying serpents hiss their eternal question: Why?

Heinrich Heine

Avoue que tu étais un grand bavard.

Voltaire, *Dictionnaire Philosophique*

Author's Preface

"If I have seen further, it is by standing on the shoulders of giants." Thus Isaac Newton, leaving the question open whether he himself was a *dwarf* on giants' shoulders (as is the case is some formulations of this ancient saying), or whether he himself was a *giant* on giants' shoulders. Fortunately the question of gigantism does not arise in the present context of a commentary on Job where the modern commentator is being perpetually cut down to size by the towering achievement of the Joban author. "*If* I have seen further" expresses nicely too my ambivalence about the novelties in these volumes, putting the decision squarely in the reader's court; *caveat emptor*, and let the reader understand. It will be a surprise to some to know that the greatest anxiety of this commentator on a biblical book has been the thought, whenever he believes he has stumbled upon a fresh and preferable interpretation of his text, that he cannot with any probability have been the first person in twenty-five hundred years to understand his author aright, and that he is consequently much more likely wrong than right.

There have been giants among commentators on Job. Not only the intrinsic quality of the book, but also the perceptiveness, ingenuity and tetchiness of scholars of heroic stature have made the exegesis of the book a titanomachic battlefield. Fohrer's commentary is to my mind the finest, in imagination and theological sensitivity head and shoulders above the nevertheless outstanding work of Dhorme (sometimes overpraised as the best commentary on any book of the Bible). In the next rank I would put Duhm, Driver and Gray, Gordis and (the most recent) Habel. After them, Andersen, Pope, Terrien, Peake, Davidson, Hölscher, Weiser, Delitzsch, Horst, and Budde all have their distinctive contributions to make and the serious commentator must read every word (well, almost) of them all. On the text I appreciated in addition de Wilde and Sicre Diaz (in Alonso Schökel's commentary). It is a matter of regret to me that my rhythm of working did not leave me leisure to read extensively in the great scholars of an earlier age, Dillmann, Hitzig, Schlottmann, and the others, though I turned to them and others often enough when either my eighteen or so desk companions or my own imagination did not supply an exegesis that satisfied me.

There have been two books more valuable to me than any commentary, and more often handled: the lexicon and the concordance. Whether this signals some grand theory of intertextuality or simply some pragmatic habit I have fallen into, I don't rightly know; but I know I was constantly surprising myself with what precisions, what assurances, what better readings, emerged almost of their own accord from the systematic study of the words themselves. Not that a commentary should remain on the level of words; single-minded concentration on words is the strength, and the weakness, of the work of Dhorme. My intent has always been to understand every detail in the context of the total book, and I can testify that to keep in motion a perpetual interplay between the part and the whole has been the greatest intellectual pleasure of the entire work.

I have always, dear reader, had an implied reader present to my mind; not you, perhaps, because my implied reader is a composite of real people, significant others, whom I would not be so unkind as to mention by name. Let us say that among them is a Hebraist eager to challenge my philological decisions, a committed Old Testament theologian, left of center, who will pick up every word to do with society, psychology, and God, a friend who will recognize immediately the sentences addressed directly to her and her religious sensibilities but published freely like messages in the personal columns of *The Times,* a picker up of trifles who will dip in here and there and whom I hope to seduce into reading on, and an enthusiast who will quite properly thank me less for what I have said than for the hares I have set running in his mind. This implied reader of the subjoined *Enigma Variations* is also of course an ideal reader, for upon none of my friends (nor, come to think of it, my enemies) would I actually wish to impose the task of reading this book right through. So along with the handful of readers, implied, ideal, or actual, who will properly speaking *read* these books, there will be a larger clientele who will *use* them; such too have been in the forefront of my mind.

Among the features of this commentary that I hope will prove to be user-friendly is the constant reference in the textual notes to several English versions. I have suspected that one of the reasons why persons in their right mind might want to pick up a commentary on Job is to find out why the standard English versions of the text under study differ so amazingly from one another, and whether at any particular instance it can be argued that one rendering is better than others. (I have inevitably found, incidentally, that to weigh the alternative renderings of fifteen English versions of every line has been a most constructive process for me as a Hebraist and critic, leading sometimes, admittedly, to a state of palsied indecision but more often to a sharpened perception of the text.) For the user's convenience too, though also out of conviction, I have most often tried to say near the beginning of the comment on any verse what I think it is in general about and how I think it connects up with what precedes it, and only then how that general sense is supported by the actual words in their actual sequence. But occasionally, and especially when I have come to a famous crux, I have written a kind of stream of consciousness commentary that starts with the problem and only by stages, like a detective story except that I lay no red herrings, moves toward my preferred solution. For one other feature of the commentary that users will, I hope, appreciate I can take no credit at all but must myself thank the editors for their conception of a piece of *Explanation* at every chapter's end (or so). Under that heading I have tried hard to stand a little way off from the text to ask what has been going on and what it all means. Any user of this commentary who reads nothing more than the *Explanations* would have the gist of the perspective adopted here.

Writing a commentary on Job is nearly as dangerous as composing a ninth symphony. Many commentators reveal in their prefaces the real losses and anguishes they have endured in the course of writing, though, like Job, most of them have not actually died in the process. But even if one does not suffer objectively any more than the average biblical commentator or the average human being, living for day after month after year with the powerful, insistent and imaginative depiction of suffering and its significance sensitizes the commentator to one's own experiences and to the signs of suffering that spring up everywhere in the world about.

Nevertheless, I am glad to report, I have rarely wished to assent to the most frequent comment made to this commentator by friends, relatives and acquaintances: How depressing to spend your days with Job, that book of unrelieved gloom! The truth is, and no one who spends more than half a hour with this commentary will be very surprised to learn it, that increasingly my response has been: On the contrary! Job represents the vitality of the human spirit which refuses to be humiliated, not even by God, and especially not by theologians! Reading and close-reading the Book of Job, the most intense book theologically and intellectually of the Old Testament, has been a perennially uplifting and not infrequently euphoric experience. The craftsmanship in the finest details, the rain of metaphor, the never-failing imagination of the poet, is surpassed only by the variety and delicacy of the theological ideas and the cunning of this most open of texts at confronting its readers with two new questions along with any answer.

What is going on in commentaries and commentary writing? I am asking myself this all the time. Reading in Montaigne one day, I chanced on this passage (Florio's translation):

> There's more adoe to enterpret interpretations, than to interpret things: and more bookes upon bookes, then upon any other subject. We doe but enter-glose [intergloss] our selves. All swarmeth with commentaries: Of Authors their is great penury. Is not the chiefest and most famous knowledge of our ages, to know how to understand the wise? . . . [The latest] is got-up but one inch above the shoulders of the last save one (bk 3, ch 13; Everyman ed., 3:327).

This is good knockabout stuff, in its last sentence incidentally taking a side-swipe at the aphorism with which, in one of its forms, this preface opened (though Robert K. Merton, in his otherwise estimable, and exhaustive, *On the Shoulders of Giants: A Shandean Postscript* [New York: Free Press, 1965] seems to know nothing of the Montaigne passage). It suitably shames the commentator, for a minute or two, and leads him (that is, me) to sobering reflections on the parasitic nature of the critic compared to the creativity of the original artist. But what it leads to wondering in the end is whether there is such a great gulf between text and comment, whether the work of the critic and the work of the artist are not perhaps of the same substance, whether the work of art does not perhaps stand in need of the commentator to ensure its survival into each new generation, and whether, religiously speaking, not just the author but also the reader must be inspired. If, as I believe, meaning comes into existence at the intersection between the text and the reader, texts need readers to become meaningful, for meaningful always means meaningful to someone. And texts, especially classic texts, Job, Dante, and Shakespeare, need commentators to become fully themselves; if they are texts capable of being commented on, they in a way include their commentaries within themselves, like the iridescent feathers of a peacock's tail, as the Irish theologian Scotus Erigena put it when he argued that Holy Scripture contains an infinite number of meanings within itself. So if a commentary is a kind of extension of the work itself, an afterglow of the text, its afterimage, or rather its afterlife, it must not be a mere pragmatic and functionalist explication of hard words and unfamiliar customs (like the books of Hölscher and de Wilde) but must worm its way into the text, replay the text, milk it, worry it—all these images for an intimate and exhausting encounter with its imagery, its structures, its ideas. All this is leading up to a justification of the rather considerable size of this commentary, perhaps the longest on the Book of Job since Gregory the Great. Most people feel that the Book of Job is already long enough, and many find it full of windy and tedious words. I of course believe that it is exactly as long as it ought to be, just as *Il Seraglio* has exactly the right number of notes, despite what the prince said to Mozart. And I of course believe that this commentary contains no redundancy, and that a commentary faithful to the spirit of the Book of Job will be, like it, ample, full and voluminous.

This is the time to express my thankfulness for the many people who have given their support to this author over the almost ten years this book has been in preparation. Perhaps the most important background to the book has been the Department of Biblical Studies in Sheffield in which I have worked since 1964, and where I have enjoyed the inestimable benefit of adventurous and creative colleagues. I name them all, because in some way each has contributed to this book. They are: Loveday Alexander, James Atkinson, Bruce Chilton, Philip Davies, David Gunn, David Hill, Andrew Lincoln, Ralph Martin, David Payne, John Rogerson, Peter Southwell, and Tony Thiselton. The University of Sheffield has granted me three terms of study leave that have been spent in the writing, as well as financial support from its University Research Fund for some of the costs of research. To the Master and Fellows of St Edmund's House (now College), Cambridge, I am deeply grateful for electing me to a Visiting Fellowship in January-April 1986, and providing the ambience for the most sustained period of writing I have ever had. My own college of St John's has given me its hospitality on numerous occasions when I have been working at the University Library in Cambridge. The residents and readers of Tyndale House, Cambridge, have often been a stimulus or a sounding board, especially at the *manche Teepausen* for which Tyndale is famous.

I am especially grateful to several people who have contributed to the text of this work. Hugh Williamson kindly gave me ready access to his extensive bibliography on Old Testament texts. Helen Orchard worked on the bibliography to the Introduction. Philip Chia brought consistency to the biblical citations. Heather McKay read the greater part of the work and made many valuable suggestions for improvements. David Deboys helped especially on Septuagintal matters.

And then there are the typists, Pauline Bates, Rosemarie Kossov, Jane Holden, Andy Davidson, Marcia Crookes, Betty Scholey, and Susan Halpern, and others I fear I have forgotten, who have spent precious hours of their lives on my neat but nevertheless difficult manuscripts.

The Old Testament editor of the series, John Watts, has given me both freedom and urging in due measure, and I thank him and Pat Wienandt of Word Books for their care and attention to many matters both large and small.

More than one large-scale commentary on Job has not progressed beyond the first volume; I hope not to disappoint readers, but to provide a second volume in a much shorter time than the first volume has taken. Whether it will "recapture That first fine careless rapture" that A. S. Peake said A. B. Davidson never could after his first volume on Job remains to be seen. In the meantime, I conclude my preface in much the same spirits as those of the first commentator on Job to have had his book published in English, Theodore Beza, and quote in sympathetic vein these lines from his preface dated January 23, 1587:

> Seeing the troubles of these times and the dangers wherein this commonwealth now standeth . . . I am . . . minded to expound the histories of *Job,* in which, as in other books of the holie Scripture, there are many darke and hard places, insomuch as I must here of necessitie sometime sayle, as it were, among the rocks: and yet I hope I shal not make any shipwracke.

D.J.A.C.

February 28, 1989

Abbreviations

PERIODICALS, SERIALS, AND REFERENCE WORKS

AASOR	*Annual of the American Schools of Oriental Research*
AB	Anchor Bible
AcOr	*Acta orientalia*
ACR	*Australian Catholic Record*
AER	*American Ecclesiastical Review*
AION	*Annali dell'istituto orientali di Napoli*
Aistleitner	Aistleitner, J., *Wörterbuch der ugaritischen Sprache* (Berlin: Akademie Verlag, 1963)
AJBA	*Australian Journal of Biblical Archeology*
AJSL	*American Journal of Semitic Languages and Literature*
Alonso Schökel	Alonso Schökel, L., and J. L. Sicre Díaz, *Job, comentario teológico y literario* (Madrid: Cristiandad, 1983)
ALUOS	*Annual of the Leeds University Oriental Society*
AmCl	*Ami du Clergé*
AnatSt	*Anatolian Studies*
AnBib	Analecta Biblica
AnBoll	*Analecta Bollandiana*
Andersen	Andersen, F. I., *Job: An Introduction and Commentary* (TOTC; Leicester: Inter-Varsity Press, 1976)
Ang	*Angelicum*
AnnInternMed	*Annals of Internal Medicine*
AnOr	Analecta Orientalia
ANEP	*Ancient Near East in Pictures,* ed. J. B. Pritchard (Princeton: Princeton UP, 1954)
ANET	*Ancient Near Eastern Texts,* ed. J. B. Pritchard, 3d ed. (Princeton: Princeton UP, 1969)
Ang	*Angelicum*
AnStEbr	*Annuario di studi ebraici*
Ant	*Antonianum*
AOAT	Alter Orient und Altes Testament
AOS	American Oriental Series
ASTI	*Annual of the Swedish Theological Institute*
ATAbh	Alttestamentliche Abhandlungen
ATANT	Abhandlungen zur Theologie des Alten und Neuen Testaments
ATD	Das Alte Testament Deutsch
ATR	*Anglican Theological Review*
AULLA	*Australasian Universities Language and Literature Association*
AUSS	*Andrews University Seminary Studies*
BA	*Biblical Archaeologist*
BAC	Biblioteca de autores cristianos
Ball	Ball, C. J., *The Book of Job: A Revised Text and Version* (Oxford: Clarendon, 1922)
BASOR	*Bulletin of the American Schools of Oriental Research*
Bauer-Leander	Bauer, H., and P. Leander, *Historische Grammatik der hebräischen Spraches des Alten Testaments* (Halle: Niemeyer, 1922)

BBB	Bonner Biblische Beiträge
BDB	Brown, F., S. R. Driver, and C. A. Briggs, *A Hebrew and English Lexicon of the Old Testament* (Oxford: Clarendon, 1907)
BCPE	*Bulletin du centre protestant d'études*
Beer	Beer, G., textual notes to Job in *BHK,* 1105–54
BeO	*Bibbia e oriente*
BETL	*Bibliotheca ephemeridum theologicarum lovaniensium*
BHK	*Biblia Hebraica,* ed. R. Kittel (3d ed.; Stuttgart: Württemburgische Bibelanstalt, 1937)
BHS	*Biblia Hebraica Stuttgartensia,* ed. K. Elliger and W. Rudolph (Stuttgart: Deutsche Bibelstiftung, 1966–67)
BHT	Beiträge zur historischen Theologie
Bib	*Biblica*
BibB	Biblische Beiträge
BibFe	*Biblia y Fe*
BibOr	Biblica et orientalia
BibRes	*Biblical Research*
BibReview	*Bible Review*
Bickell	Bickell, G., *Das Buch Job nach Anleitung der Strophik und der Septuaginta auf seine ursprüngliche Form zurückgeführt und in Versmasse des Urtextes übersetzt* (Vienna: Karl Gerold's Sohn, 1894)
BIFAO	*Bulletin de l'Institut Français d'Archéologie Orientale*
BIJS	*Bulletin of the Institute of Jewish Studies*
BiKi	*Bibel und Kirche*
BiLit	*Bibel und Liturgie*
BiTrans	*Bible Translator*
BJ	*Bible de Jérusalem*
BJRL	*Bulletin of the John Rylands University Library of Manchester*
BKAT	Biblischer Kommentar: Altes Testament
Blommerde	Blommerde, A. C. M., *Northwest Semitic Grammar and Job* (BibOr 22; Rome: Pontifical Biblical Institute, 1969)
BMik	*Beth Mikra*
BN	*Biblische Notizen*
BO	*Bibliotheca Orientalis*
BOT	De Boeken van het Oude Testament
BotAT	Die Botschaft des Alten Testaments
BSac	*Bibliotheca Sacra*
BTB	*Biblical Theology Bulletin*
Brockelmann	Brockelmann, C., *Lexicon Syriacum* (Berlin: Reuter & Reichard, 1895; 2d ed., Halle: M. Niemeyer)
Brockington	Brockington, L. H., *The Hebrew Text of the Old Testament: The Readings Adopted by the Translators of the New English Bible* (Oxford: Clarendon, 1973)
BSOAS	*Bulletin of the School of Oriental and African Studies*
BTS	*Bible et terre sainte*
BulMusBeyrouth	*Bulletin du musée de Beyrouth*
BurHist	*Buried History*
BWANT	Beiträge zur Wissenschaft vom Alten und Neuen Testament
BZ	*Biblische Zeitschrift*
BZAW	Beihefte zur ZAW
BZAW	*Beihefte zur ZAW* (when book title is not also cited)
CAD	[Chicago] *Assyrian Dictionary* (Chicago: Chicago UP, 1956–)
CahArch	*Cahiers Archéologiques*

CalTJ	*Calvin Theological Journal*
CamB	Cambridge Bible
CB	Century Bible
CBQ	*Catholic Biblical Quarterly*
CBQMS	*CBQ* Monograph Series
CCARJ	*CCAR Journal*
CCSL	Corpus Christianorum, Series Latina
CenB	Century Bible
Charles	Charles, R. H. *The Apocrypha and Pseudepigrapha of the Old Testament* (2 vols.; Oxford: Clarendon, 1913)
Cheyne	Cheyne, T. K., *Job and Solomon, or the Wisdom of the Old Testament* (London: Kegan Paul, Trench & Co., 1887)
ChrPädBl	*Christliche Pädagogische Blätter*
CiTom	*Ciencia Tomista*
CiuD	*Ciudad de Dios*
CiVit	*Città di Vita*
CJT	*Canadian Journal of Theology*
CleR	*Clergy Review*
ColBG	*Collationes Brugenses et Gandavenses*
ColcTFu	*Collectanea Theologica Universitatis Fujen*
ColctMech	*Collectanea Mechliniensia*
CommSpok	*Communio* (Spokane)
ConB	Coniectanea biblica
Conc	*Concilium*
ConcRev	*Concilium-Revue,* French edition of *Concilium*
ConsJud	*Conservative Judaism*
Cox	Cox, D., *The Triumph of Impotence: Job and the Tradition of the Absurd* (Analecta Gregoriana 212; Rome: Università Gregoriana Editrice, 1978)
CQ	*Church Quarterly*
CSCO	Corpus scriptorum christianorum orientalium
CSRBull	*Council for the Study of Religion Bulletin*
CT	*Cuneiform Texts from Babylonian Tablets in the British Museum*
CTA	Herdner, Andrée, *Corpus des tablettes en cunéiformes alphabétiques découvertes à Ras-Shamra-Ugarit* (Paris: Imprimerie Nationale, 1963)
CTM	*Concordia Theological Monthly*
CuadTe	*Cuadernos de Teología*
CurTM	*Currents in Theology and Mission*
Dahood, *Psalms I*	Dahood, M., *Psalms I: 1–50* (Garden City, NY: Doubleday, 1966)
Dahood, *Psalms II*	Dahood, M., *Psalms II: 51–100* (Garden City, NY: Doubleday, 1968)
Dahood, *Psalms III*	Dahood, M., *Psalms III: 101–150* (Garden City, NY: Doubleday, 1970)
Davidson	Davidson, A. B., *The Book of Job, with Notes, Introduction and Appendix* (CamB; Cambridge: CUP, 1884)
DB	*Dictionnaire de la Bible,* ed. F. Vigouroux (Paris: Letouzey & Ané, 1895–1912)
DBSup	*Dictionnaire de la Bible, Supplément,* ed. L. Pirot and A. Robert (Paris: Letouzey & Ané, 1928–)
Delitzsch	Delitzsch, Franz J., *Biblical Commentary on the Book of Job,* tr. F. Bolton (2 vols.; Edinburgh: T. & T. Clark, 1866)
Delitzsch, Friedrich	Delitzsch, Friedrich, *Das Buch Hiob, neu übersetzt und kurz erklärt* (Leipzig: J. C. Hinrichs, 1902)

de Wilde   Wilde, A. de, *Das Buch Hiob eingeleitet, übersetzt und erläutert* (OTS 22; Leiden: E. J. Brill, 1981)
Dhorme   Dhorme, E. *Le livre de Job* (Paris: Gabalda, 1926), tr. H. Knight, *A Commentary on the Book of Job* (London: Thomas Nelson & Sons, 1967)
DictSpir   *Dictionnaire de spiritualité ascétique et mystique*, ed. M. Viller (Paris: Beauchesne, 1932–)
Dillmann   Dillmann, A. *Hiob*, 1869 (3d ed.; Leipzig: S. Hirzel, 1891)
DJD   Discoveries in the Judean Desert
Doederlein   Doederlein, J. C., *Scholia in libros Veteris Testamenti poeticos Jobum, Psalmos et tres Salomonis* (Halle, 1779)
Driver   See Driver-Gray
Driver-Gray   Driver, S. R., and G. B. Gray, *A Critical and Exegetical Commentary on the Book of Job together with a New Translation* (ICC; Edinburgh: T. & T. Clark, 1921)
Driver, *Tenses* Driver, S. R. *A Treatise on the Use of the Tenses in Hebrew and Some Other Syntactical Questions*, 2d ed. (Oxford: Clarendon, 1881)
DTT   *Dansk teologisk tidsskrift*
Duhm   Duhm, B., *Das Buch Hiob erklärt* (KHC; Tübingen: J. C. B. Mohr, 1897)
EB   *Encyclopaedia Biblica*, ed. T. K. Cheyne and J. Black (4 vols.; London: A. and C. Black, 1899–1903)
EBB   אנציקלופדיה מקראית, *Encyclopedia Miqrait* (Jerusalem: Bialik Institute)
EchB   Echter-Bibel
EC   *Enciclopedia Cattolica* (Vatican City, 1949–)
EHAT   Exegetisches Handbuch zum Alten Testament
Ehrlich   Ehrlich, A. B., *Randglossen zur hebräischen Bibel*, Vol. 6: *Psalmen, Sprüche, und Hiob* (Leipzig: J. C. Hinrichs, 1918)
EI   *Eretz Israel*
Eitan   Eitan, I., *A Contribution to Biblical Lexicography* (New York: Columbia UP, 1924)
Enc   *Encounter*
EncJud   *Encyclopaedia Judaica* (Jerusalem: Macmillan, 1972)
EncMiq   See EBB
EQ   *Evangelical Quarterly*
ErbAuf   *Erbe und Auftrag*
ERE   *Encyclopaedia of Religion and Ethics*, ed. J. Hastings (13 vols.; Edinburgh: T. & T. Clark, 1908–26)
EstBíb   *Estudios bíblicos*
EstEcl   *Estudios Eclesiásticos*
EstFranc   *Estudios Franciscanos*
ETL   *Ephemerides Theologicae Lovanienses*
EuntDoc   *Euntes Docete*
EvT   *Evangelische Theologie*
EvErz   *Evangelische Erzieher*
Exp   *Expositor*
ExpB   Expositor's Bible
ExpT   *Expository Times*
Fedrizzi   Fedrizzi, P., *Giobbe: La Sacra Bibbia, traduta dai testi originali illustrata con note critiche e commentata* (Turin: Marietti, 1972)
FF   *Forschungen und Fortschritte*
Fohrer   Fohrer, G., *Das Buch Hiob* (KAT 16; Gütersloh: Gütersloher Verlagshaus Gerd Mohn, 1963)

FoiTemps	*La Foi et le Temps*
FolOr	*Folia Orientalia*
FOTL	The Forms of the Old Testament Literature
FreibRu	*Freiburger Rundbrief*
FRLANT	Forschungen zur Religion und Literatur des Alten und Neuen Testaments
Galling, *Reallexikon*	Galling, K., *Biblisches Reallexikon* (2d ed.; Tübingen: Mohr, 1977)
Gard	Gard, D. H. *The Exegetical Method of the Greek Translator of the Book of Job* (SBLMS 8; Philadelphia: Society of Biblical Literature, 1952)
GerefTTs	*Gereformeerd Theologisch Tijdschrift*
Gerleman	Gerleman, G., textual notes to Job in *BHS*
Gesenius-Buhl	Gesenius, W., and F. Buhl, *Hebräisches und aramäisches Handwörterbuch zum Alten Testament* (17th ed.; Leipzig: Vogel, 1915)
Gibson	Gibson, J. C. L., *Canaanite Myths and Legends* (Edinburgh: T. & T. Clark, 1978)
Gibson, E. C. S.	Gibson, E. C. S., *The Book of Job* (WC; London: Methuen, 1899)
GJ	*Grace Journal*
GKC	*Gesenius' Hebrew Grammar*, ed. E. Kautzsch and A. E. Cowley (2d ed. Oxford: Clarendon Press, 1910)
Gordis	Gordis, R., *The Book of Job: Commentary, New Translation, and Special Notes* (New York: Jewish Theological Seminary of America, 1978)
Grabbe	Grabbe, L. L., *Comparative Philology and the Text of Job: A Study in Methodology* (SBLDS 34; Chico, CA: Scholars Press, 1977)
Graetz	Graetz, H., *Emendationes in plerosque Sacrae Scripturae Veteris Testamenti libros* (Breslau: Schlesische Buchdruckerei, 1892)
Gray	See Driver-Gray
Greg	*Gregorianum*
Guillaume	Guillaume, A., *Studies in the Book of Job with a New Translation* (ALUOS Supp. 2; Leiden: Brill, 1968)
GuL	*Geist und Leben*
Habel	Habel, N. C., *The Book of Job* (London: SCM, 1985)
Hahn	Hahn, H. A., *Commentar über das Buch Hiob* (Berlin: J. A. Wohlgemuth, 1850)
HAR	*Hebrew Annual Review*
HAT	Handbuch zum Alten Testament
HDB	*A Dictionary of the Bible*, ed. J. Hastings (5 vols.; Edinburgh: T. & T. Clark, 1899)
Hen	*Henoch*
HervTS	*Hervormde Teologiese Studies*
Hesse	Hesse, F., *Hiob* (Zürcher Bibelkommentar; Zurich: Theologischer Verlag, 1978)
HibJ	*Hibbert Journal*
Hitzig	Hitzig, F., *Das Buch Hiob übersetzt und ausgelegt* (Leipzig: C. F. Winter, 1874)
HKAT	Handkommentar zum Alten Testament
Hölscher	Hölscher, G., *Das Buch Hiob* (HAT; Tübingen: J. C. B. Mohr [Paul Siebeck], 1937)
Hoffmann	Hoffmann, J. G. E., *Hiob* (Kiel: C. F. Haeseler, 1891)
Horst	Horst, F., *Hiob* (BKAT 1; Neukirchen: Neukirchener Verlag, 1960–63)
Houbigant	Houbigant, C. F., *Biblia Hebraica cum notis criticis* (Paris, 1753)

Houtsma	Houtsma, M. T., *Textkritische Studien zum Alten Testament*: I. *Das Buch Hiob* (Leiden: Brill, 1925)
HS	*Hebrew Studies*
HSAT	Die Heilige Schrift des Alten Testaments (4th ed.; Tübingen, 1922–23)
HSM	Harvard Semitic Museum; Harvard Semitic Monographs
HTR	*Harvard Theological Review*
HUCA	*Hebrew Union College Annual*
Hupfeld	Hupfeld, H., *Quaestioñum in Jobeidos locos vexatos specimen: Commentatio* (Halle: E. Anton, 1853)
IB	*The Interpreter's Bible*, ed. G. A. Buttrick (12 vols.; Nashville: Abingdon, 1951–57)
IBD	*Illustrated Bible Dictionary*, ed. J. D. Douglas et al. (3 vols.; Leicester: Inter-Varsity, 1980)
ICC	International Critical Commentary
IDB	*Interpreter's Dictionary of the Bible*, 4 vols., ed. G. A. Buttrick (Nashville: Abingdon, 1962)
IDBS	*IDB, Supplementary volume*, ed. K. Crim (Nashville: Abingdon, 1976)
IEJ	*Israel Exploration Journal*
IndJT	*Indian Journal of Theology*
Int	*Interpretation*
Interp	*Interpreter*
ISBE	*The International Standard Bible Encyclopedia*, ed. G. W. Bromiley (4 vols., rev. ed.; Grand Rapids: Eerdmans, 1979–)
ITQ	*Irish Theological Quarterly*
IZT	*Internationale Zeitschrift für Theologie*, German edition of *Concilium*
JAAR	*Journal of the American Academy of Religion*
JANESCU	*Journal of the Ancient Near Eastern Society of Columbia University*
Janzen	Janzen, J. G., *Job* (Interpretation; Atlanta: John Knox, 1985)
JAOS	*Journal of the American Oriental Society*
JBC	*The Jerome Bible Commentary*, ed. R. E. Brown et al. (London: Geoffrey Chapman, 1968)
JBL	*Journal of Biblical Literature*
JBLMS	*Journal of Biblical Literature* Monograph Series
JBR	*Journal of Bible and Religion*
JCS	*Journal of Cuneiform Studies*
JDTh	*Jahrbücher für deutsche Theologie*
JETS	*Journal of the Evangelical Theological Society*
JewEnc	*Jewish Encyclopedia*
JHI	*Journal of the History of Ideas*
JMEOS	*Journal of the Manchester Egyptian and Oriental Society*
JNES	*Journal of Near Eastern Studies*
Joüon	Joüon, P., *Grammaire de l'hébreu biblique* (Rome: Pontifical Biblical Institute, 1947)
JPOS	*Journal of the Palestine Oriental Society*
JPsychJud	*Journal of Psychology and Judaism*
JPsychTheol	*Journal of Psychology and Theology*
JQR	*Jewish Quarterly Review*
JPTh	*Jahrbücher für protestantische Theologie*
JR	*Journal of Religion*
JSJ	*Jounral for the Study of Judaism*
JSOT	*Journal for the Study of the Old Testament*
JSOTSup	*Journal for the Study of the Old Testament*, Supplement Series

JSP	*Journal for the Study of the Pseudepigrapha*
JSS	*Journal of Semitic Studies*
JTS	*Journal of Theological Studies*
Jud	*Judaica*
JüdSHRZ	*Jüdische Schriften aus hellenistischer und römischer Zeit* (Gütersloh)
KAT	Kommentar zum Alten Testament, ed. E. Sellin
KatBl	*Katachetische Blätter*
KB	Koehler, L., and W. Baumgartner, *Lexicon in Veteris Testamenti libros* (Leiden: Brill, 1953)
KB³	Koehler, L., and W. Baumgartner, *Hebräisches und aramäisches Lexikon zum Alten Testament* (Leiden: E. J. Brill, 1967–)
KEH	Kurzgefasstes exegetisches Handbuch zum Alten Testament
KHC(AT)	Kurzer Hand-Commentar (zum Alten Testament)
King	King, E. G., *The Poem of Job; Translated in the Metre of the Original* (Cambridge: CUP, 1914)
Kissane	Kissane, E. J., *The Book of Job Translated from a Critically Revised Hebrew Text with Commentary* (Dublin: Browne & Nolan, 1939)
KKAT	Kurzgefasster Kommentar zu den Heiligen Schriften Alten und Neuen Testaments
Knox	[Knox, R.], *The Holy Bible: A Translation from the Latin Vulgate in the Light of the Hebrew and Greek Originals* (London: Burns, Oates & Washbourne, 1945–49)
König	König, E., *Historisch-kritisches Lehrgebäude der hebräischen Sprache: 3. Historisch-Comparative Syntax der hebräischen Sprache* (Leipzig: Hinrichs, 1897)
KTU	Dietrich, M., O. Loretz, and J. Sanmartin, *Keilalphabetische Texte aus Ugarit* (AOAT 24; Kevelaer and Neukirchen: Butzon & Bercker, 1976)
KuD	*Kerygma und Dogma*
KV	Korte Verklaring
Lamparter	Lamparter, H., *Das Buch der Anfechtung, übersetzt und ausgelegt* (BotAT; Stuttgart: Calwer, 1951)
Lane	Lane, E. W., *An Arabic-English Lexicon* (London: Williams & Norgate, 1863–93)
Larcher	Larcher, C., *Le Livre de Job* (BJ; Paris: Cerf, 1950)
LCQ	*Lutheran Church Quarterly*
Leš	*Lešonenu*
Lévêque	Lévêque, J., *Job et son Dieu: Essai d'exégèse et de théologie biblique* (Paris: Gabalda, 1970)
Levy	Levy, J., *Neuhebräisches und chaldäisches Wörterbuch über die Talmudim und Midraschim* (4 vols.; Leipzig: Brockhaus, 1876–89)
LingBib	*Linguistica Biblica*
LTP	*Laval théologique et philosophique*
LTQ	*Lexington Theological Quarterly*
LTR	*Lexington Theological Review*
LUÅ	Lunds Universitets Årsskrift
MAA	*Medelelingen der koninklijke nederlandse Akademie van Wetenschappen, Amsterdam*
Merx	Merx, A., *Das Gedicht von Hiob: Hebräischer Text, kritisch bearbeitet und übersetzt, nebst sachlicher und kritischer Einleitung* (Jena: Mauke's Verlag, 1871)
MethQR	*Methodist Quarterly Review*
MGWJ	*Monatsschrift für Geschichte und Wissenschaft des Judentums*

Michaelis	Michaelis, J. D., "Varianten im Buch Hiob" (in his *Orientalische und exegetische Bibliothek* 7 [1774] 217–47; 8 [1775] 179–224)
Michel	W. L. Michel, *Job in the Light of Northwest Semitic*, Vol. 1 (Rome: Pontifical Biblical Institute, 1987)
MittSeptU	Mitteilungen des Septuaginta-Unternehmens
Moffatt	Moffatt, J., *A New Translation of the Bible* (London: Hodder & Stoughton, 1926)
MP	*Monatsschrift für Pastoraltheologie*
MTZ	*Münchener Theologische Studien*
Murphy	Murphy, R. E., *Wisdom Literature: Job, Proverbs, Ruth, Canticles, Ecclesiastes and Esther* (FOTL 13; Grand Rapids: Eerdmans, 1981)
Muss-Arnoldt	Muss-Arnoldt, W., *A Concise Dictionary of the Assyrian Languages* (Berlin: Reuther & Reichard, 1905)
MVAG	Mitteilungen der vorderasiatisch-ägyptischen Gesellschaft
NCB	New Century Bible
NBD	*The New Bible Dictionary*, ed. J. D. Douglas (London: IVF, 1962)
NedGTT	*Nederduitse Gereformeerd Teologiese Tydskrif*
NedTTs	*Nederlands Theologisch Tijdschrift*
NICOT	New International Commentary on the Old Testament
NIDNTT	*The New International Dictionary of New Testament Theology*, ed. C. Brown (2 vols.; Grand Rapids: Eerdmans, 1979)
NJDTh	*Neue Jahrbücher für deutsche Theologie*
NRT	*Nouvelle Revue Théologique*
NTT	*Norsk Teologisk Tidsskrift*
OBO	Orbis Biblicus et Orientalis
OED	Murray, J. A. H., *New English Dictionary on Historical Principles* (Oxford, 1888–1928)
OLP	*Orientalia Lovaniensia Periodica*
Olshausen	Olshausen, J., *Hiob erklärt* (KEH; Leipzig: S. Hirzel, 1852)
OLZ	*Orientalische Literaturzeitung*
Or	*Orientalia*
OrChr	*Oriens Christianus*
OrdKor	*Ordens-Korrespondenz*
OTL	Old Testament Library
OTS	*Oudtestamentische Studiën*
OTWSA	*Die Ou Testamentiese Werkgemeenskap in Suid-Afrika*
PalCl	*Palestra del Clero*
Payne Smith	Payne Smith, R., *Thesaurus Syriacus* (2 vols.; Oxford: Clarendon, 1879–1901)
Peake	Peake, A. S., *Job, Introduction, Revised Version with Notes, and Index* (CB; Edinburgh: T. C. & E. C. Jack, 1905)
PEFQS	*Palestine Exploration Fund, Quarterly Statement*
PEQ	*Palestine Exploration Quarterly*
Perles II	Perles, F., *Analekten zur Textkritik des Alten Testaments* (N.F.; Leipzig: Engel, 1922)
PerspRelSt	*Perspectives in Religious Studies*
PerspT	*Perspectiva Teológica*
Peters	Peters, N., *Das Buch Hiob übersetzt und erklärt* (Münster: Aschendorff, 1928)
PG	*Patrologiae Cursus Completus, Series Graeca*, ed. J. P. Migne (Paris, 1857–66, 1894)
PL	*Patrologiae Cursus Completus, Series Latina*, ed. J. P. Migne (Paris, 1844–80)

PO	Patrologia Orientalis
Pope	Pope, M., *Job* (AB; Garden City, NY: Doubleday, 1965; 3d ed., 1973)
POTT	*Peoples of Old Testament Times*, ed. D. J. Wiseman (London: OUP, 1973)
PrAmAcJewRes	*Proceedings of the American Academy of Jewish Research*
Prot	*Protestantesimo*
QDAP	*Quarterly of the Department of Antiquities in Palestine*
RA	*Revue d'Assyriologie*
Ravisi	Ravasi, G., *Giobbe, traduzione e commento* (Rome: Borla, 1979–84)
RazF	*Razón y Fe*
RB	*Revue biblique*
RBibArg	*Revista Biblica*, Buenos Aires
RBibIt	*Rivista biblica italiana*
RCatalT	*Revista Catalana de Teologia*
RE	*Realencyklopädie für protestantische Theologie und Kirche*, ed. J. J. Herzog (3d ed.; Leipzig: J. C. Hinrichs, 1896–1913)
RÉArmén	*Revue des Études Arméniennes*
RÉJ	*Revue des Études Juives*
Reiske	Reiske, J. J., *Coniecturae in Jobum et Proverbia Salomonis* (Leipzig, 1779)
Renan	Renan, E., *Le livre de Job, traduit de l'hébreu* (Paris: Calmann Lévy, 1860)
Reuss	Reuss, E., *Hiob* (Braunschweig: Schwetschke, 1888)
RevApol	*Revue Apologétique*
RevArch	*Revue Archéologique*
RevEcclLiège	*Revue ecclésiastique de Liège*
RevÉtIs	*Revue des études islamiques*
RevExp	*Review and Expositor*
RevNouv	*Revue Nouvelle*
RevQ	*Revue de Qumran*
RGG	*Die Religion in Geschichte und Gegenwart*, ed. K. Galling (6 vols.; Tübingen: J. C. B. Mohr, 1957–65)
RHE	*Revue d'histoire ecclésiastique*
RHPR	*Revue d'histoire et de philosophie religieuses*
RHR	*Revue de l'histoire des religions*
Richter	Richter, H. *Studien zu Hiob: Der Aufbau des Hiobbuches dargestellt an den Gattungen des Rechtslebens* (Berlin: Evangelische Verlagsanstalt, 1959)
RicR	*Ricerche Religiose*
RivB	*Rivista Biblica*
Rosenmüller	Rosenmüller, E. F. C., *Scholia in Vetus Testamentum: Editio secunda auctior et emendatior*, Pars V: *Jobus* (Leipzig: J. A. Barth, 1824)
Rowley	Rowley, H. H., *Job* (NCB; Thomas Nelson & Sons, 1970)
RQ	*Restoration Quarterly*
RR	*Review of Religion*
RRel	*Review for Religious*
RS	Ras Shamra
RSPT	*Revue des sciences philosophiques et théologiques*
RSO	*Rivista degli studi orientali*
RTAM	*Recherches de théologie ancienne et médiévale*
RTL	*Revue théologique de Louvain*
RUO	*Revue de l'Université d'Ottawa*
SAB	*Sitzungsberichte der Deutschen Akademie der Wissenschaften zu Berlin*

SacDoc	*Sacra Doctrina*
SANT	Studien zum Alten und Neuen Testament
SBFLA	*Studii Biblici Franciscani Liber Annuus*
SBL	Society of Biblical Literature
SBLDS	Society of Biblical Literature Dissertation Series
SBLMS	Society of Biblical Literature Monograph Series
SBLSCS	Society of Biblical Literature Septuagint and Cognate Studies
SBOT	Sacred Books of the Old Testament
SBT	Studies in Biblical Theology
ScEs	*Science et esprit*
Schultens	Schultens, A., *Liber Iobi cum nova versione ad hebraeum fontem et commentario perpetuo* (Leiden: J. Luzac, 1787)
SchwTZ	*Schweizerische Theologische Zeitschrift*
ScrHieros	*Scripta Hierosolymitana*
SEÅ	*Svensk Exegetisk Årsbok*
Sef	*Sefarad*
Sem	*Semitica*
Sicre Diaz	Alonso Schökel, L., and J. L. Sicre Díaz, *Job, comentario teológico y literario* (Madrid: Cristiandad, 1983)
Siegfried	Siegfried, C. [G. A.], *The Book of Job: Critical Edition of the Hebrew Text* (SBOT; Baltimore: Johns Hopkins UP, 1893)
SJT	*Scottish Journal of Theology*
Skehan	Skehan, P. W., "Strophic Patterns in the Book of Job," *CBQ* 23 (1961) 125–42 (= *Studies in Israelite Poetry and Wisdom*, CBQMS 1 [1971] 96–113)
Snaith	Snaith, N. H., *The Book of Job: Its Origin and Purpose* (SBT 2/11; London: SCM, 1968)
SOTSMS	Society for Old Testament Study Monograph Series
SR	*Studies in Religion/Sciences religieuses*
SSEA	Society for the Study of Egyptian Antiquities
ST	*Studia theologica*
StAns	*Studia Anselmiana*
StANT	Studien zum Alten und Neuen Testament
STDJ	Studies on the Texts of the Desert of Judah
Stevenson	Stevenson, W. B., *The Poem of Job: A Literary Study with a New Translation* (London: OUP, 1947)
Stier	Stier, F., *Das Buch Ijjob hebräisch und deutsch: Uebertragen ausgelegt und mit Text- und Sacherläuterungen versehen* (Munich: Kösel, 1954)
StLuke	*St Luke's Journal of Theology*
Strahan	Strahan, J., *The Book of Job Interpreted* (Edinburgh: T. & T. Clark, 1913)
StSemNed	*Studia Semitica Nederlandica*
SWJT	*Southwestern Journal of Theology*
Szczygiel	Szczygiel, P., *Das Buch Job, übersetzt und erklärt* (HSAT; Bonn: Hanstein, 1931)
Tarb	*Tarbiz*
TBT	*The Bible Today*
TBü	Theologische Bücherei
TDig	*Theology Digest*
TDNT	*Theological Dictionary of the New Testament*, ed. G. Kittel and G. Friedrich, tr. G. W. Bromiley (10 vols.; Grand Rapids: Eerdmans, 1964–76)

TDOT	*Theological Dictionary of the Old Testament,* ed. G. J. Botterweck and H. Ringgren (Grand Rapids: Eerdmans, 1974–)
Terrien	Terrien, S. L., *Job* (Commentaire de l'Ancien Testament 13; Neuchâtel: Delachaux et Niestlé, 1963)
Textual Notes	*Textual Notes on the New American Bible* (Paterson, NJ: St. Anthony's Guild, n.d. [pp. 325–451 of some editions])
TGl	*Theologie und Glaube*
TGUOS	*Transactions of the Glasgow University Oriental Society*
ThB	Theologische Bücherei
ThBl	*Theologische Blätter*
Theol	*Theology*
THWAT	*Theologisches Handwörterbuch zum Alten Testament,* ed. E. Jenni and C. Westermann (Munich: Kaiser, 1971)
ThEx	*Theologische Existenz Heute*
ThZ	*Theologische Zeitschrift*
TLZ	*Theologische Literaturzeitung*
TOTC	Tyndale Old Testament Commentaries
TPM	*Theologische-Praktische Monatsschrift*
TPQ	*Theologische-Praktische Quartalschrift*
TQ	*Theologische Quartalschrift*
TRev	*Theologische Revue*
TRu	*Theologische Rundschau*
TS	*Theological Studies*
TSK	*Theologische Studien und Kritiken*
TTijd	*Theologische Tijdschrift*
TTKi	*Tidskrift for Teologi og Kirche*
TTod	*Theology Today*
TTQ	*Tübinger Theologischer Quartalschrift*
TTZ	*Trierer theologische Zeitschrift*
TU	Texte und Untersuchungen
Tur-Sinai	Tur-Sinai, N. H., *The Book of Job: A New Commentary* (Jerusalem: Kiryath-Sepher, 1957)
TV(ers)	*Theologische Versuche*
TZ	*Theologische Zeitschrift*
UF	*Ugarit Forschungen*
USQR	*Union Seminary Quarterly Review*
Van Selms	Van Selms, A., *Job: Die Prediking van het OT* (2 vols.; Nijkerk: Callenbach, 1982–83)
VD	*Verbum Domini*
VF	*Verkündigung und Forschung*
VigChr	*Vigiliae Christianae*
Voigt	Voigt, C., *Einige Stellen des Buches Hiob* (Leipzig: W. Drugulin, 1895)
Volz	Volz, P. *Weisheit (Das Buch Hiob, Sprüche und Jesus Sirach, Prediger)* (Göttingen: Vandenhoeck & Ruprecht, 1911; 2d ed., 1921)
von Soden	Soden, W. von, *Akkadisches Handwörterbuch* (Wiesbaden: Harrassowitz, 1965–71)
VS	*Vie spirituelle*
VT	*Vetus Testamentum*
VTSup	*VT Supplements*
Watson	Watson, W. G. E. *Classical Hebrew Poetry: A Guide to Its Techniques* (JSOTSup 26; Sheffield: JSOT, 1984)
WC	Westminster Commentaries

Webster	Webster, E. C. "Strophic Patterns in Job 3–28," *JSOT* 26 (1983) 33–60
Weiser	Weiser, A., *Das Buch Hiob übersetzt und erklärt* (ATD; Göttingen: Vandenhoeck & Ruprecht, 1951)
Westermann	Westermann, C., *The Structure of the Book of Job: A Form-Critical Analysis*, tr. C. A. Muenchow (Philadelphia: Fortress, 1981)
WMANT	Wissenschaftliche Monographien zum Alten und Neuen Testament
WO	*Die Welt des Orients*
Wor	*Worship* (Collegeville, Minn.)
Wright	Wright, G. H. B., *The Book of Job* (London: Williams and Norgate, 1883)
WTJ	*Westminster Theological Journal*
WuD	*Wort und Dienst*
WZ	*Wissenschaftliche Zeitschrift . . .*
WZKM	*Wiener Zeitschrift für die Kunde des Morgenlandes*
Yellin	Yellin, D., חקרי מקרא איוב (Jerusalem, 1927)
ZA	*Zeitschrift für Assyriologie*
ZAW	*Zeitschrift für die alttestamentliche Wissenschaft*
ZDMG	*Zeitschrift der deutschen morgenländischen Gesellschaft*
ZDPV	*Zeitschrift des deutschen Palästina-Vereins*
ZeichZt	*Die Zeichen der Zeit*
ZKT	*Zeitschrift für katholische Theologie*
ZRGG	*Zeitschrift für Religions- und Geistesgeschichte*
ZST	*Zeitschrift für die systematische Theologie*
ZTK	*Zeitschrift für Theologie und Kirche*
ZZ	*Zwischen den Zeiten*

BIBLICAL (INCLUDING APOCRYPHAL) BOOKS

Gen	Genesis	Dan	Daniel
Exod	Exodus	Hos	Hosea
Lev	Leviticus	Joel	Joel
Num	Numbers	Amos	Amos
Deut	Deuteronomy	Obad	Obadiah
Josh	Joshua	Jonah	Jonah
Judg	Judges	Mic	Micah
Ruth	Ruth	Nah	Nahum
1–2 Sam	1–2 Samuel	Hab	Habakkuk
1–2 Kgs	1–2 Kings	Zeph	Zephaniah
1–2 Chr	1–2 Chronicles	Hag	Haggai
Ezra	Ezra	Zech	Zechariah
Neh	Nehemiah	Mal	Malachi
Esth	Esther	Tob	Tobit
Job	Job	Jdt	Judith
Ps	Psalm	Wisd	Wisdom of Solomon
Prov	Proverbs	Ecclus	Ecclesiasticus or The Wisdom of Jesus son of Sirach
Eccl	Ecclesiastes		
Cant	Canticles		
Isa	Isaiah	Bar	Baruch
Jer	Jeremiah	1–2 Macc	1–2 Maccabees
Lam	Lamentations	Matt	Matthew
Ezek	Ezekiel	Mark	Mark

Luke	Luke	1–2 Tim	1–2 Timothy
John	John	Titus	Titus
Acts	Acts	Phlm	Philemon
Rom	Romans	Heb	Hebrews
1–2 Cor	1–2 Corinthians	James	James
Gal	Galatians	1–2 Pet	1–2 Peter
Eph	Ephesians	1–2–3 John	1–2–3 John
Phil	Philippians	Jude	Jude
Col	Colossians	Rev	Revelation
1–2 Thess	1–2 Thessalonians		

Qumran and Rabbinic Literature

1QH	Hymn Scroll from Qumran	*b. Bat.*	*Baba Bathra*
1QM	War Scroll from Qumran	Gen. Rabb.	Genesis Rabbah
1QS	Manual of Discipline	Midr.	Midrash
11QtgJob	Targum of Job from Qumran, Cave 11	*Moᶜed Qat.*	*Moᶜed Qatan*
		Pss. Sol.	*Psalms of Solomon*
b.	Babylonian Talmud	*T. Job*	*Testament of Job*

Modern Translations

ASV	American Standard Version	NEB	New English Bible
AV	Authorized Version, King James Version	NIV	New International Version
BJ	Bible de Jérusalem	NJB	New Jerusalem Bible
GNB	Good News Bible, TEV	NJPS	New Jewish Publication Society Version
JB	Jerusalem Bible	RSV	Revised Standard Version
JPS	Jewish Publication Society version of the Bible	RV	Revised Version
KJV	King James Version, Authorized Version	TEV	Today's English Version, GNB
NAB	New American Bible	TOB	Traduction Oecuménique de la Bible

Hebrew Grammar

abs	absolute	inf	infinitive
acc	accusative	intrans	intransitive
consec	consecutive	juss	jussive
coh	cohortative	masc	masculine
constr	construct	niph	niphal
fem	feminine	pass	passive
fut	future	perf	perfect
gen	genitive	pers	person
haplog	haplography	pl	plural
hiph	hiphil	ptcp	participle
hithp	hithpael	sg	singular
hithpo	hithpolal	subj	subject
hoph	hophal	suff	suffix
impf	imperfect	vb	verb
impv	imperative		

TEXTUAL NOTES

Akk.	Akkadian	MH	Mishnaic Hebrew
Aq	Aquila	MT	Masoretic Text
Arab.	Arabic	OG	Old Greek
Aram.	Aramaic	OL	Old Latin
Ass.	Assyrian	Pesh	Peshitta, Syriac version of the OT
Eg.	Egyptian		
G	Greek translation of the OT, Septuagint, LXX	Q	Qere, Masoretic vocalized Hebrew text of OT
Germ.	German	Rashi	Commentary printed in Rabbinic Bibles
Heb.	Hebrew		
Hitt.	Hittite	Symm	Symmachus
K	Kethibh, consonantal Hebrew text of OT	Syr	Syriac version of the OT, Peshitta
Lat.	Latin	Tg	Targum
LXX	Septuagint, Greek translation of the OT	Theod	Theodotion
		Ugar.	Ugaritic
		Vg	Vulgate

MISCELLANEOUS

ANE	Ancient Near East	NT	New Testament
cf.	compare	OT	Old Testament
chap(s).	chapter(s)	OUP	Oxford University Press
col(s).	column(s)	opp.	opposite (to)
ct.	contrast	orig.	original, originally
CUP	Cambridge University Press	p.	page
		pl.	plate
dittogr	dittograph(y)	postbib.	postbiblical
ed(s).	edition; edited by: editor(s)	*prp*	*propositum,* suggested (of a textual emendation)
ET	English Translation	*q.v.*	*quod vide,* which see
EVV	English versions	repr.	reprinted
frag.	fragment	sc.	scilicet, that is to say
frt	*forte,* perhaps	*si v.l.*	*si vera lectio,* if the reading is correct
FS	Festschrift		
lit.	literally	*s.v.*	*sub verbo,* under that word
mg	margin	tr.	translate(d); translator
ms(s)	manuscript(s)	UP	University Press
n.	note	v(v)	verse(s)
n.d.	no date	*v.l.*	*varia lectio,* alternative reading
N.F.	Neue Folge, new series		
N.R.	Nieuwe Reeks, new series	vol(s).	volume(s)
ns	new series		

Introduction:
I. Orientation to This Book

Mega biblion, mega kakon; a big book is a big evil. The proverb is true for the reader almost as much for as for the writer. These first pages are intended to enable readers to use this book for their own purposes, and not to foreswear it for its forbiddingness.

By way of *Introduction*, there is, following this orientation to the commentary itself, an *Orientation* to the Book of Job, so that one may read, as one runs, in the space of a few pages, "what the book is all about." It will not therefore be necessary to read the entire commentary to find out what this commentator thinks, in general, the book is "all about." If a thing is worth saying, it is worth saying briefly.

There are, however, two drawbacks to finding out what the Book of Job is all about. The first is that no one can say, and certainly not this commentator, what the Book of Job is all *about*, not even given unlimited space and time. For it is a part of the Book's greatness that whenever we think we have it mastered, it surprises us with new angles that we realize we haven't yet properly taken into consideration. The second drawback is that "what the book is all about"—which is to say, its meaning—varies from reader to reader. For meanings are not properties of books, but are understandings created in the minds of readers who are intent upon reading books. And as many readers, as many readings. This realization does not have to lead to despair of making sense of Job or to abandonment of the quest for superior and more persuasive meanings. But it does put the reader and the reader's concern in a very much more prominent place than is customary. In line with this emphasis on the reader, the second part of the Orientation sketches some particular readings of Job that might be generated by a sample of readers with particular stances and commitments—for example, feminists, materialists, vegetarians, and Christians.

There is not a lot in this Orientation about the traditional questions usually dealt with in Introductions to commentaries—date, authorship, sources, and the like. This is because I regard these questions as mostly *extrinsic* to the book itself and therefore to the question of meaning or interpretation, which is always for me the primary question. No doubt there are many interesting things to be said about how the Book of Job may have developed into the book it now is. But I must confess to having spent almost all my time on the book as it now is, without thinking very much about how it came to be in its present form. Of its author or date of composition I frankly know nothing, and my speculations are not likely to be worth more than the many guesses that already exist. However, I do admit that it would be doctrinaire to rule out these questions altogether, and I agree that my reading of the book as it now stands does make some historical judgments, such as the assumptions that the book is written by a Hebrew or Jew several centuries before the Christian era. So the reader curious about such matters will find in the Orientation some few remarks on strictly historical or genetic matters.

The third part of this Introduction is an Orientation to Works about the

Book of Job—which is to say, a *Bibliography*. Unlike bibliographies in most commentaries, even those in the Word Biblical Commentary series, this is intended to be a reasonably comprehensive bibliography. It does not contain only items I have read or seen, though I think I have seen most that are in Sheffield, Cambridge University Library or the British Library in the British Museum, London. It does not usually include works in languages with which I have no familiarity. There are several reasons why I decided to compile such a bibliography.

1. There is no such bibliography anywhere in print.

2. I thought it was important to consider the quantity—and the range—of works that have been inspired by the Book of Job. There are certainly more on the Book of Psalms, but I would be surprised if there were more on any other book of the Old Testament. The existence of these works is in itself a commentary on the Book of Job.

3. I became increasingly dissatisfied with restricting my horizon to the so-called scholarly works. Scholars quote scholars and create their own canon of approved literature on the Book of Job. Those writings that are not soon cited by commentators do not generally get cited by subsequent commentators. If a writer on Job has been dead for more than a hundred years, or wrote in a language other than English, French, or German, or addressed people who were not scholars, or was published by a publishing house committed to a particular religious viewpoint—it is very unlikely that the views of that author will be taken into any account by the writer of a scholarly commentary. I should know, because that is to a large extent what I too have been doing throughout this commentary. Of course, when it comes to technical questions about philology, unscholarly remarks can be safely ignored. But when it is a matter of large-scale interpretation, of the meaning of the book as a whole and not just of a particular word or verse, one does not need to be a technically trained scholar to have valuable insights. So my "undiscriminating" bibliography, which includes sermons and works of popular devotion alongside vast works of erudition, is meant as a kind of atonement for the principle of scholarly apartheid which reigns elsewhere in the commentary.

4. The writings on Job of older commentators, including the Fathers of the Christian church and the oldest Jewish interpreters, are listed here deliberately. For I came to understand that there can be no serious distinction between "interpretation" and the "history of interpretation." At the moment of publication of this commentary it becomes part of the "history of interpretation" and no different in principle—however much in content and quality—from those of Chrysostom, Rashi, Oecolampadius, Schultens, and the others. One day I was browsing in the 1,500–page commentary of Sebastian Schmidt (1670); when I read his heartfelt comment on the last verse of Job, *Nihil in hoc v. difficultatis,* "Nothing of difficulty in this verse," that unique blend of disappointment and relief only known to long-distance commentators, I knew it would be an insult to him and a sign of small-mindedness in myself if he, and the hundreds of honest workers like him, were omitted from my bibliography. The history of a work's "reception," we are belatedly coming to realize, is part of the meaning of the work.

In the Commentary proper, the design followed is of course that of the editors, themselves standing in the tradition of the Biblischer Kommentar series. First comes the *Bibliography* to each section; in the case of the dialogues of Job, each speech forms a section. Why, I have asked myself, does the bibliography come first? To impress the reader with how much homework the commentator has done, or how much the reader would have to put in before becoming qualified to utter a sentence of one's own on the meaning of the text? I should hope not. I came eventually to regard it as a confession of the limitations of the commentator: in signaling the tradition in which the commentator stands, that is, the academic, textual, linguistic, orientalist, Christian-theological (for the most part) authorities the author has consulted, what is being silently admitted is the relative absence of influence from rhetoric, poetry, literature, psychology, philosophy, and the relative subjugation of the author's individuality in the interests of a common "objective" language of discourse. Nevertheless, the literary genre of the "confession" can also be turned to good use, and I hope it will be. On a more practical note, I should say that, on the whole, items in the pericope bibliographies throughout the book will not be found in the general bibliography of the *Introduction,* and vice versa. Bibliographical items that are referred to once only within a pericope commentary have a full citation at that place; only if an item is referred to more than once will it appear in the bibliography.

Next comes the *Translation.* It is meant to be reasonably literal. No indications of meter are given because the whole subject of Hebrew meter is too vexed for simple decisions to be made, and in any case it is hard to see any interpretational significance in the notation of meter. I have not managed to use inclusive language in the translation; committed though I am to its use in my own writing—and it is employed throughout the commentary proper—it is not always possible, in my experience, to conform the writing of another person to a gender-free style. For example, in the depictions of the "wicked man" in chap. 18, there is no reason to think that the words should refer only to males; on the other hand, there is no reason to doubt that the author so intended. One option that I have not taken is to convert all the references to the "wicked man" into plurals, for the poetic image of the evildoer would be weakened if I did so.

A word about my analysis of strophes is in order. By leaving a line of space between certain lines of the poetry, I am presenting an interpretational decision about how I view the structure of the poem. I am not necessarily affirming that the poet intended the structure or composed in strophes. Sometimes, especially when several strophes in sequence have the same number of lines, there is reason to suppose that the author was consciously shaping the poem. But on the whole, the strophic analysis is no more than a patterning device of our own that expresses our sense of coherence and difference.

In the *Notes* I have had two main purposes before me. First, to justify my own translation of the Hebrew text, noting where I have adopted emendations of the text or new suggestions for meanings of the Hebrew words. Second, to explain and evaluate the translations offered by the dozen or so English translations I have always had open before me, from the Authorized Version (King James) down to the New International Version and the new Jewish Publication Society version. Since the versions differ among themselves greatly, I thought that one of the responsibilities of a commentator on the Hebrew text was to explain to the English reader how this enormous variety in translation can have been possible, and to attempt to make judgments on the relative validity of the individual translations. On this matter, as on all the topics covered in the *Notes*, I have always tried to make a judgment rather than simply record the opinions of others. In the relatively few cases where no evaluative comment is made, the mere recording of an opinion means that I did not accept it but was too bored to go on saying so. As far as the ancient versions go, I did not attempt to explain or evaluate them in the same way, partly because they have often enough been studied in their own right (see *Bibliography*, sect. 5), and partly because their translations are necessarily of less interest to the English-speaking reader. I have therefore referred to them only when they promised to shed some light on the Hebrew text. Such a piecemeal use of the ancient versions is theoretically improper from a text-critical point of view, I know, but I hope it has not been seriously misleading.

The *Comment* proper is in constant tension between the part and the whole. Believing as I do that verse-by-verse interpretation can be an abuse of the text, and that what appears in many commentaries as a worthily thorough and detailed interpretation can be in fact a steadfast and systematic refusal to confront the primary questions of meaning, I have had to be in movement all the time between the smallest detail and the larger wholes. My normal method has been to set down first my understanding of the larger unit, whether the chapter, the strophe or the verse, and then to support that interpretation with a more detailed treatment of the individual sentences and words. At every point I have tried to be conscious of the book as a whole, and of how the sentence under consideration contributes to the total work. At every point also I have been asking how this sentence is connected, in thought, with the previous sentences, and how the argument of the speaker is being developed.

Readers of commentaries approach them with different needs, so the structure of the comment has been designed to make it easy for a reader to find what is needed, whether a detailed remark on an individual word or phrase, or a general account of the sweep of a speech.

Much of the commentary is written from the point of view of the character speaking the lines. It is valuable, I think, to attempt to sympathize with the characters, Eliphaz, Bildad, and the rest, not exactly in order to recreate them as plausible characters psychologically speaking, but to appreciate the force of their arguments. But I speak sometimes in the commentary itself with the voice of Job, or the voice of the implied author, or in my own voice.

Speaking in my own voice is what I understand the last section, the *Explanation*, to be intended for. Here I try to savor what has been going on in the speech, evaluate it as warmly and respectfully as I can, and then to make no secret about what I myself think about it. The Book of Job of course lends itself to such a degree of personal involvement by the commentator—or indeed by any reader—for it propounds many ideas that are in conflict with one another and in so doing compels the reader to make personal evaluations. Job and Zophar cannot both be right about the moral order of the universe, so the book makes a critical demand of the reader in a way that, say, Romans, does not.

The reader who wants nothing more from this book than a quick survey of what it is saying in its sequential unfolding should be able to gain that by reading the *Explanations* at the end of each section one after another. Another way of surveying the book is presented in the Orientation to the book in this Introduction; there the argument of the book is reviewed, not in the sequence in which it appears in the book itself, but from the standpoint of the individual characters in the book (including the narrator). Reading both the orientation and the expositions should then provide something of a stereoscopic view of the Book of Job as a whole. The rest is work for the microscope.

Introduction:
II. Orientation to the Book of Job

Select Bibliography of Works in English

COMMENTARIES:

Andersen, F. I. *Job.* TOTC. Leicester: Tyndale, 1976. **Clines, D. J. A.** "Job." In *A Bible Commentary for Today,* ed. G. C. D. Howley. London: Pickering & Inglis, 1979. 559–592 [2d ed. in *The International Bible Commentary,* ed. F. F. Bruce. Basingstoke, Hants: Marshall Pickering, 1986. 520–51.] **Dhorme, E.** *A Commentary on the Book of Job.* London: Thomas Nelson & Sons, 1967. **Gordis, R.** *The Book of Job: Commentary, New Translation, and Special Notes.* New York: Jewish Theological Seminary of America, 1978. **Habel, N. C.** *The Book of Job.* OTL. London: SCM, 1985. **Pope, M. H.** *Job.* AB. 3d ed. Garden City, NY: Doubleday, 1973. **Rowley, H. H.** *Job.* NCB. Thomas Nelson & Sons, 1970. **Terrien, S.** "The Book of Job: Introduction and Exegesis." In *The Interpreter's Bible.* New York and Nashville: Abingdon, 1954. 3:877–1198.

OTHER WORKS:

Barr, J. "The Book of Job and Its Modern Interpreters." *BJRL* 54 (1971–72) 28–46. **Clines, D. J. A.** "The Arguments of Job's Three Friends." In *Art and Meaning: Rhetoric in Biblical Literature,* ed. D. J. A. Clines, D. M. Gunn, and A. J. Hauser. JSOTSup 19. Sheffield: JSOT, 1982. 199–214. **Gordis, R.** *The Book of God and Man: A Study of Job.* Chicago: University of Chicago Press, 1965. **Tsevat, M.** "The Meaning of the Book of Job." In *The Meaning of the Book of Job and Other Biblical Studies.* New York: Ktav, 1980. 1–37. **Westermann, C.** *The Structure of the Book of Job: A Form-Critical Analysis,* tr. C. A. Muenchow. Philadelphia: Fortress, 1981.

As I have already said, I plan to offer first an orientation to the present form of the Book of Job, attempting to understand the book as a coherent whole. Only later in this section will other questions, about the origins and growth of the book during the time of its composition, be examined. However tentative may be our assessments of the meanings of the book in its present form, at least we are dealing with a piece of literature that has actual existence; studies of origins, influences, authorship, date, and purpose, on the other hand, no matter how technically accomplished, must be to a large extent necessarily speculative.

A. THE BOOK OF JOB IN ITS PRESENT FORM

1. SHAPE

We cannot begin to comprehend the Book of Job piecemeal, beginning at the first verse or opening the book at random. What we need to do, with this book more than many others, is to start by identifying and becoming familiar with its shape.

The shape of a book, as of anything, is not an intrinsic property of the object itself, but a design in the mind of the observer. Without any arbitrariness, different readers of the book may discern different shapes in it, esteeming and highlighting this part or that part in varying degrees. Even the one reader may see more than one way of grasping the overall shape of the work. Here are three ways of seeing shape in the Book of Job.

a. Framework and Core

We may distinguish between the *framework* of the book and its *core* or *center*, using the image of a painting surrounded by a frame. The book itself suggests this view of its shape through its use of *prose* and *poetry*. The *framework* of the book is *prose*, the *core* is *poetry*; and since the framework is naive (or so it seems) and the core is sophisticated, the distinction between the relatively cheap and unimportant frame of a painting and the painting itself sounds a convincing analogy. We can also distinguish framework from core by noticing that the *framework* of Job is *narrative* and the *core* is *didactic poetry*. The book as a whole is thus both a *narrative* and an *argument,* or, perhaps more precise, an *argument* set within the context of a *narrative.* We may represent it diagrammatically as follows:

1:1–2:13	Framework:	prose	narrative
3:1–42:6	Core:	poetry	argument
42:7–17	Framework:	prose	narrative

b. Exposition, Complication, Resolution

A somewhat different shape emerges if we pay more close attention to the narrative thread that runs throughout the book. The analysis of shape given above, though valid in general, ignored the fact that there is a certain amount of prose narrative within the poetry, and it paid little attention to the *content* of the narrative. If we now emphasize the narrative elements, noting especially the marks of closure embedded in the narrative, we may discern an alternative structure.

The narrative of the Book of Job begins with God afflicting Job in order to discover whether Job's piety depends only upon his prosperity; will Job still loyally worship God if God deprives Job of all his possessions? By 2:10 we find that Job is unshakable in his piety. "In all this, Job did not sin with his lips," says the narrator. So, to all appearances, the story is over; no further development of the plot is required by the story, and we have reached a point of closure.

The narrative continues, nevertheless. We soon learn that Job *feels* more than he has *said,* and we soon find him "curs[ing] the day of his birth" (3:1). This more aggressive behavior of Job will continue for many chapters, with Job demanding that God cease his unreasonable treatment of him. Thereafter Job challenges God to a lawsuit, that is, to justify his actions legally. When he has finally delivered his challenge, and his oath that he is innocent of any cause for which God could be punishing him, we reach a second point of closure, the narrator's sentence, "The words of Job are ended" (31:40).

In the third segment of the book, a fourth friend, Elihu, lectures Job in speeches to which Job has no opportunity to reply before a dramatic turn is taken in the narrative: God himself responds to Job—not by answering Job's challenge, but by issuing a challenge of his own to Job. What right has Job to dictate how the universe should be run? Job admits in the end that he has no right to question God's actions, and he withdraws his case against God (42:3). God shows he is free either to afflict or to bless by showering Job with wealth and extending his life. The final point of closure comes with Job's death, "an old man, and full of days" (42:17).

These three segments of the book, which we have identified from the story line and from the marks of closure, may now be analyzed as the three basic elements that are to be found in every story: exposition, complication, resolution. In the *exposition* the scene is set, the characters are introduced, and all the necessary conditions for the plot are established. In the *complication,* the characters encounter difficulties or dangers, and tensions emerge that excite the reader's curiosity as to how they can possibly be resolved. The *resolution* portrays how the narrative problem posed by the story is solved.

The three segments are further distinguished from one another by another device of the narrative: new characters are introduced at the beginnings of each of the segments. In the first it is Job (1:1–3); in the second it is the three friends who come to commiserate with Job (2:11–13); in the third it is the fourth friend Elihu, who is angered by the speeches of the other friends (32:1–5), and more especially God himself, who enters the scene in 38:1.

The shape of the book from these perspectives can now be displayed diagrammatically:

1:1–2:10	God afflicts Job	exposition	new character: Job
2:11–31:40	Job challenges God	complication	new characters: 3 friends
32:1–42:17	God challenges Job	resolution	new characters: Elihu, God

c. Prologue, Dialogue, Epilogue

Yet another way of viewing the shape of the book follows the indications given by the book itself about the speakers. The whole book may be seen as a series of *speeches,* the *narrator* speaking in prologue and epilogue, and the *characters* in the dialogue. Thus:

I Prologue (1:1–2:13)
    Narrator
II Dialogue (3:1–42:6)
    1   Job and the three friends, First Cycle
            Job (3:1–26)
                Eliphaz (4:1–5:27)
            Job (6:1–7:21)
                Bildad (8:1–22)
            Job (9:1–10:22)
                Zophar (11:1–20)
    2   Job and the three friends, Second Cycle
            Job (12:1–14:22)
                Eliphaz (15:1–35)

		Job (16:1–17:16)
		Bildad (18:1–21)
		Job (19:1–29)
		Zophar (20:1–29)
3		Job and the three friends, Third Cycle
		Job (21:1–34)
		Eliphaz (22:1–30)
		Job (23:1–24:25)
		Bildad (25:1–6)
		Job (26:1–14)
		Job (27:1–28:28)
		Job (29:1–31:40)
4	Elihu	
		Elihu (32:1–33:33)
		Elihu (34:1–37)
		Elihu (35:1–16)
		Elihu (36:1–37:24)
5	Yahweh and Job	
		Yahweh (38:1–40:2)
		Job (40:3–5)
		Yahweh (40:6–41:34)
		Job (42:1–6)

    III Epilogue (42:7–17)
        Narrator

This analysis alerts us to different realities in the book. First, the narrator's words enclose those of all the characters, at first predisposing the reader to certain views of how all of the speakers in the dialogue are to be heard, and at the end leaving the narrator's perspective uppermost in the reader's mind. Second, it is Job who for the most part initiates conversation; he speaks and the friends reply to him. Indeed, after Bildad's third speech the friends do not speak again, but Job speaks three times without any intervention by them, as if they have faltered and he has gained new energy. Elihu speaks four times, without receiving any reply from Job, as if Job is no longer listening; is he waiting for someone else to speak? When Yahweh speaks, it is he and not Job who takes the initiative; though Job has summoned Yahweh to speak, Yahweh's speeches are less a reply than a new approach. Third, all the speaking moves toward silence: Job, who has done most of the talking, in the end lays his hand on his mouth (40:4–5); the friends run out of steam and do not even finish the third cycle of speeches. The question has to be raised: what has all this talk achieved? Is the real resolution to the problem of the book a verbal one at all, or is it perhaps only a resolution when Yahweh too stops speaking and actually does something about Job's suffering by "restor[ing] the Job's condition" (42:10)?

2. ARGUMENT

We have distinguished between the narrative of the framework of Job and the argument of the poetry that forms the core of the book. But this distinction is not wholly valid. For we have been able to speak of the narrative of the book as a whole, that is, of a narrative that does not only *frame* the book, but which runs *through* it. And we can now speak of the argument not just of the *speeches* in which the characters are obviously arguing with one another, but of *the book as a whole*, narrative and speeches included.

What is "the argument" of the book? It is the view the book takes of the principal issue it is addressing. We may either suppose, with most readers of the Book of Job, that the major question in it is the problem of suffering. Or we may suggest that the chief issue is the problem of the moral order of the world, of the principles on which it is governed. Each of these issues will provide us with a different perspective from which to consider the book.

a. The Problem of Suffering

To understand the book well, it is first of all important to know what exactly *is* the problem of suffering according to the book.

Many think that the essential question about suffering is, *Why* suffering? That is to say, What is its origin and cause, or, more personally, Why has this suffering happened to me? These are serious questions, but the Book of Job gives no satisfactory answer to them. It is true that this question about the origin or cause of suffering is ventilated in the book, and partial answers to it are given by the friends. They say that suffering comes about sometimes as punishment for sins, sometimes as a warning against committing sin in the future, and sometimes, as in Job's case, for no earthly reason at all, but for some inscrutable divine reason. In the end, however, readers cannot discover from the book any one clear view about what the reason for their own particular suffering may be, nor any statement about the reason for human suffering in general; for the book is entirely about the suffering of one particular and unique individual.

A second problem about suffering is whether there is such a thing as *innocent* suffering. The intellectual background of the book is obviously one in which cut-and-dried theologies of guilt and punishment have prevailed; for all the friends of Job, in their different ways, insist that if Job is suffering he must in some way be deserving of his suffering. It is still today a natural human tendency to ask, when one is suffering, What have I done to deserve this? The Book of Job, while of course it does not deny the possibility that sometimes suffering is richly deserved by the sufferer, speaks out clearly against the idea that such is always the case. Job is an innocent sufferer, whose innocence is not only asserted by himself (6:30; 9:15), but is attested to by the narrator (1:1), and above all by God (1:8; 2:3; 42:7–8). Nevertheless, even this question about the possibility of innocent suffering and the answer to it given by the book are not the primary issue in the book's concern with suffering.

The third, and essential, problem of suffering in the Book of Job may be said to be a more existential one, namely: In what way am I supposed to suffer? Or, What am I to do when I am suffering? To such questions the book gives two different but complementary answers. The first is expressed in the opening two chapters. Here Job's reaction to the disasters that come upon him is a calm acceptance of the will of God; he can bless God not only for what he has given but also for what he has taken away (1:21; 2:10). Sufferers who can identify with Job's acceptance of his suffering, neither ignoring the reality of suffering by escaping into the past, nor so preoccupied with present grief as to ignore past blessing, are fortunate indeed. The patient Job of the prologue is a model for sufferers. But Job does not remain in that attitude of acceptance. Once we move into his poetic speeches, from chap. 3 onward, we encounter a mind in turmoil, a sense of bitterness and anger, of isolation from God and even persecution by God. Job makes no attempt to suppress his hostility toward God for what has happened to him; he insists that he will "speak in the anguish of [his] spirit" and "complain in the bitterness of [his] soul" (7:11). What makes this protesting Job a model for other sufferers is that he directs himself constantly toward God, whom he regards as the one who is responsible, both immediately and ultimately, for his suffering. It is only because Job insists on response from God that God enters into dialogue with Job. Even though Job's intellectual questions about the justice of his suffering are never adequately answered, he himself in the end is satisfied, as a sufferer, by his encounter with God.

Viewed as an answer to the problem of suffering, then, the argument of the Book of Job is: By all means let Job the patient be your model so long as that is possible for you; but when equanimity fails, let the grief and anger of Job the impatient direct itself and yourself toward God, for only in encounter with him will be the tension of suffering be resolved.

b. The Moral Order of the World

Another way of stating the argument of the book is to see it as addressing the question whether there is any moral order in the world; that is to say, whether there is any rule whereby goodness is rewarded and wickedness is punished. The belief that there is an exact correspondence between one's behavior and one's destiny is known as the doctrine of retribution. In one form or another it is shared by most human beings, not just religious people, since it is the foundation of most people's childhood upbringing: certain behavior will earn you rewards, while certain other behavior will bring pain or disaster. There is indeed a mismatch between this principle, which we seem to require in some form or other for the world to have coherence, and the realities that contradict the principle; and to this mismatch both the narrator and the characters of the Book of Job turn their attention. Each of them has a distinctive standpoint on this question of retribution or the moral order.

(1) Narrator. The narrator in fact founds the whole story upon the doctrine of retribution. Job, the wealthiest of all orientals, is equally the most pious; there is no coincidence here, the narrator means to say. "That man was blameless and upright, fearing God and turning away from evil" (1:1)—that is deed. And here is consequence: "And there were born to him seven sons and three daughters [the perfect family], and he had 7,000 sheep, 3,000 camels," and so on (1:2). Here in the first two sentences of the book we find spelled out the doctrine of retribution, wearing its more acceptable face: piety brings prosperity. Into that prosperity there then breaks on one day the most terrible of calamities: Job loses all he has—which is not only his children and his wealth, but worse than that, his social significance and, worse still, his reputation as a righteous man. For the other, and more unlovely, side of this principle of world order is that suffering is caused by sin.

Up to this moment Job himself has believed in retribution, but now, unshakably convinced that he has done nothing to deserve his misery, he is launched on a quest for another moral order. The doctrine has failed the test of reality—reality, that is, as he experiences it. Job's three friends, too, find their dogma challenged by Job's experience, for they have always taken Job at face value, as a pious man. After all, he is a conspicuous testimony to the validity of the dogma: his exceptional piety has brought about his exceptional wealth, has it not? It does not take them long, however, to decide against Job and in favor of the dogma, though they each restate it differently.

What the friends have in common is their unquestioning belief that suffering is the result of sin. Their doctrine of retribution, that sin produces punishment, is also reversible: see a man suffering and you can be sure he has deserved it. There is no doubt in their minds of the order: Job's misery is by the book. But there is room for difference of opinion over what precisely Job's sufferings signify.

(2) Eliphaz. Eliphaz, the first friend, starts from the assumption that the innocent never suffer permanently: "What innocent man ever perished, where were the upright ever annihilated?" (4:7). For him Job is essentially one of the innocent, so whatever wrong Job has done must be comparatively trivial, and so too his suffering is bound to be soon over:

> Is not your piety your source of confidence?
> Does not your blameless life give you hope? (4:6)

he asks. Job is blameless on the whole, pious in general. Eliphaz's search for order leads him to nuance in this way the concept of innocence; that is how he can explain the mismatch between theory and experience. Even the most innocent of humans, like Job, must expect to suffer deservedly on occasion.

(3) Bildad. The second friend, Bildad, is if anything even more convinced of the doctrine of retribution, for he has just now seen a compelling exemplification of it. Job's children have died, cut off in their prime; it is the classical picture of the fate of the wicked:

> Your sons sinned against him,
> so he has abandoned them to the power of their guilt. (8:4)

The very fact that Job still lives is proof that he is no gross sinner, like his children. However serious his suffering, it is not as bad as it might be; therefore his sin is not as serious as he may fear.

(4) Zophar. Now whereas Eliphaz has set Job's suffering in the context of his whole life (his suffering is just a temporary pinprick), and Bildad has set it in the context of the fate of his family (the children are dead, Job is not), Zophar, the third friend, perceives no such context for Job's pain. The fact is, he would say, that Job is suffering, and suffering is inevitably the product of sin. To contextualize Job's suffering and try to set it in proportion is ultimately to trivialize it. Zophar is for principle rather than proportion; the bottom line is that Job is a sinner suffering hard at this moment for his sin.

Since Job refuses to acknowledge his sin, claiming,

> . . . My doctrine is pure,
>   I am clean in your sight, [O God]. (11:4)

it follows that he is a secret sinner. In fact, if only the truth were known, it would no doubt transpire that Job is a worse sinner than anyone suspects:

> If only God would speak,
>   if only he would open his lips to you,
> if only he would tell you the secrets of his wisdom . . .
>   you would know that God exacts of you
>   less than your guilt deserves. (11:5–6)

For all his talk about divine secrets, "higher than heaven—what can you do? deeper than Sheol—what can you know?" (11:8), Zophar holds a theology of the essential knowability of God. God's wisdom is not of a different kind from human wisdom; it only means that he knows more about humankind than anyone realizes, and that means more about their sins. Where there is suffering but no visible reason, we can be sure, says Zophar, that God's wisdom holds the reason. What is more, it will not be some mysterious, ineffable, transcendental reason, but a reason that could easily be comprehended by a human being "if only God would open his lips." So while we cannot always be sure why God is punishing people, we can be sure that when they are suffering he is punishing them for some reason or another, never without cause or gratuitously.

Zophar has in addition a more distinctive contribution to make: it concerns the role of God's mercy in the outworking of the principle of retribution. Job might be tempted to think that even though there is doubtless no escape from the working of the law of retribution, perhaps he could appeal for mercy to soften its blows. But what you must know, says Zophar, is that "God has already overlooked part of your sin" (11:6). Any mercy that God is going to allow to temper justice has already been taken into account when the law of retribution comes into play. Discounts for mercy's sake are included in the price you pay.

(5) *Elihu.* Another participant in the dialogue enters only after the first three friends have completed all they have to say. Elihu, the young man, at first "timid and afraid to declare [his] opinion" (32:6), in the end intervenes, realizing that "it is not the old that are wise" but rather "it is the spirit in a man, the breath of the Almighty, that makes him understand" (32:8–9). His point about retribution is that it is not some balancing mechanism in the universe that operates ruthlessly and inescapably, but rather is a channel by which God speaks to humans. Suffering is not so much a mystery; it is more a revelation.

Sometimes, for example, God speaks in visions of the night, in terrifying nightmares, to warn people against committing sins they are contemplating. At other times, a person may be

> . . . chastened with pain upon his bed
>   and with continual strife in his bones. (33:19)

like Job. The purpose of such suffering is not retribution, but to lead to confession by the sinner, one's restoration by God, and one's public praise of God (33:27). The other friends, and Job, have been narrow-minded in their view of retribution as a tit-for-tat process. Look to its design, says Elihu, and you will find that it is an instrument of divine communication.

For these four theologians, the retribution principle stands unshaken by Job's experience. Eliphaz has allowed a redefinition of "innocent" to mean "well, hardly ever wicked," Bildad has stressed that the law of retribution has a certain sensitivity (if you are not extremely wicked, you don't actually die), while Zophar has declared that the principle of retribution is not at all a rigorous quid pro quo, for a percentage of the punishment that should light upon you has already been deducted for mercy's sake. Even Elihu, while recognizing that there are more important theological truths than strict retribution, still affirms its validity.

(6) Job. By contrast with the friends' singleminded and static positions, Job's mind is confused, flexible, and experimental. In every one of his eleven speeches he adopts a different posture, psychologically and theologically. In the end he admits that he has nothing to rely upon, not even God—nothing except his conviction of his own innocence.

His first religious instinct is to accept what has happened to him as God's doing, and to bless God even for calamity: "Yahweh has given, and Yahweh has taken away; blessed be Yahweh's name" (1:21; cf. 2:10). But his second thoughts are more reflective and theological, because he realizes that order has collapsed about him. When in chap. 3 he wishes he had never been born, it is not mainly because he is suffering from his physical illness and from the grief of bereavement; he is expressing a psychic reaction to disorder. Since it is too late now to strike his birthdate out of the calendar—which is the first thought that occurs to him (3:6)—in his second speech he cries out for God to kill him and so put an end to his disorientation:

> O that it would please God to crush me,
> that he would let loose his hand and cut me off! (6:8)

When nothing makes sense any longer, and especially when the most fundamental moral order of all—the principle of retribution—is subverted, and disproportion reigns, there is nothing to live for:

> Am I the sea, or a sea-monster? . . .
> I loathe my life, I would live no longer. (7:12, 16)

Even so, to have nothing to live for, and to live without order, does not mean for Job that he can have no desire. In his third speech he openly desires what he lacks: a declaration that he is innocent. It is a desire impossible of fulfillment, but it his desire all the same.

> How can a man be declared innocent by God?
> If one took him to court [to prove one's innocence]
> one could not answer one in a thousand of his questions. (9:2–3)

The problem with God is not just that he is superwise and superpowerful (9:19); it is rather that he is by settled design hostile to his creation. As Job puts it, sardonically: "Being God, he never withdraws his anger" (9:13). The ancient myths were right, thinks Job, when they recounted that the first thing God ever did was to create the world by slaying the chaos monster, in a primeval act of aggression (9:13). Not only toward creation at large but toward Job in particular God's attitude has been, since Job's conception, one of perpetual hostility and cruelty, masked indeed by an apparent tender concern:

> Your hands fashioned and made me;
>> and now you turn about to destroy me. (9:8)

It is hopeless to seek vindication, he says; so he will not do it. But in the very act of saying to God, "It is hopeless to ask you for what I deserve," Job is in reality demanding what he believes he is entitled to.

Something has happened to Job in expressing his hopelessness. For in his next speech (chaps. 12–14) he has moved to a decision: nevertheless, I will present my case to God.

> No doubt he will slay me; I have no hope;
>> yet I will defend my ways to his face. (13:15)

His decision is more startling than that, however. He cannot *defend* himself against the pain which God is inflicting on him; he can only defend himself *verbally*. But since God is not *saying* anything, Job can only defend himself verbally by creating a scenario where both he and God are obliged to speak, each in his own defense. In short, Job summons God to a lawsuit! He challenges God to give an account of himself—to explain what Job has done wrong to deserve such suffering. But of course since Job believes he has done nothing wrong, implicitly he challenges God to confess that he and not Job is the criminal.

This is a case that must be heard promptly, for Job does not believe he can have much longer to live, considering how God is buffeting him. If Job's name is not cleared now it never will be, and certainly not in any afterlife.

> For a tree there is hope,
>> that if it is cut down it will sprout again,
>> that its fresh shoots will not fail.
> Though its root grows old in the ground
>> and its stump begins to die in the dust,
> yet at the scent of water it may bud
>> and put forth shoots like a plant new set.
>
> But a man, when he dies, loses every power;
>> he breathes his last, and where is he then?
> Like the water that has gone from a vanished lake,

> like a stream that has shrunk and dried up,
> Man lies down and will not rise again,
>> till the heavens are no more he will not awake,
>> nor be roused out of his sleep. (14:7–12)

What is now certain, in all the uncertainty that surrounds him, is that his word of challenge to God has been uttered—and cannot be unsaid. It is written into the heavenly record, and stands as his witness to himself in heaven. It is his own assertion of his innocence that he is referring to when he says in his fifth speech (chaps. 16–17):

> Even now, my witness is in heaven,
>> my advocate is on high.
> It is my cry that is my spokesman;
>> sleeplessly I wait for God's reply. (16:19–20)

And it is the same affirmation of innocence that in his sixth speech (chap. 19) he speaks of as his "advocate":

> I know that my advocate lives. (19:25)

He has in mind here no heavenly figure who will defend his cause before God, since there is none—and least of all God himself, who has proved to be nothing but his enemy. He is compelled to undertake his own defense, and leave his own affidavit to speak in his behalf.

The climax to Job's defense of his own innocence and his demand upon God that he explain for what reason he has been tormenting Job comes in the last of Job's speeches (chaps. 29–31). Here Job reviews his past life in a final attempt to discover whether there can be any cause in himself for the suffering he has been enduring. Whatever area of his life he considers, he can judge himself blameless. He brings his speeches to a conclusion with a mighty oath affirming his righteousness. Still working within the metaphorical scenario of the lawsuit, he imagines himself signing a declaration:

> Here is my signature [to my oath of exculpation];
>> let the Almighty answer me!
> Oh, that I had the bill of indictment written by my adversary! (31:35)

So brief would any bill of charges against Job be, and so trivial would be the faults that could be leveled against him, that Job would be proud for all the world to see how little he had offended against God and how greatly he had fulfilled the ideal of human piety:

> Surely I would carry [the indictment] on my shoulder;
>> I would bind it on me as a crown.
> I would give him an account of all my steps.
>> Like a prince I would approach him! (31:36–37)

Job's impressive and convincing protestation of innocence poses a desperate problem for the moral order of the universe, however. For if Job is innocent, the doctrine of retribution is false. And there is no other principle available to replace it.

(7) *God*. Only God can address the problem. He is compelled, by Job's meta-

phor of the lawsuit and by the logic of the author's narrative, to enter the conversation. But what divine word can both defend Job's innocence—to which God committed himself in chap. 1—and at the same time affirm the working of a moral law in the world?

In reality, God's speeches (chaps. 38–41) are remarkable as much for what they omit as for what they contain. There is, in the first place, not a word of the retributive principle here. This must mean that it is not so fundamental to understanding the world as all the previous characters of the book have thought. But it must also mean that it is not entirely wrong, either. If God were passionately in favor of it or violently against it, would he not have had to mention it?

In the second place, the divine speeches are notorious for their insistence on asking questions rather than giving answers, quite apart from the seeming irrelevance of the questions themselves to the fundamental issues of the book.

> Where were you when I laid the foundation of the earth? . . .
> Have you entered into the springs of the sea? . . .
> Do you know when the mountain goats bring forth? . . .
> Is it by your wisdom that the hawk soars? (38:4, 16; 39:1, 26)

Those—and suchlike excursions into cosmology and natural history—are, amazingly enough, the substance of the divine speeches. The purpose of God's parade of unknown and unknowable features of the natural world can hardly be to browbeat Job with dazzling displays of his power and intelligence—for Job has not for a minute doubted that God is wise and strong, too wise and strong indeed for human comfort and for his own good. Rather, God invites Job to reconsider the mystery and complexity—and the often sheer unfathomableness—of the world that God has created.

God's questions to Job are arranged in three distinct sequences. First there is the series that focus on Job's nonparticipation in creation, such as: "Who shut in the sea with doors?" (38:8). These mean that Job is not qualified to hold views on the nature of the universe. Second, there is the series on the management of the world, among which we find:

> Have you ever in your life ordered the morning forth? . . .
> Can you bind the chains of the Pleiades
>   or loose the cords of Orion? (38:12, 31)

Job has never organized the appearance of a new day; how can he speak then about the governance of the universe? Third, there is the sequence of questions about the animals, lion and raven, goat and hind, wild ass, ostrich, war-horse, hawk and eagle. Through these questions Job's gaze is deliberately fastened upon animals that serve no purpose in the human economy but are, instead, useless to humans, their habits mysterious to us. In these chapters there is no mention of those domesticated animals, sheep, ass and camel, that Job possessed in abundance and knew the ways of. The subject here is wild animals, the purpose of whose existence is unintelligible to humans. By the end of the second divine speech (40:7–41:34) the focus has come to rest upon two animals, Behemoth and Leviathan, hippopotamus and crocodile, symbols of primeval chaos, who of all the animal creation are supremely wild and terrible.

The point must be that hippopotamus and crocodile, however alarming, are part of God's creation. God expects Job to realize, and Job is not slow at grasping the point, that the natural order—the principles on which the world was created—is analogous to the moral order—the principles according to which it is governed. In both these orders, there is much that is incomprehensible to humans, even threatening their existence, but all of it is the work of a wise God who has made the world the way it is for his own inscrutable purposes. Innocent suffering is a hippopotamus. The only sense it makes, it makes to God, for it is not amenable to human rationality.

Job has no right to an explanation for his suffering, any more than he has a right to have the purpose of crocodiles explained to him. He is not even entitled to be told whether he is being punished for some fault he has committed, or whether he is indeed the innocent sufferer he believes himself to be. The order of creation sets the standard for the moral order of the universe; and that is, that God must be allowed to know what he is doing, and lies under no obligation to give any account of himself.

What does this viewpoint expressed by the character God do to the doctrine of retribution? It neither affirms nor denies it; but it marginalizes it. In Job's case, at least, the doctrine of retribution is beside the point. We, the readers, have known from the beginning of the book that Job is innocent, for the narrator and God have both affirmed it (1:1, 8; 2:3); Job himself, though suffering as if he were a wicked man, is unshakably convinced of his innocence. We and Job, therefore, know that the doctrine of retribution is not wholly true. But God never tells Job that he accepts Job's innocence; so Job never learns what God's view of the doctrine is. All that Job learns from God is that retribution is not the issue, but whether God can be trusted to run his world.

Job capitulates. His religious instinct for reverence which prompted his initial acceptance of his misfortune (1:21; 2:10) had become overwhelmed by his more intellectual and theological search for meaning. But now his religion and his theology are suddenly able to cohere. He replies to God:

> "Who is this that darkens the [divine] design by words
>   without knowledge?" [so you have rightly said, Yahweh].
> You are right: I misspoke myself, I was beyond my limits. . . .
> I had heard of you by the hearing of the ear
>   but now my eye sees you. . . . (42:3, 5)

Which means to say: I knew you, but did not know you; what I knew of your workings (through the principle of retribution) was real knowledge, but it was not the whole truth about you. The whole truth is that you are ultimately unknowable, and your reasons are in the last analysis incomprehensible.

> Therefore I melt in reverence before you,
> and I have received my comfort,
>   even while sitting in dust and ashes. (42:6)

Religiously, Job finds this position acceptable, even actually comforting: to bow in awe before a mysterious God he cannot grasp, perceiving only the "outskirts of his ways" (26:14). This is the Job of the prologue, but with a difference: the religious instinct is now supported by a theological realignment. Now he not only feels, but also has come to believe, that it makes sense that God should not be wholly amenable to human reason. It was the theology of wild animals that convinced him, the inexplicability of whole tracts of the natural order, the apparent meaninglessness of creatures useless to humankind but unquestionably created by God nevertheless. Now he knows that was a paradigm for all knowledge of God.

(8) Narrator. The book does not conclude at this point, however. The narrator has yet to tell us of the reversal of Job's fortunes. There is more to this happy ending of the book than at first appears, for the issues of the moral governance of the world and the doctrine of retribution are still on the agenda. What this concluding episode does for these issues is, surprisingly, to reinstate the dogma of retribution as the principle according to which the world operates. For the story shows at its end that the righteous man Job is also the most prosperous, just as he was at the beginning. Job is here described as the "servant" of the Lord, who has spoken of God "what is right," unlike the friends (42:7–8), and when he has prayed for forgiveness of the friends' "folly" he is rewarded with twice the possessions he had at first (42:10).

It must be admitted that the ending of the book undercuts to some extent the divine speeches of chaps. 38–41. For although the Lord has implied that questions of justice and retribution are not the central ones, the narrator's concluding word is that after all the principle of retribution stands almost unscathed by the experience of Job. By rights, according to the principle, the innocent Job should never have suffered at all; so the principle was partially defective. Yet in the end the principle becomes enshrined in the history of Job, and he functions as a prime witness to its general validity. Even if in every instance it does not explain human fates, in the main it is affirmed by the Book of Job as the truth about the moral universe.

3. READINGS

All readers of biblical texts, as of any other texts, bring their own interests, prejudices, and presuppositions with them. While they would be wrong to insist that the Bible should say what they want it to say, they would be equally wrong to think that it does not matter, in reading the Bible, what they themselves already believe. For the combination of the reader's own interests, values, and commitments is what makes him or her a person with identity and integrity; in no activity of life, and certainly not in reading the Bible, can one hide or abandon one's values without doing violence to one's own integrity. If one is, for example, a feminist pacifist vegetarian—which are quite serious things to be, even if they are modish—it will be important to oneself to ask what the text has to say, or fails to say, about these issues; one will recognize that the text may have little concern with such matters, but if they are a serious concern to the reader they may be legitimately put on the agenda for interpretation, that is, the mutual activity that goes on between text and reader.

What usually happens, when we bring *our* questions to the text instead of insisting always that the text set the agenda, is that the text is illuminated in unpredictable ways. This means that one does not need to be a feminist or a Christian, for example, to find readings from these perspectives interesting. The more readings, the more stereoscopic our picture of the Book of Job.

a. A Feminist Reading

A feminist reading of any text, biblical or otherwise, begins from the premise that in the history of civilization women have been regarded as inferior to men and have been excluded from positions of public influence. Assuming that we are right to reject these historic attitudes, we are now in a position to examine what effect the suppression of women has had upon literature, to what extent literature has abetted their subjection or to what extent it contains materials subversive of a social order that has been unjust to women. Biblical texts come of course from male-dominated societies and reflect male interests; for a feminist reading it is interesting to focus on both the presence of women where they do occur in texts, and on their absence from texts where we would have expected them to occur.

The feminist reader of Job notes first that in this great work of literature all the five principal characters (including God!) are male. The book, not surprisingly, thus subserves the outlook of an unthinkingly male-oriented culture that weighty matters of intellectual and theological inquiry are the preserve of males, and that women have no place in such discussions. The outstanding stature of the Book of Job among world literature only reinforces the influence of its view of women.

The role of the one woman character in the Book of Job fits exactly with the overall pattern. Job's wife functions in the narrative almost entirely as a foil to the male friends. Whereas they deliver themselves of formal, rationally argued speeches, she bursts out emotionally with a question and an imperative: "Do you still hold fast your integrity? Curse God and die" (2:9). The last time we have heard such words is on the lips of the Satan, who predicted to God that when Job lost his possessions he would indeed "curse you to your face" (1:11); at least an impression is given that she stands over against Job in much the same way as the Satan stands over against God. Is it not worse, however, that anyone should encourage another to "curse" God; and what can she be thinking of that she incites her husband to a course of action that can only result in his death? It is little wonder that Job's wife has often been seen as a counterpart to Eve, the ancestral "temptress." Job himself responds to her with a statement of his piety, which the narrator certifies to be valid: "In all this Job did not sin with his lips" (2:10). Job is calm, reasonable, and praiseworthily mild-mannered in his reproof of his wife; he does not reject her invitation to curse God for the blasphemy it is, but merely invokes her sense of dignity as he comments upon her suggestion as words like those of "the foolish women," whoever they are. She is put in her place again with an unanswerable rhetorical question: "If we receive good at the hand of God, should we not also accept harm?" (2:10).

This is not all that may be said about her intervention, however. If in the second half of her speech she echoes the Satan's words, in the first half she uses God's: her husband Job is "hold[ing] fast his integrity" (cf. 2:3). It is not clear whether she is casting doubt on the reality of Job's claim to integrity, but she obviously questions the wisdom of maintaining it when the evidence of the great disasters that have befallen them is that God accounts Job a most dreadful sinner. Since she, Job himself and all the friends have been uncritical believers in the doctrine of retribution, it is nothing strange if she too should draw the obvious conclusions from recent events.

A feminist approach alerts us to a further aspect of her attitude also. Though the androcentric narrator has excluded her from parts of the narrative where she rightly belongs, as when he notes that "there were born to [Job] seven sons and three daughters" (1:2)—as though such were possible in her absence—by introducing her at all, even as a minor character, he opens the way to our rereading the whole of the narrative from her perspective. From her point of view, it must be said, despite her husband's somewhat excessive scrupulosity, rising early in the morning after his children's birthday feasts to offer sacrifices in case any of them had inadvertently blasphemed God (1:5), the net result of his way of life has been that she has now been robbed of her ten children, of her income, of her social standing, and must for the foreseeable future live with a husband afflicted with "loathsome sores" all over his body (2:7). At the moment that she speaks, no one is disputing—not even Job—that he is to blame for the calamities that have befallen the homestead. God has sent the harm, but the husband has incurred it. Job's wife has therefore, to the best of her knowledge, been terribly wronged by her husband, but must go on maintaining her loyalty to him despite the guilt by association that now attaches to her. And although the family income has been reduced to zero, she is not exempted from the responsibility of managing her household and providing hospitality for leisured friends of her husband who come to "console" him—but ignore her and her quite comparable degree of suffering (2:11–12). Her only hope of release from a life of penury and disgrace is the death of her husband and a return to the security of her parents' family.

Job's wife is not again explicitly mentioned in the book—which has led many nonfeminist readers to suppose that she has been marginalized on the ground of her misguided intervention in chap. 2. Yet her presence is indispensable in the narrative of the restoration of Job's fortunes in chap. 42. There he acquires a new family of seven sons and three daughters, and not—we must assume, though the narrator does not mention it—without the cooperation of his wife (there are no other wives or concubines in the story). We may therefore speak of the reconciliation of Job and his wife, and of her intellectual development, no less necessary than her husband's, from a blind faith in the doctrine of retribution to an acceptance of the possibility of innocent suffering.

There are several other points in the book which will catch the attention of the feminist reader. For example, the picture of domestic felicity with which the book opens has the daughters of Job being regularly invited to birthday parties in the houses of their brothers, "to eat and drink with them" (1:4), a token of recognition of females by males not always encountered in the ancient world; it is noticeable, however, that the daughters do not have parties of their own to which they invite their brothers. The more impressive feminist notation of 42:15 that the second set of daughters inherited property "along with" their brothers (a unique occurrence in the narrative world of the Hebrew

Bible) is somewhat undercut by the immediately preceding remark that "in all the land there were no women so fair as Job's daughters"; it is implied, if not explicitly stated, that their inheritance is not because they are equally with their brothers the offspring of Job but principally because they are beauties.

The major feminist question, however, for the book is whether its principal concern is in any way a gender-determined one. If it is at all difficult to imagine an alternative version of the book in which all the protagonists were female and in which at the same time the principal issue arising from the loss of family, social standing and reputation was the doctrine of retribution and the justice of God, then to that extent the book, however sublime a literary work, may be defective, as yet another expression of an uncritical androcentricity.

b. A Vegetarian Reading

Like feminism, vegetarianism is an ideology that manifests itself in various attitudes and practices. A simple vegetarianism may avoid meat on purely aesthetic grounds, or even as a matter of taste or preference; but a more reasoned vegetarianism takes as its starting point the nature of animals as living beings, and develops a philosophy of the responsibility of humans to fellow inhabitants of the planet. Since it turns the everyday matter of diet into a set of ethical decisions, and tends to become associated with larger questions about human relationship with the environment generally, vegetarianism is for its adherents a powerful philosophy that influences many aspects of life, including reading. A vegetarian reader will be concerned to see whether the text under consideration uncritically adopts the attitudes of a carnivorous culture toward animals, or whether in any way the text undermines those attitudes by a more positive estimation of animals.

There are three places in the Book of Job where animals are significant. In the first, Job is depicted as the owner and guardian of large flocks of animals, 7,000 sheep, 3,000 camels, 500 yoke of oxen, and 500 she-asses (1:3). After the restoration of his fortunes he has exactly double the number in each category (42:12). His wealth is measured almost exclusively in terms of his animals; so, although the animals are obviously kept not for their own sakes but for reasons of the agricultural economy in which Job is engaged, Job has no arms-length relationship with the animals but is involved in a relationship of mutual dependence with them. The text invites us to view Job as the center of a network of relationships, his family of wife and children immediately surrounding him, his "very many servants" standing between him and the animals which they tend, and, on the periphery, these vast herds of animals. The catastrophe that befalls Job begins on the fringes of this network, oxen, asses, sheep, and camels progressively falling prey to disaster before his own children are struck down (1:14–19). Further, the purposes for which these animals are kept are equally instructive. The flocks (the term includes both sheep and goats) are kept for their wool and their milk; the oxen for plowing (they are enumerated as "pairs" or "yoke" of oxen); the camels for riding or for carrying loads; the she-asses for milk, for riding and for various kinds of farm work. There is no eating of meat or "flesh" in the narrative world of the book. That does not mean of course that the author is preaching or assuming vegetarianism, but that an affirmative attitude to animals sits comfortably with the outlook of the book.

Animals next appear in the narrative as the material of sacrifice. After every birthday celebration by his children Job offers "whole burnt offerings," whether of bulls, sheep, or goats, as a sin-offering. He fears that his children may in the excitement of their partying have inadvertently spoken lightly of God, and so makes the sacrifice that would have been required if they had in fact sinned (1:5). Corresponding with these animal sacrifices at the beginning of the book are the whole burnt offerings of seven bulls and seven rams at the end of the book which God commands Eliphaz to offer on behalf of himself and his two friends. The three friends have "not spoken of [God] what is right" and have thus acted "foolishly" (42:8); so they need to offer a sin-offering to atone for their wrongdoing. Unlike most other animal sacrifices, the sin-offering was wholly consumed by fire, and no part of it was eaten by the offerer. Symbolically it represented the transfer of property from the realm of humans to the realm of the divine, the burning of the slaughtered animal being the means of removing the material of the animal from the earth to the sky where the deity lived. The concept of animal sacrifice is of course aesthetically, if not also religiously, disagreeable to most people today, whether or not they are vegetarians, but at least we may allow that within the cultural codes of the book the animal is not being devalued by the practice but esteemed as a mechanism for communication between the earthly and heavenly worlds. The point of most interest, however, from a vegetarian perspective, is that the convention of animal sacrifice, which is taken for granted by the book, is also called into question by the book. For the net effect of Job's sacrifices on behalf of his children is zero; despite the sacrifices, they are cut off in their youth by a whirlwind, a clear sign in Job's eyes of God's displeasure. The question is therefore implicitly raised whether the sacrifices of the friends in chap. 42 has any more efficacy than Job's sacrifices in chap. 1, and whether perhaps it is Job's prayer on behalf of his friends (42:8, 10) rather than their sacrifices that ensures their forgiveness.

The third major reference to animals is the most important of all. In the divine speeches of chaps. 38–41, the existence of animals proves to be the essential clue to the meaning of the universe. It is not the domestic animals of chaps. 1–2 that are here spoken of, but the wild animals that serve no purpose in human economy. Their existence prohibits a wholly anthropocentric view of the world, and confirms to humans that the world does not exist solely for the benefit of humankind. In a sense, wild animals are even more valuable for humans than are domesticated animals; for while tamed animals may serve to magnify humans' sense of their own importance and mastery over their environment, wild animals serve to impress humans with the fundamental inexplicability of the world as it has been created. The significance of wild animals is even more pointed in the context of the divine speeches, however. For there they function as an analogy to the existence of equally inexplicable elements of the moral order of the world, namely the existence of innocent suffering and of evidence that the principle of retribution is not wholly valid. God has created the world the way it is for his own inscrutable purposes; we can only presume that *he* knows what he is doing, for there are many things in the world we experience that make no sense to *us*. In sum, in the view of the Book of Job a proper estimation of the animal creation is essential for coping with certain of the riddles of human existence. This is a far cry from an attitude that ignores animals except as food or as pets for humans.

c. A Materialist Reading

A materialist reading of a text typically has a double focus: the first is upon the material or the socioeconomic conditions that have produced it, especially the condition of opposed social classes that may be presumed for every society. The second is upon the material realities presupposed or supported by the narrative world of the text. The former consideration is of course a historical one, and depends to some extent upon the questions of the book's origin that will be discussed in the second section of this chapter.

If we make only the simple and uncontroversial assumptions that the society in which the book originated was composed of rich people and poor people, or that some groups in the society held power and others were relatively powerless, or that some persons lived from the profits on their capital and others from wages earned from their daily labor, we have established two socioeconomic groups in ancient Israel and thus two possible socioeconomic locations for the book. Whichever location we determine as the place of origin of the book will provide an important interpretive key for understanding, not so much the verbal meaning of the book, but its total significance.

Did the Book of Job originate among the wealthy? The fact that Job is a rich man is of course no proof that the book originated among the privileged classes, for poor people often tell stories about the rich. But the fact that he is wealthy *and* pious, indeed, the most wealthy *and* the most pious, suggests it strongly. For, from the perspective of the poor, it is in general hard to believe that the rich can deserve to be rich or can be both honest and rich. Equally, in the world of the rich it is assumed that the poor either are dishonest or else deserve to be poor; it is an interesting exception if it can be said, "She was poor *but* she was honest." Indeed, the very problem of the book—the truth of the doctrine of retribution—may be said to be a rich person's problem; the poor cannot afford to believe in the doctrine of retribution, because they know all too many examples of piety that does not lead to prosperity; the rich, on the other hand, are fearful that their reputation for piety may be as fragile as the prosperity which attests it.

Furthermore, if the scholarly consensus is accepted that the Book of Job forms part of the "Wisdom" literature of ancient Israel and that such literature arose in court circles or in the educational establishments that were attached either to the court or to the religious centers, then there are historical evidences for connecting the book with the powerful rather than with the powerless in society.

A materialist approach argues that literature is written, to a greater or lesser extent, to support the interests of the social class of its author. It makes a difference to our understanding of the Book of Job if we read it not just as a work of literary quality, nor simply as a debate among theologians, but as promoting the position of the privileged. In this reading, the book functions to support those of the wealthy classes who are temporarily impoverished or powerless, and to assure them that if they have once been in a position of privilege that remains their entitlement; at the same time it reassures those whose position is currently secure against any fear of calamity. The story of Job is after all one of a wealthy man who deserves his wealth, and who, although he loses it through no fault of his own, regains it in the end—twice over. If the readers are wealthy persons, they will be likely to believe that they deserve their wealth, and will identify with Job. If the readers are the poor and have never been wealthy they will find it difficult to identify with Job even in his poverty, not only because he once was wealthy and in that way more advantaged than the poor but because he is destined to become wealthy again—which is more than the poor in general can even hope for.

If we turn now to the second focus, the world of the text as distinct from the external world in which the text was produced, we can make some observations concerning the material realities supposed or promoted by the text. We first note that the text shows little awareness of the realities of poverty. The question is never raised how Job and his wife and his domestic servants survive now that their means of livelihood, the livestock, has been lost. There has been feasting in plenty in the days before disaster struck (1:4, 13, 18), and there will be again after the restoration of Job's wealth (42:11), but even in the period of Job's calamity no one goes hungry. We know well enough, though the author never alludes to the fact, that his visitors who sit with him for a week in silence (2:13) and thereafter engage in lengthy argument with him need feeding; so too do his clients, serving girls, personal manservant, and wife who are still dependent on him (19:15–17). When he contrasts his former privileged existence (chap. 29) with his present unhappy state (chap. 30), it is striking that his principal concern in both pictures is with his *status*, as though he is not suffering at all from erosion of his means of existence. He actually depicts at one point the group of the homeless poor, who "through want and hard hunger . . . gnaw the dry and desolate ground," collect brushwood to warm themselves and live in caves (30:3–7); but he does not identify with them, but rather insists—still striking the patronizing stance of the rich—on regarding them as "a senseless, disreputable brood" (30:8), and complains that even they are despising him. The overwhelming concern of the character Job with status rather than survival betrays a narrator (and, no doubt, behind the narrator, an author) who knows nothing of real poverty and therefore cannot envisage poverty as a moral criticism of wealth. Job's suffering, mental and physical, is "real" enough and is realistically portrayed; for rich people can suffer pain as deeply as poor people. But rich authors cannot truly imagine poverty, and the depiction of Job's poverty is as a consequence unrealistic and unconvincing by comparison with the depiction of his suffering.

Another point at which we may observe an interesting attitude to material reality in the world of the text is the narrative of Job's restoration. We learn in chap. 42 that after his time of poverty, Job regains all his wealth, or rather double his original wealth. If we ask how this comes about, which is a vital question for any who can identify with Job in his poverty, since they cannot help being interested in escaping from poverty, it is disappointing, but not entirely surprising, to learn that "the Lord restored the fortunes of Job . . . the Lord gave Job twice as much as he had before" (42:10). To the poor, this *can* of course mean that anyone can be made rich by God, but is more likely to mean: if you are poor, there is no way of ceasing to be poor, *short of a miracle.*

Since in general such miracles of divine enriching are thin on the ground, the story of Job means: even if you are Job, there is no way of clambering out of poverty, there is nothing you can do about it; the story knows of no mechanism by which Job's stolen oxen and dead sheep can be regained. It only serves to rub in the point when we go on to read in 42:11 that *after* God has restored Job's fortunes, that is, when he has acquired new herds of the cattle that constitute his wealth, he is visited by all his friends and relatives, who bring him a piece of money. To him that hath is given. But when he is in need, even wealthy acquaintances do not want to know. The narrator knows his class well, and takes for granted that no one backs a loser. There is not a lot of encouragement for losers here.

A final point at which a materialist perspective yields an important consequence for an interpretation of the book lies in the conclusion of the story of Job with the narrative of his material restoration. Many readers of the book have faulted it for the so-called naivety of its "happy ending"; after the penetrating intellectual argumentation and psychological depictions of the dialogue it seems to lower the tone of the book to return to an externalized description of the newfound wealth of the protagonist. Job has in 42:2–6 pronounced himself satisfied with God's answers; he has withdrawn his demand that God give an account of himself, and he declares himself "comforted" (so the second verb of 42:6 should probably be understood) even while still among dust and ashes. But for the narrator the story must not end, and justice will not be satisfied, until Job is lifted from his ash-heap and has restored to him the goods that he has been wrongfully deprived of. Translated into more ideological language, the plot implies that questions of divine justice and human suffering cannot be adequately answered at the intellectual level but demand affirmative action. Job requires not just the mental assurance that God knows what he is doing, but a public testimonial from God that, despite the evidence, Job is a righteous man. In a culture where a dogma of divine retribution is pervasive and where material prosperity has long been regarded as the most obvious sign of divine approval, Job must get his wealth back for his own sake and for God's. At this point the interests of rich and poor come nearest to coinciding; for neither group will allow that the possession of goods is a matter of no moral or religious importance, and each will argue that the divine justice cannot be fully and properly displayed when wealth among humans is unfairly distributed. The Book of Job is thus resistant to a purely existentialist or theological interpretation; the restoration of the hero's possessions is as needful as the divine speeches for the resolution of the book.

d. A Christian Reading

There have of course been many Christian readings of the Old Testament throughout the Christian centuries, most of them building on the assumption that the Old Testament conveys essentially the same teaching as the New Testament, but in a coded form. In traditional Christian interpretation of the Old Testament, for example, attention has often been focused on predictions or hints of a messiah, and even on texts that did not ostensibly speak of a messiah but could be read in reference to Christ. Job has been read typically as prefiguring the sufferings of Christ, or the tribulations of the church. And in medieval exegesis and iconography in particular the figure of Job was essentially a symbol of the Christian virtue of patience.

It is arguably a more appropriate Christian approach to the Old Testament to forswear an exclusively Christological reading, and to allow the Old and New Testaments to confront one another, with the possibility being entertained that they may be in conflict with one another over quite important matters. The legitimacy of a Christian reading will then be on a similar footing to that of a feminist or a materialist reading: such a reading represents the personal ideological position of many readers, and it takes their concerns seriously by asking how they impinge upon the reading of the text.

A Christian perspective on the Book of Job first attends to the very first sentence of the book, which depicts Job as "blameless and upright," the first of these epithets also being conventionally translated as "perfect." For a Christian reader such language, if meant literally and seriously, is inappropriate for any human being; Christian theology and culture takes for granted that no one is perfect and that even the best of people can never be wholly free of sin. This perspective is part of what has been called the "introspective conscience of the West," fueled by the Pauline convictions that "none is righteous, no, not one" and that "all have sinned" (Rom 3:10, 23). Jesus himself is said to have refused the description "good" of himself on the ground that "No one is good but God alone" (Luke 18:19 RSV). The point is not some trivial verbal one, for it is fundamental to the story of Job that Job should be a perfectly innocent person, who deserves nothing of what happens to him. If the reader believes that such a man has never existed, Job becomes for that reader not merely a nonhistorical figure but a quite fictive and unrealistic character whose experiences lie outside the realm of normal human experience. And the Book of Job is then about nothing at all.

Since no one wants to regard the Book of Job as a kind of science fiction, the Christian reader is obliged to qualify Job's righteousness as, not moral perfection, but an innocence that deserves better treatment than Job has meted out to him. Nevertheless, the Christian conscience remains unhappy at Job's total refusal to consider the possibility that he is in some way to blame for his misfortunes, and asks whether a person so unaware of his proclivities to sinfulness can properly be regarded as a righteous person at all. Is not Job something of a sinner in insisting so unselfconsciously that he has never sinned? In short, a Christian reading relativizes the terms in which the problem of the book is posed.

A second major point at which a Christian ideology runs somewhat counter to the book is that Job's quest for *meaning* differs from the essentially Christian quest for *salvation*. If the fundamental truth about the human condition is that people are sinners alienated from God, and in need of redemption from that state, Job's concern for order in God's governance of the universe is a quite secondary matter. If Job cannot see that human sinfulness, his own or others', must be the first item on his agenda, it may be argued, he has no right to be questioning the way the universe is being run. The book could then, from this supposedly "Christian" persepctive, be read as an extended account of Job's attempt to evade the real question about suffering, which is human responsibility for human suffering. On the other hand, a more charitable Christian reading could agree to differ with the program of the Book of

Job, and allow that the issue of guilt and responsibility, however primary it may be, is not the only issue, and that the question of theodicy may be legitimately raised. In some Christian traditions (such as the mystical), indeed, some value might even be allowed to Job's perception that the alienation of humankind and God is God's doing rather than humans'. But however one handles the cleavage between a Christian orientation and the orientation of the book, it becomes clear that a Christian perspective calls into question some unexamined tenets of the book and suggests its own distinctive evaluation of the significance of the book.

A Christian reading will not by any means always find itself in tension with the book, however. It will be particularly noticed by the Christian reader, for example, that the book, in dealing with the issue of innocent suffering, establishes an indispensable prerequisite for Christian theology. For if the Christian reader feels unhappy with the unself-critical Job, such a reader can only be delighted with the way the book breaks the causal nexus between sin and suffering. If Jesus is to be judged by the conventional doctrine of retribution—which the friends of Job uphold—he is the chiefest of sinners; it is only when the conception of innocent suffering propounded by the book as a whole can be invoked that any theological significance can be attributed to the death of Jesus. From a Christian perspective, moreover, the hints of a salvific quality to Job's suffering are doubly interesting: Job is able to pray for his friends, it appears, because of his experiences (42:8–9), and the restoration of his own fortunes is associated with, if not actually the consequence of, his intercession for the three friends (42:10).

A final point at which a Christian reading of Job is illuminating is over the issue of the rationale according to which God governs the world. A Christian perspective identifies this as the issue of the principles of the kingdom of God, which is the central theme in the preaching of Jesus. Although the character of the kingdom of God is in contemporary Christianity not a high profile issue, it is interesting to the reader of Job that the parables of Jesus are at pains to show that God's rule is not always amenable to human rationality. Although Jesus never wants to say that God acts unjustly, he does insist that the operation of the kingdom defies many of the rules of human justice: in the parable of the workers in the vineyard, for example, everyone is paid the same wage though some workers have worked much longer hours than others (Matt 20:1–16). In other parables, as in that of the self-producing grain (Mark 4:26–29), the growth of the kingdom is hidden and mysterious, just as in Job the principles of God's rule are secret from the world of humans. Jesus' conviction of the presence of the kingdom of God despite the appearances, and his call for faith in a partly unknowable and partly self-communicating God, resonate with the program of the Book of Job. A Christian perspective, in some ways alien to the Hebrew book, engages the reader in critical but associative thinking and opens up a new set of significances for the book.

B. THE BOOK OF JOB IN HISTORICAL PERSPECTIVE

Naturally, for the most complete understanding of any piece of literature, we need to consider all that may be known about its background, its author, and the circumstances of its composition. Unfortunately, in the case of the

Book of Job, there is little hard evidence of this kind, and we must rely largely
on intelligent speculation.

1. ORIGINS

Most scholars today would date the composition of the Book of Job to
some point between the seventh and the second centuries BCE, with the probability that a prose folktale of a pious sufferer existed long before the largely
poetic book itself was written.

The story of the Book of Job is set in the patriarchal era depicted in Genesis:
like Abraham, for example, Job's wealth consists of his animals and his servants
(1:3; 42:12; cf. Gen 12:16), and he himself as head of his family offers sacrifices
without the intervention of any priest (1:5; cf. Gen 15:9–10). Like the patriarchs
of Genesis, who live 175, 180, 147, and 100 years (Gen 25:7; 35:28; 47:28;
50:26), Job lives 140 years (42:16). But the narrator is clearly depicting an
archaic age and not writing of his own time.

In a search for the date of composition of the book, many have observed
that the theme of the suffering of the innocent is found also in Jeremiah and
in the poems of the Suffering Servant of the LORD in Second Isaiah, both of
these prophetic texts stemming from the sixth century. Some have thought
that the inexplicable suffering of Job may have been intended to be symbolic
of the suffering of the Jews in Babylonian exile in that century, and therefore
to have been composed at about that period. But the author has so convincingly
located his narrative in the patriarchal world that there are no clear contemporary allusions of any kind to the period contemporary with the author.

The earliest reference to Job outside the book is found in Ezek 14:14, 20,
where Job is mentioned along with Noah and Danel (probably not Daniel) as
an ancient hero. This sixth-century reference may well be, however, not to
the Book of Job but to a more ancient folktale; so no inference about the
date of the book can be drawn.

There can be little doubt that the author of the book was an Israelite. It is
true that Job's homeland is depicted as North Arabia or possibly Edom, and
in most of the book Job himself does not know God by the Israelite name
Yahweh. Nor does the book refer to any of the distinctive historical traditions
of the Hebrew people. But these facts only mean that the author has succeeded
well in disguising his own age and background in his creation of the character
of his hero.

2. THE HISTORY OF THE BOOK OF JOB

There are a number of indications in the book that it was not all written
at one time, but went through a history of composition. Some of the major
elements that have been thought earlier or later than the main body of the
book are the following.

a. The Prologue and Epilogue

Since the prologue (chaps. 1–2) and the epilogue (42:7–17) form a reasonably coherent prose narrative, and since there is some evidence that a folktale

about Job existed earlier than the composition of our Book of Job, it has often been argued that the prose framework of the book existed in writing for some time before the poetic speeches were composed. Some of the differences between the prose and the poetic sections of the book might be more easily explained, it has been thought, if we could attribute them to different authors. Thus, for example, Job is portrayed as a patient sufferer in the prologue, but as a vehement accuser of God in the dialogues; in the prologue (and epilogue) God is known by the name Yahweh, but not in the dialogues; and the cause of Job's misfortunes is recounted in the prologue but unknown in the dialogues.

All these differences between the prose and poetry of the book can be better explained, however, on literary grounds. Thus, it is dramatically satisfying that Job should change from his initial acceptance of his suffering to a violent questioning of it; and, since the friends of Job are not represented as Yahweh-worshipers, it is only natural that in the dialogues the name of Yahweh should be avoided; and it is of course not surprising that the dialogues should proceed in ignorance of the events in heaven which have brought about Job's misery, for if the ultimate cause had been known, there would have been no problem for the friends to discuss. Furthermore, it is improbable that the prose narratives ever formed an independent whole; for the narrative of the arrival of the three friends in 2:11–13 is plainly designed to preface the speeches, and Yahweh's closing address to the friends (42:7–8) makes no sense unless the friends had been speaking words for which God could reproach them. If they had merely sat in sympathetic silence with Job—which is all they do according to the prose narrative (2:13)—they would not have needed to offer sacrifices to atone for their foolish words (42:8). Even if these paragraphs of narrative should be regarded merely as editorial links between the prose and the poetry, it is hard to believe that any prose tale about Job could have moved directly from Job's patient acceptance of his suffering (2:10) to Yahweh's restoration of his fortunes (42:10) without some intervening events. It is therefore more probable that the author of the prologue and the epilogue is also the poet of the dialogues, and wrote the prose framework deliberately for its present place in the book. This is not to deny, of course, that the *story* of Job may be much older than the *book*.

b. The Speeches of Elihu

The great majority of critics regard the four speeches of Elihu (chaps. 32–37) as an addition to the book after its original composition. The main reason for this judgment is the absence of Elihu from both the prologue and the epilogue. While it might be replied that it could have been to the author's dramatic advantage to have a fresh interlocutor enter after the conversation of Job and his friends seems to have concluded (cf. 31:40 "The words of Job are ended"), it is hard to explain why Elihu should not be mentioned in the epilogue. The first three friends have spoken "folly" about God and Job has spoken "what is right" (42:7), but no judgment is made on the wisdom or otherwise of Elihu's speeches. It is strange also that although Elihu's speeches intervene between those of Job and of God, God makes no allusion to Elihu when he replies to Job. The evidence that the Elihu speeches are secondary is quite strong, but it is nevertheless something of a difficulty to understand how an author wishing to expand the Book of Job would have inserted Elihu's speeches as chaps. 32–37 but failed to insert Elihu's name in chap. 42. Whatever the origin of the Elihu material, the interpreter of the book must of course come to terms with the shape of the book as we have received it, and must, if at all possible, explain the significance of Elihu's intervention (see the comments above under Argument).

c. The Poem on Wisdom

The poem of chap. 28 (28:1–28), on the theme that wisdom is hidden from humans, who must content themselves with living according to the divine commandments (28:28), has also commonly been thought to be a later addition. It is somewhat strange in the mouth of Job, because he is subsequently led to a similar position only by dint of lengthy divine argument. It may be in fact that the third cycle of speeches (chaps. 21–31) has suffered some dislocation in the course of scribal transmission; for, as the text stands, Bildad delivers an uncharacteristically short speech in 26:1–6, and Zophar makes no speech at all. But even if the poem on wisdom was originally uttered by Zophar, as some suggest—and it is interesting that Zophar has already made similar points, though more prosaically, in 11:7–20—it still seems that the poem on wisdom lessens the effectiveness of the divine speeches when they come. In that case, the solution to the problem may be that Zophar is speaking only about the impossibility of knowing the particular cause of a particular misfortune, whereas God is speaking about the impossibility of humans' knowing whether a misfortune was due to any human cause at all. However the issue is resolved, we must acknowledge the possibility that the Book of Job has been subject to expansions at various times.

3. THE BOOK OF JOB AND ANCIENT NEAR EASTERN LITERATURE

Select Bibliography

The Legend of King Keret: **Gibson, J. C. L.** *Canaanite Myths and Legends.* Edinburgh: T. & T. Clark, 1978. 82–102 (previous ed. [1956] by G. R. Driver). **Pritchard, J. B.,** ed. *Ancient Near Eastern Texts relating to the Old Testament* [= ANET, 3d ed., 1969]. 142–49.
A Dispute over Suicide: ANET. 405–407.
The Protests of the Eloquent Peasant: ANET. 407–10.
I Will Praise the Lord of Wisdom: ANET. 434–37. **Lambert, W. G.** *Babylonian Wisdom Literature.* 1960.
The Babylonian Job: ANET. 589–91.

The discovery in the present century of many works of ancient Near Eastern literature enables us to view the Book of Job within a wider context than that of the Hebrew Bible. Many individual motifs of the Book of Job are to be found in this nonbiblical literature, but no text can with any probability be regarded as a source or ancestor of the biblical book.

From the realm of Canaanite culture, we have the poetic epic of Keret, a king who loses all his family, including his wife, in a series of natural disasters. He himself is in danger of death, but at the command of the god El he finds a new wife and, like Job, begets a new family.

From Egypt, a text with some analogies to Job is the Dispute over Suicide, otherwise known as the Dialogue of a Man with His Soul, in which a man debates with himself whether in his present misery suicide is not to be preferred to life. "To whom can I speak today? I am laden with wretchedness for lack of an intimate. . . . Death is in my sight today like the odor of myrrh, like sitting under an awning on a breezy day." Like Job, the man expresses his longing for someone who will take up his case in the heavenly council. Another Egyptian text, The Protests of the Eloquent Peasant, contains the appeal of a man who is suffering social injustice for his wrongs to be righted by the Chief Steward. Like Job, he would prefer death to being oppressed by injustice, but unlike Job he is not making his plea to heaven.

From Babylonia, the most interesting parallel to the Book of Job is the work known as "I Will Praise the Lord of Wisdom" (*Ludlul bēl nēmeqi*), in which a pious man is struck down by disease; he is mocked by his friends as a wrongdoer, and his family has become hostile to him. He himself believes that he must have committed some sin, even if only inadvertently, to be so punished by God. He is troubled by his human inability to understand the gods: "What seems good to one, to a god may be evil. . . . Where have mankind learned the way of a god?" He describes his suffering in excruciating detail, and appeals for deliverance from it. In the end he is restored to health. An older text, from Sumer, called by its translator "Man and His God," differs from the Book of Job on several fundamental points, but has many elements, especially of wording, in common with Job. The sufferer here is complaining that he is being made to suffer by God and is being scorned by his friends: "You have doled out to me suffering ever anew. . . . My friend gives the lie to my righteous word." He begs God for mercy: "My god, you who are my father who begot me, lift up my face." Unlike Job, this man acknowledges that he has sinned, and the outcome is that the god "turned the man's suffering into joy."

The Hebrew tale of Job—which we may suppose to have existed before the book came into being—may be indebted to such texts, or at least to the traditional story material which they themselves draw upon, but the Book of Job itself seems to be a fresh and independent creation. The other Near Eastern texts do, however, remind us that the issues raised by the Book of Job were not unique to Israel.

4. THE BOOK OF JOB AND BIBLICAL WISDOM LITERATURE

Among modern students of the Hebrew Bible, Job is reckoned as belonging to a group of books known as "Wisdom" literature. These are the books of Proverbs, Ecclesiastes, and Job, to which may be added two other Wisdom books appearing only in the Greek Old Testament and now included in the Apocrypha or among the Deuterocanonical books: Wisdom (or, The Wisdom of Solomon) and Ecclesiasticus (or, Sirach). They are so called because of their didactic contents; they deliberately set out to be instructional about right living or right thinking.

These books are generally thought to have had their origin among the circles of the "wise" in Israel, who have been identified as a class of intellectuals or bureaucrats. Some of the "wise" will have been engaged in the education of the young, and others in the administration of government. In the Book of Proverbs, the narrator addresses the reader as "my son," in the manner of an ancient schoolmaster addressing his pupils, and Proverbs can be easily understood as a textbook for students in a scribal school. It would be a mistake, however, to limit the term "the wise" to professional wise men—in Israel as much as in any society today. So we cannot assume that Job or Ecclesiastes is the work of some professional wise man or that either reflects the views of a particular class or circle. Everything about the Book of Job, as also about Ecclesiastes, suggests that the author was writing as a unique and somewhat unorthodox individual. The Book of Job is such an intensely intellectual work that it is hard to imagine that it had a very much wider appeal to its ancient readers than it has to readers of the present day; its presence in the canon of the Hebrew Bible may be as much due to happy accidents as to any deliberate preservation of the book by a class of intellectuals or administrators for whom it spoke.

Even though there may be no common social background for the books of Proverbs, Job, and Ecclesiastes, it is instructive to compare them theologically, since Proverbs and Ecclesiastes are intellectually the nearest neighbors of the Book of Job. The Book of Proverbs is, next to Deuteronomy, the most stalwart defender in the Hebrew Bible of the doctrine of retribution. In it the underlying principle is that wisdom—which means the knowledge of how to live rightly— leads to life and folly leads to death (e.g., Prov 1:32; 3:1–2, 13–18; 8:36). Everywhere it is asserted—or else taken for granted—that righteousness is rewarded and sin is punished (e.g., 11:5–6). And the world of humans is divided into two groups: the righteous (or, wise) and the wicked (or, foolish); which group a particular individual belongs to seems to be determined by upbringing and education and there is little hope or fear that a person may move from one group to another. Thus there is a determinism about the outlook of Proverbs, and a rather rigid notion of cause and effect, which is reasonable enough in material designed for the education of the young but is lacking in intellectual sophistication and, to be frank, in realism.

Job and Ecclesiastes introduce that needed element of sophistication and realism into the philosophy of Wisdom, calling into question as they do so the universal validity of the tenets of Proverbs. Ecclesiastes does not doubt the value of the quest for wisdom: "Wisdom excels folly as light excels darkness" (Eccl 2:13). But the author insists on raising the question, What happens to one's wisdom at death? Since death cancels out all values, not excepting wisdom, life cannot be meaningful if it is made to consist of gaining something that is inevitably going to be lost. However valuable the pursuit of wisdom is, it is even better for a human being to regard life as an opportunity for enjoyment: "There is nothing better for humans than to eat and drink and find enjoyment in all their activity" (2:24, my translation). For enjoyment is not a cumulative possession or a process leading to a goal which can then be destroyed; enjoyment exists in the course of living along with the activity that produces it, and so it cannot be lost; it has already been acquired and used up. Ecclesiastes thus inscribes a challenging question mark in the margin of Proverbs.

Job confronts the ideology of Proverbs at a different point. As we have seen, the Book of Job is an assault on the general validity of the doctrine of retribution. In the framework of the thought of Proverbs, the man Job is an impossibility. If he is truly righteous, he finds life, and wealth, and health. If he is in pain, he is one of the wicked and the foolish. In the end, of course, the Book of Job does not completely undermine the principle of retribution, for Job ends up pious *and* prosperous, but once the principle is successfully challenged, as it is in the Book of Job, even in a single case, its moral force is desperately weakened. For, once the case of Job becomes known, if a person who has a reputation for right living is found to be suffering the fate Proverbs predicts for wrongdoers, no one can point a finger of criticism; the Book of Job has established that the proper criterion for determining whether people are pious or not is the moral quality of their life and not the accidental circumstances of their material existence. At the same time, the book maintains that a truly religious attitude does not consist of passive resignation to misfortune, but includes a courage to enter into confrontation with God. Even though the Book of Job dissents from the leading theological statement of Proverbs on retribution, it more than earns its place beside it within the corpus of "Wisdom" literature for its implicit instruction on how to live rightly when one is suffering.

Introduction:
III. Orientation to Books about Job

This is intended to be a reasonably comprehensive bibliography. It does not contain only items I have read or seen, though I think I have seen most that are in Sheffield University Library, Cambridge University Library or the British Library in the British Museum, London. It does not usually include works in languages with which I have no familiarity. Other remarks about the intentions lying behind this bibliography may be found in the first part of the introduction, Orientation to this Book.

Works are arranged in this sequence:
1. Bibliographies of Works on Job
2. Commentaries and Translations
   a. Patristic
      i. Greek
      ii. Latin
      iii. Syriac
   b. Jewish, before the 19th Century
   c. Christian, Medieval and pre-16th Century
   d. Christian, 16th to 18th Centuries
   e. Christian and Jewish, 19th and 20th Centuries
3. The Book as a Whole
4. Philology, Text Criticism
5. The Ancient Versions
   a. Septuagint and Other Greek Versions
   b. Targum
   c. Vulgate and Other Latin Versions
   d. Peshitta and Other Syriac Versions
   e. Arabic
   f. Ethiopic
   g. Coptic
6. Literary Aspects
7. Motifs, Theological Elements
8. Job and Its Influence
   a. General
   b. Early Jewish
   c. Contemporary Jewish
   d. Islam and Other Religions
   e. Early Christian
   f. Western Thinkers and Writers
   g. Literary Works Inspired by Job
   h. Job in Art
   i. Job in Music
   j. Job in Dance
   k. Job in Film
9. Sources and Composition
10. Date and Authorship
11. The Ancient Literary Context, Including the Hebrew Bible

Little account has been taken in this bibliography of studies of Job that form part of larger works. For example, all introductions to the Old Testament contain treatments of the book, as do commentaries on the whole Bible and works on the Wisdom literature. Thus, quite apart from errors of omission, this bibliography, for all its length, is far from an exhaustive list of what has been written about the Book of Job. It may be regarded, however, as richly representative of the writing which the Book of Job has generated over the centuries.

1. BIBLIOGRAPHIES OF WORKS ON JOB

Baker, J. A. "Commentaries on Job." *Theol* 66 (1963) 179–85. **Barr, J.** "The Book of Job and Its Modern Interpreters." *BJRL* 54 (1971–72) 28–46. **Conte, G.** "Letture di Giobbe." *Prot* 39 (1984) 93–96. **Glatzer, N. H.,** ed. *The Dimensions of Job: A Study and Selected Readings.* New York: Schocken Books, 1969. **Hausen, A.** *Hiob in der französischen Literatur: Zur Rezeption eines alttestamentlichen Buches.* Europäische Hochschulschriften 13/17. Frankfurt: Peter Lang, 1972. 212–60. **Kaminka, A.** "Neueste Literatur zu den Hagiographen." *MGWJ* 71 (1927) 289–306. **Kegler, J.** "Hauptlinien der Hiobforschung seit 1956." In C. Westermann, *Der Aufbau des Buches Hiob.* 2d ed. Stuttgart: Calwer, 1977. 9–25. **Kinet, D.** "Der Vorwurf an Gott: Neuere Literatur zum Ijobbuch." *BiKi* 36 (1981) 255–59. **Kuhl, C.** "Neuere Literarkritik des Buches Hiob." *TRu* N.F. 21 (1953) 163–205, 257–317. ———. "Vom Hiobbuche und seinen Problemen." *TRu* N.F. 22 (1954) 261–316. **Lang, B.** "Neue Literatur zum Buch Ijob." *TTQ* 160 (1980) 40–42. **Lods, A.** "Recherches récentes sur le livre de Job." *RHPR* 14 (1934) 501–33. **Mika'el, M.** "ספר איוב באספקלריה של כתבי־עת משנת 1921 עד שנת 1950". [The Book of Job in Periodical Review 1921–1950]; *BMik* 76 (1978–79) 106–15; 77, 229–40; 78, 336–46. **Müller, H. P.** "Altes und Neues zum Buch Hiob." *EvT* 37 (1977) 284–304. ———. *Das Hiobproblem.* Darmstadt: Wissenschaftliche Buchgesellschaft, 1978. **Robinson, T. R.** "The Ten Best Books on the Book of Job." *Exp* 9/4 (1925) 357–77. **Sanders, P. S.** *Twentieth-Century Interpretations of the Book of Job: A Collection of Critical Essays.* Englewood Cliffs, NJ: Prentice-Hall, 1968. **Tebbe, W.** "Predigthilfe aus Kommentaren: Neuere Literatur zum Buche Hiob." *MP* 43 (1954) 156–67. **Vold, K.** "Jobbokens problemer: Litteratur om Jobboken." *TTKi* 3 (1932) 41–56. **Waldow, H. E. von.** "Studien zum Buche Hiob." *VF* 20 (1960–62) 215–27. **Williams, R. J.** "Current Trends in the Study of the Book of Job." In *Studies in the Book of Job,* ed. W. E. Aufrecht. *SR* Supplements 16. Waterloo: Wilfrid Laurier UP, 1985. 1–27.

2. COMMENTARIES AND TRANSLATIONS

Commentaries and translations in this section of the Bibliography have been arranged principally by period: Patristic; Jewish before the nineteenth century; Christian, medieval; Christian, sixteenth to eighteenth centuries; Jewish and Christian, nineteenth to twentieth centuries.

Before the Renaissance, the Book of Job was given less attention than the more obviously Christological parts of the Old Testament. It may be that the remarkable interest in the book since the sixteenth century is related to the growth of humanism, and the comparative freeing of biblical study from ecclesiastical constraints. The Book of Job, with its presentation of divergent theological views, has obviously not been entirely congenial to the proponents of dogmatic theology.

Much of the greatness of the Book of Job has been its adaptability to the needs and interests of various ages. In the Renaissance, as in the Middle Ages, Job was often seen as an ethical model, an exemplar of fortitude and patience. In the Enlightenment, he became rational man, struggling on the side of reason and experience against dogma. The Job of Romanticism is a figure weighed down with human sadness, full of restless longings for the infinite. In the twentieth century, Job becomes rather a representative of a humanity condemned to an existence of absurdity. None of these readings of the book and of its central character is a misreading; rather, the convictions and concerns of different ages have revealed a dimension in the work that was not previously well recognized. It would be an error to suppose that the history of the interpretation of the book only teaches us that we all see in the Bible only what we want to see. It would be better to think of writings on the Book of Job as comments in a visitors' book at a historic monument, as transcriptions of an orchestral suite for the piano or flute or cello, or as gossip about a well-loved, but awkward, character of our acquaintance.

a. Patristic

In the patristic period, it was apparently the Greek writers who favored the Book of Job. Besides the fragments of the commentaries of Chrysostom, Athanasius and others, there is also the Greek Catena, a collection of comments from twenty-four Greek fathers, most of whose commentaries have not otherwise survived. The Latins seem to have been overwhelmed by the *Moralia* of Gregory the Great which exercised a vast influence in the Middle Ages not only on biblical study but on Christian ethics and theology generally.

Dhorme, E. *A Commentary on the Book of Job.* Tr. H. Knight. London: Thomas Nelson, 1967. ccxxi–ccxxiv. **Guillaumin, Marie-Louise.** "Recherches sur l'exégèse patristique de Job." *Studia Patristica* 12/1. Ed. Elizabeth A. Livingstone. Texte und Untersuchungen 115. Berlin: Akademie, 1975. 304–8.

i. Greek

Anon. [Ps.-Origen]. *In Job commentarius.* PG 17:371–522 [only known in Latin].
Athanasius (c. 296–373). *Fragmenta in Job* (excerpts from the Greek catena). *PG* 27:1343–48.
Chrysostom (c. 347–407). *Fragmenta in beatum Job* (excerpts from the Greek catena). *PG* 64:506–635. ———. *Synopsis scripturae sacrae, Job.* PG 56:361–68. ———. *In Job homilias IV.* PG 56:563–82. See also **Dieu, L.** "Le 'commentaire de S. Jean Chrysostome sur Job.'" *RHE* 13 (1912) 640–58. **Haidacher, S.** "Chrysostomus-Fragmente. A: Chrysostomus-fragmente zum Buche Hiob." Χρυσοστομικα. *Studi e richerche a S. Giovanni Crisostomo.* Rome, 1908. 1:217–34. **Samir, K.,** and **J. L. Scharpé.** "Les sermons sur Job du Pseudo-Chrysostome (CPG 4564 = BHG 939d–g) dans la version paléo-russe." *OLP* 9. Ed. M. Heltzer, 1978. 167–73. **Samir, K.** "Les sermons sur Job du Pseudo-Chrysostome (CPG 4564 = BHG 939d–g) retrouvés en arabe." *OLP* 8. Ed. H. Sauren et al. 1977. 205–16.
Didymus the Blind (c. 313–98). *Fragmenta ex catenis in Job.* PG 39:1119–54. Eds.: **Hagedorn, D., U. Hagedorn,** and **L. Koenen.** *Didymus der Blinde: Kommentar zu Hiob (Tura-Papyrus).* Vols. 3, 4. Bonn: R. Habelt, 1985. **Henrichs, A.** *Didymos der Blinde: Kommentar zu Hiob (Tura-Papyrus).* Papyrologische Texte und Abhandlungen 1, 2. 2 vols. Bonn: R. Habelt, 1968. See also **Marchal, G. W.** *Didyme de blinde en zijn interpretatie van het boek Job.* Sneek: Doevendans, 1977.
Greek Catena. Eds.: **Comitolus, P.,** ed. *Catena in Beatissimum Job absolutissima, e quatuor et viginti Graeciae Doctorum explanationibus contexta, a Paulo Comitolo e graeco in latinum conversa.* Venice, 1587. **Junius, P.,** ed. *Catena Graecorum Patrum in beatum Job collectore Niceta Heracleae Metropolita ex duobus mss. Bibliothecae Bodleianae codicibus, graece, nunc primum in lucem edita et latine versa, opera et studio Patricii Junii Bibliothecarii Regii.* London, 1637 [= *PG* 64:505–635]. See also **Bertini, U.** "La catena greca in Giobbe." *Bib* 4 (1923) 129–42.
Hesychius of Jerusalem (fl. c. 300). Eds.: **Tscherakian, C.,** ed. *Commentary on Job* [Armenian]. Venice, 1913. **Renoux, C.** *Hesychius de Jérusalem, Homélies sur Job: Version arménienne.* PO 42/1–2. Turnhout: Brepols, 1983. See also **Renoux, C.** "L'Église de Sion dans les Homélies sur Job d'Hésychius de Jérusalem." *RÉArmén* 18 (1984) 135–46.
Julian of Halicarnassus (d. after 518) (attrib.). See Julian the Arian.

Julian the Arian (4th cent.). Eds.: **Hagedorn, D.** *Der Hiobkommentar des Arianers Julian.* Patristische Texte und Studien 14. Berlin: de Gruyter, 1973. See also **Ferhat, P.** "Der Jobprolog des Julianos von Halicarnassos in einer armenischen Bearbeitung." *OrChr* 1 (1911) 26–31. **Olympiodorus of Alexandria** (6th cent.). *Commentarium in beatum Job* (excerpts from the Greek catena). *PG* 93:11–409. Eds.: **Hagedorn, U., and D. Hagedorn.** *Olympiodor, Diakon von Alexandria: Kommentar zu Hiob.* Patristische Texte und Studien 24. Berlin: de Gruyter, 1984. **Origen** (c. 185–c. 254). *Ex Origene selecta in Job. PG* 12:1031–50. ———. *Hexaplorum quae supersunt . . . Job. PG* 16/1:287–570. ———. *Ennarrationes in Job. PG* 17:57–106. **Theodore of Mopsuestia** (c. 350–428). *In Jobum* (excerpts from the Greek catena). *PG* 66:697–98.

Draguet, R. "Un commentaire grec arien sur Job." *RHE* 24 (1924) 38–65. See also **Osieczkowska, C.** "Note sur un manuscrit grec du livre de Job, no 62 du Musée byzantin d'Athènes." *Byzantion* 6 (1931) 223–28.

ii. Latin

Anon. [Ps.-Origen]. *In Job commentarius. PG* 17:371–522.

Ambrose (c. 339–97). *Liber de Interpellatione Job et David. PL* 14:793–850. See also **Baskin, J. R.** "Job as Moral Exemplar in Ambrose." *VigChr* 35 (1981) 222–31.

Augustine (354–430). *Adnotationum in Job liber unus. PL* 34:825–86. ———. *Sermo de eo quod scriptum est in Job, cap. 1,6. PL* 38:100–106. See also **Jackson, M. G. StA.** "Formica Dei: Augustine's Enarratio in Psalmum 66:3 (Job as 'God's Ant')." *VigChr* 40 (1986) 153–68.

Gregory the Great (c. 540–604). *Libri XXXV Moralium. PL* 75:515–1162; 76:9–782. ———. *Excerpta ex commentario in Jobum* (attrib. Bede). *PL* 23:1470–80. Eds.: **Adriaen, M.,** ed. *S. Gregorii Magni Moralia in Iob.* CCSL 143, 143A, 143B. 3 vols. Turnhout: Brepols, 1979–85. *Morals on the Book of Job, Translated with Notes and Indices.* 3 vols. Oxford: H. Parker, 1844–50. **Gillet, R., A. de Gaudemaris,** and **A. Bocagnano.** *Grégoire le Grand, Morales sur Job: Texte latin, introduction et notes.* 4 vols. Sources chrétiennes 32, 32b, 212, 221. Paris: Cerf, 1950–75. See also **Castaldelli, F.** "Il meccanismo psicologico del peccato nei 'Moralia in Job' di San Gregorio Magno." *Salesianum* 27 (1965) 563–605. **De Ayala, L.** *Las flores de los 'Morales de Job': Introduzione, testo critico e note.* Florence: Le Monnier, 1963. **Salmon, P.** "Le texte de Job utilisé par S. Grégoire dans les 'Moralia.'" *Miscellanea Biblica et Orientalia . . . A. A. Miller.* 1951. 187–94. **Wasselynck, R.** *L'influence des Moralia in Job de S. Grégoire le Grand sur la théologie morale entre le VIIe et le XIIe siècle.* Diss. Lille, 1956. ———. "Le compilations des Moralia in Job du VIIe au XIIe siècle." *RTAM* 29 (1962) 5–33. ———. "Les Moralia in Job dans les ouvrages de morale du haut moyen âge latin." *RTAM* 31 (1964) 5–31. See also Lathcen; Odo of Cluny; Peter of Waltham.

Hilary (c. 315–67). *Tractatus in Job* [frag.]. *PL* 10:723–24.

Jerome (c. 342–420). *Commentarii in librum Job. PL* 26:619–802. ———. *Liber Job* [a translation]. *PL* 28:1079–1122. ———. *Liber Job. Altera versio. PL* 29:61–114. ——— (attrib.; Ps.-Philip the Presbyter). *Expositio interlinearis libri Job. PL* 23:1402–70. See also **Fransen, I.** *Le commentaire au livre de Job du diacre Philippe.* Diss. Lyon, Maredsous, 1949. **Lagarde, P. de.** "Des Hieronymus Übertragung der griechischen Übersetzung des Iob." *Mittheilungen.* Göttingen, 1887. 2:189–237.

Julian of Eclana (c. 386–454). *Expositio libri Jobi. PL* Suppl. 1/1:1573–1679. Eds.: **Amelli, A.** *PL* Suppl. 1:1573–1679. **De Conink, L.** *Iuliani Aeclanensis Expositio libri Iob.* CCSL 88. Turnhout: Brepols, 1977. See also **Vaccari, A.** *Un commento a Giobbe di Giuliano di Eclana.* Rome, 1915. **Weyman, C.** "Der Hiobkommentar des Julianus von Aeclanum." *TRev* (1916) 241–48.

Lathcen (Laidcend, Laidgen) (d. 661). *Egloga quam scripsit Lathcen filius Baith de Moralibus Job quas Gregorius fecit.* Ed. M. Adriaen. CCSL 145. Turnhout: Brepols, 1969.

Walafrid Strabo (c. 808–49) (attrib.). *Glossa ordinaria . . . In librum Job. PL* 113:747–

840. See also **Datema, C.** "A Supposed Narratio on Job." *AnBoll* 103 (1985) 303–304.
Stiglmayr, H. "Der Jobkommentar von Monte Cassino." *ZTK* 43 (1919) 269–88.

iii. Syriac
Bar Hebraeus (1226–86). Eds.: **Bernstein, G. H.** *Gregorius bar Hebraeus: Scholia in librum Iobi; ex codd. MSS. emendata, denuo edidit, difficiliorum locorum interpretatione illustravit, notis criticis instruxit.* Breslau: Typis Universitatis, 1858. *Scholia in Jobum.* In **Kirsch, G. G.** "Bar Hebraei scholia in Jobum ex ejus Horreo Mysteriorum, sec. cod. Bodl. A." In *Chrestomathie syriaque.* Leipzig: K. Knobloch, 1836. 186–210.
Ephrem (c. 306–73). **Benedictus, P.** *Scholies sur Job: Edition syriaque et traduction latine.* Opera Syriaca. Rome, 1740. 2:1–20.
Ishodad of Merv (9th cent.). **Schliebitz, J.** *Išodadh's Kommentar zum Buche Hiob.* BZAW 11. Giessen, 1907. See also **Vosté, J. M.** "Mar Išo'dad de Merw sur Job." *Bib* 30 (1949) 305–13. **Van den Eynde, C.** *Commentaire d'Iso'dad de Merv sur l'Ancien Testament. 3: Livre des sessions.* CSCO 229–30. Scriptores Syriaci 96–97. Louvain: Secrétariat du CSCO, 1962–63.

b. Jewish, before the Nineteenth Century

Anon. *Bruchstücke eines rabbinischen Hiob-Commentars: Als Manuscript in einigen Exemplaren* (from 1295). Bonn: C. Georgi, 1874. ———. *A Commentary on the Book of Job, from a Hebrew Manuscript in the University Library, Cambridge.* Ed. W. A. Wright. London, 1905.
Abraham, Israel ben. ספר איוב: עם העתקה אשנזית ובאור [Yiddish translation]. Prague, 1791. **Abraham, Zeeb Wolf ben.** זה ספר פשר דבר על מקרא איוב. Berlin, 1777. **Alshech, M.** ספר איוב חלקת מחוקק: ביאור ספר. Venice, 1603. **Arama, Meir b. Isaac.** ספר מאיר איוב. Venice, 1567.
Duran, Simon. ספר אוהב משפט, and **Sforno, Obadiah b. Jacob.** משפט צדק ספר. Venice, 1589 [the two commentaries in parallel columns].
Gersonides [Ralbag] (1288–1344). **Lassen, A. L.** *The Commentary of Levi ben Gersom (Gersonides) on the Book of Job: Translated with Introduction and Notes.* New York: Bloch Publishing Co., 1946.
Ibn Ezra, A. (d. 1167). In *Biblia Rabbinica* of Buxtorf. See also **Galliner, J.** *Abraham ibn Esra's Hiobkommentar auf seine Quellen untersucht.* Berlin: H. Itzkowski, 1901.
Masnuth, Samuel b. Nissim (12th cent.). מעין גנים. In **Buber, S.** *Commentar zu Job von Rabbi Samuel ben Nissim Masnuth.* Berlin, 1889. **Meldola, J. H.** ספר איוב [Hebrew text with Spanish version by Jacob Lombroso]. Livorno, 1778. **Menahem, Jacob U. S. F.** בית יעקב אש: באיור נחמד ונעים על ספרא דאיוב. Frankfurt an der Oder, 1765. **Mendelssohn, M.** *Bible Commentary on Job.* Berlin, 1789. **Midrash.** מדרש איוב. Ed. S. A. Wertheimer. 2d ed. Jerusalem, 1953.
Nahmanides [Ramban] (1194–1270). **Chavel, C. D.** כתבי רבנו משה בן נחמן. Jerusalem, 1963. 1:19–28. See also **Silver, D. J.** "Nachmanides' Commentary on the Book of Job." *JQR* 60 (1969–70) 9–26.
Qara, David. See **Ahrend, M. M.** *Le commentaire sur Job de Rabbi Yoséph Qara': Étude de méthodes philologiques et exégétiques.* Hildesheim: Gerstenberger, 1978. See also **Arend [Ahrend], M.** "The Commentary of R. Joseph Kara on Job and Its Relationship to Rashi's Commentary." *Studies in Bible and Exegesis . . . A. Toeg.* 1980. 183–207 [Heb.].
Rashi [Itzhaki, R. Samuel] (1040–1105). In *Biblia Rabbinica* of Buxtorf.
Saadia b. Joseph Gaon (882–942). Eds.: **Goodman, L. E.** *The Book of Theodicy: Translation and Commentary on the Book of Job by Saadiah ben Joseph al-Fayyūmī, Translated from the Arabic with a Philosophic Commentary.* New Haven: Yale UP, 1988. **Qapah, J.** *Sepher Iyyob im Targum Uperuš Rabbi Sa'adia Ga'on.* Jerusalem, 1970. See also **Rosenthal, E. I.**

J. "Saadya's Exegesis of the Book of Job." In his *Saadya Studies*. Manchester: Manchester UP, 1943. 177–205. **Vajda, G.** "Quelques remarques en marge de la seconde rédaction du Commentaire de Saadia Gaon sur le livre de Job." *RÉJ* 135 (1976) 157–68. See also under Ancient Versions, Arabic (sect. 4e below).

Shoeib, Joel ibn, and **Abraham b. Mordecai Galante.** ספר כל בכים. Venice, 1589.

c. Christian, Medieval and Pre-Sixteenth-Century

Albert the Great (c. 1200–1280). *Postilla super Iob*. Eds.: **Weiss, M.** *Commentarii in Job: Postillae super Job*. Freiburg i. Breisgau, 1904. See also **Coggi, R.** "Il significato del libro di Giobbe secondo S. Alberto Magno." *SacDoc* 26 (1981) 105–22. **Jutras, A.-M.** "Le Commentarius in Job d'Albert le Grand et la Disputatio." *Études et Recherches* 9 (1955) 9–20.

Anon. *Der mitteldeutsche poetische Paraphrase des Buches Hiob*. Ed. T. E. Karsten. Deutsche Texte des Mittelalters 21. Berlin, 1910. ———. *Mystere de la Pacience de Job*. 15th cent. See **Meiller, A.,** ed. *La Pacience de Job, mystère anonyme du XVe Siècle (ms. fr. 1774)*. Paris, 1971.

Aquinas, Thomas (c. 1225–74). *Expositio in librum beati Job*. Eds.: *Sancti Thomae Aquitanis Doctoris angelici O.P. expositio in aliquot Veteris Testamenti libros et in Psalmos adjectis brevibus adnotationibus*. Parma: Fiaccadori, 1863. 1–145. ———. *Expositio super Job ad litteram cura et studio Fratrum Praedicatorum*. Opera omnia 26. Rome: Ad Sanctae Sabinae, 1965. See also **Coggi, R.** "L'insegnamento del libro di Giobbe. i. Sintesi dell'Expositio super Iob di S. Tommaso; ii. Validità perenne." *SacDoc* 27 (1982) 215–310. **Manzanedo, M. F.** "La antropologia filosófica en el comentario tomaista al libro de Job." *Ang* 62 (1985) 419–71. **Michaud-Quantin, P.** "L'édition critique de l'Expositio super Job de S. Thomas d'Aquin." *RSPT* 50 (1966) 407–10. **Kreit, J.** *St. Thomas d'Aquin, Job un homme pour notre temps*. Paris: Téqui, 1982.

Bede (673–735). See Gregory the Great. See also **Vaccari, A.** "Scripsitne Beda commentarium in Job?" *Bib* 5 (1924) 369–73.

Bruno d'Asti (Bruno of Segni) (c. 1048–1123). *Expositio in Job*. PL 164:551–696.

Denis the Carthusian [Denys van Leeuwen, Denys Ryckel] (1402–71). *Enarratio in librum Job*. In *Doctoris ecstatici D. Dionysii cartusiani opera omnia*. Monstrolii, 1847. 4:293–696. ———. *De causa diversitatis eventorum humanorum: Enarrationes in libros Job, Tobiae, Judith, Esther, Esdrae, Nehemiae, Machabaeorum*. Cologne, 1534.

Francocordia, J. de. *Commentarius super librum Job*. 1441.

Marquard von Lindau. See **Greifenstein, E.** *Der Hiob-Traktat des Marquard von Lindau: Überlieferung, Untersuchung und kritische Ausgabe*. Munich: Artemis, 1979. **Stammler, W.** *Der Job-Traktat des Marquard von Lindau*. 1965–66. **Palmer, N. P.** "Der Hiob-Traktat Marquards von Lindau in lateinischer Überlieferung." *Beiträge zur Geschichte der deutschen Sprache* 104 (1982) 48–83.

Nicholas of Lyra (c. 1270–1340). *Postillae perpetuae in Vetus et Novum Testamentum*. Cologne, 1478.

Odo of Cluny (879–942). *Epitome moralium S. Gregorii in Job*. PL 133:105–512.

Peter of Blois (c. 1130–c. 1203). *Compendium in Job*. PL 207:795–826. See also **Gildea, J.** *L'Hystore Job, an Old French Verse Adaptation of Compendium in Job by Peter of Blois II: Introduction, Notes, Glossary*. Liège: Vaillant, 1979.

Peter of Waltham (12th cent.). **Gildea, J.,** ed. *Peter of Waltham, Archdeacon of London (c. 1190–1196), Remediarium conversorum: A synthesis in Latin of Moralia in Job by Gregory the Great*. Villanova, PA: Villanova UP, 1984.

Philip the Presbyter. Sichardus [Sickart], J., ed. *Philippi Presbyteri viri longe eruditissimi in historiam Iob commentariorum libri tres*. Basel, 1527.

Roland of Cremona (13th cent.). See **Dondaine, A.** "Un commentaire scripturaire de Roland de Cremone: Le livre de Job.'" *Archivum Fratrum Praedicatorum* 11 (1941) 109–37.

Rolle, Richard, of Hampole (c. 1290–1349). *Explanationes in Job.* Oxford, 1483.
Rupert de Deutz (c. 1070–1129). *Super Job commentarius. PL* 168:963–1196.

d. Christian, Sixteenth to Eighteenth Centuries

Among this surprisingly extensive list of books on Job (over 150 items, that is, a new book on Job every eighteen months, on average), two points stand out. First, the quantity of translations, professing to be translations from the original Hebrew. Very many of these are in verse (English and French especially, but also German, Greek, Italian; such a translation could be done in a month, as Hugh Broughton's title testifies: *Iob. To the King. A Colon-Agrippina studie of one moneth, for the metricall translation: but of many yeres, for Ebrew difficulties,* 1610). For sheer nerve the tour de force by John Duport, one of the translators of the Authorized Version, who turned Job into epic verse in the dialect of Homer, deserves mention (ΘΡΗΝΟΘΡΙΑΜΒΟΣ. *Sive Liber Job Graeco carmine redditus,* 1637). The publication of so many versions is a testimony to the wide knowledge of Hebrew among the learned classes generally, and gives cause for wonder concerning the apparently insatiable appetite of the reading public for such works. Second, the number of "critical" commentaries, i.e., with detailed philological comments, often expressly based on Jewish authors, and commonly with ample evidence of knowledge of Arabic.

To look simply at the earliest entries in the British Library catalogue of sixteenth-century books of Job is both fascinating and instructive of how the book was used in this period. One is even tempted to discern reflections of national characteristics in the titles that first appear. The earliest work in English is not an independent work, but a translation of the commentary of the reformer Theodore Beza. The first work published in Scotland was the daunting series of no fewer than 316 lectures on Job given by George Hutcheson to his indefatigable congregation in Edinburgh: *An Exposition of the Book of Job: Being the sum of cccxvi lectures preached in the City of Edinburgh,* 1669). The earliest work in French is a translation from the Hebrew, with a brief commentary by the author, Jean Pélerin, who signs himself only by the rather transparent pseudonym Le Viateur; the second item is another translation (see d'Albiac), this time into "French poetry," that is, the Alexandrine verses beloved of Racine and his age. The earliest work in German is a collection of sermons, *The History of Job expounded as useful Christian Preaching* (J. Wildt, *Iobi historia Christlich und nützlich Predig weyss ausgelegt . . . Durch Johan Wildt . . . geprediget . . . 1552,* 1558).

As in all periods of interpretation, there was a lot of derivative writing, often acknowledged in the copious title pages. But the dominant impression is rather of vigorous and technically expert scholarship. The period precedes the rise of critical *historical* scholarship; but it abounded in fine examples of linguistically and exegetically critical studies, in which dogma, allegory and ecclesiastical influence are refreshingly absent. The work of J. J. Duguet and J. V. Bidel d'Asfeld, *Explication du livre de Job où, selon la méthode des saints Pères, l'on s'attache à découvrir les mystères de Jésus-Christ et les règles des moeurs renfermées dans la lettre même de l'Écriture* (1732), i.e., *Explanation of the Book of Job in which, according to the method of the Fathers, the concern is to discover the mysteries of Christ and the moral principles contained in the very letter of Scripture,* is something of an exception that proves the rule.

A prize for the most optimistically entitled book on Job should be awarded to John Brentius, the Wittenberg theologian, for his *Hiob cum piis et eruditis Iohannis Brentii commentariis ad Hebraicam veritatem ita translatus, ut nulla porro obscuritas lectorem possit offendere* (1527), i.e., *Job so translated according to the true Hebrew original, with the pious and learned comments of John Brentz, that no obscurity should any further cause the reader to stumble.* For such hybris, he should be sentenced to a posthumous compilation of a bibliography of books published on Job since 1527.

Finally, a consolation prize is justly deserved by C. Peters for his *A Critical Dissertation on the Book of Job, wherein the account given of that book by the author of The Divine Legation of Moses Demonstrated, &c. is particularly considered; the antiquity of the book vindicated; the great text (Chap. xix.25—) explained; and a future state shewn to have been the popular belief of the ancient Jews or Hebrews* (2d ed., 1757). The course of subsequent scholarship has declared him wrong on each of his primary assertions.

Among the most important scholarly commentaries of this period may be mentioned, in chronological order:

1527	Brentius	1600	Pineda	1720	Michaelis, J. H.
1528	Bucer	1612	Piscator	1734	Hoffmann
1528	Titelmann	1625	Sanctius	1737	Schultens
1573	Mercerus	1629	Bolducius	1753	Houbigant
1582	Huerga	1644	Cocceius	1779	Reiske
1584	Zúñiga	1663	Terentius	1779	Döderlein
1599	Merlin	1670	Schmidt	1789	Dathe

Abbott, G. *The whole booke of Job paraphrased, or made easie for any to understand.* London, 1640. **Anon.** *Hijr begynt dat boeck Iob.* Augsburg, 1480. ———. *Büchlein von dem heiligen Job.* Argentorati, 1498. ———. *Liber beati Job. Si patientiam, si modestiam, si constantiam in tribulationibus, infirmitatibus et adversis, si denique celibem ac beatam vitam ducere cupis librum beati Job ydumie sive Arabiā legito.* Paris, 1508. [The Lat. text preceded by Jerome's prologue.] ———. *Das Buch Hiob, nach der Hebreischen Grundsprache gottsfürchtiger und gelehrter Lehrer Auslegung: In zwölf vnd dreyzehen silbige deutsche Reime gesetzt, Sampt . . . einer kurtzen erzehlung wer dieser heilige Mann gewesen und zu welcher Zeitt ere gelebet.* Wittenberg, 1638. ———. *Jesu Christi Festum Natalitium . . . Insunt observationes ad librum Jobi.* Tübingen, 1826. ———. *Job, un drama engiadinais del 16. secul. Nouvamaing publicho da Jakob Ulrich.* Chur, 1896. **Aurelius, A.** *Iobus, sive de patientia liber, poetica metaphrasi explicatus.* London, 1632.

Barbauld, Anna Laetitia. *Devotional pieces, compiled from the Psalms and the Book of Job: to which are prefixed, thoughts on the devotional taste, on sects, and on establishments.* London, 1775. **Bellamy, D.** *A Paraphrase on the sacred history, or Book of Job, with observations from various authors.* London, 1748. **Belleau, R.** *Traduction en vers du livre de Job.* 1576. **Benserradde, I. de.** *Paraphrases sur les IX. leçons de Iob.* Paris, 1637. **Beza, T. de.** *Jobus commentario et paraphrasi illustratus.* Geneva, 1583. ———. *Iob expounded by Theodore Beza, partly in manner of a commentary, partly in manner of a paraphrase. Faithfully translated out of Latine into English.* Cambridge, 1589 (?). See also **Raitt, J.** "Beza, Guide for the Faithful Life (Lectures on Job, Sermons on Song of Songs, 1587)." *SJT* 39 (1986) 83–107. **Blackmore, R.** *A Paraphrase on the Book of Job: as likewise on the Songs of Moses, Deborah, David: on four select Psalms: some chapters of Isaiah, and the third chapter of Habakkuk.* [In verse.] London, 1700. **Bolducius [Bolduc], P.** *Commentaria in librum Job.* 2 vols. Paris, 1629, 1637. **Boullier, D. R.** *Observationes miscellaneae in librum Job.* Amsterdam, 1758. **Bravi, B. A.** *Parafrasi del sacro libro di Giobbe fatta in versi italiani.* Verona, 1763. **Brentius [Brentz], J.** *Hiob cum piis et eruditis Iohannis Brentii commentariis ad Hebraicam veritatem ita translatus, ut nulla porro obscuritas lectorem possit offendere.* Haganoae, 1527. **Brett, A.** *Patientia Victrix: or, the Book of Job, in lyrick verse.* London, 1661. **Broughton, H.** *Iob. To the King. A Colon-Agrippina studie of one moneth, for the metricall translation: but of many yeres, for Ebrew difficulties.* In his *The Works of the Great Albionean Divine, renown'd in many nations for rare skill in Salems and Athens tongues, and familiar acquaintance with all rabbinical learning.* London, 1662. 2:247–94. **Brucioli, A.** *Il libro di Iob, tradotto dalla ebraica verita, in lingua italiana, & con nuovo commento dichiarato.* Vinegia, 1534. **Bucer, M.** *Commentarii in librum Jobi.* Strasbourg, 1528. **Bugenhagen, J.** *Adnotationes in Jobum.* Strasbourg, 1526.

Cajetan, T. de V. *In librum Iob commentarii.* Rome, 1535. **Calmet, A.** *Commentaire littéral sur le livre de Job.* 1722. **Calvin, J.** *Sermons sur le livre de Job, recueillis fidèlement de sa bouche selon qu'il les preschoit.* 1554. Eds.: *Calvini Opera.* Ed. G. Baum, E. Cunitz, and E. Reuss. Vols. 33–34. Braunschweig, 1887. ———. *Sermons upon the booke of Job, translated out of French.* Tr. A. Golding. London, 1584. ———. *Sermons from Job.* Tr. L. Nixon, 1952. See also **Schreiner, Susan E.** "'Through a mirror darkly': Calvin's sermons on Job." *CalTJ* 21 (1986) 175–93. **Smid, T. D.** "Some Bibliographical Observations on Calvin's Sermons sur le livre de Job." *Free University Quarterly* (1960) 51–56. **Woudstra, M. H.** "The use of 'example' in Calvin's sermons on Job." *Bezield verband.* FS J. Kamphuis. Ed. M. Arntzen et al. 1984. 344–51. **Cappel[lus], L.** *Critica sacra, sive de variis quae in sacris Veteris Testamenti libris occurrunt lectionibus libri sex.* Paris, 1650. ———. *Commentarii et notae criticae in Vetus Testamentum.* Amsterdam, 1689. **Carpenter, W.** *A Poetical Paraphrase on the Book of Job.* Rutland, 1796. **Caryl, J.** *An Exposition with practicall Observations upon . . . the Booke of Job.* 12 vols. London, 1643–66. **Cermelli, A.** *Catena in Job ex SS. Patrum Scriptorumque ecclesiasticorum sententiis concinnata.* Gênes, 1636. **Cerutti [Ceruti], G.** *Il Libro di Giobbe recato dal testo Ebreo in versi italiani dal sacerdote G. Cerutti.* Turin, 1759. **Chapelow [Chappelow], L.** *A Commentary on the Book of Job, in which is inserted the Hebrew text and English translation; with a paraphrase from the third verse of the third chapter, where it is supposed the metre begins; to the seventh verse of the forty-second chapter, where it ends.* 2 vols. Cambridge, 1752. **Chassignet, J.–B.** *Job ou de la Fermeté* [verse paraphrase]. Bibliothèque Nationale, Ms. fr. 2381, 1592. See also **Müller, A.** *Un poète religieux du XVIᵉ siècle: Jean Baptiste Chassignet, 1578(?)–1635(?).* Paris: R. Foulon, 1951. 45–67. **Chasteignier de la Roche-Posai, H. L.** *Exercitationes in librum Job.* Poitiers, 1628. **Clericus [Le Clerc], J.** *Veteris Testamenti Libri Hagiographi. Jobus, Davidis Psalmi, Salomonis Proverbia, Concionatrix et Canticum Canticorum.* Amsterdam, 1731. **Clodius, J. C.** *Theoria et praxis linguae arabicae. Liber II. De usu linguae arabicae in libri Jobi seorsim.* Leipzig, 1729. 68–230. **Codurcus, P.** *Libri Iob versio nova ex hebraeo cum scholiis.* Paris, 1651. [= **Codercus, P.** *Scholia seu adnotationes in Jobum ad sermonem sacrum Ebreum adornata.* Paris, 1651.] **Corderius [Cordier], B.** *Job elucidatus.* Antwerp, 1646. **Cocceius [Coch], J.** *Commentarius in librum Ijobi.* Franeker, 1644. **Crommius, A.** *In Jobi historiam.* Louvain, 1632. **Cube, J. D.** *Poetische und prosaische Uebersetzung des Buches Hiob.* 3 vols. Berlin, 1769–71.

d'Albiac, A. [**A. du Plessis**]. *Le livre de Iob: traduit en poésie françoise, selon la verité Hébraïque.* Geneva, 1552. **Dathe, J. A.** *Jobus, Proverbia Salomonis, Ecclesiastes, Canticum Canticorum ex recensione textus hebraei et versionum antiquarum latine versi notisque philologicis et criticis illustrati.* Halle, 1789. **Devens, R.** *A Paraphrase on some parts of the Book of Job.* Boston, 1795. **Didacus a Stunica.** *In Iob commentaria, quibus triplex eius editio vulgata Latina, Hebraea, et Graeca septuaginta interpretum, necnon et Chaldaea explicantur et inter se cum diferre hae editiones videntur, conciliantur, et praecepta vitae cum virtute colendae literaliter deducuntur.* Toledo, 1584. **Döderlein, J. C.** *Scholia in libros Veteris Testamenti poeticos Jobum, Psalmos et tres Salomonis.* Halle, 1779. **Drusius [Van der Driesche], J.** *Nova versio et scholia in Iobum.* Amsterdam, 1636. **Duguet, J. J., and J. V. Bidel d'Asfeld.** *Explication du livre de Job où, selon la méthode des saints Pères, l'on s'attache à découvrir les mystères de Jésus-Christ et les règles des moeurs renfermées dans la lettre même de l'Écriture.* Paris, 1732. ———. *Préface sur le livre de Job.* Amsterdam, 1734. [**Du Plessis, A.**] See d'Albiac, A. **Duport, J.** ΘΡΗΝΟΘΡΙΑΜΒΟΣ. *Sive Liber Job Graeco carmine redditus.* Cambridge, 1637. **Eckermann, J. C. R.** *Versuch einer neuen poetischen Uebersetzung des Buches Hiob, nebst einigen Vorerinnerungen und einer nachstehenden Umschreibung.* Leipzig, 1778. **Erskine, R.** *Job's hymns; or, a book of songs upon the Book of Job.* Glasgow, 1753. **Estius, G.** *Annotationes in praecipua ac difficiliora Sacrae Scripturae loca. Annotationes in librum Job.* Douai, 1620. **Fernandez de Palazuelos, A.** *La divina providencia o historia sacra poetica de Job. Versio de un filopatro expatriado, dedicada al principe de la paz.* Venice, 1795. **Fer, J.** *Jobi historiae docta et catholica explicatio in CXIIII conciones eleganter distributa.* Cologne, 1558. **Forerius, F.** *Commentarius in Job.* Antwerp, 1563.

Gallo, J. *Historia y diálogos de Job, con explicación literal y moral, según las versiones de Vatablo, Pagnino, el Parafrastes y los Setenta.* Burgos, 1644. **Garcia, J.** *Job evangélico.* Zaragoza, 1644. **Garden, C.** *An Improved Version attempted of the Book of Job; a poem . . . with a preliminary dissertation and notes.* Oxford, 1796. **Garnett, J. A.** *A Dissertation on the Book of Job, its nature, argument, age and author.* London, 1749. **Gordon, J.** In *Biblia Sacra cum commentariis ad sensum literae.* Paris, 1632. **Grey, R.** *Liber Jobi in versiculos metrice divisus, cum versione latina Alberti Schultens, notisque ex ejus commentario excerptis, quotquot ad Divinum plane poema illustrandum . . . necessariae videbantur. Edidit, atque annotationes suas, ad metrum praecipue spectantes, adjecit Ricardus Grey.* London, 1742. **Grotius [De Groot], H.** *Annotationes in Vetus Testamentum.* Paris, 1644. **Grynaeus, S.** *Das Buch Hiob in einer poetischer Uebersetzung nach des Prof. Schultens Erklärung mit Anmerkungen von Simon Grynäus.* Basel, 1767.

Hardouin, J. *Le livre de Job selon la Vulgate paraphrasé avec des remarques.* Paris, 1729. **Hatcher, R.** *Jobi peroratio, pro triplici status sui colore, tribus capitulis distincta.* In his *Funus corporis.* London, 1646. 89–112. **Heath, T.** *An Essay toward a new English version of the Book of Job from the original Hebrew, with a commentary, and some account of his life.* London, 1756. **Henry, M.** *An Exposition of the Five Poetical Books of the Old Testament; viz. Job, Psalms, Proverbs, Ecclesiastes, and Solomon's Song.* London, 1710. **Hoffmann, J. A.** *Neue Erklärung des Buches Hiob, darin das Buch selbst aus der Grundsprache mit den darin liegenden Nachdruck ins Teutsche übersetzt; hienächst aus denen Altherümern und der morgenländischen Philosophie erläutert; überhaupt aber die darin verborgene tieffe Wiesheit geseiget wird. Jetzo nach des Verfassers seel. Abschiede mit Fliess ubersehen, und mit einer Paraphrasi, wie auch Vorbericht von Hiobs Person, Buche und dessen Auslegern vermehret.* Hamburg, 1734. **Hog [Hogaeus Scotus], W.** *Paraphrasis in Jobum poetica. Auctore Gulielmo Hogaeo Scoto.* London, 1682. **Holden, L.** *A Paraphrase on the Books of Job, Psalms, Proverbs, and Ecclesiastes, with notes critical, historical and practical.* 4 vols. London, 1763. **Hottinger, J. H.** *Liber Ijobh post textum hebraeum et versionem verbalem latinum, analysis simplex, sed accurata, omnium radicum.* Zurich, 1689. **Houbigant, C. F.** *Biblia Hebraica cum notis criticis et versione latina ad notas criticas facta.* 4 vols. Paris, 1753 [Unvocalized Heb. text, Latin translation, and notes]. ———. *Notae criticae in universos Veteris Testamenti libros cum hebraice, tum graecae scriptos cum integris ejusdem prolegomenis.* 2 vols. Frankfurt, 1777. [The notes only, the same as in the work above]. **Huelga [Huerga], C. de la.** *Commentaria in librum beati Job et in Cantica Canticorum Salomonis regis.* Complutum, Alcala, 1582. **Hufnagel, W. F.** *Hiob neu übersetzt mit Anmerkungen.* Erlangen, 1781. **Hutcheson, G.** *An Exposition of the Book of Job. Being the sum of cccxvi lectures preached in the City of Edenburgh.* London, 1669.

Ilgen, K. D. *Jobi antiquissimi carminis Hebraici natura atque virtutes.* Leipzig, 1789. **Isham, Z.** *Divine Philosophy: containing the Books of Job, Proverbs, and Wisdom, with explanatory notes.* London, 1706.

Janssonius, J. *In propheticum librum Job enarratio.* Louvain, 1623. **Járava, F. de.** *Liciones de Job en castellano.* Antwerp, 1550. **Johannes a Jesu-Maria.** *Liber Job paraphrastice explicatus.* Rome, 1611. **Jonghen, H. de.** *Brevis elucidatio litteralis libri Jobi.* Antwerp, 1661. **Joubert, F.** *Éclaircissements sur les discours de Job.* Paris, 1741.

Kessler, C. D. *Hiob aus dem hebräischen Original neu übersetzt und mit erklärenden Anmerkungen versehen zum allgemeinen Gebrauche.* Tübingen, 1784. **Kortum, R. A.** *Das Buch Hiob, aus dem hebräischen Grund-text auffs neue getreulich ins Teutsche übersetzt, nebst einer paraphrasi.* Leipzig, 1708.

Langhorne, W. *Job. A poem, in three books.* London, 1760. **Lausana, J. de.** *Moralitates in Iob.* Limoges, 1528. **Lavater, L.** *Liber Iobi, homiliis CXLI . . . Germanica lingua explicatus . . . ac recens . . . Latinitate donatus.* Zurich, 1585. ———. *Beati Iobi fides et confessio de resurrectione mortuorum, novissime iudicio, et vita aeterna, homilia L. Lauerteri . . . illustrata; nunc primum ex Germanico . . . conversa.* Zurich, 1587. **[Le Maistre, I. L.]** *Job traduit en françois, avec une explication tirée des saints pères, & des auteurs ecclésiastiques.* Paris, 1687. **Leon, Francisco de.** *Sobre el parce mihi.* Pamplona, 1622. **León, Luis Ponce**

de. *Exposición de Job* (1576). First published as *Exposición del libro de Job. Obra posthuma del Padre Fr. L. de León.* Ed. D. T. Gonzalez. Madrid, 1779. Also in *Obras completas castellanas de Fray Luis de León.* Ed. F. Garcia. Madrid: BAC, 1951. 791–1287. See also **Baruzi, J.** *Luis de León, interprète du livre de Job.* Cahiers de la RHPR. Paris: Presses Universitaires de France, 1966. **Arkin, A. Ḥ.** *La influencia de la exégesis hebrea en los comentarios bíblicos de Fray Luis de León.* Madrid: Instituto 'Arias Montano,' 1966. 65–182. **Lowth, R.** *De sacra poesi hebraeorum. Praelectiones Academicae.* Oxford: Clarendon, 1753. Praelectio 37. De poemati Jobi argumento et fine. [= *Lectures on the Sacred Poetry of the Hebrews.* Tr. G. Gregory. London, 1789.] **Lutz, R.** *Commentariorum, quibus beati viri Iob historia . . . breviter explicatur, libri II.* Basel, 1559.

Manley, T. *The Affliction and Deliverance of the Saints: or, the whole booke of Iob, composed into English heroicall verse, metaphrastically.* London, 1652. **Mercerus [Mercier], J.** *Commentarii in librum Iob.* Geneva, 1573. **Merlin, P.** *Iiob Petri Merlini commentariis illustratus. Analytico methodo in gratiam studiosae iuventutis conscriptus.* Geneva, 1599. **Michaelis, J. D.** *Deutsche Übersetzung des Alten Testaments mit Anmerkungen für Ungelehrte. Das Buch Hiob.* Göttingen, 1765. ———. "Anzeige der Varianten im Buch Hiob." In his *Orientalische und exegetische Bibliothek* 7 (1774) 217–47; 8 (1775) 179–224. **Michaelis, J. H.** *Notae in Jobum.* Halle, 1720. **Moldenhawer, D. G.** *Hiob. Übersetzt.* 2 vols. Leipzig, 1780–81. **Montano, Arias.** *Liber Ijob Chaldaice et Latine, cum notis.* Paris, 1632. **Morgan, W.** *Llyvyr Job* [First Welsh translation]. London, 1588. Repr. Oxford: J. G. Evans, 1888. **Morillon, G. de.** *Paraphrase sur le livre de Iob, en vers françois.* Paris, 1668.

Narhamer, J. *Historia Jobs 1546.* Ed. Barbara Könneker and W. F. Michael. Arbeiten zur mittleren deutschen Literatur 12. Frankfurt: Lang, 1983. **Nebiensis, A. J.** *Liber beati Job: quem nuper hebraice veritati restituit.* Paris, 1520.

Oecolampadius, J. *In librum Iob exegemata. Opus admodum eruditum, ac omnibus divinae Scripturae studiosis utile.* Basel, 1532. **Osorio, H. de.** *Paraphraseon in Job libri III.* Cologne, 1579.

P., R., minister of the gospel. *The Book of Job in meeter, as to several of those excellent things contain'd therein, the better to familiarize them, and to bring them the more into use, for peoples benefit, to be sung after the ordinary, and usual tunes.* London, 1700. **Patrick, S.** *The Book of Job Paraphras'd.* London, 1679. ———. *The Books of Job, Psalms, Proverbs, Ecclesiastes, and the song of Solomon, paraphras'd: with arguments to each chapter, and annotations thereupon.* London, 1710. **Pélerin, J. [Le Viateur]** *Texte de Hiob, translate selon la verite hebraique. Et bref commentaire du Viateur [Jean Pélerin] sur icelluy.* Paris, 1530. **Peters, C.** *A Critical Dissertation on the Book of Job, wherein the account given of that book by the author of The Divine Legation of Moses Demonstrated, is particularly considered; the antiquity of the book vindicated; the great text (Chap. xix.25—) explained; and a future state shewn to have been the popular belief of the ancient Jews or Hebrews.* 2d ed. London, 1757. **Pineda, J. de.** *Commentariorum in Iob libri tredecim, adiuncta singulis capitibus sua paraphrasi, quae et longioris commentarii continet.* Madrid, 1600 [usually printed in editions of the biblical commentaries of Cornelius a Lapide]. See also **García Moreno, A.** *El sentido del dolor en el libro de Job según Juan de Pineda.* Diss. Gregorian University, 1977. ———. "Juan de Pineda y el libro de Job." *EstBíb* 35 (1976) 23–47, 165–85. **Piscator, J.** *In librum Jobi commentarius. In quo, praeter novam versionem, versioni Tremellio-Junianae e regione adjectam, ordine & distincte proponuntur I. Analysis logica singulorum capitum. II. Scholia in singula capita. III. Observationes locorum doctrinae e singulis capitibus depromtae.* Herborn, 1612. **Poix, L. de.** *Essai sur le livre de Job.* Paris, 1768. **Pole, M.** *Synopsis criticorum aliorumque scripturae interpretum.* London, 1671. 2:1–498. **Presbyter of the Church of England, A.** *A Short Paraphrase on the Book of Job with arguments to each chapter.* London, 1716.

Quevedo y Villegas, F. G. de. *La constancia y paciencia del Santo Job en sus peridas endermedades y persecuciones* (1641). First published 1713. Also in *Obras Completas.* Madrid, 1969. 1:1322–86. ———. *La providencia de Dios, padecida de los que la niegan y gozada de los que la confiesan. Doctrina estudiada en los gusanos y persecuciones de Job.* Zaragoza, 1700.

See also **Piero, R. A. del.** "Quevedo y Juan de Pineda." *Modern Philology* 56 (1958) 82–91. ———. "Two Notes on Quevedo's Job." *Romanic Review* 50 (1959) 9–24. **Reiske, J. J.** *Coniecturae in Jobum et Proverbia Salomonis.* Leipzig, 1779. **Rezzano, F.** *Il Libro di Giobbe, esposto in Italiana poesia, con annotazioni, dall' Abate Francesco Rezzano.* Nizza, 1781. **Sanctius [Sanchez], G.** *In librum Iob commentarii cum paraphrasi.* Lyon, 1625. **Sander, H.** *Das Buch Hiob zum allgemeinen Gebrauche.* Frankfurt, 1780. **Sandys, G.** *A Paraphrase upon the Divine Poems. A Paraphrase upon Job.* . . . London, 1638. **Savonarola, G.** *Prediche sopra Giobbe.* In *Edizione Nazionale delle Opere di G. Savonarola.* III/1–2. Rome: A. Belardetti, 1957. **Schmidt, S.** *In librum Ijobi commentarius, in quo, cum optimis quibusque commentatoribus, tum Hebraeis tum Christianis, cohaerentia et vocabula diligenter expenduntur, et sensus studiose eruitur.* Strasbourg, 1670. **Schnurrer, C. F.** *Animadversiones ad quaedam loca Iobi.* Tübingen, 1781. **Schultens, A.** *Animadversiones philologicae in Jobum, in quibus plurima . . . ope linguae Arabicae et affinium illustrantur.* Utrecht, 1708. ———. *Liber Iobi cum nova versione ad Hebraeum fontem et commentario perpetuo, in quo Veterum et Recentionum Interpretum cogitata praecipua expenduntur: genuinus sensus ad priscum linguae genium indagatur, atque ex filo, et nexu universo, argumenti nodus intricatissimus evolvitur.* Leiden, 1737. ———. *Commentarius in Librum Iobi. In compendium redegit et observationes criticas atque exegeticas adspersit G. I. L. Vogel.* Halle, 1773–74. **Schultz, J. C. F.** *Scholia in Vetus Testamentum.* Vol. 6. Nuremburg, 1792. **Scott, T.** *The Book of Job in English verse; translated from the original Hebrew; with remarks, historical, critical, and explanatory.* London, 1771. **Senault, J.–F.** *Paraphrase sur Job.* Paris, 1637. ———. *A Paraphrase upon Job; written in French.* London, 1648. ———. *The Pattern of Patience, in the example of holy Job: a paraphrase upon the whole book.* London, 1657. **Società Clementina, Paris.** *Saggio sopra il Libro di Giobbbe secondo la nuova versione fatta su l'ebreo da' PP. della Società Clementina di Parigi.* Milan, 1774. **Sotomayor [Sotomaior], L. de.** Paris, 1610. **Sousa, J. de Mello de.** *In librum Job paraphrasis poetica.* Lyon, 1615. **Spanheimius [Spanheim], F.** *Historia Jobi, sive de obscuris historiae commentatio.* Leiden, 1670. **Steuchus, A.** *Enarrationes in librum Jobi.* Venice, 1567. **Strigelius, V.** *Liber Iob, ad Ebraicam veritatem recognitus et argumentis atque scholiis illustrata.* Leipzig, 1571. **Sylvester, J.** *A divine and true tragicomedy. Iob Triumphant in his Triall: or, The Historie of his Heroicall patience, in a measured Metaphrase.* In *The second session of the parliament of vertues royall (continued by prorogation) for better propagation of all true pietie and utter extirpation of atheisme and hypocrisie, avarice and crueltie, pride and luxurie.* In his *Du Bartas: his diuine weekes, and workes.* London, 1633. 886–950.

Talleoni, M. *Volgarizzamento in terza rima del sacro libro di Giob.* Osimo, 1764. **Terentius, J.** *Liber Ijobi, Chaldaice et Latine, cum notis, item Graece στιχηρως, cum variantibus lectionibus.* Franeker, 1663. **Thompson, W.** *A poetical paraphrase on part of the Book of Job* [chaps. 40–42] *in imitation of the style of Milton.* Dublin, 1726. **[Thou, J. A. de.]** *Iobus, sive de constantia libri IIII. poetica metaphrasi explicati.* Paris, 1587. **Titelmann, F.** *Elucidatio paraphrastica in Jobum.* Antwerp, 1547. [= *Paraphrastica Elucidatio in librum D. Iob, priore aeditione multo castigatior, adiectis annotationibus in loca difficiliora.* Paris, 1550]. **Tuccius Lucensis.** *Lectiones in Job.* Rome, 1617.

Vavassor, F. *Jobus brevi commentario et metaphrasi poetica illustratus.* Paris, 1638.

Weidenbach, K. F. *Das Buch Hiob aus dem hebräischen mit Anmerkungen von H. A. Schultens nach dessen Tode hrsg. und vollendet von H. Muntinghe. Aus dem holländischen mit Zusätzen und Anmerkungen des Herrn D. und Professor I. P. Berg.* Leipzig, 1797. **Wesley, S.** *Dissertationes in librum Jobi.* London, 1736. **Wildt, J.** *Iobi historia Christlich vnd nützlich Predig weyss aussgelegt . . . Durch Johan Wildt . . . geprediget . . . 1552.* Mainz, 1558. **Worthington, W.** *A Dissertation on the Design and Argumentation of the Book of Job.* In his *An Essay on the Scheme and Conduct, Procedure and Extent of Man's Redemption.* London, 1743. 463–527.

Young, E. *A Paraphrase on Part of the Book of Job.* London, 1719.

Zampieri, C. *Giobbe esposto in ottava rima. Poema del Conte Cammillo Zampieri.* Piacenza,

1763. **Zúñiga, D. de.** *Commentaria in librum Job, quibus triplex eius editio Vulgata Latina, Hebraica et Graeca LXX Interpretum, necnon in Chaldaea explicantur et inter se concilantur.* Toledo, 1584.

e. Christian and Jewish, Nineteenth and Twentieth Centuries

The great majority of the works included here are commentaries of the conventional kind. There are also some other works, such as chapter by chapter expositions, which also treat the Book of Job in the order of its contents. Since most of the commentaries include a new translation by the commentator, those few translations of Job that have not been accompanied by commentary are also mentioned here. No account of course is taken of translations of Job that form part of a version of the whole Bible or some large part of it.

There follows, arranged by year of publication, a personal selection of the commentaries that may be judged to have had the greatest survival value—which does not necessarily imply that they are the most important.

1851	Schlottmann	1897	Duhm	1963	Terrien
1864	Delitzsch	1904	Peake	1965	Pope
1871	Merx	1921	Driver and Gray	1970	Rowley
1874	Hitzig	1926	Dhorme	1976	Andersen
1884	Davidson	1937	Hölscher	1978	Gordis
1891	Dillmann (3d ed.)	1960–63	Horst	1981	De Wilde
1896	Budde	1963	Fohrer	1985	Habel

Abraham, Israel ben. אשכנזי ותרגום באור עם איוב ספר. Offenbach, 1807. **Adams, H. W.** *The Book of Job in poetry; or, a Song in the night.* New York: R. Craighead, 1864. **Alonso Schökel, L., and J. L. Ojeda.** *Job.* Los Libros Sagrados 16. Madrid: Ediciones Cristiandad, 1971. [Translation by Alonso Schökel and Ojeda, commentary by Alonso Schökel]. **Alonso Schökel, L., and Sicre Díaz, J. L.** *Job, comentario teológico y literario.* Nueva Biblia Española. Madrid: Cristiandad, 1983. **Andersen, F. I.** *Job. An Introduction and Commentary.* TOTC. Leicester: Tyndale Press, 1976. **Anderson, H.** "The Book of Job." In *The Interpreter's One-Volume Commentary on the Bible,* ed. C. M. Laymon. Nashville: Abingdon, 1972. 238–52. **Andreä, H. V.** *Hiob: Classisches Gedicht der Hebräer, Aus dem Grundtexte neu übersetzt und mit Andeutungen zum tieferen Verständniss versehen.* Barmen, 1870. **Anon.** *The Book of Job, illustrated with fifty engravings from drawings by John Gilbert, and with explanatory notes and poetical parallels.* London: J. Nisbet & Co., 1857. **Arnheim, H.** *Das Buch Hiob übersetzt und vollständig commentirt.* Glogau: H. Prausnitz, 1836. **Artom, E. S.** מפרש :איוב ספר. Tel Aviv: Yavneh, 1954. **Augé, R.** *Job. La Biblia.* Versió . . . i Comentari. (Montserrat) 9. Monestir de Montserrat, 1959. **Avronin, A.** See Rabinowitz, A. Z.

Baethgen, F. *Hiob deutsch, mit kurzen Anmerkungen für Ungelehrte.* Göttingen: Vandenhoeck & Ruprecht, 1898. **Ball, C. J.** *The Book of Job: A Revised Text and Version.* Oxford: Clarendon, 1922. **Baour Lormian, L. F.** *Le Livre de Job, traduit en vers français.* Paris: Lallemand-Lépine, 1847. **Barbaresi, P.** *Il Libro di Giobbe: Versione poetica.* Milan, 1894. **Barelli, V.** *Il Libro di Giobbe: Recato in versi italiani.* Como: F. Ostinelli, 1891. **Barnes, A.** *Notes, critical, explanatory, and practical, on the Book of Job, with a new translation, and an introductory dissertation.* Glasgow, 1847. **Barton, G. A.** *Commentary on the Book of Job.* New York: Macmillan, 1911. **Ben Meir, E.** *Menschenleid und Sünde? Das Buch Hiob im Lichte neuer Kommentare übersetzt und bearbeitet.* Frankfurt, 1930. [Chaps. 1–4.] **Bergant, Dianne.** *Job, Ecclesiastes.* OT Message 18. Wilmington: Glazier, 1982. **Berkholz, C. A.** *Das Buch Hiob: Ein Versuch.* Riga: E. Götschel, 1859. [Translation]. **Bernard, H. H.** איוב ספר: *The Book of Job, as expounded to his Cambridge pupils by the late H. H. Ber-*

nard . . . Edited, with a translation and additional notes, by . . . Frank Chance. Vol. 1. London: Hamilton, Adams & Co., 1864. **Bernard, V. L.** *A Sacred Poem in four books: Being a paraphrase on the Book of Job.* Norwich, 1800. **Bertie, P.** *Le Poème de Job, traduction nouvelle, introduction et notes.* Paris: Rieder, 1929. **Bickell, G.** *Das Buch Job nach Anleitung der Strophik und der Septuaginta auf seine ursprüngliche Form zurückgefürht und in Versmasse des Urtextes übersetzt.* Vienna: Karl Gerold's Sohn, 1894. **Bleeker, L. H. K.** *Job. Tekst en Uitleg.* Praktische Bijbelverklaring. Groningen: Wolters, 1926. **Blei, K.** *Job: Verklaring ven een Bijbelgedeelte.* Kampen: Kok, 1978, **Blumenfeld, B.** ספר איוב עם תרגום אשכנזי ובאור. Vienna, 1826. **Böckel, E. G. A.** *Das Buch Hiob, übersetzt und . . . kurz erläutert . . . mit einer Zugabe philologischer und exegetischer Anmerkungen.* Hamburg, 1830. **Böttcher, V.** *Das Buch Hiob nach Luther und der Probebibel aus dem Grundtext bearbeitet und mit Bemerkungen versehen.* Leipzig: J. Lehmann, 1885. **Boileau, M. J.** *Le Livre inspiré de Job: Discours de ce prince d'Idumée, des princes ses amis et de Dieu lui-même sur l'origine des souffrances et de la douleur ou du mal physique dans la vie terrestre. Paraphrase.* Paris: V. Retaux et Fils, 1893. **Bourke, M. M.** *The Book of Job: Parts 1 & 2, with a Commentary.* New York: Paulist Press, 1962–63. **Bradley, G. G.** *Lectures on the Book of Job delivered in Westminster Abbey.* Oxford: Clarendon, 1887. **Brates, J.** *Job. Traducción y comentario.* BAC 287. Madrid: BAC, 1969. 435–739. **Bridel, J. L.** *Le livre de Job, nouvellement traduit d'après le texte original non ponctué et les anciennes versions, notamment l'arabe et la syriaque; avec un commentaire.* Paris: F. Didot, 1818. **Bruges, W. E.** *Book of Job.* Bognor Regis: New Horizon, 1983. [A translation in iambic pentameters.] **Bruno, A.** *Das Hohelied: Das Buch Hiob. Eine rhythmische und textkritische Untersuchung.* Stockholm: Almqvist & Wiksell, 1956. **Buber, M.** *Ijob verdeutscht.* Frankfurt: Insel-Verlag, 1965. **Bückers, H.** *Die Makkabäerbücher, Das Buch Job, übersetzt und erklärt.* Freiburg im Breisgau: Herder, 1939. **Budde, K. F. R.** *Das Buch Hiob, übersetzt und erklärt.* HAT. Göttingen: Vandenhoeck & Ruprecht, 1896. 2d ed., 1913. **Bullinger, E. W.** *Book of Job: Part 1, The Oldest Lesson in the World. Part 2, A Rhythmical Translation* [in iambic pentameters] *with The Structure; and brief, explanatory, and critical notes.* London: Eyre and Spottiswoode, 1904. **Busch, K. A.** *Hiob: Ein Lehrgedicht in Wechselgesprächen aus dem Alten Testament in neuen deutschen Rhythmen.* Dresden: Sturm, 1935. **Buskes, J. J.** *Job.* Berne: Bosch & Keuning, 1935. **Buttenwieser, M.** *The Book of Job.* London: Hodder & Stoughton, 1922. **Caminero, F. J.** *El libro de Job: Versión directa del hebreo e introducción crítica.* Madrid: Voluntad, 1924. **Carey, C. P.** *The Book of Job translated . . . on the basis of the Authorized Version: explained in a large body of notes . . . and illustrated by extracts from various works . . . and a map; with six preliminary dissertations, an analytical paraphrase, and Meisner's and Doederlein's selection of the various readings of the Hebrew text.* London: Wertheim, Macintosh & Hunt, 1858. **Carlisle, T. J.** *Journey with Job.* Grand Rapids: Eerdmans, 1976. [Versified commentary.] **Cary, O.** *The Man who feared God for Nought, being a rhythmical version of the Book of Job.* London: Elliot Stock, 1898. **Castelli, D.** *Il Poema semitico del pessimismo. Il libro di Job. Tradotto e commentato.* Florence, 1897. **Chouraqui, A.** *Iyov. La Bible traduite et présentée 15.* Paris: Desclée de Brouwer, 1974. **Clarke, H. J.** *The Book of Job: A Metrical Translation with introduction and notes.* London: Hodder & Stoughton, 1880. **Clines, D. J. A.** "Job." In *A Bible Commentary for Today,* ed. G. C. D. Howley. London: Pickering & Inglis, 1979. 559–92. 2d ed. in *The International Bible Commentary,* ed. F. F. Bruce. Basingstoke, Hants.: Marshall Pickering, 1986. 520–51. **Clow, W. McC.,** and **W. G. Jordan.** *Job: A Little Library of Exposition, with New Studies.* London: Cassell, 1928. **Coleman, J. N.** *The Book of Job, translated from the Hebrew with notes explanatory, illustrative, and critical.* London: J. Nisbet & Co., 1869. [**Conant, T. J.**] *Book of Job: The common English version, the Hebrew text, and the revised version, with critical and philological notes.* London: Trübner, 1856. **Consolo, B.** *Volgarizzamento del libro di Job, con spiegazione e commenti.* Florence, 1874. **Coutts, F.** [**B. F. T. M.**] [**Coutts-Nevill, F. B. T.**]. *The Heresy of Job, with the inventions of William Blake.* London: John Lane, 1907. **Cowles, H.** *The Book of Job, with notes, critical, explanatory, and practical . . . With a new translation appended.* New York: D. Appleton & Co., 1877. **Cox, S.** *A Commentary on the*

Book of Job, with a translation. London: Kegan, Paul & Co., 1880. **Crampon, A.** *Job.* In *La Sainte Bible.* Paris, 1952. **Curry, D.** *The Book of Job, according to the version of 1885, with an expository and practical commentary.* New York: Phillips & Hunt, 1887. **Davidson, A. B.** *A Commentary, grammatical and exegetical, on the Book of Job, with a translation.* Vol. 1 [chaps. 1–14]. London: Williams and Norgate, 1862. ———. *The Book of Job, with notes, introduction and appendix.* CamB. Cambridge: CUP, 1884. **Davidson, A. B.,** and **H. C. O. Lanchester.** *The Book of Job, with Notes, Introduction and Appendix, Adapted to the Text of the Revised Version with Some Supplementary Notes.* CamB. Cambridge: CUP, 1926. **Dawidowicz, D.** *Hebräisches Kommentar zum Ijob-Buche: Mite einer deutschen Beilage: 'Zur Auslegung des Ijob-Buches' von Prof. A. Berliner.* Berlin: L. Lamm, 1913. ———. ספר איוב. *Das Buch Hiob: Mit Uebersetzung und Erläuterung. Deutsche Bearbeitung des* חידות מני קדם (*Rätsel aus dem Morgenlande*). Berlin: A. Schwetschke & Sohn, 1919. **Delebecque, Edmée.** *Le Livre de Job: Traduit de l'hébreu.* Paris: E. Leroux, 1914. **Delitzsch, Franz J.** *Das Buch Iob: Mit Beiträgen von Prof. Dr. Fleischer und Consul Dr. Wetzstein, nebst einer Karte und Inschrift.* Leipzig, 1864. ———. *Biblical Commentary on the Book of Job.* Trans. F. Bolton. 2 vols. Edinburgh: T. & T. Clark, 1866. **Delitzsch, Friedrich.** *Das Buch Hiob, neu übersetzt und kurz erklärt: Ausgabe mit sprachlichem Kommentar.* Leipzig: J. C. Hinrichs, 1902. **De Rossi, G. B.** *Il Libro di Giobbe tradotto dal testo originale.* Parma, 1812. **Dhorme, E.** *Le livre de Job.* Paris: Gabalda, 1926. Tr. H. Knight. *A Commentary on the Book of Job.* London: Thomas Nelson & Sons, 1967. ———. "Job." In *La Bible de la Pléiade.* Paris: Gallimard, 1959. **Dillmann, A.** *Hiob,* 1869. 3d ed. Leipzig: S. Hirzel, 1891. **Dillon, E. J.** *The Sceptics of the Old Testament, Job, Koheleth, Agur, with English text translated for the first time from the primitive Hebrew as restored on the basis of recent philological discoveries.* London: Isbister & Co., 1895. ———. *The Original Poem of Job, translated from the restored text.* London: T. Fisher Unwin, 1905. **Dimmler, E.** *Job übersetzt, eingeleitet und erklärt.* München Gladbach: Volkvereins-Verlag, 1922. **Dimnent, E. D.** *The Book of Job: The Poem, an Epic Version in English.* New York: Fleming H. Revell, 1937. **Donn, T. M.** *The Divine Challenge, Being a Metrical Paraphrase of the Book of Job in Four-Line Stanzas of Anapaestic Tetrameters in Rhyme.* Inverness: Robt. Carruthers and Sons, 1963. **Driver, S. R.** *The Book of Job in the Revised Version, Edited with Introductions and Brief Annotations.* Oxford: Clarendon Press, 1906. **Driver, S. R.,** and **Gray, G. B.** *A Critical and Exegetical Commentary on the Book of Job together with a New Translation.* ICC. Edinburgh: T. & T. Clark, 1921. See also **Compston, H. F. B.** "Marginal Notes on Driver-Gray's 'Job.'" *ExpT* 42 (1930–31) 92–93. **Duhm, B.** *Das Buch Hiob erklärt.* KHC. Tübingen: J. C. B. Mohr, 1897.

Ebrard, [J. H.] A. *Das Buch Hiob als poetische Kunstwerk übersetzt und erläutert für Gebildete.* London, 1858. **Edel, R.-F.** *Hebräisch-Deutsche Präparation zum Buch Hiob.* Lüdernscheid-Lobetal: Oekumenischer-Verlag, 1984. **Eerdmans, B. D.** *Studies in Job.* 2 vols. Leiden: Burgersdijk & Niermans, 1939. **Ehrlich, A. B.** *Randglossen zur hebräischen Bibel. VI. Psalmen, Sprüche, und Hiob.* Leipzig: J. C. Hinrichs, 1918. [Repr. Hildesheim: Georg Olms.] 180–344. **Eichhorn, J. G.** *Hiob.* Leipzig: Weidmann, 1800. **Ellison, H. L.** *From Tragedy to Triumph: The Message of the Book of Job.* London: Paternoster Press, 1958. [= *A Study of Job: From Tragedy to Triumph.* Grand Rapids: Zondervan, 1971.] **Elzas, A.** *The Book of Job, translated from the Hebrew text, with an introduction and notes, critical and explanatory.* London: Trübner & Co., 1872. **Epping, W.,** and **J. T. Nelis.** *Job.* Roermond: Romen, 1968. **Ewald, G. H. A. von.** *Das Buch Ijob übersetzt und erklärt. Die Dichter des Alten Testaments.* Göttingen: Vandenhoeck, 1836. ———. *Commentary on the Book of Job with translation.* Tr. J. F. Smith. London: Williams and Norgate, 1882.

Fedrizzi, P. *Giobbe: La Sacra Bibbia, traduta dai testi originali illustrata con note critiche e commentata.* Turin: Marietti, 1972. **Fenton, F.** *The Book of Job: Translated direct from the Hebrew text into English . . . Rendered into the same metre as the original Hebrew word by word and line by line.* London: Elliot Stock, 1898. **Fielding, G. H.** *The Book of Job: A revised text, with introduction and notes.* London: Elliot Stock, 1898. **Figueiredo, C. de.** *O Livro de Job em versos portuguezes.* Lisbon: Livraria Ferreira, 1894. [**Finch Hatton, G. J.**]

Winchilsea, Earl of. *The Poem of the Book of Job done into English verse.* London: Smith, Elder & Co., 1860. **Fischel, S. A. ben Ephraim.** ספר איוב מהכתובים: זאת חלקת מחוקק. Lemberg, 1833. **Fischmann, N. I.** איוב עם פירוש הנקרא שפה לנאמנים. Lemberg, 1854. **Fohrer, G.** *Das Buch Hiob übertragen und herausgegeben.* Krefeld: Scherpe-Verlag, 1948. ———. *Das Buch Hiob.* KAT 16. Gütersloh: Gütersloher Verlagshaus Gerd Mohn, 1963. **Fox, S. H.** *A Metrical Version of the Book of Job.* Part 1 [chaps. 1–20]. London: C. Gilpin, 1852. **Freehof, S. B.** *The Book of Job—A Commentary.* New York: Union of American Hebrew Congregations, 1958. **Fry, J.** *A New Translation and Exposition of the very ancient Book of Job; with notes, explanatory and philological.* London: James Duncan, 1827. **Gaab, J. F.** *Das Buch Hiob.* Tübingen: J. G. Cotta, 1809. **Gans, A.** *Job vertaald en ingeleid.* Leiden, 1952. **Garcia Cordero, M.,** and **G. Perez Rodriguez.** "Job." In *Biblia comentada: Libros Sapiencales.* Madrid: BAC, 1962. 16–167. ———. *Libro de Job: Introducción y comentario.* Madrid: BAC, 1972. **Garland, D. D.** *Job: A Study Guide.* Grand Rapids: Zondervan, 1971. **Genung, J. F.** *The Epic of the Inner Life: Being the Book of Job, translated anew, and accompanied with notes and an introductory essay.* Boston, 1892. **Gibson, E. C. S.** *The Book of Job.* WC. London: Methuen, 1899. **Gibson, J. C. L.** *Job.* Daily Study Bible. Edinburgh: St Andrews Press, 1985. **Gilbert, G. H.** *The Book of Job as Poesy.* Rutland: Tuttle Co., 1886. [Translation into English verse.] ———. *The Poetry of Job. Part I: A rhythmical translation of Job. Part II: Interpretation of the poem.* Chicago: A. C. McClurg, 1889. **Glotzbach, A.** *Het Boek Job: Het Hooglied.* Arnhem: Van Loghum Slaterus, 1938. **Good, E. M.** "Job." In *Harper's Bible Commentary.* Ed. J. L. Mays. San Francisco: Harper & Row, 1988. 407–32. **Good, J. M.** *The Book of Job, literally translated from the original Hebrew, and restored to its natural arrangement: with notes critical and illustrative; and an introductory dissertation on its scene, scope, language, author, and object.* London: Black, Parry and Co., 1812. **Gordis, R.** *The Book of Job: Commentary, New Translation, and Special Notes.* New York: Jewish Theological Seminary of America, 1978. See also his "Observations on Problems and Methods in Biblical Research. Writing a Commentary on Job." *PrAmAcJewRes* 41–42 (1973–74) 105–35. **Graetz, H. H.** *Emendationes in plerosque Sacrae Scripturae Veteris Testamenti libros.* Breslau, 1892–94. **Greenberg, M., J. C. Greenfield,** and **N. M. Sarna.** *The Book of Job, A New Translation according to the Traditional Hebrew Text with Introductions.* Philadelphia: Jewish Publication Society, 1980. **Greene, W. B.** *The Book of Job.* Boston: G. C. Rand & Avery, 1866. [A translation.] **Gualandi, D.** *Giobbe, nuova versione critica.* Rome: Gregorian University, 1976. **Guillaume, A.** "Job." In *A New Commentary on Holy Scripture,* ed. C. Gore, H. L. Goudge, and A. Guillaume. London: SPCK, 1951. ———. *Studies in the Book of Job with a New Translation.* ALUOS Suppl. 2. Leiden: Brill, 1968.

Habel, N. *The Book of Job: Commentary.* CamB. Cambridge: CUP, 1975. ———. *Job.* Knox Preaching Guides. Atlanta: Knox, 1981. ———. *The Book of Job.* OTL. London: SCM, 1985. **Haghebaert, P.** *Het Boek Job, vertaald en uitgelegd.* New ed. Bruges: Bayaert, 1929. **Hahn, H. A.** *Commentar über das Buch Hiob.* Berlin, 1850. **Hakam, A.** ספר איוב: מפורש [*The Book of Job, a commentary*]. Jerusalem: Kook, 1970. **Halsted, O. S.** *The Book Called Job, from the Hebrew, with footnotes.* Newark: author's own ed., 1875. **Hamblen, E. S.** *The Book of Job Interpreted, Illustrated with the Designs of William Blake.* New York: Delphic Studios, 1933. [Commentary.] **Hanson, A. T.,** and **Miriam Hanson.** *The Book of Job: Introduction and Commentary.* Torch Bible. London: SCM, 1953. **Hartley, J. E.** *The Book of Job.* NICOT. Grand Rapids: Eerdmans, 1988. **Hartom, E. S.** See Artom, E. S. **Haupt, [J.] L.** *Hiob: Ein Gespräch über die göttliche Vorsehung. Ins das Deutsche übertragen.* Leipzig, 1847. **Hauser, O.** *Das Buch Hiob: In der Übertragung von Otto Hauser.* Berlin, 1909. **Hayd, H.** *Das Buch Hiob, in gereimten Versmasse übersetzt und mit . . . Erklärungen versehen.* Munich, 1859. **Heavenor, E. S. P.** "Job." In *New Bible Commentary Revised,* ed. D. Guthrie et al. London: IVP, 1970. 421–45. **Heiligstedt, A.** *Commentarius im Jobum.* Halle, 1847. ———. *Praeparation zum Buche Hiob mit den nöthigen, die Uebersetzung und das Verständnis des Textes erleichternden Anmerkungen.* Halle, 1869. **Hengstenberg,**

E. W. *Das Buch Hiob erläutert.* Berlin, 1870. **Herrmann, J.** *Das Buch Hiob. Aus dem Grundtext übersetzt und mit Erläuterungen versehen.* Leipzig: P. Reclam, 1900. **Hertzberg, H. W.** *Das Buch Hiob übersetzt und ausgelegt.* Bibelhilfe für die Gemeinde. Stuttgart: J. G. Oncken, 1949. **Hesse, F.** *Hiob.* Zürcher Bibelkommentar. Zürich: Theologischer Verlag, 1978. **Hirzel, L.** *Hiob, erklärt.* KEH. 2d ed. Leipzig: Wiedmann, 1852. **Hitzig, F.** *Das Buch Hiob übersetzt und ausgelegt.* Leipzig and Heidelberg: C. F. Winter, 1874. **Hoffmann, J. G. E.** *Hiob.* Kiel: C. F. Haeseler, 1891. **Hölscher, G.** *Das Buch Hiob.* HAT. Tübingen: J. C. B. Mohr (Paul Siebeck), 1937. ———. *Das Gedicht von Hiob und seinen drei Freunden übersetzt.* Wiesbaden: Insel-Verlag, 1948. **Hontheim, J.** *Das Buch Hiob als strophisches Kunstwerk nachgewiesen, übersetzt und erklärt.* Freiburg, 1904. **Horst, F.** *Hiob.* BKAT. Vol. 1 (chaps. 1–19). Neukirchen: Neukirchener Verlag, 1960–63. **Hulme, W. E.** *Dialogue in Despair: Pastoral Commentary on the Book of Job.* Nashville: Abingdon, 1968. **Hunt, G.** *The Book of Job: Translated from the Hebrew.* Bath, 1825. **Hupfeld, H.** *Quaestionum in Jobeidos locos vexatos specimen. Commentatio. . . .* Halle: E. Anton, 1853. **Hurwitz (Gurvits), N.** *The Immortal Drama of Life (The Book of Job): The Mystery Book of More than 3000 Years, Translated from the Original.* Cape Town, 1944. **Hutchinson, R. F.** *Thoughts on the Book of Job.* London: S. Bagster & Sons, 1875. **Irwin, W. A.** "Job." In *Peake's Commentary on the Bible,* ed. M. Black and H. H. Rowley. London: Thomas Nelson & Sons, 1962. 391–408.

Janzen, J. G. *Job.* Interpretation. Atlanta: John Knox, 1985. **Jastrow, M.** *The Book of Job: Its Origin, Growth and Interpretation, together with a New Translation Based on a Revised Text.* Philadelphia: Lippincott, 1920. **Jennings, W.** *The Dramatic Poem of Job: A Close Metrical Translation, with Critical and Explanatory Notes.* London: Methuen, 1912. **Jones, G. T.** *Sylwadan eglurhaol ac ymarferol; neu, esponiad byr ar Lyfr Job.* Caerfyddin, 1818. **Junker, H.** *Das Buch Hiob.* EchB. Würzburg: Echter Verlag, 1951. **Justi, K. W.** *Das Buch Hiob, neu übersetzt und erläutert.* Kassel: J. J. Bohné, 1840.

Kahana, A. *Commentary on Job* [Heb]. Tel Aviv: Mekorot, 1928. **Kalt, E.** *Das Buch Job übersetzt und erläutert.* Steyl: Missionsdrückerei, 1924. **Kaplan, J.** ספר איוב: מבוא ופרוש [*The Book of Job: Introduction and Commentary*]. Tel Aviv: Mahbarot Lisparot, 1951. **Kelly, W.** *Notes on the Book of Job, with a new version.* London: G. Morrish, 1879. **Kemmler, G.** *Hiob oder die Weisheit der Urzeit.* Cannstatt: L. Bosheuner, 1858. [Verse translation with some notes.] ———. *Hiob: oder, Kampf und Sieg im Leiden, In dichterischen Form wiedergegeben.* Calw: Verlag der Vereinsbuchhandlung, 1877. **King, E. G.** *The Poem of Job: Translated in the Metre of the Original.* Cambridge: CUP, 1914. **Kissane, E. J.** *The Book of Job Translated from a Critically Revised Hebrew Text with Commentary.* Dublin: Browne & Nolan, 1939. **Kline, M. E.** "Job." *Wycliffe Commentary.* **Knabenbauer, J.** *Commentarius in Librum Iob.* Paris: P. Lethielleux, 1886. **König, E.** *Das Buch Hiob eingeleitet, übersetzt und erklärt.* Gütersloh: C. Bertelsmann, 1929. **Königsberger, B.** *Hiobstudien: Exegetische Untersuchungen zum Buche Hiob nebst einer Einleitung zum Buche.* Breslau: W. Koebner, 1896. **Köster, F. B.** *Das Buch Hiob und der Prediger Salomo's nach ihrer strophischen Anordnung übersetzt: Nebst Abhandlungen über den strophischen Character dieser Bücher, Zum Gebrauche bey akademischen Vorlesungen.* Schleswig: Königliches Taubstummen-Institut, 1831. **Kroeze, J. H.** *Paraphrase van het boek Job.* Franeker: Wever, 1946. ———. *Het Boek Job.* Korte Verklaring. Kampen: J. H. Kok, 1960. ———. *Het Boek Job.* Commentaar op het OT. Kampen: J. H. Kok, 1962. **Kunz, U.** *Hiob.* 1958.

Lambert, F. A. *Das Buch Hiob übertragen und herausgegeben.* Berlin: Furche-Verlag, 1919. **Lamparter, H.** *Das Buch der Anfechtung, übersetzt und ausgelegt.* Die Botschaft des ATs. Stuttgart: Calwer, 1951. **Langer, J.** *Das Buch Job in neuer und treuer Uebersetzung nach der Vulgata, mit fortwährender Berücksichtigung des Urtextes.* Luxembourg, 1884. **Larcher, C.** *Le Livre de Job, traduit.* BJ. La Sainte Bible. Paris: Cerf, 1950. **Laurens, H.** *Job et les Psaumes: Traduction nouvelle d'après l'hébreu, les anciennes versions et les plus habiles interprètes, précédées de deux discours préliminaires et accompagnée d'arguments et de notes.* Paris: Gaume Frères, 1839. **Le Blanc d'Ambonne, M. P.** *Le Livre de Job allégoriquement expliqué: La grande tribulation de l'Église. . . .* Nantes: E. Grimaud, 1893. [Vulgate and allegorical explanation in parallel columns.] **Lee, C.** *The trial of virtue, a sacred poem; being a paraphrase of the whole book of Job . . . interspersed with critical notes upon a variety of its passages.* Hartford: Lincoln & Gleason, 1806. **Lee, S.** *The Book of the Patriarch Job, translated from the original Hebrew . . . [with] an introduction, on the history, times, country, friends and book of the patriarch.* London: James Duncan, 1837. **Le Hir, A. M.** *Le Livre de Job: Traduction sur l'Hébreu et commentaire.* Paris: Jouby & Roger, 1873. **Leimbach, A.** *Das Buch Job, übersetzt und kurz erklärt.* Fulda: Fuldaer Aktiendruckerei, 1911. **Leroux, P.** *Job, drame en cinq actes, avec prologue et épilogue, par le Prophète Isaie, retrouvé, rétabli dans son integrité, et traduit littéralement sur le texte hébreu.* With Appendix, "Le Job des Églises, et le Job de M. Renan" (pp. 201–389). Grasse, 1866. **Lesêtre, H.** *Le livre de Job traduit et commenté.* Paris: Lethielleux, 1886. **Levavasseur, B. M. F.** *Le livre de Job, traduit en vers français avec le texte de la Vulgate en regard; suivi de notes explicatives, ainsi que des variantes tirées des plus célèbres interprètes de la Bible, et de quelques poésies françaises du traducteur.* Paris: P. Delaunay et G. Dentu, 1826. **Levi, B. G.** *Commentary on the Book of Job.* New York: Bloch, 1946. **Lewis, T.** *The Book of Job: A Rhythmical Version with introduction and annotations,* with O. Zöckler, *A Commentary.* Lange's Commentary 7. Tr. L. J. Evans. Edinburgh: T. & T. Clark, 1875. **Ley, J.** *Das Buch Hiob nach seinem Inhalt, seiner Kunstgestaltung und religiösen Bedeutung. Für gebildete Leser dargestellt.* Halle: Verlag der Buchhandlung des Waisenhauses, 1903. [Commentary.] **Lods, A.,** and **L. Randon.** "Job." *La Bible du Centenaire.* Vol. 3. Paris, 1947. **Lofthouse, W. F.** "Book of Job." In *Abingdon Bible Commentary.* New York: Abingdon-Cokesbury, 1929. 483–508. **Loisy, A.** *Le livre de Job, traduit de l'hébreu, avec une introduction.* Amiens: Imprimerie Rousseau-Leroy, 1892. **Löwenthal, M.** איוב. *Hiob: Praktische Philosophie oder klare Darstellung der im Buche Hiob obwaltenden Ideen; nebst wortgetreuer, rhythmisch gegeliederter Uebersetzung und fortlaufenden Commentar.* Frankfurt, 1846. **Lubsczyk, H.** *Das Buch Ijob erläutert.* Düsseldorf: Patmos, 1969. **Luzzatto, S. D.** *Il Libro di Giobbe volgarizzato ad uso degli Israeliti.* Trieste: F. Marenigh, 1853. [Translation.] **Luzzi, G.** *Giobbe tradotto dall'ebraico e annotato.* Florence, 1918.

MacBeath, A. *The Book of Job: A Study Manual.* Glasgow: Pickering and Inglis, 1967. **MacKenzie, R. A. F.** "Job." In *Jerome Bible Commentary,* 1968. 511–33. **Maizel, S.** ספר איוב על ספר באור הוא :ס"שבי דברי ספר עם :איוב. Warsaw, 1899. **Malet, A.** *The Book of Job in* [2146 lines of] *blank verse.* Ashcott, 1880. **Margolfo, P.** *Lamentazioni di Giobbe e di Geremia.* Naples: Banzoli, 1840. **Marinellius, P. P.** *Job, Apocalypsis, et Moysis Cantica.* Ancona, 1846. **Marshall, J. T.** *The Book of Job.* An American Commentary on the Old Testament. Philadelphia: American Baptist Publication Society, 1904. **Matinez, J. M.** *Job, la fe en conflicto: comentario y reflectiones sobre el libro de Job.* Barcelona: CLIE, 1982. **Matthes, J. C.** *Het Boek Job vertaald en verklaard.* Utrecht, 1865. **McCarthy, C.,** and **V. Huonder.** *The Book of Job/Le livre de Job. Preliminary Report on the Hebrew Old Testament Project.* Vol. 3. Stuttgart: United Bible Societies, 1977. **McKenna, D. L.** *Job.* Communicator's Commentary. Waco, TX: Word, 1986. **Meikle, W.** *The Book of Job in metre, according to the most approved commentaries.* Falkirk, 1869. **Merx, A.** *Das Gedicht von Hiob: Hebräischer Text, kritisch bearbeitet und übersetzt, nebst sachlicher und kritischer Einleitung.* Jena: Mauke's Verlag, 1871. **Millet, A.** *Le Livre de Job traduit en vers.* Lyon: Vitte & Perrussel, 1887. **Minn, H. R.** *The Burden of This Unintelligible World, or, The Mystery of Suffering: Being a Rhythmical Version of the Book of Job, Annotated.* Auckland: Whitcombe and Tombs, 1942. ———. *The Book of Job: A Translation with Introduction and Short Notes.* Auckland: University of Auckland Press, 1965. **Mitchell, S.** *Into the Whirlwind: A Translation of the Book of Job.* Garden City, NY: Doubleday, 1979. **Montet, E.** "Job." *La Bible du Centenaire.* Paris: Société Biblique, 1932. 3:215–72. **Montvaillant, A. de.** *Poètes bibliques. Le livre de Job mis en vers français.* Paris: Fischbacher, 1897. **Mosner, H.** *Hiob ins Deutsche übersetzt und mit hebräischen Anmerkungen versehen.* Halle, 1858. [Chaps. 1–11:8.] **Moulton, R. G.** *The Book of Job, Edited with an Introduction and Notes.* The Modern Reader's Bible. New York: Macmillan, 1906. **Mowinckel, S.** *Diktet om Ijōb og hans tu venner.* Kristiania: H. Aschehough, 1924. ———. "Diktet om Job." *Det*

gamle Testamentet. 1955. 293–384. **Mumford, A. H.** *The Book of Job: A Metrical Version, with an Introductory Essay: "The Significance of the Book of Job" by A. S. Peake.* London: Hodder & Stoughton, 1922. **Murphy, R. E.** *Wisdom Literature: Job, Proverbs, Ruth, Canticles, Ecclesiastes and Esther.* FOTL 13. Grand Rapids: Eerdmans, 1981. **Nairne, A.** *The Book of Job, edited with an introduction.* Cambridge: CUP, 1935. **Neiman, D.** *The Book of Job. A Presentation of the Book with Selected Portions Translated from the Original Hebrew Text.* Jerusalem: Masada, 1972. **Nesfield, V.** *Let Cockle Grow Instead of Barley.* London: A. J. David. n.d. **Neumann, R.** *The Book of Job: A Metrical Translation, with a Critical Introduction.* Burlington, IA: Lutheran Literary Board, 1934. **Noyes, G. A.** *Job. A Translation in the Hebrew Rhythm.* London: Luzac, 1915. ———. *A New Translation of the Book of Job.* 2d ed. Boston: J. Monroe & Co., 1838. **Noyes, G. R.** *An Amended Version of the Book of Job, with an introduction and notes chiefly explanatory.* Cambridge, MA: Hilliard & Brown, 1827.
Odiosus, *pseud.* ספר איוב. *Das Buch Ijob im engeren Anschluss an den masoretischen Urtext deutsch übersetzt und mit Erläuterungen versehen von Odiosus.* Lieferung 1 [chaps. 1–14]. Berlin, 1863. **Oettli, S.** *Das Buch Hiob erläutert für Bibelleser.* Stuttgart: Calwer, 1908. **Olshausen, J.** *Hiob erklärt.* KEH. Leipzig: S. Hirzel, 1852. **Osty, E.,** and **J. Trinquet.** *Livre de Job—L'Ecclésiaste—Livre de la sagesse.* Paris: Rencontre, 1971. **Ottensosser, D.** כתובים: ספר איוב [Hebrew text, Yiddish translation, Hebrew commentary by Israel b. Abraham of Lissa]. Fürth, 1805. **Ottoni, J. E.** *Job, traduzido em verso . . . Precedido primeiro, d'um discurso sobre a poesia em geral, e em particular no Brasil . . . Terceiro d'um prefacio extrahido de versão da Biblia por de Genoude.* Rio de Janeiro: F. M. Ferreira, 1852. **Owens, J. J.** See Watts, J. D. W.
Patrick, D. *Arguing with God: The Angry Poem of Job.* St. Louis: Bethany, 1977. [With translation.] **Peake, A. S.** *Job.* CB. London: T. C. & E. C. Jack, 1904. **Peters, N.** *Das Buch Hiob übersetzt und erklärt.* EHAT. Münster: Aschendorff, 1928. **Philips, T. W.** *Job, A New Interpretation.* London: Murby, 1937. **Pixley, J.** *El libro de Job; comentario bíblico latino-americano.* San José, Costa Rica: Sebila, 1982. See also **Stadelmann, L.** "O livro de Jó; a propósito de um 'comentário bíblico latino-americano.'" *PerspT* 15 (1983) 407–12. **Polotak, P. ben Judah.** ספר איוב . . . גבעת פנחס. Vilna, 1808. **Pope, M.** *Job.* AB. Garden City, NY: Doubleday, 1965. 3d ed., 1973. **Porteous, M.** *Job paraphrased; a poem.* Maybole, 1854. **Potter, R.** "Job." In *A New Catholic Commentary on Holy Scripture,* ed. R. C. Fuller et al. London: Nelson, 1969. 417–38. **Pritchard, M.** *The Poem of Job, A Version . . . with Introduction and Notes.* London: Kegan Paul, Trench, Trübner & Co., 1903.
Rabinowitz [Obronin, Avronin], A. Z. איוב. Jaffa, 1916. **Ratner, I.** ספר איוב בשם דברי אמת . . . עם פירוש. Warsaw, 1893. **Ravasi, G.** *Giobbe, traduzione e commento.* 2 vols. Rome: Borla, 1979–84. **Raymond, R. W.** *The Book of Job: Essays, and a Metrical Paraphrase.* New York: Appleton & Co., 1878. **Reichert, V. E.** *Job with Hebrew Text and English Translation, Commentary.* Soncino Books of the Bible. Hindhead, Surrey: Soncino Press, 1946. **Renan, E.** *Le Livre de Job, traduit de l'hébreu.* [with] *Etude sur l'age et le caractère du poème.* Paris: Calmann Lévy, 1860. ———. *The Book of Job translated from the Hebrew with a Study upon the Age and Character of the Poem.* Tr. A. F. G. [H. F. Gibbons] and W. M. T[homson]. London: W. M. Thomson, 1899. See also **Crelier, H. J.** *Le livre de Job vengé des interprétations fausses et impies de M. E. Renan.* Douniol, 1860. **Reuss, E.** *Hiob.* Braunschweig: C. A. Schwetschke & Sohn, 1888. [Introduction and translation.] **Ricciotti, G.** *Il libro di Giobbe. Versione critica dal testo ebraico con introduzione e commento.* Turin: Marietti, 1924. **Richardson, J. W.** *Out of the Whirlwind: A dramatized version of the Book of Job Based on Dr. James Moffatt's Translation.* London: Epworth, 1936. **Robin, E.** "Job traduit et commenté." *La Sainte Bible.* Paris: Pirot-Clamer, 1949. 4:797–868. **Rocholl, C.** *Das Buch Hiob, neu gedichtet.* Stuttgart: Steinkopf, 1922. **Rodwell, J. M.** איוב. *The Book of Job, translated from the Hebrew.* London: Williams & Norgate, 1864. **Rosenfeld, M.** ספר איוב: עם פירוש נחלק לשנים. Lemberg, 1875. **Rosenmüller, E. F. K.** *Scholia in Vetus Testamentum: Editio secunda auctior et emendatior.* Pars V: *Jobus*

latine vertit et annotatione perpetua illustravit. Leipzig: J. A. Barth, 1824. **Rowley, A.** *Ten Chapters of the Book of Job, rendered from the common translation, into verse.* Boston: J. H. A. Frost, 1825. **Rowley, H. H.** *Job.* NCB. Thomas Nelson & Sons, 1970. **Rozelaar, M.** *Het Boek Job in Nederlandse verzen.* Kampen: Kok, 1984. **Sadler, R.** *The Book of Ayub: known in the West as Job.* London: Sheppard & St John, 1897. [A translation with notes.] **Saithwell, P.** *Ezra—Job.* London: Scripture Union, 1982. **Saint-Maur, H. de.** *Le Livre de Job: Traduction en vers.* Paris, 1861. **Sarão, A.** *Giobbe, poema eroico.* Messina: Pappalardo, 1831. **Schärer, J. R.** *Das Buch Hiob, aus dem Grundtext metrisch übersetzt und erklärt.* Bern: L. R. Walthard, 1818. **Schlögl, N.** *Das Buch Hiob, aus dem kritisch hergestellten hebräisch Urtext ins Deutsche metrisch übersetzt und erläutert.* Vienna: Orionverlag, 1916. **Schlottmann, K.** *Das Buch Hiob verdeutscht und erläutert.* Berlin: Wiegandt & Brieben, 1851. **Schmidt, H.** *Hiob, das Buch vom Sinn des Leidens . . . gekürzt und verdeutscht.* Tübingen: J. C. B. Mohr, 1927. **Schmidt, N.** *The Messages of the Poets: The Books of Job and Canticles and Some Minor Poems in the Old Testament, with Introductions, Metrical Translations, and Paraphrases.* New York: Scribners, 1911. **Schröder, R. A.** *Das Buch Hiob mit Randbemerkungen.* Munich: R. Piper, 1948. **Schubert, L.** *Das Buch Hiob. Dichterische Übersetzung mit einer Erklärung.* Leipzig: Klein, 1927. **Schwarz, F. W. S.** *Das Buch Hiob. Ein Kreuz- und Trostbuch: Nach dem Holländischen des ten Kate unter Vergleichung des biblischen Textes deutsch bearbeitet.* Bremen: C. E. Müller, 1868. **Schwarz, I.** תקות אנוש: ספר איוב. Berlin, 1868. **Schweitzer, R.** *Job. La Bible et la vie.* Paris: Ligel, 1966. **Seitz, O.** *Hiob.* Berlin, 1931. **Sekine, M.** *Yob-ki chūkai* [*A Commentary on the Book of Job*]. [Japanese]. Tokyo: Kyōbunkan, 1970. **Siegfried, C.** *The Book of Job: Critical Edition of the Hebrew Text.* SBOT. Baltimore: Johns Hopkins UP, 1893. **Simon, M.** *Hiob übersetzt und herausgegeben.* Munich: Chr. Kaiser, 1925. **Smith, Elizabeth.** *The Book of Job: translated from the Hebrew . . . With a preface and annotations.* Bath, 1810. **Snaith, N. H.** *Notes on the Hebrew Text of Job I–VI.* London: Epworth, 1945. **Solomon [Baba-Jan].** ספר איוב עם עתקה בלשון פארסי [*The Book of Job with Persian translation*]. Jerusalem, 1895. **Speyr, A. von.** *Job* (*Kommentar*). Einsiedeln: Johannes-Verlag, 1972. **Spiess, M.** *Hiob metrisch uebersetzt.* Buchholz: G. Adler, 1852. **Sprague, H. B.** *The Book of Job: The Poetic Portion Versified, with Due Regard to the Language of the Authorized Version, A Closer Adherence to the Sense of the Revised Versions, and a More Literal Translation of the Hebrew Original, with an Introductory Essay Advancing New Views and Explanatory Notes Quoting Many Eminent Authorities.* Boston: Sherman, French & Co., 1913. **Stather, W. C.** *The Book of Job in English Verse. Translated from the original Hebrew; with notes, critical and explanatory.* Bath: Binns & Godwin, 1860. **Steinmann, J.** *Job. Témoins de Dieu.* Paris: Cerf, 1946. ———. *Le Livre de Job.* Lectio Divina. Paris: Cerf, 1955. ———. *Job. Texte français, introduction et commentaire.* Connaître la Bible. Bruges: Desclée de Brouwer, 1961. **Sternberg, S. Z.** ספר איוב: עם באור חקר שדי. 1872. **Steuernagel, C.** "Das Buch Hiob." *Die Heilige Schrift des Alten Testaments.* Tübingen: J. C. B. Mohr, 1923. 2:323–89. **Stevenson, W. B.** *The Poem of Job: A Literary Study with a New Translation.* London: OUP, 1947. **Stickel, J. G.** *Das Buch Hiob rhythmisch gegliedert und übersetzt, mit exegetischen und kritischen Bemerkungen.* Leipzig: Weidmann, 1842. **Stier, F.** *Das Buch Ijjob hebräisch und deutsch. Uebertragen ausgelegt und mit Text- und Sacherläuterungen versehen.* Munich: Kösel, 1954. **Stock, J.** *The Book of Job: metrically arranged according to the Masora, and newly translated into English. With notes critical and explanatory.* Bath, 1805. **Strahan, J.** *The Book of Job Interpreted.* Edinburgh: T. & T. Clark, 1913. **Strashun, A. D.** מישר נובכים: והוא באור. ———. תורת אדם: באור על ספר איוב. Vilna, 1888. על ספר איוב עם מבוא. Vilna, 1897. **Studer, G. L.** *Das Buch Hiob für geistliche und gebildete Laien übersetzt und kritisch erläutert.* Bremen: M. Heinsius, 1881. **Stuhlmann, M. H.** *Hiob, ein religiöses Gedicht. Aus dem Hebräischen neu übersetzt, geprüft und erläutert.* Hamburg: F. Perthes, 1804. **Sutcliffe, E. F** "Job." In *A Catholic Commentary on Holy Scripture.* Ed. B. Orchard et al. London: Thos. Nelson & Sons, 1953. 417–41. **Sydenstricker, H. M.** *The Epic of the Orient: an original poetical rendering of the book of Job.* Hartford: Student Publishing Co, 1894. **Szczygiel, P.** *Das Buch Job, übersetzt und erklärt.*

HSAT. Bonn: Hanstein, 1931. **Szold, B.** ספר איוב: מבואר מחדש. *Das Buch Hiob,
nebst einem neuen Kommentar.* Baltimore: H. F. Siemers, 1886.
Takamini, A. V. *Il Libro di Giobbe: Versione poetica.* Venice, 1871. **Talmid.** *The Book of
Job and the Song of Solomon: Translated into English metre.* Edinburgh, 1890. **Tattersall,
J.** *The Poem of Job, rendered in English metre.* London: B. Quaritch, 1897. **Telles, B.** *O
Livro de Job. Traducção em verso.* Porto: Lello & Irmão, 1912. **Terrien, S. L.,** and **P.
Scherer.** "Job." *IB.* New York and Nashville: Abingdon, 1954. 3:877–1198. **Terrien,
S. L.** *Job.* Commentaire de l'Ancien Testament. Neuchâtel: Delachaux et Niestlé, 1963.
Thilo, M. *Das Buch Hiob neu übersetzt und aufgefasst.* Bonn: A. Marcus & E. Weber,
1925. **Thomas, D.** *Problemata Mundi: The Book of Job, exegetically and practically considered.
Critically revised, with an introduction, by Samuel Davidson.* London: Smith, Elder, & Co.,
1878. **Torczyner, H.** *Das Buch Hiob: Eine kritische Analyse des überlieferten Hiobtextes.* Vi-
enna: Löqit, 1920. ———. ספר איוב מפורש. *The Book of Job Interpreted.* Jerusalem:
Hebrew UP, 1941. See also Tur-Sinai, N. H. **Trentepohl, K.** *Das Buch Hiob, übersetzt
und metrisch bearbeitet.* Vechta, 1860. **Turoldo, D. M.** *Da una casa di fango (Job).* Brescia:
La Scuola, 1951. [Commentary, with translation of A. Vaccari.] **Tur-Sinai [Torczyner],
N. H.** ספר איוב עם פירוש חדש. Tel Aviv: Yavneh, 1954. ———. *The Book of Job, A
New Commentary.* Jerusalem: Kiryath Sepher, 1957.
Umbreit, F. W. C. *Das Buch Hiob, Übersetzung und Auslegung.* Heidelberg, 1824.
———. *A New Version of the Book of Job with expository notes, and an introduction, on the
spirit, composition, and author of the book.* Tr. J. H. Gray. 2 vols. Edinburgh: Thomas
Clark, 1836–37.
Vaccari, A. *Il Libro di Giobbe e i Salmi, tradotti dai testi originali e annotati.* 2d ed. Rome:
Pontifical Biblical Institute, 1927. **Vaihinger, J. G.** *Das Buch Hiob, der Urschrift gemäss
metrisch übersetzt und erläutert.* Stuttgart, 1842. **Van Calcar, J. D.** *Job. Bijbels Lekespel.*
Assen: Van Gorcum, 1934. **Van Hagen, Mrs Henry.** *Evenings in the Land of Uz: Short
Expositions of the Book of Job; arranged for family reading.* 2d ed. London: W. W. Robinson,
1845. **Van Prosdij, A. C. G.** *Het Boek Job.* Amsterdam: S. J. B. Bakker, 1948. **Van
Selms, A.** *Job.* Prediking OT. 2 vols. Nijkerk: Callenbach, 1982–83. ———. *Job: een
praktische bijbelverklaring.* Tekst en Toelichting. Kampen: J. H. Kok, 1984. [Tr. J. Vriend.
Job, A Practical Commentary. Grand Rapids: Eerdmans, 1985]. **Viani, B.** *Il Libro di Giobbe,
recato in versi italiani e corredato di note.* Rome: Osservatore Romano, 1865. **Vignolo,
G. M.** *Il Libro di Giobbe tradotto in versi sciolti.* Turin, 1902. **Villa, E.** *Antico teatro ebraico:
Giobbe, Cantico dei cantici.* Milan: Poligono, 1947. **Virgulin, S.** *Giobbe . . . introduzione,
note.* Nuovissima Versione 17. Rome: Paoline, 1980. **Voigt, C.** *Einige Stellen des Buches
Hiob.* Leipzig: W. Drugulin, 1895. **Volck, W.** "Das Buch Hiob." In *Die poetischen Hagiogra-
pha (Buch Hiob, Prediger Salomo, Hohelied und Klagelied) ausgelegt.* Ed. W. Volck and S.
Oettli. Kurzgefasster Kommentar zu Heiligen Schriften Alten und Neuen Testaments.
Nördlingen: C. H. Beck, 1889. **Volz, P.** *Hiob und Weisheit.* Göttingen, 1911. ———.
Weisheit (Das Buch Hiob, Sprüche und Jesus Sirach, Prediger). Göttingen: Vandenhoeck &
Ruprecht, 1911. **Vuilleumier, H.** *Le livre de Job.* Lausanne, 1894.
Walls, A. *The Oldest Drama in the World: the Book of Job, arranged in dramatic form, with
elucidation.* New York: Hunt & Eaton, 1891. **Warren, C. B.** *A Paraphrase of Job's Dark
Days.* New York: H. Harrison, 1941. **Watson, R. A.** *The Book of Job.* ExpB. London:
Hodder & Stoughton, 1892. **Watts, J. D. W., J. J. Owens,** and **M. E. Tate.** "Job." In
Broadman Bible Commentary. Nashville: Broadman, 1971. 22–151. **Weber, J.-J.** *Le Livre
de Job. L'Ecclésiaste. Texte et commentaire.* Paris: Desclée, 1947. **Weiser, Artur.** *Das Buch
Hiob übersetzt und erklärt.* ATD. Göttingen: Vandenhoeck & Ruprecht, 1951. **Weiser,
Asher.** ספר איוב מפרש. Tel Aviv: Yehuda, 1950–51. **Weiser, L.** *Das ungekürzte Buch
Hiob: Deutsch von Lazarus Weiser. Jetzt ein Buch für jede Seele, die Kraft trinken kann vom
alten starken Geiste Hiobs, früher bei dem gekürzten Urtext ein unverstandenes Buch.* Vienna:
Ta'nach-Selbstverlag, 1931. **Weitzner, E.** *The Book of Job: A Paraphrase.* New York, 1960.
Welte, B. *Das Buch Hiob, übersetzt und erklärt.* Freiburg im Breisgau, 1849. **Wemyss, T.**
Job and his Times, or a Picture of the patriarchal age . . . a new version of that . . . poem,

accompanied with notes and dissertations. London: Jackson & Walford, 1839. **White, G. C.** *The Discipline of Suffering: Nine short readings on the history of Job. [Part 2. The Conversation* [i.e., the text of Job] *in blank verse]*. London: W. Skeffington & Son, 1880. **Wilde, A. de.** *Het boek Job, ingeleid en vertaald*. Wageningen: Veenman, 1974. ———. *Das Buch Hiob eingeleitet, übersetzt und erläutert*. OTS 22. Leiden: E. J. Brill, 1981. **Wilkinson, F. H.** *The Book of Job: Translated and Annotated*. London: Skeffington & Son, 1901. **Wilson, P.** *The Book of Job Translated into English Verse* [of various meters]. Edinburgh: James Thin, 1912. **Winterfield, von.** *Kommentar über das Buch Iob*. Leipzig: H. Walter, 1898. **Wolff, C.** *Job, traduit et commenté*. Colmar: C. Decker, 1873. **Wolfson, J.** איוב. *Das Buch Hiob: Mit Beziehung auf Psychologie und Philosophie der alten Hebräer neu übersetzt und kritisch erläutert*. Breslau, 1843. **Wray, N.** *The Book of Job: A Biblical Masterpiece Interpreted and Explained*. Boston: Hamilton Bors, 1929. **Wright, G. H. Bateson.** *The Book of Job: A new, critically revised translation, with essays on scansion, date etc*. London: Williams and Norgate, 1883. **Wutz, F. X.** *Das Buch Job*. In *Eichstätter Studien*. 3. Stuttgart: Kohlhammer, 1939 [Translation and Commentary]. See also **Schilcher, K.** "Das Buch Job und Prof. Wutz." *Klerus Bl* 21 (1940) 67–68, 76–77.
Yellin, D. חקרי מקרא—בארים חדשים במקראות:איוב. Jerusalem, 1927. **Yerushalmi, E.** ספר איוב: הקפה מדעת. Jerusalem: Eretz-Israel, 1927.
Zöckler, O. *Das Buch Job: Theologisch-homiletisch bearbeitet*. Bielefeld: Velhagen und Klasing, 1872. ———. *The Book of Job*. Lange's Commentary on the Holy Scriptures. Trans. L. J. Evans. Edinburgh: T. & T. Clark, 1875. **Zschokke, H.** *Das Buch Job übersetzt und erklärt*. Vienna, 1875.

3. THE BOOK AS A WHOLE

In this section are listed works which offer interpretations of the Book of Job as a whole but are not arranged according to the sequence of the book itself. It includes, as do all the sections of the *Bibliography*, both books and articles, and both technical and nontechnical studies. Especially in the case of this particular biblical book, the degree of technicality of a work on the subject is no kind of indicator of the value of the work for understanding the biblical text.

Works that concern only a part of the Book of Job are listed in the bibliographies to the relevant chapters, and are not mentioned here.

Aalders, W. *Wet, tragedie, evangelie: een andere benadering van het boek Job*. The Hague: Voorhoeve, 1979. **Aked, C. F.** *The Divine Drama of Job*. Edinburgh: T. & T. Clark, 1913. **Allen, F. E.** *Practical Lectures on the Book of Job*. New York: Revell, 1923. **Alonso Schökel, L.** "Toward a Dramatic Reading of the Book of Job." *Semeia* 7 (1977) 45–61. See also **Crenshaw, J. L.** "The Twofold Search: A Response to Luis Alonso Schökel." *Semeia* 7 (1977) 63–69. ———. "God's Answer to Job." *Conc* 169 (1983) 45–51. **Archer, G. L.** *The Book of Job: God's Answer to the Problem of Undeserved Suffering*. Grand Rapids: Baker, 1982. **Anderson, H.** "Another Perspective on the Book of Job." *TGUOS* 18 (1961) 43–46. **Aufrecht, W. E.,** ed. *Studies in the Book of Job*. SR Supplements 16. Waterloo: Wilfrid Laurier University, 1985. **Augé, R.** "Job." *EncBib* 4 (1965) 569–78. **Baab, O.** "The Book of Job." *Int* 5 (1951) 329–43. **Badè, W. F.** *The Book of Job and the Solution of the Problem of Suffering It Offers*. 2d ed. 1914. **Baker, J. A.** "The Book of Job: Unity and Meaning." In *Studia Biblica 1978. I.* JSOTSup 11. Sheffield: JSOT, 1978. 17–26. **Barth, K.** *Hiob*. Biblische Studien 49. Neukirchen-Vluyn: Neukirchener Verlag, 1966 [= *Kirchliche Dogmatik* 4/3, 1]. **Barthélemy, D.** "Dieu méconnu par le vieil homme: Job." *VS* 105 (1961) 445–63. **Barylko, J.** *Job*. Buenos Aires: Ejucativo Sudamericano del Congreso Judio Mondial, 1970. **Batten, L. W.** "The Epilogue of the Book of Job." *ATR* 15 (1933) 125–28. **Baumer, L.** "Das Buch Hiob, Versuch einer psychopathologischen Deutung." *Der Nervenarzt* 28 (1957) 546–50. **Baumgärtel, F.** *Der Hiobdialog. Aufriss und Deutung*. BZAW 4/9. Stuttgart: Kohlhammer, 1933. **Baumgartner, F.** "Das

Buch Job im Religionsunterricht." *ChrPädBl* 54 (1931) 87–88. **Beet, W. E.** "The Message
of the Book of Job." *Exp* 48 (1922) 111–20. **Bennett, T. M.** "When a Righteous Man
Suffers: A Teaching Outline of the Book of Job." *SWJT* 14 (1971) 57–64. ———.
When Human Wisdom Fails: An Exposition of the Book of Job. Grand Rapids: Baker, 1971.
Bergant, Dianne. "Why Do I Suffer?" *TBT* 20 (1982) 341–46. **Bickell, G.** *Job, Dialog
über das Leiden des Gerechten.* Innsbruck, 1885. **Bigot, L.** "Job (Livre de)." *Dictionnaire
de théologie catholique.* 1925. 8:1458–86. **Billheimer, P. E.** *Adventure in Adversity.* Alres-
ford: Christian Literature Crusade, 1984. **Bishop, E. F. F.** *Job, The Patriarch of East
Palestine: The Epic that Transjordan Gave to the Scriptures of the World.* Reigate, Surrey:
George J. Hieatt and Son, 1973. **Blake, B.** *The Book of Job and the Problem of Suffering.*
London: Hodder and Stoughton, 1911. **Bonnard, P. E.** "Job ou l'homme enfin exstasié."
LumVie 13 (1964) 15–33. **Bonora, A.** *Il contestatore di Dio: Giobbe.* Turin: Marietti, 1978.
Bovey, W. "The Unjust God? Job's Problem and Ours." *HibJ* 36 (1937–38) 353–64.
Bradley, G. G. *Lectures on the Book of Job Delivered in Westminster Abbey.* 2d ed. Oxford:
Clarendon, 1888. **Brandenburg, H.** *Das Buch Hiob: Der Mensch in der Anfechtung.* Giessen:
Brunnen, 1969. **Brandon, S. G. F.** "The Book of Job: Its Significance for the History
of Religions." *History Today* 2 (1961) 547–54. **Breakstone, R.** *Job: A Case Study.* New
York: Bookman Associates, 1964. **Brenner, Athalya.** "God's Answer to Job." *VT* 31
(1981) 129–37. **Brook, Peggy.** *Job: An Interpretation.* London: Foundational Book Co.,
1967. **Brunner, R.** *Der Gottesknecht: Eine Auslegung des Buches Hiob.* 3d ed. Basel: J. F.
Reinhardt.
Camhy, O. *Une trilogie biblique sur le drame de la vie: un sujet, trois conceptions: Job, Qohéleth
. . . Isaïe.* Paris: Grassin, 1973. **Cantalausa, J. de.** *Lo libre de Jòb (presentacion e causi-
das).* . . . Rodés: Cultura d'oc, 1983. **Ceuppens, F.** *De libro Iob quaestiones selectae.* Rome:
Collegium Angelicum, 1932. **Cheyne, T. K.** *Job and Solomon or the Wisdom of the Old
Testament.* London: Kegan Paul, Trench & Co., 1887. ———. "Job." *EB.* 1901. 2:2465–
91. **Claudel, P.** *Le livre de Job.* Paris: Plon, 1946. **Clines, D. J. A.** "The Arguments of
Job's Three Friends." In *Art and Meaning: Rhetoric in Biblical Literature,* ed. D. J. A.
Clines, D. M. Gunn, and A. J. Hauser. JSOTSup 19. Sheffield: JSOT Press, 1982.
199–214. ———. "Job." *The Books of the Bible.* Ed. B. W. Anderson. New York: Scribners,
1989. ———. *Oxford Companion to the Bible.* Ed. B. M. Metzger. New York: OUP (forth-
coming). ———. "Deconstructing the Book of Job." In *The Bible as Rhetoric: Studies in
Biblical Persuasion and Credibility,* ed. M. Warner. London: Routledge, 1989. 65–80.
———. "The Wisdom Books." In *Creating the Old Testament,* ed. S. Bigger. Oxford:
Blackwell, 1989. 269–91. **Cocagnoc, A. M.** "Job sans beauté ni éclat." *VS* 422 (1956) 355–
71. **Conder, C. R.** "Illustrations of the Book of Job." *PEFQS* (1898) 254–61. **Cook, A.**
The Root of the Thing: A Study of Job and the Song of Songs. Bloomington: Indiana UP,
1968. **Cook, E. D.** *The Man Who Had Everything: Job.* Glasgow: Church Pastoral Aid,
1978. **Cooper, B. Z.** "Why, God: A Tale of Two Sufferers." *TTod* 42 (1986) 423–24.
Corrado da Arienzo. "Il dolore di Giobbe." *PalCl* 37 (1958) 735–39. **Cox, D.** "Rea-
son in Revolt: The Poetic Dialogues in the Book of Job." *SBFLA* 24 (1974) 317–28.
———. *The Triumph of Impotence: Job and the Tradition of the Absurd.* Analecta Gregoriana
212. Rome: Università Gregoriana Editrice, 1978. ———. "A Rational Inquiry into
God: Chapters 4–27 of the Book of Job." *Greg* 67 (1986) 621–58. **Craigie, P. C.** "Biblical
Wisdom in the Modern World. III. Job." *Crux* 16 (1980) 7–10. **Cranfield, C. E. B.**
"An Interpretation of the Book of Job." *ExpT* 54 (1943) 295–98. **Crook, M. B.** *The
Cruel God: Job's Search for the Meaning of Suffering.* Boston, 1959. ———, and **S. A.
Eliot.** "Tracing Job's Story." *HibJ* 60 (1962) 323–29. **Cruveilhier, P.** "Pour une connais-
sance plus parfaite du livre de Job." *RevApol* 53 (1931) 641–67; 54 (1932) 5–27.
Dalzell, S.H. *Lessons in the Book of Job.* London: Stockwell, 1922. **Daniélou, J.** "Les
quatre visages de Job." *Études* (September 1955) 145–56. ———. *Les saints païens de
l'Ancien Testament.* Paris: Le Seuil. 109–28 [= *Holy Pagans of the Old Testament.* Tr. F.
Faber. London: Longmans, Green & Co., 1957. 86–102]. **Davis, H. G.** "The Message
of the Book of Job for Today." *LCQ* 6 (1933) 131–46. **Davison, W. T.** "Job." *HDB*

2:660–71. **Devine, M.** *The Story of Job: A Sympathetic Study of the Book of Job in the Light of History and Literature.* London: Macmillan, 1921. **Drucker, A. P.** "The Book of Job." *The Open Court* 49 (1935) 65–78. **Duhm, B.** "The Book of Job." *The New World* (1894) 328–44. **Eaton, J. H.** *Job.* Old Testament Guides 5. Sheffield: JSOT, 1985. **Eerdmans, B. D.** *Studies in Job.* 2 vols. Leiden: Burgersdijk & Niermans, 1939. **Ehrenberg, H.** *Hiob der Existentialist.* Heidelberg: Lambert Schneider, 1952. **Epp, T. H.** *Job a Man Tried as Gold.* Lincoln, NE: Back to the Bible Publications, 1967. **Ewing, W.** *Some Critical Observations on the Book of Job.* London, 1844. **Ewing, W. B.** *Job: A Vision of God.* New York: Seabury, 1976. **Feinberg, C. L.** "The Book of Job." *BSac* 91 (1934) 78–86. **Ferguson, J.** *Job.* London: Epworth, 1961. **Festorazzi, F.** *Gli "Scritti" dell'Antico Testamento.* Il Messaggio della Salvezza 5. Turin-Leumann: LDC, 1985. 14–28, 52–182. **Fichtner, J.** "Hiob in der Verkündigung unserer Zeit." *WuD* 2 (1950) 71–89. **Fohrer, G.** "Nun aber hat mein Auge dich geschaut. Der innere Aufbau des Buches Hiob." *TZ* 15 (1959) 1–21 [= "Der innere Aufbau des Buches Hiob." *Studien zum Buche Hiob (1956–1979).* BZAW 159. Gütersloh: Gerd Mohn, 1963. 1–18]. ———. "Das Hiobproblem und seine Lösung." *WZ der Martin-Luther-Universität* 12 (1963) 249–58. ———. *Studien zum Buche Hiob.* BZAW 159. Gütersloh: Gerd Mohn, 1963 [2d ed. *Studien zum Buche Hiob (1956–1979).* Berlin: de Gruyter, 1983]. **Foote, G. W.** "Poor Job." In *Bible Heroes.* London: Freethought Publishing Co., 1900. 37–44. **Ford, L. S.** "The Whirlwind Addresses Job." *StLuke* 24 (1980–81) 217–21. **Francisco, C. T.** "A Teaching Outline of the Book of Job." *RevExp* 68 (1971) 511–20. **Freedman, D. N.** "Is It Possible to Understand the Book of Job?" *BibReview* 4/2 (April 1988) 26ff. **Frost, G. E.** *The Color of the Night: Reflections on the Book of Job.* Minneapolis: Augsburg, 1977. **Froude, J. A.** *The Book of Job.* London: J. Chapman, 1854. [= *The Westminster Review* ns 8 October 1853.] **Gemüsch, G.** *Das Rätsel Hiob: Gemeinfassliche Gedanken über das Buch Hiob.* Karlsruhe: C. F. Müller, 1958. **Gerber, I. J.** *Job on Trial: A Book for Our Times.* Gastonia, NC: EP, 1982. ———. *The Psychology of the Suffering Mind.* New York: Jonathan David, 1951. **Gese, H.** "Die Frage nach dem Lebenssinn: Hiob und die Folgen." ZTK 79 (1982) 161–79. **Gibbs, P. T.** *Job and the Mysteries of Wisdom.* Nashville: Southern Publishing, 1967. **Ginsberg, H. L.** "Job the Patient and Job the Impatient." *ConsJud* (1967) 12–28. ———. עיונים בספר איוב: Studies in the Book of Job." *Leš* 21 (1956–57) 259–64. ———, **T. Friedman, B. Bayer** et al. "Job, the Book of." *EncJud* 10:111–29. **Girard, R.** *La route antique des hommes pervers.* Paris: Bernard Grasser, 1985. Tr. *Job, The Victim of His People.* London: Athlone, 1988. ———. "The Ancient Trail Trodden by the Wicked: Job as Scapegoat." *Semeia* 33 (1985) 13–41. **Glazner, A.** "Introduction to the Book of Job" [Heb]. *BMik* 23 (1978) 189–202. **Godet, F.** "The Book of Job." In *Godet's Biblical Studies on the Old Testament,* ed. W. H. Lyttleton. Oxford: James Parker, 1875. 183–240. **Goldschmidt, H. L.** "Hiob einst und immer." *Israel hat dennoch Gott zum Trost,* FS S. Ben-Chorin, ed. G. Müller. Trier: Paulinus, 1978. 20–30. **González, Á.** "Giobbe, il malato." *Conc* 12 (1976) 1475–82. **Good, E. M.** "Job and the Literary Task: A Response [to David Robertson]." *Soundings* 56 (1973) 470–84. **Gordis, R.** "'All Men's Book': A New Introduction to Job." *Menorah Journal* 37 (1949) 329–58. [= *Poets, Prophets and Sages.* Bloomington, IN, 1971. 280–84.] ———. *The Book of God and Man: A Study of Job.* Chicago: University of Chicago Press, 1965. ———. "The Temptation of Job—Tradition versus Experience in Religion." *Judaism* 4 (1955) 195–208. [= *Poets, Prophets and Sages.* Bloomington, IN, 1971. 305–24.] ———. "The Conflict of Tradition and Experience." In *Great Moral Dilemmas in Literature, Past and Present,* ed. R. M. McIver. New York: Institute for Religious and Social Studies, 1956. 155–78. ———. "The Lord out of the Whirlwind: The Climax and Meaning of 'Job.'" *Judaism* 13 (1964) 48–63. **Gray, G. B.** "The Purpose and Method of the Writer." In *Twentieth-Century Interpretations of the Book of Job: A Collection of Critical Essays,* ed. P. S. Sanders. Englewood Cliffs, NJ: Prentice-Hall, 1968. 36–45. [= Driver-Gray, xxv–l.] **Green, W. H.** *The Argument of the*

Book of Job Unfolded. New York: Hurst & Co., 1873. **Guillaume, A.** "The Unity of the Book of Job." *ALUOS* 4 (1965) 26–46. **Gunkel, H.** "Hiobbuch." *RGG*² 3:1924–30. **Gutiér-rez, G.** *On Job: God-Talk and the Suffering of the Innocent.* Maryknoll, NY: Orbis, 1987. Tr. by M. J. O'Connell from *Hablar de Dios desde el sufrimiento del inocente.* Lima: Centro de Estudios y Publicaciones, 1986. ———. "But Why Lord: On Job and the Suffering of the Innocent." *Other Side* 23 (1987) 18–23.
Hackmann, H. "Das wahre Gesicht des Buches Hiob." *NedTTs* 19 (1930) 25–35. **Ham-blen, E. J.** *The Book of Job Interpreted: Illustrated with the Designs of William Blake.* New York, 1939. **Hartley, J. E.** "Job." *ISBE* 2:1064–76. **Hauptmann, G.** *Buch der Leidenschaft.* Gütersloh: C. Bertelsmann, 1953. **Hawthorne, R. R.** "Joban Theology." *BSac* 101 (1944) 64–75, 173–86, 290–303, 417–33; 102 (1945) 37–54. **Heinen, K.** *Der unverfügbare Gott: Das Buch Ijob.* Stuttgart: Katholisches Bibelwerk, 1979. **Hempel, J.** "Das theologische Problem des Hiob." *Apoxysmata: Vorarbeiten zu einer Religionsgeschichte und Theologie des Alten Testaments.* BZAW 81. Berlin: A. Töpelmann, 1961. 114–74. **Hengstenberg, E. W.** "Interpreting the Book of Job." In *Classical Evangelical Essays in Old Testament Interpretation,* ed. W. C. Kaiser. Grand Rapids: Baker, 1973. 91–112. **Hirsch, N. D.** "The Architecture of the Book of Job." *CCAR Journal* 16 (1969) 22–32. **Hölscher, G.** *Das Gedicht von Hiob und seine drei Freunden.* Wiesbaden: Insel, 1948. **Höffken, P.** "Hiob in exegetischer Sicht." *EvErz* 36 (1984) 509–26. **Hoffman, Y.** "The Relation between the Prologue and the Speech Cycles in Job: A Reconsideration." *VT* 31 (1981) 160–70. ———. "The Mutual Relation between the Prologue and the Dialogues in the Book of Job." *Proceedings of the 7th World Congress of Jewish Studies* (1981) 53–61 [Heb]. **Holmgren, F.** "Barking Dogs Never Bite, Except Now and Then: Proverbs and Job." *ATR* 61 (1969) 341–53. **Howard, D. M.** *Understanding God's Plan.* London: Scripture Union, 1973. **Humbert, P.** "Le modernisme de Job." *VTSup* 3 (1955) 150–61. ———. "A propos du livre de Job." In his *Opuscules d'un hébraïsant.* Neuchâtel: Université de Neuchâtel, 1958. 204–19.
Inch, M. *My Servant Job.* Grand Rapids: Baker, 1979. **Irwin, W. H.** "An Examination of the Progress of Thought in the Dialogue of Job." *JR* 13 (1933) 150–64. ———. "Job." *Dictionary of the Bible* [New Hastings]. 2d ed. Edinburgh: T. & T. Clark, 1963. 501–5.
Jastrow, M. *The Gentle Cynic.* Philadelphia: Lippincott, 1920. **Jepsen, A.** *Das Buch Hiob und seine Deutung.* Aufsätze und Vorträge zur Theologie und Religionswissenschaft 28. Berlin: Evangelische Verlagsanstalt, 1963. [= Arbeiten zur Theologie 1,14. Stuttgart: Calwer Verlag, 1964.] **Job, J.** *Where Is My Father? Studies in the Book of Job.* London: Epworth, 1977. [= *Job Speaks to Us Today.* Atlanta: Knox, 1980.] **Johnson, L. D.** *Out of the Whirlwind: The Major Message of Job.* Nashville: Broadman, 1971. **Johnstone, C. K.** "Poetic Statement in 'Job.'" *RUO* 32 (1962) 45–59. **Jones, E.** *The Triumph of Job.* London: SCM, 1966. **Jordan, W. G.** *The Book of Job: Its Substance and Spirit.* New York: Macmillan, 1929. **Jung, C. G.** *Answer to Job: Researches into the Relation between Psychology and Religion.* Tr. R. F. C. Hull. London: Routledge, 1954. **Junker, H.** *Jobs Leid, Streit und Sieg; oder Ein Mensch ringt mit dem Schicksal und mit Gott.* Freiburg im Breisgau: Herder, 1948.
Kahn, J. *Job's Illness: Loss, Grief and Integration, A Psychological Interpretation.* Oxford: Pergamon, 1975. **Kaminka, A.** "Principles for Understanding the Speeches in the Book of Job." [Heb.] *Moznaim* 1 (1945). **Kapelrud, A. S.** *Job og hans problem—i fortid og i dag.* Oslo: Land og Kirche, 1976. **Karary, E.** ‏ספר איוב‎ [The Book of Job]." *BMik* 51 (1972) 416–27, 530–31. **Kellett, E. E.** "'Job': An Allegory?" *ExpT* 51 (1939–40) 250–51. **Kent, H. H.** *Job, Our Contemporary.* Grand Rapids: Eerdmans, 1968. **Kidner, D.** *Wisdom to Live By: An Introduction to the Old Testament's Wisdom Books of Proverbs, Job and Ecclesiastes.* Leicester: IVP, 1985. **King, H. M.** *Songs in the Night: A Study of the Book of Job, With Illustrations by William Blake.* Gerrards Cross: Colin Smythe, 1968. **Klostermann, A.** "Hiob." *RE.* 3d ed. 1900. 8:97–126. **Kline, M. G.** "Trial by Ordeal." *Through Christ's Word: A Festschrift for Dr. Philip E. Hughes.* Phillipsburg, NJ: Presbyterian & Reformed Publishing Co., 1985. 81–93. **Knietschke, M.** *Kultur- und Geisteswelt des*

Buches Hiobs. Berlin-Lichterfelde: Runge, 1925. **Knight, H.** "Job. Considered as a Contribution to Hebrew Theology." *SJT* 9 (1956) 63–76. **Knobel, A. W.** *De carminis Jobi argumento, fine ac dispositione.* 1835. **Köberle, J.** *Das Rätsel des Leidens: Eine Einführung in das Buch Hiob.* Berlin-Lichterfelde: E. Runge, 1905. **Kraeling, E. G. H.** *The Book of the Ways of God.* London: SPCK, 1938. **Krinetski, L.** "Ich weiss, mein Anwalt lebt: Die Botschaft des Buches Job." *BiKi* 20 (1965) 8–12. **Kuhl, C.** "Hiobbuch." *RGG*³ 3:355–61. **Kuhn, J.** *Warum bist du so, Gott? Hiob der Fragende.* Stuttgart: Quell, 1978. **Lacoque, A.** "Est-ce gratuitement que Job craint Dieu?" *Mélanges A. Neher.* Paris: Librairie d'Amérique et d'Orient, Adrien-Maisonneuve, 1975. 175–79. **Lang, B.** "Ein kranker sieht sein Gott; das Buch Ijob." In *Wie wird man Prophet in Israel? Aufsätze zum Alten Testament.* Düsseldorf: Patmos, 1980. 137–48. **Larcher, C.** "Job (Le Livre de)." *Catholicisme* 6,25 (1965) 899–907. **Latch, E. B.** *Indications of the Book of Job.* Philadelphia: J. B. Lippincott, 1889. **Laurin, R.** "The Theological Structure of Job." *ZAW* 84 (1972) 86–89. **Lefèvre, A.** "Job." *DBSup* 4:1073–98. **Levenson, J. D.** *The Book of Job in Its Time and in the Twentieth Century.* Cambridge, MA: Harvard UP, 1972. **Lévêque, J.** *Job et son Dieu: Essai d'exégèse et de théologie biblique.* 2 vols. Paris: Gabalda, 1970. ———. "Le sens de la souffrance d'après le livre de Job." *RTL* 6 (1975) 438–59. ———. "Sofferenza e metamorfosi: Una lettura del libro di Giobbe." *Communio* 33 (1977) 4–16. ———. "Tradition and Betrayal in the Speeches of the Friends." *Conc* 169 (1983) 39–44. ———. *Job, le livre et le message.* Paris: Cerf, 1985. ———, and **C. Kamnengiesser.** "Job (Le Livre de)." *DictSpir* 8:1201–25. **Levine, B.** "René Girard on Job: The Question of the Scapegoat." *Semeia* 33 (1985) 125–33. **Lewin, M.** "Job." *JewEnc* 7:193–95. **Ley, J.** "Characteristik der drei Freunde Hiobs und der Wandlungen in Hiobs religiösen Anmerkungen." *TSK* (1900) 331–63. **Lichtenstein, A.** "Toward a Literary Understanding of the Book of Job." *HS* 20/21 (1979–80) 34. **Lindblom, J.** *Boken om Job och hans Lidande.* Lund: Gleerup, 1940. **Lipiński, E.** "Le juste souffrant." *FoiTemps* 1 (1968) 329–42. **Loader, J. A.** "Job—Answer or Enigma?" In *Old Testament Studies,* ed. J. A. Loader and J. Le Roux. Pretoria, 1984. 2:1–38. **Long, T. G.** "Job: Second Thoughts in the Land of Uz." *TTod* 45 (1988) 5–20. **Lovelock, R. T.** *Job: A Study of the Book and Its Message.* Birmingham: Christadelphian, 1957. **Lusseau, H.** "Job." In *Introduction à la Bible,* ed. A. Robert and A. Feuillet. 2d ed. 1959. 1:642–54. **Maag, V.** *Hiob: Wandlung und Verarbeitung des Problems in Novelle, Dialogdichtung und Spätfassungen.* FRLANT 128. Göttingen: Vandenhoeck & Ruprecht, 1982. **MacDonald, D. B.** *The Hebrew Philosophic Genius.* Princeton: Princeton UP, 1936. **McKeating, H.** "The Central Issue of the Book of Job." *ExpT* 82 (1971) 244–47. **MacKechnie, J.** *Job, Moral Hero, Religious Egoist and Mystic.* Greenock: McKelvie & Sons, 1925. **MacKenzie, R. A. F.** "The Transformation of Job." *BTB* 9 (1979) 51–57. ———. "The Cultural and Religious Background of the Book of Job." *Conc* 169 (1983) 3–7. **Maillot, A.** "Job: livre païen." *FoiVie* 69 (1970) 2–15. ———. "L'apologétique du livre de Job." *RHPR* 59 (1979) 567–76. **Marböck, J.** *Das Buch Hiob.* Klosterneuburg: Österreichisches Katholisches Bibelwerk, 1980. **Marshall, J. T.** *The Book of Job.* Philadelphia: American Baptist Publication Society, 1904. **Martin, A. D.** "The Book of Job." *ExpT* 26 (1914) 75–81. **Matheney, M. P.** "Major Purposes of the Book of Job." *SWJT* 14 (1971) 17–42. **Michel, D.** "Hiob: Wegen Gott gegen Gott." In his *Israels Glaube im Wandel.* Berlin, 1968. 252–77. **Miles, J. J.** "Gagging on Job, or the Comedy of Religious Exhaustion." *Semeia* 7 (1977) 71–126. See also **Polzin, R.** "John A. Miles on the Book of Job: A Response." *Semeia* 7 (1977) 127–33. **Miskotte, K. H.** *Antwoord uit het Onweer.* Amsterdam: Uitgevers-Maatschappij Holland, 1936. See also Ridderbos, J. **Mitchell, S.** "The Book of Job." *Tikkun* 1 (1986) 56–64. **Möller, H.** *Sinn und Aufbau des Buches Hiob.* Berlin: Evangelische Verlagsanstalt, 1955. **Moore, T. W.** "The Book of Job—Revised Version Old Testament." *MethQR* 23 (1986) 261–71. **Morgan, G. C.** *The Answers of Jesus to Job.* London: Marshall, Morgan and Scott, 1934. **Müller, H. P.** *Hiob und seine Freunde.* Zurich, 1970. ———. *Das Hiobproblem: Seine Stellung und Entstehung im Alten Orient und im Alten Testament.* Erträge der Forschung 84. Darmstadt: Wissenschaftliche Buchgesell-

schaft, 1978. **Murphy, R. E.** "Job in the New Confraternity Version." *AER* 133 (1955) 16–29.
Nash, J. "Images of Job." *RRel* 42 (1983) 28–33. **Nelson, C.** "Job: The Confessions of a Suffering Person." In *Spinning a Sacred Yarn,* ed. A. Abernethy, C. Carlson, P. Carque et al. New York: Pilgrim, 1982. 144–48. **Nola, A. M. di.** "Giobbe, Libro de." *EncRel* 3 (1971) 212–22.
Orelli, A. von. "Hiob. Deutung eines biblischen Mythos." *Reform* 25 (1976) 74–82, 148–58. **Obbink, H. T.** *Over het Boek Job.* Amsterdam, 1935.
Parisi, R. *La divino libro di Giobbe esposto in lezioni teologico-critico-morali.* Palermo, 1843.
Paterson, J. *The Wisdom of Israel: Job and Proverbs.* Bible Guides 11. London: Lutterworth, 1961. **Patrick, D.** "Job's Address of God." *ZAW* 91 (1979) 268–82. **Paulsen, A.** *Hiob: Ein Buch der Bibel für unsere Zeit gedeutet.* Hamburg: Wittig, 1947. **Peake, A. S.** "The Art of the Book." In *Twentieth-Century Interpretations of the Book of Job: A Collection of Critical Essays,* ed. P. S. Sanders. Englewood Cliffs, NJ: Prentice-Hall, 1968. 109–13.
Phillips, T. W. *Job: A New Interpretation.* London: Murby, 1937. **Plank, K. A.** "Raging Wisdom: A Banner of Defiance Unfurled." *Judaism* 36 (1987) 323–30. **Polzin, R.,** and **D. Robertson,** eds. *Studies in the Book of Job.* Semeia 7. Missoula: Scholars Press, 1977. **Pope, M. H.** "Job, Book of." *IDB* 2:911–24. **Popma, K. J.** *De boodschap van het boek Job.* Goes: Oosterbaan, 1957. **Prat, F.** "Job (Livre de)." *DB* 3:1560–78. **Pury, R. de.** *Job ou l'homme révolté.* Geneva: Labor et Fides, 1955.
Quintens, W. "De boodschap van het boek Job." *ColBG* 15 (1969) 17–33.
Reid, S. A. "The Book of Job." *Psychoanalytic Review* 60 (1973) 373–91. **Retief, G. J.** *Hy het die geloof behou: Oordenkinge oor Job.* Kaapstad, Pretoria, 1957. **Rexroth, K.** "The Book of Job." *Twentieth-Century Interpretations of the Book of Job: A Collection of Critical Essays,* ed. P. S. Sanders. Englewood Cliffs, NJ: Prentice-Hall, 1968. 107–109. [= *Saturday Review,* 23 April 1966, 21.] **Reynierse, J. H.** "A Behavioristic Analysis of the Book of Job." *JPsychTheol* 3 (1975) 75–81. **Richter, H.** *Studien zu Hiob: Der Aufbau des Hiobbuches, dargestellt an den Gattungen des Rechtslebens.* Berlin: Evangelische Verlagsanstalt, 1959. **Ridderbos, J.** "Dr Miskotte over het boek Job." *GerefTTs* 38 (1937) 57–72. **Riebl, Maria.** *In Krise und Hoffnung, Arbeitsheft zum Buch Ijob.* Klosterneuberg: Österreichisches Katholisches Bibelwerk, 1981. **Robertson, D.** "The Book of Job: A Literary Study." *Soundings* 56 (1973) 446–69. See also E. M. Good. ———. "The Book of Job." In his *The Old Testament and the Literary Critic.* Guides to Biblical Scholarship. Philadelphia: Fortress, 1977. 33–54. **Robinson, T. H.** *The Cross of Job.* London, 1916. [= *The Cross in the Old Testament.* Part 1. London: SCM, 1955.] **Rolla, A.** *Job and His Friends.* London: SCM, 1954. ———. "Il libro di Giobbe." In *Il messaggio della salvezza.* 3:535–57. **Rongy, H.** "Le dialogue poétique du livre de Job: Le prologue du livre de Job." *RevEcclLiège* 25 (1933–34) 96–101, 168–71. **Rosenberg, D. W.** *Job Speaks: Interpreted from the Original Hebrew Book of Job: A Poet's Bible.* New York: Harper & Row, 1977. **Rowley, H. H.** "The Book of Job and Its Meaning." *BJRL* 41 (1958–59) 167–207. [= *From Moses to Qumran: Studies in the Old Testament.* London: Lutterworth, 1963. 139–83.] **Ruckman, P. S.** *The Book of Job.* Pensacola, FL: Pensacola Bible Institute, 1978. **Ryckmans, G.** "De scopo auctoris sacri in libro Job." *ColctMech* 17 (1928) 674ff.
Schapiro, D. S. "A Study of the Book of Job." *Tradition* 13 (1972) 81–99. **Scafella, F.** "A Reading of Job." *JSOT* 14 (1979) 63–67. **Segal, M. H.** "ספר איוב [The Book of Job]." *Tarb* 13 (1941–42) 73–91. **Sellin, E.** *Das Problem des Hiobbuches.* Leipzig: A. Deichert, 1919. ———. *Das Hiobproblem: Rede.* Berlin: Preussische Druckerei, 1931. **Seltz, O.** *Hiob: Eine Betrachtung über das Leiden.* Berlin. **Sewell, R. B.** "The Book of Job." In *Twentieth-Century Interpretations of the Book of Job: A Collection of Critical Essays,* ed. P. S. Sanders. Englewood Cliffs, NJ: Prentice-Hall, 1968. 21–35. [= *The Vision of Tragedy.* New Haven: Yale UP, 1959. 9–24.] **Sicre, J. L.** "El libro de Job (entrevista con su autor)." *RazF* 211 (1985) 621–29. **Simon, M.** "Hiob." *Zeitwende* 7 (1931) 159–74. **Singer, R. E.** *Job's Encounter.* New York: Bookman Associates, 1963. **Skehan, P.** "Job, Book of." *New Catholic Encyclopedia* 7 (1967) 999–1001. [= *Studies in Israelite Poetry and Wisdom.*

CBQMS 1, 1971. 78–82.] **Smick, E. B.** "Semeiological Interpretation of the Book of Job." *WTJ* 48 (1986) 135–49. **Smith, R. L.** "Introduction to the Book of Job." *SWJT* 14 (1971) 5–16. **Snaith, N. H.** *The Book of Job.* London: Epworth, 1945. ———. *The Book of Job: Its Origin and Purpose.* SBT 2/11. London: SCM, 1968. **Snell, P.** "A Journey of Faith." *TBT* 20 (1982) 334–37. **Snoep, H.** *Job, aanklager en gedaagde.* The Hague: Boekencentrum, 1980. **Spadafora, F.** "Giobbe." *EC* 6 (1951) 407–13. **Spalding, P. A.** "The Poem of Job." *Congregational Quarterly* 18 (1940) 290–99. **Sperka, J. S.** *The Book of Job: Mankind on Trial, A Modern Interpretation of the Most Perplexing Problem of All Ages.* New York: Bloch, 1979. **Stange, C.** "Das Problem Hiob's und seine Lösung." *ZST* 24 (1955) 342–55. **Stedman, R. C.** *Expository Studies in Job: Behind Suffering.* Waco, TX: Word, 1981. **Steinberg, M.** "Job Answers God: Being the Religious Perplexities of an Obscure Pharisee." *JR* 12 (1932) 159–76. **Steinmann, J.** *Job.* Témoins de Dieu 8. Paris: Cerf, 1946. ———. *Job, témoin de la souffrance humaine.* Foi Vivante 120. Paris: Cerf, 1969. **Stewart, Irma.** *Job. His Spiritual Value.* 2d ed. New York: North River Press, 1943. **Stewart, J.** *The Message of Job.* London: Independent Press, 1959. **Stockhammer, M.** *Das Buch Hiob: Versuch einer Theodizee.* Vienna: Europäischer Verlag, 1963. **Stockhammer, S. E.** "Job's Problem: Faith and Reason." In *Essays in Judaism,* ed. R. Gordis et al. New York: Ktav, 1973. 54–60. **Strahan, J.** *The Book of Job Interpreted.* Edinburgh: T. & T. Clark, 1913. **Straubinger, J.** *Job, el libro del consuelo.* Buenos Aires: Guadalupe, 1945. [= *Job: Ein Trostbuch in schwerer Zeit. Betrachtungen über das Geheimnis des Übels und des Leidens.* Stuttgart: Katholisches Bibelwerk, 1949.] **Strauss, J. D.** *The Shattering of Silence: Job Our Contemporary.* Joplin, MO: College Press, 1976. **Strolz, W.** *Hiobs Auflehnung gegen Gott.* Opuscula aus Glaube und Dichtung 30. Pfullingen: Neske, 1967. **Studer, G.** *Gott redet in Wettersturm: Eine Auslegung des Buches Hiob.* Witten: Bundes-Verlag, 1954. **Sullivan, K.** "The Book of Job." *Wor* 29 (1954–55) 449–61.

Terrien, S. *Job: Poet of Existence.* Indianapolis: Bobbs Merrill Co., 1958. **Thompson, K. T.** "Out of the Whirlwind: The Sense of Alienation in the Book of Job." *Int* 14 (1960) 51–63. **Torczyner, H.** "Job." *EncJud* 8:63–73. **Tournay, R.** "Le procès de Job ou l'innocent devant Dieu." *VS* 422 (1956) 339–50. **Tsevat, M.** "The Meaning of the Book of Job." *HUCA* 37 (1966) 73–106. [= *Studies in Ancient Israelite Wisdom,* ed. J. L. Crenshaw. New York: Ktav, 1976. 341–74; *The Meaning of the Book of Job and Other Biblical Studies.* New York: Ktav, 1980. 1–37; also *The Fourth World Congress of Jewish Studies.* 1967. 1:177–80.] **Tur-Sinai, N. H.** "איוב." *EBB* 1:241–57, 796.

Ulanov, B. "Job and His Comforters." *The Bridge* 3 (1958) 234–68. **Urbrock, W.** "Mortal and Miserable Man: A Form-Critical Investigation of Psalm 90." In *SBL 1974 Seminar Papers,* ed. G. MacRae. Cambridge, MA: SBL, 1974. 1:1–33. ———. "Job as Drama: Tragedy or Comedy?" *CurTM* 8 (1981) 35–40.

Van Gelderen, C. *De hoofdpunten des zielsgeschiedenis van Job.* Kampen: Kok, 1931. **Vawter, B.** *Job and Jonah: Questioning the Hidden God.* New York: Paulist, 1985. **Vischer, W.** *Valeur de l'Ancien Testament: Commentaire des livres de Job, Esther, Ecclésiaste, le Second Isaïe.* Geneva: Labor et Fides, 1958. ———. "God's Truth and Man's Lie: A Study of the Message of the Book of Job." *Int* 15 (1961) 131–46. **Vogels, W.** "Job a parlé correctement: Une approche structurale du livre de Job." *NRT* 102 (1980) 835–52. **Vries, S. de.** "Wegwijs in Job: voor bijbelstudie." Hattem: Filippus, 1980.

Walker, C. C. *Job: "Hast Thou Considered My Servant Job?" (Job 1:8; 2:3), An Attempted "Consideration" in the Light of the Later Work of God in Christ.* Birmingham: Christadelphian, 1955. **Ward, W. B.** *Out of the Whirlwind: Answers to the Problem of Suffering from the Book of Job.* Richmond: John Knox, 1958. **Weill, R.** "Le livre du 'Désesperé.' Le sens, l'intention et la composition de l'ouvrage." *BIFAO* 45 (1947) 89–154. **Welch, C. H.** *Studies in the Book of Job.* London: Berean Publishing Trust, 1953. ———. *The Book of Job.* Rev. ed. London: Berean Publishing Trust, 1975. **Wemyss, T.** *Job and His Times, or A Picture of the Patriarchal Age.* London: Jackson & Walford, 1839. **Westermann, C.** "The Two Faces of Job." Tr. G. Harrison. In *Job and the Silence of God,* ed. C. Duquoc and C. Floristán. *Conc* 169 (1983) 15–22. **Wharton, J. A.** "The Unanswerable Answer: An

Interpretation of Job." In *Texts and Testaments: Critical Essays on the Bible and Early Church Fathers . . . in honor of S. D. Currie*, ed. W. E. March. San Antonio, TX: Trinity UP, 1980. 37–69. **Whedbee, W.** "The Comedy of Job." *Semeia* 7 (1970) 1–39. **White, G. C.** *The Discipline of Suffering: Nine Short Readings on the History of Job.* London: W. Skeffington & Son, 1919. **Williams, J. G.** "'You Have Not Spoken Truth of Me': Mystery and Irony in Job." *ZAW* 83 (1971) 231–55. ———. "Deciphering the Unspoken: The Theophany of Job." *HUCA* 49 (1978) 59–72. ———. "Job's Vision: The Dialectic of Person and Presence." *HAR* 8 (1984) 259–72. **Willi-Plein, I.** "Hiobs immer aktuelle Frage." In *Der Herr ist einer, unser gemeinsames Erbe*, ed. K. Illmann et al. Meddelander frøn Stiftelsens för Åbo 47. Åbo, 1979. 122–36. **Wood, J.** *Job and the Human Situation.* London: G. Bles, 1966. **Würtemberg, G.** "Das Hiobsproblem." *Philosophie und Schule* 2 (1930) 190–203.

Yates, K. M. "Understanding the Book of Job." *RevExp* 68 (1971) 433–45.

Zenger, E., and **R. Böswald.** *Durchkreuztes Leben: Besinnung auf Hiob.* Frankfurt: Herder, 1976. ———. "Ijob—ein Lebensbuch für Leidende und Mitleidende." *Lebendige Katachese* 5 (1983) 106–10. **Zika, C.** "Ijob." *Biblia Revuo* 4 (1968) 21–34. **Zimmermann, E. H.** "The Book of Job." *MethQR* 16 (1979) 703–16. **Zorell, F.** "Ex disputatione Jobi cum amicis suis." *VD* 10 (1930) 265–68, 374–78; 11 (1931) 33–37. **Zuck, R. B.** *Job.* Chicago: Moody, 1978. **Zuckerman, B.** "Job, Book of." *IDBS.* 479–81.

4. Philology, Text Criticism

Aufrecht, W. E. "Aramaic Studies and the Book of Job." In *Studies in the Book of Job,* ed. W. E. Aufrecht. SR Supplements 16. Waterloo: Wilfrid Laurier UP, 1985. 54–66. **Baer, S.** ספר איוב. *Liber Iobi: Textum masoreticum collatis praestantibus codicibus instauravit atque ex fontibus masorae illustravit.* Leipzig: Tauchnitz, 1875. **Barr, J.** "Philology and Exegesis: Some General Remarks with Illustrations from Job." *BETL* 33 (1974) 39–61. ———. "Hebrew Orthography and the Book of Job." *JSS* 30 (1985) 1–33. **Barton, G. A.** "Some Textcritical Notes on Job." *JBL* 42 (1923) 29–32. **Beer, G.** *Der Text des Buches Hiob.* Marburg: N. G. Elwert, 1895–97. ———. "Textkritische Studien zum Buche Hiob." *ZAW* 16 (1886) 297–314; 17 (1897) 97–122; 18 (1898) 257–86. ———. *Iob.* In *Biblica Hebraica*, ed. R. Kittel. 3d ed. Stuttgart: Württembergische Bibelanstalt, 1913. 1105–54. **Bickell, G.** *Carmina Veteris Testamenti metrice: Notas criticas et dissertationem de re metrica Hebraeorum. . . .* Innsbruck: Libraria Academica Wagneriana, 1862. ———. "Kritische Bearbeitung des Jobdialogs." *WZKM* 6 (1892) 136–47, 241–57, 327–34; 7 (1893) 1–20, 153–68. **Blommerde, A. C. M.** *Northwest Semitic Grammar and Job.* Rome: Pontifical Biblical Institute, 1969. **Boadt, L.** "A Re-Examination of the Third-Yodh Suffix in Job." *UF* 7 (1975) 59–72. **Bobzin, H.** *Die 'Tempora' im Hiobdialog.* Diss. Marburg, 1974. **Buber, M.** "Zur Verdeutschung des Buches Ijob (Hiob)." *Werke.* 2:1170–74. **Budde, K.** *Beiträge zur Kritik des Buches Hiob.* Göttingen, 1876. **Byington, S. T.** "Hebrew Marginalia." *JBL* 60 (1941) 279–88. ———. "Hebrew Marginalia II. Job 28." *JBL* 61 (1942) 205–7. ———. "Hebrew Marginalia III." *JBL* 64 (1945) 339–55. ———. "Texts in Job." *ExpT* 57 (1945–46) 110–11.

Clarke, E. C. "Reflections on Some Obscure Hebrew Words in the Biblical Job in the Light of XI Q Tg Job." In *Studies in Philology in Honor of R. J. Williams*, ed. G. Kadish et al. SSEA 3. 1982. 17–30. **Compston, H. F. B.** "The Accentuation of *Wayyomar* in Job." *JTS* (1912) 426–27. ———. "Marginal Notes on Driver-Gray's Job (I.C.C.)." *ExpT* 42 (1930–31) 92–93. **Craigie, P. C.** "Job and Ugaritic Studies." In *Studies in the Book of Job,* ed. W. E. Aufrecht. SR Supplements 16. Waterloo, Ont.: Wilfrid Laurier UP, 1985. 28–35.

Dahood, M. "Some Northwest-Semitic Words in Job." *Bib* 38 (1957) 306–20. ———. "Northwest Semitic Philology and Job." *The Bible in Current Catholic Thought*, Gruenthaner Memorial Volume, ed. J. L. McKenzie. New York: Herder & Herder, 1962. 55–74. ———. "Some Rare Parallel Word Pairs in Job and Ugaritic." In *The Word in the World: Essays in Honor of Frederick L. Moriarty.* Cambridge, MA: Weston College Press, 1973. 19–34. ———. "Chiasmus in Job: A Text-Critical and Philological Criterion." In *A Light Unto My Path: Old Testament Studies in Honor of Jacob M. Myers,* ed. H. N. Bream et al. Philadelphia: Temple UP, 1974. 119–30. **Driver, G. R.** "Studies in the Vocabulary of the Old Testament." *JTS* 36 (1935) 293–301. ———. "Problems in Job and Psalms Reconsidered." *JTS* 40 (1939) 391–94. ———. "Problems in Job." *AJSL* 52 (1935–36) 160–70. ———. "Problems in the Hebrew Text of Job." *VTSup* 3 (1955) 72–93.

Ehrlich, A. B. *Randglossen zur hebräischen Bibel.* VI. *Psalmen, Sprüche und Hiob.* Leipzig: J. C. Hinrichs, 1913. **Eitan, I.** "Biblical Studies. 4. Notes on Job." *HUCA* 14 (1939) 9–13.

Foster, F. H. "Is the Book of Job a Translation from an Arabic Original?" *AJSL* 49 (1932–33) 21–45. **Freedman, D. N.** "Orthographical Peculiarities in the Book of Job." *Eretz Israel* 9 (1969) 35–44.

Grabbe, L. L. *Comparative Philology and the Text of Job: A Study in Methodology.* SBLDS 34. Chico, CA: Scholars Press, 1977. **Graetz, H.** *Emendationes in plerosque Sacrae Scripturae Veteris Testamenti libros.* 3 vols. Breslau, 1892. ———. "Register der corrumpierten Stellen in Hiob und Vorschläge zur Verbesserung." *MGWJ* 15 (1886). **Gray, G. B.** "Critical Notes on the Text of Job." *AJSL* 35 (1919–20) 95–102. **Greeff, J.** "'n Beoordeling van pogings vanuit Ugarities, Aramees en Arabies om sekere cruces interpretum in die boek Job op te los." *NedGTT* 23 (1982) 6–17. **Grimme, H.** "Metrisch-kritische Emendationen zum Buche Hiob." *ThQ* 80 (1898) 295–304, 421–32; 81 (1899) 112–18, 259–77. **Guillaume, A.** "The First Book to Come out of Arabia." *Islamic Studies* 3 (1964) 152–66. ———. *Hebrew and Arabic Lexicography: A Comparative Study.* Leiden: E. J. Brill, 1965. ———. *Studies in the Book of Job, with a New Translation.* ALUOS Supplements 2. Leiden: E. J. Brill, 1968. ———. "The Arabic Background of the Book of Job." In *Promise and Fulfilment: Essays Presented to S. H. Hooke,* ed. F. F. Bruce. Edinburgh: T. & T. Clark, 1963. 106–27.

Hamilton, W. T. "Difficult Texts from Job." In *Difficult Texts of the Old Testament,* ed. W. Winckler, 1982. 301–10. **Herz, N.** "Some Difficult Passages in Job." *ZAW* 20 (1900) 160–63. **Hoffmann, J. G. E.** "Ergänzungen und Berichtigungen zu Hiob." *ZAW* 49 (1931) 141–45, 270–73. **Houtsma, M. T.** *Textkritische Studien zum Alten Testament.* I. *Das Buch Hiob.* Leiden: Brill, 1925.

Jeffrey, J. "The Masoretic Text and the Septuaginta Compared, with Special Reference to the Book of Job." *ExpT* 36 (1924–25) 70–73. **Joüon, P.** "Notes philologiques sur le texte hébreu de Job." *Bib* 11 (1930) 322–24.

King, E. G. "Some Notes on the Text of Job." *JTS* 15 (1914) 74–81.

Lipiński, E. "Notes lexicographiques et stylistiques sur le livre de Job." *FolOr* 21 (1980) 65–82.

Michel, W. L. *The Ugaritic Texts and the Mythological Expressions in the Book of Job, Including a New Translation and Philological Notes on the Book.* Diss. University of Wisconsin, 1970. ———. *Job in the Light of Northwest Semitic.* Vol. 1. Rome: Biblical Institute Press, 1987. **Perani, M.** "Rilievi sulla terminologia temporale nel libro di Giobbe." *Hen* 5 (1983) 1–28. **Perles, F.** *Analekten zur Textkritik des Alten Testaments.* Münster: Ackermann, 1895. ———. *Analekten zur Textkritik des Alten Testaments. Neue Folge.* Leipzig: Engel, 1922. ———. "Neue Analekten zur Textkritik des Alten Testaments." *Orientalische Studien . . . Hommel. MVAG* 22 (191) 125–35. **Peters, N.** "Textkritisches zu Hiob." *TQ* 83 (1901) 208–18, 389–96. ———. "Vertikale Doppelschreibung als Fehlerquelle im Buche Job." *TGl* 14 (1922) 106–10.

Qafiḥ, J. "The Accents of Job, Proverbs, and Psalms in Yemenite Tradition" [Heb]. *Tarb* 31 (1961–62) 371–76.

Richter, G. *Erläuterungen zu dunkeln Stellen im Buche Hiob.* BZAW 11. Leipzig: Hinrichs, 1912. ——. *Textstudien zum Buche Hiob.* BWANT 3/7. Stuttgart: W. Kohlhammer, 1927. **Rignell, L. G.** "Comments on some *cruces interpretum* in the Book of Job." *ASTI* 11 (1978) 111–18.
Sarna, N. M. *Studies in the Language of Job.* Diss. Dropsie College, 1955. ——. "Epic Substratum in the Prose of Job." *JBL* 76 (1957) 13–15. ——. "Some Instances of the Enclitic *-m* in Job." *JJS* (1955) 108–10. **Selms, A. van.** "Motivated Interrogative Sentences in the Book of Job." *Semitics* 6 (1978) 28–35. **Schwally, F.** "Einige Bemerkungen zum Buche Hiob." *ZAW* 20 (1900) 44–48. **Snaith, N. H.** *Notes on the Hebrew Text of Job 1–6.* London: Epworth, 1945. ——. "The Introductions to the Speeches in the Book of Job: Are They in Prose or in Verse?" *Textus* 8 (1973) 133–37. **Stevenson, W. B.** *Critical Notes on the Hebrew Text of the Poem of Job.* Aberdeen: Aberdeen UP, 1951. **Sutcliffe, E. F.** "Notes on Job, Textual and Exegetical." *Bib* 30 (1949) 66–90. ——. "Further Notes on Job, Textual and Exegetical." *Bib* 31 (1950) 365–78.
Theile, C. G. G. אִיוֹב, *Liber Jobi ex recensione C. G. G. Theile.* New York: American Bible Union, 1857. **Torczyner, H.** *Das Buch Hiob: Eine kritische Analyse des überlieferten Textes.* Vienna: R. Löwit, 1920.
Van den Oudenrijn, M. A. "Scholia in locos quosdam libri Job." *Ang* 13 (1936) 228–40. **Vetter, P.** *Die Metrik des Buches Hiob.* Biblische Studien 2. Freiburg im Breisgau, 1897. **Voigt, C.** *Einige Stellen des Buches Hiob.* Leipzig: W. Drugulin, 1895.
Webber, H. J. "Material for the Construction of a Grammar of the Book of Job." *AJSL* 15 (1898–99) 1–32.

5. The Ancient Versions

a. Septuagint and Other Greek Versions

Edition: **Ziegler, J.** *Iob.* Septuaginta Gottingensis 11,4. Göttingen: Vandenhoeck & Ruprecht, 1982.
Bickell, G. *De indole ac ratione versionis alexandrinae in interpretando libro Jobi.* Marburg, 1862. ——. "Der ursprüngliche Septuagintatext des Buches Hiob." *ZTK* 10 (1886) 557–64. ——. *Das Buch Job nach Anleitung der Strophik und der Septuaginta auf seine ursprüngliche Form zurückgeführt und in Versmasse des Urtextes übersetzt.* Vienna: Karl Gerold's Sohn, 1894. **Cox, C. E.** "Methodological Issues in the Exegesis of LXX Job." In *VI Congress of the International Organization for Septuagint and Cognate Studies. Jerusalem, 1986.* SBLSCS 23. Atlanta: Scholars Press, 1987. **De Lange, N. R. M.** "Some New Fragments of Aquila on Malachi and Job." *VT* 30 (1980) 291–94. **Dieu, L.** "Le texte de Job du Codex Alexandrinus et ses principaux témoins." *Muséon* ns 13 (1912) 223–74. **Field, F.** *Origenis Hexapla quae supersunt; sive veterum interpretum Graecorum in totum VT fragmenta.* Oxford, 1871–75. 2:4–82. **Gammie, J. G.** "The Angelology and Demonology in the Septuagint of the Book of Job." *HUCA* 56 (1985) 1–19. ——. "The Septuagint of Job: Its Poetic Style and Relationship to the Septuagint of Proverbs." *CBQ* 49 (1987) 14–31. **Gard, D. H.** *The Exegetical Method of the Greek Translator of the Book of Job.* SBLMS 8. Philadelphia: Society of Biblical Literature, 1952. ——. "The Concept of Job's Character according to the Greek Translator of the Hebrew Text." *JBL* 72 (1953) 182–86. ——. "The Concept of the Future Life according to the Greek Translator of the Book of Job." *JBL* 73 (1954) 137–43. **Gehman, H. S.** "The Theological Approach of the Greek Translator of Job 1–15." *JBL* 68 (1949) 231–40. **Gerleman, G.** *Studies in the Septuagint. I: The Book of Job.* LUÅ 43. Lund, 1946. **Gray, G. B.** "The Additions in the Ancient Greek Version of Job." *Exp* 46 (1920) 422–38. **Heater, H.** *A*

Septuagint Translation Technique in the Book of Job. CBQMS 11. Washington, DC: Catholic Biblical Association, 1982. **Jeffrey, J.** "The Masoretic Text and the Septuagint Compared, with Special Reference to the Book of Job." *ExpT* 36 (1924–25) 70–73. **Orlinsky, H.** "Some Corruptions in the Greek Text of Job." *JQR* 26 (1935–36) 133–45. ———. "Studies in the Septuagint of the Book of Job." *HUCA* 28 (1957) 53–74; 29 (1958) 229–71; 30 (1959) 153–57; 32 (1961) 239–68; 33 (1962) 119–51; 35 (1964) 57–78; 36 (1965) 37–47. **Schaller, B.** "Das Testament Hiobs und die Septuaginta-Übersetzung des Buches Hiob." *Bib* 61 (1980) 377–406. **Tisserant, E.** "Un manuscrit palimpseste de Job." *RB* (1912) 481–503. ———. "Nouvelles notes sur le manuscrit palimpseste de Job." *RB* (1919) 89–105. ———. "Note additionelle sur le manuscrit palimpseste de Job." *RB* (1919) 500–505. **Wevers, J. W.** "Septuagintaforschungen." *TRu* 22 (1954) 85–138, 171–90 (esp. 133–34). **Ziegler, J.** "Der textkritische Wert der Septuaginta des Buches Hiob." *Miscellanea Biblica B. Ubach.* Rome: Pontifical Biblical Institute, 1934. 2:277–96. [= *Sylloge.* Göttingen: Vandenhoeck & Ruprecht, 1971. 9–28.] ———. *Beiträge zum griechischen Job.* MittSeptU 18. Göttingen: Vandenhoeck & Ruprecht, 1985. **Zimmermann, L.** "The Septuagint Appendix to Job." *The Scotist* (1960) 48–59.

b. Targum

Editions: *Miqraot Gedolot.* Vilna, 1912. **Sokoloff, M.** *The Targum to Job from Qumran Cave XI.* Bar Ilan Studies in Near Eastern Languages and Cultures. Ramat-Gan, Jerusalem: Bar-Ilan University, 1974.
Andersen, F. I. "The Qumran Targum of Job." *BurHist* 10,3 (1974) 77–84. **Aufrecht, W. E.** "Aramaic Studies and the Book of Job." In *Studies in the Book of Job,* ed. W. E. Aufrecht. SR Supplements 16. Waterloo, Ont.: Wilfrid Laurier UP, 1985. 54–66. **Bacher, W.** "Das Targum zu Hiob." *MGWJ* 20 (1871) 208–23, 283–84. **Boyarin, D.** "Aramaic Notes I: Column 36 of 11QTg Job." *JANESCU* 6 (1974) 29–33. **Brownlee, W. H.** "The Cosmic Role of Angels in the 11Q Targum of Job." *JSJ* 8 (1977) 83–84. **Caquot, A.** "Un écrit sectaire de Qoumrân: Le 'Targoum de Job.'" *RHR* 185 (1974) 9–27. **Clarke, E. C.** "Reflections on Some Obscure Hebrew Words in the Biblical Job in the Light of XI Q Tg Job." In *Studies in Philology in Honor of R. J. Williams,* ed. G. Kadish et al. SSEA 3. 1982. 17–30.
Delcor, M. "Le Targum de Job et l'araméen du temps de Jésus." In *Exégèse biblique et judaïsme* [= *RSR* 47 (1973)], ed. J.-E. Ménard. Leiden: E. J. Brill, 1973. 78–107. **Díez Macho, A.** "Le Targum de Job dans la tradition sefardie." In *De la Tôrah au Messie: Études d'exégèse et d'herméneutique bibliques offerts à Henri Cazelles,* ed. M. Carrez et al. Paris: Desclée, 1981. 545–56. **Díez Marino, L.** "Manuscritos del Targum de Job." *Hen* 4 (1982) 41–64. ———. *Targum de Job; edición principe del Ms. Villa-Amil n. 5 de Alfonso Zamora.* Bibliotheca Hispana Biblica 8. Madrid: Consejo Superiore, 1984. **Dupont-Sommer, A.** "Sur 11QtgJob, col. XXXIII." *Sem* 15 (1965) 70–74. **Fitzmyer, J. A.** "Some Observations on the Targum of Job from Qumran Cave 11." *CBQ* 36 (1974) 503–24 [= "The First-Century Targum of Job from Qumran Cave XI." In *A Wandering Aramean: Collected Aramaic Essays.* SBLMS 25. Missoula, MT: Scholars Press, 1979. 161–82.] **Fohrer, G.** "4QOrNab, 11QTgJob und die Hioblegende." *ZAW* 75 (1963) 93–97. **Garcia, F.** "Nuevas Lecturas de 11QtgJob." *Sef* 36 (1976) 241–49. **Gray, J.** "The Masoretic Text of the Book of Job, the Targum and the Septuagint Version in the Light of the Qumran Targum (11Qtarg Job)." *ZAW* 86 (1974) 331–50. **Greenfield, J. C.,** and **S. Shaked.** "Three Iranian Words in the Targum of Job from Qumran." *ZDMG* 122 (1972) 33–45.
Jongeling, B. *Een aramees Boek Job (11QtgJob) uit de bibliotheek van Qumrān.* Exegetica. N.R. 3. Amsterdam: Bolland, 1974. ———. "La colonne XVI de 11QtgJob." *RevQ* 8 (1974) 415–16. ———. "The Job Targum from Qumran Cave 11 (11QtgJob)." *FolOr* 15 (1974) 181–86. ———. "Contributions of the Qumran Job Targum to the Aramaic

Vocabulary." *JSS* 17 (1972) 191–97. ———. "Détermination et indétermination dans 11QTgJob." In *Qumran. Sa piété, sa théologie et son milieu,* ed. M. Delcor. BETL 46. Gembloux: Duculot, 1978. 131–36. **Kaufman, S. A.** "The Job Targum from Qumran." *JAOS* 93 (1973) 317–27. **Kutsch, E.** "Die Textgliederung im hebräischen Ijobbuch sowie in 4QTgJob und in 11QTgJob." *BZ* 27 (1983) 221–28. **Lewin, M.** *Targum und Midrasch zum Buche Hiob.* Bern, 1895.
Mastin, B. A. "A Re-examination of an Alleged Orthographic Feature in 4Q Targum Job." *RevQ* 41 (1982) 109; 44 (1984) 583–84. **Milik, J. T.** "Targum de Job." In *Discoveries in the Judean Desert. IV. Qumrân Grotte 4.* Oxford: Clarendon, 1977. 2:90. **Moravkeh, T.** "On the Language of the Job Targum from Qumran." In *Proceedings 6th World Congress of Jewish Studies.* 1977. 159–65. **Morrow, F. J.** "11Q Targum Job and the Masoretic Text." *RevQ* 8 (1973) 253–56. **Muraoka, T.** "Notes on the Old Targum of Job from Qumran Cave XI." *RevQ* 9 (1977) 117–25. **Ploeg, J. van der.** *Le Targum de Job de la Grotte 11 de Qumran (11QtgJob): Première communication.* Akademie van Wetenschappen, Amsterdam. Mededelingen. Afd. Letterkunde. N.R. 25/9. Amsterdam: Noord-Hollandsche Uitgevers Maatschappij, 1962. ———, and **A. S. van der Woude.** *Le Targum de Job de la Grotte XI de Qumran.* Leiden: Brill, 1971. **Ringgren, H.** "Some Observations on the Qumran Targum of Job." *ASTI* 11 (1978) 119–26. **Tuinstra, E. W.** *Hermeneutische aspecten van de targum van Job uit grot XI van Qumrân.* Diss. Groningen, 1970. **Vasholtz, R.** "Two Notes on 11QtgJob and Biblical Aramaic." *RevQ* 10 (1979) 93–94. ———. "A Further Note on the Problem of Nasalization in Biblical Aramaic, 11QtgJob, and 1QApGn." *RevQ* 10 (1979) 95–96.
Weiss, A. *De libri Job paraphrasi chaldaica.* Breslau, 1873. **Weiss, R.** "Further Notes on the Qumran Targum of Job." *JSS* 19 (1974) 13–18. ———. "Recensional Variations between the Aramaic Translation of Job from Qumran Cave 11 and the Masoretic Text." *Shnaton* 1 (1975) 123–27. ———. *The Aramaic Targum of the Book of Job* [Heb.]. Tel-Aviv: Tel-Aviv UP, 1979. ———. "Divergences from the MT Reflected in the Qumran Targum of Job" [Heb.]. In *Studies in the Text and Language of the Bible.* 1981. 240–44. **Woude, A. S. van der.** "Das Hiobtargum aus Qumran Höhle XI." *VTSup* 9 (1962) 322–31. **York, A. D.** "11QTgJob XXI 4–5 (Job 32:13)." *RevQ* 9 (1977) 127–29. ———. "*Zrʿ rwmʾh* as an Indication of the Date of 11Q Tg Job." *JBL* 93 (1974) 445–46. **Zuckerman, B.** *The Process of Translation in 11QtgJob, A Preliminary Study.* Diss. Yale, 1980. ———. "Two Examples of Editorial Modification in 11QtgJob." In *Biblical and Near Eastern Studies, Essays in Honor of William Sanford LaSor,* ed. G. A. Tuttle. Grand Rapids: Eerdmans, 1978. 269–75. ———. "The Date of 11Q Targum Job: A Paleographic Consideration of Its *Vorlage.*" *JSP* 1 (1987) 57–78.

c. Vulgate and Other Latin Versions

Edition: *Biblia Sacra juxta latinam Vulgatam versionem. IX. Libri Hester et Job.* Rome, 1951. **Barret, L.** *Job selon la Vulgate.* Toulon: Imprimerie J. d'Arc, 1925. **Caspari, C. P.** *Das Buch Hiob (1,1–38,16) in Hieronymus's Übersetzung aus der alexandrinischen Version nach St Gallener Handschrift saec. VIII.* Christiana: J. Dybwad, 1893. **Erbes, P. J.** *Die Job-Übersetzung des hl. Hieronymus.* Diss. Freiburg im Breisgau, 1951. **Gailey, J. H.** *Jerome's Latin Version of Job from the Greek, Chapters 1–26; Its Text, Character and Provenience.* Diss. Princeton, 1945. **Salmon, P.** "Le texte de Job utilisé par S. Grégoire dans les 'Moralia.'" *StAns* 27–28 (1951) 187–94. ———. "De quelques leçons du texte du Job dans la nouvelle édition de la Vulgate." *Miscellanea Biblica B. Ubach.* Montserrat, 1953–54. 177–84. **Wahl, O.** "Der Codex Rupefucaldinus—ein bedeutsamer Textzeuge des Ijobstextes der Sacra Parallela." In *Theologie und Leben: Festgabe für George Soldl,* ed. A. Bodem et al. 1983. 25–30. **Ziegler, J.** *Randnoten aus der Vetus Latina des Buches Job in spanischen Vulgatabibeln.* Sitzungberichte der Bayerischen Akademie der Wissenschaften. Phil.-hist. Kl., 1980. Heft 2. Munich: Bayerische Akademie der Wissenschaften, 1980.

d. Peshitta and Other Syriac Versions

Edition: **Rignell, L. G.** *Job: The Old Testament in Syriac according to the Peshiṭta Version.* 2/1a. Leiden: Brill, 1982.
Baumann, E. "Die Verwendbarkeit der Pešita zum Buche Hiob für die Textkritik." *ZAW* 18 (1898) 305–38; 19 (1899) 15–95, 288–309; 20 (1900) 177–201, 264–307. **Mandl, A.** *Die Peschita zu Hiob.* Leipzig, 1892. **Rignell, L. G.** "Notes on the Peshitta of the Book of Job." *ASTI* 9 (1973) 98–106. **Smith Lewis, Agnes.** *A Palestinian Syriac Lectionary Containing Lessons from the Pentateuch, Job, Proverbs, Prophets, Acts and Epistles.* London, 1897. **Stenij, E.** *De syriaca libri Jobi interpretatione quae Peschîta vocatur.* Helsingfors, 1887. **Vosté, J.-M.** "Les deux versions syriaques de la Bible d'après Mar Išoʻdad de Merw (c. 850)." *Bib* 33 (1952) 235–36.

e. Arabic

Editions: **Lagarde, P. de.** *Psalterium Job Proverbia Arabice.* Göttingen, 1876. **Bacher, W.** *Version arabe du livre de Job de R. Saadia ben Iosef al-Fayyoûmî, publiée avec des notes hébraïques par W. Bacher. Accompagnée d'une traduction française d'après l'arabe par J. Derenbourg et H. Derenbourg.* Paris: Leroux, 1899.
Bacher, W. *Moses b. Samuel Hakohez ibn Chiquitilla: Arabische Übersetzung zum Buche Hiob nebst arabischem Kommentar.* Budapest, 1909.
Baudissin, W. W. von. *Translationis antiquae arabicae libri Jobi quae supersunt ex apographo codicis Musei Britannici.* Leipzig: Dörffling & Franks, 1870. **Cohn, J.** :איוב כתאב אלמלקב בכתאב אלתעדיל. *Das Buch Hiob, übersetzt und erklärt von Gaon Saadia: Nach Handschriften der Bodlejana und der Königlichen Bibliothek in Berlin, herausgegeben und mit Anmerkungen versehen.* Altona: Bonn, 1889. **Ecker, R.** *Die arabische Job-Übersetzung des Gaon Saʻadja ben Josef al-Fajjumi nach ihrer Eigenart untersucht.* Munich: Kösel, 1962. **Ulback, E.** "An Arabic Version of the Book of Job." *The Open Court* 46 (1932) 782–86.

f. Ethiopic

Pereira, F. M. E. *Le livre de Job. Version Éthiopienne publiée et traduite.* PO 2. Paris: Firmin-Didot, 1905. 561–688.

g. Coptic

Dieu, L. "Nouveaux fragments préhexaplaires du livre de Job en copte sahidique." *Muséon* (1912) 147–80. **Porcher, E.** (ed.). *Le livre de Job: Version copte bohairique.* PO 87. Paris, 1924. Repr. Turnhout: Brepols, 1974. **Tattam, H.** *The Ancient Coptic Version of the Book of Job the Just. Translated into English and Edited.* London: W. Straker, 1846.

6. Literary Aspects

Ahroni, R. "An Examination of the Literary Genre of the Book of Job" [Heb.]. *Tarb* 49 (1979–80) 1–13. **Antolín, T.** "El género literario del libro de Job." *EstBíb* 6 (1947) 449–50.
Bowes, Paula J. "The Structure of Job." *TBT* 20 (1982) 329–33.
Ceresko, A. R. "The A:B::B:A Word Pattern in Hebrew and Northwest Semitic with Special Reference to the Book of Job." *UF* 7 (1976) 73–88. **Cooper, A.** "Narrative Theory and the Book of Job." *SR* 11 (1982) 35–44. **Cox, D.** "The Book of Job as 'Bi-Polar Mašal': Structure and Interpretation." *Ant* 62 (1987) 12–25.
Dion, P.-E. "Formulaic Language in the Book of Job: International Background and

Ironical Distortions." *SR* 16 (1987) 187–93. **Dobson, J. H.** "Translating Job—Prose or Poetry?" *BT* 23 (1972) 243–44.

Feinberg, C. L. "The Poetic Structure of the Book of Job and the Ugaritic Literature." *BSac* 103 (1946) 283–92. **Fohrer, G.** "Form und Funktion in der Hiobdichtung." *ZDMG* 109 (1959) 31–49 [= *Studien zum Buch Hiob (1956–1979).* BZAW 159. 2d ed. Berlin: de Gruyter, 1983. 60–77]. ———. "Dialog und Kommunication im Buche Hiob." In *La Sagesse de l'Ancien Testament,* ed. M. Gilbert et al. BETL 51. Leuven: Leuven UP, 1979. 219–30. [= *Studien zum Buch Hiob (1956–1979).* BZAW 159. 2d ed. Berlin: de Gruyter, 1983. 135–46.] **Frye, J. B.** "The Use of māšāl in the Book of Job." *Semitics* 5 (1977) 59–66.

Gordis, R. "Quotations as a Literary Usage in Biblical, Oriental and Rabbinic Literature." *HUCA* 22 (1949) 157–219. ———. "Virtual Quotations in Job, Sumer and Qumran." *VT* 31 (1981) 410–27.

Habel, N. C. "The Narrative Art of Job: Applying the Principles of Robert Alter." *JSOT* 27 (1983) 101–11. **Hertzberg, H. W.** "Der Aufbau des Buches Hiob." In *Festschrift Alfred Bertholet,* ed. O. Eissfeldt. Tübingen: J. C. B. Mohr, 1950. 233–58. **Herz, J.** "Formgeschichtliche Untersuchungen zum Problem des Hiobbuches." *WZLeipzig* [FS A. Alt] 3 (1953–54) 107–12 (157–62). **Hoffman, Y.** "Irony in the Book of Job." *Immanuel* 17 (1983) 7–21. **Holbert, J. C.** *The Function and Significance of the Klage in the Book of Job with Special Reference to the Incidence of Formal and Verbal Irony.* Diss. Southern Methodist University, 1975. **Holland, J. A.** "On the Form of the Book of Job." *AJBA* 1 (1972) 160–77. **Hontheim, J.** *Das Buch Hiob als strophisches Kunstwerk.* Freiburg im Breisgau, 1904.

Irwin, W. A. "Poetic Structure in the Dialogue of Job." *JNES* 5 (1946) 26–39.

Kissane, E. J. "The Metrical Structure of Job." In *Twentieth-Century Interpretations of the Book of Job: A Collection of Critical Essays,* ed. P. S. Sanders. Englewood Cliffs, NJ: Prentice-Hall, 1968. 78–85. [= Kissane, l–lx.] **Kutsch, E.** "Die Textgliederung im hebräischen Ijobbuch sowie in 4QTgJob und in 11QTgJob." *BZ* 27 (1983) 221–28.

Ley, J. "Die metrische Beschaffenheit des Buches Hiob." *TSK* (1895) 635–92; (1897) 7–42. **Lichtenstein, A.** "Irony in the Book of Job." *Dor* 13 (1984–85) 41–42. **Löhr, M.** "Beobachtungen zur Strophik im Buche Hiob." *BZAW* 33 (1918) 303–21.

Masini, F. "Observaciones al rededor de la poesia del Viejo Testamento y del libro de Job en particular." *Davar* 69 (1957) 46–53.

Nicholls, P. H. *The Structure and Purpose of the Book of Job.* Diss. Hebrew University, 1982.

Peake, A. S. "The Art of the Book." In *Twentieth-Century Interpretations of the Book of Job: A Collection of Critical Essays,* ed. P. S. Sanders. Englewood Cliffs, NJ: Prentice-Hall, 1968. 109–13. [= Peake, 41–45.] **Persons, G. W.** "The Structure and Purpose of the Book of Job." *BSac* 138 (1981) 139–57, 213–29. **Polzin, R.** "The Framework of the Book of Job." *Int* 28 (1974) 182–200. ———. *Biblical Structuralism: Method and Subjectivity in the Study of Ancient Texts.* Semeia Supplements. Philadelphia: Fortress, 1977. 57–125. **Power, W. J. A.** *A Study of Irony in the Book of Job.* Diss. Toronto, 1961.

Reynolds, Roberta M. *Piety and Paradox: A Rhetorical Study of the King James Version of the Book of Job.* Diss. University of Oregon, 1984. **Richter, H.** *Studien zu Hiob: Der Aufbau des Hiobbuches, dargestellt an den Gattungen des Rechtslebens.* Berlin: Evangelische Verlagsanstalt, 1959. **Robertson, D.** "The Book of Job: A Literary Study." *Soundings* 56 (1973) 446–69. ———. "The Book of Job." In *The Old Testament and the Literary Critic.* Guides to Biblical Scholarship. Philadelphia: Fortress, 1977. 33–54.

Sawyer, J. F. A. "The Authorship and Structure of the Book of Job." *Studia Biblica 1978: I.* JSOTSup 11. JSOT Press: Sheffield, 1979. 253–57. **Seitz, C. R.** "Job. Full-Structure, Movement and Interpretation." *Int* 43 (1989) 5–17. **Skehan, P. W.** "Strophic Patterns in the Book of Job." *CBQ* 23 (1961) 125–42. [= *Studies in Israelite Poetry and Wisdom.* CBQMS 1. 1971. 96–113.] **Smick, E. B.** "Architectonics, Structured Poems, and Rhetorical Devices in the Book of Job." In *A Tribute to Gleason Archer,* ed. W.

Kaiser and R. Youngblood, 1986. 87–104. **Snaith, N. H.** "The Introductions to the Speeches in the Book of Job: Are They in Prose or in Verse?" *Textus* 8 (1973) 133–37.
Tur-Sinai, N. H. "שירת איוב כיצרה כפרותית [The Poem of Job as a Literary Creation]." החינוך 25 (1954) 300–305.
Urbrock, W. "Formula and Theme in the Song-Cycle of Job." In *SBL Proceedings 1972,* 1972. 2:459–87. ———. "Oral Antecedents to Job: A Survey of Formulas and Formulaic Systems." *Semeia* 5 (1976) 111–37. ———. "Job as Drama: Tragedy or Comedy?" *CurTM* 8 (1981) 35–40.
Van der Lugt, P. "Stanza-Structure and Word-Repetition in Job 3–14." *JSOT* 40 (1988) 3–38. **Vetter, P.** *Die Metrik des Buches Job.* Biblische Studien 2. Freiburg in Breisgau, 1897.
Webster, E. C. "Strophic Patterns in Job 3–28." *JSOT* 26 (1983) 33–60. **Westermann, C.** *Der Aufbau des Buches Hiob.* Tübingen: J. C. B. Mohr, 1956. ———. *The Structure of the Book of Job: A Form-Critical Analysis.* Tr. C. A. Muenchow. Philadelphia: Fortress Press, 1981. **Whedbee, J. W.** "The Comedy of Job." *Semeia* 7 (1977) 1–39. **Williams, J. G.** "'You Have Not Spoken Truth of Me': Mystery and Irony in Job." *ZAW* 83 (1971) 231–55. ———. "Comedy, Irony, Intercession: A Few Notes in Response." *Semeia* 7 (1977) 135–45.

7. MOTIFS, THEOLOGICAL ELEMENTS

Aiura, T. "Wisdom Motifs in the Joban Poem." *Kwansei Gakuin University Annual Studies* 15 (1966) 1–20. **Albertz, R.** *Weltschöpfung und Menschenschöpfung, untersucht bei Deuterojesaja, Hiob und im den Psalmen.* Calwer Theologische Monographien A3. Stuttgart: Calwer, 1974. **Alonso Díaz, J.** "La experiencia de Job en la órbita del amor de Dios." *BibFe* 1 (1975) 66–81. **Ararat, N.** "Concerning Job's 'Fear of God'" [Heb]. *BMik* 29 (1983–84) 263–78. **Archer, G. L.** *The Book of Job: God's Answer to the Problem of Undeserved Suffering.* Grand Rapids: Baker, 1982.
Bakan, D. "Sacrifice and the Book of Job." In his *Disease, Pain and Sacrifice.* Chicago, 1968. 95–128. ———. "Das Opfer im Buche Hiob." In *Psychoanalytische Interpretationen biblischer Texte.* 152–66. **Balla, E.** "Das Problem des Leides in der Geschichte der israelitisch-jüdischen Religion." In *Eucharisterion.* FS H. Gunkel. Göttingen, 1923. 1:214–60.
Barron, Mary Catherine. "Sitting It out with Job: The Human Condition." *RRel* 38 (1979) 489–96. **Barthélemy, D.** "Dieu méconnu par le vieil homme: Job." *VS* 105 (1961) 445–63. **Bardtke, H.** "Prophetische Züge im Buche Hiob." In *Das Ferne und nahe Wort: FS für Leonard Rost,* ed. F. Maass. BZAW 105. Berlin: Töpelmann, 1967. 1–10. **Batley, J. Y.** *The Problem of Suffering in the Old Testament.* Cambridge: Deighton Bell, 1916. **Becker, D.** "Der Grundgedanke des Buches Job: Biblische Lehr- und Trostgedanken zur praktischen Seelsorge." *TPM* 29 (1918–19) 109–17. **Beel, A.** "De causis tribulationum juxta librum Job. De historica existentia personae Job. Interpretatio Job 7,11–21." *ColBG* 38 (1933) 321–26, 349–53; 34 (1934) 89–94. **Benamozegh, E.** "L'immortalità dell'anima in Giobbe e nei Proverbi." *AnStEbr* 8 (1975–76) 145–72. **Berg, W.** "Gott und der Gerechte in der Rahmenerzählung des Buches Ijob." *MTZ* 32 (1981) 206–21. **Bergant, Dianne.** *An Historico-Critical Study of the Anthropological Traditions and Motifs in Job.* Diss. St. Louis University, 1975. **Bič, M.** "Le juste et l'impie dans le livre de Job." VTSup 15 (1966) 33–43. **Bloch, E.** "Studien zum Buche Hiob." In *'Auf gespaltenem Pfad': FS zum 90. Geburtstag von Margarete Susman,* ed. M. Schlösser. Darmstadt: Erato, 1964. 85–102. ———. "L'uomo Giobbe." *De Homine* 24–25 (1967–68) 3–18. **Bobrinskoy, B.** "La vieillesse et la mort, drame ou bénédiction: pointe de vue de la tradition orthodoxe." In *In necessariis unitas,* ed. R. Stauffer. 1984. 25–33. **Böhles, M.** "Von der Macht

und Ohnmacht des Bösen." *OrdKor* 18 (1977) 129–46. **Brates, L.** "La esperanza en el libro de Job." *XXX Semana Bíblica Española.* 1972. 21–34. **Brown, W. E.** *The Nature of Sin in the Book of Job.* Diss. New Orleans Baptist Theological Seminary, 1983. **Cabodevilla, J. M.** *La Impaciencia de Job: Estudio sobre el sufrimiento humano.* Madrid: BAC, 1967. **Caquot, A.** "Traits royaux dans le personnage de Job." In *maqqél shâqédh. La branche d'amandier: Hommage à Wilhelm Vischer.* Montpellier: Causse, Graille, Castelnau, 1960. 32–45. **Caspar, J.** "Job, ein Held in Leid." *BiLit* 10 (1935–36) 497–98. **Cepeda Calzada, P.** "El problema de la justicia en Job: Personalidad, ley y justicia en el libro de Job." *Crisis* 20 (1973) 243–90. ———. "El Leviatán, símbolo bíblico: El Caos frente a la idea de ley en Job." *Crisis* 21 (1974) 49–68. ———. *El problema de la justicia en Job.* Madrid: Prensa Española, 1975. **Chambers, O.** *Baffled to Fight Better: Talks on the Book of Job.* London: Simpkin Marshall, 1943. **Charue, A.** "Job et le problème des rétributions dans l'Ancien Testament." *Collationes Namurcenses* 33 (1939) 251–71. **Christ, Marie-Paul du.** "Job et le mystère de la mort." *VS* 422 (1956) 392–406. **Christensen, D. L.** "Job and the Age of the Patriarchs in Old Testament Narrative." *PerspRelSt* 13 (1986) 225–28. **Cocagnac, A. M.** "Job sans beauté ni éclat." *VS* 422 (1956) 355–71. **Cosser, W.** "The Meaning of 'Life' (*hayyîm*) in Proverbs, Job, Qoheleth." *TGUOS* 15 (1955) 48–53. **Cox, D.** "Righteousness in Later Wisdom." *SBFLA* 27 (1977) 33–50. **Crenshaw, J. L.** "Popular Questioning of the Justice of God in Ancient Israel." *ZAW* 82 (1970) 380–93. ———. "Impossible Questions, Sayings and Tasks." *Gnomic Wisdom.* Semeia 17, 1980. 19–34. **Croatto, S.** "El libro de Job como clave hermenéutica de la teología." *RBibArg* 43 (1981) 33–45. **Crook, M. B.** *The Cruel God: Job's Search for the Meaning of Suffering.* Boston, 1959. **Cross, R. N.** "Shall We Reason with God?" *HibJ* 46 (1948) 125–28. **Crumbach, K. H.** "Splitter zum Problem des Todes." *GeistLeb* 43 (1970) 325–38. **Cruveilhier, P.** "La conduite de la Providence selon l'auteur du livre de Job." *RevApol* 52 (1931) 150–68.
Dedmon, R. "Job as Holocaust Survivor." *StLuke* 26 (1982–83) 165–85. **Deloches, R.** *Les sciences physiques et naturelles dans le livre de Job.* Nîmes, 1909. **Di Lella, A.** "An Existential Interpretation of Job." *BTB* 15 (1985) 49–55. **Dunn, R. P.** "Speech and Silence in Job." *Semeia* 19 (1981) 99–103. See also **Olsen, A. M.** *Semeia* 19 (1981) 121–23. **Patriquin, A.** *Semeia* 19 (1981) 87–91. **Duquoc, C.** "Demonism and the Unexpectedness of God." *Conc* 169 (1983) 81–87. ———, and **C. Floristán.** *Job and the Silence of God.* Concilium 169. Edinburgh: T. & T. Clark, 1983. **Dussaud, R.** "La néphesh et la rouah dans le 'Livre de Job.'" *RHR* 129 (1945) 17–30. **Dussel, E.** "The People of El Salvador: The Communal Sufferings of Job." *Conc* 169 (1983) 61–68. **Edelkoort, A. H.** *Het Boek Job en het probleem van het lijden.* Hague: J. V. Voorhoeve, 1946. **Eising, H.** "Alttestamentliche Sittenlehre im Buche Hiob." *Kirche in der Welt.* Munich, 1952. 255–58. ———. "Das Menschenleben im Buche Ijob." In *Memoria Jerusalem*, FS F. Sauer, ed. J. B. Bauer et al. Graz, 1977. 43–57. **Engelmann, F.** *Gerecht durch Gott: Hiobs Leidenweg durch Drangsal zur Freude, Licht des Neuen Testaments im Alten.* Wittenberg: Bundes-Verlag, 1933. **Erny, P.** "La rêve dans le livre de Job." *Présence orthodoxe* 74 (1987) 30–39.
Faur, J. "Reflections on Job and Situation-Morality." *Judaism* 19 (1970) 219–25. **Feinberg, C. L.** "Job and the Nation Israel." *BSac* 96 (1935) 405–11; 97 (1940) 27–33, 211–16. **Fichtner, J.** "Hiob in der Verkündigung unserer Zeit." *Wort und Dienst* 29 (1950) 71–89. [= *Gottes Weisheit: Gesammelte Studien zum Alten Testament.* Arbeiten zur Theologie 2/3. Stuttgart: Calwer, 1965. 52–66.] **Fine, H. A.** "The Tradition of the Patient Job." *JBL* 74 (1955) 28–32. **Fischer, W.** "Hiob, ein Zeuge Jesu Christ." *ZZ* 12 (1932–33) 386–414. **Fohrer, G.** "Dialog und Kommunikation im Buche Hiob." In *La Sagesse de l'Ancien Testament*, ed. M. Gilbert et al. BETL 51. Leuven: Leuven UP, 1979. 219–30. [= *Studien zum Buche Hiob (1956–1959).* BZAW 159. 2d ed. Berlin: de Gruyter. 135–46.] **Forrest, R. W. E.** *The Creation Motif in the Book of Job.* Diss. MacMaster University, 1975. **Frye, J. B.** *The Legal Language of the Book of Job.* Diss. King's College, London, 1973.

Garcia Cordero, M. "La tesis de la sanción moral y la esperanza de la resurrección en el libro de Job." *XII Semana Bíblica Española.* 1952. 571–94. ———. "La esperanza de la resurrección corporal en Job." *CiTom* 80 (1953) 1–23. ———. "Corporal Resurrection in Job." *TDig* 2 (1954) 90–94. **Garofalo, S.** "Il peso di Dio e l'angoscia dell'uomo Giobbe." *EnutDoc* 2 (1949) 3–30. **Gese, H.** "Die Frage nach dem Lebenssinn: Hiob und die Folgen." *ZTK* 79 (1982) 161–79. **Gibson, J. C. L.** "On Evil in the Book of Job." In *Ascribe to the Lord: Biblical and Other Studies in Memory of Peter C. Craigie,* ed. L. Eslinger and G. Taylor. JSOTSup 67. Sheffield: JSOT, 1988. 399–419. **Ginsberg, H. L.** "Job the Patient and Job the Impatient." *ConsJud* 21·(1966) 12–28. ———. "Job the Patient and Job the Impatient." VTSup 17 (1968) 88–111. **Girard, R.** "Job et le bouc émissaire." *BCPE* 35 (1983) 3–33. ———. *Job the Victim of His People.* London: Athlone, 1987. [= *La route antique des hommes pervers.* Paris: Grasset, 1985.] ———. "'The Ancient Trail Trodden by the Wicked': Job as Scapegoat." *Semeia* 33 (1985) 13–41. See also **Levine, B.** "Girard on Job." *Semeia* 33 (1985) 125–33. See also P. Watté. **Goiten, L.** "The Importance of the Book of Job for Analytic Research." *American Imago* 2 (1954) 407–15. **Gonzalo Maeso, D.** "Sentido nacional en el libro de Job." *EstBíb* 9 (1950) 67–81. **Gordis, R.** "Job and Ecology (and the Significance of Job 40:15)." *HAR* 9 (1985) 189–202. **Gordon, C. H.** "Leviathan: Symbol of Evil." In *Biblical Motifs,* ed. A. Altmann. Cambridge, MA: Harvard UP, 1966. 1–10.

Haag, H. *Ijobs Fragen an Gott.* Stuttgart: KBW-Verlag, 1972. **Habel, N.** "He Who Stretches Out the Heavens." *CBQ* 34 (1972) 417–30. ———. "Only the Jackal is My Friend: On Friends and Redeemers in Job." *Int* 31 (1977) 227–36. ———. "'Naked I Came . . .': Humanness in the Book of Job." In *Die Botschaft und die Boten: FS für Hans Walter Wolff zum 70. Geburtstag,* ed. J. Jeremias and L. Perlitt. Neukirchen-Vluyn: Neukirchener Verlag, 1981. 373–92. ———. "Of Things beyond Me: Wisdom in the Book of Job." *CurTM* 10 (1983) 142–54. **Hammer, R.** "Two Approaches to the Problem of Suffering [Job, Ruth]." *Judaism* 35 (1986) 300–305. **Hancock, E. L.** "The Impatience of Job." In *Spinning a Sacred Yarn,* ed. A. Abernethy, C. Carlson, P. Carque et al. New York: Pilgrim, 1982. 98–106. **Harper, W. R.** *The Book of Job: A Study in the Problem of Suffering as Treated in the Old Testament.* Chicago: American Institute of Sacred Literature, 1908. **Harris, R. L.** "The Book of Job and Its Doctrine of God." *GJ* 13 (1972) 3–33. [= *Presbyterion* 7 (1981) 5–33.] **Harrison, W. P.** "Christ in the Book of Job." *MethQR* 27 (1988) 390–400. **Hastoupis, A. P.** "The Problem of Theodicy in the Book of Job" [Gk]. *Theologia* (1951) 657–68. **Haught, J. F.** "The Significance of Job for Christology." *AER* 166 (1972) 579–86. **Hawthorne, R. R.** "Jobine Theology." *BSac* 101 (1944) 64–75, 173–86. 290–303, 417–33; 102 (1945) 37–54. **Hedinger, U.** "חַנֵּם oder die Infragestellung Hiobs: Dogmatische Studie und Meditation zum Zweifrontekampf Hiobs." In ΠΑΡΡΗΣΙΑ: *K. Barth zum 80ten Geburtstag.* Zurich, 1966. 192–212. **Hempel, J.** "Das theologische Problem des Hiob." *ZST* 6 (1929) 621–89. [= *Apoxysmata: Vorarbeitungen zu einer Religionsgeschichte und Theologie des Alten Testaments.* BZAW 81. Berlin: A. Töpelmann, 1961. 114–74.] ———. "Was nicht im Buche Ijob steht." *Wahrheit und Glaube,* FS E. Hirsch. Itzehoe, 1963. 134–36. **Herrmann, S.** "Grenzen der Toleranz im Alten Testament: Die Bücher Deuteronomium, Jeremia und Hiob." In *Glaube und Toleranz, das theologische Erbe der Aufklärung,* ed. T. Rendtorff. Gütersloh: Mohn, 1982. 180–90. **Hoang-van-Doan, F.** *Le sens de la souffrance dans le livre de Job.* Diss. Paris, 1944. **Holbert, J. C.** *The Function and Significance of the "Klage" in the Book of Job with Special Reference to the Incidence of Formal and Verbal Irony.* Diss. Southern Methodist University, 1975. **Hora, R.,** and **D. M. Robinson.** "Does the Book of Job Offer an Adequate Pastoral Response to Suffering?" In *Church Divinity,* ed. J. Morgan, 1981. 67–73. **Howard, D. M.** *How Come, God? Reflections from Job about God and Puzzled Man.* London: Scripture Union, 1973. **Humbert, P.** *L'Ancien Testament et le problème de souffrance.* 1917.

Jacobson, R. "Satanic Semiotics, Jobian Jurisprudence." *Semeia* 19 (1981) 63–71.
Kaiser, O. "Leid und Gott: Ein Beitrag zur Theologie des Buches Hiob." In *Sichtbare*

Kirche, FS H. Haag. Gütersloh: Mohn, 1973. 13–21. **Kapusta, M. A.** et al. "The Book of Job and the Modern View of Depression." *AnnInternMed* 86 (1977) 667–72. **Kardong, T.** "The True Image of Job—An Existentialist Who Searches Deeper Conversion." *ColcTFu* 59 (1984) 1–14. **Kinet, D.** "The Ambiguity of the Concepts of God and Satan in the Book of Job." *Conc* 169 (1983) 30–35. **King, A. R.** *The Problem of Evil: Christian Concepts and the Book of Job.* New York: Ronald Press Co., 1952. **Kleinert, P.** "Das spezifisch Hebräische im Buche Job." *TSK* 59 (1886) 267–300. **Knieschke, W.** *Kultur- und Geisteswelt des Buches Hiob.* Zeit- und Streitfragen des Glaubens, der Weltanschauung und Bibelforschung 15/9–12. Berlin-Lichterfelde: E. Runge, 1925. **Konig, E.** "The Problem of Suffering in the Light of the Book of Job." *ExpT* 32 (1920–21) 361–63. **Köpp, W.** "Vom Hiobthema und der Zeit als Leiden." *TLZ* 74 (1949) 389–96. **Köppel, M.** "Jahwe's Allmacht und Gerechtigkeit in den Reden Hiobs." *ZAW* 29 (1909) 204–14. **Kubina, Veronica.** "Ja-Sagen zur Wirklichkeit: Leiden und Leidbewältigung im Buche Ijob." *KatBl* 107 (1982) 743–53. **Kurzweil, B.** "Job and the Possibility of Biblical Tragedy." In *Arguments and Doctrines . . . A. A. Cohen.* New York, 1970. 323–44. **Kusenberg, K.** "Das Buch Hiob: Stichworte bei meiner Lektüre." *Merkur* 23 (1969) 543–46. **Kutsch, E.** "Hiob: leidender Gerechter—leidender Mensch." *KuD* 19 (1973) 197–214. **Lacocque, A.** "Job and the Symbolism of Evil." *BR* 24–25 (1979–80) 7–19. ———. "Job or the Impotence of Religion and Philosophy." *Semeia* 19 (1981) 33–52. **Lafont, G.** "L'excès du malheur et la reconnaissance de Dieu." *NRT* 101 (1979) 724–39. **Larue, G. A.** "The Book of Job on the Futility of Theological Discussion." *The Personalist* 45 (1964) 72–79. **Laurin, R.** "The Theological Structures of Job." *ZAW* 84 (1972) 86–92. **Lévêque, J.** "Job, ou l'espoir déraciné." *VS* 125 (1971) 287–304. ———. "L'argument de la création dans le livre de Job." In *La création dans l'Orient ancien,* ed. L. Derousseaux. Paris: Cerf, 1987. 261–99. **Ley, J.** "Das Problem im Buche Hiob und dessen Lösung." *Neue Jahrbuch für Philosophie und Pädagogie* (1986) 125ff. **Lichtenstein, M. H.** "The Poetry of Poetic Justice: A Comparative Study in Biblical Imagery." *JANESCU* 5 (1974) 255–65. **Lillie, W.** "The Religious Significance of the Theophany in the Book of Job." *ExpT* 68 (1956–57) 355–58. **Lindblom, C. J.** "Die Vergeltung Gottes im Buche Hiob: Eine ideenkritische Skizze." In *A. von Bulmerincq Gedenkschrift.* Abhandlungen der Herder-Gesellschaft und der Herder-Instituts zu Riga 6/3, 1938. 80–97. **Link, C.** "Die Überwindung eines Problems: Bemerkungen zur Frage der Theodizee." In *Wenn nicht jetzt, wann dann?* FS H.-J. Kraus, ed. H.-G. Geyer et al. Neukirchen-Vluyn: Neukirchener Verlag, 1983. 339–51. **Loader, J. A.** "Different Reactions of Job and Qoheleth to the Doctrine of Retribution." *OTWSA* 15 (1972) 43–48. **Long, T. J.** "Life after Death: The Biblical View." *BTod* 20 (1982) 347–53.

Macaluso, G. *Profeti e màrtiri. 1. Giobbe come uomo e come Cristo. 2. Il messaggio del Mahatma Gandhi.* Rome: Edizione "Pensiero & Azione," 1970. **MacFadyen, J. E.** *The Problem of Pain: A Study in the Book of Job.* London: James Clarke & Co., 1917. **MacKenzie, R. A. F.** "The Transformation of Job." *BTB* 9 (1979) 51–57. **Macleod, W. B.** *The Afflictions of the Righteous as Discussed in the Book of Job and the New Light of the Gospel.* London: Hodder & Stoughton, 1911. **Magonet, J.** "The Problem of Suffering in the Bible." *Month* 244 (1982) 311–16. **Many, G.** *Der Rechtsstreit mit Gott (rîb) im Hiobbuch.* Diss. Munich, 1970. **Marcus, R.** "Job and God." *RR* 14 (1949–50) 5–29. **Marie-Paul du Christ.** "Job et le mystère de la mort." *VS* 422 (1956) 392–406. **Maston, T. B.** "Ethical Content in Job." *SWJT* 14 (1971) 43–56. **Mattioli, A.** "Le ultime ragioni dell'esistenza del male e della sofferenza in Giobbe." *La Sapienza della Croce Oggi* 3 (1976) 157–87. **Meinhold, J.** "Das Problem des Buches Hiob." *NJDTh* 1 (1892) 63–109. **Michel, W. L.** "Death in Job." *Dialogue* 11 (1972) 183–89. **Milgrom, J.** "The Cultic שגגה and Its Influence in Psalms and Job." *JQR* 58 (1967) 115–25. **Möller, M.** "Die Gerechtigkeit Gottes des Schöpfers in der Erfahrung seines Knechtes Hiob." *TVers* 6 (1975) 25–36. **Moore, R. D.** "The Integrity of Job." *CBQ* 45 (1983) 17–31. **Müller, K.** "Die Auslegung der Theodizeeproblems im Buche Hiob." *ThBl* 1 (1922) 73–79. **Muntingh, L.** "Life, Death and Resurrection in the Book of Job." *OTWSA* 17–18 (1974–75) 32–44. **Murphy,**

J. *Living without Strain: Inner Meaning of the Book of Job.* London: L. N. Fowler, 1961.
Neher, A. "Job: The Biblical Man." *Judaism* 13 (1964) 34–47. **Nemo, P.** *Job et l'excès du mal.* Paris: B. Grasset, 1978. **Newell, B. Lynne.** "Job: Repentant or Rebellious?" *WTJ* 46 (1984) 298–316. **Ney, P.** "A psychiatrist's discussion of Job." *Crux* 17 (1981) 2–3. **Nowell-Rostrom, S.** *The Challenge of Calamity: A Study of the Book of Job.* London: Lutterworth, 1939. **O'Connor, D. J.** "Reverence and Irreverence in Job." *ITQ* 51 (1985) 85–104. ———. "The Comforting of Job." *ITQ* 53 (1987) 245–57. **Olson, A. M.** "The *Silence* of Job as the Key to the Text." *Semeia* 19 (1981) 113–19. **Ortiz de Urtaran, F.** "Un rico amigo de Dios." *Lumen* 34 (1985) 289–313.
Parente, P. P. "The Book of Job: Reflections on the Mystic Value of Human Suffering." *CBQ* 8 (1946) 213–19. **Payne, J. B.** "Inspiration in the Words of Job." In *The Law and the Prophets,* FS O. T. Allis, ed. J. H. Skilton. Nutley, NJ: Presbyterian & Reformed, 1974. 319–36. **Peake, A. S.** *The Problem of Suffering in the Old Testament,* 1887. Repr. London: Epworth, 1946. **Perani, M.** "Giobbe di fronte alla morte." In *Gesù e la sua morte,* ed. G. Boggio et al. Atti della XXVII Settimana Biblica. Brescia: Paideia, 1984. 267–91. ———. "Crisi della Sapienza e ricerca di Dio nel libro di Giobbe." *RivB* 28 (1980) 157–84. **Peters, N.** *Die Leidensfrage im Alten Testament.* Biblische Zeitfragen 11/3–5. Münster, 1923. **Pfeiffer, R. H.** *Le problème du livre de Job.* Geneva, 1915. **Pifano, P.** "Nel grido di Giobbe il grido dell'uomo contemporaneo." *Asprenas* 31 (1984) 497–524. **Pipes, B. R.** *Christian Response to Human Suffering: A Lay Theological Response to the Book of Job.* Diss. Drew, 1981. **Pixley, J. V.** "La ironía antesala de la teología de la liberación: el libro de Job." *CuadTe* 3 (1973) 57–80. ———. "Jó, ou o diálogo sobre a razão teológica." *PerspT* 15 (1983) 407–12; 16 (1984) 333–43. **Ponthot, J.** "Le scandale de la souffrance du juste selon le livre de Job." *Revue Diocésaine de Tournai* 13 (1958) 271–75. **Prado, J.** "La creación, conservación y gobierno del universo en el libro de Job." *Sef* 11 (1951) 259–88. **Procksch, O.** "Die Theodizee im Buche Hiob." *Allgemeine evangelisch-lutherische Kirchenzeitung* 58 (1925) 722–24, 739–42, 763–65. **Pröpper, T.** "Warum gerade ich? zur Frage nach dem Sinn vom Leiden." *KatBl* 108 (1983) 253–74. **Proskauer, W.** *Hiob und wir: Schicksalfragen und Gottesantwort.* Berlin, 1937. **Pury, R. de.** *Job ou l'homme révolté.* Geneva, 1955. ———. *Hiob, der Mensch im Aufruhr.* Neukirchen, 1957.
Raphael, D. D. "Tragedy and Religion." In *Twentieth-Century Interpretations of the Book of Job: A Collection of Critical Essays,* ed. P. S. Sanders. Englewood Cliffs, NJ: Prentice-Hall, 1968. 46–55. [= *The Paradox of Tragedy.* Bloomington: Indiana UP, 1960. 37–61.] **Raurell, F.** "Ètica de Job i llibertat de Déu." *RCatalT* 4 (1979) 5–24. ———. "Job's Ethic and God's Freedom." *TDig* 29 (1981) 133–37. **Renié, J.** "La maladie de Job." *RevApol* 60 (1935) 365–67. **Reynierse, J. H.** "A Behavioristic Analysis of the Book of Job." *JPsychTheol* 3 (1975) 75–81. **Reynolds, Roberta M.** *Piety and Paradox: A Rhetorical Analysis of the King James Version of the Book of Job.* Diss. Oregon, 1984. **Richter, H.** "Die Naturweisheit des Alten Testaments im Buche Hiob." *ZAW* 70 (1958) 1–20. ———. "Erwägungen zum Hiobproblem." *EvT* 18 (1958) 202–24. **Roberts, J. J. M.** "Job's Summons to Yahweh: The Exploitation of a Legal Metaphor." *RestQ* 16 (1973) 159–65. **Robinson, H. W.** *Suffering Human and Divine.* London: SCM, 1940. ———. *The Cross of Job.* London: SCM, 1916. R.p. in *The Cross in the Old Testament.* London: SCM, 1955. **Rodríguez Ochoa, J. M.** "Estudio de la dimensión temporal en Proverbios, Job y Qohélet: El eterno volvar a comenzar en Qohelet." *EstBíb* 22 (1963) 33–67. **Rohr Sauer, A. von.** "Salvation by Grace: The Heart of Job's Theology." *CurTM* 37 (1966) 259–70. **Rongy, H.** "La résurrection est-elle enseignée dans Job?" *RevEcclLiège* 25 (1983–84) 25–30. **Rouillard, P.** "The Figure of Job in the Liturgy: Indignation, Resolution or Silence?" *Conc* 169 (1983) 8–12. **Rowold, H. L.** *The Theology of Creation in the Yahweh Speeches of the Book of Job as a Solution to the Problem Posed by the Book of Job.* Diss. Concordia Seminary in Exile (Seminex), 1977. **Royer, I.** *Die Eschatologie des Buches Job.* Biblische Studien. Freiburg im Breisgau, 1901. **Rusche, Helga.** "Warum starb ich nicht vom

Mutterschoss weg? Mit Ijob klagen lernen." *Entschluss* 40 (1985) 32, 34–35. **Ruprecht, E.** "Leiden und Gerechtigkeit bei Hiob." *ZTK* 73 (1976) 424–45. **Rutler, G. W.** *The Impatience of Job.* La Salle, IL: Sugden, 1982. **Samuel, J. B.** *The Prophetic Character of Job; or, The Solution of a Great Problem.* Goodmayes: Hebrew Christian Testimony to Israel, 1954. **Sanders, J. A.** "Suffering as a Divine Discipline in the Old Testament and Postbiblical Judaism." *Rochester Divinity School Bulletin* 28 (1953) 28–33. **Scammon, J. F.** *If I Could Find God: Anguish and Faith in the Book of Job.* Valley Forge, PA: Judson, 1974. **Schärf, Rivka R.** *Die Gestalt des Satans im Alten Testament.* Zürich: Rascher, 1948. **Schimmel, J.** "Job and the Psychology of Suffering and Doubt." *JPsychJud* 11 (1987) 239–49. **Schmidt, H.** *Hiob: Das Buch vom Sinn des Leidens. Gekürzt und verdeutscht.* Tübingen: J. C. B. Mohr, 1927. **Schmidt, P.** "Sinnfrage und Glaubenskrise: Ansätze zu einer kritischen Theologie der Schöpfung im Buche Hiob." *GeistL* 45 (1972) 348–63. **Schmitt, E.** *Leben in den Weisheitsbüchern, Job, Sprüche und Jesus Sirach.* Freiburg im Breisgau: Herder, 1954. **Scholnick, Sylvia H.** *Lawsuit Drama in the Book of Job.* Diss. Brandeis, 1975. ———. "The Meaning of *mišpaṭ* in the Book of Job." *JBL* 101 (1982) 521–29. **Schwarz, W.** "Naturschau im Buch Hiob." *Frankfurter Israelitische Gemeindeblätter* 9 (1930–31) 337–40. **Seeskin, K.** "Job and the Problem of Evil." *Philosophy and Literature* 11 (1987) 226–41. **Seinecke, L.** *Der Grundgedanke des Buches Hiob.* Clausthal: Grosse, 1863. **Seitz, O.** *Hiob: Eine Betrachtung über das Leiden.* Berlin: O. Seitz, 1931. **Sekine, M.** "Schöpfung und Erlösung im Buche Hiob." *Von Ugarit nach Qumran,* FS O. Eissfeldt. BZAW 77. Berlin: A. Töpelmann, 1958. 213–23. **Shapiro, D. S.** "The Problem of Evil and the Book of Job." *Judaism* 5 (1956) 46–52. **Smick, E. B.** "Mythology and the Book of Job." *JETS* 13 (1970) 101–8. ———. "Another Look at Mythological Elements in the Book of Job." *WTJ* 40 (1977–78) 213–28. **Sockman, R. W.** *The Meaning of Suffering.* 1961. **Southwick, J. S.** "Job, An Exemplar for Every Age." *Enc* 45 (1984) 373–91. **Sperka, J. S.** *The Book of Job: Mankind on Trial, A Modern Interpretation of the Most Perplexing Problem of All Ages.* New York: Bloch, 1979. **Stamm, J. J.** "Gottes Gerechtigkeit, das Zeugnis des Hiobbuches." *Der Grundriss. Schweizerische Reformierte Monatsschrift* 5 (1943) 1–13. **Stockhammer, M.** *Das Buch Hiob: Versuch einer Theodizee.* Vienna: Europäischer Verlag, 1963. ———. "The Righteousness of Job." *Judaism* 7 (1958) 64–71. ———. "Theorie der Moralprobe." *ZRGG* 22 (1970) 164–67. **Susman, Margarete.** *Das Buch Hiob und das Schicksal des jüdischen Volkes.* Zurich, 1946. 2d ed. Basel: Herder, 1968. **Sutcliffe, E. F.** *Providence and Suffering in the Old and New Testaments.* Oxford, 1955. **Swain, L.** "Suffering in Job." *CleR* 51 (1966) 624–31. **Taradach, Madeleine.** "De la 'modernité' de l'absurde chez Job à la lumière de l'absurde chez Camus." *EstFranc* 81 (1980) 155–68. **Taylor, W. S.** "Theology and Therapy in Job." *TTod* 12 (1955–56) 451–63. **Tengbom, M.** *Sometimes I Hurt: Reflections and Insights from the Book of Job.* Nashville: Nelson, 1980. **Thelen, Mildred F.** "Job and the Biblical Doctrine of Man." *JBR* 27 (1959) 201–5. **Thieberger, F.** "Jona, Hiob, und das Problem der Gerechtigkeit." *Der Morgen* 2 (1926) 128–40. **Thomas, D.** "Types of Wisdom in the Book of Job." *IndJT* 20 (1971) 157–65. **Thompson, K., Jr.** "Out of the Whirlwind: The Sense of Alienation in the Book of Job." *Int* 14 (1960) 51–63. **Torrance, J. B.** "Why Does God Let Men Suffer? A Sermon on Job." *Int* 15 (196) 157–63. **Toynbee, A. J.** "Challenge and Response: The Mythological Clue." In *Twentieth-Century Interpretations of the Book of Job: A Collection of Critical Essays,* ed. P. S. Sanders. Englewood Cliffs, NJ: Prentice-Hall, 1968. 86–97. [= *A Study of History.* Abridged ed. New York: OUP, 1947. 60–67. And *A Study of History* (original ed.). New York: OUP, 1934. 1:293–98.] **Tromp, N. J.** *Primitive Conceptions of Death and the Nether World in the Old Testament.* BibOr 21. Rome: Pontifical Biblical Institute, 1969. **Urbrock, W. J.** "Reconciliation of Opposites in the Dramatic Ordeal of Job." *Semeia* 5 (1976) 111–37. **Vawter, B.** *Job and Jonah: Questioning the Hidden God.* New York: Paulist Press, 1983. **Vischer, W.** *Hiob: Ein Zeuge Jesu Christi.* Munich: Kaiser, 1934. ———. "Hiob, ein Zeuge Jesu Christi." *ZZ* 11 (1963) 386–414. **Vogels, W.** "The Spiritual Growth of Job:

A Psychological Approach to the Book of Job." *BTB* 11 (1981) 77–80. ———. "The Inner Development of Job: One More Look at Psychology and the Book of Job." *ScEs* 35 (1983) 227–30.
Wagner, S. "'Schöpfung' im Buche Hiob." *ZeichZt* 34 (1980) 93–96. **Waldman, N. M.** "Tradition and Experience in the Book of Job." *Studies in Jewish Education and Judaica,* ed. A. Shapiro and B. Cohen. 1984. 157–68. **Waldner, E.** "Das todeswürdige Verbrechen der Freunde Jobs." *Seelsorger* 7 (1930–31) 181–84. **Watté, P.** "La logique de Dieu [à propos R. Girard]." *Rev nouv* 83 (1986) 177–80. **Weiser, A.** "Das Problem der sittlichen Weltordnung im Buche Hiob: Unter Berücksichtigung seiner Entwicklung bei den Griechen und in der israelitischen Religion." *ThBl* 2 (1923) 157–64. [= *Glaube und Geschichte im Alten Testament und andere ausgewählte Schriften.* Göttingen: Vandenhoeck & Ruprecht, 1961. 9–19.] **West, M. S.** "The Book of Job and the Problem of Suffering." *ExpT* 40 (1928–29) 358–64. **Westermann, C.** "The Two Faces of Job." *Conc* 169 (1983) 15–22. **Wolfers, D.** "Is Job After All Jewish?" *Dor* 14 (1985–86) 39–44. ———. "Is Behemoth Also Jewish?" *Dor* 14 (1985–86) 220–27. **Wood, J.** "The Idea of Life in the Book of Job." *TGUOS* 18 (1959–60) 29–37. **Wright, J. H.** "Problem of Evil, Mystery of Sin and Suffering." *CommSpok* 6 (1979) 140–56. **Würthwein, E.** *Gott und Mensch in Dialog und Gottesreden des Buches Hiob.* Habilitationsschrift. Tübingen, 1938. ———. "Gott und Mensch in Dialog und Gottesreden des Buches Hiob." In *Wort und Existenz.* Göttingen, 1970. 217–95.
Young, D. M. *Fencing with the Promises: Report of a Project on Proper and Faithful Cursing—A Study of the Book of Job with Senior High Youth.* Diss. Boston University, 1981.
Zahrnt, H. *Wie kann Gott das zulassen? Hiob—der Mensch im Leid.* Munich: Piper, 1985. **Zerafa, P. P.** *The Wisdom of God in the Book of Job.* Rome: Herder, 1978. **Zink, J. K.** "Impatient Job." *JBL* 84 (1965) 147–52. **Zurhellen-Pfleiderer, E.** "Das Hiobproblem—Vom Sinn des Leidens." *Christentum und Wirklichkeit* 10 (1932) 111–18, 131–38, 154–61.

8. JOB AND ITS INFLUENCE

This section of the bibliography surveys the influence of the Book of Job on later thinking and writing. It should not be imagined that the study of the "history of interpretation," as it is often called, is merely an interesting or optional addition to the study of the book itself. For all study of the book, including the present commentary, is itself part of the history of interpretation; every item in the whole of this bibliography could equally well be registered under the heading of "Job and Its Influence." The present section, however, is focused upon the influence of the Book of Job on writers and thinkers who were not necessarily intent on interpreting the book, but who nevertheless have been affected by its theme and its imagination. Inevitably there is some overlap with other sections of the bibliography, but on the whole the attempt has been made to focus the present section on the effects the Book of Job has had upon other literatures, especially upon philosophy and imaginative writing.

a. General

Berry, D. L. "Scripture and Imaginative Literature Focus on Job." *Journal of General Education* 19 (1967) 49–79. **Besserman, L. L.** *The Legend of Job in the Middle Ages.* Cambridge, MA: Harvard UP, 1979. **Bochet, M.** "Job in Literature." *Conc* 169 (1983) 73–77. **Daiches, D.** *God and the Poets.* Oxford: Clarendon, 1984. **Eltz-Hoffmann, Liselotte von.** "Hiob in der Dichtung." *Wege zum Menschen: Monatsschrift für Seelsorge, Psychotherapie und Erziehung* 19 (1967) 184–94. **Francisco, Nancy A.** "Job in World Literature." *RevExp* 68 (1971) 521–33. **Frenzel, Elisabeth.** "Hiob." In *Stoffe der Weltliteratur: Ein Lexikon dichtungsgeschichtlicher Längsschnitte.* Stuttgart, 1962. 276–79. **Friedman, M.** "The Modern Job: On Melville, Dostoïevsky and Kafka." *Judaism* 12 (1963) 436–55. **Gerritson,**

A. "Bibliodrama about Job." In *Current Issues in Psychology of Religion,* ed. J. Belzen and J. Lans. 1986. 112–23. **Geyer, C.-F.** "Das Hiobbuch im christlichen und nachchristlichen Kontext. Anmerkungen zur Rezeptionsgeschichte." *Kairos* 28 (1986) 174–95. **Gietmann, G.** *Parzival, Faust, Job.* Freiburg, 1887. **Glatzer, N. M.** *The Dimensions of Job: A Study and Selected Readings.* New York: Schocken, 1969. **Goodheart, E.** "Job and Romanticism." *Reconstructionist* 24 (1958) 7–12. ———. "Job and the Modern World." *Judaism* 10 (1961) 21–28. [= *Twentieth-Century Interpretations of the Book of Job: A Collection of Critical Essays,* ed. P. S. Sanders. Englewood Cliffs, NJ: Prentice-Hall, 1968. 98–106.] **Hausen, A.** *Hiob in der französischen Literatur: Zur Rezeption eines alttestamentlichen Buches.* Europäische Hochschulschriften 13/17. Frankfurt: Peter Lang, 1972. **Levenson, J. D.** *The Book of Job in Its Time and in the Twentieth Century.* Cambridge, MA: Harvard UP, 1972. **Lüth, E.** "Das Buch Hiob und die Deutschen." In *Auf gespaltenem Pfad,* FS Margarete Susman, ed. M. Schlössner. Darmstadt: Erato-Presse, 1964. 63ff. **MacLean, H.** "The Job Drama in Modern Germany." *AULLA* 2 (1954). **Matthews, M. S.** *Issues and Answers in the Book of Job and Joban Issues in Three Twentieth-Century Writers: C. Jung, R. Frost, A. MacLeish.* Diss. Florida State University, 1976. **Mura, G.** "Giobbe e il pensiero contemporaneo; l'esilio della parola." *Nuova umanità* 1,6 (1979) 23–44; 2,7 (1980) 36–61; 2,10–11 (1980) 29–62. **O'Hara, M. L.** "Truth in Spirit and Letter: Gregory the Great, Thomas Aquinas, and Maimonides on the Book of Job." In *From Cloister to Classroom,* ed. E. Elder. 1986. 47–79. **Owen, J.** *The Five Great Sceptical Dramas of History (Prometheus Vinctus, Job, Faust, Hamlet, El Mágico).* London, 1896. **Pinell, J.** "El Canto de los 'Threni' en las Misas cuaresmales de la antigua liturgia hispanica." In *Eulogia: P. Burkhard Neunheuser,* ed. M. Arranz et al. 1979. 317–66. **Rabory, J.** *Le livre de la souffrance: Le livre de Job, dans l'histoire, la théologie, la liturgie.* Paris, 1917. **Ravisi, G.** "Giobbe, nostro contemporaneo." In his *Giobbe, traduzione e commento.* Rome: Borla, 1984. 185–255. **Roth, J.** "הריחס אל ספר איוב בתחום התרבות היהודית והנוצרית [Attitudes toward the Book of Job as Reflected by Jewish and Christian Thinkers: A Survey]." *BMik* 50 (1972) 306–9, 381–82. **Sanders, P. S.,** ed. *Twentieth-Century Interpretations of the Book of Job: A Collection of Critical Essays.* Englewood Cliffs, NJ: Prentice-Hall, 1968. **Schubert, Beatrix.** "Vom Umgang mit dem menschlichen Leiden: ein Versuch über Ijob in der modernen Literatur." *ErbAuf* 60 (1984) 356–75. **Strolz, W.** "Die Hiob-Interpretation bei Kant, Kierkegaard und Bloch." *Kairos* 23 (1981) 75–87.

b. Early Jewish

Testament of Job. Editions: **James, M. R.** *Apocrypha Anecdota.* 2d ser. Cambridge, 1897. 104–37. **Brock, S.** *Testamentum Iobi.* Leiden, 1967. **Kraft, R.** et al. *Testament of Job according to the SV Text.* Missoula, MT: Scholars Press, 1974. Translation: **Spittler, R. P.** "Testament of Job." In *The Old Testament Pseudepigrapha,* ed. J. H. Charlesworth. London: Darton, Longman and Todd, 1983. 1:829–68. See also **Collins, J. J.** "Structure and Meaning in the Testament of Job." In *Society of Biblical Literature: 1974 Seminar Papers,* ed. G. MacRae. Cambridge, MA, 1974. 1:35–52. **Delcor, M.** "Le Testament de Job, la prière de Nabonide et les traditions targoumiques." In *Bibel und Qumran: Beiträge zur Erforschung der Beziehungen zwischen Bibel- und Qumranwissenschaft, Hans Bardtke zum 22.9.1966,* ed. S. Wagner. Berlin: Evangelische Haupt-Bibelgesellschaft, 1968. 57–74. **Horst, P. W. van der.** "The Role of Women in the Testament of Job." *NedTTs* 40 (1986) 273–89. **Jacobs, I.** "Literary Motifs in the Testament of Job." *JJS* 21 (1970) 1–10. **Philonenko, M.** "Le Testament de Job et les Thérapeutes." *Sem* 8 (1958) 51–53. ———. "Le Testament de Job." *Sem* 18 (1968) 1–77. **Schaller, B.** "Das Testament Hiobs." *JüdSHRZ* (1979) 305–87. ———. "Das Testament Hiobs und die Septuaginta-Übersetzung des Buches Hiob." *Bib* 61 (1980) 377–406.

Baring-Gould, S. *Legends of the Old Testament Characters from Talmud and Other Sources.* London, 1871. 52–59. **Baskin, Judith R.** *Pharaoh's Counselors: Job, Jethro and Balaam in Rabbinic and Patristic Tradition.* Brown Judaic Studies 47. Chico, CA: Scholars Press,

1983. **Carstensen, R. N.** "The Persistence of the 'Elihu' Tradition in the Later Jewish Writings." *LTQ* 2 (1967) 37–46. **Fine, H. A.** "The Tradition of a Patient Job." *JBL* 74 (1955) 28–32. **Glatzer, N. H.** "The Book of Job and Its Interpreters" [mainly medieval Jewish]. In *Biblical Motifs: Origins and Transformations.* Philip W. Lown Institute of Advanced Judaic Studies. Studies and Texts 3. Cambridge, MA: Harvard UP, 1966. 197–220. ———. "Jüdische Ijob-Deutungen in den ersten christlichen Jahrhunderten." *FreibRu* 26 (1974) 31–34. **Gorringe, T. J.** "Job and the Pharisees." *Int* 40 (1986) 17–28. **Jacobs, I.** *The Book of Job in Rabbinic Thought.* Diss. University College, London, 1970. **Ravenna, A.** "Il caso Giobbe e la tradizione talmudica." *RivBibIt* 7 (1959) 61–63. **Sel, M.** "Job in Rabbinical Literature." *JewEnc* 7:195. **Wjernikowski, A.** *Das Buch Hiob nach der rabbinischen Agada.* Frankfurt, 1893.

c. Contemporary Jewish

Brinker, M. "On the Ironic Use of the Myth of Job in Y. H. Brenner's *Breakdown and Bereavement.*" In *Biblical Patterns in Modern Literature,* ed. D. Hirsch and N. Aschkenasy. Brown Judaic Studies 77. Chico, CA: Scholars Press, 1984. 115–26. **Goldschmidt, H. L.** "Hiob in neuzeitlichen Judentum." *Weltgespräch* 2 (1967) 41–55, 71–72. **Lazare, B.** *Le fumier de Job.* Paris: Rieder, 1928. **Neher, A.** "Job: The Biblical Man." *Judaism* 13 (1964) 37–47. [= *L'existence juive: Solitude et affrontements.* Paris, 1962. Chap. 5.] **Rubenstein, R. L.** "Job and Auschwitz." *USQR* 25 (1969–70) 421–37. **Sheldon, M.** "Job, Human Suffering and Knowledge: Some Contemporary Jewish Perspectives." *Enc* 41 (1980) 229–35. **Watté, P.** "Job à Auschwitz: Deux constats de la pensée juive." *RTL* 4 (1973) 173–90. **Zafrani, H.** "Une histoire de Job en judéo-arabe du Maroc." *RevÉtIsl* 36 (1968) 279–315.

d. Islam and Other Religions

Apt, N. *Die Hioberzählung in der arabischen Literatur. 1. Teil. Zwei arabische Hiobshandschriften der Kgl. Bibliothek zu Berlin.* 1913. **Castillo Castillo, C.** "Job en la leyenda musulmana." *CiuD* 195 (1982) 115–30. **Clines, D. J. A.** "In Search of the Indian Job." *VT* 33 (1983) 398–418. **Fortes, M.** *Oedipus and Job in West African Religion.* Cambridge: CUP, 1959. **Jeffery, A.** "Ayyub." *Encyclopédie de l'Islam.* 1965. 13:318. **Kohlbrugge, Hanna.** *De tijding van Job in de Bijbel en in de Koran.* The Hague: J. N. Voorhoeve, 1981. **Rao, S.,** and **M. Reddy.** "Job and His Satan—Parallels in Indian Scripture." *ZAW* 91 (1979) 416–22. **Scaltriti, G.** "Giobbe tra Cristo e Zaratustra." *PalCl* 34 (1955) 673–82, 721–28.

e. Early Christian

Geerlings, W. "Hiob und Paulus: Theodizee und Paulinismus in der lateinischen Theologie am Ausgang des vierten Jahrhunderts." In *Jahrbuch für Antike und Christentum* 24, ed. T. Klauser et al. 1981. 56–66. **Hanson, A. T.** "Job in Early Christianity and Rabbinic Judaism." *CQ* 2 (1969) 147–51. **Hanson, R. P. C.** "St. Paul's Quotations from the Book of Job." *Theol* 54 (1950) 250–53. **Kniaseff, A.** "The Theodicy of Job in the Byzantine Offices of Holy Week" [Gk.]. *Theologia* (1955) 107–23. **Michael, J. H.** "Paul and Job: A Neglected Analogy." *ExpT* 36 (1924–25) 67–70. **Naish, J. P.** "The Book of Job and the Early Christian Period." *Exp* 9/3 (1925) 34–49, 94–104. **Schaller, B.** "Zum Textcharakter der Hiobzitate im paulinischen Schrifttum." *ZNW* 71 (1980) 21–26.

f. Western Thinkers and Writers

Barth, K. See **Migliore, D. L.** "Barth and Bloch on Job: A Conflict of Interpretations." In *Understanding the Word: Essays in Honor of Bernhard W. Anderson,* ed. J. T. Butler et al. JSOTSup 37. Sheffield: JSOT, 1985. 265–79. And **Schulweis, H. M.** "Karl Barth's Job: Morality and Theodicy." *JQR* 65 (1975) 156–67.

Bloch, E. See **Chirpaz, F.** "Ernst Bloch and Job's Rebellion." *Conc* 169 (1983) 23–29. **Gerbracht, D.** "Aufbruch zu sittlichem Atheismus: Die Hiob-Deutung Ernst Blochs." *EvT* 35 (1975) 223–37. **Mottu, H.** "La figure de Job chez Bloch." *RTP* 27 (1977) 307–20. **Raurell, F.** "Job llegit per E. Bloch." *EstFranc* 81 (1980) 403–27. See also Strolz, W., in Section 8a above.

Camus, A. See **Taradach, Madeleine.** "De la 'modernité' de l'absurde chez Job à la lumière de l'absurde chez Camus." *EstFranc* 81 (1980) 155–68.

Hobbes, Thomas. *Leviathan, or The Matter, Forme and Power of a Common-Wealth Ecclesiasticall and Civil.* London. 1651.

Jaspers, K. "Hiob." *Einsichten . . . G. Krüger.* Frankfurt, 1962. 86–106.

John of the Cross, St. See **Anon.** "Job et S. Jean de la Croix, choix de textes." *VS* 422 (1956) 372–91.

Jung, C. G. See **Broadribb, D.** "Carl Jung kaj la Biblio." *Biblia Revuo* 1 (1964) 13–45. **Hedinger, U.** "Reflektionen zu C. G. Jungs Hiobinterpretation." *TZ* 23 (1967) 340–52. **Marco, N. di.** "Dio come Padre nella 'Riposta a Giobbe' di C. G. Jung." *Aquinas* 27 (1984) 33–74. **Michaëlis, E.** "Le livre de Job interpreté par C. G. Jung." *RTP* 3 (1953) 182–95. ———. "Ist Satan die vierte Person der Gottheit?" *Zeitwende* 25 (1954) 368–77. **Pascal, E.** "Risposta a Jung." *Prot* 21 (1966) 215–22. **Philp, H. L.** *Jung and the Problem of Evil.* London, 1958. 133–71. **Ryan, Penelope J.** *An Interpretive and Critical Analysis of Carl Jung's 'Answer to Job' as it Reflects his Psychological Theory, his Religious Understanding and Statements in Light of Christian Tradition.* Diss. Fordham, 1983. **White, V.** "Jung et son livre sur Job." *VS Suppl* (1956) 199–209. **Wildberger, H.** "Das Hiobproblem und seine neueste Deutung." *Reformatio* 3 (1954) 355–63, 439–48. [= *Jahwe und sein Volk.* 1979. 9–27.] See also **Matthews, M. S.,** in Section 8a above.

Kant, I. See **Strolz, W.,** in Section 8a above.

Kierkegaard, S. "'The Lord Gave, and the Lord Hath Taken Away.'" In *Four Edifying Discourses* (1843). In *Edifying Discourses,* tr. D. F. and Lillian M. Swenson. Minneapolis: Augsburg, 1942. And *Edifying Discourses: A Selection,* tr. P. L. Holmer. New York: Harper & Row, 1958. ———. [**Constantinus, Constantin**]. *Repetition: An Essay in Experimental Psychology* (1843). In *Fear and Trembling,* ed. H. V. and Edna H. Hong. Princeton: Princeton UP, 1983. 125–231. See also **Müller, H. P.** "Welt als 'Wiederholung': Sören Kierkegaards Novelle als Beitrag zur Hiob-Interpretation." In *Werden und Wirken des Alten Testaments,* FS C. Westermann, ed. R. Albertz. Göttingen: Vandenhoeck & Ruprecht, 1980. 335–72. **Mura, G.** *Angoscia ed esistenza, da Kierkegaard a Moltmann: Giobbe e la 'sofferenza di Dio.'* Rome: Città Nuova, 1982. **Wahl, J.** "Sören Kierkegaard et le livre de Job." *Etre et Penser* 27 (1948) 147–66. See also **Strolz, W.,** in Section 8a above.

Maimonides, M. (1135–1204). See **Kravitz, L. S.** "Maimonides and Job: An Inquiry as to the Method of the Moreh." *HUCA* 38 (1967) 149–58. **Laks, H. J.** "The Enigma of Job: Maimonides and the Moderns." *JBL* 83 (1964) 345–64. See also **O'Hara, M. L.,** in Section 8a above.

Milton, J. See **Fisch, H.** "Creation in Reverse: The Book of Job and Paradise Lost." In *Milton and Scriptural Tradition,* ed. J. Sims and L. Ryken. 1984. 104–16.

Ricoeur, P. See **Crossan, J. D.,** ed. *The Book of Job and Ricoeur's Hermeneutics.* Semeia 19. Chico, CA: Scholars Press, 1981. **Dornisch, Loretta.** "The Book of Job and Ricoeur's Hermeneutics." In ibid., 3–21. **Pellauer, D.** "Reading Ricoeur Reading Job." In ibid., 73–83.

Teilhard de Chardin, P. See **Franco, R.** "Job y Teilhard de Chardin sobre la problema del mal." *Proyección* 32 (1985) 27–41.

Tillich, P. See **Cranford, W. J.** *The Doctrine of God in the Book of Job and the Systematic Theology of Paul Tillich.* Diss. Baylor, 1981.

Voltaire, J. "Job." In *Dictionnaire Philosophique.* 1767–69. In *Oeuvres complètes de Voltaire.* Paris: Garnier, 19:504–7. ———. *Histoire des voyages de Scarmentado.* In his *Romans et*

contes. Paris: Garnier. See also **Senior, N.** "Voltaire and the Book of Job." *French Review* 47 (1973) 340–47.
Weil, S. *Attente de Dieu: Lettres et réflexions.* Paris: La Colombe, 1950. [= *Waiting for God,* tr. Emma Crawford. New York: Putnam, 1951.] ———. *La pesanteur et la grâce.* 1947.

g. Literary Works Inspired by Job

Angioletti, Giovanni Battista. *Giobbe, uomo solo* [drama], 1955. **Anon.** *Mystère de la patience de Job* (15th cent.). ———. *L'Hystore Job* (16th cent.). See **Bates, R. C.** *L'hystore Job: adaptation en vers français du 'Compend[i]um in Job'* [of Peter of Blois]. Yale Romanic Studies. New Haven, 1937. ———. *Historia Jobs* (1546). See **Karsten, T. E.** *Die mitteldeutsche poetische Paraphrase des Buches Hiob: aus der Handschrift des Königlichen Staatsarchivs zu Königsberg herausgegeben.* Berlin: Weidmann, 1910. **Narhauser, J.** *Historia Jobs 1546.* Arbeiten zur mittleren deutschen Litteratur 12. Frankfurt: P. Lang, 1983. **Anon.** *Job* [drama in Romansch], 1896. **Aue, Hartmann von** (13th cent.). *Des arme Heinrich.* See **Datz, G.** *Die Gestalt Hiobs in der kirchlichen Exegese und der "Arme Heinrich" Hartmanns von Aue.* Göppinger Arbeiten zur Germanistik. Göppingen: A. Kümmerle, 1973. **Baumann, Emile.** *Job le Prédestiné, roman.* Paris, 1922. **Beckett, Samuel.** *Waiting for Godot.* 1949. See also **Beckmann, H.** *Godot oder Hiob: Glaubensfragen in der modernen Literatur.* Hamburg, 1965. **Magny, O. de.** "Samuel Beckett ou Job abandonné." *Monde nouveau-paru* 97 (February 1956) 95. **Borchardt, Rudolf.** *Geschichte des Heimkehrenden (Das Buch Joram).* 1905. **Borchert, Wolfgang.** *Draussen vor der Tür* [a novel.] **Boye, Karin Maria.** *De sju dödssyndera* [The Seven Deadly Sins] [cantata], 1941. **Calderón de la Barca, Pedro.** *Autos sacramentales.* **Clements, C. C.** *Job: A Play in One Act.* New York: Samuel French, 1923. **Claudel, Paul.** "Réponse à Job." In *Oeuvres complètes.* Paris: Gallimard, 1952. 2:373–74. **Dante, A.** See **Baur, G.** "Das Buch Hiob und Dantes Göttliche Komödie." *TSK* (1856) 583ff. **Debout, J.** [**Roblot, R. I.**] *Job, maître d'école libre, comédie dramatique en trois actes.* Paris, 1932. **de Bruin, H.** *Job* [Dutch epic], 1944.
Desportes, Philippe. *Poesies Chrestiennes.* Paris. 1598. [Including 'Plainte de l'Autheur durant une sienne longue maladie']. See also **Pensec, H.** "Philippe Desportes' Poésies chrestiennes and the Book of Job." *Res Publica Litterarum* 6 (1983) 265–73. **Dostoievsky, F.** See Friedman, M., in Section 8a above.
Enriquez Basurto, D. See **Rauchwarger, Judith.** "Seventeenth-Century epic, Diego Enriquez Basurto's El triumpho de la virtud y paciencia de Job." *Sef* 40 (1980) 99–119. **Enriquez Gómez, Antonio.** See **Rauchwarger, Judith.** "Antonio Enriquez Gómez: Epistolas tres de Job, A matter of racial atavism?" *RÉJ* 138 (1979) 69–87. **Faraj, Murād.** *Ayyūb* [a prose version in rhymed Arabic], 1950. **Farrère, Claude.** *Job siècle xx, roman.* Paris, 1949.
Frost, Robert. *A Masque of Reason.* New York: Henry Holt, 1945. See also **Matthews, M. S.**, in Section 8a above. **Gelber, S. M.** *Job Stands Up: The Biblical Text of the Book of Job Arranged for the Theater.* New York: Union of American Hebrew Congregations, 1975. **Godínez, Felipe.** *La gran Comedia de los trabajos de Job.* 1638.
Goethe. *Faust.* See also **Carrière, L.** "Satan, Mephisto und die Wetten bei Hiob." *Goethe* 20 (1958) 285–87. **Matenko, P.** "Job and Faust." *Studies in Yiddish Culture.* Leiden, 1968. 75–162. **Zhitlowsky, C.** *Job and Faust: Translated with Introduction and Notes by P. Matenko.* Leiden: Brill, 1966. See also **Gietmann, G.**, in Section 8a above. **Greene, Robert.** *The Historie of Job.* 1594.
Heine, Heinrich. "Hebräische Melodien." Book 3 of *Romanzero.* In *Heinrich Heine: Sämtliche Werke,* ed. H. Kaufmann. Munich: Kindler, 1964. 3:117–64. **Hertz, Henri.** "Ceux de Job." In his *Tragédies des temps volages.* 1955. **Kafka, F.** See **Susman, M.** "Der Hiobproblem bei Franz Kafka." *Der Morgen* 5 (1929) 31–49. **Suter, R.** *Kafkas "Prozess" im Lichte des "Buches Hiob."* Europäische Hochschulschriften 1/169. Frankfurt: P. Lang, 1976. See also **Friedman, M.**, in Section 8a above.

Kochoschka, O. *Sphinx und Strohmann.* 1907. Reissued as *Hiob.* 1917. [= *Job, A Drama.* In *An Anthology of German Expressionist Drama,* ed. W. H. Sokel. New York: Anchor, 1963. 159–71.] See also **Schuly, H. I.** *Oscar Kokoschka: The Painter as Playwright.* Detroit: Wayne State UP, 1982. 67–88, 145–50. **Kysar, Hans.** *Das Blumenhiob.* 1909. **Leivick, H.** *In di Tag fun Iyov* [Yiddish poem]. c, 1953. **Leroux, P.** *Job, drame en cinq actes, avec prologue et épilogue, par le Prophète Isaie, retrouvé, rétabli dans son integrité, et traduit littérale- ment sur le texte hébreu.* Grasse, 1866. **Limentani, G.** *Le grande seduto.* Milan, 1979. **Lin- scheid, J.** "Jobia versus God: The Book of Job Revisited" [short story]. *Other Side* 23 (1987) 24–27.

MacLeish, A. *J.B.: A Play in Verse.* London: Samuel French, 1956. See also **Bieman, E.** "Faithful to the Bible in Its Fashion: MacLeish's J.B." *CSRBull* 3/5 (1972) 26. **Priest, J.** "Job and J.B.: The Goodness of God or the Godness of Good?" *Horizons* 12 (1985) 265–83. **Thelen, M. F.** *"J.B.:* Job and the Biblical Doctrine of Man." *JBR* (1959) 201– 5. See also **Matthews, M. S.** in Section 8a above.

Melville, H. *Moby Dick.* New York, 1851. See **Young, W. A.** "Leviathan in the Book of Job and *Moby-Dick." Soundings* 65 (1983) 388–401. See also **Friedman, M.,** in Section 8a above.

Milton, John. See **Fulton, Pauline R.** *Milton's Use of the Book of Job in 'Paradise Regained' and 'Samson Agonistes.'* Diss. University of North Carolina, 1984. **Teunissen, J.-J.** *Of Patience and Heroic Martyrdom: The Book of Job and Milton's Conception of Patient Suffering in 'Paradise Regained' and 'Samson Agonistes.'* Diss. Rochester, 1967.

Morax, Rena. *Job le vigneron, mystère en trois actes.* Sierre, 1954. **Ned, Edouard.** *Job le glorieux, roman.* Paris, 1933. **Obaldia, René de.** *Et à la fin était le bang: Comédie héroïque* [a play]. In his *Théâtre.* Paris: Grasset. 6:1–194. **Ponholzer, Bartholomaeus.** *Job, der fromme Idealist* [drama], 1927. **Racine, J.** "Annotations du livre de Job." In *Oeuvres complètes,* ed. R. Picard. Paris: Pléiade, 1960. 2:699–705. **Radcliffe, Ralph [Robert].** *Job's Afflictions* [drama]. c.1550. **Roth, J.** *Hiob, Roman eines einfachen Mannes.* Berlin: G. Kiepenheuer, 1930. [= *Job: The Story of a Simple Man.* Tr. D. Thompson. London: Chatto and Windus, 1933.]

Sachs, Hans [the Meistersinger]. *Der Hiob* [play]. 1547. **Simon, Neil.** *God's Favorite: A New Comedy.* New York: Samuel French, 1975. **Spark, Muriel.** *The Only Problem* [a novel]. London: Bodley Head, 1984. **Stevens, J. S.** *A Dramatization of the Book of Job: The Problem of Human Suffering.* Boston: Stratford, 1917. **Tamez, Elsa.** "A Letter to Job." In *New Eyes for Reading,* ed. J. Pobee and B. Wartenberg-Potter, 1986. 50–52.

Wahltuch, Marco. *Giobbe* [five-act tragedy], 1872. **Weege, Fritz.** *Das Spiel Hiobs* [play], 1926. **Wells, H. G.** *The Undying Fire: A Contemporary Novel.* In *The Works of H. G. Wells.* Atlantic ed. London: T. Fisher Unwin, 1925. 11:1–172. **Wiesel, Elie.** "Job ou le silence révolutionnaire." In his *Célébration biblique.* Paris: Seuil, 1975. 179–99. **Winawer, B.** *The Book of Job: A Satirical Comedy.* London: Dent, 1931.

Wojtyla, K. [Pope John Paul II]. See also **Fantuzzi, V.** "Il 'Giobbe' di Karol Wojtyla a San Miniato." *CC* 136 (1985) 500–504. **Gatta, E.** "Il Giobbe di Papa Wojtyla." *CiVit* 40 (1985) 403–48. **Wolfskehl, K.** *Hiob und Die vier Spiegel: Gedichte.* Hamburg: Hamburg- Verlag, 1950. **Zapf, Adolf Philipp.** *Hiob* [drama], 1866.

h. Job in Art

i. General

See especially **Réau, L.** *Iconographie de l'art chrétien.* Tome II. *Iconographie de la Bible.* I. *Ancien Testament.* Paris: Presses Universitaires de France, 1956. 310–18. **Leclerq, H.** "Job." In *Dictionnaire d'Archéologie Chrétienne et de Liturgie,* Paris, 1927. 7:2554–70. **Budde, R.** "Job." In *Lexikon der christlichen Ikonographie.* Rome, 1970. 2:407–14. **Ravisi, G.** *Giobbe: Traduzione e commento.* Rome: Borla, 1984. 258–74. **Weisbach, W.** "L'histoire de Job dans les arts." *Gazette des Beaux-Arts* (1936) 102–12.

See also **Durand, J.** "Note sur une iconographie méconnue: le 'saint roi Job.'" *CahArch*

32 (1984) 113–35. **Huber, O.** *Hiob: Dulder oder Rebell? Byzantinische Minaturen zum Buche Hiob in Patmos, Rom, Venedig, Sinai, Jerusalem und Athos.* Düsseldorf: Patmos, 1976. **Le Blant, E.** "D'une représentation inédite de Job sur un sarcophage d'Arles." *RevArch* (1860–B) 36–44.

ii. By theme and period

Job's Trials. *13th cent.* North Door of Chartres Cathedral; Door of Rheims Cathedral. *14th cent.* Frescoes from St. Stephen's Chapel, Westminster, now in British Museum. *15th cent.* Master of the Legend of St. Barbara, The Story of Job (1480–83), Cologne, Wallraf-Richartz Museum. *16th cent.* Peter Hugo (or Jan Mandyn), Les Épreuves de Job, Douai Museum; Window of Troyes Cathedral; Rubens, Altarpiece of Church of St. Nicholas, Brussels (destroyed in 1695). *19th cent.* William Blake, Illustrations of the Book of Job.
The Three Messengers of Misfortune. *12th cent.* Chapter house of Pamplona Cathedral. *16th cent.* Fresco in Campo Santo, Pisa.
Death of Job's Children. *16th cent.* Bernart van Orley, Brussels Museum.
Job on the Ash-heap. In Christian art, a prefigurement of Christ awaiting crucifixion. *3rd cent.* Frescoes in Catacombs, Rome, and in cemetery of St Peter and St Marcellino, Rome; Frescoes of Synagogue, Dura-Europos. *4th cent.* Sarcophagus of Junius Bassus, Rome. *13th cent.* North Door of Chartres Cathedral; Door depicting the Last Judgment, Notre Dame, Paris. *15th cent.* Jean Fouquet, Heures d'Étienne Chevalier, Musée Condy, Chantilly. *17th cent.* Giordano, Sacristy of L'Escorial, Madrid. *18th cent.* Lattanzio Querena, S. Giobbe, Venice. *19th cent.* Bonnat, Musée du Luxembourg, Paris.
Job and His Wife. *3rd cent.* Fresco of the cemetery of St Peter and St Marcellino, Rome. *4th cent.* Sarcophagus of Junius Bassus, Rome. *16th cent.* Dürer, Jabach altarpiece in Städelschen Kunstinstitut, Frankfurt and Cologne Museum; Peter Huys, Douai Museum; Windows of St Patrice and of St Romain, Rouen; Stalls of the Cathedral, Amiens. *17th cent.* J. Lievens, 1631; Murillo, Parma Pinocotheca; Ribera, Parma Pinacotheca; Georges de la Tour, Musée d'Épinal.
Job Mocked by His Friends. *12th cent.* Capital from the cloister of La Daurade, Musée des Augustins, Toulouse. *13th cent.* Bas-relief in doorway representing the Last Judgment, Notre Dame, Paris. *15th cent.* Misericord in church of Champeaux, Seine-et-Marne; Jean Fouquet, Heures d'Étienne Chevalier, Musée Condy, Chantilly. *16th cent.* Hieronymus Bosch, Douai Museum. *17th cent.* Il Calabese, Antwerp; J. Bendt, St Job's Hospital, Utrecht. *19th cent.* A. Decamps, Institute of Arts, Minneapolis.
Job at the Capture of Leviathan. *12th cent.* Window representing the Crucifixion, Cathedral of Chalons-sur-Marne.
Job as the Patron Saint of Musicians. Esp. in 15th and 16th cents. Rubens, Job on the Dunghill (1612), presented to the musicians' guild of Antwerp. See also **Denis, V.** "Saint Job, patron des musiciens." *Revue belge d'archéologie et d'histoire d'art* 21 (1952) 253–98. **Meyer, Kathi.** "Saint Job as a Patron of Music." *Art Bulletin* [New York] 36 (1954) 21–31. **Nicholson, J. W.** "Job." In *The New Grove Dictionary of Music and Musicians*, ed. S. Sadie. London: Macmillan, 1980. 9:655–56.

iii. By artist

Blake, William. Editions: **Bindman, D.** *William Blake's Illustrations of the Book of Job: The Engravings and Related Material.* London: William Blake Trust, 1987. ———. *Colour Versions of William Blake's Book of Job Designs from the Circle of John Linnell.* London, 1987. See also **Foster, D. S.** *Blake's Job: William Blake's Illustrations of the Book of Job.* Providence, RI: Brown UP, 1966. **Raine, Kathleen.** *The Human Face of God: William Blake and the Book of Job.* London: Thames & Hudson, 1982. **Wright, A.** *Blake's "Job": A Commentary.* Oxford: Clarendon, 1972. **Fronius, Hans.** *Das Buch Hiob: Illustrationen von Hans Fronius. Einleitung von J. Marböck.* Klosterneuburg: Österreichisches Katholisches Bibelwerk, 1980. [12 charcoal sketches.] **Jaekel, Willi.** *Das Buch Hiob: Mit originalen*

Lithographien. Berlin: E. Reiss, 1917. **Tongue, C. Mary.** *The Book of Job: With an Introduction by G. K. Chesterton and Illustrated in Colour by C. Mary Tongue.* London: Cecil Palmer and Hayward, 1916. **Uhrig, H.** *Hiob: Eine Bildexegese in 15 Federzeichnungen.* Kassel: J. Stauda, 1954.

i. Job in Music

Adler, Hugo Chaim. *Hiob* [oratorio]. 1933.
Bitgood, Roberta (b. 1908). *Job* [cantata]. **Burck, Joachim à** (16th cent.). Motet. **Byrd, William.** *Cunctis diebus* [motet]. In *The Byrd Edition,* ed. P. Brett. Vol. 3: *Cantiones Sacrae (1591),* ed. A. Brown. London: Stainer & Bell, 1981. 232–44.
Carissimi, G. *Job* [oratorio]. **Chiaromonte, F.** *Job: Drame biblique en trois actes, Poëme de J. Guilliaume.* Leipzig and Brussels, 1884. **Chipp. E. T.** *Job: An Oratorio.* London, 1875.
Clemens non Papa, J. (16th cent.). Motet. **Converse, F. S.** *Job, Dramatic Poem for Solo Voices, Chorus and Orchestra.* New York: H. W. Gray, n.d. **Crecquillon, T.** (16th cent.). Motet.
d'Albergatti, P. *Job* [oratorio]. **Dallapiccola, Luigi.** *Giobbe: Sacra rapprasentazione* [oratorio, also for stage performance]. Milan: Suvini Zerboni, 1951. First performance: Rome, 1950.
Engel, Lehmann. *Four Excerpts from "Job"* [for voice and piano]. 1932.
Franco, Fernando, of Mexico (1532–85). *Parce mihi, Domine* [motet]. Ed. H. Ross. New York: Peer International, 1953.
Gallus [Handl], Jacobus (16th cent.). Motet. **Gines Perez, J.** *Parce mihi, Domine* [motet].
Guerrimi, Giodo. *Il lamento di Job, per voce de basso, archi, pianoforte e tam-tam. Riduzione dall'autore per canto e pianoforte.* Milan: G. Ricordi, 1939.
Händel, Georg Frideric. "I Know that My Redeemer Liveth." Aria in *Messiah* (1742).
Herder, R. (b. 1930). *The Job Elegies* [choral]. **Hiller, H. C.** *Job's Wedding Day Song.* London: D. Davidson, 1882.
Jenkins, D. *Job: An Oratorio for Soli, Chorus, and Organ and Orchestra.* Aberystwyth, 1903.
Kósa, György. *Hiob* [cantata]. 1933.
La Rue, P. de (16th cent.). Motet. **Lassus [Lasso], Orlando di.** *Sacrae lectiones ex Propheta Iob* (c. 1560). ———. *Lectiones sacrae novem, ex libris Hiob excerptae* (c. 1582). In *Two Motet Cycles for Matins for the Dead: Sacrae lectiones ex Propheta Iob (c. 1560) and Lectiones sacrae novem, ex libris Hiob excerptae (c. 1582),* ed. P. Bergquist. Madison, WI: A-R Editions, 1983.
Manneke, D. (b. 1939). *Job* [cantata]. **Morales, L.** (16th cent.). Motet.
Nabokov, Nicolas. *Job* [oratorio]. 1932. Text by Jacques Maritain.
Parry, C. H. H. *Job: An Oratorio for Treble, Tenor, Baritone and Bass Soli, Chorus and Orchestra.* London: Novello, 1892. First performance: Gloucester, 1892.
Rabaud, H. *Job. Oratorio. Poëme de Charles Raffalli & Henry de Gorsse.* Paris: Enoch, 1900. **Russell, W.** *Job, A Sacred Oratorio . . . Adapted . . . for the Organ or Pianoforte* by S. Wesley. London, 1826.
Schütz, H. *Ich weiss, dass mein Erlöser lebt.* Cantata in his *Geistliche Chor-Musik.* 1648.
Senfl, L. (16th cent.). Motet. **Sermisy, C. de** (16th cent.). Motet.
Telemann, G. (1681–1767). *Ich weiss, dass mein Erlöser lebt* [cantata; attrib. J. S. Bach as Cantata 160).
Vaughan Williams, Ralph. *Job. A Masque for Dancing.* London, 1930. ———. *The Voice of the Whirlwind* [for choir and organ]. **Victoria, Tomas Luis de** (c. 1549–1611). *Officium defunctorum: in obitu et obsequiis sacrae imperatricis* [motet].

j. Job in Dance

Valois, Ninette de. *Job: A Masque for Dancing in Eight Scenes.* Book: Geoffrey Keynes. Music: Ralph Vaughan Williams. London, 1931. See also **Beaumont, C. W.** *Complete*

Book of Ballets: A Guide to the Principal Ballets of the Nineteenth and Twentieth Centuries.
London: Putnam. Repr. 1951. 931–35.

k. Job in Film

Collet, J. "From Job to Bergman: Anguish and Challenge." *Conc* 169 (1983) 69–72.
Fassbinder, Rainer W. *Berlin Alexanderplatz.* **Vettermann, Willy.** *Hiob. Filmdichtung.*
Chemnitz: M. Müller, 1928.

9. SOURCES AND COMPOSITION

Alt, A. "Zur Vorgeschichte des Buches Hiob." *ZAW* 55 (1937) 265–68. **Brandwein, C.**
"אגדת איוב לשלביה השונים [The Legend of Job according to Its Various Stages]."
Tarb 35 (1965–66) 1–17, i–ii. **Buhl, F.** "Zur Vorgeschichte des Buches Hiob." *BZAW*
41 (1925) 52–61. **Fohrer, G.** "Vorgeschichte und Komposition des Buches Hiob." *TLZ*
81 (1956) 333–36. ———. "Zur Vorgeschichte und Komposition des Buches Hiob."
VT 6 (1956) 249–67. [= *Studien zum Buche Hiob (1956–1979)*. BZAW 159. Gütersloh:
G. Mohn, 1963. 2d ed. Berlin: de Gruyter, 1983. 19–36.] ———. "Überlieferung und
Wandlung der Hioblegende." *Friedrich Baumgärtel Festschrift.* Erlangen, 1959. 41–62.
[= *Studien zum Buche Hiob (1956–1979)*. BZAW 159. 2d ed. Berlin: de Gruyter, 1983.
37–59.] **Foster, F. H.** "Is the Book of Job a Translation from an Arabic Original?"
AJSL 49 (1932–33) 21–45. **Fullerton, K.** "The Original Conclusion of Job." *ZAW* 42
(1924) 116–35. **Grill, W.** *Zur Kritik der Komposition des Buches Hiob.* Tübingen: Fues'sche
Buchdruckerei, 1890. **Guillaume, A.** "The Unity of the Book of Job." *ALUOS* 4 (1962)
26–46. **Hoffmann, R. E.** "Eine Parallele zur Rahmenerzählung des Buches Hiob in
1 Chr 7,20–29?" *ZAW* 92 (1980) 120–32. **Hurvitz, A.** "The Date of the Prose Tale of
Job Linguistically Reconsidered." *HTR* 67 (1974) 17–34. **Kautzsch, K.** *Das sogenannte
Volksbuch von Hiob und der Ursprung von Hiob.* Tübingen, 1900. **Laue, L.** *Die Composition
des Buches Hiob.* Diss. Halle, 1896. **Lindblom, J.** *La Composition du livre de Job.* Lund:
Gleerup, 1945. ———. "Joblegenden traditionshistoriskt undersökt." *SEÅ* 5 (1940) 29–
42. **Maag, V.** *Hiob: Wandlung und Verarbeitung des Problems in Novelle, Dialogdichtung
und Spätfassungen.* Göttingen: Vandenhoeck & Ruprecht, 1982. **Müller, H.-P.** *Hiob und
seine Freunde: Traditionsgeschichtliches zum Verständnis des Hiobbuches.* Theologische Studien
102. Zurich: EVZ-Verlag, 1970 . ———. *Das Hiobproblem: Seine Stellung und Entstehung
in Alten Orient und im Alten Testament.* Erträge des Forschung 84. Darmstadt: Wissenschaftliche Buchgesellschaft, 1978. **Pfeiffer, R. H.** "Edomitic Wisdom." *ZAW* 3 (1926)
13–24. **Reddy, M. P.** "The Book of Job—A Reconstruction." *ZAW* 90 (1978) 49–94.
Sarna, N. M. "Epic Substratum in the Prose of Job." *JBL* 76 (1957) 13–25. **Stockton,
E.** "Literary Development of the Book of Job." *ACR* 49 (1972) 137–43. **Studer, G. L.**
"Über die Integrität des Buches Hiob." *JPTh* 1 (1875) 688–723. **Terrien, S.** "Le poème
de Job: drame para-rituel du nouvel-an?" *VTSup* 17 (1969) 220–35. **Thils, G.** "De
genere litterario et fontibus libri Job." *ColctMechl* 31 (1946) 37–40. **Torczyner, H.** "Hiob-
dichtung und Hiobsage." *MGWJ* 69 (1925) 234–48, 717–33. **Vermeylen, J.** *Job, ses
amis et son Dieu: La légende de Job et ses relectures postexiliques.* Studia biblica 2. Leiden:
E. J. Brill, 1981. **Weimar, P.** "Literarkritisches zur Ijobnovelle." *BN* 12 (1980) 62–80.

10. DATE AND AUTHORSHIP

Anon. "Job a-t-il existé? Son livre n'est-il qu'un conte pieux pour montrer un beau
modèle de patience?" *AmiCl* 53 (1936) 131–33. **Bachar, S.** "על מועד כתיבת ספר איוב
[When Was the Book of Job Written?]." *BMik* 76 (1978–79) 75–76, 122. **Berger, H.**
"האם היתה חורן מולדתו של איוב [Was Hauran the Birthplace of Job?]." *BMik* 53
(1973) 228–29, 274. **Beveridge.** "The Date of the Book of Job." *JRAS* (1919) 234.
Beel, A. "Auctor et tempus conscriptionis libri Job. Analysis libri Job. De indole libri

Job." *ColBG* 33 (1922) 189–93, 241–47, 268–70. **Brenner, Athalya.** "The Language of the Book of Job as an Index to the Time of Its Composition" [Heb]. *BMik* 24 (1978) 396–405. **Endemann, K.** "Über den Verfasser des Buches Hiob." *Nach den Gesetz und Zeugnis* 26 (1926) 127–36. **Hurvitz, A.** "The Date of the Prose-Tale of Job Linguistically Reconsidered." *HTR* 67 (1974) 17–34. **Lévêque, J.** "La datation du livre de Job." *Congress Volume: Vienna 1980,* ed. J. A. Emerton. VTSup 32. Leiden: Brill, 1981. 206–19. **Ley, J.** "Die Abfassungszeit des Buches Hiob: Eine Abhandlung." TSK 71 (1898) 34–70. **Maisler, B.** *The Genealogy of the Sons of Nahor and the Historical Background of the Book of Job.* Jerusalem: Zion, 1946. **Naish, J. P.** "The Book of Job and the Early Persian Period." *ExpT* 9 (1925) 34–39, 94–104. **Pfeiffer, R. H.** "The Priority of Job over Is. 40–55." *JBL* 46 (1927) 202ff. **Schmitt, G.** "Die Heimat Hiobs." *ZDPV* 101 (1985) 56–63. **Slotki, I. W.** "The Origin of the Book of Job." *ExpT* 39 (1927–28) 131–34.

11. THE ANCIENT LITERARY CONTEXT, INCLUDING THE HEBREW BIBLE

a. The Hebrew Bible

Altheim, F., and **R. Stiehl.** "Hiob und die prophetische Überlieferung." In *Geschichte Mittelasiens im Altertum.* Berlin: de Gruyter, 1970. 131–42. **Bruston, E.** "La littérature sapientiale dans le livre de Job." *ETR* 3 (1928) 297–305. **Caquot, A.** "Traits royaux dans le personnage de Job." In *maqqél shâqédh. La branche d'amandier: Hommage à Wilhelm Vischer.* Montpellier: Causse, Graille, Castelnau, 1960. 32–45. **Crüsemann, F.** "Hiob und Kohelet: ein Beitrag zum Verständnis des Hiobbuches." In *Werden und Wirken des Alten Testaments,* FS C. Westermann, ed. R. Albertz. Göttingen: Vandenhoeck & Ruprecht, 1980. 373–93. **Dhorme, P.** "Ecclésiaste ou Job?" *RB* 32 (1922) 5–27. **Festorazzi, F.** "Giobbe e Qohelet: crisi della sapienza." *Problemi e prospettive di scienze bibliche.* Brescia, 1981. 233–58. **Frye, J. B.** "The Use of Pentateuchal Traditions in the Book of Job." *OTWSA* 17–18 (1977) 13–20. **Gese, H.** *Lehre und Wirklichkeit in der alten Weisheit: Studien zu den Sprüchen Salomos und zu dem Buche Hiob.* Tübingen: Mohr, 1958. **Gordis, R.** "Wisdom and Job." In *Old Testament Issues,* ed. S. Sandmel. London: SCM, 1969. 213–41. [= his *The Book of God and Man: A Study of Job.* Chicago: University of Chicago Press, 1965. 31–52.] **Goshen-Gottstein, M. H.** "Ezekiel und Ijob: Zur Problemgeschichte von Bundestheologie und Gott-Mensch-Verhältnis." In *Wort, Lied und Gottesspruch,* FS J. Ziegler, ed. R. Schnckenburd et al. Würzburg: Echter, 1972. 2:155–70. **Kuenen, A.** "Job en de lijdende knecht van Jahveh." *TTijd* 7 (1873) 540–41. **MacKenzie, R. A. F.** "The Cultural and Religious Background of the Book of Job." *Conc* 169 (1983) 3–7. **Maggioni, B.** *Giobbe e Qohelet, la contestazione sapienziale nella Bibbia.* Assisi: Cittadella, 1979. **McDonagh, Kathleen.** "Job and Jeremiah: Their Approach to God." *TBT* 18 (1980) 331–35. **Neher, A.** "Au-delà de l'épreuve Job et Abraham: des épreuves identiques." In המקרא ותולדות ישראל. *Studies in Bible and Jewish History,* FS J. Liver. Tel Aviv: University of Tel Aviv, 1972. 124–28. **Nestle, E.** "David in the Book of Job." *ExpT* 22 (1910) 90. **Noth, M.** "Noah, Daniel und Hiob in Ezekiel XIV." *VT* 1 (1950) 251–60. **Oberforcher, R.** "Abraham, Jeremia, Ijob. Typen des von Gott beanspruchten Menschen." *BiLit* 52 (1979) 183–91. **Pfeiffer, R. H.** "The Dual Origin of Hebrew Monotheism" [Job and Deutero-Isaiah]. *JBL* 46 (1927) 202–6. **Roberts, J. J. M.** "Job and the Israelite Religious Tradition." *ZAW* 89 (1977) 107–14. **Segal, M. Z.** " המקבילות ספר איוב [Parallels to the Book of Job]." *Tarb* 20 (1949) 35–48. **Shapiro, D. S.** "The Book of Job and the Trial of Abraham." *Tradition* 4 (1962) 210–20. **Spiegel, S.** "Noah, Daniel and Job." *Louis Ginzberg: Jubilee Volume on the Occasion of His Seventieth Birthday.* New York: American Academy for Jewish Research, 1945. 1:305–35. **Terrien, S.** "Quelques remarques sur les affinités de Job avec le Deutéro-Esaïe." VTSup 15 (1965) 295–310. **Vawter, B.** *Job and Jonah: Questioning the Hidden God.* New York: Paulist, 1985. **Vinton, Patricia.** "Radical Aloneness: Job and Jeremiah." *TBT* 99 (1978) 143–49. **Volz,**

P. *Hiob und Weisheit in den Schriften des Alten Testaments.* Göttingen, 1921. **Whybray, R.
N.** *Two Jewish Theologies: Job and Ecclesiastes.* Hull: University of Hull, 1980. **Zoller, J.**
"Giobbe e il servo di Dio." *RicR* 8 (1932) 223–33.

b. The Ancient Near East

Albertson, R. G. "Job and Ancient Near Eastern Wisdom Literature." In *Scripture in
Context II,* ed. W. Hallo, J. Moyer, and L. Perdue. Winona Lake, IN: Eisenbrauns,
1983. 213–30. **Albertz, R.** "Der sozialgeschichtliche Hintergrund des Hiobbuches und
der 'Babylonischen Theodizee' [Ludlul bēl nēmeqi]." In *Die Botschaft und die Boten,* FS
für Hans Walter Wolff, ed. J. Jeremias and L. Perlitt. Neukirchen-Vluyn: Neukirchener
Verlag, 1981. 349–72. **Ayuso Marazuela, T.** "Los elementos extrabíblicos de Job y del
Salterio." *EstBíb* 5 (1946) 429–58. **David, M.** "Travaux et service dans l'Épopée de
Gilgamesh et le livre de Job." *Revue Philosophique* 147 (1957) 341–49. **Dion, P.-E.** "Un
nouvel éclairage [Fekherye] sur le contexte culturel des malheurs de Job." *VT* 34 (1984)
213–15. **Finkelstein, C.** "ספר איוב וחכמת המזרח הקדמון [The Book of Job and the
Wisdom of the Ancient Near East]." *BMik* 51 (1972) 428–38, 532. **Fohrer, G.** "4QOrNab,
11QTgJob und die Hioblegende." *ZAW* 34 (1963) 93–97. **García de la Fuente, O.** "La
prosperidad del malvado en el libro de Job y en los poemas babilónicas del 'Justo
Paciente.'" *EstEcl* 34 (1960) 603–16. **Gray, J.** "The Book of Job in the Context of
Near Eastern Literature." *ZAW* 82 (1970) 251–69. **Griffiths, J. G.** "The Idea of Posthumous Judgment in Israel and Egypt." In *Fontes atque pontes: Eine Festgabe für H. Brunner,*
ed. M. Görg. Wiesbaden: Harrassowitz, 1983. 186–204. **Hoyos, H.** "Un texto original
de los Sumerios con entonaciones del libro de Job." *RBiLit* 18 (1956) 36–37. **Humbert,
P.** *Recherches sur les sources égyptiennes de la littérature sapientale d'Israël.* Mémoires de
l'Université de Neuchâtel 7, 1929. **Israel, S.** "Hiob: Prometheus in Judäa." *Antaios* 9
(1967) 369–84. **Jastrow, M.** "A Babylonian Parallel to the Story of Job." *JBL* 25 (1906)
135–91. **Kramer, S. N.** "Man and His God: A Sumerian Variation on the 'Job' Motif."
VTSup 3 (1953) 170–82. **Krieger, P.** *Weltbild und Idee des Buches Hiob, verglichen mit
dem altorientalischen Pessimismus.* Diss. Erlangen, 1930. **Landersdorfer, S.** *Eine babylonische
Quelle für das Buch Job? Eine literar-geschichtliche Studie.* Freiburg im Breisgau: Herder,
1911. **Loffreda, S.** "Raffronto fra un testo ugaritico e Giobbe." *BeO* 8 (1966) 103–16.
Moran, W. L. "Rib-Hadda: Job at Byblos?" In *Biblical and Related Studies Presented to
S. Iwry,* ed. Ann Kort and S. Morschauer. Winona Lake, IN: Eisenbrauns, 1985. 173–
81. **Müller, H.-P.** "Keilschriftliche Parallelen zum biblische Hiobbuche: Möglichkeit
und Grenze das Vergleichs." *Or* ns 47 (1978) 360–75. ⸺. *Das Hiobproblem. Seine
Stellung und Entstehung im Alten Orient und im Alten Testament.* Erträge der Forschung
84. Darmstadt: Wissenschaftliche Buchgesellschaft, 1978. **Murtagh, J.** "The Book of
Job and the Book of the Dead." *ITQ* 35 (1968) 166–73. **Nougayrol, J.** "Une version
ancienne du 'juste souffrant.'" *RB* 59 (1952) 237–50. ⸺. "(Juste) souffrant (R.S.
25.460)." *Ugaritica* 5 (1968) 265–83. **Preuss, H. D.** "Jahwes Antwort zu Hiob und die
sogenannte Hiobliteratur des alten Vorderen Orients." In *Beiträge zum Alten Testament-
liche Theologie,* FS W. Zimmerli, ed. H. Donner et al. Göttingen: Vandenhoeck & Ruprecht, 1977. 323–43. **Schmökel, H.** "Hiob in Sumer." *FF* 30 (1956) 74–76. **Speiser,
E. A.** "The Case of the Obliging Servant." *JCS* 8 (1954) 98–105. **Terrien, S.** "The
Babylonian Dialogue on Theodicy and the Book of Job." *JBL* 63 (1944) vi. **Williams,
P. J.** "Theodicy in the Ancient Near East." *CJT* 2 (1956) 14–26. **Wiseman, D. J.** "A
New Text of the Babylonian Poem of the Righteous Sufferer." *AnatSt* 30 (1980) 101–
7.

c. Greek Literature

Bussler, E. *Hiob und Prometheus: zwei Vorkämpfer der göttlicher Gerechtigkeit.* Hamburg,
1897. **Frieländer, M.** *Griechische Philosophie im Alten Testament: Eine Einleitung in die*

Psalm- und Weisheitsliteratur. Berlin: G. Reimer, 1904. **Fries, C.** *Das philosophische Gespräch von Hiob bis Plato*. Tübingen, 1904. **Irwin, W. A.** "Prometheus and Job." *JR* 30 (1950) 90–108. **Kallen, H.** *The Book of Job as a Greek Tragedy Restored*. New York: Moffat, Yard & Co., 1918. **Kaufmann, U. M.** "Expostulation with the Divine: A Note on Contrasting Attitudes in Greek and Hebrew Piety." *Int* 18 (1964) 171–82. [= *Twentieth-Century Interpretations of the Book of Job: A Collection of Critical Essays*, ed. P. S. Sanders. Englewood Cliffs, NJ: Prentice-Hall, 1968. 66–77.] **Lindblom, J.** "Job and Prometheus: A Comparative Study." In *Dragma: Martino P. Nilsson anno 1939 dedicatum*. Acta Instituti Romani Regni Sueciae 2/1. Lund, 1939. 280–87. **May, H. G.** "Prometheus and Job: The Problem of the God of Power and the Man of Wrath." *ATR* 34 (1952) 240–46. **Miranda, A. A. de.** "Job y Prometeo: o religión y irreligión." *Anthologia Annua* 2 (1954) 207–37. **Montefiore, C. G.** "The Book of Job as a Greek Tragedy Restored." *HTR* 12 (1919) 219–24. **Murray, G.** "Prometheus and Job." In *Twentieth-Century Interpretations of the Book of Job: A Collection of Critical Essays*, ed. P. S. Sanders. Englewood Cliffs, NJ: Prentice-Hall, 1968. 56–65. [= *Aeschylus: The Creator of Tragedy*. Oxford: Clarendon, 1940. 87–110.] **Neyrand, J.** "Le livre de Job et les poèmes d'Homère." *Études* 59 (1922) 129–51. **Paulus, J.** "Le thème du juste souffrant dans la pensée grecque et hébraïque." *RHR* 121 (1940) 18–66. **Simon, U.** "Job and Sophocles." In *Images of Belief in Literature*, ed. D. Jasper. London: Macmillan, 1984. 42–51. **Weiser, A.** "Des Problem der sittlichen Weltordnung im Buche Hiob: Unter Berücksichtigung seiner Entwicklung bei den Griechen und in der israelitischen Religion." In his *Glaube und Geschichte im Alten Testament und andere ausgewählte Schriften*. Göttingen: Vandenhoeck & Ruprecht, 1961. 9–19. **Wolfson, E. R.** "The Dialectic of Faith and Doubt in the Philosophy of Socrates and Piety of Job." *Dor* 8 (1979–80) 197–200.

The Prologue (1:1–2:13)

Bibliography

Albright, W. F. "The Name of Bildad the Shuhite." *AJSL* 44 (1927–28) 31–36. **Alter, R.** *The Art of Biblical Narrative.* London: George Allen and Unwin, 1981. **Barr, J.** "Hebrew עד, Especially at Job i.18 and Neh. vii.3." *JSS* 27 (1982) 177–88. **Berg, W.** "Gott und der Gerechte in der Rahmenerzählung des Buches Hiob." *MTZ* 31 (1981) 206–21. **Clines, D. J. A.** "False Naivety in the Prologue to Job." *HAR* 9 (1985) 127–36. ——. "In Search of the Indian Job." *VT* 33 (1983) 398–418. **Coats, G. W.**, ed. *Saga, Legend, Tale, Novella, Fable: Narrative Forms in Old Testament Literature.* JSOTSup 35. Sheffield: JSOT, 1985. **Cooper, A.** "Narrative Theory and the Book of Job." *SR* 11 (1982) 35–44. **Driver, G. R.** "Ancient Lore and Modern Knowledge: 4. Earth to Earth." In *Hommages à André Dupont-Sommer*, ed. A. Caquot. Paris: Librairie d'Amérique et d'Orient, 1971. 277–86. **Fohrer, G.** "Zur Vorgeschichte und Komposition des Buches Hiob." *VT* 6 (1956) 249–67 (= *Studien zum Buche Hiob [1956–1979]*. BZAW 159. Berlin: de Gruyter. 2d ed., 1983. 19–36). ——. "Überlieferung und Wandlung der Hioblegende." *FS Friedrich Baumgärtel.* Erlanger Forschungen A 10. Erlangen, 1959 (= *Studien zum Buche Hiob [1956–1979]*. BZAW 159. Berlin: de Gruyter. 2d ed., 1983. 37–59). **Görg, M.** "Ijob aus dem Lande ʿŪṣ. Ein Beitrag zur 'theologischen Geographie.'" *BN* 12 (1980) 7–12. **Habel, N. C.** "The Narrative Art of Job: Applying the Principles of Robert Alter." *JSOT* 27 (1983) 101–11. **Hoffmann, Y.** "The Relation between the Prologue and the Speech-Cycles in Job." *VT* 31 (1981) 160–70. **Houtman, C.** "Zu Hiob 2:12." *ZAW* 90 (1978) 269–72. **Hurwitz, A.** "The Date of the Prose-Tale of Job Linguistically Reconsidered." *HTR* 67 (1974) 17–34. **Jacob, B.** "Erklärung einiger Hiob-Stellen: 1,5; 1,22; 2,4; 2,10." *ZAW* 32 (1912) 278–87 (278–79). **Joüon, P.** "Notes philologiques sur le texte hébreu de Job 1,5; 9,35; 12,21; 28,1; 28,27; 29,14." *Bib* 11 (1930) 322–24. **Kahn, J.** *Job's Illness: Loss, Grief, and Integration: A Psychological Interpretation.* Oxford: Pergamon, 1975. **Kautzsch, K.** *Das sogenannte Volksbuch von Hiob und der Ursprung von Hiob I, II, XLII,7–17: Ein Beitrag nach der Integrität des Buches Hiob.* Tübingen: J. C. B. Mohr, 1900. **Lacocque, A.** "Est-ce gratuitement que Job craint Dieu?" *Mélanges André Neher.* Ed. E. Amado Levy-Valensi, et al. Paris: Librairie d'Amérique et d'Orient. Adrien Maisonneuve, 1975. 175–79. **Lohfink, N.** "Enthielten die im Alten Testament bezeugten Klageriten eine Phase des Schweigens?" *VT* 12 (1962) 260–77. **Maag, V.** *Hiob. Wandlung und Verarbeitung des Problems in Novelle, Dialogdichtung, und Spätfassungen.* FRLANT 128. Göttingen: Vandenhoeck & Ruprecht, 1982. 20–90. **McCormick, S.** "Someone HAD to Speak! A Sermon on Job 2:13." *Int* 20 (1966) 211–17. **Moore, R. D.** "The Integrity of Job." *CBQ* 45 (1983) 17–31. **Owens, J. J.** "The Prologue and the Epilogue." *RevExp* 68 (1971) 457–67. **Polzin, R.** "The Framework of the Book of Job." *Int* 31 (1974) 182–200. **Ricciotti, G.** "'Et nu j'y retournerai' (Job 1:21)." *ZAW* 67 (1955) 249–51. **Rinaldi, G.** "*mqnh (miqneh). Giobbe* 1,3." *BeO* 20 (1978) 60. **Rongy, H.** "Le prologue du livre de Job." *RevEcclLiège* 25 (1933) 168–71. **Sarna, N. M.** "Epic Substratum in the Prose of Job." *JBL* 76 (1957) 13–25. **Schmidt, L.** *"De Deo." Studien zur Literaturkritik und Theologie des Buches Jona, des Gesprächs zwischen Abraham und Jahwe in Gen 18,22ff und von Hi 1.* BZAW 143. Berlin: de Gruyter, 1976. **Speiser, E. A.** "On the Name Bildad." *JAOS* 49 (1929) 360. **Torczyner, H.** "How Satan Came into the World." *ExpT* 48 (1936–37) 563–65. **Ward, E. F. de.** "Mourning Customs in 1, 2 Samuel." *JJS* 23 (1972) 1–27, 145–66. **Weimar, P.** "Literarkritisches zur Ijobnovelle." *BN* 12 (1980) 62–80. **Weiss, M.** *The Story of Job's Beginning. Job 1–2: A Literary Analysis.* Jerusalem: Magnes, 1983. **Wensinck, A. J.** *Some Semitic Rites of Mourning and Religion: Studies on Their Origin and Mutual Relation.* Verhandelingen der Koninklijke Akademie van Wetenschappen te Amsterdam. Afdeeling Letterkunde, Nieuwe Reeks. 18/1. Amsterdam: J. Müller, 1917.

Translation

¹ *There was a man in the land of Uz; Job was his name. That man was blameless and upright, a God-fearer, a shunner of evil.* ² *There were born to him seven sons and three daughters.* ³ *And his substance* ᵃ *was: seven thousand sheep and three thousand camels and five hundred yoke of oxen and five hundred she-asses; and he had a great multitude of servants.* ᵇ *That man was the greatest of all the people of the East.* ⁴ *His sons would go and make a feast in the house of each on his day, and they would send and invite their three sisters to eat and drink with them.* ⁵ *And when the days of the feast were over,* ᵃ *Job would send* ᵇ *and hallow them. He would rise up early* ᶜ *in the morning and offer sacrifices in accord with the number of them all. For Job would say, "It may be that my children have sinned and cursed* ᵈ *God in their hearts!"* ᵉ *Thus did* ᶠ *Job continually.*

⁶ *Now there came a day when* ᵃ *the sons of God came to present themselves before* ᵇ *Yahweh, and the Satan also came among them.* ⁷ *And Yahweh said to the Satan, "Whence do you come?" The Satan answered Yahweh, saying, "From going to and fro in the earth, and from walking up and down in it."* ⁸ *Yahweh said to the Satan, "Have you considered my servant Job?* ᵃ *There is none like him in the earth, a man blameless and upright, a God-fearer, a shunner of evil."* ⁹ *The Satan answered Yahweh, saying, "Is it for naught that Job has feared* ᵃ *God?* ¹⁰ *Have you not put a hedge about him and about his house and about all that is his on every side? You have blessed the work of his hands, and his substance is spread throughout the land.* ¹¹ *But put forth* ᵃ *your hand now and touch all that is his; surely he would curse* ᵇ *you to your face!"* ¹² *Yahweh said to the Satan, "See, all that is his is in your hand; only upon himself do not put forth your hand." And the Satan went out from the presence of Yahweh.*

¹³ *Now there came a day when Job's sons and daughters were eating, and drinking wine, in the house of their eldest brother.* ¹⁴ *A messenger came to Job, and said, "The oxen were plowing* ᵃ *and the asses grazing beside them;* ᵇ ¹⁵ *and the Sabeans fell upon them* ᵃ *and took them; the servants they have put to the sword;* ᵇ *and I alone have escaped* ᶜ *to tell you."* ¹⁶ *But while he was still speaking, another came, and said, "The fire of God fell from heaven and burned the flocks and the servants, and it has consumed them; and I alone have escaped to tell you."* ¹⁷ *But while he was still speaking, another came, and said, "The Chaldeans formed three bands, and made a raid against the camels and took them; and the servants they have put to the sword; and I alone have escaped to tell you."* ¹⁸ *But while he was still* ᵃ *speaking, another came and said, "Your sons and your daughters were eating and drinking wine in the house of their eldest brother;* ¹⁹ *and suddenly a mighty wind came across the wilderness and struck the four corners of the house; it has fallen upon the young people, and they are dead, and I alone have escaped to tell you."*

²⁰ *Then Job rose up, and he rent his mantle, and he shaved his head, and he fell down upon the ground and did obeisance.* ᵃ ²¹ *And he said, "Naked I came forth from my mother's womb; and naked I shall return. Yahweh has given; and Yahweh has taken. May Yahweh's name be blessed."* ²² *In all this* ᵃ *Job did not sin or speak irreverently* ᵇ *of God.*

²:¹ *Now there came a day when the sons of God came to present themselves before Yahweh, and the Satan also came among them to present himself before Yahweh.* ² *And Yahweh said to the Satan, "Whence do you come?" The Satan answered Yahweh, saying, "From going to and fro in the earth, and from walking up and*

down in it." [3]*Yahweh said to the Satan, "Have you considered my servant Job? There is none like him in the earth, a man blameless and upright, a God-fearer, a shunner of evil. And he still maintains his integrity, even though*[a] *you urged*[b] *me against him to destroy*[c] *him without cause."*[d] [4]*The Satan answered Yahweh, saying, "Skin for*[a] *skin! All that a man has he will give for his life.* [5]*But put forth your hand now and touch his bone and his flesh; surely he would curse you to your face!"* [6]*Yahweh said to the Satan, "See, he is in your hand; only you must preserve his life."* [7]*The Satan went forth from the presence of Yahweh, and he smote Job with grievous sores from the sole of his foot unto the crown of his head.* [8]*And Job took up a potsherd and scraped himself with it as*[a] *he sat among the ashes.*

[9]*His wife said to him, "Do you still maintain your integrity? Curse God and die!"*[a]

[10]*Job said to her, "Would you too speak as one of the foolish women? We indeed*[a] *accept good from God; shall we not*[b] *also accept harm?"*

In all this Job did not sin with his lips.

[11]*Now when Job's three friends heard of all this misfortune that had come upon him, they set out, each from his own home, Eliphaz from Teman, Bildad from Shuah, and Zophar from Naamah, and by consent they met in order to bring him sympathy and comfort.* [12]*And when they lifted up their eyes from a distance and saw him, they hardly recognized him; then they lifted up their voice and wept. Each of them tore his robe, and they threw dust over their heads into the air.*[a] [13]*And for seven days and seven nights*[a] *they sat with him on the ground; none of them spoke a word to him, for they saw how great his suffering*[b] *was.*

Notes

1:3.a. מקנה, a collective noun generally including only cattle, most often only cows, sheep, and goats. Though the broader meaning "possessions" is not recognized by BDB, it is attested in Gen 49:32 (where מִקְנַת is not to be read) and perhaps Gen 47:18 (and the root קנה is "get, acquire"); cf. also G. Rinaldi, *"mqnh (miqneh): Giobbe* 1,3," *BeO* 20 (1978) 60. Here מקנה includes servants, so is best translated "substance" (KJV, RV), "possessions" (JPS), or "property" (Pope, Gordis) rather than "cattle" (Driver, Dhorme; cf. Fohrer).

3.b. עבדה, a rare collective noun (only elsewhere in Gen 26:14) in a position in such lists at which male and female slaves are usually mentioned. The meaning "work animals" (NAB) is unparalleled, as well as being inappropriate after such animals have been specified.

5.a. הקיפו, probably an intransitive hiph "complete a circuit, come to a full end" (so BDB, KB, Fohrer, Gordis; cf. a similar use of *nqp* in Ug.: *CTA* 23:67–68; Gibson, 127). For the view that "sons" is the subject and "days of the feast" the object, see Driver, Dhorme.

5.b. Frequentative, as the verbs in v 4.

5.c. This is the conventional translation of שכם hiph, but it is challenged by Pope, who remarks, "The notion of earliness does not appear to be intrinsic to its meaning," and translates "he would get busy" (similarly Andersen: "conscientious activity, not necessarily . . . time"). It is true that בבקר frequently accompanies שכם (as here; Judg 19:5, 8; 1 Sam 15:12; 29:10, 11; Isa 5:11), and that in some passages the sense appears to be "do quickly, eagerly" (so Jer 7:13, 25; 11:7; 25:4; 26:5; 29:19; 32:33; 35:14, 15; 44:4; Zeph 3:7), but in other places the sense of "early in the morning" is implied (Cant 7:13 [12]; Hos 6:4 [where it is parallel with "morning"]; Gen 20:8 [where it refers to telling a dream after waking]). Where "persistently" seems the most natural translation (as in the Jer passages), שכם is a dead (or almost dead) metaphor (cf. KB). On the verb, see also M. Delcor, "Quelques cas de survivances du vocabulaire nomade en hébreu biblique. Leur signification," *VT* 25 (1975) 307–22 (309–10).

5.d. ברכו, lit., "blessed," a euphemism for "cursed" (see *Comment*). It cannot be determined whether ברך is a scribal replacement for a verb that was found too offensive, or whether "the same psychological process postulated for a scribe may [not] well have operated for the author" (Gordis; similarly Duhm). J. J. Owens translates "they (i.e., the sons) blessed God in their hearts" for their father's concern (*RevExp* 68 [1971] 457–67), but the identical phrase in 1:11; 2:5, 9 cannot be so translated. The view that ברך means properly "salute" (as in 1 Sam 25:14), and that it may have been used in taking leave, hence "bid farewell to, renounce" (so Dillmann, Davidson, RV), is unsupported by clear evidence. "Blasphemed" (RVmg, JPS, NAB, NJB) is rather vague; does it mean "spoke irreverently" or "reviled, calumniated, abused" (cf. *OED, s.v.*)?

5.e. P. Joüon interestingly proposed that we should restore בְּטוּב before לבבם "in the joy of their hearts," a euphemism for "in their drunkenness" (cf. Deut 28:47; Isa 65:14). Their "cursing" would then not be silent, but, more naturally, verbal (*Bib* 11 [1930] 322–24 [322]).

5.f. Frequentative impf.

6.a. Pope, followed by Blommerde, translates "the day arrived when the gods come and present themselves," i.e., the day characterized by that event; other uses of ויהי היום, regularly followed by *waw* consec and "impf," do not support this view (see *Comment*).

6.b. In view of the usage of the phrase, the על should not be taken as adversative (as against Rashi, comparing Isa 3:13); see also on 2:1.

8.a. The connective is כי, translated "for" by RV, Gordis (similarly Horst, Fohrer), but better taken as introducing a clause forming a second complement of the verb (Dhorme); so it means "that" (which may be omitted in translation).

9.a. Word order, with ירא first, shows that the form is pf tense, not present ptcp; see Driver, *Tenses*, § 135 (4).

11.a. The use of the imperative as a hypothetical is recognized by the grammarians: GKC, § 110f, notes the use of two imperatives linked by simple *waw*, the first imperative containing a condition, the second "the consequence which the fulfilment of the condition will involve" (cf. Job 2:9; etc.). Driver, *Tenses*, §§ 150–52, offers a more thorough analysis, but does not mention our passage, perhaps because the notional apodosis is in oath form rather than a plain indicative.

11.b. Lit., "bless"; see n. 5.d.

14.a. חרשות: "the fem. cannot be very satisfactorily explained" (Driver), especially when the masc suff of ידיהם refers to them (though masc suffs referring to fem nouns are common enough; GKC, § 135o). The fem in Gen 33:13 refers specifically to female cattle. צאן also occurs inexplicably with fem adjectives in Gen 30:43. Guillaume saw in this use of the fem further evidence of a setting of the book in the Hijaz, in that in the region of Tema and Dedan C. M. Doughty (*Travels in Arabia Deserta* [Cambridge: CUP, 1888] 1:152) saw cows rather than oxen plowing; but not much weight can be put on this argument.

14.b. על־ידיהם: Driver notes that על־ידי and על־יד are more commonly followed by a geographical term (cf. BDB, 391b § 5.h.3). Dahood's suggestion (*Psalms II*, 354) that יד here means "pasture" (tr. "on their grazing plots") is unnecessary, though יד does occur in parallelism with מרעית "pasturage" in Ps 95:7.

15.a. The verb is fem because its subject is the collective שבא; the omission of *beth*, על or אל after the verb is exceptional but intelligible.

15.b. Lit., "to the mouth of the sword," "mouth" being a dead metaphor in this common idiom, but arising from the "devouring" of the victim by the sword (cf. Deut 32:42; 2 Sam 2:26). Irrelevant to the question of whether this is a "poetic figure" is the artifact referred to by Pope with the blade of a sword coming forth from a hilt shaped like a lion's mouth (T. J. Meek, "Archaeology and a Point in Hebrew Syntax," *BASOR* 122 [1951] 31–33; cf. Rev 1:16; 2:16; 19:15); the "sword of the mouth" (as in Rev 2:16) is an independent literary figure.

15.c. Ehrlich's supposition (repeated by Gordis; cf. also Duhm) that the cohortative expresses the survivor's difficulty in escaping is fanciful.

18.a. MT עַד is usually revocalized to עֹד or עוֹד, the form found in the parallel vv 16, 17. עַד does appear as a conjunction, "while," in 1 Sam 14:19; Ps 141:10 (BDB, 725 § II.2; KB, 681a § 8), and with a ptcp in Neh 7:3. J. Barr defends the reading עַד "while" (*JSS* 27 [1982] 177–82; see also the Additional Note by J. Hughes, ibid., pp. 189–92).

20.a. השתחוה, derived by the standard lexica from שחה, has been thought, in the light of Ug. ḥwy, to be derived from a root חוה (KB³). Cf. also G. I. Davies, "A Note on the Etymology of hištaḥªwāh," *VT* 29 (1979) 493–95 (cognate with Arab. ḥawā "coil up, double up"). But see J. A. Emerton, "The Etymology of hištaḥªwāh," *OTS* 20 (1977) 41–55, in favor of the derivation from שחה.

22.a. Or, possibly, "in spite of all this," *beth* concessive (cf. Driver; see BDB, 90b § III.7).

22.b. תפלה is now usually taken as "unseemliness" (KB), and is found elsewhere only in Jer 23:13 (perhaps also Ps 109:4); the occurrence in Job 24:12 requires emendation. Cf. תָּפֵל "what is tasteless" (6:6; also Lam 2:14). Some connect it with Arab. *tifl* "spittle" (Tur-Sinai, Pope). Older emendations, to עַוְלָה "wickedness" or נְבָלָה "folly" (Beer; cf. *BHK*) or to תְּפִלָּה "prayer," understood here as "protest" (Ehrlich), have been rightly abandoned, though M. Dahood ("Hebrew-Ugaritic Lexicography XII," *Bib* 55 [1974] 381–93 [390]) argued for the vocalization תְּפִלָּה meaning "curse" as well as "prayer" (cf. 1:5 where "they sinned" is balanced by וּבֵרְכוּ, "and they cursed").

2:3.a. Not a *waw* consec expressing "a logical or necessary consequence of that which immediately precedes," thus "he still holdeth fast his integrity so that thou thus (as it now appears) groundlessly movedst me against him" (GKC, § 111l), for חנם should not be linked with וַתְּסִיתֵנִי (see n. 2:3.d). More probably it is analogous to cases where "the action, or its results, continues into the writer's [here the narrative's] present" (Driver, *Tenses*, § 80), though whether Driver's translation by a present tense, "and thou art enticing me," is satisfactory is doubtful. Many versions have "although" (RSV, NAB; cf. NIV, Pope), which is not strictly a translation of *waw* consec; but Driver, *Tenses*, § 74β, notes cases where two verbs in a consecutive chain are *contrasted*, and best translated by "and yet"; so "although" is permissible.

3.b. סות, "movedst" (KJV, RV), "moved" (RSV), "provoked" (JB), "enticed" (NIV), "incited" (NEB, NAB, Pope, Gordis), is a delocutive verb, signifying an attempt to persuade rather than the act of successful persuasion; cf. פתה "attempt to deceive" (see D. J. A. Clines and D. M. Gunn, "'You Tried to Persuade Me' and 'Violence! Outrage!' in Jeremiah xx 7–8," *VT* 28 [1978] 20–27).

3.c. בלע, lit., "swallow" (cf. RVmg), is frequently a metaphor for general destruction. Mot, the Ugaritic god of death, "swallows" his victims (cf. N. M. Sarna, *JBL* 76 [1957] 13–25; and cf. also n. 8:18.a; 10:8). A. Guillaume, however ("A Note on the √בלע," *JTS* ns 13 [1962] 320–23; followed by KB³), insisted that we have here a בלע II (cognate with Arab. *balaġa* "reach, arrive at," and so "afflict"), meaning "afflict, distress, injure." The meaning is satisfactory but not mandatory.

3.d. חנם "without cause" or "without success" is linked by many with the verb תְּסִיתֵנִי (Dhorme, Hölscher, Rowley, Andersen; cf. Moffatt "it was idle of you to entice me"; similarly Terrien, *TOB*, JB). But it is not clear that the "urging" was either baseless or futile, and חנם is more naturally connected with the verb it accompanies, בלע (so Horst, Fohrer, Gordis, RSV, NEB, NAB, NIV).

4.a. Gray's suggestion to read עוֹר בְּעַד עוֹרוֹ is discussed in the *Comment*. For בעד "on behalf of" and thus equivalent to תחת, see BDB, 126 § 2; "in exchange for" must be the sense in its second use in this verse.

8.a. The final phrase should be taken as a circumstantial clause (cf. Driver, *Tenses*, § 160; GKC, § 156); so NEB, NAB, NIV, Gordis.

9.a. The second imperative most probably indicates the consequence of the first (examples in GKC, § 110f); it is most improbable that the meaning is "Curse God before dying" (Dhorme, Rowley [possibly], Andersen [perhaps]; similarly Davidson).

10.a. D. N. Freedman suggested that *gam* means "aloud" (cited by M. Dahood, "Ugaritic Lexicography," *Mélanges Eugène Tisserant* [Città del Vaticano: Bibliotheca Apostolica Vaticana, 1964] 1:81–104 [86 n. 17]); on *gm* in this meaning see also D. Beirne, "A Note on Numbers 11,4," *Bib* 44 (1963) 201–3 (203). But it is better to take it as the emphatic גַּם; see C. J. Labuschagne, "The Emphasizing Particle *GAM* and Its Connotations," *Studia Biblica et Semitica* (FS Th. C. Vriezen; ed. W. C. van Unnik and A. S. van der Woude [Wageningen: Veenman & Zonen, 1966]) 193–203 (199); and cf. already B. Jacob, *ZAW* 32 (1912) 278–87 (279–82).

10.b. לֹא "not" is taken as לָא "indeed" by F. Nötscher, "we must indeed also receive evil" ("Zum emphatischen Lamed," *VT* 3 [1953] 372–80 [375]). This is no more likely than the proposal that לא is an affirmative use of the negative particle (G. S. Glanzman, "Two Notes: Am 3,15 and Os 11,8–9," *CBQ* 23 [1961] 227–33 [231–32], and G. R. Driver, "Affirmation by Exclamatory Negation," *JANESCU* 5 [1973] 107–14).

12.a. הַשָּׁמַיְמָה "toward heaven" is deleted by some (see *Comment*). Among emendations are the logical but bookish suggestion of Szczygiel מֵהֲשַׁמָּה "because of his desolation" (hoph inf of שמם, Lev 26:34), and the interesting proposals of Tur-Sinai מְשַׁמִּים "desolate" (as in Ezek 3:15, "I sat there desolate [in mourning]"; cf. Ezra 9:3, "I sat appalled [מְשׁוֹמֵם, poel ptcp]"), and subsequently, because משמים is not plur, הַשַּׁמֵם, hiph inf abs. Though Pope finds the idea attractive, the inf abs is not likely, and there is some distance between "*sitting* appalled" and "*sprinkling dust* appalled"; Tur-Sinai therefore argued that the word stood originally after v 13a, "they sat . . . seven days and seven nights," but it is asking too much to believe that as well.

13.a. Duhm, finding "and seven nights" missing from the "original LXX" (Beer in *BHK* simply says it is lacking in LXX), would delete it as a "harmless expansion." The evidence is rather that though the phrase was missing from the MSS used by Origen (as an annotation in the margin of the Syro-Hexaplar says) all extant MSS of LXX have it (though not always the "seven") and editors regard it as genuine (perhaps deciding that its absence from Origen's MSS was due to homoeoteleuton).

13.b. כאב can be physical "pain" or mental "grief," the former in 14:22, the pain of one's body, and in Ezek 28:24, pain from a thorn; the latter probably in Job 16:6 (his grief is not assuaged), and in Prov 14:13 (even in laughter the heart grieves). Here, where the "suffering" is "seen"—which suggests it is external—we may be invited to wonder whether the friends really understand how Job feels.

Form / Structure / Setting

The *structure* of this prose prologue to the book is clearly defined. There are five scenes, alternating between earth and heaven, and a sixth, pendant to those, linking the events and the prologue with the dialogues:

1. *On earth*   Job's piety (1:1–5)
2. *In heaven*   First dialogue of Yahweh and the Satan (1:6–12)
3. *On earth*   Disasters announced to Job (1:13–22)
4. *In heaven*   Second dialogue of Yahweh and the Satan (2:1–7a)
5. *On earth*   Personal afflictions of Job (2:7b–10)

To which is added:

6.   Arrival of Job's friends (2:11–13)

This is a very stylized structure, tending toward the naive. Its simplicity is further emphasized by parallels between scenes. Most striking is the parallel structure of scenes 2 and 4:

1. Situation
   The sons of God present themselves (1:6; 2:1)
2. Complication
   a. Question by Yahweh (1:7a; 2:2a)
   b. Reply by the Satan (1:7b; 2:2b)
   c. Question by Yahweh (1:8; 2:3)
   d. Reply by the Satan (1:9–11; 2:4–5)
   e. Yahweh's authorization (1:12a; 2:6)
3. Resolution
   The Satan goes forth (1:12b; 2:7a)

The parallels here extend beyond the structure to the bulk of the wording.

The scenes are with one exception clearly marked off from one another by the recurring phrase "there came a day when" (ויהי היום, 1:6, 13; 2:1); the first scene does not of course need any marker of beginning. The exception to the pattern is at the juncture between the fourth and fifth scenes. That is, at the beginning of the final scene, the breaking of the formal pattern signals the impingement of the divine world upon the human; as the two scenes dissolve into one another, the tempo quickens for the finale. The simple and repetitive structure of the prologue may be termed one of its "falsely naive" features (see D. J. A. Clines, *HAR* 9 [1985] 127–36).

In each scene there are never more than two speakers, a sign of the naivety of the depiction (in the third scene, as each messenger gives his account of disaster, he disappears from the scene as another is superimposed).

The *genre* of the prologue (1:1–2:13) and the epilogue (42:7–17) considered as a whole should probably be designated as *legend,* in the form-critical sense of "edifying story," a narrative type in which the focus is upon character rather than strictly upon event (G. W. Coats, "Tale," in *Saga, Legend,* 63–64), in which we find "a virtue embodied in a deed," in A. Jolles' classic formulation (*Einfache Formen* [2nd ed.; Tübingen: Niemeyer, 1958] 23–61), with an emphasis on behavior and character worthy of imitation (cf. R. M. Hals, "Legend," in Coats, *Saga, Legend,* 51). This designation focuses on the depiction of Job's response to his afflictions as the appropriate response of a godly person. As Fohrer put it, "The concern of this narrative, as of the book as a whole, is not the problem of suffering, but the behavior of people in their experiencing and enduring suffering . . . not the problem of theodicy, but of human existence in suffering" (69).

It is not always possible to distinguish clearly between legend and "tale"—R. E. Murphy uses the term "edifying story" (*Wisdom Literature: Job, Proverbs, Ruth, Canticles, Ecclesiastes, and Esther* [FOTL 13; Grand Rapids: Eerdmans, 1981] 21)—and the typical features of the *tale* (Coats, "Tale," in *Saga, Legend,* 63–67) may be seen here, principally the movement from exposition, through complication, resolution, dénouement, to conclusion. Here exposition is obviously 1:1–5, followed by a double complication (the two heavenly scenes and their consequences, 1:6–21 and 2:1–10). If the prologue is read without knowledge of the epilogue (and the distance that separates them invites us to keep the ultimate resolution at the back of our minds as long as possible) then a double resolution is effected in 1:20–21 and 2:10 (similarly Habel, speaking of an "apparent resolution," p. 79). Already in 1:20–21 we are being tempted to believe that the story has reached its conclusion with Job's "arising" (cf. R. Alter, *Art of Biblical Narrative,* 65). The legend as tale is, however, further "complicated" by the episode of 2:11–13, the arrival of the friends, which locates itself in the position of a dénouement or conclusion where loose ends are tied up and reconciliations effected, but which turns out to be a further disorientation. The prologue thus concludes at the opening of a new arc of tension that will not reach its resolution before 42:9. Every appearance of simplicity in this narrative breaks apart into the most intriguing subtlety.

This prologue is a superb instance of the art of *narration through dialogue* that Alter has characterized in reference especially to 1 Sam 1 and 21 (*Art of Biblical Narrative,* chap. 4). The opening scene (1:1–5) we may designate a "pretemporal exposition," first identifying the protagonist and his character, specifying his wealth, and moving then into the "iterative tense" where a repeated action (1:4–5) will form the transition from the "actionless beginning" to the narrative proper, the "singulative" tense. Job's habitual thought, and therewith his character, is rendered by a piece of interior speech (1:5).

In the second scene (1:6–12) there is no narrative proper except for the framing sentences (the Satan came, the Satan left). The whole substance of this crucial narration that determines Job's fate is contained in a five-element dialogue, of which Yahweh has the first, the middle, and the last, and the Satan the second and fourth elements. That the speeches of Yahweh open and end the conversation (it is the same in the second heavenly scene) is a signal that he is the architect and the authorizer of Job's calamity. The first exchange ("Where have you come from?," "From going to and fro in the earth. . . .") draws into the dialogue material that is more for the readers' information than for the progress of the dialogue; we need to know that the Satan has had the opportunity and the responsibility of inquiring into the case of the man Job. The second speech of Yahweh ("Have you considered Job?") seems at first a guileless question, but hearing the response it elicits ("Does Job fear God for naught?") we come to see that it was a provocative question, pregnant with implication. The final speech confirms that although it may seem to be the Satan who has fingered Job, it is Yahweh who is truly the hard-faced one: "All that he has is in your power"; only after the general authorization to harm Job comes the rider to protect him ("only . . ."). It is the same in the second heavenly scene.

Alter has nicely remarked on how the respective speeches of Yahweh and the Satan function as "contrastive dialogue" to suggest characterization. Yahweh's first words ("Where are you coming from?") are almost brusque, and it is only when he is echoing the narrator's initial depiction of Job (1:1) that he speaks a formal language. The Satan, on the other hand, "shows a fondness for verse-insets, clever citation of folk-sayings, argumentative positioning of syntactical members for the most persuasive effect . . . he is a master of conscious rhetoric, alongside of whom God seems plainspoken" (*Art of Biblical Narrative*, 74).

In the third scene dialogue again is primary as the events that constitute Job's calamity are never narrated but reported, not shown but told. The device of the messenger speeches not only creates an atmosphere of accelerating doom, no speaker being able to conclude his report before being overtaken by the next, but also heightens the readers' expectation for Job's reaction by preventing Job from responding emotionally or verbally to any one calamity until he responds to them all. Strikingly, his response when it comes is initially silent (1:20), and thereafter is a monologue (1:21), or even perhaps an interior speech like 1:5.

The fifth scene invites comparison on several fronts with the third: it has more narration in it than any of the others (2:7b–8), the narrator himself taking the place of the messengers of chap. 1. But the weight lies upon the dialogue of Job and his wife, her speech forming in verbal mode the third trial of Job, borrowing half its material from Yahweh ("hold fast integrity") and half from the Satan ("curse God"), as if to make her the earthly counterpart of his heavenly assailants.

Dialogue in heaven and speech on earth have spelled Job's disaster; what will it signify that his friends on their arrival impose on themselves an unnaturally extended silence? Only the sequel of the dialogues will offer an answer to that little riddle with which the prologue concludes.

Comment

1:1–2:13 *The prose prologue.* The Book of Job begins and concludes with a prose narrative relating the experiences of the righteous sufferer Job. In the prologue, the two fundamental data indispensable for the book as a whole are presented. First, Job is a righteous man; second, he is suffering undeservedly, and that at God's hand, or at least with God's permission. From these data the whole issue of the book arises. But that issue appears differently to Job and to the readers of the book. To Job the issue is how to reconcile his experience of suffering with his knowledge of his innocence; to the readers the issue is rather how a righteous person is to behave when afflicted by undeserved suffering. The difference between Job and the readers of the book is that the readers are offered the twin fundamental data of the book as its unexaminable premise; whereas for Job the twin data are the object of unrelenting examination, for though he believes both implicitly, they spell out to him only a gigantic contradiction that imperils either his faith in God or his faith in himself—or both.

The prose prologue is divided into five scenes, the first, third, and fifth set on earth, and the second and fourth set in heaven:

1. Job's character and concern for his children's safety (1:1–5)
2. First confrontation between the Satan and Yahweh (1:6–12)
3. Announcements of disasters to Job's possessions and children, and Job's response (1:13–22)
4. Second confrontation between the Satan and Yahweh (2:1–6)
5. Personal afflictions of Job, Job's response, and the friends' response (2:7–13)

The scenes are, with one exception, kept clearly distinct from one another by means of the phrase "and there was a day when" (ויהי היום ו) at the beginning of the second, third, and fourth scenes (1:6, 13; 2:1). The exception draws attention to itself: not only is the introductory phrase absent from 2:7, but, for the only time in the prologue, one of the actors moves out of his proper sphere. The Satan, that is, though he is a character in the heavenly realm, eventually operates both on the heavenly plane and on the earthly plane; he goes "forth from the presence of Yahweh" in heaven and "afflict[s] Job" on earth. The breaking of the formal pattern signals the impingement of the divine world upon the human; and it further underscores the role of the Satan as the executor of the heavenly decision against Job. God remains in heaven, uninvolved directly in the affliction of Job; the very possibility of movement from the heavenly sphere to the earthly accentuates the aloofness of God, who does not engage in any such movement. So charged with implications is the fracture of the formal pattern of scenes that one is tempted to find in this structure a pattern created only in order to be destroyed for the sake of the effect. That is, the simple structure of the prologue is only falsely naive; like the unsophisticated language of these chapters, the plainness of the structure suggests, not a primitive narrative mode, but a subtle artistic severity. See further, D. J. A. Clines, *HAR* 9 (1985) 127–36.

1–5 *Job's character.* The one thing needful in the preface to the poem of Job the righteous sufferer is that "there must be no room for the misgiving that the sufferer's afflictions are the due reward of his deeds" (Peake). The opening sentence establishing Job's blamelessness is given precedence over the more external description of Job's family and wealth, since it is his moral rectitude that will be put in question by events of the narrative. Reference to his children and possessions, however, functions not as a decorative addition to the portrayal of the man, but as tangible evidence of his uprightness. The fundamental assertion of Job's blamelessness is reverted to in the last two verses of this unit, where a cameo scene depicts how scrupulous he is to ensure that his innocence extends beyond himself to the members of his family. At the same time, by bringing the children within the ambit of the story, it prepares for the third scene, in which their fate is portrayed.

1 First things first, for this storyteller. What is important about this man is not his name or his origin. The name Job is of uncertain meaning, Uz of uncertain location; was it any different in the narrator's time? Job's moral character is the theme of this scene, and the barest identification of the man is all that is needed.

A customary formula with which a biblical narrative book begins is "and it came to pass that" (ויהי) or "and there was" (ויהי); thus Joshua, Judges, 1 Samuel, (2 Samuel), Ruth, Esther (also Ezekiel). Some continuity with preceding narrative is probably implied; or, in the case of a book like Ruth, which had no doubt been an entity independent of Israel's national history, the formula forges a deliberate link with that history. Here the opening phrase is, literally, "a man there was" (איש היה), the only genuine parallels to which occur at the beginnings of Nathan's parable (2 Sam 12:1) and of Joash's fable (2 Kgs 14:9); in Esth 2:5, often cited in this connection, the similar word-order simply marks a shift of focus; similarly 1 Sam 25:2). The implication is not that what follows is a tale rather than history (Gordis) but that the subsequent narrative has no link with any stage in the course of Israel's history (thus König, *Syntax*, § 365g). The formulation of the opening words gives an advance warning that the frame of reference of this story will be other than Israel's canonical history. The name of Job's land will be a further such signal.

The importance of the name Uz lies not in where such a place is, but in where it is not. Israelites themselves may not have known its precise location, but they will have known, as we do, that it is not in Israel. The name therefore signifies that the action has a horizon that is not peculiarly Israelite. It does not mean that Job necessarily *is* a foreigner, for most Jews of the exilic period and beyond—if that is the time of the book's composition—lived outside the borders of Israel, and the patriarchs themselves—since that is ostensibly the time in which the story is set—were almost as often to be found outside the land as within it. The Book of Job simply does not say whether or not Job is an Israelite; by leaving open the question of his race, the book effectively makes his experience transcend the distinction between Israelite and non-Israelite, Jew and non-Jew. We do not know that the storyteller had such a conscious intention, but such is the effect he has created.

The clearest pointer to the location of Uz is Lam 4:21, where "the land of Uz" stands parallel to "Edom" (the only other occurrence of Uz as a place name is in Jer 25:20, where no clues to its location are given). Further support for a situation in or near Edom may be given by the occurrence of the personal name Uz in an Edomite genealogy (Gen 36:28 = 1 Chr 1:42), and by the probability that most of the personal names in Job have an Edomite origin (see on 2:11). Further, the personal name Uz is linked in Gen 22:21 with the name Buz, which appears in Jer 25:23 as a place name associated with Dedan and Tema, towns in northwest Arabia and thus not far south of Edom.

Again, the Septuagint appendix to the Book of Job preserves a tradition that the land of Job (which has become Ausitis in Greek transliteration) was located "on the borders of Idumea and Arabia" (42:17b), which indicates the same general setting (it is not clear that this tradition rests on the faulty identification of Job with the Jobab of Gen 10:29, as claimed by Fohrer, and Snaith, *Job,* 45). The name Uz has also been seen in a Lihyanite tribal name, al 'Auṣ (B. Moritz, "Edomitische Genealogien," *ZAW* 44 [1926] 81–92), and in the place name Khirbet el-'Iṣ (so A. Musil, *Arabia Petraea* [Vienna: A. Hölder, 1907] 2/1:337; cf. J. Simons, *Geographical and Topographical Texts* [Leiden: Brill, 1955] 25). Very much less probable are attempts to situate Uz in the region of Damascus or of northern Mesopotamia (cf. Gen 10:23 [= 1 Chr 1:17] where Uz is a "son" of Aram; and the tradition in Josephus, *Ant.* 1.6.4, that Ouses or Ousos son of Aram was the founder of Damascus and Trachonitis). Cf. also G. A. Barton, "The Original Home of the Story of Job," *JBL* 31 (1912) 63–68. M. Görg relates the name to the Egyptian term 'ḏ or 'ʒḏ, "land on the edge of the desert at the border of the regularly watered region," locating the friends' homes in the south, the east, and the north, as representing a global failure to comprehend Job ("Ijob aus dem Lande 'Ûṣ: Ein Beitrag zur 'theologische Geographie,'" *BN* 12 [1980] 7–12).

The name Job is not attested elsewhere in Hebrew. But it is known from several extrabiblical sources as a Semitic name. In the Egyptian Execration Texts of the nineteenth century B.C. a Palestinian chieftain whose name is probably to be read Ay(y)abum is mentioned (*ANET,* 329; so W. F. Albright, "The Land of Damascus between 1850 and 1750 B.C.," *BASOR* 83 [1941] 30–36 [36]; but cf. B. Landsberger, "Assyrische Königsliste und 'dunkles Zeitalter,'"

JCS 8 [1954] 47–73 [60 n. 126]). Longer forms Ayabi-sharri and Ayabi-ilu are identified in an eighteenth-century list of Egyptian slaves, some of whom bear Semitic names (Pap. Brooklyn 35.1446; cf. W. F. Albright, "North-west Semitic Names in a List of Egyptian Slaves from the Eighteenth Century B.C.," *JAOS* 74 [1954] 223–33 [225–26]). In eighteenth-century Alalakh and sixteenth-century Mari the name Ayyabum appears (D. J. Wiseman, *The Alalakh Tablets* [London: British Institute of Archaeology at Ankara, 1953] no. 11.35 [p. 38]; H. B. Huffmon, *Amorite Personal Names in the Mari Texts* [Baltimore: Johns Hopkins, 1965] 103, 161). In the fourteenth-century Amarna Letters, the prince of Ashtaroth in Bashan has the name Ayyâb (letters 237, 256; *ANET*, 486; cf. W. F. Albright, "Two Little Understood Amarna Letters from the Middle Jordan Valley," *BASOR* 89 [1943] 7–19 [11]). And in thirteenth-century Ugarit the form Ayab occurs in a list of personnel (*Le palais royal d'Ugarit* [Mission de Ras Shamra 7; ed. C. F.-A. Schaeffer; Paris: Imprimerie Nationale et C. Klincksieck, 1957] 2:62 [text 35 rev., line 10]). There can be little doubt, in the light of the forms attested, that the name originally meant "where is my father?"—though it is hard to see precisely how the Hebrew form אִיּוֹב (*'iyyôb*) has been derived. The name probably signifies "where is my (divine) father?" and is an appeal to a deity for help. Less likely is the suggestion that it is a name given to a child whose father has died before its birth (for such names see J. J. Stamm, *Die akkadische Namengebung* [Leipzig: J. C. Hinrichs, 1939] 284–87). The Hebrew vocalization does not suggest such a meaning, however, and there is no hint in Old Testament or rabbinic sources that any particular meaning was attached to the name, though occasional plays on the similarity of the name with the verb "to hate" (איב, *'āyab*) were made in Jewish literature (*b. B. Bat.* 16a; *Nid.* 52a).

Suggestions about what the Hebrew name might have been thought to mean by readers or hearers of the Job story have been made nevertheless. The most obvious connection is with the root איב "to hate," the form אִיּוֹב (*'iyyôb*) being analogous to the passive participial forms יִלּוֹד (*yillôd*) "born" and שִׁכּוֹר (*šikkôr*) "drunken," and so signifying "the hated one," "the persecuted one" (so, e.g., Gordis). Less likely is the idea that אִיּוֹב, *'iyyôb*, is analogous to the active participial form גִּבּוֹר (*gibbôr*) "strong," and thus signifies "the hater," or, more precisely, since the *gibbôr* formation tends to signify a profession or habitual activity, "the inveterate foe." Others have related the name to the Arabic *'awwâb* "returning, penitent," especially because the Koran describes Job (*'ayyûb* in Arabic) as *'awwâb* (Sura 38.44). But in the same chapter David and Solomon have the same epithet applied to them also. It is better to suppose that the name Job was the traditional one for the hero of the story and that it derives from a non-Hebrew origin. Perhaps when the tale was first told the West Semitic form of the name with its implicit cry for divine help was intentionally symbolic; in the Old Testament context the name has no particular significance, and nothing in the man's name, any more than in his character, presages his history.

This headline verse finally epitomizes the character of Job. The perfect tense of "that man was" is a frequentative, indicating the constant nature of the man, which is attested here by the narrator in his own person and in 1:8 and 2:3 as the assessment of God. Job's piety is described by two pairs of words, familiar in proverbial wisdom and in the Psalms, "blameless" and "upright" (in Prov 2:21; 28:10 [29:10 doubtful]; Ps 37:37; cf. 25:21 [abstract nouns]; Prov 2:7 [one abstract noun]) and "fearing God and turning away from evil" (in Job 28:28; Prov 3:7 [cf. 14:16; 16:6]). The language, though formed and shaped poetically, is not peculiar, however, to any sphere of Israelite life.

"Blameless" translates תם better than "perfect" (KJV, RV). But the often-repeated comment that the term does not mean that Job is sinless (so Peake, Rowley, Gordis) is questionable; for the contrast in the book is almost invariably between the "righteous" and the "wicked" and there is no doubt that from the viewpoint of the author and the hero himself, Job is "righteous." That the righteous are imperfect is sometimes suggested (cf. on 4:17), but in Job's case the issue is never whether his sins are serious or slight but simply whether he is a sinner or not. From perspectives other than those of the book it may seem pretentious for the author—or Job—to assert Job's blamelessness; thankfully, however, the issues of the book are posed in the simple terms of innocence and guilt, suffering deserved and undeserved, and do not become entangled in niceties about gradations of sinfulness or righteousness.

Though the cognate adjective תמים frequently describes the sacrificial animal that is without blemish (e.g., Lev 22:18–20), there is no sign that תמים in the ethical sense or תם, as here, is in any way derived from the cultic sense (as against W. Eichrodt, *Theology of the Old Testament* [tr. J. A. Baker; London: SCM, 1967] 2:394). And while the root has the connotation of "to be whole," it is misleading to insist that the adjective must mean "complete, whole, with integrity" or must indicate physical as well as moral health (cf. J. Pedersen, *Israel: Its Life and Culture I-II* [London: OUP; Copenhagen: P. Branner, 1926] 336–37, 358–59). Gray's explication of תם as implying "a character that is complete, all of a piece, not . . . one thing on the surface and another within" (similarly Gordis) falls prey to the etymologizing fallacy. The link with ישר "upright" indicates that the term has much the same generalized meaning. See also K. Koch, *THWAT* 2:1049, § 3f. The distinction proposed by Dhorme between תם as what is intrinsically perfect and תמים as what is perfect in relation to others cannot be sustained. And the argument of W. Brueggemann, "A Neglected Sapiential Word Pair," *ZAW* 89 (1977) 234–58 (238), that תם signifies what is health-giving *in relation to the community,* and characterizes a person who leads a "disciplined, coherent life according to community norms," does not strictly define the word, but offers an exemplification of it.

The term generally translated "upright" (ישר) indicates ethical propriety in the broadest sense. It is frequently found in connection with טוב "good" (e.g., Deut 6:18; Ps 25:8) and with צדיק "righteous" (e.g., Ps 32:11; 33:1). It certainly is a relational term, having to do with behavior toward others (cf. G. Liedke, *THWAT* 1:792–93), though here no specific meaning is relevant. The use of ישר in a concrete sense, for a "straight" or "level" path (e.g., Isa 26:7), misleads many into insisting upon some semantic equivalent for its moral sense, such as "straightforward" (cf. BDB, 449a, § 3). Nothing in the usage of the term justifies such specification, however.

No special distinction is made here between morality and religion, the expression denoting religious behavior being interposed among three terms for ethical behavior. So whatever may be the truth of the matter, nothing in the present text entitles us to assert that Job's fear of God was the secret of his moral and social equilibrium (as Terrien; similarly Rowley). The "fear of God" is in many texts an anxiety in face of the numinous, but here a respect or reverence for the divine will which is conceived as an aspect of ethical behavior. J. Becker has argued that the original sense of the term is numinous dread before the mighty deeds of God, and that the ethical "fear of God" is a later development in which an echo of the numinous still lingers (*Gottesfurcht im Alten Testament* [AnBib 25; Rome: Pontifical Biblical Institute, 1965] 38–39). The Psalms, however, contain many examples of the expression in a cultic and not particularly numinous context; and Elohistic passages of the Pentateuch attest the ethical usage (e.g., Gen 20:11; 22:12; Exod 1:17), so that a developmental hypothesis is doubtful. The term is of course common in wisdom literature, though more frequently in the form "fear of Yahweh," and its application to Job signifies his casting as the type of the ideal pious wise man.

Characteristic also of wisdom theology is the instruction to "turn away from" (סור) evil. The teachers of wisdom plainly see their duty not only in the inculcation of good example but in warning against bad example. The idea of "turning" belongs to the concept of life as "walking" on a "way," which should be "straight ahead" (Prov 4:25) without "swerving" (נטה) to right or left (e.g., Prov 4:27); keeping to the right way involves "turning away" (סור) from taking evil paths (the expression does not mean to abandon evil paths already followed). "The highway of the upright (ישרים) turns away from evil" (Prov 16:17). For the expression "turn away from evil," cf. also 1:8; 2:3; 28:28; Prov 3:7; 13:19; 14:16; 16:6, 17; Ps 34:15 [14]; 37:27, all typically sapiential.

2 Job's character, so the Hebrew delicately suggests (*waw* consecutive), was the precondition of his wealth in heirs and possessions. It is not a retributive theology of virtue and reward at play here, however, but the old idea of God's blessing in which the pious have a share (Fohrer). First mentioned as the finest blessing a man can have is the imposing number of sons; cf. Ps 127:3, where "sons" are a "heritage" (נחלה) from Yahweh, i.e., a grace gift, and a "reward" (שכר), almost in the sense of "boon." Cf. also Ps 128:3; 144:12. "Seven" symbolizes completeness or perfection; here (as in 42:13; Ruth 4:15; 1 Sam 2:5; cf. Jer 15:9) "seven sons" is the ideal, as often in the ancient Near East. In the Ugaritic literature, Keret has seven sons (*CTA* 15.2.23; Gibson, 91; Baal and Mot probably have seven pages, rather than sons, as is sometimes thought [*CTA* 5.5.8–9; 6.6.8; Gibson, 72, 80]); cf. the seven sons and seven daughters of Niobe in Ovid, *Metamorphoses* 6.182–83). The ratio of seven sons to three daughters reflects the superior worth attached to sons, and although the storyteller here uncritically adopts the conventional sexual ideology, in the reversal of Job's fortunes at 42:15, he breaches convention by having Job give his daughters an inheritance on an equal footing with his sons. The figure three in its own way symbolizes a perfect wholeness, groups of three female figures being familiar from many ancient legends and myths (three daughters of Baal [*CTA* 3A.1.23–25; 3C.3–4; Gibson, 46, 48]; three Graces, Hesperides, Gorgons, Fates, Furies, Horae). The proportion seven:three, amounting to another round number, ten, is seen also in v 3 (7000:3000) (cf. also 1 Kgs 11:3: Solomon's 700 wives:300 concubines).

Job's wife is not mentioned among his blessings, not so much because of her ambiguous role as because it is dramatically more effective to postpone her appearance to the crucial juncture of 2:9.

3 Job's possessions are equally the result of his uprightness and piety:

the verb shows that the enumeration of blessings in v 2 is continued. In keeping with the patriarchal flavor of the narrative, Job's wealth is described entirely in terms of his cattle and servants (cf. Gen 12:16; 26:14; 30:43; 46:32; 1 Sam 25:2). Clearly Job also possesses plowland (cf. v 14; 5:23; 31:38) and gold (cf. 22:24; 31:24; 42:11), while the quantities of oxen (for plowing) and asses (for carrying the produce of the fields) indicate forms of wealth besides the animals (for gold and silver among cattle as forms of wealth in patriarchal times, cf. Gen 24:35). Though the exclusive reference here to animals creates the impression that Job is pictured as a nomad on the patriarchal pattern, the book as a whole shows Job as a settled agriculturalist with princely rule in a "city" (cf. especially chaps. 29–31).

The term translated "sheep" (צאן) includes both sheep and goats, which customarily grazed together (cf. Matt 25:32). Camels were used for carrying loads (cf. Gen 37:25; 2 Kgs 8:9) as well as riding (cf. Gen 24:10; 31:17, 34; Judg 6:5; Isa 66:20); their presence in this list depends on the patriarchal narratives, and cannot be used as dating evidence for the story or the Book of Job (as against Fohrer, Hesse; on the date of the domestication of the camel, see K. A. Kitchen, *IBD* 1:228–30). Aristotle offers an ancient attestation that Arabs sometimes kept as many as three thousand camels, the number here ascribed to Job (*De anim. hist.* 9.50.5); but such a number would be more appropriate to Bedouin-like camel nomads than to the settled farmer Job. Oxen were yoked in pairs; and a "yoke" (צמד) of land was the area a pair of oxen could plow in a day (1 Sam 14:14; Isa 5:10). Oxen were also used for pulling (2 Sam 6:6) and for carrying loads (1 Chr 12:41 [40]). She-asses rather than he-asses are mentioned because of their superior value as milk-producers and for breeding (cf. Pliny, *Nat. hist.* 28.50.183; 8.68.167–70); in recent centuries in Syria she-asses fetched three times the price of male asses (Wetzstein, cited by Delitzsch). She-asses are also said to be better for riding. A much smaller number of he-asses would need to be kept (cf. Gen 32:16 [15]). Asses were used in various farm work, for carrying burdens (e.g., Gen 42:26), plowing (Deut 22:10; Isa 30:24), and threshing (cf. *ANEP*, 89), as well as riding (e.g., 2 Sam 17:23). The ass was unclean according to OT food laws (Lev 11:2–8; Deut 14:3–8), but ass's meat was probably eaten nevertheless (cf. 2 Kgs 6:25). Such a number of animals would obviously require a large staff of "servants" for their tending; it is probably because the servants are required by the animals that they are mentioned last in this list and not because they were thought less valuable (for servants as the last item in such a list, cf. Gen 26:14; and from Ugarit, *Le palais royal d'Ugarit* [Mission de Ras Shamra 6; ed. C. F.-A. Schaeffer; Paris: Imprimerie Nationale et C. Klincksieck, 1955] 3:57, text 15.120, lines 17–19). The servants are nevertheless classed among property, since they have no legal rights.

The numbers of animals, though perfectly realistic for a wealthy man (cf. the three thousand sheep and one thousand goats of Nabal, 1 Sam 25:2), are obviously very stylized. The "round" figures seven and three, with their sum ten, are marks of the folktale style that charges superficially insignificant detail with symbolic value.

Job's "greatness," as the simple narrative style has it, is here entirely his "wealth" (for גדול "great" as "rich," cf. Gen 26:13; 1 Sam 25:2; 2 Sam 19:33 [32]; 2 Kgs 4:8). The expression "sons of the East" (בני־קדם) is a loose term applied indiscriminately to Arameans on the northern Euphrates (Gen 29:1) and inhabitants of more southerly regions like Edom, Moab and Ammon (Isa 11:14), or even Midian (cf. Judg 6:3). No more specific location than east of Israel can be established from the term (Fohrer and Hesse believe it pinpoints the region of Safa). That Job's wealth surpassed that of all the "sons of the East" does not necessarily imply that he is one of them (cf. 1 Kgs 5:10 [4:30], where Solomon's wisdom is said to be greater than that of all the "sons of the East"), though that is a natural interpretation. Other references to these peoples are in Gen 25:6; Jer 49:28; Ezek 25:10.

4   The narrative returns to the theme of Job's piety; one impressive example says more about the character of Job than any number of approbatory adjectives. At the same time the course of the narrative is advanced by this little cameo which explains how all the children of Job could happen to be together in the one place and so suffer the one fate that meets them all (1:18–19).

The seven sons of Job are envisaged as princes, each with a house of his own, as royal princes have in 2 Sam 13:7, 20; 14:31, and with the wealth to prepare an elaborate feast of food and wine (v 13) that would last for some days (v 4). Despite the number seven, which would correspond to the days of the week, it is not meant that Job's children indulged in year-round feasting (so Duhm, Dhorme, Hölscher, Fohrer, Rowley, cf. LXX; cf. also Luke 16:19). Even if that were the case, however, no censure is implied; a life of constant festivity (Peake) would be perfectly appropriate for the idyllic character of the portrayal. But the phrase "when the days of the feast had run their course" (v 5) describes best a feast that lasts some days (cf. the seven-day feasts in Judg 14:10–18 and Tob 11:19, and the seven days of the cultic festivals of Passover-Unleavened Bread and Booths), rather than the weekly conclusion of a cycle of feasts. The invitation to the sisters also suggests irregular, occasional festivities rather than an unceasing round of high living. The "day" of each brother would most naturally be his birthday (cf. "his day" in 3:1; and Hos 7:1) or perhaps is simply equivalent to "on his appointed day, i.e., when his turn came around" (Gordis). The occasions of the feasts are unlikely to have been annual festivals like Ingathering (as Pope), since such religious festivals would have been celebrated at the parental home. On the feast day, the sons, who are probably envisaged as unmarried (despite the prosaic remark of Driver: "for seven adult sons of a single mother . . . to be all unmarried would be flagrantly out of keeping with the social customs of the time and country"), would "send" and invite their sisters who, likewise unmarried, would still be living in their father's house. The participation of daughters in the banquets is a mark of the ancient epic character of the tale, according to N. M. Sarna, *JBL* 76 (1957) 24. Certainly what is depicted is a scene of domestic harmony and high spirits which will be darkened by the tragedy soon to ensue.

5   Job's piety is scrupulous, even excessively so, if not actually neurotically anxious. It would not be absurd to see here an almost obsessional *manie de perfection*, a hypersensitivity to detail (E. Gutheil, in W. Stekel, *Compulsion and Doubt* [tr. E. Gutheil; New York: Liveright, 1949] 9; J. Kahn, *Job's Illness: Loss, Grief, and Integration. A Psychological Interpretation* [Oxford: Pergamon, 1975] 18). But to some degree, as patriarchal head of a household, even of grown sons and daughters, it is reasonable enough for him to regard himself as responsible to God for their behavior, and to take the initiative in guarding against

any sin on their part. It is not supposed that his children may have sinned openly, whether in word or deed; their festivities are obviously decorous. It is somewhat strange then that Job should fear that they may have committed the gravest sin of all, to "curse God" (a sin punishable by death; cf. 2:9; 1 Kgs 21:10). The Hebrew, indeed, uses the normal term for "bless" (ברך), but since blessing God is no "sin," without question we have here a euphemistic use of the verb such as we find in 1:11; 2:5, 9; 1 Kgs 21:10, 13; Ps 10:3, where it prevents the connection of the divine name with a term of abuse.

The difficulty, unnoticed by most commentators, can be explained in two ways. First, the verb קלל, conventionally translated "curse"—the verb for which ברך "bless" no doubt stands here—means properly "despise, esteem lightly" (see C. A. Keller, *THWAT* 2:643; and cf. on 5:3 [קבב]). Job's concern may then be that they may have neglected or disregarded God in some way (JB "affronted" is hardly right), perhaps because of their preoccupation with pleasure—that is, that they may be guilty of a sin of omission rather than commission. This explanation, however, would give to the phrase "bless God" a different signification from what it clearly bears in 1:11; 2:5, 9 (a difficulty faced and accepted by Guillaume). A second explanation is perhaps more satisfactory, that "cursing God" is not the only sin that Job imagines his children may have committed but the extreme to which they may have descended without anyone else being aware. On this understanding, it would not be the possibility of inadvertent sin (cf. Driver) that troubles him, but the possibility of secret sin. With such an expression of Job's concern, his own still-future temptation would be foreshadowed. Observe, the narrator would be saying, how the man who will inconvenience himself for his children, just in case they may have "cursed God," will himself soon fall into a state where his wife—and a heavenly being—will see his "cursing God" as his most reasonable behavior.

Job's concern for the "holiness" of his family—by which is meant their ritual purity and their security within the sphere of the divine protection—leads him to "send" and "hallow" his children. There is a formal and archaizing touch in the word "send" (as there was in the same idiom in v 4); it is certainly not a matter of Job's patriarchal dignity not permitting him to visit his sons' houses (Pope). What is probably implied is that Job summons his children to the family home in order to be present at a sacrifice intended to decontaminate them from any stain they might have incurred. No special technical term is used for sin-offering (like the חטאת of the priestly legislation, e.g., Lev 4), but a general term עֹלָה "(ascending) sacrifice" (again not in the technical sense of "whole burnt offering," e.g., Lev 1). For the story's setting in place and time lies beyond the horizon of the priestly law. For the same reason, it is not any priest but Job himself, as head of the family, who offers the sacrifice (cf. Gen 8:20; 22:2, 13; 31:54; 46:1)—ten, or (if the sons alone are meant, which seems improbable) seven, animals.

Some have thought the "hallowing" (קדשׁ) a ritual preparatory to the sacrifice, involving washing and changing garments (cf. Gen 35:2; Exod 19:10, 14; Josh 3:5; 7:13; 1 Sam 16:5); so Davidson, Peake, Driver, Horst. Others (e.g., Dhorme), following B. Jacob (*ZAW* 32 [1912] 278–79), believe that קדשׁ of itself signifies the invitation to the sacrifice about to be performed (cf. קרא "summon" parallel to קדשׁ in Joel 1:14; 2:15; 4:9 [3:9]), but this is improbable. Since the sacrifice itself is designed to remove the sin that has possibly occurred, it is most natural to find in the phrase "he hallowed them" an anticipatory statement that is immediately thereafter amplified.

In the Book of Job, sacrifice is, surprisingly, not considered as a means of communication with the deity—apart from this passage and 42:8. The nearest approach to such actions is the reference made by Eliphaz to the paying of one's vows (22:27). But in general, as Job's account of his innocent life silently testifies, relationship with God is principally a matter of right behavior and not of religious exercises. In this the dialogues of the book are wholly at one with the stance of the wisdom teaching of Proverbs and Ecclesiastes; how much this stance represents an alternative posture in Israelite religion and how much it is consciously one-sided or legitimate only within the broader Israelite framework of history, covenant, and cult, is impossible to say. What is clear is that it is only in those parts of the book most obviously folkloristic and unbegotten by the wisdom tradition (the prologue and the epilogue) that sacrifice appears—as a natural, though not primary, means of contact between the human and the divine.

This little scene, in vv 4–5, has been narrated in the typically *faux naïf* style of our storyteller. Without any appearance of extravagance in the narration (no adjectives, no adverbs of quantity) the scene is rich in every aspect. There is uninterrupted domestic felicity, to which the sisters' presence at the festivities lends a further emphasis. There is an unbroken pattern of existence, in which the children's absorption in pleasure is matched by Job's devotion to their protection. There is his extraordinary scrupulousness that must cover even unseen sin, that must bestir itself "early in the morning," that must offer not one sacrifice but ten, that must never fail in its responsibility but "do so continually." This unwavering routine, no burden to Job any more than it is to his children, is not a monotony but the ominous prelude to an irruption into the lives of all.

6–12 *The Satan and God: first encounter.* From the timelessness of the first scene the narrator transports us to a particular time: "there was a day." And from the earthly sphere of the Easterners he takes us to the heavenly sphere of the divine court or council. So on the one hand this second scene sets the whole narrative in motion, and on the other hand it motivates the subsequent course of events. Here we learn what Job never learns, that his suffering had a particular cause and that it subserved a purpose. The cause of Job's suffering is unmistakably the Satan's challenge that Job's piety is not disinterested and God's acceptance of the challenge; the purpose of the suffering is to substantiate God's assessment of Job's piety and so justify God's claim to disinterested piety from humans.

This revelation (the term is exact) of the events that lie behind Job's suffering raises very acutely the question: is the book about Job or about a suffering man? Had we only chaps. 3–42:6 we should have no doubt of the latter. Will then the traditional narrative stuff in prologue and epilogue, with its specifics of name and place and its successive particular "days" (1:6, 13; 2:1), wholly subvert our deepest impression and constrict us to a view of the book as simple biography and not "wisdom" or "instruction" except in the bygoing? Can the very indeterminacy of the man's name and place and time not point to a hermeneutical transposition of key that has already begun to take place in the book itself, a transformation of an individual into an everyman? There is "none like Job," according to the traditional tale (v 8), yet at the same time it applies to him epithets suited to every innocent sufferer. If indeed Job is everyman—and the core of the book convinces us of that—is the cause of his suffering the cause of all innocent suffering, and was the day of the heavenly dialogue not some moment of archaic time but a timeless day in which the same scene is perpetually reenacted?

The vast bulk of the book, of course, proceeds in ignorance of such causes and purposes. There is no greater mark of the writer's subtlety than that the drama of Job's sufferings unfolding from chap. 3 to chap. 42 is never impinged on by the events in heaven as they are depicted in chaps. 1–2. We have no choice but to believe that chaps. 1–2 are the truth about the origins of Job's suffering; but we never feel that the origins are relevant to the suffering, and we never conceive the tragedy of the book to be the simple ignorance on Job's part of the events of chaps. 1–2. We even suspect that Job's suffering might have been the more had he known what we are given to know. We are not ignorant, but Job is; and the ignorance of Job belongs to the human condition no less than our knowledge. Job's ignorance of the causes behind his suffering is not swallowed up in our knowledge of those causes; if anything, Job's suffering in ignorance seems more meaningful to us than our knowledge negating his ignorance.

6 From a gathering on earth (vv 4–5), the scene moves to a more momentous gathering. It is an assembly of the heavenly council, God being pictured as a king surrounded by his courtiers, other heavenly beings neither human nor divine in the full sense, but "sons of God," their being derivative from his, and their rank superhuman. The concept of the royal council in which the king would be surrounded by his courtiers, receiving reports from them, taking counsel with them, and giving directives to them, is familiar especially from Egypt (cf. A. Erman, *Life in Ancient Egypt* [tr. H. M. Tirard; London: Macmillan, 1894] 69–72, 142–44) and may be assumed equally for Israel. The common royal practice was naturally ascribed to God also, to what extent as a fictive device and to what as a matter of serious belief is hard to determine. The clearest OT analogies to this scene are 1 Kgs 22:19–22, where Yahweh is envisaged by Micaiah ben Imlah as "sitting on a throne" (the royal imagery is explicit) with his courtiers on his right hand and on his left; and Dan 7:9–14, where the "ancient of days" is seated on a throne, thousands of courtiers attend him, and a court for judgment is constituted. Other allusions to the same complex of ideas appear in Ps 7:8 [7]; 29:9–10; 82:1; 89:7–8 [6–7]; 103:19; Isa 6:1–8; 40:13–14; Job 15:8. The appropriate terms for the council are סוֹד and עֵדָה. On the divine council, see further: H. W. Robinson, "The Council of Yahweh," *JTS* 45 (1943) 151–57; F. M. Cross, "The Council of Yahweh in Second Isaiah," *JNES* 12 (1953) 274–77; R. N. Whybray, *The Heavenly Counsellor in Isaiah xl 13–14* (SOTSMS 1; Cambridge: CUP, 1971). On the same concept in ancient Near Eastern religions (e.g., the *phr ilm* or *ʿdt ilm* in Ugaritic or the *puḫur ilāni* in Akkadian), see M. H. Pope, *El in the Ugaritic Texts* (VTSup 2; Leiden: Brill, 1955) 48–49; W. H. Schmidt, *Königtum Gottes in Ugarit und Israel* (BZAW 80; Berlin: A. Töpelmann, 2nd ed., 1966) 26–28.

The "sons of God" who comprise the heavenly court are known in other Near Eastern literature, but especially in Ugaritic, where the corresponding term *bn il* "son of God" or *dr bn il* "family of the sons of God" or *dr il* "family of God" appears (e.g., *CTA* 32.16–17; 15.3.19; Gibson, 92). In Canaanite religion the sons of God (El) are envisaged as his physical descendants; but the term "sons of" could also be used in Hebrew for members of a group belonging or adhering to, or in some way participating in the nature of, their "father" (e.g., "sons of the prophets"; cf. also BDB, 121b, § 7a). In the framework of a monotheistic religion, in which a consort of the deity could not be imagined, the latter view naturally prevailed. These heavenly beings (בני [ה]אלהים, בני עליון, אלים) are paralleled in 38:7 with the morning stars, identified with the "host of heaven" in 1 Kgs 22:19 and called simply "gods" in Ps 82:1, 6 (cf. also Gen 6:2, 4; Deut 32:8 [emended]; Ps 29:1; 89:7 [6]; Dan 3:25). The same figures are known as "messengers, angels" or the "servants" of God (see on 4:18); in later Jewish and in Christian theology such references in the OT were interpreted as signifying angels (the term by which the LXX here translates "sons of God"). See further W. Herrmann, "Die Göttersöhne," *ZRGG* 12 (1960) 242–51; G. Cooke, "The Sons of (the) God(s)," *ZAW* 76 (1964) 22–47; M. Tsevat, "God and the Gods in Assembly," *HUCA* 40/41 (1969–70) 123–37; C. H. W. Brekelmans, "The Saints of the Most High and Their Kingdom," *OTS* 14 (1965) 305–29.

On one particular day the "sons of God" come to "present themselves" (התיצב) before Yahweh; the verb signifies the appearance of courtiers before their king in order to make their reports and receive instructions (cf. Prov 22:29; Zech 6:5; the same idea is represented by the more common phrase "stand before" [לפני], e.g., 1 Kgs 22:21). N. M. Sarna saw in the term a fixed traditional phraseology (*JBL* 76 [1957] 13–25 [22–23]). No particular day of assembly is envisaged by the story, although the Targum identified the day as "the day of judgment at the beginning of the year" (יומא דדינא בריש שתא) and the subsequent day in 2:1 as the Day of Atonement, these two days being in rabbinic ideology the days on which the destiny of humans is determined and then finally sealed. The phrase "there came a day when" (ויהי היום + *waw* consecutive and "imperfect") not infrequently introduces a scene without any stress being laid on the nature of the day (e.g., 1 Sam 14:1; 2 Kgs 4:8, 11, 18; see also n. 1:6.a).

Among the "sons of God" comes the Satan. Some indeed have argued that because it is explicitly said that he came "among them" (בתוכם) he cannot have belonged to their number (Terrien) or that "it is because he has no right to be there that he alone is asked his business" (Andersen; cf. Dhorme, "Among the sons of God Satan has insinuated himself"). But to be "among" frequently enough expresses membership of the group in question; thus Gen 23:10; 40:20; 2 Kgs 4:13; and cf. the common expression "from among" which regularly implies membership of the group. And the fact that the Satan is singled out for God's inquiry has no other purpose than a narrative one: in some way the dialogue of God and the Satan must be set in train; what more natural means than to have God ask of the Satan the question we may safely assume is consistently addressed to all the "sons of God" who arrive at the court with something to report? On another "day," in another story, the Satan would be lost in the crowd of courtiers; today a drama will unfold in which he is to play a principal part.

What is the character and function of this member of the "sons of God," the "Satan"? We note first that the definite article appears before the term at

each of its occurrences in the book (1:6, 7 *bis,* 8, 9, 12 *bis;* 2:1, 2 *bis,* 3, 4, 6, 7);
this fact prevents us from identifying the figure of the Satan with "Satan" of
later Jewish and Christian theology. Although the latter is clearly derived from
the former, it would be best to ignore the later development of the figure
when establishing the nature and role of "the Satan" in Job. Semantic approaches
are valuable only to a limited extent: there is a verb שָׂטַן (*śṭn*) meaning "be,
or act as, an adversary" (so BDB), or "bear a grudge, cherish animosity" (so
KB); its occurrences in Ps 38:21 [20]; 71:13; 109:4, 20, 29 all refer to human
opponents of the psalmists, and only in the manifestly quite late passage Zech
3:1 is the verb used of the activity of "the Satan." The noun itself (שָׂטָן) is
applied to human adversaries in 1 Sam 29:4; 2 Sam 19:23 [22]; 1 Kgs 5:18 [4];
11:14, 23, 25; Ps 109:6 (in a legal context). It cannot be decided whether the
verb is derived from the noun (as a denominative; so BDB) or vice versa, but
the well-attested usage of both verb and noun in secular settings confirms
that we have to do here not with a title but with a description of function.
(The verb שָׂטַם, if a variant form of שָׂטַן, makes no difference to the discussion,
since its meaning is identical with שָׂטַן; in that it is used of God's hostility to
Job [see 16:9; 30:21] it may represent an intentional differentiation from שָׂטַן.)

In general, therefore, the usage of the terms elsewhere shows that the "Satan"
here is some kind of opponent or adversary; but that much is obvious from
the narrative itself. Further precisions about his function can come only from
the story. First, is he God's adversary or Job's? Later theological development
of the figure of Satan preconditions the reader to say, "God's"; but the story
here makes it evident that the Satan is Yahweh's subordinate, presenting himself
before him as one of his courtiers, responding to Yahweh's initiatives, and
powerless to act without Yahweh's authorization. His only undelegated capacity
is to "allure, incite" Yahweh (2:3), which must mean only "attempt to allure,
etc." (like פתה "attempt to persuade"; cf. D. J. A. Clines and D. M. Gunn,
VT 28 [1978] 20–27). So the Satan of this story is *Job's* adversary. But is he
his adversary by nature, that is, because he is an adversary to humans generally,
some kind of embodiment of superhuman hostility, or is he Job's adversary
because of the way things develop? Is he perhaps called "the adversary" only
proleptically (similarly T. H. Gaster, *Myth, Legend, and Custom in the Old Testament*
[London: Duckworth, 1969] 786)? Hesse even suggests that the Job story once
called him only a "spirit" (cf. 1 Kgs 22:21), and that the term "the Satan"
became attached to him only in the course of postexilic development of demonology. The narrative does not say whether he is the "Satan" by nature or by
reason of this episode, but precisely because the latter is a possibility, we need
to be shy of typecasting the "Satan" pictured here as the archenemy of mankind,
the "adversary the devil [who] prowls around like a roaring lion, seeking someone to devour" (1 Pet 5:8). Though his question prompts the assault on Job,
and though he is the immediate instrument of Job's sufferings, his responsibility
is certainly no greater than Yahweh's—and is actually less, since Yahweh is
under no compulsion (as far as the story is concerned) to take the slightest
notice of the Satan. The Satan, in short, is Job's adversary; from the point of
view of the action, more so than Yahweh, but from the point of view of the
ethics, less so than Yahweh.

Many descriptions of the Satan offered by commentators fall to the ground
if the story itself is taken as the primary frame of reference. The Satan is not

"bad," "evil," "malevolent," "cynical" (Peake, Gordis). We cannot say that "Satan takes his duty too seriously, until it poisons his own nature" (Rowley), or that "he has lost all faith in human goodness" (Peake). Nor is he here, whatever the origins of such a figure may have been, the author of all misfortune and especially illness (Hölscher, 3). Nor is he primarily a legal "accuser" (G. von Rad, *TDNT* 2:73–74; cf. שׂטן in Ps 109:6, though Fohrer denies the existence of such a figure in Israelite judicial proceedings). In Zech 3:1 the Satan appears as a potential accuser, in 1 Chr 21:1 (cf. 2 Sam 24:1) as an inciter to evil, an *agent provocateur;* but such is not the case here. He is "rigidly subordinated to heaven, and in all he does subserves its interests" (Davidson).

When all that is said, the role of the Satan remains tantalizing. The freedom with which he can address his lord, the influence he can have upon him, and the plenipotentiary powers granted him all seem more at home in a polytheistic culture than in the world of the OT. Although in the strictest sense a belief in monotheism is in no particular challenged here, the scene echoes in spirit the assembly of the gods, whether in the Mesopotamian heaven, in the Canaanite "heights of the north," or on the Hellenic Olympus. Whether or not the scene is borrowed from non-Israelite storytelling, it gives us a rather unusual glimpse into the mythic and imaginative possibilities for depicting and understanding the divine world that are still open even when the door has been firmly closed on polytheism.

Viewed as a method, whether conceptual or purely literary, whether deliberate or unconscious, for grasping the pluriformity of the divine, the conceptualization of the "sons of God" (or, "angels," as later Christian theology would term them) is profound. Whether "sons of God" exist or not is beside the point; the point is that human experience of authoritative persons taking counsel and devolving functions requires a parallel arrangement in the heavenly sphere if God is to be viewed as knowledgeable and wise and as deciding rather than merely executing, delegating authority rather than being enmeshed in trivialities. Such a vision of God can of course become utterly one-sided, and the dignity of the divine ruler can petrify into a stubborn unapproachableness; but Old and New Testaments alike are remarkably successful in handling the ambivalence of the official and the personal in God. Everywhere, the antinomies of transcendence and immanence present themselves in an unaccountably random pattern (e.g., the "transcendent" God of the priestly history "makes" animals and reptiles and "shuts the door" of Noah's ark, while the "immanent" Lord of the early church "sends" an "angel" to rescue Peter from prison), so that far from permitting evident lines of development to be traced, the material demands a constant bifocal perception.

All in all, distinctions between God and God's "angel" are rather arbitrary (see also W. Eichrodt, *Theology of the Old Testament* [tr. J. A. Baker; London: SCM, 1967] 2:23–27), as is witnessed by the several occasions of angel-appearances that turn out to be theophanies, and—within the Book of Job—by the superficial contradiction between the narrative's affirmation of the Satan's causality of Job's suffering (1:12; 2:6–7), and the dialogue's insistence that God is directly the author of Job's misfortunes (e.g., 6:4; 7:14; 9:17). Without invoking the suspect concept of "corporate personality" or of servants as the "extensions" of their master's personality (as A. R. Johnson, *The One and the Many in the Israelite Conception of God* [Cardiff: University of Wales, 1961]; cf. J. W.

Rogerson, "The Hebrew Conception of Corporate Personality: A Re-examination," *JTS* ns 21 [1970] 1–16), we can suggest that "sons of God" or "angels" are manifestations of the divine personality, the means of execution of divine decisions, the source of the divine acquisition of knowledge of human affairs. That they are *only* personifications of divine attributes, powers, or dispositions is beyond the competence of any human to tell; but they are that at least.

If this is so, the "sons of God" have theological value as an embodiment of God's accumulated wisdom, continuing self-deliberation, and multifarious acts of decision. How does the "Satan" fit into such an interpretation? His function is primarily twofold: he raises the question of whether Job's piety is disinterested, and he puts into effect the divine authorization to afflict Job. Neither function is in the least inappropriate to God himself. Perhaps it puts it overdramatically to represent the Satan as a manifestation of divine doubt, an embodiment of the demonic wrath of God, an expression of the "dark" and sinister side of the divine personality (as R. R. Schärf, "Die Gestalt des Satans im Alten Testament," in C. G. Jung, *Symbolik des Geistes: Studien über psychische Phänomenologie* [Psychologische Abhandlungen 6; Zurich: Rascher, 1948] 151–319). But Job himself experiences his suffering as manifestations of God's wrath (see especially chap. 9), and the notion of divine uncertainty and doubt is not foreign to the OT (see further D. J. A. Clines, "Story and Poem: The Old Testament as Literature and as Scripture," *Int* 34 [1980] 115–27 [126]; J. G. Janzen, "Metaphor and Reality in Hosea 11," *Sem* 24 [1982] 7–44). Seen in this light, the book shows Job performing for God a signal service (is he not repeatedly called by God "my servant Job"?; cf. on v 8): he justifies God in the sight of God. It is not primarily the Satan that God has to convince that a human's piety may be disinterested, but God himself.

That is a theological reading of the story; it is not—we may suppose—the storyteller's intention. For him, there are two heavenly personalities in uneasy confrontation; two personalities who are not equals but able to converse freely, who are neither enemies nor conspirators, neither friends nor rivals. The tension of these two personalities can be simply accepted as a datum of the narrative, or it can be probed theologically for its hidden resonances. What may be stressed is that the theological reading presented here is not some fanciful psychological extrapolation from the story, but meshes with it at all its significant points. Thus if it is difficult to imagine a God who doubts himself and must test the loyalty of Job to restore his own self-confidence (theological interpretation), is it any more difficult than to imagine a God who needs to allow a "Satan" to afflict Job to see whether Job's piety is disinterested (story-line)? The "God of the philosophers" (in Pascal's phrase) could in an instant dismiss the question of the Satan by a categorical assurance about Job's motives; but the God of this story needs to wait for the infliction of the suffering to know Job's response. The God of the story is more "human" than many would care to admit; any appropriate reading of the story will preserve that flavor. On the figure of the Satan, see further G. von Rad, *TDNT* 2:73–74; A. Brock-Utne, "'Der Feind': Die alttestamentliche Satansgestalt im Lichte der sozialen Verhältnisse des nahen Orients," *Klio* 28 (1935) 219–27; H. Torczyner (Tur-Sinai), *ExpT* 48 (1936–37) 563–65; A. Lods, "Les origines de la figure de Satan, ses fonctions à la cour céleste," in *Mélanges Syriens* (FS René Dussaud [Paris: P. Geuthner, 1939]) 2:649–60; M. J. Gruenthaner, "The Demonology of the Old Testament," *CBQ* 6 (1944) 6–27; R. Schärf Kluger, *Satan in the Old*

Testament (Chicago: Northwestern UP, 1967); G. Wanke, *THWAT* 2:821–23; T. H. Gaster, *IDB* 4:224–28.

7 It belongs to the naivety (superficial though that may be) of the narrator's style that Yahweh asks the Satan from where he comes. Such a question does not imply ignorance on God's part (as Duhm thought); Exod 4:2, where God asks Moses, "What is that in your hand?," is often cited as a similar case where there can be no doubt that God already knows the answer. The question has a dramatic function in focusing upon the Satan as the one significant member of the "sons of the gods"—for this narrative at any rate—and in providing an impetus for the ensuing conversation and its sequel; and it has a role-establishing function in making Yahweh the initiator of the conversation and the action that follows. Cf. especially H. Rouillard, "Les feintes questions divines dans la Bible," *VT* 34 (1984) 237–42; and also L. Koehler, "Archäologisches. Nr. 16–19," *ZAW* 40 (1922) 15–46 (38); B. O. Long, "Two Question and Answer Schemata," *JBL* 90 (1971) 129–39.

It is easy to read too much into the Satan's reply. The false naivety of the style indeed permits, and perhaps even encourages, various subtleties among interpreters. Duhm saw in the Satan's response a sign that he is "the vagabond among the heavenly beings," the one with no fixed purpose but a roving commission. Peake, to similar effect, contrasted the assignment of fixed regions to some at least of the "sons of God" (cf. Deut 32:8; Dan 10:13, 20–21; Ecclus 17:17) with the unrestricted function of the Satan. Pope notes that the verb for "roam" (שׁוּט) is applied in Akkadian to the evil eye and evil spirits that roam around looking for trouble or the opportunity to do evil; this connects with his identification of the Satan figure as analogous to the secret police of the Persian government, known as the "eyes" and "ears" of the king. Gordis sees in the short staccato reply an expression of the Satan's "impudence before his master," while Andersen finds the Satan's reply "non-committal" and "evasive."

But the language of his reply supports none of this. The verb שׁוּט refers predominantly to going about for a particular purpose (Num 11:8, to search for manna; 2 Sam 24:8, to take a census; Jer 5:1, to see if a righteous man can be found in Jerusalem; Amos 8:12, to seek a word from Yahweh; cf. 2 Chr 16:9; Ezek 27:8, 26; Zech 4:10; only Dan 12:4 [polel] and Jer 49:3 [hithpolel] appear to be exceptions). The translations "roaming" (NAB, NIV, cf. JB) and "strolling about" (Pope) for the next verb are altogether too casual. This second verb התהלך, though conventionally translated "walk to and fro," very frequently means no more than its simple form הלך "go, walk"—for example, in the sense "live, behave" (e.g., Gen 17:1; 24:40)—and it certainly does not necessarily denote aimless or haphazard movement (cf., e.g., Gen 13:17 "walk through the length and breadth of the land").

Whether the implication is that the Satan's particular mission has been to assess the piety of humans, as may appear from the next verse (so Fohrer, Hesse), is hard to determine. Most probably the reason for the Satan's movement throughout the earth is simply not specified for dramatic reasons: he has nothing to report, nothing to advise, nothing to initiate; but he has nevertheless been abroad on earth with his eyes wide open, amassing the reserve of observations which his sovereign can use as he wills. His one task has been to "set [his] mind" upon human affairs, as will transpire from v 8.

8 The heavenly convocation almost seems to have as its chief function this narrowing of the focus of attention to the one figure Job. In the first scene, Job first appeared alone in the center of the stage (v 1); around him accumulated his possessions (vv 2–3). The children then moved to center stage (v 4), but only to illuminate the character of Job, who eventually stepped back into the center again (v 5). In this second scene, a multitude who do not include Job occupy the stage (v 6), and a dialogue ensues between the two principal characters (v 7) and focuses ultimately upon the (absent) character of Job (v 8), revolves about him (vv 9–12a) and concludes with the spotlight upon the Satan (v 12b), whose function has now become wholly Job-directed. In the first scene, the movement has been from the one to the many to the one again; in the second scene, from the many to the one. And whether the scene is set on earth or in heaven, Job is at its center.

Job is God's boast. Not only does God endorse the author's characterization of Job in v 1, using exactly the same words, "a man blameless and upright, a God-fearer, a shunner of evil," but also denominates Job "my servant" and declares "there is none like him in the earth." (It is of course equally the author's evaluation of Job whether he expresses it in his own person in v 1 or sets it in the mouth of God in v 8, but he means to dispel any shadow of doubt that Job's piety may be only seeming and to have the God from whom Job's afflictions will stem affirm his own cognizance of Job's character.)

The term "my servant" is frequently applied to individuals by God, but not indiscriminately to all kinds of pious persons. Most often Moses is the one designated God's servant (forty times in all), perhaps principally because of his prophetic role (cf. Num 12:7–8), the prophets also often being called servants of Yahweh, especially in Deuteronomistic phraseology (e.g., 1 Kgs 14:18; 15:29). But perhaps the use of this term for Job belongs with its application to the patriarchs, Abraham (Gen 26:24; Ps 105:6, 42), Isaac (Gen 24:14; 1 Chr 16:13 [*si v.l.*; contrast RSV]), Abraham, Isaac, and Jacob (Exod 32:13; Deut 9:27); it would be a further example of the "patriarchal" shading of the narrative. In any case, the term signifies the "obedience, loyalty and piety of Job towards his divine master as well as God's bond with him and claim upon him" (Fohrer). See further W. Zimmerli, *TDNT* 5:665–66; C. Westermann, *THWAT* 2:191–93.

One phrase, however, in God's description does not identify Job, but apparently isolates him: "there is none like him in the earth." "None like him" is a phrase usually applied to God; only here and in 2:3; 1 Sam 10:24 to humans. Here it is the rhetoric of epic; it does not mean that Job's piety is qualitatively different from that of others. This claim that there is none to compare with Job in point of piety is at bottom no more than what the narrator has already made out in his account of Job in the first scene.

Again, it is possible to read this question of God's as a taunt or provocation (Pope), as if in Job he has found the final rebuttal of the Satan's hostile attitude to humankind (similarly Fohrer). But if, as has been argued above, the Satan has no specific purpose in his earthly rovings except to see and hear all he can, and if the Satan is not necessarily predisposed to enmity, God's question can be heard as a "straight," unloaded question arising from God's pleasure in Job. Of course, once the next sentence is uttered, it becomes plain that the matter of Job's piety is not as simple as it sounds; herein lies the "false" naivety of the storyteller's style: God's question is both guileless and pregnant

with implication. To hear it simply as a challenge to the Satan is too sophisticated;
to take it purely at its face value is to fall prey to the artful naivety of the
narrative.

Little should be made of the fact that it is (or appears to be) a non-Israelite
who is thus described by God as his servant (as is Nebuchadrezzar in Jer 25:9)
and beyond comparison. Hesse, for example, remarks how strange such compli-
ments about a non-Israelite must have sounded in the ears of a pious Hebrew;
he attributes them to the influence of the international "wisdom" tradition
that knew no national boundaries. Certainly Job is human being simply rather
than specifically an Israelite (though the latter is not excluded), and in the
ambience of the book as a whole, matters specifically Israelite are conspicuous
by their absence. But the question of Job's national identity has in all probability
receded into the background by this point, where the spotlight falls on the
relationship of a man and his God.

In all his comings and goings, has the Satan "given his attention" (שִׂים לֵב,
lit., "set the heart") to Job? Of course he has, not just because of Job's exemplary
life (Gordis), but because of the Satan's diligence.

9 The Satan also implicitly assents to the assessment of Job expressed by
the narrator (v 1) and God (v 8)! He cannot call into question Job's incomparable
piety. Nor does he doubt its sincerity, its genuineness. What he must question—
and what *must* be questioned (there is nothing "satanic" about the question)—
is what the link between Job's godliness and his prosperity is. In the "false
naivety" of the epic story it has not been questioned—rather taken for granted—
that Job's piety has been the source of his prosperity (see on v 2); the link is
causal, from piety to prosperity. In the heavenly realm, where it is the business
of all to *know*, and not to be taken in by naive assumptions, the question is
entirely proper: is the causal link perhaps rather in the reverse direction,
from prosperity to piety? In a word, does Job "fear God" gratuitously (חִנָּם,
"for nothing, for no reward," as in Gen 29:15; Isa 52:3)?

Here is "wisdom" thinking at work. If the causal connection between sin
and suffering can be radically examined in the book as a whole, with the
result that the popular, naive preconception is overturned, why cannot the
supposed causal connection between piety and prosperity be subjected to the
same scrutiny? Cynicism it may seem to ask "Doth Job fear God for naught?"
(KJV), and diabolical cynicism is what most commentators insist on ascribing
to the Satan here. But we do not yet know, and the characters of the narrative
do not yet know, whether Job's piety is disinterested or not; it is a question
that we all, in company with the heavenly court, would like to hear settled.
Job has indeed "feared" (יָרֵא, perfect tense) God up to this point, but will he
prove to have the character of a "God-fearer" (יָרֵא, participle) in the future?

The Satan indeed means to imply in this speech (vv 9–11) that Job's piety
is not disinterested, and in this respect is properly functioning as the "Satan,"
the accuser. Not the "devil" himself, he is remarkably analogous to the function-
ary in Christendom known as *advocatus diaboli* whose task is to raise objections
to the canonization of a saint; his office and his appointment owe their existence
to the body that actively supports the canonization, and his role is to ensure
that no potential criticism of the candidate remains unheard and unanswered.
The Satan in Job speaks more dramatically and rhetorically than a canon
lawyer designated devil's advocate, but his function may be no different. Is

there anything at all that can be said against the exceptional piety of Job? Yes, says the Satan, his piety may be conditioned by self-interest. He does not suggest that he knows human nature better than God does, that he is less naïve than the deity (Terrien); he voices the doubt that exists long before it is uttered. And it is a doubt, as will be shown by the reaction of Yahweh (v 12) to the Satan's speech, that exists also in the divine mind. It will be some time before it is revealed whether Job's piety is truly gratuitous and without motivating reasons. In the end, his piety is revealed to be a kind of *imitatio Dei*, whose workings are equally gratuitous and inexplicable (cf. A. Lacocque, "'Est-ce gratuitement que Job craint Dieu?'" in *Mélanges André Neher*, ed. E. Amado-Valensi, et al., 175–79).

10 The previous question has not been a rhetorical question (as against Fohrer and others), and the questions of this verse are motivations for that serious query. God has so prospered Job that piety and prosperity are inextricably entangled. Job has been surrounded as if by a thorn hedge protecting him from all manner of harm (in Hos 2:8 [6] Yahweh uses a thorn hedge [the same verb שׂוך] to block the way of idolatrous Israel toward her Baal-lovers). The metaphor is rich in psychic undertones: the act of encompassing that can be experienced as protection can be felt as constriction and stiflement (cf. on 3:23; and see Lam 3:7; and with different terminology, Job 6:9; 7:12, 15, 19; 9:18a; 12:14; 13:27; 19:6, 8, 12; etc.). Within the security of the perimeter fence about Job and his possessions there has persisted a divine blessing on the "works of his hands" (the result of agriculture, cf. Gen 5:29), such as is promised in Deuteronomic parenesis to those obedient to Yahweh (Deut 14:29; 16:15; 24:19; cf. 2:7; 15:10; and cf. Ps 90:17) and—as if to block out the negative resonances of the term "hedge"—within the hedge there has been a "breaking forth" (פרץ "break out," hence "overflow") into abundance of "possessions" (מקנה, primarily the flocks of v 3) such as is narrated of the patriarchs (the same term is used of Jacob, Gen 30:30, 43; cf. also 28:14; Exod 1:12). The "you" is emphatic, not to criticize God in some way—as if to say that God has made piety altogether too easy for Job (so Fohrer, Andersen)—but to affirm the absolute security afforded Job.

11 The Satan's language is abrupt, peremptory. He uses the imperative voice in addressing God; he makes his prediction of Job's behavior in colloquial fashion with a "self-imprecation" ("I'll be damned if he doesn't curse you to your face"); above all "he refuses to use the conventional courtesies of court etiquette which avoided the personal pronouns by addressing a superior as 'my lord' instead of 'you' and using the deferential 'your slave' instead of 'I'" (Andersen). Andersen finds in these marks of insulting speech, as he sees them, further evidence that "the Satan does not belong to the circle of God's respectful servants."

But we must recall what kind of court scene is depicted here. There are none of the trappings of the oriental imperial states: no throne, no heavenly temple, no seraphim, no incense (as in Isa 6:1–4); not even a throne with the host of heaven arrayed before Yahweh on right and left, as in the much humbler portrayal by Micaiah (1 Kgs 22:19–23). It belongs to the naivety of the Joban story, in which not one word descriptive of the heavenly scene appears, except the presence of the "sons of God," that courtly deference is uncalled for and direct language the order of the day. It is the court of Saul rather than of

Solomon (and certainly not of the Egyptian or Assyrian empire) that forms the model for the conversational etiquette of these scenes; perhaps even more accurately, it is the court of the chieftain Job himself (depicted hyperbolically in chap. 29) that is the earthly analogue of the scene. So nothing consequential can be inferred from the style of the Satan's language.

What of its content? The dynamic of the conversation has the Satan propose that Job should be deprived of his prosperity and assert that Job's piety will forthwith be transformed into hatred of God. The proposal is cruel and unnatural, the prediction malicious speculation. Surely here is the firmest ground for calling the Satan purely hateful, cynical, and, in short, wicked. That is the "naive" reading of the story (and "naive" is not pejorative, for the narrative clearly engages our sympathies with Job and against the Satan).

But here too a "false" naivety is in play. For the "problem" of the prologue is the relation of piety and prosperity, and it is in no other way possible to prove that piety is not the product of prosperity than by removing the prosperity. True, if some poor man had been singled out for his exemplary piety, there would have been no point in depriving him of what he did not possess in order to establish a point; yet, if such had been the tale, the "problem" might well have been whether piety is not causally related to poverty (perhaps, after all, the poor trust God because they have nothing else to trust), and the dramatic move would then have to be an enrichment of the poor man, to see whether his piety survived his new wealth. In either case, the "problem" can be solved dramatically only by a reversal of fortunes.

So the proposal of the Satan is, on a slightly more sophisticated reading, a necessary part of the dramatic machinery, and is not eligible for moral approval or disapproval. There is indeed no "cause" in Job to provoke the horrible train of events that will unfold: his suffering is, on the narrative level, gratuitous (cf. on 2:3). But on the conceptual level, his suffering is indispensable if the archaic doctrine of piety leading inevitably to prosperity (as in v 2) is to be upset. And the abruptly imperative language is not the mark of disrespect, but the idiom of colloquial speech that puts the hypothesis (protasis) as an imperative and the consequence (apodosis) as an affirmative statement. Suppose the Satan to have said, "If you should simply put forth your hand . . . then you would find he would forswear his piety"; the proposition would have been the same, but the dramatic impact much weakened (on the syntax, see further n. 1:11.a). All that need be recognized is that the Satan is not bullying God, and certainly not offering him a wager.

The idea of a heavenly wager has often been seen here by commentators (Hölscher, 2–3; Fohrer; Weiser; H. Gunkel, *The Folktale in the Old Testament* [tr. M. D. Rutter; Sheffield: Almond, 1988] 84–85), but there is nothing that is obviously at stake, such as Job's soul (Andersen). The often-cited Indian tale of King Harischandra, a pious king who suffers afflictions not dissimilar to Job's, can hardly be part of the background, but in some of its forms may itself reflect the biblical story of Job. For a full review of this and other alleged Indian parallels to the Job story, see D. J. A. Clines, *VT* 33 (1983) 398–418.

Is the Satan then *challenging* God? On the level of the story he challenges God to a trial of Job because God has taken for granted what popular thought takes for granted, that piety and prosperity are not independent of one another. On the conceptual level, the challenge is directed against this naive assumption.

In the story as such the Satan is not more clever than God, nor does he
know more than God (Driver, Fohrer); and he does not score off God; conceptu-
ally, however, the question he voices demands to be asked, and on the conceptual
level it makes no difference who asks it. The conceptual dynamic requires
God to agree to the proposal, because conceptual problems cannot be shoveled
underground; the narrative dynamic of itself could have elicited all kinds of
different responses from God, but here the conceptual dynamic has got the
upper hand, for this point is the hinge of the whole prologue.

The link between Job's piety and his prosperity has never been tested. It
needs only God to "stretch out" (שלח) his hand (a picturesque detail [Duhm];
for the hand as symbol of God's power, cf. Exod 13:3; Deut 4:34; for the
phrase "stretch out the hand" in order to smite, cf. Exod 3:20; 9:15) and to
"smite" (נגע, not merely "touch" as in many versions; cf. *Comment* on 4:5) all
that is Job's, and Job will not only abandon his scrupulous piety but turn
upon God and "curse" him "to (his) face," i.e., directly, impudently, and certainly
not "in his heart, secretly" (cf. v 5). The language is heightened, of course;
Job cannot be, in this story, a man of moderate piety, nor can he lapse into
lukewarm impiety. Again it is the naivety of the style that determines the
content, and that has the Satan affirm Job's inevitable "curse" with a speech-
form that originated as a self-imprecation (sc. "if he does not curse you, may
I myself be cursed by some dreadful [unspecified] fate"). The "falseness" of
the naivety lies in the fact that what is at stake is not the behavior of this one
man Job, but the validity of the principle of reward and of the causal nexus
between ethics and success.

So the "test" is proposed. We are reminded of the "testing" of Abraham
(Gen 22), where the "test" is of Abraham's loyalty to God's command *and* to
the countermanding of God's command. Here the test only appears to be a
test of Job's piety; it is in reality a test of whether Job's piety stems from his
prosperity. The narrative level for a moment merges with the conceptual.
The test is not exactly a test of Job's motives, for despite the opinion of many
commentators, it is not suggested, not even by the Satan, that prosperity is
the motive of Job's piety (cf. *Comment* on חנם "gratuitously" in v 9); rather, it
is because the prosperity is intertwined with the piety that the prosperity must
be removed in order to uncover the relationship between the two.

12   So naturally does Yahweh's agreement to the proposal follow that we
are compelled to pause in order to ponder its implications. Are we to condemn
the figure of Yahweh here for his alacrity and cold-bloodedness (Duhm) in
assenting to such a scheme? And do we find in the prohibition of harm to
Job's person the one lingering sign of Yahweh's affection for his servant? Or
is it that God himself does not need to be convinced of Job's disinterested
piety, but is prepared to allow the Satan to satisfy himself of its reality (Rowley),
or, to put it more positively, accepts the challenge in order to vindicate his
servant against the insinuations of the Satan (Peake)? Or are we to say, most
improbably of all, that God assents to the trial of Job's piety in order to refine
or deepen Job's faith?

All these suggestions attribute to the narrative a subtlety it does not bear,
at least in its essential story-line. God can agree to the proposal to "smite" all
that is Job's only because he too, like everyone else, does not know what the
outcome will be. The Yahweh of this tale is not the absolutely omniscient

God of later systematic or speculative theology. He is wise beyond human comprehension, for his "eyes" and "ears," like the spies of the Persian kings, are everywhere abroad, and report to him on days of assembly (cf. v 6). But not even Yahweh knows what has not yet happened; his knowledge does not encompass all possible hypothetical situations. He has confidence in Job, but not a confidence that would enable him to use Job as an object lesson to refute the Satan's aspersions. He too has taken it for granted that he will bless the pious man; but that benign reciprocity has obscured the true relation of piety and prosperity. The Satan has the right to ask the question, and Yahweh is in the right in having the problem probed.

The alternative to such a reading of the story is worse. Affirm that Yahweh is infinitely omniscient, and you assert that Job's suffering serves only to prove God right in the eyes of one of his subordinates. Affirm that Yahweh knows that Job will not waver, and you cannot explain why Yahweh takes the slightest notice of the Satan's questions or why he does not dismiss them out of hand from superior knowledge.

If now we move beyond the story-line and essay a probe into the theological resonances of this element of the story along the lines sketched in the *Comment* on v 6, the uncertainty in the divine world presses for a resolution. Is the problem one of heaven's making or of earth's? Suppose that an immutable law of retribution were heaven's design; the question would always wait to be posed whether the retribution was no simple single process of cause and effect, but an endlessly revolving circle, with no possibility of discerning what was cause and what effect. That is, if the godly were always rewarded with earthly blessings which in turn promoted greater godliness, heaven would be confronted with the perennial chicken-and-egg conundrum, and heaven itself would not know what was really happening on earth. But suppose the immutable law of retribution were only a human inference on the part of the "wise" (or the naive) about the manner of heaven's working, would not those shy of immutability in the deity crave some heaven-inspired drama to cripple the dogma and open up space in heaven and on earth for personal freedom? In either case the trial of Job is as necessary for loosing the causal nexus between piety and prosperity as it is for establishing the independence of suffering and guilt.

Yahweh delivers into the Satan's "hand" all that Job possesses (but not the man himself). It is understood that Yahweh has agreed to "stretch forth [his] hand" and "smite" what is Job's, and the delegation of the actual task to the Satan is entirely what we should expect given the scene of a monarch and his courtiers. Nothing is to be made of the fact that "Yahweh himself will not smite. He permits the Satan to do it" (Peake). This for three reasons: first, delegated permission is delegated authority and the ultimate delegator has the ultimate responsibility; second, the story does not distinguish between command and permission; third, if there is any significant difference between God's part and the Satan's part in the affliction of Job, Job's complaints against God in the speeches (always against God and never against the Satan) would be to that extent wide of the mark, a conclusion the book as a whole does not allow us to entertain.

The Satan "goes forth" (יצא, the correlative of התיצב "present oneself" in v 6) from the heavenly council in order to perform his task (cf. יצא in 1 Kgs 22:22; Zech 6:5). That he goes "swiftly" (Duhm), "without delay" (Weiser), "eager" (Andersen), or "intent, like Judas, on his ghastly errand" (Peake), is what the narrator has no concern to say; it will indeed be another day (v 13) when the disasters strike Job's possessions (contrast perhaps 2:7). Nor is this simple notation of the Satan's exit a mere narrative link, though it is obviously that at least. The Satan is obedient to what he perceives as his master's will, be it expressed directly or apparently as only "permission."

13–22 *Announcement of disasters to Job, and Job's response.* The storyteller reaches the perfection of his art in this central scene of the five that form the prologue. The contrast between the "before" and "after" of Job's state is depicted in truly dramatic fashion; for it is the simple train of events and not some convoluted chain of consequences that spells out the disaster. The opening sentence of the scene depicts afresh the carefree life of Job's children already portrayed in v 4, and "leaves us to think of Job still tranquil and unexpectant of evil up to the very point when the first messenger of ill comes" (Driver).

The focus is entirely upon Job, and not upon the disasters themselves, for the issues of the prologue revolve entirely about this man. Dramatically, the spotlight remains fixed upon Job, since the narrative advances only to the measure in which Job himself becomes aware of the disasters. The device of the messengers admirably focuses concentration upon Job rather than upon the scenes of disaster, and at the same time creates an atmosphere of accelerating doom: each messenger after the first arrives before his predecessor has told his tale; each messenger is the sole survivor of the disaster he describes. The unbroken succession of messengers further heightens the tension the hearer feels concerning Job's reaction; he cannot respond emotionally to any calamity until he responds to them all; for, after all, they are in reality one and the same calamity in design and in effect.

The pattern of four disasters is also artistically conceived. There is not only the alternation of human and "natural" (or "supernatural") calamities (Sabeans, lightning, Chaldeans, whirlwind); the disasters strike from all points of the compass (south, east, north, west), and (probably) increase in intensity (one thousand oxen, five hundred asses, servants; seven thousand sheep or goats, servants; three thousand camels, servants; Job's children). Cumulatively, the disasters eliminate all of Job's possessions mentioned in vv 2–3; the very number four symbolizes the completeness of the ruin (on the pattern of "ascending numeration" [here 3+1], see *Comment* on 5:19). Enumeration of four punishments or calamities is especially well attested: in the Gilgamesh epic, four plagues that diminish mankind are the lion, the wolf, famine, and the god of plague (11.177–85; *ANET*, 95); in Ezek 14:12–23 there appear famine, wild beasts, the sword, and plague (cf. also the four horns of Zech 2:1–4 [1:18–21]; the four angels of Rev 9:13–15; and the seven calamities of Job 5:19).

The naivety of the style is apparent in the simplicity of the narrative and especially in its repetitiveness, the same device of the messenger being used four times, each of the reports ending with the same formula, all but the first of the reports beginning with the same formula, and the first and the last report balancing one another in contrasting a scene of tranquillity with a moment of disaster. The "falseness" of the naivety lies in the dramatic impact that is only heightened by the formality of the narration.

Conspicuous by their absence from this catalogue of disasters are both God and the Satan. It is true that lightning is conventionally called "fire of God" (v 16) and that it fell "from heaven," but the implication is not that God is directly responsible for this calamity as contrasted with the others. On one level the reason for the absence of the heavenly figures is that the (almost) rigidly enforced distinction between the divine and earthly spheres in this prologue forbids their appearance in this episode; on a deeper level, the calamities are mute and it is for Job to discern their origin (v 21).

13 Like the "day" of v 6, this is a day of no special import in itself, a day that will develop its meaning as it progresses. It is the day when the children of Job are gathered in the house of the eldest; those commentators who saw in v 4 a weekly cycle of feasts culminating in the purgative sacrifice by Job (v 5) are specially impressed by the disaster falling immediately after the sacrifice had been offered and the children had therefore been made ritually innocent: "Job's godliness and his calamity are brought into the closest contrast" (Davidson). But even if irregularly occurring feasts are supposed by v 4, it is far from clear that the Satan chose the first opportunity on which all Job's children were assembled. For it is of no consequence *when* the blow fell; all that we are unquestionably supposed to understand is that no cause for the disaster lay in the behavior of any of the human actors. No such thought occurs to Job, either.

It may seem curious that the grammatical antecedent for "his" sons and daughters is "the Satan" of v 12; the Septuagint clearly felt it necessary to specify "Job's sons and daughters." There is no hint here that the heavenly scenes are a later insertion into the story of Job, simply a further sign that it is the figure of Job about whom the whole story revolves.

14–15 Gordis correctly notes that "the impact of the narrative is heightened by its compression." The message begins with news—which is no news—of the farmer's routine: in the early winter, after the early rains, the oxen are plowing and the asses (not here used for plowing; cf. on v 3) are grazing in the fields; they will have carried the plowing gear and the seed to the fields. For illustrations of modern Palestinian plowing, see G. Dalman, *Arbeit und Sitte in Palästina* (Gütersloh: Bertelsmann, 1932) 2: pl. 24–26, 28–29, 31–39; for the ass, see pl. 27 and cf. pp. 160–61. Cf. also E. Nielsen, "Ass and Ox in the Old Testament," in *Studia Orientalia Ioanni Pedersen . . . dicata* (Copenhagen: Einar Munksgaard, 1953) 263–74.

Into this scene breaks an event, a destructive "falling" (the verb נפל is used in three of these scenes, vv 15, 16, 19). The marauders who drive off oxen and asses and slay the servants tending them are "Sabeans." Most identify this group with the inhabitants of Sheba, the prominent city of southwestern Arabia (mentioned in 1 Kgs 10:1; Isa 60:6; Jer 6:20 ["a distant land"]; etc.; cf. also on Job 6:19) and identified as modern Marib in present-day Yemen. However, the inhabitants of Sheba are nowhere else referred to as brigands, and a plundering expedition some one thousand miles north of their home (if indeed the setting of the story of Job is in northern Arabia; cf. on v 1) stretches the bounds of plausibility even for the hyperbole of the folktale. Pope (as previously Budde, Szczygiel) argues that the Sheba here is some closer region; in 6:19 it is parallel to Tema, and in Gen 10:7 and 25:3 (both genealogical lists) it is associated with Dedan, both names clearly to be linked with north Arabia. He even suggests that the stream name Wadi eš-Šaba in the region of Medina may preserve the ancient name. Fohrer, on the other hand, thinks that the depiction of the Sabeans as brigands witnesses to the antiquity of the narrative in representing them as still at an early nomadic stage of their development. The designations of "Sabeans" and "Chaldeans" may indeed be traditional, and the merchantmen Sabeans of 6:19 may be a different group. See further, on Sheba in the Yemen: Wendell Phillips, *Qataban and Sheba: Exploring Ancient Kingdoms on the Biblical Spice Routes of Arabia* (London: Gollancz, 1955); G. W. Van Beek, *IDB* 4:144–46; idem, "South Arabian History and Archaeology," in *The Bible and the Ancient Near East* (FS W. F. Albright; ed. G. E. Wright; Garden City, N.Y.: Doubleday, 1961) 229–48.

Since plunder is the object of the Sabeans' raid, their killing of the farm-workers is an unexpected detail that obviously arises from the dramatic necessity to eliminate all of Job's possessions, including his "great household" (v 2). Only one survivor is left from each of the four disasters; his escape is also dramatically required. This stock narrative feature is turned to good effect here in concentrating the attention upon Job rather than upon the scenes of disaster (for the stock element "one alone left," cf. Gen 44:20; Josh 13:12; 1 Kgs 18:22; Isa 49:21; Ezek 9:8; in inverse mode, 2 Sam 13:32–33; for "the survivor bringing news," cf. Gen 14:13; 1 Sam 22:20; 2 Sam 1:3; Ezek 24:26).

16 In creating a sense of the relentlessness of the unfolding series of disasters, a further stock narrative device is used to good effect: "while he was still speaking" (also Gen 24:15; 1 Kgs 1:42; Dan 4:28 [31]; cf. also the Ugaritic text *1 Aqht* [*CTA* 19] 113–16; Gibson, 117). Lightning is regularly called the "fire from heaven" (2 Kgs 1:10, 12, 14) or "the fire from Yahweh" (Num 11:1; 16:35; 1 Kgs 18:38) or "fire from Yahweh from heaven" (Gen 19:24). While the divine name does not simply function as a superlative ("a great fire," i.e., "lightning"; as Gordis; cf. D. Winton Thomas, "A Consideration of Some Unusual Ways of Expressing the Superlative in Hebrew," *VT* 3 [1953] 209–24 [210]), the normality of the phrase prevents the reader (or Job) from presuming that this has been a direct divine visitation. Indeed, other terms for lightning existed (בָּרָק, e.g., Exod 19:16, though this occurs chiefly in poetry [BDB]; and אוֹר, in Job 36:32; 37:3, 11, 15 [and cf. Hab 3:11], though this is the general term for "light" and its meaning in chaps. 36–37 is specified by the context). "Fire" (אֵשׁ) by itself (as LXX has here and as in Exod 9:23) or "fire from heaven" would have been natural terms to use, but the narrator may have been constrained by the "archaic" aspect of his style; certainly a disaster of nature (like the whirlwind in v 19) seems to be intended.

It is, nevertheless, a preternatural strike of lightning that consumes seven thousand sheep and all their attendant shepherds. The folkloristic hyperbole serves yet again to emphasize the totality of the destruction of Job's possessions.

It may be that this disaster is represented as coming from the west, from where—from a Palestinian standpoint at least—most violent thunderstorms emanated. From the viewpoint of a north Arabian setting, however, thunderstorms may be more usually from the south.

17 The agents of the third catastrophe are Chaldeans (כַּשְׂדִּים, *kaśdîm*), but not the imperial race of the neo-Babylonian empire of the late seventh and the sixth centuries B.C. Kaldai are known from Assyrian annals as early as the tenth century B.C. as inhabitants of southern Mesopotamia, and nomadic peoples of the same name may have roamed the deserts between north Arabia and the Persian Gulf. Certainly we have here unsettled marauders, perhaps descending upon Job from the north, as the Sabeans had from the south;

the northern connection may be attested in some way by the presence of Chesed (כֶּשֶׂד) among the children of Nahor (Abraham's Aramean brother) and as an uncle of Aram in Gen 22:22. The use of the well-known imperial name Chaldeans may be an archaic or archaizing note in the narrative. Wherever Job's home is to be located, attacks by both Sabeans and Chaldeans are as hyperbolically folkloristic an element as the bolt of lightning in v 16. On the origin and use of the name Chaldeans, see A. R. Millard, "Daniel 1–6 and History," *EvQ* 49 (1977) 67–73 (69–71); A. L. Oppenheim, *IDB* 1:549–50.

The stratagem of dividing one's forces into three bands is attested also in Judg 7:16; 9:43; 1 Sam 11:11; 13:17. This disaster also is one that "falls" upon Job's possessions (cf. kjv "fell upon the camels"), even though a different verb (פשט) is used from that in vv 15, 16, 19. It would be indiscreet to say that the term "falling" hints at the heavenly origin of Job's losses, but trouble does not sprout from the ground (5:6), and the reader will sense that the image carries the appropriate resonances.

18–19 Like the first messenger, the fourth begins by depicting the tranquillity of the scene before disaster struck, but now the tonality of the report of good news is changed. In the first message, the contrast between the news of peace and the announcement of disaster was the focus; now the expectation is exclusively upon the inevitable disaster that is surely to be reported, and the good news merely increases the tension.

Like the other disasters, this fourth one is both natural and preternaturally heightened. A violent wind, the sirocco or khamsin, sweeping in from the eastern desert, "from the other side (מעבר) of the wilderness," is no rare occurrence (cf. the "east wind," 15:2; 27:20–23; Hos 13:15; the "hot wind from the desert," Jer 4:11; and "the desert wind," Jer 13:24; cf. R. B. Y. Scott, "Meteorological Phenomena and Terminology in the Old Testament," *ZAW* 64 [1952] 11–25 [20]); but a wind that strikes all four sides (lit., "corners") of a house at once (on the significance of "four" see on vv 13–22) is the kind of wind that blows in the heroic world of folktale. A whirlwind could perhaps be said to strike all corners of a house, but "true whirlwinds or tornadoes are rare and occur chiefly near the coast" (R. B. Y. Scott, *IDB* 4:841; cf. D. Nir, "Whirlwinds in Israel in the Winters 1954–55 and 1955–56," *IEJ* 7 [1957] 109–17), admittedly in the early winter, which is the season suggested by the narrative (cf. on v 14). Nothing among the disasters is a "special intervention of God" (as Habel says of the whirlwind), but their enormity and concentration direct Job's attention unhesitatingly to the activity of God (v 21).

Each time it has been the "young men" or "young people" (נערים) who have been slain; Hebrew, like many languages, can use terms meaning "boy, lad" for "servant" (as has been the case in the previous scenes). In this scene it is the children of Job who are meant; on looking back over the passage, we realize that it is for the sake of this announcement that the term נערים has been used throughout. These are the נערים that really matter, though no doubt their attendant servants also have died.

The "house" of the eldest brother is obviously not a tent; this "patriarchal" story, we are reminded, is not set in the world of nomadic shepherds, but of settled pastoralists and farmers, even though the archaic language of an earlier style of life is often employed (see, e.g., on 5:24; 29:4).

20 What we have been waiting for is Job's reaction to the news. The narrator has artfully kept us waiting; though the spotlight has been upon Job from the beginning of the scene, we have not heard one word from him or had an inkling of how the news registers with him. All that survives to him of his former prosperity and rank are four anonymous messengers, whom even a quite unsophisticated audience will easily recognize as owing their survival entirely to the exigencies of narrative art (the manner of their escape is of no interest whatever); for the purposes of this story, Job is alone and unattended by house servants when he receives the messengers, and even his wife is kept out of sight until her significant appearance in 2:9.

Up to this point, Job has been sitting, as is still the custom in many Middle Eastern societies when receiving visitors. His reaction to the news is most empathetically perceived if we conjure up some countertexts; for example, that the story had him burst into vigorous lament (like that of chap. 3), cry out for vengeance, or in a frenzy seek to discover whether the reports of the messengers were in fact not some horrifying joke. Such imaginative alternatives to the story highlight three facets of the story we actually have: acts precede words; acts and words are deliberate and few; acts and words are conventional and external.

The ritual acts of mourning delay even further Job's verbal response to the messengers' speeches (Job himself has not spoken since v 5, and there the "speech" may be only a thought). The narrative by no means suggests "rapidity of movement" (which Dhorme infers from the initial וַיָּקָם "and he rose up"). Rather, the acts are deliberate, and, though conventional, deeply symbolic.

The tearing of garments, a frequently attested rite of mourning (Gen 37:29; Josh 7:6; cf. 2 Sam 13:19; Lev 10:6; whatever its origins may have been (according to W. O. E. Oesterley, *Immortality and the Unseen World* [London: SPCK, 1921] 143–49, as a palliative of self-mutilation; cf. also W. Robertson Smith, *Lectures on the Religion of the Semites* [London: A. C. Black, 3rd ed., 1927] 687), its symbolic value is rich. Perhaps it symbolizes that the pain reaches the heart of the survivor (Fohrer); perhaps it expresses the mourner's identification with the destruction of the one dead; perhaps it marks a recognition that a significant element of one's own life has been irredeemably ended; perhaps it seeks relief from shock or horror in violent physical action (E. F. de Ward, "Mourning Customs in 1, 2 Samuel," *JSS* 23 [1972] 1–27, 145–66); certainly, some such strong muscular activity is, physiologically speaking, an appropriate response to the release of adrenaline into the bloodstream. It is the outer mantle or robe (מְעִיל) that is torn, a garment worn by persons of distinction or by others on special occasions over the ordinary tunic (כֻּתֹּנֶת); cf. 2:12; Exod 28:31; 1 Sam 15:27; 18:4; 24:5, 12 [6, 13]; 28:14; Ezra 9:3, 5. It corresponds generally to the modern Palestinian *qumbaz,* a long, loosely fitting robe worn over other garments (J. M. Myers, *IDB* 1:870; illustration, G. Dalman, *Arbeit und Sitte in Palästina* [Gütersloh: Bertelsmann, 1937] 5: fig. 58). In an exceptional case, the tunic itself may be torn (as in 2 Sam 15:32).

Shaving the head as a mourning symbol was also common in ancient times (Isa 15:2; 22:12; Jer 7:29; 16:6; 41:5; 47:5; 48:37; Ezek 7:18; Amos 8:10; Mic 1:16); it was forbidden by the Deuteronomic law (Deut 14:1), as apparently was the shaving of the head for any purpose by the Holiness Law of Lev 19:27 (cf. Jer 9:25 [26]; Ezek 44:20). Examples occur of tearing out the hair

(Ezra 9:3; cf. also Gilgamesh 8.2.21, *ANET,* 88), and clipping the beard (Isa 15:2; Jer 41:5; 48:37). A large collection of parallels from other cultures to shaving or cropping the hair may be found in T. H. Gaster, *Myth, Legend, and Custom in the Old Testament* (London: Duckworth, 1969) 590–602.

The origins of the custom are probably irrelevant, even if they could be determined. A "primitive" anthropological approach, like Frazer's, suggested purposes such as disguising oneself from the ghost of the dead, or offering the strength supposed to reside in the hair as energy for the spirit of the departed. For strictures upon such approaches, see J. W. Rogerson, *Anthropology and the Old Testament* (Oxford: Blackwell, 1978), esp. 46–53. Note also that Jer 7:29 speaks of cutting off the hair in mourning and throwing it away, which suggests that no special significance attaches to the disposal of the hair. A psychological interpretation of the function of such a practice is likely to be nearer the truth; the self-mutilation or disfigurement involved in hair rituals is analogous to the rending of garments: the living identifies with the dead. The common practice of putting dust on the head (cf. on 2:12) is the most convincing sign that the suffering survivor identifies with the dead. In the narrative here, this is a ritual act that plainly is no impulsive hasty reaction, but one which necessitates preparations and a rather lengthy activity.

In the same way, Job's falling to the ground is not, as Driver points out, "some immediate half-involuntary physical reaction against the distressing news" (contrast 1 Sam 28:20). Unlike the former two mourning rites, whose conventionality cloaks any individual expression of feeling, this third act makes Job's inner attitude plain. Falling to the ground (not itself a mourning rite; contra Gordis) and "worshiping" or "doing obeisance" (הִשְׁתַּחֲוָה) are here the same act of conscious and deliberate piety before God. Job falls to the ground not in despair but in reverence (Rowley), no doubt touching the face to the ground in a silent act of submission. E. W. Lane described the Islamic custom of religious obeisance thus: "He . . . drops gently upon his knees . . . places his hands upon the ground, a little before his knees, and puts his nose and forehead also to the ground (the former first), between his two hands" (*An Account of the Manners and Customs of the Modern Egyptians* [London: John Murray, 5th ed., 1860] 77, with illustration; for illustrations from the ancient Near East of postures in prayer, see *ANEP,* pl. 355, 45, 46; *IBD* 3:1259). Other biblical examples are found in Gen 24:52; Josh 7:16; Isa 44:17. While a technical term for verbal prayer is only seldom connected with this word for "worship" (הִשְׁתַּחֲוָה) (cf. J. Herrmann, *TDNT* 2:788–80), the word itself does not denote prayer, but one of the postures of prayer, reverence, or supplication (to a superior or even to an equal also; cf. Gen 23:7; Exod 18:7; 1 Sam 25:23); it is often followed, as here, by "and he said" or its equivalent. See also D. R. Ap-Thomas, "Notes on Some Terms Relating to Prayer," *VT* 6 (1956) 220–24; H.-P. Stähli, *THWAT* 1:530–33.

Job's actions in response to the news have been few: there has been no gashing of the body, no donning sackcloth, no scattering dust, no lamentation, no weeping, no fasting. Is this simply the economy of the "naive" narrative style, or does it signal a disproportionate restraint that will be burst open in the passion of the dialogue? On mourning rites, see further A. J. Wensinck, *Semitic Rites,* esp. 5–55; E. Kutsch, "'Trauerbräuche' und 'Selbstminderungs-riten' im AT," *ThSt* 78 (1965) 25–42.

21 The purely conventional acts of mourning have been performed, and narrated, first because the real issue, of whether Job will curse God, must for the sake of the dramatic tension be postponed as long as possible. In the event, the Satan is proved both right and wrong. He has said that if all that Job has is "struck," Job will "bless" (ברך) God (v 11)—but he means "bless" as a euphemism for "curse." Job indeed "blesses" (ברך) God; verbally the Satan has been proved right, though on the level of intention he has been proved wrong. And what of the Satan's prognostication that Job will "bless" God "to [his] face"? Is there any significance in the fact that neither here nor in 2:10 (nor in chap. 3) does Job address God directly? It will only be in the ensuing dialogue with the friends that Job will say anything at all "to [God's] face"; have we met once more with the "false naivety" of the narrator in this tiny narrative thread that is not tied up in the narrative itself but cries out for further resolution in the book as a whole?

But blessing will not be Job's first word. First he utters a sentiment entirely in tune with the generalizations of pessimistic "wisdom": "Naked I came from my mother's womb, and naked shall I return [there]"; cf. Eccl 5:14 [15] "As [a man] came from his mother's womb he shall go again, naked as he came." This is "pessimistic" only in the sense that it takes into account the reality of death, which "optimistic" wisdom does not generally do. There is a tension, indeed, between the idea that earthly possessions are the natural fruit of a life of piety, and the idea that death negates everything positive, and strips one "naked" of all that life has brought; the reports of the messengers have in a day translated Job from the sphere of "piety and reward" attested in vv 1–2 into the sphere where Qoheleth stands. That is not a sphere of fatalism or nihilism, or even of resignation or despair (contrast Duhm, who found this inactive "resignation" so alien to "the more energetic spirit of the European" [!]); it is a sphere where the boundary situation is encountered, and where the rest of life is evaluated from that perspective. Job feels himself now already as good as dead; stripped naked of his possessions, he is as if he were already prepared for burial. His words simply verbalize the psychological identification with the dead that he has already made by his ritual acts of mourning.

The interpretive difficulty raised by this line is the phrase "I shall *return thither*." For it is evidently not to his mother's womb that Job expects to return at death (cf. John 3:4). Two exegetical moves are usually suggested.

(i) That the "mother's womb" is the womb of Mother Earth; Ps 139:15 speaks of the human body as being formed in the "depths of the earth," and Ecclus 40:1 explicitly refers to the grave as the "mother of all the living"; the origin of humankind in general from the "mud of the ground" (Gen 2:9; cf. 18:27; Job 4:19; Ps 103:14; 1 Cor 15:47–49) lies of course in the background of this image. G. R. Driver refers to Arab. *ʾummu* "mother" as meaning also "abode, habitation, tomb," and cites the Arab. phrase *buṭûnu-ʾllarā* "wombs of the earth" for "graves" ("Ancient Lore and Modern Knowledge," in *Hommages à André Dupont-Sommer,* ed. A. Caquot, 277–86); but these must be self-conscious literary usages. On the concept of "Mother Earth" in Semitic thought, cf. M. Eliade, *RGG*[3] 2:548–50.

(ii) That "thither" is a euphemism for the underworld; there is an Egyptian phrase "those who are there" for the dead (cf. N. Herz, "Egyptian Words and Idioms in the Book of Job," *OLZ* 16 [1913] 343–46 [343–44]), and Greek ἐκεῖ "there" (e.g., Euripides, *Medea,* 1065) is paralleled as a term referring to the underworld (see also G. R. Driver, "Ancient Lore and Modern Knowledge," 286). Gordis sees in שָׁם in Eccl 3:17 a similar usage ("There is a proper time for everything and for every deed—over there!"), and also compares שָׁם in Job 3:19. But this view does not entirely dispose of the difficulty of "I shall *return*," since Sheol is not the mother's womb. It may simply be that "return" (שׁוּב) is not to be pressed too literally; cf. Ps 9:18 [17], where the wicked "return" to Sheol, and 146:4, where a prince who is no more than a "son of man" "returns [שׁוּב] to his earth" once his breath departs. There is certainly no adequate evidence for arguing, with Dahood, *Psalms III,* 295, that the human body is regarded as created and preexistent in the netherworld; the passages he cites (Gen 2:7; 3:19; Ps 90:3; Eccl 3:20; 5:14 [15]; 12:7; Ecclus 40:1 [to which Job 34:15 could be added]) speak of no more than the creation of humankind as such from the earth.

The best clue to the crux lies in Ps 139, where v 13 speaks of an individual's creation in the mother's womb, and v 15 of that same individual's creation in the depths of the earth. The images surrounding the origin of humankind and that of the individual are fused, and it would be a wooden exegete who would find the metaphors self-contradictory. So here too the imagery of the individual's birth is silently fused with the imagery of humankind's creation, so that "thither" is indeed the earth, not as a technical term or a euphemism for it, nor because it is precisely identified as "Mother Earth." (Jorge Luis Borges draws attention to the critics who found a similar "fallacy" in Keats' "Ode to a Nightingale" ["The Nightingale of Keats," in *Other Inquisitions* (tr. J. E. Irby; Austin: University of Texas Press, 1964) 121–24].)

Two further points need to be added: (i) G. Ricciotti's interesting suggestion (*ZAW* 67 [1955] 249–51), that the point of comparison is the fetal position assumed by the child in its mother's womb and the same position assumed by the corpse in the grave, distracts attention from the primary comparison between nakedness at birth and nakedness at death; (ii) Ecclus 40:1, often cited as illumination of our present text, is indeed inspired by it, but its greater explicitness differs significantly from the fused images of our text; it reads ". . . from the day man comes forth from his mother's womb, until the day he enters [not "returns to" as RSV, JB, NAB] the mother of all living."

The second element of Job's speech voices his response not in the language of reflection upon life ("wisdom") but in the language of religious feeling (praise): "Yahweh has given, and Yahweh has taken away; blessed be the name of Yahweh." Indeed, like the first sentence, it has a conventional or traditional air about it; some Arab tribesmen are said to utter the formula *rabbu jābu, rabbu aḫadu,* "His Lord gave him, his Lord has taken him away," upon the death of a kinsman (A. Musil, *Arabia Petraea* [Vienna: A. Hölder, 1908] 3:427), and for the sentiment, cf. 1 Sam 3:18, "It is from Yahweh; let him do what seems good to him" (Eli to Samuel); Ecclus 11:14. But the temper of the saying is not so much the learned wisdom of a Qoheleth, as the piety of the congregation at worship.

Again, following a lead from S. Kierkegaard's brilliant exposition of this verse (*Edifying Discourses: A Selection* [London: Collins, 1958] 78–94), we may expound it against the varying backdrops of alternative countertexts. Job does not say, "Yahweh has given and the Sabeans, the Chaldeans, the lightning and whirlwind, have taken away"; he sees his human enemies and the natural forces as secondary to the one who must be ultimately responsible. This sense will be a navigation aid for him in the dark waters of the chapters that follow. He does not allow the anger inevitable in bereavement to vent itself upon secondary causes; in time we shall see that anger expressed in just the direction this initial reaction has set for him. Nor does Job say, "Yahweh has taken away"; the sudden awareness of loss as it has been dramatically presented has not closed his mind to everything but his immediate sensation; at the moment of his loss he is wholly conscious that what has been lost was God's gift. Nor yet does Job say simply, "Yahweh has given," as if, like many victims of loss, to expel the hurt of the present by dwelling exclusively on the joys of the past, wishing the hurt away by refusing to accept its reality. He can balance the gift and the loss, the joy and the hurt, and accept them both as "from the hand of God." And yet further, Job does not merely say, "Yahweh has given, and Yahweh has taken away." That in itself is the utterance of psychological maturity and thoughtful piety; but even yet it does not make patent the feeling with which the words are uttered. The next phrase, however, does: "Blessed be the name of Yahweh!" Yahweh is blessed not for the giving or for the taking away but for the totality of what he has been to Job. His bounteousness and his inexplicable hurtfulness are equally manifestations of his personal reality; and in the face of that Job knows no other response than "blessing." In a rabbinic text from the Mishnah (*m. Ber.* 5.3) the cryptic sentence occurs: "If anyone says, For blessings be thy name praised, we silence that man." That is to say, such a praise could disguise a *sotto voce* "but for calamities may your name be cursed." Job needs no such warning; his instincts direct him to a dignified, tightly reined, sober, balanced piety. (It is not clear that Job thinks especially of the right of God to "take away" what he has "given," the gift being merely a loan, and God being entitled to take back what is really his own; Fohrer and Hesse, among others, emphasize this aspect.) There is no authorization in this text for the common view that in the OT God is regarded as the author of everything that occurs in the world. Job is making no global statement of divine causality, but a pious utterance of his sense of how entirely his fate lies in the hands of God. See further F. Lindström, *God and the Origin of Evil: A Contextual Analysis of Alleged Monistic Evidence in the Old Testament* (tr. F. A. Cryer; Lund: C. W. K. Gleerup, 1983) 137–57.

In this sentence, then, of response to the disaster that has befallen him, the Book of Job reaches—for the first time—what I argue in this commentary to be its primary aim: to portray how one should behave under suffering. No more sudden or catastrophic suffering could easily be imagined; how should a human being respond? Precisely as Job, without recrimination, self-pity, or rejection of reality, and with praise to the Lord of his being. Job is unarguably here set forth as an exemplar of faith in crisis. Nevertheless, the vast bulk of the Book of Job will depict a different Job, who is nevertheless the same man, a Job who finds such a response, though genuinely willed and in every respect real (and not to be misjudged as "unnaturally calm"; cf. Hesse), does not begin to match the turmoil of emotion that the events of this chapter come to awaken in him. There is no doubt that Job's behavior here is *right,* and therefore exemplary; whether it is *possible*—at least to persist in—is another matter. For some it may be, and they are to be congratulated. For the others, the rest of the book will portray another—though ultimately congruent—way.

We may note as of less pressing significance the fact that Job here for the only time (but see on 12:9) employs the name Yahweh; indeed all the speakers in the book (including the Satan) use one or other term for "God" (statistical table in Driver-Gray, xxxv), though the narrator himself in prologue and epilogue speaks of "Yahweh" ("sons of God" [1:6; 2:1] is a fixed phrase, as also apparently in the idiom of this writer "fearing God" [in 1:8 in the mouth of Yahweh!]). Nothing about the literary origins of the book can be deduced from these facts; what may be suggested by the use of the name Yahweh here is that the phrases are adaptations of familiar Israelite formulae (cf. Ps 113:2, "Blessed be the name of Yahweh from this time for evermore"). (T. H. Gaster, *Myth, Legend, and Custom in the Old Testament* [London: Duckworth, 1969] 2:787, cites a similarly formed sentence from a Mesopotamian text, "The king gave, and the king has taken; long live the king!" [A. Pohl, "Akkadische Sprichwörter," *Or* 19 (1950) 382]; there is no connection of dependence, however.) Our narrator writes for alert readers, and no simplistic generic explanation of why "Yahweh" is used will satisfy; the point is that Job, Israelite or no, behaves and speaks at the crisis moment as if bound by covenant with Yahweh, God of Israel. Even if only temporarily—and certainly *sub rosa*—this "pagan saint" (J. Daniélou, *Holy Pagans of the Old Testament* [tr. F. Faber; London: Longmans, Green, and Co., 1956] 86–102) becomes a Jewish proselyte.

The form of the blessing (יהי שם יהוה מברך, "may Yahweh's name be blessed") is an unusual one, the normal formula being "blessed be Yahweh" (ברוך יהוה) or "blessed be thou" (ברוך אתה). But exactly the same wording occurs in Ps 113:2, suggesting that Job's utterance is to be recognized as a conventional liturgical formula. Job himself does not simply "bless" God, but expresses the wish that wherever the news of his suffering spreads people may display their reverence for the deity (the form functions like the imperative summons to praise; see C. A. Keller and G. Wehmeier, *THWAT* 1:353–76 [363]), and not, moved by sympathy with Job, make of Job's suffering a reason for hostility toward God (cf. again Ps 113:2–3: "May Yahweh's name be blessed . . . praised from east to west"). While it is comparatively easy to understand the concept of a "blessing" as some kind of wish or gift directed toward humans by God or by others, or, as J. Scharbert (*TDOT* 1:303) emphasizes, "to strengthen *solidarity* with individuals and groups with whom [the one blessing] has or seeks particularly close social, racial, and religious relationships," what does it mean to "bless" *God*, who must be assumed to stand in no need of blessing? While some, working with a "magical" view of Israelite thought, have imagined that a blessing actually increases the power of Yahweh, the most natural view is that the "blessing" is a means of expressing gratitude and respect (cf. J. Scharbert, *TDOT* 1:305), "an ascription of praise and gratitude for blessing received" (W. Harrelson, *IDB* 1:446). See further S. Mowinckel, *Segen und Fluch in Israels Kult und Psalmdichtung* (Psalmenstudien 5; repr. Amsterdam: P. Schippers, 1966 [orig. 1924]), esp. 27–30; J. Hempel, "Die israelitischen Anschauungen von Segen und Fluch im Lichte altorientalischen Parallelen," *ZDMG* 4 (1925) 20–110 (= BZAW 81 [1961] 30–113); J. Pedersen, *Israel: Its Life and Culture I-II* (London: OUP; Copenhagen: P. Branner, 1926) 182–212; J. Scharbert, *Solidarität in Segen und Fluch im AT und in seiner Umwelt* (BBB 14; Bonn: Hanstein, 1958); idem, *TDOT* 1:279–308; S. H. Blank, *HUCA* 32 (1962) 85–90; H. Mowvley, "The Concept and Content of 'Blessing' in the OT," *BiTrans* 16 (1965) 74–80; J. Guillet, "Le langage spontané de la bénédiction dans l'AT," *RSR* 57 (1969) 163–204; F. Horst, "Segen und Segen-shandlungen in der Bibel," *EvT* 7 (1947–48) 23–37 (= *Gottes Recht: Gesammelte Studien zum Recht im Alten Testament* [TBü 12; Munich: Kaiser, 1961] 188–202); W. S. Towner, "'Blessed be YHWH' and 'Blessed Art Thou, YHWH': The Modulation of a Biblical Formula," *CBQ* 30 (1968) 386–99.

On the "name" of God as essentially a synonym for God himself in psalmic language, cf. Ps 5:12 [11]; 96:2.

22 In no way has Job "sinned" by cursing God. "In all this" may refer to all the circumstances that have been narrated (Horst), or, more probably, to what Job has spoken (Dhorme). Misfortune has led Job to "bless" in the true sense, not to speak words that are only euphemistically called "blessing." Nothing that God has done is open to criticism; the exact meaning of תפלה (rsv "wrong"; neb "unreason") is uncertain (see n. 22.b); but the context shows that to "attribute תפלה to God" (the phrase is patterned on the more common idiom "to give, attribute praise or glory to Yahweh," e.g., 1 Sam 6:5) must be the most modest form of "cursing" God (cf. nab "nor did he say anything disrespectful of God"). It is not so much that God has a right to do whatever he pleases, or that his gifts remain his own property and he is therefore entitled to take them back at any time; no such grand generalizations determine Job's response. It is prompted entirely by his persistent attitude of reverence toward God (cf. v 5).

2:1–6 *The Satan and God: second encounter.* This fourth scene of the prologue is modeled very closely upon the second, with much verbal repetition. The doubling heightens the dramatic expectations, for the hearer or reader, in the process of realizing that a scene is being repeated, becomes at the same moment more alert for the novelties in the second presentation.

Here the chief novelty to attract the attention is heaven's reaction to Job's behavior: is it now satisfied, or must the earthly scene be replayed with greater violence? If the latter, what then of Job's response? Once that is established, this fourth scene must rapidly give place to the fifth, which will be climactic and final.

Some have doubted that this second cycle of testing originally belonged to the Job narrative. Hesse, for example, points out that the testing of Job has already proved effective; the point in question has been decided. To afflict Job now with illness, after all his losses, is to add nothing new. Furthermore, the epilogue to the book in chap. 42 speaks of the restitution of Job's possessions, but not a word of the healing of Job's disease—as if that had never been an issue in the story. Hesse attributes the story of the second phase of Job's trial to a purely narrative "law of doubling" or "law of heightening," which was employed in order to form a bridge to the figure portrayed in the dialogues—the Job who is smitten by illness.

Horst, on the other hand, sees the image of the suffering Job as the essence of the narrative, especially because of the Mesopotamian analogues to the figure of the "righteous sufferer" (in the Mesopotamian text known as "I will praise the Lord of Wisdom" [*Ludlul bēl nēmeqi;* W. G. Lambert, *Babylonian Wisdom Literature* (Oxford: Clarendon, 1960) 21–62; *ANET,* 434–37]; the Righteous Sufferer [see J. Nougayrol, "Une version ancienne du «juste souffrant»," *RB* 59 (1952) 239–50]; and *Man and His God* [see S. N. Kramer, "'Man and His God': A Sumerian Variation on the 'Job' Motif," VTSup 3 (1955) 170–

82]). Fohrer, however, though distinguishing several stages in the composition of the book, finds no need to discriminate between the two trials of Job; and the whole discussion perhaps only reflects the tendency in OT scholarship to project horizontal or synchronic tensions within a narrative onto a vertical, diachronic, developmental grid (which is generally hypothetical).

1–2 The wording is repeated exactly from 1:6–7 with one purely verbal difference (the word for "whence" [אֵי מִזֶּה] in v 2 is different from that [מֵאַיִן] in 1:7), and one difference that may perhaps be significant: at the end of v 1 the Satan comes among the sons of God "to present himself before Yahweh"— precisely the same phrase that has already just been used of the sons of God themselves. The Septuagint translators omitted the last phrase "to present himself before Yahweh," but we do not know why; they may have followed a different Hebrew manuscript; they may have omitted the phrase accidentally or intentionally because it had already occurred in the verse; or they may have omitted it intentionally because the term for "before" God (עַל) could have been misunderstood as "against" (D. H. Gard, *The Exegetical Method of the Greek Translator of the Book of Job* [SBLMS 8; Philadelphia: Society of Biblical Literature, 1952] 28). Many translations omit the phrase (JB, NEB, NAB, though not RSV, NIV). Gordis speculates that the phrase has a different significance here: while in the first half of the verse it means "stand in God's presence, like courtiers," when used of the Satan it means "stand over against God" in insolence and rebelliousness (cf. the phrase in Num 16:27; Deut 7:24). But the obvious explanation lies ready to hand: the Satan is the only one of the "sons of God" who, in our narrative, has been sent out from the last assembly of the heavenly council with a specific task. Attention is therefore directed to him as the one who must give some report of his mission.

On repetition as a feature of Hebrew narrative style, see W. Baumgartner, "Ein Kapitel vom hebräischen Erzählungsstil," in *Eucharistērion: Studien zur Religion und Literatur des Alten und Neuen Testaments* (FS H. Gunkel; FRLANT 36; Göttingen: Vandenhoeck & Ruprecht, 1923) 145–57; J. Muilenburg, "A Study in Hebrew Rhetoric: Repetition and Style," VTSup 1 (1953) 97–111; Alter, *Art of Biblical Narrative*, 88–113.

Why does the Satan answer Yahweh so vaguely, so cagily? Gordis wryly remarks: "In accordance with the immemorial practice of subordinates vis-à-vis their superiors . . . the Satan offers the Lord as little information as possible. He makes no reference to Job or to the effect that his trials have had upon him." But perhaps this reading is oversubtle. The prior question is, why does Yahweh say, "From where do you come?" Why does Yahweh not get to the point directly himself? Unless Hesse is right in seeing these verses as the work of a clumsy supplementer, the answer can only be that the formalities (modest though they are) have to be gone through; or else, that the naivety of the narrative style demands as close a repetition of the first heavenly scene as possible. Nevertheless, we are entitled to wonder whether there is here also not a little "false" naivety: is there a little "fencing" about the subject, a disinclination to plunge into the topic of primary concern?

3 What are we to make of the fact that Yahweh already knows how Job has responded to the test before the Satan appears again before him? Perhaps it is a simple foreshortening of the narrative for the sake of the movement of the dialogue; or more probably, it is important that the attestation of Job's continued piety should be set in the mouth of Yahweh rather than of the Satan. We are not to assume that Yahweh has no need to learn what has taken place because he is all-knowing (Gordis). Such a presumption about God's omniscience would destroy the whole rationale of the heavenly court. No, Yahweh has discovered, whether from some other member of the "sons of God" or from the present conversation with the Satan, that "Job maintains his integrity." How Yahweh has come to know this is of less importance than his announcement of Job's integrity to the Satan; for Yahweh's statement is flaunted before the Satan; it requires a response from him; it implicitly invites the very kind of reply the Satan has made in 1:9.

Job "still," despite the calamities depicted in 1:13–19, "maintains his integrity," i.e., "his life continues blameless as ever" (JB). "Maintains" (חזק ב) means "hold fast to" (cf. Exod 9:2); "integrity" (תֻּמָּה) occurs outside Job (2:9; 27:5; 31:6) only in Prov 11:3; but the root תמם is common, and the adjective תם "blameless" has already just been used of Job. Later in the book Job's "maintaining" his integrity will have the different sense of "continuing to affirm" his integrity (cf. on 27:6).

And if Job still maintains his integrity, what does that prove? It could mean that the issue has been settled, that piety is not simply the result of prosperity. If that is so, the trial has not been "without cause" or "without effect" (the two possible meanings of חנם): the cause has been the question hitherto untested of the relation between prosperity and piety; the effect has been to establish that in the case of one human at least, piety did not depend on prosperity.

But Job's maintaining his piety could have a more unhappy meaning: it could signify that the trial had not been severe enough. Indeed, it has been settled that deprivation of his material possessions and of his children has not shaken his piety; but suppose that "prosperity" includes physical and mental health; what then? The fact is that once the question of the causal nexus between piety and prosperity has been raised, it must be probed to the utmost extent.

There has indeed been no "cause" in Job himself why he should be the object of this examination of the relation of piety and prosperity. It is truly gratuitous (חנם) that he should have been fastened upon, quite fortuitous that he should be both the most upright and the most prosperous man of his time. But that does not mean that the suffering is meaningless or gratuitous. His suffering has not been decreed in order to settle a divine wager, or to provide an object lesson for some second-rank heavenly being—but in order to lay bare a truth that lies at the heart of the moral universe (a truth that has been badly misconstrued by popular religion and professional wisdom alike), and even more perhaps (to put the matter in the frankly anthropomorphic language that suits the narrative) in order to lay to rest a doubt in the mind of God himself (cf. on 1:9). The assault upon Job has not been some "abortive attempt" and the Satan is not "mortified at its failure" (Peake). The experiment—cruel though the term is—has not yet yielded a conclusive result because the conditions in which it was carried out were not rigorous enough.

The experiment, however, has even by this inconclusive stage brought into the open—at least to the observant reader—one striking fact about the moral universe as perceived by the narrator: it is indeed possible for a righteous person to suffer gratuitously. We first became aware of this perception from the course of the narrative of the first heavenly scene (1:6–12), but now for the first time it is with a single word explicitly granted that Job has been smitten "for nothing" (חנם). That means to say: the law of retribution has been broken! This admission does not amount to a virtual self-reproach on the part of Yahweh (as Hesse maintains, shocked by the audacity of the "supplementer"—to whom he ascribes these verses—in attributing such an admission to Yahweh); and this is not the moment in the flow of the narrative for the development of a questioning of the nexus of suffering and sin—that will be treated amply in the dialogue. Here the nexus under the microscope is that of piety and prosperity; but the one nexus is the obverse of the other, and it is not surprising that in this phrase "destroy him without cause" we should have a premonition of the pivotal issue of the dialogue. Here it is stated from God's point of view; in the dialogue, it will be from Job's point of view, and it will take the form "destroy *me* without cause."

In reminding the Satan that he "urged" Yahweh to "destroy" Job, Yahweh is by no means repudiating responsibility for Job's former trial (Peake), nor giving him credit for instigating the experiment (Pope). Rather, Yahweh invites Satan's agreement to the apparent success of the experiment in which the Satan and Yahweh have together been implicated.

4–6 That agreement the Satan will not give. The real test of the relationship of Job's piety and his prosperity has not yet begun, he means to say; it is only when the man himself, his own "bone" and "flesh," is smitten that one can determine the truth about the piety of Job.

The no doubt proverbial saying "skin for skin" is difficult of interpretation; but the import of the Satan's speech is made entirely clear by what follows: Job has been willing to bow to Yahweh's "taking away" all he possessed because his own life has been spared. Prosperity of a kind he still has: his own life and health. So may it not be *that* prosperity that is inextricably linked with his piety?

Several suggestions have been offered for the meaning of the phrase "skin for skin." If we suppose, as most do, that it sums up Job's reaction to the blows that have fallen on him, the most natural view is that the saying comes from the world of bartering, where "one skin for another skin" could well be a phrase for a fair exchange. Fohrer mentions a similar phrase *bîta kima bîti* "house for house" in a legal document from Ugarit (*Le palais royal d'Ugarit* [Mission de Ras Shamra 6; ed. J. Nougayrol; Paris: Imprimerie Nationale et C. Klincksieck, 1955] 3:164 [text 16.383, line 9]); and Hölscher cites an Arabic phrase *ra's bira's,* "one head [of cattle] for another" (from R. Dozy, *Supplément aux dictionnaires arabes* [Leiden: Brill, 1881] 1:494), surmising that the phrase originated in tribal bartering where pelts were used as a staple article of currency. The German phrase "Wurst wider [*or,* um] Wurst," "a sausage for a sausage" is also often cited. The difficulty raised against this suggestion is that "the exchange of one skin for another is not a likely commercial transaction" (Andersen), since barter does not involve exchanging one thing for another of the same kind (Tur-Sinai, followed by Rowley). But proverbial expressions are often tautologies, and the phrase may well have had to do originally with what was *fair:* proverbially speaking, the only indisputably fair exchange for one pelt is another pelt. That does not mean that the saying must always have precisely that sense. In the present context, it would mean that Job has judged his possessions (including his children) and his own life (including his health) to be of equal value to him; he can afford to forgo his goods to save his life—and indeed he must, for if he refuses to afford to, he loses his life. True, Job has not been asked to relinquish his prosperity in order to secure his life in return (Andersen); yet the only means he has of securing his life is to give up his possessions with good grace—and not curse God.

A variant of this view, taking "skin" more literally, is that the "skin" that Job gives up is the skin of his family, servants, and animals, in order to save his own skin (cf. B. Jacob, *ZAW* 32 [1912] 279); on this understanding, the proverb means that "a man will give anyone else's skin on behalf of, i.e., to save his own skin" (Gordis). Gray was even tempted to a slight emendation in the Hebrew (see n. 2:4.a) that would yield: "[Another] skin for his [own] skin." It is no argument against this view that "Job had never been confronted with this choice, and can scarcely be said to have sacrificed his children and his possessions" (Rowley); for Job indeed had the choice whether or not to accept the death of his family and animals, or to protest it and thereby lose his own life. It is interesting that all that Job has lost are living beings (whether human or animal), and for them the term "skin" would be appropriate. But once it is admitted that the first "skin" stands for the totality of Job's possessions, this variant becomes virtually identical with the interpretation first mentioned. In either of its forms, this understanding is quite acceptable, though another interpretation to be put forward below may be preferable.

Less probable, however, is the quite common view that the idea of a "double skin" is in mind, as in Arabic literature, viz. the concept of an outer skin (*bašarat*) and an inner skin (*ʾadamat*). Here the sense would be that only Job's outer skin, so to speak, has been touched, the man himself remaining unscathed; thus we might translate: "[There is one] skin beyond (בעד) [another] skin." To use an earlier metaphor, the "hedge" (1:10) surrounding Job has been breached, but he himself has not been struck (1:12). Rowley and Andersen incline to this view, following Schultens, Merx, Budde, and others. Gordis objects that there is no evidence for Heb. עור "skin" having this twofold meaning and that for such a distinction Arabic uses two different words. Pope's objection is that since Job's person has not been touched, there is no skin off him as yet; though this is an overliteral reading, "skin beyond skin" would be more apt in a context of inflicting greater physical hardship upon one already suffering in this way. Pope's own suggestion, "skin after skin" (following Tur-Sinai), i.e., there are layers of skin protecting his heart and life, actually seems little different.

Less acceptable still is the interpretation of the Targum and Rashi, followed by Driver and others, that a person will sacrifice one part of the body to save some other part, e.g., an arm to save the head. The obvious objection to this view is that עור "skin" is never used for a *part* of the body.

A quite different route to a solution, and one which leads to the most attractive interpretation, lies in supposing that "skin for skin" does not refer to the immediate past (how Job has reacted) but to the immediate future (how he will *treat Yahweh* if Yahweh should touch his bone and his flesh). If Yahweh scratches Job's skin, it will be Yahweh's skin that is put at risk. "Skin for skin" would be a saying appropriate to a situation of conflict, a rule or observation about redress for injury; it would be very similar to the formulae of Exod

21:23–25, "life for life, eye for eye, . . . hand for hand . . ." (though the preposition there is תחת rather than בעד as here; see n. 2:4.a). On this interpretation, the Satan's speech means: "Only when you strike at the man's life will you see of what temper his piety is. He has given up his possessions in exchange for (בעד) his life (נפש, *nephesh*), but now that he has only his life, attack that and you will find that he attacks *you*—in the only way he knows how, by 'cursing' you, i.e., assaulting your life, your skin for his skin." Olshausen pointed the way to this interpretation, but his view is seldom referred to by recent commentators, no doubt because neither he nor they saw how "skin for skin" relates not to Job's reaction to past calamity but to his expected reaction to any future assault from heaven (v 5).

However the phrase is understood, there is no need to see the Satan's speech as "insolent and vulgar" (Duhm), or to agree with Peake that "the rather vulgar language . . . is not exactly a sign of impudent familiarity, but the free speech of an old servant, who does not wish to see his master imposed upon." It is colloquial speech, no doubt, but, after all, the heavenly court of this tale is a rather rustic and informal assembly.

What is needed to resolve the heavenly question of the connection between Job's piety and his prosperity (now reduced to his own personal existence) is to remove what prosperity remains to him. But if Job is deprived of existence altogether the question will remain for ever unsettled; for everything hangs upon Job's reaction. So the man himself must be smitten, and smitten so severely that he despairs of life and feels himself in the grip of death, but he must not actually die. His "bone" and "flesh" will be smitten, but his "life" (נפש, *nephesh*) must be "preserved" (שמר) (v 6).

The distinction between "flesh" (בשר) and "life, vitality" (נפש) usually runs along different lines from what we encounter here. "Flesh" in the OT normally denotes the human being in its entirety, but may be used for the physical, external being of a person as distinct from the inner being (e.g., Prov 4:21–22; 14:30). When "flesh" (בשר) is linked with "life" (נפש), the terms collectively express the whole of a person's being (cf. Ps 63:2 [1]; 84:3 [2])—each term then, by the principle of the "break-up of stereotype phrase," individually expressing the totality (on this principle, see further E. Z. Melamed, "Break-Up of Stereotype Phrases as an Artistic Device in Biblical Poetry," *ScrHieros* 8 [1961] 115–53; M. Dahood, *Psalms III,* 413–14). The distinction between the two terms—which is implied by a phrase like "from 'life' (נפש) as far as 'flesh' (בשר)" (Isa 10:18; RSV "wholly")—is usually much less important than their similarity. Whether or not N. P. Bratsiotis's formulation is correct, that they are to be understood as "different aspects of man's existence as a twofold entity" (*TDOT* 2:326), the fact is that they are not normally set in opposition to each other (as against G. Gerleman, *THWAT* 1:378) or even significantly differentiated (see also on 12:10; 13:14; 14:22). Here, however, "life" (נפש) must mean simple existence, as contrasted with "bone and flesh" as the bodily structure of the human individual.

"Bone" (עצם) and "flesh" frequently indicate family or kin relationship (as in Gen 2:33; 29:14; Judg 9:2; 2 Sam 5:1 [= 1 Chr 11:1]; 19:13–14; cf. W. Reiser, "Die Verwandtschaftsformel in Gen 2,23," *ThZ* 16 [1960] 1–4; W. Brueggemann, "'Of the Same Flesh and Bone' (Gen 2,23a)," *CBQ* 32 [1970] 532–42). The bones, however, frequently appear as the seat of disease (30:17, 30;

Ps 6:3 [2]; Prov 12:4; contrast Job 20:11; see also on 19:20), and clearly it is the physical infliction of illness that the Satan proposes here. There may be an intentional allusion, in rather poor taste, to the fact that it is Job's "bone and flesh" (his children) who have already been "smitten," just as the sparing of Job's "life" (v 6) may allude to Job's own instinct for survival which has led him to give everything "for his life" (v 4; if that is indeed the meaning of that verse).

As in 1:11–12, the Satan will act as Yahweh's agent; the "hand" that is "put forth" against him is Yahweh's, and at the same time the "hand" which will smite Job is the Satan's.

7–13 *Job's affliction, Job's response: scene 2.* The scene in heaven "dissolves" (as Gray puts it; the term is yet more apt if understood cinematically) into the final scene on earth. The absence of a formal notation of the transition from heaven to earth not only signals the impingement of the divine world upon the human and the delegation of authority by Yahweh (see above on 1:1–2:13), but also quickens the pace of the narrative.

As in the first scene of Job's affliction, Job's reaction to the suffering is an unvoiced act. As if to press more rapidly toward the resolution of the issue at stake, the narrative does not have Job spontaneously utter an expression of acceptance; rather, it quietly assumes his attitude of acceptance and moves immediately into a probing of it and a pressure upon it in the form of his wife's question. And even under that pressure, his stance persists, and with the utterance of v 10 it would seem that the issue of the prologue ought to be settled for good and all.

Thereafter, what is demanded of the narrative by the dramatic logic is that the focus should shift again to heaven, and a scene of resolution should be played out between the Satan and Yahweh. It is their dialogue that has set in train this twofold testing of Job; so what passes between them now that the testing is completed? Yet it is of the essence of the Book of Job that from this critical moment onward heaven is sealed off and silent; God himself will not speak again before there have been thirty-four chapters of human speech (discursive and inconclusive, they render, on reflection, the direct decisiveness of heavenly speech in this prologue almost brutal); and earth will determinedly remain the locus of speech and action until the final sentences of the book. Not until the concluding verses will it be allowed by Yahweh that "my servant Job" has "spoken what is right of me" (42:7, 8) despite the long-continued— and even then still unrelieved—sufferings of Job. Yet while in these words no reference is made to the heavenly question at stake in chaps. 1 and 2— how could it be, unless earth were made privy to the inner workings of heaven?— they presuppose that the issue has indeed been resolved. And the restoration of Job's fortunes (42:10–17) forms a final, though indirect, testimony to the nature of the question about which chaps. 1 and 2 revolve; for it is only if it has been decisively established that Job's prosperity is not the cause of his piety that his fortunes can be restored (42:10) without permitting the initial question of 1:9–11 to be raised afresh, so setting in motion again the whole tragic cycle.

The remainder of the present scene, vv 11–13, is a link passage between the prologue and the dialogue: in it are introduced the three friends of Job with whom the conversations of chaps. 3–31 will be conducted. So this passage, and especially its depiction of the pregnant silence in which they sit with him, looks toward what is to follow. But it also forms a conclusion to what has gone before: the three friends are a promising counterpart to Job's three "enemies" (the Satan, Yahweh, Job's wife); the "evil" that has "come" (בוא) upon Job now begins to take on a less devastating aspect when it causes the friends to "come" (בוא) to Job, "each from his own place"—as earlier the four calamities had come. They make an appointment to assemble; and this earthly assembly for the consolation of Job promises to counterbalance the heavenly assembly which has brought him only harm. Finally, this narrative of silence, coupled with ritual activities of sympathy, coming at the end of the prologue, corresponds with Job's nonspeaking but sympathetically active role (1:1–5a; and his "speaking" [אמר] in 1:5b is perhaps only "thought") at the beginning of the prologue, as well as with his repeated (and therefore characteristic) response to events that precedes speech by action (1:20–21; 2:8–10). The speaking in this prologue has been *about* Job and *to* Job; apart from the brief utterances in 1:21 and 2:10 (1:5 may be passed over), which have expressed only acceptance of the suffering, Job is silent. Over against the heavenly conversations and the constantly interrupted succession of messages that bombard Job in 1:13–19, Job has been silent, and now, to conclude the prologue, the silence of the friends matches that of Job.

The original connection of this episode, vv 7b–10, with the Job story is denied by Hesse, who observes that Job's illness, and Job's wife, are not mentioned in the epilogue (chap. 42). See the *Comment* on vv 1–6 above.

7 In this second trial of Job, the Satan is named as the direct source of Job's affliction whereas in the first trial the Satan's part in the calamities is not spelled out. It is difficult to assess the significance of this difference. It may be that the immediate causes of the four calamities in chap. 1 made any reference to the Satan's activity (which is implied in 1:12) superfluous. Here, the infliction of illness can hardly be attributed to any human or physical cause, and the ascription of illness to the hostile activity of a supernatural being, whether demon (cf. Ps 91:6), heavenly messenger (cf. 1 Sam 16:14; 2 Sam 24:15–17; 2 Kgs 19:35; Ps 78:49), or God himself (cf. Exod 11:4; 12:23; Deut 28:22), is a common occurrence in the OT. But we may also have here a deliberate intensification of the immediate link between the heavenly decision and Job's suffering; the same intensification may be suggested also by the "dissolving" of the heavenly scene into the earthly, without a formal marker that the locus of events has changed.

This second affliction of Job resembles the first group of calamities in its suddenness and completeness. Just as he must lose *all* his possessions, so too he must be smitten with a disease that afflicts the *whole* of his body, "from the sole of his foot to the crown of his head" (for the phrase cf. Deut 28:35; 2 Sam 14:25; similarly Isa 1:6). This is not simply the typical hyperbole of the folk story; it is (theo)logically necessary for the question to be probed to the utmost, and therefore for Job's disease to be as widespread as possible. The reader knows that it cannot be a fatal disease, but Job will not know the difference between chronic and terminal illness. There were skin diseases that could be healed (Lev 13) and skin diseases that could not be healed (Deut 28:27, 35), and there was probably no way of distinguishing between them, at least in their early stages. For this very reason it is futile to argue (as Fohrer;

similarly Hesse) that the original Job story, followed by the prologue and the epilogue of the present book, depicted a curable disease, whereas the speeches depict a fatal disease. For the prologue and epilogue necessarily regard the disease from the narrator's standpoint (and he knows the disease will be healed), while the speeches necessarily represent Job's viewpoint (and he, getting no relief, can only suppose that his illness is incurable). C. Barth has suggested that for the Hebrews death and life were often regarded as distinct but overlapping spheres, death constantly encroaching upon life; so those who were still physically alive might nevertheless be regarded, and might regard themselves, as being in the sphere of death and under its power (*Die Errettung vom Tode in den individuellen Klage- und Dankliedern des Alten Testaments* [Zollikon: Evangelischer Verlag, 1947]). More simply, since "life" so often means total well-being including prosperity and health, death is the loss of that total well-being (W. Brueggemann, *IDBSup*, 220).

The identification of Job's disease has been a matter of continuing speculation. The term used (שְׁחִין) is a general one that could cover various diseases of the skin. Since it is mentioned in Lev 13:18–23 as a boil which may be an initial sign of leprosy, leprosy has been a common identification; however, there is in Hebrew a special word for leprosy (צָרַעַת)—though this is a vaguer term than the current medical term, which denotes infection by *Mycobacterium leprae*. Another common identification is elephantiasis, a disease producing swollen limbs and blackened skin. But it is better to admit our ignorance of the precise malady. For further discussion, see H. H. Rowley, "The Book of Job and Its Meaning," *BJRL* 41 (1958) 169–70 n. 4; Gray, 23–24 (probably elephantiasis); G. N. Münch, "Die Zaarath (Lepra) der hebräischen Bibel," *Dermatalogische Studien* 16 (1896) 135–37 (chronic eczema); D. Schapiro, "La maladie de Job: Étude clinique et exégétique," *Hippocrate* 7 (1940) 281–88; KB, 960b (smallpox); Dhorme, 18 (malignant, infectious ulcer); Terrien, 59 n. 3 (a skin disease, *pemphigus foliaceus*); Pope, 21 (ulcerous boil known as the "Baghdad Button" or "Jericho Rose"); Librarian, Army Medical Library, "Morbus Jobi," *The Urologic and Cutaneous Review* 40 (1936) 296–99 (syphilis, Job's reference to the "sins of [his] youth" [13:26] being held in evidence); S. G. Browne, *Leprosy in the Bible* (London: Christian Medical Fellowship, n.d.); J. V. Kinnier Wilson, "Leprosy in Ancient Mesopotamia," *RA* 60 (1966) 47–58 (56) (pellagra, scurvy, vitamin deficiency); C. Brim, "Job's Illness—Pellagra," *Archives of Dermatology and Syphilology* 46 (1942) 371–76; K. P. C. A. Gramberg, "'Leprosy' and the Bible," *BiTrans* 11 (1960) 10–23; D. H. Wallington, "'Leprosy' and the Bible," *BiTrans* 12 (1961) 75–79; R. G. Cochrane, "Biblical Leprosy," *BiTrans* 12 (1961) 202–3; E. V. Hulse, "The Nature of Biblical 'Leprosy' and the Use of Alternative Medical Terms in Modern Translations of the Bible," *PEQ* 107 (1975) 87–105; on the term, see J. F. A. Sawyer, "A Note on the Etymology of *sāraʿat*," *VT* 26 (1976) 241–45. Several more recent writers regard Job's skin disease as psychosomatic in origin; W. Guy, for example, thinks Job's dermatological condition "appeared, lasted for a time, and then suddenly disappeared, just as do many cases of widespread lichen planus, psoriasis, atopic eczema, chronic urticaria, dermatitis herpetiformis, and generalized exfoliative dermatitis. The comings and goings of such dermatoses are enigmatic" ("Psychosomatic Dermatology *circa* 400 B.C.," *Archives of Dermatology* 71 [1955] 354–56; similarly J. Kahn, *Job's Illness: Loss, Grief, and Integration. A Psychological Interpretation* [Oxford: Pergamon, 1975] 10–11).

Many references are made in the course of the book to Job's illness. While attempts to use these references to pinpoint the illness are not on principle to be ruled out (as Horst), the poetic language makes it a risky undertaking. It is best to translate the term שׁחִין here with some general phrase like "running sores" (NEB), "severe boils" (NAB) or "painful sores" (NIV); the repeated eruption of pustules (7:5) and blackening and peeling off of the skin (30:30) are the most definite signs in the poem of a skin disease, and correspond to the itching purulence mentioned here. Other symptoms are more general: emaciation (19:20), fever (30:30b), nightmares (7:14) and sleeplessness (7:4), weeping (16:16); 19:17 in all probability does not contain a reference to putrid breath, though this is commonly said (see *Comment*). Many commentators note as a further symptom maggots breeding in his sores (7:5), but the reference is probably to the discharge of pus (see n. 7:5.a). References to the aching or rotting of his bones (30:17) and to their burning (30:30) probably reflect only the common idea of the bones as the seat of disease (cf. above on vv 4–6) and are not to be regarded as literal descriptions of his symptoms. Similarly the reference to strangulation in 7:15 is not to be seen as a symptom of elephantiasis (as Gray) but as a psychic dread of the suffocating closeness of God's presence.

The root שׁחן, from which the term for Job's illness is derived, means in some cognate languages (Ug., Akk., Aram., Syr., Arab.) "be hot" or "be inflamed," and the noun may therefore be a general term for any kind of inflammation of the skin. In a Ugaritic text, the god Baal is "feverish" (*šḥn*) in the loins (*CTA* 12.239), and in the Qumran text known as the "Prayer of Nabonidus," this neo-Babylonian king is said to have been "smitten with grievous sores [שׁחנא באישא, the Aram. equivalent of שׁחין רע here] at the command of the Most High God" (4QPrNab; J. T. Milik, "'Prière de Nabonide' et autres écrits d'un cycle de Daniel: Fragments araméens de Qumrân 4," *RB* 63 [1956] 407–15 [408]).

Nothing is said explicitly about the rapidity with which the disease struck Job, but the implication is that the blow was sudden and devastatingly complete. While skin diseases generally take some time to spread (elephantiasis, for example, "develops slowly, and often lasts some years before death ensues" [Gray]), the time-span is irrelevant to the narrative.

8 Job is already sitting among the ashes when the disease is inflicted upon him (see *Translation*). The narrative economy and the vivid picture that results are remarkable.

Nothing has been said in the previous scene of Job's affliction (1:13–22) concerning Job's subsequent action after his blessing of Yahweh (1:21). Many versions, including KJV, RV, RSV, JPS, JB, imply that only after this second affliction did Job go to sit on the ash-heap; but the Hebrew rather suggests that since his first affliction he has been sitting there in mourning. Ashes appear to have the same ritual significance as dust (cf. the expression "dust and ashes" to denote worthlessness, Gen 18:27; and cf. Job 30:19; 42:6 [*q.v.*]). The words sound very much alike, *ʿāpār* and *ʾēper*, עָפָר וָאֵפֶר. As a sign of mourning they were thrown on the head (2 Sam 13:19; cf. Isa 61:3; like dust, Job 2:12) or on the clothes (Esth 4:1), or were lain in (Esth 4:3) or rolled in (Jer 6:26; Ezek 27:30; Mic 1:10). See E. F. de Ward, *JSS* 23 (1972) 1–27, 145–66, esp. 6–8; M. Jastrow, "Dust, Earth, and Ashes as Symbols of Mourning among the Ancient Hebrews," *JAOS* 20 (1904) 133–50 (136–41). For sitting as a posture of weeping, cf. Ezek 8:14; 26:16; Neh 1:4; 1 Macc 1:27; in Ugaritic texts, *CTA* 5.6.11–14 (Gibson, 73); see de Ward, *JSS* 23 (1972) 3–4. As with many mourning rituals, the use of ashes was also a penitential ritual (Jonah 3:6; Dan 9:3; Isa 58:5; Matt 11:21; Luke 10:13) or supplication ritual (1 Sam 2:8; Ps 113:7).

It is by no means clear from the text whether Job has performed this ritual in his own house or has gone out to a public place to display his grief. Certainly in the dialogue, 19:15–18 and 30:28b suggest that Job is not permanently outcast, voluntarily or otherwise, from his house. But it is almost universally assumed by interpreters that the ashes in which Job sits are in the public ash-heap outside the town, the resort of outcasts and persons with infectious diseases, as well as, in cases like the present, those who psychically identify themselves with the rejected and destitute. The Septuagint in fact explains "ashes" by its translation "the dungheap outside the city" (τῆς κοπρίας ἔξω τῆς πόλεως), perhaps with a recollection of Priam's mourning for his son Hector, and "rolling himself in the dung" (κυλινδόμενος κατὰ κόπρον) (*Iliad* 22.414). Such rubbish dumps, termed *mezbala* (cf. postbib. Heb. *zebel* [זֶבֶל], "dung"), outside Arab villages in the Hauran were described by Wetzstein: "The dung . . . is carried in baskets in a dry state to that place outside the village, and there generally it is burnt once a month . . . . The ashes remain . . . . If a place has been inhabited for centuries, the *mezbele* attains a height far greater than that of the place itself. The rains of winter reduce the layers of ashes to a compact mass, and gradually convert the *mezbele* into a solid hill of earth . . . . The *mezbele* serves the inhabitants of the place as a watch-tower, and on sultry evenings as a place of concourse, for on this height there is a breath of air. . . . There lies the outcast who, smitten by loathsome disease, is no longer admitted to the dwellings of men. . . . There lie the dogs of the village, gnawing perhaps some fallen carcase, such as is often thrown there" (cited from Gray). Cf. also A. Musil, *Arabia Petraea* (Vienna: A. Hölder, 1908) 3:413. Sitting or dwelling among rubbish forms part of several Near Eastern cursing formulae; see P.-E. Dion, "Un nouvel éclairage sur le contexte culturel des malheurs de Job," *VT* 34 (1984) 213–25.

The potsherd Job picks up would be easily found on such an ash-heap. Most think that that he uses it as a counterirritant to relieve or distract his attention from the itchiness of his skin. The Septuagint, which is rather expansive in this scene, adds that Job took the potsherd to scrape away the pus (ἵνα τὸν ἰχῶρα ξύῃ). It is less likely that he uses it to lacerate his skin (as Pope, Owens), a well-attested symbol of mourning, though it is forbidden in Pentateuchal law (Lev 19:28; 21:5; Deut 14:1; for the practice, see Jer 16:6; 41:5; 47:5; 48:37; and in Ugaritic texts, *Aqht* (*CTA* 19) 4.172–73; 5.6.17–18 (Gibson, 120, 73). Pope notes that in Akkadian the term "place/mound of potsherds" is apparently used to designate the realm of the dead.

The two trials of Job have now coalesced; and the one place, the ash-heap, is, as the site of ashes for his mourning ritual and potsherds for his sores, the single appropriate place for his situation of alienation and displacement.

9 Job's wife plays an ambiguous role. In purely narrative terms, her intervention functions as the means of drawing from Job a verbal response to his affliction. That response is delayed both by the characteristic silence of Job and by the challenge of his wife's utterance; and at the same time response in the vein we have come to expect of Job is threatened by her suggestion. Her presence thus introduces delay, tension, and finally resolution into this tiny segment of the narrative.

But how is her intervention to be seen, ethically or religiously speaking? On the one hand, her invitation to "curse God and die" can certainly be seen as a further "temptation" of Job; it cannot be accidental that such have also been the words of the Satan—not, indeed, as his recommendation to Job but as his prediction of Job's ultimate response to being deprived of possessions and health. Her taking up these words implies that she too belongs in the camp of those who believe in the causal nexus between piety and prosperity (like the majority, and like the "falsely naive" narrator in 1:1–2); she has a firm belief in what is, in heaven, only a question. She does not believe in gratuitous piety, in fearing God for naught (1:9). Not surprisingly, many have cast her in the role of "devil's assistant" (Augustine: *diaboli adjutrix*); Calvin called her "Satan's tool," and Thomas Aquinas thought that the Satan spared her, in the calamities of chap. 1, precisely in order to use her against Job. The parallel with Eve and thus with the archetypal "woman as temptress" has also naturally often been drawn. (The rabbis note, however, that Job, unlike Adam, did not accept his wife's suggestion; *Midr. Gen. Rab.* 19:12.)

On the other hand, however, Job's wife does not doubt his "integrity" (תמה; cf. on 2:3), and if in the second half of her speech she echoes the words of the Satan, in the first half she echoes the words of Yahweh (2:3). And if she recommends Job to "curse" God and so bring death upon himself (see n. 2:9.a), it can only be because she feels that sudden death must be better for Job than lingering pain from which no recovery seems possible. It is an impious suggestion she makes, but it does not arise out of impiety; it is humane and entirely for Job's benefit, this "theological method of committing euthanasia" (Terrien). "Job's wife is a realist," says Habel; whereas Job, we must add, is nothing if not an idealist—and he will suffer for it.

There is more yet to the intervention of Job's wife, however. Rarely has the scene been viewed through her eyes (though even the merely psychologizing expansion of the Septuagint noted below moves in that direction). Through no fault of her own, but solely because of the social structures of her time, her own well-being has been wholly dependent on Job's. She has relied on him for her economic existence, for her social status, and for her moral standing in the community. But now, at a stroke, she has lost everything. Her income is gone, now that the cattle and servants have been destroyed, her position as matriarch and wife of a prince has been lost, and she is open to the obloquy of guilt by association. All this in addition to the sudden loss of her ten children. And who is to blame? No one but her husband. All that rising early in the mornings to offer sacrifices in case the children had sinned (1:5) was nothing but the scrupulosity of the hypocrite. It is not the children but the husband who has brought disaster upon the household. And Job has uttered no word of regret for his unarguable responsibility for the destruction of the family, but insists on "maintaining his integrity." The only honorable act from this guilty man now would be for him to call down the wrath of God upon his own head.

In fact, not to put too fine a point upon it, Job continues to wrong her by his submissiveness to the act of fate. By accepting his suffering he brands *her*

children as wrongdoers. As Sarah, the wife of the Job character in Archibald
MacLeish's play *J.B.*, puts it:

<blockquote>

They are
Dead and they were innocent: I will not
Let you sacrifice their deaths
To make injustice justice and God good!
</blockquote>

J.B.:   [covering his face with his hands]
     My heart beats. I cannot answer it.

Sarah: If you buy quiet with their innocence—
     Theirs or yours . . .
       I will not love you.

J.B.:   [softly]
     I have no choice but to be guilty.

Sarah: [her voice rising]
     We have the choice to live or die
     All of us . . .
      Curse God and die . . .

        (A. MacLeish, *J.B.* [Boston: Houghton Mifflin, 1956] 110)

She has immediately, or (shall we say?) instinctively, seen what Job will take
some time to realize, that he cannot *both* hold fast his integrity *and* bless God;
either Job or God must be guilty. Though Job never does "curse" God, strictly
speaking, his railing, taunting, protesting, and summoning of his divine assailant
is nothing like "blessing" God either. Though he does not follow his wife's
advice to the letter, he is from this point onward entirely infused by its spirit.

Certainly, the narration is suggestive rather than explicit. An open text
like this invites divergent approaches, of which a particularly appealing example
may be here mentioned. Muriel Spark, in her novel *The Only Problem,* which
must surely be the only novel to have as its central character a man who is
writing a monograph on the Book of Job, has her hero fascinated by a painting
of Georges de La Tour, the seventeenth-century French artist. It is called
"Job Visited by His Wife," and it is done in the manner of the Dutch candlelit
pictures of the time. She describes it thus: "Job's wife, tall, sweet-faced, with
the intimation of a beautiful body inside the large, tent-like case of her firm
clothes, bending, long-necked, solicitous over Job. In her hand is a lighted
candle. It is night, it is winter; Job's wife wears a glorious red tunic over her
dress. Job sits on a plain cube-shaped block. He might be in front of a fire,
for the light of the candle alone cannot explain the amount of light that is
cast on the two figures. Job is naked except for a loin-cloth. He clasps his
hands above his knees. His body seems to shrink, but it is the shrunkenness
of pathos rather than want. Beside him is the piece of broken pottery that he
has taken to scrape his wounds. His beard is thick. He is not an old man.
Both are in their prime, a couple in their thirties. . . . His face looks up at
his wife, sensitive, imploring some favour, urging some cause. What is his
wife trying to tell him as she bends her sweet face toward him? What does
he beg, this stricken man, so serene in his faith, so accomplished in argument?
. . . Job and his wife are deeply in love" (*The Only Problem* [London: Grafton,
1985] 76–79). Suppose this to be a "true" representation, and the text gains
new and surprising resonances. It is certainly not a reading forbidden by the
text.

Nevertheless, we must admit, for the narrative it is not the psychology or morality of Job's wife that is the central issue: it is Job's behavior. And for that very reason, any wrong in her suggestion is not accented; the "temptation," if that is what it is, is easily resisted by Job (Duhm), and Job's reply to her is remarkably mild (see further on v 10).

The Septuagint, which expands vv 8–10 considerably, here inserts a long speech in the mouth of Job's wife, probably not because it was in its Hebrew original (Ball), and hardly because the translator felt "nature and propriety outraged, that a woman should in such circumstances say so little" (Davidson). Rather, it appears to be an example of the midrashic tendency to provide details about minor characters and to elaborate brief speeches (the same tendency is seen in the concluding Septuagintal expansion in 42:17) and in the present passage at least may be a secondary addition in the Septuagint itself, since the words for "hold fast" and "bless (= curse)" are differently translated from their occurrences in vv 3, 4 (Duhm). The addition may reflect the tendency in Jewish tradition to portray Job's wife sympathetically (cf. *T. Job* 21–25, and for the rabbinic sources, see R. Gordis, *The Book of God and Man: A Study of Job* [Chicago: University of Chicago Press, 1965] 226).

Here the Septuagint adds, at the beginning of the verse, "When a long time had passed," perhaps as if to emphasize that the reaction of Job's wife is no hasty impulse. Then follows her speech, which both testifies to her concern for her husband, and, by dwelling on her own grief, explains to some extent how she can come to offer such advice. It runs: "How long will you endure, saying, Behold, I will wait yet for a little time, looking for the hope of my salvation? Behold, the memory of you has been blotted out from the earth, [namely] the sons and daughters, the travail and pain of my womb, whom with toil I reared for nothing. And yet you yourself sit in the decay of worms, passing the nights under the open sky, while I am a wanderer and a servant, from place to place and from house to house, waiting until the sun goes down, so that I may rest from my toils and from the pains that now grip me. Now, say some word against the Lord, and die. But he, looking at her, said to her. . . ." Cf. also *T. Job* 24, where part of this addition is repeated, and where also she humiliates herself by selling her hair to buy bread. See also N. Peters, "Zum Charakter der Frau Jobs [Job 2,9s]," *ThGl* 11 (1919) 418–23.

The name of Job's wife appears in the Targum and some rabbinic references (*Gen. Rab.* 19.2; 57.4; *b. B. Bat.* 15b) as Dinah, perhaps because Job says (v 10) that she speaks as one of the "foolish women" (נבלות) and Dinah the daughter of Jacob was one with whom "folly" (נבלה) had been done (Gen 34:7). In the *Testament of Job* she is called Sitis, a name derived from Ausitis, the LXX translation of Uz.

10 Job rejects his wife's suggestion with the retort that she speaks "like one of the foolish women." The reticence of his reproach is noteworthy; she is not herself a foolish woman but is speaking as if she were; "he implies that she has spoken, under momentary stress, as any one of a class to which she did not belong" (Gray). But who are the "foolish" women? The term נבל, conventionally translated "foolish," may have not only an intellectual-moral connotation, but also an ethical-religious or a social connotation. Thus, in the first sense, it can be contrasted with חכם "wise" (Deut 32:6) and, as a noun, with "a man of experience" (Ecclus 21:22); in the second sense, it can be effectively identical with רשע "wicked" (cf. Ps 14:1 with 10:4; 39:9 [8] with 39:2 [1]); and, in the third sense, it can be linked with the phrase בלי־שם "nameless," i.e., disreputable, without reputation, and contrasted with נדיב "noble" (Isa 32:5; Prov 17:7) (a similar sense is probable in 2 Sam 3:33; Prov 30:22). We therefore cannot simply state that "the fault of the *nābhāl* was not weakness of reason but moral and religious insensibility" (Driver, cited by Gray), nor that the cognate noun נבלה (*nᵉbālâ*) essentially denotes "serious disorderly and unruly action resulting in the break up of an existing relationship" (A. Phillips, "NEBALAH—A Term for Serious Disorderly and Unruly Conduct," *VT* 25 [1975] 237–41 [241]), nor that "the oldest meaning of the adjective . . . [is] *outcast*" (W. M. W. Roth, "NBL," *VT* 10 [1960] 394–409 [402–3]). Since Job appears to be referring to a *group* of "foolish" women, the adjective should probably be taken here essentially in its social sense as "low-class" or "common," with the unambiguous overtone of disapproval on moral or religious grounds. It is in keeping with the aristocratic hauteur of the story's world that the lower orders of society should be imagined as the least religious—on the other end of the spectrum from Job, who is rich and God-fearing. So his retort to his wife means, "You talk like a low-class, irreligious woman; such words are beneath you." On the term נבל, see further P. Joüon, "Racine נבל au sens de bas, vil, ignoble," *Bib* 5 (1924) 357–61; A. Caquot, "Sur une désignation vétéro-testamentaire de 'l'insensé,'" *RHR* 155 (1959) 1–16; M. Saebø, *THWAT* 2:26–31.

To his wife's question Job responds with a counterquestion, "If we accept good from God, shall (*or*, should) we not also accept harm?" The term translated "harm" (הרע) is the correlative of "good" (הטוב), and in an ethical context means "(moral) evil" (hence the use of that term by many translations). But Job speaks only of blessing and its opposite, deprivation of blessing, or harm. For Job, there is no question about God, about whether God is the source of all happenings; the only question for Job concerns human behavior toward God (Weiser). It is not some passionless rationality that prompts the symmetry of Job's attitude ("if good, then harm also"), as if to say: God being God, we are bound to have whatever he chooses to give us, good or bad; protest is therefore idle, resignation the only reasonable response. Nor is it some high-minded sense of fair play, that says: If God has had the goodness to grant us blessings, would it not be churlish to refuse him the right to send us calamities (cf. Peake)? It is rather some kind of trustfulness that God knows what he is doing, and the very same piety we have witnessed in Job's blessing the Yahweh who had given and taken away (1:21). It is not the expression of a rational theological position or of some long-standing habit of life; Job has never before encountered "harm," at least as far as we know from the story. What we read of here is religion on the hoof, a faith that instinctively fashions new stances for new crises out of a trust that goes deeper than any theology (for an opposite view, see R. D. Moore, "The Integrity of Job," *CBQ* 45 [1983] 17–31 [20]).

Though the word for "receive" (קבל) has sometimes been thought to be "stronger" than the ordinary word for "take" (לקח) and so to signify "accept" (so Horst), it is probably only the context that gives the term this flavor, making it "an active word, implying co-operation with Providence, not mere submission" (Andersen). Certainly קבל, though it is common in Aramaic, and is found in the Hebrew Bible mostly in later texts, is no sign of the date of the Book of

Job, as is sometimes argued; for it is attested in Canaanite as early as the fourteenth century B.C. (W. F. Albright, "An Ancient Hebrew Proverb in an Amarna Letter from Central Palestine," *BASOR* 89 [1943] 29–32 [31]; but cf. also S. Wagner, *Die lexicalischen und grammatikalischen Aramaismen in alttestamentlichen Hebräisch* [BZAW 96; Berlin: A. Töpelmann, 1966] 99–100).

The rabbinic exegesis that understood the plural of the verb as specifically including Job's wife rather than as a general statement of human obligation (*Gen. Rab.* 19.12) is no doubt on the right lines; this understanding would fit with Job's earlier response that in v 9 she had been speaking out of character.

But rabbinic exegesis of the clause, "Job did not sin with his lips," as implying that "in his thoughts he pondered on words" (Targum; cf. *b. B. Bat.* 16a) is today universally thought to be beside the mark. It is sin with the lips that the Satan has predicted of Job (v 5), and it is just such sin that Job repudiates. The narrative takes for granted here that speech is the outward sign of inner feeling, that "thinking and speaking hardly differ in the East" (Davidson). No doubt the narrator means nothing as unsubtle as Rashi's interpretation: "Job did not sin with his lips, but in his heart he did." But we have seen enough signs of false naivety in this narrative to suspect that ibn Ezra may have been more on the right track when he saw here a hint that although Job had not at this point sinned with his lips he was about to do so. Or at least, we might say, genuine enough though Job's pious speech may be, the full truth about his reaction to his calamity is not yet revealed. The narrative remark about Job's lips leaves him in the clear morally at this point; but it foreshadows the very different turn the narrative will take when Job opens his mouth again (3:1). Job's experience will not be so very dissimilar from that of the psalmist of Ps 39: "I said, I will guard my ways, that I may not sin with my tongue; I will bridle my mouth . . . I was dumb and silent; I held my peace to no avail; my distress grew worse, my heart became hot within me. As I mused, the fire burned; then I spoke with my tongue" (39:2–4 [1–3]). Job's experience, as the following chapter will show, is not dissimilar. His sores are his body's recognition of how gravely he suffers, even before he has truly comprehended intellectually what it all means. "His body is already speaking for him; the damaged and broken skin represents the onset of Job's breakdown" (Kahn, *Job's Illness*, 35). The boils are personal; they loosen his tongue, says Muriel Spark.

11–13 This scene, of the arrival of the friends, forms a bridge between the prologue proper and the dialogue. The friends will be Job's conversation partners throughout the dialogue, and will remain on stage, though silent toward the end, right through to the epilogue. But they do not appear in the prologue until the transactions of heaven with earth have been completed; they are mere commentators on events that have transpired.

This assembly of the friends invites comparison structurally with the two assemblies we have already been presented with: that in heaven of the sons of God and that on earth of the messengers to Job. This assembly gathers round Job as the heavenly council gathered around Yahweh (Habel), but here the purpose is more humane. And the friends, more considerate too than the four messengers, who "appear in hurried procession," in formal and stately fashion "first arrange to meet before they intrude on Job's grief" (Habel).

An interval of some weeks or, more probably, months, is supposed between

Job's calamities and the arrival of the friends. There must be time for the
news to reach them, for them to communicate with one another and to arrange
to meet one another, and then to journey together to Uz. Certain allusions
in the dialogues agree with such a depiction: in 7:3 Job speaks of months of
pain he has already endured, and the tenor of chap. 30 is that the onset of
his suffering is of no recent date (cf. Gray).

In that this episode is tied in closely both to the prologue and the dialogue,
all those scholars who regard the prologue as having a separate origin from
the dialogue have occasion to explain the presence of this scene. Fohrer, for
example, believes that the Job story originally told at this point of the arrival
of friends and relatives, intending to comfort him but in fact leading him
into the same temptation as his wife, a temptation he resists. For their speeches
to Job, they would have been rebuked by God in the words now addressed to
the three friends in 42:7–8 (Fohrer, 32). Such a narrative, Fohrer believes,
can be reconstructed on the basis of 42:11. A redactor has replaced the friends
and relatives with the three friends of Job, 2:11 being formed as an imitation
of 42:11.

De Wilde, on the other hand, thinks that yet another testing of Job, by his
relatives, would have been otiose, and supposes that 2:10 was originally followed
by 42:11, 10ac, the introduction of the three friends in these verses 11–13
being due to the Joban poet (similarly Gordis).

11 The narrative becomes very compressed, but hardly "parsimonious,
summary, and restricted to essentials and externals" (Weiser); for these verses
do not merely consist of dramatic machinery for bringing Job's partners in
conversation to him. They also convey very empathetically the effect the sight
of Job's suffering has on the friends.

They have heard from messengers, each in his hometown, the story of
Job's plight, and they have communicated with each other, again by messengers
no doubt, their desire to visit him. "The fact that they met by *appointment*
shows that they were already acquaintances who felt it would be better to
come *together*" (Andersen). It is left to the reader to conjecture how such a
plan could have been organized (Hesse thinks the practical difficulties well-
nigh insurmountable) or indeed why they might have felt it "better" to come
together. It does sound as though they are each in need of support from the
others, for Job's calamity is a shocking event that alerts his peers to their
own vulnerability, and Job himself is now, as a man afflicted by God with
"evil" (physical calamity, רעה), a dangerous person to associate with. Perhaps
there is safety in numbers. Amos 3:3 may serve as a fine illustration of this
narrative: "Do two walk together unless they have trysted [יעד]?" says the
prophet; G. A. Smith comments, "Hardly in the desert; for there men meet
and take the same road by chance as seldom as ships at sea" (*The Book of the
Twelve Prophets* [London: Hodder and Stoughton, 1896] 1:82). Cf. also Josh
11:5 of kings in alliance meeting at the start of a campaign. The stress here
of course is on their simultaneous arrival, in parallel to the virtually simultaneous
arrival of the four messengers in chap. 1.

The problem of how the friends of Job learned of his misfortune was already
raised in Jewish interpretation: the Targum has it that when they saw the
trees in their gardens withered, that the meat they were eating turned into
raw meat, and their wine into blood, they realized that a misfortune had befallen

Job. In *b. B. Bat.* 16b it is said that they had wreaths that withered (Rashi: a crown on which a portrait of each was engraved, which changed if trouble came on any one of them), thus enabling them to enter Job's town simultaneously by the same gate, even though they lived 300 parasangs apart (see L. Ginzberg, *The Legends of the Jews* [Philadelphia: Jewish Publication Society of America, 1925] 2:237; 5:387).

Their purpose in visiting Job is wholly supportive in intention; it is only when they find him recalcitrant and unteachable, as they see it, that they become his enemies, "torturer-comforters" as he calls them (16:2). The verb "console" (נוד) is often used in its concrete sense "move to and fro, wander, flutter (of a bird)" as well as in its transferred senses "show grief" by shaking or nodding the head (e.g., Jer 22:10) or "show sympathy, condole" (also 42:11; Ps 69:21 [20]). For the practice of visiting mourners to condole with them, cf. Gen 37:35 (2 Sam 10:2, messengers are sent to condole). Jer 16:5, 7 speaks of comforters sharing bread and wine with the mourner. On comfort to mourners in Judaism and its etiquette and rituals, see O. Schmitz and G. Stählin, *TDOT* 5:791. The term conventionally translated "comfort" (נחם) suggests rather more than a mere soothing; it often expresses an encouragement, whether with promises (Gen 50:21; Isa 40:1–2), or with actual gifts (Job 42:11), or help from a situation of distress (as with the formulaic "there was none to comfort," Lam 1:2, etc.); cf. H. J. Stoebe, *THWAT* 2:61–62.

The names of Job's friends and of their places of origin probably indicate an Edomite background, as is the case also with the place-name Uz. The place-name Teman is the most certainly identifiable: it is several times referred to as an important town of Edom, and sometimes stands by synecdoche for the whole country of Edom (Amos 1:12; Obad 9; Jer 49:7, 20; Ezek 25:13; Hab 3:3; cf. "the land of the Temanites," Gen 36:34; 1 Chr 1:45). As a personal name it appears as the name of an Edomite ruler (son of an Eliphaz!) in Gen 36:15; cf. v 42. The place has commonly been identified as Ṭawilân, a site roughly half-way between the southern end of the Dead Sea and Elath (cf., e.g., Y. Aharoni and M. Avi-Yonah, *The Macmillan Bible Atlas* [New York: Macmillan, 1968], map 52), following N. Glueck, who described it as the largest Edomite center in the area of Petra (*The Other Side of the Jordan* [Cambridge, Mass.: ASOR, 1940] 24, 26). But Glueck has now withdrawn that identification (*The Other Side of the Jordan* [Cambridge, Mass.: ASOR, 1970] 32), and R. de Vaux has questioned whether Teman was ever a town and not rather a region ("Téman, ville en région d'Édom?" *RB* 76 [1969] 379–85; followed by C.-M. Bennett, "Ṭawilân (Jordanie)," *RB* 77 [1970] 371–74 [374]). But there is no doubt that it is Edomite (we may ignore the suggestion of W. F. Albright, *AJSL* 44 [1927–28] 36, followed by V. R. Gold, *IDB* 4:534, that "Temanite" here means from Tema in N. Arabia).

The name Shuah does not appear in the OT as a place-name, but it is possible that the reader is supposed to recall that one of Abraham's sons by Keturah was called Shuah, and he and his brothers (including Midian and Jokshan, father of Dedan, a name with some Edomite connections) apparently lived in the "east country" (Gen 25:1–6; 1 Chr 1:32). Many commentators refer to a country named *Suḫu* located on the middle Euphrates and mentioned in cuneiform sources (so originally Friedrich Delitzsch, *Wo lag das Paradies? Eine biblisch-assyriologische Studie* [Leipzig: J. C. Hinrichs, 1881] 297–98 but withdrawn by him in *Das Buch Hiob* [Leipzig: J.C. Hinrichs, 1902] 139), and some would even locate Bildad the Shuhite there (Peake, Fohrer, Terrien, Andersen; J. Simons, *The Geographical and Topographical Texts of the Old Testament* [Leiden: Brill, 1959] 90). See further, B. Moritz, "Die Könige von Edom," *Le Muséon* 50 (1937) 101–22 (112); idem, "Ergänzungen zu meinem Aufsatz: Die Könige von Edom," *ZAW* 57 (1939) 148–50. It may be doubted whether the author of Job or his readers had ever heard of such a place, or that Job was "an international" figure in quite the sense Andersen suggests.

Naamah, the home of Zophar, is less certainly connected with anything. It can hardly be the town of Naamah in Judah, in the Shephelah near Lachish (Josh 15:41) (de Wilde). Some have thought of Jebel el Naʿameh, in northwest Arabia (so A. J. Jaussen and R. de Savignac, *Mission archéologique en Arabie* [Paris: E. Leroux, 1914] 1:64; for other possible locations, cf. F.-M. Abel, *Géographie de la Palestine* [Paris: Gabalda, 1933], 1:287 n. 4). Naamah is attested as an Ammonite personal name in 1 Kgs 14:21 (mother of Rehoboam), and, nearer to the Edomite context, as the name of a descendant of Esau (through the Edomite Eliphaz!) in 1 Chr 4:15. But that genealogical relationship is very complicated; readers could hardly be meant to infer that Naamah as a place-name signified Edom because a person called Naamah figured in a genealogy of Esau's descendants (which is in 1 Chr 4 ostensibly of Judahites, anyway, Kenaz being the Edomite link). It is best to admit that we do not know what significance Naamah had or was meant to have. LXX by changing the order of the consonants made Zophar a Minean, from S. Arabia, more than a thousand miles from Edom.

The names of the friends may also have some Edomite connection. The name Eliphaz occurs in Gen 36:4, 10–11, 15; 1 Chr 1:35–36 as the eldest son of Esau and father of Teman; so he is quite unmistakably an Edomite. The name has variously been explained as "God is fine gold" (cf. BDB), "God is agile" (cf. פזז II; E. Meyer, *Die Israeliten und ihrer Nachbarstämme* [Halle: Niemeyer, 1906] 347), but most probably "God conquers" (cf. Old S. Arab. *fawwâz;* B. Moritz, *ZAW* 44 [1926] 84; KB³). H. L. Ginsberg and B. Maisler saw here a Hurrian ending *-izzi* (*JPOS* 14 [1934] 258–59); though the Eliphaz of Gen 36 is indeed said to have had a Horite concubine (36:12, 22), the Horites of Edom seem to have nothing to do with the Horites who are Hurrians (E. A. Speiser, *IDB* 2:645; H. A. Hoffner, *POTT,* 225).

Bildad is a name not found elsewhere in the OT. Its first syllable probably means "son" and its second is the divine name Hadad (cf. the Nuzi form Bil-Adad [for Apil-Adad], "son of Hadad," like Ben Hadad); so E. A. Speiser, "On the Name *Bildad*," *JAOS* 49 (1929) 360; idem, "The Name Bildad," *AfO* 6 (1930) 23; KB³, Fohrer. W. F. Albright, *AJSL* 44 (1927–28) 31–36; idem, *JBL* 54 (1935) 174 n. 3, saw in it an Amorite name: *Yabil-Dad, "Dad [Hadad] brings increase." More important than the correct etymology of the name, however, is the association it would have conjured up for a Hebrew reader. The *Bil-* element would remind such a reader of Balak, king of Moab (Num 22:2–4; etc.), of Balaam who is not himself a Moabite but is hired by the Moabite king (Num 22–24), of Bela, the first king of Edom (Gen 36:32; 1 Chr 1:43), and perhaps also of Bilhan, yet another Edomite descendant of Esau in Gen 36:27 (= 1 Chr 1:42); the name of Bilhah, Jacob's concubine, is also perhaps regarded as a non-Israelite name (so Gordis). (Not all these names

may be etymologically related, but the point is that they sound alike.) The
-*dad* element is reminiscent of Bedad, father of the Edomite king Hadad, also
in Gen 36 (v 35; 1 Chr 1:46), though also of Eldad and Medad who prophesied
(Num 11:26). Eldad etymologically has often been thought to be connected
with Akk. *Dādi-ilu*, "Dadi is god" (though this meaning is not certain; cf.
K. L. Tallqvist, *Assyrian Personal Names* [Helsingfors: Societas Scientiarum Fen-
nica, 1914] 67); M. Noth would take it to mean "God has loved" from a root
דוד (*Die israelitischen Personennamen im Rahmen der gemeinsemitischen Namengebung*
[Stuttgart: Kohlhammer, 1928] 123; see also J. J. Stamm, "Der Name des Königs
David," VTSup 7 [1960] 165–83 [178]), from which root also Meded is probably
derived (מידד "beloved"; Noth, *Personennamen*, 223; KB³).

The name Zophar also occurs only here, but it is reminiscent of Zippor
("bird"), father of Balak king of Moab (Num 22:2; etc.). The Esau genealogy
of Gen 36 has a Zepho (vv 11, 15 צְפוֹ; צְפִי in 1 Chr 1:36), grandson of Esau
and son of Eliphaz and brother of Teman, and the LXX there and in 1 Chr
1 has Sophar (Σωφάρ), which perhaps forms another link with Edom. We
may safely ignore the place-name ʿAin Ṣōphar on the road from Beirut to
Damascus as irrelevant (despite B. Moritz, "Ergänzungen zu meinem Aufsatz:
'Die Könige von Edom,'" ZAW 16 [1939] 148–50, followed by Fohrer, Hesse).

All six proper names in this verse have therefore a stronger or weaker
Edomite connection (that of Naamah being the weakest), as does the name
Uz in 1:1 and the name Buz in 32:2 (as against, e.g., Fohrer, who thinks
Edom, N. Mesopotamia, and Syria are in view). So Job's friends seem to be
represented as countrymen of his, sharing the same values and traditions,
not the historical and cultic traditions of Israel, but the religious views one
might expect from descendants of Abraham, that is, for practical purposes,
general Israelite religious and social ideas shorn of whatever might strike the
hearer as distinctively Israelite.

The significance of the Edom connection is not far to seek. Two prophetic
texts (Jer 49:7; Obad 8; cf. also Bar 3:2–3) witness to a tradition that Edom
was renowned for its "wisdom." Of what nature that wisdom was we cannot
now say; R. H. Pfeiffer went too far in attempting to identify traces of Edomite
wisdom in one source of Genesis, certain psalms and proverbs as well as in
the Book of Job as a whole ("Edomite Wisdom," ZAW 44 [1926] 13–25; cf.
J. R. Bartlett, "The Moabites and Edomites," in POTT, 229–58 [246–47]). It is
perhaps significant that this book that portrays a debate of the wise is set in
an Edomite location, that is to say, just outside Israel, in order not to be
distracted by Israelite distinctives, but just next-door to Israel because it is an
Israelite audience that is being addressed.

12 Everything in the previous verse was external and objective, and the
false naivety of the style encourages us to believe that what we have here too
is merely an externalized depiction of rites of consolation. The intent goes
deeper, however, to establishing the nature of the relationship between the
friends and Job.

While they are still some way off, the friends catch sight of Job and are
amazed at how unlike the Job of their acquaintance he is. To "lift up the
eyes" (נשׂא עינים) is one of the commonest Hebrew idioms (35 times, BDB,
670b); generally it is followed by a verb of seeing, but here exceptionally by
the opposite. The writing is so compressed that it must be filled out in translation.

When they lifted up their eyes from afar, they saw a figure on the ash-heap; it is not surprising that from afar they did not recognize it to be Job, because it is quite normal not to recognize someone from a distance. So what is implied is: when they came closer, close enough to see his face, they still did not at first recognize it to be Job; but in the end, of course, they must have. Therefore, pedantic though it may seem, we can hardly write in a translation, "when they saw him from afar they did not recognize him" (RSV), far less "when, at a distance, they lifted up their eyes and did not recognize him, they began to weep" (NAB), for, if they didn't recognize him, why should they have wept? GNB makes a determined effort to reconstruct the narrative sequence: "While they were still a long way off they saw Job, but did not recognize him. When they did, they began to weep." But this is still not really right, because the point must be that even when quite close they still did not recognize him because he was so disfigured by his suffering; it is almost meaningless to say that when they were still a long way off they did not recognize him, because that is usually the case for people with normal eyesight. NIV boldly says, "When they saw him from a distance, they could *hardly* recognize him" (my italics), which means that they did in fact recognize him, but with difficulty. This makes reasonable sense, but can it be what the Hebrew means? Perhaps so, if we may allow that "not" in Hebrew, as in other languages, may mean not only "not at all" but "not often," "not usually," "not principally," "not easily," etc. (cf. Gen 32:29 [28]; 45:8). But this rendering of course implicitly says that "from a distance" they *did* recognize him; so why then is the distance mentioned? Would it not be much more to the point to say that even when they came close to him they could hardly recognize him?

In brief, none of the standard translations offers a satisfactory rendering of the Hebrew. One would hesitate to say that the Hebrew was overcompressed and that this degree of brevity is a stylistic fault; one can say, however, that we would not naturally permit ourselves such concision in a narrative sentence in English. In Hebrew to see from afar off is not at all a common phrase, and it invites reflection on the circumstances: in Gen 22:4 Abraham "lifts up his eyes and sees" (as here) the mountain of sacrifice afar off and leaves his attendants at that very point as if to signify their absolute exclusion from the coming event; in 37:18 the plot against Joseph's life is stylishly depicted as developing between the time his brothers "saw him afar off" and the moment that he "came near to them"; cf. also Luke 15:20 where the distance between the prodigal and the seeing father is consumed by the running of the father. (Seeing [נבט] from afar in Job 36:25; 39:29 is not relevant to the point here.) So the seeing from afar here is likely here also to have a significance that needs savoring. Their being able to discern a single figure from a distance suggests the isolation of Job, who is not now at his usual place in the city gate (29:7) but outside the city, alone on the ash-heap (cf. on v 8), his whole circumstances now completely changed (cf. Horst). There is a reticence in the text in that the reason for their not recognizing him is not stated; for the idea of the appearance being so altered by suffering as to make someone unrecognizable, we might of course compare Isa 52:14 where the servant's face and body (מראה, תאר) are changed, beyond human semblance.

An interesting new suggestion arises from N. Lohfink's comparison of a ritual of lament from Sardinia (*VT* 12 [1962] 260–77). The mourners, as if suspecting nothing, enter the room where the dead person is lying, and then as though by accident catching sight of the corpse they burst into their laments; the nonrecognition would thus be a ritual or customary refusal to recognize what is before their eyes, as when we say (less formally, of course), "I don't believe my eyes," when in reality we don't really doubt them. In this case the "from afar" only means that at a distance they could tell it was Job, which only goes to strengthen their "disbelief" at what had happened to him. There was no difficulty in *telling* it was Job (they could tell that from afar); the difficulty lay in *believing* it was Job.

Attractive though this line of interpretation is, there is a better solution yet. נכר does not necessarily refer exclusively to a mental action of "recognizing" but also often includes a verbal consequence such as "acknowledging" or some other act that translates the mental recognition into reality. When Jacob's sons bring him Joseph's coat they ask him to "recognize" (נכר) whether it is Joseph's, which he does with the words, "It is my son's robe" (Gen 37:32–33). In Gen 38:25–26 Tamar calls upon Judah to "recognize" whose property it is that she holds, and Jacob "recognizes" or rather "acknowledges" the objects, verbally (cf. Gen 31:32). To "recognize" a king (Dan 11:39), or to be "recognized" by one's fellow-countrymen (Isa 63:16) or by God (Jer 24:5) or by a well-wisher (Ruth 2:10), inevitably involves far more than visual or mental recognition. Here too, the friends "lifted up their eyes" and thus saw Job, but did not "recognize" (נכר) him, that is, did not acknowledge him as Job or greet him as Job. Rather, as the text immediately says, they began to perform mourning rituals, treating Job as a person already dead. The fact is, as the next verse says, that they do not say a word to him for seven days—which is explanatory of what not recognizing him implies. Their identification with Job's suffering is no doubt sincere, but expressed in an wholly alienating way since they treat him as one already dead and not as a living man. The ambivalence in the portrayal of them in the dialogues, friends who are traitors (6:15), comforters who are torturers (16:2), is already foreshadowed here.

The remarkable turn the narrative takes is that when the friends behold Job, they abandon their stated purpose in coming to Uz, to "condole with him and comfort" him, and do not address to him a single word, but treat him as if he were already dead. Their conventional acts are properly speaking rituals of mourning; since there is no explicit mention of his dead children, and the focus is unambiguously on Job himself, we must suppose that their mourning is not primarily because of his bereavement but because of the death-like situation they find Job himself in. "Weeping" (בכה) is different from crying (דמע); weeping comes from the mouth as sound, crying from the eyes (V. Hamp, *TDOT* 2:117). The phrase "the voice of weeping" (קול בכי, Ps 6:9 [8]; Isa 65:19) shows that weeping is primarily a vocal activity, being thought of as generated by "the same violent disturbance of the intestines which causes tears to flow" (T. Collins, "The Physiology of Tears in the Old Testament," *CBQ* 33 [1971] 18–38, 185–97 [37]). While בכה can of course signify the expression of emotional grief, it not infrequently indicates ritual wailing or lamenting, and such is in all probability the case here. To "lift up the voice" in weeping is not an empty idiom signifying merely to speak, but probably refers to the higher pitch of the voice in wailing. A normal accompaniment of wailing was the lament (see E. Jacob, *IDB* 3:453; H. Jahnow, *Das*

hebräische Leichenlied im Rahmen der Völkerdichtung [BZAW 36; Giessen: A. Töpelmann, 1923] esp. 40–57), and here, though no words are spoken to Job himself
(v 13) we may also assume the presence of verbal laments. For examples of
traditional laments, see *b. Moʿed Qaṭ.* 28b.

The tearing of the outer garment (מְעִיל) is a ritual Job has already performed
(1:20, *q.v.*), and in performing it themselves the friends identify with Job's
present state. Far less clear is the act of sprinkling or throwing (זרק) dust
"upon their heads toward heaven." If this simply means that they threw dust
in the air so that it would fall on their heads (e.g., Peake, Andersen), it is not
only a curious way of saying so (one might expect "heavenwards" before "upon
their heads") but a strange way of putting dust on one's head. Putting dust
or ashes upon one's head is a well-attested mourning rite (Josh 7:6; 1 Sam
4:12; 2 Sam 13:19; 15:32; Ezek 27:30; Lam 2:10; ? Esth 4:1; ? Dan 9:3;
rolling in the dust and in that way putting dust on one's head: Mic 1:10; Jer
6:26; Ezek 27:30 [ashes]; Job 16:15; cf. Neh 9:1 [penitence ritual]; see E. F.
de Ward, *JJS* 23 [1972] 6–8; and cf. the mourning rituals of Ugaritic El in
Baal and Mot [*CTA* 5] 6.12–24; Gibson, 73–74). But never is the verb "sprinkle"
(זרק) used in this connection. The only time ashes are said to be "sprinkled"
(זרק) is when they are sprinkled or thrown "toward heaven" (as here) by
Moses, becoming boils upon humans and animals (Exod 9:8–10). Dhorme
thought that two separate rituals had become accidentally amalgamated in
the narration, that of throwing dust toward the sky and the more usual custom
of putting dust on one's head; he advised deleting "toward heaven" (as JB,
NAB, NIV, Ehrlich, Hölscher, Fedrizzi; see also n. 2:12.a). Gordis saw here an
apotropaic rite of throwing dust over the head (i.e., backwards, like over the
shoulder) toward heaven, so as to ward off from themselves the evil that had
befallen Job from that direction (similarly Buttenwieser; M. Weiss, *Job's Beginning*, 76: "a magical act of self defence"; see also Weiser: "perhaps originally
apotropaic"; Fohrer: "to repay a malicious person, perhaps a sorcerer").
Habel also thinks the Exodus passage the clue, but more daringly suggests
that "the friends perform a rite which symbolically calls forth the same sickness on themselves as an act of total empathy. They are one with the dust
of death and one with Job in his diseases" (p. 97). They are thus "patriarchal examples of true friendship just as Job is the paragon of ancient piety"
(N. C. Habel, "'Only the Jackal Is My Friend.' On Friends and Redeemers in
Job," *Int* 31 [1977] 227–36 [228]). He is surely right that their action, whatever
precisely it signifies, is an act of identification with the suffering Job, like the
tearing of garments and sitting in silence; it does seem improbable, though,
that throwing dust skyward symbolized something so precise as wishing boils
on oneself. The close parallel in Acts 22:23 where a hostile crowd demanding
Paul's death tear off their clothes and throw dust in the air has also never
been satisfactorily explained (cf. H. J. Cadbury, in *The Beginnings of Christianity*
[London: Macmillan, 1933] 269–77; H. D. Betz, *Lukian von Samosata und das
Neue Testament* [TU 76; Berlin: Akademie Verlag, 1961] 72; E. Haenchen,
The Acts of the Apostles [Oxford: Blackwell, 1971] 633), though the context is
also of death (anticipated); there may be some allusion to our passage, though
not to the Septuagint version of it, which lacks the phrase "toward heaven."

However uncertain we may remain about the meaning of the act of throwing
dust upon the head toward heaven, there are certain interpretations that we

may safely reject. It cannot simply be a "token of distress" (Gray). It is not a symbol of the rain of dust that has metaphorically laid waste Job's prosperity (Duhm). The height of the throwing of dust ("heavenwards") does not signify the immensity of Job's suffering (Budde), nor does the gesture intimate that they themselves felt laid in the dust by a calamity sent from heaven (Davidson). Nor is it an incitement to heaven to bring such an evildoer as Job down to the dust (G. Hoffmann, "Ergänzungen und Berichtigungen zu Hiob," *ZAW* 49 [1931] 141–45 [141]). Nor is the most recent suggestion by C. Houtman persuasive, that the throwing of dust heavenwards constitutes an appeal to God to slay the originator of Job's sufferings and to cover him with dust (*ZAW* 90 [1978] 269–72).

13 The posture of sitting on the ground during mourning is often attested (cf. 2:8; Lam 2:10; Isa 3:26; 47:1; Ezek 8:14; Ezra 9:3; Neh 1:4; cf. El who comes down from his throne to sit on a stool, and from the stool to earth, *Baal and Mot [CTA* 6] 6.11–14; Gibson, 73). "On the ground" (לָאָרֶץ) is presumably specified because one usually sits on carpets or cushions, and not directly on the earth. The symbolic value of the posture is plain, though not perhaps precise: it signifies humiliation (in sympathy with the dead person; here it is said explicitly "with him" [אִתּוֹ]) and a closer than usual attachment to the earth as the surface of Sheol (see de Ward, *JJS* 23 [1972] 3–4; Wensinck, *Some Semitic Rites of Mourning and Religion*, 12–18).

The silence of the friends is multivalent. Perhaps this is the final element in the prologue that we should identify as "falsely naive" (cf. Clines, *HAR* 9 [1985] 127–36), for there is the stylization of the naive ("seven days and seven nights"), there is the extremism of depiction that we have found characteristic of the prologue (a whole week's silence must demand almost superhuman reserve!), and there is the hint that the "silence" is not all that it seems (see below). The period of seven days is a standard time for mourning (Gen 50:10; 1 Sam 31:13, a mourning fast; Ecclus 22:12 "Mourning for the dead lasts seven days"; Jdt 16:24; cf. Gen 50:3, Egyptian mourning for Joseph seventy days; Ezek 3:15, Ezekiel is "appalled" for seven days). On the symbolism of "seven," see J. Hehn, *Siebenzahl und Sabbat bei den Babyloniern und im Alten Testament* (Leipziger Semitische Studien 2/5; Leipzig: J. C. Hinrichs, 1907); idem, "Zur Bedeutung der Siebenzahl," *Vom Alten Testament* (FS K. Marti; BZAW 41; Giessen: A. Töpelmann, 1925) 128–36; E. Kutsch, "Erwägungen zur Geschichte der Passafeier und des Massotfestes," *ZTK* 55 (1958) 1–35 (25–28). Nowhere else is mourning said to be for seven days *and seven nights;* this emphasis belongs to the extreme character of the depiction (like "blameless," "greatest," "from the feet to the head," 1:1, 3; 2:7). It is often remarked that the period of seven days is in fact determined by Job (so, e.g., Fohrer) and indeed we shall discover in the next verse that it is Job, not the friends, who breaks the silence (3:1), the implication being seen that if Job himself had spoken, say, on the second, or the fourteenth, that is how long the silence of the friends would have lasted. But at this moment in the narrative we do not know that the length of the period of silence hangs upon Job, for here in vv 12–13 everything else hangs upon the perspective of the friends. In fact, at this juncture the length of their silence is noted entirely from the friends' point of view: "they sat seven days . . . not speaking, *for* [from their perspective, of course] they saw his suffering was very great." Here the seven days are not of Job's making; in 3:1 they are. It would be better to speak of a complicity between the friends and Job, in which he understands the symbolic value of their silence, and waits till that symbolism is fully realized before he will speak.

So what is the symbolism? Everything in their actions treats him as one already dead (not as one on the point of death, as Terrien thinks), and the seven days and nights fit in as a period of mourning. It is possible, of course, that mourning rituals were regarded as appropriate for one in great distress, but it is hard to avoid the impression that such a way of showing grief would be experienced as alienating. For he is not yet dead; and although, when he opens his mouth, he will say that to be dead is his dearest desire, there must be for him a particular poignancy in seeing that fate externalized in the ritual behavior of his acquaintances. It is one thing to know one has an incurable illness, it is another to witness the reaction of friends to the news.

It is fascinating to read how variously the friends' silence has been explained. Some have thought it due to their inability to find any appropriate words (Terrien), or remark that, "overwhelmed by the greatness of his suffering, they speak no word" (Gray). Ewald comments, "They do honour by profound silence to his vast grief," and Peake, "His pain and the reverse of his fortunes strike them dumb, for when grief is so crushing, what form but silence can sympathy take?" Andersen writes, "They were true friends, bringing to Job's lonely ash-heap the compassion of a silent presence" (similarly Horst). Such psychological interpretations may well have truth in them, though it is interesting that those quoted all put the friends in the most favorable light. Delitzsch stands alone in remarking that "their long silence shows that they had not fully realized the purpose of their visit" and in thinking it "a pity that they let Job utter the first word, which they might have prevented by some word of kindly solace." Rather than such psychologically inspired readings, however, it is preferable, in view of the clearly ritual actions of the friends in v 12, to suspect some conventional custom as the ground of their long silence.

N. Lohfink has argued that a period of silence was customary in Hebrew mourning (*VT* 12 [1962] 260–77; similarly E. Haulotte, *Symbolique du vêtement selon la Bible* [Paris: Aubier, 1966] 128) and he quotes an interesting passage from A. Musil's depiction of a Transjordanian Bedouin custom at the turn of the present century: "As soon as the news of an illness circulates, relatives and friends come to pay a visit, and they form a circle around the ill person; in silence, without saying a word, they listen to his groans and cries. Only when he addresses them, do they answer him and lament his state" (*Arabia Petraea* [Vienna: A. Hölder, 1908] 3:413). Cf. also *b. Moʿed Qat.* 28b: "Comforters are not permitted to say a word until the mourner opens [conversation]" (Job 2:13 is then quoted). Cf. also Gilgamesh, 11.126, where the gods sit mourning silently when they see the destruction wrought by the flood (*ANET,* 94b). If such a custom lies behind our text, we can only say that to wait a whole week for the sufferer to speak seems to carry the convention to the height of absurdity, and to transmute a reasonable reticence into an all-too-plain identification of the sufferer with the dead. This of course may be exactly what is intended. It needs to be said that the evidence for a formal phase of silence in the mourning ritual is not textually strong (see de Ward, *JJS* 23 [1972] 17–20).

One further factor needs to be considered. Since oriental mourning was not a silent activity but typically contained much lamenting, both articulate and inarticulate, we should not perhaps suppose that Job's ash-heap was a place of utter silence during this week of mourning. Indeed, it is said explicitly that "none was speaking a word *to him*" (cf. "did not acknowledge him" in v 12), which does not preclude laments as if he were no longer present. The friends' refraining from speech with him (and we learn how Job feels about that in general in 19:16; cf. 12:4) might perhaps only have been exacerbated by their laments that assumed his death.

Given that we know, at the second reading at least, in what terms the friends are going to address Job, we cannot naively suppose that these days and nights of silence are nothing but the most refined expression of sympathy. Unusually among commentators, A. B. Davidson remarks that "from the sentiments which the three friends gave utterance to afterwards we know that very mixed feelings may have led to their silence and dismay"; however customary a short period of silence with a sufferer may have been, this hugely extended silence provokes reflection in the readers on what they may be being told *sotto voce* by the narrator.

Explanation

In these two chapters of seemingly artless prose, the problematic of the book has been exposed. It is that while the doctrine of retribution is initially taken for granted—as in the depiction of Job's piety and his consequent prosperity in 1:1–3—it has in the course of the narrative been first questioned and then overturned. It is questioned in 1:9 where it is asked whether Job serves God gratuitously, i.e., whether his piety may not be the result of his prosperity rather than the other way about—as has always been assumed; and it is overturned by the heavenly decision to decide that question by removing his prosperity. Once that is done, the retributive principle has been broken; for now the most pious man on earth is among the most wretched. It is irrelevant that 40 chapters later he will be restored to his wealth, for the bulk of the book revolves about what it signifies that a righteous person can be in such misery. What counts now is that in a world where it is believed and taught that actions have appropriate consequences (despite the many evidences to the contrary), heaven itself has now sabotaged that doctrine with a most shocking infringement.

This attack on the doctrine of retribution has both an intellectual and an existential dimension. The intellectual dimension has hardly been broached in the prologue, and innocent readers of the book may actually be deceived into thinking the prologue nothing but a simple folktale forming the machinery for the real intellectual issues of the dialogue. This is not so, of course, because here we have heard not some apparent and fictive exception to the doctrine that we may hope to find reconciled with it ultimately, but a categorical reversal of it which is certified by the narrator to be no misprision, and which no less a character than God authorizes explicitly. All the same, it will be much more the business of the dialogue than of the prologue to probe the intellectual conundrum of the innocent's suffering. What the prologue first turns its attention to is the existential dimension.

The existential problem is not the question, Do the innocent suffer?—that is, If they are suffering, can they indeed be innocent? Nor is it the question,

Why do the innocent suffer?—that is, What reason can be given for such suffering?, which is to say, How can innocent suffering be comprehended or explained within some other set of concepts? These are all intellectual questions, and the book as a whole does indeed address them, even if it does not resolve them. But here what is posed is the existential question: What should innocents do when inexplicable suffering comes upon them? The portraiture of Job contains the answer the narrative seeks to convey: in mourning for his loss Job blesses the Lord who gave and who has taken away, never sinning in his speech or speaking irreverently of God (1:21–22; 2:10). This is not the only answer the book gives to the existential question, for the moment we turn the page (literally, as it happens, in my RSV) into chap. 3 we find the selfsame Job, who has abandoned neither his piety nor his integrity, first wishing he had never been born and then by stages moving to the most formal accusation of God a human can mount. In case we should be supposing that Job from chap. 3 onwards is making false moves, unworthy of imitation by readers, or losing his faith, or at the least failing to maintain the moral and religious standards he exemplifies in the prologue, the end of the book has Job praised by God for speaking of him "what is right," and to such a degree in tune with the divine disposition that only through his prayer are the friends relieved of the consequences of their "folly" (42:8–9). There are not two Jobs, but there is more than one right way of coping with innocent suffering: when Job cannot bow in pious submission to the divine theft of his children, his property and his reputation he can still, with a piety equal but different, assert that it is with God and no other that he must treat and demand that from God and no other his innocence be vindicated, since not even his own complete assurance of his innocence can satisfy him. This attitude too, aggressive and febrile in contrast to the compliant and almost catatonic Job of chaps. 1–2, will in the dialogue be presented as an answer to the existential question, How can I endure suffering? But while we are still in the prosaic, formal, and antique world of the prologue, the more conventional piety prevails.

Job's First Speech (3:1–26)

Bibliography

Barr, J. "Philology and Exegesis: Some General Remarks, with Illustrations from Job." In *Questions disputées de l'Ancien Testament: Méthode et théologie. XXIIIᵉ session des Journées Bibliques de Louvain.* BETL 33. Louvain: Leuven UP, 1974. 39–61. **Blank, S. H.** "The Curse, Blasphemy, the Spell, and the Oath." *HUCA* 23/1 (1950–51) 73–95. ———. "'Perish the Day!' A Misdirected Curse (Job 3:3)." *Prophetic Thought: Essays and Addresses.* Cincinnati: Hebrew Union College Press, 1977. 61–63. **Bratsiotis, N. P.** "Der Monolog im Alten Testament." *ZAW* 73 (1961) 30–70. **Brichto, H. C.** *The Problem of "Curse" in the Hebrew Bible.* JBLMS 13. Philadelphia: SBL, 1963. **Clines, D. J. A.** "The Etymology of Hebrew אָדָם." *JNSWL* 3 (1974) 19–25. **Cox, C.** "The Wrath of God Has Come to Me: Job's First Speech according to the Septuagint." *SR* 16 (1987) 195–204. **Cox, D.** *The Triumph of Impotence: Job and the Tradition of the Absurd.* Rome: Università Gregoriana Editrice, 1978. **Dahood, M.** "Denominative *riḥḥam*, 'to conceive, enwomb.'" *Bib* 44 (1963) 204–5. ———. "Hebrew-Ugaritic Lexicography VII." *Bib* 50 (1969) 337–56. ———. "Northwest Semitic Texts and Textual Criticism of the Hebrew Bible." In *Questions disputées de l'Ancien Testament: Méthode et théologie. XXIIIᵉ session des Journées Bibliques de Louvain.* BETL 33. Louvain: Leuven UP, 1974. 11–37. **Day, J.** *God's Conflict with the Dragon and the Sea.* University of Cambridge Oriental Publications 35. Cambridge: CUP, 1985. **Driver, G. R.** "Problems in the Hebrew Text of Job." VTSup 3 (1955) 72–93. **Fishbane, M.** "Jeremiah IV 23–26 and Job III 3–13: A Recovered Use of the Creation Pattern." *VT* 21 (1971) 151–67. **Freedman, D. N.** "The Structure of Job 3." *Bib* 49 (1968) 503–8 [= *Pottery, Poetry and Prophecy.* Winona Lake: Eisenbrauns, 1984. 323–38]. **Guillaume, A.** "The Arabic Background of the Book of Job." *Promise and Fulfilment.* S. H. Hooke Festschrift. Ed. F. F. Bruce. Edinburgh: T.&T. Clark, 1963. 106–27. **Katz, R. L.** "A Psychoanalytic Commentary on Job 3.25." *HUCA* 29 (1958) 377–83. **Kinnier Wilson, J. V.** "Biblical and Akkadian Philological Notes." *JSS* 7 (1962) 173–83. **Lipiński, E.** "Notes lexicographiques et stylistiques sur le livre de Job." *FolOr* 21 (1980) 65–82. **Loretz, O.** "Ugaritisch-hebräisch in Job 3,3–26. Zum Disput zwischen M. Dahood und J. Barr." *UF* 8 (1976) 123–27. **Moore, R. D.** "The Integrity of Job." *CBQ* 45 (1983) 17–31. **Rendsburg, G.** "Double Polysemy in Genesis 49:6 and Job 3:6." *CBQ* 44 (1982) 48–51. **Ṣmudi, Y.** "The Beginning of Job's Protest (Chapter 3)" [Heb.]. *BMik* 27 (1981–82) 229–32. **Snaith, N. H.** "The Introductions to the Speeches in the Book of Job: Are They in Prose or in Verse?" *Textus* 7 (1973) 133–37. **Stade, B.** "Miscellen. 15. 'Auf Jemandes Knieen gebären' Gen 30,3, 50,23, Hiob 3,12 und אֶבְנָיִם Exod 1,16." *ZAW* 6 (1896) 143–56. **Tromp, N. J.** *Primitive Conceptions of Death and the Nether World in the Old Testament.* BibOr 21. Rome: Pontifical Biblical Institute, 1969. **Ullendorff, E.** "Job III 8." *VT* 11 (1961) 350–51. **Webster, E. C.** "Strophic Patterns in Job 3–28." *JSOT* 26 (1983) 33–60.

Translation

¹ *After that, it was Job who broke the silence, with a curse on his day.*
² *And Job said:* ᵃ
³ *Perish the day I was born,*
    the night that said, ᵃ *"A boy is begot!"* ᵇ
⁴ *That day* ᵃ *would it had become darkness!*
    that God above had taken no thought for it,
    that no light had shone on it!

⁵ *Would that gloom and death's shadow*^a *had claimed it for their own,*^b
    that cloud had settled upon it,
    that eclipses^c *had affrighted it!*
⁶ *That night*^a*—would that deep darkness had carried it off,*^b
    that it had not been counted^c *among the days of the year,*
    not found its way into the reckoning of the months!
⁷ *If only that night*^a *had been barren,*^b
    and no cry of joy been heard in it!
⁸ *Would that the cursers*^a *of days*^b *had laid a spell*^c *on it,*
    those skilled at rousing^d *Leviathan!*
^{9a} *Would that the stars of its dawn had been darkened,*
    ^b*that it had waited in vain for the light,*
    and never seen the eyelids^c *of the morning!*
¹⁰ *Because it did not shut the doors of the womb,*^a
    nor^b *shield*^c *my eyes*^d *from trouble.*

¹¹ *Why did I not die*^a *new-born,*^b
    perish as I left the womb?
¹² *Why did the knees receive me,*
    or a mother's breasts suckle me?
¹³ *Then*^a *I should have laid myself down in tranquillity,*
    then I should have slept and taken my rest,
¹⁴ *with*^a *kings and ministers of state,*
    who rebuilt ruined cities^b *for themselves,*
¹⁵ *with princes rich in gold,*
    who filled their houses with silver.
¹⁶ *Why*^a *was I not buried*^b *like a stillborn child,*
    like an infant^c *that never saw the light?*
¹⁷ *There the wicked*^a *cease to rage;*
    those who have spent their powers^b *rest.*
¹⁸ *Captives are at utter*^a *ease;*
    they hear no slavedriver's shout.
¹⁹ *Small and great alike*^a *are there;*
    and the slave is free^b *from his master.*

²⁰ *Why is light given to the troubled,*
    and life to those bitter in spirit?
²¹ *They yearn for death, and yearn in vain,*^a
    would dig for it rather than^b *for hidden treasure;*
²² *they would rejoice exultingly*^a
    and delight to attain^b *the grave.*
^{23a} *Why is light given to one whose path is hidden,*
    one whom God has hedged about?
^{24a} *For my sighs are*^b *my daily bread,*
    groans^c *pour from me like water.*
²⁵ *For what I most feared*^a *has befallen*^b *me,*
    all that I dreaded has come upon me.
²⁶ *I have no repose, no quiet, no rest.*
    Turmoil has come.

Notes

2.a. Lit., "answered and said"; ענה "answer" does not necessarily imply any previous speech, but can mean "beginning to speak as an occasion required" (Driver), "respond to an occasion, speak in view of circumstances" (BDB, 773a § 2), e.g., Judg 18:14; 1 Sam 9:17.

N. H. Snaith has observed that the introductions to the speeches, beginning with this verse, bear verse accents in Masoretic texts, that is, either accents that distinctively indicate verse or accents shared by prose and verse ("The Introductions to the Speeches in the Book of Job: Are They in Prose or in Verse?" *Textus* 7 [1973] 133–37).

3.a. Grammatically it would be possible to translate "the night in which one said" (KJV "in which it was said"; similarly NIV), but it is harder to imagine who the "one" could be than to ascribe supernatural knowledge and speech to the night (cf. Ps 19:3–5 [2–4]). The emendation to אֻמִּי (*BHK, frt*), הֹרָה being understood as the fem ptcp, or else הָרָת being read (*BHK*), is quite implausible.

M. Dahood, "Northwest Semitic Texts and Textual Criticism of the Hebrew Bible" (in *Questions disputées de l'Ancien Testament* [BETL 33; Louvain: Leuven UP, 1974] 11–37 [22–23]), sees here the אמר he maintains means "see"; but no improvement in sense is apparent. Tur-Sinai argued that אמר means "refused (to let a man be conceived)," perhaps as an aphel of מרה "rebel," but the syntax is unsupportive (cf. also H. H. Rowley, *JSS* 3 [1958] 84). A. Ehrman ("A Note on the Verb אמר," *JQR* 55 [1964–65] 166–67) argued on the basis of one medieval text that אמר can mean "curse," and translates "and the night be cursed wherein a man had coition," but this would involve two emendations to the MT which he does not specify.

3.b. LXX Ἰδού ἄρσεν "behold a male" probably read הרה as הָרָה (= הֲרִי) "behold." This is followed by Duhm, Gray, Stevenson, de Wilde. NAB "The child is a boy" does not claim to follow this reading, but it manages to give the impression that birth, not conception, is in view. Gray's argument carries little conviction, that "Job's quarrel is not with his conception, but with his birth, with the fact that he had issued from the womb living into the world with its life of trouble and pain"; it is true that in v 16 he can envisage being stillborn, i.e., having conception but not birth, as a preferable state to life, but acceptance of conception in that context should not be read into the present verse where conception is simply the natural precursor of birth. הֹרָה is taken as pual by BDB, KB³, qal pass by Driver, GKC, § 52e.

4.a. "That day" is projected to the beginning of the line as a casus pendens (cf. GKC, § 143b–c). Dahood ("Northwest Semitic Texts," 23–24) gives some interesting Ugaritic examples of casus pendens with a special solemnity.

Hölscher deleted the line as the writing of a pedantic glossator who did not realize that the day and night of v 3 were the same (conception being poetically equivalent to birth), and who tried to distinguish between "day" in vv 4–5 and "night" in vv 6–10; all the lines refer to the same complex day-and-night (so too Stevenson, Fohrer). LXXᴮ is sometimes called upon in testimony, since although it does have the first colon it has "night" (νύξ) instead of "day." Duhm eliminated two tricola from the chapter by bringing v 9b up to follow v 4a (reading "night" for "day" as LXX), which otherwise is a line without a parallel (he writes some unconvincing comments about marginal notes in old manuscripts).

5.a. צלמות should probably be understood as a compound noun, "darkness of death" (cf. NJB "shadow dark as death") and not revocalized to צַלְמוּת "darkness" (as NEB, NAB, JB, NJPS, NIV, Dhorme, Gordis) as if derived from a צלם II "be dark," since it is doubtful that such a root is attested in West Semitic (see D. J. A. Clines, "The Etymology of Hebrew צֶלֶם," *JNWSL* 3 [1974] 19–25; W. L. Michel, "ṢLMWT, 'Deep Darkness' or 'Shadow of Death'?" *BR* 29 [1984] 5–20; idem, *Job in the Light of Northwest Semitic* [BibOr 42; Rome: Pontifical Biblical Institute, 1987] 1:42–46; against, e.g., KB). See also D. Winton Thomas, "צַלְמָוֶת in the Old Testament," *JSS* 7 (1962) 191–200, though his view that the "death" element in the word should be regarded as a "superlative" should probably not be adopted. See further n. 10:21.b; and see J. Barr, "Philology and Exegesis," in *Questions disputées* (BETL 33) 39–61 (50–55); Grabbe, *Comparative Philology*, 27–29.

5.b. גאל "redeem," that is, claim as a kinsman property belonging to one's clan. Dhorme thought this admittedly subtle sense too artificial, and derived the word here from גאל II "defile" (so already Targum, Aquila, Rashi, Ehrlich; cf. KJV "stain," NEB "sully") perhaps vocalizing יִגְאָלֻהֻ (Ehrlich) since גאל II is not attested in qal. But "defile" is not a wholly appropriate verb to govern "day," especially because גאל II elsewhere is usually of cultic defilement (e.g., Ezra 2:62; Mal 1:7) or, less specifically, of staining garments with blood (Isa 63:3) or hands with blood

(59:3). See *Comment*. A. R. Johnson ("The Primary Meaning of גאל," VTSup 1 [1953] 67–77) argued that both "redeem" and "defile" as meanings of גאל derive from a common meaning "cover," and proposes that meaning here, "let utter blackness cover it"; but there is no OT parallel to such a sense.

5.c. A favored interpretation of כמרירי has been to suppose a root כמר "be black" and read כַּמְרִירֵי "blackness of (day)" (so BDB, KB³, kjv, rv, rsv, nab, njps, niv, and most commentators), sometimes understood as "eclipses" (jb, Pope), or by Dhorme as "fogs," though these are hardly terrifying. A difficulty is that *kmr* as a Semitic root "be black" is attested only in Syriac, and even there J. Barr has argued that this may be only a secondary meaning to a principal meaning "be sad" ("Philology and Exegesis," 55–56; cf. Grabbe, *Comparative Philology*, 29–31; O. Loretz, "Ugaritisch-hebräisch in Job 3,3–26. Zum Disput zwischen M. Dahood und J. Barr," *UF* 8 [1976] 123–27 [125]). But it is enough that the meaning "be black" is well attested in Syr. (cf. Brockelmann, Payne Smith), and we may note that in the case of the semantically similar קדר the movement seems to be from "be dark" to "mourn" (Jer 8:21; 14:2; cf. also on Job 30:28). There will hardly be any connection with Hitt. *kammara* (as M. L. Modena Mayer, "Note etymologiche IV," *Acme* 20 [1967] 287–91 [290]).

It is no real objection to this view that the phrase במרירי יום occurs in two extrabiblical passages where the preposition ב requires a derivation of the noun from מרר "be bitter." In Ecclus 11:4 "Do not mock at a worn cloak, and do not despise anyone in the bitterness of a day" (cf. nab; the Greek, followed by rsv, jb, is very different), and 1QH 5.34 "My eyes are dimmed because of vexation and my soul by the bitterness of the day," it is a psychological state that is suggested, which would not fit our present text. Pope argues that a "day of bitterness" is associated with an eclipse of the sun in Amos 8:9–10, but it is rather that "a bitter day" (יום מר) is parallel to "mourning for an only son." And this still does not explain the locution "bitternesses of day."

Gordis has recently revived the explanation of Rashi and ibn Ezra as "demons of the day," comparing Deut 32:24 where קטב מרירי "a bitter (?) destruction" is understood as "a destruction of demons" because of the parallel with לחמי רשף "eaten by pestilence," רשף being taken as the name of the Semitic plague-god Resheph (cf. on 5:7). Gordis further derives מרירי not from מרר "be bitter" but from Arab. *marr* "pass by," hence "the passing, flitting being," and decides that the initial כ is "asseverative *kaph*." The whole argument is a tissue of implausibilities.

6.a. Some read הַיּוֹם "(that) day," on the grounds that darkness already has sway over night (Terrien, de Wilde; E. Ullendorff, "Job III 8," *VT* 11 [1961] 350–51), and that it is strange that the night should be counted "among the days" (Pesh adds "that day" as the subject of "be counted"). Duhm, Hölscher, Horst, Fohrer omit the colon on similar grounds.

6.b. neb "Blind darkness swallow up that night" apparently reads nothing other than the MT.

6.c. יחד is juss of חדה "rejoice" (so rv, rsv), but it is hard to see why being among the days of the year should be a particular matter for rejoicing by the night (we know nothing of a "festive band" of nights, as Peake envisages; similarly Strahan, Driver). Most versions, from Tg onward, through kjv, and niv, and most commentators, assume a revocalization to יַחַד "let it [not] be joined" (neb "count it not among," nab "let it not occur among" are variant expressions of the same Heb.). The parallelism between יחד niph "be joined" and בוא "come" in Gen 49:6 is further evidence for the revocalization here. Without defending the originality of MT, Grabbe puts up a sympathetic case for it (*Comparative Philology*, 32–35). M. Dahood ("Northwest Semitic Texts," 24; also Blommerde) saw in יֵחַד a Canaanite form of יֵחָז "let be seen," claiming that יחד in Gen 49:6 is the same word. Though KB³ notes Dahood's conjecture, it does not lend it support. H. L. Ginsberg (VTSup 16 [1967] 71–72) is appropriately scathing. A similar suggestion had been made by O. Wintermute, *Studia Biblica et Orientalia* (AnBib 10; Rome: Pontifical Biblical Institute, 1959) 26–36 (35). Gordis attempts to argue that both meanings are intended, by the figure of *talḥin* (others prefer the term *tauriya;* cf. G. Rendsburg, *CBQ* 44 [1982] 51 n. 19); but this is quite implausible, and his argument that v 6b is chiastically parallel to 7b fails on the fact that it is not night that is joyful in 7b but a cry that is heard in it. G. Rendsburg's claim ("Double Polysemy in Genesis 49:6 and Job 3:6," *CBQ* 44 [1982] 48–51) that not only does יחד mean "be united" and "rejoice," but also יבא means "enter" and "desire" (from אבה) is doubly doubtful (and what would "in the number of the months let it not desire" *mean*?).

7.a. Hölscher deleted "that night," and de Wilde alters it to "that day," thinking that it is still the day of Job's birth that is the subject.

7.b. Dhorme translates "sorrowful" (jb "dismal") claiming that גלמוד has this sense in 30:3, but this is dubious (njb "sterile"). Since the context is of conception, Gordis's "lonely as a crag," aiming to reproduce the metaphor of stoniness, is out of place. "Solitary" (kjv) and "desolate" (njps) are also beside the point.

8.a. Gordis, accepting the reading of יָם "sea" (n. 8.b) and the criticism that anyone desiring an upheaval of order would not *curse* Sea, emends אֹרְרֵי "cursers of" to עֹרְרֵי "rousers of," preempting criticism of an emendation that leaves the same verb in two parallel cola by referring to 8:3; 11:7; 12:23; 38:22, and others (see his Special Note, pp. 508–13). The question is not whether such repetition is possible but whether, in view of its rarity, it is likely to provide the solution to a textual problem. Actually, there is no textual problem; see *Comment*. G. R. Driver saw here a new Heb. root עיר "revile" cognate with Arab. *ʿāra*, Eth. *taʿayyara* (VTSup 3 [1955] 72; followed by J. V. Kinnier Wilson proposing an Akk. cognate *āru/awāru* ["Biblical and Akkadian Philological Notes," *JSS* 7 (1962) 173–83 (181–83)]); see J. Barr, *Comparative Philology and the Text of the Old Testament* (Oxford: Clarendon, 1968) 125–26; idem, "Philology and Exegesis," 56–57. NEB "those whose magic binds even the monster of the deep" accepts the emendation to "sea" as a personified being, but otherwise retains the MT; but "binding" the sea-monster and "taming" Leviathan seem to be just the opposite to the loosing of disorder that is here in view (cf. also Day, *God's Conflict*, 47). M. Fishbane's comment in *VT* 21 (1971) 163 n. 6 is unintelligible, since there is no Akk. verb *arrātu* "bind with a curse."

8.b. On the proposal to read יָם "sea" for יוֹם "day," see *Comment*. Grabbe argues that a standard mythological formula paralleling Sea with Leviathan lies behind the line, but that the poet altered "sea" to "day" for his own purpose (*Comparative Philology*, 35–38); ingenious but unconvincing. M. Dahood believed it was Sea here, but retained the MT punctuation on the ground that *yôm* may be the Phoenician pronunciation of Heb. *yām* "sea" ("Northwest Semitic Texts," 24–25); this is less ingenious than perverse. J. Barr has an interesting methodologically slanted discussion of the problem, concluding with hesitation in favor of "day"; but he does not see that v 8 is primarily about the *night* ("Philology and Exegesis," 56–57).

8.c. E. Ullendorff, *VT* 11 (1961) 350–51, took יקבהו from נקב "pierce" and אֹרְרֵי as pl const of אוֹר "light"; thus, "Let the light-rays of day pierce it (i.e., the night) apt even to rouse Leviathan." Quite apart from the tameness of such a malediction (the worst it can mean is, Let the night be cut short by the approach of day), the interpretation does not begin to explain how the rays of day can rouse Leviathan (the reference is surely not to his rising from sleep each morning but rather to his being roused to angry activity); cf. also Day, *God's Conflict*, 48.

8.d. For the proposal to find a new עיר "revile" here, see n. 8.a.

9.a. Dhorme removes the verse to follow v 6; "the cursed night must not be allowed to see the light of day."

9.b. The colon is omitted by Hölscher, Horst and Fohrer as a prosaic interruption of the metaphorical cola before and after. Duhm moved it to follow v 4a, de Wilde to follow v 6a.

9.c. The arguments for עפעפים as "eyelids" or "eyeballs" are rather finely balanced. "Eyelids" is perhaps supported by an etymology from עוף "fly," thus "flutter." The meaning is well attested in postbib. Heb. Except in 16:16 where it is parallel with "face," עפעפים is always parallel to or associated with eyes (41:10 [18], eyes like the עפעפים of dawn; Ps 11:4; 132:4; Prov 4:25; 6:4, 25; 30:13; Jer 9:17 [18]), which may mean either that they are distinct from eyes, or that the term means nothing else but eyes. BDB reckons all these occurrences "eyelids," KB translates the Heb. as *Wimpern* ("eyelashes") but offers the Eng. translation "eyelids," KB³ also has *Wimpern*, even though Heb. has a special term for eyelashes (שְׂעִיר עפעפים "hair of the eyelids" [Levy]; perhaps עפעפים includes both), but thinks "eyes" is preferable for Job 41:10 [18] and Prov 6:26 along with 4Q184.1.13 (the harlot raises her עפעפים; J. M. Allegro [ed.], *Qumrân Cave 4* [DJD 5; Oxford: Clarendon Press, 1968] 82–83). Fohrer translates "beams" (*Strahlen*), understanding the imagery as of the flashing eyes of a person.

In the one place in Ug. where *ʿpʿp* occurs (*Keret* [*CTA* 14] 3.147; parallel in 6.295; Gibson, 86, 90) a beautiful young woman has "eyeballs (*ʿq*) [that] are gems of lapis lazuli (and) her eyelids (*ʿpʿp*) bowls of onyx" (Gibson's translation). H. L. Ginsberg thought *ʿpʿp* here must be "eyes" (*The Legend of King Keret* [BASOR Supplementary Series 2–3; New Haven: ASOR, 1946] 39), in which he was followed by M. Dahood, *Bib* 50 (1969) 272; idem, "Hebrew-Ugaritic Lexicography VII," *Bib* 50 (1969) 337–56 (351–52), arguing that both 4Q184.13 "she raises her *ʿpʿp* to gaze upon a just man" and Jer 9:17 where עפעפים stream with tears prove they are eyes. This view is followed by E. Jenni, *THWAT* 2:261; C. Brekelmans, *BO* 23 (1966) 308; H.-P. Müller, *VT* 21 (1971) 562; T. Collins, *CBQ* 33 (1971) 36; Pope; and JB "the opening eyes of dawn." The evidence may be judged short of convincing, for eyelids may equally well as eyes be seen as bowls (viewed from the outside). J. M. Steadman, "'Eyelids of Morn': A Biblical Convention," *HTR* 56 (1963) 159–67, discusses the translation of the imagery in early European Bible versions as a background to Milton's line, "Under the opening eyelids of the Morn" (*Lycidas*, 26).

10.a. Lit., "my womb," i.e., the womb that carried me and gave me birth; cf. on 19:17. Dahood's view that the suff is 3rd fem sg ("Northwest Semitic Texts," 25) is unnecessary.

10.b. The negative of the first colon does duty for the second also (GKC, § 152z; Dahood, *Psalms III*, 438), as in v 11.

10.c. Dahood found ויסתר to be from סור "turn aside," with infixed *t* ("Northwest Semitic Texts," 25–26; Blommerde), claiming the support of LXX ἀπήλλαξεν "removed" (LXX uses the verb several times for סור hiph). But quite apart from the problem of ambiguity, the image in MT makes better sense.

10.d. Andersen reads מֵעָי "from my belly," i.e., from the womb of my mother, מֵעִים being in parallelism with בֶּטֶן "womb" also in Gen 25:23, and synonymous with "womb" in Ruth 1:11. Then עמל would be the "labor" of his mother's childbearing. The difficulty with this suggestion is that the stanza would then come to rest not on the self-regarding note of the MT, which seems appropriate, but on the pain his birth caused his mother, which is beside the point, however generous. Strict parallelism does not rule everywhere.

11.a. Is אמות an incipient imperfect (Driver), and not rather a preterite?

11.b. Lit., "from the womb" (מרחם). The parallel colon, if indeed it does not represent a distinct possibility which Job is suggesting, makes it necessary to understand מן as "immediately after." Usually מן temporal means "continuously after," as with מרחם in Ps 22:11 [10]; 58:4 [3] (in the closest analogue to our passage, Jer 20:17, מרחם "from the womb" is unusual, but it is probably not an error for ברחם, "in the womb," as *BHS* claims; cf. NJB "still-born"). מרחם "from the womb" is the *min* of separation, not temporal *min*, in Jer 1:5. Others think we have here מן in the sense of ב "in" (Andersen refers to such a "locative" sense of מן, presumably alluding to M. Dahood, "Hebrew-Ugaritic Lexicography V," *Bib* 48 [1967] 421–38 [427]; cf. *Psalms III*, 395–96; note that N. M. Sarna, in discussing the "interchange" of *beth* and *min,* speaks only of the use of *beth* in place of *min,* not vice versa ["The Interchange of the Prepositions Beth and Min in Biblical Hebrew," *JBL* 78 (1959) 310–16]; but sufficient persuasive examples are supplied by G. Schuttermayr, "Ambivalenz und Aspektdifferenz: Bemerkungen zu den hebräischen Präpositionen ב, ל und מן," *BZ* 15 [1971] 29–51). M. Dahood revocalized to מְרֻחָם "enwombed," as also in the analogous Jer 20:17 ("Denominative *riḥḥam,* 'to conceive, enwomb,'" *Bib* 44 [1963] 204–5; also Blommerde); if this is correct, which is doubtful, the first colon would not be strictly parallel with the second.

13.a. עתה usually "now," but also "in this case" or, as we say, "then," עתה "pointing to a condition assumed as a possible contingency" (BDB, 774b § 2g; cf. Driver, *Tenses,* § 141). In the second colon, אז, usually temporal "then," has exactly the same sense, "expressing logical sequence strictly" (BDB, 23a § 2).

14.a. עם is perhaps to be understood as "like" (cf. BDB, 768a § 2f, for examples); so Fohrer, Dahood ("Northwest Semitic Texts," 26, comparing Ug. ʿm "like," and citing M. Held, "The Action-Result (Factitive-Passive) Sequence of Identical Verbs in Biblical Hebrew and Ugaritic," *JBL* 84 [1965] 272–82 [280 n. 36]).

14.b. חרבות is well attested as "ruins of cities," e.g., Isa 58:12; 61:4 חרבות עולם "ancient ruins," with בנה "build," as here); Ps 109:10; Ezek 26:20; 36:4, 10, 33; Mal 1:4; cf. Dan 4:27 [30]. To the objection that "kings do not usually attain fame by *re*-building ruined sites" (Driver) it can now be easily evidenced how prestigious Mesopotamian kings thought it was to rebuild cities of their ancestors, and especially to improve them, in particular their fortifications and temples (e.g., Nabonidus of Babylon, *ANET,* 312a; cf. Sargon on Samaria, *ANET,* 284b; and from Phoenicia, Yhmlk of Byblos (J. C. L. Gibson, *Textbook of Syrian Semitic Inscriptions* [Oxford: Clarendon, 1982] 3:18). Dwelling in ruined towns in 15:28 is a quite different image.

Rather popular has been the suggestion to see here a trace of an Egyptian term for pyramid (cf. Arab. *hirâm;* but the Eg. is *mr*); so Ewald seems to have read חֲרָמוֹת "pyramids," so also Budde (apparently), Driver, Stevenson, *BHK* (*prb*). Others, while not actually emending the text, nevertheless have seen in חרבות an allusion to pyramids (Delitzsch, Hölscher, Weiser, Fohrer, Moffatt "pyramids," JB "vast vaults") (there are a lot of faulty attributions of views on this point to be found in the commentaries).

Among emendations may be noted T. K. Cheyne's קַבְרוֹת עוֹלָם "everlasting tombs" ("More Critical Gleanings in Job," *ExpT* 10 [1898–99] 380–83 [380]; followed by Peake), and banal suggestions like אַרְמְנוֹת "palaces" (Dillmann), הֵיכָלוֹת "palaces" (Beer; and so apparently NEB, though not acknowledged by Brockington). Avoiding emendation, S. Daiches ("The Meaning of חֳרָבוֹת," *JQR* 20 [1980] 637–39; followed by G. R. Driver, "L'interprétation du texte masorétique à la lumière de la lexicographie hébraïque," *ETL* 26 [1950] 337–53 [349]), saw here an Old S. Arab. *mḥrb* "fortress, city"; though neither Biella's dictionary nor that of Beeston et al. acknowledges such a meaning (p. 187), R. B. Serjeant, "*Miḥrāb*," *BSOAS* 22 (1959) 439–53 (441–43), argues that the term originally signified a row of columns, and hence a castle or palace in which they featured. This means that Daiches's suggestion remains possible (as acknowledged by J. A. Emerton, *VT* 34 [1984] 492–93), but no more than possible.

Some have thought "ruins" refers to the present state of the cities built by kings, the end result of their building rather than their objective (Habel; similarly Rowley; NAB, Pope "built themselves ruins," NIV); but such an irony seems out of place here (Hölscher). Dhorme has "in desert places," seeing an allusion to the Egyptian pyramids built in the desert; thus also NJB.

16.a. MT begins with אוֹ "or." If this connects back to the אוֹ of v 15, it makes the line dependent ultimately on v 13: "Then I should have laid myself down . . . with kings . . . or with princes . . . or like a stillborn child." If that is so, the negative in the first colon is superfluous; it should rather be "or become like a hidden stillborn child" (so Wright, Budde, Hölscher, Fohrer, Sicre Díaz). But it is better to regard v 16 as connecting back to the "why?"-questions of vv 11–12 (so Duhm, Freedman, *Bib* 49 [1968] 505, Andersen, and of course those who move the verse to follow vv 11 or 12). Gordis attempts to solve the difficulty by revocalizing לֻא "if, if only"; but this is a somewhat desperate solution. Sicre Díaz reads אָז "then." Hitzig and Kissane suggested לֹא הָיָה "[which] never came into being." But MT is satisfactory though awkward.

16.b. M. Dahood has made the interesting suggestion ("Northwest Semitic Texts," 27) that טָמוּן is actually a noun designating the underworld as "the Hidden Place," or, as he puts it, "the Crypt" (נָפֶל is then a construct, "a stillborn in the Crypt"). With the article in 40:13 the term certainly means the underworld. His further argument that such a place-name gives the שָׁם "there" of v 17 something to refer to carries some weight, though the same argument will recur in v 19 without the same degree of persuasiveness. It is not a serious objection that the term here does not have the article (Sicre Díaz), nor is it correct that the point of the comparison is being in darkness rather than being in Sheol (as against Loretz, *UF* 8 [1976] 126). The decision lies between reading "Why was I not like a stillborn child in the Hidden Place?" and "Why was I not hidden like a stillborn child?"; the lack of specificity in the second rendering inclines me to favor it in the present allusive context.

16.c. עֹלְלִים, lit., "infants," a common enough noun with a general sense. Dahood ("Northwest Semitic Texts," 27) suggests that it has the specific sense of "fetus," as in Aram. and Syr. עוּלָא; but in both those languages only context can determine this sense for a word of more general reference, and the context here (even with the parallelism) is not specific.

17.a. A curious emendation of רְשָׁעִים "wicked" to רְעֵשִׁים "tremblers" was made by Beer (cf. *BHK*), Ehrlich and Tur-Sinai, so "those who tremble cease to be troubled." Indeed, this achieves "synonymous" parallelism in the verse, and keeps the focus of vv 17–19 on the small by contrast with that of vv 14–15 on the great. Sicre Díaz also suggests that the mood of the child's entrance into the world in v 12, a welcomed birth, fits with the theme of the powerful, whereas the hidden birth of v 16 would fit with the powerless of the following verses. But the emendation fails on the fact that רעשׁ "tremble" is never used elsewhere of persons (Ezek 31:16, of nations, is the nearest use, and there the imagery is rather cosmic), but of the earth, heavens, mountains, etc.

17.b. Lit., "exhausted of strength." Dahood makes the outlandish suggestion that כֹּחַ here means "wealth" rather than "strength" (as it does in 6:22; and perhaps Prov 5:10; but not Job 36:19), and translates "those wearied by wealth"; on the contrary, in the vicinity of "weary" כֹּחַ must surely mean "strength."

18.a. יַחַד "together," can be "all together" or "altogether"; the latter is more appropriate here, for there is nothing particularly desirable for slaves to find themselves "all together" in Sheol, since on earth they never had a great deal of private life. Dhorme can hardly be right that "the prisoners form a group with those previously enumerated." BDB, 403a § 2b, notes that the adverb often in poetry begins a clause with emphasis (cf. 24:4; in 16:10; 19:12; 21:26 it is "all together"). Contrast with KJV, RV, RSV, NAB, Pope "together" the more appropriate rendering of NJPS, "Prisoners are wholly at ease." NIV "captives also" is hardly right.

Dahood ("Northwest Semitic Texts," 28) thinks יַחַד a noun, "community." BDB and KB³ see the noun only at 1 Chr 12:18 [17], and KB adds Deut 33:5 (which is dubious). J. C. de Moor, "Lexical Remarks concerning *yahad* and *yahdaw*," *VT* 7 (1957) 350–55, doubts even these occurrences (as against S. Talmon, "The Sectarian יחד—A Biblical Noun," *VT* 3 [1953] 133–40). The noun occurs frequently in the Qumran texts, but Dahood's claim that it appears in Ugaritic is not substantiated (and it is not to be found in Gibson or Aistleitner). True, a noun here would give שָׁם in v 19 something to refer back to, but that is not really necessary (cf. n. 16.b above). What makes this suggestion of Dahood's unacceptable is that he claims "community of prisoners" is a term for Sheol, when it is self-evident that where the people in question were prisoners was on earth, where their taskmasters were.

19.a. This may be a reasonable addition to the Heb. (Moffatt, NJPS, Pope, Habel) but not the insistence that small and great are "the same" (Strahan, Peake, NAB) or "equal" (Gordis). It is sometimes urged that the phrasing קָטֹן וְגָדוֹל שָׁם הוּא cannot mean "the small and the great are there" since that would be שָׁם הֵם; it can only be replied that the pronoun agrees with *one* of the subjects, as if to say, "The small is there, as also the great." It is certainly not true that הוּא means "the same," Ps 102:28 [27] "Thou art the same (אַתָּה הוּא) and thy years shall not change" being quoted as a parallel (so, e.g., Dhorme, Horst, Gordis); אֲנִי הוּא in Isa 41:4; 43:10, etc., is also said to mean "I am the same." Driver, however, already put his finger on the point: אַתָּה הוּא may be *paraphrased by* "I am the same," but הוּא nowhere in itself *means* "the same." E. Lipiński made the interesting suggestion ("Notes lexicographiques et stylistiques sur le livre de Job," *FolOr* 21 [1980] 65–82 [65–70]) that the first *waw* is emphatic and that חֹפְשִׁי means "powerful" (cf. 1 Sam 17:25); thus, "There, the small is great, and the servant more powerful than his masters." But of course the theme is not the *reversal* of social distinctions, but their abolition (v 18); and in any case, this is a most unnatural way of reading קָטֹן וְגָדוֹל.

19.b. Blommerde translated the line, "namely, slave, freedman [see *Comment*], his master," taking the initial *waw* as *waw explicativum*, and the *mem* of מֵאֲדֹנָיו as enclitic *mem* on חֹפְשִׁי. This unattractive suggestion, followed by Dahood ("Northwest Semitic Texts," 28–29), relies on a nonbiblical sense of the well-attested חֹפְשִׁי, and fails to explain why a freedman should interpose between the slave and his master (cf. also Andersen).

21.a. Lit., "and it is not"; Dahood's proposal to read *'nn* plus pl *-û*, "that they be no more" ("Northwest Semitic Texts," 29) is eccentric.

21.b. Beer, Duhm read *kaph* "like" instead of comparative *min* "more than" before מִטְמֹנִים (LXX and Pesh also have "like"), because, says Duhm, those embittered in soul do not dig for treasures. True, but they dig for death more (enthusiastically) than they *would* for treasures, or more than anyone would for treasures (Strahan), so the מִן is quite intelligible. Not so intelligible is the comment of Budde and Driver that the emendation is necessary only if חפר is taken to mean "dig"; for on Duhm's reasoning they do not "seek for" treasures either.

22.a. Lit., "to the point of exultation" (אֱלֵי־גִיל); the phrase occurs also at Hos 9:1, with שְׂמֹחַ "rejoice," as here. But in both places it has excited the suspicions of commentators ("a bizarre expression," says Pope) who often would read here גָּל, lit., "heap" (NEB "tomb," JB "grave-mound"), to parallel קֶבֶר "grave"; so Houbigant, Duhm, *BHK*, Hölscher, Fohrer, Pope. But גל means any kind of heap and never without specification means anything like "tomb"; in Josh 7:26; 8:29; 2 Sam 18:17 a גַל אֲבָנִים, a "heap of stones," covers a dead body, but principally as a memorial rather than as a mere burial, whereas here those who seek death have no particular desire to have their names perpetuated. Furthermore, such a burial mound is not to be found by digging (Dhorme)! Not much better is Hölscher's suggestion גּוֹלָל, postbib. Heb. for "the stone placed on top of a burial cave" (Levy), which hardly seems the right kind of object of desire (unless perhaps it is thought to be metonymic for the tomb as a whole).

A. Guillaume ("The Arabic Background of the Book of Job," *Promise and Fulfilment* [S. H. Hooke Festschrift; ed. F. F. Bruce; Edinburgh: T.&T. Clark, 1963] 106–27 [110]) agreed that גל should be read, but saw in it the Arab. *gâl* "the inner side of a grave" (followed by Pope and perhaps by NEB), but Grabbe notes that this sense may well be peculiar to Arab. (*Comparative Philology*, 38–41). Dahood ("Northwest Semitic Texts," 30) connects גִיל with a Ug. *gly* "arrive" (parallel to מצא); but it is doubtful that that is the specific meaning of *gly*.

And all these proposals run up against the difficulty that שׂמח אל does not elsewhere mean "rejoice over" but "rejoice against" (Ezek 25:6), ב being the normal preposition. A. A. Macintosh ("A Consideration of the Problems Presented by Psalm ii, 11 and 12," *JTS* ns 27 [1976] 1–14 [3–4]) saw here another sense of גִיל, "distress," the root meaning "be agitated" either in joy or sorrow; hence "rejoice when they come to (mortal) distress." But there is no need to insist on such exact parallelism.

The conjunction of גִיל and שׂמח is well attested (C. Westermann, *THWAT* 1:415–18; D. W. Harvey, "'Rejoice Not, O Israel!'" in *Israel's Prophetic Heritage* [J. Muilenburg Festschrift; ed. B. W. Anderson and W. Harrelson; London: SCM, 1962] 116–27; P. Humbert, "'Laetari et exultare' dans le vocabulaire religieux de l'Ancien Testament," *RHPR* 22 [1942] 185–214 [= *Opuscules d'un hébraïsant* (Neuchâtel: Secrétariat de l'Université, 1958) 119–45]), and the MT is to be retained.

Guillaume sees here the poetic device known in Arabic poetry as *taurîya* whereby a word deliberately plays on the two meanings it has; so גִיל "exultation" is the natural and expected sequel to שׂמח "rejoice," but the context requires mention of a grave ("Arabic Background," 110); similarly Gordis, calling the device *talḥin*. There is indeed more than one level in the imagery here (the grave-digging treasure hunter and the "troubled" who seeks death) but that is different from a mere play upon the accidents of homonymy.

22.b. מצא, usually "find," here perhaps with the nuance "reach" (cf. KB³), as in 11:7.

23.a. MT has only "to a man. . . ."; לְמָה יִתֵּן אוֹר "why is light given?" is understood from v 20.

24.a. Duhm deletes the verse, believing that it and v 25 cannot both stand, and that it is a marginal annotation on v 25. Hölscher too thinks it merely a line in conventional psalm style that interrupts the connection between vv 23 and 25. Dhorme acidly observed that if this verse is no more than a commentator's remark we should have to abandon the attempt to distinguish poetry from what is not.

24.b. Lit., "are before" (לִפְנֵי), but it is hard to believe this means "before I eat, before every meal," still less "as a side-dish" or "vegetable" (Hölscher). It is rare (and dubious) for לִפְנֵי to mean "as, like, instead of," but the parallelism with "like water" confirms this; cf. 4:19 and 1 Sam 1:16 (BDB, 817b § 4f); and so G. R. Driver, "Linguistic and Textual Problems: Jeremiah," *JQR* ns 28 (1937–38) 97–129 (121–22); and thus RSV, NEB "sighing is all my food" (similarly JB).

Others have "instead of" (NIV), but that sounds as if Job is starving, whereas the text must mean that it is sighs that nourish, or rather, fail to nourish him. NAB "Sighing comes more readily to me than food" attempts to convey a temporal dimension, but what does it mean? Is it "I find it easier to sigh than to eat"?

Dahood ("Northwest Semitic Texts," 31) reads לְפָנַי "[when my bread is] before me [sighing comes]"; the meaning of that is rather cryptic. Emendations to כְּפִי "like" (Budde), לְפִי "in proportion to" (BDB, 805b § 6c), are unnecessary.

Tur-Sinai took לִפְנֵי as temporal, understanding לַחְמִי as "my threat, the threat to me" (a new Heb. word cognate with Syr. *lhm* "threaten"), and referring it to Job's apprehension of misfortune, as expressed also in v 25. But while Job could say that so long as he was still prosperous he was "afraid" that something would go wrong, he can hardly say that in those days he was already "sighing" and "groaning."

24.c. Thinking the image too weak, Andersen reads for כמים "like water," כְּמוֹ־יָם "[my bellowings cascade] like the Sea." But see *Comment*.

25.a. Lit., "I feared a fear and it came upon me." Driver says "the sentence is *virtually* hypothetical, though no hypoth. particle is used" (see also Driver, *Tenses*, 111 § 80). But it seems preferable to regard this as a narrative sequence: then I feared, now it has come (cf. Gordis). The initial כי "for" may perhaps be "when" (cf. Hos 11:1), but more naturally prefixes the reason for the sighing of v 24. But the connection is not to v 23 (as Horst and others), for to have one's fears realized is not a reason for wishing to die (v 23), whereas for grief to be one's only sustenance (v 24) may well be.

25.b. וַיֶּאֱתָיֵנִי, "met me," preterite, like יבא, "came" in the next colon.

Form / Structure / Setting

The *structure* of this speech, to which the strophic structure corresponds exactly, is among the most clear and uncontroverted in the book. After the prose headline of v 1 and the introduction of the speaker in v 2 we find three strophes: vv 3–10, 11–19, 20–26. The "why?"-questions of vv 11 and 20 are formal demarkers of beginnings, and the subject matter corresponds to these markers. Job's malediction on the days of conception and birth (vv 3–10) is followed, in the next strophe, by the wish that, if he had to be born, he could have died at birth (vv 11–19), and in the next, by the wish that, since that did not happen, he could die now (vv 20–26).

Habel would divide simply vv 3–10 (curse) and 11–26 (lament); see below on genre. P. W. Skehan divided the speech into seven strophes (vv 3–6, 7–10, 11, 16, 12, 13–15, 17–19, 20–23, 24–26; = NAB); apart from the unnecessary rearrangement of v 16 (see *Comment*), it is reasonable to see minor divisions like these within the major strophes. Thus vv 3–5, maledictions on the day, may be distinguished from vv 6–9, maledictions on the night, with a pendant (v 10). The second strophe obviously divides vv 11–15 from 16–19, each introduced by a "why?"-question; and in the third there is a distinction between vv 20–22 on the (mostly plural) weary ones, and vv 23–26 on the (singular) sufferer who is Job. E. C. Webster, "Strophic Patterns in the Book of Job," *JSOT* 26 (1983) 33–60 (37), thinks, less persuasively, that v 23 should form part of a unit 20–23, but this seems only in order to find a concentric (a–b–b–a) pattern. Terrien also sees the three primary strophes, but further divides them into (i) 3–7, 8–10; (ii) 11–

12, 13–16, 17–19, (iii) 20–23, 24–26; in this analysis only the connection of v 16 with
what precedes is questionable.

The marks of closure in the poem are very definite. The stanza 3–10 concludes
with a "motive" line as a pendant (v 10), giving the ground for the lament, and the
whole poem ends with three lines (vv 24–26), tightly integrated into the preceding
material, giving the ground for the lament. Within the three strophes there is in each
case a diptych arrangement, differently organized in each strophe:

Strophe I	3–10
Theme (day and night)	3
1. Day	4–5
2. Night	6–9
Motive ("for")	10
Strophe II	11–19
Theme ("why?")	11–12
1. Portrait of Sheol	13–15
Theme reśumed	16
2. Portrait of Sheol	17–19
Strophe III	
Theme ("why?")	20
1. Those seeking Sheol	21–22
Theme resumed ("why?" understood)	23
2. I, Job, lacking Sheol	24–26

For a rather similar analysis, see D. N. Freedman, "The Structure of Job 3," *Bib* 49
(1968) 503–8.

The presence of five tricola in the first strophe (but nowhere else in the poem) is
remarkable (vv 3–6, 9); it can only signify a relentless aggregation of the maledictions,
one tricolon concerning the day and the night, then two about day, and two about
night.

In *genre* the poem is a *complaint* (*Klage*) (so, e.g., Murphy, *Wisdom Literature*, 22–
23). The literary *forms* that it draws upon are almost wholly two: the curse and the
lament. Vv 3–9, with its motive clause v 10, adopts many features of the *curse*, though
it is questionable whether we should recognize it as a curse proper (as Murphy, *Wisdom
Literature*, 22–23; Habel)—not because the word "cursed" (אָרַר) does not occur—for
in the somewhat parallel Jer 20:14–18 it does, and that text is hardly a regular curse—
but because it is directed against something that cannot be cursed, the past. Features
of the passage typical of the curse (of the composite type or freely composed; see S.
Blank, "The Curse, Blasphemy, the Spell, and the Oath," *HUCA* 23/1 [1950–51] 73–
95 [75–83]) are: the identification of the one cursed (here the day and night), the
motive clause or condition (here v 10), and several clauses each constituting a curse
(vv 4–9); the agent of the execution of the curse is concealed. But, as Blank remarks
(p. 82), the form of the curse here is very elastic; and it might be better to call these
maledictions rather than curses proper (Fohrer speaks of "a poetically expanded cursing-
wish"). It might even be said that the cursing corresponds to the lament against enemies
(Westermann, *Structure*, 58), so loose are the forms.

The *lament* is also a free variation on the conventional lament (*Klage*, "complaint")
form; normally a lament is cast in the second person and addressed to God, but here
this is avoided, and God is spoken of only indirectly (Westermann, *Structure*, 37). Normally
also a lament has the aim of improving the lamenter's lot, but nothing could be further
from Job's purpose here. Two types of lament are drawn on: the self-lament in vv
11–19 and vv 24–26 (where it is a description of mourning) and the God-lament in
vv 20–23. Characteristic of the lament are the "why?"-questions (vv 11, 12, 16, 20; also

implied in v 23), the depiction of the lamenter's sorry state (vv 24–26), what Westermann (*Structure*, 38, 61 n. 14) calls the "primordial individual lament," comparing for example Rebekah's laments (Gen 25:22; 27:46), such laments being "too untamed to allow for incorporation into the prayer book of the community." So the lament here, like the curse, draws upon conventional forms but goes its own way. Both the curse and the lament are here denatured in such a way as to reflect the futility of the speaker's existence: the curse is no true curse, for it fastens itself upon what cannot be altered, and the lament is no true lament, for it addresses no one, and what purpose can a lament serve if it is spoken into thin air?

The poem also draws upon the form of the *monologue,* a genre found in all parts of the Hebrew Bible (see N. P. Bratsiotis, "Der Monolog im Alten Testament," *ZAW* 73 [1961] 30–70), and favored naturally for the expression of the speaker's inmost thoughts and feelings. Although Job's friends are present and overhear the speech, and will respond to the speaker of it, it is not addressed to them. Nor is it addressed to God, even though he too may be presumed to overhear it. This monologue is of the type Bratsiotis calls "the lament-monologue" (cf. also Gen 25:22; Ps 42:3–6, 11–12 [2–5, 10–11]; 1 Macc 2:7–13; Jer 15:10; Mic 7:1–6), which contains self-imprecations, and questions the value of continued existence. Westermann rejects the term "monologue" for this speech (*Structure,* 60 n. 5) as belonging to a quite different mentality, but it is hard to see the reason for his sharply expressed view. It is true that the formal similarities with other lament monologues are rather general.

The *function* of the speech is suggested by the forms it employs together with its position in the book. The force of the curse and the lament is tempered by the evident avoidance of an addressee for the lament and by the futility of the curse; the form of the monologue indicates that from Job's point of view the speech is designed for no function at all. From the author's perspective, however, such a deliberately uncommunicative speech functions as the springboard for the whole of the ensuing dialogue, for while it does not divulge the whole gamut of Job's attitudes to his suffering, it makes plain by its very reticence that the one thing Job will not allow is that his suffering proves his guilt. To refuse to acknowledge that presumption in the presence of these friends is a launchpad for controversy.

The *nodal verse* of this chapter should be identified as v 26: it contains in both positive and negative form the dominant image of the poem, the presence of "turmoil" and the absence of "ease," and as well it summarizes the stance of Job, as a distressed sufferer pure and simple and not as one who has been drawing intellectual and theological inferences from his suffering.

The *tonality* of the poem is determined also by the primary image; though the theme of the poem is death and the desire for death, nevertheless the image of restlessness rather than, say, of resignation advises the reader that this cannot be Job's last word and prepares us for further developments of Job's quest for order and orientation. The man says he wishes he were dead; but with such violence (especially vv 3–9) that the reader's expectations of impending action and controversy are stimulated. Y. Ṣmudi ("The Beginning of Job's Protest (Chapter 3)" [Heb.], *BMik* 27 [1981–82] 229–32) remarks on the fading of the aggressive note in the course of the speech; but there is more to this speech than a mere diminution into quietude.

Comment

1–26 In this speech we are suddenly plunged out of the epic grandeur and deliberateness of the prologue into the dramatic turmoil of the poetry, from the external description of suffering to Job's inner experience. This beautiful and affecting poem is built upon a dynamic movement from the past to the future and from the experience of the man Job outwards to the experience of humankind. There is first a curse on the days of his conception and birth (vv 3–10), then, since that must inevitably fail, a wish that he had died at birth (vv 11–19), and finally the question why suffering humanity cannot be relieved of its suffering by an early death (vv 20–26).

1 The opening line of the chapter is more than a simple narrative transition from the prose prologue to the poetic dialogues. Job's curse is, as Habel has well written, an *event*, integral to the plot of the narrative of the book as a whole. In chaps. 1–2 we saw an accepting sufferer, urged indeed by his wife to "curse God and die" (2:9); now Job's curse intrudes upon the depiction of his piety. It is "a catalytic action which provokes reactions from other characters in the narrative. . . . From the moment [his curses] are uttered, Job is under a shadow; he has called for his origins to be negated, invoked forces of darkness, and set himself against God" (Habel). We are not meant to understand that Job has indeed cursed God, but he has cursed "his day" (see below).

Someone had to speak, after those seven days and seven nights of silence; "in the end it was Job who broke the silence," as JB puts it so well, linking the chapter firmly back into the narrative of chap. 2, and making the routine phrase "after that" (אחרי כן) carry its usual significance as a conjunctive rather than a disjunctive expression (cf. Gen 23:19; 25:26; 32:21 [20]; 41:31; 45:15; mainly in 2 Sam "and it came to pass afterwards" [ויהי אחרי כן] marks a major transition or disjunction, as 2:1; 8:1; 10:1; 13:1). Similarly in the Ugaritic texts *aḫr* does not so much "introduce the transition to a new episode" (M. Dahood, "Northwest Semitic Texts," 22; similarly Pope) as link a new episode to the preceding; it means "whereupon" at *The Palace of Baal* (*CTA* 4) 3.23 (Gibson, 58), and *Aqhat* (*CTA* 17) 5.25 (Gibson, 107).

Job's "opening his mouth" first is a narrative hint that the speech cycles are to be construed as responses of the friends to Job, not responses of Job to the friends (we shall note that the narrator shows us Elihu as regarding the friends' speeches as "answers," 32:3, 5). They have come to "comfort" him (2:11), and at times that is what he understands to be their purpose (16:2; 21:34), however ineffectually it may be carried out. But all the real progress in the drama is made by Job, and he challenges the friends much more than they comfort him. The phrase to "open the mouth" is no conventional phrase merely equivalent to "say," or a literary device to draw attention to what follows (Pope), but generally points to the breaking of silence or dumbness (Dan 10:16; Ps 51:17 [15]; cf. Job 32:20 "open lips"; of opening another's mouth: Num 22:8; Ezek 3:27; 24:27; 33:22; in the negative: Ps 38:14 [13]; 39:10 [9]; Prov 24:7; Isa 53:7; in the NT at Matt 5:2 it seems to signify the beginning of solemn speech, but in Acts 8:35 and 10:34 it looks like a false Septuagintalism [18:14 is different]). Ps 39:3–4 [2–3] depicts a similar situation where the psalmist is finally unable to hold his peace. The parallel of the Egyptian *Dispute over Suicide* in which the speaker "opened my mouth to my soul" and "my soul opened its mouth to me" (*ANET*, 405, lines 1, 56, 86) is fortuitous.

Job's "day" (יומו) that he cursed is almost universally taken to be the day of his birth (so, e.g., RSV, NEB, JB, NIV), in view of the subsequent verse. But the normal Hebrew for one's birth-day is יום הִוָּלְדוֹ (Eccl 7:1; cf. Hos 2:5 [3]; Gen 40:20) and "day" by itself nowhere else means the day of one's birth; it is perhaps better to regard his "day" as equivalent to his life (cf. 30:25 "one hard of day," one whose life is hard, BDB, 399a § 4a), or his unhappy fate (similarly Budde), perhaps even as meaning the day of his disaster (as 18:20; Jer 50:31; 1 Sam 26:10; Ezek 21:30 [25]; Ps 37:13). The curse upon the day of his birth is only one aspect of his curse (Fohrer).

What is the significance of a "curse"? At one extreme it may be thought to set in train an inescapable doom, the word of curse itself having a power of its own (cf. S. Gevirtz, *IDB* 1:750) or being imbued with the potency of the curser (cf. J. Pedersen, *Israel: Its Life and Culture I-II* [London: OUP; Copenhagen: Branner, 1926] 441–42). At the other extreme it may be stressed that the term here used, קלל piel, strictly means to "make light, esteem as light, or worthless" (cf. C. A. Keller, *THWAT* 2:641–47 [643]; J. Scharbert, "'Fluchen' und 'Segnen' im Alten Testament," *Bib* 39 [1958] 1–26 [8]; H. C. Brichto, *The Problem of "Curse" in the Hebrew Bible* [JBLMS 13; Philadelphia: SBL, 1963] 105, 129, has "railed at"); it is thus not so categorical as ארר "curse" (cf. Exod 22:27 [28] where קלל is used of "reviling" God, and ארר of "cursing" a ruler). Can קלל be just "a less offensive synonym" of ארר (S. H. Blank, "The Curse, Blasphemy, the Spell, and the Oath," *HUCA* 23/1 [1950–51] 73–95 [84])? Certainly, too much has been made of the power of words in the ancient world; see A. C. Thiselton, "The Supposed Power of Words in the Biblical Writings," *JTS* ns 25 [1974] 283–99, who shows that the power resides not in the words themselves but in the authority, status, or office of the one who utters them. From this perspective, Job's curse is doomed from the outset, for he is quite deprived of social or psychic power. And there is no reason to suppose that the poet means that some harm objectively falls upon either Job's present state or upon a particular date in the calendar (whichever "his day" means). The meaning of "cursed" here cannot in the end be derived from the lexicon or the theological dictionary but only from the contents of the poem of which it is a headline—including a poetic wish for a curse (ארר) in v 8, but also "why"-questions of reproach against God (vv 11, 12, 20), and simple lament (vv 24–26).

It is strange that nowhere else is קלל used with a thing as its object, but this fact can hardly mean that God himself is in some way the object of the curse (Cox, *The Triumph of Impotence*, 38–39).

3–10 The point of this first stanza is to utter the vain wish that he had never been born. It is a vain wish and the curses it includes are inconsequential and ineffective because it is too late to do anything about it. It is absurd therefore to treat this text as solemnly portraying Hebrew conceptions of the nature of the curse, as Rowley, for example: "In Hebrew thought a curse was not the mere expression of a wish; it was charged with power to work for its own fulfilment, and once uttered it had passed beyond the power of its utterer, and gone forth on its evil errand." That is probably not true even of a genuine and credible curse, but this malediction is a parody of a curse in that the past cannot be changed; and that is the point of the stanza. The language is fierce, but the curse has no teeth and the wish is hopeless. Its power is wholly literary, its extravagance the violence of Job's feeling. Because he has been injured in life he would have, if he could, the whole of that life annihilated. The form is the form of a curse, but the function is to bewail his unhappy lot, "when in disgrace with fortune and men's eyes [he] all alone beweep[s] his outcast state" (Shakespeare, *Sonnets*, 29). May we go further and say with Andersen that the purpose of such a cry is to evoke pity, human and divine? Or should we hear it simply as a cry of pain, the sufferer himself being conscious of no further purpose than the need to give expression to his grief?

The similarity of these verses with Jer 20:14–20, likewise a curse on the day of one's birth, needs to be explored and explained. First there is the issue of resemblances and differences. The structure of the Jeremiah text is similar, moving from a curse on the day of one's own birth, through the announcement of a male child's birth, to the blocking of the womb, to a wish that the sufferer had not been born to see "trouble" (עָמָל) (Jer 20:14, 15, 17, 18; cf. Job 3:3, 10). But the bulk of the two passages differs: in Jer 20 a curse is laid upon the messenger (no doubt still alive) who announced the birth, both for bringing the news and for not having killed the mother before she gave birth (20:15–17); though somewhat surprisingly J. Lundbom ("The Double Curse in Jer 20:14–18," *JBL* 104 [1985] 589–600) finds it hard to accept that the messenger could be blamed for that failure. The focus on the messenger is further developed by wishing his fate to be like that of Sodom and Gomorrah (v 16). In Job 3, on the other hand, the futile malediction is laid upon no human subject but exclusively upon the day of the birth and, at greater length, on the night of the conception (vv 4–5, 6–10); and the only reason for the curse is that conception was not prevented (v 10), not, as in Jer 20, that the birth itself was not prevented.

Are the two texts literarily related? Duhm (1897), confident as ever, affirmed that independent though the poet of Job was elsewhere, here he clearly borrowed from Jeremiah. "Generally," he wrote, "a greater poetic power is found in Job 3:3ff. than in Jer 20:14ff.; but the unadorned and more naive explosions of grief in Jeremiah have a more compelling effect on me than the more artful imitation, which is more self-conscious but somewhat over-heavy and cold." E. Renan, on the other hand, had found in the Jeremiah passage a "flabbiness, heaviness, lack of vibrancy and parallelism" (*Le Livre de Job* [Paris: Michel Levy, 2nd ed., 1860] xxxv–xxxvi = *Oeuvres complètes de Ernest Renan* [ed. H. Psichari; Paris: Calmann-Levy, 1955] 7:324–25). Clearly the matter cannot be decided by a purely aesthetic judgment.

Dhorme, scrutinizing the details, judges Job to be the imitator but the greater poetic talent: the poet of Job has "ingeniously lightened" the Jeremiah text, eliminating the unpoetic relative pronoun אֲשֶׁר "that" from his v 3 and substituting for the perfect pual יֻלַּדְתִּי "I was born" the imperfect niphal אִוָּלֵד. Job "deepens and adds a sinister touch to the malediction" by introducing the idea of the night of conception, while the series of questions, provoked by a single verse in Jer 20:18, is "prolonged with many reverberations in the development of Job's lament. . . . Inspired by the malediction launched by the Prophet, the author of Job at once soars on his own wings and circles the mountain peaks of the purest poetry. The clumsier phrases are lightened and surge upwards. The hesitating style becomes firm and vigorous" (Dhorme, clx–clxi).

The fact is that we cannot determine which passage is the earlier, whether either author was aware of the other, or which piece is the greater poetry. The very great difference of focus (the messenger vs. the night) together with the similarity of structure suggests if anything that each poet was creating his own variations on a familiar theme. Certainly each is a very considerable poem and it is otiose to regard them as competitors. In view of the probability that the Jeremiah passage is not to be read as a transcript of the prophet's feelings but as a somewhat conventional utterance of distress accompanying a judgment-speech or woe oracle (D. J. A. Clines and D. M. Gunn, "Form, Occasion and Redaction in Jeremiah 20," *ZAW* 88 [1976] 390–409 [406–407]; cf. also D. R. Hillers, "A Convention in Hebrew Literature: The Reaction to Bad News," *ZAW* 77 [1965] 86–90), and the fact that the Job passage is of course a highly literary piece, the probability is that neither author was aware of the other's writing. J. Bright's conclusion is the best we can manage: "The two texts certainly reflect a common tradition; but it is probably futile to talk of literary dependence, one way or the other" (J. Bright, "Jeremiah's Complaints: Liturgy, or Expressions of Personal Distress?" in J. I. Durham and J. Porter, eds., *Proclamation and Presence*, FS G. Henton Davies [London: SCM, 1970] 189–214 [213 n. 61]).

In structure, this stanza is built upon the disjunction of "day" and "night," linked in v 3, and then developed separately, the day in vv 4–5, the night in vv 6–9, with a pendant in v 10. Day and night are to be denatured, day becoming dark as night, night to yield no pleasure and give place to no dawn.

M. Fishbane has argued ("Jeremiah IV 23–26 and Job III 3–13: A Recovered Use of the Creation Pattern," *VT* 21 [1971] 151–67) that the thrust of this text (he says 3:1–13), a "counter-cosmic incantation," is toward a systematic *bouleversement* or reversal of the world-ordering events of Gen 1: "Job, in the process of cursing the day of his birth (v. 1), binds spell to spell in his articulation of an absolute and unrestrained death wish for himself and the entire creation." He attempts to parallel the events of Gen 1 with these verses, but although it is true that the darkening of day (v 4a) reverses the act of the first day of creation, there are few other genuine correspondences (e.g., the reference to Leviathan in v 8 is not a *reversal* of the creation of sea-monsters on the fifth day, and the rest Job longs for in the grave in v 13 is no kind of parallel to God's rest on the seventh day). Job's concern is not with the created order as a whole but with those elements of it that have brought about his own personal existence.

3 Strictly speaking, this is not a curse, but a wish or malediction, directed essentially against the two events that made his life possible, his conception and birth, and directed on the verbal level against the "day" and "night" when those events occurred. It is part of the surrealism of the wish that its object is the "perishing," not of the conditions of his existence, but of the conditions for the conditions of his existence. Job is not someone to settle for half-measures (Weiser); he would like to root up his present life out of the world, carrying with it the causes of it, the moments of his conception and birth, and along with them the very calendrical time that made them possible.

Day and night are superficially a standard word-pair (Gen 1:5; Job 2:13; 17:12; Ps 19:3 [2]), but here they are not on the same footing; for the day of his birth must be a day of 24 hours, the night of his conception a mere night. Day and night are depicted as living beings (cf. Ps 19:3–5a [2–4a]), which can "perish" or "speak," since otherwise a curse against them is ineffectual.

Does Job mean that he wishes that date could be struck from the calendar? Peake supposed that "a day did not cease to be when it was succeeded by the following day. The same day would return in the following year" (similarly Fohrer, Horst). Now of course if Job wishes he had never been born, every recurring birthday will be a potent reminder to him of his unhappy lot, and it would not be absurd for him to wish his birthdate expunged from the calendar (similarly Delitzsch). But it is hard to imagine him so far anticipating his continued existence that he should be concerned about his next birthday. The day that really matters is the one in a past year when he was actually born; that is the day he wishes could have perished, or, because he is trapped in a grammar of the absurd, wishes *would* perish even though it is past (Rashi and ibn Ezra also noted here a past conditional or past optative sense; cf. Brichto, *The Problem of "Curse,"* 107; Fishbane, *VT* 21 [1971] 154). Peake regarded this interpretation as depicting a "mere sentimental cursing of something which has passed into a nonentity where no curse can reach it," and preferred to see here "something which each year returns to work its malignant will." But Job has nothing to fear from the return of his birthday; his animus is wholly against his birth. Nor is it that he regards the day of his birth as a baneful day that doomed him to misery, and thinks that if he had been born on a more fortunate day life would have been more happy for him (Peake). The fault lies not in his stars but in his birth. The recipe of cursing the day as a means of coping with a disaster is different again in Constance's speech in *King John* (3.1.84–88): "A wicked day and not a holy day! / What hath this day deserv'd? What hath it done, / That it in golden letters should be set / Among the high tides in the calendar? / Nay, rather turn this day out of the week, / This day of shame, oppression, perjury."

It has seemed an oddity to many that the day of his birth should be mentioned (v 3a) before the day of his conception (v 3b), and some have adopted the LXX rendering, "See, a boy," to make the second colon refer also to the time of birth, not conception (see n. 3:3.b). But it easy to see how Job's mind is here working backwards from his own present state to the moment of his birth and then beyond that to the moment of his conception (cf. the same sequence of birth and conception in Ps 51:7 [5]). The night is personified as "a mysterious soothsayer" (Habel), "busy with her spells" (Strahan), making an announcement about the sex of the child just conceived, as in the similar passage in Jer 20:15 a man brings news to the father that a male child has been born (a Ugaritic parallel in *Shachar and Shalim* [*CTA* 23] 52–53; Gibson, 126). Like a messenger who brings bad tidings, night is cursed for the message it delivers, though it is hardly responsible.

The term here translated "male-child" (גבר) normally means an adult male (as distinct from women and children; cf. Jer 43:6; Deut 22:5; Prov 30:19); it is doubtful that it has any special overtones of "strength," like the verb גבר "be strong," or of a man in relationship with God (against H. Kosmala, *TDOT* 2:377–81). It is not elsewhere used of a child, and especially not of a just-conceived child; it must be that the term is "looking at what he essentially is, not at the stage of developments he has reached" (Peake).

To whom would the night have announced its news of the conception of Job? Not to the parents, who do not reckon on knowing the sex of the child before it is born, but to the subsequent nights, just as the nights in Ps 19:3 [2] pass on the "knowledge" acquired by the nights of creation week. There is an air of excitement or joy presumed in the speech of the night (cf. also vv 6b, 7b) because the subject matter is the conception of a male child (cf. Isa 9:5 [6] "unto us a child/son is born"; Jer 20:15, news of a son makes a father glad; John 16:21, where the woman in labor is joyful because a human being [ἄνθρωπος, *anthrōpos*] has been born into the world; 1QH 3.7–10, where the joy is implicit). Job wishes that joy could have perished.

There is an allusion to our verse at Ecclus 23:19 [14]: if you speak improperly in the presence of nobility, you will come to regret it, and "wish you had not been born, and curse the day of your birth" (JB).

Several have suggested that Job's malediction is deliberately "misdirected" to day and night, since they are of course not responsible for what happens in them, and that the implied or real objects of his curse are his parents, or God, who are indeed responsible. So, for example, S. H. Blank (*HUCA* 23/1 [1950–51] 85 n. 44; and "'Perish the Day!' A Misdirected Curse (Job 3:3)," *Prophetic Thought: Essays and Addresses* [Cincinnati: Hebrew Union College Press, 1977] 61–63), who argues that Job "avoids" cursing his parents by cursing the day of his birth. But it seems more correct to find here a malediction of Job upon his own existence. Because it is not exactly a curse, and especially because his words do not lead to his death, this malediction can hardly be called suicidal; it is of the same kind as several other despairing expressions of the OT: Rebekah: "If it is thus with me, why do I live?" (Gen 25:22); and "If Jacob marries one of the daughters of Heth . . . what meaning is there left in life for me?" (27:46 JB); Elijah: "It is enough, now, O Lord; take away my life" (1 Kgs 19:4); Jonah: "Take my life from me, for it is better for me to die than to live" (Jonah 4:3); Tobit: "Command my spirit to be taken up, that I may depart and become dust; for it is better for me to die than to live" (Tob 3:6); Sarah, who "thought of hanging herself" because all her seven husbands had died but desisted because it would bring disgrace on her father, asks God: "Command that I be released from the earth . . . Why should I live?" (Tob 3:10, 13, 15); cf. also 1 Macc 2:7, 13. Of course the most striking parallel is Jer 20:14–18, "Cursed be the day on which I was born . . . ," discussed further on vv 3–10 above. These authentic Israelite parallels to Job's mood make it quite unnecessary to seek the original of the present depiction in Egyptian wisdom literature (as Fohrer). Of course Job is out of character with the typical Israelite attitude toward life, and of course there is pessimistic wisdom literature from Egypt, notably the *Dispute over Suicide* (*ANET*, 405–7) and *The Admonitions of Ipu-wer* (*ANET*, 441–44); but there is no reason to suspect cross-cultural influence.

Is this Job who "curses" life a different Job from the Job of the prologue who accepts life along with its inconcinnities? R. D. Moore argues ("The Integrity of Job," *CBQ* 45 [1983] 17–31 [25]) that this chapter "does not represent a mere shift in attitude or fluctuation in mood but rather a complete reversal of the narrative Job." In its sequence of the womb, the tomb, and the giver of life, chap. 3 is "a step-by-step rebuttal of Job's manifesto of faith in 1:21," the poet simply contradicting the traditional portrait of Job in the prologue. It is an even more interesting depiction of character if we assume that the same author is responsible for the Job of the prologue and the Job of the poem.

4 Particular maledictions now follow, upon the day (vv 4–5) and the night (vv 6–9), with a concluding pendant (v 10). The day in question is the day Job was born, and it is of course absurd to wish anything of the past; that is the measure of Job's disorientation and sense of disproportion. Most commentators think the day is his birthday as it recurs annually (cf. *Macbeth*: "Let this pernicious hour / stand aye accursed in the calendar"), because then the malediction can be on something that lies in the future. It could of course be that Job regards any future occurrence of his birthday as a standing testimony to the fact of his birth which he wishes had never happened; but in v 3 the focus is inescapably on the past day of his birth and it is best understood as remaining there. The potency of his imagination is not weakened by the impossibility of his wish.

Job begins his maledictions with a parodic reversal of the first divine word at creation, "Let there be light" (Gen 1:3). "As for that day," he says, "let there be darkness" (יהי חשך), using the same phrasing exactly as Gen 1. This is not a defiant gesture against God but the anguish of a man who has found the creation of himself the very opposite of the "good, very good" of Gen 1.

In wishing that God may not "seek out" (דרש) the day, Job supposes that each day comes into being only when God summons it into existence with his renewed command, "Let there be light!" Or, as Gerard Manley Hopkins has it: "And though the last lights off the black West went, / Oh, morning, at the brown brink eastward springs— / Because the Holy Ghost over the bent / World broods with warm breast and with ah! bright wings" ("God's Grandeur," in *Poems of Gerard Manley Hopkins* [ed. W. H. Gardner; London: OUP, 3rd ed., 1948] 70). In 38:12 Yahweh depicts the dawn as his "commanding the morning" and "making the dawn know its place"; the image is very similar in Isa 40:26 of God bringing out the stars into the night sky by calling their names. דרש is "seek out" (iniquity in 10:6, food in 39:8, God in prayer in 5:8) and more generally, "be concerned about," "care for" (Deut 11:12; Jer 30:14, 17; Ps 142:5 [4]); the implication is that if God does not actively "seek out" a day and will it into existence it remains shrouded in darkness.

M. Fishbane suggests (*VT* 21 [1971] 155) that the verb "belongs in a magical context," one of its principal meanings being to "consult an oracle"; but this can hardly be the case here when God is the subject. Certainly there is no simple curse here; Job and his words have no power to effect change in the cosmic order, and only if God could be prevailed on to abandon a day would it fail to appear.

To say "may light not shine upon it" does not mean "may there be no light in the course of that day" since "on" a day is normally ב, not על. It rather implies that light is in the possession of God, who grants it to each day in succession; light is not an inherent part of day, but shines from elsewhere "onto" each day as God's gift to the day; cf. 38:19, 24 envisaging light being "distributed" from its dwelling place. G. Rinaldi raises the question whether the language here may not be borrowed from psalmic language about Yahweh's revelation ("Affulge, Deus," *BeO* 2 [1960] 40).

5   If day is granted no light by God, it remains in the power of darkness, that is, of the chaotic powers presiding over the world in primeval times (Gen 1:2). Changing the image slightly, Job can say that darkness would "redeem" (גאל) or win back its rights over day, wishing that "the old masters might . . . reclaim the fateful day on which he was born" (Strahan). Tur-Sinai thought that darkness cannot be said to have a blood relation's right of redemption over the day; but that is just the point: day is in cosmogonic terms the offspring of night.

Primeval "darkness" (חשך) is shown up in its true color as "the shadow of death" (צלמות, see n. 3:5.a), since light is life (cf. vv 16, 20, 23) and darkness is death (10:21–22; 23:17). If clouds (עננה, a collective noun, only here) "alight" or "settle" upon it (שׁכן, of the cloud resting on the tabernacle, Exod 40:35; Num 9:17), no light breaks through; cf. the making of clouds and thick darkness the swaddling bands of the sea (38:9).

As a climax to the tricolon, Job wishes that day might be overwhelmed by another form of darkness, "the blackness of day," i.e., the eclipse (see n. 3:5.c), which not only obscures the light but brings terror (בעת; cf. 7:14) to humans and so metaphorically to the day itself (for terror at an eclipse, cf. Isa 13:6–10; Joel 2:10–11; Rev 6:12–17; and see further on v 8a).

6 The maledictions, now directed to night, still concern the past day of Job's birth. It is not that he wishes his birthday may in future drop out of the calendar (as Fohrer and others) so that he may no longer be reminded of the unhappy event that occurred on it, but rather that he wishes that the particular night of his conception had never been.

If "deep darkness" (אפל) had carried off or seized the night, darkness would never have given place to day and so that night would have had no existence as a typical calendrical night. Or, if אפל means here, as in some other places in Job, the darkness of Sheol (10:22; 28:3; perhaps also 23:17; 30:26), a "sinister darkness greater than night itself" (Habel), the idea may be that the night would have been hijacked by the blackness of the underworld, and so never been able to encompass a life-affirming event like a conception (it is not that the night is to be so dark that it cannot turn into day, as Delitzsch suggested). The verb לקח, often translated "seize" (RSV, NIV), is better attested in the sense "carry away" (so NJPS; as in 15:12), the removal of the night from existence being the point at issue, not a forcible laying hold of it.

If the night of Job's conception had not been included among the "days" of the year—and there is no oddity here, because the night is the first half of the day—his conception would have been impossible. He wants to snap all the chains that bind him to existence (Fohrer). Of course, the night enters the number of the months by being included in a day; the number of the months must be the number of days in a month, not the number of months in a year (LXX saw the little logical problem and translated the last colon, "let it not be numbered among the days of the months"). The parallelism of "year" with "months" is found only here in the Hebrew Bible, but may be paralleled in a Ugaritic text, where to have immortality is "to count the years with Baal, with the sons of El count the months" (*Aqhat* 2 [*CTA* 17] 6.28–29; Gibson, 109).

7 Job is not so hostile to humanity in general as to give voice to a malediction upon the recurring date of his birth, nor is he so generous toward the human race as to wish that "it shall do to no others the wrong it did to him" (Peake). His anguish remains directed exclusively to the conditions of his own existence, and now he wishes, another hopeless wish, that the night of his conception had been "barren" (גלמוד, perhaps literally "stony"; cf. on 15:34), his mother's conception being regarded as the personal act of the night on which it took place, or, perhaps better, the night being a fertile being who produces as its offspring human conception. The "cry of joy" (רננה, not "triumphing" as in 20:5) he wishes had never been uttered is the sound of his parents' lovemaking that resulted in his conception (so also Terrien), or perhaps the joyful singing of the epithalamium or wedding ode, if it is to be assumed that the wedding night is the night of conception (Fohrer); for the "sound of joy" associated with the wedding, cf. Jer 7:34; 16:9; 25:10; 33:11. The rejoicing is obviously not over the birth of the child (as against most commentators), since it is the night of conception, not the day of birth, that is in view.

8 The night of Job's conception is still the subject, Job now wishing that it had been laid under a spell or had been declared an unlucky day by magicians or astrologers so that no conception could have occurred on that day, or at least that only a ill-destined pregnancy could have been begun.

Since H. Gunkel (*Schöpfung und Chaos in Urzeit und Endzeit* [Göttingen: Vandenhoeck & Ruprecht, 1895] 59) it has often been thought that instead of those who curse the "day" (יוֹם) we should, by a simple revocalization, read those who curse the "sea" (יָם) (so *BHK*, Ehrlich, Horst, Gordis, Pope). G. R. Driver (VTSup 3 [1955] 72) cited an Aramaic incantation, "I will enchant you with the spell of the sea and the spell of Leviathan the sea-monster" (text and translation now to be seen in C. D. Isbell, *Corpus of the Aramaic Incantation Bowls* [SBLDS 17; Missoula: SBL, 1975] 2:3–4 [p. 19]). Since in the second colon of our verse there is a definite mythological reference to Leviathan, some have thought that "Sea" in the first colon should refer to the sea-god Yam of Canaanite mythology (so, e.g., W. F. Albright, *JBL* 57 [1938] 227); we read of Baal's battle against Prince Sea (Yam) in the Ugaritic text *Baal and Yam* (*CTA* 2.1, 4; Gibson, 40–45), where the weapons used to defeat Sea had been "rendered ineffective by incantations tantamount to curses pronounced by the [craftsman] god Koshar who specialized in magic as well as metallurgy" (Pope).

However, this view contains the inescapable problem that anyone who "curses" the sea must be on the side of order and goodness, since the sea is a chaotic and evil power, whereas in the second colon the rousing of Leviathan is obviously for the sake of destructive activity; and it is impossible to see how partisans of order could be invoked to lay spells on the night of Job's conception (so Dhorme, Gordis, Day, *God's Conflict*, 46–47). It is preferable, then, to retain the Masoretic reading, even if it is "flatter" (Rowley), and see those who curse a day as "enchanters or magicians reputed to have the power to make days unlucky" (Driver), perhaps specifically by producing eclipses, which is what is referred to in the second colon. They can hardly be simply those who, like Job, curse the day of their birth (Dhorme), for such curses— being *ex eventu*—are by definition ineffectual. In wishing that the "cursers [אֹרֵר]" of days had laid a spell [קָבַב]" on that night Job perhaps uses milder words (אֹרֵר "enchant, lay a magic spell on" [E. A. Speiser, "An Angelic 'Curse': Exodus 14:20," *JAOS* 80 (1960) 198–200] and קָבַב "revile" [J. Scharbert, *TDOT* 1:415; Brichto, *The Problem of "Curse*," 200–202]) than we might have supposed; in that case the meaning of קָבַב is like its sense at 5:3 "despise as something cursed." Job wishes that the night of his conception had been ugly and ill-omened. It is no difficulty that it is "cursers of *days*" who are spoken of, for nights are parts of days; and they do not curse a particular day, but "certain days" (NJB).

Leviathan usually figures in the OT as a violent sea-monster subdued by God in primeval times (Ps 74:14; Isa 27:1), but here it is plain that by incantations known to those "skilled" (עָתִיד) in magic the normally dormant monster is still regarded as capable of being roused to activity (see C. H. Gordon, "Leviathan, Symbol of Evil," *P. W. Lown Institute Studies* 3 [1966] 1–9). The particular activity, though not explicit, may well be the swallowing up of the sun or moon, i.e., the causing of eclipses; see T. H. Gaster, *Myth, Legend, and Custom in the Old Testament* (New York: Harper and Row, 1969) 787–88, for evidence of such a belief from several cultures (and J. Day [*God's Conflict*, 45] for a Ugaritic text [*CTA* 6.6.44–52; Gibson, 81] showing the sun and the sea-dragon to be enemies). Gaster discriminates between the popular belief in the dragon that swallows the sun and the literary mythology of the primeval monster who threatens order again in eschatological times (cf. Isa 27:1; Rev 20:1–3); it may be rather that the two ideas coalesce here (cf. further M. Fishbane, *VT* 21 [1971] 158–60). Leviathan is a monster that has only to be awoken from sleep or stirred into activity (עור can mean either, but not "control" [GNB] or "tame" [NEB]) for its destructive power to be felt; the same verb is used in 41:2 [10] of the danger of "stirring up" Leviathan, where it is the crocodile that is depicted in mythological terms rather than the mythological creature itself. Any magician who can summon up the superhuman power of this unamiable being is a true professional. He would surely have the power to curse a day. But of course the day that Job wants to be cursed is long past, and his wish for professional assistance is entirely futile.

It is a mistake to see here Job invoking forces of chaos to destroy the created order (Habel) or articulating an "absolute and unrestrained death wish for himself and the entire creation" (Fishbane, *VT* 21 [1971] 153; similarly Cox, *The Triumph of Impotence*, 43). As J. Lévêque puts it, "Job makes no appeal to nothingness, to primordial chaos, in order to give himself the Promethean satisfaction of seeing the whole world perish along with himself; rather he appeals to those who could, if required (העתידים), conjure up these forces from the depths. At no time does Job claim to deregulate the creation or reduce the cosmos to the same state of night as his soul experiences at this moment; it should be stressed that his malediction relates only to *one* particular day and *one* particular night" (*Job et son Dieu* [Paris: Gabalda, 1970] 1:336).

It might be, of course, that the skill to rouse Leviathan is only a certificate of competence Job would require of any sorcerer he would engage to lay spells on a night. But it is perhaps more probable that rousing Leviathan is a second skill that Job would have wished employed on his behalf against the night of his conception. For if the dragon had swallowed up the moon, the night would have belonged unequivocally to the realm of the underworld and conception of a life would have been either impossible or ill-omened.

9 If the night of his conception had been consigned to the power of the underworld by the ministrations of Leviathan (by the activities of the sorcerers, Weiser thinks), it could have remained dark for ever, never giving place to day (it is not a "punishment" upon the night, as de Wilde thinks, but a constraint). It would then have been no ordinary night, one in which a mortal could be conceived, but would have taken on a wholly new quality as a monstrous manifestation of the dark powers of Sheol. On such a night Job's life could never have begun. Here is quite the opposite of "rage against the dying of the light" (Dylan Thomas, "Do Not Go Gentle into That Good Night").

The stars of the twilight (נשף "evening twilight" in 24:15; Prov 7:9; etc.; "morning twilight" in 7:4; Ps 119:147) are the morning stars (38:7), Venus and Mercury to us, that appear as harbingers of the coming of day. If they are darkened, day cannot come, and night becomes an endless night waiting for a dawn that never breaks (Driver). Boldly and unmetaphorically the poet writes, "(that) it longed for light and there was none." Then in a delightful image, the "eyelids" (עפעפים; see n. 3:9.c) of the morning that the infinitely extended night will never see (or be regaled with, take pleasure in; ראה ב as in 20:17) are the light in the eastern sky that heralds sunrise. If perhaps the term refers to the "eyelashes" rather than the "eyelids" (see n. 3:9.c), the image may be of the rays of the rising sun. In either case the dawn (שחר) is personified, probably as a beautiful woman, the eye being the sun and the lids or lashes being the accompaniments or harbingers of the full splendor (cf. also Sophocles, *Antigone,* 102–3, "eyelid of the golden day"). The (male) Canaanite god of dawn bears the same name, Shahar, but it would be a mistake to see here a mythological allusion, as is the case in Isa 14:12, where Helel (Daystar) is "son of Shahar." See further, especially for the argument that in the OT Dawn is envisaged as a woman, J. W. McKay, "Helel and the Dawn-Goddess: A Re-examination of the Myth in Isaiah xiv 12–15," *VT* 20 (1970) 451–64. If by any chance the view is correct that we have here not the lids or lashes but the "eyes" of Dawn (see n. 3:9.c), the meaning must be that a night entirely shrouded in darkness would never see the light in the sky, the "opening eyes of dawn" (JB), a less interesting image. The "wings of Shahar" (Ps 139:9) are a quite different image of the dawn as a winged creature that flies away as the sun rises; "awaking Shahar" in Ps 57:9 [8] is another personification of Dawn.

10   Why all these maledictions upon the night of his conception? After so many lines of imaginative cursing, the poet takes only one line to state night's crime: it is simply that on that night the conception took place, without any hindrance by night, and Job was launched upon a life that has led only to turmoil and distress. God is the one who "opens" or "closes" women's wombs, enabling or preventing conception (to "open" the womb in Gen 29:31; 30:22; to "close" it in 1 Sam 1:5, 6 [סגר as here] and Gen 16:2; 20:18 [עצר in both]); whether or not the "doors of the womb" suggest the labia, it is not simply the act of intercourse that produces a child but a supernatural "opening" as well. But it is night, not God, that is the subject here (against Andersen). What superhuman powers like Night can give they can also take away; Night had it in its power to prevent Job's conception, but failed to use its power. Therefore Job has wished Night could have had the gift of life taken out of its hands and have been swallowed up by the pitch darkness of Death, transformed from a natural and benign being into a manifestation of the dark power of Sheol. The shutting of the doors of the womb unquestionably refers to the conception of the child, as the attachment to "night" in the present context (vv 6–9) and the parallels show, not the birth of the child from the womb (against, e.g., JB "it would not shut the doors of the womb on me," NIV, and Gordis, who thinks "day" must be the subject of the verb, and Freedman [*Bib* 49 (1968) 503] who thinks the composite day and night is). It is, as Driver says, scarcely more than an accident that the closing of doors in the OT is generally to prevent entry rather than exit (Gen 19:10; Neh 6:10; Isa 45:1; as against Job 38:8), but that happens to be the purpose here also.

The "trouble" (עמל) or "labor" that it has become Job's lot to behold is not an internal subjective "misery" (Gordis) or "sorrow" (JB) but an objective state of affairs that is burdensome and productive of grief (cf. עָמָל in 5:6, 7; 7:3; 11:16; 16:2). It is Job's term for the sum of the afflictions that have come upon him, and is echoed by the similar term רֹגֶז in vv 17, 26. It is the opposite of the tranquillity he desires in v 13. The phrase is cited in 1QH 11.1, 19.

11–19 In this second stanza we find no longer maledictions, but a lament. The malediction is given up because it is futile; it doesn't alter the fact, Job is alive, and his life is turmoil (Driver). Unlike the typical OT "lament" (*Klage*), however, whose function is *appeal*, this lament sets its heart not on some improvement of the sufferer's lot, but on the dissolution of his life (Fohrer). Developing his theme forward in time from the moments of vv 3–10, Job asks why, if his conception and birth could not have been prevented, he could not have died so soon as he was born. Then he should have had "rest" and "quiet" (v 13), the opposite of the turmoil that now engulfs him—which is the theme that will be picked up finally by the third stanza as it draws to its close (v 26). So filled is his mind with this single thought that he can disregard "not only the long years of happiness that he had previously enjoyed, but also the drearier aspects of Sheol, which elsewhere he could vividly portray" (Driver). Davidson well observes on these lines: "The picture of the painless stillness of death fascinates him and he dwells long on it, counting over with a minute particularity all classes, kings and prisoners, slaves and masters, small and great, who there drink deep of a common peace, escaping the unquietness of life."

The structure of the stanza is twofold, vv 11–15 mirroring vv 16–19. In the first panel of the diptych, two lines prefixed by "why?" are followed by three depicting the peace of Sheol; in the second, one line prefixed by "why?" is followed by another three continuing the depiction of the underworld. Recognition of this simple pattern (similarly Freedman, *Bib* 49 [1968] 505; Habel) persuades one that a removal of v 16 to follow v 11 or v 12 is needless (see further on v 16).

11 Would that he had died the moment he was born! The rhetorical "why?"-question does not seek an answer, here there is no spirit of curiosity of an ontological kind (Terrien), but just as the maledictions of vv 3–9 draw the eye to their futility, this unanswerable question that does not even sincerely seek a response focuses the attention on the hopelessness of the lamenter's plight. Indeed, such a question must have an addressee, even if it is only thin air, and Job's question or rather complaint is uttered in the direction of God (not the friends), though only implicitly; see further on v 20.

The first colon is made more precise by the second. In the first, he asks, "Why did I not die from the womb?" and "from the womb (רֶחֶם)" is expanded and specified by "I came forth from the womb (בֶּטֶן)" in the second. It may be that the "from" in the first colon means immediately after leaving the womb (see n. 3:11.b), or perhaps that the verb of the second colon, "I came forth" is implied here (cf. Horst, Andersen). The parallelism of "die" (מוּת) // "expire" (גוע) occurs also at 14:10, and of רֶחֶם "womb" // בֶּטֶן "belly" at 10:18–19; 31:15 (בֶּטֶן is the A-word); Ps 22:11 [10]; 58:4 [3]; Jer 1:5 (בֶּטֶן is the A-word). If the language is conventional, the thought too is easily paralleled both in Jewish literature and beyond. Cf. 2 Bar 10:6 "Blessed is he who was not born, or he, who having been born, has died" (Charles, 2:485; he thinks Eccl 4:2–3 may be the origin of the wording); *4 Ezra* 7.116 "Better had it been that the earth had not produced Adam, or else, having once produced him, (for thee) to have restrained him from sinning" (Charles, 2:591); Ecclus 30:17 "Better death than a wretched life, and everlasting rest than chronic illness" (JB); Theognis, *Elegies* 1.425–28 "Best of all for mortals is never to have been born, but for those who have been born to die as soon as possible"; Sophocles, *Oedipus at Colonus,* 1224–27 "Not to be born at all / Is best, for best that can befall, / Next best, when born, with least delay / To trace the backward way " (F. Storr, Loeb edition); Menander, *The Double Deceiver* (frag. 125K) "Whom the gods love dies young." Cf. also Herodotus 1.31, and other classical references by G. Stählin in *TDNT* 5:787–88. An elegant review of the theme in Greek and Hebrew literature is made by D. Daube, "Black Hole," *Rechtshistorisches Journal* 2 (1983) 177–93.

12 It is uncertain whether the knees that received the newborn child were the mother's or the father's knees. The presence of the mother in the second half of the line cannot decide the issue (against de Wilde). From Roman society we know well the practice of legitimation of a child by the father taking it on his knees, while A. Musil has testified to the custom among certain Bedouin (*Arabia Petraea* [Vienna: A. Hölder, 1908] 3:214); thus too the expression "the children of Machir b. Manasseh [i.e., Joseph's great-grandchildren] were born upon Joseph's knees" (Gen 50:23). Duhm, Peake, Driver, Stevenson saw here the father's act. But Dhorme, Horst, Fohrer and others (cf. also NEB, GNB) argue strongly that it is the mother's act of taking the child on her knees in order to suckle it (second colon); cf. Isa 66:12 where the child sucks as it is dandled on the mother's knees. Often quoted in this connection is an Assyrian text in which Ashurbanipal is addressed by the god Nabu: "You were weak, Ashurbanipal, when you sat in the lap (on the knee) of the goddess, Queen of Nineveh. As for the four nipples placed at your mouth, two you sucked, and in two you hid your face" (M. Streck, *Assurbanipal und die letzten assyrischen Könige bis zum Untergange Nineveh's* [Leipzig: J. Hinrichs, 1916] 2:348–49).

To somewhat different effect, B. Stade ("Miscellen. 15: 'Auf Jemandes Knieen gebären' Gen 30,3; 50,23; Hiob 3,12 und אֶבְרַיִם Exod 1,16," *ZAW* 6 [1886] 143–56 [148–54]) reported a custom among Bedouin women of being seated upon the knees of a midwife while giving birth; this may be the precise significance of Gen 30:3, where Bilhah is to give birth upon the knees of Jacob, using his knees as a kind of birthing chair (cf. further H. H. Ploss, M. Bartels and P. Bartels [ed. E. J. Dingwall], *Woman: An Historical, Gynaecological and Anthropological Compendium* [London: Heinemann, 1935] 2:728). In this case being received by the midwife's knees would be a moment intermediate between being born and being put to the breast. Ecclus 15:2, often cited in this connection, though it contains the word "receive" (קדם), of a mother, has nothing to do with the legitimation or suckling of an infant.

Tipping the balance in favor of its being the mother's knees is the consideration that legitimation by the father is not so directly a means of ensuring the life of the child as its being suckled by the mother; if sitting on the mother's knees is essentially only an alternative depiction of the child's being fed, the point would be clearest: Job wishes that, since his birth could not have been prevented, he had not been nourished as an infant but left to perish.

13 What Job's state in Sheol would now be if he had died at birth is now portrayed in three lines (vv 13–15); the depiction of Sheol is continued further in vv 17–19. It is crucial for the poem as a whole that the dominant image of existence in the underworld he presents is of peace and rest: he would have lain down (שׁכב) as in a bed, been quiet, undisturbed (שׁקט), have slept (ישׁן), and have rested (נוח), since (vv 17–19) Sheol is a place of cessation from "troubling" or agitation (רגז), a place of rest (נוח) for the weary, of taking one's ease or finding security (שׁאן) and finding freedom (חפשׁי). These images portray in inverse mode Job's present experience, which he will not once express directly in the whole poem except in its closing three lines (vv 24–26). We may guess indeed what it feels like to look upon "trouble" (עמל, v 10), but "trouble" is an external reality, not a psychological truth. The method of the poet is first to project Job's longings, his vision of an ideal state, so that at the poem's close Job may resile to the reality of his present state of restlessness and anxiety. The imagery is so precise and the psychological depiction so authentic that we may miss the surprise here. For if we consider the man Job, afflicted with some terrible skin disease, we might suppose for him feelings of irritability, sheer pain, disgust, or, as he reflects on the significance of his illness, self-pity, anger or hopelessness. And if we consider him as one who has lost his goods, honor, children, wife (to speak truly), we might suppose for him feelings of grief, loss, meaninglessness, futility, worthlessness. The last thing we would imagine for him is anxiety and restlessness. For it seems, from our perspective, though not yet perhaps from his, that all that can befall him has befallen him and that the certainty of his present state has become all too evident. Restlessness, even anxiety, emerges (does it not?) from a state where good and bad, fear and hope, are mixed. What has Job to hope for now, or what to fear? His death? Here he welcomes death as the most desirable state, and when he next opens his mouth it will be to voice his desire that God would crush him to death, let loose his hand and cut him off (6:8–9); it is hard to believe that here the fear of death is the focus of this pervasive mood of restlessness. Rather, we should regard the anxiety as arising from the intellectual-existential significance of what has happened to him. The suffering and the loss is one thing, but it is not on the same level as the mind-blowing and foundation-shaking threat that the exceptional suffering of the exceptionally pious poses to notions of cosmic order, divine justice and human values. Dermot Cox in his original book, *The Triumph of Impotence: Job and the Tradition of the Absurd* (Rome: Università Gregoriana Editrice, 1978), observes that "the setting established in Job 1–2 is a stock situation in the literature of the absurd, from Sophocles to Beckett and Ionesco" (p. 31). And he quotes from Camus' *The Myth of Sisyphus:* "It happens that the stage-sets collapse . . . [O]ne day the "why" arises and everything begins in that weariness tinged with amazement (*cette lassitude teintée d'étonnement*)" (A. Camus, *Le Mythe de Sisyphe. Essai sur l'absurde* [Paris: Gallimard, 1942] 27; *The Myth of Sisyphus* [London: Hamish Hamilton, 1955] 19). This collapse of the stage-set, this weariness tinged with amazement, is, in a different language, Job's experience of restlessness.

The idea of the underworld as a place of rest by comparison with the turmoil of life seems a very obvious one, but it is in fact rather hard to parallel in the Hebrew Bible. A quick overview of N. H. Tromp's *Primitive Conceptions of Death and the Nether World in the Old Testament* (BibOr 21; Rome: Pontifical Biblical Institute, 1969) shows no section in a most comprehensive study allotted to this aspect, despite very many sections on Sheol as a hidden place, the depths, waters, pit, corruption and ruin, destruction, silence, dust, forgetfulness, darkness, as a city, prison, river, mountains, with a personal god, his terrors and demons, and so on. The only truly comparable OT text is Eccl 6:5 where one untimely born finds more rest in Sheol than someone who has no joy from their possessions or lacks burial—which on any interpretation must be counted an idiosyncratic text. Ecclus 30:17, often quoted in this connection, portrays death as better than a bitter life and the "rest" of death as preferable to chronic illness, but this too is to be accounted a specialized view. In general, Job's words here must be judged eccentric by OT standards, a "desperate reversal of traditional understandings of that unhappy domain" (Habel). Things are different of course in Egyptian literature (which doesn't mean that Job is influenced by such ideas; against Fohrer); death "à l'égyptienne" (Terrien) is often depicted as something desirable; in one text the inhabitants of the underworld say "'Welcome, safe and sound!' to him who reaches the West [the afterlife]" (*The Good Fortune of the Dead,* in *ANET,* 33–34); better known are the beautiful lines from the *Dispute of a Man with His Soul over Suicide:* "Death is in my sight today, / Like the recovery of a sick man, / Like going out into the open after a confinement. / . . . Like the odor of myrrh, / Like sitting under an awning on a breezy day / . . . Like the odor of lotus blossoms, / Like sitting on the bank of drunkenness. / . . . Like the longing of a man to see his house again, / After he has spent many years held in captivity" (*ANET,* 407a). But this is in a culture where death is regarded as a continuation and fulfillment of life. From the classical world we may compare Aeschylus, frag. 141 (255); Sophocles, *Trachiniae,* 1173; *Oedipus at Colonus,* 955, 1224–26; Euripides, *Trojan Women,* 636–37. The inscription on the tomb of Sennacherib, "Palace of sleep, tomb of repose, eternal abode of Sennacherib, king of the world, king of Assur" (L. Messerschmidt, *Keilschrifttexte aus Assur historischen Inhalts* [Leipzig: J. C. Hinrichs, 1911] 1:49, no. 47), is a somewhat analogous text from a Semitic milieu.

14–15 The poem suddenly moves in an unexpected direction. Duhm, ever alert to logical problems, is one of the few to have doubted whether the depiction of kings and nobles in the underworld is necessary to the subject matter; he draws the conclusion that vv 14–15 are purely dramatic decoration. Indeed, we may well ask, what does having the high-born in Sheol contribute to the restfulness of the place, which is the one thing Job finds desirable about it? Davidson must be entirely wrong, that Job means that "instead of lying in squalor and being the contempt of the low-born race of men as he now is (ch. xxx), if he had died he would have been in company of the great dead who played famous parts in life" (similarly Driver). Would he really rather be dead than déclassé? Is having one's status recognized in Sheol supposed to be one of its attractive features? Is that what Job expects from the restfulness of Sheol, a segregation of its citizens by the social rank they enjoyed, or suffered, on earth? Dante's Inferno was infinitely more discriminating.

A route to a new interpretation of the picture of Sheol is to observe first that there are two groups of inhabitants of Sheol, to be identified in v 17 as the "wicked" and the "weary," with whom the "taskmaster" and the "captives" of v 18 are aligned, as well as the "great" and "small" and the "master" and "slave" of v 19. These two groups were in life locked together in a bitter social relationship, described from the perspective of the exploited as an absence of rest or ease, compulsion to work, absence of freedom, inferior status, and from the perspective of the "narrator" as a "troubling" on the part of the exploiters. In Sheol the social distinction and thus the control of one group by the other has been annihilated, and that is what makes Sheol a restful place. Life above ground is by contrast a matter of "trouble" (עָמָל, v 10) or "troubling" (רֹגֶז, vv 17, 26), in the social sense of class conflict.

Why should Job, who is one of the privileged members of society, look upon life as essentially social turmoil and upon death as a desirable state of abolition of social distinctions? We can hardly imagine that while he was "the greatest of the sons of the east" (1:3) he looked at life this way; but in the course of the days of the prologue he has become both economically deprived and socially outcast. His social perspective has altered, perforce, from that of the "great" to that of the "small." It is only those who suffer from social oppression that think its abolition in death a good thing; those who benefit from systems of economic and social control always think of it as the inevitable order of things or even as a God-given structure, and they never desire its annihilation.

This outlook on the social order, dictated by the wording of vv 17–19, must form the inexplicit background of vv 14–15. In these verses, the kings, ministers of state, and princes seem at first to be described quite objectively as "rebuilding ruins" (v 14) or "having gold" or "filling their houses with silver" (v 15), the only authorial comment apparently being the implicit irony that now they possess nothing in Sheol. Viewed against the picture of Sheol that gradually unfolds in this poem, however, these rulers can only be aligned with the "great," the masters, and so with the wicked. Seeing that, we observe that the wording of vv 14–15 already points in the same direction. For the references to gold and silver are to be taken in a pejorative sense (as all but well-to-do readers see immediately); and even the wealthy Job intends that sense, for his riches consist exclusively in livestock and servants (1:3), the (uncoined) silver and gold rings he is given at the time of his restoration being tokens of esteem rather than monetary gifts to increase his wealth. Job's own exculpation also specifically abjures reliance upon gold and silver (31:24–25), which carries with it at the very least a hint of the questionableness of gold and silver as a measure of wealth and perhaps contains an implicit rejection of the wealth typical of the despot. And if Eliphaz means in 22:24–25 that once Job has been restored he will become so wealthy that he will "count gold as dust, gold of Ophir as stones in the wadi," he means gold only metaphorically, just as Shaddai also is to be "your gold, and your precious silver." So Job does not fancy himself among the hoarders of precious metals, and no more, we may presume, does he equate himself with kings who "rebuilt ruins for themselves," for Job has always found his significance in personal relations and the maintenance of justice in a village society (chap. 29) and would be intolerant and judgmental of the ambitions of oriental potentates who built vast cities (largely on the backs of unpaid-for labor) to satisfy their egos (the לָמוֹ "for themselves" means exactly this). These men, with an inflated sense of their own importance, are the "wicked" of v 17. These are the "troublers" of the social order (cf. 1 Kgs 18:17–18, where also the identity of a "troubler" [עֹכֵר] depends on one's point of view and social position). Job has no desire to endure his underworld existence in their company, but in Sheol their power is spent, and they, the disturbers of life on earth, are as quiet now as those they once disturbed. Indeed, the quietness of erstwhile troublers is more impressive a feature of Sheol existence than even the quietness of the formerly troubled; so the troublers make their entry into Job's depiction of the restfulness of Sheol as exemplars of its "trouble"-reducing power. The remark of Duhm that vv 14–15 are not necessary to the sense is thus controverted. For Job the turmoil or "trouble" (עמל) of life is, indeed, not exclusively due to the inequalities of power in human societies, for there is the pain of bereavement and Godforsakenness and physical illness which can fall on all regardless of social position. But having experienced, for at least a week plus the time his friends took to reach Uz (2:11, 13), life at the bottom of the social pyramid, he has acquired a certain feeling for the lot of the oppressed and unquestionably sets himself on the side of the weary, the captives, the small, and the slave (vv 17–19). At the very least, the "trouble" they experience is paradigmatic of human trouble in general. "Life is a form of slavery and enforced labor" (Habel); cf. 7:1–2.

The name of Sheol is in this poem never mentioned ("to *suggest* the object, that is the poet's dream" [Mallarmé]), but its reality looms all the larger for the assumption that we all know, from the moment those potentially ambiguous verbs "lie down," "be quiet," "stop," "rest" (v 13) are spoken that there is no ambiguity at all about their reference here.

The graduated series, kings, counselors, princes, appears also in Ezra 7:28; 8:27 (princes, counselors in Isa 19:11), suggesting a Persian background, since in Israel officials of the title counselor are not mentioned in the lists of 2 Sam 8:16–18; 20:23–26; 1 Kgs 4:1–6 (Horst). On the counselor, see P. A. H. de Boer, "The Counsellor," VTSup 3 (1955) 42–71; W. McKane, *Prophets and Wise Men* (SBT 44; London: SCM, 1965), esp. 55–62. The continued identity and social status of the inhabitants of the underworld is alluded to at Isa 14:9–10 (where perhaps Sheol is a landlord rousing his royal guests to greet the arrival of the king of Babylon; cf. Tromp, *Primitive Conceptions,* 103), Ezek 32:27 (where warriors descend to Sheol with their weapons), and 1 Sam 28:14 (where the shade of Samuel is an old man in a robe). But our passage is much subtler and richer in its depiction not just of "weakness" (as Isa 14:10) but of the cessation of "troubling." It is not wholly adequate to say that here "the fundamental equality of all men in death is stressed" (Tromp, *Primitive Conceptions,* 193 n. 80), nor even that the text "carries the reflex that already in this life all men are equal" (Andersen). For it is Job's point that in this life people are *not* equal, and that what is desirable about Sheol is not its egalitarianism as an abstract principle, but the absence of the strife between unequal humans that constitutes "trouble" in the upper world.

Some have seen in these verses a reference to the pyramid-builders of Egypt, building mausoleums for their future existence (note למו "for themselves"), great structures that already in Job's day had come to look like "ruins" from the depredations of later tomb-builders or else situated in the desert "wastes" (Dhorme), and filled with the treasures that popular imagination—not unjustly—believed those pyramids contained (so Duhm, Hölscher, Fohrer, and others). In that case the "houses" of v 15 would be the pyramids themselves or other sepulchres (cf. "house" in Isa 14:18). But there is no specifically Egyptian coloring in these verses, and it fits the total picture better to see the princes as hoarders of wealth during their lifetime (cf. 22:18 for the filling of the houses of the wicked with good things [טוב]; Deut 6:11 and Neh 9:25 for Israel's capture of Canaanite cities full of good things).

Andersen sees in these verses four categories of persons, corresponding to four categories in vv 17–18: here kings, counselors, builders, and princes, there the wicked, the overworked, criminals, and the exploited. But in v 14 the builders are not a group separate from the kings and counselors (as the article of הבנים makes clear), and in vv 17–18 there seems to be nothing about criminals, but there are eight groups of persons, who are perhaps to be seen as exemplifications of just two categories, oppressors and oppressed.

16 Is this verse misplaced? Certainly, it breaks the link of v 17 with v 15, for the "there" that opens v 17 can only refer to Sheol as depicted in vv 13–15, and not to anything in v 16. And does not the subject matter of v 16, the immediate burial of a premature child, belong with vv 11–12, the fate of the child that dies at birth? NEB, Driver, Dhorme, Rowley, de Wilde therefore transpose this verse to follow v 12; NAB, JB, Beer, Duhm, *BHK*, Stevenson, Moffatt, Pope to follow v 11 (either is a suitable place); Weiser and Horst to follow v 13 (less probably); and Fohrer, Fedrizzi, and Hesse omit the verse entirely as destroying the connection of thought.

There is no doubt that v 16 belongs logically with vv 11–12; the question must rather be whether there may be any reason why it is to be found in its present place. An adequate reason (see also on vv 11–19) is that the resumption here of the topic of vv 11–12 sets up two (three-line) depictions of Sheol existence (vv 13–15, 17–19), which would otherwise be one, but which need to have their individuality preserved. For the first deals only with the holders of power, and speaks from a seemingly neutral position, while the second constantly juxtaposes the powerful and the powerless and identifies with the latter. In that vv 17–19 are separated from vv 13–15 by the interposition of v 16, they can constitute comment on them more effectively.

The image in this verse is slightly different from that of v 11; there it was the child who dies soon after birth, here it is the stillborn fetus (as in 10:18–19, carried from the womb to the grave). The נפל, lit., "what falls (sc. from the womb)," is not strictly a miscarriage or abortion (as Germ. *Fehlgeburt*, and cf. Num 12:12, the flesh being "half consumed" at birth) but a stillborn child (also at Eccl 6:3; Ps 58:9 [8]), for whom the term "hidden" (טמון) is immediately appropriate even before we know its exact reference. Probably the term "hidden" suggests the burial of the child, perhaps as a source of dread because of its unnaturalness (cf. L. Koehler, *Hebrew Man* [London: SCM, 1956] 51); but see also n. 3:16.b. Eccl 6:3 evokes the reality: "It comes in vain and goes into darkness and in darkness its name is covered; moreover it has not even seen the sun or known anything" (Podechard's translation, quoted by Dhorme). There is a pathos here that is excluded from the Jeremiah text by the violence of its idea of death in the womb leaving the mother's womb for ever great (20:17).

For the expression "to see the light" meaning to live, cf. 33:28; Ps 49:20 [19]; Isa 53:10 (emended).

17 Nothing here explicitly binds together as correlatives the "raging" of the wicked and the state of exhaustion experienced formerly by those who now rest. In the same way there is no explicit connection of the "small" with the "great" in v 19a. But v 19b with the slave free from his master reminds us that just as "slave" and "master" are mutually self-defining (if there are no slaves there are no masters, and vice versa), so also "small" and "great" are, and v 18 puts beyond question the correlation of the captive laborers and their shouting taskmaster. We are encouraged therefore to find here also in v 17 a relation between the "raging" of the wicked and the exhaustion of the weary.

What is meant by "raging" (רֹגֶז)? In a physical sense the verb denotes earthquakes (9:6; 1 Sam 14:15; Amos 8:8), and in the emotional sense it signifies fear (Jer 33:9; Hab 3:16), strong surprise (Isa 14:9), violent grief (2 Sam 19:1 [18:33]) or anger (Isa 28:21; 2 Kgs 19:27, 28; Job 39:24 [noun]). The verb does not take an object, so the English term "troubling" (KJV, RV, RSV, NAB) is not appropriate since it implies an object. There are indeed victims of the "raging" of the wicked but the word itself does not say so (Driver). Their "raging" is expressive of their wickedness; it is not simply the turmoil of life (as in v 16; 14:1). In Isa 57:20 the wicked are similarly said to be like the tossing of the sea that cannot rest but throws up mire and dirt—which cannot refer only to the inward mental state of the wicked but also to their effect on society; if there is dirt being thrown around, it is going to land on someone. The wicked in psalmic language are typically not just the opposite of the righteous, but their oppressors (Ps 17:9; 36:12 [11]; 37:12; 55:4 [3]; 82:4; 119:95); being wicked is not simply a matter of being in a state of sin or of living in a state of emotional disturbance (Andersen), but of actively desiring the harm of others, acting antisocially (Horst). The wicked always have "victims" (Moffatt, Gordis). Correlative then to the violent and oppressive anger of the wicked is the exhausted powerlessness of those who are "exhausted of power" (יְגִיעֵי כֹחַ), those who have been exhausted by the powerful, their own power drained from them for the greater power of the strong. Cf. Eccl 4:1 "I considered all the acts of oppression here under the sun; I saw the fears of the oppressed, and I saw that there was no one to comfort them. Strength was on the side of the oppressors" (NEB). The turmoil that exists in life is created by the oppression of the weak by the powerful, and for Job there are only those two classes, just like great and small (v 19). In Sheol that turmoil "ceases" (חָדַל), which is why Sheol becomes a desirable residence. It is not the abolition of differences or the instituting of equality that gives the underworld its particular character for Job, but the removal of the possibilities for turmoil. This "lovely picture of Sheol's calm, untroubled peace" (Peake)—if that is what it is—is nonetheless, *sub rosa,* a protest at the institutionalized rage that torments humans in the upper world.

18 The image here is of captives, prisoners-of-war (not criminal or civil "prisoners" [as KJV, RV, RSV, JB, NJPS, GNB]), who by long custom formed the forced labor gangs of the ancient Near East (cf. I. Mendelsohn, *IDB* 4:389 [bibliography]; add I. Mendelsohn, "On Slavery in Alalakh," *IEJ* 5 [1955] 65–72). They were principally employed on state works like building temples and palaces (2 Sam 12:31; cf. R. de Vaux, *Ancient Israel: Its Life and Institutions* [London: Darton, Longman and Todd, 1961] 88–90), and it is tempting to harmonize these various vignettes of Sheol existence by seeing the captives as the laborers on the city-building referred to in v 14. But since the slave of v 19 is evidently a domestic slave, a totally unified picture should not be sought for.

The "ease" (שַׁאֲנַן) that captives feel in the underworld is not liberty, but perhaps release from fear, since the verb in three of its other four occurrences (Prov 1:33; Jer 30:10; 46:27) is directly contrasted with fear. The נגש is in Exod 3:7; 5:6, 10, 13, 14 the Egyptian taskmaster of the Israelites who are engaged in state building projects. In Isa 9:3 [4] the taskmaster is equipped with a rod, and at Zech 9:8 he metaphorically tramples (עבר) on the workers; in Job 39:7 the נגש is the "driver" who shouts at the unwilling ass. So the term suggests vividly the humiliation of the slave-laborer.

Fohrer argues that the reference to the taskmaster (with its reminiscences of Egyptian slavery), coupled with the similarity of the imagery to that in an Egyptian text, indicates influence from Egypt upon the poet. But the text known as *The Dispute over Suicide* bears only a superficial resemblance to our text, in its words "Death is in my sight today like the longing of a man to see his house again after he has spent many years held in captivity" (*ANET*, 407a).

19 Even here, we do not have what is fundamentally a statement of the equality of humans in Sheol (as against Fohrer, Andersen and most). For there is nothing in such an equality in itself that would make Sheol desirable for Job. He has never been a doctrinaire egalitarian (cf. 29:7–10, 21–25), and even now, at the bottom of the social heap, he does not hope to regain some status by bringing everyone down to his level. "Small" and "great" are classes that define each other and, because they are not equals, are in life necessarily in conflict ("trouble" is Job's word). Why Sheol is so desirable is that though small and great are there (as they are in the upper world!) the conflict between them is at an end. Just one example says it all: the slave is free of his master. The first colon is intelligible only in the light of the second. Job identifies with the slave, of course, for he has come to feel that life is a form of slavery, and so the image is presented from the point of view of the slave (not, for example, "the master no longer beats the slave"); but the image has a wider reference, to the cessation of conflict.

This makes the poet's depiction quite different from and more subtle than the ubiquitous cliché of world literature that in death all are equal. Dhorme cites the recurrence of this commonplace in Lucian's *Dialogues,* and Seneca's famous phrase that death *exaequat omnia,* levels everything (*On Consolation,* 20.2). Cf. also *The Greek Anthology,* 7.342, 538.

The slave who is free from his master (contrast the singulars with the plural "captives" of v 18) sounds like a domestic slave rather than a state slave (against Fohrer). No special social significance attaches to the word "free" (חפשי), which is here used of a freed slave, though the term in extrabiblical contexts commonly signifies a freeborn person (I. Mendelsohn, "The Canaanite Term for 'Free Proletarian,'" *BASOR* 83 [1941] 36–39; idem, "New Light on the *Ḥupšu,*" *BASOR* 139 [1955] 9–11; O. Loretz, "Ugaritisch-hebräisch *ḥb/pt, bt ḥptt–ḥpšj, bjt hḥpšj/wt,*" *UF* 8 [1976] 129–31). See also n. 3:19.b.

There may be some chiastic arrangement in this stanza, as Andersen suggests: he sees the sequence of privileged (vv 14–15) and underprivileged (vv 17–18) to be mirrored by the sequence "small"–"great" and "slave"–"master" in v 19. Gordis, however, notes that the sequence "small"–"great" is normal in Heb. (cf. Deut 1:17; 1 Sam 5:9; 30:2, 19; etc.).

20–26 The suffering of the man Job is not the only suffering in the world. Through his identification of his life with "trouble" (עמל, v 10) and his desire for the "rest" of Sheol where the "trouble" (רגז, v 17) of earth has come to an end for all the inhabitants of earth, he looks out beyond his own experience to the unhappy lot of all those of humankind who are "troubled" (עָמֵל, v 20). But we must not think that the pain of his experience that provoked the maledictions of vv 3–10 is in the end mollified by the elegiac direction the poem takes here; for beneath the surface of vv 20–23, purportedly about troubled humanity in general, the principal concern is still the troubled individual Job, who in the last verses (vv 24–26) speaks again directly of himself. And here finally the *Leitmotiv* of the whole poem is stated in its most explicit form: unlike the ease of Sheol which he desires, he has here in life no "ease" (נוּחַ) at all, but only "trouble" (רֹגֶז) that comes, and keeps on coming, against him.

. It is a nice question whether he regards the "troubled" as only a segment of humanity or whether perhaps he has come to feel that this is the truth about human existence in general (cf. Cox, *The Triumph of Impotence*, 48: "As Job sees it, then, man's essential condition is one of misery and bitterness"). In what follows it will be assumed that Job means only to describe those who have suffered like himself, but the wider possibility is not ruled out. Terrien remarks on how different Job's desire for death is from the individualist style of romanticism; Job speaks not of himself alone but in the name of a suffering humanity.

It is remarkable to us that Job never contemplates suicide. The only occasions when suicide is mentioned in the Hebrew Bible are in circumstances of acute military or political disaster, in order to avoid a more disgraceful death: Judg 9:54 (Abimelech); 1 Sam 31:4–5 (Saul and his armor-bearer); 2 Sam 17:23 (Ahithophel); 1 Kgs 16:18 (Zimri); cf. also 2 Macc 14:37–46; Matt 27:5. This is not to say that it was unknown for people in personal distress or suffering to take their own lives, for such events are not often dramatic enough to find their way into narrative. So it remains somewhat uncertain whether we may speak of a Semitic inhibition against suicide (as, for example, Duhm), or whether perhaps the silence of Job on this issue may be evaluated as an expression of his tenacity upon life that will manifest itself ultimately in a unquenchable desire for vindication. On suicide in Babylonia ("only when it is clear that one is about to fall into the hands of enemies"), cf. B. Meissner, *Babylonien und Assyrien* (Heidelberg: C. Winter, 1920) 1:424; and cf. J. Leipoldt, *Der Tod bei Greichen und Juden* (Leipzig: G. Wisand, 1942). Articles on suicide in Hastings' *Encyclopaedia of Religion and Ethics*, by G. Margoliouth and G. A. Barton (12:37–39) contain many unbelievable statements, e.g., "The ancient Hebrews were, on the whole, a naive people, joyously fond of life, and not given to tampering with the natural instinct of self-preservation" (Margoliouth). The more authoritative articles of L. I. Rabinowitz and H. H. Cohn in *Encyclopaedia Judaica* (15:489–91) show that, among Jews of most periods when historical evidence exists, suicide is well attested (cf. 6:8–9).

20 The peace of Sheol is assuredly the opposite of what Job experiences; every sentence about the underworld has been *sotto voce* a protest about this life. So it is no surprise that the focus should now shift to the pain of existence in the upper world. Having first wished he had never been conceived or born (stanza 1, vv 3–10), and secondly wished that, since he was born, he could have died at birth or been stillborn (stanza 2, vv 11–19), Job now wishes that, since he has had to live, he could cease to live (stanza 3, vv 20–26).

S. Terrien has called this a movement from hatred of life to love of death (*Poet of Existence,* 46). It is not "Why should the sufferer be born to see the light?" (NEB), but rather "Why should one who is suffering continue to live?"

Who is it that gives light (life, cf. on v 16) to the troubled? Obviously God, who slays and makes alive (1 Sam 2:6), but is the verb here impersonal and more or less passive (KJV, RV, RSV, NAB, NIV, Gordis), or referring to God though not explicitly (NJPS, Fohrer, Pope, Habel)? We cannot tell (similar cases in 12:13; 16:7; 20:23; 22:21; 25:2; 30:18). But the absence of the divine name is less probably because "the speaker still avoids [it], all the instincts of a lifetime holding him back from challenging his Maker" (Strahan), than because his emphasis lies on the sheer fact of the inescapability of life, no matter how distressful it may be, rather than upon the one who is responsible for this state of affairs (so also Horst).

The familiar equation of light with life (cf. v 16; 18:5–6; 33:30; Ps 56:14 [13]; Isa 53:11 [emended]; 1QS 3.7; John 8:12) has a special significance here, for Job's desire has been for darkness, the day of his birth becoming darkness, and the night of his conception becoming darker still through being seized by the darkness of the underworld (vv 4–6, 9). The term "troubled" (עָמֵל) is in its two other occurrences an unemotive term for a worker or laborer (Judg 5:26; Prov 16:26; in Job 20:22 the adjective is probably to be emended to the noun), but here of course it is the *mot juste* for the state of humankind as Job perceives it, a state of עמל, turmoil, conflict, unease. At first we think Job is speaking (in the singular) about himself, but then the plural in the second colon alerts us to realize that now in this stanza he will speak also for others. Those who suffer עמל are מרי נפש, lit., "bitter of soul, spirit" or "sour, disappointed, aggrieved" (Driver), as in Judg 18:25 ("angry," RSV); 1 Sam 1:10 (Hannah, "deeply distressed," RSV); 22:2 (the socio-economically marginal in the cave of Adullam; cf. Job 21:25, where the "bitter of soul" has never had prosperity): 30:6 (bereaved parents); 2 Sam 17:8 (men enraged like a bear robbed of its cubs); Prov 31:6 (give wine to such to forget their "trouble" [עמל]); Isa 38:15 (Hezekiah is sleepless because "bitter of soul"); Ezek 27:31 (mourners wailing); and especially Job 7:11 and 10:1 (Job will speak out in the "anguish of his spirit"). So the term does not suggest a silent depressiveness but a vigorous and often vocal response to misfortune, such as Job's proves to be.

The "why?"-question belongs to the psalmic language, where it never signifies a desire to discover a reason intellectually, but always forms part (typically the first part) of a complaint, modeled on the speech forms of the legal and the semiformal accusation (cf. H. J. Boecker, *Redeformen des Rechtslebens im Alten Testament* [WMANT 14; Neukirchen-Vluyn: Neukirchener Verlag, 1964] 30–31). It is not a question about the meaning of life (Weiser: "the human question about existence is at root the question about God"), nor even about the meaning and value of a life of suffering (Horst). Like the questions of vv 11–12, this rhetorical question or charge is uttered in the direction of God, who is certainly in Job's mind as v 23b will make plain; but that is not to say that Job is here accusing God of anything. The reality of his suffering occupies his horizon totally, even excluding the thought of the undoubted originator of the suffering.

21 Because those oppressed by the turmoil of life are embittered by their suffering, they long to be released from life (it is not that they are embittered because death is denied them). They "yearn" (חכה) for death (the verb is stronger than merely "wait for" [NEB]; cf. the "yearning" for Yahweh in Isa 8:17; Ps 33:20; cf. 106:13). The emotional intensity of this yearning is brilliantly suggested by the striking metaphor of those who "dig for hidden treasures." W. M. Thomson has a lively account of treasure hunting in nineteenth-century Palestine, concluding that "there is not another comparison within the whole compass of human actions so vivid as this. I have heard of diggers actually fainting when they have come upon even a single coin. They become positively frantic. . . . There are, at this hour, hundreds of persons thus engaged all over the country. . . . This country abounds, and ever has abounded, in hid treasure" (*The Land and the Book* [London: T. Nelson, 1890] 135–37). For biblical references to hidden treasure, usually hidden in the ground and thus having to be dug for, cf. Josh 7:21; Prov 2:4; Jer 41:8; Matt 13:44; 25:18, 25; Col 2:3. Jorge Luis Borges appositely for these verses describes the Orient as "a world of extremes in which people are very unhappy or very happy, very rich or very poor. A world of kings, of kings who do not have to explain what they do . . . There is, moreover, the notion of hidden treasures. Anybody may discover one" (*Seven Nights* [London: Faber and Faber, 1986] 51). Treasure indeed has often to be "dug" for (חפר), and death, because the underworld lies below the ground, is in a magnificent image equally presented as dug for in the earth out of desperation. The two images merge even more closely when we realize that perhaps most hidden treasure in the ancient world was in tombs; so the grave-robbers are in a way themselves digging into Sheol! Many commentators of course observe that digging is not likely to be a successful way of finding death, and think חפר is being used in its secondary meaning "search for" (NAB, NJPS, NIV; cf. NEB, JB, Budde, Hölscher, Fohrer, Pope, Habel). At the very least the verb must carry the two meanings (de Wilde), because the seekers for hidden treasure are no doubt literally digging for it; but it seems best to see the embittered also as metaphorically digging for death (KJV, RV, RSV, Dhorme, Moffatt, Rowley).

22 Those submerged in the troubles of life do not succeed in reaching their goal of the grave, but must endure their unhappy lot. Suicide is evidently out of the question (see further on 3:20–26 above). They have no opportunity to "take arms against a sea of troubles and by opposing end them" (*Hamlet* 3.1.59–60). So they do not in fact "rejoice" (RSV, NAB; cf. NEB, NIV), but "*would* rejoice" (Moffatt) or "*would* exult" (Gordis). Behind this potent image of yearning for death there perhaps still lies that of the treasure-seekers, who are themselves in many cases grave-robbers who are overjoyed to reach the tomb where buried treasure lies. In the same way the troubled would rejoice "to the point of jubilation" (Dhorme) if they could "attain" (מצא; see n. 3:22.b) the grave. "Their vain longing for the restfulness of death, which is never met, only makes their torment the keener, and that in turn quickens their yearning" (Fohrer). On the longing for death, cf. Jer 8:3; Rev 9:6; Sophocles, *Electra* 1007–8 "The truly hateful thing is not death but desiring it and never attaining it"; Ovid, *Ibis* 123–26, pronouncing against an enemy the imprecation that he might have reasons for dying but not the means; Cicero, *Tusculan Disputations* 1.48.

23 Still not speaking directly of himself in the first person, Job begins to move the focus of his speech back to himself as he talks now not of the (plural) "bitter in spirit" but of the (singular) "man" (גבר) whose way is hid. The man is Job, no doubt, but he is also every suffering person, not yet the "I" of vv 24–26. Job too is one of those who desire death and reject life (7:15; 10:1). As in vv 21–22, the image here can be read on two levels. On the one hand it is an image of a person who has lost sight of the path ahead as darkness falls, or who finds himself shut in by a hedge or wall that constricts the path. The conventional metaphorical code of "spaciousness" for salvation, "narrowness" for distress and danger shines through. At the same time the "path" is one's destiny ("way of life" as an objective genitive, the way that leads to life) or one's state of being on the way to reaching one's destiny ("way of life" as a subjective genitive, the way surrounded by life, the way constituted by life). For the way to be hidden, sc. to the one who walks on it, means that one feels oneself to have lost control of one's destiny and to have lost one's grasp on its present significance ("way" is "a kind of outward realization of self-awareness," says K. Koch, *TDOT* 3:285). These are disorientating experiences that provoke the desire for a death that prescinds from all questions of order. (Israel's fear in Isa 40:27 that its "way" is "hidden" [דרך and סתר as here] from Yahweh is a rather different matter.)

Yet another circle of meaning impinges upon this text, and moves the focus more unmistakably back toward Job himself; there is more than a reminiscence of the Satan's observation in 1:10 that God had "put a hedge" (שוך, equivalent to סוך here) about Job—there was no malice or cynicism in that remark, but a frank recognition of God's protectiveness. But what the Satan, God and Job once felt as a protection, Job now finds a restriction (Andersen). In itself, what is wrong with having a hedge about one? It is not an image derived from the chase, as against G. Gerleman, "Contributions to the Old Testament Terminology of the Chase" (*Årsberrätelse 1945–1946. Bulletin de la Société Royale des Lettres de Lund 1945–1946* [Lund: Gleerup, 1946] 89). It is not something Job elsewhere complains of. Indeed, the only objection to an encircling (בעדו) hedge arises if one wants to travel. It is the juxtaposition with the "way" in the first colon that makes of the hedge a prison, or makes it an obstacle across the "way" of life. In 19:8 God's barring (גדר) Job's way forms part of a catalogue of recriminations against God (cf. Hos 2:8 [6] where barring [שוך] a way is an act of divine punishment, and Lam 3:7 where walling about [גדר] is an act of imprisonment, but where, by contrast with Job, there are strong expressions of hope [Lévêque, *Job et son Dieu*, 340–41]). Whether a hedge is a protection or an obstacle depends only on one's point of view. So what is the hedge whose function has changed in Job's altered perspective? It is his continued existence. Previously God's protection has ensured that his life was safe (and within chaps. 1–2 God still makes sure of that: "only spare his life," 2:6). But for a man who wants to die God's sustaining of his life is a hostile and constrictive act. Job wants his life-support to be switched off but God insists on keeping him alive.

We should note that the emphasis here lies upon the reality of Job's experience, not upon the author of his suffering. Continued existence is "given" (passive), indeed, by God, but he is not being blamed (it is not that the lament has sharpened into an accusation against God, as Hesse); the path is constricted by God, indeed, which is not to accuse him of hostility (against Weiser: the worst of his plight is that it is God who has blocked his way) but to stress the inescapable reality. When your path is hedged by God, it stays hedged.

24 Now the "I" speaks, for himself, of what is real to him. The "for" (כי) that introduced this verse links it back to v 23 and thence to v 20: here is a reason why Job would rather be dead, and why he deplores a continued existence that has its permanence underwritten by God. A normal human life is sustained by food and drink, but when all that one consumes is insubstantial and disagreeable, sighs and groans, life has become unlivable and not worth sustaining. *Der Mensch ist, was er isst* (Feuerbach), what you eat, you are; and if Job feeds on sighs his life becomes one mass of "trouble" and bitterness. The image is subtle: no sustenance from outside him enters Job's life now, he feeds on himself, "the self-consumer of [his] woes" (John Clare), he is locked into a food chain of ever-decreasing nutritiousness. Andersen thinks "sighing" and "groaning" too feeble a depiction of Job's misery and seeks ways of strengthening their force (see n. 3:24.c); but the power of the imagery lies not in the nouns themselves but in what these feeble and insubstantial breathings have become for Job: his food and drink.

It is actually a familiar psalmic image to depict one's tears as being one's food or "bread" (Ps 42:4 [3]; 80:6 [5] "the food of tears"; 102:10 [9] "I eat ashes like [or, in place of] food, and mix my drink with weeping"; it is a standard description of mourning (Westermann, *Structure*, 37). In those places, however, they are in the context of an appeal to God for deliverance; they do not lead to a rejection of life. The term for "sighing" (אנחה) is used both in the context of grief and of physical suffering (23:2; Ps 6:7 [6]; 31:11 [10]; 38:10 [9]; etc.), in many cases it being impossible to distinguish the two; in this chapter Job's physical sufferings are not so much as mentioned, and the stress lies exclusively on his mental and psychological anguish. "Roaring" (שאגה), like its verb (שאג), is often used specifically of lions (4:10; Ezek 19:7; Judg 14:5; Amos 3:4, 8; Ps 104:21) or metaphorically of the roaring of lions (Isa 5:29; Jer 2:15; Ps 22:14 [13]; etc.). But that image is not necessarily present when it is used of human cries of distress in Ps 22:2 [1]; 32:3; 38:9 [8], and here (KJV, RV, JPS, Habel have "roarings" or similar, but other versions prefer "groans").

The image of groans being poured out like water is complex. נתך "pour out" happens to be most often used of pouring out wrath (e.g., 2 Chr 12:7; Jer 42:18), but also of rain being poured upon the earth (Exod 9:33; 2 Sam 21:10) and of milk being poured out (Job 10:10). So groans too can metaphorically be poured forth from the mouth like water, just as (rather more concretely) in the Keret epic, the hero's tears "pour down [*ntk*, as here] like shekels to the ground" (*CTA* 14.28–29; Gibson, 83). The complicating factor here is that the groans become the lamenter's drink. Although the sighing is only "like" (כלפני; see n. 3:24.b) bread (as לחם probably means here, rather than food in general) and the groans only "like" water, the conjunction of bread and water impels us to see here also an image of sustenance; the irony is that Job's only sustenance is self-produced and as insubstantial as sound and breath. What is more, bread and water are images not simply of food but of minimum levels of subsistence (1 Kgs 22:27, bread and water of oppression; Ezek 12:18; differently in Ecclus 15:3).

25 The question about this verse is whether it describes Job's present experience or his past. Most commentators and versions believe him to be saying that at the present time whatever fear his imagination presents him with he finds turning into reality (as JB "Whatever I fear comes true, whatever I dread befalls me"); "he has only to think of some new evil and it is sure to come upon him" (Rowley). Perhaps if Job's present includes the events of chap. 1 he could speak of a succession of fears becoming realities, but if he is describing his feelings since his afflictions came upon him, it hardly rings true to say that new waves of affliction overtake him. It is often argued that the fear cannot have been felt in his time of prosperity; so Davidson: "it would be contrary to the idea of the poem to suppose that Job even in the days of his golden prime was haunted with indefinite fears of coming misfortune" (and cf. 16:12; 29:18–20). That puts it too strongly, for what the narrator presents in the prologue is a man of scrupulous piety who is up early to offer sacrifices on behalf of his children in case they have perhaps cursed God. Without living in trepidation (contrast NEB "Every terror that haunted me has caught up with me"), Job evidently was aware that calamity was a possibility even for the most exemplary person. And now the worst he could ever have imagined has become literal reality (similarly NJPS, NIV, Pope, Gordis, Andersen, Habel [?]).

Job's expression of his anxiety harmonizes well with the depiction of him in 1:1–5, and invites a psychoanalytic reading. R. L. Katz, "A Psychoanalytic Commentary on Job 3:25," *HUCA* 29 (1958) 377–83, sees in Job a man who has "a need for punishment," whose success has aroused guilt to an intolerable degree, and has induced free-floating anxiety. The figure of the Satan, psychoanalytically speaking, is a projection of a conflict within Job himself. "It is Job who doubts himself and it is Job who must make the test and inflict punishment on himself. It is Job's unconscious speaking . . . He was wrecked by success, to use Freud's term" (p. 382). Of course, from a narrative point of view the calamity is entirely external to Job in its origin, but one does not have to be a very subtle analyst even of one's own dreams to see how this interpretation imposes itself, reading what the narrative represents as a conflict between Job and others as a conflict within the person of Job.

26 What is it that Job has dreaded and that has now come upon him (v 25)? Andersen answers, "the loss of God's favour," which is true, but not what Job says. Habel replies, "his suffering," which is nearer the mark, but not yet precisely Job's point. The present verse is the answer: it is loss of ease, of quiet, of restfulness; it is the advent of turmoil. Reading the prologue again, we are impressed by the tranquillity of the portrayal of Job's condition before disaster struck. There is a tidy inevitability about the prosperity that flowed from his piety, and a decent regularity about the partying of Job's children and his picking up the tab for any delinquency of theirs. But now his worst fear has been realized: order has descended into chaos and therewith tranquillity into turmoil.

First, negatively, he says what he longer has: no repose (שׁלו, perhaps including physical as well as mental well-being; cf. 16:12 where he was "at ease" before God attacked him; Ps 122:6 where the lovers of Jerusalem should "prosper"), no quiet (שׁקט, as in v 13, often of a land being at rest, undisturbed by war, e.g., Josh 11:23, and of persons, the opposite of being afraid, Jer 30:10; 46:27; cf. Ps 94:13), and no rest (נוח, the most general word). Then positively,

what he experiences is "turmoil" (רֹגֶז, as in v 17), the keyword of the entire
chapter (along with its near synonym עָמָל "trouble," v 10, and the adjective,
v 20). It is of course significant that רֹגֶז is the very last word of the speech,
because it sums up what for Job is wrong with life and what is desirable about
Sheol. It is possible that he means that trouble keeps on coming against him
(יָבוֹא taken as an imperfect, "comes"), but more likely that he refers to the
one climacteric of his existence, the onset of misfortune that "came" (יָבוֹא
preterite) upon him, as narrated in the prologue.

Explanation

This poem, one of the great masterpieces of the work, is striking above all
for its restraint. Not for the restraint of Job's emotions, which are deep, raw,
and terrifying, as he showers with maledictions every aspect of the world that
gave him existence or continues to support it. That excessive and surreal rejection of life that imagines the night of his conception being swallowed up by
the underworld (v 6) or that depicts the world-weary as grave-robbers desperately digging their way into Sheol as into a treasure-house (vv 21–22) is a
quintessential instance of the vitality of the human spirit when freed from
the bounds of custom, decorum and prosaic reality. The restraint that makes
this a poem of world stature is the exclusive concentration on feeling, without
the importation of ideological questions. For a book that is so dominated by
intellectual issues of theodicy, it is amazing to find here not one strictly theological sentence, not a single question about the meaning of his suffering, not a
hint that it may be deserved, not the slightest nod to the doctrine of retribution.
All that will come, in its time, but here we are invited to view the man Job in
the violence of his grief. Unless we encounter this man with these feelings
we have no right to listen in on the debates that follow; with this speech
before us we cannot overintellectualize the book, but must always be reading
it as the drama of a human soul.

What are Job's friends, who have sat silently with him seven days and seven
nights (2:13), to make of this utterance with which Job breaks the silence?
Trained themselves, as Job too must have been, in the doctrine of exact retribution, they must be astonished to hear from Job not the faintest concession to
that fundamental explanation of human fortunes, nor the slightest admission
of a guilt that had brought him to this point. This poem is not only powerful,
it is improper. They have been wondering, no doubt, and their subsequent
speeches confirm it, how to behave like friends at all when the evidence before
their eyes marks Job out as a man who has deeply sinned, and whom it is
not entirely safe to associate with. To hear Job speak, it sounds as if he knows
of nothing to blame himself for, and so, whether gently or astringently, they
will feel it their duty to point out to him in their speeches that the suffering
that has brought him to this extreme of turmoil can have only one meaning:
that he is nothing but a sinner being punished for his sin.

Another restraint, on the poet's part, that surprises us the more as we read
further in the book is that God is not blamed, nor even especially held responsible, for the suffering Job is encountering. It is God indeed who continues to
give life to those in "trouble" (v 20), but that fact is mentioned only to wish
that he wouldn't, not to blame him for doing so. And Job himself is a man

"hedged in" by God (v 23), overprotected, and not allowed to sink toward the grave; but that too is not said in order to charge God with cruelty, but to stress how inescapable a hold life has on Job. Even in the prologue, Job's responses to the double calamity had been to see God behind everything that had befallen him (1:21; 2:10), but here there is no word of that, simply the naked feelings. The accusations against God will begin in Job's next speech (6:4), and thereafter will fall thick and fast; but at this moment the poet shuts us up to a contemplation of Job's inner life that will only hereafter breed harsh words against God and the friends and will involve Job ultimately in a metaphorical lawsuit against God.

Yet another surprise in this poem has been referred to on v 13. It is that the dominant note of the poem has been Job's restlessness or turmoil (vv 10, 17, 20, 26) contrasted with the restfulness of Sheol (vv 13–15, 17–19). This is not self-evidently the emotion people in Job's position would feel about their suffering: self-pity, anger, disgust, hopelessness, yes; but anxiety and turmoil, hardly. The reason can only be that it is the intellectual-existential implications of his suffering that "disturb" Job; though he will not ventilate them here, we are to understand that already he has been meditating on the religious significance of the disasters. His anxiety is not because of his foul skin disease, nor even because he fears he may soon be dead, but rather because he is experiencing a shaking of the foundations of cosmic moral order. He is disoriented by the anomie of his experience and longs for Sheol as a place where order reigns, the order, indeed, of inactivity and effacement of earthly relationships, to be sure, but an order where the conflicts of the absurd have been swallowed up by a pacific meaninglessness.

Eliphaz's First Speech   (4:1–5:27)

Bibliography

Asensio Nieto, F. "La visión de Elifaz y su proyección sapiencial." *EstBíb* 35 (1976) 145–63. **Beer, G.** "Zu Hiob 5:23." *ZAW* 35 (1915) 63–64. **Cheyne, T. K.** "Job V.7." *ZAW* 11 (1891) 184. **Clines, D. J. A.** "Job 4,13: A Byronic Suggestion." *ZAW* 92 (1980) 289–91. ――――. "Verb Modality and the Interpretation of Job iv 20–21." *VT* 30 (1980) 354–57. ――――. "Job 5,1–8: A New Exegesis." *Bib* 62 (1981) 185–94. **Coggan, F. D.** "The Meaning of אטח in Job v.24." *JMEOS* 17 (1932) 53–56. **Crenshaw, J. L.** "The Influence of the Wise upon Amos: The 'Doxologies of Amos' and Job 5,9–16; 9,5–10." *ZAW* 79 (1967) 42–52. ――――. *Hymnic Affirmations of Divine Justice: Doxologies of Amos and Related Texts.* SBLDS 24. Missoula, Mont.: Scholars Press, 1975. **Dahood, M.** "Northwest Semitic Philology and Job." In *The Bible in Current Catholic Thought* (Gruenthaner Memorial Volume), ed. J. L. McKenzie. St Mary's Theology Studies 1. New York: Herder and Herder, 1962. 55–74. ――――. "ŚʿRT 'Storm' in Job 4,15." *Bib* 48 (1967) 544–45. **Driver, G. R.** "On Job V.5." *TZ* 12 (1956) 485–86. **Eitan, I.** "Biblical Studies." *HUCA* 14 (1939) 1–22. **Fullerton, K.** "Double Entendre in the First Speech of Eliphaz." *JBL* 49 (1930) 320–74. **Gibson, J. C. L.** "Eliphaz the Temanite: Portrait of a Hebrew Philosopher." *SJT* 28 (1975) 259–72. **Gillischewski, E.** "Die erste Elifaz-Rede Hiob Kap. 4 und 5." *ZAW* 39 (1921) 290–96. **Gordis, R.** "The Biblical Root ŚDY-ŚD: Notes on 2 Sam. i.21; Jer. xviii.14; Ps. xci.6; Job v.21." *JTS* 41 (1940) 34–43. **Gray, J.** "The Massoretic Text of the Book of Job, the Targum and the Septuagint Version in the Light of the Qumran Targum (11QtargJob)." *ZAW* 86 (1974) 331–50. **Herz, N.** "Some Difficult Passages in Job." *ZAW* 20 (1900) 160–63. **Horst, F.** *Gottes Recht: Gesammelte Studien zum Recht im Alten Testament.* Munich: Kaiser, 1961. **Koch, K.** "Gibt es ein Vergeltungsdogma im Alten Testament?" *ZTK* 52 (1955) 1–42. ――――. *Um das Prinzip der Vergeltung in Religion und Recht des Alten Testaments.* Wege der Forschung 125. Darmstadt: Wissenschaftliche Buchgesellschaft, 1972. **Kopf, L.** "Arabische Etymologien und Parallelen zum Bibelwörterbuch." *VT* 8 (1958) 161–25. **Lust, J.** "A Stormy Vision: Some Remarks on Job 4,12–16." *Bijd* 36 (1975) 308–11. **Paul, S. M.** "Job 4,15–A Hair Raising Encounter." *ZAW* 95 (1983) 119–21. **Rimbach, J. A.** "'Crushed before the Moth' (Job 4:19)." *JBL* 100 (1981) 244–46. **Winckler, H.** "Maṣpan keller." *Altorientalische Forschungen.* Leipzig: E. Pfeiffer, 1902. 3/1:235–36.

Translation

4:1 *Eliphaz the Temanite replied:*

> 2 *Are we to speak*[a] *to you one word? You cannot bear*[b] *it.*
> *But who can bear*[c] *to hold back his words?*
> 3 *Think back!*[a] *You have instructed*[b] *many*[c] *in wisdom.*
> *You have given vigor to feeble hands.*
> 4 *Words of yours raised the fallen;*[a]
> *you strengthened failing knees.*
> 5 *And now,*[a] *when it meets*[b] *with you, you cannot bear*[c] *it!*
> *It strikes at you, and you are dismayed!*[d]
> 6 *Is not your piety*[a] *your source of confidence?*[b]
> *Does not your blameless life*[c] *give you hope?*[d]

> 7 *Recall now: What innocent man ever perished?*
> *Where were the upright ever annihilated?*

⁸*As my experience goes,^a those who plant^b iniquity*
  and those who sow mischief reap due harvest.
⁹*By a breath from God they perish,*
  by the wind of his fury they are shriveled.
¹⁰*The roar of the lion,^a the growl of the young lion,^b are cut off,^c*
  and the teeth of the maned lions^d are broken;
¹¹*the strong lion^a perishes^b for lack of prey;*
  and the whelps of the lion^c are scattered.

¹²*Now there came to me a secret word,^a*
  my ears caught only a fragment^b of it.
¹³*In the anxious visions of the night,^a*
  when heavy sleep had fallen upon men,
¹⁴*terror and trembling^a came upon^b me*
  and set every^c bone^d shaking.
¹⁵*Then a wind^a swept past^b my face,*
  a whirlwind^c made my body quiver.^d
¹⁶*There stood a figure,^a unrecognizable;^b*
  a form was before my eyes, and I heard a thunderous^c voice:

¹⁷*"Can a man^a be righteous^b before^c God?*
  Can a man^d be pure^e in the sight of^f his Maker?"
¹⁸*If^a God mistrusts his own servants,*
  and can charge^b his angels with folly,^c
¹⁹*how much more those who dwell in houses of clay*
  which are founded^a on dust^b
  and can be crushed^c like^d a moth.^e
²⁰*Between dawn and dusk^a they can^b be stamped to death;*
  they can be utterly^c exterminated, and none may ever know.^d
²¹*Their tent-cords^a have only to be loosened^b*
  and they can die^c without ever gaining wisdom.^d

^{5:1}*You may call;^a but is there any to answer you?*
  To which of the Holy Ones^b could you turn?
²*For^a the fool is slain by his resentment,*
  the stupid killed by his anger.
³*Indeed, I have seen the fool firmly rooted,^a*
  but forthwith^b I have declared his home^c accursed.^d
⁴*His children are abandoned, far from any help;*
  at the gate^a they are crushed, with no defender.
⁵*^aWhat he has sown^b the hungry eat,*
  the shriveled sheaves they carry off,^c
  ^dand the thirsty^e pant after^f their possessions.^g
⁶*For it is not from the ground that affliction^a springs,*
  not from the soil that suffering sprouts;
⁷*it is man who begets^a suffering^b for himself,*
  and^c the sons of Pestilence^d fly high.^e

⁸*But I myself seek God in prayer,^a*
  and to God I address my speech.^b

⁹ᵃ*He it is who works great deeds, past human reckoning,*
who performs wonders, beyond all numbering.
¹⁰ᵃ*He it is who sends rain upon the earth,*
who pours down water ᵇ *upon the fields.* ᶜ
¹¹*He raises* ᵃ *the lowly to the heights,*
and lifts ᵇ *the bereaved* ᶜ *to safety.* ᵈ
¹²*He thwarts the plots of the crafty,*
so that their hands win no success. ᵃ
¹³*He ensnares the cunning in their own craftiness,*
and the counsel of the wily runs to ruin. ᵃ
¹⁴*By daylight they meet with darkness,*
and at noonday they grope as though it were night.
¹⁵*But the poor he saves from the sword of their mouth,* ᵃ
from the hand of the mighty,
¹⁶*so that the crushed can hope again,*
and injustice must shut its mouth. ᵃ

¹⁷*Consider!* ᵃ *Happy is the man whom God reproves!*
So do not spurn the discipline of the Almighty. ᵇ
¹⁸*For* ᵃ *he may wound, but he binds up the sore;*
he may smite, but his hands ᵇ *heal.*
¹⁹*From* ᵃ *six calamities he will rescue you;*
and in the seventh no harm will touch you.
²⁰*In famine he will ransom you from death,*
in battle from the stroke ᵃ *of the sword.*
²¹*From* ᵃ *the lash of the tongue* ᵇ *you will be hidden;*
you need not fear destruction ᶜ *when it comes near.*
²²ᵃ*At ruin and blight* ᵇ *you will mock,*
and you will have no fear of the wild beasts.
²³*For* ᵃ *you will be in covenant with the stones of the field,* ᵇ
and the wild animals ᶜ *will be at peace with you.*
²⁴*You will know that your dwelling* ᵃ *is secure;*
you will take stock of your estate ᵇ *and miss* ᶜ *nothing.*
²⁵*You will know that your offspring will be many,*
your descendants like the grass of the earth.
²⁶*In ripe old age* ᵃ *you will come to your grave,*
as a sheaf comes up to the threshing floor at its season.

²⁷*Behold! This is what we have discovered; it is true.* ᵃ
Take heed, ᵇ *and know it yourself.*

Notes

2.a. הֲנִסֹה taken as orthographic variant for הֲנִשָּׂא (interrogative הֲ + 1 pl impf of נשׂא). נסה is sometimes written for נשׂא (cf. Ps 4:7); נשׂא "lift up" can have as object "proverb" (Job 27:1) or "psalm" (Ps 81:3 [2]), and Aq, Symm, Theod took the verb in this sense. Alternatively, it can be parsed as הֲ + 3 sg piel pf of נסה "attempt, venture" (so most EVV).

2.b. תלאה, usually translated "you will (or, will you) be impatient." But לאה more properly means "be unable," viz., to bear something (Gordis; cf. JB). The interrogative particle of הנסה does not belong to this verb, contrary to most EVV (e.g., RSV "will you be offended?"). There is a contrast between Job's presumed incapacity to listen, and Eliphaz's incapacity to be silent.

2.c. יוכל "be able, be able to bear," "be strong," is the opposite of תלאה. Cf. יכל in Isa 1:13; Jer 20:9.

3.a. הנה followed by כי עתה (v 5) introduces a lengthy conditional clause: "If you, Job, have been able to help others in their suffering, will you now abandon hope of help?" (for the construction, cf. 3:13; Fohrer).

3.b. יסר, a technical term for the teaching of the wise (cf. JB "schooled"), often accompanied by physical punishment (Prov 19:18; 29:17; Deut 22:18); cf. מוּסָר "lesson, chastening" (5:17; 20:3). Some feel this sense fits poorly with the sequence of verbs in vv 3–4 (תְּחַזֵּק "strengthen," יְקִימוּן "establish," תְּאַמֵּץ "make strong") and have proposed emendation to עָזַרְתָּ "you have helped" (Driver) or to יָסַדְתָּ "you have established" (Perles), though יסד is not used elsewhere in this metaphorical sense. G. R. Driver saw here an Aramaism, יסר being equivalent to Aram. אֹשַׁר "strengthen" ("Studies in the Vocabulary of the Old Testament," *JTS* 36 [1935] 293–301 [295]); this is reflected in NEB "encouraged." Gordis's solution is that יסר is a "metaplastic form" (by-form) of אסר "bind, strengthen." The occurrence of יסר and חזק in conjunction in Hos 7:15 is no real parallel, since it is there a matter of "training" and "strengthening" of arms for battle (if indeed יִסַּרְתִּי is textually sound). יסר "instruct, counsel" is after all probably the most fitting sense for the first of the verbs describing Job's former activities (see *Comment*). Y. Hoffmann, "The Use of Equivocal Words in the First Speech of Eliphaz (Job IV–V)," *VT* 30 (1980) 114–19 (114), stresses the potential ambiguity between "chasten" and "strengthen," suggesting that Eliphaz may be portrayed as hypocritical in saying one thing but hinting at another. But the collocation with the other verbs of vv 3–4 adequately removes the ambiguity. Hardly a sentence in any language is unambiguous if collocation is ignored.

3.c. רַבִּים translated "the aged" by M. Dahood, "Hebrew-Ugaritic Lexicography V," *Bib* 48 (1967) 421–38 (425); cf. on 32:9; "those who faltered" by NEB, vocalizing רָבִים or רֹעֲבִים (Brockington) from רבב "be weak, afraid" (cf. Arab. *rwb*; Tur-Sinai).

4.a. Tg moralizes כשל and כרעות by a reference to falling into sin. כשל, conventionally translated "stumble," probably has a stronger meaning (Ehrlich); cf. 2 Chr 28:15.

5.a. Not "because," introducing the reason for Eliphaz's speech (as Driver).

5.b. תבוא: indefinite fem subj, "not mentioned, but before the mind of the speaker" (GKC, § 144b); see *Comment*. Vg adds the understood subject *plaga*, "blow."

5.c. *Waw* consec + impf, after תבוא which is preterite or else virtually perfect (so GKC, § 111t). לאה is not "lose patience" (NEB, JB; cf. RSV, NAB), but in contrast to the verbs for "strengthen" in vv 3–4; see *Comment*.

5.d. KJV, ASV "troubled" is used in the stronger sense common in sixteenth- and seventeenth-century English: "harmed, molested, oppressed" (cf. 3:17 and *OED*, 10:405).

6.a. Lit., "your fear" (יראתך), for יִרְאַת אֱלֹהִים (e.g., Gen 20:11) or יִרְאַת יהוה (e.g., Prov 1:29); also in 15:4; 22:4 in Eliphaz's mouth. "Fear of God" is best represented by "religion" (NEB) or "piety" (JB); cf. on 1:8.

6.b. "Source of confidence," lit., "confidence." כִּסְלָה and כֶּסֶל can be "stupidity" (as taken here by LXX, Jerome) or "confidence," clearly the latter here. It is hardly a "considered ambiguity" (Hoffmann, *VT* 30 [1980] 114). "Comfort" (NEB) is not forward-looking enough.

6.c. Lit., "purity of your ways."

6.d. תִקְוָתֶךָ parallel to כִּסְלָתֶךָ. Line structure (3+3) suggests transferring *waw* of ותם to preface תקותך (so, e.g., *BHS*). MT may be saved by taking *waw* as introducing an apodosis, sc. "as for your hope, it is the integrity of your ways" (GKC, § 143d; E. Vogt, "Wāw emphaticum," *Bib* 34 [1953] 560; Fohrer) or as emphatic *waw* (Pope; idem, "'Pleonastic' Wāw before Nouns in Ugaritic and Hebrew," *JAOS* 73 [1953] 95–98 [97]; bibliography: Blommerde, 29, 40; add Ehrlich, 193). The simple emendation is preferable. On LXX deviation, see Fullerton, *JBL* 49 (1930) 342.

8.a. Poetically, the caesura comes after "iniquity" (אוֹן); logically, the caesura seems to come after "as my experience goes" (וכאשר ראיתי). It is unlikely that חֹרְשֵׁי אוֹן "plowers of iniquity" should be taken as the object of ראיתי "I have seen" (as Franz Delitzsch), unless וזרעי עמל "sowers of mischief" is also taken as part of the object; so Gordis: "Wherever I have seen those who plow iniquity / and sow trouble—they reap it!"

8.b. Nowhere else is the object of חרש "plow" the seed sown; parallelism with זרע makes this certain here; however, English "plow," despite most EVV, cannot have the seed as its object (note NAB "plow for mischief").

10.a. Five different words are used for lion in vv 10–11; it is probably futile to attempt to distinguish them (see *TDOT* 1:374–77). The first term is אַרְיֵה, the most common term for lion, often claimed, but without adequate justification, to designate strictly the African lion (following Koehler's derivation; see KB, 86b). On אריה as the generic term, see E. Ullendorff, "The Contribution of South Semitics to Hebrew Lexicography," *VT* 6 (1956) 190–98 (192–93); for a proposal that לביא and כביא are etymologically identical, cf. J. J. Glück, "*ʾarî* and *laviʾ* (*labiʾ*)—An Etymological Study," *ZAW* 81 (1969) 232–35.

10.b. שַׁחַל, by derivation perhaps "noisy one"; cf. Arab. *sahala* "bray" (so W. S. McCullough and F. S. Bodenheimer, *IDB* 3:136a); hence RSV "fierce lion"; or "young lion," cf. Arab. *hisl* "young one" (metathesis of consonants; cf. Arab. personal name *Sheili*), or *sahlu* "young one" (of any animal, cf. Guillaume, 81), hence NEB "cubs"; or "leopard" (Lat. "lion-panther") because of the parallel with נָמֵר in Hos 13:7 (Dhorme).

10.c. The verb נִתָּעוּ at the end of the verse must have as its subject "roar," "growl" and "teeth." But the *hapax* נתע, if an Aramaism equivalent to נתץ "break," can be used most properly only of the teeth (as נתץ in Ps 58:7 [6] of the fangs of lions), and only by extension (or zeugma) of the "roar" and "growl." A translation needs to introduce a verb for these nouns (so NEB "fall silent").

Less probable is the suggestion that v 10a is an independent colon, "Roaring of the lion and growl of the young lion!" (Dillmann, Friedr. Delitzsch, Duhm, J. C. L. Gibson, "Eliphaz the Temanite: Portrait of a Hebrew Philosopher," *SJT* 28 [1975] 259–72 [265]), or that the two cola are contrasted (e.g., Pope: "The lion may roar, the old lion growl, / But the young lion's teeth are broken"; similarly Terrien, Gordis, Horst, NIV). Driver denies that נתע is an Aramaism, because (i) it does not occur in this meaning in Aram., and (ii) Aram. ע = Heb. צ only when cognate Arab. has *ghain*. Driver consequently emends to נִצְּצוּ (as *BHS*). But it is probably needless to debate whether נתע is an Aramaism; it may be regarded as a genuinely Heb. by-form of נתץ, and can be argued to be attested in מַלְתָּעוֹת "teeth," i.e., those that break, crush. For this view and a possible connection with Akk. *natû* "beat" and Ug. *ntʿ*, see M. Dahood, "The Etymology of *Maltaʿot* (Ps 58,7)," *CBQ* 17 (1955) 180–83.

10.d. כְּפִיר, by derivation perhaps "covered one" (with mane) or "concealed one," cf. Arab. *kapara* "cover" (KB, 450b); less probably "young lion," cf. Arab. *ġafr* "four-month-old lamb" (J. Blau, "Etymologische Untersuchungen auf Grund des palästineschen Arabisch," *VT* 5 [1955] 337–44 [342]). Some uses of כפיר in the Psalms (see *Comment*) may be repointed to כֹּפֶר or כָּפִיר "unbeliever"; cf. Arab. *kafara;* D. Winton Thomas, *The Text of the Revised Psalter* (London: SPCK, 1963) 12; Gordis.

11.a. לַיִשׁ cognate with Arab. *laiṯ,* etymologically perhaps "the strong one." "Old lion" (KJV) depends on a traditional Jewish interpretation (*EB* 3:3802).

11.b. Less probably, "wanders about," אבד being taken as more strictly equivalent to פרד hithp, as also in Ps 92:10 [9] (Gordis, 42, 48). Clearly אבד does mean "be lost" (e.g., 1 Sam 9:3, 20; Ps 119:176), perhaps also "wander" (cf. Deut 26:5). More probably the picture in this colon is that of the young of the lion (בְּנֵי לָבִיא) being scattered because of (not: in parallel to) the death of their parent (cf. the image of the scattering of sheep for lack of a shepherd: Ezek 34:5; Zech 13:7; Matt 26:31; Mark 14:27).

11.c. לָבִיא, argued by Koehler to designate the Asian lion (see KB, 472b), and by S. Bochart (*Hierozoicon sive bipertitum opus de animalibus S. Scripturae* [London: T. Roycroft, 1663] 1:719) to be the lioness (hence RSV, JB, NEB). But there was apparently a separate vocalization לְבִיָּא for the fem (Ezek 19:2).

12.a. "came . . . a secret word." Most take this יְגֻנָּב as pual of גנב "steal," hence "be brought by stealth" (BDB). But elsewhere in Job the verb is used of the storm (סוּפָה) which carries humans away. J. Lust, "A Stormy Vision: Some Remarks on Job 4,12–16," *Bijd* 36 (1975) 308–11 (309), therefore argues that in Job גנב means "transported violently," and translates here, "A word was hurled upon me." The lexica compare Arab. *janaba* "put aside, removed" (cf. also L. Kopf, "Arabische Etymologien und Parallelen zum Bibelwörterbuch," *VT* 8 [1958] 161–215 [169]), which does not contain any notion of stealth. But since Heb. גנב is the normal word for "steal," I prefer to retain some idea of stealth, secretness, suddenness, or unexpectedness. R. J. Zwi Werblowsky, "Stealing the Word," *VT* 6 (1956) 105–6, maintains that גנב in reference to prophetic revelations both here and in Jer 23:30, where false prophets are said to גנב Yahweh's word from one another, is a pejorative term for the nocturnal reception of a דבר, as distinct from the reception of an authentic word from Yahweh. This view, though followed by Fohrer, leaves unexplained why the oracles in Jer 23:30 should be said to be Yahweh's words and why bogus prophets should bother to take over the words of their colleagues. It also negates the authenticity of Eliphaz's audition, for which there is no good reason.

12.b. שֶׁמֶץ occurs elsewhere only in 26:14, though שִׁמְצָה is in Exod 32:25. Most lexica and commentaries translate "whisper." In later Heb. it meant "a little" (Ecclus 10:10; 18:32); so also in medieval Heb., hence KJV (cf. also Tg); this meaning is preferred by Rowley, Gordis ("echo"). Similarly Lust, *Bijd* 36 (1975) 309, 311, "only a little of it"; however, on the basis that LXX of Ecclus 10:10 has μακρόν and of 18:32 πολλῆ, he suggests (rather improbably) that here we should translate "my ear received the fullness of it."

13.a. Lit., "in the anxious thoughts arising from visions of the night." שְׂעִפִּים only here and 21:2, but שַׂרְעַפִּים (with epenthetic *resh*, Pope) occurs in Ps 94:19; 139:23. סָעִיף (or סָעִיף), also with epenthetic *resh* סַרְעַפָּה, "branch," occurring several times, is the same word. What the two meanings probably have in common is dividedness: "Just as the boughs branch off from the trees, so thoughts and opinions can branch off in more than one direction, leading to bewilderment and indecision" (Rowley); cf. Arab. *šaġifa* "be disquieted." The *mem* of מֵחֶזְיֹנוֹת is the מִן of origin.

14.a. Perhaps פַּחַד and רְעָדָה are a hendiadys for "a shuddering dread" (Fullerton, *JBL* 49 [1930] 347).

14.b. קְרָאָנִי for קָרָנִי, from קרה; GKC, § 75rr.

14.c. Lit., "the multitude of" (רֹב). There are c. 200 bones in the human body; but G. R. Driver, ignoring this fact, and arguing that one does not have enough bones to call them a "multitude," proposed finding here רֹב "quaking," probably attested in 33:19 and cognate with Akk. *rîbu* (*VTS* 3 [1955] 73). Hence NEB "the trembling of my body [= bones] frightened me." Ehrlich already suggested repointing to רֹב "anxiety" (cf. Arab. *raib*); and J. C. L. Gibson apparently reads רֹב (for רִיב, "contention"): "strife struck terror to my bones" (*SJT* 28 [1975] 266). However, apart from the problem of homonymity caused by postulating other Heb. words pronounced *rîb* (cf. in general J. Barr, *Comparative Philology and the Text of the Old Testament* [Oxford: Clarendon, 1968] 134–45), it is less probable that the "quaking" or "trembling" of Eliphaz's own bones should cause his fright rather than vice versa.

14.d. Lit., "my bones," עַצְמוֹתַי. G. R. Driver, prior to the proposal mentioned above, suggested a new word עַצְמָה "calamity" ("Hebrew Roots and Words," *WO* 1 [1947–52] 406–15 [411]), but Eliphaz was not at the time of this uncanny experience suffering from a *multitude* of *calamities*.

15.a. "Wind," רוח. Though usually fem, רוח when masc always refers to a wind or breath (1:19; 41:8 [16]; Exod 10:13; Num 5:14; Eccl 1:6; 3:19; etc.; see KB, 877b; Terrien). It is therefore not likely to mean a "spirit" (KJV, RSV, NAB, NIV, Duhm); ghosts are called רְפָאִים, אוֹב, or אֱלֹהִים (2 Sam 28:13). Nor is it likely to be the "Spirit" of God (as against Andersen), which appears in Job only in 32:8 (// נִשְׁמַת שַׁדַּי) as the ultimate source of human understanding.

15.b. חלף, used of the sweeping by of the wind (רוח, Hab 1:11; סוּפָה, Isa 21:1), but also of the swift passing by of God (Job 9:11; 11:10).

15.c. שַׂעֲרַת, constr of שַׂעֲרָה, elsewhere "a single hair," as in 1 Sam 14:45. Here it may be collective; it is unnecessary to emend to pl שַׂעֲרוֹת (Rowley, NAB). One Jewish tradition has taken שערת here as related to שְׂעָרָה "storm," and as parallel with רוח (Tg עלעולא, and ויקא for רוח); similarly Gordis, "a storm made my skin bristle" (cf. also Merx, Tur-Sinai). S. M. Paul suggests that a double entendre on both meanings may be intended, with overtones of the storm-theophany of chap. 38 ("Job 4,15—A Hair Raising Encounter," *ZAW* 95 [1983] 119–21). But this is improbable. Rather than emending to שְׂעָרָה (Ehrlich), Gordis and M. Dahood ("Ŝ'RT 'Storm' in Job 4,15," *Bib* 48 [1967] 544–45), followed by Blommerde, vocalize שַׂעֲרָת, as the older form of the absolute; this is an attractive suggestion, though it is supported by Joban parallels of fem abs in *-at* only in 27:13; 41:25–26 (Blommerde, 11). See also G. Janssens, "The Feminine Ending –(a)t in Semitic," *Orientalia Lovaniensia Periodica* 6–7 (1975–76) 277–84.

15.d. סמר in qal at Ps 119:120 is intransitive, "bristle up, or creep" (BDB) (of flesh). If שערת בשרי is subject here, תסמר must be an intrans piel. תסמר is a true causative if שערת "whirl-wind" is taken as the subject. NEB "made the hairs bristle on my flesh" improbably takes רוח as subj of masc יַחֲלֹף *and* fem תְסַמֵּר. But the exact sense of סמר is unclear. BDB regarded Arab. *šamara* "contract" as cognate, while KB compares *šammara* "raise." It is just as possible that some more general word like "tremble" (RSV) or "shudder" (NAB) as in Ps 119:120 is appropriate here.

16.a. Lit., "(one) stood," indefinite subj. תמונה may be the subject; cf. Vg. *stetit quidam cuius non agnoscebam vultum imago coram oculis meis*.

16.b. Lit., "and I did not recognize its appearance (*or*, face)." The phrase is deleted by Fohrer, Lust, *Bijd* 36 (1975) 310 n. 8. The shortness of the line (3 words) is probably accidental; Duhm was reminded of significant half-lines in Shakespearean monologues, and no doubt the debated intentionality of half-lines in the Aeneid could be produced as a parallel. Rowley is overimaginative in supposing that "the breaking off of the line suggests the sudden catch of the breath, as the horror of that moment returns to Eliphaz."

16.c. If דממה is derived from דמם I "be dumb, silent" (so BDB, KB), it may be either dissociated from or linked with קול; i.e., "there was silence; then I heard a voice" (so MT accentuation; RSV, JB), or as a hendiadys, "a still, low voice" (so apparently MT vocalization of וקול; cf. NEB, NAB, NIV "a hushed voice"). But following J. Lust, "A Gentle Breeze or a Roaring Thunderous Sound? Elijah at Horeb: 1 Kings xix 12," *VT* 25 (1975) 110–15, I take דממה from דמם "moan, roar" (דמם II in KB; cognate with Akk. *damāmu*, "mourn, moan" [*CAD*, D, 59–61], Ug. *dmm*); cf. G. V. Schick, "The Stems *dûm* and *damám* in Hebrew, 2," *JBL* 32 (1913) 219–43 (222); M. Dahood, "Textual Problems in Isaia," *CBQ* 22 (1960) 400–409 (400–402); N. Lohfink, "Enthielten die im Alten Testament bezeugten Klageriten eine Phase des Schweigens?" *VT* 12 (1962) 260–77 (275 n. 1 [bibliography]); M. Dahood, "Hebrew-Ugaritic Lexicography II," *Bib* 45 (1964) 393–412 (402–403); T. F. McDaniel, "Philological Studies in Lamentations. I," *Bib* 49 (1968) 25–52 (37–39); S. Abramson, "The Historical Dictionary" [Heb.], *Leš* 42 (1977) 9–16 (medieval Heb. evidence). Thus דממה וקול is to be taken as the sg obj of אשמע: "I heard a roaring voice."

17.a. אֱנוֹשׁ in the first colon and גֶּבֶר in the second. Attempts to distinguish between the semantic meaning of the various nouns for "man" on the basis of their etymologies are probably misguided, though reflected in the versions, e.g., "mortal man" (KJV, RSV, NEB) for אנושׁ, "un homme brave" (Terrien) for גבר; cf. E. Jacob, *Theology of the Old Testament* (tr. A. W. Heathcote and P. J. Allcock; London: Hodder and Stoughton, 1958) 156–57: "*'enosh* . . . stresses the feeble and mortal aspect of man . . . *geber* lays stress on power." For reasons why אנושׁ is frequently used in statements of human weakness (without that being necessarily implied by the noun), see C. Westermann, *THWAT* 1:43–44. For further argument for the connotation "strong one" for גבר, see H. Kosmala, "The Term *geber* in the OT and in the Scrolls," VTSup 17 (1969) 159–69 (esp. 164–67).

17.b. יִצְדָּק. Or, "be declared righteous by" God. צדק in hiph is "declare righteous," but it is not used in hoph, so qal may function as pass of hiph.

17.c. In both מאלוה and מעשׂהו the *mem* appears to be the מן of comparison, so "more just or righteous than God" (KJV, RV, ASV, NEB, NIV). For a defense of some such translation, see Horst. Broader considerations (see *Comment*) make it more probable that מן here means "in the sight of" (cf. RSV, JB) or "as against God" (NAB); cf. Num 32:22, "free of obligation before [מן] Yahweh"; Jer 51:5 "their land is full of guilt before [מן] the holy one of Israel." See BDB, 579b § 2d: מן "of the source or author of an action"; KB, 536a § 9. And see further on 32:2 for another possible use of מן in this sense. Dhorme argues that the use of עם rather than מן in the very similar verses 9:2 and 25:4 shows that מן must have that sense here; but see the *Comment* on those verses.

17.d. See n. 4:17.a.

17.e. יִטְהָר. Or, if יצדק is a declarative, יטהר may be assimilated to the same function, viz. "be declared pure." טהר piel is "pronounce clean," and although pual is used (rarely), it is not in the declarative sense; hence qal may function as pass of declarative piel. The impfs denote "obvious truths known at all times" (Dhorme).

17.f. See n. 4:17.c.

18.a. הֵן, when followed by אַף or אַף כִּי, states a premise, and must be equivalent to Aram. אִין, Arab. *'in* (BDB, 243b; Blommerde, 28).

18.b. שִׂים ב, "charge with, impute"; cf. 1 Sam 22:15 (BDB, 963a § 1a). Blommerde's translation "ascribe to" is an attempt to preserve the idea of "write" which שׂים may have in 22:22; 38:33; Ps 56:9 [8] (// ספר) (M. Dahood, "The Metaphor in Job 22,22," *Bib* 47 [1966] 108–9); but there is no reason to suppose that שׂים means "write" here, and the possibility of a play on the English "ascribe" is fortuitous.

18.c. תָהֳלָה, a hapax. See Grabbe, *Comparative Philology*, 41–43. Probably from הלל (הלל III in KB³) "be deceived, be made a fool" (so also Rashi, ibn Ezra, Kimchi, Dhorme, Gordis); cf. הלל II (BDB: qal "be boastful"; poal "be mad"). Note 12:17, and Eccl 2:2; 7:7, 25; 10:13 where "folly" translates the root well. The form with *t-* preformative is paralleled in double *'ayin* verbs (Bauer-Leander, 497zη), so not impossible (as against Driver).

Dillmann regarded Eth. *tähälä* (or preferably a by-form *tähälä*) III "wander" as cognate (hence many translate as "error"; so RSV, NIV). But a root *thl* occurs nowhere else in Semitic. Could a cognate be Arab. *wahila* "err" (J. Barth, *Nominalbildung in den semitischen Sprachen* [Leipzig: J. C. Hinrichs, 2nd ed., 1894] 278)? This seems to be rather a rare sense in classical Arabic.

Emendations and revocalizations are numerous: תָּלָה "folly" (as 1:22: what Job did *not* charge

God with) (so Hupfeld, Driver); הַתָּלָה "deception" (Delitzsch); תְהִלָּה "praise" (applying the force of לֹא to both halves of the line; so Ehrlich, Blommerde, though his claimed parallel with Ps 106:12 is illusory).

19.a. יְסוֹדָם "their foundation" refers to בָתֵי "houses," not סכני "dwellers" (against Ehrlich, Horst). The phrase is perhaps alluded to at 1QH 12.26 (M. Mansoor restores בעפר [ויסודו], in *The Thanksgiving Hymns* [STDJ 3; Leiden: Brill, 1961] 175 n. 15).

19.b. It is tempting to regard the *beth* of בעפר "in dust" as equivalent to *mem*, i.e., "whose foundation is (made) of dust/mud" (bibliography: Blommerde, 19), especially in view of Gen 2:19. For מן of material, see BDB, 579a § 2b. But not much is gained for the sense; it is all the same whether foundations stand in dust or are made from dust.

19.c. ידכאום, lit., "they [indefinite] crush them."

19.d. לפני, probably "like" (as LXX σητὸς τρόπον); cf. on 3:24. Temporal "before" is also possible; all depends on how עש is taken, and on the general sense (see *Comment*).

19.e. עש "moth" (Arab. *ʿuššun*, Akk. *ašāšu*, B; cf. עשש "waste away." For possible interpretations, see *Comment*. Some propose a עש II cognate with the rare Akk. *ašāšu*, A (*CAD*, A/II, 422), attested, like *ašāšu* "moth," only in lexical texts, and meaning "bird's nest" (as probably in 27:18); Friedr. Delitzsch translated "nest of reeds" (cf. Ehrlich), and G. R. Driver, "Linguistic and Textual Problems: Jeremiah," *JQR* 28 (1937–38) 97–129 (121), "bird's nest" (hence NEB; and Fohrer, who, however, omits the half line as a gloss). The reading is attractive, but the linguistic support is not strong.

The emendation by N. Herz, "Some Difficult Passages in Job," *ZAW* 20 (1900) 160–63 (160), was יְדֻכְּאוּ מִלִּפְנֵי עֹשָׂם "they are crushed (from) before their Maker." This idea has been resurrected in new garb by Blommerde, reading יְדֻכְּאוּ מִלְּפָנַי עָשׂ: ידכאו is from דכא = זכי "be pure," the *mem* of מלפני results from new word division (or may be enclitic *mem* on וידכאום), while עש is defective writing of עָשׂה, the pl suff of יסודם doing double duty for עָשׂה; thus "would they . . . be pure before their Maker." The emendation by Herz was more convincing, but equally unnecessary. It is followed by J. A. Rimbach, "'Crushed before the Moth' (Job 4:19)," *JBL* 100 (1981) 244–46.

20.a. מבקר לערב, i.e., in the course of a single day (cf. Isa 38:12); cf. GNB "A man may be alive in the morning, but die unnoticed before evening comes." NAB "Morning or evening they may be shattered" is not what is meant, nor is it likely that "morning" and "evening" refer to birth and death, as Fohrer implies: "Life is regarded as the span of one day, man as the creature of a single day" (similarly Gordis).

20.b. Taking the verb as expressing the modality of possibility; see D. J. A. Clines, "Verb Modality and the Interpretation of Job iv 20–21," *VT* 30 (1980) 354–57.

20.c. לנצח may well be "for ever," as is usual; but the superlative sense "utterly" (cf. NEB "perish outright") may be more appropriate here (cf. also 14:20). See D. Winton Thomas, "The Use of נצח as a Superlative in Hebrew," *JSS* 1 (1956) 106–9; P. R. Ackroyd, "נצח—εἰς τέλος," *ExpT* 80 (1968–69) 126; Kopf, *VT* 8 (1958) 186; P. P. Saydon, "Some Unusual Ways of Expressing the Superlative in Hebrew and Maltese," *VT* 4 (1954) 432–33; P. Joüon, "Notes de lexicographie hébraïque," *Bib* 7 (1926) 162–70 (162).

20.d. מבלי משים, probably lit. "without anyone setting it (to heart)." מֵשִׂים would be the hiph ptcp, otherwise unattested, but perhaps explicable as an anomalous back-formation from יָשִׂים thought of as hiph rather than qal of שִׂים/שׂוּם (יָשׂוּם does occur in Exod 4:11 as qal impf). Less probably, מֵשִׂים may be emended to שָׂם, qal ptcp (Fohrer), and the initial *mem* may be regarded as enclitic *mem* on מבלי (cf. Blommerde). In either case, most argue that the participle abbreviates the phrase שִׂים לֵב "lay to heart, pay attention" (so in 23:6; Isa 41:20); thus מבלי משים is parallel to ולא בחכמה in v 21. Horst, followed by Gerleman (*BHS*), suggested מֵשִׂים is a noun, "attention," formed like מָרוֹץ "running" from רוץ.

Some, however, find the ellipsis "rather too violent" (Dhorme; cf. Rowley), and propose emendations. Merx read מִבְּלִי מוֹשִׁיעַ "without a savior, with none to help" (cf. LXX παρὰ τὸ μὴ δύνασθαι αὐτοὺς ἑαυτοῖς βοηθῆσαι ἀπώλοντο); he is followed by Dhorme, Rowley, J. C. L. Gibson, *SJT* 28 (1975) 266 n. 4; parallels in Ps 18:42 [41]; Isa. 47:15; see also J. F. A. Sawyer, "What was a מוֹשִׁיעַ?" *VT* 15 (1965) 475–86.

N. Herz (*ZAW* 20 [1900] 160) read בְּלִי שֵׁם "without a name," and this interpretation, judged "very much worthy of consideration" by Nöldeke, has been revived by M. Dahood, taking the initial *mem* of משים as enclitic to מבלי ("Northwest Semitic Philology and Job," in *The Bible in Current Catholic Thought* [Gruenthaner Memorial Volume, ed. J. L. McKenzie; St Mary's Theology Studies 1; New York: Herder and Herder, 1962] 55–74 [55]); followed by Pope,

Blommerde; it is also adopted by Rimbach, *JBL* 100 (1981) 244–46. Cf. the phrase בְּנֵי בְלִי שֵׁם
(30:8), "nameless men" (NAB). Human failure to achieve dignity ("name") seems beside the point
here, however, and the parallelism with v 21b is destroyed.

Ehrlich emended to מֵשִׁיב "restoring," comparing Isa 42:22 וְאֵין אֹמֵר הָשַׁב; so too Kissane,
NJB.

21.a. "Tent-cord" (יֶתֶר), as here, is never the object of נסע; though several commentators
assert that cords and pegs alike can be "pulled up" (Horst, Fohrer, Pope), tent-cords (מֵיתָר, יֶתֶר,
חֶבֶל) are "loosed" (פתח, as 30:11) or "snapped, torn apart" (נתק, as Isa 33:20; Jer 10:20), and it
may be better to read יְתֵדָם "their tent-peg," from יָתֵד (so Olshausen et al.; JB, NAB).

KJV "their excellency" takes יתרם from יֶתֶר I (BDB, 451b) "remainder, excess, preeminence"
(so Tg and one Pesh rendering, as also some medieval Jewish commentators, followed by Kissane).
Similarly NEB "their rich possessions" (cf. יֶתֶר in 22:20; Ps 17:14), though NEB transposes
הֲלֹא־נִסַּע יִתְרָם בָּם to follow 5:4 (after Dhorme). NEB's transposition and translation follow G. R.
Driver ("On Job V.5," *TZ* 12 [1956] 485–86), who suggested that יתרם בם was a scribal error
for בְּמוֹתָרָם "in their abundance" (from מוֹתָר).

Terrien ("Ne leur arrache-t-on pas leur éminence comme un pieu de tente?") apparently
translates יתרם twice over. Dhorme also takes יתרם from יֶתֶר I "abundance," and translates
"Has not their superfluous wealth been taken away from them?," and transposes to follow 5:5b.
Despite Rowley, this does not seem the most satisfactory treatment of the line, involving as it
does an unnecessary transposition.

21.b. נסע "pull up" (often, tent-peg), thus "remove, move away." After the verb, MT adds
בָּם, lit., "in them." Gordis takes this as "by themselves, *per se*, by virtue of their own nature,"
comparing Ps 90:10 יְמֵי שְׁנוֹתֵינוּ בָהֶם שִׁבְעִים שָׁנָה, "the days of our years are of themselves seventy
years" (though here Dahood, *Psalms II*, 325; *Psalms I*, 122, translates בהם "then"). A simple
solution would be to take בם as equivalent to מֵהֶם "from them," *beth* and *min* being interchanged
(see N. M. Sarna, "The Interchange of the Prepositions *beth* and *min* in Biblical Hebrew," *JBL* 78
[1959] 310–16 [esp. 313–14]; followed by Fohrer; see further Blommerde, 19; and cf. esp. Z.
Zevit, "The So-Called Interchangeability of the Prepositions *b, l,* and *m(n)* in Northwest Semitic,"
JANESCU 7 [1975] 103–12). Tg, Pesh, Vg all preserve this interpretation; see also on 5:21; 20:20;
and Duhm, following their lead, proposed emending בם to מֵהֶם. Horst interestingly emends to
בַיּוֹם "in a day, i.e., suddenly" (as in Prov 12:16; Neh 3:34 [4:2]), which would parallel מבקר
לערב in v 20.

21.c. The question introduced by הֲ at the beginning of the verse is not in fact v 21a, but
only v 21b, and v 21a is a conditional clause (see GKC, § 150m; and cf. 4:2). RSV is correct as
against RV (cf. KJV, NIV).

21.d. ולא בחכמה. With מות "die," *beth* usually signifies cause (e.g., thirst, Judg 15:18; Isa
50:2; sword and famine, Jer 11:22). Hence Terrien translates, "They die, and that is not [by
excess] of wisdom," similarly Dhorme, "They die and it is not of wisdom," following this verse
immediately with 5:2, "For it is vexation which kills a senseless man"; i.e., grief and anger, from
which Job is suffering, are the true causes of death; it is not wisdom that kills a man. This
rearrangement is ingenious, but it destroys the parallelism that Gordis has correctly noted between
מבלי משׂים and ולא בחכמה. He renders "while they (the victims) are unaware" (similarly Budde,
"they know not how"; and Fohrer). But חכמה can hardly signify simple awareness of a state of
affairs; for this reason a translation such as "without anyone else being aware" (which would be
strictly parallel to v 20b) is also unacceptable. See further, *Comment*.

5:1.a. The imperative קְרָא־נָא is, as Davidson said, "not ironical, but merely a very animated
way of putting a supposition"; cf. NEB, NIV "Call if you will" (similarly Moffatt).

1.b. Gordis translates the colon "To whom rather than to the Holy One can you turn?,"
taking קדשׁים as an epithet for God. This is an improbable construction of the Heb., and Esth
6:6 is no real parallel.

2.a. The prefixed *lamed* is a sign of the direct accusative, possibly an Aramaism, but too frequently
attested in Bib. Heb. to be so regarded (cf. n. 5:7.b below).

3.a. משׁרישׁ hiph, emended to מְשֹׁרָשׁ pual "uprooted" by Hoffmann, Duhm, NEB.

3.b. Gordis makes the ingenious proposal to revocalize פתאם to פְּתָאִם "fools," reading נְוֵה
פתאם "the dwelling of fools (*or*, folly)." פתאם would then form a neat parallel to אֱוִיל, but an
emendation of נוהו is also required. Some have found פתאם "suddenly" rather unexpected (cf.
Duhm) and on that ground have attempted to find in ואקב an external event which suddenly
befell the fool (see n. 5:3.d); but פתאם can well express the rapidity with which the fool met his
fate and with which therefore Eliphaz was able to pronounce him accursed.

3.c. נוה originally signified grazing land, though the man depicted here is a farmer rather than a shepherd. No more than the "dwelling" (rsv), "home" (neb) or "House" (jb) is covered by the term; Driver notes places in poetry (Prov 3:33; Isa 33:20) where the term obviously means "habitation" in general. On the term, see Andersen; D. O. Edzard, "Altbabylonisch *nawûm*," *ZA* 19 (1959) 168–73.

3.d. MT וָאֶקּוֹב] appears difficult if translated "and I cursed" since that makes the fate of the fool lie in Eliphaz's hands. The solution may simply be that קבב does not mean "curse" in the formal sense, but "despise," and especially "despise as (something) cursed" (cf. קלל "curse, despise as cursed"); see J. Scharbert, *TDOT* 1:415. Gordis takes וָאֶקּוֹב as a declarative verb, "I declared cursed," though it must be admitted that hiph and piel are much more common as declaratives. The verb does not quite fit the criteria for "delocutive" verbs as sketched by D. R. Hillers, "Delocutive Verbs in Biblical Hebrew," *JBL* 86 (1967) 320–24, though Gordis is tempted to think so. The parallelism of וָאֶקּוֹב with רָאִיתִי suggests that emendations of the 1st person verb to a 3rd person form with וְנָוֵהוּ as the subject are probably wrong. But among consonantal emendations may be mentioned וַיִּרְקַב "and (it) rotted away" (Duhm, Ehrlich, Fohrer, nab; some cf. LXX ἐβρώθη for support, but βιβρώσκω never renders רקב); וַיֹּאבַד "and (it) perished" (Ball); בְנָוֵהוּ "and a wild beast [is] in his dwelling" (J. J. Slotki, "The Re-emergence of an Akko," *ExpT* 43 [1931–32] 288). Gerleman suggests וָאֶקּוֹב is an Aram. inf for וְהָקוֹב "and (it) dried up" (cf. Arab. *qabba*). I. Eitan, "Biblical Studies," *HUCA* 14 (1939) 1–22 (12–13) read וַיִּקֹּב from a verb קוב (cf. Arab. *qāba*) "dig; V be uprooted"; he is followed by neb (cf. Brockington) with "his home in ruins about him." For other emendations, see Driver, Rowley, Fohrer.

4.a. Andersen reads שַׂעַר for שַׁעַר, sc. "in the tempest," and sees here "a cruel reference to Job 1:19"; but the language is typically forensic (see *Comment*). Others (e.g., Bickell, Duhm, Fohrer) omit it as metrically superfluous; it may be, but is at least implied by the sense (Horst).

5.a. neb transfers 4:21a to this point.

5.b. MT קְצִירוֹ "his harvest," sc. of the fool, is intelligible, though many would revocalize to קָצְרוּ, yielding "what they (the children) have reaped" (so jb, neb, nab, Dhorme, Fohrer; cf. LXX ἃ γὰρ ἐκεῖνοι συνήγαγον).

5.c. MT is extremely difficult—lit., "and unto from thorns he takes it." Seven different moves are possible: (i) Reference to some supposed custom, such as covering harvested grain with torn bushes to protect it from animals (so W. M. Thomson, *The Land and the Book* [London: T. Nelson, 1890] 348; followed by Fohrer, though he regards the phrase as a gloss); or robbers breaking through the thorn hedge surrounding the field to harvest the grain for themselves (so tob) (but why find the hardest way into a field open to public view in order to thieve?). The combination of עַל־מִן) "and unto from" remains a difficulty; it is an improbable way of saying "and even." (ii) Emendations of the text have convinced few. Budde proposed וְאֶל מָתָם עָנִי יִקָּחֵהוּ "and their sheaf a poor man will take" (followed hesitantly by Driver). Dhorme quite plausibly developed a suggestion of H. Winckler ("Maspan keller," *Altorientalische Forschungen* [Leipzig: E. Pfeiffer, 1902] 3/1:235–36) to emend מצנים to מַצְפֻּנָיו (cf. Obad 6), "hiding-places"; tr. "and carry away to hiding-places." Gerleman notes the proposal וְאֶל צְנָמִים יִקַּח הוּא "and their withered sheaves he takes away"; this suggestion has the merit that צְנֻמִים is applied to "ears" (שִׁבֳּלִים) of grain in Gen 41:23. (iii) Simple deletion of the phrase (Hölscher; cf. Horst ["perhaps"], Fohrer, Moffatt; nab encloses in square brackets). J. Reider deletes the colon as an Arabizing gloss on צמים in the next colon ("Some Notes to the Text of the Scriptures," *HUCA* 3 [1926] 109–16 [111–12]). (iv) The homonymic approach of G. R. Driver (*TZ* 12 [1956] 485–86) yields "a strong man snatches it from the baskets" in which the grain is being carried from the field; אֵל is אֵל "strong man" (cf. Ezek 31:11; 32:21), and צנים is cognate with Aram. צנא, Arab. *ṣannu(n)*. neb follows Driver with "the stronger man seizes it from the panniers." (v) A different word-division led Tur-Sinai, followed by Gordis, to the proposal וְאֵלָם צָנִים יְקָחֶה "and their wealth [אוּל "strength," hence "substance, wealth"] the starving [צָנִים being a *qātîl*-type noun form from צנם "be shriveled up"] will seize." (vi) A different revocalization produces וְאֵל מְצַנֵּם יִקָּחֵהוּ "and he [God] takes it away by drought" (צָנֵם from צנם "dry up, harden"); so nab "or God shall take it away by blight," but the phrase is enclosed in square brackets as a gloss. Certainly reference to direct divine intervention seems out of place here. (vii) jb emends to מִשִּׁנֵּימוֹ "from [their] teeth," i.e., from their mouths (though the pl form שִׁנַּיִם does not actually occur anywhere).

5.d. Dhorme transfers 4:21a to this point (cf. n. 5:5.a above).

5.e. MT צַמִּים "snare" (parallel to פַּח in 18:9) does not yield a very satisfactory sense, though preferred by rv. Most read צְמֵאִים "the thirsty," a good parallel to רָעֵב in the first colon (so, e.g., rsv, jb, neb, nab, niv; cf. Aq διψῶντες, Symm διψῶν, Vg *sitientes*). Less probably, Gordis takes צַמִּים as a *qattil* form from צמם ("bind, contract"; cf. צָמָה "veil"; צָמִים, "trap"), meaning "one contracted through lack of food; lean." KJV "robber" followed the Tg reading ליסטיסין (from λῃστής).

5.f. שָׁאָף is usually emended to שָׁאֲפוּ (cf., e.g., *BHS*) to harmonize with the pl צמאים (see n. 5:5.e). But the sg verb is not indefensible (see GKC, § 145o). Duhm emended to the phrase וְשָׁאַב צָמֵא מֵגְּלָם "and the thirsty (sg) drew water from their spring"; NAB builds on this suggestion with וְשָׁאֲבוּ צְמֵאִים "and the thirsty (pl) shall swallow their substance"; שאב does not mean "swallow," but this is perhaps a legitimate metaphorical use. The MT is still more probable.

5.g. חֵילָם, "their wealth" (sc. of the fool's children), is a quite satisfactory reading, though RSV, NIV prefer "his wealth." Less probable is the reading חלקם "their portion" in one Kennicott Heb MS (cf. *BHS*), or the emendation חֲלָבָם "their milk" (Hoffmann, Beer, followed by Moffatt).

6.a. אָוֶן, "(moral) evil," or "(physical) evil" (cf. on 4:8, where both meanings of און and עָמָל are employed).

7.a. יוּלָּד "is born"; the passive (perhaps the word was sometimes read as יֻלַּד) is read by the ancient versions. But the verb ילד (niph or pual) with ל usually means "be born to," i.e., as the child of; and that will not fit the context here. Further, the best way of connecting v 6 (which denies that the earth is the origin of human suffering) with v 7 is to see in v 7 the real origin of suffering. A simple revocalization to יוֹלִד (for hiph יוֹלִיד) yields "begets." This change is adopted by Beer, Budde, Duhm, Dhorme, Rowley, Weiser, Gordis, Hesse, 57 (contrast 52), Terrien, Moffatt, JB, NAB, GNB.

7.b. On the prefixed *lamed*, see n. 5:2.a above. It is unnecessary to explain it as "emphatic" *lamed* (as Dahood, cited by Blommerde, 44).

7.c. The *waw* is generally regarded as the *waw adaequationis*, or *waw* of comparison, though in such cases the second half is usually compared with the first (cf. Prov 25:25) rather than the reverse, as here (cf. Driver). On the translation here suggested, *waw* is a simple *waw* linking two (almost) contemporaneous actions.

7.d. For the translation of בני רשף, see *Comment*.

7.e. Some versions refer to the flight of birds; so NEB "as surely as birds fly upwards"; JB "as surely as eagles fly to the height" (cf. Terrien). These follow the ancient versions that saw in the "sons of Resheph" a reference to a bird, probably under the influence of the final verb עוף "fly" (for details, see Dhorme). The "eagle" comes entirely from Job 39:27 where what is said to "rise high" (יַגְבִּיהַ) is explicitly the "eagle" (נֶשֶׁר).

8.a. On this meaning of דרש, see *Comment*. Certainly the legal language of NEB, "I would make my petition to God," or of JB, "I should appeal to God" (cf. NAB), seems out of place.

8.b. דְּבָרָה is a rare noun, occurring 3 times in the phrase עַל־דִּבְרַת in Eccl, and elsewhere only in the unusual phrase "a priest after the order of (עַל־דִּבְרָתִי) Melchizedek" (Ps 110:4). Many modern versions translate with "cause" (KJV, RSV, NEB, NIV) or "case" (Moffatt, JB), or "plea" (NAB). Fullerton, *JBL* 49 (1930) 360, argues convincingly that Eliphaz would be unlikely to concede that Job had any "case," legally speaking, to argue; it would be better to regard דברה as semantically equivalent to אָמְרָה "utterance, speech." The semantic analogy with Akk. *awātam šakānum* "to put a case," a juridical idiom, is interesting (S. M. Paul, "Unrecognized Biblical Legal Idioms in the Light of Comparative Akkadian Expressions," *RB* 86 [1979] 230–39 [235–36]), but falls a long way short of establishing such as the meaning here.

9.a. NAB omits the line as an "expansionist transposition from 9,10" (*Textual Notes*, 373).

10.a. V 10 is deleted as a gloss by Duhm, Fohrer, Hesse, because the theme of rain seems irrelevant to the hymn of praise. Horst protests that anything that praises the majesty of God is relevant in a doxology; for a further suggestion about its relevance, see *Comment*.

10.b. Or, perhaps, "sends waters over the countryside" (so Dhorme). Ps 104:10 uses שלח of God's sending forth a spring to become a brook.

10.c. חוּצוֹת "open places," usually refers to the streets and squares of a city as contrasted with the houses. In Prov 8:26 and Ps 144:13 (as the place where flocks abound) the reference must be to the countryside.

11.a. The inf לָשׂוּם is not attached in sense to what precedes (as Duhm, Peake, Weiser, TOB) or to what follows (as Dhorme, JB), but as an inf abs "takes on the same tense as the finite verb preceding it" (Gordis), here the ptcps of v 10.

11.b. NAB reads שַׂגֵּב and translates "he exalts"; the piel would be more probable.

11.c. קֹדְרִים, lit., "those who are dark," hence "the mourners," or perhaps more generally, "the afflicted." קדר "does not denote a state of mind (sorrowing or grieving), but . . . has reference to the squalid person and dark attire . . . of a mourner in the East" (Driver).

11.d. NAB reads וַיּוֹשַׁע "and he saves" for MT יֶשַׁע "(in, to) safety"; the change is unnecessary since ישע can be regarded as an adverbial accusative (Gordis, GKC, § 118q).

12.a. תּוּשִׁיָּה, usually in a good sense, "sound counsel" or its consequence, "effectiveness, success." See Driver; J. F. Genung, "Meaning and Usage of the Term תושיה," *JBL* 30 (1911) 114–22; H. Bauer, "Die hebräische Eigenname also sprachliche Erkenntnisquelle," *ZAW* 48 (1930) 73–80 (77–78); H. A. Brongers, "Miscellanea Exegetica. III. Tûšîyyâ," *Übersetzungen und Deutung: Studien zum Alten Testament und seiner Umwelt Alexander Reinard Hulst gewidmet* (ed. H. A. Brongers et al.; Nijkerk: Callenbach, 1977) 30–49 (37–47), arguing for a sense more like מחשבות "plots." The term, like several in vv 12–13, is typical of the vocabulary of the wisdom literature.

13.a. If נִמְהָרָה is from מהר "hasten," it literally means "is hurried," sc. away, or to destruction; "is carried headlong" (Pope), "routed" (NAB), "swept away" (NIV), "thrown into confusion" (NEB), "brought to a quick end" (RSV). Gordis's suggestion that מהר is a denominative from מֹהַר "gift," thus "is sold out, betrayed," is interesting, but not very plausible.

15.a. MT מֵחֶרֶב מְפִיהֶם "from the sword of their mouth" is judged by most to be corrupt. Gordis regards the two words as a hendiadys equivalent to "from their sharp tongue"; but the only parallel he cites (Isa 53:8: מֵעֹצֶר וּמִמִּשְׁפָּט) is open to question. The simplest alteration is a revocalization of מחרב to מָחֳרָב "the desolated [one]" (hoph ptcp of חרב "be waste, desolate"); so Dhorme, Rowley, NEB; similarly Reider, *HUCA* 3 (1926) 112 (though he wishes to read מפי הָם "from the mouth of the ambitious" [cf. Arab. *hm*]—an unlikely proposal).

Emendations either (i) omit the initial *mem* of מפיהם, thus "from the sword of their tongue" (as some Heb. MSS, Tg, Pesh), or omit מפיהם altogether (as, apparently, LXX) (is מפיהם a gloss on מחרב, since the sword is not likely to be used literally against the poor?); or (ii) replace מפיהם by a synonym for אֶבְיוֹן, viz., עָנִי (so Siegfried, Duhm, GNB; cf. JB "the bankrupt"), or יָתוֹם "the fatherless" (Budde, Driver), or פֶּתָיִם "simple ones" (Pope), or מַפָּח "the ensnared" (Horst; cf. *BHS*); or (iii) read מִפִּי חֶרֶב "from the mouth (edge) of the sword" (NAB); or (iv) emend מחרב to יָתוֹם, repositioned after מפיהם (so also Budde, Driver, RSV). However, is not the MT tenable: viz. "from the sword [that proceeds] from their mouth"? It is not a literal sword, but calumny, that strikes the poor; in Ps 59:8 [7] (*si v.l.*) swords are "in (בּ)" their tongues; in 64:4 [3] they sharpen their tongue like (כּ) a sword; and in 57:5 [4] their tongue is a sharp sword. There is no standard idiom linking חרב and פה (or לשׁון) in a construct chain, so the present phrase is not unnatural. NIV's "from the sword in their mouth" seems the most acceptable rendering.

16.a. NEB "and the unjust are sickened" I cannot explain.

17.a. הנה marks the beginning of a new train of thought (cf. v 27), an example of anacrusis (Gordis). Even though LXX, Pesh, Vg and some MSS have nothing corresponding to it, it certainly should not be deleted (as Duhm, Fohrer, NEB [effectively], NAB).

17.b. שַׁדַּי, here used for the first time in Job; see *Comment.*

18.a. כי is not concessive (as Blommerde), but introduces a reason for the previous verse.

18.b. Q יָדָיו is clearly to be preferred to K ידי, since the verb is pl. JB's and GNB's use of the sg is probably due to English idiom, and does not reflect a textual decision.

19.a. Does the *beth* mean "from"? So Blommerde, 19 (bibliography on the interchange of *beth* and *min;* and cf. n. 4:21.b). In the second half of the line *beth* must be translated "in," so parallelism might suggest this meaning for the first half too. Driver notes that at one stage in the development of the Heb. script *beth* and *min* resembled one another, but he does not suggest emending the text.

20.a. יְדֵי־חֶרֶב "the hands [power] of the sword" is a phrase attested in Jer 18:21 (// רַע) and Ps 63:11 [10]; פִּי־חֶרֶב "the mouth of the sword" is more common, however.

21.a. בְּשׁוֹט: Most read with 1 MS, LXX, Pesh, Vg מָשׁוֹט "from the scourge," or perhaps מִשּׁוֹט "from the scourging" (inf) (Gordis, *BHS*). Cf. n. 5:19.a. Here the emendation is more probable, but equally probable is the use of *beth* for *min.*

21.b. לְשׁוֹן: Ehrlich, Gordis, and apparently Andersen, see this as an ellipsis for לְשׁוֹן אֵשׁ "tongue of fire" (Isa 5:24), just as לָשׁוֹן appears in Josh 15:2 as an ellipsis for לְשׁוֹן יָם (Josh 15:5; 18:19; Isa 11:15). But the use of לשׁון *simpliciter* in a geographical notice is no real parallel. The suggestion arises only because "the scourging of the tongue" or slander is thought to be out of place in the present list of calamities, as distress experienced by an individual rather than by the community. "Scourge of the tongue" is sufficiently attested by μάστιγ γλώσσης in Ecclus 26:6 and שׁוֹט דבת לשׁון in Ecclus 51:2. Duhm wanted to emend לשׁון away altogether by a word for plague like רֶשֶׁף, which appears in other catalogues of calamities as דֶּבֶר (Ezek 5:17; 14:21; Ps 91:6); but the emendation, though followed by Peake, Ball, Moffatt, is arbitrary.

21.c. שֹׁד "destruction": since the same calamity appears in the next verse, some have suggested an emendation of the word to שֵׁד "demon" (Hoffmann, Pope) (cf. Ps 91:5) or to שׁוֹאָה "desolation" (Driver) or better "devastating storm" (as in Ezek 38:9 where it is parallel to עָנָן and associated with the verbs עלה and בוא, and in Prov 1:27 [Q] where it is parallel to סופה and associated with בוא). JB translates "brigand," apparently reading שֹׁדֵד. Gordis argues for the meaning "flood, torrent" from a root *שׁוד־ד (cf. Aram., Arab.) "pour, flow" (cf. Ps 91:6 יָשׁוּד [usually from שדד "devastate"] // יִּדֹּל; Isa 13:6; Joel 1:15). This suggestion would be more convincing if his interpretation of לשׁון in the first line as "fire" (see n. 5:21.b above) were acceptable. Guillaume suggests a new Heb. noun שׁוד "calumny," cognate with Arab. *sawwada* "blackened his character, disgraced him"; this would create an acceptable parallelism in the line.

22.a. The whole verse is deleted by some (Duhm, Budde, Hölscher, Fohrer, Horst, Hesse) on the grounds that it increases the number of calamities mentioned beyond the "seven" of v 19 and that it consists of two calamities mentioned elsewhere: שׁד in v 21 and (השׂדה) חית הארץ in v 23. On the seven calamities, see *Comment* on v 19. The omission of v 22 would make the initial כי of v 23 fit very awkwardly with v 21, and the verse should be retained. But see further n. 5:23a.

22.b. כָּפָן is generally thought an Aramaism; Gordis thinks it a particular form of famine, that due to bad crops rather than drought or enemy attack. JB "drought and frost" reads for שׁד "ruin," שָׁרָב "burning heat," and for כפן "blight," כְּפוֹר "hoar frost," following the lead of LXX ἀνόμων, which was presumably based on a reading כְּפֹר (Dhorme).

23.a. כִּי is omitted by Duhm, Fohrer (cf. Horst), only because their deletion of v 22 entails it. Fohrer argues that the security in v 22 is not dependent on the compacts of v 23 but on the help of God. On the contrary, while all the promised security no doubt depends ultimately on God, it is precisely because Job will have a covenant with the stones (not to ruin his crops) and will be at peace with the wild animals (so that they will not damage his crops) that he will be able to afford to "laugh" at shortage of food (cf. also Dhorme).

23.b. אבני השׂדה: This unusual concept of a "covenant with the stones of the field" has led to suggested alternative readings. Rashi has a variant noun אֲדֹנֵי השׂדה "lords of the field" (cf. Midrash Koh. R. on 6:11; Sifra on Lev 11:27), viz., satyrs, gnomes, or sprites who would keep the fields clear from stones that interfere with planting (cf. Isa 5:2; 2 Kgs 3:19 "ruin every good piece of land with stones"; 3:25). So K. Kohler, "Das Erdmännlein," *ARW* 7 (1910) 75–79. To similar effect G. Beer, "Miscellen. 4. Zu Hiob 5:23," *ZAW* 35 (1915) 63–64, read בְּנֵי השׂדה "sons of the field" (the reference to *m. Kil.* 8.5 is, however, a mistake; see K. Albrecht, "Kil VIII 5," *ZAW* 36 [1916] 64); similarly, without emending the text, Blommerde regarded the initial letter of אבני as a prosthetic *aleph* (cf. on אכפי in 33:7; אזרעי in 31:22). These figures would be the "earth-folk" (*ʾahl el-ʾarḍ*) believed by Arabs to need placating to preserve the fertility of the soil (Pope). One might, however, have expected such sprites to be called בַּעֲלֵי השׂדה (Fohrer, Rowley). Andersen, following Blommerde's suggested reading and adding new examples of אב equivalent to בן (Gen 49:24; Isa 14:19; Ezek 28:14, 16), argues that the אבני השׂדה are simply untamed beasts, a proposal that unfortunately destroys the parallelism of v 22a with v 23a. J. Gray, "The Massoretic Text of the Book of Job, the Targum and the Septuagint Version in the Light of the Qumran Targum (11QtargJob)," *ZAW* 86 (1974) 331–50 (336 n. 10), regards שׂדה as cognate with Arab. *sada(n)* "forsaken, useless," translating אבני השׂדה as "the waste stones"; the repetition of שׂדה in the two lines is an example of *taurîya* ("deliberate ambiguity").

23.c. The חית השׂדה is assumed by most commentators to be identical to the חית הארץ in v 22, viz. "the wild animals." G. R. Driver, however, proposed that חית here is cognate with Arab. *ḥayyu(n)* "plant" ("Studies in the Vocabulary of the Old Testament. V," *JTS* 34 [1933] 33–44 [44]); he is followed by Guillaume, J. Gray, *ZAW* 86 (1974) 336 n. 11, and by NEB "weeds."

24.a. אהלך, lit., "your tent"; the antique pastoral language is used as in v 3.

24.b. נוך, lit., "your fold" (JB "your sheepfold") (cf. n. 5:3.c above). F. D. Coggan read נָוָתְךָ, the fem form of נוה attested in 8:6 (though נוה usually means "pasture, meadow"), and took it as the subject of תחטא: "thou shalt visit the abode of thy flock and it shall not be missing" ("The Meaning of חטא in Job v.24," *JMEOS* 17 [1932] 53–56). But the chain of 2nd person sg verbs tells against this suggestion; the difficulty raised by Fohrer, that a place cannot be "missing," is perhaps overcome by the temporary nature of an encampment of shepherds.

24.c. חטא, often "sin" (as in KJV, RVmg), means in secular contexts "miss" (the way, a goal, something desired; cf. Prov 19:2; 8:36; and an illuminating use in Isa 65:20). NEB "find nothing amiss" is not quite correct; it is rather "find nothing missing, lacking."

26.a. The precise meaning of בְּכֶלַח is unknown. Arab. *kalaḥa* "be (or appear) hard, stern" suggests to Driver "firm strength, vigour" (cf. RVmg, Moffatt, NEB, NIV), but the connection is rather remote; the supposed Syr. cognate *klḥ* is an error (see Pope). Dahood regarded it as a "congeneric assimilation" of כח "strength" and לַח "freshness" ("Northwest Semitic Philology," 56), but evidence of such assimilation is scanty (cf. Blommerde). KJV "a full age" (cf. RSV, JB) followed the medieval

Jewish tradition (e.g., Rashi, ibn Ezra) of connecting it with כלה "be complete." "Old age" has recently been cogently argued for on the basis of the Arab. roots *klḥ* and *qlḥ* by Grabbe, *Comparative Philology*, 43–46. Among emendations, none of which is convincing, may be mentioned בְחֵילָךְ "in your strength" (Beer), בְלֵחָךְ "in your sap, freshness" (cf. Deut 34:7, where rsv translates לֹח "natural force") (nab); בְלָח (Merx). Guillaume regards the Arab. cognate as *kulāʿu(n)* "strength," which would suit the context well, but offends against the normal laws of Semitic philology: Arab. *ʿain* does not usually correspond to Heb. *ḥeth*.

27.a. Lit., "it is so."

27.b. שְׁמַעֲנָּה: Many (including neb, nab) revocalize to שְׁמַעֲנֻּה "we have heard it," partly on the ground that the adversative particle *waw* and the emphatic pronoun אתה are linked with the subsequent verb, and partly because LXX apparently vocalized it this way. Gordis also sees a distinction between what the sages have "discovered" (חקר) on the basis of their own observation, and what they have learned or "heard" (שמע) from the past. The revocalization, adopted by Duhm, Driver-Gray, Horst, Fohrer, Hesse, is appealing but not compelling, since the emphatic personal pronoun links naturally with the final לָךְ, viz., "*you* must know it *for yourself.*"

Form/Structure/Setting

The *structure* of Eliphaz's speech is fairly self-evident, though several slightly varying strophe divisions may be suggested. Verse 1 is plainly a prose introduction. Thereafter, the speech itself is divided into five major units, of which the first and the second may be subdivided into two smaller units:

	4:1	Introduction
1.	4:2–11	Address to Job
	2–6	Job's personal situation
	7–11	Contrast between fate of righteous and wicked
2.	4:12–21	Account of a revelation
	12–16	The circumstances
	17–21	The content and its implication
3.	5:1–7	Discourse: Fate of the fool
4.	5:8–16	Discourse: God's contrasting dealings with righteous and wicked
5.	5:17–26	Discourse: Fate of the righteous
	5:27	Peroration/Concluding address

Among versions and commentators, the only significant variations from some such analysis are: the creation of a separate strophe for 4:10–11 (neb, as if to suggest that these verses are secondary); the linkage of 4:12–5:7 as Eliphaz's visions and its message (so Rowley); and the attachment of 5:6–7 to what follows (Fohrer) rather than to what precedes.

The speech, like all those in the dialogue, does not follow any fixed *form*, but contains a great variety of *form-critical elements*. In the first major strophe (4:2–11), we have first a conventional "speech preface" (cf. 8:2; 9:2a; 11:2–3; 15:2–3; 16:2–3; 18:2; 20:2; 21:2a; 32:6–33:3; 34:2; 36:2; 38:2), where reference is made to "words," either the imminent words of the speaker, or those of his interlocutor. Frequently in this element the effect of words (trouble, aggravation) or non-effect of them (ignoring, depreciation) is mentioned (so here; and, e.g., 16:2–3; 18:3; 19:2; 20:3). A reference to the impossibility of not speaking is also a gambit in this form (4:2b; 11:2; and esp. 32:6–20). These elements will have been characteristic of all conversational speech, not necessarily of the debates of the wise or of legal opponents (as Fohrer).

The contrast between Job's former life and his present behavior is somewhat reminiscent of cross-examination in legal disputations, but belongs to a wider ambit than that, and need not be interpreted as unsympathetically disputatious.

In the second part (vv 7–11) of Eliphaz's personal address to Job (vv 2–11), we meet with a highly stylized description of the fate of the wicked, such as recurs frequently in the book (5:2–5; 8:13–19; 15:20–35; 18:5–21; 20:5–29; 27:13–23). We term such stylized passages *topoi,* i.e., traditional set-pieces. Their function has to be carefully scrutinized, since it varies from case to case. See *Comment* on 4:7–11, for the view that the *topos* here functions as an *assurance* to Job. In vv 7, 8, as also in 5:3, 27, there is an appeal to experience, which reflects a wisdom orientation. The lion scene in vv 10–11 is thought by Fohrer to belong to psalmic tradition, though that may itself have been indebted to wisdom speech-forms in such instances; one may in fact speak here of "proverbial" material (Horst).

The second major strophe (4:12–21) recounts Eliphaz's experience of a nocturnal vision and audition. The prophetic experience of the vision, and especially of the hearing of a word from God, must stand in the background of this depiction; see M. Sister, "Die Typen der prophetischen Visionen in der Bibel," *MGWJ* 78 (1934) 399–430; F. Horst, "Die Visionsschilderungen der alttestamentlichen Propheten," *EvT* 20 (1960) 193–205; B. O. Long, "Prophetic Call Traditions and Reports among the Prophets," *JBL* 95 (1976) 353–65. But also the theophany traditions of the Sinai experience or the Jerusalem cult may have been drawn upon here (see especially *Comment* on v 16), and it must not be overlooked that accounts of dreams are widely spread through many forms of ancient Near Eastern literature. The external manifestations of a theophany are depicted here from a quite unusually psychological aspect (cf. vv 14–15). The second half (vv 17–21) of this strophe is wisdom material through and through; even the revelatory word is in the form of a question (rhetorical or otherwise; see *Comment*). The remainder follows a typically wisdom pattern of inference *a maiore ad minus,* and is concluded with psalmic material on the topic of death and the mortality of humankind.

The third major strophe (5:1–7) again makes use of a *topos* on the fate of the fool. A proverb (v 2) forms its preface, and its condemnation of the "fool" (not here the "wicked") as well as its theology of the "fate-determining deed" (vv 2, 6–7) and its proverb-like conclusion (vv 6–7) confirm its wisdom derivation.

By contrast, the fourth strophe (5:8–16) has a hymnic cast. After its introductory "confession" (v 8), which functions as advice rather than as testimony, the strophe has the form of a "doxology" (see on 5:8–16). No particular cultic use of this passage need be supposed, but the cataloguing of the activities of Yahweh (with ample employment of the participial forms) is adequate evidence of the sources of such a passage. Especially noteworthy is the presentation of the "reversal of fortunes" motif (especially vv 11, 13), familiar in hymns of this kind (12:16–25; 1 Sam 2:7–8; Ps 113:7–8; Luke 1:51–53). The "doxology," like the "confession" of v 8, serves as advice to Job rather than directly as praise to God. On the doxology form, see further on 5:9–16.

The fifth strophe (5:17–26) again stems from wisdom traditions, being cast in the form of a *topos* on the good fortune of "the man whom God reproves." The initial verse (v 17) is directly parallel to Prov 3:11–12, while v 19 makes use of the traditional form of the "number" proverb (see *Comment*). Further marks of the conventional wisdom background are the dogma of the divine deliverance of the righteous (vv 19–26), and the conclusion of the speech in a sentence of personal advice based on the collective experience of the community of the wise (v 27).

The role of *direct address* in the speech is a noteworthy feature of its form. Indeed, as will be noticed throughout the Commentary, much of the speeches, both of Job and of the friends, is not directed to those engaged in the dialogue but has, so to speak, a life of its own, and can at the most be regarded as only indirect address. Often the distinction between second person usage and third person material is sufficient marker of the comparative role of direct and indirect address. In this speech, however, this formal grammatical distinction may be misleading, since it would appear that 5:19–26, though cast in the second person singular, is a didactic *topos* without special reference to Job (note, for example, the inappropriateness of vv 25–26 to Job's situation). Job is directly addressed by Eliphaz only in 4:2–7; 5:1, 8, and 27. These passages are especially significant (as are direct addresses throughout the book) compared with the somewhat decorative and expansive *topoi* with which the speech is filled out.

From these passages we are best able to discern the *mood* of the speaker. The hesitant opening (4:2), the positive assessment of Job's former life (4:3–4), the affirmation of his present piety and integrity (4:6), and the concluding note of advice (5:27), all show Eliphaz as well-disposed and consolatory toward Job. That mood being established, some passages more uncertain in their intent shed their ambiguity. 4:5, for instance, is to be read not as a smug and hostile criticism, but at the worst as a mild reproof and at the best as a sympathetic encouragement. 5:1 is not a satirical jibe, but an almost purely rhetorical question, while 5:8 expresses no "holier than thou" superiority but comradely advice. Similarly, larger units like those describing the fate of the wicked (4:8–11; 5:2–5) contain no innuendo against some pretended virtue of Job's, but rather are designed to serve as further encouragement to Job by presenting the lot of the wicked as a contrast to what Job is entitled to expect. Such assessment of mood does indeed have a subjective element in it, and it would be possible to read the speech as much more coldly critical of Job; but it is submitted that the reading here presented makes a coherent interpretation of Eliphaz's speech possible and accounts best for the windings of the thought.

Concentration on the passages directly addressed to Job leads us to single out in this speech (as also in most others) *nodal verses* in which the thrust of the speech as a whole is encapsulated. These may be suggested to be 4:6 and 5:8. In the former, Eliphaz presents his own evaluation of Job as an encouragement: Job may be sure of restitution, sooner or later, because of his exemplary life. In the second, Eliphaz goes a step further: while awaiting a happy outcome to his suffering, Job should be patient and rest his claim to restitution with God. In short, his message to Job is: Take heart, and wait for God to restore you.

Comment

2 Eliphaz's speech begins in the most conciliatory manner possible (but cf. 15:1; 22:1). Not only is it introduced, like most of the friends' speeches, by a rhetorical question, which Job is not expected to answer, but it shows Eliphaz's sensitivity to Job's present anguish. Job's self-curse in chap. 3 has arisen out of silence (2:13), and Job should perhaps be allowed to lapse back into the silence of self-pity. Eliphaz is in a dilemma: he fears that Job is "unable to bear" (לאה) a weight of words and arguments in addition to his grief; yet, on the other hand, he is, like any friend, "unable" (מי יוכל) to sit there and say nothing. Weakness is confronted by weakness; the weakness of Job that may find "one word" (דבר) more than enough to bear is overwhelmed by the weakness of Eliphaz, who cannot "restrain" (עצר) his torrent of words (מלין) (cf. the use of עצר ב in 12:15). It is not simply a question here of Eliphaz's fearing that his speech may be felt by Job as an intrusion (cf. rsv "will you be offended?"; nab "will you mind?"; neb "will you lose patience?"), but an awareness, at least at the rhetorical level, that the sufferer and the counselor are equally helpless. Restraint in speech is urged by the wisdom teachers (e.g., Prov 10:19; 12:23), of whom Eliphaz is a representative (see above on *Form*), and his incapacity to hold back his words is a triumph of humanity over principle (cf. also Elihu, 32:18–20; Jer 20:9).

3 Job himself has in the past suffered no such dilemma when faced with depressed and helpless people. Eliphaz pays him the tribute of having known how to speak to the condition of the "weak" and "stumbling." He has no

fault to find with Job's past life, and, without being aware of it, confirms
both God's testimony to Job given in the prologue (1:8; 2:3) and Job's own
account of his life before disaster struck (29:11–17; 31:3, 16–20). He has given
counsel (יסֹר); the term "denotes not the instruction of the intellect (הֹודִיעַ,
לִמַּד), but the discipline or education of the moral nature . . . the discipline
with which a parent trains his child" (S. R. Driver, *Deuteronomy* [ICC; Edinburgh:
T. & T. Clark, 3rd ed., 1902] 76), or, as Horst writes, "the correction of a
person by corporal chastisement or by censure or judicial admonition, but
also by teaching, instruction and direction." Chastisement is out of the question
here, of course, but otherwise this is the very image of the patriarchal Job,
diligent for his family's right behavior (1:5; 2:10), and endowed with the authority of the desert sheikh (cf. 29:7–10, 25). In the particular setting of Job's
suffering, the "instruction" Job has offered may have a very particular meaning:
Job has taught others how to understand and come to terms with their own
suffering. Such "counsel" has been his special gift to the distressed; now is
the moment when his experience may be applied to his own case.

The symptoms of physical exhaustion, feeble hands and weak knees (v 4),
almost invariably function in biblical literature as images of depression and
loss of psychic energy or morale; see 2 Sam 4:1; Isa 13:7; Ezra 4:4; 2 Chr
15:7; cf. Ecclus 2:12; Lachish ostracon 6 (*ANET*, 322b) (weak hands); Isa 35:3
(weak hands, stumbling knees); Ezek 7:17; 21:12 [7] (weak hands, knees turned
to water); cf. Ecclus 25:23; and Nah 2:11 [10]; Heb 12:12 (trembling knees);
Ps 109:24 (stumbling knees); 1QM 14.6 (tottering knees); contrast Judg 9:24;
2 Sam 2:7; Jer 23:14 (strengthened hands).

4 Job's words have had the same efficacy as Eliphaz hopes his own will
have. "Words are the physicians of a spirit (ὀργή, variant ψυχή) diseased," says
Aeschylus (*Prometheus Bound*, 378; cf. Milton, *Samson Agonistes*, 184–85), and
Job's friends certainly have faith in the power of words to heal mental distress.
Job is of a different mind when he is at the receiving end of words (19:2),
but only because he hears unjust and unrealistic words. "Windy words" (16:3)
there may be in abundance in the book, but it is through the words of the
divine speeches (chaps. 38–41) that Job comes to the resolution of his crisis.
Silence can be sympathetic (2:13), silence can be the sign of conviction (6:24),
but what Job demands is to speak (7:11; 9:35; 10:1; 13:3, 13) and to be addressed
(13:22; 14:15; 23:5). Silence is damnation for Job (19:7, 16; 24:12; 30:20;
31:35).

5 What is "it" that has come to Job? The use of the indefinite feminine
subject may be a way of avoiding explicit mention of misfortune, the very
words for which may have seemed ill-omened (cf. Terrien). Clearly it is the
adversity (cf. NEB) that in vv 3–4 Job has energetically resisted on behalf of
others. Now he, from whom strength moved outwards, has himself become
the weak and cannot "bear" it (לאה, the same word as in v 2). He contradicts
himself in giving way to helplessness. The "nearer neighbourhood of misfortune
unmans" him (Knox). Were he in the friends' place, he will later say, he could
speak like them and "strengthen" (אמץ) them with his mouth (16:5). But he
is in his own place.

What has impelled Eliphaz's sympathy—for sympathy it is, and not sarcasm—
is Job's mental suffering, his dismay (בהל "terrify," "affright"; cf. Pope: "you
are aghast"), rather than his physical pain. This is a mark of Eliphaz's discern-

ment, and a response in some measure to the mood of Job himself in chap. 3, where he presents himself as one of the "bitter in soul" (מרי נפש, 3:20), as one "hedged in" by God (3:23). Job has not simply been "touched" by suffering (as KJV, RV, RSV, NAB, JB, NEB); for though נגע can signify "touch," when the subject is affliction or any calamity the verb almost invariably means "strike, smite"; the desert wind that "touched" (נגע) the four corners of the house of Job's eldest son (1:19) did more than merely "touch"; cf. also 1:11; 2:5; 5:19; 19:21. Nor is he simply "troubled" (KJV, RV); rather he is "overwhelmed" (JB).

The question of the mood of Eliphaz's speech becomes crucial at this point (as also at 4:8–11; 5:2–5; for a survey of commentators' opinions, see conveniently Fullerton, *JBL* 49 [1930] 340 n. 9). One translator comments on vv 3–5: "All who labour for men lay themselves open to this reproach. But how cruel it is! 'He saved others: himself he cannot save'" (King, 10 n.). Proverbial sarcasm about the difference between spectator and player could perhaps be seen here (cf. Weiser); cf. Terence's lines: 'How easy we all find it, so long as we're well, to give sound advice to the ill; but once you're in his state, you'd feel differently' (*facile omnes, quom valemu', recta consilia aegrotis damus. tu, si hic sis, aliter sentias* [*Andria*, 2.1.9–10]). Peake finds Eliphaz's words an irritant, not an emollient. Fundamentally, however, Eliphaz is well-disposed to Job, as the general consolatory tendency of this speech makes plain (note especially v 6 and the climax to which chap. 5 moves). Fullerton accurately assesses Eliphaz as "simply a rather stupid good person, blundering into words that would cut Job to the quick because he did not have a sufficiently sympathetic imagination to realize what impression he was likely to make by them" (*JBL* 49 [1930] 340).

6 Here the substratum of Eliphaz's theology is clearly visible: those who fear God and conduct themselves with moral probity will in the long term— if not at once—enjoy God's visible favor and deliverance. It will be 5:8 before Eliphaz actually makes any positive recommendation to Job—and even then only indirectly; but in the present verse he not only states, but takes for granted that Job also accepts, the basis on which alone his whole speech hangs together. So sure is he of his ground that he begins with a not-to-be-answered rhetorical question, "is not . . . ?" (הלא), which Gordis aptly terms a "petrified interrogative, best rendered nearly always as 'indeed.'"

Eliphaz speaks as the representative of a broad consensus in the wisdom tradition: the "fear of God" is the principal part of wisdom (Prov 1:7), i.e., it is the chief requirement for anyone who would live well and long, since life is the aim of wisdom (see R. E. Murphy, "The Kerygma of the Book of Proverbs," *Int* 20 [1966] 3–14). See also on 15:24, and cf. Prov 9:10; Ps 111:10; Job 28:28. Reverent piety ensures confidence and security. But the essence of this piety of the wisdom teachers is, as Duhm vigorously argued, the behavior of humans themselves. While elsewhere in Hebrew religion the initiative lies primarily with God, in the wisdom tradition religion is seen essentially as adherence to divine prescriptions for life. Whoever carries out these regulations has "integrity of way," and is "correct" (תם). God's role is to establish the standards, to react to obedience or disobedience appropriately, and to ensure the ultimately unfailing consequences of right behavior; so the God-fearing may be encouraged through thick and thin to have confidence in their piety.

Implicitly, Terrien writes, Eliphaz subscribes to the thesis of salvation by works. To say that today, however, is to put Eliphaz in the wrong. We must ask what else any of the friends or Job himself could have affirmed. To have denied Eliphaz's theology would have been to suggest that moral struggle is a waste or that God is essentially unjust (Andersen).

Eliphaz fails to help Job because his theology does not allow for the reality of a Job, of a righteous man who has no longer any ground for confidence, whose reverent piety has led him only away from assurance and toward despair. The only help a Job can be offered is the possibility of living, at a time of loss of assurance and abandonment of hope for life and weal, still in the confidence of the reality of God's goodness and wisdom. Rational wisdom finds that position impossibly self-contradictory. Only the encounter with the unavoidable but mysterious God can give Job, or the readers of the book, a firmly grounded confidence that does not negate the confidence of which Eliphaz speaks, but extends it beyond school wisdom to the case history of humankind.

7   Eliphaz's appeal to Job takes for granted Job's fundamental agreement with him. It is only a matter of Job's "recalling" and reflecting upon a truth that is as self-evident and well known to him as to Eliphaz; that will be enough to restore Job's equilibrium. This unquestionable truth, as it is in Eliphaz's eyes, is not that the righteous never *suffer,* but that they never wholly "perish" (אבד) nor are "annihilated" (כחד "be hidden, effaced, destroyed"; also used by Eliphaz in 15:28; 22:20). Eliphaz does not use any explicit term for death (neither in this verse nor in its counterpart, the description of the fate of the wicked, in v 9), but death is fairly clearly what he has in mind. In a word, Eliphaz's message is: the righteous do not die prematurely; Job is not dead; *ergo,* he is among the righteous and can afford to have hope (as v 6). (Pope regards an interpretation of Eliphaz's speech such as that here offered as "casuistry surpassing that of the friends"!)

It may appear quite improbable that Eliphaz's opinion, that the righteous are never "cut off" in the midst of their days, could ever have been seriously maintained. Yet, however cruel such a doctrine may be, its strength lies in the fact that it is unfalsifiable. If one already believes the doctrine, every instance of premature death is proof of the wickedness (however secret) of the victim, and serves only to support the validity of the original premise. Certainly, such a view is met with frequently, especially in texts influenced by the wisdom tradition (cf. Ps 37:25; 1:3; Ecclus 2:10) though also in popular superstition (cf. Acts 28:4), and the thought has been a consolation to many sufferers; cf. R. E. Prothero, *The Psalms in Human Life* [London: J. Murray, 1903] 257 (on Ps 37:25), and J. Bunyan, *Grace Abounding to the Chief of Sinners,* § 63–65 (*The Works of John Bunyan* [ed. G. Offer; London: Blackie and Son, 1862] 1:13) (on Ecclus 2:10).

However crude or cruel Eliphaz's view may be in the abstract, in the present circumstances it is doubly hurtful. In the first place, it is no consolation to Job to be reminded that as a righteous man he need have no fear of being cut off before his time; for Job not only has no wish to live out his appointed days but numbers himself among those "who long for death . . . who rejoice exceedingly . . . when they find the grave" (3:21–22). In the second place, Eliphaz's theology implicitly attributes the death of Job's seven sons and three daughters (1:2) to some sinfulness of theirs. That is hard enough for any father to have to listen to, but is even worse in Job's case since he had constantly gone out of his way to ensure that any shortcomings on their part had been adequately atoned for by sacrifice (1:5). Job has therefore failed his children as much as they have failed him. Now it is true that in the dialogues Job makes no reference to the loss of his children as one of the calamities that have befallen him; there may be reasons for this omission in the history of the growth of the book, but in the context of the book as it now stands the fate of Job's children is in the mind of its readers, and it is impossible not to see such implications in Eliphaz's speech even if its original author did not intend them. The "double entendre" elsewhere in Eliphaz's speech so elegantly analyzed by Fullerton is particularly ironic here: from Eliphaz's viewpoint he is being nothing but consolatory; heard with the ears of Job, though, his words only rub salt into Job's wounds. Our author's sympathies lie wholly with Job, and in putting these words into the mouth of Eliphaz, the kindliest representative of the orthodox dogmatic position, he damns that position for its (no doubt unintentional) heartlessness. The irony lies not in Eliphaz's words themselves—they are meant in a kindly spirit—but in their significance within the book as a whole.

8–11 In launching upon this elaborate and rhetorical set-piece (*topos*) on the fate of the wicked, Eliphaz does not for a moment mean to imply that Job is—or may perhaps be—in the company of the wicked. On the contrary, in his experience, those who "perish" (אבד) and are "shriveled" (כלה) are the wicked. Job is not among the wicked; therefore he may take comfort from Eliphaz that he will suffer no such fate (even if appearances are to the contrary).

8 In v 7 Eliphaz had appealed to Job's experience (though it was experience that he only assumed Job and he had in common); now he appeals to his own experience: "as I have seen" (כאשר ראיתי). He likes to put himself on the stage (Dhorme; cf. 4:12–21; 5:3, 8). But even if in speaking of what he has himself seen he is not deceiving himself, it is not objective observation—as if there were any such thing—that has given him this insight, but the traditional antitheses of the wisdom teachers (e.g., Prov 17:7, 8, 12, 13, 21) that have shaped his perception of reality. There is a false modesty and a false pride in Eliphaz here. He speaks only for himself, only out of his own experience, and yet at the same time he expects Job to accept that his experience is universally valid.

It is not that Eliphaz's vision is thoroughly warped. In its simplest form his principle is taken up by Paul: "Whatever you sow, that you will reap" (Gal 6:7). But there it is transmuted into a principle of eschatological dimensions: "The one who sows to please his sinful nature, from that nature will reap destruction; the one who sows to please the Spirit, from the Spirit will reap eternal life" (6:8 NIV; cf. also Rom 2:9–11). In Synoptic language, "the harvest-time is at the close of the age" (Matt 13:39). But in a setting bounded by birth and death, Eliphaz's principle may be allowed to function as a warning or encouragement (cf. its use in Ecclus 7:3), but it cannot be immutable law. To transpose the language of natural law ("sow/reap") to the sphere of human morality and fortune is a confidence trick. It supposes a deterministic nexus between act and consequence, and thus robs both God and humans of their freedom. Though it is often true that act and consequence correspond (cf. Hos 8:7; 10:13; Prov 22:8), it is also often untrue.

An important treatment of this topic was offered by K. Koch, "Gibt es ein Vergeltungsdogma im Alten Testament?" *ZTK* 52 (1955) 1–42, in which he argued that the OT is more familiar with the idea of the "fate-determining deed" (*schicksalentscheidend Tat*) than with a doctrine that God personally judges each misdeed and awards fitting retribution. By one's actions, Koch argues, one creates for oneself a sphere of woe or weal which surrounds one perpetually and belongs to one in the same way as does one's property (see also briefly Koch, *THWAT* 2:517). However, against this view, full allowance must be made for those criticisms of Koch which have stressed the personal involvement of Yahweh in retribution, not simply as "guarantor of the moral order" and as "a workman who oversees the regular running of his machines" (Koch, *ZTK* 52 [1955] 14). Most of these criticisms have been collected in a volume edited by Koch, *Um das Prinzip der Vergeltung in Religion und Recht des Alten Testaments* (Wege der Forschung 125; Darmstadt: Wissenschaftliche Buchgesellschaft, 1972), to which reference is made where appropriate below. See F. Horst, "Recht und Religion im Bereich des Alten Testaments," *EvT* 16 (1956) 711–74 (= Horst, *Gottes Recht. Gesammelte Studien zum Recht im Alten Testament* [Munich: Kaiser, 1961] 260–93; = Koch, *Prinzip,* 181–212); J. Scharbert, "Das Verbum PQD in der Theologie des Alten Testaments," *BZ* 4 (1960) 209–26 (= Koch, *Prinzip,* 278–99); idem, "ŠLM im Alten Testament," in *Lex Tua Veritas* (H. Junker Festschrift, ed. H. Gross and F. Mussner [Trier: Paulinus, 1961] 209–29 [= Koch, *Prinzip,* 300–324]); H. Graf Reventlow, "'Sein Blut komme über sein Haupt,'" *VT* 10 (1960) 311–27 (= Koch, *Prinzip,* 412–31). Further note Koch's modification of his position when in response to Reventlow he allowed that God is regarded as actively involved in the operation of bloodguilt retribution, and that the outworking of the "fate-determining deed" is not purely mechanical: "Der Spruch 'Sein Blut bleibe auf seinem Haupt' und die israelitische Auffassung vom vergossenen Blut," *VT* 12 (1962) 396–416 (= Koch, *Prinzip,* 432–56 [446]). For a convenient review and further critique, see J. G. Gammie, "The Theology of Retribution in the Book of Deuteronomy," *CBQ* 32 (1970) 1–12. Further literature: P. Zerafa, "Retribution in the OT," *Ang* 50 (1973) 464–94; J. K. Kuntz, "The Retribution Motif in Psalmic Wisdom," *ZAW* 89 (1977) 223–33.

The formulation of Eliphaz's thought is assisted by the dual significance of the Hebrew nouns אוֶן and עמל. Both can indicate either an act of wrongdoing or its consequence: אָוֶן "iniquity" (perhaps lit. "worthlessness"; cf. Driver) is sown and אָוֶן "punishment, misery" is reaped; עמל "mischief" or "trouble" for others is sown and עמל "sorrow, trouble" is reaped. See further on 15:35. Job has already described himself as one who has been brought into the world only to see "trouble" (עמל, 3:10), but Eliphaz is not intentionally insulting Job by assuming him to be the cause of his own misfortune (as against Dhorme, Weiser). But this is a prime example of the ironic difference between what Eliphaz intends and the effect he is likely to have produced in his auditor. Fullerton perceptively argued that this verse in the mouth of Eliphaz is the author's hint of a certain flaw in his character. "Eliphaz is pictured as so obsessed by the orthodox doctrine of rewards and punishments that, having formulated the comforting side of it [v 7], he almost unconsciously and automatically adds the threatening side as well, unmindful of the unfortunate inference Job might draw from it with regard to himself. . . . This unmindfulness [is] to be explained by the fact that Eliphaz, in the author's conception of him, is so addicted to general formulas as solvents for life's problems that he has lost all sense for reality" (*JBL* 49 [1930] 332–33).

9 Premature death for wrongdoers who have studiedly set about acquiring habits of evil (the metaphor of sowing may suggest the deliberate cultivation of sin or sinning of set purpose; so Rowley) is not produced wholly mechanically, by an inevitable and impersonal process. Nor is disaster produced by the wrong-doers themselves, as the symbol of harvest (v 8) may suggest. No, God is the agent of humans' annihilation when it occurs before the due time. True it is that the wicked have prepared their punishment for themselves; but without the active volition of God their crimes would lie hidden. God is not only the architect of the moral processes of the universe, but consciously their executor. The "breath" of God betokens his personal involvement in retribution.

The "breath" of God and the "wind of his fury" (lit., "spirit [*or*, breath, wind] of his nostril") play the part of the hot desert wind that consumes the Palestinian vegetation (cf. Hos 13:15; Isa 40:7; 2 Sam 22:16; Exod 15:7–8; and cf. 2 Thess 2:8). The "breath" (נשמה or רוח) of God is a mirror of his dynamic activity. It appears as a creative force in its own right (Gen 2:7; Job 34:14; Ps 104:29–30; Eccl 12:7; Ezek 37:5–6, 9–10; cf. Num 16:22; 27:16), and as token of God's creative power (Amos 4:13; Jer 10:13), as well as the means by which mighty acts of salvation are accomplished (Exod 14:21; Num 11:31). But it is also a destructive force (as here, and Isa 40:7; Hos 13:15), since God's power is not always exercised beneficently. See R. Albertz and C. Westermann, *THWAT* 2:726–53; N. H. Snaith, *The Distinctive Ideas of the OT* (London: Epworth, 1944) 143–58. Snaith's distinction between רוח as "hard, strong, violent breathing" and נשמה as "ordinary, quiet breathing" can hardly be sustained, but a good case can be made that נשמה is restricted to the breath of God that is also imparted to humans (T. C. Mitchell, "The Old Testament Usage of *nešāmâ*," *VT* 11 [1961] 177–87). Whether the "wind of [God's] fury" hints at the idea of eschatological judgment by fire (Terrien; E. Jacob, *Theology of the OT* [London: Hodder and Stoughton, 1958] 115) is open to question (see further *IDB* 2:269b).

Is the imagery of v 9 homogeneous with that of v 8? In v 8 there is to be a harvest of some sort; in v 9 there is to be no harvest at all (Fullerton, *JBL* 49 [1930] 345). But in v 8 the harvest is of consequences; in v 9 the destruction is of perpetrators of wickedness. The two images are distinct, and v 9 does not (as against Driver) describe what the harvest of v 8 is. And though v 9 may be a "rather vague generalization," its lack of strict attachment in imagery is no reason to delete it (as Fullerton, *JBL* 49 [1930] 345; cf. Duhm).

10–11 This portrayal of the destruction of lions is not syntactically connected with the fate of the wicked; many commentators have judged it irrelevant, the work of an inferior poet, or an insertion from a different poem (cf. Duhm, Fohrer, Weiser). Yet the wicked are frequently compared to lions in psalmic literature (Ps 7:3 [2]; 17:12; 22:14 [13], 22 [21]; 35:17; 58:7 [6]; 1QH 5.9–10); and cf. J. J. M. Roberts, "The Young Lions of Psalm 34,11" (*Bib* 54 [1973] 265–67), for Akkadian parallels suggesting the lion was a proverbial figure of self-assertion. No grammatical link with what precedes is needed to bring to a climax this triple-imaged description of the fate of the wicked (vv 8–11). It is all the more effective that the unrighteous whose destiny Eliphaz is envisaging

have by the end of his sketch (or *topos*) been metamorphosed *into* lions; they
are not *like* lions, but *are* lions, and as lions they may at any time perish for
lack of prey, or even break their teeth and so starve to death. What is at
issue is not the eventual death of the lions, as if that could be paralleled with
the eventual decay of the wicked (as Habel), but the unforeseeable calamity
that can strike at any moment: that is the already determined destiny of the
unrighteous.

Terrien seems to be wrong in finding in the lions' "roar" (שְׁאָגָה) a sly reference
to Job's cries of distress (Job has indeed spoken of his groaning as his "roarings,"
שַׁאֲגֹתַי, 3:24), as though to say that anyone who "roars" has put himself in
the company of lionlike evildoers. For the psalmist of Ps 22 also confesses to
"roaring" (שַׁאֲגָתִי, v 2), and it is Eliphaz's point that it is the wicked—and
therefore not people like Job—who come to such ultimate disaster.

12–21 The purpose of this remarkable and evocative passage is essentially
to explain how, though the distinction between righteous and wicked is firm,
the righteous can never be *perfectly* righteous, and therefore must expect to
experience—at least to some small extent—the misfortunes of the wicked.
Though the righteous will never "perish" in the sense of being cut off in
their prime, nevertheless they do suffer—as Job is witness. Eliphaz elaborately
impresses upon Job that the cause of such—temporary—suffering lies not in
Job alone: all created beings, even heavenly creatures, share in imperfection.
Since Job may not have realized this, in the absence of such experience as
Eliphaz has had, Eliphaz at once excuses Job and instructs him (Driver).

This second section of Eliphaz's speech falls into two parts: (1) a description
of his nocturnal experience (vv 12–16); (2) its content and the inferences to
be drawn from it (vv 17–21).

12–16 The knowledge that Eliphaz has to impart to Job about the quality
of righteousness is not gained by human learning. Eliphaz pushes beyond
the wisdom of the schools in maintaining that the distinction between righteous
and impious is not a black-and-white one; he must therefore appeal to some
supernatural insight for authority to make such a pronouncement. This is
not to deny the sincerity of Eliphaz's claim to extraordinary experience—though
its content raises some problems (see on v 17). It is indeed a most dramatically
evocative recollection of experience, not perhaps ranking with "the most wonderful triumphs of genius in the world's literature" (Peake), but indeed "wonderfully graphic" (E. C. S. Gibson), "one of the most uncanny in the OT" (Pope),
and at least "very spooky" (Andersen), and hardly "comic" (Terrien).

12 The revelation was made to Eliphaz personally: "to me" (אֵלַי) is in
emphatic position at the beginning of the sentence (cf. Eliphaz's self-assurance
in 15:17; 22:22). Although what he experienced was primarily an audition (a
"word" [דבר] and a "voice" [קוֹל, v 16]), it was accompanied by a vision (v 16)
and physical sensation (v 15). What reached him under cover of darkness
came, like a thief, "stealthily" (as in English, Heb. גנב "steal" can be used
metaphorically [cf. 2 Sam 19:4 (3)] though not, as against Fohrer, as a technical
term for the reception of supposed prophetic oracles). It was most like a prophetic experience, in which the combination of vision and audition is common
(e.g., Amos 7:7–9). Have we here then a wise man who pretends to be a
prophet? See on v 17. The mysteriousness (and also the exclusivity) of the
vision is further hinted at by his being able to catch only a fragment of heavenly

conversation. Clearly, even for Eliphaz the question of the suffering of the righteous can be answered, if at all, only by a "word" that brings a communication from the divine sphere. On this point see further F. Asensio Nieto, "La visión de Elifaz y su proyección sapiencial," *EstBíb* 35 (1976) 145–63.

13 It is difficult to know whether what Eliphaz describes is a dream or a waking vision. A "vision of the night" (חזיון לילה) need mean nothing other than a "dream" (cf. 7:14; 20:8; 33:15), but the experience of "waking visions" is also well attested (cf., e.g., W. James, *The Varieties of Religious Experience* [New York: Longmans, Green, 1902] 59–62, 481–83), and it may be such that Eliphaz is depicting (so Fohrer). See further E. L. Ehrlich, *Der Traum im Alten Testament* (BZAW 73; Berlin: Töpelmann, 1953).

It is usually assumed that the "deep sleep" (תרדמה) Eliphaz here speaks of is his own sleep or state of trance in which he received his vision, and it is commonly argued that the very term signifies the supernatural source of his sleep and vision. Thus we read of Eliphaz's "trance more deep than sleep" (Fullerton, *JBL* 49 [1930] 347), of "trancelike, hypnotic, mantic sleep" (S. Terrien, *The Elusive Presence* [New York: Harper and Row, 1978] 78). It is said to be not natural refreshing sleep, but an extraordinary supernatural mood of anesthesia, in which a person feels and perceives nothing (as in Gen 2:21; 1 Sam 26:12; Isa 29:10) or else is sensitized to experiencing a divine revelation (Gen 15:12; Job 33:15); it is an atmosphere propitious for divine revelations (Terrien). It must be emphasized, however, that there is nothing in the term itself that requires such a significance, and the noun and its related verb are in fact frequently enough used of perfectly natural, though especially deep, sleep. In Prov 19:15, for example, it signifies the deep sleep induced by slothfulness. Elsewhere the verb רדם "sleep" is used of natural sleep in Judg 4:21; Jonah 1:5, 6; Prov 10:5; probably also Job 33:15; possibly also Dan 8:18; 10:9. The fact that it "falls" (נפל) upon people (as here, and Gen 2:21; 15:12; 1 Sam 26:12; Job 33:15; cf. Prov 19:15) or is "poured out" (נסך) upon them (Isa 29:10) does not mean necessarily that it is supernaturally induced. These observations enable us to suggest that the sleep Eliphaz here speaks of is not some supernatural trance of his own but the ordinary sleep of other mortals: while they slept soundly in their beds, he was subject to a terrifying waking vision. See further D. J. A. Clines, "Job 4,13: A Byronic Suggestion" (*ZAW* 92 [1980] 289–91), citing the line of Byron, "Deep sleep came down on ev'ry eye save mine" (T. L. Ashton [ed.], *Byron's Hebrew Melodies* [London: Routledge and Kegan Paul, 1972] 145). No doubt in ancient times, also, night terrors were known; much worse than nightmares, and sometimes fatal, they are termed today the "nocturnal death syndrome" in which healthy young males die in their sleep.

14 "First of all comes the terror, with no apparent cause; . . . the sudden sense of the presence [is] felt before it has made itself manifest to ear, eye, or touch" (Peake). This terror in the presence of the numinous is frequently portrayed (e.g., Gen 15:12; Dan 8:17; 10:8, 10), and on numerous occasions meets with the divine response "Fear not!" (e.g., Gen 15:1; 26:24; Isa 40:9; 44:8). On the formula as an element in the typical salvation-oracle, see W. E. March in J. H. Hayes (ed.), *Old Testament Form Criticism* (San Antonio: Trinity UP, 1974) 163; H. Gressmann, "Die literarische Analyse Deuterojesajas," *ZAW* 34 (1914) 254–97; L. Köhler, "Die Offenbarungsformel 'Fürchte dich nicht!'

im Alten Testament," *SchwTZ* 36 (1919) 33–39; J. Begrich, "Das priesterliche Heilsorakel," *ZAW* 52 (1934) 81–92; J. Becker, *Gottesfurcht im Alten Testament* (AnBib 25; Rome: Pontifical Biblical Institute, 1965) 50–55; S. Plath, *Furcht Gottes. Der Begriff* ירא *im Alten Testament* (Stuttgart: Calwer, 1963) 114–22; H. M. Dion, "The Patriarchal Traditions and the Literary Form of the 'Oracle of Salvation,'" *CBQ* 29 (1967) 198–206; E. Conrad, *Fear Not, Warrior: A Study of ᵓal tîrā᾽ Pericopes in the Hebrew Scriptures* (BJS 75; Chico, Calif.: Scholars Press, 1985).

Eliphaz's fear of the uncanny or supernatural is manifested in physical symptoms. "The *bones*, as the supporting framework of the body, are often in Heb. poetry taken as representing it; and affections, and even emotions, pervading or affecting strongly a man's being, are poetically attributed to them, or conceived as operating in them" (Driver). Starting from the message that entered the ear, the whole body is activated (H. W. Wolff, *Anthropology of the Old Testament* [tr. M. Kohl; London: SCM, 1974] 75).

15 Eliphaz's description of physical terror in the presence of the supernatural continues. The change of tense from the descriptive perfects of v 14 to the historical presents of v 16 adds to the vividness of the scene. He could have had the uncanny experience of a draught of air from an unknown quarter brushing past his face and making the hair of his whole body—not just his head, as our idiom has it—stand on end in his fright. The bristling of body hair, known as pilo-erection, is a well-known physiological reaction to fear; it is brought about by the *arrectores pilorum* muscles and contributes to the thermal insulation of the body (H. Davson and M. B. Segal, *Introduction to Physiology* [London/New York: Academic Press/Grune and Stratton, 1976], 3:68). S. M. Paul cites several Akkadian medical texts referring to hair standing on end when a person encounters a demon ("Job 4,15—A Hair Raising Encounter," *ZAW* 95 [1983] 119–21). And Gilgamesh, waking in the middle of the night in terror, asks, "Why am I startled? Did some god go by? Why is my flesh aquiver?" (*Gilgamesh* 5.4.11–12; *ANET*, 83).

There is no question that his experience has been terrifying, but rather than describing a mysterious wind, it seems more likely that Eliphaz is describing a theophany. The "wind" (רוח) and the "whirlwind"—if that is how שְׂעָרַת (or, emended, שְׂעָרָה) is to be taken—are elsewhere also an accompaniment of a divine appearance (cf. 1 Kgs 19:11, "a great and strong wind [רוח]"; Ezek 1:4, "the wind of a storm [רוח סערה]"; cf. 2 Sam 22:11, Yahweh rides "upon the wings of the wind [רוח]"; in Nah 1:3 his way is "in storm and whirlwind [בסופה ובשערה]"; and note especially Yahweh's speaking from the "whirlwind" [סערה], elsewhere in Job, 38:1; 40:6). See further on v 16. On the whirlwind as a natural phenomenon in Israel, see D. Baly, *Geography of the Bible* (London: Lutterworth, 1957) 65–66; D. Nir, "Whirlwinds in Israel in the Winters 1954–55 and 1955–56," *IEJ* 7 (1957) 109–17; R. B. Y. Scott, "Whirlwind," *IDB* 4:841.

16 The vagueness with which the supernatural visitor is introduced heightens the terror (Peake). rsv "It stood still" would refer us back to the "spirit" of v 15, but since reason has already been shown for rejecting that translation of רוח, we are left with the anonymity of the subject of יעמד "he/it stood." Like the disaster in v 5, such a terrifying apparition must not be identified by a concrete word (Terrien). Lust (*Bijd* 36 [1975] 310 n. 8) takes תמונה "a form," which comes in the next line of the verse, as the subject; this is possible, for though the noun is feminine, the gender of the verb may be determined *ad sensum* (cf. GKC, § 145o).

The "figure" that Eliphaz saw was "unrecognizable" (לֹא־אַכִּיר מַרְאֵהוּ, "I did not recognize its/his face/appearance"). This is no doubt because we are meant to suspect that the "form" (תְּמוּנָה) and the "appearance" (מַרְאֶה) are those of God himself. Strikingly, תְּמוּנָה always refers to God or to some representation of God: in Num 12:8 Yahweh says that with Moses he speaks "mouth to mouth, clearly, and not in dark speech; and he beholds the form of Yahweh (תְּמֻנַת יְהוָה)." This is a privilege reserved to Moses; Israel at Horeb "heard the sound of words, but saw no form (תְּמוּנָה); there was only a voice" (Deut 4:12; cf. 4:15). In Ps 17:15 the "form" of Yahweh is parallel with his "face" (פָּנִים). Elsewhere תְּמוּנָה refers to representations of God (Exod 20:4; Deut 4:16, 23, 25; 5:8). Thus Eliphaz is claiming that he has both seen (v 16) and heard (vv 15, 17) God. It is not surprising that he couches his report in cryptic language, nor that some of the earliest translations negated the sentence (LXX οὐκ ἦν μορφή; cf. Pesh).

As already noted, several features traditionally associated with theophanies appear here: the sense of terror in the presence of the numinous (v 14), the violent storm-wind (v 15), and the thundering sound (v 16). See J. Jeremias, *Theophanie. Die Geschichte einer alttestamentlichen Gattung* (WMANT 10; Neukirchen-Vluyn: Neukirchener Verlag, 1970) 105–8; F. Dumermuth, "Biblische Offenbarungensphänomene," *TZ* 21 (1965) 1–21; J. Lindblom, "Theophanies in Holy Places in Hebrew Religion," *HUCA* 32 (1961) 91–106. The storm theophany as distinct from the earthquake theophany is analyzed (though without reference to Job) by E. C. Kingsbury, "The Theophany *Topos* and the Mountain of God," *JBL* 86 (1967) 205–10. On the relation between the prohibitions of representations of Yahweh, which may be traced to the Sinai traditions, and the references to the visibility of Yahweh (especially in visions), which belong to the desert traditions (Exod 24:9–11) and those of the Jerusalem temple, see H. Schmid, "Gottesbild, Gottesschau und Theophanie," *Jud* 23 (1967) 241–54. H.-P. Müller ("Die kultische Darstellung der Theophanie," *VT* 14 [1964] 183–91) explores the relationship between the Sinai traditions and the portrayal of theophany in the Jerusalem cult. On the whole topic of theophany, see especially J. K. Kuntz, *The Self-Revelation of God* (Philadelphia: Westminster, 1967).

Several Near Eastern parallels to Eliphaz's dream experience exist. A dream of Gilgamesh in the Cedar Forest is thus recounted:

> Sleep, which is shed on mankind, fell on him.
> In the middle watch, he ended his sleep.
> He started up, saying to his friend:
> "My friend, didst thou not call me? Why am I awake?
> Didst thou not touch me? Why am I startled?
> Did not some god go by? Why is my flesh numb?
> My friend, I saw a third dream,
> And the dream that I saw was wholly awesome!
> The heavens shrieked, and earth boomed,
> [Day]light failed, darkness came.
> Lightning flashed, a flame shot up . . ."
> —(Gilgamesh, 5.4.7–17; *ANET,* 83a).

17 Almost every reader of Eliphaz's speech is struck by the apparent banality of the utterance that forms the climax of the scene portrayed in vv 12–16. Especially if the more straightforwardly grammatical translation is accepted ("Can a man be more righteous than God?"), the comment of Peake is wholly appropriate: "So trivial a commonplace as that man is not more righteous than God needed no vision to declare it; and it is quite irrelevant in this connexion," since it is only later that Job questions the justice of God (e.g., 9:19–20; 10:2–7; 16:20; 19:7; 24:1), and in each of these places an exposition of Job's attitude has to be subtly modulated. There is never a question in Job's mind of humans being *more* righteous than God.

To save the reputation, therefore, of both Job and Eliphaz, as well as that of the author of the book, the broader context must be allowed to prevail, and the words מאלוה and מעשהו must be translated "before God" and "before his Maker" (see n. 4:17.c). Even so, can we affirm that this supernatural utterance, preceded by the panoply of theophany, is worthy of the occasion? Up to a point, yes. This insight, which Eliphaz is at such pains to impress upon Job, does indeed break out of the usual categories in which the wisdom movement, and the Book of Job itself, usually conducts its debates. Fundamental to the typical OT statements of the principle of retribution (however that is nuanced; see on v 8 above) is that humanity is divided into two camps, the righteous and the wicked. Eliphaz himself, as if in disregard of this divinely vouchsafed truth, has already addressed Job as one of the righteous—without any qualification: Job's piety (יראתך) and blameless life (תם דרכיך, v 6) should give him grounds for hope, while the rhetorically developed contrast between the innocent and the evildoers (vv 7–11) makes the same assumption of a hard-and-fast distinction (cf. also in the same speech, the contrast between 5:2–5 and 5:17–26). So in this respect, that Eliphaz has been made aware that terms like "righteous" and "innocent" are simply rule-of-thumb designations that do not correspond to the reality of a universe where only God is truly "righteous," v 17 is a more profound statement than most of the OT finds it necessary to make (though cf. Ps 14:2, 3; 53:3, 4 [2, 3], where there seems, however, to be no more than a rhetorical overstatement; see, however, the use made of these passages in Rom 3:9–12).

The force of this verse is easy to see. If Job, like all humans, is less than perfectly righteous, he must expect to share to some degree in the suffering that is meted out to the unrighteous. His present suffering is therefore no more than a marginal element in his assured and generally consistent good fortune which, as a pious man, he is entitled to expect. Eliphaz here, as throughout this speech, is entirely consolatory.

It is exactly here, however, that one begins to consider more closely the author's intention in putting these words into Eliphaz's mouth. However true they may be in theory—and we are not meant by the author to doubt that these are divinely inspired words—they are plainly inappropriate to Job's case. For, in the first place, Job is not suffering some trifling misadventure that can be blamed on his falling short of absolute perfection, but is devastated entirely; and though he has not in fact been "cut off," as one may have expected a wicked man to have been (vv 8–9; cf. 5:3–4), he is in an even worse plight than that, since that very fate is what he desires but is denied (3:20–23). And in the second place, the question of human imperfection over against divine perfection is quite outside the ambit of the book as a whole; God's power, wisdom, and mystery are issues in the debate between Job and the friends or between Job and God, but not God's righteousness *as contrasted to* Job's. It may be true that no creature is sinless, but sinfulness is not a logical necessity inherent in creatureliness; and since the righteousness of Job is on all sides admitted (1:1, 8; 2:3; 4:6; 8:20; 42:7–8; etc.), the fact that Job is only a creature of God's is irrelevant to the question whether he has deservedly suffered.

Is this then not the author's supreme irony in this speech of Eliphaz, that at the very point where Eliphaz dares to press beyond the conventional school wisdom and to question a simplistic dogma of retribution, his tenor becomes even more alien to Job, and the dogma is doubly hurtful because it both makes light of Job's suffering and casts doubt on Job's integrity? It is indeed Job's only hope to maintain his integrity (as Eliphaz has in fact seen, v 6) *and* to insist upon the severity of his suffering (6:2–3, 11–13). Eliphaz, says Fullerton, is "a type of a certain kind of dogmatic theologian whose presuppositions are supposed to be divine revelation . . . and whose eyes are therefore blind to all that does not fit into the preconceived pattern. Now the difficulty with such persons is that they are *unintentionally* cruel. . . . They may have sympathy, but it is an abstract sympathy. . . . They are unable to feel their way into ideas or experiences alien to their own. Dogma has a terrible power to dull the imagination, and without imagination sympathy is unable to help" (*JBL* 49 [1930] 336–37). The author does not mock the dogma of Eliphaz; he mocks the presumed efficacy of dogma to alleviate suffering. And the heightening tension of vv 12–16, climaxed with this thunderous word from God out of the whirlwind, only demonstrates the inadequacy of dogma, humanly conceived or divinely revealed, to suit Job's case.

What Job wants is not to *be* righteous, since he is—for a human, at any rate—righteous enough already, but to be *declared* righteous by God (see 9:2, "How can a man be declared righteous by God?") by being delivered from suffering and restored to prosperity. What Eliphaz has offered him is an apparently unequivocal divine statement that denies both the possibility of human beings' actual righteousness when judged from God's perspective and the reasonableness of expecting from God a public certification of unqualified righteousness.

Eliphaz understands the divine rhetorical question of this verse as equivalent to a categorical negative (cf. Prov 20:9; Eccl 7:20). But what does the author of the book—assuming that he is not leading us on in claiming this as an oracular revelation—understand by the question? God only asks a question. Who says it is a rhetorical question? It is a question worth considering if one has never doubted the possibility of righteousness before God, but it does not have to be answered negatively. Our author tells of a man who not only is righteous before God (42:7–8), but actually "justifies" God by proving God in the right in his contest with the Satan (1:8–12; 2:3–6). In the story of Job, a human acts *more* righteously, not less, than the "sons of God" can manage. So if it is God's question, it is a provocative question that calls for further thought and debate, and not an emptily rhetorical question.

18 Almost all commentators and versions that indicate quoted speech regard vv 18–21 (or vv 18–20 if v 21 is secondary) as part of the divine speech heard by Eliphaz. With Weiser (and perhaps Andersen), however, I regard v 17 alone as the divine word of revelation, and vv 18–21 as wisdom's extensions of it.

It may then be asked from where Eliphaz derives his idea of the untrustworthiness and "folly" of the "messengers" or angels, if not from some divine revelation. Certainly, it is agreed by commentators, there is no reference here to the fully developed idea of "fallen angels" as found in the intertestamental literature (e.g., *1 Enoch* 6–9; 15; 64; *Adam and Eve* 12–16; see J. A. Sanders, "Dissenting Deities and Philippians 2:1–11," *JBL* 88 [1969] 279–90 [284–88]; P. D. Hanson, "Rebellion in Heaven, Azazel, and Euhemeristic Heroes in 1 Enoch 6–11," *JBL* 96 [1977] 195–233). But the story of the union of the "sons of God" with the daughters of men in Gen 6:1–4 is adequate traditional background for this assessment of angels' reliability. It should be noted that a similar indictment is made by Bildad (25:5) without reference either to Eliphaz or to supernatural revelation. Pope mentions a case in the Ugaritic Baal myth where some such (female) servants of the gods are reproached for gross misbehavior.

Heavenly beings are referred to in Job relatively infrequently. Apart from the prologue, two scenes of which are set in the heavenly court of Yahweh and his "angels," they are referred to in the dialogue by the term "holy ones" (קדשים, 5:1; 15:15—a passage in a speech of Eliphaz, and directly parallel to the present one, where the term מלאכים is used). Elsewhere the heavenly beings are known simply as קדשים in Deut 33:3; Ps 89:6 [5], 8 [7]; Zech 14:5; see M. Noth, "The Holy Ones of the Most High," in *The Laws in the Pentateuch* (Edinburgh: Oliver and Boyd, 1966) 215–28 (= *Interpretationes ad Vetus Testamentum pertinentes Sigmundo Mowinckel septuagenario missae* [Oslo: Forlaget Land og Kirche, 1955] 146–61); H.-P. Müller, *THWAT* 2:589–609 (601–2); but for the meaning "heathen gods" in Hos 12:1 [11:12]; Ps 16:3; Prov 30:3, see M. Pope, *El in the Ugaritic Texts* (VTSup 2; Leiden: Brill, 1955) 13–14. They are not "holy" in virtue of their own moral perfection, for they are open to criticism and judgment (Job 21:22; Isa 24:21); rather "holy" has its usual meaning of "belonging to God." Their "holiness" resides solely in their closeness to Yahweh. See further on holiness J. Milgrom, "The Compass of Biblical Sancta," *JQR* 65 (1975) 205–16; O. R. Jones, *The Concept of Holiness* (London: Allen and Unwin, 1961).

19 The familiar rhetorical argumentation *a maiore ad minus* (Heb. קל וחמר) is put to good use by Eliphaz, for whom the fragility and mortality of human beings seems some kind of evidence for their lack of moral reliability. Humankind is portrayed, in clear reminiscence of Gen 2:7, as "dwellers in houses of clay," themselves founded on dust. They are "built of earth, derived from earth, limited to earth. The accumulation of terms enhances the material nature of man" (Davidson). Their "foundations" signify their "conditions of existence" (Budde; cf. 22:16; Prov 10:25). If the "houses" are human bodies, as most commentators think, this would be the first reference in Hebrew literature to the idea of the body as the residence of the human being (but see later texts: Wisd 9:15 "the earthen shelter [γεῶδες σκῆνος] weighs down the mind" [NAB]; 1QH 3.23–24; 18.12; 2 Cor 5:1; 2 Pet 1:13). Certainly human origin from clay or dust is mentioned elsewhere in Job (10:9 [Job]; 33:6 [Eliphaz]). But if Ehrlich is right in seeing here simply a reference to literal clay houses in which humans dwell as contrasted to the heavenly dwelling-places of the angels, Eliphaz would be arguing that humans are more likely to sin than are the angels, not only because they are mortal but because they live in inferior accommodation! Like George Herbert, they would be "guilty of dust *and* sinne" ("Love. III," *The English Poems of George Herbert* [ed. C. A. Patrides; London: Dent, 1974] 192). In either case it is taken for granted that matter is inferior to "spirit" (רוח), that "nobler, more fine substance" (Duhm), a sentiment one would have thought less at home with a Hebrew view of creation than with a Gnostic conception of the world. See K. Rahner, "The Unity of Spirit and Matter: A Christian Understanding," in *Man before God,* ed. D. Burkhard et al., 25–51; O. Schilling, *Geist und Materie in biblischer Sicht. Eine exegetischer Beitrag zur Diskussion um Teilhard de Chardin* (Bibelstudien 25; Stuttgart: Verlag Katholische Bibelwerk, 1967) esp. 18–34.

What does "crushed before the moth" (rsv) mean? The moth is a ready image for the instantly destroyable, though it so happens that elsewhere in the Bible the moth is proverbial not for its fragility but for its destructiveness (13:28; Isa 50:9; 51:8; Matt 6:19, 20; James 5:2). That is no reason to deny that "moth" may present a different image here. "Before" (לפני) may indeed mean "like" (as in 3:24) rather than "before" temporally, i.e., "sooner than"—which would be rather excessive hyperbole. We should notice at this point a distinct change that has come over the flow of the logic. The first two cola of the verse depict a universal truth about humankind: they all dwell in houses of clay whose foundation is in the dust. But they do *not* all get crushed like a moth or perish forever without anyone noticing (v 20b) or die without gaining wisdom (v 21b). Vv 19c–21b present therefore not the universal fate of humans, but the *danger* their precarious existence lays them open to: they *can* be crushed like a moth, they *may* die and never be noticed, they *can* live and die without ever acquiring wisdom. See further D. J. A. Clines, "Verb Modality and the Interpretation of Job iv 20–21," *VT* 30 (1980) 354–57.

20 The exposure of humankind to sudden and unpredictable death, described in v 19c with the image of the crushing of a moth (or perhaps, bird's nest; see n. 4:19.e), is further pictured in these two verses. Whether the sudden crushing or beating to powder (כתת) resumes the metaphor of the clay houses (Fohrer) is not clear; the image may be that of the smashing of a clay vessel, like that in Isa 30:14: "smashed (כתות) so ruthlessly that among its fragments not a sherd is found with which to take fire from the hearth, or to dip up water from the cistern" (rsv).

Not only are human creatures liable to rapid annihilation, between a dawn and a dusk, but their life can be so cheap that they may perish utterly or forever (לנצח will support either rendering), without their passing being noticed. Noticed by whom? is a question that arises. It is not that God does not notice, though Eliphaz has not covered himself very well against that possible interpretation of his words. Andersen, for example, writes: "Eliphaz's well-meant exaltation of God has led to a horrible result. If He cannot be bothered with angels, how much less would He care about men" (similarly Terrien). But it is not a question of God's "bothering about" angels, and Eliphaz is not concerned to deny that God has any interest in the fate of human being; that would be contrary to his whole philosophy. A more likely interpretation is that the victims of sudden disaster do not themselves foresee nor are they aware of what is happening to them; in this case the phrase מבלי משים "without setting it to heart" would continue the emphasis of v 20a: "between dawn and dusk." Thus Gordis translates, "While they pay no heed, they are destroyed forever," and v 21b yields a parallel sense, "they die, having gained no wisdom." An interesting view was propounded by Horst, that it is the power of death itself that blindly sweeps mortals away without consideration and without any discrimination (v 21b). That would suit the sense well, except that death is not here personified or the subject of any verb. However, the best understanding is to assume that v 20b and v 21b are not parallel, and to take מבלי משים as "without any one (else) taking any notice"; cf. KJV, RSV "without any regarding it"; "unheeded" (NEB), "unnoticed" (NIV) ("and no one remembers them" [JB] is not quite the point).

21 The image here is of death as the uprooting of a tent, in which tent-pegs are pulled up and ropes loosened, in order for the occupant to move to another place. The human being is the tent, the focus and hub of varied and incessant activity. The apparently minor action of pulling up the pegs collapses a whole world of activity into a piece of inert material. The image is not of the tent as the body "in" which the person lives (as was perhaps the case with the "clay houses" of v 19) but rather the person itself; hence there is no serious conflict between the metaphors of vv 19 and 21. Cf. Isa 38:12, "My dwelling is taken from me, pulled up like a shepherd's tent"—where Hezekiah speaks of his impending death (cf. v 12b "you have cut short my life").

The merest tinkering with the fabric of human existence, and the person is *dead;* for the first time, in the very last line of this half of the speech, Eliphaz uses *the* word that elsewhere he has avoided by euphemism, vaguer term, or metaphor. And there is a sting in the tail, also. Humans not only die, but die without gaining wisdom. Various interpretations of this phrase are discussed in n. 4:21.d, but it seems improbable that חכמה, "wisdom," can be used in any sense of mere "awareness." "Wisdom" is true insight—into the way one should live, into the nature of things, into the ways of God and humankind. Death without knowledge (דעת) is the fate of the wicked who will not listen to God's reproofs, according to Elihu (36:12), whereas the godly, conscious of the brevity of life, pray that they may be taught to "number" their days so as to acquire a heart of "wisdom" (חכמה). Wisdom in Proverbs is the source of salvation from crooked behavior (2:10–15); it bestows long life (3:13, 16); it preserves from the "strange woman," Lady Folly and false religion (7:4–5); it is the mark of the righteous (14:32–34; 10:31).

To die without being noticed (v 20) is unfortunate; to die without ever having obtained wisdom is culpable. If Eliphaz were speaking of the wicked, as Elihu is in 36:12, his sentence would be understandable. But he is speaking of humankind generally, and it is going too far to assert that humanity at large dies without wisdom. Can it be that Eliphaz's rhetoric has led him beyond his intention; once embarked on his theme of the feebleness and mortality of the human race, has he forgotten where to stop? Can he, in his desire to affirm that no one is thoroughly righteous, have asserted that all humans are thoroughly lacking in wisdom? The rhetoric of these speeches has a potent effect, even more upon the interlocutors than upon their hearers; but it is not necessary to believe that Eliphaz has so far forgotten himself as to conclude by destroying his original premise: that there exists a distinction between the righteous and the wicked (vv 7, 8), and that Job's hope derives solely from knowing to which camp of humanity he is attached (v 6).

Let us take our clue from v 20. Eliphaz cannot be saying that human beings universally die "between dawn and dusk," for some suffer lingering deaths, and others (to be prosaic) die between dusk and dawn. Nor can he be asserting that all die without being noticed, or, if the translation is otherwise, without being aware of what is befalling them. His point is the fragility of humankind: they *can* be crushed between morning and evening; they may not, for the fragile can survive beyond expectation. Here in v 21, it is not to his purpose to claim that humankind as a whole (himself included!) invariably dies "without wisdom," but that it is possible for someone to live and die without ever having acquired the rudiments of what the schoolmen of his time regarded as essential for a truly human existence. It is enough that such should be a possibility for *some* human beings to call in question the quality of human existence. Nuanced in this way, Eliphaz's speech is fully coherent.

5:1 Job's cry hitherto has been a cry against life (3:3, 11, 16, 20–22) and so it will be also in the speech that responds to Eliphaz (chaps. 6–7; cf. 6:8–9; 7:16). But Eliphaz supposes, since he cannot bring himself to believe that anyone would really want to die, that Job may be nurturing an appeal for the healing of his suffering. Job may indeed number himself among those who "long for death" (3:21) and who "rejoice exceedingly . . . when they find the grave" (3:22), but Eliphaz has convinced himself that Job's real desire is for a calm and peaceful existence such as he pictures in 5:19–26. Now if such a cry for deliverance is in Job's heart, Eliphaz says, he may as well stifle it, for there is no power, not even among the heavenly beings, that can release Job from the nexus of sin and punishment in which he is caught.

Eliphaz's attitude toward Job has been made clear in the previous chapter: Job is essentially a righteous man, but—like any human (or angel; cf. 4:18)—he has his faults and is suffering for them. Job's goodness has long been evident (4:3–4), and his fear of God and personal integrity are rightful grounds for confidence that his suffering will not last for long (4:6). He may rest assured that he will never perish utterly, for every righteous person has found ultimate deliverance (4:7). However, Job shares the moral frailty of all created beings (4:17–19); so his sinfulness—not specified in this speech, but see on 22:6–9—must be recompensed, and no appeal can get him off the hook of retributive justice. These lines have been the inspiration for the powerful opening lines of Rainer Maria Rilke's *Duino Elegies:* "Wer, wenn ich schreie, hörte mich denn aus der Engel/Ordnungen? und gesetzt selbst, es nähme/einer mich plötzlich aus Herz: ich verginge von seinem/starkeren Dasein. . . . Ein jeder Engel ist schrecklich." ("Who, if I called, would hear me from among the ranks of angels? Even if one should clasp me suddenly to its heart, I should perish from its stronger being. . . . Every angel is terrible" [*Duino Elegies* (tr. C. F. MacIntyre; Berkeley: University of California Press, 1961) 2–3].

Other understandings of this verse have been plentiful. It is often supposed, for example, that any appeal to the "holy ones" would be an act of wrath such as is said in v 2 to slay the fool; several commentators similarly propose that Eliphaz is likening Job's behavior to that of the "fool" whose fortune will be described in vv 2–5. But it seems improbable that an appeal for deliverance from suffering should be regarded by Eliphaz as a fatal form of anger (impatience is not the topic in v 2), and unlikely that Eliphaz should regard Job's reaction to his suffering as anger when the only feelings he has ascribed to Job are "weakness" and "dismay" (4:5; cf. ותבהל, ותלא). More persuasive is the suggestion that any appeal to the "holy ones" is futile because they too are morally frail (4:18); but there seems to be no good reason why the intercession of angels should be wholly nullified by their lack of perfection. The futility of any appeal Job makes lies not in the quarter to which he directs it but in the fact of the appeal itself; he has no right to do anything but bear with fortitude (contrast his "weakness" [לאה] in 4:5) the suffering that has come upon him. For further discussion, see D. J. A. Clines, "Job 5,1–8: A New Exegesis," *Bib* 62 (1981) 185–94.

The heavenly beings or angels are called "holy ones" (as also in 15:15; Deut 33:3; Ps 89:6, 8 [5, 7]; Zech 14:5; Dan 4:14; 8:13; Ecclus 42:17; *1 Enoch* 1.9; etc.) "not on account of moral perfection (ct. 4:18), but of their proximity to God" (Driver). The idea of angels as intercessors or as mediators between humanity and God here makes an untimely appearance; for further discussion, see on 33:23 (Elihu). Some have seen Eliphaz's statement of the hopelessness of appeal to any divine being as a polemic against the Mesopotamian idea of a "personal" god to whom one could turn to speak on one's behalf in the assembly of the greater gods (so Pope; cf. Andersen). Such a background need not be supposed, since Eliphaz's view follows naturally from his conception of the gulf between heavenly beings and God. Others have regarded the verse as a late addition, the theory being that the concept of intercessory angels developed only late in Israel's history (so, e.g., Duhm); but we may be skeptical of efforts to date concepts like this, especially when we cannot date the book itself with any accuracy.

2 This sentence sounds like an aphorism from the Book of Proverbs. Its subject is the "fool," who is encountered rarely in Job (apart from the present passage, we can note only 30:8; 2:10 [נָבָל, נְבָלָה]) though he makes numerous appearances in Proverbs.

The word used for "fool" (אֱוִיל) does not denote one who is only unwise but one who is positively unrighteous, "always morally bad" (BDB, 17a); the "fool" of Ps 14:1 who says "There is no God" is no different from the "wicked" of Ps 10:4 who says just the same thing; see also the description of the activities of the fool (נבל) in Isa 32:5–6 (cf. *THWAT* 2:29–30). In parallelism to אויל is the term פֹּתֶה, often translated "simple" (so RSV). However, it is not the related adjective (פֶּתִי), which usually means the "innocent" or "inexperienced" or "untutored youth" (W. McKane, *Prophets and Wise Men* [SBT 44; London: SCM, 1965] 265, 342), but rather the participle of the verb, the strength of which is determined here by the key term "fool" (אֱוִיל).

Eliphaz can hardly be classing Job among such impious "fools," since he has affirmed Job's general—though not absolute—innocence. Neither can the fate of the fool's children (v 4), who suffer because they are deprived of a father, be at all apposite to Job's case, in which it is the children who have died while the father remains alive. (It is true that Eliphaz is sometimes insensitive to Job's calamities, as in 5:25 where he assures him that his "descendants will be many"; but if Job is the fool in v 2, Eliphaz is not just insensitive but thoroughly illogical.) A somewhat more likely possibility is that Eliphaz means Job *would be* a fool if he allowed his "resentment" and "anger" to slay him.

But quite apart from the fact that he has not previously attributed these emotions to Job (cf. on v 1 above), the inappositeness of the reference to the fool's children would still remain, and it would be simple folly, not impiety (as implied by אֱוִיל), to allow his "weakness" (cf. 4:5) to harden into "resentment."

The case of the "fool" who comes to some unspecified ruin is therefore not directly applicable to Job (as against, for example, H. A. Brongers, "Der Eifer des Herrn Zebaoth," *VT* 13 [1963] 269–84 [278–79]) but illustrative of some broader principle Eliphaz is trying to convey. That principle is spelled out very clearly in vv 6–7: affliction, or suffering, is not self-produced but human-produced. "It is man that breeds trouble for himself" (JB, v 7; for the translation, see n. 5:7.a). The fool brings about his own death by his anger. Job is no fool, and he is not in danger of death, not at least as Eliphaz sees it. But Job's suffering is self-induced, the result of his relative impurity in the sight of his Maker (4:17). Therefore there is no escape from the suffering Job is undergoing at the moment; it will no doubt be temporary (cf. 5:8), and there is no reason to think it will be fatal (cf. 4:7). It is, however, real and unavoidable. Thus this sentence about the fool (v 2) begins with "for" (כִּי): it is pointless to appeal to the "holy ones" for premature relief from self-induced suffering, *for* the principle of the causal nexus between sin and suffering must be allowed to work itself out.

We may wonder how passions like resentment and anger can "slay" a person. Terrien indeed regards the anger as the *divine* anger that the fool has incurred (cf. also Tg), but Horst fairly points out that when God's anger is referred to, the context usually makes it quite clear (cf. Deut 29:19 [20]; Ezek 5:13; etc.). In Prov 27:3, where the fool's resentment (כַּעַס אֱוִיל) is again referred to as something heavier than a stone or sand, it seems to be the effect of the fool's anger upon others that is in mind. Most commentators who consider the question decide that the fool is slain by allowing his suffering to cause him to murmur at his lot and so bring down upon himself further calamities (so Davidson, Driver; cf. Peake). A much less far-fetched explanation lies close at hand: it is a well-known piece of proverbial wisdom that "A tranquil mind gives life to the flesh, but anger [קִנְאָה, the same word as here] makes the bones rot" (Prov 14:30). A psychological insight that may be, but neither improbable nor unworthy nevertheless. Anger is produced by a human being personally, and when it is not constructively channeled its effect is ultimately death, whether physical death or the effectual death of the personality. No intervention by God is required; it is a natural law.

3 As he has previously done (4:8), Eliphaz appeals to his own experience: "I myself have seen" (אֲנִי רָאִיתִי); cf. also his closing words in 5:27. But whereas his observation in 4:8 was so generalized that its objectivity was questionable, here at least it is possible that Eliphaz is reporting an event known to him personally. Nevertheless we cannot be sure that this is no fictionalized proverbial utterance.

In this case, Eliphaz claims he has seen a fool "taking root," i.e., becoming prosperous and flourishing, like a plant or tree (this image of human life is common in Job; cf. 8:16–17; 15:32–33; 18:16; 19:10; 24:20; 29:19). That this fool was a victim of anger we are no doubt meant to presume, though Eliphaz's account is somewhat cryptic. What befell the "fool" is not entirely clear: it looks at first sight as though it was Eliphaz's curse that laid him and his house low. But this incident would then show that "the disaster that befell the fool was not self-entailed, but was brought about by Eliphaz" (Rowley). Such a course of events would contradict Eliphaz's general argument in vv 1–7, that disaster is produced by the one who suffers; and further, it would make this verse no illustration at all of the more general statement of the preceding verse. For v 2 has claimed that a fool is, or may be, slain by his own anger; the present verse can hardly mean that Eliphaz's curse had in any way brought about the fool's fate. One way of handling the difficulty is to see Eliphaz's curse as a curse on the fool's children and not upon the fool himself. Vv 4–5 would then be translated, "May his sons be removed from safety! May they be crushed in the gate, with no one to deliver them! May the hungry eat what they have reaped . . ." (so Dhorme, Terrien, TOB; cf. LXX πόρρω γένοιντο οἱ υἱοὶ αὐτῶν ἀπὸ σωτηρίας). The Hebrew allows such a translation, but on this view Eliphaz's curse would be irrelevant to the one person whom we would expect to be the subject of v 3, viz. the fool himself.

A more satisfactory solution to the difficulty is to regard Eliphaz's "curse" not as the cause of the fool's downfall but as his reaction to the sight of the fool's self-induced destruction (cf. Davidson). A curse was not necessarily a fate-producing word, but could be a spoken recognition that a person was already under a curse. J. Scharbert has in fact suggested that the "curse"-formula אָרוּר אַתָּה, "cursed are you," was intended by the one uttering it to keep himself vigorously aloof from the person and action of the accursed one (*TDOT* 1:408). Even if that is not the function of the curse here, it is plausible that the verb קבב here used, not one of the regular verbs for "curse," really means "to express contempt for" rather than "to curse" in the formal sense (cf. Scharbert, *TDOT* 1:415); we may compare the dual sense of the verb קלל, which means both "to curse" and "to despise as one cursed" (cf. on 3:1; and see further C. A. Keller, *THWAT* 2:643; cf. also Gordis: "I declared cursed"). The agent of the cursing is neither Eliphaz nor, explicitly, God; the fool has by his behavior laid himself under curse (contrast Prov 3:33, "Yahweh's curse is on the house of the wicked").

4 The focus of attention shifts in this and the next verse to the children of the fool, since he himself is apparently dead, and no more can be said of him—except that by his own wrong he has left his children in a miserable position. If it is not exactly a case of the sin of the father being visited on the children (cf. on 21:19–20), it is at least an illustration of the crippling effect of sin on all that belongs to the fool, his "habitation" (נָוֵהוּ, v 3) and his children (בָּנָיו, v 4). "What a Semite dreads more than anything is the desolation of his family, so that its members all perish or come to ruin" (Wetzstein, quoted by Driver). His children are, as orphans, without a strong protector to ensure them justice in the legal and business transactions that take place in the city gate (NEB "court" narrows the range unduly). On the activities that occur there, cf. 29:7; 31:21; Deut 25:7; Ruth 4:1–12; Amos 5:10; Isa 29:21.

The language is conventional and formulaic. Prov 22:22 instructs: "Rob not the poor because he is poor, and do not crush [דכא, as here] the needy at the city gate [בשער, as here]." And the phrase "with none to deliver" (וְאֵין מַצִּיל) is also found in Isa 5:29; Ps 7:3 [2]; 50:22. The conventionality of the language simply evidences how commonly the underprivileged were further deprived of rights and privileges.

No reference to the fate of Job's children is intended (as against Driver, Andersen), for in Job's case it is the children who have died and the father who is unprotected by them (cf. Ps 127:5, where it is the sons who protect the father at the gate). No doubt Eliphaz's phrase "his children are far from safety" is heard by Job rather differently from Eliphaz's intention (cf. Fullerton, *JBL* 49 [1930] 359; Fohrer), but Eliphaz, though insensitive, is not intentionally cruel (contrast Andersen).

5 Despite difficulties in the Hebrew, the sense of the verse is plain: the fruits of the fool's labors are enjoyed by others, and his own children are left in want. If the "thirsty" and "hungry" who take over the fool's possessions are themselves genuinely needy, no great harm seems to result; perhaps then we should regard those who take over the fool's possessions as the greedy, perhaps even, as some suggest, the seminomadic Bedouin plunderers who live on the edge of the cultivated land and ravage the farmers' crops (cf. Peake, Fohrer). A contrast with the fortune of the children of the righteous remains the unstated background of the present picture; cf. Ps 37:25, "I have never seen the righteous forsaken and his offspring searching for food" (cf. also Prov 13:22; 20:7). The unfortunate fate of the children of the wicked is a well-known theme in *topoi* such as this: cf. 18:19; 20:10; 27:14; Prov 13:22.

6 The particular illustration (vv 2–5) is complete; the general principle can now be stated. What happened to the fool took place "because" (כִּי) suffering is not self-producing and natural, like vegetation or weeds (v 6), but human-produced (v 7). Though human beings themselves are created from dust (עָפָר) and soil (אֲדָמָה), it is not human origins that are in mind here; the language is that of the growth of vegetation (for "spring" [יָצָא], cf. 14:2; 31:40; Deut 14:22; for "sprout" [צָמַח], cf. Gen 2:5; 41:6). There may perhaps be an allusion to the doctrine that human troubles stem from our hostile environment (as in Gen 3:17–19; cf. Andersen); but if so, such a doctrine is denied (as against Pope, who vocalizes לֹא "not" as לָ "assuredly"). It is not nature that is the source of suffering in the world but humanity itself. Job himself will of course agree with Eliphaz that his own trouble is not "natural" but will dissent vigorously from Eliphaz's corollary that it is due to himself. And it is ironic that he must implicitly agree with Eliphaz that trouble does not come from below, from the ground; the real trouble for Job comes from above (cf. 6:4; etc.).

Those commentators who interpret the following verse (v 7) in the traditional sense, "Man is born to (*or,* for) trouble," may indeed find in v 6 a hint that God is in fact the immediate cause of human suffering. The poem that soon follows (vv 9–16) puts God's activity in human affairs very much in the forefront (cf. vv 12–14), so that it is possible that Eliphaz is "insinuating that the Lord is the hidden cause of the fool's troubles, even though they are so universal that they might appear to be natural" (Andersen). A further possibility is to take the verse as a question: "Does not trouble grow out of the soil . . . ?" (so Pope, 1st ed.; Habel). But the interpretation of v 6 presented above seems preferable.

7 Everything since v 1 has been building up to this climax of an astounding and provocative generalization. It may be, to our mind, logically a little perverse to begin with a particular exemplification of the principle (v 2), to continue with an even more particular illustration of the principle (vv 3–5), to deny thereafter any alternative to the principle (v 6), and only finally to enunciate the principle itself (v 7). But the principle is so fundamental to Eliphaz's whole outlook that it matters little to him by what devious route he finally achieves explicit statement of it.

The principle is that the suffering (אָוֶן, עָמָל) that humans undergo is "begotten" by themselves. In this Eliphaz is at one with all the friends of Job, and with Job's own worst fears about the reality of the moral universe (see on 4:8). This is no pessimistic view of humankind, which makes them inherently incapable of good, or which views their life as given over to suffering. In this respect, the alteration of the Masoretic vocalization from "man is born (יוּלָּד, yûllād) for trouble" to "man begets (יֹלִד, yôlid) trouble" (see n. 5:7.a) lightens the load Eliphaz places on the shoulders of human beings. We should not fail to note the purpose to which Eliphaz turns this nevertheless unhappy principle: he develops it solely in the cause of alleviating Job's pain by explaining to him its cause. Job need not feel the victim of a capricious universe, or of a fatal flaw in the human constitution; no, there is a particular fault in Job's behavior that has brought upon him his present trouble, and the very particularity of the fault should ensure that any corresponding suffering will be short-lived. Behind this unbending principle stands the warm-hearted assurance of Eliphaz that Job is essentially a righteous man (4:6), and that as an innocent man Job cannot be "cut off" (4:7).

The second colon of the verse is much debated. The usual interpretation of the "sons" of Resheph (רֶשֶׁף) is "sparks" of fire; רשף = "flame" in Cant 8:6, and metaphorically the "sparks of the bow" (רִשְׁפֵי קָשֶׁת) in Ps 76:4 [3] are "arrows." A perfectly satisfactory sense for the present verse is gained if v 7b means "as surely as the sparks fly upward" (cf. RSV, NAB, NIV). Human sin and its concomitant suffering have the same inevitability about them as the upward dance of sparks from a fire (so, e.g., Weiser, Fohrer, Rowley). A complication in this interpretation is raised by our knowledge of a Phoenician god Resheph who is attested as a god of the arrow and as a god of pestilence. Some have wondered whether we may not have in this reference to the "sons of Resheph" some reflection of an otherwise unattested myth of their upward flight (like Phaeton or Icarus) to wrest power or privileges from high gods. This view is rather too problematic, and it is more likely that Resheph is here mentioned in his role as god of pestilence (cf. the use of the same word for "pestilence" in Deut 32:24; Hab 3:5 [parallel with דֶּבֶר]). A list of Ugaritic gods equates him with the Mesopotamian Nergal, god of pestilence and the netherworld. Since in Joban language the deity Death (Mot) has a "firstborn" (18:13) and is entitled "the king of terrors" (18:14), who are underworld demons, it is entirely likely that the "sons of Resheph" had the same function. On this view, Eliphaz is saying that when humans beget trouble for themselves they let loose (metaphorically speaking) the underworld demons of pestilence to fly high to earth in order to attack mortals. V 7b is not then strictly parallel to v 7a, but rather its consequence.

On the god Resheph, see J. Gray, IDB 3:36–37; S. B. Parker, IDBSup, 224–25; J. B. Burns, "The Mythology of Death in the Old Testament," SJT 26 (1973) 327–40; F. Vattioni, "Il dio Resheph," AION 15 (1965) 39–74; D. Conrad, "Der Gott Rescheph," ZAW 83 (1971) 157–83; A. van den Branden, "'Reseph' nella Bibbia," BeO 13 (1971) 211–25; J. C. de Moor, "The Semitic Pantheon of Ugarit," UF 2 (1970) 187–228; W. Fulco, The Canaanite God Rešep (AOS 8; New Haven: American Oriental Society, 1976).

8–16 This doxology in praise of God (vv 9–16), prefaced by a confession by Eliphaz (v 8), functions as advice to Job. Eliphaz does not address Job or directly describe his situation (except perhaps in v 11); but the confession and the doxology are equally *for* Job, who may identify himself with this orthodox posture of praise and so be able to "bear" (cf. on 4:5) his present misfortune. (Weiser compares the use of what he calls the hymn form for parenesis in the case of the Egyptian Instruction for King Meri-ka-re [*ANET*, 414–18].)

8 Having advised Job that appeal for deliverance from his affliction is futile (v 1), since his suffering is his own fault (v 7) and must therefore be endured, what can Eliphaz now say that is more positive? He can only testify to what he himself does: "I myself pray to God and leave my case in his hands." Many modern versions and commentators (but contrast Dhorme) translate the verbs as hypothetical, i.e., as indicating what Eliphaz would do if he were in Job's situation. JB, for example, actually says, "If I were as you are, I should appeal to God." But it is a sign of Eliphaz's attempted delicacy, as also of his self-assuredness, that he speaks only of himself and does not presume to tell Job what to do.

What he does is "pray to God" (דרש "to seek" often has this significance; see S. Wagner, *TDOT* 3:298–304; E. Ruprecht, *THWAT* 1:462–66; C. Westermann, "Die Begriffe für Fragen und Suchen im Alten Testament," *KuD* 6 [1960] 2–30) and "address [his] speech" to God. He does not mention an "appeal" or even a "case" that he may advise Job to submit to God's judgment. The language is not judicial but religious (see n. 5:8.b on דברתי). Particularly striking is Eliphaz's failure to reproduce a prayer of lament or appeal or implicitly to recommend such a prayer to Job. He has in v 1 already ruled out the efficacy of such an appeal—to whatever quarter; sinners must bear their sin, but they *can* entrust themselves to God as the reverser of fortunes. It is to God as the almighty wonder-worker that Eliphaz prays, not primarily by way of appeal to exert himself on the petitioner's behalf, but by way of praise for the divine qualities that are already the subject of communal praise. No doubt the ultimate purposes in a prayer of appeal and in a prayer of thanksgiving at a time of distress are very similar, but the effect upon the worshipers themselves is very different. For Job, as for himself, Eliphaz implies, appeal is futile but praise is becoming.

In directing Job's attention to God, Eliphaz little knows how fixed Job's concentration already is upon God and God's responsibility for Job's fortunes. Job has not yet addressed God directly, but when he does, in virtually every one of his subsequent speeches, it will be no thanks to the well-intentioned words of Eliphaz, but a necessity that arises out of Job's own perception of how things stand (cf., e.g., 6:4; 7:11–21).

9–16 The activities of God mentioned in this doxology are described in very stereotyped language; Eliphaz has nothing novel to present to Job (as he did in the account of the night-vision, 4:12–21), but simply the conventional cultic praise of God, with which Job must be familiar (the indication of Job's non-Israelite origin in 1:1 is irrelevant in the bulk of the book).

It is quite possible that some of the elements in the doxology have no application to Job and his situation, and are found here simply because they belong to the conventional language of worship. But of the two strands that typically compose such a doxology, (i) God's creative and world-sustaining activity, and (ii) his readjustment of the moral and social order, the latter predominates in this doxology. It is possible, in fact, that the one element in strand (i) that appears here, the giving of rain (v 10), carries with it the overtones of strand (ii), namely the role of God as reverser of fortunes. (For a doxology where the two strands are inextricably intertwined, cf. Ps 147, where vv 4, 8–9, 14–18 belong to strand [i], and vv 2–3, 6, 10–11, and perhaps 19–20, belong to strand [ii].) It is inconceivable that the content of the doxology is not meant to have any applicability to Job and his circumstances apart from the general purpose of encouraging Job to turn himself toward God (so, e.g., Hesse). It seems much more plausible that it is precisely the image of God as the reverser of fortunes that is intended by Eliphaz to appeal to Job. In using the doxological form, Eliphaz can avoid any specific promises to Job, and especially any indication of how long he may expect his suffering to last. No doubt there is not much else that Eliphaz can do, and it cannot hurt Job—though it may well irritate him—to be reminded of the ability and tendency of God to reverse situations of distress.

On the doxology form see F. Horst, "Die Doxologien im Amosbuch," *ZAW* 47 (1929) 45–54 [= *Gottes Recht. Gesammelte Studien zum Recht im Alten Testament* (ThB 12; Munich: Kaiser, 1961) 155–66]; T. H. Gaster, "An Ancient Hymn in the Prophecies of Amos," *JMEOS* 19 (1935) 23–26; J. D. W. Watts, "An Old Hymn Preserved in the Book of Amos," *JNES* 15 (1956) 33–39; idem, *Vision and Prophecy in Amos* (Leiden: Brill, 1958) 51–67; J. L. Crenshaw, "The Influence of the Wise upon Amos: The 'Doxologies of Amos' and Job 5:9–16, 9:5–10," *ZAW* 79 (1967) 42–52; idem, *Hymnic Affirmations of Divine Justice: Doxologies of Amos and Related Texts in the Old Testament* (SBLDS 24; Missoula, Mont.: Scholars Press, 1975). For a Babylonian analogy to the doxology form, see W. G. Lambert, "Three Literary Prayers of the Babylonians," *AfO* 19 (1959–60) 47–66 (56).

9 This first element in the hymnic doxology is a very general and comprehensively summarizing one, almost exactly repeated by Job in 9:10: that God does "great" things is commonly said (cf. 9:10; 37:5; Ps 71:19; 136:4 "great wonders"; 145:6; Deut 10:21); likewise that his greatness is "unsearchable" (cf. Ps 145:3; Isa 40:28; cf. Job 36:26). His "wonders" (נפלאות) are connected with the exodus (Ps 78:4; 106:22), with other acts in history (Ps 105:5; 106:7), and with his works in creation (Ps 107:24; 136:4). That his deeds of greatness are "numberless" is said also in 9:10. What *Leitmotif* in this praise of God will emerge is not yet made clear, though by the end of the praise it will be plain that the "wonders" (נפלאות) are the linking theme in all the "mighty acts" (גדלות) of God here mentioned.

10 Not even in the first example of God's great deeds is the thrust of this doxology completely apparent. True it is that rain is "a mysterious commodity" (Habel), but Gordis more perceptively notes that in the East rainfall is often regarded as one of the greatest of wonders. He observes that in the ʿAmidah of the Jewish liturgy, the praise of God as the one who "causes the wind to blow and the rain to fall" (מַשִּׁיב הָרוּחַ מוֹרִיד הַגֶּשֶׁם) immediately follows the praise of God as the raiser of the dead. His power over the rains is referred to in Mishnaic language as גבורת הגשמים "the power of rains" (*m. Ber.* 5.2). Also in the thanksgiving of Ps 147 the rain is the first element in the catalogue of God's beneficent deeds. The production of rain can certainly be used as an illustration of the unfathomable knowledge of God (as in 36:27–28; 38:26–27), but it can also demonstrate the power of God to *change* the appearance of nature; thus Ecclus 43:22–23: "When the mountain growth is scorched with heat, and the flowering plains as though by flames, the dripping clouds restore them all, and the scattered dew enriches the parched land" (NAB).

What is specially remarkable about rain, then, is its *transforming* power. This aspect of rain is not so obvious in climates where rain is a regular component of every season; but in countries that experience the monsoon, a similar image is conjured up by the word "rain." In Palestine, the former and latter rains transform the face of the countryside and mark the change of the seasons. If the theme of the present doxology is God as the reverser of fortunes, his gift of the rain is an obvious illustration in the natural sphere of his character as it will be portrayed in the subsequent verses. In Amos 5:8 God's sending of water upon the earth is mentioned in a doxology as an illustration of his judging activity (cf. Crenshaw, *Hymnic Affirmation,* 128); this does not seem to be the significance here.

11 Even if the previous verse illustrates solely the *power* of God, and not specifically his *transforming* power, it is certain that with this verse a veritable catalogue of God's powers as a reverser of fortunes sets in.

The reversal of outward fortune or estate is a motif greatly beloved by biblical doxologists. The "wonder" is that God can overturn the social stratification that humans have developed in the name of social order. It is not that God constantly or habitually upsets the social pattern, any more than that he constantly sends rain upon the earth. It is rather that the unexpected elevation of the oppressed and toppling of the oppressing classes is thought of as an act worthy of God and one that is ultimately his own doing. So we find that hidden within the apparently cloistered and other-worldly confines of the language of worship is a view of the nature of God that threatens every human-made social order with revolution.

To be economically "poor" and socially "afflicted" is more often than not in biblical literature a sign of piety, but it is not an ideal (Hesse), and in the context of praise (and not just in the context of law or prophetic preaching or political action) it is affirmed that it is of the nature of God to challenge the equation of the "pious" with the "poor." There *are* those who deserve to be poor; and so God executes judgment, "putting down one" and stripping one person of wealth or position while "lifting up another" (Ps 75:8 [7]).

For parallels to the reversal of "high" and "low," cf. 22:29 (Eliphaz); 1 Sam 2:8; Ps 18:28 [27]; 75:8 [7]; 113:7–8; 147:6; Luke 1:52; cf. Ps 138:6. For deliverance of the afflicted, cf. 36:15 (Elihu); Isa 61:2–3. The idea of lifting mourners "to safety" may reflect some such danger to widows and father-less as is described in 2 Kgs 4:1.

12–14 We pass now to the negative side of "reversal of fortunes." This is delicate ground for any would-be "comforter" of Job to be treading; the sufferer could all too easily identify his own fate with the disaster of the "crafty," "cunning" and "wily." But the rhetoric of wisdom teaching leads Eliphaz on, far beyond what can be relevant to Job. Neither the crafty nor the wily have brought about Job's downfall, but only God himself; there is no consolation for Job, then, in these assurances of God's judgment against the unrighteous. No humanly created situation of distress, such as those suffer who are the object of crafty schemes laid against them, is irreversible by God. But who is to undo the plots laid by God himself?

It is indeed a particular point of superiority in God that he can use the very schemes of the crafty as a means to ensnare them. This is not the only time in OT literature that the wicked are described as hoist with their own petard (cf. Ps 7:15–16 [14–15]; 10:2; 35:8; 57:7 [6]; Prov 26:27; 28:10); and cf. Ps 18:27 [26] [= 2 Sam 22:27] "with the crooked thou dost show thyself perverse"). On the "craftiness" of the divine outside Israel, cf. for Islam I. Goldziher, *Vorlesungen über den Islam* (2nd ed.; Heidelberg: C. Winter, 1925) 25–26, 305–6; and for Greece, K. Deichgräber, *Der listensinnende Trug des Gottes. Vier Themen des griechischen Denkens* (Göttingen: Vandenhoeck & Ruprecht, 1952) 108–41.

When Paul is contrasting human wisdom (ἡ σοφία τοῦ κόσμου τούτου) with the wisdom of God (1 Cor 3:19), it is natural for him to cite v 13a: human wisdom is caught by God in its own artfulness, and proves to be not wise enough by half. This is the only passage of Job expressly cited in the NT; the form of the citation (ὁ δρασσόμενος τοὺς σοφοὺς ἐν τῇ πανουργίᾳ αὐτῶν) differs from that of the LXX (ὁ καταλαμβάνων σοφοὺς ἐν τῇ φρονήσει [αὐτῶν]), but it is not known whether Paul is translating directly from the Hebrew himself, or using another Greek version.

The criticism of the "wise" found in these verses has suggested to some (e.g., Hesse) that the author of this hymnic doxology at least can hardly have stemmed from the circles we know as the "wise" or the "wisdom movement." Without entering upon the question whether there is much value in postulating a religious or social "movement" that we might call "wisdom," we may nevertheless affirm that an important part of wisdom, in whatever guise, lies in recognizing its boundaries. Within the so-called "wisdom" books of the OT, Ecclesiastes—which must be reckoned to any "wisdom" movement—plainly asks radical questions about the limits of human wisdom (cf. W. Zimmerli, "The Place and Limit of the Wisdom in the Framework of the Old Testament Theology," *SJT* 17 [1964] 146–58). Gen 3 invites yet more searching questions about "wisdom," the serpent being more "wise" (עָרוּם) than any other of God's creatures, and the quest for the "knowledge of good and evil" being so fraught with danger and prohibition. Yet here too we are in the presence of "sapiential" language (see L. Alonso Schökel, "Sapiential and Covenant Themes in Genesis 2–3," *Studies in Ancient Israelite Wisdom,* ed. J. L. Crenshaw [New York: Ktav, 1976] 468–80, and J. de Fraine, "Jeux de mots dans le récit de la chute," *Mélanges bibliques rédigés en l'honneur de André Robert* [Travaux de l'Institut Catholique de Paris 4; Paris: Bloud et Gay, 1957] 47–59 [53]). We have to do here, then, not with cultic or religious ideas and language that clash with the wisdom ideology, but with a normal expression of the dark side of wisdom.

The function of wisdom is to give orientation to life: "dark" wisdom removes the signposts that wisdom in the fear of God has set up, and those who employ the techniques of wisdom for their own selfish ends find their enlightenment becomes darkness. Elsewhere the image of darkness for lack of understanding may be seen in 12:25; Deut 28:29; Isa 59:10; Jer 13:16; cf. 23:12.

15–16 With v 15 we return to the central theme of the doxology: God as the reverser of fortunes. The "poor" (אֶבְיוֹן), who may be the economically poor or those maltreated in various ways (see L. E. Keck, *IDBSup,* 672–73; G. Botterweck, *TDOT* 1:27–41), are at the mercy of the "strong" (חָזָק), who may oppress them verbally ("by the sword of their mouth") or physically. Their fate seems hopeless, but God is their "savior" (מוֹשִׁיעַ; see on v 4), and his acts of salvation, though not universal—the poor are always among us—are sufficient to give "hope" to the languishing "poor." The concluding note of the doxology repeats the theme: if unrighteousness stops its mouth, it not only means that the tumult and noise that betoken rebellion against justice (e.g., Ps 2:1; 10:2; 12:4 [3]; 22:14 [13]; 31:21 [20]; 65:8 [7]; Isa 13:4) are silenced, but also that "wickedness" experiences amazement. To "shut the mouth" is a mark of astonishment (as in Isa 52:15), in this case because of the reversal God has achieved on behalf of the "poor" (v 16b is closely paralleled by the wording of Ps 107:42, in a similar context of the reversal of fortunes).

For the image of the tongue as a sword (v 15), cf. Ps 57:5 [4]; 64:4 [3]; cf. 52:4 [2] (tongue as sharp razor); 55:22 [21] (words as swords); 59:8 [7] (swords in lips); Job 5:21 (tongue as whip); and cf. Prov 5:3–4; 25:18.

The note of hope on which this doxology concludes evidences again Eliphaz's general attitude toward Job. As a righteous, though necessarily imperfect, human creature, Job can look to God as the reverser of fortunes to release him from his unhappy situation. Nevertheless, Eliphaz has spoken wholly in generalizations, and Job can have at the end of the doxology no better sense of how or when such a reversal of fortune might be achieved. Worse than that, Eliphaz has not begun to plumb the depths of Job's despair (as revealed in chap. 3) if he can talk blandly of hope, exaltation to safety, and the deliverance of the poor. The only kind of deliverance Job wants is to be freed of his suffering by death.

17–27 Here, for the first time since v 1, Eliphaz directs his speech to Job. The theorizing is (almost) over, and his good intentions shine through in his determination to end his speech to Job on a positive, up-beat note. For all the characters or the readers know (if the dramatic fiction may be allowed for a moment), this will be Eliphaz's final word to Job, and in it he will paint a future for Job that ought to transform Job's mood to patient optimism.

This fifth and final major element in Eliphaz's discourse begins in v 17a with a macarism ("Happy is he . . ."), that sets the tone by telling Job how well off, in fact, he is. The irony, of course, lies barely below the surface. Following the macarism, there is a negative command to Job (v 17b), "Spurn not the instruction of the Almighty," which will be balanced by the positive command with which this fifth section of the speech concludes: "Hear, and know it for yourself" (v 27b). These imperatives are doubtless not intended to convey an authoritarian attitude on Eliphaz's part, but they certainly take the bloom off the rosy picture of Job's future that is framed by them. The didacticism of the imperatives sounds a note of uncertainty; that is, there *is* a blessed future for Job, but *only if* he will meet certain conditions. True, they are not, on the surface, conditions of any difficulty; one commentator gladly notes that "there are no conditions mentioned that must be fulfilled before salvation can become a reality" (Hesse). Job has only "not to spurn" God's chastening, and only to "hear, hearken to" the experience of Eliphaz and the community of the wise he represents. Yet these are precisely the conditions Job cannot possibly meet. How can he accept God's chastening if for him his suffering is not chastening but rank injustice? How can he accept Eliphaz's experience when it has been filtered through the sieve of a retributionist theology that Job knows from his own case to be defective?

The irony is tragic: what Eliphaz believes will surely encourage Job must in fact only re-echo his fate; Job cannot retain his integrity and allow himself to fall in with Eliphaz's blinkered perspective; and so any assurances about the future can only be gall to Job. And above all, what is the meaning of a speech of salvation to a man who desperately desires the very opposite of salvation? It can only add to his anguish, and it is without surprise that we read the first words of Job's reply in the following chapter: "Ah, could my anguish but be measured and my calamity laid with it in the scales, they would now outweigh the sands of the sea!" (6:2–3 NAB).

But the rhetoric of "wisdom" has borne Eliphaz along. The "number saying" of v 19 launches him upon what must be described as a delightful and fervent account of the blessings of the one who enjoys God's favor. These verses constitute a *topos* on this theme; like the many set-piece *topoi* of the book, it strays at times from relevance to the need at hand, even at times almost callously ignoring it (cf., e.g., v 25). Whether or not the seven disasters (v 19) that God delivers from are systematically set out in the subsequent verses (cf. on v 19), the very form of the "number saying" lays claim to a comprehensiveness that in itself can be most cruel. In its very assuredness of God's deliverance from conventional plights, it leaves out of account the particular and deeply personal disaster of Job—whether we call that a denial of his integrity, or a sense of isolation from God, or a state of utter depression. Job can hear in Eliphaz's assurance nothing he wants to hear; and its silence about his real needs is deafening.

17 With the initial "behold" (הנה), Eliphaz introduces a new and striking idea at this, the beginning of the fifth major element of his discourse. He takes an important step forward in explaining the significance of suffering as the "discipline" or "instruction" (מוסר) of God (the word is characteristic of the wisdom teaching). No longer is suffering merely the inevitable consequence of human imperfection, as it has been in 5:7 (cf. 4:17). Now suffering can be regarded as a positive act of God for the education of the sufferer (the father-child relationship is in mind). The two ideas are not contradictory, but their tonality is very different. Now suffering may be seen not as something that puts a gulf between a human being and God but as something that binds them together. There is a personal dimension that makes human suffering far less mechanistic than Eliphaz had previously allowed. Of course, how that personal dimension is experienced will depend on the sufferer's view of the cause of the suffering. If one is willing to accept that one deserves it, it will be a consolation to know that one's suffering is not the outworking of some blind natural law, but the personal act of the "Celestial Surgeon" (Stevenson): "he who wounds is he who soothes the sore." But if, like Job, the sufferer cannot believe that the suffering is "discipline," it is even worse to think of oneself as on the receiving end of "discipline" indiscriminately dispensed by God than to imagine oneself the victim of a blind and inflexible law of nature.

The macarism ("Happy is . . . ," אשרי) is the secular counterpart to the blessing ("Blessed is . . . ," ברוך). It appears a number of times in the "wisdom" literature (Prov 3:13; 8:32, 34; 14:21; 16:20; 28:14; 29:18; Eccl 10:17), but more frequently (26 times) in the Psalms, and only five times elsewhere. It is probably impossible to determine whether the macarism had a cultic or wisdom origin (the point is debated by E. Lipiński, "Macarismes et psaumes de congratulation," *RB* 75 [1968] 321–67 [357]); but it does appear that our present text depends upon such sentences as we find in Ps 94:12 or Prov 3:11–12, which are reflected in *Pss. Sol.* 10.1–3 and quoted in Heb 12:5–6. In neither the Psalms nor Proverbs passage cited is it plain that God's "correction" takes the form of suffering, though this may be implied. In Job there is no question of what Eliphaz means, especially in the light of v 18 (it is not legal correction [as against Horst], as it is elsewhere in Job; cf. on 9:33). As often, however, the partial insight into truth hardens into a universal principle, and Eliphaz is proved in the wrong by Job—and other sufferers—to the extent that he claims that suffering is necessarily divine education. (For the difference between the views of Eliphaz and Elihu on this subject, see on 33:14–30.) Lipiński has observed that the macarism is generally a form of congratulation that assumes some good fortune already realized or at least in course of realization. But also it easily takes on a hortatory or parenetic tone, since it invites its hearers to rank themselves with the "happy." To Job, therefore, Eliphaz not only offers his congratulations on his suffering, but urges him to count himself happy, even if such a thought has not crossed Job's mind! The author of Job again knowingly addresses us from behind Eliphaz's back, observing how so harmless an idiom as the macarism, when set among other general hortatory material, can become, when addressed directly to a person's face, an unfeeling rebuff. Job, says Eliphaz, should not "spurn" or "reject" (מאס) the discipline of God, but what else can he do if he believes it is not discipline but arbitrary cruelty?

On the macarism, see further: W. Janzen, "ʾAšrê in the Old Testament," *HTR* 58 (1965) 215–26; W. Käser, "Beobachtungen zum alttestamentlichen Makarismus," *ZAW* 82 (1970) 225–50; H. Cazelles, *TDOT* 1:445–48 (bibliography).

The divine name *Shaddai* (שַׁדַּי) occurs here for the first time in Job (30 other occurrences). The etymology most favored currently is that proposed by W. F. Albright ("The Names Shaddai and Abram," *JBL* 54 [1935] 173–204), who saw a connection with Akk. *šadû* "mountain," thus "he of the mountain." This view was further supported by F. M. Cross (*Canaanite Myth and Hebrew Epic: Essays in the History of the Religion of Israel* [Cambridge, Mass.: Harvard UP, 1973] 52–60). M. Weippert (*THWAT* 2:873–81) concisely reviews eight proposed etymologies and leans to that of Albright and Cross. The characteristic rabbinic etymology was *še-day*, "the one who is (self-)sufficient"; Aquila and Symmachus accordingly translated the name by ἱκανός "the sufficient one." LXX and Vg were probably not far from its *meaning*, as distinct from its *etymology*, in rendering it παντοκράτωρ (or κύριος) and *omnipotens*, "the Almighty." Since we can have no certainty about the etymology, and since etymology would not guide us necessarily to the meaning of the name as used, the conventional translation "Almighty" is here preferred. The use of a divine name that is common in the patriarchal narratives (e.g., Gen 17:1; cf. Exod 6:2–3) may suggest that the poet wished to preserve the atmosphere of patriarchal times that prevails in the prologue to the book (Habel).

18 The two-sided character of God, positive and negative, has in the previous strophe of this discourse been illustrated by Eliphaz; by God's act the lowly are elevated, the crafty are frustrated (vv 11–12). But here it is one and the same person who experiences the dual aspect of God's nature; it is the one who is wounded by God in "chastisement" (v 17) who has that wound bound up by God as healer. The same idea appears in Deut 32:39 "I kill and I make alive; I wound and I heal"; and in Hos 6:1 "He has torn, that he may heal us; he has stricken, and he will bind us up" (cf. also Isa 30:26).

The language finds a striking analogy in the Akkadian text from Ugarit known as "The Righteous Sufferer," a hymn of a man who praises his god Marduk: "I praise the work of Marduk, I praise the work of my angry god, I praise the work of my wrathful goddess. . . . He smote me and he took pity on me; he has cut me in pieces and torn me away; he has dissolved me, and he has gathered me. He rejected me, and he has welcomed me, he had abandoned me and he has exalted me" (RS 25.460, lines 29–31; *Ugaritica V* [Mission de Ras Shamra 16; ed. J. Nougayrol et al.; Paris: Imprimerie Nationale et P. Geuthner, 1968] no. 162, pp. 268–69; also in Lévêque, *Job et son Dieu*, 44; cited by J. Gray, "The Book of Job in the Context of Near Eastern Literature," *ZAW* 82 [1970] 251–69 [264]; translation above follows the improvements of W. von Soden, "Bemerkungen zu einigen literarischen Texten in akkadischer Sprache von Ugarit," *UF* 1 [1969] 189–95). In Vedic mythology, too, Rudra, the god of storms, both inflicts and heals disease (M. Leach and J. Fried [eds.], *Funk and Wagnall's Standard Dictionary of Folklore* [New York: Funk and Wagnall, 1949–50] 2:960).

This theology at least avoids an appearance of dualism: the God of death and suffering is not in conflict with the God of life and weal. Yet the parallel in Hos 6:1 offers another perspective on such language, "exquisite in simple beauty, but . . . lacking in moral depth, as the poetry which Hosea (6.1) puts into the mouths of the shallow optimists of Northern Israel" (Strahan). To move too rapidly from the experience of God's abrasiveness to the sense of his restoration may be to make grace too cheap. On the theme of God as healer, see J. Hempel, "Ich bin der Herr, dein Arzt (Ex 15,26)," *TLZ* 82 (1957) 809–26.

19 An elevated air is lent to this catalogue of the blessings of the one whom God educates by the use of the rhetoric of "ascending numeration" (see W. G. E. Watson, *Classical Hebrew Poetry: A Guide to Its Techniques* [JSOTSup 26; Sheffield: JSOT, 1984] 148). In this device, a number that would be regarded as sufficient is increased by one, as if to remove all shadow of doubt. Clearly, the general sense is: There is no trouble from which the Almighty will not deliver you.

The device is a doubtless ancient technique in wisdom instruction, perhaps deriving from the use of questions in the process of education. But it is already well attested in the Ugaritic epic and mythic texts (for details, see Pope) and in the OT is found not only in "wisdom" literature (Prov 6:16–19; 30:15–16, 18–19, 21–23, 24–28, 29–31; Eccl 11:2; Ecclus 23:16; 25:7; 26:5, 28; 50:25) but also in prophetic literature (Isa 17:6; Amos 1:3–13; 2:1–6; Mic 5:4 [5]) and in psalmic literature (Ps 62:12–13 [11–12]) that is not necessarily influenced by "wisdom." Though in some cases the particular items are named (in Prov 6:16–19; 30:15–16, 18–19, 21–23, 24–28, 29–31), the device is rhetorically effective even if specific items are not referred to. See W. M. W. Roth, *Numerical Sayings in the Old Testament: A Form-Critical Study* (VTSup 13; Leiden: Brill, 1965). Dhorme, Rowley, and Pope do not believe that seven particular disasters should be sought in the verses that follow, while Driver thought that seven instances were certainly not given by the writer but may have been intended by the interpolator of v 22 (if indeed that is an interpolation).

If we attempt, as some do, to identify seven distinct calamities from which Job is promised deliverance, we first observe that *nine* appear to be mentioned: famine (רעב), war, the scourge of the tongue, destruction (שׁד, twice, in v 21 and v 22), famine (כפן), the wild animals of the land, the stones of the field, and the wild animals of the field. One solution is to count two of the apparent pairs of equivalents as one. The problem is further complicated, however, by the possibility that we should distinguish between apparent equivalents; thus one שׁד may be taken as "calumny" (though then it may form an equivalent to "the scourge of the tongue"); or כפן may be a different kind of famine from רעב; or the חית השׂדה in v 23 may be "weeds" and not wild animals. Deleting v 22 as an insertion to make the number of items up to seven (see n. 5.22a) is a strange move, since the removal of v 22 decreases the items from nine to six. Gordis confidently finds seven items, but at the cost of (i) identifying the "beasts of the field" (v 23) with the "beasts of the earth" (v 22) (very reasonable); (ii) distinguishing between the hunger of רעב (v 20) and that of כפן (v 22) (no evidence); (iii) regarding לשׁד ולכפן (v 22) as a hendiadys for "the devastation of drought" (unlikely); (iv) taking שׁוט לשׁון, the "scourge of the tongue" (v 21) as an ellipsis for "the scourge of the tongue of fire" (very unlikely; see n. 5:21.b); and (v) taking שׁד (v 21) as "flood" (possible).

Two new ways of counting to seven may be suggested: (a) the calamities are (1) famine; (2) war; (3) tongue; (4) wild animals; (5) loss of property; (6) loss of offspring; (7) premature death; or (b), since hunger is so frequently alluded to and so may be the climactic seventh disaster, (1) war; (2) tongue; (3) destruction (? or flood); (4) wild animals; (5) loss of descendants; (6) premature death; (7) hunger. In either case v 23 can hardly be relevant, for it is a *reason* for v 22; and repetition of significant items is only to be expected in this discursive style. The general point is in any case totally unaffected by our ability to determine seven distinct calamities.

20–21 Perhaps we should see in these verses a little self-contained group of four calamities, whether or not they are incorporated in a larger group of seven. A group of four calamities in Ezek 14:13–20 (famine, wild beasts, sword, pestilence) appears as a set of punishments for Israel. Here the promise is apparently so unconditional and comprehensive that for all its charm ("the thrilling language . . . of a truly pious man," Peake) it takes on an air of unreality. And of course, since Eliphaz is launched upon a *topos*, Job's particular circumstances have quite faded from this picture of collective salvation.

The "ransom" paid by God for the life of an individual (the question of to whom that ransom might be paid is beside the point) is regarded as already paid; the perfect tense פָּדְךָ "he has ransomed you" is reproduced in no modern versions, and even the Septuagint employed a future tense. The Targum, following its habit, referred such general statements to particular moments in the history of Israel, seeing here the redemption from death in Egypt. But what we have is a use of the verbal system that may be called the "perfect of certitude" (Driver, *Tenses*, 14γ; GKC, § 106n). The term belongs to the realm of the law and of psalmody, not to the wisdom material. Salvation of all kinds is of course the substance of much psalmody, so it is not surprising to find parallels to deliverance from famine in Ps 33:19; 105:16–17; to deliverance from death in Ps 49:16 [15]; 103:4 (cf. Job 33:28); and note especially Ps 49:8–9 [7–8] "the ransom of life is costly"; to deliverance from the sword in Ps 22:21 [20]; 144:10; to protection from the tongue of false witnesses or sorcerers in Ps 31:21 [20]; 52:4, 6 [2, 4]; 64:4 [3]; 120:2; to protection from the pestilence that "wastes" (שׁוּד, cf. שׁד here) at noonday in Ps 91:6 (the whole of Ps 91 is in fact reminiscent of these verses). This imagery is not exclusive to the Psalms, but evidences the blend in the Joban poetry of "wisdom" and "psalmic" material.

22–23 The note of the security assured by the Almighty to one under his "discipline" becomes stronger. Not only would such a person be "ransomed" (v 20), "hidden," and "not be afraid" (v 21), but that individual will positively "scorn" (שׂחק "laugh in derision at") dangers that may cross the path, not unlike the prudent housewife of Prov 31 who "can afford to laugh at tomorrow" (v 25 NEB). Perhaps also the form of the negative used (אל־תּירא, "you need not fear") as contrasted with that in v 21 (לא־תּירא, "you shall not fear") further strengthens the note of security (cf. Peake; and n. 6:29.b). Above all, though, this verse marks a shift of emphasis from *deliverance* from potential disasters (vv 20–21) to assurance of *protection* and safety.

An idyllic picture of harmony between humans and nature is drawn (an ironic picture when the reality is that Job's life is being confronted by chaotic powers). In Hos 2:20–24 [18–22] and Isa 11:6–9 such harmony features in pictures of an eschatological era; Eliphaz finds the rhetoric of divine protection so persuasive that he tends to overrealize Hebrew eschatology, and so adds further to the air of unreality of this *topos*. The promises of Lev 26:3–10 which are to ensue if Israel walks in Yahweh's statutes are by comparison distinctly less lavish; and though they include the absence of threat from "evil beasts" (חיה רעה, v 6), the removal of that threat takes place by the elimination of these wild animals rather than, as here, by the creation of an atmosphere of peace that permits humans and wild animals (חית השדה, v 22; חית הארץ, v 23) to live in a state of harmony (שלום) with each other. There may be overtones also of a paradisal harmony (Terrien, Habel).

The "covenant" (ברית; RSV "league") with the stones of the field is a remarkably anthropomorphic image for human assurance that one's soil will produce its crops richly (cf. NEB "a covenant with the stones to spare your fields"). In Matt 13:5 the stony ground is infertile soil, while in 2 Kgs 3:19, 25 to cast stones into the fields of a defeated enemy is a practical and symbolic gesture of ensuring its total destruction. Job, says Eliphaz, will be in "covenant" with the stones; perhaps it is a covenant of equals imposed by a stronger third party, God, but the image is so vivid that it may even be a treaty-covenant between a greater (the stones, which have the power to render Job's activity futile) and a lesser (Job) (so Fohrer). On the distinction between various forms of covenant, see G. E. Mendenhall, *IDB* 1:714–23 (esp. 716–17). The "covenant" is purely metaphorical, of course, for an assured relationship; cf. 31:1; 40:28 [41:4]; Isa 28:15, 18 (a covenant with death); Hos 2:20 [18] (a covenant with the beasts of the field, the birds of the air, the creeping things of the ground).

24 The unintended irony, which Eliphaz does not stop to consider because he is carried along by his rhetoric, becomes more heavy-handed. For the person under divine protection, the dwelling, lit. "tent" (the term from a more archaic lifestyle heightens the dignity), and "estate" (or perhaps "pasture") will be secure. Life at its center and on its fringes will be equally secure (we are reminded by contrast of the disaster that swept in upon Job from the periphery to the center in chap. 1).

25 The same assuredness is emphasized by the repetition of the simple "and you will know." Beyond the individual personally, that person's offspring (lit., "seed") will flourish like the grass of the earth; the twin metaphor from plant life is found also in 21:8; Isa 44:3; 48:19; and the comparison of descendants to the "grass of the earth" may be seen also in Ps 72:16. "From the conventional list of earthly blessings a numerous posterity could not be absent" (Peake). Eliphaz's tact and sense of occasion has totally deserted him here, for if there is one thing Job cannot be certain of, it is a numerous posterity. Some scholars indeed argue that the speeches betray little knowledge of the prologue of the book, but the book as it now stands forces upon its readers the unhappy juxtaposition of Job's actual situation and the grandiose claim Eliphaz is making here. For Eliphaz the rhetoric is all; for the author the cruel irony is the essence (see further, Fullerton, *JBL* 49 [1930] 339 n. 8).

Of course, we may respond that Eliphaz speaks more truly than he knows, since the outcome of Job's bereavement will ultimately be the provision of a numerous progeny (cf. 42:13, 16). That is correct, but only on a level that is relevant neither to Job nor to Eliphaz at the present moment; and the poet surely wishes us at this time to savor the bitterness of the contrast between conventional words of encouragement and the reality of suffering.

26 Finally, the crowning blessing on a life protected by God is death at a ripe old age. Death before the proper time (cf. 20:11; 22:16) and being "cut off" before life has run its full course (cf. 4:8) is a curse, and a sign of divine disapproval. Death at "the right time" (עתו "at its time") is no punishment, but itself a blessing (cf. Ps 1:3; Prov 15:23 for the idea of the right time). It is not long life as such that is the blessing, though that is promised to those who heed the teaching of the wise (Prov 3:2, 16; 4:10; 9:11; 10:27); it is rather the patriarchal experience of being "gathered to one's fathers" (cf. Gen 25:8; 49:33) that is the final blessing. If the obscure word כלח ("in ripe old age," RSV) means "in full strength, with vigor unabated" (see n. 5:26.a), a bonus to death at the right time is promised: it is death without the loss of strength and fading of powers that usually accompany extreme old age (cf. Moses, 120 years old when he dies, yet "his eye was not dim, nor his natural force abated," Deut 34:7; and contrast Eccl 12:1–7 for the gradual fading of one's powers).

The image that parallels such a death is strikingly positive: the sheaf of corn that "comes up" from the field to the elevated threshing floor has survived through its many moments for this particular moment; "its time" (עתו) for gathering in has arrived. Qohelet would add: "God has made everything beautiful in its time (בעתו)" (Eccl 3:11). The sheaf has not come to the end of its usefulness; that is only beginning when it mounts to the threshing floor. There is no thought here, though, of any future existence for the person under God's protection: the fullness finally achieved is the whole.

Again, as with v 25, it will turn out that Eliphaz's promise is amply fulfilled in the final restoration of Job's fortunes in 42:16, where he lives to the age of 140, exactly double the normal span of threescore and ten (Ps 90:10); but in the present circumstance, scenes from a patriarchal idyll are desperately irrelevant to a man who craves immediate death to end his sorrow.

27 The conclusion of Eliphaz's speech, in the form of a "summary appraisal," proffers the final clue to its tonality and purpose. All that he has said has been "for your good" (RSV; lit., "for yourself"). It has not been judgment

or criticism, nor have the doxology of 5:9–16 or the description of the one
protected by God (5:19–26) been spoken for their own sake. They all form
parts of a many-sided encouragement to Job.

But equally, all that Eliphaz has spoken has not arisen from himself; though
he has several times testified to his own experience (4:8, 12–17; 5:3, 8), the
essence of his speech has resulted from the communal experience of the wise.
Perhaps he adds together what the wise of his own generation have observed
and experienced for themselves ("this is what we have discovered") and what
the wise of former generations have passed down ("this we have heard," NEB).
But the concluding line in the MT vocalization is wholly addressed to Job,
encouraging him to "take heed" (שְׁמַע, "hear, hearken") and apply the teaching
of the wise to himself ("know it for yourself"). It is up to Job now to align
himself with common experience; it is not in order for Job to search on the
basis of his own experience for a satisfying perspective on his suffering.

Explanation

Eliphaz has in this speech intended to offer Job nothing but assurance and
encouragement to patience. To this end he has contrasted Job with the wicked,
and has directed Job's attention to the power of God to reverse fortunes. In
all that he says, he has drawn upon experience, whether his own (4:12–17)
or that of the teachers of wisdom as a group (explicitly in 5:27). But it has
been obvious throughout the speech that the "wisdom" Eliphaz offers, though
sometimes unexceptionable, has been developed within very narrow categories,
and the "experience" of which he speaks is not raw experience of life, but
observation filtered through the distorting spectacles of a retributionist theology.
He speaks from a theoretical position that cannot really allow the possibility
of a Job, and it is only by dint of deviation from the traditional orthodoxy, in
questioning the absoluteness of the concept "righteous," that he is able to be
as accommodating to Job as he is. All the while, however, there runs beneath
Eliphaz's attitude the author's sense of irony at Eliphaz's dogma, and the reader
becomes aware that the speech operates on two levels. Occasionally the two
levels merge, as when Eliphaz's conventional piety and rhetoric lead him into
remarks that are totally inappropriate or even positively painful to Job (cf.
on 4:7; 5:4, 19, 25, 26). On the upper level, then, these chapters present a
speech of encouragement to Job; on the deeper level, they are an indictment
of the cruelty of narrow dogma.

Nowhere sharper, yet nowhere more subtle, is the irony in the account of
Eliphaz's night vision. We cannot be meant to overlook the strange similarity—
and difference—between the single sentence from a divine voice out of the
whirlwind here reported in the opening response to Job's plaint, and the lengthy
speeches of a divine voice out of the whirlwind that address Job directly at
the end of the book. "Can a man be righteous before God?" asks the divine
voice Eliphaz hears (4:17), whereas the divine voice Job hears (chaps. 38–41)
says, in effect, "That is not the question here. The question is, Can a man
find God wonderful in all he does?" (cf. 42:3–4). On the difference between
these two divine utterances hangs the message of the Book of Job and the
irony of the conflict between theology and theophany.

Job's Second Speech (6:1–7:21)

Bibliography

Dahood, M. "Mišmār, 'Muzzle,' in Job 7:12." *JBL* 80 (1961) 70–71. ———. "Northwest Semitic Philology and Job." *The Bible in Current Catholic Thought.* M. J. Gruenthaner Memorial Volume, ed. J. L. McKenzie. New York: Herder and Herder, 1962. 55–74. ———. "Ugaritic Lexicography." *Mélanges Eugène Tisserant.* Vol. 1. Studi e Testi 231. Città del Vaticano, 1964. 81–104. ———. "Chiasmus in Job." *A Light to My Path: Old Testament Studies in Honor of Jacob M. Myers,* ed. H. N. Bream, R. D. Heim, C. A. Moore. Gettysburg Theological Studies 4. Philadelphia: Temple UP, 1974. 119–30. **Doniach, W. S.** and **W. E. Barnes.** "Job vi 25: √מרץ." *JTS* 31 (1929–30) 291–92. **Driver, G. R.** "Hebrew Notes." *JRAS* (1944) 165–68. ———. "Problems in the Hebrew Text of Job." *VTS* 3 (1955) 72–93. **Fontaine, C. R.** "'Arrows of the Almighty' (Job 6:4): Perspectives on Pain." *ATR* 66 (1984) 243–48. **Habel, N. C.** "'Only the Jackal Is My Friend': On Friends and Redeemers in Job." *Int* 31 (1977) 227–36. **Jacob, B.** "Erklärung einiger Hiob-Stellen. 7:10. 7:16." *ZAW* 32 (1912) 282–83. **Kopf, L.** "Arabische Etymologien und Parallelen zum Bibelwörterbuch." *VT* 8 (1958) 161–215. **Mers, M.** "A Note on Job VI 10." *VT* 32 (1982) 234–36. **Millard, A. R.** "What Has No Taste? (Job 6:6)." *UF* 1 (1969) 210. **Reider, J.** "מְדֻדָּ in Job 7:4." *JBL* 39 (1920) 60–65. ———. "Some Notes to the Text of the Scriptures: 9. Job 6.7." *HUCA* 3 (1926) 112–13. ———. "Etymological Studies in Biblical Hebrew." *VT* 4 (1954) 276–95. **Riggans, W.** "Job 6:8–10: Short Comments." *ExpT* 99 (1987) 45–46. **Selms, A. van.** "Motivated Interrogative Sentences in the Book of Job." *Semitics* 6 (1978) 28–35. **Skehan, P. W.** "Second Thoughts on Job 6:16 and 6:25." *CBQ* 31 (1969) 210–12. (= *Studies in Israelite Poetry and Wisdom.* CBQMS 1. Washington, D.C.: Catholic Biblical Association, 1971. 83–84.) **Sutcliffe, E. F.** "Further Notes on Job, Textual and Exegetical: 6,2–3.13; 8,16–17; 19,20.26." *Bib* 31 (1950) 365–78.

Translation

⁶:¹ *Then Job spoke:*

> ² *If only my anguish* ᵃ *could be weighed*
>   *and my misfortune* ᵇ *set* ᶜ *with it on the scales,*
> ³ *then they would outweigh* ᵃ *the sand of the sea!*
>   *No wonder that my words are unrestrained.* ᵇ
> ⁴ *For the arrows of the Almighty are in me,* ᵃ
>   ᵇ*and my spirit drinks in* ᶜ *their poison.*
>   ᵈ*The terrors of God stand arrayed* ᵉ *against me.*
> ⁵ *Does the wild ass* ᵃ *bray when he has found green grass?*
>   *Does the ox low when he has his fodder?*
> ⁶ *Can one eat tasteless foods* ᵃ *without salt?*
>   *Is there flavor in the juice* ᵇ *of mallows?* ᶜ
> ⁷ *I* ᵃ *refuse to touch them;* ᵇ
>   *they are no better than rotten food.* ᶜ
>
> ⁸ *Would that my request should find fulfillment,*
>   *that God should grant me what I hope for!* ᵃ
> ⁹ *that God should decide to crush me,*
>   *to let loose* ᵃ *his hand and cut me off!* ᵇ

10 *Then this consolation could still*[a] *be mine*
　　(even while I recoiled[b] *in unrelenting*[c] *pain),*
　　that I have not denied[d] *the ordinances of the Holy One.*
11 *What strength have I for waiting*[a]*?*
　　what end in store that I should prolong my life?
12 *Is my strength the strength of stone,*
　　or is my flesh bronze?
13 *I have no power in myself at all;*[a]
　　all help[b] *has been thrust from me.*

14 [a]*A friend*[b] *does not refuse*[c] *his loyalty,*
　　nor[d] *does he forsake the fear of the Almighty.*
15 *But my brothers*[a] *have been as treacherous as the wadis.*
　　They are like seasonal streams that overflow,[b]
16 *that are dark with ice,*
　　swollen[a] *with thawing snow;*
17 *but no sooner are they in spate*[a] *than they dry up,*
　　in the heat they vanish away.
18 *Caravans*[a] *turn aside*[b] *from their routes;*
　　they go off[c] *into the desert and are lost.*
19 *The caravans of Tema search for water;*[a]
　　the travelers of Sheba raise their hopes.
20 *But they are disappointed*[a] *despite*[b] *their confidence;*[c]
　　they arrive, only to be frustrated.

21 [a] *Thus*[b] *have you become for me;*
　　you have seen a calamity and have taken fright.
22 *Have I said, "Make me a gift!"?*
　　"From your wealth offer a bribe for me!"?
23 *"Rescue me from my enemy!"?*
　　"Ransom me from from brigands!"?
24 *Tell me plainly,*[a] *and I will say no more;*
　　show me where I have erred.[b]
25 *How distressing*[a] *are words of right judgment!*[b]
　　but what do your reproofs[c] *amount to?*
26 *Do you think mere words settle matters,*[a]
　　when you disregard[b] *the speech of a man in despair?*
27 [a] *Would you cast lots*[b] *for an orphan,*[c]
　　or barter over[d] *a friend?*

28 *But now, come, if you will, look at me.*
　　I swear[a] *I will not lie to your face.*
29 *Turn*[a] *to me; there is no*[b] *iniquity here!*
　　Turn[c] *to me; my integrity is still*[d] *intact!*[e]
30 *Is my tongue a liar?*[a]
　　Can my palate not discern falsehood?[b]

7:1 *Has not man only hard service on earth?*
　　Are not his days like a hired laborer's?

²*Like a slave he longs for the evening shadow,*
    like a servant awaiting his wages.
³*I too have been allotted months of futility,*
    and nights of misery have been assigned^a *to me.*
⁴*When I lie down, I think,*
    "How long before^a *I arise?"*^b
  But the night^c *drags on,*^d
    ^e*and I have more than my fill of restlessness till dawn.*^f
⁵*My flesh is covered with pus*^a *and scabs;*^b
    my skin grows firm^c *and then oozes.*^d

⁶*My days have been swifter than a weaver's shuttle,*^a
    they have reached their end,^b *and there is no*^c *thread*^d *left.*
⁷*Remember that my life is a mere breath;*
    my eyes shall never again see good fortune.
⁸^a *Eyes that see me now*^b *shall see me*^c *no more;*
    your^d *eyes will turn to me, but I shall be gone.*^e
⁹*For*^a *like*^b *a cloud that dissolves*^c *and vanishes*^d
    is he who descends to Sheol;^e *he will not again come up.*
¹⁰*He returns to his home no more;*
    his place^a *knows him no longer.*^b

¹¹*Therefore*^a *I cannot restrain my utterance;*
    I must speak in the anguish of my spirit;
    I must protest^b *in the bitterness of my soul.*
¹²^a *Am I Sea,*^b *am I the monster Tannin,*
    that you keep me under guard?^{c,d}
¹³*When*^a *I say,*^b *"My bed will comfort me;*
    my couch will relieve^c *my protestations,"*^d
¹⁴*then you terrify me with dreams,*
    affright me with^a *visions.*
¹⁵*I*^a *should choose strangling;*^b
    death, rather than this existence.^c
¹⁶*I have rejected*^a *life; I shall not live*^b *long.*^c
    Leave me alone; for my days are a mere breath.^d

¹⁷*What is man that you make so much*^a *of him,*
    fixing your mind^b *upon him,*
¹⁸*inspecting him every morning,*^a
    at every moment testing him?
¹⁹*Will you never*^a *take your gaze from me,*
    or let me be till I swallow my spittle?
²⁰^a *If*^b *I have sinned,*^c *how do I injure you,*^d
    O Man-Watcher?^e
  Why have you set me up as your target?^f
    Why have I become a burden^g *to you?*^h
²¹*Why do you*^a *not tolerate any sin of mine?*
    Why do you^a *not overlook any fault of mine?*
  For soon I shall lie in dust;
    if you^a *should seek me then, I shall be no more.*

[2] *Like a slave he longs for the evening shadow,*
    like a servant awaiting his wages.
[3] *I too have been allotted months of futility,*
    and nights of misery have been assigned[a] to me.
[4] *When I lie down, I think,*
    "How long before[a] I arise?"[b]
  But the night[c] drags on,[d]
    [e]and I have more than my fill of restlessness till dawn.[f]
[5] *My flesh is covered with pus[a] and scabs;[b]*
    my skin grows firm[c] and then oozes.[d]

[6] *My days have been swifter than a weaver's shuttle,[a]*
    they have reached their end,[b] and there is no[c] thread[d] left.
[7] *Remember that my life is a mere breath;*
    my eyes shall never again see good fortune.
[8] *[a] Eyes that see me now[b] shall see me[c] no more;*
    your[d] eyes will turn to me, but I shall be gone.[e]
[9] *For[a] like[b] a cloud that dissolves[c] and vanishes[d]*
    is he who descends to Sheol;[e] he will not again come up.
[10] *He returns to his home no more;*
    his place[a] knows him no longer.[b]

[11] *Therefore[a] I cannot restrain my utterance;*
    I must speak in the anguish of my spirit;
    I must protest[b] in the bitterness of my soul.
[12] *[a] Am I Sea,[b] am I the monster Tannin,*
    that you keep me under guard? [c,d]
[13] *When[a] I say,[b] "My bed will comfort me;*
    my couch will relieve[c] my protestations,"[d]
[14] *then you terrify me with dreams,*
    affright me with[a] visions.
[15] *I[a] should choose strangling;[b]*
    death, rather than this existence.[c]
[16] *I have rejected[a] life; I shall not live[b] long.[c]*
    Leave me alone; for my days are a mere breath.[d]

[17] *What is man that you make so much[a] of him,*
    fixing your mind[b] upon him,
[18] *inspecting him every morning,[a]*
    at every moment testing him?
[19] *Will you never[a] take your gaze from me,*
    or let me be till I swallow my spittle?
[20] *[a] If[b] I have sinned,[c] how do I injure you,[d]*
    O Man-Watcher?[e]
  Why have you set me up as your target?[f]
    Why have I become a burden[g] to you?[h]
[21] *Why do you[a] not tolerate any sin of mine?*
    Why do you[a] not overlook any fault of mine?
  For soon I shall lie in dust;
    if you[a] should seek me then, I shall be no more.

Notes

6:2.a. כַּעַשׂ in 5:2 is parallel to קִנְאָה and probably means "anger." That is a possible meaning here (cf. RSV "vexation"), but the parallel with הַיָּתִי (see n. 6:2.b) suggests "misery" (JB) or "anguish" (NAB, NIV). NEB "grounds for my resentment" is an interpretative paraphrase. For כַּעַשׂ as the feeling produced by an external calamity, cf. e.g., Ezek 32:9. See further on *Comment.*

2.b. וְהַיָּתִי, from הוה "befall," hence "what has befallen me, my calamity," is to be read. Cf. S. D. Goitein, "*YHWH* the Passionate: The Monotheistic Meaning and Origin of the Name *YHWH*," *VT* 6 (1956) 1–9 (5 n.1).

2.c. Indefinite 3 pl verb functions as a pass.

3.a. The sg יִכְבַּד serves both כַּעַשׂ and הַיָּה, since the former is the inward expression of the latter.

3.b. לָעוּ was derived by KJV "swallowed up" from לוע "swallow," but by most now from לוע II or לעע "talk wildly" (cf. Arab. *laġâ* "make mistakes in speaking"). Hence RSV "have been rash," JB, NEB "are wild," NIV "have been impetuous," NAB "I speak without restraint." Dhorme took לעו from a verb לעה "chatter," and translated "are stammered out," but has found no followers. NEBmg somewhat inexplicably has "words fail me"; but words are one thing that does not fail Job! E. F. Sutcliffe ("Further Notes on Job, Textual and Exegetical: 6,2–3.13; 8,16–17; 19,20–26," *Bib* 31 [1950] 365–78 [367–68]) translated "charged with grief" (cf. Arab. *lāʿ* "be anxious"). M. Dahood (*Bib* 43 [1962] 225) supposes a root לעע (cf. לֹעַ "throat") "gush, overflow."

4.a. Most translate עִמָּדִי in some such way (cf. JB "stick fast in me," NEB "find their mark in me"; Blommerde's "are directed toward me" to parallel the third colon is unlikely since Job's spirit already drinks in their poison, and עם for "against" is rare (Blommerde). For עִמָּדִי as a parallel to בִּי, see 28:14.

4.b. Hesse deletes as a secondary addition.

4.c. Most take רוּחִי as subj of שָׁתָה "drinks"; but NEB apparently regards חֲמָתָם as subject ("their poison soaks into my spirit")—rather improbably.

4.d. Fohrer deletes as a gloss on v 4a.

4.e. יַעַרְכוּנִי is a perfectly acceptable reading, the suffix being datival (GKC, § 117x); for a recent study, see J. J. Stamm, "Das hebräische Verbum *ḥākar*," *Or* 47 (1978) 339–50. Nevertheless, various emendations have been made: to יְעָרְכֻנִי (privative piel; M. Dahood, "Northwest Semitic Philology and Job," *The Bible in Current Catholic Thought* [M. J. Gruenthaner Memorial Volume, ed. J. L. McKenzie; New York: Herder and Herder, 1962] 55–74 [57]); to יַעַכְרוּנִי (Dillmann, Duhm, Fohrer) "trouble, undo me"; to יַכִּירוּנִי "they recognize me" (Ehrlich). Alternatively, a second Heb. root עָרַךְ "wear down" is proposed by G. R. Driver ("Problems in the Hebrew Text of Job," *VTS* 3 [1955] 72–93 [73]) and P. P. Saydon ("Philological and Textual Notes to the Maltese Translation of the Old Testament," *CBQ* 23 [1961] 249–57 [252]) and followed by NEB, *BHS* (probably).

5.a. פֶּרֶא, usually translated "wild ass," was thought by L. Köhler ("Archäologisches. Nr. 20.21," *ZAW* 44 [1926] 56–62 [59–62]) to be the zebra, depicted in the Ptolemaic period with the inscription ὀνάγιος (onager) (J. P. Peters and H. Thiersch, *Painted Tombs in the Necropolis of Marissa (Marêshah)* [London: Palestine Exploration Fund, 1905] pl. XIII). But P. Humbert has argued again in favor of the traditional identification, noting the parallelism with עָרוֹד "wild ass" in 39:5 ("En marge du dictionnaire hébreu," *ZAW* 62 [1950] 199–207 [202]).

6.a. תָּפֵל, usually "what is insipid, tasteless"; in Lam 2:14 it is linked with שָׁוְא "emptiness" to describe false and misleading oracles. The noun תִּפְלָה means "unseemliness, impropriety" in 1:22.

6.b. רִיר "spittle" in 1 Sam 21:14 (13), so "slime, juice, liquid."

6.c. חַלָּמוֹת is probably some vegetable, the word being cognate with the unidentifiable *ḥilimitu* of the Alalakh texts (A. R. Millard, "What has no taste? (Job 6:6)," *UF* 1 [1969] 210). Hölscher, Horst, Fohrer, NEB, JPS identify as "mallows," a "wild plant . . . having hairy stems and leaves and deeply-cleft reddish-purple flowers; it is very mucilaginous" (*OED, s.v.*)—hence "the juice of mallows." RSV, following RVmg, and Driver have "purslane" (purslain), a leguminous plant exuding mucilage. Pope, following A. S. Yahuda, connects it with Arab. *ḥal(l)ūm* "soft cheese." AV, RV, JB, NAB, NIV retain the ancient interpretation of רִיר חלמות as "white of an egg"; this follows the rabbinic explanation (e.g., in Rashi) that חלמון is the yolk of an egg, its "slime" being the white of the egg.

7.a. נַפְשִׁי, either "my soul" (KJV), "my throat" (NEB) (hence "my appetite" [RSV]), or simply "I" (NAB, NIV).

7.b. No obj for לִנְגּוֹעַ is expressed; I assume it is the foods mentioned in v 6 (so also NAB). JB "The very dishes which I cannot stomach" is loosely equivalent; NEB "Food that should nourish me sticks in my throat" is unintelligible as a translation. G. R. Driver ("Hebrew Notes," *JRAS* [1944] 165–68 [168]) translated "my soul refuses to rest," comparing an Arab. verb "was comfortable" and LXX.

7.c. This difficult colon is lit. "they are like the sickness of my food," which may be taken as "they are as food that is loathsome to me" (rsv). The complaint of Driver that "they" (המה) has no proper antecedent can be answered by pointing to the pl חלמות or to the implied pl of תפל together with ריר חלמות. Many, however, emend the text, with a lead from LXX βρόμου "foul odor," to זֵהֲמָה from זהם "loathe," translating, "It [my life, נפשי] loathes it like the sickness of my food," or, reading דוי for כדוי, "It loathes the sickness of my food" (Driver). Similarly NAB reads זֲהֲמָה כַדָּוֶה לַחְמִי (lit. "my food is loathsome like sickness [?]") "they are loathsome food to me." JB emends כדוי to בְדָי (?): "these are my diet in my sickness." NEB "my bowels rumble with an echoing sound" follows suggestions by I. Eitan ("An Unknown Meaning of Raḥamîm," *JBL* 53 [1934] 269–71 [271]) and G. R. Driver (*JRAS* [1944] 168) and reads הֹמָה "growls, roars" (ptcp), כְדָוִי "echo" (cf. Arab. *dawiyyun*), and לְחֵמִי or לְחֵמָי from לְחוּם "bowels." J. Reider ("Some Notes to the Text of the Scriptures: 9. Job 6.7," *HUCA* 3 [1926] 112–13) took המה as Arab. *hm* "waste away" or *hama* "wear out." The suggestion reported in *BHS* (בָדֵי =) זֲהֲמָה כְדֵי must mean "it (my soul) loathes them as (for) my food"; this yields a satisfactory sense, especially in parallel to v 7a. Further suggestions are made by Dhorme and Terrien.

The translation adopted here understands the MT thus: "They (such food) are like diseased food to me" (for דְוַי לַחְמִי equivalent to לֶחֶם דְּוָי, cf. עֶרֶשׂ דְּוָי, Ps 41:4 [3]).

8.a. "My hope" (תקותי) is thought by some (e.g., Driver) to be less what Job means than "my desire." Since LXX has αἴτησις "request," several commentators have emended to תַאֲנָתִי "my desire" (cf. rsv), but this suggestion is rarely followed now.

9.a. נתר hiph "unfasten, set free"; יָדוֹ appears to be the obj, though "hand" is nowhere else the obj of this verb. NEB "snatch me away with his hand" follows G. R. Driver, comparing Arab. *natara* "drag violently, tear," and arguing that the acc is being used to indicate the organ or instrument of action ("Difficult Words in the Hebrew Prophets," *Studies in Old Testament Prophecy Presented to Professor Theodore H. Robinson* [ed. H. H. Rowley; Edinburgh: T. & T. Clark, 1950] 52–72 [70–71]).

9.b. בצע appears explicitly in connection with cutting cloth from the loom only in Isa 38:12; it is also a more general verb for "to cut off," and it cannot be proved that the image of the weaver is in view here.

10.a. עוֹד "still," untranslated by rsv, NEB, and not well translated by JB "at least," points to a "consolation" that Job presently has and would continue to have if God would proceed to "cut him off."

10.b. סלד occurs only here. Driver shows good reason why the conventional translation "exult" is untenable, whether the root is related to Arab. *salada* "be hard" (cf. kjv, rvmg) or to rabbinic Heb. סלד "draw back." Gordis, however, adduces a metaphorical use of סלד with נפש as subject, the sense being "recoil" (נפשו סולדת לאחוריה, *Pesiq. Beshallah* 103a), and some such sense fits well here (similarly Grabbe, *Comparative Philology*, 45–47). NEB "leap for joy" depends on Levy's assumed translation (3:531), which seems satisfactorily disposed of by Driver.

10.c. חילה may be fem, and while it is possible that a fem noun may have as predicate a masc verb (cf. GKC, § 145o), it is also possible that the sense is "pain, in which he (?God, one) spares not." The verb חמל elsewhere always has a personal subj. M. Mers ("A Note on Job VI 10," *VT* 32 [1982] 234–36) removes the final *he* of בחילה to form the interrogative particle הֲ attached to לא, "Shall he [God] not spare?"; he divides the verse into two bicola, but the resultant sense is unintelligible to me.

10.d. כחד, usually "to hide," a rendering defended by Horst (cf. 15:18; 27:11) as Job's protestation that he has never failed to declare God's judgments in matters of right and wrong, a declaration of the "words of God" alluded to already by Eliphaz in 4:3 "you have instructed many" (cf. also Dhorme). This meaning would relate to a comparatively small area of Job's life—as purveyor of divine decisions—and it is not surprising that virtually all translations have "deny," which would relate to the whole of his life. Gordis suggests how the semantic shift may have occurred, and certainly the Eth. cognate means "deny," but that proves little. BDB, 470a, suggest "be effaced, destroyed" for the niph, so the piel here could well have the active meaning "disregard" or "disown" (as proposed by BDB for this passage).

11.a. Lit. "What strength have I that I should wait?" This and the next colon are examples of what A. van Selms has called "motivated interrogative sentences" ("Motivated Interrogative Sentences in the Book of Job," *Semitics* 6 [197] 28–35 [30]).

13.a. הַאִם is a rare collocation, elsewhere only in Num 17:28 [13], where it is either a simple interrogative or else requires the response "Surely not!" In the present context, a rhetorical question equivalent to an affirmation is required, though some regard הַאָם as an acceptable reading as effectively equivalent to הֲלֹא (*BHS*, Horst, Fohrer). Gordis, following Yellin, takes אם as an emphatic particle (also in 8:4; 14:5; 17:2), like Arab. *ʾanna* "indeed"; this seems the most acceptable solution.

Among emendations, there is Duhm's variant word-division הָא מָאַיִן, "Behold, of nothing [is my help]," adopted, with a revocalization of הָא to הָא, by NEB, which then translates, "Oh how shall I find hope within myself?" Graetz attached the ה of האם to the preceding word, yielding the acceptable noun נחושה in v 12 and leaving a direct question in v 13; hence NAB "have I no helper . . . ?" For other less probable emendations, see in Rowley, Dhorme, Fohrer.

13.b. תֻּשִׁיָּה "effective aid" (Gordis); cf. on 5:12. For a range of proposed translations, cf. Rowley. H. A. Brongers (cf. n. 5:12.a) accepts the emendation to תְּשׁוּעָה "deliverance."

14.a. The whole verse is deleted by some, either as an explanatory gloss on v 15 (Fohrer), or because it is impossible to translate with confidence (cf. Hesse). Dhorme, translating it "His friend has scorned compassion and has forsaken the fear of Shaddai," regarded it as a marginal note intended to explain what follows, viz. the attitude of Job's friends as seen by Job.

14.b. This translation accepts the emendation of מרעהו "from his friend" to מֵרֵעַ "friend," making מרע the subject of the first verb.

14.c. MT לַמָּס is here emended by the addition only of two vowel letters to לֹא מָאַס (as *BHS*, Horst). לַמָּס is sometimes taken as an adj מָס (found only here) "despairing, lit. melting" (BDB) from מסס "to dissolve." This is not very probable, and it requires the addition of some such sense as "is due" (loyalty). An unashamed emendation of למס to מֹנֵעַ, "the one refusing," is based on Tg, Pesh, and Vg, and is adopted by RSV and presumably JB. Pope achieves "sick" for מס via Arab. *muss* "be seized with madness, possessed with a demon," which is no more persuasive than BDB's suggestion. See also on מאס in 7:16; 36:5; 42:6.

14.d. No negative appears in the second colon, but the carrying forward of a negative is well attested in e.g., 3:10; 28:17 (cf. GKC, § 152z).

15.a. אחי presumably refers to the friends of the dialogue, since no other kinsfolk are mentioned in the book. 19:13 may be a parallel use. Pope and GNB translate by "friends."

15.b. יעברו can either be "overflow" (as of streams in Isa 23:10; 8:7–8) or "pass away, vanish" (as Isa 29:5 [chaff]; Ps 144:4 [shadow]). The former is the more natural sense, but forms no parallelism with v 15a and is rather linked with vv 16–17; it is supported by NIV, JPS, Moffatt, Duhm, Peake, Pope. The latter is quite possible, though the link with v 16 is more awkward; it is preferred by most translations and commentators. It is less probable that אחי is the subj of יעברו (as in KJV), despite the chiasmus that thereby results (M. Dahood, "Chiasmus in Job," *A Light to my Path: Old Testament Studies in Honor of Jacob M. Myers* [ed. H. N. Bream, R. D. Heim, C. A. Moore; Gettysburg Theological Studies 4; Philadelphia: Temple UP, 1974] 119–30 [121]); עבר is rarely used of persons "perishing" (cf. BDB, *s.v.*, § 6.c.).

16.a. יתעלם "hides itself" (RSV, cf. KJV, JPS), is not very plausible; Driver-Gray's explanation, "falls upon them and disappears into them," evidences the difficulty. Many emend to יתערם "is piled up" (following עלימו "on them"), or else maintain that יתערם and יתעלם are simply phonetic variants (Dhorme, Gordis); P. W. Skehan sees the variation as due to the assonance of the liquids *l* and *m* in the second half of the line ("Second Thoughts on Job 6:16 and 6:25," *CBQ* 31 [1969] 210–12). Nevertheless, unless the picture is of snow being heaped up on top of frozen rivers (as NAB), which would be a rather rare occurrence in a Palestinian climate (in Ecclus 43:21, adduced by Skehan as a parallel, ice forms "water," not rivers), the "heaping up" is the swelling of the stream by the melted snow; hence JB "they swell with the thawing of the snow" (cf. NIV). NEB translates twice-over, with "hidden with piled-up snow"! Pope follows Dahood in taking עלם as "be dark" (cf. 42:3 מעלים equivalent to מחשיך in 38:2), and so renders "darkened with snow." The parallelism is neat, but it is difficult to see why snow as well as ice should "darken" the water; and the issue is confused by Pope's citation of the Arab. cognate *ẓlm* "be dark" in the phrase *ẓalama al-wādī* "the wadi overflowed." Grabbe (51–54) rightly argues against the supposition of a Heb. root *ʿlm* "be dark" (cf. also D. J. A. Clines, "The Etymology of Hebrew צֶלֶם," *JNWSL* 3 [1974] 19–25; and cf. n. 3:5.a).

17.a. בעת ירזבו, lit. "at the time [when] they flow," assuming that the *hapax* זרב is cognate with the well-attested Semitic root *zrb* "flow" (cf. Arab. *zariba;* and see Grabbe, *Comparative Philology,* 54–55). G. R. Driver ("Some Hebrew Medical Expressions," *ZAW* 65 [1954] 255–62 [261]) urged this sense, but also referred to Akk. *zarābu* "press, squeeze," which must now be abandoned (Grabbe). NEB following Driver assumes a Heb. זרב "flow"; hence "the moment they are in spate"; cf. NAB "once they flow." Most other versions assume זרב to be a by-form of צרב "burn."

18.a MT אָרְחוֹת is const pl of אֹרַח "way" and is lit. translated "the paths of their way [sc. the wadis] turns aside," i.e., the course of the wadis winds about in the desert and eventually loses itself in the sand (or less probably, as Rowley explains this view, "the courses of the streams wind about the stones in their beds and finally disappear in the ground"). This interpretation is adopted by KJV, JPS, Weiser, Gordis. Almost all modern interpreters slightly revocalize אָרְחוֹת to אָרְחוֹת "caravans," a change that must be made in any case in v 19, thus e.g., RSV "The caravans turn aside from their course." Andersen takes אָרְחוֹת דָּרְכָּם as a const phrase, with a final enclitic *mem*, "highway caravans"; this is possible, but the usual view is preferable.

18.b. לפת, only elsewhere in Judg 16:29 (Samson "rings" the temple pillars), Ruth 3:8 (the man "turns over"). So cognate Arab. *lafata* "twist, wring; turn aside, divert" (Lane, 2665) is compared. Most think the caravans turn aside from the usual trail (cf. JB "leave the trail"), but NEB, less probably, translates "winding hither and thither."

18.c. עלה "go up" also means "depart" (cf. BDB, *s.v.*, § 2.e.).

19.a. The verse ends with לָמוֹ "for them," referring to the "streams" (נחלים) of v 15. If the referent is not made explicit (as by NEB, NIV), it may appear that the caravans of Tema and Sheba are searching for the lost caravans of v 18.

20.a. בוש, conventionally translated "be ashamed," very frequently refers not to the sense of shame but to the disappointment of expectation. See F. Stolz, *THWAT* 1:269–72; J. W. Olley, "A Forensic Connotation of *bôš*," *VT* 26 (1976) 230–34. H. Seebass (*TDOT* 2:50–60) could perhaps have distinguished more clearly between the obj and subj senses of בוש.

20.b. The difference in meaning between causal כי "because" and concessive כי "even though" (Andersen) is minimal here.

20.c. בטח is sg where a pl is plainly necessary. Most read בָּטָחוּ, but whether this is an emendation or the normalization of spelling is hard to say.

21.a. The whole verse is deleted by Bickell and Duhm, on the grounds that there is nothing to suggest that the friends are afraid; but see *Comment*.

21.b. Most emend the initial כי to כֵן "thus," and לֹא (Q לוֹ) to לִי "to me" (cf. RSV, JB, NAB), which seems the most natural sense. Attempts to preserve MT are less successful; לֹא as a noun "nothing" (as KJV, Blommerde) is poorly attested, if at all; the difficulty with Gordis's "now you have become it (the stream)" is that all references to the wadis since the נחל of v 15 have been in the pl. It is not clear what text is rendered by NIV "Now you too have proved to be of no help"; perhaps לְאַל "(to) nothing" (as in 24:25); so also Horst. Nothing can be said to recommend J. Reider's idea that לֹא is an abbreviation for לָאִים = לָאֵם "hesitating" from לאה ("Etymological Studies in Biblical Hebrew," *VT* 4 [1954] 276–95 [288]).

24.a. הוֹרוּנִי lit. "teach me," a typical term from educational instruction (wisdom) (cf. 8:10; 12:7, 8; 33:33). See *Comment*.

24.b. Technically, שׁגה/שׁגג denotes sins of negligence or ignorance (as Lev 4:13; Num 15:22 [cf. 24]); see J. Milgrom, "The Cultic שׁגגה and Its Influence in Psalms and Job," *JQR* 58 (1967) 115–25, and R. Knierim, *THWAT* 2:869–72. But it is used in its more general sense here.

25.a. מרץ, usually niph "be sick, grievous," in Mic 2:10 of destruction (חָבָל), in 1 Kgs 2:8 of a curse (קְלָלָה), hence NIV "painful." This meaning is often thought unsuitable here; some cf. Akk. *marāṣu* "be difficult, inaccessible." KJV "forcible," RSV "forceful," derive from the definition by ibn Ezra and Qimchi as חזק. Cf. N. S. Doniach and W. E. Barnes, "Job vi 25: √מרץ," *JTS* 31 (1929–30) 291–92. Many follow Tg מַה־נִּמְלְצוּ "how pleasant [to my palate are your words]," and either simply emend נמרצו to נמלצו (Duhm), or else see an interchange of *mem* and *resh* (cf. on יתעלם, v 16) (so Dhorme, Pope; similarly Skehan, *CBQ* 31 [1969] 210–12, observing the assonance of *m* and *r*). Hence NAB "agreeable." G. R. Driver ("Some Hebrew Words," *JTS* 29 [1927–28] 390–96 [394]) sees מרץ as cognate with Akk. *marāṣu* "be ill, displeasing," and translates "are bitter"; hence probably NEB "how harsh." Driver himself took the colon as a question, "How are honest words bitter?" which amounts to saying they are "sweet." Gordis unpersuasively argues that the verb מרץ "be ill" here means, by the principle of *addad* (opposite meaning), "be strong, vigorous." JB "Fair comment can be borne without resentment" is too paraphrastic to be helpful.

25.b. יֶשֶׁר "straightness; uprightness; what is due, right" (BDB, 449b), in the phrase דִּבְרֵי יֹשֶׁר, often rendered "honest words" (RSV, NAB, NIV, GNB). The nuance "right judgment" is determined from the context; see *Comment*. NEB "the upright man" revocalizes to יָשָׁר (so also Duhm), thus creating a parallel to חכמים in the next colon (see n. 25.c).

25.c. The straightforward הוֹכֵחַ מִכֶּם is unnecessarily emended by some to הַחֲכָמִים, hence NEB "the arguments of wise men" (cf. Brockington).

26.a. יכח hiph, usually here translated "reprove," may be better understood as "convict, convince" (cf. BDB, 407a). NIV unconventionally translates: "Do you mean to correct what I say?" but יכח hiph apparently has only a personal object in the sense of "correct."

26.b. It is debatable whether אמרי נאשׁ is a second obj of תחשׁבו (as JPS, Gordis), or whether "is" should be supplied in the second half; the translation is not affected. חשׁב with לְרוּחַ could be "reckon as wind" (cf. RSV, NIV, NAB), i.e., presumably, emptiness (not, as Rowley, "soon blown away, and so should not be taken seriously"; cf. JB "desperate speech that the wind blows away"). Some have sought in רוח a parallel to לְהוֹכַח; MT is satisfactory, however, though NEB reads וּלְרֻוַח "and to sift." Guillaume, with the same reading, compared Arab. *rawwaḥa* "gave rest to" and translated "and to silence."

27.a. The verse is deleted by, e.g., Fohrer because "these strong reproaches against the friends are at this point quite unjustified," but this is to ignore any modal use of the verbs, e.g., "would you," or the possibility that it is a question (Bickell). Peake suggested that the verse would be more suitable after v 23; in this he is followed by Moffatt, with "(Ransom? You fall upon a blameless man, you would make capital out of a friend!)." This spoils the rhythm of the development of the argument from v 22 to v 27.

27.b. תַּפִּילוּ "you (would) cause to fall" has no obj expressed, so most assume that the idiom הִפִּיל גּוֹרָל "cast lots" is employed (גורל is omitted also in 1 Sam 14:42, though there the doubled prep בֵּין makes the meaning sure). NJB "haggling over the price of" presumably bases itself on the parallel תכרו. An alternative adopted by some involves reading עַל־יָתוֹם as עֲלֵי־תָם (see n. 27.c), rendering תפילו "will you fall upon?" The hiph hardly allows this rendering, so a minor emendation to תִּפְּלוּ (cf. LXX) is required (so Duhm; NEB "assail," allowing יתום to stand in the text, and admitting תם in mg). KJV "ye overwhelm" perhaps follows LXX ἐπιπίπτετε, registering the lit. sense of תפילו in mg: "cause to fall upon."

27.c. MT עַל־יָתוֹם can be divided differently to yield עֲלֵי־תֹם "upon innocence" or more probably עֲלֵי־תָם "upon an innocent man." This suggestion is usually combined with the correction of תפילו to תפלו (see n. 27.b), and is followed by Duhm, NEBmg, Andersen. This is a reasonable alternative to MT.

27.d. תִּכְרוּ is usually "buy," and with following על once occurs in the sense "make a bargain over, barter over" (40:30 [41:6]); the point is that it would be extremely callous to regard any person, but especially a friend, not as a human being but as a commodity to be traded in, bargained over (cf. RSV), and made merchandise of (cf. RV); cf. Dhorme, "treat your friend as a subject for speculation." "Barter away" (NAB, NIV) is not the issue, still less is "selling your friend at bargain prices" (JB). KJV "dig *a pit*" connected תכרו with כרה "dig" (cf. Vg *subvertere nitimini*); but כרה always has the obj expressed; and the על would be rather meaningless. NEB "hurl yourselves" vocalizes וַתָּכֹרוּ, comparing LXX ἐνάλλεσθε "rush against" (perhaps with כרר "dance, whirl" in mind); this reading follows Schultens, Merx, Beer, but is judged "very precarious" by Driver.

28.a. For אם introducing oaths, see M. R. Lehmann, "Biblical Oaths," *ZAW* 81 (1969) 74–92 (87–91). Most versions have an emphatic particle (e.g., NAB "surely") or a question (NIV "Would I lie to your face?"; cf. NEB). This is certainly weak; Gordis calls it "banal," and recommends an inversion to ואל פניכם אם אכזב, a very idiosyncratic move.

29.a. שֻׁבוּ, lit. "return," translated "Think again" (NEB), "Think it over" (NAB), "Relent" (JB, NIV). Gordis argues for "Stop, stay" (cf. R. Gordis, "Some Unrecognized Meanings of the Root *Shub*," *JBL* 52 [1933] 153–62).

29.b. אַל used in poetry as more emphatic than לֹא; cf. BDB, 39a *s.v.* אַל a.(c); Gordis.

29.c. Following Q שֻׁבוּ for K שבי.

29.d. עוֹד is linked by the Masoretic punctuation to the preceding ושבו, but a good case is made by Dhorme for linking it with what follows (so JB, NAB, NIVmg).

29.e. צִדְקִי־בָהּ, lit. "my righteousness is in it," taken by some to mean "in the matter under discussion" (cf. KJVmg); hence NEB "in question," RSV, NIV "at stake"; cf. JB "my case is not yet tried"; Moffatt "no guilt has been proved against me." Others understand, "My right is still in it," i.e., is present, and so I have a righteous cause; hence RV, JPS: "my cause is righteous." Gordis more persuasively argues for the meaning "my integrity is still in itself," i.e., is intact. Ps 90:10 and Gen 24:14 may be analogies. Others emend בה to בִּי "in me" (Hitzig, Driver).

30.a. הֲיֵשׁ־בִּלְשׁוֹנִי עַוְלָה lit. "is there iniquity on (or, in) my tongue," translated by most versions fairly literally, but unidiomatically in English. NEB "Do I give voice to injustice?" is rather irrelevant to Job's present claim.

30.b. הַוּוֹת, usually understood as "calamities" (cf. conjectured הַוָּתִי in v 2); cf. RSV, JB. But most seek a parallel with עולה in the first half of the line; KJV "perverse things," RV "mischievous things," NIV "malice," perhaps look to the other meaning of הוה as "evil desire" (cf. BDB, 217b). Gordis argues to better effect that הוה here means "deceit, falsehood" as in Mic 7:3; Ps 5:10 [9] (opp. to נְכוֹנָה); NAB also translates "falsehood." Pope less convincingly argued that הַוּוֹת here is equivalent to Ug. *hwt* (cf. Akk. *awatu*, normally *amatu*) "word" (though he advances no other OT parallels), translating "Can my palate not discriminate words?" Such a suggestion probably gives rise to the periphrastic NEB "Does my sense not warn me when my words are mild?" This takes us too far from the thrust of Job's purpose at this point.

7:3.a. מָנוּ, lit., "they (indefinite) have numbered." It is unnecessary to emend to the passive מֻנּוּ (so Hölscher) or to regard the form as a phonetic variant of the pual (Gordis).

4.a. מָתַי is simply "when," but since the mood is one of impatience "how long before" serves better, as also in, e.g., Amos 8:5; Ps 41:6 [5]; 42:3 [2]; 94:8. עַד־מָתַי "how long" refers to an action now going on; מָתַי to one anticipated.

4.b. Conjectural emendation to מָתַי יוֹם וְאָקוּם (e.g., Duhm, NEB "When will it be day that I may rise?") or מָתַי יֵאוֹר וְאָקוּם (Horst, *BHS*) "when will it be light that I may rise?" partly follows LXX ἐὰν κοιμηθῶ, λέγω Πότε ἡμέρα; ὡς δ' ἂν ἀναστῶ, πάλιν Πότε ἑσπέρα; More thorough retroversion of LXX leads to יוֹם וְאָקוּם וְאָם קַמְתִּי מָתַי (Hölscher, Dhorme); hence JB: "Lying in bed I wonder, 'When will it be day?' Risen I think, 'How slowly evening comes!'"; similarly Terrien, Hesse. The resemblance to Deut 28:67 should not dominate discussion. Most probably the whole verse concerns Job's "nights," elaborating v 3b (so RSV, NAB, NIV).

4.c. עֶרֶב is usually "evening" rather than "night," the nearest parallel being the dubious Prov 7:9. The combination with מְדֻד strengthens somewhat the case for emending the latter (see n. 4.d). But a word for "evening" can surely apply, in poetry at least, to the whole night.

4.d. מְדֻד piel from מדד "measure" is used only here for "extend, continue" (BDB, 551a), but hithpo וַיִּתְמֹדֵד in 1 Kgs 17:21 also clearly means "stretched." This makes the suggestion of Perles II, Driver-Gray, וּמְדֵי for מדד "as often as evening (comes)" (so also Fohrer, Rowley) needless. The view of J. Reider ("מְדֻד in Job 7:4," *JBL* 39 [1920] 60–65) that דד means "breast," thus "from the breast of evening, i.e., from early evening," is quite unconvincing in the absence of Heb. parallels and the strained nature of the Arab. parallels he adduces.

4.e. The line is bracketed as a gloss by Hesse.

4.f. נֶשֶׁף is twilight of morning or evening; so RSV "dawn," JB "[evening] twilight."

5.a. רִמָּה is now almost universally translated as "worm(s)" (as in 17:14; 21:26). A homonym of רמה as a medical term may be proposed, cognate with Arab. *ramaya* VI "be sluggish; [of wound] become putrid, corrupt" (similarly Guillaume, comparing Arab. *rimmatun*, "rottenness, decay"). רמה is probably chiastically connected with ימאס, so the term "pus" suggests itself. Cf. LXX ἐν σαπρίᾳ σκωλήκων "in corruption of worms" and Jerome *putredine vermium*, both translating רמה twice, and aware of the sense of "rotting (flesh)." Vg has simply *putredine*.

5.b. גּוּשׁ, a *hapax* form of גּוּשׁ "clod," probably has a medical sense (cf. LXX βώλακες "clods") like "pustules" (G. R. Driver, *VTS* 3 [1955] 73) or "scabs" (JB, NEB, NAB, NIV); cf. Arab. *jas'u(n)* "rough skin." The following word עָפָר appears to be in constr relation, hence "clods of dust" (KJV, RV), "dirt" (RSV); עפר is understood metaphorically by Dhorme, thus "dirty scabs"; cf. BJ "croûtes terreuses" (so also Terrien), JB "loathsome scabs"; but the literal and the metaphorical senses are both rather implausible. It is perhaps better to see עפר as a gloss on the very rare גּוּשׁ; so e.g., Fohrer, Horst, *BHS* (prb). G. R. Driver takes עפר as a new root cognate with Arab. *jafara* "covered"; cf. *jafira* (of a wound) "cracked and reopened." He then links גוּשׁ עפר עוֹרי together as "scab covers my skin" (which NEB follows) and regards רגע וימאס "it is cracked and gapes open" as an "obvious gloss" on the former phrase (hence NEB relegates רגע וימאס to a footnote). It is doubtful that רגע means "cracked" (see n. 5.c), and improbable that a phrase denoting open sores should be a gloss on "scab," which indicates the healing of a sore.

5.c. רָגַע, often taken as "harden" (BDB, 921b, RSV; cf. RV "closeth up"), cognate with Eth. *raga'a* "congeal" (see Driver-Gray). Others note רגע in parallelism with מחץ in 26:12, and translating מחץ as "break, shatter," take רגע as "crack" (cf. NEBmg, NAB, JB, NIV). But מחץ more probably means "strike, smite," and רגע in 26:12 is not a strict parallel but means "congeal," as does קָפָא in reference to the same event in 10:10; Exod 15:8. Guillaume's comparison with Arab. *raja'a* "returned" (translate "grows again") is implausible. L. Kopf's recourse to the same cognate (*VT* 8 [1958] 202) leads to the unconvincing proposal to understand רגע as "becomes," thus "my skin becomes a clod of earth that breaks apart" (in reference to the decomposition of the body after death); but Job is not here envisaging his postmortem state.

5.d. Most take וַיִּמָּאֵס as a by-form or "metaplastic" form of מסס niph "flow, drip": thus e.g., NEBmg "discharging," NIV "festering," JB "oozes pus."

6.a. אֶרֶג is plainly a "loom" in Judg 16:14, and though BDB, 71a, translates it thus here, most take it as "shuttle."

6.b. It is debatable whether וַיִּכְלוּ means "[my days collectively, viz. my life] have reached their end" (cf. JB; TOB; Dhorme or "[my days individually, viz. every day] reaches its end" (so most). KJV, RV "are spent" means "are finished," not "are lived through."

6.c. בְּאֶפֶס is usually translated "and [that] without." Those who take תקוה as "thread" (see *Comment*) take באפס as "for lack of," which, despite Driver-Gray's objection, is adequately paralleled by Prov 26:20. However, this translation (as Dhorme: "have come to an end for lack of thread") is unsatisfactory; for what is the "thread" from which life is woven? There is no answer offered by the metaphor. We should assume that ובאפס תקוה transposes into the metaphoric key of v 6a the idea of conclusion (ויכלו), and translate "and there is no thread."

6.d. See *Comment.* If there is a play on the senses of תקוה as "hope" or "thread," the literary device may be termed a *taurīya* (Guillaume) or *taḥīn* (Gordis). Most probably, "thread" alone is meant.

8.a. The verse is missing from LXX; for that reason and also because it is somewhat repetitive of v 8, it was deleted by Bickell; but it is today generally retained (Moffatt enclosed it in square brackets; Driver-Gray set it in smaller type). LXX's omission of the verse may have been theologically motivated, as avoiding the inference that God cannot see Job at all times (Gard, *Exegetical Method of the Greek Translator,* 77).

8.b. ר אי "of the one seeing me," viz., anyone who now sees me. J. Weingreen proposed that ר אי was a noun, "sight," translating אין ר אי as "no seeing eye" ("The Construct-Genitive Relation in Hebrew Syntax," *VT* 4 [1954] 50–59 [56–57]); it would not then be necessary to supply "no more" with "shall see me." The proposal is not very convincing (cf. Fohrer), and is contrary to the Masoretic vocalization (Gordis). NEB apparently adopts Weingreen's proposal but nevertheless supplies "no more." Andersen moves athnach to ע'ני and translates "(Your) eye(s) will [assertative *l*] gaze for me; your eyes will look [reading ראֹ, inf abs] for me; but I won't be there." This is possible, but MT is satisfactory, despite Andersen's claim that the first colon is too long and the second incomplete.

8.c. NEB takes תְּשׁוּרֵנִי as 2 sg, which is possible only by adopting Weingreen's suggestion for ר אי (see n. 8.b), or by regarding the second verb as addressed by Job's wraith to his "visitor" (ר אי) (Stevenson).

8.d. Gordis improbably regards the 2 sg suff as impersonal, viz. "you, anyone," parallel to the indefinite אין ר אי of the first colon.

8.e. For אֵינֶנִּי and other forms of אין signifying nonexistence, cf. Ps 39:14 [13]; Job 3:21; 23:8; 24:24; 27:19. Blommerde revocalizes to וְאֵינֶנִי as a "denominative piel" from אין, translating the phrase "Your eyes are against me and annihilate me" (cf. also on 27:19). The conventional use of ויאנני and ויאננו for the final outcome of some action is much more probable here, however.

9.a. Supplied; v 9 is the reason that no eye will be able to see him (v 8).

9.b. With ancient versions (cf. Dhorme) and some modern versions (JB, NEB, NAB, NIV; Terrien) "like" is added to make the comparison explicit. כַאֲשֶׁר correlative to כֵן is sometimes omitted in poetry (e.g., Isa 55:9; cf. BDB, 486b, § 2.d.).

9.c. כלה "cease"; of smoke being dispersed, Ps 37:20.

9.d. Lit., "goes" (וַיֵּלַךְ); used of the vanishing of clouds or dew in Hos 13:3. For the pausal vocalization, see GKC, § 69x.

9.e. A major pause here is required by the sense, since the comparison is between the vanishing of a cloud and a human's descent to Sheol.

10.a. מְקֹמוֹ, effectively equivalent to "his abode" (cf. Dahood, *Psalms I,* 162; *Psalms III,* 29; "Hebrew-Ugaritic Lexicography V," *Bib* 48 [1967] 421–38 [431]).

10.b. NEBmg "and he will not be noticed any more in his place" no doubt takes the subject of יַכִּירֶנּוּ as indefinite, and מקמו is perhaps understood adverbially. But reading מקמו as subject is quite acceptable.

11.a. גַם would make good sense as "therefore" (so KJV, RV, NIV; Dhorme, Horst). Ps 52:7 [5] is quoted as a parallel, but it is equally well explained as adversative (cf. BDB, 169b, § 5); so "therefore" is perhaps not sufficiently well attested. "I also" for גַם־אָנִי is possible if it is thought that Job is comparing himself with Eliphaz. It hardly seems that he compares himself with God; the explanation of Driver-Gray is far-fetched: "As God shows no regard for man . . . so he [Job] also will show no regard for him by restraint of speech" (similarly Gordis). Regard in either quarter is not the issue. See C. J. Labuschagne, "The Emphasizing Particle *gam* and its Connotations," *Studia Biblica et Semitica Th. C. Vriezen . . . dedicata* (ed. W. C. van Unnik and A. S. van der Woude; Wageningen: H. Veenman & Zonen, 1966) 193–203 (198 n.1).

11.b. שִׂיחַ is not primarily a mental activity (e.g., "muse"), but a verbal one; in this context, of speech with complaint (cf. also Ps 55:18 [17]; 77:4 [3] [in both cases parallel to המה "moan"]; Isa 53:8). Even where usually rendered "muse" (e.g., Ps 77:13 [12]), verbal activity is involved (similarly with הגה); cf. also on 9:27. S. Mowinckel ("The Verb *śiaḥ* and the Nouns *śiaḥ, śiḥā,*" *ST* 15 [1961] 1–10) wants to stress the relation of שׂיח to "inner, mental activity, to the emotional thinking and musing" (8), but H.-P. Müller ("Die hebräische Wurzel שׂיח," *VT* 19 [1969] 361–67) rightly stresses the verbal aspect ("loud, enthusiastic or emotion-laden speech").

12.a. This verse is another example of the motivated interrogative sentence (van Selms, *Semitics* 6 [1978] 30–31).

12.b. Without the article; it is effectively a proper name.

12.c. M. Dahood ("Mišmār, 'Muzzle,' in Job 7:12," *JBL* 80 [1961] 270–71) takes מִשְׁמָר here and in Ps 68:23 [22] (reading אשבם מצלות ים for ישוב ממצלות ים) as "muzzle." Pope, while accepting the suggestion for Ps 68:23 [22], rightly objects that there is nothing in the present passage that suggests that God is trying to silence Job; in Ps 39:2 [1]; 141:3 "guarding" the mouth prevents wrong speech, so it is not even possible to picture Job here as a wild beast muzzled to prevent its viciousness. It is rather God's constant surveillance that Job is protesting; see *Comment*. In any case, the existence of a Semitic root *šbm* "muzzle," upon which Dahood's suggestion for our verse was based, has been shown to be highly doubtful by J. Barr ("Ugaritic and Hebrew *šbm?*" *JSS* 18 [1973] 17–39; cf. also Grabbe, *Comparative Philology*, 55–58).

Dhorme's translation, "that Thou shouldst erect a barrier against me" (as also he understands משמר in Jer 51:12) also suffers from the difficulty that God does not appear to be pushing Job off. Ehrlich thought to solve the difficulty of the relation between v 12 and v 13 (see *Comment* on v 13) by translating משמר "wakefulness" (cf. Arab. *samara* "was awake"; Gordis accepts this as a *talḥin* (double entendre), but the phonetic correspondence is suspect.

12.d. NAB transposes to this point v 20c, d.

13.a. כִּי frequentative, as in 1:5 (GKC, §§ 112hh, 164d): "whenever."

13.b. אמר "say" is not infrequently well translated "think" (BDB, 56 § 2); so here Moffatt, NEB, NIV, Duhm, Fohrer, Gordis.

13.c. נשא ב "share the burden of" (cf. Num 11:17).

13.d. שִׂיחִי: see n. 7:11.b. "My complaint" (KJV, RSV, NAB, NIV) could misleadingly suggest "my illness." JB "my pain" (BJ "mes souffrances") is hardly defensible.

14.a. מן of cause equivalent to ב of means prefacing חמלות. It is unnecessary to classify this as an example of the alternation of *beth* and *min* (on the issue, see N. M. Sarna, "The Interchange of the Prepositions *Beth* and *Min* in Biblical Hebrew," *JBL* 78 [1959] 310–16 [313]; and cf. on 4:21), still less to regard *beth* as actually denoting "from" (cf. Dahood, *Psalms II*, 33; Blommerde, 19, 49).

15.a. נפש sometimes means "throat, neck" (e.g., Ps 69:2 [1]) (cf. KB, 626b; C. Westermann, *THWAT* 2:74–75), a sense not recognized by BDB. It is hazardous to regard this concrete sense as the "original" or "primitive" meaning, as some do. The combination of נפש with מחנק "strangulation" tempts one to translate by "throat" here (so Pope; M. Dahood, "Ugaritic Lexicography," *Mélanges Eugène Tisserant* [Studi e Testi 231; Città del Vaticano, 1964] 81–104 [93]; Blommerde; Andersen), but this move is not necessarily correct.

15.b. Andersen sees in מַחֲנַק, a *hapax* usually translated as an abstract noun "strangulation," an epithet of the deity Mot, "the Strangler"; he would translate: "And the Strangler has selected my neck, Death my bones," viz., Death the strangler has chosen the bones of my neck. Presumably the verb וַתִּבְחַר is understood as a 3 pl *tqtl* form (bibliography: Blommerde, 16; add Dahood, *Psalms III*, 387), despite "the Strangler" and Death being the same person. Some comparative textual evidence for Death as a strangler (Andersen cites iconography) is needed to make the suggestion more than merely possible.

15.c. A somewhat free rendering of עַצְמוֹתָי, lit., "my bones," viz., "my being" (cf. BDB, 782b, § 1d); cf. KJV "my life." If נפשי is taken as "throat," עצמותי would be more naturally "bones," but most feel that "death rather than my bones" is a strange phrase, which would hardly signify that Job had wasted away until he was a mere bag of bones ("this skeleton," Guillaume). On the contrary, if עצמותי signifies the whole person, נפשי is likely to have the same meaning.

Certainly emendation of עצמותי to עַצְבוֹתַי (as in 9:28) is unnecessary (though adopted by Moffatt, JB, NAB; Driver-Gray, Dhorme, Terrien, Rowley, Hesse). Little can be said for the translation of J. Reider (*VT* 2 [1952] 126) "my defensive arguments," reading מַעֲצָמוֹתַי (cf. עֶצְמָה "defense" in Isa 41:21, as Arab. *ʿiṣmat*. Avoiding emendation, G. R. Driver ("Mistranslations," *ExpT* 57 [1945–46] 192–93 [193], 249) proposed a new word עַצָמָה, cognate with Arab. *ʿaẓm* "great," and translated "great misfortunes, sufferings" (so too NEB; Horst, Fohrer). But, as Rowley remarked, the vital word "sufferings" has to be supplied.

Another approach is to regard the initial *mem* of מעצמותי as enclitic *mem* attached to מות (so N. M. Sarna, "Some Instances of the Enclitic *-m* in Job," *JJS* 6 [1955] 108–10 [109]; Dahood, "Ugaritic Lexicography," 93; Pope, Andersen [implied]). This permits the translation "My neck prefers strangulation, my bones death," which makes reasonable sense but flattens out an interestingly crafted line into a bland synonymous parallelism.

16.a. The natural translation of מָאַסְתִּי requires an obj, which is not expressed. "Death" is a possibility, and some even transfer the verb to the end of v 15 to render "I despise death more than my pains" (reading מעצבותי; see n. 7:15.c). Driver-Gray, however, rightly object that מאס is to "despise so as to *reject*, not to despise while *accepting*." "[My] life" (either חַיַּי understood [cf.

9:21] or in reference back to עצמותי) is much more probably the implied obj (and is supplied by rsv, niv); and מאסתי is to be understood not as a feeling in the present (kjv, rsv "I loathe") but as a decision already taken. Dhorme's difficulty, how this verb is linked with the following clause, is thus overcome.

Another possibility, though it is denied by Driver, is that מאס is a metaplastic form of מסס "melt; despair"; hence probably Vg *desperavi;* cf. rvmg, jb, nab "I waste away"; neb "I am in despair"; similarly Dhorme, Rowley. Emendation to מַסּוֹתִי (as Bickell, Driver, *BHS*) is unnecessary.

The word is not rendered by LXX, and Fohrer rejects it as a gloss on v 15; Pope is tempted to do likewise.

16.b. rsv "I would not live" (cf. neb) balances the next colon less well than an acknowledgment that "I shall not live."

16.c. לְעוֹלָם, traditionally translated "for ever" (rsv, niv) is a litotes that sounds too exaggerated in that form.

16.d. הֶבֶל, probably with the sense of transitoriness and fleetingness (cf. יָמַי קַלּוּ, v 6) rather than worthlessness (as niv "my days have no meaning"; cf. gnb "My life makes no sense") (cf. K. Seybold, *TDOT* 3:317).

17.a. Pope renders תְגַדְּלֶנּוּ "rear" (similarly Stevenson ["breed up"]; Horst, Fohrer, comparing 1 Sam 1:2 and remarking on the significance of successful rearing of a child in a culture where infant mortality is high). The translation is possible, but it spoils the parallel with Ps 8, and the link with v 12 (see *Comment*).

17.b. תָשִׁית לָבָּ, translated by the old EVV "set thine heart," which may suggest affection. But לב is rather understanding or attention (cf. 8:10; 36:5).

18.a. L. Delekat's argument that בקר here and elsewhere in poetry must mean "day" rather than "morning" is unconvincing ("Zum hebräisches Wörterbuch," *VT* 14 [1964] 7–66 [8]); it is not even so by merismus, for the picture is of Job under inspection the moment he wakes (cf. v 14, where his sleep is equally troubled by God).

19.a. Lit. "how long will you not" (כַּמָּה לֹא). The question-form is frequent in psalmic petitions (cf. H. Gunkel and J. Begrich, *Einleitung in die Psalmen: Die Gattungen der religiösen Lyrik Israels* [Göttingen: Vandenhoeck und Ruprecht, 1933] 229–30).

20.a. Duhm, Hölscher, Fohrer, Hesse, omit the whole of this line as far too long. See also n. 20.c.

20.b. On the implied hypothesis, see *Comment*.

20.c. חטאתי is omitted by Pope on metrical grounds.

20.d. Lit. "What do I do to you?"

20.e. LXX has ὁ ἐπιστάμενος τὸν νοῦν τῶν ἀνθρώπων "the one who understands the minds of humans," which leads some to propose inserting לֵב before הָאָדָם (so Ball; cf. *BHS*; followed by neb). But LXX may be paraphrasing to remove the irony of נצר האדם (cf. Gard, *Exegetical Method of the Greek Translator*, 48). Certainly there is little reason for following Pesh in connecting נצר with יצר and translating "creator of man" (cf. *BHS*).

20.f. מִפְגָּע, lit. "thing hit," is suitably rendered "target" (cf. 6:4; 16:12), despite Peake's preference for "something against which one strikes" ("Job is, so to speak, always in God's way"); similarly Driver, Rowley, Moffatt. neb "butt" is "a mark for archery practice; properly a mound or other erection on which the target is set up" (*OED* 1:1216a).

20.g. Some find מַשָּׂא "burden" out of place here (cf. Pope: "what seems desiderated is a synonym for target"). Beer suggested מַטָּרָה, "target" (in 16:12; Lam 3:12); cf. *BHK*; so too Hesse; neb, nab (transferred to v 12).

20.h. MT עָלַי "to myself" (as kjv, rv, jps) is generally recognized as one of the 18 *tiqqune sopherim*, "corrections of the scribes," made in order to avoid using improper language of God. See *IDBS*, 263–64; C. D. Ginsburg, *Introduction to a Masoretico-Critical Edition of the Hebrew Bible* (New York: Ktav, repr. 1966), 347–63; W. E. Barnes, "Ancient Corrections in the Text of the Old Testament (*Tikkun Sopherim*," *JTS* 1 (1899–1900) 387–414 (412); C. McCarthy, *The Tiqqune Sopherim, and other Theological Corrections in the Masoretic Text of the Old Testament* (OBO 36; Freiburg/Göttingen: Universitätsverlag/Vandenhoeck und Ruprecht, 1981) esp. 79–81; and for another possible example, cf. on 9:19. The original text probably read עָלֶיךָ "to you" (as also LXX). Driver, following Budde, nevertheless thought עליך anticlimactic, and preferred MT. Blommerde strains probability in revocalizing עלי to עֵלִי "Most High" (bibliography: Blommerde, 24; see further, n. 10:2.a) and supposing that לֶךְ in the second colon does duty in this colon also.

21.a. The addressee is surely God, not an indefinite person equivalent to "anyone" (as Gordis).

Form / Structure / Setting

The *structure* of this speech may be best determined from the directions in which Job turns his address. (i) In 6:2–13 he is evidently uttering a monologue, speaking neither to the friends nor to God. He ignores the friends entirely and speaks of God in the third person. Even his questions (vv 11, 12) are purely rhetorical questions, addressed to no one in particular. (ii) In 6:14–30, on the other hand, he is clearly addressing himself to the friends. Vv 14–20 are not indeed cast in the second person, and he even refers to the friends in the third person (v 15a) as though they were not present; but there can be no doubt that these lines are directed to them, since the first explicit address to them (6:21) identifies the treacherous friends who have been objectively portrayed in vv 14–20 as no other than Job's three interlocutors. From that point on to the end of the chapter the friends are addressed directly in every verse, except for the last (v 30), where the question hovers between the direct and the rhetorical. (iii) 7:1–21, by contrast, are wholly directed toward God. Although vv 1–6 do not explicitly state the addressee, the imperative "remember" of v 7, unquestionably directed to God, makes clear that vv 1–6 have been for his benefit, even tempting us to read v 1 as a true questioning of God and not just a rhetorical question. From v 7 onward the presence of God as the object of Job's address is strongly marked, the "thou" appearing in vv 7, 8, 12, 14, 16–21.

Other scholars, with the exception of Terrien and Webster ("Strophic Petterns," 39), do not tend to recognize this clearly marked threefold structure. Murphy, for example, finds two parts to the speech, (1) 6:2–27, containing such disparate items as a complaint (6:2–4), the justification of the complaint (6:5–7), affirmation of loyalty in the form of a deathwish (6:8–10), and various motifs from the complaint (6:11–27); and (2) 6:28–7:21, Job's challenge to his friends to hear him (6:28–30), together with a complaint addressed to God (7:1–21). Murphy (*Wisdom Literature*, 25) seems to be influenced in his analysis of the structure of the speech by the detection in it of a double "alphabetizing poem," i.e., two poems of 22 lines and 23 lines respectively (6:2–23; 7:1–21), joined with two transitions (6:24–27, 28–30); in this he follows Skehan ("Strophic Patterns," 102–3). But even if such a feature could be detected, it would be no more than a purely formal structural device, and could hardly have more significance than the matter of who is actually addressed by the speech.

Fohrer finds a fourfold structure to the speech: (1) 6:2–13; (2) 6:15–30 (he omits v 14); (3) 7:1–11; (4) 7:12–21. This pattern is influenced by desire to discern a balance in the smaller strophic divisions and the larger sense divisions, but it unnecessarily divides the address to God into two parts. Habel sees only two major parts, an address to the friends in chap. 6 and to God in chap. 7; but it is hard to see 6:2–13, with its wishes of vv 2, 8, as in any sense addressed to the friends.

The *strophic structure* tends to display strophes of three lines. In part 1 we have 6:2–4, 5–7, 8–10, 11–13; in part 2, after an opening line that stands independent (6:14), 6:15–17, 18–20, 21–23 (with a pendant, v 24), 25–27, 28–30. In part 3 we have 7:1–3, 4–5 (v 4 contains two bicola), 6–8, then, exceptionally, four two-line strophes, 9–10, 11–12, 13–14, 15–16, reverting to three-line strophes in 17–19, 20–21 (v 20 contains two bicola). Strophes 1 and 2 hang together (6:2–7), as do 3 and 4 (6:8–13), 5 and 6 (6:15–20), and 7, 8, and 9 (6:21–29 [30]). In chap. 7 strophes 10 and 11 hang together (7:1–5), as do strophes 12–16 (7:6–16) more or less loosely, and strophes 17–18 (7:17–21), more tightly.

This analysis corresponds quite closely to that of Webster ("Strophic Patterns," 39–40) who, however, identifies as strophes 6:14–17, 24–27; 7:11–15, 16–19. A not dissimilar strophic structure is advanced by Terrien, who, however, takes 6:21 as an independent line that, together with v 14, frames the two three-line substrophes of vv 15–17 and 18–20. Vv 22–24 then become the following substrophe. In chap. 7 he finds substrophes in vv 13–15, 16–18, 19–20a, 20b–21. Fohrer differs from my analysis in discerning 6:18–

21, 22–25, 26–30, and 7:1–4, 5–8, 9–11, 12–15, 16–19, 20–21. This produces four four-line strophes in chap. 7, and two three-line strophes. This also has a lot to recommend it, except that to link vv 16 and 17 seems a little weak, since v 16 has to do with Job personally, and v 17 extends the thought to humankind generally.

In *form* the speech as a whole belongs to the *appeal* (often called the *lament*). In chap. 7, which is directed solely toward God, it conforms in many points to the psalmic models of the appeal; and chap. 7 also, where the friends are addressed in vv 14–30, is formally speaking an appeal to them to disclose what they believe to be the sin for which he is suffering (6:24). Murphy (*Wisdom Literature*, 25) differs from this analysis, regarding the speech as essentially a disputation speech, with elements from the appeal prominent. It seems rather the other way around: it is an appeal, with a prominence of elements from the disputation. Fohrer will allow only that appeal and disputation alternate.

Typical of the *appeal* form are the following elements. There is the *appeal* proper, couched either in the imperative (6:24, 28–29; 7:16b, 7) or in a wish formula (6:2, 8; an allusion to a wish in 7:15) or in a negative rhetorical question (7:21); in all these elements there is at least an overtone of the reproach, which belongs equally to the disputation form. There is the *complaint*, in which the speaker sets forth particulars of his sorry state as a ground for the fulfillment of his appeal; thus his depiction of the arrows of the Almighty (6:4), of the futility of his life (7:3), of his sleeplessness (7:4), physical affliction (7:5), nightmares (7:14). A particularly developed motif is the depiction of the enemies (6:14–21); the fact that those who function as enemies to the lamenter are supposed to be his friends, or have turned from friends into foes, is itself a common psalmic motif (cf. Ps 38:12 [11]; 41:10 [9]; 55:13–15 [12–14]; 88:9 [8], 19 [18]; 109:4; but there are significant differences here from the psalmic examples, as Westermann, *Structure*, 43, points out). Another characteristic motif is the framing of the depiction of the speaker's affliction with a generalized description of the human condition (7:1–6; cf. Ps 39:6–8 [5–7]); such is "an intrinsic aspect of lamentation" (Westermann, *Structure*, 47). There is also the use of the *rhetorical question* with "how long?" (7:19; cf. "when?" v 4) and "why?" (7:20, 21); 7:17–18 also may well be regarded as functioning as a "why?" question. Such questions are characteristic of the psalms of appeal (e.g., Ps 74:1, 10; 80:5 [4], 13 [12]). It is important to notice that, as distinct from the psalmic models, Job's appeal is not for deliverance from his distress by restoration to life, but for death as the only means of escape from his suffering. And he does not appeal to God to pay attention to him, but to "look away" from him (7:19).

Elements from the *disputation* are also frequently encountered in this speech, especially prominently in 6:22–30. There are the speech of reproach (6:21, 22–23, 27), the dismissal of the arguments of the opponent (6:26), and the intensive use of rhetorical questions addressed to the opponent (6:22–23, 25b, 26, 30).

From the sphere of *wisdom* we find in 6:5–6 two interesting *proverbial sayings*, introduced as justification of the appeal; 6:14 also, whatever precisely it means, has the form of a proverbial utterance. Some at least of the disputation language belongs rather to the *intellectual disputation;* thus, for example, the demand that the opponent "teach" one, though at 6:24 it does not carry the irony it usually does, and the references to "reproofs" in 6:25–26.

A particularly striking form is the *parody* in 7:17–18, where the familiar words of Ps 8:5–6 [4–5] are turned to a different, and systematically negative, effect.

In *function*, the speech has a double focus. On the one hand, in its address to the friends, it offers them the opportunity of convincing Job that he does in fact deserve what is happening to him, and on the other, in its address to God, it calls upon God to desist from attacking him so that he may live out his few remaining days in comparative peace.

The *nodal verses* in this speech may then be identified in two places; for chap. 6, it is Job's demand to the friends to "show [him] where [he] has erred" (6:24) that is crucial; for chap. 7, it is the cry to God to "Leave me alone" (7:16b) that is quintessential.

In *tonality* there is an interesting mixture in the speech. Opening with a somewhat wistful deathwish, "Would that . . . God should decide to crush me" (6:8–9), a wish that Job clearly has no confidence will be fulfilled, the speech concludes on a rather more peevish and aggressive note, demanding of God that he abandon his attacks on Job for the short time Job feels he still has to live (7:19–21). To God he addresses himself with candor and force; he "must speak in the anguish of [his] spirit . . . protest in the bitterness of [his] soul" (7:11), highlighting with a distinct note of grievance the disproportion in God's treatment of him (7:12). To the friends he is sarcastic (6:22–23), but at the same time he is bitterly disappointed and desperate for their attention (6:29). In the same speech he can be sardonic (6:21–23) and despairing (7:21b), didactic (6:14), enfeebled (6:11), assertive (6:30), and reproachful (7:19–20). He is buffeted by the array of emotions that his new circumstances have conjured up in him.

Comment

6:2–4 Job sees that Eliphaz's words of encouragement have not touched the fringe of his problem. He therefore ignores Eliphaz's speech, and reverts to the point at which he left off in chap. 3. He will begin by explaining why his words have been "unrestrained": his calamity makes it impossible to speak or listen with the cool confidence of an Eliphaz.

2 In the sharpest contrast to the hesitant manner of Eliphaz's opening words (4:2), Job bursts out with a cry for understanding: if only others could recognize the burden of his suffering, they would understand the violence of his language!

Eliphaz has already brought the term כעש "anger, vexation, misery" into the conversation as one of the causes of the fool's death (5:2). It may be thought that by acknowledging his כעש Job numbers himself among those who let their passions get the better of them, the "fools." He would be acknowledging his כעש but excusing it at the same time by stressing how heavy it is to bear (v 3) (so Peake, Driver, Rowley, Andersen). But it is unnecessary to see here a reference by Job to the כעש of the fool of 5:2; כעש in itself is no crime but entirely excusable if one's circumstances are unhappy enough: cf. 17:7; Deut 32:21 (of God); Ps 6:8 [7]; 10:14 (God takes note of the sufferer's כעס [= כעש] in order to take action for the sufferer; 31:10). So we may translate it here as "misery" (JB) or "anguish" (NAB, NIV) (see n. 6:2.a).

Some have thought that Job protests that if the anger (כעש) he expresses could only be set in one pan of the scales, and the provocation he has suffered from his misfortune (היתי) could be weighed against it, it would be immediately seen that his anger in no way matches the provocation, in fact that the provocation outweighs it as decisively as if the sands of the seas were to be weighed against it (so Duhm, Driver).

But it is more likely that Job's wish is that his כעש and his היה should be weighed in the same scale-pan against the heaviest object he can imagine: the sands of the seas. He does not mean by his כעש the passion of anger that Eliphaz had reckoned to be the cause of the fool's death (5:2). It is the inner sorrow, grief which weighs down or oppresses people because of the external calamity (היה) that has befallen them. Job's sufferings have not only been the losses depicted in chaps. 1–2; they have also been what he has experienced psychically. Together they form an unimaginable burden. If only that burden could be physically demonstrated on some cosmic scales, an Eliphaz would be convinced that Job's outburst is not in the least excessive.

The hopeless wish that begins this speech of Job's carries us back immediately to the hopelessness with which his first speech (chap. 3) began. The metaphor of overwhelming weight that cannot be borne takes us back to the opening of Eliphaz's speech (4:2) where Eliphaz showed some awareness that speech itself might be felt as a further burden, and that what had befallen Job was something he was too weak to bear (לאה, 4:5).

3 It would be unreasonable to expect Job to speak dispassionately about his anguish. The weight of the bereavement he has been suffering, together with the implications of unrighteousness that his bereavement carries, is heavier than the sand on every sea-shore. (For the image of sand as what cannot be weighed, cf. Prov 27:3; Ecclus 22:15; Ahiqar 8.111 [*ANET*, 429]); more commonly sand is an image for what cannot be counted: cf. e.g., Gen 22:17; 32:13 [12]; Josh 11:4; 1 Kgs 5:9 [4:29]; Jer 15:8.) It is not surprising that his words, in his lament of chap. 3, or in the renewed cry in the present speech, have been "unrestrained"; they have been squeezed out of him, so to speak, by the weight that presses down upon him.

Job is not apologizing for anything, far less confessing to any indiscretion (contrast rsv "my words have been rash"), not even to the form of his language rather than its substance (as Duhm, Peake). He simply wishes that it could be demonstrated how words of such misery have been forced out of him. He cries out for an understanding of his incapacity for restraint to a man who has done nothing but urge restraint (in the form of patience) upon him.

Has the similarly worded proverb (Prov 27:3), "A stone is heavy, and sand is weighty, but the anger (כעס) of a fool (אויל, as in 5:2) is heavier (כבד, as here) than them both," any connection with the present verse? Fohrer believes that the poet has here adapted the proverb. If indeed Job appears to his friends as a "fool" whose "anger" is heavier than sand (but see *Comment* on 5:2 above), he will here invite them to consider his "calamity," which will more than adequately justify his "anger." But if 5:2 has nothing directly to do with Job, we may regard the proverb simply as a parallel to the idea of the "weight" (כבד) of "anger" or "anguish" (כעס).

4 For the first time, Job explicitly names God as the ultimate (and immediate) cause of his suffering. Of course, he knows nothing of the events that have taken place in heaven that make his complaint only all the better founded. He simply knows that what happens to him does not arise from any guilt of his own, and since he presumably agrees with Eliphaz that trouble is not self-generating (5:6–7), there is only one direction in which he can look for the origin of his suffering. It is remarkable that Job does not develop this insight further at this point, for it is a crucial insight, and one that forms the basis of later speeches (7:12–21; 9:13–35; 13:19–27; etc.). But points are not developed systematically in these speeches; a slow process of accretion and continual reversion to the central issues focuses the attention no less effectively than a more systematic rhetoric.

We notice too that Job does not directly accuse God of causing his suffering: by employing the picture of the archer shooting his poisoned arrows, he effectively assumes that it is agreed on all sides that Shaddai is his opponent. Whether there is any deliberate reference back to the image of Shaddai as the reverser of fortunes and preserver of the poor portrayed by Eliphaz in 5:17–26 it is impossible to say. The fact remains that his experience of Shaddai is poles apart from Eliphaz's "research" (חקר) and "hearsay" (שׁמע; but cf. on 5:27). Shaddai for Job is effectively the Near Eastern deity Resheph, god of plague and war. This Resheph is known in a Cypriote inscription as "Resheph of the arrow" (*Corpus Inscriptionum Semiticarum* [Paris: Imprimerie Nationale, 1881] 1/1:36, 38 [text no. 10, line 3; cf. also *Comment* on 5:7, with bibliography). As god of the underworld, he commands the allegiance of demons, here known as the "terrors" (בעותים) (cf. on 18:11–14), and, like Apollo, to whom he corresponds, spreads diseases as arrows from his bow.

God is of course, for Job, not Resheph; yet he acts like him. Elsewhere too in the OT, elements of this mythological correspondence appear: for the image of humans as the targets of the archer god, see 7:20; 16:12–13; Deut 32:23 (note רשׁף and חמה in v 24); 32:42; Ps 7:13–14 [12–13]; 38:3 [2]; 64:8 [7]; Lam 2:4; 3:12–13; Ezek 5:16 ("arrows of famine"). The poisoning of arrowheads is not elsewhere clearly attested in the ancient Near East, so the "poison" could perhaps be metaphorical for the effect of the arrows themselves (so Tur-Sinai); but Dhorme cites classical allusions to the practice (Virgil, *Aeneid*, 9.773; Ovid, *Epist. ex Ponto*, 1.2.17–18), and it is probably to such a custom that Job alludes. M. Dahood sees such a reference in Gen 49:23 (*Psalms II*, 104). For חֵמָה, usually "anger," as "poison," cf. Deut 32:24, 33; Ps 58:5 [4]; 140:4 [3]. Peake makes the interesting, but not very probable, suggestion that the fevered or "wild" utterances of v 3 are because of the poison of the arrows.

The "terrors" of God are, on one level, various diseases that can be sent by God; on another level, they are the battery of devices God has of demonstrating his hostility to Job. G. R. Driver argued that the notion of "suddenness" was present in the root בעת and rendered "sudden assaults" (*VTS* 3 [1955] 73) (cf. NEB "onslaughts").

Above all, this sentence crystallizes the nature of Job's suffering. It is neither the physical pain nor the mental anguish that weighs him down, but the consciousness that he has become God's enemy. His life-force or vitality (רוח) has been enfeebled by drinking in the venom of God's bitterness against him, and he feels himself beleaguered by the terrifying hostility of God. He does not as yet protest the injustice of his fate; God's attack upon him still remains only a reason for his "unrestrained" words in the face of his friends' sympathetic silence (2:13) and Eliphaz's consolatory speech (chaps. 4–5).

5–7 Job's reason for speaking unrestrainedly (v 3b) out of his anguish is further developed by a twofold proverb-like rhetorical question, followed by a reinforcing statement, which explains why he is unable simply to endure the fortune that has befallen him.

5 In this rhetorical question, the affirmation implied is that if one receives what is appropriate one does not complain about it. Animal imagery is used as so often in proverbial material, a wild animal here being paralleled with a domesticated one. If the wild ass (פֶּרֶא, see n. 6:5.a) finds the "soft grass" (JB) that is its natural food, it does not bray (contrast Jer 14:6); if the domesticated ox is given its regular provender (cf. also Isa 30:24), it does not low. Job receives the very contrary of what is due to him as a righteous man; what wonder then if he cries out?

It is not a question of whether the animals find *enough* food (as many commentators think, e.g., Hesse, Weiser), but whether they find what is usual and *right for them* (cf. Fohrer).

6 In the next question, the underlying affirmation is that there are substances too unappetizing to be eaten. One might be offered them as food but reject them with revulsion. This again is Job's situation: he is refusing to swallow the pill that God has prescribed. His protests arise wholly from the revolting nature of what he has been offered in place of the wholesome nutriment of life.

Job is not describing what is simply insipid or unappetizing, but what is inedible. It is unnecessary therefore to refer this remark to Eliphaz's argument, even though the figure of taste is a natural one for reason and sense (Pope).

7 The rhetorical question of v 6, which needs no answer, is nevertheless followed up by an emphatic and explicit response. The dish that has been served up to Job is sickening, and he must say how it makes him feel. He has spoken without restraint (v 3b) in calling upon God to end his life (chap. 3); but he makes no apologies for his "impatience," as it must seem to Eliphaz, for he speaks out of the compulsion of his circumstances. He will not give his assent to a situation that wrings from him the cry of "No!"

This reiterated justification of his earlier speech (chap. 3) forms a perfect prelude for the nodal sentence that immediately follows: "O that I might have my request . . . that it would please God to crush me, that he would let loose his hand and cut me off!" (vv 8–9). Again, it is not the consolations of Eliphaz that taste loathsome to him (as Duhm, Rowley, Habel) but the events that have befallen him (especially the implied attack upon his integrity) that are more than he can stomach.

8–10 This is the speech in which presumptions become visible. In v 4 Job had openly declared that the sufferings he endures are the arrows of the *Almighty*. Here he says, for the first time explicitly, that his wish is for *death*. In chap. 3 he had uttered futile wishes that he should not have been born (vv 3–10) and that he should have died at birth (vv 11–19) and had asked forlornly why the lives of those who would rather be dead are prolonged (vv 20–23). But it is not until now that he speaks explicitly of himself in this connection.

8–9 Hitherto, Job has asked for nothing for himself. In the prose prologue he has simply accepted: "Yahweh gave and Yahweh has taken away; blessed be the name of Yahweh" (1:21). He has received good at the hand of God and will accept harm also (2:10). In chap. 3 he has expressed futile wishes that only reflect his despair, and cannot possibly be fulfilled; so from that speech also he expects nothing. But now he will ask for something for himself: death. It is not exactly death as a relief from his suffering, but death to mark the futility and hopelessness of his situation. Such a death he can even perceive as a "hope" (v 8). Quite the contrary to Eliphaz, who envisages hope for Job as a prosperous future (4:6) or as a reversal of fortune for Job as the "poor, afflicted one" (5:16), Job's hope is for death. Has Job at last followed the counsel of his wife, urging him to "curse God and die" (2:9)? The end is the same, but Job here has no wish to die in the isolation of a curse against God. "Since Job can no longer see any possibility of life with God, his last wish is that he should at least die at his hand!" (Weiser).

Will God decide to do something, undertake to act (this is the force of יאל, RSV "it would please"; but better JB "decide")? It is inaction, unaltering and seemingly unalterable suffering existence, that Job cannot bear (cf. vv 11–13). Even yet he will not address God directly; he says only "O that . . . [Heb. "Who will give that . . ."]" and "Would that God should undertake. . . ." Heaven is silent, and he has not yet gained the courage to speak directly to God (cf. 7:12). But there are two things God could do, if he would: he could "crush" him (דכא, the word used already in 4:19 for the fate of fragile humanity; cf. also 5:4; 19:2; 34:25; Ps 143:3; Isa 53:5, 10), i.e., stamp out his life, or, to change the metaphor, he could "give his hand free play" (JB) and "cut [him] off." Hitherto, despite loosing off his arrows against Job, God has been holding himself back, holding himself in reserve, withholding from Job the real strength of his hand. What God could do with his hand is cut the threads of Job's life: we seem to have an image from weaving (so Duhm, Driver, Dhorme, Horst, Fohrer, Pope), where the weaver brings to an irreversible conclusion his intricate work with loom and shuttle by cutting across the warp (for the picture, cf. Isa 38:12 "he cuts me off from the loom"; and see below on 7:6).

Job gives no thought to suicide. Such an act does not appear to have been commonly considered as a real option by Israelites (cf. on 3:20–26). Occasionally, heroes mortally wounded in battle asked to be dispatched quickly. Saul has eventually to fall on his own sword (1 Sam 31:3–4); Abimelech, wounded by a woman, has his armor-bearer kill him out of male pride (Judg 9:53–54); Zimri burns his citadel down upon himself when he sees his capital taken by Omri (1 Kgs 16:18); and the spurned counselor Ahithophel hangs himself (2 Sam 17:23). Heroic suicide is attested in Hellenistic times, doubtless under Greek influence (Josephus, *War* 3.7.5; 7.8.6–7; 2 Macc 10:13; 14:41–46). See F.W. Young, "Suicide," *IDB* 4:453–54. If Job were to kill himself because of his depression, his case would be most like that of Ahithophel. But Job is not simply depressed: although he has not yet expressed a realization that he has a *case* against God that demands resolution (cf. chap. 9), he recognizes even here that his life is in God's hands, for good or ill. If he is to die, and that is his deepest desire, it must be God who strikes the blow. God has created this kind of existence for Job; it is God, not Job, who must end it.

10 Some have seen the "consolation" Job envisages for himself as the assurance that God has not utterly abandoned him, even if he breaks his silence only to end Job's life. The mysterious darkness of such a death would give him a final glimpse into the mercy of God (so Weiser). Others have seen death itself as the "consolation." Thus N. C. Habel, "'Only the Jackal Is My Friend': On Friends and Redeemers in Job," *Int* 31 (1977) 227–36 (229): "Job's yearning is for meaningful compassion (*nahāmāh*). . . . If I died, insists Job, "I would have comfort (*nehāmātî*) again' (v 10a). Death would indeed be a friend. For a friend knows the art of *nahāmāh*." Yet if such readings are correct,

the last line of the verse, "for I have not denied (or, concealed) the words of
the Holy One," is rather irrelevant and has, not surprisingly, been deleted by
many scholars.

It is better to regard Job's "consolation" as the assurance he would have, if
God were to "cut off" his life immediately, that he has never yet infringed
the ordinances of the Holy One (cf. NIV). He is like a prisoner under torture,
who fears the moment when he will break; the possibility that he will "curse
God and die" has become a vivid one for him. His hope (v 8) is that he may
still remain loyal to the unfathomable God, the "Holy One," who has inexplicably
become his enemy, until the moment of his death. No greater boon could be
granted a doomed man, no greater comfort in the agony of death, than to
know that he has not betrayed his God.

The sentiment may sound to us a little self-righteous, a little "insolent" (cf.
Andersen); is it not hypocritical, perhaps, to speak of preferring "death with
honor"—for that is what it is—when we all know that life with honor, even a
sometimes tarnished honor, is what we would choose? It makes all the difference
in the world, though, to know that Job has set his face against life; for life to
him means only the dishonor of undeserved suffering. So in this seemingly
extravagant cry for God to bring him death, Job is at his most heroic. As in
31:37, he approaches God "as a prince"; and it is the man, not the god, who
earns our regard. Davidson felt a somewhat different difficulty with such an
interpretation: it "gives a prominence to the innocence of Job which is not
suitable in this place, and makes his words too reflective and self-possessed
for the rest of the passage." The difficulty disappears when it is recognized
that this is not merely a protestation of innocence by Job, but a desperate
appeal for a speedy end to his life because he fears he cannot maintain his
right behavior much longer (cf. vv 11–13).

The significance of v 10c, "For I have not denied (or, concealed) the words
of the Holy One," has been variously understood. Dillmann saw it as giving
the reason that God should grant Job's request, with the subsidiary purpose
of justifying his "vexation" (כעש) in 6:2 and his refusal to listen to Eliphaz's
admonitions. It is more probable, as has been suggested above, that the righteousness of Job's life is the ground (כי) for his "comfort" in the agony of
death (so Delitzsch, Hitzig, Budde), but with the subsidiary purpose, in the
light of vv 11–13 which follow, of urging God to act now while Job can still
make a claim to righteousness. Duhm follows Siegfried in deleting the line,
viewing it as an interpolator's attempt to give content (כי = "that") to the
comfort. Duhm could not see why Job should be comforted at the prospect
of death unless he believed in an afterlife, and such a belief is not evidenced
by the book as a whole (similarly Peake). The line is deleted also by Hesse,
Moffatt, NEB, and Fohrer on the ground that Job is not portrayed as a witness
to God's words (wisdom teaching not being divine word).

What the "words of the Holy One" (אמרי קדוש) are in particular is uncertain;
but since Job is characterizing his life as a whole, he probably refers to the
range of divine commands by which he as a godly man has lived. The language
is neither specifically cultic, legal, nor sapiential.

11–13 The feeling of weakness (cf. on 4:2, 5) under the weight (cf. on
6:2–3) of suffering returns. This is a psychic lassitude, no doubt felt physically
as well; it is essentially a conviction of a complete lack of inner resources (cf.

v 13). It is not that he suffers so badly from his physical diseases and is so enfeebled by them that he no longer sees anything to live for and can only hope for death as a relief from his sufferings. On the contrary, his self-worth has been so radically undermined by the absence of desert in his suffering that his psyche or spirit has been totally drained of strength; he is as good as dead physically. Death would be just an outward and visible sign of his inward feeling.

11 Job's plea is for immediate death. He has no strength to wait. It is not that he has not the strength to endure the suffering, though that may also be true. It is that he has no strength to endure the reality of not having died. To wait, to have patience, itself requires an energy that he no longer possesses. He does not at this moment feel the driving force of impatience, though he will know that experience too (cf. 7:11, 19). Even waiting for Godot takes doing, and he is past doing.

Many think he asks what end could possibly be achieved from waiting: "What is my end?" i.e., what real future (as distinct from the visionary future Eliphaz has projected in 5:17–26) lies in store for me? "What end have I to expect?" (NEB). But NAB offers the rendering, "What is my limit that I should be patient?" which suggests that the "end" here is the end of his resources that he has already reached. A nearer exegesis may perhaps be reached by considering Ps 39:5–6 [4–5], "Yahweh, give me to know my end [קץ, as here], and what may be the measure of my days be, that I may learn how transient I am. The days you have made for me are a few handbreaths; my whole being is a nothing before you." The psalmist does not seek to know what the outcome (קץ) of his life may be, nor yet precisely how many days he still has to live, in order that he may be assured that he is a transient being. He wants to be reminded of his *limitations* as a human being, "each man that stands on earth is only a puff of wind, every man that walks, only a shadow" (vv 6–7 [5–6] JB). Job knows his limitations: he has no strength for waiting, he has the limitation that prevents him from "prolonging his life" (אאריך נפשי). The psalmist indeed can say "What have I to hope then, Lord? My patience (תוחלתי, same root as יחל here) is in thee" (v 8 [7]). Job has not the strength for patience; nor can he break through his limitations to hope that his life should be prolonged (for a contrast, cf. Isa 53:10).

12 The weakness that Job feels persists as the theme. He has not the strength of stone (cf. 41:16 [24]); he is bound by the weakness of "flesh" (בשר; contrasted with רוח "spirit," Isa 31:3); he does not know in himself the strength of bronze. (It is not the insensitivity of stone and bronze that is the point, but Job's feeling of weakness compared with these commonplace natural symbols of strength.)

13 Job concludes this triplet of verses with the most complete confession of his weakness. In v 11 he had no strength for waiting, no power for sheer patience. The reality is that he has no strength of any kind. It is as though his strength has been "thrust" or "driven" (RSV) from him by an external power. All he knows is that such a weakness is properly matched only by death, the state of ultimate absence of energy.

14–30 That such a moving confession of utter helplessness should be immediately followed by a biting and sarcastic attack on his friends has nothing unreal about it. Job's depression, that has expressed itself in vv 2–13 as a desire for immediate death and a feeling of extreme lassitude, now expresses itself in anger against those from whom he expected support.

We do not detract from our essential sympathy with Job if we find this address to his friends overcritical. Job can allow that they have traveled far to visit him in his distress (2:11), have been silent when silence was appropriate (2:13), have recognized that his suffering is heavy (2:13), have showed themselves willing to speak—at length—with him (chaps. 4–5)—and, at the same time, give vent to his anger that their well-meant intentions are worthless to him. He cannot be expected to weigh up their support against their incapacity; we hear from his lips only of their failure, but his sense of disappointment cannot be our only measure of their value. Job has no resources left in himself (v 13), so it is natural that he should look beyond himself to those from whom he might expect support. They have in fact already disappointed him in not offering whatever kind of support it is he needs, and the realization of their unreliability or "treachery" as he calls it (v 15, perhaps 21) is no doubt partly the reason for his own inner sense of weakness and hopelessness. Indeed, it may seem too early in the dialogue for Job to reach such a conclusion (so Hesse), but he knows already that he has no hope of finding in the friends the kind of support he needs.

The structure of this section of the speech is in some respects plain: vv 14–21 are one unit, revolving about the image of the seasonal wadi, not directly addressed to the friends, beginning and ending with distinctive couplets (vv 14, 21) and containing as a center two clearly defined triplets (vv 15–17, 18–20). The second unit, vv 22–30, revolving about Job's relationship to his friends (the imagery is minimal), is addressed to the friends themselves, beginning and ending with rhetorical questions (vv 22–23, 30); within that framework there are two less clearly defined triplets (vv 24–26, 27–29).

14 Job prefaces his reproach with a proverbial type of sentence expressing the expectation a person in distress is entitled to have of one's friends. The Hebrew is unfortunately very difficult, and probably corrupt, and no translation can be offered with confidence. But certain key terms are plain.

There is the quality of "loyalty" (חסד) that a person has a right to expect from one's friends. This is a characteristic frequently ascribed to God (usually translated "stedfast love" by RSV, "lovingkindness" by KJV), and combined with qualities of "faithfulness" (אמת or אמונה, e.g., Ps 25:10; 88:12 [11]) or "justice" (משפט or צדקה, e.g., Ps 101:1; 36:11 [10]). It is particularly related to his keeping covenant, which demands "loyalty" (e.g., Deut 7:9; Neh 1:5; Isa 54:10). In the human sphere it is also combined with similar qualities, faithfulness (e.g., Hos 4:1; Prov 3:3) and justice (Hos 10:12; Prov 21:21). See N. Glueck, *Hesed in the Bible* (tr. A. Gottschalk; Cincinnati: Hebrew Union College Press, 1967); K. D. Sakenfeld, *The Meaning of Hesed in the Bible: A New Inquiry* (HSM 17; Missoula, Mont.: Scholars Press, 1978) esp. 216–17; H. J. Stoebe, *THWAT* 1:600–621.

What Job means by "loyalty" is plainly different from what the friends mean by it. He is looking for unqualified acceptance that takes his side whether he is in the right or the wrong. They offer sympathy and support, but only from what seems to them a realistic point of view; it is absurd, they would argue, to take the stance "my friend right or wrong" when the evidence (Job's suffering) proves that—to some extent at least—Job is in the wrong. Are they to disregard the evidence of their eyes and their learning, and prop Job up in what they believe to be a falsely self-righteous position? Eliphaz has done his utmost to emphasize Job's essential goodness, but he had to point out as delicately as he knew how that even the righteous are not perfect. Could any more be expected of a "loyal" friend?

The other quality Job expects to find is "the fear of God," i.e., true religion, a phrase particularly prominent in the wisdom literature (in the form יראת יהוה 14 times in Prov; cf. H.-P. Stähli, *THWAT* 1:765–78 [776]). See S. Plath, *Furcht Gottes: Der Begriff* ירא *im Alten Testament* (Stuttgart: Calwer, 1963); J. Becker, *Gottesfurcht im Alten Testament* (AnBib 25; Rome: Pontifical Biblical Institute, 1965) 210–61.

How these two qualities are held together in the verse is unclear; but on general grounds of what is appropriate in OT thought, it is more likely that they are compared rather than contrasted. Job's special concern is the loyalty (חסד) that he believes he is owed, so a plausible sense is:

> A friend does not refuse his loyalty,
>   nor forsake the fear of the Almighty.

The meaning would be: he is *no more likely* to be disloyal than to abandon his faith in God. The point may be put more strongly by defining loyalty as *involved in* the fear of God:

> A friend who does not refuse his loyalty
>   does not forsake the fear of the Almighty.

The most similar linkage of the loyalty of friendship with right religion is seen in Prov 14:21: "he who despises his friend sins (חוֹטֵא)"; cf. also Hos 4:1; Mic 6:8. A yet stronger form of the sentence defines the fear of God as *consisting in* loyalty to a friend. Thus:

> He who withholds kindness from a friend
>   forsakes the fear of the Almighty (RSV).

or:

> Grudge pity to a neighbor,
>   and you forsake the fear of Shaddai (JB).

Such a translation states hyperbolically that loyalty is a *necessary part* of religion by affirming that it is *equivalent to* true religion.

Less appropriate, though no doubt more striking, are versions that see the second colon as descriptive of the one who is owed devotion:

> A friend owes kindness to one in despair,
>   though he have forsaken the fear of the Almighty
>   (NAB; similarly GNB, NIV).

or:

> Devotion is due from his friends
>   to one who despairs and loses faith in the Almighty (NEB).

or:

> A sick man should have loyalty from his friend,
>   though he forsake fear of Shaddai (Pope).

or:

> To him that is ready to faint kindness is due from his friend
>   even to him that forsaketh the fear of the Almighty (JPS).

Several commentators point out that such a sentiment cannot be paralleled in the OT; this is an important, though not perhaps overwhelming, objection to it. Even if this understanding is correct, there is of course no admission on Job's part that *he* has forsaken the "fear of the Almighty" (as against Habel, "Only the Jackal," 230).

The most remarkable translation is that of Gordis:

> He who pleads for kindness from his fellow man
>   has forsaken the reverence due to the Almighty.

There is a superficial attractiveness about this rendering (which reads the first word as לֹמֵס "desiring," cognate with Arab. *lamasa* VIII): Job would be saying that anyone who trusts in human goodness shows a lack of faith in God. The sentiment can be paralleled in hymns of praise to God (Ps 118:8; 146:3 [where it is expressed in the sapiential form of a command]), but here it would have to mean that Job's bitter experience of his friends' "treachery," as he calls it (v 15), has borne in upon him that he should not have been expecting support from them at all. Why then should he berate them at length (vv 15–30) for what he himself now recognizes was wrong to expect of them?

However the verse is translated, it is clearly the friends' lack of "loyalty" (חֶסֶד), as Job sees it, that is central, for he proceeds to describe how they have been "treacherous" (בָּגַד) to him, the very opposite of loyal.

15–17 In the first of two closely related triplets, Job compares his friends' unreliability with that of the desert wadis whose water cannot be relied on from one season to the next.

15 Job feels himself deceived by those he regards as his "brothers" or "kinsfolk." The three friends are not related to him by blood but by some mutual obligation. The contrast between the two words "brothers" and "have been treacherous" could not be sharper, for brotherhood implies an agreement, and "treachery" (בָּגַד) denotes precisely the dishonoring of an agreement (S. Erlandsson, *TDOT* 1:470–73 [470]). The "treachery" here is not some objective act, but the feeling is none the less real to Job for all that. The experience of desertion by one's kinsfolk is always expressed as particularly distressing (cf. 19:13; Ps 38:12 [11]; 88:9, 19 [8, 18]).

The natural image for such unreliability is the seasonal wadi of Palestine, full to overflowing (see n. 6:15.b) in the rainy season, and a dry watercourse in the heat of summer (cf. Jer 15:18; Isa 58:11; cf. 33:16). The wadis overflow when their water is not needed; when it is needed they have nothing to offer. So it is with Job's friends and their loyalty.

16–17 The image is further expanded by two couplets depicting the wadi in winter and in summer. In winter and early spring, the melting snow and ice from the mountains transform the wadis into muddy torrents that may then be said to be "dark with ice," and "swollen with [melted] snow." It is quite different when the heat of summer comes. The water retreats into its channels, and then ultimately dries up altogether, and vanishes (the verb דעך is "to be extinguished" [usually of light]). The round of the seasons may be a long time, but the annual disappearance of a valuable resource almost deserves to be counted reliable when compared with the sudden evanescence of the friends' loyalty (חסד, cf. v 14).

18–20 In this triplet the image of the wadi is employed again from a somewhat different aspect. In the previous triplet (vv 15–17) the unreliability of the friends' loyalty was compared with the sudden disappearance of the water of the wadi. Here it is Job's own disappointment at their unreliability that is compared with the experience of the thirsty caravaneers who find the wadi dried up. The image now, with the introduction of human beings into the scene, reflects the feeling of Job more personally. The focus is more evidently upon Job himself than upon the friends (though even in vv 15–17 it was upon the friends only as Job saw them).

18 Caravans of merchantmen are tempted by their knowledge of a nearby wadi to leave the regular track in search of water. They go off into the unmarked desert, find only dried-up streams, and perish before they can reach the next watering-place.

19–20 Caravans from two famous trading centers are mentioned. Tema (modern Teima) is an oasis in northern Arabia, c. 250 miles southeast of Aqaba, and a station on the route from Medina, 200 miles to the south, to Damascus in the far north. Further references to Tema occur in Isa 21:14; Jer 25:23; see also *IDB* 4:533. Sheba (or Seba) is an even better known market city specializing in precious commodities and located in southwestern Arabia; see on 1:19 where Sabeans appear as marauders, rather than traders, and cf. Ps 72:10, 15; Isa 60:6; Jer 6:20; Ezek 27:22–23; 38:13; see also *IDB* 4:144–46.

Even experienced caravaneers can have their hopes of finding supplies of water on the long caravan trails falsely aroused and then frustratingly disappointed. (Horst suggests that the caravaneers of Tema and Sheba would not be so foolhardy as those of v 18 who lose the trail, but could be disappointed nonetheless by finding already dried-up wadi beds.) If the Book of Job is set in northern Arabia, Job's friends, who would themselves have traveled in caravan to visit him, would no doubt know the truth of Job's depiction from their own experience.

21 The double image of the dried-up wadi applies to Job's experience with his friends: not only has he found them unreliable and inconsistent (cf. vv 15–17), he has felt himself deceived by them (cf. vv 18–20). He suffers, like the traveler in the desert, not only a disappointment of expectation, but a danger to life. Job knows the reason that they have adopted their "stand-offish" position: they have "seen" (תִּרְאוּ, *tirʾû*) his misfortune and been frightened (תִּירָאוּ, *tîrāʾû*). The word-play is familiar (cf. Ps 40:4 [3]; 52:8 [6]; Isa 41:5; Zech 9:5; and cf. G. R. Driver, "Problems and Solutions," *VT* 4 [1954]

225–45 [242]), but the sense here is different from its conventional use. Generally people see some marvel and consequently fear the mighty one who has achieved it. Job's friends, on the other hand, have seen the calamity that has befallen him and have feared to come too close to it because of the contagion. He speaks metaphorically, of course: the danger is that anyone associating too closely with a person obviously suffering divine displeasure may himself incur God's wrath. On a deeper level yet, Job means that his friends lack the courage to identify themselves with him; "loyalty" (חסד, v 14) would demand that, but Job feels that they intend to be observers and commentators rather than taking his part.

With this concluding sentence, balancing the opening sentence of v 14, the vignette of the seasonal wadi is concluded, and Job will turn to address the friends more directly.

22–30 Job moves from the relatively objective portrayal of a scene in which neither he nor his friends were apparently involved, but which nevertheless bore its meaning on its face and which was in any case unmistakably applied to the present situation (v 21). He will now address his friends directly, and speak, with a minimum of imagery, expressly of his expectations of them and of what he perceives to be their response.

22–23 Job disclaims any excessive demands upon his friends; the little he asked from them is the "loyalty" (v 14) of friendship. If only Job knew that what he in fact desires from them, namely to take his part in a struggle against God for vindication, is a far more demanding test of loyalty than any of these four sarcastically worded requests he says he might have made! It seems that the first two claims that Job denies, in his battery of rhetorical questions, have to do with money. There would be nothing dishonorable in asking for money with which to "bribe" some official, but it would be an imposition upon the generosity of his friends. As Pope observes, "Lending and borrowing among friends was a sure way to spoil friendship long before Shakespeare put the famous observation in the mouth of Polonius." Cf. Jer 15:10 "I have not lent, nor borrowed, yet everyone curses me." The second pair of claims Job says he has never made (v 23) is to have asked his friends to expose themselves to danger in order to rescue him from some adversary (whether at law or in battle) or from some tyrant or brigand.

24 In this crucial sentence Job leaves off his bitter bantering (vv 22–23) and asks the friends in all seriousness to point out what his guilt is. All the time it is understood that the guilt in question is the crime for which he is suffering, the wrongdoing which Eliphaz at his most sympathetic must argue lies at the basis of Job's present predicament. In inviting them to "teach" or "instruct" (הורוני) him, a term from the vocabulary of wisdom, he defers— not without a touch of irony—to their discernment. Everything that Eliphaz has said has assumed guilt, however slight, on Job's part. Now, for the first time, Job asks the friends to say without any beating about the bush, what they believe his sin (שגה) to be. That is all it would take to "silence" Job; he speaks out only in defense of his impugned integrity. But we know, as Job knows, that no real grounds for his suffering can be discovered, and it will be only after many words that Job falls into "silence" (40:4–5).

Fohrer errs, I believe, in his interpretation of this verse by supposing that Job refers only to a minor error that he may have committed in his speech hitherto (especially in chap. 3); what is it, Job asks, about his attitude to suffering that so repels them and prevents them from entering into his distress? This interesting interpretation hangs, however, on taking the verb שׁגה "err" in its most narrow and technical sense: to commit an unwitting sin. There is nothing in the present context that requires such a sense.

25–27 The tone of Job's speech takes another turn in this triplet. While in v 24 Job speaks straightforwardly—almost—here the note of sarcasm becomes strong again. The theme of this triplet is "words." Words of right judgment against evildoers have force, but the banal generalities of the friends signify nothing. What is more, words are mere prattle if the tone of the speaker is ignored; and Job's words matter less than the mood of despair from which he speaks. Such inattentiveness to what is real for Job is an egregious species of callousness (cf. v 27).

25 "Words of right judgment" (דברי ישׁר) are the sentences that any wrong-doer flinches from hearing. If the friends of Job could catalog his faults and pronounce his crimes, he would of course find that a distressing experience. But the reproofs of the friends as expressed, up to this point, only by Eliphaz are vague generalities about the inevitability of human sin. Eliphaz has never been specific, and so for all his talk he has never addressed Job's sense that he is innocent and unjustly treated.

Many versions and commentators do not see this point and have Job remark, "How forceful (*or,* pleasant) are honest words." This is a platitude that can hardly be disputed, but it would not be advancing Job's argument. Far from acknowledging that he would be pleased to hear his friends speak their minds, he confesses that the last thing he would choose to hear said of himself is that he is unrighteous in any way. And judging by what he has heard so far he can well remark, "But what do your reproofs amount to?"

26 This verse reads literally, "Do you think to convince [with] words, and [to regard] the words of a despairing man as wind?" There is apparently a contrast between the words (מלין) of the friends' reproof and the words (אמרי) of Job, the man in despair. But this contrast is perhaps more apparent than real; the essential contrast, as is clear from the whole attitude of Job to his friends, is between what they *say* and what he *feels*. Hence the translation offered above: "Do you think mere words settle matters?" There has been in Eliphaz's speech of chaps. 4–5 no criticism of Job's words in chap. 3 (contrast Rowley); this is a remarkable enough circumstance in itself, but Job's point is that the friends, as represented by Eliphaz, seem to think that talk by itself will reach convincing conclusions (יכח hiph "show to be right; convince; reprove"; BDB, 407b). Against mere words (מלין) are ranged the "words of a man in despair (יאשׁ niph)," which do not signify themselves but the man and his state of mind. To let them go "into the wind" without creating any impression is callousness.

27 Such callousness would be the equivalent of the friends' casting lots for the orphan of a man who had been their debtor in order to sell it into slavery (cf. the situation depicted in 2 Kgs 4:1), or "selling" their friend as if he were a commodity. Job does not, we presume, accuse his friends of doing any such thing; rather, he says that they are behaving like people who would do such things (cf. Hesse). These are probably proverbial examples of hard-heartedness. The analogies are not particularly apt, and many commentators

delete the verse as inappropriate here (see n. 6:27.a). But what it conveys is
a mood of bitterness, of disappointment and unfulfilled "loyalty" (חסד), which
would otherwise be muted by the plain language of vv 25–26. This verse
then forms a climax to the triplet (vv 25–27) on the theme of the friends'
words: Eliphaz, who speaks for the friends, has not simply disappointed or
misled Job (as the images of vv 15–20 have showed) but has treated him with
callousness. This is strong talk, and justified only from Job's perspective; it
doubtless must sound bewildering to Eliphaz. The reason for Job's anger will,
however, be clearly spelled out in the final triplet of this chapter: Job's "integrity
is at stake" (v 29). Job is not simply suffering, discouraged, depressed, impatient;
worse than that, he is falsely accused—by God!—and no one gives a moment's
thought to the possibility that he might be in the right.

28–30 The kernel of this triplet lies in v 29b: "My integrity is at stake!"
All criticism of the friends' ineffectualness is here put aside for the time being
while Job pleads with them to "look" at him, "return" or "turn" to him so
that the most significant communication can occur. His death-wish is also stifled
temporarily, so that his protestation of innocence may dominate the discussion.
Job's mood is not hopeful; he does not expect anything much of his friends
beyond listening to him; but he must make this protestation of innocence. It
will be many chapters before Job's final grand protestation (chap. 31) concludes
the dialogue with the three friends. But what we have here is enough, if it
were taken seriously, to dispense with all the posturing of the intervening
speeches. Job speaks as loyal friend to loyal friends, swearing that he tells no
lie, affirming to their faces that there is in him no cause for the suffering he
endures. This is no mere protestation that he truly suffers greatly (as Duhm,
Horst), but reaches to the very nub of the whole issue that divides him and
God. It is true that his proper dealings are with God himself, and it will be
in that direction that he will immediately hereafter turn. But he purposes to
enlist his friends' support, and to win them to his conviction that he deserves
nothing of what he suffers.

28 "But now," he says, indicating that the speech is taking a radically
new turn, "be pleased" (הואילו) to pay attention to *me* as a person, to listen
to me as friends to a friend. In his last angry sentence (v 27b) Job had reproached
them as ready to treat a friend as an object, a commodity to bargain with.
Now, he says, let rhetoric be put aside, and let us speak as persons. Some
have supposed that during his angry tirade since v 14 the friends have turned
their backs on him (so Duhm, Driver); but whether or not that is so, it is
their attention he craves. He has been disappointed in them, deceived by them,
but they are the friends he has. If they cannot recognize his innocence, no
one can. With a solemn oath, not usually recognized by the translations (except
Moffatt), he swears that he does not lie to them (for the particle אם introducing
an oath, cf. Duhm, Rowley, Andersen).

29 The "turning," lit. "returning" (שוב) may involve physical movement,
but it certainly involves a change of attitude: turn "from the unfair course
you have adopted: do not unjustly assume my guilt" (Driver). It is far more
than that his lament is justified (Fohrer): it is that his integrity or innocence
is still intact (so בה should probably be understood; see n. 6:29.e), and that
he demands that they should recognize it.

30 This triplet concludes, like the previous one (vv 25–27), with a double rhetorical question, "Is my tongue a liar? Can my palate not discern falsehood?" In the previous case it was the *coup de grâce* in Job's indictment of his friends' callousness; here it is the final affirmation that Job speaks the truth when he denies that he suffers deservedly. If we follow RSV's translation, "Cannot my taste discern calamity?" a tolerable meaning can be extracted from the line, viz. "'Am I unable to discern the true flavor of my misfortune?' i.e., to know whether it is deserved or not" (Rowley). But if we adopt the alternative sense of הוה as "falsehood" (see n. 6:30.b), Job affirms, as this strophe concludes, that he alone, and not the friends, is in a position to judge whether he has just cause for complaint, and he challenges them to deny that he has an unquestionably sharp sense ("palate") for the difference between right and wrong. It follows, according to his logic at least, that he is best qualified to know whether he is speaking the truth.

Job asks a great deal of his friends! They must not only suffer his abuse, but must take his word that he is speaking the unvarnished truth (v 28)— and that he is the best judge in his own cause (v 30)! But what is his alternative? To allow that men who know little of his personal life can insinuate or assume that he is guilty of God's punishment when all they have to go on are their theological generalizations about sin and suffering? Such an alternative would be even more intolerable! It is not surprising that Job's address to his friends concludes with this unanswerable sentence, and that a new theme is taken up in 7:1.

7:1–10 God is first directly addressed in v 7, and it is not until vv 12–21 that Job speaks consistently to God without indirect ruminative remarks. But it seems most reasonable to take vv 1–6 as a prologue to the direct address to God (so also Fohrer, Weiser); if these words are not spoken *to* God, they are spoken *in the direction of* God: they are for God's hearing. Job has moved from the phase of monologue in 6:2–13 through the phase of address to the friends in 6:14–30; he will not now lapse into monologue again, but moving still further outward from himself, will address himself to the most distant, most silent, but most significant, interlocutor: God. (It is noticeable how in the case of the direct address to the friends in 6:21–30 there are prefatory words spoken *for* their hearing [6:14–20] but not explicitly addressed *to* them.)

In this chapter Job's death-wish, so strongly affirmed in chap. 3, presents itself again. Now he will motivate it with his experience of the futility and misery of life. He projects upon the human condition his own experience, finding it now impossible to doubt that suffering, not joy, and futility, not fulfillment, are the ultimate truths about life. Yet Job is not really presenting a philosophy of life—and far less is the author of the book depicting some form of Hebrew pessimism (contrast Duhm); he suffers so deeply that he cannot imagine that anything else can truly be said about life for anyone. So while his speech is a profoundly moving expression of depression, it is that, and not some "contribution" to the Biblical "doctrine" or "view" of humanity. For a different approach, cf. Weiser, Peake.

1 Job's depression finds its expression now not in anger so much as in painful lament over the drudgery of life, drudgery that is all to no purpose. Human beings, he says, generalizing his own experience because that has become his horizon, are bound to "hard service" (צבא). The word is frequently used of military service (cf. Dhorme: "Is not man's life on earth a term of military service?"); the "hireling" too (שָׂכִיר) could be a mercenary soldier (Jer 46:21). But it is more probable that צָבָא here refers to hard service of any kind (cf. Isa 40:2; Dan 10:1), and that the "hireling" is a hired laborer. Job has been compelled to reject the optimistic view of the wisdom teachers that the lot intended for humans is happiness and success; on the contrary, it is "hard labor," and that not even for the satisfaction of some tyrant (as against Hesse, Habel, who think it is implied that God is the slave-master), but for sheer futility (v 3). Like the work of the "hireling" (שָׂכִיר) it is necessitous, often subject to abuse, and without security.

The "hired laborer" in Israel was a free man, an Israelite or a foreigner, but inevitably "poor" by comparison with a landowner (Deut 24:14), though earning twice the wage of a "slave" (Deut 15:18). According to the law, a hired servant was to be paid at the end of each day (Lev 19:13; Deut 24:15; cf. Matt 20:8), but the law will have been often abused (cf. Jer 22:13; Mal 3:5; Ecclus 34:22; James 5:4).

2–3 The image of the laborer is viewed again from a somewhat different angle. In v 1 life is seen simply as hard labor. In v 2 it is seen as labor that strives to reach its end. The slave working in the field as farmer or shepherd (cf. Gen 31:40) eagerly awaits the shadow of evening, when he can rest from the "heat and burden" of the day (Matt 20:12); and the hired laborer who works through all the day for the necessities of life longs for the end of the day, when he will be paid.

If Job asks to what end the labor of his life is tending, he finds there is no end in sight. His "hard service" is meaningless. If he feels himself a hired laborer, he knows he will not have the satisfaction of receiving his wages at the end of the day; on the contrary, he finds he is contracted for months of "hard labor" for no wages at all! The reward of his life is futility (שָׁוְא). Or if he feels himself a hard-pressed slave whose only pleasure is to anticipate the shade of evening, he finds that his evenings are no welcome relief, but rather "nights of misery." The only relief from his days of toil are nights of "toil" or "suffering" (עָמָל is used in both meanings; cf. also on 4:8). Vv 2 and 3 are arranged chiastically, 2a being parallel to 3b, and 2b to 3a.

4 The "nights of misery" (v 3b) are now depicted. His sleeplessness that subverts rest like that of the laborer into yet more "toil" (עָמָל, v 3b) is, on one level, no doubt due to the irritation of his skin by the disease he is suffering (see on 2:7), but it is also a normal symptom of depression. He dreads the night, thinking only as he lies down, "How long will it be till morning?" for he knows what "tossings" (נְדֻדִים, the plural perhaps for an abstract, "restlessness") he will endure until daylight. Peake remarked that the poet must have known "with how much greater slowness time seems to move through a night than through a day of pain."

5 His sleeplessness (v 4) stemmed no doubt from both psychic and physical causes. He now describes, in unpleasant detail, the symptoms of his physical complaint. His body is covered either with open sores that exude pus or with scabs of sores that are apparently in the course of healing. The skin grows firm and then breaks out again as if the healing process were set in reverse. In itself, the scab could be a hopeful sign, but it has deceived him too often; this is a man who is now "without hope" (v 6).

V 4 developed the phrase "nights of misery" in v 3b; it may be that the present verse develops the thought of "months of futility" in v 3a. For the disease that afflicts him makes no progress: it neither leads him back to health nor is continually aggravated so as to proffer him some hope of approaching death. Even his disease runs in a futile cycle: the scab that covers the sore and the growth of firm new flesh are counterbalanced by the opening up of new purulent sores, so that nothing is achieved for all his "hard labor" (v 1).

The image of a skin disease (whether leprosy itself or some other ailment) as clothing is met with also in more than one Babylonian text. We find, "May Sin, the lamp, . . . wrap him in leprosy as with a garment" (F. E. Peiser, *Texte juristischen und geschäftlichen Inhalts* [Keilinschriftliche Bibliothek. Sammlung von assyrischen und babylonischen Texten im Umschrift und Übersetzung; ed. E. Schrader; Berlin: Reuther und Reichard, 1896] 80–81, col. 3, lines 18–19); and "May the god Sin, illuminator of the high heavens, clothe all his limbs with incurable 'leprosy' until the day of his death" (J. V. Kinnier Wilson, "Leprosy in Ancient Mesopotamia," *RA* 60 [1966] 47–58).

6–10 Job's thought moves from the depiction of the misery of his existence (vv 1–5) to a reflection upon its brevity: it is certain now that his life is about to peter out.

Formerly (3:21–23; 4:8–9, 11) he had cried out for sudden death; now he seems to reflect regretfully upon the brevity of the days still left to him. The circumstances here, however, are different. He is not lamenting the imminence and certainty of his death, but grounding upon his inescapable end (vv 6–10), as well as upon his present misery (vv 1–5), his ensuing appeal to God to cease tormenting him (vv 11–21).

The nodal sentence in this strophe is v 7a, the direct request to God to "remember" that his life, viewed as a whole, is an insubstantial breath that will rapidly be spent; vv 7b–8 develop the thought of his imminent end, while vv 9–10 develop further the picture of his "vanishing" in vv 7b–8.

6 A new turn to Job's thoughts (contrast the strophic division of RSV) is taken by the theme of the brevity of his life which is now fast approaching its inevitable end. He speaks now of "my days" rather than "his [humankind's] days" as he did in v 1. There he spoke of the drudgery of human existence as he saw it through his own experience; here he speaks of his sense that he himself is nearing his end. So there is no contradiction between the "months of emptiness" (v 3) that have dragged on, and the present awareness of the swiftness of his life taken as a whole. He is, after all, a man who expects to be "cut off in the midst of his days": a whole life-span has been compressed into mere "days." In this verse he looks back over his life, in v 7a he considers it as a whole, and in vv 7b–10 he looks toward his future fate.

His image here for the swiftness of life comes from the craft of weaving (see *IDB* 2:652–53; G. Dalman, *Arbeit und Sitte in Palästina* [Gütersloh: Bertelsmann, 1937] 5:100–102). As rapidly as the shuttle flies from one side of the web to the other, so rapidly have the days that have made up his entire life passed (not the days that still remain for him; as against Fohrer). He feels that he stands effectively at the end point, his present existence having no more substantiality than a "breath" (v 7); from this point he can look back over them as having "reached their end."

The final phrase באפס תקוה has been traditionally translated "without hope," which is a slightly surprising note in that Job's hope hitherto in his speeches has been precisely that his days *should* come to an end. In 17:15 and 19:10, indeed, he will speak of "hope" as hope of life, but that does not yet appear to be the mood. A quite different translation is possible if תקוה is taken not as "hope" but as "thread," the image from weaving being continued. The weaver has exhausted his thread and the cloth is ready to be cut from the loom (cf. on 6:9; 8:13 NEB) (so NEB, TOB, Dhorme, Horst, Rowley, Andersen). Dhorme aptly quotes the lines of the eleventh-century Spanish Hebrew poet Moses ibn Ezra:

> Man weaves as a weaver in the world,
>   and it is his days that are the thread.

The same word (תקוה) is used. The metaphor of life as the weaving of a cloth appears also in Hezekiah's prayer (Isa 38:12): "You have folded up my life like a weaver who severs the last thread" (NAB; text uncertain).

Other images of the brevity or insubstantiality of life that appear in Job are the cloud (v 9), the breath (vv 7, 16; cf. Ps 78:39; 144:4), a fleeting shadow (8:9; 14:2; cf. Ps 102:12 [11]; 109:23; 144:4; 1 Chr 29:15), a runner (9:25), swift reed boats, an eagle (9:26), a flower that withers (14:2; cf. Ps 90:5–6; 103:15–16; Isa 40:6–7), a dream (20:8; cf. Ps 39:7 [6]).

7 Reflection upon the brevity of his life leads Job to appeal to God that he too should "remember" this fundamental truth about Job as he goes about his daily business of mounting guard over him (v 12), oppressing him (vv 16b, 19b), testing him (v 18b), attacking him (v 20b), terrifying him (v 14). Such a cry to "remember" is conventional in the language of prayer (cf. Judg 16:28; 2 Kgs 20:3; Ps 74:2; and cf. Job 10:9; see W. Schottroff, *THWAT* 1:507–18 [516–17 on its use in the Psalter]; and cf. B. S. Childs, *Memory and Tradition* [SBT 1/37; London: SCM, 1962]). It always implies that God's concentration is elsewhere, and that, if he would for a moment simply take note of the fact or condition that is so overwhelmingly obvious to the one praying, he would immediately set about changing the situation.

God must have temporarily overlooked, Job says—not without a hint of the sarcasm that will become the dominant mood in vv 12–20—that his life is no more substantial than air (רוח), whether as breath or as wind. Sometimes life is compared to the exhaled breath (הבל; cf. v 16; Ps 78:33; 39:6, 12 [5, 11]; 62:10 [9]; 144:4; see K. Seybold, *TDOT* 3:313–20). Sometimes it is compared to a "wind" (usually רוח), especially "a wind that passes and returns not again" (Ps 78:39; cf. Eccl 1:14). The parallel with Ps 78:39 is especially close ("He remembered [זכר] that they were . . . a wind [רוח]"), but either sense is appropriate here. The point is that Job's life is bound to cease at any moment. His grasp on life is uncertain; the one thing certain is that he will never again return to his former happy state: he will never again "see" (i.e., experience, cf. Ps 4:7 [6]; 34:13 [12]) "good," or "happiness" (NAB, NIV), "joy" (JB), "good days" (NEB) (elsewhere in Job in this sense at 9:25; 21:13; 36:11; and cf. 17:15). This cry to God to "remember" the brevity of his life is no indirect appeal to God to restore him to health (contrast Fohrer), but an appeal to God to ignore him; that is the only relief to his pain that Job can envisage (see further on v 16).

8 Not only will "good fortune" never "return" to Job (v 7); he is destined for death. Those who see him now, his acquaintances and the friends themselves, will soon—it is assumed—find he has departed. Even if God should look for him, he will already be dead. He does not hold out any hope that God should look upon him with favor; he does not urge God to come quickly to his rescue or else it will be too late. He simply expresses his sure conviction of his imminent end by affirming that soon not even God will be able to set his eyes on him.

9–10 What that "nonexistence" (cf. אֵינֶנִּי, v 8) will mean is here spelled out. It is the dissolution of his being (כלה, "be at an end, be spent, vanish"), a departure (הלך), a descent (ירד) from which there can be no ascent (עלה). The familiar pattern of return to one's house at the end of the day, to be recognized and welcomed by one's household, will have disappeared. Death is not spoken of as violent or acutely painful, but—so appropriately for a person who feels his extreme weakness (cf. 6:11–13)—as a vanishing and a sinking. His life will end in the way that clouds "break up and disperse" (NEB); he will sink into the nether world in a weakness that forbids any thought of "rising up."

For the image of clouds as what is fleeting, cf. 30:15; Isa 44:22; Hos 13:3. The phrase "his place knows him no longer" recurs in Ps 103:16, again in the context of the brevity of human life (there are minor parallels also with vv 7, 8); the language is conventional.

Whether or not the Egyptian doctrine of life beyond death is being deliberately rejected (cf. Terrien), Job's views of the underworld are typical of the OT and indeed of much of the ancient Near East. The abode of the dead, here named Sheol for the first time in the book (also in 11:8; 14:13; 17:13, 16; 21:13; 24:19; 26:6), has already been described in 3:13–15, 17–19 as a place of rest and of the annihilation of earthly distinctions. Elsewhere we read of it as a dwelling-place deep in the earth (11:8), and, behind its gates (38:17), full of deep darkness (10:21–22; 17:13) and covered in dust (17:16); it is the destiny of all the living (30:23). Above all, it is a land from which no traveler returns (10:21; cf. 2 Sam 12:23; Gen 37:35). It is perhaps not surprising that it is only outside the Book of Job, especially in the psalmic literature, that its significance is expressed as absence from God and the worship of God (cf. Isa 38:11; Ps 6:6 [5]; 30:10 [9]; 88:11–13 [10–12]; 115:17); for in Job the presence of God is not regarded as unambiguously desirable (cf. vv 16, 19). See further, T. H. Gaster, *IDB* 1:787–88; and on the theological significance of death, W. Brueggemann, *IDBS*, 219–22; and cf. on 10:21. The conception of the nether world portrayed in Job is paralleled closely in Babylonian literature where the nether world is known as "the land of no return" (*erṣet lā tāri;* cf. *CAD*, E, 310b). Note especially the depiction of that land in the myth of Ishtar's descent to the nether world (*ANET*, 107a).

11–21 Job has two grounds for this astonishing request that God should leave him alone. The first is the misery of his pain-ridden life (vv 1–5), the second the imminence and inevitability of his death (vv 6–10). His present misery is due to God's attack on him (cf. 6:4), so if only God would leave him alone he could be more comfortable. Not that he would have anything to hope for, even if the "arrows of the Almighty" (6:4) should be held back; for he is marked down for death, and does not question that such is his immediate destiny. This fact again leads him to beg God to leave him alone; he craves the last boon of a dying man.

The passion of Job's speech makes us hesitate to examine its logic; but we will better understand him if we do. If God were to accept Job's plea on the first ground, and desist from torturing him because his pain is too great to bear, would Job not then be relieved of his suffering, and would he not then have reason to doubt that his death is at hand? Would he not then have to abandon his plea on the second ground, that his death is certain and imminent? Yes, indeed; but what conditions this speech is not the pure logic of the situation but the fact that Job has already despaired of hearing any answer to his plea on any ground.

Further, we may ask, If God accepted his plea on the first ground, and if Job then felt less certain of his death, would he not be in large measure restored, enough at least to say that his eyes again beheld good fortune (v 7)? No, not even so; for quite apart from the loss of his children—which Job might feel himself responsible for (though the point is not brought out explicitly)—his honor is still besmirched by the undeserved suffering he has already undergone. He has been publicly humiliated by God's punishment, and the stain on his character remains. How that could possibly be expunged he is in no mood for considering; at this moment he *wants* nothing—except to be left alone.

This final segment of the speech contains two strophes. The first (vv 11–16), after an introductory announcement (v 11), complains of God's harassment of him, especially by nightmares (v 14), and comes to rest on the sentence "Let me alone" (v 16b). The second (vv 17–21), again after an introductory element consisting of a quotation (v 17), pleads for God to desist from his harassment (v 19), and then takes a bold step in challenging the rationale for God's behavior toward him (vv 20–21a), before coming to rest finally on the sentence "Now I am about to lie in the dust of death" (v 21b).

11 Eliphaz knew the experience of being unable to restrain his words (4:2); Job too ("I also," גם־אני) finds it impossible not to burst forth—in a passionate, sarcastic, but deeply despairing, speech to God. Others have the luxury of speaking their mind; Job in his turn will not let propriety restrain him. Peake exaggerates when he says that Job "comes perilously near to fulfilling the Satan's prediction that he would curse God to his face"; but Job admits that he does not speak the language of humble devotion or unquestioning praise. Eliphaz may "seek" God in a spirit of happy resignation (5:8), but Job is forced to speak by his anguish. He speaks from the distress of his spirit (רוח) and the bitterness of his soul (נפש), for it is the psychic torment rather than the physical pain that goads him.

Job speaks as one who has nothing to lose; he "hopes nothing from Him, soon he will have no more to fear from Him; he will have the relief of utter frankness" (Peake), even if he speaks in an unaccustomed mode to God.

12 The doctrine of retribution, which the friends and Job alike turn to instinctively as the only explanation of his suffering, has at its heart a sense of proportion. A person is requited *according to* one's works. But in Job's case there is, as it seems to him, a ludicrous and hugely unjust lack of proportion. Job feels that he is being treated by God as if he were one of the monster enemies of God whose primordial battles against him were recounted in the old myths. But Job's own evaluation of himself is a "passing wind" (רוח, v 7) or "mere breath" (הבל, v 16), as insubstantial as a cloud (v 9), and wholly without strength (6:11–13). It is this cruel disproportionateness that evokes Job's savage irony.

There may be another thread also in Job's indignation: to treat him as a monster is to overvalue him as a power ranged against God; but it is to undervalue him as a human being (cf. Habel). Subhuman monsters deserve the kind of treatment Job is receiving; a human being has other needs: joy (cf. 6:2), the loyalty of friends (cf. 6:14), fulfillment (cf. 7:3), hope (cf. 7:7). Job has been dehumanized by being ranked with the monsters. Worse than the inhumanity of humans to one another (6:14–30) is God's "inhumanity" to the human race (7:12–21).

The mythical figures here mentioned, Sea (Yam) and the Dragon (Tannin) are identified by the older commentators with the sea-monster of Babylonian myth, Tiamat, whose defeat by Marduk is recounted in the creation epic *Enuma elish* (*ANET*, 60–72 [67]). Since the impact of the Ugaritic texts on OT scholarship, however, it has become widely acknowledged that the allusion here is to a West Semitic form of the myth of the conquest of the sea-deity (probably embodying chaos or sterility) by the high god. So in the Baal cycle of myths, Yam the sea-god (cf. Heb. ם׳, *yām*, "sea") is destroyed by the Ugaritic high god Baal. The monster Tannin is also known by that name in the Baal myths, where the name occurs in parallel with Leviathan (see on 3:8). Whatever the precise symbolic value of the sea-deities may be—and there is no hint in the Ugaritic texts that the conflict with them was directly connected with creation, as is the case with Tiamat in the Babylonian myth—Job's point is unaffected: he is God's prisoner, as if he were some threat to the sovereignty of God!

For other OT references to deities of the sea, cf. 9:13 (Rahab); 26:12 (Yam, Rahab); Isa 51:9 (Rahab, Tannin); Ps 74:13–14 (Yam, Tannin, Leviathan); Isa 27:1 (Leviathan); perhaps Ps 68:22 [21] (Bashan; cf. Isa 27:1); some would say Gen 1:2 (Tehom). Other allusions may exist in Isa 17:12–13; Jer 5:22; Nah 1:4; Hab 3:4; Ps 46:3–4 [2–3]; 65:8 [7]; 77:17–19 [16–18]; 93:3–4; 104:6–9; 114:3; 124:4–5; 144:7. Tannin, like Leviathan, is sometimes the term for a nonmythological creature, a reptile of sea or land (e.g., Gen 1:21; Exod. 7:9), and Yam is of course also the term for the "sea"; so it is not always certain where reference to the mythological beings is intended. See further: O. Kaiser, *Die mythische Bedeutung des Meeres in Ägypten, Ugarit und Israel* (BZAW 78; Berlin: Töpelmann, 1959); J. Day, *God's Conflict with the Dragon and the Sea* (University of Cambridge Oriental Publications 35; Cambridge: CUP, 1985).

These hostile forces, though soundly defeated by God in primordial times, are nevertheless sometimes viewed in the OT as still in existence though safely under control by God. Thus for the sea Yahweh has set the sand as a "perpetual barrier which it cannot pass" (Jer 5:22 RSV), and "shut [it] in with doors . . . and prescribed bounds for it, and set bars and doors, and said, 'Thus far shall you come and no farther, and here shall your proud waves be stayed'" (Job 38:8, 10–11). Here too there is an allusion to the "guard" (משמר) or "watch" set upon the sea. The Ugaritic myth of the defeat of Yam by Baal is fragmentary at the point where such a guard may have been depicted; but it does mention that Yam has been made "captive" (*CTA* 2.4.29–30; Gibson, 44). More explicit is the Babylonian myth of the slaying of Tiamat, where a bar and guard is set to prevent that part of her that has become the "waters above the firmament" from flooding the earth (*Enuma elish* 4.139–40; *ANET,* 67). The Joban allusion is nevertheless more probably to the West Semitic myths than to the Babylonian.

For Job the sense of oppression by God to the point of suffocation is among the most dominant of his feelings (cf. 3:23b; 7:19b; 9:18a; 10:3; 13:21, 27; 19:6b, 8). It will issue in his cry, "Let me alone!" (v 16).

13–14 One way of viewing Job's deepest longing is as a need for "comfort" (נחמל). He himself has known what it is to be a comforter, "smiling" on the despondent when they lacked confidence, like one who "comforts" mourners (29:24–25). Now that his time of distress has come, he should be able to expect comfort from the loyalty of his friends (cf. 6:14). Indeed, the three friends had set out to bring him consolation and comfort (לנוד־לו ולנחמו, 2:11). And in the prose prologue they are in some respects the very exemplars of comfort: "They weep in empathetic response to his tragic condition; they join him in abject self-negation by throwing dust on their heads and flinging it heavenwards. . . . They identify with Job as a man reduced to the dust (cf. Ps 35:13–14). . . . While Job is stunned into patient silence, they have the strength to say nothing, nothing at all" (Habel, "Only the Jackal," 228; a somewhat different reading in the *Comment* on these verses). Yet in the reality that emerges in the dialogue they are nugatory comforters, offering empty comfort (21:34) or, worse, "comfort" that turns out to be greater woe: they are "comforters of misery" (16:2), a contradiction in terms. Job, though every resource has been thrust from him (6:13), has to find his own consolation. One comfort he can at least envisage is that if God would rapidly bring his life to an end, he would have the comfort (נחמתי) of knowing that he has "not denied the ordinances of the Holy One" (6:10). While his death remains an unfulfilled wish, the only "comfort" he can seek from his friends is that they should at least listen to what he is saying; "let that be the consolation you offer" (תהי תנחומתיכם, 21:2). But that seems a forlorn hope, just as the hope of "comfort" he holds before himself when he considers the oblivion of sleep is wrested from him by God: "If I think, my bed will comfort me (תנחמני), . . . you terrify me with dreams" (v 13). He can grasp no comfort of any kind (see also on 42:6).

Comforters human or divine he has none. Perhaps the inanimate "bed" may play the personal role of "comforter," at least to a man reckoned by his God as subhuman (see on v 12). But it is debatable whether the imagery of v 12 is continued into vv 13–14. Driver certainly regards the recurrent nightmares (v 14) as a method used by God to keep harmless the dangerous monster Job imagines he must be. Horst, however, finds the metaphor of the monster to be abruptly abandoned in v 13, with a reversion in vv 13–14 to the thoughts of vv 3–4. Others still, while agreeing that the image of the sea-monster is not continued beyond v 12, find a connection of thought between v 12 and vv 13–14: Fohrer, for example, sees a parallel between the perpetual captivity of the sea-monster and the incessant suffering of Job. Most probably, however, Duhm is nearer the mark in designating the nightmares of vv 13–14 as another token of God's enmity (it is less sure that they are also a herald of further suffering to come, as he suggests). Better still would be to see in both Job's perpetual imprisonment as a dangerous monster (v 12) and the constant interruption of his sleep with nightmares (v 14) signs of God's hostility indeed, but more specifically of God's "suffocation" of him—God's being too close for comfort (as we say)—that lead to the cry, "Let me alone" (v 16b; cf. v 19). (For the quite different view of Ehrlich, see n. 7:12.c.)

Any expectation of "comfort" he may have is soon dashed, for in the hours of rest he is the victim of the most terrifying of God's assaults: nightmares and frightening visions. No matter whether these are normal symptoms of Job's elephantiasis (if that is what his disease is; see Hölscher, 24); they are for him entirely God's means of attacking him. It is not that "Lacking our modern conception of secondary causes, Job sees in these sufferings not the natural accompaniment of his disease, but direct acts of God" (Peake), but that Job rightly understands, to whatever extent he recognizes secondary causes, that he is a man afflicted not by disease but by God.

Eliphaz has recounted the experience of a terrifying auditory vision of the night (4:13–16), but that, unlike Job's dreams, was educative; Job's are an extension of the miseries of the day. See also E. L. Ehrlich, *Der Traum im Alten Testament* (BZAW 73; Berlin: A. Töpelmann, 1953) 145–46. Among other ancient references to the terrors of the night can be mentioned Ecclus 40:5–6; Ovid, *Epist. ex Ponto*, 1.2.43–44; Plutarch, *De virtute et vitio*, 2.100.

15 Better than a life in which one is unaccountably persecuted day and night by God is death itself. It is not the misery of sleepless nights or terrifying nightmares that makes Job's being (נפשׁ) "prefer strangling," but the knowledge that these are the manifestations of a divine hostility (cf. 6:4) which is not so much inscrutable as perverse. It seems almost irrelevant that "strangling" or suffocation is a symptom of elephantiasis (Driver), for the significance of the disease lies wholly in its author, and any suffocation that resulted in death would be the personal act of God rather than the climax of the disease.

16 In the previous verse, Job makes his choice (בחר) for death; here he seems to say, in the same vein, that he has turned his back on and rejected (מאס) life (the object is not expressed; see n. 7:16.a). The man who has no strength for anything (6:11–13) has not slipped into feeble despair, and let happen what will happen: he has the strength to make choices, and he knows what he is doing in choosing death.

To reject life and to say to God "Leave me alone!" amount to the same thing. What any psalmist in distress fears as the worst disaster of all—the absence of God (cf. references to "forsake," "be far," "hide," "forget," "hearken," "answer," "arise," "turn" and so on)—is what Job craves. No cultic psalmody can encourage individuals or community to beg God to "desist," for that spells death, and the cult is oriented toward life in fellowship with God. Job has reached the bottom of despair in finding that God is part of the despair, indeed, its larger part. He has rejected life and he has rejected God.

The dreadful extremity to which Job is driven by the "anguish of [his] spirit" (v 11) is too often underestimated by commentators. Many do not even remark on the phrase "leave me alone," while others think that it has to do solely with the suffering God is inflicting (so e.g., Davidson: "i.e. cease from paining me with such afflictions"), or see it as a plea to be left in peace (so e.g., Hesse). But Job's words are categorical, and their import is unmistakable in its further development in vv 17–19.

Job uses similar language in 10:20 (*q.v.*); the only parallel outside Job is found in Isa 2:22.

Two facts have been moving Job toward the cry "Leave me alone": his harassment by God, and the certainty of his own imminent death (see on vv 11–21). In this strophe (vv 11–16), as in the next (vv 17–21), the focus is upon God's attack upon him; but the strophe ends on the more plaintive note of his assurance that he "will not live long (lit., forever)" and that his "days are a mere breath." If God will not altogether forbear to close-guard him like a monster (v 12), or to disturb his sleep with terrifying visions (v 14), can he not grant Job some short intermission from these assaults? By the time God is ready to resume them, Job will certainly be dead.

17–18 In this bitter parody of Ps 8:5–6 (4–5) (cf. also 144:3; and cf. P. E. Dion, "Formulaic Language in the Book of Job: International Background and Ironical Distortions," *SR* 16 [1987] 187–93), Job returns to the theme of disproportion which emerged in v 12. There Job felt his significance so exaggerated that he was treated like some threat to the cosmos that must be kept in close confines by God. Now he complains that this is God's attitude to humankind in general, not just to himself. But, as in v 1, the horizon of his own experience and of his perception of the human condition have merged, and it is patent that "humankind" (אנוש) of v 17 is not really different from the "I" of v 19. It is a particularly unhappy manifestation of depression when the sufferer believes that everyone else must be, in reality, equally miserable; for it removes any possibility of hope.

Ps 8:5 [4] asks, "What is man that you should be mindful of him (תזכרנו)," Job "that you should magnify him, *or* esteem him highly (תגדלנו)"; the idea in Job's תגדלנו is modeled on the description of the exalted rank of human beings in Ps 8:6–9 [5–8]. "You set your mind [לב, lit. heart] upon him" in Job recalls the תזכרו, "be mindful," of Ps 8:5 [4]. The "inspecting" (פקד) by God in Job is equivalent to the "visiting" (פקד; "dost care for him," rsv) of Ps 8:5 [4]; the verb פקד can have both a positive sense of "care for" (cf. on 10:12) and a more negative sense of "visit in order to execute judgment" for some misdeed (cf. Exod 20:5; 32:34; see W. Schottroff, *THWAT* 2:475–84 § 4a-b).

In every respect the language of the psalm is reapplied ironically by Job (cf. also M. Fishbane, *Biblical Interpretation in Ancient Israel* [Oxford: Clarendon, 1985] 285–86). In Ps 8, in the context of praise to the majesty of God's name (vv 2, 10 [1, 9]), "What is man?" expresses thankful wonderment that humankind, apparently so insignificant on the scale of the universe (v 4 [3]), should be the object of the almighty God's concern, and, most especially, should be dignified with the status of lords of the earth. In Job, "What is man?" prefaces a reproof that God's elevation of humankind to a position of significance has not been for its good, but has only drawn down upon mortals God's merciless scrutiny and perpetual examination. In the psalm, God's "magnifying" human beings is reverently accepted; in Job it is an unwelcome intrusion. In the psalm, God's "mindfulness" (זכר) of humans is an inexplicable favor; in Job God's "mindfulness" (שית לב) is an inexplicable cruelty: "the unsleeping care of God [is distorted] into a maddening espionage" (Peake). In the psalm, the "visiting" by God is for care, in Job for harm. In psalmic language, the morning is especially treasured as the time of God's deliverance (Ps 5:4 [3]; 46:6 [5]; 90:14; 143:8; cf. Isa 33:2; Lam 3:23; Zeph 3:5), the time when joy comes (Ps 30:6 [5]) (see J. Ziegler, "Die Hilfe Gottes 'am Morgen,'" *Alttestamentliche Studien Friedrich Nötscher . . . gewidmet* [ed. H. Junker and J. Botterweck; BBB 1; Bonn:

Hanstein, 1950] 281–88), with the critique of C. Barth, *TDOT* 2:226–28). Job now knows the morning only as the time of God's visitations in wrath (cf. uniquely in the Psalms, 73:14), despite his long habit of associating the morning with sacrifice (1:5). Even "testing" (בחן) is a neutral term; whether the one tested is rewarded or suffers is determined by what is found by the test, and it is not the fault of the test if punishment follows. Psalmists sometimes even invite God to "test" them (e.g., Ps 17:3; 26:2; 139:23), for they are confident of their righteousness (see M. Tsevat, *TDOT* 1:69–70; E. Jenni, *THWAT* 1:273–75). Job has become embittered about divine testing, however, even though he has (unbeknown to himself) passed it with flying colors (1:8; 2:3, 10). What he suffers points only to unredeemable failure in God's examination of him. It is possible also that in the language of these verses there is a faint echo of Yahweh's song of his vineyard (Isa 2:2–5), which Yahweh "keeps" (נצר; cf. Job 7:20) watering it "every moment" (לרגעים, as in Job 7:18), guarding (נצר) it night and day lest any one "visit" (פקד) it with harm. Whatever, in short, can be said positively about the relationship of humankind with God is negated by Job; he has rejected life itself and God too, and the conventional encouragements have lost their meaning: the "consolations of God [are] too small for [him]" (15:11, Eliphaz).

19 As with the cry "Leave me alone" (v 16), Job takes the opposite attitude to that of the sufferers who speak in the Psalms. They earnestly beseech God to "see" (ראה) them (e.g., Ps 25:19; 59:5 [4]; cf. Lam 1:9) or "consider" (נבט hiph) them (e.g., Ps 13:4 [3]; 80:15 [14]) or not to "hide [his] face" (סתר פנים hiph) from them (e.g., Ps 27:9; 69:18 [17]); Job asks with despairing impatience how long it will be (see n. 7:19.a) before God looks (שעה) away from him. Outside the Book of Job (where 10:20; 14:6 are parallels) such a wish is expressed only in Ps 39:14 [13]; even there, however, the tonality is more positive, since the same psalm says "My hope is in you" (v 8 [7]), and an appeal has just been made to Yahweh to "hear," "give ear," and "be not silent" (v 13 [12]). Whether this means simply that the psalmist "desires to be spared further punishment, not to be relieved of Yahweh's presence or help" (A. A. Anderson, *Psalms* [London: Oliphants, 1972] 1:313) (cf. v 11 [10]) is difficult to say; certainly Job's rejection of God's gaze is in its context much more categorical.

The force of Job's appeal is evidenced by the vivid phrase "let me be till I swallow my spittle." One commentator of a former generation wrote: "One would be glad to think the poet wrote something different" (Peake); but undecorous as the phrase may be, it powerfully represents Job's sense of the "majestic instancy" (Francis Thompson) of God's assaults upon him. Similar phrases are well known in Arabic, e.g., *'abli'ni riqi*, "let me swallow my spittle," i.e., "wait a moment" (cf. also 9:18).

20 Job nears the climax of his speech with an immensely provocative line: "If I have sinned, how do I injure you?" It is true that the Hebrew here has no word for "if" (cf. KJV), and Andersen strongly insists that the word should not be supplied: "Job knows that he is a sinner. . . . It gives Job a quite undeserved air of self-righteousness to make this [clause] hypothetical by adding the word *if*. . . . [It] makes Job's speech rather insolent, implying that human sin makes no difference to God." Indeed, it is not grammatically necessary to supply the "if," but it is perfectly legitimate: cf. Prov 18:22, (lit.) "One has found a wife, one has found a good thing," i.e., "If one has found. . . ." (see also on Job 4:2, 21; and cf. GKC, § 159hh). This understanding, which is adopted by most versions (including LXX and Syriac) and commentators, is further supported by an almost identical line in the mouth of Elihu (35:6), which is introduced by "if" (אם). On the broader issue of Job's righteousness, nothing has happened since the beginning of the book to change the author's announcement that Job is an innocent man (1:1), or God's declaration that Job is "blameless and upright" (1:8; 2:3), or the narrator's comment that "Job did not sin with his lips" (2:10)—or to refute Job's claim that he has "not denied the words of the Holy One" (6:10). It is hard to see that protestation of innocence by an innocent man is "self-righteous" or "insolent."

Job is not arguing that the sins of mere human beings are so trivial as to be unworthy of God's consideration; he has no deist inclinations. Elihu comes closer to that position in 35:5–8; but Job is making an *ad hoc* argument that concerns himself alone. It is not that human sin is trivial, but that any sin Job may have committed is hardly worth retribution since he will in any case soon be dead. Surely no harm can come to God if he staves off the execution of punishment for a little, for Job's days are now so few that God will very soon have the satisfaction of ultimate retribution.

The irony of disproportion (cf. on v 12) strikes Job again. Can the alleged sin of one dying man be so harmful to God that he must bend all his energies to the harassment of that man? Out of all the objects that deserve God's wrath, is it not absurd that Job has been set up as the target (cf. 6:4; and see further on 16:12)? Is it not ironic that the man who is so light and insubstantial that his days are a breath (vv 7, 16) seems to have become a "burden" to God? Is not God's preoccupation with Job, in short, totally disproportionate to Job's significance?

Again the conventional language about God is twisted to ironic shape: often the verb "keep watch" (נצר) is used of God's protection of the righteous (e.g., Ps 12:8 [7]; 31:24 [23]; cf. KJV's translation here, "thou preserver of men"), but here the term designates God as spy or scrutineer of humans, with allusion back to v 12. Not so differently, H. G. Wells's Mr. Polly had been educated to think of "the Divinity as of a limitless being having the nature of a schoolmaster and making infinite rules, known and unknown, rules that were always ruthlessly enforced, and with an infinite capacity for punishment, and, most horrible of all, of limitless powers of espial" (*The History of Mr Polly*, chap. 1).

21 It may appear that Job, in the very last verse of his speech, makes a fundamental admission of guilt when he asks, "Why do you not pardon my sin?" Yet if Job considers himself a sinner in need of divine forgiveness, we may well wonder why he has not sought such forgiveness from the very beginning of his suffering rather than proclaim his desire for death and protest God's assaults on him. Indeed, the supposition that Job acknowledges that he is guilty makes nonsense of the whole course of the book hitherto. It must rather be that Job means by "my sin": my sin as you (God) reckon it. Job is suffering; and unless God's dealings with human beings are quite arbitrary—a possibility that Job will only later seriously entertain (cf. 9:22)—God must have something against Job to make him suffer as he does. Very well, says Job; I will not debate whether God is right in counting me a sinner; I will only ask that he should overlook and "forgive" (i.e., not punish) the sin of a feeble dying man like myself. The verse lies entirely in the shadow of the hypothesis of v 20, "If I have sinned"; that is, "my sin" means "my (hypothetical) sin," the sin that must be hypothesized if my suffering is to be explained.

The emphasis, then, lies not upon any admission of guilt (cf. my translation: "Why do you not pardon any sin of mine?" sc., assuming I have committed some sin), but upon Job's plea for toleration. The verbs נשא (lit. "lift up") and עבר (hiph) (lit. "cause to pass away") could signify forgiveness in its usual sense of remission, but here may mean only "tolerate" and "overlook" (as e.g., Dhorme, JB). For to Job, at this point at least, what is more important than either forgiveness or recognition of his righteousness is relief from his suffering until death brings the final relief. Cannot God let his supposed sin pass (עבר)?

Job's point is not that any sin he has committed must be an inadvertent one—since he is not aware of any sin—and is therefore relatively insignificant and the more easily forgivable; though most commentators assume that inadvertent sin is in mind (e.g., Driver, Fohrer, Rowley), nothing hangs upon its inadvertence or otherwise. What matters is that, however gross the sin may be, it can surely do God no harm to forego the punishment of it for the remaining brief span of Job's life (see also on 12:26).

Soon, says Job, or rather, "immediately" (עתה, "now"), he will be lying in the dust of Sheol (cf. also 17:16; 20:11; 21:26). Should God "seek" him then, he would find Job was no more in being. Why, though, does Job imagine that God would wish to "seek" him? It reads too much into the word to suppose that "Job still believes . . . that God is a God of love, who will one day seek earnestly to renew his former communion with His servant . . . but he will have passed into Sheol, and it will be too late!" (Driver; similarly Duhm, Peake, Rowley). It is rather an emphatic way of affirming that he will no longer be; even God cannot find that which does not exist (a similar expression in v 8b). See further on 14:15.

It is tempting to regard Job's cry for an undemanding and unconditional "forgiveness" as the token of a view of the relationship of God and humans that does not put the question of sin at the center (so Fohrer). Could it be "a protest against the view of those who make sins the primary factor in religion and the determinant of the relationships between God and men," an affirmation of the possibility of friendship between God and humankind that is unassailable even by the undeniable fact that humans in their weakness sin (Duhm)? Such a view is by no means foreign to the OT (see G. Fohrer, "Action of God and Decision of Man," *Biblical Essays* [Die Outestamentiese Werkgemeenskap in Suid-Afrika, 1966] 31–39) but it seems out of place here; Job's cry is an *ad hoc* one, arising not from a principle but from his pain and his certainty of imminent death. He asks for no readjustment of relationship between God and humankind in general but rather that he himself should be left alone (v 16b)—both for good and ill.

Explanation

The most remarkable aspect of this speech has been the direction in which it has been addressed. Far from replying decorously to the encouragements of Eliphaz, Job has burst out again in lament over his suffering and has, for the first time, begged for sudden death (6:1–13). The man is in the grip of his anguish, which neither reason nor consolation can touch. In ignoring Eliphaz's speech, Job shows not only that his psychic and physical pains form his whole horizon, but that talk like Eliphaz's must miss the mark when deep hurt is being suffered.

So when Job comes to address the friends (6:14–30) his attitude is unsurprising: they have cheated him of the one thing he might have expected from them: an understanding sympathy. The bitterness of his irony arises from their denial of the essence of friendship: loyalty (*ḥesed*, 6:14). All that anyone could offer Job is support and acceptance; but they have found the sight of suffering too frightening, and despite their physical nearness and their verbal communication they have backed away from Job psychically. For Job, friendship has issued in isolation.

The third movement of Job's speech (7:1–21) is, by contrast to the address to the friends, quite unexpected. Direct address to God in the midst of formal debate with his interlocutors may be out of place and inappropriate, but, all considered, it is only in that direction that speech has any value for Job. The monologue of chap. 3 was impotent, dialogue with the friends has already proved distressingly disappointing; where else can Job turn his words than toward God? His instinct to do so, his single-minded assurance that it is God with whom he has to do, will prove his salvation in the end. For the present, though, he asks nothing of God but that he should let him alone (7:16) so that his few remaining days may be free from pain. Yet in the very act of begging God to desert him he approaches him; the ambivalence in Job's attitude to the presence and absence of God that will be laid bare in the developing drama has already been signaled.

Bildad's First Speech (8:1–22)

Bibliography

Dahood, M. "Hebrew-Ugaritic Lexicography." *Bib* 46 (1965) 311–32. **Habel, N. C.** "Appeal to Ancient Tradition as a Literary Form." *ZAW* 88 (1976) 253–72. **Irwin, W. A.** "The First Speech of Bildad." *ZAW* 51 (1953) 205–16. **Löhr, M.** "Die drei Bildad-Reden im Buche Hiob." *Beiträge zur alttestamentliche Wissenschaft* (FS K. Budde), ed. K. Marti. Berlin: A. Töpelmann, 1920. BZAW 34. 107–12. **Reider, J.** "Etymological Studies in Biblical Hebrew." *VT* 2 (1952) 113–30. **Sarna, N. M.** "Some Instances of the Enclitic -*m* in Job." *JJS* 6 (1955) 108–10. **Sutcliffe, E. F.** "Further Notes on Job, Textual and Exegetical: 6,2–3.13; 8,16–17; 19,20.26." *Bib* 31 (1950) 365–78.

Translation

[1] *Then Bildad the Shuhite spoke:*

[2] *How long will you speak thus,*
    the words of your mouth a tempestuous[a] wind?
[3] *Can God pervert justice?*
    Can the Almighty pervert[a] what is right?
[4] [a]*Your sons sinned against him,*
    so he abandoned them to the power[b] of their own guilt.
[5] [a]*As for you, if you would make your prayer to God,*
    and seek the favor of the Almighty,
[6] [a]*if you are pure and upright,*
    he will surely[b] now rouse himself[c] for you,[d]
    and restore[e] your righteous abode.[f]
[7] *Then, lowly though your former state was,*
    your future will be very great.[a]

[8] *Question now the former generation,[a]*
    apply[b] your mind to the discovery of their fathers,[c]
[9] *For we ourselves are but of yesterday and know nothing,*
    our days on earth a mere shadow.
[10] *But they[a] can teach you and tell you,*
    they can speak[b] out of their understanding.
[11] *Can papyrus grow high where there is no marsh?*
    Can reeds flourish where there is no water?
[12] *While it is still in flower,[a] and even if it is not[b] cut,*
    it can[c] wither faster than any other plant.[d]
[13] *Such is the fate[a] of all who forget God;*
    and[b] so does the expectation[c] of the godless perish.
[14] [a]*His confidence is cut off,[b]*
    his trust proves a spider's house.
[15] [a]*Let[b] him lean upon that house[c]; he will not stand.*
    Let him grasp hold of it; he cannot arise.
[16] *A lush plant is he in the sun's warmth,[a]*
    spreading its shoots[b] over the garden.

¹⁷ *Its roots twine about the heap of stones,*^a
   it takes firm hold^b *among the rocks.*
¹⁸ *But if it is once torn* ^a *from its place,*
   that place disowns it with "I never saw you."
¹⁹ *That is the dissolution of its life* ^a*;*
   and others ^b *spring from the ground to take its place.*^c

²⁰ *Behold, God will not reject a blameless man,*
   nor will he uphold the evil-doer.
^{21 a} *He will yet again* ^b *fill* ^c *your mouth with laughter;*
   shouts of joy will be on your lips.
²² *Your enemies will be covered in confusion,*
   and the tent of the wicked will be no more.

Notes

2.a. כַּבִּיר, lit. "mighty." NEB rather improbably regards it as elliptical for כַּבִּיר יָמִים, "aged," as in 15:10; unlikely too is G. R. Driver's translation "The breath of one who is mighty are the words of your mouth" ("Hebrew Studies," *JRAS* [1948] 164–76 [170]).

3.a. The same verb יְעַוֵּת as in the first colon, a relatively infrequent type of repetition (see Gordis, 508–11, for other examples in Job). Whether or not the repetition is for emphasis (as Driver, Fohrer), emendation of the second verb to יְעַנֶּה, "bend" (Duhm, Hölscher, Dhorme), reflected in JB, NAB, is unnecessary. LXX's use of two verbs was probably simply stylistic (Gordis).

4.a. The sentence begins with אִם, lit. "if," but the context shows it is not a purely hypothetical "if" but equivalent to "since" (a use not recognized by the lexica; but cf., e.g., Fohrer and Gordis, though it is unnecessary to regard אִם as a different word cognate with Arab. *'inna*). For the translation as a statement, cf. NEB.

4.b. Lit. "into the hand" (בְּיַד). Gordis unnecessarily suggests the word is a phonetic equivalent for בְּעַד "because of"; similarly S. Rin, "Ugaritic-Old Testament Affinities," *BZ* 7 (1963) 22–33 (32–33).

5.a. Beer and Duhm replace אִם אַתָּה by וְאַתָּה, retroverted from LXX σὺ δέ (so *BHK*). BJ, JB adopt this, moving אִם־זָךְ וְיָשָׁר אַתָּה from v 6 to follow אַתָּה.

6.a. This clause is deleted by many (e.g., Duhm, Dhorme, Horst, Fohrer, Hesse), as a moralizing gloss on v 5; the line is then reduced to two cola. But the phrase is quite intelligible as a secondary condition.

6.b. כִּי emphatic (cf. BDB, 472b § 1e; bibliography: Blommerde, 30).

6.c. יָעִיר, usually taken as a "declarative or exhibitive" hiph, "act in an aroused manner, awake" (intrans; BDB, 735b); so KJV, RSV, NAB, NIV. Others take it as "watch over (עַל), guard" (Dhorme, Gordis, NEB), which offers a possible parallel to שָׁלַם (see n. 6.e); similarly H. L. Ginsberg, "Two North Canaanite Letters from Ugarit," *BASOR* 72 (1938) 18–19 (19); H. N. Richardson, "A Ugaritic Letter of a King to his Mother," *JBL* 66 (1947) 321–24 (322) (with Ug. and Arab. parallels); S. Loewenstamm, "Ugaritic Formulas of Greeting," *BASOR* 194 (1969) 52–54; B. Hartmann, "Mögen die Götter dich behüten und unversehrt bewahren," *VTS* 16 (1967) 102–5; J. J. Stamm, "Ein ugaritisch-hebräisches Verbum und seine Ableitungen," *TZ* 35 (1979) 5–9 (7–9). JB has "he will restore his favor to you," perhaps following LXX δεήσεως ἐπακούσεταί σου "he will hearken to your request" (preferred by Peake), but it is probably only LXX's avoidance of a too striking anthropomorphism (Gard, *Exegetical Method of the Greek Translator*, 45–46). NJB "his light will shine on you" reads יָאִיר, hiph of אוֹר. J. Reider, "Etymological Studies in Biblical Hebrew," *VT* 2 (1952) 113–30 (126), suggested "will bestow wealth on you," adducing Arab. *ġâr* as cognate. The psalmic parallels of language (see *Comment*) make "awake" still the most probable rendering.

6.d. M. Dahood, *Psalms II*, 318, vocalizes עָלֶיךָ to עֻלָיךְ from עוּל "suckling" and translates: "Even now he would be safeguarding your little ones."

6.e. שָׁלַם is usually taken here as "restore, reestablish" with the abode as the object (so NAB; cf. JB; Dhorme, Pope). Others take שָׁלַם as "reward (you)," with the accusative of person (understood) and of thing (so RSV, NIV). Gordis, following Rashi, Delitzsch, translates "keep whole, safeguard" which he regards as synonymous with יָעִיר. NEB "and see your just intent fulfilled" is unintelligible.

6.f. Lit. "the abode of your righteousness." The righteousness of Job is regarded poetically as inhabiting his "estate" (נָוֶה). This interpretation makes the subtlety of Driver unnecessary: "the habitation which, by its prosperity, will be evidence of the righteousness of its possessor" (cf. KJV, RV "make the habitation of thy righteousness prosperous"). RSV "rightful habitation" (cf. NIV, NAB) means "the house you deserve" (cf. Hesse), but this meaning is improbable. "Your righteous dwelling" (Gordis) is a legitimate translation, but fits the context less well.

7.a. יִשְׂגֶּה: the anomalous masc form is probably assimilation to the masc verb וְהָיָה in the first colon (cf. König, 3:§ 251i; Driver). Alteration to תִּשְׂגֶּה (fem) (e.g., BHK, NAB) or יַשְׂגֶּה "shall make great" (e.g., Duhm) is unecessary.

8.a. See *Comment*.

8.b. כּוֹנֵן, "fix," sc. לְבָּךְ "your heart," a phrase that occurs nowhere else. Some suggest therefore the emendation בּוֹנֵן "considering" (so e.g., Duhm, Fohrer, BHK, NAB; support of Pesh *wᵉtbyn* and LXX ἐξιχνίασον is sometimes claimed, though the verb in LXX probably corresponds to חקר [Dhorme]. But כּוֹן לְ in Isa 51:13 means "is determined to," and a connection of the roots *šᵊl* and *knn* occurs in Ug. (cf. M. Dahood, "Hebrew-Ugaritic Lexicography," *Bib* 46 [1965] 311–32 [329]); for omission of לְ, see König, 3:§ 209c.

8.c. אֲבוֹתָם is emended to אָבוֹת by Duhm, Hölscher, Fohrer, Hesse; see *Comment*. Others consider the final *mem* an enclitic (N. M. Sarna, "Some Instances of the Enclitic *-m* in Job," *JJS* 6 [1955] 108–10 [109]; M. Dahood, *Bib* 46 [1965] 329). Very improbable is J. A. Fitzmyer's reading אֲבוֹתָם, "their ghosts" (in W. F. Albright, *Yahweh and the Gods of Canaan* [London: Athlone, 1968] 124). Budde read אֲבוֹתֵינוּ "our fathers" (so also Moffatt), Stevenson אֲבוֹתֶיךָ "your fathers."

10.a. Lit. "is it not that they [emphatic]."

10.b. Lit. "put forth words" (יוֹצִאוּ מִלִּים), the noun, according to GKC, § 125c, being indeterminate for the sake of emphasis (*indeterminatio ad augendum*), "important words." But it is preferable to link מִלִּים and מִלָּבָם (cf. also König, 3:§ 293d).

12.a. בְּאִבּוֹ לֹא redivided to בְּאָב לֹא by BHK, NAB.

12.b. לֹא taken as emphatic (= לֻא) by I. Eitan, "La particule emphatique 'la' dans la Bible," *REJ* 74 (1922) 1–16 (8–9); F. Nötscher, "Zum emphatischen Lamed," *VT* 3 (1953) 372–80 (374); G. R. Driver, "Affirmation by Exclamatory Negation," *JANES* 5 (1973) 107–14 (110). Hence JB "Pluck them even at their freshest: fastest of all plants they wither" (cf. NEBmg). But this sense is unacceptable, since it makes cutting down rather than deprivation of water the cause of their withering.

12.c. Clearly a modal use of the imperfect verb, equivalent to "can"; for papyrus *as a rule* does not wither (cf. on 4:20).

12.d. Or, "any grass" (כָל־חָצִיר).

13.a. אָרְחוֹת "ways" or "paths" (RSV), in the sense of "tracks of fate" (Dhorme) or "destiny" (as NIV); for a similar use of דֶּרֶךְ, cf. Isa 40:27; Ps 37:5. Most, however, emend to אַחֲרִית "end," as suggested by LXX τὰ ἔσχατα (so Merx, Duhm, Driver, Fohrer, Pope, Gordis, NAB, JB "fate"). Nevertheless, the formal identity of Prov 1:19 (despite the recommendation of BHS to read אַחֲרִית there too) tends to confirm MT (so Dhorme), which is followed by Horst.

13.b. Emphatic *waw*, according to Blommerde.

13.c. NEB "life-thread" sees here not תִקְוָה "hope" but תִקְוָה "thread" (as also in 7:6; Prov 11:7 "thread of life"). In a similar phrase in 27:8 NEB has "hope" (mg "thread of life"), and simply "expectation" or "hope" in Prov 10:28; 11:23. The "hope of the wicked" is unexceptionable, nevertheless.

14.a. W. A. Irwin's wholesale reconstruction of the verse to וישר יקום כסנה ותם כעשב במדבר, "But the righteous shall rise up like a thorn bush, and the innocent like a plant in the desert" ("The First Speech of Bildad," *ZAW* 51 [1933] 205–16 [218–10]) is of an arbitrariness no longer entertained, and is in any case woefully banal.

14.b. יְקוֹט is *hapax*, perhaps impf of *קוֹט (BDB, 876b) or *קטט (KB³); cf. Arab. *qatta*, "cut, carve." Thus KJV, RV "break in sunder"; cf. RSV mg "be cut off" (and cf. TOB). This was also how Tg and Pesh took it. Parallelism suggests יְקוֹט is a noun; hence BDB also suggests "fragile thing" (hence NIV). BHS proposes a root קטט "be short" (cf. Arab. *qatta*). Saadia's Arabic translation is attractive: *habl eš-šams* "thread of the sun," especially if this means "gossamer" (cf. R. Ecker, *Die arabische Job-Übersetzung des Gaon Saadja ben Josef al-Fajjûmi. Ein Beitrag zur Geschichte der Übersetzung des Alten Testaments* [Munich: Kösel, 1962] 37). Saadia presumably saw in יקוט the Aram. קַיְט "summer" (= Heb. קַיְץ) (J. Reider, "Etymological Studies in Biblical Hebrew," *VT* 4 [1954] 276–95 [288–89]), and his version is an interpretive expansion. It is doubtful also whether the Arab. phrase means "gossamer." H. Derenbourg, *Version arabe du Livre de Job de R. Saadia ben Iosef al-Fayyoûmî* (Oeuvres complètes 5; Paris: Leroux, 1899), *in loc.*, translated "a trail (*trainée*) of dust in the sunlight," and Fleischer denies such an expression in Arabic (see Grabbe, *Comparative Philology*, 58–60). Nevertheless, many adopt "gossamer" (so NEB, NAB), sometimes comparing with Saadia's phrase German *Sommerfäden*, "summer-threads," viz. gossamer" (see also *OED*, 6:310). This leads to emendations of MT to conform to Saadia's understanding: thus קוּרִים "threads" (Beer, Duhm; followed cautiously by Driver, Hölscher); קַיִם "threads" (Gordis); קוּרֵי קָיִט "threads of summer" (Budde, *BHS* [prp]); or, to replace אֲשֶׁר־יִקוֹט, קָיִט שָׁרֵי קִשְׁרֵי "bands of summer" (Peters, KB, Fohrer, Horst, Terrien, Pope, *BHS* [prp]); or חוּט קָיִץ, "thread of summer" (Bickell); or simply חוּט "thread" (Beer, *BHK*, JB). Grabbe wisely concludes that emendations based on Saadia's translation lack a sound philological basis (*Comparative Philology*, 60).

15.a. Budde, Hölscher, Hesse, delete the verse as a mistaken gloss on v 15.

15.b. LXX rightly saw the hypothetical aspect of the sentence, and introduced ἐάν "if" (cf. JB "Let him lean").

15.c. Lit. "upon his house" (עַל בֵּיתוֹ); Horst deletes the phrase (the absolute use of שָׁעַן is attested in 24:23); so too *BHS* (*frt*).

16.a. Dhorme took לִפְנֵי־שֶׁמֶשׁ as "before the sun rises" (similarly NAB), but this is improbable. Gordis' version, "even under the hot sun," may be appropriate but is not supported by LXX, as he claims.

16.b. Collective sing (Andersen).

17.a. גַּל so understood by most; but Merx, Duhm, followed by Moffatt, and E. F. Sutcliffe, "Further Notes on Job, Textual and Exegetical. 6,2–3.13; 8,16–17; 19,20.26," *Bib* 31 (1950) 365–78 (371–75), took it as "well" (cf. Cant 4:12, where the text is, however, dubious), the most favorable spot in the garden.

17.b. בֵּית אֲבָנִים יֶחֱזֶה lit. "it sees a house of stones." יחזה "sees" is represented by KJV, RV; cf. NIV "it looks for a place among the stones." The image requires something like יֶחֱז (= יֶאֱחֹז), "grasps" the stones as a source of support. So Budde; Bickell יַחֲזֶנּוּ; NAB, Pope יֶחֱזֶנּוּ; NAB, יֶחֱזַק to similar effect. Less convincing are attempts to follow LXX ζήσεται "will live"; thus יִחְיֶה (Siegfried, Duhm, Dhorme, RSV, JB). Also somewhat improbable in sense is יָחֹז (cf. Arab. *hazza* "cut, pierce," i.e., pushes its roots down between stones (Budde; cf. Driver); similarly Gordis' equation of יֶחֱזֶה with יֶחֱצֶה "cleave, piece." G. R. Driver found a cognate in Arab. *hāḍa* "was opposite" ("Studies in the Vocabulary of the Old Testament," *JTS* 34 [1933] 375–85 [381]; idem, "Problems in Job and Psalms Reconsidered," *JTS* 40 [1939–40] 391–94 [391]), hence NEB "run against." בֵּית can be equivalent to בֵּין "among" (as *byt* in Syr.) (cf. Prov 8:2; Ezek 41:9), though some emend to בֵּין (e.g., Hölscher); or it could be a contraction of בְּבֵית (GKC, § 118g).

18.a. יְבַלְּעֶנּוּ, indefinite subject, lit. "one swallows it" (less probably God is subject; as Ehrlich); בלע can be a metaphor for general destruction or annihilation, though Pope translates "When his place swallows him," taking the initial *mem* of מְקוֹמוֹ as an emphatic enclitic attached to the verb (so Sarna, *JJS* 6 [1955] 109–10); Gordis simply deletes the initial *mem*.

19.a. מְשׂוֹשׂ דַרְכּוֹ, lit. "the joy of its way" (so KJV, RSV, TOB), sc. way of life. If this reading is correct, the phrase must be ironic (Driver, Pope). More straightforward is to read מְסֹוס דרכו "the dissolving, dissolution of his way (= life)," from מסס (so Fohrer, Horst, Hesse). Dhorme took מְשׂוֹשׂ from a supposed root סוס "rot" (cf. סָס "moth") and revocalized דרכו to דַּרְךְּ (pausal) "(on the) way"; hence JB "he rots on the roadside" (cf. NAB). NEB, NIV "its life withers away" presumably reckon with the same root. Gordis has "thus he departs on his way," taking מְשׂוֹשׂ as the polel ptcp (initial *mem* elided) of מוּשׁ "depart"; the sense is rather tame. Guillaume suggested a cognate to Arab. *sawwasa* "threw into disorder, confounded."

19.b. אַחֵר "another" is sg, יצמחו apparently plur. יצמחו may be an *ad sensum* plur (as GKC, § 145d) or, less probably, a sg *yaqtulu* form (Pope, Blommerde). Others emend to יִצְמָח (Duhm, Driver, Fohrer).

19.c. Lit. "after (it)."

21.a. The whole verse is deleted by Hölscher on the ground that it is too friendly a sentence for Bildad!

21.b. Read with most עַד for עַד (against König, 3:§ 387l); cf. also n. 1:18.a.

21.c. Dhorme, overinfluenced by the parallel in Ps 126:2, read the passive יִמָּלֵא instead of יְמַלֶּה (for יְמַלֵּא).

Form/Structure/Setting

The *structure* of the speech is dominated by the content: vv 1–7 concern the application of the doctrine of retribution to Job and his children, vv 8–19 the fate of the wicked, vv 20–22 the happy future in store for Job. The conclusion of each section is signaled clearly: in v 7 by the pronouncement of joy for Job, in v 19 by the announcement of doom for the wicked (note the introductory ‏הן‎), and in vv 21–22 by a diptych representing respectively the fates of Job and of the wicked.

Within this broader structure, triplets, or, units of three two-line verses predominate: vv 2–4, 5–7, 8–10, 11–13, 20–22 are clearly independent sense units. Only vv 14–19 break the scheme with an elaborated image that divides naturally only after v 15, not v 16 as strict strophic regularity would require. Fohrer achieves such regularity by transferring v 19 to follow v 15, thus creating two units: vv 14–15 + 19 (where there is a natural pause), and vv 16–19; but the reconstruction is purely conjectural. Hesse deletes v 15, and divides vv 11–19 into two four-verse units (vv 11–14, 16–19). Horst prefers to regard the units of the middle section as two six-verse units (vv 8–13, 14–19), of which only the first is composed of two three-verse units; but it seems slightly more probable that the appeal to traditional wisdom in vv 8–10 is a preface to the whole of the middle section (vv 8–19) and not just to the image of the papyrus and reed (vv 11–13).

From the point of view of *form,* the speech exhibits elements familiar from the disputation, sapiential teaching, and cultic psalmody. Elements of the language of *disputation* appear in v 2, where the "speech preface" makes reference to the "words" of the previous speaker (see on chaps. 4–5, *Form*), and perhaps in v 3 (a question of judicial examination?); it is doubtful that vv 20–22 show the form of the "decisive conclusion" in the speech disputation (as Fohrer). Clear examples of typically *sapiential* forms occur: the appeal to tradition formulated with an imperative (v 8; cf. Ecclus 8:9, though this is also employed in the formal public speech; cf. Deut 4:32 and 32:7 [a verse speech, the "song of Moses"]); the rhetorical question about instruction (v 10; cf. Prov 8:1; 1:22); the proverbial utterance about the papyrus (v 11), and the extended imagery from the natural world (vv 11–12, 14–19). Comparable with forms typical of *psalmody* is the exhortation to prayer (v 5; cf. Ps 88:10 [9]; 143:6; though this is equally a prophetic form, cf. Amos 5:4–6 [Hos 6:3 is more cultic language]), and the announcements of salvation (vv 6b–7; 21–22; see *Comment* for parallels).

These are simply elements reminiscent of or borrowed from forms in other literature. The speech as a whole has the form of *exhortation* or *conditional assurance* (see on vv 5–6). The *tonality* of the speech is, to begin with, more severe than Eliphaz's (cf. 8:2, 4); but it ends on a note of unconditional assurance. Its *nodal verses* are 8:4–5.

Comment

2–7 Bildad, like the other friends, believes firmly that suffering is punishment. But in the way he applies that belief to Job's case he differs from the other friends. Eliphaz takes it for granted that Job is essentially a righteous man (4:6), and only temporarily chastised by God (5:17–18) for some imperfection inevitable in any mortal (4:17). Bildad, on the other hand, leaves the matter of Job's righteousness more in doubt when he rests the whole of his encouragement to Job upon the condition "if you are innocent and upright" (v 6). Job's continued existence is *prima facie* evidence of his innocence, indeed, and Bildad wants to offer Job hope (cf. vv 6–7, 21–22); he is far from hostile to Job, despite the reproachful opening of his speech (v 2) (cf. M. Loehr, "Die drei Bildad-Rede im Buche Hiob," *BZAW* 34 [1920] 107–12 [108]).

This first strophe of Bildad's speech contains its essential point; vv 4–5 are the nodal sentences of the whole. Job's children have sinned; therefore they have been struck dead. Job himself *may* be innocent; if he is he will be rewarded. The doctrine of retribution is the sole and sufficient explanation of human fortune.

2 Bildad's opening sentence certainly strikes a different note from the

diffident beginning Eliphaz made to his speech (4:2). But two things have
changed. First, the ice has been broken by Eliphaz's speech and it is now
clear (as it was not at the beginning of chap. 4) that Job is ready to engage in
dialogue with his friends. Secondly, Job has been much more explicit in his
last speech (chaps. 6–7) than in the speech of chap. 3 that preceded Eliphaz's
intervention. In chap. 3 Job expressed his death wish by lamenting the lot of
those in misery to whom light is given (3:20)—and thereby attracted sympathetic
attention. In chaps. 6–7, however, what has most impressed his auditors is
not his explicit desire that God should "cut him off" (6:8–9), not even his
sarcastic criticism of his friends' "treachery" (6:14–30), but his protests against
God that go so far as to put God in the wrong. It is one thing to say, "the
arrows of the Almighty are in me" (6:4)—a fact that anyone suffering deservedly
might well lament; it is quite different to suggest that God's hostility has exceeded
all due bounds and that the disproportion of God's assaults upon him amounts
to wrongful harassment, not to say lack of any pity (7:11–21). That is criticism
of God, and Bildad must protest.

Picking up Job's "how long?" (כמה) of 7:19, the cry of one oppressed (cf.
Ps 35:17), Bildad himself cries out "how long?" (עד־אן)—as if he now felt
himself oppressed on behalf of God! (Cf. the further exchange of "how long?"
[עד־אנה] questions between Bildad and Job in 18:2; 19:2.) "Such words" (lit.
"these things") of reproach against the Almighty must be unjustified (v 3).

In describing Job's words as a "mighty wind," Bildad is not mocking their
emptiness, as most suggest (contrast "words of wind," 16:3), but recognizing
them as tempestuous and devastating (cf. "mighty waters," Isa 17:12; 28:2).
They threaten to uproot cherished beliefs (Peake); they make assault upon
heaven. Bildad is shocked, not sardonic.

3 The rhetorical question conveys Bildad's surprise and dismay: How could
it ever be thought that the Almighty ("God" and "the Almighty" are in emphatic
position in the sentence) could "pervert" the right ordering of the world?
The moral universe, in Bildad's theology, is founded upon the principle of
retribution; any deviation from that would be injustice, and "God and injustice
are mutually incompatible terms" (Rowley). Job's protestation of innocence
(6:10c) and complaint at God's arbitrary and disproportionate treatment of
him (7:12, 17–18, 20) have implicitly charged God with injustice; and even
though Job is concerned only with his own case, the whole principle is called
into question. Bildad feels his theology endangered, but fails to see it is Job—
his integrity, self-esteem, and personhood—that is in danger (cf. Fohrer).

For a very similar statement that "the Almighty does not pervert justice,"
see 34:12b (Elihu), where the affirmation is tied up closely with the principle
of retribution (v 11) and with God's establishment of the world order (v 13).
On the juridical sense of the term, see also S. H. Scholnick, "The Meaning of
Mishpaṭ in the Book of Job," *JBL* 101 (1982) 521–29 (522–23). Bildad, like Elihu,
has a static view of God as guarantor of the world order. Job's sense that
it is God and not himself who has changed threatens that view of God.

4–6 Bildad invites a sympathetic engagement with his argument on Job's
part by the subtle uses of the particle "if" (אם). In v 4, there is no question
but that Job's sons and daughters are dead, so the "if" introduces a reason
rather than a hypothesis. But Bildad does not bluntly say, "Your children
sinned against him"; by casting his sentence in hypothetical form he strives

for Job's renewed assent to the principle of retribution. What of the "if's" in vv 5, 6? Are they hypothetical, or are they too equivalent to "since," as if to say "since you are a devout man, since you are upright . . ."? Job is left to be the judge of that himself; Bildad is covering himself, and at the same time opening up Job's innocence to question.

4 Bildad's argument proceeds from the result to the cause: if there was premature death, there must have been prior sin. So wedded is he to the sufficiency of the doctrine of retribution as an explanation for all human fortune or misfortune that he even states the result in terms of the cause. He does not say, "Your children have died," but "[God] has abandoned them to the power of their own guilt." If that is the result, the cause is already obvious: they "have sinned against him." He does not say, "If your children have died, it can only be because they have sinned against God," but the other way around. The doctrine of retribution is so fundamental to his world-view that he has actually perceived the death of Job's sons and daughters as God's punishment; he does not know he is deceiving himself, he does not know how to distinguish between perception and inference, he does not acknowledge that to deny the universal applicability of retribution is not to deny the righteousness of God (v 3).

He probably does not think he is telling Job anything new; he assumes that Job himself will have drawn the same conclusion, and have seen in the death of his children further proof of the reliability of the doctrine of retribution. He raises the matter of Job's children simply to remind Job of the contrast between their fate and his.

It need hardly be remarked how callous doctrinal rigidity is made to appear by the poet. To ensure the innocent standing of his children had been Job's most urgent duty, according to the prologue (1:5), since he himself had always feared that they might have "sinned in their hearts," and had "continually" offered sacrifices to decontaminate them from sin. There is no reason in the narrative to suppose that the fate of Job's sons and daughters was the result of their behavior; for Job, his children's fate and his own are equally inexplicable.

Bildad, like the other interlocutors, does not recognize the possibility of forgiveness or the validity of sacrifice. No one ever urges Job to offer sacrifice in atonement for the sins they suspect or accuse him of, even though sacrifice belongs to the praxis of the prose framework (1:5; 42:8). Forgiveness likewise generally lies outside the ambit of the friends' theologies (though cf. 22:21–26). The reason is no doubt the affinity of the speeches with the relatively cult-free "wisdom" outlook; but the case of Job, who by the black and white standards of Proverbs or according to a simplistic dogma of retribution must be reckoned among the "wicked," points up the superficiality of "wisdom's" generalizations.

For the idea of the "fate-determining deed," here in the form of one's iniquity being personified as the agent of one's destruction ("victims of their own iniquity," NEB) (cf. Isa 64:6 [7]; Num 32:23), cf. on 5:2.

The reference to Job's children is one of the relatively few direct connections between prologue and dialogue (cf. on 5:25), evidence that the two are not entirely independent works.

5 Job, unlike his sons and daughters, is still alive; as yet therefore there is no evidence that he has sinned irremediably against God. The emphatic "you" (vv 5, 6) stresses the difference between him and his children. Hope need not be lost if he fulfills two conditions: devout prayer and a blameless life (v 6a). The justice of God (v 3) can then be displayed in a positive light.

Bildad's counsel on this score is more directive than Eliphaz's who contented himself with presenting his own "seeking" of God (5:8) as an example for imitation (5:8). Bildad's attitude is not authoritarian, nevertheless, for he couches his advice not in the form of a command (contrast LXX) but as a condition (which might even be construed as a description of how Job actually behaves). If indeed Bildad's "ifs" are genuinely hypothetical, the poet is indulging in quiet irony at Bildad's expense. For Job has been presented to us in the early verses of the prologue precisely as a man who is "perfect and upright" (תם וישר, 1:1; cf. וישׁר זך here) and as one who would "rise early in the morning" (השׁכים, 1:5; cf. שׁחר here, lit. "seek early") to perform his devotions. Bildad's advice, in short, is that Job should be what Job knows, and we know, he already is. Now the second friend also has shown how out of touch he is with the real Job, while the poet mocks the impersonality of the dogmatic theology that governs Bildad.

Bildad nowhere in this speech expressly says that Job is a sinner, but what else can be inferred from his doctrine? Nevertheless, it is a sign of delicacy, not always recognized in Bildad, that he will not make an issue of Job's sinfulness, but will try to direct Job toward God and toward the future. Bildad's advice is first that Job should "seek" (here שׁחר) God. In prophetic language that often involves repentance (cf. Hos 5:15; similarly with דרשׁ "seek" in Amos 5:4–6; Isa 9:12 [13]; on the latter verb, see S. Wagner, *TDOT* 3:301–2). In Job the notion of repentance may appear in 22:23, but here the verb has a more general sense of "pray" or "worship"; as became normal from the exile onward, the phrase "to seek Yahweh" referred not to a particular act but to the habitual practice of the devout (E. Ruprecht, *THWAT* 1:464). The second term Bildad uses is "seek favor" (הִתְחַנֵּן), a verb often associated with "pray" (פלל hithpa) or "call upon (God)" (קרא). It is a verbal request for mercy, not so much for God's free undeserved grace, but for a just recompense for right behavior (Fohrer); the favor of God here is "a reward for righteousness, not a pardon for penitence" (Andersen).

6 The opening conditional clause, "If you are pure and upright," is deleted by many commentators (see n. 8:6.a). It is sometimes argued that Bildad's view cannot allow the possibility of Job's righteousness, since Job is undoubtedly suffering and must therefore be a sinner. Yet Bildad's "if" could be a kindly avoidance of what he infers to be the case; or better, Job's purity and uprightness may be viewed by him as qualities Job should now exhibit in order to deserve future happiness (vv 6–7). On זכה "pure," see on 15:14.

If Job meets the double condition of vv 5 and 6, linking devoutness and moral purity, Bildad's dogma of retribution, in the positive sense now, assures him that God cannot fail to respond to Job's behavior with signs of favor. As we have seen (on v 4) an unbending doctrine of retribution makes the sinner the victim of his own guilt; now we note that it chains God also, and compels him to respond with favor to any human merit.

Using the language of psalmody, Bildad affirms that God will "rouse himself" (cf. Ps 35:23; 44:24 [23]; 59:5 [4]) in order to bring him salvation. Psalmists who lament the apparent absence and inactivity of God call upon him to "rouse himself"; it is a signal of how little of Job's feeling has touched Bildad that he should proffer this expectation, for Job has already had more than enough of God's unfriendly presence and incessant activity (7:12, 16b–19). No less insensitive is the promise that God will "restore" Job's "habitation," his home and household, for even if the outlying "house" occupied by Job's eldest son (1:19) and forming part of Job's estate should be restored, how can his dead children be restored? And it is unfortunate that what Bildad sees being restored to Job is "the habitation of your righteousness," that is to say, the home where Job's righteousness is depicted as dwelling. For Job has no wish to believe that *in the future* he will find himself dwelling in a house recognized as the abode of righteousness, since at this very moment Job is maintaining both his piety and his integrity (6:10c), and he must wince afresh at Bildad's reminder that to all who know him the present state of his home and family is, on the contrary, proof positive of his unrighteousness.

7   Like Eliphaz (5:19–26), Bildad holds out before Job hope of a prosperous future; unlike Eliphaz, he does not elaborate the details of such a future, and a larger portion of his speech will be devoted to an elaboration of the fate of the wicked (vv 11–19) by way of warning to Job. Nevertheless, he does not offer to Job a hope that he believes to be unreal. No doubt the phraseology of this verse is traditional, for it is a little strange to describe Job's "former state" (lit. "beginning") as "lowly" or "a trifle" (מִצְעָר) when Job has been pictured as "the greatest of all the people of the east" (1:3). But it is by comparison with Job's future (lit. "end") that his "beginning" will seem lowly. The rhetoric is, from the viewpoint of Bildad the character, who can hardly imagine greater prosperity than Job's former state, rather hollow; but from the viewpoint of the author, Bildad speaks more truly than he knows, for in 42:12 Yahweh will bless the "end" of Job more than his "beginning" (ראשית, אחרית, the same terms as are used here).

8–19   This elaborated *topos* on the fate of the wicked consists of two units (vv 11–13, 14–19), each drawing upon imagery from the natural world, and each brought to a conclusion by a verse in "summary appraisal" form (vv 13, 19). They are prefaced by an appeal to the accumulated wisdom of former generations as validation of the import of the *topos*.

What is intriguing about this section of Bildad's speech is not what it means in itself but what he means by it. Does he suggest that Job will probably suffer the fate of the wicked (Duhm saw the strophe as the first open suspicion of Job's guilt), does he warn Job against "godlessness" by depicting the doom of the ungodly, or does he encourage Job by describing a fate that Job will no doubt not suffer? Nothing in this strophe can answer the question; only the general tonality of the speech as a whole can suggest the answer. The key elements in pinpointing the tonality of the speech are v 2, which is not so rough or sarcastic as is often imagined, vv 5–6a, where it is hard to know how likely Bildad thinks Job is to fulfill the conditions for restoration, and vv 21–22, where words of apparently unconditional assurance are spoken directly to Job. The note on which the speech concludes is the strongest indication that the *topos* on the wicked is not meant to be any threat to Job; it is perhaps only the mildest of warnings and functions partly as encouragement (cf. also on 5:12–14). Nevertheless, a speech of encouragement pure and simple would have no room for such a *topos* as this, unless by way of explicit contrast to the expected future of the one being encouraged. It is the lack of explicitness in Bildad's speech that permits varying readings of it—a situation quite probably intended by the author.

8 The validity of Bildad's assurance that if Job will "seek" God and if he is pure and upright he will be rewarded (vv 6–7) will now be supported by appeal to the wisdom of the fathers (note "for"); they have observed that the hope of the godless perishes (v 13) and that God does not reject a blameless man (v 20). Job will have to discern for himself which of these observations is best applicable to himself, though Bildad's concluding direct address to Job (vv 21–22) suggests that the observations are to be taken *ad bonam partem*, despite the expansiveness of the description of the godless (see above on vv 8–19).

Unlike Eliphaz, who has appealed to his own experience (4:8; 4:12–17; 5:3) and that of his contemporaries (5:27; but see 15:18–19) in support of his argument, Bildad, a professor without charisma (Terrien), invites Job to consider ("inquire," שְׁאַל, and "fix the mind on," כּוֹנֵן) the experience of former generations (for the formulation, cf. Deut 4:32; 32:7; and cf. Ecclus 8:9; see further, N. C. Habel, "Appeal to Ancient Tradition as a Literary Form," *ZAW* 88 [1976] 253–72 [254–61]). Pope sagely comments that "Bildad's assertion that the wisdom of the ancients is in accord with his doctrine and counsel is quite correct, as confirmed by much of Mesopotamian Wisdom Literature." The wisdom of the ancients is, of course, in Bildad's conception nothing other than the doctrine of retribution in its most simplistic form. It is this that the "research" (חֵקֶר) of generations of wisdom teachers has amounted to. The "former generation" (דֹר רִאשׁוֹן) is, as the MT stands, the immediately preceding generation(s) (not some long-lived generation like the patriarchs or even the antediluvians), who have passed down the experience of "*their* fathers" (אֲבוֹתָם); thus JB, NEB, NIV. Ecclus 8:9 envisages a handing down of wisdom to the "aged" from "their fathers." But if LXX is correct in reading the last word אָבוֹת "(the) fathers" instead of אֲבוֹתָם "their fathers," the two halves of the line will be parallel, and the term "former generation" may be understood as a collective expression for all former ages; thus RSV, NAB.

9 The case for the supremacy of tradition could not be more crisply put. Creatures of yesterday, whose whole life-span can be likened to a fleeting shadow (cf. 14:2; 1 Chr 29:15; Ps 102:12 [11]; 109:23; 144:4; Eccl 6:12; and cf. Sophocles, *Ajax*, 125–26), humans cannot hope to acquire for themselves the wisdom and experience accumulated over the ages. Job and Bildad share the same sense of the extreme brevity of life (cf. 7:7, 16), but while it wrings from Job an elemental cry to God, Bildad experiences it intellectually, as a ground for adherence to traditional wisdom. The commentators show their hand, and their age, at this point. Duhm (1897) found the respect for tradition similar to that of his own age for books and the written word. Peake (1905) remarked with turn of the century optimism: "It is not quite clear on what principle Bildad considers the wisdom of the ancients to be superior. . . . Surely it is the heirs of all the ages who are 'the true ancients,' and each generation adds its own quota to the stock, the former age being less wise than the most recent." Driver (1921) observed acidly in the spirit of objective science: "[Bildad] conveniently forgets, after the manner of traditionalists, that the past, too, was composed of individuals, that the oldest doctrine was once

new, and that novelty and antiquity are alike irrelevant as tests of truth."
Perhaps it is not uncharacteristic of our own age that Andersen (1976) should
remark not upon the validity or otherwise of Bildad's statement, but about its
function in the book: "There is a delightful touch of satire. . . . The author
of Job seems to hint at one of the purposes of his work: to question such
tradition and to upset the people who hold it unthinkingly."

10 The truth about human existence, according to Bildad, is to be learned,
and learned from others. The truth is knowledge, not experience. Job knows
the force of traditional doctrine (9:2a; 12:3; 13:1–2; 16:4), but his own experience is every bit as real to him as the learned dogma, and it contradicts the
dogma. In appealing to knowledge rather than to personal experience Bildad
talks straight past Job, and deserves the name of "traitor" that Job has already
applied to the friends (6:15). His assurance that the "former generation" can
address Job "from their understanding" (lit. "heart," as the seat of intelligence)
almost formally distinguishes between the knowledge of the wise and the mere
feeling of Job. Bildad's respect for the wisdom of the past is admirable (despite
the remarks of commentators cited above on v 9), as is his conviction that
God does not pervert justice (v 3). It is because he allows the doctrine of
retribution to fill the whole horizon both of human wisdom and divine justice
that he is both unappealing and unconvincing, and because he insists on abso-
lutizing the doctrine that he must be both unjust and unkind to Job.

11–13 In this first scene depicting the fate of the godless—which Bildad
sets forth as the teaching of the fathers—the ostensible subject is at first the
papyrus plant, and it is only with v 13 that we learn that the papyrus is a
symbol of the godless person. In the second scene (vv 14–19), it is plain from
the beginning that it is the godless man who forms the subject, and the imagery
from the natural world is secondary.

Gordis's suggestion that vv 11–20 depicts two plants, representing the wicked
(vv 11–15) and the righteous (vv 16–19) to whom God's reaction is spelled
out in v 20a and v 20b respectively is at best ingenious, and fails to note the
structural significance of the summary appraisal form in v 13 which enables
a fresh set of imagery to be employed in the lines following v 13. W. A.
Irwin, "The First Speech of Bildad," *ZAW* 51 (1933) 205–16, had a similar
idea, but was compelled to reconstruct the text ruthlessly to prove it (see e.g.,
n. 8:14.a).

11 The rhetorical question form and the fact that its force depends upon
some piece of knowledge of the natural world are a double indication of the
"wisdom" origin of the saying. This is exactly the kind of shape in which the
wisdom of the fathers would have been transmitted: the question-form inviting
the hearer's participation, the mildly "learned" character of the detail, and
the indirect presentation of the truth. The teaching has of course nothing to
do with papyrus plants; but the wise will immmediately recognize that it is a
message in code. In fact, by itself this question-proverb would more naturally
convey a message about cause and effect, like our "no smoke without a fire"
(cf. also Hesse). Bildad, however, uses the image as a peg on which to hang a
conventional *topos* on "sudden reversal."

The papyrus plant (גֹּמֶא) is a perennial aquatic rush that grows to a height
of ten or fifteen feet; hence the verb that is used is גָּאָה, "be lofty." Common
in lower Egypt in Biblical times, it is now extinct there, though it is found on

the banks of the Blue and the White Nile, as well as in the Huleh valley in northern Israel and on the coastal plain (illustrations: *IBD* 2:1144–45). The "rush" (אָחוּ) is a marsh grass, attested for Palestine by a Ugaritic text (*CTA* 10.2.9, 12; Gibson, 132) that apparently locates it (*aḥ*) in the Huleh valley. Both terms (גֹּמֶא and אָחוּ) are Egyptian in origin (אָחוּ appears in an Egyptian context in Gen 41:2, 18), and some have inferred that the author of Job had at least visited Egypt (Gordis); note also the Egyptian coloring in the depiction of Behemoth and Leviathan (40:15–41:26 [34]). But it is fallacious to suppose that such references can tell us anything of the author, especially when the details have so obviously come to him as traditional learning.

12 The crucial event for the life of the papyrus is left to be inferred: the drying up of its water supply. If that should happen, it will rapidly wither away, even though it was in the full vigor of growth and not destroyed by cutting.

13 The intention of the image in v 12 is explained, somewhat pedantically, as applying to the "godless" (חָנֵף, "profane," a term used 8 times in Job), those who "forget God" (cf. Ps 50:22). In forsaking God they deprive themselves of the source of their life, and so any expectation they may have for the future "perishes"—just like the papyrus or reed when deprived of the water which is its sustenance. This is the fundamental order in the natural and moral worlds alike. To "forget" God suggests not a lapse of memory but practical behavior that opposes God or acts as if there were no God (cf. Ps 10:4; 14:1; 53:2 [1]) or as if God could not see (cf. 22:13–17; Ps 94:7) or will not act (Zeph 1:12) (cf. W. Schottroff, *THWAT* 2:902–3). The image of the human being as plant has appeared already in 5:3.

14–19 In this second scene on the fate of the wicked two sets of imagery appear. The first, in vv 14–15, is imagery of impermanence and unreliability; they are metaphors of the confidence of the godless man. The second, in vv 16–18, is imagery of final extermination after seeming permanence and stability; here the ostensible subject, a plant or tree, is a metaphor for the godless man. The two parts of this scene are so distinct that Fohrer's proposal to move v 19 to follow vv 14–15 as a summary appraisal for that set of images has its attraction, though textual evidence is entirely lacking.

14 Just because the godless man has cut himself off from the source of his life (vv 11–13), his future is insubstantial and unreliable. Unlike the confidence (כֶּסֶל) Job is entitled to in Eliphaz's opinion (4:6), whatever confidence the godless may feel must rest upon "what is fragile" (NIV; see n. 8:14.b), and can have only as much solidity as a "spider's house." For the image, cf. 27:18; Isa 59:6; also in the Koran, 29.40 "Those who take for themselves a protector other than God are like the spider that builds a house for himself; surely the spider's house is the weakest of all houses"; the phrase "weaker than a spider's house" has become proverbial in Arabic literature. The verse has only said metaphorically what was expressed directly in v 13 ("perish" is no doubt a dead metaphor); so there is a close link with v 13. However, the metaphor of this verse extends into v 15, which in turn cannot be separated from the extended image that follows in vv 16–18, so a division after v 13 is reasonable though not absolute.

15 Though the "house" upon which the godless man rests his confidence may be his own house "including his family, establishment, and the resources implied in the possession of an estate" (Driver, similarly Fohrer; NAB "family"), it is better to see the image of the spider's "house" continuing through this verse (as NIV). It is then self-evident why any confidence on the part of the godless man is disastrously misplaced. The verbs "stand" (עמד) and "arise, stand" (קום) could refer either to the godless man himself who finds he cannot be supported by the object of his confidence (as *Translation*) or to the house (cf. JB, NEB, NIV, Dhorme).

16–18 A second image is presented to us in this scene: a plant or tree that flourishes, only to be uprooted and disowned. The metaphor signals the psychological state of displacement, and the elaboration of rootedness in vv 16–17 only serves to render the displacement more shocking. The initial picture of prosperity persuades some that the original text here described the righteous man (cf. Gordis who remarks on the emphatic personal pronoun "he" [הוא] in v 16), and Saadia actually prefixed to v 16 the caption *as-saliḥ*, "the righteous." But there can be little doubt that vv 16–18 comes to a climax with the devastation (בלע) of v 18.

16–17 What kind of plant this is does not matter, whether a vine or a gourd (Budde), a tree (Ehrlich), some noxious plant (Duhm; cf. v 18a), a creeper or climber (Fohrer). Being well watered allows it to flourish in the sun and take advantage of its warmth rather than be withered by it; its shoots spread out "over" or "beyond" (על) (cf. Gen 49:22) the garden in which it grows. Stones are no obstacle to its growth: it simply twines itself about them and makes itself more firmly rooted. Dislodgement of this plant seems impossible; it seems to have in its assurance of water the security that the papyrus plant of vv 11–12 lacked.

The view that v 17 pictures the tree as failing to find nourishment when its roots run into stony ground (as in NEB) is less probable; the first sign of disaster comes with v 18. In any case the doctrinaire retributionist Bildad allows that effect may not immediately follow cause, that the godless may prosper, and not only seemingly. It does not occur to him, apparently, that if that is so it may also be that the righteous may suffer; if he had realized that—and the poet of course intends his readers to see through Bildad's dogma—he would not have had to attach conditions to his assurances to Job (vv 5–6).

18 However firmly rooted the plant that images the godless may seem, it can be uprooted and annihilated. Perhaps the one who uproots ("he") is God (as Ehrlich, Fohrer), or it may be an indefinite subject. So final is the extermination that "its place," viz. "its garden" (v 16), loses all memory of it (cf. 7:10) and, in the formal language of repudiation (see Deut 33:9) says, "I have never seen you" (cf. Matt 7:23). There is an especial bitterness in the denial of any memory, for in Hebrew thought a memorial that survived one was, like one's children, the only kind of immortality conceivable.

19 The image comes to an end with a summary appraisal, either in ironic form "this is the joy of its way," or more straightforwardly, "so its life comes to dissolution" (see n. 8:19.a). In the place where it grew, others will spring up, so that even the memory of its uprooting will fade. The image is still that of the plant, but there is nothing here now that applies only to the plant and not to the godless person. The metaphor and the reality coalesce. The godless man's fate is to be exterminated; not only will what is dear and meaningful to him (his "place," v 18), forget him, it will forget that it has forgotten him. That is the meaning of dissolution (משוש read מסוס).

Bildad's purpose in presenting this extended imagery of the fate of the godless is not entirely certain, as has been remarked above (on vv 8–19). One thing that he does not mean, however, is that Job should recognize his own experience in the fate of the godless—as against Driver: "The fall of the godless man . . . resembles that of Job; and Bildad . . . no doubt desires Job to consider whether his own misfortune may not be due to the same cause."

20–22 To these images of the fate of the wicked is appended now a scene depicting the fate of the innocent, Job himself included. The positive side of the doctrine of retribution is, despite his concentration on the fate of the godless, not ignored by Bildad. Even so, he must begin this brief upbeat movement with a generalizing proverb-like utterance that yet again states the principle in both its positive and negative forms. More to Bildad's credit is his willingness to lapse back into the address form of speech (vv 21–22) when he speaks of good fortune; he could so easily have stayed in the groove of descriptive speech (as in v 20a and as LXX does with vv 21–22) and have left his attitude toward Job very ambiguous.

20 The sentence crystallizes the whole retributionist theology, and presents a positive statement of the principle of moral order that lay behind the questions of v 3. At its heart stand two assertions: the one that humankind is sharply differentiated into "innocent people" and "evildoers," the other that it is God himself, and not some abstract principle of justice, who ensures that each group gets its just deserts. The only concession this simple dogma makes to the complex reality of the world is to admit the concept of "seeming good fortune" or the prosperity of the wicked. This apparent counter to the validity of the dogma has been developed in the imagery of vv 16–19; now, when the dogma is to be stated in summary form, all concessions and modifications to its naive simplicity are set aside.

The reader cannot be meant to overlook the fact that the "blameless" (תם) man has already been designated in this book: he is Job, "blameless and upright" (תם וישר, 1:1, 8). Did Bildad but recognize that—and indeed he knows nothing for which Job could be blamed—he could have saved himself this speech. Yet again, the author shares his inside knowledge with the reader at the expense of a character who represents traditional wisdom.

To "support" is literally to "grasp the hand of," i.e., in order to lead (as Gen 19:16), and so to support with solidarity (cf. Isa 41:13; 42:6). Weiser's opinion that the term derives from the royal ritual in the cult (cf. Ps 73:23) ignores the widespread use of the phrase throughout the OT; but cultic language may be used in the following verses.

21 Bildad does not preface this happy conclusion he predicts for Job's suffering with the conditions of v 5, but allows the promise of salvation itself to carry its own reminder of the necessary conditions (Fohrer)—if such a reminder is necessary. The language of salvation naturally echoes the Psalms: Ps 126:2a especially is verbally very close. For "laughter" as a symbol of assurance, cf. also 5:22; 29:24; Prov 31:25; for the "shout" of triumph, cf. 33:26; 1 Sam 4:5, 6; 2 Sam 6:15; 2 Chr 15:14; Ezra 3:11–13; Ps 33:3; 47:6 (5); and P. Humbert, *La "Terou'a." Analyse d'un rite biblique* (Neuchâtel: Secrétariat de l'Université, 1946) (in Ps 126:2 רנה is used).

22 The conventional language used often in psalmody, of salvation for the pious and destruction for his enemies, now takes over completely. Job might well be puzzled to know who these "enemies" of his are (lit. "those who hate you"). No one can now envy him his fortune (contrast 31:29); and neither he nor Bildad will be thinking of the Sabeans or Chaldeans who attacked his property in 1:15, 17, since they have faded into the scenery of the story, and they are never the objects of animosity on the part of Job or his friends. The enemies here are those conventional figures, "workers of iniquity," whom we meet with frequently in the psalms of individual appeal. They symbolize, in all probability, the many faces of death with which the psalmists sense they are confronted (see G. W. Anderson, "Enemies and Evildoers in the Book of Psalms," *BJRL* 48 [1965–66] 18–29; C. Barth, *Introduction to the Psalms* [tr. R. A. Wilson; Oxford: Blackwell, 1961] 49–55). For the language, cf. Ps 9:14 [13]; 18:18 [17]; 21:9 [8], etc. (the "haters"); 35:26; 132:18 ("clothe with shame"); 84:11 [10] ("tents of wickedness," cf. "tent of the wicked ones" here; and contrast 118:15, "the tents of the righteous").

There is another possible interpretation of "your enemies." The enemies of the psalmist are frequently those who "on the basis of the doctrine of retribution infer from his misfortune some sin which has caused it, and set themselves against him as one who has been punished by God" (Fohrer). Those who act like this in the Book of Job are none other than the friends! Can the poet mean Bildad's final sentence as a mordant criticism of the friends themselves? It would not be the first time that one of Job's interlocutors has served as a vehicle for the author's irony (cf. on v 5). Similarly, J. J. M. Roberts has remarked generally about the Book of Job that it shows that "the traditional wisdom theology, pushed uncritically to its logical limits, would end by transforming would-be comforters into the slandering enemies so well-known from the individual laments" ("Job and the Israelite Religious Tradition," *ZAW* 89 [1977] 107–14 [113]).

The "shame" (בשׁת) with which Job's enemies will be "clothed" (for a similar use of the verb לבשׁ see 7:5) is not the subjective feeling of shame, but an objective being put to shame or being reduced to insignificance (cf. F. Stolz, *THWAT* 1:270; similarly קלון in 10:15). The end to which Bildad sees the adversaries of Job being brought is that they should "be no more" (איננו). This final note of his speech echoes the last word of Job's preceding speech, אינני "I shall be no more" (7:21). The implication is clear: Job sees annihilation (אין, "non-being") as his goal (cf. also 7:8) and presses eagerly to that consummation (cf. 6:8–9); Bildad sees annihilation as the desert of the wicked and has never for a moment accepted—any more than had Eliphaz—that Job could genuinely desire what is properly the destiny of the wicked. This last word of Bildad's proves all over again how out of touch he is with Job's mood in proferring hope to a man whose only desire is to be ignored by God (7:16a, 19) until his imminent death (cf. "now," 7:21b) takes place. Job himself will come to desire vindication more than death, but what he needs now is not advice or encouragement that ignores his feelings, but a loyal being-with that does not back off in fear when it sees his calamity (6:21).

Explanation

In all essential respects, Bildad's perspective on Job and his suffering is little different from Eliphaz's. Like Eliphaz, he is a theologian of retribution (8:3–6, 13; cf. 4:7–8; 5:2–3), he venerates the wisdom of the past (8:8–10; cf.

4:7, 27), and he addresses Job with a mixture of instruction (8:3–6, 8–10, 20; cf. 4:12–21; 5:9–16) and encouragement (8:5–7, 20–22; cf. 4:6; 5:19–26). Yet there is a more distinct air of severity in Bildad's speech. It is apparent in 8:2 where Bildad professes himself shocked by Job's tempestuous words against God; it is seen again in the brusque statement of the reasons for the death of Job's children. It shows itself also in the single-mindedness with which Bildad expounds the doctrine of retribution; for him (unlike Eliphaz), no other considerations are relevant to Job's condition. Above all, it is plain in the retributionist theology itself which he espouses: the behavior of God and humans alike is rigidly schematized, and the moral universe is conceived entirely in black and white.

Compared with Bildad's uncompromising theology, the message he has to give Job is strangely ambiguous. Does he believe Job is a pious man, or does he leave the question of Job's innocence entirely open? Do the "if's" of vv 5–6 carry with them an encouragement since it is plain that Job "seeks" God and is "pure and upright," or are they a severe warning to Job that his future depends wholly upon his fulfilling certain conditions? Is the apparently unconditional assurance of vv 20–22 colored by the conditions of vv 5–6, or, contrariwise, does the tonality of those last verses soften the demanding character of vv 5–6? Since we find it hard to see just where Bildad stands, is it perhaps because the author himself wished to portray how imperfectly the doctrine fitted Job's situation?

Certainly the naively simple dogma Bildad presents, that divides humanity into "innocent" (תם, 8:20) and "godless" or "wicked" (חנף, 8:13; מרעים, 8:20, and רשעים, 8:22), is none too gently guyed by the author in this speech. And, assuming that the conditions Bildad lays before Job in vv 5–6 are genuine conditions that Job may fulfill or fail to fulfill, a further irony presents itself (cf. Fohrer): if Job does what Bildad tells him to, the doubt raised by the Satan in chap. 1 will have been justified. For Job will have proved that he does not "fear God for naught" (1:9); he will have allowed his desperate need to determine his behavior toward God and made piety into a means for improving his sorry lot.

Job's Third Speech (9:1–10:22)

Bibliography

Bergmeier, R. "Zum Ausdruck עצת רשעים in Ps 1:1; Hi 10:3; 21:16 und 22:18." *ZAW* 79 (1967) 229–32. **Crenshaw, J. L.** "Wᵉdōrēk ʿal-bāmŏtē ʾāreṣ." *CBQ* 34 (1972) 39–53. **Dahood, M.** "The Root ʿZB II in Job." *JBL* 78 (1959) 303–309. **Day, J.** *God's Conflict with the Dragon and the Sea: Echoes of a Canaanite Myth in the Old Testament.* Cambridge: CUP, 1985. **Driver, G. R.** "Problems in the Hebrew Text of Job." *VTS* 3 (1955) 72–93. ———. "Two Astronomical Passages in the Old Testament." *JTS* ns 7 (1956) 1–11. **Fullerton, K.** "On Job 9 and 10." *JBL* 53 (1934) 321–49. ———. "Job, Chapters 9 and 10." *AJSL* 55 (1938) 225–69. **Herz, N.** "The Astral Terms in Job IX 9, XXXVIII 31–32." *JTS* 14 (1913) 575–77. **Hess, J.-J.** "Die Sternbilder in Hiob 9:9 und 38:31f." *Festschrift Georg Jacob.* Ed. T. Menzel. Leipzig: Harrassowitz, 1932. 94–99. **Jacob, B.** "Erklärung einiger Hiob-Stellen. 10:15." *ZAW* 32 (1912) 278–87 (287). **Kellett, E. E.** "A Suggestion." *ExpT* 44 (1932–33) 283–84. **Paul, S. M.** "An Unrecognized Medical Idiom in Canticles 6,12 and Job 9,21." *Bib* 59 (1978) 545–47. **Pope, M. H.** "The Word *šaḥat* in Job 9:31." *JBL* 83 (1964) 269–78. **Reider, J.** "Some Notes to the Text of the Scriptures. 10. Job 10.8." *HUCA* 3 (1926) 113. **Roberts, J. J. M** "Job's Summons to Yahweh: The Exploitation of a Legal Metaphor." *RestQ* 16 (1973) 159–65. **Sacchi, P.** "Giobbe e il patto (*Giobbe* 9,32–33)." *Hen* 4 (1982) 175–84. **Stec, D. M.** "The Targum Rendering of *WYGʾH* in Job x 16." *VT* 34 (1984) 367–68. **Watson, W. G. E.** "The Metaphor in Job 10,17." *Bib* 63 (1982) 255–57. **Xella, P.** "*ḤTP,* 'uccidere, annientare' in Giobbe 9,12." *Hén* 1 (1979) 337–41. **Zimmermann, F.** "Note on Job 9:23." *JTS* ns 2 (1951) 164–65. **Zurro, E.** "Disemia de *brḥ* y paralelismo bifronte en Job 9,25." *Bib* 62 (1981) 546–47.

Translation

¹ *Job answered, saying:*

² *I know that this is so;*
  but how [a] *can a man* [b] *be justified* [c] *by God?*
³ *Should one wish to dispute with him,*
  one could not answer him once [a] *in a thousand times.*
⁴ *He is wise* [a] *and he is powerful* [b];
  who ever argued [c] *with him and succeeded?* [d]

⁵ *He* [a] *moves mountains, though they do not know it* [b];
  [c] *he overturns them in his wrath.*
⁶ *He shakes the earth from its place*
  and its pillars quiver.
⁷ *He gives command* [a] *to the sun so that it does not shine,* [b]
  and on the stars he sets a seal.

⁸ *He alone stretches out the heavens,*
  and tramples upon the sea-monster's back. [a]
⁹ *He is the maker* [a] *of the Bear* [b] *and Orion,*
  of the Pleiades and the circle of the southern stars. [c]
¹⁰ *He works great deeds, past human reckoning,*
  he performs wonders, beyond all numbering.

¹¹ *Should^a he pass near me, I would not see him^b;*
   should he move past me, I would not perceive him.
¹² *Should he take away,^a who could dissuade^b him?*
   Who could accuse him for what he is doing?
¹³ *Being God,^a he does not withdraw his anger;*
   beneath it^b even Rahab's supporters^c were laid prostrate.

¹⁴ *How then^a could I respond to him,*
   how choose words with which to answer him^b?
^{15a} *Even if I were in the right, I could not defend myself^b;*
   I could only appeal for mercy to my adversary.^c
¹⁶ *Even if he should respond to my summons,^a*
   I could not be sure that he would really listen to me.

¹⁷ *For a trifle^a he crushes^b me,*
   for no reason^c he wounds me again and again.
¹⁸ *He will not let me catch my breath,*
   but makes me drink deep of bitter poison.^a
¹⁹ *If it is a matter of strength,^a behold, he is the mighty one^b;*
   if a matter of justice, who can arraign him?^c
²⁰ *Though I am innocent, my own mouth^a would condemn me;*
   though I am blameless, it^b would prove me guilty.^c

²¹ *I am blameless;*
   I do not care about myself;
   I have rejected my life.
²² *It is all one.^a Therefore I say:*
   Blameless and wicked alike he brings to an end.
²³ *Should the plague^a bring sudden^b death,*
   he mocks at the calamity^c of the innocent.
²⁴ *If^a a land^b falls^c into the power of a wicked man,^d*
   then God blindfolds^e its judges.
   If it is not he, who then is it?^f

²⁵ *My days^a have been swifter^b than a courier;*
   they have fled^c away without beholding joy.
²⁶ *They have slipped past like skiffs of reed,^a*
   like an eagle swooping on its prey.
²⁷ *If I say,^a I will forget my moaning,^b*
   I will lay aside my sadness^c and be cheerful,
²⁸ *I become afraid of all I must suffer,^a*
   for I know you do not hold me innocent.
^{29a} *Come what may,^b I shall be accounted guilty;*
   why then should I strive in vain?
³⁰ *Though I wash^a myself with soap,^b*
   and cleanse my hands with lye,^c
³¹ *you would only plunge me in a pit,^a*
   so that my very clothes would abhor me.^b

^{32a b} *He is not a man like myself, that^c I should answer^d him:*
  "Let us go^e to court together!"
³³ *If only there were (but there is not!)^a a mediator^b between us,*
  who could lay his hand on both of us,
³⁴ *who^a could remove God's rod from my back,*
  so that fear^b of him should not unnerve me.
³⁵ *Then I should speak out, with no dread of him—*
  for in myself I am not fearful.^a

^{10:1} *I have rejected my life;^a*
  so I can give vent to^b my complaint,
  speak out of the bitterness of my soul.
² *I will say to God, Do not hold me guilty;*
  but tell me why^a you are my adversary.
³ *Do you take pleasure in oppression,*
  in rejecting the work of your own hands,
  ^awhile smiling on the plans^b of the wicked?
⁴ *Have you a mere man's eyes?*
  Do you see things as men see them?
⁵ *Are your days like the days of a mortal,*
  your years^a like the life of a man,
⁶ *that you must seek out some iniquity in me,*
  and search for some sin of mine?
⁷ *Because you know that I am not guilty,*
  there is no escape from your hand.
⁸ *Your hands fashioned^a me and made me;*
  and now you have turned^b and destroyed^c me.
⁹ *You molded^a me like clay,^b do you remember?*
  Now you turn me to mire^c again.
¹⁰ *Did you not pour me out like milk?*
  did you not curdle me like cheese?
¹¹ *With skin and flesh you clothed me,*
  with bones and sinews knit me together.
¹² *Life and loyalty^a you have favored me with;*
  your attention has preserved my life.

¹³ *Yet this was your secret intention,^a*
  this was your purpose, I know,
¹⁴ *that, if I sinned, you would be watching^a me*
  and would not acquit me of my guilt!
¹⁵ *If I am guilty, woe to me!^a*
  and if I am innocent, I dare not lift my head,
  ^bI am filled with shame and sated^c with affliction.
¹⁶ *And if I lift myself up,^a like a lion you hunt me,*
  so that you are marveled at^b afresh^c—because of me!
¹⁷ *You renew your hostility^a toward me;*
  you increase^b your wrath against me;
  release^c—then hard struggle—is my lot.^d

> ¹⁸*So why did you bring me out of the womb?*
> *I should have died then and never been seen.*
> ¹⁹*I should have been as if I never lived,*
> *carried from the womb to the grave.*
> ²⁰*Are not my days few? Let me alone!*^a
> *Turn away from me, so that I may find a little comfort*
> ²¹*before I go—I shall not return!—*^a
> *to the land of darkness and deep shadow,*^b
> ²²^a*the land of gloom*^b *like blackness,*^c
> *of deep shadow without order,*^d
> *where the light*^e *is as darkness.*^f

Notes

9:2.a. For מה "how," cf. מה־נצטדק "how shall we justify ourselves?" (Gen 44:16); cf. BDB, 553b *s.v.* מה § 2.(a): "(*a*) *how?* especially in expressing what is regarded as an impossibility."

2.b. אנוש is a mainly poetical term for "human"; it does not have a special connotation of "weak" or "mortal" (as e.g., Terrien), despite its possible connection with אנש "be weak"; cf. F. Maass, *TDOT* 1:347.

2.c. For the qal as equivalent to the passive of the hiph, cf. *Comment*.

3.a. The proposal by E. E. Kellett ("A Suggestion," *ExpT* 44 [1932–33] 283–84) to read אֶחָד (masc) for אַחַת (fem), "not even one of the thousand [cf. 33:23, the thousand angelic mediators] will become man's advocate" is interesting, but arbitrary.

4.a. Lit. "wise of heart," the heart as the seat of intelligence.

4.b. Taking the colon as a *casus pendens*, resumed by אליו (so e.g., Driver). Others suppose it a modifier of מי; thus "however wise and mighty a man might be" (Gordis; similarly Terrien, Pope).

4.c. הקשה "hardened," usually regarded as an ellipsis for הקשה ערף "hardened the neck" (as Deut 10:16; Jer 7:26) or perhaps for הקשה לבו "hardened his heart" (cf. Exod 13:15; Prov 29:1); hence "stubbornly resisted" (NEB), "withstood" (NAB), "defy" (JB, Pope). Gordis' suggestion is here followed that קשה hiph means "argue, dispute, raise a question" as in Mishnaic Heb.; the forensic imagery is continued.

4.d. וישלם "remained safe" (Dhorme), "survived" (NEB), "remained unscathed" (NAB; cf. NIV, Moffatt, Pope), or, better, "prepared" (KJV, Driver), "succeeded" (RSV); cf. JB "successfully [defy]." שלם is rare in qal.

5.a. The ptcps of vv 5–7 have the article, those of vv 8–10 lack it. No significant difference can be observed.

5.b. ידעו emended to יֵדָע by Bickell, Duhm, Gray, Moffatt, *BHK*; similarly Pesh, "and he does not know it," viz. without being aware of it, so slight is the difficulty. But if he overturns them "in his anger," he must be aware of so doing (Guillaume). To avoid the anthropomorphic language, D. Winton Thomas connects ידעו with Arab. *wada'a* "be still," thus "so that they are no longer still" ("Additional Notes on the Root ידע in Hebrew," *JTS* ns 15 [1964] 54–57 [54–55]); hence NEB "giving them no rest." On the root ידע II "be still, humiliated," see J. A. Emerton, "A Consideration of Some Alleged Meanings of ידע in Hebrew," *JSS* 15 (1970) 145-80 (170); D. F. Payne, "Old Testament Exegesis and the Problem of Ambiguity," *ASTI* 5 (1967) 46–68 (60–62, 67); P. R. Ackroyd, "Meaning and Exegesis," in *Words and Meanings. Essays Presented to David Winton Thomas* (ed. P. R. Ackroyd and B. Lindars; Cambridge: CUP, 1968) 1–14 (10–14). ידעו has also been understood as "and men know it not" (Tur-Sinai) or "before one knows it" (Rashi, Pope). It is best to retain the MT as signifying "without their being aware of it (because it happens suddenly)"; cf. Ps 35:8; Isa 47:11; Jer 50:24. The suggestion of M. Dahood, "New Readings in Lamentations," *Bib* 59 (1978) 174–97 (190–91) that ולא ידעו is "without sweating" (ידע III, a dialectal form of יזע, cf. זֵעָה), though noted by KB³, must be accounted implausible.

5.c. אשר could be "that," viz. "that he has overturned them in his wrath" (Dillmann, Driver), or "when" (RSV), or "who," sc. "they do not know who has overturned them" (Dhorme, Gordis). Hölscher, Fohrer prefix *waw* to אשר (lost by dittography).

7.a. אָמַר here "command," as not infrequently (BDB, 56b, § 4); cf. 36:10.

7.b. זָרַח is normally "shine" (so NIV) but also "rise" (of the sun) as KJV, RSV, JB, NEB, NAB, Pope; the latter meaning does not fit the context, however.

8.a. בָּמֳתֵי יָם, formerly understood as "the heights of the sea," is now generally taken as "the back (בָּמֳת) of Sea," following W. F. Albright, *JBL* 57 (1938) 227; idem, "The Psalm of Habakkuk," in *Studies in Old Testament Prophecy* (ed. H. H. Rowley; Edinburgh: T. and T. Clark, 1950) 1–18 (18); F. M. Cross and D. N. Freedman, "The Blessing of Moses," *JBL* 67 (1948) 191–210 (196, 210); so too RSVmg, NEB. But NAB, NIV retain references to "waves"; J. L. Crenshaw also would prefer to retain "the crest of the sea" ("W⁽ᵉ⁾dōrēk ʿal-bāmōtê ʾāreṣ," *CBQ* 34 (1972) 39–53 (46–48); similarly J. Day, *God's Conflict*, 42. Fohrer and Hesse follow the reading of a few MSS, עָב "cloud" (collective), as more suited to the context (vv 8a, 9).

9.a. Gordis finds here a second עשׂה "cover, conceal" (cf. Arab. ġašawa), as in 23:9; Prov 12:23; 13:16; Isa 32:6. This would parallel v 7b, but would not fit the identical phrase in Amos 5:8, and is therefore unacceptable.

9.b. *BHS* reads עָיִשׁ as in 38:32; Hölscher suggests עָיֵשׁ, corresponding to Syr. *'eyūtā*.

9.c. To the suggestions mentioned in the *Comment* may be added Hoffmann's ingenious revocalization of תמן to תֹמֶן (= תְּאֹמִים), "the twins, Gemini."

11.a. הֵן "if" (BDB, 243b § b).

11.b. Redivision to אֶרְאֶהוּ יַחְלֹף (Ehrlich, Gray, *BHK*, Dahood, *Psalms III*, 135) is possible; other ways of accounting for the absent suffix of אראה are to vocalize אֶרְאֶה or to invoke the principle of double duty suffix (Blommerde).

12.a. Most connect the verb חתף (*hapax*) with חטף "catch, seize," and some even emend to יַחְטֹף (cf. *BHK*, NEB). That is unnecessary, since we also find חֶתֶף "prey" in Prov 23:28, and forms meaning "rob, plunder, ravish" in Ecclus 15:14; 32:22; 50:4 (cf. 1QH 5.10), which is identical with חטף. See further, Grabbe, *Comparative Philology*, 60–62. Most improbable is Dahood's suggestion ("Some Northwest Semitic Words in Job," *Bib* 38 [1957] 306–20 [310]), followed by Blommerde: יַחַס פָּמִי "[if] he should snatch away [חתף] then . . ." (the alleged Heb. conjunction -פָּ); for bibliography, see Blommerde, 32–33; and see n. 9:20.a). P. Xella, "*ḪTP* 'uccidere, annientare' in Giobbe 9,12," *Hen* 1 (1979) 337–41, none too convincingly explains חתף as "kill, annihilate," on the basis of Ug. *htp*, an animal sacrifice (*KTU* 1.119 [= RS 24.266].32).

12.b. Lit. "turn him back" (שׁוב hiph) or "turn back, repel, refute" (cf. BDB, 999b § 5); TOB "qui l'en dissuade?" "Who can make him return it?" (Gordis) is a superficially attractive translation, but שׁוב hiph does not mean "cause to cause to return."

13.a. Pope: "a god could not turn back his anger"; followed by J. J. M. Roberts, "Job's Summons to Yahweh: The Exploitation of a Legal Metaphor," *RestQ* 16 (1973) 159–65 (163). But אלוה in Job invariably refers to the one God (except 12:6, where it is parallel to אל) and outside Job means "a god" only in literature probably later than Job (Chronicles, Daniel).

13.b. Most translate תחתיו as "beneath him," though JB, NEB, NIV have "at his feet," a rendering advocated by Dahood, *Psalms II*, xxvi, and *Psalms III*, 330, who claims שׁחחו תחתיו is the Heb. equivalent of El Amarna *ana šēpē šarri lu ištahahin*.

13.c. H. L. Ginsberg, "A Ugaritic Parallel to 2 Sam 1:21," *JBL* 57 (1938) 209–13 (210–11 n. 5), and M. Dahood, *Bib* 43 (1962) 226, saw in עָזֵר Ug. *ġzr* "hero, warrior." But a more nuanced assessment of a root *ʿzr* in Heb. makes the suggestion questionable; see P. D. Miller, Jr, "Ugaritic *ĠZR* and Hebrew *ʿZR* II," *UF* 2 (1970) 159–75 (164); A. F. Rainey, *Ras Shamra Parallels* (AnOr 50; Rome: Pontifical Biblical Institute, 1975) 2:74–75, 105–106.

14.a. אַף כִּי "how much more" or "how much less," clearly the latter here. English idiom is better served by "then." Gordis takes אַף as an emphatic interrogative particle, "Can I indeed . . . ?" (cf. Gen 3:1).

14.b. Lit. "with him" (עמו); for עם suggesting "in a contest with," cf. vv 2, 3; 10:17 (?); 16:21; Ps 94:16 (Driver). Examples of עם meaning "like" (BDB, 767b § e) are too dissimilar from the present verse to allow "like him" for עמו (as Blommerde).

15.a. The verse is deleted by Hesse as destructive of the connection between vv 14 and 16.

15.b. Lit. "answer" (אענה). Many read אֶעֱנֶה "I will be answered" (cf. LXX οὐκ εἰσακούσεταί μου; similarly Pesh, Theod; but perhaps they read יענה); so *BHK*, Hölscher, Dhorme, Fohrer, NEB. Terrien reads יַעֲנֶה לֹא. MT is, however, quite satisfactory (cf. v 3 יעננו).

15.c. מְשֹׁפְטִי is usually regarded as poel ptcp, "my adversary," "my opponent at law," though Fohrer, following R. Meyer, "Spuren eines westsemitischen Präsens-Futur in den Texten von Chirbet Qumran," in *Von Ugarit nach Qumran* (O. Eissfeldt Festschrift; ed. J. Hempel and L. Rost; BZAW 77; Berlin: A. Töpelmann, 1958) 118–28, takes it as a mistaken form of the *yaqātal* conjugation. Roberts, *RestQ* 16 (1973) 163, divides שֹׁפְטִי לֹם, with an enclitic *mem* on the preposition. Revocalization to מִשְׁפָּטִי "[for] my right" (Hitzig, Budde, RSVmg; cf. NAB) is unnecessary, especially with the further supposition that the *-y* suffix is third person (as Blommerde: "to his justice").

16.a. Lit. "If I should call and he should answer." LXX^B has a negative before "answer"; hence Duhm read וְלֹא יַעֲנֵנִי (so also *BHK*). Dahood, "Hebrew-Ugaritic Lexicography IV," *Bib* 47 (1966) 403–19 (408), followed by Blommerde, achieves a similar sense by taking לֹא as a noun, "nothing," object of וַיְעַנֵּנִי.

17.a. The revocalization of בְּשַׂעֲרָה "with a tempest" (elsewhere spelled סערה in Job) to בְּשַׂעֲרָה "for a hair" is adopted by Hitzig, Ehrlich, Dhorme, Rowley, Terrien, Pope, Andersen, Gordis, JB, NEB. Tg had seen שערה "hair" here already (as also Pesh), rendering "who deals exactly with me even to a hair's breadth"; for a Talmudic appearance of the same phrase, cf. *b. Yeb.* 121b.

17.b. שׁוּף "crush"; G. R. Driver, "Some Hebrew Verbs, Nouns and Pronouns," *JTS* 30 (1928–29) 375–77, translated "swept close over"; but recognition of שׁערה as "hair" (n. 9:17.a) makes this rendering implausible, as also Blommerde's understanding of שׁוף as "watch" (cf. discussion by Dhorme): "He watches me from [ב] the whirlwind." Implausible is E. Lipiński's suggestion ("Notes lexicographiques et stylistiques sur le livre de Job," *FolOr* 21 [1980] 65–82 [70–71]) that the picture is of a serpent spitting out poison (v 18b) which paralyzes the victim and makes him lose his breath (v 18a); for נשׁף in postbiblical Heb. means not "spit" but "blow" (Levy), the suffix would be odd, and the reference to multiple "wounds" would be out of place.

17.c. חנם understood by Dahood, *Psalms III*, 201, and Blommerde as "stealthily" (cf. Prov 1:17; Dahood, *Psalms I*, 211); contrastive parallelism between "tempest" and "stealthily" is noted.

18.a. ממררים only here. Some revocalize to מְמֹרְרִים (Driver, Ehrlich) or emend to בְּמרֹרִים (Beer, Hölscher). Dahood, "Hebrew-Ugaritic Lexicography V," *Bib* 48 (1967) 421–38 (427), followed by Blommerde, attached the initial *mem* to the preceding word.

19.a. Lit. "if it is for strength."

19.b. אמיץ הנה is taken together (so e.g., Gordis), and with many, הנה is read as הִנֵּה (or הֵנָּה) "behold him" (cf. Tg, NEB "see how strong he is"; similarly JB, NIV). Driver understood "He saith" before each half of the line, and took הנה as equivalent to הִנְנִי (so RVmg); KJV understood "I speak" and RV "we speak" in the first half, while *BHK* actually emended הנה to הִנְנִי. NAB read הוּא "he" for הנה.

19.c. Most emend יועידני "will arraign me" to וִידִיעֶנּוּ "will arraign him" (the form יוֹעִידֵהוּ suggested by Brockington does not occur). Blommerde reads יוֹעִידֶנִּי, with a 3rd pers suff (bibliography: Blommerde, 8). Gordis plausibly regards the MT reading as a deliberate scribal alteration for reverential reasons, though he should not, strictly speaking, call it a *tiqqun sopherim*, since it is not one of the standard list (see C. McCarthy, *The Tiqqune Sopherim, and Other Theological Corrections of the Masoretic Text of the Old Testament* [OBO 36; Freiburg: Universitätsverlag, and Göttingen: Vandenhoeck und Ruprecht, 1981] 168; and cf. also on 7:20).

20.a. For the sake of the parallelism, some read פִּיו "his mouth" (Hölscher, Fohrer, Hesse), and Dahood so renders פִּי ("Nest and Phoenix in Job 29, 18," *Bib* 48 [1967] 542–44 [543], apparently abandoning his previous suggestion [*Bib* 38 (1957) 311] that פִּי is the conjunction *pa-* "then"— which K. Aartun, "Textüberlieferung und vermeintliche Belege der Konjunktion *pᵛ* im Alten Testament," *UF* 10 [1978] 1–13 [8–9], rightly judges to be unjustified). MT is far more expressive, and the parallelism is easily preserved (n. 9:20.b).

20.b. Parallelism favors "it" (the mouth) as the subject (so KJV, RV, TOB, NIV, Dhorme, Terrien).

20.c. וַיַּעְקְשֵׁנִי, i.e., "if I am perfect, it (he) will have proved" (Driver), possibly to be pointed וְיַעְקְשֵׁנִי (Budde, Beer, NAB), i.e., "it (he) will prove," is clearly a declarative hiph of עקשׁ "twist," parallel to the more usual judicial term יַרְשִׁיעֵנִי. NEB "he twists my words" is very improbable.

22.a. Transferred by Duhm to the end of v 21, with which indeed it belongs in sense (see *Comment*). Dhorme transposes אחת היא and אמרתי to על־כן to make אחת היא relate more obviously to v 22b. LXX omits אחת היא.

23.a. שׁוֹט "whip, scourge," is a symbol for a natural disaster, probably plague, possibly flood (Fohrer, Horst, NEB; cf. Isa 28:15, 17–18). Hölscher proposed שׁוֹטוֹ "his scourge," following Pesh (so too Weiser; but see *Comment*).

23.b. Rather unlikely is F. Zimmermann's interpretation, "Note on Job 9:23," *JTS* ns 2 (1951) 165–66, though favored by Terrien; he reads פְּתָאִים "simple ones, young," and translates "If mockery could kill innocents, why He would indeed mock at the trials of the guiltless."

23.c. מסה may be from נסה "test," hence "trial" (KJV, RV) or, more probably, since the point is not testing but destruction, from מסס "melt," hence "despair" (NAB, NIV, Pope) or what brings about despair, "calamity" (RSV, JPS) or "plight" (JB, NEB).

24.a. Not in the Heb., but the two clauses are related sequentially.

24.b. Or, "a land" (Dhorme); no particular land is in mind (NEB "the land" may also be indefinite).

24.c. Lit. "is given" (נתנה).

24.d. This and the following line were omitted by LXX, perhaps for reverential reasons (Gard, *Exegetical Method of the Greek Translator*, 72–73), but were taken into MSS of the Gk. Bible from Theodotion. Fohrer deletes v 24b as an explanatory gloss; similarly Moffatt, NEB.

24.e. It is not clear why NEB has "are blindfold." Gordis translates the line permissibly "who [the wicked man] is able to bribe [lit., cover the faces of] the judges," but wrongly supposes that the niph in the first line makes it unlikely that "God" is the subject here.

24.f. Lit. "if not, then who is it?" Transposing אפוא and הוא makes for a smoother reading: "if not he, then who?" The phrase is hardly an abbreviation of a line similar to 24:25, ואם־לא אפו מי יכזיבני "and if not, who will prove me a liar?" (24:25) (Tur-Sinai, following ibn Ezra).

25.a. Lit. "and my days." Horst notes that the copula in an adversative sense is also a mark of a new topic in the style of the laments, where also the subject of the sentence appears in first position (cf. C. Westermann, *The Praise of God in the Psalms* [tr. K. R. Crim; London: Epworth, 1965] 70–72). Some omit the initial *waw*, which is not represented in Pesh or Vg: so BHK, NAB, Driver, Hölscher, Fohrer, Hesse. M. Dahood sees a vocative *waw* here: "O, my days are swifter" ("Vocative *kî* and *wa* in Biblical Hebrew," in *Mélanges offerts au R. P. Henri Fleisch, S. J.* [Mélanges de l'Université Saint-Joseph 48; Beirut: Imprimerie Catholique, 1973–74] 49–63); though strictly speaking "O" is not here a vocative.

25.b. With NEB, but against most other versions, the perf tense of the verses should be insisted upon: "have been swifter," "have fled away," "have not seen."

25.c. Quite unpersuasively E. Zurro finds here a play on the meaning of ברח I "flee" and ברח II "be troubled, suffer" ("Disemia de *brḥ* y paralelismo bifronte en Job 9,25," *Bib* 62 [1981] 546–47), since the reference to speed in the first colon ensures that ברח will be taken as "flee," and will not be read in connection with "have not seen good." The existence of ברח II, though acknowledged by KB³, is in any case open to doubt (it was proposed by G. R. Driver, "Proverbs xix.26," *TZ* 11 [1955] 373–74, and C. Rabin, "*Bāriaḥ*," *JTS* 47 [1946] 38–41).

26.a. אֵבֶה, though *hapax* in OT, is attested in Akk. *apu*, Arab. *ʾabā* "reed." KJVmg "ships of desire" followed Symm in connecting with אבה "be willing."

27.a. The inf אמרי after אם is unparalleled, and usually emended to אָמַרְתִּי. G. R. Driver, "Problems in the Hebrew Text of Job," *VTS* 3 (1955) 72–93 (76), reads אֹמַר (cf. 1 Sam 20:21).

27.b. See n. 7:11.b. It is not a matter of forgetting the situation that causes the complaint (Fohrer) but of being so distant from the former (verbal) complaining that it is forgotten.

27.c. אעזבה פני, lit. "I will forsake my face," is not an obvious way of saying "I will abandon my sadness," which is what the sense requires. Gordis compares 1 Sam 1:18, where פנים without qualification apparently means "sad countenance, sadness," but the reading is uncertain. G. R. Driver, *VTS* 3 (1955) 76, saw in עזב a cognate to Arab. *ʿadaba* IV "made agreeable," pointed the word אֶעְזִיבָה, and translated "I will make pleasant my countenance," i.e., "put on a cheerful look"; hence NEB "I will show a cheerful face." Lane, 1981, however, gives a very restricted range of meanings for *ʿadaba* IV, thus: "the people became in the condition of having sweet water," and the existence of a cognate עזב, for which no other OT examples are cited, is problematic. M. Dahood, "The Root *ʿZB* II in Job," *JBL* 78 (1959) 303–9, compared Ug. *ʿdb* "make, arrange" (cf. also on 10:1), and translated "I shall arrange my face," i.e., "I shall wash and anoint my face." This is followed by Pope ("fix my face"), and Fohrer "prepare another visage" (*ein anderes Gesicht machen*). It is no improvement to use the sense "repair, restore" of Ug. *ʿdb* (claimed for עזב in Neh 3:8, 34 [4:2]; etc. by KB³), and translate "resume my (normal) countenance"; for it is doubtful that this עזב I exists in Bib. Heb., and it is uncertain whether Ug. *ʿdb* is truly cognate with עזב (see H. G. M. Williamson, "A Reconsideration of עזב II in Biblical Hebrew," *ZAW* 87 [1985] 74–85). The number of homonymous roots עזב (G. R. Driver notes five!) is a problem, and a straightforward translation "I will forsake my (present) countenance" is not impossible. The translation given above is *ad sensum*.

28.a. NEB "I tremble in every nerve" follows G. Perles, "The Fourteenth Edition of Gesenius-Buhl's Dictionary," *JQR* 18 (1905–1906) 383–90 (387), on the basis of postbiblical עצב, "nerve."

29.a. The whole verse is deleted by Hölscher and Fohrer as a prosaic gloss which nevertheless is not misleading.

29.b. The future ארשע "I shall be accounted guilty" denotes what will inevitably be the case, expressing "an obligation or necessity according to the judgment of another person. . . . I am to be guilty" (GKC, § 107n). Alternatively, the first clause אנכי ארשע is to be taken as a hypothesis (like the opening clause of v 24) (so LXX, Pesh, KJV, JB, NEB, NAB, Dhorme); some insert before אנכי a particle of hypothesis, הֲ (*BHK* [prp]). The sense is essentially the same.

30.a. V. Sasson wants רחץ here to refer to "inner purification and moral refinement" ("ŠMN RHṢ in the Samaria Ostraca," *JSS* 26 [1981] 1–5 [4]); but the parallel with cleansing the hands in the second colon rules this out.

30.b. Pesh, Tg read, as Q בְמֵי־שֶׁלֶג "with snow water" (so too KJV, RV), but since the water of melted snow is not especially white, K במו־שלג (= בְמוֹ) "in snow" is preferable. There may be some allusion to a folk-belief in the efficacy of snow to cleanse; Hölscher refers to an Arab fable of a black man rubbing himself with snow to make himself white, and to Mohammed's prayer, "Lord, wash me white from my sins with water, snow and ice." In Ps 51:9; Isa 1:18 snow serves not as the means of purification, but as a symbol of purity. But in view of the parallel with בר "lye," the suggestion of J. Preuss, *Biblisch-talmudische Medizin. Beiträge zur Geschichte der Heilkunde und der Kultur überhaupt* (Berlin: Karger, 2nd ed., 1921) 431, that שלג is equivalent to Mishnaic אֶשְׁלָג and Talmudic שַׁלָּגָא "soap, soapwort" is better still (cf. Akk. *ašlāku*). So NEB, NIV, Gordis, H. R. Cohen, *Biblical Hapax Legomena in the Light of Akkadian and Ugaritic* (SBLDS 37; Missoula, Mont.: Scholars Press, 1978) 140. Fohrer reads בְמֵי־שֶׁלֶג as "in water of soapwort."

30.c. בר, probably *hapax* (since Isa 1:25 is dubious), is elsewhere בֹּרִית "lye," an alkaline solution made from the ashes of wood or vegetable matter (pot ashes); chemically it is caustic potash. Modern lye is generally caustic soda (sodium hydroxide).

31.a. שׁחת "pit"; KJV probably used "ditch" in the old sense of "any hollow dug in the ground; a hole, pit, cave, den" (*OED*, 3:541); the rendering is adopted by RV, NAB. A pit would normally be muddy (Gen 37:24 has to specify that the pit in question here was "waterless"). Though the term is used of the nether world (cf. 33:22), and the abode of the Ugaritic Mot is a miry city and his throne a pit (*CTA* 4.8.11–12; Gibson, 66), there is no reference to the nether world here (as against Pope; cf. also idem, "The Word *šaḥat* in Job 9:31," *JBL* 83 [1964] 269–78). Many, with LXX's ἐν ῥύπῳ "in filth" in mind, emend to שֻׁחֹת (Hoffmann, Dhorme, Hölscher, Horst, Fohrer, Hesse, *BHS* [prb], NEB) or סוּחָה "offal" (cf. Isa 5:25; so Beer, Duhm) or סְחִי "refuse" (cf. Lam 3:45; so G. Hoffmann, "Ergänzungen und Berichtigungen zu Hiob," *ZAW* 8 [1931] 141–45 [142]; *BHK*), or "dung" (JB). But LXX may well have read the Heb. exactly as MT, which should be followed (so too Gordis).

31.b. Surprised at the metaphor, some commentators have emended שַׂלְמֹתַי "my clothes" to שֶׁלְמָי (Duhm) or מְשַׁלְּמָי "my friends" (Lagarde), or changed תעבוני to תְעָבְתַנִי "you would make [my clothes] loathsome for me" (Gordis). But the personification of clothing is not strange in poetry (Pope), and Calmet (cited by Dhorme) well said: "This way of speaking which endows clothes with feelings, such as those of horror and aversion from a sullied body, has about it something most striking, something which seizes the attention and gives the idea of terrible corruption."

32.a. Initial כי is probably the emphatic particle "surely," since "for" does not connect with what precedes.

32.b. "He" is supplied; Hölscher's proposal to insert אַתָּה "you," following LXX, is attractive (so also Duhm, deleting יענני); but the 3rd pers is used in vv 34–35.

32.c. The verb is a voluntative without the usual *waw* (Driver, *Tenses*, § 64).

32.d. Pope's rendering of ענה as "challenge" points in the right direction for the understanding of v 32b, but can hardly be justified as a translation.

32.e. Or, with most versions, "[and] that we should go . . ." The absence of *waw* before נבוא, which is a little strange (cf. Duhm), is accounted for by the translation above.

33.a. לֹא יֵשׁ "there is not" is not found elsewhere in OT (אֵין is normal). Probably read therefore לֻ אֵ or לוּ "would that there were" (as some MSS); so LXX, Pesh, RSVmg, NEB, NAB, NIV, TOB, *BHK*, Terrien, Pope, Gordis); cf. also C. F. Whitley, "Some Remarks on *lû* and *lo'*," *ZAW* 87 (1975) 202–204.

33.b. KJV "daysman," i.e., umpire or mediator, comes from the obsolete verb "to day," meaning to submit a matter to arbitration, or, to decide by arbitration (cf. "dayment," arbitration) (*OED*, 3:51–53).

34.a. אשׁר understood, as before ישׁת (v 33b). Equally possible is "Let him (God) remove."

34.b. M. Dahood, "Hebrew-Ugaritic Lexicography I," *Bib* 44 (1963) 289–303 (295) translates "his arm" (אֲמָתוֹ) from אַמָּה).

35.a. Similarly JB "I do not see myself like that at all" [sc. fearful]. Lit. "since I am not thus with me/myself." NAB "Since this is not the case with me" refers to the possibility of unfearful speech with God. NEB "for I know I am not what I am thought to be," i.e., guilty. Others regard כֵּן "thus" as the adjective "right, honest" (cf. LXX ἄδικον for לֹא־כֵן; on LXX cf. P. Joüon, "Notes philologiques sur le texte hébreu de Job," *Bib* 11 [1930] 322–34 [322–23]), emending either

הוּא, "he is not honorable with me" (Ehrlich, Fohrer, Hesse, Gordis), or עִמּוֹ "I am not honest (= just) with him." Blommerde has "though [כִי] I am not just before him [עֹמְדִי] with -*i* suffix of 3rd pers]"; followed by J. J. M. Roberts, *RestQ* 16 (1973) 160. Dhorme reverses the order of vv 35a and 35b: "Since it is not so [there is no arbiter], I with myself will commune and will not fear Him."

10:1.a. Blommerde takes the suffix of חַיָּי as 3rd pers, thus "my soul (נַפְשִׁי) is sick of *its* life."

1.b. Lit. "let loose" (עָזַב) (jb, neb "give free rein to"), עָלַי "upon myself" (kjv) being used "to give pathos to the expression of an emotion, by emphasizing the person who is its subject, and who, as it were, feels it acting *upon* him" (BDB, 753b § d). Dahood saw here the root עזב "prepare" (cf. n. 9:27.c) and translated "I shall prepare on my behalf my complaint" (*JBL* 78 [1959] 305); so too Pope, who finds this preferable to Dahood's later suggestion that עָלַי is "to him" (*Psalms I*, 257). Others emend to עָלָיו "to, before him" (*BHK* [?], Merx, Duhm, Terrien), claiming the support of LXXᴮ ἐπ' αὐτόν, which is, however, probably an inner-Greek corruption of ἐπ' ἐμαυτόν (as LXXᴬ). The usual interpretation is quite satisfactory, however. On the pattern of this verse, see M. Dahood, "Hebrew-Ugaritic Syntax and Style," *UF* 1 (1969) 15–36 (32–34).

2.a. Blommerde sees in עַל, usually taken as a phrase עַל מֶה "on account of what, why," the supposed divine title עַל "Most High" (cf. n. 7:20.h), which certainly yields a parallelism with אֱלוֹהַּ "God" in the first line, though it is doubtful whether it can explain the absence of a maqqeph between עַל and מֶה.

3.a. Deleted as a gloss by Duhm, Gray (perhaps), Hölscher, Fohrer, Hesse. But see *Comment*.

3.b. עֵצָה "counsel," less probably in this context "council" (Dhorme, Dahood, *Psalms I*, 2). G. R. Driver saw here עֵצָה "disobedience" (*WO* 1 [1947–52] 411), while R. Bergmeier translates "fellowship, circle," as in 21:16; 22:18 ("Zum Ausdruck עצת רשעים in Ps 1:1; Hi 10:3; 21:16 und 22:18," *ZAW* 79 [1967] 229–32.

5.a. MT כִימֵי "like the days of," as in the first colon. Though the repetition of a word in parallelism is not uncharacteristic of Job (see Gordis, 508–13) and MT is retained by some (Dhorme, Gordis), כִימֵי may well be a scribal error for שְׁנוֹת "years of." English style in any case prefers a variation, and most render "years of" even if not emending the text.

8.a. BDB relates עָצַב to Arab. *'adaba* "cut off," hence "carve, fashion" (thus עָצָב "idol" is "what is cut off"); KB connects with Arab. *'aṣaba* "twist, bind," hence neb "gave me shape"; עָצָב is then "what is shaped."

8.b. MT יַחַד סָבִיב lit. "together round about" (kjv, rv, jps, cf. tob "ensemble, elles [tes mains] m'avaient façonné de toutes parts"; Weiser, Gordis). Suspicion of the text is aroused by the fact that the logical caesura does not coincide with the metrical caesura (though that is not unparalleled; cf. n. 4:8.a), and by LXX's reading אַחַר (μετὰ ταῦτα) for יַחַד. Most follow LXX, and further find in סָבִיב some form of סבב "turn": תָּסֹב "you turn" (Delitzsch, Driver, nab; cf. *BHK*), סַבֹּתָ "you have turned" (Beer, cf. *BHK*, Fohrer, Pope), סָבוֹב (inf abs) "turning" (Duhm, Hölscher, Horst, *BHS* [frt]), or סֹבֵב "turning" (neb, סוֹבֵב Terrien). Dhorme retains סָבִיב as meaning "utterly" (cf. 19:10), qualifying וַתְּבַלְּעֵנִי, but the existence of postpositive *waw* is dubious.

8.c. A. Guillaume, "A Note on the √בלע," *JTS* ns 13 (1962) 320–22, argued that the verb must here (as also at 2:3; 37:20) mean "afflict, distress," not "swallow up," comparing Arab. *balaġa* "reach, arrive at," thus "afflict"; so too KB³. The meaning is unexceptionable, but there is no need to depart from the admittedly more dramatic "swallow up."

9.a. neb "you modeled me" assumes a revocalization to עֲשִׂיתָנִי, derived from עשה pi "press, squeeze."

9.b. Since clay is often said to be the material from which the first human was created (cf. *Comment*), some read simply חֹמֶר, i.e., as the acc of the material (cf. LXX; GKC, § 117hh) or בְּחֹמֶר (Ehrlich; cf. Exod 38:8). Dhorme thought כַחֹמֶר equivalent to כ + בְּחֹמֶר "as it were with clay," *beth* being unacceptable after the *kaph* of comparison (GKC, § 118w).

9.c. עָפָר is earth wet or dry; wet mire or mud also in Gen 2:7; 3:19.

12.a. חַיִּים וָחֶסֶד "life and loyalty" is an unusual combination, so several emendations have been proposed: for חַיִּים, חֵן "mercy" (*BHK*, nab, Gray, Hesse); or for חֶסֶד, חֶלֶד "length of life" (Duhm, Hölscher); or delete חַיִּים (Ehrlich). Dhorme takes it as a hendiadys, rendering "the favor of life"; similarly Andersen, and Gordis, with "a life of free grace, i.e., . . . out of your freely bestowed love." The phrase חֶסֶד עָשִׂית עִמָּדִי is clearly primary.

13.a. Lit. "these things you hid in your heart."

14.a. Gordis finds "watch" an inept rendering of שָׁמַר here, since God watches him even if Job does not sin. He therefore urges that שָׁמַר be rendered "bear a grudge, keep in mind" (similarly Ehrlich), like נְטֹר "keep, keep one's anger" (Lev 19:18; Jer 3:5). But there is no other example of שָׁמַר in this sense.

15.a. Horst's proposal to reverse the order of this line and the following provides a clear subject for יגאה in v 16a; but see n. 10:16.a.

15.b. This third line, together with v 16a, is omitted as a citation by Duhm, and by Hölscher and Fohrer as destroying the sequence of ideas and images (deletion also by Hesse, and of v 15c alone by Moffatt, NEB).

15.c. וּרְאֵה עָנְיִי apparently "and look on my affliction" (cf. KJV) is rightly rendered by most "and satiated with my affliction"; רָאֵה is construct of רָאָה, an orthographic variant of רָוֶה (for רָוֶה = רוה; cf. Ps 91:16 [ראה], שָׂבַע // ראה], and perhaps Isa 53:11; see also G. R. Driver, "Notes on the Psalms," *JTS* 36 [1935] 147–56 [152]; idem, "L'interprétation du texte masorétique à la lumière de la lexicographie hébraïque," *ETL* 26 [1950] 337–53 [351]; D. Winton Thomas, "A Consideration of Isaiah 53 in the Light of Recent Textual and Philological Study," *ETL* 44 [1968] 79–86). Emendation of ראה to רוה (*BHK, BHS*, Duhm, Driver, Hölscher, Fohrer, Horst) is therefore unnecessary, as is also the deletion of the suffix of עניי to yield עֲנִי "affliction." NEB "steeped in" (as in Isa 53:11 "bathed in") is not the appropriate image for ראה/רוה which means "be satiated, drink deeply" (referring to imbibing rather than being soaked).

16.a. Reading וְאֶגְאֶה (as Driver-Gray, Weiser, Terrien, RSV, JB, NEB, TOB, following Pesh) for MT יגאה "and it (he) is proud, lifts itself up." A close examination of the Tg suggests that it too supports the emendation (D. M. Stec, "The Targum Rendering of WYG'H in Job X 16," *VT* 34 [1984] 367–68). Some think "my head" (v 15a) is the subject (so RV "if *my head* exalt itself"; cf. JPS, NAB, perhaps NIV), but this seems most improbable. For not only is the subject of the verb rather far removed, but the sense is strained if in v 15b Job cannot lift his head and in v 16 he recounts what happens when he does lift his head. Pope suggests וְגָאֶה and Gordis וְגָאֶה [error for וְגֵאֶה] "proudly You hunt me," the adjective modifying the subject, but the claimed parallels in 9:4 and Ps 107:5 are too dissimilar to support this syntax. Dhorme proposes וְיָגֵעַ "and exhausted (as I am)," but his idea that the adjectives in the last line of v 15 are linked with this word and v 16 is improbable. Several commentators omit v 16a altogether (see n. 10:15.a).

16.b. Lit. "you again show yourself wonderful, *or* extraordinary" (תשב תתפלא); the exceptional, and perhaps, inexplicable, character of God's behavior is at issue, rather than the result of his handling of Job. But "win fresh triumphs" (cf. JB "adding to the tale of your triumphs") or "dost not cease to glorify Thyself" (Dhorme) is not impossible, as also "again display your awesome power" (NIV; similarly NEB, NAB) or "repeat your exploits" (Pope; similarly TOB).

16.c. Lit. "you return and make yourself marveled at": וְתָשֹׁב is juss, as are תצודני and תתפלא, following the hypothetical ויגאה or ואגאה (see Driver, *Tenses*, § 152 iii). Emendation to וְתָשׁוּב (NEB) is needless.

17.a. עֵדֶיךָ in Masoretic vocalization is "your witnesses" (cf. KJV, RV, RSV, NIV, Gordis); see *Comment.* Slightly preferable is Ehrlich's proposal to see here a new word עֶדְיּ (read עֶדְיְךָ) "hostility, attack," cognate with Arab. 'adiya "was hostile" (cf. ḥadāwa "hostility"); the image of the attacking lion is hardly still in view, though an Arab. epithet for the lion is al-ḥādî "the attacker" (Guillaume). Cf. LXX ἔτασιν, which usually translates נגע "blow." Thus JB, NEB, NAB, TOB, Dhorme, Terrien, Pope. W. G. E. Watson, "The Metaphor in Job 10,17," *Bib* 63 (1982) 255–57, takes עדי as "troops," claiming that Ug. 'dn in *CTA* 14.2.85–87 (Gibson, 84) is really 'dy plus an afformative -n. This is not entirely convincing. Dahood (*Psalms I*, 197), followed by Blommerde, relates the word to Ug. ġdd "swell up, be irritated," and translates "your petulance"; the root is insufficiently attested in Ug., however (cf. Grabbe, *Comparative Philology*, 64, whose dismissal of the Arab. is too hasty).

17.b. Jussive, indicating that the apodosis after the hypothesis of v 16a continues.

17.c. חֲלִיפוֹת, lit. "exchange," in connection with צבא "hard service" or "military service," will most probably signify "release" from that service (as in 14:14). Pope sees a hendiadys: "successions and hardship," i.e., incessant hardship. Since חליפה has other military meanings, however, like "relays" (1 Kgs 5:28 [14]), and "reserve" (1QM 16.10), some have seen here two complementary terms: thus Dhorme, "reliefs and army," a hendiadys for "relief troops," Watson (*Bib* 63 [1982] 255–57, citing a neo-Bab. text where cognates of the two terms appear in one sentence about troop replacements), and Gordis, "changes and [= of] the military guard are upon me," i.e., one blow succeeds another. But this is very strained, and it is doubtful whether there is a *military* metaphor, properly speaking, in this verse at all. Emendations are improbable: וְתַחֲלִף (cf. LXX ἐπήγαγες; *BHK*, Hölscher; similarly Driver) וְתַחֲלִף "and thou wouldst renew thy hosts (= bring fresh hosts)" (thus RSV; and NEB, reading חֲלִפָת).

17.d. Lit. "is with me" (עמי).

20.a. K יחדל "let it (or, it will) cease" is unintelligible, but Q וַחֲדָל "(and) cease!" (similarly KJV, RV, Pope) makes good sense, echoing 7:16 חֲדַל מִמֶּנִּי, though the sense caesura is different from the metrical caesura. The initial *waw* of the next word (see n. 10:20.b) also supports taking this as imperative. Many, however, see in יְמֵי חֶדְל יְמִי a single phrase, probably an error for יְמֵי חֶלְדִּי "the days of my life" (*BHK, BHS* [prp], RSV, JB, NAB, KB; cf. LXX^A ὁ χρόνος τοῦ βίου μου). D. Winton Thomas ("Some Observations on the Hebrew Root חֶדְל," *VTS* 4 [1957] 14) and Gordis think to avoid the need for emendation by regarding חֶדְל as a metathesis for חֶלְד (cf. Isa 38:11; Ps 39:5 [4]). The combination of "days" with חֶלְד occurs nowhere else, however. NEB "is not my life short and fleeting?" reads וְחָדֵל "and lacking," which is, however, not in agreement with יָמַי. NAB reads יְמֵי שְׁנוֹתַי חֲדַל "the days of my life (lit. years) . . . let me alone," ingeniously transforming יָשִׁית into שָׁנוֹת.

20.b. Read Q וְשִׁית "and put" (sc. yourself or your hand, face) from me (K יָשִׁית again impossible). Such an ellipsis cannot be paralleled, not even by מִשִּׁים in 4:20 (see n. 4:20.d), so many read "look (away)," citing LXX ἔασόν με "leave me," which represents שְׁעַה in 7:19.

21.a. The clause, unrelated grammatically to the rest of the sentence, is a kind of interjection.

21.b. D. Winton Thomas, "צַלְמָוֶת in the Old Testament," *JSS* 7 (1962) 191–200, argued influentially that צַלְמָוֶת incorporates the term מָוֶת "death" used as a superlative, and so means "(a) very deep shadow, thick darkness"; there is thus "no intrinsic reference in צַלְמָוֶת to physical death, or to the underworld of Sheol" (p. 197). RSV likewise has just "deep darkness," without any reference to *death*. It seems to me, however, that if using מָוֶת is a way of expressing the superlative (as Winton Thomas, "A Consideration of Some Unusual Ways of Expressing the Superlative in Hebrew," *VT* 3 [1953] 209–24 [219–22]), it does more than simply express a superlative: it does so by using "death" as the intensifier. So therefore should the translation. See also n. 3:5.a.

22.a. Some unnecessarily omit the whole verse as a marginal expansion (Duhm, Hölscher, Hesse).

22.b. עֵיפָתה, elsewhere only Amos 4:13, usually "darkness" (cf. מוּעָף and מָעוּף, Isa 8:22–23, and תְּעָפָה [*si v.l.*], Job 11:17). Gordis suggests the word means "light," which would suit in Amos 4:13, but this translation would spoil the climactic final phrase וַתֹּפַע כְּמוֹ־אֹפֶל; but cf. TOB "au pays où l'aurore est nuit noire."

22.c. כְּמוֹ אֹפֶל צַלְמוּת "like darkness, deep shadow" is omitted by many, as glosses on the rare word עֵיפָתה (so *BHK*, Budde, Dhorme, Fohrer, Horst, RSV, NAB). Driver omitted only כְּמוֹ אֹפֶל.

22.d. See n. 10:21.b.

22.e. סֵדֶר "order" is only here in Bib. Heb. G. R. Driver found in סְדָרִים a new sense, "line, beam of light" (cf. Arab. *sadira* "was dazzled by the glare") and translated לֹא־סְדָרִים as "without ray of light" (*VTS* 3 [1955] 76–77); hence NEB (perhaps cf. LXX φέγγος). A similar translation is offered by those who think the reference to chaos out of place, and read נְהָרָה "light" (so Peters, Fohrer). But the term is well attested in later Heb., including the Qumran texts; cf. J. Carmignac, "Précisions apportées au vocabulaire de l'hébreu biblique par la guerre des fils de lumière contre les fils de ténèbres," *VT* 5 (1955) 345–65 (352).

22.f. תֹּפַע "it shines" (on the fem gender for natural phenomena, see GKC, § 144c), is thought by G. R. Driver, *VTS* 3 (1955) 76–77, to be from another root יפע "show dark clouds" (cf. Arab. *yafʿu(n)* "cloud foreboding rain"); hence NEB for וַתֹּפַע כְּמוֹ־אֹפֶל "dark upon dark." This is quite improbable.

Form / Structure / Setting

The *structure* of this speech can best be analyzed as twofold, the division being indicated by the direction of the address. In 9:2–24 it is not clear whether we have a monologue or an address to the friends, but obviously God is spoken of in the third person. In 9:25–10:22, with the sole exception of 9:32–35, God is consistently addressed in the second person. This most basic form-critical distinction overrides the more subtle and more debatable distinctions made by Fohrer and Hesse, who find three main sections, 9:2–24; 9:25–35; 10:1–22. Horst less plausibly regards the address to God as beginning properly only in chap. 10. Terrien's division into four "poems," 9:2–13; 9:14–24; 9:25–10:6; 10:7–22, recognizes the important transition between 9:24 and 9:25, but a major disjunction at 9:13 is improbable, and 10:1–7 should be more closely attached to what follows in 10:8–17.

Within the sections, certain *strophes* are clearly marked, though at some points the division is uncertain. In section 1, the doxology of 9:5–10 is a definite unit, while 9:21–24 is also clearly integrated. Six strophes can thus be recognized: vv 2–4, 5–10, 11–13, 14–16, 17–20, 21–24. In section 2, the most evident units are 10:8–12 and 10:18–22; hence a further six strophes should probably be distinguished: 9:25–31; 9:32–35; 10:1–2; 10:3–7; 10:8–17; 10:18–22. The triplet prevails as the most common strophic unit in the first section of the speech: thus 9:2–4, 11–13, 14–16, and (as a double triplet) 9:5–10. In the second section of the speech the 5-line strophe is most frequent: thus 9:25–31; 10:3–7, 18–22, and (as a double 5-line strophe) 10:8–17. This last example is sure evidence that detection of strophic structures is not an arbitrary exercise; for the obvious 10-line unit, 10:8–17, is clearly jointed at 10:13 where the mood changes and a transition marker (ואלה "but these things") appears. Two strophes of a single couplet appear (9:25–26; 10:1–2) and three of 4 lines (9:17–20, 21–24, 32–35) which may, except for the last, really be double 2-line strophes.

Different strophic divisions are made by Horst, viz. 9:2–10, 11–17, 18–24; 10:1–7, 8–12, 13–17; by Fohrer, viz. 9:11–14, 15–18, 19–21, 22–24, 25–28, 29–31; by Hesse, viz. 9:19–24, 25–28a, 28b–31; 10:1–7, 8–12, 13–17; by Terrien, viz. 9:17–21, 22–24, 25–29, 30–35; 10:1–6, 7–12, 13–17.

From the point of view of *form*, we find the usual combination of elements from various forms, here principally the legal controversy, the hymn, and the psalm of appeal. Despite the persistence of terminology from the legal sphere, comparatively few of the speech-forms of the *legal controversy* appear, except by way of allusion. The reason is no doubt the fact that this speech is not itself a legal speech, but tentative thoughts about the possibility of entering into controversy with God. In the second part of the speech, addressed directly to God, the protestation of innocence (9:21a), the "why" question (10:2b) and the question "Does it seem good to you?" (10:3) are characteristic of the controversy (though Fohrer sees the origin of the last in the prophetic reproof). The call to "remember" (10:9a), though fitting in the hymn-like context in which it appears, also makes sense in a controversy setting.

Among allusions to the procedures of legal controversy are the references to "summoning" and "answering" (9:16a, 3b, 14, 15a, 19b, 32a), to words of invitation to trial (9:32b), to the demand to know the charges made by one's opponent (10:2b), to the oath of self-exculpation (metaphorically described as a cleansing ritual, 9:30), to the possibility of self-incrimination (9:20), to the plea for mercy to one's opponent (9:15b), to the figure of the arbitrator who mediates between the parties and prevents intimidation of the weaker by the stronger (9:33–34), to the declaration of guilt by one's opponent (9:28b, 29; 10:14b; 9:30 [metaphor]), to the lifting up of the head as a token of acquittal (10:15). Legal speech forms are used incidentally in 9:12b (accusatory question) and 9:22 (legal "sentence").

Related to the language of controversy are the "if" clauses of this speech. "If" clauses belong to the formulation of law, and also, as here, to the contemplation of legal steps to be taken. Explicit "if" clauses in such a context are seen in 9:2, 15, 16, 19, 20, 30; 10:14, 15, creating a marked impression of the experimentation of the speaker's thoughts and the tentative character of the legal procedures here alluded to.

From among the forms of psalmic poetry, the *hymn* form is attested here by the doxology in strict hymnic form, each line introduced with a participle (9:5–10). The description of the creation of an individual person (10:10–12) perhaps represents a further employment of hymnic style. More common are elements of the *appeal*, expressing the plaint of the sufferer (9:17–18; 10:15b, 16–17) or his determination to express his complaint (10:1), his sense of the brevity of life (9:25–26; 10:20a), the appeal to God to "remember" (10:9a), the desire for God to leave him alone (10:20b), and reproach for allowing him to be born (10:18a).

The *wish* form, in this case a wish to be dead, is also used (10:18b–19).

Viewed from the aspect of function, the speech as a whole has the form of *controversy with oneself*, Job debating the wisdom or possibility of legal disputation with God (9:2–24), and of *reproach* against God (9:25–10:22).

The *tonality* of the speech is probably despairing, rather than bitterly ironic (see *Comment* on 9:25–10:22). The *nodal verse* is 9:2 "How can a man be justified by God?"; of almost equal importance for the speech as a whole is 9:13a "God does not withdraw his anger."

Comment

9:1–10:22 Intense though the mood of Job's previous speeches has been, a new level of intensity and poignancy is reached in these chapters. We observe the most developed statement of Job's powerlessness before God so far made (e.g., 9:3–4, 14–20, 30–31), his sense of being trapped (9:15, 20, 27–31), and—most poignant of all—his growing awareness that all God's unremitting care for him, from the moment of his conception onward, was not for his good, but in order to fasten guilt upon him: "This was the secret purpose of thy heart . . . that, if I sinned, thou wouldst be watching me" (10:13–14, NEB). The sarcasm with which he spoke of God's close watch over him in 7:17–20 has now turned entirely to a pathetic sense of having been profoundly deceived (10:8–17). The concluding note is, unsurprisingly, a reiteration of the life-denying wish that he had never been (10:18–19, as in 3:3–13) and of the God-denying wish that he would leave him alone until his imminent death (10:20b–22, as in 17:16b).

From the conclusion of the speech it may appear that Job is condemned to move forever only around the same Dantean circle of his own private hell. But the most significant feature of this speech is that Job has shifted, temporarily at least, out of his preoccupation with sheer suffering, away from his life-denial and his overwhelming sense of bitter disappointment, to ventilate the question of his vindication. From the start he envisages it as a lost cause (9:2b), but he explores it nevertheless. And while the hopelessness of seeking vindication from God throws him, by the end of the speech, back into black despair, he has allowed the thought to play in his mind. It is a thought that he never rejects, one that only intensifies its attraction for him in subsequent speeches (cf. 13:13–23; 16:18–21; 19:23–27; 23:2–14).

Does Job charge God with "cosmic injustice" (R. Gordis, *The Book of God and Man. A Study of Job* [Chicago: University of Chicago Press, 1965] 80)? Some lines in the speech seem to suggest that strongly (e.g., 9:16, 20, 22b, 24, 30–31; 10:15), and several commentators find Job to be arguing that might is right with God, and rejecting Bildad's assertion that God does not pervert justice (8:3). Thus Gordis sees the speech as "a vigorous attack upon the moral government of the world . . . a searing attack upon God's irresponsible and unjust power" (p. 95), and Fohrer comments that according to Job "the human is never right; God is always right since for him might is right. Because he possesses all power, he can make his will his law and carry it out without the possibility of hindrance. Thus his law is wholly injustice."

Despite the apparent support given to this view by the lines referred to (on which the *Comment* should be consulted), it seems rather that the speech is best read as a protest that it is hopeless for a person to seek *vindication* from God. For—if God is withholding vindication, as he is in Job's case—no one can be in a position to compel God to give one anything, not even the vindication one deserves.

We should note that the hopelessness of the quest for vindication is not felt by Job so radically that he forthwith abandons the search. Not only does he revert to the quest at various points in this speech, but also he develops the rather tentative thoughts of 9:3, 14, 19–20, 32–33, in which he simply toys with the possibility of bringing God to trial, into the outright summons to God of 13:22 and 31:35. Indeed, we may well ask what this wondering aloud—in the presence of God, who will be addressed without formality in vv 28, 31—about the possibility of impeaching God really is, unless it is in some way an indirect and hesitant impeachment.

The quest for vindication has only just begun. His previous speeches have not given the possibility a moment's thought, but once he has been prompted to it—perhaps through a delayed reaction to Eliphaz's words in 4:17 (Terrien)—he immediately sets about exploring its ramifications, though his instincts warn him it is a dangerous and futile enterprise. It is perhaps not unnatural, since vindication is a legal concept, that his mind should turn first to legal remedies; but he is dimly aware also that there are other routes he could follow. Only very briefly does he hint at the possibility of simply throwing himself upon God's mercy (9:15b), or of seeking some mediator (9:33), or of attempting to understand God's reasons for so treating him (10:2). But these alternatives remain in the background and do nothing more than create anxiety and indecisiveness about how he should behave.

Finally, we may consider what vindication might mean for Job. As the epilogue will show, only a public restoration of fortunes (42:10), including presumably recovery from illness and the restoration of his progeny and possessions or their equivalent, will ultimately count as vindication worth the name. But what Job wants now is not his good health or possessions but the personal sense of worth and divine acceptance that is symbolized by them. He needs vindication not because he is suffering, but because he has lost his self-esteem and assurance of God's protection (cf. 1:10; 10:8–12).

2–4 Job needs vindication, and he deserves it; his distress here is because he has no way of compelling God to give him vindication. For God is too powerful for humans to compel him to do anything. The issue is Job's vindication rather than God's righteousness, though the two are not entirely distinct.

2 Most commentators believe that Job's opening words, "Truly I know that it is so," refer specifically to Bildad's assertion that God does not pervert justice (8:3). Many regard the "truly" as ironic, since they see Job's speech as an indictment of God on that very ground (cf. Driver, Fohrer, Hesse, Gordis). But it may well be that Job is not disposed to question the righteousness of God (as Weiser argues strongly); his concern is not with the moral governance of the universe but with his own yearning to be vindicated as a righteous man. He can assent in all seriousness to the principle that God does not pervert justice (if that is indeed what v 2a is referring to) and at the same time complain that he cannot gain vindication from God. The issue is not whether God is just but whether he can be prevailed upon. Job knows of no reason why God should be punishing him (cf. 10:2b) but he is so overwhelmed by the majesty (to be precise, the power and the wisdom) of the one who is assailing him that he has no hope of being in the right (cf. v 20).

Another way of taking this sentence has been to see v 2b, "How can a man be just with God?" as the truth to which v 2a assents (so Davidson, JB, NEB). The reference of v 2b is primarily, on this understanding, to the very similar sentence of Eliphaz in 4:17; Job's meaning, however, will be different. For while Eliphaz spoke of the impossibility of anyone's being perfectly righteous, Job speaks of the impossibility (as it seems) of anyone's gaining vindication from God (not exactly as Davidson has it: "How shall man substantiate his righteousness, and make it to appear"; nor as Terrien: "Man cannot be in the right against God" [similarly Peake, Fohrer, Hesse]).

In whichever way the two parts of the verse are related, the primary interpretative issue remains the same: what is it to be "just (יִצְדַּק) with God"? In the context of the whole speech that phrase means: to be "vindicated by God." The active (qal) voice of the verb here functions as the passive of the causative (hiphil) and means "be justified" (as BDB, 842b; cf. 11:2; 40:8; Isa 43:9, 26); to be justified "with" (עִם) God is to be regarded as just by him and to be treated as such. It is possible that the forensic imagery common throughout the speech dominates here also, and that NEB is correct in translating "no man can win his case" (similarly Andersen) but it is misleading to continue: "against God" (as NEB, TOB, Terrien, Horst, Fohrer), for Job is not lamenting the impossibility of *defeating* God in a lawsuit, but of *defending himself* in such a way as to *compel* God to vindicate him (cf. 9:15a, 20, 28).

The form of the rhetorical question, and especially the initial "how" (מַה) is not without significance. The question does not have to be read as a categorical denial, and the stress is upon the hopelessness of discovering *means*. The means that Job naturally thinks of, since the issue is one of justice, are forensic means; but his formulation prompts the question whether there are not other possible means and whether his despair at winning vindication from God is not premature. 9:15b has him raise the possibility of an appeal for clemency rather than insistence upon his rights, while the book as a whole suggests—since Job is successful in the end—that it is not exactly a forensic process that will lead to the desired end but persistent address to God.

One approach to Job's meaning which appears misconceived is to envisage Job as despairing of being in the right because God has the power to make or break the rules of right and wrong at whim. So Fohrer: "Job regards God's being in the right as based upon the inability of anyone to oppose him"; or Driver: "What chance has [Job] to prove himself innocent, when God, who sets himself the standard of righteousness, and is irresponsible and omnipotent, is resolved to prove him guilty?"; or Horst: "God is no doubt always in the right as against man—but only because he has the power." For Job's hopelessness stems not from a sense that God is arbitrary but from a sense of his own powerlessness against the divine decision and his own incapacity to refute the divine judgment (cf. 9:3, 14, 19).

3 It is not affirmed by Job that the only possible way of gaining vindication from God would be by entering into a legal dispute or lawsuit (רִיב) with him. It is rather being said that should one choose that method of approach—and it is a natural one to consider, since Job feels he has been deprived of what is justly his—there is no possibility of success. What is envisaged is a lawsuit in which a person lays charges and one's adversary (in this case God) counters them with questions of cross-examination until the position of one or other of the disputants falls to the ground through inability to give satisfactory answers (ענה, a term from legal language). The dominant legal metaphor in Job has Job as the defendant and God as the plaintiff; here Job envisages changing roles by laying a counter charge (see M. B. Dick, "The Legal Metaphor in Job 31," *CBQ* 41 [1979] 37–50 [40 n. 17]). Cf. 13:22 for a picture of a disputation that consists of speech and counterspeech; the whole dialogue of the Book of Job has the same form, with the position of Job gaining the upper hand in chap. 31, only to be vanquished temporarily by Elihu and decisively by God in chaps. 38–41. Job knows in advance that such a disputation would be futile, for God could in response make a thousand charges or pose a thousand questions to every one a human could devise. Peake's observation is to the point, that when God finally speaks to Job out of the storm his speeches are composed almost entirely of questions to which Job can give no answer. For the futility of disputation with God, cf. 2 Chr 13:12, and for the use of "one" against "a thousand" to indicate impossible odds, cf. Deut 32:30; Josh 23:10; Eccl 7:28 (cf. also Job 33:23; Ecclus 6:6). There is no clear sign that God is regarded in the imagery of this speech as judge (except perhaps for vv 28–31; משפטי in v 15 probably means "opponent"); for a contrary view, seeing a conflict between God's "dual role as litigant and judge," cf. J. J. M. Roberts, "Job and the Israelite Religious Tradition," *ZAW* 89 (1977) 107–14 (111); idem, "Job's Summons to Yahweh: The Exploitation of a Legal Metaphor," *RestQ* 16 (1973) 159–65; the same is true for 13:20–22.

The Hebrew of the verse is equally susceptible of the rendering "if he [God] wished to dispute with him [the human], that person could not answer one in a thousand" of God's questions. So Duhm (though mistakenly arguing that חפץ "be pleased, deign," would not be used of a human; cf. 13:3), Hölscher, Pope, RV, Moffatt, NEBmg. Alternatively, some have understood the second colon as "God would not answer one question in a thousand" (so NEB, TOB, Dhorme, Gordis) (cf. perhaps v 16; 33:13), God refusing "to appear at the bar in answer to so wretched an adversary as man" (Dhorme). The general thrust of the verse is unaffected.

4 Developing the thought of v 3, Job voices his despair of gaining vindication from God through legal disputation by affirming that no one has ever successfully brought God to law. He does not know this from experience, of course, but simply infers it from what he knows of the wisdom and power of God. God is so immeasurably superior to humans that they cannot hope to come off best if they formally make God their adversary.

Again, we do not have here the bitter sarcasm that several commentators find (e.g., Fohrer, Hesse); Job's tone is that of the lament rather than the reproach. Indeed, he does not speak purely out of reverence for the absolute right of God (so Weiser), but rather in all seriousness (cf. Andersen) laments the impossibility of a successful prosecution of God. His grievance is not that God is unjust but that he is inaccessible and rigorous.

We should not fail to notice that Job's despair of gaining vindication from God or of arguing successfully with him is not so radical as to prevent his continuing his plea for vindication and addressing the language of legal disputation to God.

The language of v 4b is thought by Fohrer and Hesse to have a hymnic cast (cf. perhaps Isa 40:26), but the strophic structure which calls for a break after the triplet of vv 2–4, as well as the content of v 4b, show that the verse is to be kept distinct from the hymn of vv 5–10.

5–10 This hymnic doxology to the power of God in nature is formed from two triplets, the former (vv 5–7) depicting destructive or negative acts of God, the latter (vv 8–10) depicting his creative acts and concluding with a "summary appraisal" sentence (v 10; cf. 8:13, 19). The function of the doxology is to elaborate the statement of God's wisdom and power in v 4a by images of his exercise of this wisdom and power (the two are inseparable, as often in Job) in the natural world. The implications of this picture of God are particularly spelled out in the succeeding triplet (vv 11–13); its general effect is to show the impossibility of successful litigation with a God who is so mighty and so capable of violence and anger (vv 5–7). The doxology presents some important contrasts with that of Eliphaz (5:9–16) despite the virtually identical summary sentences (5:9 at the beginning of Eliphaz's doxology and 9:10 at the end of Job's). Eliphaz's doxology has revolved about the *beneficent* acts of God as reverser of human fortunes; Job's will revolve about God's *powerful* acts of creation and upheaval in the natural world. Indeed, destructive acts are included here among God's deeds of power, but Job's theology is hardly novel: Eliphaz also, in speaking of God's behavior toward human beings, had spoken of its more negative aspect when he dwell on God's humiliation of the "crafty" (5:12–14).

Several commentators, especially those who detect an ironical tone in vv 2–4, regard the doxology as a kind of reproach; they emphasize particularly vv 5–7, dealing with the destructive acts of God, even to the extent of denying the authenticity of vv 8–10, which do not share that emphasis (so Beer, Duhm, Budde). Habel calls this a satirical hymn, a hymn to the King of chaos. Davidson sees here "the mere un-moral play of an immeasurable Force." K. Fullerton ("On Job 9 and 10," *JBL* 53 [1934] 321–49 [331]) and Gordis find in v 10, which they take to be a quotation of Eliphaz's words (5:9), an irony that stamps the whole passage with its mark. While it is hard to disprove the existence of irony in many passages, such comments overlook the fact that similar language to Job's in these verses occurs in praises in the Psalter where irony cannot be suspected.

5–6 The doxology exhibits the usual participial style, each verse from v 5 to v 10 beginning with a participle, lit. "the one removing," etc. (for bibliography, see on 5:9–16). The mountains and pillars of the earth form a fundamental part of the cosmic order; their upheaval is therefore very threatening (in Ps 82:5 the threat to the moral order posed by unjust demigods is symbolized as a shaking of the foundations of the earth). The motif of the shaking of the mountains normally appears either (i) as the worst possible calamity which nevertheless cannot terrify the pious (so Ps 46:3–4 [2–3]; 75:4 [3]) or (ii) as accompaniments and signals of the coming of Yahweh for deliverance (so Ps 18:8 [7]; cf. v 16 [15]; 97:4; 114:5–7; Isa 13:13; 29:6; Hab 3:6, 10; Judg 5:4; cf. Exod 19:18). With the latter significance, the anger of Yahweh (against evildoers and oppressors of his people) is several times specified, as here. The language is characteristic of OT accounts of theophany, perhaps deriving in part from descriptions of the appearance of the storm-god (see J. Jeremias, *Theophanie. Die Geschichte einer alttestamentlichen Gattung* [WMANT 10; Neukirchen-Vluyn: Neukirchener Verlag, 1965] esp. 23–24, 88–89). The frequent occurrence of the upheaval motif in descriptions of Yahweh's deliverance makes it impossible to see the main thrust here as depiction of God's *destructive* activity. Indeed, the focus in the Psalms is upon *deliverance* whereas here it is upon God's sheer *power*, but this emphasis, though perhaps one-sided, is not a satirical reversal of the psalmic motif (as is claimed by Fullerton, *JBL* 53 [1934] 330–31; Gordis; W. Whedbee, "The Comedy of Job," *Semeia* 7 [1977] 1–39 [15–16]: "[Job] catalogues examples of the pervasive chaos in creation. . . . What results is an ironic parody of a doxological hymn, which is used only in order to twist its intention . . . [it] portrays [God] as a God of terror who revels in destruction.").

The pillars (עמוד) of the earth here are conceived of as supporting pillars beneath it (cf. Ps 75:4 [3]; 1 Sam 2:8 [מצק]). For the "bases" or "pedestals" (אדן) of the earth, cf. 38:6; and for the "foundations" (מוסד) of the earth more generally cf. Ps 18:16 [15] (= 2 Sam 22:16); 82:5; Prov 8:29; Isa 24:18; Jer 31:37; Mic 6:2; cf. Ps 104:5 (מכון). A similar cosmology is found in Seneca, *Quaestiones naturales,* 6.20. The pillars (עמוד) of heaven (26:11) are different: they support the sky.

7 Envisaged here is the obscuring of the light of sun or stars by eclipses, clouds (cf. 3:5), sandstorms, or preternatural darkness (cf. Exod 10:21–23). This may seem at first a negative display of God's power, but it is remarkable that the bringing about of darkness (sometimes including specifically the absence of sidereal light) is a typical element in the upheaval motif mentioned above; see Ps 18:10b [9b], 12 [11]; 97:2; Isa 13:10; Hab 3:11 (?); cf. also Ezek 32:7–8 where the emphasis is wholly upon the destruction (of Egypt) rather than upon any deliverance for Israel; Joel 2:10 where earthquake and darkness are the accompaniments of the locust plague that is Yahweh's army (against Israel!); 3:15–16 (earthquake and darkness prefacing the day of Yahweh). While the darkness motif sometimes depicts divine hostility, it most commonly develops the theme of God's majesty as witnessed by his control over the most powerful of cosmic phenomena. There is no need to doubt that this is its function in the present passage also.

The idea of sealing up the stars may be that they are restrained by God in their abode and not brought out by him into the night sky (cf. Isa 40:26). Sealing up is the final act of making secure something that is already restrained.

8 Though the participial style is continued, the reference in vv 8–9 is plainly to creation. The phraseology of v 8a was well known in hymnic language and is probably not a late concept displacing that of the fixed firmament (as Fohrer).

A close verbal parallel is Isa 44:24 "I stretch out the heavens, I alone"; cf. also Isa 42:5; 51:13; Jer 10:12; 51:15; Zech 12:1; 1QH 1.9; and Isa 40:22 and Ps 104:2b, where the image is explicitly that of stretching out the heavens "like a tent" or "curtain."

The second half of the line alludes to the myth of the conquest of the sea-monster or dragon in primeval times (not necessarily at creation). As in 7:12, it is the northwest Semitic mythology that is drawn upon, Yam (ים) being the name of the sea-god in Ugaritic literature. Most probably it is the "back" of the sea-monster (NEB) rather than the "waves" of the sea on which God treads (see n. 9:8.a). The same idiom for trampling on the backs of defeated foes occurs in Deut 33:29; Amos 4:13; Mic 1:3 (cf. also Isa 63:3).

9 These three constellations, although they cannot be identified with certainty, were undoubtedly recognized in the ancient world as outstandingly splendid. In Hebrew psalmody reference to these stars was a conventional motif in doxology (cf. Amos 5:8; cf. Job 38:31–32). On the identification of the names, see G. Schiaparelli, *Astronomy in the Old Testament* (Oxford: Clarendon, 1905); N. Herz, "The Astral Terms in Job ix 9, xxxviii 31–32," *JTS* 14 (1913) 575–77; S. Mowinckel, *Die Sternnamen im Alten Testament* (Oslo: Grøndahl, 1928); J.-J. Hess, "Die Sternbilder in Hiob 9:9 und 38:31f," *Festschrift G. Jacob* (ed. T. Manzel; Leipzig: Harrassowitz, 1932) 94–99; R. Mesnard, "Les constellations du livre de Job," *Revue belge de philosophie et d'histoire* 30 (1952) 1–11; O. Neugebauer, "The History of Ancient Astronomy," *JNES* 4 (1945) 1–38; G. R. Driver, "Two Astronomical Passages in the Old Testament," *JTS* ns 7 (1956) 1–11.

The first constellation (עָשׁ, עַיִשׁ in 38:32) has most commonly been identified with Arcturus, the Bear (also known as the Wain). In 38:32 its "children" also are referred to, which would be the three stars that form the tail of the Bear or the pole of the Wain. In Syriac literature, however, the term Iyutha, with which the Syriac version here translates עָשׁ, and no doubt derives from עַיִשׁ, is used of the Hyades, which form a constellation in Taurus, and whose brightest member is the red star Aldebaran (so Schiaparelli, G. R. Driver; hence NEB). Others connect עָשׁ/עַיִשׁ with an Arabic cognate meaning "lion"; some of the stars of Virgo are called in Arabic literature the dogs barking after the Lion (so KB, Fohrer, Hesse).

There is less doubt that the second constellation is Orion. LXX translates with "Orion," and Tg and Pesh have "the giant," which in Arabic is the term for this constellation. In classical mythology Orion was a giant who after his death was bound to the heavens in chains. The Heb. name is כְּסִיל "fool," so the Hebrew myth concerning this constellation may have been of "a giant who, confiding foolishly in his strength, and defying the Almighty, was, as a punishment for his arrogance, bound for ever in the sky" (Driver). 38:31 speaks of the "cords" of Orion, so in one essential respect the Hebrew and classical myths are identical. For myths of Orion as the giant Nimrod, see T. H. Gaster, *Thespis. Ritual, Myth, and Drama in the Ancient Near East* (rev. ed.; New York: Doubleday, 1961) 320–27; idem, *Myth, Legend, and Custom in the Old Testament* (London: Duckworth, 1969) 790.

The third constellation (כִּימָה) is agreed to be the Pleiades (as LXX, though Vg has Hyades). These are a group of seven stars mentioned also in 38:31 and Amos 5:8. In classical mythology (Apollodorus, 1.4.3–4) the Pleiades were pursued by the hunter Orion until the gods changed them into doves and set them among the stars (R. Graves, *Greek Myths* [Harmondsworth: Penguin, 1955] 1:152). The three constellations, the Bear, Orion, and the Pleiades, were well known to the Greeks also in early times (e.g., Homer, *Iliad*, 18.486–88), partly no doubt because of their conspicuousness, and partly because their risings and settings marked the seasons (Driver).

The "chambers of the south" (RSV) (חַדְרֵי תֵמָן), if correctly read, must be a reference either to southerly constellations generally (Driver, NAB, NIV), or to the chambers where wind, snow, and hail are stored, as in 37:9; 38:22 (Peake, Pope), or perhaps to the southern zodiacal circle of stars (Horst, Fohrer). G. R. Driver, following a translation in Origen's Hexapla, revocalized חַדְרֵי to חֹדְרֵי, "the encirclers (of the south)," i.e., the southern band of stars (*circulus austrinus*), further south than the zodiacal circle; hence NEB "the circle of the southern stars." Reference to the southern sky indicates knowledge (whether from personal observation or report) stemming from as far south as the Yemen or Upper Egypt (Mowinckel).

Although the allusions to the trampling of the back of Yam, the sea-god (v 8b), and to Orion, the bound giant, may conjure up a picture of primeval conflict between the creator and mighty adversaries, it is doubtful that the note of hostility or violence is strongly marked; it is rather that all these ancient stories combine in their praise of the might of God.

10 This summary verse presents, in almost identical words to 5:9, a conventional statement of praise. Job is of course not simply a bemused or reverent spectator of the wonderful deeds of God; he knows from his own experience how God's power is used against him in unfriendly and hostile ways (cf. 6:4; 9:34; 10:3, 16). But his mood is one of dismay (cf. what follows in vv 11–13), rather than of the bitterness of irony (as Dhorme, Fohrer, Gordis). Certainly the whole of God's cosmic activity, at creation and in the realm of nature, is viewed by Job entirely from the perspective of how that activity impinges on him. He is not concerned with questions of God's governance of the universe, but wholly with God's treatment of him. The tonality of this verse is quite other than in Eliphaz's speech (5:9).

11–13 These lines on the inapprehensible, unrestrainable God are, in reality, as much about Job as they are about God. That is, they concern God as experienced by Job, and Job as experiencing God. It is not a matter of the "amorality of omnipotence" in general (Terrien), but of Job's sense of incapacity to apprehend God (v 11), to hold him back from his determined action (v 12a), to reproach him (v 12b), and to withstand his anger (v 13).

11 Any attempt to gain vindication from God is doomed to founder on the impossibility of establishing contact with him. The traditional description of theophany, that is, of self-disclosure by God that creates such contact, only serves to reinforce Job's despair; for it is a striking feature of the primary theophany at Sinai that Moses is unable to see God's face as he and his "glory" "pass by" (עבר, as here); Moses can see only God's back (Exod 33:22–23; cf. also 1 Kgs 19:11–13). Job does not expect to see even God's back; the nearest encounter he can have with God is a hurried (חלף) passing by of a figure he cannot see (ראה) or recognize (בין).

12 A second thought makes the likelihood of gaining vindication from God even more remote. He cannot be brought to court for any deprivation he may have caused. No one is in a position to say to him, "What are you doing?" (מה תעשה), the regular words of accusation or reproof (see H.-J. Boecker, *Redeformen des Rechtslebens im Alten Testament* [WMANT 14; Neukirchen-Vluyn: Neukirchener Verlag, 1964] 26–31). This is no novel insight peculiar to Job; Zophar says the same thing (11:10; cf. also 23:13 [Job]), and it is indeed a truism that few religious people could dissent from. But Job is not dealing in generalities; what has just now struck him with force is not that no one can successfully reprove God, but that he, Job, cannot. In these verses (vv 11–13) Job has moved from the more general level, as in vv 2–10, to the level of his own existence. It may even be that God's "theft" ("he snatches away") against which he cannot win an action is really the theft of Job's own reputation, if not the "theft" of Job himself (cf. NAB "should he seize me forcibly . . ."; Fullerton, *JBL* 53 [1934] 323: "he clutcheth (at me).")

13 Indeed, the aspect of God that Job most closely experiences is not his righteousness or creative power but his mighty anger, the anger of a god (אלוה is in emphatic position). That is the final barrier to any move to wring vindication from God: his permanent hostility, as it seems to Job. God does not "turn back" his anger; anger has been his predominant impulse ever since primordial times, when it was unleashed against the sea-monster Rahab, symbol of chaos, and her "partisans" (NEB). There is no one who can hold God back (יְשִׁיבֶנּוּ) from his acts of theft against Job (v 12); and in any case, he on his part makes no effort to hold back (יָשִׁיב) his own rage that drives him to assault Job and frightens off Job from any encounter or confrontation.

For other references to Rahab as God's adversary in a primeval battle, see 26:12; Ps 89:11 [10]; Isa 51:9. The name is probably connected with a root meaning "be boisterous, agitated" (cf. Akk. *raʾabu* "storm at," in reference to the raging waves). Other allusions to the conflict have been noted at 9:8; 8:12; 3:8. In the Babylonian creation epic, *Enuma elish*, the chaos monster Tiamat is also depicted as being subdued along with her helpers: "And the gods, her helpers who marched at her side, trembling with terror turned their backs about in order to save their life" (4.107–109; *ANET*, 67).

The myth of a conflict of Yahweh and the sea-monster is never recounted in the OT; but the number of allusions to it makes it certain that it formed a part of Hebrew literature (oral, if not written). See further, J. Day, *God's Conflict with the Dragon and the Sea. Echoes of a Canaanite Myth in the Old Testament* (Cambridge: CUP, 1985); on Rahab's helpers, see p. 41. There is nothing in the OT to suggest that the battle was a stage in or precondition for creation (the reference to Tehom, the "deep," in Gen 1:2 is not to Tiamat, and does not indicate conflict); but obviously it was regarded as an event of ancient, or rather, primordial times.

14–16 In these lines on the impossibility of legal disputation with such a God the thought is: If God is determined upon anger (v 3), what hope is there of a successful disputation with him? If the cross-examination should focus on Job, he could not withstand the strength of God's interrogation (v 14); even if he has nothing but right on his side, he could not withstand God's verbal onslaught any more than he has withstood his physical assaults (v 15). And if on the other hand Job should be the interrogator, he could have no confidence that his voice could be heard above the roar of the divine anger. It is not that Job fears the perversion of justice—although no doubt it is a perversion of justice to be denied access to justice—but that his sense of God's anger directed against him utterly unnerves him.

14 If the primordial powers of chaos could not withstand the wrath of God, how much less (אף כי) can a mere mortal (אנכי, "I" emphatic)? Any legal disputation over the question of Job's vindication is foredoomed to failure. For if God should take the part of prosecutor or judge, Job would be no match for his questions (cf. v 3) which would inevitably wear him down and result in his losing his case (cf. on v 3). The fury of his opponent would render Job tongue-tied, so that he would be incapable of choosing the right or effective words with which to defend himself. The wrath of God that Job shrinks from encountering further is not a divine characteristic for which Job is reproaching God; he is not protesting that the world is ruled by an amoral and arbitrary wrath (contrast Fohrer), but that God's wrath, which is for him a given fact of experience, is bound to sabotage any attempt at reasonable argument—for which the processes of law here present themselves as a symbol.

15 Job does not doubt that he is "in the right," "innocent" (צדקתי), even though he uses the hypothetical form. But mere innocence is unable to fashion "answers" (the term is forensic) to the hostile interrogation of an angry God. Job is so outclassed by God (cf. also v 32) that he can approach him only as a suppliant, for Job and the one he would make his legal opponent (מְשֹׁפְטִי) by issuing a summons to him (v 3a) are not on the same footing. The same idea of being forced to beg for what one is actually entitled to is found in a different setting in 19:16.

Why then does Job not abandon what he recognizes to be a futile endeavor, and plead for mercy—which he admits is the only posture worth adopting toward God? Bildad has already counseled such an act of supplication (התחנן) to the Almighty (8:5). The answer is that Job cannot see how he can plead for mercy without abandoning his integrity; and he will not abandon the truth as he knows it even in order to win release from his sufferings. So he says, "I could only appeal for mercy," and not, "I must appeal for mercy" (RSV), nor "I plead . . . for mercy" (NEB).

16 Throughout the chapter, Job has been envisaging a formal summons to God that would compel him to vindicate Job or at least to show good cause why he will not vindicate Job. In vv 14–15a he has contemplated the paralysis that would overcome him if God were to respond to his summons by counter-questions, and in v 15b has realized that he could conjure up the strength only to beg for mercy. Now he considers a less frightening prospect, but no less hopeless: even if he should "call" (i.e., issue a summons) and if God should "answer," i.e., should agree to disputation with Job, and if then Job himself should enjoy the luxury of cross-examining (rather than being interrogated), what confidence could he have that God was listening to his questions? It is not that God can be expected to behave unrighteously and ignore the due processes of justice, but that the majestic God hymned by the doxology of vv 5–10, who is also the inapprehensible, unrestrainable God depicted by vv 11–13, is hardly likely to concern himself too seriously with the protests of Job. Human "calling" (קרא) and divine "answering" (ענה) are a familiar pair in the psalmic language of appeal (e.g., Ps 3:5 [4]; 17:6), but here in Job we do not have the address to the judge as deliverer but the summons to a party in a lawsuit.

Andersen finds it improbable that Job should here express such skepticism about God's listening to his arguments, since elsewhere in the book a hope for a hearing is at the basis of all his speeches, and is what he insists upon until the end: "Let the Almighty answer!" (31:35). Andersen therefore suggests that "not" (לא) is in fact the assertative particle "certainly" (לְ; cf. on v 33). Alternatively, Dahood argues that לא is a noun meaning "nothing," and the object of "answer"; the verse would then read: "if I call he answers me nothing: still I am convinced that he hears my voice" (so also Blommerde). But such a supposition is unnecessary, for we have already noted in this speech (cf. on v 4) the tension between Job's practice and what he declares to be impossible or hopeless.

17–20 Job and God are not equal before the law: God's assaults upon Job make it impossible for Job to reach even the first phase of a formal attempt to gain vindication. And even supposing a lawsuit could be started, the majesty of God would surely overawe Job into misspeaking himself (v 20).

17–18 These verses do not depict what will happen to Job in the lawsuit, but present a reason why Job cannot believe that God would take his case seriously enough to listen to his interrogations: Job has in the past experienced God too often as one who rides roughshod over him, cares nothing for him, and treats him with disproportionate hostility (cf. 7:12, 20). The language of the lawsuit is temporarily abandoned while Job depicts with the imagery of physical conflict his prior experience of God on which is based his expectations for any forensic disputation with God.

Since it is somewhat inappropriate to speak of a tempest "crushing" someone (see n. 9:17.a), we should surely read בְּשַׂעֲרָה "for a hair" instead of בִּשְׂעָרָה "with a tempest," and thereby improve the parallelism as well (see n. 9:17.b). For a mere trifle (a "hair"), or indeed for nothing at all (חנם, "gratuitously"), God crushes him and "rains blows" (NEB) on him. So relentless is the assault that Job has no chance to catch his breath (cf. 7:19); the imagery of attack with poisoned arrows (cf. 6:4) may also appear here in God's compelling him to "drink bitterness" (ממרור) or poison. For bitterness (מְרֹרָה) as poison, cf. 20:14; and for the association of "drinking" (שׂבע, lit. "being satiated with") poison with being pierced by arrows, cf. Lam 3:12–13, 15.

19 The two halves of the verse sum up in turn Job's experience of God and his expectation of God. Hitherto his experience has been of the domineering might of God, which can be properly recognized only when it is felt or suffered; the fact that "he is the mighty one" (cf. v 4) negates every other force. Transfer the sheer strength of God to the judicial sphere, and Job's hopelessness is confirmed: no one can compel God into any kind of debate or litigation. Job's quest for vindication from God is as futile as resistance to God's power (cf. v 13a).

Job does not mean that he expects that a "summons" to God would be met with the kind of physical violence he has been suffering; he simply realizes afresh that his experience of God's power makes absurd any ambition to constrain God in the way a legal disputation "binds" the parties. For the same idea, see Jer 49:19 (= 50:44).

20 This verse, though connected by the assertion of Job's innocence (צדק) and blamelessness (תם) with what follows (vv 21–22), still has in mind the lawsuit setting. It climaxes the sense of futility voiced in v 19 by imagining what would happen should the impossible be achieved and should God allow himself to be constrained into legal disputation. Earlier, when Job had envisaged that stage in a judicial process, he had bitterly predicted that either he would be unable to answer the divine interrogation (vv 14–15a) or else he would be unable to believe that God was paying any attention to his cross-examination (v 16). Now, in a noble excess of despair, he reckons on an even worse outcome than silence, whether his own or God's: overcome by the divine sovereignty, his own mouth would condemn him (cf. 15:6), innocent though he is. God would not have to win the case; Job would lose it single-handed. Rowley remarked, reasonably enough, that "Job is afraid he will be overawed and confused by God's presence and will argue against himself," but Duhm's more subtle comment is perhaps more appropriate: "'my own mouth' condemns me, since I can do nothing but implore God (as if I were a sinner), and cannot maintain my right." The Heb. permits the translation of v 20b, "*he* would prove me perverse" (so e.g., RSV), and some have read "his mouth" for "my mouth" in the first line (see n. 9:20.a), but it is not to Job's purpose in this speech to argue that God is unjust or "perverts the right" (8:3), however unjust it may be for God to treat Job with such hauteur and rage.

21–24 Job puts aside for the time being his dream of a satisfactory confrontation with God, and muses on his present sorry state and what it proves about God's attitude to humankind. The facts about Job are two: he is blameless, and he is in despair. A God who can allow that combination of conditions can only be cruelly disposed toward humankind. Two examples follow of how God only exacerbates the misery brought about by natural (v 23) and social (v 24) calamities.

21–22 The rather cryptic phrases of v 21 have an unusual staccato rhythm of three two-beat phrases, perhaps suggesting the intensity of Job's emotions (so Pope and others). The key to the two verses must be the phrase "it is all one" (lit. "it is one thing"). At first sight, what is "one" is the fate of the blameless and the wicked (v 22b; cf. Tg "it is one measure," i.e., good and bad are requited alike; so too Gordis). But the position of "therefore I say" rules that interpretation out, and requires us to find the "one" thing in what precedes. What is "all one" is not, as Duhm thought, God's wrath whether Job is without cause hounded to death or whether he is struck down precisely because of his obstinacy in maintaining his integrity. Rather, what is "one" in v 21 is the man Job—in his contrasting states: on the one hand, he is "blameless"; on the other, he despises his life. No blameless person should feel so hopeless; it is the wicked who should hold their life cheap, for it is they who are likely to be cut off at any moment. Only if God treats the blameless in the same way as the wicked can the contradictories in Job's experience be true. And they *are* true, which goes to show that indiscriminate hostility to humans, good and bad alike, is the settled disposition of God.

As so often, Job extrapolates from his own experience to large statements about God and the world; but what else is he to do? When the only comprehensive theological theories find no room for him, must he not reject them and use his own experience as a paradigm? In the end, his experience must be accommodated within a more comprehensive, and more humane, theology; but this is not yet the end, and the experience has still to be lived through.

Savage and wild, or perhaps rather, quietly bitter and desperate, though Job's indictment of God may be, no more than in other verses does Job accuse God of moral arbitrariness or perversity. No, it is precisely God's undeviating principle of anger and his unbending position of superiority over mortals that engenders Job's complaint. It is not that God destroys the blameless and makes the wicked to flourish; that would be moral perversity. Nor is it that one never knows whether rewards or punishments will be visited on the good or the bad; that would be moral arbitrariness. Nor it is that God treats good and wicked alike with equal beneficence (cf. Matt 5:45); that would be morally defensible. Rather, in unremitting hostility toward humans (cf. vv 13, 17–18, 34), he visits the innocent and the unrighteous alike only with destruction; and that is morally inexcusable. The participial construction (מְכַלֶּה) perhaps echoes the style of the doxology (vv 5–10), as if this were another of God's regular attributes (cf. P. E. Dion, "Formulaic Language in the Book of Job: International Background and Ironical Distortions," *SR* 16 [1987] 187–93).

One phrase, in the middle of v 21, remains obscure: literally, "I do not know myself." The meaning is probably not that Job is a riddle to himself, nor that he mistrusts his own integrity (cf. Dhorme: "Am I perfect? I do not know myself!"; similarly JB), but that he does not care about himself; cf. the similar use of "know" in Gen 39:6; Deut 33:9; and see D. Winton Thomas, "The Root ידע in Hebrew," *JTS* 35 (1935) 298–306 (300–301); idem, "A Note on וַיֵּדַע אֱלֹהִים in Exod. II 25," *JTS* 49 (1948) 143–44. Gordis offers the interesting rendering "I am beside myself [with misery]" (cf. Cant 6:12 where the verb seems to mean "I am beside myself [with joy]"). S. M. Paul comes close to clinching this interpretation by noting the expression in an Akkadian medical text, "he does not know himself" (*ramānšu la îde*), describing a loss of consciousness ("An Unrecognized Medical Idiom in Canticles 6,12 and Job 9,21," *Bib* 59 [1978] 545–47). It is not clear, however, that this yields a better sense in the context than "I do not care about myself." In any case the phrase seems parallel to what follows, "I despise my life." Life is not for him the highest good, since it is in any case foreshortened (cf. vv 25–26). His honor is all that matters to him now; "he clings to his integrity as the last vestige of meaning" (Habel).

23 The cruelty of God goes further still. Not only is destruction God's goal for the good as well as the wicked, but he mocks derisively at the fate of the innocent when they are overtaken by some calamity. The evil too perish in the natural disaster implied by the word "scourge" (שׁוֹט), but God's special sadistic pleasure lies in the fate of the righteous.

The tradition of psalmic rhetoric felt no discomfort with the idea of Yahweh's mocking (לעג) the wicked, whether rebellious nations destined for subjugation (Ps 2:4), or the persons or nations who oppose the pious psalmist (Ps 59:9 [8]). In the wisdom tradition also, the righteous rejoice with scorn over the sudden doom of the wicked (Job 22:19 [Eliphaz]), and, in a close analogy, wisdom announces that she will mock at the calamity and panic of fools who have neglected her counsel (Prov 1:26). But to rejoice at the unhappy lot of the righteous is another matter: "He who mocks the poor insults his Maker; he who is glad at calamity will not go unpunished" (Prov 17:5). On that principle, God, according to Job, ranks himself among the godless and will suffer the consequences of his lack of innocence (לֹא יִנָּקֶה).

How does Job know that God mocks the innocent? Of course he knows nothing but what he infers; and he infers from the hideous suffering of the innocent that only a sadist could be responsible for what happens. It is again his own situation that is the touchstone: "his conception is but the reflection of his own case, as he conceived it, flung over the world" (Davidson). Both here and in v 24a the primary disaster is a sheer event, for which God is not held responsible (the still-current view of a "Shemitic mind which had no conception of second causes" [Davidson] is incidentally refuted by the text). It is God's response that forms the gravamen of Job's charge, and it is his response, rather than the disasters themselves, that may be referred to by the words of v 22 "He destroys blameless and wicked alike" (NEB). The reason must be that it is not primarily the justice of God that is on trial in this speech, but his sympathy. While many commentators have read the whole speech as an indictment of "cosmic injustice" or of the moral arbitrariness of God, a closer reading suggests that the nub of Job's resentment is the divine aloofness (9:4–12, 16, 19, 32) which terrifies humans and is experienced by them as cruelty and anger (9:5b, 12a, 13, 17–18, 22–24, 34–35; 10:3–17).

How surprising that such radical criticism of God's character should forswear attributing to his direct intervention the sudden disaster that sweeps away both guilty and innocent!

24 Again, it is not Job's point that God is the cause of social injustice and oppression. How a land comes to be delivered into the power of a wicked man is not the issue. Rather, it is what God does, or does not do, about such a calamity. As with the former example of God's cruelty in v 23, God not only fails to relieve the plight of the innocent, but makes it more bitter or more oppressive: in v 23 he mocks the innocent by not intervening to deliver them from natural disasters, in v 24 he abandons an innocent population to the caprices of a tyrant by "covering the faces" of its judges so that the people are denied justice.

Nothing in Job's speech comes so close as this sentence to a direct accusation of injustice on God's part. It seems to some that Job is indeed formally rebutting Bildad's affirmation that God does not pervert justice (8:3). Nevertheless, that is not really Job's point. The parallelism with the preceding verse shows clearly that God's behavior is being looked at, not from the standpoint of objective ethics, but from the perspective of those in suffering, here the people subject to a wicked ruler and corrupt officials. The accent of Job's charge lies on the cruelty of God's attitude toward those who are wrongfully oppressed by a tyrannous state. All that Job really knows is that unjust societies actually exist and that God does not do anything about them; that is a further sign, he infers, of how God "mocks at the calamity of the innocent" (v 23b). He must be "covering the faces" of the judges who could otherwise alleviate the people's lot.

The expression "to cover the face (or, eyes)" of judges would most naturally refer to the giving of bribes; cf. Exod 23:8 "a bribe blinds (עור) the officials"; and Gen 20:16, where a "covering of the eyes" (כסות עינים) is a pacification gift so that the wrong done will not be regarded and prosecuted (see further, M. Greenberg, "Bribery," *IDB*, 1:465; Job 6:22). Here a specific reference to bribery is unlikely, and what is meant is a blinding of subordinate officials to the misery of people living under a tyrannical ruler.

The Hebrew permits the rendering, "The land is given over into the hand of the wicked one, who covers the face of its judges" (so Gordis), which would remove the most shocking utterance from this speech. But on this interpretation, v 24c would be an unintelligible sequel, and the parallel with v 23, in which the second line also has God as the subject of the verb, makes the usual interpretation of v 24 almost certain.

The exemplary nature of vv 23–24 should be noted; Job is not saying that the earth is in general given into the power of the wicked, as if in protest against the conventional theology that the pious will inherit the earth (Ps 37:9;

Prov 2:21; 10:30; Matt 5:5) (so Pope), but illustrating God's behavior in a particular situation. Some have seen here an allusion to a historical event (Duhm), to an oppression of the Jews (Peake), or even specifically to the Babylonian exile (Terrien), others merely a stock sentence from skeptical wisdom (Horst); there is no way of knowing where the truth lies.

The last line, "If it is not he, who then is it?" draws special attention to itself as the only third colon of a verse in the whole chapter (cf. however 10:1, 3, 15, 17, 22 [?]). It can only be seen as a reservation, however slight, to the angry or desperate dogmatism of vv 21–24, and as an acknowledgment of the necessarily inferential character of that critique of God. We do not have here some general statement of divine responsibility for all that happens in the world of humans, but the expression of a distressing conviction that the cruelty that life exhibits can only reflect a divine sadism. Such is the understandably distorted view Job has obtained through a single-eyed extrapolation from his own bitter experience of God. It is as one-sided as the statement of v 22b, that God "destroys both the blameless and the wicked"—that is, only destroys and never prospers. But it does at least betoken a radical monotheistic faith in Job: it does not occur to him to blame the Satan for life's miseries. And that radical monotheism that leads from every aspect of life ultimately to God will in time lead Job to the point of encounter with the one whom he can now only regard as his enemy.

25–31 The monologue gives way to the address: with some echoes of the lament form Job turns himself toward God, and addresses him in the second person. A brief reflection on the brevity of his life centers upon the perpetual misery of his days (vv 25–26). He cannot pretend his misery does not exist, for his sufferings are a constant reminder that God regards him as guilty (vv 27–28), and is determined to continue doing so, regardless of Job's efforts to exculpate himself (vv 29–31).

The themes of this strophe are tightly woven together: the "no good" that is the focus of vv 25–26 is the point of departure for the proposal in v 27 that he should put his plight to the back of his mind. That proposal in turn is introduced only as the hypothesis (protasis) which is overturned by the remainder of the sentence (v 28), in which his present plight becomes more evidently the expression of God's judgment of him. That judgment is then the ground for the sense of the hopelessness of self-exculpation (v 29), whereupon the theme of the futility of self-defense is further elaborated (vv 30–31).

Two moves are here contemplated by Job that could lead him out of the cul-de-sac: each is introduced by "if." He could attempt to banish the sense of suffering from his mind (v 27), or he could attempt to purge himself of any conceivable guilt, by an oath of exculpation (to which the symbolic language of ritual washing probably points). Neither of these avenues, he realizes, offers any real escape, and he is thrown back afresh on the necessity for a forensic settlement of his case (vv 32–35).

25–26 With these verses we reach the major turning point of the speech, for we encounter here the transition from the monologue of 9:2–24, in which God is a distant figure, referred to generally simply as "he," to the personal address that is sustained, with the exception of vv 32–35, to the end of the speech, reaching new intensities of emotion in 10:8–17. It is characteristic of Job's speeches to move from monologue or address to the friends to address to God in the latter half of the speech; this example is exceptional in acknowledging the interlocutors only in 9:2a. Admittedly, the first verb of address does not occur until v 28b, but the sentence that contains it begins with v 27, and vv 25–26 are unquestionably connected with what follows them.

It has seemed strange to many commentators that so soon after declaring that he cared nothing for his life (v 21), Job should be lamenting the brevity of his days. Some have seen in the sudden shift of mood the hand of "a master of the psychology of suffering" (Terrien; similarly Duhm), others evidence of Job's inconsistency. But as we have noted on 7:1–3, 6 (and cf. the apparent contradiction of mood between 7:6 and 7:16), the theme of the brevity of life can be employed for various purposes; here the only purpose that blends with the context is uncovered if we regard the phrase "they have seen no good" as the center of this sketch. The days of one's life may be expected to yield varying experiences; Job, unlike other people, must affirm that the rapid succession of days that has unfolded before him have brought to him only one experience: no good. Every day the same deprivation of joy lies in store for him; no matter how quickly one day gives place to the next, the one unvarying aspect marks them all. The theme of this vignette, then, is not the brevity of life as such but the misery of life that is in no way relieved by the progression of the days. In 7:7 Job had predicted that his eye would never again see good (טוב; cf. also 17:15); here, in reviewing the past, he reckons that he has never seen good (טובה) (is this the same Job who, on his own admission, has received "good" at the hand of Yahweh [2:10]?). The connection of this thought to what follows is obvious.

Three striking images of the swiftness of the days of one's life are used (for others, cf. on 7:6). The runner is the swift carrier (KJV "post") who brings news (cf. 2 Sam 18:19–23; Isa 41:27; 52:7). The reed boats are no doubt are the Egyptian papyrus skiffs (כלי גמא) mentioned in Isa 18:1–2 as transporting "swift messengers" and perhaps alluded to again in Job 24:18; Pliny and other ancient authors note the use of papyrus for building light boats (*Nat. hist.* 23.22; 6.24; Plutarch, *De iside et isiride,* 18; Lucan, 4.136; Heliodorus, 10.460; Herodotus, 2.96) (for illustration, see *ANEP,* pl. 109).

The eagle's swoop (or rather, "stoop," the technical term in falconry for the swift descent on the quarry) is a familiar image of speed; see also 39:27–30; Deut 28:49; 2 Sam 1:23; Prov 23:5; Jer 4:13; Hab 1:8; Lam 4:19; cf. *Baal and Yam (CTA* 2) 4.15, 21, 24 (Gibson, 44); *Aqhat (CTA* 18) 4.17, 20, 30 (Gibson, 112–13); *ANET,* 131a, lines 14, 16, 21. The eagle (נשר) is also the vulture. Gordis remarks on the ascending order of speed in the three similes—the runner, the skiff, and the eagle; but his further observation that the runner represents speed, the papyrus skiff adds the idea of fragility, and the eagle as vulture the theme of cruelty is less persuasive. The three similes happen to come from three spheres—land, water, and air (Fohrer)—but their collocation may be accidental. The similes of the boat and the bird as images of the brevity of life are developed in Wisd 5:10–11, where a third simile, of the arrow, is added.

27–28 Is there any way of escaping the constant misery of a man refused vindication (cf. v 2b)? As in 7:13, Job contemplates a means of relief, only to realize immediately its futility. If he resolves to have done with his moaning to the point where he has forgotten it entirely ("forget my moaning" is a compressed phrase), and to put a brave face on things (בלג, lit. "brighten my face") his resolve is undermined by the fear of what new sufferings may lie in store for him, for he is convinced that God does not regard him as an innocent man and is certain to prolong his agony.

The "pains" of which he is afraid are the inevitable punishments for a person held accountable by God; it is not that the attempt to be cheerful will itself provoke further divine hostility (Rowley). The verdict of God that pronounces him guilty is not one that he dreads will be passed upon him (contrast most versions, e.g., RSV "I know that you will not hold me innocent"), but one that he already knows to have been passed against him. The same verdict that has resulted in his recent sufferings still holds, and fills him with disquiet for the future. Elsewhere in the chapter the forensic imagery has envisaged God as a fellow litigant (cf. vv 3a, 32) whether defendant (v 16) or prosecutor (vv 3a, 14). Here the language may suggest that God is seen as the judge who has delivered a verdict, but not necessarily so; the other party to the lawsuit may properly be said not to hold his adversary innocent (לא תנקני), and he is certainly in a position, if his arguments reduce his opponent to silence, of declaring him "guilty" (v 29). In any case, with v 32, the imagery of the bipartisan disputation is resumed.

29 This verse is a bridge from the collapse of the first possible move to the contemplation of the second, v 29a linking with v 28b, and v 29b with v 30.

The conviction that he will be treated as being in the wrong, no matter what happens, sabotages the second possibility (vv 30–31) before he even puts it into words. But his sense of the "futility" (הבל), lit. "breath," the word frequently translated "vanity" in Ecclesiastes, is not so overwhelming as to dry him up in mid-speech. The feeling of hopelessness that he expresses is real enough, but he knows other feelings as well, which we sense not through his explicit utterances but through the sheer fact that he continues to speak and argue.

30–31 Is there another way for Job to establish his innocence? A solemn oath of exculpation (such as in fact he will use in chap. 31 as his last line of defense) is indeed a possibility. He speaks of such an oath metaphorically, as a "washing" of himself with the finest cleansing agents of his world, soapwort, the roots of the plant *leontopetalon*, and lye, an alkaline solution. Personal cleanliness was probably much more commonly effected by covering the skin with oil which was then scraped or rubbed off. To apply soap or lye to the body is a rather extreme and certainly very thorough form of cleansing. But no matter how energetically Job should attempt to clear himself, the outcome would inevitably be confirmed presumption of guilt on his part, since God has obviously not forsworn his determination to afflict Job.

The washing of hands was a well-known ritual means of purification, a symbolic declaration of innocence (cf. Deut 21:6; Ps 26:6; 73:13 [where also it is "in vain" (ריק)]; Matt 27:24). In prophetic theology, it is recognized that some sins are too serious to be purged by purely ritual means; hence in Jer 2:22 Israel's guilt will still be apparent even if it washes itself with lye (ברית), and in Isa 1:18 and Ps 51:4, 9 [2, 7] (influenced by prophetic theology); only God can perform adequate cleansing from sin. Job envisages a similar washing to that described in Jer 2:22, but the verb he uses is more emphatic (התרחצתי, the hithpael probably being iterative [Andersen]). On the issue of the influence of prophetic theology on Job, cf. J. J. M. Roberts, "Job and the Israelite Religious Tradition," *ZAW* 89 (1977) 107–14 (111).

The image Job uses for God's expected ignoring of his claim to innocence is a striking one: God will take him, as he stands freshly clean from his washing, and will plunge him mother-naked into a filthy pit or cesspool, so that his very clothes will shun him. (It is improbable, as against Pope, Habel, that there is a reference to a custom of providing clean clothes for the acquitted, as in Zech 3:3–5.) The savagery of the image reflects the bitterness of Job's feeling that no matter how he strives to gain vindication, it is in vain (v 29b), since God will not give up accounting him guilty. The sequential narrative of the metaphor ("if I . . . , then God") is not to be correlated with some actual sequence of events that Job foresees; it is a dramatization of the conflict he feels between his claim to innocence and God's "guilty" verdict upon him which are present realities.

32–35 Since the possibilities reviewed in vv 25–31 are without promise, Job reverts to the idea of a legal disputation. Because he and God can never be disputants on the same footing (v 32), what Job needs is an arbitrator who can mediate between the two parties (v 33). But since no such arbitrator exists, Job is cast back on his own resources; he will have to argue his case with God single-handed. Very well, says Job; but I do not have the courage to enter upon such a dispute with God unless he promises me safe conduct. It is hard enough (nay, impossible!) to contend with him in words; to contend with his strength, and to argue from a position of weakness and terror (v 34), is unthinkable. Take away from me the numbing fear he inspires in me, and, yes, I believe I have it in me to engage in controversy with him.

Chap. 10 contains the words he would use (no, the words he *does* use) in the confrontation he here steels himself for.

32 The legal recourse open to any wronged human is denied to Job because his adversary is God (the imagery of the bipartisan conflict presumed in vv 3, 14–16, 19 is reverted to). Job cannot respond to God's handling of him by the challenge that they should go to court together, each of them equal before the law. The expression "to enter into litigation with" (בוא במשפט עם/את) or "to bring to litigation" (הביא במשפט) usually designates an experience to be avoided if possible when God is one of the parties (cf. Roberts, *RestQ* 16 [1973] 160). A psalmist prays to be delivered from such a lawsuit (Ps 143:2), Isaiah uses its imminence as a threat (Isa 3:13–14), and Qoheleth uses it as an ultimate sanction against excessive self-indulgence (Eccl 11:9). Job however now realizes that, given only some relief from his present anxieties, there is nothing that he would like better than a confrontation with God.

Job first says that since God is not a human he is unable to "answer" (ענה) him (v 32a). But God has not in fact questioned him, and Job is not at this moment imagining a future scene where God will have initiated a disputation (as in vv 14–15a). We must suppose that the "answer" Job would like to make would be in response to God's present attitude toward him. By applying his "rod" (v 34) to Job, God has declared that he has already judged Job to be a sinner (cf. v 28b). Job would "reply" to this hostile judgment by voicing a challenge, "Let us go to court together!" But no, formal disputation is out of the question, and Job will have to be content with an informal, do-it-yourself controversy (chap. 10) that may yield no satisfactory result or no result at all.

33 The figure of a mediator or arbitrator (מוֹכִיחַ, lit. "one who judges, reproves") is introduced. It is not clear whether he is "a mediator who settles the quarrel by reconciliation, a negotiator who brings both parties together" (Andersen), or an arbiter superior to both the parties and able to impose his authority (as NEB) upon them both. He places his hands on the two parties either to symbolize his power or jurisdiction over both of them (for a similar expression, cf. Ps 139:5) or as a gesture of reconciliation (Terrien). While the figure of the mediator derives ultimately from the practice of law, it is conceivable that in the ancient Near East one might also appeal to a personal god to mediate between oneself and one of the high gods who was distressing one (cf. "one of the holy ones," 5:1; so Pope, Habel); whether this is in the background of Job's thought is hard to say, but plainly Job expects nothing from any quarter. N. C. Habel, "Only the Jackal is My Friend: On Friends and Redeemers in Job," *Int* 31 (1977) 227–36 (232–33), interestingly relates this figure to the vision of the ideal friend which Eliphaz and the others have failed to realize, and to the "redeemer" figures (16:19–21; 19:25). It is not entirely à propos to introduce here the idea of a covenant between God and humans which has now been abrogated (as P. Sacchi, "Giobbe e il Patto," *Hen* 4 [1982] 175–84), but Job is certainly expressing his alarm at the realization that normal relations between God and humankind cannot any longer be relied upon.

The MT has Job say that there is no such person—which is undoubtedly the case—but it is more probable that we should read the negative particle לֹא as the wish particle לוּא or לוּ (see n. 9:33.a), as RSVmg, NEB, NAB, NIV. Those who have resisted this alteration have done so on the ground that v 32 has already effectively ruled out any possibility that such a person could exist, and v 33 is based on the assumption that no such arbitrator exists. But לוּ can express a wish contrary to fact (cf. GKC, § 151e, Pope)—hence the translation given above—so no real objection to taking the sentence as a (hopeless) wish remains. And perhaps the link with the following verses is as follows: Would that there were such an arbiter! He could remove God's "rod" from me. Then I could speak out without any fear (so NIV). Strahan nicely observes that "the man who uses such language is ostensibly pleading for justice; but deeper down he is seeking reconciliation, he is thirsting for love."

34–35 The Heb. of v 34a can mean either "let him (God) remove his rod," or "who (the mediator) would remove (God's) rod." On balance the latter seems more probable (so too JB, NAB, NIV, Dhorme, Terrien); it would be the mediator's responsibility to see that one party to a dispute was not intimidated or overawed by the other. God's "rod" is the instrument of his anger which engenders fear (cf. 21:9; Lam 3:1; cf. Isa 10:5); it is experienced by Job as God's rejection of him which his suffering at God's hands signifies. If the anxiety that his suffering causes him—not least because it is psychic suffering as much as physical—could cease and relations with God could be normalized, Job now feels strong enough to imagine himself engaging in controversy with God without fear (v 35a) despite God's majesty and wrath (vv 4, 19), so firm now is his confidence in his innocence. Difficult though v 35b is, the most straightforward reading of "for I am not so in myself" is "I am aware of nothing to make me afraid of Him, if He acts not in might, but in right" (Gray; similarly Peake). What has made Job lose his nerve is not a fading of his conviction of his innocence, but the sheer terror induced by God's anger—of which this chapter has been full. The appeal, "let not dread of thee terrify me," will be made again later, in a direct second person address (13:21), again as a desired precondition for a legal disputation (cf. also Elihu's assurance that [unlike God?] no fear of him need terrify Job, 33:7).

But all of this new strength and confidence stems from a wish contrary to fact (introduced by לֹא, v 33). There *is* no arbiter, so God's rod will not be removed, the fear will not be quieted, and a formal controversy with God will not (as yet) be entered upon. But strangely enough, the mere contemplation of a nonexistent possibility has in reality injected a resilience into Job; if he will not embark upon a formal controversy with God, he has surprised himself by the announcement (v 35b) that he does not feel in his inner self the kind of numbing dread of God that would foreclose dialogue with him; it is God's wrath, and what an angry God can do even to a righteous man, that has clouded his mind to the possibility that is indeed still open to him. Even if he risks his life to do so (10:1a), he can—and he will—open his mouth, "give free utterance to (his) complaint" (10:1b RSV), ask God why he holds him guilty, why he oppresses him. No matter that God would never agree to a court hearing, that Job could have no hope of a response to his challenge, "Let us go to court together" (v 32b); he can still ventilate his grief, he can still "speak to God" (10:2a).

10:1–22 Continuing the second major section of the speech, Job returns (after 9:32–35) to the second person form of address, and throughout persistently addresses God (there are 40 grammatical markers of the address in vv 2–17). Is this address to be designated a "prayer of lament" (Weiser) or an "accusation" (Fohrer)? There is no doubt that a number of elements of the accusation appear here (see *Form*), but the speech contains such a mixture of forms and motifs that no closer form-critical classification than "address" is possible. Its tonality is sometimes that of the accusation (vv 2–7), sometimes that of lament (vv 15–17), or appeal (vv 20–22), but its form is all its own.

The structure of these verses is fourfold: (1) program for the speech (vv 1–2); (2) possible motivations for God's treatment of Job (vv 3–7); (3) the contradiction between the apparent and the hidden purpose of God in creating and sustaining Job (vv 8–17); (4) appeal for release from God's oppressive presence (vv 18–22).

1 The language of this announcement, establishing the tonality of the whole speech, is reminiscent of 7:11 which also led into the most radical and ironic challenge of God's intentions toward Job. In one point, however, Job's fresh decision to speak his mind is different: in 7:16 (and 9:21) he had declared that he had "rejected" (מאס) life; now he speaks of his life not as something he has decided against, but as something he abhors or loathes (קוט). The injection of this feeling of disgust, obscured by the tendency of our versions to translate מאס and קוט alike, may even be a positive sign, a token of a somewhat less nihilistic attitude; it will be some time before Job lapses again into his death-wish (vv 18–22).

Whatever the nuance, his loathing for his life is the necessary condition for his free utterance. Only a person who finds no joy in life would dare to speak as Job will of God. The announcement signals a deliberate heightening of the intensity.

2 A disputation or controversy (רִיב, *rîb*) with God is what in chap. 9 he has longed for but seen no hope of commencing. Now it would appear that the controversy is already in progress, for he says, "Tell me why you are in controversy with me!" ריב must be used here not in the strictly technical sense of the face to face confrontation, but of the situation of conflict that precedes and precipitates a legal controversy. For the distinction, cf. G. Liedke, *TWHAT* 2:771–77. In asking for the grounds of God's hostility, Job in fact is initiating a legal *rîb*. God will now be obliged—if only he would conform to conventional processes of law!—to verbalize his hostility to Job, and give him reasons, some of which Job may dispute, why he already regards him as guilty. In saying, "Do not condemn me," Job does not refer to any future condemnation, but means "do not go on treating me as guilty"—for there is no doubt that guilt in God's eyes is the only implication Job can draw from God's persecution of him. (On the LXX, see H. S. Gehman, "The Theological Approach of the Greek Translator of Job 1–15," *JBL* 68 [1949] 231–40 [237].)

3–7 In three questions Job now speculates about the motives that lie behind God's treatment of him. If God were a human being, his actions would be intelligible, though not necessarily excusable. But Job is convinced enough that God does not act for human reasons. And so the question must be put: Why does God act *as if* he were a human?

3 The first question asks whether God's treatment of him is in any way for God's profit. "Is it good for you?" (הֲטוֹב לְךָ) does not focus on the justice of God's behavior, but on the possible gain that God may hope to have from it. Obviously it can be to no one's gain to destroy what they have made with hard toil (יְגִיעַ כַּפֶּיךָ "[the product of] the toil of your hands" rather than the usual phrase מַעֲשֵׂה כַפֶּיךָ "the work of your hands"). Perhaps "good" (טוב) means "pleasing" (so Terrien); cf. Gen 2:9; 6:2; Exod 2:2; 2 Sam 11:2. In that case, Job would be asking if God is not something of a masochist, to take pleasure in damaging and rejecting his own handiwork. Some perverted intention in Job's creation is ascribed to God again in vv 13–14. As so often, Job regards his own lot as the general human condition. The "toil" of God's hands is intended to signify humankind, but it is of himself that Job is really speaking.

Recognizing that fact makes the last line of the verse intelligible. For if "the toil of your hands" signified humankind generally, it would include the wicked, and we would be hard put to see the contrast between the second and third lines. As it is, Job is not particularly interested in the fate of the wicked, and certainly not in any specific plans of theirs—except in so far as they and their fortunes are the counterpart to him and his. Here I am, he means, toiled over by you, and faithful to you, but rejected by you, while those who scheme to do evil are looked on by you with approval (a theme that will be much developed by Job in chap. 21). The term translated "smiles on" (הוֹפָעְתָ), lit. "shines on," is used in psalmic language of God's self-manifestation in order to bring salvation (cf. Deut 33:2; Ps 50:2; 80:3 [2]; 94:1); there is a deliberate irony therefore in applying it to his attitude to the wicked.

4 The second question asks whether God has simply the vision and outlook of a mortal, which is necessarily short-sighted and may see error where there is none, or take a small error for a large (Duhm). To treat a righteous man as if he were guilty suggests some defect of vision, to say the least. But Job raises the question only to negate it. Of course he presupposes, like all the

OT, that God is not "flesh" but "spirit" (Isa 31:3; cf. 40:6; Ps 56:5 [4]). God's vision is not superficial like humans' but penetrates to the inner realities: "Yahweh sees not as man sees; man looks on the outward appearance, but Yahweh looks on the heart" (1 Sam 16:7). Similarly the wisdom teachers stress the supra-human sight of God (Prov 16:2; 21:2), and Job (26:6; 31:4) and his friends (34:21) themselves represent the same tradition (for the idea in extrabiblical wisdom, cf. Amenemope 18; *ANET*, 423b). But if that is so, how then can the puzzle of God's behavior be explained?

5–6 The third question asks whether God has so limited an expectation of life, no more than a mere human's, that he feels himself under pressure of time to discover some fault in Job before he (God) is dead. The question is a reflex of Job's sense of the unrelenting pressure of God's persecution of him; were his enemy a human, Job reflects, such impatient insistency could perhaps betray an overblown sense of the brevity of life. His opponent behaves like those whose desperate rush to get things done stems from their fear of approaching death, or more exactly whose drive toward cruelty is a symptom of their fear of death (Terrien). Of course Job would acknowledge that God's life is not so bounded, that he is "from everlasting to everlasting" (Ps 90:2) and that his "years have no end" (Ps 102:28 [27]). Then such behavior, explicable and therefore excusable in a human being, is inexplicable in God—unless perhaps in an unspeakably sinister manner (cf. v 13).

A less probable interpretation of v 5 is to see in it a closer parallel to v 4, as if it asked whether God is short-lived and therefore limited in experience or "shortsighted" like those with "eyes of flesh" (so Horst). The verse is certainly no mere marginal note to v 4 (as Duhm, Hölscher), since it explains the determination in v 6, which the thought of v 4 alone cannot.

In speaking of "my iniquity" and "my sin" in v 6, Job does not of course acknowledge that there is indeed some sin hidden in him that God by persistent probing could uncover. Hebrew has no convenient way of expressing the nuance of "some (supposed) sin in me" other than by the word "my sin," and Job's reiterated clear affirmation of his guiltlessness must determine how the apparent reference here to his guilt should be understood. The implication is that God knows *a priori* that Job (being a human) must have some sin attaching to him; therefore, because God's days are short (so the hypothesis runs) he must urgently search out the sin (and punish it) lest his victim should outlive him.

7 The verse is usually thought to be linked grammatically with what precedes, viz. ". . . although (עַל) you know that I am not guilty, and [that] there is none to deliver from your hand." On this reading, v 7a relates most closely to v 6, and v 7b to v 5: v 7a claims that God is so stubborn as to insist on searching him for sins (v 6) even when he knows he is guilty of none; v 7b apparently claims that God is overanxious to discover Job's guilt, since (in view of Job's impending death) Job cannot outlive his persecutor (cf. v 5), so there is no doubt that even with patience God will achieve his goal; there is "none to deliver from (his) hand." Similarly Peake explained: "[God] knows that no one can deliver Job from His power, yet He overwhelms him with suffering as if at any moment he might slip through His fingers." Verse 7b would then turn on the issue of God's *haste* in prosecuting Job, a theme that is explicit neither in v 5 nor in v 7b.

Perhaps a less strained reading can be gained by taking v 7 as an independent sentence, and rendering the initial על by the usual "because," thus: "Because you know that I am not guilty, there is no escape (lit., none to deliver) from your hand" (Ehrlich recognizes על as "because," Terrien, Pope and Blommerde agree that v 7 is independent of vv 5–6 and that the first line is a subordinate clause). The sense is: You are in a desperate hurry to discover some guilt in me (vv 5–6); but deep down you know as well as I do that you will find none, so I am caught (v 7), for your frantic search will never reach its goal.

Job here reaches a new milestone in his confrontation with God: while in chap. 3 he laid no claim to guiltlessness, and in chaps. 6–7 he had stressed his unhappiness more than his innocence (though cf. 6:10c, 30), in this speech he not only vigorously protests his innocence (9:15, 20, 21), but here—for the first time—asserts that *God also* knows that he is innocent. It would be much more comfortable to believe that God had overlooked his suffering, or even that he had made a mistake about Job's innocence; to believe that God knows he is innocent and punishes him all the same is to feel utterly trapped. To an absent-minded or mistaken God one could appeal, but from one who knows what he is doing there is indeed "no escape."

8–17 The superb depiction of God's creative action with which this strophe begins (vv 8–12) leads only to a bitter conclusion (vv 13–14) further developed in the final verses (vv 15–17). The worst possible construction is put by the nodal verses (vv 13–14) on all the care God has lavished upon Job: everything has been done to meet God's sinister purpose of fastening guilt upon Job and making him suffer for it. Wicked or innocent, his life has one purpose: to serve as God's target (vv 15–17). "All the kindness was but intended to make his present suffering the more acute" (Rowley). The truth about God, as the whole speech has been asserting, is that he uses his power only to sustain his anger, and his attitude toward his creation is one of unremitting hostility and cruelty.

8 Job understands his conception and formation in the womb to have been the personal activity of the creator God. Like a potter or craftsman with his raw materials, God formed and shaped the embryo with care and skill. The tension, or rather the contradiction, between God's tender concern in the past and his ruthless destructiveness in the present is the theme of this strophe, and spelled out already in this opening verse. The sequel to this skillful fashioning has been a change of heart ("you have turned about," if the text is to be so understood; see n. 10:8.b) to an act of unmotivated cruelty. We may well wonder whether the poet, in choosing for "destroy" the term בלע (lit. "swallow, engulf"; also at 8:18), intends—at this critical point of Job's attack on the perverseness of God's destruction of his handiwork—to refer us to 2:3 where Yahweh uses the same somewhat unusual term in a very similar context: "[Job] still holds fast his integrity, although you moved me against him, to destroy (בלע) him without cause[!]." What Job does not know is not only the circumstances that have brought about his suffering, but that God himself is pained by the unjustifiable suffering Job has been exposed to.

For other ascriptions of the processes of birth to the personal activity of God, cf. Ps 22:10 [9]; 119:73; 139:13; Eccl 11:5.

9 The line of thought is identical to v 8, with the contrast between the creative and the destructive acts. But in this verse the pathos is heightened by an appeal to God to "remember" (cf. on 7:7) what his past relationship to

Job has been. "The figure is that of the potter who has lavished infinite care upon his vessel, and now reduces his work of elaborate skill and exquisite ornament into dust again" (Davidson).

The common concept of the human being as clay (cf. 4:19; 33:6; Gen 2:7; Isa 64:7 [8]; cf. Isa 45:9; Jer 18:5; Rom 9:20–21), made into some vessel that returns to earth (cf. Gen 3:19; Ps 90:3; 104:29; 146:4; 1 Macc 2:63; 1QH 3.21, 23–24; 12.24–27; 1QS 11.21–22) when it is smashed, is here applied not to the natural lot of mortals but to Job's particular treatment at God's hands ("wilt thou grind me into dust again?," Moffatt). Job is not of course lamenting that humankind is destined to return to the dust, but that God is reducing Job to his native earth (cf. 1:21) before he has lived out his life (cf. on 5:26). For this reason the second line is not subordinate to the "remember" of v 9a (as Terrien, Gordis, though Gordis is no doubt right not to take the line as interrogative).

10–11 Luther said, "To believe in God the Creator means to believe that he created me along with all other created beings. Few have progressed so far as to believe this in the fullest sense." It is not some form of egocentricity that leads Job to view the creative work of God entirely in terms of his own personal procreation and birth, but a reverent sense, unsurpassed in Biblical literature, of God's meticulous and intimate craft in bringing him into being. The fact that the beauty of the description is soured by the sinister motivation ascribed to God in vv 13–14 can ultimately be set aside, since neither Job nor the poet finally believed that vv 13–14 expressed a more settled truth about God than vv 10–12.

Without any theological portentousness, it can here be taken for granted that in and behind the human acts of procreation and conception lies the attentive activity of God. Semen, the milk-like substance, is poured into the womb; like cheese it coagulates (KJV "cruddled" is an archaic dialectical form of "curdled") in the mother's womb into the embryo, and finally flesh and bones are woven together into "this knot intrinsicate of life" (*Anthony and Cleopatra* 5.2.296). A similar picture is drawn in Ps 139:13–16; 2 Macc 7:22–23; cf. Eccl 11:5; Wisd 7:1–2; Koran, Sura 22.5; 36.76; 40.69; 80.19; 96.2; Pliny, *Hist. nat.,* 7.13; *m. 'Abot* 3.1. The term for "knit together" (סכך, JB "weave") occurs elsewhere in the OT only in Ps 139:13, in the same connection, though nouns from the root are well attested.

12 And after Job's birth, God's attention to him has been wholly supportive: in his loyalty (חסד; cf. on 6:14) to his handiwork, God has continued to sustain the life that he created; his gracious attentiveness has ensured (שמר "keep") his existence. That is, one should almost say, his *former* existence, that fullness of life depicted in 1:1–3. "Life" (חיים) will not here refer to his birth (as Peake), nor even to mere physical existence, but to healthy, full life (cf. KB, 294a §3; G. Gerleman, *THWAT* 1:551). "Attentiveness" (פקדה) is elsewhere used negatively for "visitation (for punishment)" (cf. KJV, RV; Hos 9:7; Isa 10:3 and the verb פקד in Job 7:18), but it cannot mean that here.

13–14 All God's tender care pictured in vv 8–12 was in reality, says Job, a façade: his purpose (the repeated "this" in v 13 must refer forward) was quite other, and utterly perverted. No wonder that he kept "hidden" (צפן) in his heart his intention of nurturing a man only to find fault in him. Behind a smiling providence, God hid a frowning face. God's "preservation" (שמר) of Job's life (v 12b) was but a means to his true end of "watching" (שמר; see

n. 10:14.a) him as a spy (cf. the "guard" [משמר] that God sets over him in
7:12). In the name of protection God has staked out a "hide," ever watchful
to pounce on his victim. What would please this "Man-Watcher" (7:20) is not
Job's enjoyment of a full life (cf. חיים, v 12a) but the discovery of some sin
in Job that would justify cruel handling (there is no distinction between slight
and serious sins [as against Rowley], though any sin would be sufficient grounds).
Job has disappointed God, for he has proved to be innocent; but God has
not let himself be cheated of his ambition: he has treated Job as guilty nevertheless.

This shocking thought, which Job is not shy of developing at length, arises
not unnaturally from the assumptions that form his horizon. If God does not
harass him simply accidentally or automatically, he knows well enough what
he is doing (cf. v 7a); and since God's behavior is too consistent to be accounted
a caprice, it follows that hostility is a settled intention of his; and since God is
the sovereign creator (cf. 9:4–13 as well as 10:8–11) and can afford to wait
for his plans to mature (which is what vv 5–6 ultimately affirm), it follows
that what Job is now experiencing is the success of some old plot of God's,
hatched long since. The theme of God's hostile anger, so dominant a leitmotif
in this speech, comes to the surface here yet again.

These verses give the lie to the reading of the strophe advanced by Andersen,
for example, that Job is "basically confident that God's intentions were
good . . . in making man. . . . The affirmation of life by God through creation is . . . an expression of struggling faith." Yet though it seems clear
that God's hostile purpose embitters the whole of vv 8–12, it remains a nice
question whether the tonality of Job's words is the irony of 7:17–21, or bitter
reproach, or a depth of despair that has made itself willing to believe the
worst.

At such a point as this we should no doubt warn ourselves of the danger
of taking everything Job says *au pied de la lettre*. Of course he means what he
says in the utmost seriousness, but his seriousness is provoking and experimental
as well as—for all the crafted rhetoric—an elemental instinctive cry of pain,
"wild words" (6:3). Nothing here is his last word; nothing is here that must
not be viewed afresh from the perspective of the resolution of the story. And
Job is ill, also. Not just his sores but his bruised psyche provoke these words.
He speaks with the language of the paranoid, who "brood over grievances,
and then project or rationalize their aggression, hatred or longing. Ideas of
reference insidiously become delusions of persecution. Plots, they believe, are
hatched against them: their thoughts, their persons and their property are
interfered with" (*Henderson and Gillespie's Textbook of Psychiatry*, rev. I. Batchelor
[London: OUP, 10th ed., 1969] 295). But even so, just because you're paranoid
doesn't mean they're not out to get you; and Job's mental illness has its grounds.

15 It is not that God does not discriminate between the just and the unjust
(Dhorme) in general but that he is determined to afflict Job and thus declare
him a guilty man whether he is or not. Just as in 9:22, where blameless and
wicked had indeed been spoken of in more general terms, the criticism of
God's dealings is not that he acts arbitrarily but—precisely the opposite—that
he executes one unhesitating design: destruction of life and reputation. If
Job is in fact a wrongdoer, he is destined for punishment; and if he is innocent,
he cannot lift his head high with justifiable pride in his innocence (cf. 11:15;
to "lift up the head" is generally a signal of boldness and independence; cf.

Judg 8:28; Ps 83:3 [2]; Zech 2:4 [1:21]). For he is already pronounced guilty by the shame and affliction which he has been made to drink (קָלוֹן, "shame," has an "objective" sense, like בֹּשֶׁת in 8:22).

16 Even if Job has the energy to assert himself by stubbornly maintaining his innocence ("lift myself up"; on the reading, see n. 10:16.a), he is assailed by God's savagery. Like the persecuted psalmists, he will be hunted down by a lion of an enemy (cf. Ps 7:3 [2]; 10:9; 17:12; 22:14 [13]; 35:17; 57:5 [4]); but unlike the psalmists, his enemy will be God. The metaphor of the lion is used of God in Hos 5:14; 13:7, for his wrathful punishment of guilty Israel. But here in Job the point is that it is against an innocent person that God's wrath is directed.

On the animal imagery used for God, cf. J. Hempel, "Jahwegleichnisse der israelitischen Propheten," *ZAW* 42 (1924) 74–104. In view of the parallels, it is not likely that it is Job who is the lion, hunted by God (as Ehrlich, Stevenson, Gordis); צוד "hunt" does indeed usually indicate human activity, but 38:39 shows it can be used of the lion. NEB links "like a lion" with "I am proud." On the term for "lion" (שַׁחַל), cf. n. 4:10.b.

All God's resources are used against Job. "Marvelous" (נפלאות) have been God's deeds in creation (5:9; 9:10; 37:14); "marvelous" too have been his deeds in Israel's history (Exod 3:20; 15:11; 34:10; Ps 77:15 [14]; 107:8; etc.); now he uses Job's case as an opportunity to "display himself once again as marvelous" (תשב תתפלא). Humans are astounded at the show of majesty in God's handling of Job. A prophet can describe the humiliation of Israel as God's "dealing marvelously" with them (Isa 29:14), that is, in astonishing and frightening wrath. Here it is a lone individual against whom God pits himself in order to achieve a notable victory; the irony of disproportion is evident (cf. on 7:12).

17 The strophe concludes on a note of heightened intensity. If Job dares to assert himself (v 16a), God renews the vigor of his hostility against him. The Heb. has "you renew your witnesses (עד) before me," i.e., "you bring new witnesses against me" (NIV); the witnesses could only be Job's "sufferings regarded as so many proofs of his guilt" (Driver). Cf. 16:8, where Job's emaciation is a "witness" (עד) against him. But despite the prevalence of legal metaphors in this speech, this rendering does not fit well in its immediate context; nor is the personification of his sufferings as witnesses seen elsewhere in the chapter. It is preferable to render "you renew your hostility against me" (see n. 10:17.a), which displays synonymous parallelism with the second line. God's anger, a leitmotif throughout the speech, appears again in the words עדי "hostility" and כעש "anger" (rather than RSV "vexation"; cf. on 5:2; 6:2), only in intensified form: Job's protestations of innocence serve only to multiply God's outbursts against him. And if he has any respite from the divine assaults (perhaps he is thinking of moments when he is "proud" in his innocence, v 16a), the sequel is inevitably the imposition of the "hard labor" (צבא) that is his lot (cf. 7:1 "Has not man only hard service [צבא] on earth?").

18–22 Job's need for vindication (9:2) has foundered on his inability to force God's hand (9:3–4, 14–20). Now, that need has come to appear impossible of achievement even if God could be compelled into a courtroom; for God is determined to mark him down as guilty, no matter what (10:14–15). It is bad enough to feel that God cannot be reached out to (9:11), but worse to know oneself a righteous man in the hands of an angry God, with "no escape from (his) hand" (10:7). Doubly hopeless, Job lapses into his initial mood of chap. 3. But here that old despair is mixed with the new appeal for the absence of God (v 20b) that first arose at the end of his previous speech (7:16b, 19).

18–19 The lament takes up the theme of the middle section of Job's cry in chap. 3 (vv 11–19), where also, with the introductory "why?" that marks off the reproach or appeal, he voiced his vain wish that he could have been still-born, not "brought forth from the womb" alive. Here, though not in chap. 3, he ascribes his birth to God's personal activity. This is a natural development of the thought of chap. 3, in line now with the exposition of vv 8–12. But it also signals how far Job has moved since chap. 3: there God was mentioned only in the passive voice, and none of Job's hurt was laid to God's account. Here the self-curse has become a reproach directed at God, and his unwished-for existence has become but the outworking of the perverse divine plan (vv 13–14). And here Job's anguish arises not simply from his calamity and suffering, as in chap. 3, but from the consciousness that has now developed in him that the suffering is no accident but the long-standing grisly design of God.

20 Now the theme of chap. 3 merges with the theme of the last half of chap. 7. So "few" (מעט) are Job's remaining days that any "cheer" he can find will be "little" (מעט) enough. The verse begins and ends on the same note of the "little" that is all he can expect. "Cheer" he cannot induce in himself because he knows his divine enemy is brooding over him (9:27, בלג as here); it is only God's absence that would cheer him. The mood is the same as in 7:16.

21–22 The wistful or turbulent speculations of Job on the question, "How can a man be justified by God?" (9:2), have now entirely subsided and his imminent destiny of utter deprivation wholly occupies him. His existence has become a perversion of creation; his fate lies in a land where creation is undone. Instead of a world in which light is God's first creation and in which order is apparent in every detail, the "land" he is bound for is monotonous gloom without order, like the formless black void before creation began (Gen 1:2), "death's dateless night" (Shakespeare, *Sonnets* 30), without any possibility of alteration. Job's life, like the universe according to the second law of thermodynamics, tends always toward irreversible disorder. On the motif of Sheol as the land from which one does not return, cf. on 7:9–10; and cf. also Callimachus 15(13).3–4 "How is it in the underworld? Deep darkness. How about return to us? All a lie. And Pluto? A myth. So we are lost."

Like other speeches of Job's, this one comes to an end with a prospect of death. Here the particular characteristic of death is not that it provides a release from pain (as in 3:20–22) or as a permanent hiding from God (as in 7:21b), but that it envelops one in darkness (see H. Ringgren, *TDOT* 5:255–56). Job has cried out for darkness ("Would that I had died before any eye had seen me," v 18b); he knows that darkness is for the moment denied him. But he desires the darkness; life before death can be "comfortable" only if God's gaze can be turned away from him (v 20b), if he can secrete himself from the glare of the divine attention or rather inquisition.

Explanation

The language of this address has been rich in the metaphors of legal disputation. Job has—hesitatingly and adventurously—contemplated means of winning legal vindication from God. The futility of the undertaking becomes only the more apparent as the speech progresses, so that it may appear that the whole subject is in danger of coming to a complete dead-end.

Something is in motion, however; and that is Job's growing recognition of the divine hostility. What thwarts Job's ambitions, he comes to recognize in this speech, is not so much the majesty and omni-competence of God which dooms any attempt to compel him, but the divine anger that cannot be deflected, a studied hostility that flings into battle against Job all the resources of a God.

On the level of rationality, then, the whole line of approach toyed with by Job in this speech—a legal confrontation on a grand scale—seems to fall to the ground, and only a mood of sour resignation can be expected to survive. But on the level of feeling, the conflict has only just begun; for the fact is that, for the first time, Job has brought to the surface his sense of the anger of God. And that anger, whether or not it is a reality, must be met by a radical anger within Job. Intellectually the game may be at stalemate; but emotionally everything is still at stake.

Zophar's First Speech (11:1–20)

Bibliography

Jacob, B. "Erklärung einiger Hiob-Stellen. 11:11." *ZAW* 32 (1912) 278–87 (283). **Slotki, J. J.** "Job XI 6." *VT* 35 (1985) 229–30. **Sutcliffe, E. F.** "Notes on Job, Textual and Exegetical. 6,18; 11,12; 31,35; 34,17.20; 36,27–33; 37,1." *Bib* 30 (1949) 66–90.

Translation

¹*Zophar the Naamathite answered:*

²*Should a multitude of words* ᵃ *go unanswered?*
Should a man win vindication by mere talk? ᵇ
³*Will* ᵃ *your pratings silence* ᵇ *men*
so that ᶜ *you may mock on without any to shame you,*
⁴*so that you may say, "My doctrine* ᵃ *is pure,"*
and "I am ᵇ *clean in your* ᶜ *sight [O God]!"?*
⁵*But if only God would speak,*
if only he would open his lips to you,
⁶*if only he would tell you the secrets of wisdom;*
for there are mysteries ᵃ *in his working.* ᵇ
Then ᶜ *you would know that God overlooks* ᵈ *part of your sin.*

⁷*Can you uncover* ᵃ *the mystery* ᵇ *of God?*
Can you attain ᶜ *to the perfection of Shaddai's knowledge?* ᵈ
⁸*It is higher* ᵃ *than heaven—what can you do?*
It is deeper than Sheol—what can you know?
⁹*Longer than the earth is its measure,* ᵃ
and broader than the sea.

¹⁰*If as he passes by* ᵃ *he shuts a man up* ᵇ *in prison,*
or if he calls him to account, ᶜ *who can dissuade him?*
¹¹*For he recognizes worthless men,*
and when he sees guilt he marks it well. ᵃ
¹²*A hollow* ᵃ *man will gain understanding* ᵇ
when a wild ass ᶜ *is born* ᵈ *tame.* ᵉ

¹³*Yet* ᵃ *if you direct* ᵇ *your mind toward him* ᶜ
and spread out ᵈ *your hands to him—*
¹⁴*if there is wrongdoing in your hand, renounce* ᵃ *it,*
and do not let iniquity dwell in your tent— ᵇ
¹⁵*then you will lift up your face, free of fault,*
you will be firmly established, ᵃ *and have no fear.*
¹⁶*You* ᵃ *will forget your suffering,*
remember it only as water that has flowed past.

¹⁷*Then your* ᵃ *life will be brighter than the noonday;*
its darkness ᵇ *will be as morning light.*

18 *You will be secure,*ᵃ *because there is hope;*
    *you will be protected*ᵇ *and lie down in safety.*
19 *You*ᵃ *will take your rest with none to disturb you;*
    *and many*ᵇ *will entreat*ᶜ *your good favor.*
20 *But the eyes of the wicked will fail,*
    escape there will be none for them,
    *their only hope very despair.*ᵃ

Notes

2.a. LXX, Tg, Symm, Vg vocalize רֹב as רַב, viz. "great of words, garrulous," a closer parallel to אִישׁ שְׂפָתִים, "man of lips, man full of talk"; so also Duhm, Fohrer, Horst, van Selms, NAB. Tur-Sinai unconvincingly argues that רֹב is a variant Masoretic orthography for רַב. MT is quite satisfactory (cf. JB, NEB); see Gordis for other examples of an abstract noun parallel to a concrete noun.

2.b. Lit., "Should a man of lips be vindicated?"; perhaps אִישׁ שְׂפָתַיִם means "a glib talker" by contrast with אִישׁ דְּבָרִים, "a fluent speaker" (Exod 4:10).

3.a. There is no interrogative particle in this line; it may be carried forward from v 2. Alternatively, vv 3–4 may be statements (Gray), in which case יַחֲרִישׁוּ should probably be understood modally ("your pratings try to silence"). NJPS takes vv 3–4 as a virtual hypothetical: "your prattle may silence men. . . . But would that God might speak!"

3.b. חרשׁ is usually intransitive, "be silent" (except perhaps at 41:4).

3.c. Representing the *waw* consecutive of MT, against proposed revocalization to וְתִלְעַג (cf. *BHK, BHS*); consequent action is effectively *resulting* action: if others are silenced, Job can continue speaking his blasphemies.

4.a. MT לִקְחִי to be kept as against the common emendation to לָכְתִּי "my way of life" (Beer, Duhm, *BHK*); LXX ἔργοις is no evidence, since it never translates לכת (Dhorme). Though לֶקַח is obviously related to לקח "receive," there is nothing in its usages that suggests it is *primarily* "received" wisdom (as e.g., Horst, Fohrer).

4.b. Pope (cf. also Ehrlich, *BHK*, Tur-Sinai) reads הָיִיתָ, "you have been," as Zophar's address to Job. The emendation is unnecessary; see *Comment*.

4.c. עֵינֶיךָ, not to be emended with LXX to עֵינָיו, "his eyes" (Merx, Beer), much less to עֵינַי, "my eyes" (Siegfried, Duhm, Terrien).

6.a. כִּי־כִפְלַיִם לְתוּשִׁיָּה is lit., "for there is double to understanding/effectual working." Hence "double to the understanding," i.e., ambiguous (Duhm), "there are two sides to wisdom," the manifest and the hidden (Pope; similarly NIV), "[the secrets of wisdom] are twice as effective" (NAB). These are strained interpretations. Certainly כפלים can hardly mean "manifold" (RSV). It is better to read כְּפִלְאִים, "like wonders" (cf. omission of *aleph* in צמים, 5:5) (so Merx, Duhm, Fohrer, Horst), or perhaps better just פְּלָאִים, "wonders" (Driver, *BHK*, Rowley), though God's secrets could be rightly said to be *like* miracles, wonders. The *kaph* of כפלאים is unlikely to be asseverative *kaph* (Gordis). De Wilde reads כְּפוּלִים, "folded," thus "hidden." A very tempting conjecture has been made by J. J. Slotki, "Job XI 6," *VT* 35 (1985) 229–30, that כפלים should be transposed from being the first word of the first כי clause to being the first word of the second כי clause, and that לתושיה should be read לוֹ תושיה; thus כִּי לוֹ תוּשִׁיָּה וְדַע כִּי־כִפְלַיִם יַשֶּׁה לְךָ אֱלוֹהַּ, "for sound wisdom is his. And know thou that double (punishment) shall God exact of thee."

6.b. תושיה is usually "successful working" (as in 6:13; cf. 12:16), though it cannot often be distinguished from "wisdom" (cf. שכל, "understanding," and cf. H. A. Brongers in n. 5:12.a). NEB has "wonderful are its effects," NAB "twice as effective." I suggest it is not simply parallel to חכמה but refers to the method of divine working, blending mercy and justice (see *Comment*).

6.c. Lit., "and know!" an imperative expressing the certainty of the consequence; cf. GKC, § 110i.

6.d. RSV "God exacts of you less than your guilt deserves" (similarly NEB) is unjustifiable, apparently resting on identification of יַשֶּׁה with נשׁא/נשׁה "to be a creditor." יַשֶּׁה is rather from נשׁה "forget," thus "God causes to be forgotten for you [= overlooks] some of (מִן partitive) your guilt" (thus Driver-Gray, Fohrer, KB³). NAB "will make you answer for your guilt" adopts the needless and weak emendation to יִשְׁאָלְךָ "will inquire of you" (Ehrlich, Dhorme, E. F. Sutcliffe,

"Notes on Job, Textual and Exegetical," *Bib* 30 [1949] 66–90 [67]; similarly JB). Equally unpersuasive are the emendations to יְשַׁלְחֶךָ, "pursues you" (Terrien), and יֶשְׁנָה . . . מֵאֱלֹוהַּ בַּעֲוֹנֶךָ, "there comes from God what is equivalent to your sin" (Duhm; cf. Bickell יְשַׁוֶּה, "he makes equal, requites to you"). Houtsma's conjecture יִשָּׂא, "he forgives," is the most attractive of the emendations, yielding a good sense. Few now (except NEB, which puts v 6c in square brackets) follow Duhm and Hölscher in deleting the line, difficult though it is. A. R. Ceresko, "The Chiastic Word Pattern in Hebrew," *CBQ* 38 (1976) 303–11 (308) argues that recognition of an A:B::B:A pattern confirms the authenticity of the colon; but such a "pattern" would cut across the strophic boundaries, and, furthermore, seems entirely accidental.

7.a. Lit., "find out" (תִּמְצָא).

7.b. חֵקֶר, "object of research, inquiry."

7.c. תִּמְצָא as in v 7a, but the meaning is perhaps slightly different, as with its semi-cognate Aram. מְטָא, "reach" (similarly Ehrlich, Dhorme, KB³, M. Dahood, "Northwest Semitic Philology and Job," in *The Bible in Current Catholic Thought* [Gruenthaner Memorial Volume, ed. J. L. McKenzie; New York: Herder and Herder, 1962] 55–74 [57]). A. R. Ceresko notes this as an example of antanaclasis (repetition of a word with a different meaning), in "The Function of *Antanaclasis* (mṣ' "to find" // mṣ' "to reach, overtake, grasp") in Hebrew Poetry, Especially in the Book of Qoheleth," *CBQ* 44 (1982) 551–69 (560–61). Simple repetition is, however, well attested in Job (see Gordis, 508–13).

7.d. Lit., "to the perfection (תַּכְלִית) of Shaddai"—but it is only his perfect *knowledge* that is in view.

8.a. גָּבְהֵי שָׁמָיִם, lit., "the heights of heaven"; but the parallelism with עֲמֻקָּה מִשְּׁאוֹל, "deeper than Sheol," suggests that we should emend to גָּבְהָה מִשָּׁמַיִם, "higher than heaven" (so Vg, NAB, NEB, JB, Fohrer, Gordis, Horst and most). Some older scholars rather forcedly translated as an exclamation: "Heights of heaven! what canst thou do?" (Davidson). The similar form in 22:12 is no analogy (as against *BHS*).

9.a. Q מִדָּה presumably means it is to be read as מִדָּתָהּ, "its measure," the antecedent being חכמה (v 6) or more probably תַּכְלִית (v 7). Cf. GKC, § 91e. Alternatively מִדָּה, without any suffix, could be an "adverbial accusative": "as far as measure is concerned."

10.a. For יַחֲלֹף many read יַחְטֹף, "seizes" (so NAB, Gordis) or יַחְתֹּף "snatches away" (as in 9:12) (so *BHK*, Driver, de Wilde). But LXX καταστρέψῃ, often quoted in support, could well represent יַחְלֹף hiph (Horst). "Overlook" (Pope) is hardly appropriate.

10.b. וַיַּסְגִּיר with simple *waw* because the action is contemporaneous with the preceding verb. NEB "he may keep secret his passing" is not probable, and unnecessarily conflates the thought with that of 9:11.

10.c. The legal interpretation of קהל hiph, "call to account," is best (see *Comment*), though some relate it to Arab. *qâla*, "speak"; hence Gordis "speak out against, arraign"; NEB "proclaims it [his passing]." E. Ullendorff, "The Meaning of קהלת," *VT* 12 (1962) 215, also takes קהל as "rebuke, argue."

11.a. לֹא יִתְבּוֹנָן, lit., "he will/does not ponder it." Thus Driver-Gray render, "without considering it," i.e., he knows about sins instantaneously and without effort. Similarly ibn Ezra: "he does not need to observe closely"; Rowley. This is a lot of weight to lay on the verb, since v 10 has asserted that God does in fact act upon his knowledge. Perhaps the best interpretation is to take the phrase as a question (RSV "will he not consider it?"; similarly NJPS, Pope).

Alternative interpretations are: (i) "and he is himself unobserved" (so B. Jacob, "Erklärung einiger Hiob-Stellen. 11:11," *ZAW* 32 [1912] 278–87 [283]; Fohrer)—but it is rather the guilty men who seem to be the subject. (ii) Reading לוֹ, "to it (evil)," for לֹא (so Reuss, Duhm, Dhorme); the objection (Horst) that בִּין hithpolel is never construed with ל is weak. (iii) Reading לֹא as an emphatic particle (I. Eitan, "La particule emphatique 'la' dans la Bible," *RÉJ* 74 [1922] 1–16 [9–10]; F. Nötscher, "Zum emphatischen Lamed," *VT* 3 [1953] 372–80 [375]; G. R. Driver, "Affirmation by Exclamatory Negation," *JANES* 5 [1973] 107–14 [110]; *BHK*). (iv) Taking לֹא as a noun, "nothing," viz. "considers them nothing" (Tur-Sinai; Blommerde, comparing Isa 53:3 as understood by M. Dahood, "Hebrew-Ugaritic Lexicography," *Bib* 47 [1966] 408)—but this does not fit the sense. (iv) Emendation to יִתְבּוֹנֶנּוּ, "they do not understand it" (Szczygiel). (v) Altering אָוֶן to אִישׁ אָוֶן, "man of iniquity," and translating "though he (the wicked man) does not notice" (Horst; similarly de Wilde, comparing 9:11). Next to the suggestion I have adopted I would rank (iii). It is uncertain how NEBmg "he does not stand aloof" is derived.

12.a. נָבוּב, "hollowed," used metaphorically only here, and no doubt chosen because of the assonance with יְלָבֵב (Dhorme). German has the term "Hohlkopf," "hole-head."

12.b. יְלָבֵב can hardly be privative, as RV "vain man is void of understanding" (see Driver). Tur-Sinai reads the first four words as וְאִישׁ נָבוֹב יִלָּבְבוֹ עַיִר, "Man is an offspring which a donkey produces," נבוב from נוב, "flourish" (cf. polel יְנוֹבֵב, Zech 9:17), and לבב meaning "to sprout" (cf. MH, Aram. לבלב, Akk. *lippu*). Similarly H. Rosenrauch, "Critical Notes. II. The Hebrew Equivalent to Accadic *lib(lib)u*," *JQR* ns 36 [1945–46] 81, comparing Exod 9:14. The point would be that compared with God's wisdom, humans are the offspring of donkeys—an intriguing possibility, but too far removed from the MT to be seriously entertained.

12.c. פֶּרֶא "wild ass." E. F. Sutcliffe read (for פרא אדם) פֶּרֶד, "stallion," translating, "A witless wight may get wit when a mule is born a stallion" (*Bib* 30 [1949] 70–71), a suggestion judged worthy of inclusion in *BHS*. P. Humbert, "En marge du dictionnaire hébraïque," *ZAW* 21 (1950) 199–207 (201–2), understood the line as "Is an empty head endowed with reason? Is a mortal born to command?" (lit., born the stallion of a wild ass).

12.d. Ball vocalized יוֹלֵד, "begets." Many have emended to יְלֻמַּד, "is taught, tamed" (Budde, Hölscher, Fohrer, JB, NAB). It is no objection (against Pope) that למד is not used in hiph; it does not occur in pu.

12.e. Pope follows M. Dahood in equating אדם, "human," with אֲדָמָה, "ground, steppe" ("Zacharia 9,1, 'ÊN 'ĀDĀM," *CBQ* 25 [1963] 123–24; idem, "חָדֵל 'Cessation' in Isaiah 38,11," *Bib* 52 [1971] 215–16; and KB³ *s.v.* אדם IV). Sicre Diaz makes the same proposal as Pope, apparently independently. Similarly also NIV mg, GNB.

13.a. Added to mark the transition.

13.b. Though perf, הכינות is not to be taken as referring to the past (as NEB "if only you had . . ."), but as a future perfect, "If you shall have . . ., once you . . ." Cf. Driver, *Tenses*, § 138i (β*).

13.c. "Toward him" is to be understood from אליו of the second half of the line. Many take "direct your mind" as meaning "direct your behavior or intentions *aright*" (cf. RSV, NEB, JB, NAB), "to strengthen one's heart, i.e., take a difficult decision and stick to it" (Terrien), but the phrase is not used absolutely (not even in Ps 78:8, properly speaking).

13.d. Part of the "if"-clause, and not itself the apodosis (as RSV "[then] you will stretch out"). On the meaning of פרש "spread out," see *Comment*.

14.a. Retaining MT impv הרחיקהו, we must regard v 14 as a parenthesis (as JPS shows), not as a simple continuation of the "if's" of v 14 (as NAB, NIV). Emendation to תַרְחִיקֵהוּ, "[if] you put far," is offered by Dhorme.

14.b. Lit., "tents," but names for dwellings are often in the plural (cf. 18:21; 21:28; 39:6; M. Dahood, *Ugaritic-Hebrew Philology* 37 [Rome: Pontifical Biblical Institute, 1965] § 13.17; Blommerde). Emendation to אָהֳלְךָ (as *BHK*) is unnecessary, though the ancient versions apparently read a sg.

15.a. מֻצָק, generally taken as hoph ptcp of יצק "pour (e.g., molten metal)." But NJPS has "when in straits," from צוק; similarly Sicre Diaz.

16.a. It is hard to see why "you" (אתה) should be emphatic here, and the emendation to עַתָּה, "now, i.e., in that case," is attractive (being pronounced similarly); so Merx, Fohrer, Horst. But it is purely conjectural (not supported by Pesh; see Driver), and not to be accepted (so also Driver, Gordis, Alonso Schökel-Sicre Diaz).

17.a. It is not necessary to add the suffix to חלד (as *BHK*); LXX σοὶ ζωή need not presuppose it.

17.b. תָעֻפָה is 3 fem sg impf of עוף, "be dark," viz., "[though] it be dark" (so Gray, Fohrer; RV; cf. JB "will make a dawn of darkness"). But most revocalize to תְעֻפָה, a noun, viz. "the darkness [of your life] will become like the morning."

18.a. Attractive is the proposal to take בטח in the sense "lie down" (as in Jer 12:5; Prov 14:16; cf. KB³, 116a). So Gordis, L. Kopf, "Arabische Etymologien und Parallelen zum Bibelwörterbuch," *VT* 8 (1958) 161–215 (167), comparing Arab. *bataha*, "lie down." But this makes the repetition of "lie down" (שכב, רבץ) in vv 18-19 rather weak.

18.b. חָפַרְתָּ is apparently "you will dig," hence "search" (cf. 39:29), though this is a rare meaning. Gray understood: "Searching around, before going to rest for the night, finding nothing amiss, Job will lie down with a sense of security" (this must be intended also by NAB, NIV). But such an interpretation is strained, and it is better to adopt Ehrlich's proposal (accepted by KB³) of a verb חפר III, cognate with Arab. *hafara*, "protect," and vocalize חֲפַרְתָּ, RSV, NEB, NJPS ("entrenched"), Dhorme, Terrien. Quite improbable is a connection with חפר II "be ashamed" (as Fohrer); so too NJB "after your troubles," lit., "even if you have been confused," reading וְחָפַרְתָּ. E. Lipiński, "Notes lexicographiques et stylistiques sur le livre de Job," *FolOr* 21 (1986)

65–82 (71–73), sees here a Sem. root *ḥpr* "provide for oneself" (cf. Akk. *epēru* "provide," Arab. *ḥafara* "be provided for"; thus "you will be provided for" (if the verb is reflexive) or else read pu. חֻפַּרְתָּ or pass qal חֻפַרְתָּ. But Akk. *epēru* is not well attested, not being recognized by CAD.

19.a. Deleted as repetitive of v 18b by Duhm, Hölscher, Fohrer, Hesse, NEB.

19.b. רבים could of course equally well mean "great ones" (NEB "great men")

19.c. חלה, "be weak, ill," piel "to make soft" (so KB³; cf. D.R. Ap-Thomas, "Notes on Some Terms Relating to Prayer," *VT* 6 [1956] 225–41 [239–40]) rather than from a חלה II, "be sweet" (as BDB, Gordis).

20.a. For this meaning, see *Comment.* Alternatively, the sense "sigh" or "sorrow" (as in Ecclus 30:12; so KB³) are possible translations, but do not suit the context so well.

Form / Structure / Setting

The strophic structure of Zophar's speech is self-evident, and is accurately indicated by the RSV's typography:

    2–6 (6 lines)
    7–12 (6 lines)
    13–20 (8 lines)

Each strophe, however, can more accurately be perceived as containing two smaller units ("sub-strophes," Terrien): vv 2–4 (3 lines), 5–6 (3 lines), 7–9 (3 lines), 10–12 (3 lines), 13–16 (4 lines), 17–20 (4 lines).

The three-strophe structure corresponds to the content of the speech: in vv 2–6 Zophar reproaches Job for his claim to innocence; in vv 7–12 he affirms the inscrutability of God; in vv 13–20 he counsels Job on the right way to behave and offers him hope if he will take Zophar's advice. The divisions within these three strophes are less strongly marked, but correspond first, at v 5, to a transition from direct address to Job to an expressed wish ("O that!," אולם), secondly, at v 10, to the transition from a statement of the inscrutability of God to an affirmation that God invariably punishes the wicked (a kind of contradiction of the previous sub-strophe!), and thirdly, at v 17, to the transition from a conditional statement of hope to an amplification of the blessed future awaiting Job.

This last sub-strophic division (put forward by Fohrer, Hesse) is not wholly clear-cut, however, and, not surprisingly, alternative analyses are often proposed, Terrien, for example, dividing the third strophe into three sub-strophes, vv 13–15, 16–18, 19–20. Others regard vv 13–20 as an undivided strophe.

As for *genre,* the chapter is evidently a *disputation speech,* as several features make clear. First, Zophar accuses his opponent of long-windedness and filibustering; Job's speech is empty of content, yet at the same time constitutes blasphemy ("mockery," לעג) (vv 2–3). Second, he quotes words of his opponent (v 4) in order to refute them. Third, he cites authority for his case over against Job: the traditional teaching about the wisdom of God in which, Zophar presumes, lies hidden the reason for Job's suffering (vv 5–6). Fourth, he interrogates Job in the style of a cross-examination, asking questions which cannot fail to leave Job in the wrong. (They are not exactly the pre-trial questions [*Verhörfragen vor Gericht*] that Fohrer envisages, but unanswerable questions within the course of the trial itself; cf. Horst, 169.)

Other genre elements drawn upon, as so often in these speeches, are hymnic, wisdom, and prophetic elements. Of a *hymnic* cast are vv 7–8, extolling the unfathomable wisdom of God in the form of rhetorical questions (cf. both for form and content Ps 139:8–9; and for the form Isa 40:12–14). The most obvious *wisdom*-like element is the proverb-saying of v 12 (see the Explanation below for its exact interpretation). But equally at home in wisdom teaching is the contrast between the righteous and the wicked (esp. vv 19–20) echoing the doctrine of the "two ways" (as in the wisdom Ps 1). The pastoral counsel, "If you set your heart aright . . ." (vv 13–15), also reflects the didactic function of wisdom (cf. e.g., Prov 1:10–15). Of the *prophetic* elements the most striking is the description of future happiness (vv 15–19), markedly reminiscent of the salvation oracle but also, it must be allowed, of psalmic language.

The *nodal verses* are evidently vv 6c and 15. In v 6c is contained the essence of Zophar's view of Job's guilt: it is not less than it appears, but worse, and if God were not so merciful Job would be suffering even more severely than he is at this moment. V 15 is nodal because it encapsulates Zophar's recommendation to Job and at the same time holds out promises of how different his future can be from his present state.

The *mood* of this speech seems at the first contemptuous of Job and aggressive (vv 2–4). But at least it is directed toward Job himself, and does not spend itself in disquisitions about the fate of the wicked like Bildad's (8:11–19). Quite distinctively, only vv 10–12 (and the concluding v 20) in this speech are not cast in second person address to Job, and at v 13 there is a marked transition to positive and upbeat advice to Job (vv 13–14), accompanied by a delightful elaborated portrayal of the possibilities for his latter days (vv 15–19). Even if Zophar's theology is the cruelest of all the friends', and even though at his most winsome he is making recommendations to Job (vv 13–14) which only serve to emphasize how grossly Job—who has followed all such advice from his youth up—has been maltreated by God, Zophar's intentions are of the best. He is only being cruel to be kind.

Comment

1–20   The major thrust of this opening speech of Zophar is conveyed precisely through its nodal sentence: "know then that God overlooks part of your sin" (v 6c). Whereas for Eliphaz Job's suffering is brought about by some relatively trifling sin and is therefore bound to be soon relieved (4:5–6), and for Bildad also Job's essential righteousness is confirmed by the fact that he, unlike his children, has not been cut off from life (8:4–6), for Zophar Job's suffering is *nothing but deserved suffering.* Both Eliphaz and Bildad set the suffering of their friend in a particular context: Eliphaz in the context of Job's evidently near-blameless life, Bildad in the context of the fate of Job's children. From either perspective, Job's suffering is qualified and thus—to the satisfaction of the first two friends—suitably mollified.

Zophar perceives no such context for Job's pain. The fact is, he would say, that Job is suffering, and suffering is inevitably the product of sin. To contextualize Job's suffering and try to see in it proportion is ultimately to trivialize it. If, like Eliphaz, you compare it with his many years of prosperity this calamity is a mere pinprick, however painful at the instant; and if, like Bildad, you compare Job's continuing life with the unalterable fact of his children's death, whatever discomfort Job is experiencing is negligible. Those were reasonable points of view; but Zophar is for principle rather than proportion, and that is reasonable too. For the bottom line in each friend's accounting is that *Job is a sinner*—not much of a sinner, perhaps, in Eliphaz's book and Bildad's, but a sinner suffering hard at this moment for his sin. Every other consideration is extraneous to Job's present condition.

Zophar strikes the readers as the least sympathetic of the friends; but it is just because he so determinedly refuses to take other factors into account that he actually stands closest to Job. For Job also rejects out of hand any argument that does not address itself directly to his present situation; and though he cannot for a moment assent to Zophar's analysis, he must agree with him that sin is the principal—or rather, the only—issue.

2 On the surface, Zophar begins with the conventional language of disputation, in which the opponent's arguments are decried as mere words, but needing reply by the present speaker nevertheless. Yet Zophar's rhetoric has its own special point to make, especially in distinction from Eliphaz (cf. on 4:2) and Bildad (cf. on 8:2). Whereas Eliphaz professed himself hesitant to intrude upon Job's grief, and Bildad had gone no further than to pronounce himself affronted, on God's behalf, by Job's tempestuous speech, Zophar judges it his moral duty to silence Job. The more aggressive tone of Zophar's speech is designedly climactic to the friend's addresses: Eliphaz and Bildad, he implies, should have said enough to quiet Job's ravings against heaven. Since Job nevertheless has gone on answering back, stronger measures are called for. We note that the stylized pattern of chaps. 4–11—a speech by a friend, followed by a speech by Job—is not a simplistic literary structure but, under cover of its "false" naivete, builds tension toward a climax of anger on the friends' part.

Zophar's first assessment is that he has heard nothing but "a multitude of words." This does not only mean that he has not heard the *man,* has been unable to penetrate beyond Job's words to his real self, but also that he has taken Job's refusal to fall silent as itself evidence of guilt. He may indeed have in mind the principle of Prov 10:19, "In a multitude of words [רֹב דְּבָרִים, as here], sin is not lacking" (cf. also Eccl 5:2; there is no contrast here between words and action, as at 2 Kgs 18:22; Prov 14:23). It is not so much the length of Job's previous speech (chaps. 9–10), which is little longer than his first (chaps. 6–7) or than Eliphaz's speech (chaps. 4–5), that earn Zophar's disapproval, but his continued speaking. That is what requires to be "answered"— or rather, since it is the legal idiom that is in place here, "rebutted," proved to be in the wrong.

Likewise, on his conventional principles, Zophar cannot allow that a man should win legal acquittal ("be vindicated," rsv) if he will not be silenced by convincing proofs of his guilt. It is not a question whether "the garrulous man [must] necessarily be right" (nab; similarly neb), but whether anyone should be allowed to put himself in the right by going on talking after his guilt has been established. That is contrary to natural justice. Of course, the setting of the Joban speeches is not a law court, but the friends not unnaturally use the formal idioms and rhetoric of the lawsuit in their arguments against Job, and Job—even more naturally—views his controversy with God as essentially a legal one, since he is serving a sentence when no crime has been committed and no due process of law against him has even been set in train.

3 Moving from the general (v 2) to the particular (a similar rhetorical move in 5:17–18; 7:1–3; 8:20–21), Zophar continues his point: it is outrageous that Job should not be silenced by the refutations proffered by the friends. The whole process of legal argument is that the disputants should continue talking until one or other concedes the issue. If Job has not conceded the points of Eliphaz and Bildad, but has gone on speaking, he must be attempting to reduce *them* to silence, putting them in the wrong. Zophar's complaint is not that Job simply talks too much, speaks lies, or even filibusters in an attempt to drown out all arguments but his own; it is rather that he is not playing fair by the rules of legal disputation.

Job's speaking is of course wrong not just because he does not accept the friends' position: it is wrong in itself. It is "prattle," "babbling" (בד), a term used elsewhere in the context of proud boasting (Isa 16:6; Jer 48:30)—which is just the term in Zophar's book for Job's defense of his innocence against God. But more, it is "mockery" (לעג) against God; for not to accept the rightness of God's punishment is to challenge God's morality, to belittle God. Such impiety should not be allowed to pass unchallenged, "with none to rebuke"; Zophar believes he owes it to God to take up the cudgels on God's behalf and to defend God's integrity. The impropriety of Job's arguments against God convinces Zophar of the propriety of his speech against Job. In the name of theological correctness and the avoidance of blasphemy, Job's "friend" becomes his legal opponent whose endeavor will be to "shame" or "humiliate" him by proving him in the wrong (for the use of כלם in a legal context, cf. Prov 25:8; see also Job 19:3).

4 If no one takes up God's cause, says Zophar, Job will continue his mockery of the divine honor (v 3), protesting both to humans (v 4a) and to God (v 4b) that it is he—and not God—who is in the right.

It is a characteristic of the legal speech of controversy that the opponent's words are cited (cf. Isa 40:27; Ezek 12:21–22, 26–27; see H. W. Wolff, "Das Zitat im Prophetenspruch," in *Gesammelte Studien zum Alten Testament* [Munich: Kösel, 1964] 36–129; A. S. van der Woude, "Micah in Dispute with the Pseudo-Prophets," *VT* 19 [1969] 244–60). Job has not used these particular phrases, but the protestation of innocence Zophar puts into Job's mouth is—with one important exception—a reasonable summary of the stage Job's self-consciousness has reached by the time of his speech in chaps. 9–10, just concluded. In his opening lament in chap. 3 the question of his innocence was never raised, and in his reply to Eliphaz in chaps. 6–7 he had affirmed his sense of innocence relatively indirectly (6:10, 24, 26, 29–30; 7:20–21). But in chaps. 9–10 he has unambiguously asserted, "I am innocent. . . . I am blameless" (9:20, 21), "You [God] know that I am not guilty" (10:7) (also in 9:14–19).

Where Zophar wrongs Job is in the word, "my *doctrine* is pure." "Doctrine" (לקח) is a familiar term in wisdom literature (Prov 1:5; 4:2; 9:9; 16:21, 23; Ecclus 8:8; cf. Isa 29:24), and Job has indeed been pictured by Eliphaz as a "teacher" who has "instructed" many and whose "words" have upheld the despondent (4:3–4). But the Job of these agonized speeches has been anything but didactic or professorial, and it is the gravest misapprehension for Zophar to cast Job's speeches as classroom lectures or theoretical disquisitions. This term "doctrine" by itself is enough to show how little empathy Zophar is capable of. Our readerly indignation against the professional theologian who uses human misery as the raw data for academic point-scoring has to be tempered somewhat (does it not?) by the irony that the author of the book is no less guilty than Zophar of using Job's suffering as "doctrine"; for he too has his theological purpose to maintain. And we, his readers, inasmuch as we find the book "instructive," have also deflected our attention from the religious and physical extremity of the man Job to our own theological extrapolations.

Presumably it is to the friends that Job has been addressing—according to Zophar—his first affirmation, that "my doctrine is pure" (though NIV, inserting "to God," thinks otherwise: "You say to God, 'My beliefs are flawless.'"). But certainly the second line is represented as addressed to God: "I am clean in your sight." At first reading, this is a strange claim, for, as Pope remarks, Job "does not know that God reckons him as just; this is his complaint, that God treats him as the wicked ought to be . . . treated." But while Pope is quite correct in seeing that Job has no evidence that God recognizes his innocence, Job believes it all the same. Job's argument has been, in fact, that God treats him as wicked *even though* he knows Job is innocent (9:15–21; 10:15b). In Zophar's view, it is a blasphemy for Job to address God thus; for it implicitly charges God with gross dishonesty.

5–6 Job's assertion of his innocence (v 4) would be silenced if God could tell Job the truth about himself and about Job. It is that God is merciful as well as righteous. If he were to be merely righteous, who can doubt that Job would be suffering even more? "Use every man after his desert, and who should 'scape whipping?" (*Hamlet*, 2.2.561).

It has been left to Zophar, the last of the friends, to direct Job to the mercy of God, but of course that is the cruelest thing of all to do. For the import is that not only is Job being treated fairly—as Eliphaz and Bildad have argued—but more than fairly: he is actually getting off lightly (Andersen), with less than his guilt deserves.

5 Zophar says straight out what Job has been feeling his way toward: a clearly expressed wish that God would himself speak. In chap. 3 Job has voiced rhetorical questions (e.g., "'Why is light given to him that is in misery?'" v 20) which expect no answer, but are nevertheless questions directed toward heaven. In chap. 7 he has more openly addressed God with questions that are not purely rhetorical but carry reproof ("Am I the sea . . . that thou settest a guard over me?," "What is man, that thou dost make so much of him, . . . test him every morning?," "How long wilt thou not look away from me?," vv 12, 17, 19). In chap. 9 he has contemplated the anguish of a legal disputation that would compel God to speak (vv 3, 14, 16, 35), and in chap. 10 he has announced that he "will say to God, 'Do not condemn me'" (v 2), and has directed disputatious arguments toward God (vv 3–22). But nowhere has he seriously envisaged the possibility of God addressing him. That is yet to come, in 13:22, where he will invite God to "call" him to disputation, in 23:5, where he imagines God "answering" him, and ultimately in 31:35 where he will call on the Almighty to "answer" his protestation of innocence (chap. 31).

In the end, Job will rest his case and challenge God to answer him. But at this point in chap. 11, though Zophar wishes it could be *God* who speaks ("Eloah" in emphatic position, as Gordis notes), he does not for a moment imagine that God actually will address Job. There is no need for that, in fact, for Zophar has appointed himself God's spokesman.

6 The secret wisdom of God, with which he could put Job in his place, is a rather open mystery. For Zophar knows it, and he here communicates it to Job. It is that God, being merciful as well as just, allows his mercy to temper his just retribution against sinners. The balance between mercy and justice is not for humans to determine, however; it lies in the unfathomable freedom of God to "pass over" transgression and not exact the full punishment that is deserved (cf. Amos 7:1–9; Mic 7:18; Ezek 11:3; 20:17; Jer 4:27; 5:10, 18; 30:11; 46:28; Ezra 9:13). See further G. von Rad, *Old Testament Theology* (tr. D. M. G. Stalker; Edinburgh: Oliver and Boyd, 1962) 1:262–64; K. Koch, "Sühne und Sündenvergebung um die Wende von der exilischen zur nachexilischen Zeit," *EvT* 26 (1966), 217–39; H. Thyen, *Studien zur Sündenvergebung im Neuen Testament und seinem alttestamentlichen und jüdischen Voraussetzungen* (FRLANT 96; Göttingen: Vandenhoeck und Ruprecht, 1969); J. J. Stamm, *Erlösen und Vergeben im Alten Testament. Eine begriffsgeschichtliche Untersuchung* (Berne: Francke, 1940); H.-P. Stähli, *THWAT*, 2:204; H. Vorländer, "Forgiveness," *NIDNTT* 1:697–703.

It is noticeable that the idea that the nexus of sin and punishment can be interfered with by God's mercy is largely confined to the prophetic traditions, and certainly appears nowhere else in the wisdom literature. Indeed, in Prov 19:11 it is said of a wise *man* that "it is his glory to overlook (עבר) an offense," but such a perception is not transferred into a theological dimension. Job himself has expressed the forlorn wish that God would forgive (lit. "make pass over," עבר hiph) his presumed transgression (7:21), but on the whole it is evident that Zophar is appealing to a tradition outside the normal parameters of wisdom. Perhaps it is because the concept of the forgiving mercy of God is alien to the wisdom thinker but at home with the visionary prophet that Zophar depicts it as one of the "secrets" (תעלמות) of God's wisdom (חכמה here the divine wisdom) and understanding (תושיה). It is a bold move for Zophar to pick up Job's plea (7:21) that his "transgression" should be pardoned, and to answer it—from the prophetic tradition, not his own—with the assurance that it *has* been pardoned, in part at least. It is bold because in so saying Zophar implicitly abandons the confident standing of the wisdom theologian with his ability to pinpoint the way in which the moral order operates, the way in which God will act, and casts himself adrift on the unknowable "secret wisdom" of God in which a maverick mercy disturbs the tidy causal nexus.

Zophar is the most original theologian of the three friends of Job, and has been saved up by his creator (the author of the book) for third and climactic position in the speech cycle because of his wider-ranging theological formation (not because he comes last alphabetically, as Fohrer supposes!). But more original does not necessarily mean more correct, and the conclusion he reaches is self-evidently absurd (at least to readers who have begun with 1:1 and 1:8). Neither God's mercy nor his justice has much to do with the case of Job, and it is precisely to the extent that Zophar believes he can fathom the unfathomable God that he goes astray in deciding that "God overlooks part of your sin." Zophar is right in locating the cause of Job's suffering in the mystery of God, and for Job that will be the only explanation he ever gets, even from God. But Zophar is wrong—and so comes nowhere near preempting the divine speeches of chaps. 38–41—in supposing that the only mystery in God is how he mixes justice and mercy in his dealings with humans.

7–12 But Zophar is not going to dwell on the subject of how far God's mercy has shielded Job from the full effects of his sinfulness. The crucial fact is, for Zophar, that no matter how great or how small Job's sin is—and it is no doubt greater than Job imagines—it is sin. And however much mercy has tempered justice, justice is still the principle upon which the moral universe runs, and God is fundamentally the regulator of retribution. Zophar embarks upon this *topos* (vv 7–12) on the unfathomable wisdom of God with one particular aspect of God's wisdom specifically in mind: God knows who is guilty and who not. Whether God knows absolutely everything is neither here nor there at the present moment for Zophar—though his language is of the most extreme generality; what matters is that God has an unerring ability to ferret out wrong-doing. And that means, when the generalities have been stripped down, that God knows that Job is a guilty man despite Job's every protestation (v 4).

This "Panegyric on the Divine Wisdom" (Davidson), especially vv 7–9, which looks like a conventional formulation, has no exact parallel in the book. Job's own "hymns" of praise to the divine wisdom focus rather upon that wisdom as subversive and destructive (9:4–10; 12:13–25). In the wisdom poem of chap. 28, ascribed to Job in the MT but perhaps to be allotted to Zophar (see the *Comment* on chap. 28), "wisdom" is not explicitly described as God's own wisdom, but it is undiscoverable by humans (28:12–13) and it is pictured as beyond the knowable world of the sea or land (28:14, 21; cf. 11:8–9). A further linguistic analogy to the undiscoverability of the divine wisdom lies in 23:8–9, where God is described as undiscoverable (cf. 23:3), not behind nor before, not on the left hand nor the right.

7–9 Job is of course not in the least interested in discovering the totality of God's knowledge; and it comes as no surprise to him to learn that it is beyond human comprehension. "High as heaven is that wisdom, and thy reach so small; deep as hell itself, and thy thought so shallow" (Knox). The only relevance of this statement of God's unfathomable wisdom is that God's knowledge must be presumed to contain specific knowledge of Job's guilt. Zophar does not himself lay claim to any superior acquaintance with God's wisdom than Job has; he only argues that, since God's knowledge is immense, there is room in it for knowledge of sins which Job himself does not remember or acknowledge.

It would be going too far to insist that Zophar preaches a doctrine of God's "omniscience." God's is a knowledge beyond human knowledge, one that cannot be probed to its fullest extent (cf. 5:9, where God does "marvelous deeds, that cannot be fathomed"; there it was said that there was no possibility of fathoming it [אֵין חֵקֶר], whereas here חֵקֶר means the *object* of fathoming). Humans can "do" nothing to acquire full knowledge of God's wisdom; they cannot "know" God's wisdom in its entirety (though they can of course know it in part). But that does not mean that God's knowledge is viewed primarily as an accumulation of data (though obviously it must include that); in the book generally "knowledge" is so often linked with "power" that we must suppose that "knowledge" is primarily "know-how" (cf. 5:9; 9:4; 12:13; 42:2–3).

Neither is it true that Zophar affirms that God is unknowable. It is unfair to him to say that in vv 7–9 he enunciates a general truth which he then proceeds to contradict in his application of it (so Terrien). Zophar's awareness of the ultimate mystery of God does not preclude him from practicing his craft as a teacher of wisdom in affirming that he knows how God acts toward wrongdoers (vv 10–11). Neither also is Zophar affirming the incomprehensibility of God's essence or nature (as Fohrer thinks), but simply his *wisdom*.

The dimensions of the human world are here fourfold: heaven, underworld, sea, land (elsewhere usually threefold; cf. Fohrer, 517–19). They represent the totality of human space, in three dimensions (unlike north, south, east and west); the numeration is evidently based on, though not identical to, the creation narrative (heaven/firmament, "deep," sea, land, Gen 1; cf. also Hag 2:6, heavens, earth, sea, dry land; Ps 135:6, heaven, earth, seas, deeps; and cf. Ps 139:8–9 for the list heaven, Sheol, sea). If humans cannot reach to these extremities of their own natural world, how much less can they attain something that is beyond them in scope? The similarly worded passages, Jer 23:24; Amos 9:2–4; Ps 139:8–10 are not to do with the *wisdom* of God but his presence and capacity for intervention in human affairs.

The question form used by Zophar, with its fourfold short unanswerable interrogations, seemed to G. Fohrer ("Form und Funktion in der Hiob-dichtung," *ZDMG* 109 [1959] 31–49 [37]) to be, or at least to imitate, the interrogation process in a legal trial (*Verhörfragen vor Gericht*); but it seems more probable that these are the questions of an academic disputation (cf. Horst: typical *Disputationsfrage*) such as wisdom teachers will have engaged in. At the same time their content is reminiscent of hymnic traditions, in which also the form of the rhetorical question is used to extol the majesty of God (cf. Ps 113:5–6; 139:7).

10–12 The implication of God's superhuman knowledge is that God knows the truth even about secret sinners—like Job. Humans may not be able to find any fault in Job, but if God is punishing him it proves simply that he has—in his superior wisdom—discovered something.

10–11 What kind of "hindering," "dissuading" or "restraining" of God has Zophar in mind? Job has already used the same word in 9:12 (יְשִׁיבֶנּוּ, lit. "turn him back"), but there it concerned the impossibility of preventing God—by legal means or otherwise—from exercising the anger to which he is perma-nently committed: "If he should snatch away, who could restrain (or, dissuade) him?" Zophar, who is not exactly refuting Job but rather setting him straight, refers rather to the impossibility of proving that God has no right to act as he does; no one can hinder or dissuade God from his acts of rightful judgment because he operates on the basis of superhuman knowledge, to which every human's is inferior. He knows who is righteous and who "worthless," and judges on the basis of that knowledge. We note, incidentally, that the concept of God's mercy tempering the process of retribution (as in v 6c) seems to have faded from Zophar's consciousness; if reminded of it he might respond that even mercy must know the facts. Though to know all would certainly not be to forgive all, in Zophar's book, to forgive anything at all God would need to know all that was deserved.

So locked into the retributionist dogma is Zophar that he cannot see Job as a sufferer but only as a guilty man. His language to describe what is happening to Job is legal because he has moved instantly from his perception of Job's distress to a theological interpretation of that distress as divine judgment. And though he speaks quite generally of what God habitually does with "worthless" individuals it is evident that he is directing his attention primarily to Job and proffering Job an explanation for his suffering.

God's passing by (חלף) is in itself of no special consequence: it is part of his routine governance of the world that he passes to and fro among humans, his eyes ever open for misdemeanors—just like the Satan of chaps. 1–2, whose existence Zophar does not recognize but who even in chaps. 1–2 does nothing but perform a divinely assigned task. Job has just now used this word "pass by" (חלף) of God (9:11), but he has invested the term with a special significance: for him the God he craves to enter into dialogue with will never stop to listen or reply. He hurriedly "passes by" without Job gaining so much as a glimpse of a figure he cannot "see" or "recognize." From Job's perspective, when God "passes by," Job suffers personal loss and deprivation of the one relationship that would be meaningful for him; from Zophar's perspective, when God "passes by" in the course of his unceasing scrutiny of human affairs, Zophar rejoices that the moral order of the universe is being faithfully upheld by God's diligence.

In the course of such investigation, God's far-seeing wisdom may have cause to call someone to account. It will not be his unbridled power (as Horst suggests; cf. 9:4) but here his "wisdom" (cf. 11:6–9) that will bring the guilty to book. Legal processes are duly observed by this wise ruler comparable to an "intelligent and conscientious sheikh" (Terrien): first he "shuts up" (סגר) the guilty man in custody until it should be plain what is to be done with him (as in Lev 24:12 and Num 15:34, in the cases of a rebellious man and of a man found breaking the sabbath [the term is ינוח במשמר]) or until the fault should be confirmed (as in Lev 13:4 where leprosy is suspected [the verb is סגר, as here]).

Then, as part of the same proceeding (the connective is simple *waw*, "and"), he summons a legal assembly (NIV "convenes a court") to inquire into the facts and make a legal judgment (as in Neh 5:7; Ezek 16:40; 23:46 [NAB]).

That is all metaphor, of course. In fact God is himself investigator, prosecutor, legal assembly and judge, and needs no earthly court nor lengthy process of law before he can act upon what he has discovered. For by himself (הוא, "he," in emphatic position) he recognizes an evildoer when he sees one, and wherever he lights upon iniquity he marks it well. Probably the particular kind of iniquity Zophar has in mind as detected by God is lying, for the term "men of worthlessness" (מתי־שוא) is elsewhere used in parallelism with "deceitful" (נעלמים, Ps 26:4 [5]; cf. Ps 24:4 "he does not lift up himself to what is false [שוא] // nor swear deceitfully"). It is improbable that the iniquity is magic (as M. A. Klopfenstein, *Die Lüge nach dem Alten Testament. Ihr Begriff, ihre Bedeutung und ihre Beurteilung* [Zürich: Gotthelf, 1964] 315–16) or misuse of magical powers (J. F. A. Sawyer, *THWAT* 2:882–84), since such crimes are alien to Job's situation. Certainly this "worthlessness" belongs to the semantic realm of falsehood. The implication is that Job is a dissembler, knowing well enough what his sins are for which he is suffering God's punishment.

Not for the first time in the book, a generalization is uttered not for its own sake but primarily for its applicability to Job (cf., e.g., 8:20; 9:22). This sentence of praise for the unflagging watchfulness of God over the moral order is in function a sentence of condemnation against the man who has dared to affirm "I am clean in your sight!" (v 4b). Job, in challenging the universal doctrine of retribution, has challenged the moral order, and in so doing put himself in the wrong as a "hollow man" ("man of emptiness," שוא). Nonetheless, as Hesse points out, Zophar is not as savage as a man of his principles might be: he does not speak of the *end* of the wicked (as e.g., 8:11–19) but only of the beginning of the end, not of the *destruction* of the wicked but of their detection. And we may note that he will not indeed utter a word about their end until he has done his best—given the unprepossessing resources

his dogma allows him—to encourage Job to move into the sphere of the blessedness of the righteous (vv 13–19).

12 But first a proverb-like saying will conclude Zophar's excursus on the
wisdom of God. On the surface it is not a very difficult proverb: "A 'hollow'
man will get understanding; and the colt of a wild ass will be born a man" or
preferably, following Pope, ". . . and a wild ass will be born tame." Formally,
the sentence has something in common with 5:7, "Man begets suffering for
himself, and the sons of Pestilence fly high"—another proverbial utterance in
which the relationship of the two halves of the line (joined simply by "and")
is rather problematic. Here rather than an act and its consequence we seem
to have two statements of impossibility which we could well represent as RSV
does: "A stupid man will get understanding, when a wild ass's colt is born a
man"—"when pigs fly," "dans la semaine des quatre jeudis," that is. Peake
objected that "a hollow man is void of understanding" is a mere tautology;
but we must stress that the verb is not a statement of a generalized present,
but refers to a future acquisition of wisdom: an "empty" man *will* as soon
gain understanding as a wild ass be a tame donkey.

The exact meaning of the Hebrew has been variously understood, but one
suggestion commends itself as superior to the conventional interpretation (as
in RSV). Pope's rendering, "a wild ass will be born tame," is admittedly not as
striking as " . . . born a man." But he has rightly pointed out that the phrase
usually translated "a wild ass's colt" (עַיִר פֶּרֶא) can mean no such thing, since
עַיִר is always used for the domesticated ass (e.g., Gen 32:15; Judg 10:4; Zech
9:9) and does not indicate the *young* animal, while פֶּרֶא is always used for the
wild ass (e.g., Job 24:5; Isa 32:14; Jer 2:24). He also notes that the phrase
פֶּרֶא אָדָם, usually translated "wild ass of a man" (Gen 16:12) appears to be a
fixed phrase; if אָדָם, *'ādām*, "man" in this context is understood as אֲדָמָה,
'ªdāmâ, "earth, land, steppe" (as seems to be the case in several other passages),
the "man" disappears from the verse, and the "wild ass of the steppe" takes
its place. See n. 11:12.e for details.

The more difficult issue is how the proverb is related to the context. If
Job is a "hollow" man, the proverb means that there is no hope for him; but
the verses that immediately follow (vv 13–19) show that Zophar believes there
is. What we must note is that Zophar has not actually called Job a morally
"hollow" man. He believes Job has committed some wrong, and that God is
punishing him for it as he punishes all wrongdoers (v 11); but he also retains
more than a streak of confidence in Job, as his acceptance of the possibility
of Job's repentance (vv 13–14) makes plain. So Job cannot be wholly "worthless,"
morally "hollow." To tell the truth, says Zophar, wrongdoers are generally
beyond redemption, incapable of gaining that moral "understanding" that leads
to right behavior. But you, Job (note the emphatic "you" in v 13), are not so
stupid; you are teachable, and I will teach you!

13–20 Zophar now offers to Job conditional advice, persuading him of
the blessings of repentance. Both Eliphaz and Bildad have already offered
similar encouragement; it is in the conditions they attach to their promise of
future restoration that they differ. Eliphaz in 5:8–26 approaches Job so delicately
that he does not even presume to tell Job that he must "seek" God, but simply
testifies to what he himself does, as some kind of model for Job's imitation:
"I myself seek God in prayer, and to God I address my speech" (5:8). And

even when he utters a negative or positive imperative ("Do not spurn the discipline of the Almighty," "Take heed, and know it for yourself"), he does not lay upon Job conditions too hard to bear—from his perspective, at any rate (see *Comment* on 5:17–27). Bildad, for his part, sees only two conditions as indispensable for God's favor: devout prayer and a blameless life (8:5–6: "if you will seek God . . . if you are pure and upright"). Now Zophar, more assured than either of the other friends of Job's sinfulness, speaks plainly of prayer *and* of extirpation of evil.

And whereas Eliphaz and Bildad have both contrasted the fate of the wicked with that of the pious man such as they hope Job will prove himself to be, they each conclude their speech on the upbeat note of Job's well-being (cf. 5:25–26; 8:20–22). Zophar, on the other hand, manages, despite the general optimism of these verses, to conclude on a note of baleful warning—as if he fears that his promise of virtue rewarded will not be truly efficacious without an annexed threat of vice requited.

13 Job, for all his undoubted sinfulness, is not a reprobate. Even he, he also (the "you" is in emphatic position), can attain restoration to God's favor. Of course, as with Bildad (8:5), the restoration envisaged by Zophar is "a reward for righteousness, not a pardon for penitence" (Andersen on 8:5).

It matters little whether we detect here two conditions (directing the mind in prayer, removing iniquity) or primarily that of v 13, regarding v 14 as a parenthesis (Budde, Weiser). The structure is similar to that of 8:4–6 ("if . . . if . . . if . . . then" [כי־עתה]) with its "if . . . if . . . then" (כי־אז). But here the first "if" is unquestionably a hypothetical, and the second, in view of v 6c, surely means "since."

First Job is to "direct [his] mind" toward God since true righteousness stems from the inner self, and is not simply an outward matter of "spreading out hands" in prayer. The deliberate act of turning one's attention to a religious duty is reminiscent of the Rabbinic teaching on "intention" or "concentration" (כַּוָּנָה, *kawwānâ*, from the verb כון used here) regarded as the essential element in prayer. The pious men of old, says the Mishnah (*m. Ber.* 5.1), used to sit quiet for an hour before praying, so that they might "direct their minds toward God" (כון לב, as here). See further G. F. Moore, *Judaism in the First Centuries of the Christian Era, the Age of the Tannaim* (Cambridge, Mass.: Harvard UP, 1930) 2:223–26; C. G. Montefiore and H. Loewe, *A Rabbinic Anthology* (repr. New York: Schocken Books, 1974) 272–94. The directing of the mind toward God is connected in 1 Sam 7:3 with commitment to serving Yahweh alone (cf. 2 Chr 20:33) and in Ps 78:37 with faithful loyalty to him (cf. 112:7).

Next Job should spread out his hands in prayer. To judge from ancient Near Eastern iconography, this conventional gesture of prayer consisted of raising the hands, palms outwards and close together, to face level. The symbolic significance of the gesture, despite confident assertions by commentators (it is a sign of expectancy, innocence, or abandonment of weapons), remains unknown. The "historical" explanation of Keel that originally it expressed "the attempt to restrain a superior, numinous opposite by means of conjuring, thus rendering it serviceable or averting it" is equally speculative (O. Keel, *The Symbolism of the Biblical World: Ancient Near Eastern Iconography and the Book of Psalms* [New York: Seabury, 1978] 313). There may be some connection, however, with the gesture of surrender (still well known in some Middle Eastern cultures), in which the hands, with palms forward, are held at shoulder level, and the head is turned slightly to one side; see R. A. Barakat, *Journal of Popular Culture* 6 (1973), 749–87 (778 no. 104). See Keel, fig. 422, for a fine line-drawing of the posture (from an Egyptian context); and *ISBE* 2:450, for a photograph of a carved ivory casket with a similar depiction (from Hazor, 9th–8th centuries B.C.). The verbs used for this gesture with the hands are principally פרשׂ, "to spread out" (as in Ps 143:6; Ezra 9:5) and נשׂא, "to lift up" (as in Ps 28:2; 63:5 [4]); it is not a matter of *stretching* out (as RSV, JB, NAB, NIV), which is a gesture of appeal (Prov 1:24). And it is the *palms* (כף) specifically and not the hands (יד) generally that are normally mentioned because it is the palms that are presented to the person addressed. (A. Parrot, in his "Gestes de la prière dans le monde mésopotamien," *maqqél shâqédh. Hommage à Wilhelm Vischer* [Montpellier: Causse, Graille, Castelnau (1960) 177–80], deals mainly with the gesture of the folded hands.)

It goes without saying that this well-intentioned advice is superficial. Can Zophar be unaware that Job's impassioned speech to God (chap. 10) evinces just that "concentration" upon God that he is now demanding of Job?

14 Hands that are unclean cannot be presented to God in prayer (cf. Isa 1:15). Despite the "if," Zophar obviously believes Job to have iniquity in his hand. How does Zophar propose Job can get rid of his sin? Not by sacrifice or atonement, not even by repentance, but by a renunciation of it, a distancing of himself from it, putting himself far from it. This is wisdom theology speaking. Sin is not something to be covered up or cleansed or forgiven, but to be avoided, departed from, disassociated from (cf. Ps 1:1; Prov 1:10–15; 4:14, 24; 5:8; 30:8). Once sin has been committed there is nothing that can be done about it except suffer the inevitable future. (This distinctive attitude to sin is overlooked in the scholarly literature, e.g., S. Porubčan, *Sin in the Old Testament: A Soteriological Study* [Rome: Herder, 1963]; K. Koch, *TDOT* 4:309–19; R. Knierim, *Die Hauptbegriffe für Sünde im Alten Testament* [Gütersloh: Mohn, 1965]; idem, *THWAT* 1:541–49.) Job can only "renounce" (JB) his present wrongdoing, and, to use a metaphor familiar to the world of oriental hospitality, give it no house room as a guest ("let iniquity not dwell in your tent"). Elsewhere "to dwell in the tent" of someone means to appropriate that person's property (Gen 9:27; 1 Chron 5:10; Ps 78:55; cf. Job 18:15), but it does not seem (against Fohrer) that here there is an image of a personified "iniquity" having taken over Job's home and forced him out of it. The image is rather that of Jer 4:14, where evil thoughts "lodge" within Jerusalem. The reference to Job's "tent" (singular; see n. 11:14.b) does not of course imply that he is a tent-dweller; it is a metaphor from a more archaic life-style (as in 5:24; 8:22; 19:12; 29:4; etc.).

15 The consequence of renunciation of evil, in wisdom theology, is righteousness of life—with the rewards that brings. This three-verse sentence (vv 13–15) concludes on the positive note of the confidence of the righteous. Job will "lift up his head (lit. 'face')" with justifiable pride in his innocence (this is not the "lifting up of the head" of victory, as in Ps 110:7; Judg 8:28) but more probably the expression of a good conscience (as 2 Sam 2:22; cf. F. Stolz, *THWAT* 2:112. On the possible forensic use of such a phrase, see I.L. Seeligmann, "Zur Terminologie für das Gerichtsverfahren im Wortschatz des biblischen Hebräisch," *VTS* 16 [1967] 251–78 [270–72]). Gordis may be right, however, in understanding the idiom as "to be happy," which would parallel well the last words "you will not fear" (cf. the opposite idiom, "his face fell" [Gen 4:6], i.e., "he became sad").

He will become "firm," lit. "cast" (as of metal); hence NEB "a man of iron"; the metaphorical sense is rarely attested, but cf. 41:23 [15], 24 [16]. His firmness lies simply in his freedom from fear (cf. 5:21, 22) in that he knows he has done nothing to call down upon him the divine retribution (for the imagery of the steadfastness of metal for fearlessness, cf. Jer 1:17–18; Ezek 3:8–9).

In all this delightful picture the reader cannot miss an irony, however far it may be from Zophar's intention; for everything that he has been commending to Job has, according to the prologue, been entirely true of Job from the very beginning (1:1).

16 The climactic element in feeling secure is being able to contrast it with the experience of insecurity, says Zophar. Job will "remember" his "suffering" (עמל, physical and mental; cf. 3:10; 7:3) only as a pain that is past and gone; he will "forget" it not in the sense of losing it completely from his memory, but in the sense of its no longer having any power to affect him. There is a close parallel in Gen 41:51 where Joseph, in naming his first born Manasseh (מְנַשֶּׁה, *menaššeh*) "[God] causes to forget," explains the name as meaning "God has caused me to forget (נַשַּׁנִי, *naššanî*) all my suffering (עמל, as here) and all my father's house." Of course, in the very act of naming the child "Forgetting" Joseph is remembering. Here, the very parallelism of "forget" with "remember" is a striking confirmation of a psychological truth, that pain that has been thoroughly worked through is not totally forgotten—as it might be if it were merely repressed—but is remembered as powerless. "Remember" is of course often paralleled to "*not* forget" (e.g., Ps 9:13 [12]; 74:18–19, 22–23) and "forget" to "*not* remember" (Job 24:20; Prov 31:7; Isa 17:10; 54:4), but here only are these polar opposites in *synonymous* parallelism.

Waters, especially flood-waters, waves or deep waters are frequently images for trouble; but the time when they "pass by/over" (עבר) is itself the very time of distress (cf. Ps 124:4–5; 42:8 [7]; 88:17). So the picture here is not of "flood-waters" (NEB, Fohrer, Horst); nor is it of the wadis that "pass away" (עבר, 6:15) as they dry up (so de Wilde), for the "passing away of such waters" is a disappointment. Here it must be water that has flowed past (so NJPS), out of sight, out of mind, and gone irrevocably.

17 Job has pictured himself as bound for the "land of darkness and deep shadow, the land of gloom like blackness" (10:21–22), but Zophar dismisses such extravagance, projecting a future of light, the most evident symbol of life. Not just the life he now lives, but his life as continuing and enduring (חלד), will be bright as midday—no, so bright that midday by comparison will itself be deadly gloom. The sentence is built on the pattern of Isa 58:10, "Then shall your light rise in the darkness and your gloom become as the noonday" (cf. 58:8), but the metaphor is much heightened; for here it seems to be not so much a question of present darkness becoming bright, but rather that the darkest phase of the life that still lies ahead of Job will be like morning light—which is to say that he will be perpetually bathed in light.

18 There is no real security in the present that does not include the confidence that it will continue: "you will be secure because there is hope." Hope is an important principle in the Book of Job, but it is not quite the hope of psalmic piety, in which the suffering worshiper appeals to God for deliverance and waits patiently—in hope—for God to act (e.g., Ps 62:6 [5]; 71:5). This is a confidence in the right order of a just world governed by exact retribution: "The hope of the righteous ends in gladness, but the hope of the wicked comes to nothing" (Prov 10:28).

Such a concept of hope is modulated differently by Job's three conversation-partners. Eliphaz has located a ground for "hope" in the universally acknowledged Godfearingness and uprightness of Job: "Is not your piety your source of confidence? Does not your blameless life give you hope?" (4:6). Eliphaz means: Trust in the righteousness you already have. Bildad in more cautious mood depicts in metaphors of papyrus reeds and spider's web the hope that the wicked have, which is doomed to be frustrated: "so does the hope of the godless perish" (8:13). He means: Hope exists wherever a person is righteous; but where there is wickedness there is truly only room for despair. Zophar, convinced of Job's present sinfulness, can only project "hope" as a concomitant of future righteousness; if, conditionally, Job enters the sphere of blessedness, he will be "secure because there is hope." He means: Hope is available to you. It simply depends upon your becoming righteous. See further, W. Zimmerli, *Man and his Hope in the Old Testament* (SBT 2/20; London: SCM, 1971) 16–25—to whom some of the wording in the foregoing paragraph is indebted; C. Westermann, "Das Hoffen im Alten Testament," in *Forschung am Alten Testament. Gesammelte Studien* (ThB 24; Munich: Kaiser, 1964) 219–65; J. van der Ploeg, "L'espérance dans l'AT," *RB* 61 (1954) 481–507.

Perhaps in focusing upon the time of sleep as the moment when security is best enjoyed (cf. Ps 4:9 [8]) Zophar has in mind Job's confession in 7:13–14 that at that very time he is beset by nightmares.

19 *Security* is obviously the chief attraction of the blessed life, as far as Zophar is concerned; for the image is continued for yet another line, in language of the most conventional kind; the same wording, "lie down (רבץ) with none making afraid (אין מחריד)" occurs in Isa 17:2; Zeph 3:13, and "none making afraid" in Lev 26:6; Deut 28:26; Jer 7:33; 30:10; 46:27; Ezek 34:28; 39:26 (the last two with "dwell in safety" [וישב לבטח] as well); Nah 2:12. The poet surely wants us to reflect on how the pious Job of chap. 1, "none like him on earth," and fulfilling to the last detail Zophar's prescription, had had his security shaken to the foundations.

What is the connection of the picture of security (vv 18–19a) with that of the image of the revered patriarch being flattered and deferred to (v 19b)? It must be that security for a princeling or sheikh like Job and his friends cannot consist in the mere absence of assault upon one's property or person, but must also involve the esteem of those whom they have been accustomed to leading. Job suffers at the moment not only from the assaults of Sabeans and Chaldeans (1:15, 17) but from the disgrace into which his afflictions have cast him (cf. his own description of his disgrace in 30:1–15 compared with his former standing [29:7–17]). There is no security without honor, without full appreciation of one's rank and quality. It is therefore climactic in Zophar's depiction of the good fortune that awaits a truly converted Job that "many will seek your favor," lit. "will make soft, or, sweet, your face." The idiom is found in Prov 19:6 ("Many seek the favor of a generous man") while Ps 45:13 [12] ("The people of Tyre will entreat your favor with gifts") reminds us that oriental flattery is not merely a verbal matter, but includes the presentation of gifts as tokens of esteem (a practice frequently misunderstood by westerners as "bribery"). The phrase is used also of entreating the favor of God (e.g., Exod 32:11; Jer 26:19; 1 Kgs 13:6) and here also the giving of gifts (sacrifices) is sometimes explicit (1 Sam 13:12; Mal 1:9). At Job's restoration, indeed, such a scene will be enacted, with all his relatives and acquaintances bringing gifts as tokens of congratulation and also, no doubt, as a means of self-ingratiation (42:11). No one becomes prosperous through the gifts of such clients (in 42:10 Job had already had his fortunes restored to twice their former worth *before* the arrival of the *bakshish* money), but they are the icing on the cake for the man of wealth and dignity, and more: they are the outward and visible sign of social worth—which is what everyone wants, but Job more than most, considering that he has started at the top of the social ladder.

20 Zophar is not quite done, however. Since his whole speech functions as an incentive to Job to forsake his present evil-doing, Zophar cannot conclude simply by expatiating on the happiness of the pious but must also allude to the dark alternative: the fate of the wicked (it is not quite the motif of the "two ways" [Weiser, Hesse]). This theme, expanded on by Eliphaz (4:8–11) and Bildad (7:11–19), in the latter case explicitly by contrast to the theme of the fortune of the righteous, is here briefly stated. This does not mean that Zophar is less severe than Bildad, however; for his attitude to Job has already been stated clearly in the nodal verse 6: Job is indeed already headed for the fate of the wicked.

That fate is the absence of security. For Zophar in this speech, it is not death, not even premature death, not divine punishment, not physical illness that is the true punishment they endure. It is that, unlike the righteous man of vv 18–19, they lose confidence. Their eyes fail, which is to say, they abandon hope for what they had looked for longingly (for the idiom, cf. 31:16, where it is parallel to "withheld desire"; Deut 28:32, 65; Ps 69:4 [3]). Flight or escape "perishes" from them: with all security gone the merest trifle can pose a life-destroying threat (for the phrase, cf. 5:4; Jer 25:35; Amos 2:14; Ps 142:5). In sum, their hope can have no substance: it is merely despair, lit. "the breathing of breath." It is not that their only hope is death, the breathing of their last (as RSV, NAB, NIV); this idiom for despair recurs in 31:39 and probably also Jer 15:9 (so Gordis, de Wilde).

It is in the crucial sphere of *security,* in Zophar's reckoning, that the unrighteous receive their retribution and are most strongly differentiated from the pious of vv 16–19.

Explanation

Zophar's speech is, from one perspective, nothing but a further variation on the retributionist theme extensively developed by the two former friends. Guilt will find its punishment, and right doing its reward (vv 11, 13–16, 20). Nothing can stay the hand of inflexible justice.

Nevertheless, Zophar's theological standpoint is quite distinctive. Where Bildad had appealed to the impossibility of God's perverting justice (8:2) and Eliphaz had appealed to the impossibility of a mortal's being entirely righteous in the sight of one's maker (4:17), Zophar appeals to the impossibility of fathoming the divine knowledge (11:6–9). This seems a more mystical, perhaps more prophetic, move—but that is a misleading impression. For Zophar is at bottom the product of the academy, and as such holds a theology of the essential *knowability* of God. The "secrets of wisdom" and "mysteries in his working" (v 6) are not so much the ground for a silent and reverent awe as a datum about God with implications that can and must be drawn for a practical theology of God's dealings with humankind. In plain language: God knows more about humans than will ever be discovered, and that means more about their sins. Where there is punishment without any visible reason, we can be sure that God in his wisdom knows the reason. What is more, it will not be some mysterious, ineffable, unfathomable, transcendental reason, but a reason that could easily be comprehended by a human "if only God would open his lips" (v 6). So while we cannot always know exactly why God is punishing someone, we can be sure that he is punishing that person *for some reason or other,* and never without cause or gratuitously (Zophar has never heard the divine confession in 2:3!). Which all goes to show that God is knowable and indeed quite adequately known, that his dealings with humankind follow a strict but simple pattern, and that if we cannot trace his workings from cause to effect, why then we can reconstruct them from effect back to cause. And that leaves Zophar where he has always been—in the academy of the wise—but, as against Eliphaz and Bildad, with his own personal chair in Divine Epistemology. Has the author of Job not drawn his dramatis personae from life?

There is another theological distinctive in Zophar's speech. It is the role of divine mercy. This divine attribute, so frequently appealed to by Hebrew sufferers in their psalmic prayers, and so often the backcloth of prophetic denunciations, transforming their totalitarian violence into anguished cries of divine longing, has been cruelly denatured in the wisdom theology of Zophar. For, far from being a counterweight to the principle of retribution, mercy has been subsumed under it. No one may hope that God will exercise his mercy to temper his justice, for he has already done so! Any mercy that God is going to show has already been allowed for before the law of retribution is called into play. God exacts from humans less than their guilt deserves, and, wherever he punishes, has already overlooked part of their sin (v 6). Human suffering, which is always punishment (according to Zophar), has already had a percentage deducted for (divine) good will. That means to say that Job can plead for no mitigation, but in his suffering can only be thankful for the mercy that has already remitted part of his deserved punishment.

Finally, Zophar deserves our attention for the advice he gives Job on what his future conduct should be. Eliphaz has, a trifle more delicately, not presumed to give Job direct advice but has spoken only of what he himself does (5:8). Bildad has been somewhat more explicit and directive in his advice to "make [his] prayer to God" and to "seek the favor of the Almighty" (8:5); but even so has cast the advice in a conditional form that might even be construed as a description of what Job's habitual practice actually is (see *Comment* on 8:5). Zophar similarly chooses the "if"-form, but makes it plain enough (comparing v 6 and v 14) that there is for him no question of Job's guilt. What Job has done wrong he must suffer for; it cannot be atoned for, forgiven or prayed away. Only by a fresh start, renouncing sin and embarking anew on a life of piety, can Job hope for a blessed future. Even judged by the canons of theological options open to him in his own time, Zophar has done an injustice to God in leaving him no space for any further exercise of mercy or forgiveness. In that regard he is a worse theologian than the other friends, although in his incapacity to conceive any explanation for suffering other than guilt he is on an even footing with them.

Yet even Zophar, for all his shortsightedness, is an orthodox theologian with something of value to teach. Picture his position thus: Whatever is (suffering, for example), is; and whatever is past (sin, for example) is past. There is no point in crying over spilled milk—nor even over spilled blood. It is from the present moment onward that a life of godliness is to be lived, the mind directed in concentrated intention toward God, the hands spread out in an attitude of prayer, and sin henceforth banished from the life (vv 13–14). And simplistic though his theology of reward is, it is a striking affirmation of the truths that "God rewards those who seek him" (Heb 11:6), and that "the prayer of a righteous man availeth much" (James 5:16). However alien to Job's situation Zophar may be, his word is "draw near to God and he will draw near to you" (James 4:8)—which is not only orthodox truth but a personal assurance.

Job's Fourth Speech   (12:1–14:22)

Bibliography

Blenkinsopp, J. "The Prophetic Reproach." *JBL* 90 (1971) 267–78. **Boecker, H. J.** *Redeformen des Rechtslebens im Alten Testament.* WMANT 14. Neukirchen-Vluyn: Neukirchener Verlag, 1964. ———. "Anklagereden und Verteidigungsreden im Alten Testament: Ein Beitrag zur Formgeschichte alttestamentlicher Prophetenworte." *EvTh* 20 (1960) 398–412. **Cohen, A.** "Studies in Hebrew Lexicography." *AJSL* 40 (1923–24) 153–85. **Davies, J. A.** "A Note on Job XII 2." *VT* 25 (1975) 670–71. **Dahood, M.** "Two Pauline Quotations from the Old Testament." *CBQ* 17 (1955) 19–24. ———. "Northwest Semitic Philology and Job." In *The Bible in Current Catholic Thought*, M. J. Gruenthaner Memorial Volume, ed. J. L. McKenzie. New York: Herder and Herder, 1962. 55–74. ———. "Ugaritic *ušn*, Job 12,10 and 11QPs Plea 3–4." *Bib* 47 (1966) 107–8. **De Gugliemo, A.** "Job 12:7–9 and the Knowability of God." *CBQ* 6 (1944) 476–82. **Driver, G. R.** "Problems in Job." *AJSL* 53 (1935–36) 160–70. ———. "Hebrew Roots and Words." *WO* 1 (1947–52) 406–15. ———. "Problems in the Hebrew Text of Job." *VTS* 3 (1955) 72–93. ———. "The Resurrection of Marine and Terrestrial Creatures." *JSS* 7 (1962) 12–22. ———. "Affirmation by Exclamatory Negation." *JANES* 5 (1973) 107–14. **Eitan, I.** "Two Unknown Verbs (איד, חלש)." *JBL* 42 (1923) 21–28. ———. *A Contribution to Biblical Lexicography.* New York: Columbia UP, 1924. **Gard, D. H.** "The Concept of the Future Life according to the Greek Translator of the Book of Job." *JBL* 73 (1954) 137–43. **Gemser, B.** "The RIB or Controversy Pattern in Hebrew Mentality." *VTS* 3 (1955) 120–37. **Gordis, R.** "Quotations as a Literary Usage in Biblical, Oriental and Rabbinic Literature." *HUCA* 22 (1949) 157–219. (= *Poets, Prophets and Sages; Essays in Biblical Interpretation.* Bloomington and London: Indiana UP, 1971. 104–59.) **Guillaume, A.** "A Contribution to Biblical Lexicography." *BSOAS* 16 (1954) 1–12. ———. "The Use of חלש in Exod. xvii. 13, Isa. xiv. 12 and Job xiv. 10." *JTS* ns 14 (1963) 91–92. **Halpern, B.** "Yhwh's Summary Justice in Job XIV 20." *VT* 28 (1978) 472–74. **Harvey, J.** *Le plaidoyer prophétique contre Israël après la rupture de l'alliance.* Studia travaux de recherche. Montreal: Editions Bellarmin, 1967. **Habermann, A. M.** "The Tomb of Rachel and the Term נפש" [Heb]. *Tarbiz* 25 (1956) 363–68. **Herz, N.** "The Exaggeration of Errors in the Massoretic." *JTS* 15 (1914) 258–64. **Jacob, B.** "Erklärung einiger Hiob-Stellen: 12:6; 14:11; 14:16; 14:22." *ZAW* 32 (1912) 278–87 (284–86). **Joüon, P.** "Notes philologiques sur le texte hébreu de Job 12,21." *Bib* 11 (1930) 322–24. **Katz, P.** "Notes on the Septuagint. V. Job xv.2." *JTS* 48 (1947) 194. **Limburg, J.** "The Root *RIB* and the Prophetic Lawsuit Speeches." *JBL* 88 (1969) 291–304. **Mejia, J.** "El lamed enfático en nuevos textos del Antiguo Testamento." *EstBíb* 22 (1963) 179–90. **Michael, J. H.** "Paul and Job: A Neglected Analogy." *ExpT* 36 (1924–25) 67–70. **Milgrom, J.** "The Cultic שגגה and its Influence in Psalms and Job." *JQR* 58 (1967) 115–25. **Nielsen, K.** *Yahweh as Prosecutor and Judge: An Investigation of the Prophetic Lawsuit (Rîb-Pattern).* JSOTS 9. Sheffield: JSOT, 1978. **Orlinsky, H. M.** "The Hebrew and Greek Texts of Job 14.12." *JQR* 28 (1937–38) 57–68. **Reider, J.** "Etymological Studies in Biblical Hebrew." *VT* 2 (1952) 113–30. ———. "Etymological Studies in Biblical Hebrew." *VT* 4 (1954) 276–95. **Sarna, N. M.** "איתנים, Job 12:19." *JBL* 74 (1955) 272–73. **Seeligmann, I. L.** "Zur Terminologie für das Gerichtsverfahren im Wortschatz des biblischen Hebräisch." *VTS* 16 (1967) 251–78. **Skehan, P. W.** "Strophic Patterns in the Book of Job." *CBQ* 23 (1961) 125–42 (= *Studies in Israelite Poetry and Wisdom.* CBQMS 1. Washington, D.C.: Catholic Biblical Association, 1971. 96–113). **Thompson, J. G. S. S.** "Sleep: An Aspect of Jewish Anthropology." *VT* 5 (1955) 421–33. **Ziegler, J.** *Iob 14,4–5a als wichtigster Schriftbeweis für die These "Neminem sine sorde et sine peccato esse" (Cyprian, test 3,54) bei den lateinischen christlichen Schriftstellern.* Bayerische Akademie der Wissenschaften, Phil.-hist. Klasse, Sitzungsberichte, Jahrgang 1985.3.

Munich: Verlag der Bayerischen Akademie der Wissenschaften und C. H. Beck. **Zink, J. K.** "Uncleannness and Sin. A Study of Job xiv 4 and Psalm li 7." *VT* 17 (1967) 354–61.

Translation

^{12:1} *Then Job answered and said:*

² *Truly you are the last of the wise!* [a]
With you wisdom will die! [b]
³ *But I have intelligence as much as you;*
I am not inferior to you.
Who does not know such things? [a]
⁴ *For* [a] *I have become a laughingstock to my friends,* [b]
I, a man who would call upon God and be answered,
I, an innocent man, a blameless man—a laughingstock.
⁵ *"Add insult to injury!"* [a] *think the secure,*
"Strike the man down now he is staggering!" [b]
⁶ *Yet the tents of brigands are left in peace,*
those who provoke God live in safety— [a]
those whom God has in his own power! [b]

⁷ *And yet [you say]:*
Ask the cattle, and they will teach [a] *you,*
the birds of the sky, they will tell you.
⁸ *Or speak to the earth,* [a] *and it will instruct you,*
the fish of the sea, they will inform you.
⁹ *Which among all these* [a] *does not know*
that Yahweh's [b] *hand has done this?—*
¹⁰ *He, in whose hand is the life of every living thing,*
and the breath of every human [a] *being.*
¹¹ *Does not the ear test words*
as the palate tastes its food?
¹² [a] *Wisdom is found with the aged,*
understanding comes with length of days.

¹³ *With him is wisdom and might,*
counsel [a] *and understanding is his.*
¹⁴ [a] *What he destroys will not be built,*
whom he imprisons will not be freed.
¹⁵ *He holds back the waters, there is drought;* [a]
he lets them loose, they overwhelm the earth.

¹⁶ *With him is strength and wisdom;*
in his power are the deceiver and the deceived.
¹⁷ [a] *Counselors he leads away barefoot,* [b]
judges he drives to folly. [c]
¹⁸ *He loosens the belt* [a] *of kings,*
and binds [b] *a rope* [c] *about their loins.*

¹⁹ *Priests he leads away barefoot,*^a
   and brings to ruin^b *men long established,*^c
²⁰ *depriving reliable men of their speech,*
   taking away the discretion of the elders.
²¹ *Upon nobles he pours disgrace,*
   and loosens the belt^a *of the mighty.*^b

²² *He uncovers mysteries hid in darkness*
   and brings deathly shade^a *to the light.*
²³ *He makes nations great,*^a *and he destroys them;*
   he disperses^b *nations*^c, *and he leads*^d *them.*
²⁴ *He deprives a country's leaders*^a *of their reason,*^b
   and leaves them to wander in a trackless waste.
²⁵ *They grope in darkness*^a *without a light;*^b
   he leaves them to stagger^c *like drunkards.*

^{13:1} *All this*^a *I have seen with my own eyes;*
   with my own ears I have heard it and understood.
² *My knowledge is a match for yours;*
   I am not inferior to you.
³ *But it is to the Almighty that I would speak;*
   it is with God that I crave to enter dispute.

⁴ *And as for you,*^a *you are lying soothers;*^b
   worthless physicians,^c *all of you.*
⁵ *If only you would be utterly silent!*
   That is what would count as wisdom for you.
⁶ *Listen, if you will, to my disputation,*
   attend to the arguments I will utter.

⁷ *Is it on God's behalf that you speak falsehood?*
   Is it for him that you utter lies?
⁸ *Will you favor God's side?*
   Do you propose to argue his case for him?
⁹ *Would it be well for you if he were to examine you?*
   Could you deceive^a *him as a man is deceived?*

¹⁰ ^a *He would be sure to begin proceedings against you*
   if even in secret^b *you were partisan.*
¹¹ *Will not the fear*^a *of him terrify you?*
   Will not the dread of him fall upon you?
¹² ^a *Your reminders*^b *would become*^c *maxims*^d *of ash,*
   your sayings^e *words of clay.*

¹³ *Be silent, let me alone!*^a *I must speak!*
   Let what may^b *befall*^c *me.*
¹⁴ ^a *I will take my flesh in my teeth,*
   and put my life in my hand.
¹⁵ ^a *He may slay me; I am without*^b *hope.*^c
   Yet I will defend my conduct^d *to his face.*

16 *And*[a] *this is what I take refuge in:*
   A godless man dare not approach him.

17 *Listen closely to my words;*
   let my declaration be in your ears.
18 *You will see that I have drawn up my case.*[a]
   I know that I am in the right!
19 *If*[a] *any one can make out a case against me,*
   then[b] *I will hold my peace till*[c] *I breathe my last.*

20 *Grant me these two favors only, O God,*[a]
   so that I need not hide myself from you.
21 *Withdraw your hand*[a] *far from me,*
   and let not fear of you unnerve me.
22 *Then summon me, and I will answer;*
   or let me speak first, and you shall reply to me.

23 *How many iniquities and sins are laid to my charge?*[a]
   Show me my offense and my sin!
24 *Why do you hide your face from me?*
   Why do you count me your enemy?
25 *Would you strike with dread a leaf driven by the wind?*[a]
   Would you pursue a withered straw?

26 *You ordain me to suffer bitterness;*
   you make me inherit the faults of my youth.
27 *You set my feet in the stocks;*
   you keep a watch on all my paths;
   you take note of my footprints.
28 *And this to one like a worn-out*[a] *wine-skin,*[b]
   like a garment eaten by the moth.

14:1 *Man, born of woman,*
   is few of days and full of turmoil.
2 *He blossoms*[a] *like a flower, and he withers;*[b]
   like a shadow he is gone and will not stay.
3 *Is it upon such a one that you fix your eyes?*
   Is this the one[a] *you will bring into dispute with you?*

4 *Who can make the unclean*[a] *into the clean?*[b]
   No one![c]
5 *Since man's days are determined,*
   and the number of his months is known to you,
   and you have set[a] *the bound*[b] *that he cannot pass,*
6 *look away from him and let him be,*[a]
   till he has enjoyed[b] *his day—like a hired laborer!*

7 *For a tree there is hope,*
   that if it is cut down it will sprout again,
   that its fresh shoots will not fail.

8 *Though its root grow old* [a] *in the ground*
  and its stump begin to die in the dust,
9 *yet at the scent of water it may bud*
  and put forth shoots like a plant new set.

10 *But a man, when he dies, loses every power;* [a]
   he breathes his last, and where [b] *is he then?*
11 *Like the water that has gone from a vanished lake,*
   like a stream that has shrunk and dried up,
12 *man lies down and will not rise again,*
   before the heavens are no more [a] *he will not awake,* [b]
   [c]*nor be roused out of his sleep.*

13 *If only you would hide me in Sheol,*
   conceal me there till your wrath is passed, [a]
   set a time when you would call me to mind!
14 *If a man could die and then live again,* [a]
   I would wait, all the days of my hard service,
   till my relief should come.
15 *You would call, and I would answer you,*
   you would yearn for the work of your hands.
16 *You would indeed count* [a] *my steps,*
   but not watch for any sins of mine;
17 *My transgressions would be sealed up in a pouch,*
   and any fault you would cover over.

18 *Yet as* [a] *a mountain slips away* [b] *and erodes,* [c]
   and a cliff is dislodged from its place,
19 *as water wears away stone*
   and torrents [a] *scour the soil from the land—*
   so you destroy man's hope.
20 *You overpower him once for all,* [a] *and he is gone,*
   you disfigure [b] *him and then you banish him.*
21 *His sons may come to honor, but he does not know it;*
   they may sink into obscurity, but he does not perceive it.
22 *He feels only his own pain;*
   he grieves only for himself.

Notes

12:2.a. עַם by itself can hardly mean "the people" or even "the gentry" (as Pope), still less "the voice of the people" (JB, NJPS, GNB), "everybody," viz. "the only people who count" (Rowley, Gordis), "the rightful people" (*die rechten Leute*) (as KB, KB³, Fohrer). NEB "perfect man" rests upon J. Reider's proposal (*VT* 4 [1954] 289–30) that עַם corresponds to an Arab. root "to be complete"; the absence of any other Heb. example makes this very dubious. Unbelievable is Dahood's "you are the Strong One" (*עָם, from a proposed root עמם) (*Psalms I*, 113; so too Blommerde). Emendation to הָעָם, "the people," is not successful, for that would be a strange way to say "the only people who have wisdom." Most other (conjectural) emendations try to incorporate such a meaning, but otherwise are unconvincing: יֹדְעִים, "knowing ones" (A. Klostermann; BH³), עֲרֵמִּים, "wise ones." The almost certainly correct solution to this long-standing problem was given by J. A. Davies, *VT* 25 (1975) 670–71, that the second clause is a paratactic relative clause, viz. "You are the people with whom wisdom will die" (for the use of *waw* to introduce a relative clause, cf. 29:12). I have translated "last of the wise" in order to give content to הֶעָם.

2.b. Not unattractive is the suggestion of Tur-Sinai and Reider (*VT* 4 [1954] 289) to read תֻּמַּת "completeness, perfection"; cf. Aq τελειώματα σοφίας, Symm ἡ τελειότης τῆς σοφίας.

3.a. Lit., "with whom are not [things] like these?"

4.a. Added in translation for the connection; see *Comment*.

4.b. Lit., "to *his* friend," a little strange when the verb is "I am." Fohrer firmly emends אֶהְיֶה to יִהְיֶה, "he is," to bring the grammatical persons into agreement, but the sense is spoiled, for Job must be speaking of himself. To similar effect C. D. Isbell argued that אהיה is an orthographic variant of יִהְיֶה "is," viz. a person who does not know "these things" (v 3c) "would be a laughingstock to his friends" ("Initial ʾAlef-Yod Interchange and Selected Biblical Passages," *JNES* 37 [1978] 227–36 [233–34]). kjv "I am *as one* mocked of his neighbour" (similarly jps) is a valiant attempt to retain "I" and "his" in the same sentence. The Hebrew is not difficult, however: "A 'mockery-to-his-neighbor' I am"; see the *Comment* for references to this standard motif. rsv, neb, niv have "to my friend(s)," which is the smoothest translation.

5.a. So, excellently, jb, lit., "derision for calamity."

5.b. Lit., "a blow to those whose steps are faltering," taking נָכוֹן as a noun, "blow," from נכה (so Schultens, Dhorme, Gordis, KB³; cf. jb, neb); not as נכון "fixed, ready" (as rsv, nab).

6.a. בטחות, "security" (plural of intensity) is indeed not parallel to "tents," but the attempt of J. Reider (*VT* 2 [1952] 126–27) to find a parallel noun ("inhabited valleys," on the basis of an Arab. cognate) is unconvincing (though followed by KB³). Siegfried and others had equally arbitrarily created exact but banal parallelism by emending ישליו "one at ease" to שָׁלוֹם "peace."

6.b. Fohrer deletes this line as a gloss (so too nab). niv mg "secure in what God's hand brings them" seems an impossible translation. Gordis's "all those who have deceived Him" carries no conviction, being based on the idiom in Elizabethan English "to bear someone in hand," meaning to "deceive." nebmg translates "He brings it in full measure to whom he will," which the Hebrew can hardly mean, and removes the line to follow 21:17. D. Winton Thomas surprisingly approves the improbable emendation of לְמַרְגִּיזֵי אֵל "for the provokers of God" to לְמוֹ רָגְזֵי־אֵל "in the face of violent disturbances," אֵל being nothing but a superlative ("Some Further Remarks on Unusual Ways of Expressing the Superlative in Hebrew," *VT* 18 [1968] 120–24 [121–22], following T. H. Gaster, "Some Emendations in the Text of the Bible," in *Semitic Studies in Memory of Immanuel Löw* (ed. A. Scheiber; Budapest: Hungarian Libraries Board, 1947) 284–87 (287n.) who offers an interesting but strained rendering of vv 5–6 as a whole. For more plausible interpretations, see *Comment*.

7.a. Sg vb with pl coll subj (see GKC, § 145k), not to be deleted as dittogr of v 8 (as Merx, Dhorme, Fohrer), nor emended to pl וְתֹרֻגֶּךָ (as nab).

8.a. Many emend, in order to find an animate object to parallel cattle, birds, and fish. Thus, for שׂיח לארץ we find חַיַּת הָאָרֶץ "the animals of the earth" (Ewald, Fohrer, Horst, Hesse, KB), שֶׁרֶץ הָאָרֶץ "reptiles of the earth" (Hitzig, Peake), or זוֹחֲלֵי אֶרֶץ (cf. Deut 32:24; Mic 7:17; but nowhere else) "creeping things of the earth" (Duhm, Dhorme, neb, nab, jb). rsv "plants of the earth" (similarly Weiser) sees in שׂיח the word for "shrub" (as in 30:4, 7). Dahood sees אֶרֶץ as "underworld," and thus finds allusion to a fourfold division of the universe: earth, sky, netherworld, sea ("Northwest Semitic Philology," 58). The Ug. passage cited in illustration (*CTA* 3C.19–22 [Gibson 49]) does not attest such a meaning (against Pope also), and it would have been totally out of place for the netherworld to be mentioned, since obvious and accessible sources of knowledge are being referred to. The MT should stand.

9.a. The Hebrew could mean "by means of all these," i.e. "who (among humans) does not know by observing all these (creatures)?" (cf. NEB "Who cannot learn from all these?"). But since the animals have been represented as having knowledge which can be communicated (v 7), it is more appropriate to see them as "knowing" what they will communicate.

9.b. Three mss of Kennicott and two of de Rossi have אֱלוֹהַ, "God," a reading adopted by Dhorme, Pope, jb, nab.

10.a. Dahood revocalizes אִישׁ "man," to אוֹשׁ, a new word supposedly cognate with Ug. *ušn* "gift" (*Bib* 47 [1966] 107–108). This has nothing to recommend it; the context requires an easily paralleled cliché. The phrase "all flesh of humankind" is unusual, but obviously distinguishes humans from animals; "all flesh" by itself can include animals (see A. R. Hulst, "*Kol baśar* in der priesterlichen Fluterzählung," *OTS* 12 [1958] 28–68).

12.a. To avoid the oddity of these words in Job's mouth jps and njps translate them as a question, but this is unnecessary in view of the interpretation proposed in the *Comment*. Beer, Stevenson, Fohrer, Rowley, and Hesse transfer לו "to him" from the end of v 11 to the beginning of v 12 and read it as לֹא "not" (see *Comment*). The view of Blommerde, following W. Quintens, that יְשִׁישִׁים means "the Old One" and אֹרֶךְ יָמִים means "the Long-lived," both divine titles, is to be rejected as based on a faulty interpretation of a Ugaritic text (see Pope).

13.a. To create exact parallelism, Budde emended עצה to עֹצֶם or עׇצְמָה, "strength." For the same reason G. R. Driver found another עצה here meaning "endurance" (*WO* 1 [1947–52] 410–11; followed by NEB's "firmness"). Neither proposal has gained much acceptance.

14.a. הֵן is probably not the Aram. particle for "if," but the alternative Heb. for הִנֵּה, "behold"; but its use here is as a hypothetical.

15.a. Lit., "they dry up," but it is strictly illogical to say that the *withheld* waters dry up; it is rather the streams in which they would be flowing. No emendation is required (contra Duhm וְיִבַשׁ, "and he dries up [the earth]").

17.a. The similarity with v 19a leads many to question the correctness of this line. Duhm's emendation to יוֹעֲצֵי אֶרֶץ יְסַכֵּל, "counselors of the earth he makes foolish," creates a more close parallelism with v 17b (for [סכל] שכל // הלל cf. Isa 44:25), and has been widely followed (e.g. Fohrer, Pope, de Wilde, KB, JB); Duhm notes that LXX^A has γῆς after βουλετάς, but that proves little about the Heb. Vorlage, since LXX also has a translation of מוֹלִיךְ (διάγων). Horst suggests a graphically more plausible emendation, מְלַכֵּי יוֹעֲצִים יְשׁוֹלָל, "he plunders the advice of counselors"; but this leaves a lot to be desired by way of sense. There is nothing wrong with the MT if we allow that such repetitions, jejune to Western ears, were permissible within Hebrew poetry; for an argument similar in principle, see Gordis, 508–13, showing that the 43 instances of repetition of the one root in two parallel lines cannot all be due to scribal error, but must form a feature of Joban poetic style.

17.b. KB and BDB agree in translating שׁוֹלָל as "barefoot," apparently only in dependence on LXX ἀνυπόδετος for שׁלל in Mic 1:8. G. R. Driver, *AJSL* 53 (1935–36) 160, proposed a root שׁגל "be mad" (hence NEB "makes counsellors behave like idiots"), but the word is nowhere else attested, and it is a strained way of achieving a strict parallelism. Less persuasive is A. Guillaume's equation with Arab. *tafalfala*, "took short steps," hence "led in fetters" (*BSOAS* 16 [1954] 1–9).

17.c. הלל III; cf. n. 4:18.c.

18.a. מוּסָר, spelled thus, is "instruction"; here it must be vocalized מוֹסֵר "bond."

18.b. Gordis takes וַיֶּאְסֹר as a variant spelling of וַיָּסַר "he removes [the girdle from their loins]." It is simple to follow JB's hint that אֵזוֹר is here the prisoner's rope (see *Comment*). Blommerde would read the verb as a privative piel, וַיְאַסֵּר, "he loosens," which indeed forms an exact parallel with the previous line; but it makes one wonder how a reader is supposed to know that "bind" (אסר) here means "loose."

18.c. Duhm, Peake and others emended to אֵסוּר "bond."

19.a. See n. 12:17.b.

19.b. סלף "twist, pervert, overturn" (BDB), "twist, lead astray, bring to ruin" (KB^3), also "cause to run dry" (KB), comparing Arab. *salafa* "pass away"; hence NAB "lets their waters flow away," connecting v 19b with v 21a (*q.v.*); a similar translation is offered by Fohrer.

19.c. אֵיתָן "constant, unfailing," usually of waters (Amos 5:24; Ps 74:15), but also of an "unmoved" bow (Gen 49:24), an "impregnable" dwelling (Num 24:21), an "enduring" nation (Jer 5:15). N. M. Sarna, *JBL* 74 (1955) 272–73, ingeniously discovered here the name of a class of temple servitors analogous to the Ugaritic *ytnm* (cf. the Hebrew Nethinim); so also Gordis, NJPS "temple-servants." But, as Horst remarks, they would be a too lowly order of society to figure in these verses.

21.a. מֵזִיחַ for מֵזַח "girdle, belt." P. Joüon, "Notes philologiques sur le texte hébreu de Job: 1,5; 9,35; 12,21; 28,1; 28,27; 29,14," *Bib* 11 (1930) 322–24 (323), conjectured a מֵזַח meaning "impudence"; hence NEB "abates the arrogance of nobles."

21.b. אָפִיק elsewhere means "stream" (e.g. Joel 1:20; Ps 18:16 [15]), or the hollow bones of the crocodile or the rows of his scales (Job 40:18; 41:7). Some therefore think this line is about rain, and therefore misplaced. So NAB "He breaks down the barriers of the streams," connecting this line with v 19b. But the root אפק "to be strong" is well attested (cf. also Akk. *epēqu* "be massive, solid"), and אָפִיק is a normal adjectival formation. There is no need to see a direct relation with Arab. *ʾafiqa* "excellent" in order to achieve good parallelism with נדיבים, as Guillaume thought, followed by Pope. The well-meaning emendations to אַמִּיצִים "the strong" (Budde), אַבִּירִים "the strong" (Duhm), and תַּקִּיפִים "the powerful" (Beer) are equally needless.

22.a. On צַלְמָוֶת, see n. 10:21.b.

23.a. מַשְׂגִּיא "makes great," a common verb in Aram., attested in Heb. only here and 8:11; 36:24. Some mss have מַשְׁגִּיא, which would imply derivation from שגה "lead astray" (a by-form of שגג in v 16). LXX omitted the line, possibly objecting to the idea that God destroys nations (Gard, *Exegetical Method of the Greek Translator*, 77), but Aq Symm have πλανῶν, obviously seeing שגה here. This is followed by NEB.

23.b. J. Reider (*VT* 4 [1954] 290–91) rather unconvincingly understood שטח as Arab. *šataḥa* "flatten, prostrate," but he is followed by NEB "lays them low." Ball ingeniously suggested an emendation to שחט "slaughter," used in Num 14:16 of the nation of Israel being "slain" by Yahweh in the wilderness.

23.c. The noun גוים "nations" is repeated, thogh 5 mss have לְאֻמִּים "peoples." Duhm emended to עַמִּים and Dhorme to לְעַמִּים for the same sense, but such repetitions are obviously not avoided by our poet (cf. Gordis, 508–13).

23.d. וינחם is from נחה "lead, guide," which never means "lead away" (as RSV, NJPS, Pope; NIV "disperses them"), nor has it ever a negative connotation (cf. Ehrlich). Many therefore argue that it should be vocalized וַיַּנִּחֵם, hiph B of נוח "rest," hence "abandon" (so NAB, Hitzig, Driver-Gray, Gordis). But this verb would be ambiguous, since when its object is "nations" it means "leave in peace" (Judg 2:23; 3:1) or "settle" (Isa 14:1). An emendation often adopted is וַיְמַחֵם "and he destroys them" (Ball, Dhorme, Fohrer, Horst, JB). Perhaps Blommerde is on the right track in finding the second line to be antithetically parallel to the first (though his claim that נחה means "lead to paradise" is preposterous); נחה would then have a positive connotation here, as it does when Israel is "led" by God (Exod 13:17; 15:13; Ps 77:20 [21]; cf. also Ps 107:7), and שטח would have a negative connotation, "disperse, scatter," cf. also RV "spreadeth abroad . . . bringeth in"). Emendation and revocalization are here equally unnecessary. It might be argued, however, that if שטח is negative, it predisposes us to a negative reading of נחה, thus "lead away" (into exile), "enslave" (Moffatt). For וינחם NEB has "there they lie," presumably as hiph B of נוח "set down."

24.a. ראשי עם־הארץ "chief of the people of the earth" seems to overload the line, and עם is usually deleted (so Duhm, Dhorme, Gray, Fohrer). But see *Comment.*

24.b. Lit., "heart."

25.a. Driver claimed מסס חשׁך must mean "*feel* darkness" rather than "grope about *in* darkness," but Gen 31:34 is no support.

25.b. "Darkness and not light": for examples of litotes used for emphasis, see E. König, *Stilistik, Rhetorik, Poetik in Bezug auf die biblische Litteratur* (Leipzig: Dieterich, 1900) 45–46; I. Lande, *Formelhafte Wendungen der Umgangssprache im Alten Testament* (Leiden: Brill, 1949) 60–62.

25.c. The hiph ויתעם is unexceptionable, but the inclination to emend to qal וַיִּתְעוּ is understandable, especially because the pattern of a verse of closure (cf. 10:22) requires no further statement of God's causation. Cf. Dhorme: "What is here being described is no longer the divine action itself but its effects" (similarly Horst). LXX πλανηθείησαν apparently read ויתעו (as niph); thus too Duhm, Driver-Gray, Horst (mostly for the sake of stricter parallelism). Dahood and Blommerde too, interestingly, want to find a niph or qal here—but at the price of an enclitic *mem* (Dahood, "Northwest Semitic Philology," 58).

13:1.a. ראיתי means "I have seen [it] all"; there is no need to correct the text to כָל־אֵלֶּה, "all these things," as some mss, or כָל־זֹאת, "all this" (as Horst, NAB; cf. Pope); "all this" is nevertheless the best translation.

4.a. וְאוּלָם, strongly adversative again, as at the beginning of v 13.

4.b. For this translation, see *Comment.* RSV "whitewash" depends on the context of תפל/טפל in Ezek 13:10–12.

4.c. This occurrence of רפא, everywhere else "to heal," was thought by Dillman to be cognate with Arab. and Eth. roots "to mend, stitch" (so Rowley, NEB). See P. Humbert, "Maladie et médicine dans l'AT," *RHPR* 44 (1964) 1–29.

9.a. חָתַל and תְּהָתַלּוּ from תלל or perhaps the alternative form התל (see F. C. Fensham, "The Stem *HTL* in Biblical Hebrew," *VT* 9 [1959] 310–11).

10.a. Gordis takes the verse as continuing the questions of vv 7–9; he translates, "Will he declare you in the right . . . ?," claiming that הוכיח can be used "declaratively" (he compares 13:15; 19:5; Gen 24:14, 44). This is doubtful.

10.b. Gordis takes סתר "sever" as a variant writing of סטר "side," hence "if you show partiality to one side" (cf. סתר in 1 Sam 25:20). But his reasoning, that "there has been nothing clandestine about the Friends' defense of God," overlooks the future or hypothetical aspect of the sentence.

11.a. שאת usually taken as inf const of נשׂא "lift up," hence "excellency" (RV), "majesty" (RSV, NEB), "splendor" (NIV). It occurs in Gen 49:3 (parallel to עז "strength"), Ps 62:5 [4] (RSV "eminence"), Hab 1:7 (RSV "dignity"), Job 31:23 (again parallel to פחד), but in all these cases its meaning has been doubted. In Job 41:17 [25] it perhaps means simply (Leviathan's) "rising up" (RSV "when he raises himself"). The suggestion is to be preferred that we read שְׂאֵתוֹ "his fear" (NJPS "his threat"; similarly Pope, Gordis).

12.a. A thoroughly difficult verse. The settled point in it is the parallelism of אפר "dust" and חמר "clay" (as in 4:19; 10:9; both in the reversed order). משלי cannot be anything other than "proverbs, (wisdom) teachings," which means that גבי and גביכם must also be terms for words spoken, "replies" or simply "sayings" (see n. 13:12.e).

12.b. זכרון is "memorial," what provokes memory, and "memorandum," something worthy of being remembered (Exod 17:14; Esth 6:1). Here it must be the sayings of the friends that call on Job to remember teachings he has previously held to.

12.c. The ל in the second half of the line indicates a becoming or a "transition into a new state or condition" (BDB, 512a); the transition is equally valid for both halves of the line.

12.d. Not to be connected with משל "to be like" (as AV, JPS "your memorials shall be like unto ashes").

12.e. גב II "answer," a homonym of גב I "back," etc., cognate with Arab., Aram. and Syr. g(w)b "answer," recognized by KB³, NJPS "responses," JB "retorts"; Dhorme, Gordis, Horst. The older view was that it was a use of גב I, usually "back," but also "mound," "(eye)brow," "rim (of wheel)," and here thought to be "boss (of a shield)" (as in 15:26), or "bulwarks, breastworks" (so BDB). Hence RV, RSV, NEB, NIV "defenses." But this would be a strange parallel to "proverbs." Shields (of leather or wickerwork) often had a boss of metal at the centre (see *ANEP*, pl. 164, for a·depiction of a shield with a boss and a bound rim); in the present image that center of security would be of clay. NAB "your fabrications are mounds of clay" apparently connects the word with גבב in rabbinic Heb., "bring together"; cf. A. Cohen, "Studies in Hebrew Lexicography," *AJSL* 40 (1923–24) 153–85 (165). AV "your bodies" derives from LXX σῶμα, presumably connecting גב with גופה "body."

13.a. Lit., "be silent from me" (cf. 1 Sam 7:8; Jer 38:27; Ps 28:1), a "pregnant construction" implying "stand away from me in silence" (GKC, § 119ff).

13.b. מה "whatever," "what may"; cf. 2 Sam 18:22.

13.c. עבר על "come upon" expressing the coming of a misfortune, as Nah 3:19. NAB "I will give vent to my feelings" apparently finds חֵמָה "anger" here (so too KB; cf. LXX θυμοῦ; cf. also Ball).

14.a. The opening words על־מה "why" are probably to be deleted as a dittogr of the closing words of v 13 (so RSV, NEB, NAB). There is little to be said for the view that מה על מה means "whatever may," as Bickell, Duhm, Fohrer (contra Gray, Horst), and even less for taking על־מה as עולם plus adverbial -â, "for ever" (Dahood, "Northwest Semitic Philology," 58).

15.a. הן may be "behold" or "if."

15.b. So K; on Q לו "to him," see *Comment.* Dahood's proposal that לא is a divine title לֵא, "the victor" (root l'y) is far-fetched (*Psalms I*, 144). More probable is his suggestion (*CBQ* 17 [1955] 24) that it is an asseverative particle "surely" (so too J. Mejia, "El lamed enfático en nuevos textos del Antiguo Testamento," *EstBíb* 22 [1963] 177–90 [183]; Andersen), but this fails the test of "homonym probability" (cf. D. F. Payne, "The Old Testament and the Problem of Ambiguity," *ASTI* 5 [1966–67] 48–68).

15.c. The emendation of Graetz and Ehrlich, אֲיַחֵל to אָחִיל "I will tremble," though supported by Dhorme and Pope, has little to recommend it. Dhorme's argument that the verse should express the feeling Job will experience if God kills him (i.e., he will not tremble) is not cogent.

15.d. I. L. Seeligmann, rightly observing that הוכיח usually means "accuse, reproach" rather than "defend," proposed reading דְּרָכָיו "his ways" instead of דְּרָכַי "my ways" ("Zur Terminologie für das Gerichtsverfahren im Wortschatz des biblischen Hebräisch," *VTS* 16 [1967] 251–78 [267–68]). That is, Job would be reproaching God rather than defending himself. This is an attractive suggestion, but "argue my case" perhaps translates both terms fairly.

16.a. גם "also"; "and" shows that this phrase relates to the defense of his conduct in v 15b. It is not גם as emphatic particle "surely" (Gordis).

18.a. Emendation of משפט "a case" to מִשְׁפָּטִי "my case" (Duhm, Driver) is unnecessary, though that is what the text means.

19.a. Lit., "Who will . . . ?," expecting the answer "no one"; the עתה in v 19b makes clear this is a hypothetical.

19.b. Heb. has ועתה, not "and now" but "and then, in that case." Cf. also on 14:16.

19.c. On the relationship between the two verbs "be silent" and "die," see *Comment.*

20.a. "O God" not in the Hebrew, but inserted to indicate that the verbs are now 2d pers sg (so also Moffatt, NIV).

21.a. Some find כַּפְּךָ "your hand" too loose a parallel to אֵמָתְךָ "your fear" and vocalize the latter as אַמָּתְךָ "your arm" (Dahood, *Psalms II*, 331). But אַמָּה "forearm, cubit, ell" is used only as a measurement of length. Pope achieves closer symmetry by reading אֲכָפְּךָ "your pressure" (cf. 33:7), but there is quite adequate parallelism already: the hand of God is clearly an object of terror, and no emendation is needed.

23.a. Lit., "are mine"; see *Comment*.

25.a. "By the wind" is supplied for the sake of the sense. A. Guillaume, "A Note on Isaiah xix. 7," *JTS* ns 14 (1963) 382–83, makes the attractive suggestion that נִדָּף is not "driven" from נדף I (Arab. *nadafa* "strike") but a new נדף II "dry up" (Arab. *nadifa* "was dried up, waterless"; *nadafa* "was exhausted," of a well). A "dried leaf" appears also in Lev 26:36, and a dry, hot wind (הבל נדף) in Prov 21:6. Of course, a *driven* leaf is a *dry* leaf, so there is no way of knowing which is meant, except by the rule of thumb that homonyms are not to be multiplied *praeter necessitatem*. Guillaume rather undercuts his own proposal by allowing that נדף is actually "equivocal," combining both meanings by the figure of *tauriya*.

28.a. Supplying the relative אֲשֶׁר, "like a skin that is worn out," as in the next colon also (so also NEB; contrast NAB "he wears out like a leather bottle").

28.b. רָקָב "rottenness" is not entirely appropriate; how can something "waste away" "like rottenness"? It does not mean "rotten thing" (RV, RSV, NJPS) or "rotten word" (JB). It is better to emend to רֹקֶב "(wine-)skin" (as LXX ἀσκῷ and Syr) with Beer, Fohrer, Tur-Sinai, de Wilde, Gordis, NEB, NAB. רָקָב "rottenness" is parallel, it is true, with עָשׁ "moth," which also occurs here, though not strictly in parallelism. רֹקֶב "skin" does not occur elsewhere in the Heb. Bible, but is attested at Ecclus 43:20, and is acknowledged by KB (cf. also Aram. רָקְבָּא, Syr. *rabkā*).

14:2.a. יצא "comes out," of plants in 1 Kgs 5:13 [4:33]; Isa 11:1; Ps 104:14. Emendation to יִצְמָח "springs up" (Beer) or יָצִיץ "blossoms" (Wright) is unnecessary. So too Dahood's equation with Ug. *wdʾ* "shine," as a contrast to "shadow" in the next colon ("Northwest Semitic Philology," 60).

2.b. מלל taken as "languish, wither" by BDB (מלל III) and KB³ (מלל I), but as "cut off" (BDB מלל IV; KB³ מלל II) by KB, RV, Fohrer.

3.a. Lit., "is it me you will bring. . . ?" Many read וְאֹתוֹ "and him" for אֹתִי "and me," which suits the logic better, but then Job himself is principally what is intended by "humankind" (v 1), and Job "frequently oscillates between his own tragic lot and that of all men" (Gordis).

4.a. Blommerde reads מְטַמֵּא "unclean" for MT מִטָּמֵא "from an unclean" to provide an example of the construction of נתן with two accusatives, "to make something into something else." The Hebrew as it stands can adequately mean that, however.

4.b. Lit., "Who will give pure from impure?" An alternative translation is: "Who can find the pure among the impure?" (see *Comment*).

4.c. Blommerde's reading of לָא אֶחָד "the Mighty One alone" (following Dahood's supposition of לָא "mighty one" [see n. 13:15.b]) has little to commend it, though it is toyed with by Andersen. Vg "Is it not you who are alone?" and Tg "none except God" are so obviously theologically motivated corrections as to be worthless text-critically.

5.a. עָשִׂיתָ "you have made" is emended by some to שַׁתָּ "you have set," the same verb as in v 13. But the renderings of LXX, Symm, Vg do not necessarily point in this direction.

5.b. K חֻקּוֹ "his limit" is to be preferred to Q חֻקָּיו "his limits," since the reference is to the total lifespan.

6.a. In view of 7:16 and 10:20, where Job urges God to "desist" from him (חֲדַל impv), an emendation to this form seems desirable here (so Dhorme, Driver-Gray, Fohrer, Gordis, Pope, RSV, JB, NEB, NAB, NIV). MT וְיֶחְדָּל is sometimes translated "that he may be at ease" (NJPS; cf. RV, JPS, Horst) but this meaning cannot be paralleled. Nor will "that he may cease" (a legitimate rendering) suit the context; God's looking away from the human being is not in this verse to enable him to die. Another interpretation, preserving the MT, sees here a חדל II "be fat, prosperous" (P. J. Calderone, "HDL-II in Poetic Texts," *CBQ* 23 [1961] 451–60 [454–55]; "Supplementary Note on HDL-II," 24 [1962] 412–19; see also D. Winton Thomas, "Some Observations on the Hebrew Root חדל," *VTS* 4 [1957] 8–16). This requires the postulation of a word עַד "food" or עַד "lifetime" (so Blommerde), yielding "that he may be fat with food" or "that he may enjoy his lifetime." The former seems unbelievable in the context, the latter is superficially parallel to the next colon; but the present bicolon with a small emendation is greatly to be preferred to this reconstructed tricolon. KB³ accepts the sense "become fat" (though contrast חדל I § 2d), but not apparently the word עַד "food" for this context (and עַד III "food" does not appear in its proper place).

6.b. See *Comment* for keeping the usual sense of רצה. A רצה II "pay off, count, reckon" has been widely recognized since the time of BDB (see KB); Dhorme thinks "day" means "work due for the day," so that the phrase means "finishes his day's work" (does it?). Gordis takes the verb to mean "count, complete" (i.e., presumably, count completely), and translates "complete his day" (cf. Lev 26:34 and 2 Chr 36:2, where the land "completes" ["enjoys" ?] its sabbaths). But it seems that the object of "complete" in the sense of "count completely" must be pl; here we have the sg "his day." Nevertheless, several versions have "finish" (JB; cf. NJPS), "complete" (NAB); NEB's "counting the hours day by day" is the logical meaning of רצה II but is an impossible translation of the Hebrew; it demonstrates that the verb cannot be רצה II. Some older lexica and versions took רצה I here as "accomplish" (AV, RV; cf. Isa 40:2), as a secondary meaning of the verb, but this is very doubtful.

8.a. Inchoative hiph (Gordis; cf. GKC, § 53e), which imparts an inchoative nuance to the next verb ימות "begins to die."

10.a. For reasons mentioned in the *Comment*, some emend וְיֶחֱלָשׁ "is, becomes weak" to יַחֲלֹף "passes on, away" (cf. 9:11; Ps 90:5) (so Wright, Graetz, Budde, Driver-Gray, A. Guillaume, taking יחלש as an alternative writing of יחלף, claiming that שׁ and ף are often interchangeable in Heb. ["The Use of חלש in Exod. xvii. 13, Isa. xiv. 12, and Job xiv. 10," *JTS* ns 14 (1963) 91–92]) or יַחֲלֹף "goes away" (Dillmann, Beer, Driver-Gray). I. Eitan found a homonym of חלש here, cognate with Arab. *ḥls* "rob" ("Two Unknown Verbs: Etymological Studies. II. חָלַשׁ," *JBL* 42 [1923] 22–28 [25–28]), or *halaša* "reap with a sickle" (*A Contribution to Biblical Lexicography* [New York: Columbia UP, 1924] 42–44). G. R. Driver connected it with Arab. *halaša* "carry off suddenly" ("The Resurrection of Marine and Terrestrial Creatures," *JSS* 7 [1962] 12–22 [16]), reading niph וְיֵחָלֵשׁ "is taken away" (so also KB[3]); hence NEB "disappears." See further the *Comment*.

10.b. M. Dahood, "The Conjunction *wn* and Negative *ʾi* in Hebrew," *UF* 14 (1982) 51–54 (54), finds here the (rare) negative particle אי "not" (cf. 22:20, and KB[3], 37b *s.v.* אי III), presumably with suffix, thus אִיוֹ. It is hard to see any "improvement" here.

12.a. עַד־בְּלָתִי is quite intelligible, "until not"; but it is tempting to emend to עַד־בְּלוֹת "until the wearing out of" since בלה is used elsewhere of the wearing out of the heavens (Ps 102:27 [26]; Isa 51:6) and Aq (κατατριβῇ) and LXX[A] Theod Symm (παλαιωθῇ) read it in this way (so too Geiger, Duhm, Dhorme, Horst, Pope, JB, Moffatt, *BHK*). Blommerde preserved the consonantal text, pointing בְּלֹתִי or בָּלֹתִי, at the cost of detecting a gen ending on the inf.

12.b. יקיצו is pl, because the subject אִישׁ is viewed as a collective. H. M. Orlinsky ("The Hebrew and Greek Texts of Job 14:12," *JQR* 28 [1937–38] 57–68 [65]) and G. R. Driver ("Problems in the Hebrew Text of Job," *VTS* 3 [1955] 72–93 [77]) saw a verb קוץ II "split open," cognate with Arab. *qāḍa*, Akk. *kâṣu*, and claimed also for Isa 7:6. This is accepted by KB, KB[3], Fohrer, NEB.

12.c. Orlinsky (*JQR* 28 [1937–38] 57–68) regarded the third colon as a mistaken gloss on לא יקיצו.

13.a. Andersen thinks אף שוב, lit., "turn back the nose" means "revive (Job)," an allusion to God's breathing life into the human's nostrils (אפים) in Gen 2:7; but the use of שוב meaning, in reference to anger, "to pass away," is well established. See *Comment*.

14.a. Reading וְיִחְיֶה "and live"; see *Comment*.

16.a. Syr adds "not" (לא) to this verb; similarly Gray, and most recently Pope, to achieve formal congruence between the two cola. But this is not necessary; see *Comment*. The לא of the second colon is certainly not an affirmative (as G. R. Driver, "Affirmation by Exclamatory Negation," *JANES* 5 [1973] 107–14 [110]).

18.a. The indicator of the simile is the *waw* beginning v 19c, a *waw adaequationis* (GKC, § 161a; cf. also v 12). JB and NIV give advance notice of the comparison with "as" before each of the four depictions.

18.b. Lit., "falls" (נוֹפֵל ptcp). Many doubt that יִבּוֹל "decay" could be used of a mountain, and emend to נָפוֹל יִפֹּל (inf abs) "will finally fall" (Dhorme), "falls at last" (NAB); Theod, Syr read likewise (not LXX, as often stated, for it omitted the verse), and Lagarde, Beer, Dhorme, Horst, Fohrer.

18.c. נבל is usually "to fade," of flowers, grass (so Isa 1:30; 28:1, 4; 34:4; 40:7, 8; Jer 8:13; Ezek 47:12; Ps 1:3; 37:2), but at Isa 24:4 it is used of the earth (ארץ and תבל). "Crumble away" (RSV; cf. NJPS, NIV) would probably be appropriate; less so "cometh to naught" (RV). NEB, JB "is swept away" depends on the revocalization to יָבֵל = יוּבָל "is carried away." For an emendation, see n. 18.b.

19.a. Doubtful. MT סְפִיחֶיהָ "her aftergrowths" (cf. Lev 25:5, 11; 2 Kgs 19:29; Isa 37:30) makes no sense here, neither the noun nor its pronoun suff. "Its overflowings" (RV) is no more meaningful. Almost universally the emendation to סְחִיפָה "rainstorm" is adopted; it occurs nowhere else, but rain (מטר) is called סֹחֵף in Prov 28:3; and the term has been thought to be related to Arab. *sahīfeh* (as cited by Dhorme) "rainstorm, torrential rain" (so Budde, Ball, Dhorme, Fohrer, Gordis, de Wilde, KB, KB[3]). "Torrents" (RSV, NJPS, NIV) and "floods" (NAB) may have the streams formed by such rainstorms in mind. It is more than doubtful, however, whether there is any such Arab. word; *sahīqah* is attested for "a great rain that sweeps away that along which it passes," from the verb *shq* "bruise, pound, wear out"; *saḥîfah* is known only from an Arabic lexicographer who claimed that the third root letter should be written with one dot (*f*) rather than two (*q*) (see Lane, 1319c); the root *shf* "peel off" has no connection whatsoever with rain. The one certain cognate to סחף is Akk. *saḥāpu* (von Soden, *AHW* 1004), a general word, "cast down, destroy." S. R. Driver rightly observed that there is no evidence that סחף was confined to the prostrating effects of rain.

20.a. לנצח, probably meaning "utterly" rather than "forever"; cf. n. 4:20.c. Translate "once for all" (JB, NAB, NIV). At 4:20 and 20:7 it is connected with the verb "to perish" (אבד), but here it must be connected with תתקפהו "you prevail" (against Blommerde, who thinks the *waw* of ויהלך is emphatic, not consecutive); Andersen likewise thinks לנצח "post-positive"; Vg indeed links "forever" with "he goes."

20.b. The ptcp משנה obviously has God as its subject (though Dhorme thought it was "man"; cf. NEB). Many think it syntactically awkward, and emend to תְּשַׁנֶּה "you change" (so Graetz, Driver-Gray, Gordis). B. Halpern, "Yhwh's Summary Justice in Job XIV 20," *VT* 28 (1978) 472–74, makes the unconvincing proposal that משנה פניו means "he (man) acts (once) with treasonous intent"; the supposed parallel, *panū(tu) šanūtu* in the Amarna letters, does not clearly mean "have *treasonous* intent," and the claimed chiasmus in the verse is illusory.

Form / Structure / Setting

The importance of this speech of Job, standing at the threshold between the first and second cycles, is marked by its length. It is the longest of all his speeches so far, and only his closing speech in chaps. 29–31 will be longer. At this position, the speech serves both as a first reply to the friends collectively and as the precipitating cause of the ensuing cycle of speeches. There are no compelling reasons for connecting the speech with the second cycle (as do most scholars) rather than with the first, and it is preferable to regard it (and similarly chap. 21) as transitional.

Questions of form are influenced to some extent by decisions about the integrity of the text. It is necessary therefore to note here the numerous excisions, often very substantial, that have been proposed for this speech, usually on the ground of seeming irrelevance to or even contradiction of Job's position as it is stated elsewhere. Fohrer and Hesse, for example, omit 12:7–11 and 12:12–25 as later expansions, and Gray 12:4–12. Duhm regarded 12:4–6 and 12:7–10 as extraneous, while Siegfried omitted 12:4–13:1, and Volz transferred 12:4–10, 13–25 and 13:1 to Zophar's speech of chap. 11. More recent commentators like Rowley, Pope, Andersen, and Horst tend to be skeptical of such drastic excisions, and Gordis in particular argues vigorously in favor of the Masoretic text. As the *Comment* will show, a thoroughly persuasive interpretation of these admittedly strange parts of chap. 12 can be made; and it will be argued that the speech has suffered no significant distortion.

The *structure* of the speech has seemed plain to most commentators, who have analyzed it into *three* sections, usually corresponding to the chapter divisions (so, e.g., Rowley, Davidson, Andersen). Murphy displays a similar structure, though he designates 13:1–5 a transition between sections 1 and 2. Skehan saw three poems of "alphabetic length." Fohrer and Hesse, though excising 12:7–25, also find three sections (12:2–13:12; 13:13–28; 14:1–22). It is far better, however, to see only two main sections, making the transition from Job's address to the friends to his address to God the major dividing-line in the speech; and that line should be drawn between 13:19 and 13:20. Fohrer indeed describes his first section as "to the friends" and the second and third as "to God"; but 13:13–18 is certainly not addressed to God (note the plural in v 13), and a third section is unnecessary if the first is allowed to stretch from 12:2 to 13:18. Terrien analyzes four poems: (1) 12:2–25 "experience against dogma"; (2) 13:1–19 "the risk of death"; (3) 13:20–28 "invocation of God's presence"; (4) 14:1–22 "prayer for eternal life." This at least recognizes the break at 13:19, but, quite apart from the misleading captions given to the four sections, does not sufficiently express the flow of the poem.

The *strophic structure* is best understood thus:

I	1	12:2–6	5 lines (3 + 2)
	2	7–12	6 (3 + 3)
	3	13–15	3
	4	16–21	6 (3 + 3)
	5	22–25	4 (3 + 1)
	6	13:1–3	3
	7	4–6	3
	8	7–9	3
	9	10–12	3
	10	13–16	4 (3 + 1)
	11	17–19	3

(43 lines in all)

II	1	13:20–22	3
	2	23–25	3
	3	26–28	3
	4	14:1–3	3
	5	4–6	3
	6	7–9	3
	7	10–12	3
	8	13–17	5 (3 + 2)
	9	18–22	5 (3 + 2)

(31 lines in all)

The basic strophic pattern in this speech is thus of three lines (14:1–3, 4–6, 7–9, 10–12 are particularly clearly marked examples), which are sometimes extended by one line (12:22–25; 13:13–16) or two (12:2–6; 14:13–17, 18–22). In one of the five-line strophes, the basic three-line pattern is suggested by the form of the third line as a tricolon, which is often a mark of closure (12:4). In two cases at least the unit seems to be an undifferentiated six lines (12:7–12, 16–21).

Skehan, "Strophic Patterns," 106–8, identifies in chaps. 12–13 a series of nine strophes, alternating between five and six lines each: 12:2–6 (5 lines), 7–12 (6), 13–18 (5), 19–25 (6), 13:1–5 (5), 6–11 (6), 12–16 (5), 17–22 (6), 23–27 (5). In chap. 14 he marked out six strophes, 1–3 (+ 13:28) (4 lines), 4–6 (3), 7–9 (3), 10–12 (3), 13–17 (5), 18–22 (5). His pattern for chaps. 12–13, however, was achieved at the cost of several rearrangements of lines and half-lines: in chap. 12, v 18 follows 15, 21b (understood differently from the present commentary) and 19b (also differently understood) follow 18, 19a + 17b follow 16, and 24b is a gloss. 13:28 is moved to follow 14:3.

Webster, "Strophic Patterns," 42–43, sees in this speech three poems roughly equivalent to the present chapters. He tends to see strophes of three lines, less frequently four lines, thus: 12:2–3, 4–6, 7–9, 10–13, 14–16, 17–21, 22–25; 13:1–3, 4–6, 7–9, 10–12, 13–16, 17–19, 20–22, 23–27; 13:28–14:2, 3–6, 7–9, 10–12, 13–17, 18–22.

There are ten tricola in this poem (12:3, 4, 6; 13:27; 14:5, 7, 12, 13, 14, 19), sometimes in a concluding position (12:6; 13:27; 14:12, 19; perhaps also 12:4).

The elements of *form* that appear here are various, as is usually the case (cf. on chaps. 9–10). The principal spheres from which the form-elements are drawn are the legal controversy, the wisdom dispute and the hymn.

The *legal controversy* has supplied much of the material of this speech, almost exclusively in chap. 13. The principal controversy is of course between Job and God, but a subsidiary controversy between Job and the friends, who are cast as witnesses of the principal controversy, is also evidenced.

In 13:3 we have the decision to enter controversy with God, repeated in 13:13 and expanded by the plaintiff's resolution in face of the difficulties of the lawsuit (vv 14–

15a) and his avowal and personal belief of innocence (vv 15b–16). The friends are summoned to act as witnesses (v 17), the plaintiff asserts that he is legally in the right (v 18) and undertakes to desist from disputation if he is proved to be in the wrong (v 19).

In 13:20–22 address is made directly to the legal opponent; first, conditions for the rightful management of the dispute are stipulated. Then in v 23 the legal complaint is preferred: the plaintiff requests a statement of the charges on which his opponent has already begun to execute extra-judicial sanctions upon him. The "why?"-questions of v 24 are a legal reproof, though they also contain overtones of the psalmic lament. The question of v 25, stressing the disproportionateness of the opponent's reaction to the defendant's behavior, is also a legal reproof. The statements of God's actions in vv 26–27 are further accusations of unreasonable behavior on God's part. The lament-like generalizing statement about the human condition in v 28 functions similarly to the question of v 25 as a reproof.

In 14:3 the form of the legal controversy is again drawn upon for an accusation of God's unreasonableness (Fohrer thinks the accusation is directed to God as judge rather than as legal opponent; but the distinction is too subtle). The form of the accusation appears again finally at 14:20, and we may therefore gather that it is best to take the whole of chap. 14 as part of the legal controversy. Indeed, it makes good sense of the elegaic poetry of chap. 14, in which the lament and wisdom are drawn upon, to see it as an elaboration of the substantive charge against God that his persecution of Job as an example of the species "mortal" is unreasonable and disproportionate.

The subsidiary controversy with the friends occupies 13:4–12. We notice the elements of insult of the opponents (v 4), demands that they be silent (v 5; there is a reflection of the wisdom dispute in v 5b) and listen to his arguments (v 6, with the third party, God). The series of rhetorical questions (vv 7–9) charges Job's opponents with the injustice of favoring one of the parties in a dispute instead of acting as unprejudiced witnesses. The prediction of v 10 is used as a threat against being partisan; the rhetorical question of v 11 is a further reproof, and v 12 is a further threat (the wisdom aspect of the friends' unjust behavior is strongly marked in the terms used here for their speech).

From the realm of wisdom the *wisdom disputation speech* is drawn upon in 12:2–3, where his academic (not legal) opponents are mocked for their previous words and the speaker stresses the superiority of his own wisdom; it is the same in 13:1–2.

Wisdom instruction is well represented in 12:7–12, where Job employs this form to paraphrase, and so parody, the manner of the friends' address to him. The use of the second person singular indicates that the verses are cast as address to Job, that is, as Job's depiction of how he imagines the friends addressing *him*. The formal indicators of such instruction are the imperatives "ask," "speak" (vv 7, 8), the rhetorical question (vv 9, 11), and the proverb (vv 11, 12). From the point of view of content, the interest in animal wisdom, the "teachings" of the natural order, the issue of discrimination by the physical senses (v 11) and the ascription of "wisdom" to the aged are further indicators of the "instruction" form. Another example of wisdom instruction is found in 14:7–9, where the detailed description of the life of the tree belongs to the "encyclopedic" interests of wisdom. The presence of several similes from nature in the vicinity of this passage (vv 11, 18, 19) is probably also due to the conventionalities of wisdom teaching.

Of the psalmic forms, the *hymn* is strongly represented in 12:13–25. The participial style is used in vv 17, 19–23, though without the article (contrast 9:5–10). There is obvious dependence upon Ps 107 (esp. in vv 15, 21, 22, 24) but in each case the material is turned to quite different use, in that no moral purpose is discerned behind God's acts of social upheaval. 12:13–25 is a parody of the hymn.

The *appeal* (commonly called the "lament" form-critically) is the form of 12:4–6;

we note the speaker's description of himself as a laughingstock (cf. Ps 22:8 [7]; 44:14–15 [13–14]; 79:4), and his quotation of the enemies' words of self-encouragement to further assault the speaker (cf. Ps 71:11). These are not natural elements of the disputation speech (against Fohrer), but a typical element of the appeal form. The appeal form is also noticeable in the questions of reproof in 13:24–25.

The bulk of chap. 14 may be designated an *elegy* (Horst), though there are traces of wisdom teaching in vv 7–9 and there is the appeal form in v 3. Quite distinctive is the elaborated *wish* of vv 13–17, in which an impossibility is lingeringly entertained.

From the point of view of *function*, the speech as a whole is first a (wisdom) *disputation speech* addressed to the friends (12:2–13:19), and then a (legal) *disputation speech* addressed to God (13:20–14:22). The elegy of chap. 14 functions not as an independent poem, on the theme of brevity of life, but as the reason why God's concern to punish sin is disproportionate (13:25 picked up in idea by 14:3).

The *tonality* of the speech varies from the sarcastic (12:2) and the angry (13:4) in address to the friends, to the bold (13:20; cf. v 19) and reproachful (13:24; 14:3) in address to God. The movement in chap. 14 from the individual Job to humanity as the focus of attention distances the content from Job to some degree, but also extends the scope of the sadness here voiced. The concluding note of the isolated, hurting individual, cut off equally from God and from humanity, resembles the note on which previous speeches of Job have finished.

The *nodal verse* is 13:3 "But it is to the Almighty that I would speak; it is with God that I crave to enter dispute"—a sentence that is elaborated by the actual disputation begun at 13:20.

Comment

12:1–14:22 It has already been noted (see *Form*) how this speech stands at the threshold between the first and second cycle of speeches. In addition to taking stock of its position in the book, we should also chart its position relative to other speeches of Job himself. Where it stands in the progress of his drama is that it sets up a new milestone in his movement toward dialogue with God in that here for the first time Job directly invites God to enter into disputation with him (13:22) and specifies the question which the disputation is intended to resolve (13:23–24), "How many are my iniquities? . . . Why dost thou . . . count me as thine enemy?"

2–3 In speaking again after all his friends have addressed him, Job is directing himself to them all collectively, not to Zophar in particular. This speech begins with his comment on their collective wisdom. They have put themselves forward as purveyors of wisdom, but they have had nothing to teach Job.

2 For the first time in the book, Job is contemptuous of his friends. Earlier he had expressed his disappointment in them (6:15–21), had even pronounced them disloyal (6:14), and had angrily inveighed against their callousness (6:26–27). But he had not previously accused them of laying exclusive claim to wisdom. That they have not of course done. They have only spoken the conventionalities of wisdom teaching, and though they have occasionally appealed to personal experience (cf. 4:12–19; 5:3, 8, 27), their stance has been typified by Bildad's encouragement to "question the former generation, apply your mind to the discovery of their fathers, for we ourselves are but of yesterday and know nothing" (8:8–9). They have never represented themselves as the people at whose death wisdom will pass away, the last of their race (a similar charge is made by Aeschylus against Euripides in Aristophanes' *Frogs*, 868–69). But it feels like that to Job, who, with mock seriousness, allows for the moment the truth of this claim: unquestionably (אמנם, in itself not necessarily a sarcastic term; cf. 9:1) they must be wholly in the right and he wholly in the wrong.

It may not be thought entirely to Job's point to represent the friends as believing that wisdom will *die* with them, since it is surely bad enough that they regard themselves as the epitome or embodiment of the wisdom of the ages—the validity of which will undoubtedly survive them. Yet the rejoinder can well be made that the more they regard themselves as the embodiment of wisdom the better their pomposity can be punctured by declaring, "So much so that wisdom will perish with you!"

3 Perhaps with reference to Zophar's proverb about the "hollow-headed man" who will never acquire "heart" (לבב) (11:12), Job protests that he is a man of intelligence no less than they. "Heart" (לב, לבב) is the seat of understanding (as in 8:10); "in by far the greatest number of cases it is intellectual, rational functions that are ascribed to the heart—i.e. precisely what we ascribe to the head, and more exactly, to the brain" (H. W. Wolff, *Anthropology of the Old Testament* [Philadelphia: Fortress, 1974] 46; see also F. Stolz, *THWAT* 2:862–63). His intelligence is higher than theirs, he really means, for while they utter nothing but commonplaces, which the mass of humanity also knows, he can discriminate between platitudes and serious talk. Of course he is referring principally to the doctrine of retribution—the strength of which lies as much in its popular acceptance as in any intrinsic truth it may have. He has moved outside the realm of the conventional on this issue, and as an outsider has to defend himself. He is "not inferior" to the friends; in fact he reckons himself superior by virtue of his greater experience.

This line, "I am not inferior to you," recurs at 13:2b, where it is indispensable to the metrical structure; many have thought it an intrusive repetition in the present verse, creating a rather unusual three-line verse. But when we observe that immediately after 13:2b there begins a quite new development in the speech, "But I would speak with the Almighty," we realize that 13:2b is a deliberate repetition, by way of "inclusio," of a line with which chap. 12 began. Between 12:3 and 13:2, in other words, Job presents his evidence that he is not only his friends' equal in wisdom but indeed their superior.

4–6 These verses are a great difficulty, both in what they contain and in how they relate to their context. Many commentators (e.g., Siegfried, Duhm, Gray) regard them as misplaced or secondary. No one doubts that the words are suitable in Job's mouth, but why should Job *at this point* complain that he is a "laughingstock" to his friends, and that "those who provoke God are secure"? The answer can only be that these lines present the *reason* why Job is "not inferior" in wisdom to his friends (v 2b). "Not inferior" by litotes actually means "superior"; he is not just the friends' equal in knowledge of conventional wisdom, but he by his own experience has gained a higher wisdom, a knowledge contrary to conventional theology, namely that a righteous man can be afflicted by God, *and*—as a corollary—the reverse of that, namely that the deeds of the wicked can go unrequited.

4 Job has become a potential laughingstock, or object of derision, to his friends in that he has been smitten by God. The phrase need not mean that his friends—whether those of the dialogue or others of his acquaintance—

have actually been deriding him, but that his affliction is a sign that he has
been humiliated by God and is therefore fair game for the taunts of the pious.
This nasty habit, as it appears to us, of laughing at the afflictions of others
perhaps originates in a desire to disassociate oneself from the victim of a curse,
divine or human; by taunting or mocking the sufferer one distances oneself
from the disaster and thus protects oneself from its baleful influence. It is
not, from this perspective, simply a heartless expression of self-righteous *Scha-
denfreude* to do so; the truly righteous can rightly laugh when calamity strikes
the boastful wicked, saying, "See the man who would not make God his refuge
but trusted in the abundance of his wealth" (Ps 52:9 [7]). The motif of laughing
at the calamity of others is a frequent one in the OT, especially in psalmic
and prophetic literature: e.g. Ps 31:12 [11]; 35:15; 69:11–13 [10–12] ("when
I made sackcloth my clothing [as a symbol of distress or deprivation] I became
a byword, a taunt"); Jer 20:7–8; Lam 1:7; 3:14; Job 30:1, 9. Usually it is enemies
who are the deriders or taunters, but the sufferer's complaint is especially
poignant when—as here—it is his erstwhile friends or his relatives that have
become his mockers; so e.g. Ps 55:13–14 [12–13]; 88:9 [8]; cf. also on 9:23.

The Job who thus suffers is the man who proves in his own person the
inadequacy of the doctrine of exact retribution and thus is wiser than, "superior"
to, simple believers in uncomplicated theology; the sufferer is the man, "righteous" and "perfect," whom we have met in the narrative preface (צדיק and
תמים here, תם and ישר in 1:1). He is morally blameless, but also religiously
faultless, enjoying reciprocal communion with God, a man who would call
(the participle קרא indicates recurrent action) upon God and invariably be
answered. We have had a glimpse of such a person, from the outside, in 1:5,
where Job is pictured in constant petition to God on behalf of his children—
petition that evidently met with favor on every day except that fateful day of
the divine assembly. Here we are invited into that man's experience of "calling"
and "being answered" as a natural, unfretful, satisfying relation with the divine.
But of course that was a *former* experience; now he is the man whom God
has *not* answered and will *not* answer. Now Job is a caller without an answerer:
"I cry to thee and thou dost not answer me . . . thou hast turned cruel to
me" (30:20–21). Should he "call" to heaven, Eliphaz has warned him, there
would be no one to "answer" him with escape from the web of retributive
fate (5:1). What he longs for is that he could again approach God and learn
what he would answer him (23:5); every speech of his is implicitly a cry to
God, an attempt to restitute that dialogue he had enjoyed, and his last speech
will be climaxed by the cry, "Let the Almighty answer me" (31:35). If God
were to call upon *him*, he, mere mortal that he is, could not answer God
(9:3, 14–16, 32); yet such an ill-matched dialogue would be better than nothing,
if only there could be dialogue of some sort again (13:22). Even to wait a
whole life long for a "call" from God would be worth it: "all the days of my
hard service I would wait . . . then thou wouldest call, and I would answer
thee" (14:15). But as it is, he is in the position of the godless man whose
"cry" God does not "hear" (27:9); and even ordinary human and domestic
dialogue with Job has been stifled: "I call to my servant but he gives me no
answer" (19:16). Heaven and earth alike have become deaf, and Job hears
nothing but the echo of his own cries.

5 What it means to be a laughingstock is now developed. The innocent

Job is the butt of those secure in their piety, like the Zophar who has just now been busy picturing a future for the "converted" Job, a future when he will be secure, confident, and fearless (11:15–19; cf. also 8:13–15). For their security is grounded upon their convictions of exact retribution: they cannot be harmed, for they are righteous. And they maintain their security by instantly designating any sufferer an evildoer; if anyone suffers injury, that person deserves moral condemnation as well ("add insult to injury" is their principle); and if anyone is staggering beneath misfortune, that person is an apt target for censure ("strike him down" with social disapproval, for his misfortune has already marked him out as impious). Cf. Ps 123:4 "Too long our soul has been sated with the scorn of those who are secure (שַׁאֲנָן, as here), the contempt (בּוּז, as here) of the proud"; but whereas in that passage the "secure" are the unrighteous oppressors, here they are the genuinely righteous, who are oppressors nevertheless, sitting in judgment on the insecure. It is an irony, of course, that Job should use the word שַׁאֲנָן, "at ease, secure" for well-nourished theologians, for such a term often denotes the godless who are secure in their prosperity (Amos 6:1; Isa 32:9; Zech 1:15).

The expression "the feet slip" refers to the coming of misfortune or the succumbing to danger (cf. 4:4; Ps 37:31; a more literal sense in Ps 18:37 [36] and Prov 25:19; it is uncertain if it ever has a moral connotation, not even in Ps 26:1).

6 In the last two verses Job has spoken out of his own experience; now he draws an implication which he cannot personally testify to: that while a godly man like him is being afflicted, the godless sleep sound in their beds. It is not a logical inference from his own experience, and he has not previously drawn it; but it is no doubt a psychological correlate. For if Job feels that God is so distant and aloof as to let him suffer undeservedly, he must also feel that God cares nothing about the prosperity of the wicked (cf. also on 9:23–24). They are here specifically "brigands" (JB), professional plunderers (as שָׁדַד in 15:21; Jer 6:26; 12:2; 48:8; etc.), not "robbers" simply (RSV, NAB). Perhaps Job has in mind those marauders who have brought disaster to him (Sabeans and Chaldeans, 1:15, 17), though he does not know what fate may have befallen them, and cannot without guesswork affirm anything about their present state.

The next line has caused much debate. The commonest view, represented by RSV "who bring their god in their hand," understands it as further descriptive of the wicked. Perhaps they are idolators who carry about their gods with them (Doederlein, Andersen), or else their god *is*, metaphorically speaking, their own hands (cf. JB "make a god of their two fists"). There are similar, but not identical, expressions in Mic 2:1 and Gen 31:29, which may mean "their hand serves as their god" and "my hand serves me as a god" (Dhorme), though many see here not אֵל, "god," but a separate word for "strength" (KB[3]; cf. BDB). Virgil's phrase *dextra mihi deus*, "my right hand is my god" (*Aeneid* 10.773) is often quoted in this connection. The major difficulty with these interpretations is that the verb and noun suffix of the line are singular, "he brings . . . in his hand," whereas the brigands and God-provokers of the previous lines are plural. It seems necessary, therefore, to see God as the subject of the verb, as the one who has evil-doers in his power but does nothing whatever about their wickedness. They then are "those whom God has brought into his own hand," and thus protects (cf. Sicre Diaz). Job has already voiced similar sentiments, in declaring that God ignores the oppression of wicked judges (9:23–24).

7–12 To many readers these verses have seemed decidedly out of place, so much so that they are omitted as later additions by Fohrer and Hesse among others. Superficially the connection of thought might seem to be: The wisdom of the friends, which they claim as their exclusive possession (so says Job in v 2, but he misrepresents them), is so commonplace that even the animals share it. But, as Gray writes, such a thought is strangely stated: "for Job's charge is not that the friends lack the particular knowledge in question, and *need to be taught*, which is the point emphasized in vv 7–8, but that they have *no need to teach* things so universally known, v 3c."

There are other aspects of these three verses also that call them into doubt. (a) The questions of vv 7–8 are addressed to an individual, not to the friends collectively, as is Job's normal practice. (b) The idea that wisdom is the prerogative of the aged (v 12) sounds more at home in the mouth of the friends (cf. 8:8–10; 15:10) than of Job. (c) The use of the name Yahweh in v 9 is unparalleled in the whole of the dialogues. (d) The reference of "this" at the end of v 9 is unclear. (e) The whole passage begins (v 7) with the strongly adversative conjunction וֿאוּלָם, "but assuredly," which suits the sense very poorly, since Job has just now been speaking of his own superior insight and depth of experience (vv 4–6), not of commonplace knowledge.

These difficulties are comfortably resolved by the view, strongly advocated by Gordis, that vv 7–12 are a quotation ("Quotations as a Literary Usage in Biblical, Oriental and Rabbinic Literature," *HUCA* 22 [1949] 157–219). Developing Gordis's argument, I would suggest that these verses are not Job's address to the friends but an ironic statement by him of what he imagines they have been saying to him, or might well say to him. They may thus be thought "a satirical adaptation of the appeal to ancient tradition employed by Bildad in 8:8ff." (N. C. Habel, "Appeal to Ancient Tradition as a Literary Form," *ZAW* 88 [1976] 253–72 [266]). The thrust of the verses would then be that the friends have a simplistic view of divine activity, conceiving God's way of dealing with the world as obvious and well-known throughout creation (vv 7–9), and as a matter of traditional lore (v 12) that admits no novel adjustments to suit the whim of a theological parvenu like Job. No doubt it would be unwise to attempt to resolve many difficulties in the Biblical text by supposing that they are ironic quotations of a point of view opposite to the speaker's—and all of Gordis's claims to have identified such quotations are not equally convincing— but there is one important clue in the present text that clinches the argument. It is the presence of the second person singular verbs and pronouns, "Ask . . . they will teach you . . . they will tell you . . . they will teach you . . . will declare to you." This is not Job addressing the friends, but paraphrasing the way *they* address *him*. It is *they* who pretend that God's ways with the world are essentially simple, comprehensible even to animals, plants and fish; it is *they* who regard the law of retribution as fundamentally a *natural* law, a law like those according to which life is lived throughout the created order. It is *they* who utter the platitudes of vv 10–11. And it is *they* who assert that wisdom is with the aged (v 12), that is, that it is a matter of traditional learning and not of ideological novelties founded by a distraught and sinful man upon his own experiences. It is an interesting irony that if these verses are used to teach a doctrine of natural revelation (as by A. De Guglielmo, "Job 12:7–9 and the Knowability of God," *CBQ* 6 [1944] 476–82), their setting in the chapter actually undermines that doctrine, branding it not wrong, exactly, but simplistic.

7–8 Ironically, Job pretends to quote the friends. The introductory particle, "but nevertheless" (וֹאוּלם, a strong adversative) indicates clearly that what follows is contradictory to Job's own views that he has been expressing in vv 4–6. His friends have been insulting his intelligence (cf. vv 2–3), and now he protests by putting his words into their mouth. There is no mystery about your situation (they are saying to Job); it is obvious, and if you do not know it already, you have only to consult the lower orders of creation, the earth itself, if you like, and they will tell you what you seem not to know—or perhaps have willfully forgotten.

The friends have, to be sure, never uttered such words. Their advice to Job has been to "enquire" (שְׁאָל־נָא as here) of the former generations, of the fathers (8:8), who will "teach" Job (יוֹרוּךָ; cf. תרף here) from their wisdom. But so unsubtle is the teaching of the ages on the present question—for it is nothing but exact retribution pure and simple—that Job parodies the friends' advice by casting it as equivalent to asking subhuman creation for its wisdom.

9 Animals, of course, have intelligence below the human; thus when Nebuchadrezzer lost his reason and was driven from his throne, the decree was, "Let his mind be changed from that of a man, and let a beast's mind be given him" (Dan 4:13 [16]; cf. 5:21). Yet a human may learn from an animal, as when a prophet is blind to the presence of the Lord's angel with drawn sword and must be rebuked by an ass (Num 22:21–35), or when the sluggard is urged by the wisdom teacher to "go to the ant . . . consider its ways and become wise" (Prov 6:6). Cf. also M.-L. Henry, *Das Tier im religösen Bewusstsein des alttestmentlichen Menschen* (Sammlung gemeinverständlicher Vorträge und Schriften aus dem Gebiet der Theologie und Religionsgeschichte 220/221; Tübingen: Mohr, 1958) esp. 44–46.

Job reproaches his friends by insinuating that they treat him as a mental defective or a moral delinquent, needing the most elementary lessons from the world of nature. It is a deep irony—on the poet's part, not Job's—that in the end it will be to the book of nature that God will direct Job's attention, and that by considering the animals, mountain goats, hawks, and suchlike, with Behemoth the earth monster and Leviathan the water monster, that Job will be brought to his ultimate insight. Creation, indeed, contains the secret of its own existence within itself, and the natural order will prove itself a soulmate of the moral order (see *Comment* on chaps. 38–41). But Job does not see that yet, and for him at this moment the wisdom of nature is of the most elementary kind, and he has certainly nothing to learn from it.

What exactly is it that all creation knows? "That the hand of Yahweh has done this" is a rather enigmatic clause. The line occurs also in Isa 41:20 and is reminiscent too of Ps 109:27, which leads many to suppose it an interpolation in the present verse. In Isa 41:20 it concludes an oracle of salvation, in which "has done this" refers to the imminent preparation of the way for the returning exiles. In Ps 109:27, "Let them [my accusers] know that this is your hand; you, O Yahweh, have done it," it is not clear whether "this" refers to the act

of deliverance the psalmist envisages (Gunkel) or the suffering which has come
upon the psalmist. The latter view is taken by A. Weiser, for example, writing
that "God himself must intervene and make his enemies realize that it was
he, God himself, who caused the sudden death of that poor man, and not
dark, magic machinations which are laid to the charge of the worshipper"
(*The Psalms* [OTL; Philadelphia: Westminster, 1962] 691). In Isa 66:2 we have
"The hand of Yahweh made all these [things] (כל־אלה, as here) when all of
them came into being," in clear reference to the creation of heaven and earth,
and in Jer 14:22 "You have done all these things," in reference to the sending
of rain. The wide range of contexts suggests the common sense conclusion,
that the phrase does not point to any one signification (creation, for example)
but it is an all-purpose phrase.

Here, the elementary lesson that all created things can teach is that whatever
is done is done by God; that is their own mute testimony to the reality of
their own being. And this is the lesson—Job says that the friends say—that
Job refuses to learn. It is as if, says Job, the friends had declared, with an
airy wave of the hand to the world of nature, "All this, dear Job, is God's
doing; and your suffering is nothing but a natural, inevitable, ordered, prescribed, intelligible, rational and coherent part of 'all this.'" And why, we may
ask, is Job cynical about such an attitude? Because what he has encountered
is an untidy, arbitrary and cruel world order, in which the just person is a
laughingstock (v 4), an order of affairs in which God is experienced not as
some tidy-minded watchmaker but as the one who tears down, withholds,
overthrows, deprives, despises, and destroys (vv 14–25). The friends think
everything in the garden is lovely, all created things being neatly arranged
according to their kinds (there may be overtones of the cosmic ordering in
Gen 1 in the language of vv 7–8); for Job the garden of nature is a bear-
garden and nature (whether physical or moral) is red in tooth and claw. For
the friends the wisdom of the ages has been melted down into a cliché, a
saying for all seasons, "Yahweh's hand has done this"; for Job raw experience,
not mulled theology, is true wisdom.

Strangely enough, Job too agrees that "Yahweh's hand has done this," but
he can not consent to the friends' conception of what "this" is: it is not for
him the inexorable outworking of a moral law of nature but the willful act of
a malign deity.

What is the significance of the use of the name Yahweh here? It never
occurs elsewhere in the poetry of the book. Most commentators see it as a
sign that the line has been secondarily inserted here by a scribe, probably as
a quotation from Isa 41:20. But it is not an accidental intrusion; Job is "citing"
the words of his friends, whom he envisages as deploying religious clichés.
So it *is* a quotation, not directly of Isa 41:20, no doubt, but of a well-worn
idiom that is used there also (cf. Weiser). It is true that the friends themselves
in their speeches never use the name Yahweh, but Job is not noticeably careful
to do justice to the friends' exact theological position on other matters. It is a
little more surprising that the poet allowed himself the freedom to use "Yahweh"
here; the reason must be that "hand of Yahweh" is a fixed phrase (over thirty
occurrences); while "the hand of God" (Elohim) is very rare (1 Sam 5:11; 2
Chr 30:12; Ecclus 9:1; Job 19:21 has "the hand of Eloah" and 27:11 "the
hand of El"). Some mss indeed have Eloah (used 41 times in Job for God),

and it is possible that "Yahweh" here is a scribal slip, and not the poet's own term.

10   The argument is little advanced here. It is another obvious truth that both animals ("every living thing") and humans (lit., "all the flesh of human-kind") are in the power of God. (No special distinction is being made between נֶפֶשׁ "life principle" [RV, NAB "soul"] and רוּחַ "breath"; both terms are appropriate for animals and humans.) The implication of such a statement, as set in the mouth of the friends by Job, is that everything that has happened to Job has been by divine arrangement. Job also believes this, but his point is that to speak of God's "control" of his creatures so glibly is to disregard the *character* of that control as destructive (vv 14–25). "He's got the whole world in his hand" would be the theme song of the friends, says Job; but the question is whether that hand is an open palm or a clenched fist.

11   Here is another self-evident truth, cast in proverbial form, and, like all of vv 7–12, attributed to the friends by Job (it is used again by Elihu at 34:3, though not in question form). A similar proverb occurs in Ecclus 36:19 [24], "As the palate tastes the kinds of game, so an intelligent mind detects false words." The point is that "just as the palate discriminates between foods and accepts only what commends itself to it, so the ear discriminates and receives only what commends itself" (Rowley). The function of the mouth is not only to eat but also to decide some things are not worth eating; so too the function of the ear is not only to receive messages, but to discriminate among them. The saying invites the hearer to agree with what is being said, though under the guise of opening up the subject to discriminating decision. It is a somewhat disingenuous way of saying, "I'm right, amn't I?" or "This is unquestionably true, isn't it?" Job resents such an attitude because truth for him is far from self-evident; what is deeply true is disturbing and subversive of superficial truth.

12   Undoubtedly this is not the opinion of Job, as many scholars recognize (e.g. Budde, Gray, Rowley) even if they have not seen that vv 7–12 as a whole does not represent him; cf. RV mg "With aged men, *ye say*, is wisdom." The speech Job attributes to the friends concludes with a sentence that epitomizes what is wrong with their position: the appeal to tradition, the experience of the ages, and conventional wisdom. Reality has jolted Job out of adherence to the wisdom of the aged; we may suppose that before his suffering he would have spoken the same language as the friends.

The "old men" are perhaps the living elders to whose judgment younger men defer (cf. 29:8; 15:10); but they also by reason of their age are the living representatives of the former generations, appeal to whom ("the former generations" together with "their fathers") has already been made by Bildad (8:8–10).

Some regard v 12 as the beginning of the hymn to the wisdom and might of God (vv 12–25), and in attributing v 12 to the persona of Job see it as the backdrop of v 13 (cf. GNB "Old men have wisdom, but God has wisdom and power"). This is not an impossible view, but it is not very probable to have Job conceding that the aged have wisdom, even if he is quick to assert that it is little by comparison with God's. It is better to see v 13 as Job's response *in propria persona* to the friends' position represented in v 12. Less probable is the view of Fohrer and Hesse, emending the text slightly (see n. 12:12.a), that v 12 is a strong denial by Job of the wisdom of the aged and is set in counterpoint to the praise of God's wisdom.

13–25 These verses constitute a hymn to the power of God in the human world. The poem invites comparison with what I have called a "hymn to the power of God in nature" in the previous speech of Job (9:5–10). There the theme had been God's power, no less destructive than benevolent, in the natural order; here again it is God's power, but principally as it operates in the social sphere, and principally in its subversive or destructive aspect. Formally there are differences and similarities with 9:5–10: in both places there is a generalizing introductory sentence (12:13; cf. 9:4), though in chap. 9 it seemed to be part of the preceding strophe. In chap. 9 the obvious grammatical marker of the hymnic style, the participle with the article, was evident; here there are nine participles referring to God's activity (vv 17, 19, 20, 21, 22, 23) but none of them with the article. There is no "summary appraisal" sentence (as there is in 9:10). The formal features of the hymn should also be compared with the doxology of Eliphaz (5:9–16; see further on 9:5–10).

The purpose or significance of the hymn is not immediately evident (it is thought secondary by Fohrer and others). It cannot simply be a hymn of praise, for Job has no call to *praise* God. Nor can it be a mere *acknowledgment* of God's power, since God's power is usually the object of *complaint* on Job's part (cf. 9:3–4, 17, 34). Its purpose rather is to convey Job's "wisdom," his understanding of the *true* nature of God's activity. The God he has encountered is no placid governor of a universe of order, but an eccentric deity, equally inapprehensible and untameable whether he stands aloof from humans or frenetically and obnoxiously interferes in their lives. This is the deeper wisdom, the higher knowledge, that calls forth a hymn—half-serious because Job is truly awed by this revelation of a God beyond theological entrapment and half-ironic because Job deeply despises a God who does not play fair.

This hymn presents many examples of the *topos* of the reversal of fortunes. As has been noted in connection with Eliphaz's doxology in 5:9–16, such praise of God usually revolves around his readjustment of the social order into a more just pattern. Such readjustment often involves cataclysmic upheavals, like raising the lowly to the heights, and ensnaring the cunning in their own craftiness (5:11, 13), but it is no less salvific (5:15), and its purpose is essentially rectification of an already disturbed social order. Job's modulation of the theme fastens exclusively on acts of reversal, and it is notable that at no point in these verses is any moral purpose served by the upheavals (cf. Andersen). Job's concentration is wholly upon the upsetting of expectations, for his motive is to speak the theology of a righteous man who is a laughingstock (v 4). That is the degree of his disenchantment with conventional theology, and to that degree his depiction of God is skewed by his own experience.

It needs to be stressed, nevertheless, that throughout this unflattering account of God's activity not a hint of injustice is breathed. It is not Job's purpose to speak of injustice, though that may be a reasonable inference from what he says. His concern rather is to assert that God does not act in accord with strict retributive ethics, but in pursuit of some principle of disorder. There is an amoralism in such behavior, of course, but the gravamen of Job's critique of God is not that God is unethical, but that he is destructive and subversive (cf. on 9:1–10:22 where it has been argued that Job is not accusing God of "cosmic injustice," but protesting that it is impossible to win vindication from God).

The arguments of some scholars (e.g. Fohrer) that these verses are intrusive are unpersuasive. Fohrer finds in them "general hymnic ideas, not to be found elsewhere in the book of Job," but the parallels in 5:8–15 and 9:5–10 (the latter passage he has judged secondary) put that notion to rest. He believes that they contradict 12:6, but there the claim is that God ignores wickedness while here the claim is that (regardless of ethical values) he interferes in the social order—which is no contradiction. And he judges them to be part of an independent hymn, reminiscent of Ps 107 and Isa 44:24–28; but he overlooks the fact that there is nothing salvific about God's activity in these verses—in sharp contrast to Ps 107 and Isa 44. These verses must rather be seen as a deliberate reworking (perhaps even "parody," Andersen) of conventional hymnic material, blocking out the positive aspects of reversal of fortune.

The connections with Ps 107 are so close and numerous that it seems right to term it a "source" of the present hymn, in the way that Ps 8 was the "source" of Job 7:17–18 (*q.v.*). For comments on the quite different atmosphere of the Joban hymn, see on vv 15, 21, 22, 24.

The *structure* of the hymn is fairly straightforward. There are three general statements of God's wisdom (vv 13, 16 and 22) each introducing a strophe of the hymn. The first is of six lines (like the six-line unit of vv 5–6), the second is of twelve lines (like the twelve-line unit of vv 7–12), and the third is of six lines plus a two line closure (cf. on v 25). The content of the strophes also is a distinguishing feature: most single-minded is the second strophe (vv 16–21), with ten verbs having God as the subject and some group of leaders of society as the object. The first strophe, by contrast, has a more indeterminate or metaphorical content, and the third concerns nations as a whole, together with their leaders.

P. W. Skehan, "Strophic Patterns," 106–7, however, saw major dislocation here. He could not accept that the very similar vv 17a and 19a could both be original, so he deleted v 19a (his translation claims, by error, to omit v 17a). He moved v 18 to follow v 15 on the understanding that it develops the idea that God "imprisons" (v 14a); but the only imprisoning done in v 18 is by kings, not God. Then, taking v 21b as referring to streams (see n. 12:21.b), he transferred it to follow v 18 and develop the idea of God's control of waters (v 15); v 19b understood as descriptive of "never-failing waters" (see n. 12:19.c), follows. Verses 21a and 24b are omitted as repetitious of Ps 107. The result is two strophes of ten and twelve (+ one) lines which fits into his general view that chaps. 12–14 present a sequence of nine stanzas, alternating between ten lines and twelve; the general view seems to have overinfluenced the treatment of the particular verses. This idiosyncratic and unconvincing reconstruction could perhaps be allowed to fade into obscurity were it not that it is adopted wholesale, without comment, into the NAB.

13 Job reverts to speaking in his own person. The friends have been urging (he claims) that the truth about God is what has been traditionally believed ("wisdom is found with the aged," v 12); on the contrary, he says, the truth about God is with God: he is the only one who knows what he is doing. Job lays claim, of course, to a superior knowledge about God, but, Socrates-like, what he knows about God is really *less* than the friends claim to know. For they pretend to know the principles on which God acts, whereas Job only knows that there are no principles on which God acts—none, at any rate, that could be called rational or ethical.

This is a most intriguing situation, because it is not so far distant from the position Job will adopt at the end of the book, after the divine speeches. In the end he will be left with the ungainsayable truth that God does what he likes, and has his own reasons. But that is a statement that can be uttered either in bitterness or with a believing acceptance. And at this moment Job is not ready to reflect on the creative values of such an idea; he is still shocked by how discordant the idea is with a traditional theology that shrinks from mystery and calmly purports to justify the ways of God to man.

It is difficult to tie down precisely what "wisdom" includes. On the one hand, it seems to be the highest wisdom, insight into the divine nature, its motives and ways of working—which only God himself possesses. On the other hand, it is also "know-how," a practical sort of wisdom, as its conjunction with "might" shows. Wisdom cannot be understood in the Hebrew Bible as a purely theoretical knowledge; it presses always towards action, so that ability to act and knowledge of how to act effectively are rarely contrasted. Here the parallelism might suggest that the accent is on wisdom rather than strength (Horst), but perhaps rather the four abstract terms in this verse refer collectively to God's capacity to act according to his own (mysterious and disturbing) principles.

14 With this verse the catalogue of divine activities begins. Job is not claiming that this is the whole truth about God's dealings with humankind, as if to say, God's might "frustrates all human endeavour, and overthrows all human institutions" (Driver). Especially if the "all" were emphasized, such a statement would be so palpably false that we cannot imagine it being uttered. Rather, these verses portray *some* scenes of divine involvement with humans. What gives this selection its potency is that all the scenes show God acting destructively, negatively or in the cause of chaos. And of course Job and the poet never add the qualifications to this portrait that the commentator must; it is enough that such a catalogue can be prepared for Job's belief to be reinforced that through his experience of God's persecution he has come to a deeper insight into the divine nature, to a knowledge "not inferior" to that of the friends (v 3).

There may well be a contrast here between objects, like walls or cities, that are "destroyed" and persons who are "bound." The verb "destroy" (הרס) is generally used of destroying material objects (e.g. altars, Judg 6:25; cities, Isa 14:17; walls, Ezek 13:14), though occasionally also of persons (Exod 15:7; Jer 42:10; etc.); it is often paired with "build" (בנה, as in Jer 45:4; Prov 14:1). To "shut up" (סגר) is also used mostly in reference to objects, like doors, but plainly here in reference to "a person" (איש); its regular contrast is with פתח, "open," as here.

The sentence is in its structure reminiscent of 9:11–12 and especially 11:10. In 11:10 Zophar has used God's shutting up of the wicked as an example of his "wisdom." In form, the sentence is gnomic, which makes it unlikely that specific historical events are referred to, whether the flood and the fall of Sodom and Gomorrah (cf. "shut up," Gen 7:16), as Andersen; or the flood ("shut in") and the tower of Babel ("not built"), as Tur-Sinai; or the destruction of Jericho, destroyed and not rebuilt (cf. Alonso Schökel). It matters little whether what is stressed is the impossibility of countering God's measures (Horst) or the simple fact that no one actually does.

15 The lord of human history is the lord of nature equally. But to what effect? He restrains life-giving water and sends devastating torrents. The contrast with the praise of God in Ps 107 is striking: there (vv 33–37) he turns rivers into a desert, and watersprings to dry ground *because of the wickedness of the inhabitants*; and he turns a desert into pools of water, a land of drought into watersprings, *in order to provide a dwelling place, fields and vineyards for the hungry*. Abstract the motivation of these two actions—and Job has good reason to suspect divine motivation—and an arbitrary and aimless exercise of divine power becomes apparent. Transpose the sending of rain into a minor key—which corresponds to Job's mood—and the sending of rain signals not salvation but catastrophe. Either there is too little water or there is too much—that is the cry of a depressed oriental. It is the cry too of a man whom God has blessed overabundantly (1:1–3) and has made to suffer gratuitously and excessively (1:9, 21a; 2:3, 7); there is a dreadful disproportion in what God does (cf. 7:17–21). Note also the contrast with Eliphaz's picture of God's gift of rain, the transforming substance, perhaps also the substance that restores social equilibrium (cf. 5:10–11).

16 A new sub-strophe begins with a repetition of the thought of v 13. The terms for wisdom (on תושיה see on 11:6) and strength are reversed, and perhaps the focus is here somewhat more on God's power or ability to dismantle the normal social institutions. Zophar has pointed to God's תושיה as a confidential data bank containing information on human activities licit and illicit. But Job has his own alternative perception of the divine תושיה: it is God's skill in wreaking chaos in human affairs.

Humankind is here grimly divided by Job into two classes: the deceivers and the deceived. Often the term שׁגג or שׁגה refers to inadvertent sin in the cultic sphere (cf. J. Milgrom, "The Cultic שׁגגה and Its Influence in Psalms and Job," *JQR* 58 [1967] 115–25; R. Knierim, *TWHAT* 2:867–72). Here it must be a moral term for deliberate error, as in Prov 28:10, where "he who misleads (שׁגה) the upright into an evil way" is contrasted with "the blameless." God makes no evident distinction between the morally culpable and the blameless; this has been Job's argument in 9:22, "blameless and wicked alike he brings to an end," and it is equally his point here, that the just man is a laughingstock while the tents of brigands are left in peace (vv 4–6). This is Job's wisdom, newly born of his own unhappy experience.

The phrase "deceived and deceiver" is reminiscent of phases indicating totality, such as "bond and free" (Deut 32:36; 1 Kgs 14:10), "small and great" (Job 3:19; Esth 1:5). But the phrase here does not primarily indicate the totality (contra Rowley, Fohrer), but rather the two distinct ethical groups. Several commentators deny that moral error is involved, arguing that it is the inadvertent leading astray of peoples by their rulers (so, e.g., Gray). This view is argued in order to provide some connection with the following specific cases; but there is in fact nothing to suggest that the leaders of society in vv 17–21 are "deceivers," and the connection of the present verse is rather with the distinction between the good and the evil.

There is a bitter force in Job's analysis: people are either deceived or deceivers.

Either way they are wrapped in illusion and truth is inaccessible. It is a perspective that fits well with Job's belief that conventional theology is a bundle of deceptions.

17 Anyone who gives advice may be a counselor, of course; but here, in parallelism with "judges," they must be professional counselors, court officials like David's counselor (יוֹעֵץ) Ahithophel (cf. 2 Sam 16:23), that are here referred to. On the office of "counselor" see W. McKane, *Prophets and Wise Men* (SBT 44; London: SCM, 1965); see also on 3:14; and cf. Isa 19:11; 1 Kgs 12:6; 2 Kgs 6:8; 2 Chr 25:16; 32:3. Since his responsibility to the king is for the security of the state, his function is proved a total failure should the state he serves fall prey to another and he himself be taken away in a procession of captives. Literary and archaeological evidence combine to illustrate the custom of leading captives barefoot; see Isa 20:2–4; Mic 1:8 (where captives are also naked); and *ANEP*, pls. 205 (three barefoot captive lyre players), 321 (the inhabitants of Lachish).

Parallel to the failure of the counsel of the wise is the making foolish of the sage decisions of the judges. "Sober as a judge" is our own idiom; but judges too lose their wits if God so decrees. The idea of God making fools of the wise is found also in Isa 44:25 (also in a doxological context) and 19:11, 13, though not in reference to judges specifically.

18 The dissolution of royal power is a further sign of the chaos-creating power of God. The "bonds" (RSV) of kings are most probably not bonds but some regal garments (*BHS*) or the "belt" (JB) as symbol of authority (Gordis); the common view, that God loosens the bonds that kings have imposed on others (Gray, Rowley, NEB, NAB, NIV), is inappropriate to a depiction of the king's own loss of power.

The meaning of the second line is not certain, but the picture may well be of kings being led captive (as of counselors in v 17a). See *ANEP*, pls. 249 (Darius's Behistun inscription, showing nine princely rebels roped together, with hands tied behind their backs), 305 (Mari shell inlay, showing naked prisoners with ropes around arms and waist), 311 (Asiatics bound with ropes being led off by Egyptians), 332 (Megiddo ivory with naked bound prisoners). Binding captives with ropes is plentifully attested in literary texts also: e.g., Judg 15:13; and metaphorically, Ps 2:3. The interpretation of אֵזוֹר as "belt" is open to question, since the term generally denotes an article of clothing, "waistcloth" (RSV, NAB) or "loincloth" (NIV), an undergarment of skin or linen (2 Kgs 1:8; Jer 13:1); cf. L. G. Running, *ISBE* 2:403, who identifies it as the short wrapped skirt depicted, for example, in *ANEP*, pls. 1, 2, 8, etc. But in Isa 5:27 the אֵזוֹר appears to be the Assyrian soldier's belt, and in Ezek 23:15 the Babylonian belt; such is no doubt the best interpretation here. But if in fact the term must mean "loincloth," God's binding a garment on the loins of kings must mean that they are already stripped of their regal robes, and must wear only rudimentary clothing.

Among the leaders of most societies are the professional religious men. Priests are nowhere else mentioned in Job, and cultic matters are in general ignored within the dialogue. Those who are "long established" could be any kind of noblemen or officials, but the phrase may be especially descriptive of the priests of the first line; priesthoods are generally hereditary institutions (cf. Moffatt: "He marches priests away barefoot, their ancient orders he o'er-throws"). Priests, like kings, counselors and judges, are guardians of the *status quo*, and for them to be led into exile "barefoot" implies that their cultic office has lost its efficacy. This is a further illustration of the subversiveness of the divine governance of the world.

20 The "reliable" men are probably the same as the "elders," those who have a less formal position in the society than the groups mentioned in vv 17–19, but in their own fashion supportive of social order. They contribute discretion (טעם, lit., "taste," thus "judgment") and sound speech (שפה, lit., "lip"; cf. on 11:2).

21 The first line is taken from Ps 107:40a, the source of several phrases in the present verses; 107:40b forms Job 12:24b. In the psalm, however, the princes who are made contemptible are those who have oppressed the "redeemed of the Lord"; those princes are exiled to trackless wastes so that the needy may be restored from affliction (Ps 107:39–41). Here, on the other hand, no purpose in the humiliation of princes is apparent, apart from displaying God's destructive power (cf. esp. on v 15). "Contempt" (בוז) probably refers to an objective humiliation rather than to a subjective feeling on God's part or on the part of human bystanders (in v 5 "contempt for calamity" was the subjective sense). It is thus like "shame," which often has an "objective" sense (cf. on 8:22). See also M. Görg, *TDOT* 2:60–65.

The "mighty," if the Hebrew word is understood correctly (see n. 12:21.b), are very probably fighting men. If their "belt" is "loosened" or "relaxed," they are no longer girded for war—that is, with their sword tied to their girdle and hanging on their left side (cf. 2 Sam 20:8; Judg 3:21). The "nobles" who are humiliated may well be military leaders; although נדיבים is often used in contexts without any military connotation, the term does seem to be related to the verb נדב "to volunteer" (cf. e.g. Judg 5:2, 9 of the leaders and the people volunteering for war; and Ps 47:10 [9]; 83:12 [11]; Cant 6:12; Isa 13:2, where a military connection might exist). Military leaders and fighting men are of course a conventional sign of national security; they are humiliated if they lose a battle and the chaos of invasion occurs.

22 The abstract content of the verse makes its presence in this catalogue of concrete examples somewhat suspect. Duhm, Fohrer and Pope omit it as a gloss, Horst as a "theological expansion," and NEB transposes it to follow v 25, presumably because the list of specifics has ended by that point. If the verse is original it may refer to God's disclosing men's secrets that for safety's sake would best be kept hidden "in deep shade." And those that have such secrets are presumably the counselors and elders of former verses. We meet such "shady" characters in Isa 29:15 who "hide deep" (root עמק, as here) from Yahweh their counsel (עצה, root יעץ, as in v 17), whose deeds are in the dark (root חשך, as here).

It is curious that rather similar language is found in Ps 107:10, 14, a psalm with many other affinities to these verses. There the ones who sit in "darkness" or "deep shade" (חשך and צלמות, as here) are not leaders but captives, and what is "brought out" (יצא, as here) is not secrets but prisoners, by Yahweh's deliverance. Here again the poet of Job may be reshaping some traditional language to yield the kind of perverse sense Job is here promoting. There may, for that matter, be something in Duhm's alternative suggestion that the reference is to lower strata of society gaining the ascendancy when men of rank have been deposed (vv 17–21); but it is not easy to see how the Hebrew wording can actually mean that.

Others of course find no difficulty in interpreting the passage as a reappearance of the cosmic motifs of v 15, "because the poet wishes to show the contrast that separates the omnipotence of God, before whom even the depths of the cosmos are laid bare, and the blindness of the great ones of the earth, who grope about in obscurity (v 25) and are lost in trackless deserts" (Terrien). But *contrast* between God and humans is not really the theme of the hymn of vv 13–25.

Perhaps the best interpretation is to see here God's revealing, not the hidden secrets of human leaders, but his own depths and bringing into open view, not captives, but his own "shadiness," the dark side of God. This fits well with Job's present purpose, which is to expatiate upon the hidden or unregarded character of the divine nature, namely his chaotic destructiveness. The language of "deepness" and "hiddenness" for God's wisdom ("know-how") is doubly appropriate: it is what Job has been trying to say, and it is language that Zophar has just now used—though to signally different purpose! Zophar has expressed his wish that God would make known the "secrets" (תעלמות, "hiddennesses") of his wisdom, and has declared that wisdom more "deep" (עמקה, as here) than human comprehension. Job agrees on the words, though not their sense. In Job's view, God's wisdom (which includes his might) is hidden only because few have had the opportunity to penetrate like Job to the God beyond God; God makes that deep wisdom visible ("uncovers" it, יגלה), for those have eyes to see, by his chaos-creating acts in the world of humankind; his "deepness" is not in principle beyond human comprehension but—to Job at least—as clear as day, however unfamiliar to the mass of humanity.

This interpretation may be supported by the strophic structure of the present speech. In the acknowledged unit formed by vv 13–25, there have been two statements of God's "wisdom and might," the first (v 13) introducing a three-line strophe (vv 13–15), the second (v 16) introducing a couple of three-line strophes (vv 16–21). The focus of vv 13–15 is clearly distinct from that of vv 16–21, and so too is the focus of vv 22–25, upon nations rather than just their leaders. Verses 22–25 also is a three-line strophe, with a "hanging" or attached couplet (v 25) rounding off the whole poem of vv 13–25. In this setting it makes sense for the introductory v 22 to repeat the orientation of v 13 and v 16: it too affirms the nature of God's wisdom, and it too will be followed by supporting examples.

The final evidence that it is God's wisdom that is the subject of this sentence is the very close analogue in Dan 2:20–22, itself a doxology. There God is praised as the one who possesses "wisdom and might" (Aram. חכמתא and גבורתא, the same terms as in v 13); he "removes kings and sets up kings" (cf. the removal of kings from office in v 18); and he "reveals" (גלא = גלה here) "deep things" (עמיקתא = עמקות here) and "hidden things," he knows what is "in darkness" (בחשוכא; cf. מני־חשך here), and the "light" (נהירא; cf. אור here) dwells with him. In the context in Dan 2, it is evident that it is to Daniel as a Hebrew wise man that the mysteries are revealed (2:19, 23); here, by analogy, it is Job who beholds the unveiling of mysteries. In Daniel, the mystery is nothing more subtle than the meaning of a dream; here in Job the revelation is of the deepest reality of the character of God—as Job perceives it, that is. The language of "darkness," which Zophar had had no call to use in chap. 11 even when speaking of the mysteries of God's wisdom, is specially appropriate for Job's view of the divine. On the whole, in the Hebrew Bible, it is light rather than darkness that is associated with God, but Job is not entirely alone in seeing God wrapped in darkness; cf. Exod 19:16; 20:21; Deut 4:11; 5:19, 20 [22, 23] (Sinai in darkness); 2 Sam 22:10, 12 (= Ps 18:10, 12 [9, 11]); Ps 97:2; Joel 2:2 (?); Zeph 1:15 (theophany); 1 Kgs 8:12 (= 2 Chr 6:1) (Yahweh dwells in thick darkness).

23 Yet another form in which the chaos-creating power of God can be portrayed is here presented. In v 14 there were two destructive acts of God (he destroys, he imprisons) which cannot be reversed. In v 15 there were two mutually contradictory acts of God and their consequences. In vv 17–21 there was a simple succession of ten verbs describing his activity toward society's leaders (eight or nine groups being specified). Here there are two sets of mutually contradictory acts, chiastically arranged, in reference to the same object, nations generally. He makes them great (or, numerous) but (then, or, equally) wipes them out of existence; he scatters them abroad, but (then, or, equally) guides them to a homeland. By itself, this verse would be typical of the doxological depiction of God's reversal of fortunes (cf. Ps 107:33–34; 1 Sam 2:6–7; Luke 1:51–53). But in its context here, the emphasis must be on the destructive verbs, acts of chaos-making not palliated by the life-affirming acts of "making great" and "leading."

The focus in this verse is no longer the leaders of society (vv 16–21) but nations generally, whose rise and fall are susceptible of no adequate natural explanation but must be attributed to God. To what end is their increase in numbers or land, to what end is God's guidance of a wandering people to a homeland? Nothing is meaningful; there is no plan in history, no universal *Heilsgeschichte* or teleological purpose. Every movement of growth in the history of nations is followed inexorably by destruction or dispersion.

An alternative translation would make all four verbs of God's activity negative: "He leads nations astray and destroys them, he disperses them and carries them into exile." This would convey the general mood of this perverse doxology quite well, but without the more subtle nuances of the reading proposed here.

24 Some have thought that this sentence belongs rather with vv 16–21 than in its present place, since it depicts the downfall of leaders of society. But it can well be understood as appropriate here, in that it sets out the cause (Horst), or at least an accompanying aspect, of a nation's destruction. The movements of nations (dispersal, perhaps "being led away," perhaps "being led astray") are reflected in the movements of their leaders (wandering, staggering). To be precise, they are the leaders of "the people of the land" (*ʿam hāʾārets*), the heads of the propertied families, the yeomen-farmers, perhaps distinct from the professional classes of vv 16–21.

Ps 107:40 is drawn upon again here; the "nobles" upon whom God pours disgrace (Ps 107:40a = Job 12:21a) are made to wander by God in a trackless waste. In the psalm, they were apparently oppressive princes guilty of the affliction of the needy; here, however, as throughout the doxology of vv 13–25, there is no hint of any wrongful action on their part that may account for their dispersal to chaos. The term for "waste," *tōhû*, is one of the terms used for the chaos preceding creation; the breaking down of the physical

created order is envisaged in Jer 4:23 as a return to that primal chaos, but
here the annihilation of the social order has no evident connections with creation
motifs. The desert is described as *tōhû* also in Deut 32:10. Such a breakdown
of order occurs, in social actuality, when peasants have to abandon their small-
holdings because of adverse climate, trade or politics and have to adopt a
more nomadic life-style; such movement, from the viewpoint of the settled
farmer, who dreads the loss of social and economic order, is nothing better
than an aimless "wandering" or "staggering" from place to place. It may be,
however, that the language here does not correspond directly to any social
reality.

25 The elaboration of the fate of the leaders signals the closure of the
poem (vv 13–25). The verse adds no new item to its catalogue-like depiction
of God's destructive acts, and the one verb in it expressing his activity (but
see n. 12:25.c) is identical with the verb of v 24b. A similar closure is found
in 4:11 and 10:22. Closure can also be indicated by a summary appraisal (5:16;
6:19; 20:29), by the addition of a third line (5:5c; 10:17c), by an affirmation
of the truth of what has been said (5:27; 24:25), or by a brief contrast (8:22;
11:20).

The note on which this poem ends is of the desperate plight of men who
have lost their way; there is a strong contrast with God who in all human
affairs displays his "effectual working," the irresistible combination of wisdom
and might (vv 13, 16).

Throughout this unarguably one-sided portrait of the ways of God with
humans, his subversive acts have been hymned. Only perhaps in v 23 are
there allusions to any positive act of his (see n. 12:23.a, d), but they are immediately negated.

13:1–3 This strophe both forms an *inclusio* with 12:2–3, and introduces a
new direction in which the speech will move. In referring back to "all" that
has just now been said, and especially in repeating the clause "I am not inferior
to you" (= 12:3b), Job indicates that the subject of chap. 12 is now at a close:
he has now completed his demonstration that his knowledge of God's ways is
superior to that of the friends.

1 What Job has "seen" and "heard" (for the word-pair, cf. Isa 52:15; Ezek
40:5; Eccl 1:8; in the inverse order, Job 29:11) is not "everything"; it is not
that he "has himself observed everything relating to God's rule of the world"
(Gray). Rather, it is the examples of God's destructive acts catalogued in 12:14–
25 to which Job claims to bear personal testimony. They have not just presented
themselves to his organs of sense, but their significance has imprinted itself
upon Job's mind. On the whole, the friends have appealed to the wisdom of
the wise of generations present and past (5:27; 8:8–10; 15:9–10, 17–18; 20:4)
rather than to their own experience (though cf. 4:12–17; 5:3), but Job takes
his stand upon his own observations and upon his assessment of their meaning.
To tell the truth, Job must have had a remarkably rich experience if he has
personally witnessed the many disastrous events he has just now described.
We may, however, allow him a little poetic license, for his emphasis lies principally upon the inner meaning of events known by tradition and naively re-
hearsed in the communal praise.

2 Contrary to the impression given by most translations (as for example
RSV, NEB), "What you know, I also know," Job's claim does not concern the

quantity but the quality of his knowledge. The Hebrew is literally, "according to your knowledge I know," that is, my understanding is qualitatively on a par with yours. For the issue is not facts but meaning: it is the question of what divine intention is revealed in the course of human affairs. On this score Job is not "inferior" to them—which is to say, his insight is actually superior to theirs. The phrase "to fall from" (נפל מן) does not occur elsewhere in this sense, but it is similar to נפל לפני, "to fall before" as in Esth 6:13.

3 But in the end, what really matters to Job is not the truth in general about the divine character but the particular confrontation with God in which he, Job, is involved. Job's uncovering of the divine cruelty has not been an end in itself, as if it were the exposé of an investigative theological journalist. It was undertaken primarily to demonstrate that his plight could not be ameliorated by recourse to hackneyed formulae of retribution, that the wisdom of the ages had nothing to offer a righteous man who had been made a laughing-stock by God (12:4).

As for himself, he says, using the strong adversative אולם, "but for my part" (NEB), he would be glad to be rid of theoretical justifications for his attitude and be free to get on with his principal business: to resolve his dispute with God. What he wants to do, and what he shortly will do (v 20), is to direct his speech toward God—not indeed as a monologue, for Job's ideal is reciprocal conversation, a calling and a being answered (cf. on 12:4; and note 13:22). The friends, for all their talk, are no real partners in dialogue, but mere eavesdroppers on the one meaningful conversation, that between Job and God.

What Job wants (he uses the quite strong word חפץ, "to desire"; cf. 33:22) is to "argue" (הוכיח) "with" (אל) God. The preposition "with" indicates that the verb does mean not "reproach" or "reprove," as it generally does when followed by a direct object or by the preposition על, but "argue" a case. The language is thoroughly legal and formal, but, as in Israelite legal practice generally, the point of the legal process Job envisages here is not so much the winning of a dispute as the settlement of a disagreement. Its aim is reconciliation rather than victory (cf. Andersen); Job's longing in 14:15 for a fully reciprocated relationship with God is momentarily foreshadowed. (On הוכיח as a technical term, see further I. L. Seeligmann, "Zur Terminologie für das Gerichtsverfahren im Wortschatz des biblischen Hebräisch," *VTS* 16 [1967] 251–75 [266–67].)

At this point we become aware of a certain shift in Job's position since his last speech (chaps. 9–10). There he had deplored the impossibility of winning vindication from God (9:2), and in that context had recognized that there was no hope of God and himself coming to trial under the eye of an impartial judge (9:32–33). That being so, he has now abandoned the idea of "legally" compelling God to vindicate him (he regards it as a lost cause from the beginning in any case). He still envisages a "legal" disputation, but now rather than accusing God of the injustice of withholding vindication from him, he will invite God to accuse him, to tell him what he has against him (cf. especially v 23). Job still believes that he is innocent, and that any disputation with God can only result in his own vindication (v 18b), but he is now opening himself up to divine challenge. It is a less strident position, and one that leads more naturally into a hope for a renewed dialogue with God (14:13–15).

It is misleading therefore to think that Job contradicts himself in 9:32–33 (cf. Horst), or that he goes back on his categorical statement of 9:2–3 of the impossibility of bringing God to justice (cf. Fohrer). It is rather that he has moved on from the stance he took there.

4–12 Before Job will begin his address to the Almighty, he has something to say to the friends as interlocutors who believe they have already been addressing Job on God's behalf. They have not, indeed, claimed to be God's spokesmen—the nearest Eliphaz came to that was to report a supernatural voice that spoke in his presence, perhaps not even directly addressing him (4:12–17); they would not aspire to such intimacy with the divine as to deliver, in prophetic fashion, a "Thus saith the Lord." Yet they have taken their stand for theological truth, which in their eyes must in the end be nothing other than a stand for God that ranges them against Job.

Job regards the friends as bearing false witness against him (accusing him of wrongdoing) on behalf of God, whose side they believe they have taken in this dispute. Job, for all his doubts about the divine generosity, believes that God must disapprove of such behavior and will surely punish them for their "partiality" towards himself (v 10) and their lack of objectivity.

A triplet of three-line strophes can easily be distinguished in the nine lines of vv 4–12: the central strophe consists entirely of rhetorical questions addressed to the friends. Verses 4 and 12 are manifestly the boundaries of this unit in view of their similarity of subject matter and structure (cf. Andersen).

4 What exactly is Job's criticism of the friends? The imagery of the verse is not clear. To call them "plasterers of falsehood" would mean, if Ps 119:69 ("The godless plaster me with lies") is any analogy, that they have been falsely accusing him of guilt, "smearing" him as we would say (NIV; cf. also Ecclus 51:5 "those that plaster lies"). The "falsehood" would consist in their "plastering." If, on the other hand, a thought such as that of Ezek 13:10–12 lies in the background, the image is of a workman giving the impression that a poorly built wall is strong and secure by plastering over it so that the reality cannot be seen. The friends would then be "plastering falsehood" over the truth, that is, perhaps, denying the evidence for divine malignancy (12:13–25) by repeating theological platitudes. That image certainly conforms to Job's attitude to the friends, but then how does the picture of "worthless physicians" in the second half of the verse parallel this? Some have claimed that the verb רפא "heal" here means "stitch together" (see n. 13:4.c) and that the "stitchers together of worthlessness" (NEB "stitching a patchwork of lies"; cf. Dillmann) are strictly parallel to the "plasterers of falsehood." A more convincing way of finding parallelism here would be to take the "plastering" as an anointing with oil or ointment (for which the verb סוך is admittedly usually employed), and regard the friends as "false soothers" and "worthless physicians."

If then the "plasters" of the friends are medicinal plasters, what is the disease or sore which the friends have thought themselves to be treating? It is not Job's physical ailments, for the friends hawk words, not ointments. The "illness" is Job's conviction of maltreatment by God; the friends have failed to "heal" this conviction by insisting that it is mistaken and that there has been no undeserved suffering.

5 The friends' words, which they saw as the solution or "medicine" (v 4) for Job's mistaken theology, are so foolish in Job's eyes that they would be better left unspoken. He perhaps alludes to a familiar proverb, "If he keeps quiet, even a fool is reckoned a wise man" (Prov 17:28; cf. also Ecclus 20:5–6). The *via negativa* of silence about God is preferable to cheap theologizing that ignores the dark side of God. Better, indeed, than any talk *about* God is dialogue *with* God, even if it must be painful and bitter disputation (v 6).

6 They would do better to listen to him, not so much to what he will have to say directly to them in the next few verses (vv 7–12)—that is parenthetical—but to what he will have to say about God and to God (13:13–14:22). It is a matter of listening to his "disputation" (תוכחתי from הוכיח as in v 3) and his (legal) "controversies" (רבות) which he proposes engaging in with God. The Hebrew "controversy" (*rîb*) can be any quarrel in everyday life (e.g., Exod 21:18), or, more specifically, the exchange of arguments engaged in by legal opponents in private before their case comes to public adjudication (e.g., Gen 31:36), or, most formally, the lawsuit itself in which plaintiff and defendant argue their case in the hearing of a "reprover" (*môkîaḥ*) or judge. Throughout most of the book, Job envisages himself in the "pre-trial" phase of his conflict with God. On the *rîb*, see further: G. Liedke, "ריב streiten," *THWAT* 2:771–77; B. Gemser, "The RIB- or Controversy Pattern in Hebrew Mentality," *VTS* 3 (1955) 120–37 (122–25); J. Harvey, *Le Plaidoyer prophétique contre Israël après la rupture de l'alliance* (Studia travaux de recherche 22; Montreal: Les Editions Bellermin, 1967); J. Blenkinsopp, "The Prophetic Reproach," *JBL* 90 (1971) 267–78; J. Limburg, "The Root *RIB* and the Prophetic Lawsuit Speeches," *JBL* 88 (1969) 291–304; K. Nielsen, *Yahweh as Prosecutor and Judge: An Investigation of the Prophet Lawsuit (Rîb-Pattern)* (JSOTS 9; Sheffield: JSOT, 1978); H. Richter, *Studien zu Hiob. Der Aufbau des Hiobbuches, dargestellt an der Gattungen des Rechtslebens* (Berlin: Evangelische Verlagsanstalt, 1959).

Against Horst, this verse does not seem to be an example of the well-attested "opening formula used by a teacher" (*Lehreröffnungsformel*), as in Prov 4:10; 7:24; Ps 49:2 [1]. For in this context the friends are called on, not to *hear*, but to *overhear*, what Job is saying to God.

7–12 God would not be too pleased to find out (v 9) that those attempting to justify his ways to Job have resorted to lies to keep God in the clear. Job has a higher opinion of God than do the friends! Any theology that does not accommodate Job's experience (a righteous man who is a laughingstock, 12:4) is simply a lie, and it is shocking that lies should be spoken about God. The series of rhetorical questions (vv 7–9, 11) expresses Job's (ironic) amazement that anyone will use falsehood in the service of truth.

The whole of vv 7–12 is probably to be regarded as referring to the immediate future. The friends have already, in Job's view, been "lying" in their speeches about God. But now, events are about to take a more serious turn. Job is about to enter the formal judicial process with God, strictly speaking in its "pre-trial" phase when the disputants will declare what they have against one another. Once that process begins, the friends' status will change: they are about to become witnesses at the trial between God and Job; but that means witnesses to the facts, not witnesses on behalf of either the prosecution or the defense, since Hebrew law does not recognize such a role. If they continue in their present vein, they will be siding with one of the litigants against the other, which is not permitted, and they will be uttering "lies" on his behalf, which is a crime. They will be, legally speaking, false witnesses. Job therefore challenges them, asking whether they realize what their role will become and whether they are prepared for the consequences of testifying untruthfully.

7 Job does not ask whether the friends are speaking lies. He assumes they are, because they stand opposed to his experience of the truth. What he asks, in astonishment, is whether they think they are doing God a service by uttering lies on his behalf. Surely God, even though he is in the wrong (in Job's opinion), would wish himself defended according to the rules of fair argument. For the parallelism of "falsehood" (עוֹלָה) with "deceit" (רְמִיָּה) see also 27:4.

8 To have favorites and to be partisan are normal behavior in everyday life, and the expression "to favor," lit., "to lift up the face of" (נְשָׂא פָנִים), is often enough used without any criticism being implied (Gen 19:21; 1 Sam 25:35; of God, Job 42:8, 9). But in a legal setting things are different. Strict impartiality is the requirement of justice. It is wrong (עֶוֶל, injustice) to be partial (נְשָׂא פָנִים) even to the poor, just as it is wrong to defer to the great (Lev 19:15)—that is to say, in the lawsuit; the practice of "positive discrimination" in favor of the poor, often urged in the OT, is not at issue here. Yahweh himself is not partial in judgment (Deut 10:17). Questions of justice must be settled evenhandedly, without consideration of the person of the disputant; that would be "respect of persons" (הִכִּיר פָנִים) (Deut 1:17; 16:19; Prov 24:23; 28:21), which in the legal sphere is equivalent to נְשָׂא פָנִים (cf. A. S. van der Woude, *THWAT* 2:441; E. Lohse, *TDOT* 6:779–80; M. I. Gruber, "The Many Faces of Hebrew נְשָׂא פָנִים 'lift up the face,'" *ZAW* 95 [1983] 252–60 [256]).

The friends must from now on play the part of unprejudiced witnesses, committed to truth-speaking (v 7), to impartiality (v 8a), and to a subsidiary role as onlookers. Once the debate between Job and God is joined in earnest, God must conduct his own case; it would be improper for witnesses, who are meant to be impartial, to argue the case of one of the disputants.

9 To display partisanship in a legal dispute—even on behalf of God—is against the rules of justice; if the friends continue to argue on God's behalf they run the risk of God beginning to investigate *them*. There is an irony here, that Job has now adopted the friends' pastoral or didactic role, and gives them warning of the dangers of tangling with God. There is a deeper hint here also that to speak in defense of God lays oneself open to a divine scrutiny that can more easily be avoided by taking up one's stand as a detached observer of the ways of God.

What indeed is the friends' motivation for volunteering for the defense of God? Job actually seems to question their integrity by using the phrase "favoritism" or "respect of persons" (נְשָׂא פָנִים, v 8). No doubt Davidson put it too strongly in suggesting that, according to Job, the friends "merely took part for God against him out of servility to God . . . a superficial religiousness, allied to superstition, which did not form its conception of God from the broad facts of the universe." But certainly Job implies that they are over-respectful of God (unlike Job himself!), and act, whether out of fear or for the sake of praise, in disregard for truth. Theirs is, as Fohrer puts it, a self-seeking piety less concerned with God than with their own teaching about God, and open to criticism as a piety that is not disinterested. What the Satan alleged against Job (1:9–10) is here being alleged by Job against the friends.

The secret motives of the heart are open to God's examination (חָקַר); thus

"If we had forgotten the name of our God, or spread forth our hands to a strange god, would not God examine (חקר) this?" (Ps 44:21 [20]; cf. also Ps 139:1, 23 "search the heart"; Jer 17:10, Yahweh searches the heart to reward everyone according to their deeds). Such inquisition could not be deflected; such an examiner could not be "deceived" (תלל, Gen 31:7; Exod 8:25 [29]; Jer 9:4 [5]). The outcome would only be shame for the friends; "would it be good for you if he examines?" means "would it go well for you?," "what have you to gain?" (cf. on 10:3).

10 The warning continues, and with it the legal language. Even if the friends' partiality for God and respect of his person is harbored only secretly, the all-seeing judge who investigates judicial malfeasance will "begin (legal) proceedings" against them. הוכיח could perhaps be simply "rebuke" (RSV, NIV) (cf. on v 3), but the more technical sense is probable in this context.

The friends, of course, will not heed Job's warning, for they do not believe there is any question of partisanship: God is wholly in the right and Job is wholly in the wrong. The irony is that, at the end of the day, it will be Job who is in the right and the friends who are in the wrong; the divine wrath will be kindled against them because they have not spoken of God what is right (42:7).

11 But, in the manner of the friends themselves, Job expresses the not entirely disingenuous hope that it will not come to a confrontation of God with the friends, and that a moment's sensibility of the divine wrath will be enough to drive from their minds every partisan thought together with all self-serving piety. The "fear" (פחד) of God, that is, the numinous terror his coming inspires, is frequently connected with his visitation, as judge, upon wrongdoers (Isa 2:10, 19, 21; Jer 49:5; Ps 119:120; cf. 36:2 [1]) or his enemies (Exod 15:16; Gen 35:5). On the term, see H.-P. Stähli, *THWAT* 2:411–13.

Many writers have found strange paradoxes in this address of Job to the friends. Thus Stevenson (*Critical Notes*, 52): "If God intervened in their debate he would condemn the friends and so, implicitly, would justify Job. But . . . if God sides with Job against the friends, he admits Job's condemnation of himself." Peake commented: "It is noteworthy as showing the conflict of feeling in Job, that while he attacks with the utmost boldness the unrighteousness of God's conduct he should have such deep-rooted confidence in His righteousness as to believe Him incapable of tolerating a lying defence even of Himself."

But what has emerged from the text as commented upon here is that any intervention by God would not be an intervention *between* Job and the friends. Job hopes for his part that God will tell him what he has against him, and believes, as far as concerns the friends, that any intervention by God would show them to be swayed by considerations external to the subject of Job's argument. The friends would be convicted not for bad arguments but for bad faith; and that is what indeed happens in chap. 42, where Job, contrariwise, is praised, we may perceive, not for what he has said but for the direction in which he has said it. The fact that Job addresses himself to God is the proof that he is a godly man (as he himself recognizes even at this juncture; see v 16).

As for the question of God's righteousness, there are certainly the makings of a paradox here. But we must observe that Job's stress has been on the cruelty, hostility, anger, and disproportionateness of God's treatment of him rather than upon its injustice. To be sure, we may well say, if such behavior is not an unjust way of treating an innocent person, what is? Yet divine *injustice* is not what Job is talking about, at least in so many words; and so there is no overt conflict between his previous criticisms of God and his present assertion that God will be fairminded enough to punish the friends' partisanship. A more striking conflict in Job's thinking is over the question whether God cares very much about the right governance of the world. If those who provoke God by their criminality manage to live in safety from the divine wrath (12:6), why does Job suppose that the friends' legal misdemeanors will be unfailingly punished by God? Is it because God's own honor is more intimately involved if the friends for impure motives set themselves up as advocates for God?

12 With this sentence Job's direct attention to the friends (vv 4–12) is concluded. It is not to his point here to disparage the friends' arguments generally as "proverbs of ashes," "words of clay," though no doubt that is what he believes. His present concern is more precise: it has been to warn them that he is now putting his disagreement with God on a legal footing, and that they are now in danger of provoking God's wrath as false witnesses if they continue to show themselves partisan to God. That is, the context is much more specific than generalized irony at the friends' expense, and it is directly related to the dynamic of Job's speeches, which have here taken a decisive turn (cf. on v 3).

What he warns the friends of here is what will happen to them if even in secret they should be partisan (v 9b): God would begin legal proceedings against them and all their wise sayings would become clay and ashes, that is, would be worthless before the divine anger. Ash, when not in a funereal context, is clearly a symbol for what is light, superficial, insubstantial, negligible (cf. Isa 44:20; Gen 18:27)—rather than transitory (Fohrer; cf. Dhorme). Peake's little flight of fancy, however charming, is hardly exegesis: "their traditional maxims . . . are ashes, dead, obsolete relics of what may once have been glowing convictions at which men warmed their hands." The insubstantiality of the friends' arguments forms a striking contrast to the image, to be encountered a little later, of Job's words that should be graven on the rock that Job envisages (19:24). Clay has several metaphorical connotations, but here as in 4:19 it is viewed as the substance of brittle pottery; it is what is easily and irremediably destroyed. That will be the fate of the friends' "reminders"—words to Job like those of 12:7–12, the maxims of 8:11–14 and 11:12, or the "remember" of 4:7—should God decide to "investigate" (v 9) the arguments of the friends.

13–19 Job is not yet quite ready to address God. This strophe is addressed to the friends ("be silent," v 13; "listen," v 17), but the subject-matter is no longer the friends (as it was in vv 4–12); it is the significance of his new address to God upon which he is about to launch himself (13:20—14:22). Twice before in the speeches he has addressed God (7:7–21; 10:1–22), but whereas in chap. 7 he had appealed to God to cease paying attention to him, and in chaps. 9 and 10, although expressing a forlorn hope for the dialogue of controversy with God, had equally begged for release from the divine scrutiny, here he deliberately summons God to disputation (v 22). It is a dangerous undertaking (v 14)—or rather a hopeless, suicidal one (v 15); but hopelessness engenders its own kind of courage, and Job is convinced that right is with him (v 18).

The strophe divides into two sub-strophes (vv 13–15, 16–19), each introduced by an imperative addressed to the friends ("be silent," "listen").

13 After the digression that warned the friends of the dangers of becoming false witnesses (vv 4–12), Job now returns to where he was in v 3: "It is to the Almighty that I would speak." The friends must not interrupt him when he is "speaking," i.e. formally addressing God in legal controversy, even though they believe he is blaspheming. He himself recognizes the dangers of embarking upon a legal dispute with God (cf. 9:4, 14–16).

14 But he will risk all. He has nothing to lose, everything to gain. He uses two proverbial and somewhat obscure expressions of risk, the second of which is at least attested elsewhere. In Judg 12:3; 1 Sam 19:5; 28:21 (cf. Ps 119:109) "I set my life in my hands" can only mean "I risked my life," "I went defenseless into danger." It is not likely that *nephesh* (נֶפֶשׁ), "life," means "throat" in this context, though Pope adduces the Akkadian phrase *napištam lapātum,* "to touch the throat" in the Mari letters; the act of touching the throat symbolized either strangulation or cutting the throat, in either case representing the jeopardy of one's life as sanction when taking an oath. Here, however, there is no oath-taking, and Job is not offering his life as a guarantee of good behavior. The idiom is also found in a Greek text, Athenaeus, *Deipnosophistae* 13.569c (cf. also Hölscher's citation of an Egyptian text). Alonso Schökel notes that it is known in Spanish, especially in the form found in *Don Quixote,* "su alma en su palma."

To put one's life in one's hand is obviously a risky business: human hands are not safe places for the long-term protection of precious objects! Taking one's flesh in one's teeth, the first proverbial expression, must have an identical meaning, "flesh" parallel to "life" and "teeth" parallel to "hands." Though teeth can hold small objects quite satisfactorily for a short time, they are incapable of holding anything large for any length of time. We may note that though "flesh" (body) and "life" (life-principle, soul) are usually distinguished from one another, it is obviously permissible, as in our text, that each should refer to the whole person and so can have the same significance and stand in parallel (cf. 14:22; Ps 63:2 [1]; 84:3 [2]; cf. N. P. Bratsiotis, *TDOT* 2:325–26).

Other interpretations of the proverbs are numerous. Dhorme envisages Job carrying off his flesh in his teeth as a wild animal, especially when threatened (cf. Schlottmann, Dillmann), makes off with its prey (cf. 27:17 "I tore the prey from his teeth"; Jer 38:2 "you shall have your life as booty"). Rowley thinks of an animal that fights with flesh in its mouth and so risks losing it. Buttenwieser compared an Arabic saying, "he escaped with his life between his jaws," which seems more to the point. N. Herz thought that the idiom meant to take extra care of one's life ("Egyptian Words and Idioms in the Book of Job," *OLZ* [1913] 343–36 [344–45]; "The Exaggeration of Errors in the Massoretic," *JTS* 15 [1914] 258–64 [263]), the first colon meaning the same, since animals "carry off their prey in their teeth for fear of another animal taking it from them"; but it is hard to see how this can yield the meaning, "Why should I take extra care of my body and soul? I do not mind risking them." Not even if these images signify that Job is running a great risk will they be appropriate, for his point is not that he will take care of himself although he runs a risk, but that the will indeed recklessly risk his neck. Rashi took it to mean that Job would force himself to be silent, which is inappropriate (similarly Tur-Sinai: "Why should I hold my tongue with my teeth?"). Most improbable is the suggestion of A. M. Habermann, "The Tomb of Rachel and the Term נפש [Heb.]," *Tarb* 25 (1956) 363–68, that a pagan practice is alluded to of taking sacred objects, e.g., the limbs of the dead, with one's hand in order to acquire strength from them. Nor does there seem to be any connection with the idiom "the skin of the teeth" in 19:20.

If the "Why?" at the beginning of the verse in the MT is to be retained (see n. 13:14.a), the question is best explained, not as expressing a genuine doubt on Job's part as to why he is engaging in such a dangerous adventure, but as a rhetorical question posing an objection such as the friends might advance: "Why, you may ask, do I. . . ?" Gordis calls this an example of an "indirect quotation." The answer is given in v 15. If, on the other hand, the "Why?" should be deleted, Job is saying that he knows very well what he is doing, hazardous though his undertaking against God is.

15 The primary difficulty in this famous verse is whether the לא is to be read as "not" or as "to him." The consonantal text (Kethiv) has לא "not," but the Masoretic vocalization (Qere) is לו "to him." So is it "I will *not* hope" or "I *will* hope in (= to) him"? Gordis notes that both renderings were recognized as possible in a passage of the Mishnah (2d century A.D. or earlier), *Soṭah* 5.5: "the matter is undecided—do I trust in him or not trust?" Only one's sense of the context can determine an answer.

(a) If we accept the Masoretic vocaliztion of the Qere (as Dhorme, Horst, Andersen, Fohrer, AV, RV, NAB, NIV), and understand that Job has hope, or, will wait for (another possible nuance of the verb) God, we must ask, What does he expect God to do? We know that he nurtures a hope that God will vindicate him (though of course he has no hope of wringing vindication out of God). But if God slays him, when will he vindicate him? Posthumously? Then Job will not know. Unless, perhaps, Job envisages a conscious afterlife. But that would be out of step with Israelite thinking. Even in 14:14–15, when he actually imagines a release from the underworld, he has already negated that very possibility (cf. 14:7–12). Perhaps the Hebrew could be squeezed to mean, "Even if he should end up killing me, I should continue to hope, *till then*, in him that he will vindicate me." The objection to this line of interpretation is that the context stresses, not any hope on Job's part, but rather the futility and danger that surrounds his approach to God. Any positive "salvation" he sees arises from his own innocence and his own courage (v 16), not from the justice of God. In his own case he does not expect justice from God, though he has assumed it as far as the friends are concerned (vv 9–10). There is also the difficulty that the next half of the line begins with אך which normally has an adversative or restrictive meaning, "however," "nevertheless." How can Job's determination to go on arguing his case for vindication be in contrast with a conviction that God will vindicate him? RV shows the problem up well: "Though he slay me, yet will I wait for him: Nevertheless I will maintain my ways before him." The "nevertheless" is meaningless.

There is another possible way of reading the text in a "positive" sense: "Behold, he will slay me—I wait for him [to do so]; nevertheless I will defend. . . ." (so Delitzsch; RV mg), but this interpretation has attracted little support.

(b) If, on the other hand, we follow the consonantal text (Kethiv), and take it that Job means that he does *not* have hope, or will *not* wait, it is conceivable that he means that even at the moment of God's slaying him he would not hesitate to continue arguing his case (so NEB). Stevenson took it that Job intends to persist in his challenge, he will not "wait" or "delay" it, in spite of all its dangers. It is more probable, however, that the sentence is more disjointed or staccato, as in RSV, "Behold, he will slay me; I have no hope; yet I will defend my ways to his face." In that translation, however, there is one phrase that does not ring true: "he *will* slay me." How would Job know that?

Hitherto Job has made it a matter of complaint that God has not already slain him and put him out of his misery (cf. 3:20–23; 6:9). So from where could this conviction come now, that God will indeed slay him? Some have thought that he believes that the mere sight of God will strike him dead (cf. Exod 33:20; Judg 6:22–23; 13:22) (so Fohrer, Horst), but there is no hint that the legal encounter Job desires will involve the *sight* of his divine opponent, nor is it obvious that within Job's thought-world the sight of God would necessarily be fatal. A psalmist can express a longing to see God's face (Ps 42:3 [2]; cf. Isa 1:12; Deut 16:16; Exod 24:10), and no danger is involved in that. If Job is indeed confident that God will slay him, that could be an expression of his hopelessness (the very next words will be, in fact, "I have no hope"), or, better, a token of his bitterness that regards God as eternally malign. At this moment, when Job is actually purposing some action that could alter his present parlous state, the divine hostility would display itself by cutting off his life and his tiny ambition; at another moment, when Job is truly hopeless and wishes for nothing other than death, his heavenly persecutor sustains his life and thereby prolongs his misery. It may be, however, that the verb יקטלני is not to be rendered "he *will* slay me" but rather "he *may* slay me" (so NJPS; for such a modal use of a verb, cf. on 4:20). Job could simply be allowing the possibility that God would foreclose the disputation by slaying Job; Job has no real hope of success, because with God nothing can be predicted; nevertheless he intends to go on arguing his case all the same.

However that first verb should be translated, there is a strong case to be made for taking this line as an expression of Job's hopelessness. The traditional translation of AV, "Though he slay me, yet will I trust in him," must regretfully be set aside as out of harmony with the context. As Peake says, "It is very beautiful in itself, and no doubt what Job ought to have said, and what he would have said after the vision of God. But it is singularly unfortunate, since it is one of the few widely known fragments in the poem and has thus created an entirely false impression as to Job's real attitude." Job does not have much faith in God, compared with his faith in himself; but how could a person so obsessed with God be called in the least irreligious? For Job, faith is not a matter of whether he believes in God, but of whether God believes in him.

Job's "ways" are his innocent "conduct" (NAB, JB), "way of life," as דרך often means in the wisdom literature (cf. 17:9; 31:4; Prov 3:6; 4:18–19). The verb הוכיח must mean "defend" rather than "dispute" (as in v 3) or "begin proceedings against" (v 10). There is the possibility, however, that דרך means "cause, case" (so NEB, NJPS; cf. Isa 40:27, parallel to משפט, "right"), in which case הוכיח will mean "argue."

16 Job is so conscious of the dangers he runs, and so hopeless about the outcome—though confident that he is taking the right course—that it is strange to hear him speaking, at this point, about "salvation." It cannot be God who is Job's "salvation" here (against RVmg, Peters, Gordis) since "the fact that a godless man does not dare to appear before God is not a reason why God should be the salvation of Job" (Dhorme). The "salvation" must consist in what is affirmed in the second half of the line. An evil person would not willingly approach God; Job's boldness must argue his innocence. But how will that be his "salvation"? Salvation from what? In the context, not from death, because God, who deals death, does not adhere to principles of retribution (cf. 12:4–6), and in any case Job has no hope (v 15). Not from God either, because God is set on a collision course with Job, and Job has no reason to expect that God will suddenly "save" him from Himself. The only person Job has any faith in is himself, the one certain conviction he has is that he is innocent. Therefore the one person he has to fear is himself. If he loses his nerve and ceases to believe in himself, his case crumbles and God wins. What he needs "salvation" from is self-doubt, loss of confidence in the rightness of his cause. Now what will preserve or "save" him from such doubt is the very course on which he is embarked, approaching God. The disputation with God is an objective verification—beyond his own memory of past events and his own self-consciousness—of his innocence.

If that seems too psychological an interpretation, we have only to reflect that a similar sense would be obvious if the term was "consolation"—as it is in 6:10. Salvation is nothing more than effective consolation. "Salvation" here is "source of salvation," "support" or, as in the translation above, "this is what I take refuge in." NEB "This at least assures my success" and NIV "this might turn out for my deliverance" both have too positive a note; Job expects nothing, hopes for nothing, but he does want to be sure that he is on the right course, that this argument with God is right, even if it is dangerous (v 14), even if it is hopeless (v 15a). This is not a "noteworthy expression of Job's conviction of God's righteousness" (Peake). His confidence is not in the justice of God, for he has no reason to revise his deep skepticism (though never outright denial) of that, but in himself and his own integrity. It is a Promethean stance, to be sure, but what honor does it do God to vilify his creation without cause?

The wording of v 16a has been thought by some to have been borrowed by Paul in Phil 1:19 (J. H. Michael, "Paul and Job: A Neglected Analogy," *ExpT* 36 [1924–25] 67–70; followed by Horst).

17–19 Job now expresses his confidence in his own cause, that is, in its rightness. He has never doubted that; that is his "refuge" or "salvation" (v 16b). It is not that "Job has a sudden surge of new confidence" (Habel). He has no new hope of acquittal by God, the impossibility of dragging God into court has not disappeared.

17 The verse is omitted by Dillmann, Bickell and Fohrer as a prosaic gloss, duplicating in part 21:2, and erroneously continuing the address to the friends. But it can be better seen as introducing a strophe parallel to vv 13–16, expanding Job's request to the friends from "be silent" to "listen," and invoking their attention as witnesses to his argument with God which will begin in v 20.

18 Job has already, in his mind, "drawn up" his case, "marshalled" his arguments. The term is perhaps used metaphorically with its military sense, "draw up" lines of battle (עָרַךְ, Judg 20:22; 1 Sam 17:8); in a legal context it appears also in 6:4; 23:4; 37:19 (cf. also 32:14; 33:5). Military metaphors are, not unnaturally, common enough in legal language. Despite his passion, Job recognizes that a certain methodicalness advantages any legal disputation (מִשְׁפָּט, the case itself rather than the decision; so also 23:4). Yet more important than the "preparation" or orderedness is the underlying conviction, which he cannot cease to reiterate: "I know that I am in the right." Although the verb צָדֵק in a legal context can mean "be justified, be acquitted" (so 9:2; 11:2; 40:8), the context makes it clear that Job is expressing, not a hope of acquittal (cf. v 15b), but his conviction of innocence (v 15a). It is not being said that "if he can finally bring his case to court God will acquit him" (Habel). It is a matter of actually being in the right to start with (as RV, NAB, JB) rather than being vindicated or acquitted in the end (RSV, NEB, NJPS, NIV).

19 The cry, "Who will dispute with me?," may well have been a formal expression initiating a legal controversy; cf. Isa 50:8, where also a parallel challenge is found, "Who is my adversary?" But here in Job the meaning must be other, for Job is not proposing to conduct his lawsuit by "being silent and expiring"! Nor can the phrase be simply the rhetorical question, "Who will dispute with me?"—which would imply: no one can dispute with me; for he acknowledges that God is in fact already in dispute with him. The second half of the line, where he promises to hold his peace, points unambiguously to the time beyond the conclusion of the lawsuit; before that time, Job will be "silenced" by nothing except being found at fault by an objective tribunal.

The meaning of the whole verse in its context can only be that Job does not believe that anyone, not even God, can convict him of wrongdoing, and that in the unlikely event of that being so, he would abandon his case, submit to the facts and die. The verb רִיב must mean "argue successfully," "make out a case" (cf. NAB "make a case against"), "defeat in argument" if the sentence is to have any meaning. But it must be acknowledged that such would appear to be a unique sense of רִיב, which, as G. Liedke points out in his admirably lucid article in *THWAT* 2:771–77, elsewhere always refers to a lawsuit as a whole, or to certain elements of it, but never to elements having to do with its conclusion (for which שָׁפַט and דִּין are used). The present usage must be an extension of the general sense of רִיב, which in covering the whole lawsuit naturally also includes the final decision.

If Job is worsted in the confrontation, he will forever hold his peace. The two verbs, "be silent," "die," are not on the same footing, for while Job has it in his power to be silent, he has no say over whether he dies or not (actually, according to him, God is mercilessly prolonging his life in order to extend his suffering). Job's response rather will be to be silent till the day of his death (whenever that may be), to be silent and so (i.e., in that state) die, to be as silent in that portion of life that remains as in the grave. For גָּוַע "expire, perish," always of physical death, and usually of humans, cf. also 3:11; 10:18; 14:10; 27:5; 29:18; 34:15; 36:12.

The irony is that when, in the outturn of the book, Job *is* worsted by his heavenly interlocutor, he is as good as his word; he lays his hand on his mouth, and promises to proceed no further with his lawsuit (40:4–5). But, contrary to his expectation, he does not die: he is restored to full health and vitality.

13:20–14:22 After the great build-up of 13:3, 13–19, and the emphasis on the legal forms to be followed, it comes of something of a surprise to find nothing systematic (contrast v 18a) about the remainder of this speech, and little new matter compared with Job's earlier speeches. An example of what we might have expected to see emerging when the poet is having Job use a legal form occurs in the extended oath of innocence in chap. 31; cf. also the systematic arguments of God in chaps. 38–41.

Are we to surmise then that Job's nerve has failed him here, or that he forgets to carry out his expressed intention? Hardly. It is surely significant that after this speech, in which God is constantly addressed (there are 39 grammatical markers of the address to God; cf. on 10:1–22) Job never again directs a word to God until his closing speech, and there only briefly (30:20–23), and of course in his responses to God (40:4–5; 42:1–6). He will cry that the judge is inaccessible (23:3), but he will not speak to him again. This can only mean that 13:20–14:22 says all he wants to. However unprepossessing, this speech is Job's formal legal plea.

Its thrust is twofold. Its first concern is to require God to give an account of the supposed sins for which he, Job, is being punished (the principal topic of 13:20–28). The second is a paradoxical plea for God to ignore him, a plea which contains an undisguised expression of longing for renewed intimacy with God (14:1–22, esp. vv 13–17). The first concern is easily recognized as a legal matter; the second is not so evidently such, but in appealing to a principle of proportionateness it portrays God's "looking away" from Job (14:6) as a matter of justice in the broadest sense, and in envisaging renewed fellowship with God it reaches to the intention of the legal process as such: the reconciliation of the divided and disputant parties.

As the speech to God progresses the legal veneer wears thin. The more Job thinks about the significance of his suffering, the more he is inclined to cast it in terms of a miscarriage of justice and to seek legal redress; and he is never more litigious than when he is expatiating to bystanders on the wrong done to him (as in 13:4–19). But the more Job becomes involved in address to his heavenly opponent, the more personal and less formal his language and tone become. And the speech ends not with the flinging down of a gauntlet but with a whimper for the lot of humankind which implicitly craves the divine mercy rather more than it questions divine justice. He had never (*pace* Fohrer and others) conceived of himself as *winning* this dispute (cf. 13:15a), however confident he was of the rightness of his cause (cf. 13:18b); the speech he makes in defense of his right shifts imperceptibly from assurance (of innocence) to hopelessness (of victory). He does not modify his position in this speech, but works it out thoroughly in its double dimension.

It is remarkable how few commentators even allude to the significance of this address to God within Job's fourth speech. Not many even see 13:20 as the major point of disjunction in the speech as a whole, and some do not even recognize 13:20–14:22 as an address to God at all; Habel, for example, calls chap. 14 "Job's Soliloquy [*sic*] on Mortality."

20–21 The stipulation of "two things" as a condition of the legal dispute has something of an air of formality about it such as we might expect in a legal speech. Job actually says "do *not* do two things to me" and then expresses the first of them positively, "remove your hand from me." This is formally inconsistent, but the sense is plain enough, for both halves of v 21 have in view essentially negative acts of God.

Already in 9:34 Job has expressed his hope for the removal of God's rod,

so that fear of God should not unnerve him (the same phrase as here), but
there is a significant difference. There he uttered a wish, contrary to fact, of
a "mediator" or arbiter who, standing between the parties, or, perhaps, over
them both, could ensure a fair disputation. That forlorn hope has now become
a plea for justice addressed to God himself. Job does not say so in as many
words, but there is obvious injustice in a lawsuit if one of the parties is intimidated
by the other. "Truth can thrive only in the air of mutual freedom" (Weiser).
Perhaps Job's call in v 21 for God to stop threatening him is a customary
phrase in legal disputes; Elihu uses almost the same words in 33:7 in assuring
Job that he has no intention of putting undue pressure on him.

What exactly does Job want God to do or not to do? Does he ask him to
stop the suffering with which he is now afflicting him (so Hesse, Horst)? The
"hand" of God is indeed what has afflicted Job (1:11; 2:5; 19:21), but it can
hardly be the case that Job makes the removal of his suffering a condition
for his lawsuit. For Job will in fact continue his speech without the slightest
adjustment to his condition. The answer must lie in the fact that the "hand"
of God can be envisaged as the instrument of even severer suffering than
Job is at present enduring (cf. 6:9 "let loose his hand and cut me off"), and
here must be seen as conveying punishment for Job's temerity in entering
into dispute with God. He wants assurance of safe conduct through this disputation, and a guarantee of no recriminations hereafter.

It may seem strange that Job makes not "hiding" from God conditional
upon these requests being met. As Andersen says, "Job has never hidden
from God and has no intention of doing so." So the point must be, not that
Job is hiding from God now, but he realizes that if God were to lay his hand
on him more heavily his will to defend himself could break and he could
find himself, against all his inclination, running for cover. He knows also, no
doubt, that it is impossible in fact to hide from God (cf. 7:12; 10:7; 14:6),
but he is speaking now of an instinct to hide from danger. It is an instinct, in
the long run, for self-preservation, which Job does not care too much about;
but it is an instinct, in the first place, that is merely a reflex action.

22 It does not make much difference, legally speaking, in such a dispute,
who is plaintiff and who defendant. God has already effectively taken the
plaintiff's role by initiating punishment against Job. And Job has also adopted
a plaintiff's role in uttering reproach and accusation against God (7:11–12, 17–
19, 21; 10:3–7, 18–19). The language of "calling" and "answering" is not always
used in this book of legal accusation and defense (cf. on 12:4); at 14:55 it is
the reciprocal conversation of intimates that Job desires. This reminds us that
from Job's point of view the legal dispute is not an end in itself as if justice
were his main aim; it is not, and the dispute about justice is only a means
towards a better end, that of reconciliation. Meanwhile, even a legal disputation
is better than no contact at all.

As it is, of course, God will not "call" as plaintiff—not yet. So Job must be
"first to speak," on the understanding that the words now to be uttered will
not be words spoken into the air but words eliciting a reply. In 9:16 things
were different, we may note; for there Job doubted that, even if God were to
reply to any summons issued by Job, God would take any notice of arguments
and complaints advanced by Job. There is a contradiction here, but only between
what Job preaches and what he practises. He doubts that God is listening to

him but he goes on speaking, he mistrusts God's disposition toward him but he goes on opening himself up before God nevertheless. This is a thoroughly human and admirable attitude, even if it is strictly speaking illogical.

On the terminology of the legal speech, cf. H.-J. Boecker, *Redeformen des Rechtslebens im Alten Testament* (WMANT 14; Neukirchen-Vluyn: Neukirchener Verlag, 1964) 58 n. 1; and cf. on 9:3, 15, 16.

23 God of course does not intervene at this moment in Job's speech to play the role of plaintiff. But what follows does not do so on the basis that "because God remains silent, Job decides immediately to adopt the second method [of v 22]: he attacks" (Terrien). Nor is it exactly that "God failing to respond to Job's invitation in 22a to formulate His charges, Job speaks on" (Gray). All this talk of legal niceties is something of a smoke screen; the fact is that both parties are each plaintiff and defendant, and there is no evidently correct point at which the legal controversy should be commenced. Job happens to be speaking now, so he may naturally set forth his side of the case. God has not spoken, and still shows no signs of speaking, so the question whether he should most properly speak first has from the beginning been rather academic.

What Job says is shaped as a formal legal phrase (as against Gray); one or other party to a dispute may ask for clarification or explanation of wrongs alleged. In the two closest parallels to our text, Yahweh asks Israel, "What wrong did your fathers find in me that they went from me?" (Jer 2:5), and Jacob asks Laban, "What is my offense, what is my sin (מה־פשעי מה חטאתי, two of the terms used here) that you have hotly pursued me?" (Gen 31:36). Neither example belongs to the setting of the formal lawsuit, and in both cases the speaker may well be regarded as plaintiff rather than defendant (contrast H.-J. Boecker, "Anklagereden und Verteidigungsreden im Alten Testament. Ein Beitrag zur Formgeschichte alttestamentlicher Prophetenworte," *EvTh* 20 [1960] 398–412 [405]). And we should note that such questions are not necessarily intended to be answered directly; they are sometimes purely rhetorical questions, implying that no wrong at all has been committed (this is certainly the case in Jer 2:5). Even in this more legal setting in Job (and perhaps even here the setting is really metaphorical), the question "how many sins are mine?" may well be a kind of affirmation of innocence. Job asks for a catalogue of his sins, but he does not believe that catalogue will contain any items. So is his question genuinely seeking information, or is it a rhetorical form?

The answer depends upon whether the Hebrew means, "How many sins have I committed?," or "How many sins are laid to my charge?" If it is the former, it is a rhetorical question; if the latter, he is asking for an itemized bill of particulars, which may contain many items, all of them false charges. One thing we may be certain of is that, in asking "how many are the iniquities and sins that are mine?," Job does not for a moment admit to any wrongdoing. As against Gray ("Job, though 'perfect,' does not deny that he has sinned"), Gordis ("Job does not pretend to be free from all guilt") and Andersen ("Job never pretends that he is sinless"), I argue that it is essential to realize that his case is that he is completely innocent, in accord with the view of the narrative prologue in 1:1, 8. Apparent exceptions to this view can easily be accounted for: the "iniquities of his youth" (v 26) are either misdeeds for which he is not responsible, committed before he had reached an age of accountability, or sins which have already been atoned for (cf. 1:5) and should not be brought into any reckoning now. Cf. also on 10:6; 14:17.

Strictly speaking, the first half of the line concerns the *quantity* of sins (כמה, "how many"; and the nouns are in the plural), and the second half the *character* of the sins (the nouns are in the singular). There is a rhetorical distinction here that has more form than substance, but no doubt the question is more precise here than in 10:2, where the dispute was in its "pre-trial" stage. The differences that can be made out in other contexts between עון "iniquity," חטאה "sin," and פשע "rebellion, transgression" (see, e.g., R. Knierim, *THWAT* 2:493) are probably nugatory here.

Job's anguish depends very largely upon his total ignorance of the crime for which he is suffering. The situation is uniquely depicted in our own age by Kafka's novel *The Trial*. See also Dermot Cox, *The Triumph of Impotence: Job and the Tradition of the Absurd* (Rome: Università Gregoriana Editrice, 1978), who is particularly alert to the signs of the absurd in Job. Job's failure to understand what is going on is a frightening experience (v 25) that must lead to the brink of mental exhaustion and breakdown. His situation is strictly absurd; normal logical rules do not apply, and the brain cannot accept an excess of meaningless and unanalyzable data without damage. Some order can perhaps be introduced into this theatre of the absurd by the production of a catalogue of crimes, even if each one is imaginary. Kafka's Joseph K. would think himself well off if he could take in his hands such a list.

24 This is the reproachful "why?"-question (in the Heb. there is only one למה, "why?" here) we meet with often in the Psalms. Its concern is not to elicit a reason, but to reproach the one addressed in the hope of changing the situation. Cf. Ps 10:1; 22:2 [1]; 74:1; and see C. C. Broyles, *The Conflict of Faith and Experience in the Psalms: A Form-Critical and Theological Study* (JSOTS 52; Sheffield: JSOT, 1989), on these psalms in which the inaction of God is lamented. The hiding of God's face means not the covering of his face so that it cannot be seen, but the covering of his sight so that he cannot see (A. S. van der Woude, *THWAT* 2:452). The image, as Fohrer notes, can be an expression of wrath (34:29; Deut 31:17–18; 32:20; Isa 8:17; 54:8; 59:2; 64:6 [7]; Jer 33:5; Ezek 39:23–24; Mic 3:4; Ps 27:9) or a sign of forgetfulness (Ps 13:2 [1]; 44:25 [24]), but also a mark of God's refusal to be friendly and well-disposed (cf. Ps 30:8 [7]; 69:18 [17]; 102:3 [2]). Both the first and the third senses are appropriate here, in that Job feels himself to be God's "enemy" (v 24b), frightened, accused and imprisoned by God (vv 25–27). See also S. E. Balentine, *The Hidden God: The Hiding of the Face of God in the Old Testament* (Oxford: OUP, 1983).

The occurrence of Job's question at this point has been thought to signify a pause after v 23, as if Job had waited to hear the charges against him and then, hearing no word from God, has burst out with this protest. More probably, though, the point is not God's refusal to meet his challenge, but his harsh treatment of him in general (Peake).

It is not a contradiction of thought that here Job complains that God is hiding his face, whereas in 7:19 he had complained that God scrutinizes him too closely, and had cried, "Will you never take your gaze from me?" For in both places, whether by investigative scrutiny or by disinterest, God is playing the role of "enemy"; in chap. 7 by treating Job as the sea or a sea monster (7:12), here by the hostile acts of vv 25–27. It is possible that there is play on the words "Job" (אִיּוֹב, *'iyyôb*) and "enemy" (אוֹיֵב, *'ôyēb*), as if God had mistaken Job's identity and has taken to treating him as a personal threat to himself, an *'ôyēb*, instead of the mere man *'iyyôb* (cf. Terrien).

Verses 24b and 27a–b are quoted by Elihu as Job's words in 33:10–11.

25 This is how being God's enemy feels from Job's point of view. Job himself is physically and psychically powerless; his vigor is dried up. Two images of plant life that is cut off from its source of vitality and so desiccated, feeble and insubstantial capture his sense of his own state. The image of the driven leaf, light enough to be blown along by air, among the most insubstantial of natural objects, recurs in a somewhat different usage in Lev 26:36, "the sound of a driven leaf shall pursue (רדף, as here) them"; dry straw is a more common image for what can easily be driven away (Ps 83:14 [13]; Isa 40:24; Jer 13:24) or easily burnt (Exod 15:7; Isa 5:24; 33:11; 47:14; Joel 2:5; Obad 18; Nah 1:10; Mal 3:19 [4:1]), or what is weak (Job 41:28–29 [20–21]) or what is trifling and fragmented (Isa 41:2). It is more often the wicked who at the time of their destruction by God are compared with a leaf that fades (Isa 64:5 [6]) or falls (Isa 34:4); the righteous, on the contrary, might have expected to be like a tree whose leaf does not wither (Ps 1:3).

God, for his part, acts with power. ערץ "act ruthlessly, violently" is used in the noun form עריץ of the wicked enemies of the psalmists (Ps 37:35; 54:5 [3]; 86:14) who rise up against them and seek their lives. The verb itself means "terrify" (though also "fear"). רדף is "pursue," especially with hostile purposes, thus "harass, persecute" (e.g. Ps 69:27 [26]; 119:86, 161); elsewhere in Job the friends "persecute" him (19:22, 28) "like God" (19:22), and his honor is "pursued" (30:15 emended).

God's wielding superhuman power against such a weak creature is preposterous and grotesque; there is a dizzying lack of proportion about it (cf. on 7:12). It even betrays a lack of self-respect on God's part. And to harass what is already robbed of life, to chase after what is already at the mercy of the breeze is ludicrous. In plain language, Job is already as good as dead; the most God can do with his punishments of Job is to kill him altogether, an achievement that hardly seems worth expending any energy on.

26 As in 7:12, 17, the sentence beginning with "for" (כי) elaborates the reasons for which the question has been posed. God's harassment (ערץ, v 25) consists in his "writing bitter things," punishments (NEB), against him. The image, continuing the prevailing legal depiction, is of a judge prescribing a sentence (for כתב "write," as meaning "ordain, prescribe," cf. Isa 10:1, where it is parallel to חקק "decree"; and cf. also L. Kopf, "Arabische Etymologien und Parallelen zum Bibelwörterbuch," *VT* 8 [1958] 160–215 [180]), rather than of a physician prescribing a bitter medicine (Hitzig), though an allusion to "water of bitterness" in which curses are dissolved (Num 5:23–24) is not entirely impossible. There is no evidence among the Hebrews of written prescriptions of medicine for individual patients, though Egyptian medical texts with diagnoses and standard prescriptions, as well as the Ugaritic hippic texts with prescriptions for ailing horses, are known (Pope). Here the context is judicial retribution, without any suggestion of remedy or healing. It is certainly bitter in Job's experience of it; whether it is bitter in God's intention as well is something he does not at this moment judge.

The sins of one's youth are presumably sins for which one is not morally culpable, since they were committed before an age of responsibility. They are faults nevertheless and according to the strictest justice deserve punishment. A psalmist can ask God therefore to be mindful of his mercy and so not remember the sins of the psalmist's youth (Ps 25:7). There is of course nothing in the phrase itself to indicate that the "sins of one's youth" are not sins for which one is fully responsible. It would be surprising, however, for Job to admit to misdemeanors he could properly blame himself for, even if long past, in the context of his unrelenting protestation of innocence.

The overriding point, nevertheless, is the issue of disproportionateness. "The mature man is not responsible for those trifling sins. It would indicate rancour on the part of God to persecute Job on account of these youthful errors, supposing them to have existed" (Dhorme). That last phrase reminds us that Job is not exactly confessing to such sins. He does not know that God is punishing him for the sins of his youth, but in the absence of any sin of his adulthood that he can remember he presumes that there must be some dark secret from his boyhood which God is unable to forget. It is doubtful whether the sins he presumes his children are capable of (1:5) are the sorts of sins he has in mind here; but if they are, the Job of the prologue would surely have been scrupulous enough to offer sacrifices in atonement for any childhood demeanors of his own. Is there still something unremembered and unforgiven, he wonders.

To "inherit" (ירש hiph) is to "inherit the consequences of" (for the rare metaphorical use, cf. Hos 9:6; Ecclus 15:6). The child has been father to the man, and what he has "inherited" from his childhood has been the vengeance of God, an inheritance that is no blessing (contrast Ps 127:3; and see also Job 20:29; 27:13; 31:2; 42:15).

27 What is described here is not a legally determined punishment, but the kind of oppressive behavior engaged in by a powerful person against his adversary at law. Such a person could arrest or imprison his opponent, without trial, but in the expectation of a formal trial to resolve the matter at issue. God has been acting like the עריץ "oppressor" of v 25.

The סד is generally thought to be "stocks," two notched beams of timber between which the legs of criminals are fastened. No ancient example of such stocks survives, but Dhorme refers to the use of stocks to confine prisoners of war in twentieth-century Arabia, and Horst cites earlier Middle Eastern examples (from J. L. Burckhardt, *Notes on the Bedouins and Wahabys* [London: H. Colburn and R. Bentley, 1830] 2:146; J. Barth, "Zu den Papyri von Elephantine [ed. Sachau]," *OLZ* 15 [1912] 10–11). The term occurs nowhere else in Hebrew, except at 33:11 where much of the present line is duplicated; but the term is attested in Syriac (where it is used for the Roman stocks at Acts 16:24) and in Aramaic (*b. Pes.* 28a "the stocks-maker sits in his own stocks").

The "stocks" of Jer 20:2–3; 29:26 and 2 Chr 16:10 (מהפכת) are probably some other device of punishment, perhaps, as is suggested by the root verb הפך "bend," a frame for holding a prisoner in bent position (KB[3]; cf. H. A. Fehr, *Das Recht im Bilde* [Erelenbach-Zurich: E. Rentsch, 1923] 110, pls. 139, 143). If the צינק is the "pillory" (Jer 29:26; so NAB; RSV "collar") some similar device to the stocks may be meant.

One does not need great acuity to observe that if Job's feet are held fast in the stocks, he makes no "paths" for God to observe. Some have therefore argued that the "stocks" must rather be fetters which permit movement of a kind (cf. NIV "shackles"; similarly Peake); God's disproportionate cruelty would then consist in his making Job unable to move without difficulty of pain, and then adding insult to injury by keeping close guard over his movements as if he was a prisoner attempting to escape custody. But there is no evidence that סד signifies fetters of this kind. Fetters of iron or bronze are called חֶבֶל or נְחֹשֶׁת (Ps 105:18; 149:8; Judg 16:21; 2 Sam 3:24; 2 Kgs 25:7).

Other commentators omit the second line of the verse as incompatible with the first line (so Jastrow, Fohrer, NEB), but the same words occur also at 33:10 (where Fohrer and Jastrow find no difficulty, and NEB translates "keep a close watch on all I do"); the objection to them at this point is primarily because they create a tricolon, something of a rarity in Hebrew poetry. (But of course if this verse is the last in the chapter [see on v 28 below], a tricolon would be quite natural.)

Others again emend סד "stocks" to סיד "lime," following the Targum, "he puts my feet in mortar, cement"; Fohrer envisages Job's feet being coated with lime so that his footsteps can be more easily traced; this improbable suggestion involves also the supposition of a verb סמם "besmear, color" (so too KB, KB³).

Yet another solution is to understand Job's "paths" as simply his way of life or behavior (cf. Pope; LXX has "my works" rather than "my ways"). But perhaps the best solution is to regard the actions of v 27 not as a sequence but as a set which God performs at various times. No prisoner is kept in the stocks for days or weeks on end; sometimes he is let loose, but still kept within close bounds, his steps "watched." Taken as a whole, the verse presents a mixed and self-contradictory metaphor; but since to have one's movements closely spied upon must feel like having no free movement at all, the inconsistency is not very deep.

The last colon is literally "you engrave a mark on the roots of my feet." חקה is a rarely used byform of חקק "cut in, inscribe," the hithpael signifying here "inscribe for yourself" (GKC, § 54f). This is taken by many to be a reference to a supposed custom of the slave-owner branding his name upon the soles of his slave's feet (NEB "setting a slave-mark on the arches of his feet"; similarly NIV, KB³, Tur-Sinai, Pope, Gordis, de Wilde; the interpretation goes back to J. A. Dathe). But the only evidence we have of slave-branding is upon the hand (Isa 44:5; 49:16) and the forehead, and it seems rather foolish to put such a brand in so inconspicuous a place. Tur-Sinai's explanation is unbelievable: "the master's name [was] inscribed on the sole of the foot in such a way that the mark of the inscription was left by the footsteps of the fugitive slave, so that he could be traced by them." And the two photographs reproduced by Tur-Sinai from E. Ben-Dor, QDAP 18 (1947) pl. 27, showing the name of the owner (is it?) on jar handles, enclosed in a cartouche in the shape of a foot sole (is it?), are too remote from the practice of slavery to have any probative value.

The "roots" of the foot (an expression encountered nowhere else) have alternatively been understood as the tracks made by the feet, i.e., the spot where the feet press into the ground. The verb would then mean "mark, note for oneself," with some such translation as "my footprints dost Thou examine" (Dhorme; similarly Terrien, Sicre Diaz, Horst, NAB, GNB). This seems the best solution.

Another not improbable sense of the phrase could be "you make a line about the soles of my feet" (so Delitzsch; cf. RV, RSV "settest a bound," NJPS "hemming in"), עַל meaning not "upon" but "as regards, concerning, for" (BDB, 349a). A rather unlikely interpretation is to understand the "roots" of the "feet" as the ankles, רֶגֶל "foot" being understood to include all the leg beneath the knee; thus Jastrow: "stocks, which press against my ankles"; but it does not appear that סַד is feminine, which this rendering would require. The three cola depict an investigation of Job by God and a restriction on his movement. Such acts of close arrest carry legal implications: God should follow up his arrest with the formulation of charges, but if that does not happen he is behaving like a gangster (עָרִיץ).

28 It is hard to see the connection of this verse with what precedes, and it is apparently taken more naturally with 14:1–2. It begins "and he" (וְהוּא), without any indication of who the "he" might be. Some suggest that the verse describes "humankind" referred to (as אָדָם) at the beginning of 14:1 (Gordis); RSV, NJPS, NIV insert "man" at the beginning of the verse, and Terrien speaks of "pronominal anticipation." But such a feature is hard to exemplify (Gordis's example from 8:16 is only appropriate on his own interpretation of the passage).

For this reason many commentators decide that the verse has been accidentally transposed from its original place in chap. 14, after v 2b according to most (e.g., Siegfried, Dhorme, Pope, Horst, NEB), though others place it after v 2a (Merx), v 1 (Stevenson), v 3 (Bickell; cf. Beer, NAB, Moffatt), v 6 (Kissane) or delete it altogether (Budde, Hölscher).

All the evidence does not point in the same direction, however. The strophic structure at this point in the speech is very regular: 13:20–22, 23–25; 14:1–3, 4–6, 7–9, 10–12 are indisputable triplets, and it would make sense that 13:26–28 should also be a triplet and that v 28 should not be grafted on to some other triplet (cf. also Terrien). There is also the question whether this verse is really appropriate following 14:2, since there the theme is the brevity of human life, whereas here it is the insubstantiality of human existence. Admittedly, these would not be strong objections if no other sense could be made of the verse in its present context.

Gordis interestingly suggested that the verse be regarded as the conclusion of the question of v 25, vv 26–27 being a long parenthesis; that is, "Will you terrify a leaf . . . which wastes away?" This gives us the clue that the "he" or "it" of our verse is not "Job" or "humankind" but the leaf or straw of v 25. But rather than take vv 26–27 as parenthesis, the strophic structure encourages us to take vv 23–25 and 26–28 as parallel. Each strophe in its first two verses speaks of God in his relation to Job, and in its last verse portrays Job thus harassed as something feeble and insubstantial. The former strophe means "Why do you think I am your enemy when I am something so weak?"; the second, "Why do you take such close note of me when I am something so worn out and worthless?"

This particular object of God's arrest and close scrutiny is surely unworthy of divine attention. It is like skins that wear out (see n. 13:28.a, b), that can indeed be mended (cf. Josh 9:4 where also בָּלָה "wear out" is used of wineskins) but are not very reliable (Matt 9:17) and will not last. On the term "wear out" of humans, cf. Gen 18:12; Isa 50:9; Ps 32:3; 49:15 [14]; Lam 3:4. Or, changing the picture, it is like a garment already eaten into holes by moths (on the image of the moth's destructiveness, cf. on 4:9). Fohrer sees the second colon as derived from the psalm-style phraseology encountered in Isa 50:9; 51:8; Hos 5:12; Ps 39:12 [11].

14:1–3 The focus changes here from Job specifically (as in 13:20–28) to humankind generally. Job is of course still speaking of himself, but not for the first time has projected his own experience onto the wider canvas of all humanity (cf. on 3:20; 7:1–10). The point of this strophe is that humans in their insignificance do not merit the kind of divine surveillance Job himself is being subjected to.

1 Of humankind generally he will now speak, as the introductory word אדם shows by its prominent position. The life of humans is so fleeting that it seems undignified for God to consecrate so much effort to investigating and judging it. There is no conflict or contradiction (against Andersen) in Job's thought between his desire for a speedy death and his complaint that human life is fearfully brief. For himself, a swift death often seems the most desirable escape from his intolerable position (cf. 3:20–23; 6:8–9; 7:21b; 9:21); but in any case, the lifespan of humans, himself included, is so tiny even when life is fully lived out, that the amount of attention God has given him seems hugely disproportionate (cf. 7:7–10, 16b–19; 10:20–22).

Unlike 7:1–3, where in lamenting the brevity of life, his emphasis lay upon the laboriousness and aimlessness of life, here it lies strictly upon its brevity, not as a cause of complaint in itself (after all, what counts as brevity is an arbitrary or at least relative matter) but by way of background for the question of v 3, "Is it upon such a one that you fix your eyes?"

The expression "born of woman" is unique to Job in the Hebrew Bible (see also 15:14; 25:4; Ecclus 10:18; 1QS 11.21; 1QH 13.17; 18.12–13, 16, 23–24; Matt 11:11; Luke 7:28). Perhaps it has the connotation of weakness, though women are rarely referred to as weak in the OT (cf. Jer 50:37; 51:30 where warriors become women; and Isa 19:16, Egyptians tremble like women); there may be some folk etymology at work here, connecting אשה "woman" with the verb אנש "be weak." It certainly does not seem to have any connotation of uncleanness, which would be beside the point in this context; even in 15:14 and 25:4, where the concept of uncleanness is in the immediate context, it still seems to be weakness that birth from a woman signifies. Ritual uncleanness of woman at certain times, including childbirth, would lie outside the comparatively non-cultic thoughtworld of the dialogues of Job. De Wilde has recently suggested that "born of woman" means nothing more than "mortal," which is certainly the case in the NT passages cited and in Ecclus 10:18, and may be for all the occurrences.

Human life is poor in days, but rich in turmoil; Job's aphorism is almost a reversal of the standard phrase "full of days, riches, and honor" (1 Chr 29:28). The conventional expression "full of days" (Gen 25:8; 35:29)—which will be said of Job himself at 42:17!—can be negated easily enough for etiquette's sake (Jacob, at 130 years: "few and evil have been the days of the years of my life," Gen 47:9), and here out of profound depression about the human condition. "Turmoil," which רגז signifies (not simply "trouble" as RV, RSV, NAB, NJPS, NIV), is the "tumult of feeling and the onslaught of sufferings" (Fohrer); cf. also on 3:17, 26. Job is full of, "satiated with" (שׂבע), restlessness (7:4) and shame (10:15); it is this fullness that makes him empty, dried up, and feeble.

2 Two conventional images of the brevity of life follow. "Nothing is so ephemeral as the flower, nothing so fugitive as the shadow" (Dhorme). For the image of the flower as short-lived, cf. Ps 103:15–16; Isa˙28:1, 4; 40:6–8; James 1:10, 11; 1 Pet 1:24 (grass: 2 Kgs 19:26; Ps 37:2; 90:6; 102:12 [11]; 129:6). The picture is generally of the fresh growth in the spring which comes to an untimely end before the hot east winds of summer. Here, however, it is possible that the verb מלל means "cut off," not "fade" (see n. 14:2.b); the image is that of the spring flowers being cut down by the reaper's sickle along with the grain in May or June (Fohrer). For the image of the shadow as swift, cf. 8:9; Ps 102:12 [11]; 109:23; 144:4; Eccl 6:12; 1 Chr 29:15. Schopenhauer rightly praised this verse as an example of the impressiveness of simple language (*Parerga und Paralipomena,* in *Arthur Schopenhauers sämtliche Werke,* ed. P. Deussen [Munich: R. Piper, 1913] 5:570–71).

3 Such human frailty and impermanence is contrasted with the divine inquisition, which is of course thorough and long extended. The amazing disproportion is highlighted by the introductory particle אף "surely, indeed" (introducing intensive clauses, GKC, § 153). There is a similar train of thought in 7:17–19. To "open the eye(s)" (פקח עין) is here to pay attention to; what is elsewhere met with as an appeal for God's care (Isa 37:17; Jer 32:19) is here turned against him (Fohrer): too close attention is only for humanity's harm—which is to say, specifically, for Job's.

Such close attention by God is exercised only for the sake of finding fault with humankind and so being able to put them in the wrong legally. The point resembles that of 10:12–14. The "disputation" (משפט) into which God brings people is not some future judgment but the conflicts between God and a human being that occur from time to time, begun by God as the plaintiff who "brings" or hales his opponent to trial (cf. 13:27). Such trials (Job's is the model of all such trials) *begin* with punishment, presumably in the form of pre-trial "arrest" of the defendant by the plaintiff. Job himself certainly wants a trial with God now that he finds his character blackened; but without self-contradiction regards the whole concept of God willfully entering into legal disputation with humans as inappropriate and disproportionate to the relative power of humanity and God. A psalmist could contrast the brevity of human life with God's greatness in order to stress his goodness (Ps 103:15–17), but Job is made of sterner stuff—or, should we say, more sensitive matter.

4 The connection of this verse to the context is hard to discern, but there is no good reason to delete it (as Bickell, Budde, Driver-Gray, Pope, NEB, Horst); it can hardly be "the sigh of a pious reader, written on the margin, and mistakenly introduced into the text" (Peake). The problems are: (1) that it is the *brevity* of human life, not its "uncleanness," that is in the rest of vv 1–6 the reason for begging God to turn his gaze from humankind; (2) that these sound more like the friends' words (cf. 4:17) than Job's; (3) that the second colon is abnormally short, which may suggest textual corruption.

These problems are soluble, however. The mention of human uncleanness is not itself the *reason* for asking for God to "look away"; the point is that since humans are short-lived, God could reasonably ignore the sins of humankind, since the sins of such creatures can hardly be on a scale to threaten cosmic order or divine honor. The line of thought is exactly parallel to 7:19–21, though there Job spoke exclusively of himself, and here of humankind generally. There he asked, "How long before you look away (שעה, as here) from me? If I sin, how does that harm you? Why do you not just overlook any sin I am supposed to have committed, because very soon I shall be dead and nothing will matter any more." Here he says, "We both know that human beings commit sins. But why spy on them and persecute them for the sake of their wrongdoing? Soon they will all be dead, so why make such a fuss about it?"

There is a little logical difficulty in this argument, of course. If humans generally are "unclean," is not Job himself also "unclean"? Surely he does not admit that? Yes, in principle he has always admitted that he is capable of sin ("if I sin," 7:20); it is only that as a matter of fact he does not allow that he is guilty of any sin for which his present suffering can be a punishment. And his point about humankind does not depend upon all human beings being always sinners; it has to do with the potential sinfulness of humankind, whose moral fallibility is a kind of correlate of their physical frailty and impermanence. In some respects Job would not dissent from Eliphaz's words, "Can a man be pure in the sight of his Maker?" (4:17); he agrees that humankind is, as a whole, unrighteous compared with God, but he denies that it therefore follows that he, Job, is a sinner.

Job has no concept of "original" or inherited sin (against W. Eichrodt, *Theology of the Old Testament* [tr. J. A. Baker; London: SCM, 1967] 2:410, and the church fathers generally, who cited this verse—more frequently than any other in Job—in support of the Christian dogma; see further, J. Ziegler, *Iob 14,4–5a als wichtigster Schriftbeweis für die These "Neminem sine sorde et sine peccato esse"* [*Cyprian, test 3, 54*] *bei den lateinischen christlichen Schriftstellern* [Bayerische Akademie der Wissenschaften, Phil.-hist. Klasse, Sitzungberichte, Jahrgang 1985.3; Munich: Verlag der Bayerischen Akademie der Wissenschaften und C. H. Beck, 1985]). Job speaks only pragmatically, of what actually turns out to be the case. Some have thought the phrase "a clean from an unclean" points to the impossibility of "cleanness" in the offspring of a contaminated parent. But there is no allusion to any uncleanness attaching to conception, childbirth or women (against Dhorme, Rowley). For the expression is not "Who will *bring* a clean out of an unclean?" but "Who will *give* . . . ?," the phrase expressing a hopeless wish (GKC, § 151b) that human nature could be otherwise, and that one example of a "pure being" (generally speaking) could be distinguished from the mass of the "impure" (cf. NAB "Can a man be found who is clean of defilement?"); Horst cites by way of analogy Deut 15:7, "a poor man, from one of your brothers" (אביון מאחד אחיך), i.e., a poor man from among the category of your brothers.

The use of terminology that is, strictly speaking, cultic ("clean" and "unclean," טהור and טמא) in the dialogues of Job and in Job's mouth especially is remarkable, since the cult is rarely alluded to in the book. There can hardly be said to be a concern about cultic impurity here, as is argued by J. K. Zink, "Uncleanness and Sin: A Study of Job xiv 4 and Psalm li 7," *VT* 17 (1967) 354–61. The context makes clear, however, that the terms are being used metaphorically of moral "cleanness," i.e., righteousness, and not ritual cleanness at all (טהר elsewhere in Job of gold [28:19], of the wind clearing the sky of clouds [37:21] and of ethical "cleanness" [4:17; 17:9]; טמא "unclean" is not used elsewhere in Job).

Nothing definite can be said of the reason for the shortness of the second colon; the effect is certainly an impressive statement of the absence of any fulfilling of the wish.

5–6 The three cola of v 5 are best taken as the threefold reason for the demand of v 6. The initial אִם is not the hypothetical "if," but "if, as is the case," which means "since." The emphasis in this triple description of the prescribed length of human life is not that it has been fixed at a particular span, nor that God himself has fixed it, but that God well knows how brief a span it is; this is so evidently the general reference that it is not expressly stated. Instead, what is stated is the impossibility of the assigned span being exceeded. The number of human days is "determined" (חָרוּץ), the accent being on the irrevocability of the divine decree (Horst; cf. חרץ in Isa 10:22; Joel 4:14 [3:14]; Dan 9:26, 27; 11:36). Likewise the months of human life are "known" to God, lit., "with you" (אִתָּךְ), in your knowledge or memory; for such a meaning of אֵת "with," cf. Isa 59:12; Prov 2:1; Gen 40:14 (BDB, 86 § 3b). Days and months together add to a total which is humankind's "limit" (חֹק "prescribed thing"); the term is used in v 13 of a prescribed time, and elsewhere of the prescribed limit of the sea (26:10; 38:10; Jer 5:22; Prov 8:29), of the heavens (Ps 148:6) and of the land of Israel (Mic 7:11). To "pass over" (עבר) a "prescribed limit" (חֹק) sounds like a legal expression meaning to "transgress a decree" (the exact phrase is not actually attested in the Hebrew Bible); some play may be made with the idea that any "overstepping" (עבר) the divine prescription of one's fixed span of life would be like a "transgression" (עבר) of a divine law. There is no thought here of the lifespan of any individual being predetermined, but simply that humankind's allotted span (at whatever number of years it may be set) is a trifling period.

Job has twice urged God to "desist" (חדל) from him, to leave him alone (7:16; 10:20), so that he may have some relief in the days that remain for him. The thought is apparently a conventional form of lament; cf. Ps 39:14 [13] "Look away (שעה, as here) from me, that I may be cheerful (בלג, as in 9:27; 10:20), before I depart and be no more." Here of course it is humankind, not Job personally, that is the ostensible object of God's unremitting attention, which Job experiences as hurtful and undesirable. Failure to recognize the conventionality of an expression for "joy" in such a sombre context has led many to seek here a different sense for רצה from "enjoy" (see n. 14:6.b). The point is rather that the little "pleasure" or "comfort" (10:20) that remains for a person in Job's position is comparable to the necessitous lot of the day-laborer. Who ever heard of a "hired laborer" "enjoying" his work? The term has an irony in it, as if Job were to say, I will snatch what pleasure I can—if any!—from the days that are left to me. Of course it will be a relief to be rid of the oppressive burden of God's scrutiny, once he has taken his eyes "from off" (מֵעָלָיו) humankind—which is to say, Job.

The view has little to commend it that the hireling enjoys his "day" only at its end, when his work is over (so Gray, Rowley); that would be an unnatural sense to give to the word "day"; cf. also Delitzsch, who aptly cites Hahn: "[Job] desires that God would grant man the comparative rest of the hireling, who must toil in sorrow and eat his bread in the sweat of his brow, but still is free from any special suffering, by not laying extraordinary affliction on him in addition to the common infirmities beneath which he sighs."

7–12 Two strophes, each of three lines, contrast the "hope" of a tree and the hope of humankind for a life beyond death. On the formal relationship between strophe and antistrophe (as also in 14:13–22), cf. J. Krašovec, *Antithetic Structures in Biblical Hebrew Poetry* (VTS 35; Leiden: Brill, 1984) 112–15. This exceptionally beautiful little poem has connections both to what precedes and what follows. It provides an elaboration for the thought of v 5, that human life has a fixed bound that cannot be transgressed, which is the ground of the plea in v 6 for God to "look away." And it leads into the hopeless wish of vv 13–17 that things were otherwise, and that Sheol, rather than being a place of no return, could be a place of safe hiding from the divine wrath.

7 The tree, if we speak anthropopathically, can be said to have "hope" (תִּקְוָה), a rare commodity in Job's life (17:15; 19:10; and cf. on 7:6; contrast 4:6; 8:13; 11:18, 20) and in human life generally if the hope is for resuscitation or revivification (see v 19, "so you destroy the hope of man"). There may be some allusion to a practice noted by J. G. Wetzstein (cited by Franz Delitzsch, p. 175) in Transjordan and around Damascus of cutting down old fig trees, walnuts and pomegranates, as well as vines that have ceased to bear good fruit; the stumps if watered put out new shoots the following year and subsequently bear good crops. Pliny speaks also of the laurel as keeping its life even when the trunk is cut down (*Hist. nat.* 15.30). For a tree, death brings new life—at least that is the hope. The old stump (cf. Isa 6:13; 11:1) may sprout new shoots (חלף hiphil; cf. 29:20; Ps 90:5–6; perhaps Isa 9:9 [10]; 40:31; Ecclus 46:12), which may grow strong and not "fail" (חדל, "desist" in v 6).

This three-colon line begins the unit vv 7–12, which is concluded by another three-colon line.

8–9 The picture of the felled tree is presumably continued. It is possible that the tree here is another tree to that of v 7, one that simply withers and dies of old age; גִזְעוֹ could be "its stem, trunk" rather than "its stump." More likely, however, the picture is of a tree cut down, which thereafter begins to decay and wither by natural process. Even that deadness needs only a "whiff" or hint of water to revive it. The רֵיחַ "scent" of water is of course itself metaphorical, as in Judg 16:9 a rope of tow snaps when it "scents" (verb רוח) the fire. The revived tree will put forth (עשה; cf. 15:27) shoots as if it were a new plant freshly set.

No doubt Rowley goes too far in commenting: "Why, Job asks by implication, should man be denied what is granted to a tree?"—as if Job were hinting that human destiny must surely be to survive death. Cf. Peake: "We may well think that the poet, by placing in Job's mouth this reference to the tree's indomitable vitality, meant subtly to suggest that it is irrational to think that what is granted to a tree can be denied to a man." For it is not that Job is protesting that there is no afterlife for humankind, but that he is urging that since there is no such hope for human creatures God should ignore their petty failings.

10 In contrast to the fate of a tree is the fate of humankind: the person that is felled (to use the imagery of v 7) by death has no hope, but is "weak." The verb is חלש which means "be weak" (cf. Joel 4:10 [3:10] for חַלָּשׁ contrasted with גִּבּוֹר "mighty"), not "be prostrate" (cf. RSV, NIV, "is laid low") and it has seemed strange to some that first the person "dies," and thereafter is "weak." Gordis thinks it is the figure of *hysteron proton*, the verbs being reversed in sense, "man dies and grows faint" signifying "man grows faint and dies." Others have suggested a different meaning for חלש, such as "snatch away" or "disappear" (see n. 14:10.a), and others again emend the verb to yield the meaning "pass away" or "is driven away." These suggestions can be set on one side when it is recognized that חלש refers to human loss of power after death as contrasted with the tree's continuing vitality after it is cut down, and that the stress is on this verb, not upon "dies." M. Dahood likewise comments that "the poet is evoking the motif of Sheol as the dwelling of weaklings, those of diminished vigor" ("The Conjunction *wn* and Negative *ʾi* in Hebrew," *UF* 14 [1982] 51–54 [54]). Thus we should translate: "a man, when he dies, loses every power." The first term for "man," גבר, though it does not mean "strong man" as distinct from other terms for male (see n. 4:17.a), has overtones from its root גבר "be strong" which contrast with the weakness the human male is reduced to in the end. On "breathes his last, expires" (גוע), cf. on 13:19.

The question "Where is he then?" is not a "rhetorical" question which would have to be answered with "nowhere"—in the spirit of Ecclesiastes' question, "Who knows whether the spirit of man goes upward?"—a question expecting the answer, "No one!" It is a question intended to evoke in the hearer's mind the image of Sheol, a place of extreme weakness and lassitude (3:17; Ps 88:5 [4]; cf. the Egyptian expression *wrd ʾib* "weary of heart" as a euphemism for the dead), and, moreover, a place from which return to new life is impossible (cf. 10:21; 16:22).

11–12 These verses draw a comparison between water that evaporates or drains away and the human being who sinks down into the dust of death. The waters of a lake (ים "lake" as well as "sea"; BDB, 411 § 3, 4) can vanish in the heat of summer, and a stream "dry up" (חרב of flood waters, Gen 8:13; of deep waters, Isa 44:27; of the Reed Sea, Ps 106:9; and יבש, of water at Gen 8:7; 1 Kgs 17:7 [נחל "brook"]; Jer 50:38; Joel 1:20 [אפיקי ים "streams of water"]). It is never seen again. Just so humankind.

The comparison is not, as is generally thought, between the lake or stream and humankind. For, as Peake and Rowley observe, dried up streams and lakes generally become full again when the rains come, and their drought is not permanent like the fate of humans.

A quite different interpretation is offered by Dhorme, Terrien and Horst (also JB): that is, the image presents an impossible situation, like that in v 12b of the heavens' disappearance. The waters of the sea (ים in its usual sense) may disappear and a mighty river (נהר, used of the Nile and Euphrates) dry up, but even then the human person, once at rest in the grave, will never rise. This attractive interpretation is, however, ruled out by the "and" at the beginning of v 12, which can only be the "and" of comparison (*waw adaequationis*; see GKC, § 161a); it has just now been used to mark the comparison/contrast between a tree and humankind at the beginning of v 10.

The verse is identical with Isa 19:5 (with the substitution here of אזלו "have gone" for נשתו "are dried up"). The line is perhaps borrowed from Isaiah, but used in a different setting. There it had to do with the drying up of the Nile, called ים "sea," (as also in Isa 27:1 and Nah 3:8) as well as נהר "river," in the course of divine punishment upon Egypt. Here there seems to be no specific reference to the Nile, and it is possible that the more proverb-like form of the line, such as we have here, is the more original. Fohrer thinks

only the first colon of v 11 is appropriate here, and refers it to the water of
the underworld ocean which is dissipated when absorbed into the streams of
earth; both points are unconvincing.

Humans stay dead so long as the heavens remain, a familiar image for
perpetuity (Deut 11:21; Jer 31:35–36; Ps 72:5, 7, 17; 89:30 [29], 38 [37]; 148:6).
There is indeed a tradition in OT literature of an end to the universe in a
cosmic catastrophe or exhaustion (Isa 34:4, the stars rot and the skies are
rolled up like a scroll; 51:6 the heavens vanish like smoke, the earth wears
out like a garment; Ps 102:26–27 [25–26], the heavens perish, the foundation
of the earth wears out like a garment; cf. Heb 1:10–12); but it is doubtful
whether this represents a genuine belief (as in 1 Enoch 45:4–5; 51:1–2) and
is not rather a hyperbolic statement of the permanence of God, as if to say
"even if heaven and earth were to cease to exist, God and his salvation would
not." In any case, there can be no thought in the present passage of the
downfall of the universe, since the point is wholly the finality of human death.

The final term used of death in this passage, "sleep," is not to be misunderstood as signifying some temporary state. That is never the case when this
image occurs (cf. "eternal sleep" [Jer 51:39, 57]). See J. G. S. S. Thompson
"Sleep: An Aspect of Jewish Anthropology," *VT* 5 (1955) 421–33; T. H. McAlpine, *Sleep, Divine and Human, in the Old Testament* (JSOTS 38; Sheffield: JSOT,
1987).

13–17 For a little Job drops the fiction that he is speaking in the name
of humanity (אדם [v 1] or גבר [v 10] or איש [v 12]) and speaks solely of
himself; for here we have feeling rather than ratiocination, an impossible dream
rather than an all too evident reality. In these verses, it will be "hide me,"
"conceal me," "set me a time," "remember me," and so on, as it was in the
highly personalistic dialogue of 13:20–28.

13 In no way is Job's denial of the possibility of awakening from the sleep
of death weakened by his immediate expression of a passionate longing that
it could be otherwise. Hopeless though this particular wish is, that Sheol could
be an asylum from God's wrath and that a human being could emerge from
it to enjoy renewed intimacy with God, a radical move is made in the utterance
of it. For not once before this moment has Job envisaged the possibility of
God's present disposition toward him of anger and hostility being replaced
by a more friendly, not to say positively yearning (v 15b), attitude. We have
noticed before (cf. on 9:4) how the ventilation of an impossible wish proves
to be no waste of words but a way of expressing what is really of value to the
one speaking.

In other OT passages God "hides" people from the danger of enemies
(Isa 49:2; Ps 27:5; 31:21 [20]); for hiding until wrath is past, cf. Isa 26:20;
Amos 9:3). Here Job imagines God hiding someone from God himself. The
very thought of a God beyond the God he is now experiencing is a concession
to the possibility that God is not all he seems to be, and that the future does
not have to be a simple extension of the past. At 9:13 Job was convinced that
God would never "turn back" (שוב hiph, not significantly different from שוב
qal here) his anger which has been his studied posture since primordial times.
Job does not deny that conviction here, but by injecting into his impossible
dream the depiction of a future in which God's anger would have been laid
to rest he opens up a space for himself to contemplate change. It is possible

to imagine a time when God's anger will have "passed," "been appeased" (שׁוּב,
lit., "turned back"; of anger at Gen 27:44–45; Isa 5:25). Job has not used the
word "anger" of God in this speech as he had in his previous speech (9:5, 13);
but we are apparently meant by this verse to infer that God's hostility pictured
in 13:25–27, as perhaps also his upheavals of the social order recounted in
12:13–25, are motivated by that same passion that dominated God's dealings
in chaps. 9–10 (cf. on 9:13).

Job has come a long way from the simple self-cursing hopelessness of chap.
3 and the demand for death and the absence of God in chaps. 5–6 to the
wish, absurd though it might be, of a future when God could "remember"
him kindly, in wrathless tranquillity. There is a dynamic in the Joban speeches
that stands in marked contrast to the static dogmatism of the friends.

Previously Job has asked God to "remember" (זכר) that his life is a mere
breath (7:7), with the implication that God has in his treatment of him overlooked an elementary and elemental fact about him; and he has called on
him to "remember" or take cognizance of the disparity between his early creation
of Job from clay, by his care preserving Job's life, and his present attempts to
undo his creation by attacking him (10:9). Here, in his impossible dream, he
envisages a "remembering" more intimate than those, a "remembering me,"
not as mere human, nor as a divine creation, nor as a wretched sufferer, but
simply as the man Job in his naked personhood. If only the "land of forgetfulness" (Ps 88:13 [12]) could become at some "fixed time" (חק, as in v 5c, though
there of the span of life, here of an appointed moment) a land of "remembering"! On זכר as signifying the resumption of relations between God and man,
see W. Schottroff, *"Gedenken" im Alten Orient und im Alten Testament: Die Wurzel
zākar im semitischen Sprachkreis* (WMANT 15; Neukirchen-Vluyn: Neukirchener
Verlag, 1964, ²1967).

Where does Job get the idea that God's wrath could "pass away"? It can
hardly be that he thinks "no one's anger lasts forever" (contrast Horst), since
he has already spoken of the settled "anger of a god" (9:13). Can there be an
allusion to the psalmic assertion that "His anger is but for a moment, and his
favor is for a lifetime" (Ps 30:6 [5])? Cf. Isa 54:8 "In overflowing wrath for a
moment I hid my face from you, but with everlasting love I will have compassion
on you." Weiser and Fohrer detect some allusion to the flood story, where
the flood as an expression of God's anger (though the term "anger" is not
used) is concluded with God's "remembering" Noah (Gen 8:1). More probably
the idea is generated simply from Job's present experience; the simple absence
of the wrathful God was the first alternative he could imagine (7:19; 10:20b),
his transmutation into a "remembering" God the second.

14 The initial colon, translated as "If a man die, shall he live again?"
(RSV, RV; cf. NEB, NJPS, NIV), seems distinctly out of place. At best it is an interjection, expressing—in the middle of Job's vision of an impossible future—his
conviction of its impossibility; at worst it is a misplaced line rightly belonging
after v 19 (Dhorme) or v 12a (Steuernagel, NEB), or a gloss modeled on v
10a (Ehrlich, Stevenson, Fohrer). These latter suggestions are far from persuasive: it is equally feeble to have the striking question needlessly answered by
"he shall never be roused from his sleep" (NEB) as to have the definitive statement
"you destroy the hope of man" (v 19) followed by a reiteration of the principle
upon which the preceding strophes have been constructed.

It is very much more satisfactory to see the "dying" and "living" as both belonging to an "if"-clause, stating the condition upon which Job would be willing to await a "release." If he could die and then live again, he would be willing to go through that process if at the end he could be assured of God's loving concern for him (*not* of the expectation of a fair trial, as against Habel). So Terrien translates, "If man, once dead, could live again . . . ," and NAB "When a man has died, were he to live again. . . ." Unfortunately, it is not certain that the Hebrew actually means this. To be sure, a small emendation from הֲיִחְיֶה "will he live?" to וְיִחְיֶה "and will live" (so Duhm, though he connects the colon with v 13) would yield the required sense. LXX does not have the question, but that does not mean that the translators did not read it in their Hebrew (as Duhm), for their affirmative statement might be a dogmatic correction of the Hebrew (cf. D. H. Gard, "The Concept of the Future Life according to the Greek Translator of the Book of Job," *JBL* 73 [1954] 137–43 [137–38]), and Aq and Theod certainly read the interrogative particle.

The "hard service" (צבא) that Job is prepared to endure is the time he would spend in the shadowy existence of the underworld. צבא (cf. on 7:1) perhaps has military overtones of the soldier consigned to uncomfortable or wearisome duties (cf. Moffatt "my weary post"), the term "relief, release" (חליפה, lit., "exchange") possibly meaning concretely "my replacement" (NJPS), the one who relieves me of my duty. Such a (concrete) "replacement" would of course have value for the metaphor only in as much as he brings (abstract) "relief, release" for Job (cf. the use of צבא and חליפה together in 10:17). It is no less possible that the "service" is that of the hired laborer, who equally longs for release from his "drudgery" (NAB). In either case, the emphasis here is on enduring a disagreeable lot rather than upon actually fighting or working, since Sheol is not the place for that.

The last time Job used the verb "hope" (יחל) he was expressing his entire absence of hope for a favorable outcome to his lawsuit (13:15). Nothing has changed here; it is only in the context of his impossible dream that he can imagine himself waiting in hope. Only if there could be some assurance of renewed intimacy with a God who had turned about face could "hope" be entertained. But, of course, there is no such assurance, and its likelihood is as great as that of a corpse coming back from the dead!

Fohrer argues strongly that the protection from God's wrath that Job seeks must be in this life, and the "release" he awaits is release from his sufferings while he still lives. The "dying" can only be metaphorical, for it is unnecessary for those in Sheol to be hidden from God's wrath, since they are beyond the touch of it there. However, this seems a mistaken interpretation, since Job is too hopeless to seek anything like release from his present sufferings; it is only in the framework of an impossible vision that he can allow himself to speak his real desires. And it is not a question of "hiding" those already dead since the dying and remaining dead would for Job constitute the act of hiding which he would so welcome.

15 This thought, however impossible of realization, of a life beyond death is not due to Egyptian influence or philosophical speculations about theodicy, but may more properly be accounted for as "directly inspired by a spiritual perception of the love of God. . . . [Job's] fleeting vision is not of immortality; it is the fruit of a specifically religious questing. . . . Once again, the sufferer

rises from the level of meditation to that of the dialogue of love" (Terrien).
What would be truly worth desiring—were it to be even remotely possible—
would be a renewed communion with God, in which there would be a reciprocal
"calling" and "answering." The legal language of calling (summoning) and
answering (9:15–16; 13:22a) has been entirely dispensed with, and the language
is wholly that of personal relationship, indeed of *the* relationship that Job had
enjoyed with God as "a man who would call upon God and be answered"
(12:4, *q.v.*; cf. also 19:16; 30:20). Since it is God who has broken off the relationship, it will need his initiative for it to be resumed; hence in this text it is
God who would call and Job who would answer.

In such a renewed relationship, the God who had hidden Job from his
wrath (v 13b) would remember him and seek him out after that wrath had
abated (cf. Esth 2:1; and from the tale of Ahiqar: "until afterwards Esarhaddon
the king remembers Ahiqar and desires his counsel and grieves over him"
[A. E. Cowley, *Aramaic Papyri of the Fifth Century B.C.* (Oxford: Clarendon
Press, 1923) 222 (line 64; cf. 53)]). Despite the lexica, there is no reason to
connect כסף "desire, long" (also Ps 17:12; 84:3 [2]; Gen 31:30) with any Semitic
root "be pale" (as the color of silver [כסף], according to Pope). The phrase
"work of your hands" (מעשה כפיך) alludes to the similar phrase in 10:3 (יגיע
כפיך) and the elaboration of it in 10:8–12; it expresses God's protective concern
as creator and sustainer of life.

All this wishfulness is founded upon an unreality; humans do not rise from
the dead, nor will God seek out the work of his hands. At 7:21 Job had imagined
the possibility of God "seeking" (שחר) him after his death, and, of course,
being unable to find him because "I shall be no more." That is still Job's
belief, and any concern God may feel for him after Job is dead will be wholly
futile.

16–17 These verses have often been taken as referring to the present
situation (so Dillmann, Delitzsch, Duhm, Beer, Driver-Gray, Fohrer; RV, NEB,
JPS), the most ready understanding of the initial כי־עתה "for now" being in
reference to the present. "You do not keep watch over my iniquities" (v 16b)
is a problem on this view, since that is precisely Job's complaint (10:14 where
also שמר "keep watch" is linked with חטא "sin"; cf. also 7:20; 13:26). So it
has had to be emended to תעבר "pass over" (with the doubtful support of
LXX; similarly Duhm, Beer), or else the clause has to be read as a question
(Fohrer), without an interrogative particle.

It is far better to see vv 16–17 as continuing the "dream" of vv 13–15 (so
Merx, Budde, Horst, Pope, Gordis, RSV, NAB, NIV). The present speech of Job
would then conclude with two extended strophes, of five lines each (vv 13–
17, 18–22) separated by the strongly contrastive particle ואולם "but now" (v
18). It is most improbable that only v 16a refers to the present (as Dhorme,
Terrien, JB).

For God to count someone's steps signifies the closest possible scrutiny of
that person's behavior (cf. 31:4, 37; 34:21), the kind of attention that Job
now suffers and would think himself well rid of (7:17–19; 10:6, 14; and especially
13:27 "you watch all my paths"). But in this dream of renewed friendship
with God Job professes himself ready to accept such scrutiny since the spy-
God would *ex hypothesi* be favorably disposed to him and would not be primarily
looking for faults in Job. The psalmist found God's scrutiny a mark of God's

esteem for humankind (Ps 8:4); so too could Job, provided that there were no negative consequences. The numbering of one's steps is, as Fohrer observes, never a mark of God's mercy, but the point here is that if the absence of God's wrath could be envisaged, every kind of danger from the side of the divine could be viewed with equanimity.

Any transgression Job might have committed (he is not admitting to anything! [against Terrien]) would in the circumstances be safely locked away and not used in evidence against him. Elsewhere the sins of the enemies of Israel are said to be "sealed up" (חתם, as here) in God's storehouses against a day of recompense (Deut 32:34–35), and the iniquity of Ephraim is "bagged" (צרר, cf. צרור "bag" here) and his sin "hidden" or "treasured up" (צפן) for future punishment (Hos 13:12). Here the meaning is quite other: any sins that Job may have committed are "sealed up" so that they may never be visible. The image is not just of objects like coins put in a bag which is then tied about the neck (cf. the צרור of money in Prov 7:20; Hag 1:6; Gen 43:35 [thus Fohrer, Horst]), but of a "bag" or "bundle" that is "sealed" (חתם). That term usually signifies a seal on a written document (cf. 1 Kgs 21:8; Isa 8:16; 29:11; Jer 32:10, 11, 14, 44; Esth 3:12; 8:8, 10; Dan 12:4, 9; Neh 10:1, 2 [9:38; 10:1]), so it is best to envisage here (papyrus) documents detailing Job's sins, which are folded and tied (צרור would refer to the tie, sometimes in the form of a napkin ring) and then sealed up with wax over the tie. Tur-Sinai reproduces an illustration from E. G. Kraeling's *The Brooklyn Museum Aramaic Papyri* (New Haven, 1953), pl. 21, showing such a document. It is much less likely that the sins are envisaged as pebbles in a bag, a device that does seem to have been used as a form of accounting; Pope has a lengthy treatment of the evidence for such (see A. L. Oppenheim, "On an Operational Device in Mesopotamian Bureaucracy," *JNES* 18 [1959] 121–28), but it does not fit the present picture because no *sealing* is involved. It does indeed seem to lie behind the image of the "bundle of the living" (1 Sam 25:29) which is envisaged as a collection of (tally) stones (cf. O. Eissfeldt, "Der Beutel der Lebendig: Alttestamentliche Erzählungs- und Dichtungsmotive im Lichte neuere Nuzi-Texte," *Berichte über die Verhandlungen der Sächsischen Akademie der Wissenschaften zu Leipzig*, Phil.-hist. Klasse, Band 105, Heft 6 [Berlin: Akademie-Verlag, 1960]).

The term "cover over," literally "plaster over" (תפל), has already occurred in 13:4, perhaps as a metaphor of concealing the truth. Here it certainly has to do with concealment (as did the "sealing" of the documents), but truth is less the issue than survival and the friendship of God. To be fair to Job, he doesn't believe he has committed any wrong, so the "cover-up" he would entertain would be no affront to truth; it would only serve to divert God's attention, which at the moment seems fixated on the question of Job's guilt. Tur-Sinai thinks תפל should mean "daub" with soft warm wax, allowing the seal to be imprinted; but we do not know for sure that the verb can have such a meaning; and there is no reason why a different metaphor should not be used in v 17b from that in the first half of the line.

As things are, of course, God counts Job's steps in order to find him out in some sin, and stores up his presumed iniquities in order to make him suffer for them.

18–19 A different music is heard in these verses. In the world of reality as distinct from the dream-world of vv 13–17 (the contrastive particle ואולם

marks the break) there is *no hope* for humans (v 19c). We are taken back in thought to v 7, where the life of nature could be seen as open to renewal, and to v 13, where for a few moments Job tantalized himself with the thought of what could be hoped for if human life were like a tree's.

What is the function of the four pictures from the world of nature? Dhorme thinks that they portray "phenomena which could not take place before an indefinite lapse of time, in order by this means to symbolize poetically the fate of man after death" (similarly Horst). Hahn finds here a contrast between the vast changes that are possible in the natural world and the impossibility of change in human destiny. Duhm thinks of a simple comparison between the destruction of mountains, stones, and earth and that of humankind. Habel takes the images to signify that the reality of the universe, however solid it may appear, is toward decay rather than new life, more like a crumbling mountain than a tree. But is it not human *hope* rather than human *fate* that they symbolize?

It must first be asserted that these verses make no statement about physical reality, but rather about human hope. If they were a statement about the world order, they would conflict with v 7. Secondly, what is in view in the fourfold image is the *gradual* destruction of what appears immovable, with the implication that no matter how firm anything is, it cannot resist persistent wearing down. That is how it is also with human hope. Even if humankind should hope against all hope for a life beyond the grave, even if their hope should tower to mountain size, be rock hard and stable as the earth itself, God erodes that hope by the simple actuality that leaves them a long time dead. Any hope they may have of a tree-like renewal is worn down by the never-changing reality of human death.

Mountains do not "fall" down, not even gradually (contrast RV, RSV); the picture must be of the weathering away of the mountainside. Mountains of course are symbols of the immovable and unshakable (though cf. 9:5; Ps 46:3 [2]), but even they can over time be worn down. The "rock" that falls is probably the outcrop of rock on a cliff that is dislodged ultimately by the elements. The image of water wearing away stone is not met with elsewhere in the Bible (on Prov 19:13 cf. 27:15), but cf. Lucretius 5.306–307, 313–15 ("Do we not see lumps of rock roll down, torn from lofty mountains, too weak to bear and endure the mighty force of time finite?"). The last image in v 19b is apparently of soil being gradually eroded from fields, or possibly from the banks of rivers.

20 Death is depicted now as God's victory over human hope for life. Death, that is to say, is not a mere natural process that could perhaps in principle be stalled or cheated; it is direct divine activity that causes a person's death, and God's attributes of masterfulness and destructiveness (cf. 12:13–24) are what bring death about. Dealing death is no more than the last item in the history of God's hostile dealings with a human being from the moment of conception (cf. 10:8–14); in the end God inevitably "prevails" (תקף; cf. 15:24) against the human, who then has no choice but to "go" (הלך)—one of the many euphemisms for death (cf. 19:10; Ps 39:14 [13]; perhaps Gen 15:2). It is God also who disfigures human beauty with the ravages of old age and death itself (משנה פניו, lit., "[you] change his face," i.e. for the worse; שנה piel in such a sense in Prov 31:5; cf. Ecclus 13:25); Gordis, following ibn

Ezra, thinks the reference is specifically to *rigor mortis,* but the language is
not so precise. The final phase in life is not death itself, but what death signifies
of the expulsion of the person from the land of the living; God's last assault
on the human creature is "banishment" (שלח pi, lit., "send away"). The language
of "going" and "sending" is of the simplest; the reality is the unequivocal
destruction of hope and the permanent impossibility of renewed communion
between the human individual and God once God has invoked his fatal power.
There is no wistfulness in Job's language here; Job has no intention of going
"gentle into that good night"; to the last he will be "rage against the dying of
the light" (Dylan Thomas).

21 "Dismissed to Sheol, the dead no longer have knowledge of what would,
if they were alive on earth, most intimately concern them" (Gray). Job feels
for humankind, and not solely for himself. For he himself knows what has
become of his children, and will not die with uncertainty on that score. But
for humans in general, death is a deprivation of contact with those who are
dear to them, a withholding of knowledge of whether it goes well with them
or ill; "the dead know nothing" (Eccl 9:5), "there is no knowledge in Sheol"
(9:10). What is lost is knowledge of whether one's descendants become great
persons (כבד "be honoured") or insignificant (צער) rather than whether they
are many or few (cf. Jer 30:19) (against F. Perles, "A Miscellany of Lexical
and Textual Notes on the Bible," *JQR* 2 [1911–12] 97–132 [118]).

22 Even if it were possible for those "overpowered" (v 20a) by God to
know of the fate of their family, such persons would not have the will or the
capacity to care about them, so preoccupied would they be with their own
suffering. It is unparalleled in the OT to attribute feelings to the dead (18:13
and Isa 66:24, referred to by Pope, concern only the bodies of the dead),
and Fohrer suggests that "pain" and "grief" should not be taken too literally
as actual feelings but (presumably) as a kind of anthropopathism for the experience of the dead. We could also suggest that any sharp distinction between
"death" and "life" is not always appropriate for the OT; for a person in the
grip of death, "overpowered" by the divine "murderer" but not yet actually
dead, is more in the realm of death than life, but is still capable of experiencing
pain. That makes it easier to attribute such feelings to the physically dead.
What we do not have here is the expression of a belief about the nature of
existence in Sheol (against Peake, Rowley, and others).

Not too much emphasis should be put on the terms "flesh" (בשר) and
"life, vitality, soul" (נפש, "self"). The terms *can* be contrasted (Gen 9:4), but
they both can well signify the whole person (cf. 12:10; Ps 63:2 [1]; 84:3 [2]).
It is the person as a unity that experiences pain and grief, though perhaps
"flesh" is more appropriate for pain and "soul, spirit" for grief.

More subtle exegeses are unconvincing. Dillmann saw here the suffering
of soul and body as they are separated from one another at the moment of
death. Tur-Sinai thought "only with his soul upon him (עליו)" must mean
"only while he is still alive"; but the "upon" (על) is the "pathetic" על, emphasizing
the person who is the subject of the emotion and who feels it acting *upon* the
self (BDB, 753b; cf. also 10:1).

The speech concludes, as Job's last two speeches have, on the note of death
and the underworld. Whatever vigor they have displayed has weakened itself
in the expressing, and in each case Job resiles to his emotional nadir. Left to

himself he loses all energy; the friends, for all their faults, goad him by their errors into vital anger and disputatiousness and keep alive in him the sense of divine cruelty under which he labors.

Explanation

Something quite new and dramatic has happened in this speech. Standing as it does at the junction between the first and second cycles of speeches it signals a climax in the progress of Job's emotions and lays down a marker for the future development of the plot of the work as a whole.

The dramatic development in this speech is that after all his desire to be put out of his misery as soon as possible (6:8–9), after his acknowledgment of the danger—not to say to the impossibility—of calling God to account (9:3, 14, 16), after his conviction that if he goes to law with God he is bound to be found guilty (9:29), after his demand for an assurance of safe conduct if he is to approach God (9:34–35), here he does the unthinkable and acts as he had not imagined himself acting. Here, at the center of the speech, he unequivocally calls on God to provide the evidence on which God would justify his severity toward him. It matters not which of them is to be plaintiff, and which defendant (13:22); what Job seeks is a formal judicial process, in which an obligation is laid upon God to supply a catalogue of Job's supposed crimes (13:23). This is an utterance which, once made, cannot be unsaid; Job is now committed to confrontation with God, whatever the risks.

What outcome to this legal battle does Job expect? He has no illusions, and no hope; of one thing he is confident, that his temerity will issue in his death (13:15). But he has not gone to court to plead for his life or to beg for mercy, but to clear his name. He has no faith in the goodness of God, and not a lot in his justice; but he believes so strongly in the rightness of his own cause that he cannot doubt that in the end, whether before or after his death, he will be vindicated (13:18). He seeks the triumph, certainly not of God, and not even of himself, but of truth.

All this talk of lawsuits and summonses is metaphor, of course. But that does not make it decorative language gilding some plainer truth. The language of the metaphor is the language of feeling; the terminology of plaintiff and defendant, cases, crimes, deposition, affidavit and subpoena signals what it feels like to be involved in dispute with God. Job has a lifetime behind him of godfearingness (1:1), of calling upon God in reverent prayer and being answered (12:4), of harmonious relation with the divine. In a moment, that harmony has been shattered, and he has had to learn a new and more abrasive language to embody the discord in his universe. Now it must be the language of compulsion and division, of contest and defeat. The grimmest irony of all is that the quintessential phraseology for the old harmony, the calling and the answering, turns out to be the technical terminology for the power struggle of the lawsuit ("call, and I will answer," 13:22); what he had known as the language of personal reciprocity has been denatured into a language for isolation and conflict, plaintiff against defendant and defendant against plaintiff.

This is the heart of Job's fourth speech; and by itself this movement in the drama would be rich enough. But there are two further elements enlarging the scope of its significance.

The first concerns the friends. Now that they each have spoken, it is time that Job tell them, and us, what he has made of their words. Hitherto, we have learned from him that he thinks little of their loyalty (6:14, 20), and that he feels disregarded by them (6:26); we have seen him agreeing, on one point at least, with them (9:2). But on the whole he has ignored them; while they have addressed him throughout, he has tended either to soliloquize or to address himself to God. Here, on the contrary, he addresses them directly in 12:2–3 and 13:1–12, and parodies their speeches to him in 12:7–12. His tone is assertive, sarcastic, disputatious. He does not here speak of his feelings about them (as in 6:14, 20), but contrasts himself with them on the intellectual plane. When he says his wisdom is not inferior to theirs (12:2; 13:2), he means that his is superior; he has abandoned the idea of them as friends and he is treating them as conversation partners, colleagues at a theological seminar. It is a token of his greater psychic stability, now that he has made his decision about confronting God, that he speaks of looking to them not for solidarity but for explanation, and can even esteem himself their superior for his greater experience of reality. In the end, he can even become patronizing toward them, proffering them good advice (13:9) and laboring the point that now a legal process is in motion between himself and God their status has changed. No longer can they delude themselves that they speak for heaven against Job; now that they have become nothing but witnesses, partisans for neither party in the dispute, they can testify only to the facts, not to theological theories. But of course they have scant acquaintance with facts, having always believed that wisdom is inherited from one's elders (12:12) rather than fashioned in the crucible of experience; so on pain of having their stupidity exposed, or worse, of falling foul of the deity for unbecoming partisanship, their best course of action is to fall silent (13:5, 13).

The friends are characters in the drama of the book, and it is instructive, not to say entertaining, to see how their role develops—not through any changes internal to themselves, but in step with the forward march of Job's psychological and religious progress. But there is more: they are also Job's alter ego, representations of what Job would be without his calamity. In struggling with them, Job is struggling with the Job of yesteryear; and in affirming his superior intelligence to theirs, Job is committing himself all the more irrevocably to his new religious orientation.

The further weighty element in this speech is to be found in Job's elegy on the human condition in chap. 14. This is not the first time that he has made of his own unhappy state a paradigm for the lot of humanity at large (cf. also 3:20–23; 7:1–2, 17–18), but this is his most extended meditation on the significance of his own experience for what may be said about human life as such. Only in vv 13–17, in the center of this chapter, does he focus on himself; at beginning and end his thought is for "man born of woman" (14:1). There is nothing new, and nothing unconventional, in his assumption that there can be no life beyond death, that there is more hope for a tree than for a human being (14:7). All the wistful lines about death perhaps being a kind of refuge in which a human could be protected from the divine wrath and from which one could, after an appointed time, arise, into a life of renewed communion with God, a restored intimacy of a calling and answering (14:15), are nothing but an impossible dream, and Job knows it. Human experience goes only to show that, time upon time, "thou destroyest the hope of man" (14:19). What Job, or even the poet, does not acknowledge is that impossible dreams have a surprising habit of coming true; and that even if they never do come true, they can create shape and structure for their dreamers. What this impossible dream will do for Job is impel him into taking action here and now against a wrathful God; would he have been better off if he had believed his dream were possible?

Eliphaz's Second Speech   (15:1–35)

Bibliography

Dahood, M. "Northwest Semitic Philology and Job." In *The Bible in Current Catholic Thought*, M. J. Gruenthaner Memorial Volume, ed. J. L. McKenzie. New York: Herder and Herder, 1962. 55–74. ———. "The Value of Ugaritic for Textual Criticism." *Bib* 40 (1959) 160–70. ———. "Hebrew-Ugaritic Lexicography I." *Bib* 44 (1963) 289–303. ———. "Hebrew-Ugaritic Lexicography VII." *Bib* 50 (1969) 337–56. **Driver, G. R.** "Misreadings in the Old Testament." *WO* 1 (1947–52) 234–38. ———. "Problems in the Hebrew Text of Job." VTSup 3 (1955) 72–93. **Heater, H.** *A Septuagint Translation Technique in the Book of Job.* CBQMS 11. Washington, D.C.: Catholic Biblical Association, 1982. **Hoffmann, G.** "Ergänzungen und Berichtigungen zu Hiob." *ZAW* 49 (1931) 141–45. **Köhler, L.** "Miscellen. 6. Die Septuagintavorlage von Hi 15:28." *ZAW* 31 (1911) 155–56. **Lipiński, E.** "Notes lexicographiques et stylistiques sur le livre de Job." *FolOr* 21 (1980) 65–82. **Reider, J.** "Etymological Studies in Biblical Hebrew." *VT* 2 (1952) 113–30.

Translation

¹ *Then Eliphaz the Temanite answered and said:*

² *Would a wise man answer with violent notions,*
  would he fill[a] his belly with the east wind?
³ *Will he argue with useless[a] talk,*
  with words that are nothing worth?

⁴ *You do worse:[a] you abandon[b] proper reverence,*
  and slight[c] meditation before God!
⁵ *It is your sin that inspires your words,[a]*
  so that you adopt the language of the crafty.[b]
⁶ *It is your own mouth that condemns you, not I;*
  your own lips testify against you.

⁷ *Were you the first human ever born?*
  Or were you brought into the world before the hills?
⁸ *Are you a listener at God's secret council?*
  Are you the only one with wisdom?
⁹ *What do you know that we do not?*
  What understanding have you that we do not share?
¹⁰ *Among us is one who is gray-haired and aged,*
  older indeed than your father!

¹¹ *Are God's encouragements too little for you,*
  and speech that deals gently[a] with you?
¹² *Why let your thoughts carry you away,[a]*
  why let your eyes fail you,[b]
¹³ *that you turn your anger against God,*
  and pour out such words from your mouth?

¹⁴ *What is humankind, that it could be blameless,*
  one born of woman, that such a one could be innocent?

¹⁵*If God puts no trust in his holy ones,*^a
  and the heavens themselves are not clean in his eyes,
¹⁶*how much less can humanity be, that is loathsome and foul,*^a
  that drinks wrongdoing like water?

¹⁷*I will show you, if you will listen to me;*
  what I have seen, I will recount—
¹⁸*it is what the sages have reported,*
  what their fathers have divulged,^a
¹⁹*those to whom alone the land was given,*
  when no stranger passed among them.

²⁰*The wicked is in torment all his days,*
  the ruthless one through all the years^a *stored up for him.*
²¹*The sound of the Terrors is in his ears,*
  in the midst of peace he imagines the Destroyer's attack.
²²*He cannot hope to escape*^a *the darkness;*
  he is marked down^b *for the sword.*

²³*He is cast out as food for vultures;*^a
  he knows that his ruin^b *is certain.*^c
²⁴*The day of darkness terrifies him,*^a
  distress and anguish overwhelm him,
  ^b*like a king*^c *poised to attack.*^d
²⁵*For he has raised his arm against God,*
  and has played the hero against the Almighty,
²⁶*defiantly*^a *running against him*
  behind his stout bossed shield.^b

²⁷*Though his face is covered with fat,*
  and his loins are gross^a *with blubber,*
²⁸*he will dwell in ruined towns,*
  in houses that are deserted,
  destined to be heaps of rubble.
²⁹*He will have no riches, and his wealth will not endure,*
  his possessions^a *will not spread over the land.*^b

³⁰*[He will not escape from the darkness;]*^a
  a flame will wither his shoots,
  and his blossom will be swept away by the wind.^b
³¹*Let him not trust in his height,*^a *deceiving himself,*
  for his branch^b *will be as nothing.*
³²*It will wither*^a *before its time,*
  and his branches will not be green.

³³*He will be like a vine dropping its grapes while still unripe,*
  like an olive tree shedding its blossom.
³⁴*For the band of the godless is unfruitful*
  and fire consumes the tents of bribery.

³⁵ *They conceive mischief and breed disaster;*
   their womb has produced deceit.

Notes

2.a. Andersen suggests that מלא is used privatively, i.e., "empties the east wind from his belly." Eliphaz's language has turned coarse, in that case!

3.a. E. Lipiński ("Notes lexicographiques et stylistiques sur le livre de Job," *FolOr* 21 [1980] 65–82 [73–74]) argues that סכן here is סכן II "incur danger" as in Eccl 10:9 and postbib. Heb., and translates "does not run risks with a word." But the parallelism is against this.

4.a. אף emphatic, "indeed."

4.b. פרר; "break, frustrate" is a satisfactory rendering. But G. R. Driver finds a different root פרר "expel, banish" (VTSup 3 [1955] 77), with cognates in Arab. and Syr.; hence NEB "you banish the fear of God from your mind."

4.c. Lit., "diminish" (גרע), i.e., esteem as insignificant.

5.a. The Heb. could mean "your mouth teaches your iniquity," but אלף pi can hardly mean "reveal, evince," which is what "teach" would signify. Dahood (*Bib* 44 [1963] 294), Blommerde, and Andersen translate, "your mouth increases your iniquity," comparing אלף hi "increase a thousandfold" (Ps 144:13).

5.b. To achieve parallelism with v 5a, Blommerde and Andersen translate "your tongue chooses deceptions," but this involves revocalizing לְשׁוֹן, supposing a double-duty suffix on פִּיךָ, and taking ערומים as an abstract noun—none of which is impossible, but collectively it is very improbable. ערומים is taken as an abstract also by Sicre Diaz.

11.a. לאט "with gentleness"; not connected with the verb לאט "be secret," as KJV "is there any secret thing with thee?"

12.a. יקחך "takes you away." Tur-Sinai, Pope and Blommerde attractively suggest that the suffix is datival, hence "What has taken from you your mind?" (לב = "reason," not "passion," JB); the phrase also in Hos 4:11, and cf. also לבב in Cant 4:9. The objections are that מה is unlikely to mean "what?" in the first colon and "why?" in the second, and that parallelism would suggest that "your heart" and "your eyes" are both subjects (cf. I. Eitan, *A Contribution to Biblical Lexicography* [New York: Columbia UP, 1924] 21). G. R. Driver unconvincingly proposed a root יקח cognate with Arab. *waqiḥa* "be bold" (read יִקַּח) (*WO* 1 [1947–52] 235), comparing G ἐτόλμησεν "dared"; hence NEB "what makes you so bold at heart?" See also J. Barr, *Comparative Philology and the Text of the Old Testament* (Oxford: Clarendon Press, 1968) 17–19.

12.b. רזם only here, and with no evident cognates. With metathesis to רמז it becomes the postbib. Heb. "hint," cognate with Arab. *ramaza*, Aram. רמז "make a sign," hence perhaps "wink, flash" (cf. Grabbe, 66–67). Less probable is the feeble emendation to יְרוּמוּן "are high, haughty" (cf. Prov 6:17; 30:13) (Reiske, Budde; cf. *BHK*)—which LXX indeed reads. Tur-Sinai's explanation on the basis of Arab. *razama* "dwindle away, become weak" (followed by Pope), perhaps best suits the context; cf. NJPS "how have your eyes failed you, that you could vent your anger. . . ."

15.a. Reading בְּקֹדֶשׁ as בִּקְדֹשָׁיו.

16.a. אלח, according to G. R. Driver, means "debauched with luxury, corrupt" ("Some Hebrew Words," *JTS* 29 [1927–28] 390–96).

18.a. Reading כַּחֲדֻם אֲבוֹתָם, the *mem* of the verb being an emphatic enclitic (Pope, Blommerde, Gordis). Perhaps the *mem* could be the suffix equivalent to "from them" (the sages), כחד being exceptionally construed with direct object rather than מן (cf. GKC, § 117x); Ehrlich compared מנע in 31:16. Probably this is how RSV read it. Others read כחדו מֵהֶם אֲבוֹתָם (Bickell, Szczygiel, Horst), which is certainly sound grammatically, or simply omit the troublesome *mem* (Duhm). The MT is not impossible: "from their fathers" could be construed with "they have reported" (יגידו) and mean "according to the tradition of their fathers" (Dhorme; cf. NIV, and Sicre Diaz) or "since the days of their fathers" (NAB); but this is very awkward.

20.a. מספר שנים, lit., "the number of years," must be "all the years [that are laid up]" (RSV; cf. NEB); "limited years" (NAB; cf. JB, NJPS) would be שְׁנֵי מספר (cf. 16:22; Num 9:20) (so Driver-Gray, Dhorme). אֲשֶׁר is to be understood before נצפנו, pl because of the collective idea in מספר.

22.a. For לא יאמין שׁוב Duhm read לא, the same phrase as begins v 30. He is followed by Peake and half-heartedly by Gray. De Wilde has a complex reconstruction.

22.b. צָפוּ "spied out" (K) is perhaps just another (older?) form of the qal pass ptcp צָפוּי (Q); so Gordis. There is no call to emend to צָפוּן "treasured up," as Ewald, *BHK*, Fohrer, Hesse, de Wilde, or to צוֹפֶה "he looks out for" (Ball, Rowley; NAB "he looks ever for the sword").

23.a. The colon, though translatable, makes very awkward sense: "He wanders about for bread,

Where [is it]?" Most commentators and versions follow the lead of LXX, who saw in אֵיה not אַיֵּה, "where?," but אַיָּה, "black kite, vulture" (so Michaelis, Merx, Duhm; NEB, JB, NAB, NIV). This leads to revocalization of לְלֶחֶם, "for bread," to לְלֶחֶם, "for bread of" (LXX εἰς σῖτα γυψίν). The verb נֹדֵד, "wandering" is retained by NAB, NIV, Fohrer, Pope, but the revocalization of NEB to נֻדָּד (hoph), "is flung out," is to be preferred, since it conveys better the wicked man's dramatic anxiety. Dhorme equally well vocalized נֻדָּד, "thrown out," niph ptcp of ידד, "throw" (cf. ידה "throw"). Emendations to נֻתַּן "is given" (Siegfried) or מוּעָד, "is appointed" (Beer; cf. perhaps LXX κατατέτακται) are uncalled for. נַעַד "is destined" (JB, following Duhm, Hölscher) is improbable, since יעד in niph is always reflexive, never passive.

23.b. Emending בְּיָדוֹ "in his hand" to פִּידוֹ "his ruin" (cf. 12:5) (Wright, Peake, Dhorme, Horst, Fohrer, Pope, Rowley, de Wilde). בְּיָדוֹ is unlikely to be the phonetic spelling of בַּעֲדוֹ, "for him" (Gordis). Emendations of נָכוֹן "ready" to גֶבֶר "disaster" (Duhm), and of בְּיָדוֹ to לְאֵיד "for calamity" (Beer) are now of historical interest only.

23.c. The last two words of the colon, יוֹם־חֹשֶׁךְ, are transferred to the beginning of v 24, since they make v 23b too long (so also JB, NEB, NAB, following LXX [ἡμέρα δὲ αὐτὸν σκοτεινὴ στροβήσει]; thus too Duhm, Fohrer, Terrien, Rowley, Pope, Sicre Diaz, de Wilde). Horst deletes the two words as a gloss on פִּידוֹ.

24.a. Reading pl יְבַעֲתָהוּ as a sg יְבַעֲתֻהוּ "terrifies him" (so BHK, NEB, NAB, as also LXX).

24.b. Deleted by Duhm as a gloss on v 26 (so also Fohrer); NAB transposes to follow v 26, NEB puts the line in square brackets.

24.c. The emendation of כמלך "like a king" to כְּמֹהֲלָךְ, "like a soldier [or perhaps, highwayman] marching on" (G. Hoffmann, "Ergänzungen und Berichtigungen zu Hiob," *ZAW* 49 [1931] 144) is not to be accepted; but the image of a "king" is a little strange.

24.d. כִּידוֹר, only here; perhaps to be connected with Syr. *kudrā* "bird of prey" (KB[3]), or with Arab. *kadara* VII "rush down" (of a hawk but also rain); from the same Arab. root J. Reider, *VT* 2 (1952) 127, suggests "perturbation." "Siege" (NJPS) makes the phrase apply to the wicked man, not to his anxieties.

26.a. Lit., "with a neck," RSV "stubbornly," NJPS, NIV "defiantly," JB "blindly," NEB "head down," NAB "sternly." The translation is not secure; the well-known phrase "with a stiff neck" is quite different, referring rather to unteachableness and disobedience. Nearest in sense is Ps 75:6 [5], "do not speak with arrogant neck" (צַוָּאר עָתָק), parallel to "do not boast," "do not lift up your horn on high." Tur-Sinai's instinct is sound, to see here an item of military equipment parallel to גַבֵּי מָגִנָּיו "the bosses of his shields." But it is more than doubtful whether his solution of "hauberk" is correct; in medieval armor it was a protective covering for the neck which soon developed into the chain-link coat of mail. We do not have any ancient evidence of such a term for such a piece of armor. Pope, however, follows him, and so too Andersen, "charging against him in full armour, neck-mail and thickly-bossed shield." Emendations to כְּעָרִיץ "like a violent man" (cf. Beer, BHK), כְּגִבּוֹר "like a warrior" (Graetz), "like an enemy" (Ehrlich), are otiose.

26.b. Lit., "with the thickness of the bosses of his shields," but of course he has only one shield.

27.a. According to D. Winton Thomas, "Translating Heb. ʿāsāh," *BiTrans* 17 (1966) 190–93, this is the sense "cover" (as Arab. ġašā) of עשה.

29.a. מֶנְלָם is a *hapax*, now most commonly taken as cognate with Arab. *manāl* "possession, acquisition" (so Saadia, Zorell, KB[3], Pope, Gordis, Dahood, "Northwest Semitic Philology," 60–61, NIV), and vocalized מֶנְלָם, the pl suff referring to the group of the wicked (like מבניו in v 26), or, less probably, being an enclitic *mem* (Pope, Blommerde). Other, less plausible, solutions are: (i) read צַלְמוֹ or צִלּוֹ "his shadow" or צֶלֶם "their shadow" (following LXX σκιάν) (JB, NAB, Houtsma, Dhorme, Terrien); (ii) read שִׁבֳּלָם (= שִׁבֳּלִים) "ears of grain" (Dillmann, Driver-Gray); (iii) read מְלָם, also "ears of grain" (*hapax* at Deut 23:26 [25]) (Hitzig); (iv) read אָצְלִים "[their] roots" (Wellhausen, following Vg *radicem suam*; hence RSV, NEB "strike no root in the earth"); (v) read חֲבָלִים "measuring-line" (de Wilde).

29.b. Dahood, "Northwest Semitic Philology," 60–61, translates "his possessions will not go down to the netherworld," נטה being well attested as "decline" as well as "spread out" (BDB, 640a), and ארץ being "underworld" (Dahood, *Bib* 40 [1959] 164–66; *Psalms I*, 106; this meaning is recognized for a few passages also by KB[3], 88a). This translation has the immediate advantage of giving sense to v 30a (on which see *Comment*), by making it refer to the darkness of Sheol. Dahood compared Ps 49:18 [17], where the wealth of the rich does not descend to Sheol with them; but this is not at all the point here, where it is the continuance of the wicked's wealth on earth that is at issue. Cf. also Grabbe, 67–69.

30.a. The colon is omitted by NEB, NAB, Pope (perhaps), Driver-Gray, Dhorme, Fohrer, Horst. See *Comment*.

30.b. A difficult clause, lit., "and he shall turn away by the breath of his mouth" (cf. KJV, RV), i.e. presumably God's mouth, though God has not been referred to since v 26, and then in a quite different connection. ויסור is very feeble, so it is usually emended to a form of the verb סער "drive away (like a storm)," ויסער (poel) "and will drive away" (cf. NIV, JB) or וְיִסָּעֵר (niph) "and will be driven away" (Beer, Budde, Driver-Gray) or ויסער (poal) "and will be driven away" (KB³, de Wilde, Duhm, Dhorme, Fohrer, Horst; cf. NEB). Beer (*BHK*) read וְיִשּׁוֹר from the postbiblical root נשר "fall" (cf. LXX ἐκπέσοι); LXX may, however, have read the MT exactly, but may have harmonized it with the image of v 33 (see H. Heater, *A Septuagint Translation Technique in the Book of Job* [CBQMS 11; Washington, D.C.: Catholic Biblical Association, 1982] 61–62). MT is retained by NAB "will disappear," NJPS "will pass away" and ברוח־פיו is kept by NJPS, NIV, Gordis, Pope. Gordis proposes that יָסוּר is a noun, "branch" (i.e. the part that "separates" itself from the trunk), but תיבש would have to be revocalized to תִּיבָשׁ and *beth* prefixed to שלהבת to achieve his translation.

פיו "his mouth" is best emended to חֹ פֶּרַח "his blossom" (Driver-Gray, Dhorme, Fohrer, Horst, Sicre Diaz, de Wilde, RSV, JB, NEB, NAB, GNB, following LXX ἄνθος which translates פֶּרַח at Isa 5:24; 18:5). Less attractive is the emendation to פֶּרְיוֹ "his fruit" (Duhm, Pope [1st ed.]). Dahood's thought (*Bib* 50 [1969] 343), to read רֶוַח "expanse" for רוח "breath," and translate "nor will he escape from its massive mouth," i.e., the mouth of the underworld, assumes sympathy with his view that "Darkness" and "Flame" are terms for the underworld (cf. *Comment* on 18:13), and also takes for granted that the initial לֹא of the verse serves also as the negative for this colon (though it has not been for the second).

31.a. בשו is emended by Dhorme to בְשִׂיאוֹ "in his stature, loftiness" (שִׂיא at 20:6, of the wicked); he is followed by Terrien, JB, NEB "his high rank." This would create the dissimilarity between שו and שוא that the verse seems to demand. Others suggest בְעָשְׁירֻתוֹ "in his riches" (Beer) or בְשׂוֹא נִטְעוֹ "in the bearing (fruit) of his plant" (שׂוֹא a rare inf of נשא) (Beer, *BHK;* de Wilde).

31.b. תרומתו "his exchange, recompense" (the act or the thing acquired as recompense) seems a commercial metaphor (not to be buttressed by ימלא in v 32), out of place in the depiction of the wicked as a plant. Some suggest תְּרוּמָתוֹ "his yield, profit, produce" (cf. *BHK,* de Wilde), though תרומה generally has a cultic connection and is not a general word for "produce." More popular is the reading תִּמוֹרָתוֹ or תְּמָרָתוֹ "his palm-tree" (Beer, Budde, Driver-Gray, Tur-Sinai, Pope, NEB); but since the wicked man *is* a plant, he cannot "have" a palm-tree, neither does it make sense, for the same reason, to transfer "his palm-tree" to the beginning of the next verse (as Driver-Gray, Rowley, Pope, NEB). Far superior is Dhorme's emendation to זְמוֹרָתוֹ "his branch" (so JB "his boughs," NAB "his stalk"). NAB cuts several knots by omitting the first colon and transposing the second to follow v 29a.

32.a. A rather certain emendation of תִּמָּלֵא "it will be paid in full" (RSV, NIV), a commercial metaphor out of place here, to תִּמַּל "it will wither" (so LXX φθαρήσεται, Dhorme, Fohrer, Horst, Rowley, Pope, NEB, NAB, JB, GNB). Gordis argues for the MT word as a metaplastic form of מלל. The subject may be זְמוּרתו, the last word of the previous line.

Form / Structure / Setting

The *structure* of the speech is self-evidently twofold. In the first part Job is directly addressed (vv 2–16); in the second (vv 17–35) there is a description of the wicked man and his fate, which is indeed for Job's instruction—the point being that Job is *not* such a man and therefore has good reason for confidence—though Job is not addressed except in the introductory sentence advising him to listen (v 17). These elements, of address and description, are common, in that order, to all the friends' speeches (except perhaps defective speeches in the third cycle); but in the first cycle there is a concluding address to Job (5:19–27; 8:20–22; 11:13–19), whereas in the second cycle each speech concludes with the description of the fate of the wicked. This structural novelty in the second cycle may be a mark of a greater severity of depiction of the friends' attitudes, but it must not be overlooked that the description of the wicked serves a different function in the mouth of each of the three friends: for Eliphaz, it is a picture of what Job is not; for Bildad (chap. 18) it is a picture of what Job may become; for Zophar (chap. 20) it is a picture of what Job must avoid. The *strophic structure* can be analyzed thus:

I	1	15: 2–3	2 lines
	2	4–6	3
	3	7–10	4
	4	11–13	3
	5	14–16	3
II	1	17–19	3
	2	20–22	3
	3	23–26	4
	4	27–29	3
	5	30–32	3
	6	33–35	3

The basic strophic pattern in the poem is thus the three-line strophe (vv 4–6, 11–13, 14–16, 27–29 are particularly clearly marked examples); this is extended twice to a four-line strophe (vv 7–10, where six rhetorical questions in three lines are followed by an affirmation as a pendant; and vv 23–26, where the fourth line extends the strophe by developing the matter of the third). The initial two-line strophe, vv 2–3, can perhaps be paralleled at the beginning of other speeches (8:2–3; 6:2–3; 4:2–3; 20:2–3), though it might be better to recognize initial five-line strophes both here and elsewhere.

The strophic structure presented here is similar to that discerned by Fohrer, though he makes 23–25 one strophe, and 29–32 another, eliminating v 31. This arrangement does not accord so well with the content, since v 26 more naturally belongs with v 25, and v 29 with v 28.

Skehan finds six strophes of five lines, together with one of three, and one of one line (vv 2–6, 7–11, 12–16, 17–19, 20–24, 25–29, 30–34, 35) (similarly NAB); but he transposes vv 29a and 31b to follow v 29b. Webster, on the other hand, agrees fundamentally with the present analysis, though he recognizes as strophes vv 2–6, 20–23, 24–26, 27–30, 31–35. Terrien also sees mostly five-line strophes, usually composed of a triplet followed by a couplet; thus vv 2–6, 7–11, 12–16, 17–21, 22–26, 27–30 (four lines), 31–35.

The elements of *forms* that appear in this poem are, exceptionally, derived mainly from one sphere: that of wisdom.

The *wisdom disputation speech* form is evident in the rhetorical questions about how a wise man should behave (vv 2–3, 12–13) which function as a reproach of Job's behavior (rhetorical questions serve such a function also in legal disputation). A second set of six rhetorical questions in vv 7–9 reproach Job for claiming superior wisdom to the friends'.

The *wisdom instruction* form appears in the rhetorical question of v 14, "What is man, that he can be clean?," which is in function not a reproach like the other questions, but a wisdom statement that invites the hearer's assent to the proposition it incorporates. Direct statements of an instructional kind are seen in vv 15–16 about the "corruption" of humanity (an argument *a maiore ad minus*), and above all in the description of the anxious life and ultimate fate of the wicked (vv 20–35). The function of this description is not to reproach Job (against Fohrer, who thinks it depicts Job's suffering as that of the godless), but to contrast Job's experience of recently begun and hopefully only temporary suffering with the continuous mental anguish of the wicked. Another element that belongs to the wisdom instruction is the teacher's announcement of personal experience (v 17; cf. 4:8; 5:3).

The *function* of the speech as a whole may be said to be encouragement. Eliphaz makes no criticism of Job's behavior prior to his suffering, and holds against him only what he has said in this dialogue (v 5; see the *Comment*). He does not condemn Job (v 6a), for he believes he is fundamentally innocent; Job's own words, however, put him in the wrong (v 6). Eliphaz views his own interpositions as "speech that deals gently" with Job, and sees himself as conveying "the encouragements of God" (v 11). The assertion that humankind cannot be morally pure in God's sight (vv 14–16) intends to be excusatory of Job: even the best of people are bound to sin at some time. Read in this light, the depiction of the wicked in vv 20–35 can only be essentially encouragement to Job, since the experience of the wicked is so alien to Job's own experience.

The *tonality* of the speech, in line with its function, is sympathetic but firm; Job has spoken unwisely (vv 2—3), self-importantly (vv 7–9), and aggressively (vv 12–13), and he has adopted a position that ill becomes his piety (vv 4–5). He has abandoned proper reverence before God (v 4). He ignores fundamental truths about human nature (vv 14–16) and needs clear correction. There is some sarcasm in the speech, in the questions whether Job has not mistaken himself for the First Man, possessor of superhuman wisdom (vv 7–8), but the very extravagance of the sarcasm blunts its edge, and it seems that Eliphaz is administering a douche of cold water to Job to bring him to his senses rather than essentially attacking Job or attempting to humiliate him.

The *nodal verse* may be designated v 20: "The wicked man writhes in pain all his days"—in which the crucial phrase is *all his days*; the thought is the obverse of 4:6, but it serves the same function of encouraging Job to have confidence in his innocence.

Comment

1–35   Is there any inherent reason in the dynamics of the book why a second and a third cycle of speeches should unfold? The friends have no new points to make, so their speeches are in themselves otiose. But Job, ever divergent and exploratory, has yet a lot of ground to cover, and the immovability of the friends' theologies is a necessary backdrop to his perpetual shifting of position and perspective. As far as the overt plot goes, however, it is somewhat unexpected that the dialogue should continue any further now that each friend has said his piece. Job has called on them in his previous speech to be quiet and to listen as witnesses to his disputation with God (13:13, 17), and it is perhaps to be regarded as a kind of interference on their part that they should continue addressing Job (from their perspective, of course, it must be seen as a necessity laid on them by Job's extravagant language). Hesse on the contrary thinks that Job asked for silence only so long as he needed for his own speech; that being concluded, Eliphaz must feel justified in opening his mouth again.

There is no question but that the friends adopt a harsher tone toward Job in the second cycle; but their basic attitudes and theological positions remain unchanged. It is indeed essential to recognize that it is the same Eliphaz speaking here as in chaps. 4–5, for outside that context this chap. 15 could seem to be far other than it really is. Fohrer, for example, maintains that in this chapter Eliphaz abandons his former attitude of kindliness toward Job, and, addressing no word of promise to him, now only threatens him with the dreadful narrative of the fate of the wicked; chap. 22, however, in which Eliphaz repeats his consolation of Job and holds out a happy future before him, shows that there has been no change of mind, or heart, in Eliphaz.

2   As always, Eliphaz begins with a question (cf. 4:1; 22:1; so also Bildad at 8:2; 18:2; and Zophar at 11:2). The question is usually, from a formal point of view, the introduction to a disputation speech. Eliphaz's tone is not apologetic, as in chap. 4, nor even so placatory; but neither is he scornful or rude. He simply challenges Job—man to man, straight from the shoulder, we may suppose—over Job's claim to wisdom (12:3; 13:2), indeed to wisdom superior to the friends'. That, we recall, was the essence of Job's immediately preceding address to the friends (12:2–13:2). In referring to Job's speech as "knowledge of wind" he dismisses it as tempestuous and violent, not the kind of calm sagacity expected from the kind of "wise man" he and Job both regard themselves as (cf. also v 18, and cf. "wisdom" in v 8). "Wind" does not here symbolize what is empty, insubstantial and impermanent (against Rowley, Horst, Fohrer and most versions), but, as in 8:2, what is violent; the parallelism with the "east wind" (as also in Hos 12:2 [1]) in the next colon makes that clear. Eliphaz can hardly characterize Job's speech as "empty" when he, Eliphaz, must agree with a good deal of it. But he can criticize it as not sober enough.

The east wind (קדים) is the sirocco or Khamsin, the hot violent wind from the desert that brought the destruction of Job's family and possessions to a climax (1:19). Tactless though it may be for Eliphaz to suggest that Job has allowed himself to be invaded by such a wind, hot (Exod 14:21; Hos 13:15; Jonah 4:8) and violent (Job 27:21; Jer 18:17), it well expresses his sense of Job's intemperate passion, so unbecoming in a sage, and his outrage at how destructive to sound theology Job's words are. That Job has "filled his belly" with the wind suggests that he speaks too much from his feelings and not discriminatingly from his heart, the seat of reason. (The idiom is slightly different at 32:18.)

The real objections Eliphaz raises to Job's speech will become apparent in vv 4, 14–16. The issue at the moment is whether he has behaved like a "wise man"—which is of course what Job has in his previous speech claimed to be.

3 Eliphaz's objection to Job's words is, curiously, that they are not "profitable" (סכן, only in Job, at 22:2; 34:9; 35:3 [see n. 15:3.a]; and יעל hiphil). Gray thought they were "useless" because his words directed against God had not helped to establish his case; more exactly it may be that Eliphaz thinks it "useless" to argue (הוכיח, Job's verb in 13:3, 15) with God, certainly not in a formal, legal disputation. It is a sentiment that Job does not disagree with, but he argues nevertheless! "Uselessness" belongs to the vocabulary of the executive, the efficiency expert; but "Eliphaz does not reckon with the fact that Job does not speak as a learned and sterile academic, but as a witness to his own living death" (Terrien). It is not utility but passion that dictates his language.

4 There is more wrong with Job's speech than the spirit in which it is uttered. That violence was not the mark of a wise man, but even more damaging is Eliphaz's charge that it betrays an improper attitude to God. Job's speech is not sufficiently respectful of God, lit., "you break, violate (פרר) fear, reverence (יראה)"; "fear" is not simply, as most commentators think, an abbreviation of the expression "fear of Yahweh" or "fear of God," which is the "principal part" of wisdom (Ps 111:10; Prov 9:10; in Job 28:28 the "fear of Adonai" *is* wisdom), and which often means roughly "religion." In each case when Eliphaz uses "fear" by itself (4:6; 22:4) he seems to have in mind specifically reverence for God. Parallel to that is "meditation" before God; שׂיחה usually means "musing aloud," sometimes with complaint (as שׂיח in 7:11 [see n. 7:11.b]; 7:13; 9:27; 10:1), but here simply in the process of theological study and reflection (as in Ps 77:13 [12]; 104:34; 119:15, 23, 27, 48, 78). The term would describe the contemplative activity of the pious wise man. Job's criticism of God, and especially his lawsuit against him (13:3, 19–24), is an abandonment of the respect due to God, and a rejection, or at least a minimizing (גרע "diminish"), of the patient meditative posture of the truly pious. NEB's translation of the second colon, "usurping the sole right to speak in his presence," implies that Job is rejecting other people's "meditation" before God, but that can hardly be meant.

Is there any particular feature of Job's speech that has triggered Eliphaz's reaction? Weiser thinks that it is the fact that he has called God's justice into question, Lamparter that the depiction of God's "demonic" qualities (12:13–25) has perpetrated a slander on God, H. Richter that Job's determination upon a lawsuit with God is unworthy (*Studien zu Hiob: Der Aufbau des Hiobbuches, dargestellt an den Gattungen des Rechtlebens* [Berlin: Evangelische Verlangsanstalt, 1959] 81–82). Horst remarks that the text leaves the door open to all these possibilities, but since it would be hard for Eliphaz to disagree with much that Job has said, it does seem that it is the boldness of Job's lawsuit with God that has affronted Eliphaz; it is certainly this that seems to be in Eliphaz's mind at v 13a.

Eliphaz reproaches Job for not living up to his own high standards, just as he had in 4:5–6. It is not that he is accusing Job of having abandoned religion, or having become positively irreligious (Gray), whether in inward sentiment or outward observance. Still less is Eliphaz's reproach that Job is undermining religion as such (Fohrer), or other people's religion (cf. GNB "If you had your way, no one would fear God"), as if "the tendency of his conduct and principles must be to diminish and do away devoutness and religion among men" (Davidson), or as if Eliphaz were "brand[ing] Job's dangerous ideas as a menace to society" (Rowley). Eliphaz remains basically sympathetic to Job, and convinced of his essential goodness, though he is not a little horrified by what he has heard from Job's lips.

5 Rightly nuanced, the sentence is still partly affirmatory of Job, and excusatory of his words. It is not that Job, with his eyes wide open, has willfully embarked upon this wrongful line of speech. It is rather that the sin which even he, a righteous man, cannot wholly avoid has fueled his anger and dictates (NEB, NJPS; "prompts" [JB, NIV]; lit., "teaches") his words (lit., "mouth"). The result (the *waw* is consecutive) is that he adopts a manner of speech that does not come naturally to him: the speech (lit., "tongue") of the "crafty" (ערומים). These are "wise" men of a sort (indeed, in Proverbs the term is always in a good sense), but unlike the pious wise, they use their wisdom for evil ends (cf. 5:12; Gen 3:1). What has been "crafty" about Job's speech in chaps. 12–14? Unless this is just an unspecific smear against Job, the reference may be to Job's argument in 12:13–25 that God's activity is essentially destructive; it could rightly be called "crafty" to use traditionally orthodox language about God to make a far from orthodox point—to God's disfavor. Job's sin would be "prompting" such craftiness in the sense that it is because he is being punished (for sin that he will not acknowledge) that he allows himself to be led into this unflattering portrait of God.

6 It is fundamental to Eliphaz's attitude that he is not intent on proving Job a sinner; he never desires to "condemn" Job or put him in the wrong (רשע hiphil). His motive is to encourage Job (cf. 4:6). But Job's speech is disrespectful of God and is inevitably putting Job, who is essentially an innocent man, in the wrong. It is not that when Job opens his mouth he shows, even without intending it, that he was a sinner all along, and so deserves what is happening to him. Rather, Eliphaz is dismayed to see his righteous friend putting himself in danger by his wild words. If only Job could hear himself talking, he would realize that this is no way for a pious man to behave!

It is ironic that Job himself has foreseen such a turn of events. At 9:20 he has said that what he fears about a formal lawsuit with God is that "though I am innocent, my own mouth would condemn me; though I am blameless, it would prove me guilty." He was thinking that he would misspeak himself, terrified by God's majesty; here Eliphaz says that Job has already erred against his own best principles of behavior and has put himself in the wrong, by setting himself up as an opponent of God even though it is in the sober environment of a (metaphorical) law-court.

It will be noted that the reading here offered of Eliphaz's words in vv 2–6 is rather more soft on Eliphaz than most commentators are. Rowley, for example, summarizes these verses thus: "Eliphaz declares that Job's words are ill-considered and irreverent, and that they only demonstrate the rightness of the charges made against him [by God]" (p. 133). But this is to suppose that Eliphaz has changed his basic attitude since chaps. 4–5. Davidson wrote that "such language as [Job] uttered could be inspired only by deep evil in his heart; and was proof enough without anything more of his wickedness. . . . The charge of Eliphaz is that Job's complaint of unrighteousness in God's treatment of him and his assertions of his own innocence . . . were mere crafty pretences put forward to cover his own wickedness." On the contrary, Eliphaz is not the man to invent such a fabrication; he believes in moderation. He has had no anxiety about Job's eventual, even soon, restoration, but these recent words of his friend's are, frankly, sinful.

7–10 Eliphaz replies to Job's assault on the friends' wisdom (12:2–3; 13:1–2; and the words put in the friends' mouth in 12:7–12). Eliphaz is no more tender to Job than Job himself has been to his interlocutors. Job has claimed superior wisdom; Eliphaz rejects any implication that Job alone is wise (v 8b) and resists the possibility of Job's wisdom being higher than the friends' (v 9).

7 There is sarcasm here, but it is not bitter. Eliphaz is a moderate man, and he asks Job not unkindly what kind of wisdom he can expect to acquire for himself in comparison with the accumulated wisdom of the ages (cf. v 10). Surely he has not so far forgotten himself as to imagine himself to be the First Man—who is not the Adam of Genesis, but a mythical figure endowed with supernatural wisdom. The myth of the First Man (never actually narrated in the OT) has formed the quarry for the depiction of the king of Tyre in Ezek 28:11–19 and perhaps also for the portrait of Wisdom in Prov 8. It apparently told of his creation before the world, his perfect wisdom and beauty, and his participation in the council of God, and possibly of a theft of divine wisdom by him. The figure of the First Man (*'ādām haqqadmôn*) played a significant role in apocryphal and rabbinic literature. See H. Gunkel, *Schöpfung und Chaos in Urzeit und Endzeit: Eine religionsgeschichtliche Untersuchung über Gen 1 und Ap Joh 12* (Göttingen: Vandenhoeck und Ruprecht, 1895); H. Schmidt, *Die Erzählung von Paradies und Sündenfall* (Tübingen: J. C. B. Mohr [Paul Siebeck], 1931) 287, 352, 489–90; I. Engnell, "Die Urmenschvorstellung und das

Alte Testament," *SEÅ* 22–23 (1957–58) 265–89; R. Gordis, "The Significance of the Paradise Myth," *AJSL* 52 (1936) 86–94; S. Mowinckel, "Urmensch und 'Königsideologie'," *ST* 2 (1949) 71–89; idem, *He That Cometh* (tr. G. W. Anderson; Oxford: Blackwell, 1956) esp. 422–24; H. L. Strack and P. Billerbeck, *Kommentar zum Neuen Testament aus Talmud und Midrasch* (München: C. H. Beck, 1926) 3:477–78; cf. also R. N. Whybray, *The Heavenly Counsellor in Isaiah xl 13–14: A Study of the Sources of the Theology of Deutero-Isaiah* (Cambridge: CUP, 1971) 54–56.

The First Man was evidently "born," perhaps, according to the myth, from a divine being; the verb shows that Eliphaz cannot be referring to the Adam of Gen 1 or 2, who is not "born" but made. "Brought forth before the hills" also indicates the mythical background of this figure; the phrase is borrowed from Prov 8:25b where it is used of Wisdom. There can be little doubt that the direction of literary dependence is from Proverbs to Job (with Dhorme, and against Fohrer), a fact of some value for the (relative) dating of the Book of Job. But the connection with the primal man (as here) is undoubtedly more primitive than that with the figure of Wisdom. For the notation "before the hills" cf. Ps 90:2 (in reference to God's eternity).

8 The Hebrew could mean "Have you listened?," i.e., in the primeval past when creation was being planned (Peake), or "Do you listen?" now. In either case it is assumed that the First Man has the right of entry to the heavenly council (סוֹד), a group of divine beings such as we have encountered in 1:6–12; 2:1–6 (cf. also 2 Kgs 22). In a prophetic context it is understood that a true prophet is privy to the deliberations of the divine council, and that false prophets claim attendance there (Jer 23:18, 22; cf. Amos 3:7); but the question here is not whether Job is giving himself prophetic airs (as Eliphaz did in 4:12–17!) but whether he is arrogating to himself the functions of the First Man, who presumably derived his wisdom from his participation in the heavenly assembly. On the divine council, see on 1:6.

It is doubtful whether the second colon refers to a *theft* of wisdom from heaven (as Fohrer, Tur-Sinai); the verb גרע means properly "to diminish" (cf. v 4) and so "to limit," rather than to diminish in the sense of taking from others (but see KB[3]). The Prometheus myth, in which an archetypal man steals fire from the gods to bring it to humankind, and the idiom of Phil 2:6, where Jesus does not consider equality with God a thing to be seized, have been compared. The present context, however, has no room for the idea of a theft of wisdom; its concern is solely with Job's claims to superior knowledge, which is represented as a "limiting" of genuine wisdom to himself.

9 "Returning from this lofty flight of the sarcastic imagination, Eliphaz asks Job in what respect his knowledge surpasses theirs" (Peake). Far from possessing superhuman wisdom, Job does not even surpass the friends in insight. It is a little strange that Eliphaz should seriously ask, "What do you know that is superior to our knowledge?," for Job has been at pains to make the content of his superior knowledge clear in 12:2–6: it is that the doctrine of retribution is not always true. It is likely that Eliphaz means "What *can* you know. . . ?," i.e., how can a lone individual hope to push back the frontiers of human knowledge unaided? Wisdom for Eliphaz is fundamentally a matter of consensus, a consensus that has accumulated over the generations; it is— more to the point of v 10—a body of knowledge that one encompasses progressively through the course of a long life.

It becomes evident that Eliphaz has little, if any, personal animus against Job; he is affronted rather by the threat Job poses to the intellectual values of his day. The set of rhetorical questions in vv 7–9 do not begin to join argument with Job, but declare, by their very form, that Job's claimed breakthrough in theological thought is impermissible and impossible. As rhetorical questions, they assume that the hearer is in sympathy with the speaker and has only to be reminded where truth lies to instantly fall in line with it. It is hopeless to argue with such a warrior for the status quo.

10 The words for "gray-haired" and "aged" are singular, and while it is possible that they are to be taken as collectives (so RSV, NAB, NIV), it is much more likely that Eliphaz is still speaking of the three friends as a group, as he was in v 9. Most plausibly, Eliphaz is understood as referring in particular to himself (Duhm, Gray, Pope); the fact that he is the first to speak may suggest he is the oldest. There is no need to solemnly calculate whether Eliphaz could be eighty years of age and so literally older than Job's father (Fohrer, de Wilde); seniority of a mere ten years or so would be adequate for this oriental hyperbole.

Eliphaz does not say directly what he means: the point of mentioning his age is to affirm that he must necessarily be wiser than Job. Eliphaz has the delicacy not to say so in as many words; Job of course also had deferred to etiquette in saying "I am not inferior" (12:3; 13:2) when he meant "I am superior." And Job cannot be surprised by what he hears, for he has already attributed this very attitude to the friends: "Wisdom is found with the aged, understanding comes with length of days" (12:12). It is a corollary, not a distinct belief, that wisdom is the heritage of the ages (cf. 8:8–9).

Eliphaz forgets, Peake exclaims, "that it is not mere length of days, but the intensity with which they have been lived that counts for wisdom, just as the grey-headed may become so not simply by lapse of time, but in a single night in which years seem to have been packed. . . . Ripe as he was in many ways, [Eliphaz's] placid career had known no such tragic break as had taught the much younger Job." The poet is on Job's side in this dispute, naturally; he must be very conscious of swimming against the theological current.

11–13 Eliphaz has dealt in vv 7–10 with Job's reaction to the friends (he claims superior wisdom to theirs); now in vv 11–13 he deals with Job's reaction to God (he rejects what is positive from the divine side and insists on angry argument).

11 Eliphaz evidently refers to his own earlier speech (chaps. 4–5). He has spoken not just as a friend, or a fellow member of the company of the wise, but as a practical theologian, from God's side. Most commentators think the "encouragements of God" are specifically the words of the supernatural audition which Eliphaz has recounted in 4:17. Those words, though on the surface a divine condemnation of human righteousness, can readily be perceived as encouragement; for they demonstrate that all humans, even the most righteous, are bound to sin occasionally, and that therefore, by implication, a righteous man should not draw devastating consequences from a bout of suffering; his essential righteousness is not in doubt. It may be, however, that Eliphaz regards not just 4:17 but the whole of his speech as "divine encouragement," since every word is "encouragement," being founded on the belief that Job is fundamentally righteous and so may soon expect relief from his suffering, and every word is "from God, divine" since it is nothing but orthodox theology

that he teaches. Terrien remarks that Eliphaz, "the pompous orator," here
falls into "the same error of pride as that which the rebel Job has just been
accused of" (v 8); indeed, dogmatism is not generally thought immodest if it
is orthodox. Job has to shout to get a hearing, and so he cannot fail to be
thought a self-important agitator.

Eliphaz's first speech, with its hesitant introduction (4:2), its non-directive
counsel (5:8), its dramatic picture of the fate of the wicked—which Job is *not*
suffering (4:8–11; 5:2–5)—and its loving depiction of the blessedness of the
righteous man chastened by God (5:17–26), can rightly enough be called "speech
that deals gently with you." If Job could accept Eliphaz's approach, if it were
not "too little," that is, unsatisfying for him, he could no doubt learn to live
with his pain in the hope of ultimate if not speedy deliverance from it and
could cast from his mind the numbing thought that his affliction was the
sign of unquenchable divine anger. It is such a shame that Job has to be so
black and white over the issue of his innocence.

Horst and others think Eliphaz includes the other friends' speeches along
with his own as "encouragements"; but it is hard to know how Eliphaz regards
the other friends' positions, since he does not share their views in every particular.

12–13 It is still the moderate man speaking. Nothing in Eliphaz's experience
justifies Job's opinions or his behavior, so Job must be the one who is out of
line. The heart is usually the "mind," rather than the seat of feeling, and
Eliphaz certainly believes that wild ideas have "carried [Job] off," diverting
him from the path of the godly; Job's problem is a rational one as much as
an emotional, and he needs to be taught again what he surely knows already,
the wisdom of the ages (cf. 4:7; 5:27; 15:17–18). Job may think God counts
him an enemy (13:24), but let him realize that by his protestation and dispute
he is treating God as *his* enemy. It is a failure of insight (v 12b) that is behind
Job's anger and his words of accusation against God. We observe that Eliphaz
does not accuse Job of bad faith or of simple passionateness, but of an ideological
defect.

Ehrlich thought that the first colon of v 13 should be translated "you return
your spirit to God," as in Eccl 12:7; but Dhorme rightly remarks that "the
words which Job utters are not the last sighs of a dying soul, but manifestations
of his state of mind."

14 Job has over-reacted to his suffering, so the moderate man Eliphaz
judges. Instead of accepting that all are to some degree unrighteous and therefore deserve some amount of punishment, Job has insisted unreasonably on
his claim to perfect innocence. Eliphaz still takes his stand on the heavenly
words he reported in 4:17; though he does not quote them again verbatim,
he clearly alludes to them and their import, that no mortal being is entirely
clear of sin. In 4:17 it was "righteous in the sight of God, pure in the sight
of his maker"; here "in the sight of God" is entirely implied (as is perhaps
indicated by the fact that "God" is the unexpressed subject of the verbs of v
15). זכה "be pure, clean" is the ethical term, most frequent in wisdom contexts
(cf. 25:4; Prov 20:9; Ps 51:6 [4]; 73:13; 119:9), to which צדק "be righteous"
corresponds in the legal sphere (though L. R. Fisher proposed that זכה was
primarily a legal expression: "An Amarna Age Prodigal," *JSS* 3 [1958] 11–
22, esp. 15). See also the adjective זך in 8:6; 11:4, and the verb in the literal

sense "make clean" at 9:30. "Born of a woman" refers only to human mortality (as at 14:1); there is no hint that the woman or birth itself is the origin of uncleanness (against Dhorme; Rowley, "the low oriental estimate of woman"; similarly Peake).

As in 4:17–19, the connection between mortality and moral weakness is merely assumed; they need not of course be correlative. It is noteworthy that Eliphaz makes no condemnation, specific or general, of Job's way of life; he speaks of the faults common to humankind rather than of Job in particular.

15 The thought of 4:18 is repeated here, though we now have "his holy ones" for "his servants," and "the heavens" in parallelism, rather than "his servants." For the "holy ones," cf. on 5:1. There is little reason to see here an allusion to a fully developed myth of a primeval rebellion and fall of heavenly beings, but the narrative of Gen 6:1–4 is perhaps the traditional background (see on 4:18; and cf. P. Humbert, "Démesure et chute dans l'Ancien Testament," in *Maqqél shâqédh: La branche d'amandier. Hommage à Wilhelm Vischer* [Montpellier: Causse, Graille, Castelnau, 1960] 63–82 [75–76]).

The "heavens" may of course be the material heavens (so Dhorme, Fohrer), whose "cleanness" (זכה) could only be literal, not figurative (cf. Exod 24:10, under the feet of God was a pavement, "like the very heavens for cleanness"). In that case the physical cleanness of the heavens would be contrasted with the ethical uncleanness of humans—an illogical but not impossible connection for a speaker who equates mortality with sinfulness. But it is perhaps more likely that the heavens here signify the heavenly bodies (so Targum), who are regarded as beings, the "host" or "army" of heaven, morally imperfect and unclean like the "holy ones." We note that in the closely parallel 25:5 it is the moon and the stars, envisaged as sentient beings, which are ethically unclean.

16 If heavenly beings are morally imperfect, how much more so (אף כי, introducing an *a fortiori* argument) must humankind be! איש "man" is not the particular man Job, but any person at all from among humankind. It is not that it is "impossible for Job, who deliberately soaks himself with unrighteousness, to escape the fate of the wicked" (Gray), or that it is specifically Job who is "loathsome" (נתעב) and "foul" (נאלח) (against Gordis, Pope); for in Ps 14:3 (= 53:4), the only other places where אלח occurs, it is humankind generally that is stamped "foul" (cf. תעב "act abominably" in Ps 14:1; 53:2). On the verb תעב, see P. Humbert, "Le substantif *tōʿēbā* et le verbe *tʿb* dans l'A.T.," *ZAW* 72 (1960) 217–37.

To "drink (something) like water" is a self-explanatory idiom, appearing again at 34:7, where Elihu says that Job "drinks up scoffing like water." The application of the proverbial formula to Job there by no means suggests that it must be Job who is principally spoken of here. Presumably the image of drinking of water does not portray drinking in full gulps, with "uncontrollable avidity" (Terrien), stronger liquids being drunk more cautiously (so Duhm, Rowley), nor does it suggest eager, thirsty drinking, but rather that it is as natural for humans to sin as to drink "Adam's ale."

But is this not all rather excessive language to use about humankind's inevitable moral weakness? Does that make them "loathsome and foul," and is it true of all humans that they "drink wrongdoing like water"? In particular, how can a member of the guild of the wise denigrate humanity (himself included)

so categorically when he believes that there are righteous people, sharply differentiated from the wicked, and when he will indeed immediately hereafter
depict the fate of the wicked as a destiny distinct from that of the righteous?
Hesse thinks he must be led into such speech by thinking specifically of Job
though speaking generally of humankind. But this is in conflict with Eliphaz's
settled and stated attitude to Job. It is much more likely that Eliphaz here
represents what he imagines to be the divine perspective on mortals: from
the standpoint of a perfectly righteous God who finds fault even in heavenly
beings humankind must be truly disgusting. But such an absolute standard
does not always have to be applied, and it does not obliterate the long acknowledged distinction between good persons and evil.

Job is of course included with the rest of humanity in its incapacity not to
sin (*non posse non peccare*). This is not exactly an inborn defect, for all individuals
are, in Eliphaz's view, responsible for their own faults; it is simply a correlate—
not a consequence—of humans' physical frailty. It needs to be emphasized
how exculpatory of Job this affirmation of Eliphaz is. Job has sinned, to be
sure, but then so has the rest of humanity (cf. Ps 143:2). Let him not be
fazed at being discovered by God in an uncharacteristic fault; let him accept
the common lot of humankind—and reflect with thankfulness upon the fate
that awaits the persistently wicked (vv 17–35), among whom Job certainly is
not!

17–35   The second part of the speech consists of a *topos* devoted to the
fate of the wicked. Here Eliphaz uses the traditional material such as is drawn
upon for the same purpose by himself in 5:12–14 and by Bildad in 8:8–19.
But it is important to note for what end Eliphaz paints this picture. In the
light of the first half of his speech (vv 2–16) as well as his stance adopted in
his first speech, it is unthinkable that he can mean that it is now impossible
for Job to escape the fate here portrayed (Gray). Nor is it even just a warning
(Weiser), still less a threat (Fohrer). It is not even "instruction" (Hesse), for
what end would such an instruction serve? No, it is an account of what the
life-history of Job will *not* be. It is the wicked, not Job, who writhes in pain
all his days (v 20), who has stretched out his hand against God (v 25), whose
heart conceives mischief and deceit (v 35). To be sure, Eliphaz is not a master
of tact (cf. on 5:25) and in his easy flow of conventional phrases unwittingly
lets slip some that might be thought tailor-made for Job (vv 21b, 22a). But
that is not his intent (he is not devious); his purpose is solely to encourage
Job by displaying a negative image of what he foresees as Job's own destiny.

17   The *topos* begins with an elaborate introduction (vv 17–19) appealing
to the wisdom of the ages, similar in form and content to the introduction
(8:8–10) to Bildad's *topos* on the same theme (8:11–22); cf. also 4:7–8, 12. It
is the "opening formula of a teacher" (*Lehreröffungsformel*) (cf. on 13:6). Again,
as in 4:8, 12–17, and 5:3, 27, Eliphaz appeals to his own experience, what he
has "seen" (not what he has seen in vision [Terrien], despite the use of חזה
for "see," often used of prophetic visions); yet, as is obvious in his first speech,
what he has personally experienced (like the nocturnal audition) is not distinguished from what he has learned (as with the proverbial type of utterance
in 4:8 and 5:3). In the same way, the "we" who have investigated the workings
of the moral universe (5:25) are both the fathers and the contemporary generation of the wise. The identity of the two sources of knowledge is expressed

formally by the apposition of the two clauses "what I have seen" and "what wise men declare" (v 18). He is not lacking in candor when he calls the observations of the fathers his own; he finds truth in collective and well-matured wisdom, and is suspicious of upstart claims to knowledge (cf. vv 8b–9).

Job has asked for silence on the part of the friends (13:13) and for them to "listen" to him (13:17); Eliphaz on the contrary thinks that Job is the one who should be in the listener's position, with the wisdom of the ages ranged against him.

18 Eliphaz's experience is wholly of a piece with traditional wisdom. He has sold his soul to tradition, and has so ensured that he will never have any experience that runs counter to it; everything that happens to him will be interpretable in wisdom categories, for he will perceive everything from its viewpoint. He is buttressed by the living community of the "sages" (חכמים), to which he and Job (informally) belong, and by the previous generation(s) of sages, here called "their fathers." They are not necessarily their physical fathers, nor are they their teachers just of the former generation; "fathers" includes everyone in the tradition of the wise (cf. the well-known rabbinic treatise *Pirqe Abot,* "The Sayings of the Fathers"). The two stages of tradition are visible again at Ecclus 8:9, "Do not disregard the discourse of the aged, for they themselves learned from their fathers."

There is nothing especially mysterious about wisdom teaching, though he says the fathers have "divulged" it (lit., "not withheld it"); the term is simply an elegant variation on the lackluster "reported" (יגידו). In the similar phrase at Isa 3:9, "not withheld" is much more significant.

19 This verse, with its references to the giving of the land to the fathers, and to the absence of foreigners from the land in a former age, has seemed to some to reflect the interests of a Jewish scribe rather than maintaining the viewpoint of the Temanite Eliphaz. De Wilde would delete it, and NEB encloses it (and v 18) in square brackets as being a secondary addition. Others think the author's concentration has slipped, and he has put into Eliphaz's mouth words not really appropriate to him. Against these views, it can be affirmed that the second half of the line could not have been truthfully uttered by a Jewish writer (author or copyist) at any historical time about Jewish ancestors; for biblical tradition is unanimous that from patriarchal times to post-exilic the people of Israel shared their land with other races. Certainly it is impossible to use this verse in attempting to date the Book of Job (against Duhm and others).

Some specific allusion, now beyond our grasp, may be made to Temanite traditions of the origins of their people; but the sense is plain. As the first occupants of their land, the ancestors possessed a primal, pristine wisdom, a wisdom that was as internally consistent and unadulterated as the social framework of their community. No disintegrating or falsifying influence from outside sources had disturbed the comprehensive pattern of their perception of life, just as no foreign infiltrators had interfered in the social fabric. There is appeal in Eliphaz's words to a primitive ideal time as the *fons et origo* of the wisdom he now teaches. With that appeal goes a haughty disdain for the newfangled and the foreign—which is by definition the inferior; this attitude fits so well with the picture of the conservative and orthodox sage and sheikh we imagine Eliphaz to be.

On זר, "foreign," see L. A. Snijders, "The Meaning of זר in the OT,"
OTS 10 (1954) 1–154; idem, *TDOT* 4:52–58; R. Martin-Achard, *THWAT* 1:520–
22. Of course it does not need to mean "non-Israelite" here; Snijders describes
the זר here as one who does not share ancestral traditions.

Joel 4:17 [3:17] bears an interesting similarity to our passage; it describes
the idyllic future, with Jerusalem holy and free from strangers passing through
it (עבר, as here), in the same terms as are used here for the idyllic past (Pope).
Perhaps the naivety of the racism in both passages makes it relatively excusable.

20–35 This *topos* on the fate of the wicked is the wisdom handed down
from ancient times (vv 18–19), to which Eliphaz lends his supernumerary support. The theme of this depiction is not the untimely though inevitable *end*
of the wicked, as it was in Bildad's 8:11–19 (cf. 18:7–21; 20:4–29), but the
whole *life experience* of the wicked, which he envisages as full of terror and
insecurity. In so saying, Eliphaz gives voice to a somewhat more penetrating
form of wisdom theology than do his friends, for it can always be objected to
the conventional picture of the unrighteous man's unhappy end that in ordinary
experience wicked men often prosper and live long, thus calling into question
any naive version of the principle of exact retribution. Eliphaz goes deeper,
by professing to tell us the truth about the inner life of the wicked: which is
to say, despite all that external prosperity, the ungodly man is inwardly suffering
already for his unrighteousness and the principle of retribution is already at
work; indeed it makes its mark on the wicked his whole life long. There is no
doubt more than a grain of truth here, but as a comprehensive statement it
is frankly silly. No matter; Eliphaz's point is simply to differentiate Job and
his short-lived suffering from the life-long pain of the wicked. In his previous
speech he has stressed the confidence and security the righteous can enjoy
(5:19–26; cf. 11:15–19), by way of encouraging Job to expect a bright future;
here he depicts the misery of the wicked by way of encouraging Job to believe
that his misery is of a quite other kind. It is ironic, and unfortunate, that Job
could easily identify the sufferings he is at this moment undergoing with those
of the wicked; but he is not meant to do that, the crucial difference between
his experience and that of the wicked being the length of time such suffering
may last.

The strophic structure is not easy to discern. Perhaps the basic three-line
strophe is continued, with just one extension to four lines in vv 29–32; thus
vv 20–22, 23–25, 26–28, 29–32, 33–35 (similarly Fohrer, though omitting v 31).
Terrien finds four major strophes encompassing vv 17–35: vv 17–21, 22–26, 27–
30, 31–35, each of five lines except for the third, and each dividing into two
sub-strophes of 3 lines + 2, except for the third; hence vv 17–19, 20–21, 22–
24, 25–26, 27–28, 29–30, 31–33, 34–35. An emendation of the first word of
v 28 is required to achieve an independent sub-strophe in vv 27–28.

20 The subject of this extended depiction is the "wicked" (רשע, as in 8:22;
11:20) and the "oppressor," whether brigand or tyrant (עריץ, as in 6:23; of
God in 13:25 *q.v.*). They are the same figure, the characteristics of the high-
profile tyrant or brigand being applied to the wicked in general (against Horst,
who thinks that it is not the wicked in general but the specific type of the
"oppressor" that is here in view). The terms make clear that Eliphaz cannot
be speaking of Job (against Fohrer and many others), for whatever Job's sins
may be in Eliphaz's eyes he cannot be called a "gangster" (עריץ)! The type

of person here depicted is one of the "godless" (v 34), who stretches out his hand in defiance against God (vv 25–26), hatching trouble and wickedness and inventing deceit (v 35).

The "torment" (חלל hithp; cf. Esth 4:4) is a mental torture, to be specified in v 21. The emphasis in the second colon is equally on the continuance of the torment throughout the years of the tyrant's life, however many they may be (see n. 15:20.a).

21 The torment is mental, a dread of the loss of security because the wicked man knows well that punishment is deserved. It is not the pangs of remorse in his conscience (Dhorme). The "terrors" (פחדים) are not simply the plural of the abstract noun "terror" but the personified spirits of vengeance, denizens of the underworld, whom we meet at 18:14, ruled over by the "king of terrors" (מלך בלהות). The sound of their approach is not physical; the wicked man hears them in his inner ear. Parallel to the Terrors is the Destroyer (שודד), who is not any human assailant, though a human being may sometimes be the agent of supernatural vengeance; the Destroyer is a demonic power.

In the second colon, the text says at face value that "the destroyer comes upon him (= attacks him)" while he is at peace; but this does not fit the context very well, since it is the inner torment rather than external attack that seems to be uppermost. The "destroyer attacking him" (שודד יבואנו) should be taken as parallel to the "terrors" (פחדים) in the first colon, and "in time of peace" (בשלום) belongs in sense to both halves of the line. Fully expanded, the line would read, "When all is (outwardly) well for him, in the ear of his mind sounds the Terrors, that is, the Destroyer who is coming to attack him."

There are some close correspondences between this picture and what Job has said of his own experience. So in 3:25 he says that what he fears (lit., "the fear [פחד] that I fear") comes upon him, and what he dreads "comes upon" him (יָבָא לִי; cf. יְבוֹאֶנּוּ here). But this does not mean that Eliphaz is here made by the author to pick up Job's words, and to use them as proof that Job exemplifies the fate of the wicked. For the idea that the wicked live in a state of neurotic fear because of their wickedness is a common proverbial idea and no novelty here; cf. Prov 28:1, "The wicked (רשע) flee when no one pursues"; and cf. also Wisd 17:3; Deut 28:66. Job's complaint in 3:25 is that he is being compelled to live in a state of anxiety *as if* he were a wrongdoer.

22 Literally, the first colon reads, "He does not trust to return from darkness" (cf. RSV). To "return" (שוב) suggests that he is already *in* darkness, which would be an unexceptional metaphor for the inner suffering that torments him (cf. Ps 112:4). To be in darkness must mean to be already as good as dead; for to "see the sun" is to live (Eccl 7:11; cf. Isa 53:11 emended). There are a few examples of שוב, "return," used in the causative (hiph), where the sense seems to be "keep away from" rather than "cause to return from" (so perhaps 33:30; Ps 35:17 "rescue"). Added to this, the fact that in v 30 a very similar clause to the present colon means "he will not *avoid* (סור rather than שוב) darkness" leads some to think that here too the "darkness" is what is not *avoided* by the wicked, and is therefore the darkness of death (so Horst; cf. 10:21–22); cf. JB "no hope of fleeing from the darkness," NEB "cannot hope to escape from dark death." The parallelism of "darkness" with "sword" suggests to some also that "darkness" must signify death (so Fohrer). The translation "he despairs of escaping the darkness" (NAB, NIV) leaves it unresolved whether the "darkness" is what he awaits or what he presently experiences; perhaps that is the best way to leave it.

The wicked man is truly "hopeless"; he "does not trust" (לֹא יַאֲמִין) to escape his fate, unlike the righteous psalmist who "trusts" (הֶאֱמַנְתִּי) to "see the goodness of Yahweh in the land of life" (Ps 27:13). He is "spied out" (צָפוּה) or "marked down" (NEB, following G. R. Driver, VTSup 3 [1955] 78) for the sword, that is, a violent end. This second colon expresses his fear, just as the first does; he will not necessarily meet a violent death, but he daily imagines that "somewhere a sword is waiting to kill him" (GNB).

23 It seems that the anxieties of the wicked are still being described in the first colon, as they clearly are in the second. No one has actually "cast him out" as yet; he is still outwardly "in the midst of peace" (v 21b). But he already senses himself "cast out" from the security of his home as carrion is thrown out for vultures to feed on. He lives as if his life were over, as if he was good for nothing, not even deserving burial, but mere garbage. Fohrer, retaining the MT vocalization, envisages him darting restlessly about (נֹדֵד), like a small animal pursued by birds of prey; but, against Fohrer, we do not seem to have the "external suffering" of the wrongdoer here, but his own perception of his own state of being.

The "vulture" is properly the kite, *milvus*, of the hawk family. De Wilde describes two types, *milus milvus*, a slender bird 70 cm long, brown with white flecks on the wings and breast, and *milvus migrans*, brown and black, with a smaller tail. They feed on carrion, small animals, reptiles, frogs and larger insects. Their far-sightedness is alluded to by the saying in the Talmud (*Ḥullin* 63b), "A kite in Babylon saw carrion in the land of Israel."

Throughout his uncertainty and anxiety there is one thought that constantly recurs to the wicked man: his "downfall" (פִּיד; also 12:5; 31:29) is the one certainty he has, the sole fixed point in his future. The word "certain" (נָכוֹן) often has the sense of "ready" or imminent (18:12; Ps 38:18 [17]; Exod 19:11, 15; 34:2), which it may here also.

24 The "day of darkness" that terrifies the wicked man is the day of his death that awaits him. He already lives in darkness (v 22a), but he nevertheless lives, and therefore dreads death. The day is certainly not the eschatological day of darkness in Amos 5:18–20, Joel 2:2, Zeph 1:15 (as Dhorme).

Job has said in 14:20 that it is God who "prevails" (תָּקַף, as here) against humans and their hope, or "overwhelms" them. Here the more rationalistic teaching of the wise appears, that it is the wicked man's own fears and anxieties that finally prove his undoing. For all the mythological language of the demonic Terrors and the Destroyer in v 21, it can equally well be said that the evil man is brought to death by the working of his own psyche. Anxiety (צַר and מְצוּקָה, together also at Zeph 1:15, both metaphors of narrowness) plays the imperious role of the chieftain ("king") who is armed for an assault.

25 The root of the wicked man's anxiety is his consciousness that his wickedness has been an assault not just on his fellow-humans but on God; the "for" introduces the reason for his fears in vv 20–24. To "raise the arm against" (Heb. "stretch out the hand against") is an image of the warrior; often it is found of Yahweh, acting in judgment (Isa 5:25; 23:11; Ezek 6:14; 14:9, 13; 16:27; 25:7, 13, 16; 35:3; Zeph 1:4; 2:13), like the conventional phrase, "with outstretched hand," used of Yahweh's leading Israel out of Egypt in the teeth of Egyptian hostility (Exod 6:6; Deut 4:34; 5:15; Ps 136:12; etc.). (Contrast "spread out the hands" in 11:13.) The phrase occurs nowhere else of human hostility to God; it is heightened language that Eliphaz speaks.

It is foolhardy heroism to set oneself against God as the wicked do; the verb (התגבר, hithpael) signifies to "act the hero, play the role of a warrior" (cf. התנבא, "play the prophet"). In Isa 42:13 Yahweh "shows himself mighty" against his foes, and in Ecclus 31:25 one is warned not to "play the hero" where wine is concerned (cf. also Job 36:9). It is the "Almighty" (Shaddai) whom the wrongdoer assaults, so foolishly unaware is he of his own puny stature.

Some find here a clear allusion on Eliphaz's part to the attitude of Job (so Fohrer, Pope), who has indeed challenged God to a disputation. But it is fundamental that Eliphaz here concerns himself with the life experience of the wicked man—which Job assuredly is *not*. Any resemblance to any living person is purely coincidental; or at least, if Eliphaz were to speak his whole mind, though it is shocking for him to find his old friend behaving like one of the wicked, he nevertheless firmly believes that such behavior, like Job's misfortune itself, is only a temporary aberration.

It is not easy to decide whether the "for"-clauses (vv 25–27) are linked to what precedes (v 24) or what follows (v 28); the overall sense is much the same. The strophic pattern of the chapter suggests that at least v 25 belongs with the foregoing. Verse 26 then seems best to take with v 25 because of its similar content; and it can hardly begin a new strophe as the fact for which v 27 is the reason (כי) (against Fohrer). Verses 23–26 should probably be regarded as an extended strophe, four lines instead of the three-line pattern common in this speech. Horst, however, thinks vv 25–28 an independent strophe.

Siegfried, Duhm and Beer thought vv 25–28 (vv 25–28b) were secondary additions, and indeed v 29 could follow v 24 quite naturally. But the depiction of these verses, that the wicked man's wrongdoing is actually defiance of God, is nothing exceptional (cf. 8:13; 21:14–15), and should be retained.

26 The picture of the attacking warrior, running against his opponent (lit., "runs against him with a neck"), is continued. Some rabbis, followed by Ehrlich, thought that it was *God* who was rushing against the ungodly man (cf. NAB "One shall rush sternly upon him"), but the similarity of this verse to the preceding makes it more natural to see the wicked man as the subject; moreover, it does not appear elsewhere in this depiction that God himself intervenes in the downfall of the wicked, the causes being self-induced (v 24) or else semi-natural (vv 30, 34). It is an act of hybris to stick one's "neck" out against God, to play the "red-neck" with him. No defensive shield, massive though its "bosses" may be (cf. on 13:12; and *Iliad* 4.448, 7.266–67 for bossed shields) provide a guilty man with protection against an assaulted God. It seems doubtful that the shield is envisaged as a weapon of offense, for all its weightiness (against Fohrer, NEB "charging him head down, with the full weight of his bossed shield"); there must be more effective weapons than a shield. But neither does it seem to be the covering of shields held protectively above the head, like the Roman tortoise (*testudo*) (against Horst). A "comical picture" (Andersen) perhaps; but it is not an underhand depiction of a Job who, "by virtue of his frontal attacks of God, deserves the fate he is experiencing" (Habel).

27 The evildoer's fatness is not a sign of his unfitness for battle, and thus a further evidence of the folly of his defiance of God (Rowley). There may well be some allusion to a tale of a gargantuan warrior like Goliath (so Gordis), though nothing is said in 1 Sam 17 of fatness as such, and it may well be that the image of the warrior has been abandoned at the end of v 26. Rather, the wicked man's fatness is a mark of strength and sound health (Fohrer). Fatness or sleekness in the OT is certainly ascribed to the arrogant (Deut 32:15; Ps 73:4, 7; Jer 5:28), and "fatness of heart" is wickedness (Ps 119:70) or fecklessness (Isa 6:10) (cf. G. Münderlein, *TDOT* 4:396–97). It is not clear, however, that fatness is here seen as the result of self-indulgence and luxury ("a bloated egoist who in his greed puts on fat" [Dhorme]; or "a practical materialist, for whom eating and drinking are the all-important things" [de Wilde]); rather it is the result of good nurture (as in Neh 9:25, where fatness is no fault).

It is therefore not a criticism of the ungodly that he has run to fat; it is rather that despite his enjoyment of health and prosperity, he ends up as an inhabitant of ruined cities (v 28). The initial כי is not "because" but "although" (cf. NEB, NIV).

To be precise, he has "covered his face with his fat"; כָּסָה can mean "hid," but no improper concealment is here apparently in view. It is rather that he has covered his face with fat as one covers one's body with clothes (the verb is rare, perhaps only Jonah 3:6, for covering with clothes because there is a special verb for "clothe"); it is the sign of prosperity that he wears. Something deliberate about his acquisition of "healthy" fat is suggested by the piel verb; so also in the second colon he has "made" fat upon his waist or loins (i.e., lumbar region, כסל).

Tur-Sinai fancifully saw in vv 24–27 a set of allusions to a mythological warrior, a titanesque figure, who battled against God in the past and who forms the model for the depiction of the wicked man in these verses. V 24b he translates "He braceth himself like a king-hero for the fight," and in v 27, since the titan is a partisan of the sea-monster Leviathan, he smears his face with fat and puts grease on his hips to protect him from the sea in his marathon swim across the sea to the help of Leviathan. Tur-Sinai has no followers, but Terrien, apparently independently, also saw here fragments of a myth of a battle between God and a mythic warrior. His starting point is the word "act the hero" in v 25, and in the present verse he is intrigued by the Syriac rendering that saw in the word for "blubber" (פימה, a *hapax legomenon*) the Pleiades (כימה) and in כסל "loins" the word כסיל "Orion." Orion was often regarded in the ancient world as a giant who is also a fool (כָּסִיל "fool"). "His fat" (חלבו) then disguises the term חלבנה, a resin used in incense and cosmetics; and one knows that ancient warriors decorated their face so as to give themselves a fierce appearance. . . . Hence v 27 becomes, "Because he has covered his face with a warrior's mask, and has (?) the Pleiades above Orion." This interpretation cannot be pronounced an exegetical success, but not for lack of trying. It is not impossible that the present typifying depiction of the evildoer borrows traits from a historical or legendary account of a particular tyrant (so Horst); but we are in no position to reconstruct such a tale.

28 Given that v 27 describes the present healthy state, physically speaking, of the wicked man as a type, this verse is best understood as a depiction of the lonely and accursed future that awaits him. While the first two strophes in this *topos* (vv 20–22, 23–26) recounted the dreadful *present* state of the wicked (emphasis on his inner suffering), the last three strophes (vv 27–29, 30–32, 33–35) recount his dreadful *future* state (emphasis on his outward destruction). In Israelite tradition at least, cities laid under the ban of holy war are perpetually an anathema (Deut 13:17 [16]; Josh 6:26; cf. 1 Kgs 16:34); but that idea is not necessarily at work here, for the concept of ruined cities as the abode of demons and wild animals, avoided by decent people, is commonplace in the ancient world and adequate to explain the present verse. See Isa 13:19–22 for such a depiction of Babylon, and 34:9–17 (Bozrah). Those who pass by such a ruin are "appalled" and hiss in token of their dissociation from the doom that has befallen the place (1 Kgs 9:8; Jer 19:8; Lam 2:15). Why should the prosperous ungodly man live in such surroundings? Everywhere in these verses the fates that fall on him are rather mysterious. Here it is probably that he is cast out from the society of other people when they recognize him as accursed by God; only half-alive, psychically speaking, he can find shelter nowhere but in "ghost"-towns. They are cities destroyed (lit., "effaced," כחד; also used by Eliphaz in 4:7) for whatever reason, not necessarily because of divine judgment, uninhabited by humans just because they are ruins, and "destined" (lit., "made ready," עתד hith) to become nothing but heaps of stones because they will never again be rebuilt.

Other interpretations are less plausible. Dhorme believed that "the tyrant has ravaged and reduced to barrenness the regions around him in order that he may settle in the room of others"; the verse would then describe his crime rather than his punishment (cf. GNB "That is the man who captured cities and seized houses whose owners had fled"). But a tyrant would not willingly live in a still ruined city (Hab 1:6 is no real parallel, no more than Job 20:19), one moreover destined to become a heap of rubble. If this is his crime, we would expect it to be said that he rebuilt the homes of others for his own use. Others (e.g., Fohrer, Gray, Peake) think that he rebuilds devastated cities which have God's curse on them and so are danger zones (cf. Josh 6:26). This is a sign of his indifference to God (Gray), of his self-confidence in the face of demons and divine commands (Fohrer). De Wilde cites a divine oracle in a letter to Zimri-lim, king of Mari, forbidding him to rebuild a ruined house (*ANET*, 624a), and Horst thinks there may be some allusion to the building activities of Nabonidus in Harran and Teima (cf. *ANET*, 312–15). But there is nothing in our text about rebuilding, only about dwelling in, ruined cities—which makes it more than likely that it is punishment, not crime, that is the subject (in 3:14 there is an allusion to rebuilding ruined cities, but there it is no crime). Equally the suggestion of ibn Ezra that the wicked man and his followers hid in ruined towns in order to raid passers-by puts the whole interpretative weight upon an action not mentioned in the text. Some think that it is his own city and house that will be ruined (so NEB); yet it is not the act of ruin that is the focus (as it is, e.g., in v 30) but his dwelling among ruins.

29 The wrongdoer's fatness (v 27) was the work of his prosperity, but his fate is to lose his wealth, and therewith his good health. Job has of course already lost all his wealth in the catastrophes of chap. 1, but Eliphaz does not for a moment imagine that Job has reached his life's end. Close to the bone though this allusion to the loss of wealth may be, in Eliphaz's mind Job's future is the very opposite of the fate of the wicked; it is a future full of security and blessing (5:19–26). The wicked man's fate will be to lose his riches (לֹא־יֶעְשַׁר does not mean "not become rich," against JB). The word translated "wealth" (חַיִל) could equally well be rendered "strength," for the function of the wicked man's wealth is to ensure his vitality. The thought in the third colon, of his possessions no longer "spreading" (נטה) over the earth, assumes that the wicked man is a pastoralist (like Job), his wealth consisting in his flocks and other animals ranging over wide tracts of land.

30 In this new strophe, the image of the short-lived plant is taken up (RSV, and others found it already in v 29b, but see n. 15:29.b). It is a trite image (cf. 8:11–12, 16–19; 18:16), obviously more meaningful to inhabitants of the Middle East than to dwellers in more temperate zones. It is in its present place not a wholly satisfying image, for it appears that the thrust of Eliphaz's description up to this point has been that *no matter how long the evildoer lives*, he lives in an undisclosed misery. Now we suddenly find that the accent seems to be on the *brevity* of the wrongdoer's life. Perhaps we should say that the plant figures not primarily the brevity but the insubstantiality of the evil man's life. But also in speaking of "shoots" (יוֹנֶקֶת) and "blossom" (פֶּרַח) the metaphor is not entirely apt, for the evildoer may well be a hardened sinner, not in the first flowering of his crime. "Shoots" denote what is young and tender (8:16; 14:7; Ezek 17:22; Hos 14:7 [6]; Ps 80:12 [11]), just as the "blossom" precedes the flower which itself precedes the fruit (Isa 18:5). The image is clearly more suited to the theme of the sudden perishability of the wicked (cf. Isa 40:24), and its exploitation here is conventional rather than masterly.

The "flame" that "dries up" or "withers" (יָבֵשׁ) is not fire from heaven (lightning) (as Gray) or some freak firestorm sent as divine punishment (as שַׁלְהֶבֶת is in Ezek 21:3 [20:47]) (so Fohrer), nor the fire that devours stubble (Isa 5:24), but more probably the scorching sun. The "wind" (רוּחַ), which is probably not "the wind of his [God's] mouth" (see n. 15:30.b), is also the perfectly natural though destructive wind of the desert. No special divine intervention is here spoken of, though doubtless the retribution that is being meted out has the justice of God standing behind it.

The first colon, which repeats some words from v 22a, has nothing to do with the image of the plant. Mixed metaphors are nothing improbable, though it may be oversubtle to suppose them "intended by the author to make Eliphaz's ornate peroration somewhat ludicrous" (Andersen). We could see the phrase as a meaningful repetition of the darkness theme, as if to stamp "destined for darkness" over the two strophes that conclude the speech, or else—more probably—we could delete the colon as an erroneous repetition.

31 The verse seems to have nothing to do with the metaphor of the plant, and to be a feeble moralizing generality, lit., "Let him not trust in emptiness, deceiving himself, for emptiness will be his recompense" (RSV). Many (e.g., Duhm, Fohrer, Horst, NAB) therefore omit it entirely. The warning form ("let him not trust") is also somewhat out of place in an extended metaphorical description but perhaps "not impossible in the heightened liveliness of the dialogue" (Weiser). Dhorme and others are probably right to search for some continuance of the plant image, and the rendering in the *Translation*, though tentative, may represent the original more nearly than the MT. The wicked man would be depicted as a plant (or tree) that shoots up rapidly from the soil because of the heat but, without water, it has no staying power and does not develop strong branches; for (v 32) it quickly withers. He is a contrast to the righteous man of Ps 1, who is a long-lived tree whose leaf does not wither (1:3).

32 We have now moved into the theme of the sudden and premature end of the ungodly, cut off in the midst of his days (Ps 55:24 [23]; 102:25 [24]), when it is not yet time (Job 22:16; cf. Prov 10:27; etc.). He is a rank plant, that shoots up unnaturally and alarmingly, only to be withered and yellowed by the sun while still in the season of growth; his branches will not be green (רענן, "fresh, luxuriant"). No particular tree or plant is in mind in v 32, though in v 33 two specific plants will be exploited as examples.

33 The image of the plant is now developed differently: the wicked man is like a plant that behaves unnaturally (חמס) in not bringing its fruit to complete ripening. It would only be a diseased or unnatural vine that dropped its grapes while they were unripe (בסר "sour grapes," as in Jer 31:29; Ezek 18:2); normally the less ready grapes are the harder they are to pick (or to fall off). If the image has the identical significance in the second colon, it would be of an olive tree that shed *all* its blossom and had nothing left to develop into fruit. So olives are said to do in alternate years (Wetzstein; but see the demurrer of L. Bauer, "Einiger Stellen des Alten Testaments bei Kautzsch: 4. Aufl. im Licht des heiligen Landes," *Theologische Studien und Kritiken* 100 [1927–28] 426–38 [434–35]). W. M. Thomson, *The Land and the Book* (London: T. Nelson, 1890) 54–55, remarks that "The olive is the most prodigal of all fruit-bearing trees in flowers. It literally bends under the load of them. . . . The tree casts them off by millions." The point however is not the profusion of blossoms, nor even the quantity in which they are shed, but the effect of a tree shedding all its blossoms.

Such a vine and olive have brought themselves to an abrupt and untimely end in the course of the natural cycle; the vine is said to "do violence" (חמס) to its grapes by dropping them (cf. חמס in Prov 8:36). Cf. Isa 18:5 where the unripened grape is removed by destructive interference, not by the vine itself. The evildoer's end is to be cut off in the middle of his life cycle, none of his plans coming to fruition.

34–35 The metaphor from plant life is abandoned for the final two lines of the *topos*. Now the evildoer is viewed as a member of a group of evildoers, who are now not envisaged as a plant that fails to attain its natural end of producing fruit and are self-destroyed in mid-life, but as sterile or barren persons who fail to attain the goal of producing progeny. Or, if they are not actually sterile, they see their dwellings, in which their children live, consumed by fire, and they are without progeny as certainly as if they had been sterile. Seen differently, though the wicked are literally speaking sterile, they are in another sense anything but sterile, for they "conceive" and "are pregnant" and then "bear" harm and deceit. Theirs is a wholly negative, an unlovely and uncreative progeny. These two severely conflicting uses of the metaphor of barrenness and fecundity are very striking, and serve well as a closure for the *topos* on the wicked.

The "band" or "company" (RSV, NIV) of the godless is not his family, but the group of persons that can be designated ungodly—even if they do not act or gather as a social group. עדה is used of such groups or entities within the community in Ps 22:17 [16]; 86:14; 106:17; the "congregation (עדה) of the righteous" in Ps 1:5 is especially parallel, since it never constitutes itself as a gathering but is rather a conceptual grouping.

It is not entirely certain that the term translated "sterile" or "barren" (גלמוד, also at 3:7; 30:3; Isa 49:21) strictly means that and not rather "desolate" or "stony" (of ground) (as the cognate in Arabic). If it does refer to sterility, it is not clear whether the "company of the ungodly" are represented as a sterile man or an infertile woman, though the female metaphors of v 35 would suggest the latter. The point of this image can hardly be, as it has been in the preceding verses (27–32), that the ungodly man is cut off before his time. It is rather that he is visibly under a curse (of sterility) even before he dies; there is a similarity with the opening depiction in this *topos*, of the wicked man writhing in pain all his days (v 20), where also the accent was wholly upon the quality of his life and not upon his end, untimely or otherwise.

In parallel to the "company of the ungodly" are "the tents of bribery." "Bribery" here of course refers to attempts to pervert justice; in itself, a bribe is only a gift, and as M. Greenberg notes, "since giving gifts was viewed as a perfectly legitimate means of getting ahead" (Prov 18:16), and was even recommended to pacify antagonists (21:14), "the distinction between gifts and bribes must sometimes have been extremely subtle" (*IDB* 3:465; cf. also Job 6:22). But in the context of the legal court, gifts are outlawed (Exod 23:8; Deut 16:19; cf. 1 Sam 8:3; Prov 17:23) as perverting the course of impartial justice; those who give and take them in that setting are "sinners" (חטא, Ps 26:10), "wicked" (רשע, Prov 17:23). The thought here is not that such men have grown rich on the proceeds of bribes (against Gray, Horst, Fohrer) but simply that such malpractice is an illustration or example of wickedness. The fire that destroys the "tents" (a formal archaizing idiom; cf. 5:24; 8:22; 11:14; 12:6) of these representative wicked men is not here to be seen as a direct divine punishment (it is not lightning, "fire of God," as in 1:16) but as a purely natural phenomenon (as in 22:20; 20:26 seems different). Of course the destruction of their homes is a token of divine displeasure and judgment, just as their sterility in the first half of the verse was. What they lose in the fire is not primarily their wealth, but their offspring; for in the context this colon depicts the line of the wicked being brought, during his lifetime, to an end, and the man himself undergoing, during his lifetime, the pain his wickedness deserves (the theme of v 20).

It may at first be judged an unhappy mixture of metaphors to ascribe procreativeness to the sterile and childless; but the point is that though the wicked is fated to die without natural progeny he nevertheless begets an unnatural disreputable brood. The opening phrase of v 35, "They conceive mischief and give birth to evil," is evidently a proverbial expression, as the use of the two "vivid" infinitive absolutes (GKC, § 113ff) may suggest, and as its appearance, with variants, at Ps 7:15 [14] and Isa 59:4 confirms. The verbs הרה, "conceive," and ילד, "bear," are literally used properly of the mother (though ילד is used of the father "begetting" about 20 times); but here they obviously are the (metaphorical) act of wicked *men*; their "belly" (בטן) is plainly also not the "heart" (rsv) but their womb (neb, niv; as also in 3:10), speaking metaphorically, in which the embryo is "prepared" (כון hiph, not otherwise used in this connection). Birth (ילד) is mentioned before pregnancy because "conceive" and "bear" belong to the proverb-like phrase.

The nouns used for the progeny of the wicked, "trouble" (עמל; cf. 4:8), "iniquity" (און; cf. 4:8) and "deceit" (מרמה), are not to be differentiated here; the child that is conceived and the child that is born is one and the same. There may be some thought that what the wicked gives birth to is his own downfall; this may be suggested also in the parallel Ps 7:15 [14] (though not in Isa 59:4), where the succeeding image is of the wicked man falling into the pit he has dug. If this is so, it would link up with the image Eliphaz has used previously, at 4:8, that those who plough iniquity (און) and sow trouble (עמל) reap the same (cf. 5:6–7, where humans beget iniquity [און] and trouble [עמל]). The harm begotten by the wicked is not just harm done to others, but ultimately a harm that strikes him himself. That, in the end, is the thrust of Eliphaz's present depiction: the wicked man lives his life long in constant torment—self-inflicted. Job's suffering, too, is due to no one but himself (for humans beget their own suffering, 5:7), but he is not one of the wicked, and his present pain is assuredly only temporary (cf. 4:5a).

Weiser, who speaks for many, thinks it significant that Eliphaz has "no room any more for a word of consolation" and judges Eliphaz's depiction of the fate of the wicked to be some kind of warning to Job. But it is only necessary to observe the "happy" ending to his first *and* third speeches (5:17–27; 22:21–30) to recognize that Eliphaz stands on Job's side, in this speech also.

Explanation

The fundamental key for the interpretation of this speech is the recognition that the depiction of the wicked in vv 20–35 is a depiction of what Job is *not*. It opens the way to see the speech as a whole as an encouragement to Job, in essential accord both with Eliphaz's first speech (chaps. 4–5) and with his third (chap. 22). From Eliphaz's point of view, Job's present rash and, frankly, sinful words apart, Job is at bottom a righteous man whose innocence Eliphaz admires. Job has nothing to fear from the present suffering he endures at God's hand, for it is but an epiphenomenon upon the ordered course of a prosperous and devout life. The mental anguish that the godless suffer all their days (vv 20–22) is not Job's experience, nor can their end, "marked down for the sword" (v 22), "cast out as food for the vultures" (v 23), their "blossom swept away by the wind" (v 30), ever be his.

Job has two faults, nevertheless—an intellectual one and a moral one. The intellectual wrong is not to recognize that even the most upright of humanity is tainted in God's sight (vv 14–16). Perfect innocence such as Job lays claim to, innocence that can admit no cause at all in oneself for divine punishment, is not within the grasp of humankind; and Job as a member of the theological guild ought to know that and recognize its bearing upon himself. As it is, he is victim of the sin of intellectual pride, which imagines itself more gifted than the commonality (v 9) and which in the fever of supposed new insights abandons the meditative and consensual habits of his class (v 4).

Job's moral fault is not to bear the suffering that has come his way with fortitude and patience. The fault that has earned him his suffering is insignificant by comparison with the wrong he now perpetrates by his present behavior.

It is a wrong against himself (v 6) and against God (v 13) to speak so one-sidedly and perversely about God. The animation of Job's language is its own condemnation, it appears (vv 12–13); the truly wise is prudent and calm in speech. It is not as though from Eliphaz's point of view what Job says about God is wholly wrong; for has not Job quoted the traditional language of piety in 12:13–25, for example? It is the perverse design in Job's speeches, that care for nothing but evidences of divine hostility, and the intemperate language, which rejects the values of the academy, that trouble Eliphaz and call forth this firm rejoinder.

He does not, according to his own lights, reject Job the man. But what he cannot see is that Job the man is not a man to be reasoned with, but a hurting, brawling individual to whom a call for patience is an invitation to dishonesty: for Job to suffer in silence would be to accede to the divine judgment against him, and Job could do that only at the price of his own integrity. From the perspective given us by the prologue, we can only be on Job's side in this struggle.

Job's Fifth Speech   (16:1–17:16)

Bibliography

Arnold, W. R. "The Interpretation of קרנים מידו לו." *AJSL* 21 (1904–1905) 167–72. **Curtis, J. B.** "On Job's Witness in Heaven." *JBL* 102 (1983) 549–62. **Dahood, M.** "Northwest Semitic Philology and Job." In *The Bible in Current Catholic Thought*, M. J. Gruenthaner Memorial Volume, ed. J. L. McKenzie. New York: Herder & Herder, 1962. 55–74. ———. "Hebrew-Ugaritic Lexicography IV." *Bib* 47 (1966) 403–19. ———. "Hebrew-Ugaritic Lexicography V." *Bib* 48 (1967) 421–38. **Driver, G. R.** "Studies in the Vocabulary of the Old Testament VI." *JTS* 34 (1933) 375–85. ———. "Problems in the Hebrew Text of Job." VTSup 3 (1955) 72–93. **Finkelstein, J. J.** "Hebrew חבר and Semitic *ḤBR*." *JBL* 75 (1956) 328–31. **Gordis, R.** "A Rhetorical Use of Interrogative Sentences in Biblical Hebrew." *AJSL* 49 (1933) 212–17. ———. "'My Mother and My Sister'—A Note on Job 17,14 and the Name AḤʾAV" [Heb]. *Leš* 36 (1971–72) 71–72. **Greenfield, J. C.** "Lexicographical Notes." *HUCA* 29 (1958) 203–28. **Hempel, J.** "Jahwegleichnisse der israelitischen Propheten." *ZAW* 42 (1924) 74–104 (= BZAW 81 [1961] 1–29). **Jacob, B.** "Erklärung einiger Hiob-Stellen. 17:6." *ZAW* 32 (1912) 278–87 (286). **Loretz, O.** "*ḤBR* in Jb 16,4." *CBQ* 23 (1961) 293–94. **Perles, F.** "A Miscellany of Lexical and Textual Notes on the Bible." *JQR* 2 (1911–12) 97–132. **Rin, S.** "Ugaritic–Old Testament Affinities." *BZ* 7 (1963) 22–33. **Sarna, N. M.** "Some Instances of the Enclitic *-m* in Job." *JJS* 6 (1955) 108–10. **Speiser, E. A.** "The Semantic Range of *dalāpu*." *JCS* 5 (1951) 64–66. **Tromp, N. J.** *Primitive Conceptions of Death and the Nether World in the Old Testament*. BibOr 21. Rome: Pontifical Biblical Institute, 1969. **Vella, P.** "Il redentore di Giobbe (Nota a *Giob.* 16,20)." *RivB* 13 (1965) 161–68. **Winton Thomas, D.** "מלאו in Jeremiah IV.5: A Military Term." *JJS* 3 (1952) 47–52.

Translation

16:1 *Then Job answered and said:*

> 2 *I have heard many such things;*
>   *torturer-comforters* [a] *you all are!*
> 3 *Will there be no end to windy words?*
>   *What so agitates* [a] *you that you must reply?*
> 4 *I also could speak as you do,*
>   *if you were in my place.*
> *I could harangue* [a] *you,*
>   *and shake my head at you.*
> 5 *But no! I would strengthen you with my encouragements,*
>   *the consolations of my lips would soothe* [a] *your pain.*
> 6 *Yet if I speak, my pain is not soothed;*
>   *if I am silent, it will not* [a] *leave me.*

> 7 *But now:*
> *He* [a] *has worn me out;*
>   *he has appalled the whole company of my acquaintance.* [b]
> 8 *He has shriveled me up* [a]*—it is a witness against me.*
>   *My gauntness* [b] *rises up to testify against me.*

⁹ *His anger* ᵃ *has torn me, and his hatred assaults me;* ᵇ
  he gnashes his teeth at me.
  My enemy ᶜ *whets his eye* ᵈ *against me.*
¹⁰ *Men laugh in open mockery of me,*
  they strike my cheeks in insult, ᵃ
  and band together against me. ᵇ
¹¹ *God has abandoned me to evil men,* ᵃ
  he has thrust ᵇ *me into the clutches of the wicked.*

¹² *I was untroubled, but he shattered* ᵃ *me;*
  he seized me by the neck and dashed me to pieces.
  He made me his target;
¹³   *his bowmen* ᵃ *surrounded me.*
  He pierced my kidneys; he was pitiless;
  he spilled my gall on the ground.
¹⁴ *He battered me down, breach upon breach;* ᵃ
  he rushed against me like a champion.

¹⁵ *I have sewn sackcloth to* ᵃ *my skin;*
  I have buried my glory ᵇ *in the dust.*
¹⁶ *My face is red from weeping,*
  and on my eyelids is the darkness of death. ᵃ
¹⁷ ᵃ *For in my palms is "non-violence,"*
  and my prayer ᵇ *is undefiled.*

¹⁸ *O earth, cover not my blood,*
  and let my outcry ᵃ *find no rest.* ᵇ
¹⁹ *Even now my witness is in heaven,*
  my advocate is on high.
²⁰ *It is my cry* ᵃ *that is my spokesman;* ᵇ
  sleeplessly I wait ᶜ *for God's reply.*
²¹ *It will argue a mortal's case before God*
  as a man ᵃ *argues for his friend.* ᵇ
²² *For when a few years* ᵃ *have come*
  I shall take the road of no return.

¹⁷:¹ *My spirit is crushed,* ᵃ
  my days ᵇ *have been snuffed out,* ᶜ
  the graveyard ᵈ *awaits me.*
² *Is there not* ᵃ *mockery* ᵇ *around me?*
  Are not my eyes weary ᶜ *from men's antagonism?* ᵈ
³ *Keep my pledge* ᵃ *close by you* ᵇ *[O God];*
  for there is no one who will stand surety ᶜ *for me.*
⁴ *You have shut their minds to reason;*
  therefore you will win no honor ᵃ *on that account.*
⁵ ᵃ *[They are like] a man bidding* ᵃ *his friends to a feast* ᵇ
  while his children are starving.

⁶ *He has set me up as a byword* ᵃ *of peoples;*
  I have become something to spit at. ᵇ

⁷*My eyes have grown dim with grief;*
　*and my limbs*ᵃ *have wasted*ᵇ *to*ᶜ *a shadow.*
⁸*At this the upright are appalled;*
　*the innocent*ᵃ *are roused against the ungodly.*
⁹*The righteous*ᵃ *maintain their way;*ᵇ
　those whose hands are clean grow stronger still.
¹⁰*But, attack*ᵃ *me again, all of you!*ᵇ
　I would not find a single wise man among you.

¹¹ᵃ*My days have passed;*ᵇ
　*broken are my plans,*ᶜ
　*the desires*ᵈ *of my heart—*
¹²ᵃ*which had turned night into day,*ᵇ
　*brought light nearer than*ᶜ *darkness.*
¹³*If*ᵃ *I look for*ᵇ *Sheol to be my home,*
　if I have spread my couch in the darkness,
¹⁴*if I have cried to the Pit,*ᵃ *"You are my father!,"*
　and to the worm, "My mother!," "My sister!,"
¹⁵*where then is my hope?*
　*and as for happiness,*ᵃ *who can see any for me?*
¹⁶*Will they descend*ᵃ *with me*ᵇ *to Sheol?*
　*Shall we go down*ᶜ *together into the dust?*

Notes

16:2.a. Lit., "comforters of woe." Gordis thinks עמל is "worthlessness" because it is parallel to און in 15:35; but there און does not mean "naught" but (physical) "harm." D. Winton Thomas argued that since "the primary meaning" of נחם is "make to breathe" (cf. Arab. *naḥama* "breathe pantingly or hard [of a horse]"), the phrase means "breathers out of trouble," i.e., mischief makers ("A Note on the Hebrew Root נחם," *ExpT* 44 [1932–33] 191–92); against this is the fact that the friends have come to "comfort" (נחם piel) him (2:11; cf. 42:11).

3.a. Gordis improbably translates מרץ "force, compel"; cf. n. 6:25.a.

4.a. Following J. J. Finkelstein's proposal ("Hebrew חבר and Semitic *HBR*," *JBL* 75 [1956] 328–31) of a verb חבר II "make a sound," cognate with Ug. *ḥbr* (cf. also Deut 18:11; Ps 58:6 [5]; Prov 21:9; 25:24); similarly O. Loretz, "ḤBR in Jb 16,4," *CBQ* 23 (1961) 293–94, comparing Akk. *ḥabaru*; so also NEB, perhaps NJPS, Pope, Terrien. Less likely is the suggestion of a חבר II "make beautiful" (which would occur only here) cognate with Arab. *ḥabara*, used of speech, but probably only in later Arabic (Gray); thus KB³, Fohrer, Horst, de Wilde. The traditional understanding is of חבר "join," i.e., "join words together, compose"; so Gordis, Sicre Díaz. Among emendations, the most attractive is אַכְבִּירָה "I would multiply" (Dhorme); cf. מִלִּין יַכְבִּר "he multiplies words" in 35:16.

5.a. There is no object for יחשך, which indeed usually means "withhold, restrain, refrain." So many emend to לֹא אֶחְשֹׁךְ "I will not restrain," following LXX οὐ φείσομαι (so Merx, Bickell, Budde, Dhorme, Rowley, Hesse, de Wilde). Others agree in inserting the negative, and translate "would not be lacking" (Fohrer). G. R. Driver also thought the verb intransitive (also KB³) but did not read the negative ("Studies in the Vocabulary of the Old Testament VI," *JTS* 34 [1933] 375–85 [380]). Ehrlich, Gordis and Sicre Díaz take ניד as subject and שפתי as object, "sympathy would restrain my lips" from harsh words (cf. "lips" and "words" as objects of חשך in Prov 10:19; 17:27). All these are plausible suggestions, but it is arguable that what should be determinative is the use of חשך in the next line, where it fairly clearly means "be assuaged, soothed" in the niph (cf. 21:30 "is spared"); the implied object of the verb is therefore "your pain" (Horst; cf. Pope). Emendations to אֲחַזֵּק "I would strengthen" (Duhm) or יְחַזֶּקְכֶם "would strengthen you" (Hölscher, cf. *BHK*) can be dismissed.

6.a. מה is thought by Dhorme, Pope and others to be equivalent to Arab. *ma* "not" (cf. 1 Kgs

12:16); the interrogative used rhetorically amounts to the same meaning, and it is unnecessary to postulate מה as a negative particle.

7.a. The subject is God, not "my pain" (ibn Ezra, Peters; cf. Vg *oppressit me dolor meus*), nor Eliphaz (Merx), nor "the jealous or malicious man" (Dhorme and NEB ["my friend with false sympathy"], revocalizing השׁמות to הַשְׂמוֹת, a noun from the postulated root שׂמת "rejoice at the misfortunes of others," cognate with Arab. *šamita*; cf. also F. Perles, "A Miscellany of Lexical and Textual Notes on the Bible," *JQR* 2 [1911–12] 97–132 [110]). JB apparently follows Dhorme in translating "ill-will drives me to distraction." NAB reads הֲשִׁמֹּתַנִי "I am stunned" (שׁמם hithpo). De Wilde emends to מְשַׁמָּתִי "my ruin," subject of הלאני, to be emended to the fem הֶלְאָתַנִי. If the second verb is to be emended to a third person form (see *Comment*), הֵשַׁם it must be (Fohrer), or הֲשִׁמַּנִי if כל־עדתי is to be transferred to the next line (see n. 7.b).

7.b. Lit., "my company." JB "a whole host molests me" takes עדה as the subject and presumably emends רָעָתִי "my calamity, woe" as the subject of השׁמות; so too Driver-Gray, Hölscher, Pope. Among emendations may be mentioned the following: E. G. King, "Some Notes on the Text of Job," *JTS* 15 (1914) 74–81 (74–76), read נִצְדֵּיתִי "I am wasted." De Wilde emends to another word for misfortune (parallel to משמתי)—עֹנָתִי—and Horst reads בְּעוּתָיו "his [God's] terrors." Sicre Díaz finds here עֵדָה II (KB³) "testimony" (as in Gen 21:30; Josh 24:27), and takes Eliphaz as the subject of the verb: "you reduce my testimony to silence"; but would Job admit that? Dhorme, followed by NEB, read עֲדָתוֹ, "his company," i.e., of Job's friend-opponents (NEB "he and his fellows"). The noun is often taken as the subject of יתקמטני in v 8 (JB, NEB, NAB, Duhm, Dhorme, Rowley, Horst, Pope, de Wilde).

8.a. קמט only here and 22:16, properly "seize, grasp" (cf. Arab., Aram.), but also "wrinkle" (Rabb. Heb., Syr.; cf. Driver, Gordis). So AV "filled me with wrinkles," Pope "wizened"; but BDB, KB³ do not recognize this sense. Aq had "you have wrinkled me" (ἐρρωτίδωσάς με).

8.b. כחשׁ usually "lie, deceit," but the verb in Ps 109:24 does mean "be lean"; "leanness" is here accepted by RV, RSV, NJPS, NIV, Gordis, Pope, Horst, Fohrer, de Wilde. Revocalization to כֶּחָשִׁי (F. Delitzsch, Dhorme) would yield "my liar" (cf. the pl in Isa 30:9), which could perhaps mean "the one who slanders me" (the false friend of v 7); Symm (καταψευδόμενος) and Vg (*falsiloquus*) did indeed take the word thus, but that is not surprising, and it does not amount to strong support.

9.a. אפו is evidently the subject (as it is of טרף in Amos 1:11); it is improbable that אף has the concrete meaning "nose, snout" (against Ehrlich, Andersen)—since the snout is not naturally used for tearing—and so also unlikely that the *beth* of בשׂניו is double-duty.

9.b. שׂטם "hate" (RSV) is thought by many illogical here, in that the hating ought to precede the fearing. Many therefore emend to וַיִּשְׁמְטֵנִי "and he dropped me," sc. from his mouth to the ground (so perhaps LXX κατέβαλέν με; cf. Syr; Hölscher, Horst, de Wilde); that retains the image, but unsuitably suggests the idea of escape. Two parallels make clear that שׂטם refers to ongoing hatred as expressed in action (not merely "harbored" or "cherished," against BDB and KB): Gen 49:23 where it is used immediately after "the archers . . . shot at him," and Amos 1:11 where the verb is not used but the same thought occurs: "his wrath tore (אפו . . . יטרף) and he kept his wrath (MT his wrath kept) for ever." "Persecute" (RV, NJPS), though a little vague, is more correct than "hate"; Gordis's suggestion that it is a case of *hysteron proteron* is unnecessary (cf. also on 14:10).

9.c. Not to be altered to צָרַי "my enemies," with consequent pluralization of following verbs and suffixes, though evidenced by Symm (οἱ ἐναντίον μου) and Syr (so Duhm, Stevenson, de Wilde; NEB, JB, NAB). Dahood thought צָר was "his blade," צר for צֻר, "flint-knife" (*Psalms I*, 46), the suffix -*i* being third person (cf. Ball עֵינָיו צָרֵי "the blades of his eyes").

9.d. Lit., "sharpens his eyes," לטשׁ of whetting a sword at Ps 7:13 [12], a razor at Ps 52:4 [2]. Our idiom "look daggers at" (NEB) is now too dead a metaphor; JB "whet their eyes on me" suggests Job is the whetstone. NAB's emendation to עָלַי יִלְטֹּשׁ "lord it over me," omitting עֵינָיו, "their eyes," has nothing to commend it.

10.a. It is not clear why NEB has "they slash my cheeks with knives."

10.b. The phrase "they mass themselves against me" (יחד עלי יתמלאון), probably a military metaphor (D. Winton Thomas, "מלאו in Jeremiah IV.5: A Military Term," *JJS* 3 [1952] 47–52; cf. NAB "they are all enlisted against me"), does not occur in the Psalms, but the language of plotting "together" (יחד) is found in 31:14 [13]; 83:6 [5] (cf. 2:2), and whispering "together" at 41:8 [7] and especially "closing in upon" (נקף hiph) "together" at 88:18 [17]; and allusions to bands of numerous enemies are of course frequent (e.g. Ps 3:7 [6]; 17:11; 22:13, 17 [12, 16]; 31:22 [21]; 56:6). Such depictions are real as depictions of the sufferer's feeling, but are not necessarily statements of objective reality.

11.a. עֲוִיל is "boy" (19:18; 21:11; from עול "suckle"); emendation to עַוָּל "evildoer" (parallel to רשע in 27:7) is obvious, since it is unlikely that there was a by-form עויל of that word (against Gordis).

11.b. Probably יְרְטֵנִי from ירט "thrust" (KB³; cf. BDB)—or perhaps יְרְטָנִי, pf piel (*BHK*), or יְיְרְטֵנִי, impf piel (Brockington, 106)—rather than יְרְטֵנִי from רטה "wring out."

12.a. From פרר "break" (BDB, Dhorme); the existence of a פרר II "shake," though recognized by KB³ (so too Horst, Fohrer), is questionable.

13.a. In view of Jer 50:29 we should take רַבָּיו as "his archers" (BDB, NJPS, NIV; Gordis, Pope, Andersen) rather than "his arrows" (as LXX, Vg, Tg, Pesh; KB, NEB, NAB, JB; Dhorme, Horst, Fohrer).

14.a. Dahood, *Psalms I*, 308, read פֶּרֶץ עַל־פְּנֵי־פ־רוֹץ, "[he rends me] rift upon rift, // Rushes at me like a warrior," seeing here the emphatic particle *pa*. K. Aartun has rightly protested at the arbitrariness of this proposal, "Textüberlieferung und vermeintliche Belege der Konjunktion *pᵛ* im Alten Testament," *UF* 10 (1978) 1–13 (9–10).

15.a. A more dramatic image than NEB's "I stitched sackcloth together to cover my body"; see *Comment*.

15.b. So NJPS, lit., "I have dug my brow into the dust"; there is no corresponding native English idiom, and קרן, "horn," should not be transmuted to "brow" (JB, NAB, NIV). NEB "I buried my forelock in the dust" depends upon a suggestion of W. R. Arnold ("The Interpretation of קדנים מידו לו," *AJSL* 21 [1904–1905] 167–72 [170]) reported by S. R. Driver, who found the cognate Arabic noun could signify the forelock and noted that among Bedouin "horns" could refer to long sidelocks. The older view that עלל meant "defiled" (AV, RVmg, following Rashi) is abandoned now in favor of "insert" (cognates in Aram., Syr.), or perhaps "lower, dip" (S. Rin, "Ugaritic–Old Testament Affinities," *BZ* 7 [1963] 22–33 [23]; J. Gray, *The Legacy of Canaan* [VTS 5; Leiden: E. J. Brill, 1957] 195).

16.a. On צַלְמָוֶת see n. 10:21.b.

17.a. Duhm and de Wilde transpose this verse to follow v 14; but even the strong connection of thought with v 14 and the preceding verses (see *Comment*) does not justify the transposition.

17.b. תפלתי, emended by Duhm to נְתִיבָתִי, "my way," or perhaps אִמְרָתִי, "my speech." See *Comment*.

18.a. Strictly it is the blood that cries out; hence some emend to זַעֲקָתוֹ "its outcry" (*BHK*, *BHS*, de Wilde). But the change is unnecessary.

18.b. "Place" (מקום) must mean resting-place or stopping place, though it is difficult to parallel either of these uses. It is impossible that מקום means "tomb" (Dahood, "Northwest Semitic Philology," 61–62; followed by Rowley, Pope, Blommerde), since the evidence for such a specific meaning has been misinterpreted (see Grabbe, 69–72). "Let there be no room for my outcry" would be a more natural understanding of the words (cf. RVmg "have no more place"), but this does not fit the context.

20.a. Taking רֵעִי from רֵעַ III, according to BDB "purpose, aim," and KB "will, intention, thought," but better explained as equivalent to רְעוּת "longing, striving" (Eccl 1:14; 2:11, 17, 26; etc.) from the same root רעה III. This sense suits the other occurrences of רֵעַ in Ps 139:2, 17 better than "thought" (RSV). Pope gives the right lead by translating "interpreter of my thoughts," but "thoughts" does not suit the context well. Almost as attractive is Dhorme's translation "clamor," רֵעַ II from רוע (the noun is in 36:33; Exod 32:17; Mic 4:9); hence JB "My own lament is my advocate with God" (also Kissane). Most versions and commentators see רֵעִי here as "my friends" (רֵעַ I), though they can hardly be Job's "intercessors" or "interpreters" (see n. 20.b). J. B. Curtis, "On Job's Witness in Heaven," *JBL* 102 (1983) 549–62 (554), vocalizes מְלִיצִי רֵעִי אַל־אֱלוֹהַ "[my intercessor is] my shepherd," a parody of Ps 23:1, since it is the personal god, not the high god, who is Job's shepherd; but this would be an amazing way to introduce, for the first time in the book, the idea of a "personal god."

20.b. Reading מְלִיצִי "my spokesman" for MT מְלִיצַי "my spokesmen" (a reading possibly due to thinking the word is from ליץ, hence "scorners," the friends in the pl). מֵלִיץ "spokesman" is well attested (see *Comment* and KB³), no doubt as a root different from ליץ "scorn" (against BDB, KB³); see further N. H. Richardson, "Some Notes on ליץ and Its Derivatives," *VT* 5 (1955) 163–79; idem, "Two Addenda to 'Some Notes on ליץ and Its Derivatives,'" *VT* 5 (1955) 434–36. Tur-Sinai, Irwin, Pope, Gordis, JB, NAB, NIV, NJPS adopt this interpretation. Reference to "my friends" (רֵעַי) as "scorners" is out of place here, and can only be understood as parenthetic or contrastive. RSV "my friends scorn me" is not impossible, but the "spokesman" figure fits better into the immediate context. Emendations, e.g. to מָצָא "has reached" (מֹטה = מצא) (Dhorme), or יִמָּצֵא לִי רֵעִי "my Friend will make an appearance on my behalf" (Duhm, Fohrer), or יִמָּצֵא רֵעִי "my appeal will reach" (NEB; cf. LXX "may my request reach the Lord"), or מִלִּבִּי יָצָא רֵעִי "from my heart goes out my cry" (de Wilde), are certainly wrong.

20.c. דלף, though obviously "leak" at Eccl 10:18, is best connected here and at Ps 119:28 with Akk. *dalāpu* "be sleepless" (KB, KB³, Horst, Fohrer, G. R. Driver, "Studies in the Vocabulary of the Old Testament," *JTS* 34 [1933] 375–85 [384–85]; perhaps cf. also Ug. *dlp* "exhaust"). For precisions on the Akk., see E. A. Speiser, "The Semantic Range of *dalāpu*," *JCS* 5 (1951) 64–66; J. C. Greenfield, "Lexicographical Notes I," *HUCA* 29 (1958) 203–28 (207–10), resists this connection for דלף here, comparing its use for dripping eyes in *b. Bek.* 44a and זלף "pour out, sprinkle" in postbib. Heb., Aram., Syr. Curtis, *JBL* 102 (1983) 555–59, supports the sense of דלף as "be restless," but wants to read דְּלְפָה עֵינִי "he who watches over me harasses him" (דלף piel with masc suff *-oh*, עין as verb "watch," as Q of 1 Sam 18:9 and Hos 10:10 perhaps suggest). The whole proposal is forced. J. Vella, "Il redentore di Giobbe (Nota a *Giob.* 16,20)," *RivB* 13 (1965) 161–68, reads הָעַיִן (or, דְּלף) מְלִיצִי יָרַע אֵל־אֵלוֹהַּ דֶּלֶף "my advocate will harm God, whose eye will drip tears," a totally improbable interpretation (the noun דֶּלֶף in any case does not seem to mean "dripping of water" but a "leaking roof").

21.a. The reading of a few MSS וּבֵין "and between" (so *BHK, BHS*, and many) is to be rejected (though cf. J. Barr, "Some Notes on *ben* 'between' in Classical Hebrew," *JSS* 23 [1978] 1–22 [12]); see *Comment*. On the "and" of comparison (*waw adaequationis*) see GKC, § 161a, and cf. 12:11; 14:12; contrast 5:7 (*q.v.*). Pesh, Vg, Tg took the *waw* thus (they did not read וכב(ן), as against *BHK*).

21.b. De Wilde's emendation of רעהו to עשֵׂהוּ "his Maker" is an effort to create synonymous parallelism, but it overlooks the precise significance of the prepositions.

22.a. שְׁנוֹת מִסְפָּר, lit., "years of number"; the idiom is common (= "a few men," Gen 34:20; Deut 4:27; Jer 44:28; 1 Chr 16:19; Ps 105:12; Ezek 12:16) and the bound phrase should probably not be split apart, as in JB "the years of my life are numbered" (cf. NAB). It is attractive (see *Comment*) to emend מספר to מִסְפֵּד "mourning" (Lagarde, Bickell), except that mourning does not last for *years*. Bickell, Hoffmann and Peake therefore read שׁנוֹת "(female) repeaters of (mourning)," i.e., wailing women, but the phrase is unparalleled, and it can be objected that the journey to Sheol (v 22b) takes place before the arrival of the wailing women (v 22a)—though in reply it can also be argued that the journey to Sheol does not properly occur before the burial. Dahood's proposal (*Bib* 48 [1967] 429) to read מִסְפָּר (so Blommerde, Pope), "years without number, innumerable years," also has the disadvantage that the years spent in Sheol are mentioned before the journey there.

17:1.a. To create a more usual line, Duhm read חִבְּלָה רוּחוֹ יָמַי "his anger has destroyed my days"; so too Hölscher, KB³, but it is not an improvement on the MT, as Rowley remarks.

1.b. Not עִמִּי, "my spirit is broken within me" (*BHK*, Fohrer); this is an attempt to remove the pattern of 2+2+2 in the line.

1.c. Some MSS have נדעכו, with the same meaning; *lectio difficilior* is to be preferred. Duhm read נֶעֱזָב קְבָרִים לִי "the grave is left to me" (so also *BHK*, Fohrer); but it makes poor sense to say that the grave is "abandoned" for him (Driver). Klostermann, JB, de Wilde prefer נִזְעֲקוּ קְבָרִים לִי "the gravediggers are assembled for me"; but זעק niph means "are assembled" only in a military context, i.e., "are called out, summoned" (Josh 8:16; Judg 6:34, 35; 18:23; 1 Sam 14:20).

1.d. קְבָרִים, lit., "graves," probably the graveyard as the place where graves (pl) are found. This would be a plural of extension (GKC, § 124c), rather than an intensive pl, sc. "a stately tomb." There is no need to hypothesize an enclitic particle *-m* on the sg form (as Pope). Others vocalize קֹבְרִים "gravediggers" (see n. 17:1.c).

2.a. אִם־לֹא functions as an emphatic positive particle (GKC, § 149b).

2.b. הֲתֻלִּים, an abstract noun, "mockery." Tur-Sinai and NEB read הֹתֵלִים "mockers" (as Tg) because of the pl suff on המורתם, but Gordis argues that קָבְרִים is itself a *qatûl* participle "mockers" (like זָכוּר "remembering"). N. Tromp, *Primitive Conceptions of Death and the Nether World in the Old Testament* (BibOr 21; Rome: Pontifical Biblical Institute, 1969) 54–55, followed by Dahood, *Psalms I*, 279, read הַתֻּלָּם "the two mounds" (at the edge of Sheol, bounding the earth, as in *The Palace of Baal* [*CTA 4*] 4.8.4 [Gibson, 66]; cf. Ezra Pound, *Canto* 16: "And before the hell mouth; dry plain / and two mountains" [*The Cantos of Ezra Pound* (London: Faber & Faber, 1954) 72]). Similarly also Pope, though construing the noun as pl.

2.c. Reading תֵּלָא וְ עֵינִי (= תִּלְאֶינָה), "my eyes are tired" (Hölscher, G. R. Driver [VTSup 3 (1955) 78], Fohrer, *BHK*, de Wilde) for MT תָּלַן עֵינִי "my eye dwells." לין is "stay the night," thus "dwell," but the sense is strained. Budde read וְ עֵינִי תִּכְל (= תִּכְלֶינָה) "my eyes fail" (as in 11:20); so too NAB "my eyes grow dim" and perhaps also NEB "my day is darkened" (though Brockington says the text presupposed is תֶּחְלָאֶנָה [*sic*]); cf. *BHK*.

2.d. הַמְּרוֹתָם, "their antagonism, refractory behavior," from הָמָרָה "complaint." G. R. Driver supposed a הַמְרָה, cognate with Arab. *hamratun* "angry words" and *hammârun* "garrulous old man," and rendered "your stream of peevish complaints" (VTSup 3 [1955] 78); so NEB "their sneers." Tromp, *Death and the Nether World*, 54–55, read הַמָּרְתֵם "the twin miry deeps"; Pope, "the Slime-Pits," as characteristic of the underworld (cf. 9:31).

3.a. Reading עֶרְבֹנִי "my pledge" for MT עָרְבֵנִי "take me on pledge" (so most, following Reiske).

3.b. Lit., "set my pledge with you."

3.c. Lit., "who will be struck with my hand?" The gesture of striking (תקע) hands was a ratification of an agreement to stand surety (Prov 11:15; 17:18; 22:26). The niph (only here in this sense) must be *niphal tolerativum*, "who will allow himself (= his hand) to be struck (in conclusion of a bargain) with my hand?" (not "*give* a pledge," as Gordis explains the niph). Emendation to יִתְקַע "will strike" (Fohrer) is unnecessary. The rhetorical question expects the answer "no one"; and the question functions as the reason for the imperative שִׂימָה.

4.a. תֵּרֹמֵם to be taken as a pass pilel (so KB), "will be exalted," as in Ps 75:11 [10]; Neh 9:5; Ps 66:17 (text emended), or perhaps the polal (reading תְּרֹמָם, so Gordis). But most regard it as an active polel, "you will exalt (them)," perhaps a contracted form equivalent to תְּרֹמְמֵם (GKC, § 72cc; Horst); some actually emend to תְּרֹמְמֵם or else vocalize as hiph תָּרֵם (Merx, *BHK*, KB). Dhorme suggested "their hand is (not) raised" (so too Hölscher, Terrien, JB) but in the absence of evidence that the hands were raised in striking a bargain the emendation is too precarious. NAB's emendation to יָבִינוּ "they do (not) understand" is arbitrary.

5.a-a. יַגִּיד, lit., "announces, informs" cannot easily mean "invite" (as, e.g., Dhorme, Gordis, Horst), but given the proverbial character of the line it is perhaps possible. "Denounce" is supported by Jer 20:10, but it cannot have been a very common thing for a man to "denounce friends for a portion" (cf. NIV; RSV "informs against his friends to get a share of their property"); so could this have been a proverb? And surely Job does not seriously mean that those who "denounce" him as unrighteous do so for hope of some benefit from his property? De Wilde supposes another noun חֵלֶק "destruction," from חלק III (KB³) "destroy" (cognate with Ug. *ḥlq*; cf. Dahood, *Bib* 47 [1966] 405), hence "he who denounces his friends [goes] to destruction"; but the attestation of this root in Heb. is uncertain.

5.b. Similarly Moffatt, Peake, Dhorme, Horst, Fohrer, Gordis. חלק is a "portion" of food (Lev 6:10 [17]; Deut 18:8; Hab 1:16) but the proverb would mean much the same if it is taken as "possession," a more common meaning. Some revocalize to לְחַלֵּק "to give a portion to" (Budde, Hölscher, Peake, KB³). A connection with חֵלֶק III (BDB; I, KB³) "flattery," as in Prov 7:21, cannot be sustained (against KJV "he that speaketh flattery to his friends"). See n. 5.a-a.

6.a. Reading, with most, לִמְשֹׁל, the construct of the noun, rather than לִמְשֹׁל, inf constr.

6.b. Lit., "a spitting in the face," i.e., one in whose face people spit. It is more than doubtful that תֹּפֶת is derived from the place Topheth as a symbol of shame (Blommerde); NJPS suggests "I have become like Tophet [that swallowed children; Jer 7:31] of old [לפנים]," but the connection with Job is not very evident. KJV "tabret" ("aforetime I was as a tabret") took the word as equivalent to תֹּף "drum" (following Rashi). Blommerde took עַמִּים as "my relatives" and לְפָנִים as "for my ancestors," which is more ingenious than convincing. Others read מוֹפֵת "a portent" (Perles, Budde, Terrien, claiming support from Vg *exemplum*; cf. Deut 28:46; Ps 71:7); but the parallel in 30:9–10 confirms the present text (Dhorme).

7.a. יְצֻרָי only here; obviously from יצר, "form," it is taken as "limbs" by most (BDB, RSV, NEB), but as "form" by L. Delekat ("Zum hebräischen Wörterbuch," *VT* 14 [1964] 7–66 [49]) (cf. NIV "my whole frame"; cf. NAB). Others follow Pesh "my thoughts, imaginations" (cf. יֵצֶר, Gen 6:5; 8:21; Deut 31:21); so Hoffmann, Budde. Terrien suggests ("all my thoughts dissolve like a shadow") that his illness makes him lose the thread of his ideas. These suggestions are perhaps too subtle, and the parallelism with "eyes" suggests we need here a word for parts of the body.

7.b. Reading כָּלִים, ptcp of כלה "are wasting" as in v 2, emended text; cf. also 33:21 (flesh); Ps 71:9 (strength); 73:26 (flesh and heart); 143:7 (spirit); Prov 5:11 (flesh and body). So Houbigant, Dhorme, Fohrer, NEB, NAB. N. M. Sarna ("Some Instances of the Enclitic -m in Job," *JJS* 6 [1955] 108–10 [110]) achieved the same sense by vocalizing כָּלָם, "they have wasted" plus enclitic mem (followed by Blommerde).

7.c. Lit., "like a shadow."

8.a. The Heb. is sg, but the same persons are referred to as in v 8a.

9.a. The Heb. is sg, but the same persons are referred to as in v 8a; see *Comment*.

9.b. Blommerde, following Dahood, *Psalms I*, 2, takes דרכיו as "his force," parallel to אמץ "strength" (so also Pope).

10.a. Lit., "return (juss) and come" (תשבו ובאו); שוב with a following verb signifies repetition (e.g., Gen 26:18); cf. GKC, § 120d–e; BDB, 998a § 8.

10.b. כֻּלָּם "all of them"; the lack of concord is not an occasion for emendation to כֻּלְּכֶם "all of you" (as 5 mss, *BHK*, Gordis); though Mic 1:2 and Mal 3:9 are not exact parallels (cf. GKC, § 135r), the principle is clear enough.

11.a. A very difficult verse, subject to many emendations. A tricolon (as MT punctuation has it) is comparatively unusual, especially when the third colon has no verb. But a very similar verse opens the strophe vv 1–5; there also, there is no verb in the third colon, and the general sense is similar.

11.b. Gordis takes עברו as transitive, "my days have passed (i.e., outstripped) my hopes," i.e., my life has lasted longer than my hopes. An ingenious suggestion, but the image is unparalleled, and it is not well supported by עבר (quite rare in the sense "pass beyond," and not found at all in this metaphorical sense).

11.c. It is no real difficulty that זמה elsewhere means "evil plan, plot," for מזמה also means both "evil plan" and "discretion" or (Yahweh's) purpose. Horst's emendation to מְזִמּוֹתַי is unnecessary. Fohrer reads בְזִמָּה "in shame," but זמה hardly means that. Interesting is the suggestion of Tur-Sinai (following ibn Ezra) that the term means "my cords," from זמם in late Hebrew, Aram. and Syr. "bind, esp. muzzle" (cf. NJPS "my tendons severed") since this could form a parallel to "the strings of my heart" (see n. 11.d). But there is no evidence that the noun זמה in any language meant "cord." The nouns from this זמם mean "muzzle" (זמום, זְמָם). De Wilde draws attention to the Aram. זמה "whisper," and argues that זמה means "groaning" (whence LXX ἐν βρόμῳ), reading בְזִמָּתִי, "(my days run their course) with my groanings." NEB "my days die away like an echo" also depends on LXX's βρόμος, any loud noise. These renderings are unconvincing. JB's "My days have passed, far otherwise than I had planned" (uncharacteristically prosaic!) presumably supposes some such reading as מְזִמָּתַי, and, like many others, endeavors to create a bicolon of the verse. Blommerde's rendering "the days of my plans have gone by," reading יְמֵי as a construct separated from its absolute (cf. also his "The Broken Construct Chain, Further Examples," *Bib* 55 [1974] 549–52 [549–50]) is something of a curiosity (despite the apparent analogies of 29:18; Isa 27:9; Hos 8:2; 14:3).

11.d. מוֹרָשׁ, not "possession," from ירשׁ (KJVmg, RVmg, BDB), but "desire," from *ארשׁ (KB; RSV, NAB, NIV). LXX ἄρθρα "joints, limbs" is supposed by some (e.g., Dhorme) to result from a connection with Aram. מרשׁא, Syr. *marša* "rope" (Heb. מֵיתָר, with נתק at Jer 10:20); hence NEB "heart-strings," JB "every fibre of my heart," NJPS "strings of my heart," i.e., the sinews, veins of the heart (cf. Saadia). Budde actually emended to מֵיתְרֵי (cf. *BHK*). This interpretation would be more attractive if there were good reason for joining the verb נתק to the phrase; in any case the explanation of LXX on these grounds is questionable.

12.a. LXX lacks this verse, which is supplied from Theodotion; perhaps LXX found the connections of thought as difficult as we do, and omitted it.

12.b. Elsewhere the idiom שים + ל means to turn A into (ל) B (see BDB, 964, § 5). NEB "Day is turned into night," though at first sight more appropriate to Job's lament, is not justifiable. There is no hint here of the moral perversity implied by the similar phrase in Isa 5:20.

12.c. The idiom "near from the face of" (קרוב מפני) is unparalleled and somewhat uncertain. Gordis thinks קרוב means "excellent, praiseworthy" (followed by Sicre Díaz), but the epithet would be weak, and the quoted analogies are unconvincing.

13.a. "If" here means "since." Dhorme thinks אם is interrogative ("Can I hope again? [Certainly not, since] Sheol is my house"). But such a use of אם is rare if not actually unattested (GKC, § 150f claims that apparent examples are "really due to the suppression of the first member of a double question"); 6:12 is no parallel, against Dhorme, since there we have the double אם. Gordis insists that אם is an emphatic particle, like Arab. *'inna* (I have accepted his view on 6:13, but not on 8:4; 14:5); but it cannot be positive and emphatic here unless we also accept his idiosyncratic view of אקוה (see n. 13.b). אם as an emphatic is normally *negative* (BDB, 50a § 2; GKC, § 149b). Hence Fohrer, Horst, de Wilde translate "I have nothing to hope for," or "What do I hope for?" But it seems better to contrast the *actual expectation* Job has (קוה, v 11) with the *impossibility of real hope* (תקוה, v 13).

13.b. Gordis, following Yellin and Tur-Sinai, takes אקוה as a denominative from קו "line," and translates "have marked out my home as Sheol," patently in order to avoid the apparent platitude of "if I hope . . . where is my hope?" Similarly NEB "If I measure Sheol for my house." The *Comment* shows good reason why such a move is unnecessary.

14.a. שחת is to be taken as a concrete object, because it is parallel to the "worm" (RSV, NEB), rather than a personified abstract "corruption" (RV, NAB, NIV). It seems to derive (BDB, KB) from שוח "sink down" rather than שחת "destroy," though no doubt the Hebrew speaker readily associated it with the latter verb. Andersen, following Tromp, *Death and the Nether World*, 69–71, would rehabilitate the old translation "corruption."

15.a. Lit., "my hope." Many have found the repetition of תקותי improbable. Considering that LXX has τὰ ἀγαθά for the second תקותי and that the pl verb תרדנה of v 16 implies *two* referents in v 15, it is hard to resist the emendation to טוֹבָתִי "my well-being, happiness" (Merx, Duhm, Dhorme, Driver, Fohrer, Horst; JB, NAB) (cf. טובה in 9:25). Wright's תַאֲנָתִי is much less probable. A. Guillaume rather implausibly attributes an Arabic sense to the word and translates "my steadfast piety" ("The Arabic Background of the Book of Job," *Promise and Fulfilment*, ed. F. F. Bruce [Edinburgh: T. & T. Clark, 1963] 113); hence NEB. If the MT stands, the first "hope" is psychological and the second more concrete, the object of hope, as suits the verb ישׁורנה "will see."

16.a. Most probably a fem pl verb, with תקותי and טובתי of v 15 as subjects. Dahood, followed by Pope, Sicre Diaz, vocalized תֵרְדֶנָּה as a 3 sg with an energic *nun*; this device is called into play principally to avoid the emendation in v 15.

16.b. בדי as it stands can only be "poles of" Sheol, which is hardly a natural way of referring to its "gates" (NIV) or even their "bars" (RSV). LXX ἦ μετ' ἐμοῦ suggests to most that we should emend to הֲעִמָּדִי "will they [descend] with me" (Duhm, Driver, Fohrer; JB[?], NEB[?], NAB [despite *Textual Notes on the NAB*, 374]). Less attractive is Dhorme's הֲבְיָדִי "is it that by my side," בְיַד corresponding to Akk. *ina idi*. Dahood's view that it is a contraction of בְיָדִי "into the hands of" ("Northwest Semitic Philology and Job," 62–63; followed by Pope, Blommerde) has little to recommend it, since the power of Sheol is not especially in view.

16.c. Revocalizing MT נָחַת "rest" (cf. RV) to נֵחָת "we shall descend," as is quite universally done.

Form / Structure / Setting

The *structure* of this fifth speech of Job is not so clear as in other speeches. As often, the direction of *address* is a helpful clue to structure.

In 16:2–5 Job plainly addresses the friends ("you"), in 16:7–14 he addresses no one but speaks of God and his assaults on him ("he" and "I"), in 16:15–17 he speaks only of himself ("I"), in 16:18 he addresses Earth, in 16:19–22 he speaks principally of his witness ("it"), in 17:1–5 he seems to be addressing God ("you" in vv 3–4), in 17:6–10 the friends ("you" in v 10), in 17:11–16 no one. We may then perhaps display the structure thus:

A. To the friends	16:2–6
B. To himself	16:7–17
C. To Earth	16:18(?–22)
C'. To God	17:1–5
A'. To the friends	17:6–10
B'. To himself	17:11–16

Fohrer finds, on the basis simply of content, three principal sections: (1) rejection of the friends (16:2–6), (2) controversy with God (16:7–22), (3) lament over his fate (17:1–16). But the structure seems more complex than that. Habel sees the following structure:

A. Exordium	16:1–5
B. Complaint against God as the Enemy	16:6–17
C. Cry of Hope amid Despair	16:18–17:1
B'. Complaint against the Friends	17:2–10
C'. Cry of Despair about Hope	17:11–16

It is not clear that 17:2–10 is as a whole concerned with the friends, since the mockers of 17:2, 4 are not the friends, and v 4 is addressed to God. Habel is certainly right to relate the "hope" of 16:18–21 to the "despair" of 16:11–16, though he does not stress clearly enough that the object of hope and despair is the same in each case, Job's vindication.

The *strophic structure* is plain:

Strophe	1	16:2–6	6 lines
	2	16:7–11	5 (v 10 a tricolon)
	3	16:12–14	4
	4	16:15–17	3
	5	16:18–22	5
	6	17:1–5	5 (v 1 a tricolon)
	7	17:6–10	5
	8	17:11–16	6 (v 11 a tricolon)

The speech thus exhibits basically the five-line strophe. Strophe 1 is really 5 lines + 1, since v 6 is an appendage to it. Strophe 3 appears according to the MT versification a strophe of 3 lines, vv 12 and 13 being bicola; it seems better, however, to regard vv 12c and 13a as forming one line with the single image of the archer(s). Strophe 8, like Strophe 1, is really 5 + 1, 17:16 being a pendant to 17:15.

Inevitably, other strophic divisions remain possible. Webster ("Strophic Patterns," 45–46) makes them 16:2–5, 6–9 (3 tricola), 10–14, 15–17 in the "poem" of 16:2–17; 16:18–21, 16:22–17:2, 17:3–7, 8–12, 13–16 in the "lament." Against this it may be argued that a disjunction between 17:12 and 17:13 is rather weak, and that the assault on the friends of 17:10 sits none too well in a strophe of 17:8–12. Skehan ("Strophic Patterns," 108–9) finds strophes of 16:2–4b, 4c–6, 7–9b, 9c–12b, 12c–14, 15–17, 18–21, 16:22–17:2, 17:3–6 (omitting 5b and making 5a, 6 a tricolon), 7–9, 10–12, 13–16— thus principally three-line strophes, as he finds also for Job's "reply" to Eliphaz in the first cycle (chaps. 6–8). This is not the most persuasive of Skehan's analyses, since disjunctions between 16:9b and 9c, and between 16:12b and 12c seem implausible, and the connective "for" (כִּי) that begins 16:22 argues against the separation of 16:21 and 22. NAB's decision to collapse Skehan's 12 strophes into six (16:2–6, 7–12b, 12c–17, 16:18–17:2, 3–9, 10–16) is more acceptable.

The *form* of the speech as a whole is again the *disputation speech;* in this speech Job's hostility to the arguments of the friends is very evident. The *forms* drawn upon within the speech are varied (contrast the previous speech, Eliphaz's in chap. 15, where the forms are derived almost exclusively from wisdom). Here we find materials from the wisdom controversy, from legal controversy, from the lament, and from the cultic sphere.

From the *wisdom controversy* comes some of the matter of the opening strophe (16:2–6)—which is not surprising since that is the form of the speech cycles of the book. In the sphere of the ridicule of the opponent (which would be also at home in the legal controversy) there is the speaker's claim that nothing new has been said (16:2a; cf. 9:2a; 12:3c). The argument that the speaker could equally well take his opponents' place (16:4), implying that because he does not choose to do so he has a stronger case than they, reeks of the atmosphere of the academic disputation. The proverb of 17:5, though obscure in meaning, is a further instance of a wisdom-oriented form.

The *legal sphere* provides the formal background to the crucial verses 16:18–21. The cry of the murdered for blood-vengeance (16:18) belongs of course to a deep-rooted form of justice that is hardly judicial; in vv 19–21, however, the image of the "advocate" who presses for a declaration of Job's innocence is presented with the language descriptive of the lawsuit.

By far the greater part of the material in this speech, however, is drawn from the *lament.* Two principal types of lament here are the "I"-lament and the "enemy"-lament. In the former the speaker laments his pain (16:6, 15–16), his lack of vitality (17:7, 11–12), his hopelessness (16:22; 17:1, 13–16). In the latter he protests against the attacks of his enemy, depicted here as an oppressor (16:7–8), an angry beast (16:9), a traitor (16:11), a wrestler (16:12), an archer (16:12c–13a) and a swordsman (16:13b–14). A secondary target of his protest is the human mockers who insult him as a man under divine punishment (16:10; 17:2, 4–5, 6). These motifs are familiar from the psalms of lament. As in the psalms, the laments of whatever kind function as an appeal or accusation against the source of the suffering, which is understood to be God himself.

The *cultic* sphere provides the material of the oath of exculpation alluded to in the reference to the clean hands and the pure prayer (16:17).

The *function* of this speech is to urge a prompt response from God to the demand for a lawsuit made in Job's previous speech (chaps. 12–14). On the trajectory of Job's developing argument, this speech adds no new matter to his complaint against God, but serves—in the absence of any divine reply to his summons in 13:22—to stress the urgency of a reply. "Sleepless I wait for God's reply," he says (16:20b). He has nothing further of substance to lay before God; his legal cry for justice of chap. 13 has been uttered in heaven's presence, and can now be assumed to be awaiting its turn to be heard: "it is my cry that is my spokesman . . . it will argue a mortal's case before God" (18:20–21).

The *nodal verses* of the speech are therefore 16:19–21, affirming Job's assurance that all that can be done on his side to win his vindication has been done, and that his "witness is in heaven" (16:19).

The *tonality* of the speech resembles that of Job's previous speech in chaps. 12–14. There is the same combination of sarcasm directed to the friends at the opening (16:2–5), though less pugnacious, less intellectualist, and the same hopeless conviction of the imminence of death at the close (17:11–16). The middle of the speech exhibits a self-pitying expression of exhaustion (16:7), dryness (16:8), weeping (16:16), extinction of the life-force (17:1), destruction of hope (17:11). The "laments" that protest at God's ferocious behavior display, strangely enough, a sense of keen vitality on Job's part; it is as though when he considers himself in his suffering his spirit droops, but when he considers how his suffering has come about and what it proves about the God who has caused it his anger rouses him to fresh élan. Distinctive in this speech are: the defiant cry to Earth that his death should not go unavenged (16:18), a cry of great potency that shows Job's mood is far from a settled depressiveness; and the stolid conviction, emphatically prefaced ("even now behold," גם־עתה הנה), that his plea is firmly entrenched in heaven. Unlike chaps. 12–14 the subject matter of the speech is persistently Job himself and never the suffering of humanity in general; there is nothing elegiac here, but rather an overflowing of the language of intensity.

Comment

16:1–17:16 This fifth speech of Job's is the most disjointed of all the speeches in the book up to this point. His previous speeches had built to a climax in chaps. 12–14, where he had formally summoned God, in the language of the law court, to disclose the charges against him (13:23). From that point on, Job has nothing novel to say, and essentially waits for God's reply. The rest of Job's speeches (here in chaps. 16–17; also 19; 21; 23–24; 26–31) fill out many themes already adumbrated in the earlier speeches, but they make no further logical or dramatic developments of importance. This recapitulatory and elaborative character of the speeches may account for their less strongly marked coherence.

There seem to be five major divisions within this speech. (1) In 16:2–6 Job addresses the friends with criticism of their words. (2) In 16:7–17 he begins to soliloquize, first lamenting the attacks of God. (3) In 16:18–22 he envisages the possibilities for vindication. (4) In 17:1–10 the lament (which seems to enclose an address to God, vv 3–4) concerns the friends. (5) In 17:11–16 the lament concerns his death without vindication.

2–6 The dominant motif in this opening rejection of the foregoing speech(es) by the friends, which we have now come to expect, is that of "words" and their lack of efficacy. In Job's previous speech, the initial denigration of the opponent had been more sarcastic and aggressive, and was integrated with an assertion by Job of his superior wisdom (12:2–4). The tone here is much less pugnacious, and it is Job's *feeling* of helplessness that is evident (v 6), by contrast with the more intellectual confrontation in 12:2–4. It is a sign of the movement inward towards feeling that Job for a moment envisages what it must be like to be in the friends' shoes (v 4); in acknowledging that he would treat them no differently from the way they are treating him he lapses from a mode of angry sarcasm into disappointment (cf. 6:15–21).

2 Job evidently replies directly to Eliphaz, at least in the opening lines of this speech. It is unusual to find direct reference to the preceding speech within the Book of Job; and we should not exaggerate the extent to which Job's speech is directed to refuting that of Eliphaz. Andersen finds in the structure of this speech a deliberate contradiction to the structure of Eliphaz's speech, but his analysis is not entirely convincing. In this verse at least it seems that "these" things that Job has often heard (i.e., before the dialogue began) are the conventional picture of the fate of the wicked which Eliphaz has elaborated in 15:20–35.

Eliphaz and, by association, all the friends are literally "comforters of woe, trouble" (עמל), i.e., comforters who increase trouble instead of ministering comfort (Rowley). There does not seem to be any significant allusion to the term "trouble" (עמל) in Eliphaz's last sentence (15:35), despite its proximity, for there it had a moral sense ("wrong") and here it means mental suffering (cf. 3:10). Eliphaz had indeed portrayed himself as a channel of (divine) consolation (15:11), and the prologue had designated the friends collectively as "comforters, consolers" (2:11; cf. 7:13; 21:34; 42:11). Job expects of comforters that they will take his part; how can there be sympathy (*feeling* with) if they position themselves theologically over against him? In a more overtly legal context, Job had sneered at the friends for their partisanship of God (13:8), but here, when those legal overtones are absent, he expects them—not entirely unreasonably—to be partisans for him. A professed comforter who will not share one's point of view but sits in judgment on it is indeed a comfortless comforter, or rather, a comforter who increases the sufferer's distress, a torturer of a comforter. To speak concretely, inasmuch as they have found in Job's suffering proof of guilt they have only magnified his suffering. The thought is closely similar to that of 13:4, where also the shape of the line is parallel: "healers of worthlessness, all of you" there, "comforters of woe, all of you" here; the resonance is perhaps designed.

3 Eliphaz has just now reproached Job for his "windy knowledge" (15:2), by which he meant his tempestuous speech. Job apparently characterizes Eliphaz's speech as "windy words" in the sense that they are empty and thus lacking any efficacy. Genuine words of comfort are more substantial. It is a matter of some wonderment to Job that Eliphaz has chosen to speak again if he has so little to say. In ironic mood, Job determines that Eliphaz himself must be experiencing some inner agitation, some nervous complaint, that compels him to open his mouth; what can it be that "disturbs" him or "makes him ill" (מרץ, "be ill")?

Attractive though this reading is, it is unusual to find Job addressing just one of his friends, and using the second person singular. So it is perhaps better to see this sentence as put by Job into the mouth of the friends, who have indeed been addressed in the plural ("all of you") in v 2. This is exactly what we can imagine them saying to *him*: Is there an end to (your) words of wind, your tempestuous utterances? The answer "No!" is expected to the rhetorical question. Or, to put the question differently, What has got into you, Job, what disease has infected you, that you must go on answering back? For a previous case where the use of the second person singular marks an imagined address by the friends to Job, see on 12:7–8. It is an even nicer irony (though on the part of the author rather than of his characters) that the friends should now imagine that Job's angry words must arise from some illness; for that is surely true!

On the form of the rhetorical question, in which a negative is perhaps expected, see Gordis's commentary, and his article, "A Rhetorical Use of Interrogative Sentences in Biblical Hebrew," *AJSL* 49 (1933) 212–17.

4 Not for the first time Job compares himself with the friends—to his own advantage. In 7:11 "I also" (גַם־אָנִי, as here) cannot restrain my words; in 12:3 "to me also" (גַם־לִי) there is intelligence at least as high as theirs; in 13:2 "I also" (גַם־אָנִי) have insight the equal, or rather the superior, of theirs. This is not the claim of self-importance or arrogance: it is the cry of a disappointed man who has looked for aid—intellectual, moral, or psychic—from outside himself, only to find no more resources in his friends than he already has in himself. What they can offer is common coinage; it is not worth offering, for Job himself is already familiar with the conventional modes of consolation. If their places were to be changed, his and the friends, he could so easily offer the same mixture of shallow encouragement and superficial criticism as he has been hearing; he does not say that he *would* speak such words (contrast NJPS), for then he could hardly complain at the treatment he is now receiving (Gordis).

"Shaking" or "wagging" the head is a gesture used both in sympathetic mourning (2:11) and in mockery (2 Kgs 19:21 = Isa 37:22; Ps 22:8 [7]; 44:15 [14]; 109:25; Ecclus 12:18; 13:7; Matt 27:39), as well as an expression of distancing from an afflicted object (Lam 2:15; Jer 18:16; cf. the gesture of laughing, on which see on 12:4). Job plays on the ambiguity: from the friends' points of view their gesture, like their words, has been sympathetic, but from Job's point of view that same gesture, and those very words, are expressions of scorn; the comforters are torturers (v 3). And that is solely because they insist collectively and individually on interpreting his suffering as divine punishment.

5 What he *could* do is not what he *would* do. Given the occasion to bring comfort to a sufferer, he would use his words not—as the friends do—to make mere noise (as חֲבֹב probably means in v 4) but for the constructive purpose of "strengthening" and "soothing." Eliphaz has indeed testified to Job's ability at giving vigor to feeble hands and strengthening failing knees (4:3–4). "Strengthening" (אָמֵץ) is what comforting is all about (we might recollect the etymology of "comfort" from Lat. *fortis*, "strong," though that does not tell us what the word is now used to mean); and that is what this powerless man needs, whose strength is not the strength of stones, whose flesh is assuredly not bronze, who has no power in himself at all (6:11–13).

Some have thought that the tone here is still ironic (so Peake, Gray, Rowley,

Hesse); Gray, for example, remarks that "if Job had been turning from irony
to a statement of what he would actually do, he would not lay stress on *mouth*
and *lips*." For this reason he rejects the RV "*But* I would strengthen you with
my mouth" (cf. also NIV) as "virtually an emendation, and a bad one." But he
overlooks the fact that the only consolation that either Job or the friends
could conceivably offer is a verbal one, and what is criterial is whether the
words spoken are supportive or destructive. There is no contrast here between
words spoken "with the lips" and words "from the heart" (against Fohrer);
on the power of words, cf. on 4:4. We should therefore translate the verbs of
this verse as "*would* strengthen," "*would* soothe," not "*could*" (as RSV, JB, NAB,
GNB).

6 But to what end is all this talk of talk, these words about speaking?
Job's experience is that speech and silence are both alike incapable of assuaging
his suffering. He has experimented with silence and with speech; he has restrained his mouth (2:10) and he has opened it (3:1); he has spoken in the
anguish of his spirit (7:11), but he would as well be silent since his own mouth
condemns him in God's presence (9:20). And he has experienced also the
friends' silence (2:13) and their speeches; and he now knows from their speech
that their silence was not the silence of sympathy but the amazed silence of
horror at the enormity of his crime. Silence and speech from them have been
equally ineffectual, equally judgmental, equally misdirected.

Some critics have found the connection of thought difficult. There can be
little doubt that the line is to be taken with what precedes, where the topic is
very much that of speaking, rather than with what follows (vv 7–14), which is
entirely about aggressive actions against Job. But of course the line does not
harmonize with the argument of vv 4–5, for Job rejects not only the friends'
speech and silence, but no less his own speech and silence. It is quite improbable
(against Duhm, Ehrlich, Fohrer) that he should be continuing the depiction
of how he would speak if he were in the friends' place, as if to say, "if I
should speak, my pain (= sympathy) would not be withheld (or, assuaged); if
I should be silent [and listen], how would I let it leave me?" For it is unnatural
to have Job mean by "my pain" the fellow-feeling he would have in a hypothetical
setting, when it is more than obvious what his present actual pain is (on כאב
"pain, grief," cf. on 2:13).

Job is being difficult to please, of course. He wants consolation, but he
also calls it useless. The problem is that even the most determined espousal
of his perspective on his suffering, even wholehearted cooperation with Job
in his assault on heaven, will not satisfy his real need, which is to be pronounced
innocent by God and therewith to have the burden of his suffering and his
presumed guilt lifted. There is nothing the friends can do that will truly alleviate
Job's situation.

Nor is it at all probable that the speaking and silence is vis-à-vis God. Thus
Gray: "If I say to and of God what I think about his treatment of me, it is
true He remains deaf to my appeals, and I get no alleviation[;] neither do I,
however, when I keep silence; therefore, I will repeat my case against Him."
This reading does establish a connection with the following verses, but there
is no reason whatever in the present verse to think that Job has anything but
human discourse in mind.

7–17 In this strophe we meet with a powerful account of the aggressive acts of God against Job. The transition to this principal topic from the introductory verses concerning the friends and Job (vv 2–6) is marked by the words "But now" (אָךְ־עַתָּה). The ironic and aggrieved tone of vv 2–6 gives way altogether to a lament of an oppressed and persecuted man, who thinks to drive home the enormity of his maltreatment by drawing up a catalog of assaults as they would be perpetrated by many different kinds of opponent, a wild animal (vv 9–10), a traitor (v 11), a wrestler (v 12), an archer (vv 12c–13a), a swordsman (vv 13b–14). Robert Alter has drawn attention to the depiction here of narrative movement: ". . . a series of linked actions which, acccording to the poetics of parallelism, are approximate equivalents but which prove to be, on closer inspection, logically discriminated actions that lead imperceptibly from one to the next. A sense of temporal progression is thus produced in a manner analogous to the illusion of movement created in the cinema, where a series of still photographs flashes on the retina with sufficient speed so that one seems to flow into the next, each frozen moment in the visual sequence fusing into temporal flux" ("From Line to Story in Biblical Verse," *Poetics Today* 4 [1983] 615–37 [626]).

7–8 These verses contain many difficulties. The transition from third person, "he/it has worn me out," to the second person, "you have made desolate," "you have shriveled me up," followed by "he has torn me" (v 10) is suspicious. Though many such changes of person are attested in the Hebrew Bible, Gordis goes too far in describing the phenomenon as "virtually normal in biblical Hebrew." Whether or not there has been corruption of the text here, perhaps through a scribe's supposing that these verses should have been addressed to God directly, there can be little doubt but that these lines are not principally such an address but a depiction, which we ourselves would most naturally represent by third person verbs throughout.

Because the first half of v 7 is short, and v 8 is long, we sometimes find a redivision and emendations along these lines: "But now he has worn me out and made me desolate; my calamity (רעתי instead of עדתי, "my company") has shriveled me up. As a witness it has risen against me; my leanness testifies to my fate" (thus Pope). This fairly cautious reworking has a lot to commend it, though in the translation given at the head of this chapter a rendering of the MT has been retained.

Though the first verb has no specified subject, it seems clear that it must be God, for the action of "wearing out" (לאה), i.e., making weak, exhausted (cf. on 17:1), functions as the accumulated effect of the specific assaults catalogued in the following verses. Some have thought, following the Vulgate, that "my pain" is the subject (e.g., Sicre Diaz), but the fact that the second verb, whether emended or not, has God as its subject makes this improbable.

The "company" (עדה) of Job which God has "devastated" or "ravaged" (שמם hiph) may be his household, comprising both his children and his servants (so, e.g., Gordis; cf. NJPS "You have destroyed my whole community"; NIV "you have devastated my entire household"). There can be little doubt that the events of the prologue are presupposed by the dialogue (cf. 8:4), and though the word "company" in 15:34 has referred to the (ideological) group of the godless, it is quite reasonable to give it here a much more concrete connotation. It is perhaps most natural to regard the "company" here as Job's friends, whether those of the dialogue or a wider circle of acquaintances (19:13), who have been "made appalled" (as שׁמם hiph can mean; cf. Ezek 32:10; Jer 49:20; 50:45) by the suffering inflicted on him. There would then be an identity of thought with v 8; in v 7 God so wears him out that his acquaintances are appalled at this signal of divine displeasure; in v 8 God so shrivels him up that his leanness becomes a self-evident proof of his iniquity.

Verse 8, despite some uncertainties (reflected in the variant translations of RSV, JB, NEB and NAB, for example), seems to mean that Job's emaciated condition, for which God is responsible, serves as proof—to everyone but Job—that Job is a dreadful sinner. His "leanness" is a witness against his innocence so long as the doctrine of exact retribution is operative. Job's gauntness, of which we hear nowhere else, is hardly to be explained clinically as a result of his skin disease; it is a mark of his mental suffering, and is perhaps more something felt by Job than observed by his companions. The thought belongs to that complex of ideas in which fatness signifies prosperity which in turn signifies divine pleasure (cf. 21:23–24; 15:27) and thinness signifies what is dried up, devoid of life. The psychic sense of being dried up has previously come to expression in the images of the wind-driven leaf and withered straw (13:25) and, by contrast, in the image of the tree whose root decays but may nevertheless burst into new life at the scent of water (14:7–9).

Job is helpless against the criticism of his friends if his own physical appearance is testimony of his wrongdoing. His cause is lost if anything but his own inner conviction of his integrity is taken into account; God, the friends, his speech, his suffering and even his own body are witnesses against him.

For false witnesses "arising" (קום), probably specifically rising to speak in the legal process, not just a general "rising up" against in hostility, cf. Ps 27:12; 35:11; Deut 19:16 (of a champion "arising," cf. Job 19:25). For "testifying against" (ענה ב), cf. 15:6.

9 God's attack on him has been that of a wild beast. It is a conventionality of the psalmic lament to depict one's (human) opponents as animals (e.g., Ps 7:3; 10:9; 17:12; 22:13–14 [12–13]), the point of comparison being their super-human power and death-threatening assault. Not for the first time, Job borrows cultic language depicting enemies to apply to God (cf. 10:16). It is God's anger that motivates this assault upon him (the theme notably of chaps. 9–10; cf. especially 9:5, 13), tearing him as a lion or wolf tears its prey (Deut 33:20; Gen 49:27; etc.), making his attack incessant (שׂטם, cf. Gen 49:23), grinding his teeth, a sure threat to the prey of its imminent devouring (the gnashing of teeth in rage, not elsewhere attributed to animals; cf. Ps 35:16; 37:12; 112:10; Lam 2:16; Acts 7:54), and piercing him with the sharp look of a murderous intent. Theriomorphic language about God's anger is rare, but can be seen in Hos 5:14; 6:1 (טרף "tear" as here); cf. J. Hempel, "Jahwegleich-nisse der israelitischen Propheten," ZAW 42 (1924) 74–104 (= BZAW 81 [1961] 1–29).

Some want to transfer the third colon to the beginning of v 10, thus creating two couplets in v 10; this suggestion is bound up with the emendation of "my adversary" to "my adversaries," which is to be rejected (see n. 16:9.c).

10 Now for a moment it is not God's hostility that is catalogued, but humans'; they are not specified as the "godless" or "my enemies," but that is what they obviously are (cf. 24:2 for similar lack of specificity). There is no real change of subject, for human hostility is the direct consequence of divine attack. God has marked Job out as a sinner, so every righteous person feels it a religious duty to take God's side by affronting Job (cf. the "laughingstock" idea in 12:4). The language Job uses is of the utmost conventionality: it does not describe with literal accuracy what Job is suffering at the hands of his fellows. It is not easy to determine exactly what the attitude of others to Job was (cf. 16:20; 17:6; 19:13–19; 30:1, 9–14)—and in any case the only truth we have access to is the poet's depiction of the feelings of his character Job—but it seems plain that he is drawing upon the traditional language of the psalmic lament without precise regard to its applicability.

The "gaping" mouth (for which the terms פער, as here, and פצה are used) can be an image of the wild beast ready to devour (Ps 22:14 [13]), but more frequently it is a gesture of mockery, probably simply of opening wide the mouth in laughter (Ps 35:21; Lam 2:16; 3:46; Isa 57:4); the latter is more likely here (cf. NIV "open their mouths to jeer at me," as against JB "open gaping jaws," NAB "bare their teeth to rend me"). It is a human gesture (as against the animal metaphor of v 9), as the act of smiting the cheeks is a human act of derision; though לחי can mean "jaw" as well as "cheek," the insult is to slap the face, not to give a punch on the jaw (as Andersen thinks); cf. Ps 3:8 [7]; Lam 3:30; Mic 4:14 [5:1]; Isa 50:6; 1 Kgs 22:24; Matt 26:67. Delitzsch remarked that since slapping the cheeks is itself the insult, "with scorn" must refer to derogatory words that accompany the act.

Several commentators have wished to remove vv 9c–11 as a later addition on the ground that these verses depict a *plurality* of *human* adversaries (on this view "my adversaries" is usually read in v 9c; cf. n. 16:9.c), whereas vv 9a–b and 12–14 speak solely of God (so Duhm, Driver-Gray, Hölscher, Horst, Fohrer, Hesse, de Wilde). But it is equally probable that the action of human opponents has been deliberately inserted by the poet within a frame of divine hostility, not so much because the human enemies are viewed as the emissaries of God (Gordis) but because God's humiliation of Job through compelling him to suffer gives those surrounding Job occasion to mock his downfall.

11 The language of the psalmic lament is continued. In Ps 31:9 [8] the psalmist thanks God that he has not "yielded him up" (סגר hiph as here) into the hand of his enemy, and in Lam 2:7 the Lord has "yielded" (סגר hiph) into the hand of the enemy the walls of the palaces of Jerusalem (cf. also Ps 78:48, 50, 62). The ungodly who have Job in their power are not the friends, of course, for however they denigrate Job's righteousness and fail to recognize the truth about the divine character (cf. chap. 12), they cannot be called godless. But neither are the ungodly to be seen as criminals or oppressors who literally have Job in their power; they are rather any who openly scorn him as a victim of divine displeasure. Job never lets far from his consciousness the thought that such human injustice does not arise from purely human motivation, but is merely a reflex of God's willful putting him in the wrong; it is God's own treatment of him that has laid him open to every kind of humiliation at the hands of others.

12a–b At the beginning of the new strophe Job reverts in thought to his former condition before the hostility of God assailed him. Throughout vv 12–14 there is one consistent image, that of God as warrior. There is nothing splendidly heroic about such a God, who brings the force of a whole army to bear upon a lone and unsuspecting individual. The motif of gross disproportion between Job's crime, whatever it may be (if anything), and God's vengeance here comes to the surface again.

To be "quiet," "untroubled" (שָׁלוּ) sometimes occurs in a political-military context (1 Chr 4:40; Zech 7:7; of a land or a city; differently in Dan 4:1 [4]); the thought is reminiscent of Judg 18:7, 27 where the people inhabiting Laish are said to have been "at ease (שֶׁקֶט) and unsuspecting" before they were attacked by the Danites. The verbs "shattered" and "dashed in pieces" are the reduplicated (pilpel) forms, probably iterative or intensive in force; פרר "shatter" is used in a context of combat in Ps 74:13 (cf. Isa 24:19), and likewise פצץ in Hab 3:6 (of a hammer shattering, Jer 23:29). To "seize" (אחז) is of course a normal term in depictions of warfare (Judg 1:6; 12:6; etc.), the "neck" (ערף) being the most vulnerable part of one's fleeing opponent (cf. Gen 49:8 "your hand shall be on the neck of your enemies"; Exod 23:27; Ps 18:41 [40]).

G. R. Driver believed that the image in v 12a–b returns to that of the wild beast (as in v 9), and calls upon Arabic cognates to yield meanings for the two reduplicated verbs of "worried" and "mauled" (as of an animal) (VTSup 3 [1955] 78); hence these translations, though in the reverse order, in NEB. But it is preferable to see military imagery consistently throughout those three verses. Fohrer and Hesse saw some allusion to Ps 137:9, "happy shall he be that seizes (אחז) your little ones and dashes (נפץ; cf. פצץ here) them against the rock"; but this also misses the image of warfare, for the act against the children is not itself a combat, even though it is carried out in the context of war.

12c–13 There follow two couplets in which a more specific image of warfare is developed, that of archery. Job is "designated" by God as the mark (cf. also 7:20) at which his archers are to aim, and they let fly. That Job is God's "target" (מטרה) does not mean that the attack is not for real but only practice (as with Jonathan's archery, 1 Sam 20:20; cf. GNB "uses me for target-practice"); to "set up" (קום) a target evidently means to mark something or someone out as a target (cf. נצב "station, set" a target in Lam 3:12). God as the field commander (cf. also 19:12) details his bowmen to concentrate their fire upon Job; they "surround" him, more like a firing squad than a military engagement of matched forces. Peake paints a dramatic picture, which unfortunately rests on the assumption that "target" means only a practice mark: "Having set Job up as a target, God shoots at him, first letting his arrows whistle all about him, thus keeping him in suspense, dreading that every shaft would strike its mark, then sporting with him no longer, but sending every arrow home into his vitals, till he has strewed the ground with them."

The effect of the archers' attack—since they act under God's direction, he personally is the subject of the verbs of v 13—is to strike at the vitals. Just as the hunter's arrow pierces (פלח) the stag's liver (Prov 7:23), and God's arrows are driven into the lamenter's kidneys (כליות) (Lam 3:13), so here also his arrows pierce Job's kidneys (פלח כליות). The kidneys are at once a most sensitive and vital part of the human anatomy and a seat of emotion and affection (cf. BDB); God's assault on him has been not only lethal but directed against Job's affections. This is truly the "unkindest cut of all," and it is wholly appropriate that the narration of it should be accompanied by the phrase "and he was without compassion" (לא יחמול). Apparently the verb "to spare" was used in a technical sense of to spare or economize on arrows (cf. Jer 50:14), so there is doubtless an ironic double entendre here: in not sparing any arrows but ordering that his bowmen's quivers be emptied against Job, God has not been "sparing" Job either. Cf. also 6:10, where it is pain that does not "spare" (חמל) Job, and pain that he does not spare himself from undergoing. Parallel to the kidneys is the "gall" (מררה; cf. 20:25), the secretion of the liver, which God "spills" or "pours out" on the ground as he punctures the gall bladder with his arrows. This organ too has a symbolic significance, for "gall" or bile has always been known as something bitter (the term is derived from the root מרר "be bitter"). If the affections and sympathies are assaulted, it is bitterness that spills out.

14 The final military image is of the ultimate stage in any assault on a city: the breaching of its walls and the storming in of the enemy troops. After the archery that assails him from a distance (in 12c from the archer's perspective, in 13b–c from the target's) comes the nearer approach of his enemy to batter on his very self. Job is the besieged city, God the stormtrooper intent upon breaching his defenses. For the imagery, cf. 30:14; Ps 80:13 [12]; 89:41 [40]; Amos 4:1; 1 Kgs 11:27; Isa 5:5; Neh 3:35 [4:3]. First God acts like an overwhelming army, inflicting one breach after another upon the city's walls (for the idiom, cf. "disaster upon disaster," Jer 4:20). Then he acts like a champion in single-handed combat, like a Goliath or "mighty warrior" (גבור; cf. 1 Sam 2:4; Jer 46:12; Hos 10:13) rushing upon his individual foe (for the realia, see R. de Vaux, "Les combats singuliers dans l'Ancien Testament," *Bib* 40 [1954] 495–508 [= "Single Combat in the Old Testament," in *The Bible and the Ancient Near East* (tr. J. McHugh; Garden City, N.Y.: Doubleday, 1971) 122–35]). The sack of the city has one man's defeat as its object. Job is both the city and its lone inhabitant; the flow of the imagery mirrors the onward rush of the invader. Eliphaz has depicted the ungodly man "running" (רוץ) as a warrior against God; whether or not Job deliberately reverses that depiction, he here affirms the contrary in his own case: the aggression is all from God's side, it is God who makes the "running" (רוץ). In every other passage where God is called a "mighty warrior" (גבור), it is his salvific power that is being hymned (Isa 42:13; Jer 20:11; Zeph 3:17; Ps 24:8; 78:65). Here, in a shocking reversal of Israelite piety, he has the character of the enemy of the psalmists, the mighty man who boasts of mischief done against the godly (Ps 52:3 [1]; cf. 124:4, where the "warrior" is specifically an archer).

15 Job reverts now from the catena of metaphors depicting the assaults of God and humans upon him (vv 7–14) to the description of his present state that was being given in v 6. The subject is now not the immediate effects of the attacks upon him, but the necessity for lamentation that they impose upon him. His response to these unjustified assaults has not been to resist or defend himself in like manner; but with words and tears he will argue for his disregarded rights (cf. vv 18, 20–21).

The language of the horn laid in the dust is metaphorical, of course; so also is that of the sackcloth being "stitched over the skin." The prose narrative of Job, it is true, never speaks of him wearing sackcloth; but the death of his children would make it unnatural to suppose that he was not wearing this most conventional symbol of mourning. Opinions differ over whether the garment of sackcloth was a large piece of cloth in essentially the shape of a grain sack (cf. references to being "covered" or "clothed" with sackcloth, 2 Kgs 19:1–

2; 1 Chr 21:16; Esth 4:2–3; Ps 69:12 [11]; Isa 37:1–2) or a smaller garment
in the form of a loincloth (cf. references to girding the loins with sackcloth, 2
Sam 3:31; Isa 15:3; 22:12; Jer 4:8). There are no other references to sackcloth
being stitched, and indeed it seems unlikely that much stitching would be
involved in making such a simple garment, and less likely still that the mourner
would represent himself as stitching the sackcloth for his own mourning. Either
Job means that, speaking metaphorically, he has stitched himself into his garb
of mourning in that (like Jacob, Gen 37:34–35) he never expects to take it
off before the day of his own death, or else that, in a more striking metaphor,
he has sewn the garment onto his very skin, so permanent and inseparable
from his being have grief and its symbols become. Certainly, the phrase does
not refer to some concrete reality, as J. V. Kinnier Wilson thought when he
saw in it a reference to the coarse, rough skin of a sufferer from pellagra,
supposedly Job's illness ("Leprosy in Ancient Mesopotamia," *RA* 60 [1966]
47–58 [56]).

This ritual of mourning is properly a ritual of self-abasement. The mourner,
in a display of psychic affinity with the one dead, wants to signify his own
absolute loss of worth (cf. on 1:20), and so dresses himself in cloth of the
cheapest quality, fit rather for bagging objects than for human adornment.
Job's mourning is of course not only for his dead children but perhaps even
more for himself; for he has suffered a dissolution of powers and a disruption
of relationships akin to what may be expected in death itself, and his longing
for death, so often expressed, has been not so much a suicidal wish for release
from unendurable suffering as a desire to move wholly into that realm of
Sheol which has already laid so enfeebling a hold upon him.

In parallel with the clothing of self-abasement is the wholly metaphorical
action of "thrusting his horn in the dust." The image may perhaps be of the
wounded bull that droops its head and sinks its horn into the ground (Pope,
de Wilde), but is perhaps rather merely the reverse of the more frequent
image of exalting the horn, as of a bull or wild ox, a metaphor of heightened
power, pride, or status (1 Sam 2:1; Ps 75:5–6 [4–5]; 89:18 [17], 25 [24];
92:11 [10]; 112:9; 148:14); the reverse is usually expressed as horns being
cut off (Jer 48:25; Ps 75:11 [10]) or cast down (Zech 2:4 [1:21]). The symbolism
here goes further, however. It is not just that Job's standing in his community
as an exemplary righteous man has been overturned, but that it has merged
with the dust, which signifies both his abasement and also the context of mourning, dust being upon the heads of the mourners (2:12; and cf. Lam 3:29,
"mouth in the dust").

16 Job's weeping, though no doubt real enough, is here primarily metaphorical of his grief (see further T. Collins, "The Physiology of Tears in the Old
Testament: Part I," *CBQ* 33 (1971) 18–38 [36]). His red cheeks are very possibly
not discernible by the natural eye, but the grief which they signify cannot be
mistaken. Equally, the darkness of death upon his eyelids can be perceived
only by the inner eye. There is a physical correlate of these psychic realities,
but the essential fact is Job's sensation that the outcome of the divine (or
divinely engineered) assaults upon him is to put him within the sphere of
the influence of death, its deep darkness already weighing down upon his
eyelids.

More naturalistic interpretations of this verse are commonly advanced: Davidson, for example, remarks that involuntary weeping is said to be a symptom of elephantiasis, identified by many as the skin disease from which Job is suffering (cf. on 2:7). And the English versions tend to eliminate "death" from the term "darkness of death" (צלמות; cf. on 3:5; 10:21; 12:22), presumably because death is not physically visible, and to translate "my eyelids" (עפעפי) by "my eyes" because literally speaking it is eyes and not eyelids that become dark (NIV "deep shadows ring my eyes"). Yet however valid these readings may be, the symbolism reaches deeper. What happens to a man whose eyelids are shadowed over by the darkness of death is not simply that he does not look a pretty sight but that he can no longer with ease "see the light," which is to say, live. He is already beginning to experience the gloom of the land of deep darkness that he is bound for (10:21–22).

17 A crucial point here is how the conjunction *ʿal* (על) is to be translated. Commentators and modern versions are unanimous in translating "although [on my palms there is no violence]," which means that what Job is suffering is contrasted with the absence of any moral grounds for such suffering. There are, however, no convincing parallels for taking this common conjunction as anything other than "because" (cf. on 10:7; 34:6). That is to say, we have here the *reason* why Job is grief-stricken: it is not the loss of his children or his own pain, but the fact of his innocence. The contrast is not between the weeping and the innocence, but between the divine assaults (of vv 7–14) and the innocence. His weeping results from God's refusal to acknowledge his innocence. The interesting similarity with Isa 53:9 "because he had done non-violence (על לא־חמס עשה) and there was no deceit in his mouth" is not to be explained as a case of dependence of one text on the other, but more probably as a matter of common dependence on a ritual declaration of innocence, probably in the cult, and perhaps in the ritual of the ordeal (cf. also 1 Chr 12:17 [18]).

The palms (כפים) are often thought of as signifying innocence, if they are clean (cf. 9:30; 31:7; Ps 7:4 [3]; Gen 20:5; contrast Isa 59:3); a righteous person has clean palms and a pure heart (Ps 24:4), washes the palms in innocence (Ps 26:6; 73:13), and is delivered through the cleanness of the palms (Job 22:30). Violence (חמס) can be "on" or "in" the palms (Isa 59:6; Jonah 3:8), since it is the work of human hands, and so too is its contrary, the absence of violence, or rather, "non-violence." The hyphenation of the words "non" and "violence," and the use of the negative לא rather than אין, show that the contrary of violence is regarded as a positive entity, a goal capable of pursuit, and not just the mere absence of violence. The servant of Yahweh in Isa 53 has "practised non-violence" (לא־חמס עשה), while Job bears the (non-)marks of non-violence upon his palms. Of course violence is not the only form of wrongdoing, but it powerfully symbolizes all kinds of wrong. חמס is properly not just acts of physical violence but also "abandonment of an order laid down or guaranteed by God" (G. von Rad, *Old Testament Theology* [tr. D. M. G. Stalker; Edinburgh: Oliver and Boyd, 1962] 1:170; cf. H. J. Stoebe, *THWAT* 1:583–87), "unscrupulous infringement of the personal rights of others, motivated by greed and hate and often making use of physical violence and brutality" (H. Haag, *TDOT* 4:478–87 [482]).

Some critics of a former generation thought it strange that "my prayer" should be parallel to the absence of violence (so e.g. Gray), and proposed emendations to "my way" (see n. 16:17.b); but since the point at issue is not primarily the contrast between Job's grief and his innocence, but between God's treatment of him and his innocence, it is only right that he should make his religious purity a principal part of his complaint.

Job's protestation of innocence is an implicit response to Eliphaz's charge in 15:4–5, and Bildad's assumption in 8:6, that Job is not already pure (דַּ‍, as here) and upright. It would be wrong, however, to imagine that Job's language is generated by his friends' criticisms; in this regard they do nothing but embody an interpretation of his distress that Job is the first to recognize: that is, his suffering is a testimony against his innocence (v 8). What is ironic is that he, the practitioner of non-violence, has been set upon by a hostile God (vv 9, 12–14), and as an undefiled man of piety, pure of hands, has been abandoned by God to the vile hands of the wicked (vv 10–11).

18–22 The legal challenge to God that he will declare the bill of particulars against Job (13:20–23) still stands unsatisfied. Job does not abandon that approach, but here adopts a second line of argument in his attempt to win redress. In that he has been attacked by God (vv 7–14), with consequences that will no doubt prove fatal, he appeals for blood vengeance to be wreaked—upon God!—on his behalf by a heavenly "vindicator." A difficulty in the text that will need resolving is that v 18a seems to envisage Job's death before his vindication, whereas v 22 assumes that Job demands vindication before his death, and that the nearness of his death is a reason why vindication is urgent.

18 Job is not yet dead, but he expects the sufferings he presently endures to prove mortal, as we have already heard (7:7, 21b; 10:20–22; cf. 14:1–2). The course of events up to this point leaves him little hope for vindication this side of death. When he had first ventilated the question of winning vindication from God (9:2) he had immediately concluded that the task was hopeless (9:3, 14–16, 19–20). But he nevertheless determined to embark upon it, and formally called upon God to tell him what the crimes were for which a penalty was being exacted (13:23). But heaven has remained silent, and any hope of eventual reconciliation with God is an impossible dream (14:13–17). Job's imminent death will put paid to any hope of his seeing his own vindication; but his innocent death will nevertheless demand satisfaction. Earth and heaven, the "sleepless watchers of men's actions and guardians of ancient covenants" (Andersen; cf. Isa 1:2) must be pressed into service in the cause of establishing his innocence—even if posthumously. (Earth is addressed in Jer 6:19 and Mic 1:2 in a different context.)

It is something of a difficulty for this reading that v 22—if it is rightly connected with the preceding verses—suggests that it is only vindication before death that interests Job and that the imminence of his death is a reason for urgency in pressing for vindication. However, v 18b cannot be a cry for this-worldly vindication (as against Fohrer) because it assumes Job's death: Job's blood must be spilled before it can be avenged! The solution to the difficulty is this: the urgency is not for vindication itself but for setting in train the processes of vengeance. Job must cry to earth *now*, and must affirm the existence of a testimony in heaven to his own innocence *now*, for soon he will be dead, and then it will be too late forever. A posthumous vindication will be small comfort to Job who in Sheol will know nothing but feel only his own pain and grieve only for himself (14:22). But Job's own sense of justice is so affronted—indeed, the moral order of the universe is so threatened—by his innocent death that justice must sooner or later be satisfied.

The thought behind the cry to earth, "Cover not my blood," is that the spilled blood of an innocent person cries out to God for vengeance, at least so long as the blood remains uncovered (Gen 4:10; 37:26; Isa 26:21); in Ezek 24:7–8 the guilt of Jerusalem remains to be punished because the blood shed in it (by violence, murder) has lain upon the unabsorbent rock and not upon the earth where it could be covered with dust. There may be vestiges of a dynamistic view of the power of blood behind the language; but it is equally susceptible of explanation as metaphor. So long as the evidence of murder remains visible, so long is there a case to be answered and a culprit to be apprehended. Job, born from the earth (cf. 1:21) and destined to lie in it (7:21), touches the roots of human existence when he calls on the earth to allow no covering up of his murder at the hands of God. Spilled blood that has not been avenged by a human kinsman must of course necessarily cry to God for vengeance (Gen 4:10); here it is not at all God himself who is the kinsman avenger, for God is the murderer, but a figure who will take up his case before the heavenly court (see v 19). On "blood," see B. Kedar-Kopfstein, *TDOT* 3:234–50, and literature cited there.

The "cry" is here not a cry for deliverance (as against Fohrer) but is wholly explanatory of the cry for vengeance in v 18a (the verb צעק is similarly used of the cry for vengeance by Abel's blood, Gen 4:10). זעקה/צעקה does often signify a cry for help, often for help against "violence" (חמס, cf. v 17), as, e.g., in Hab 1:2 and Jer 20:8, but here Job expects no deliverance from his suffering, and focuses exclusively upon his need for a post-mortem vindication. May his appeal never rest, "let the cry of it wander through the world" (Moffatt), until vindication is won. On the "cry," cf. G. Hasel, *TDOT* 4:112–22; R. Albertz, *THWAT* 2:568–75.

19 By saying that "even now" (גם־עתה) he has a "witness" to his character in heaven, Job must be meaning that his vindication need not wait upon his death. Heaven already knows the facts about his innocence, and could clear his name here and now if it wanted to. Who or what is this "witness"? A "witness," as Davidson remarked, "does not mean merely one who *knows* Job's innocence, but one who will testify to it and see it recognised"; who in heaven plays that role?

Many would say, God. All agree that in the end that is who Job's effectual "witness" will turn out to be (cf. 42:7–8), but is that what Job thinks now? If it is, Job would be expressing a subtle thought, that God is both his unprincipled assailant and his ultimate avenger against that very assailant. On this view, God will rise up as "witness" against God, and avenge the Job he will not give justice to (similarly Dhorme, Rowley, Fohrer). Thus, it may be said, "Job appeals, against the enemy God whose destructive activity he has just now described, to the selfsame God in his character as witness and surety of the pious" (Hesse). But even if we could allow such paradoxes we may well ask, Whence comes this confidence in Job? Everything we have heard from Job previously has displayed a striking lack of confidence in God's will to repair the damage he has done to Job, and nothing in his present speech suggests that he has had any second thoughts about that. It is even more upsetting for the identification of the "witness" as God that in v 21 it seems that the witness's function is to *mediate* between God and mortals (see further on v 21).

And yet, it is hard to believe that, if the witness is not God, it can be some other heavenly being. Eliphaz has scoffed at the idea that there could be any heavenly being who might extricate Job from the nexus of retribution (5:1), and Job himself probably believes that Eliphaz is in the right. An even more crucial sentence on the subject is Job's own unequivocal statement (in the form of a wish contrary to fact) that there is no mediator who could stand between God and a human being and lay his hand in reconciliation upon them both (9:33). Such a role is very close, if not identical, to the function of the effectual witness here, and Job has had no new revelation about the heavenly bureaucracy to make him believe now that there is such a person. As against J. B. Curtis, "On Job's Witness in Heaven," *JBL* 102 (1983) 549–62, there is no reference here to a personal god who will prosecute Job's cause against the high god (see also n. 16:20.a).

The fact is (so it may be suggested) that there is *no* personal "witness" in heaven. What is in heaven "now" and had not been before the dialogue began is Job's own protestation of innocence and his formal deposition that requires God to give an account of himself. (JB "My own lament is my advocate before God" is on the same lines; but it is not precisely his *lament* but rather his affirmation of innocence that stands as his witness in God's presence.) By addressing himself to heaven Job has ensured, even though he has not been answered and expects no answer in his lifetime, that the truth about his innocence has been placed on record in the heavenly court. It is lodged there, and remains Job's perpetual witness to his character. His shed blood, his murder by God, when it happens, will be the final piece of evidence that he has been victim of a miscarriage of justice. See also on the "champion" of 19:25.

20 Despite the extreme difficulty of the Hebrew, a coherent sense may be discerned. The theme of the heavenly "witness" continues, only now the witness is called an "interpreter" or "middleman," a spokesman (מליץ as in Gen 42:23; 2 Chr 32:31; Isa 43:27; Ecclus 10:2; and especially Job 33:23, where the spokesman is a heavenly being). This spokesman represents Job's cause, and continues to press for a declaration of his innocence from God. And who is this spokesman? God himself has no interest in the case or in the question of Job's righteousness; and there is no heavenly mediator or umpire who can act on God's behalf (9:33). It is only Job's own cry, his "clamant word" (Dhorme), as רעי seems to mean here (see n. 16:20.a), that can speak for him, and that is what is happening in the heavenly sphere whether or not anyone there is interested in listening. It is his cry for justice, his legal cry of chap. 13, which now pleads for him; it is not the cry for vengeance of v 18, which will not be heard until his death. Job has no hope for vindication, either before or after death, but that does not mean that he has no right to it nor that he will cease demanding it.

Until his right is won Job waits in sleepless anticipation. He does not "pour out tears" (RSV, NIV) to God in entreaty nor even now weep because of the pain he endures (contrast v 16); rather he is ever watchful and alert for the recognition he deserves—even though he believes he has no hope of attaining it! Like the eyes of servants that look to the hand of their master, like the eyes of the maid to the hand of her mistress (Ps 123:2), Job looks to God— though not for mercy; for justice, rather.

21 The purpose and consequence (ויוכח has final *waw*) of the entry of Job's cry into the presence of God is that it will continue to argue a mortal's case in the divine sphere just as a man could argue his own case in the human realm. Job cannot enter heaven, he cannot by force bring God into legal debate with himself, he cannot find him or come to his seat (23:3), but he can put his deposition (13:23) on record—not with an iron pen and lead admittedly (19:23–24)—and let it plead his case for him (on "argue," cf. on 13:3). He has no confidence that God will listen (9:16; contrast 19:25), but the words of challenge to God have been spoken and cannot now be withdrawn. They have a kind of independent existence of their own; they are facts, they exist whether or not Job himself exists. And they, poor substitute though they are for a personal confrontation with God, will have to carry his case forward.

This interpretation of the verse thus develops the picture of the "spokesman" in the immediate context (vv 19–20), and does the best justice to the syntax of the verse. The spokesman "argues" (יוכח) "on behalf of a man" (לגבר), who is Job, "in his dispute with God" (lit., "with God," עם־אלוה); that arguing is comparable with ("and" of comparison; see n. 16:21.a) the arguing of "a man" (בן־אדם), any man, "on behalf of his friend" (לרעהו). Compare NIV "on behalf of a man he [my intercessor] pleads with God as a man pleads for his friend"; JB "Let this plead for me as I stand before God, as a man will plead for his fellows"; similarly Pope. In the first half of the verse there are three parties, the man, his advocate, and the opponent; in the second half there are two, the man and his advocate. Many, however, have seen the dispute there as *between* the man and his "neighbor" (רעהו can be "friend" or "fellow"); so RV, RSV, NEB, NAB, NJPS, Duhm, Driver-Gray, Dhorme, Horst, Weiser, Fohrer, Rowley, Gordis, Hesse, Terrien, Sicre Diaz and Alonso Schökel). This is an implausible reading because it is not the heavenly advocate (no matter its identity) that decides between a man and his neighbor, and because "for his neighbor" more naturally parallels "for a man" in the first half of the line. The view that the "neighbor" in question is one of the friends (Eliphaz, according to Peake) or the friends viewed collectively (Gray) fails on the same grounds, as also on the fact that Job is not engaged in a legal suit with the friends as he is with God.

Those who believe the heavenly witness of v 19 is God are compelled to see here Job putting his trust in a God who will plead Job's case against God himself, a "daring thought," says Rowley, but an improbably paradoxical one rather. Fohrer, believing that Job "demands of God that he should give thought to his own character and recognize his true duty as protector of justice," suggests that Jer 31:20 and Hos 11:8–9 offer parallel statements about God; but in both those cases the tension is portrayed as God's own expression of the competing desires he feels within himself. That is very different from the situation here; for if Job should give over the prosecution of his case to the God he has uniformly depicted as hostile to him he would abandon it forthwith. And that is impossible for him to do.

22 It is because of his imminent death that Job has had to set his "cry" (v 20) on record now. If he had left it much longer there would have been no legal case to be answered by God, nor any cry for vengeance (v 18) ascending to heaven after his death. The urgency that provokes the reference to the "few years" is not Job's impatience for vindication, but his certainty that anything he can do to clear his name will have to be done in the short space of time before his death.

It is strange to hear Job speaking of "years," even "few years" (lit., "years of number"), that remain of his life, when on other occasions he has given us the impression that he regards his life as effectively over, his days having reached their end, with no thread left (7:6), his days a mere breath (7:16); soon he will lie in the dust (7:21); his days have fled away more swiftly than a courier (9:25); they are few (10:20). Emendations are unsatisfactory, and we must simply accept that Job regards his diseases as not immediately fatal, though doubtless mortal (Davidson).

The way along which he will not return is of course the path to Sheol, perhaps conceived of as the way on which the corpse is carried to the burial place. The phrase is paralleled in a Babylonian hymn to Tammuz, *uruḫ lā tāri*, "the road with no return" (H. Zimmern, *Sumerisch-babylonische Tamūz-Lieder* [Leipzig: Teubner, 1907] 204, no. 1, line 12); cf. the Babylonian phrase for the underworld, *irṣit lā tāri*, "the land of no return" (*ANET*, 106), and see Job 7:9–10; 10:21.

17:1–16 Job has confidence in the rightness of his cause, but he has no expectation that he will live to see his innocence vindicated. As in all his previous speeches, he moves in the end to the contemplation of death, for that is the one certainty in his future, and he feels its near approach. The whole of this chapter revolves about the contrast of "hope" and "death": in v 1 the absence of hope is expressed by the language of the imminence of death, in vv 13–16 its absence is explained by his feeling of being kin with death. There is, intermixed with these prevailing expressions of hopelessness, some caustic criticism of the friends and the sanctimoniously righteous in general; the train of thought is at several points obscure, and the exact sense of several lines remains a mystery.

1 Job does not regard himself as being literally and physically on the point of death, if we have rightly understood 16:22, where he envisages some years of life still ahead of him. But quite apart from his physical suffering, which appears irremediable and which can lead only to death whether sooner or later, he is psychologically in the grip of death. For however vociferous his protestation of innocence, every external reality—God, his friends, humanity at large, the teachings of wisdom, and even his own physical appearance (16:8)— are ranged against him as witnesses of his guilt; and the unequal conflict in which he is willy-nilly involved has so sapped his pyschic energy that he experiences a living death. His life-force is no more literally spent than is his grave already dug; but what matters the banal literal truth when the reality that constantly imposes itself upon him is his sense of being already dead?

His spirit (רוח) is "crushed" (חבל pu, lit., "destroyed"); this does not simply mean that he has lost hope, as RSV, NAB, NIV "my spirit is broken" may suggest. Rather, the רוח is the life-force, breath as expressing the dynamic vitality of humankind (R. Albertz and C. Westermann, *THWAT* 2:726–53 [735]). The רוח can be "low" (שפל, Isa 57:15 [not "humble"]), "crushed" (דכא, Isa 57:15 [not "contrite"]; Ps 34:19 [18]), "smitten" (נכאה, Prov 15:13; 17:22; 18:14), "broken" (שבר, Isa 65:14; Ps 51:19 [17]; Prov 15:4), and "dim" or "faint" (כהה, Isa 61:3; Ezek 21:12 [7]). The present usage belongs with this group as signifying a loss of élan expressed metaphorically as a stamping out of the life-force. The image of life as something intrinsically weak, that can be crushed out of existence, we have met before in 4:19; 5:4; 6:9 (דכא; cf. also 19:2;

34:25), and 9:17 (שׁוּף). To the same effect is the image of the days being "snuffed out" (זעך only here, a by-form of דעך, used of the light of the wicked being extinguished in 18:5, 6; 21:17; Prov 13:9; 20:20; 24:20, and of enemies being extinguished and "quenched like a wick" in Isa 43:17; in Job 6:17 it referred, unusually, to waters being dried up). Darkness is closing in upon him, a foretaste of the darkness of death (cf. on 16:16, and on the imagery bound up with light and darkness, cf. 3:4–6, 9, 16, 20, 23; 5:14; 10:21–22; 11:17; 15:22, 23, 30).

2 The glance at the mockery that surrounds him forms a reason for his loss of spirit. For Job to endure mockery, which is specifically a castigation of him as a hypocrite and a denial of his righteousness (cf. on 12:4–5), is a debilitating experience. He does not refer particularly to the friends of the dialogue as his mockers, but to any whom he has previously counted as his friends (as at 12:4). Nor is it to be supposed that the mockery he endures is necessarily expressed in any gross form (though cf. 30:1–15); he takes it for granted that the company of the godly must be despising him, as he himself had no doubt in happier times despised those whom suffering had marked out in his eyes as the wicked. The weak and the stumbling he supported (4:3–4), indeed, but as one of the wise he must have shared the common belief in that very retributive justice from whose operation he is now—in the eyes of others—smarting.

His reference to the "mockery" and "antagonism" that surrounds him is the language of the lamenting psalmist. It is different in the ideology of wisdom, where the "mockers" or "scoffers" are the wicked who scorn right behavior (Prov 1:22; 9:7; 14:6; Ps 1:1; etc.; and so Zophar regards Job, 11:3). In the idiom of lament, however, mockery is usually the response of the wicked to the distress of the righteous (Ps 22:8 [7]; 35:15–16; cf. Job 12:4 *q.v.*). The idea of the weariness that results from sustained weeping also has its home in the lament (יגע, Ps 6:7 [6]; 69:4 [3]; cf. also Job 16:7 [לאה, as here]).

3 If all around him are mockers, who insist on regarding him as justly punished, the only quarter in which he can protest his innocence is toward heaven. Though he does not name God, and though these verses are probably the only address to God in the speech (though see on 16:7–8), it does seem that vv 3–4 are indeed directed toward God. His way of affirming his innocence now is to offer a "pledge" which will be forfeit if he is proved guilty.

A pledge (עֵרָבוֹן, also חֲבֹל, עֲבוֹט, or עֲבָטִיט) was a piece of personal property, such as a ring or garment, which a borrower would deposit with his creditor as a guarantee that he would repay his debt (cf. Gen 38:17, 18, 20; Deut 24:10–14; Exod 22:25–26 [26–27]). A person also could be a "surety" and be held legally responsible for the debt of another; such a surety could be a child, whose labor would pay off the debt if it were defaulted on, or else it could be a brother (cf. Gen 43:9; 44:32, where Judah is surety for the life of Benjamin) or any well-wisher (cf. Prov 6:1; 11:15; 17:18; 20:16; 22:26; 27:13, where one is warned not to become a surety for others). See G. A. Barrois, "Debt," "Surety," *IDB* 1:809–10; 4:446; A. Abeles, "Der Bürge nach biblischem Recht," *MGWJ* 66 (1922) 279–94; 67 (1923) 35–53.

Job has not incurred a debt, but he has been assaulted by God (16:7–14)—which is prima facie evidence of guilt. He is in the unenviable position of having no one, on earth or in heaven, who will take his side and offer himself

as a guarantor of his innocence. Only he himself, and his declarations of innocence (cf. 16:17a), can serve as guarantors (it is not his suffering that is his
pledge, as Dhorme thinks); for no one else will let himself be used as a surety,
or will offer a pledge on Job's behalf (v 3b). Therefore he must ask God to
accept him as his own guarantor—a very unlikely possibility, but Job has no
alternative.

Of course, those who saw in 16:19, 21 an allusion to God taking sides against
himself, the God of mercy in conflict with the warrior God, are inclined to
find here an appeal to God to be himself the guarantor for Job (NEB "Be
thou my surety with thyself"; NJPS; similarly Fohrer, Rowley, et al.); but it
would be whistling in the dark for Job to hope that the hostile God he has
experienced would play that protective role; it is adventurous enough for him
to demand that his affidavit of innocence should be allowed to plead his case
at the heavenly court, whether or not he Job is still alive (cf. 16:21–22). Thus
JB's translation is to be followed: "You [yourself] must take my own guarantee."
It needs to be stressed (against Horst) that the purpose behind the motif of
the pledge here is the eventual declaration of Job's innocence; it is not to be
viewed as some kind of bail money that will lift the wrath of God from him
at least temporarily. For although Job longs here and now to be free of divine
suffocation and assault (7:16b, 19; 9:34; 10:20b; 13:21; 14:21b) he longs even
more to have his name cleared (9:2; 10:2; 13:15b, 23)—even though he has
no real hope that he will live to witness such an event.

4 The reason why no one will take Job's part but will one and all abandon
him to his fate is that all who know him (not just the three friends of the
dialogue) have lost their reason. And that can hardly be their fault entirely.
For if they cannot accept the truth about him that he is a misjudged and
innocent man, the explanation can only be that a hostile God has deliberately
isolated him from the natural sympathy he could have expected. At 6:15–21
he had blamed the friends for their lack of fellow-feeling and loyalty, but
now he believes he has hit on the explanation for their failure as friends:
their reason has been perverted by God. The MT, "you have hidden their
heart from understanding," uses the figure of hypallage for "you have hidden
understanding from their heart." The motif drawn upon is that of God's blinding
the eyes or hardening the heart or otherwise depriving people of their natural
senses (cf. Isa 6:10; 44:18; Job 39:17). The understanding Job's acquaintances
lack is of Job's true innocence; to recognize that and affirm it, despite the
evidence against it, has been called by Job a sign of wisdom higher than that
possessed by his friends (12:3; 13:2).

It is far from clear how God's closing human minds to understanding forms
any reason (עַל־כֵּן, "therefore") why God will "not let them triumph" (RSV,
etc.) over Job. Why should God prevent others from recognizing Job's righteousness (presumably through their attachment to the doctrine of exact retribution),
yet ensure that their mockery of Job (v 2) as unrighteous should fail? And
why, especially, should the fact that God has done the former be a reason
why he should do the latter? It must be said that a completely unmotivated
expression of confidence in God's ultimate defense of him against all comers
seems out of place in Job's mouth at this point. And the verb itself, "not let
them triumph, or, exult" seems strange in reference to those who "surround"
him (v 2); it would not even be completely appropriate in reference to the

outcome of the disputation of the three friends. For these reasons it seems better to take the phrase (לא תרמם) as meaning "you [God] will not be (or, are not) exalted, glorified," viz. God's honor is not advanced by his engagement of bands of "mindless" scoffers in his assault on Job.

5 The best interpretation of this obscure verse is to take it as a popular proverb of the boastful man who calls his friends to a banquet when his larder is so empty that his children are starving. But who is the "he" against whom the proverb is directed? All those who mock Job claim to have knowledge of the true situation, but their intellectual cupboard is bare, for their minds have been closed. But it is also possible that it is God who is represented as the boaster who summons his "friends," i.e., all who take the side of retributionist dogma, to luxuriate in righteous indignation against Job, whereas the "children" (viz. Job!), to whose support God should be committed, are starved of what they most need, which is hope (similarly Budde, Kissane, Fohrer). For the idiom, "the eyes fail," cf. on 11:20.

6 The verse returns to the theme of v 2, while the next verse resumes the theme of v 1. There may be some contrast between the rightful expectation Job could have had of support from God (v 5) and the reality of being turned loose and exposed to mockery (so Fohrer). The form of the lament is drawn upon again to present Job's distress. The lamenter in the Psalms depicts himself as a byword (משל, *māšāl*) among the wicked, the topic of conversation among those who sit idly at the city gate and the butt of the mocking songs of drunkards (Ps 69:12–13 [11–12]; cf. 44:15 [14], a communal lament, where the "byword" is parallel to "a shaking of the head" [cf. on Job 16:4]). "Job comes to rank among neighbouring peoples, to whom the story of his sufferings spreads, as a great sinner, so that they say 'as great a sinner as Job'" (Gray); for similar phrases, cf. 30:9; Deut 28:37; 1 Kgs 9:7; 2 Chr 7:20; Jer 24:9. His ill fame spreads beyond his own acquaintance to the "peoples" (עמים); cf. NEB "a byword in every land." To spit in the face of someone, or perhaps simply, in the presence of someone, was evidently the strongest expression of contempt (30:10; Deut 25:9; Isa 50:6; Matt 26:67; 27:30; Mark 10:34; 14:65; 15:19). It is God who has devised this fate for Job through inflicting suffering upon him; though there is no subject expressed for the verb "he has set," and some take it as an impersonal verb meaning "I have become" (cf. JB, NEB, NAB), it is best to regard God as the subject.

7 In 16:16 Job's eyelids were shadowed over by the darkness of death; here the image is rather of the waning of the natural physical powers as a result of his inner stresses (כעש is "anguish" as at 6:2, not "anger" as at 5:2; 10:17). Elsewhere the eyes become dim (כהה; perhaps rather "become weak, expressionless" [KB³]) because of advancing age (Gen 27:1; Deut 34:7), but the verb is used also of eyes that have been violently blinded (Zech 11:17). This is still the language of the lament (cf. Ps. 6:8 [7], "my eye wastes away [עשש] because of grief [כעס]" = 31:10 [9]). The weakness of his eyes matches the weakness, almost the insubstantiality, of his limbs (cf. also on v 1). They have become (or perhaps, "wasted away to," NEB) a shadow, an image commonly used of brevity (8:9; 14:2; Ps 102:12 [11]; 109:23; 144:4; Eccl 6:12) but not unnaturally expressive of unreality or insubstantiality. We had an earlier reference to his gauntness in 16:8. An interesting possibility is the translation "all shapes seem to me like shadows" (NJPS), the line carrying on the thought of the preceding line: "his eyes are so dim that the objects he sees flit before them like shadows" (Peake); see further n. 17:7.a.

8 Many commentators regard vv 8–10 (or vv 8–9) as out of place because they sound completely out of character for Job, and they interrupt the lamenting train of thought (note how well v 11 could follow v 7 directly). Thus Duhm, Peake, Gray, Fohrer, Hesse, de Wilde. They are right in what they discern but wrong in what they propose (deletion or removal to another place). Words that are out of place in Job's mouth may be still his words if he is quoting an opponent or if he is speaking ironically. It is surprising that so few (Ehrlich, Andersen, Habel) recognize the irony here. There is indeed a subtlety in the irony: the "ungodly" man, who is the target of the scorn of the godly, is an ironic reversal of Job's unblemished innocence, whereas the "upright" and the "innocent" are not ironic terms: the double irony is that these *are* appropriate terms. The bearers of these epithets are decent people, whose defect is in their head rather than their heart; Job has nothing against their piety, but he despises their lack of intelligence (v 10).

What the upright and innocent are appalled at is Job's present condition ("this"). They experience the conventional pious reaction of horror to a disaster that evidences God's judgment like the "many" who are "appalled" at the suffering of the servant of Yahweh in Isa 52:14 (on שׁמם cf. on 16:7; and see F. Stolz, *THWAT* 2:970–74). We are still in the world of the "byword" and the spitting of v 6. The difference here is that now it is plain who the mockers are: not just people in general, or "peoples," but righteous persons. Not the self-righteous, who only "claim to be honest" (GNB), but genuinely "honest" people (NEB, JB) who have never questioned the retributive nexus and rely on "shocking" tragedies like Job's to keep their moral universe intact. They need the stimulation of the crime and punishment of others to assure them that the moral system remains in good working order. They are "roused" with righteous indignation against the godless; the verb (התערר) does not mean the indignation believers feel in their heart when they notice that the workers of iniquity prosper (as Dhorme, comparing התחרה in Ps 37:1, 7, 8; Prov 24:19) nor even the "exultation" of the righteous when evil overtakes their enemy (as התערר means in 31:29), but the excitement of being in the right when deserved doom is falling on the godless.

The point of view in the verse is that of Job's opponents; so he is the one designated by their term "the ungodly" (חנף, as in 8:13; 13:16; 15:34). Though "the upright" was in the plural (ישׁרים), "the innocent" is in the singular (נקי) because it is correlative with "the godless" man Job.

9 Most versions and commentators assume that there is a contrast between vv 8 and 9 (RSV "Upright men are appalled. . . . Yet the righteous holds to his way"; cf. NAB, NIV). If this is a contrast between the upright (plural) of v 8 and the righteous (singular) of v 9, it would be Job who, despite universal disapproval, nevertheless "holds to his way," i.e., maintains his integrity. This is an improbable interpretation, because the singular has already been used in v 8 (נקי) of those who oppose Job, and because (more tellingly) Job is unlikely to speak of himself as "gaining strength" in the very speech in which he bewails his loss of vitality and energy (see 16:7–8; 17:1, 7). Perhaps the contrast intended in RSV and similar translations is between the momentary shock righteous people experience on beholding Job and their deliberate maintenance of right behavior. But that too is an unsatisfactory interpretation, because the "appallment" they feel does not for a moment threaten their habitual way of life, but rather confirms it.

We should suppose, therefore, that v 9 continues the description of the righteous begun in v 8. He "keeps" (אחז) his way, i.e., maintains his upright manner of life, perhaps by more carefully guarding himself against any sin that could call down on him a calamity of Joban proportions (cf. Ps 39:2 [1] "I will guard [שמר] my ways from sinning with my tongue"). It does not seem to be God's way (as in 23:11) but the righteous person's own chosen way. The sight of the suffering of the godless, far from unsettling them, only serves to "strengthen" them in their righteousness. Job is weakened by his suffering (vv 1, 7), but righteous people are strengthened by it! There is irony here, not against the honesty of the righteous who are genuinely provoked to greater godliness by the fate of the wicked, but against their intelligence, which will not let them question their conviction that any sufferer must be a godless person. But is not such an adamant assertion of theory over fact an evil in itself, an intellectual dishonesty? Job does not actually say so here; elsewhere his complaint against humanity—as represented by the friends—has generally been grounded in their disloyalty (6:15), uselessness (13:4), and insight inferior to his own (12:3). But at 13:4, 7–8 he has accused them, and all those who take their intellectual position, of a lying partisanship of God; and such a thought may be in the background here too.

It is important to affirm that Job is not in this verse describing his own position. Davidson, for example, thought otherwise: "It is his own sentiments and resolution that he gives expression to, and the passage is perhaps the most surprising and lofty in the Book. . . . No mysteries or wrongs shall make him falter in the way of righteousness. And the human spirit rises to the height of moral grandeur, when it proclaims its resolution to hold on to the way of righteousness independently both of men and God." Delitzsch also had spoken of these words in a fine phrase as "a rocket which shoots above the tragic darkness of the book, lighting it up suddenly, although only for a short time." They are indeed words so surprising in Job's mouth that we may beg leave to doubt that he means them of himself.

10 The strophe concludes with an address. Though commentators almost universally see the verse as directed to the friends, it is more in keeping with the immediate context to take it as a challenge to the righteous in general, who have found in Job's distress a signal of his guilt. In their number are the three friends, of course; they may be strengthened (v 9) in their moral judgment of Job, but that will be a sign of their theological shallowness. True wisdom in this affair is, as Job has said, to see that his case proves that the standard theology is in error. Because he has seen that, he has wisdom superior to the friends' (12:3), and because they—and everyone else—have not seen it, their reason must have been perverted by God (17:4). The righteous may assault him ("come" against him) for all they are worth, but they will only prove their lack of insight ("I will not find a wise one among you").

In this invitation to renew their assaults on him (lit., "return and come"; see n. 17:10.a) the words are defiant but the mood is hopeless; for there is little likelihood that people will see things Job's way or that God will openly vindicate him and so compel others to acknowledge that Job was in the right after all. This is a very specific hopelessness, this hopelessness of vindication; it does not inhibit Job's conviction of his innocence and of his superior insight. To say "I shall not find a wise man among you" puts himself in the position of the teacher or examiner of the theological perceptions of others. The invitation ("attack me") is of course a rhetorical presentation of the conditional ("if you attack," i.e., no matter how often you attack; GNB's dynamic equivalence translation has seen that correctly: "if all of them came. . . .").

11 This lapse into a mood of hopelessness is not a contradiction of the aggressiveness of v 10. For we have come now to a clearer sense of where Job's despair lies. He is not so debilitated by his depression as to give up caring about anything. He still believes passionately in his own innocence, and in the superior insight into the workings of the moral universe he has gained by his own experience. He can be cynical and patronizing towards his friends (16:2–5), haughty towards the conventionally pious (17:8–10). But at the same time he is in despair because he knows himself to be in the grip of death and has no hope that his innocence will be vindicated this side of death.

His life he regards (as in 7:6; 17:1) as already over (as against Fohrer, "the days he still has to live"); עבר in reference to time will mean "be past, over" (Gen 50:4; 1 Kgs 18:29; Amos 8:5). His plans for the future have been broken off or snapped (נתק, used of snapping cords, or of tearing up roots, Judg 16:9; Ezek 17:9). The theme for this strophe, loss of hope, has been established.

12 The Hebrew is obscure, as the RSV margin notes, not because of any difficulty in the words themselves, but because the connection of the whole line is unclear. RSV, with RV, JB, NJPS, GNB, NIV, NAB, think the verse represents the attitude of the friends to Job's distress: he will soon emerge from the darkness of his suffering into the light of life. JB takes the whole line as a quotation of their words: "Night, they say, makes room for day, and light is near at hand to chase the darkness." RSV, with NJPS, takes the first colon as descriptive of their attitude ("They make night into day"), the second as their words ("'The light,' they say, 'is near to the darkness'"). NIV, with NAB, regards only the words "light is near" as the suppositious quotation ("in the face of darkness they say, 'Light is near.'").

Now it is true that the friends have in general encouraged Job to believe that his misery will, or may, soon be over, and Zophar has actually spoken of Job's life becoming brighter than the noonday, even its darkness being as morning light (11:17). Yet Job does not upbraid the friends for encouraging him, but only for failing to recognize his innocence. And in any case, it is not the friends who are the imaginary bystanders in this chapter, but upright persons (vv 8, 9) who mock his suffering (v 2), ignorant of its real cause (v 4). They are appalled at Job's ungodliness (v 8), and not in the least concerned to proffer encouragement to Job. So the line cannot represent the viewpoint of others.

It is better to suppose that the line elaborates the "plans" and "desires" of v 11 (similarly Dhorme, Gordis, Habel), i.e., the natural human hopes for the future that count on night giving place to day. All such plans have been "broken" (v 11); Job has abandoned hope that he will see the light, i.e., live; his hope is invisible and non-existent (v 15). That is what it means for his days to have passed away (v 11): the night surrounds him now, a night that will never yield to day (cf. his wish concerning the day of his conception, 3:6, 9).

Dhorme ingeniously argued that the changing of night into day was part of Job's lament, the longings of v 11 being his present unfulfilled desires that haunt his mind and keep him sleepless, so making his nights into a veritable day. But it is inconceivable that darkness should in v 12 be the desirable time of sleep but in v 13 the symbol of death. More persuasive is Horst's understanding of v 12b as meaning that "light comes only from the darkness" (cf. 10:22, where the light is as the darkness), but this involves an unidiomatic reading of v 12a, "the night has been determined as day for me" (cf. n. 17:12.b).

13–15 These lines appear to be one long sentence, introduced by three "if"-clauses (though אִם stands only before the first); so RSV, NEB, NAB, NIV. Duhm, Dhorme and others object that it is too trite to say, "If I hope for Sheol . . . where is my hope?" but the point is that Job has indeed an *expectation* (hope in v 13)—of imminent death—which deprives him of *hope* (hope in v 15).

For Job, normal human hope arises from social significance; in his earlier life his standing in the community as a respected and compassionate leader (29:7–17) gave him cause to hope for a long and prosperous future, multiplying his days as the sand, and dying peacefully at the end, "in his nest," with his family surrounding him (29:18–20). Now he has lost both his family and his status: the only intimacy he can imagine is with the forces and denizens of the underworld (Corruption is his father, worms are his mother and sister), and, as one whose dwelling-place is already designated as Sheol, he no longer has any firm footing in this world. For these reasons he can have no hope.

13 The idea of Sheol as a house is doubtless old and widespread (cf. also 30:23 "the house appointed for all living" and Ps 49:12 [11], Eccl 12:5). The Palestinian practice of secondary burial of bones in an ossuary, sometimes in the shape of a house, reflects and supports the idea (see E. M. Meyers, "Secondary Burials in Palestine," *BA* 33 [1970] 2–29). One such ossuary from Jerusalem (L. Y. Rahmani, "Jerusalem's Tomb Monuments on Jewish Ossuaries," *IEJ* 18 [1968] 220–25 [222] and pl. 23) actually bears the inscription *šʾwl*, "Sheol." Spreading one's couch in Sheol is reminiscent of Ps 139:8; the image is of the final activity of the day or, in this case, of life. The verb רִפֵּד properly means "support" (cf. Cant 2:5), i.e., with cushions, perhaps suggesting a curled up or fetal position (the evidence for posture in sleep is meager; see T. H. McAlpine, *Sleep, Divine and Human, in the Old Testament* [JSOTSup 38; Sheffield: JSOT, 1987] 85–106).

14 What Job has to look forward to is something worse even than his present situation. Here on earth he has lost the solidarity of the family; in Sheol he will not be reunited with them (contrast Jacob's "I shall go down to Sheol to my son, mourning," Gen 37:35), but will enter a new macabre community (Horst) of the grave and its worms. He calls "Corruption," which is Sheol personified, his father—as a sign of his close relationship to death (E. Jenni, *THWAT* 1:6) and its power over him. The formula, "You are my . . . (father, son, etc.)," has a legal ring to it; cf. the divorce formula of Hos 2:4 [2], "She is not my wife, and I am not her husband," and the legitimation formula of Ps 2:7, "You are my son," with its counterpart in Ps 89:27 [26], "You are my father." In Jer 2:27 we have the closest parallel to this parent-recognition formula, when Israel says to a tree, "You are my father," and to a stone, "You gave me birth" (cf. also Prov 7:4 "Say to wisdom, 'My sister,' and call insight your familiar friend"). The formula is always used to signify a newly acquired status; Job has come to recognize his future familials. The "pit" is a common term for Sheol (33:18, 22, 24, 30; Ps 16:10; Jonah 2:7 [6]), or perhaps a burial pit lying within the land of Sheol (cf. Prov 9:18). To call the pit one's father may suggest its authority over one (Andersen), but in the context of home and bed and mother and sister it more naturally indicates Job's sense of belonging to the world of Sheol, and what is more, being kin with it and sharing its essence. "Mother" and "sister" primarily express the family relation but also signify affection, as in Cant 4:9–10, 12, where the lover calls his beloved "my sister, my bride"—a common Semitic idiom (see M. Pope, *Song of Songs* [AB; Garden City, N.Y.: Doubleday, 1977] 480–81).

15 If his *expectation* (אקוה, v 13) is wholly of joining the company of worms, what kind of *hope* (תקוה, v 15) is that? It is important to remind oneself that Job is not simply despairing that his life seems to be drawing to a close. The sting of death for him is that it will prevent him from witnessing his own vindication, and will make him powerless to have any hand in bringing it to pass. And as for "happiness" or "well-being" or "good" (טובה), that for him in this speech consists of vindication; of course he mourns his lost prosperity and dead children, but wealth and family happiness were above all certifications of his piety. What can now be no longer envisaged (שׁור, "behold, regard") is the restoration of his public honor as a righteous man. In 7:7 he had said that he would never again "see" or experience good (טוב), in 9:25 that his life never had seen "good" (טוב); here he doubts that anyone will ever see his honor restored. The vigor of his cry to Earth to demand vengeance for him (16:18), and his confidence that his oath of innocence is even now pleading for him in heaven (16:19) are somewhat abated. But he does not deny that strength he momentarily had; the very use of rhetorical questions here suggests a certain wistfulness on his part, an inability to put the hope entirely from his mind.

16 He appeals to the traditional phrase, exemplified in Ps 49:18 [17]: "When one dies one carries nothing away; one's glory (or, possessions, כבוד) will not descend after him." Hope and well-being belong only to the upper world, the land of the living; they have nothing in common with the world of Sheol. There is no "hint that this hope will support him in his home in Sheol" (Habel), for the wish that Sheol could be a refuge, though he expresses it in 14:13–17, he rejects as an impossible dream. But neither is this a moment of total loss of self-sufficiency that opens the way for him to look to God alone (Weiser), for he finds himself wholly abandoned by God, and deprived by God of his right.

The dust of Sheol is a conventional enough image (cf. 7:21; 20:11; 21:26; Ps 22:16 [15], 30 [29]; 30:10 [9]; Isa 26:19; Dan 12:2); it is peculiarly apt here when a predominating idea has been of his being shriveled up (16:8). The dryness he feels makes him already kin with the dust of the underworld.

As in his previous speeches, it is death that is the closing note (7:21b; 10:21–22; 14:20–22). But that is not because he is suffering so badly that he believes he must soon die, nor because he has been unable to gain the support he had a right to expect from his friends, but because there is no sign of the vindication he demands, no hint that his judicial appeal to God (13:20–22) has penetrated the court of heaven. It is the perpetual ignoring of his right that has worn him down, crushed his spirit (v 1), wasted his limbs (v 7), broken his hopes (v 11).

Explanation

This speech of Job's comes from a limbo-land between calling and being answered, between the outright summons to God to vindicate him (chaps. 12–14) and any assurance that he has indeed been heard (chaps. 38–41). There is nothing really new to say, for all that matters has been comprehended in the catalogue of grievances against God that Job's previous speeches have contained. Yet it is a new situation in which Job finds himself, now that what had to be said has been said, now that he has committed, irrevocably, an act he had indecisively contemplated for long. Now that the summons against God has been issued, and now that God himself has not responded but, on his behalf, Eliphaz has spoken again, with easily imagined consequences for the resumption of the routine the first cycle of speeches had established— what is to be said?

One thing that can be said, perhaps the most positive thing that Job has said so far, is that his protestation of innocence and his demand for vindication now stand as his "witness" in heaven (protestation and demand are of course the same thing, for only a man convinced of his own innocence could have the courage to demand vindication from God). It is one thing to come out with it and say, I appeal to God for justice; it is another to live with the knowledge that those are the words that stand to one's account in the heavenly court of law. That emphatic statement, "Even now my witness is in heaven, my advocate is on high" (16:19), signals that Job's case has been moved to a higher plane; it is out of his hands, his very cry itself having acquired a sort of existence of its own, "argu[ing] a mortal's case before God as a man argues for his friend" (16:21). The cry, now that it has formally been uttered, has become a standing reminder to God that he has a piece of unfinished business on his hands; though Job waits "sleepless for God's reply" (16:20), he has no fear now that his death, which he still expects, will remove his case from the heavenly agenda. His cry has become his spokesman (16:20).

The pressure of the short time that remains before he dies of his pains has been much relieved; perhaps it is significant that here he now envisages his death in a matter of "years" (16:22) rather than days or weeks—as we had earlier been led to expect (7:6, 21; 10:20). Indeed, he does not really *hope* for vindication before death, although he *desires* it. Rather, he believes that he will die a victim of God's murderous design, but he intends that even that should not stifle his cry. So, while he still lives, he calls upon Earth not to cover his blood when it has been shed, but to cry ceaselessly for vengeance till his vindication is assured (16:18).

Now that the die has been cast and he himself no longer has to struggle with the decision, two interesting touches of objectivity towards his own suffering appear in his speech; he becomes able to distance himself a little from the experience of his pain. At the opening of the speech Job so far forgets his own immediate pain as to envisage himself in the friends' shoes. What would it be like, he asks himself, if the roles were reversed? It is an act of vicarious imagination that any therapist would be delighted to see in a depressive as a sign of returning health: the patient, however fleetingly, exchanges his couch for the psychiatrist's chair. Better still, Job can imagine himself doing rather more satisfactorily than his therapist "comforters." *They* are "torturer-comforters" (16:2), so directive in their counsel that they cannot begin to hear *him*, mishearing all his cries as mere "tempestuous words," finding his compulsion to cry out a clinical symptom, an "agitation" or "illness" (16:3b), a logorrhea that should be staunched rather than encouraged to well forth purgatively. He for his part knows the formulas and techniques of their learned, directive counsel: "I also could speak as you do if you were in my place" (16:4). But no! If the chairs were changed, he would "strengthen you with my encouragements," the consolations of his lips soothing their pain (16:5). This is suddenly the old Job again, the Job whose words would raise the fallen, strengthening feeble knees (4:4); and for a moment he knows he is the same man, still with the same capacities. The suffering has for a time been beaten back from occupying the whole of his imagination. For a time the Job of the prologue treads the boards with him as his Doppelgänger.

In another moment of objectivity Job takes a look at himself from the viewpoint of the conventionally righteous. Even within this speech those who have found his suffering a token of divine displeasure have been scorned by him as "mockers," the "ungodly" who jeer at the lamenting sufferer (17:2; cf. 12:4). But at 17:8–9 he allows that those who are appalled at his misfortune and are "roused" with indignation against him may indeed be the "godly," whose determination to stick to the straight and narrow is only reinforced by what they see as Job's terrible punishment. Job does not deny the piety of those who scorn him as a sinner; he thinks them bereft of reason, indeed (17:4a, 10), for not recognizing that conventional theology is too narrow to comprehend his case, but he wryly admits that his opponents (among whom are his "torturer-comforters") are not all of the devil's party. It is ironic that the truly upright are finding their righteous indignation against sin roused by the suffering of one who is truly innocent; and the irony brings its own special pain of isolation for Job, an isolation from the company and consolation of the godly. But at the same time, he has wrenched himself free momentarily from the moral simplism that was overwhelming him, that all that was right and good was on his side, and all that was on the other side was malign, perverse and unreasonable. In allowing that even the godly see him as a deserving sufferer, not an innocent, he has accepted a reality outside of himself, and that can only be good for a man so imprisoned by his experience; his healing, when it comes, will be through a not dissimilar though vastly more comprehensive recognition that only an unfaltering gaze upon the whole universal reality external to humankind can discern a meaning in suffering that is acceptable religiously and theologically (see on chaps. 38–41).

Bildad's Second Speech (18:1–21)

Bibliography

Burns, J. B. "The Identity of Death's First-Born (Job xviii 13)." *VT* 37 (1987) 362–64. **Dahood, M.** "Some Northwest-Semitic Words in Job." *Bib* 38 (1957) 306–20. ———. "The Root עזב II in Job." *JBL* 78 (1959) 303–309. **Driver, G. R.** "Some Hebrew Medical Expressions." *ZAW* 65 (1953) 255–62. ———. "Reflections on Recent Articles. II. Hebr. *môqēš*, 'Striker.'" *JBL* 73 (1954) 125–36, esp. 131–36. ———. "Problems in the Hebrew Text of Job." *VTS* 3 (1955) 72–93. **Irwin, W. A.** "Job's Redeemer." *JBL* 81 (1962) 217–29. **Moran, W. L.** "**taqtul*—Third Masculine Singular?" *Bib* 45 (1964) 80–82. **Reider, J.** "Some Notes to the Text of the Scriptures. 11. Job 18,3." *HUCA* 3 (1926) 113–14. **Sarna, N. M.** "The Mythological Background of Job 18." *JBL* 82 (1963) 315–18. **Williamson, H. G. M.** "A Reconsideration of עזב II in Biblical Hebrew." *ZAW* 97 (1985) 74–85.

Translation

¹ *Then Bildad the Shuhite answered and said:*

² ᵃ *How long before* ᵇ *you will end* ᶜ *your speeches?*
   You must reflect; only then can we talk.
³ *Why are we regarded as cattle,*
   thought of as stupid ᵃ *by you?* ᵇ
⁴ *You* ᵃ *may tear yourself to pieces in your rage,* ᵇ
   but is the earth to be unpeopled ᶜ *on your account?*
   are the rocks to be dislodged?

⁵ *Truly, the lamp of the wicked will be snuffed out,*
   the flame of his fire will shine no more.
⁶ *The light in his tent will be darkened,*
   the lamp above him ᵃ *be quenched.*
⁷ *His vigorous stride* ᵃ *will be hobbled,*
   his own counsel will hurl him down. ᵇ

⁸ *For he is thrust headlong* ᵃ *into a net,*
   he walks over a lattice.
⁹ *A trap grips him by the heel,*
   a snare closes tight on him.
¹⁰ *A noose lies hidden for him on the ground,*
   a gin across his path.

¹¹ *On every side terrors affright him,*
   they harry ᵃ *him at his heels.*
¹² ᵃ *Calamity* ᵇ *is hungry* ᶜ *for him,*
   Disaster waits only for him to stumble. ᵈ
¹³ ᵃ *By Disease* ᵇ *his skin is devoured,* ᶜ
   the firstborn of Death consumes his limbs.

[14a] *He is torn from the shelter of his tent,*[b]
and haled[c] *before the King of Terrors.*

[15] *Fire*[a] *lodges in his tent,*
over his dwelling is scattered brimstone.
[16] *Beneath, his roots dry up,*
above, his branches wither.[a]
[17] *His memory perishes from the farmlands;*
he leaves no name in the grazing lands.

[18] *He is driven*[a] *from light into darkness;*
he is expelled[b] *from the world.*
[19] *He leaves no posterity, no progeny*[a] *among his own kinsfolk,*
not a survivor wherever he sojourned.
[20] *They of the west*[a] *are appalled at his fate;*
they of the east are seized with horror.
[21] *Such indeed is the dwelling*[a] *of the evildoer,*
such the place of one who knows not God.

Notes

2.a. LXX has sg verbs, though it is uncertain how close its *Vorlage* was to the MT; it has "How long will it be before you [sg] cease (speaking); stop now, so that we ourselves may speak" (see Gray). 11QtgJob also has the sg for the first verb; the other forms in question are lost from the fragmentary text. Terrien explains the pl תשׂימה as having arisen from a dittogr of the *waw* in תבין ואחר (to תבינו ואחר), followed later by harmonizing corrections in vv 2–3.

2.b. Can עד־אנה תשׂימון mean "how long *before* you set . . . ?" Delitzsch and Peake thought this would require the negative לא. NJPS recognizes the difficulty and renders "How long? Put an end to talk!" and Gordis allows that the *paseq* after עד־אנה may be a Masoretic indication of a pause. No doubt the phrase occurs everywhere else without a following pause (Gordis), but עד־מתי, which means the same thing, is found as an interjection on its own (Ps 6:4 [3]; 90:13).

2.c. קנצי, constr pl (for abs; cf. GKC, § 130a) of a *hapax* קֵנֶץ is often explained as "snare, net" (cf. Arab. *qanaṣa* "capture, ensnare"); so BDB, RV, JPS, Gordis. This could mean "hunting for words" (cf. RSV) in the sense of seeking words to cover up deficiency in the argument (cf. Gray), making subtle and artificial attempts at finding arguments (Davidson), or, less probably, setting snares with words (Pope), i.e., playing word games (Habel). A supposed Akk. cognate *qinṣu* "bridle" (Gesenius-Buhl) was the source of JB "Will you never learn to check such words" and, curiously, of NEB "How soon will you bridle your tongue" (similarly Hölscher, Dhorme, Terrien, de Wilde), though G. R. Driver had pointed out the non-existence of *qinṣu* ("Problems in the Hebrew Text of Job," VTSup 3 [1955] 72–93 [79]; cf. *CAD*). There is an Akk. *qinnazu* "whip" (Fr. Delitzsch; hence Tur-Sinai), but no good sense emerges. The preferred suggestion is to take קנצי as a by-form (an Aramaizing dissolving of the gemination by the insertion of an *n*, according to KB³) of קֵץ "ends." So medieval Jewish commentators, NAB "put an end to words," NJPS, NIV, Horst, Fohrer, Andersen. The 11QtgJob reading תשׂוא סוף למלי[ן] virtually clinches the argument (cf. E. G. Clarke, "Reflections on Some Obscure Hebrew Words in the Biblical Job in the Light of XIQTg Job," *Studies in Philology in Honour of Ronald James Williams* [ed. G. E. Kadish and G. E. Freeman; Toronto: Beuben, 1982] 17–30 [20–21]).

3.a. נטמינו seems at first a form of טמא "be unclean," hence "are [reckoned] unclean" (so Vg, RV, Fohrer). This fits poorly with the idea of the stupidity of animals (though cf. Grabbe, 72–74). Most derive the form from טמם (Aram., postbib. Heb.), "stop up" (eyes, ears, etc.), i.e., "be stupid"; 3 mss actually have נָטַמֹנוּ "we are stupid." LXX apparently read a form of דמם "be silent," but that does not harmonize well with "in your eyes." Less probable still is Blommerde's suggestion that the root is טמן "hide" ("must we hide from your sight?") since that does not connect at all with the idea of stupidity. The conjecture of Dhorme נִדְמִינוּ כַבָּעַר "[Why should we be] likened to cattle [in your eyes]?" (followed by Terrien, JB[?], de Wilde [reading more correctly בְּעֵיר]) is unnecessary. NAB "their equals in your sight" similarly reads נִדְמֵינוּ "we are likened." On the Qumran targum see E. C. Clarke (n. 18:2.c above).

3.b. Reading בְּעֵינֶיךָ "in your [sg] eyes"; see *Comment* on v 2.

4.a. Lit., "[O] one who tears himself in his rage"; for the 3rd pers clause in a 2nd pers address cf. Obad 2–3.

4.b. The line is omitted by Fohrer as breaking the train of thought. Others thought a linking line had been lost before it (Driver-Gray, Hölscher), and have filled the gap with a line like 5:2 (Volz, Tur-Sinai) or 17:8–10a (Duhm).

4.c. Lit., "abandoned." M. Dahood's suggestion ("The Root עזב II in Job," *JBL* 78 [1959] 303–9 [306]; followed by Andersen, and perhaps NJPS "will earth's order be disrupted") that a עזב I "arrange, rearrange" appears here is at first attractive since it suggests the idea of order; but it is not clear what concrete image could be intended by "rearranging the earth." More compelling still is the strong probability that Heb. has no עזב II (see H. G. M. Williamson, "A Reconsideration of עזב II in Biblical Hebrew," *ZAW* 97 [1985] 74–85). LXX has the interesting interpretive paraphrase, "What then? If you die, will the earth beneath heaven be depopulated?"; but the issue is rather, "if you have your way over the doctrine of retribution."

6.a. Taking עליו literally as "above him." NIV makes it into a table-lamp ("the lamp beside him"; so also RV mg). NAB has "in spite of him," a very doubtful sense of על (BDB, 754 § II.f.(f) recognizes only two occurrences; and see *Comment* on 10:7, one of the supposed occurrences). NEB "his lamp dies down and fails him" and NJPS "his lamp fails him" take the על as referring to the lamp itself.

7.a. Lit., "steps of his strength," taking אונו from אָן "vigor, wealth." NJPS "his iniquitous strides" takes it from אוֹן I "trouble, wickedness." G. R. Driver reads אונו יָצֵר צעדיו "his wickedness encompasseth his steps" ("Mistranslations," *ExpT* 5 [1945–46] 192–93); hence perhaps "in his iniquity his steps totter," reading יָצוּרוּ (Brockington, 107).

7.b. MT ותשליכהו "and shall cast him [down]" (rarely in this sense, cf. BDB, 1021 § 1.e) is emended by metathesis of consonants to וְתַכְשִׁלֵהוּ "and will cause him to stumble" (Driver-Gray, Dhorme, Hölscher, Fohrer, Terrien), following LXX. The translation is not greatly affected.

8.a. Following, with NEB, NAB, *BHS*, Horst, the suggestion of G. Gerleman ("ברגליו as an Idiomatic Phrase," *JSS* 4 [1959] 59) that ברגליו, lit., "at his feet" is an idiom for "immediately" (cf. Judg 5:15; Num 20:19; Deut 2:28). It must be admitted that Ps 25:15; "he delivers my foot (רגלי) from the net (רשת)," suggests that the literal sense may not be wholly inappropriate here.

11.a. Lit., "scatter" (פוץ hiph); it is a difficulty that here only is a single individual the object (BDB "and drive him" is not easily defensible). *BHK* mentioned the emendation וַהֲדָפֻהוּ "they thrust, drive"; others include הֱאִיצֻהוּ "they rush him off" (from אוץ) and הֱצִיקֻהוּ "they oppress" from צוק I. Gordis thinks פיץ a by-form of פצץ "crush," but the meaning is not very appropriate; Horst thinks it may be a by-form of פוז "be supple, hasty," in hiph perhaps "scare away," but this is not so convincing. Improbable was Ehrlich's suggestion that it means "urinate over his feet" (cf. Ezek 7:17; 21:12 [7]), involuntary micturition in fear being a well-known experience; G. R. Driver gave the view support ("Some Hebrew Medical Expressions," *ZAW* 65 [1953] 255–62 [259–60]), supposing a Heb. פיץ "make water," cognate with Arab. *fâḍa*; this is incorporated into NEB as "and make him piss over his feet" (a concession to the Zeitgeist, says de Wilde). Grabbe, *Comparative Philology*, 74–76, thinks a similar meaning could be derived from Arab. *fâḍa* "overflow." The objection is not the earthiness of the idea, but its comparative unsuitability in a context where the focus is the assaults of enemies, not the reaction of the assaulted.

12.a. NAB omits line as dittogr of v 7a (!).

12.b. Taking אוֹן as אָן rather than אוֹן "vigor" (as in v 7); so JPS, Moffatt, NIV. Alternatively, "his strength is hungry" (RSV "hunger-bitten"), NJPS "his progeny hunger" (so Tur-Sinai, Gordis, arguing that "strength" means "offspring" in Gen 49:3, a traditional Jewish interpretation which seems, however, out of place here, where it is the wicked man himself who is spotlighted).

Among emendations the simplest is Dhorme's, בְּאוֹנוֹ "[he is hungry] amid his wealth" (so too Terrien; and *BHS* thinks this should perhaps be read). *BHK*'s proposal יִרְעָב אָוֶן לוֹ, "(his) trouble is hungry for him" (cf. Jer 42:14), apparently adopts a throw-away suggestion of Driver-Gray, יִרְעָב לוֹ אוֹנוֹ. JB's "hunger becomes his companion" (אָחֹתוֹ, following Larcher) is weak.

A new line of approach was started by Dahood, claiming that "the Hungry One" is a standard epithet of Mot (*Psalms I*, 203); this is followed by Pope and Habel. Pope also follows Dahood's view (*Psalms I*, 237) that אנו is from his אנה III "to meet," with suff, thus "the Ravenous One confronts him" (Pope). Dahood and Pope do not say how they understand יהי, and Habel's translation "the Hungry One will be his strength" does not have an obvious meaning (Habel says it is satirical, but is Death depicted as weak?). It is true that Death is depicted in the next two verses, but that is no reason why calamity and disaster should not be personified here.

12.c. NEB "For all his vigour he is paralysed with fear" derives from G. R. Driver's suggestion (*ZAW* 65 [1953] 260), otherwise unaccepted, of a new root רעב "was bewitched" (cf. Arab. ra‘aba "uttered incantations; terrified") (so too A. Guillaume, "Paronomasia in the Old Testament," *JSS* 9 [1964] 282–90 [289]). Wetzstein, cited by Delitzsch, has a graphic portrayal of the phenomenon of paralyzing fright among Bedouins of Syria: "If the . . . idea of some great and inevitable danger or misfortune overpowers the Arab, all strength of mind and body suddenly forsakes him, so that he breaks down powerless and defenceless. Both European and native doctors have assured me that the ro‘b in Arabia kills, and I have witnessed instances myself. Since it often provides a stiffness of the limbs with chronic paralysis, all kinds of paralysis are called ro‘b." The only question is whether our Heb. text can mean this.

12.d. The parallels cited in the *Comment* put beyond doubt the derivation of צלעו from צלע "stumbling" (so RSV; cf. JPS, NIV), though the term may perhaps mean "stray" rather than "stumble" (G. R. Driver, "Theological and Philological Problems in the Old Testament," *JTS* 47 [1946] 156–66 [162]). A long Jewish tradition saw here, however, צֵלָע "rib," used for "wife" (cf. Gen 2:21–22). Hence NJPS "disaster awaits his wife" (similarly Tur-Sinai, Gordis), a most improbable divergence of attention from the wicked man himself. Others have taken "rib" to mean "side" (though it never means the "side" of a person elsewhere), and translate "disaster is ready at his side" (NAB; cf. JB, GNB, Dhorme, Terrien, Pope, Sicre Diaz, Habel), but this has nothing to recommend it. Andersen has an impressive picture, "His plump body becomes emaciated, his ribs stick right out," but it cannot be seen how all this derives from the Heb.

13.a. The line is omitted by NAB as a dittogr of v 13b.

13.b. Revocalizing to בְּדָוָי, "by disease" as Wright, Driver-Gray, Dhorme, Terrien, Fohrer, de Wilde, RSV, NEB, JB), and to יֵאָכֵל "is eaten." MT בַּדֵּי עורו, lit., "parts of his skin" is rendered literally by NIV (RV, JPS "the members of his body" can hardly be right); painful indeed but hardly thoroughgoing enough to bring the man to Sheol in the next verse. NJPS "the tendons under his skin" probably is thinking of the בדים "poles" for carrying the ark, but the disease sounds unconvincingly specific, especially when it is "tendons" again in the remainder of the line.

An interesting conjecture (N. M. Sarna, "The Mythological Background of Job 18," *JBL* 82 [1963] 315–18 [317]), taken up by Pope and Habel, makes both בדי and בדיו "with his two hands"; but the strict repetition is more Ugaritic than Hebrew, and there are problems involved with the translation "Firstborn Death" (see *Comment*).

13.c. Reading יֵאָכֵל (cf. *BHS*).

14.a. NAB exchanges the places of vv 14a and 15a.

14.b. Lit., "from his feet, i.e., his shelter"; a similar apposition in Isa 32:18, "dwellings, securities." This parallel renders unnecessary the suggestion of Blommerde, 85 (followed by Habel), that מבטחו is a genitive.

14.c. ותצעדהו seems to be 3 fem sg (as is תשכון in v 15) but no fem subject appears available. NJPS offers an attractive rendering, "Terror marches him to the King," presumably taking בלהות as an intensive pl (GKC, § 124e) and an *ad sensum* subject of the sg verb (so too Pesh); this will also explain the fem in v 15, but למלך (anarthrous) seems very bald (NJPS itself feels it necessary to supply a footnote, "Viz. of the underworld," while NEB glosses with "Death's terrors escort him to their king"). W. A. Irwin thought ("Job's Redeemer," *JBL* 81 [1962] 217–29 [222]) that the fem may refer to a *queen* of the underworld like Ereshkigal; but a person of her status would hardly be doing the escorting. N. M. Sarna imagined the anomalous forms were a rare masc with *t*- preformative (*JBL* 82 [1963] 318), the subject being Death's firstborn, but W. L. Moran denied there was adequate support for a **taqtul* masc sg in Canaanite and proposed וְתַצְעִידֻהוּ "they march him," as indefinite pl or having the denizens of the underworld as subject ("**taqtul*— Third Masculine Singular?," *Bib* 45 [1964] 80–82, esp. 82 n. 1), taking this as an example of the 3 masc pl *taqtulū* form (cf. Moran, "New Evidence on Canaanite *taqtulū(na)*," *JCS* 5 [1951] 33– 35; and see now M. Dahood, *Psalms III*, 387). H. J. van Dijk responded with several examples from Ugaritic and the OT where a **taqtul* form seems in evidence ("Does Third Masculine Singular **taqtul* Exist in Hebrew?," *VT* 19 [1969] 440–47). Certainly the **taqtulū* pl form is better attested, which perhaps gives the preference to וְתַצְעִידֻהוּ "and they march him" (Moran, Blommerde).

Gordis and Sicre Diaz point to GKC, § 144b for support for taking the fem sg as impersonal, but the parallel evidence is not strong. Dhorme unconvincingly took the forms here and in v 15 as 2 sg, "You [i.e., anyone] may lead him away . . . You may dwell in his tent" (so NEBmg). Driver thought the subject was the doom previously described (so too Hesse, van Selms), but was open to an emendation to יַצְעִדֻהוּ "they escort him." Others simply emend to the 3 masc pl, used indefinitely (Duhm, Horst). Fohrer, following Stier, reads מבטחותו צעדהו "from his security, his step [goes]."

15.a. MT מבלי־לו is intelligible as "what is none of his" (RV, RSV; cf. BDB, 116a), and בלי is quite frequent in Job (4:11, 20; 6:6; 8:11; 24:7, 8, 10; 30:8; 31:19, 39; 33:9; 34:6; 35:16; 36:12; 38:2, 41; 39:16; 41:25; 42:3). But if brimstone is scattered over his house, it is unlikely that anyone, even strangers, should live in it, and a parallel with "brimstone" is perhaps expected. G. R. Driver ("Problems in the Hebrew Text of Job," VTSup 3 [1955] 72–93 [79]) ingeniously suggested "mixed herbs," supposing a Heb. מַבְלִיל or similar (from בלל "mix"), and noting the use of mixed herbs, sometimes mingled with spices, in an Assyrian rite of exorcism (and hence NEB "magic herbs lie strewn about his tent"). Most, however, agree that Dahood has solved the difficulty with his proposal ("Some Northwest-Semitic Words in Job," *Bib* 38 [1957] 306–20 [312–14]) of a Heb. מַבֶּל "fire" cognate with Akk. *nablu*, Ug. *nblat* (pl) (so too Pope, Habel, Sicre Diaz, Gerleman in *BHS* [*frt*], NAB, NIV). For a further possible occurrence, see on 20:23. Grabbe's objection (*Comparative Philology*, 76–77) that the cognate nouns do not have a *mem* prefix is not very serious. Fire and brimstone are a natural pair (Gen 19:24; Ps 11:6; Ezek 38:22). Dahood's further suggestions, to read תֻשַּׁכַן "is set" (pu), and the emphatic *lamed* before the next verb יזרה, are not necessarily to be followed. Gordis came to a similar conclusion in proposing to read מַבּוּל "flood (of fire)" (cf. Akk. *nabālu* "destroy"). De Wilde's complaint that fire does not "dwell" and Rowley's objection that "dwell" is not a very good parallel to "is scattered" may be ignored. Quite attractive was the older proposal to find here לִילִית, Lilith, the night-hag that haunts waste places (Isa 34:14), which would also explain the fem of תשכן (Voigt, Beer, Fohrer, Terrien, Hölscher, Rowley, de Wilde; JB "The Lilith makes her home under his roof").

16.a. On מלל, cf. on 14:2.

18.a. Subject of the pl verb no doubt the demons; emendation to the sg to make God the subject (Duhm, Ball) would be quite wrong, as also the insertion of אלוה into the second half of the line *metri causa* (BHK).

18.b. From נדד hiph "chase away, make to wander." Dahood (followed by Habel) supposes a נדה "hurl, cast" with Akk., Ug. cognates (also at Ps 31:18 [17]; *Psalms I*, 190); the image is rather of the chase.

19.a. Not "grandson" (NAB; cf. RV, JPS); KJV "nephew" means "son's son."

20.a. אחרנים, lit., "those behind," contrasted with קדמנים "those before." Older commentators often understood these as "later generations" and "predecessors" (i.e., present inhabitants of Sheol [Budde]); so AV, RV, NAB, JPS, NJPS, Tur-Sinai, Gordis. But how can later generations know anything about him if the memory of him is exterminated? The terminology seems built upon the expressions הים האחרון for the "Western" Sea (Deut 11:24; etc.) and הים הקדמוני for the "Eastern" Sea (Dead Sea; Ezek 47:18; etc.).

21.a. Lit., "dwellings" (משכנות, as also in 21:28), obviously a single dwelling parallel to מקום "place"; perhaps a plural of "local extension" (GKC, § 124b). Dahood has noted a number of cases where habitations are pl in form, sg in meaning (*Psalms III*, 384), e.g. משכנות in Ps 43:3; 84:2 [1]; 132:5, 7 (49:12 [11] not so convincing).

Form / Structure / Setting

The *structure* of the speech is clearly two-fold: an exordium addressed directly to Job (vv 2–4) and a wisdom-type instruction on the fate of the wicked (vv 5–21). The absence of explicit links between the two parts of the speech makes its overall intention somewhat cryptic (see *Comment* on vv 2–21).

The strophic structure is on the whole easy to discern; in particular, the three-line strophes of vv 2–4 and 8–9 are clearly marked. This fact predisposes one to look for three-line structures throughout the speech, and such do become evident, though those of vv 11–13 and 18–20 have a pendant line. Verse 14, the pendant to 11–13, both concludes the narrative of the wicked man and is a bridge between 11–13 and 15–17 which cover the same ground, and v 21 is a concluding pendant in the form of a summary appraisal. The strophes may be outlined thus:

2–4	(3 lines)	address to Job
5–7	(3 lines)	the end of the wicked
8–10	(3 lines)	he is trapped
11–14	(4 lines)	he is brought to the underworld

15–17   (3 lines)   on earth memory of him perishes
18–21   (4 lines)   his story recapitulated; appraisals

Fohrer sees a very similar strophic structure, but divides 11–13, 14–16, 17–19, 20–21 (a two-line strophe). This is open to the objection that v 14 properly belongs to the narrative of the wicked man's downfall (vv 11–13), not to what follows. Verses 16 and 17 also belong together because the reason why memory of him perishes (v 17) is because his descendants are destroyed (v 16). Webster differs from the proposed analysis by dividing 11–13, 14–17 ("Strophic Patterns," 47). Skehan reduces 11–14 to three lines by excising 12a, 13a as dittographies (cf. NAB). Horst has a quite different result, through connecting v 7 with the "traps" passage, 8–10; but it seems exegetically incorrect to understand the traps as pitfalls of the wicked man's own making. Horst's distinction between vv 11–12 (terrors, calamity) and 13–14 (disease, king of terrors) is also unpersuasive. Terrien finds in all four five-line strophes, vv 2–6 (3 + 2), 7–11 (3 + 2), 12–18 (2 + 3), 17–21 (2 + 3); but it is hard to see that the strongest disjunction in the poem (between vv 4 and 5) can be enclosed within one strophe.

In *genre* the speech as a whole is a *disputation speech* which includes a lengthy *instruction* on the fate of the wicked. Elements from the disputation speech form proper, but principally from its exordium style, are confined to vv 2–4, where we find rhetorical questions implying that the other speaker should stop talking (v 2; cf. 8:2; 16:3) and that he is insulting the present speaker's intelligence (v 3; cf. 12:2–3). There is also the exhortation to the opponent to use his intelligence (v 2b; cf. 12:7; 8:8). These elements relate principally to the performance of the opponent in debate, and not to the substance of the controversy between the speakers.

The *topos* on the fate of the wicked has the character of *instruction,* with its closest analogues in wisdom and psalmic literature. The whole *topos* can be seen as an elaboration of proverbial sentences like Prov 10:24a "what the wicked dreads will come upon him"; cf. 11:5b; 12:13; 13:9b; 14:11; 21:12; 22:5; 24:16b, 20. The *narrative* of the fate of the wicked is particularly a psalmic feature (e.g. Ps 7:15–17 [14–16]; 10:2–11; 49:14–15 [13–14]; 64:2–10 [1–11]; cf. 37:35–36; 109:6–20; and contrast the narrative of the righteous man, e.g. 32:3–5; 34:5–7 [4–6]; 35:11–14; 39:2–4 [1–3]; 116:1–4). Among the proverb-like materials and motifs are these: the "lamp" of the wicked (vv 5, 6; cf. Prov 13:9; 20:20), being thrown down by one's own schemes (v 7b; cf. 5:12–13; Prov 26:27; 28:10; Ps 7:15–16 [14–15]; 10:2; 35:8; 57:7 [6]), "root and branch" (v 16; cf. Ecclus 10:16; 23:25; 40:15; mainly attested in the prophets, but surely proverbial), "progeny and posterity" likewise (v 19; cf. Ecclus 41:5; 47:22). But the images of the extinguished fire, of the snares, and especially of the terrors is much more elaborated than elsewhere.

The *function* of the speech as a whole, it will be argued below, is, by depicting the fate of the wicked, to *encourage* Job to amend his life.

The *tonality* depends on how the instruction of vv 5–21 is understood. If it is thought to depict Job as himself the wicked man it will inevitably be much different from the understanding advanced here. But even if it is entirely instruction, designed to encourage Job away from an avoidable fate, the exordium establishes a tone that is not merely impatience. Job speaks before thinking (v 2), and, adding insult to injury, regards the friends as the unintelligent ones (v 3); that is an attitude that Bildad, naturally enough, can stand no longer; but more serious is his perception of Job as a man who is tearing himself to pieces, and demanding that the natural order be upset. This is deeply disturbing for Bildad, and the anger of his speech reflects his anxiety.

The *nodal verse* is clearly v 4: it reveals the psychological position of the speaker, and explains why the speech is almost wholly taken up with an exposition of conventional dogma. It is because Bildad counts on keeping the mountains in their proper places (v 4c), which is to say, on defending the *status quo ante* by maintaining the unshakeability of the moral order of retribution.

Comment

2–21 The primary interpretive question for this speech is whether Bildad casts Job as one of the wicked, who will inevitably suffer the fate here portrayed, or whether the picture here drawn is of what precisely Job is *not*. R. E. Murphy, typically for many commentators, simply writes: "The implication, of course, is that Job is the wicked person" (*Wisdom Literature*, 32). He allows that "the tenor is not unlike Bildad's earlier speech (cf. 8:8–19)," but continues, "*but now* judgment has been passed on Job" (my italics). Gray too believed that the particular application of Bildad's words are suggested plainly enough: "Job is not prosperous, Job is wicked" (158; similarly Hesse). For Habel too, "the mood of Bildad has changed from being positive but defensive to being negative and condemnatory . . . his portrayal of the wicked is an unconditional announcement of the fate Job can expect" (282–83). Davidson had put it well, as usual: "Every sentence of Bildad's speech carries with it the charge, Thou art the man."

The interpretation here offered is different. It is that Bildad has perceived in Job's claim for his innocence to be recognized—despite the evident signs of his guilt—an affront to the stable moral order in which he has always found his own security. He needs for his own sake as well as Job's to reiterate that "the laws of the universe remain unshaken, and retribution will ultimately overtake the evildoer" (Gordis, 187). He does not mean to imply that Job is himself the man here depicted, though he would not be embarrassed to admit that there are certainly similarities. His principal aim, already established in his first speech, is to encourage Job to "seek" God with a "pure and upright" life; he cannot now be coolly informing Job that it is too late for any of that. The few words that Job has spoken, unwise and hostile against heaven though they may have been, cannot outweigh the simple fact that Job is still alive; and that for Bildad is the difference between a rescuable sinner and a doomed one (cf. on 8:4–6). That is part of what is meant by God not perverting justice (8:3). If he were to "cut off" the man Job for less than a fatal sin he would be no less unjust than if he failed to punish Job for the sin he has evidently committed.

2–4 The usual exordium confronting the arguments of the opponent begins this speech, but textual and linguistic problems present a formidable obstacle to a satisfactory interpretation. We would expect Bildad to address himself exclusively to Job, for that is the direction of all the friends' speeches. Instead, we find him using the plural "you" form in vv 2–3 ("you set," "you understand," "your eyes"), and addressing Job in the singular only in v 3.

Various solutions to this puzzle are proposed.

(i) It is the other friends, not Job, whom Bildad addresses in vv 2–3 (Fohrer). But this cannot be right because in v 3 "we" who are "reckoned like cattle . . . in your [plur] eyes" must be the friends, so the friends cannot also be "you." Translating "Do you think that we are unclean" (Fohrer), whereby the "you" presumably means Eliphaz and Zophar, and the "we" means all the friends, is a very forced way of taking the Hebrew.

(ii) Bildad addresses the friends in v 2, but Job in v 3 (so Murphy, *Wisdom Literature*, 32: v 2 is Bildad's "exhortation to his peers," v 4 his "exasperation with Job"). This is possible, though it implies an emendation of "your [plur] eyes" to "your [sg] eyes" in v 3, and it has still to be resolved what accusation is being made against the friends in v 2.

(iii) Bildad addresses the friends in v 2, the "audience" in v 3 (Dhorme; cf. Sicre Diaz); is there an audience?

(iv) Bildad is "quoting" or paraphrasing Job's words to the friends in v 2; so Tur-Sinai, translating "How long will you put the whip to the words?," which means "How long will you urge words onwards, as it were, with a whip? Gently! Let us not talk until you have understood." Bildad's reponse in v 3, says Tur-Sinai, links up with the image of driving on animals with a whip, "Wherefore are we counted as animals?" Among the difficulties with this reading are: (1) it is unparalleled in Job for a speech to *begin* with a "quotation" of an opponent's words; (2) the point of the comparison with animals is their stupidity, not their being whipped; (3) the emendation of "your eyes" is still required in v 3. Even if Tur-Sinai's proposal is only loosely adopted, namely that v 2 "quotes" Job, there is still the small difficulty that "how long" (עד־אנה) does seem to be a phrase of Bildad's (8:2) (though Job himself uses it at 19:2), and that it is hard to see how v 3 forms any riposte to the "quotation" of v 2.

(v) Verse 2 should be removed to the beginning of chap. 19, where Job speaks (de Wilde). This is a desperate solution.

(vi) Bildad addresses Job not as an individual in his own right but as a representative of the class of the impious (Ewald, Pope; cf. GNB "Job, can't people like you ever be quiet?"); why then the change to the singular in v 4?

(vii) Job identifies himself with the class of righteous sufferers (Davidson); is there such a class?

(viii) Bildad "emphasize[s] his sarcasm by echoing the plural language used by Job (12:2; 19:2)" (Habel); this seems weak.

(ix) The plural is used for courtesy's sake to Job alone (Sicre Diaz); what does the singular mean then in v 4?

(x) The plural could be used in address to one person (Gordis); but it is very doubtful whether the parallel cited (Cant 5:1) is at all apposite.

(xi) The three plural forms should be emended to the singular. This apparently arbitrary solution (for possible support from LXX and the Qumran Targum, see n. 18:2.a) may be adopted *faute de mieux*, and indeed several commentators do accept it (Duhm, Driver, Peake, Terrien; cf. *BHK*); so do most English versions, implicitly, since they do not distinguish between "you" singular and plural. It must be admitted that it is very difficult to see why the presumed corruption of the text would have occurred (but see n. 18:2.a).

What has to be determinative in the end is not what sense may be wrested out of the detail of the wording as it stands, but what the flow of the book entitles us to expect. Usually the detail and the flow can be read in harmony, but when they are in as irreconcilable conflict as they are here, perhaps the flow must win. On the purely linguistic difficulties, see the *Notes*.

2 Bildad's opening line sounds as tetchy as the question with which he began his first speech, "How long will you speak thus, the words of your mouth a tempestuous wind?" (8:2). But what lies behind his question is not principally impatience with Job, nor even resentment at Job's disdain for the friends' intelligence (v 3), but rather his sense of outrage at Job's calling into doubt the moral foundations of the universe. This wish for Job to stop speaking arises from the concern of v 3, "Will the earth be forsaken on your account?," the same concern as surfaced in chap. 8, "Can God pervert justice?" (8:3).

Job had begun his last speech with a complaint against the inefficacy of words, and had called for an end to "windy words" without substance (16:3).

Bildad on the contrary has much to fear from words; for Job's words threaten to upset his notions of universal order. His is a more nervous response than Eliphaz's, who had merely reprimanded Job for unprofessional behavior, that is, uttering "tempestuous" words unbecoming to a sage (15:2).

Job has claimed wisdom superior to the friends' (12:3; 13:2); he has "understood" (בין) all the conventional theology of retribution but has pressed beyond it in his attempt to account for his own calamity. Eliphaz for his part has challenged Job's claim to "understand" (בין) what the friends do not (15:9), and now Bildad too asserts that all the "understanding" still needing to be done must be on Job's part. Not to have interpreted one's experience in the light of the dogma is a failure of intelligence. Until Job does that there is no hope of dialogue: first he must "understand" (בין) and then they can talk. Talk about what, we may well wonder, if the precondition for conversation is agreement! Talk about Job's future, talk about what he can do to extricate himself from the disaster, talk, that is, along the lines of Bildad's advice to Job in 8:5–6. Bildad is not so much the pedagogue as to believe that all the talking that needs to be done is on the friends' side and that the better part of wisdom for Job would be silence. That was Job's rude remark to them in 13:5, but Bildad, very decently, envisages dialogue ("let's talk," נדבר) as the route to Job's recovery. He has not noticed that Job's last remark on that subject has been that speech is no better than silence: "if I speak, my pain is not soothed; if I am silent, it will not leave me" (16:6).

3 Job's claims to superior knowledge of the ways of God relegate the friends' theology to the subhuman level, so Bildad feels. Job had indeed represented the friends as regarding his intelligence as even below that of the animals (12:7), and we witness here a rather unattractive trading of insults. But Bildad's real problem is not that he and his friends feel their intelligence compared by Job to that of animals (cf. Ps 32:9; 73:22), but that he fears that Job knows something his theology does not.

4 If the retributive order of the moral universe is abandoned, as Job demands it should be for his sake, the cosmic order of stability goes with it. It is not that there is a mere analogy between the cosmic order and the moral order; it is rather that the moral principle of retribution is a organic part of the world order. Job's assault on retribution for his own sake (למענך), i.e., so that his claim to inocence may be sustained, is an assault on cosmos and an invitation for chaos to invade. Without a justice guaranteed by heaven the foundations of the earth tremble (Alonso Schökel, quoting Ps 82:5; cf. 11:3).

Distancing himself from Job by his use of the grammatical third person and objectivizing Job by calling him "a man who tears himself in his rage," Bildad puts the blame for Job's suffering squarely where it belongs: on Job's shoulders. Job has made out that it is God's anger that has "torn" him (16:9, טרף, as here); on the contrary, says Bildad, it is not God's wrath against Job but Job's wrath against God that is the cause of his suffering (Weiser). Rightly understood, Job's injuries are self-inflicted! *He* treats himself like a beast, mauling and savaging himself by his refusal to bow to the decision God has made against him, yet he insists on regarding the *friends* as beasts for their subhuman intelligence.

With a sarcasm that barely conceals his own anxiety, Bildad poses two proverb-like questions. The question, "Is the earth to be deserted on your account?" (for עזב, "desert" a city or land by emptying it of its population, see Lev

26:43; Isa 6:12; 7:12; Zeph 2:4), implies that the readjustment of the moral order Job requires would be a chaotic upheaval equivalent to depopulating the earth and bringing to ruin its God-given character as the inhabited realm. God did not create the world to be a chaos, he formed it to be inhabited (Isa 45:18); Job has become so full of his own importance that he demands a reversal of the divine design (38:2 will assure us that the worst Job does is to *obscure* the divine design, not subvert it). Rosenmüller quotes an Arabic proverb used of a person who has grown too big for his boots: "the universe will not be emptied on his account." Just as people have fixed places on earth, so too the elements of the physical order: Job will no more rearrange the moral law to suit his convenience than will the rocks shift from their place. Bildad, not surprisingly, has a thoroughly static view of the world, physical or human; another thinker with a more flexible theology could have a dynamic view of the natural world as being perpetually in flux (cf. Eccl 1:5–7).

There are parallels in Bildad's speech to phrases Job has used: the idea of words having an end (18:2; cf. 16:3), the imagery of the beast (18:3; cf. 12:7), the action of "tearing" (18:4; cf. 16:9), and now the rock being moved from its place (14:18, צור יעתק ממקמו, as here, with the first two words in reversed order). Such intertextual references do not necessarily imply that the character Bildad is deliberately referring to Job's speech and satirizing it. The poet indeed invites us to consider how differently the same phrase can sound on different speakers' lips, but the relationship between the several occurrences may be more subtle than those suggested by the terms "retort," "rebuttal," "modification," "allusion" (veiled or open), "parody" or "satire" that appear in some commentaries.

Given Bildad's premise that the doctrine of retribution belongs organically to the divinely established world order, and that Job's suffering proves him a sinner though his continued life proves him a less gross sinner than his children (8:3–4), Bildad's next move can only be to reiterate the dogma that Job seems bent on ignoring, leaving Job to draw the appropriate conclusions.

5–21 There is a certain indeterminacy in Bildad's description of the wicked. This was also true in chap. 8, which was neither a speech of encouragement pure and simple, nor yet a severe prediction of Job's fate as a wicked man. There at least there was a concluding note of assurance (8:20–22), consisting not only of a proverb-like generality ("God will not reject a blameless man") but a specific promise to Job ("He will yet again fill your mouth with laughter") which was nothing if not positive, no matter how many conditions may have hedged it round (cf. 8:5–6). Here, though there is no such explicit assurance, we may well suppose that nothing has happened to change Bildad's initial diagnosis of Job's situation: Job has sinned, no doubt about it, but the beauty of the doctrine of strict retribution is that there is nothing arbitrary about it (so Job will suffer not a moment longer than he deserves to) and it works to a person's advantage as well as one's hurt (so amending one's ways inevitably leads to blessing). In a word, Job has the choice of whether this depiction of the wicked will be true of him or not; Job will create the determinacy the portrayal lacks. There are some lines that seem all too painfully applicable to Job's present state (vv 11, 13, 15b, 19 especially), but there is no reason for Job to believe that he is locked into this fate. Those readers who think Bildad is describing Job and those who think he portrays the opposite to Job are both wrong: what he sets forth is an avoidable possibility. (The Septuagint translators thought that Bildad was only uttering a pious wish for the destruction of the wicked, but that is wrong too; see G. Gerleman, *Studies in the Septuagint: I. Book of Job* [Lunds Universitets Årsskrift: N.F. Avd. 1. Bd 43. Nr 2; Lund: Gleerup, 1946] 50–52).

By comparison with Eliphaz's depiction of the fate of the wicked in 15:20–35, this *topos* concentrates not on the wicked man's life-long experience of insecurity and terror, but on the ultimate fate that inevitably awaits him: the truly wicked is destined to be cut off, to be trapped by death, to perish in the underworld. The flow of the description is from the final experience of entrapment to the fate of the wicked after death; the pivot between these two elements is v 14 where he is torn from his tent and brought before the lord of the underworld.

Weiser has pointed out that throughout this depiction God is not mentioned; his name occurs only as the last word of the chapter: "such is the place of him who knows not God" (18:21). This is as it should be, for what is at stake in Bildad's eyes is the world-order as a self-regulating mechanism. God stands behind it as its sanction, to be sure, and it is he who has established the order in the first place, but its workings are immutable, and that is what the deviant theologian Job needs to know.

The form and content of the *topos* is clearly sapiential. There are many conventional thoughts and ready-made phrases in it, the whole "studded with sententious and proverbial sayings" (Davidson). But the poetic imagination breaks through at several points, and the intensity of focus makes the depiction very memorable.

The three-line strophe pattern prevails. Verse 21 is evidently a summary verse lying outside the pattern, and v 14 the pivot between the living and the postmortem experience of the wicked. The strophes are:

5–7		key metaphor: lamp
8–10		: trap
11–13		: disease
14	Pivot	
15–17		: dryness
18–20		: annihilation
21	Summary	

5–6 Nothing could be more conventional than the phrase, "the light of the wicked will be put out"; see 21:17; Prov 13:9b; 20:20; 24:20; and on "light" for "life" see on 3:20. The lamp (אוֹר) burning in the house, like the fire (אֵשׁ) on the hearth, are "symbols that the fortunes of the owner are still intact" (Gray). But the symbolism goes deeper, of course: darkness is the signal of death, the pervading condition of the underworld (10:21–22); the wicked, as Eliphaz has said, "cannot hope to escape the darkness" (15:22), since he already lives under its power. "When the light in the abode of the wicked becomes darkness, that dwelling becomes the domain of death even if its inhabitants are still living" (Habel). An Arabic proverb quoted by Schultens runs, "An unhappy fate has extinguished my light."

The reference to "tent" does not imply a nomadic mode of existence, so Terrien's remark that a lamp in a nomad's tent is something of a luxury is beside the point. It is a dignified term from a more archaic life-style (as in vv 14, 15; cf. on 5:24; 11:14; 15:34). Along with the metaphor of the "tent" comes the image of the lamp suspended from the roof ("above him"; cf. also 29:3). There is indeed no archeological evidence (how could there be?) of suspended lamps, though the author of a comprehensive study of lamps in the OT period thinks it is not impossible they existed (R. H. Smith, "The Household Lamps of Palestine in Old Testament Times," *BA* 27 [1964] 1–31). The silver cord and golden bowl in Eccl 12:6 have sometimes been thought to allude to a hanging lamp (L. E. Toombs, *IDB* 3:64), though obviously one of high quality. Lamps in a house would often have been set in niches in the wall: most lamps did not have a flat enough base to stand on a table, unless perhaps they were set inside a bowl. Domestic lampstands are not attested archeologically, though 2 Kgs 4:10 may be a literary reference.

7 Another image for the destruction of the wicked person's well-being is the shortening of the stride; taking small steps tends to lead to tripping up. (It may be, however, that there are two distinct images, signifying collectively that both the vigor and the cleverness of the wicked will end their serviceableness; so Horst.)

The background to the image may well be the failing powers of old age, the hobbling gait of an elderly person contrasted with the free and confident movements of someone in the vigor of youth ("His athletic pace becomes a shuffle," Andersen), but the implication is not that the wicked will age prematurely or will be crippled by disease. The image is primarily of decay and an ultimate laying low, like the image of the extinguishing of lamp and fire in vv 5–6. The symbolism of narrowness is of trouble and danger, while spaciousness signifies salvation; for "narrowness" (צר) of spirit, cf. 7:11; for strength being "narrow," cf. Prov 24:10; for spaciousness, cf. Ps 18:20 [19], 37 [36], and see J. F. A. Sawyer, "Spaciousness (An Important Feature of Language about Salvation in the Old Testament)," *ASTI* 6 (1967–68) 20–34.

There is a connection elsewhere too between narrow steps and stumbling: Ps 18:37 [36], "You widened my steps under me, and my ankles have not slipped"; Prov 4:12, "When you walk, your steps will not be narrowed (צרר as here); and if you run you will not stumble" (כשל, which is read here also by some; see n. 18:7.b). No concrete image is discernible here, however, for the idea of the wicked man's "plan" (עצה) "casting" him down (שלך hiph). The wicked typically have "plans" (עצה; cf. 5:13; 10:3; 21:16; 22:18; cf. Ps 1:1; 33:10; 106:43), which are connected with their "craftiness" (cf. 5:13; Ps 83:4 [3]), and that, ironically, often proves their own undoing (see on 5:12–14).

8–10 In this elaborated metaphor of the trap, six different words being used for the trap as if to express its unescapability, the point is that—by whatever precise means—the wicked man is inevitably ensnared *by death*. The whole issue in this *topos* is that the wicked is set on a collision course with death; it is not that he is taken in the snares he has set for others (Fohrer, Habel), nor that he and not God is the cause of his own downfall (Terrien), nor that "the world is full of traps to catch the feet that stray from the right path" (Peake), but rather that "all things hasten on his ruin; the moral order of the world is such that wherever he moves or touches upon it it becomes a snare to seize him" (Davidson). The imagery is drawn not from the heroic hunting of big game, like lions and wild oxen, such as is depicted in Mesopotamia and Egypt, but from the devices used by ordinary people for the snaring of game, especially birds.

8 The opening "for" is explicative; there follow the details of the ways in which the wicked man's happy and prosperous state comes to an end. The "for" (כִּי) does not connect specifically with v 7 (against Dhorme), for there was no image of the trap there.

The net (רֶשֶׁת) into which he rushes is used to catch either birds or animals; it is suspended above the ground and collapses when the prey enters it (cf. Ps 9:16 [15]; 31:5 [4]; 35:7–8; 57:7 [6]; 140:6 [5]; and especially Prov 1:17; Hos 7:12; for taking a lion, see Ezek 19:8; and a crocodile, 32:3). An alternative method of snaring is to dig a pit over which lattice-work or toils (שְׂבָכָה) of boughs and earth is constructed (in 2 Kgs 1:2 of a window-lattice); in Ecclus 9:13 a person in danger of death is said to "walk" (הִתְהַלֵּךְ as here) "over a net" (רֶשֶׁת).

The verse does not suggest that the wicked brings his own retribution down upon himself (though Bildad no doubt believes that), but that, do what he may, he is beset by snares. The verb "is thrust" (שׁלח pu) may allude to the battue system of hunting in which a large group of hunters shout, bang sticks and create alarm in the prey as they drive them into a defile where they can be more easily netted or killed with arrows or javelins (see L. E. Toombs, *IDB* 2:662–63). See also G. Gerleman, "Contributions to the Old Testament Terminology of the Chase," in *Årsberättelse 1945–1946: Bulletin de la Société Royale des Lettres de Lund 1945–1946* (Lund: Gleerup, 1946) 79–90; and cf. the many references to the dead being trapped in nets (though in these cases specifically in the afterlife) in J. Zandee, *Death as an Enemy according to Ancient Egyptian Conceptions* (Studies in the History of Religions; Supplements to Numen 5; Leiden: E. J. Brill, 1960) 226–34.

9–10 The "trap" (פַּח) is generally used of a bird-trap (as in Amos 3:5; Ps 91:3; 124:7; Prov 7:23; Eccl 9:12; Hos 9:8), perhaps made from wood, since it can be "broken" (Ps 124:7); but fowlers' traps do not catch either birds or humans by the heel, and we may suppose that the word here is just a general term for "trap" (cf. G. R. Driver, "Reflections on Recent Articles. II. Hebr. *môqēš*, 'Striker'," *JBL* 73 [1954] 125–36 [131]). The "snare" (צַמִּים, occurring only here) seems to be a trap that closes tight on its prey (if from a verb "to bind together" and noting that it seizes hold "upon" [עַל] its victim [the verb חזק usually has בְּ]). This or the following "noose" may be equivalent to the modern Egyptian noose which "the victim pulls round its neck when it takes the bait" (Driver, *JBL* 73 [1954] 133).

The "noose" is a cord (חֶבֶל) that catches its victim unawares (such a noose is set by wicked men, Ps 140:6; in Ps 119:61 the "cords of the wicked" surround the psalmist; in Prov 5:22 the wicked is caught in the cords of his own sin). The "gin" (מַלְכֹּדֶת, occurring only here though its root is common) is equally something that "seizes hold."

This depiction of the snares laid for the wicked has the impact of representing him as perpetually surrounded by danger. While he lives, he lives a charmed life, but at any moment one of the traps will spring and his life will be over. T. H. Gaster supplies some comparative material for the idea of the nets of death: "In Hindu belief, Yama, the god of death, comes equipped with nets, and among the Iranians the demon Astoridhotush stalks abroad in this fashion. A Mandean text speaks in the same way of 'the bands and toils of death'" (*Myth, Legend and Custom in the Old Testament* [London: Duckworth, 1969] 745).

11 "The preceding [three] verses described how he walked on snares unwitting that they were there; now he awakens to the perception of his condition" (Davidson). These terrors he experiences are not the fearful imaginings that Eliphaz ascribed to the wicked troubled by a bad conscience, as we would say (15:21); they are rather the evident signs of the encroachment of death, namely, hunger and disease (vv 12–13). The terrors that afflict humans this side of death are nothing other than the terrors who are the minions of the lord of the underworld, himself the "king of terrors" (בלהות also in v 14). They are not exactly the avenging spirits of those murdered or robbed by the wicked (Fohrer), nor are they the remorse that assails the conscience of the wicked (Dhorme).

12 Despite difficulties in the Hebrew, the sense seems to be a continuation of the vivid personification of v 11. Calamity and disaster are perhaps pictured as two of the "terrors" that surround the wicked man; just like the terrors that actively affrighted and harried him in v 11, they are represented as wild animals that actively hunger to take him in their maw, or alternatively wait only for the moment when they can overcome him with least resistance, the moment when he stumbles. The language is formed on the pattern of the lament, "I am ready (נכון, as here) for stumbling (צלע, as here)" (Ps 38:18 [17]). There it is the innocent man who is ready to or about to stumble, here it is the demons who are waiting for the wicked man to stumble; cf. also Ps 35:15 "at my stumbling (צלע) they gathered in glee" and especially Jer 20:10 where the prophet is surrounded by "terror on every side" (סביב, as here) and believes his erstwhile friends are "watching for my fall" (צלע). The wicked in these passages are the enemies of the righteous, but here the wicked also have their enemies, the emissaries of death. They go in pairs, like the attendants of a god (cf. "distress" and "anguish" in 15:24; Ps 23:6; 25:21; 43:3; 89:15 [14]; and perhaps Hab 3:5 [plague and pestilence]; see H. L. Ginsberg, "Baal's Two Messengers," *BASOR* 95 [1944] 25–30).

What is not said is that the wicked man grows hungry (cf. Terrien; RSV "his strength is hunger-bitten"), for that is not a great disaster for a strong man; it is rather than in the midst of his good health and good fortune the forces of death waylay him and may pounce on him at any moment; the more static image of the trap has been transformed into the dynamic image of the devouring animal. Traps should be to catch animals, but these supernatural and demonic animal forces are themselves the snares for the wicked.

13 This is more a picture of death than of illness. It is not a matter of "Death's First-Born gnaw[ing] his limbs" (JB) or "eat[ing] away parts of his skin" (NIV), but of the total devastation wreaked upon the body of the wicked by death. The focus is not a gradual process of decaying disease (e.g., "eats away") but on the overwhelming result ("consumes"). Not all wicked people die of lingering illnesses, of course, and Bildad does not want to maintain they do; whatever the specific cause, the result is the same; the lamp of the wicked is snuffed out (v 5). "Skin" and "limbs" are equally terms for the body as a whole, so no specific diseases affecting in turn skin and then limbs are in mind. Fohrer and Hesse thought the disease so indicated must be leprosy, and that Bildad is making a grim reference to the precise medical condition of Job. Not only does this misapprehend Bildad's purpose in his depiction of the wicked, but it also ignores the universal character of the impact of death upon the wicked.

Who is the First-Born of Death? Or is First-Born a title of Death himself? Both translations are possible. Older scholarship thought the First-Born of Death was some particular disease or affliction, whether starvation (Hitzig) or the plague (Dhorme, noting that the Babylonian plague god Namtaru is not exactly the firstborn but at least the vizier of the underworld), or the deadliest form of disease (Gray, comparing Arab. *bint el-maniyya*, "daughter of fate," for "fever").

Our whole understanding, however, has been greatly enhanced by the article of N. M. Sarna ("The Mythological Background of Job 18," *JBL* 82 [1963] 315–18) which, following U. Cassuto, *The Goddess Anath* [Hebrew] (Jerusalem: Bialik Institute, 1951) 49 (= *The Goddess Anath: Canaanite Epics of the Patriarchal Age* [tr. I. Abrahams; Jerusalem: Magnes Press, 1971] 63), drew upon the Ugaritic mythology to explain our text (cf. also N. Tromp, *Primitive Conceptions of Death and the Nether World in the Old Testament* [BibOr 21; Rome: Pontifical Biblical Institute, 1969] 162–65). Mot (Heb. מָוֶת, *māwet*, "death") is the ruler of the netherworld in Canaanite mythology; "a pit is the throne on which (he) sits, filth the land of his heritage" (*CTA* 5.2.16–17 [Gibson, 70]; 4.8.13–14 [Gibson, 66]). Such a figure is undoubtedly what is meant by "the king of terrors" (v 14). The Firstborn of Mot (Death) is not referred to in the Ugaritic texts, but it is not unreasonable to believe that there was such a being, occupying the same position in Canaanite mythology as did Namtar, the vizier of the underworld and son of Ereshkigal, queen of the netherworld, in Mesopotamian mythology. Like Hermes Psychopompos in Greek mythology, the First-Born of Mot would have the function of driving souls into Sheol and bringing them before its ruler. Here, however, the function of the First-Born of Death is to consume the bodies of the wicked as the means of transporting them from the earth into the underworld.

More recently it has been suggested that Death is himself the First-Born (W. L. Michel, *The Ugaritic Texts and the Mythological Expressions in the Book of Job,* Ph.D. Diss. University of Wisconsin, 1970; Pope, Habel), since in the Ugaritic texts Mot is called "son of El"; whether he literally is El's firstborn we do not know, but "firstborn" is primarily a title of rank which would be appropriate for him. The language used of Mot would fit here well, for his voracious appetite is well known (cf. also Isa 5:14; Hab 2:5): one lip reaches to earth, the other to the heavens, and his tongue reaches to the stars (*CTA* 5.2.2–3 [Gibson, 69]). He says, "My appetite is an appetite of lions (in) the waste" and "If it is in very truth my desire to consume 'clay,' then in truth by the handfuls I must eat (it)" (*CTA* 5.1.14–15, 18–20 [Gibson, 68]). A former translator had Mot eating "mud" by the handfuls (G. R. Driver, *Canaanite Myths and Legends* [Edinburgh: T. & T. Clark, 1956] 103)—presumably as the most available sustenance in the underworld. But if J. C. L. Gibson's revision (which may incorporate Driver's second thoughts) is correct, that the reference is to eating *humans,* made of "clay," the parallel to our text is closer. It can even be suggested that the rather unusual words בַּדֵּי, emended to בְּדַוָּי, "by disease" and בַּדָּיו, usually translated "his limbs," are both contracted spellings of the word "with both hands" (see n. 18:13.b); i.e., "He [Death] consumes his [the wicked's] skin with both hands; First-Born Death consumes with both hands" (Habel). Further evidence of Mot's hunger for human flesh may occur at *CTA* 6.2.17–19 (Gibson, 76) where Mot speaks of himself scouring the face of the earth for his prey: "My appetite did lack humans, my appetite (did lack) the multitudes of earth." At least, so he does in Gibson's translation, but the translation given by Driver in his first edition (*Canaanite Myths and Legends* [Edinburgh: T. & T. Clark, 1956] 111) seems no less plausible: as Mot scours the earth for Baal, wherever he passes, naturally enough, since he is the god of death, "Life did fail amongst men, the life of the multitudes of earth." That is to say, of course, death consumes life, but it is doubtful whether in the Ugaritic texts Mot is represented as eating human flesh, and whether therefore the texts cited are a specific background to our passage.

Here at 18:13 the parallelism is best served if "Disease" is parallel to "the Firstborn of Death," as two underlings of Death that go out in the world looking for victims. Like Calamity and Disaster in v 12, they are demons, a little more specific, but equally portrayed as wild animals. The dramatic flow of the depiction also requires that Death itself, who sits enthroned in the underworld, should not make his appearance until his minions have made full work of their prey. Only at the end of v 13 does the wicked man pass from life to the underworld, an event expressed again in different terms in the first half of v 14.

The Ugaritic texts are seductive, but they do not always lead unhesitatingly to appropriate exegetical solutions. In this case it seems clear that Death is personified and that various demons, all perhaps offspring of Death and the last mentioned (in climactic position) certainly his firstborn, are portrayed as wild beasts, individually enough to deserve capitalization. But it is not Death precisely who is the ravenous one, and we do not find the sobriquet the Hungry One used of him in v 12. See also J. B. Burns, "The Identity of Death's First-Born (Job xviii 13)," *VT* 27 (1987) 362–64, rejecting the equation of the First-Born with Mot himself, and seeking rather comparison with Namtar, Mesopotamian god of plague.

14 These powerful images build to a climax with the picture of the man being prised from his home and frogmarched before the underworld king. His enemies are now portrayed not as (impersonal) traps, nor as (animalistic) beasts, but as (human) agents of a malign power; their knock on the door would be readily recognized in many countries as the sign of the secret police. The "tent" has a multiple metaphoric significance: it is the man's shelter, if not exactly his castle, where he has a right to feel secure; it is his own property, where he has a right to invite his own guests (cf. 11:14) and turn away unwelcome visitors like these emissaries of Death; it is the symbol of his well-being and of the security of his existence. (It is not here a symbol of his body from which he is wrested, as against Andersen.) The tent *is* the security. No criticism is being made of him for "trusting" in his tent (as if perhaps he would have done better to trust in God); the poet becomes even more sympathetic as the man hastens to his fate. On "tent" as a dignified, because antique, word for "dwelling," "house," see on v 6.

To be "torn" (נתק) or "plucked" (NAB) from his tent is language that can be used of a human; but the root metaphor perhaps still persists, of a rope being snapped (Judg 16:9, a string of tow when it touches the fire; Eccl 4:12, a threefold cord not easily snapped; Isa 33:20, no tentcords of Zion will be broken [cf. Jer 10:20]; 5:27, not a sandal-thong is broken). In 17:11 it was the desires of Job's heart that were broken. Of humans, the verb is used of (with)drawing defenders from a city, and so separating them from their security

(Josh 8:16; Judg 20:32). The wicked man has been part and parcel with security, he and his house and his well-being have been a threefold cord; when he is sent for, he has to be torn away. A relevant image may be the sending out of messengers to escort a guest to a party (cf. Esth 6:14 "the king's eunuchs arrived and brought Haman to the banquet that Esther had prepared"; cf. also Luke 14:23). When Death's messengers arrive at the house of the wicked man, it is a wrench for him to leave.

They "hale" him before the king of the underworld; the verb is sometimes used in a military context (Judg 5:4; Ps 68:8 [7]; Hab 3:12, all in reference to Yahweh's marching, hence "march him" in NAB, NJPS, NIV), but since its noun means "step" in all kinds of contexts, it would be wrong to insist on a specifically military sense. But the causative form of the verb ("made him walk") is enough to show that this is no voluntary jaunt, but a compelled and unwelcome journey the wicked must make, the descent to the underworld, into the power of its lord.

As for the "King of Terrors": it would be a crime to tamper with that magnificent phrase, but the "terrors" that are his minions and agents of destruction are not terrors in the psychological sense, as if their task were principally to strike fear into their victims, but are themselves the very calamities that bring humans into the clutch of Death. There is no good reason to give a mainly psychological or emotional sense to the term בלהות, generally translated "terrors"; in Ezek 26:21; 27:36; 28:19 it clearly refers to a climactic disaster (RSV "a dreadful end"), and in all other references an objective disaster rather than a subjective experience is most appropriate (Isa 17:14; Ps 73:19 [the wicked are brought to an utter end by בלהות]; Job 27:20 [parallel סופה, "storm-wind"]; 30:15). Since disaster is experienced as terrible, it is no error to objectify the experience, and name its objective cause with the term properly used of the subjective result (as "joy" is a feeling, but "a joy" can also be a "thing of beauty"). On the "King of Terrors" as the equivalent of the Canaanite Mot, god of the underworld, see on v 13. The "Terrors" are those personified beings that have been mentioned in vv 11–13. The King is known in Babylonia as Nergal, among the Greeks as Hades, in Virgil as Pluto, the fearsome king (*rex tremendus, Georgics* 4.469), the infernal king (*rex infernus, Aeneid* 6.106). In the OT he is also represented as the "shepherd," i.e., ruler, of the inhabitants of the underworld (Ps 49:15 [14]). In Sumerian texts Nergal is called "king of the land of terror" (*CT* 24.36.52; 47.10), and his realm "the terrible house" (E. Ebeling, *Tod und Leben nach den Vorstellungen der Babylonier* [Berlin: de Gruyter, 1931] 166.14.

15 In this new strophe attention turns from the wicked man himself and the path by which he meets with his destiny in Sheol to his "tent" that had symbolized his well-being. He has been "torn" from it (v 14), so who is now its occupant? Not some descendant of his, not a kinsman, and not even a stranger, but an inhuman force that will prevent the house that gave him shelter ever being a home again for humans or animals. Now that "fire" (see n. 18:15.a) has taken up residence in his home, no one else can approach it. Habel wants to maintain that the fire is not the rain of destruction sent from above as in the case of Sodom and Gomorrah (Gen 19:24), but fire that erupts from below, as a further agent of Death. He finds the fire that consumed the company of Dathan and Abiram (Ps 106:17–18) to be an instance of such infernal fire; but the Num 16:35 account says specifically that the fire was "from Yahweh" and it is difficult to suppose that the psalm has a different image. The parallel here with brimstone also makes clear that in the present image the fire comes from above. Nevertheless, the point here is not the origin of the fire (God is not mentioned in the whole depiction except as the last word of v 21), but what it does to the wicked man's continued existence. If the only immortality he could have hoped for is the continuance of the family line and the family possessions, the fire writes finis to that.

Brimstone ("burning-stone") was once the common name for sulphur, but is now chiefly used in reference to its inflammable character. It burns easily in air, forming the noxious and suffocating sulphur dioxide gas. In the eastern Mediterranean environment it is found in regions of volcanic activity (cf. D. R. Bowes, *Zondervan Pictorial Encyclopedia of the Bible* [ed. M. C. Tenney; Grand Rapids: Zondervan, 1975] 1:655) such as the valley of the Dead Sea. Together, fire and brimstone depict an extraordinary natural disaster such as is inevitably ascribed to divine wrath (Ps 11:6; Isa 30:33; Ezek 38:22; cf. Isa 34:9). Land affected by brimstone is infertile (Deut 29:23). The restoration of "fire" to the first half of the line (see n. 18:15.a) rules out a reference to the disinfectant property of sulphur such as is well known from the ancient world (Pliny, *Natural History* 35.50; Homer, *Odyssey*, 22.481, 823, where it is used for cleansing a room defiled by corpses). Even though the brimstone is said to be "scattered" or "sprinkled" (יזרה), which sounds like a human act (Dhorme), the immediate context makes this interpretation less acceptable (against Ehrlich, Hölscher, Weiser, Fohrer, Horst, Terrien, de Wilde).

The language of supernatural destruction does not necessarily mean that Bildad envisages a divinely sent disaster falling upon the wicked; for there cannot in reality have been many wicked people who suffered such a fate. This is a dramatic phrasing of what he hopes and believes may happen to the posterity of the wicked.

16 Total destruction, root and branch (Ezek 17:9; Mal 3:19 [4:1]; Ecclus 10:16; 23:25; 40:15) or, root and fruit (Amos 2:9; Hos 9:16; cf. Eshmunazar, king of Sidon, in a curse [*ANET*, 662b]), is a common and proverb-like image (for the phrase in a favorable sense, cf. Job 29:19; 2 Kgs 19:30; Isa 27:6; 37:31; Jer 17:8; Ps 1:3). Some have deleted this verse as inappropriately portraying the wicked man as still alive (Budde, de Wilde), but it is not the wicked man himself who is here destroyed—that has happened when he descended to Sheol—but his family and possessions (a similar thought more prosaically in v 19). His roots and branches are what he has put forth, both as progeny and as the material evidence of his existence; when he himself is "torn away" (v 14), all that has "ramified" from him must of necessity perish also, "above" and "below" being the extremes that include the totality (the figure of merismus). It is possible that the image of the fire (v 15) continues into this verse, the fire that now "inhabits" his dwelling causing the withering up of all that was green and vital about his existence. "Wither" and "dry up" may sound like gradual processes, but what is in mind is "the immediate and simultaneous destruction of branch and root" (Gray).

17 Total annihilation is the destiny of the wicked. It is not that when he himself dies his name is forgotten, or even that God somehow eradicates the memory of him from the consciousness of others (as H. Eising seems to suggest,

TDOT 4:76). The "memory" (זכר) is much more concrete than that; it consists in a memorial surviving one's death and in the testimony it gives to the existence of the one it memorializes. Rulers who have inscriptions engraved with accounts of their exploits ensure that their "memorial" or memory of them will endure (cf. 2 Sam 18:18; Isa 56:5); failing that, a written account of one's deeds may stand as a "memory" (as "remember" in Neh 5:19; 6:14, 13:14, 22, 29, 31 refers to the achievements recorded in his book); alternatively, and more often, one's "memorial" is the perpetuation of one's self (and name) in one's children. It is not that the descendants themselves remember the dead ancestor, and respect his name, though of course they do, but that they are a continuing "reminder" of his existence, whether because they bear his personal name or whether simply their present existence is a testimony to his earlier existence. The levirate marriage, for example, is represented as a "raising up" or perpetuating of the "name" of a dead man, by creating a legal line of descendants for him (Deut 25:7). To destroy one's "memorial" (זכר) is to destroy one's post-mortem existence (however shadowy that may have already been), and so to render a person as if that one had never been. For this reason cutting off the "memorial" or "mention" (זכר) of an enemy is a means of his destruction (Exod 17:14; Deut 25:19; 32:26; Isa 26:14; Ps 9:7 [6]; 34:17 [16]; 109:15; 112:6). See further, B. S. Childs, *Memory and Tradition in Israel* (London: SCM, 1962) esp. 70–73; W. Schottroff, *"Gedenken" im Alten Orient und im Alten Testament* (WMANT 50; Neukirchen-Vluyn: Neukirchener Verlag, 1964) esp. 287–92.

In the present case it is the destruction of his progeny and possessions that annihilates the "memory" or "name" of the wicked. They do not perish automatically when he dies; but the effects of his wickedness reach beyond himself and involve the whole of his family. Their extermination spells his annihilation. The memory or mention of him disappears from the "earth" or "land" (ארץ) and from the "open place" (חוץ), i.e., probably the inhabited, cultivated land on the one hand and the steppe country used for grazing flocks on the other (the pairing of ארץ and חוץ in 5:10 is not so precise).

Bildad has come as close to Job's own situation as it is possible to come; Job has already experienced the loss of his offspring, before his death, and therefore suffers worse than the person depicted here, who has already died. Job himself has described the bitterness of death as an ignorance about what may be happening to one's descendants: "His sons may come to honor, but he does not know it; they may sink into obscurity, but he does not perceive it" (14:21). It is a greater bitterness by far to know before one's own death that one's posterity has been destroyed. Nevertheless, it is not Bildad's intention to identify Job with the wicked, and this is not simply "a transparent allegory which is singularly cruel in its obvious reference to Job's bereavement" (Andersen). Job is suffering for some sin, to be sure, and therefore much of his experience will parallel that of the typical wicked person; but whether his fate will be in every way the same is still an open question. Job may do what he likes with this depiction: if the cap fits, he can wear it, but he is not yet dead (which signifies: wicked beyond hope of change) and the way is still open for a reformation of life (cf. 8:5–6).

18–20 The movement of this strophe recapitulates that of the last (vv 15–17), but its focus is again the man himself, rather than "his tent," "his roots," "his branches," "his memory," "his name." Verse 18 corresponds to v

14 (the actual death of the wicked), v 19 to vv 16–17 (no descendants), while v 20, pressing towards a conclusion for the poem, moves beyond the point of view of the whole poem hitherto to portray the wicked's fate from the perspective of the world of onlookers. Finally, the point of view of the narrator (poet) himself will become visible in v 21.

18 The metaphor is of the simplest: the light is life (3:20 [life parallel to light]; 33:20 "the light of life"; cf. Ps 56:14 [13]), the darkness is death (10:21–22 "the land of darkness and deep shadow"; 17:13 [Sheol parallel to darkness]; and cf. also 19:8), and these two are the only possible states of being. The imagery links back to the opening picture of the snuffing out of the light (v 5). The righteous also die, but they are not "driven" out of life (הדף, like Canaanites out of Canaan [Deut 6:19] or an official from his office [Isa 22:19]). Who does the "driving"? Not God (as Duhm thought; cf. Pope), at least not directly, since it is the inexorable workings of the law of retribution that Bildad is dilating upon here; nor is it humans (Horst), as if humankind itself were expelling the sinner from its midst (Davidson), but precisely those emissaries of Death pictured before us in vv 11–13 (the verbs, translated here by the passive, are actually active plurals). When the wicked man took to flight (v 11b) in the hope of escaping the demons, he never realized that he was running in the direction of darkness. Like an animal being driven into a trap (perhaps a resonance from the trap imagery of vv 8–10 here), his flight is exactly what his hunters want: it is to his own doom that he has been hastening himself. It is the demons too who "expel" (נדד; NEB, NIV "banish" sounds like a human activity) him from the world (תבל) of living beings.

19 In plain terms Bildad now says what he previously said metaphorically (v 16): the wicked man's children suffer the fate he has brought on them. The phrase "progeny and posterity" is alliterative in the Heb. (נין, נכד, nîn, nēked, always used together: Gen 21:23; Isa 14:22; Ecclus 41:5; 47:22); we might say "seed or breed" (NJPS), "son nor scion" (Moffatt), "chit nor child" (Ball), "kith or kin" (Pope), "breed nor brood" (Tur-Sinai). But perhaps, even though his family in general has been exterminated (עם, "kinsfolk, family, people"), some fortunate individual from his kin may have escaped, a survivor (שריד) from the ruined homestead, and found safety in some other community that had once given the family guest-rights and shelter as resident aliens (in מגוריו "his place[s]" of sojourning). Not so; every last kinsman of the wicked man's is, like him, marked down for destruction, no matter where he may think to hide himself. For the ultimate truth about the wicked man, the end to which the whole depiction of vv 5–19 has been moving, is his annihilation, which carried with it the annihilation of any memory of him that could contrive a quasi-existence for him after death. Bildad has moved to the same concluding point as he did in chap. 8, but via a whole new network of images, no less memorable and compelling. There the wicked was a lush plant spreading its shoots over the garden; but "if it is once torn from its place, that place disowns it with 'I never saw you'" (8:18); here the wicked is equally forgotten, equally unacknowledged, equally annihilated as if he had never been.

20 Both this verse and the next are conclusions, but from different perspectives. Here Bildad stands back from the description of the wicked's fate to imagine its impact on observers. Wherever the news reaches, people are "appalled" (שמם), the conventional term for reaction to the hearing of bad news (cf. 16:7, God has "appalled" the whole company of Job's acquaintance; 17:8, the upright are "appalled" at Job's calamity; 21:5, Job invites the friends to "look at me and be appalled"). Cf. also D. R. Hillers, "A Convention in Hebrew Literature: The Reaction to Bad News," *ZAW* 77 (1965) 86–90. The wicked, as Habel puts it, "do not fade away unnoticed"; easterners and westerners, the two groups into which the human race is divided (or perhaps, two groups standing by merismus for all humankind) alike hear the news; cf. Ps 50:1, "the earth from the sun's rising to its setting"; 113:3; Mal 1:11; Matt 8:11, "many will come from the east and the west" (the whole earth). To see the "day" (יוֹם) of the wicked is to see the day of his calamity or death (cf. 1 Sam 26:10; Ps 37:13, the Lord sees that the wicked's "day" is coming; 137:7, the day of Jerusalem is the day of its destruction; Jer 50:27; Ezek 21:30 [24], 34 [29]). One's "day" can of course also in different contexts mean the day of one's birth (cf. on Job 3:1; E. Jenni, *THWAT* 1:714). In describing the horror felt by those who behold his fate, the Heb. idiom here is "they seized hold of terror" (as 21:6; Isa 13:8) (the figure of hypallage), rather than "terror seized hold of them" (as Exod 15:14; 2 Sam 1:9; etc.).

21 Bildad has modulated the point of view of the speech from his own (unabashedly in vv 2–4), to an objective and distanced narrator's perspective in the bulk of the speech (vv 5–19), and now via the point of view of onlookers (v 20) back to his own personal stance (these are not the words of onlookers, against Targum, Ball, NJPS). The form of the sentence is the "summary appraisal" (as 5:27; 8:19; 20:29; cf. also 8:13), introduced by "surely" (אַךְ asseverative; cf. 16:7; Ps 58:12 [11]), and forming a closure of the poem that had opened with another global statement (v 5).

Bildad in summary does not say directly that this is the fate of the wicked man himself but of his "dwelling" (מִשְׁכְּנוֹת; see n. 18:21.a) or "place" (מָקוֹם). This shows how preoccupied he is with externals, says Andersen, while Ehrlich thought the terms could not be understood literally, but signified the wicked himself and his fate. On the contrary, it is a sign of Bildad's striving for rationality and objectivity that he focuses on the dwelling: what happens to the wicked in the underworld is a matter of belief, not observation; the unseen powers that trap a man for Death are postulates of the imagination; but the house, that is concrete reality, that is the ungainsayable fact that validates everything else about the fate of the wicked. See a ruin, witness the annihilation of a family, and you have gained unarguable confirmation of the doctrine of retribution. With the blandest and least specific word "place" Bildad has evacuated the wicked man's life of all significance: where he has spent his days is in the end not a house, not a tent, not a dwelling, but no more than a mere "place."

Does Bildad make reference, direct or indirect, to Job's own personal circumstances? All through his depiction, there are indeed parallels between the fate of the wicked and the fate of Job (cf. vv 13, 15, 19, 20) and such parallels cannot be coincidental. But, as against most commentators, it may be suggested that it is not Bildad's purpose to rub in the point that Job's experience bears the hallmarks of the punishment of a sinner; that was his point of departure, and Job for his part wholly agrees that that is how things look (e.g., 16:8, "My gauntness rises up to testify against me"). Bildad's purpose is less cruel, as well as less specific, than that: rather than predicting Job's future, he warns him of what it might be if he does not amend his life; rather than describing

Job's present, he invites him to judge for himself what meaning his experiences may have by reading synoptically his own history alongside Bildad's *Life and Times of Mr. Badman*.

Morality and religion go hand in hand for Bildad, of course: the evildoer is none other than "the one who knows not God." This is the assumption too of the naive prologue (cf. 1:1), where, however, it is certified that Job is flawless in both spheres. Whatever Bildad's intention, the reader knows (and Job no less assuredly) that the one person Bildad has *not* been describing is Job himself.

Not to "know" God is of course not a sign of genuine atheism, which as a theoretical position is hardly to be met with in the ancient world, but "an evidence of insufficient piety" (Fohrer). The "knowledge of God" is a characteristic prophetic phrase (Hos 4:1, 6; 5:4; 8:2; Jer 2:8; 4:22; 9:2 [3], 5 [6]) and not typical of wisdom, it is true. Perhaps the multitude of proposals for the background of the phrase only goes to prove that it was common to all streams of Israelite tradition (cf., e.g., 1 Sam 2:12). It is thought to originate in a priestly setting by J. Begrich, *Die priesterliche Tora* (BZAW 66 [1936] 68–72), H. W. Wolff, "'Wissen um Gott' als Urform von Theologie," *EvTh* 12 [1952–53] 533–54, J. L. McKenzie, "Knowledge of God in Hosea," *JBL* 74 [1955] 22–32, W. Schottroff, *THWAT* 1:696; from the relationship of marriage by E. Baumann, "*yadaʿ* und seiner Derivate," *ZAW* 28 [1908] 22–41, 110–43; W. Eichrodt, "'The Holy One in Your Midst': The Theology of Hosea," *Int* 15 [1961] 259–73, esp. 264; and from treaty terminology by H. B. Huffmon, "The Treaty Background of Hebrew *yādaʿ*," *BASOR* 181 [1966] 31–37). On the phrase "not to know God," see G. J. Botterweck, *THWAT* 4:500.

Explanation

There is nothing new in Bildad's speech, of course, but how finely it is said! There is passion (v 4), there is careful brushwork (vv 8–10), there is a dramatic imagination (vv 11–14), there is pace. The author does not believe in giving the opponents of Job all the best lines, indeed, but neither will he make their poetry as flat-footed as their theology.

The theology, of course, is what counts. And it is a theology without nuances, this simplistic retributionist theology. Bildad's moral world is divided into two camps, the righteous and the wicked, as distinctly as his geographical world is peopled only by easterners and westerners (v 20). The case of Job ought to be enough, one would have imagined, to warn anyone off commitment to such simplism, for however gravely Job must have sinned to deserve, by retributionist thinking, the state he now experiences, no one who has known him of old could surely doubt that he has also been a man of notable piety. Even the strictest of retributionists is not obliged to maintain that humans are either wholly good or wholly bad; would not the cause of retributionist theology be better served by arguing that the mixed fortunes of Mr. and Mrs. Average are best explained as the result of their partial goodness, partial wickedness?

What is most striking about Bildad's portrayal of the wicked is its air of unreality. When did he last see what he has here described, or is his depiction little more than a fantasy of what he would like to happen? Is this what makes something traditional doctrine, the fact that no one has ever witnessed it for oneself? Is it true that the grossly wicked who find fire and brimstone raining down on their homesteads get forgotten by the world, or do they not rather become the stuff of folklore and saga? And do the righteous stand any better a chance at having themselves remembered and their existence perpetuated than the wicked do? Or had Ben Sira a point when in praising famous men of the past he acknowledged that "Of others there is no memory, for when they ceased, they ceased. And they are though they had not lived, they and their children after them" (44:9 NAB). These are godly persons, but forgotten! Is that not closer to reality?

Bildad has been projecting a fantasy because that is the way he needs the world to be. To be sure, some evidence crops up from time to time to give color to the fantasy, and the case of Job with its story of instantaneous devastation bids fair to be such a piece of evidence—were it not for the fact that all the world knows that Job is a righteous man, to say nothing of the further fact, that Job will no doubt be maintaining his innocence to his dying day with a conviction that is in the end hard to ignore. But Bildad needs a dogma of exact retribution and of black-and-white morality because order is fundamental for his own psychological well-being (see further, *Explanation* on chap. 8). How do I know this? By his imagery in v 4. He can only see in Job, a man assailed by (well-grounded) theological doubt and fighting a battle between dogma and experience, someone "tearing himself to pieces." That is how intellectual conflict feels to Bildad: it is mental self-abuse, deeply destructive, intuitively repugnant, and above all, wholly unnecessary. And he can only see in Job's demand for a rethinking of conventional theology a challenge to the world-order that he himself finds profoundly disturbing: "Is the earth to be unpeopled on your account? are the rocks to be dislodged?" He cannot face the upheaval of thought Job invites him to any more than he can contemplate the depopulation brought about by a war or the convulsion of an earthquake. Now we all know what is wrong with people who cannot with equanimity say to mountains, "Get up and throw yourself into the sea" (Matt 21:21 JB). Faith and the need for order do not make good room-mates. Bildad is a man of dogma, not of faith, and he will run no risks. He mistrusts even himself. He is "yesterday's child, and knows nothing" (8:9).

In the circumstances, his attitude to Job is very decent. Not for him Zophar's line, "Know then that God exacts of you less than your guilt deserves" (11:6 RSV). Bildad never directly says that Job is a sinner, and, if his second speech has been rightly interpreted in the foregoing pages in the light of his first, his dearest wish for Job is that he will come to his senses, give up his controversy with God, amend his life and live happily ever after (8:6–7, 21). There is a kind of poetic justice in a retributionist dogmatician being able to envisage no futures except a fairy tale happiness or a sci-fi extermination. It is ironic too that Bildad should think himself to be doing Job a favor by announcing that the fate of the wicked is something Job can choose to avoid, when the reality is that Job, the most blameless man on earth, has come perilously near, without the least effort on his part, to suffering the fate of the archetypal sinner.

Job's Sixth Speech (19:1–29)

Bibliography

Baker, A. "The Strange Case of Job's Chisel." *CBQ* 31 (1969) 370–79. **Blumenthal, D. R.** "A Play on Words in the Nineteenth Chapter of Job." *VT* 16 (1966) 497–501. **Burkitt, F. C.** "On *celtis* 'A Chisel': A Study in Textual Tradition." *JTS* 17 (1916) 389–97. ———. "On *celtis* 'A Chisel': A Further Note." *JTS* 22 (1921) 380–81. **Conder, C. R.** "Notes on Biblical Antiquities: 3. Writing with Lead." *PEFQS* (1905) 155–58. **Dahood, M.** "Hebrew-Ugaritic Lexicography IX." *Bib* 52 (1971) 337–56. **Driver, G. R.** "Problems in the Hebrew Text of Job." VTSup 3 (1955) 72–93. ———. "Ugaritic and Hebrew Words." In *Ugaritica VI*. Mission de Ras Shamra 17. Paris: Mission Archéologique de Ras Shamra, 1969. 181–86. **Fisher, L. R.** "*šdyn* in Job xix 29." *VT* 11 (1961) 342–43. **Galling, K.** "Die Grabinschrift Hiobs." *WO* 2 (1954–59) 3–6. **Gehman, H. S.** "סֵפֶר, an Inscription, in the Book of Job." *JBL* 63 (1944) 303–307. **Guillaume, A.** "The Arabic Background of the Book of Job." In *Promise and Fulfilment: Essays Presented to Professor S. H. Hooke*. Ed. F. F. Bruce. Edinburgh: T. & T. Clark, 1963. 106–27. **Kutsch, E.** "Text und Textgeschichte in Hiob XIX: Zu Problemen in V. 14–15, 20, 23–24." *VT* 32 (1982) 464–84. **Penar, T.** "Job 19,19 in the Light of Ben Sira 6,11." *Bib* 48 (1967) 293–95. **Smith, W. T.** New Rendering of Job xix.23–27." *ExpT* 3 (1891–92) 60. **Stamm, J. J.** "Versuch zur Erklärung von Hiob 19,24." *TZ* 4 (1948) 331–38. ———. "Zu Hiob 19,24." *ZAW* 65 (1953) 302. **Sutcliffe, E. F.** "Further Notes on Job, Textual and Exegetical." *Bib* 31 (1950) 365–78. **Winckler, H.** "סלה ? Threni 1,15; Hiob 19,12; 30,12." *Altorientalische Forschungen*. Leipzig: E. Pfeiffer, 1903. 242–44.

On vv 25–27:

Barré, M. L. "A Note on Job xix 25." *VT* 29 (1969) 107–9. **Beaucamp, E.** "Le goël de Jb 19,25." *LTP* 33 (1977) 309–10. **Brates Cravero, L.** "La esperanza en el libro de Job." In *XXX Semana Bíblica Española* (Madrid, 1972) 21–34. **Bruston, C.** "Pour l'exégèse de Job 19,25–29." *ZAW* 26 (1906) 143–46. **Clines, D. J. A.** "Belief, Desire and Wish in Job 19:23–27. Clues for the Identity of Job's 'Redeemer'." In *"Wünschet Jerusalem Frieden": Collected Communications to the XIIth Congress of the International Organization for the Study of the Old Testament, Jerusalem 1986*. Beiträge zur Erforschung des Alten Testaments und des antiken Judentums 13. Ed. M. Augustin and K.-D. Schunk. Frankfurt a.M.: Peter Lang, 1988. 363–70. **Davidson, A. B.** "Job xix.25–29." *ExpT* 9 (1897–98) 192. **Driver, G. R.** "Problems of the Hebrew Text and Language." In *Alttestamentliche Studien: Friedrich Nötscher zum sechzigsten Geburtstag*. Ed. H. Junker and J. Botterweck. Bonn: Hanstein, 1950. 46–61 ("I. Scenes in Court," pp. 46–47). **Droste, O.** "Hiob 19,23–27." *ZAW* 4 (1884) 107–11. **Garcia Cordero, M.** "La tesis de la sanción moral y la esperanza de la resurrección en el libro de Job." In *La encíclica Humani Generis*. XII Semaña Bíblica Española. Madrid: Librería Científica Medinaceli, 1952. 571–94. ———. "La esperanza de la resurrección corporal en Job." *Ciencia Tomista* 80 (1953) 1–23. **Gaster, T. H.** "Short Notes: Job xix 26." *VT* 4 (1954) 73–79 (78). **Hölscher, G.** "Hiob 19:25–27 und Jubil 23:30–31." *ZAW* 12 (1935) 277–83. **Hudal, A.** "Textkritische und exegetische Bemerkungen zu Job 19:25–27." *BZ* (1916–17) 214–35. **Kuhl, C.** "Neuere Literaturkritik des Buches Hiob." *ThR* 21 (1953) 163–205, 257–317. **Lévêque, J.** *Job et son Dieu: Essai d'exégèse et de théologie biblique*. Paris: Gabalda, 1970. 2:467–89. **Martin-Achard, R.** *From Death to Life. A Study of the Development of the Doctrine of the Resurrection in the Old Testament*. Tr. J. P. Smith. Edinburgh: Oliver & Boyd, 1960.

166–80 (= *De la mort à la résurrection d'après l'Ancien Testament*. Neuchâtel, 1956). **Meek, T. J.** "Job xix 25–27." *VT* 6 (1956) 100–103. **Mombert, J. I.** "On Job xix.25–27." *JBL* (1882) 27–39. ———. "Job xix.25–27." *JBL* (1883) 154–55. **Mowinckel, S.** "Hiobs gō'ēl und Zeuge im Himmel." *BZAW* 41 (Marti Festschrift), 1925. 207–12. **Neubauer, A.** "Job xix.25–27." *The Athenaeum* 3000 (June 27, 1885) 823. **Prado, J.** "La perspectiva escatológica en Job 19,25–27." *EstBíb* 25 (1966) 143–53. **Rose, V.** "Etude sur Job XIX, 25–27." *RB* 5 (1896) 39–55. **Speer, J.** "Zur Exegese von Hiob 19,25–27." *ZAW* 25 (1905) 47–140. **Sutcliffe, E. F.** "Further Notes on Job, Textual and Exegetical." *Bib* 31 (1950) 365–78 (377–78). **Tournay, R.** "Relectures bibliques concernant la vie future et l'angélologie." *RB* 69 (1962) 481–505 (489–95). **Waterman, L.** "Note on Job 19:23–27: Job's Triumph of Faith." *JBL* 69 (1950) 379–80. **Zink, J. K.** "Impatient Job: An Interpretation of Job 19:25–27." *JBL* 84 (1965) 147–52.

Translation

[1] *And Job answered and said:*

[2] *How long do you mean to* [a] *torment me?*
   How long will you try to [b] *crush me with your words?*
[3] *Ten times now you have tried to humiliate me;*
   you have shamelessly attacked [a] *me.*
[4] *Even if it be true that I have sinned,*
   my fault should harm me only.
[5] *But since you must get the better* [a] *of me,*
   using my suffering in evidence against me, [b]
[6] *understand that it is God who has put me in the wrong;*
   he it is who has thrown up siegeworks around me. [a]

[7] *If* [a] *I cry out "Violence!," I am not answered;*
   I shout for help, but there is no justice.
[8] *He has barred my way so that I cannot pass;* [a]
   he has veiled [b] *my path in darkness.*
[9] *He has stripped me of my honor,*
   taken the crown from my head.
[10] *From every side he has ruined me, and I have perished;*
   he has torn my hope [a] *up by the roots.*
[11] *He has kindled* [a] *his anger against me,*
   he counts me his enemy. [b]
[12] *His troops have advanced in force,*
   they have built a rampart against me,
   they have laid siege to my tent on every side.

[13] *My kinsfolk he has put* [a] *far from me;*
   my acquaintances are wholly estranged. [b]
[14] *My clansmen and my intimates have forsaken me;*
   my retainers [a] *have forgotten me.*
[15] *The serving girls* [a] *treat me as a stranger;*
   I have become to them [b] *an alien.*
[16] *My own servant I summon, but he will not answer,*
   not even if I beg him for pity's sake. [a]

17 *My very life*[a] *is repulsive*[b] *to my wife,*
   I have become loathsome[c] *to my brothers.*
18 *Even young children*[a] *reject me;*
   when I rise,[b] *they turn their backs*[c] *on me.*
19 *All my intimates loathe me,*
   those I have loved have turned against[a] *me.*
20 [a]*My bones hang from my skin and my flesh;*
   [b]*I am left with only the skin of my teeth.*

21 *Spare me! do spare me! you are my friends!*
   for the hand of Eloah has struck me.
22 *Why must you persecute me like God?*[a]
   Will you never be finished with your calumnies?[b]

23 *O that*[a] *my declarations could be written,*
   O that they could be inscribed[b] *on a monument,*[c]
24 *with an iron chisel and with lead*[a]
   graven into the rock in perpetuity![b]
25 *But I know that my champion lives*[a]
   [b]*and that he will rise*[c] *last*[d] *to speak for me on earth,*[e]
26   [a]*even after my skin*[b] *has thus*[c] *been stripped*[d] *from me.*
   Yet, to behold[e] *Eloah while still in my flesh—that is my desire,*
27   *to see him for myself,*[a]
   to see[b] *him with my own eyes, not as a stranger.*[c]
   [d]*My inmost being is consumed with longing!*

28 *When you say, How*[a] *we will persecute him!*[b]
   and, The root of the trouble[c] *lies*[d] *in him,*[e]
29 *you should tremble at the sword yourselves*
   (for yours[a] *is an anger*[b] *worthy*[c] *of the sword),*
   [d]*and realize*[e] *there is a judgment*[f] *to come.*[g]

Notes

2.a. Taking the impf as modal (cf. GKC, § 107m).
2.b. Modal impf again.
3.a. הכר occurs only here. Older connections with Arab. *hakara* suggested "made to wonder," but this hardly suits the context. Three Heb. mss have תחכרו; an otherwise unattested Heb. חכר "illtreat" (cf. Arab. *hakara*, ?Akk. *ḥakāru* "break to pieces") may be postulated (Duhm, Driver, Dhorme, Fohrer, Rowley, de Wilde, KB³, RV, RSV, JB, NIV "attack"). This is a satisfactory sense, and emendations are gratuitous. Eitan and Gordis compare Arab. *haqara* "abuse, insult" (NJPS "abuse"), which indeed forms a closer parallelism, but not necessarily a preferable one.
5.a. Gordis unnecessarily supposes another Heb. גדל here, and in Jer 48:26, 42 and several other places, cognate with Arab. *jadala* "quarrel."
5.b. Not "try to justify the reproaches levelled at me" (NEB), for the "reproach" is Job's state, not other people's words.
6.a. Most have connected מצודי with ציד "hunt," taking the noun as "net" (BDB, KB³). More appropriate in the light of vv 7–12 seems the image of siegeworks thrown up round a besieged city (so Gordis, Habel, NJPS), a meaning of מצוד that may be attested in Eccl 9:14. The usual word for siegeworks is מְצוּרָה, which perhaps should be read here by a small emendation.
7.a. As in 9:11; not "behold" (RV, RSV, JPS).

8.a. NEB "break away."

8.b. Guillaume (and before him Reiske) supposed a noun חָשָׂךְ cognate with Arab. *ḥasak* "thorn hedge" ("The Arabic Background," 114); hence NEB "has hedged in the road before me." The parallelism is neater (cf. also Hos 2:8 [6] for blocking the way with a thorn hedge) but less expressive (Sicre Diaz).

10.a. NEB "my tent-rope," as תִקְוָה seems to mean at 7:6; but it is absurd to pluck up a tent-rope "like a tree" since tent-ropes are quite easily pulled up, no matter how devastating the consequences, metaphorically speaking (cf. 4:21). And tent-ropes are always pulled up for good and all, whereas trees seldom are; one could perhaps pull up a tree "like a tent-rope" but not vice versa.

11.a. Emendation to וַיַּחַר (Driver-Gray, Fohrer, Sicre Diaz) is unnecessary; see *Comment*.

11.b. Reading כְּצָרוֹ "like his enemy" rather than MT "like his enemies" (so Dhorme, Rowley, Pope, de Wilde), though Weiser suggests that the plural might be original as a traditional element from cultic recitation of Yahweh's deeds against enemies. Fohrer thinks a pl would refer to primeval chaos monsters. Gordis defends the pl as a distributive, "as one of his foes."

13.a. The sg of the MT should be retained as forming a link between the actions of God in vv 7–12 and of Job's acquaintances in vv 13–19 (so too Habel). Many, however, emend to הִרְחִיקוּ "they are distant" (Duhm, Hölscher, Horst, Fohrer, Gordis, de Wilde, Sicre Diaz, NEB, NAB, JB).

13.b. Or perhaps, "have gone far from me"; cf. KB³ "sich abwenden," L. A. Snijders, "The Meaning of זוּר in the Old Testament," *OTS* 10 (1954) 1–154 (9).

14.a. Transferring גָּרֵי בֵיתִי "the household retainers" from v 15, which is overloaded, to v 14 which is too short. So *BHS* and most translations except KJV, RV, NJPS, NIV. This change also makes "my intimates" (מְיֻדָּעִים) into a second subject of "have ceased" (חָדְלוּ). The transfer seems supported by 11QtgJob which has no "and" preceding "my servant-girl(s)"; so E. Kutsch, "Text und Textgeschichte in Hiob XIX: Zu Problemen in V. 14–15, 20, 23–24," *VT* 32 (1982) 464–84 (466–67).

15.a. E. Kutsch proposes on the basis of the sg אמתי "my serving-girl" in 11QtgJob that the MT originally had the sg (*VT* 32 [1982] 467–68), as it does for the (masc) servant in v 16, meaning a typical servant of either sex; but it is perfectly understandable that Job should refer to (pl) serving-girls and a (sg) personal manservant.

15.b. Masc pl suff referring to fem pl noun; cf. GKC, § 135o.

16.a. Lit., "with my mouth I entreat him"; the two halves of the line may be co-ordinated (as RSV, JB) or sub-ordinated, the concessive "though" being implied (NEB, NIV).

17.a. רוּחַ can mean "breath" (BDB, 924b) as humankind's vital principle; indeed R. Albertz and C. Westermann call this, along with the sense "wind," one of the fundamental meanings (*THWAT* 2:734) and most translate it so here. But see *Comment*. Some suggest we emend to רֵיחִי "my smell, odor" (cf. *BHK*; KB³, 256b, NJPS, Wernberg-Møller [see n. 19:17.b]). Gordis, following a hint from Ehrlich, thought רוּחִי meant "my passion, desire," but parallels are lacking. See further, *Comment*.

17.b. From זוּר II "to stink" (BDB, KB³ and most versions and commentators), attested only here. L. A. Snijders, *OTS* 10 (1954) 14–16, following Driver, RV, denies the existence of this verb, and relates it to זוּר I "be strange," as in vv 14, 27 (as also Habel). P. Wernberg-Møller, "A Note on זוּר 'to stink,'" *VT* 4 (1954) 322–25, refers to an Arabic poem in which of a wife whose husband had become repulsive to her it is said that "into her nose the smell of *diyār* had come," *diyār* being "camel-dung" or anything stinking, and cognate with Heb. זוּר II. (This does not of course mean that her husband was literally foul-smelling; see *Comment*.) The parallelism with חנן II "be loathsome" supports the existence of זוּר "stink."

17.c. From חנן II "be loathsome" (only attested here in Heb.), rather than חנן I "supplicate" (as in v 16) (RV "my supplication").

18.a. Not "my children" (עֲוִילַי) as Gordis suggests to bring it into harmony with the other nouns of vv 13–17.

18.b. Cohortative for an "if"-clause; cf. 16:6; GKC, § 159e.

18.c. Accepting, with NEB, Fohrer, de Wilde, KB, KB³, derivation from a דבר (I, in KB³) "turn aside from, turn one's back on" (cf. Ps 76:6 [5]; Cant 5:6), cognate with Arab. *dabara* "be behind"; so Eitan, 33–34; idem, "Studies in Hebrew Roots," *JQR* 14 (1923–24) 31–52 (38–41); so also G. R. Driver, "Studies in the Vocabulary of the Old Testament I," *JTS* 31 (1930) 275–84 (284 n. 3), T. Penar, "Job 19,19 in the Light of Ben Sira 6,11," *Bib* 48 (1967) 293–95 (294 n. 2). This involves taking ב as "from" (which KB³, 101a § 13 approves), which makes the case fairly weak philologically. But the sense benefits!

19.a. Penar, *Bib* 48 (1967) 293–95, argued that ב means "from," thus "turn away from" rather than "turn against." Despite N. M. Sarna, "The Interchange of the Prepositions *Beth* and *Min* in Biblical Hebrew," *JBL* 78 (1959) 310–16, and Dahood, *Psalms III*, 391–93, the evidence is not strong; cf. n. 7:14.a.

20.a. Some interpretations alternative to that proposed in the *Comment* should be noted here. Commonly, v 20a is thought to picture emaciation (so Driver-Gray, Rowley, Fohrer, Gordis). This results from a hasty confusion of the present image with the distinct images of Ps 22:18 [17] and others, detailed in the *Comment*. NEB "my bones stick out through my skin" is a sad example of a presumption about the imagery; no better is NIV "I am nothing but skin and bones," which fails completely to translate דבקה. Equally blithely, D. Blumenthal, "A Play on Words in the Nineteenth Chapter of Job," *VT* 16 (1966) 497–501, translated "my skin and my flesh cling to my bones," noting that common usage in English is to speak of skin and flesh adhering to the bones and not the other way round (!). The Syriac made the same transposition. Several have noted that "flesh" and "bones" often signify one's relatives (e.g., Ehrlich, and cf. on 2:4–6), and van Selms has made the interesting proposal that the verse be translated, "To my relatives I have inwardly cleaved, but they have given me nothing," i.e., omitting בעורי as a gloss, understanding עצמי as "I myself, I inwardly," and "skin in the teeth" as the small portion of an animal a wild beast can run off with when the shepherd chases him, that is to say, virtually nothing. This has the merit over all suggestions other than that proposed in the *Comment* of linking closely with the preceding verses, but the interpretation of the second half of the line is unpersuasive, and it would be strange to find "flesh" and "bone" together metaphorically in *distinct* senses ("I" and "they"); in metaphorical use they are equivalent (Gen 2:23; 29:14; Judg 9:2; 2 Sam 5:1; 19:13, 14 [12, 13]; 1 Chr 11:1). C. A. and E. G. Briggs had the bright idea on the same phrase in Ps 102:6 that it was because the bones were burning from fever and so lacking in moisture that the bones cleaved fast to the flesh (*A Critical and Exegetical Commentary on the Book of Psalms* [Edinburgh: T. & T. Clark, 1909] 2:319), but they did not ask what bones do under normal circumstances. Szczygiel divined in the phrase a kind of paralysis, a loss of elasticity of the flesh, which is perhaps not severe enough for the circumstances. The suggestion of Tur-Sinai that בשׂר means not "flesh" in general but "tongue" and that עצם means not "bone" in general but "palate-bone," thus "my palate bone cleaveth to my tongue," has little to recommend it, especially because the cleaving would have to be the other way round. There is a lack of plausibility too in Janzen's more existential interpretation, that Job, "deserted by the wider community (human and divine) . . . seeks solace and companionship in his embodied self, in a covenant loyalty which seeks at least to keep soul and body—or bones and flesh—together"; he translates, "I cleave loyally to my skin and my flesh."

An approach relying on Semitic philology is that of E. F. Sutcliffe, "Further Notes on Job, Textual and Exegetical," *Bib* 31 (1950) 365–78 (375–77), observing that it is quite normal for bone and flesh to adhere (he and Merx and Siegfried are the only writers to do so), argues that בשׂר means "skin," like Arab. *bašarat*, which has been glossed with בעורי in the margin; thus "my bones cleave to my skin"; so too G. R. Driver, "Problems in the Hebrew Text of Job," VTSup 3 (1955) 72–93 (80); "Ugaritic and Hebrew Words," *Ugaritica VI* (Mission de Ras Shamra 17; Paris: Mission Archéologique de Ras Shamra, 1969) 181–86 (185). This sense of the Arabic cognate had been called on by E. F. C. Rosenmüller, *Scholia in Vetus Testamentum* (Leipzig: Barth, 1823) 4/3:1585, F. Delitzsch, *Biblical Commentary on the Psalms* (London: Hodder & Stoughton, 1889) 3:80, and by T. Witton Davies, *The Psalms* (CB; Edinburgh: T. C. and E. C. Jack, 1906) 2:164, in explaining Ps 102:6 [5], and by Gesenius-Buhl (120), as well as by Kimchi, and had been rejected by H. Hupfeld and W. Nowack, *Die Psalmen* (3rd ed.; Gotha: Perthes, 1888) 419.

The most minor emendation is בעור-בשׂרי "to the flesh of my skin" (*BHS*, Horst), a surprisingly redundant phrase, attested indeed in Lev 13:2–4, 11, 38–39, 43; but the context there is rather technical and not in the least poetical; so the emendation is not very probable.

Among emendations, perhaps the most acceptable is the deletion of ו בעורי "to my skin and," absent from the parallel Ps 102:6 (so Ehrlich, Hölscher, Stevenson, Tur-Sinai), though this leaves an apparently banal phrase. Others delete ובשׂרי "and my flesh" (Bickell, Budde, Peake, Driver-Gray, *BHK*, Fohrer, Hesse, Sicre Diaz, NEB, NAB, Kutsch, *VT* 32 [1982] 464–84).

Michaelis and Merx also proposed בעורי בשׂרי רָקָבָה "in my skin my flesh has rotted away," noting LXX ἐν δέρματί μου ἐσάπησαν αἱ σάρκες μου "in my skin my flesh (pl) has rotted" (so too Duhm [less probably reading בשׂרי], Dhorme, Kissane [reading רָקָב (masc)], Budde, Siegfried, Pope, Szczygiel [reading רָקָב "rottenness"], de Wilde [reading בעורי רקב בשׂרי], JB "beneath my skin, my flesh begins to rot")—difficult to justify medically, comments Sicre Diaz.

20.b. Other interpretations, some undeniably bizarre, are: (i) Leaving the MT as it stands and taking מלט as "escape," the skin of the teeth is taken as the gums (ΝΙνmg "only my gums"); some scholars have been seduced by the German for "gums," *Zahnfleisch* (lit., "teeth-flesh"), which means that the rest of his flesh has wasted away (Rashi, Dillmann) or that the only sound part of his flesh not attacked by leprosy are his gums (Delitzsch, Weiser). Peters thought the lips were the skin of the teeth (cf. Vg *et derelicta sunt tantummodo labia circum dentes meos* "only the lips about my teeth are left") and that Job meant, "Nothing is left to me except the possibility of speech." Renan and Buttenwieser, observing that teeth have no skin, understood "I will escape [coh] with the skin of my teeth," i.e., never, "dans la semaine des quatre jeudis." Terrien, noting that although adult teeth have no skin, milk teeth of children are covered by a pseudo-cutaneous tissue, wondered if that skin could be a symbol of innocence, Job meaning, "If only I could escape [coh] with my integrity intact."

(ii) Supposing a different verb מלט, either (a) "become bald," cognate with Arab. *malaṭa* (and cf. מרט "be bald"), as Michaelis, Hölscher, Fohrer, Fedrizzi, KB³, meaning "I am bald on the skin of my teeth," which is supposed to mean that the lips or cheeks are emaciated or else that he has lost or pulled out the hair of his moustache or beard (cf. Symmachus, quoted at the end of this note). This is wildly implausible. E. Kutsch has recently argued elaborately ("Text und Textgeschichte in Hiob XIX," *VT* 32 [1982] 464–84 [473–81]), that the skin of the teeth are the gums, and to be bald on the gums is to have lost one's teeth; he does not for a moment consider whether this may be appropriate to the context. Alternatively, (b) a root מלט "rub, bite" cognate with Akk. *marātu* "rub," Arab. *marata* "pluck out hair, grow," Syr. *mraṭ* "pluck out," Eth. *malaṭa* "pluck out hair" has been postulated by G. R. Driver, VTSup 3 (1955) 80–81, and followed by Gerleman in *BHS* (though the diacritics have there been mistakenly omitted from three of the cognates). (c) A further alternative is that a root מלט, attested in the noun מֶלֶט "mortar, cement," may be supposed meaning "to cleave, stick" (thus parallel with דבק in the first half of the line; so Doederlein, explaining that Job's teeth would have fallen out if the skin had not held them in place—a phenomenon unknown to dental science). Tur-Sinai suggests, "I cleave to the skin of my teeth (with my tongue) as if by means of cement, so that I am no longer able to speak"; but of course it is not Job himself that so cleaves, but only his tongue. Furthermore, it is more than doubtful that מלט means "cement" in its one occurrence at Jer 43:9, and not rather "loamy soil" (KB³; Kutsch, *VT* 32 [1982] 476); and of course the fact is that Job seems to have little difficulty in continuing speaking.

(iii) Seeking a Semitic cognate for עור, G. R. Driver further proposed that עור in the second half of the line is not "skin" but a second עור cognate with Arab. *garu(n)* "bottom of palate, pit of chin" (VTSup 3 [1955] 80–81); hence NEB "I gnaw my under-lip with my teeth," which Driver explained as a sign of "acute or harassed perturbation." Quite apart from the fact that this seems a very mild problem for Job to be encountering, it is more than doubtful that the comparative Semitic evidence is adequate. For it is only in Arab. that the root *mrt* seems to mean "gnaw," and the "under-lip" is not what the supposed cognate Arab. term actually means. Blumenthal, *VT* 16 (1966) 499, drew on the same Arabic cognate to translate, "I am left with (only) my skull," i.e., the bone within which my teeth are set; but this is a willful extension of the meaning of the Arabic, and the resultant sense tends to the absurd: what kind of a creature is Job depicting himself as?

(iv) Emending the text, (a) Bickell[1], Budde, Peake, Driver-Gray, *BHK*, NAB, read ואתמלטה בשני בשרי "and I have escaped with my flesh in my teeth," like a wild animal running off with a piece of savaged goat or sheep (13:14 is often compared but the sense is quite different). (b) Duhm read וַיִּתְמַלְּטוּ שִׁנָּי "and my teeth have fallen out" (followed by Moffatt), which can hardly be thought germane to the context; Pope has "my teeth drop from my gums," retaining עור as "gums." A rabbinic commentary of the 13th or 14th century took the same view (*A Commentary on the Book of Job*, ed. W. A. Wright, tr. S. A. Hirsch [London: Williams & Norgate, 1905] 56, 130). (c) Dhorme read בְּשִׁנָּי "with my teeth" instead of בעור שני "with the skin of my teeth," transferred עצמי "my bone" to the second half of the line, and translated "I have gnawed my bone with my teeth," which means that his bones are visible under the skin; this certainly sounds like hunger, but that is not the point of the line, as has been argued above. (d) For Merx, Job had escaped with his bones in his teeth, ואתמלטה בשני עצמי, whatever that means. (e) Kissane read ועצמי הִתְמַלְּטוּ בָשִׁים "and my bones protrude in sharp points" (lit., as teeth); hence presumably JB "my bones stick out like teeth." (f) De Wilde rather rashly emends to עַצְמוֹתַי תְמַלֶּאנָה בְּעִיר שַׁדַּי "and my bones are full of the wrath of the Almighty" (which is not the point in this description of desertion by his friends). (g) The proposal may be made to read ואתמלטה עור בשני "I made my skin bald with my teeth," i.e., "I ate the hair of my body for hunger." This is exactly what Symmachus has: ἐξέτιλλον τὸ δέρμα μου ὀδοῦσιν ἐμοῖς, "I stripped bare my skin with my teeth." With this we might compare the Phoenician inscription of Kilamuwa in the translation of C. C. Torrey ("The Zokar and Kalamu Inscriptions," *JAOS* 35 [1915–17] 353–69 [365]): "And I was in the midst of kings as though I were eating my beard, or even were eating my hand" (lines 6–7) (similarly M. Dahood, "Textual Problems in Isaia," *CBQ* 22 [1960] 400–409 [404–5]). It is true that in the more recent translations of F. Rosenthal (*ANET*, 654b) and J. C. L. Gibson (*Textbook of Syrian Semitic Inscriptions* [Oxford: Clarendon, 1982] 3:34) the sentence is rendered "I was in the hand(s) of the kings like a fire that consumes the beard or like a fire that consumes the hand" (Gibson), but this translation is not fully convincing. For the imagery of eating one's own flesh (though not necessarily because of hunger) cf. v 22 and Isa 49:26; Jer 19:9 clearly depicts the hunger of a siege. It nevertheless needs to be stressed that it is more than doubtful whether hunger is at all the theme in this verse.

22.a. As Dhorme says, it is a "pure whim" to emend כְּמוֹ־אֵל "like God" to כְּמוֹ־גֹּאֵל "like an avenger" (A. Neubauer, "Job xix.25–27," *Athenaeum* 3000 [June 27, 1885] 823) or כְּמוֹ־אַיָּל "like a stag" (Reiske, *BHK prps*).

22.b. Lit., "will you not be satisfied with my flesh?" See *Comment*.

23.a. Some grammatical aspects of the phrase מִי יִתֵּן are discussed by B. Jongeling, "L'expression *my ytn* dans l'Ancien Testament," *VT* 24 (1974) 32–40. Cf. also C. J. Labuschagne, *THWAT* 2:133–34.

23.b. Horst, thinking וְיֻחָקוּ "that they should be engraved" fits better with v 24, removes it to there and deletes the second מִי־יִתֵּן from this verse. Duhm also deletes the second מִי־יִתֵּן and transfers מִלִּי to the second half of the line, translating "that my words should be marked in his book [reading בְּסִפְרוֹ יֻחָקוּ]." Beer (*BHK*) thought a verb had been lost after the second מִי־יִתֵּן. The position of בַסֵּפֶר before the verb that logically begins its clause is of course no mistake, nor is the *waw* an emphatic *waw* (Blommerde); "the arrangement of the words is extremely elegant, בַסֵּפֶר stands *per hyperbaton* emphatically prominent" (Delitzsch; K. Galling, "Die Grabinschrift Hiobs," *WO* 2 [1954–59] 3–6 [5]).

23.c. An attractive suggestion is made that we should understand סֵפֶר as equivalent to Akk. *siparru* "copper" and Arab. *sufr, sifr* (so Perles II, 70; Dhorme, Hölscher, Sicre Diaz, Terrien, Richter, 89); other possible occurrences are at Isa 30:8 where also the verb חקק is used, and Judg 5:14, where the "ruler's staff" (שֵׁבֶט סֹפֵר) may be a staff of bronze. The use of copper or bronze sheets for writing is rarely attested in the ancient world, but is known from such disparate periods as the tenth century B.C. (six items from Byblus mentioned by G. R. Driver, *Semitic Writing* [London: OUP, rev. edn., 1954] 92–93; text and translation of one text: H. Donner and W. Röllig, *Kanaanäische und aramäische Inschriften* [Wiesbaden; Harrassowitz, 1962–64] 1:1; 2:5; cf. W. F. Albright, "A Hebrew Letter from the twelfth century B.C.," *BASOR* 73 [1939] 9–13; M. Martin, "A Preliminary Report after Re-Examination of the Byblian Inscriptions," *Or* 30 [1961] 46–78 [46–63]), the second century B.C. (1 Macc 8:22; 14:18, letters on bronze tablets), and the first century A.D. (the celebrated Copper Scroll from Qumran; cf. J. M. Allegro, *The Treasure of the Copper Scroll* [London: Routledge & Kegan Paul, 1960]). In view of the poor attestation of the supposed סֵפֶר "copper" in Heb., it remains preferable to take the word as meaning "inscription" or the stele or monument on which the inscription is engraved (cf. H. S. Gehman, "סֵפֶר, an Inscription, in the Book of Job," *JBL* 63 [1944] 303–7; J. A. Soggin, "Osservazioni a due derivati della radice *spr* in ebraico," *BeO* 7 [1965] 279–82). For סֵפֶר "inscription," cf. the Phoenician inscription of Ahiram, line 2 (J. C. L. Gibson, *Textbook of Syrian Semitic Inscriptions* [Oxford: Clarendon, 1971, 1975, 1982] 3:14; translated differently in *ANET*, 661b); of Kilamuwa (i 15) (Gibson, 1:34–35; *ANET*, 655a), and the Aramaic inscription of Sefire, i C 17; ii C 2 (Gibson, 2:32–33, 44–45); Exod 17:14 and Isa 30:8 may have the same sense (so KB³). We may ignore Duhm's proposal to read בְּסִפְרוֹ יֻחָקוּ "that they may be inscribed in his book" (cf. 14:17), though he rightly questions why Job should find this so impossible a wish. It is not technically impossible, or even difficult, to carve letters in stone, but for Job it is logistically impossible, and so the equivalent of an impossible dream. The article of בַסֵּפֶר of course indicates the stele that is to be devoted to the inscription, or alternatively, the inscription in question (GKC, § 126s).

24.a. The translation given implies that the *beth* of בָּעֵט does double duty for עֹפָרֶת (König, *Syntax*, § 319mβ; Blommerde); emendation to בָּעֹפֶרֶת (Beer) is unnecessary. עֹפָרֶת "lead" is quite well attested in Heb. (and cf. Akk. *abāru*). Hölscher's view in the first edition of his commentary that it means magnesite, a soft whitish chalk, has been given up in the second edition. JB "engraving tool" derives from the Vulgate reading *celte*, supposedly a "chisel," but now shown to be an error for *certe*; see A. Baker, "The Strange Case of Job's Chisel," *CBQ* 31 (1969) 370–79.

The parallel phrasing in Jer 17:1 led Budde (J. J. Stamm's support in *TZ* 4 [1948] 331–38 was withdrawn in *ZAW* 65 [1953] 302), to emend here to בְּצִפֹּרֶן "with a stylus point" (Jer 17:1 has בצפרן שמיר "with a diamond point," the עט presumably being for the rough work, the צפרן for the fine work). The parallel, however, could only support the substitution of a phrase like צפרן שמיר, not צפרן on its own.

24.b. Theod. εἰς μαρτύριον and Vg *in testimonium* read לעד "forever" as לְעֵד "for a testimony," which suits the context well enough, and is followed by Merx and Duhm, as well as by Weiser, who remarks that Job is not interested in a *perpetual* witness to his innocence by the inscription since he hopes before long to be declared innocent by God. "Forever," however, contrasts with Job's imminent death, not with the time that must pass before his vindication. So while the emendation perhaps gives a better sense than the MT, there is nothing wrong with the MT and the emendation, though supported by ancient versions, seems a little arbitrary.

25.a. M. C. Barré ("A Note on Job xix 25," *VT* 29 [1969] 107–9) takes a false track by assuming that we have here a word-pair קום // חיה "live" // "rise," and by going on to translate "I know that my redeemer can restore life/health, And that (my) guarantor can raise up from the dust." The proposal includes the improbabilities that *gᵓlyhy* has a consonant "shared" between *gᵓly* and *yhy* (understood as a defectively written piel of חיה "cause to live"), that יקום is to be read יקם (a defectively written hiph of קום "raise up"), and that על means "from."

25.b. There is little reason to accept a concessive sense here, as Gordis: "though He be the last to arise upon earth."

25.c. M. Dahood suggested for יתום "he shall stand" יָקוּם "he will take vengeance," the motif of Yahweh's victory over Sheol ("Hebrew-Ugaritic Lexicography IX," *Bib* 52 [1971] 337–56 [346]); the revocalization was already suggested by Bickell. Arbitrary is Neubauer's emendation to ואחרון כל עפר יקיץ (*Athenaeum* 3000 [1885] 823).

25.d. Less probably appeal may be made to the Mishnaic and Talmudic word אַחֲרָאִי "surety, guarantor, sponsor, afterman" (S. Mowinckel, "Hiobs gōʾēl und Zeuge im Himmel," BZAW 41 [1925] 207–12 [211], reading אַחֲרוֹנִי; Beer [*BHK*]; Pope). The suggestion is "neither proved nor probable" (Gray).

25.e. G. R. Driver thought "on dust" simply meant "in court," "since justice was done in the threshing-floor or in the gate, both very dusty places" (VTSup 3 [1955] 47); hence NEB "rise last to speak in court." The logic is defective: the fact that a place is dusty is no reason why "dust" should signify that place, any more than that "rain" should signify "England." N. H. Ridderbos rejects the fairly clear evidence of 41:25 [33] to insist that "upon dust" never means "upon earth," and argues that it here means "above the dust of Sheol" (עָפָר als Staub des Totenortes," *OTS* 5 [1948] 174–78).

26.a. Among the simplest and therefore most elegant emendations (as Lévêque puts it, p. 477) is that of E. F. Sutcliffe, "Further Notes on Job, Textual and Exegetical," *Bib* 31 (1950) 365–78 (377–78), who rearranged the words of the MT to read וְעֵרִי נקפו מבשרי ואחר זאת אחזה אלוה, "And shall my skin be stripped from my flesh, Even after that I shall see God." R. Tournay improved on that by bringing ומבשרי to the beginning of the verse, "and if my skin is stripped from my flesh" ("Relectures bibliques concernant la vie future et l'angélologie," *RB* 69 [1962] 481–505 [489–95]; so too Lévêque, 477, 486.

Beer suggested וְאַחַר עֵדִי נִצָּף אִתִּי "and I shall see [חור not elsewhere in Heb., but cognates in Akk. and Aram.] my witness standing erect beside me" (cf. *BHK*), and G. R. Driver (VTSup 3 [1955] 47) follows this, adding that מְבַשְּׂרִי (= מבסרי) "my refuter," i.e., the one who refutes for me (this verb is not elsewhere in Heb., but a cognate in Aram.) should be so read. Hence NEB "I shall discern my witness standing at my side, and see my defending counsel, even God himself." This conjectural emendation, further weakened by the supposition of two verbs not attested in Hebrew, has not a chance of being what the poet wrote; yet the NEB mg has the nerve to say that the MT is "unintelligible"!

Duhm, transferring יקום from v 25, reads וְיָקוּם אַחַר עֵדִי וְזֶה זֶה אֹתוֹ "and another shall arise as my witness, and will raise up his sign," viz., over Job's dead body to show that his murder will be avenged; this is an emendation that may safely be "left to itself" (A. B. Davidson, "Job xix.25–29," *ExpT* 9 [1897–98] 192). Dhorme reads נִצָּפְתִּי "I shall stand up" and translates אחר עורי as "behind my skin" as if looking from behind a curtain, parallel to "from my flesh" as the position from which Job will look. Gordis seems to approve this understanding, translating "deep in my skin." De Wilde even less convincingly suggests וְאַחַר זֹאת יָקְרָא שַׁדַּי "and then Shaddai will call (me)." Skehan ("Strophic Patterns," 109) felt confident that v 26a was a "crude, meaningless and manifest dittography," mainly for the half-line that preceded it; he then rearranged the order to 27a, b, 26b, 27c (as displayed in NAB).

26.b. JB "After my awaking" (similarly NIVmg, Janzen) takes עוֹרִי as עוּרִי, inf of עוּר "awake" (so too Terrien). D. R. Blumenthal ("A Play on Words in the Nineteenth Chapter of Job," *VT* 16 [1966] 497–501) invented a new Heb. עוּר with an Arab. cognate, meaning "disgrace, abuse," thus "when the period of my abuse is at an end."

26.c. Taking זֹאת as an adverb (to which there are no real parallels) or else emending to כָּזֹאת "thus," with or without reading נֶקַּף; so Budde, Fohrer, Sicre Diaz.

26.d. Larcher reads וְקָפֵנִי אִתּוֹ "he will raise me up beside himself"; this is followed by Terrien and JB. Gordis derives from נקף II "go around" and so "mark off," and translates "this has been marked." Janzen takes נקפו from נקף II "go around," and translates "things will come around to this (זֹאת)," comparing 1:5; but we would need a subject such as "days" (cf. also Isa 29:1), and how can the *perfect* be explained? T. H. Gaster read וְאַחַר עֵדִי נָזְקַף אִתִּי "(?) and after my testimony is vindicated," explaining זקף as "vindicate," as Akk. *zaqāpu* ("Short Notes: Job xix 26," *VT* 4 [1954] 73–79 [78]).

26.e. L. Waterman suggests that אחזה should be taken as a present, as though Job already "sees" that God is on his side and already *is* his vindicator even though the vindication may only come after Job's death ("Note on Job 19:23–27: Job's Triumph of Faith," *JBL* 69 [1950] 379–80); this largely follows C. Bruston, "Pour l'exégèse de Job 19,25–29," *ZAW* 26 (1906) 143–46. Similarly Gordis: Job "is experiencing the mystic vision." F. Nötscher denies that this is a "mystical" sight of God, but ignores the legal significance of the term entirely (*"Das Angesicht Gottes schauen" nach biblischer und babylonischer Auffassung* [Würzburg: Becker, 1924] 158–59). Kissane's interesting translation suggests that the whole idea of "seeing God" in an afterworld is simply one great impossible dream (cf. 14:13–17): "And after my skin is stripped off, did I but see Him, without my flesh were I to behold God, He whom I should see would be on my side"—that is, v 26 is a conditional clause. This fits Job's general attitude better than interpretations that find here a leap of faith; but it is a somewhat awkward reading of the Heb., and it remains preferable to read vv 25b–26 as expressing Job's desire for an encounter in this life.

27.a. לִי could of course mean "on my side" (cf. Ps 66:10 [9]; 118:6–7; so here RSV, JB, Duhm, Gray, Lévêque [477 n. 4], Pope). Of course Job wants to see God vindicate him, and so be "on his side," but the point here is his desire for the face-to-face encounter itself, as "I" emphatic, "my eyes," and "not a stranger" make clear; so "for myself" (RV) or "myself" (NAB, NIV).

27.b. The "perfect" form of ראה can equally well be a permansive, and so strictly parallel to אחזה. Emendation to יִרְאוּ (Budde, Hölscher, Fohrer) is not needed.

27.c. Similarly NEB "I myself and no other," NAB, NJPS, NIV. An alternative grammatical possibility is to take "stranger" (זָר) as the object of the verb, as Driver-Gray, "And mine eyes shall see (to be) unestranged"; so too JB "These eyes will gaze on him and find him not aloof." Gray argues strongly that Job is "not . . . interested in what will not happen to some one else [a stranger will not see], but in what will happen to himself . . . he will see God—God once more his friend." This is quite true, but the issue in the text is rather the difference between Job's being vindicated after his death and his seeing God for himself before his death. L. A. Snijders finds a rather more substantive meaning for "stranger": Job "has been treated as a *zār*, one that has turned away from the community and from God, an outsider . . . [who] will dwell in the presence of God as 'one initiated,' a friend" ("The Meaning of זָר in the Old Testament," *OTS* 10 [1954] 1–154 [70–71]).

27.d. Many think a half-line is missing after these words (so Hölscher, Fohrer, Pope). Pope thinks it "a lame conclusion," but Gordis "the sad aftermath to Job's ecstatic vision." T. J. Meek less persuasively thought Job "so astounded by the prospect of coming face to face with God that he is completely exhausted emotionally" ("Job xix 25–27," *VT* 6 [1956] 100–103 [103]). NEB regards this line as introductory of vv 28–29 ("My heart failed me when you said. . . ."; similarly GNB), which solves the problem of what to do with the half-line; but it would be strange if the expression of intense emotion should attach to the friends' hostility rather than to Job's desires about God. E. G. King, "Some Notes on the Text of Job," *JTS* 15 (1914) 74–81 (76–78), translated, "I fully trust in my bosom," supposing that כלה means "hope" (cf. Vg *reposita est haec spes in sinu meo*), a sense not otherwise attested in Heb., though כלי in Targ. Aram. is normal.

28.a. מה exclamatory (BDB, 553b § 2.b).

28.b. Sicre Diaz rather unconvincingly proposes that לו refers to God, Job meaning that to attack him is to attack God.

28.c. Lit., "matter" (דבר); cf. 1 Kgs 15:5, the "affair" of Uriah; 1 Sam 4:16, "how went the matter (the battle)?" It is not a specifically legal use, as against Dhorme (citing Exod 18:16; 24:14).

28.d. Lit., "is found." Grammatically possible is "we will find" (Duhm, Peake, Hölscher, Fohrer, de Wilde), but if so, perhaps a stronger verb than "find" would have been used, such as "search out" (Gray).

28.e. Most (not Pope) emend בִי "in me" to בוֹ "in him" (so also c. 100 Heb. mss and the ancient versions). The sense is attainable without emendation, however; it is simply a question of point of view. M. Dahood ("Qoheleth and Northwest Semitic Philology," *Bib* 43 [1962] 349–65 [353]) and Blommerde find here the *-i* suff of the third person, but this is more than unlikely.

29.a. Not expressed in the Heb.; cf. njps "For [your] fury is iniquity worthy of the sword." Gordis "for yours are crimes deserving the sword." This interpretation, which seems almost self-evident, goes back to Rashi; Dhorme among others thought it awkward, and agreed with Ball in finding the MT "ungrammatical and untranslatable."

29.b. חמה is frequently emended to הֵמָּה "these acts (or slanders) [are sins worthy of the sword]" (Dillmann, Budde, Driver-Gray, Fohrer, Gordis), but this is rather feeble. More radical emendations, like חמה עֲנָלִים יָבוֹא "wrath comes upon wrongdoers" (Siegfried, Hölscher, de Wilde; cf. LXX θυμὸς γὰρ ἐπ᾽ ἀνόμους ἐπελεύσεται; Merx חמה עונות תבוא "wrath comes upon sins"), or alternatively reading the last word as תַחֲרֵב "fury will destroy wrongdoers" (Duhm; Pope: "wrath will destroy iniquity") or חמה בַעֲוֹנוֹת תֵּחַר "wrath will be kindled against wrongs" (Dhorme) do not recommend themselves. jb "there is an anger stirred to flame by evil deeds" presumably accepted Dhorme's reading, though not his exact interpretation. rsv "wrath brings the punishment of the sword" (similarly niv) read MT. neb "the sword that sweeps away all iniquity" is hard to understand, especially since it read חַמָּה "heat, sun" (so Brockington). Sicre Diaz suggests חֲמַת עֲונות "the sentence for crimes," "anger" signifying "sentence of condemnation"; but there seem to be no parallels for this. Alternatively he proposes an interpretation that reads חמה as חֲמֵה "see, take care" (Aram. חמי), as Gerleman does on 36:18.

29.c. On the idiom, see the *Comment*.

29.d. The line is a gloss, according to Hölscher.

29.e. Lit., "so that you may realize"; see *Comment*.

29.f. MT שַׁדִין, Q שַׁדּוּן, is unintelligible. Though the relative pronoun שׁ, sometimes שׂ (as here), "which," occurs nowhere else in Job, it provides the simplest solution. דין can be read דִּין "judgment" or דַּיָּן "judge" (so neb, Driver-Gray [cf. *BHK*], gnb); the former is preferable because God is far from prominent here as the personal avenger. Some insert יֵשׁ "there is" (Budde). Others have seen here the divine name Shaddai (שַׁדַּי, Dillmann, Beer), or perhaps a byform of the name, *Šdyn* (L. R. Fisher, "*šdyn* in Job xix 29," *VT* 11 [1961] 342–43; followed by Pope with "Shaddayan"), or else a nunated form (N. Walker, "A New Interpretation of the Divine Name 'Shaddai'," *ZAW* 72 [1960] 64–66); the same objection as for the reading דַּיָּן applies.

29.g. Implied.

Form / Structure / Setting

The *structure* of this fifth speech of Job is unusual. Analysis of the direction of *address* shows the friends are spoken to both at the beginning and end (vv 2–6, 28–29) as well as in the course of the speech (vv 21–22), a pattern that has not previously occurred. Here too, for the first time since chap. 3, Job does not address God. The major blocks can be displayed thus.

> A.   2–6 Address to the friends
>   B.   7–20 Complaint
> A'.   21–22 Address to the friends
>   B'.   23–27 Wish, Belief, and Desire
> A''.   28–29 Address to the friends

The addresses to the friends are well integrated with the contents of the other blocks. Job's protest against the friends' "persecution" of him in vv 2–6 has its reason in the last verse of that address (v 6), whereupon the reason (God has put him in the wrong; it is not Job who is the cause of his own downfall) is developed in vv 7–12 and 13–20.

The second address to the friends, calling on them to stop persecuting him (vv 21–22), links back in topic to the exordium of vv 2–6, and the reason why they should desist is presented in vv 23–27 (Job is innocent and one day will be declared so). The peroration, the third address to the friends, picks up the "persecution" theme again, deploys again the friends' argument that Job gets what he deserves, and extends the note of confidence in his eventual exculpation into Job's final warning of the judgment to come that will give them what they deserve, a judgment that will be the obverse of Job's vindication.

The *strophic structure* does not display a regular pattern, but junctures between strophes are generally strongly marked. The address analysis set out above determines disjunctions between vv 6 and 7, 20 and 21, 22 and 23, 27 and 28. The one major remaining block, 7–20, is clearly divided into two on the grounds of theme and the use of metaphor: 7–12 depict God's attacks, with many metaphors, while 13–20 depict Job's ostracism by friends and relatives with no metaphors except in the concluding v 20. We may therefore identify six strophes:

1.	2–6	5 lines
2.	7–12	6 lines, a tricolon as the last
3.	13–20	8 lines
4.	21–22	2 lines
5.	23–27	5 lines, with two tricola and one monocolon concluding
6.	28–29	2 lines, a tricolon as the last

The stichometry of vv 25–27, here analyzed as two tricola followed by a monocolon on the grounds of content and parallelism, is the one element open to question.

Horst's analysis of the strophic structure is identical to that set out above, except that he does not separate out vv 21–22; Skehan's analysis is similar but for distinguishing 13–17, 18–22 ("Strophic Patterns," 109). Fohrer's strophic analysis (vv 2–4, 5–8, 9–12, 13–16, 17–20, 21–24, 25–27, 28–29) wholly ignores an analysis of address, running across boundaries set at vv 6 and 22. It is unconvincing too to separate 23–24 from what follows in 25–27, for while it is true as he says that 23–24 envisage a scene after Job's death, that is probably also true for 25–26a. Webster's analysis ("Strophic Patterns," 47–48) of seven strophes (vv 2–6, 7–9, 10–12, 13–16, 17–19, 20–24, 25–29) may be faulted on a lack of distinction between 7–9 and 10–12 and on his ignoring of the persons addressed from v 20 to the end. Terrien, marking out vv 2–6, 7–12, 13–18, 19–24, 25–29, unpersuasively separates the summarizing v 19 from what precedes it, and vv 23–24 from what is clearly attached to them in the following verses (25–27). Habel rather strangely attaches v 6 to the following strophe, at the cost of some difficulty in the syntax.

Habel has pointed to evidence of a chiastic design in vv 21–29, where plainly the important statements of vv 23–27 are ringed by two couplets addressed to the friends. With some modification of Habel's analysis the pattern may be displayed thus:

A	Admonition	21	Pity me!
B	Indictment	22	Why persecute me like God?
C	Wish	23–24	If only my words were recorded!
D	Conviction	25–26a	I know that my *gōʾēl* lives.
C′	Desire	26b–27	From my flesh I would see God.
B′	Indictment	28	You say, How we will persecute him!
A′	Admonition	29	Fear the sword for yourselves.

The Wish of vv 23–24 is of course not identical with the Desire of vv 26b–27.

In *genre* the speech as a whole is another *disputation speech,* with several strongly accented forms from other settings being drawn upon. The *forms* that appear in the speech are, first, from the *disputation speech* itself, more perhaps from the legal sphere than from a wisdom setting. We find the rhetorical questions ("how long?," "why?") implying that the other speakers should stop talking (vv 2, 22), the imperatives urging understanding ("know," v 6), doing the favor of ceasing to accuse ("spare me," v 21), or giving instruction ("fear," v 29). The accusation that a wrong has been done "ten times" (v 3) is met with also in a disputation context at Gen 31:7, 41. In general, the language of vv 2–6 is characteristic of a defendant replying to accusers and asserting his innocence (Murphy, *Wisdom Literature*, 33). The final warning to the friends, including a quotation of their words as a charge against them (v 28), and reminding them of an impending judgment (v 29), obviously belongs to the disputation speech.

A substantial amount of the material in the speech is derived from the *lament*. As in chaps. 16–17, both the "enemy"-lament and the "I"-lament are extensively used, the former in vv 6–13a, the latter in vv 13b–20. In the former the speaker depicts his enemy God under a controlling metaphor of assault: the enemy misjudges him as wicked (6a), refuses to answer his cries for justice (7), blocks the path of his journey (8), humiliates him as an alien ruler does a prince (9), uproots him like a plant (10), engages him in single-handed combat (11), besieges him like a city (6b, 12). In the latter, the lamenter portrays almost exclusively his abandonment by his friends and relatives, with many specific examples depicted realistically (13–18), and a summary line in conclusion (19), followed by a corporal metaphor expressing the psychic reality (20). The sufferings of the "I"-lament are very clearly portrayed as the work of the "enemy" (v 13, "he has put them far from me"). Most of the material of these laments is easily paralleled from the Psalms. The function of the lament is, untypically, not as an indirect appeal or accusation but as an elaboration and explanation of the assertion, "God has put me in the wrong" (v 6a). This way of reading the laments here as a kind of narrative epexegetic of Job's legal situation is encouraged by the introduction of the key metaphor of "siegeworks" in v 6 in the first strophe. That is to say, the "siegeworks" envelope (vv 6b, 12 b–c) contains a sheaf of metaphors for the act of assault that Job calls "putting me in the wrong." The "kinsfolk-acquaintances" envelope (vv 13, 19) similarly encloses a set of snapshots portraying the effects of so being "put in the wrong" by God.

In vv 23–27 we have a wish, a conviction, and a desire. The *wish* (impossible of fulfillment) is that Job's testimony to himself should be engraved on a mountainside to bear witness to him until the day of his vindication (vv 23–24). The *conviction*, which sounds like a legal affirmation ("I know . . ."), is that his case will in the end be won even if it must be after his death (vv 25–26a). His *desire* (more in the language of the lament, as is the depiction of the inner feeling, v 27c), despite that conviction, is that he could confront God here and now with his claim for vindication (vv 26b–27). See further, D. J. A. Clines, "Belief, Desire and Wish in Job 19:23–27: Clues for the Identity of Job's 'Redeemer'," *"Wünschet Jerusalem Frieden": Collected Communications to the XIIth Congress of the International Organization for the Study of the Old Testament, Jerusalem 1986* (Beiträge zur Erforschung des Alten Testaments und des antiken Judentums 13; ed. M. Augustin and K.-D. Schunk; Frankfurt a.M.: Peter Lang, 1988) 363–70.

The *function* of the speech is nearer to its *form* than has often been the case in Job. It seems primarily to be directed towards the friends, who are explicitly addressed in vv 2–6, 21–22, 28–29, and functions as a demonstration to them that Job's apparent guilt is something imposed on him by God (v 6a), he himself being wholly innocent and bound to be vindicated ultimately (vv 25–26a). Further remarks on the function of the chapter are made in the *Explanation*.

The *nodal verses* of this speech must therefore be vv 25–27, though not primarily because of the conviction—that is only the context for the reiterated desire.

The *tonality* of the speech bears marked similarity to, but one striking difference from, Job's previous speech in chaps. 16–17. There we had the conventional sinking towards death at the close of the speech that cast its shadow over even the more vigorous sarcasm against the friends. Here for the first time in Job's speeches, there is no such concluding note; even though in v 26a he envisages his skin being stripped from him, that moment of dissolution is not to be the last act in the drama of Job. For after his death his case will be raised again and again in the heavenly court until "in the end" (v 25b) it receives its full and favorable adjudication. And the concluding note is of a self-possessed vitality that can afford to affect concern for the friends, holding over their heads the threat of a judgment of death upon *them!* Looking back over his address to the friends in this speech, we find a note of stubbornness and of counter-accusation that does not always come out in our English versions. In vv 2–3, for example, Job is not wilting under the tortures his interlocutors have been inflicting on him, but exposing them and their intentions as cruel and evilly meant. In vv 21–22 likewise, what reads like a plea for simple pity in many versions is at the least a blunt demand for the friends' silence and perhaps even a cutting irony at their expense ("you are my 'friends,'" v 21a).

Nonetheless, there is another tone also that sounds in this speech. The two strophes depicting God's assault (vv 7–12) and Job's abandonment by human companions (vv 13–20) are unexcelled in the book for the intensity with which they convey his sense of loss, vv 7–12 by tumbling image over image of gratuitous assault, vv 13–20 by piling instance upon painful instance of the withdrawal of intimacy. Psychically he has become boneless and spineless, a heap of unstructured flesh, his bones cleaving to his flesh (see *Comment* on v 20); psychically he has been flayed alive by the divine animosity, being left with no more skin than the skin of his teeth. But these are not the images of exhaustion, dryness, devitalization we met with in chaps. 16–17; as if to match the spirit that will go on desiring (v 26c) though it takes every last ounce of his energy, his inmost self being consumed with longing (v 27c), the metaphors are plastic and raw. The conviction of vv 25–26a and the unabated desire of vv 26c–27b do not represent a radical and unmotivated shift of mood out of some deep despondency in earlier verses; rather we see set against one another, still at stalemate but now in a more equal struggle, the reality of divine hostility and the reality of the human self-assurance.

Comment

2–29 In this brilliant and powerful poem the presence of the friends is strongly felt by Job. They, of course, are addressed by Job in the exordium we have come to expect (vv 2–6), but they are addressed also with important lines in vv 21–22 and vv 28–29.

2 Bildad is not the only one who is short on patience. Job begins with the same phrase as Bildad: "How long?" (עד־אנה) (18:2; cf. 8:2). That does not necessarily mean that he is "quoting" Bildad, making a "direct hit" at him (Dhorme), "making sport" of him (Terrien). It may only mean that the poet invites us to recognize how tempers on both sides become frayed by impatience in this *conversation des sourds,* this debate that can never reach a conclusion so long as the participants cannot agree on the premises. It is significant that Job does not address Bildad in the singular, but directs his speech to the friends generally.

What is Job's mood here? It affects greatly the way we translate the verbs. Duhm saw here a "pained note, so different from earlier rejections of the other speakers, and evidencing Job's engagement in the most bitter spiritual struggle." Terrien on the other hand found in Job's reply a hitherto unexpressed violence, and Habel sees here a "new pitch of intensity." Which is right? Other lines in the speech suggest strongly that Job speaks less in sorrow than in anger here. Note especially "are you not ashamed to abuse me?" (v 3), the self-confidence of v 4, the reproach of v 5, the threat of vv 28–29. Job's appeal, "have pity, my friends" (v 21), seems in the context of the whole speech more the irony of a proud though bitter man than the plea of a helpless sufferer. Above all, the completely new point of confidence Job reaches in v 25, that his innocence will ultimately be recognized, as well as the fact that his speech, for the first time, does not end with the theme of death but with a threat against the friends, suggests a relatively aggressive attitude toward his interlocutors throughout the chapter. If this reading is appropriate, we should understand "torment" and "crush" in v 2 as Job's perception of what the friends are trying to do to him, not as what he acknowledges to be his own experience. That is, the friends are (objectively) *trying* to torment, *trying* to crush him, but he is not in fact (subjectively) being crushed by them. Similarly in Lam 1:5, 12; 3:33 (ענה "afflict"); Isa 51:23, the focus of יגה "afflict, torment" is upon the (objective) action rather than upon the subjective experience (as also with the noun יגון "sorrow," but more properly "affliction," in Jer 20:18 at least). The verb דכא "crush, pulverize" does not generally have a psychological sense, being used of the action of enemies against the psalmists, for example (Ps 94:5; 143:3), or of God against hostile powers (e.g., Ps 89:11 [10]); the metaphor is of threshing (see H. F. Fuhs, *TDOT* 3:195–208 [202]). So it is unlikely to mean here that Job *feels* crushed, psychologically speaking (as against Rowley, for example: "how crushed Job feels at the bitter and unfeeling words of his friends"); it is rather that he regards the friends as treating him like an enemy (not like real friends who would by contrast "comfort" and "strengthen"), attempting to "pulverize" him and his arguments with their arguments. The "arguments" (מלים, not just "words") are of course entirely over the question of his innocence or otherwise; any resistance to his affirmation of innocence or any reiteration of the doctrine of retribution is an enemy action against him designed to put him down or "pulverize" him. As Job grows more vigorous, though more disappointed in them, the less they are able to see things from his perspective. The last thing about his attitude is that he is about to succumb to the forcefulness of their rhetoric (against Fohrer).

3 To "how long?" in v 2 corresponds the "ten times" here; "ten, from being the number of the fingers on the human hand, is the number of human possibility" (Delitzsch), a full measure (also in Num 14:22; cf. Gen 31:7; Lev 26:26). By their insistence that Job is a sinner they have tried to humiliate (כלם) him; but only "tried to," because unless he confesses he is not humiliated. One is humiliated before one's enemies when one is defeated (Ps 35:5; 40:15 [14]); so, like the verb "to shame" (בוש), "humiliate" can have an objective meaning, focusing upon the intention of the humiliator (in parallel with בוש in this sense at Isa 45:16; 50:7; Jer 22:22). In a more affective or subjective sense כלם appears at Ezra 9:6; 2 Chr 30:15; Jer 6:15; but this is clearly not the sense here. The friends have not actually confuted or confounded or humiliated Job.

Since "humiliate" is so often parallel to "shame" (11 times; see E. Jenni, *THWAT* 1:270), it is strange to find it paralleled here to "*not* be ashamed." In trying to humiliate Job, the friends have *ipso facto* been trying to put him to shame; but, says Job, that attempt to (objectively) humiliate him is so disgraceful that he would expect them to be (subjectively) ashamed. It is those who humiliate who ought to be ashamed, and especially those who try to humiliate the innocent. As it is, the friends do not realize their guilt, they do not recognize they are doing Job a gross injustice, and so they are not ashamed of their ill-treatment (חכר; see n. 19:3.a) of Job. Job doesn't exactly want them to be ashamed of what they are doing, but to stop their arguments and accept his assurances.

4 One thing we can be sure of in this much disputed verse is that Job is not admitting to any sin, or, at the very least, not to any that could be the cause of his present state (there may be a little difficulty about the "sins of my youth," 13:26). In 9:21; 10:7; and 16:17 he has stated unequivocally his certainty of his own innocence, and he is not giving that up here. This can only be a hypothetical statement, then, like 7:20, which was addressed to God: "If I have sinned, how do I injure you?" (so too Rowley). The point there was that God's affliction of him is totally disproportionate to any sin he can possibly have committed, and that thought may be the most relevant to the present verse. Here the friends have felt constrained to attempt to humiliate him, an utterly disproportionate reaction; since Job has not harmed them in any way, why should they be trying to harm him? If I have sinned, he says, my sin has not invaded their personal space, their guest-rooms, and "it is with myself that my sin lodges"; the "with myself" (אתי) is in emphatic position. If it "lodges" (לון) it remains with him like a house-guest (cf. 11:14) (for evil thoughts "lodging" in a city's "heart," cf. Jer 4:14; for righteousness "lodging" in a city, cf. Isa 1:21). It does not damage the friends, it harms Job only; therefore they should not react as if they themselves had been the victims of Job's hypothetical sin.

Other interpretations are: My error is my own concern (Dhorme); it is no business of yours. But of course if Job expects the friends to comfort him they cannot make his guilt none of their concern; for that is the whole reason why they are in dialogue with him. Some say Job is rejecting the interference of the friends in a matter that should be strictly between a man and his God (Andersen; cf. Habel). If that were his position, he should have stopped the dialogue long ago; however much he resents the line the friends have taken, he does not for a moment think his case is a private matter; how can it be, when the evidence for his guilt is a matter of public record and visible to any visitor to his ash-heap? Others take the clause to mean, "I should be aware of it [but I am not]" (cf. Pope), but that seems a strained sense for "lodge." Pope suggests it means, "Does the error lodge with me?" as if Job is foreshadowing the statement of v 6 that it is God who has "subverted" him; but again, "lodge" is a strange word to indicate "origin" (though we say in English, "Does the fault *lie* with me?").

Another approach is to find some special significance in the word for "err" (שגה, noun משוגה), arguing that it is a mild word, as if to say, I am willing to admit I have sinned lightly, and that the penalty for that sin comes home to me ("lodges with me"), but that is no ground for you to argue that I have *greatly* sinned, in proportion to my present suffering (Gray). It is true that the noun שגגה is used normally for sins of inadvertence, as distinct from intentional sins, those done with a "high hand" (Num 15:29–30), but the verb

שגה is used more generally also as well as having a specific sense of committing an inadvertent sin (Lev 4:13); so in 1 Sam 26:21; Ps 119:21, 118. Cf. R. Knierim (*THWAT* 2:869–72) and J. Milgrom ("The Cultic שגגה and Its Influence in Psalms and Job," *JQR* 58 [1967–68] 115–25), defining שגגה as either a negligent or ignorant sin ("either the offender knows the law but accidentally violates it or he acts deliberately without knowing he did wrong").

5 Though he has done them no harm, the friends treat Job as an enemy (v 4). So, since they are evidently determined to act the enemy toward him (v 5a) by maintaining that his suffering is proof of his sin (v 5b), they need to recognize that they have got it all wrong, and that the aura of guilt that surrounds Job is not of his own making, but has been put upon him by God (v 6a), with the result that he cannot escape (v 6b) the implication of guilt. So runs the argument of these verses.

The friends are in fact, from Job's perspective, "magnifying" (rsv; גדל hiph) themselves against him, i.e., "set[ting themselves] forth as great illegally, presumptuously and arrogantly" (R. Mosis, *TDOT* 2:405; differently at 7:17). They do that solely by continuing to regard him as guilty, in the process making themselves Job's moral and intellectual superiors. The language is typical of the psalmic laments against oppressors (Ps 35:26; 38:17 [16]; 41:10 [9], if "heel" is deleted; 55:13 [12]; cf. Lam 1:9). There is no doubt but that this is their attitude, so the opening "if" (אם) in the Hebrew cannot be taken as conditional; it means "since" (the "if" of argument). Job does not admit, of course, that they *are* superior to him, so we must translate: "you try to, you have to, get the better of me." Their superiority rests upon a false premise, that Job is the author of his own guilt; to this v 6 responds that it is God who has made Job look like a sinner. The theme of superiority has already been developed in 12:2–13:2 (especially 12:3; 13:2). Although the language sounds like the intellectual machismo of the seminar room, and there is perhaps an element of authorial playfulness in the strictly disputational lines, life and death matters are at stake here. God for his part is not honored by the efforts of the friends on his behalf: he is not "exalted" (רמם) by people closing their minds to the possibility that Job is after all a righteous man (17:4).

Job's "reproach" (rv, nab; חרפה) is the condition of disgrace in which he finds himself, that is, his "humiliation" (rsv, niv) in being treated as a sinner, the actual state of suffering he experiences. The friends use the suffering as an "argument against him," and they have a prima facie case (cf. Job's admission in 16:8).

6 This is not news, that Job believes it is God who has (unjustifiably) put him in the wrong and not some sin of his own—though he has never used just these words. But this is the headline for his extensive charges against God for grievous bodily harm (vv 7–12) and for alienating the affections of everyone he knows (vv 13–19). It is not that he means that God has "wronged" him (as njps, niv), "dealt unfairly" with him (nab) or become his "oppressor" (jb)—though that is also true. What he means specifically is that by causing him to suffer God has destroyed his reputation for innocence and in a moral or legal sense branded him a sinner (cf. rsv, neb "put me in the wrong"). Bildad has used the same word עות "pervert, wrong, declare wrong," but in a different sense; so it is hardly correct to say that the verb is chosen deliberately in reply to Bildad (Dhorme), or that we have here a delayed reply to a point

Job has long pondered (Terrien). In 8:3 Bildad denied that God "perverts" justice or right order (צדק) (cf. also 34:12), and no doubt to declare an innocent man guilty is a perversion of justice. But Job is not saying exactly that, so he cannot be thought to be replying to Bildad; he simply means that God is the author of his bad reputation (as against Rowley and others: "Job solemnly declares that in his case God has . . . perverted [justice]"). What is for the friends a matter of ethics is for him a question about God. It is uncertain whether there is a further allusion to twisting or perverting a way in the context of a siege (as Habel, comparing Lam 3:9).

The following metaphor is somewhat unexpected, but it can be explained as introducing the imagery of the next strophe. Siegeworks took the form of an earthen wall surrounding the besieged city, affording some protection for the besiegers, especially their archers, and making exit from the city impossible. Cf. J. W. Wevers, *IDB* 4:804; Y. Yadin, *The Art of Warfare in Biblical Lands* (London: Weidenfeld and Nicolson, 1963) 18, 98. The metaphor applies to the inescapable logic in which Job is trapped: he has no more chance of winning vindication than a besieged city has of breaking through walls thrown up around it. Job is one of history's earliest victims of the catch-22 principle: if he accepts his suffering, it proves he is a sinner; if he doesn't accept it, he makes himself a sinner by questioning God's justice. He has virtually said this himself at 10:15a-b.

The metaphor of the net, which most commentators and versions find here (RSV "closed his net about me"), is thoroughly out of place, though having a superficial connection with Bildad's extended image (18:8-10). The metaphor is rather that of the siege.

There is pain in this speech, but there is also an assurance of the kind we only first began to hear in chap. 16. This forceful and unapologetic "understand!" (lit. "know then," דעו־אפו) elsewhere introduces a sentence like "know then that there shall fall to the earth nothing of the word of Yahweh which he spoke concerning the house of Ahab" (2 Kgs 10:10). It resonates with the confident "I know that my champion lives" of v 25—which is something for the friends to know as well—and with the plainly hostile "so that you may know there is a judgment" of v 29.

7-12 There is a veritable kaleidoscope of images here, all images of assault; the hapless citizen set upon by thugs and unable to summon any passer-by to his aid (v 7), the traveler who finds his path blocked and nightfall overtaking him (v 8), the prince who is humiliated by an alien lord (v 9), the plant that is pulled down or pulled out of the ground (v 10), the warrior compelled into single-handed combat (v 11), the king or city surrounded by hosts of besieging enemies (v 12). There are close similarities with Lam 3:7-9, where also the lamenter feels "walled about" (גדר, as v 8 here) by God so that he cannot escape, where he "cries" (זעק, equivalent to צעק in v 7 here) and "shouts" (שוע, as v 7 here) but has his prayer shut out, where he feels God has "blocked" (גדר as v 8 here) his "path" (דרך, equivalent to ארח in v 8 here) and has "made crooked" (עוה, as in v 6 here) his "paths" (נתיבות, as in v 8 here). There is no more fixity in the imagery of Lam 3 than there is here, where God is also pictured as a beast (v 10) and an archer (v 11). These images must belong to a conventional stock available to both poets.

7 The imagery here is from the dangers of urban life. The "cry" (צעק) is in the first place the cry of the assaulted for deliverance; its content in Israel is the word "Violence!" (חמס), just as we cry, "Help!" (cf. Jer 20:8; Hab 1:2; Deut 22:24, 27; Job 35:12 with the noun צעקה, 27:9; 34:28; for זעק, with identical meaning, cf. 31:38; 35:9). But here, as in 16:18 (where the spelling is צעקה), it is not a cry for deliverance but for vindication. The problem with God's "putting him in the wrong" (v 6) is that he is *keeping* him in the wrong; Job's protest, which has now been made in formal style (13:20–23), has so far been ignored. The oppressed person has a right to expect support from his community—it is not a favor they do him—but when Job is oppressed by God he suffers the same lack of reciprocity he has expressed before: there is calling but no answering (cf. 9:16; 12:4; 13:22; 14:15; and note the same lack of response on the human level in v 16). The metaphor has moved from the sphere of the street to the sphere of the lawcourt; but from God's lawcourt, despite Job's "shout" (שוע), there comes no legal decision (משפט in its strict sense)—which means there is no justice (משפט in its broader sense). Job is not exactly saying without qualification that God is unjust; his concern is primarily with himself rather than with the character of God, and with the fact that he has not yet been granted justice, not so much with the injustice of delaying justice.

8 This metaphor of walling up a road does not refer to any everyday concrete reality; the use of walls suggests that the image is not from the hunting of animals into a defile (as against G. Gerleman, "Contributions to the Old Testament Terminology of the Chase," *Årsberättelse 1945–46. Bulletin de la Société Royale des Lettres de Lund 1945–46* [Lund: Gleerup, 1946] 89). "Walls" (גדר) usually enclose vineyards (Isa 5:5) or sheepfolds (גדרה, Num 32:16; 1 Sam 24:3 [4]), and a road may have walls on either side (Num 22:24). But in normal circumstances no one would build a wall *across* a path. In Hos 2:8 [6] indeed, in an exceptional metaphor, Yahweh builds a wall (גדר גדרה) across his unfaithful wife's path to prevent her pursuing her lovers. In the present context it is a deliberate act of frustration of Job's legitimate intentions; cf. Lam 3:9 where Yahweh blocks the lamenter's path with hewn stones. His path is his normal course of life (cf. 13:27; Ps 139:3), which is hindered from developing. The image in 3:23 of a man on a path being hedged in is quite similar, though there the emphasis lies upon Job's feeling rather than upon God's responsibility.

The traveler on the path finds his way forward blocked, and at the same time becomes aware that no alternatives are possible because the way is veiled in darkness (lit. "he has set darkness upon my path") at the onset of night. The darkness thus functions to extend the metaphor but also, of course, carries its own symbolic value, that death has overshadowed his life (cf. most recently 18:18; and for the image of light shining on one's path, see 22:28; Prov 4:18).

Delitzsch thought that the image was that of a prisoner, confined to a narrow dark space (cf. Lam 3:7); but prisoners are not on "paths." Habel sees here the imagery of the siege (cf. v 6b), God setting up a blockade to prevent Job's free movement; but the connection of the "darkness" is then not clear.

9 The image now is of fine clothes being stripped from an honored person as an act of humiliation (less convincingly, Habel argues that the siege metaphor is being continued, Job being imprisoned like a king in a besieged city and stripped of his capacity to rule; cf. Mic 4:14 [5:1]). Job's honor (כבוד) is his righteousness, which he has worn like a garment (29:14); by being visited with calamity and clothed instead in sackcloth (16:15), Job has been marked out as an evildoer for all the world to see. He has been "clothed with shame," like the enemies in 8:22. The "crown" (עטרת) is equally his honor or reputation as a righteous man; cf. Ps 8:6 [5] "crowned [עטר] him with glory and honor." These metaphors do not make Job into a royal personage (against Terrien, referring to A. Caquot, "Traits royaux dans le personnage de Job," *maqqél shâqédh. La branche d'amandier. Hommage à Wilhelm Vischer* [Montpellier: Causse, Graille, Castelnau, 1960] 32–45, though Caquot does not mention this passage). They depict him *as* a prince, but a prince among men for his moral quality. For another metaphorical use of such language, cf. Lam 5:16; and for a literal use, see Jer 13:18, "your crown has come down from your head." For Job, innocence that is not recognized is not true innocence; it is not that he is fixated upon outwardness, but he has a sense of the social dimension of moral worth, which cannot conceive of goodness and godliness as simply matters of inner disposition. The epilogue to the book evinces the same concern.

10 The first figure here is of a building that is demolished, נתץ being used for destroying a house (Isa 22:10), a city wall (Jer 39:8), an altar (Judg 2:2). The destruction comes "from every side" (סביב, cf. 10:8; 18:11), which does not necessarily imply that the metaphor of the besieged city is being resumed (against Weiser, Fohrer, Habel). He means to say that "God reduces all Job's efforts to defend his integrity to the rubble of unanswered protestations" (Habel). It is not the building but Job himself who as a result "passes away" or "perishes" (הלך "go" in general, but also specifically "perish, die," as BDB, 234a recognizes; so also in 14:20).

The second image is of an even more final destruction. We have heard of rebuilding ruins as good as new (3:14) and of the hope that remains for a tree that has been cut down (14:7–9). But for a tree that is uprooted (for the image, cf. 31:8; Ps 52:7 [5]), the hope is forever destroyed, as in 14:19 God destroys the hope of human beings. Job's hope which God has extirpated is not a hope for deliverance—he gave that up long ago—but for vindication this side of death. Job still believes he will be vindicated in the end (v 25), but what he really wants is to "see" God declaring his innocence while he is still alive to see it (v 26). He desires that, but he hopes for it no longer (17:15).

11 Now we find the language of hostility, preparing for the specifically military imagery of v 12. In a graphic variant on the common phrase, "one's wrath was hot" (e.g., 32:5), Job says, "He has made hot (חרה hiph) his wrath," to show more clearly it is God's deliberate action (on God's anger, see 9:5, 13; 16:9). To consider a person as one's enemy comes from the language of personal relations, not from the language of warfare (against Peake, Rowley et al.); one does not "reckon" or "esteem" (חשב) one's literal enemy to be an enemy, but only "reckons" someone an enemy who, properly speaking, is not or previously has not been so (cf. 13:24; 18:3; 19:15; 33:10; Gen 31:15; Num 18:27, 30; Neh 13:13 is different). In Lam 2:5 it is God who has become like an enemy to Israel (אויב); here he regards Job as the enemy—there is not very much difference.

12 The last word of the line gives the clue to the irony in this depiction. The object of this massing of the divine hordes is the lonely *tent* of Job! This accumulation of metaphors has been leading up to the theme of the disproportion of God's treatment of Job (cf. already 7:12, 17–20; 10:16–17; 13:25); "God's grand assault is a bitter example of divine overkill" (Habel).

The "troops" (גְדוּדִים) of God do not have to be specified as personified powers that bring disaster or as demons of disease (Fohrer); they arise simply from the metaphor of God as warrior and assailant. Whereas in 16:12–14 God's assault was depicted as an attack on a lone champion, here Job is imaged as a city ringed by siege-troops, who build a rampart up to his gate so as to wheel up their battering rams (for the realia see, e.g., Y. Yadin, *The Art of Warfare in Biblical Lands* [London: Weidenfeld and Nicolson, 1963] 314–15); similar imagery, but used of human opponents, occurs in 30:12. The "rampart" or "mound" (סֹלְלָה is the usual term; here "they cast up their way," וַיָּסֹלּוּ דַרְכָּם) is a commonly attested feature of warfare (2 Sam 20:15; 2 Kgs 19:32 [= Isa 37:33]; Jer 6:6; Ezek 4:2; 17:17; 21:27 [22]; 26:8; Dan 11:15).

So unexpected is the last word of the line, "my tent" (Rowley, e.g., commenting, "A rampart would hardly be required to attack a tent"), that some commentators have felt there must be some mistake. Shall we delete "they have built a rampart against me" (so Houtsma, Fohrer, Hesse, Moffatt, NEB), noting that the phrase occurs again in a variant form at 30:12 and so may be here an inappropriate gloss? Or shall we suppose that a colon more suitable to the image of the tent has been lost immediately after the troublesome phrase (so Duhm, Hölscher), or after the reference to the tent (Merx)? Or shall we see here a reference to the Bedouin *razwas* (H. Winckler, "סֹלְלָה? Threni 1,15. Hiob 19,12; 30,12," *Altorientalische Forschungen* [Leipzig: E. Pfeiffer, 1902] 3/1:242–44)? None of these proposals is necessary, of course, once we recognize that disproportion is the point. There is the grimmest of humor here.

It is hard to say whether the present or the past tense should be used in translating the variegated imagery of vv 7–12. The English versions veer between past and present, typically producing past tense verbs in vv 8–9, present in v 10, past in v 11a, present in vv 11b–12. The Hebrew perfect and imperfect "tenses" do not of themselves indicate time, though the *waw* consecutive forms in vv 10, 11, 12 do suggest that we have the form of a narrative before us. Perhaps it is best to take v 7, with its introductory "if" (הֵן "if and when," "whenever") as an umbrella or headline over what follows; vv 8–12 then furnish instances that have occurred of the divine violence against which v 7 protests. Vv 8–12 could then be catalogued in the English past tense, as in the above translation. In the following strophe (vv 13–20) the focus is more clearly on the present state of affairs (except for v 13), but there also the English past tense may have something to recommend it as presenting a list of indictments.

13–20 The sudden transition from the wholly metaphorical speech of vv 7–12 to the wholly concrete speech of vv 13–19 is breathtaking. In vv 7–12 there has been artistry and there has been passion, but suddenly in vv 13–19, notwithstanding the artistry and the conventionality, we hear the cry of an isolated human being, a cry that is wholly credible as literal truth. In vv 7–12 there is nothing but images of physical violence; in vv 13–19 no one raises a hand or a weapon or a voice: there is nothing physical, nothing violent. Or is there? Does Job want us to understand that the withholding of affection and esteem is a kind of violence, and does he mean that the principal form in which God's violence presents itself to him is the alienation of his acquaintance and the denial of intimacy? In vv 7–12 there was nothing specific, anything could refer to anything; here in vv 13–19 everything is specific, every line is charged with the felt pain of the disintegration of his human relationships.

It would be easy to say that vv 7–12 refer to Job's physical sufferings imposed on him by the hand of God, and that vv 13–19 are simply the consequence of his physical state, with his bad breath (v 17a), his repulsive appearance, and his evident loss of significance (v 18). There is truth in that, but for Job everything is one great act of divine violence against him: the loss of human intimacy and esteem are for him here nothing other than the sharp end of the divine hostility, and it has become otiose to talk of cause and consequence, or to parcel out blame to the various conspirators about him.

In surveying his circle of acquaintance, Job moves inward from kinsfolk and acquaintances (vv 13–14) to domestic servants (vv 15–16) to his wife and brothers (v 17), and outward again via the children of the neighborhood (v 18) to the whole company of his confrères and intimates (v 19). Nowhere does Job portray his sense of human isolation more compellingly than here (Lamparter).

13 The whole sorry catalogue of Job's losses of human intimacy is laid at God's door: "he" is the one who has alienated Job's kinsfolk. No matter that the act has been indirect, mediated by the suffering that God has inflicted on Job, which has made him not just not nice to know but positively dangerous. Secondary causes fade into the background when the primary cause is at hand; and so it must be, when the issue is the matter of blame. And how God has acted is as the destroyer of community. It is true that Job will not explicitly accuse him of the kind of perversity that destroys harmonious human relationships such as he himself epitomized as the "perfect" man (תם), characteristically acting in the interests of community (see W. Brueggemann, "A Neglected Sapiential Word Pair," ZAW 89 [1977] 234–58 [255]). But the import of Job's words is not obscure.

Job's "kinsfolk" (אחים, lit., "brothers") are not here his blood brothers who appear in v 17 as the "sons of my mother," but members of his "clan" (משפחה, cf. 32:1), if the term is precise, or, more generally, "relatives." Much of the language of these verses is paralleled in the psalms of lament; for the idea of kinsfolk being "afar" (רחק) see Ps 38:12 [11] (רחוק); 88:9 [8], 19 [18] "you have put far away my friends"; Prov 19:7; and for the lamenter as "stranger" to his brothers, see Ps 69:9 [8]. Here Job's "acquaintances" (ידעים, cf. 42:11) have become like strangers (זור) to him.

14 These terms for friends and relations perhaps had precise meanings which we no longer have access to. His "clansmen" (קרובים, lit. "near ones") are perhaps equivalent to the "kinsfolk" of v 13 (they seem to be defined in Lev 21:2–3 as closest family; cf. 25:25; Num 27:11), the "intimates" (מידעים, lit. "known ones") being the same as the "acquaintances" of v 13 (and cf. 2 Kgs 10:11). The "near ones" or "known ones" who now stand at a distance from the sufferer are found also in Ps 38:12 [11], 88:9 [8], while in 31:12 [11] the psalmist in his terrible suffering becomes an object of dread to his "known ones" (cf. also Ps 55:14 [13]). These acquaintances of Job's own neighborhood have "forsaken" him simply by fading away (חדל "cease"; cf. 14:7 of the branches of a tree; 7:16; 10:20 of leaving Job alone) at the onset of his calamity, as have those who owed him a debt for his hospitality in conferring on them status and privilege, the resident aliens (גר, here גרי בתי, "the sojourners of my house"). The resident aliens occupied an intermediate position between natives and foreigners; as not related by blood to the people whose territory they inhabit, they need the patronage of an influential person who is native-born (see D. Kellermann, *TDOT* 2:439–49 [443]). They are not his house guests, as rsv, jb and others suggest (31:32 is different); they belong institutionally to his household (בית), but they reside on land allotted to them (cf. Gen 23:4; Exod 2:22; 12:19; 20:10; cf. also on Job 18:19). The obligations of these "clients" or "retainers" (the terms are not at all strictly parallel to "resident alien") are less intimate than those of friends but no less binding.

15 "The tables are now so completely turned that the very persons who owed their places in the household to Job now look upon him as one outside the family" (Gray). "Serving girls" (אמה) are female slaves or servants, whether maids or concubines (A. Jepsen defined an אמה as an "unfree woman," "Amah und Schiphchah," *VT* [1958] 293–97; on concubinage see E. Neufeld, *Ancient Hebrew Marriage Laws* [London: Longman, Green & Co., 1944] 121–29). 31:13 shows that אמה is the female equivalent of an עבד, "servant, slave." The exact meaning of "stranger" (זר) has to be established by the milieu, whether it is the family, the nation, the company of priests or the circle of the devout (L. A. Snijders, *TDOT* 4:52–58 [57]); here it is obviously a stranger to the family (see also vv 13, 27; 15:19). The "alien" (נכרי), however, is generally a person of another race (Deut 17:15; Judg 19:12; 1 Kgs 11:1; cf. R. Martin-Achard, *THWAT* 2:66–68). "Alien" thus is a heightening of "stranger" here.

16 There is a reversal of the normal order here too. Generally servants are expected to look to the gesture of their master or mistress to translate their merest hint into action (Ps 123:2 "as the eyes of servants look to the hand of their master"). But Job's personal attendant, a male servant (עבד; the singular shows that he has a special status, cf. Gen 15:2–3; 24:2; 39:19), has become so neglectful of him that Job must verbalize his every need (במו־פי "with my mouth" in emphatic position). More than that, he must "beg" (חנן hithp) of his servant what he has a right to demand of him. And even this is ineffective. This goes against the grain for Job; he is a proud man who stands on his rights. He has even resented—and rejected—the idea of having to beg God for the justice he is entitled to (9:15, חנן as here).

But even the humiliation of begging from a servant is not the worst of it. Job actually has a refreshingly egalitarian attitude toward his servants: the question, "Did not the same One fashion us before our birth?" (31:15), is used as a motivation for ensuring justice for his servants (31:13). Job may be in fact less patronizing toward the "lower classes" than was his commentator A. B. Davidson in 1884, remarking, "Very soon the reflection of one's fall is thrown from the countenances of those higher in rank down upon the faces of the servants, where it shows itself without any delicacy or reserve." It is not the reversal of the social order in itself that bothers Job; it is what that says about his innocence and what it says about his own personal worth. For Job the worst thing is the loss of reciprocity, of speaking and answering, the human interchange that arose from the social network surrounding Job and that in every hour of Job's life proved his worth and indispensability to his family and community. For the significance of this theme of "calling" and "answering," already surfacing in v 7, see on 12:4; and cf. also 5:1; 9:16; 13:22; 14:15; 23:5; 30:20. An Akkadian medical text cites as a symptom of what we would call a pathological anxiety state the condition of a householder who feels he is "constantly giving orders with no (one) complying, calling with no (one) answering" (E. K. Ritter and J. V. Kinnier Wilson, "Prescription

for an Anxiety State: A Study of *BAM* 234," *Anatolian Studies* 30 [1980] 23–
30). But Job is describing a reality, not a mere anxiety.

All Job's friends and household, even his valet, became theologians at the
moment of his calamity. All of them saw in his suffering the finger of God,
and each has taken God's part against him.

17 Most commentators are confident that Job is here complaining that
his bad breath, caused by his disease presumably, repulses his wife (and, apparently, his blood brothers). If this is the correct reading, the emphasis must be
not on the means by which his intimates are repulsed but upon the effect
(their abandonment of him), for hitherto in this strophe there has been no
specific word of why precisely his acquaintances have come to disown him.
Hitherto it has seemed that what has alienated people from him has been
the evidence of divine displeasure presented by the enormity of his sufferings;
it would be something of a disillusionment then to find that the chief problem
is his halitosis. We may doubt that this is what the text means, especially because
there are no parallels to the idea of רוּחַ as sweet or bad breath.

It may be that רוּחִי, lit. "my spirit, vitality, breath," does not refer so specifically to the breath and its odor as some versions suggest (e.g., NEB "My breath
is noisome to my wife," and GNB, dynamically equivalent as ever, "my wife
can't stand the smell of my breath"). Some older commentators thought רוּחִי
was really equivalent to נַפְשִׁי "my life," and so to "myself" (perhaps we could
compare רוּחִי in 6:4, "my spirit [= I?] drinks in their poison," but there and
in 10:12; 17:1 Job's "vitality, vital spark" seems to be more the point). Then
Job might be "repulsive" to his wife and brothers not for some physical reason
but because of his evident sinfulness ("repulsive" would be metaphorical). Preferably, however, רוּחַ should be taken as his "life," his continued existence,
that his closest relatives find repugnant, for they must be suffering guilt by
association with him so long as he still lives. It would suitably heighten the
tension of these verses if, whereas mere acquaintances have deserted Job, his
wife and brothers should prefer him dead. We need not imagine that his
wife's "curse God and die" (2:9) was entirely altruistic.

Perhaps a parallel can be drawn with lines in the Egyptian text known as
"A Dispute over Suicide" (*ANET*, 405–7). Addressing his soul, who resists
death, the suicidal man says that if he follows the soul's advice, his "name
will reek"—more than the stench of bird-droppings, more than a fish-handler
on the day of the catch when the sun is hot, more than the stench of crocodiles,
more than a married woman against whom a false accusation of adultery has
been made, more than a boy of whom it is whispered that he is the child of
his father's rival (lines 87–104). Continued existence is thus spoken of as a
repulsive odor.

Job's "brothers" are literally "the sons of my belly" (בֶטֶן, more often "womb,"
but in Deut 28:53; Ps 132:11; Mic 6:7 of the father). Many have argued that
the phrase must mean "my own sons" (NJPS; cf. Gordis), airily brushing away
the problem that according to the prologue Job's sons are all dead; writes
Dhorme, "Since he is using hyperboles, the poet does not bother to reconcile
this allusion with the Prologue" (similarly Duhm, Pope, Habel). There is, however, no parallel lapse on the part of the poet anywhere in the book; the
friends may be allowed to let their rhetoric carry them away into thoughtless
generalities that contradict the realities of Job's experience (e.g., 5:25; 8:7;

18:19), but Job himself, so particular in recounting his past in chap. 29, is not going to have utterly inappropriate allusions put in his mouth (and the death of his children *is* alluded to in the dialogues: 8:4; cf. 29:5). Some have thought the children of concubines are meant, though there is no direct reference to concubines at all in the book (though cf. on v 15). Grandchildren are even more unlikely, since Job's children in chap. 1 seem to be unmarried. The further suggestion that בטן should be understood from the cognate Arabic *baṭn* "clan" (Wetzstein; W. Robertson Smith, *Kinship and Marriage in Early Arabia* [new ed.; ed. S. A. Cook; London: A. and C. Black, 1903] 34; Hölscher, de Wilde) founders on the lack of Heb. parallels. There is no probability at all in the idea that the Heb. means "*her* womb," the suffix being third person (M. Dahood, *Or* 32 [1963] 498–500; *Psalms I,* 11; Blommerde). The best solution is clearly that the "sons of my womb" are the sons born from the same womb as Job, i.e., his uterine brothers (so Peake, Driver-Gray, Fohrer, Rowley) (elsewhere such are specified as "my brother[s], the son[s] of my mother" [Gen 43:29; Judg 8:19]).

18 This verse is a pendant to a series that reached its climax with v 17. To be rejected by those emotionally and physically closest to him is the cruelest element in the total isolation he experiences; that children too, who are "often still free from the bias of social opinion" (Habel), but whose cruelty can be distressingly frank, should also reject him, instinctively and without the color of justification the doctrine of retribution provides for adults, only serves to drive home his real isolation from human sympathy. It is hard to tell whether the children (עוילים, only here and at 21:11) are the urchins of the street (Habel), or small children of Job's own household. That they should "despise" him (RSV, NEB) or "disdain" him (NJPS) he can stand; the humiliation of being esteemed as worthless when once he had "dwelt as a king among his troops" (29:25) is nothing compared with the elemental human "rejection" (מאס) he now encounters. For this more vigorous sense of מאס throughout Job, cf. 5:21 "do not reject the discipline of the Almighty"; 7:16 "I have rejected [my life]"; 8:20; 9:21; 10:3.

When does Job "rise" (קום)? In 30:28 he rises in the assembly to call for help, in 1:20 he rises from the sitting posture in which he has heard the news of the messengers, in 7:4 he arises from sleep. Here the arising makes best sense if it is rising from sitting, in order to approach and address. It is not that the children "laugh at the grotesque figure he cuts when he tries to get up and hobble about" (Peake; cf. Gray, Fohrer, Weiser); that is to overconcretize what is essentially a psychological portrayal.

If the philological decision taken here is correct, that the children "turn their backs" on Job (see n. 19:18.b), rather than that they "talk against" him (RSV), "ridicule" him (NIV), or are "ever ready with a jibe" (JB), the dominant impression Job conveys is of the silence that surrounds him. In former days, the silent withdrawing of the young men when he would go into the city gate (29:7) was a welcome mark of respect, for it was only a prelude to a rich interchange of words (29:11–13); now the silence of children signifies not respect, but only his isolation.

19 The catalogue of rejection concludes with a summarizing line, a summary appraisal. His "intimates" ("men of my council") and "loved ones" are perhaps roughly identical to the groups we distinguish as "friends and relatives" (cf.

vv 13–14, kinsfolk and clansmen as distinct from acquaintances and intimates; and cf. Esth 5:10; 6:13). One's "council" (סוד) is "a company or circle who talk confidentially to and exchange secrets with one another" (Driver); cf. Jer 6:11; 15:17; Ps 89:8 [7]; 111:1; and 55:14–15 [13–14], where סוד is the "counsel" exchanged.

20 This famous crux is one of the most problematic verses of the whole book. The initial difficulty is that after speaking for seven verses about his isolation from his fellow humans it is strange that Job should suddenly be concerned about his physical distress (as nowhere else in the whole speech; cf. on v 17). Second, it is curious that he should complain that his bones are "cleaving to his flesh," since that seems to be a very satisfactory situation anatomically. Third, the first half of the line seems overlong (four stressed words instead of the usual three). Fourth, it is strange that Job should say that he has "escaped" (מלט hithp), since that seems to be the last thing he would claim has been his experience.

There is moreover some conventionality and some proverbial language in this sentence. For one's bone (עצמי sg) cleaving (דבק) to one's flesh (בשרי), we must compare Ps 102:6 [5], where the same words occur. For the unparalleled phrase "the skin of my teeth," we must observe that the teeth are the one part of the body (the nails excepted) that are not covered by skin; so we may suspect we have some ironical proverb-like phrase here.

The crucial word in the first half of the line is דבק "cleave." It never means two things sticking to each other, but always *one* thing sticking or clinging *to another*, or depending on another, the weaker to the stronger or the less significant to the more significant. Thus a waistcloth "clings" to the loins (Jer 13:11), little fish to the scales of a dragon (Ezek 29:4), leprosy to Gehazi (2 Kgs 5:27), pestilence or disease or famine to the disobedient (Deut 28:21, 60; Jer 42:16), a spot to the hands (Job 31:7), the work of evildoers to a psalmist (Ps 101:3), Ruth to Naomi (Ruth 1:14) or to Boaz's maidens (2:8, 21, 23), Israel to Yahweh (Deut 10:20; 11:22; 13:5 [4]; 30:20; Josh 22:5; 23:8), Hezekiah to Yahweh (2 Kgs 18:6), the tongue to the roof of the mouth (Job 29:10; Ps 22:16 [15] [jaws?]; 137:6; Lam 4:4; Ezek 3:26), Shechem's *nephesh* to Dinah (Gen 34:3), Solomon to his foreign wives (1 Kgs 11:2), and a man to his wife (Gen 2:24, no exception to the general rule!). Possible exceptions are Job 41:15 [23], where the folds of the crocodile's flesh simply "cling" (דבקו, no object expressed), similarly 41:9 [17] of the row of shields that make up his back (but this is passive [pual]) and 38:38 of the clods of earth (also pual); but the idea could well be "cling [dependently] to one another." An interesting play on the sense of דבק is made at 2 Sam 23:10 where the warrior Eleazar keeps on smiting the Philistines "until his hand grew weary and his hand clung to his sword"; usually it would be the sword that would "cling" to one's hand, not the hand to the sword, but in the warrior's manic or supernaturally heightened state the hand can be thought of as an appendage to the sword!

Here in our text there is the same kind of inversion of the normal. In the healthy body, the flesh and the skin "cling" to or hang on the bones, the framework of the body. But if the bones are weak, without vigor, diseased, rotten, it is the flesh and skin that support the bones, as if the human body has become a shapeless lump of meat so different from Theodore Roethke's "woman lovely in her bones." Thus Job's complaint is that "my bone(s) cling to my flesh and my skin" (עצמי sg is collective, as in 2:5; Gen 29:14; Lam 4:7). (My interpretation was suggested by a sentence in E. W. Hengstenberg, *The Book of Psalms* [Edinburgh: T. & T. Clark, 1853] 3:216 on Ps 102:6 [5]: "That state of weakness and relaxation of the bones is manifestly described, which is brought on by severe pain and long-continued distress, when they lose their force and vigorous power of motion . . . they cleave on, hang upon the flesh." I find that for the Job text I was anticipated by Dillmann, and in part by Peters). BDB always use words like "cling, cleave, keep close" in their article on דבק, but without the concept of *dependence* introduced here; German translations such as "hangen an" in KB and KB[3] may suggest the idea of dependence, but not necessarily so (G. Wallis, *TDOT* 3:79–84, and E. Jenni, *THWAT* 2:431–32, do not present such an idea). The concept of "rotten" or "decayed" (רקב) bones is attested in Prov 12:4; 14:30; Hab 3:16. In Ps 31:11 [10] the psalmist's bones are "wasted away" (עשש), in 32:3 "worn out" (בלה). The opposite is for bones to be "made strong" (Isa 58:11, חלץ) or "flourish (פרח) like the grass" (Isa 66:14).

This image of rotten bones that cannot support the human body but on the contrary are weaker than the flesh is quite distinct from other images of flesh and bones. It is an image of the decay of vigor, rather than of emaciation, where the sufferer can count his bones (Ps 22:18 [17]) which stick out (Job 33:21). Compare the limestone relief from Saqqara showing the chest bones of starving nomads, *ANEP*, pl. 102; O. Keel, *The Symbolism of the Biblical World* (New York: Seabury, 1978), fig. 88. Cf. also the sufferer's depiction of himself in the Babylonian "I Will Praise the Lord of Wisdom" (*Ludlul bēl nēmeqi* 2.93): "My bones look separated [Lambert: "have come apart"] and are covered [only] with my skin" (*ANET*, 598a; W. G. Lambert, *Babylonian Wisdom Literature* [Oxford: Clarendon, 1960] 44–45), or where the skin shrivels over one's bones (Lam 4:8); for the "gauntness" of emaciation, cf. Job 16:8; Ps 109:24. Different again is the image of bones being "burned" (with heat, Job 30:30; like a hearth, Ps 102:4 [3]; with fire sent from above, Lam 1:13; with a fire shut up in them, Jer 20:9), which is probably an image of pain rather than of fever. Different yet again is the idea of bones being "dried up" (Ezek 37:11; and cf. the whole chapter on the "dry bones"), as distinct from being "full of vigor" (Job 20:11), their marrow moist (21:24), the bones in that sense being "fat" (Prov 16:30) and thus healthy.

This review of the metaphorical network related to "bones" enables us to suggest, as against all commentators, that Job is not referring to any specific physical malady here. Such should already have been evident from the juxtaposition with the phrase "the skin of my teeth," which can hardly be taken literally. We have already noted several places where language about the physical body is metaphorical for a mental state; no one, for example, imagines that 16:13 means that Job suffered from a ruptured gall bladder, though many suppose that 16:16 means that his face was literally red from weeping. We have argued that such language is primarily metaphorical of a psychic reality, and the same may be suggested here. The collapse of his bones is not a physical symptom of his disease, but the expression of the overpowering sense of weakness and being worn out that has surfaced in the poetry on many occasions (6:12–13; 13:25, 28; 16:7–8; 17:7).

This explains how the present verse is related to the preceding verses. The absence of his friends and relations and the deprivation of human intimacy have not of course induced some recurrence of his malady, but have weakened his spirit and sapped his vigor. The psychic sense of isolation has been experienced as an interior loss of structure; he has "collapsed in a heap," as we say. Perhaps not surprisingly the psalmist of Ps 102:6 [5] who also has his bones clinging to his flesh has had the same experience of abandonment as Job; he is like a desert owl, like a sparrow alone on the housetop (7–8 [6–7] NAB). The parallel shows that the language is conventional, not freshly minted to express Job's particular physical distress.

The above interpretation solves the first three difficulties mentioned at the beginning of this *Comment*. First, there is no sudden break from the theme of abandonment to the theme of his malady; v 20 is his *psychic*, not physical, reaction to the experience of desertion. Second, the problem of the verb "cleave" has been solved. Third, the question of the overlong first half of the line can be settled. The present interpretation, like no other, makes sense both of "flesh" and "skin," since it is essentially the same image to have the bones supported by the "flesh" or by the "skin." That is not to say that both nouns belonged in the poet's text, but it explains why one has been added to a half-line that presumably had only one of them originally. Since it is "flesh" and not "skin" in the parallel Ps 102:6 [5], "skin" is the term that should probably be deleted here.

The remaining difficulties concern "escaping" and "by the skin of my teeth." The only thing that Job has "escaped" from (מלט hithp) is what he has not yet suffered, death. If the phrase is to have any meaning remotely parallel to "my bones hang on my skin and flesh," i.e., that he feels deprived of vigor, it must mean that the "escape" is not worth having, that it is no real escape at all (as distinct from the common English usage of the phrase, in which it refers to a genuine though narrow escape). He means that he has been delivered from death but in such a state that he might as well be dead. The "escaping" is thus ironic, it is no more an escape than a Pyrrhic victory is a victory; it is not "I have lost everything, but I have escaped alive" (Terrien), but rather "The only escape I have achieved is to have lost everything." In being delivered "with" (not "by," RSV, NIV) the skin of his teeth, he has no skin left on him except the skin on his teeth (which of course does not exist, as Janzen also recognizes), for he has been flayed alive, the skin of his body stripped off; the image is used in Mic 3:3 of tyrannical rulers who like butchers "flay" (פשט) or "tear off" (גזל) the skin from the bodies of the people (Wyclif has the phrase, "Thus, as god seiþ of tyrauntis, þei taken here skyn fro þe bak, & eten & drynkyn mennus blood" ["Of Prelates," chap. 9, *The English Works of Wyclif* [London: Trübner and Co., 1880] 73). In English to "flay alive (or, quick)" is the punishment of beating so that the skin is damaged and so stripped off (first attested in Leyland, c. 1205), but here the image is more probably that of Mic 3:2–3, where the images of the wild animal, the butcher, and the cook all contribute to the metaphor of flaying. Job's existence is a living death, not of course in the present context primarily because of his physical suffering, but because of his sense of abandonment. Other interpretations of the verse are catalogued in n. 19:20.a.

21–22 A strikingly new note is sounded here, "a strain we have not heard previously" (Delitzsch), when Job calls upon his friends to "pity" (חנן) him.

He has never before asked for their pity. Indeed, having berated them for their treachery (6:15), their callousness (6:27), their stupidity (12:2–3; 13:2), their worthlessness (13:4), their lies (13:7), their partisanship (13:7–9), their torture (16:2), and their attempts to destroy him (19:2), having done everything wrong if he had been trying to win friends and influence people, it is truly amazing that he should suddenly fall into a supplicative mood, and that for only two verses, to be followed shortly by as aggressive an address to the friends as we have heard (vv 28–29). (6:28–29 is not such an appeal; see *Comment*.)

Gray's comment is typical of how this change of mood is viewed by most: "Ruthlessly assailed by God and abandoned by other men, even those nearest to him, Job, yearning for some support, appeals to the compassion of the three friends who, unlike others, were at least physically still near him: for the moment all thought of argument is abandoned; he no longer seeks to convince them, or asks them to be just to him; he asks them to be *kind*." This seems so out of character for Job that our first inclination must be to wonder whether these words can indeed be addressed to the three friends of the dialogue. The preceding verses, from v 13, have depicted his rejection by every category of friend and relation, and it is at first attractive to find him here begging *them* to restore him to their intimacy (cf. 17:10 for another place where "you" does not refer to the three friends). But in fact it cannot be those acquaintances of vv 13–19, for they have done nothing that could be called "persecution" (רדף); there is an attachment of a kind between persecutors and their victims, but from his acquaintances Job has experienced not even that kind of interest, but rather a silent ostracism. What is more, "persecution" is explicitly attributed to the three friends—only they can be meant—in v 28. These three are the רעים "friends," a term not used in vv 13–19 of his other acquaintances and relatives, but used of his three interlocutors in 2:11; 32:3; 35:4; 42:7, 10 (which is to say, however, only in the prose and once in a speech of Elihu).

Given that it is his conversation partners that he addresses, what does Job mean? Habel is the only other commentator to feel unable to take Job's cry for "pity" at its face value; he finds Job's words ironic: "Job's appeal to his friends to exhibit compassion is a sharp sarcastic barb . . . . With tongue in cheek, Job solicits their sympathy." There is indeed something ironic in making the reason for his appeal for pity the fact that "the hand of Eloah has struck me"; for it is precisely because they regard God as the origin of Job's suffering that the friends feel themselves justified in withholding their pity. But that is not to say that the appeal for pity is itself ironic. Our first step must be to recognize that "have mercy, take pity" does not ask for a mood of sympathy and compassion in the hearer so much as for an objective act of mercy or favor (cf. חנן in Gen 33:5; 2 Sam 12:22; Ps 102:14 [13]; 119:29). Job can hardly be asking his friends here to do him the favor of accepting his self-assessment as a righteous man (as against Fohrer), though that is of course his ultimate objective; the biggest favor he can believably ask of them now is to stop hounding him or persecuting him by continuing their speeches (so also H. J. Stoebe, *THWAT* 1:592). He does not want their pity so much as their silence. The repeated verb is indeed a depiction of the anguish of his soul (Duhm); cf. the repetition of the same verb in Ps 123:3, addressed to

God. And there is a poignancy in Job's use of this phrase in address to his friends when he has rejected the idea of begging God for mercy (9:14): to have done that would have been to abandon his claim for justice, and to have surrendered his integrity in the face of the overpowering might of God. He would be grateful for a small mercy from his friends, though, as he would have been for the mercy he begged from his servant (חנן again) for a normal human responsiveness (v 16). All the same, even if they were to stop their verbal persecution of him, which is all he asks here, his principal suffering would remain unhealed: he still suffers the pitiless ferocity of God's violence. This understanding of the cry for pity links up vv 21–22 with the opening lines of the speech (vv 2–3). It explains also why the reason for his appeal is that the hand of Eloah has "struck" him (נגע, as in 1:11, 19: 2:5; 4:5; 5:19; it has of course not been a mere "touch" [as RSV, NEB]), and that means there is no need for any humans to cause Job to suffer further. The "hand of God" means his might (cf. the Akk. phrase qāt ili "the hand of God," referring to illnesses), and cf. Ps 32:4; 39:11 [10]; 1 Sam 5:6; 6:3, 5, all in reference to illness (cf. A. S. van der Woude, THWAT 1:671). For God's hand as destructive or terrifying, cf. 6:9; 10:7; 13:21.

The persecution (רדף) of the righteous by the wicked is a familiar psalmic theme, suggesting sometimes verbal abuse, sometimes physical assault (Ps 7:2 [1], 6 [5]; 31:16 [15]; 35:3; 69:27 [26]; 71:11; 109:16; 119:84, 86, 157, 161; 142:7 [6]; 143:3; cf. Jer 15:15; 17:18; 20:11). Here we are at two removes from that conventionality, for first the role of the persecutor is transferred to God (as in 13:25 where he acts as an aggressor) and second to the friends, who become imitators of the savage God (they are not depicted as demons, as Fohrer thinks). They for their part by "telling it like it is" believe they are playing the role of avengers, like God pursuing his enemies with his tempest (Ps 83:16 [15]) or the Angel of the Lord pursuing the enemies of the righteous on a dark and slippery path (Ps 35:6); they would not resist the word "pursue" (see v 28), but whether or not they should be ashamed of themselves (cf. v 3) depends on the question of Job's innocence. He does not mean perhaps that they take upon themselves God's work and usurp a divine judicial authority (Delitzsch), or that at the moment when they believe themselves almost divine they become monsters (Terrien).

The last clause, "will you never have enough of my flesh?" (JB), could be simply a metaphor of wild beasts devouring an animal (so Gordis, Pope), but since animals do not "pursue," it is more likely that a second metaphorical meaning is superimposed. In Akkadian and Arabic the expression "to eat the pieces" of someone can mean to defame or accuse (cf. G. Gerleman, THWAT 1:140); in Dan 3:8; 6:25 [24] we have the phrase "to eat the pieces (קרצין) of" used in that sense in biblical Aramaic, and in Ps 27:2 "to eat the flesh of" may well mean "to slander" (so RSV, and cf. NJPS, though BDB and KB³ do not acknowledge this sense); Eccl 4:5 is more difficult. This would suit the present context perfectly because it is the friends' persistent denunciation of Job as a sinner that he cannot stand and that is the respect in which they are behaving like God. Not to be "satisfied with [his] flesh," as the Heb. runs literally, means that they cannot stop asserting his guilt—which is the exact point of his appeal for mercy in v 21, and the very issue uppermost in his reproaches of vv 2–3. It goes without saying that the more concrete image of being devoured is still visible. It goes too far to discern a "flesh" motif in this chapter (as Habel), since "flesh" means very different things in vv 20, 22, 26.

23–27 Job's forlorn hope is that his asseveration of innocence could be inscribed in some permanent medium that will last beyond his death; for he has no hope of vindication before his death, and while he believes that his protestation stands written into the heavenly record, that remains, deep down, only a metaphor. He would feel more secure that his case will some day be decided if he knew that his words were preserved imperishably on earth.

For whose eyes is his self-testimony to be written? Not primarily, perhaps not at all, for posterity—as though he cherishes a hope that a later generation will recognize his innocence despite the calumnies of his friends (against Fohrer, Terrien and others). There is only one person whose endorsement Job craves, for without God's declaration of his innocence no human assessment is worth anything. Job's thought here is no extraordinary and unparalleled leap of faith; his stance is no different from what it was in his previous speech: there he said that even now his declaration of innocence is present in heaven as his witness or advocate (16:19); his cry for vindication is his spokesman, and he awaits God's reply with sleepless anticipation (16:20). But he does not expect that he will see his vindication before his death, so he calls upon earth not to let his murder at God's hand go unavenged but rather to permit his blood to go on crying for his vindication (16:18). So also here: his declaration of innocence "lives" as his champion in heaven (v 25a), and his anxious (v 27c) desire is that he should "see" God enter the courtroom to judge his case while he is still alive (vv 26b–27). But he does not, frankly, expect that he will be vindicated before his death, so despite his conviction that he will "in the end" be adjudged innocent (v 25) he voices the wish that the record of his case should be committed to permanent writing (vv 23–24). The written words he here envisages would serve a similar function to the earth's refusal to cover up his murder in 16:18; earth and inscription alike would keep his cause alive.

The center of gravity in this strophe is therefore not the hopeless wish of vv 23–24, nor even the unshaken conviction that he will eventually find vindication even after his death, but the reiterated desire that "from [his] flesh," i.e., while he is still alive, he should come face to face with God, the two of them parties in a legal contest that will issue in Job's full vindication.

23 Job's wish for a record of his case that will outlast him is a forlorn hope, like all those wishes of his beginning with the phrase "O that . . ." (lit. "who will grant that . . . ?" מי־יתן; see Cox, 33–35); in 6:8–9 it introduced the wish that God would kill him as a sign of the futility of his existence; in 13:5 that his friends would keep their peace; in 14:13 that God would hide him in Sheol until his wrath was past; in 23:3 that he could discover where God is located so that he could argue his case personally with God; in 29:2 that he could be restored to his former life "as in the months of old," in 31:35 that he had a legal opponent who would respond to him (14:4 and 31:31 are different; the phrase is only used elsewhere in the book by Zophar at 11:5). It is of course not an impossible wish that his words should be "written," but he does not mean written on a scroll or on parchment (against, e.g., Peake, who thought he first wishes them written in a book, and then corrects himself by desiring a more permanent record); his vindication is likely to be so long delayed that his testimony to himself would need to take a more durable form.

So the meaning of the general term "write" (כתב) is specified by the terms "engrave" (חקק) and "cut" (חצב).

What are his words (מלין)? Not of course the words that immediately follow (vv 25–27) as if this were the high point of the book, an affirmation of faith (among other reasons, such an "inscription" could hardly begin with "and"), nor the Book of Job itself (contrast Strahan: "Yet how splendidly his idea has been realized! His singular fancy of a testimony 'in the rocks' could not be gratified, but he has his *apologia* . . . 'in a book' which is the masterpiece of Hebrew poetic genius"). The language throughout the strophe is judicial, and here too the "words" are Job's depositions that have been referred to in 13:3, 6, 13, 17, 18 and are stated more or less directly in 13:23–24.

The Heb. of v 23b could perhaps means "inscribed on a scroll" (cf. NIV; RSV "book") for ספר is the normal word for a document on leather or papyrus, and "inscribed" (חקק) is sometimes used for writing on such a medium (Isa 30:8, of writing "upon" [על] a ספר; Ezek 23:14, of paintings on a wall; though such examples may use the verb in a metaphorical sense). Such materials will hardly serve Job's requirement for a permanent record, however, and especially in view of the "iron" and "rock" of v 24 it is best to see here either a hard substance, copper (see n. 19:23.c), or a general term for an enduring record such as "on a stela" (Pope), "in an inscription" (NEB), "on some monument" (JB; cf. Gordis). The technology of KJV's "printed in a book" is a trifle anachronistic!

24 There is one composite image here, of an inscription being carved on a rock with an iron tool. The term עט "pen" is used of a reed pen or brush for writing with ink (Ps 45:1 [2]; Jer 8:8) but also of an iron stylus or chisel for use on stone (Jer 17:1, the sin of Judah is written with a "pen of iron"). It is more difficult to discover what the function of the "lead" is. Some have thought that the chisel was made of an alloy of iron and lead, but it is hard to believe that lead would improve the hardness of the iron. Dhorme thought that the alloy was used not for engraving as such but for marking the outline of the letters before the stone was cut; but a term for the chisel itself is much more likely to have been combined with the verb "engrave" (חצב). Others note the use of lead tablets in classical antiquity, μολύβδινοι χάρται or *tabulae plumbae* (cf. Josephus, *Apion* 1.307; Pausanias 9.31.4; Pliny, *Nat. Hist.* 13.669; Tacitus, *Ann.* 2.69) and also among the Hittites (G. R. Driver, *Semitic Writing* [new ed; London: OUP, 1976] 84 n.11, 241); but the text would have to be altered to read "with a pen of iron on lead" (so Moffatt, NIV) rather than "and lead." Such lead tablets were frequently used for curses (cf. A. Deissmann, *Light from the Ancient East* [tr. L. R. M. Strachan; London: Hodder and Stoughton, 1910] 304–5). There is wide support for the explanation first given by Rashi that the lead was used to fill in the incised letters (so too Dillmann, Delitzsch, Duhm). C. R. Conder ("Notes on Biblical Antiquities," *PEFQS* [1905] 155–58 [156]) thought the letters were painted with red lead paint after being incised, and referred to the case of the Phoenician inscription of the fifth century B.C. (now no. 15 in H. Donner and W. Röllig, *Kanaanäische und aramäische Inschriften* [Wiesbaden: Harrassowitz, 1962–64] 1:3; 2:23–24) on which the incised characters were painted red (according to M. Lidzbarski, *Ephemeris für semitische Epigraphik* [Giessen: Töpelmann, 1908] 49). Only one example of this technique, however, is known: in the inscription of Darius at Behistun (text and translation: R. G. Kent, *Old Persian* [New Haven: American Oriental Society, 1953] 116–34) the names of the king in the small inscription above the king's head were formerly inlaid with lead in the cuneiform signs, presumably so that the names might sparkle in the sunlight (E. Weidner, "Ausgrabungen und Forschungsreisen," *AfO* 15 [1945–51] 146–50 [147]; J. J. Stamm, "Zu Hiob 19,24," *ZAW* 65 [1953] 302; Galling, *WO* 2 [1954–59] 3–6). De Wilde even suggests that the poet of Job had Darius' Behistun inscription in mind; but since the inscription is located more than 200 feet higher than the road that passes it and only the king's names appear to have been treated in this way, it seems more than doubtful that the facts about this particular inscription would have been well known. If such a practice existed, however, it would perhaps provide the most plausible interpretation of the verse (so NEB "cut with an iron tool and filled with lead"). For a suggested emendation, see n. 19:24.a.

Whatever may be the precise technology of inscribing Job's words, what is the background of the idea of having one's words inscribed at all? K. Galling has seen here a tomb inscription hewn in the rock and bearing not Job's name but his plea ("Die Grabinschrift Hiobs," *WO* 2 [1954–59] 3–6). But Job's plea for vindication is not addressed to casual passers-by but to God, and Weiser's proposal is more persuasive, that the votive inscription set up in a temple is the conceptual background of the image; cf. Ps 102:19 [18], where Yahweh's salvation is recorded (כתב) for a future generation. That is not to say that Job or the poet has a cultic setting in mind, for here the inscription is undoubtedly in the living rock, but that the image perhaps presupposes a concrete reality in which a person's words may be permanently on record in the presence of God. Even if in Israelite temples such votive inscriptions were nonexistent (as Richter argues), Ps 102:19 [18] presents a metaphorical construct on which we may lean. Richter himself thinks of written prayers from Egypt in which the individual begs a favorable decision at the last judgment (pp. 28, 90); but there of course we are not dealing with *engraved* inscriptions on stone. It remains possible that the concrete background is the ancient Near Eastern practice of engraving royal inscriptions (usually of a propagandistic nature) on cliffsides, as attested in Egypt, Syria, and Persia (cf. F. H. Weissbach, *Die Denkmäler und Inschriften an der Mündung des Nahr el-Kelb* [Wissenschaftliche Veröffentlichungen des Deutsch-Türkischen Denkmalschutz-Kommandos 6; Berlin: de Gruyter, 1922]; F. Sarre and E. Herzfeld, *Iranische Felsreliefs* [Berlin: Wasmuth, 1910]).

25–27 Basic to the interpretation here presented of these celebrated and much debated verses is a distinction between what Job *knows* or believes and what he *desires*. This is a distinction we have been able to discern throughout Job's speeches, and while it is theoretically possible that here he should break with what he has said previously and make a great leap of faith into the unknown, it is more convincing to read these words in the light of what we have already heard from him. What Job *knows*, or believes, is that God is his enemy (6:4; 10:8–14; 13:24; 16:7–14; 19:7–12), that he will never again see good (7:7), that he will soon be dead (7:21; 10:20; 16:22), that he will be murdered by God (12:15; 16:18), that though he is innocent of any wrong for which he could be suffering (6:10c, 29; 9:15, 17, 20, 21; 12:4; 13:18) he can have no hope of wresting vindication from God (9:2–3, 20, 28–33; 13:15; 19:7), and that his own innocence which is known to God even if unacknowledged by him is the one thing in which he can have confidence (13:16; 16:19–21). What Job *desires*, on the other hand, once he has overcome his initial desire to be put to death immediately (6:8–9) and his subsequent misgiving that all desire is simply futile (chaps. 9–10), is to enter into dispute with God (13:3, 22) in the hope of winning vindication before his death. Now that his protestation of innocence stands in the heavenly court as his witness, advocate, spokesman, and pledge, prepared to argue his case before God (16:19–20a, 21; 17:3), Job's only desire is that God should respond; his strongest positive desire has been expressed at 16:21: "sleeplessly I wait for God's reply."

Here, his desire is exactly the same: it is that he should "see" God as the respondent in his court case while he is still alive (lit. "from my flesh"). The next time he speaks of his desire, it will be in the same terms: he will wish that he knew where he could find God, that he could reach his judgment seat and lay his case before him so as to receive the vindication he deserves (23:3–7). The desire remains constant.

Here too, what he knows or believes is also of a piece with what he has said before and will say again, though what he says here makes an important advance. Hitherto he had never expressed any conviction that he would in the end be vindicated. Of course, his unquenchable desire for vindication and his engagement in legal controversy with God prove his confidence in the ineluctable rightness of his cause, but he has never yet said straight out that he "knows" that he will in the end receive his desire. Once he has decided to argue his case with God (13:3), he says strongly, "I know that I am in the right" (13:18). "This is what I take refuge in: a godless man does not approach him" (13:16). And he believes that his declaration of innocence will go on arguing his case before God as a man argues for his friend (16:21). But he never has said that he believes he will in the end be successful in his lawsuit: that is the breakthrough here. And that is what he still believes in chap. 23 too: "When he has tried me, I shall come forth as gold" (23:10). It is a breakthrough for him to voice that confidence, but it is not an entirely new idea, and it is not the same thing as a confidence that he will actually be publicly vindicated—how can he be after his death? It springs from his long-felt conviction of innocence, and it rests for its actualization entirely upon the truth of that conviction. He has no beliefs about any future act of salvation or mercy, only about an inevitable and ultimate recognition of his blamelessness. The person (if person it is) who declares him innocent is of less significance than the fact of his innocence which alone makes any such declaration possible.

Now to a closer look at the words. The opening "but" (*waw*) is of course contrastive with vv 23–24, but in what sense exactly? In vv 23–24 he wishes there could be a permanent record of his innocence on earth, but, no matter, quite apart from the fact that such would be difficult or impossible, it is unnecessary because there is an enduring witness to him in heaven. Job's phrase "I know" (ידעתי), usually in forensic contexts, means "I firmly believe," "I am convinced" (Habel). In 13:18 he "knows" that he is in the right, in 9:28 that God will not count him innocent, in 10:13 that God's purpose was to mark him down as a sinner, in 30:23 that God will bring him to death, in 42:2 that God can do everything, in 9:2 that God does not pervert justice or else that it is impossible to compel God to vindicate anyone (13:2 is different). It will be seen that the fact that Job "knows" something does not prove it is true. But these are all rather fundamental convictions of Job's, and we cannot forget when we hear next of the "champion" that "lives" that Job is equally convinced that God will not regard him as innocent, and that divine hostility is the story of Job's life.

Who then (or, what) is Job's "champion" (גאל *gō'ēl*, usually translated "redeemer"; Pope: "vindicator")? The *gō'ēl*, apparently a person's nearest relative at any particular time, whether brother, uncle, cousin, or some other kinsman, could have the responsibility of buying back family property so as to keep it in the family inheritance (Lev 25:25–34; Jer 32:6–15); redeeming a kinsman from slavery (Lev 25:47–54); marrying a widow to provide an heir for her dead husband (Ruth 3:12; 4:1–6); avenging the blood of a murdered relative (Num 35:12, 19–27; Deut 19:6, 11–12; Josh 20:2–5, 9; cf. 2 Sam 14:11). Nowhere is there legislation or narrative about the role of a *gō'ēl* in the lawsuit, though the application of the term to Yahweh in metaphorical legal contexts (Prov 23:11; Jer 50:34; Lam 3:58; Ps 119:154) suggests strongly that the *gō'ēl* would also be active on his kinsman's behalf there. See further, H. Ringgren, *TDOT* 2:350–55; A. R. Johnson, "The Primary Meaning of √גאל," *VTS* 1 (1953) 67–77; N. H. Snaith, "The Hebrew Root G'L (I)," *ALUOS* 3 (1961–62) 60–67 (65–67); E. Beaucamp, "Le goël de Jb 19,25," *LTP* 33 (1977) 309–10; J. J. Stamm, *THWAT* 1:383–94.

So who is Job's *gō'ēl* who "lives" and whose assistance will establish Job's innocence in the end? Hardly God, as Ringgren puts it succinctly: "Since the lawsuit here stands in the context of a dispute with God, it seems unlikely that God himself would appear as vindicator and legal attorney against himself, unless a very loose train of thought is to be assumed" (*TDOT* 2:355). In view of the similarities between this passage and 16:18–21, it seems certain that the *gō'ēl* here is the same as the "witness" (עד), the "advocate" (שהד), and the "spokesman" (מליץ) there. In that place, Job's "cry" (רע) is explicitly identified with his "spokesman" and so by implication with the "witness" and the "advocate." That is to say, there is no personal being in heaven to represent Job; only his cry, uttered in the direction of God, speaks on his behalf. If in chap. 16 his "cry" is personified as witness, advocate, and spokesman, it is perfectly intelligible, though it remains a bold metaphor, that it should here be called his "kinsman" or "champion" ("redeemer," as well as having inappropriately divine connotations, is in many contexts unsuitable for the functions of the *gō'ēl*). So this affirmation is nothing different from the asseveration of 16:19, "even now, behold, my witness is in heaven." Here indeed it is not said that Job's "kinsman" or "champion" is in heaven; it is a reasonable assumption, but it can only be inferred from the parallel in chap. 16, and perhaps from an implied contrast with the announcement of Job's vindication "on earth" in v 25b.

Why should Job here call his deposition of character (which is the content of his "cry") his *gō'ēl*, when in chap. 16 he had used more exclusively legal terms? The reason is plain from the context. This is the chapter in which he has most extensively elaborated his desertion by his relatives and acquaintances (vv 13–19). Not one of them wants anything to do with him, and he is bereft of any personal *gō'ēl* who might defend his cause. God is his enemy, so he has no one to rely on except himself. He has to be his own *gō'ēl* just as in

17:3 he had to be his own surety. Indeed, he objectifies his protestation of innocence into an entity that has something of an existence of its own and now dwells in the heavenly realm where there is a better chance of encounter with God. But that is no more than an image for the fact that Job himself has spoken, has challenged God to a lawsuit, and has presented his own affidavit of innocence. This remains a fact, whatever happens to Job himself; his words cannot be unspoken, and they indeed go on speaking for him as his kinsman-champion.

Why, next, should Job use such personal language in saying that his cry "lives"? We note first that the adjective "live" (חי) and the verb "to live" (חיה) are not used exclusively of animate beings, though of course that is the most normal sense. Water is often called "living" (Gen 26:19; Lev 14:5, 6, 51, 52; 15:3; Num 19:17; Cant 4:15; Jer 2:13; 17:13; Zech 14:8), as is "raw" meat (1 Sam 2:15); God's "work" can be "made to live" (Hab 3:2), as can the stones of a city (Neh 3:34 [4:2]) or a city generally (1 Chr 11:8) or grain (Hos 14:8 [7]). But that is not wholly relevant, for it is not a special use of "lives" here; for Job's cry is personified as a living being, a kinsman-champion, and it is entirely appropriate to say that a kinsman "lives." The real reason for the presence of the term "lives" is Job's conviction that he himself will soon be dead (cf. v 10; so also Gray) and that to have any chance of being vindicated he needs some testimony to himself to survive his death. Furthermore, "lives" is more than "exists" (יש); it points to the champion as ready to act on Job's behalf. There is, incidentally, an Ugaritic line in which El says, "I know (yd‘) that mightiest Baal lives (ḥy), that the prince lord of earth exists" (CTA 6.3.8–9 [Gibson, 76–77]). There is here a surface similarity to our text, and it is quoted by most recent commentators, but no one has shown any relevance it may have to the interpretation of Job.

In the next clause it seems clear that legal language is being used. Job's "champion" will be the "last" to "rise" (cf. NEB "he will rise last to speak in court," following G. R. Driver, "Problems of the Hebrew Text and Language: I. Scenes in Court," Alttestamentliche Studien: Friedrich Nötscher . . . gewidmet [BBB 1; ed. H. Junker and J. Botterweck; Bonn: Hanstein, 1950] 46–61 [46–47]). The "last" (אחרון) to rise in a lawsuit is presumably the winner of the dispute; we have no real parallels to this usage, and it is true that in the dispute with God in this book, it is Job himself who literally has the last word (42:2–6). But if we have rightly assumed that the procedure of the rîb was for the two disputants to keep arguing until one conceded the case of the other, clearly the concluding speech of concession is not the "last" substantive argument, and if it is the "final" speaker (like God in Job) who wins the day, Job here believes that it will be *his* defense counsel who will have the last word. The verb "rise" (קום) is quite well attested in a legal setting: in 16:8 Job's leanness "rises up" as a witness against him (of false witnesses in Ps 27:12; 35:11; Deut 19:16; of a judge in Ps 76:10 [9]; 94:16; and perhaps in Job 31:14; Isa 2:19). "Upon dust" (על־עפר) is more difficult: it could perhaps mean Job's dust, the dust where he lies (as in 7:21; 17:16; cf. 20:11; 21:26; so Duhm; and Janzen: "a graphic reference to Job-gone-to-dust"), but it is more likely to mean "on earth" (cf. "upon dust" in 41:25 [33] where there is none "on earth" that can be compared to Leviathan; and cf. 28:2; 30:6 for "dust" equivalent to "earth").

Does Job indeed believe that he will be vindicated? He believes that his defense counsel will have the last word, that he will win his case, but does he trust God to do anything about carrying that vindication into effect? And what form does he imagine a postmortem vindication can take, for if he is dead and his children too, and his property remains destroyed, how will anyone be able to believe that Job was an innocent man after all, even if God were to broadcast it from the whirlwind? "Vindication after his death would be a meager and bitter comfort" (J. K. Zink, "Impatient Job: An Interpretation of Job 19:25–27," *JBL* 84 [1965] 147–52 [151]), too little and too late. So is this certitude of Job's all rather nugatory? No, but only if we recognize that it is much more a conviction that he is innocent than a conviction that he will really be vindicated. And certainly, vindication *in heaven* is not Job's aim. Though God must be the one to testify to Job's innocence, it is "on earth" among the company of humans that Job's righteousness must be acknowledged if vindication is to be worth anything; for it is in the eyes of humankind that he has been defamed, by God.

The next clause is almost certainly corrupt, lit. "and after my skin (masc.) they have stripped off (or, beaten; or, cut down) this (fem.)." The verb נִקְּפוּ occurs elsewhere only at Isa 10:34 where it refers to cutting down (? or trimming) thickets in a forest and the derived noun נֹקֶף only at Isa 17:6; 24:13 where it refers to the shaking of olives from an olive tree; KB³ suggests "flay" for our passage. The subject here must be "persons unknown," equivalent to a passive (GKC, § 144g). "This" (fem.) is mysterious; it can hardly mean "thus" (though 33:12 provides a partial analogy); but a simple emendation to כָּזֹאת, "thus," yields a reasonably satisfactory, though not secure, sense: "even after my skin has been thus flayed from me" (cf. NJPS "after my skin will have been peeled off"; RSV "and after my skin has been thus destroyed"; similarly NIV; Pope: "flayed"). If he regards his disease as consuming his skin, by the spread of sores over the skin, it is natural enough to call this a "stripping off" or "flaying" of the skin (cf. the language of 7:5; 30:30). He may, however, be referring to the destruction of the skin (standing for the whole body) in the grave; in which case the KJV "worms destroy this body" may not be so far from the mark, though the Heb. has no word for "worms." However we understand the details of the clause, it fairly clearly indicates that Job expects his case to be resolved only after his death.

In sharp contrast to Job's *expectation* is his *desire:* he wants to see his name cleared while he is still alive. "From my flesh" (מִבְּשָׂרִי) is by anyone's reckoning a rather strange way of saying "while I am still alive"; but the only alternative meaning, "without my flesh" (RSVmg), i.e., after my death, not only contradicts Job's frequently expressed desire but raises the problem of how Job can "see" if he has no body. The "imperfect" verb אֶחֱזֶה, conventionally translated "I shall see," should be taken either as a modal imperfect (GKC, § 107m–n) or as a cohortative (GKC, § 48b–e), expressing a will or desire rather than a simple prediction, "my desire is to see God." Thus NJPS "But I would behold God while still in my flesh"; similarly Zink, *JBL* 84 (1965) 149; Tur-Sinai: "I want to see [my] God"; Habel: "I would behold Eloah"; Fohrer: "I would see God" (v 27; but v 26: "I will see God"). Job has nowhere previously said in so many words that he wants to "see" God, but at many points his language has implied a yearning for face to face converse: so, for example, his desire to come to trial with him (9:32), his regret that there is no arbitrator who could lay his hands on both Job and God (9:33), his wish to speak to the Almighty (13:3), and especially his ambition to defend his behavior "to [God's] face" (13:15), his promise not to hide himself "from [God's] face" (13:20), and his complaint that God "hides [his] face" (13:24). Now that he has come out with the unambiguous word "see" (חזה), he can say it again more openly and expansively in chap. 23 where he wishes he could find the way to God's "seat" (23:3) and bemoans the fact that he cannot perceive (בין), see (חזה), or behold (ראה) God; such, however, is his desire. The metaphor of the lawsuit is entirely sufficient to account for this language of "seeing" God (it is not a question of a theophany, as Fohrer; A. Jepsen, *TDOT* 4:289); but it is not irrelevant that despite the widespread belief in the danger of seeing God (Exod 33:20; Judg 13:22) some OT passages speak of it as a desirable occurrence (e.g., Ps 11:7, where the upright see his face; 17:15; 63:3 [2]; cf. also Exod 24:10).

The next line says in the most emphatic manner that it is with God that he desires to treat (we note "I" emphatic, "for myself," "my eyes," and "no stranger"). Even if the "kinsman-champion" were a personal being, and not, as argued here, simply the personification of Job's plea, such a being fades immediately into the background. The champion has no significance in himself, but functions only to keep Job's cause alive before God. It has to be God's vindication if it is to be vindication at all. And of course if Job himself, and not someone else ("a stranger"), is to witness God vindicating him, Job himself has to be alive. So v 27a must belong to Job's desire of v 26b, not to his "belief" of vv 25–26a. A "stranger" (זר) means simply anyone else other than Job himself (cf. on v 15); all, including his family, have made themselves strangers to him.

Finally, v 27c somewhat enigmatically conveys the emotion with which this desire has been expressed. Andersen's despairing translation, "my kidneys have ended in my chest," shows the extent of the difficulty. But if we allow that the kidneys, as a most sensitive part of the anatomy (cf. on 16:13) and as the seat of the emotions and affections, stand for the feelings in general (Ps 73:21; Prov 23:16), that "come to an end" (כלה) means particularly to be exhausted by longing (as of the נפש, "soul, vitality" in Ps 84:3 [2]; 119:81), and that "in my chest, bosom" (חק) means simply "within me" (which is, admittedly, more commonly בקרבי, Jer 23:9; 1 Sam 25:37), Job means that he is emotionally exhausted, psychically drained, by the intensity of his feelings (cf. NAB "my inmost being is consumed with longing"). This is his prevailing experience, not "the profound dejection that follows the exaltation of the mystic experience" (R. Gordis, *The Book of God and Man: A Study of Job* [Chicago: University of Chicago, 1965] 207; cf. Janzen).

It needs perhaps to be said that the foregoing exegesis has proceeded on the basis of "the story so far," and has presented a reading "as if for the first time." A second reading, in which the end of the book is allowed to resonate here also, superimposes a new level of author's meaning above the meaning intended by the character Job. It is an irony, though not a bitter one, that Job's words have a meaning other than he intends. The truth is that, though he expects God would be the last person to vindicate him, God does indeed become his vindicator, and that on earth (42:10, 12). Job's desire to "see" God is fulfilled to the letter (42:5), and the knowledge and the desire of these verses, here so opposed to one another, are shown in the end to be identical. Job does not see his hope fulfilled, for he has no hope; but he sees his words, hopeless but desirous, fulfilled with unimaginable precision.

Up to this point in the exegesis, opposing interpretations have generally not been mentioned. For a review, see J. Speer, "Zur Exegese von Hiob 19,25–27," *ZAW* 25 (1905) 49–107; and cf. H. H. Rowley, "The Book of Job and Its Meaning," in *From Moses to Qumran: Studies in the Old Testament* (London: Lutterworth, 1963) 141–83 (180–81). Some of the most favored interpretations may now be outlined.

1. These verses have long been regarded as teaching a doctrine of the resurrection. The influential KJV translation of v 26, "And though after my skin worms destroy this body, yet in my flesh shall I see God," took its cue from Jerome's Vulgate: "For I know that my redeemer lives and that on the last day I will be raised from earth; and I will again be surrounded by my skin, and in my flesh I will see my God; whom I myself will see, and my eyes will behold, and not another; this hope is fixed in my breast." Already *1 Clement* 26.3 presents a similar exegesis, and similarly Origen, *Commentary on Matthew*, 17.29 (on Matt 22:23). For the history of interpretation see J. Speer, "Zur Exegese von Hiob 19,25–27," *ZAW* 25 (1905) 49–107; A. Hudal, "Die Auslegung von Job 19,25–27 in der katholischen Exegese," *Der Katholik* 95 (1916) 331–45; and earlier, H. P. C. Henke, *Narratio critica de interpretatione loci Jobi c. XIX vers. XXV–XXVII in antiqua ecclesia* (Helmstedt: Schnoor, 1783); G. L. Eyrich, *Tentamen historicum circa diversas de spe et expectantione quam Jobus 19,25 sibi facit opiniones et sententias* (Würzburg, 1791).

The idea that Job expresses a belief in a resurrection still finds its defenders (see a list in Lévêque, 480 n.10). E. J. Young, for instance, wrote of "this magnificent statement of a bodily resurrection" (*An Introduction to the Old Testament* [London; Tyndale, 1949] 317), and G. L. Archer would translate, "And from the vantage point of my flesh, I shall see God" (*A Survey of Old Testament Introduction* [Chicago: Moody, 1964] 449). Janzen too has recently offered an intelligent defense of the traditional view, arguing that only its perspective does justice to many conceptual and rhetorical details of the speeches. M. Dahood breathed somewhat spurious new life into this ancient interpretation by revocalizing מבשרי "from my flesh" as מְבֻשָּׂרִי (a pual participle with suffix), which he translated as "refleshed by him [I will gaze upon God]," a doctrine, he says, "of the creation of a new body for the afterlife" (*Psalms II*, 196). Surprisingly, Pope seems to be cautiously attracted by this philological curiosity. Without referring specifically to Dahood, Andersen notes the "much recent research that shows interest in the after-life as an ancient concern for Israelite faith," and finds here "the hope of a favorable meeting with God after death as a genuine human being," a hope, however, that "falls short of a full statement of faith in personal bodily resurrection."

A somewhat whimsical modulation of the resurrection view was advanced by Larcher (1957), followed somewhat by Terrien: Larcher thinks of a momentary and tailor-made resurrection at which Job will have his innocence recognized, and then presumably sink back into Sheol. Terrien too thinks that the Hebrew does not depict a disincarnated spirit, but a Job whose "personality, not for eternity but for the specific instant of his encounter with his creator, will be truly alive, endued with fleshly vitality . . . the same individual." Habel apparently has a similar idea: "Job is not proposing the idea of a universal resurrection, but the radical hope that he will see his divine adversary face to face, in person, 'from his flesh,' even if that seeing is a postmortem event . . . not in some visionary, mystical or metaphorical manner, but physically." Perhaps this is not so very different from Gray, who, however, does not use the term "physical": "There is still no belief here in a *continued* life of blessedness after death . . . in a moment after death it will be given to Job to know that he was not deluded in maintaining his integrity."

Against any view of bodily resurrection it need only be noted that it contradicts everything the book has said previously about the finality of death (7:9; 10:21; 14:10, 12) and, in case it should be argued that this is some kind of new revelation of an existence beyond death, it needs to be noted that it is totally ignored in the remainder of the book (cf. 21:23–26; 30:23). Among the early fathers, Chrysostom already refuted the resurrectionist interpretation by quoting 14:12 (*PG*, 57:396).

2. The currently prevailing view can probably be said to be that Job expects a postmortem encounter with God, but in a disembodied state (cf. RSV "without my flesh I shall see God," taking the מן as *min* privative). Thus Ewald: "the spirit of the deceased must behold its own justification . . . the idea of the indestructability of the spirit comes clearly out. . . . I shall behold . . . with spiritual eyes, not with my present ones." And Duhm: "Job will rise from the earth as a spirit, rather like Samuel (1 Sam 28)." So too Dillman, Lamparter, and Weiser, the last of whom writes that for Job the fact of his sight of God after his death is more important than its manner. "It is the faith that does not see and yet believes." G. Hölscher attempted to answer the question of how an Israelite could be conceived as "seeing" after his death by referring to *Jub.* 23.19–31 where the bones of the just rest in the earth but they nevertheless "see" that God is repelling their enemies ("Hiob 19,25–27 und Jubil 23,30–31," *ZAW* 53 [1935] 277–83; see too G. J. Streeder, "G. Hölschers Exegese von Job 19,25–27," *NTT* 22 [1939] 98–104). For Hölscher, death in Job is represented as a kind of sleep (3:13–18; 14:12) in which the dead have no knowledge of their descendants on earth but nevertheless have a certain capacity to know and to feel. It is easy to see, however, that the text in *Jubilees* hangs on a more developed idea of an afterlife than appears anywhere in Job, and it may be supposed that the idea of encountering God in a postmortem existence would have seemed less than plausible to Job.

3. A third approach is to see the restoration of Job as something that is to happen before his death. C. J. Lindblom, for example, thought Job was here envisaging simply his healing and return to prosperity ("'Ich weiss, dass mein Erlöser lebt': Zum Verständnis der Stelle Hi 19,25–27," *Studia Theologica* (Riga) [1940] 65–77. Similarly Ball: "the God of righteous Retribution will appear to right his lamentable wrongs in the present life, before his disease has run its fatal course." Fohrer seems to adhere to this view, regarding "without my flesh" as an indication simply of Job's emaciation (T. J. Meek: of the putrefaction of his flesh by his disease ["Job xix 25–27," *VT* 6 (1956) 100–103]).

The difficulty here is that is is entirely inappropriate to suppose that Job "knows" that this will be his lot. And if he "knows" that he will be restored before his death, he has no reason still to contemplate death (as in 23:17). Fohrer indeed refers to a restoration as "Job's hope and wish" (p. 320), but in his translation (p. 307) he has Job "know" it—and that is a far different matter.

All the interpretations mentioned above have assumed that the "redeemer" (gō'ēl) is God. So, e.g., Duhm, Driver-Gray, Dhorme, Rowley, de Wilde. Among the arguments that have been adduced for this view, which Habel has lucidly analyzed (and convincingly refuted, pp. 305–6) are the following: (a) The gō'ēl Job expects to rise on his behalf must be the same figure as the God he expects to see; (b) In the Psalms and Isa 40–66, especially, God is invoked as the gō'ēl of the afflicted (e.g., Ps 78:35; Isa 49:7, 26; so Dhorme, Lévêque, 479); (c) The "uncompromising monotheism" of the book prevents the supposition of an intermediary "kinsman" between God and Job (Gordis); (d) "The Last" (אחרון) is to be understood as a title for God, "the Ultimate," as in Isa 44:6; 48:12 (Dahood, *Bib* 52 [1971] 346). Against these points it can be argued: (a) The God whom Job describes throughout the book has not been acting as his "witness" or "kinsman"; and the "witness" of 16:19–20 is very clearly winning justice for Job *from* God; (b) The allusions elsewhere to God as Redeemer are beside the point; "the context here is forensic, not cultic, and the need is for deliverance from God, not by God" (Habel); (c) It may not indeed be necessary to postulate an intermediary between God and Job if the view taken in this commentary is accepted, that it is Job's own cry that is his spokesman and kinsman; (d) There is no reason to suppose that "the Last" was a standard OT title for God.

The major argument against identifying God as the gō'ēl is that "it would mean a complete reversal in the pattern of Job's thought. . . . Job has portrayed God consistently as his attacker not his defender, his enemy not his friend, his adversary at law not his advocate, his hunter not his healer, his spy not his savior, an intimidating terror not an impartial judge" (Habel). At the very end of his speeches he is still calling God "my adversary" (31:35).

Habel, for his part, follows the line taken by S. Mowinckel ("Hiobs gō'ēl und Zeuge im Himmel," *BZAW* 41 [1925] 207–12) and W. A. Irwin ("Job's Redeemer," *JBL* 81 [1962] 217–29; cf. also T. J. Meek, "Job xix 25–27," *VT* 6 [1956] 100–103; E. G. Kraeling, *The Book of the Ways of God* [London: SPCK, 1938] 89; Terrien, Pope), that the gō'ēl is a heavenly being, not perhaps like a personal god in Babylonian religion (Pope) but, more to the point, a defense attorney who is a counterpart of the Satan. Elihu certainly envisages the existence of a mediator "angel" (מלאך), a "spokesman" (מליץ, as in 16:20), who can appeal to God for the healing of a person (33:23–25) or, according to Habel, can vouch for his righteousness (cf. also Zech 3:1–5; Gen 48:16). But Elihu's view is not necessarily Job's: Eliphaz has denied that there is any angel who will take up Job's case (5:1), and Job himself has regretted (in a wish contrary to fact) that there is no intermediary between himself and God (9:33). Especially in view of the exegesis of 16:19–20, it is better to see Job's champion not as some heavenly being but as his own declaration of innocence.

Most of the implausible interpretations reviewed here are swept away by the recognition (i) that there is a contrast between what Job *believes* will happen (his death before vindication, but vindication thereafter) and what he *wishes* would happen (a face to face encounter with God this side of death); and (ii) that what pleads for Job in the heavenly realm is nothing but his own protestation of innocence.

Given such a plethora of interpretations of the words as they stand, more or less, conjectural emendations of the text seem *de trop;* but the evident obscurity and almost certainly corrupt nature of the text invites them, and a selection of the more suggestive—and of the more bizarre—is reviewed in the *Notes.* When the result is obviously in contradiction to the exegesis here presented, the objections to the emendations have not usually been repeated.

28–29 The closing sentences addressed to the friends are, at first blush, exceedingly curious both for their tone and their content (some find them more or less unintelligible; a "jumble of verbiage," says Pope). After the note of exalted confidence in vv 25–27—as many see it—it is surprising to hear this sharp and supercilious tone here. Terrien, reminding himself that the Job of the dialogues is never the saint of the prologue and epilogue, nor the humble creature who prostrates himself before Yahweh (42:1–6), finds Job's attitude "faithful to the psychology of uncomprehended suffering," but not, admittedly, satisfactory morally or theologically. As for the content, it is at first astonishing to find Job asserting that there is a judgment that punishes wrongdoing; Pope not unreasonably feels that v 29 "appears to smack of the argument of the friends rather than of Job." There is the further oddity that in every one of his previous speeches Job has concluded on the note of death and Sheol (3:20–26; 7:21b; 9:18–22; 14:20–22; 17:13–16).

A close attention to Job's words and to their context will, however, dispel most of the surprises. First, we recollect that the keynote of vv 25–27 has not been Job's unconditioned hope in God or his expectation of a beatific vision, but rather a reiterated conviction of the rightness of his cause and the impatient desire to confront God with the wrongs Job believes God has done him. The note of exasperation here in vv 28–29 is not so very far from the note of self-assured impatience in vv 25–27.

Second, the term "persecute, pursue" (רדף) carries a lot of freight. As was noted on vv 21–22 above, the word is applied to the friends in this speech as imitators of the savagery of God, while in the background lies the thought that typically those who "pursue" the righteous are themselves the wicked. Those who "pursue" have to be very sure of their ground, for *prima facie* they declare themselves criminals in so doing, and even if they can claim that they are siding with God and carrying out his vengeance for him, that will hardly earn them a certificate of blamelessness from a man who has been experiencing only the cruelty of God.

What does "persecution" of Job by the friends mean, concretely? Since they are obviously not offering him physical violence, it can only be their false accusation that he refers to (see again on vv 21–22). They have each in turn made their accusation, and here Job warns them (as he begged them in vv 21–22) to leave off the repetition of this false testimony, and so do themselves, as well as him, a favor. So these verses become intelligible as the peroration of the speech, inviting the friends to desist from further talk, warning them that they are putting themselves into the role of wrongdoers (false witnesses against the innocent) by so doing, and reminding them that they cannot hope to escape punishment if they insist on playing this part.

The false accusation is: "The root of the matter lies in him," i.e., Job is the cause of his own suffering; the persecution of v 28a consists of making the judgment of v 28b. The truth is, as Job has said in this very speech, that "it is God who has put [him] in the wrong" (v 6). That was the climax of the exordium addressed to the friends (vv 2–6), and to that issue the speech now returns at its close.

The "anger" (חמה) must here be the friends' own anger (not God's, as in 21:20) expressed in their hostile "persecution" of Job. We have already heard from Eliphaz how "anger" (כעש) can kill (5:2), but here it is rather different: the anger that persecutes an innocent man is a capital offense (the phrase "crime of the sword" [עונות חרב] must be modeled on חטא־מות, "sin worthy of death" [Deut 22:26]; cf. [עון פלילים] עון פלילים "sin deserving judgment," lit. "of judges" [Job 31:11, 28]). No doubt this is not literally true about anger, though we recall that bearing false witness against one's "neighbor" (or "friend," רע) is prohibited by the ten commandments, which perhaps carry the death penalty (A. Phillips, *Ancient Israel's Criminal Law* [Oxford: Blackwell, 1970] 23–27), and curses were often laid upon potential witnesses to ensure that the truth was spoken (Prov 29:24; Judg 17:2; cf. also Prov 14:25; 19:5, 9; 21:28). To pursue their line of argument against Job is a risky business; if they knew what they were doing they would fear for their lives. Once we have read to the end of the book we will know from what other quarter "anger" can prove the friends' undoing; for at 42:7 Yahweh's "wrath" (אף) is kindled against the friends and needs to be averted. But here, even though Job believes that he will in the end be proved to be the innocent one (v 25), he does not yet go so far as to imagine that the divine wrath under which he has been laboring will come to light upon the friends.

The last clause is the most difficult, lit. "so that you may know that there is a judgment" (on the last word see n. 29.f). The syntax seems strange; how could they "fear" to argue with Job "in order that" (למען) they should know that judgment may overtake them? Is it not rather the other way round: they should recognize that there is a judgment "in order that" they may be afraid to persecute Job? BDB notes, however, that sometimes (though this passage is not mentioned) "in rhetorical passages, the issue of a line of action, though really undesigned, is represented by it ironically as if it were designed" (cf. Isa 30:1; 44:9; Jer 7:18; 27:10, where RSV finds it necessary to translate למען as "with the result that"). So too here NEB and NIV have "then you will know," since the syntax is hard to convey.

More troublesome is Job's appeal to a belief about vengeance or retribution, since we have come to recognize how fundamentally unrealistic he believes the doctrine of retribution to be. He has yet to protest that "times of judgment" and assize days are not kept by the Almighty (24:1), but we have already heard him complain that "blameless and wicked alike [God] brings to an end," that he "mocks at the calamity of the innocent" and that he "blindfolds [the] judges" (9:23–24). Job's position on the moral universe is, however, actually quite finely nuanced. In 9:23–24, for example, there is no categorical rejection of the idea of moral order but a protest against a recurrent refusal of God to act in accord with his own norms, and the last line, "If it is not he, then who is it?" contains enough of a trace of self-doubt to make us realize that we are hearing a cry of grief rather than a settled philosophy. In 13:7–11, a passage even closer in theme to the present, Job assumes that partiality on the friends' side will inevitably lead to their punishment—even at the moment when he is calling God to account for the way *he* has treated Job! Here too, in chap. 19, he has expressed the strongest conviction that right will prevail in the end, even if he never lives to see it. So he does not believe that God is fundamentally unjust and that evil will always win; but he has had too bad an experience of God to have more faith in God than he has in himself. This conviction that the friends stand to suffer if they go on "persecuting" him is of the same stuff as his conviction that his "champion" lives: it is God who in the end would have to be moved by the appeals of Job's champion or by the wickedness of the friends, but justice for the future lies more in the respective merits of the cases than in the person of God himself.

Explanation

Still in the waiting room between issuing the summons and having his case called, Job has time for reflection on the significance of what he has done and where he now stands. There is plenty of feeling here, but it is not the raw uncensored cry we have earlier overheard. Now it manifests itself in a more ordered exploration of what has happened to him at God's hand and at his friends' hands; it is a more structured statement too of what he wants and what he expects.

Matching this lowered level of intensity is the fact that here for the first time since his opening soliloquy (chap. 3) Job does not address God; nor will he do so again until his closing speech (30:20–23). All that he says is still for God's ears, of course; but since his formal indictment of God in chap. 13 he has no new matter to lay before God, for it is God's turn to respond. Even his most vivid depictions of God's violence against him are cast in the third person (vv 6b–12); they are not now cries of protest directed at his assailant, but the accumulation of evidence that confirms the wrongfulness of his suffering.

As God becomes less present in the speech, the friends' presence imposes itself more strongly. It is a distinctive of this speech that the friends are addressed directly at the beginning, middle, and end, and the whole matter of the speech can be read as supportive and elaborative of what Job requires of the friends. What he wants of them, in short, is to cease their speeches against his innocence. Reflection on the point he has reached in his lawsuit has convinced him ever more strongly that he stands or falls before God solely on the question of his innocence; that the friends should go on assuming and arguing his guilt is now not only in bad taste but otiose. "Ten times now" they have "tried to humiliate" him (v 3), but the time has come when they must "understand" that it is God who has "put him in the wrong" (v 6a), that the "root of the trouble" lies not in Job but in God (v 28b). Were they to understand that, they would cease their speaking altogether, for every word they utter is built on the premise of Job's guilt. Their attempts to "pursue" Job (vv 22, 28), to "torment" and "crush" him (v 2), to "humiliate" and "abuse" him (v 3), run up against the rock of his inalienable innocence, and by maintaining their stand they are doing themselves as great an injury as they would do him; for they have made themselves into false witnesses who should themselves stand in fear of judgment (v 29) if they knew what was good for them. To cease their accusations against Job would be to do themselves a favor at the same time as sparing Job (vv 21–22).

The more powerful parts of Job's speech function as evidence in Job's battle with the friends. While, first, vv 7–20 can be read as depictions of his painful experience or as accusations against its author—and such they no doubt are—their textual placement makes them even more definitively part of the argument with the friends. For the stream of images of God's violence in vv 7–12 exists as an amplification of the general statement, "it is God who has put me in the wrong," which is directed to the friends as the substance of what they must "understand" (v 6). Vv 7–12 are not a case of Job licking his wounds nor of him yet again reproaching God for them, but of Job defending his innocence to the friends by fastening upon God the blame for what is *prima facie* evidence of his guilt. This reading is confirmed by the introduction of the "siegework" metaphor into v 6, which is strictly addressed to the friends; since the "siegework" imagery will occur again at v 12, the poet has created an envelope of vv 6b–12, the whole an elaboration of the headline, "it is God who has put me in the wrong."

Vv 13–20 are in their turn linked back into the preceding strophe by the first verb of v 13, "he has put far from me my kinsfolk"; this shows that the whole of the strophe vv 13–20 is to be understood logically as a pendant to vv 7–12, and, like those verses, an elaboration of the blameworthiness of God.

The last and most potent portion of the speech (vv 23–27) is for its part enclosed within two addresses to the friends (vv 21–22, 28–29; see under *Form /Structure/Setting* for the plan of these lines), as if to ensure that Job's wish, conviction, and desire of vv 23–27 will be read in the context of his debate with his friends. For reasons that the poet could not have anticipated, in the history of the transmission of his text and in the history of Christian doctrine, these verses have practically never been read in their designed context, but have been excised from their setting as a testimony to an erratic leap of faith into the unknown. In their context, the primary intellectual stress is on Job's innocence which, first, he is convinced will one day be recognized, second, he wishes for safety's sake could be engraved on the rock, but, third, he desires above all to be acknowledged here and now. The primary emotional emphasis lies on his desire, so intense that it exhausts him (v 27c), to encounter God face to face, not indeed for the sake of the beatific vision, but so as to confront God with his unanswered claim for justice. But these are not matters strictly between God and Job; sandwiched between the addresses to the friends, Job's words of vv 23–27—even though not perhaps envisaged as spoken directly to the friends—function for their sake especially. Job's conviction of his innocence is not a soliloquy uttered for the sake of keeping his spirits up, still less a long-wave broadcast to latter-day readers of his book, inaudible in the land of Uz but coming through loud and clear to believers in a resurrection. It is for the friends' benefit and to convince them of their wrongheadedness that he says, "I know that my champion lives"; and it is not for his own consolation but because they cannot believe that God could do anything but punish him that he affirms, "To behold Eloah while still in my flesh—that is my desire."

From the dramatic point of view, there are two novelties in this speech that move forward the depiction of this ever-labile man, Job. The first, and perhaps the more important, certainly the most striking, is the closure of his speech not, as in every previous speech, with the theme of death, but with a vigorous and sarcastic reversal of the friends' aggression back toward themselves: "You should tremble at the sword yourselves" (v 29a). Waiting in the anteroom before the divine tribunal, Job has studied his own innocence until it has become not simply his plea and his defense but the redoubt from which he can assail his critics.

The second novelty lies in the expression of his conviction that his "champion lives." Understood not of God himself nor of some heavenly being but (as here) of Job's own protestations of innocence, this is not the cry of faith it has commonly been thought to be. Yet it *is* a cry of faith—of faith in himself, which is, in the circumstances, when his innocence is being denied by everyone, perhaps more an act of pure faith than the most reverent piety toward God. Job's conviction, "I know that my champion lives," is not the core of this speech, but it is among the boldest of his metaphors, exposing for the first time his complete assurance that even heaven must in the end accept that he is an innocent man undeservedly suffering.

Zophar's Second Speech (20:1–29)

Bibliography

Chajes, H. P. "Note lessicali a proposito della nuova edizione del Gesenius-Buhl." *Giornale della Società Asiatica Italiana* 19 (1906) 175–86. **Dahood, M.** "Some Northwest-Semitic Words in Job." *Bib* 38 (1957) 306–20. ———. "The Root עזב II in Job." *JBL* 78 (1959) 306–7. ———. "Northwest Semitic Philology and Job." *The Bible in Current Catholic Thought,* ed. J. L. McKenzie. New York: Herder and Herder, 1962. 55–74. **Delcor, M.** "De l'origine de quelques termes relatifs au vin en hébreu biblique et dans les langues voisines." *Actes du premier congrès international de linguistique sémitique et chamito-sémitique: Paris 16–19 juillet 1969,* ed. A. Caquot and D. Cohen. The Hague: Mouton, 1974. 228–30. **Driver, G. R.** "Hebrew Notes on the 'Wisdom of Jesus ben Sirach.'" *JBL* 53 (1934) 273–90. ———. "Hebrew Studies." *JRAS* (1948) 164–76. ———. "Glosses in the Hebrew Text of the Old Testament." *L'Ancien Testament et l'Orient: Etudes présentées aux VIᵉˢ Journées Bibliques de Louvain (11–13 septembre 1954).* Orientalia et Biblica Lovaniensia 1. Louvain: Publications Universitaires, 1957. 123–61. ———. "Problems in the Hebrew Text of Job." *VTSup* 3 (1955) 72–93. **Gordis, R.** "A Rhetorical Use of Interrogative Sentences in Biblical Hebrew." *AJSL* 49 (1933) 212–17. **Guillaume, A.** "The Arabic Background of the Book of Job." *Promise and Fulfilment: Essays Presented to Professor S. H. Hooke,* ed. F. F. Bruce. Edinburgh: T. & T. Clark, 1963. 106–27. ———. "Notes on the Roots ריע, ידע, and רעע in Hebrew." *JTS* ns 15 (1964) 293–95. **Holbert, J. C.** "'The skies will uncover his iniquity': Satire in the Second Speech of Zophar (Job xx)." *VT* 31 (1981) 171–79. **Joüon, P.** "Etudes de morphologie hébraïque." *Bib* 1 (1920) 353–71. **Kelly, B. H.** "Truth in Contradiction: A Study of Job 20 and 21." *Int* 15 (1961) 147–56. **Loretz, O.** "Hebräisch tjrwš und jrš in Mi 6,15 und Hi 20,15." *UF* 9 (1977) 353–54. **Pardee, D.** "*mᵉrôrät-pᵉtanîm* 'Venom' in Job 20:14." *ZAW* 91 (1979) 401–16. **Rabin, C.** "Eytmological Miscellanea." *ScrHieros* 8 (1961) 384–400. **Reider, J.** "Contributions to the Biblical Text." *HUCA* 24 (1952–53) 85–106. **Williamson, H. G. M.** "A Reconsideration of עזב II in Biblical Hebrew." *ZAW* 97 (1985) 74–85. **Winton Thomas, D.** "The Root ידע in Hebrew, II." *JTS* 36 (1935) 409–12. ———. "The Text of Jesaia II 6 and the Word שפק." *ZAW* 75 (1963) 88–90.

Translation

¹ *Then Zophar the Naamathite answered and said:*

² ᵃ *Truly,*ᵇ *my troubled thoughts compel me to give answer,*ᶜ
  because ᵈ *of the feeling* ᵉ *within me.*
³ *I have had to hear* ᵃ *a word of instruction* ᵇ *that defamed me;*
  but an impulse ᶜ *from my understanding* ᵈ *prompts my reply.* ᵉ

⁴ *Do you not* ᵃ *know that* ᵇ *since ancient times,*
  since man was first set ᶜ *on earth,*
⁵ *the triumph cry of the wicked has been of the briefest,*
  the rejoicing of the godless has lasted but a moment? ᵃ
⁶ *Though his height* ᵃ *may reach the heavens,*
  his head touching the clouds,
⁷ *he perishes forever like his fire-fuel,* ᵃ
  and those who once saw him say, "Where is he now?"

⁸*Like a dream he takes wing and will never be found,*ᵃ
   *banished*ᵇ *like a vision of the night.*
⁹ᵃ*The eye that saw him will glimpse*ᵇ *him no more;*
   *his dwelling will not again behold*ᶜ *him.*
¹⁰ᵃ*[His children must beg*ᵇ *the poor for mercy,*
   *when his hands have relinquished their strength.]*ᵃ
¹¹*Youthful vigor may fill his bones,*
   *but it*ᵃ *lies down in the dust with him.*

¹²*Though evil tastes sweet in his mouth*
   and he rolls it under his tongue,
¹³*loath to let it go,*
   making it linger on his palate,
¹⁴*yet it turns sour*ᵃ *in his stomach;*
   it is the venom of asps that is within him.
¹⁵ᵃ*The wealth he swallowed he must vomit up;*
   *God makes him disgorge*ᵇ *it from his belly.*
¹⁶*It was the poison of asps that he sucked;*
   the snake's tongue will slay him.
¹⁷*He will enjoy*ᵃ *no*ᵇ *streams of oil,*ᶜ
   torrents flowing with honey and cream.
¹⁸*He disgorges*ᵃ *the gains*ᵇ *he cannot keep swallowed,*ᶜ
   *and takes no pleasure*ᵈ *from the fruit of his commerce.*ᵉ
¹⁹*For he has defrauded and disregarded*ᵃ *the poor,*
   *and seized by force houses he did not build.*ᵇ
²⁰*He has known no contentment*ᵃ *in his belly,*
   *he has let nothing that he desired*ᵇ *escape him,*
²¹ᵃ*There is nothing left*ᵇ *after he has eaten;*
   *therefore*ᶜ *his prosperity cannot endure.*
²²*When in full abundance,*ᵃ *he suddenly is thrown into distress,*ᵇ
   *all the strength*ᶜ *of misfortune*ᵈ *assails him.*
²³ᵃ*If [God] would*ᵇ *fill the wicked's*ᶜ *belly to the full,*
   he will send his burning wrath against him,
   *rain*ᵈ *it down on him*ᵉ *as his food.*ᶠ

²⁴*Though*ᵃ *he flee*ᵇ *from a weapon of iron,*
   an arrow of bronze will pierce him through.
²⁵*When*ᵃ *he pulls*ᵇ *it out of his back,*ᶜ
   *the arrowhead*ᵈ *from his liver,*ᵉ
   *terrors come*ᶠ *upon him,*
²⁶   *the depth of darkness lies in wait*ᵃ *for his treasures.*ᵇ
   *A fire unfanned*ᶜ *consumes*ᵈ *him,*
   *it feeds*ᵉ *on any survivor left in his tent.*
²⁷*Heaven declares his guilt;*
   earth rises to denounce him.
²⁸*A flood*ᵃ *sweeps away*ᵇ *his house,*
   *torrents*ᶜ *on the day of [God's] wrath.*
²⁹*Such is the fate God*ᵃ *allots to the wicked,*ᵇ
   *such the inheritance appointed*ᶜ *him by God.*

Notes

2.a. NAB reverses the position of vv 2a and 3a, to create a more exact parallelism.

2.b. לָכֵן can hardly be "therefore" as it usually is, since it is not referring back to what precedes, nor even "in reference to the preceding" (Hölscher, Fohrer). KB³ allows the meaning "truly," as at 1 Sam 28:2 (Jer 2:33 is not so convincing), and this seems most suitable here (so Gordis "indeed"; NJPS, Habel "in truth"). JB "To this my thoughts are eager . . ." is not a very probable rendering. Emendation to לֹא כֵן "not so!" (LXX οὐχ οὕτως, but they apparently always treated לָכֵן thus in Job and some other books) suits the line very poorly.

2.c. יְשִׁיבוּנִי might be expected to mean "make answer to me" (cf. RV, RSV), but, as Peake observes, the idea of a conversation between Zophar and his thoughts is rather artificial. The obvious solution is to take the hiph as doubly causative, "*cause* me to *make* answer" (similarly KJV, NEB, NJPS, NIV), though such a usage does not seem to be recognized by the grammars, the lexica, or most commentators (it is explicitly denied by Delitzsch).

2.d. Lit. "and because," which suggests that a verb should follow. Thus Hölscher read וּבַעֲבוּרה "and because of that they meditate in me." Duhm, Driver-Gray, Beer (*BHK*), Fohrer, de Wilde, NEB insert זֹאת "this" after בַּעֲבוּר; NAB reads וּבַעֲבוּרוֹ "and because of it." Others find the word so difficult that they feel compelled to emend; Duhm's proposal, יַרְהִיבוּנִי "they disturb me," has been widely applauded (followed by Driver-Gray, de Wilde). Kissane proposed יְשִׂימֻנִי "appall me."

2.e. חוּשִׁי used to be taken as inf of חוּשׁ "hasten," thus "my hastening" (cf. RV, RSV) or "my inward excitement" (BDB); NEB somewhat differently, "this is why I hasten to speak"; cf. JB "no wonder if I am possessed by impatience." More commonly now it is reckoned to חוּשׁ II "feel" (especially pain), only elsewhere at Eccl 2:24; thus KB³, reading יָחֻשׁוּ "they (my thoughts) are painful." Gordis retains MT as "my feeling, pain," which seems perfectly satisfactory; the *waw* of בַּעֲבוּר could well be epexegetic (explanatory, says Dhorme). Alternatively, a conjectural emendation is made to רָחַשׁ לִבִּי "my heart is astir" (as in Ps 45:2 [1]) (Beer, Fohrer, NAB "I am disturbed"; NIV's very similar "because I am greatly disturbed" presumably reads the MT).

If חוּשׁ means "feel," it is still an open question whether it means "feel painful." In Eccl 2:25 an obvious sense is "feel joyful," and we should perhaps compare Akk. *ḫašāšu* "feel joyful"; but in postbib. Heb. it is "feel painful, be troubled," and that sense is by no means ruled out for Eccl 2:25 (so A. Lauha, *Kohelet* [BKAT 19; Neukirchen: Neukirchener Verlag, 1978] 58, following F. Ellermeier, *ZAW* 75 [1963] 197–217; but note to the contrary R. Braun, *Kohelet und die frühhellenistische Popularphilosophie* [BZAW 130; Berlin: de Gruyter, 1973] 110–11).

3.a. A modal use, "I must hear," noted by Delitzsch.

3.b. Despite the standard translation of מוּסָר as "correction, rebuke, reproach" (here "censure," RSV, Gordis; "reproach," NEB; "reproof," RV, NJPS; "rebuke," NAB, NIV; "check," KJV, an obselete word for "rebuke," deriving from "check" in chess, as do all meanings of "check" ultimately), there is little evidence that the term has this sense of contradicting someone or putting them right. It is rather a term for instruction, teaching, education in general which may of course involve correction or warning, but not necessarily (Sicre Diaz rightly has "una lección," and Ravisi "una lezione," "un insegnamento magistrale").

3.c. Dhorme's word; lit. "wind, spirit" (רוּחַ), but it is hard to understand "a spirit out of my understanding" (NJPS; cf. NAB). "A spirit beyond my understanding" (NEB) can hardly be meant, since Zophar is not given to supernatural revelations. Driver thought it was "a spirit answer[ing] me out of my understanding, i.e., a higher spirit, speaking in, and out of, my understanding"; but this is confusing.

3.d. Dahood's revocalization to מַבָּנִיתִי "my frame" ("Northwest Semitic Philology," 63), followed by Pope, has nothing to recommend it; but it is at least preferable to his previous emendation to בִּינוֹתַי "within me" (*Bib* 38 [1957] 315–16). Duhm, Terrien, de Wilde have "a wind without intelligence," taking מִן as privative; Terrien calls LXX (πνεῦμα ἐκ τῆς συνέσεως "a spirit from the understanding") in support; but though LXX lacked the pronoun it certainly did not regard the *min* as privative.

3.e. יַעֲנֵנִי should be taken as a hiph "causes me to reply" (cf. יְשִׁיבוּנִי in v 2); so NJPS, NIV, Dhorme, Fohrer, Gordis, Habel, rather than RSV "answers me" (NEB "gives me the answers," Driver-Gray, Pope). Duhm's emendation to תַּעֲנֵנִי "you answer me" (with a wind without intelligence; see n. 20:3.d), though followed by de Wilde, is no more than a rewriting of Job.

4.a. Absent from the Heb., but fairly clearly demanded, as the EVV recognize. Gordis explains that "where the speaker's certitude is overwhelming, he dispenses with the negative," and parallels from 1 Sam 2:27 and Jer 31:20 are rather convincing (2 Kgs 6:32 is different); see his "A Rhetorical Use of Interrogative Sentences in Biblical Hebrew," *AJSL* 49 (1933) 212–17 (followed by Fohrer). Emendation to הֲלֹא (Duhm) is unnecessary, and still more is Merx's יָדַעְתִּי "I know."

4.b. In the Heb., the "that" (כִּי) does not come until the beginning of v 5, a literary feature well enough attested to be unsurprising. Gordis calls it "anticipation" and compares Gen 1:4 and, better, Deut 31:29 "I know after my death that you will act corruptly" (cf. also Isa 40:21). Clearly it would be absurd to ask Job whether he knows something from primordial times. NEB, JB, NIV successfully negotiate the difficulty by advancing the position of the "that"; RV, RSV, NAB do not.

4.c. שִׂים, apparently an uncommon inf form (usually שׂוּם), with indefinite, though transparent, subj—or else perhaps a pass qal (P. Joüon, "Etudes de morphologie hébraïque," *Bib* 1 [1920] 362–63; Dahood, "Northwest Semitic Philology," 64; Blommerde).

5.a. עֲדֵי־רָגַע lit. "until a moment," i.e., it will last only for a moment; though עַד could be "while" here (cf. J. Barr, "Hebrew עַד, Especially at Job i.18 and Neh. vii.3," *JSS* 27 [1982] 177–88 [184]).

6.a. שִׂיא is generally thought to be a *hapax* (but possibly occurs also at 15:31); it is clearly from נשׂא "lift up," so is probably "height," "loftiness" (BDB), not specifically "pride" (Hölscher, NAB, NIV). Guillaume compared an Arab. *šawā* "head, skull" in order to create an exact parallel ("Arabic Background," 114–15). C. Rabin compared Arab. *šāʾa* "wish," and translated "his desire" ("Etymological Miscellanea," *ScrHieros* 8 [1961] 399).

7.a. גְּלָלוֹ is pretty certainly from גָּל, "dung, dung-cake." Dhorme's supposition that we have here a cognate of Akk. *gallu* "evil demon" (hence presumably JB "like a phantom") fails because demons do not perish (Dhorme translates, "like a ghost, he vanishes for ever," but Akk. *gallu* is not a ghost, and certainly not a vanishing one, as the entries in *CAD* witness). Ewald read "according to his greatness"; cf. Arab. *jaʾlal* "greatness" (so too Gordis). E. G. King ("Some Notes on the Text of Job," *JTS* 15 [1914] 74–81 [78–79]), alarmed at the vulgarity of the usual rendering, proposed taking גלל as "roll, *so* trust" (as Ps 22:9 [8]), thus "while he is confiding, i.e., building himself up in self-confidence."

8.a. Indefinite pl subj.

8.b. Lit. "he is chased away." De Wilde reads וְיָדֹד "and he flees away," but the form is dubious, and the proposal unnecessary.

9.a. Duhm deleted the verse on the grounds that v 9a repeats the thought of v 7b, v 9b is a citation of 3:10, and the verse was omitted by the original LXX. Moffatt presumably followed him. These are insufficient reasons, especially because LXX omitted several verses in the vicinity.

9.b. Lit. "the eye that glimpsed him will not again." If שׁוּף actually means "glimpse" (BDB "catch sight of, look on")—it occurs elsewhere only at 28:7; Cant 1:6—the point must be not that those who only glimpsed him will not see him again (as NEB, NJPS) but that those who *saw* him will never so much as glimpse him again.

9.c. Emendation to the masc יְשׁוּרֶנּוּ (Duhm, Driver, Hölscher, NAB) is probably unnecessary, since מָקוֹם "place" is fem also at Gen 18:24; 2 Sam 17:12; and perhaps also Job 28:6. NEB and NJPS, with Tur-Sinai, take עַיִן "eye" as the subj of the fem verb, understanding מְקוֹמוֹ as "in his place"; but the MT phrasing is conventional (7:10; Ps 103:16; cf. Job 8:18). N. M. Sarna ("The Mythological Background of Job 18," *JBL* 82 [1963] 315–18 [318]) argued that the verb is actually masc with *t*- preformative (thus a *taqtul* form); but it is doubtful whether such a form existed in Heb. (cf. n. 18:14.c). It is strange that in the very similar phrase וְלֹא־יַכִּירֶנּוּ עוֹד מְקֹמוֹ "and his place shall not again know him" in 7:10 (cf. Ps 103:16), מָקוֹם is masc whereas we can only suppose that here it is, exceptionally, fem.

10.a-a. De Wilde offers a conjecture: בָּדָּיו יֵרְזוּ וְיִדְלוּ וִידָיו תִּשְׁבֹּנָה אוֹנָן "his limbs grow lean and languish, and his hands lose their strength." It fits the context much better than MT, but it is hard to believe it was original.

10.b. See *Comment* for the two principal possibilities. There is little likelihood that we should see here רצץ "crush" (as the ancient versions, Budde, BDB, reading יְרֻצַּצוּ niph), i.e., "his children are crushed [as] poor ones"; alternatively יְרַצְּצוּ "the poor crush his children" (Rosenmüller).

11.a. עֲלוּמִים, an abstract pl, can take a verb in the 3 fem sg (cf. Ps 103:5; GKC, § 145k). Contrast NJPS "his bones . . . lie down in the dust."

14.a. "The bare perfect, introducing the apodosis, expresses the suddenness of the change" (Driver; cf. Driver, *Hebrew Tenses*, 204 § 135γ). As he points out, in English the *present* is sometimes used for the same purpose: "If thou say so, villain, thou *kill'st* thy mistress" (*Antony and Cleopatra* 2.5.26).

15.a. Fohrer and de Wilde remove this verse to follow v 16 so that the two verses on snake poison will lie together. Andersen finds a concentric structure in vv 12–18, with v 15 as the pivot and vv 14 and 16 balancing one another with similar material; but he does not explain how v 12 is parallel with v 18, or v 13 with v 19. Actually v 15 is most closely parallel to v 18.

15.b. ירש hiph, usually "possess" or "dispossess" (BDB), but KB³ recognizes a ירש II "tread, press" in Mic 6:15, following P. Haupt ("Critical Notes on Micah," *AJSL* 26 [1909–10] 201–52 [215, 223]) and others. Tur-Sinai and M. Delcor ("De l'origine de quelques termes relatifs au vin en hébreu biblique et dans les langues voisines," *Actes du premier congrès international de linguistique sémitique et chamito-sémitique: Paris 16–19 juillet 1969,* ed. A. Caquot and D. Cohen [Janua Linguarum. Series Practica 159; The Hague: Mouton, 1974] 223–33 [228–30]) see this same root here. O. Loretz has denied the existence of ירש II, probably rightly ("Hebräisch *tjrwš* und *jrš* in Mi 6,15 und Hi 20,15," *UF* 9 [1977] 353–54).

17.a. ב ראה has always been recognized to mean sometimes "look at with pleasure" (BDB, KB³), but Blommerde has correctly noted that "enjoy" is a more precise meaning in certain places (as NJPS, NIV here). NEB "Not for him to swill down rivers of cream" perhaps takes ראה as equivalent to רוה "be satiated." JB "He will know no more of streams that run with oil" takes ראה in its most elementary meaning.

17.b. The juss with the negative, אל־ירא, lit., "let him not enjoy," is used sometimes to express a strong negation, a "conviction that something cannot or should not happen" (GKC, § 109e); cf. 5:22.

17.c. פלגות נהרי נחלי דבש "streams of rivers of brooks of honey" has seemed to most an implausibly long chain of consts. There is support for having two adjacent consts in apposition (Isa 37:22; 1 Sam 28:7; GKC, § 130e), but the text is usually emended to read יצהר "oil" instead of נהרי, thus "streams of oil" (so Driver-Gray, Dhorme, Fohrer, Pope, de Wilde, JB, NAB). There is something to be said for the suggestion of H. P. Chajes ("Note lessicali a proposito della nova edizione del Gesenius-Buhl," *Giornale della Società Asiatica Italiana* 19 [1906] 175–86 [181–82]), followed by Blommerde, Gordis, Sicre Diaz, that we have a noun *נהר "oil" derived from the root נהר "shine" as יצהר is from *צהר "shine" (cf. also צהל). Heb. already has שמן and יצהר for "oil," so the proposal is not overwhelmingly convincing. NEB reads for נהרי, דהן (Brockington, 107) which it apparently thinks means "milk" (cf. LXX ἄμελξις "milking"), but the word is not attested in Heb.

18.a. משיב, lit., "causing to return"; in the context it is still the metaphorical food that is being spoken of (cf. בלע "swallow," עלס "eat, drink, enjoy"), and the only way he can cause food to "return" is to vomit it up, the same image as in v 15a. Duhm's emendation to מָשָׁךְ "he increases, extends (his labor)" is poor. De Wilde's מֵשִׁיב יְגִיעוֹ "the profit of his work" is unsupported. JB "Gone that glad face at the sight of his gains" is quite mysterious.

18.b. יגע, only here, but patently "gain" as the product of labor (root יגע "toil"). Many suggest adding a suffix, יְגַעוֹ "his toil" (*BHK,* Fohrer, Sicre Diaz), the suffix perhaps being omitted by haplography, or else reading יָגֵעַ (Dhorme; Hölscher, de Wilde: יְגִיעוֹ), or יָגַעוֹ (Brockington), with the same meaning.

18.c. Lit. "he disgorges (his) gain and does not swallow it"; but if he does not swallow it, how can he vomit it? Perhaps it means he doesn't swallow it again, since it is vomited food, or better, that he never manages to swallow successfully in the first place, he cannot keep his food down. Of course, if משיב does not mean "disgorge" there is apparently no difficulty, as NIV "What he toiled for he must give back uneaten"—except that the image of the strophe is consistently on his actually eating and swallowing (Gray acknowledges the inconsistency with v 15). We should say that he doesn't "swallow" or consume *in the sense that* he vomits up his food.

18.d. For עלס, taken by BDB, KB as "rejoice" (elsewhere only 39:13, of the ostrich's wings flapping, and Prov 7:18 of delighting oneself in love), we should more probably distinguish a עלס I (cognate with Arab. *ʿalasa* "eat, drink") "taste, enjoy (*geniessen*)" from a עלס II (Arab. *ʿaliza*) "be restless" for 39:13 (so KB³; Gordis finds the idea of enjoying "both anticlimactic after stich *a* and completely lacking in parallelism." He avers that יעלס is a "scribal metathesis for יְלְעס "he chews," not indeed in biblical Heb. but in Mishnaic Heb.; the suggestion is doubly precarious. לא יעלס has a *waw* prefixed; many delete it (cf. *BHK*), but it could be an example of the postponed *waw* (cf. 23:12, 25:5; Driver, *Tenses,* § 124).

18.e. Lit. "according to the strength, or, wealth of his trading" (כְּחֵיל תְּמוּרָתוֹ). If the *kaph* is correct, it must mean that his (non)enjoyment is out of proportion to his wealth. Many mss have בְּחֵיל, which *BHK* and others recommend to read, i.e., he does not enjoy his wealth. תְּמוּרָה is properly "exchange, thing acquired by exchange," hence "trading" (Dhorme, NIV); but v 19 suggests that it is not regular business activity that brings him to such straits. Gordis, reading בְחֵיל, vocalizes it בְּחֵל "loathes" and translates "will spew forth his gain" (so too NEB), but loathing and vomiting are not quite the same idea. NEB "undigested" is hard to understand, as is its reading כֹּחַ לְתמוּתוֹ. How JB gets "those comfortable looks when business was thriving" is unknown.

19.a. עֻזָּב "neglected" has commonly been thought suspicious, mainly because it seems too general and anticlimactic (Gray) (but see *Comment*). Ehrlich proposes a new word עֻזָּב "hut," on the basis of Mishnaic מַעֲזִיבָה; but that word means precisely "a concrete of stone chippings, clay &c., used for paving floors, pavement covering the ceiling of the lower story and serving as flooring to the upper story" (Levy)—which is hardly the same thing as "hut." Dahood approved this view ("The Root עֻזָּב II in Job," *JBL* 78 [1959] 306–7), observing that רצץ "crush" is the perfect verb to use of destroying a reed-hut (cf. "a crushed reed," קנה רצוץ in Isa 42:3). So too JB "Since he once destroyed the huts of poor men," Terrien. But the meaning is hazardous, as Rowley says. J. Reider ("Contributions to the Biblical Text," *HUCA* 24 [1952–53] 86–106 [103–4]) read עֲזֵב, meaning like postbiblical עֲזִיבה the "leavings" of the poor, what the rich are supposed to leave for the poor as in Lev 19:10.

Kissane suggested a word עֻזָּב "hovel" which he presumably derived from BDB's עֻזָּב II "restore, repair"; it is true that LXX has οἴκους "houses," but the existence of this עֻזָּב II should now be abandoned (see H. G. M. Williamson, "A Reconsideration of עֻזָּב II in Biblical Hebrew," *ZAW* 97 [1985] 74–85). G. R. Driver saw in עֻזָּב the Arab. 'aḏḏaba "punished, tormented," and regarded רצץ as an explanatory gloss upon it ("Glosses in the Hebrew Text of the Old Testament," *L'Ancien Testament et l'Orient: Etudes présentées aux VIᵉˢ Journées Bibliques de Louvain (11–13 septembre 1954)* [Orientalia et Biblica Lovaniensia 1; Louvain: Publications Universitaires, 1957] 123–61 [138]). Tur-Sinai, following Yellin, derived the word from the same root; hence probably NJPS "tortured."

Among emendations may be mentioned: זְרֹעַ "(crushed) the arm of (the poor)" (Beer; cf. *BHK*; Fohrer, de Wilde; cf. 22:9; 38:15; Jer 48:25; Ezek 30:21–22, 24; Ps 10:15; 37:17, though never with רצץ); עֶצֶב "pain" (Hoffmann, Duhm, Hölscher), but that does not seem to mean "profit gained by pain"; and the ingenious בְעֹז "with strength, violence" (Dhorme).

19.b. Lit. "a house, and he did not build it." בית "a house" is no doubt intended collectively for "houses" (so JB, NEB, NIV). Andersen maintains that בית here means "land," not a building (cf. NAB "patrimony"); but בנה "build" would suggest otherwise. The last clause is taken by some to mean "and goeth not on to build it," i.e., through being impoverished (if that is how v 18 is to be read) he cannot renovate it or add to it or otherwise fit it for his own use (so Delitzsch, Driver). That is indeed what the impf יבנה, apparently "does build," suggests, coming after the quasi-hypothetical גזל in the pf (cf. Driver, *Tenses*, § 85). But that is no kind of crime, and even if he did renovate the house he had seized, that would hardly excuse his seizing it. NJPS takes the second half of the line as a threat, "He will not build up the house he took by force," but this spoils the idea that taking someone else's house is explicative of the verbs of the first half of the line. Duhm emended יבנהו to בָּנָה "he built it" and deleted the *waw* before לא "not," to make it clear that "he did not build" is a relative clause.

20.a. שלו is properly an adj, "quiet, at ease." BDB accepts that here it appears to be an abstract noun, but many read the usual noun שַׁלְוָה "ease" (KB³, Driver-Gray, Fohrer, de Wilde) or else שַׁלוֹ (cf. Ps 30:7 [6]) with the same meaning (*BHS* [*frt*]). The similar phrase in Isa 59:8, לא ידע שלום "he has not known peace," suggests strongly that we have a noun here. D. Winton Thomas saw in ידע the root ידע II "be quiet, at ease" (Arab. *waduʿa* "was chastened, quiet") and so deleted שלו as a gloss explanatory of the rare verb ("The Root ידע in Hebrew, II," *JTS* 36 [1935] 409–12; followed by G. R. Driver, "Glosses in the Hebrew Text of the Old Testament," 137). This is quite possible (for a positive evaluation of the proposal of ידע II see J. A. Emerton, "A Consideration of Some Alleged Meanings of ידע in Hebrew," *JSS* 15 [1970] 145–80) but hardly obligatory, since the text is quite intelligible. *BHS* proposes שָׁלוֹ בֶן־בִּטְנוֹ "[he cares nothing for] the prosperity of his brother," lit., "the son of his womb" (cf. 19:17), but the theme seems to be rather the inner state of the wrongdoer (de Wilde). NJPS "he will know no peace with his children" sounds like an emendation to שלום, but is perhaps an attempt at שלו "contentment, tranquillity"; בטן never means "children" though perhaps בְנֵי־בטן can (cf. 19:17). Duhm's conjecture לא שָׁלוּ בְמַטְמֹנוֹ "he has no rest in his hidden treasure" is only doubtfully a back-translation of LXX, and need not be considered.

20.b. חָמוּד, qal pass ptcp "desired," usually denotes the thing desired, as Ps 39:12 "what is dear to him," and this is possible here: "he will not save anything in which he delights" (RSV). The *beth* is then partitive (GKC, § 119m; BDB, 88b § I.2.b), "some of what is desired"; cf. הרג ב "kill some of" (Ps 78:31), ב הכה "slay some of." NIV "he cannot save himself by his treasure" presumably understands נפשׁ "his self" (as Kimchi) as the obj; but the clause is a כי clause and should be one of the reasons why his prosperity will not endure (v 21; note כן על), not itself a statement of his doom. N. M. Sarna, arguing that *beth* is often interchangeable with *min*, translated "of his most cherished possession he shall save nothing" ("The Interchange of the Prepositions *Beth* and *Min* in Biblical Hebrew," *JBL* 78 [1959] 310–16 [315–16]), but this is open to the same syntactic criticism as NIV's version. NJPS on the same lines has "he will not preserve one of his dear ones." NAB emends to בַּחֲמוּדָיו "of his goods" (pl).

If the verb is revocalized to יִמָּלֵט "he will be delivered" (Budde, Driver-Gray, Hölscher) a rendering like JB becomes possible, "now his hoarding (NAB treasures) will not save him," i.e., literally "he will not be saved by his hoarding." NEB "he cannot escape his own desires" claims to accept this vocalization (Brockington, 108), but it is hard to see how they construe the Heb. unless they take *beth* as "from."

A different approach was taken by Dhorme, who argued that חָמוּד means not "thing desired" but "appetite" (followed by Habel), thus "by his appetite he allows nothing to escape"—which gives a good sense. Unfortunately, Dhorme did not explain how the pass ptcp can mean this. De Wilde gains the same meaning by emending to בְּחָמוּדוֹ (late Heb. חָמוּד "desire").

21.a. Duhm omits as a gloss. NAB arbitrarily transposes v 21b to follow v 19, and v 21a to follow v 22a.

21.b. Lit. "survivor," elsewhere only of persons; hence NJPS "with no survivor to enjoy it," but that is at the cost of ignoring עַל־כֵּן.

21.c. Gordis thinks this עַל־כֵּן may simply be emphatic, but it is much more evidently the "therefore" that introduces a judgment. Because of his translation "indeed," Gordis mistakenly views vv 20b–21a as further statements of the wrongdoer's punishment.

22.a. Lit. "in the fullness of his sufficiency." סֶפֶק "sufficiency" is only here in the OT, and the verb is rare, but occurs several times in Ecclus (cf. D. Winton Thomas, "The Text of Jesaia II 6 and the Word שֶׂפֶק," *ZAW* 75 [1963] 88–90).

22.b. Lit. "there is straitness for him."

22.c. יָד to be taken as "strength, power" (BDB, 390a § 2). "Blows" (Dhorme) is a little too specific.

22.d. עָמֵל is "laborer, sufferer," as in 3:20; hence Gordis "every embittered sufferer will attack him"; but LXX, Vg read an abstract noun עָמָל here, and so do most commentators and modern versions, for it is hard to believe in a depiction of the wicked man being brought to ruin at the hands of those he has defrauded. The MT pointing is probably due to the presence of יָד, leading the Masoretes to regard עמל as personal (Budde).

23.a. This colon is omitted by LXX, Merx, Bickell, Duhm (as gloss on v 22a), Driver-Gray, Hölscher, Fohrer, de Wilde), JB, NEB, NAB (as dittograph of v 20).

23.b. יְהִי is juss, and some try to preserve this; so Driver-Gray, "His belly must be filled"; NJPS, "Let that fill his belly"; Andersen. Driver rightly insists that strictly "יהי can only mean *may it be* . . . , and if original, must indicate that the poet's feeling leads him to express the *wish* that such may be the fate of the ungodly." We note too the juss וימטר (see n. 20:23.d), and that ישלח too could equally well be juss. But the thought does not allow us to see three independent juss clauses; the second (and the third in some sort of parallelism with it) must depend on the first for the first is not self-contained; thus "May it be, to fill his belly to the full, that God should send . . . and rain. . . ." Another possibility is that the juss יהי is the sign of the protasis of a conditional sentence (see GKC, § 109h–i); thus "if he [God] should be about to [היה with ל, cf. BDB, 227b § 5.b] fill his [the wicked's] belly to the full, [what he will do is that] he will send . . ." Perhaps it is the wicked who is about to fill his belly (cf. Dhorme "when he is occupied in filling his belly," NIV "when he has filled his belly"). However it is taken, the Heb. is awkward (the juss with the negative in v 17 was much easier). Many simply assume that יהי is equivalent to יִהְיֶה "it will be"; so Gordis, "It will happen, in order to fill his belly to the full."

23.c. "Of the wicked" added for clarity.

23.d. ימטר is juss, which NJPS preserves, "Let Him loose . . . and rain down." Most, however, read a simple ind וְיַמְטֵר; the juss has probably been introduced incorrectly to harmonize with יהי. See further n. 20:23.b.

23.e. The suffix of עלימו is poetic, and generally pl; it is sometimes attested as sg, however (see GKC, § 103f, n.), and must be so here. Dhorme read עָלְמָיו "his arrows," presuming a Heb. עֶלֶם cognate with Ass. *ulmu* (hence JB "a hail of arrows," Terrien); but *ulmu*, formerly explained as simply the name of some sharpened weapon (cf. Muss-Arnoldt), is now known to be "ax" (von Soden), and the suggestion must be abandoned. Others emend to עָלָיו (Duhm, NAB), but this is strictly unnecessary.

23.f. MT בלחומו should probably be rendered "on, against his flesh," לָחוּם elsewhere only Zeph 1:17 (cf. Arab. *lahm*). It seems strange, however, to have "upon him" (עלימו) as well as "on his flesh," especially since the "flesh" seems to have no special significance (it can hardly be in parallelism with "his belly," as Sicre Diaz). "Upon his corpse" is a possibility (so Tg בשלדיה), but the idea of post-mortem punishment seems strange. Gordis's view that the word means "his anger," parallel to חֶרוֹן אַפוֹ, is unsupported. G. R. Driver supposes a לְחוּם II cognate with Arab. liḥamu(n) "buffeting" from laḥama I "struck" and suggests LXX understood this with their ὀδύνας "pains" (VTSup 3 [1955] 72–93 [81]); hence NEB "rains on him cruel blows"; similarly NIV.

The simple emendation to בְּלַחְמוֹ "as his food" provides an excellent sense and is adopted by many (Dillmann, Budde, Peake, Driver-Gray, Habel, RVmg, RSV). Among other emendations we find חֲבָלִים "pains" (cf. LXX ὀδύνας) (so Merx, Hölscher, Fohrer, de Wilde); בַּלָּהוֹת "terrors" (Bickell, Ball, elsewhere translated ὀδύναι); עָלָיו חֲמָתוֹ "upon him, his anger," later expanded to מַבֵּל חֲמָתוֹ "upon him the flood of his anger" (Duhm, Weiser); עָלָיו מַבֵּל חַמּוֹ "upon him the fire of his wrath" (M. Dahood, "Some Northwest-Semitic Words in Job," *Bib* 38 [1957] 306–20 [314–15]; followed by Blommerde, Pope), מבל equivalent to Akk. *nablu,* Ug. *nblat* "fire" (so also at 18:15; see n. 18:15.a), and חַמּוֹ, apparently the inf of חמם "be hot, angry" with suff (but the form should be בְּחָמּוֹ as 6:17). Ps 11:6 has the Lord raining on the wicked coals of fire (אֵשׁ) and brimstone, so the idea is reasonable, though not convincing. NAB proposes כְּלֵי לַחְמוֹ "missiles of war," lit., "weapons of war," which is presumably the rare and doubtful לָחֶם (only Judg 5:8; cf. BDB, 535b; not acknowledged by *BHK*); similarly NJPS "His weapons."

24.a. The formulaic nature of the sentence (cf. *Comment*) makes plain that this is a conditional clause (so JB, NAB, NIV, Gordis). A simple parallelism (as RSV) is very flat.

24.b. G. R. Driver argued that ברח cannot here have its normal meaning of "flee" because that is not parallel to "pierce"; he proposed a ברח II cognate with Arab. *baraḥa* "bruised," *barḥu(n)* "blow of a sword"; he also finds the root at 27:22; 41:20 (VTSup 3 [1955] 81); hence NEB "he is wounded." This shows an excessively mechanical attitude to parallelism.

25.a. It seems best to construe the first two cola as a single action, followed by (and causing) the coming of the terrors in v 25c and (in parallel) the darkness of v 26a; somewhat similarly NJPS, Gordis. Hölscher regards v 25a (to מִמְּרֹרָתוֹ) as a gloss which, with v 24, breaks the connection of the thought of God's judgment on the evildoer.

25.b. שֶׁלַף, though it makes excellent sense, is very generally emended to שֶׁלַח "missile, weapon," reversing the order of ויצא and שלף "a spear comes out of his back" (Duhm, Dhorme "a shaft," Fohrer, Rowley, Pope, *BHK*, NAB "the dart," JB "an arrow"). They claim as support LXX διεξέλθοι δὲ διὰ σώματος αὐτοῦ βέλος "let an arrow come out through his body." Quite apart from the satisfactory text of MT, this rendering destroys the connection ("arbitrary," according to Duhm) between v 24 and v 25; for if the arrow strikes the evildoer as he flees, i.e., in the back, it cannot "come out through" his back (as NEB, NAB, JB). NJPS thinks it refers to the withdrawal of a blade from a sheath ("Brandished and run through his body, the blade . . ."); but again it is weak to introduce a new weapon here when the arrow of v 24 still fits. Habel's "Flying forth and penetrating his back; the flashing arrow . . ." keeps the image, but "fired" (i.e., shot) or "flying forth" seems a bit strained for שלף.

Hölscher read שֶׁלֶף יֵצֵא "the knife (cf. Syr. *šelāfā*) comes out." So too G. R. Driver (VTSup 3 [1955] 82), supposing a Heb. שֶׁלֶף (Brockington, 108); hence NEB "the point." Driver allows that שלף ויצא may stand in that order as an example of a postponed *waw.*

25.c. מִגֵּוֹה "from the back" is almost universally revocalized to מִגֵּוָה "from his back" since the form גֵּוָה occurs nowhere else. KB³ suggests a second גּ "insides" (Aram. loanword), as in the Qumran Hymn to Zion (11QPsᵃZion, 7). This makes no difference to the meaning. De Wilde thinks מִגְּוִיּוֹ "from his corpse" possible, but the form attested is גְּוִיָתוֹ.

25.d. ברק, lit. "shining, flashing object," used normally to denote lightning, but several times of the flashing of a metal weapon (Deut 32:41, of a sword; Nah 3:3; Hab 3:11, of a spear; Ezek 21:15 [10], 20 [15], 33 [28] of a sword polished so as to flash; cf. Zech 9:14, an arrow goes forth like lightning). NAB omits "the arrowhead from his liver" as a dittogr of v 14b.

25.e. Lit. "gallbladder."

25.f. יהלך "goes" is by some mss attached to the preceding, by others to the following words. It seems preferable to take it as the verb of אמים (sg verb with pl subj, as GKC, § 145o). Inevitably some emend to pl יַהֲלֹכוּ "they go" (*BHK*, Hölscher, Fohrer, NAB). Others complain that הלך "go" is not the right verb for "attack," which is rather בוא "come" (cf. on v 22), neglecting to observe that in Hab 3:11 God's arrows "go" (הלך), their flight rather than their hostility being in view. Duhm wanted to read יֵהָפְכוּ "(terrors) are turned (against him)" (so too Driver-Gray), comparing 19:19, where it is Job's intimate friends who are "turned" against him (!), and 1 Sam 4:19, where the wife of Phinehas finds her pains "turned" against her; Duhm might more profitably have compared Job 30:15 where Job's "terrors" (בלהות) are "turned" against him.

Others link יהלך with what precedes (NEB), and then perhaps omit "upon him terrors," as NEB, following G. R. Driver's fancy that the words are "a sympathetic scribe's or reader's exclamation meaning 'how awful for him!'" and can be relegated to the margin (VTSup 3 [1955] 82). Dhorme too thought we should render "a sword-flash comes (יַהֲלֹךְ) out of his liver," but then "terrors upon him" is without a verb; he supplied יִפָּלוּ "fall," which is idiomatic enough (Gen 15:12; Exod 15:16; Josh 2:9; Ps 55:5 [4]), but none the less arbitrary; he is followed by JB, NAB, de Wilde.

26.a. טָמוּן "is hidden"; the verb is often used of snares that lie hidden (18:10; Ps 9:16 [15]; 31:5 [4]; 35:7, 8; 64:6 [5]; 140:6 [5]; Jer 18:22) and thus lie in wait for someone to fall into them. It is strange that the next word here, צְפוּנָיו, also comes from a verb "to hide," so that many suspect the text. But the Heb. is intelligible though not limpid: "darkness lies hidden, i.e., lies in wait (NIV), for what lie hidden, i.e., his treasures" (cf. JB "all that is dark lies in ambush for him").

26.b. צפן "hide," often means "treasure up" (knowledge, Prov 10:14; a father's commandments, 2:1; God's goodness, Ps 31:20 [19]; retribution, Job 21:19). In Ps 17:14 the wicked should have their bellies filled with what God has "treasured up" (probably read צְפוּנְךָ, qal pass ptcp as here) for them (a text closely parallel to v 23a above). צפן should not be emended into Job 15:22 (see n. 15:22.b). So the meaning would clearly be "his treasures" were it not that Ps 83:4 [3] has God's צְפוּנִים as "his treasured ones," his saints; some think therefore that it may be the evildoer's children in view here (so Ehrlich). Certainly the שָׂרִיד "survivor" in v 26c seems to be human, but the translation "treasures" is more natural here.

Some delete טָמוּן and emend לצפוניו to לוֹ צָפוּן "is laid up for him" (Hölscher, Dhorme, Rowley, de Wilde), while Duhm, Budde, Fohrer, Sicre Diaz, NAB regard צפון as the variant. These suggestions are needless.

26.c. נָפְחָה might be expected (as Duhm, BHK; cf. BHS [prp], Hölscher), אֵשׁ "fire" being fem. Equally well, the verb could be taken as impersonal (Fohrer, citing GKC, § 145u; G. R. Driver, "Hebrew Studies," JRAS [1948] 164–76 [169]), or אֵשׁ could be masc, as apparently at Jer 48:45; Ps 104:4. For the idiom "fire not kindled (by humans)," "unlit by man" (JB), cf. 34:20 "removed by no (human) hand"; similarly Lam 4:6. It is not exactly a "fire that *needs* no fanning" (NEB; similarly NAB). G. R. Driver once thought to read נָפְחָה "quenched" from a Heb. פחה = Ass. *pahū* "damp down (fire)" ("Hebrew Notes on the 'Wisdom of Jesus ben Sirach,'" JBL 53 [1934] 273–90 [288–89]), but this root does not seem to be attested in the Akk. dictionary (von Soden).

26.d. Vocalizing תֹּאכְלֵהוּ (see Driver); Gordis thinks it a form of the piel.

26.e. ירע most naturally taken as from רעה "graze," so parallel to אכל "eat." The form is juss, but modern versions do not attempt to reproduce it. Avoiding the masc verb with fem subj, some have read יֵרַע niph (Dillmann, Budde) or יֵרָעֶה (BHK [prp]), but "the pass. does not read naturally" (Driver). Much less probable is יֵרַע (juss) or יֵרַע (impf) (Fohrer, BHS [prp], Pope) "fares ill" from רעע. Nor is יָרֹע "breaks" (from רעע II) any improvement (suggested by de Wilde). Duhm's emendation יְעַר שַׁדָּד "the Destroyer [15:21] stirs himself (against his tent)" has nothing to recommend it. NEB translates the last clause, "Woe betide [root רעע I] any survivor in his tent!" and puts it in square brackets. NAB omits the whole clause as a dittogr of v 21a (!). D. Winton Thomas read for ירע, ידע, which in fact some mss have, and saw in that his ידע II, "be humiliated"; taking שָׂרִיד as the subj, he translated "every survivor in his tent is brought to humiliation, disgrace" ("The Root ידע in Hebrew, II," JTS 36 [1935] 409–12 [411]); this suggestion was made in order to surmount the problem of the change of gender, but it destroys the parallelism. A. Guillaume ("Notes on the Roots ירע, ריע, and רעע in Hebrew," JTS ns 15 [1964] 293–95) connected the word with ירע "be faint-hearted" (BDB "quiver"), and translated "the survivor in his tent is terrified"; but we expect something more drastic than terror.

28.a. יבול is usually "produce," of the soil (e.g., Lev 26:4; Judg 6:4); it does not fit well in this context, because a "house" in whatever sense does not elsewhere have "produce," and translations like "possessions" (RSV) cannot easily be justified. Ehrlich, Dhorme, Beer, and most subsequent commentators (and NEB, NAB, JB, NJPS, NIV) have read נָבָל "stream, flood" (recognized by BDB at Isa 30:25; 44:4; cf. יוּבַל "stream" at Jer 17:18; אוּבָל "river" at Dan 8:2; KB³ adds Ecclus 50:8, and Ps 18:5 [4] and our text by emendation). We may compare Akk. *biblu, bubbulu* "flood" from *abālu* "carry off."

28.b. יגל is juss of גלה "may it go into exile" (RSV "be carried away"); if it is accepted that יבול means "stream, flood" (n. 20:28.a) we must read here יָגֹל "will roll away" from גלל "roll" (so most recent commentators and translators).

28.c. Formerly נִגָּרוֹת was taken as "(things) dragged away" (cf. RSV), fem pl ptcp niph of גרר, or "poured away" (RV "shall flow away"), from נגר. It is now almost universally recognized as the pl of a noun *נֶגְרָת "torrent" (KB³) or else the ptcp used as a noun (cf. נֹזְלִים "the flowing ones," which means "springs"), parallel to "stream, flood" in the first colon.

29.a. מֵאֱלֹהִים "from God" seems to overload the first colon, and is sometimes deleted (Pope; cf. Gordis).

29.b. אָדָם "human" seems unnecessary, and some delete it, Duhm for example suggesting it was a gloss to show רשע is to be read רָשָׁע "evildoer" and not רֶשַׁע "evil," though it seems improbable that anyone would have imagined the latter.

29.c. אמרו "(the inheritance of) his appointment," lit., "word," is difficult; אֹמֶר (BDB) or אֵמֶר (KB³) is "promise" at Ps 77:9 [8], "command" at Ps 68:12 [11], perhaps "plan" at Job 22:28, but these are not quite the same as "appointment." Pope says firmly that "there is no problem whatever with the expression," "his" command being the wicked man's command, i.e., the command he receives from God; and Driver finds no difficulty with "the heritage of his appointment" for "his appointed heritage" (cf. GKC, § 135n), which Gordis, however, thinks far-fetched. אמר nevertheless hardly seems the appropriate word; but no convincing emendation has been offered. Beer (*BHK*) suggests מֹרֶה = מֹרָא "rebellious one" (so also Terrien); Graetz, עָרִיץ "ruthless one" (cf. 27:13); Ehrlich מַמְרֶה "rebellion" or מַמְרוֹ "his rebellion," though the word is not attested; Duhm, אוֹנוֹ "his wickedness" (perhaps אוֹנוֹ is represented by LXX ὑπαρχόντων αὐτοῦ "his possessions," understanding אוֹנוֹ as "his wealth"); J. Reider, אִישׁ מֶרִי "man of rebellion" (*HUCA* 24 [1952–53] 104; followed by Fohrer, de Wilde). No more persuasive is Dhorme's argument that "his word" means "his person" (as Aram. מימרי "my word" can mean in Tg of 7:8; 19:18; 27:3), nor Eitan's proposal to see here the Arab. ʾamrun "man," nor Gordis's to find here the Arab. ʾamîr "prince," in the sense "bad prince, wealthy evildoer" (as נדיב means at 21:28); he has to explain the *waw* of אמרו as "the petrified suffix of the original nominative case," which stretches the credulity.

Form / Structure / Setting

The *structure* of Zophar's second speech is of the simplest: a brief exordium (vv 2–3) is followed by a disquisition or *topos* on a single theme, the doom of the wicked (vv 4–28), and ended by a summary appraisal (v 29). Beginning, as usual, with an exordium in which, unusually, Job is not directly addressed (vv 2–3), Zophar addresses Job in the second person only in the opening line of the body of his speech ("Do you not know . . . ?" v 4a). The exordium is alienating, from Job's point of view, and it indicates to the reader, in the way Zophar speaks only of his own feelings, his dismay at the course the dialogue has taken. But the direct address to Job in v 4a leaves us in no doubt that the speech as a whole is a speech to Job, even though, characteristically of the speeches of the friends in the second cycle, it comes to an end without any further address to Job (contrast in the first cycle, 5:19–27; 8:21–22; 11:13–19).

The *strophic structure* also is plain. After the exordium (vv 2–3), a two-line "signature," we find three long strophes, vv 4–11, 12–23, 24–29, of 8 lines, 12 lines, and 7 lines, the longest being concluded by a tricolon (v 23), and the last containing a pendant (v 29). The central strophe of vv 12–23 is marked out by the unity of the image of food, which does not occur in the previous strophe and is only alluded to in the following strophe (v 26b–c); the tricolon (v 23) also functions as a device of closure (cf. Watson, 183). We could well further discern smaller substrophes of 4 lines each; thus vv 4–7, 8–11, 12–15, 16–19, 20–23, 24–26 (the two apparent tricola of vv 25–26 being better understood as three bicola), and 27–29 (3 lines). Fohrer analyzes the structure similarly, but he does not see the larger strophes and he reverses the position of vv 16 and 15. The substrophes concluding at vv 15 and 19 would contain marks of closure: v 15b has a novel reference to God; v 19 is a "for"-clause pendant to vv 16–18.

Habel's strophic division (vv 12–22, 23–29) differs slightly because he wants to have the term "full" in each of the three strophes; but linking v 23 with what follows transports the food imagery into a strophe where it does not otherwise occur. Webster ("Strophic Structures," 48) finds eight strophes, vv 2–3, 4–7, 8–11, 12–16, 17–19, 20–22, 23–25, 26–

29; but despite the similar subject matter of vv 14 and 16 there is no need to keep v 16 within the same strophe, and v 23 need not be assimilated to vv 24–29 as one of the terrors that await, since v 22 also contains that theme. Skehan ("Strophic Patterns," 110) has vv 2–3, 4–9, 11–16, 17–22, 23–28, 29 (omitting v 10 as a dittograph), i.e., strophes of 6, 6, 6, and 7 lines plus a one-line pendant; similar objections apply as to Habel and Webster. Terrien's strophic division is: vv 2–5, 6–11 (omitting 10), 12–16, 17–20 (including 10 after 19), 21–25b, 25c–29, that is, exactly five lines in each strophe except for the first, which has 4; the removal of v 10 to follow v 19 is not absurd, though unsupported by any external evidence; but a division between vv 20 and 21 is unpersuasive since vv 20–21a seem to be three conditional clauses of which v 21b is the apodosis, and vv 25c–26a is better read as the conclusion of the sentence that began with v 25a.

The *genre* of the speech is of course the *disputation speech*. The bulk of the speech (vv 4–29) has been designated the *appeal to ancient tradition* (cf. also 8:8–13; 12:7–12), following N. C. Habel's pioneering analysis of the form ("Appeal to Ancient Tradition as a Literary Form," *Society of Biblical Literature. 1973 Seminar Papers* [ed. G. MacRae; Cambridge, Mass.: SBL, 1973] 1:34–54; followed by Murphy, *Wisdom Literature*, 33). It is not clear, however, that it is desirable to regard all the material contained in vv 4–29 as proper to that appeal form, since the majority of the material could readily be regarded as *wisdom instruction*. It might be preferable to regard the appeal to ancient tradition as a structuring device, with its own introductory language ("Ask now . . . ," "Do you not know from of old . . . ?"), rather than as a genre description for the traditional material that it evokes. An exegesis of the speech also tends to militate against Habel's (not unreasonable) view that the first words cited after the appeal proper are a "citation of the tradition" and constitute the theme of the following material to which the tradition is applied; for in the case of v 5 here, there seems to be good reason to suggest that the thrust of this verse, that the rejoicing of the godless is "of the briefest," is not the primary emphasis of the remainder of the poem, which is first on the disappearance of the wicked, then upon the fruitlessness of his life, and finally upon the inescapability of his doom (cf. on vv 4–11 and on vv 2–29). However we designate vv 4–28, it is obvious that the speech concludes with a *summary appraisal* in v 29 (cf. 18:21; 27:13).

The *wisdom instruction* is mostly very conventional and not wholly integrated, though some main lines of thought can be discerned. Fohrer thought that the depiction of the fate of the evildoer does not form a coherent composition, the sequence of the strophes being arbitrary and giving a strong impression of disunity. Often, he says, disparate wisdom sayings seem to be taken up without being shaped into a harmonious whole; and this certainly seems to be true of vv 14–16, for example, where at first incompatible images of the regurgitating of food seem to be used; a more close reading, however, perhaps may find a harmony of images even here (see *Comment*). The majority of the wording of these lines may be paralleled from wisdom instruction in Proverbs or Psalms; even in the case of the narrative of inescapable doom (vv 24–25), which is paralled only in the prophets, we may suspect an origin in folk wisdom. One line that comes from a quite distinct genre, however, is v 27, which recalls the *legal controversy*.

The exordium (vv 2–3) belongs to the *disputation speech* proper, though with the unusual feature that the opponent is not addressed, and the speaker dwells entirely on his own feelings about what he has heard in the disputation and on his own decision to reply (cf. 32:6 and 32:17–20 respectively).

The *function* of the speech is, as is suggested in the *Comment* on vv 2–29, to encourage Job into a change of life that will prevent him suffering the fate of the evildoer here depicted.

Its *tonality* is only apparent in the exordium, which untypically represents the speaker as disturbed by what he has heard (the wording is stronger than Job's in 19:2–3), which is to say, personally threatened by Job's attack on the world-view he himself relies on for security. The extravagance of the depiction and perhaps also its grossness (vv 15, 18), certainly the cosmic dimension it attains in v 27, signal the agitation of the speaker. The speech says more about the ruffled dogmatician than it does about his ostensible subject matter.

The *nodal verses* are, as is evident from the structure of the poem, vv 4–5, although (as argued in the *Comment* on vv 4–11) it is not precisely the *brevity* of the evildoer's success that seems to be the major emphasis of the speech.

Comment

2–29 Zophar's second speech is neatly structured. After the conventional exordium (vv 2–3), his traditional material on the fate of the wicked falls into three sections: (a) How thorough is the annihilation of the wicked! (vv 4–11). (b) There is no lasting profit from wrongdoing (vv 12–23). (c) The inescapable end of the wicked (vv 24–29). Like the other friends, Zophar confines himself in this speech of the second cycle almost exclusively to a depiction of the fate of the wicked, though to a different purpose and effect from the other friends. Whereas for Eliphaz (chap. 15) the fate of the wicked is a picture of what Job is not, for Bildad (chap. 18) it is a picture of what Job may become, and for Zophar it is a picture of what Job will not avoid without a radical change. As usual, we do not find Zophar explicitly responding to what Job has just said, though reminiscences of earlier phrases of various speakers are quite plentiful. Habel believes that "ironic barbs adorn Zophar's portrait," but the examples cited fail to persuade one that this is so.

Throughout the entire depiction, which is almost wholly metaphorical, only one verse gives any specifics of the wicked man's wrongdoing: in v 19 we learn that he has crushed the poor and seized the houses of others (but cf. also v 15a). This is confirmation enough that Zophar is not speaking expressly of Job. It is a signal too, since there are more kinds of wickedness than this, that what we are reading in this speech is a *topos*, an illustrative portrait of a single but typical individual.

2 Zophar's opening words of psychological distress may be, for all we know, utterly conventional phrases from the language of the dispute, as when we speak of a "concern" when we mean only a subject or say that X "feels" when we mean he thinks, or profess ourselves "worried" when we are simply intellectually puzzled. But even if they are quite conventional, it is interesting that the poet should employ them at this point, for they convey to us the impression— if only by indirection—that Zophar is rattled. His opening word "my troubled thoughts" (שְׂעִפַּי; NEB "distress of mind"), the noun before the verb in emphatic position, conspicuously conveys the same sense of disorientation as Bildad had expressed more obliquely in 18:4 (the term also at 4:13, of troubled thoughts in night visions; also Ps 94:19; 139:23). Likewise, to say that his thoughts compel him to return answer (שׁוּב hiphil) signifies that he is not in perfect control of himself. Which is no more than he freely admits when he gives as his reason "the feeling [perhaps, painful feeling; see n. 20:2.e] within me."

What has disturbed Zophar, as it gave Bildad the sensation of an earthquake (18:4), is that if Job is right everything Zophar stands for is wrong. While

Job was crying out at the disproportionateness of his suffering and the cruelty of God (chaps. 9–10), Zophar could roll his eyes heavenward and ask in mock despair whether owning a never-ending story of woe was any way to win acquittal (11:2). But now that Job, in calmer and more reflective mood, has pronounced himself ready and equal for a one-on-one encounter with God and has unswervingly—or more to the point, quite convincingly—maintained his innocence over against God, Zophar is flustered. "His violence is the measure of his fear" (Terrien). He now knows that Job seriously means to overthrow the retributionists' world-order.

3 Job has seen the friends' insistence on his guilt as a defamation (כלם, 19:3), and now Zophar protests that he for his part feels equally defamed by an "instruction of my defamation" (מוסר כלמתי), i.e., an instruction that defames, as מוסר שלומנו "chastisement of our health" in Isa 53:5 is a chastisement that heals us, an appositional genitive (Gordis). The term מוסר in the wisdom vocabulary means first chastisement (sometimes physical; cf. 5:17; Prov 22:15), but more often "instruction" (parallel to "wisdom" at Prov 1:2, 7; etc.). In calling Job's speech an "instruction," Zophar intellectualizes Job's words as he did in 11:4 when he called them "doctrine," as well as criticizes Job for taking a superior position (it is always a father, a schoolmaster, or God who gives "instruction"; equals do not "instruct" or "educate" one another; cf. 4:3). The defamation lies in Job's presumption to offer his friends "instruction" (cf. his claims to superior wisdom in 12:2–3; 13:1–2), and perhaps also in the particular implication that they are false witnesses who need to be in fear of judgment themselves (19:29).

Zophar's response to Job's new theology is an appeal to reason. The "impulse from his understanding" that supplies him with the words of this chapter is something he fondly imagines is the product of pure reason. Unfortunately for him, his very next words (v 4a) show the source from which his "reason" has been fed: it is the wisdom of the ancients, undiluted and uncontaminated by any truly original thought of his own. "Unlike the suffering Job, who has had everything shattered to pieces, and who feels himself crushed and exhausted, Zophar remains rooted in the native soil of his rationalist wisdom teaching, and draws strength from it" (Fohrer).

4–11 This is fairly evidently a self-contained unit, partly because it moves to a point of closure with v 11b ("lies down in the dust") and partly because a new sustained metaphor of food begins in v 12. But what precisely is the point of this strophe? Rowley labels it "the brevity of the triumph of the wicked," Habel "Rapid Fall of the Wicked," Fohrer "The early and utter fall of the evildoer" (vv 4–7) and "The apparent good fortune of the evildoer" (vv 8–11), Terrien "The disappearance (*évanescence*) of the wicked" (vv 6–9, 11), Szczygiel "The brief good fortune of the godless, even of the greatest" (vv 1–6) and "Sudden loss of wealth and health" (vv 7–12). Perhaps it is unreasonable to expect that a strophe will develop a single primary thought, but we may surely ask what is the dominant metaphor here. If we do, we shall not fasten on "brevity" but on the visual image of "absence" or "disappearance," since that is obviously the most sustained image, through vv 7–9. The wicked man ceases to exist like fuel for the fire (v 7a), like a dream that can never be found (v 8), like a person who disappears from the sight of friends and family forever (vv 7b, 9). This evanescence occurs despite the high visibility of the wicked in life: he may be as tall as heaven (v 6)—a visual metaphor. So the evanescence is set up against its opposite, an appearance of solidity, of occupying space. That visual contrast is then depicted temporally: now you see him, now you don't. The prominence of the wicked turns into the invisibility of the wicked. Drastic change is commonly represented as sudden change; and since the second state of the wicked (low profile) is longer lasting than the first (high profile), the first state can be represented as of the briefest (v 5). So then the statement of the brevity of the triumph of the wicked can be set down as the first and arresting affirmation of the strophe, and v 5 could justifiably be regarded the principal point if vv 4–11 were a paragraph of prose. Here, however, we may take it as a dramatic preface to the real matter of the strophe, the destiny of the wicked as annihilation. The final line again presents in a different metaphor the same contrast that is worked out in vv 6–7: there, though he is visible, he disappears; here (v 11), though he is strong, he becomes weak.

4 This rhetorical question stands as a headline not only for the strophe it introduces (vv 4–11), but also for the remainder of Zophar's speech (vv 4–29). All that Zophar has to say is traditional wisdom, which he pretends to be as old as Adam, and he marvels ironically that Job has not yet learned it. Like Bildad (8:8–9) and Eliphaz (15:18–19), he appeals to the past as the source of authority. Is it not ironic that at 15:7 Job was upbraided for imagining himself the First Man, and here reproached for not knowing what has been known ever since humankind was set on the earth?

It is not perhaps a direct rebuff to Job's conviction that a champion for his cause yet lives ("I know," יָדַעְתִּי, 19:25) that Zophar puts his question, "Do you (not) know?" (יָדַעְתָּ); there are too few contacts between Zophar's speech and the preceding to believe we are dealing with a genuine reply (cf. further on 19:2). But the contrast is there all the same, and it points up the difference between the two characters. Job knows what he knows by experience and conviction, even if it is wrong (on the phrase cf. on 19:25–27); Zophar knows what he knows because he has been taught it.

The idiom of the sentence is common Israelite rhetoric, and it is interesting to see that its closest analogue is not from the wisdom literature, but from Deut 4:32, "Ask now [שְׁאַל־נָא, as in Job 8:8; 12:7] of the days that are past- . . . from the day when God created man on the earth . . . ," meaning from time immemorial; the verb "set" (שִׂים) here probably echoes God's "setting" Adam in the garden (Gen 2:8). The knowledge Zophar transmits is "from perpetuity" (מִנִּי־עַד), עַד curiously being used here of the past when in its 48 occurrences elsewhere it is exclusively of the future (E. Jenni, *TWHAT* 2:207–9; but perhaps Hab 3:6 could be of the past). Perhaps there is a hint here of the permanent validity as well as the antiquity of the wisdom.

5 First Zophar states thematically what ancient wisdom has to teach; in vv 6–11 he will depict examples of the truth, with greater emphasis on the disappearance of the wicked than on the brevity of his prior existence. He means of course that the good fortune of the wicked or "godless" (חָנֵף; cf. on 8:13) is swiftly brought to an end by his death, but he dramatizes that a little by speaking more concretely of the "shout of joy" (רְנָנָה, as at 3:7; Ps 100:2; 63:6 [5]) and the "rejoicing" (שִׂמְחָה, as in 1 Sam 18:6; 1 Kgs 1:40) lasting but a moment. Some in fact think that מִקָּרוֹב, lit. "from near," means his rejoicing is "from recent (time)," so that the whole extent of the wrongdoer's triumph is so to speak "from" a second ago "until" (עדי) the next "moment" (so Fohrer). But even if we should just take the *min* as comparative, and translate "of the briefest" (BDB), we recognize a familiar thought; cf. 8:13–15 (Bildad, though his point is rather that of "sudden reversal"); 15:31–33 (Eliphaz, though his point is rather that of "untimely end"); Ps 37:2, 9, 10, 35–36; 73:18–20.

Zophar concedes that the wicked may indeed prosper, having something to shout or sing about, but the proper perspective on his well-being is to recognize how short-lived it is. This is even more unarguable than Eliphaz's claim that the wicked "is in torment all his days" (15:20) or Bildad's that he is surrounded by snares (18:8–10). For Zophar's truth about the wicked corresponds to no psychological reality within the wicked (as Eliphaz's), nor to any metaphysical reality that surrounds the wicked (as Bildad's), but solely to the observer's own estimation of time: if you can be as patient as the wisdom of the ages would have you be, you will see that however long the wicked prospers it is only for a moment, for this is the kind of time that is weighed, not measured. Once the chronometer is left out of the calculation of the duration of the wicked's prosperity, it is easy to see, as Terrien puts it, that "the dogma of retribution is the object of continual verification." Andersen most interestingly suggests that Zophar's concession, that the present experience of the godless may be anything but tragic, moves Zophar "nearer to Job's position that confidence in God's justice is not based on observation, but is a matter of trust and hope." But this is overgentle with Zophar, for Zophar has knowledge, not trust, and leans for his support upon the wisdom of the ages, not upon hope. Zophar is not a materialist; he does not measure time by the clock. But is a quixotic idealism that ignores concrete and social reality preferable to materialism?

6–7 The wicked in this chapter is represented exclusively as an agent of social wrong who dispossesses the poor (v 19). He is not specifically immoral or irreligious. But his social power is felt by himself—and by others—to be godlike in its control over others; so it is natural for the poet to depict him as making an assault on heaven. The wicked man would recognize in himself no such ambition, and would no doubt pride himself rather for being merely shrewd or successful. Zophar's depiction, however, means that being shrewd or successful at the expense of other people's livelihood is a hybris that will earn an inevitable doom.

The similar account of the wicked in Ps 37:35–36, "towering [?] like a cedar of Lebanon" and then suddenly not to be found, might suggest that here too the backgound image is simply of a huge tree. But the words "heaven" and "cloud" are different, and incline us to see a mythological background of the assault on heaven (as attested in Isa 14:12–20; differently in Ezek 28:2–19). For the conventional language of the "height" of the wicked's pride, cf. Ps 73:8–9; Obad 4.

The wicked perishes כגללו, lit. "like his dung," which most versions think is "his own dung" (KJV, RV, RSV, NEB, JPS, NIV). The coarseness (by some standards) is no problem, but the image is strange, for human excrement is not notably perishable. The reference could be to its noisomeness, comparable with the stench of a decaying body; but we would have expected rather some picture of total destruction. That is readily supplied if we take the dung as the animal dung used as fuel (cf. NAB "like the fuel of his fire"). Wetzstein in Delitzsch's commentary has a fascinating account of the use of *gelle* (the same word as in our text) by Syrian peasants of the last century: the cow-dung, free from smell even when fresh, is collected from the fields, mixed with chopped straw and formed into round cakes. Thoroughly dried out during the summer, the cakes are built into domes as high as 25 feet, and gradually used up as winter fuel. Wetzstein's own exegesis of our verse is cryptic and probably mistaken; the image is simply of fuel that is totally consumed in a short space of time.

For the phrase "those who saw him," cf. 7:8 "the eye of him that saw me," and for "where is he?" cf. 14:10; Isa 33:18. The sense is of the disappearance into insubstantiality of the all-too-visible (his head reaching the sky) wrongdoer, a theme sustained in vv 8–9. A little conventional wisdom-like narrative is presupposed here: the acquaintances of the wicked pass by his house, look for him but fail to find him; the scenario is more developed at Ps 37:35–36. At 14:10 Job used the same question to depict the hopeless fate of all mortals; in using it just of the wicked, Zophar cannot be contradicting him, for he also must believe there is no life after death. The parallel simply points up the irony that the fate of the wicked is in the end no different from anyone's fate.

8 Here too the language is conventional, both psalmic and prophetic texts depicting enemies as phantoms of a dream (Ps 73:20; Isa 29:7). Such a designation does not only mean that wrongdoers are as quickly exterminated as dream-images are at the moment of wakening (though this seems to be the connective thread in the present strophe), but also that they have no substantive reality and in the broad light of day are shown up to be mere appearance. The wicked man certainly does not come across to the poor and dispossessed of v 19 as a mere phantom, for he is the concrete reality that more than anything else dominates their lives; but to the wise man who can afford to acquire the wisdom of the ages (v 4), since he does not have to spend too much time keeping the wolf from the door, the wicked are nothing more than figments of his imagination, their prosperity a temporary blemish on the doctrine of retribution that can be removed by the simple expedient of rubbing one's eyes awake.

The "night vision" (חזיון לילה) is here certainly a dream though in 4:13 it seems to be a waking vision. For "fly away" (עוף) used of dying, cf. Ps 90:10. Not being "found" implies the narrative lying behind v 7 (and cf. also 7:21).

9 The thought links back to 7b (it is not that the eye that saw him in dream-vision no longer sees him when morning comes, as Fohrer, Hesse). For the conventional phraseology of the eye of one's acquaintances (not, God) no longer seeing one, cf. 7:8a (Job); Ps 37:10; and for one's place no longer knowing one, cf. 7:10b; 8:18; Ps 103:16b.

It is hard to accept Habel's claim that there are repeated references in these verses to Job's speech of chap. 7. He argues that the disappearance of the wicked "like a dream" (v 8) "recalls Job's complaint that God was terrifying him with nightmares" (7:14), that the reference to "those who see" (v 7) is a sharp jibe by Zophar with "allusion to the recurring surveillance motif" (the "Seeing Eye" of God in 7:8), and that picturing the wicked as "lying in the dust" (v 11) is a way of branding Job a sinner because in 7:21 Job acknowledges he will soon lie in the dust. None of these parallels in language can carry such a weight.

10 No truly satisfactory interpretation of this awkward verse exists. The very reference to the wrongdoer's "children" seems out of place in a strophe dealing with his own annihilation, especially since the children, however impoverished they may become, live on and so in a way perpetuate his name. This is not quite the annihilation of the wrongdoer we have been hearing of. Many critics think the verse misplaced, Dhorme and Terrien transferring it to follow v 19 and others (NEB, Moffatt) placing it after v 11. Problems still remain, as Duhm remarked; if the text speaks of the restitution of stolen wealth by the children of the wrongdoer, who, may it be supposed, compels them to make amends, and why should this be regarded as such a bad thing? So both subject matter and the lack of connection of thought brand the line as doubtful, and no proposed conjectural emendation recommends itself. The square brackets in the translation indicate that the verse seems unsuitable. Duhm and NAB simply omit it.

Two distinct lines of interpretation have been advanced. (a) Taking רצה in the generally postbiblical sense "satisfy (a debt), make up for" (Levy; but also "pay off" in biblical Heb.), we could translate, "his children will compensate the poor" (Dhorme) or "make amends to the poor" (NIV; cf. JB). In that case the second half of the line should mean that they "return his wealth" to those from whom he has stolen it. But the text says "*his* hands" return it; hence emendations to יְדֵיהֶם "their hands" (cf. *BHK*, NEB) or יְלָדָיו "his children" (Hölscher, JB; emendation of the gender of the verb is also required, to יָשִׁיבוּ). Gordis thinks that MT ידיו "his hands" can actually mean "his offspring," but his parallels are unconvincing. It is something of a difficulty with this view that we have hitherto learned nothing of the source of the evildoer's wealth (and v 19 does not exactly tell us either), and to have his children restoring his ill-gotten gains does not seem to be on the same level of destruction that vv 7–9 portrayed.

(b) A no more plausible sense arises if we take רצה as "seek the favor of" (RSV), and suggest that the children of the wrongdoer, as the poorest of the poor, are reduced to begging their bread from the poor (NEB "pay court to the poor," NJPS "ingratiate themselves with the poor"; Driver-Gray, Fohrer). This is presumably because "he" has had to restore the property of the poor to them, so that there is nothing left for his children to inherit (so Fohrer). This view adds to the difficulty of the previous view the improbability that the evildoer is envisaged as restoring the goods of the poor in his own lifetime ("*his* hands"). A weaker version of this interpretation is to take the two halves of the line as parallel, describing both the children's act and the father's (cf. NJPS); but why in that order?

If any sense is to be made of the verse, it seems that the father's act must precede the children's (Sicre Diaz also sees that we have a case of *hysteron proteron* here.) I would suggest that the father's hands "relinquish" (as BDB translates שׁוב hiphil here) their "strength" (as אוֹן generally means; MT "his strength" since of course the hands' strength is the man's strength). This at least fits well with v 11. Now although the simple connective *waw* is used, the loss of the father's strength in death must be the cause of the children's needy state. His property is not at all in view here; they are in reduced circumstances just because he has prematurely perished.

11 The thought of the *premature* death of the wicked is appended to the strophe, which otherwise has concerned simply his disappearance from earth:

he vanishes, and that before his time. The first clause should be understood concessively, "though his bones are full of vigor." Zophar's theology stresses that the wicked does not live out his days (cf. Ps 55:24 [23], "not half their days"; cf. 102:25 [24]) because retribution overtakes him. There may be some delay in the execution of justice, as v 6 allows, but his fate is the grave (the wording is reminiscent of 17:13–16 where Job's hope does *not* descend to Sheol to the couch he has spread). Terrien curiously thinks that Zophar "makes a bizarre personification of the sexual vigor of the wicked and has it go down with him into his tomb like a lover"; but עלומים no more signifies sexual vigor (cf. 33:25; Ps 89:46 [45]; Isa 54:4) than does שכב typically mean "lie with sexually"; the Arab. cognate of עלם cannot determine the meaning of the Heb.

The strophe has been differently understood as demonstrating that sin brings its own retribution, God "us[ing] a person's own wickedness to bring about his downfall" (Andersen; cf. Rowley, "The self-entailed retribution of sin"). That is indeed the significance of the food being "turned about" in his stomach (v 14a), but the dominant theme of "no lasting profit" is more clearly indicated by vv 18, 21.

12–23 This second strophe defines itself by the sustained metaphor of eating: we have the mouth (v 12), the tongue (v 12), the palate (v 13), the stomach (v 14), the innards (v 14), the belly (vv 15, 20, 23); there is savoring (v 12), swallowing (v 15), vomiting and disgorging (v 15), sucking (v 16), disgorging (v 18), not swallowing (v 18), eating (v 21); there is sweetness (v 12), oil, honey, and cream (v 17), food (v 23); above all, there is fullness of abundance (v 22) and filling to the full (v 23). Not surprisingly, the metaphor is deployed in a variety of ways.

The primary theme appears to be that the sinner gains no lasting profit from his wrongdoing. This links back into the primary image of the previous strophe (vv 4–11), the ultimate disappearance of the evildoer. The food he eats leads to his death, not his life. In the first place, the image is of food that is pleasant to the taste but sours the stomach and is vomited up (vv 12–15), so that it does not function as life-supporting food. In a second version of the image, the food that he eats is itself actually deadly poison, which prevents him enjoying real food and compels him to vomit it up (vv 16–19). The third use of the image has him eating as a glutton and consuming all available food so that he possesses no further stocks of food and thus through his appetite is brought to starvation (vv 20–22). Another dimension to the image is provided by the notations that God makes him vomit up his food (v 15b) and that the food he believes is sustaining him is actually the anger of God that is bloating him (v 23). Throughout these varying deployments of the controlling metaphor is the idea that there is no lasting profit from his eating (v 18b).

12–14 In this long sentence, of which vv 12–13 are two conditional clauses and v 14 the principal clause, the wrongdoer's wickedness is depicted as sweet food that becomes bitter in the stomach. The tasty morsel is sweet to the mouth, the tongue, and the palate. It is a conventional enough picture of sin as enticing; cf. Prov 9:17, "stolen water is sweet, bread eaten in secret is pleasant"; 20:7 "bread gained by deceit is sweet"; Gen 3:6. But there is the more developed thought here of keeping the sweet food in the mouth as long as possible in order to extract the maximum pleasure from it.

The term for "sweet" (מָתוֹק; here the verb מתק, intransitive hiph) can be applied to water (Exod 15:25) as well as to sugary things (honey, Judg 14:14; Ps 19:11), and may here not mean specifically sweet but simply "pleasant." The epicurean evildoer "hides" his sin under his tongue, not of course in this image to conceal it but to savor it (cf. Cant 4:11 "honey and milk under your tongue"). He is loath to let go of his pleasure: the Heb. is literally "he spares it" (חמל, as at 6:10; 16:13; 27:22), used only here in this transferred sense, perhaps ironically suggesting the evildoer's protective attitude toward his wrongdoing. To "forsake" (עזב) a morsel of food is also an extravagant idea, implying that it is some object of worth, like wisdom, the law, or God, which is what people generally do or don't forsake. Letting the food linger on his palate is literally "withholding" it (מנע), the palate jealously and selfishly holding the morsel back from being swallowed.

But evil deeds, "no matter how pleasurable the sensation involved when they are committed, have an inherent destructive capacity which discloses itself at a later stage" (Habel). It is not the sweetness in itself that is the problem, though Prov 25:27 warns that it is not good to eat much honey. When the food of the evildoer is swallowed it proves its true character; the man suffers food poisoning as his delicay is "turned" (הפך ni.), as we say of milk that has become sour (the wording is not that it is turned "into" the venom of asps [as Gordis, NJPS], for the second half of the line is an independent clause). In his stomach (as מעים is at Ezek 3:3; 7:19; Jonah 2:1, 2 [1:17; 2:1]; not "bowels," as KJV, RV, Pope) his evil becomes metaphorically the venom of asps (v 15 will say somewhat differently that it was snake's venom he has been eating all along). D. Pardee has shown how מררה (16:13; 20:25) from the root מרר "be bitter" is in the first place "gall" (bile) as the bitter-tasting secretion of the liver and secondarily as the poison emitted by snakes, their venom, which was thought by the ancients to be their gall ("mᵉrôrăt-pᵉtanîm 'Venom' in Job 20:14," *ZAW* 91 [1979] 401–16). On the snake, see on v 16.

This depiction is, next to vv 24–25, the most interesting part of Zophar's rather tepid speech, but even it is excessively conventional. Cf. Prov 23:31–32 where wine that goes down smoothly bites in the end like a serpent and stings like an adder; 20:17 where food gained by deceit is sweet in the mouth but is afterwards gravel in the mouth; and Deut 32:32–33 where the grapes of the Lord's enemies are grapes of poison and clusters of venom (מררה as here), their wine is the poison (ראש = רוש, as in v 16) of serpents and the venom (ראש) of asps (פתן, as here). Cf. also Rev 10:10, where the scroll is honey in the mouth but bitter in the stomach. The snake's poison is of course seen as fatal (Num 21:6; Deut 32:24; Amos 5:19).

15 The next stage, once the stomach has become full of bile, is vomiting. It is the same image extended; but in continuing the metaphor the poet says in plain language what the food of the image is: it is "wealth" (חיל) that the evildoer has swallowed, and that can only be other people's wealth, though the poet will not explicitly say so until v 19. There is no such thing as a free lunch, and no one becomes rich except at the expense of other people. The Egyptian *Instruction of Amenemope* warns: "Be not greedy for the property of a poor man . . . it is a blocking to the throat, it makes a vomiting to the gullet" (chap. 11; *ANET*, 423a). It is strange to find here God as the admininstrator of an emetic, not because the figure is coarse ("as befits Zophar," says Peake) for it occurs also in Jer 51:44, but because in wisdom teaching generally God does not so often personally execute vengeance. It could well be that Zophar simply means that God so orders the world that bitter and poisonous food irritates the stomach to the point of vomiting it up; in that case God would be doing nothing at all directly (and talk of a divine emetic would be misleading), but would be simply allowing the natural moral order to take its course. This sounds, it must be said, more like the Zophar of 11:13–20. The LXX, incidentally, found the idea of God causing a man to vomit too distasteful and either had an "angel" do it, or transformed the vomiting into an "expulsion" from the evildoer's "house," or both (see Gard, *Exegetical Method of the Greek Translator,* 26).

Gray and Pope are worried by the idea that the emetic will rid the man of the poison and so in the end do him a good turn, so they sever this verse from the image of vv 12–14; but of course the poison *is* the unjustly gained wealth, and to be rid of the poison is to be rid of the wealth. Sin disagrees with the human constitution as bad food disagrees with the stomach.

16 It is hard to see what this verse adds to v 14, and some more resolute commentators delete it (Budde, Driver-Gray, Hölscher). It does indeed say that the evildoer *dies* of the poison—which v 14 left at most implied. But when does he "suck" the poison? Not *after* the eating and vomiting of vv 12–15, as most translations seem to imply. It can only be that the sweetmeat in his mouth in vv 12–17 was actually poison, and that while he thought he was savoring a delicacy, he was in fact absorbing more and more poison into his system; hence the translation "it was poison that he sucked" in vv 12–13 (cf. JB). This image does not square too well with a common understanding of v 14, that his food *turns into* poison in his stomach, for v 16 seems to be saying that it has been poison all along. But if v 14b describes not what happens in the stomach but what the stomach as distinct from the mouth recognizes to be harmful food, the two images cohere, and v 16 tells us that the stomach was right to heave. It also tells us that vomiting solves nothing, for the fatal poison is already at work. In plain language, making money is destructive to those who make it, and not only to those they make it from. More theologically, the results of sin develop according to an inexorable but natural logic.

On the zoological front, the פתן that appears here and in v 14 is not precisely the asp, the Egyptian cobra not found in Palestine, but any large snake; the אפעה is usually taken as the Carpet Viper (F. S. Bodenheimer, *IDB* 2:246–56 [254]), with illustration). No snakes sting or kill with their tongue, but with the poison discharged through the front teeth or fangs; nevertheless, the darting tongue of the viper (actually in constant motion because it is the organ of smell) was not unreasonably regarded as the means by which the poison was delivered. Cf. Ps 140:4 [3] for a tongue as sharp as a viper's, and 1QH 5.27 for lying tongues like the venom of adders fitfully spurting forth (translation, T. H. Gaster, *The Scriptures of the Dead Sea Sect* [London: Secker and Warburg, 1957] 153).

17 Food is still the image, but there is a new twist, for here it is not the poisonous food that the evildoer eats but the wholesome food that he will never eat because he has died of his eating. This is quintessential Palestinian food that he will not "enjoy" (ראה ב, see n. 20:17.a): oil, honey, and cream are the regular symbols of plenty in the land of Canaan. Olive oil (see n. 20:17.c) literally flowed in "streams" from the oil press (cf. 24:11; 29:6 where the rock-hewn press pours out streams [פלג like פלגה here] of oil; Joel 2:24 where the vats overflow with wine and oil). It is strange that there are not more references to the use of oil in cooking, since we may assume a widespread use; but cf. Num 11:8; Jdt 10:5. There never have been "torrents" (נחל) of honey and curds, so we must readjust our reading of "streams" of oil to see that also as hyperbolic. Honey is typically in OT times not the honey of domesticated bees but wild honey (Judg 14:8; 1 Sam 14:25–26) or a thick grape or date syrup (Arab. *dibs*) (J. F. Ross, *IDB* 2:639). Cream or curds (חמאה) is not butter (KJV, RV), but a fermented milk product, today called leben, and similar to yoghurt, "prepared by churning fresh milk in a goatskin containing left over clots from the previous supply" (J. F. Ross, *IDB* 1:749); it is fed by Abraham to his visitors (Gen 18:8), by Jael to Sisera (Judg 5:25), and by Barzillai to David's troops (2 Sam 17:29). In Isa 7:14 curds and honey are perhaps a basic diet, but more often milk and honey are a symbol of plenty, especially if the land is flowing with them (Exod 3:8, 17; 13:5; 33:3; Lev 20:24 and often). In the Baal myth, a celebrated passage has El dreaming that Baal has returned to life and the earth's fertility is reawakened; he sees that "the heavens rained oil, the ravines (*nḥl*, as נחל here) ran with honey" (*CTA* 6.3.12–13 [Gibson, 67]). Fohrer strangely maintains that the images in our text belong to an old nomadic formulation and have nothing to do with the Ugaritic text; but even if these depictions of plenty represent in the first place the longing of the unsettled for the lifestyle of the Palestinian peasant, the images stem from the experience of the peasant, not the nomad.

18 The strophe concludes with this summary verse, to which v 19 forms a pendant. V 18a reiterates the image of v 15, while v 18b picks up the theme of v 17. In brief, because the evildoer must vomit up his gains, he never experiences the enjoyment of them. There is no explicit word yet of the source of his wealth (despite the hint in v 15 and the renderings here of many versions, e.g., NEB "he must give back his gains without swallowing them," implying that he has robbed others and must repay them). The emphasis is solely on how it feels from his point of view to lose possession of what is dear to him. He restores nothing to anyone; and no one benefits from his loss, though, as we shall see, his gain had been loss for others. Even good gifts are contaminated by the poison of his person.

19 Here at last the metaphors drop away, and we learn some specifics of the actual wrongdoing of the wicked. Granted, these crimes are only exemplary, and in a way even this description functions metaphorically for the whole range of evils that can brand a person one of the wicked. But it is of unmistakable significance that the crime that comes most readily to Zophar's mind as the quintessence of wickedness is a social and economic crime. Not a sin against God, nor a cultic offense, not the infringement of some state law, but the perhaps perfectly legal exploitation of the poor is the crime above crimes. "Attitudes and actions toward the underprivileged is a fundamental gauge of integrity and righteousness in Job" (Habel); uncaring rejection of their needs will be the unwitting sin Eliphaz will accuse Job of (22:5–9) and will be later the subject of Job's most passionate self-exculpations (29:12–17; 31:13–23).

And what precisely has the wicked done? רצץ, though a common word "to crush," seems to be here no metaphor but a semitechnical word from the practice of law meaning "defraud" (contrast NEB "hounded," NIV "oppressed,"

RSV, NJPS "crushed"). Cf. 1 Sam 12:3–4 where Samuel denies having taken anyone's ox or ass (parallel to עשׁק "extort" as also Deut 28:33; Amos 4:1; Hos 5:11); in 2 Chr 16:10 where Asa imprisons the seer Hanani he also רצץ some of the people, presumably supporters of Hanani—again the word may have a much more specific meaning than "oppressed" (NAB) or "inflicted cruelties" (RSV). Of course "defraud" can cover a multitude of sins, not all of them objectively illegal acts; what the buyer thinks is a fair price the seller may rightly believe defrauds him because he is forced by economic necessity to sell his goods or his labor cheap. The wicked person of this depiction is clearly in the position of economic power, ranged over against the "poor" (דלים). There can be no "free" markets when those who meet in the market square are not economic equals but rich and poor.

Next, the wicked has "forsaken" (עזב) the poor. This too seems at first a vague term (as NEB "harassed," NJPS "tortured"), and Gordis suggests that the figure of *hysteron proteron* is being used, "the order of two sequential acts [being] reversed because the more important [and here the more specific] intrudes upon the consciousness of the speaker or writer" (cf. Exod 24:7; Esth 9:27); he translates "He has forsaken, indeed crushed, the poor" (though in his translation proper he has "oppressed and tortured"). That is not unreasonable, but comparison with Deut 12:19; 14:27 where Israel is enjoined not to "forsake" (עזב) the Levite suggests that it is "neglect" (as BDB) or disregarding of the legitimate demands of a social group that is at issue. Here it is probably the ignoring of the cry of the poor for justice, perhaps specifically in the matter of their property rights spoken of in the next half of the line.

More specifically still, perhaps on the principle of the "parallelism of greater precision" (D. J. A. Clines, "The Parallelism of Greater Precision: Notes from Isaiah 40 for a Theory of Hebrew Poetry," *New Directions in Biblical Poetry*, ed. E. R. Follis [JSOTS 40; Sheffield: JSOT, 1987] 77–100), the crime of the wicked is to "seize a house that he has not built" (lit. "and he has not built it"), that is, a house that someone else built. This act of violence (גזל is "tear away, take violent possession") is not necessarily seen as such by its perpetrators, for whom it may be simply a paper transaction; the rich, who may for example be "rent capitalists" or money-lenders (see B. Lang, "The Social Organization of Peasant Poverty in Biblical Israel," *JSOT* 24 [1982] 47–63), may simply regard themselves as enforcing agreed contracts and acting entirely aboveboard. Even if they have inherited the property or money that gives them power over others, and have not set out to aggrandize themselves, their use of that power inevitably leads to loss, experienced as violent deprivation (גזל), by those they have power over. A person can become one of the wicked by simply complying with the given economic system (contrast Job himself in 29:12–16; 31:16–21). On גזל as an antisocial act, see J. Schüpphaus, TDOT 2:456–58, and cf. Prov 28:24 and 22:22 where revealingly the poor are in danger of being violently robbed (גזל) just because they are poor. This does not mean that the rich are so foolish as to think robbing the poor is more profitable than robbing a bank, but that the poor are always the victims of the economic system. From those that have not is taken even that which they have.

20–21 In these lines, the opening "for" (כי) clause looks forward and is picked up by the "therefore" (על־כן) of v 21 (contrast the כי of v 19 which looks back to the preceding); the two intervening clauses (vv 20b, 21a) are best understood as further reasons for the "therefore." The image of food is continued, but a new aspect is developed here: here it is the greed for eating, where the key terms are "not content," "belly," "desired" (v 20), "eat," "produce" (טוב) (v 21), "be full," "sufficiency" (v 22), "fill," "belly," "rain down," "food" (v 23). Earlier in the strophe the stress had been on the reversal and disappointment of expectation when the sweet food turns sour and when what is eaten is vomited up. Here the all-consuming greed of the wicked feeds on itself and so self-destructs. The behavior of the wicked is the cause of his doom.

Food is a finite resource that may be used up completely; so too the desire of the wicked for self-aggrandizement leads ultimately, if it is not checked, to the consumption of all that it fed on till nothing is left. Because he is insatiable he can never feel satisfied (Fohrer). He knows no "quietness" or contentment (שלו) in his belly. Prov 17:1 "Better is a dry morsel with quiet (or, contentment, שלוה), than a house full of feasting with strife," presents an objective, externalized view of the value of quietness for eating; here the disturbance is wholly internal, not through lack but through surfeit. Wisdom more typically features the wicked as starving (Prov 13:25 "the belly of the wicked suffers want"); here the evildoer's greed is the cause of his want.

The second half of v 20a is often taken as a statement of the punishment for his greed; e.g., RSV "he will not save anything in which he delights." But the structure of these verses is best understood as three clauses (vv 20–21a) giving reasons for the judgment of v 21b ("therefore . . .") (so also Fohrer, Pope). Seen in this light, the present phrase means that he consumes everything his appetite desires, like a glutton or scavenger; "he has let nothing that he desired escape him," as though his food were hunted animals or humans that he does not save or deliver (as מלט piel usually means) from the consequences of his greed. The result is that, when this trencherman has done eating, no food is left in the cupboard, or, as it runs literally and more anthropomorphically, "there is no survivor of his eating." שריד is elsewhere always used of human survivors of battle or disaster (e.g., 18:19; 27:15; Deut 2:34; and cf. also v 26 below). The lines sketch a grossly amusing picture of a cannibalistic decimation of comestibles by a gargantuan evildoer.

His property (טוב), or probably specifically the edible "produce" of the land (cf. Gen 45:18; Ezra 9:12; Neh 9:35) since the food metaphor is still dominant, does not continue, lit. "stay firm" (חול elsewhere at Ps 10:5), not because God brings vengeance upon him (though he does), but because the greedy evildoer has consumed everything that came into his hands.

In the light of the food metaphor in vv 12–19, where it transpired in vv 15 and 19 that the crime of the evildoer was not really gluttony but avarice for the possessions of others, we may be sure that the same is the case here also, though nothing says so explicitly.

22 What the wicked robs from others makes its possessor not rich but poor (Weiser). The reversal theme emerges here: at the moment when he is most satiated, "at the fullness of his sufficiency" (the language itself is overblown; either word alone would do), he suddenly "becomes straitened" (צרר; on the symbolism of "narrowness" and "spaciousness" see on 36:16), or in distress. It is a bald and blunt phrase, lit. "there is narrowness for him," the straits being objectified like a package that is delivered to him. It is hard to know whether the term connotes the state of mind of a person in anxiety and distress

(Dhorme). Certainly, this is a more dramatic image than we have had in vv 20–21, where the wicked gradually consumes all earth's resources; here, when he is indeed full he is (suddenly) brought into judgment; the "full force" of misery (NIV) assails him like a warrior (בוא "come [against]" in the military sense, "attack" [BDB, 98b § 2b], as in 3:24; 5:21; 15:21). "Misery" (עמל) is the wicked man's fate because it is the opposite of his wealth and sufficiency; עמל is not generally, perhaps never, the emotional feeling of misery, but typically the objective situation of being hard at work or being oppressed (see respectively Eccl 2:10; Deut 26:7 with Job 3:10, 4:8 [by implication]; 5:6, 7; 7:3; 11:16; 16:2) or the objective act of oppressing (4:8; 15:35; Ps 10:7; Isa 59:4 [this emphasis is lacking in S. Schwertner's entry in *THWAT* 2:332–35]). In Prov 31:7 it is directly parallel to "poverty," and here too it signifies the deprivation of his ample means.

23 The wicked person thinks that he has been satisfying his greed; but he will not know what satisfaction really is until he is filled by the wrath of God. There is more of that available, in unlimited supply, than all the victuals he has ever laid his hands on. There is a grim humor here, both in the idea of the bloated glutton being further force-fed (God's wrath is "sent into" him and he has no choice about ingesting it), and in the parody of the manna story, where God "rained" (מטר hiph, as here) "food" (לחם, cf. לחום here or לחם by emendation; see n. 20:23.f) upon the people (Exod 16:4; Ps 78:24; cf. v 27). The background is not (as against Fohrer) the breaking in of the chaotic waters of heaven as at the flood (Gen 6:11) or of the raining down of fire and brimstone on Sodom and Gomorrah (Gen 19:24; cf. Ps 11:6).

Fohrer sees here in the picture of the "sending" of God's wrath an almost personal figure who executes God's vengeance, "on the way to a hypostasis as a kind of bad angel." Even if that goes too far, there is unmistakably here the idea that the law of retribution under which the evildoer is rewarded like for like, filled with God's wrath as recompense for filling himself with the goods of others, is no mechanical and self-effecting principle but the deliberate act of God (cf. also v 15b). God is so evidently the promoter of the moral order that he does not need to be mentioned by name: "he" sends his burning anger against the wrongdoer. For a similar thought in which God's action is equally prominent, cf. Ps 17:14, a curse upon the wicked: "May their belly (בטן) be filled (מלא) with what you have in store for them."

24–29 This third strophe has as its principal theme the inescapability of the end of the wicked. That is the significance of the military narrative (vv 24–25b): even if he escapes one weapon, he will fall to another that will prove fatal. There is then a depiction of the arrival of death itself, which he experiences as terror and as darkness. More objectively, his death is described as being consumed by divine wrath (v 26), and then a cosmic imagery of a legal procedure presses home the point that he has no defense against a death sentence (v 27). Parallel to the consuming fire of v 26 is the overflowing waters that "roll away" him and his house (v 28). Finally, a summary appraisal (v 29) draws together the twin strands of the evildoer's fate as both his own creation (cf. "inheritance") and as divine punishment (cf. "portion").

The imagery here is almost exclusively violent; apart from the lawcourt images of v 27, there is the battlefield image of v 24, focusing down to the close-up on the wounded man pulling the arrow from his body only to lose his vitals in the process (v 25), the fireball (v 26b–c), the flood (v 28). The language is conventional, and, apart from the battle images of vv 24–25—which even so are not so interestingly developed as analogues elsewhere in the OT—the depictions are somewhat jejune. But the cumulative effect is not unimpressive, and it invites speculations on the psychology of a theologian who finds it necessary to invest his belief in retribution with such lurid imaginings.

24 It is a familiar thought here of the inescapability of doom, one avenue of escape leading inexorably only to a worse or more certain end. Cf. Isa 24:18 where we have the sequence: flee from the sound of terror, fall in a pit, climb out of a pit, be caught in a snare; and Amos 5:19 where we have: fled from a lion, met by a bear, went into a house, a serpent bites (cf. also 9:1–4). Though encountered in the prophets, the idea is obviously part of popular wisdom (so too Hölscher). The present formulation is less picturesque than those cited: If he flees from a weapon of iron, an arrow of bronze pierces him through. We recall that Zophar is a traditionalist (cf. v 4) even in the images of his speech. It would be extremely tame if the sense were: if he escapes from an iron weapon, he will be slain by a bronze. Though נשק is a general word for weapon (as Ezek 39:9–10, where the types are specified), it may well be that a "weapon of iron" is understood as specifically a sword (so Gordis). If that is so, the point is, more interestingly, that if the wicked escapes from destruction at close quarters (by sword), he will be caught up from afar (by arrows). The Heb. actually says "bronze *bow*" (קשת), as at Ps 18:35 [34], but of course only arrows from a bow can "pierce" (חלף "pass through," and so pierce, as Judg 5:26, of a tent-peg), so "bow" must be used by synecdoche (part for whole) or some such figure (as at Isa 13:18) (surprisingly JB, NAB, NJPS still have "bow"). Moreover, a bow of bronze would be an impossible weapon, lacking flexibility or resilience (G. R. Driver, VTSup 3 [1955] 82; Y. Yadin, *The Art of Warfare in Biblical Lands* [London: Weidenfeld and Nicolson, 1963] 6–9); the only bronze bows known from antiquity are dedicatory gifts to temples and not for practical use (K. Galling, *Biblisches Reallexikon* [2nd ed.; Tübingen: Mohr, 1977] 50), and there is no evidence of bows with metal coverings or decoration (as Hölscher, R. de Vaux, *Ancient Israel: Its Life and Institutions* [tr. J. McHugh; London: Darton, Longman and Todd, 1961] 243). Even arrows would not be primarily of metal but of reed or wood, and we should understand "bronze-tipped" (as NEB, NIV). Perhaps bronze was used along with horn as a strengthening element in the manufacture of a "composite" bow; but more probably the bronze in question may simply have been the points on the arrows. B. Couroyer ("L'arc d'airain," *RB* 72 [1965] 508–14) argued that a "bow of bronze" means only a strong bow, but the fact that this bow is parallel to what is clearly a metal weapon (of iron) puts that explanation out of court.

There is no call to follow Habel's suggestion here that Zophar "intends a satirical allusion to Job's earlier portrayal of Shaddai as the Archer who fires his poisoned arrows into Job" (6:4; 16:13); see the general comments on allusion at v 9.

25–26 These two tricola, as they appear in the MT, are probably to be redivided as three bicola (so also Terrien, NIV). For despite many uncertainties in translation, it is plain that "from his back" (מגוה) in v 25a is parallel to "from his gall" (מִמְּרֹרָתוֹ) in v 25b, and "fire eats" in v 26b is parallel to "it consumes" in v 26c; it seems then that the "terrors" that "come upon him" in v 25c are parallel to the "darkness" that is "hidden" or "hides" to harm him.

The image in v 25a–b, if we retain the MT, is fairly clearly a development of v 24. There the wicked man is fleeing from punishment but is overtaken by an arrow, which obviously strikes him in the back. He attempts to withdraw it from his body (שׁלף being the precise term for drawing a weapon from a wound, Judg 3:22), or to be more exact, from his gallbladder (מררה), with the result that the gall spills on the ground (the image of the arrow puncturing the gallbladder or liver is the same as in 16:13), a fatal injury. In a way, he kills himself; in his attempt to extract the divine arrow, he spills his own vitals. As he sees what has been done to him and what he is doing to himself, the "terrors" (אמים) come upon him; these, in the plural (contrast the more abstract "dread" in the singular at 9:34; 13:21; 33:7), are the same as the "terrors" of 18:11 (בלהות), the minions and messengers of Death. The depth of darkness, "darkness unrelieved" (NEB), "utter" (NJPS) or "total" (NIV) darkness, lit. "all darkness" (כל־חשׁך) like "all force" (כל־יד in v 22), lies hidden in waiting (טמן, see n. 20:26.a) for what he has hidden (צפן), i.e., accumulated in his greed. This all goes to say that Sheol is the only net gainer for all his activities, and, by way of poetic justice, lies hidden to swallow up what he had hidden. The "terrors" of Death and the "darkness" of Sheol stand in parallel.

The image changes again: after the images of warfare and of Sheol, the fire comes into play as another symbol of annihilation. This is supernatural fire, a fire not fanned or kindled (נפח, 41:12 [20]) by human hands but divine in origin like the fire from Yahweh that destroyed the family of Korah (Num 16:35); God is involved directly or indirectly in the fate of the wicked at several points in Zophar's speech (vv 15, 23, 28b, 29). In v 26a the darkness of death takes over his material possessions; here in v 26c the heavenly fire devours (אכל "eat," of fire from heaven at 1:16) any descendants he may have (שׂריד as usual means human "survivors" [so NEB, NJPS]; contrast v 21 above, and RSV, NIV "what is left"). This fire is not exactly lightning (as 1:16) but a more supernatural fire, the fire of God's wrath (contrast 15:34; 22:20), as the fire kindled by God's anger (Deut 32:22; Jer 15:14; 17:4). God's anger has destroyed his property (v 26a), his person (26b), and his household (26c) (Habel).

The belly is the core of the evildoer's being, his center of gravity, so it is fitting that the arrow of destruction strikes him there. He has sought to fill his belly (v 15) and has never known contentment in his belly (v 20); God therefore sends his wrath on him to fill his belly to the full, or, changing the image, to penetrate his gallbladder with his deadly arrow. Gall (מררה) proves his undoing in both strophes, in vv 12–19 and 20–29: at v 14 he finds his dainty food soured by the "gall" or poison of serpents within him, here the gall-sac as a vital organ is pierced and destroyed. His life long, he has been turning sweet into bitter; his death ensues when the souring organ that controlled his mode of being is ruptured. The biter is bit.

And the consumer is consumed. It is a nice irony that the man who lived for eating dies from being eaten. He himself is "devoured" (אכל) by fire; his descendants are "grazed on" (רעה).

27 As we approach the climax of the speech, the imagery becomes cosmic.

The focus is now not upon the inward minutiae of the evildoer's digestive system nor even upon the external facts of his dramatic but ineffectual flight from retributive justice, but upon the most public realities of all, heaven and earth that have witnessed every misdeed. In those most formal documents of the ancient world, the international treaties, heaven and earth are frequently called as witnesses, among other theogonic gods and gods of cultus (e.g., the Egyptian-Hittite treaty of Rameses II, *ANET,* 201a; the Hittite-Amurru treaty of Mursilis, *ANET,* 205a). That convention was adopted, so it seems, by the prophets for solemn declarations (Isa 1:2; cf. Mic 6:1, mountains) (cf. D. R. Hillers, *Treaty-Curses and the Old Testament Prophets* [Rome: Pontifical Biblical Institute, 1964] 4; and P. A. Riemann, *IDBS,* 192–97 [196a] for a well-nuanced statement, with bibliography), but it is also intelligible as a natural rhetorical move, uninfluenced by legal formulas, of invoking the cosmos as witness (cf. Deut 32:1). In the present context there is no specifically covenant or treaty overtone, but there is a generalized legal setting. The implication is that the crimes of the evildoer are on such a scale that heaven and earth have been compelled to take cognizance of them; they can then be called upon to testify to what they have seen and heard (cf. Ps 19:2–3 [1–2] where the heaven "recounts" God's glory and one day "shows knowledge" to the next of what it has learned). Heaven and earth also function as enduring witnesses (like a cairn, Gen 31:48; a traditional song, Deut 31:19, 21; a law-scroll, Deut 31:26; an altar, Josh 22:26–28, 34; the moon, Ps 89:38 [37]; the appeal to the moon in the *Instruction of Amenemope* 4:19 [*ANET,* 422a] to establish the crime of the wicked against him is somewhat different in that the moon-god Thoth has an official capacity as the barrister of the gods). The heavens "disclose" before the tribunal of God what they have witnessed of the wrongdoer and what he would wish to keep hidden (the language links back to v 26a and his "hidden treasures"); גלה is to "lay bare" deep mysteries (12:22), secret places (Jer 49:10), secrets (Prov 11:13; 25:9), a city's foundations (Mic 1:6), and when the object is transgressions it points to the element of hearing (Hos 7:1; Lam 2:14; Prov 26:26; Ezek 21:29 [24]; Isa 26:21), a legal situation always being assumed in which the hidden crime is discussed (H.-J. Zobel, *TDOT* 2:476–88 [480]). To the same legal context belongs the idea of a witness "rising up" (קום hithpo; more commonly in qal); for references to the rising of witnesses or a judge in court, see on 19:25–27. The two cosmic entities provide the legally required minimum for a verdict, for, as the old law has it, "A single witness shall not prevail against a man for any crime or for any wrong in connection with any offense that he has committed" (Deut 19:15).

At least since Budde, commentators have toyed with the speculation that Zophar is satirizing Job's appeal in 16:18 that the "earth" should not "cover" his blood, and his conviction in 16:19 that his "witness" is in "heaven" and in 19:25 that his champion will "rise" to speak in court on his behalf. Recently J. C. Holbert ("'The skies will uncover his iniquity': Satire in the Second Speech of Zophar [Job xx]," *VT* 31 [1981] 171–79) has argued that satire against Job is the clue to the whole speech: "The satiric technique is the same throughout. Zophar speaks what sounds like a general *Klage* on the fate of the wicked. However, the speech is filled with descriptions of the wicked which are clearly borrowed from *all* Job's earlier speeches" (p. 178). But it is inevitable, if Job is suffering and if traditional theology believes the wicked suffer, that there should be overlap in language; what has to be determinative is the overall purpose of each speaker, and we cannot assume too readily that we know what Zophar's aim is in depicting the fate of the wicked. And on the detail, there is not such a closeness of language as might be expected if direct allusion were being made to Job's speeches; for here it is *heaven* that discloses the wicked's *iniquity* whereas in 16:18 it was *earth* that was summoned not to cover Job's *blood*, and here it is earth itself that rises against the wicked whereas in 16:19 (and 19:25) it was a witness to Job who would rise in heaven.

28 Traditional versions of this verse made it sound rather anticlimactic, RSV for example having the possessions of the evildoer's house merely carried away and dragged off. Some commentators therefore thought the positions of vv 27 and 28 should be reversed (Budde, Dhorme, Driver-Gray [possibly], Moffatt). The prevailing view now, however, is to see here a reference to a devastating flood, which, in conjunction with the fire of v 26, annihilates the evildoer's "house" (see n. 20:26.e). The "streams" (יְבַל) that carry it away are in Isa 30:25 and 44:4 and Ecclus 50:8 beneficent streams, but also in Ps 18:5 [4] (emended text, reading יִבְלֵי for חבלי "cords," as NAB, parallel to נחלי "torrents"), the streams of the underworld. The torrential waters, like a swollen river in Palestine, sweep away the evildoer's physical dwelling (בית), built of earth or clay, but of course symbolically they are also the unmanageable waters of the underworld that annihilate his "house," that is, both his own body ("house of clay," 4:19) and his progeny.

The day of God's wrath (lit. "his" wrath, but God is implied as in v 23) is sometimes the eschatological day of God's wrath against a nation (Ezek 7:19; 22:24; Lam 1:12; 2:21, 22) but also a day of retribution against an individual (21:30; Prov 11:4), as here. God's wrath is depicted as an overflowing stream in Isa 30:28, and it is often the subject of verbs for pouring out (e.g., Hos 5:10, like water). In v 23 God's wrath had been "sent into" the man as a food substitute, he in his greed gladly taking in anything that will pass through his mouth but surprised at finding himself bloated on the divine anger. Here God's wrath is an external force that "rolls away" the evildoer and his house. The end of the wicked has been pictured in increasingly supernatural terms. In vv 5–11 there was no hint of *how* his end comes about; we heard only that when he perishes, he perishes for good. In vv 12–19, we heard something more about the causality: he comes to an end through his own greed, his favorite foods being turned sour in his stomach and being vomited up. But at the same time we hear of a divine causation of this apparently natural sequence: "God" makes him disgorge his food (v 15b). In vv 20–28 there is natural causation also, in that he consumes everything and presumably starves because he has nothing left to eat. At the same time we learn more definitively of the divine part in his annihilation: his end comes about through God sending upon him his wrath, which is first a bogus food that deceptively "fills" him, then a fire unfanned by human hands, consuming him and his, and finally a flood that sweeps him and all he possesses away. The poem has been moving gradually from the externally perceivable reality to the issues of the rationale and the mechanism of the evildoer's death.

29 Zophar's speech ends with a summary appraisal, like Bildad's at 18:21 (cf. for the wording 27:13, which however stands at the beginning not the end of a depiction; cf. also Ps 109:20). The portion (חלק) and the inheritance (נחלה) that are allotted to the evildoer are of course metaphors derived from the life of the clan, "portion" referring to the agricultural land assigned to an individual by the community, often by means of the lot (cf. M. Tsevat, *TDOT* 4:449), "inheritance" to that same land viewed as a possession of the family through its generations (cf. Num 26:53–54; 33:54). Though the "portion" is by definition only a part of the whole, for the family that earns its livelihood from the land it represents the whole material condition of its existence. From that sense it is a simple metaphorical shift to the idea of the total reality of a life, including its end or destiny, as apportioned by God (so also 27:13; 31:2; Isa 17:14; Eccl 3:22; 5:17 [18], 18 [19]; 9:9). The term "inheritance," on the other hand, views a life diachronically, as something that is handed down and in process of becoming; in this metaphor the destiny of a person does not derive directly from God, but is determined by one's ancestry, which in the metaphor means one's prevailing quality of life. One's "inheritance" is ultimately "from God" since he has established the retributive nexus, but it is more directly determined by oneself, the self as it ages "inheriting" the younger self (cf. for example "inherit the faults of my youth," 13:26).

As with Bildad's speech in chap. 18, Zophar's concludes with the word "God." Zophar has not so rigorously excluded God from his depiction of the fate of the wicked as did Bildad, for in the middle of the second strophe, that is, at the midpoint of the poem, God's role in the retributive process is explicit (v 15b), and at vv 23 and 28, though his name is not used, it is unmistakably God's anger that spells doom for the wicked. When the metaphors are decoded, we are probably to understand from Zophar that God does nothing to the wicked that the wicked do not already do to themselves; God's role is to establish the moral order and to ensure that it operates.

Terrien makes the intriguing remark that the evildoer is here compared with the אדם, the Adam of the primeval rebellion (for an allusion to the myth, cf. 15:7–8). Habel further sees the reference to Adam here as an inclusio linking up with v 4, where Man (אדם, *'adam*) was first placed on earth. Other elements of the poem may belong to the Adam image: the hybris of the man whose head reaches to the clouds (v 6), the food that is delightful to the taste but poison in the belly (vv 12–14), like the death-dealing fruit of Gen 3:6 that was delightful to the eyes, and his separation from the rivers that brought fertility (v 17).

Explanation

Zophar has done nothing in this speech but portray the fate of the wicked; what he means by this portrayal is not easily discerned. He has felt Job's refusal to accept the advice of his friends a reproach (v 3a), and he has probably been nettled by Job's last words that have declared the friends liable to judgment (19:28–29). But such annoyance would not justify him in pronouncing Job one of those wicked whose doom he delineates here. For Job has not evidently been one of the godless proud (v 6) who have savored wickedness (vv 12–13) and lived off its gains (vv 18–19). To what end would the poet have Zophar inform Job that his wickedness is quintessential, that Job will suffer the inescapable doom of the most nefarious of his class? What can be Zophar's meaning then?

If we may judge by his stance in his previous speech—and in the absence of any clear position here that seems an entirely reasonable procedure—Zophar believes that Job is guilty and deserves what he suffers, and no doubt more than he suffers (11:6c). If he does not adjust his way of life he will find a future unfolding for him identical to that of the wicked: the loss of hope and the absence of security will lead to an inescapable doom (11:20). Job however has the opening for a quite different life, a life of piety that will bring security (11:15, 18–19).

This too is how Job relates to the wicked in the present depiction. If Job refuses to eradicate from his life the evil his present suffering bears witness to, his fate will be the inheritance of the wicked (v 29). But it is up to Job to decide where his destiny lies; and Zophar, in a genuine effort to be constructive, paints the grimmest picture he knows how of the wicked's fate in the hope that Job will remove himself with all due haste from any shadow of identification with it.

Zophar's most distinctive rhetorical move in this speech has been the gradual unfolding of truths, a rhetoric that perhaps coheres closely with his view of life. It was noticeable in vv 14 and 16, for example, where first he told us that the wicked man has the poison of serpents in his belly, and only afterwards revealed how that poison got there: he had been sucking it in. Again, in vv 15 and 19 we learned first that it is characteristic of the wicked to swallow down wealth, but only later that the wealth is the wealth of others. In v 23 we learned that the evildoer's food, which we had been contemplating since v 12, has in some sense been the wrath of God all along. And in v 15b we found that the apparently natural process of vomiting up food that is sour in the stomach was after all a divine initiative.

This is Zophar's perception of the moral order: deeds and events do not wear their significances on their sleeves, but only gradually, or only by the discernment of the wise, can be persuaded to show themselves in their true colors. Wickedness may raise a man high as heaven (v 6), fill him with youthful vigor (v 11), taste sweet in his mouth (v 12), nourish him to full abundance (v 22), but the truth of it is, not primarily that God will one day bring the wickedness into judgment, but that these very benefits are already imbued with the opposite significance. It is not just that they carry the seed of their own destruction in them, but that they, rightly perceived, are themselves negativities. So when the wicked man greedily fills his belly with everything his eye desires, he is not only displaying his prosperity by his conspicuous consumption but at the same time eating away his prosperity to the point of extinction (vv 20–21). And the sweetness of evil that is savored on the tongue does not somehow suddenly become bitterness once the food has dropped to the stomach; the sweetness itself, rightly understood, is the poison of asps. It is not quite that "there is nothing either good or bad, but thinking makes it so" (*Hamlet* 2.2.259), but that wisdom sees the bad in what is generally accounted good, and, presumably, vice versa.

These thoughts are not developed for Job's sake; for when the speculative philosopher in Zophar begins to speak it is the internal logic of his thought that drives him on, not the pragmatic question of its applicability to Job. Job does not need to be warned that wickedness is its own recompense, especially wickedness under the figure of food, for he is in the condition where "sighing" is his food (3:24), and he is plotting nothing. Zophar's huge metaphysical system stands at some remove from reality, and it is with some surprise that we find him descending in v 19 to the level of the concrete, specifying one typical crime of the godless, a crime in the sphere of economic relations.

THE
SILENCE
CALLING

Perhaps when on my printed page you look,
　Your fancies by the fireside may go homing
To that lone land where bravely you endured.

　And if perchance you hear the silence calling,
The frozen music of star-yearning heights,
　Or, dreaming, see the seines of silver trawling
Across the ship's abyss on vasty nights,

　You may recall that sweep of savage splendor,
That land that measures each man at his worth,
　And feel in memory, half fierce, half tender,
The brotherhood of men that know the South.

apologies to Service —
D. M.

THIS ORIGINAL POEM BY SIR DOUGLAS MAWSON WAS DISCOVERED BY CHANCE BY
JONATHAN CHESTER WHEN HE WAS RESEARCHING HIS BOOK ON ANTARCTICA,
GOING TO EXTREMES: PROJECT BLIZZARD AND AUSTRALIA'S ANTARCTIC HERITAGE. IN
1985 HE VISITED THE SYDNEY HOME OF MARY DAVID, DAUGHTER OF MAWSON'S
MENTOR PROFESSOR SIR T W EDGEWORTH DAVID. MISS DAVID, THEN IN HER
NINETIES, SHOWED HIM AN ORIGINAL EDITION OF MAWSON'S TWO-VOLUME WORK
HOME OF THE BLIZZARD, FIRST PUBLISHED IN 1915. INSIDE THE FLYLEAF WAS THIS
POEM, WRITTEN BY MAWSON TO HIS OLD FRIEND WITH THE PHRASE THAT INSPIRED
THE TITLE FOR THIS BOOK. TODAY THE SILENCE IS STILL CALLING AUSTRALIANS TO
ANTARCTICA.

THE
SILENCE
CALLING

Australians in Antarctica 1947–97

THE ANARE JUBILEE HISTORY

TIM BOWDEN

ALLEN & UNWIN

First published in 1997 by
Allen & Unwin
9 Atchison Street
St Leonards NSW 2065
Australia
Phone: (61 2) 9901 4088
Fax: (61 2) 9906 2218
E-mail: frontdesk@allen-unwin.com.au
URL: http://www.allen-unwin.com.au

National Library of Australia
Cataloguing-in-Publication entry:

Bowden, Tim, 1937-.
The silence calling: Australians in Antarctica 1947–97.

   Bibliography.
   Includes index.
   ISBN 1 86448 311 3 (hbk.)
   ISBN 1 86448 406 3 (limited ed.).

   1. Australian National Antarctic Research Expeditions -
   History. 2. Scientific expeditions - Antarctica - History.
   3. Antarctica - Research - Australia - History. I. Title.
507.20989

Designed by Textart
Set in 11pt New Baskerville
Printed by Brown Prior Anderson Pty Ltd, Burwood, Vic.
10 9 8 7 6 5 4 3 2 1

For the men and the women of ANARE

FOREWORD

In 1947 the Australian Government established the Australian National Antarctic Research Expeditions (ANARE) and, for the first time in Australian history, assumed full responsibility for Antarctic exploration and research and for financing all the operations. From this small and tentative beginning, the ANARE has developed rapidly into a large and complex organisation, maintaining Antarctic and sub-Antarctic stations and carrying out extensive exploration and scientific research.

ANARE activities were directed to the 6000 kilometre coastline of the Australian Antarctic Territory (AAT) and the vast, almost completely unexplored hinterland. The sheer magnitude of the ANARE task produced a breadth of approach and an attitude of mind rather different from those of nations whose fields of operation in Antarctica were much more circumscribed.

Fortune favoured the Australian endeavours. An early start gave ANARE time to consolidate before the advent of the International Geophysical Year (IGY), with consequent benefits in scientific achievements during that momentous period. Moreover, being the first post-war expeditions to seek bases in AAT, the ANARE had the pick of the accessible sites.

The selection of the Mawson and Davis sites was fortuitous. I was not to know of the existence of the Prince Charles Mountains inland from Mawson or that of the huge Lambert Glacier. These, together with the Amery Ice Shelf and the ice-free areas of the Vestfold Hills, the Larsemann Hills and the islands of Prydz Bay, presented fascinating fields for exploration and scientific studies.

The Americans had discovered the Windmill Islands and built Wilkes Station in that region for the IGY. When Australia took over this base from the USA, another extremely interesting complex was opened to Australian researchers, while the inland ice plateau and Law Dome paid handsome dividends for ANARE glaciologists.

The mountainous regions of Kemp Land and Enderby Land at the western, and Oates Land at the eastern, extremities of AAT completed the vast canvas across which ANARE operations over a fifty-year period were to extend.

Patterns of Antarctic adventure had been set in the early years of this century, but those men had no monopoly of heroic endeavour. Countless numbers of young people from many nations have, over successive decades, risked their lives and achieved prodigious accomplishments in the face of the extreme hazards and difficulties of the Antarctic environment.

Amongst them the men and women of ANARE stand proudly and Tim Bowden's history is a monument to their efforts.

Phillip G Law
AC, CBE, MSc, DAppSc(Hon.Melb), DEd
(Hon.Vic), DSc(Hon.LaTrobe), Hon.
FRMIT, FANZAAS, FAIP, FRSV, FTSE,
FAA and Director, Australian
Antarctic Division 1949–66

CONTENTS

PREFACE

In November 1994, while filming an ABC documentary on Australians working in Antarctica, I stood alone on the top of an iceberg just off the coast of Princess Elizabeth Land near Davis Station. The helicopters that landed me had flown away. There was utter silence. The scene was breathtaking. To my left was the great tumbled mass of the Sørsdal Glacier glistening in the spring sunshine. Below me the sheer cliff of the iceberg plunged down into the frozen sea. In such an incredible location, I was gripped with a heady mix of exhilaration and fear. I have never felt so isolated and insignificant—a human speck in the vast emptiness of Antarctica.

Humans do not belong in Antarctica. We go there like astronauts entering deep space, taking with us everything needed for survival—accommodation, food and fuel. Every visitor is a transient, staying for limited periods, a few weeks or months, or wintering for a whole year. No one lives indefinitely in Antarctica.

Although ANARE—Australian National Antarctic Research Expeditions—has been in existence for half a century, I am in no doubt that almost all those who venture south, for short or longer periods, do so because they are still motivated by a strong sense of adventure. For those lucky enough to go there, Antarctica becomes a magnificent obsession, drawing them back again and again. My own journeys to Antarctica in 1989, 1994 and 1995 have made me an enthusiastic polar recidivist. All travel to ANARE's four permanent Antarctic stations is by ship, and to go on one of these polar voyages is the ultimate travel experience. It would have been extremely difficult, I think, to have attempted to write the history of ANARE without experiencing the classic stages of a journey south by sea, visiting Macquarie Island, Casey, Davis and Mawson Stations, and meeting a variety of expeditioners while they were 'on the ice'. Each small party not only works in and copes with an implacably hostile environment but has to endure living in isolation, with attendant passions, personal idiosyncrasies, occasional medical emergencies and some grinding routine. Inevitably there are 'good' years and 'bad' years on the sociological front.

My feelings on beginning to write the history of ANARE were rather akin to standing alone on the iceberg—a mixture of excitement and fear. How much of the human drama of actually living in Antarctica should the ANARE historian pursue? Indeed for whom is the history designed—the general reader who may want to know what Australians have been doing down south for the last fifty years, or the professionals for whom a corporate history might be more appropriate? What proportion of this history should be devoted to the adventure/action stories of basic exploration, the raw realities of human interaction in isolation? What of the evolving importance of Antarctic science, Australia's influence on international politics in Antarctica, the changing emphasis from exploiting resources to conservation? And what of the new awareness of the importance of Antarctica in assessing global climate change, and the Antarctic Division's own struggles to survive against a backdrop of changing governments, contracting budgets and some inevitable internal dissension?

For better or worse, I have tried to involve all these elements in *The Silence Calling*. I have selected events that are not only interesting in themselves but illuminate the most important themes. Some events and good stories have therefore had to be dropped in favour of others. For example, there were many epic tractor-train journeys onto the ice cap and the interior of Antarctica during the last half century, but it is simply not possible to feature them all. So the Vostok Traverse of 1962 out of Wilkes Station is dealt with in some detail as a contrast to the more modern Davis–Mawson–Davis glaciological traverses around the head of the Lambert Glacier in 1993–94 and 1994–95.

I have attempted to describe people and events which give an overview of the feel and flavour of the ANARE experience without duplicating themes already explored. Many ANARE expeditioners who have taken part in notable events are not mentioned, but such omissions are an inevitable consequence of tackling a broad canvas and sweep of history.

A great deal of the primary research for *The Silence Calling* has been gleaned from direct testimony and personal interviews with ANARE expeditioners and Antarctic Division staff whose memories extend from 1947 to the present day. These testimonies and interviews are intended to enlarge and enlighten the value of the written records. Through these accounts, the voices of ANARE participants can speak directly to the reader. Where possible, transcripts of interviews have been checked with the people concerned and drafts made available to many of the key players for verification and comment. Lists of those interviewed are included in the endnotes and transcript material is held in the Antarctic Division Library at Kingston.

The Silence Calling is a commissioned work. I was obliged to show drafts to the Antarctic Division's Jubilee Working Group as the manuscript progressed and they had the right to correct matters of fact, and to make suggestions. But, in fact, I was given autonomy over the writing of the ANARE history.

ANARE's history is a chronicle of life on a frontier, not only an important Australian frontier, but a significant international one. In the past, Australians have been very conscious of frontier life and pioneering, particularly in areas like the Northern Territory and Papua New Guinea. But Antarctica, far removed from broad-brimmed hats and sunburned faces, remains unfamiliar to most Australians. Mawson, in his balaclava, still seems an uncharacteristically alien image.

My hope has been to do justice to the story of half a century of endeavour by ANARE expeditioners, whose enthusiasm, bravery, sense of adventure, patriotism and endurance have helped to keep Australia a world leader in scientific research and related Antarctic activities.

They are the men and the women of ANARE—to whom *The Silence Calling* is dedicated.

ACKNOWLEDGMENTS

This project began in 1993 when I was selected by the Antarctic Division's Jubilee Working Group to write the history of ANARE from 1947 to 1997. The working group has been unfailingly supportive, its members cheerfully ploughing through many thousands of words of early chapter drafts, offering helpful comments and suggestions. Des Lugg and Martin Betts (whose corporate memory goes back to the 1960s), Patrick Quilty, Andrew Jackson, Liz Haywood and Phil Wood were particularly generous with their time and expertise. Peter Boyer, the chair of the group, has steered the project through all its phases with deft diplomacy and unfailing good humour—as well as rescuing the author from occasional lapses into the slough of despond during the manuscript's four years gestation. The division's legal officer Wendy Fletcher was extremely supportive.

I was able to interview all but two of the Antarctic Division's leaders and directors—Stuart Campbell, Phil Law, Don Styles (who acted as director for nearly seven years), Ray Garrod, Jim Bleasel and Rex Moncur. Phil Law was unfailingly patient and helpful despite a blizzard of phone calls and letters over the last four years. He also contributed many photographs from his personal collection.

It is simply not practicable to list here all those members of ANARE who were helpful with reminiscences, papers and photographs. They are, however, acknowledged in the text and in the captions. In addition we have been able to publish a list of all wintering expeditioners from 1947–97 as an appendix to the history, as well as Polar Medal and Antarctic Medal recipients, voyage leaders and ships' captains. I hope that will atone to some extent for any omissions. Ian Teague made available his unpublished manuscript *Polar Medals Awarded to Australians for Service in Antarctica* for reference purposes — for which I thank him.

The ANARE Club has been a tower of strength in many ways throughout the writing of the history, not only giving permission to quote from the club journal *Aurora*, but helping me to amass an enviable collection of back copies. Max Corry, who has been compiling a list of ANARE winterers for many years, made his records available to me at the beginning of the project, which was deeply appreciated. Martin Betts, who took on the herculean task of preparing the final list of winterers for the ANARE history, was able to rationalise division records provided by the librarian Evlyn Barrett with Corry's independent research. Kathryn Barker keyed the final list on to the computer.

As I live in Sydney, it was essential to have a researcher operating from the division in Hobart. Alison Alexander, a noted Tasmanian historian, got the project off to a tremendous start before leaving the project after a year to pursue her own writing career. Her expert preparation of source material and oral history interviews—particularly the preparation of a list of key dates and events—was an enduring legacy.

Enter Annie Rushton who quickly mastered a complex brief and became a powerhouse of productivity, combining basic research with oral history interviews recorded in Hobart, Melbourne, Canberra, Brisbane, Adelaide and Darwin. Annie Rushton's input has been prodigious. I cannot think how I could have written the ANARE history without her.

With office space at the division at a premium, Annie was given a desk in the multimedia unit. This was a bonus when it came to selecting photographs for the history. My personal thanks to Kevin Bell, Rene Wanless, Glenn Jacobsen, Wayne Pepps and Beverley Wood for their help in accessing and processing images from the division's collection. Rene Wanless in particular worked well beyond the call of duty on this project. Dave McCormack, Judith Wolters and Nick Lovibond assisted mightily, identifying and coordinating contributions from private sources.

Research into the early years of ANARE was facilitated by Gillian Redmond at the Australian Archives in Canberra and Chris Taylor, archivist at the Department of Foreign Affairs, both of whom helped me access key original documents. John Pepper and Moira Smythe at the Australian Archives in Canberra were also extremely helpful to Annie Rushton. My thanks also to Kathleen Ralston, then writing her PhD thesis on the early life of Phil Law, for her generosity with her original research. Geoff Munro was similarly obliging in making available the text of interviews he recorded with ANARE Heard Island veterans.

At the eleventh hour, Andrew Jackson prepared the excellent 'time line' of ANARE history for which general readers and researchers will thank him down the years, as well as the author.

ANU historian Hank Nelson provided a knowledgeable and friendly shoulder to lean on in the early stages of planning the ANARE history— as he has done with most of my major projects since 1980.

I thank Patrick Gallagher of Allen & Unwin for backing this project before a line had been written, and senior editor Rebecca Kaiser for her cheerful and continuing counsel. Nina Riemer (who has edited all but one of my books) took on the unfamiliar topic of the Antarctic with her usual unflappable aplomb, and was not dismayed when asked to cut my first draft by 30 000 words. Thank you Nina. I don't begrudge even one of them. And Nora Bonney was equally equable about casting her astute proofreading eyes over the remaining 200 000 words, for which I remain extremely grateful. Designer Mark Davis has created a very fine artefact. Clodagh Jones indexed this volume with speed, erudition and great competence.

My father, John Bowden, inculcated into his teenage son growing up in Hobart a love of polar literature, and sowed the seeds of future interest in Antarctic history. This was confirmed by the head of ABC Radio National's Social History Unit Jenny Palmer in 1986 when she suggested I undertake a major radio oral history project 'Australians in Antarctica'. See what you started, Jenny? My wife Ros has been amazingly tolerant and supportive during my long periods of withdrawal from family life over the past four years.

But above all, I am grateful to all those who have shared their experiences so frankly during the research and writing of *The Silence Calling*.

Jubilee Working Group: Evlyn Barrett, Kevin Bell, Martin Betts, Peter Boyer, Rob Easther, Liz Haywood, Jo Jacka, Andrew Jackson, Des Lugg, Harvey Marchant, Rex Moncur, Richard Mulligan, Pat Quilty, Phil Wood.

ACRONYMS AND ABBREVIATIONS

AANBUS	Australian Antarctic Building System
AAE	Australasian Antarctic Expedition
AAT	Australian Antarctic Territory
ACAN	Australian Committee for Antarctic Names
ACAP	Advisory Committee on Antarctic Programs
ACOA	Administrative and Clerical Officers' Association
ACS	Australian Construction Services
AGSO	Australian Geological Survey Organisation
ANARE	Australian National Antarctic Research Expeditions
ANCA	Antarctic Names Committee of Australia
ANCOSPAR	Australian National Committee for Space Research
APIS	Antarctic Pack Ice Seals (Project)
APTS	Antarctic Policy and Transport Studies
ARPAC	Antarctic Research Policy Advisory Committee
ASAC	Antarctic Science Advisory Committee
ASOC	Antarctic and Southern Ocean Coalition
ASS	Antarktis und Spezialfahrt Schiffartsgesellschaft GmbH
ATCM	Antarctic Treaty Consultative Meeting
BANZARE	British Australian and New Zealand Antarctic Research Expedition
BIOMASS	Biological Investigations of Marine Antarctic Systems and Stocks
CATSA	Cooperative Air Transport System for Antarctica
CCAMLR	Convention for the Conservation of Antarctic Marine Living Resources
CEMP	CCAMLR Ecosystem Monitoring Program

COMNAP   Council of Managers of National Antarctic Programs
CRC   Cooperative Research Centre for the Antarctic and
            Southern Ocean Environment
CSIR   Council for Scientific Industrial Research
CSIRO   Commonwealth Scientific and Industrial Research
            Organisation
DASETT   Department of the Arts, Sport, the Environment, Tourism
            [and Territories]
DEA   Department of External Affairs
DUKW   WWII Vintage Amphibian—D (date of manufacture),
            U (utility), K (front-wheel drive), W (with winch)
EAAN   East Antarctic Air Network
EEO   Equal Employment Opportunity
EPC   Executive Planning Committee
ERC   Expenditure Review Committee
FIBEX   First International Biomass Experiment
GLOCHANT   Group of Specialists on Global Change and the Antarctic
GPS   Global Positioning System
IAGP   International Antarctic Glaciology Program
IASOS   Institute of Antarctic and Southern Ocean Studies
IBEA   International Biomedical Expedition to the Antarctic
ICSU   International Council of Scientific Unions
IGY   International Geophysical Year
IPCC   Intergovernmental Panel on Climate Change
IPY   International Polar Year
JATO   Jet Assisted Take Off
JMR   Joint Management Review
LARC   Lighter Amphibious Resupply Cargo
LCVP   Landing Craft Vehicle and Personnel
LIDAR   Light Detection and Ranging
LST   Landing Ship Tanks
NAVSAT   US Navy Satellite Navigation System
NBSAE   Norwegian British Swedish Antarctic Expedition
NGO   Non-government Organisation
NRAC   National Radiation Advisory Committee
PAC   Joint Parliamentary Committee of Public Accounts
PCM   Prince Charles Mountains
PSI   Public Service Inspector
PWC   Parliamentary Works Committee
SAB   Special Antarctic Blend
SAE   Soviet Antarctic Expeditions
SANAE   South African National Antarctic Expedition

SCALOP   Standing Committee on Antarctic Logistics and Operations
SCAR   Special Committee for Antarctic Research (later Scientific
            Committee for Antarctic Research)
SCM   Special Consultative Meeting
SIBEX   Second International Biomass Experiment
SPRI   Scott Polar Research Institute
STOL   Short Take Off and Landing
WOCE   World Ocean Circulation Experiment
WRE   Weapons Research Establishment

ANARE TIME LINE

20 December 1946	To build on Mawson's earlier work and consolidate interest in the Australian Antarctic Territory, Cabinet agrees to refit *Wyatt Earp* for Australian exploration and research in Antarctica.
March 1947	In the lead up to the 1947–48 expedition, RAAF makes three long-range observation flights in modified bombers over the Southern Ocean including reconnaissance flights over Macquarie Island.
May 1947	Executive Planning Committee established and Stuart Campbell appointed to lead the Australian expedition.
7 July 1947	Phillip Law appointed as senior scientific officer.
9 July 1947	Executive Planning Committee decides on the title of Australian National Antarctic Research Expedition.
17 November 1947	HMALST *3501* sails from Melbourne for Heard Island arriving 11 December 1947.
26 December 1947	*Wyatt Earp* leaves Hobart for the Antarctic on a voyage that is thwarted by mechanical problems, weather and ice. On the same day, Heard Island is claimed for Australia and Atlas Cove Station opens with fourteen winterers.
28 February 1948	LST *3501* sails from Melbourne for Macquarie Island, arriving on 7 March 1948. The station opens on 21 March 1948 with fourteen winterers.

3 January 1949	Phillip Law appointed as director of the Antarctic Division, which was formed in the Department of External Affairs and which, by year's end, had a staff of eleven.
13 July 1950	Cabinet decides to establish a permanent station in Antarctica, but progress is thwarted by lack of a suitable ship.
22 October 1951	Inaugural meeting of the ANARE Club in Melbourne provides a focus for returning expeditioners to maintain contact.
6 February 1953	The availability of *Kista Dan* leads to Government approval to establish the proposed continental station in the 1953–54 summer.
4 January 1954	*Kista Dan* sails from Melbourne to seek a site for a permanent station in the AAT, arriving in Horseshoe Harbour on 11 February.
13 February 1954	Mawson Station commissioned with ten winterers who spend the first year erecting buildings, taking meteorological observations, and commencing coastal and inland exploration.
9 March 1955	Heard Island Station closes.
March 1956	Aircraft hangar erected at Mawson. The first RAAF Antarctic flight photographs 1600 km of coastline.
Summer 1956–57	Discovery of coal in the Prince Charles Mountains.
13 January 1957	Davis Station established for the International Geophysical Year with a winter complement of five.
1–17 February 1957	Wilkes is built by the USA for IGY in just 17 days.
30 June 1957	Official start of IGY with twelve nations having established Antarctic expeditions.
3 January 1958	*Thala Dan* commences a voyage which explores almost the entire coast of AAT and Terre Adélie and establishes Antarctica's first continuous automatic weather stations on Lewis Island and Chick Island.
1958	Overland explorations from Mawson reach the southern limits of the Prince Charles Mountains.
4 February 1959	Australia takes over Wilkes from the US.
1 December 1959	Antarctic Treaty signed by Australia and eleven other nations.
21 December 1959	The first four women to visit an ANARE station

	arrive at Macquarie Island on *Thala Dan* to take part as scientists in the summer program.
Summer 1959–60	Helicopters used by ANARE for the first time.
Summer 1960–61	Using dog teams, a journey from a camp in the Prince Charles Mountains travels south and makes the first ascent of Mt Menzies, the highest peak in the western sector of the AAT.
8 February 1961	*Magga Dan* arrives at Mawson carrying, as a guest of the ship, Nel Law—the first Australian woman to visit the AAT.
23 June 1961	Antarctic Treaty comes into force.
17 September 1962	Six expeditioners set off from Wilkes for a 17 week, 3000 km traverse to Vostok and back.
May 1963	In Melbourne the Antarctic Division moves from Collins St to St Kilda Rd.
25 January 1965	Davis Station closes for four years as construction of Repstat begins to replace Wilkes which has been buried by snow.
April 1966	Phillip Law resigns and is replaced by Don Styles as acting director.
1967	Australian Academy of Science conducts a review of Antarctic research.
Winter 1968	Amery Ice Shelf project—four men winter on the ice shelf in ANARE's smallest wintering party.
Summer 1968–69	Prince Charles Mountains Survey commences an extensive field program that continues for another five summers.
February 1969	Davis Station reopens on 19 February 1969 following completion of Repstat and is renamed Casey.
2 October 1970	Bryan Rofe commences a short term as Director of Antarctic Division until his death in August 1971.
25 November 1970	LARCs replace DUKWs at Macquarie Island and then, in the same summer, are introduced into Antarctica.
27 January 1971	First recorded landing on the McDonald Islands.
1971	Radio telephone system introduced to improve communication between Australia and Antarctica.
18 February 1972	Underground cosmic ray observatory opens at Mawson.

8 May 1972	Ray Garrod commences as Director of Antarctic Division.
Summer 1972–73	Deep drilling commences on the Law Dome ice cap.
Early 1974	Government decides to relocate the Antarctic Division to Kingston in Tasmania.
December 1974	Advisory Committee on Antarctic Programs reports on its review of the ANARE program.
19 January 1976	Four women arrive at Casey on *Thala Dan* to become the first women to visit a continental station as part of ANARE.
1976	On Macquarie Island, Dr Zoë Gardner is the first woman to winter with ANARE.
26 February 1977	Geologists land at Gaussberg for the first Australian visit since 1912.
2 March 1977	First visit of an Australian field party to the Bunger Hills.
13 February 1977	Qantas operates the first of a series of one day charter tourist overflights from Australia to Antarctica.
1977	Federal budget provides for rebuilding the stations, additional staff for the Antarctic Division, commencement of a marine research program, and planning studies for an Australian Antarctic ship.
Winter 1977	Rod Ledingham (OIC) and Jean Ledingham (doctor) on Macquarie Island become the first husband and wife team to winter with ANARE.
18 January 1978	Granholm hut erected at Cape Denison to support a summer program at Mawson's Hut.
16 October 1978	Construction of new ANARE headquarters begins at Kingston.
December 1978	As the first stage in plans for a cooperative air transport system, RAAF flies four flights on the Christchurch–McMurdo route.
Summer 1978–79	US Hercules lands at Lanyon Junction to deliver scientists and summer support staff to work at Casey.
2 April 1979	Clarrie McCue becomes acting director following Ray Garrod's retirement.
November 1979	Antarctic Research Policy Advisory Committee

	recommends that Antarctic research place greater emphasis on resources and environmental effects of their exploitation.
Summer 1979–80	For the first time it is necessary to charter a third ship, *Nanok S*, to carry cargo for rebuilding. New living quarters commissioned at Davis, the first of the AANBUS buildings.
Summer 1979–80	Six people camp on McDonald Island for four days in March to complete the first survey of the island.
20 May 1980	Convention on the Conservation of Antarctic Marine Living Resources is agreed at a diplomatic conference in Canberra. Australia signs the Convention on 11 September 1980.
December 1980	Kingston buildings completed and transfer from Melbourne commences.
Summer 1980–81	Following her modification for marine research, *Nella Dan* supports FIBEX, ANARE's first dedicated marine biology cruise and the start of a long-term commitment to Antarctic offshore research.
	In Terre Adélie ANARE participates in the International Biomedical Expedition to Antarctica—the first expedition solely for medical research.
January 1981	Dr Louise Holliday arrives at Davis to become the first woman to winter at an ANARE station in the AAT.
22 April 1981	New Antarctic Division headquarters opened by Prince Charles. Later that year in Tasmania's Central Highlands the Bernacchi Antarctic Training Centre opens—named after the Tasmanian who was the first Australian to winter in Antarctica.
January 1982	*Nella Dan* commences a 35-day cruise in Prydz Bay for ANARE's first marine geophysical survey.
1983	Joint Management Review recommends significant restructuring of the permanent staffing of the Antarctic Division.
18 February 1984	Jim Bleasel commences as acting director.
5 November 1984	*Icebird* departs Cape Town for Mawson on its maiden voyage for ANARE. The advent of *Icebird* allows a large number of expedition staff to be

carried, opening up ANARE to many more participants.

Summer 1984–85 Fossil dolphin bones discovered at Marine Plain near Davis, proving this site to be of great palaeontological significance.

1985 Antarctic Science Advisory Committee established.

Summer 1985–86 Installation of ANARESAT satellite communications terminals commences at the Antarctic stations.

27 October 1985 *Nella Dan* becomes beset and, unable to be freed by *Icebird*, waits until 14 December to be released by the Japanese icebreaker *Shirase*. Some research is deferred and *HMAS Stalwart* relieves Macquarie Island.

Summer 1985–86 Edgeworth David summer base established in the Bunger Hills.

Summer 1986–87 Summer base established at Cape Denison near Mawson's Hut.

Two school students win the inaugural Antarctic School Science Prize and visit Antarctica on *Icebird*.

18 January 1987 Law Base in the Larsemann Hills opens as a summer scientific station.

3 December 1987 *Nella Dan* grounds in Buckles Bay, Macquarie Island, and is subsequently scuttled in deep water off the island on 24 December 1987.

17 December 1987 Government announces its intention to negotiate a charter for an Australian-crewed and constructed icebreaker.

1 January 1988 First live television broadcast from the AAT—a link-up with Davis during Australia's bicentennial celebrations.

5 February 1988 As design of the new Antarctic ship proceeds, the prime minister announces a competition among young Australians to choose a name for it.

June 1988 Convention for the Regulation of Antarctic Mineral Resource Activity is agreed by the Antarctic Treaty nations.

29 October 1988 Keel laid for *Aurora Australis*.

Summer 1987–88 Dovers Base established providing support for a five-year study in the northern Prince Charles Mountains.

20 December 1988 New Casey opened.

1989 The first woman station leaders, Alison Clifton

	at Macquarie Island and Diana Patterson at Davis, take up duty.
22 May 1989	Prime Minister announces that Australia will not sign the Convention for the Regulation of Antarctic Mineral Resources but instead explore the prospects for a comprehensive environmental protection convention.
June 1989	Inquiry into the Antarctic Division's management by the Joint Parliamentary Committee on Public Accounts concludes and recommends an increase of staff for the Antarctic Division.
18 September 1989	*Aurora Australis* launched at Newcastle to be completed in time for a winter voyage to Heard Island in 1990.
21 December 1989	Rex Moncur appointed as director after acting in the position following Jim Bleasel's resignation.
Summer 1989–90	A compressed snow-ice runway is constructed at Casey, but heavy snowfalls prevent the trial flights planned for February 1990.
3 March 1990	Governor of Tasmania Sir Phillip Bennett visits Macquarie Island.
4 October 1991	Antarctic Treaty meeting adopts the Madrid Protocol which bans mining and designates Antarctica as a natural reserve devoted to peace and science.
Summer 1991–92	A temporary station is established at Spit Bay to accommodate five people in the first wintering party on Heard Island since 1954.
August 1992	Antarctic Science Advisory Committee recommends that Antarctic science be restructured into six priority areas.
November 1992	Twenty-two huskies removed from Mawson in accordance with the Madrid Protocol and taken to the USA.
Summer 1992–93	Inland from Casey, while the old station is being removed, drilling through the Law Dome ice cap yields a 1200-metre ice core containing climate records going back 15 000 years.
Summer 1992–93	ANARE continental stations receive their first tourist visits by US-chartered Russian vessel *Kapitan Khlebnikov*.

February 1993	ANARE enters a partnership with NASA for cooperative research into human adaptation to isolation.
August 1993	Federal budget decides that ANARE should go to a one-ship operation supported by long-range helicopters.
December 1993	A review of ANARE head office staffing and structure commences.
Summer 1993–94	Completion of the first traverse around the head of the Lambert Glacier, the world's largest, to measure ice movement.
	LARCs are used for the last time in Antarctica ending a 46-year association with army amphibious transport.
6 April 1994	Australia ratifies the Madrid Protocol.
1994	New science strategic plans completed, setting the direction for Antarctic research into the next century. A human impacts research program is established.
Summer 1994–95	ANARE operates with one ship for the first time since the summer of 1963–64. Long-range aircraft, S76 helicopters, are used to directly link the continental stations by air.
31 December 1994	Tourist charter flights to the AAT are re-introduced using Qantas aircraft. Over 2100 passengers see the AAT on six one-day flights.
September 1995	ANARE's first voyage into winter sea ice.
December 1995	Australian Antarctic Data Centre established to integrate ANARE data sets and make data more widely accessible.
Summer 1995–96	With *Polar Bird* (formerly *Icebird*) on charter for the summer, this season supports 241 scientists and 116 days of marine research, the highest ever.
June 1996	Government nominates Macquarie Island and Heard Island for inclusion on the World Heritage List.
May 1996	Nineteen of the older buildings at Mawson, the oldest continually occupied station south of the Antarctic Circle, are placed on the Interim List of the Register of the National Estate.
9 July 1997	The 50th anniversary of the naming of ANARE sees Australia developing plans for the Antarctic program into the next century.

INTRODUCTION

FLYING THE FLAG

A Gypsy Moth biplane droned south over the vast sweep of the Antarctic ice sheet. It was 25 January 1930. Sir Douglas Mawson was sitting in the front cockpit, a leather flying helmet and goggles replacing his usual woollen balaclava. His lips were moving as he read aloud from a document on his knees, but the words, whipped back by the slipstream, were not heard by pilot Stuart Campbell in the rear cockpit:

> In the name of His Majesty King George the Fifth, King of Great Britain, Ireland and the British Dominions beyond the Seas, Emperor of India. Whereas I have it in command from His Majesty King George the Fifth to assert the sovereign rights of His Majesty over British land discoveries met with in Antarctica. . .[1]

The reassuring roar of the Moth's engine at full cruising revolutions became a puny spluttering as Campbell eased the throttle to idling speed, at the same time holding the joystick back to keep the nose of the Moth up as the air speed decreased. It was the classic way to induce a stall. In seconds the nose of the aircraft dropped with a gut-wrenching lurch as the Gypsy Moth literally began to fall out of the air. At that precise moment Campbell flung a Union Jack tied to a wooden pole from the cockpit. The Moth's engine roared as the aircraft dived briefly to regain flying speed, then circled as the two Australians confirmed they could see the splash of imperial red lying on the crystalline whiteness below.[2]

Twelve days before, on 13 January, Mawson had read the proclamation under more conventional circumstances beside a cairn of rocks on the quickly named Proclamation Island. On behalf of Great Britain

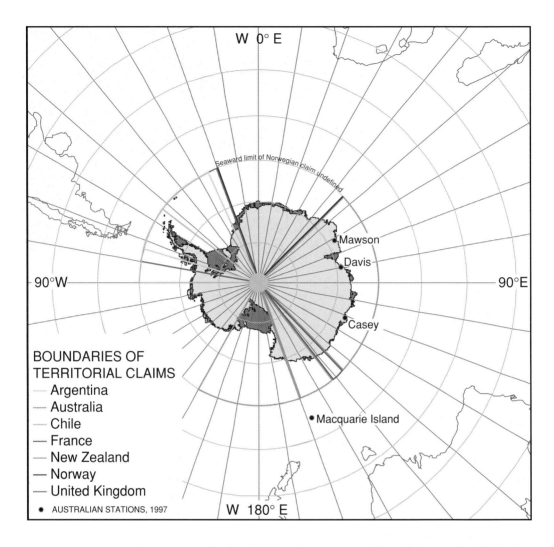

W 0° E

Seaward limit of Norwegian claim undefined

•Mawson

Davis

90°W

90°E

•Casey

BOUNDARIES OF
TERRITORIAL CLAIMS
---- Argentina
---- Australia
---- Chile
—— France
----- New Zealand
—— Norway
—— United Kingdom
• AUSTRALIAN STATIONS, 1997

•Macquarie Island

W 180° E

MAP OF ANTARCTICA
SHOWING NATIONAL CLAIMS.

he had claimed a generous slice of Antarctica: Enderby, Kemp and Mac. Robertson Lands. While he had not been on the Antarctic continent itself—as the annexing protocol laid down—it was a distinct improvement on occasional sightings of the Antarctic coastline from the ship *Discovery,* unable to penetrate barriers of pack ice.

Sir Douglas Mawson's first BANZARE (British Australian and New Zealand Antarctic Research Expedition), supported by the three governments, was to raise the British flag on the long coastline between Enderby Land and Oates Land with the understanding that Australia should control the whole of this enormous segment of the Antarctic continent.[3] Although Mawson rated the scientific aims of BANZARE voyages highly, he was equally keen to ensure that Norway, France and the USA did not encroach on what both the British and Australian

Governments regarded as their own. There were commercial as well as territorial interests to safeguard, with Norwegian whaling ships active in the area.

Australian territorial interest in Antarctica began in the late nineteenth century with the scientific and commercial plans of the Australian Antarctic Exploration Committee, supported at first by Australian learned and scientific societies, but with little encouragement at all from colonial legislatures. The Royal Society of Tasmania was particularly active in making a case for Antarctic exploration, but the first Australian Antarctic Exploration Committee was set up by the Royal Society of Victoria in Melbourne in 1866. It tried unsuccessfully for twenty years to lobby for an Antarctic expedition and to raise the necessary funds.

SIR DOUGLAS MAWSON IN HIS CABIN ON *DISCOVERY* DURING THE BANZARE VOYAGES OF 1929–31.
(F HURLEY)

The first party to winter on Antarctica, led by Carsten Borchgrevink aboard *Southern Cross*, established a base at Cape Adare during 1899. Tasmanian physicist Louis Bernacchi, who was among the wintering party, also accompanied Captain R F Scott on his first (1901–04) expedition.

Australian scientists seem to have been popular recruits. Ernest Shackleton's first Antarctic expedition in 1909 included geologist Douglas Mawson and his professor at Sydney University, T W Edgeworth David, who even then recognised the potential of his student:

> Just as Shackleton was the general leader, so, in all sincerity and without the pride that apes humility, I say that Mawson was the real leader who was the soul of our expedition to the Magnetic Pole. We really have in him an Australian Nansen of infinite resource, splendid physique, astonishing indifference to frost.[4]

Mawson was a towering figure in every way and his Antarctic achievements over half a century are his greatest legacy. Australia's claim to almost 42 per cent of the Antarctic continent is based mainly on his exploratory and scientific voyages in 1911–14 and the summer season BANZARE of 1929–31.

Most territorial claims in Antarctica extend from the coast to the South Pole, the boundaries between the sectors radiating from the pole and dividing the continent like giant slices of a cake. The British, New Zealand and Australian claims are based on priority of discovery, followed by what has been termed 'a sufficient display of authority' such as the issuing of whaling licences, the policing of the area and the establishment of scientific and survey bases. Formal territories were defined on these grounds from 1903 onwards.

Britain had granted a Norwegian whaling company a licence to operate in Antarctic waters between 45° east and 90° east in 1928 and it was at the end of 1928 that the British, Australian and New Zealand governments decided to support a combined expedition. Britain agreed to provide Scott's old ship *Discovery*, at no cost, for an expedition to leave Australia in the summer of 1929–30. Sir Douglas Mawson accepted the leadership and immediately began raising funds. On 12 March 1929 a newly appointed Antarctic Committee held its first meeting in Melbourne to define the territorial and scientific aims of what were to be the BANZARE voyages from 1929 to 1931.

The first BANZARE voyage reunited Sir Douglas with Captain J K Davis, who had skippered *Aurora* on the 1911–14 expedition. In contrast with the harmony of their earlier collaboration, the BANZARE voyage of 1929 was marked by tensions between them. Both men were in their late forties, both in the prime of their professional lives. Relations between them were strained even before Mawson joined *Discovery* in Cape Town in October 1929. Davis thought Mawson's expedition untidy, badly organised, haphazard and ill prepared, while Mawson found Davis 'very difficult. . .a confirmed pessimist, curt, surly, extremely rude and bad tempered'.

Davis felt that Mawson did not understand the stresses and pressures a captain had. He found it difficult to get Mawson to make up his mind. Mawson used his diaries on the first BANZARE voyage to rail against Davis's uncooperative attitude and even wondered if Davis's lack of stamina and unpleasant disposition were caused by an inadequate diet 'of pickles and beef'. It says a great deal for their underlying mutual respect—or tolerance—that Mawson and Davis maintained a cordial relationship in later years.

On his return to Australia in March 1930 Mawson immediately began lobbying and planning for the second BANZARE voyage. It was fortunate for his ambitions that four Norwegian ships returned to their Australian and New Zealand bases that month with valuable cargoes of whale oil: the international interest in and the economic potential of the Antarctic were on opportune display. The Australian Prime Minister,

J H Scullin, told the House of Representatives on 22 May that a further Antarctic expedition would take place in the coming summer season, and that 'work in the Australian sector of the Antarctic. . .is of considerable national interest and importance to the Commonwealth for economic, scientific and other points of view. . .'

Discovery was to be skippered this time by the chief officer of the first BANZARE voyage, K N MacKenzie, who left Mawson and his scientists in no doubt that he would be a much more reasonable and indeed bold skipper. But the burden of command fell heavily on MacKenzie; he became nervous and irritable and made it clear to Mawson in the latter stages of the voyage that his whole future depended on getting *Discovery* back to port safely.

Although the difficult relations between Mawson and both captains with whom he sailed put some limitations on what was achieved, the BANZARE voyages were strategically and scientifically important. Few landings and flag raisings were possible, but Mawson's voyages and his advocacy of Australia's Antarctic interests were strongly instrumental in the British Government making the Order in Council of 7 February 1933 establishing the Australian Antarctic Territory. The Australian Government responded by passing the Australian Antarctic Acceptance Bill through the House of Representatives in May 1933 and the Senate on 1 June—although it was not proclaimed until August 1936.[5]

Attorney-General J G Latham cited the indiscriminate slaughter of female whales, whale calves and immature whales by the various whaling industries as a prime reason for Australia to take over and administer the territory. The area was close to Australia and might prove embarrassing in the hands of another power. It also had 'considerable and potential economic importance'. He left the House of Representatives

THREE CHEERS FOR THE KING
ON 13 JANUARY 1930 AS SIR
DOUGLAS MAWSON AND HIS
COMPANIONS TAKE
POSSESSION OF MAC.
ROBERTSON, ENDERBY AND
KEMP LANDS FROM
PROCLAMATION ISLAND.
MAWSON IS FIFTH FROM LEFT.
(F HURLEY)

in no doubt as to the significance of Mawson's BANZARE voyages in claiming the AAT: 'As a result of the voyage of *Discovery*, the area had been so thoroughly visited and British sovereignty so completely established, that. . .there was no longer need for delay in providing for the administration of the territory, and for taking it over on behalf of the Commonwealth.'[6]

In summarising the achievements of BANZARE, Mawson gave more space to the scientific achievements than geographical discovery. The dredging and specimen-collecting activities alone resulted in 'the amassing of an immense amount of data regarding the region lying south of Australia and the Indian Ocean'.[7]

Although the outbreak of World War II delayed the publication of the scientific results of BANZARE (some 2700 pages in two series) and forced a pause on all Australian Antarctic work, Mawson lived long enough not only to be able to reflect on the achievements of his two major expeditions and the claiming of two and a half million square miles [six million square kilometres] of Australian Antarctica, but to be a key influence in Australia's Antarctic policies in the late 1940s and early 1950s.

He continued to lobby and take an active interest in future plans, and was influential in getting the Australian Government to establish bases in the AAT and to continue scientific programs, exploration and mapping. Largely as a result of his efforts, the Australian National Antarctic Research Expeditions—ANARE—was formed in 1947, and has operated continuously for half a century.

Sir Douglas Mawson died in 1958. Mawson Station, named in his honour, was the first Australian settlement to be built on continental Antarctica and remains today the longest continuously operated station inside the Antarctic Circle.

THE BEGINNING
1947–1953

ONE

BIRTH OF ANARE

As soon as World War II ended Sir Douglas Mawson resumed lobbying the Australian Government to consolidate claims to the Australian Antarctic Territory. In October 1945 the Australian press reported that he was making preliminary moves to organise—but not to lead—an expedition. By then he was 62.

Others were also interested in Antarctica. Scientific bodies, particularly the National Research Council, were anxious to renew work there, public interest was stirred by press hints about uranium deposits and there was talk of renewing the Antarctic whaling industry. The activity of other nations meant that if Australia did not do something to consolidate her hold on the territory she claimed, she risked losing it. The British and Americans were active on the Antarctic Peninsula and in 1946–47 Admiral R E Byrd led a large expedition—the biggest ever mounted in Antarctica—to explore, photograph and map the continent and to extend American influence. Byrd's 'Operation Highjump' succeeded in photographing almost the entire coastline of the continent, as well as several hundred thousand square kilometres of the interior—a tremendous achievement even though it was a massive assault organised on military lines, using 4700 men and 13 ships (including an aircraft carrier).[1] Photographs taken of the coastline of the AAT were to be crucial in locating and establishing Mawson Station in 1954.

The massive United States operation was regarded with suspicion by Australian diplomats, aware that 'the State Department had always reserved the position of the United States Government regarding all Antarctic claims'. Australian concerns were heightened by the legal opinion that discovery followed by annexation was insufficient for claiming territory if that were not followed by a subsequent continuity of 'effective occupation'.[2]

A top secret note from the Australian Embassy in Washington dated 6 December 1946 informed the Department of External Affairs that despite Admiral Byrd's refusal to be drawn into any discussion of claims to sovereignty in the area, there were grounds for thinking that 'the United States, standing firm on its refusal to recognise any other nation's claims to Australian [Antarctic] territory, might seek to lay the foundations for claims of its own to any part of the subcontinent which might turn out to be useful'. This note also expressed concern that the Americans were planning to enter the AAT and had made no formal approach to the Australian Government to do so.[3] It was clearly time for Australia to think seriously about its claim to 42 per cent of the Antarctic continent.

The key to the post-war activity was the prestige and personality of Sir Douglas Mawson. Later, ANARE's first director, Phillip Law, said that only Mawson could have talked the Government into an Antarctic expedition when its resources were stretched with post-war reconstruction:

Mawson was fundamental in persuading the government to set up the ANARE in 1947. . .It was Mawson who revived the whole business of Antarctica post-World War II and said, 'Look, the war interrupted what we were trying to do, now let's get back onto it and get it done'. And then he persuaded them to set up a committee. . .which later became the Executive Planning Committee. He was a strong influence.

On 2 December 1946 the Department of External Affairs had convened a committee of interested government departments—Defence, Fisheries, Mineral Resources, Supply and Shipping, Meteorological Service and the Council for Scientific and Industrial Research (CSIR)—and Mawson himself. The committee recommended that plans for an Antarctic expedition should be made using a naval ship equipped with aircraft, and with the aim of finding a site for a base. Mawson suggested that *Wyatt Earp* be used as it had sailed to Antarctica before and was made of 'stout timbers'. Cabinet accepted the recommendation and on 20 December 1946 the Australian public was told that a short reconnaissance voyage coordinated by the CSIR was to be sent to Antarctica 'this summer'.[4]

'This summer' was far too optimistic, but the departments concerned did act quickly. Scientific and practical concern with weather made it obvious that meteorological observations and research should be part of the scientific program. In meteorological terms there was a complete *terra incognita* south and west of Tasmania. In January 1947 the South-West Pacific Regional Commission of the International Meteorological Organisation recommended that meteorological stations be established on Macquarie Island and various other islands. As a result, RAAF flights went far to the south to complete a photographic reconnaissance of Macquarie Island, to investigate conditions in waters south of Australia, and to test aircraft performance and crew fatigue.[5]

By early May 1947 much had been resolved. The Government had agreed to provide £100 000 [$200 000] towards the Antarctic expedition and £50 000 [$100 000] to refurbish HMAS *Wyatt Earp*.[6] An Antarctic policy committee called the Executive Planning Committee and chaired by the Permanent Head of External Affairs, John Burton, had been set up consisting of representatives of the Navy, Air Force, Treasury, CSIR and Fisheries Department, plus Commander Oom, the captain of *Wyatt Earp* (and a veteran of BANZARE), Mawson and J K Davis. On 5 May this committee decided that Group Captain Stuart Campbell, a third veteran of BANZARE, was the most suitable leader, that he and other team members should be obtained at once, and that another ship would be needed as well as *Wyatt Earp*. Work the following summer should be limited to reconnaissance of a site for a base on the continent and setting up a station on Macquarie Island.[7]

The meeting was followed by a conference on the proposed expedition. There was concern whether *Wyatt Earp*, 28 years old and rather small, could do the job. The aims of the expedition were necessarily limited. Discussion took place about who would have command—a seaman while at sea, and the expedition leader on shore.[8] It all sounded unpromising, particularly for those who remembered the clashes between ship's captain and expedition leader on the BANZARE voyages.

The fragile nature of these plans was not made known to the public, but on 7 May there was an announcement that Group Captain Stuart Campbell had been offered the position of leader. At first undecided whether he would accept the leadership, Campbell eventually did so and set about organising the expedition.[9]

Later that month the Executive Planning Committee had firmed its ideas. There were to be two island bases and the continental reconnaissance party, with eleven or twelve people in each island group—meteorologists (from the Meteorological Bureau), physicists (from universities), geologists and geomagneticians (Mineral Resources), radio operators (RAAF), surveyors, cooks and diesel mechanics (Army, Navy or civilian).[10] Men were to be recruited from government departments as far as possible, then universities and the armed services. As a last resort, advertisements would be placed for the remainder. A scientific liaison officer and a medical officer were needed, and an LST (Landing Ship Tanks) would be used as well as *Wyatt Earp*.[11] Davis, consistent with his nickname 'Gloomy', advised Campbell that LSTs were unsuitable for the Southern Ocean because of their shallow draught and box-like design, but Campbell told him that the seaworthiness of the LSTs could not be questioned.[12]

By July the Executive Planning Committee had ordered scientific equipment, appointed an advisory scientific committee to coordinate scientific activities, and decided on a title: the Australian National Antarctic Research Expedition, with the pleasing acronym of ANARE.[13]

The Antarctic was not in the forefront of the Australian Government's post-war thinking, although strategic concerns were evident—there was always the chance of other nations moving in on an empty AAT. The Government, with an eye to revenue, was interested in exploring the commercial possibilities of fishing, whaling and any mineral resources that might be found, and the need for meteorological and other scientific observations in the Antarctic was also acknowledged.[14] But there was the usual reluctance to begin spending large sums of money.

Because of Mawson's lobbying of the Minister for External Affairs, Dr H V Evatt, to take some action to buttress Australia's Antarctic claims, the ANARE office was loosely attached administratively to the DEA. The executive officer of the fledgling ANARE, Stuart Campbell, was appointed in May 1947, knowing that the first expedition to Heard Island on HMALST *3501* would have to leave before the end of that year.

Campbell came from the Department of Civil Aviation, where he was the Director of Air Navigation and Safety. He was reputed to be a good administrator and one of few people with Antarctic experience—he had directed flight operations during Mawson's two BANZARE voyages in 1929–31. His flying experience was extensive, including a period in Papua New Guinea in the 1930s, after which he was made a Fellow of the Royal Geographic Society. During World War II he commanded the famous Catalina squadron from Darwin, and flew many missions against the Japanese. He was a man of action, an adventurer and a hands-on administrator. Campbell had no intention of flying a desk in Melbourne while all the action was elsewhere. He planned not only to accompany the Heard Island team on LST *3501*, but to stay on the island for four months and be picked up by *Wyatt Earp* on its way back from its voyage to pick a site for a permanent Australian station on the Antarctic mainland.

He set up the ANARE office in a suite of rooms in Victoria Barracks, St Kilda Road. His small staff consisted of administrative officer Trevor Heath, storeman George Smith and several typists. Smith worked at

Tottenham, a suburb thirteen kilometres west of the city of Melbourne, where the RAAF had provided a building in their No. 1 Stores Depot as a packing and storage area for the Antarctic venture.

Smith's interview with Stuart Campbell consisted of Smith putting his head round Campbell's door and Campbell saying, 'Oh, you're George Smith. All right, you're to go back to Tottenham and work with the RAAF till I tell you we want you.' Six weeks later he told Smith, 'We've got a bit of work for you.' Smith said, 'Well I've been around for about six weeks—is there any chance of getting a bit of pay?'

George Smith stood six foot four inches in his socks [193 centimetres] and possessed a voice that could eclipse that of any sergeant major on parade. He was to be the indispensable storeman for ANARE for the next 31 years. With Norm Jones (his clerk) and Trevor Heath he had to organise supplies for an unknown number of men going to an unknown destination in the south.

THE ANTARCTIC DIVISION'S LEGENDARY STOREMAN GEORGE SMITH IN RELAXED AND CONVIVIAL MODE.
(P LAW)

Smith and Heath went through RAAF catalogues, choosing anything they thought might be needed. Smith, who understood RAAF procedures, wrote out his own vouchers, typed them up, put them through the RAAF process, and withdrew the material he wanted on the basis that 'if you wanted it, there and then you took it'. It was ten years before the RAAF caught up with him.

Physicists came from the universities, particularly Melbourne University where Dr Henry Rathgeber had his postgraduate students making equipment to study cosmic rays. Four of them became so interested that they joined the expedition.

Melbourne University also provided another recruit. Phillip Law, a Victorian and the son of a schoolteacher, had always been interested in bushwalking, skiing and the outdoor life and had read all he could about Antarctica. After finishing school he studied physics at Melbourne University and in 1947 was a lecturer there. His professor, Leslie Martin, was often in Canberra, and one day as Martin and Law were walking down a passage Martin commented that the forthcoming Antarctic Expedition was having trouble finding a chief scientist:

I stopped in my tracks and said, 'Did you mention my name?' and he said, 'Oh, you wouldn't be interested in that, Law, would you?' I said, 'I'd give my right arm to go on that'. He said, 'Good gracious me, I'll go and ring up'. And within a few weeks I had an interview and I was appointed the senior scientist for the expedition.

Phil Law (who would take over the reins of ANARE within two years) was, like Campbell, a born adventurer and a fitness fanatic. A short, vigorous man, clean shaven in those days, Law was then 35 years of age and crackled with energy and enthusiasm for what lay ahead. He was appointed senior scientific officer on 7 July 1947. Two days later the Executive Planning Committee decided that the official title of the expedition should be the 'Australian National Antarctic Research Expedition 1947'.[15]

Law was to coordinate the scientific programs and carry out cosmic ray observations during *Wyatt Earp's* proposed voyage to the Antarctic. Setting up major expeditions from scratch in six months was difficult and compromises, acceptance of second bests, were inevitable. While the practical problems were being solved, Law had to put in place a scientific program that not only would yield useful results immediately, but would look towards the future of Australian scientific research in Antarctica—if there was one.

He was aware that meteorology and geology were the priorities from the Government's point of view. Australia's weather was profoundly influenced by the Antarctic, and any advance warning of what was coming would be clearly and immediately beneficial. If there were valuable mineral resources available for easy picking, naturally they would not only benefit Australia, but would help justify the millions of dollars to be spent. There were also longer term scientific objectives to be considered:

> As a physicist I was familiar with various aspects of geophysics—meteorology, gravitation, seismology, geomagnetism, upper atmosphere physics and cosmic rays—and it was obvious that Heard Island and Macquarie Island would provide opportunities for unique observatory studies in those fields. Even more obvious was the need for investigation of the zoological and biological species and general ecology of these sub-Antarctic islands and of their geology.

Law took up his duties as senior scientific officer at the ANARE office at Victoria Barracks on 1 August 1947. Later, he said that his job was to sit at a desk and think up all the possibilities, then try to get appropriate people interested. Law believed that the main scientific interest lay first in meteorology, followed by geology, biology (because of the abundant animal life), geophysics 'and anything else you could think of'. He knew that the Government's priority was to establish a territorial claim on Antarctica.

Having said that the main purpose is political, one must realise that they used science as a pseudo reason for going—as all the nations did—in order to cloak the real reason. No one likes to come out and say, 'Oh, politically we're colonialists, we want to go out and grab another bit of empire'. So you say, 'Well, we're going down for scientific purposes'.

Later on it became pretty clear that Antarctica—apart from the Falkland Islands area—has no strategic importance. But in those days there was a possibility that it *might* be strategically important, but that's political, it's not scientific. So I had to design a scientific program for two reasons: first to produce the facade behind which all the rest could be carried out, but second to try to get some pay-off. . .and get as much scientific work out of it as we usefully could for the big money being spent.

Stuart Campbell set about finding personnel. He did this as far as possible by the 'old boy' network, interviewing men who were suggested by their government departments, especially ex-servicemen who could be recommended by their commanding officers. He liked strong characters, people he thought could cope well with the conditions they were likely to meet. For most positions he had plenty of people to choose from. Many jobs were not advertised; however, even limited publicity brought over 500 applications, mostly from men, but also from two schoolboys and one woman. People of several nationalities applied to go to Antarctica, but only Australians were chosen as it was an Australian venture. There was no thought in those days of taking women to the Antarctic, so the woman applicant missed out.[16] Nor was there any psychological screening, later an important part of the selection process. Campbell:

> If they looked like good kids, I put them on. . .you've got to make a judg-ment. Most people are all right—give them a job and they'll stick to it. Psychological screening came in during the war to screen people to see if they were going to be successful pilots, but it couldn't be done. You can't tell what a man is going to be like until you give him a job and he goes and does it.

ANARE expeditioners were recruited by formality, association and random collision. Stuart Campbell told applicants there were to be three parties, one for Macquarie Island, one for *Wyatt Earp* and one for an unknown destination. Heard Island was being kept a secret. Phil Law:

> The Heard Island bit was put in at the specific request of the British Government who said Heard Island—our claim on it—was disputed by

the Americans because they reckoned they discovered it. The British say it was first sighted by an Englishman. But certainly the first person to ever go there was an American. And the French island of Kerguelen is just a few hundred miles to the north-west. . .the Germans had used it as a base for raiders to raid allied shipping in the Indian Ocean during World War II. So you see, Heard Island was pretty important. And the secret instruction or request from London to our government asked that we do something about it. It was all kept very hush-hush in the early part.

Alan Campbell-Drury read an article about the expedition in the newspapers. He was in Japan with the navy but wrote to Mawson, whom he had known in South Australia, asking to go on the expedition. Mawson told him to come to Australia, so he did 'the quickest exit from the navy ever!' Mawson also recommended John Abbottsmith to Campbell. He was taken on as a diesel fitter. Alan Gilchrist, a young doctor, heard at a British Medical Association meeting that the expedition was having trouble finding medical staff. He loved the snow country, so applied to go.

The next essential was equipment, and here George Smith's expertise and the expedition's needs came together. If the RAAF did not have what the storemen wanted, they 'scrounged'. Some cold-weather gear, including heavy white high-necked sweaters made from unscoured wool smelling faintly of lanoline, came from Royal Navy disposals (the Royal Navy having sent warm clothing designed for the North Sea with its Pacific ships). Huts also came from disposals; the best were the fourteen-sided American buildings designed for Alaska. The Australian models, designed for the tropics, were not as successful, despite modifications. Food came from the RAN and landing pontoons from the Army.

There were still shortages, and Smith had to forage around Australia for many essential items such as valves for transmitters. As cargo space was not a problem—the LST had plenty of room—he took everything that might possibly come in handy on the stations. Across the road was an old building containing tent pegs, mallets and mallet handles, so he put them in the store. If they could not be used as mallets, they could always be used as firewood, he reasoned.

Wood itself was also a problem but, fortunately, the huts at Tottenham stood on wooden supports which were stayed by four-by-two struts. 'I don't think there was one left within any of the sheds within two hundred yards of us by the time we finished. How the place didn't fall down, I don't know', Smith said.

Many items could be obtained for nothing, but when things had to be paid for there was a problem—money. As a start, firms were asked to donate goods, and many were generous: MacRobertsons (as they had done for Mawson's BANZARE voyages) gave chocolate and confectionery, and Commonwealth Oil Refineries supplied fuel. Other goods were obtained as cheaply as possible. Rather than buy expensive huts the expedition built its own, using the doctor as carpenter's assistant. In later years Phil Law persuaded MacRobertsons to donate the four-gallon [18.18 litres] tins in which nuts arrived from South America. They became polar toilets—and expeditioners sometimes scored the bonus of a few handfuls of cashew nuts before the containers were pressed into sanitary service.

As their work would be finished when the expeditions left—or so it was thought—Campbell asked George Smith and Norm Jones if they would like to join an expedition south. Smith was only just out of the army and did not feel fit enough, but Jones agreed to go and was taken on as a cook.

By July the itinerary of *Wyatt Earp* was fixed. She was to go to Commonwealth Bay in December for scientific work and reconnaissance of the Cape Freshfield area, then to Princess Elizabeth Land to look for a site for a continental station, and refuel at Kerguelen on her return to Australia. LST *3501*, meanwhile, would set down the shore parties, first on Heard Island, then on Macquarie Island.[17]

The Executive Planning Committee held few meetings after July. It had decided the main outlines of the expeditions and the rest was up to Campbell to organise and implement. The Minister for External Affairs, Dr Evatt, then had the pleasure of reporting to Cabinet in August 1947 that scientific and meteorological stations were to be established on the two sub-Antarctic islands, reconnaissance was to be done in Antarctica itself, and a ship was to be obtained for Antarctic work.[18]

Meanwhile the new chief scientific officer, Phil Law, found he did not have to spend much time in his bleak office at Victoria Barracks. By a fortunate coincidence earlier in the year, Law had been invited by Leslie Martin, his professor at the Melbourne University Physics Department, to join a research team to develop a program of cosmic ray research. Working in conjunction with Dr Henry Rathgeber of Melbourne University's Cosmic Ray Research Group, the team decided to send cosmic ray equipment on *Wyatt Earp* and to Macquarie and Heard to study longer term variations in the composition and intensity of the rays. Law, on *Wyatt Earp*, would measure latitude variations between Australia and Antarctica. Most cosmic rays—charged particles from outer space—are deflected by the earth's magnetic field, but they occur at much greater frequency near the poles. The measuring equipment to be used had to be tested in the snow, in a hut specially built at Mt Hotham in the Victorian Alps.

The Cosmic Ray Group included six postgraduate students, David Caro, Ken Hines, Fred Jacka, Jo Jelbart, John Prescott and Charles Speedy. Getting the cumbersome scientific apparatus to 'Cosray Hut' in August was difficult, involving not only vehicles but also packhorses. On the way one packhorse slipped on slushy snow and rolled fifteen metres down a steep slope, neighing shrilly and losing its load. Fortunately the horse was not hurt nor were the instruments irreparably damaged, and by 23 August 'mechanical counters clicked intermittently and neon bulbs flashed as the incoming mesons of the cosmic rays triggered off the Geiger counters'.[19]

During the trips to and from Mt Hotham, often under dangerous conditions, Law established a leadership style in field work that changed little over the years. Fred Jacka, a 22-year-old physicist who was to join the Heard Island party, was impressed by Law's knowledge of the mountain conditions and his capacity to get things done:

> Phil was a small man but extremely energetic and fiery. His drive, his energy and his determination were very apparent in the beginning. He was very much the leader in the field exercises. . .very effective, very sympathetic, but there was no letting up at all.[20]

Sometimes the scientists in Cosray Hut were snowed in for days, and Fred Jacka remembers another facet of Law's leadership style that was to be a hallmark of later years and many Antarctic voyages:

> Phil took charge in a very masterly way and entertained the gathering very well with a clarinet. . .he played and we sang songs and he told stories. He was very much the centre of the whole social scene at that time.[21]

Law's own discipline was physics. Oceanography and marine biology would be attempted during the voyages of both LST *3501* and *Wyatt Earp*, but he could find no professor in an Australian university prepared to take responsibility for the Island biology programs—seals, penguins, flying birds and plants. A young biology graduate, Ron Kenny, was found for the pioneer Macquarie Island party, but no one for Heard Island. It was hoped that Alan Gilchrist, the medical officer, would carry out bird observations in addition to his other duties, with Law acting as his supervisor for the biological work.

By September the cold weather testing of the cosmic ray equipment was over and ANARE had more recruits. Jacka and Jelbart had been appointed to take one set of cosmic ray equipment to Heard Island—Hines and Speedy would go to Macquarie. Law would operate the third set on *Wyatt Earp*.

On 6 November 1947 the Prime Minister, the Rt Hon. J B Chifley, publicly announced that Australia had organised an Antarctic expedition. There was a good deal of media interest which must have pleased the Department of External Affairs bureaucrats who had drafted a top secret Cabinet minute recommending such publicity, 'with a view to consolidating Australian territorial claims in Antarctica. . .'.[22]

It was hoped regular broadcasts would be made from Heard and Macquarie Islands—and indeed from *Wyatt Earp*. Photographers would accompany each party to ensure a wide pictorial coverage of expedition activities, including a flag-raising ceremony to be conducted by Campbell on arrival at Heard Island. The Postmaster General's Department would also arrange for the special postmarking of envelopes posted from Heard Island.

The Government was determined to get maximum publicity and Clause 4 of the Cabinet minute left no doubt as to the real reasons behind the venture:

> That the leader of the Expedition be directed that in the event of a landing by any other party during the Expedition's stay on Heard Island, he should peacefully assert Australian rights over the islands [ie Heard and the neighbouring McDonald Island].[23]

Expedition members did not undertake any special training for the Antarctic; they were meant to know their jobs already. The two cooks worked for a couple of days in a bakery to look at bread making, but there was no fire drill or any other specialist work. The men did have medical tests and Abbottsmith remembered that he had his teeth specially done with different fillings—porcelain, gold and amalgam—so dentists could see which were most successful in low temperatures. All worked well, he said.

With no other training to do, the men were sent to Tottenham to organise their own gear, practise assembling huts and other pieces of equipment and help with the packing. This last was an advantage—when they came to unpack the material on the stations, they had some idea of how things had been packed, and they all got to know each other in the packing process.

When the radio operators arrived back in Melbourne late in October after training at the RAAF wireless school in Ballarat, they found Headquarters working at full pressure to make the sailing date in the middle of November. They joined the others in choosing gear and packing, and Arthur Scholes was fascinated by one piece of equipment he was given—a silk combination suit, 'a neck-to-ankle affair'—but without the holes where combinations usually have holes. He never solved the mystery of what to do with it.[24]

Every morning the men reported to Victoria Barracks where Campbell had his office. Two luxurious hire cars with uniformed drivers, the usual transport for the Department of Foreign Affairs, would arrive. Instead of their normal passengers in dark suits they carried expedition members, dressed in an assortment of old uniforms and overalls, out to Tottenham. There the men crated bags of cement, loaded trucks, boxed and stored different items all day, and then climbed back into the luxury cars for the ride home.[25]

Already some members of the expedition were standing out. Dr Alan Gilchrist rode to Tottenham each day on his beloved motor cycle. On wet days he wore the expedition clothing to test it, but these tests came to an abrupt end when he skidded off his machine in wet concrete in the middle of Melbourne. Despite this incident, he planned to take his motor bike to Heard Island.[26]

Expeditioners Bob Dovers and Johnny Abbottsmith were sent to a Melbourne record store to buy records for the Heard and Macquarie parties. Abbottsmith:

> We said, 'Look, we want 200 records'. The girl nearly fainted on the spot. She said, 'Oh, I'll take you to the manager. . .' He said, 'What do you want?' We said we didn't know. I wouldn't know a record from a record in those days. So we left it to them and they made two parcels up, one for Heard and one for Macquarie.

The physicists were still working frantically on the cosmic ray equipment. Fred Jacka remembered reading a great deal about Antarctic matters and studying the subject he was to work on. J K Davis told him Heard Island was 'the most God-forsaken place I've seen in all my days', but this only made Fred all the more anxious to see it.

On 6 November Prime Minister Ben Chifley announced the expedition's aims: to maintain Australian and British interests in Antarctica, to find a site for a permanent base and to undertake scientific work.[27]

Commander Karl Oom was to command the recently commissioned HMAS *Wyatt Earp*. Of Swedish ancestry, he had served in the RAN during the war. All the stories about him were untrue, he said cheerfully when interviewed. Oom had experience in Antarctic waters as a hydrographer on Mawson's second BANZARE voyage in 1930–31. The wooden-hulled *Wyatt Earp* had been further strengthened against the ice. She would carry radar, echo-sounding gear, instruments to measure cosmic rays, fifteen months' food supply and the carcasses of thirty sheep. The ship would also carry an aircraft, flown by Squadron Leader Gray, who had never seen the snow and hated the cold.[28]

The captain of LST *3501* was Lieutenant Commander George Dixon, an experienced and popular skipper. Dixon had extensive seagoing experience, including rounding Cape Horn in a sailing ship before the mast.

Someone, probably Campbell, had drawn up advice to station leaders. They were to delegate responsibilities and give the men as much freedom as possible, always treating them as equal members of a team. They were to remember that the aim was the success of the expedition, 'nothing else!'. They were to be fair and impartial, and especially nice to the cook, who had a 'lousy job'. To keep morale up, they should not allow too much spare time, and should break the monotony with celebrations, such as special Saturday nights, birthdays, Christmas, and a sweep for the Melbourne Cup. Spirits were to be limited to a nip a day, and port was provided for the Royal Toast.[29]

PHIL LAW MAINTAINING HIS ELABORATE COSMIC RAY MEASURING EQUIPMENT ON BOARD *WYATT EARP*, 1948. (E McCARTHY)

Preparations for the Heard and Macquarie expeditions continued at the Tottenham store where the men were loading trucks until two days before the first departure. There was no guarantee that the stores, carefully packed and checked by George Smith, would all get on board. According to Heard Island radio operator Alan Campbell-Drury:

> There was a lot of pilfering on the wharf. One morning just before we sailed, old Alf Hayter, the bosun on the LST, was in the middle of having a shave. I went up onto the bridge and Alf was waving a shaving brush at the wharfies down below and shouting, 'I don't know what's wrong with you blokes. You get twice our pay and half the cargo, and you're still not happy!' And that sort of stuck in my mind. They were getting into our chocolate and what grog we had. And, mind you, some of this chocolate was our emergency rations! But anything sort of went in those days.

Arthur Scholes remembered how excited and tired the men were as the last truck, loaded to capacity, left the depot. Then the Heard Island party was sworn in and signed statutory declarations of allegiance, and everyone headed for the LST, berthed at Station Pier, dwarfed beside two large overseas liners.

LST *3501* had been built in Canada in 1943. Before she left for the south on 17 November 1947 she was inspected by the Minister for the Navy, W J F Riordan. Members of the expedition lined up in front of the ship, facing a naval guard of honour, and newsreel and press photographers were busy while Campbell introduced each man to the minister. Arthur Scholes was standing beside Norm Jones, the cook. 'Ah, the most important man in the party!' said the minister. 'How right he was!' commented Arthur.[30] Once this formality was over, the first Australian National Antarctic Research Expedition was ready to leave.

TWO

HEARD ISLAND

Heard Island is a very threatening place, the sheer malevolence of it
hits you when you go there. It is essentially black and white, stark, because
the black volcanic rock cliffs rise out of a grey seething sea, the wind is
blowing, and the birds are just floating around in the gale and screaming. The tops of the island's black cliffs are coated with a thick, 50-foot
or so layer of glacier white ice, and this disappears up into the swirling
mists that are engulfing this great mountain. I've brought men who have
wintered in Antarctica into Atlas Cove, and they lean over the rail and
say, *'Jesus what a place!'*

Phil Law

F inding a ship capable of carrying passengers and heavy cargo
and able to combat the wild seas and hurricane-strength winds
of the Southern Ocean was difficult in post-war Australia but the
Naval Board, after some collective soul searching, decided that
an LST (Landing Ship Tanks) could do the job.

Landing Ship Tanks were substantial vessels mass-produced during
the war as multi-purpose, cargo-carrying work vessels. They were designed
to run up on to the beach and discharge tanks, troops, and heavy equipment through their blunt bow doors, over a big steel ramp which dropped
down for that purpose. (It was unavoidable, considering the speed of construction, that some LSTs were jerry-built. Numbers of them had broken
in half in Atlantic storms while ferrying goods from America to England
during the war.) They were essentially vast cargo holds with engine, bridge
and accommodation tacked on the back, so there was no shortage of
cargo space on HMALST *3501* for the Heard Island operation.

Heard Island has a unique record in the history of exploration. It was 'discovered' no fewer than eight times.

An active volcano, rising sheer out of the sea to 2745 metres, its peak, Big Ben, is seldom seen through the constant swirling clouds. Situated south of the Antarctic Convergence, where the chilled Antarctic waters of the Southern Ocean meet the warmer waters of the Indian Ocean, it is 4000 kilometres south west of Western Australia and some 1500 kilometres from the Antarctic coastline. A 42-kilometre-long island running north-west to south-east, it is heavily glaciated and ice cliffs form much of the coastline. The climate is Antarctic, while the vegetation and animal populations are sub-Antarctic. Winds in excess of 130 kilometres per hour are common throughout the year.

The first person claiming to sight it was Englishman Captain Peter Kemp, who in 1833 was exploring the area in his ship *Magnet*, looking for sealing and whaling opportunities. The island appeared on his track chart.[1]

Sixteen years later an American, Captain Thomas Long, also reported sighting land, but neither he nor Kemp published his discovery. This was left to another American, Captain John Heard, who saw the island on a trip from Boston to Melbourne in his ship *Oriental*. If discovering a place means publishing its location so that others can find it, Heard's discovery of

Heard Island was the basis for America's claim to ownership.[2] News moved slowly, however, and the following year four British captains thought they had discovered the island, as did a German in 1857.[3]

The importance of discovery lay in the promise of wealth from the thousands of seals found on the island's beaches. By the 1850s, whaling and sealing had been established in the Southern Ocean for 70 years and in many places the supply of animals was declining. Heard Island was plundered from then on by visiting gangs of sealers for its fur seals and blubber from elephant seals.

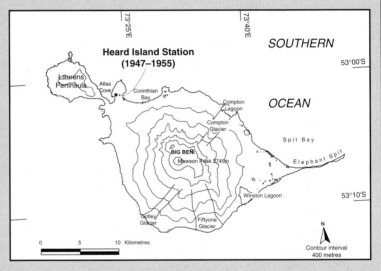

After the 1880s, due to indiscriminate slaughter, it was difficult to find enough seals. Few further voyages were attempted and in 1902, when a German group under Professor von Drygalski visited, the island had been deserted by humans for some years.[4]

In the early years of the twentieth century Heard Island was deserted and little interest was taken in it until in 1908 a Norwegian asked the British Government whether they had claimed the island and if so, whether he could operate a floating whaling factory there. Some whaling was carried on for a short period, and the island was claimed for Britain.[5] Whaling was revived in 1926 when a South African firm obtained a licence to operate in the area and in January 1929 one of its ships, *Kildalkey*, visited Heard Island under the command of Captain H O Hansen. *Kildalkey* also landed a French geologist, E Aubert de la Rue, who carried out a survey on the northern part of the island.[6] Later in 1929 nine members of the BANZAR expedition under Sir Douglas Mawson stayed for eight days and undertook surveying, photography, biology, and exploration. Elephant seal carcasses were abundant, they observed, and had been stripped a few weeks previously, so some sealing continued.[7]

In the 1930s all sealing and whaling finally ceased on Heard Island as the price of oil crashed during the Depression, and the next phase in the island's history was as a possible base for submarines. During World War II the Australian Navy checked it to see if the Germans were operating there. They were not, but German raiders did use the nearby Kerguelen Islands on a number of occasions to shelter, make running repairs, take on fresh water, and change the identity of individual ships.[8]

After the war the British Government, aware of the American interest in Heard Island based on historical precedent and its strategic importance, asked the Australian Government to occupy the island as part of its post-war Antarctic activity.[9]

The Captain, Lieutenant Commander Dixon, had encouraged his ship's surgeon, Peter Blaxland, to put his MG sports car in the cargo space so that the two men could have transport from Fremantle to Perth during a stop-over there. Even with the prefabricated huts, a year's stores, and a bulldozer, there was plenty of spare cargo space. The expedition's doctor, Alan Gilchrist, put his prized 500 cc Indian motor cycle on board and took it south.

Dixon had selected LST *3501* for the Antarctic expeditions from the LSTs available after the Australian Government had acquired a flotilla of six in 1946. Allegedly the pick of the bunch, she had lost her bow doors in an accident in the Coral Sea in 1946, and without them (they were designed to give the bow a modest convex shape to help steer the ship) looked even more like a shoe box. Dixon, with the help of naval architects, redesigned the devices which held the bow doors in place at sea, enabling them to be opened and closed more quickly in emergencies. This was to be a blessing later at Heard Island.

On 17 November 1947, LST *3501* passed through Port Phillip Heads and turned her reconstituted bows to the west. Bass Strait was relatively calm, with a slight swell. 'Doc' Gilchrist began the time honoured ANARE tradition of breaking out sea sickness pills for the landlubber expeditioners. He thought they might help 50 per cent of sufferers, but fell foul of his own statistics. He was one of the first to succumb.[10]

25

HMALST *3501*—LATER
LABUAN.
(P LAW)

As the ship neared Fremantle the royal wedding of Princess Elizabeth and the Duke of Edinburgh was celebrated with loyal toasts. The party practised landing with an LCVP (Landing Craft Vehicle and Personnel) and were entertained at the Fremantle Town Hall with beer and sandwiches. ANARE leader Stuart Campbell joined the party, and LST *3501* sailed for Heard Island on 28 November 1947. Dr Peter Blaxland's MG sports car had to remain on board, as Dixon was told by the navy that he might have to return directly to Melbourne from Heard.

For the first four days south the weather was warm and calm, the nights tropical and balmy, and everyone enjoyed the trip. Expeditioners were allowed a full run of the ship—even access to the bridge at any time, a privilege that became a cherished part of the ANARE experience in later years, with most polar captains allowing expeditioners to come and go at will, except while entering or leaving port.

Fine weather left with December, and the Roaring Forties struck. The flat-bottomed LST not only rolled alarmingly (40 degrees from the upright was not uncommon), but the whole vessel flexed and twisted. Dixon was heard to say that they were the biggest seas he had ever seen and later he wrote:

> An enormous green wall of water would appear ahead. Up the bows would rise, and the white top of the oncoming sea would break angrily and disappear beneath them. Occasionally when the sea had passed, the bows would fall unsupported and pile-drive an oncoming sea with a resounding crash.
>
> Seeing is believing the way an LST can bend. The whole structure quivers like a spring board after a diver has jumped off. The decks bend in ripples like a caterpillar in progress. Bulkheads pant with a loud banging noise as the ship gathers for another attack. And so it goes on, making sleep out of the question.[11]

With no land masses to break the onrush of wind and waves around the globe, 30-metre-high waves are not uncommon in the Southern Ocean. When the trough is taken into consideration as well, the towering

walls of water are higher than substantial ships. Sub-Lieutenant John
Lavett remembered that first storm:

> We made only 50 miles [93 kilometres] one day, which would have been
> even better if it had been in the direction we really wanted to go. The
> wind shrieked. The swell ahead of us was immense to the point where
> the waves had separate breakers, of say seven feet [2.23 metres], on top
> of them. The overall size of the seas was difficult to measure because
> they towered over the ship. Our height above sea level on the bridge
> was about 36 feet [10.9 metres], and we were still looking up at walls of
> water. Fifty feet [15.2 metres], seventy feet [21.3 metres]? Who knows?

At the height of the tempest came a dramatic call over the loud-
speaker system: 'All hands and expedition personnel muster on the
foredeck! Deck cargo is loose forward!' A particularly venomous wave
had crashed over the forecastle, and washed aft over the main deck. A
bridging pontoon, torn from its lashings, stove in the bows of a motor
boat. Drums of aviation fuel broke loose and began rolling about the
heaving deck. Stuart Campbell, in tennis shoes and overalls, worked
beside navy and ANARE men, slipping and sliding over the oily main
deck securing the cargo. Expedition radio operator Arthur Scholes wrote
in *Fourteen Men*:

> Once I paused in the middle of heaving on a drum, my stomach muscles
> exhausted with strain. I glanced at the rising and plunging bows. It was
> an awe-inspiring sight! Magnificent, yet dreadful. Great mountains of
> turbulent water lay ahead. Down in the trough the water surrounded
> the ship like the grey walls of a prison. The water walls were higher than
> the funnel. . .we worked with the energy born of despair.[12]

Fears that the LST might actually break in two were fuelled by a crack,
about one metre long, which developed in the steel deck near the bridge.
Johnny Abbottsmith, the expedition's diesel mechanic, recalled how they
watched this crack open and close as the LST bucked and twisted, riding
over the huge seas. It could not be welded because of the continual
expansion and contraction. The ship's chief engineer came up with an
ingenious solution. Holes were drilled in a steel plate big enough to
straddle the fracture:

> Then when all the holes were drilled everybody stood by. The people
> under the bulkhead were ready with the nuts, and the sailors up on top
> had the bolts ready to drop into the holes when they lined up. And when
> we were down in the trough of a wave they banged in the bolts and they

had the nuts on the bolts from underneath before we hit the top of the wave again. Then they tightened them up and stopped the crack from developing right across the boat and breaking it in half.

After four days of full gale, the weather began to ease, but it was still very rough. At 9.45 pm, Sub-Lieutenant John Lavett was on the bridge when the engine room telegraph rang. The engines were about to be stopped as there was a problem with the fuel. Lavett said his first thought was: 'Gee, you can't stop here!'

But stop we did. The lights went out and the only sound was the loud ringing of the gyroscope alarm bell in the bowels of the ship, working off its temporary emergency supply. We began to wallow and broach. If this had happened a few hours earlier, I do not think our chances would have been better than minimal, but again we were lucky. The enormous pounding the ship had experienced had started a couple of plates, and salt water had entered a fuel tank.

Landfall was made on 11 December, with a rare sighting of Big Ben, the 2745 metre volcano almost permanently cloud covered. Johnny Abbottsmith:

When we first saw the island we just looked at it in amazement! We were forty miles [74.4 kilometres] out to sea and all we could see was this big ice-cream cone sticking up in the air, out of the clouds.

With only rudimentary maps and charts available, Dixon approached Heard Island with extreme caution. The first plan was to run down the eastern, more sheltered side of the island and land the expedition at Spit Bay on the extreme south of the island. Then it was hoped to establish a cache of stores at Atlas Cove in the north (where a small dwelling, Admiralty Hut, already existed, built in January 1929 by the crew of the whaler *Kildalkey* to shelter shipwrecked sailors). With depth sounder pinging and engines at dead slow, the LST nosed towards the inhospitable shoreline of Spit Bay.[13]

Campbell began to organise a landing party to find a suitable camp site. Aub Gotley, the senior weather man and OIC of the first Heard Island ANARE wintering party, was posted on the bridge to warn of sudden changes in the weather. So sudden and violent are the changes in those latitudes that after one hour Gotley warned the captain the barometer was falling and a change in the weather was imminent. Arthur Scholes:

The captain did not hesitate. Preparations for the landing party were abandoned and the order was given to up-anchor. With her bows pointing to the NE, the LST steamed out of the bay. The departure was not a moment too soon. The wind came tearing in from the west, whipping up the waves. Grey clouds turned to black ones. Fog descended round the rugged coastline, as if nature herself was laying a smoke screen to hide the secrets of her wild stronghold.[14]

Several hours later the LST steamed cautiously into the relatively sheltered waters of Atlas Cove flanked by the bulk of Rogers Head to the east (thought to have the profile of a Red Indian) and Cape Laurens to the west. Again Campbell began to assemble a shore party. An LCVP barge—a mini version of the LST with a drop-down landing ramp—was used, and Arthur Scholes was included to operate the walkie-talkie radio between shore and ship.

As penguins watched impassively from the shore, the LCVP ground to a halt some twenty metres from dry land. The bow ramp went down, and they were free to land. Scholes said no one seemed to want to make the first move. Eventually David Eastman, the official photographer, took the initiative. 'Well I'm supposed to get the pictures. I might as well be the bloody hero.' With his movie camera slung over his shoulder he jumped off and sank to his thighs, shouting over the laughter of the rest of the party that 'it's as cold as charity'. Campbell was next, and then they all splashed ashore. Scholes:

> The barking of the elephant seals in the nearby tussock and the shrill protesting cries of the birds, flying inches above our heads, were the only sounds which greeted the first visitors to the island in many years. The absence of other noises was almost disturbing to ears accustomed to the shipboard cacophony. It was the strange mysterious silence of an unknown land.[15]

Two hundred metres from the water's edge stood the tiny Admiralty Hut, still in good condition. Two elephant seals lay wallowing outside the door, but were persuaded to move by Campbell, who belted their tails with a piece of driftwood. Inside, he found seven bunks, emergency rations and a Union Jack left by the Mawson BANZARE party in 1929. After an hour the weather closed in again, and the shore party was asked to return to the ship.

The next day the LST again steamed south down the east coast of Heard Island to Spit Bay to try to find a site for the main camp. The weather was fine and clear and an LCVP and a dinghy were sent off to attempt a landing. But a heavy surf was breaking onto the rocky beach. Wide open to the north-easterly winds, without shelter for the landing barges, Spit Bay was clearly not suitable for the main station. The LST

returned again to Atlas Cove.

Taking advantage of the fine clear weather, the Walrus amphibian aircraft was winched over the side and at 4 pm on 13 December the amphibian took off, circled LST *3501* twice in salute, and flew down the east coast to Spit Bay. It was piloted by Flight Lieutenant Mal 'Smithy' Smith, and his crew included Warrant Officer Peter Swan to take still photographs, radio operator Warrant Officer C Dunlop, and David Eastman with a movie camera.[16] During the first part of the flight they saw and photographed an unknown lake on the west side of the southern extremity of Heard Island.

The big surprise was Big Ben, thought to be only about 7500 feet [2286 metres] high. Smithy reported that when his cockpit was level with the top of Big Ben's dome, his altimeter read 10 000 feet [3048 metres]. 'But that was nothing! We saw another peak about a thousand feet [305 metres] higher. It was mostly hidden by clouds, but we could see the top sticking up like a pimple.'[17]

The existence of this second 'pimple' peak was unknown, and hidden from view at ground level. At a confirmed 2745 metres Big Ben did not measure up to Smithy's enthusiastic first observations, but it was significantly higher than first thought. It had been a good day's work and the historic flight had lasted an hour and a half. Smithy was disappointed not to be able to fly over Big Ben's summit—he was recalled by radio because of bad weather moving in. David Eastman suffered a frostbitten right hand operating the camera trigger without a glove as he filmed the summit of Big Ben.

The Walrus was taxied onto the beach at Atlas Cove and tied down to large stones and concrete blocks brought ashore from the LST. In navy parlance, Walrus aircraft were known as 'ducks', and Captain Dixon went ashore to check on 'the duck's' security. Dixon noticed under the aircraft a large almost perfectly oval stone resembling an egg, and ordered it to be taken back on board where it was painted the same colour as the 'duck'. In the ward-room that night he presented it to pilot Mal Smith and sent a whimsical signal to the presumably bemused Australian Commonwealth Naval Board: 'Duck has laid an egg. Is this unique?' There was no immediate reply from Melbourne.

Campbell was still undecided where to put the main camp. Admiralty Hut on the western side of the Atlas Cove beach had obviously survived Heard Island's worst weather, but it was well away from any sources of fresh water and besieged by elephant seals wallowing and belching in the high tussocks surrounding it. An alternative site (later known as 'Windy City') at the eastern end of the bay needed to be checked, and a seven-man party, including Fred Jacka, one of the expedition's physicists, was sent off in the LST's work boat with a tent and camping gear to check out the site, make tide measurements, and establish a site for magnetic observations. Two LCVPs were sent to take the party to Windy City, and the first of many near disasters to plague unloading operations took place: one LCVP began to take water and sink, and had to make a run for the shore.

TETHERED WALRUS
AMPHIBIAN AIRCRAFT AT
WHARF POINT, HEARD
ISLAND.
(A CAMPBELL-DRURY)

At Atlas Cove, the plan was to unload heavy cargo on to pontoons and tow them to shore, augmented by the two LCVPs. But the plyboard pontoons were hopeless in the swells rolling in to Atlas Cove, and the LCVPs were plagued with mechanical breakdowns. One of the expedition's main radio receivers was badly damaged on a pontoon and after a week's activity at Heard Island, very little cargo had reached the shore. LST *3501* was burning up so much fuel that there was concern that she might not have enough oil to get back to Australia. The weather, in typical Heard Island style, was capricious and vicious.

Dixon made the courageous decision to run the LST up on to a rocky beach so that the heavy cargo could be unloaded directly and quickly—otherwise there would be no wintering party at Heard Island that year. The beaching was made without incident and a party of navy personnel and expeditioners cheerfully plunged up to their waists in freezing water,

31

UNLOADING THROUGH THE
BOW DOORS OF LST *3501*—A
RISKY BUT NECESSARY
OPERATION.
(A CAMPBELL-DRURY)

shifting rocks to try to make a primitive jetty to the lowered ramp of the LST. There was a gap between the ramp and the beach, making the manoeuvre to drive the expedition's tractor ashore a critical task. When a gangway of planks was built Doc Gilchrist decided it was time to get his prized Indian motor bike ashore. The duty officer in charge of unloading refused permission, so Gilchrist waited until he went to lunch and the more amenable Captain Dixon took over:

> I revved her up and Captain Dixon turned his navy cap back-to-front, grabbed the carrier, and pushed like mad. I zoomed across the bridge and up the beach, and then I hit a grass tussock and the bike went over and I was ashore.

That was Gilchrist's sole Heard Island motor cycle excursion. The Indian was no trail bike and simply bogged down in the volcanic sand. He claimed to be the first man to ride a motor bike in the Antarctic.

LST *3501* had beached early in the morning and unloading went on furiously all day. The most backbreaking task was to roll the 44-gallon [200 litres] drums of oil up over the rocks of the landing beach. The uphill shove became known as 'The Burma Road', after the famous wartime supply route from Burma across the Himalayan foothills towards China. Abbottsmith bulldozed a track through the tussocks to Admiralty Hut and at the end of the day 300 drums and tonnes of food were on shore.[18]

By 8 pm Aub Gotley warned of approaching bad weather and the LST prepared to pull back from the beach. She came off the rocks, but swung around and went aground broadside to the beach. The port and starboard engines were juggled to no avail. Nothing would shift the ship and it was getting dark. All available boats were launched to take out extra anchors to try and winch the ship to safety. It was decided to take the stern anchor farther out in the hope that the extra pull might move her off the rocky bottom. The officers on the bridge signalled to the work boat to take the stern anchor out; there was no response. They hooted irritably on the ship's siren several times, but the work boat's engine had failed.

The situation was verging on desperate. Even with the stern anchor moved further out and both engines straining, the LST could not be budged. John Lavett recalled that there was nothing more they could do:

THE 'BURMA ROAD'— HAULING STORES ASHORE, WHARF POINT, HEARD ISLAND, DECEMBER 1947. (A CAMPBELL-DRURY)

> George Dixon went below for a cup of coffee and no doubt to contemplate our next move, leaving me on the bridge alone. I stood there for some time, in a somewhat melancholy state, when I heard a 'click', then another, and after a while another. It was the gyro compass. I took the two flights to the wardroom in two bounds to shout to George: 'She's swinging sir'. He was half a pace behind me on the way up again. Indeed she was. She came off gently, by herself, evidently as the result of a very soft wind and tide change. We quickly got ourselves further out to anchor, tired but elated.
>
> Half an hour later a full gale burst on to the area we had just left. Had we still been there, we should certainly have been finished. We had been very lucky again.

But in weather terms Heard Island had only been toying with the first ANARE expedition. On the morning of 20 December Gotley told Dixon that the weather was changing rapidly and warned against either beaching the LST or attempting another flight. There were two expedition groups on shore; one had access to the Admiralty Hut but the other, at Windy City on the eastern side of the bay and living in tents, was more exposed. By 8 pm a 50 knot gale was blowing in Atlas Cove and so steep was the barograph fall that Gotley decided to keep an all-night vigil on the bridge. By 3 am on 21 December, the pressure had fallen to 28.14 inches [71.47 centimetres], lowering by half an inch [1.27 centimetres] the record for those latitudes, and was still falling. Dixon ordered that LST *3501* be prepared for sea. The two anchors began to drag and, even with both engines at full speed, the ship was being driven on to the rocks.[19]

Dixon later described the gale as the most violent he had ever experienced in a lifetime at sea. No sooner had he cleared Atlas Cove than his radar failed. His dilemma: to ride out the storm at sea, or to nose blindly into the lee of the unknown, shoal infested western shore of the Atlas Roads peninsula to seek some shelter from the 200 kilometres per hour westerly winds:

> If I remained at sea it was inevitable that, sooner or later, the upper deck would be swept clean. Boats, rafts, precious drums of lubricating oil—would all be swept away or destroyed.
>
> The wooden structure of the bridge house quivered and shook. Its sides bulged so that the doors flew open, and one wondered if it would collapse altogether. Ears drummed as though one were at high elevation in an aircraft. At every moment we expected the glass windows to blow in.[20]

When Captain Dixon stepped out of the chart room on to the rear of the bridge, the wind immediately knocked him down and hurled him against a gun platform. He decided it would be less risky to seek shelter under the lee of the island and nosed his ship blindly towards Heard Island to ride out the hurricane.

Meanwhile, at Windy City, Campbell and his small party piled up cases of supplies around the walls of their army tent on the windward side, but it wasn't long before their canvas shelter was shredded by the screaming wind. They finished up huddled behind the cases. It was a long night. In the morning when the wind eased so that they could actually stand up, Fred Jacka noticed something that they had failed to appreciate before about the effect of wind on their camp site.

> All the stones that were partly buried in the sand had very clean-cut faces, abraded by the blasting sand. They were three-sided with sharp edges—corresponding to the three directions of the wind. So Stuart Campbell didn't need any more convincing that it wasn't a suitable site for us to build a station.

Back at Atlas Cove, the Walrus amphibian plane tethered on the beach was completely wrecked after its one successful flight. It had survived 150 kilometre per hour gales in its operational life, but the hurricane had converted it into a sad mess of twisted spars, floats and fuselage. It had not completely outlived its usefulness, however. Fred Jacka and his co-physicist Jo Jelbart found it a treasure trove of fittings and spare parts

for their experimental cosmic ray work during the year.

Faced with the task of telling the Naval Board that the amphibian was no more (it was also the last Walrus in RAN service), Dixon returned to his previous theme of the 'duck's egg' and cabled Melbourne: 'If egg is not fertile, species is now extinct'. The penny dropped, and signals began to fly back and forth. 'Vintage Dixon', according to John Lavett.

The LST risked two more beachings before the last of the supplies were lugged up 'the Burma Road' to the growing settlement around Admiralty Hut. Heard Island even turned on a white Christmas. On 26 December 1947 Campbell conducted an official proclamation ceremony to claim Heard Island for Australia. He had been instructed to do this by the Department of External Affairs, but was unsure exactly how to proceed. 'I looked through books and books and books and a huge volume of External Affairs papers on how to claim land. We put up a flag, and buried a capsule with the proclamation.' Sailors from the LST built a cairn of rocks and Campbell and Dixon signed the declaration, claiming the island (and the adjacent McDonald Islands) for the Commonwealth of Australia.

On 29 December LST *3501* steamed out of Atlas Cove, and blew a 'cock-a-doodle-doo' on the siren as her yellow superstructure disappeared around Rogers Head. She was bound for Kerguelen to land fuel supplies for *Wyatt Earp* on her return from probing the Antarctic coast of George V Land. LST *3501* would then set a course for Melbourne.

Campbell elected to stay with the fourteen Heard Island winterers and help them build huts and settle in, until he could be picked up by

'THE SPECIES IS NOW EXTINCT.' WRECKED WALRUS AIRCRAFT AFTER HEARD ISLAND HURRICANE, 1947. (AAD ARCHIVES)

THE HEARD ISLAND POST OFFICE, OPEN FOR BUSINESS DECEMBER 1947. THE POSTMASTER IS ANARE LEADER STUART CAMPBELL. (D EASTMAN)

Wyatt Earp in late February or early March. There had been no time, during the frenetic unloading activity, to begin to build the prefabricated huts. Admiralty Hut was too small to accommodate everyone and was used to shelter from the elements and have a cup of tea or coffee. Army tents were pitched among the tussocks and hummocks nearby, competing with the elephant seals which used the area as a wallow. The prospect of being rolled on by three tonnes of bull elephant seal was frightening and also likely, as they came in from the sea at night. Johnny Abbottsmith recalls lying in bed hearing the huge creatures coming towards the tents, making 'galumphing' noises as their great bodies compressed the wet sand and tussocks:

> They got cranky because we were on their spot. We were worried because if one came through the tent he'd squash the lot of us to death. So we tried to shoo the big bull elephant seals away, but they wouldn't take 'no' for an answer and kept coming on. We wondered how the hell we could stop them.
>
> We tried firesticks, but they weren't worried about those, they'd never seen fire, and didn't know what it was. You couldn't get near them because when they reared up they would stand eight feet tall [2.4 metres], leaning back on their tails. And then they'd lunge at you. If you were caught, they'd crush you into the sand.

The senior radio supervisor, Louis E Macey ('Lem'), and one of his operators, Alan Campbell-Drury, got together and contrived an electric prod which proved the most effective deterrent.

The first radio broadcasts to be sent from Heard Island were unofficial. Campbell-Drury had bought a war disposals Marconi transceiver, Type A, Mark III for £10 [$20]. It was built into a suitcase, transmitted Morse code only, and operated on very low power—four watts.

> I set it up in one of our tents, among the elephant seals, got the battery from the Doc's motor bike—because we had no power on at that stage—and I called Australia and got an answer. I think I can rightly say I'm the first radio ham to work from Heard Island.

This channel of communications did not escape the notice of journalist Arthur Scholes. One night Alan Campbell-Drury heard Scholes tapping away on the Morse key of the little Marconi, and was able to 'read' his key clicks as he sent his message. He realised Scholes was sending an unofficial story to a Sydney newspaper about the success of the Heard Island landing: 'I said: "Cut it out Arthur. I'll lose my licence!"'

No scientific work could begin at Heard until huts had been constructed, concrete slabs poured for the diesel generators and radio masts erected. Building materials were scarce in post-war Australia and a mixed collection of prefabricated huts had been obtained. Four US Signal Corps huts with heaters, light fittings and shelves had been brought to the island. Each hut had fourteen plywood sides, held together by nuts and bolts.[21] Some of the other huts had been designed for the tropics and needed to be insulated and lined. By New Year's Eve the 'met' and radio hut was finished, and celebrations were held inside.

HUT ERECTION AT ATLAS COVE. THE 14-SIDED US SIGNAL CORPS HUTS WERE A WELCOME CHANGE FROM THE TENTS PITCHED IN THE TUSSOCKS AMONG ELEPHANT SEALS. (A CAMPBELL-DRURY)

Several nights later, most members of the party were enjoying the warmth and comfort of the new hut in the middle of a rain storm, when there was a knock at the door. This was as unlikely as a car horn or telephone bell, and Campbell-Drury said they did a quick head count:

> Well, we opened the door, and there stood Captain Dixon from LST *3501*! We couldn't believe our eyes. He was soaking wet, and said, 'Quick, let me in and give me some dry clothes. I've fallen arse over head out of the boat.'

Dixon later recalled saying that when Macey's pale and anxious face peered out of the hut door, he said: 'Don't worry, the ship's sunk, but we're all saved'. Then, 'Group Captain Campbell forgot his toothbrush, and we've brought it back'.

Stuart Campbell was in fact still sleeping in one of the tents among the tussocks and elephant seals. He thought Macey was pulling his leg when he was told Captain Dixon was there to see him. But at Kerguelen Dixon had received a radio message that *Wyatt Earp* (which was to pick up Campbell on its return from exploring the coast of George V Land) had been forced to go back to Melbourne. That meant that Campbell, the leader of ANARE, might be marooned on Heard Island for a whole year unless special arrangements were made to pick him up. As there

37

was a great deal of organising to be done in Melbourne for the fledgling ANARE, Dixon had been ordered back to Heard Island to get Campbell and return him to HQ.

Before leaving Heard, Campbell officially handed over to Aub Gotley, the senior meteorologist, and on 4 January 1948 LST *3501* again headed away from Atlas Cove—but she was still not finally away. Lem Macey had lent his one and only set of long woollen combination underwear to the sodden captain. Macey asked Dixon to return them before the ship sailed, but he forgot. Campbell-Drury radioed the ship, on Macey's urging, that Dixon had absconded with his underpants.

Dixon responded: 'Terribly sorry, we'll bring them back to you.' The LST was some miles out to sea, but she turned about and came back in. The combinations were attached to a buoy, and thrown over the side. Lem and I both sat patiently on the beach at Atlas Cove for an hour waiting for them to drift in. When we went back up to the radio shack, Macey pulled them out of the box and said: 'Look at that. You'd think he'd have cleaned them first—look at the skid marks in them!' That was the final straw for Macey.

The fourteen Heard Island expeditioners were finally on their own.

THREE

MACQUARIE ISLAND AND PUSHING SOUTH

Macquarie Island is 'wet cold'. The wind hardly ever stops. There's generally fog too. You don't often see the plateau top exposed, and with the wind comes driving rain—very much like the weather you get in a Melbourne winter. When Melbourne has wild south-easters blowing one minute, then heavy showers of rain I call them 'Macquarie Island days'. The wind is so strong it blows the clouds aside and the sun breaks through—and then there's another rain squall.

Phil Law

LST *3501*, battered and holed during the Heard Island landings, went into dry dock for repairs at Williamstown on its return to Melbourne on 18 January 1948. It was ready to transport the 13-man Macquarie Island party and 400 tonnes of supplies (including sheep and goats) from Melbourne on 28 February. There was not time to fix everything. Some holes remained in the ballast tanks, and those game enough could lift covers on the floor of the tank deck and gaze directly down into the green depths of the Southern Ocean. The LST called in to Hobart briefly, then set course for Macquarie Island on 3 March.

In November and December at Atlas Cove, Heard Island, rigid floating pontoons and LCVP craft had been unable to cope with the demands of unloading cargo, so the LST, in addition to its complement of barges and pontoons, carried two DUKWs (an army code for World War II vintage amphibians), which were essentially 2½-tonne trucks, encased in steel hulls, which could carry cargo directly from ship to shore. Their presence on the LST was due to the persistence of Captain Laurie Stooke.

Situated to the south-east of Australia, approximately halfway to the Antarctic continent, Macquarie Island is so permanently shrouded in mist and rain that it remains 'the least adequately mapped part of Australia'.[1] The small, elongated island, permanently battered by the prevailing westerly winds, is just north of the Antarctic Convergence, and therefore free of pack ice. Snow falls at any time of the year but at sea level seldom lasts on the ground for more than a few hours, or a week up on the plateau. While Heard Island to the west is distinguished by an active volcano nearly 3000 metres high, Macquarie is a long, low-lying island 34 kilometres long, up to 5.5 kilometres wide and no more than 433 metres at its highest point, Mt Hamilton. Much of the island is a plateau, 250–350 metres above sea level.

The geology of Macquarie is as fascinating as the dramatic heights of Heard. It is a slice of the oceanic crust elevated above sea level in almost pristine condition, an exposed fragment of the Macquarie Ridge complex which runs south from New Zealand towards the Balleny Islands. Its ice-free shores and proximity to Antarctica make it a haven for wildlife, with a profusion of breeding colonies of seals, penguins, and other sea birds.

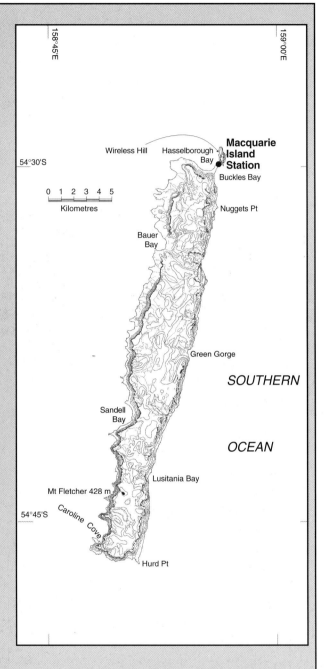

Australia's European settlers were quick to realise that seals and other marine life on nearby offshore islands were valuable commodities and from the 1790s seals were killed for fur and oil. As nearby resources were worked out, merchants were forced further afield. On 11 July 1810, *Perseverance* under Frederick Hasselburg was taking a sealing gang south to Campbell Island when he discovered another island which he called after Governor Lachlan

Macquarie. Hasselburg's landing led to the island's exploitation. Its beaches and rocky shores were thick with seals, and it was obviously a potential commercial goldmine.[2]

Hasselburg left a sealing gang on the island and returned to Sydney. He tried to keep his discovery a secret, but news leaked out and soon six ships left for Macquarie Island.[3] This was the beginning of several years of intensive slaughter when up to 100 000 fur seals were clubbed to death indiscriminately in a season. But the kill dropped dramatically, and by 1815 the harvest was only about 5000.[4]

The sealers then turned their attention to killing elephant seals for their copious blubber, which was boiled down to produce oil. When the Russian explorer von Bellingshausen visited Macquarie Island in 1820 he found two gangs of sealers working there. They lived in huts lined with sealskins and grass, used blubber for lighting and ate sea birds and penguins, eggs, the flippers of young elephant seals and wild cabbage—an effective remedy for scurvy. Bellingshausen noted there were wild dogs and cats on the island.[5] Many visiting groups left exotic specimens on Macquarie until it was declared a sanctuary in the 1930s. The list includes ducks, fowls, geese and wekas, goats, sheep and rabbits. They were destined for the pot. Dogs, cats, rats and mice arrived by ship. The wekas (flightless birds native to Stewart Island, New Zealand) did particularly well, as did the rabbits. They soon outbred the sealers' ability to eat them. The dogs ran wild for a while, but died out.

Unclaimed in the early years of exploration, in 1825 Macquarie Island was included in the jurisdiction of Van Diemen's Land (later Tasmania) when it became a separate colony from New South Wales. But for decades the Tasmanian Government made no attempt to assert its authority there.[6]

Sealing gangs continued to kill elephant seals, as their numbers waxed and waned, until as late as 1919. When they ran out of seals, they herded the penguins into the digesters and boiled them for their oil. In 1915 Sir Douglas Mawson—among others—was pressing for Macquarie Island to be declared a sanctuary, and in 1919 the Tasmanian Government refused to renew any sealing leases. Macquarie Island was left to the seals and penguins.[7]

In 1929 Mawson led the BANZAR expeditions to Antarctica, and in December 1930 visited his old base on Macquarie Island built during his 1911–14 Australasian Antarctic Expedition. He found the hut in fairly good condition and the wireless masts still there. His party explored and studied the wildlife, and decided that there had been a marked increase in numbers since they were last there. In 1933, Mawson's original suggestion bore fruit, and the Tasmanian Government declared Macquarie Island a wildlife sanctuary.[8]

As well as being a haven for wildlife Macquarie Island is a geological curiosity. It represents a piece of the ocean floor that has been pushed to the surface of the Southern Ocean by tectonic plate action—in this case the Pacific plate folding down under the Australian plate. The area is unstable and strong earthquakes occur regularly—sometimes causing rock and mud slides along the cliffs that circle the coast. Geological studies of Macquarie are continuing to the present day. The movement on the island is complex, with various sections moving relative to each other—making it the best place on earth to examine the sea floor above sea level.

SOME OF THE 1948
MACQUARIE ISLAND PARTY ON
THE WHARF AT HOBART, 3
MARCH. FROM TOP LEFT:
N LAIRD, Y VALETTE
(FRENCH OBSERVER),
C DU TOIT, W MONKHOUSE,
A MARTIN (OIC),
G MOTTERSHEAD,
DR R BENNETT, R KENNY.
FROM BOTTOM LEFT:
L SPEEDY, J IVANAC
(GEOLOGIST RETURNED ON
LST), R CHADDER,
G MAJOR, C SCOBLE.
(COURTESY HOBART *MERCURY*)

Stooke had been at the Puckapunyal army camp when he read newspaper reports of the difficulties experienced unloading cargo at Heard Island:

> I contacted a senior officer at army headquarters and suggested that maybe there was a role for us in this business. He put it to various people at HQ, but then the bureaucracy bought in, of course, and I was reprimanded for having the temerity to suggest that we could tell the navy how to do anything. Anyhow, through perseverance and contacts behind the scenes, it was agreed that the army would provide two DUKWs to go down to Macquarie Island.

This link with the Australian Army provided amphibious vehicles for ANARE operations from 1948 until 1994.

On the morning of 7 March 1948 Lieutenant Commander Dixon navigated LST *3501* into the relatively sheltered waters of Buckles Bay on the north-eastern end of the low hills of Macquarie. In contrast to the Heard Island voyage, it had been a quick, comparatively calm passage. As the ship dropped anchor the mist lifted and bright sunshine highlighted the green slopes of Wireless Hill and the plateau, where Mawson's wintering party had erected aerials in 1911.

It was immediately clear that it would not be possible to beach the LST. The shoreline was guarded by rocks above and below the water, meshed with great strands of kelp, and this barrier extended 150 metres out from the beach. Before leaving Australia it had been decided that the Macquarie Island station would be located somewhere on the low isthmus joining the northern end of the main island to Wireless Hill. One of the LCVPs was launched to take a reconnaissance party to shore.[9]

Staying outside the kelp, the crew of the LCVP took soundings as they moved parallel with the main beach, but there was no sign of a suitable channel until they came to Garden Bay, a small bay between Camp and Wireless Hills. Here the water was calmer and the party, including OIC Alan Martin, was able to make a landing. (Having been to Heard Island, John Lavett from LST *3501* was determined to secure his moment in history. As the LCVP hit the beach he jumped over the side to be first ashore.) They were greeted by elephant seals and penguins. The only sign of past human habitation was the derelict hut which had housed Mawson's 1911 party and those manning the meteorological station until 1915. Martin's party also looked at an old sealers' camp in the lee of the Razorback at the southern end of the isthmus, but bogs and elephant seal wallows made the transport of equipment down there impractical.[10]

A LONG-BOAT BATTLES BUCKLES BAY SURF DURING UNLOADING OPERATIONS TO AND FROM THE LST *3501* AT MACQUARIE ISLAND, MARCH 1948. (S CAMPBELL)

It was decided to establish the new camp on the site of Mawson's old AAE hut, straight up the beach from Garden Bay, where channels between the rocks offered the least obstructions to landing craft. Then came the tricky job of actually launching the DUKW from the tank deck of the LST. With good reason Stooke attempted this on his own:

> You've got to come out backwards with a DUKW because, if you drive straight out, the wheels are floating so you get no steerage. The back of the vehicle is still on the boat, so you have no steerage from your rudder—you would just be at the mercy of the seas.

With the bow doors of the LST open, and the ramp lowered, there was another problem. Even in a gentle swell, the bow door was moving up and down two to three metres:

> So I had to sit there and get the rhythm, because you don't get any second chances. Once you commit yourself to go, you've got to keep going. If you dropped the wheels off the ramp as it was rising, it would be a disaster—it would just lift the bows of the DUKW up, and you'd just spear straight to the bottom.

43

MACQUARIE ISLAND OIC
ALAN MARTIN SEEMS
REMARKABLY RELAXED IN THE
COMPANY OF A TRUCULENT
LEOPARD SEAL, 1948.
(N LAIRD)

With the DUKW safely launched, Stooke drove it alongside the LST. The DUKW had been loaded with tents, survival gear, and rations—essential if the wind swung around to the east, at which point the LST would have to up anchor and leave within minutes or run the risk of being blown on the rocks. The sudden departure of the LST was to become an unwelcome and regular feature of the first Macquarie Island unloading operation in Buckles Bay.

Mawson's old hut, apart from not having a roof, was in fair condition. When the remains of the collapsed roof were cleared away, a case of metal polish and boxes of canned tea, pickles and sauce were found, including a cheese too 'high' to sample. On a shelf stood a rusty tin of tapioca, with the contents in perfect condition. (This was later sent to Lady Mawson, wife of the AAE's leader.)[11]

Fairly soon a temporary tarpaulin provided a roof and tents were pitched ready for use at any time. Laurie Stooke recalled that the first meal in the hut, after seal and bird dung had been shovelled out, was a stew of M & V (army rations, meat and vegetables) plus half a bottle of rum tipped in by French chef Carl (Charlie) Du Toit to give extra flavour.

Serious unloading began the next day, 8 March, using DUKWs (which could carry loads up to five tonnes) and LCVPs towing pontoons. Stooke had located a better route to the shore for the DUKWs which could carry stores straight to the camp site, but the LCVPs could not reach the beach. A buoy was laid 200 metres from the shore, and a wire rope, kept taut, ran to an anchorage point on the beach. The LCVPs towed pontoons and other craft to the buoy where they were linked up to the wire running ashore. They were then hauled ashore by the D4 bulldozer when it was landed.[12]

Charlie Scoble, who had driven the bulldozer ashore, noted a certain cheerful chaos in his diary.

11 March. The first sheep and goats came ashore & wandered round enjoying the grass & getting in the way. Snowy [the dog] nearly went mad & wanted to round them up all the time. . .We drifted off to sleep as 'Rocky' John read Ulysses' Odyssey.

13 March. Sea roaring in Hasselborough Bay, mountains wreathed in mist, goats baaing, sea elephants fighting, & the flap of the tent in the wind.[13]

Although Stooke had located a better run in through the partially submerged rocks and kelp in Garden Bay for the DUKWs, it was not without its hazards:

I found a track through the rocks in which the DUKW could manoeuvre, protected on each side by virtually a wall of rock. Once you got into this crevice you had to curve around a bit, but you could get in. Unfortunately, right at the end of it, there was one [rock]. You wouldn't believe it, but we chopped two propeller shafts on that same rock. The DUKW would be lifted up by the surge and dumped right on it.

Some craft were lost. One LCVP, disabled by kelp around its prop, was waiting for a tow when a sudden squall drove on to the rocks both the LCVP and the pontoon it was towing and they were completely wrecked.

When on 21 March an LCVP began to sink, LST's bosun, Alf Hayter, had to scramble on to a rock just out of the water. Jack Cunningham edged a DUKW towards him and shouted for him to jump aboard. Hayter, a dyed-in-the-wool navy man, considered DUKWs an abomination—neither boats nor trucks. He told Cunningham in lurid language what he could do with his DUKW. 'I'd sooner die than get on that so-and-so thing!'

Cunningham brought the DUKW back out to the LST and unloaded the stores that had been on their way to the camp. Not only was the weather worsening, but it was getting dark. A searchlight was rigged on the LST to illuminate the figure of Hayter, stuck on the rock, and turning the chilly air blue with a magnificent stream of invective. Laurie Stooke said:

Jack went back, and in a display of beautiful seamanship, put his DUKW right in there amongst the rocks, so that Alf just had to step off. He'd changed his mind about being rescued by us after being there for about an hour. But Alf wouldn't have a bar of DUKWs. He loved his barges, although he was losing them more quickly than they could be replaced. The rock is now known, of course, as Hayter Rock.

On land, the road from the beach to the camp site became churned up into a river of grey mud into which men sank to their knees. Constant delays were caused by either the bulldozer or the DUKWs getting bogged in the soft peaty soil, and having to pull one another out. It was hard, gruelling work, carried out in constant rain and gusts of biting wind.

Peter King, a radio operator, recalled one night when a sudden wind change marooned a large party on shore:

> There were sixty of us altogether, including the naval crew, and the cook had to make a meal for us. He had a big copper that he boiled water in [fired] with bits of timber and stuff, and then he heated up cans of food on little tins filled with sand with metho poured in. And he fed sixty of us that one night, just at the drop of a hat. It was fantastic. We had about four tents and we had to sardine all these blokes in.

It was decided to dismantle the old AAE hut, as it was in a prime sheltered spot. The new fourteen-sided prefabricated huts were supposed to be put up in two hours, but in fact it took much longer. The second hut, 'Chippy's Church', was built by the ship's carpenters from scrap material. (Chippy's Church is still in use as a hydroponics hut growing fresh vegetables.)

On 20 March the LST returned to Buckles Bay and an eager watch was kept for *Wyatt Earp*, due to arrive that day after the unsuccessful push to reach the Antarctic mainland. She was sighted at noon, and Geoff Mottershead and Gersh Major climbed Camp Hill with an Aldis lamp to signal her.

W*yatt Earp* had been commissioned at Port Adelaide on 17 November 1947 in the presence of the Governor of South Australia, Sir Willoughby Norrie, Sir Douglas Mawson, and other dignitaries. Her master was Commander Karl Oom RAN, who had experienced Antarctic waters on Mawson's BANZARE voyages. The refurbished herring trawler slid stern first into the water, surged back across the Torrens and smashed her spoon-shaped stern into the side of a tramp steamer moored directly opposite. It was an unfortunate start.

The fact that a small wooden sail-assisted ship was being sent down to the Antarctic on a voyage of national exploration was an indication of the shortage of suitable vessels in the post-war period. *Wyatt Earp* had been used by the American millionaire explorer Lincoln Ellsworth as a support ship in his attempts to be the first to fly across the Antarctic continent from 1933 to 1939. After succeeding in this ambition, Ellsworth gave *Wyatt Earp* to his friend and co-adventurer Sir Hubert Wilkins, who sold her to the Australian Government for £4400 [$8800]—with the

support of Sir Douglas Mawson. Although a wooden vessel, she was stoutly timbered and able to cope, to a modest degree, with the pressures of pack ice. Round-bottomed, like all ships designed for polar ice navigation, *Wyatt Earp* was reputed to be able to roll violently 'on wet grass'.

Defying superstition, *Wyatt Earp* sailed on 13 December 1947 and battled through what seemed like one continuous storm all the way to Port Phillip. Able Seaman Norm Tame recalled that Phil Law, ANARE's new chief scientist, was very seasick:

> On one occasion he was flaked out in a coiled rope, and you could see the marks in his face like the pattern of the rope. We carted him inside with one on each arm and one of us on each leg, and he said he didn't remember anything about it. He was really out to it, and he was as green as a cabbage leaf.

In Melbourne, navy dock workers were busy for several days making repairs. A Vought-Sikorsky VS-310 Kingfisher float plane was mounted on the deck and the final members of the ship's company came on board. Captain Karl Oom was so concerned about Law's chronic seasickness that he recommended he not be allowed to go on the expedition—which would have cut off his Antarctic career there and then. But Stuart Campbell supported Law, and he was allowed to continue.[14]

Wyatt Earp got away on Friday 19 December 1947, but outside the Heads went smack into a Force 10 easterly storm and suffered a heavy bashing. Almost everyone on board was seasick. All this not even a day's sailing from Melbourne, and far away from the expected fury of the Southern Ocean and Antarctic waters.

SHARING TERRITORY WITH THE LOCALS. BABY ELEPHANT SEALS AROUND THE RADIO AND METEOROLOGICAL HUTS, MACQUARIE ISLAND ISTHMUS, 1948.
(N LAIRD)

WYATT EARP AFTER RECOMMISSIONING FOR ANTARCTIC SERVICE, 1947.
(AAD ARCHIVES)

HMAS *WYATT EARP*
MOORED AT ICE EDGE TO GET
SNOW FOR DRINKING WATER.
(P R WHITE)

Captain Oom sheltered in the lee of Flinders Island, but the next day the ship's gyrocompass failed and it was back to the ministrations of shipwrights and engineers when they put in to Hobart on 22 December. They still hoped to get away before Christmas, but as they left the wharf on Christmas Eve to swing the compasses before final departure, salt water was found emulsifying with the engine lubricating oil.

Wyatt Earp again left for Antarctica at 1310 hours on Friday 26 December. An hour later they stopped to replace a faulty engine valve and eight hours later ran into a Force 9 south-westerly gale and hove to in the lee of Eddystone Rock.

By 30 December the engines had to be stopped to repair a fuel pump. In addition, the engine revolutions had to be reduced because the gland where the tail shaft passes through the hull astern was running hot. A large rectangle of heavy canvas was nailed over the hull just above the waterline—a tricky operation at sea—to reduce the amount of water getting into the starboard cabins and the radio room.

On 1 January the engines were stopped again. The new diesel engines had sunk on their beds, causing the propeller shaft to bend. Chief Engineer Freddie Irwin had loosened the tail gland to relieve the distortion, but water leaked into the bilges and soon rose above the deck in the engine room.

That afternoon Captain Oom was ordered by the Naval Board to return to Melbourne. *Wyatt Earp* was by then well on the way to Antarctica and had reached the Antarctic Convergence. Despite the obvious good sense of the recall, the ship's company was disappointed and wanted to continue, but by 7 January *Wyatt Earp* was back in dry dock at Williamstown. It was two weeks before the ship returned to Nelson Pier, Williamstown.

It was now very late in the season, and the voyage plans were amended yet again. The Executive Planning Committee recommended that *Wyatt Earp* go to that part of the Australian Antarctic Territory closest to Australia, and examine the coastline of George V Land.

ANARE Leader Stuart Campbell (who had returned from Heard Island early on LST *3501* after his option of being picked up by *Wyatt Earp* seemed doubtful) decided to sail south with the expedition. Phil Law asked for an assurance that he and his geomagnetician colleague Ted McCarthy could land at Commonwealth Bay to make observations of the earth's magnetic field, but Campbell opposed the idea of putting scientists on shore in case *Wyatt Earp* could not get back to pick them up. Although Law's request was supported by Mawson and Davis, the matter was left unresolved.

A LANDING ATTEMPT AT THE BALLENY ISLANDS. FROM LEFT, SEAMAN W WALLACE, SEAMAN NORM TAME, PHIL LAW AND AN UNIDENTIFIED CREWMAN.
(COURTESY P LAW)

The expedition finally got away from Williamstown on Saturday 7 February 1948. On Wednesday 18 February, the first icebergs were sighted, always a significant moment on an Antarctic voyage. Even Stuart Campbell, who was somewhat blase about icebergs following his BANZARE experiences with Mawson, noted in his diary:

> About 0900 I found everyone on deck getting their first thrill out of the sight of an Antarctic iceberg. And though I've seen lots before I must confess that I, too, get a thrill out of that first sign of the Antarctic. They were all around us, at least six of them. Huge flat slabs of gleaming white ice with vertical sides rising 150 feet sheer out of the sea.[15]

As *Wyatt Earp* cruised along the fringe of the pack ice zone it became clear to Law that the captain had no intention of pushing into the pack ice itself. Law:

> The captain tried charging one of the smaller floes to test the ship. I had thought we might crack it and go through, but the ship had neither the weight nor the power and merely bounced off. As an ice-breaker this ship was a gnat.[16]

On Sunday 22 February *Wyatt Earp* steamed in the vicinity of the Mertz Glacier hoping to find clear water, but without success. By 24

THE VOUGHT-SIKORSKY
VS-310 KINGFISHER FLOAT
PLANE WAS FAR TOO BIG AND
CUMBERSOME FOR THE TINY
WYATT EARP, AND ONLY FLEW
TWICE (ON ONE DAY) IN
ANTARCTIC WATERS.
(J WATTS)

February they were near the Ninnis Glacier Tongue, but conditions were ideal for a 'freeze up' and Captain Oom was determined to stay clear. There was to be no landing at Mawson's old base at Commonwealth Bay, and by 27 February *Wyatt Earp* had turned away from the coast towards the Balleny Islands, where a brief and extremely hazardous landing was attempted on a rocky shore on 29 February. Campbell, Law and Seaman Wallace were ashore for only a few minutes before jumping back on board the ship's whaler, which was being buffeted by a rolling surf and was already half swamped. The expedition managed, however, to carry out an accurate running survey of the coasts of the Balleny Islands (except for Sturge Island which was surrounded by heavy pack ice).

For the next two weeks *Wyatt Earp* headed west towards Commonwealth Bay again, but hopes of a landing continued to fade. On 13 March they managed to fly the Kingfisher float plane for the first and only time on the voyage. The procedures to put it together, winch it over the side and fly it were simply too cumbersome to be practical. RAAF pilot Flying Officer Robin Gray managed two short test flights.

Despite the many difficulties of keeping the complex cosmic ray equipment in operation, Law and McCarthy felt they had achieved good results, but Law was angry about the lack of interest shown in scientific work.

By Tuesday 16 March any thought of making a landing on the continent was abandoned and *Wyatt Earp* headed for Macquarie Island. Southern Ocean gales enabled the little wooden ship to attempt new records for severe rolling and when engine trouble stopped her for four hours, the crew trailed a sea anchor and hoisted the fore trysail to try to stabilise their wildly lurching ship. Then a new surprise—a following wind and great swells astern caused *Wyatt Earp* to achieve an all-time record speed of just on ten knots.

Early on the morning of Saturday 20 March the watch sighted the Bishop and Clerk Islands, south of Macquarie, and by 1230 *Wyatt Earp* had anchored in Buckles Bay, dwarfed by the great bulk of LST *3501*. Displaying an appropriate sense of occasion, the LST signalled: 'THE WYATT EARP I PRESUME'.

CAPTAIN LAURIE STOOKE EASES HIS DUKW THROUGH THE ROCKS AND KELP OF GARDEN BAY, MARCH 1948. (S CAMPBELL)

Wyatt Earp might have been dwarfed by the size of LST *3501*, but the final triumph was hers. Because Commander Oom outranked Lieutenant Commander Dixon, the LST had to dip its ensign and defer to the smaller vessel. Laurie Stooke described what happened:

> When they came into sight, the LST crew had to dress ship—stand to on the deck. Commander Oom sailed by and they saluted him. He then anchored some distance away, and because George Dixon was the junior officer, he had to pay the official visit to *Wyatt Earp*. Here's this thing which looked like a raft compared with the LST—but tradition, that's what it's all about.

Stuart Campbell was 'most satisfied' with the general progress made on the island in his absence, and at dusk the next afternoon, the last load went ashore from the LST. Charlie Scoble noted in his diary: 'Party with Campbell's lot (on the LST), singing bawdy songs and drinking hard'. A southerly swell kept the LST from its last planned job, carrying reserve supplies and fuel to an emergency base at Lusitania Bay. On the morning of 25 March the wintering party of thirteen went aboard the LST for a last hot bath and a beer in the wardroom and she sailed at 3 pm, signalling as she went: GOOD LUCK TO YOU, SEE YOU AT THE Y & J [Young and Jacksons Hotel].

ANARE's first two sub-Antarctic stations had been established on Heard and Macquarie Islands without loss of life or serious injury, but the hoped-for establishment of a permanent Australian station on the mainland of Antarctica remained a practical impossibility until a suitable ship could be found.

FOUR

THE FIRST OPERATIONAL YEAR

As the 27 expeditioners on Heard and Macquarie Islands assembled their prefabricated huts and prepared for the winter of ANARE's first operational year, they had little time for scientific work. Radio masts had to be erected before any meteorological results could be Morse coded back to Australia, and buildings constructed in which to inflate the balloons to carry aloft radiosonde equipment which would measure temperature and pressure in the upper atmosphere. The cosmic ray scientists had to have a hut (to assemble their elaborate measuring equipment) and a reliable power supply. In reality the men on both stations were concentrating on building shelter, and not spending much time thinking why they were there. According to Phil Law, it was occupation first and science second:

> There's no doubt that everyone interested in Antarctica in those days was in it because of the territorial acquisitions, the value of possible minerals, the whaling industry, the fishing rights—all the commercial interests of colonialism. And that was accentuated, of course, by the fact that seven nations had claims in the Antarctic [hence] all this fuss about whether other people would recognise them or not. The scientific work was literally put in as a bit of softening of that hard approach. It was to convince people you were there for good purposes as well as grabbing territory.

Each island team had a scratch selection of huts to erect, the best and toughest of which were fourteen-sided American buildings. By contrast, the Australian huts, designed for the RAAF in New Guinea, were difficult to put up. The masonite and hardwood sections were not insulated and the wall panels were fitted with opening flaps at the top and bottom so that 'hot tropic nights would be cooled by the soothing breezes'.[1]

The scientists pitched in as labourers and builders. Cosmic rays from deep space bombarded Heard Island unrecorded while Fred Jacka and his fellow physicist Jo Jelbart heated water to stop concrete mixes (for the diesel generator pads) from freezing. Jacka was also an enthusiastic competitor in ANARE's first recorded beard-growing competition:

> We were using a dreadful thing called a blubber stove, which we fed with seal blubber and any bits of wood and other combustibles we could find. I opened a little door in the front to see how things were going and there was a mighty blast of flame that practically enveloped my whole head, and dealt with my beard very effectively.

After the living quarters were finished, Jelbart and Jacka built their own laboratory. Huts were separated so that a fire would not wipe out the entire station. All structures were guyed with wire cables against Heard Island's tremendous winds. The radio aerials represented the biggest challenge. Four 20-metre-high sections were to be erected in rhombic pattern for the transmitting aerials. They were designed to withstand a wind of 200 kilometres per hour. Rock under the camp site was so hard it blunted crowbars and picks; blasting with gelignite was also ineffective. Lem Macey had a brainwave and suggested 44-gallon [200.2 litre] drums filled with stones and gravel as anchorages above the ground. Arthur Scholes said they tried to bash in the tops of the oil drums with picks, but after two weeks of cacophonous labour only a few drums were without tops. Bob Dovers tried blowing the tops off with cortex explosive with great success and the mast was hauled into position using the tractor. The rigidity of the Kelly and Lewis mast and its supports was soon tested by a 100 kilometres per hour wind. As the wind built to gale force, the mast and its wire stays reverberated with great booming sounds, like sustained notes on a giant organ. After a time the Heard Island men could accurately judge wind strength by the pitch of the notes from the aerial.[2]

Similar building was going on at the settlement at Macquarie Island. Thirty sheep and some goats were let loose. Peter King, radio operator, said the smooth-haired Saanen goats from Queensland were unimpressed by Macquarie's cold, windy, rain-drenched climate and clustered around a fire used to heat hot water kettles, burning their hides in the process. The Border Leicester sheep, more at home in their new surroundings, moved off to graze on the tussocky grass. Charlie Scoble noted the birth of the first lamb in his diary on 24 May.[3]

To combat the wet cold, the expeditioners were issued with clothing originally designed for British submariners—oiled cloth with a thick blue

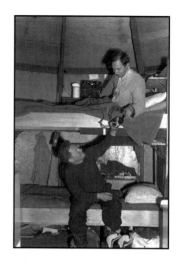

THE HEARD ISLAND
'HILTON' PHOTOGRAPHED
FROM THE TOP OF THE RADIO
MAST, SUMMER 1948.
(A CAMPBELL-DRURY)

ALAN CAMPBELL-DRURY (TOP
BUNK) AND AUB GOTLEY
SHARE HEADPHONES TO ENJOY
THE SHORTWAVE RADIO
PROGRAM 'HOT JUICE' FROM
MOZAMBIQUE. NOTE THE
PENGUIN EGG ON TOP OF THE
COCOA TIN.
(A CAMPBELL-DRURY)

linen lining. Camouflaged British Army windproof parkas and trousers and wool-lined, knee length flying boots as well as tan leather army boots completed their ensemble. The Macquarie party also had to adapt the RAAF tropical huts to the conditions by securing the ventilation flaps and insulating them against the cold.

Later ANARE policy ensured that every expeditioner had some private space, even if it was just a curtained-off cubicle within a communal hut, with a bunk, desk and a few shelves. But in the first year there were only two sleeping huts for the thirteen Macquarie men.

As the expeditioners settled into their living and working routines in both sub-Antarctic camps, ANARE rituals that were to endure were already being created. Saturday night was 'ding' (party) night, the time to relax and have a few drinks to mark the end of the working week and let off steam. 'Ding' was RAAF slang for a party and it has persisted in the ANARE vocabulary. At Macquarie Charlie Scoble noted in his diary on 7 May:

> The ding party getting more & more furious. They were starting a game of table tennis when Ken [Hines] switched [the power] off. . .they were furious. . .There was a free for all for a while, followed by a pillow fight, a letting down of beds & so on. Peace about 1.30.[4]

Both Macquarie and Heard settlements had a piano, radiogram and records and a selection of feature films and a projector. Cigarettes, sweets, toffees and chewing gum were available for issue to each man and a limited amount of spirits and liqueurs.

The Heard Island party had a piano, but after 'Lem' Macey spent about four hours unpacking it and getting it into the rec room, Johnny Abbottsmith remembers him asking an important question: '"Who can play?" Dead silence. "Can't anyone do anything?" Dead silence.' As it happened, Campbell-Drury was a classical organist, but he showed little interest in the piano, and 'didn't play it much'.

NORM JONES COOKING MORNING PORRIDGE ON THE EIGHT-BURNER KEROSENE PRESSURE STOVE, HEARD ISLAND, 1948.
(A CAMPBELL-DRURY)

Scholes reported that drinks were available before the evening meal and on party nights, but half the party were non-drinkers and the grog ration began to accumulate. Eventually it was just put out in case anyone wanted it. Occasionally an individual would spend an evening getting quietly and slowly drunk—remaining in the recreation room with everyone else, but drinking alone. Johnny Abbottsmith said that everyone did this at least once, even those who weren't interested in alcohol. 'It was a way of letting off a bit of tension.' But like the Macquarie crew, they often 'let off steam' on Saturday nights with a few grogs.

Food supplies in the pre-refrigeration era were ample, but basic. The sheep and goats taken to Macquarie were expertly dismembered and served by French chef Carl 'Charlie' Du Toit, who spared the party the obligatory bully beef and tinned food whenever he could by using local resources. Rabbits and the flightless wekas, thoughtfully provided by the sealers in the previous century, were often on the menu and Du Toit even ran to the occasional Chinese meal. The men also ate penguin breasts, skuas and elephant seal liver.

Fresh meat taken to Heard and kept in snowdrifts near the camp was buried in a small crevasse in the nearby Baudissen Glacier by Doc Gilchrist. But the sub-Antarctic environment was not cold enough. Fred Jacka reported that 'only a month after the ship had left we noticed a brown stain developing on the glacier. That was the end of the fresh meat.'

55

Compared with the Gallic sophistication of Carl Du Toit on Macquarie, Norm Jones was a fairly basic Aussie cook who dished up tinned rations on Heard Island to a group of mostly ex-servicemen who had been eating similar tucker for the past six years. Tinned stew was tinned stew, whether it was curried or buried under a pie crust.

The most frequently eaten local food on Heard was penguin and elephant seal. 'Penguin was more popular', wrote Gilchrist, 'as elephant seal was rather coarse, but both were delightful. The chops taken from an eight week old sea elephant pup were as delicious as anything I have ever tasted.'[5] The station log recorded meals of braised penguin, penguin steaks 'better than rump steak', elephant seal brain fried in breadcrumbs, 'very tasty', and elephant seal liver and kidney.[6]

In summer Jo Jelbart caught fish which were enjoyed, but fishing was difficult in winter and by spring everyone was too busy to fish. Birds were also eaten. Roast skua was 'not unlike duck', and petrels were edible 'apart from the fishy flavour', but it took a good number of birds to feed fourteen men, so they were an occasional treat.[7] Norm Jones was not keen on cooking the local wildlife and those who could not bear to eat it kept to tinned food. Those expeditioners who wanted to experiment did so on Sundays, the cook's day off. Abottsmith said that penguin breasts were not too bad. 'They were quite big, like a half-pound steak—black meat—but it was good eating.'

The locally plentiful Kerguelen cabbage, which Gilchrist was keen for the men to eat as a vegetable supplement, was a useful source of vitamin C. It had a very strong flavour and was not popular, but the men were cooperative about eating a spoonful occasionally. Gilchrist ate penguin eggs raw and said they were delicious, but other people preferred them made into omelettes. The eggs had a peculiar feature—the whites would not set when cooked, even when Norm Jones fried one for twenty minutes.[8]

Although elephant seals were easy enough to shoot through the brain, penguins presented a more elusive target. Fred Jacka decided to cook penguin breasts on one of his Sunday cooking days, and asked OIC Aub Gotley for a revolver:

I went to a nearby gentoo penguin rookery and sat there for a little while till the penguins sort of settled down, carefully aimed and fired, but no penguin fell over. I really found it an extremely difficult thing to hit a penguin in the head. There was no point in shooting them through the body—they'd just squawk and walk away.

It was a pretty awful, brutal business, but I finished up by grabbing them and sawing their heads off with a carving knife. If you have a decent, large, sharp knife you can saw through the neck and kill them fairly quickly.

In general the weekly fare was predictable. Alan Campbell-Drury:

> Norm used to get so heartily tired of standing there at the servery in the little kitchen, having thirteen men come up to him, one after the other, every night of the week, saying, 'What's on for tea tonight, Norm?' Norm used to reply, 'Well, tonight we've got shit with sugar on—what do you think?'
>
> One Sunday night Bob Dovers was the cook. And he must have anticipated Norm, who said to Bob, 'What's on for tea tonight, Bob?' And Bob said, 'Shit with sugar on, Norm,' and he handed him a plateful of seal shit with sugar on! And Norm was taken aback a little bit, I don't mind telling you. That phrase was never used again.

At both Heard and Macquarie Islands the meteorologist was appointed officer-in-charge. There were no formal selection procedures for such a position at that stage. Stuart Campbell had intended to appoint Bob Dovers as OIC at Heard, but George Smith had noticed, during preparations in the store and packing for the voyages, that 'the blokes were not going to be happy under Dovers'. Phil Law would later appoint Dovers OIC of the first wintering party on the Antarctic continent at Mawson, but that was six years away. Law: 'So Campbell delayed making a definite appointment, went down on the ship and apparently sensed enough of it so that during the erection of the Heard Island station—while Campbell was there—he nominated Aub Gotley as OIC.'

The 'met' men and radio operators tended to outnumber any other group in those early days because there had to be enough of them to make observations round the clock. On both Heard and Macquarie there were two weather observers and a meteorologist, a radio supervisor and two operators.

The parties on both islands seem to have survived any major personal upsets despite bunking and living close together. On Heard, communal harmony was ruffled in November after Doc Gilchrist decided to investigate a sealer's grave in nearby South West Bay to see if he could establish the cause of death. He lashed a kerosene tin to his back at the camp, causing Norm Jones (a big but rather nervous man) to express anxiety and opposition to the prospect of any human remains returning to base. Gilchrist said he thought he might find out a little bit about diseases on Heard Island:

> So I sneaked out one fine Sunday morning about 6 am with a shovel and excavated the skeleton. And I'd got the skull and most of the thorax exposed when I was interrupted by three men who had decided after

ALAN GILCHRIST
INVESTIGATING A SEALER'S
GRAVE, SOUTH WEST
BAY, HEARD ISLAND,
NOVEMBER 1948.
(A CAMPBELL-DRURY)

breakfast to take a stroll over to South West Bay. They were absolutely furious with me for having disturbed this sealer.

Gilchrist thought he had discovered why the sealer had died—as a result of a depressed fracture of the temple bone on one side of his skull. Eyewitness accounts of what happened next differ. Campbell-Drury says that OIC Aub Gotley objected when Gilchrist began putting some of the bones and the skull into his kerosene tin for later examination. Gilchrist says that no bones, other than the skull—and that only temporarily—were lifted from the grave. Campbell-Drury:

> This was when things flared up, because Gotley got the kerosene tin and emptied all the bones back into the grave. The doctor came up out of the grave and punched Aub Gotley on the nose—and Gotley decided to suspend the doctor [from duty] at once.

Gilchrist says he has no memory of being suspended, and agrees that 'an alteration did occur and an intense dispute did arise as a result of me having done the forensic investigation, but I'm not prepared to give any details'.

Suspension or no, Gilchrist obligingly stitched up a gash in Alan Campbell-Drury's leg shortly afterwards. There is no mention of suspension in the station log where Gotley wrote on 24 November, 'Organised expedition to South West Bay where we noticed a grave. Found male skeleton, buried at least 10 years. All was replaced and covered.'[9] But personal relations had been badly strained. Fred Jacka, one of the youngest of the party, became the peacemaker:

> I somehow managed to persuade both of them to come over to the cosmic ray lab to have a quiet talk. They drank a cup of coffee I brewed on the spot and talked civilly to each other and to me. Then, when things had simmered down a little, I introduced a little alcohol into the proceedings. Somewhere near midnight they were patting each other on the back. We were all pretty weary by then. I had a bit of difficulty getting these two guys safely down the snow bank and into the door of the living hut.

On both island stations there was an eagerness to explore and there was much basic work to be done. Bob Dovers was a surveyor, and 'Swampy' Compton was his assistant. On the basis of one astrofix, Dovers discovered that by his calculations Heard Island was 60 miles [100 kilometres] away from the position shown in the one atlas at the camp. Dovers, Compton and the geologist Jim Lambeth began climbing the nearby peaks and started a comprehensive survey and geological examination of the island. At the end of the year they produced the first accurate map of Heard. Lambeth concluded that Heard Island was not continental, but oceanic (an active volcano like Hawaii built up from the ocean floor) and had never been part of Australia.[10]

GLACIER TRAVEL, HEARD ISLAND STYLE.
(A CAMPBELL-DRURY)

The field work was dangerous. The tent was too small, and the three men were plagued by wet sleeping bags and inadequate field equipment. On one field party to the western face of Mt Olsen in April it got so cold that Dovers' theodolite froze. They built an igloo to supplement their meagre tent, but a sudden thaw collapsed it.

Some of the most risky travel was by sea in a three-metre dinghy (named ANARE) that had been left with the Heard party. It was powered by a capricious outboard motor and a small auxiliary sail. Jim Lambeth suggested to Abbottsmith that they forget about the emergency survival equipment complete with tents and rations that weighed them down in the bow. Abbottsmith:

> 'If we get swamped we'll be alive for two minutes and dead in five', he said, 'so what's the use of all that?' I said, 'Well if that's the case, chuck it out.' So we got rid of all our emergency crates and it used to be a little lighter in the boat.

One of the jobs with the dinghy was to take soundings in Atlas Cove and its approaches to make entry safer. On one such outing Abbottsmith watched wide-eyed while a huge white whale swam slowly under their cockleshell craft. On another occasion, Lambeth said, 'Look behind you quickly, Johnny':

> There was a sea leopard—oh, six feet out of the water—with his mouth open, coming towards us. He could've swallowed that outboard motor and spat out the bits. He just kept on coming at us. I always used to carry a revolver in my belt, loaded and ready. I fired a couple of quick shots into him, into his mouth, and I must have hit him in the back of the spine—a fluky shot—and he just keeled over back in the water. When we got to shore this leopard was just a mass of foam where the others came in to get a piece of him. I reckon that was one of the closest shaves we had.

There was no biologist on the 1948 Heard Island party, and Doc Gilchrist agreed to do what he could:

> When we arrived in December it was obvious that this island was the breeding ground for millions of penguins and sea elephants and several species of petrels [but] no provision had been made to study them. I had no idea of what was scientifically important, so we kept a biology log. We just wrote down the day the first gentoo penguins arrived to make their nests, the day the first eggs appeared, when the sea elephants arrived to start breeding, when the first pups appeared and the location of the albatross rookeries. We had a lot of fun exploring the cliffs to define the location of the very, very beautiful black and brown and light-mantled sooty albatrosses. The biology log was of real assistance to the [later] biologists when they arrived.

Gilchrist, a doctor in charge of a group of healthy, fit men, was delighted to turn his medical and research skills to biology. He was particularly proud of his identification of *Mawsonotrema eudyptala*—the liver fluke in the gentoo penguin—and noting the presence of snow petrels, previously unreported on Heard Island.

Some individuals found the isolated wintering experience more difficult to cope with than their fellow expeditioners. Norm Jones was intimidated by Heard Island, and never went more than 500 metres from the huts the whole year he was there. He did his job, but was often under stress. However his vulnerability did not prevent the kind of cruel practical jokes that were to be the hallmark of ANARE service for the next 50 years. Alan Campbell-Drury said that at Christmas the station had a telegram from Melbourne asking if the party would mind staying till March 1949 because of problems with shipping. There was no choice whatever of course, and everyone was relaxed about it—except Norm Jones. Campbell-Drury:

Lem Macey made something in the radio shack—a stick of wood about four feet long [1.21 metres], with a cross piece, to which he was attaching little lights, one red, one green and one white. He said, 'Norm Jones is in bed. I want you to go right over there in the dark, amongst the sea elephant mounds, over in the direction of the entrance of Atlas Cove. I'll light this thing up and you go and tell Norm Jones there's a ship in the bay, coming into Atlas Cove.'

This is exactly what I did. Norm Jones couldn't get out of bed quickly enough. We stood outside the sleeping hut and, sure enough, it just looked for all the world like a ship coming into Atlas Cove. Then all of a sudden Macey walked out of the darkness—and Jones nearly killed him. He never ever forgave Macey or myself for that effort. But it was fun.

On Macquarie Island the year was reasonably tranquil in personal terms, although chef Carl Du Toit was at times temperamental. Scoble was late for lunch one day and there was no hot food left:

> Carl reckoned I should have come and got it. Told him that last time I did I was told to sit down and be waited on. He got wild and brandished a sharpening iron and told me if I went on like that, he'd cut my throat.[11]

Scoble ignored Du Toit and dined on bread and currant jam.

Doc Gilchrist had only a few occasions on which to practise his medical skills on Heard Island. He filled some teeth when hard sweets broke fillings, and removed a papilloma from Gotley's foot using a special instrument made by Jacka. Towards the end of the year Gilchrist had his surgery in good shape and when one man asked to be circumcised, the doctor was persuaded to perform the operation with the versatile cosray scientist Fred Jacka as anaesthetist. A significant first for ANARE field medicine, although by no means the last. (In later years ANARE medical officers performed many circumcisions while in Antarctica. Expeditioners who had been considering the operation took advantage of their period of enforced sexual abstinence to have the procedure performed.)

As soon as radio masts were erected on both Macquarie and Heard, regular weather data was passed on to Sydney. Some reports went to Marion Island and on to South Africa. Reports from Australia's sub-Antarctic stations filled a valuable gap in assessing weather fronts moving up from Antarctica. Four balloons were released a day, the first at 4 am. They were filled with hydrogen, generated in long cylinders from a mixture of ferro-silicon, caustic soda and water, and gave information about wind speed and direction. Some of the balloons carried a radiosonde to transmit information on temperature, pressure, humidity and wind speeds in the upper atmosphere.

A SPECTACULAR LENTICULAR
(LENS-SHAPED) CLOUD FORMS
IN THE LEE OF BIG BEN,
HEARD ISLAND, 1948.
(A CAMPBELL-DRURY)

Sometimes the work of the Heard weather men was not taken seriously by their colleagues. Swampy Compton decided to boost one day's rainfall by peeing in the rain gauge. The artificially boosted results were radioed to Sydney and had to be corrected later by the unimpressed weather observers.

Cosmic rays were to be measured not only on Heard and Macquarie Islands but by Phil Law on *Wyatt Earp* on its 1948 voyage to the Antarctic coastline. The equipment was bulky and complicated to operate. It also involved the use of a photographic darkroom to develop the film on which the cosmic ray intensity had been captured. Fred Jacka:

> We were basically recording the variations of the cosmic ray intensity with a number of different systems of Geiger counter telescopes and a device called an ionisation chamber, for measuring different components of the cosmic ray intensity. The cosmic rays come dominantly from outer space, from the galaxy and beyond. A small component comes from the sun. At that time very, very little was known about these cosmic rays except that, as the name implies, they were thought to come from somewhere beyond the solar system.

On Macquarie Island Leigh Speedy and Ken Hines were complementing the work of Fred Jacka and Jo Jelbart, but had problems with the cosray measuring equipment. They were also plagued by an erratic power supply, but achieved some worthwhile results. Jacka, on Heard, became so scientifically interested in Antarctic auroras, which fascinated all the expeditioners, that he changed direction and devoted the remainder of his scientific career to upper atmosphere physics:

> The study of the aurora gives us information about the structure and the dynamics of the upper atmosphere, the atmosphere above the levels that usually interest meteorologists. And it enables one to get a better understanding of the interaction between the outer fringes of the earth's magnetic field and the so-called solar wind, the outflowing plasma from the sun. These studies have relevance to the whole field of so-called space research, and possible relevance also in the field of meteorology. They have also very considerable importance in radio communications, both by high-frequency—involving reflection from the ionosphere—and by UHF and direct satellite communication.

Expeditioners on both Heard and Macquarie Islands had trouble with power supply in 1948. Although there were three second-hand army Lister 15-kVA diesel generators provided for each island, mechanical problems meant that electric power sometimes had to be rationed. On Heard, Johnny Abbottsmith earned the ire of his OIC and the scientists by restricting generating time, but had it not been for Abbottsmith's ingenuity all those diesel generators might have ground to a halt. The storage of diesel fuel in 44-gallon [200 litre] drums in the open caused condensation and rust inside. Rust particles came through the filters into the injectors, causing mayhem with the starting and general running of the Listers. After talking with the scientists (who provided a small jeweller's lathe), Abbottsmith decided to try the sensitive and difficult job of regrinding the plungers in the barrels of the injectors.

> But we were stuck for a grinding paste. One of the boys said, 'John, what about trying toothpaste?' I watered it down a bit and that overcame the injector trouble. But I had to keep half a dozen injectors ready, because as soon as one started to dribble out I had to replace it and clean the old one up. That's how we kept the diesels going. I believe the Macquarie boys blew their diesels up completely.

There was a tragic reason for the Macquarie Island power crisis. On 4 July diesel engineer Charles Scoble (a keen outdoors man) went for a skiing excursion up on the plateau with one of the cosmic ray physicists, Ken Hines. Scoble, a big heavy man, skied over a frozen lake and broke through the ice. When Hines went to help he fell through too, and got back to shore by using his stock to crash a path through the ice and rest on it. But Scoble disappeared. Hines later wrote:

> We were close enough to talk to one another and Charlie was of the opinion that we had no chance of getting out and could not retain our

BURIAL

The day we found him was a memory
Of all the cold stones of the earth,
A reminder of discovery
And of adventure, and of the history
Of men in the endless searching.
We crunched up the side of the mountain
With a fog that always touched our sides.
Where he lay, spigots of moss were
Encased in ice, and around as though
For the occasion golden Azorella
Formed bright wreaths.
Mottershead bowed his fierce face
The monkish cowl of his wind cheater
Giving him an aspect out of character.
He put his strong arms to the spade
And turned reluctant sods
Where none had turned before, while
Bennett and Kenny laced his shroud.
When all was done we returned him
From whence he came;
In a quiet and level voice Speedy
Read the Service for the Dead,
Then offered up a simple prayer
As clean as the cool grass about,
And some of us unaccustomed to raw tombs
And the words of God,
Hung our heads in that wild place
And felt the shuddering sea below.

(Previously unpublished poem by Norman
Laird, fellow expeditioner and photographer
on Macquarie Island, 1948.)[13]

hold on the ice much longer. We knew that the nearest human beings were several miles away and separated from us by a thousand foot [304.8 metre] climb, and it was no use shouting for help.

. . .I frequently relaxed my grip on the ice and rested by treading water very slowly, whereas Charlie, perhaps unable to swim, seemed never to relax his hold, but had to waste energy in his efforts to cling to the ice when too tired to make further progress. He became exhausted before covering half the distance to the bank and shortly afterwards disappeared below the surface of the ice. I finally reached the bank and after lying on the ice at the edge until I could walk, somehow stumbled across the plateau, down the cliff and back to the camp.[12]

Scoble's body was recovered the next spring and buried beside the lake. He was the first expeditioner to die in the service of ANARE and his death shocked the small party. Many of them were ex-servicemen and that, Peter King believes, helped them to adjust: 'We just coped with it. It's the same in the army. You lose mates fighting wars, and carry on. You have to.'

Scoble had a wife, Marjorie, and two small daughters. Excerpts from his diary reflect a hard worker who was enjoying life on Macquarie. On 2 June he recorded his daughter Heather's second birthday—'we have a birthday cake'. On 30 June 'telegram from Marjorie & Mother gave away about my birthday unfortunately'.[14] Four days later he died.

After his death the Federal Government gave £1100 [$2200] compensation to his wife and daughters, provided they took no further action against the Commonwealth.[15]

After Scoble's death the situation with Macquarie's Lister diesels worsened. Two of the three generators broke down and the emergency Lister was unreliable. Gersh Major, one of the radio operators, took over as engineer and did what he could.

In Melbourne, Stuart Campbell approached the RAAF to fly down a replacement diesel mechanic, Frank Keating. Macquarie Island could be reached by air—just. The only aircraft capable of making the flight was a Catalina which would have to carry fuel for the return journey of 3750 kilometres. The amphibious Catalina could use a conventional airstrip from Cambridge Airport, near Hobart, but would have to land on and take off from the choppy waters of Buckles Bay at Macquarie. Because of the prevailing swell off the island there were doubts that the heavily laden amphibian would be able to take off at all.

As luck would have it the RAAF was testing JATO (Jet Assisted Take Off) units at Point Cook. It was decided to fit four units on Catalina A24-104, each giving 1000 pounds of thrust for twelve seconds. The flight crew, commanded by Squadron Leader Robin Gray, and captained by Flight Lieutenant A E Delahunty, went to Point Cook for JATO experience. (Robin Gray had flown for ANARE earlier that year. On 13 March he flew the Sikorsky Kingfisher amphibian carried on *Wyatt Earp* on two brief test flights off the coast of George V Land.)

Flight Engineer Jack Vercoe reported that the rockets gave the stately Catalina a performance comparable to a Sabre jet for a memorable twelve seconds. 'Unfortunately this only endured to about 500 feet when the old girl returned to her true performance of about 90 knots. End of exhilaration!'[16]

The flight to Macquarie Island had to be made in the middle of winter, in the most unfavourable conditions imaginable. Campbell (a former wartime Catalina pilot) decided to go along for the ride, and the aircraft flew to Cambridge Airport, Hobart, on 22 July to wait for suitable weather conditions.

65

The first attempt was made on 25 July, but the aircraft was forced to return because of thick, low cloud and poor visibility. After another false start, Campbell returned to Melbourne and was not on board the successful flight which left Tasmania on 4 August at 5.13 am. It was a long, hard haul south, fighting the prevailing westerlies which made navigation 'even more difficult if that were possible'. Flight Engineer Jack Vercoe said that the fuel range did not allow much time to find 'this miserable speck in the Antarctic Ocean'. When they sighted Macquarie Island, Flight Lieutenant Delahunty ordered all crew not actually involved in the landing to adopt crash positions. The sea conditions were so bad that the commander of the flight, Squadron Leader Gray, made it clear that the pilot did not have to land and gave him the option of returning to Australia. Jack Vercoe:

> The captain elected to land. This he did in a most professional manner (at 12.50 pm). We taxied very close to a sandy beach where, with the aid of two anchors and running engines, we managed to hold the aircraft into the wind whilst we unloaded Gray and the engineer into the waiting boat. Survival time in the sea at that particular time of the year was estimated at two minutes.[17]

The Catalina's two anchors failed to hold against the prevailing wind and the courageous decision was made to allow the aircraft to drift three kilometres out to sea. Vercoe said they then taxied back to shore on one engine: 'This procedure was followed, using alternate engines, until Gray came aboard bringing with him first day covers of the first airmail to Macquarie Island.'[18]

Vercoe said that Gray's insistence on going ashore to get the first day covers franked cost them three hours, and it was almost dark when he boarded the aircraft for the return journey. The westerly winds had increased in that time, preventing any chance of a return direct to Hobart. The four JATO rockets catapulted the Catalina into the air with startling efficiency and the aircraft made for the Royal New Zealand Air Force base at Wigram, near Christchurch, New Zealand. Doubtless the Catalina's crew were comforted by the thought that the only back-up aircraft available was a Lincoln bomber, standing by on search and rescue readiness at the RAAF base at East Sale. Unable to land on the water, it could only have dropped life rafts and survival gear had the Catalina come down in the Tasman Sea.

Frank Keating 'regenerated' the Lister diesels, which powered the Macquarie Island station successfully until the 1949 relief party arrived in late March 1949. He was further challenged by a drastic shortage of lubricating oil, which he overcame by using any grease he could find on the station, including tinned butter and elephant seal blubber.[19]

FIVE

EARLY DAYS

B ack in Melbourne the politics of the bureaucracy of ANARE were becoming as turbulent as the waters of Macquarie Island's windswept Buckles Bay.

In April 1948 DEA Secretary John Burton had expressed reservations about the ability of his department to undertake detailed supply work of ANARE and thought that other government departments should contribute, with the Public Service Board being responsible for staff appointments in Melbourne. The Council for Scientific and Industrial Research was also reluctant to take overall responsibility for Antarctic activities, although it was prepared to do much of the 'collation, coordination and distribution of scientific data'.[1]

On 4 May 1948 an Antarctic Section was set up in the Department of External Affairs, and by 18 May the Antarctic Division was more formally incorporated into the DEA with Stuart Campbell as officer-in-charge. A new ANARE Planning Committee was formed consisting of representatives of the various departments and organisations that were involved with the expeditions' activities.

One of the committee's first priorities was to recommend that Campbell go overseas to try to find a suitable ice-strengthened ship to replace the wooden *Wyatt Earp*. He had no success locating a ship and, faced with the prospect of simply running the Heard and Macquarie Island operation, with no immediate prospects of getting to mainland Antarctica, the restless Campbell began to consider other options.

Chief scientific officer Phil Law had been overseas on a visit to Japan in connection with his cosmic ray work and when he arrived back in Sydney from Japan on 20 August 1948 his attention was drawn to an advertisement for the job of Assistant Officer-in-Charge (Scientific) for the Antarctic Division that had appeared in the Commonwealth Gazette while he was away. With two sub-Antarctic island stations established and the Government committed to a five-year program to maintain them, it was necessary to formalise ANARE's structure. Law was uneasy about working with Campbell:

> He would always try and obstruct or oppose and contradict and you had to justify yourself tremendously strongly in order to get anything through. It was the antithesis of my optimistic approach of encouraging people to come up with ideas and do things. So I couldn't have worked under Campbell personally.[2]

Law was encouraged to apply for the new position following a conversation with Colin Moodie, Counsellor-in-Charge of Antarctic Affairs in the DEA, who told him Campbell was considering leaving the Antarctic Division to return to his permanent position with the Commonwealth Department of Civil Aviation. Moodie also indicated that the assistant OIC (scientific) would very likely be appointed as acting officer-in-charge when Campbell left. This was splendid news for Law, who had decided that a pivotal role in the Antarctic Division was the career he wanted:

> I was fascinated, of course, like all adventurers are, with the exploration and discovery aspects of it, and my interest in mountaineering and snow and ice gave me a strong adventure motivation. But as well as that, I was fascinated by the research potential of the islands and Antarctica, so I was deeply interested as a scientist.[3]

What Law did not know was that Campbell was determined that Law would not succeed him. Before he left for Japan, Law had asked Campbell to let him know of any positions becoming vacant with the reorganisation of the division, but Campbell always told him nothing had been decided. In fact, three days after Law had left for Tokyo, Campbell had written to the DEA and advised that Law's appointment would terminate on 1 August, adding that 'in view of the pending reorganisation of this Division, it is not proposed to recommend an extension of Mr Law's appointment'.[4]

Fortunately for Law, he had allies in the DEA such as Moodie, while John Burton, the DEA Secretary, had reservations about Campbell.[5] On 20 August Burton wrote to Campbell on Moodie's advice, suggesting a panel of three scientists should sit on the selection committee with Campbell to consider the applications for the OIC (scientific) position. Professor Martin from Melbourne University, who had supported Law's move to the Antarctic Division originally, was one, and all three knew

Law well. Campbell objected to having scientists on the panel but Burton insisted, although he compromised by allowing Martin to be replaced. He also insisted that Sir Douglas Mawson (who lived in Adelaide) should be invited on to the selection committee.

On 12 October Campbell attempted to skew the job description towards his favoured candidate, Wing Commander H W Berry of the RAAF. Influenced by Berry's service background, Campbell believed that ANARE needed someone as second in command who could 'hack it when things got tough'. He did not believe that Law, from a civilian background, had that degree of toughness compared with someone who had seen military action. Berry was older than Law, had no scientific qualifications, but had good technical and administrative experience making him well suited to the new requirements.

When Campbell wrote to Mawson inviting him to Melbourne for the interview, he added: 'Personally, I very much doubt if it would be worth your while coming'. He also told Mawson that he would soon return to the Department of Civil Aviation, that the new appointee would take over his job and that wide general experience and organising ability were more important for the assistant OIC (scientific) position than academic or scientific qualifications. Mawson decided against going to Melbourne, but arranged to see the interview documentation.[6]

At his interview, Law was 'staggered' to find he had been ambushed, and began a spirited campaign to make sure he got the job. He was unimpressed both by Campbell's ingratiating friendliness to his face and by his apparent disregard for science. In a long letter to Moodie, setting out his distaste for the way Campbell was working against him, he said what Campbell was trying to do was quite obvious:

> He never at any time gathers together the whole committee. They write their opinions which he then takes around personally to each. . .in turn, coloring, distorting and twisting the facts to suit his plan.[7]

Law told Moodie he was pleased that Mawson had apparently refused to be talked around by Campbell and was properly concerned at the short shrift being meted out to science. He ended his letter with an offer:

> Look, if they appoint a 'pure administrator', even the Island programmes will degenerate into routine, unimaginative exercises in 'logistics'. . .and the Antarctic show itself will just never materialize. . .Pick a good reputable scientific bloke for this job and I'll withdraw my application. But I'll fight 'pure administrators', particularly heavy-handed ex-service administrators who believe in handling a scientific expedition like a military exercise, as long as I have any breath left.[8]

STUART ALEXANDER CAIRD CAMPBELL, BENG, FRGS

When it became obvious that the establishment of an Australian station on mainland Antarctica was at least several years away, Stuart Campbell quickly lost interest in his job as leader of ANARE. A man of action, when Campbell saw things that needed to be done, he did them, and worried about the bureaucratic proprieties later. But his autocratic style was causing problems with the Department of External Affairs. He was impatient with his superiors, who in turn were more used to senior officers who observed diplomatic niceties. Campbell decided to return to his job with the Department of Civil Aviation and resigned as leader of ANARE on 31 December 1948.

Shortly afterwards, DCA sent him to Thailand with the International Civil Aviation Organisation to design Bangkok's Dom Muang international airport. Interviewed in 1987 in Townsville, Campbell said:

I liked Thailand, so then I resigned after another year with DCA, and went back to Thailand for twenty years, running my own business, importing everything from peas and matches, wine, cement, beds—everything.

The confirmed bachelor even overcame his shyness. 'I got married in Thailand to an Australian girl, and we had seven years of it there.'

When he first arrived in Thailand, Campbell wanted to learn the Thai language but could not find any textbooks so he wrote one—*The Fundamentals of the Thai Language*, published in 1957.[9] The man whom Law felt was not particularly sympathetic to science then wrote another book, *A Guide to the Hard Corals of*

Thai Waters—illustrated with his own underwater photographs and published in 1980.[10] He returned to Australia in the late 1970s.

GROUP CAPTAIN STUART CAIRD CAMPBELL,
THE FIRST LEADER OF ANARE.
(A CAMPBELL-DRURY)

Years after his ANARE experience Campbell told a friend, Hugh Philp, that he had resigned as leader of ANARE because he felt he could not work with Law, and their personality clash would not be good for ANARE. He also told Philp he had misjudged Law's calibre, and that, in the end, Law's appointment was well justified.

Stuart Campbell died on 7 March 1988 aged 85.

Campbell finally got the selection committee together on 8 November and recommended that the assistant OIC (scientific) 'not be filled at present'.[11] Burton, well aware of what was happening, intervened, advising the Public Service Board that the appointment be proceeded with and that Law was the most suitable applicant. On 13 December Burton finally advised Campbell of the decision to appoint Law. Campbell continued to fight against the decision right up to 21 December when Law was advised his application had been successful.

Mawson's role in this manoeuvring is unclear. Moodie felt that 'Campbell had him in his pocket to some degree'. He thought Mawson may not have been 'sure' about Law. This may have been partly based on the difference in physical size between the two men. Mawson had been—and still was—a big, strong man, and Moodie had the impression he thought the short, slightly built Law was 'a bit cautious, not intrepid enough'.[12] Campbell was not a tall man either, but he projected a tough, macho image, and shared a long association with Mawson.

On 29 and 30 December Law went to Canberra for a briefing. By 31 December Campbell had returned to the Department of Civil Aviation and Law had resigned from Melbourne University. On 1 January 1949, Law was appointed Acting Officer-in-Charge of the Antarctic Division, including the responsibilities of leader of ANARE. He had just twenty-one days to prepare for his first voyage as expedition leader.[13]

In keeping with the kind of formality he felt should be observed when ANARE ships were leaving and arriving in port, Law ordered all the new Heard Island party to be present at a departure ceremony on 21 January 1949. Three were late, and had been drinking. One resented having to present himself at the ceremony, and it was not until Law 'made an outright order of it that he came to heel'.[14] The new ANARE leader was making it clear who was boss right from the start.

As LST *3501*, now renamed *Labuan*, headed south for Heard, Law discovered that the bigger ship made little difference to his chronic seasickness and he experienced for himself the extraordinary behaviour of the LST in the Southern Ocean:

> It was a unique vessel in a storm. An LST is about 300 feet [91.4 metres] long, and all the works are at the back. It has blunt bows, so as you hit a wave it's like bashing into it with a brick wall. There'd be this tremendous crash like a thousand kerosene tins being bashed. Then the whole of the front part of the ship would bump up and down like a springboard, and as it flapped waves would come back through the steel decking.

On Heard, waiting for *Labuan* had become unbearable, and there was much conjecture in the Heard Island rec room who would be the first to see the relief ship. Campbell-Drury wrote in his diary on 5 February:

> After tea, I strolled over to Corinth Head with Macey and took the Aldis lamp with which to exchange words of welcome with the ship as she first hove into view. We learnt by radio that it had first put into Spit Bay, to establish a food dump, and was now bound for this end of the island. As I stood watching out to sea, suddenly, almost magically, through the slight mist, the form of *Labuan* almost indistinguishable at first, grew, as it were, and became a solid thing. It was all too difficult to realise—the first ship we had seen in fourteen long months. I flashed the words of welcome to her captain, Lieutenant Commander Dixon: 'Welcome, George. This is Heard Island. Please don't miss us.'

After the flurry of greetings and delivery of mail, Law—mindful of Heard Island's tempestuous climate—was keen to begin the changeover. He could not believe his luck—a high barometer and calm weather enabled unloading to start at 4.30 am the next day, and with the advantage of the DUKW's capacity to take loads from the ship directly to the camp, the changeover was completed in record time. This lesson was not lost on Law, who made it a rule to capitalise fully on every skerrick of fine weather that the Antarctic could provide when unloading stores, or exploring new territory—even if it meant working around the clock.

Fred Jacka was impressed with the way Law handled the whole unloading operation:

> It was just amazing to see them lower these things [DUKWs] over the side and people climbed into them and they just drove over and landed on shore.
>
> It was like the Messiah coming. He [Law] was in control of the situation. He came there with a definite idea of what he wanted to get done, and it was done expeditiously.

The dramatic nature of Heard Island, with its towering volcano, glaciers, ice cliffs and savage winds, had a curious psychological effect on some people. One of the three biologists assigned to Heard for 1949 found it so unnerving after one day that he decided he could not cope. He went to Phil Law:

> He said, 'Phil, I'm sorry, I can't stay here, I want to go back to Australia'. He knew he would have to face the contempt of all the other ocker Australians that were there. Thank God he did, because the average bloke would have been too proud to admit that he was frightened, and he would have had a terrible year down there. I thought he showed great moral courage.

After calling briefly at the Kerguelen Islands, *Labuan* returned to Melbourne on 26 February to prepare to relieve the Macquarie Island first wintering party. Trevor Heath, the Secretary of the Antarctic Division, and Law's deputy, was the voyage leader on the *Labuan* on this occasion, and the changeover was completed by 14 April.

Costs of the first year's Antarctic operations had exceeded the original estimate of £150 000 [$300 000] and were in excess of £215 000 [$430 000] with £327 000 [$654 000] being allocated for the second year.[15] Law had inherited a dog's breakfast of bureaucratic procedures:

> The finances on the scientific side were run by CSIR. . .all purchasing was done through the RAAF system, except for victuals which were purchased by the navy. What I did was cut through all those strings and set up our own supply department in the new Antarctic Division.

The main objectives of the newly formed division were to develop the scientific work at Heard and Macquarie Islands, looking towards the eventual establishment of a station on the Antarctic continent.[16] Law threw himself into the administration of the division, which consisted then of an administrative officer, two typists and a storeman. He was aware of the importance of an efficient home-based organisation, but he wanted it to be as unlike a public service department as possible. He was later to complain that 'the thing you never get credit for is the administration'. His desire for independence immediately irritated public servants while he campaigned for the Antarctic Division to have distinctively painted premises and its own letterhead. His wife Nel designed an emblem depicting a map of the Antarctic surrounded by a border of Antarctic flora and fauna which was later used on all stationery, official reports and publications, despite continuing DEA disapproval.

The fibro-cement premises at Albert Park Barracks had the standard drab olive-green and brown public service interior. Law battled with Department of Works officers to get the offices painted with white woodwork and pastel coloured walls. Later he was amused to see Department of Works officers proudly showing visitors 'the new look that they had introduced'.[17] He continued to ignore official requests to stop using his maverick notepaper.

The need for the Antarctic Division to control its own purchasing was paramount. Ordering supplies through the Department of Air could mean a delay of eight weeks for a particular piece of equipment. Had it not been for the continuing ingenuity and unconventional approach of storeman George Smith, the expeditions could not have been equipped in time for sailing:

> You've got to beat the system. . .If the boat is sailing tomorrow and you need [something] first thing tomorrow morning, it's necessary to have contact with people in the right places who are prepared to turn around and put their necks out a little bit and give you the stuff on the basis that you will honour your promise and get the paperwork through in due course. I left after many years with none of them looking for my blood.

Law had complete confidence in Smith's ability to manage the all-important business of supply:

> He had a memory like an elephant, he could remember every article he'd packed in a case and what the case numbers were, and he didn't ever forget to put anything on the ship. He ran the Tottenham Store with an iron hand. He'd make the blokes work, and stand over them—belt them into action. He'd sort out the weedy ones, stimulate the slow ones and annihilate the lazy ones. He had a tremendous role out at Tottenham Store.

Faced with a motley collection of World War II cold-weather clothing gleaned from the British Navy and other services, George formed the idiosyncratic notion that if any of this clothing actually fitted the expeditioner concerned, 'he must be deformed'. His methods of dealing with complaints endured into the 1960s, according to Des Lugg who was recruited as a medical officer:

> George, standing behind the counter, would throw you an immense array of clothing and suggest you tried it on. And as a newcomer, you'd come back and say: 'Well, this doesn't fit. This is too short, or too long.' And George would invariably say, 'You're pathological, you bastard!'

It became standard procedure for selected expeditioners to work at the Tottenham Store to help prepare the stores for the coming year. This also saved money. According to Smith:

Everything was done as cheaply as possible. There was no money what-soever. I can remember the days when we built our own huts; we estimated, including the carpenter's wages, we were building prefabricated huts for about £350 [$700] each. We were using the doctor as chief assistant to the carpenter for weeks and weeks on end.

To get anywhere you broke every rule in the book as far as getting on with the job. You had to. You just couldn't run with that system because you had only weeks to do a job, not months or years. The money wasn't there, so we learnt to live with the little we got.

Work in the store made it clear that the specialists, scientists, 'met' men and even the doctor were expected to pitch in where necessary down south to assist with essential practical tasks like building huts, digging latrines or helping the diesel mechanic and, of course, the all-important cook.

Although scientific work was acknowledged as a priority (and an important element of establishing national sovereignty over the Australian Antarctic Territory),[18] Law had problems developing programs over and above the obviously useful meteorological data being gained and trans-mitted from the sub-Antarctic stations:

Scott, even in his earliest, first expedition, did a tremendous amount of scientific work. . .it helped them get better public support and general acclaim, publicity and money. In our case, I had the greatest difficulty in selling the scientific side of things. There were many people who just thought putting a hut down there with some men was occupation [enough] and that was all you needed to do for your claims. But I had to keep pointing out that the Argentinians and Chileans and British were competing in the Falkland Islands Dependencies area of the Antarctic Peninsula. The British were doing meteorology and one or two other things and the Argentinians and Chileans were not doing nearly as elaborate programs and their prestige and the sort of pay-off, in terms of territorial occupation, were substantially lower than that of the British for this reason. So I had to keep saying, 'If we don't do scientific work, our position in the pecking order just won't be good enough.'

From the time he became acting officer-in-charge of ANARE in 1949 Law had his sights set on gaining a foothold on the Antarctic continent itself. He knew this would have to wait until an ice-strengthened ship was either built or chartered, but he was content to continue projects of sci-entific research on Heard and Macquarie Islands while the Antarctic Division was built up and consolidated. Sir Douglas Mawson, who remained on the Executive Planning Committee (EPC), was also keen for Australia to establish a continental station. Mawson was generally supportive of Law's plans, but he was not always predictable. During the EPC meeting of 3 June 1949, the veteran Antarctic explorer threatened the continuing existence of ANARE and the sub-Antarctic program. It was the first time Law had chaired an EPC meeting.

Sir Douglas asked the chairman whether it was the Government's intention to pursue the present Antarctic research indefinitely. He felt there should be some limit to the activities of ANARE unless it could be made to pay for itself. Perhaps before more money was allocated for scientific exploration in the Antarctic, a critical analysis should be made in order to discover if the money 'might be more usefully expended elsewhere'.[19]

Law deflected this attack on the sub-Antarctic program by saying that the question of continuity had not yet arisen in his various discussions with the DEA in Canberra. The Government was already committed to an island program of at least five years, and had set up a permanent Antarctic Division in Melbourne for this purpose and to prosecute plans for establishing a base on the Antarctic continent.

But Sir Douglas persisted, saying he wanted to make it clear that when he had first suggested an Antarctic expedition to the Government he had not contemplated the present large expenditure, but had considered that part of the cost should be met by proceeds from associated commercial undertakings such as whaling. Whaling expeditions could finance an Antarctic program and, in addition, 'their ships could take with them aircraft capable of surveying large areas in the interior'. Failing attention to the commercial side, it would, in his opinion, 'be too expensive to maintain base camps indefinitely'.[20]

Law, from the chair, turned this sally aside by saying that in his view recommendations for a whaling industry lay outside the functions of the Executive Planning Committee.

Dr F W G White of the CSIR weighed in at this point and reminded the committee that, at their last meeting, members had requested direction from the Government as to its future policy on the exploration and development of the Antarctic. The resolution made the point that if, for political or other reasons, the Government wanted to embark on a long-range, extensive program of Antarctic development, the committee could draw up such a program but 'does not consider that this scientific work alone could justify the despatch of a major expedition'. Had any reply to this resolution been obtained from the DEA?

Law said it had not, but 'the department had been given all possible information and must be presumed to realise the position'. In his opinion the question of the period of operation of ANARE was a matter for his department but that in any case 'further consideration of this matter should be postponed until near the end of the five-year period to which the Expedition was committed'.[21]

It had been a tough first meeting of the EPC for the new chairman, but it demonstrated Law's determination to make sure the committee operated only as an advisory body, while he ran the Antarctic Division and called the shots. The committee's comment that scientific work could not justify a major expedition was an acknowledgment of the territorial imperative driving Australian Government Antarctic policy at the time.

Ever since the beginning of his Antarctic career Law had believed that the future of a continuing Australian Antarctic program lay in carrying out a vigorous program of scientific research:

> In a number of speeches I had to hammer the point that governments don't operate by taking money from you and putting it into something else. If they cut it out of one thing, they just cut it—it doesn't go anywhere else. I used to say to the scientific community in Australia: 'You ought to be jolly glad that we're spending this money, because that's money being spent on science that otherwise would not be spent'.

In June 1950, conscious of the importance of public support for the ANARE program, Law wanted to brief two journalists on Australia's proposed plans for Antarctica. As public service rules dictated, he applied for permission from the DEA to do so. But there had been a change of government in 1949 to a Liberal–Country Party coalition. Alan Watt had replaced Burton as secretary of the DEA and Richard Casey was the minister. Charles Kevin was made assistant secretary (administration), with responsibility for the running of the Antarctic Division. Even Watt admitted that Kevin's position was a 'thankless post' and concluded that 'no one in this position ever achieves fame or glory. . .'

Although Law had no problems with Watt, who seemed reasonably well disposed towards the Antarctic Division, he had most of his dealings with Kevin and their relations were at best cool—mutual animosity only lightly masked by the stilted, impersonal language used in their memoranda.[22] Kevin knocked back Law's request to brief the two journalists on future ANARE plans.

On 20 July 1950, Law received a message from Jim McCarthy, OIC at Heard Island, that the medical officer, Serge Udovikoff, had diagnosed himself as having appendicitis. Udovikoff had had an eventful year. First he broke his ankle skiing, put it in plaster himself and spent three weeks in bed.[23] Then followed a violent episode of food poisoning. Udovikoff was one of the 'refugee doctors', medical practitioners from Europe who were not registered with the State Licensing Boards but who, through a special arrangement, were allowed to practise in Antarctica. (Many of these doctors with European qualifications also worked in Papua New Guinea after the war.)

With no other expeditioner capable of performing an appendicitis operation, Udovikoff's plight was serious. Law requested assistance from the Royal Australian Navy who refused point blank. It was the middle of winter, 'they had no suitable ship and they couldn't spare one anyway'. He then arranged for an SOS to be sent to all ships within a certain distance of Heard Island asking if they could divert to the island.

The story was front page news all over Australia and by 21 July it was reported that a passenger steamer, *Port Phillip*, travelling from Australia to London, had answered the call and was heading towards Heard Island.

Despite this development, Law was horrified when he heard that Udovikoff was planning to operate on himself:

> I was of course in touch with the Medical Adviser at Royal Melbourne Hospital. Our strong advice. . .was, 'Certainly don't try that. Use every conservative method you have and hope the thing will go away. . .you'll kill yourself if you try to operate on yourself.'

Expeditioner Peter Wayman noted in his diary on 23 July that Udovikoff was marking his stomach and reading medical books, and had fresh symptoms all the time. On 26 July a home remedy for relieving the symptoms of appendicitis was received by radio: mix 1 teaspoon coffee grounds with 1 dessertspoon of castor oil in half a pint [0.3 litre] of warm water and drink every four hours.[24]

Ignoring advice to concentrate on palliative methods, Udovikoff got ready to operate on himself. Phil Law:

> He prepared everything down there—the boys helped rig up everything—to the point I believe of actually lying on the operating table and beginning to have them shave his pubic area and then he lost his nerve and decided not to.*

---

* On 30 April 1961 a Russian doctor, L I Rogozov, successfully removed his own appendix in Antarctica, at Novolazarevskaya Station on the coast of Queen Maud Land.[25] With self-diagnosed signs of possible perforation of his appendix and localised peritonitis and no help possible, Rogozov decided the only solution was to operate on himself. He prepared local anaesthetic and instructed a meteorologist in the use of surgical retractors while another expeditioner held a mirror so Rogozov could view what he could not otherwise see. The resourceful doctor was back on duty within two weeks.

Rescue by ship was looking more and more unlikely. The captain of *Port Phillip* radioed that he could not continue the dash to Heard Island in dangerous weather conditions—the passengers were all complaining, the furniture was getting broken, and the grand piano had broken loose.[26]

Another ship, *Perthshire,* responded to the call with two doctors on board standing by 'day and night to broadcast detailed directions to the expedition should Dr Udovikoff decide to remove his own appendix'.[27] The press was in a high state of hyperbole. On 22 July the Sunday Telegraph headlined: DOCTOR WITH KNIFE POISED, STOPS OWN OPERATION.[28]

Meanwhile the biologists Peter Young and Les Gibbney were practising removing appendixes from seals. OIC McCarthy thought that Young was capable of doing the operation with a bit of advice from a Melbourne surgeon, but Udovikoff did not choose that option.[29]

Gales raging in the Southern Ocean forced *Perthshire* also to give up attempts to reach Heard Island. Law was having such a hectic time that his wife Nel shifted all his clothes and personal gear out to the lounge room at his Canterbury home, and he lived beside the phone for two weeks snatching catnaps as the Udovikoff affair gained momentum.[30]

Eventually the navy decided to help, and on 27 July it was reported that HMAS *Australia* would be sent 'on her 3200 mile [5120 kilometres] mercy dash to Heard Island' with two doctors aboard.[31] Law had been contacted two days before by the navy and told to arrange cold-weather clothing for the entire ship's company:

> We descended on Myers, and Buckley and Nunn's, and London Stores. We bought all their long johns and their woollen singlets. . .and tried to get everything done in a period of 36 hours.

Meanwhile on Heard Island things were less hectic. Peter Wayman wrote in his diary that Udovikoff was still reading medical books, 'but unfortunately he read the wrong one and developed symptoms of childbirth'. By 27 July there were signs that Udovikoff's condition was easing and, three days later, Jim McCarthy was relaxed enough about the situation to go on a short mountaineering expedition.[32]

The press was still in a frenzy of excitement. 'A thin white line of hope for a man in danger was cut through the Southern Ocean today as HMAS *Australia* sped towards Heard Island' was typical of the coverage even though the big cruiser was making heavy weather of the Southern Ocean gales.[33]

On 2 August Heard Island reported one of the year's worst blizzards with wind gusts reaching 160 kilometres per hour. But by 7 August the seas were calm enough for the Australian flagship to take Udovikoff on board for the return journey. The *Canberra Times* of 11 August reported that HMAS *Australia* was speeding to Fremantle. No immediate operation was necessary. The doctor, a thin grey-eyed man, 'clenched his teeth as he was helped to the ship's surgery, but said he felt fairly strong and had little pain'. Law said the voyage back was very rough:

> They were struck by an immense wave that stove in about six frames on the side of the ship. By the time they got back to Fremantle the conservative measures taken by the doctor had proved effective.

The arrival in Fremantle was a public relations disaster, with Udovikoff walking ashore unaided. Law thought the least that could have been done was carry him off on a stretcher:

> There was an uproar by ignorant people and the media, querying whether he had ever been sick. This was during the cold war with Russia and some even went so far as to suggest that Udovikoff was a Russian agent and he'd deliberately designed this illness so he could divert Australia's main flagship away from Australia! It was a tremendous drama. But I might just say Udovikoff was [later] qualified for medical service and he had a long and quite distinguished career as a medico in Western Australia.

One immediate outcome of the Udovikoff crisis was that the Minister for External Affairs, Richard Casey, made it clear to Law that the navy would not be available in the future to attempt this kind of rescue (HMAS *Australia* had sustained expensive structural damage). He also told Law that no doctor could go to an Australian Antarctic station in future without his appendix being prophylactically removed. The British Medical Association, however, considered it was unethical to operate on a person to remove a healthy appendix.

Law solved this problem by simply ignoring the BMA's concerns, but it did add to the problems of finding doctors for Antarctic service, because 'not everyone is prepared to walk "cold" into a surgery and have his appendix out just to get a job in the Antarctic'.

The Udovikoff affair underlined the pressing need for Australia to have its own Antarctic ship. *Labuan* was not available for the emergency dash to Heard Island to bring back Dr Udovikoff and whether she could have managed the journey in winter is doubtful.

Law had hoped to mount an expedition to the Antarctic continent in the summer of 1951–52, but the prospect of chartering an overseas ship was complicated by the outbreak of the Korean War and the uncertain international situation. Law urged the Executive Planning Committee to discuss the practicality of a plan already drawn up by the Antarctic Division to design and build an Antarctic ship in Australia. The committee resolved to recommend to the Government that a ship be chartered in 1951 and that a sub-committee be appointed to prepare detailed specifications for the new vessel.[34]

Cabinet agreed and on 13 July 1950 decided 'that an expedition should be sent to the Antarctic to establish a permanent station in the Australian sector' and 'that a new ship should be built for this purpose'. Costs of the ship were estimated to be in the region of £700 000 [$1.4 million] to £800 000 [$1.6 million].[35]

For two years from December 1950, a sub-committee including Law, Sir Douglas Mawson, Captain J K Davis and Commander Peter Peak RAN met and worked painstakingly with the chief naval architect from the Australian Shipbuilding Board, Claude Barker.[36] The general requirements for the proposed ship were that it be capable of breaking three-foot-thick sheet-ice [91.4 centimetres], carry 50 passengers and 50 crew, and have a helicopter deck and space for an aircraft, amphibious vehicles, laboratories, oceanographic winches and other equipment. Specifications for this Antarctic ship were actually completed 'right down to the furniture and the crockery'. The vessel was never built. Australia would not have its own Antarctic ship until the launch of the Newcastle-built *Aurora Australis* in 1989.

SIX

TESTING TIMES

I n February 1951 the whole sub-Antarctic program was thrown into chaos by the breakdown and removal from service of HMAS *Labuan* on her way back to Fremantle while relieving the 1950 Heard Island party and landing the 1951 expeditioners and their supplies. This was something Phil Law had feared from the time of his first Southern Ocean voyage on *Labuan* in 1949:

> There's no doubt that the Naval Board in Australia had great misgivings about sending an LST to Heard Island. They argued about it for a long while and finally agreed reluctantly to send an LST because there was just nothing else. The thing that will always amuse me is that, having argued for so long and worried so much about the chance of survival of the LST. . .when it returned successfully from Heard Island everyone threw their caps in the air and said: 'Hooray, we made it. Good old LST. A wonderful job.'

The voyage to Heard had been rough, with *Labuan* performing her usual remarkable twisting and corkscrewing motion through heavy seas that Law estimated were twelve metres high. On the night of 28 January it was blowing up to hurricane force, '60 mph [96 kilometres per hour] with gusts up to 90 mph [144 kilometres per hour], a pitch black night with mountainous seas'. It was so bad that Law thought he would check on how the ANARE men were faring in the cabins on either side of 'this great flapping foredeck':

> They were all sitting up very worried, and they said, 'Phil, the crew's all gone.' I said, 'What do you mean?' They said, 'Well, there's no one next

door.' So I went to the crew's quarters and sure enough there was no crew there. . .So I went back aft and there in the mess decks were all the crew with their knapsacks packed with all their personal belongings. I said, 'What goes on?' They said, 'Well, if this ship is going to break in half, we're going to be in the half that's got the works in it!'

The steering gear failed before they got to Heard Island and while there the ship ran short of drinking water after cracks in the hull polluted the fresh water with salt. The captain, Lieutenant Commander I Cartwright, insisted on taking *Labuan* to neighbouring Kerguelen Island to replenish the fresh water stocks before the Heard resupply was completed. They got back to the island on 13 February and completed the resupply, to Law's great relief. The first day out on the return journey the steering gear failed again, but one of the crew devised an impromptu gadget with belts and pulleys from a refrigeration electric motor to maintain steerage. Law said later that the ingenious young engine artificer was later court martialled for drilling holes in the deck without the approval of the Naval Board.

JO JELBART (LEFT) AND 'SHORTY' CARROLL WITH A HAUL OF ANTARCTIC COD, HEARD ISLAND 1948. JELBART DIED IN AN ACCIDENT WHILE ON THE NORWEGIAN-BRITISH-SWEDISH ANTARCTIC EXPEDITION IN 1951. (A CAMPBELL-DRURY)

On Wednesday 21 February *Labuan* wallowed without power for eight hours in mid-ocean while engine repairs were attempted. Law was also told that a crack (by no means the first in the LST's Antarctic history) had opened up right across the steel foredeck—a reminder that LSTs had broken apart in the Atlantic during World War II—and sea water had entered the fresh water tanks and the condenser tubes.

During this dismal time Law was shocked to get a radio report that the physicist Jo Jelbart (who had been one of the original Heard Island party in 1948) had been killed while working as an Australian observer with the Norwegian-British-Swedish Antarctic Expedition. Jelbart and two other men had driven over the ice cliffs in thick fog into the sea near the base camp of Maudheim in a Weasel over-snow vehicle. This was a double blow for Law. Apart from his personal friendship with the bright young physicist, Law had been grooming Jelbart to succeed him if ever he left the Division.[1]

In 1948 when Phil Law returned from the voyage of *Wyatt Earp* with his newly-grown beard, he believed himself to be one of only three men in Melbourne to sport one, and it excited comment wherever he went. In 1951, little had changed:

> The breakdown of *Labuan* and her diversion to Fremantle meant that men of the returning Heard Island party were in a strange city, far from home, with no money. I had radioed from the ship to Canberra requesting that the Public Service Inspector's office in Fremantle be authorised to pay the men a fortnight's salary upon their arrival. So, as soon as we berthed, I gathered the men and we all trooped along to the PSI's office.
>
> We entered the building and I found the office. Saying, 'Wait here till I check', I left the men in the corridor and went in to speak to the girl at the reception counter. Behind her was a large room with numerous typists working in an 'open plan' layout—about twenty in all. I asked the girl was the money for the Heard Island men available. After she had enquired and answered 'Yes', I went to the door and said, 'All right men, come in.'
>
> Into the space before the reception counter trooped eighteen men, almost all wearing beards. The beards were all types, sizes and colours, and some men with long, black, luxuriant growths looked very fearsome indeed.
>
> Every typist stopped work and there was a deathly, wide-eyed hush. After a few moments of shocked silence, there erupted a few giggles and a murmur of excited conversation; then the heads bent again over the typewriters and work resumed. I never again was to see beards have such an impact.[2]

On Tuesday 27 February a tug finally reached *Labuan*, but she was finished. After some weeks undergoing repairs in Fremantle she limped back to Melbourne for further work, and then to Sydney where she was tied up. She never put to sea again.

The 1950 Macquarie Island party was following these events with more than average interest, because the men were effectively marooned, with no suitable vessel available to relieve them despite Law's efforts to contact every organisation controlling shipping around the Australian coastline. They had a difficult year in many ways. There was friction over the management style of OIC Dick Cohen, which caused four members of the party to write to Phil Law complaining about his behaviour.[3] The letters were able to be delivered because of a visit to Macquarie Island in September 1950 by a New Zealand naval frigate, *St Austel Bay*. This caused the unexpected departure of the cook, Norman Figg, who arrived on the beach at Garden Cove with his kitbag just before the frigate was due to sail. Weather observer Reg Frost said:

'Where are you going Norm?' 'I'm going home' said the cook, all done up in his best clothes. And he did! We couldn't stop him, providing the captain of *St Austel Bay* was prepared to take him.

Figg had injured his leg playing a particularly robust form of Macquarie Island football—a melange of rugby and Australian Rules 'with no written rules', played on the soft fine sand of the isthmus. That became the official reason for his 'repatriation', but the reality was he just decided to quit, having received some disturbing news from home. Fred Doutch, the assistant cook/storeman, took over culinary duties for three months until the British oceanographic research ship *Discovery II* dropped in a replacement chef.[4]

Another member of the party became so depressed during the year that he used to sit on top of Camp Hill near the station and shoot any seals 'that put their heads up' with a .303 rifle. The rest of the men thought it best not to interfere. According to weather observer Trevior Boyd, one of the enduring station slogans was, 'Every bastard down here is mad except me'. Dissatisfaction with the OIC reached the point where a palace coup was actually planned. Biologist Bill Taylor:

> We had a series of informal meetings, and we were going to have a new King, Eric Shipp [the other biologist]. Nobody disagreed, but there were two or three who wouldn't vote in favour of it, so we decided that unless we were all unanimous, we wouldn't do it. But [the OIC] got a big scare and behaved himself a bit better after that.

All these group tensions were overtaken by the illness of meteorologist John Windsor, who developed severe symptoms of appendicitis in December 1950.

Windsor was not keen to have an operation on the island. The doctor, Kostos Kalnenas, was a Displaced Person with European qualifications (like Serge Udovikoff) not recognised by Australian medical authorities. Kalnenas was an ear, nose and throat doctor without much general surgical experience.[5] Windsor knew that the surgical instruments were in poor shape, as Bill Taylor recalled, 'because [when we arrived] Kostos made the mistake of showing us the state of some of the instruments. They were all rusty, which Windsor didn't like one bit.'

According to Taylor, Windsor delayed reporting his symptoms because he had heard a French polar ship, *Commandant Charcot*, was due to sail past Macquarie Island, and could call in to pick him up.

> When it got fairly close to Macquarie he reported sick and wanted the ship to come in. But the doctor said, 'You have no time. You have delayed reporting it, and it's obviously burst.' And he still would not agree to an

operation. It wasn't until there was an exchange of cables and he was told that the ship wouldn't be coming—because he would be dead by the time the ship got there—that he agreed to an operation.

Kalnenas operated on 2 January 1951, but it was too late. Windsor's appendix had ruptured, and the incision revealed 'one big pussy mess'. There was little Kalnenas could do other than clean up the infected area, put in a drain and administer antibiotics. Windsor died on 5 January and his widow agreed to her husband's burial on Macquarie Island.[6]

To compound these traumatic events, Cyril Park, the diesel mechanic, also developed symptoms of appendicitis. Bill Taylor:

> Cyril was a real tough mechanic, a good guy. Everybody liked old Cyril. But for some reason he started to get the same vomiting and pains. . .it was a combination of gall bladder and appendix symptoms.

By this time the French polar vessel *Commandant Charcot* that Windsor had hoped would rescue him was close enough to Macquarie to be diverted to pick up Park, who was evacuated on 12 February.

The 1950 Macquarie Island party was depending on Phil Law to find a suitable ship for them. The rumour mill had it that a ship would actually have to be built to relieve the island, and that could take twelve months. But a more conventional solution was at hand. The Australian Shipping Board finally offered ANARE *River Fitzroy*, a 9000-tonne ship used for transporting iron ore for BHP, then about to load iron ore at Whyalla. It was far from suitable, but at least it was a ship, and Law accepted it gratefully. The Shipping Board offered the seamen's union £1 a day [$2], and the union responded with a 'take it or leave it' offer of £2/10/0 [$5] a day. Law took it.[7] This was the first time ANARE had worked with a merchant crew, rather than the navy.

Fortunately the army was able to provide two DUKWs to replace the beaten-up vehicles that were still on *Labuan*. The landing of stores from *River Fitzroy* was organised by Dick Thompson, ANARE's new supply officer. Thompson was an ex-navy man with wide experience, a good organiser and widely respected by those who worked with him.

It was 1 May before *River Fitzroy* cleared Hobart for Macquarie Island, arriving in Buckles Bay on Friday 4 May. By then it was late in the season, dark each day at 4.30 pm and unloading from the ship was illuminated by floodlights. Beacons were also lit on the beach to guide the DUKWs in. Gales and snow storms interrupted the unloading, and pontoons and a disabled DUKW were blown out to sea and had to be rescued. On 13 May *River Fitzroy* sailed down the coast of the narrow island to Lusitania Bay to land emergency supplies for a hut there. One of the two DUKWs was stranded on rocks just off the beach where it was pounded by a heavy swell and had to be abandoned. Law, Thompson and the landing party were rescued by a whale boat from *River Fitzroy* after a cold and uncomfortable night in a small shelter hut. Eleven men trying to sleep in a hut only 2.4 by 2.6 metres reminded Law of 'sea elephants in a wallow'.[8]

Despite the odds, however, the 1950 party had been relieved—even though it seemed at one stage that they might have to sit down to their second mid-winter dinner in 1951. But the problem of finding a suitable ship to support ANARE activities remained.

After the Udovikoff evacuation from Heard Island in 1950, and John Windsor's death early in 1951, Antarctic Division staff in Melbourne were alarmed to hear from Heard Island in October about another medical emergency. Jack Starr, the cook on Heard Island, had been diagnosed with acute appendicitis. There were no ships available for a rescue, so after an exchange of cables with the division and the consultant surgeon of Royal Melbourne Hospital an urgent operation was recommended.

The medical officer on Heard Island was Dr Otto Rec who, like Udovikoff and Kalnenas, had European qualifications not recognised in Australia. He was a physician and had never performed an appendicectomy. Law's insistence that certain expedition members from each wintering party had three weeks' training at the Royal Melbourne Hospital as a theatre assistant and anaesthetist was about to be put to the test again. The radio supervisor on Heard Island, Nils Lied, noted in his diary:

Dr Rec wanted the following assistants: biologist Ken Brown as assistant surgeon to help him underbind the tissues and arteries etc; myself to hold Jack's guts open while he and Ken did the digging; biologist Max Downes to be in charge of instruments; OIC Frank Hannan to be the anaesthetist, and Kevin Johnson, radio operator, to be general 'sister' to fetch and carry.[9]

87

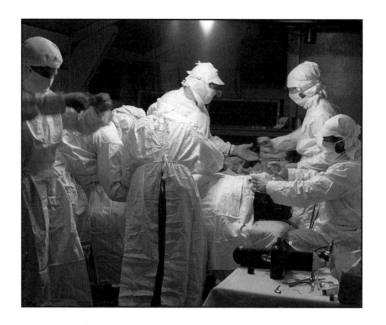

Photographs taken at the time show a professional-looking gowned and masked operating team gathered round an operating table in the gale-buffeted recreation hut. The table was hastily knocked up by radio operator Dave Cheffins from scrap timber and a masonite desk top. The whole area had been scrubbed with lysol. Nils Lied:

DR OTTO REC (CENTRE) AND HIS ANARE THEATRE ASSISTANTS OPERATING ON JACK STARR FOR APPENDICITIS, HEARD ISLAND, 1951. (R DINGLE)

It took us all hours and hours to get scrubbed up. . .at first we used sandsoap, then ordinary soap, then when seemingly all the skin had been thoroughly removed from hands and arms, we held our hands in pure alcohol for ten minutes. This was, of course, considered a terrible waste by several of the party.[10]

The cook, by general ANARE consensus then and now, is the indispensable person on a wintering station. Rec began the operation with the words of diesel mechanic Peter Lawson ringing in his ears: 'If you kill the bloody cook, they'll kill you!'

Starr was brought in, putting on a bold front. He told his masked and gowned colleagues that their appearances were much improved. Lied:

We made a mask from gauze and we had ether. We kicked him off with Pentothal, and he got very drowsy. Somebody said, 'Where are you Jack?' And he said, slurring, 'Sydney Cricket Ground'. I said, 'Oh he's all right' so we slapped the mask on him. Even so, it took an hour to get him under because. . .he had such a bushy beard that oxygen got through the beard and mixed with the ether. But we got him under in the finish. We tried several times, but every time Doc touched his belly with a knife, he'd draw his knees up.

Anyway we finally got into him, and Doc said, 'I cannot find the bloody thing!' We had all Jack's entrails spread over his stomach and finally we found the appendix, and that was not in the best of condition.[11]

The discovery of the elusive appendix triggered a muffled cheer from the operating team and the anxious spectators. Lied said the job was finished just in time:

> The last stitching was as fast as possible, and soon after the last stitch was in and a dressing clapped on his belly, Jack came out of the anaesthetic and said 'Shit'!—which may well have been appropriate under the circumstances.[12]

Radio contact with Melbourne was lost during the operation and it was some hours before Cheffins could get a message through to the Antarctic Division (relayed through Scandinavia on an amateur band) to a relieved Phillip Law that the operation had been successfully completed. Starr made a slow recovery, but managed to return to duty.

SHE WAS SMALL, BUT SHE DID THE JOB. *TOTTAN* IN ATLAS COVE 1952.
(P LAW)

At the end of 1951 the absence of a suitable ship to recover the Heard and Macquarie parties and replace them with the 1952 winterers was still the most urgent practical problem confronting the Antarctic Division. It was thought a motor ship, *Kabarli*, would be available for charter from the Government of Western Australia, but the offer was withdrawn 'at the last moment'.[13] The charter of vessels from overseas was ruled out as too expensive. Law pinned his hopes on a Norwegian sealer, MV *Tottan*, used by the French to resupply their station on Adélie Land.

There were some difficulties to be overcome. *Tottan* was scheduled to take the French expeditioners back to Europe and its owner-master, Captain Engebretsen, was returning to Norway to take part in that season's sealing operations off Newfoundland. Law sent administrative officer Jerry Donovan to Adelaide to sound out Captain Engebretsen on his way south, and asked Westralian Farmers Transport Ltd in London to act as agents for the Antarctic Division and open negotiations in Norway.

After prolonged negotiations between London and Oslo, a charter was arranged to relieve both Heard and Macquarie Islands within Law's budget estimate of £50 000 [$100 000]. There were no objections by the French, because they found it cheaper to fly their expeditioners home rather than continue their charter.[14]

Tottan was a small vessel of 500 tonnes, not ice-strengthened but—although about the same size as the wooden-hulled *Wyatt Earp*—at

89

least with a steel hull. She was not big enough to carry army DUKWs, and alternative methods of getting cargo ashore at Heard and Macquarie islands had to be worked out. Supply officer Dick Thompson and scientific officer Lem Macey chose inflatable pontoons. They were US wartime stock, they came in 10×2 metre sections, had timber decking on top of them, and were originally used as a quick method of bridging rivers. Thompson:

> Lem Macey and I became the masters of pontoon technology. . .these big inflatable pontoons proved to be a lifesaver for the Antarctic Division for a long, long time.
>
> We cut our teeth on *Tottan* because we didn't have the navy any more. Before [on the *Labuan*] there were sailors to do things. *Tottan* had a small crew, and they would handle the cargo in the hold, we'd load it on to the pontoon, the ship's motor boat would tow us in—we had no more than four people on a pontoon—and then when we got on to the beach all our troops would unload it.

Tottan sailed for Heard Island on 9 February 1952 under the command of Captain L Frederiksen. Law rated her on a par with *Wyatt Earp* for comfort, which was not a ringing endorsement. Peter Lancaster Brown, a Heard Island expeditioner, wrote that Melbourne harbour regulations forbade the dumping of foodstuff into the river and a week's accumulation of galley scraps lay rotting on the burning hot steel decks:

> Little imagination is required to visualise the scene, and with the putrid odours percolating through from the old, leaking blubber tanks in the ship's hold, it was only too easy to realise that we were in for no luxury cruise.[15]

Law described the seventeen-day voyage to Heard Island as 'not enjoyable', with most of the ANARE men being sick all the time. A pen containing twelve sheep was stove in by a heavy sea and the bedraggled beasts were moved on to one wing of the bridge—courtesy of the captain—for the rest of the voyage.[16]

The new pontoons proved effective in moving cargo and, anxious to take advantage of calm weather on the evening of 27 February, Law decided to throw 44-gallon drums [200 litres] of fuel overboard to float ashore.

> After the first twenty-five drums had been put over I noticed that they were floating alongside the ship and not moving towards the shore, so I stopped the unloading and work ceased. Soon afterwards the wind went around to the south-west and most of these twenty-five drums were

not seen again. They will probably turn up on one of the adjacent beaches.[17]

RUBBER PONTOONS CARRY CARGO ASHORE FROM *TOTTAN*, MACQUARIE ISLAND 1952. (P LAW)

The next morning the experiment was tried again and 'drums now put overboard floated ashore rapidly and were dragged by the men above high-water mark'. The unloading and change-over was completed by 2 March and Law was extremely impressed with the cooperation ANARE had from the master Captain Frederiksen and the crew of *Tottan*.

Before leaving Heard, Law gave his permission for the crew to do some sealing as a bonus for their good work. A score of bull elephant seals were lying up on the rocks near Wharf Point, near the camp. All of them were youngsters not more than four or five years old but, even so, they were over three metres long and each weighed about a tonne. Peter Brown described the scene:

> Armed with long flensing knives and rifles, the Norwegians approached the dozing seals that lay shoulder to shoulder in a wallow of stinking ooze and rotting faeces. . .An old sealer called Thorsen picked up a length of driftwood. Whacking the unfortunate beasts about the head, he tried to separate them to give the men more room for flensing.
>
> With thunderous, raucous bellows, the victims arched their bodies as they scattered to avoid the rain of blows. Some tried to lollop back into the sea to escape their tormentor, but a snap shot by the riflemen quickly ended their flight. It was horrible to witness the great seals die. The huge masses of flesh quivered in the death agonies and spouted plumes of bright red blood. As life became extinct their eyes glazed over—turning green and expressionless.[18]

The dead seals were quickly flensed and within half an hour the strips of white blubber were deposited into *Tottan*'s rusting blubber tanks. Law was impressed by the operation and its commercial possibilities and noted in his voyage report:

As a result of discussions on board this sealing ship and (later) at Kerguelen, together with observations of these men at work, I am convinced that the time is ripe to commence sealing operations at our Islands.[19]

Within five days of her return to Melbourne on 10 March *Tottan* was on her way to Macquarie Island where the technique of unloading cargo on inflatable pontoons was to be put to its toughest test. With the beach at Buckles Bay guarded by rocks and kelp, and a surf to contend with as well, the pontoons could not be towed straight to shore as they had been at Heard Island. Instead a buoy was anchored just beyond the breaker line, near a narrow strip of open water about twelve metres wide and leading into the beach between the rocks and kelp. The pontoons were towed to this buoy by the ship's motor boat and then were hauled from the buoy to the shore by a continuous line running from the buoy to the beach—a method devised and rigged by the ingenious duo, Macey and Thompson. Law later wrote that *only* the flexible pontoons could have operated in the heavy surf in Buckles Bay.

Tottan left for Melbourne on 9 April. It had taken two weeks wrestling with cargo, cold, surf and gale-force winds to complete the changeover. Back in Melbourne, a smooth rhythm of annual expedition administration was now operating, tied irrevocably to the shipping schedule that took men and supplies to the sub-Antarctic islands. In 1951 Law requested that his title 'officer-in-charge' be changed to 'director'. He was not confirmed in his job, however, until 27 March 1952, more than three years after he had taken up the acting position.

On 11 June 1952 the Antarctic Division moved from its Victoria Barracks location to 187 Collins St, Melbourne. From a complement of four in 1949 when Law first took over, there were now eighteen permanent staff including Law, director; Jeremiah (Jerri) Donovan, administrative officer; Fred Jacka, physicist (in charge of a small staff of scientists); Dick Thompson, supply officer; George Smith, storeman at Tottenham; Alan Campbell-Drury, photographic officer; Mynwe (Mrs Mac) McDonald, cables officer; a librarian and other support staff.

The Antarctic Division's planning system was set out in a monthly time line beginning in April when Law returned from overseeing the last changeover voyage of the summer season. Plans, forward estimates of costings and budgets were prepared for the next expedition. Staff positions were created and approvals sought. Ordering of overseas supplies began in May and vehicles, aircraft, radios and general equipment were overhauled or purchased. Advertising for expeditioners for the following year began in June and the budget was prepared and presented to Treasury. In July Law travelled to State capital cities to interview expeditioners who had applied to go south. In the latter half of the calendar year the island stations ordered food and equipment for the resupply. The all-important operations manuals were written or updated during September and ship itineraries and passenger lists finalised. The selected expeditioners began training in October. Trial erection of new huts was an important element and the men began packing stores under the 'guided democracy' of George Smith in the Tottenham store. This work went on through November and into December when the first ship sailed.

In the first few years of island operations there was little training for expeditioners. Two men went to the Royal Melbourne Hospital to learn basic anaesthetic and nursing techniques to help the doctor in an emergency, and the cook was checked out and further trained if necessary in the all-important art of baking bread. The doctor also did a quick (but essential) course in basic dentistry at the Dental Hospital. After Dick Thompson joined the division in 1950 he suggested to Law that a properly designed training program be set up for all expeditions, to enable them to handle better the extreme conditions in Antarctica.

It became the practice for all expeditioners to attend a week-long program at the University of Melbourne in November. There they had lectures on the aims and ideals of the expedition, survival and first aid, hygiene, fire precautions and the use of fire extinguishers, Antarctic clothing, how to travel by tractor and dog sled (when the Antarctic stations were established), films of life at a station, photographic techniques, supply problems, reordering, stores procedures, administration and how to deal with morale problems. An expedition member was selected as station photographer, trained by Alan Campbell-Drury, and issued with cameras and film to undertake moving as well as still photography during the year. While every photographer was credited, the film exposed remained the property of the Antarctic Division and the release of any publicity material was controlled by the director.

The dangers of Antarctic (and sub-Antarctic) life were many and a trap for the unwary. Getting there involved a potentially dangerous voyage fraught with cyclones, pack ice, submerged rocks and unknown coasts. Loading and unloading stores under risky conditions could and did cause injuries to those taking part. Those who ventured away from the stations faced risk of exposure, frostbite, snow-blindness, slipping on ice and breaking a limb, white-outs, being lost in a blizzard, falling into crevasses or being killed or injured by aircraft, vehicles or machinery. On station there could be fire, carbon monoxide poisoning (an insidious danger in huts warmed by burning fossil fuels) or industrial accidents.

93

Weather observers manufacturing hydrogen for balloon launches were vulnerable to explosions.

These dangers were no less potent on the sub-Antarctic islands than on the yet-to-be-attained Antarctic continent. Heard Island, with its 2745 metre volcano Big Ben, generated a full range of polar conditions. Savage blizzards, glaciers, snow and ice posed grave risks for those undertaking pioneering field work. Those who broke established rules or took unacceptable risks through inexperience could pay a terrible price.

In April 1952 radio operators Jim Carr and Peter Brown set out to walk from the station at Atlas Cove to conduct a seal count at Saddle Point along the coast—only about ten kilometres as the metaphorical crow flew, but considerably longer in practice because of the steep slopes and glaciers of Heard Island. When they came to a feature sometimes called the Baudissen Glacier (later renamed the Little Challenger Glacier) it looked easier to walk along the beach in front of its ice cliffs, instead of climbing over. Carr:

> These glaciers have ice walls at the shore, 150 feet [45.7 metres] or so high, and then a beach as wide as the average lounge room, twelve or fifteen feet [around 4 metres]. So we thought we'd take a risk because it would be quicker.[20]

Brown agreed that the short cut would save 'hours of back-breaking toil', and they began to walk across. Brown wrote: 'I felt uneasy—like a kind of foreboding. The sand strip was terribly narrow and forced us to walk directly under the vertical ice wall looming menacingly above. . .'[21]

Carrying packs weighing over 30 kilograms, the two men began running and fast walking along the front of the glacier. Halfway across they went down to their knees in soft wet sand. In Carr's words: 'As though there were some malignant force guiding it all. . .a wave leapt up in the air and ran straight in. Now that water's very cold, and it just engulfed us.'[22] Driven back against the ice cliff, the two men drove their ice axes in and held on as the next wave surged over them. 'This is the end', thought Brown. But the waves held back, and they scrambled to safety, 'lucky to be alive'.

On 26 May, impatient to get away from base camp for an excursion, dog handler Alastair 'Jock' Forbes, radio operator Dick Hoseason and weather observer Laurie Atkinson decided to walk to Saddle Point to conduct another seal count, over the same route Carr and Brown had pioneered. The three men had not done a great deal of field work, and Brown and two companions walked with them for part of the way. After seeing them over the worst of the Baudissen Glacier, Brown and his party decided to turn back. Brown recalled saying to Forbes:

'Don't be tempted to cross beneath the ice cliffs—no matter how easy it looks.' Forbes said he understood and gave me a look which made me feel rather pompous.[23]

Next morning Brown was about to enter the mess hut for morning tea when the door burst open and medical officer Jeff Faulkner rushed out 'with his face as white as a sheet':

> 'Lorry's back!' was all he could utter. 'Lorry's back. . .Dick's dead for certain!'
>
> I dashed into the kitchen where Teyssier and Ingall were supporting Lorry Atkinson on a chair. He was almost unconscious; his hands puffed and white—utterly lifeless. His eyes were bloodshot, and his bare dishevelled head dripping wet like the rest of his body. Teyssier was trying to pour some hot soup down his throat, and the scalding liquid burnt his lips—jarring him back into consciousness.
>
> He looked at us vaguely and said, 'I'm damned sorry. . .I'm damned sorry. . .Dick's drowned under the Little Challenger Glacier. . .Jock set off last night. . .to cross the Baudissen. . .Haven't you seen him'? Then he lapsed into incoherency.[24]

Despite being warned, the three men had tried to take the short cut under the ice cliff, and been overwhelmed by the surf. Like Carr and Brown earlier, they had managed to hold on to the ice cliff with their ice axes, but a second wave caught Forbes off balance. When he recovered, Atkinson described what happened:

> Hoseason and I grabbed hold of him [Forbes] and held on until the water receded. . .then we threw away our packs and ice-axes and ran for it—trying to reach the safety of the next moraine before any more rollers broke. . .But another one smashed clean over our heads. We held on to each other, but poor Hoseason was dragged away by the undertow—we were powerless to stop him. He shouted to us to save him, then I saw him disappear and we didn't see him again. . .
>
> Forbes and I managed to hold on, then we dashed towards the moraine. Our clothes were soon frozen solid; I was terribly cold and frightened. We couldn't believe that Hoseason had really 'bought it' and we expected him to show up at any moment. Everything was lost when we threw away our packs. Hoseason carried the emergency chocolate inside his windproof.[25]

Atkinson collapsed and Forbes started over the Baudissen Glacier to get help. Atkinson came to and dozed through the night. He decided

DIGGING ALASTAIR FORBES'
GRAVE AT ATLAS COVE,
HEARD ISLAND, 1952.
(A CAMPBELL-DRURY)

to return along the beach, risking the waves, knowing that he had no strength to climb over the glaciers.

Forbes's body was recovered from the Baudissen Glacier on 28 May but Hoseason's remains were not found until spring. Forbes was buried near the station on 31 May. OIC Les Gibbney noted in his log that there was no prayer book 'so we are forced to make up a burial service. Perriman did this'.[26]

The twelve remaining Heard Island expeditioners gathered in the mess-room for a prayer, and then carried the coffin to the prepared burial mound. Brown:

As we paid our last respects, the wind screamed through wireless masts, and two sledge dogs broke out into a mournful chorus, accentuating the scene of utter desolation. There could never have been a more fitting 'Last Post'.[27]

ESTABLISHMENT AND EXPLORATION 1954–1966

SEVEN

BREAKING THE ICE

By 1953 there was still no Australian presence on continental Antarctica and the lack of a suitable ice-strengthened ship remained an insuperable obstacle to ANARE's main aims in the Antarctic. During the summer of 1949–50, Phil Law gained valuable Antarctic experience when he travelled as an Australian observer on the Norwegian British Swedish Expedition (NBSE) to Queen Maud Land on a 700-tonne diesel-powered ship *Norsel*, sailing from Cape Town. *Norsel* had only fair icebreaking capacity but managed to deliver the wintering party to the Maudheim base through the pack ice. Law was particularly impressed by the use of Auster aircraft carried on board to assist navigation through the ice, and carry out general reconnaissance and mapping work, using floats and skis. And he always had his future plans in mind:

> They had to leave one of their major huts behind, and I persuaded them to sell it to me so I could put it in store [and] if we ever went to Antarctica we would have a major hut. [Also] I got them to promise that they'd sell me the two Austers.

As well, he acquired first-hand experience of the stores and equipment needed and an understanding of the conditions to expect when setting up a base in Antarctica. From Cape Town he travelled on to Europe to visit people and institutions involved with polar work. He was particularly interested in a warm cotton windproof cloth called 'Ventile' manufactured in England, ideal for polar tents and clothing. From the French polar explorer Paul-Emile Victor he learned about the availability of Weasels, the over-snow tracked vehicles he had seen used on the NBS

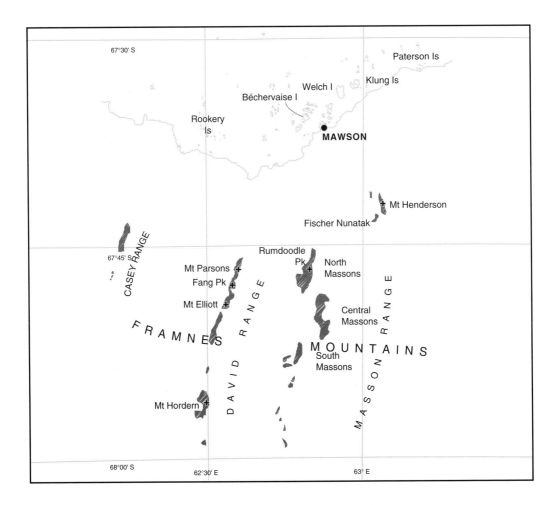

MAWSON STATION ON
MAWSON COAST

expedition, and investigated dog and cargo sledges used by the Norwegians. He also visited shipbuilders in Glasgow, studied plans of ships, and wrote specifications for Australia's requirements. Buoyed by the whole experience, he wrote to his wife Nel, 'I am more and more certain that the thing to do is to BUILD A NEW SHIP! And I think I can sell the idea to the Govt!'[1]

Law's advocacy was effective. On 13 July 1950 Cabinet decided that in order to establish and maintain a permanent Antarctic station, 'a new ship should be built for this purpose'.[2] But the availability of icegoing vessel *Kista Dan*, just built by Danish shipping firm J Lauritzen Lines, put the Australian project on indefinite hold. Law was alerted to the existence of *Kista Dan* by Westralian Farmers Transport Ltd, the Antarctic Division's shipping agents in London who had previously arranged the charter of the Norwegian sealer *Tottan*.

Why was a company called Westralian Farmers Transport in London assisting the Antarctic Division in Melbourne in the chartering of Antarctic ships from Denmark?

Westralian Farmers Transport (Wesfarmers) was one of the few companies that represented Australian interests on the Baltic Exchange in London—essentially the centre of world shipping. It has handled the Antarctic Division's foreign charters for almost half a century.

Westralian Farmers began in the 1920s, in the depression years when farmers realised they would do better as a cooperative. John O'Rourke was managing director of Westralian Farmers Transport from 1960 to 1987:

John Thompson was the general manager of Westralian Farmers from the late twenties through to 1957. In the early days there wasn't a great deal known about shipping in Australia. We relied on England for everything—the mother country—and companies such as the P&O ran regular shipping lines here, and you had to dance to their tune. They had the ships, we had the produce; we had no ships, they had the bulk of the market. And there was a time when the farmers were suffering dreadfully. John Thompson went to the overseas shipping representatives and said: 'Look, unless you do something to stabilise wool and wheat freight rates, we're going to have to do something for ourselves'.

They looked at him rather benignly and said, 'Well, precisely what did you have in mind?' So he said, 'We'd have to charter ships of our own'. And, of course, they all thought this was rather a joke—an Australian farming cooperative chartering ships. What would they know about shipping? But that's precisely what he did when they wouldn't listen to him.

One of his first ventures was with refrigerated ships. He went out and chartered three Swedish refrigerated ships to carry the Western Australian apple crop to Europe. The ships were superb; they were new, they were fast, they were well-controlled. So Wesfarmers got its fruit to market quicker, cheaper, and got the best of the market. This was an enormous shock for the established shipping lines out here and they really sat up and started to take notice of this little company, Westralian Farmers Transport.

Kista Dan was built for voyages between Denmark and Greenland in the Northern Hemisphere summer. Despite the Australian ship on the drawing board, Law could see advantages in chartering a good new ice ship with an experienced ice captain and crew. He was also relieved he would not have to work in Antarctic conditions with an Australian crew who were likely to want to work to rule, whereas he knew a foreign crew would labour round the clock, if necessary, to take full advantage of short periods of good weather. (He had experienced problems with an Australian crew on the ship *River Fitzroy* at Macquarie Island in 1951.) Law went to the Government about *Kista Dan*:

I said, 'Look, I can get *Kista Dan*. We can now go down and set up an Antarctic base on the continent, I can arrange it so it won't cost you much, we'll only put ten men ashore. . .and if you like I'll close down Heard Island Station so that the money can be applied to the Antarctic continent. Further, I'm prepared to pick up the radio sets and the diesel engines and the tractor and various things from Heard Island, and one or two of the huts. . .so it really won't cost you much at all and then we'll get a foothold on the Antarctic.'

Law had little difficulty in carrying the Executive Planning Committee—and Sir Douglas Mawson—with him in abandoning plans to build an Australian ship, and deciding to get down to Antarctica quickly with the chartered *Kista Dan*.[3] The sweetener for the Government was to trade off the station at Heard Island for the first continental base—saving an estimated £40 000 [$80 000]. Keeping both sub-Antarctic stations open and getting to the continent would have cost an extra £100 000 [$200 000].[4] There was opposition from the Meteorological Branch who argued that the whole system of weather forecasting in Australia's southern States had been profoundly influenced by the results from Heard Island.[5] The reports from Macquarie Island, to the east, were of more benefit to New Zealand than to Australia.

This objection was not significant and Law's Antarctic plans were enthusiastically embraced by the Minister for External Affairs, Richard Casey. During 1951 Casey had succeeded Percy Spender as Minister. Antarctica was, according to Casey's biographer W J Hudson, one of his lifelong interests. He was involved with Antarctic work when he was stationed in London during the late 1920s as Australian political liaison officer when Mawson's BANZARE voyages were being planned. In 1937, when he was Australian Treasurer, Casey was chairman of a polar committee that recommended to the Imperial Conference in London that the dominions cooperate in setting up one or more permanent meteorological stations in the Antarctic.[6] A qualified pilot, he keenly supported Law's use of aircraft in the Antarctic and because he had an office in Melbourne, Law saw him on a regular basis.[7]

On 21 March 1953 it was announced in the press that the Government had decided to send an expedition to the Antarctic continent during the next summer to set up a scientific research station in the Australian Antarctic Territory.[8] Casey outlined the plans and ended: 'Today the Antarctic is a challenge—which cannot be ignored—to Australian courage and imagination, and the proposed expedition shows that we will grasp our opportunity.'[9]

The Government's plans were also endorsed by the leader of the Opposition, Dr H V Evatt, who said 'this territory is of great strategic importance in the confused state of the world today'.[10] 'Such unanimity of political opinion', the Antarctic historian Robert Swan commented, 'boded well for the future of Australian Antarctic activity'.[11] The Cabinet submission of 6 February 1953 pointed out: 'It would demonstrate that Australian statements during the last five years concerning our intentions in Antarctica were not hollow boasts. . .', and concluded: 'Australia would be in a good position to build up the station to a full-scale scientific observatory in time to participate in the International Polar Year 1956–57.'[12]

There was some argument in the Executive Planning Committee of ANARE about where the new station should be. Sir Douglas Mawson had a nostalgic attachment to King George V Land and the region around Cape Freshfield, near the site of the base he occupied during the 1911–14 Australasian Antarctic Expedition. There was unfinished exploration work to be done there and he believed this location, near the Magnetic Pole, would be interesting to the physicists.

Law argued in favour of Mac. Robertson Land, to the west. Mawson's BANZARE voyage had sighted Mac. Robertson Land and Kemp Land from the sea and landings had been made at the Scullin Monolith, Proclamation Island and Cape Bruce. The Norwegians had been active in the region, and the United States had conducted aerial mapping during 'Operation Highjump' in the summer of 1946–47:

> If Australia's claim to its Antarctic territory were to stand up, the original reconnaissances of Mawson's BANZAR Expedition would have to be consolidated. Sightings of Mac. Robertson Land from the sea had shown interesting mountain ranges inland, contrasting with the featureless ice plateau of George V Land, while comparatively close was Prydz Bay and the fascinating ice-free rock of the Vestfold Hills.
>
> . . . I and my fellow physicists of the ANARE. . .considered that the Auroral Zone (an annular belt of maximum auroral display surrounding the Magnetic Pole at a radial distance of roughly 22½ degrees) was a more interesting phenomenon than the Magnetic Pole itself, and this zone intersected the coast of Mac. Robertson Land.[13]

Once the Planning Committee decided on Mac. Robertson Land, Sir Douglas Mawson supported the collective decision. Law managed to get sets of the 'Operation Highjump' photographs of the coast of Mac. Robertson Land through the Australian Embassy in Washington, and with the aid of a magnifying glass was able to observe possible sites for an Australian base: 'Mawson would often come to my home in Melbourne

THIS PHOTOGRAPH OF THE
COAST OF MAC. ROBERTSON
LAND, TAKEN BY THE US
NAVY DURING OPERATION
HIGHJUMP IN THE SUMMER OF
1946–47, WAS INVALUABLE IN
HELPING TO LOCATE THE SITE
OF MAWSON STATION.
HORSESHOE HARBOUR CAN
BE SEEN IN THE ROCKY
OUTCROP IN THE TOP THIRD
OF THIS PHOTOGRAPH.
(US NAVY)

and we'd have dinner together. One of my wife's keenest remembrances of Mawson is he and I kneeling down on the floor in our flat in South Yarra peering at photographs and maps of Antarctica on the floor.'

Outcrops of rock were of particular interest, because if an Antarctic station were built on ice, it would inevitably be pushed out to sea and float away on an iceberg. From the American aerial photographs Law picked out a little outcrop of rock in the shape of a horseshoe on the coast of Mac. Robertson Land which looked as though it might be a natural harbour, if the water proved to be deep enough. It was decided to make that the first choice for a landing.

Kista Dan arrived in Melbourne from Europe on Friday 11 December 1953. Law watched her berth at No. 3 North Wharf just south of Spencer St Railway Station. He was impressed with the look of her, mindful of the polar ships he had been used to like *Wyatt Earp* and *Tottan*. Built in 1952 in Lauritzen's shipyards at Aalborg, Denmark, *Kista Dan* was 65 metres long and 11.2 metres broad with a gross tonnage of 1250 tonnes. Her diesel engines produced a maximum of 1560 horsepower. She was strengthened for navigation in ice to the standard of Finnish Ice Class 1A, had a range of 14 500 nautical miles, and accommodation for 24 passengers—twelve of whom were in the forecastle.

For cargo the ship had two large holds and a heavy lift derrick and the larger hold could accommodate one of the two Auster aircraft. *Kista Dan* had already been to the Antarctic and the Weddell Sea the previous summer (making a feature film starring Alan Ladd called *Hell Below Zero*) and Law was anxious to meet the captain, Hans Christian Petersen:

> He was a large man, with a round face and blue eyes. He laughed easily and was a good raconteur. We were to find that he was an immensely competent person. He was highly intelligent and prided himself on his technical ability. He had come up the hard way and had seized every possible opportunity to learn how to operate and repair the equipment with which he had to deal—engines, winches, motor boats, radios, echo sounders, gyro compasses and so on.[14]

He and Law were both strong-willed people, and were about to test each other's authority—Law as the voyage leader, and Petersen as the ship's master. The complex details of a ship's charter were new territory for Law and the Antarctic Division:

> I rapidly became familiar with the intricacies of chartering ships, in which meticulous attention to detail and the instincts of a bush lawyer were required. I conducted long negotiations with Knud Lauritzen, the head of J Lauritzen Lines, through our agents, Westralian Farmers Transport Ltd, in London. Up to three or four months would be involved each time a new charter was arranged, that being every year at first and, later, every two or three years.
>
> We stood in a weak bargaining position, for the Lauritzen ships were the only ones in the world that really suited our purposes, and Lauritzens knew it. Nevertheless, by hard argument we were able to wring from the company a number of important concessions. I gained the impression that Knud Lauritzen thoroughly enjoyed the negotiations, treating them like a kind of chess game, which added savour to an otherwise pretty routine set of operations.[15]

Mindful of the appalling food he had endured with the Norwegians on *Norsel* during the NBS Expedition, Law included a clause specifying that the Australians would not only supply their own food on board, but their own cook. His other main aim, which he endeavoured to spell out in an additional clause to the charter, was 'to have a ship and captain completely under my control'.[16] This was wishful thinking.

Kista Dan was to resupply Macquarie Island before heading to Heard Island and then the coast of Mac. Robertson Land on the western side of the AAT. The Macquarie cargo included 24 Border Leicester sheep, and the army amphibious DUKWs—now back in action with a ship large enough to carry them. This operation was completed efficiently in three weeks during December 1953. After some hectic loading of supplies in Melbourne, *Kista Dan* sailed for the Antarctic on 4 January 1954—four

THE HISTORIC 1954
DEPARTURE FROM
MELBOURNE. FROM LEFT:
PHIL LAW, MRS CASEY,
RICHARD CASEY (MINISTER
FOR EXTERNAL AFFAIRS),
DICK THOMPSON (BACK TO
CAMERA), LEM MACEY,
FLIGHT LIEUTENANT DOUG
LECKIE, FLIGHT SERGEANT
RAY SEAVER.
(A CAMPBELL-DRURY)

days earlier than planned—farewelled by Minister for External Affairs Richard Casey, Mrs Casey and an enthusiastic crowd of 300, including press, radio reporters and photographers. The Point Lonsdale lighthouse flashed a good luck message as they headed out through the Rip.[17]

Nine Australians had been selected to pioneer the first Australian Antarctic station. The OIC was Robert Dovers, a surveyor who had been a member of the first Heard Island party in 1948, had spent six months on Macquarie Island and a further twelve months in Adélie Land as an observer with the third French Antarctic Expedition. Lem Macey, the Division's technical officer, had been a member of the same Heard and Macquarie parties. John Russell, an engineer, had also been on both sub-Antarctic stations. Robert Dingle, a weather observer, had been on Heard Island, and William Storer, a radio operator, had been on Macquarie Island. Robert Summers, the medical officer, was a University Ski Club member; Bruce Stinear, a geologist, had experience in the New Zealand Alps; Jeff Gleadell, the cook, born at South Georgia, had accompanied Sir Hubert Wilkins' expedition to Graham Land; and William Harvey, a carpenter, was from Scotland. The tenth member of the party, a French observer and dog handler, Georges Schwartz, would join *Kista Dan* at the Kerguelen Islands. Schwartz was an experienced polar traveller with experience in Greenland and Adélie Land.[18]

The rendezvous at Kerguelen was necessary for another reason. There was simply too much cargo for *Kista Dan* to carry. After the Heard Island resupply, the ship would load water, petrol and diesel fuel taken to Kerguelen earlier by the French. A second French observer, André Migot, would also join *Kista Dan* for the round trip to write a book on the expedition.

As well as stores and food for a possible two years' stay on the continent, *Kista Dan* also had on board the two Auster aircraft (with skis and floats) and the prefabricated wooden hut obtained from the NBSE, other prefabricated huts, three over-snow Weasel vehicles, and 30 huskies picked up from Heard Island. The RAAF had taken responsibility for the operation

KISTA DAN HEADING SOUTH
IN ROUGH SEAS, 1954.
(COURTESY P LAW)

of the Auster aircraft and provided two pilots and two mechanics. They were under the command of the principal pilot, Flight Lieutenant Douglas Leckie. The aircraft and the RAAF personnel were to return to Australia on *Kista Dan* at the end of the summer.

As *Kista Dan* headed south, Law knew that he had guaranteed funding for only one year, but was optimistic: 'I hoped that, with a toehold on the Antarctic continent, I could persuade the government to expand the bridgehead in 1955, and gradually build up a full program of research.'[19]

With such a small party and a new station to establish, Law was aware that building and establishing the station would take priority. There would not be much time for science in the first year:

> The scientific work was limited to survey and cartography, geology, meteorology and biology. It was not possible to include programs of observatory work in geomagnetism, seismology and cosmic rays similar to those at our island stations, although Stinear was briefed to carry out spot observations on the earth's magnetic field and gravity at points visited by field parties.[20]

Kista Dan reached Heard Island on 9 January and, despite the usually atrocious local weather, managed to change over the 1953 and 1954 parties, unload stores and take on board thirty vociferously quarrelling huskies—all in three days. Unfortunately the weather broke before a Caterpillar tractor could be loaded and it was left behind.

Shortly before midnight on Friday 22 January the French lit beacons to guide *Kista Dan* into their station at Port aux Français, Kerguelen Islands. There, over the next five days, also in foul weather, the hospitable French assisted in the loading of fuel, water, and a third Weasel. Law wrote in his voyage report:

> Not only did the French bring all our supplies, including fuel, freight free from France, but they completely disrupted their normal routine of work at Kerguelen to provide men and equipment to load these supplies and water into the *Kista Dan* even though this involved working on a Sunday. No charge was made for any of these services. Finally, as our aviation fuel was of the wrong octane value, the French gave us eight 44-gallon [200.2 litres] drums of 100 octane aviation spirit. I cannot speak too highly of their friendliness, cooperation and generosity.[21]

It was a good start, and typical of the unique international fraternity in Antarctica to be experienced in the decades ahead.

On 27 January 1954 *Kista Dan* turned her specially strengthened steel bows towards an unknown destination on the coast of Mac. Robertson Land. The first ice—a small bergy bit—was sighted on 30 January, followed by icebergs and Antarctic petrels. A sense of excitement was palpable. The French observer André Migot was even a little disappointed that they had arrived at latitude 64° south so soon:

> If we kept up the same speed we should be in sight of Mac. Robertson Land the next day and ready to land. . .I had been looking forward so much to the prospect of steaming through the pack ice, to the splendid scenery, to the difficulty and excitement of it all, and to the adventure of a polar expedition that I should be cheated if we arrived too quickly and met no obstacles on the way.[22]

The expression 'A-Factor' (the Antarctic Factor—meaning unexpected difficulties or disasters) had not then been coined, but M. Migot was about to experience it. That evening they encountered scattered pack ice which became gradually more thick. Already it was clear that *Kista Dan* was a vast improvement on ships like the wooden *Wyatt Earp*, which Law once said had the icebreaking capabilities 'of a gnat'. Cameras clicked as the ANARE men delighted in their first experience of steaming through pack ice, although the more experienced Law cautioned them not to waste too much film as better opportunities lay ahead. André Migot joined in the general delight of the new ship's performance:

The *Kista Dan*'s bow was specially shaped in a gentle curve just above the water. When she hit small floes or lumps of iceberg she merely brushed them aside without trouble, but when she came upon a more solid mass of ice, she slid up on to it like a sledge. When the ice was thin she broke it with her own weight, but when it was too thick the ship was jammed in the ice and could go no further. So she went astern and charged the ice again, gradually driving a sort of furrow across the floe, until finally it gave way and broke in pieces, letting the ship subside heavily into her natural element.[23]

THE ABILITY TO OPERATE AUSTER AIRCRAFT ON FLOATS FROM *KISTA DAN* WAS CRITICAL TO THE SUCCESS OF THE 1954 ANTARCTIC EXPEDITION.
(AAD ARCHIVES)

The next morning, 2 February, Captain Petersen called to Law from *Kista Dan*'s protected crow's nest control platform above the bridge that he could see some islands ahead. Law joined him, and immediately recognised the Henderson, Masson, David and Casey Ranges he had studied in the 'Operation Highjump' photographs in Melbourne. By 0745 he could see 'the cream slopes of the Antarctic plateau'. A long line of grounded icebergs was a spectacular feature, flanking a deeper channel that led towards the coast—later familiar to visitors to Mawson Station as Iceberg Alley. At midday the ship entered a long open lead and Law suggested to Captain Petersen that the Auster seaplane carried on deck be used for reconnaissance:

> He was most reluctant to comply. I think he probably would have pre-ferred to find his way in without aerial assistance, but I insisted and he finally agreed. (Later the captain became an enthusiastic supporter of aerial reconnaissance as an aid to ship navigation.)[24]

The Auster carried on the deck could be quickly lowered over the side. With Law as his passenger pilot Doug Leckie climbed to 1000 metres. There, Law's earlier optimism about reaching the coast was tempered by the reality of what he saw. Only about three nautical miles of open water lay ahead. Then an unbroken stretch of winter 'fast' ice continued for some sixteen miles [25.6 kilometres] to the shore. As they approached the coast Law noted that the horseshoe rock formation he had been aiming for seemed ideal for the proposed station—if the ship could get in. After a flight lasting 1 hour and 35 minutes, with Law furiously photographing, sketching and note taking, they returned to the ship for a safe landing on the water. Before the end of that day Law asked the captain to experiment by breaking some of the unbroken fast ice he had seen from the air:

> The captain tried charging it with the ship and found he would break through it for a distance of about half a ship's length on each charge, and this gave me some comfort. Although it would be a slow business, we would eventually break through to the coast.[25]

On the morning of 3 February ice-breaking began in earnest, and *Kista Dan* began to forge a narrow channel towards the coast. As the ship progressed, Law described a remarkable sight he was not to see again in the rest of his Antarctic experience, as hundreds of Adélie penguins approached over the ice, and dived into the channel made by the ship:

> We were later to discover that the fast ice had remained unbroken much later in the season than usual, and that instead of being able to feed in open water close to their island rookeries, the penguins were forced to march about 16 miles [25.6 km] to reach the sea. Back at their rookeries their chicks were starving to death. . .
>
> The open wake gave the penguins close access to food and the churning up of the ice and water by the propeller had provided planktonic material for them to eat. Whatever the reason myriads of the creatures were porpoising in the wake of the ship. The limited area of water was entirely black and boiling with them. . .
>
> Their method of leaving the water was itself intriguing. With a last powerful sweep of their flippers they would propel themselves out of the water and land on their feet, vertical, on the ice. They were popping out like champagne corks, in scores, along the edge of the channel.[26]

Had the ice broken out, as it normally did, in late January (the conventional wisdom is around Australia Day, 26 January), *Kista Dan* could have sailed straight in to what would be known as Horseshoe Harbour. In 1954 the 'A-Factor' was well in evidence.

As *Kista Dan* was now well and truly in the fast ice, Law asked the RAAF crew to fit skis to Auster 201 and pilot Ray Seaver flew Bob Dovers in to have a look at the coast. The Auster 'behaved splendidly' on skis.[27]

On 4 February Leckie flew Dovers in to Horseshoe Harbour for the first landing on the polished blue sea ice. They broke a tail wheel in the process. On the next flight, Captain Petersen squeezed his bulk into the cockpit of the Auster to inspect the ice ahead. He estimated it would take him a week to break in, and he had the fuel to do it.[28]

Law conferred with Dick Thompson and Dovers about the best way to use that time. They agreed to push on with the program of aerial mapping of the coast and nearby mountains, but to unload stores onto the ice to cargo sledges and use Weasels No. 1 and No. 3 to transport them to Horseshoe Harbour over the fast ice. They would also establish a shore party and begin erecting the first hut. The huskies would be camped on the ice, as they were bored with life on deck.

The next day Law flew in for his first landing at Horseshoe Harbour to inspect the proposed site for the station from the ground:

> We landed just outside Horseshoe Harbour, on this polished blue sea ice, and there was an iceberg about half a mile [0.8 kilometres] ahead, in the line of direction of our landing. We didn't take much notice because we [thought we'd] stop in a couple of hundred yards [182 metres]. But skis on polished blue ice had practically no friction at all and we went careering on and on. We were showing no signs of slowing down and this iceberg was looming closer and closer. When we were about a hundred yards [91 metres] off it, Leckie put the plane into what he called 'a ground loop'. He just spun it and it went forward in a series of spinning circles. And the friction of the skis side on was much greater than the friction when they're pointing straight ahead. We finished up about thirty [27.3 metres] or forty yards [36.4 metres] off the vertical face of this iceberg!

The Auster was also used to direct the ground party, led by Dovers, to the best route over the ice. He was accompanied by Macey, Russell, Schwartz and Harvey. Some of the cracks in the ice were so wide they had to be bridged with timbers carried for the purpose. Schwartz was supposed to have taken the 30 huskies with the shore party, but for some reason had not done so. When Law asked Captain Petersen to take them on board again there was a heated altercation:

> He complained about the time wasted unloading which prevented him going ahead, although I had discussed the whole plan with him the night before. . .As he had just succeeded in jamming the ship, wasting an hour and necessitating work alongside with crowbars as well as winching on ice anchors in order to free her, his bad temper was understandable. He said he was not going to unload and load things again, but when I

reminded him sharply that it was my place to decide when and where cargo was to be unloaded he calmed down. He had on a number of occasions used obstructive tactics, but I had refused to be provoked and this was the first time our relations had deteriorated into a verbal exchange.[29]

THE EMERGENCY CAMP ON DOVERS' ISLAND, MARCH 1954, WITH LEM MACEY IN FOREGROUND.
(P LAW)

The second aircraft, Auster 200, was brought out of the hold and assembled for its first flight that afternoon but, with no space for it on board ship, Seaver and Leckie flew in tandem to an offshore island near Horseshoe Harbour where it was tied down on the ice. Auster 201 was hoisted back on *Kista Dan.* On the 2300 radio schedule with Dovers, Law was dismayed to hear that No. 1 Weasel had broken through the ice about half a mile from its destination, but fortunately had floated. Dovers asked for a 2-tonne chain block to be flown to him to help salvage the half-floating Weasel.[30]

The next day, 6 February, the weather deteriorated and flying was out of the question. Dovers radioed that he had hauled up his caravans on to an island 'a mile north of the horseshoe' and that men and vehicles were safe. No. 1 Weasel had now frozen into the sea and was secure. By nightfall it was blowing a 60-knot blizzard. Law was mindful of Auster 200, unattended and tied down on the sea ice.

French observer André Migot's earlier fears that he would feel cheated of a polar adventure if they got to their destination too quickly were now assuaged. Early on the morning of 7 February Law was wakened by a sailor who said: 'The ice is breaking up'. The storm had caused the fast ice to move:

> Ahead on the port side cracks were appearing in the fast ice, running out as far as the eye could see. A report like a shotgun would be followed by the appearance of a great crack. . .The ship began to shudder as the pressure built up around her. The question in our minds was, 'What will break first, the ice or the ship's hull'? I peered over the side and was somewhat reassured to see slabs of ice cracking, sliding up the steel hull and collapsing back in great heaps of jagged pieces.[31]

Even at that stage, Law saw possible benefits from the ice break-up. If they could sail straight into Horseshoe Harbour it would even balance the probable loss of the Weasels. At 0700 the Captain requested all expeditioners on deck as he was worried about the safety of the ship. Law:

> The shuddering of the ship increased, as did the noises of groaning, creaking and grating accompanying the movements of the ice. At this stage the ice cracking against the sides of the ship had piled up so high that pieces were falling over the bulwarks onto the foredeck. The ship was slowly rising and listing as the pressure forced ice down under her keel. Pressure ridges of rafted ice ran out for hundreds of yards to starboard from our bows and to port from our stern.[32]

At 0800 the movement suddenly ceased, and one of the major hazards to an Antarctic ship, sideways pressure by moving ice, had been overcome. 'Thank God for a welded steel ship with close frames and thick plates', commented Law. They were effectively stranded, however, until the ship could be extricated. How long this would take was unknown; it could be a week. Law hoped the islands off Horseshoe Harbour would hold the fast ice in place long enough to rescue the Dovers party and Auster 200. At 1600 hours a faint Morse message came through from Dovers to say that they and the Auster were safe.

KISTA DAN LISTING HEAVILY DUE TO THE PRESSURE OF THE PACK ICE FOLLOWING A VIOLENT STORM NEAR THE COAST OF MAC. ROBERTSON LAND, FEBRUARY 1954. (J BROOKS)

Fine weather the next day enabled Leckie to fly to the island where the field party had taken refuge, and bring back Dovers to give his report. Dovers told Law he thought the winds at Horseshoe Harbour would be too strong for a permanent camp and was pessimistic about even being able to erect the six huts brought from Australia. He suggested instead that he haul all the stores on to his island, stay there for a year with a couple of huts and explore the coast the following year to find a better site for a permanent station. Law:

> Then there was an interesting psychological problem. The morale was very low—this storm really knocked the stuffing out of these boys who were camped on that island and they were very timid and worried. I just had to bulldoze them through and say, 'No, I'm going to get ashore at

Horseshoe Harbour. That's the spot, and we'll bend every effort to do it. There's no use being on an island. We want to get onto the continent so we can go inland. If you're on an island all through the summer months you've got water around you and you can't get ashore.'

I said I would not agree to the island proposal under any circumstances and asked him to move everything at the earliest opportunity to Horseshoe Harbour. He agreed to do this after he had rescued Weasel No. 3.

KISTA DAN IN HORSESHOE HARBOUR, THE ONLY NATURAL HARBOUR ON THE ENTIRE COAST OF GREATER ANTARCTICA, FEBRUARY 1954.
(P LAW)

It took two days to dig out *Kista Dan* from the rafted slabs of ice that had nearly crushed her. A combination of crowbars, shovels and dynamite—exploded as a last resort under the ship's hull—finally broke her free. Good weather and clear sunlight lifted the morale of those who had been stuck on the off-shore island, and both No. 1 and No. 3 Weasels and their sledges and caravans made it across the sea ice to Horseshoe Harbour, where work was begun on erecting the first hut at the selected site.

Late on Thursday 11 February *Kista Dan* nosed her way between the encircling arms of the 'horseshoe', into the harbour still covered with fast ice. This was a critical moment. It was thought there might be a reef across the entrance that would stop a ship getting in. The depth was an adequate 15 metres. Inside the harbour the bottom fell away to a surprising 90 metres. The Auster aircraft had been invaluable in charting a course through the islands that masked the entrance to the harbour. Law felt the expedition had much to be thankful for:

> Captain Petersen had done a splendid job of ice navigation and had managed to extricate the ship from its desperate situation in the pressure ice. Doug Leckie and the RAAF Flight had provided us with invaluable reconnaissances, without which the whole approach exercise would have been more difficult and time consuming.[33]

EIGHT

EARLY EXPLORATION

ista Dan had arrived in the only natural harbour on the whole coastline of Greater Antarctica. In later years visiting ships would lay out mooring lines directly to the encircling West Arm of the 'horseshoe'—tying at first to large rocks, later to bollards sunk into the solid rock, thereby being able to ride out the most severe Antarctic blizzards and cyclones. Phil Law later described it as 'one of the best sites for 4000 miles' [6400 km]:

> Not only is there this lovely enclosed harbour where a ship can just run cables out fore and aft to the shore and hold itself, but it's an amphitheatre. The arms of the horseshoe are elevated, then it comes around like the curve of a horseshoe—saucer shaped—sloping up to a high ridge at the back. In this hollow we built the station so it got semi-protection from the ridge at the back. . .and it was on hard polished rock, no sand, no earth, just hard granitic type rock, polished by glacier action thousands of millions of years ago. And there was good access [to the interior]. The permanent ice cap started just behind the station. [When] you got onto that you'd go straight inland with a lot of crevassing for the first ten miles because of the rising slope, but once you were ten or fifteen miles in, the crevasses stopped and away you went. It was a perfect choice for a station.

Behind Horseshoe Harbour the peaks of the Framnes Mountains broke clear of the ice cap, thrusting through like the backs of great dinosaurs, curving down towards the coast.

No one was admiring the view early on the morning of Friday 12 February 1954. Law was woken by Dick Thompson at 0415 with the unwelcome news that the two Auster aircraft secured on the top of No. 2 hatch were apparently damaged beyond repair. Overnight the wind had built up to over 70 knots and, with *Kista Dan* broadside to the wind, the aircraft were exposed to its full fury. This had not been the case when Law retired to his cabin the previous evening:

> The captain didn't want to leave the ship pointing into the wind [towards the land]. He wanted to turn the ship and face out the other way because he was frightened that the ice might freeze up and he'd like to be pointing out towards the entrance so that he could get out—rather than have to back and turn. That worried me because I would have preferred him to just stay where he was. He'd got into a very good position. I didn't think the ice would cause trouble for the next month. Anyway he charged around a bit and broke up the fast ice in the harbour and then he tried to turn his bows to face out, and he only managed to get it half way around and had to give up. And that left us with two aircraft on board. . .with the wind blowing side on and under the wing of the aircraft, so overnight both were very severely damaged. And it was all because the captain wouldn't leave the ship the way I wanted him to leave it. So I was furious.

Relations between voyage leader Law and Captain Petersen had been patchy at best. Now they were icy. Both men had reason to regret the loss of the aircraft. For Law it meant the end of hoped-for coastal exploration and photographic surveys. Petersen, now a convert to aerial reconnaissance, was worried about navigating his way back to the open sea once the new station had been established.

The wind had picked up Auster 201 and dumped it on Auster 200. At first sight it seemed both aircraft were damaged beyond repair. All starboard mainplanes, stabilisers and rudders were damaged. Flight engineer Frank Morgan inspected the situation and said 'Well, that's it'. Law glumly recorded in his diary: 'Fridays are not our lucky days', cancelled all activity and went to his cabin to sleep until 11 am.[1]

When he woke Law had a flash of inspiration, and asked the RAAF team whether they thought they could cannibalise the two Austers and make one serviceable aircraft out of the two. This was a tall order. The aircraft were second hand when Law obtained them from the NBS expedition in 1951. Leckie thought it would have been more economical to buy new aircraft, because they were badly rusted and corroded when they came to Australia:

> I think the Australian Government thought they were getting something on the cheap, and they certainly weren't because they had to be rehabilitated at Richmond [NSW] and it was a pretty big job.

Bob Dovers' penchant for breaking through sea ice with Weasels achieved legendary status before *Kista Dan* left Horseshoe Harbour in 1954. A song, composed at the time by Bill Harvey, and sung to the tune of 'My Bonnie lies over the ocean' was enthusiastically performed by expeditioners and crew:

Bob Dovers has ditched his new Weasel
Bob Dovers has done it again;
Three times he has been in the ocean,
It's odds on he'll be there again!

CHORUS
Chain blocks, chain blocks,
Oh bring back my Weasel to me, to me
Chain blocks, chain blocks,
Oh bring back my Weasel to me.

Bob Dovers he's crash hot on sea ice,
He's good on the land and the sea.
He's what you might call the new version,
Of the good Lord on Lake Galilee.

'BOB DOVERS HAS DONE IT AGAIN.' RESCUING THE FRENCH WEASEL WHICH BROKE THROUGH THE SEA ICE DURING UNLOADING OPERATIONS IN HORSESHOE HARBOUR, FEBRUARY 1954.
(P LAW)

(Chain blocks are portable winches used for field emergencies. This song, and variations, has been popular at ANARE reunions ever since.)[2]

Fortunately Frank Morgan was the man who had made the Austers airworthy at Richmond and he and his RAAF colleague Sergeant Ken Duffell began to reassess the wreckage to see what could be done. Meanwhile, some progress towards unloading was made when Dovers came out and took the huskies ashore, although on his second trip from the ship to shore at about 2300 hours he broke through the ice again with his Weasel—but again it floated. As he was alone at the time Law made a rule that no Weasel was to run after 2000 hours.[3]

Before retiring that evening, Law sent off telegrams to Minister for External Affairs Casey, HRH Queen Elizabeth (still on tour in Australia) and Sir Douglas Mawson announcing their arrival at Horseshoe Harbour.[4]

Law's relations with Captain Petersen soured again the next day when he asked that *Kista Dan* be positioned so there was good strong ice beside the holds to support Weasels and sledges for unloading, but his relations with the officers and crew were 'never anything but excellent'. First

KISTA DAN UNLOADING THE
RAW MATERIALS TO BUILD
MAWSON STATION OVER THE
SEA ICE IN HORSESHOE
HARBOUR, FEBRUARY 1954.
(P LAW)

UNLOADING STORES AT
MAWSON STATION SITE,
FEBRUARY 1954. DONATED
MAC. ROBERTSON
CHOCOLATES SUSTAINED SIR
DOUGLAS MAWSON'S
BANZARE VOYAGES
AS WELL AS ANARE.
(P LAW)

Officer Mikkelsen offered his crew to help with the unloading from the ship to the ice, an offer which was gratefully accepted.[5]

The ship's derricks unloaded cargo onto sledges which were pulled to shore by Weasels Nos 1 and 2. Weasel No. 3 (the only vehicle with rubber tracks, picked up from the French at Kerguelen) manoeuvred the loads over the jumbled ice and tide cracks that separated the fast ice from the shore. The Ferguson tractor was useful in transporting loads over bare rock. *Kista Dan* had to be moved from time to time to stronger ice, as the unloading weakened it.

The ice conditions in 1954 were unusual. Horseshoe Harbour is generally free of ice by the end of January or early February. Law wrote later, 'It is interesting to note that never again in my subsequent twelve years of operations at Mawson did we have to unload over fast ice'.[6]

The wind dropped to almost twenty knots by lunchtime on Saturday 13 February, enabling the two mangled Auster aircraft to be lifted on to the fast ice beside *Kista Dan* where Morgan and Duffell stripped the wings and salvageable fittings from the fuselages.

By late afternoon Law decided it was time for the official ceremony to celebrate the commissioning of Australia's first post-war station on the Antarctic continent. He was unsure just what he was supposed to do or say on such an occasion, but composed a form of words and conducted a ceremony he hoped was appropriate. A flagpole was rigged on one of the barge caravans that served as living quarters while huts were

being built, and in the presence of all the ANARE men Law raised the Australian flag and made the following declaration:

> In the name of Her Majesty Queen Elizabeth II and the Government of the Commonwealth of Australia I raise this Australian flag on Australian Antarctic Territory; and I name the site of this new ANARE station 'Mawson' in honour of the great Australian Antarctic explorer and scientist, Sir Douglas Mawson.

Then they sang the national anthem and gave three hearty cheers. Law wrote that the gathering was duly photographed by all those who had cameras and it then dispersed. The work of clearing the cargo heaps continued until 2230 hours.[7]

André Migot was moved by the occasion:

> Everyone was in working clothes, having worked hard and uncomplainingly, with no thought but to get the job done. The glistening ice cliffs around this little corner of the frozen continent lent beauty and splendour to the ceremony.

THE FUSELAGE OF AUSTER 201 TETHERED NEAR HORSESHOE HARBOUR. BACK IN AUSTRALIA IT WAS REBUILT AND EVENTUALLY RETURNED TO ANTARCTICA TO FLY FOR MANY YEARS.
(P LAW)

RAISING THE FLAG AND NAMING MAWSON STATION, 13 FEBRUARY 1954. PHIL LAW IS STANDING AT THE FOOT OF THE FLAGPOLE.
(R THOMPSON)

Before the end of that day, the wings of both aircraft and the fuselage of Auster 200 were hoisted back on board into the now free 'tween-decks space of No. 2 hold. The fuselage of 201 was tethered to a large boulder on shore. Law retired to bed that night 'suffused with an emotion compounded of immense relief and considerable satisfaction'. The job was not finished, but he felt the most difficult part of establishing a permanent Australian Antarctic station had been achieved.

There was little time to dwell on that historic occasion. Law and Thompson had the ANARE men up and unloading cargo by 0500 the following Sunday morning, which prompted Dovers to complain about the early start, saying that Law would 'tire out my men'.[8] Law would not budge, acting on his firm belief that the Antarctic gave few windows of opportunity with the weather, and when it did the occasions should be exploited to the full. There would be time for rest later.

The RAAF team had worked miracles and had actually constructed a composite Auster that looked as though it might fly—but it would not have qualified for an airworthiness certificate in Australia. The left wing had a bracket of struts on it reminiscent of framework used to tie down the roof of an outback bark hut. There were no flaps and no tail fin. The hybrid was now officially Auster 200. Captain Petersen said it should have been called Auster 200.5![9] On 17 February, Leckie flight-tested it on skis, taking off from the fast ice:

> We just got through by the skin of our teeth. I took a longer run than normal to get it airborne because there were no flaps to give you lift off. You landed much faster naturally because you didn't have flaps to slow you down on approach, and without a [tail] fin you lost a lot of stability as well, so you required more rudder to get the aerodynamics to work. . .but we were operational, that was the main thing.

The fast ice provided plenty of runway, and over the next five days aerial photography, scintillometer (to check for radioactivity) and reconnaissance flights were made along the coast, east and west of the new Mawson Station. Each sortie became more difficult and exhausting for the RAAF crew because the aircraft had to be pushed physically three kilometres to the take-off point. No more than two flights a day were possible. Flying was intensely uncomfortable. Temperatures of −39°C at 2400 metres caused co-pilot Ray Seaver to suffer from cramps.

At Horseshoe Harbour, Mawson Station was taking shape as prefabricated huts were erected. The main living hut, purchased by Law from the NBS expedition in 1951, was in wooden sections to be put up by the expeditioners like a jigsaw puzzle after the *Kista Dan* left. That proved a daunting and difficult task even with an instruction manual. The works hut, fabricated by the firm of Explastics Ltd in Melbourne, had been designed in consultation with Law, Dovers, Macey and Thompson so it could be erected in one day to avoid the dangers of being blown down by a sudden storm when half built. Law:

> The process resembled that used by a child in building a house of playing cards. The secret of success was the highly accurate machining of the panels and the boring of the tubes that took the tie rods. Explastics Ltd had done their job well and the pieces fitted together with perfect precision.[10]

One day was spent laying foundations, uncrating panels and setting out the floor. Next day six men completed the hut and it was occupied the same evening. (All furnishings and fittings, including electric wiring and lights, were installed during erection.)[11]

The only limitation on these excellent aluminium clad, insulated huts was cost. More were to grace the rocky shores of Horseshoe Harbour in coming years when they could be afforded.

The scientific program at Mawson Station got off to a shaky start. Finding the site and establishing the station were obvious priorities, but Law was keen to advance a scientific program as soon as possible. Meteorology was to be the first priority as the station was established, with regular weather data radioed back to Australia by three observers. Geophysicist Jim Brooks had been included on *Kista Dan* as a round tripper, however, and his main task was to make a magnetic survey of the station site. The 'A-Factor' was against him. He was a late addition to the expedition and had to rely on the Instrument Section of the Bureau of Mineral Resources to check, pack and dispatch his equipment to the ship. Law was disgusted with the result:

First, the tent provided was quite unsuitable for the work concerned, apart from the fact that no supporting poles had been provided! The chronometer they had supplied stopped when placed outside the tent in the cold wind. The magnets were a disgrace—rusted and pitted and correspondingly unbalanced. The magnet box of the magnetometer would not come down cleanly to sit on the two pins that positioned it and Brooks therefore had difficulty in levelling it. The small subsidiary magnet usually supplied to damp the oscillations of the suspended

HYBRID 'AUSTER 200.5' ON THE SEA ICE IN HORSESHOE HARBOUR, FEBRUARY 1954. NOTE THE ROUGH FRAMEWORK ON THE UPPER EDGE OF THE LEFT WING AND THE 'FROZEN' TAIL PLANE. (AAD ARCHIVES)

ERECTING THE COMBINED RADIO, METEOROLOGICAL AND OIC'S HUT AT MAWSON, FEBRUARY 1954. (P LAW)

magnet system was missing. Finally there was no spare thermometer, and the one supplied read only as low as 0°C![12]

The two men persevered and obtained readings. Law's conclusion—that a basic precept for all Antarctic science was to make sure all equipment sent had in fact been tested for environmental conditions and checked in every detail—was to be ruefully endorsed by all field scientists in Antarctica similarly nobbled by the 'A-Factor' over the next half century.

By Wednesday 17 February unloading was completed and all available hands helped with the building of huts. On 20 February Law was delighted to receive congratulatory cables in response to his reports on their arrival and landing at Mawson Station from Minister for External Affairs Richard Casey, from Brian Roberts, a friend at the Scott Polar Research Institute, Cambridge, England, and from Mawson's old captain J K Davis. Law was especially delighted to hear from Davis who had a reputation for meanness. 'He is a nice old boy—fancy spending a couple of pounds on a long cable!'[13]

The weather held while building and scientific work continued and by 22 February Law was relaxed enough with progress achieved to declare a half-day holiday. The crew of *Kista Dan* built crude toboggans for the icy slopes behind the Mawson Station site and one enterprising lad even produced a makeshift ice yacht for runs on the sea ice outside Horseshoe Harbour. Dovers was grateful for the extra meat for the huskies (now staked out on the western side of the station) from seals shot by some of the crew on a hunting expedition. That night a celebratory party was held on *Kista Dan*. Law made hot, spiced *glühwein* for the occasion, and played his piano accordion during the festivities.

Captain Petersen was concerned about the refreezing of his track in through the fast ice and it was decided to leave at 0530 on Tuesday 23 February. Many photographs were taken as the ice anchors were hauled on board, the engines started and the propeller began to churn. It was an anticlimax—the ship refused to budge and the chilled expeditioners retreated to their new huts. It took until 1115 to break her clear with picks and crowbars. As the siren blew, the 1954 wintering party emerged to wave farewell and *Kista Dan* slowly began to break her way out towards open water.

The next objective was to reach the spectacular Scullin Monolith on the coast of Mac. Robertson Land, some 160 kilometres to the east of Mawson Station. The Scullin and the nearby Murray Monoliths are the only rock outcrops of any significance on the stretch of coast between Mawson Station and Cape Darnley, at the western extremity of Prydz Bay. The Scullin Monolith had been visited by Sir Douglas Mawson in 1931 and on 30 January 1937 by the Lars Christensen Expedition from Norway. Neither party had been able to take an astrofix to locate its position accurately, but Christensen had photographed the coast, resulting in the Hansen Atlas which Law and Petersen had used during the approach to Horseshoe Harbour.

THE FIRST WINTERING PARTY
AT MAWSON STATION, 1954.
FROM LEFT: G SCHWARTZ
(FRENCH OBSERVER),
L MACEY, W HARVEY,
R DOVERS, W STORER,
J GLEADELL, J RUSSELL,
B STINEAR, R DINGLE,
R SUMMERS.
(P LAW)

Law was anxious to pinpoint the correct position of the Scullin Monolith in order to correct errors in the Hansen Atlas, and to position the coastal photography taken during the 1954 ANARE voyage.

On Thursday 25 February *Kista Dan* anchored about a kilometre off the massive bulk of the Scullin Monolith, and a ship's boat was launched to attempt a landing. Second Mate Bill Pedersen and Dick Thompson (an ex-navy man) were on board with Phil Law, Jim Brooks and Arthur Gwynn.

Law was very keen to get ashore, but while Law the ANARE director was uncompromising in enforcing safety procedures for his expeditioners, Law the adventurer did not always apply the same standards to himself:

It was windy as usual, the sea was rough and at the foot of this great wall of rock there was a surge—waves breaking and smashing onto the rocks. We found a place where there was a sloped rock rising sharply out of the sea but the surge would hit it and sweep up and then suck back again. That looked like the only place one could get ashore but there was no way of getting the boat on to it.

So we got up within ten yards [9.14 metres] of this and had a look at it surging back and forth and finally I said, 'Look I'm going to jump, I reckon I can jump and claw my way up onto that rock and at least say we've been ashore. Then I can jump back into the water and swim out to the boat and you can haul me back.' Dick Thompson, my lieutenant, was very harsh on me. He cursed me and said, 'You stupid so-and-so, you'll kill yourself. I won't allow you to do it—it's too damn risky.'

Then I cogitated and realised there's not much point in one man getting ashore if you can't take your theodolites and instruments ashore and get an astrofix.

Thompson aborted the landing and they returned to the ship where he and Law had a stand-up argument on the deck. Thompson reiterated that there was no way Law could have landed without endangering his own and others' lives.

The next day *Kista Dan* headed north and then west towards Prydz Bay. Always the keen explorer, Law wanted to survey as much of the coast of Princess Elizabeth Land as possible and make a landing at the ice-free Vestfold Hills. He calculated there were six days in hand before returning to Melbourne within the agreed time for the charter.[14] His enthusiasm was not shared by Captain Petersen, who considered his job effectively done and was anxious to turn his bows homeward to avoid any possibility of being caught in pack ice so late in the season.

Kista Dan passed over the Fram Bank, which extends out from Cape Darnley, on 26 February. The line of grounded icebergs, detached from the Amery Ice Shelf, is one of the most spectacular sights along the coast of the AAT. Later that day the ship encountered new pack ice, and Law was not surprised to have Captain Petersen tell him at dinner that 'he was sorry, but he reckoned we had seen the end of Antarctica for this year'. Law deflected Petersen by suggesting they proceed during the night in open water, and then follow the ice edge to see if a landing on the coast of Princess Elizabeth Land was possible. The captain agreed, but when Law went to the bridge at 0630 the next morning, Petersen told him he believed survey work was not included in the charter, and he had cabled his owner for advice on whether the ship was covered by insurance for such work. Although he was still heading south-east, *Kista Dan* was at half speed. Law wrote: 'I suspected that he intended to commit the ship as little as possible on a southerly course until he obtained an answer to his cable.'[15]

Law decided to call Petersen's bluff and sent his own cable to ANARE's shipping agents, Westralian Farmers Transport Ltd in London:

WESTAUST LONDON.

CAPTAIN KISTADAN HAS REFUSED SURVEY MACKENZIE SEA AREA AS REQUESTED BY ME NOT ON GROUNDS OF SAFETY TO SHIP BUT BECAUSE HE STATES CHARTER DOES NOT COVER THIS TYPE OF WORK AND INSURANCE WOULD BE VOID STOP HE HAS CABLED OWNERS FOR INSTRUCTIONS STOP PENDING REPLY

MY TIME IS BEING WASTED AT £375 STERLING DAILY STOP AS I
SUPPLIED OWNERS BEFORE LEAVING WITH MY ITINERARY
STATING MY INTENTION OF PROCEEDING EASTWARD AFTER
LANDING WINTER PARTY I TAKE STRONGEST EXCEPTION TO
CAPTAIN RAISING THIS QUIBBLE AT THIS STAGE STOP I CON-
SIDER VESSEL SHOULD BE DECLARED OFF CHARTER FOR PERIOD
WASTED AWAITING OWNERS INSTRUCTIONS

(Signed)
LAW[16]

It took two days to sort out the disagreement. On Sunday 28 February
Law prepared a formal statement for Petersen outlining what he wanted,
and 'summoned' the captain to his cabin to give it to him. Petersen's
demeanour was conciliatory:

He told me he had received during the night a cable from the owners
stating that survey work was in line with the charter. I told him I considered he had been stalling yesterday and that I strongly objected to
being messed around. He replied that now the insurance was cleared
up he would go anywhere I wished. Everything after that was so smooth
I could hardly believe it. He turned south and proceeded at good speed
and by nightfall we were further south than the latitude of the ranges
south of Mawson![17]

That same day, following some good leads through the ice but in
overcast indifferent weather, Kista Dan moved in towards the Vestfold
Hills. The next day, 1 March, the weather was overcast and very cold with
new, black ice forming on what had been open water only a few days
before. At the end of the day Law was elated to see the brown rock of
the Vestfold Hills loom up, and Kista Dan anchored near a group of small
rocky islands. It was very cold and Law's hopes of a quick landing were
dashed the following morning by strong winds and bad weather.

Conditions improved on Wednesday 3 March. There was no wind
but it was overcast, extremely cold and snowing steadily. The shore party
set off at 0945, Law dropping Jim Brooks and Fred Elliott on a nearby
island (soon to be named Magnetic Island) to take an astrofix and magnetic observations and make notes on the bird population. Law, Thompson,
Gwynn and Shaw (and a coxswain John Hansen from the ship) set off
towards the mainland, weaving their way through scattered offshore
islands and aiming for a small sloping beach. They moored against an
area of fast ice joined to the shore and carefully stepped on to the mainland at 1030 hours. Law reflected that there had been only two previous
landings in the Vestfold Hills, which comprise about 300 square kilometres

of ice-free rock on the eastern side of Prydz Bay. The first landing was by the Norwegian Klarius Mikkelsen on 20 February 1935; the second was by the American explorer Lincoln Ellsworth and his Australian adviser, Sir Hubert Wilkins, on 11 January 1939. Ever conscious of making history, Law ordered Thompson ashore with an Australian flag, while he took pictures with a cine camera. Thompson:

> We struggled ashore, built a cairn out of rocks, planted the flag on its pole while Phil took our picture. Then I took photos of him with the flag, and a cine film of the three of them waving their caps like a trio of scat singers.[18]

Because overcast conditions had prevented Law from obtaining an astrofix to pinpoint their position precisely, on Thursday 4 March a survey party was put ashore at Magnetic Island. Law and Thompson had to row them there because the boat's engine had seized. It was decided to attempt a final flight in the patched-up Auster for photographic and scintillometer runs over the Vestfold Hills.

Captain Petersen was champing at the bit to be away, but Duffell worked on a jammed starter cartridge for four and a half hours and at 1100 hours the battered Auster was lowered into the water on floats. When it drifted away towards some nearby icebergs before it could be secured, two sailors chased it in a dinghy but could not tow it back against the wind. The ever-resourceful Leckie climbed down from the wing into the cockpit, managed to start the engine, and taxied back to the ship.[19]

Leckie's takeoff was almost certainly the most risky of the voyage. A previous effort to take off from floats near the Scullin Monolith had to be aborted when he could not break free from the water. Only too aware that the Auster was without flaps and tail fin, and with ice drifting in to the takeoff area, Law watched from *Kista Dan* with trepidation:

> For a long while [Leckie] could not get the aircraft up on the 'step' of the floats, and ahead of him we saw a strip of sludge and new ice.[20]
>
> We called to him over the radio to stop his run, but apparently he felt he was almost airborne and so stuck to it. He finally made it, after a run of 83 seconds, pulling up off the water only a few yards short of the black ice. He told me later he didn't stop sweating until he was 4000 feet [1219.2 metres] up![21]

Leckie had pushed his luck to the edge and had actually hit a chunk of floating ice which fortuitously broke his floats clear of the water at the crucial moment. He was the first to see the remarkable lakes and fjords of the Vestfold Hills, later to be the site of Australia's second mainland establishment, Davis Station: 'The inland lakes were of a different colour from the ones near the coast. The former were a bright emerald green, the latter were the same colour as the sea, which is nearly black from the air. The emerald green lakes inland were completely ice free. I could see the rocks around

these lakes extend about a hundred yards into the water, which was crystal clear.'[22]

It was the last flight of the voyage. As soon as the hybrid Auster was lifted on board, Captain Petersen weighed anchor and headed for the open sea.

Law was a happy man. Although the weather was now deteriorating badly, he could reflect on considerable gains. There had been a landing on the Vestfold Hills, Brooks had fixed the position of Magnetic Island accurately and this fix, allied with Leckie's photographic runs in the Auster, would help to correct the Hansen Atlas's depiction of this part of the coast. Rock specimens had been gathered and navigational knowledge had been gained of the approach to 'this fascinating area'.[23] He was not to know that the next day would be the most frightening of his life—and that of every living soul on *Kista Dan*. They were heading out into a full-blown hurricane.

At 0130 on Friday 5 March, Leckie woke Law to tell him that the Auster, lashed down on the deck, had been wrecked:

The wind was now blowing at Force 14 (more than 100 knots) and the ship was hove to into the wind and rolling and pitching violently in heavy seas. Doug and I stumbled along the heaving passage and pushed through the door at the end on to the boat deck. It was wild out there. We clung to the handrails as the wind buffeted us and freezing spray lashed our faces. The scream of the wind and the flapping of our parka hoods around our ears made conversation impossible. . .The aircraft certainly was a mess. Gusts of wind under the starboard wing had caused the main strut, connecting the port float to the fuselage, to collapse and the plane had lurched over on one side, crumpled and twisted, with the port wing tangled up in the lifeboat davits.[24]

They climbed up to the bridge to tell the captain. He was having great difficulty holding the ship into the wind. *Kista Dan* was bow light and stern heavy after having discharged her cargo at Mawson Station. Her bows were riding so high in the water that the helmsman could not hold her into the wind, now blowing at 160 kilometres per hour. Great waves were sending sheets of water and spray over the foredeck and against the bridge windows, and turning into sludge ice. Law asked the chief engineer whether the forward tanks had been ballasted to keep the bows lower in the water. He said they had tried, but the pipes had frozen up. Law:

> There was little conversation on the darkened bridge. The helmsman's repetition of the Captain's steering orders and an occasional comment by the First Mate or myself were the only words spoken. The radar shone green under its hood and the First Mate seldom left it . . .
>
> About 0200 hours the Captain lost control of the ship. No combination of rudder and engine revolutions could counteract the force of the wind on the bows, and *Kista Dan* broached to. Lying over on her port side, she drifted helplessly, pounded by every breaking wave and held in a permanent list by the hurricane.[25]

That spelt the end for Auster 200, which was blown over the side. The second mate cut the lashings to let the wreckage drift away, carrying with it—to Law's chagrin—the valuable scintillometer which could not be retrieved. (It was not, however, the end of the Auster contribution to ANARE service. The fuselage of Auster 201, cannibalised to augment Auster 200, was safely stowed in the hold, and was rebuilt to return to the Antarctic to fly in 1955.)

The situation was critical. *Kista Dan* lay on her side held to a permanent list of 30° by the force of the wind and rolling from that point, so that the limits of the rolls were vertical or 10° to starboard, then 60° or 70° to port. Law was aware that the stability of the ship left a lot to be desired. He had noticed on the voyage to Macquarie Island that 'the ship feels top-heavy' and tended to 'hang over' at the end of a roll. (After she returned to Denmark at the end of this voyage the owners added 70 tonnes to her keel.)[26]

In his book *You Have to be Lucky—Antarctic and Other Adventures,* Law wrote:

> There have been a number of occasions in my life when I have been afraid, but never have I experienced, before or since, terror extending

unrelieved over such a long period of time. I don't think anyone on the ship really expected to survive and, over a period of 12 hours, each large roll seemed likely to be the last.[27]

With no steerage, Captain Petersen could only use his engines to move ahead or astern with limited effect to try and avoid icebergs and large bergy bits. After *Kista Dan* sideswiped one iceberg, Doug Leckie joined other volunteers to go on deck to try and throw ice off the ship. Frozen spray on the deck and rigging was making the stricken vessel even more top-heavy and unstable:

> We had to use crowbars, anything we could to break ice off the decks and the rigging—one of the boys got quite nastily hurt with falling ice off the rigging.

Law said later that neither he nor anyone else on the ship took a photograph during the next twelve hours—and he was the official photographer—because they all thought they were going to die. Doug Leckie shared a cabin with his three RAAF colleagues:

> I remember saying to Ray Seaver and Frank Morgan that it might be an idea to say a quick prayer, because I thought this might be the end. I heard a muffled voice saying, 'What do you think I've been doing for the last two and a half bloody hours'. That was Ken Duffell, my flight engineer.

The ship's professionals were not immune from raw fear. One engineer was so distressed he had to be given sleeping tablets. His job was cleaning the strainers of ice slush to get cooling water to the engine. He later had a nervous breakdown, could not work for a year, and never went back to sea again.[28] Like most of the passengers, Law could do nothing but lie in his bunk most of the time and hope for the best:

> The most horrible moment of the whole night was when I stood in my cabin, in semi-darkness, leaning against the bulkhead, with my face pressed against the porthole, peering out on the port side over the tormented water. . .Suddenly, struck by a fierce gust of wind and a particularly

129

high wave, the ship heeled over until I was lying on my stomach on the bulkhead, practically horizontal, with my nose flattened against the submerged glass of the porthole, gazing down into the green-black depths. There I waited and waited for the recovery that would not come, as successive waves ground the ship further and further down on its side as my terror mounted. . .

Law remembers that, when confronting what seemed like certain death, he felt mostly anger and intense resentment. There he was, a successful expedition leader, returning home with a story of accomplishment and a load of important scientific records and photographs. Was all this to be lost? And would anyone ever know what had happened?

Captain Petersen, during the twenty-four hours he spent on the bridge, was also resentful at finding himself in this situation. During one of Law's visits to the bridge, Petersen shouted at him: 'Have you now got enough?'[29] Law later reflected that had the captain not procrastinated for two days on the way to the Vestfold Hills about the charter, they would have been well on their way home by that point.[30]

Daylight on Friday 5 March brought little relief, except that later in the day *Kista Dan* drifted into an area of brash ice—pulverised pack ice with the consistency of a thick concrete mix. But giant swells persisted, and remnants of larger ice floes bumped and grated against the ship's sides 'with horrible menacing sounds'.[31] During the next night the crew managed to free the frozen pipes that had prevented the captain at the beginning of the storm from pumping sea water into his forward tanks, and there was a noticeable improvement in draught and stability. By Saturday morning 6 March the worst was over, normal watches were resumed and the captain at last retired to his bunk after forty hours continuously on the bridge.

Kista Dan returned to Melbourne via Heard Island and, after taking on fresh water at Kerguelen Islands without any further major dramas, berthed at North Wharf on the morning of 31 March 1954. Despite the triumph of establishing Australia's first permanent continental station on the Antarctic continent against considerable odds, the return was oddly anticlimactic in contrast to the hoopla of the departure. One reason was the press preoccupation with the visit of the Queen and the Duke of Edinburgh to Australia. However, one journalist did comment that 'a handful of Australians have been taking part, almost unnoticed, in an exploit which, under normal circumstances, would have made headline news'.

The DEA had irritated Law by cabling him on 28 March that he was to limit any press interviews with himself and the expeditioners on arrival to 'events, personal experiences and sidelights'. Statements on achievements and the value of the expedition would be preserved for a report to the minister 'and may be the subject of a later statement'.[32]

Law wrote in his diary: 'This is typical. The first chance to give the newspapers some *serious* scientific stuff, and I am reduced to nattering about penguins!'

Apart from the Heard Island expeditioners' relatives there was no great crowd to welcome the explorers on 31 March. The Minister, Richard Casey, was there though, and came on board to chat informally with Law and Captain Petersen. Conscious that Mawson Station was far from 'permanent', Law took the occasion to remind Mr Casey:

RICHARD CASEY, MINISTER FOR EXTERNAL AFFAIRS, TALKS TO CAPTAIN HANS CHRISTIAN PETERSEN AFTER *KISTA DAN*'S RETURN TO MELBOURNE ON 31 MARCH 1954. (I FOX)

. . .that although we had ten men now at Mawson, we had no government approval for a relief expedition to pick them up in 1955, or for the appointment of a new party to replace them. One quarter of the year had passed, and we in the Antarctic Division would need an immediate decision by the government if we were to be ready in time to sail in January.[33]

Casey told Law there was a meeting the next day to talk about all this. However, Law was surprised to hear from administrative officer Jeremiah Donovan that it was not a full meeting of the Executive Planning Committee—the principal Antarctic policy-making body. He suspected that there were moves afoot to undermine the role of the EPC and determined to fight for its retention. As it happened, Law's domination of Australia's Antarctic agenda had been under attack on a number of fronts while he had been down south. Despite the fact that the establishment of Mawson Station fulfilled the final requirement set down by the Government in 1947 for Australia's involvement in Antarctica, Law—fatigued and drained by his long and arduous voyage—would have to act quickly to retain his control of Antarctic-related events.

NINE

VIRGIN TERRITORY

Although supportive and influential in promoting post-war Australian Antarctic activity, Sir Douglas Mawson thought that more attention should be paid to the eastern sector of the AAT, near Cape Freshfield, and Commonwealth Bay where he had his base in his 1911–14 Australasian Antarctic Expedition. There were also scientific benefits, he felt, in being near the South Magnetic Pole. Phillip Law, on the other hand, favoured the western sector of the AAT near the Amery Ice Shelf, where there were coastal ice-free areas and interior mountain ranges to be explored. The Norwegians had also been active in this area and Australia's claims needed to be strengthened.

During the Executive Planning Committee meeting in November 1953, Law convinced the committee (including Mawson) that the *Kista Dan* expedition in 1954 should go west, to the coast of Mac. Robertson Land. Law regarded the EPC highly. It brought together the main players in ANARE—the Commonwealth Scientific and Industrial Research Organisation (formerly CSIR), Bureau of Mineral Resources, the armed forces, Treasury, National Mapping, the Australian Academy of Science, the universities and ANARE's parent department, the Department of External Affairs, as well as influential Antarctic experts like Sir Douglas Mawson and John King Davis. The committee was chaired by Law who valued its role in breaking down 'selfish' departmental barriers, creating long and short-term Antarctic policy and playing a powerful role in getting government acceptance of that policy. He orchestrated it skilfully to support his Antarctic plans, and made sure he always drafted the minutes of its meetings:

▲ King penguins at Lusitania Bay, Macquarie Island.
(P Haddock)

▶ Grey-headed albatross at Petrel Peak, Macquarie Island.
(C Baars)

▼ Light-mantled sooty albatross and chick, Macquarie Island.
(O Ertok)

▲ WINSTON LAGOON SPIT, HEARD ISLAND, FROM
MACARONI PENGUIN COLONY.
(K GREEN)

◀ ROCKHOPPER PENGUIN, MACQUARIE ISLAND.
(C BAARS)

▶ BLACK-BROWED ALBATROSS CHICK, MACQUARIE ISLAND.
(C BAARS)

▲ King penguins and old digesters at
The Nuggets, Macquarie Island.
(AAD Archives)

▶ Fur seal at Macquarie Island.
(T Everett)

▲ KING PENGUINS WITH CHICKS,
MACQUARIE ISLAND.
(C BAARS)

◀ ELEPHANT SEAL 'WEANER' PUP,
MACQUARIE ISLAND.
(K BELL)

▼ ROYAL PENGUINS AT BAUER BAY,
MACQUARIE ISLAND.
(G JOHNSTONE)

▶ GENTOO PENGUIN AND CHICKS NEAR EAGLE
CAVE, MACQUARIE ISLAND.
(G JOHNSTONE)

▲ Elephant seal and royal penguins competing for beach space, Macquarie Island. (C Baars)

► Leopard seal, Macquarie Island. (C Baars)

▲ *Stilbocarpa polaris* — Macquarie Island cabbage. (M Price)

▼ Kelp in Buckles Bay, Macquarie Island. (J Bennett)

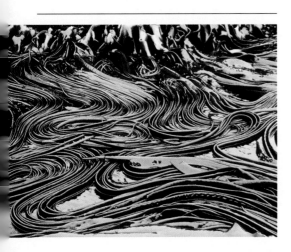

◄ The isthmus and a modern ANARE station at the northern end of Macquarie Island. The more sheltered waters of Buckles Bay are to the left. Hasselborough Bay on the western side gets the full fury of the Roaring Forties.
(J Hösel)

▲ Icebergs and floes in low light near Davis Station.
(T Bowden)

► Reminders of a grim past — boiling-down vats used by early sealers on Heard Island.
(G Johnstone)

▲ MALE EMPEROR PENGUINS HUDDLING FOR
COLLECTIVE WARMTH IN SUB-ZERO
TEMPERATURES AT AUSTER ROOKERY.
(K SHERIDAN)

◄ WANDERING ALBATROSSES PERFORMING A
COURTSHIP DISPLAY AT CAROLINE COVE,
MACQUARIE ISLAND. THE MALE, WHICH HAS
LIGHTER PLUMAGE, IS ON THE RIGHT.
(M CRAVEN)

▲ THE NUMBER OF ALBATROSSES DROWNED
ON LONG LINES SET FOR TUNA BY FISHING
FLEETS AROUND THE WORLD IS THREATENING
THE SURVIVAL OF THE SPECIES.
(COURTESY G ROBERTSON)

It is terribly important that the Minutes are written in such a way that they contribute constructively to the direction in which you want to go. . .I didn't believe in falsifying Minutes or 'rigging' them in any way but I am sure that if you write the Minutes with an object in view you can, over the years, influence the way a thing goes.[1]

Sir Douglas Mawson was well aware of Law's strong guiding hand on the EPC. On Wednesday 20 January—while Law was heading towards Antarctica on *Kista Dan*—External Affairs Minister Richard Casey asked Sir Douglas to see him in Canberra to discuss future Australian plans in Antarctica. Mawson pressed his views on the importance of the Cape Freshfield area of the AAT as a site for a future base and told Casey that the Government should abandon the Heard Island station and ask New Zealand to take over the ANARE station on Macquarie Island, or at least share the expenses of maintaining it, as the meteorological data was of interest 'only to New Zealand'. In a confidential minute to the DEA Casey wrote:

I asked Mawson what sort of a body the Antarctic Committee [EPC] was. He told me confidentially that he did not think it was a very active or useful body—as it only met once or twice a year—and then largely to be *told* by P G Law what it had been decided to do.[2]

This struck a chord with the DEA's Keith Waller (who had vexed Law by cabling him on *Kista Dan* to stop him making press statements of substance on his arrival in Melbourne). Waller wrote to DEA Secretary James Plimsoll on 22 February 1954:

Minister is concerned at the lack of control over Law's activities. I have suggested (and Minister agrees) that Law is playing the Department off against the Antarctic Committee [EPC] and vice versa. Minister has agreed that we should set up a small executive Committee of the main Antarctic Committee, consisting of Law, White (CSIRO), Treasury representative, J K Davis (an Antarctic expert) and me, under his Chairmanship.[3]

In March when Law returned from Antarctica and was alerted by his administrative assistant, Jeremiah Donovan, he moved to counter-attack. He rang the chief geophysicist of the Bureau of Mineral Resources, Jack Rayner, whom he regarded as one of the important figures on the EPC, and found he had not been invited to the meeting:

I then rang Keith Waller in Canberra, who admitted that the Minister was thinking of replacing the [EPC] with a much smaller committee consisting of a few selected men from the present committee. I told him

PHIL LAW SHOWS SIR
DOUGLAS MAWSON THE FIRST
PUBLISHED PICTURE OF
MAWSON STATION AFTER HIS
RETURN TO MELBOURNE IN
MARCH 1954.
(MELBOURNE *AGE*)

to inform the Minister that if he proceeded with this idea I would immediately resign.[4]

The meeting on 2 April passed smoothly with Casey in the chair. At the end, Law asked the minister bluntly how often he intended to call this small committee together and whether it was intended that it should usurp the functions of the EPC. He received Casey's assurances that this would not be so. Law, who had chaired the EPC since 1949, continued as its chairman until 1963, when it was allowed to lapse.[5]

The next EPC meeting, on 16 June 1954, was extremely important. Law, once again with his hands firmly on the reins of Antarctic policy, presented a draft five year plan to ensure stability and continuity of the Antarctic and sub-Antarctic stations. A submission to Cabinet sought approval for expanded activities at Mawson Station with a fifteen-man party for 1955. The Heard Island station was to be closed to help pay for the expanded activity on the Antarctic mainland. Exploration was stressed, with qualified surveyors and aircraft provided by the RAAF to investigate and chart territory within 100 miles' [160 kilometres] radius of Mawson, supported by coastal exploration from *Kista Dan*.

Law also spelled out his proposed scientific program: a boosting of meteorological activity (including experimental automatic weather stations), geology, geomagnetism and seismology, cosmic ray and ionospheric work, biology and glaciology. As no glaciologist was available in Australia, Law hoped to recruit from overseas.[6]

At Mawson, blissfully unaware that the station was not yet assured of a future, Bob Dovers and his nine companions continued to build huts and prepare for their first winter on the Antarctic continent. All were without their appendixes. Bob Dingle, a weather observer, was one of eight team members operated on by the doctor, Bob Summers, for prophylactic reasons before embarking on *Kista Dan*. 'He said it was a good idea for him to do the operation because it would give us faith in him.' A certain amount of faith in Summers was lost, though, after he buried their entire year's supply of fresh meat in the ice. Dingle: 'The first blizzard came down and removed the marker flag. . .When you bury something in a featureless bit of ice or snow, unless you take bearings on it, you never find it again.'

Fortunately for all, Summers located the cache two months later—but there was still only enough meat for one meal a month plus birthdays.[7]

However, there was plenty of tinned meat, and the choicest cuts of seal killed for the huskies also found their way on to the expeditioners' table.

The prefabricated wooden hut Phil Law had obtained from the NBS Expedition was the main living quarters and mess. Five sleeping bays and bunks on each side of the hut meant little privacy—although towards the end of the year plyboard partitions were put up to create minimal personal space. A communal dining table filled the centre of the hut and, at the end, a slow combustion Aga stove was presided over by the cook, Jeff Gleadell.

MEDICAL OFFICER BOB SUMMERS IS THE MAN IN THE ICE MASK AFTER RETURNING FROM THE MAWSON DOG LINE IN A BLIZZARD, WINTER 1954. (R DINGLE)

Despite the cramped living conditions, personal relations remained cordial despite 'a few grouches' and there were agreed ground rules to avoid friction. Bill Storer: 'We had a policy that we would not discuss religion or politics while we were there. In other words, that was our own little private affair. We could pray in our little cubicles if we wanted to.'

Talk about women was allowed but, according to Storer, did not dominate conversations in the NBS hut. For recreation the ten men played cards (canasta), listened to gramophone records or read from the excellent polar and general library provided by the Antarctic Division. There was little time to relax. The huskies had to be fed and looked after each day, snow had to be continuously carted to the snow melter for fresh water, and equipment prepared for field trips. Everyone did a day's turn as 'slushy' for the cook and cooked for the rest on Sunday, Gleadell's day off. Night watches were kept to guard against fire—a very real hazard in a wooden hut with a combustion stove and pressure lamp lighting. Dingle, the sole weather observer, began his daily weather reports and balloon launches in April. He had no radiosonde apparatus to send aloft, but measured the upper winds by sighting the released balloon with his theodolite. Any spare time remaining was often spent instructing other expeditioners in specialist tasks, in case of death or injury. Storer:

> I taught the guys how to operate the radio, the surveyor [Dovers] taught us how to take bearings and things like that. [Bob Dingle] taught us all how to read the weather. We all had our little lectures—not every night—but at least once a week.

135

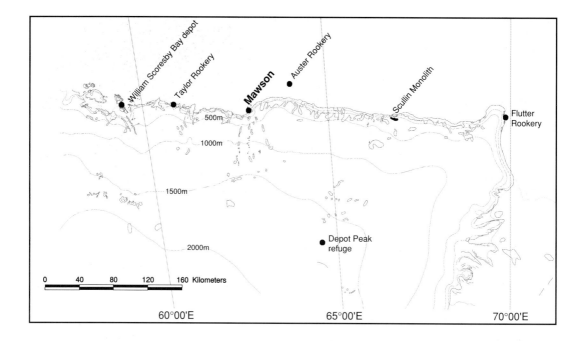

OIC Bob Dovers was keen to begin exploring the virgin territory surrounding them and in April led a party of five on a four-day field trip up to the plateau behind Mawson Station into the Framnes Mountains, to find a safe route onto the ice cap towards Mt Henderson. This was a preliminary canter to test equipment and vehicles for a much more ambitious journey—Dovers wanted to push east along the coast to the Scullin Monolith. He proposed to travel along the sea ice with two Weasels each towing a wooden barge caravan and a sledge loaded with fuel. Dovers would lead a party of four, including the carpenter Harvey, geologist Stinear and radio operator Storer:

> The sledge [barge] caravans were ordinary caravans with a roof on the top like a triangle or diamond, and in this we stored all our equipment. One caravan had all our survival gear and the other had our scientific equipment.

They set off on 17 May and made such good progress over the sea ice that they sighted the bulk of the Scullin Monolith two days later. But on the morning of 20 May a gale burst upon them. That night Dovers was forced to camp on the sea ice in front of the sheer rock face of the monolith. He was uneasy about camping on the ice but noted in his log that it was two feet [0.61 metres] thick and that he 'was not unduly worried about our situation'.[8]

The Australians woke early on the morning of 21 May to find themselves in a desperate position. The sea ice was heaving up and down in a heavy swell and breaking into floes. Dovers started the motor of No. 1 Weasel and alerted Stinear and Storer in No. 2 to do the same. Unfortunately neither vehicle had been refuelled the night before, but there was no time now for that. Dovers:

> We tried to make the eastern tip of the bay which was lower lying. . .however the rapidity with which the ice was breaking up precluded this. Already the floes were individual sections heaving up and down in the swell. The Weasels were truly magnificent scrambling from floe to floe. As the weight came on a floe it would sink and tilt leaving a gap and step to the next, but the Weasels managed to proceed, dragging their loads.[9]

They could not make it to shore, and were stopped by open water and brash ice about 200 metres out. Survival, uppermost in their minds, necessitated securing the barge caravan containing their food and emergency supplies to the shore. Leaving the Weasels and all the other equipment on ice floes, the four men began to winch the vital barge caravan towards the land by hand, precariously balanced on a tongue of non-tidal ice, clinging to hollows in the ice hummocks. Dovers:

> How we managed to cling on there in that merciless wind was a mystery. We saw the manhandled sledge fully loaded flying through the air before crashing into the tide crack near us, narrowly missing Stinear in its trajectory. Our heavy bridging timbers wafted about the bay like matchsticks. The second barge caravan was turned completely over in a gust. Then a few minutes later a subsequent gust righted it again. Even the sledges each carrying a ton and a half [1½ tonnes] of petrol were moved about.[10]

137

THERE WAS A DESPERATE
STRUGGLE TO MANHANDLE
THE REMAINING BARGE
CARAVAN ASHORE, 1954.
(W HARVEY)

By this time all four men were suffering badly from exposure. Not only that, the survival barge caravan had a large hole punched in the side, and certainly would not float. Dovers asked carpenter Harvey and Storer to patch it. While this was going on, No. 1 Weasel heeled over on its side on its ice floe and started to sink. Fortunately Storer had already removed all their sleeping bags from both Weasels, and put them in the caravan. Dovers realised that they could not survive on land without shelter, and their only hope was to get in the caravan tethered on the ice for the night and hope for the best:

> A very worrying night. . .The caravan was under constant bombardment by ice fragments that rattled on the plywood walls. The floes outside were all detached and moving. We could hear water lapping against the hull and the caravan was continually bumped by moving floes that scraped loudly against the thin plywood hull. No water came through the patch.[11]

At 0400 hours conditions eased a little, and they even managed some sleep. All had minor frostbite, and Harvey had a badly cut hand he had jammed in a Weasel door. Dovers had a deeply frostbitten hand. They dressed their wounds and next day managed to winch the caravan closer to the shore and make a cache of emergency food on land.

On 28 May after five days in this desperate situation, Dovers decided to take advantage of better ice conditions to try and winch the survival caravan to shore. It was resting on ice, but they succeeded in tethering it to a rock face in such a way that if the ice did move out to sea, they would be left suspended like a lifeboat in ship's davits. They slept better that night, Dovers noting in his log that 'the gentle rocking motion of the ice under the swell was not missed at all as an aid to sleep, and the groaning and growling of the tide crack had lost its sinister significance'.

On 2 June 'there was a frightful crash' and the barge caravan gave a sideways lurch as the ice bank beneath it collapsed, and left the four men hanging in mid-air. Dovers noted laconically in his log: 'Radio contact [with Mawson Station] interrupted by the foregoing episode. We will have to find a new home, this is no place for anyone who likes a quiet life.'[12]

HOME AWAY FROM HOME. THE BARGE CARAVAN WAS SUSPENDED OVER THE SEA ICE BY CABLES GUYED INTO THE ROCKY CLIFFS OF THE SCULLIN MONOLITH, 1954. (W HARVEY)

By 4 June the party was in its best shape since the ice break-out. The surviving No. 1 Weasel had been able to drag the barge caravan from its precarious position to dry land at a location nearby dubbed 'Weasel Beach'. No. 2 Weasel and the second barge caravan were lost on the sea ice. However, the party had ample food, fuel, accommodation and a working Weasel to get them back to Mawson Station if and when the sea ice froze again. If not, there was still an option. Storer:

We knew we could survive at that particular place even if we had to be rescued by ship in nine months' time. While we were there we couldn't do anything because the sheer cliffs were too steep to climb up. Our only exit was via the way we came—by sea.

Bruce Stinear made good use of the enforced stay by collecting geological specimens, later received with great joy by Sir Douglas Mawson, who had not been able to land at the Scullin Monolith during his BANZARE voyages in 1929 and 1931.

By the second week in June the sea ice seemed strong enough for an escape attempt, but the Scullin seemed unwilling to let them go. On 10 June a blizzard struck with such ferocity that it tipped over both the barge caravan and No. 1 Weasel. At last, on 13 June Dovers and his three companions set off with the battered Weasel towing the barge caravan and two sledges, and were back at Mawson Station by the evening of 19 June. The saga was not quite over. Dovers:

At 2300 hours just as everybody was settling down to bed, Schwarz burst into the hut reporting that No. 1 Weasel was on fire. Despite our best efforts the fire damaged the machine beyond repair before it was put out. This was the crowning blow of an ill-fated venture.[13]

The loss of two of the three Weasels caused a rethink on plans for further exploration.

The huskies had not been brought to Mawson to be cuddly canine companions for expeditioners. They were working dogs, on the cutting edge of existing polar technology. The vulnerability of heavy tracked vehicles running over sea ice had been demonstrated during the Scullin Monolith venture. Both George Schwarz and Bob Dovers had experience driving huskies and after much discussion it was decided to take two dog teams along the coast to King Edward Gulf, 230 kilometres to the west of Mawson, and carry out scientific work along the way.[14] Apart from filling in blanks in the map, they planned to take tidal observations, astrofixes from rocky features, magnetic observations, collect geological and botanical specimens and make a 'rough' survey of animal and bird life along the way.[15]

They set off on 12 October and in comparison with the Scullin Monolith debacle had a smooth run, proving the advantage of dogs over machines on sea ice—the first of many such journeys that would be made by ANARE expeditioners until 1992. Dovers planned to be away for six weeks, but only fourteen days' rations of dog pemmican were carried—they planned to kill seals to feed the huskies. On 21 October they saw many emperor penguins, and followed these magnificent birds in to the coast to discover what was later named Taylor Rookery. Radio contact was maintained with Mawson during the coastal run. Dovers' dog team led and he reported little trouble, 'but George was furious with his undisciplined crew tonight'.

Dovers summed up the Western Coastal Journey as workmanlike—'nothing extraordinary except remarkable in the smoothness of events'. They were out for 41 days, and had run 880 kilometres with the dogs, which had set out a rabble and returned as well-trained teams, with 'all objects achieved'.[16]

This was a valuable training run for the Southern Reconnaissance—the major field journey for the year—that Dovers was itching to begin. The territory inland from Mawson Station was totally unexplored and he was aware that 'Operation Highjump' aerial photographs taken by the Americans in February 1947 had shown a tantalising glimpse of what might be a mountain range to the south of Mawson.

This expedition was carried out in three stages. The surviving Weasel No. 3 now sported a wooden cabin, ingeniously constructed by John Russell.[17] Dovers, Russell and Jeff Gleadell, the cook, began by taking the Weasel on a route reconnaissance past Mt Henderson to 69°40'S, where it broke down. Leaving it there, the three men went back to Mawson and Dovers returned with Dr Bob Summers, Lem Macey and two dog teams to survey the terrain further as well as find a track south.

On 13 December, Dovers, Summers and geologist Bruce Stinear left Mawson with the repaired Weasel and one dog team and pushed into the unknown.[18] Again the dogs proved more reliable than the Weasel, which plagued them with fuel blockages. On Christmas Day the three explorers sat in the Weasel cabin to enjoy their specially provided Christmas dinner. Dovers wrote: 'A Xmas present to Summers from his people was opened and it contained some gum leaves which were ceremoniously burnt, filling the Weasel cabin with the nostalgic fragrance of the Australian bush.'[19]

On 27 December the party sighted five peaks about 240 kilometres south southeast of Mawson Station—later named the Stinear Nunataks after the expedition's geologist. The excitement of raw discoveries in virgin territory was palpable. Summers later wrote:

> The culmination of my year at Mawson was the Southern Journey. I found it extremely satisfying putting my big feet down on to territory that one knew no one had ever trod before and wondering what the next day would bring.[20]

The following day the Weasel, followed by the dogs, laboured up a great snow drift to the peak of one of the Stinear Nunataks, and a major discovery could be claimed. Dovers:

> A most interesting surprise awaited us here. As soon as we topped the crest we saw a great range of mountains leading away to the south-east. Up to this time we had not the least suspicion of the existence of this range. It was a magnificent spectacle and a very fitting climax to the journey; well worth the petty annoyances of the Weasel.[21]

Dovers, Stinear and Summers were the first to see the northernmost ranges of the Prince Charles Mountains, extending about 300 kilometres southwards in an arc from their northern extremity. These great mountains form a barrier through which streams the Lambert Glacier, which in turn feeds the vast Amery Ice Shelf. The Lambert Glacier drains a third of the AAT as its immense rivers of advancing ice move inexorably off the Antarctic continent and into the surrounding ocean. It is an area of great drama, beauty and scientific importance, and major ANARE summer programs are carried out there to this day.

The Dovers party could go no further. They did not have enough fuel or supplies to go on, and time was running out as *Kista Dan* was due to pick up the Mawson party in a matter of weeks. They returned reluctantly to Mawson Station by 7 January 1955—the same day *Kista Dan* left Melbourne for Heard Island and Mawson.

It had been an important year for ANARE. Dovers and his men had made significant discoveries along the coast and inland from Mawson. They had tested, in the field, methods of travel that would be adopted and adapted by the ANARE parties that were to follow, exploring and conducting research in the AAT.

The relief voyage was led by Phil Law, assisted by Dick Thompson, with *Kista Dan* again skippered by Captain Hans Christian Petersen. This time the ship was carrying two amphibious army DUKWs to help with the cargo operations at Heard and Horseshoe Harbour, but no aircraft. Law was eager to continue exploring the fascinating ice-free Vestfold Hills, so briefly visited the previous year. The party was astonished at the first sight of the outlying islands, now snow free, with their rocky terrain teeming with rookeries of Adélie penguins. Captain Petersen was seeking Magnetic Island, but approached another island by mistake. Instead of retreating and coming back along last year's track, he tried to edge over to Magnetic Island directly. Mariners in uncharted Antarctic waters usually try to keep to corridors of known safety, and Petersen's sideways move nearly led to disaster. Law:

> At 1140 hours there was a grinding jar, the ship lurched and bucked several times before the way could be taken off her, and we found ourselves stranded on top of a sharp pinnacle of rock which had passed to one side of the echo-sounders without registering and had struck the ship amidships. It took half an hour's manoeuvring by the Captain to get clear again.[22]

The DUKWs made landings easier, although both machines became bogged inland and had to be winched out. Land parties were able to explore the remarkable lakes, frozen fjords and ice-free extent of the Vestfold Hills for two days, although Law regretted not having aircraft to assist in an overview of the area. On 1 February, *Kista Dan* sailed towards the Larsemann Hills 100 kilometres to the west, until the ship was stopped by fast ice 20 kilometres from the coast. Law judged the ice to be much stronger and thicker than that across which they had unloaded cargo at Horseshoe Harbour the previous year. An attempt to reach the Larsemann Hills over the fast ice to take an astrofix was abandoned after the Weasel

in which Law and his companions were travelling nearly broke through on several occasions.[23]

On 3 February Law decided to risk a sledge journey over the sea ice to the nearby Bolingen Islands with a six-man party. John Béchervaise (the incoming OIC at Mawson) took part in this expedition, which managed to get an astrofix from one of the small rocky islets amongst icebergs and highly unstable sea ice.

At 0300 hours on 5 February, Law woke to a fresh north-east wind and an ominous outlook. 'The prospect of a hurricane setting the whole area into heaving motion. . .was not pleasant.' He woke the rest of the party and they moved camp onto the rocky islet the Norwegians had named Lorten Island. By later that day surveyor Bob Lacey completed his observations and geologist Peter Crohn had gathered samples of a rich profusion of both rock and lichen samples. Perhaps because of Adélie guano deposited there over the years, the Norwegians had named it Lorten—literally 'The Turd'. Law decided to change the islet's name to Lichen Island, which he thought more aesthetically pleasing.[24] The weather looked threatening, and the party set out to return to the ship over the sea ice on skis, towing a sledge. As they did so, they realised the ice was beginning to break up around them. Béchervaise:

> This is a very unhappy prospect, to cover some miles over ice floes which are breaking up. . .the floes were up to 30 feet [9.14 metres] across and we had to wait till they moved together and then make a crossing from

A PRECARIOUS OVERNIGHT CAMP ON SEA ICE AMONG GROUNDED ICEBERGS IN PRYDZ BAY NEAR LICHEN ISLAND, FEBRUARY 1955.
(P LAW)

PHIL LAW LEADING A PARTY MANHAULING A SLEDGE TO LICHEN ISLAND, PRYDZ BAY, FEBRUARY 1955.
(J BÉCHERVAISE)

143

The OIC of the 1955 Mawson party, John Mayston Béchervaise, was a man of many accomplishments. School teacher, classicist, poet and mountaineer, 'Béch' was 45 years old when he arrived at Mawson. He had been co-editing the travel-adventure magazine *Walkabout* when Law asked him to go to Heard Island as OIC in 1953. With the magnet of a major unclimbed peak drawing him to it, Béchervaise led two attempts in August and November 1953 to climb Big Ben, but the notoriously wild weather around the 2745 metre volcano beat them back. On the first attempt Béchervaise and his two companions, Peter Shaw and Fred Elliott, sheltered in a snow cave and were nearly killed by carbon monoxide poisoning when their ventilator shaft was blocked by drift.

Béchervaise was not a scientist and in later life seemed mildly puzzled why he, a generalist, should have been selected to lead parties of scientists in Antarctica. His strengths were in leadership, and he represented a break from the policy of appointing a senior scientist—often the head meteorologist—as the OIC of an ANARE station. This emphasis on management rather than scientific expertise became more evident in later years when the administration of a modern station became a far more complex logistical and staffing exercise. John Béchervaise had that rare combination of infectious enthusiasm and an instinctive ability to motivate people. 'Perhaps', wrote fellow bushwalker Graham Wills-Johnson of Béchervaise in 1981, 'the very first qualification of an Antarctic leader, therefore, is to be a good generalist. Good generalists are in much shorter supply in the twentieth century, the age of the specialist, than they were in the eighteenth.'[25]

POET, SCHOLAR AND EXPLORER JOHN BÉCHERVAISE RELISHED THE EXCITEMENT AND PRIVILEGE OF 'FIRST FOOTING' UNDISCOVERED FEATURES IN ANTARCTICA. PHOTOGRAPHED ON HEARD ISLAND, 1953.
(A CAMPBELL-DRURY)

In the 1940s and 1950s keen climbers could still find new peaks to conquer in remote areas of Australia. Béchervaise had led the first ascent of Federation Peak in the south-west of Tasmania in January 1949. His delight in finding himself in virgin territory at Mawson was palpable:

We were extraordinarily fortunate. . .all round the horizon were these mountains which had never been climbed. And some of them had been named from the sea by Douglas Mawson in 1930. There was the Casey Range, for instance, named after young Richard Casey, who was Official Secretary in London and was a big help to Mawson. We had all these virgin peaks. . .we were very lucky in having them.

one to the other—sort of floe-hopping. It's a slow and anxious business. The nearer we got to the ship the happier we were.

Petersen, an experienced ice captain, was aware of their problem and was moving towards them as fast as he could with the ship. As they got closer Béchervaise realised that the ship itself was helping to compress the ice floes they were traversing, 'And when we got to within hailing distance, over the very clear, still Antarctic air came the skipper's voice through his megaphone: "Make straight for zee ship! I am holding the floes together!".'

Béchervaise said it sounded 'like God Almighty making a pronouncement that he had control of everyone's destiny'.

After further coastal survey work along the western end of the Amery Ice Shelf, *Kista Dan* arrived off Mawson Station on 9 February to find Horseshoe Harbour free of ice. Law was delighted with what had been achieved at Mawson, which he found 'in immaculate condition—orderly,

THREE MEMBERS OF THE ANARE PARTY THAT MADE THE FIRST ASCENT OF MT HENDERSON IN FEBRUARY 1955. FROM LEFT: PHIL LAW, JOHN BÉCHERVAISE AND PETER SHAW. THE FOURTH MEMBER, TONY HALL, TOOK THIS PHOTOGRAPH ON THE SUMMIT.
(A HALL)

ROB LACEY (USING
THEODOLITE) AND ERIC
MACKLIN (WITH
CHRONOMETER) SURVEYING IN
THE PRINCE CHARLES
MOUNTAINS, 1955.
(J BÉCHERVAISE)

clean and attractively laid out'. He was concerned, though, to find OIC Dovers far from well:

> The strain of his various field journeys and of his responsibilities at the Station had told heavily on him and he had been under treatment for some time for a chronic gall bladder. All told me he had driven himself without respite for months.[26]

Dovers was ordered onto *Kista Dan* for complete rest and he improved rapidly. The incoming doctor, Bob Allison, did not agree with the gall bladder diagnosis but said the affliction was a psychosomatic condition. After Dovers had made a rapid recovery on the ship Law formed the view that extreme stress had been the cause.

The DUKWs handled the cargo easily and the changeover was smooth. Ten extra huts were built, a radio mast erected, and '40 seals killed and stored for winter dog food'. Law even found time to achieve the first ascent of Mt Henderson with Béchervaise (a keen mountaineer), Peter Shaw and Lieutenant A W Hall, officer in charge of the DUKWs. In contrast to the first *Kista Dan* voyage, Law lavished praise on Captain Petersen who, he said, 'had been cooperative in every way'.[27]

From Mawson it was back to Heard where Law had the sad task of closing down the station, sacrificed to help finance the development of Mawson and an expanded continental program.

With Mawson Station now well established, an expanded program of science and exploration was begun. Cosmic ray research was a priority and during 1955 two large meson telescopes comprising 150 Geiger counters (which had been built at the University of Tasmania under the direction of Drs G Fenton and N R 'Nod' Parsons) were assembled on converted anti-aircraft gun mounts set in concrete piers weighing four tonnes, and screened with one tonne of lead. The cosmic ray building was designed to withstand winds of up to 250 kilometres per hour. Nod Parsons wintered at Mawson to establish the cosmic ray laboratory. By the end of 1955 there were nineteen buildings in use, and the station operated the most elaborate scientific establishment the Antarctic had seen to that date.[28]

In August Béchervaise with five companions and a dog team inspected the emperor penguins at Taylor Rookery west of Mawson in what was becoming an annual Mawson Station ritual. Dogs were not used on the follow-up expedition to reinforce Dovers' sighting of the Prince Charles Mountains (PCMs). After a depot-laying exercise early in November 1955, Béchervaise, with six companions and two Weasels towing sledges, set out for the PCMs on 14 November. Important geological and surveying work was achieved, but the Weasels were not equal to the task and the party was plagued with breakdowns. They did, however, reach the northernmost range of the PCMs, enabling Béchervaise to write in his diary of 26 November:

> The Weasel was a World War II vintage vehicle, originally built as an all-terrain Bren gun carrier and designed for only a short operational life. It was not really adequate for Antarctic field work, although ANARE engineers nursed them past the limits of the possible. It could be fitted with a demolition charge to allow its destruction in combat. (Surveyor Syd Kirkby thought that was its best design feature.)

> This was a good day, containing our longest outward run of the expedition so far. It ended with us being first-footers in the Prince Charles Ranges; with our having gone further south in Mac. Robertson Land [than] any previous party.[29]

Leaving one ailing Weasel abandoned in the field (but retrieving its engine) the PCMs party returned to Mawson on 7 December.

TEN

SPREADING WINGS

Phillip Law had little difficulty in persuading DEA Minister Richard Casey to approve the purchase of aircraft (to assist exploration) and the construction of a hangar at Mawson Station. The RAAF agreed to send an Antarctic Flight which would remain at Mawson during 1956 to carry out flying operations.

The Antarctic Flight would again be led by Squadron Leader Douglas Leckie, supported by Pilot Officer John Seaton and two engineers, G Sundberg and G Johansen, but the choice of aircraft was more difficult than selecting personnel. The Auster aircraft were under-powered for Antarctic work, with minimal cargo-carrying capacity. The RAAF briefly considered using a World War II vintage Wirraway training aircraft but then decided to import a de Havilland DHC2 Beaver from Canada. This single-engined high-winged monoplane had a roomy cabin, could operate on wheels, skis or floats, and had been used successfully in the Canadian Arctic. Leckie:

> The Beaver was an ideal aircraft for the job. It could carry trimetrogon cameras for taking vertical and oblique [photographs] which is absolutely necessary for detailed aerial mapping and surveying. . .and when stripped down it was an ideal transport aircraft. We used to carry 44-gallon [200 litre] drums of fuel and also take passengers and field crews around to their various locations. It had a good range—with extra petrol tanks it would fly well over 1000 miles [1600 kilometres].

A back-up aircraft was needed to rescue the pilot in the event of a forced landing or crash and, with light aircraft in short supply in post-war Australia, Leckie remembered that the fuselage of Auster 201 had been

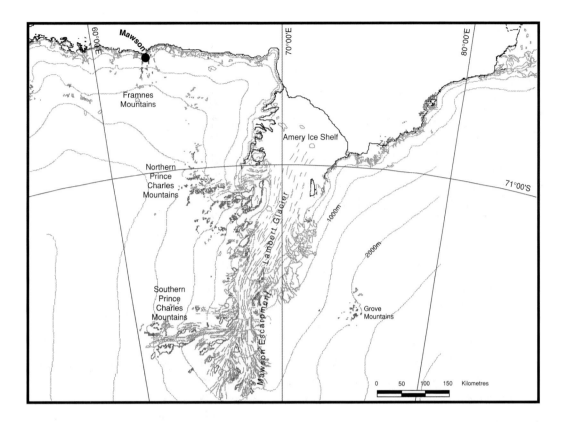

returned to Australia after its wings and other fittings were cannibalised in February 1954:

> It was now owned by the Royal Victorian Aero Club. So after quite a bit of negotiation we purchased [it] back, with skis and floats. We'd also [need] a hangar to erect at Mawson to keep the aircraft serviceable for all-year-round flying.

NORTHERN AND SOUTHERN PRINCE CHARLES MOUNTAINS SHOWING THE LAMBERT GLACIER AND AMERY ICE SHELF

A prefabricated steel and corrugated iron hangar was designed by the Department of Works and loaded on *Kista Dan* with the two aircraft.

Kista Dan left Melbourne on 27 December 1955 and by 5 January reached Davis Bay close to the French Antarctic sector, Adélie Land. The Beaver was launched on floats and Law accompanied Leckie on its first flight in good weather, reporting the new aircraft 'steady as a rock'.[1]

During the voyage along the coast of Wilkes Land, Law reported that he and Leckie managed to photograph 1600 kilometres of coastline. On 21 January the Australians on *Kista Dan* visited the Russians who were building their first Antarctic station at Mirny (on Australian territory situated half way between the present Davis and Casey Stations). This was the start of a friendly association that was to continue through the years ahead.

149

Despite being beset in heavy pack ice for ten days, Law was reasonably happy with what had been achieved—'Many valuable soundings were taken throughout the voyage and important magnetic, gravity, geological and biological observations were made whenever we landed'—although disappointed that the delay made it impossible to visit the Prydz Bay area.[2]

Kista Dan reached Mawson on 17 February and work began immediately on building the hangar at the water's edge near the east arm of Horseshoe Harbour. This construction work was supervised by the incoming medical officer, Dr Don Dowie, a man of many talents. Dowie's construction expertise came from his experiences as a prisoner-of-war of the Japanese during World War II, building timber bridges on the Burma Railway. He was also a pilot. Law reported that the hangar site was on one of the most exposed areas of rock at Mawson where conditions were so bitter the men christened the area 'Siberia'. He later wrote:

BEAVER AIRCRAFT FITTED WITH SKIS BEING OFF-LOADED FROM *KISTA DAN* ON THE SEA ICE OFF THE COAST OF MAC. ROBERTSON LAND FOR A RECONNAISSANCE FLIGHT, 1956.
(M CHRISTENSEN)

The men who bolted cross-braces to the arches 30 feet [9.14 metres] above the ground, sitting astride the steel girders and working with gloved hands while the freezing wind plucked savagely at them, carried on hour after hour uncomplaining, working in ten-minute bursts up aloft and then thawing out before a coke brazier behind a packing case wind-break.[3]

The ever present 'Antarctic Factor' made their task more difficult. A contractor's error caused them to be short of 250 bolts for the frame and 300 hook bolts for attaching the corrugated iron sheeting.[4] Fortunately Dr Dowie's genius for making do on the Burma Railway was no less effective in colder climes. Dowie:

The problem of erecting the pylons and getting them to stand up in 40 knot winds was considerable. We had guy ropes everywhere with a tractor on one side and an army DUKW on the other, holding things vertical, while a few idiots like myself were climbing up these things with nuts and bolts trying to put in the arches.

Swaying precariously eight metres above the granite rocks, Dowie found that the only way it was possible to bolt cross-members to the arches forming the hangar roof was for men to feed a rope over their shoulders, haul up the new girder and wait for the wind to blow it into position—at which point a bolt was slammed through as the two holes became aligned:

THE FIRST HANGAR EVER BUILT IN ANTARCTICA UNDER CONSTRUCTION AT MAWSON STATION, FEBRUARY 1956. (P LAW)

> Bolting on the corrugated iron sheeting was worse. Initially the thing had been designed to have neoprene rubber discs [as washers]. I pointed out to Phil Law that this was probably not going to work and that the snow—it's like powdered salt down there, not nice fluffy flakes—would seep through. The idea was to have a snow-free hangar. I suggested we dice this neoprene washer idea and use piano felts, which we did, and it worked like a charm and never gave any trouble.

Since the aircraft could not be put in the hangar until the sea ice froze on Horseshoe Harbour, keeping them from being bashed to bits by Mawson's notorious katabatic winds was a challenge. They were tethered in the lee of the new hangar, with wire mesh suspended above to stop ice falling on them and a three metre wire netting fence to act as a windbreak. They successfully weathered winds of up to 160 kilometres per hour before the sea ice formed and they were moved inside in April 1956. This was the first hangar ever built in Antarctica and it is still standing.

The 1956 party had great hopes of air-supported exploration because the number of huskies at Mawson had been reduced following a decision to donate the best of them to a planned Trans-Antarctic Expedition as part of the International Geophysical Year in 1957–58. Don Dowie was critical of this decision, which left only one rather poor team on the station:

> The program for the year was looking a bit thin on the ground if we were to rely entirely on tracked vehicles, and the huskies were very

depleted. . .I think it was a miscalculation really, in Melbourne, where the huskies were looked on as not being useful any more, when in fact they were vital.

Surveyor Syd Kirkby was more scathing, describing 'the motley collection' as 'three strong, mature dogs, two old, old men, a village idiot, a shiftless lurk-merchant, one old lady and two breeding bitches'.[5] Pups were eagerly awaited. Nils Lied, a radio operator who had wintered with huskies on Heard Island in 1951, took a special interest. As a boy growing up in Norway, Nils had an Eskimo friend who taught him how to handle sledges, harnesses and dogs. When one of the bitches did whelp in 1956, a blizzard was blowing, and the six puppies were almost snap frozen as they were born:

> There was only one thing to do. I bundled all these little pups into my parka and raced up to the surgery and brutally woke Doctor Don Dowie from a deep sleep and said, 'This is important! What can you do?' So Doc Dowie eased his bottom over and lifted his blankets and said, 'Put them in here'. Two looked very dicky—lifeless and cold. He said, 'Now you knead this one like a piece of dough and let him get the temperature of your hands into him.'
>
> I did this, and he slowly warmed up and jack-knifed and squeaked like a mouse and he was right. Under the blankets with him too! The last one we thought we'd lost, but Doc took two bowls of water, one cold and one hot. He dipped this pup into cold water, then into the hot and rubbed him with a piece of old towel. And, so help me, he blew down his mouth and got life back into him!

Fortunately Sunday was the cook's day off. 'Jock' Mackenzie was adamant there would be 'nae dawgs in ma kitchen!' Lied alleged the obliging medical officer 'slipped him a mickey' and the cook slept blissfully through his day off while the bitch and six puppies enjoyed the sustaining warmth of the Aga combustion stove during that vital first 24 hours. This building up of the husky population would be of benefit to expeditioners in the following years. The scratch collection of adult dogs available was nevertheless to play a vital part in the 1956 exploration program, backing up the mechanically fragile Weasels in the field. The pilots, surveyors and geologists waited impatiently for the sea ice in Horseshoe Harbour to form so that flying could begin. This was the first time flying with fixed-wing aircraft had been attempted during the winter. Mawson Station at 67°36' south has an hour or two of twilight each day, even at midwinter.

On 20 April flying operations began with the Beaver, and ambitious probing flights were made in the available daylight to the south and south-west. Drawn by the lure of fresh geographical discoveries, Leckie and Kirkby flew on occasions much further south than was officially notified. Correctly calculating that they were beyond any search and rescue capabilities by the back-up Auster aircraft anyway, a practice developed of switching off the radio and pushing on to the limits of fuel consumption. Kirkby:

> We would get to the maximum range and then we would switch the radio off and say, 'We're just going to stooge in this area for a while. . .' and we would fly on. It was one of those unsaid things because the minute anyone knew it, then Bill Bewsher the OIC would have had to stop it.

Not all the sightings, however, could be verified. Syd Kirkby is ribbed to this day about the sighting of the 'Princess Anne Mountains' during one of these early winter flights:

> In April 1956 we set out on a long flight south-west of Mawson, 'trudged' along for a couple of hours—went quiet on the radio—and trudged on a bit further. Lo and behold, what should we see coming up to the front of us and to our right but mountains, quite extensive mountains. They looked to be about 40 to 50 miles [64 to 80 kilometres] away. A big discovery, the 'Princess Anne Mountains'!

They flew back to Mawson in high excitement and radioed a report to Phillip Law in Melbourne, who suggested further flights to confirm their location. The problem was they never found them again. Kirkby believes that the American navigator Charles Wilkes had a similar problem in 1840 when he reported sighting various features, which later explorers could not verify, on the coast that now bears his name. Under certain weather conditions and low light a phenomenon occurs a bit like over-the-horizon radar:

> The Russians subsequently quantified it. They named it the 'Novaya Zemlya Effect' from the island in the Arctic where they did a lot of work on it. It's a situation where you get very, very dense cold air over plateau, and relatively warm air over sea ice or sea—and you get lensing. You're actually looking right over the horizon. And what we had seen when we saw the 'Princess Anne Mountains' apparently 40 to 50 miles [64 to 80 kilometres] away were the Scott and Napier and Nye [Mountains] way, way over the other side of Enderby Land 150 miles [240 kilometres]

153

away. I was somewhat pleased when the Russians quantified it and came up with shifts of this sort of order. . .many years later.

Later that year the quirky Antarctic light deceived Kirkby again during a dog sledge run through the southern Prince Charles Mountains with geologist Peter Crohn. Emerging from their polar tent one morning, he was elated to see a great range of black and brown mountains in the distance. The weather was clear, but 'whiteout' conditions prevailed with high cloud and reflected light off the snow. No horizon was visible. 'You just have a bowl of white' said Kirkby:

> We were in a high state of excitement until someone walked a little way away and realised that the mountains were moving very much relative to the tent. . .They were actually husky turds about 30 or 40 metres away, and we had no idea. They looked for all the world like mountains 80 kilometres away. So it wasn't a great discovery. It was almost as bad as the Princess Anne Mountains that Doug Leckie and I didn't discover.

They were exciting, pioneering times. John Seaton flew the Beaver 300 miles [480 kilometres] along the 63rd meridian and noted a continuation of the Prince Charles Mountains (PCMs) swinging gradually westward.[6] Although in May there were only four hours of daylight, field work supported by aircraft continued west of Mawson at Stefannsson and Scoresby Bays where Syd Kirkby and Peter Crohn were doing a survey. Crohn was wintering for the second consecutive year, and had accompanied Béchervaise's party into the northernmost reaches of the PCMs the previous year. The Beaver and Auster were used to lay fuel and food depots at Edward VIII Gulf in preparation for the exploration of the Amundsen Bay area, on the western extremity of the AAT, in the coming spring and summer.

Flying into the interior of Antarctica means climbing up the ever-rising ice sheet. The Beaver carried no oxygen, and on one of the autumn exploratory flights Leckie was flying at 4500 metres above sea level, but only 600 metres above the ice cap. He noticed that Syd Kirkby's fingernails and lips were turning purple:

> I looked at my fingers and they were going purple, so we were running out of oxygen. I said to Syd, 'We've got to do an about turn and head for the coast as quickly as possible and lose height, otherwise we're going to pass out.' So we turned, but it seemed so gradual. We were trying to go down but we couldn't beat the rate of the contour of the ice sheet, otherwise we would have flown onto the ice surface.

Syd Kirkby queries Leckie's version and says he was the first to pick Leckie's hypoxia. 'I looked over his shoulder and saw him resolutely flying along, wing down about ten to fifteen degrees and I raised the alarm.' (Syd's notes taken at the time show an illegible scrawl!)

As the daylight merged into twilight, landings on the ice at Mawson were interesting. Leckie:

> We'd drop a scientific group about 60 or 70 miles [96 or 112 kilometres] away at a penguin rookery. . .and then we'd come back, and Corporal Cooper would turn on the headlights on the Ferguson tractor and we'd land over the headlights with our lights [showing] on to Mawson harbour. So it was quite dicey flying all the year round.

(Corporal Noel 'Toby' Cooper was an army man, not RAAF. He had sailed on *Kista Dan* as an engineer with the army DUKW team for the 1955–56 changeover, and had volunteered at Mawson to stay down for the 1956 year to help with the flying program.)

Flying continued until 25 May and then closed down for winter maintenance. As soon as the daylight began to lengthen in July flying resumed and by August both pilots had made a series of flights west to the Amundsen Bay area, photographing previously unseen mountain peaks, a new glacier and many islands. Some flights were of more than seven hours' duration. Leckie recorded that he and Seaton were sometimes notching up seventeen hours' flying in a twenty-four-hour period.

While acknowledging that Antarctic flying is conducted in the world's most extreme weather conditions, and that a certain amount of good fortune is necessary, 28 October 1956 was nevertheless a frightening day in the history of Australian Antarctic aviation.

Seaton (in the Auster) and Leckie flying the larger Beaver were laying fuel dumps to assist a field trip to Amundsen Bay, an area not previously visited by ANARE scientists. They met at King Edward VIII Gulf, 300 kilometres west of Mawson, because Leckie needed Seaton to help him lift two 44-gallon [200 litre] drums of fuel into the Beaver. It was too cold to risk switching off their engines and they left the motors of both aircraft running while they worked. Seaton then took off to return to Mawson to the east, and Leckie (with his two drums of fuel) headed further west to Amundsen Bay.

Some 130 kilometres out from Mawson, just after passing Cape Wilkins, Seaton realised that his elevator controls were jammed, although he was able to maintain straight and level flight by juggling his engine power:

> I considered the position for some fifteen minutes. . .and decided to attempt a landing in an area a few miles west of Taylor Glacier. A very long final approach had to be made. . .every time power was reduced the nose dropped and it was impossible to hold up due to the state of the elevator controls.[7]

What Seaton had to do was to fly the Auster on to the ice at full cruising speed. Only then could he reduce power, and he had no brakes.

> A dead calm existed at the time and as a result the aircraft continued to run over the blue ice for what seemed miles; however the speed was dropping off enough to see that the end result would not be particularly hair-raising. Even so, avoiding action had to be taken when approximately 150 yards from the glacier tongue, and eventually the aircraft came to rest amid a [group] of Weddell seals.[8]

Seaton found that the rear support of the radio compass control box had snapped, dropping it down on the control system beneath the instrument panel. He removed the control box and took off again for Mawson 'without further trouble'.

Meanwhile Doug Leckie in the Beaver was going through one of the most traumatic incidents of his flying career, and which was not logged on the official record at the time. As he approached Amundsen Bay he climbed to clear the Napier and Tula mountain ranges ahead. The tops of the mountains were poking through cloud, and there was a higher level of cloud which Leckie decided to climb above also. The party at Amundsen Bay had reported quite good weather there, so he pressed on:

> I'd been flying for an hour or so and I looked at my radar-altimeter. It indicated zero—that I was over sea ice—and I thought, 'I must have struck a tail-wind'.

Leckie was not over the sea ice at all. His radar-altimeter had actually broken at that very moment, and his eye had been caught by the sinking indicator. Thinking he had to get down quickly or he would overshoot Amundsen Bay, he let down through the cloud beneath him:

> There was another bank of cloud below me. . .and as I broke through, there was a sheer rock face coming straight at me. Well, my heart nearly stopped. So all I could do was a violent turn to the left. . .and there was rock facing me on the left. I finished up doing a complete 360° [turn] and I had rocks running straight up into the cloud all round me. I thought, 'This is it!'

It was a pilot's ultimate nightmare. Leckie's only chance was to go on instruments and try to climb out of those rock-filled clouds, but he was 'a bit rusty' on instruments:

> It was no good delaying things. I could have stayed until I ran out of fuel. . .or just climb and face the music. If I climb out of it clear, I climb out of it clear. If I go into a rock—well, I'll know nothing because I had two 44-gallon [200 litre] drums at my back and it would've just been a ball of flame against a rock.

Going back into the cloud was 'more than flesh and blood can almost stand'. Leckie was flying blind and had to concentrate on maintaining his climb on instruments to the exclusion of all else:

> That was more frightening than before, because of the varying changing shades of the cloud. You feel it start to get dark and you would think it could be the rock face, but you'd have to trust your instruments that your turn was accurate. . .and then it would start to lighten until eventually I could see the blue sky above me. Then you are inclined to do what all seats-of-the-pants pilots do and go for the blue sky and then, of course, your instruments start toppling and you start losing control.

Leckie was so shaken by the time he climbed clear that he set course back home to Mawson Station without delivering his drums of fuel to Amundsen Bay, and did not speak of the incident publicly for 37 years.

Despite flying on the edge of operational limits, the aircraft not only dramatically expanded the ability to map and explore the surrounding coastline and interior of Enderby, Kemp and Mac. Robertson lands but were able to support wide-ranging field parties. Original discoveries were being made. For instance it was found that Amundsen Bay was really two bays and not one.[9]

The major field operation for the year was a journey from Mawson into the Prince Charles Mountains in November to extend the work done in 1954. Depots of food and fuel were established first by Weasel and air-craft. Picking a landing spot from the air was extremely hazardous as crevasses covered in snow could not be seen. On 4 November, Leckie flew the Beaver 200 miles [320 kilometres] south with OIC Bill Bewsher and geologist Peter Crohn. The aircraft was laden with food, fuel and dog food to establish a supply depot for the ground party. Ice flowing around mountains is invariably heavily crevassed but Leckie thought he saw a fairly smooth stretch of ice and landed. Before he switched off his engine, he asked Crohn and Bewsher to get out and check the area:

> Peter Crohn stepped straight into a crevasse. Well, that was it. I then told them that they had to unload the aircraft, all the spares and every-thing they could, and I would take off with an empty aircraft and while I was away refuelling at Mawson they could put down an airstrip for me with lots of flags.

Leckie was confident they could probe and explore the ice sheet nearby to find a safe landing area. While he was away, though, a bliz-zard blew up and he could not find any trace of them when he returned. Bewsher and Crohn were sitting in a grey pyramid tent almost impos-sible to see from the air, and with flapping of the fabric in the high wind, they did not hear the aircraft. It took three flights from Mawson to locate them.

The supplies off-loaded from the Beaver in the crevassed area remained there deep frozen in perfect condition for 30 years. The alternative site, located on a stretch of stable blue ice, was named Aerial Depot (or 250 Mile Depot).

On 19 November 1956, Bill Bewsher, Syd Kirkby, Peter Crohn, John Hollingshead and Lin Gardner left Mawson with two Weasels, two cargo sleds, one man-hauling sledge and a wooden 'Nansen' sledge pulled by a small team of six dogs—Mac (leader), Oscar, Horace, Streaky, Brownie and Dee. Plagued with the usual Weasel mechanical troubles and delayed by having to winch them out of crevasses, they did not get in to Aerial Depot until mid December. There, the dogs came into their own as Bewsher, Kirkby and Crohn sledged through crevassed areas of the PCMs the Weasels could not have negotiated. Syd Kirkby:

> We used the dogs fairly ruthlessly—as we used ourselves pretty ruthlessly. But it's bloody hard work. Any of this precious nonsense about dog-sledg-ing being. . .you know, lovely and beaut and fun. . .Serious dog-sledging is about as hard a bloody thing as you can find to do. You run the best part of a marathon distance in 30 lbs [14 kg] of clothing day-in, day-out, and then climb a mountain at the end of that. . .You stand up on top of

it, do some work for anything up to eight hours and then on your way back—just in case you might break into a run in your enthusiasm —you and your geologist mate pick up a half a hundred-weight of rocks to keep you from breaking into a canter. It's hard, it's very hard work.

Surveying was crucial. Kirkby climbed mountains to take an astrofix from a point other than moving ice. Distance travelled was theoretically measured with a wheel trailing behind the sledge. But the wheel seldom worked for more than a few days:

> We measured distance by pacing as we ran beside the sledge (in my case 900 double paces to the nautical mile). After a while one becomes very adept at counting paces while simultaneously assessing the terrain, yelling at the dogs, noting features for inclusion on the map and perhaps carrying on a conversation.[10]

The downside of this technique, Kirkby noted, was a tendency to count paces in your sleep.

Some idea of the pioneering nature of the work being done on this field trip can be gauged by the fact that all five members of the expedition have major peaks in the Prince Charles Mountains named after them. The names of the six huskies were put forward as well, but the Australian Committee for Antarctic Names (ACAN) was not convinced. ACAN did accept an alternative suggestion and Husky Dome is on the map a few kilometres southwest of the Aramis Range—their furthest point south.[11]

This 'poor old mob', as Kirkby described the huskies, certainly merited the honour, as he, Crohn and Bewsher pushed on through the mountains, while Gardner and Hollingshead remained with the Weasels for weeks at a time, qualifying in Kirkby's opinion for 'leather medals' for their fortitude (although Hollingshead did go on the second of the three main dog sledging runs). During this enforced wait, two more verses of the ANARE 'Chain Blocks'* song were composed and 'written in tears of blood on the walls of the Weasel':

(Tune—'My Old Man's A Dustman')

We sat in the Weasel for hours and hours,
We stuck it as long as we could
We stuck it, we stuck it, and then we said: 'Blow [?] it!
Our arseholes are not made of wood!'

CHORUS   (Tune—'My Bonnie Lies Over The Ocean')
Chain Blocks, Chain Blocks,
Oh bring back my Weasel to me, to me.
Chain Blocks, Chain Blocks,
Oh bring back my Weasel to me.

The tracks are in very good order
The springs they are right on the dot,
The engine it goes tick-tock,
But the lot's down a bloody great slot.[12]

Unlike the previous year in the PCMs with no aircraft available, Weasel spare parts could at least be dropped by the Beaver on the way in, and helpful notes were dropped to Bewsher after aerial reconnaissance indicating that it would be unsafe to take the Weasels near the eastern end of the PCMs due to extensive crevassing.[13]

Syd Kirkby recalls the pioneering dog sledging runs at that time:

We sledged up and down the ranges, Peter geologising and I doing astrofixes and rounds of terrestrial photographs from the mountain tops and triangulating. We had a glass plate camera that mounted on top of the theodolite but we had a limited number of plate holders, so every 24 plates you had to change plates somehow. We had no [photographic] dark bag, there had been one at Mawson but it was moth-eaten and ratty and let in the light and everything else.

So I used to climb into the bottom of my sleeping bag inside the double sleeping bag to load fresh plates into the plate holders. You probably can't imagine what a sledging sleeping bag is like. After you've been sledging for a while and the dogs pee on you to show they like you, and you get filthy and grotty (and of course, you're going to bed virtually fully booted and spurred all the time) the bottom of the sleeping bag

---

* Chain blocks are a portable winching system used to extricate vehicles from crevasses, and a 'slot' is ANARE parlance for a crevasse.

gets absolutely foul! I always reckoned that if you put a pit canary in there it would've died instantly!

Aerial reconnaissance in September had convinced Kirkby that the ice flowing down from the PCMs joined the Amery Ice Shelf, which extended inland some 250 kilometres from its seaward edge. This was later found to be so. The second major sledging journey of the PCMs field trip was to run down the Charybdis Glacier between the Porthos and Aramis Ranges right down to the Amery:

> We'd come down from high cold to relatively warm, down near sea level, and we were pretty tired by that stage of the game. It was very, very hard going down the glacier, a lot of crevassing and broken-up country. We had a couple of days down at the bottom of the glacier there. We did a lot of walking, and we walked over to Jetty Peninsula and Peter discovered the coal there—which was the first location of coal in the AAT. Then we went around on the east of what came to be known as the Amery Peak and I have a diary entry of the day we saw Beaver Lake for the first time—with no name then, of course—saying that it was so wonderful to sit there beside this fresh water in the amphitheatre. The sun was shining on the rock behind us and it was warm and relatively calm. We ate a block of chocolate and everything was beautiful and sweetness and light.*

A HUSKY TEAM RESTS, PONDERING THE STUPIDITY OF THE HUMANS WHO HAD STEERED THEM INTO IMPOSSIBLY ROUGH TERRITORY. PRINCE CHARLES MOUNTAINS SOUTHERN JOURNEY, 1956–57. (S KIRKBY)

RESCUING BROWNIE FROM A CREVASSE DURING THE EXPLORATION OF THE PRINCE CHARLES MOUNTAINS, 1956–57. (S KIRKBY)

---

* Curiously enough Beaver Lake has never been seen as open water since. It is regarded as a perennially frozen, tidal, freshwater lake.

161

A quiz question might well ask: 'Who has explored and surveyed the most Australian territory?'. The answer is not Burke or Wills or even Charles Sturt. It is Sydney L Kirkby, surveyor in the service of ANARE, in Antarctica.

Kirkby wintered at Mawson in 1956 and 1960 and was OIC Mawson (at the ripe old age of 47) in 1980. First into the Prince Charles Mountains with dogs in 1956–57, he again used dogs for a remarkable 400 kilometre journey through Enderby Land from the Napier Mountains to Mawson Station in the autumn of 1960. He went south on coastal exploration and resupply voyages in the summers of 1961–62 (including a visit to Oates Land on the eastern extremity of the AAT), 1962–63 to George V Land (on the east of the French sector, Adélie Land) and to Enderby and Kemp Lands (on the western extremity of the AAT) in 1964–65.

There are features named after Syd Kirkby along 6000 kilometres of the coast of the AAT, inland at the PCMs—Mt Kirkby—and even outside the AAT. Kirkby Glacier in Victoria Land is actually just within the New Zealand sector. Kirkby Shoal can be found near Casey Station (off the coast of Wilkes Land) and, to the extreme west, Kirkby Head on the Tange Promontory is near the Russian station Molodezhnaya, just on the Australian side of the border with Norway's Queen Maud Land claim. He has personally surveyed more Antarctic territory than any other explorer—including Scott, Shackleton and Mawson.

Syd Kirkby was an unlikely candidate for Antarctic exploration. At the age of five, growing up in Fremantle, Western Australia, he developed poliomyelitis and was severely disabled for years. His father (who admired the pioneering work that Sister Kenny was achieving with an exercise program for polio victims) quit his job to help Syd, and 'rebuilt' him:

He would take me down to the South Fremantle baths—it was a sandy beach—and unstrap the irons from my legs and sit me on the beach. He'd then go in and swim. I hated anyone to look at me—the cripple—so I would crawl down in the water and splash around. My upper body was always fine. We'd swim and swim, and then he'd rush out saying, 'Oh, see you later, son'.

It was a deliberate ploy to force the crippled boy to crawl up the beach, or stay in the water. Either way he had to exercise to the limits of his endurance. Later, standing beside Syd at the pool, he would often stumble against his son and knock him back into the water, so that he would have to do another half lap.

I hated being a cripple. I really hated it. I loathed it. Don't let people tell you that suffering ennobles you and makes you a better person. It doesn't at all, it makes you ratty and cranky.

This treatment was effective, however, and Kirkby recovered his strength. He could not run and jump as fast as other boys, so his father suggested boxing, saying it 'was the most mental and least physical of all sports'.

It's a matter of dominating your own fear and thinking about your opponent carefully. And if you look through boxing you'll find quite a number of famous boxers over the years who have been people with some level of physical disability. In my case, my most severely impaired movement was with my right leg. Boxing in an orthodox style meant that leg was behind me. So I always found it relatively difficult to retreat in the ring, which was something of an advantage. It's one of nature's incentives—you keep punching or you get into trouble.

In 1960 the Commonwealth Medical Officer examining Syd Kirkby picked up that he walked with a limp, as a legacy of his polio, and was not going to pass him medically fit for Antarctica. He bluffed his way through, saying to the surprised medico that he had already been to Antarctica. This doctor would have been even more surprised to learn later that shortly before leaving Mawson in 1961, Syd Kirkby and his companion Graham Dyke ran 67 nautical miles [124 kilometres] with a dog team from Depot A, behind the Framnes Mountains, back to Mawson Station in one day. That is more than a double marathon!

In 1956, during his first year at Mawson, surveyors were beginning to develop the technique of using daylight stars to make an astrofix from rocky features in Antarctica—essential for accurate mapping:

The few brightest stars are visible through a theodolite telescope in full daylight, in conjunction with sights to the sun to determine position. Before this it had been the practice, by surveyors from all nations, to use only sun sights, which gave rise to many problems.[14]

Surveying in Antarctica was heavy work, often involving rock climbing on virgin peaks with heavy packs. By 1964–65 astrofixes had been replaced by electronic distance measuring, but it was still necessary to reach the pinnacle of the peak to be measured, carrying batteries, theodolite and other essential gear. The 'hardest and longest' climb of Syd Kirkby's career was on Leckie Range in Kemp Land in early 1965. He had to hang off the peak with a rope around his waist to sight his theodolite. During the six-hour climb a rope broke on a steep pinch and Kirkby dropped some nine metres with a 40 kilogram pack on his back. At the time he was concerned about spraining his ankle, but the more serious injury was a whiplash which broke two vertebrae in his neck. He managed to climb Leckie Range a further three times, however, and finish his work.

The discomfort was offset, in his view, by being awarded an MBE for his services in Antarctica, to complement the Polar Medal awarded in 1957. He maintained his contact with Antarctica by working with the Division of National Mapping (NATMAP) full time from 1965 until 1980, when he returned to Mawson Station, this time as OIC. He hopes to return to Mawson in the year 2000 but has been told he is ineligible because of heart bypass surgery. Perhaps this will not stop him.

While Syd Kirkby seized all the Antarctic pioneering opportunities available to him with great gusto, he never ceases to marvel at his good fortune:

We'd climb a mountain peak and look out and say: 'Wow! In all time, certainly no human being and probably no creature has ever seen it.' It's a funny feeling. It's not a possessive feeling, it's a privileged sort of feeling—'How did I get this lucky?'

THE HUSKIES HAD TO BE FITTED WITH MAKESHIFT BOOTS OF LEATHER AND CLOTH TO PROTECT THEIR FEET FROM THE SHARP-EDGED GRANULAR ICE NEAR THE JUNCTION OF THE AMERY ICE SHELF AND THE PRINCE CHARLES MOUNTAINS, 1956–57 SOUTHERN JOURNEY. (S KIRKBY)

This euphoria was balanced by the necessity to climb back up the glacier, over crevassed territory, into the high country again with a heavily laden sledge and exhausted dogs. By that time Mac had died in harness and the other dogs were weakening. The three explorers took turns helping to pull in harness with the dogs. Falling down crevasses became so common that one photograph taken by Kirkby at this time shows the overturned sledge straddling a large 'slot' on the Charybdis Glacier, while one of the huskies, Streaky, rests seemingly unconcerned, taking full advantage of the delay. As they climbed back up the glacier, the dogs' feet were cut by the granulated ice caused by rock dust blowing off the mountains. Kirkby: 'We made them little boots of leather and ventile and strapped them on to protect their feet. Then you had to watch the dogs constantly to stop them eating the boots because they were starving.'

On the way back to Mawson, on 4 February, Dee died after eating a lump of cotton waste with oil or grease on it, to the great sadness of the PCMs party. It is part of a husky's nature to work and work, literally to death if need be. Syd Kirkby recalls the final moments of Brownie during the third major PCMs sledging journey:

> He got very tired and very weak, so much so that he couldn't run in the traces and we let him off hoping that he could just follow us along for a day or two and then with a bit of rest maybe he'd pick up. It was fairly early in the morning and by the time we'd been travelling for a few hours, he was maybe half a mile back behind us and repeatedly falling over. It was quite clear that he wasn't going to be able to keep up with us, so I took the pistol and walked back to him.

I'll never forget this old fellow as I came up. He'd been struggling and trying to walk and falling and struggling. . . and when I got within twenty or so metres of him, he sat down and waited for me. While I patted him and talked to him he looked at me with these bloody great eyes and you could see him saying, 'Oh, gee, everything is right now, me old mate's come back to look after me'. His old mate put a pistol to his head and shot him. So, it's not all sweetness and light. But they're fantastic things.

LEAD DOG STREAKY, WEAK BUT DEFIANT, HOMEWARD BOUND AT THE END OF THE 1956–57 SOUTHERN JOURNEY.
(S KIRKBY)

The PCMs party did not return to Mawson until 10 February 1957—eight days after the arrival of *Kista Dan* to relieve them. Their return journey had seen the chain block winches in constant service, winching the battered Weasels out of the crevasses into which they had crashed. On their return to the Framnes Mountains just behind Mawson they had the unusual experience of being greeted by the director of ANARE, Phil Law, fresh from *Kista Dan,* who had driven up by Weasel for that purpose. Law described how they appeared over a rise—'two battered Weasels hauling four sledges followed by a dog sledge drawn by [three] lean huskies with a man running beside':

> They drew up beside us and five bearded, grimy, gaunt men strode towards us amidst much laughing, back-slapping and affectionate abuse. These men had been in the field for three months. . .[15]

While the PCMs party was away, John Seaton flew the last major Beaver flight of the year on 28 November. Seaton flew a passenger to Aerial Depot to undertake magnetic observations and then, with radio operator Pat Albion as his 'key man' (to handle communications while he concentrated on navigation, photography and flying), headed southeast until at 74°south he could see the southernmost peaks of the PCMs beyond which 'only the eternal white of the plateau could be seen':

165

THE LAMBERT GLACIER,
LOOKING SOUTH, 1960. THE
WORLD'S BIGGEST GLACIER, IT
WAS SEEN FIRST FROM THE AIR
BY RAAF PILOT JOHN
SEATON, FLYING A BEAVER,
ON 28 NOVEMBER 1956.
(R RUKER)

In this position I could see the gentle sweep of the stream onto the eastern end of the Prince Charles Mountains and finally the Amery Ice Shelf. The small subsidiary glaciers flowing into the main stream from the west were very clearly outlined from this position; their stream lines and crevasses stood out distinctly.[16]

Returning to Aerial Depot to refuel, and without the necessity to take trimetrogon photographs, Seaton altered course to observe some of the western mountains, noting vast tributaries of ice running through them into a main glacier:

From my observations on this flight, I would say that the glacier is roughly 200 miles [320 kilometres] in length, varying in width from 15 [24 kilometres] to 40 miles [64 kilometres]. At 73° south its height is approximately 3200 feet [975.3 metres]. . .The mountains on the east are upwards of 6000 feet [1828.8 metres] while those to the west go to an estimated 8000 feet [2438.4 metres].[17]

Seaton had been the first to fly across and observe the whole of the Lambert Glacier, the largest glacier in the world, draining one-third of the entire AAT.

The advent of the RAAF flight based at Mawson had lifted the horizons of Australian science and exploration in Antarctica. During the year the robust Beaver and the smaller but essential Auster had transported 11 tonnes of food, fuel and equipment on depot-laying flights, and transported some 150 passengers, mostly scientists and support staff on field excursions. The trimetrogon camera had been flown on 27 sorties, capturing 12 000 photographic exposures over an area of one million square kilometres, including 2000 kilometres of coastline. The RAAF pilots had logged a remarkable 1200 flying hours.[18] Using fuel depots, the Beaver had on several occasions flown 800 kilometres from Mawson.

Law was delighted with the success of the scientific program, noting in his report that the cosmic ray and magnetic observatory work—and the marine biological investigations—had been meticulously carried out and some excellent results obtained, as well as the expanded exploration, geology and field geophysics made possible by the use of aircraft.[19]

This was a useful and timely prologue to the most ambitious science program yet attempted in Antarctica—the International Geophysical Year of 1957–58.

ELEVEN

ANTARCTICA INTERNATIONAL

The International Geophysical Year (IGY) of 1957–58 not only raised the profile of Antarctic science worldwide but was an important stepping stone to the Antarctic Treaty negotiated in 1959.

The first International Polar Year (IPY), held in the Arctic in 1882, concentrated on the gathering of magnetic, auroral and meteorological data. The second IPY of 1932–33, again confined to the Arctic, had similar scientific aims but suffered considerably from cutbacks caused by the Great Depression.

On the evening of 5 April 1950, in the United States, a notable group of scientists attended a dinner party at the Silver Spring, Maryland, home of James A Van Allen (for whom the radiation belts around the earth were later named). Although the tradition was for an international polar year every half century, the scientists felt that science was moving too fast to wait that long and the concept of a new IPY was suggested by Dr Lloyd B Berkner who had been a radio engineer on the first Byrd Antarctic expedition.[1] After some discussion the concept was broadened to include simultaneous observations of geophysical phenomena over the entire planet—on the land, in the seas, and in the atmosphere.

This proposal went before the International Council of Scientific Unions (ICSU) which set up a committee to organise what had now been named the International Geophysical Year.[2]

For Antarctica, the major geophysical questions were defined as the volume and structure of the ice sheet, the nature of the land beneath the ice, the influence of the ice cap on global and southern hemisphere weather, the aurora, and the high atmosphere with emphasis on the ionosphere. For instance, it was not known what happened to the ionosphere—an electrified region of the upper atmosphere which supposedly formed only in sunlight—during the long polar night.

The plans for the IGY came at a critical time for the Antarctic Division. Director Phil Law (who began his Antarctic career as the division's senior scientific officer) had been pushing science as the enduring reason for Australia's activity in the AAT, but his sense of priorities was not shared in Canberra. On 24 March 1955 Keith Waller of the DEA wrote to him: 'As you know I do not think of our Antarctic effort as a scientific expedition. To me the scientific work is secondary to the political consideration of maintaining our claim to this territory.'[3]

Waller was simply stating the obvious, for the DEA view at that time was that occupation was more important than scientific work. Australia's claim in Antarctica of nearly 42 per cent of its land mass was ambitious to say the least, and while the AAT was considered strategically important, there was little evidence of Australian activity to bolster its sovereignty other than one scientific station on the western extremity of the AAT's 6000-kilometre coastline. Australia did not even possess a ship capable of reaching Antarctica, so the IGY was the trigger for a flurry of increased activity. Law:

> The advent of the International Geophysical Year solved my major political problems. Up until then it had been a great battle trying to persuade politicians that we should be doing something in Antarctica. But when the IGY occurred, the Russians set up three stations in Australian Antarctic Territory. This embarrassed the Australian Government in relation to the Australian claim.
>
> Naturally there was nothing they could do to prevent the Russians going in, so they saved face by sending the Russians an official invitation to do what they had done. The Russians, of course, couldn't acknowledge that, otherwise they'd be acknowledging the Australian claim, which they didn't recognise.

Law, who had been closely involved with international conferences set up to organise the IGY, saw the opportunity to put an Australian station on what he considered one of the choicest sites in Antarctica—the ice-free Vestfold Hills on the eastern end of Prydz Bay. He had visited the area briefly after establishing Mawson Station in 1954 and managed a more thorough reconnaissance in 1955:

> This gave us the opportunity to approach the Government and say, 'Look, Australia must have a second station in order to try and neutralise the activities of the USSR', and I said, 'There's that wonderful

site. If we don't get in quickly to the Vestfold Hills, the Russians will put their station there.'

Approval for a small station was obtained, despite an earlier suggestion by Waller that it would be politically more advantageous to have six extra stations each staffed by 'two or three men', as effective occupation was the important thing. Law's view prevailed after he explained that finances limited ship charter to 100 days and it was impossible for one ship to visit and relieve so many stations in one season.[4]

In 1957 Antarctica was about to be visited on a scale not seen before or since. Argentina, Australia, Belgium, Chile, France, Japan, New Zealand, Norway, South Africa, United Kingdom, United States and USSR planned some 60 stations on the Antarctic continent and sub-Antarctic islands. Not to be outdone by the American decision to build a station at the symbolic heart of Antarctica, the South Pole, the Russians proposed a station at the Pole of Inaccessibility—the point on the ice cap most distant from the coasts.[5]

In order to take advantage of the aim of simultaneous observations of meteorological, magnetic, and upper atmosphere phenomena, the stations in Antarctica were distributed as widely as possible over the continent. As it happened, all of the IGY stations planned by the USSR were in the Australian claim, giving rise to increased Australian concern about Russia's real aims on the continent.

An Antarctic radio communications network was set up to coordinate the sharing of meteorological and other scientific data from all stations using a 'mother–daughter' model. For example, Australia's 'mother' station was Mawson, and the various 'daughters' included Norway Station, Syowa (Japan) and Roi Baudoin (Belgium). Smaller outlying bases were 'granddaughters', like Shore Base (Norway) and Advanced Base (Japan), in this case all reporting by Morse code through to 'mother' Mawson.

The IGY was the first big test of Antarctica as a zone of peace and cooperative science and it is a tribute to the scientists and support staff of all the nations involved that the 'Cold War' never invaded Antarctica.

In Australia, anti-communist, anti-Soviet sentiments were fuelled by the Petrov Affair in 1954, following the defection of Vladimir Petrov and his wife from the Russian Embassy in Canberra and their request for political asylum. The Soviet Union broke off diplomatic relations with Australia until 1959. Remarkably, none of these international tensions seemed to impinge on the IGY.

On 30 January 1956, on his way to relieve Mawson Station, Phil Law called in to the Russian station, Mirny, then being built on the coast just east of Cape Filchner, about halfway between the present Australian

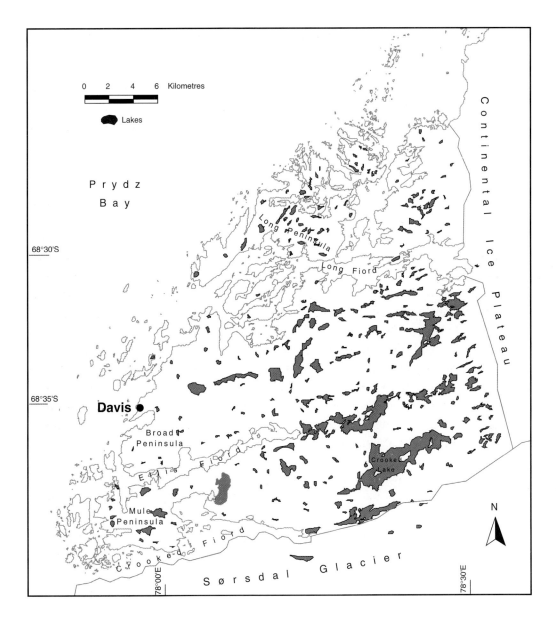

stations of Casey and Davis. There was an initial awkwardness in that first meeting between Australians and Russians in Antarctica:

> This was the period of the 'cold war'—we were not
> sure how the Russians would react, and they were
> not sure how we would react—so there was a sort of inhibition on both
> sides. We were both standing off looking at each other very warily.

The Russian expedition was led by a distinguished Arctic explorer, Mikhail Somov, whom Law considers one of the greatest leaders he ever

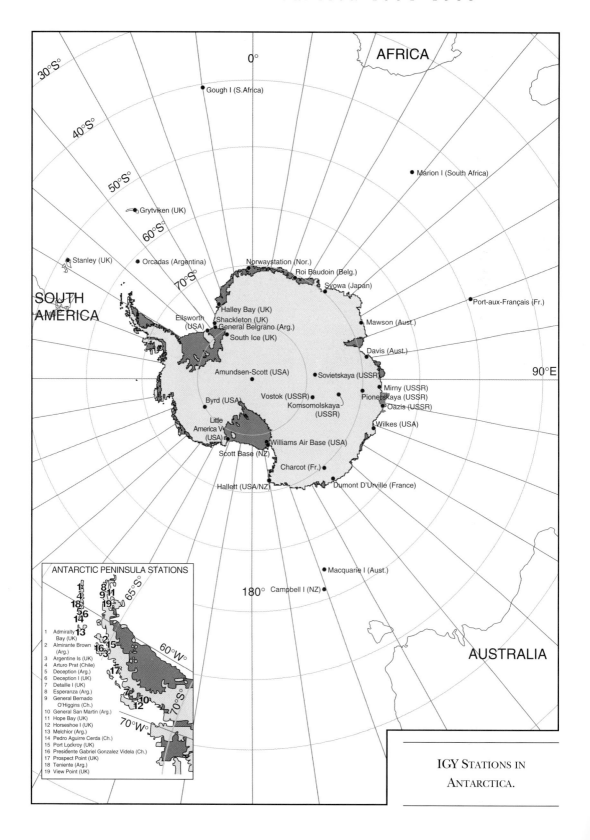

ANTARCTIC PENINSULA STATIONS

1 Admiralty Bay (UK)
2 Almirante Brown (Arg.)
3 Argentine Is (UK)
4 Arturo Prat (Chile)
5 Deception (Arg.)
6 Deception I (UK)
7 Detaille I (UK)
8 Esperanza (Arg.)
9 General Bernado O'Higgins (Ch.)
10 General San Martin (Arg.)
11 Hope Bay (UK)
12 Horseshoe I (UK)
13 Melchior (Arg.)
14 Pedro Aguirre Cerda (Ch.)
15 Port Lockroy (UK)
16 Presidente Gabriel Gonzalez Videla (Ch.)
17 Prospect Point (UK)
18 Teniente (Arg.)
19 View Point (UK)

IGY STATIONS IN ANTARCTICA.

met, and the two men quickly established a rapport. Somov was keen to get Law's opinion of their site, which left a lot to be desired. There were a few pimples of rock sticking through the ice, but some of the huts were on ice, which meant they would eventually have to be replaced. Law's main message to Somov was to work non-stop building the station while the good weather lasted. He said, 'The curtain comes down at the beginning of March and the station must be ready by then. Later Somov told him the weather did break up on 3 March and it had been good advice. Law:

THE MINISTER FOR EXTERNAL AFFAIRS RICHARD CASEY IS ADDRESSING THE CROWD FROM THE DECK OF *KISTA DAN* BEFORE ITS DEPARTURE FROM MELBOURNE IN 1955. PHIL LAW IS STANDING ON A FUEL DRUM JUST BEHIND CASEY. (A CAMPBELL-DRURY)

During that time our scientists mingled very closely with the Russians and there were some furious arguments, because we had some young 23-year-old scientists and they had some young vigorous scientists. They were each representing a different doctrine, and the arguments pro and against communism and other forms of government became very heated. I remember once going in to visit some of the men and finding one of these furious arguments raging. I kept telling my men, 'Cool it, cool it, we must preserve good relations with these people'. . .and we got through without any eruption or any great problem.

173

The advent of the IGY saw an increased Australian Government financial commitment to Antarctica. In 1955, £67 000 [$134 000] was made available to the Australian Academy of Science to enable universities and other interested organisations to take an active part. Government organisations such as the CSIRO and the Commonwealth Government departments of National Development, Supply and the Interior undertook to expand their normal functions during the IGY. In 1955 External Affairs Minister Richard Casey announced that a new Antarctic station, staffed by four to six men, would be set up in the Vestfold Hills as recommended by the Executive Planning Committee. Law had told the meeting of 29 August 1955 that if the Vestfold Hills area was not occupied by Australia it would be by some other nation.[6] The final Australian commitment to an IGY project in 1955 was £25 000 [$50 000] towards the cost of the Commonwealth Trans-Antarctic Expedition in 1957–58. This traverse of the entire continent was based on the plan of Shackleton's failed attempt in 1914–16. A British party led by Sir Vivian Fuchs would travel overland from the Weddell Sea to the Ross Sea via the South Pole, using 'Sno-cat' tractors and dog teams. The party would include one Australian, geologist Dr Jon Stephenson (who became the first man since Amundsen to drive dogs to the South Pole).

Plans for 1957 were the most ambitious and complex ever attempted by ANARE. They were previewed at a symposium to publicise the work of ANARE held by the Royal Society of Victoria in Melbourne on 3 December 1956 and opened by the Duke of Edinburgh. Among the speakers were Sir Douglas Mawson, still taking an interest in Australia's Antarctic program as an active member of the Antarctic Executive Planning Committee (EPC), and the Antarctic Division's Director Phil Law.[7]

With so much cargo to load on *Kista Dan* in December 1956 (including the huts and stores for the new Vestfold Hills station) arrangements were made for the US Antarctic Expedition to pick up seven Australians and the USA observer in New Zealand and a rendezvous was organised at the Windmill Islands, on the eastern side of Vincennes Bay, after *Kista Dan* had established what would be named Davis Station at the Vestfold Hills. Even so, Law was disappointed to have to leave an automatic weather station on the dock at the last minute. *Kista Dan* carried a Beaver aircraft to augment the RAAF flight (commanded by Flight Lieutenant Peter Clemence) at Mawson Station for the IGY-associated field activities. The master of *Kista Dan* was Captain Kaj Hindberg. It was the first time for three years that Law had sailed on a Lauritzen charter without Captain Hans Christian Petersen.

Finding a suitable site for a station at the Vestfold Hills was extremely difficult. The Norwegian-style fjords that looked so spectacular from the air were too shallow for ships to enter, and the approaches to the coast shelved gradually so that ships could not get closer than two or three kilometres to possible landing sites. The Vestfold Hills in high summer is reminiscent of a chunk of the Simpson Desert transplanted to Antarctica. In January 1957 Law was dismayed to find no snow banks remaining on the brown rocks and hinterland, a source of water for the station being essential. For three days from 10 January he and the ANARE expeditioners searched unsuccessfully for a suitable site.

Law had earlier sent a radiogram to his minister, Richard Casey, following an aerial reconnaissance, saying that if the Vestfold Hills were blocked by fast ice, there was a possibility the site for a station could be established in another similarly rocky region nearby—the Larsemann Hills. Casey became concerned and consulted Sir Douglas Mawson in Adelaide. A radiogram was sent to Law relaying Mawson's advice, which was that the Larsemanns would not be as good as the Vestfold Hills but would do if that were the only alternative. Law:

> This was amusing on two counts. First, neither man had any idea of what the new land was like. Secondly, I was the only living [Australian] to have detailed first-hand experience of Prydz Bay; yet Casey had sent me advice from Mawson who had never been there! I did not blame Mawson—he was just trying to be helpful. But I thought Casey should have had more sense.[8]

On 12 January Law returned to *Kista Dan* in the ship's motor boat from yet another search of the coastline, tired, cold and disconsolate:

> I began to turn over in my mind two other possibilities—making do with one of the outer islands of the Vestfold Hills, or abandoning the region altogether and trying the Cape Ann region in Enderby Land. However, we passed another small sandy beach and decided to land and examine it as a last resort.[9]

Although far from perfect, this site looked as though it could be reached by the army amphibious DUKWs. *Kista Dan* could probably approach within two kilometres of the shore. Law, accompanied by the incoming OIC Bob Dingle and four others, landed on the beach:

> There was a flat terrace about halfway up the steep headland on the left of the cove which looked promising for huts. We clambered up to it and decided that it would be possible to clear enough boulders away to make a rough track for the DUKWs. The terrace was very flat and obviously

the site of a great snow drift, for the pebbles constituting its floor were flattened as though from a giant steam roller. The outlook to the horizon on every side from the top of the rise was perfect.[10]

On the down side, water would have to be found somewhere during the summer. There was no time for further searching, and unloading began on the same day. By 1600 hours the next day, 13 January, a remarkable amount of cargo had been landed. Work stopped and all hands assembled around a flagpole which had been strapped to the wall of the first hut being erected. Law:

> All our party and Captain Hindberg attended. I made a short speech in which I stressed the importance of the new station in IGY research and wished it and its men under Bob Dingle success and good luck. I then broke out the flag and officially named the station 'Davis'. There followed a short account of the achievements of Captain John King Davis. . .We then sang God Save the Queen, gave three cheers, and returned to work again.[11]

By 20 January Davis Station was established enough for *Kista Dan* to sail. Five men only were to winter there. The weather observer Nils Lied, who had wintered at Mawson the previous year, volunteered to double up, and was dropped in (with a small team of huskies) by *Kista Dan* on her return trip. The station had no doctor, but there was the possibility of evacuation by air to Mawson Station. The first flight from Mawson to Davis by Beaver took place on 1 May. One of the passengers was an extra husky for Nils Lied's dog team.[12] In August the geologist Bruce Stinear was flown by Beaver aircraft 637 kilometres from Davis to Mawson to continue his geological work. (The ability of ANARE to transfer people between stations by air ended in 1960 when fixed wing aircraft capable of extended flights were no longer stationed in the AAT. Long distance flights did not resume until more than 30 years later with the advent of twin-engined Sikorsky 76 helicopters in 1994.)

The use of two Beavers and the seemingly indestructible Auster based at Mawson during the IGY enabled an impressive program to be completed. The Beavers ranged as far east as the Russian station at Mirny, south beyond the southernmost ranges of the Prince Charles Mountains, and west to Enderby Land near the Norwegian sector, as well as supporting parties in the field. Pilots Peter Clemence and Doug Johnston flew all through the winter, clocking up 213 flights. Some were on the edge of safety. During August, one of the Beavers landed at Davis with only six gallons [27 litres] of fuel remaining in its tanks.

The modest dog team at Davis was used to good effect. On 10 May 1957, Nils Lied, Bruce Stinear and a visiting surveyor from Mawson, Morris Fisher, sledged along the coast of the Vestfold Hills and located the proclamation canister left by Sir Hubert Wilkins on 11 January 1939, claiming the coastline for Australia. The proclamation note inside was wrapped in a copy of *Walkabout* magazine dated 1933 and between the pages was a typewritten note signed by Sir Hubert referring to the Order of Council of 7 February 1933 which established the AAT, and recording his landing at several places in the vicinity.[13] Lied, Stinear and Fisher signed their own names and replaced the canister at the site now known appropriately as the Walkabout Rocks.

International Polar Years only take place during cycles of maximum solar activity. Australia was able to contribute to the recording of upper atmosphere phenomena with both Macquarie Island and Mawson Station ideally placed for magnetic, auroral and other associated observations. Phil Law believes there has not been adequate recognition of the immense amount of exploration and scientific work achieved by Australia during the IGY:

> Australia, I think, produced more of significance than any other nation, including the Russians and Americans, mainly because we were the only ones, apart from the British, who'd had enough experience beforehand to set up a decent scientific program. Even the British and Chileans and Argentinians in the Peninsula area were only minuscule stations, literally only doing a bit of biology and meteorology. They hadn't got stuck into the hard core science—geophysics and so on.
>
> So then the IGY came on. Here was Australia with its experience in geophysics at Heard and Macquarie for a number of years, and Mawson for three. We'd ironed most of the bugs out of the equipment and the procedures. So we just flowed on and produced a lot of good, solid data. And almost every other nation that went down in the IGY produced a bit of a shambles in the first year because their equipment broke down, their people were not properly trained, and so on. After the IGY, of course, the Russians and Americans just left us for dead with their immense power. But power itself was not enough, in the IGY, to put them ahead of us.

That was on the ground. In space, the rockets and satellites of the US and the Soviet Union made fundamental discoveries during the IGY, the most spectacular of which was the discovery of the Van Allen radiation zones around the earth. Yet Australia from the ground could claim some success in space research which had more relevance in later years—when the break-up of the ozone layer over Antarctica in the winter was first measured by British scientists in 1981. In something of a victory for the principle of pure as opposed to applied science, ANARE scientists were among the first people in the world to do ozone measurements, now a source of global concern in Antarctica. Law:

> In 1950 I was looking for a program of something to do, and I heard there was a man in England called Dobson who had invented an ozone spectrophotometer, so I bought one and put it down on Macquarie Island. Then Fred Jacka [ANARE's chief scientist] arranged for it to go down to Mawson. We had results. . .[but] we had no idea what these measurements meant. And from being about the purest form of science, you now find that it's fundamentally important to mankind.

The IGY work mapped and assessed the structure of Antarctica in a way that changed our perceptions of it dramatically. Seismic traverses revealed the details of mountain peaks and troughs hidden below the great Antarctic ice cap. Only a little more than 2 per cent of Antarctica's bedrock is visible as mountain peaks or coastal 'oases', but intensive geological studies during the IGY provided strong evidence in favour of continental drift—an unpopular hypothesis before the IGY but now generally accepted by the great majority of scientists.

So successful was the IGY that—by mutual consent of all the nations involved—it was extended for a further year into 1959, known as the Year of International Geophysical Cooperation. Clearly the evaluation of so much primary data needed even more time, and it was agreed that three World Data Centres would be set up, one each in the United States and the USSR, with the third being spread over a number of institutions in Western Europe, Australia and Japan.

THE ANTARCTIC TREATY

Neither the USA nor the former USSR has ever claimed any part of Antarctica or recognised other nations' claims. The US made its position clear in 1924 under the Hughes Doctrine, and in 1939 when Norway claimed territory in Queen Maud Land, the USSR announced that it did not recognise any Antarctic claims. Both the superpowers, though, had historical precedents. The United States could cite the extensive explorations of Greater Antarctica by Wilkes, Admiral Byrd and aviator and explorer Lincoln Ellsworth, who in 1939 flew in his Northrop Delta aircraft 300 kilometres into the interior of Princess Elizabeth Land (already claimed by Australia) and dropped a copper cylinder and proclamation claiming 43 000 square kilometres for the US, naming the area the

American Highlands. Although these territorial initiatives were never formally advanced by the US Government, the possibility of an Antarctic claim at some future date could not be ruled out. The Soviet Union had the historical basis for an even more sweeping claim, following the exploratory voyages of Captain T von Bellingshausen—who actually circumnavigated the Antarctic continent between 1819 and 1821.

The sector under the tip of South America, and encompassing the Antarctic Peninsula, became the most hotly contested part of Antarctica, with overlapping claims by Britain, Argentina and Chile during World War II. The establishment of two bases on Gamma Island and Greenwich Island by Argentina and Chile was countered by formal protests from Britain in December 1947—followed by further British indignation about an Argentine base begun on Deception Island in the same month. Britain suggested that the disputes over Antarctic claims between the three countries be brought before the International Court of Justice at The Hague for settlement—otherwise Britain reserved its right to take 'appropriate action' to ensure its territory was respected.[14]

Both Argentina and Chile rejected this option and called for an international conference to settle claims over the entire Antarctic continent. Argentina and Britain sent warships to the region, and 1948 looked like ushering in a warm time indeed on the coast of the coldest continent.

The United States was keen to mediate between Britain and Argentina and suggested the internationalisation of Antarctica in the form of a United Nations trusteeship. After advice from Britain, the US Secretary of State George C Marshall suggested an eight-power condominium (joint sovereignty over a territory) made up of the seven nations with Antarctic claims plus the US as an intending claimant—and excluding its superpower adversary, the Soviet Union. Britain and New Zealand were the only supporters of the condominium idea. Argentina, Australia, Chile, France and Norway were against.[15] Dr Evatt, then Australia's Minister for External Affairs, was keen to retain Australia's own sovereignty over the AAT so as to be able to exploit any minerals that might be found there.

In July and August of 1948, Professor Julio Escudero (a legal adviser in the Chilean Foreign Ministry) put forward another suggestion to solve the dilemma of competing national claims in Antarctica, known as the *modus vivendi* proposal, to effectively freeze all claims so that nations could proceed with their scientific programs. Eventually this ingenious compromise was taken up and became a key element of the final draft of the Antarctic Treaty eleven years later.

In January 1949 the All-Union Geographical Society in the USSR made a public statement that no agreement on Antarctic sovereignty without the participation of the Soviet Union was going to be legitimate—an assertion taken seriously by the US, which began to explore Professor Escudero's *modus vivendi* idea as a basis for an international Antarctic agreement in discussions between 1949 and 1952 with nations claiming territory in Antarctica.

The outbreak of the Korean War on 25 June 1950 distracted attention from attempts to formalise an international regime in Antarctica, and the *modus vivendi* concept being explored by the US suffered a severe setback when its own Department of Defence opposed it.

In 1952 tensions between Argentina and Britain over their Antarctic claims were further exacerbated when a party of armed Argentinians fired over the heads of a British party attempting to re-establish a survey base at Hope Bay.[16] There were further incidents in 1953. In February two Argentine nationals were deported from Deception Island (part of the South Shetlands) by British authorities, and several Argentine and Chilean buildings were dismantled.

In 1954 the USSR announced it would participate in the IGY.

There is a view that the noble cause of science in Antarctica led to the agreement known as the Antarctic Treaty, but there is compelling evidence that although scientific cooperation was a useful practical lubricant, the primary reason for negotiating the Treaty was a negative one—fear of chaos. Unless an international solution for the Antarctic could be found, a confrontation on a world-wide scale could easily have erupted in that area.[17]

The Antarctic Treaty has been described as 'an elegant mixture of US self-interest and international high-mindedness'.[18] So the question is why the Soviet Union supported it at the height of the so-called 'cold war'. The answer is a blend of pragmatism, the tyranny of distance and perhaps just a dash of idealism.

The Soviet Union's decision to take part in the IGY had spelt the end of US attempts to quarantine the Russians from Antarctica. The US, together with Britain, Australia and New Zealand in particular, was concerned that the Russians might establish military bases in Antarctica during and after the IGY. By the early 1950s both superpowers were concerned to find ways and means of avoiding flashpoints that might involve sudden escalation into nuclear war. This was difficult enough in the Northern Hemisphere. The prospect of extending this tension to remote Antarctica was unattractive to both superpowers. By establishing a presence in the Antarctic without the risk of conflict, the Russians could demonstrate their global reach—as well as establishing themselves as a legitimate force in future Antarctic developments.[19] On the other hand, the Soviet Union was prepared to concede the dominance of the US in Antarctic affairs. Considering the state of the cold war at the time, it was remarkable that anything was agreed at all.

Negotiations for the Antarctic Treaty lasted eighteen months. There were sixty preparatory meetings held in Washington between June 1958 and October 1959. Then there was the full-scale conference which concluded with the signing of the Treaty on 1 December 1959 by the representatives of the governments of Argentina, Australia, Belgium, Chile, the French Republic, Japan, New Zealand, Norway, the Union of South Africa, the Union of Soviet Socialist Republics, the United Kingdom of Great Britain and Northern Ireland, and the United States of America.

Australia played a key role in the negotiations leading to the Antarctic Treaty through the diplomacy of Richard Casey, the Minister for External Affairs. The crucial objectives for Australia were freedom of scientific research, non-militarisation of the area, and the freezing of territorial claims. Clearly, without the last two points any treaty would be worthless. As it happened, Australia was extremely influential in convincing the Soviet Union that it should accept the freezing of all territorial claims. The Russian position at the beginning of discussions was that the Treaty should say nothing at all about territorial claims and that any reference to those claims placed claimant countries in a superior position—indeed 'if Russia was required to renounce the right to make a claim, other countries, in fairness, should renounce the claims they had already made'.[20] This position was totally unsatisfactory to Australia and the other claimant states.

Malcolm Booker was Australia's chief negotiator in the preliminary negotiations for drafting the Treaty. He was aware that 'Australia's absurd territorial claims' of 42 per cent of the Antarctic continent were very weak in international law:

> My problem was to get the Government to realise this and insist that the Treaty should embody their claim. We had the same problem with the Chileans and the Argentinians. Their original position—like our original position—was that these claims must be respected. Then we had the bright idea (I'm not sure that I can claim the authorship of it) but. . .with my Chilean and Argentinian colleagues, we said: 'Why don't we put these claims on ice?' And we thought that was a funny thing to say.

The ingenious formula of Article IV—in essence to agree to disagree on the freezing of national claims—was the cornerstone of the success of the Antarctic Treaty, but it was by no means certain it could be achieved in the early stages of negotiation.

Yet Russia's flexibility on other aspects of the Treaty was surprising Australia's diplomats who had been expecting a harder 'cold war' line. Diplomacy away from official discussions was vital to progress towards the Treaty. Malcolm Booker was keen to explore the possibility of the Antarctic being a nuclear-free zone:

> ... that in spite of the 'cold war' there could be areas of the world that could be kept free from nuclear competition and from any possible nuclear conflict. It was accepted, of course, that this wouldn't really solve the nuclear problem, but that it would establish a principle that might later be applicable in wider circumstances. And interestingly, the other delegate who was keen on this idea was a Russian.

Booker had known one of the Russian delegates, Andrei Ledovski, when they were both posted to the Nationalist capital Chonqing in China in 1943 and 1944. They had become friends during this chaotic time, when the USSR was an ally of the West. While in Washington the Australian diplomat bent the rules to sound out Ledovski on the Russian position on Treaty matters in a series of private conversations and meetings:

> The Government requirement on us all was to report whenever we met a Russian, or Soviet, official, and give details of what they said and what I said...Well, this was absurd in this situation, because we were meeting regularly discussing the Antarctic treaty and it was very much the matter of achieving a successful combination between him and myself in getting acceptance for the idea of a nuclear-free zone. So sometimes I reported when I met him, and sometimes I didn't.

Booker and Ledovski would arrange to have lunch together in one of Washington's busier restaurants, confident that they were totally secure:

> Nobody could have known you were there and nobody could hear—because of the background noise—anything that was said. And it often struck me how all these enormously expensive spy services could easily be evaded by anybody who wanted to evade them.
>
> But anyway our meetings were entirely innocent...we were serving our governments loyally and there was no possibility of any espionage on his part. Of course there wasn't on mine...he was a very intelligent, witty, cultivated bloke ...

Ledovski worked for the principal Soviet representative, Grigory Tonkin, an international lawyer who, Booker maintained, dominated the final Treaty conference intellectually.

The problem for me was that the Americans did not want the Antarctic as a nuclear-free zone, they. . .felt they had to have the option of using the Antarctic for nuclear defence, nuclear surveillance—at the worst, nuclear war. And the Australian Government in those days was, of course, entirely subservient to the United States—more subservient than at any other time probably. So it was very difficult to persuade our Government that, in effect, they should oppose the American wish to reserve the right to use the Antarctic for nuclear weapons.

In fact Australia enthusiastically supported the use of the Antarctic for 'peaceful' nuclear explosions in Antarctica—a concept not ruled out by the Russians at first, although later they hardened their position. In October 1959 Argentina was pushing for a total ban on nuclear tests or explosions of any kind in Antarctica and Casey was advised by the DEA to oppose the Argentinians on this point. Commonwealth Attorney General Sir Garfield Barwick cabled Casey on 24 October:

Taking into account our best scientific advice, I would think on balance, the potential scientific and technical advantages of peaceful nuclear explosions in the Antarctic outweigh the possible risks (i.e. the fallout hazard if adequate precautions are *not* taken and the possibility that some information of military value might be gained from an essentially peaceful explosion).[21]

Correspondence between the DEA and the National Radiation Advisory Committee (NRAC) at that time also gives an interesting insight into the more relaxed attitudes of the day towards the disposal of nuclear waste. On 2 October, NRAC Secretary J R Flanagan advised that it could be reliably stored in deep stable ice away from the seaboard for long periods:

It may be unnecessary to separately contain the radioactive material when depositing it in the ice, but this aspect would need very careful examination before being put into practice. If it were proven acceptable, it would probably constitute a considerable saving in cost.[22]

On the nuclear explosions issue, however, the USSR won the day during the final conference, with the banning of both nuclear explosions and disposal of radioactive waste material in Antarctica being enshrined in Article V of the Treaty.

Looking back, Booker believes that the Soviet premier, Nikita Khruschev, intended to use the nuclear issue in Antarctica as a signal to the west that he wanted to improve relations between the Soviet Union and the United

States—an early expression of *glasnost* and *perestroika*. But he faced resistance from his hardline generals who favoured continuing an ironclad Stalinist policy of isolation. Booker:

> Khruschev was hoping, I believe, to achieve a settlement in the nuclear area which would relieve the Soviet Union of the enormous burden of constantly having to keep pace with the American developments. I can only believe that when Ledovsky at these negotiations surprised us all with his readiness to see the nuclear free zone apply to Antarctica—this was a reflection of Khruschev's own policy of a more cooperative relationship with the west.

The Cuban missile crisis of 1962 ended any immediate prospects of détente on the question of nuclear weapons, and the arms race between the USSR and the US continued for another two decades.

In early 1959 prospects for agreement on Article IV (the freezing of claims) seemed remote, despite some encouraging remarks by Ledovski to Booker in Washington that 'he still felt sure that something could be worked out'.[23]

The breakthrough occurred at an unlikely location—Broadbeach in Queensland. The occasion was a meeting of the Economic Commission for Asia and the Far East, and the leader of the Soviet delegation was Deputy Foreign Minister Nicolai Firubin. On 12 March the Australian Minister for External Affairs, Richard Casey, had a private conversation with Firubin about the mutual reinstatement of their embassies in Moscow and Canberra (following the break in diplomatic relations in 1954 caused by the Petrov affair). He also raised the issue of Antarctica and 'explained Australian objectives and interests in orthodox but forceful terms'.[24]

Firubin responded by outlining the Soviet position—that the matter of territorial rights and claims in the region should not be dealt with as part of the current debate—but agreed to study a letter from Casey outlining the Australian position. In his letter, delivered the next day, Casey made two main points—that the freezing of claims would have the effect of keeping all national differences 'quietly in abeyance', and that it would create a legal situation in which no activity in Antarctica by any country, claimant or non-claimant, would improve its legal claim to sovereignty.[25] He also stressed that he was seriously apprehensive about the risks of future cooperation between nations operating in Antarctica if the Treaty was not concluded.[26]

Firubin's verbal response to Casey 'that all would be well' was confirmed on 11 May when, at a luncheon at the Russian Embassy in Washington, the Soviet Ambassador to the United States, Mikhail Menshikov, made it clear to US Ambassador Paul Daniels that there was no basic disagreement between the two states on the peaceful use of Antarctica, that there had been an apparent misunderstanding in regard to the US draft article on the subject of rights and claims, and that he and his colleagues were 'willing to get along with the conference'.

Confirmation of Casey's contribution to this breakthrough was received in early June in a letter from Firubin, through the British Embassy in Moscow, in reply to his Broadbeach letter of 13 March. Firubin went on to say that he was pleased to be able to tell Casey 'at the present time that the Soviet side is prepared to agree to the text of Article IV in the form indicated. . .[and] the representative of the Soviet Union at the talks in Washington has been given instructions to agree to Article IV of the draft Treaty'.[27] The breakthrough had been made.

Richard Casey's diplomatic skills were to be needed again, however, on the persistent issue of the freezing of claims. Three days before the final conference to negotiate the Antarctic Treaty was due to begin in Washington on 15 October 1959, the French representative, Ambassador Pierre Charpentier, dropped a bombshell, saying that his instructions were 'positive and definite' that 'under no circumstances was France to agree to an article such as Article IV. . .'[28]

Casey and Charpentier met to discuss 'the devastating French decision'. In his diary, Casey wrote:

> I made no attempt to hide my feelings on this. . .I suspect it is a de Gaulle decision. Charpentier showed signs of personal disagreement with his instructions. I said if the decision was an unalterable one, it would destroy the Conference and the Treaty.[29]

Casey immediately sent a long telegram to the French Foreign Minister, M. Couve de Murville, explaining that Australia would not have attended the conference unless an understanding among all twelve parties had been reached on Article IV, and detailed the role he had played in convincing the Russians to accept it. He concluded:

> If, therefore, the conference fails, the responsibility might well seem to rest solely upon France.
> . . . It would therefore cause me great personal regret if it were to appear to the Australian people that the French Government, at the eleventh hour, refused to accept a treaty that would provide such valuable protection for Australian national interests. I would therefore most earnestly hope that you might feel able, in advance of the conference on Thursday, to reconsider the French position on Article IV.[30]

This appeal had no immediate effect. On 20 October, the French moved to delete the paragraph of Article IV relating to the freezing of territorial claims. They did not, however, pursue this opposition following the US announcement that it was accepting the Soviet formula on Article IV, with the agreement of most of the other nations involved.

Charpentier did tell Casey on 26 October that Couve de Murville had said that if he had had copies of the correspondence with Firubin at the time, his attitude about the freezing of claims would have been different.[31] So it is reasonable to assume that Casey's intervention was influential. Twelve nations signed the Treaty on 1 December 1959.

International recognition of Richard Casey's role in the successful resolution of the Antarctic Treaty was marked by the selection of Canberra for the first scheduled Antarctic Treaty Consultative Meeting which began on 23 June 1961.

The Treaty has been successful in keeping Antarctica insulated from frictions generated between member countries elsewhere. It has also ensured a peaceful mechanism for growth, with 43 states adherent to the Treaty by 1996. Its consensus decision-making system has remained intact and although there is no permanent secretariat, its consultative arrangements have been able to accommodate questions not addressed in 1959—like pollution control, tourism, political status, and living and non-living resources.[32]

Sir Douglas Mawson retired from academic life in Adelaide in 1953. He was 70, and his interests had ranged far beyond Antarctica. For 30 years he headed the Geology Department of the University of Adelaide, and was also active in the fields of conservation, farming and forestry.

He died unexpectedly on 14 October 1958, following a cerebral haemorrhage, survived by his wife Paquita and two daughters. His role in establishing ANARE in 1947 had been pivotal, and he lived to see Australians established in two permanent stations on the mainland of Antarctica, and a third on Macquarie Island—which he had been instrumental in having declared a sanctuary in 1933.

The Mawson Institute for Antarctic Research was established within the University of Adelaide in 1959. Its library incorporates Mawson's collection of polar literature, his Antarctic diaries, and a substantial collection of papers, photographic records and objects of historical importance. The Douglas Mawson chair of geology was created in 1983.

TWELVE

1959—A YEAR TO REMEMBER

I f any year in the half-century of ANARE operations can be singled out as momentous, 1959 is a good candidate. Events included the occupation of Australia's third continental station at Wilkes, a tragic death midway through the year, mental illness involving visits by Russian and United States aircraft, disastrous fires at Macquarie Island and Mawson stations, and the total destruction of two aircraft at Mawson in a violent storm.

The curtain-raiser took place on 16 January 1959 when *Thala Dan* ran onto an uncharted pinnacle of rock approaching Davis Station. John Béchervaise (who was on his way to Mawson Station as the incoming OIC) recalled that it was an absolutely still sunny day, 'with all that marvellous calmness that comes inside the pack ice':

> Suddenly we struck a rock. This was really a tremendous shock, in every sense of the term. I can remember the masts quivering and making a strange noise, as though they were vibrating, and a few men were almost thrown off their feet.

The master, Captain Hans Christian Petersen, immediately signalled the engine room for full astern, but without success. It became clear that *Thala Dan* was impaled on a pinnacle of rock and had been holed. Oil gushed from a pierced fuel tank and spread over the surface of the sea. Béchervaise noted at the time that it had a singular effect on the penguins, and this was not a pleasing sight: 'I think it caused a change in the refractive index of the sea surface—for they started leaping straight out of the water, as though onto invisible ice floes.'[1]

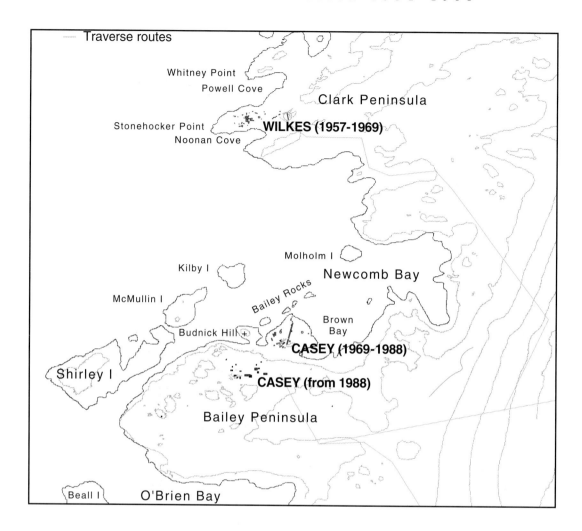

Traverse routes

Whitney Point
Powell Cove

Clark Peninsula

Stonehocker Point
WILKES (1957-1969)
Noonan Cove

Molholm I

Kilby I

Newcomb Bay

McMullin I

Bailey Rocks

Brown
Bay

Budnick Hill

CASEY (1969-1988)

CASEY (from 1988)

Shirley I

Bailey Peninsula

Beall I
O'Brien Bay

WILKES STATION ON THE
COAST OF VINCENNES BAY,
WILKES LAND.

Thala Dan was not in immediate danger, but the ship had grounded near the top of the tide, so it would be 24 hours at least before any realistic efforts could be made to free her. Half an hour after hitting the rock, Captain Petersen called the ship's company. Béchervaise recalled that moment: 'To prevent rumours an' all 'dat sort of bullshit, I will tell you what we now know. The ship she is not in danger.'[2]

Petersen said he was confident that he could get *Thala Dan* off the rocks. There was little the ANARE men could do, so they marked that evening by having a shipwreck party. Béchervaise later wrote: 'It lasted until well after dawn. The oily water, almost motionless round the ship, carried scores of floating beer cans.'[3]

Over the next fifteen days, Captain Petersen displayed remarkable seamanship in extricating his ship from this isolated and dangerous situation. After shifting ballast to raise the bow, Petersen took the same traditional course of action that Captain Cook had taken on the Great Barrier Reef in 1770, and 'fothered' the ship. Béchervaise:

> A sail was passed under the hull which prevented the inflow of water, the water was pumped out of the tank, and the captain prepared a number of wooden wedges to be driven into the gash from the oil tank just inside the hull, which had taken the strain.

The next day, Captain Petersen prepared for high water. His plan was to put out a stern anchor and then winch *Thala Dan* off the rock, with engines full astern. The most immediate practical problem was how to get the anchor—weighing more than a tonne —to its position. None of the ship's boats could possibly carry it. The ingenious solution was to suspend the anchor underneath a dinghy, where it would weigh less under water. Béchervaise:

> This allowed perhaps an inch or two inches [2½ to five centimetres] free-board. The captain and the second mate rowed very cautiously—with this great anchor hanging below—until they got to the position astern.
> Then he took a broad axe, and with one swipe cut through the rope that held the anchor. . .the ship's boat fairly leapt out of the water with the sudden relief of the strain.

Everything went according to plan. At high water the engines went full astern and the ship's winches began pulling against the ingeniously placed anchor. *Thala Dan* came off the rock to the cheers of all on board. But it would be twelve more days before the ship could continue her journey a further five kilometres to Davis Station. Ship's boats ferried rock and sand from nearby Magnetic Island as aggregate for concrete, which was poured in to reinforce and seal off the damaged tank. The repair was successful, but the waiting was taking its toll on the Davis Station people, desperate for their mail. On 20 January, a Beaver aircraft on floats was launched from *Thala Dan* and an airdrop of mail and a well-padded crate of Carlsberg beer was made by RAAF pilot Jim Sandercock.[4]

At the same time, the second Lauritzen Line ice-strengthened ship *Magga Dan* was approaching Vincennes Bay with the ANARE wintering party for Wilkes Station to establish Australia's third base on the Antarctic continent. Law had assigned his deputy Don Styles as voyage leader on *Thala Dan* to relieve and resupply Davis and Mawson, while he oversaw events at Wilkes, as well as continuing the yearly program of coastal exploration.

Wilkes had been established by the United States Government in 1957 as part of its contribution to the IGY. Although built in a mere seventeen days, it was a lavish complex compared with the simple frugality of any of the Australian stations. Because it was constructed in a hollow, even in its first year of operation its buildings were buried under a relentless accumulation of ice and snow. Nevertheless the heated buildings and enormous supply dumps were an eye-opener to the Australians when they first saw it.

As the IGY wound down in 1958 American scientists were hopeful that the scientific observations carried out at Wilkes could be continued. Phil Law:

> The Americans found themselves over-committed. . .and their scientists came to me and said: 'Look, Wilkes is a good station, scientifically it's extremely valuable. It fills an important gap as an observatory for meteorology, geomagnetism, seismology and scientific work generally. It would be a great pity if it just closed down. We are going to be forced to close down; what say we come to an agreement where you take it over. We would love to see the Australians continue to run it, because we're just as interested in the results that come out of it as you are.'

Law said he would try to persuade the Australian Government that resources could be stretched to this extent, particularly as nothing had to be built—a ready-made station was just sitting there. As early as January 1958 the US State Department was pressing the Australian Government for a response. There were two alternatives: to hand over Wilkes to Australia as a going concern, or to share its operations.

The Department of External Affairs recommended the first option. The secretary, Arthur Tange, wrote:

> I would believe that it would not be practicable for us to share the operation of the Wilkes Station with the United States. The political future of the Antarctic is at present uncertain and probably will remain so for some months at least. I believe our best policy in the interim would be to continue to consolidate our sovereignty. Granted this, the opportunity of replacing the last United States base in our territory by an Australian base presents obvious political advantages. The advantage might be lost if we only participated in the operation of what would still be a United States base.[5]

This reflected Law's preferred position on Wilkes and he urged his minister, Richard Casey, to take a tough line with the US on the issue:

> I had stressed to him that we were in a powerful position to impose our complete demands on the situation. They wanted the stations preserved—not us. It was either us or nothing! The Americans knew it, and we knew it.

The US State Department argued that there could be trouble with Congress (and the American taxpayer) if it was all just handed over, and proposed it should be a joint station, 50 per cent Australian and 50 per cent American. Law: 'At least I managed to get an assurance that the leader would be an Australian, but they had a deputy put in who was an American, so you had almost a dual control of the station'.

The awkwardness of this arrangement was evident from the very first contacts with the Americans at Wilkes. Law and Dick Thompson, his chief supply officer, had spent three weeks in Washington organising the logistical arrangements and examining lists of equipment at the station. But External Affairs had not briefed Law about the protocol of taking over a station from another nation:

> The first thing I ran into was the question of what we do about flags. I was going to pull down the American flag and put the Australian one up [but] they promptly reminded me that that wasn't on. So on our ship I was going to fly the Australian flag with the American flag on the same mast. And someone said: 'You can't do that Phil—protocol. You can't put some nation's flag underneath one of ours.' So we had to fly the Australian flag on the foremast and the American flag on the aftermast.

On 3 February 1959 Law signed a document accepting custody of all the American buildings and equipment at Wilkes for use without charge or liability, and guaranteeing the eventual return of the property to the United States.[6] This was impractical, and the whole Wilkes complex, with all the stores, abandoned equipment and spent fuel dumps now lies entombed in the ice. What to do about the historic rubbish at Wilkes remains one of the unsolved Antarctic environmental dilemmas to this day.

191

The changeover ceremony at Wilkes went smoothly on Wednesday 4 February, with Australian and American flags on separate poles, but the dual arrangements between the Australians and the Americans soon led to diplomatic difficulty. The senior US member of the Wilkes party, Herbert Hansen, a meteorologist (who had objected to the way the flags were flown during the changeover) demanded the right to radio his communications direct to the US base at McMurdo and not through Antarctic Division channels.[7] This caused a bureaucratic flurry within External Affairs as officers in Canberra tried to unravel the complex web of events that led to the joint facility. As Law had predicted, it all got too hard for both the Americans and the Australians:

> After two years it was obviously so unworkable that the State Department devised a formula where they lent all the equipment to us on long-term loan, indefinitely, and without payment. . .the divided operation ceased and we took over as we should have done right from the beginning.

On 5 February 1959 *Magga Dan* left Wilkes, with Law hopeful of voyaging east to the extreme edge of the AAT to attempt the first ever Australian landing on the coast of Oates Land. At the last moment he was able to arrange for Corporal John 'Snow' Williams, the RAAF air-frame fitter, to remain at Wilkes for the winter. Law was concerned that it would be impossible for the two Australian mechanics adequately to look after all the technical equipment at the station.[8] This turned out to be an extremely fortunate decision in view of later happenings at Wilkes during the year.

The day before *Magga Dan* left Wilkes, the damaged but still serviceable *Thala Dan* broke through the fast ice into Horseshoe Harbour at Mawson to resupply the station and change over the personnel. On 11 February unloading was halted to cope with a sudden personal emergency. One of the incoming meteorologists, Ian Widdows, developed acute appendicitis. The recreation room in Weddell Hut was scrubbed and draped with polythene sheeting. Two medical officers were available, due to the changeover. Incoming Grahame Budd was the surgeon and Grey Channon the anaesthetist, assisted by four other expeditioners.[9] Widdows made a good recovery.

It was now the turn of Macquarie Island to hit the headlines and for that ANARE station to play its part in the year's bizarre events. On Friday 13 March, the lead item in the Hobart *Mercury* revealed that the gaff-rigged schooner *Patanela* would voyage to Macquarie Island in a bid to start a sealing industry there.[10] Mr Alan Powell (described by the *Mercury* as the 'key man' of the syndicate), a former consultant to the Australian Whaling Commission in Western Australia, explained to readers that he hoped to establish a modern plant in Hobart for the packaging and flash-freezing of fresh seal meat for export to America.

Macquarie Island had been declared a sanctuary in 1933 because of the slaughter of the fur and elephant seal populations by sealers in the early nineteenth century. Nevertheless the new sealing venture was enthusiastically supported by Tasmania's Minister for Agriculture, Mr Jack Dwyer, who said that 'the establishment of a sealing industry on Tasmanian-controlled Macquarie Island' would not be opposed by the Commonwealth or the State Government or the Fauna Board.

As *Patanela* buffeted heavy seas and high winds on her way to Macquarie Island, public opinion in Hobart erupted. The reaction was led initially by Norman Laird, a former expeditioner on Macquarie during the first year of ANARE occupation in 1948. Laird worked in the Tasmanian Government's film unit and wrote under the *nom de plume* 'Antarcticus'. Laird reminded readers of the Hobart *Mercury*'s Letters To The Editor columns of Sir Douglas Mawson's efforts to have the island declared a sanctuary in 1933: 'Now we may wonder whether Mawson's work is to be in vain, and whether we are to be the unhappy witnesses of a convenient adjustment to the law which made the island a sanctuary?'[11]

Laird alerted Frank Hurley, the photographer on Mawson's 1929–31 BANZARE voyage and a ferocious anti-sealing activist, who wrote from Sydney pointing out that he had assisted Mawson in ensuring that the sealing licence of Joseph Hatch was cancelled by the Tasmanian Government in 1919.

The Antarctic Division and ANARE were by no means passive participants in the sealing affair. On 24 December 1958 the Tasmanian Premier, Eric Reece, had asked Phil Law for his view, and Law (in an era when commercial opportunities in Antarctica were seen as positive revenue-raising) replied:

> My own view is that, properly supervised, exploitation of the elephant seals at Macquarie Island would have no harmful effect upon the seal population of the island. . .The presence at the Australian National Antarctic Research Expedition station of an official curator would enable such supervision and control to be exercised.[12]

The officer-in-charge at Macquarie Island was Tom Harwood, who also wore another hat. He was the Tasmanian Fauna Board's representative on Macquarie, obliged to show the sealing syndicate's Alan Powell around the elephant seal populations on the Macquarie beaches. However, on 30 March Harwood had more urgent matters to attend to. While the syndicate's chartered schooner *Patanela* was anchored in Buckles Bay, one of her crew yelled: 'There's smoke pouring from one of your huts!'

The ionospheric and cosmic ray laboratories were sited away from the main camp, on the shores of Hasselborough Bay, and it was the cosmic ray section that was well alight when the alarm was raised. All expeditioners available rushed to the fire with extinguishers and buckets and some fairly desperate measures were attempted, according to John Munro, one of the physicists on Macquarie:

> In an effort to isolate the fire efforts were made to break through the partition joining the huts and Brian [Bell] brought the tractor to try to pull the Ionospheric Hut away completely. But all to no avail. The wire rope burned through—white hot each time.[13]

Little could be salvaged and much valuable scientific equipment was lost, including a brand new ionospheric recorder, Whistler recorder, cosmic ray telescope and the highly prized Dobson ozone spectrophotometer. Much of this equipment had been an important element in the success of ANARE's contribution to the International Geophysical Year of 1957–58. Essentially the upper atmosphere and cosmic ray programs for 1959 were wiped out by the fire.

Powell and *Patanela* were able to help ANARE by giving Brian Bell, the physics radio-technician, a stormy ride back to Hobart, to save him a year's professional inactivity. *Patanela* arrived in Hobart on 7 April with Powell claiming the Tasmanian Government had already issued him with a sealing licence. He was publicly gung-ho about his plans on Macquarie and contemptuous of the 'storm of protest from animal protection societies', saying: 'The public is ill-informed and doesn't understand conditions at a sealing station. If the public is still against it, we'll go ahead just the same. They haven't had the experience we've had.'[14]

Powell reassured his critics that killing methods would be humane:

> In the old days they got a 4 foot [1.21 metres] pole with an iron spike on the end, hit them on the snout, then cut their throats.
>
> These days we shoot them in the brain with a .303 rifle or a .45 revolver. They roar when you walk up to them, and you shoot them through the mouth and into the brain. They drop dead instantly.[15]

Powell's grasp of the scientific biological program on Macquarie being carried out by Stefan Csordas, the medical officer, seemed rudimentary. The ANARE team there made a 'hobby of studying seals and other animals', he said. Mixing his metaphors rather unfortunately given the subject, the sealing entrepreneur said there were plenty of seals available and concluded: 'We're going to put in a big investment and we're not going to kill the goose that lays the golden eggs'.[16]

Powell was wrong about public opinion. The issue had become so politically heated that six days later it was all over. The Premier, Eric Reece, admitted publicly that the popular opposition and concerns about sealing had won the day, and that no licence would be issued.[17] The Hobart *Mercury* commented that the Government had 'shown good sense in bowing to the weight of public opinion'. Its editorial was scathing in its criticism of the Tasmanian Fauna Board for its apparent 'readiness to ignore the wishes of the public and views of zoologists alike'.

In fact the board opposed the sealing plans, but seals were not under its jurisdiction. They came under the Sea Fisheries Act. Eric Guiler, a lecturer in zoology at the University of Tasmania, was a board member at that time:

> The board was under heavy Government pressure to revoke all or part of the sanctuary, but steadfastly refused to do so. It agreed to 'consider' a lease of one acre for a factory-cum-residence, fully aware that the area was too small for the sealers' purpose. The board was determined to resign in a body if their views were overridden by Government.

Public opinion had had little influence on Antarctic policy before the Tasmanian sealing imbroglio. The making of Antarctic policy was traditionally the preserve of public servants and governments. The routing of the aspiring sealers was a sign that the traditional thinking on Antarctica as a resource to be plundered could no longer be taken for granted, and was a pointer to the conservation politics of the 1980s and 1990s.

Any outbreak of fire on Antarctic stations is greatly feared. At Macquarie Island the science buildings were separated from the main camp. On continental stations, isolated in winter unlike Macquarie which can be reached by ship at any time of the year—the outbreak of fire in moisture-free, tinder-dry flammable structures (heated by internal combustion stoves in the early years) could be catastrophic. The concern about fire was the main reason behind the ANARE night watches, instituted at all stations so that someone was on duty to take action and give the alarm in the event of fire. Lack of water is an added hazard and fire drills and awareness of extinguishers have been, and still are, drummed into all ANARE expeditioners.

On 3 April, four days after the Macquarie Island physics laboratories succumbed to fire, work was proceeding as usual at Mawson Station on one of the year's most essential projects. This was the construction of a new powerhouse which was being built over the old one, so that that powerhouse could keep operating until the bigger overall structure was

195

roofed and finished. With hindsight this was not such a good idea, because diesel fuel from the original hut had soaked into the ground beneath for the previous five years. Work on the new powerhouse was popular because it meant enjoying the warmth from the operating generator. The interior of the larger structure was being lined with Caneite insulating panels, and the whole job was nearly finished.

RAAF pilot Jim Sandercock recalls that he was having lunch in the mess when the alarm was given that a fire had broken out: 'People raced for fire extinguishers. We grabbed some from our hangar, some were taken from the other buildings—but of course they were entirely useless.'

Heat had built up in the smaller, older powerhouse, enclosed by the new, and had caused the fire. The problem was to get at the seat of the blaze through or around the new building. OIC John Béchervaise recalled that one of the greatest problems was that the doors of the two buildings did not coincide:

> We put smoke masks on, crawled in one door, and then had to turn left, and then turn another way to get to the seat of the fire. This was very dicey and very hard to see. . .you just felt your way. Finally you saw a flare and did what you could.

But it was far too dangerous and the outer building was sealed. When flames broke through the roof Béchervaise ordered a bucket brigade. Holes were punched in the sea ice and a human chain formed. Sandercock:

> A chap would dip his bucket in and run madly up the line, hand it up to that part of the building that was not on fire, and the chaps would throw the bucket of water through the now partly burnt roof. But we were wasting our time.

Desperate measures were employed. At one stage Béchervaise had men punching holes through the roof with crowbars, to pour in salt water.

> But we weren't winning, and in the end I heard a sound which was very unpleasant. . .a bubbling of something down below. As I knew that was diesel fuel, I got everybody off the roof—fortunately before it blew up.

Anything useful close by was dragged away either by hand or by D4 tractor. Fortunately one of the new diesel generators had not been moved into the new shed and was saved. Finally, at 5 pm, Béchervaise ordered everyone away from the scene and they watched the powerhouse burn:

> There were tremendous flames, huge columns of smoke, many explosions. One explosion shot a column of flame and burning oil nearly a

hundred feet [30.5 metres] in the air; it was from a drum containing only about fifteen gallons [68.1 litres] of lubricating oil finally bursting under pressure . . .

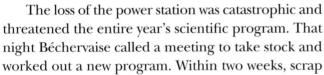

I treasure old Bert Evans' remarks from the roof just before we gave the job away. 'Hey! Anyone got a smoke? Haven't had one for hours. . .it's good to have one's feet warm for a change.'[18]

THE MAWSON STATION POWERHOUSE ON FIRE, 1959. (M KIRTON)

The loss of the power station was catastrophic and threatened the entire year's scientific program. That night Béchervaise called a meeting to take stock and worked out a new program. Within two weeks, scrap timber was used to build a small shelter for the one remaining big generator: 'There is nothing like a crisis like that to get everybody very close together. It may have been part of the great success of the year that everybody was so very helpful.'

Those at Mawson were to experience more challenges in this extraordinary year of 1959. But April also had an unwelcome surprise for ANARE expeditioners on Macquarie Island. On 30 April a tremendous storm sent waves surging across the narrow isthmus separating Hasselborough Bay from Buckles Bay, near the station. Reporting gusts of up to 170 kilometres per hour, OIC Tom Harwood noted in his log that flying debris had punched holes in three of the water storage tanks. With their fuel dump on the isthmus at risk, the station bulldozer was used to shift drums of fuel to a safer location:

[A] large wave washed right across and moved whole fuel dump eight feet. . .arrested only by the loaded sledge—even so 15 drums were carried towards Buckles Bay; 11 rescued, but 4 swept out to sea. Retainer wall construction commenced immediately and second sledge hauled to east side of dump and loaded. [It] was now dark and the tide still rising. Dozer with headlights worked overtime and 3 feet high [0.91 metres] retainer wall built by 1900 hours fortunately when largest wave. . .crashed across. . .By 2000 hours washes small and infrequent so organised night

197

watch whilst everybody bitterly cold and wet had welcome mugs of brandy and then dinner. The battle was won—thank God.[19]

Four days after the powerhouse fire at Mawson, the combined Australian and American wintering party at Wilkes was confronted with an emergency never before encountered on an ANARE station. On 7 April one of the two diesel mechanics, German national Henry Brandt, had a nervous breakdown, became violent, and had to be restrained.

Brandt's behaviour had been causing concern ever since the departure of *Magga Dan* in February. He was not self-motivated and, if not supervised, tended not to finish the jobs he was given. On 4 April, OIC Robert Dingle wrote in the station log that Brandt was 'a most unsatisfactory type for expedition life' and that he had been obtaining drugs from the medical officer for a 'nervous disorder'. Dingle canvassed options to try to motivate him:

> It has been suggested to [senior diesel mechanic Hartley] Robinson that he spend a little more time with Brandt where they complete each major job as a team instead of applying themselves as individuals to different phases of the engineering program.[20]

There was an enormous amount of engineering work to do. The Americans at Wilkes had run their vehicles, tractors and diesel generators until they dropped, and if they could not get a replacement from reserve stores, they cannibalised parts from other working machines. For economy-conscious Australians like Hartley Robinson, it was an eye-opener:

> The engines in the powerhouse had run continuously for two years with absolutely no maintenance whatsoever. . .these engines had all done anything from 5000 to 8000 hours—which says something for the Caterpillar engine. I don't know of any other engine that would work under these conditions and still give satisfactory service.[21]

Besides keeping the vital powerhouse going, all the other machines—tractors, Weasels, fork-lifts and trucks—were run down and needed extensive repair and reconditioning. Brandt's expertise was urgently needed. But on 7 April Brandt entered the mess with a knife in his hand and had to be disarmed. He was young and fit and Snow Williams recalled:

> His craziness made him even stronger. We wrestled with him, but whether he intended to use the knife or not, who can say. Five or six of us had to hold him down to get the knife out of his grip. . .his hand was cut in the struggle.

After this incident the medical officer, John Boda, sedated Brandt and decided that he would have to be confined while under treatment. Robinson:

> The boys were all perturbed about it and none of us slept for a couple of nights. We had to stand guard over him and manhandle him and it was really a very, very unhappy occurrence. It was obvious that the man had gone out of his head. We didn't know what to do so we cleared out a little bit of a storeroom and I got to work and made some wire grilles for the windows. We took all the stuff out of it, and stripped it, and made a cell and locked him in.[22]

Boda diagnosed manic depression with suicidal tendencies, and Dingle sought advice from Melbourne. Don Styles, deputy director of the Antarctic Division, contacted the Victorian Mental Hygiene Department where the psychiatric consultant thought it likely Brandt was suffering from incipient schizophrenia and recommended medication—there was even talk of radioing instructions to make a simple machine at Wilkes to administer electroconvulsive therapy. Meanwhile the RAAF made it clear that an evacuation by air was impossible.

An added problem for Dingle at Wilkes was the necessity for secrecy:

> You couldn't send these messages back to Melbourne in plain language, you had to break them down into a code so that the rest of the world didn't know what was happening down at Wilkes at that time. . .They were decoded in the Antarctic Division and taken out to the Kew mental asylum in Melbourne so they could do their diagnosis there. . .it would come back to us in code. . .oh, it was a trying business.

It was not practical to confine Brandt in his makeshift cell all the time, and Snow Williams recalls that everyone was on edge when he was free:

> A door opening, or the rattle of the buckles of the type of boots that Henry wore was enough to turn all heads in the room. Henry was quite strong, and until the medication took effect it would need five or six people to hold him down for an injection.[23]

After some official soul-searching in Canberra and Melbourne, it was decided to request medical assistance from the Soviet station at Mirny, 800 kilometres to the west. Don Styles was handling the situation from Melbourne:

> The Russians became aware of the situation and flew the 600 miles [960 kilometres] across from Mirny to Wilkes with some stimulants to keep the man in reasonable condition until the end of the season.

While this was an excellent example of the kind of international goodwill becoming the norm in Antarctica, local politics at Wilkes were more intense. The medical officer, John Boda, was a refugee from the Russian invasion of Hungary, and his attitude to a Russian visit was 'a red rag to a bull'.

The Russians had finished flying for the year, but cheerfully agreed to attempt a flight to Wilkes and land on the ice cap behind the station on a hastily graded airstrip prepared by the Australians. They landed on 4 May and anchored their Dakota-style aircraft to 'dogs'—wire ropes attached to baulks of timber melted into the ice by Robinson.

While the two doctors conferred on Brandt's condition the Russians, Australians and Americans inspected the station and then cemented good international relations by throwing a party. On the second day, the leader of the Russian party became concerned about the weather and asked to be taken back up on the plateau to inspect the tethered aircraft. Robinson, accompanied by Dingle, drove them up in a Sno-cat:

> We went inside and they boiled a billy and made a cup of tea and put a drop of jungle juice in it, 'aerovodka' as they call it, which is actually de-icing fluid for the wings. It's about 200 per cent alcohol so I declined.[24]

Robinson's excuse was that he had to drive back, but Bob Dingle, 'a non-drinking man', accepted an 'aerovodka' out of politeness. During this short time in the aircraft a strong wind blew up, creating white-out conditions. The two Australians became lost within 200 metres of the aircraft when they tried to return to Wilkes and it took them twenty minutes to find the Russians again. There was nothing to be done but ride out what was rapidly becoming a blizzard with wind speeds of 65 to 70 knots. Dingle:

> It [the aerovodka] didn't agree with me because I threw up all over the inside of this aircraft. And they put me to bed in one of their bunks in the aircraft and I slept right through the blizzard—I didn't know a damn thing about it. It was quite embarrassing actually, just trying to be sociable with these people. . .and I went out like a light!

Robinson recalled that during the worst of the storm the aircraft was vibrating 'just like a plane revving up on full power prior to a take-off', and both he and the worried pilot hoped that the anchors in the ice would hold. Next morning the wind dropped and Bob Dingle woke 'full of beans' and curious about what had happened during the night. They returned to Wilkes for another party and film night before the Russians finally took off for the flight back to Mirny on 6 May. Their visit had brought minor drama and jollity, but not much joy for the continuing problem of what to do about Brandt. The Russian doctor and Boda had consulted and, with extra drugs provided for treatment, Brandt did show some improvement. He began at least to correspond with his parents in Germany but he still had to be kept in isolation for most of the time. His condition affected everyone at the station, but Snow Williams (the RAAF engineer Phil Law had asked to stay at the last minute to help Robinson and Brandt) had particular praise for the medical officer:

> Reading my notes now that thirty years have passed, I realise again the tremendous job John Boda did medicating, feeding, exercising and looking after the welfare, generally, of his patient. John also had to learn English at Wilkes, as his skills in that direction were rudimentary.[25]

Back in Melbourne, Law radioed his thanks to the Russians at Mirny for their assistance in flying to Wilkes, but when the Minister for External Affairs, Richard Casey, wanted to add his message of appreciation to the Soviet Ministry of Foreign Affairs, he was advised against it by the DEA secretary Arthur Tange:

> . . .we feel that such a message would need to be very carefully drafted if it is to avoid providing the Russians with a useful document which [they] might produce at a later stage to demonstrate Australian acceptance of their presence in the Australian Antarctic Territory.[26]

At that time, international negotiations leading towards the Antarctic Treaty were still complex and unresolved.

The stations were able to enjoy their midwinter dinners and associated celebrations, although an attempt to fly back two scientists studying the aurora at Taylor Glacier, 80 kilometres west of Mawson, for midwinter dinner could have ended badly. A Beaver aircraft, piloted by Geoff Banfield, flying in twilight conditions and extremely low temperatures, had to return to Mawson for an emergency landing after its port aileron failed in flight. After repairs the field party was retrieved safely.

At Wilkes, a growing ANARE penchant for cross-dressing at midwinter saw the normally reticent OIC Bob Dingle shave off his moustache and arrive at dinner resplendent in a steel wool wig and velvet dress as Mrs 'Obbs of commercial radio serial fame. Others adopted the personae of Red Indians (with mohawk haircuts) and Australian Aborigines, while Hartley Robinson dressed as a penguin with flashing torch globes for eyes:

Another chappie, one of our big fellows here, carrying a lot of weight, dressed up as a baby in a napkin. Another put a brassiere on and slipped his backside into a big red lampshade and came as a ballet girl.[27]

Wilkes was a treasure trove of stores and equipment—if they could be found under the ice. There were odd shortages, though. Snow Williams:

We had ten years supply of beer and spare parts, but hardly any light globes. They were all Edison screw bulbs. But we had countless thousands of indicator bulbs out of washing machines. Harvey Nye, one of the US weather observers, would solder them into the brass base of the broken bulbs. It saved the day. Those indicator bulbs used to light the corridors with a dim glow.[28]

Light in the corridors was necessary because by the end of the year most of the Wilkes buildings had iced up to roof level and the 1959 party were living like troglodytes below the surface. One of Williams' jobs was to cut trapdoors through the roofs of the huts for emergency exits in case of fire.

On 9 July at Wilkes, a tragic accident took the life of Hartley Robinson who was working long hours keeping Wilkes Station functioning, with no help available from Brandt. 'Robbie', as he was known, was excavating some oxy-acetylene bottles using a tractor. Snow Williams went to give him a hand and jumped into the hole Robinson had dug with his excavator shovel, while the machine reversed up a short, steep ice slope. Williams dropped to his knees trying to free one of the gas cylinders and Robinson came to help him:

Instead of getting to the top and parking, he parked on the slope. I didn't know that. . .he'd hopped out and come around behind me to give me a hand. And I heard the tractor rattle and roll, and I looked up and saw it bearing down and shouted and jumped at the same time. He was coming behind me and was caught by the track.[29]

It is thought Robinson slipped on the ice as he tried to jump and was killed instantly. He was moderately deaf and may not have heard the runaway tractor.[30]

His death had a shattering effect on the Wilkes party. 'Robbie' Robinson was a popular expeditioner. He had been a prisoner-of-war of the Japanese in Malaya during World War II, and at 48 was one of the older expeditioners. He showed the films on Saturday nights and could turn his hand to any engineering job that needed attention.

Now, with Robinson dead and Brandt incapacitated, the station was without its two diesel engineers. It was fortunate that Phil Law had asked

Snow Williams at the eleventh hour to winter at Wilkes, otherwise the station could have been left without any power. Williams:

> The biggest hassle was that I had a three-phase powerhouse to look after. . .I'd done a little bit of electricity in the Air Force, but never touched three-phase power. Luckily the Caterpillar generating set had books with them, and I had observed 'Robbie' do one or two changeovers when those engines were due for an oil change.[31]

It was a case of utilising all skills. Radio supervisor Alan Marriner had some electrical knowledge, and the cook, a young Englishman, 'Alby' Giddings (formerly second chef at Menzies Hotel in Melbourne), had trained as a motor mechanic. Bob Dingle had to rearrange the list of station duties:

> When we needed things done on the engineering side, we'd take him off the cooking roster. . .and he'd move into the workshop and somebody else would do the cooking. Young Williams and Giddings kept the station going mechanically.

By early August another occurrence was about to be added to the 1959 catalogue of unwanted emergencies. David Norris, the auroral physicist at Mawson, had returned to Taylor Glacier after the mid-winter break accompanied by weather observer Les 'Wacky' Onley. OIC John Béchervaise became concerned when radio contact with the field party was lost, and an emergency flight was organised from Mawson. The

HARTLEY ROBINSON'S GRAVE (LEFT) AT WILKES. (T BOWDEN)

WILKES RADIO ROOM, 1964. (A CAMPBELL-DRURY)

two aircraft reached Taylor Glacier on 4 August and Béchervaise experienced his worst moments ever in Antarctica when pilot Geoff Banfield said, 'I can't see the [field] station. The station's not there. The station is gone!' As Béchervaise described it:

> We banked steeply. Long snowdrifts ran down from a meteorological mast on a rocky outcrop. There was a black scar near the tide cracks. 'There's been a fire!', Geoff said. 'God, the place has been burnt down!'[32]

Both Beaver aircraft banked for a second circuit. Béchervaise feared the worst. Survival without shelter, food and bedding during the Antarctic winter was problematical at best. The second, smaller stores hut was still standing, but there was no sign of life. Jim Sandercock was the pilot of the second Beaver:

> We circled round, came in and landed. Very slowly, and virtually with tears in our eyes, we walked towards the hut expecting the worst. From behind us came a shout: 'Hey, you blokes!' We turned around. . .the chaps had been out walking. They'd seen the aeroplane coming back in. . .came racing back and came up behind us. We were very pleased to see them.

Norris and Onley were equally delighted. A sudden, violent fire had burnt down their hut four days earlier, leaving them time only to snatch a few blankets and rush out on to the ice. All their scientific records, auroral observing equipment, radios and personal gear were lost. They had sheltered in the second hut, unable to make contact with Mawson. It had been a near thing.

On 8 August, there was another near miss. One of the RAAF team, fitter Sergeant Hedley McIntyre, was running a Beaver engine in the Mawson hangar. Snow drifts built up against the structure made it almost completely airtight, and McIntyre collapsed with carbon monoxide poisoning. Luckily, pilot Jim Sandercock noticed him lying prostrate under the aircraft and pulled him to safety.

The day before this incident, Mawson's sole diesel power generator (rescued from the earlier powerhouse fire) broke down, leaving the station on emergency power supplied by a tractor and one small portable generator. The situation was extremely serious as a spare part needed to be manufactured and the workshop with its essential lathes had perished in the fire. An ingenious solution was devised—Joe Lawrence, Mawson's assistant diesel engineer, would fly to Davis Station in a Beaver aircraft, manufacture the vital part in the workshop there, and fly back.[33]

On 12 August weather conditions lifted, and the engineering mission began. Twelve days later Mawson went back on to its main generator and

no major power problems were experienced for the rest of the year.

Mawson's flying program continued with flights to Davis alternating with the support of field parties in the Prince Charles Mountains and Kemp and Enderby Lands. On 3 November, a cross-wind gust caused a Beaver aircraft to scrape a wingtip on the ice at Beaver Lake in the PCMs, but despite damage to the starboard aileron it was flown safely back to Mawson.[34]

In early December, the unhappy situation with Brandt at Wilkes was finally relieved when the United States agreed to send an aircraft from McMurdo Station in the Ross Sea to pick him up. On 3 December, Snow Williams wrote in his diary:

> A Neptune landed, spent two hours on the ground refueling, while a Constellation circled overhead. We brought our firefighting Weasel. . .to pump the fuel into the Neptune. All went well and the Neptune,

with a subdued Henry on board blasted off to the roar of about a dozen JATO [Jet Assisted Take Off] bottles, giving extra thrust.[35]

AIRCRAFT NEAR THE HANGAR AT MAWSON AFTER A BLIZZARD, 1959.
(J BÉCHERVAISE)
JATO (JET ASSISTED TAKE-OFF) BOTTLES FITTED ON A UNITED STATES NEPTUNE AIRCRAFT TO PROVIDE EXTRA THRUST FOR EMERGENCY TAKE-OFFS FROM ICE RUNWAYS. THIS AIRCRAFT EVACUATED HENRY BRANDT FROM WILKES IN DECEMBER 1960.
(R DINGLE)

Despite an improvement in Brandt's condition after nine months of treatment and confinement at Wilkes, the Americans insisted that the unfortunate man be restrained for the flight. From McMurdo, Brandt was flown to Christchurch in New Zealand. Don Styles arranged for the Antarctic Division's medical officer in Melbourne, Frank Soucek, to take care of him: 'He flew back with him to Melbourne and there we gave

The entire division was saddened by the death of the popular chief medical officer Frank Soucek, who collapsed with a heart attack during unloading operations at Macquarie Island on 24 December 1967. Soucek was one of the refugee doctors who came to Australia from Europe during World War II. He worked cheerfully in the only locations permitted by the medical authorities—Papua New Guinea and the Antarctic. He wintered on Macquarie Island in 1952 and emerged with a fluent but idiosyncratic command of the English language.

There are many affectionate stories told of the enthusiastic and gregarious Hungarian. Shortly after his Macquarie Island year, he worked in Papua New Guinea. On one occasion he was showing Lady Slim, the wife of the Governor-General of Australia, through one of the outlying hospitals. 'This is the bloody dispensary', explained the ebullient Soucek, 'and this is the bloody operating theatre'. After taking in the 'bloody' casualty section and the 'bloody' wards, Lady Slim asked her guide where he had learned his English. 'From those bloody bastards on Macquarie Island', replied Soucek.

him the medical treatment that ensured his recovery. We spoke to the German Consul about this before we became too involved and he was quite aware of what we were doing, because the man concerned was a German migrant.'

Phil Law confirmed that after treatment Brandt returned to his home town in Germany and settled down to a normal life. One of the immediate results of the Brandt affair was a move to ensure psychological screening of ANARE expeditioners before sending them south to winter.

December and the lengthening days of the Antarctic summer saw all stations hurrying to complete their annual programs and preparing for the changeover voyages. But with only a few weeks to go, the demons that controlled events in this extraordinary ANARE year of 1959 were still active.

The RAAF flight stationed at Mawson in 1959 had flown almost continuously through the year, although one of the disadvantages of the hangar at Mawson was the dependence on sea ice in Horseshoe Harbour for ski-equipped operations. As the ice weakened before its annual breakout—usually in late January—aircraft were not able to exploit the best flying conditions of the year when there were almost 24 hours of daylight and periods of comparatively settled weather. With that in mind, permission had been obtained from the RAAF to move the two Beaver aircraft on to the plateau behind Mawson Station to operate on an ice strip with skis and so be available to support summer field work. Flying operations began from the plateau from 5 December. The aircraft were tethered to 'dead-men'—wooden railway sleepers dug into the ice sheet—by half-tonne breaking strain steel cables.

On the morning of 28 December, Squadron Leader Jim Sandercock and engineer Sergeants Stewart Bell and Hedley McIntyre set out from Mawson Station in a Weasel over-snow vehicle to perform routine maintenance on the two Beavers anchored up on the plateau.[36] The weather was fine, and the katabatic wind—a regular feature of the Mawson environment—was not unduly strong. But as they moved further up on to the plateau, it became stronger. When they neared the area where the two Beavers were tethered, Sandercock was astonished to see one of the aircraft well away from its anchored position:

> Seeing this [Beaver 203] put a lump in our throats. Obviously it had broken free and glissaded down the slope till it got itself into a little bit of a hollow, and there it sat. . .The second aircraft was still in its place.

Sandercock decided to climb aboard the straying Beaver, start its engines and taxi it back to where it could be secured. The rudder and aileron chocks were removed, and he began to taxi back up the ice slope while engineers Bell and McIntyre went ahead in the Weasel. As he did so, the wind increased to gale force and Sandercock found himself becoming airborne:

> There was nowhere I could go. I had no elevator controls to control the up and down movement of the aeroplane, and it was a matter of juggling power against the wind and using the rudder to keep it as much as possible into the wind. . .

By this stage the wind was gusting up to 120 knots, dropping back at times to 70 and 80 knots. Sandercock had committed himself to an untethered aircraft which was becoming airborne, but which he could not fly

RAAF PILOT JIM SANDERCOCK FLYING A BEAVER AIRCRAFT OUT OF MAWSON STATION IN 1959. THE AIRCRAFT WAS LATER DESTROYED ON THE GROUND DESPITE SANDERCOCK'S HEROIC EFFORTS TO 'FLY' THE UNTETHERED BEAVER AGAINST THE BLIZZARD. (COURTESY J SANDERCOCK)

207

The stress and strain of trying to save the Beaver aircraft may have contributed to the unusual situation confronting Jim Sandercock in January 1960. In the supposedly germ-free environment of Antarctica, he had apparently contracted poliomyelitis!

He had, however, visited the Russian ship *Ob* which called at Mawson on 10 January and may have picked up an infection. By the time the ANARE relief ship *Thala Dan* arrived on 25 January the diagnosis of a poliomyelitis-like illness had been confirmed. The medical officer, Grahame Budd, faced a potentially disastrous situation. Poliomyelitis is highly infectious, and during the changeover period at Mawson there were 90 people potentially at risk. Any winterers incubating the disease would not develop symptoms until after *Thala Dan* left for Australia. Budd decided not to alarm Mawson's population—fear of illness in isolated situations can lead to great anxiety—but stressed that Sandercock's illness was 'a particularly debilitating virus infection' and scrupulous attention to personal hygiene was essential to prevent further cases. Budd did tell three men about to set out on a long sledge journey about the possibility of polio, and they elected to continue.[37]

Budd's next problem was whether to risk allowing Sandercock to embark on *Thala Dan*, but the alternative was to leave him at Mawson with limited access to physiotherapy. Sandercock tackled the journey strapped down and firmly wedged in his bunk with pillows:

> I was hospitalised at No. 6 RAAF Hospital, where they treated me for some nine or ten months before they would let me out, back up on my feet. I made a pretty good recovery after that, with physiotherapy. . .resumed light duties back in the RAAF and eventually got back to flying duties.

because his elevators were immobilised. He tried not to think about what would happen when his fuel ran out:

> The aeroplane was sliding backwards, power was being applied to get it back up the hill, and no decision was being made as to what was going to happen or when the wind was going to stop. I do remember looking at the fuel gauge and calculating that, at the rate I was using fuel, I could do this for 2½ hours as long as the fuel hung out, but I wasn't so sure of myself.

As he juggled the nobbled Beaver, his plight was radioed back to the station and a D4 tractor and additional Weasel were driven (with difficulty) up to the area. Meanwhile the other tethered Beaver pulled its 'dead-men' out of the ice, and Bell and McIntyre, with great presence of mind, chased the aircraft in a D4 Caterpillar tractor (kept on the plateau for power generation) and dropped its blade on the cables and railway sleepers as the aircraft began to career down the slope.

The arrival of the second D4 tractor would serve as anchor for the Beaver being manoeuvred by Sandercock. But OIC John Béchervaise, driving the comparatively light two-tonne Weasel, was worried that it might not get there before the Beaver's fuel ran out. The Weasel could not hold the Beaver by itself, but might do so—just—if anchored to iron stakes hammered into the ice. Getting a steel cable to the half-flying aircraft was a tricky and highly dangerous exercise and Sandercock watched their efforts with more than average interest:

> With great skill and resourcefulness, they placed the [Weasel] ahead of me. . .and I attempted to control the aeroplane while they tied steel cables and worked their way towards the wheels of my air-craft. You've got to remember the propeller was spinning at this stage of the game. . .how they did it I don't know, but they managed to put cables around it and secure the aircraft. It was only after that that I was able to leave the aircraft.

According to Mawson OIC John Béchervaise, the elated and relieved pilot climbed down from the Beaver cockpit and greeted his rescuers with the immortal words, 'Ow yer goin', mate? Orright?'[38]

Sandercock was safe for the moment, but the wind was relentless. All the eight men on the plateau could do was crawl on their hands and knees to a caravan secured nearby and hope that it, too, did not blow away. Sandercock remembers looking out the window 'and seeing the aeroplane absolutely thrash itself to pieces, like a balloon on a stick':

THE REMAINS OF THE RAAF ANTARCTIC FLIGHT'S TWO BEAVER AIRCRAFT, TETHERED NEAR THE ICE AIRSTRIP BEHIND MAWSON STATION AFTER HURRICANE-FORCE WINDS IN DECEMBER 1959. (J BÉCHERVAISE)

> First it went over on one side and knocked a wing off, then back to the other, and the next thing you'd see a wing go past. Both aeroplanes eventually went that way. The second one tore out of its ice tie-down pit and it too was destroyed. It was only several days later that we were able to go out and recover what we could. They were complete wrecks. We brought the two fuselages back, merely because they contained radio wiring and instruments. . .it was a most unfortunate business.

It was not a good omen for the 1960 flying program when, for the first time, a twin-engined DC3 Dakota aircraft would be used by the RAAF in Antarctica. It would also be parked out on the plateau.

The last three days of 1959 elapsed with no further dramatic events.

THIRTEEN

ANARE LIFE

From 1952 to 1963, the Antarctic Division had its headquarters in the Theosophical Building at 187 Collins Street, Melbourne, which also housed ASIO. Those who experienced life at 187 Collins Street regarded it as a vintage period of ANARE history when a zest for the pioneering phase of Australia's Antarctic activities was reflected in the enthusiasm and dedication of its staff. Law tried to keep the division insulated from the 'stereotyped attitudes' of the public service generally:

> For example, it was a number of years before staff in the Division claimed overtime. Men would gladly work all Christmas Eve or New Year's Day to get a ship away on time without any concern for payment.[1]

Des Lugg, who later became the Antarctic Division's head of polar medicine, believed that the division was regarded as a front for ASIO:

> When I arrived, ASIO had moved out, but their paraphernalia was still there. . .massive armaments and window shutters and safes. In fact Phil Law kept the Law collection of Antarctic slides in probably the safest safe in Australia.

Lugg recalls that the eccentric mix of activities in the Theosophical Building was enhanced by the caretaker, who built himself a yacht on the roof and had it lowered into Collins Street one Sunday morning.

Within the Theosophical Building, Phil Law involved himself in all aspects of ANARE operations. He was a 'hands-on' director in a way never again possible because of the sheer numbers of staff in later years. Law

The Antarctic Division shared the Theosophical Building with the Australian intelligence service ASIO—a hive of activity during the Petrov affair in 1954. The first floor belonged to the Theosophical Society and housed their library and meeting room. The lift was driven by a formidable elderly theosophist, Miss Phillips, who was known to try to convert visitors to the doctrine of theosophy during their brief ascent to the upper floors. Susan Ingham was the Antarctic Division's biology secretary:

On the ground floor there was a frock shop. The second floor was an up-market hairdresser's which the Governor's lady went to. The third floor was the Antarctic Division and the fourth floor was ASIO.

We didn't see much of the ASIO people. Sometimes they used the fire escape instead of the lift—possibly to avoid Miss Phillips!

Miss Phillips' enthusiasm for theosophy was matched by her fanatical campaign against those who dared to smoke in her lift. But the large sign PLEASE REFRAIN FROM SMOKING was often ignored by her passengers, who would conceal their cigarettes as they entered. Des Lugg:

When confronted, they would say: 'We are refraining from smoking'. So Miss Phillips would drive the lift very slowly to the top so that they were in danger of burning their fingers.

formulated major policy and often chaired the Executive Planning Committee:

> One of the problems of leading ANARE has always been that of creating a spirit of corporate endeavour and of breaking down the selfish departmental barriers. If departmental loyalties override the allegiance to the umbrella ANARE concept, fragmentation occurs and conflict disrupts the harmony of the enterprise both at the stations and in Australia. . .
>
> I found the Planning Committee exceptionally valuable. It helped me generate long-term policy and short-term programs, and when these were decided, it played a powerful role in gaining government acceptance for them. No major step was ever taken without the support of this body.[2]

The EPC was allowed to 'wither on the vine' at the end of 1962 and did not convene again until July 1965. It surfaced briefly in 1966 and then disappeared. Law believed it was never popular with ministers or senior bureaucrats because it had so many powerful and influential people suggesting how Australia's Antarctic expeditions should be run. No similar advisory body existed until 1979 when ARPAC (Antarctic Research Policy Advisory Committee) was set up to advise the Minister for Science and the Environment—then the parent department for ANARE.

Law tended to have a combative approach towards the Canberra-based DEA bureaucrats charged with overseeing the Antarctic Division. He was dealing with diplomats often between postings. Most of them were unused to a logistics-based operation like ANARE and accustomed to more deference than they received from ANARE's director. Law's personal files reveal constant conflict over budgets and expenses, departmental and personal publicity (Law was well aware of the importance of publicity and public relations to ANARE), and attempts to have his own public service status upgraded.

Despite the paper war and few face-to-face meetings—bureaucrats were not keen on return train trips from Canberra to Melbourne in the winter with a change of trains at Albury—Law respected most of the DEA people with whom he dealt, and this was largely reciprocated. Arthur Tange became secretary of the DEA in 1954:

> Everybody who needs government money. . .has to be a petitioner, it is just in the nature of things. . .[Law] was pretty blunt with me. . .blunt about what he wanted. An enthusiastic advocate for it. . .he naturally tended to see things from the point-of-view of the Antarctic Division and Antarctic expeditions. That's the sort of enthusiasm that gets people places. It sometimes has to be curbed because of other prior claims for money and staff.[3]

Once in 1956 Law's single-mindedness on advancing ANARE's cause so exasperated James Plimsoll (then Deputy Secretary of the DEA) that he dashed off a handwritten note with an instruction to have it placed on Law's personal file:

> I must tell Law one day that, in everything he writes and says to me, he leaves the distinct impression that he does not *want* to act as a servant of the Government; he *wants* only to explore the Antarctic.[4]

Until ANARE managed to get permission from the DEA to set up its own supply section, there were endless wrangles. Law recalls one particularly torrid session with a senior Treasury official over the division's budget. The Treasury man queried the victualling of the stations, saying that a migrant hostel in Canberra could feed its residents for half the figure being claimed for Antarctic expeditioners. He was unimpressed by Law's explanation that Mawson Station was a little more isolated than a Canberra migrant hostel, and threatened to send a Department of Immigration victualling officer to investigate the division's food costs:

This was too much for me. I said: 'If providing strawberry jam instead of plum jam at threepence a tin more will help to keep an Antarctic expeditioner happier, then that is what I will supply. . .The day that any victualling officer arrives to investigate the Antarctic Division's system I shall send my resignation to the Department of External Affairs.'

I then walked out, followed by my very concerned departmental colleague saying, 'Phil you shouldn't speak to senior Treasury officials like that'. However, that was the end of the matter; it was not brought up again during my long period of office.[5]

LEM MACEY (LEFT) AND DICK THOMPSON DURING CARGO OPERATIONS AT HEARD ISLAND EN ROUTE TO ESTABLISH MAWSON STATION, 1954. (R THOMPSON)

Law was ably backed up in his dealings with Canberra by his administrative assistant Jeremiah Donovan and supply officer Dick Thompson, who were experienced public servants and knew how to put up credible, detailed budgets. Thompson understood the two major principles on which 'hung all the Laws and the Prophets—the Public Service Act and the Treasury Regulations and Instructions':[6]

Phil used to go there [Canberra] and argue and fight and scream and say they were destroying Australian science. They didn't care about science, or hospitals, or academics—it was the Gladstonian thing of not spending money. So then we used to walk away with the money and Phil began to think I was the administrative marvel. What I did was to subvert the buggers—work out how the system worked, then make it work for you.[7]

Law not only involved himself with every aspect of ANARE operations, but played an activist role in defining its culture. This included creating rules of behaviour for expeditioners and officers-in-charge, personally selecting winterers, designing Antarctic clothing and buildings, overseeing cultural amenities, creating an ANARE uniform, and even choosing the vintages and varieties of the wine to be sent south.

In Melbourne he constantly encouraged informal debates on how things could be improved—procedures streamlined or equipment made

Alan Gilchrist, medical officer for the first wintering party on Heard Island in 1948, claims to have introduced the term 'slushy' to ANARE. He says the word is defined in some dictionaries as a slang term for 'cook's assistant' on nineteenth century sailing ships, although it is not used by the RAN today. Gilchrist:

In the typed instructions composed by Group Captain Campbell for the first expedition to Heard Island it was laid down that the messing officer (medical officer) should maintain a roster of 'assistant cooks' so that every member of the expedition would take a turn to help the regular cook during the week and relieve him completely at the weekends.[8]

Gilchrist posted the roster as soon as the kitchen at Heard was reasonably operative. He titled it 'Slushy Roster' because of his professional concern that the correct disposal of all waste and observance of good kitchen hygiene would prevent any infectious diarrhoea.

The 'assistant cooks' on ANARE stations have been 'slushies' ever since.

lighter, faster, safer or more cost effective. Collective food tastings were held to sample and judge rations to go south. To ensure staff were aware of Antarctic conditions, he began a policy of including HQ staff on resupply voyages—a tradition which has endured to the present.

The station 'bibles'—operations manuals—were constantly revised and updated. These documents not only set out the work program for the year, but covered all aspects of station organisation and administration, health, hygiene, field equipment and survival. Geologist Bruce Stinear recalls that in his three expeditions, no one ever queried any of the regulations. One of the rules specified there was to be a roster for 'slushy' duties—an expeditioner to help the cook. The only person on station who never acted as slushy was the cook.[9] That is still the case. In the classless ANARE society even the officer-in-charge takes his turn at washing up, setting tables and sweeping out. Jack Field, a cook who wintered five times with ANARE, agreed that the slushy roster was a great leveller for the 'boffins'—scientists: 'They [the scientists] had to clean up the camp and do all the painting, not just the ordinary fellows. . .so it was an equaliser.'

Each expeditioner was issued with a personal manual covering all aspects of ANARE service from pre-departure procedures and use of Antarctic clothing to advice on interpersonal relations. The OIC had a confidential leader's manual which included hints on leadership and how to cope with personality problems that might occur during the year.

One of Law's innovations that did not stand the test of time was the ANARE uniform, designed to be worn at formal mess dinners in the

Antarctic and to give a smart corporate look to departing ANARE personnel on the wharf. The second version was a green gaberdine jacket with a belt, leather buttons, four pockets and matching trousers. Peter Lancaster Brown, about to sail to Heard Island in 1952, described it as a cross between a ski suit and a prisoner's outfit. Others likened it to a coach driver's uniform.

Law was also determined that there would be an adequate library for expeditioners (including an *Encyclopaedia Britannica* 'to settle any arguments'), a wide selection of gramophone records, and a stock of 16mm feature films. He thought it particularly important to have polar literature in the station libraries. Medical officer Grahame Budd recalls:

> Whenever he was overseas he would pick up second-hand copies of the polar classics, and both Heard Island and Mawson had marvellous collections—first editions of Shackleton and Mawson. We didn't have much time to read, but when you do, it is a very good place to read about your predecessors.[10]

Law gave a lot of thought to ANARE policy on alcohol. There had been some difficulties with the 'ration per man' system in 1948 and 1949, and with hard liquor. In 1950 he forbade spirits and brought in a system where the OIC would issue a rationed amount of sherry, dry red and white flagon wines for evening meals:

> On Saturday nights ('ding' nights), good quality bottled dinner wines would replace flagon wines. After dinner on such nights there would be port, and for the rest of the evening during which cine films would be shown, beer would be available as well.[11]

The home brewing of beer was introduced to augment the limited stocks of bottled beer that could be taken south. The only exception to the rule on spirits concerned the officers-in-charge. Law contacted the chief distiller of CSR at Bundaberg in Queensland and arranged for a special brew of rum at 180 proof strength that would, when mixed with an equal quantity of water, be of standard strength. The OP rum was stored in specially constructed two-gallon oak casks:

> I then gave one cask to each OIC, and advised him to use it. . .for semi private occasions and not for general station use. The casks were beautiful and the rum of quality I have never tasted before or since. This experiment proved well worthwhile, the OICs appreciated this special privilege, and so far as I know, it was never abused.[12]

The tradition of a general ration of supplied liquor has continued although winterers are now permitted to take down personal stocks as well. In the 1950s Australia was not a very multi-cultural country, and wine was regarded with suspicion by many Australians. Grahame Budd recalls that wine bars were places where 'old plonks' and 'deros' would go:

> On one occasion when we had some nice wine on the table [at Heard Island] one of the men looked at me very sternly and said: 'Jeez Doc, I likes me drop of piss as well as the next man, but I draws the line at plonk!'[13]

Unwilling to impose his own sophisticated tastes in wine on the stations, Law instituted wine tastings at the division with those who had wintered and those who were about to, to get a consensus. He felt that his beer and wine policy paid dividends. Heavy consumption of spirits on Antarctic stations had led to quite awkward and dangerous situations. One man formed the habit of charging out and smashing the cinema screen down on Saturday nights:

> Another. . .would wander off outside on his own and pass out in a snow drift. When he was missed a search would be instituted and he would be rescued, half frozen, and put to bed. Still another man had the habit, when heavily intoxicated, of piling papers on his bunk and setting fire to them. In an environment where fire is the greatest single hazard, this was a frightening performance.[14]

As an administrator, Law was demanding and insistent on punctuality and on deadlines being met. If they were not, his response was always controlled—curt, abrupt or dismissive. Those who worked with him for ten years or more could never recall seeing him angry and he had a genuine 'open door' policy for any staff member who wanted to see him.[15]

Dick Thompson believed that Law added 'an atmosphere, a dimension of excitement' into what was happening by having everyone involved one way or the other. 'You had no doubt you were working in a very, very interesting organisation compared to elsewhere in the Public Service.'[16]

Those who worked with Law at the Antarctic Division HQ in Melbourne believed he did not hold grudges against those who, for one reason or another, had failed his expectations. Having selected his team, he let them get on with their jobs, and backed them with the kind of loyalty he expected (and got) in return.[17]

This tolerance did not extend to expeditioners who had caused trouble or failed to do their jobs properly on ANARE stations. It was widely believed that those individuals were logged in Law's mental black book, and were never selected to go to Antarctica again.[18] Some were not even named in the official list of expeditioners.

216   ANARE's first leader, Stuart Campbell, had selected the 1948

expeditioners through a combination of the 'old boy network' and a belief that anyone who applied to go to Antarctica 'would be the right type anyway'. As soon as Law became director he established a formal application process which began with Australia-wide advertisements and ended with a personal interview before a panel. Law chaired these interview panels and effectively selected all ANARE expeditioners himself. He was impressed by applicants who were keen bushwalkers or skiers and who he thought would have some appreciation of what the elements in Antarctica could unleash. He often approved an applicant on a 'gut feeling', but admits some of his early judgments were flawed:

> I used to be impressed with enthusiasm. . .the sort of man who would say, 'I will do any job. . .so long as you take me'. I thought that was a wonderful sign of enthusiasm.
>
> . . . Antarctica is so isolated, so many things in life are removed from your environment [that] really all you have down there is your job. If you don't like that job, or you're not good at it, your chance of success is heavily reduced. So the most important thing, I think, in picking an Antarctic person is that he should love his job, because he's got to be at it fourteen or sixteen hours a day for a whole year. . .And if he's good at it then he gets the respect of the other men, regardless of his personality, and that's a plus.

On several occasions, in the 1950s and 1960s, ships were able to evacuate expeditioners with psychological and medical problems from sub-Antarctic islands which could be reached comparatively easily in ice-free seas. The Antarctic continent was not so accessible. The tragic situation faced by Henry Brandt at Wilkes in 1959, following his mental breakdown and isolation in a makeshift cell for six months, caused Minister for External Affairs Richard Casey to instruct Law to arrange psychological tests for ANARE expeditioners before they were selected:

> Casey had the simplistic view that you develop a questionnaire with thirty questions and you give that to every applicant, and the sheep go out one door and the goats go out the other. . .

Law consulted the Professor of Psychology at Melbourne University, Oscar Oeser, and asked him to design a suitable test for choosing Antarctic men:

> He said: 'Well, Law, what are the qualities of the men that are successful?' In other words, how do you define the qualities of a good expeditioner? I said: 'That's what I want you to tell me.'
> 'No', he said. 'You tell me what they are and I'll design a test for them.'

Even if ANARE did design a test, Law realised he did not have the budget to fly a psychologist around Australia every year to conduct interviews with prospective expeditioners. Oeser suggested he approach the Australian Army Psychological Service for assistance. He did and Lieutenant Colonel George Owens was selected to carry out the project. Owens was delighted to be involved:

> It was good for the army. . .because it would also help us to get some insight and get some scientific work done in relation to the performance of people in isolation. . .which was becoming more evident in these days with long range penetration. . .and small groups operating in isolated territories.

Owens steeped himself in Antarctic literature and accounts of the activities of Mawson, Shackleton and Scott, and began travelling to Antarctica on the annual resupply voyages, interviewing expeditioners on the spot, and debriefing them on the way home. (This procedure is still carried out by army psychologists.)

The only published material available at that time on the psychology of Antarctic service was a paper by Law to the *Medical Journal of Australia*, 20 February 1960, 'Personality Problems in Antarctica'. In it, Law identified some of the difficulties faced by a group of men surviving for a year in close proximity and total isolation, without the company of women, and in a community ranging from biologists and upper atmosphere physicists, through to diesel mechanics, carpenters and cooks.

Although 'trifling personal peculiarities' could cause mounting exasperation and tension, there were many compensations in Antarctic life—apart from the adventure and magnificent scenery. He wrote:

> The existence of an expedition member is socially uncomplicated. . .there is no money, and therefore no financial anxiety. One has no concern about financial status—the Joneses have been left far behind. . .There is no time wasted in travel, social engagements or in holidays and weekends. A scientist can accomplish two years work in one at an Antarctic station.[19]

Although Law never wintered on an ANARE station he was aware of one of the greatest dangers facing an isolated group—the forming of cliques—and the need for the officer-in-charge to keep that situation in check, while not joining any faction himself. He also charted the entirely predictable graph of morale at a wintering station. Morale is down at the beginning, during the uncertainty of the changeover period, with the former party still there. It surges to its highest point as soon as the ship sails, for about two months, then dips as the long winter nights, lack of

The advent of midwinter, the night of the solstice, has been a high point of celebration for all polar wintering expeditions since the era of Scott, Shackleton and Mawson. It is an occasion usually marked by a formal dinner, an elaborate menu, special wines and spirits hoarded for the occasion and speeches. As the evening progresses formality is abandoned. There may be recitations, songs, burlesque sketches and almost invariably a fancy dress party.

At Scott's last midwinter dinner in his hut at Cape Evans in 1911, Admiral Sir Edward Evans later wrote of the 'only Antarctic dance we enjoyed. . .I remember dancing with the cook whilst Oates danced with Anton'. Fueled by brandy punch, the cook, Clissold, so far forgot himself as to call Scott 'good old Truegg'. (Truegg was the name of a dried egg powder used in cakes and puddings.) Scott's response to this indiscretion is not recorded.

Men dressing as women on these all-male midwinter occasions has been an enduring Antarctic tradition enthusiastically perpetuated by many ANARE winterers over the years. Photographs taken at these occasions feature

AN INTREPID/LUNATIC ANARE EXPEDITIONER
DIVES INTO SUB-ZERO WATERS FOR A MIDWINTER
SWIM AT MAWSON, 1961.
(R McLEAN)

A MIDWINTER PARTY AT MAWSON STATION,
1960. FROM LEFT: TERRY 'CHEDDAR'
ELKINS, JIM KICHENSIDE
AND GEORGE CRESSWELL.
(G NEWTON)

INTREPID ANARE EXPEDITIONER
BILL BREEZE PADDLING HIS HOME-MADE
RECREATIONAL CANOE AT CASEY, 1976.
(W BREEZE)

bearded 'ladies' with improbably prominent chests and hairy legs appearing under extremely short skirts. While psychologists might be tempted to theorise about repressed homosexuality, ANARE winterers regard it simply as a joyous joke. Or as David Luders, an OIC at Casey and Mawson in the early 1970s put it: 'I don't think the thought of homosexuality crossed our minds.'

Luders was aware, however, of a general level of frustration at the lack of women on the stations. He can only recall one occasion when that manifested itself in any overt way during a midwinter celebration:

> At around midnight one of the fellows came into the recreation room dressed as a woman. His girlfriend had given him a wig. He had a pinkish complexion and he only had a very small black moustache. He had a miniskirt and stockings on, and the wig transformed him into a passable female.

His/her unexpected arrival stopped the party in its tracks, and a great shout went up.

Luders was aware of a deal of horseplay and coarse male jokes, but not long afterwards he was alarmed to see the 'girl' lying on his back, with another expeditioner miming sexual intercourse with him. Although it was a burlesque, the OIC felt things were getting out of hand:

> I was fairly famous for unusual ways of dealing with situations and I turned around to a water fire extinguisher on the wall and sprayed them. They wouldn't speak to me for three days afterwards. But I did that because it broke the tension. It certainly made them seem foolish. . .it gave people something to laugh about, because if I'd given them a dressing down everyone would have felt uncomfortable.

A midwinter swim has become a more robust tradition for the extremely hardy—some of whom have to smash a hole in the coastal sea ice to indulge. The urges to celebrate the longest night, looking forward to the return of the sun, are powerful indeed.

sunshine and the need to stay indoors lower morale. The graph rises when the sun returns and the expeditioners prepare for summer field trips. Another high point is reached in the last two months when the prospect of relief and a return home acts as a spur to finish uncompleted programs.

By the 1960s there was a realisation that the stations needed a core of solid professionals who just went about their work without flamboyance and great displays of ego. In 1960 Law bravely attempted to define the qualities of a good expeditioner as someone who was good at their job, unselfish (willing to pitch in and help in general station work), tolerant, capable of self control, optimistic, possessing 'stickability' (in carrying a work program through), and with a sense of adventure and curiosity. He believed that whether an expeditioner was married or unmarried was not particularly relevant and nor was age.[20]

As the army-related psychological screening began in the early 1960s Law and Owens found they had less flexibility in vetting the personalities of the specialist scientists, although it was hoped a preoccupation with their work would overshadow any anti-social qualities. Owens believed that made it even more important to have maintenance and support staff who were confident, energetic, motivated and conscientious:

> Most of the mechanics had their funny little ways of making motors work under any circumstances and their acceptability to the other members was based on their ability to make those damn machines run, and to keep the electricity going.

It is universally accepted in ANARE culture that a happy and competent cook makes a good station. Law remembers receiving a requisitioning cable in Melbourne near the end of one year reading: SEND ONE GOOD COOK, PACK WELL IN COTTON WOOL.[21]

Stefan Csordas, medical officer on Macquarie Island, who spent three winters there in the late 1950s, faced a potentially serious situation when an expedition cook broke three front teeth from his upper denture:

> As he was a little bit on the alcoholic side, I thought that having a cook who can't eat and doesn't have enough to drink, will [give us] a horrible time. So I had to improvise something for him.

With typical ANARE ingenuity Csordas ground down an elephant seal's tusk with a pedal dental drill, repaired the cook's dentures and preserved group happiness.

In the 1950s Csordas, like the other ANARE medical officers, had half a day's training at the Royal Melbourne Dental Hospital to help cope with dental emergencies. In later years this was increased to two weeks after it became clear that doctors in Antarctica spent quite a lot of their professional time attending to cracked or broken fillings and other dental work.

Most expeditioners knew their medical officers had only rudimentary knowledge of dentistry and visited them reluctantly. At Mawson in 1956 Don Dowie experimented with a pedal-operated drill which sometimes went unexpectedly into reverse, generating heat, and pain to his unfortunate patient.

Once, while Dowie was taking his turn at cooking on Sunday, he attempted ice cream and caramel sauce. But the sauce turned into toffee.

> It was the chewiest stuff you've ever seen in your life, and fillings were coming out like machine-gun bullets—you could hear them popping! The next morning I had a line-up outside the surgery for dental work

while I put in temporary fillings. I'm quite sure they thought I'd done it on purpose to get a bit of practice.

Often expeditioners (and cooks) had their own ways of curing individuals of annoying mannerisms which disrupted the community. Bob Dingle was a weather observer at Macquarie in 1956 and remembers one winterer being obsessive about his food:

> He would examine all dishes put in front of him for little bits of hair. . .and if he found something he would hold it up and expose it to the whole group, saying: 'Look, here's another short and curly'.

NECESSITY IS THE MOTHER OF INVENTION IN ANTARCTICA. MEDICAL OFFICER PETER GORMLY DRILLS HIS OWN TOOTH ABSCESS. (COURTESY P GORMLY)

This upset the cook, Jim Morgan, who waited till someone had their hair cut, then collected the results. The next day he baked individual fruit pies and completely filled one with hair:

> So when this fellow faced up to the counter for his dessert he was given the hair pie, with a nice layer of crust over it, smothered in custard. Everybody else in the party had been warned this was going to happen, so when he got back to the table and put his spoon into the pie, all the hair fluffed out. . .He was certainly cured from ever mentioning again that he'd found a hair in his tucker.

Sometimes serious tensions would build up between individuals to a degree not always evident to the rest of the party or the OIC. RAAF pilot Doug Leckie wintered at Mawson in 1956 and late one night—as duty night watchman—walked into the mess to check that the fires in the kitchen stove were safe. He found two young men on the kitchen floor with their hands around each other's throats. Leckie was sure they were out to do each other in:

> I had to break them apart and order them off to bed because [I think] they'd have killed each other if I hadn't turned up at that psychological moment. They were very serious and dead silent—dead silent. . .From then on they kept apart and had very little to do with each other.

It has been estimated that the chance of a cerebral haemorrhage occurring in a small group of fit men is one in ten thousand. Yet that was the situation facing Russel Pardoe, the ANARE medical officer at Mawson in 1961.

On 2 November 1961, the station's senior diesel mechanic Alan Newman collapsed after lifting a bag of coal briquettes on to his back, suffering a haemorrhage from an artery at the base of the brain.[22] Over the next 27 days his condition deteriorated, and Pardoe, who had been consulting with a Melbourne neurosurgeon by radio-telegram, was advised that if the pressure inside Newman's skull was not relieved, he would almost certainly die.

Pardoe had no previous experience in neurosurgery. Two Mawson expeditioners had attended the Royal Melbourne Hospital for two weeks before sailing for Antarctica. The cook, Ted Giddings, had been trained in the duties of a theatre sister, and the geophysicist Rod Hollingsworth as an assistant anaesthetist. Pardoe was given advice by cable from Melbourne on what he should do, but essential equipment had to be manufactured first. Pardoe:

> With the aid of some illustrations in an instrument catalogue, a brain cannula 6 centimetres in length and 2 millimetres in internal diameter was improvised from a dental dry-air bulb syringe. The tip of the syringe was closed with silver solder and a lateral opening was filed in the shaft. . .A second dental dry-air syringe was modified to make a sucker.[23]

In order to test these and other instruments needed for the operation, a Weddell seal was shot in the skull with a .38 revolver, and 'the resultant cerebral haematoma was aspirated

RUSSIANS TO THE RESCUE. ALAN NEWMAN, SUFFERING FROM A CEREBRAL HAEMORRHAGE, WAS EVACUATED FROM MAWSON STATION IN A RUSSIAN ILYUSHIN 18 AIRCRAFT ON 30 DECEMBER 1961.
(R WYERS)

by the technique to be used on the patient'.

On 29 November, 28 days after Newman became ill, the Mawson surgical 'team' gathered in the main room of the surgery hut. Pardoe drilled through Newman's skull and managed to aspirate some of the blood clot and relieve the intracranial pressure.

However, Newman's condition deteriorated further, and a second operation repeated this procedure on 3 December. This time Newman's condition improved. But on 16 December he collapsed again, and by 23 December Pardoe was planning to operate once more. Newman rallied a little, and the operation was postponed.

At this stage Pardoe was not optimistic about his patient's chances. The relief ship was not due at Mawson until mid-January 1962 and would not be back in Australia until March after a long, rough sea voyage. However, in late December it was learned that two long-range Soviet aircraft were making an inaugural flight from Moscow to the Russian Antarctic station at Mirny, via Australia and New Zealand. The Antarctic Division asked for Soviet aid which was willingly given. Pardoe accompanied his critically ill patient on the flight, leaving Mawson on 30 December in a Russian Ilyushin 18 aircraft (not the long-range aircraft that had first been discussed), and

flying to Mirny—then on to the Americans at McMurdo, who flew Pardoe and Newman to Christchurch, New Zealand, in a Hercules.

Ten days after leaving Mawson Station, Newman was admitted to St Vincent's Hospital in Sydney, where he was operated on again. Remarkably, he made a complete recovery, apparently suffering no intellectual impairment when he was tested several years later. He went back to work and resumed a normal life.

On 1 January 1963 Russel Pardoe was awarded an MBE for his remarkable medical efforts in Antarctica.

No murders have occurred on any Australian stations in half a century of ANARE operations, although records do not reveal whether any were planned. The total isolation of wintering parties in the early years was emphasised by the problem of communication with the outside world. Radio transmissions between ANARE stations and Australia were difficult, due to ionospheric disturbances and auroral activity, and all official correspondence was hand keyed in Morse code. Radio blackouts could occur for some days at a time, and even the Morse transmissions were frequently interrupted.

Great care was taken in the selection of the radio operators and communications personnel because the radio shack tended to be a social hub and even though much of the incoming administrative cables came in code, there was always the chance of finding out something from the outside world. George Owens said they tried to select radio operators who were sociable and amenable—but also able to keep their mouths shut and not pass on sensitive or personal material relating to other expeditioners.[24]

Personal messages to and from Antarctica were transmitted by Morse radiogram through the Overseas Telecommunication Commission's beam radio stations at special rates. The cost to each expeditioner was subsidised, with a free of charge wordage allocated each month. Messages which exceeded this limit were charged to the expeditioner in Australia. Phil Law quickly realised that the free communications allowance was inadequate, and that winterers would face a heavy financial burden when they returned to Australia:

Trevor Heath [ANARE's first administrative officer] had the idea of using Bentley's Complete Phrase Code, an international code for cable and radio communications.[25]

A supplementary code of five-letter words was drawn up specially designed for ANARE, with useful phrases like:

YOGIP   Please send details of bank account.
YASEL   We've just had a blizzard.
YAYIR   Fine snow has penetrated through small crevices in the buildings.
YIHKE   I have grown a beard which is generally admired.[26]

Any personal communications were known as 'Whizzers', after the much used code grouping WYSSA—'All my love darling'. While the five-letter code was useful for keeping down cable costs, it was not well suited to intimate communication. Geoff Butterworth wintered at Wilkes in 1963 and at Mawson in 1966. He and his wife Fay prearranged a more personal channel of communications as well as the conventional messages like 'Kids are well'. The key to this intimacy was the code grouping YOHNA—'My message is contained in the following quotation'. Fay and Geoff each had a copy of Palgrave's *Golden Treasury of Verse*:

> We went through that, and boy, there's a lot of good stuff in that book of poetry. We really kept ourselves going for the whole year with that. And my husband wasn't a big poetry reader, but he knew Palgrave by the time he came home.

In 1949, realising how important personal cables were in maintaining morale at ANARE stations, Phil Law appointed Mrs Mynwe McDonald as cables officer to oversee not only communications, but all kinds of personal problems concerning expeditioners and their partners or families in Australia:

> Mrs Mac, as she was always called, reminded men of their wives' birthdays, ordered gifts and anniversary flowers (often at her own expense), smoothed out misunderstandings, visited wives in times of family misfortune, and operated on a wide involvement that went far beyond the call of duty. I cannot imagine how we could have managed without her.[27]

One morning Mrs Mac received a cable from Sydney to be sent on to Antarctica: BY THE TIME YOU RECEIVE THIS I SHALL HAVE

Radio Australia's Mary Adams recalls some difficult diplomatic moments. Once she inadvertently read out a letter from a lover and received an angry phone call from the expeditioner's wife. Mary believes 'Calling Antarctica' broke new ground in radio:

I think we broadcast the first *ever* birth on radio. The wife insisted that the birth be recorded and we took up a good quarter-hour of a program with somebody going 'UURGH! ERGH!' and the baby was actually born on Radio Australia. The guys asked for that to be replayed two or three times, so I can only assume it was important to them.

COMMITTED SUICIDE. Law told her to be on the night train to Sydney. Fay Butterworth later wrote:

Arriving in Sydney next morning, she hurried out to the address and found the house empty. The occupant, a neighbour informed her, had gone off to work. She settled down to wait. Toward evening a smart young woman came through the front gate and Mrs Mac rose to her feet and introduced herself explaining why she had come. The woman was astounded. Coming all that way! But yes, thank you, she had quite recovered from her attack of midwinter blues.[28]

Mynwe McDonald 'mothered' ANARE expeditioners for nineteen years. In January 1967 Shelagh Robinson took over that role until her retirement in 1981. The Antarctic Division still continues this practice. Since 1987 Mary Mulligan has been the expeditioner training and family liaison officer at the division, which adheres to strict privacy legislation requirements.

The only other contact with the outside world (apart from occasional amateur radio transmissions) was via short wave broadcasts from the ABC's Radio Australia. 'Calling Antarctica', a special program for ANARE winterers, was first broadcast in 1948 and ended in the mid 1980s after satellite links revolutionised Antarctic communications and expeditioners could simply pick up the phone and ring home. Always compered by women, 'Calling Antarctica' relayed letters, personal messages and request records. The presenters most associated with the program were Jocelyn Terry and Mary Adams, and their voices and personalities were appreciated by communities of lonely men. Mawson OIC John Béchervaise wrote in his diary on 15 April 1955:

At a quarter to three, for the first time since our arrival, the Radio Australia program 'Calling Antarctica' came in 'loud and clear'. Jocelyn Terry's pleasant, youthful voice, gave us news of home, a brief, well made summary of my own press report and two or three 'request' records (asked for by men on Macquarie Island).

It is good not to take radio for granted. Outside the surgery windows, grey drift ebbed and flowed and with it all vision of other buildings and the world. On the windows, miraculous silver palms were etched in frost. . .and Jocelyn went on talking, thousands of miles beyond the racing drift. . .where it was already night. Little items of news—the arrival in Melbourne of the Italian Opera Company, new parking laws and so on, were laced with personal messages. Men sat down to tea with new and pleasant conversational topics.[29]

Even in 1960 Phil Law argued that there was some merit in not having too much communication between those wintering in the Antarctic and the home front. At Wilkes Station the United States authorities had a system whereby an expeditioner could make voice contact home through amateur radio enthusiasts:

Some men who have spoken directly by radio-telephone to their wives tend to be disturbed and depressed for several days after the initial exhilaration of the personal communication fades. Also there are wives whose regular telephone conversations to their isolated husbands would degenerate into catalogues of petty worries which the husband could just as well do without.[30]

Only men wintered at ANARE stations until 1976 on Macquarie Island and 1981 on the Antarctic continent. In 1960 Phil Law wrote in his paper 'Personality Problems in Antarctica' that 'little was known of the sexual disturbances and abnormalities caused by the deprivation of women's company':

In our experience, men seem to accept the absence of any sex life realistically; their attitude can be summed up by the sentence: 'There is nothing you can do about it, so the less you think of it the better.'[31]

Law believed this philosophical acceptance of Antarctic celibacy was partly due to the 'absence of constant sexual stimulants which abound in a civilised environment'—pretty girls, advertisements, sexy magazines and films—and speculated that much sexual energy was sublimated in hard work:

Men do miss wives and sweethearts, and at times they miss them desperately—particularly in moments of emotional stress, and particularly when family events at home worry them; but for the greater part of the time the men appear untroubled . One wonders whether the cold climate provides some sedative influence.[32]

OUTDOOR CHRISTMAS CELEBRATIONS AT MAWSON, 1957. SURVEYOR MORRIE FISHER WAITED NINE MONTHS FOR THE CHANCE TO WEAR HIS DINNER SUIT, WHILE THE BEMUSED PENGUIN IS ALWAYS FORMALLY DRESSED. THE SECOND PENGUIN (LEFT) SEEN LEAVING BAR ANTARCTICA IS A NON-DRINKER.
(AAD ARCHIVES)

In 1960 Law wrote that he was not aware of any overt cases of homosexuality in the all-male Antarctic communities, but some incipient tendencies had been noted:

> For example, one older man could not resist running his fingers through the blond hair of a young, good-looking lad each time he passed him, which finally provoked the youth into threatening to cut his throat if he did it again. I heard that one man—an ex-seaman—did some soliciting on one occasion, but there were no takers.[33]

The showing of feature films provided some outlet for sexual frustrations. As the plots and stories became well known, winterers would shout bawdy interjections, or turn the sound down completely and provide their own dialogue. Often the most turgid and predictable feature films, newsreels or magazines were re-edited in an unexpected and bizarre manner. Trevior Boyd, who wintered at Macquarie Island in 1950, remembers there was a lot of general talk about women and sex, and at times 'we used to stop the film and burn the lamps out in the projector to examine women closely'.

Sometimes the films had a markedly civilising effect on the community. *Pride and Prejudice* was the most popular film shown on Macquarie Island in 1950, and the entire station took on the elaborate manners and courtly language of Jane Austen's genteel nineteenth century England. Trevior Boyd recalls that asking someone to pass the butter at dinner would elicit the invariable response: 'Such affability, such graciousness—you overwhelm me!' When Law arrived to relieve the station he was at a loss to account for the quaint mid-Victorian quality of the men's everyday dialogue until he was told of the profound influence of *Pride and Prejudice.*

All wintering communities were exclusively male for the first 29 years of ANARE. Phil Law said he tried to have a woman sent to Macquarie Island in 1953, when a physicist engaged to carry out auroral observations at Hurd Point on the southern tip of the island asked to take his wife: 'As he would be spending most of the year isolated in a small hut, I sought permission from my Department, but it was refused.'[34]

The first women to visit an Australian station officially did so in the summer of 1959–60, at Macquarie Island. Susan Ingham, biology secretary at the Antarctic Division, claims part credit for the breakthrough when she marched into Phil Law's office and said:

> 'I want to go to Macquarie Island on the changeover, please.' Rather to my surprise, because I thought it might take a long campaign, he said: 'Well, it might be possible. We'd have to get a cabin of four.'

Other women had applied—Mary Gillham (an English botanist) and Isobel Bennett and Hope Macpherson who were both biologists interested in the geographical distribution of species in coastal tidal zones. Bennett and Macpherson were experienced travellers, used to sailing on coastal vessels in rough seas, getting in and out of small boats and landing on small islands and remote coasts around southern Australia and Bass Strait.

The announcement about the women on 24 November 1959 triggered a media flurry of reporters and photographers and a newsreel film crew. Susan Ingham:

> I did an interview which was rather fun. Later we successfully foiled an attempt by the [Melbourne] *Herald* to photograph our underwear—saying firmly that it was just ordinary winter stuff. *Women's Weekly* came, and *Woman's Day* wanted a story on our return. In fact it got to such a point that my bread shop (who didn't know my name or where I worked) inquired if I was a good sailor and my dentist wrote 'Bon Voyage' on a receipted bill.

229

THE FIRST WOMEN MEMBERS
OF ANARE TO VISIT
MACQUARIE ISLAND PREPARE
TO SAIL ON *THALA DAN* IN
DECEMBER 1959. FROM
LEFT: SUSAN INGHAM,
MARY GILLHAM,
HOPE MACPHERSON,
ISOBEL BENNETT.
(COURTESY I BENNETT)

NEL LAW, SEEN WATCHING
A CHESS GAME AT MAWSON
IN FEBRUARY 1961, WAS
THE FIRST WOMAN TO
VISIT AN ANARE
CONTINENTAL STATION.
(R MERRICK)

Isobel Bennett, one of Australia's foremost marine scientists, was unamused when she was told during an interview with Phil Law at the Antarctic Division that 'on our behaviour rested the future of our sex with regard to ANARE voyages'.[35] But all the women were aware that the spotlight was on them. The voyage in *Thala Dan* was unexceptional and the scientists suffered the usual frustrations at Macquarie of weather-interrupted sessions of field work snatched when possible during the unloading and resupply operations.

The visit was productive. Between them the first women to accompany an ANARE expedition produced two books on general aspects of the island and a series of scientific papers on various aspects of island biology. Their presence was not immediately noted. Although all male members of the Macquarie Island changeover party were named in a report written for the *Polar Record* by Phil Law, the women's contribution was summarised:

> Four women biologists carried out work in littoral ecology, the effects of nesting sea birds on plants, and the ANARE bird and seal programme.[36]

The women must have behaved impeccably. Isobel Bennett later wrote:

> On that initial trip, it behoved the four women to tread warily. We were invaders in a man's realm and were regarded with some suspicion. . .The venture inevitably made headlines. Today [1971] our presence on a polar ship south-bound for Macquarie does not even warrant a press mention, and we have become an accepted part in the scheme of things—though only for changeover voyages.[37]

The distinction of being the first woman to visit an Australian continental Antarctic station went to Nel Law, Phil Law's wife, who sailed on *Magga Dan* to Mawson and Oates Land in February and March 1961. She departed amid some controversy. Mrs Law was invited on *Magga Dan* as a guest of the Lauritzen Line and the captain, but when the story got into the press there was resentment by journalists who had been denied access to Antarctic resupply voyages due to lack of available berths. The DEA became involved and Ralph Harry, First Assistant Secretary, telephoned Law in Perth on 24 January—the day of sailing:

> I said I thought we had to consider. . .we had refused facilities to the press and that other personnel on the expedition would not be able to have their wives with them.
>
> He said that he supposed that in the circumstances he should not take his wife.[38]

Senator John Gorton, representing the Minister for External Affairs, came to the rescue at the last moment. He went to the Fremantle docks to farewell *Magga Dan* and saw Nel Law 'walking disconsolately up and down the wharf':

> Phil Law introduced me to his wife, and I said, 'Well, you are going, no doubt'. She said she couldn't go, and I said 'Why can't you go?' She said, '[External] Affairs won't let me'. And I said, 'Well go. Get on the bloody boat and go now.'

Gorton's support was needed in the coming weeks when questions were asked in Federal Parliament about 'the presence of a woman' aboard *Magga Dan*. The press had a field day after it was reported *Magga Dan* was caught in pack ice for eleven days near Chick Island off the coast of Wilkes Land after servicing an automatic weather station there. ICE GRIPS SHIP: WOMAN ABOARD—MP'S TO ASK QUESTIONS trumpeted the Sydney *Telegraph*.[39] On 18 March the *Canberra Times* reported the ship 'caught in the jaws of crushing ice'. Then: '*Magga Dan*, which has a woman on board, has freed itself from the perilous massed ice packs off Chick Island'.[40]

Phil Law's official voyage report did not mention his wife's presence on the voyage. An accomplished artist, Nel Law produced a magnificent series of oil and water colour paintings of her Antarctic voyage. Her visit to Antarctica had been a milestone of sorts, but had not 'broken the ice' for her sex in ANARE service. Twenty years were to elapse before an Australian woman expeditioner wintered on an Australian continental station.

FOURTEEN

FILLING IN THE MAP

When Australia established its first permanent settlement—Mawson Station—on the Antarctic continent, there was little accurate detail available of the coastline and interior features of Australia's vast Antarctic claim. During his time as director of the Antarctic Division from 1949 to 1966 Phillip Law oversaw a program of basic exploration to fill in the dotted lines on more than 5000 kilometres of unexplored coastline and to locate and fix the mountain ranges and peaks breaking through the Antarctic ice cap in the interior of the AAT. Law and the surveyors, geologists, pilots and other ANARE expeditioners shared in the delight of raw adventure and discovery during these pioneering years. But exploration had to be fitted in between the essential resupply and changing over of personnel each summer.[1] Law called it 'Hit and Run Exploration':

> You'd sail along the coast generally in lousy weather, just praying that when you got to a certain place you'd get that odd spot of one or two days of good weather. You'd hang around until you got it. . .then you'd have everyone on board drilled on what they were to do, with people allocated to various duties. The surveyor would go here and he'd get an astrofix. The geomagnetician would go there and he would take his geomagnetic observations, and you'd have a number of men deputed to make a census of all the birds on the island, the flying birds and the penguins.
>
> So the fine day would dawn. We'd anchor the ship immediately. As soon as the anchor dropped the boats would go, and the pontoons full of men and they'd land. Within half an hour everyone would be working

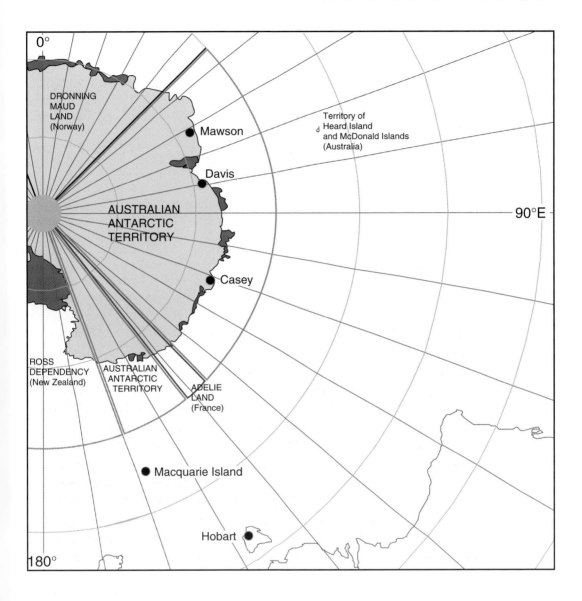

0°

DRONNING
MAUD
LAND
(Norway)

Mawson

Davis

Territory of
Heard Island
and McDonald Islands
(Australia)

AUSTRALIAN
ANTARCTIC
TERRITORY

90°E

Casey

ROSS
DEPENDENCY
(New Zealand)

AUSTRALIAN
ANTARCTIC
TERRITORY

ADELIE
LAND
(France)

Macquarie Island

Hobart

180°

furiously, and they'd work around the clock without
stopping for food or anything more than cups of tea
and biscuits—no sleep and 24 hours' daylight—just
go for your life until the weather broke.

AUSTRALIAN ANTARCTIC
TERRITORY AND NEARBY
NATIONAL CLAIMS.

Each summer Law designated new areas of the
AAT coast to be explored. He regarded the investigation of the Oates
Land coast—on the extreme eastern end of the AAT close to the Trans-
Antarctic Mountains—as the most rewarding and exciting of his career.
On 20 February 1959 *Magga Dan* reached a large pool of open water 90
kilometres from the Oates Land coast, and an Auster aircraft was lowered

233

In 1956 Dick Thompson, ANARE's supply officer from 1950 to 1960, was directing the unloading of equipment from *Kista Dan* to build an automatic weather station on Lewis Island, a small lump of rock near Adélie Land. Incoming OIC at Mawson, Bill Bewsher, Law and a New Zealand observer, Harry Ayers, decided to practise some climbing on an ice cliff nearby, across a stretch of open water. They were roped together, but only had two ice axes. Law said he would manage without one. The three men were out of sight of the ship as they began to climb. Ayers (an accomplished alpinist) was leading, followed by Law and Bewsher. Law heard Bewsher call out:

Mountaineers are taught that if you fall, you scream immediately to let everyone else know. Luckily Bill called, but I was too busy. I thought, 'God, I haven't got an ice axe to belay myself with. The best I can do is squat down in the step that Harry had dug, get the rope around my shoulder and try and belay him.'

Law was plucked from his position and he and Bewsher fell helplessly down the ice cliff which dropped sheer into the sea.

As he fell he analysed the situation:

'Well, I guess that's finished it. Harry won't know we've gone, and when he comes out also that'll be the three of us. We'll finish in the water, there's no place to scramble out, and no one knows we're here and we've got five or ten minutes and then we're gone.' Bill screamed again [as I fell] and Harry, who was very well used to taking amateurs up Mount Cook, didn't even look to see what was happening, he just banged his ice axe into the side of the cliff, wound the rope around and lay down on it, and he held the two of us. And then he brought us up one at a time.

'Doing a Boys' Own Annual' was Thompson's later comment about this escapade, which might well have ended Law's career then and there and killed his companions. Yet a certain amount of more calculated risk-taking was endemic in Antarctic coastal exploration, which involved taking ships into uncharted waters, landing on areas of exposed rock to fix a position by astronomical determination, and using aircraft to run photographic flights east and west to the limit of the aircraft's range.

over the side to attempt a coastal reconnaissance and photography flight. The Auster was underpowered at the best of times, particularly when operating on floats. On this occasion they were also 150 kilograms overweight, and the aircraft, piloted by Doug Leckie, broke free from the water only metres from brash ice. The plan was to fly in an equilateral triangle, with each leg 100 kilometres. As they had taken off from a large stretch of open water, neither Law nor Leckie took much notice of distinctive icebergs to act as markers for their return. Law:

I remember winding the window down and holding this great clumsy Air Force F24 camera, which is hand-held. You had to crank a handle to turn on each frame.

My hands are freezing off holding this out, but at least I'm getting a continuous run of photos of this sixty miles [100 kilometres] of coast, and then thankfully I can put the window up and thaw out my frozen hands and head back to the ship. But when we get back we start looking for the ship and we can't find it. We've got radio contact with the ship but we haven't got a radio-compass, because this aircraft is too small to fit these refined things into.

Captain H M Pedersen radioed the unwelcome news that the lake of open water they had taken off from was no longer there—the pack ice had moved back in. Law asked them to make smoke, but a diesel engine can produce very little. Leckie reported fuel was running low. They were looking for a small ship among innumerable ice floes. Even if they found it, Law said, there was nowhere to land on floats:

Even if we did survive a crash the ship couldn't possibly find us, they wouldn't know whether to turn the ship to go north, south, east or west and if we couldn't find the ship from the air, how could they find a little plane from the surface? So by this time things are getting desperate; then I had an idea which to this day I think was one of my brighter ideas.

I said, 'Get every pair of binoculars on the ship, issue one to each individual man, send the men up on to the monkey island (which is the flat space of top of the bridge), divide the sky into sectors and give each man a sector to scan with binoculars'. And some bloke scanned his sector of the sky and found us as a little spot and they talked us back to the ship.

Bruce Coombes, an engineer from the Department of Civil Aviation, was the man who spotted them as a speck against an iceberg about 50 kilometres to the east and gave them the correct bearing to return. With no open water available, the only hope of getting down was to have *Magga Dan* steam full speed ahead into the pack, and use the thrashing propeller to push back the ice floes to try to create enough open water for a very hazardous landing. All that could be managed was a pool about 40 metres long:

Luckily in a float plane the drag of the floats acts like very severe braking and you stop very quickly. But it needed a very good pilot with a lot of courage to land in that 40 metres of water, because it really meant you had to aim the plane right up the tail of the ship and put it down exactly on the edge of that ice. We did that and finished with the propeller still rotating just practically touching the stern of the ship.

Law said later he thought that was a good example of modern hazards in a modern era, and 'about as hairy as anything you can get in the old literature'.

Phillip Law regards the 'cracking' of Oates Land—on the eastern extremity of the AAT—as the pinnacle of his summer 'hit and run' exploration programs. His first attempt in 1958 (with *Thala Dan* and Captain K Hindberg) had to be abandoned because of heavy ice conditions.

But in 1959 with Captain H Moller Pedersen in *Magga Dan*, successful photographic flights and a landing were achieved and the Australian flag raised on 21 February 1959 near a mountain which Law named Magga Peak. A return visit and further pioneering exploration in 1960 had to be abandoned because of a shortage of food on board *Thala Dan*—a costly mistake by the ship's steward.[2]

He was back in the summer of 1961 with *Magga Dan* (Captain Vilhelm Pedersen), a Beaver aircraft and two helicopters. Law named one impressive peak Mount Gorton, after Senator John Gorton, then Minister Assisting the Minister for External Affairs on Antarctic matters.

Further work was done in February 1962 with *Thala Dan* (again with the Beaver aircraft and two helicopters), this time voyaging further east into the New Zealand sector of Oates Land, naming features and mapping the coast. (Law raised the New Zealand flag as a courtesy.)

Surveyor Syd Kirkby remembers the 1961 and 1962 voyages to Oates Land as two of the finest and most economical exercises in basic exploration he experienced with ANARE:

> It's always been the source of some satisfaction to me that I have the easternmost Australian astrofix near Cape North in the New Zealand sector, just outside the AAT, and I have the westernmost Australian astrofix

'HIT AND RUN EXPLORATION.' BELL 47-G HELICOPTER AT GREGORY BLUFFS, OATES LAND, 1962. (P LAW)

GRAVITY READINGS BEING TAKEN ON THALA ISLAND, OATES LAND, 1962. (P LAW)

> on the other end, near where the Japanese built Syowa station in later years. Oates Land is marvellous country—the mountains go up out of the sea for ever and ever. . .as far as you can see inland, there are just snowcapped mountains.

There were hazards to the coastal exploration of Antarctica not associated with ice, blizzards or uncharted rocks. On 1 February 1958, *Thala Dan* put in to the Russian station at Mirny which Law had first visited in January 1956, when it was being constructed. The first meeting between the Australians and the Russians, led by Mikhail Somov, was friendly but restrained. Since then it had become apparent that the 'cold war' had no place in Antarctica. Law's second visit was a hilarious and convivial affair that threatened to demolish the Australians because of Russian hospitality:

> The parties were always pretty desperate from a drinking point of view because the Russians drink with a different purpose from ourselves—they literally drink to get drunk. And for us it's a bit of a disgrace to finish up under the table. To the Russian it's an honour to finish up under the table with one of your friends, and of course they drink vodka and we're not used generally to such heavy spirits.

There seemed to be an unending supply of vodka, poured from large white enamel teapots. (Fred Elliott, from the ANARE party, noticed they were replenished from jerrycans—possibly the first Australian realisation that the Russians often boosted their liquor stocks by drinking 'aerovodka'—aviation de-icing fluid, which was close to pure alcohol. The ceremonial toasts were made with conventional vodka.)[3] Law was conscious that he had to combine participation with his responsibilities as leader of the Australian visitors:

> I wasn't exactly emptying my drinks into the aspidistras, but I was sipping them pretty cautiously rather than tossing them off in the Russian style. However, it became pretty heavy going. We had a lot of drinks over lunch, and I played the piano accordion and they sang Russian songs.

The Russian OIC, Dr Tolstikov, led their singing with a magnificent voice. They sounded like the Red Army Choir. The Australians responded with 'Waltzing Matilda', the only song they collectively knew 'other than 'God Save The Queen'—and the 23rd Psalm, as Fred Elliott reflected later:

> We were not in the same vocal league as our hosts, although the story of the proletarian swagman being hounded to death by the capitalist landowner and his police lackeys was a hit.[4]

The ceremonial toasts went on and on—to the Queen of England, the President of the USSR, the Prime Minister of Australia, the Premier of the USSR, the leaders of both Russian and Australian expeditions, the members of the expeditions and so on. One of the Australians—a keen follower of the BBC's radio comedy program 'The Goon Show'—raised his glass in the spirit of all these toasts and said, 'Rhubarb!'. Phil Law:

> The Australians managed to keep a straight face somehow. Another Australian stood up and proposed a toast to 'more rhubarb'. Everyone stood up and toasted 'more rhubarb'. Then a very drunk Australian who was fed up with the whole business stood up and said, 'more piss'.

Law, terribly embarrassed, was aware that matters were getting out of hand:

> I was wondering how to get out of it, when the Russians sprang to their feet and said, 'Da! Da! More peace! Peace and friendship!'

The Australians were keen to see what equipment the Russians had at Mirny and Law scribbled copious notes, having asked his men to do the same. Despite the Antarctic-engendered bonhomie there were national concerns about what the Russians were doing. It was alleged in Federal Parliament that the Russians were building submarine pens at Mirny, from where they could control vital shipping lanes to Australia.[5] While this seemed improbable, Minister for External Affairs Richard Casey had asked Osmar White, an Australian journalist accompanying the 1958 ANARE voyage on *Thala Dan,* to have a good look around while he was there.*

No one was told of White's extra-curricular activity, which was 'top secret', but the Soviet Union's penetration of the Australian intelligence scene must have been impressive despite the breaking off of diplomatic relations after the Petrov spy affair in 1954. While White was photographing a bust of Lenin outside the headquarters hut, retiring Russian OIC Treshnikov came up and patted him sympathetically on the shoulder:

> Flashing his gold fillings, he asked: 'Have you found no guns and submarines? Too bad!'[7]

By late afternoon Law, whose slight build, balding head and goatee beard gave him a startling resemblance to Lenin (noted by his delighted Russian hosts), desperately needed a respite from Mirny hospitality. American observer Gordon Cartwright was sympathetic and lent Law his quarters for a brief nap:

> He took me into his hut and laid me down on his bed and put a bucket beside me in case I was sick and I passed out for a couple of hours. Then

---

* The possibility of the Russians establishing a submarine base on the Antarctic coastline was canvassed in a report to Cabinet by the Joint Intelligence Committee in March 1957.[6]

I awoke and I realised that we'd invited the Russians back to our ship for dinner. So I walked half a mile back across the snow and ice to our ship where it was tethered against the ice edge and went on board and supervised the preparations for the big dinner for the Russians.

Law was not looking forward to dinner at all, but decided to handle the Russians in a different style. He noted that their leaders were late arriving, and conjectured they'd had a brief nap as well.

> But instead of giving them the sort of liquor routine that they were used to—which was the spirits and beer—we turned on the English system. We gave them sherry and then white wine, red wine, and champagne. . .and boy, did we lay them out! So honours were even at the end of the day.

THE RAAF DAKOTA ON
THALA DAN, 1960.
(G BANFIELD)

THE DAKOTA COMES ASHORE
AT MAWSON STATION.
(C ARMSTRONG)

While the annual voyages of the *Dan* ships (*Kista, Magga, Thala* and *Nella*) combined with flights on floats and skis by Auster and Beaver aircraft helped to fill in details of the coastline, aircraft were also used to support scientific parties in the field. Until 1960 they were able to fly between Mawson and Davis Stations, exchanging personnel and on occasions some urgently needed mechanical spare parts. Two Beavers were destroyed on the ground by hurricane force winds in December 1959, despite heroic efforts to try and save them. But the RAAF persevered with its Antarctic flying program and shipped another Beaver and a Dakota DC3 to Mawson for the 1960 season.

Due to mechanical problems and several on-ground mishaps the Dakota did not fly until 2 July but when it did, its undercarriage would not retract. On 9 July pilot Graham Dyke flew the Dakota, named 'Ann Cherie', successfully. Despite being plagued by a succession of mechanical problems, Ann Cherie played a useful part in air operations. On 16 July, in midwinter gloom, the Dakota was flown on a south-west reconnaissance mission 700 kilometres inland over the plateau. At that point the ice cap was 2900 metres above sea level. No rocky features were sighted in seven hours' flying.[8]

Other successful flights were made to Beaver Lake and Mt Meredith in the Prince Charles Mountains, Davis Station, and Amundsen Bay in Enderby Land. By early December the sea ice at Mawson was too thin to support flying operations and the Dakota was landed at the ice airfield named Rumdoodle on the plateau 24 kilometres south from Mawson.*

The smaller Beaver and the Dakota were tethered behind a wind fence, near a fuel dump and several caravans used as an engineering workshop and living quarters for the RAAF crew. On 8 December with a blizzard forecast, the stage was set for a rerun of the 1959 disaster. When Jim Kichenside, Graham Dyke, Kevin Felton and Mick Murphy fought their way to the aircraft the next morning, they found the fuselage of the Beaver—without its wings—a tangle of wreckage against the wind fence. There was no sign of the Dakota at all. It's two tie-down cables with a 15-tonne breaking strain had been snapped like cotton. Radio communication with Mawson Station was lost, and the RAAF crew retreated into their buffeted caravan. Sergeant Kevin Felton wrote in his diary:

> The rocks on which we are camped are littered with packing cases smashed to pieces and 44-gallon [200 litres] drums, some empty, some full. At about 4 pm 'Baz' Rutter looked out the window of our van and called our notice to the extent of the wind. Drums of diesel fuel and petrol weighing 350 pounds [157.5 kilos] were moving at a fast walking pace along the ice standing on their ends. The caravan nearest us shifted four feet [1.21 metres] sideways in one gust, stretching steel guy wires like rope.[9]

The blizzard blew for 42 hours and it was not possible to return to Mawson Station until Sunday 11 December. The mystery of the missing Dakota was solved that day when radio operator Graeme Currie rode his motor cycle sixteen kilometres along the sea ice down the coast from Mawson:

---

* The airfield was named after a prominent peak in the north-western part of the North Masson Range, which overlooks the airstrip. Rumdoodle was the name of a fictional mountain in the novel *The Ascent of Rumdoodle* by W E Bowman and since 1960 the name has been used locally by Mawson personnel to refer to the airstrip. There is now a recreation hut nearby also named Rumdoodle.

There was the whole aircraft sitting on the side of the hill. . .it was sitting with the nose up the slope, on its belly, as though it was just ready to take off. So I parked the bike and crawled up this ice slope, and it looked fairly stable so I crawled in. Everything inside was just as nice as it was the day it was parked. . .[10]

Ann Cherie had been whisked away by the wind down the ice sheet to the coast twenty kilometres from Rumdoodle. Currie might have thought it looked nice inside but structurally it was a write-off. What could be salvaged was returned to Mawson, but RAAF all-year-round operations in Antarctica were over. The members of the 1961 Flight were officially disbanded on 20 December 1960. In April 1961 concerns were raised in the Australian press that the safety and viability of ANARE operations would be compromised by not having air support in Antarctica.[11]

The Air Board was concerned about the RAAF's Antarctic activities, weighing the public relations gains against operational hazards, but public relations lost out.[12] In July 1961 the Board did give permission for a RAAF team to go south for the annual relief expedition and *Thala Dan* carried a single Beaver aircraft. A growing RAAF commitment to the Australian presence in Malaysia and Vietnam was a contributing factor to pulling back from Antarctic operations and the RAAF support to summer ANARE Antarctic programs ended in March 1963.[13] It is worth noting that despite the destruction of an Auster, three Beavers and a Dakota in Antarctica, not a single life was lost in the nine years of RAAF association with ANARE. All the wrecked aircraft were destroyed by storms, either on the ground or on ships.

THE RAAF DC3 ON THE SLOPE OF A COASTAL ICE CLIFF AFTER IT HAD BEEN BLOWN AWAY FROM ITS TETHERS ON THE ICE PLATEAU BEHIND MAWSON STATION, DECEMBER 1960. (P LAW)

THE WRECKED DAKOTA AIRCRAFT. (P LAW)

Significantly, helicopters were carried on ANARE resupply voyages in 1960 and 1961 to supplement the solitary Beaver. They were chartered by ANARE and flown by civilian pilots—a pointer to the future of air operations in the AAT. The machines used were Hiller 12C models, leased from Trans-Australia Airlines.[14] Compared with modern machines they were toys—but useful nevertheless. A single piston engine mounted behind the bubble cabin gave the Hillers a cruise speed of 55 knots, and they could lift 159 kilograms (including survival equipment).

The advantages of helicopters were clear. Most Antarctic field work takes place near rocky features around which the moving ice sheet fractures into crevasses. Landing fields for conventional aircraft have to be located well away from this type of terrain—if they can be found at all. A helicopter, on the other hand, can land a geologist or surveyor on a mountain peak, or within a badly crevassed area if that is necessary. With their rotors removed, they can be streamlined and tethered to withstand high winds and can land relatively easily on ships and ANARE stations.

The helicopter was developed in the closing years of World War II and used more extensively during the Korean War from 1950–1954. It was still new technology in the late 1950s and few helicopters were available in Australia. The Antarctic Division was cautious in the use of helicopters and experimented with a Hiller 12C from a small helideck on *Thala Dan* at Macquarie Island on 1 December 1958. Piloted by Keith Cotter (who had flown helicopters in the RAAF) it did not have floats, so there must have been some anxious moments during over-water flights.[15]

Two Hillers were loaded on to *Magga Dan* in 1960 for the voyage to resupply Wilkes and Davis Stations, visit Mawson and Macquarie Island Stations and carry out coastal exploration of the AAT. The pilots, both from TAA, were Ray Hudson (who had an RAAF background) and Peter Ivanoff. The two machines were successfully test flown on 15 January near the French station Dumont d'Urville and, as the voyage progressed, did useful work in concert with the Beaver flown by Wing Commander Cresswell.

The vulnerability of the under-powered Hillers was demonstrated dramatically on Sunday 13 February when both machines were on their way to get astrofixes from a group of small rocky islands 100 kilometres west of Wilkes Station, near the Vanderford Glacier. A violent downdraft, so severe Ray Hudson thought it would tear the rotors right off his machine, gripped both aircraft. Hudson made a spur of the moment decision to turn away from the coast for the sea, much as he disliked the idea, and shot away from under Ivanoff's machine 'like a rocket':

As soon as we were under control again I had a quick look around for Peter and was horrified to see his helicopter slam into the ice about 50 yards [45.7 metres] up-slope from the ice cliff. Pieces flew out in all directions, only to slide away down the slope and over the cliff into the sea. I looked away, sick at heart, fearing that the whole machine. . .would follow.[16]

ANARE's MOST SERIOUS HELICOPTER CRASH. SALVAGING EQUIPMENT FROM THE HILLER 12C THAT WAS FORCED DOWN ON THE EDGE OF A COASTAL ICE CLIFF BY A DOWNDRAFT NEAR THE VANDERFORD GLACIER IN FEBRUARY 1960.

(P LAW)

Despite climbing on full power, Ivanoff had found himself descending at a relentless twenty knots and attempted a forced landing on the ice. At the last moment he threw the Hiller on its side, hoping that the crosstubes of the landing gear and the remains of the rotor would grip the ice and stop the aircraft sliding over the cliff into the sea.[17]

Hudson 'almost cried out with relief' when he saw that the helicopter had not slipped over the cliff. His passenger was Ian McLeod, an ANARE geologist. The two men were even more relieved to see Peter Ivanoff's passenger, sur-veyor David Cook, appear and Ivanoff also crawl out of the smashed cabin.

Still fighting a 50-knot wind, Hudson managed to put down on an Adélie penguin rookery on a spur of land within sight of the crashed helicopter. He radioed *Magga Dan*, which set sail immediately from Wilkes. While McLeod set off with an ice-axe to climb up the ice cliff towards the crash site, Hudson set up the survival tent carried in the Hiller.[18]

When *Magga Dan* arrived Law took a rescue party in the motor boat, against a 50-knot katabatic wind, to land near Hudson. Law and two other men fitted crampons and climbed the ice slope to reach the helicopter. It was three hours before they and McLeod returned with the injured men. Both Ivanoff and Cook had head cuts and were spattered with blood. In fact, blood from Ivanoff's head wound had temporarily blinded him and made his traverse across the ice even more difficult. It had been

243

The first ANARE automatic weather station was built on Lewis Island, a small rocky islet off the eastern coast of Wilkes Land (near Adélie Land) in January 1958. The Department of External Affairs, through its representative on the Executive Planning Committee, Keith Waller, had been urging Law repeatedly to occupy more sites in the Australian Antarctic Territory. Law:

> I don't know whether it was this that influenced [Richard] Casey, but he eventually proposed that the Weather Bureau should examine the possibility of establishing small automatic weather stations at isolated spots along the coast of the AAT.

Law had led the first party ever to visit Lewis Island in 1956 and he returned in 1958 with electronic equipment manufactured by a French company to build the automatic station on the highest point on Lewis Island, 60 metres above sea level. He left three men behind to assemble the station and test it, and sailed east exploring the coast towards Oates Land—returning on 23 January to pick them up. By then the first automatic weather station ever set up in Antarctica was transmitting data to Wilkes and on to Australia.

In February 1961 Law led an expedition to another remote speck of rock, off the coast

MAC. ROBERTSON LAUNCH AT THE DIBBLE ICEBERG TONGUE, NEAR LEWIS ISLAND, 1958. (P LAW)

of Wilkes Land, to set up a second automatic weather station on Chick Island—some 1000 kilometres to the west of Lewis Island. Due to heavy ice conditions, *Magga Dan* could only approach to within ten kilometres of the island and helicopters played a vital role in transporting the equipment, flying 224 sorties in four days. This station transmitted weather data continually to Wilkes for seven months in 1961—a remarkable technical achievement for that time.

a near thing, and the worst operational crash in ANARE's history. As *Magga Dan* came closer, Dick Thompson, elated with the news that both men had survived the crash, radioed to Ivanoff that they proposed to name the 'island' after him.[19] As it happened, the rookery was on a promontory. Ivanoff Head was later ratified by the Antarctic Names Committee of Australia.

In spite of this accident, the helicopters had proved their worth and the surviving machine was used to ferry men and spare parts to Lewis

Island, off the eastern edge of Wilkes Land, to repair the automatic weather station there.[20]

Law had hoped to continue on to explore the coast of Oates Land but he found himself frustrated not by weather, lack of aircraft, or even time—but by lack of food. To his intense annoyance he found the chief steward had miscalculated and they had barely enough provisions to get back to Melbourne via Macquarie Island:

> Here we were, just at the right time of the season, with ice and weather favourable and with the best opportunity which I had probably ever had to proceed past Cape Freshfield and into the Oates Land area, and now carelessness and negligence on the part of the chief steward were to prevent me from taking advantage of our situation.

It was always difficult to forecast the hazards waiting for those attempting to explore Antarctica.

The use of helicopters became an established tool of ANARE operations from 1960. In 1961 a contract was signed with Helicopter Utilities Pty Ltd, Sydney, and their work continued for the next eight years. The company's initials led to their nickname 'Hupple'. Hupple flew Bell 47 piston-engined helicopters similar to those which had seen service in the Korean War and later in Vietnam. They were slightly larger than the Hillers and could lift a payload of around 200 kilograms, including survival equipment.

Russian interest in exploring remote areas of the AAT using helicopters was used by Law as an argument to support the expanded use of helicopters by ANARE. The Russians were active in the summer of 1962–63 in Enderby Land, carrying their scientists into the field with STOL (Short Take Off and Landing) aircraft and helicopters. In a letter to Ralph Harry of the Department of External Affairs in March 1963, Law emphasised that ANARE could not match the Russians in Enderby Land field work and said:

> It needs little imagination to realise the repercussions in Australia if Russian geologists found important mineral deposits in the Prince Charles Mountains, which Australians discovered in 1955 and started to examine but stopped because of lack of suitable aircraft.[21]

In the course of his 1959–60 *Magga Dan* voyage, Law and his ANARE surveyors, pilots, and scientists had ranged along almost the entire coastline of the AAT. Their exploration ventures from the *Dan* ships were complemented by land-based expeditions as the main features of the AAT were slowly inked in on the map.

In 1964–65 a Beaver aircraft returned to Antarctica on *Nella Dan*, not with the RAAF, but a private charter. Its pilot, John Whiting, flew a useful 66 hours during the season, but on 7 February 1965 there was an unfortunate accident. Whiting was flying the Beaver from sea ice near *Nella Dan*, north-east of Cape Boothby, about 150 nautical miles west from Mawson Station. As he began to taxi to the beginning of his selected runway, the aircraft's skis broke through a weak part of the floe. Law:

The three men inside scrambled out and had only just emerged when the weight of the fore part of the aircraft broke the ice still further and the nose plunged down until the whole engine and most of the cabin of the aircraft were submerged beneath the sea. The only thing that prevented the aeroplane from plunging to the bottom of the sea was the fact that it rested with its wings flush on the surface of the surrounding ice.[22]

It was a narrow escape—and a savage blow to the flying program. The Beaver was salvaged and sent down the following year, but its fuselage was damaged on the way down and it never flew in Antarctica again. There were no more fixed-wing flights during Phil Law's time as director of ANARE, to 1966.

On 1 February 1960 Law flew from Davis Station to Mawson in a Beaver piloted by Wing Commander Cresswell. The second resupply ship *Thala Dan* was already there for the annual changeover, with Law's deputy director Don Styles as voyage leader. On 3 February there was a vigorous discussion about a proposal put by Syd Kirkby for a late summer dog sledge journey from Enderby Land back to Mawson. Kirkby's plan involved being dropped off near the Napier Mountains in Enderby Land by *Thala Dan* on her way back to Australia. He and two companions with two dog teams planned to sledge 560 kilometres east to Edward VIII Gulf, mapping and taking geological samples in this unexplored region on the way. They would then be picked up by Beaver aircraft and returned to Mawson.

The outgoing Mawson OIC John Béchervaise and surveyor Chris Armstrong opposed the expedition, but Law approved Kirkby's plan—providing food dumps could be landed at Edward VIII Gulf.[23] There was concern about whether a search and rescue could be mounted if needed, and before leaving Melbourne Law himself had given the scheme the thumbs down. Kirkby believed what happened then was typical of the way Law worked:

There was always a sort of veiled antagonism between many expeditioners who'd wintered and Phil, who hadn't. I suppose I was a bit young and feisty, so I thumped the table and said: 'Well bloody well listen and then you might know!' Anyway he said, 'Well, go on'. I went right through what I was proposing to do, where we'd go, and all our fallbacks. He suddenly stopped me in mid sentence and said, 'Good, do it'. It wasn't until some time later that I realised that Phil's style was to force other people to push their views. . .to be sure he wasn't going to go along with any half-baked scheme that the proponent hadn't thought through.

Thala Dan was skippered by Captain Hans Christian Petersen, whose temper was not improved by nearly running his ship up on an uncharted pinnacle of rock while laying the emergency depot at Edward VIII Gulf. Finding a landing place with access to the plateau was difficult, and late in the afternoon of 22 February, near Cape Batterbee, a low rocky platform was sighted, although it was not clear how easy it would be to move inland from it. Petersen was champing at the bit to be heading home as it was late in the season. He told Kirkby: 'This is it. I've just got to get out. You either go ashore here or you go ashore nowhere.'

Kirkby had sixteen dogs, two sledges and some two and a half tonnes of supplies to land in the ship's boat *Dingo Dan*. It was nearly dark when the last load went in. Petersen was so anxious to leave that he headed the ship away from the coast before the ship's boat had returned. Kirkby's last sight of them was *Thala Dan*, hull down on the horizon with the *Dingo Dan* chasing it frantically into the gathering gloom.[24]

It was too steep to drive the dogs up on the plateau from the coast, so Kirkby and his companions Rick Ruker (geologist) and Ken Bennett (radio officer) had to lump all the supplies on their backs to establish a depot three kilometres from the shore. This took two weeks, in some of the most miserable circumstances Kirkby ever experienced in Antarctica. Freakish warm weather by polar standards kept the temperatures hovering just above and below freezing. It snowed continuously for a fortnight:

> Snow fell on the tent and melted, and it fell on our clothing and melted. We'd wake up in the morning literally in a bath of water, because our own body heat in the tent would melt a puddle. The dogs were not enjoying these conditions, they were getting knocked about by being wet. So we were getting up every hour or two during the night to move the dogs to keep them dry.

When they climbed to 1500 metres the temperature dropped to −20°C and they could dry their sopping gear. The unusually heavy powder snow was so deep that the loads on the sledges could hardly be seen above the surface. Kirkby recalled that the dogs had to push through blind, with the lead dogs having to jump up to see ahead. Sledging conditions gradually improved as they moved east around the Napier Mountains and headed towards the coast.

There were unexpected hazards. Travelling one day in a near white-out, Kirkby heard the wooden sledge runners clattering on blue ice, and realised that his team had run on to the down slope of an ice dome, possibly leading to crevasses or even ice cliffs. He yelled at the dogs to stop. They could hear the sledge roaring and threatening to overrun them, so they ran faster and faster. Kirkby wanted to get to the front of the sledge to throw over the rope friction brake, but as he leant down to kick off his skis, the sledge bucked and gave him 'an almighty thump in the head':

> I reckon about that stage—like the Hoffnung insurance claim man and the bucket of bricks—I must have lost my presence of mind, because I let go of the handlebars of the sledge and the dogs were gone.
>
> In the team, running towards the rear, was a dog called Snipe. He was a snapping, snarling, horrible creature—he hated everyone and he bit everyone—just a nasty personality. Anyway poor old Snipe, thank God, fell and went under the runners of the sledge. Because he was in harness he couldn't be spat out the back, and he actually acted as the friction brake.

Snipe was killed instantly, but his accident saved the day. The sledge was stopped, and Kirkby was able to warn the other team travelling a kilometre behind. They ran safely down to the coast towards Edward VIII Gulf and their rendezvous with the Beaver aircraft from Mawson.

On the coast the dogs surprised a Weddell seal near its blowhole in the ice and attacked it. Kirkby and his companions beat them off and killed the seal—a welcome and necessary addition to their supplies. The dogs had been fed pemmican blocks during their overland run, but not the black Norwegian product usually supplied.

> The new Australian stuff was mainly cereal, not the sort of stuff dogs can work on, and they were hungry, tired and in bad shape. Of course we couldn't let the dogs eat the seal meat because it was fairly early in the day and we'd have got no more work out of them.

They staked out the dogs well away from the seal and butchered it, then loaded the meat on to a sledge. The huskies were frantic, with the smell of warm meat and blood in their nostrils. Kirkby turned to speak to his companions Rick Ruker and Ken Bennett, but tripped and fell. As he hit the ice, the second team fell on him:

> They were going to eat me! I had blood on my clothes and I smelt warm. Fortunately I fell face down and I had my hood on, but they hit me hard

and started biting around my neck. I was yelling at them and I was sure that when the dogs knew it was me they would stop. But then the others kept going.

Ruker and Bennett pulled the dogs away. It was the only time Kirkby ever felt he was in danger from huskies, who were ferocious with each other but famously friendly to humans.

From time to time there is debate about how useful the huskies were in exploration and field work in the early years of ANARE, particularly after the techniques of using D4 Caterpillar tractors to pull heavy caravans and sledges long distances over the polar ice cap were introduced. The evidence is that they remained very useful indeed. Dogs remained the safest way to travel over sea ice and crevassed territory and, as veteran dog handler Nils Lied once pointed out, you cannot eat a tractor when it runs out of fuel, and dogs are much easier to start in the morning. When all-year flying operations ceased out of Mawson in 1960, following the destruction of the Dakota and Beaver aircraft on the ground, the dogs re-established themselves as a useful back-up for field parties plagued by over-snow vehicles with mechanical problems. In the Amery Ice Shelf glaciological investigation in the summer of 1963–64, the tractors travelled 1450 kilometres and the dog sledges 1700.[25]

In 1961 Dave Trail, Dave Keyser and Jim Seavers drove a dog team to the Prince Charles Mountains and climbed Mt Menzies, a 3313 metre peak then thought to be the highest mountain in the AAT—a round trip of some 1000 kilometres.*

The first two D4 tractors went to Mawson Station in 1957 for the International Geophysical Year. They towed caravans and sledges south to measure the ice thickness with equipment supplied by the Bureau of Mineral Resources, using explosives and an echo-sounder. Neville 'Gringo' Collins was the diesel engineer at Mawson:

> We discovered that the tracks had to have 'ice-grousers' fitted. We'd never seen them. It was an American term, and no one was keen to put them on. So I decided to go up on to the ice with one of the tractors, and it acted like it was on so many pairs of ice skates. The first slope it came to, it went whizzing down sideways and broke through the melt-water lake in West Arm and lay over on its side.

---

* Recent research has established that the highest point of the AAT is not a mountain at all but a high point on the ice cap on the eastern Antarctic plateau now known as Argus Dome, at 4270 metres. The highest mountain in the AAT is Mt McClintock (3492 metres) in the eastern sector. The highest point on the Antarctic continent is the Vinson Massif (4897 metres) in the Ellsworth Mountains.

The grousers were bits of metal at right angles to the tracks designed to stop sideways movement. When fitted, the D4s were ready for ice work. On the first traverse a Weasel went ahead to pick a path, but was light enough to bridge crevasses into which the D4s fell. No successful crevasse detector has yet been devised. Collins:

I suppose the D4 would be about the best crevasse detector there is. The first fairly big one we struck, the tractor almost got across, and the back fell in with a big 'whoomph', but it had enough momentum to grip the other side and got out again and went on. Then the following sledges fell in, and it was enough to say, 'Well, this is going to be a bit of a hazard'.

The practice evolved of marking known, safe routes with canes flying a small black flag. The wind soon whipped these to bits, so pieces of tin were substituted and in later years they could be picked up by radar. Every time a tractor train moved into new, unknown territory, crevasses ('slots' in ANARE parlance) were an ever present danger.

After nearly losing the Weasel in a bad crevasse, Collins came up with what he thought was a good idea. A heavy snowfall had made crevassing even more difficult to detect, and he rigged up an ingenious system of ropes tied to the Weasel's steering levers, so that he could sit on the sledge being towed, ready to jump off in case of another serious slotting:

If I wanted to go right I'd pull on the right rope. The dogs are following behind me. Suddenly the back of the Weasel falls in with a big 'whoomph', and the sledge dives down to follow it. So at this stage I bail off the back. But for some reason the Weasel got a grip on the far side of the crevasse and got out!

One of the most spectacular 'slottings' in ANARE history took place during an exploratory expedition to the southern Prince Charles Mountains in late September 1960 near Mt Cresswell, about 600 kilometres from Mawson. Diesel engineer Neville 'Gringo' Collins knew he was in doubtful territory and was not really surprised when his D4 lurched and fell over to one side with one track down a small crevasse. Established procedure was to probe around with crowbars to find out which way the crevasses were running. Henrick 'Hank' Geysen, OIC at Mawson, who was in the second D4, decided to 'whiz round the back and hook on to my last sledge and pull us all out backwards'. Collins:

Now this didn't seem to be a real good idea at the time, but he was manoeuvring to get hooked on to the back of my sledge, and he suddenly disappeared—and I mean disappeared. Just a cloud of snow flurries coming up and dead silence.

The second D4 had broken through and smashed right down a 'slot' with only the top of the cabin pressed against a lip of ice, stopping it from dropping out of sight into the blackness of unknown depths below. Syd Kirkby, who was riding on a sledge behind an accompanying Weasel, had climbing ropes and an ice axe. He smashed the back window out of the D4 and hauled a dazed but not seriously hurt Geysen five metres to the surface.

There seemed little prospect of salvage, but they all climbed into the living caravan, had a meal and considered their options. ANARE

A D4 TRACTOR WELL AND TRULY 'SLOTTED' IN THE PRINCE CHARLES MOUNTAINS, SEPTEMBER 1960. THE DRIVER, 'HANK' GEYSEN, ESCAPED WITH A BUMPED HEAD. (COURTESY N COLLINS)

USING THE SECOND D4 AND CHAIN BLOCK WINCHES, THE DEEPLY 'SLOTTED' TRACTOR IS PULLED OUT OF THE CREVASSE. DIESEL ENGINEER NEVILLE COLLINS SAID LATER THAT THE THOUGHT OF WHAT PHIL LAW WOULD SAY IF THEY LOST SUCH A VALUABLE PIECE OF EQUIPMENT ENABLED THEM TO ACHIEVE THE IMPOSSIBLE. (R RUKER)

was run on such a tight budget that Phil Law believed Australians rescued vehicles from situations that any other nation working in Antarctica would have written off. They could not get through to Mawson by radio to request that some lifting gear be flown in. Collins decided to try to recover the D4 with what they had. First he dug some hydrogen gas cylinders into the ice as 'dead-men' so that neither D4 could slip down any further. Then they set about cutting a ramp in the side of the crevasse, hoping to pull the stranded D4 out with a chain block winch. The only tools available were one shovel and Syd Kirkby's ice axe. There was no trouble getting rid of the spoil, they just let it tumble down the crevasse. Collins:

We were doing fine until the shovel disappeared out of somebody's gloved hand and went down the crevasse. By this time we'd cleared a fair bit, so we got into it with bare hands and so on, cutting into the ice.

Four days later they slowly winched the battered, draughty but still operational D4 to the surface and resumed their journey to set up a base camp in the southern Prince Charles Mountains. The Dakota flew in from Mawson with a dog team, and Kirkby flew out to work in another area. Collins and geologist Rick Ruker set off with a dog team and a Weasel to further survey the region.

Collins found himself on the wrong side of a crevasse with his Weasel and sledge disappearing into the dim distance at a steady four knots. He ran desperately along the lip of the crevasse hoping it would narrow enough for him to jump over. The snow bridge crumbled under him as he jumped, but he threw himself on his stomach and tobogganed forward like a penguin:

> I took off after the sledge and managed to jump on to it. When I got my breath back I ran around to the front and switched off the engine. That was a good try, but I knew I'd have to think of something better after that.

Improvisation was an important element of ANARE's low budget existence. There had been almost no exploration inland from Wilkes Station in the first year. The 1960 OIC, Harry Black, convinced Phil Law that he should explore and mark a safe route up on to the plateau, using Weasels, in preparation for a major traverse planned for 1962 when D4 tractors would be available. Black was concerned about navigation, as the two sextants at the station were not only marine instruments (which needed a watery horizon conspicuously lacking on the Antarctic ice cap) but were also faulty:

> So what to do? I'd read in the literature that people had made a dish of strong coffee and put it down and retreated backwards till the image of

the sun was sighted in [it], and you shoot them both and halve the angle and away you go. I tried that, but of course the coffee froze in a few seconds, so [it] was useless. Then I tried dieseline, but it didn't work.

Although Black could find out where he was on the ice cap with a sextant, the problem of steering a straight course over the ice cap remained. He devised a system of mirrors mounted on the Weasel so that the driver could view the tracks left in the rear and line them up with the intended route ahead to keep a straight line. It worked so well that Robert Thomson, leader of the Vostok Traverse in 1962, used it with great success.

Neville Collins returned to Wilkes in 1962 as senior diesel mechanic. He took part in the Vostok Traverse—the most ambitious over-ice journey then attempted by ANARE. He and fellow 'dieso' Desmond 'Pancho' Evans were responsible for keeping two D4 Caterpillar tractors (towing a train of sledges and caravans) and two vintage 1944 Weasel over-snow vehicles operational in temperatures that at one point fell to –63°C. Led by Thomson, a New Zealander and OIC of Wilkes Station, the party also included Don Walker (geophysicist), Alastair Battye (glaciologist), and American Danny Foster (weather observer). They left Wilkes on 17 September 1962 and returned on 14

NEVILLE COLLINS TESTS HIS INGENIOUS BUT HAZARDOUS REMOTE-CONTROL STEERING, BEHIND HIS ADVANCING WEASEL AND SLEDGE IN THE PRINCE CHARLES MOUNTAINS, 1960. (R RUKER)

AN INGENIOUS SYSTEM OF MIRRORS ENABLED THE DRIVER OF THIS WEASEL TO HEAD INLAND OVER THE FEATURELESS ICE CAP IN A STRAIGHT LINE DURING THE VOSTOK TRAVERSE OF 1962. (A BATTYE)

January 1963. The main purpose of the traverse was to take ice core samples and to fire seismic charges to plot the thickness of the ice sheet, travelling as far into the interior of Antarctica as fuel stocks would allow.

That would limit their farthest south at around 800 kilometres from the coast. In 1961, Wilkes OIC Neville Smethurst had pushed out some 400 kilometres and laid two fuel dumps. On 18 May 1962 Thomson received a cable from Law advising him that the Americans at McMurdo had agreed to air drop fuel to the Australians which would enable them to push on to Vostok, the Russian station at the South Geomagnetic Pole, known as the coldest place on earth. (On 21 July 1983 the lowest temperature ever recorded in the world was noted −89.6°C.)

To get to Vostok, the Australians would have to climb up the polar ice cap to 3488 metres, adding oxygen deprivation (for man and machine) to the challenges of isolation and paralysing cold. The Weasels ran on petrol and the D4 Caterpillar tractors used diesel. One ingenious method of carrying fuel was to fill up the hollow sledge runners on the main living caravan with 1000 litres. It took from three to four hours each morning to heat up the engines of the vehicles so they could be started—seven hours on some extremely cold days. The cooling systems of D4s and Weasels were filled with ATK (aviation turbine kerosene) instead of water because of its low heat transfer and anti-freeze qualities.

Gringo Collins and Pancho Evans worked miracles to keep machinery going in temperatures which made metal as brittle as glass. The most serious breakdown was a broken oil pump on one of the D4s just as the traverse neared the 800 kilometre mark, short of where they were scheduled to get their air drop of fuel from the Americans. The temperature had not risen above −45°C all day and sank to −58°C at night. Collins and Evans dug a pit under the D4 and went to work for as long as they could before returning to the caravan to warm frozen fingers. (Another diesel mechanic, Snow Williams, who was working on the Amery Ice Shelf that same year, claimed that a little frostbite under those circumstances could be an advantage, and that one of the joys of Antarctic 'mechanicing' was to have dead skin on your fingertips to lessen the pain![26]) Evans and Collins pulled the oil pump out, and diagnosed a sheared steel pin. No spare existed. Thomson:

> I drew out my best screwdriver from my pocket. Its shaft proved to be the exact size required, so a few hacksaw strokes later I was less one screwdriver—but we had one good pin for the oil pump.[27]

The 'diesos' performed miracles of improvisation welding broken tracks and snapped couplings, but sometimes even they were defeated by the conditions. The lowest temperature recorded on the Vostok traverse was –63°C on Saturday 27 October. It was not possible to travel. Collins:

> Our old tractor just couldn't run at that temperature, it lost so much power. On the Weasel, the little bogie-wheels would not go round—they were just skidding along on the tracks. So we camped until some warmer air came along.

AN AIRDROP OF FUEL AND SUPPLIES FROM A US GLOBEMASTER, 900 KILOMETRES INLAND, ENABLED THE ANARE TRAVERSE TO REACH VOSTOK AND RETURN TO WILKES IN 1962. (R THOMSON)

Odd things happened in those conditions. One evening Thomson was standing near one of the Weasels when he heard loud, crackling explosions:

> It took me some moments to identify the cause, a really uncanny occurrence; the thick paint on the shaded rear of the vehicle was rapidly forming large blisters which exploded, depositing hard skin many feet away. In the extreme cold the [paint] must have been contracting at a substantially different rate to the body metal underneath, which was receiving some warmth from the interior of the vehicle. After about a minute the explosions ceased, though by this time the Weasel showed a clean, clear unpainted rear.[28]

A successful air drop from an American Globemaster aircraft gave the party fuel reserves to press on with the final 500 kilometres to Vostok. The station was unoccupied, but the Russians had given the Australians permission to use it. The Russians were also pleased to have access to the scientific data recorded on the traverse, to link up with their own—particularly the gravity and magnetic readings.

When the Australians reached Vostok on 18 November they found the buildings snowed in, but managed to climb in through a roof hatch to the living quarters. Pushing aside polar bear skins hung in the doorway, they found the main living quarters. When they managed to start generators

255

for power and heat, they discovered the last Russians there had left in a hurry. Collins:

> On the stove there was a big pan of steak and onions, and on the table places laid out for three people. They'd made a pot of tea in a beautiful china teapot, but the tea had frozen and busted the pot. Some of the plates had steak and onions on them.

The Australians switched on the stove, finished cooking the snap frozen steaks, and warmed up water for their first bath since leaving Wilkes.

The outside temperature—even in full sun—never rose above –45°C during the six days spent at Vostok, called by the Russians the 'Pole of Cold'.

The return to Wilkes was not without its difficulties but, in contrast to the journey out, was downhill all the way. Glaciology investigations (drilling and seismic explosions) were made at regular intervals by Alastair Battye to calculate the thickness of the ice sheet above the bedrock and sample the annual rates of accumulation. Don Walker was able to take gravity readings at those same sites.[29]

This remarkable journey confirmed the feasibility of ANARE tractor train travel on the Antarctic ice sheet over long distances and provided the practical experience that led to the traverse establishing itself as the preferred method of transporting heavy cargo and equipment to support field work in areas like the Prince Charles Mountains and Law Dome. The pioneering work led to the great Lambert Glacier–Amery Ice Shelf glaciological traverses of 1994 and 1995, covering 2250 kilometres from Mawson Station to the Larsemann Hills near Davis Station and back.

By 1965 the principal features of the AAT had been named and identified following exploratory journeys by land, sea and air. The first comprehensive attempt to rationalise the names of new and formerly named features was made in the Gazetteer of the Australian Antarctic Territory, compiled by Graeme McKinnon for the Antarctic Names Committee of Australia (ANCA), and published by ANARE in 1965.

ANCA was established in 1952, on Phil Law's suggestion, to advise the Minister for External Affairs on names in the AAT. Before that there was no formal procedure for approving Antarctic names. In his day, Douglas Mawson had simply decided what names to put on the map and when the map was published these names automatically became official.[30] The original ANCA committee comprised Sir Douglas Mawson, B P Lambert (Director of National Mapping), Captain G D Tancred (Hydrographer, Royal Australian Navy), A A Wilcock (Senior Lecturer in Geography, University of Melbourne), and chairman Phil Law (Director of the Antarctic Division). Later Graeme McKinnon, the Geographical

Officer of the Antarctic Division, became secretary. Apart from one eighteen-month break, Phil Law chaired ANCA until 1981.

Historically it was accepted that the explorer who discovered a feature had the right to name it. But it was not always clear which explorer had seen it first. Australian, Norwegian, American, British and French explorers had been active on and around the AAT. Which nation's names should be accepted? ANCA became involved in a great deal of historical research.

Was it fair, for instance, for a nation conducting the first aerial survey of a significant area of coastline to 'saturate' that area with instant names from the photographs? Phil Law believed that some sense of proportion had to be maintained in applying personal names:

> Major features should be named after major personalities in Antarctic work, or those who have made major contributions in finance or administration or politics to the success of an expedition. Names should not be applied purely because of relationship or friendship with the explorers, nor should names of commercial enterprises designed to gain publicity or commercial gain be suggested.[31]

Mac. Robertson Land, named by Sir Douglas Mawson in recognition of one of his major sponsors (and supplier of chocolate and confectionery) Sir MacPherson Robertson, was so called before ANCA was set up. The first diesel mechanic on Heard Island in 1948, John Abbottsmith, has Abbottsmith Glacier named after him. Geologist Bruce Stinear has four features to his credit—Stinear Island near Mawson, Stinear Lake at Davis, Stinear Mount near the Lambert Glacier, and Stinear Nunataks south-east of Mawson. Auster Rookery near Mawson and Beaver Lake in the Prince Charles Mountains are named after aircraft, Foggydog Glacier because it looks like a dog's head, and Numbat Island, near Enderby Land, named after the Australian marsupial.

Despite Law's hope that friends and relatives of explorers would not be immortalised in Antarctica, there are plenty of examples. John Béchervaise has his own Mount Béchervaise and Béchervaise Island at Mawson. His wife, Lorna Fearn Béchervaise scored a double behind Mawson—Fearn Hill in the North Masson Range near a glacial lake, Lake Lorna. Pilot Peter Clemence's daughter (born while he was in Antarctica in 1957) has Amanda Bay near Prydz Bay, and Amanda Rookery on the western side of Amanda Bay.

Sometimes the origin of a name remains the subject of debate. Platcha, originally a remote weather station in the Vestfold Hills is officially linked to an abbreviation of 'Plateau Chateau'.[32] But according to former radio operator Patrick Moonie, 'Platcha' was the nickname of Harry Redfearn, the 1961 diesel mechanic at Davis who was primarily responsible for hauling materials to this site 31 kilometres east of Davis, and building the hut:

> The dieso was a man of immense energy, enthusiasm, flamboyance and direct language. His standard salutation to his fellows, for whatever cause, was 'go plait your shit'—abbreviated to 'go platcha'. . .[33]

This is not quite as elegant as 'Plateau Chateau', but an interesting example of usage triumphing over decorum.

Although Phil Law voyaged to Antarctica 28 times and led ANARE for seventeen years, he had comparatively few features named after him in Antarctica. Since he chaired ANCA it was awkward to approve features named after himself. When someone nominated a place be named after him, he would leave the committee room while the matter was discussed. Law Promontory and Law Islands are near Stefansson Bay, Kemp Land, and there is a Law Plateau behind Mawson—all comparatively modest features. The ingeniously designed incinerating toilet at Mawson was always known as Law Hut, an honour deeply appreciated by the former ANARE director. In 1966 an ice feature behind Casey was officially named Law Dome. It is an almost circular ice cap, 200 kilometres across, but not a particularly spectacular-looking site. It has since—to Law's delight—proved to be of enormous scientific significance. A deep-drilling program through 1200 metres of accumulated layers of snow has produced ice cores with precise evidence of climate changes dating back 20 000 years to the last ice age. Bedrock was reached in February 1993 through a layer of compressed ice, providing evidence back as far as 120 000 years ago. Doubtless because of Phil Law's undeniably bald pate, glaciologists working in the area generally referred to the ice dome as 'Law's Head'.

FIFTEEN

WHY ARE WE THERE?

The Australian Government developed its Antarctic stations from 1948 with one aim firmly in mind—to establish Australia's claim on its Antarctic territories. Although the International Geophysical Year in 1957–58 encouraged nations operating in Antarctica to pool their knowledge and avoid obvious duplication of scientific programs, the emphasis was on exploitation. There was more interest in the possibility of finding valuable deposits of minerals or in whaling and fishing rights than in exploring the boundaries of pure science.

In contrast to the internationally coordinated scientific programs of the 1980s and 1990s, scientific activity in Antarctica from 1948 through to the 1960s is described by the Antarctic Division's chief scientist Patrick Quilty as 'reconnaissance science', essentially trying to cover the continent and find out what was there.[1]

The Antarctic Treaty that came into force on 23 June 1961 did not resolve the competing territorial claims in Antarctica, it just set them aside—in 'cold storage' as it were. As Phil Law told the Parliamentary Sub-committee on Europe, the Commonwealth and Antarctica on 1 May 1963:

> I think most nations are playing it safe at the present time and saying, 'Well, whether we have got a Treaty or not, we will keep our finger in the pie down there'.[2]

Although Law told the committee that science in its own right was a very good and strong reason for Australia being in Antarctica—the 'search for truth, pure science' argument—in reality it was being carried out on an *ad hoc* basis when experts and opportunity coincided.

Certain results were of immediate practical benefit. Law addressed a science symposium in Melbourne in August 1963 and said data received from meteorological and ionospheric observations on their own were 'of sufficient value to justify quite a high level of Antarctic effort'.[3] Significant mineral resources might be found, and there was always the chance that 'some discovery may lay bare a second Kalgoorlie, Ballarat or Broken Hill'.

The opportunities to make use of Antarctica in any possible practical way were canvassed enthusiastically. Law told the same symposium that he had personal reservations about the Antarctic Treaty forbidding the dumping of atomic wastes in Antarctica which could be an ideal place for disposal of radioactive materials of long life:

> Impregnated in concrete blocks or even dissolved in water which would freeze into blocks, the wastes could then be deposited in remote regions in the interior of Antarctica or in deep inland crevasses in the ice where they would be safe for many thousands of years, well beyond their active life.[4]

Getting the finance to enable research in the many disciplines involved in Antarctic research was a constant struggle during Law's seventeen years as director of the Antarctic Division. Some Government departments—like the Bureau of Mineral Resources—could immediately contribute to geology and minerals research as well as geomagnetism and gravity work. Meteorologists went south from the Bureau of Meteorology—but under the umbrella of ANARE. Law's problem was to keep this Antarctic work sufficiently quarantined from the parent departments.

Many of the new scientific disciplines needed in the Antarctic simply did not exist in the established bureaucracies and had to be developed by the Antarctic Division—disciplines like glaciology, upper atmosphere physics and biology. The Antarctic was virgin territory. Law: 'I tried desperately to get someone in 1949–51 to take over the biology, and believe it or not I couldn't interest any professor in any university to take it on.'

The first priority with sub-Antarctic biology was to find out what was there. This involved gathering fairly basic data on the populations of animals and birds and their breeding success rates. Law encouraged the medical officers, such as Alan Gilchrist on Heard Island in 1948, to begin keeping biological records in their spare time, to get valuable data on 'dates of penguins [laying] eggs, dates of hatching', seal and bird observations. The first trained biologists, Graham Chittleborough and Tim

A DOG TEAM IN FRONT OF MT KIRKBY, PRINCE CHARLES MOUNTAINS, 1956–57. (W BEWSHER)

▲ AERIAL PLANKTON NETS ON
MAGGA DAN, DECEMBER 1960.
(COURTESY ISOBEL BENNETT)

▶ A LONGITUDINAL SECTION
OF AN ICE CORE SHOWING
ICE CRYSTALS UNDER
POLARISED LIGHT.
(D CHEESEMAN)

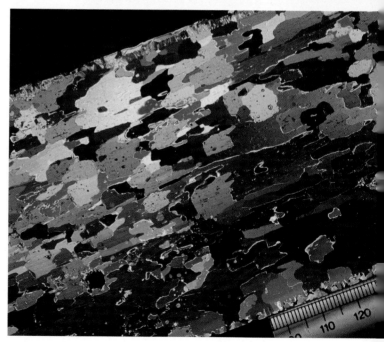

▲ A Nodwell over-snow vehicle returning to Casey Station, 1972. (D Luders)

▼ A brisk breeze at Dovers Base in the Prince Charles Mountains, 1989. (R Ledingham)

▲ Nel Law, the first Australian woman to visit Antarctica, painting in front of *Magga Dan* at Chick Island, 1961. (P Law)

▼ A rare sight — *Magga Dan* and *Thala Dan* in Mawson Harbour, February 1961. (P Law)

▲ A Bell helicopter landing on Lewis Island to assist with repairing the automatic weather station, 1962.
(J Field)

◄ HMAS *Wyatt Earp* being refitted in dry dock at Port Adelaide, 1947. She was the only ship in Australia deemed capable of reaching Antarctica.
(P Law)

▲ HEARD ISLAND STATION, 1952 — AND A
RARE GLIMPSE OF BIG BEN.
(P LAW)

▶ *NELLA DAN* AT THE ICE EDGE NEAR DAVIS
STATION WITH AN OBLIGINGLY PHOTOGENIC
EMPEROR PENGUIN, 1974.
(R BROOKES)

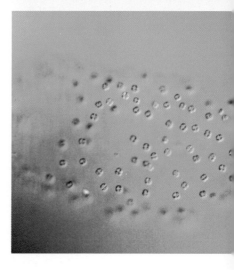

▲ EMPEROR PENGUIN AND CHICK, AUSTER ROOKERY.
(G ROBERTSON)

◀ SNOW PETRELS NESTING IN A ROCK CREVICE.
(M PRICE)

▼ ADÉLIE PENGUINS AT GARDNER ISLAND, NEAR DAVIS
STATION, GOING FISHING.
(M HESSE)

▶ *PHAEOCYSTIS ANTARCTICA* IS ONE OF THE MOST ABUNDANT
OF THE SINGLE-CELLED PHYTOPLANKTON SPECIES WHICH FORM
THE BASIS OF THE ANTARCTIC FOOD CHAINS.
(COURTESY H MARCHANT)

▲ Icescape near Davis.
(R Easther)

▶ Ralph 'Noddy' Fletcher taking a
midwinter dip at Casey Station in 1976 —
air temperature minus 6 degrees Celsius.
(W Breeze)

Ealey, went to Heard Island in 1949 for ANARE, and Law (a physicist) acted as their supervisor.

The opportunities were there for young scientists eager to make their names. Bill Taylor was the first trained botanist to winter at Macquarie Island, in 1950, and the first to study the vegetation and the soils—although botanical collections had been made by visitors in the nineteenth and early twentieth centuries and sent to London. Unfortunately these collections were all destroyed by bombing raids on Kew in World War II. Taylor, later to write his PhD thesis based on his work at Macquarie, spent a fascinating year noting the island's five principal vegetation formations—grassland, herbfield, fen, bog and feldmark:

> The interesting thing about it was that, being on an island like this, isolated [and] which had been glaciated, there were very few species—so that in some ways, things got simplified. I simply walked all over the island, dug all over the island, to try to understand everything that I could about what was growing [there].

Later studies accepted Taylor's five classifications but expanded the range of vegetation noted.

Not all young scientists were able to take full advantage of their Antarctic opportunities. Entomologist Tom Manefield, fresh out of university, went to Macquarie Island in 1949. He was ambivalent about going as his alternative was to begin a Master's degree at Cambridge University:

> Professionally I could only regard it as a total waste of time. It was quite negative, actually. . .I was undertrained, I had no program of work and no supervision. . .
>
> As an entomologist, I think there are only six or eight species of insect on the island: a moth that came out for about a fortnight a year on the kelp; another little moth that came out on the tussock grass for about a week; a few little carrion beetles on the carcases; some fleas on penguins and the kelp flies.
>
> Mostly, I suppose, we were builders. The [expedition] was grossly underplanned at that stage of the game, and buildings just had to be built. Mostly I just built or loafed. . .from a [professional] point of view it was awful.

As a result of that year on Macquarie Island, Manefield says, he moved away from science as a career.

Other biologists, though, found a great richness of fauna available to them. Max Downes followed Ealey and Chittleborough on Heard Island in 1950. They were pioneers in techniques and ingenious innovation as well as taking their discipline to a new location. There were no rings available for bird banding, so Max Downes had to get the bands made himself: 'I got sheep marking tags and had them stamped ANARE *Australia* and a number. The only banding had been done on mutton birds in Tasmania by Dr Serventy with the CSIRO.'[5]

Law's problems getting even quite modest scientific equipment for his field staff were illustrated by a letter received in June 1951 from Francis Ratcliffe, officer-in-charge of the Wildlife Survey Section of the CSIRO in Canberra:

> I cannot guarantee the swift acceptance and implementation of a bird banding scheme, and the approval of funds that will enable us to place orders for stocks of bands, and hope to see them come to hand before the end of 1951.[6]

Dr Grahame Budd, who was OIC and medical officer at Heard Island in 1954 and on later expeditions, believes Phil Law was a very fortunate choice for those formative years of the Antarctic Division's science program:

> Phil had that combination of drive and personal vision as to what it should be like. He was ready to do battle with his masters in Canberra for what he thought was right, which probably did him no good in the long run. They were very necessary battles. . .he also had this conviction that the scientific program must go on. This became a bit of a joke. . .a catch phrase, 'the scientific program must go on' (when you are climbing out of the water). . .[but it's] very important. When conditions are trying it is very easy to think, 'Oh well, gosh, it is hard enough just surviving at the moment, forget about the science'. In fact many people did go to great lengths to see they made their observations on time. That is why we were there.[7]

Arthur Gwynn, medical officer on Macquarie Island in 1949 and in 1953, was also a talented ornithologist and carried on the tradition established by Alan Gilchrist on Heard Island by running biological programs. Stefan Csordas, MO on Macquarie in 1955, 1957 and 1959, was a keen naturalist. He was introduced to Macquarie by Gwynn and Robert Carrick, a senior biologist at the CSIRO. According to Law, Carrick was an Antarctic enthusiast.

> But he used to go down there as an adventure to do his bird work, and I could never get him to write his stuff up. And till the day he died, he'd never written it up properly. He just loved the field work and hated the hard yakka of sitting at a table and writing papers. So he went back to

Scotland and left us a bit of a vacuum there. . .Continuity in biology was always difficult.

In 1955, Csordas was able to combine his work as a naturalist with some practical psychology. One of the radio operators became frustrated with life on the island and began harassing the Macquarie wild life, chasing every living creature—penguin or elephant seal—down the beach into the water. As this neurotic behaviour coincided with the time Csordas was about to begin noting nests and banding birds, he asked the radio operator to help him with his light-mantled sooty albatross program. The two men climbed the cliffs, and Csordas gave him the numbered tags to put on the nests:

> There was an enormous change in my friend's attitude. He fell in love with the birds, and spent every spare moment climbing up to them—even during the night. He got to know every bird, so I got exact dates when the eggs were laid and when the chicks started to hatch. They were his own property.

Csordas said the radio operator began taking fellow expeditioners to task if they came too near 'his' birds. He helped with banding the chicks, and his whole behaviour pattern became much more socially acceptable.

By 1965, graduate students like Michael Bryden were wintering at Macquarie working on PhD projects. Bryden, a veterinary surgeon, worked intensively for sixteen months on the growth and development of elephant seals. The growth rates of baby elephant seals are phenomenal. During their first three weeks of life they put on ten or twelve kilograms a day. Elephant seals are born on land, then quickly adapt to a life in the water. How their muscle structure and blood adapt to the change provided a fascinating study for Bryden, who was attracted to the project through an interest in the development of meat production in cattle.

Bryden was encouraged by Robert Carrick and by Fred Jacka, the assistant director (scientific) at the Antarctic Division. Apart from adding to the knowledge of elephant seal physiology and development, Bryden's project produced some interesting results for the meat industry:

> It's fairly clear that fat distribution in the body is controlled almost entirely by genetic factors, whereas the distribution of muscle and meat across the body is controlled by functional factors. Attempts had been made for some years to increase the amount of meat on, say, the rump of an animal because that's where all the expensive cuts were. It's not possible to do that. All you can do by changing the shape of animals is

263

to change the distribution of fat in their bodies—and you can do that just by careful genetic selection. . .I think that was a fairly important contribution to the meat industry at the time.

Such practical results were a useful boost to ANARE's lobby for more resources for Antarctic science.

As biologists such as Downes were the first to admit, upper atmosphere physics was the glamour science of the early 1950s. Antarctica was an ideal location for experiments in solar terrestrial physics due to the orientation of the earth's magnetic field there.

Scientists on Heard and Macquarie were interested in recording the intensity of cosmic rays (high energy particles) bombarding the earth from outer space, and lower energy particles, the effects of which can actually be seen as auroras—the aurora borealis in northern latitudes, and the aurora australis in the southern hemisphere.

Australia was fortunate that the location of ANARE stations permitted the investigation of a range of phenomena outside, under and inside the auroral regions. Pioneering work in this field was done in 1948 on Heard by Fred Jacka and Jo Jelbart, and on Macquarie by Ken Hines and Leigh Speedy. Later physicists Peter Fenton and 'Nod' Parsons continued to observe both aurora and cosmic rays from Macquarie Island.[8]

Field trips to band birds or count seals also involved other members of the stations, particularly on Heard Island. Going anywhere was difficult and involved climbing and crossing glaciers. Biologists and volunteers were subjected to the vagaries of Heard Island's sudden and violent weather changes and personal survival was the first priority of field work. Downes recalls that the adventures of field trips on Heard in 1950 were often the principal topic of conversation in the evenings.

Biologists Graham Chittleborough and Tim Ealey, who went to Heard before Downes in 1949, found the fleecy lined cold weather clothing issued to them was fine for keeping warm while sitting around, but totally unsuitable for energetic field work. They experimented and soon realised that warm inner clothing and a windproof outer layer was better. The close-weave jungle greens they had were light and fairly windproof, but needed waterproofing:

> Tim and I experimented with latex and solvent, dipping the jungle greens with fair success. As we were dissecting seals in the course of our research, I suppose we could have waterproofed with seal oil, but the rest of the party said we already carried a distinctive air with us.[9]

As it happens, biology has become one of the strongest branches of Antarctic science but in the early years biologists like Max Downes were well aware that physics had priority in ANARE:

Biology wasn't looked on as a science vital to man's future—it was good for publicity. It used to amuse me that all the press releases were about the terrific things that were happening in biology and no one used to talk about the physics. . .I think biology was the icing on the cake. Because it involved field work and because the visual effect of the wild life was so great, it was the thing that impressed people. . .[10]

'THIS MAY HURT A LITTLE.'
BIOLOGIST MICHAEL BRYDEN
IMMOBILISING A SURPRISED
ELEPHANT SEAL ON
MACQUARIE ISLAND, 1965.
(COURTESY M BRYDEN)

The two major areas of innovation in early ANARE science were glaciology and cosmic rays. After Law returned from his *Wyatt Earp* voyage in 1948, Professor Leslie Martin—who had headed the Physics Department of the University of Melbourne—decided to transfer his interests from cosmic rays to nuclear physics. Cosmic ray measuring equipment, which had gone with Law on *Wyatt Earp* and to Macquarie and Heard Islands, at the end of 1948 was brought back to be overhauled and restructured. Law:

I was able to interest Professor 'Lester' McAulay [Professor of Physics] at the University of Tasmania to take this over, and he had two very keen young physicists, Geoffrey Fenton and his younger brother Peter. After the cosmic ray equipment had been rebuilt and redesigned, Peter Fenton took one set down to Macquarie Island. We started sending equipment to Mawson after 1954. A Hobart man, Bob Jacklyn, was one of the earliest and he carried on for the next 30 years.

Australia has no permanent ice so there were no glaciologists in Australia, and although Law contacted several glaciologists in the United States and Britain he was not successful in persuading them to take charge of the ANARE glaciology programs:

Then I realised that glaciology is really physics and mathematics, and thought, 'Why can't I just get a good physicist or a good mathematician and turn him into a glaciologist?'

265

Law enlisted the aid of Dr Fritz Loewe, a German aviator and polar explorer who was chairman of the Department of Meteorology at the University of Melbourne. Also a glaciologist, Loewe had Antarctic experience with the French in 1951 and he could be used as an expert: Law:

> One of the first men I chose in this way was a British physicist called Malcolm Mellor. We sent him up to work with Loewe [and his assistant Uwe Radok] to give him the basics of glaciology—and being a good physicist and a reasonable mathematician he was able to turn himself into a glaciologist. Later he went to the United States and had a very successful glaciological career over there.
>
> But our best accomplishment was to pick William Budd, and he was chosen because he was a good mathematician. And we turned him into a glaciologist and he became one of the world's leaders.*

Glaciologists went south with ANARE every year from 1960. Bill Budd wintered at Casey in 1961 and in 1964 at Mawson, where he completed a study of the dynamics of the Amery Ice Shelf begun in 1961. These and other early glaciological studies were coordinated by Uwe Radok, who took over from Loewe as chairman of the Department of Meteorology in 1961. The first sea ice research program was undertaken by glaciologist Gunter Weller from Mawson in 1965. On the continent, one of the biggest continuing projects of ANARE glaciologists is their work on and around the Lambert Glacier—the world's largest—which drains over one million square kilometres of Antarctica through the Prince Charles Mountains into the Amery Ice Shelf, which is 200 kilometres wide where it meets the ocean.

In the early years of ANARE, geologists and surveyors often worked together. The surveyor established the true position of areas of exposed rock, and the geologist collected samples for later analysis. Law's 'second Broken Hill' was never found, but significant geological discoveries were made. Peter Crohn accompanied Syd Kirkby into the Prince Charles Mountains, having requested a second year at Mawson from 1955 through 1956. On the edge of the Amery Ice Shelf he found some fascinating sediments in rocks now called the Amery Formation. There were also seams of coal, but that was of lesser significance to the geologist. Crohn:

> The sedimentary rocks are very similar in their appearance and composition, and in the presence of fossils in the coal seams, to a much bigger [formation] in the Victoria Land area which is called the Beacon

---

* Professor W F Budd is the program leader of Polar Atmospheres at the Cooperative Research Centre, University of Tasmania.

Formation. That has been known for a long time. The earliest Scott and Shackleton expeditions brought back specimens from that.

Crohn's discovery showed that when these rocks were deposited, some 200 to 300 million years ago, there were roughly similar conditions prevailing over a very large proportion of the Antarctic continent:

> That has implications for theories of continental drift and ancient climates and so on. So that was a bit of a surprise. Nobody, I think, before we went down there, expected to find that.

Another particularly valuable combination of geologist and surveyor was that of Ian McLeod and Syd Kirkby which extended over several years.

One of Law's earliest campaigns was to unify all science under the ANARE banner. Early difficulties arose because of the inclination of departmental scientists to owe allegiance to their departments (the Bureau of Meteorology, Bureau of Mineral Resources or National Mapping) when down south instead of ANARE. With the sympathetic attitudes of the heads of these departments, Law's aims were realised. Some areas of Antarctic work had no obvious connection with existing institutions—particularly research into cosmic rays, glaciology, upper atmosphere physics, sub-Antarctic and Antarctic biology and oceanography. In November 1960, with the support of the EPC, a submission was put to Cabinet requesting that the Antarctic Division be authorised to conduct scientific research in these specialist areas 'provided

TWO ANARE TRAVERSE TRAINS MAKING SEISMIC SOUNDINGS MEET ON THE ICE CAP NEAR THE PRINCE CHARLES MOUNTAINS, 1957. (S WHEELER)

THESE COAL SEAMS WERE FIRST DISCOVERED NEAR BEAVER LAKE IN THE PRINCE CHARLES MOUNTAINS IN 1956 BY GEOLOGIST PETER CROHN. (J MANNING)

WILKES STATION ALMOST
COMPLETELY UNDER
ICE, 1966. IT WAS
ABANDONED IN 1969.
(P LAW)

there is no duplication with the functions of other Government organisations'.[11]

Law wanted the Antarctic Division scientists to have parity with salary scales in the CSIRO, but Cabinet was unsympathetic—perhaps suspicious of the growth of yet another scientific bureaucracy. The Division was told to keep on going as they were—working in conjunction with other agencies—but was specifically forbidden to 'develop its own capacity in scientific research'.[12]

This decision was a blow and was criticised by EPC members at their meeting on 19 May 1961. Law felt that it was tantamount to a lack of confidence being expressed in the division, with no investigation into its capabilities and record, and was 'quite unjust'. The External Affairs representative, Colin Moodie, agreed, noting that Cabinet was probably bewildered as to why scientific programs should come under External Affairs—the last time Cabinet had considered this matter was in 1948. The meeting decided to resubmit the matter to Cabinet.[13] This was done on 7 June 1961, but without success.

By 1962, a major concern was not so much the employment conditions of ANARE scientists, but where they might be housed. Wilkes Station was not only disappearing under an accumulation of ice, but was an extreme fire hazard. Law told an EPC meeting in December 1962 that Wilkes would only be habitable for a few more years and that the government would have to decide whether to abandon it or rebuild it.[14] The station had been thrown together by the Americans in seventeen days and was not built to last. It seemed a good idea in 1957 to build Wilkes in a sheltered hollow, but that decision doomed the settlement to a remorseless buildup of drift snow and ice.

Most of the buildings were buried to roof level and internal heating caused a dangerous mix of melt water and diesel fuel which impregnated the timbers and made the risk of fire even more dire.[15] Any practice fire alarm at Wilkes had expeditioners leaping from their bunks with genuine apprehension. The haphazard design of the station and its disappearance under the snow led to local treasure hunts. Many of the original American huts were Jamesways—a temporary version of a Nissan hut, except that instead of corrugated iron, fabric was stretched over wooden hoops. In 1963 weather observer Kevin 'Torch' Gleeson found one when he drove a D4 tractor over it and fell in, according to seismologist Malcolm Kirton:

> A rumour was put about by the 1962 party that there was a lost Jamesway full of American beer. We spent many hours probing the snow around the station with crowbars without success.[16]

In 1963 Wilkes ceased to be a shared station between the United States and Australia. The station had been essentially an Australian-run operation since its establishment in 1959 although two flags had been flown. In the house magazine *Wilkes Hard Times,* January 1964, the outgoing senior US Representative Rod Mallory paid tribute to the easy relationship enjoyed by the Americans and Australians during the years of joint operations, including the benefits of so many national holidays:

> I have enjoyed eating foods I never would have discovered anywhere else, and I believe that we Americans have converted a few of you to our dishes (like fartable beans). My vocabulary has accrued many new words that no one at home will understand, I hope!. . .We Americans think fondly of Wilkes, Australia and Australians—and that's fair dinkum! Goodbye you mob of happy bastards. . .![17]

Cabinet approval to build a new station was given on 4 July 1964.[18] The project was given the code name REPSTAT—a contraction of 'Replacement Station'. A site was selected on a rocky peninsula 2½ kilometres south of Wilkes, and the Antarctic Division threw itself into a frenzy of planning. Avoidance of the kind of problems that plagued Wilkes was high on the agenda. A general committee and five subcommittees were set up, under the umbrella of the Repstat Design Group, to design a radically different Antarctic station. The group included specialists from the Antarctic Division, Department of Works, Aeronautical Research Laboratories, University of Melbourne and Monash University. Its chairman was Don Styles, then assistant director of the Antarctic Division. As logistics officer Geoff Smith recalled, Repstat's design required:

- siting and design to inhibit accumulation of drift snow
- resistance to high winds
- weatherproof construction
- fire resistance
- durable exterior cladding
- adequate services.[19]

Maps and a contour model of the site were prepared in 1964 by surveyor Keith 'Soupy' Budnick, and data telexed back to Melbourne. A contour model of Repstat was made and subjected to tests in the wind tunnel at the Aeronautical Research Laboratories. The design which emerged was of a long single line of buildings, located across the direction of the prevailing winds, and elevated above the ground on a network of scaffold pipes. The most dramatic and distinctive feature of the design was a long curved tunnel on the upwind side to deflect drift snow well away from the construction and provide covered access to the line of buildings. (The designers would have preferred solid angle-iron supports, not scaffold piping, but could not afford it.)

Work on the site began during the 1964–65 changeover when a small team of division engineers and expeditioners (including several engineers from the Department of Works) began blasting offshore approaches and built an access road to the site. They erected one building and began work on the shells of two more. A member of the 1964 Wilkes party commented that so much building equipment was stockpiled on the shore 'it resembled the Normandy beachhead just after D-Day'.[20]

While this looked impressive to an onlooker, the reality was that Repstat was being built on a modest budget—estimated at £165 000 [$330 000] by the EPC in 1963.[21] The decision to build Repstat had meant a compromise on ANARE's programs—a decision to close down Davis Station for an indefinite period to save an estimated £50 000 [$100 000] a year.[22] Shipping space was also needed for the Repstat construction.

One of the arguments used by Law to get Davis established in the first place for the International Geophysical Year in 1957–58 was that if we did not move in, the Russians almost certainly would. But by 1964, international cooperation in Antarctica was so entrenched that Law—about to go overseas in July to Paris and Moscow—asked External Affairs whether he should approach the French, Japanese or even the Russians on whether they might like to occupy Davis Station and continue the scientific work there.[23] No one wanted to lose the continuity of meteorological and other scientific observations from Davis.

External Affairs bridled at the thought of the Russians moving in and told Law not to mention the availability of Davis to them.

Law was asked to explore whether France, Belgium or Japan might be interested—or even a country which was not a signatory of the Antarctic Treaty, like Canada.[24]

In September, the possibility of the United States moving into Davis was canvassed by External Affairs:

> Occupation of the station by the Americans would mean that we would avoid the possible embarrassment of having to refuse the Russians if (as seems unlikely) they would ask for permission to use the empty station. . .[25]

The Japanese were sounded out by the Australian Embassy in Tokyo early in 1965 but declined the offer. That ended diplomatic feelers to find a friendly occupying nation for Davis Station and on 25 January 1965 Phil Law—who had led the party which established Davis in 1957—had the melancholy duty of shutting it down:

> The last hut doors were sealed at 1430 hours. I gathered all the men who were ashore and officially pulled down the Australian flag and the ANARE pennant at 1500 hours to declare the station closed.[26]

The closure had been preceded by press publicity about the twenty husky dogs that were due to be put down before Davis closed. Quarantine regulations precluded them from being brought back to Australia and Mawson Station, with its own teams, could only accommodate a few of the Davis dogs. Headlines like DOGS TO BE SHOT prompted inquiries from the Prime Minister's Department to External Affairs.[27] In its response, EA defended the decision, noting that the dogs would not be shot 'but will be given an intramuscular injection such as morphine'.[28] Melbourne journalist Peter Michelmore commented: 'That is the wretched state of a husky as far as officialdom here is concerned—a dog without a country'.

Scientists working on Antarctic-related projects might well have described themselves as researchers without an organisation since Cabinet had refused to sanction the Antarctic Division's running its own research programs outside the umbrellas of the universities or specialised agencies like the CSIRO. In June 1964 Dr Fred Jacka, Assistant Director (Scientific) at the division, resigned to take up an appointment as Director of the Mawson Institute for Antarctic Research in Adelaide—a position that carried with it the salary and status of a university professor. Jacka had been with the division since its first year of operation, 1947, and Law, sympathetic to Jacka, was hopeful that the Mawson Institute would augment the Antarctic Division's scientific programs.

The Mawson Institute (attached to the University of Adelaide) was inaugurated on 15 April 1961 by Prime Minister Robert Gordon Menzies and its constitution drew on the Scott Polar Research Institute at Cambridge as a model. Jacka had high hopes for it and, in a discussion paper before he left the division, proposed that:

> The Mawson Institute for Antarctic Research be given the necessary government responsibility for the scientific research program which is presently the responsibility of the Antarctic Division of the Department of External Affairs. This would include, as current projects are rounded off, responsibility for research in fields which are now the joint province of the Antarctic Division and other university departments and CSIRO.[29]

But Jacka's plans were too ambitious for Law, the University of Adelaide, and the Commonwealth. On Monday 9 November 1964 Law met with the Vice-Chancellor of Adelaide University, Mr Henry Basten, to discuss working arrangements between the institute and the division. Law reported to External Affairs that Basten 'had not himself envisaged anything so radical and extensive'. Law made it clear to the vice-chancellor that the division saw merit in keeping science and logistics under its ANARE umbrella:

> The Division would not be prepared to relinquish its control of programs in cosmic rays, aurora, glaciology, terrestrial biology, human physiology and medical sciences.[30]

Law told Basten, however, that the Mawson Institute could contribute to ANARE science in the same way that other universities and agencies did. The two men then lunched with Jacka and agreed that the institute could play a significant role in oceanography, marine biology and 'certain aspects of upper atmosphere physics'.

At the time Law backed Jacka's move to Adelaide in 1964, he had no plans to leave the Antarctic Division, but by 1965 he was becoming increasingly frustrated by the Government's refusal to allow the division to be responsible for its own research. On 5 November he went to Canberra to make his views known to Sir Laurence McIntyre. He told the deputy secretary that as well as an assistant director (scientific) to replace Jacka he needed:

> . . .a chief physicist, or chief glaciologist, and a chief biologist. No permanent positions existed for these men and the chances of obtaining classifications adequate to attract men of sufficient quality were at present

Jacka took up his new job as head of the Mawson Institute in Adelaide on 28 June 1965, but his hopes for the scale of its contribution to Antarctic science were never realised. Law was supportive and tried to involve the institute in an oceanography program for the 1965–66 season, but the Government refused to grant the modest £12 900 [$25 800] requested—taking the view that the University of Adelaide should support the institute and fund its programs from its share of Commonwealth grants. Law spelled out the realities to Jacka in a letter on 11 October 1965 after discussions with the Prime Minister's Department and Treasury specifically on the oceanography issue:

> It was pointed out that when a new chair of some branch of science is established, the university accepts the fact that a substantial amount of money for research must be made available to enable the new professor to pursue his research interests. In the case of physics a new professor might bargain for several hundreds of thousands of pounds before he accepts the chair. In the case of oceanography the amounts concerned are quite modest and it was felt that if the university were really interested in such a program the money involved might well be provided by the university.[31]

Jacka was able to pursue his own research interests in upper atmosphere physics from Adelaide with ANARE assistance, but the Prime Minister's Department remained adamant on the issue of funding oceanography. The failure of the Mawson Institute to flower was noted by Sir Douglas Mawson's widow, Paquita, who wrote to the Governor-General, Lord Casey, in April 1966:

PIONEERING ANARE UPPER ATMOSPHERE PHYSICIST AND LATER DIRECTOR OF THE MAWSON INSTITUTE, FRED JACKA, PHOTOGRAPHED IN 1956.
(A CAMPBELL-DRURY)

> The Mawson Institute for Antarctic research is only a Director and a name. (I'm rather disappointed but can do nothing. I have no money. £20 000 [$40 000] was given by the Commonwealth for a building and now a few rooms are being added to an extension of the Physics Dept.)[32]

Casey passed Lady Mawson's letter on to Sir Laurence McIntyre, Deputy Secretary of External Affairs, who replied:

> Unfortunately we have the same impression of the Institute as has Lady Mawson—that it is not much more than a director and a name. (Privately we have been a bit worried about it, and particularly about the Adelaide University's apparent reluctance to provide it with any worthwhile funds.)[33]

remote. Without clearing up this situation we could not plan three years ahead, as was essential in terms of logistic and scientific support for the programs we had in mind.[34]

Law was due to sail on *Nella Dan* in December for the annual resupply voyage to relieve Wilkes and Mawson Stations, inspect the abandoned Davis Station and carry out coastal surveys and exploration. He was keen to resolve the uncertainty over the future of the division's scientific activities, which had dragged on for five years, before he left:

> I was concerned at the general indications of lack of Government interest in Antarctic achievement and our scientific programs [and] apprehensive lest mounting defence expenditure resulted in cuts to our budget. Even if our budget remained at £1 million [$2 million], the annual rise in costs of about four to five per cent would result in our activities gradually being reduced.[35]

There were personal irritations too. Law's discontent was aggravated by his annual salary of £4600 [$9200] and senior officer classification compared with directors of other Commonwealth agencies like the Bureau of Meteorology, £5020 [$10 040] and CSIRO, £5980 [$11 960]. Though his senior staff had been reclassified the previous year, his own position had not, and he felt he had 'been treated with scant consideration':

> All in all I was despondent about the future. I was 53 years old and had twelve useful years of public service ahead of me. If no real opportunity for achieving worthwhile results were given to me in the Antarctic field I would seek some other avenue for my energies. In short I was seriously considering resigning [the] next April if nothing were accomplished before then in regard to the Division's problems.[36]

Law had seriously considered leaving the Antarctic Division in 1959 when he applied for several vice-chancellorships at Australian universities. He maintained his interest in tertiary education and by the time he boarded *Nella Dan* on 29 December 1965 he knew it would be his last voyage as director of ANARE—Sir Laurence McIntyre was not able to give him any assurances about the future of the scientific program, or the status of the division.

Law's last ANARE voyage was marked (as was his first sailing in *Kista Dan*) by a hurricane—this time at Mawson Station.

On the evening of Saturday 12 February 1966 *Nella Dan* was moored in Horseshoe Harbour. Fourteen of the ship's officers and crew were ashore with all the incoming and outgoing expeditioners for the traditional

PHILLIP GARTH LAW, AC, CBE, MSC, DAPPSC (HON. MELB), DED (HON. VIC), DSC (HON. LA TROBE), HON. FRMIT, FANZAAS, FAIP, FRSV, FTSE, FAA.

They called Phil Law 'Mr Antarctica' and the conjunction of his career and that of the fledgling Antarctic Division was fateful. Appointed as senior scientific officer in July 1947, he was with ANARE right from the beginning, sailing on the wooden *Wyatt Earp* in 1948 on its attempt to find a site for the first ANARE continental station. By 1949 he became the Antarctic Division's first director (taking over from Stuart Campbell, the original leader of ANARE), and continued in that role for the next 17 years.

While Mawson's work led directly to the establishment of the Australian Antarctic Territory, it was left to Law to consolidate Australia's reputation in Antarctica. As a tireless promoter of Australia's Antarctic interests, he secured substantial and continuing national commitment to Antarctica.[37]

Law led the expeditions that established the Mawson and Davis Stations and negotiated the transfer of Wilkes Station from the USA to Australia. Later he initiated the construction of the first Casey Station.

Over his nineteen years as an Antarctic explorer, Law made 28 voyages to Antarctic and sub-Antarctic regions. His coastal exploration achieved 28 landings at previously unvisited sites, and under his direction over 5000 kilometres of AAT coastline was accurately charted for the first time. Winter parties working inland from the stations extended the total area mapped to more than one million square kilometres.[38] By the time he retired from the Antarctic Division in 1966, the main geographical features of the AAT were known,

PHIL LAW, ANTARCTIC EXPLORER, PHOTOGRAPHED IN 1956. (G LOWE)

and important scientific programs had been set in place, many of which continue to this day.

He was 55 when he left the Antarctic Division to return to academe and a new career, taking up the newly created position of Vice-President of the Victoria Institute of Colleges (VIC). Essentially this meant building up another organisation from scratch, designing and fostering an educational group that at its maximum totalled sixteen Colleges of Advanced Education. He retired in 1977.

▶

Law was awarded a CBE in 1961 for his 'substantial contribution to Australian achievement in the Antarctic'. In 1975 he was made an Officer of the Order of Australia (AO), and in 1995 received the highest award in the Australian honours system—a Companion of the Order of Australia (AC)—a more adequate recognition than the knighthood many ANARE colleagues thought he should have received immediately after his Antarctic service in the 1960s. In May 1996 he travelled to London to an investiture at Buckingham Palace to receive the Polar Medal originally offered to him in 1965, but not accepted then because two other nominated ANARE expeditioners at that time had not been awarded Polar Medals.

On Law's eightieth birthday in 1992, the Royal Society of Victoria held a symposium in Melbourne to honour him and his work in Antarctica, education and marine science.

Law's interest in ANARE affairs has never flagged and he continues to comment forcefully on Antarctic Division and Government policies in Antarctica, through the ANARE Club and its journal *Aurora* as well as in newspapers and scholarly journals and at public forums. It is an ANARE Club joke that 'Phil never really retired as director of the Antarctic Division'. Now well into his eighties, he travels widely and plays tennis several times a week when his schedule allows.

changeover party. At the last moment the master, Captain Wenzel Gommesen, and the chief engineer, Hugo Larsen, decided to stay on board as the wind began to gust at 50 knots. It was a wise decision. Had they gone ashore for the festivities they would have been unable to return to *Nella Dan*. As the hurricane intensified, the crew, marooned at the station, bunked down in the mess with emergency mattresses and blankets. At 2.30 am on Sunday Law was contacted by the radio room to hear that the ship's port mooring lines had parted. Law:

> The Captain had put the engines full speed ahead and had wedged the nose of the ship into a rim of shore ice. The forepart of the ship was resting on the rocks, but the stern was afloat and was being prevented from swinging ashore on West Arm by the stern nylon rope, which still held.[39]

Law decided to make his way from the OIC's hut to the mess to see how the rest of the party was faring. It was not a wise move. After being blown over twice in the blizzard he was forced to crawl on his hands and knees towards the door of the mess hut:

> The wind strength was now 85 knots with gusts to 100 knots the strongest that I have ever had to proceed against. My face and hands were bitterly cold, and the confusion of mind, produced by the stinging, blinding

NEW AND COASTAL LANDINGS IN AAT 1954–1966

Expeditions led by Phillip Law

1954	Mawson Station
	Vestfold Hills, Magnetic Island
	Vestfold Hills, flag-raising
1955	Vestfold Hills, first reconnaissance
	Prydz Bay Lower, on Polar Record
	Glacier Tongue
	Prydz Bay Lower, on Lichen Island
1956	Lewis Island, Wilkes Land
	Davis Islands, Wilkes Land (east of
	Vincennes Bay)
	Nelly Island, Vincennes Bay
	Donovan Island, Vincennes Bay
	Unnamed Island, Vincennes Bay
1957	Rauer Islands, Prydz Bay
1958	Larsemann Hills, Prydz Bay
	Enderby Land, island at NW corner
	of Amundsen Bay
	Mt Riiser-Larsen, Enderby Land
1960	Browning Island, Petersen Island,
	Vincennes Bay
	Magga Peak, Oates Land
	Chick Island, Wilkes Land
	Henry Islands, Wilkes Land
1961	Davies Bay, Oates Land
	Aviation Islands, Oates Land
	At base of peak, east of Davies Bay,
	Oates Land
1962	Cape Carr, Wilkes Land
	Cape Mikhaylov, Wilkes Land

Penguin Point, King George V Land
Thala Island, Nella Island, Oates Land
Cape North, Oates Land
Arthurson Ridge, Oates Land
1210 metre ridge, NE of Mt Gorton,
    Oates Land
Cooper Bluffs, Oates Land
Mt Kostka, Oates Land
Sputnik Island, Oates Land

1963	Amery Ice Shelf, Mac. Robertson Land
1965	Jagar Island, Kemp Land
	Mt Kernot, Kemp Land
	Fram Peak, Kemp Land
	Rayner Peak, Kemp Land
	Abrupt Point, Edward VIII Gulf
	Mt Mueller, Enderby Land
	Schwartz Range, Kemp Land
	Mt Storegutt, Kemp Land
1966	Island N of Mt Clarius Mikkelsen,
	Prydz Bay

Expeditions led by Donald Styles

1960	Kloa Point, Kemp Land
	Mainland, near Enderby Land
	Proclamation Island, Enderby Land
1961	Thala Hills, Enderby Land
	McMahon Islands, Enderby Land
	Tange Promontory, Enderby Land
	Survey of White Island, Enderby Land

snow, the buffeting of the hood of my parka against my ears and fore-head, the roar of the wind and the difficulty of peering out around the funnelled parka hood is impossible to describe.[40]

Law could not help thinking what it must be like to have no shelter or to be lost under such conditions. An effort of will was required in order to think at all and to resist panicking. He reached the door of the mess, but could not be heard by those inside:

> With all my strength I could open it no more than about ten centimetres against the wind. After several attempts I got my hand inside, then my arm, then my shoulder and, risking what seemed probable decapitation, my head and the rest of my body.[41]

The crew managed to get back on board by 5.30 pm that Sunday. The captain reported that during the storm the moorings of the helicopter rotor blades had parted and the blades had been spun by the wind at about 100 revolutions per minute. As the engine was not running, no oil was pumped to the rotor system and after several hours they seized up. The helicopter was unserviceable for the rest of the voyage.[42] *Nella Dan* endured another hurricane at sea in early March as Law left Antarctica for the last time—testing his propensity for seasickness to the end.

Nella Dan returned to Hobart on Friday 11 March. Seven days later, Law chaired a meeting of the EPC (which never met again) and explained he had resigned as director to take up a position as vice-president of the Victoria Institute of Colleges. He told the EPC that it was essential for the director to be involved in expedition activities, to visit the stations and mix with the men he was leading. After nineteen years he felt he could not keep up this activity until he reached retiring age. He had no desire to run the division from a desk and thought that if he were going to make a change he had to do it now; his greatest regret was leaving the men whose loyalty and friendship he had enjoyed for so many years. His decision was also influenced to some extent by the health of his wife.[43]

Law left the Antarctic Division in April 1966. During his time with ANARE he led the expeditions which established all the continental stations, oversaw a program of exploration which filled in virtually all the dotted lines along the coastline of the AAT, and located its principal interior features. And he had set up a broadly based scientific program of Antarctic-related research.

But now the 'Law Era' of ANARE was over.

TESTING TIMES
1967–1981

SIXTEEN

FROM PILLAR TO POST

D on Styles became acting director of the Antarctic Division when Phil Law left. He had been Law's deputy director and he was still running the division as acting director four years later. No one in Canberra seemed in a hurry to replace Law, whose aggression on behalf of ANARE's interests and exasperation with the bureaucratic process had long irritated the mandarins of Treasury and External Affairs.

The rhythm of ANARE field operations ran smoothly under Styles, although he had the embarrassment of a double besetment in January 1967 when both *Thala Dan* and *Nella Dan* were stuck in pack ice only 120 kilometres apart near Wilkes Station. *Nella Dan* (with Styles as voyage leader) was delayed for 26 days, and completely beset for sixteen days. The two ships were carrying building materials and a special construction team for the Replacement Station (Repstat) near Wilkes Station in Vincennes Bay. Both ships required assistance from the American icebreaker *Eastwind* which began breaking them out on 4 February. It took two days to free them. Much of the cargo destined for Repstat could not be unloaded and had to be returned to Melbourne because of the lost time.[1]

The besetments of *Thala Dan* and *Nella Dan* showed how fragile were Australia's links with its Antarctic stations through the use of chartered ships with limited ice-breaking capacity and flying foreign flags. Even with Davis temporarily closed, Styles was having problems juggling shipping schedules to support field programs and resupply the stations in conjunction with the building of the replacement station at Vincennes Bay near Wilkes Station. These concerns were being addressed at External

Affairs in Canberra on two fronts. If aircraft could be used to reach Antarctica, scientists could be flown in and out for their summer programs quickly and efficiently, and the pressure for berths on the *Dan* ships reduced. Secondly, serious thought was being given to building an Australian ship with a full ice-breaking capacity and able to carry 56 passengers.

From 1965–68 John Lavett headed the Southern Section at the Department of External Affairs, which was responsible for formulating Antarctic policy. Although Lauritzens (who chartered the *Dan* ships to Australia) were an efficient and cooperative firm, Lavett believed that a system which depended on another nation's ships was 'fundamentally unsound':

> The Lauritzen arrangement can have done nothing to advance our alleged uniquely Australian interest in Antarctica and in particular our Australian claim there. . .In the second place, the Lauritzen ships necessarily possessed only limited capacity for oceanographic research work, and yet this area of study was clearly becoming of increasing importance.

Lavett again canvassed the idea of building the new ship in Australia—an idea eagerly embraced by the Australian Shipbuilding Board. Its chairman, Dudley C L Williams, was well aware that it would be 'the most complex and sophisticated shipbuilding project ever undertaken in Australia'. Preliminary plans were prepared, and even a model constructed. The ship would be around 12 000 tonnes and cost $15 million. Lavett:

> I must confess that, even allowing for the lower figures of those days, I was always a bit sceptical about that $15 million estimate, but they insisted they could support it for the purposes of my Cabinet submission—and discussions with Treasury—so who was I to wonder?

Construction was to be carried out at the Newcastle State Dockyard, which had the only equipment in Australia capable of handling the very heavy, thick steel plates involved. If necessary it was intended to seek design advice from the respected polar ship-building firm Wartsila, in Finland.

Next Lavett was concerned with the manning of the ship and was determined to rule out regular Australian merchant seamen because of the industrial conditions at that time. The Royal Australian Navy might man the ship, Lavett thought, but he was quickly disabused of that idea:

> I received a straight rejection—in writing. The navy, they said, did not go in for things like that, so push off! This quite brief and abrupt broadside surprised me from one point of view—namely the no doubt naive belief that the navy was supposed to defend Australian territory. . .

DONALD FRANKLIN STYLES, MBE, BSc, MIE (AUST), FRGS

Styles was a respected Antarctic professional who joined the division in 1957 from the Postmaster General's Department. An engineer, he first assisted Law with engineering operational matters, having a special interest in communications. Quietly spoken, reliable and competent, Styles was the ideal deputy and was soon leading most of the annual voyages of survey and resupply not personally handled by Law. He shared the excitement of the early exploratory years and in 1960–61 led a number of important voyages—including an expedition in *Thala Dan* west of Mawson to Kemp and Enderby Lands, where the first sea landings were made at a number of points, and where the western border region of the AAT was surveyed.

Although never confirmed as director, Styles acted in that job for almost six years during difficult times for the division, including the sudden administrative switch from the Department of External Affairs to the Department of Supply in 1968. Like Phil Law, Styles revelled in the field work and until he retired, in 1977, specialised in coordinating the changeover operations and the summer field work. Eric Macklin, who worked closely with Styles on many resupply voyages, remembers his skills as a diplomat, consulting with Danish captains and with experts within the division and from the other agencies that make up ANARE:

> Don took a leading active part in all operations. He was first over the side to assist with mooring the ship at the ice edge, on occasions dangling precariously from a rope ladder over the bow of *Nella Dan*. Several times he got freezing wet when he

DON STYLES, WHO ACTED AS THE DIRECTOR OF THE ANTARCTIC DIVISION FOR NEARLY SIX YEARS, SUPERVISING UNLOADING OPERATIONS AT MAWSON STATION, 1964.
(A CAMPBELL-DRURY)

> broke through rotten ice while inspecting prospective areas for an ice airfield. . .He engendered a spirit of team work that saw men prepared to work long hours in trying conditions. He was a man who saw the good in people—if there were faults he kept them to himself.[2]

He was passed over for the director's position twice, in 1970 and again in 1972. He retired in June 1972 after nineteen years with the division. If he was bitter about not being confirmed in the top job despite doing it for so many years, he did not show it.

He was awarded an MBE in 1968 and a Polar Medal in 1974. He represented Australia at international Antarctic Treaty-related conferences from 1961 through to 1976. Don Styles died on 21 May 1995 in Melbourne after a long illness.

Although Lavett knew that the navy would have to get on with the job if Cabinet so decreed, he explored further possibilities with the Department of Shipping and Transport and was told a crew could be provided from the Lighthouse Service.

Meanwhile the Antarctic Division was pushing for the acquisition of two ski-equipped LC130 Hercules aircraft which could theoretically operate from Australia direct to a runway to be built at Davis Station—and then around the continent as required. Lavett:

> They much preferred this to the priority which we in Canberra wished to give to the ship, and it became apparent pretty quickly. . .they [the division] didn't want a ship at all—at least not one of their own. . .
>
> As I put it to Don Styles one day in Melbourne, 'Without a ship, how were the heavy supplies going to be handled? How was the fuel to get the aircraft round the continent and back to Australia to be transported?' Don's reply was, 'If we have the aircraft, they'll have to give us a ship.'

This attitude was not well received in Canberra and, according to Lavett, 'really damaged our confidence in the quality of advice we were likely to get from the division'.

While these options on shipping and air transport were being explored by External Affairs in 1967, Sir Laurence McIntyre, the Deputy Secretary of External Affairs, was keen to have an 'audit' of the Antarctic Division's scientific program. He approached the president of the Academy of Science, Sir Frederick White, who agreed to chair a committee to evaluate what the division had been doing, and whether it was worthwhile.

The Academy committee reported in August 1967 and recommended—perhaps not surprisingly—that Australian scientific research be continued. The report praised what had been done in Antarctica, finding that the scientific programs 'have been well conceived and excellently carried out'. Planning and logistic support had been effective:

> Australia has as a result gained a prominent place in Antarctic science; the performance of the expeditions both scientifically and generally stands out conspicuously when compared with that of other nations.[3]

The committee did not, however, support Law's ambitions to have the Antarctic Division employ its own scientists: '[The committee] believes that the scientific work could be directed adequately by scientists in Commonwealth Government instrumentalities and in the universities.'[4]

The report strongly recommended that the next director of the Antarctic Division should be a scientist, 'having adequate abilities to manage the logistics operations'.

In September 1967 Sir Laurence McIntyre—aware that Don Styles had been acting as director of the Antarctic Division for more than a year—asked John Lavett whether he thought Styles should be confirmed in the position. By that time it had been established that a full review would be carried out into the future of the division, and Lavett argued against appointing Styles until the review had been completed:

> I said that, even leaving aside comparisons with Phil Law, which were inevitable, it did not seem that he had the necessary charisma or drive, despite his undoubted personal likeableness—or that he would be well enough regarded by the scientific or international communities to ensure that our Antarctic effort retained its status and reputation. . .we should also be cautious about committing ourselves to someone whose essential qualifications were those of a good, straightforward public servant.

McIntyre accepted this advice and Styles continued to mind the shop. The position of assistant director (scientific) was also left open, with the incumbent, Phil Sulzberger, continuing to act in it. Lavett continued with planning the review of the division and exploring options for air links with Antarctica. He was encouraged by conversations with the US scientific attache in Canberra, Paul Siple, a veteran American Antarctic scientist who had one of the US stations named after him. Siple told Lavett the US (under the umbrella of Antarctic Treaty cooperation) would probably be able to carry small numbers of Australian expeditioners between Christchurch and McMurdo Station, on the edge of the Ross Ice Shelf, from where American LC130 flights could carry them on to Australian stations when space was available during the summer flying program.

In late October 1967—on Siple's recommendation—Lavett consulted Qantas in Sydney to see if they could help get ANARE people to McMurdo. Qantas were interested and Lavett felt he was close to nailing down a summer program which could get Australian scientists to Antarctica and back by air. He was aghast when the *Australian* newspaper published a series of three articles canvassing the need for proper air support in the Antarctic, and tracking the course of his review 'with absolute accuracy'.

Paul Hasluck, who was Minister for External Affairs at the time, was furious. He accused Lavett of leaking the information:

> Hasluck was generally a model of charm in person, but in writing, which is how he preferred to deal, he could really be abominably rude. [He]. . .said he would simply not accept a situation where a public servant—by implication me—was trying to bring pressure on the Government by leaking material to the press. . .giving the direction that we were not to take any further action about aviation in Antarctica.

Stung by this attack on his probity, Lavett needed to track down the leak. He had consulted Phil Law thoroughly during his aviation research, and flew to Melbourne to see him:

Phil readily agreed that it was indeed he who had made the leak and that he had done it to bring pressure on the Government. The possibility that it could have disastrously opposite results never occurred to him, and disastrous they were.

Lavett, concerned about his career, reported the source of the leak to Hasluck, who simply returned Lavett's letter with one word gracelessly scribbled on it—'noted'. The whole affair was symptomatic of Hasluck's impatience with his Antarctic responsibilities. It may well have been the last straw as far as the acerbic Minister for External Affairs was concerned. Unlike Richard Casey who had a strong and enduring interest in Antarctic matters and who had played a pivotal role in establishing the Antarctic Treaty, Hasluck's interests were firmly to the north. He was passionately interested in the politically emerging Papua New Guinea and preoccupied with the deteriorating situation in Vietnam. Lavett:

> He disliked in particular having to deal with the nitty-gritty of Antarctic Division work, such as approving detailed ship charters. He would have seen in this context the potential for severe political embarrassment.

Hasluck's irritation with the *Australian* articles on the Government's plans for Antarctic aviation and shipping came at an awkward time. His cooperation was needed to take the results of the review of the Antarctic Division (still being prepared) to Cabinet as a formal submission. The secretary of External Affairs, Sir James Plimsoll, made an informal approach to Prime Minister Harold Holt to sound him out on the basics of the review. Lavett:

> Apparently Holt responded in a very positive way and I dare say that one cause of this would have been the opportunity obviously provided to allege active, even adventurous, forward-looking courses of action by his government at a time when that government was running into serious difficulties for exactly the opposite reasons.

Unexpected, tragic circumstances intervened. On 17 December 1967 Harold Holt disappeared while swimming in heavy seas off Mornington Peninsula, Victoria. By 10 January 1968, Senator John Gorton had become prime minister of Australia. These were turbulent times for the Liberal–Country Party Government and Antarctic Division policy matters were overtaken by events. But not for long.

On a Sunday afternoon in March 1968 John Lavett recalls he was working back at External Affairs on the Antarctic Division review he planned to present to Hasluck in six weeks:

My telephone unexpectedly rang. It was McIntyre. His advice rocked me totally. He had received a telephone call. . .from Hasluck to tell him that, following a discussion between himself and the new prime minister, John Gorton, it had been decided to transfer the Antarctic Division from External Affairs to the Department of Supply.

To his astonishment Lavett was told the transfer was to take place the following day—Monday:

> McIntyre told me that he expostulated with Hasluck, but that it was apparent that the decision was irrevocable. However McIntyre did get Hasluck to see that such a small time frame for the transfer was quite impractical. Hasluck therefore agreed on a deferment of just one week, which was, of course, still bad enough.

The reasons for this extraordinary haste remain unclear but the simplest explanation may be the obvious one—Hasluck decided to offload an area of responsibility which, Lavett said, 'had turned out to be almost nothing but a nuisance and a headache' to him. When McIntyre and Lavett went across to the Department of Supply the next day to see Secretary Alan Cooley, Deputy Secretary Tom Lawrence and Assistant Secretary Ian Homewood to discuss details of the transfer, they discovered Supply knew nothing about the move, or any reasons for it. But having been approached, those running Supply were enthusiastic and 'raring to go'.

The Department of Supply was a vastly different organisation from External Affairs. Whereas the transportation and stores side of ANARE operations always sat somewhat uneasily with the diplomatic functions of the DEA, logistics was what Supply was all about. Its main job was to support the defence forces. The deputy secretary, Tom Lawrence, was put in charge of Antarctic affairs:

> The department was quite used to—for instance through its contracts branch—hiring anybody, anywhere, to do anything, or buy anything, anywhere in the world for anybody. So organising logistics exercises down to the south didn't really frighten us as being something new or strange. . .

The handover went smoothly, although a week was scarcely more practical than the original day allocated.*

---

* The official transfer of the Antarctic Division to the Department of Supply did not take place until 1 May 1968 when there was a Public Service Transfer, which was not formally effected until 7 June[5] and gazetted on 20 June 1968.[6]

Lavett thought that Supply was a factotum department, not a policy originator, and much more bureaucratic in its outlook and methods than External Affairs: 'I think with justice that if Phil Law had found it possible to complain about the bureaucratic hand of External Affairs—as he did—he would have had a stroke in dealing with Supply.'

External Affairs retained an interest and role in relation to Antarctic Treaty matters, as the renamed Department of Foreign Affairs does to this day. Lavett also briefed Tom Lawrence, who was an Antarctic enthusiast, on the progress of the DEA review of the division:

> Sadly, though, I could not get him to see the need for a ship of our own, and it soon became apparent that this proposal was going to be dropped. He felt that the aircraft part of it was 'not on' at that particular time. . .and, in the end, the division—as I had feared—got nothing at all [from the review].

Don Styles continued to act as director while those who ran Supply came to grips with the sudden Antarctic addition to their responsibilities. One of the most urgent practical problems was to complete the building of Repstat at Casey. The temporary closure of Davis Station was of some assistance, but the target of 1969 for occupation seemed unlikely after the besetment of *Thala Dan* and *Nella Dan* in 1967 and the effective loss of that season for building. The need for Repstat was urgent, with the ice-bound Wilkes Station a nightmare of decaying buildings, all at grave risk of fire.

It was decided to recruit a special Repstat construction party of four men to winter over on the site. They would be helped by tradesmen from the Wilkes wintering party when they could be spared. There had been another unforeseen technical problem. The first section of the distinctive connecting tunnel (which was to connect all the buildings and act as an aerofoil to prevent drift building up around Repstat) did not perform as its designers had hoped. It was redesigned and during 1968 the entire length was erected—a herculean task. Most of this work was

There was no cook on the Repstat building site. Mackenzie alternated his plumbing with bread-making:

I used to bake about, over thirty two pounds [13.9 kg] of bread a week for six and they used to eat it so fast I threw a screwed up Band-aid in a batch one time and that slowed the production down a little.[7]

It was said Mackenzie volunteered for the baking job because it gave him a chance to get his hands clean. He attributed his baking success—and the unique piquancy of his product—to his custom of wearing his 'lucky' sewerage overalls while he baked.[8] The cooking was shared. No one ever complained about the food, because their turn was next.

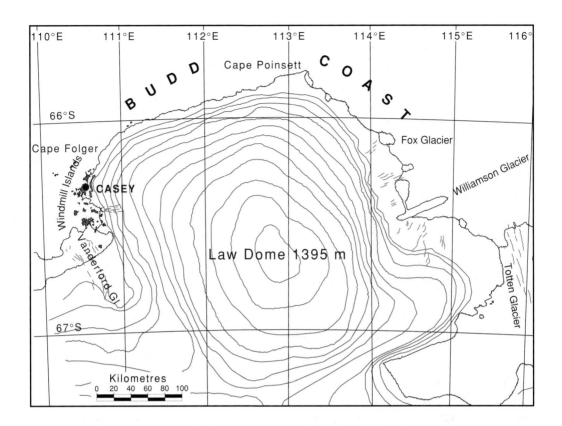

done by plumber Rod Mackenzie, assisted by Don Loades from Wilkes. The leader of this pioneering Repstat wintering construction party was carpenter Bob Nicholson. The other two on-site winterers apart from Mackenzie were Terry Kelly (electrician) and Brian Rieussant (supervising radio technician). They were given a good start by a break of fine weather during the first seven weeks of the summer program, when extra help was available. Work went on without pause, and a saying on the site was: 'Rome wasn't built in a day'. The stock reply: 'That's because ANARE wasn't running the job'.[9]

> REPSTAT WAS BUILT ON AN ICE-FREE PROMONTORY 2.5 KILOMETRES SOUTH-WEST OF WILKES STATION.

Repstat was finished on time for its official naming ceremony on 19 February 1969. It was to be called 'Wilkes ANARE Station' after the original Wilkes Station built by the United States in 1957 and named after the American naval lieutenant Charles Wilkes who explored the coastline in 1840. The Department of Supply was unhappy about calling Repstat Wilkes, because of the confusion between 'old' Wilkes and the different geographical location of the new station. It would have to be Wilkes II. The department put a submission to Cabinet, suggesting it be named 'Casey' after the then Governor-General, Sir Richard Casey, to

289

THE DISTINCTIVE REPSTAT/CASEY TUNNEL UNDER CONSTRUCTION IN 1968.

(J SILLICK)

mark his long association with Australia's Antarctic program. But Cabinet had decreed it be named Wilkes to mark the original association with the US. An extra complication was the protocol for flying flags during the naming ceremony and afterwards.[10]

Tom Lawrence was grappling with the name problem and wondering how he could convince Cabinet to change its decision. He heard that the Minister for External Affairs, Paul Hasluck, was going to address a meeting of the Royal Institute of Public Administration in Canberra. Lawrence went to the meeting and met Sir James Plimsoll, the Secretary of External Affairs: 'I knew Jim, so I explained to him the background and asked, "Is the Minister approachable? Can he be talked to?".'

Plimsoll agreed to help and introduced Lawrence to Hasluck after the meeting. He explained the dilemma and Hasluck was sympathetic: 'I said, "How do we go about it? Do we put in another Cabinet submission?" And he said, "No, no—don't embarrass Cabinet. Write me a letter, I will argue".'

Only ten days before 'Wilkes' was due to be opened, Roy Spratt, the acting director of works, sent a cable confirming that 'Repstat will be opening under the name of Casey'.[11] The Governor-General's wife was also honoured, but not on the same scale. Spratt cabled to Wilkes that 'it seems appropriate to name the new barge *Lady May* after Lady Casey'.

On 15 February 1969, four days before Repstat became Casey Station, Davis Station (closed down since January 1965) was reopened and reoccupied. The incoming OIC and medical officer Des Parker reported that the mothballed station was in surprisingly good condition:

The huts were un-
sealed and found to
be in fairly good
shape: some drift
had occurred in sur-
gery cold porch and
in cold porch at the
back of main build-
ing. Some water was
found in surgery and
main corridor of the
sleeping quarters
and the lino had
lifted, buckled and
cracked.[12]

Within half an hour of landing from *Nella Dan* the emergency diesel chugged into life for the first time in five years and provided light and power to the station. Australia's three ANARE continental stations were operational once again.

One of the first policy decisions the Department of Supply had to make on taking over the Antarctic Division was the enduring question of who was to control the scientific program. Tom Lawrence was concerned that the division had been taking scientists down south for years to do biological work, but there were few actual reports. In Lawrence's view, the division should be more forthright about its contractual arrangements with indi-vidual scientists and the CSIRO, Bureau of Mineral Resources, or university departments responsible for

OPENING STATIONS IS FAR PREFERABLE TO CLOSING THEM. A CHEERFUL INCOMING GROUP CELEBRATES THE RECOMMISSIONING OF DAVIS STATION IN 1969. CENTRE: VOYAGE LEADER ERIC MACKLIN (LEFT) HANDS THE KEYS OF DAVIS TO INCOMING OIC AND MEDICAL OFFICER DES PARKER.
(J R HAYNE)

supervising their research: 'It seemed to me that the division had got itself into the position of being a servant to these organisations.'

The Department of Supply was used to running organisations with scientific staff—like the Weapons Research Establishment in South Australia—and were aware of the need for a structure of properly graded public service positions. Lawrence:

First of all we had to establish a cast-iron case. Supply had been through this years earlier to get scientific categories for its research and devel-opment staff, and it was very important to us that standards—CSIRO-like standards—be maintained.

Dr Des Parker, OIC and medical officer of the Davis 1969 wintering party, reported that the expeditioners did themselves proud with a hydroponic indoor garden and greenhouse, growing cress, radish, lettuce, spring onions, cabbage and tomatoes—and even a few flowers.[13]

The cress, radish and lettuce were the most successful, Parker said, as an ample supply could be kept up for the small wintering party of ten people. But on Saturday 30 August the green-fingered OIC wrote sadly in the station Log:

Tragic news in the garden. Inadvertently, while Paul Watts (diesel mechanic) was draining the hot water service tank into various receptacles—urging us to put it to good use—among the filled vessels was the slop bucket from the dark room. I carried this lethal load to the garden and gave the plants a good dose of developer and fixer. Initially I thought the dilution and subsequent watering would reduce the acidity and had hoped that the fixer and developer would neutralise each other, but it was otherwise, and slowly the plants have wilted including a couple of lettuce ready for the table. It will be necessary to discard the tank contents and start again from scratch.

Lawrence was concerned that not all the scientists at the division would 'unarguably meet the standard':

Having said that, one thing that would cause as much destruction—dislocation, disturbance, loss of morale—as anything else is to split the so-called existing scientific staff down the middle [where] some go over and some don't.

Lawrence nominated glaciologist Bill Budd as someone—through his publications and demonstrated performance—who could be moved over into an established position without argument. He was less sure about some scientists occupying senior positions but felt it was essential that a new director of the Antarctic Division should be a scientist who would understand the significance of the whole Antarctic program:

We didn't think Don Styles was the person to take that attitude and that position. . .We then advertised, and it was a little while before we got some response because we were advertising overseas as well as in Australia.

An overseas candidate, a distinguished New Zealand-born glaciologist Colin Bull, was brought to Australia from the Polar Research Institute of Ohio State University. After having investigated the division, he refused the position and returned to the United States. Lawrence then turned to an Australian, Bryan Rofe, who was then principal research scientist at the Weapons Research Establishment in South Australia.

Rofe was surprised when Lawrence rang him one day and asked him if he would like a change of career. Rofe later told the division's head of polar medicine, Des Lugg: 'Lawrence asked me what I knew about Antarctica and would I like to be the director of the Antarctic Division'.

Bryan Rofe, a stockily built man with a forceful personality, took up duty at the Antarctic Division in Melbourne on 2 October 1970. At first he was viewed with some suspicion from within as 'the man from Supply' but quickly disarmed internal critics with his friendly personality and positive plans for the division and its science programs. It was felt he would push the division's position with vigour—even if that meant challenging Tom Lawrence if the occasion demanded. Martin Betts said Rofe's personal style made division staff feel that their contributions were valuable: 'I would have climbed mountains for Rofe. He was a good organiser. . .he knew what he was there for and where he was going. He was a very good communicator.'

DES PARKER, MEDICAL OFFICER, OIC AND HYDROPONIC GARDENER, TAKES HIS TURN AS 'SLUSHY' AT DAVIS, 1969.
(R MCLEAN)

As an outsider, Rofe looked at the division with fresh eyes. In 1970 it occupied a number of buildings in different parts of Melbourne, with Cosmic Ray Studies at the University of Tasmania. He planned to use the Commonwealth Government Clothing Factory site in South Melbourne to house the Antarctic Division in one place. On the science front, he planned to rearrange the programs, dividing them into broad categories—Life, Atmospheric and Earth Sciences. But first he needed to familiarise himself with the Antarctic stations, so went south on *Nella Dan* during the 1970–71 summer season.

During this voyage Rofe became ill and returned jaundiced. Liver cancer was diagnosed, and he died in Melbourne on 27 August 1971. He had been director of the Antarctic Division for less than a year.

Don Styles, who had felt rather bruised about being passed over for promotion and the suddenness of Rofe's original appointment, took over the division yet again as acting director for the next nine months until Tom Lawrence tapped the next chief executive on the shoulder.

Ray Garrod—like Bryan Rofe before him—was not expecting Lawrence's call in early 1972. Garrod headed the Science Division of the Department of Education and Science in Canberra at the time, although his earlier career had been with Supply.

In 1966 he went to Washington for the Department of Supply as the defence research and development attaché at the Australian Embassy in

BRYAN ROFE, MBE, BSc

Bryan Rofe was a physics graduate from Adelaide University. In World War II he joined the RAAF as a meteorologist and played an important role in the Australian action in Timor. Rofe was awarded the MBE for his leadership of a group during the retreat from that island. After a difficult time—during which four men died—he got his party away in an American submarine, which caught fire before it reached Fremantle.[14]

After the war, Rofe joined the newly formed Weapons Research Establishment and in 1958 was appointed to begin and develop a program to investigate the upper atmosphere by using rockets fired from Woomera. A member of the Australian National Committee for Space Research (ANCOSPAR), Rofe represented Australia on the United Nations Scientific Committee on Space Research and on a working group to detect pollution of the earth and its environment from space.[15] His meteorological and space interests were useful background for his appreciation of Antarctic science and Tom Lawrence knew him well through his work with the WRE—which was run by the Department of Supply.

As director, Rofe brought biology into the Antarctic Division, believing it should rank alongside upper atmosphere physics and

DES LUGG, ANTARCTIC DIVISION DIRECTOR
BRYAN ROFE AND LEM MACEY AT GWAMM ICE
AIRSTRIP BEHIND MAWSON, 1971.
(AAD ARCHIVES)

glaciology. In the opinion of senior biologist Knowles Kerry, this was an important and far-sighted decision for a physicist to make.

Bryan Rofe's sudden illness and death in 1971 meant that few of his planned reforms were implemented. There are long-serving people in the division today who feel that Rofe's death robbed the organisation of one of its most talented and inspirational directors.

Bryan Rofe was survived by his wife and five children.

Washington. In 1968 he was 'poached' from Supply by the secretary of the Department of Education and Science, Sir Hugh Ennor, to head the Science Branch (later Division). Ennor was one of Canberra's most formidable public service mandarins. He had impeccable connections and a reputation for achieving his bureaucratic aims.

In 1971 Garrod was somewhat restless in his job with Education and Science, 'not happy with being caught up in the policies and politics of

Australian science'. He wanted to move from developing a broad range of national policy to managing a specific area of operational science and gladly accepted Tom Lawrence's offer to return to the Department of Supply to head the Antarctic Division. It was a straight public service transfer as a Level 2, Second Division officer. Garrod does not recall ever applying for the director's position. He took up his new post at the Antarctic Division in Melbourne on 8 May 1972.

The new director agreed with Lawrence on immediate priorities: 'First to expand and develop a new structure for the Division with more emphasis on scientific effort. Second to consider a larger home head-quarters for the Division. . .'

Yet again, however, external events were to have a profound effect on plans for the Antarctic Division. On 19 December 1972, only seven months after Garrod became director, the Labor Party led by Gough Whitlam won the Federal election after 23 years of unbroken Liberal and Country Party coalition government. In the shake-up of ministerial responsibilities, the Department of Education and Science was split into two new departments—a Department of Education and a Department of Science. Sir Hugh Ennor chose to become Secretary of Science, which included the Antarctic Division along with the Bureau of Meteorology, the Ionospheric Prediction Service, the Government Analytical Laboratory, the Patents Office and responsibility for the NASA tracking stations in Australia.

Now Garrod found himself reporting again to Ennor. While personal relations between the two were cordial, Garrod had to start from scratch to try to get policies accepted. Unfortunately for Garrod and the Antarctic Division, Ennor's first reaction put a damper on these plans. Garrod:

> He was lukewarm on both the research scientist structure I had been aiming for, and the move to new premises at the Clothing Factory. He seemed to regard Antarctic science as not high in the scale of national scientific effort and he was unimpressed with the calibre of some of the division's scientific staff.

Things became less inhibited for Garrod about a year later, when a policy division was created in the Department of Science headed by Jack Lonergan. Ennor passed over responsibility to Lonergan for liaison with Garrod—a development Garrod found extremely helpful in putting forward the division's initiatives. (A research scientists' structure for the Antarctic Division was not finalised until 1983.)

With his efforts to reorganise the division largely stalled by the trans-fer to the Department of Science and an unsympathetic Public Service Board, Garrod became aware of another planned major disruption for

Raymond Ivan Garrod, ARCS, BSc (Lond.), PhD (Lond.), DSc (Melb), FIP, FAIP

Dr Raymond Ivan Garrod was 54 when he became the director of the Antarctic Division. He was a distinguished research physicist with a background in electrical engineering and metallurgy.

Garrod was born in Wellingborough, Northamptonshire, England, of Australian parents. He spent his early boyhood in Sydney but returned with his parents to England in 1924 and completed a Bachelor of Science degree (with first-class honours) in physics at the University of London in 1939. He obtained a PhD in physics from the University of London in 1947 and his research interests in crystallography resulted in a Doctorate of Science from the University of Melbourne in 1966.

For two years from 1966 he was defence research and development attaché at the Australian Embassy in Washington, returning in 1968 to head the newly created Science Branch at the Department of Education and Science in Canberra, before returning to the Department of Supply (and the Antarctic Division) in 1972.

His time at the helm of the division was marked by great change—much of it outside his control. Three changes of government, two departmental shifts and working to four different federal ministers between 1972 and 1979 meant working within a climate of constant administrative disruption. The Federal Government's determination to move the division to Hobart was an additional difficulty.

During the Garrod years the division also began its massive rebuilding program to replace the prefabricated huts built in the 1950s and

Ray Garrod, Director of the Antarctic Division from 1972–79. (J Hösel)

1960s. While debate still goes on over whether those plans should have been so ambitious, Garrod is unapologetic:

> Although [the building program] did have detrimental effects on the expansion of the science activities, nevertheless it was a 'must' that had to be undertaken.

The establishment of the Advisory Committee on Antarctic Programs (APAC) in 1974, and a subsequent report by its chairman, Sir Frederick White, paved the way for a Green Paper, 'Towards New Perspectives for Australian Scientific Research in Antarctica', released by

Bill Morrison in March 1975. Garrod was pleased that this report agreed with the Australian Research Policy Advisory Committee (ARPAC) that there was a need for greater involvement by the universities in ANARE's summer programs. In 1977, the Department of Science gave formal agreement that the Antarctic science program be extended to include marine science. Garrod:

In 1977, and at long last, the Government authorised a design study for an Australian-owned and -constructed Antarctic ship.

Garrod is remembered at the division for his friendly and consultative management style. He took a great deal of interest in planning direct flights to Antarctica using ski-equipped Hercules transport aircraft—after intense negotiations with the US National Science Foundation, the RAAF and the departments of Treasury and Science—to get scientists into the field quickly for summer programs. Several proving flights were made in to Casey in early 1979, shortly before Ray Garrod retired from the Division in April due to ill health.

the division. Within weeks of the election of the Whitlam Government, he was told that the Tasmanian Labor MHR for Denison, John Coates, had put a proposal to Bill Morrison, the new Minister for Science, that the division's headquarters be relocated to Hobart. Morrison, a former diplomat, called Garrod to Canberra not long afterwards and 'made a peremptory demand that we go to Hobart'.

Coates was a senior tutor in Biochemistry at the University of Tasmania before entering politics. He was in close touch with the Antarctic Division's cosmic ray scientists, working in Hobart at the university, who were appalled at the prospect of having to move to Melbourne if Garrod's plan to combine all division staff at the South Melbourne Clothing Factory site were carried through. After some discussions with Neil Batt, then Chief Secretary and Minister for Transport in the Tasmanian House of Assembly, Coates decided to push for the whole of the Antarctic Division to move to Tasmania. Coates:

Tasmania deserves its share of Commonwealth activities and expenditure. If centralisation of the division was important, there was no particular reason why it had to be in Melbourne. . .it could just as easily develop as a centre of scientific excellence. . .in Tasmania.

Immediately after the election, Coates lobbied Bill Morrison, with the assistance of Patti Warn, a Tasmanian then working on the minister's staff. Coates:

Bill Morrison was very receptive, keen to take up a good idea and make it happen. In 1973 it was easier to achieve such a thing, given the climate of decentralisation. There was furious reaction in Melbourne from within the division. . .there were arguments put on scientific grounds, [and] 'taking us out of a major city to an outpost of civilisation'.

Garrod, when he was called to Canberra to see Morrison, recalls that Coates was in the Minister's office at the time—which he thought was odd—but Coates did not take any part in the discussion.

Garrod says that both then and subsequently he argued consistently and strongly against the proposed move, 'almost to the point of losing my job', until it became clear in 1975 that further opposition was useless and indeed counter-productive. Earlier, Ennor asked Garrod to make a case about the pros and cons of a move to Hobart:

We prepared a position paper analysing the advantages and disadvantages, including I might say some financial estimates and costs associated with the move. In this paper, which was set out on a purely objective basis, it was quite clear that there were a number of penalties associated with the move which far outweighed any advantages from the operational viewpoint.

Political considerations could not be taken into account by Garrod. The new Whitlam Government was keen to shore up its electoral stocks in Tasmania. News of the move had Phillip Law weighing in to the Antarctic agenda again, urging all members of the ANARE Club (composed of past expeditioners) to write to their Members of Parliament to protest.

The form of words Law suggested for these letters included:

Hobart has not the technological resources needed to support a complex expeditionary headquarters; it has not the sources of supply; it has not the variety of scientific support facilities (universities, CSIRO laboratories, instrument makers, government departments, etc.). . .

In addition the transfer to Hobart would result in the resignation of a number of key personnel upon whose long period of polar experience the logistic effectiveness of the ANARE depends . . .

The move would, moreover, be expensive and so would the operations in Hobart as compared with those in Melbourne.[16]

The Government was adamant. By early May 1974 a fifteen-acre site had been chosen at Kingston to the south of Hobart.[17]

The Liberal–Country Party opposition was initially sympathetic to the stay-in-Melbourne lobby, but by May 1974 the shadow spokesman on Education and Science, Senator Peter Rae (a Tasmanian), 'guaranteed' that a Liberal Government would not reverse the Labor commitment to move the division to Hobart.[18]

Meanwhile the Antarctic Division was again subjected to a shift of parent department—although not a major one—when the Whitlam Government was returned to power after a double dissolution in May 1974, and the Department of Science became the Department of Science and Consumer Affairs.

With all the administrative changes to cope with, it was January 1975—almost three years after he took on the job—before Ray Garrod could make his obligatory new director's tour of all the Antarctic stations and actually see what he was administering. He barely had time to catch his official breath before the constitutional crisis reached its cataclysmic conclusion on 11 November 1975. The Governor-General, Sir John Kerr, sacked the Whitlam Labor Government and installed Malcolm Fraser as caretaker prime minister. Once again the Antarctic Division not only had a new Government, but a change in the name of the parent department from Consumer and Science back to Science again, and a new minister, James Webster.

Ray Garrod could be excused for being somewhat administratively shell-shocked. In his first three years as director of the Antarctic Division he had experienced three Governments, worked to three ministers and tackled the prospect of a difficult and unpopular move from Melbourne to Hobart. Within weeks of the Fraser-led Federal Government taking office he became aware that the new conservative Government was not going to reverse the Labor commitment to send the Antarctic Division to Hobart, although the new minister, James Webster, gave him a good hearing. Unlike

---

The inaugural meeting of the 'ANARE Ex-Members Association' took place at J Block, Albert Park Barracks, on Monday 22 October 1951. The meeting was convened by Alan Campbell-Drury, following discussions with Phillip Law, director of the Antarctic Division. Law was elected president, Campbell-Drury secretary, and Lem Macey assistant secretary. A further meeting on 29 October decided the organisation would be called the 'ANARE Club'. In 1953 its news bulletin to members was called *Aurora* and it has been produced regularly since then—usually four times a year.[19]

Tasmania was not the first State to bid for the Antarctic Division. In 1968—at the time the division was being moved from the Department of External Affairs to the Department of Supply—the premier of South Australia, Steele Hall, said he would offer 'every assistance towards the establishment of the Australian Antarctic Division headquarters in South Australia'.

He was responding to a speech in the Senate by SA Senator Keith Laught in early May, when he said South Australia was already the centre of oceanographic studies at Flinders University. The Department of Supply also had its own laboratories at Salisbury, as well as the Australian Mineral Research Laboratories.

The South Australian bid for the division was never seriously developed.

Morrison who had summoned Garrod to Canberra, Webster called in to see the Antarctic Division's director at 568 St Kilda Road in late 1975 and introduced himself: 'I raised the question of the division's move to Hobart. Webster was sympathetic to our opposition. I felt my arguments were not falling on deaf ears.' The new minister suggested Garrod come to his office in Canberra for a full briefing. 'I recall Webster saying: "I'll talk to the PM about it and see what I can do".'

In February 1976, as part of a program of cuts to Government spending, Webster announced that the $7 million complex planned for Kingston had been 'shelved indefinitely' thereby claiming a saving of $700 000 in the new financial year. John Coates (who had lost his Federal seat of Denison to Michael Hodgman in 1975) described it as the 'kiss of death' for the Antarctic Division move to Hobart. 'Obviously Mr Fraser and his Melbourne Establishment friends had no intention of proceeding with it.'[20]

Hodgman was quick to respond, lambasting the Whitlam Government for 'dragging its feet' on the Hobart move and saying that the move had only been deferred, not abandoned.[21] By June that year the Minister for Science—doubtless reacting to heavy lobbying from Melbourne—was again prevaricating on the Hobart move, saying it 'might be reviewed'.[22] Hodgman, again on the defensive, assured readers of the Hobart *Mercury* that Prime Minister Fraser had given 'unequivocal support' to the Hobart move, during the election campaign.

The political agenda was by then well and truly set. The Antarctic Division would move to Tasmania. It did not do so, however, until 1981.

SEVENTEEN

BUILDING AND MOVING

The Antarctic Division's assistant director, Don Styles, retired on 23 June 1976 after nineteen years of service, seven of them as acting director. Styles took a particular interest in organising the logistics for major projects in the field and represented Australia at Antarctic Treaty and Scientific Committee on Antarctic Research (SCAR) meetings around the world.

He led many exploration and resupply voyages south and helped to refine the techniques that are now standard practice for ANARE—the use of helicopters in ship-to-shore work and to support summer field parties, and the use of tractor-powered traverses to shift large quantities of fuel and supplies to remote locations. By 1975 the basic features of the western sector of the Australian Antarctic Territory had been mapped and surveyed. The area extended from the Vestfold Hills, Larsemann Hills, Amery Ice Shelf and Mawson, down through the northern and southern Prince Charles Mountains and west from Mawson through Kemp and Enderby Lands to the western extremity of the AAT.

Particularly interested in transport, Styles tried to interest the Australian Government in experimenting with hovercraft. Quite often ships were held up at the ice edge some 60 or 80 kilometres from the stations. Styles:

> I often thought how very much simpler it would have been—in the case of Mawson, Casey and Davis—to simply moor the ship to the ice edge, unload on to the hovercraft and have them shoot off at 50 or 60 miles per hour [80 or 96 kilometres per hour] to the continent. But we were always frustrated in trying to let a contract by intervention from Canberra.

One of Don Styles' long term aims was for ANARE to establish an air strip on the ice-free rock of the Vestfold Hills, near Davis Station, to support direct flights from Antarctica to Australia. He pushed this concept from 1958 until his retirement. In 1973–74 he headed an Advisory Committee on Air and Sea Transport for Antarctica:

> We found it would be quite feasible to build an airport there of inter-national standard, 10 000 feet [3048 metres] long—or more if necessary—in the direction of the prevailing wind, which is always in the same direc-tion. . .

Leading off the proposed site for the main runway were gullies in the rock, where Styles believed hangars and workshops could be con-structed. Smaller aircraft—like Twin Otters—could then fly to adjoining stations. They could leapfrog around the coast of Antarctica—east from Davis to the Russians at Mirny, to Casey and on to the Americans at McMurdo near the Ross Sea, or west from Davis to Mawson and on to Molodezhnaya (USSR) and to the Japanese at Syowa near the western extremity of the AAT:

> Thus an airfield at Davis would be a point of entry to Antarctica for several kinds of aircraft from many other places, and it could distribute the traffic to other stations on the coast around Antarctica.
>
> Remember that we have medical emergencies occasionally and when we want to get somebody out in a hurry, we can't. . .Scores of scientists want to get down there and can't. If they do get a place on the ship they have to spend weeks at sea, wasting their professional time coming and going and waiting to get back.

It was, said Styles, the greatest disappointment of his Antarctic career that the Davis airfield was not built. Australia could have virtually con-trolled direct access to the continent by aircraft, but increased environmental concerns now make it unlikely the all-weather airport will ever be built.

Don Styles' retirement coincided with the beginning of a significant change in ANARE culture. Until 1976, the only Australians to winter on Heard, Macquarie, Casey, Davis and Mawson had been men. No women had visited the continent as official ANARE expeditioners, although a number of women scientists had been going regularly to Macquarie Island during changeover voyages since the summer season of 1959–60.

In 1974, the traditional 'no facilities' argument was still being used to keep the Antarctic continent an Australian 'Boys' Own' affair. On 30 January, the Antarctic Division's director, Ray Garrod, said he believed women would go to the Antarctic with ANARE 'within ten years. . .but Australia's Antarctic stations did not have the facilities to cope with mixed communities'. He thought it best, if women did go, to start by sending married couples, and he looked forward to the day when ANARE would be able to do it.[1]

As it happened, he did not have to wait ten years. Six months after Garrod's comments, Minister for Science Bill Morrison said women could go south to do research work —but would be restricted to summer visits. COLD GIRLS headlined the *Melbourne Observer* of 6 October, while the Sydney *Sunday Telegraph* had THAW ON GIRLS IN FROZEN SOUTH: 'Several women scientists are being tested by doctors and physiologists to see if they can stand the rigours of the frozen south.'

On October 15—with International Women's Year well under way—an editorial in the *Australian* newspaper slammed the Antarctic Division's policy towards women, saying it was dictated by a mixture of male superiority and a touching concern for the 'weaker sex':

> Such anachronistic sentiments could not hold out against the onslaughts of the women's movement, so the official excuse for the ban on women working at the bases became the lack of suitable accommodation, lavatories and showers. . .

THE FIRST ANARE WOMEN OFFICIALLY TO VISIT THE ANTARCTIC CONTINENT. FROM LEFT: JUTTA HÖSEL, SHELAGH ROBINSON, ELIZABETH CHIPMAN AT CASEY IN JANUARY 1976. BUDNICK HILL CAN BE SEEN IN THE BACKGROUND. (G FOOTE)

The three women making history as the first official ANARE visitors to the AAT (Nel Law's 1960–61 visit to Antarctica was 'unofficial' as a guest of the Lauritzen shipping company) were Jutta Hösel (photographer), Shelagh Robinson (expedition liaison) and Elizabeth Chipman (information and scientific administration). They had 'proved' themselves by long involvement with the Antarctic Division and on previous voyages to Macquarie Island.[2]

With the 'no dunnies' argument dismissed there remained the attitudes of the male community about to be visited. The following message was received at the Antarctic Division from the officer-in-charge at Casey, Bert Jagger, on behalf of his men:

MEN OF CASEY 1975 DELIGHTED TO HEAR YOU VISITING US NEXT CHANGEOVER STOP FEW ONLY MUMBLES ABOUT INVASION OF MANS LAST DOMAIN BUT GRINS GIVE THEM AWAY AND KNOW DEEP IN THEIR STONY HEARTS THEY HAPPY TO EMBRACE YOU ALL ON ARRIVAL STOP[3]

More history was in the making. By the early 1970s the Antarctic Division was finding it increasingly difficult to recruit expedition doctors. Appeals to Australian doctors to undertake 'the adventure of a lifetime' were falling on deaf ears.[4] It is not possible to have an isolated community in Antarctica's winter without a doctor and there were fears that one or even two stations would have to be closed for at least a year.

In 1975 serious consideration was being given to abandoning the 1976 Macquarie Island program. Dr Des Lugg, the division's head of polar medicine, believed the only way to get enough doctors was actually to recruit women. It was, after all, International Women's Year. Lugg remembers attending a meeting in the office of the Minister for Science and Consumer Affairs, Clyde Cameron, shortly before the fall of the Whitlam Labor Government in 1975, to discuss the shortage of doctors and what might be done:

Finally, reluctantly, I said, 'Well, Minister, I do have an application from a woman'. And all the eyes of the bureaucrats fell on me, [indicating] 'You have committed the unpardonable'. But I felt duty bound to tell the minister that a woman had applied. Cameron more or less said, 'What's your problem?'

The doctor Lugg referred to was Dr Zoë Gardner, an Englishwoman then on a working holiday in Australia. Two male doctors were recruited from Switzerland and South Africa. Lugg told Cameron Dr Gardner was a most interesting woman who had done a lot as a surgeon 'and would be quite suitable as the first woman to winter on Macquarie Island'.

Cameron said 'Done!', and agreed. Then the newspapers, the press and radio had a field day saying it was tokenism because of International Women's Year. But really, it was going to happen at some stage and it happened then. . .and it has changed the expeditions.

Zoë Gardner was not interested in publicity then or later on. Press reports of 12 January 1976 have her taking part reluctantly in the official

Toilet arrangements on Antarctic stations—before the rebuilding program introduced flush lavatories, heated water pipes and a sewerage system—were perhaps more environmentally sound, but practically more hazardous.

'Law Hut' at Mawson had an ingenious arrangement of a number of metal drums, each with a fire set inside and ready for ignition, underneath each individual toilet seat and cubicle. During the all-male era, expeditioners were expected to separate their toilet arrangements by using a 'pissaphone', a strategically-placed funnel just inside the entrance door. (Peeing into the drum was a major breach of 'Law Hut' etiquette.) It was the lot of the station nightwatchman to pour a litre or two of distillate down the dunny, add a few more bits of kindling, burn out the day's doings and then shovel out the incinerated residue.

Law Hut was a warm and cosy environment inside—but best approached upwind.

Mawson expeditioner John Gillies reports that in 1967 one nightwatchman, who had been doing some painting, decided—unwisely as it turned out—that paint thinners would be a good substitute for distillate.

It was lucky he did not look down the long-drop as he chucked the lighted match in, as the resulting explosion would have taken his head off. Gillies:

THE AFTERMATH OF THE 1967 GREAT MAWSON DUNNY EXPLOSION—A HOLE BLASTED THROUGH THE ROOF OF LAW HUT. THE UNNAMED CULPRIT IS ON THE RIGHT. (COURTESY J GILLIES)

[The lid of the dunny]—Mawson's attempt to place an object into orbit—exited through the roof and landed some time later about twenty metres downwind.[5]

The explosion attracted a number of photographers to record the hole blown through the roof. That, as well as several inadvertent fires, eroded the structural integrity of Law Hut, which surprisingly survived into the 1990s—but due to its dilapidated state failed to make the list of buildings on the Register of the National Estate.

line-up on the dock at Melbourne before ducking down below into the sanctuary of *Thala Dan* to avoid reporters and photographers and declining to shake hands with the Minister for Science, James Webster, who had come to farewell the expedition.

While she was publicity-shy, she was no shrinking violet. Legend has it that during pre-expedition training, her motor cycle was locked inside the car park at the Antarctic Division's headquarters in St Kilda Road.

Gardner dismantled it, threw its component parts over the fence, reassembled it and rode away.

An individualist who did not take kindly to restrictions on her personal freedom, Zoë Gardner found many aspects of the 'team' approach to group living on Macquarie Island irksome. On 30 April 1976 OIC Peter McKenzie wrote in his log:

> Zoë off skiing on plateau on her own contrary to instructions. Terry [Hegerty] and I went to look for her at 3.30 pm (dark by 4.30 now). . .arrived at station in darkness. She was cautioned about foolhardy exploits, but it's like water off a duck's back. She is the most uncooperative person that I have ever encountered. . .I have great tolerance but I never cease to wonder what she will do next.[6]

She did, however, throw herself enthusiastically into projects which interested her and building the women's quarters was an obvious priority. She did not shirk dirty jobs and later described her role (in addition to her medical duties) as 'Catering Officer, Librarian, Dustman, Biologist'.[7] She helped Tasmanian Parks and Wildlife representative Nigel Brothers shoot rabbits around the island.

Dr Gardner certainly put paid to any worries about women being able to tackle the rigours of field work and Antarctic life. She was as tough as elephant seal hide, and gave as good as she got. During a fire drill on 10 June, the station log recorded:

> Zoë hit Chas [Cosgrove] with fire hose and he promptly threw her into Buckles Bay—all in good spirits. Chas was dyed with Gentian Violet later by Zoë—a bit over the fence I think—but a truce has been declared.[8]

Zoë Gardner slept in the surgery but shared the toilet block with the men. She put her boots under the shower curtain as a sign that she was having a bath, but often someone would sneak up and take them away so that people would continually barge in. There seems to have been more horseplay than sexual harassment—like throwing a cup of cold water into the shower recess; 'taken in good spirit' according to the station log.[9]

Certainly her professional patience was tested when Nigel Brothers broke his arm and refused to rest it:

> She threatened to send me back [to Australia] because I kept on damaging it. It kept getting knocked about when I caught it on tussocks and things and it didn't mend properly. It still gives me trouble, and that was twenty years ago. . .

Because of the necessity of having a medical officer on station, Zoë Gardner collapsed official resistance to women wintering over on Macquarie Island. The following year, in 1977, the first married couple, medical officer Dr Jean Ledingham and OIC Rod Ledingham, wintered, as did another woman, Sarah Stephens, a communications officer. But the wintering parties on the Antarctic continent remained all male until 1981.

ANTARCTIC DIVISION AT CROSSROADS

A RARE PHOTOGRAPH OF PUBLICITY-SHY ZOË GARDNER, ANARE'S FIRST WOMAN MEDICAL OFFICER, HELPING OUT WITH HUT CONSTRUCTION AT MACQUARIE ISLAND, 1976. (P GIDLEY)

The mid 1970s were a difficult and uneasy time for those responsible for running the Antarctic Division back in Australia. There was continuing uncertainty about the move of the division to Hobart, although Malcolm Fraser's Liberal–Country Party coalition remained committed to the original Labor initiative. Following a 'Dorothy Dix' question by Tasmanian MP Michael Hodgman in the House of Representatives on 18 May 1976, the prime minister cleared the matter up once and for all:

> The Antarctic Division will be transferred to Hobart. . .There are some financial stringencies upon us at the moment. Therefore the transfer will not be taking place forthwith or in the forthcoming financial year. . .But it is going to take place.[10]

The financial stringencies were also cramping the division's operations. The preliminary allocation for the 1976–77 financial year was $5.4 million—up $822 300 from the initial appropriation of the previous year. Allowing for inflation, that represented a mere 4 per cent increase in spending power.[11]

In February 1974, the (Labor) Minister for Science Bill Morrison announced yet another review of Antarctic science by a committee to be headed by Sir Frederick White, the former chairman of the CSIRO. Morrison went on to say that 'it was important that research in Antarctica should be directed towards goals that would benefit the Australian people'.[12] This infuriated former Antarctic Division director Phil Law,

307

who wrote to the Melbourne *Herald* saying that this approach was based on a false premise:

> It is a matter of answering the fundamental, simple question: 'Should Australia maintain a physical presence in Antarctica for political purposes at a cost of about $3 million a year?' If the answer to this is 'no', then we should think seriously of pulling out and saving our money.
>
> If the answer is 'yes' then we should get as much value out of our 'presence' as we can. Such value is measured mainly in national prestige, and the prestige is determined by the international standard of the research carried out.[13]

Law had identified a key difficulty about Australia's ongoing Antarctic policy. There was little purpose in claiming 42 per cent of the continent if Australia did not make its presence felt not only by occupying territory, but by pursuing an active scientific program, thereby showing 'a sufficient display of authority' which is the only realistic basis for a territorial claim.

On 5 March 1975 the Minister for Science published a Green Paper 'On Antarctic Activities—Towards New Perspectives for Australian Research in Antarctica' which was circulated to relevant government departments for comment. It incorporated Sir Frederick White's ACAP (Advisory Committee On Antarctic Programs) report, recommending a change of emphasis in some of the Antarctic science programs—skewing them more towards earth sciences and ocean studies:

> These subjects acquire some urgency due to the increased international interest in exploitation of resources, which gave rise to considerable discussion at the recent consultative meeting of the Antarctic Treaty partners. A further reason for greater emphasis in these areas is the inadequate attention they have received to date.[14]

Antarctic waters abound in krill—a small crustacean and the most abundant single species on earth—which is the basic food for whales, seals, penguins, sea birds, fish and squid. With fish stocks in the northern hemisphere declining, a number of nations are now harvesting krill. The Russians began in 1961 and have marketed krill in a number of forms. By 1977, Japan, Poland, Taiwan, East and West Germany, Chile and Argentina were also carrying out krill studies in Antarctic waters. Australia was unable to participate because it lacked a suitable ship.

Clearly the harvesting of krill was of international concern to the Antarctic Treaty nations, and it was taken up by SCAR—the Scientific

Committee for Antarctic Research. (There was a useful model. In 1972 SCAR had negotiated an agreement with Treaty nations resulting in the drawing up of the 'Convention for the Conservation of Antarctic Seals'.) Principal research scientist Knowles Kerry recalls how little was known about krill in 1976:

> The realisation came that krill was a very, very important organism in the marine food web, that it was being harvested in fairly large amounts and there seemed to be no great knowledge on how much krill was there, how much could be harvested. But since it was the central organism in the marine food chain, harvests could possibly affect the whole of the higher trophic levels—whales, seals, seabirds and so on.[15]

Following a meeting at Woods Hole, USA, in August 1976, a group of scientists (including David Tranter, a senior principal research scientist with the CSIRO) proposed an ambitious program of oceanography in Antarctic waters to be known as BIOMASS—Biological Investigations of Marine Antarctic Systems and Stocks. Knowles Kerry was keen for the Antarctic Division to be involved, but Australia did not have a history of deep sea research—nor any real capability for it:

> I managed to convince our director, Ray Garrod, of the need to do marine research—which was good. But we. . .had to convince governments and put up Cabinet submissions for approval to undertake marine research, and for extra funds to get *Nella Dan* modified to do research-scale trawling and so be involved in the BIOMASS program. This was a major change in scientific direction.

While the biologists could consider an expanding role in Antarctic science, other scientists were far from content. In a response to the Green Paper of 1975, division physicist John Reid (speaking from twelve years of ANARE experience) wrote to the Minister for Science calling for a realistic statement of our national ambitions in Antarctica and a clarification of the relationship between the division and other agencies:

> Otherwise the situation which now prevails where the division does one thing and purports to be doing another will continue. In my opinion it is this 'institutional schizophrenia' which has been most responsible for the low morale within the division over the last few years.[16]

Reid criticised the 'heavily logistic orientation' of the division as a 'habit of mind' which was embedded in every aspect of its activity. While this might have been appropriate for the mid-1950s when Australia was struggling to establish a foothold in Antarctica, it was inappropriate twenty years on.

309

There is little elasticity in employment. We employ scientists as expeditioners to man stations, rather than as experts to carry through programs. The whole orientation is wrong. . .within the public service everything militates in favour of time-serving and against task orientation. . .true research happens despite the system rather than because of it.[17]

In the 1977–78 Federal Budget the Minister for Science, James Webster, announced some significant Antarctic initiatives. These included spending $1 million on 'many of the 200 buildings' at Australia's three continental stations; the building of the first Australian-owned Antarctic research ship, to cost up to $20 million, in time for the 1981–82 relief operations; and the proposed declaration of a 200-nautical-mile 'zone of economic interest' for Australia and all its Territories—including the Antarctic.

Despite these promises, discontent in the Antarctic Division's ranks surfaced in a rash of newspaper articles the following year with headlines like CINDERELLA ON ICE and INDECISION ON THE ANTARCTIC. An increase of the division's science budget from $6.5 million to $8.7 million was dismissed by the *National Times* as '0.6 of a per cent of the cost of replacing Australia's Mirage fighters. There have been no improvements in logistics and transport to and from the ice for the last 20 years.'[18]

Division scientists, through the press, claimed that Australia's efforts in the Antarctic were more 'disorganised and uninspired' than at any time since 1954. In 1978 the *National Times* of May 20 reported that a White Paper detailing Australia's future Antarctic policy had still not been released—and there was doubt it ever would be. By December that year there was still no sign of it and the *National Times* claimed it had been cancelled, alleging that in place of the White Paper a 'Government statement' would be issued instead early in 1979:

> The Cabinet rifts which led to the demise of the White Paper have been mainly between 'hawks' and 'doves' on how strongly Australia should implement its territorial claims to the territory and the closely related issue of how much money and other resources should be committed to it.[19]

On 20 March 1979 Senator Ken Wriedt, Labor leader in the Senate, claimed that the Government had no intention of fulfilling a commitment to issue the White Paper on Antarctic policy:

> There is divided opinion in the Government on the formation of Antarctic policy between the Department of Science and the Department of Foreign Affairs.[20]

While the White Paper remained elusive, expenditure on the Antarctic program was significantly boosted in the 1979 Federal budget—almost doubling from $12.2 million in the previous year to $21.5 million. Of this $6 million was to be spent on the construction of the new Antarctic Division headquarters at Kingston, Tasmania, and $100 000 for a design study for a new Antarctic ship. It was tangible evidence that Australia intended to be serious about the future of its Antarctic activities.

It was high time. The Antarctic stations themselves were an urgent problem. By the mid 1970s they were a hodge-podge of prefabricated huts in poor repair and dating back to the 1950s. Plant, vehicles and equipment were also badly run down. Mechanical supervisor at the Antarctic Division Robert Sheers thinks of that period as 'the Dark Ages'. Sheers wintered at Casey in 1977:

> I was quite aghast at the condition of some of the equipment and the maintenance programs, or lack of. The whole thing was pretty ad hoc—very Heath Robinson. We did our best during that year but some of the equipment was really run down, and some of it really quite inappropriate. . .I began to wonder whether there was any proper planning done at head office.

THE REBUILDING PROGRAM

No single issue in the history of ANARE has polarised opinion more than the rebuilding of the continental stations. The contrast between the old and the new is best seen at Mawson where the two-storey metal-clad 'red' and 'green' sheds tower over the original huts, many of which still survive, anchored to the rock by steel cables and scattered across the landscape. They range from the aluminium clad 'Explastics' huts dating back to the 1950s and composed of prefabricated insulated panels, to traditional wooden structures of varying shapes and sizes—all erected by the expeditioners themselves.

Many of the early expeditioners believe that this policy of self-erected buildings should never have been altered—that the cause of economy and science would be better served by pulling down and replacing old huts with new prefabricated structures. This activity would have a minimum impact on the environment and maximum flexibility. Expeditioners then *know* they are in Antarctica—hauling themselves along blizzard lines in full Antarctic cold-weather gear to visit long-drop non-flushing toilets in a blizzard, and being suitably intrepid.

This view is articulated by critics like Ian Bird, who wintered at Mawson in 1960, and worked with the division from 1963 to 1975:

Expeditioners expect some hardships and privations, not a holiday style sojourn in air-conditioned comfort. The development of comradeship, initiative and high morale within an Antarctic expedition appears to depend upon the group facing and overcoming the many daily challenges of life within the most inhospitable environment on earth.[21]

But by 1976 something had to be done. The panels of the old huts had become permeated with frozen water vapour. Ian Holmes, then technical officer (buildings) with the Antarctic Division, recalls the problem:

> The panels became water-logged, frozen and corroded on the inside. The adhesives which were holding them together started to become undone. The panels were just disintegrating. . .

The only way to replace a damaged panel was to take the whole building apart. Holmes consulted with Phil Incoll, a senior architect at Australian Construction Services (then the Commonwealth Department of Housing and Construction in Melbourne), to discuss new options: 'We came to the conclusion that, within about ten years, virtually every building down there would have to be replaced completely!'

The biggest building project since the 'Law Era' had been Repstat (later Casey Station), built when Wilkes Station became hopelessly iced up, and occupied in 1969. The problem of drift had been tackled by building Casey on a birdcage of steel scaffolding and creating an aerofoil with a connecting corrugated-iron tunnel linking all the buildings in the complex. By the mid-1970s it was not wearing well. Salt spray driven from the ocean had corroded not only the supports but the superstructure. In addition, the water vapour migrating through the panel insulation—unforeseen by the designers—was corroding through from the inside. Casey had been built by teams of ANARE tradesmen over a number of years as a single project. In Phil Incoll's view it signalled the end of the 'heroic do-it-yourself era'.[22]

Information on Antarctic buildings was not easy to come by in Melbourne in 1976. Holmes gleaned what he could from Arctic sources and SCAR reports, and the Antarctic Division and Australian Construction

Services (ACS) began experimenting to build more appropriate build-ings in the Antarctic.

The first try was the yellow, fibreglass-panelled, igloo-shaped Davis biology building. However, the curved shape was hard to fabricate, inef-ficient in terms of internal space and did not seem to be any more effective than the existing 'boxes', as it also attracted accumulations of drift snow. They returned to timber panels coated with resin for the Davis power-house, the Casey trades workshop, the Mawson science building (Wombat) and the Mawson transmitter building.[23]

Meanwhile Phil Incoll was appointed by ACS as an Antarctic design officer to continue working on the rebuilding program. Ian Holmes was surprised by his next plan:

> The first thing he did was come out with a two-storey building. Most people down at the Antarctic Division just fell over, they couldn't believe it. We can't have two-storey buildings. How do we build them? What happens if we have a fire? We'd never had integrated fire services in buildings before.

Incoll felt there was no need to stick with 'little boxes' and there was no reason why Antarctic expeditioners should not live and work com-fortably in Antarctica:

> We could see that if you could get Caterpillar tractors off the ship onto the shore, you could get a reasonable crane. We looked at all different sorts of foundation systems and most people had gone in for all kinds of odd Meccano-like things which bolted together and so on, to avoid using concrete.

Summer temperatures on the Antarctic coast were not all that extreme and although concrete foundations had never been used by Australians on the continent, Incoll calculated that concrete could be poured. But what about drift? Winds in the Antarctic blow predictably with a varia-tion of only 30 degrees:

> Study of photographs of buildings at Davis showed that building sides parallel with the wind appeared to be swept clear of snow by the wind itself. . .It was accordingly proposed that buildings should be oriented with their long sides running parallel to the prevailing wind rather than across it.[24]

This hypothesis proved to be accurate. The modern two-storey metal-skinned structures in Antarctica build up a large plume of drift at the downwind end during the winter, while the long sides with entrances and windows stay clear.

The need for expeditioners to go outside was considered by the planners and work areas—like the science buildings—were situated away from the main living and accommodation block. Holmes said there was evidence that building complexes which removed the necessity of going out added to the 'cabin fever' syndrome experienced during the long winter night. Low morale was not the only concern. Holmes:

> There's a famous paper from the US Army which shows that the level of internal maintenance on their stations was much worse when they didn't have to go outside. If they had to go outside there was a high level of maintenance—not just internal but external as well.

Thought was also given to the balance of privacy and shared recreational space. US research indicated that if a recreation room was isolated from the main traffic areas, it got little use. Phil Incoll:

> There was one station in particular where the lounge and recreation areas were all gathered right in the middle of the traffic—they were on the main circulation routes of the station—and you more or less *had* to go past them. This room got very much more use and they also stated that the morale of the station benefited as a result of this.

Incoll believed it was important to create natural meeting places in the accommodation buildings—to make sure that the sleeping quarters were at one end and the kitchen and mess at the other, with the recreation and lounge area in between. Although expeditioners can have privacy in their own rooms, it is important to make sure depressed individuals cannot isolate themselves from the group:

> If you're already around the twist, you can sneak out the back door, go around and come in the kitchen door, and there's nothing [anyone] can do about that. But in the normal course of events you would walk through the lounge areas to get to the mess, and this means that if there are people sitting around they can say 'G'day' as you go past. And when you leave the mess, you are passing through this area and it's kind of natural to sit down for a minute or two and talk to somebody.

(Other old hands like Syd Kirkby, who returned to the Antarctic in 1980 as OIC Mawson, believe that the sheer scale of the modern two-storey structures made it easy for depressed people to isolate themselves.)

Before the new building plans could be put into effect the ANARE's administrative culture had to be changed. When Holmes joined the division in the early 1970s, he recalls the buildings maintenance budget was around $30 000 a year:

We were strangled. We weren't allowed to buy more than five tubes of silicone adhesive because it was too expensive. It was ludicrous. [Management] had never actually addressed the problem of what was required to run an Antarctic station properly.

The acronym AANBUS was coined—Australian Antarctic Building System—to carry through the rebuilding program. The most immediate problem was how to get building materials down to the Antarctic. The Lauritzen *Dan* ships had done yeoman service for ANARE since the 1950s, but their limited cargo and passenger-carrying capacities were stretched even to resupply the stations each year and transport vehicles, aircraft and scientific equipment for the field programs.

By 1977, the projected expenditure on the rebuilding program went over $2 million, which meant it had to be referred to the Federal Parliamentary Works Committee (PWC) for approval. Additional money was made available separately from core funding to the division but only on an annual basis. However, in 1981 the PWC approved the complete rebuilding of all three of Australia's continental stations. It agreed with a proposal for Australian Construction Services (then the Department of Housing and Construction) to be responsible jointly with the division for recruiting, training and supervising the building workers needed for Antarctica.[25]

In the summer of 1979–80, *Nella Dan* and *Thala Dan* were joined by a third ship, *Nanok S*, chartered from A E Soerensen of Svenborg in Denmark, to assist in the rebuilding program. *Nanok S* was a modest

THE CONSTRUCTION OF THE NEW TWO-STOREY RED SHED ACCOMMODATION BLOCK IN 1991 DWARFS THE ORIGINAL HUTS AT MAWSON STATION. (N LOVIBOND)

PLUMBING ANTARCTIC-STYLE. INSULATED AND HEATED ABOVE-GROUND PIPELINES UNDER CONSTRUCTION DURING THE MAWSON REBUILDING PROGRAM, 1991. (N LOVIBOND)

addition to the fleet—an ice-strengthened vessel of a mere 3000 tonnes accommodating only twenty passengers.

Ray Garrod retired as director of the Antarctic Division on medical grounds on 2 April 1979 after seven years in the job. It had been a difficult stewardship. The division had been shifted from the Department of Supply to the Department of Science, there had been a change of government in 1975 and he had worked to four different ministers. Although he had opposed plans to move the division from Melbourne to Hobart, work had started on the Kingston site by 26 February 1979. His term as director had seen the first women winter on an ANARE sub-Antarctic station, the rebuilding program get under way, and an ambitious program of marine science and oceanography begun.

Marine biologist Dick Williams recalls Minister for Science Senator Webster coming to the St Kilda Road HQ in Melbourne for Garrod's farewell:

> He gave a little speech of appreciation, and I couldn't believe it. He said: 'I've got a very high opinion of Ray Garrod. He's never given me any trouble in all the time we've worked together!'

Williams felt this was insulting to the retiring director—treating him as though he were a little schoolboy.

Garrod's successor, Clarrie McCue, came to the Antarctic Division from his former position as director of the Ionospheric Prediction Service in the Department of Science. The deputy secretary of the department, Jack Lonergan, invited him to take up the position of acting director:

Clarrie had done very well in the IPS. He was very highly thought of in academe and around the traps. . .So I rang him and put the hard word on him, and he wasn't too keen at all. So I kept at him and after quite a bit of persuasion he agreed to do it for the time being.

McCue's style was informal. Dick Williams recalls he would walk round the corridors and 'stick his head in the door and talk to you'—the only director, in his experience, who did that. Although reluctant to take the job in the first place, McCue enjoyed his work at the division, and decided to apply for a permanent appointment.

Patrick Quilty, also an applicant for the director's job (and a close friend of McCue's after he was appointed) recalls that McCue had the disconcerting habit of falling asleep if he was sitting for any length of time. This may have been due to a medical condition:

> Clarrie was a short, portly man who bustled around—as well as having this incredible ability to fall asleep! During the 1980s the RAAF conducted a review of aviation options to resupply Antarctic stations. John Whitelaw, then in charge of operations, took the results of the review to show Clarrie in his office. While he was doing so, Clarrie fell asleep. Whitelaw later said he felt like putting the clock forward and walking out. When I wanted to see him in his office, I'd always knock and wait a minute before going in, to give him time to wake up properly and not embarrass him.

The major challenge for the new director's diplomatic skills following his appointment in 1979 was overseeing the division's move to Hobart. A fierce and uncompromising Melbourne-based ANARE lobby opposed the shift to the bitter end. One of the most passionate and vocal critics was former director Phil Law who, in 1973, forecast the loss of key experienced personnel who had stated they would resign rather than move from Melbourne.[26]

The Liberal Member for Denison, Michael Hodgman, embraced the division's move to his electorate with enormous enthusiasm, taking over the running from his Labor predecessor John Coates. In 1977 Hodgman had asked the Government to change the name of the Department of Science to add the phrase 'and the Antarctic', a suggestion that was not adopted.[27]

Even before the Whitlam Government fell, sensitive documents relating to the move to Hobart had begun falling off trucks. A 'Note to the Minister' of 19 April 1974 referred to a proposed Antarctic Division exhibit on the history of ANARE to be mounted in Tasmania and opened by John Coates. The Minister for Science Bill Morrison had written in

CLARENCE GORDON MCCUE, MSc, FIP, FAIP

McCue had a distinguished scientific career, specialising in ionospheric and radio physics. He was born in Sydney in 1927, and did a Bachelor of Science (Hons) degree at Sydney University before joining the Australian public service in 1949. Shortly afterwards he gained a Master of Science from research he conducted on geomagnetism.

His research skills in physics were applied to many fields, including radio wave propagation for the Department of Supply's research station at Slough in England from 1951–53. He worked in 'classified' areas such as long-range, over-the-horizon radar (the Jindalee project) for the Weapons Research Establishment from 1953–58, and lectured in physics at the Royal Military College at Duntroon from 1958 to 1960.

He came to the Antarctic Division from the Ionospheric Prediction Service (where he was director from 1967–79) at a time when the division faced many challenges—the move to Hobart, the rebuilding of the Antarctic stations and the need to respond to the recently established Antarctic Research Policy Advisory Committee (ARPAC) and its directions for the division's science policy.

Immediately after leaving the Antarctic Division he was given the position of Principal Adviser on Antarctic matters. In 1984 he retired

CLARRIE McCUE, AUSTRALIAN ANTARCTIC
DIVISION DIRECTOR, 1979–84.

from the Australian public service to return to two of his greatest interests—consultancy work on aerodynamics and involvement with religious activities for community groups and schools.

He died on 15 June 1992.[28]

response: 'I would want a panel with photo of me and decision to have Headquarters in Hobart. The display should be reoriented in terms of the decision.'[29]

Supporters of decentralisation were also evident. In a letter to the ANARE Club's magazine *Aurora* in May 1974, physicist Dr John Reid wrote:

If some of the senior people leave a little earlier is that such a disaster? Who knows, with a younger team the division may come to regain much of the sense of excitement and adventure it had in the heyday of the 'Law Era'. At the moment Head Office is starting to take on tones of 'Dad's Army'.

By mid-1977 a ten-hectare site at Kingston had been selected, ten kilometres south of Hobart. The Kingston property was one of eleven possibilities investigated around Hobart, including the old Henry Jones & Co. warehouses on the Hobart waterfront. While this would have been convenient for shipping purposes, space was limited, and as most of the buildings dated back to 1820 they were classified by the National Trust. A site on Mount Nelson, about four kilometres

WORK BEGINS ON THE RURAL BLOCK ACQUIRED FOR THE ANTARCTIC DIVISION'S HEADQUARTERS, KINGSTON, TASMANIA, 11 JANUARY 1979. (G MCKINNON)

from the city, was ruled out because of the high cost of building on sloping land, and the adverse effect of tall buildings on the skyline.[30]

After tenders for construction were called, a $6.9 million contract was awarded to a Tasmanian firm, Watts Construction Division Ltd, on 6 October 1978. Work on the site began on 16 October.[31]

Prime Minister Malcolm Fraser unveiled a plaque on the Kingston site on 26 February 1979 to mark the official commencement of work on the new headquarters. It was hoped the division would move from Melbourne in 1981.

To ease the pain of Melbourne staff considering a shift to Tasmania, Clarrie McCue appointed Graeme Manning as a liaison officer in Hobart early in 1980. All staff members considering a transfer from Melbourne were given a trip with their families at public expense to have a look at the Hobart environment. Manning escorted them around to help them with all the information they needed.

Phil Law's prediction that many staff would not be prepared to make the move to Hobart was fulfilled. By August 1980 Clarrie McCue revealed to the press that half the division's staff had decided to resign. He said

319

44 staff would be transferring, 31 would not be moving, and four were still undecided. Another 18 people had left the division recently, and about 15 of those positions would be filled before the transfer. McCue said the mass defection would create 'large difficulties' but he was sure the division could overcome them and survive.[32]

Those who moved faced a Spartan office regime in their new steel and glass headquarters. There was a public service scale of furniture for each office. One desk, two visitors' chairs, one office desk and a glass bookcase were the bare essentials provided. Graeme Manning, who had the unenviable job of overseeing these arrangements, was aware that most of the new arrivals needed more furniture than was allowed:

> One day you'd look into a vacant office and it was fully fitted with all its furniture. The next day you'd look in and the bookcase had gone, and a couple of chairs. There were hassles trying to get them back from the people who'd taken them. One of our scientists, Harvey Marchant, had to make bookcases out of wooden packing cases because his issue had been 'lifted' before his arrival.

Manning was also on the task force created for the official opening of the new Antarctic Division Headquarters on 22 April 1981 by Prince Charles:

> It was quite a job because people from the prime minister to Departmental secretaries, Departmental ministers, ex-ministers, directors and assistant directors, state protocol and police all got involved at various stages. My most vivid memory of the preparation was that the itinerary for the visit of the Prince went through 24 drafts before there was any finality.

Prince Charles (then being spoken of as a future Governor-General of Australia) spent about 2½ hours at the Kingston complex, including the opening ceremony, tour of the $8.9 million site and afternoon tea. With sunshine streaming in through the uncurtained glass walls, the Prince told his sweating audience of Federal and State politicians and other dignitaries that the new Antarctic HQ 'is more like a tropical research centre' before continuing with his speech.[33]

Speaking at the opening, Prime Minister Malcolm Fraser reflected on the concentration of Federal Government-funded maritime activities in Tasmania—the Antarctic Division in Hobart, the Australian Maritime College in Launceston opened the previous year, and the proposed multi-million dollar CSIRO Division of Fisheries and Oceanography and a marine science complex at the Hobart wharves.

The prime minister said many of the priority recommendations of the Antarctic Research Policy Advisory Committee set up in 1979 had been implemented, including the recommendation to develop the Antarctic Headquarters as a centre of excellence in southern ocean marine biology. In 1980–81, $1.2 million would be spent on the first stage of this program. Mr Fraser also used the occasion to announce a ten-year, $58-million program to rebuild all the Australian continental stations.[34]

While the move to Hobart had been an obvious disruption, it was difficult to recall a time in the previous 30 years of ANARE when an Australian Government had been so supportive of and generous to the Antarctic program. With a state-of-the-art new HQ, the rebuilding of the stations assured, and a commitment to build Australia's first ice-breaking research and resupply ship, the Antarctic Division seemed (in the words of a former Conservative British prime minister Harold Macmillan) to have 'never had it so good'.

EIGHTEEN

FIELD WORK

I t says much for the professionalism of the operational staff of ANARE that an ambitious scientific field program on the Antarctic continent was carried through despite the leadership baton-changes and morale-sapping uncertainty the division faced in the period from Law's resignation to the early 1980s.

GLACIOLOGY

Even though Davis Station had to be closed in 1965 so that Casey Station could be built, pioneering field work continued to be done. In 1968 four men wintered on the Amery Ice Shelf—the smallest overwintering party in the history of ANARE. They were there in the winter to drill through the ice shelf, which is fed by the Lambert Glacier, and measure its speed and flow.

Much of the glaciological work undertaken by ANARE centres on this region, which drains a million square kilometres of Greater Antarctica. Only 2 per cent of the Antarctic continent is exposed rock. The rest is a great dome of ice, constantly on the move. The ice dome of Antarctica has been built up slowly, over hundreds of thousands of years, from the quite modest snowfalls that are generated over the world's biggest, windiest, coldest and driest desert. The ice sheet is 2.5 kilometres thick in the higher areas and gravity causes it to slip slowly down towards the coasts—eventually breaking off and floating away as icebergs.

Glaciologists are trying to establish whether Antarctica is in balance or whether more or less ice is coming off the continent than is being deposited as snow. Areas like the Lambert basin are important and dramatic places for research, because although the high polar ice moves at only about ten metres a year, the Amery Ice Shelf is moving much faster than that. ANARE glaciologist Jo Jacka:

> The front of the Amery Ice Shelf is moving at 1.2 kilometres per year. Now that's hiking along. There are a few spots, but not very many, around the Antarctic coastline that are moving that fast. The southern [inland] end of the Amery is moving at about 380 metres a year, and the Lambert Glacier would be travelling at about 150 to 250 metres a year.

THE EDGE OF THE GREAT
AMERY ICE SHELF.
(P LAW)

In modern times, satellite technology and the Global Positioning System have made it much more convenient to plot the movement of Antarctic glaciers from markers embedded in the ice. But in the 1960s the position of markers could only be established by astrofix calculations—sighting a grid of stars by theodolite as reference points. The first 'movement line' markers were established on the southern end of the Amery Ice Shelf by a team from Mawson in 1962, using tractors and dogs.

From 1963 to 1965 expeditions were mounted from Mawson Station to create 'strain grids' and lines of marker poles, crisscrossing and 'boxing' the entire Amery Ice Shelf. (In 1963 the front of the Amery broke away, creating a gigantic iceberg 150 kilometres long and 60 kilometres wide. This giant berg was measured from *Nella Dan* off the coast of Kemp Land in early 1965).[1]

An ambitious plan was devised in 1966 to study the Amery Ice Shelf intensively during 1968. A wintering party would not only drill right through the ice thickness of the shelf, but visit and measure all the strain grids placed on the surface to plot the movement of the ice shelf from the time, 1962, when ANARE teams first placed markers. The leader of

323

THE 'AMERY TROGLODYTES'
BEFORE THEIR CARAVANS
WERE BURIED IN DRIFT SNOW.
FROM LEFT: N COLLINS,
A NICKOLS, M CORRY,
J SANSOM, FEBRUARY 1968.
(COURTESY N COLLINS)

BY SPRING 1968, THE 'AMERY
TROGLODYTES' WERE
COMPLETELY BURIED. NEVILLE
COLLINS EMERGES FROM A
SNOWED-IN CARAVAN.
(COURTESY N COLLINS)

the group was Max Corry (surveyor/glaciologist), with Neville 'Gringo' Collins (diesel mechanic), Alan Nickols (electronics engineer) and Dr Julian 'Sam' Sansom, who answered a world-wide plea for a medical officer.[2] It was by no means certain that the party, with its sledges, vehicles and caravans, could be landed on the precipitous 40-metre high front of the Amery Ice Shelf. It was vital to establish a base far enough up the shelf to avoid the possibility of floating out to sea if a section of the shelf broke out during the year.

Early in February 1968 *Nella Dan* nosed cautiously into the uncharted waters of Sandefjord Bay at the south-eastern end of the shelf. Here, near some small rocky outcrops now known as Landing Bluff, the ice edge was only a few metres high. In a nine-hour operation, seventy tonnes of equipment was unloaded and quickly hauled three kilometres up the shelf. This was a fortunate precaution as the ice edge at the landing broke up some hours later.

The 'shelf-dwellers' had two fibreglass caravans for accommodation. Transport and haulage were by two Nodwell RN 25 tracked vehicles (with cabins) and three OMC motor toboggans. After a reconnaissance by helicopter, Max Corry chose a site near where markers from the 1964 expedition were thought to be, 100 kilometres from the front edge of the shelf. He named it G1. Helicopters began shuttling equipment from Sandefjord Bay while the Nodwells and their sledges began moving the heavy items. It took Gringo Collins 4½ days to get there. He quickly discovered that the Nodwells were not equal to the task. On the second run in, one broke down 30 kilometres from the base camp. The Nodwells had been fitted with the biggest engines possible, but their weak point was the differential which had remained unchanged. This was a serious setback. Fortunately *Nella Dan* was able to return to Sandefjord Bay after visiting Mawson and drop off a smaller Snowtrac which was not designed for heavy hauling, but was at least operational.

On their own by the first day of autumn, the four men realised that the 25-knot katabatic wind sweeping down the shelf was an almost permanent feature, and overcast conditions and heavy snow caused them to rename G1 'Lower Slobbovia'. For three weeks in March they had low cloud and winds up to 130 kilometres per hour. The Lower Slobbovians had to change their names again, to the 'Amery Troglodytes', as they became totally buried in snow.

They had expected about 50 centimetres of snow during the year. Instead there was some five metres of drift accumulation. Their ventilation chimneys just kept getting higher and higher. Even so, there was an ever-present danger of carbon monoxide poisoning. In the first few weeks under the snow the exhaust from an auxiliary generator got into the ventilation system and Max Corry became quite ill. Collins:

> We had all sorts of tubes—ones like the police use now to breathalyse you—to test for carbon monoxide. The doctor said, 'We've got to check this'. He broke one open, took one look at the colour and said: 'Right, all out!'

A vent had blocked up with ice. Another hour could have been lethal.

Autumn storms prevented any field work to search for and survey previous marker poles on the shelf. The 'Amery Troglodytes' began their drilling program using a thermal drill, obtained from the US Army Cold Regions Research and Engineering Laboratory. This literally melted its way down around a core of ice 100 millimetres in diameter and allowed ice cores of up to 1.2 metres long to be brought to the surface. The power plant was installed in the surviving Nodwell. Drilling went on in two 12-hour shifts with two men on each shift. One unexpected problem was that the surface temperature, between minus 20°C and minus 30°C, was much colder than the ice being drilled and sometimes caused the ice cores to shatter as they were brought up. Most, however, were recovered successfully.

After several months of drilling, the troglodytes reached a depth of 310 metres, calculating they were about 50 metres away from the bottom of the shelf when their drill head finally jammed. They had some 200 litres of ethyl alcohol to stop the thermal drill from sticking. The melted water from the drilling process—containing the ethyl

STRAIN GRIDS AND 1968
TRAVERSE ROUTES ON THE
AMERY ICE SHELF.

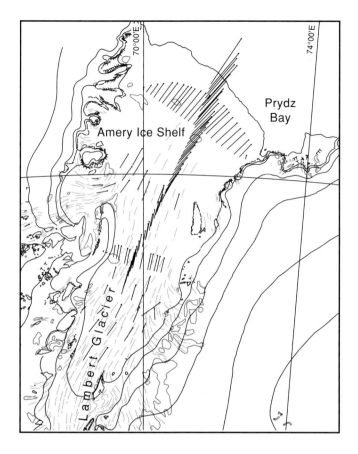

alcohol in only small quantities—was drinkable, so it was used for domestic purposes.[3]

They did have regular radio contact with Mawson Station and ham radio contact with the outside world. A favourite pastime was listening to the regular Thursday skeds between the Antarctic Division in Melbourne and the other stations, which they dubbed 'the circus of the air', presided over by 'ringmaster' Doug Twigg. Radio Australia's 'Calling Antarctica' was hard to get at times, but reception was achieved after lassoing the main wind generator to stop the major source of interference.

In such cramped and confined circumstances, personal relations have to be worked at. Corry says that the four rubbed along pretty well, 'with the usual amount of disagreement and unrest'. They were certainly all delighted to be liberated from their troglodyte lair when spring arrived. The first challenge was to dig out their vehicles from the deep drift before setting out to find and survey the lines of poles monitoring the movement of the Amery Ice Shelf.

The one surviving Nodwell only ran for 40 kilometres pulling sledges before its transmission disintegrated. Collins, one of ANARE's legendary 'diesos' (and veteran of the 1962 Vostok Traverse) worked miracles with the Snowtrac, which is basically a people-carrier not designed for heavy towing. Collins nursed it for over 1000 kilometres, while the three motor toboggans were used to range out over the length and breadth of the Amery Ice Shelf to search for and remeasure all the markers. This was done during spring and summer before *Nella Dan* plucked them from the Shelf in late February 1969. One surprise from the drilling was that the underside of the shelf was not melting as had been previously thought, but was growing due to water freezing underneath it. This growth has since been found beneath many of the major ice shelves, causing a significant revision of the estimated overall balance of the Antarctic ice sheet.[4]

Although the 1968 survey work on the Amery was done with simple techniques compared with the satellite technology available in later years, ANARE glaciologist Ian Allison makes the point that the measurements were very accurate:

> That 1968 work forms an excellent baseline [against which] we can directly look at any changes that have occurred in this part of Antarctica. It is one of the few accurate surveys we have anywhere on the continent, where you can go back and remeasure and have some confidence we'll be measuring realistic changes. (During the 1995–96 season, a survey party found eight of the original 80 steel marker poles left by the Amery Ice Shelf wintering party in 1968. The poles were first remeasured in 1969–70, and then not for 26 years.)

Just how testing the experience of the four 'Amery Troglodytes' was is hinted at by Neville Collins reminiscing after more than twenty years:

> It was maybe three years before I got around to developing my films. . .I just wanted to forget about the Amery—that's how it was. It was more than two years before I could even look at those films. It was such a difficult year. . .a small party, poor food and hard yakka.

THE PRINCE CHARLES MOUNTAINS

As Corry's party prepared to leave the Amery Ice Shelf in early 1969 they helped unload stores and equipment at Landing Bluff for the first major summer survey of the Prince Charles Mountains using fixed wing aircraft and helicopters, led by Graeme McKinnon.

The Lambert Glacier is the largest in the world. It streams down towards the Amery Ice Shelf, held back by the Prince Charles Mountains, which extend in an arc of some 1200 kilometres from their northern extremity 300 kilometres south-east of Mawson Station. These rocky peaks

327

jut up from the huge rivers of ice flowing past them, creating one of the most spectacular features in the Australian Antarctic Territory.

It is an area of continuing interest to ANARE glaciologists, geologists and, more recently, biologists. The 1969 expedition set the pattern that continues to this day for later summer PCM expeditions with air support. Using a fixed-wing Beaver aircraft and three Hiller turbine helicopters, geologists and glaciologists worked on the coast, as well as flying deep into the PCMs. The first party out into the field flew by Beaver, appropriately, to Beaver Lake, a club-shaped area of smooth ice at the eastern extremity of the Aramis Range, connected to Radok Lake by a narrow steep-sided valley. The metamorphic rocks there had been discovered first in 1956 by Peter Crohn, but had not been studied in detail. The rocks contain coal seams nearly two metres thick and about 250 million years old (the same age as coal found in Newcastle, New South Wales), with well-preserved fossil leaves and fossil wood. The Beaver Lake bivouac had an unusual feature for Antarctic field work, a coal-fuelled camp fire.[5]

Major summer expeditions to the PCMs continued for the next five years until 1973–74. Fuel, supplies and portable huts were dragged in by tractor trains operating from Mawson Station to support each summer program—at Moore Pyramid in the Northern PCMs and Mt Cresswell in the Southern PCMs. In 1969 the ANARE helicopter contract was awarded to Jayrow Helicopters and three Hughes 500 machines went south on *Nella Dan* for the second year in the PCMs. One of the pilots was Peter Clemence, a former RAAF officer who had wintered at Mawson in 1957, then flying fixed wing Beavers and an Auster. It was also the first time a fixed wing Pilatus Porter short take off and landing aircraft had been used by ANARE.

In the 1970–71 season former RAAF pilot Doug Leckie (who wintered at Mawson in 1956) returned to fly the Pilatus Porter in the PCMs. Scientist and film maker David Parer recalls how Leckie could land the Porter virtually on a postage stamp behind Mawson Station where there was no airfield at all:

> West Bay has quite steep slopes but it's got a short area just near the doglines where Doug would come in. He'd swoop down right next to the ice cliffs and do these amazing 30 metre landings.

The use of helicopters made it possible to move geologists quickly to a number of different locations through the PCMs in the limited summer season, although in 1973 geologist Bob Tingey admitted that it gave rise to the expression 'cut lunch explorers' from those who wintered on the ANARE stations:

This refers to the rations and the bars of chocolate we used to take with us for refreshments during the working day. We got the impression that we were not [considered] 'the real thing', we were not 'bona fide heroes'. But it was a very efficient way of working and instead of having a lot of geologists isolated on peaks never speaking to each other, you used to come home in the evening and have a meal cooked at the Mt Cresswell base camp. . .

Phase Six of the PCMs survey ended in the summer of 1974. Fortunately there had been no loss of life in the field, although there had been some close calls. On 17 January one of the Hughes 500 helicopters crashed on a rocky pinnacle at Burke Ridge. The machine was a complete write-off, but the pilot and surveyor passenger escaped with a few scratches.[6] In that situation other helicopters were available for a quick retrieval, but accidents during field work in remote locations remain a test of human endurance and logistical ingenuity. In February 1971, two Hughes 500 helicopters supporting the PCMs program were called away suddenly to *Nella Dan* for an emergency dash to the remote sub-Antarctic Heard Island, where an expeditioner, Ian Holmes, lay alone on a glacier after having broken his leg during a field expedition.

RESCUE OF IAN HOLMES FROM HEARD ISLAND

Summer parties had visited Heard in 1963, 1965, 1969 and 1971 for scientific work and attempts to climb Big Ben (2745 metres), then thought to be the highest mountain on the Australian Antarctic Territory. Former Heard OIC and medical officer Grahame Budd was a member of all three parties which went to Heard in the 1960s. News that the French planned to visit Heard Island in 1971 to conduct experiments into atmospheric physics alerted him to the possibility of getting to his beloved Heard Island again. The French expedition was led by a geophysicist, Roger Gendrin, who asked the Antarctic Division if they could use the ANARE huts at Atlas Cove. They invited some ANARE observers and director Bryan Rofe approved five—glaciologist Ian Allison, physicist Hugh Thelander, medical officer Grahame Budd, and two field assistants, Iain Dillon and Ian Holmes.

Sailing south on the French ship *Galliéni*, the party of sixteen landed at Atlas Cove on 25 January 1971 for a stay of six weeks. Using a French helicopter, Budd and Thelander made the first ever visit to the nearby Macdonald Islands on 27 January. Budd had been trying to get there for years, but Thelander pipped him to the first-footing post: 'Hugh stepped

329

out first. I couldn't work out why he was in such a hurry to get out. Putting his foot down first was the thing.'

The two scientists found that the Macdonald Islands were rich in breeding colonies of sea birds and fur seals, and that there were only three islands, not five.

Back on Heard, Budd and the other Australians assisted Ian Allison with measurements of ice movement on the Baudissen and Vahsel Glaciers. Budd:

> You're jumping crevasses all the time and I'd landed badly after one jump and damaged my knee. I'd in fact partly dislocated the upper tibiofibular joint. That meant the knee was a bit painful, but it was a bit weak too. And this had repercussions.

Budd and his two field assistants, Iain Dillon and Ian Holmes, planned to walk around the island to obtain further evidence of glacier fluctuations, of the increase in fur seals and king penguins, and of their own responses to cold. They also planned to survey unvisited areas on the west coast such as Cape Arkona. This entailed crossing two of Heard's biggest and most difficult glaciers, the Abbottsmith and the Gotley. For reasons of weight and convenience they did not carry radios which, in Budd's experience, were useless on Heard because of its mountainous terrain. Before they left he briefed Gendrin and the rest of the party at Atlas Cove: 'We made a very detailed map of our route and we had fixed locations where we were going to leave messages.'

To their surprise they crossed the heavily crevassed Abbottsmith Glacier relatively easily and pressed on to the Gotley, which Budd found in terrible shape:

> It was far worse than it had ever been before. This was a consequence of glacier retreat. So one mile took us three days to cross and involved all sorts of fancy Alpine techniques.

On 10 February they hoped to spend only one more night on the Gotley. Unfortunately Holmes was without his ice-axe, which had fallen down a crevasse. They were carrying bamboo poles to keep fur seals at bay and Holmes was using one as a substitute ice-axe. The surface of the glacier was a frightful mess of fractured, unstable ice and while crossing an ice ridge Holmes slipped and fell into a crevasse—dangling several metres down on the end of his climbing rope. His crampon hit the wall on the way down and broke his leg. Budd:

> When his fall stopped we called out 'Are you OK?' He said, 'Yeah—but I think I've broken my leg'. I was appalled. My first question was, 'Above

or below the knee?' He probably thought it was very heartless, but if it was a tibia and fibula at least that was a local problem, but if it was the femur, then he was likely to have shock and all sorts of problems. So I was very relieved to hear that at least it was below the knee.

The accident could not have happened in a worse spot. The whole area was 'practically vertical'—narrow ice ridges with deep crevasses in between them, like a maze. The glacier was also moving all the time, with sounds of nearby ice avalanches and the cracking and groaning of moving ice under pressure. When Budd and Dillon hauled Holmes to the surface there was barely room to lie him down on a ridge of ice between two crevasses.

After giving Holmes an injection of morphine to dull the pain, Budd cut up the bamboo pole to make some splints. At that stage of their journey the three men were running short on food, intending to replenish their supplies from a cache at Long Beach left there in 1963.

There was just room on the ice ridge to put up their small three-man tent; then Budd and Dillon left Holmes while they climbed off the glacier and down to Long Beach to bring back extra food—and also some tins of plaster of Paris. Budd hoped to set Holmes' broken leg in a cast and then move him off the Gotley Glacier to a more stable area where they could, if necessary, await the return of *Galliéni*.

Unfortunately Heard Island damp had ruined the plaster even though it was in a soldered tin. Without a cast, it was impossible to move Holmes off the glacier, but leaving him on the ice was an unattractive alternative as the glacier was not only thawing but moving quite fast.

The only option was to leave the 24-year-old Holmes in the tent on the glacier so Budd and Dillon could return to Atlas Cove to raise the alarm—and hope that the ice he was on stayed intact. Budd knew a helicopter would be needed to lift Holmes out:

331

We reckoned it would be the best part of a week before we could get back. We discussed this with Holmes, and he said he'd be right. The tent was now stocked with enough food to keep him going, and he had enough fuel. We left him with everything and just went off with what we were wearing and a block of chocolate. . .

The two men decided to continue around the island in an anti-clockwise direction. It avoided having to renegotiate the Gotley and Abbottsmith Glaciers, but was a distance of 64 kilometres, over extremely rough terrain. They planned to pick up some supplies at a depot at Spit Bay.

Ian Holmes lay in his tent—which subsequently collapsed and lay over him like a tarpaulin—with food, a primus and painkillers within reach. When he had to get water or go to the toilet he put steel crampons on his hands and levered himself out onto the sloping ice. He had a down sleeping bag, but it was impossible to keep it dry. Holmes:

> I was lying on the ice, and during the day my body heat melted a hole in the ice and I was just lying in a big puddle. The sleeping bag got wet, and then at night it all froze solid. . .one night the whole thing froze and I woke up and couldn't breathe.

He realised the zip on his sleeping bag had frozen, banged it until the ice fractured, and got his head out to gasp in urgently needed air.

The days passed slowly as the Gotley Glacier crashed and creaked around him. Once a day he would brew some soup on a fuel stove, and he tried to pass the time by reading a detective novel. The effort became too much through his fog of pain and boredom, and he used the book as a marker of time by turning a page for each passing day.

It was just as well Holmes did not know that Budd was quite seriously injured himself. Budd's injured knee was still weak as he began the Heard Island circumnavigation. Jumping one crevasse, it gave way under him as he landed. So he evolved the technique of landing stiff-legged. Eventually this cracked his pelvis in three places. Budd:

> I was a bit unstable walking, because part of the trouble with a cracked pelvis is that your normal stabilising reactions get slowed down because you know it's going to hurt—although the pain mostly refers to the lower back. And in the process of one of these falls I'd also cracked some ribs. . .the only way I could walk was to arch my back firmly and then waddle along like Donald Duck.

By the time they made it back to Atlas Cove three days later, Budd could scarcely walk at all. The French station leader Roger Gendrin met them and asked about Holmes: 'We said, *"Jambe cassée, mais il est OK"*

[He's broken his leg but he's all right]. The French took us into the mess and fed us mug after mug of scalding hot coffee, and got the story out of us.'

The first priority was to get on the radio to find out what ships were about. With the damage to Budd's pelvis sending his back muscles into spasm, it took him five minutes to move twenty metres to the radio hut. Contact with Melbourne was achieved via Mawson Station on the amateur radio band.

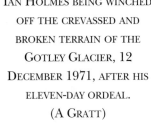

IAN HOLMES BEING WINCHED OFF THE CREVASSED AND BROKEN TERRAIN OF THE GOTLEY GLACIER, 12 DECEMBER 1971, AFTER HIS ELEVEN-DAY ORDEAL.
(A GRATT)

There were no ships with helicopters other than *Nella Dan*, which had just reached Davis en route for Mawson. Voyage leader Eric Macklin was instructed by the Antarctic Division's acting director Don Styles in Melbourne to go immediately to Mawson and pick up two Hughes 500 helicopters then supporting the 1971 Prince Charles Mountains survey and geological party, and head for Heard Island to attempt Holmes' rescue. The helicopters were taken on board *Nella Dan* on 16 February—six days after Holmes' accident.

The news that an injured young ANARE scientist was lying alone on a glacier at Heard Island captured the nation's attention. INJURED MAN FIVE DAYS ALONE ON GLACIER, headlined the Sydney *Daily Telegraph*.

Nella Dan was steaming at full speed from Mawson, but a day out on 18 February the ship's engine broke down. A cracked connecting rod on one cylinder could not be repaired so the ship continued at reduced speed on six of its seven cylinders 'and jumped all the way to Heard Island'. A makeshift winch was installed in one of the helicopters and *Nella Dan* made it to Atlas Cove by 21 February to pick up three ANARE men—Ian Allison, Iain Dillon and Grahame Budd—then steamed on down the coast to the Gotley Glacier. The operational plan called for a landing at Long Beach by amphibious LARC if the winds were too strong for flying. As *Nella Dan* steamed closer to the coast, the high winds moderated and a helicopter was able to take off from the ship. Holmes was located after a five-minute search, and was seen to be not only alive, but waving furiously.

It was not possible to land and Grahame Budd (then unaware of the extent of his own injuries) was winched down to Holmes from a hovering Hughes 500 with crampons, a stretcher and a VHF radio strapped to his back.

Holmes remembers Budd saying, 'Hello boy. You've had a pretty lousy week, haven't you?' The injured man was winched up dangling on a stretcher and flown off the glacier to a better landing site. Within minutes he was safe on *Nella Dan*, amazingly fit after his eleven days on the Gotley.

Ian Holmes estimated there was about one day a month in that area when it was possible to fly a helicopter and 'see where you are going, and it just happened to be one of those days'.

MACQUARIE ISLAND

While low-lying Macquarie Island lacks the initial drama of Heard Island's soaring volcanic peak, its wet-cold, windy weather and unstable cliffs demand it be treated with respect. More ANARE expeditioners have died on Macquarie Island than any other Antarctic station.*

The field manual reminds expeditioners that snow may fall at any time of the year and hypothermia is a real risk. Other hazards are unstable rock outcrops and cliffs, freak waves on the coastline and the possibility of being swallowed up by 'quaking bogs' on the coastal terraces and inland areas.[7]

To those dangers can be added rampaging elephant seal bulls (during the mating season) which are capable of crushing someone to death with their four-tonne bulk, or raking them with their fighting canine teeth. Skuas, the vultures of the Antarctic, will attack any injured animal and the field manual recommends that no injured or unconscious person ever be left alone on the island unless absolutely essential—and then well covered by clothing and rucksacks.

Yet this misty, windy, wet, green island is a wonderful zoo, a haven in the tempests of the 'Furious Fifties'. Macquarie literally teems with wildlife, with many species of sea birds, penguins and seals. Those who spend time there are passionate in their love of the place. Unlike their colleagues on the Antarctic continent, Macquarie winterers can get out at any time of the year, walk the 34-kilometre length of the narrow island to spend time alone, or with a few selected companions in the field huts

* (Refer to table of ANARE deaths in Appendix IV)

at Bauer Bay, Caroline Cove, Sandy Bay, Green Gorge, Lusitania Bay, or Hurd Point in the extreme south. The low-lying island is also of enormous interest to geologists, as it is the only known place in the world where sea-floor rocks of a major ocean basin are exposed above sea level in a marine environment.

The area is unstable and strong earthquakes occur regularly—sometimes causing rock and mud slides along the cliffs that circle the coast. On 7 February 1980, OIC Rod Ledingham reported a strong earthquake well over six on the Richter scale:

> The shuddering of the buildings was considerable, lasting for about 15 seconds. . .Everybody exited from the buildings at speed. About 100 books fell from the shelves in the mess and the 30 ANARE photographs by the bar were all hanging at odd angles. The area by the kitchen was a sea of broken glass, ketchup and assorted sauces.[8]

There was similar chaos in the scientific laboratories, but no one was injured either at the main station on the isthmus at Buckles Bay or in any of the field huts. The wildlife was not so lucky. Mud slides and rock falls killed penguins and seals under the coastal cliffs between Hurd Point and Lusitania Bay. Ledingham:

> Several colonies of penguins had been wiped out, and seals crushed by falling rocks. Between the station and Nuggets were numerous rock falls which had buried penguins on the beach. About eight seals had been killed by falling boulders, inland above Red River near Bauer Bay.[9]

Big cracks in the ground were reported at different places on the island. The fact that remains of ships wrecked in relatively recent times were now 50 to 100 metres inland from the high tide level caused Ledingham to speculate that the island might be rising at a rate faster than first thought:

> The recent discovery of marine beaches 760 feet [231.6 metres] above sea level on North Mountain, Perseverance Bluff and elsewhere add weight to this hypothesis.[10]

Although geology, upper atmospheric physics and ozone studies continue to be explored on Macquarie Island, it is really a biologist's paradise.

Much of the early work of observation, bird banding and marking of seals was done by the expedition doctors. Arthur Gwynn, the doctor on Macquarie in 1949, had a biology degree as well as a medical degree and continued his association with ANARE (briefing those who followed him) until 1955. Stefan Csordas (MO on Macquarie in 1955, 1957, and 1959) continued this tradition.

Csordas was the outstanding example of the medico-naturalist. He not only organised the mass banding of giant petrels (which produced some spectacular recoveries), but was out counting elephant seals and looking for branded ones in all weathers except actual blizzards.

It has been recognised that there are three species of fur seal at the island—the New Zealand fur seal which is a visitor only, the Antarctic fur seal and the sub-Antarctic fur seal.[11] The return of the fur seals to breed was confirmed by Csordas in 1955 when he saw a pup which, instead of lolloping into the water as fur seals usually do, retreated up the beach into a cave. Csordas realised that the pup could not swim—fur seals (unlike elephant seals) have to be taught to swim by their mothers. At that stage breeding fur seals had not been reported on Macquarie Island for more than 100 years: 'So you can imagine that, when the end of the year came, I practically spent every day around that cave area to see whether the mother returned to have another pup.'

Csordas was worried that the ship would arrive to take him back to Australia before he could confirm that the fur seals were breeding.

> One day I went there and a little furry ball was in the entrance of the cave. . .big black eyes and the poor little fellow didn't know what to do—to be friendly with me or escape into the cave. So I made a few steps closer and then Mama appeared on the scene. So I just sat down and I nearly cried, because it was such a beautiful picture—that after a hundred years, they finally came back.

When Robert Carrick took over the Antarctic Division's biological work in 1955, he arranged for technical officers from the CSIRO Wildlife Survey Section to go to Macquarie while remaining on the CSIRO payroll. Graduate biologists went to Macquarie on a regular basis after 1960.

The importation of exotic species by the sealing gangs from the nineteenth century placed stress on the vegetation and the wildlife. Rabbits, cats and wekas were the most damaging. Before myxomatosis was introduced to the island in 1978, rabbit numbers were estimated to be around 150 000. (The European rabbit flea was introduced to Macquarie in 1968 to prepare for the virus.) The rabbits are still not fully eradicated. Feral cats eat rabbits and also continue to prey on birds. The wekas (flightless birds from New Zealand's Stewart Island, about the size of a bantam hen) wreaked havoc on the burrowing petrels, eating the young birds as well as the eggs.

All wekas were eliminated from Macquarie Island by the end of 1988. Their numbers had been thinned by feral cats attacking them after the rabbit population dwindled because of myxomatosis. The cats remain the hardest pest to eliminate. Even with their reduced numbers in the

Wekas were audacious scavengers with little fear of human activity. Their many escapades have been recorded in ANARE song, poetry, and station log books. Ken 'Cagey' Simpson, a CSIRO technical officer who wintered in 1965, later wrote that all wekas trained their young as delinquents:

They eat everything whether it be food or not. They fight, swear and steal. All wekas are compulsive kleptomaniacs and collect things they do not need. . .Respectability is feather-deep and their hides are thick. No weka walks. It sneaks, skulks or snoops. The legs are good eating—the rest is a waste of time.[12]

Simpson records that two weka families actually ate an entire concrete doorstep at Bauer Bay—but admits that through lack of cement the sand had been bonded with egg powder and self-raising flour. Another CSIRO

expeditioner, Trevor Gadd, records a harrowing close encounter of a weka kind in 1964. He had taught a weka to take food from his hand. Early one brisk Macquarie morning, while he was relieving himself outside a field hut, Gadd sleepily became aware of his pet weka approaching. At that instant he recalled the weka's most accurate seizure of titbits held between his fingers 'by that sharp and pointed beak'. Gadd shut off quickly and painfully in midstream and beat a strategic retreat.[13]

The most poignant weka story is undoubtedly the one detailed in the essay 'There's A Weka In The Bottom Of Our Thunderbox' —again by Ken 'Cagey' Simpson. He seemed to have a thing about wekas. The full account can be read by the scatalogically curious in the ANARE Club journal *Aurora*, of November 1966, describing how Ken descended into the malodorous depths of the one-holer to extricate the screaming and ungrateful bird.

early 1990s, they are estimated to kill at least 65 000 prions, petrels and shearwaters each year. A concerted attempt to rid the island of exotic unwanted species began in 1972 when the Tasmanian National Parks and Wildlife Department took over the running of Macquarie Island from the State Animals and Birds Protection Board. Before then the island had seen a veritable farmyard of domestic animals introduced, including sheep, goats, pigs, ducks, geese, fowls, cows and horses. In 1956, ANARE expeditioners even planted fruit trees.

Most of the edible livestock was shipped down in the days when refrigeration was not available. A steak or leg of lamb was deemed preferable to eating the wildlife—particularly when expeditioners tried their hand on the cook's day off.

One of the most elaborate exercises to bring introduced species to Macquarie Island took place in the summer of 1969–70 when three horses, Brandy, Lime and Soda, were unloaded for use as draught animals. It was hoped the horses could help resupply the field hut at Caroline Cove on the extreme south-west corner of the island, which had proved

SHEEP AND TWO YOUNG
ELEPHANT SEALS ON
MACQUARIE ISLAND, 1957.
(S CSORDAS)

UNLOADING HORSES BRANDY,
LIME AND SODA AT
MACQUARIE ISLAND, 1969.
(R LANGTIP)

extremely dangerous to reach by amphibious DUKWs from the sea. The Antarctic Division's engineer in charge of transport, Alan Browne, took this challenge in his stride when it came to loading the horses on to *Nella Dan*. Purpose-built horse-boxes were hired easily, because as late as 1970 Australia was shipping horses to India for Indian Army remounts. The boxed horses were lifted on to the aft hatch of *Nella Dan* and winched off onto army LARCs (the first time they had been used at Macquarie instead of the older DUKWs) for the run ashore. Brandy was a bay, Lime a grey and Soda was a black.

They never made it to Caroline Cove because it proved impossible to get them up onto the plateau anywhere near the main station on the isthmus. They could not manage the usual route up the cliffs to the plateau through Gadgets Gully and attempts to walk them down the east coast to Sandy Bay were unsuccessful. According to Knowles Kerry, the horses could not get past rocky outcrops along the way:

> It took three months to bridge the more unsurmountable sections with a single horse track. Once at Sandy Bay, they were able to get the horses up onto the plateau. However, there they promptly sank in the bogs up to their bellies!

Brandy, Lime and Soda ended up having a most relaxed year on the isthmus, with a few expeditioners having an occasional gallop along the beach, before being returned to Australia.

Although the population of seals and penguins has built up since they were ravaged by the sealers in the nineteenth and early twentieth centuries, more recent studies have shown that the elephant seals on Macquarie have declined by 50 per cent in the last 30-odd years.[14] Current research is investigating the causes of that decline.

Macquarie Island is now a State nature reserve, administered by the Tasmanian Department of Environment and Land Management. From the late 1980s the department instituted strict quarantine regulations for all visitors to Macquarie to try to prevent unwanted seeds getting to the island. Boot washing and sterilisation is compulsory for all ANARE personnel and tourists arriving there. Even so, vigilance is essential. In 1984 wildlife management officer Geoff Copson found a thistle on the isthmus and an apple seedling sprouting near the hut at Sandy Bay. The following year two European wasps arrived in bundles of timber and several exotic moths were discovered. An adventurous Queensland green tree frog also made it to Macquarie via a bunch of ANARE bananas in August 1995.

KNOWLES KERRY INTRODUCES A HORSE TO AN ELEPHANT SEAL PUP AT MACQUARIE ISLAND, 1969.
(R LANGTIP)

COSMIC RAY LABORATORY AT MAWSON STATION

Measurements of cosmic rays were undertaken from the very beginnings of ANARE. Phil Law himself began as a cosmic ray physicist, and cosmic ray scientists were active on Macquarie and Heard Islands from 1948 onwards. When Mawson Station was established in 1954, cosmic rays were measured continually from 1955.

As the distinguished ANARE physicist Bob Jacklyn is the first to admit, 'cosmic ray' is a misnomer for the charged particles of matter bombarding the earth from deep space. One-third of the radiation received by human beings on this planet comes from cosmic rays. These intriguing particles pass through our bodies continually—and then plunge deeper into the earth. Cosmic ray activity is intensified in the Arctic and Antarctic as the earth's magnetic field deflects them towards the poles.

The problem in the Arctic is that there are no significant land masses near the North Pole for observatories. In the Antarctic Mawson Station is extremely well placed to observe cosmic rays because not only is it far south, but the uniform structure of the granitic rock on which the station

339

is built is ideal for studying the composition of higher energy particles as they penetrate deeper into the earth. In the mid-1960s the Antarctic Division's senior cosmic ray physicist, Bob Jacklyn, pushed for the only under-rock laboratory ever to be built in polar latitudes.

The plan called for an eleven-metre shaft to be sunk into the rock at the foot of which two vaults would be excavated, leading off in opposite directions. One would contain the high energy 'telescopes' that would receive the cosmic rays after they had been measured first above ground in a laboratory. Work began in 1971 and a miner, John 'Clem' Cruise, wintered at Mawson to carry out the blasting and excavation work. OIC Lem Macey later wrote that there were some unforeseen problems to be overcome:

The blasting became a regular and alarming feature of the Mawson routine. Only one large rock reached the station, crashing through the roof of Biscoe Hut, to the surprise of carpenter Bill 'Slipta' Cartledge who was working there. Lem Macey recalled:

As the wind generally carried the small stones down over the dog lines, the huskies became very cunning and would all jump up and look skywards when the shooting started—no doubt to take a bit of evasive action should it be necessary.[15]

Owing to a slight oversight, a parcel of special detonators for firing the centre shots in a predetermined sequence, were not available for the project.[16]

In other words, they had not been sent down on the ship. ANARE improvisation was called for:

One notable experiment, recommended not to be repeated, was for one chap to hold twelve fuses in the hand while Clem Cruise lit them. A wonderful idea, but the time involved in lighting the fuses had not been taken into account. . .after five of the twelve had been lit, molten tar was commencing to affect the hands of both the holder and the lighter. Then visibility became a problem when the lighted fuses emitted great volumes of smoke obscuring both lighter and holder from each other.[17]

At that point, Macey said, the fuse-holder moved a motion that 'the operation be abandoned and evacuation by climbing out of the shaft up the ladder be immediately adopted'. A more effective method of lighting the fuses in sequence was devised, and the shaft deepened daily, with no problems that could not be solved by the help of ANARE expeditioners and 'that ever present Mexican veteran Manual Labour'. By 31 May, 68 days after work began, the eleven-metre shaft was sunk and work could begin excavating the underground rock chambers.

Both the vaults and the building above were supposed to be completed by the early summer of 1971–72, but when Attila Vrana came in to Horseshoe Harbour on the relief ship to install the detecting and recording systems with ANARE physicist David Parer, they anxiously scanned the hillside with binoculars. All they saw was a crane lowering materials and people into a shaft, surrounded only by bare hillside. When they left Melbourne, the division management had assured them the building would be finished by the time they arrived.

The plan was for Vrana to install the cosmic ray measuring equipment and return with the last ship in late summer 1972. But by then, with the laboratory unfinished and much of what had to be done in his head, Vrana decided to overwinter to finish the job, assisted by David Parer. By the time Vrana returned to Australia at the end of summer in 1973, he had spent sixteen months at Mawson. He left behind a working cosmic ray observatory—at 67° south, the highest latitude station in the world. It has operated continuously ever since.

THE RISE OF BIOLOGY—THE DAVIS LAKES

Through the 1950s and 1960s biology had remained the poor cousin of Antarctic science. Although a great deal of work had been done on the sub-Antarctic islands, there was no coordinated program for the continent. At the recommendation of Robert Carrick, who oversaw ANARE's biological activities from the CSIRO, the newly appointed director Bryan Rofe contacted Knowles Kerry after he had wintered on Macquarie in 1970 and asked him to establish a mainland biology program. Only two ANARE biologists had ever worked on the continent, John Bunt who studied microbes in sea water near Mawson in 1963, and Rowan Webb (also at Mawson) in 1969, who investigated lichens and mosses. Kerry:

> I'd read a lot but I didn't know much about it, so I said, 'Well, the first thing we ought to do is go and have a look at our stations'. So I went to Mawson, Gavin Johnstone was sent to Davis, and Durno Murray went to

Casey. . .The idea was that we would have a look and see what was there, and then we'd come back and discuss it.

The most interesting area seemed to be in the Vestfold Hills, near Davis, which had an unusual array of lakes ranging from the hypersaline—which did not freeze in winter—through to all the freshwater lakes which were virtually frozen to the bottom. Kerry established a program to see if there were living organisms in most of the lakes.

Investigating biologists were nothing if not versatile. When Dick Williams arrived at Davis in 1973 to study zooplankton, he could not find any. So he changed tack to studying the phytoplankton of Deep Lake. Since then the Davis lakes have continued to provide an enormously complex and exciting area for research. Kerry:

> Everybody's still excited about the lakes. . .People like Peter Franzmann [formerly] at the University of Tasmania are finding organisms with interesting and unusual properties. Any organism which can survive in a lake which gets down to a temperature of minus 19°C but doesn't freeze, has got to have something going for it.

Knowles Kerry was keen to use films to popularise the cause of Antarctic biology and encouraged David Parer—then at Mawson as a cosmic ray physicist in 1972—to take wildlife footage during the winter. Parer continued filming the following summer and two films, *Antarctic Winter* and *Antarctic Summer*, were produced in conjunction with the Australian Broadcasting Commission.

'A Close-run thing'

As the study of the lakes gained momentum there was an urgent need for field huts away from Davis Station, deeper into the Vestfold Hills. During 1972 and 1974, Ray Brookes—the first carpenter to winter at Davis—built what is now known as Brookes Hut at Long Fjord, 15 kilometres to the west of Davis. He had to improvise with panels fabricated from scrap timber scrounged from around the station.

To get this material to the hut site, Brookes used a Willys Jeep towing a sled around the coast on the sea ice, and to guard against breaking through, he rigged eight-metre-long Oregon beams underneath the vehicle and cut an escape hatch in the roof. The Willys and sled were used without incident. But in the early summer of 1972–73 both Ray Brookes and Davis medical officer John Jackson were extremely lucky to make it back to the station.

Jackson was helping Brookes build the hut. They had a radio message from the station to say that warm weather was starting to melt the sea ice and they had better get back quickly.

The two men had skidoos—motorised toboggans—and set off quickly for the fifteen-kilometre run around the coast. All went well as they rode down the ice-covered fjord, until they turned the corner for the final run to Davis Station. Brookes:

> We were sort of in the open sea, about three-quarters of a kilometre from the base. The ice was cracking. . .and in places only an inch thick. . .because of the reflections, you couldn't see whether you were over a hole in the ice or you weren't.

The two men stopped their machines on a patch of firm sea ice and considered their options. There was really only one: 'I said to the doctor, ''Well, we've got to get back and

BROOKES HUT, DAVIS, 1986.
(COURTESY R EASTHER)

SNO-TRAVELLER ON SEA ICE WITH *NELLA DAN* IN THE BACKGROUND, 1965. (AAD ARCHIVES)

if we leave it any later we're not going to get back—we're going to be floating out to sea''.'

Brookes and Jackson checked they had enough fuel, revved their engines and shook hands. Brookes:

I said, 'Well, we have to have rules about this. If one goes in, the other keeps going, because you won't get out. . .he who hesitates is lost.' So we got in line abreast, and flattened them.

With their fellow expeditioners waving and shouting encouragement from the shore, Brookes and Jackson surged forward at 25 kilometres an hour. As they hurtled over the ice, open water broke out behind their skidoos. The party in the mess that night was a good one.

Parer built his film around a winter dog sledge journey, including filming emperor penguins out on the sea ice among grounded icebergs at Auster Rookery, near Mawson. Parer:

> The males were incubating the eggs. It was one of the most extraordinary things I have ever seen—in that just pink twilight of midwinter when the sun is not even coming above the horizon—to see 25 000 of these animals, all with eggs, surrounded by these grounded bergs in this exquisite pink pastel light. . .

The films were well received, and set David Parer on his way to a distinguished career as a wildlife film maker.

Just how much influence Parer's films had on the rising fortunes of biology is difficult to gauge, but by 1980 a growing awareness of the importance of the biological diversity of Antarctica and its surrounding seas saw a big jump in the commitment to marine sciences, with a $3.5 million allocation in the Federal budget. The comparative decline in the resources allocated to physics during the late 1970s reflected Sir Frederick White's APAC report of 1975 which suggested that 'upper atmosphere physics and cosmic ray physics take up too large a proportion of the written program'.[18] Biology was booming.

ICE DRILLING AT LAW DOME

In February 1960 a survey party of Americans and Australians led by OIC Harry Black set out to find a route from Wilkes up on to the ice cap. Unknowingly they tracked across the western slope of an isolated feature now known as Law Dome. Thinking they were safely on the main, slowly rising ice sheet, they were surprised to find themselves heading downhill again. In 1961 another major traverse led by OIC Neville Smethurst (and including glaciologist Bill Budd) noted that the 1200-metre-high ice dome was an isolated feature, a fact confirmed by seismologist Don Walker in 1962.

Due to the underlying bedrock, the ice of the dome is moving radially out from its centre, and its separation from the main ice cap and its almost circular shape make it a model in miniature of the larger Antarctic ice cap. There is a static area where very little movement occurs at the very top of the dome. Glaciologist, Jo Jacka:

> Law Dome is particularly interesting because it's divided to the north, of course, by the ocean. To the south there just happen to be two large glaciers which feed the Antarctic ice sheet to the north-east and north-west around Law Dome. . .It's almost like an island. . .and we can learn an awful lot about glaciology—about how ice flows, about climate change—just by studying Law Dome.

As soon as the significance of the 'Wilkes ice cap' was realised, Budd was determined to make the most of it and designed a scientific program. The first drilling attempt was by Fred Jacka in the summer of 1963, but he had no equipment to recover an ice core—essential for a proper study of the annual accumulated layers of ice.

A thermal drill, bought from the US Army Cold Regions Research and Engineering Laboratory (used by the Amery Ice Shelf 'troglodytes' in 1968) did produce a core, and a variation of the drill was designed and produced by the Antarctic Division's first electronic engineer, Ian Bird, in Melbourne. This was used for the first time in 1969 on the dome's summit and at Cape Folger. Drilling continued out of Casey Station through the 1970s. Ice cores were recovered and returned to Australia for detailed analysis. Ian Allison:

> If you take a sample of ice from several hundred metres you'll find very small bubbles of air in there that are basically sealed capsules of the air that was in the earth's atmosphere when that snow fell. . .so you can start looking at these atmospheric samples and determine what the carbon dioxide content was before the Industrial Revolution.

By going deep enough, it is possible to sample what the carbon dioxide content of the air was before the last Ice Age and build up a record of how natural changes have occurred before humanity came on the scene. The dust from known volcanic eruptions is used to check the dates of the annual layers of ice. Law Dome provides an accurate record of the world's climate for 30 000 years—and less precise measurement back as far as 120 000 years.

It is not possible to drill more than 500 metres with a thermal drill before the ice deforms and closes the drilling hole.*

THE CASEY 'TUNNELLERS'

The investigation and drilling of Law Dome, begun from Wilkes Station, continued from Casey Station when Repstat was completed in 1969. Those who wintered at Casey encountered an entirely new Antarctic experience. In all the other stations, ANARE expeditioners lived in separate buildings. That meant donning cold weather gear to move from sleeping hut to the mess, or to workshops and laboratories. The unique design of Casey—elevated on stilts to minimise drifts—and its long line of thirteen buildings connected with its distinctive corrugated-iron tunnel running down the entire length of the station, meant that it was theoretically possible to spend the entire year there without going outside.

IT WAS AS COLD INSIDE THE CASEY TUNNEL AS OUTSIDE.
(R WILLIAMS)

The tunnel was 260 metres long and unheated. Diesel engineer Dave McCormack recalls that it was not properly sealed in the early years, and sections of the corridor filled up with snow. It was common practice to shovel it up, carry it into a nearby room and throw it out a window. The tunnel could be extremely cold:

> I remember jumping out of the shower one night there. You'd quickly towel yourself down and you'd race up the corridor to get to your donga. I had long hair in those days. I remember it was a bit of a surprise getting back to your donga with your hair frozen solid.[19]

The sleeping 'dongas' were small—barely two by two-and-a-half metres. There were eight dongas to a sleeping block, and rudimentary privacy was provided by a curtain. ACS electrician Shane Hill:

---

* In February 1993, using an Australian-made, computer-controlled mechanical drill, ANARE scientists finally reached bedrock 1200 metres below the summit of Law Dome.

It was a sort of unspoken law that if anyone had their curtain closed in their room you certainly didn't just barge in. You'd use the normal habit of knocking on the wall. But basically whatever went on in the donga area everyone knew about it anyway.[20]

THE DISTINCTIVE SHAPE OF THE OLD CASEY STATION AND ITS FAMOUS TUNNEL, 1969. (R INNES)

The tunnel looked forbidding from a distance, a great grey tube following the contour of the hill like the leading edge of a broken aircraft wing. Plumber Rod MacKenzie, who worked on its construction, thought it looked depressing. 'People coming ashore, seeing it for the first time, used to say it looked like Alcatraz sitting up among the rocks.'[21]

Graeme Manning, OIC in 1979, thought the tunnel design, connecting work, living and community areas, was good for morale:

I don't think a day ever passed, in the fourteen months that I was there, that I didn't see every one of my expeditioners. If not at the breakfast table or the dinner table, at least in the tunnel, walking along, and with doors open, looking into their work places. In the old tunnel, you couldn't help but pass them. There was more sense of being with other people.[22]

Manning was contemptuous of the view—generally expressed by those who had never lived at Casey—that you could spend the entire year there and never go outside:

347

Those people didn't know what they were talking about. As station leader [I found] one of the problems was keeping people indoors to do their work—because one of the attractions of going to Antarctica is the elements, the beauty, and actually getting out in the cold and the wind and the snow and everything else.

Although Casey Station did avoid the build-up of drift, it was an alarming place during a blizzard. Because it was constructed on scaffold tubing and tied down with guy wires, it used to vibrate and rattle and was extremely noisy. On 1 October 1969—only nine months after it was opened— a blizzard blew away six corrugated-iron sections of the tunnel. Assessing the condition of Casey Station ten years later, Antarctic Division engineer Ian Holmes wrote: 'As an engineering exercise, Casey has proven to be a lot less than successful'.[23] The most serious structural problem was the gradual disintegration of the wall panels by high winds and blizzards, augmented by water vapour getting into the insulation in the winter, and then melting during summer. Another disadvantage was the enormous heat loss caused by the raised structure. Yet most 'tunnel rats' who wintered there over its nineteen-year existence maintained a cheerful affection for the 'old' Casey Station. Construction of 'new Casey' began in 1979 with the erection of the operations building.

AIR TRANSPORT TO ANTARCTICA

One of the continuing frustrations of scientific work in the Australian Antarctic Territory is the inability of researchers to fly in and out of the continent during the relatively short summer season. The only alternative is to go down by ship during the annual resupply and personnel changeover voyages. This involves long periods at sea (sometimes being beset for quite long periods) and often means that three or four months are needed to complete a task that might only require a week, or even days. While fixed wing aircraft and helicopters were regularly used from ANARE stations to support field work, an air link with Australia remained elusive.

A rock airstrip at Davis Station was mooted in the 1950s and 1960s. Other plans involved a compressed snow airstrip on the ice cap behind Casey Station, and a 'blue ice' strip near the Framnes Mountains behind Mawson Station. All these sites could accept flights direct from Australia—or via the United States ice airfield at McMurdo, near the north-western edge of the Ross Ice Shelf. At the 14th meeting of SCAR in Argentina in 1976, a logistics group discussed an ambitious air transport plan for

Antarctica with yet another of the acronyms so beloved of polar bureau-cracy, CATSA (Cooperative Air Transport System for Antarctica). The plan called for three 'trunk' terminals on the coast of Antarctica—prefer-ably with rock runways—to accept long-range aircraft with payloads of some twenty tonnes. Then smaller STOL aircraft (e.g. Twin Otters) or helicopters would ferry personnel and equipment to the various stations, which would be provided with the necessary fuel.[24]

In January 1977, a preliminary cost study on constructing a rock airstrip at Davis was made by John Manning (Division of National Mapping), Dick Gurevich (Department of Housing and Construction) and Gavin Bailey (Department of Transport). The most promising site seemed to be in a broad glacial valley running from Lake Dingle westwards to a large bay to the north of Davis Station.

A runway of 2000 metres was feasible—increased to 2500 metres if the strip was extended into the shallow waters off the coast. There was plenty of loose rock available for fill and it was estimated that the airfield could be built for $8 million over three years.[25]

A more immediate and cheaper option was explored in conjunction with the United States when, from 30 November 1978, the RAAF flew four Hercules flights from Christchurch, New Zealand, to McMurdo and back. In return, the National Science Foundation provided two flights from McMurdo to Casey, where an ice runway had been prepared at Lanyon Junction. The first proving flight took place on 24 January 1979. Passengers included the Antarctic Division's Director Ray Garrod, two visiting Chinese scientists, and a female husky, Rita, from New Zealand's Scott Base, to replace a dog at Casey which had died the previous year. The US Hercules LC130 spent only one hour on the ice strip at Lanyon Junction and did not shut down its engines, to guard against any diffi-culties restarting in such a remote location.[26]

A second Hercules flight from McMurdo landed at Lanyon on 31 January with the first Federal Minister ever to visit an ANARE continental station, James Webster, accompanied by Tasmanian ALP Senator Don Jessup. They were accompanied by the Secretary of the Department of Science, John Farrands, and the Director of the New Zealand Antarctic Division (and former Casey OIC), Robert Thomson, who had led the remarkable Vostok Traverse from Casey and back in 1962. The VIPs were whisked from Lanyon for a necessarily brief inspection of Casey Station by two Bell helicopters that had just arrived on *Thala Dan*. The US Hercules that had brought them waited at Lanyon, engines idling for two-and-a-half hours, before taking off to complete the 4300-kilometre round trip back to McMurdo.[27]

Back in Australia, both the Minister and Senator Jessup were enthusiastic about the prospects of this US-aided air service, with Senator Webster saying air transport might be 'about to usher in a new era in Australia's Antarctic operations', and that the proving flight to Casey showed the feasibility of air access to Australia's three mainland stations. Demonstrating the remarkable bi-partisanship on Antarctic activities that has continued ever since Australian politicians first set foot on the continent, Senator Jessup (chairman of the parliamentary committee on Science and the Environment) called for greater scientific efforts to be made by Australia—particularly in marine biology.[28]

After the formalisation of the 'Cooperative Air Transport Agreement between Australia, New Zealand and the United States', the RAAF flew six flights from Christchurch to McMurdo in the summer of 1979–80, carrying 94 passengers and over 100 tonnes of cargo. In return, a US ski-equipped Hercules made two flights to Casey in November and January. The November flight took nine scientific and construction personnel to enable summer science and construction programs to begin two months earlier than would have been possible by ship.[29]

In January 1981 the new director of the Antarctic Division, Clarrie McCue, flew in to Casey with Minister for Science David Thomson and eleven members of the Parliamentary Works Committee to inspect the rebuilding program. The seventh and final US Hercules flight to Casey was made in November 1981. There is no official explanation for the demise of the air transport agreement, but the original intention had been to fly in scientists, and the Americans were unimpressed by the number of Australian construction workers and politicians flown in to Casey on their aircraft. This view is shared by ANARE chief scientist Patrick Quilty:

> Where we ran foul of the Americans—and many of us were given messages on this which we passed on to the director at the time—was that Australians were not using these flights specifically for the support for science. They were using them basically to get support people into the stations—builders, plumbers and so on.

The straw that broke the Hercules' back was almost certainly the flying in of the eleven members of the Parliamentary Works Committee. They had four hours to inspect the Casey building site, before reboarding the aircraft that was waiting at Lanyon—again with its engines idling.

Quilty was acting director of the Antarctic Division while Clarrie McCue was away with the eleven parliamentarians. After the Hercules took off for the return to McMurdo, Quilty received a radio message from Casey that the aircraft had slewed off the marked runway and hit some of the steel marker poles. People could see hydraulic fluid on the snow and Quilty had to get a message through to the plane so they were aware of any problems when they landed at McMurdo.

> My immediate response—and I've always felt guilty about it afterwards—was that we might lose eleven politicians. . .and have to have eleven by-elections and perhaps change the government, just on the basis of an accident in the Antarctic.

There were no more US Hercules flights to Casey after November 1981. The long-running debate on whether or where to have an airstrip in the Australian Antarctic Territory suitable for direct flights from Australia continued.

A potent argument for a direct air service to an all-weather airstrip in Antarctica is to repatriate seriously ill or injured expeditioners. When the darkness of the Antarctic winter comes down, the Australian stations remain as isolated as were the classic expeditions of Scott, Shackleton and Mawson, and the Antarctic remains an extremely dangerous place to live and work.

RESCUE OF ROGER BARKER FROM MACQUARIE ISLAND

Although Macquarie Island can be reached by sea all year, the inability of aircraft to land there means the rescue of injured expeditioners cannot be achieved quickly.*

The evacuation of biologist Roger Barker from Macquarie Island in January 1979, following serious injuries he sustained in a fall from a cliff, was one of the most complex and involved ever attempted by ANARE.

When Barker, who was researching nest sites of the light-mantled sooty albatross, failed to return to camp on 3 January, a search and rescue operation was begun immediately. He was found lying at the base of a cliff at Smugglers Cove with serious injuries to his head, spine, left leg and right arm. Barker later said:

> I was unconscious for a while. When I woke I found that skuas [large predatory gulls] were pecking at my legs. All I could think was that I had to keep awake and keep the skuas away from me.[30]

---

* On Wednesday 7 September 1977 an RAAF Orion from Edinburgh, South Australia, made the first successful air drop on to the isthmus. Two storpedos landed safely on dry land—including the all-important mail, donated chocolates and a cake from the Science Minister.

Medical officer Bob Millard did what he could on the spot. Barker was strapped into a stretcher and carried to the top of the cliff—a two-hour exercise. Back at the station it was clear he was critically ill, in urgent need of hospital care and that his leg might have to be amputated. The Antarctic Division's acting senior medical officer, Peter Gormly, arranged a radio-telephone link with a team of specialists from Melbourne's Alfred Hospital and Monash University Medical School to advise Millard on Macquarie Island.[31]

The Department of Defence was asked if a navy vessel could carry out the evacuation. HMAS *Hobart* was undergoing a refit at Garden Island dockyard but quickly made ready for the voyage to Macquarie Island. Unfortunately *Hobart* had no capacity for carrying a helicopter to get Barker from shore to ship. Luckily the supply ship *Thala Dan* was only twelve hours' steaming from Hobart returning from the French Antarctic station at Dumont d'Urville. It was agreed she would put into Hobart, disembark her passengers and take on a helicopter chartered by the Antarctic Division.

Thala Dan and *Hobart* arrived in Buckles Bay within fifteen minutes of each other on 8 January. While the division's medical officer Des Parker helped Bob Millard prepare Roger Barker for the evacuation, naval ratings built a small temporary helipad on *Hobart*. The narrow-gutted destroyer was rolling up to 12 degrees from vertical in the heavy seas and the maximum roll a helicopter could safely handle was 8 degrees. Barker:

> The chopper pilot [Nigel Osborn] had only one practice run using the prefabricated helipad. He wanted to get on and off as quickly as possible.[32]

Fortunately Osborn was an ex-Royal Navy pilot with plenty of experience flying onto oil rigs in the North Sea. Barker was landed safely and *Hobart* took off at 27 knots towards her namesake port, completing the journey in a record 39 hours. On 10 January Barker's left leg was amputated below the knee, and he was transferred to the Austin Hospital in Melbourne five days later. Although the rescue had been successful and Barker seemed cheerful and on the road to recovery, he unexpectedly suffered a massive stroke on 6 February and died two days later.

Enderby Land

Following six summers of activity in the Prince Charles Mountains from 1969 to 1974, the Antarctic Division prepared to look to the extreme west of the Australian Antarctic Territory—Enderby Land. With its extensive mountain ranges (and proximity to the Russian's Molodezhnaya Station) Enderby Land represented the last major investigation by ANARE of a region where most of the mountains and coastal features had been named and noted, but much detailed survey work, glaciology and geology remained to be done. From the 1974–75 summer season until 1979–80, ANARE transferred its major field effort from the PCMs to the Enderby Land region.

MT KING BASE CAMP, ENDERBY LAND, 1976. (AAD ARCHIVES)

In the spring of 1974 a tractor train from Mawson dragged supplies, fuel and living huts to Knuckey Peaks, 350 kilometres to the west of Mawson, to support the summer program. It was an unfortunate choice. By some meteorological mischance and local effect, the weather at Knuckey Peaks was almost always foul. Pilots leaving the base camp in marginal conditions would often find clear weather 50 kilometres to the north. The Enderby Land program began with three Hughes 500 helicopters and the trusty Pilatus Porter fixed-wing monoplane, but it was not to be a good year in the annals of ANARE aviation.

On 29 December 1974, one Hughes 500 was wrecked when the pilot attempted to take off with one skid still tied down. On 22 January the Pilatus Porter was flown to Mawson and was secured on the exposed Gwamm ice runway eight kilometres south of the station. A blizzard developed and destroyed the aircraft.[33] The remaining two Hughes helicopters did what they could to battle Knuckey Peaks' appalling weather and the competing demands of the geologists, glaciologists and surveyors. By 21 February, the remaining choppers made it back to the helideck of *Nella Dan*, where their respective rotors collided, rendering all the summer season's aircraft unserviceable. No one was hurt.

Despite the chapter of accidents, the helicopter pilots managed to fly a creditable 536 sorties from the inclement camp. But it had been an expensive start to the Enderby Land program and in the summer of 1975–76, Mawson tractors hauled supplies further west to a site near

353

Mt King, 400 kilometres from Mawson, which remained the base for the Enderby Land programs until 1980.

MAWSON'S HUT AT COMMONWEALTH BAY

Concern about the deteriorating condition of Sir Douglas Mawson's Australasian Antarctic Expedition hut at Commonwealth Bay (towards the eastern extremity of the AAT) and a growing debate about whether the whole hut should be removed to Australia or restored *in situ* prompted the Antarctic Division to arrange a field party to investigate what might be done. An ANARE party of four on *Thala Dan* landed at Commonwealth Bay in January 1978. The leader was Rod Ledingham, accompanied by his wife Jean Ledingham (medical officer), Guy Macklan (engineer) and Ray Brookes (carpenter). They took with them a small 4 × 3 metre prefabricated hut to live in and to house any subsequent restoration parties.

The AAE hut had been built in three weeks and finished by late February 1912. Days after it was completed it was partially buried by drift snow and has been lashed almost every day since by the fierce katabatic winds that characterise the climate at Commonwealth Bay, 'The Home of the Blizzard'. As it was constructed from tongue and groove boards, Rod Ledingham thought it was remarkable the hut was still there at all:

> The wind had just scoured the surface off the timber and left all the nails exposed. Grains of snow had shot up the cracks, just like grains of sand would, and they'd etched away all the grooves in the roof and left small gaps between each of the boards. But the inside boards were virtually untouched and pretty well intact.

The roof hatch had been gone for many years and drift snow and ice had filled up most of the structure. Ledingham and his party began excavating their way into the building from the western winter entrance of the workshop using a powered ice chisel, chain saws and ice-axes. It was a wet, uncomfortable job as the ice chips melted on their clothing. There was no trace of the lathe, sewing machine, generator engine and wireless equipment that once were there. Not much of significance was dug out of the workshop, just objects like bottles, rusty tins, old batteries, a dog collar, newspapers and lengths of timber. And they did find the badly rusted and battered tail plane from the body of the Vickers aeroplane that Mawson tried to use as a motor sledge. Once the workshop was cleared of ice, the artefacts were replaced in their original positions and photographed.[34] On the rare calmer days, carpenter Ray Brookes tried to seal the cracks in the main roof.

With the workshop clear, the party began tunnelling into the main living area of the Australasian Antarctic Expedition hut on 20 February. After pushing in for about three metres, they broke through to find, to their surprise, that two-thirds of the main room was clear of ice. Ledingham:

MAWSON'S HUT AT COMMONWEALTH BAY, BUILT IN 1912. (AAD ARCHIVES)

> The whole of the upwind end, funnily enough, was a big air pocket. . .it looked as though the pressure of the wind blowing in there had somehow managed to keep the snow out. So Mawson's room and the shelves around his bunk were completely clear of snow, apart from icicle-like chunks hanging down from the roof.

Eric Webb's bunk and bedside shelves were also ice-free. Webb was the magnetician with Mawson's party and, as luck would have it, visited the Antarctic Division in December 1977 just before Ledingham's party left to go south. Ledingham knew the old man would be fascinated by the photographs taken of the interior which was a remarkable time capsule. Ray Brookes:

> Items found included bottles, jars, earthenware containers, old boots, a pair of wind proof trousers—belonging to Mawson?—bins of white flour, unopened tins with labels intact, crates of food still wired and with AAE written on them, bottles of pure Nitric Acid (for geological and other scientific work) books and magazines.[35]

Ledingham's team was not equipped, nor did they have the time, to begin any major restorative work. The roof presented the most immediate problem, with the softwood boards worn thin by the abrasive particles of ice continually whipped up by the almost continuous blizzards. As the Oregon frame and rafters of the hut were still in good condition, Brookes thought the best technique would be to use them to support a false timber roof above the old cladding. Then the hut could at least be sealed to prevent further drift getting in.

Brookes was keen to get back the following year to begin work, but the shipping schedules were disrupted by Roger Barker's evacuation from Macquarie Island. Mawson's hut was visited again in 1981, then left untouched until a private expedition, 'Project Blizzard', sailed down to Commonwealth Bay in the summers of 1984–85 and 1985–86 to investigate further the problem of conservation. Ledingham:

> These expeditions went down partly supported by ANARE—and rightly so, I think, because we're responsible for the hut, being a government organisation. It's now been classified as an historic building. . .The private expeditions were unable to do anything, because they were told to report back to the [Australian] Heritage Commission at great length, and nobody would make a decision. So, in fact, it's just slowly blowing away and falling down, year by year.

Nella Dan had sailed to the hut in 1986–87 and put in a base to support future work, but the sinking of *Nella Dan* put an end to the planned 1987–88 visit. Heavy sea ice stopped *Lady Franklin* in 1988–89 and in 1990–91 the notorious weather at Sir Douglas Mawson's 'Home of the Blizzard' prevented a landing from *Icebird*. The perennial logistic difficulties and the cost of getting to the site led to the Government's conclusion in 1992 that it should put no more funds towards conserving the hut. Antarctic Division policy manager Andrew Jackson:

> It's the cornerstone of our Antarctic heritage. . .but the best bet now is privately-funded conservation work. The division will happily work with anyone else who can find the money to make it happen.

ICEBERG BLOCKS MAWSON HARBOUR

The story of the rogue iceberg at Mawson Station in 1980 is a splendid illustration of the 'A-Factor' (ANARE's own Murphy's Law) and its effect on ANARE field activities. The saga appropriately involves one Sydney L Kirkby, who returned to Mawson as OIC in 1980—twenty years after he had last wintered there in 1960—although he had made summer visits in later years helping to survey and chart vast areas of the Australian Antarctic Territory.

Horseshoe Harbour, at Mawson, is the only protected anchorage on the entire coast of Greater Antarctica. Since the station was established in 1954 its annual resupply has taken place in late January when the fast-ice obligingly breaks out, enabling barges to carry heavy cargo to shore over open water. (There have been good and bad 'ice years', but the resupply has always been achieved.)

In mid-January 1980 unusual currents caused a small iceberg to drift into the narrow entrance to Horseshoe Harbour and ground itself between East Arm and West Arm. With a gap of only 30 to 40 metres between berg and rocks, the master of *Nella Dan* , John Jensen, decided against trying to navigate in to the harbour. The consequences of this decision were drastic. *Nella Dan* carried the bulk fuel for heating and powering the station, and while it was possible, using helicopters and ships' boats, to move in enough food, Kirkby realised the station could not support more than about ten people for the coming year—and only if a number of buildings were 'winterised' and left unheated.

AERIAL VIEW OF THE ROGUE ICEBERG BLOCKING THE ENTRANCE TO HORSESHOE HARBOUR AT MAWSON, 1980. (COURTESY S KIRKBY)

Thirty people were due to winter. With the probability of no fuel coming in, Kirkby made an executive decision and ordered twenty people to be transferred to the ship:

> The voyage leader wasn't very happy about this. I think he could probably understand the logic of what I was saying. I wouldn't let the people back into the station for a feed or anything because I figured that as soon as I did that it would be a case of who blinks first. If I blinked, we'd lose.

This 'Mexican stand-off' was solved by the weather. A 50-knot gale blew up, and *Nella Dan*'s master decided to run the gauntlet between the iceberg and the rocks to get shelter in Horseshoe Harbour. That meant the fuel could be pumped ashore, and all thirty people were able to winter. *Nella Dan* managed to squeeze her way out, but the iceberg remained.

Although it was a small iceberg by Antarctic standards, it was a substantial mass of ice—Kirkby estimated it at around 300 000 tonnes. During the rest of the year the Mawsonites tried to work out ways of getting rid of it. Explosives were spectacularly unsuccessful. Kirkby:

> You'd get this noise and a marvellous displays of chips of ice—and a little blackened hole about the size of a bathtub, from a case of explosives. We tried depth-bombing it, filling twelve-gallon drums with explosives

and lowering them down on ropes on the rock floor against the iceberg's side—completely without effect.

The iceberg stayed where it was. In the early summer of 1980–81, *Nella Dan* called by but did not enter the harbour. Helicopters flew in four conventional agricultural stump-pullers and a length of heavy-duty polypropylene rope. There was no hope of moving the iceberg until the sea ice around it could be broken up. The ice was marked out with grids of dark material to attract extra warmth from the sun—engine oil, rock flour and tea leaves, among other substances.

A sturdy bollard was sunk deep into the rock 50 metres from the aircraft hangar on East Arm. As soon as there was clear water between the berg and the bollard, the 12-centimetre diameter rope was wrapped around the recalcitrant iceberg and the stump-pullers began to take the strain. Kirkby:

> We just cranked tension into the polypropylene rope until it was down to about half its original diameter, singing like a G string. Of course everyone was terrified of it, because if it broke and hit anyone it would have cut them straight through. Interestingly, the rope would slip a bit on the berg from time to time and. . .there'd be twenty fellows pancake-flat on the rock.

Using the tide and a little bit of swell, the iceberg was gradually pulled across the harbour and 'tied' to the bollard on East Arm. Kirkby was uncertain what would happen next. At least it was out of the way for the resupply ship to enter the harbour:

> The ship came in. Everything was sweetness and light. Then we had a blizzard one night and the bloody rope snapped and the berg went 'pop' straight back out and put the plug in the hole at the entrance—with the ship inside the harbour this time. But at least we now knew we could move it.

This time bulldozers on land and the army amphibious LARCs pushing from the harbour were used to spin the berg back to be tied up again near the bollard on East Arm. Kirkby:

> We went to bed one night with it there, and woke up the next morning to find there had been another freak current change and the berg had taken itself for a little excursion around East Arm and into East Bay—in the process wiping out all the aerials, before going back to where it had been.

By late February 1981 nature took over and the errant berg, well festooned with ropes and cables, disappeared overnight the way it had come —out through the entrance to the harbour. It was not quite the end of the story. Later in 1981 Syd Kirkby had a cable from Paul Butler, the OIC who took over from him, that he had been along the coast 120 kilometres east of Mawson, near Fold Island, at Stefansson Bay, and found 'a gift-wrapped iceberg, still with its rope around it'.

LASSOED ICEBERG, MAWSON HARBOUR, 1980. (COURTESY S KIRKBY)

LIVING DANGEROUSLY 1982–1988

NINETEEN

LIVING DANGEROUSLY

As the head office staff of the Antarctic Division began settling in to their brand new $8.9 million headquarters at Kingston, Tasmania, in the early 1980s, parts of the building also began settling down into marshy reclaimed ground on the eastern side of the complex.[1] In July 1983, staff in the supply section temporarily refused to work in offices where floor-to-ceiling plate glass windows had developed large cracks, and where pressure caused some panes to bulge in ominously. Training officer Graeme Manning:

> They put wooden studs inside the glass and put chicken wire on them so that the staff working there were safer. The danger to them was reduced. . .if the glass did break at any time it'd fall in against the wire. . .rather than falling on the staff at their desks.

Pressures were also building up on the division itself—senior bureaucrats in the Department of Science and Technology were concerned about the general condition of the Antarctic Division. Former departmental deputy secretary Roy Green:

> My impressions were that they were back in the Phil Law days—almost the explorer days. They were really quite amateurish in many ways—not in the science—but more in the management, in the strategic planning, financial planning and reporting. . .a very significant chunk of money was going into the [division] and I have often told the story that I think they did the budgeting on the back of an envelope!

This view was and is contested by division scientists and managers who were responsible for international liaison on Antarctic Treaty matters and associated scientific committees. Green was aware of a drop in morale largely caused by the division's move to Hobart and the loss of skilled staff who stayed in Melbourne. But he was also aware of alleged 'doubtful practices' concerning the purchase of supplies. And while he was not critical of the quality of scientific work being done by ANARE, he believed the programs could be better focused:

> There was a need to make sure [the science program] was really serving the purposes of Australia's efforts in the Antarctic rather than meeting the whims of particular scientists. . .it needed to be more planned.

Green also thought the Antarctic Division should have a higher profile in the international arena—at Antarctic Treaty and SCAR meetings:

> A lot of Australia's research programs were designed on an international basis, but we wanted to have more say on what that international plan was—to actually influence what other countries were doing, in line with our priorities.

The Department of Science and Technology initiated the Joint Management Review (JMR), which began the most comprehensive investigation of the Antarctic Division's activities ever attempted. The JMR began in August 1983 and was conducted by officers from the management consultants John P Young and Associates, and representatives of the department, the division and the Public Service Board.

The JMR report was released in February 1984 by the secretary of the Department of Science and Technology, Greg Tegart. Its 86 recommendations outlined a raft of fundamental organisational changes and was highly critical of the way the Antarctic Division was run. The review found that management had become task-oriented, that there was little if any long or even short term planning and that management had failed to adequately 'consult, plan and direct as well as ensure effective communication at all levels. . .with a resultant degree of confusion, dissipation of effort and frustration'. The consultants went on to say:

> At present there is, in our view, a lack of clarity as to the role of each Branch and Section, and little attempt or opportunity to establish priorities, to identify real costs and implications, or to ensure effective communications. These deficiencies have led to the present poor use of the available resources. Policy and strategic planning have been neglected, and there has been a failure to create and communicate a clear objective throughout the Division.[2]

In its reshaping of the division's functions, the JMR recommended the formation of five branches: executive, resource management, operations (including logistics and engineering), science, and polar medicine. There would also be a new advisory body, ASAC (Antarctic Science Advisory Committee) to replace the existing ARPAC (Antarctic Research Policy Advisory Committee) and to oversee and approve all scientific projects carried out under the ANARE umbrella.

Reaction to the review from within the division was predictably mixed. As it progressed there was a perception by senior staff like John Boyd that the management consultants were marching to preconceived orders, and that the demonstrated professionalism of those in the division who organised the complex web of logistics, shipping and air support to sustain ANARE scientific programs and stations in Antarctica was disregarded. Boyd:

> It makes it look as though we're just a bunch of idiots who couldn't plan a Sunday school picnic—and I think it was just an appalling bit of work. . .to say that we had no operational plans verges on the idiotic.

The Department of Science and Technology wanted more than evidence that the division could carry out its functions. The JMR was designed to drag ANARE, kicking and screaming if necessary, out of an era of perceived *ad hoc* decision-making and disparate scientific projects, to a 'system of accountability for program performance in terms of scientific merit, relevance and results achieved'.[3]

(To show it meant business the department instigated an Implementation Review of the JMR in December 1986, by which time 51 out of the 86 of the JMR's practicable recommendations had been implemented, with 24 more either proceeding or implemented in part.)[4]

An immediate casualty of the JMR was the division's director, Clarrie McCue. Former deputy secretary Roy Green:

> Certainly the view we had at a senior level in the department was that he was not the right manager for the time. That wasn't to say he hadn't done a respectable job in getting the division finally moved [to Hobart], but we weren't convinced that Clarrie had the management capabilities to carry on the sort of business that the Antarctic Division represented at that point in time.

McCue had not been enthusiastic about the JMR process. He was sidelined as an adviser on Antarctic affairs with the Department of Science and Technology. On 18 February 1984, Jim Bleasel, an electrical engineer and formerly director of the National Materials Handling Bureau, was given two days' notice by department secretary Greg Tegart to take over as acting director. Bleasel had been aware of pressure on him to take the job, and wasn't keen. He had read the JMR report and knew whoever headed the Antarctic Division was in for 'a nightmare ride':

> So I didn't wish to go down there. In fact one of the first assistant secretaries of the department at that time said that 'the only thing that will fix that place is World War III'! I knew what happened to people sent in to clean up difficult situations—they always demand the sacrifice of the person that causes the changes. And while that wasn't exactly what happened in my case, it was somewhat close.

Bleasel was attracted to what he believed could be a wonderful and interesting job, but he didn't want to be the initial head-kicker. 'I'd been around a long time. I didn't need lessons in this.' He hoped the department would choose someone else to do that, and he could 'go and be the good guy later'. He was asked to reconsider, and refused the position. So when he was rung by Tegart's personal assistant to say he was to move to Hobart and take over the Antarctic Division immediately he was 'really shocked' because he thought there was no possibility of going.

The new acting director hit the deck running—determined to be the agent of change in his first year:

> 'I wanted to increase Australia's international Antarctic standing and the amount of ANARE science being done. . .even if I had to create lots and lots of woes and cause lots of trouble to people in entrenched positions. It had to be done, there was no choice. So naturally I wasn't number one on the popularity poll down there, and there were constant letters going off to head office about me and phone calls and all sorts of rumours. . .my position became controversial.

Bleasel's new-broom approach was welcomed by some staff. Martin Betts, then information officer, thought he was a breath of fresh air. 'He wanted to shake up the Antarctic Division by its roots and make it do something.' Policy manager Andrew Jackson thought he was a person with lots of energy and a man of vision. 'He really tried to be a charismatic leader, rather than just a bureaucrat. But he had great difficulty in changing the attitudes of his key staff.'

Even those who later agitated to get rid of Bleasel, like acting shipping manager and union activist Geoff Dannock, cautiously welcomed him as an agent of change at first. Dannock:

> It was obvious when I came here from the Public Service Board that the place had been overlooked by just about anybody that had any responsibility for running it. There were illegal employees. . .some people—a minority—had been getting away with too much for too long.

While he continued to have his supporters in the division, Bleasel's honeymoon was short lived. Andrew Jackson had his reservations about Bleasel's management style, but was sympathetic to his plan literally 'to put Australia on the map in the Antarctic', by creating new bases away from the four existing stations, and giving Australia a more prominent profile at international meetings. Jackson: 'Although Bleasel was a visionary leader, and appointed because he was a mover and shaker. . .some of the existing staff didn't want to make his ideas work.'

Two of Bleasel's former colleagues in the National Materials Handling Bureau—Jack Sayers and David Lyons—were appointed to senior positions in the division over the first two years, leading to perceptions that he was creating his own management team of 'outsiders'. Bleasel denies this. 'It was inevitable people would say that somehow or other I'd smuggled [them] in'—in fact they were outstanding candidates chosen by independent panels.

Bleasel to this day is unapologetic about criticisms that he did not consult his senior officers sufficiently on major decisions and policy changes:

> These were the people that had been running the place and got it into this mess. I needed their experience, I needed their input. I didn't need them to make the decisions for me. At one management meeting, a senior executive said, 'I thought we were all going to get a vote on this'. So I had to point out that I was responsible for the place now, and they all got a vote—it was just that I had one more vote than all of them combined . . .

One of Bleasel's management concerns was that heads of specialist departments often took part in decisions in areas outside their responsibilities—particularly in operational matters. He was also appalled at the way the government's money was being used:

> The division didn't always get its goods at the appropriate price, they paid more than they should have, or they bought more things than they should have—and this was later taken care of within the division, the surplus stock. These were serious matters. It was frightening for auditors when they saw what was going on down there.

Bleasel acknowledged that there was a solid core of dedicated people who were working huge hours and giving their all to keep the division operating, but people were 'working all around it from the side'. Bleasel believed rorts were taking place where people were appointed to positions without the appropriate advertising and interviews. 'Other people would get their friends off to Antarctica on trips—"jollies" as they were called—with no proper authorisation. The division was run as a series of personal fiefdoms, actually.'

Another of Bleasel's concerns was the number of division staff who travelled overseas to arrange or finalise contracts for equipment and stores. When he inquired, he was told those trips were paid for by the supplier:

> I thought this was a bit unusual in that it wasn't costing us anything. When it kept happening over a couple of months, I asked for a look at the contracts and then found that this was written into the contract. . .so of course the Australian Government paid for it because this was added onto everybody's price. . .There were more rorts than I could imagine—and it took me a long time to discover them all.

The new director resolved to move quickly to stamp out irregularities in his first year, aware that his actions would inevitably bring much unhappiness. The staff union was aware that some changes were inevitable, but were concerned about Bleasel's activist style.

Bleasel was keen to see the ANARE stations first hand. He decided to join the new, purpose-built, ice-strengthened cargo- and passenger-carrying *Icebird* on her maiden voyage to Antarctica from Cape Town in November 1984. *Icebird*, a German built and designed ship, was fast-tracked and completed in nine months. Because of the massive rebuilding program, the Antarctic Division had augmented the long-serving *Nella Dan* with another ice-strengthened ship, *Nanok S*. More cargo space was needed for building materials, and negotiations were begun with the German company Antarktis und Spezialfahrt Schiffartsgesellschaft GmbH (ASS), headed by Guenther Schulz, while Clarrie McCue was still director. John Whitelaw (Acting Assistant Director of Operations) had been looking for a suitable Antarctic ship through the international chartering company Wesfarmers, but was interested to see a sister ship of the yet-to-be-built *Icebird* in Brisbane during a visit there with colleague Ian Marchant. Whitelaw:

> It was the standard box construction, superstructure aft with side cranes. But it gave you tremendous capability—you just opened the top of the ship and. . .just dropped everything in and closed it up and off you went. Then, in negotiations with the shipbuilders, we got several design features put in that we wanted for our operation.

Whitelaw signed the contract for *Icebird* on behalf of the Antarctic Division in June 1984 and it was due to be delivered in time for the 1984–85 summer season. One of the modifications was the addition of an accommodation module—positioned just in front of the bridge—which would enable the ship to carry about 100 passengers. It was agreed *Icebird* should arrive in Cape Town, South Africa, by 30 October to qualify for a bonus payment of approximately $A100 000 to Guenther Schulz's company. Although *Icebird* arrived several days late, the bonus was paid because it was judged that extra work asked for by the division had caused the delays.

When *Icebird* sailed from Cape Town on 4 November it carried an abundance of 'chiefs' as well as the usual complement of 'Indians'—expeditioners and crew. The ebullient owner, cigar-puffing Guenther Schulz, was joined by acting director of the Antarctic Division Jim Bleasel, and the division's acting assistant director of operations John Whitelaw. *Icebird* was officially Voyage Two of the ANARE season (Voyage One was undertaken by *Nella Dan*). The master of the ship was Captain Ewald Brune, a blond-bearded, piratical-looking seafarer in his early thirties. Brune was no stranger to polar waters; indeed he had the misfortune of losing a ship, *Gotland II*, crushed by pack ice in 1982 near Cape Adare in the Ross Sea while taking a German expedition to Antarctica. There was time to take all passengers and crew to shore by helicopter and no lives were lost. Brune was officially exonerated of any blame and Schulz, also owner of *Gotland II*, put it down to valuable experience gained in a hazardous environment.

While Brune was the master of *Icebird*, voyage leader Ian Marchant (the division's logistics manager) was in charge of all the ANARE aspects of Voyage Two. His deputy voyage leader was Andrew Jackson.

Icebird made good time, arriving at the ice edge off Mawson on 14 November, changing over some personnel and delivering mail, fresh fruit and vegetables by helicopter before heading east along the coast to Davis Station. No serious problems had been encountered with pack ice and the new ship was performing well. Marchant was pleased when *Icebird* left Davis on 19 November, four days ahead of schedule, bound for ANARE's easternmost station, Casey.

Bleasel, full of energy as always, was on a steep Antarctic learning curve. He took an intense interest in Marchant's job as voyage leader. Marchant:

> It seemed like every hour, he'd say, 'What are you doing now?' and I'd basically say, 'Thinking'. And he'd want to know, 'What are you thinking about?' I'd say, 'What the ice conditions are like and what we're going to do tomorrow'. And he said, 'But surely there's a book that you've got'. I said, 'Yes, there's an operations manual'.

Bleasel had not seen the operations manual and retired to his cabin with it, later telling Marchant he intended to rewrite it.

ICEBIRD AT THE ICE EDGE
NEAR MAWSON, 1985.
(A URIE)

In *Icebird*'s hold was a box marked 'Russian Base' put on board by the ship's owner Guenther Schulz, containing fresh fruit and vegetables. If the occasion presented itself, Schulz wanted to show off the ice–breaking capabilities of *Icebird* to the Russians by visiting one of their stations on the coast of the Australian Antarctic Territory rather earlier in the summer season than normal. However *Icebird* was under charter to the Antarctic Division and both Bleasel and voyage leader Marchant were mindful that any delays on Voyage Two would have a flow-on effect on the whole 1984–85 ANARE shipping program.

But with *Icebird* now ahead of schedule, and due to pass by Mirny station on the coast approximately halfway between Davis and Casey, Schulz stepped up pressure on Bleasel and Whitelaw to divert to Mirny to visit the Russians, deliver his box of produce (which Bleasel says he did not know about until a year later), and show off his new ship. To this day, John Whitelaw and Jim Bleasel disagree over recollections of who supported the diversion to Mirny. Voyage leader Ian Marchant says he was overruled by the 'chiefs' he had on board. However, someone from the Antarctic Division had to authorise the captain of *Icebird*, Ewald Brune, to turn to starboard from his track to Casey and set a course for Mirny.

Traditionally that person should have been Marchant as voyage leader. In fact it was Whitelaw who told Brune to head for Mirny on 22 November. Brune said later that he did not know then that the voyage leader 'was the boss':

> I was just following the word of the person who had signed the Charter Party [Whitelaw]. He said to turn, and I did it. Ian Marchant actually hadn't said anything to me—whether to go there, or not to go there.

Whitelaw says he had considerable sympathy for the pressures being exerted on Marchant by having so many VIPs on board and confirms he gave the instruction to Brune to head for Mirny. Marchant noted in his official diary on 23 November that he would 'not contemplate such a diversion, without formal approval from the [head] office'. Bleasel did not know that *Icebird* had turned towards Mirny, as he 'had not developed the habit of going up on the bridge and checking our position on the chart'. Whitelaw, according to Bleasel, put the argument that it was in Australia's interests to demonstrate that ANARE's new vessel could get in to Mirny earlier in the season than the Russians ever had. Bleasel eventually supported the Mirny visit 'convinced by the foreign affairs-type argument'.

Captain Brune estimated the diversion to Mirny would only take two days, and the weather forecast was good. When *Icebird* arrived some 30 kilometres offshore from Mirny the next day, they could not raise the Russians on the radio. The decision was made to send in three helicopters with some fresh fruit, vegetables and other gifts from the ship, and arrive unannounced. Whitelaw:

> It was like something out of *Apocalypse Now*—these helicopters flying in line in to Mirny. . .and of course there's nothing, because Mirny isn't expecting anyone till March, and this was November. We did a couple of circles, and eventually this guy popped outside—probably for a leak—and looks up and the sky is full of helicopters, and it must have given him a bit of a start.

The surprised Russians made the Australians very welcome, and the only English-speaking Russian invited Bleasel and Whitelaw upstairs to the Mirny commander's office. Emerging an hour later, the VIP party was given a guided tour of the station.

Bleasel was about to experience Russian hospitality, Antarctic style:

> The Russian base commander was sitting near a table with us and he brought out three vodka glasses, filled them all up—he spoke no English—and he looked at us for a while and then he said; 'Australia',

tossed it straight down and he turned his glass upside down and hit it on the table. So we did the same. He then said; 'Russia'! We waited about three minutes and then we all looked at each other. . .so, 'Russia'! Down the hatch, upside down glass, whack it on the table.

After toasts to Australia and Russia again, plus peace, friendship, and back to Australia again, Bleasel thought, 'Oh God, I'm out of here'. He left a senior ANARE colleague to match the Russian drink for drink with a 'walkie talkie' to call for help. (He had to be carried, moaning and desperately drunk, to a helicopter later that day.)

On the morning of Sunday 25 November all *Icebird* passengers who wanted to go ashore were flown by helicopter to Mirny and back. To return Russian hospitality, Schulz and Bleasel asked the Russian commander and his KGB deputy to bring some of their men to *Icebird* for lunch. About eighteen Russians arrived. Marchant was worried about the deteriorating weather, but the Russians were soon incapable of worrying about anything. Marchant wrote in his diary:

> Unfortunately the lunch on the ship became a very drunken party. . .All in all a very unfortunate day, although it was lucky no one was killed, simply because of the abundance of alcohol. The helicopter pilots and engineers played a vital part in maintaining sanity and preventing accidents (although there were some close shaves).[5]

Some of the Russians were so drunk one had to be carried to a helicopter. Another attempted to open the door of an aircraft and get out before it had landed, and was restrained by the pilot with one hand, while he was landing the helicopter with the other. Andrew Jackson wrote in his personal diary:

> Ian [Marchant] at Mirny and me on ship very worried about how to sort it all out. Pilots refusing to fly dangerously drunk passengers. Russians immovable and most of ship's crew in poor state. . .Some Australians hopelessly drunk—heaving clothes etc overboard—one had to be subdued. Much anger expressed by self and other sober ones over. . .the confusion.[6]

Icebird set sail from Mirny at 1900 hours on 25 November for Casey. The later discovery of what seemed to be an unconscious Russian in one of the toilets raised the spectre of having to return yet again to Mirny—but it turned out to be a practical joke by an Australian dressed in traded Russian Antarctic clothing.

Captain Brune's estimate of two days for the Mirny diversion proved optimistic. Bad weather and heavy ice conditions prevented *Icebird* from

getting away from the Mirny area for a further five days. Marchant estimated that the 'slight diversion to Mirny occupied an estimated seven days!' This would have put *Icebird* three days behind schedule at this stage.

THE ORIGINAL ANARE LOGOS WERE DESIGNED BY NEL LAW (LEFT AND CENTRE). THE CURRENT LOGO (SINCE 1985) IS ON THE RIGHT.

Although it was unfair to sheet home to Bleasel all responsibility for a very complex web of circumstances, the Mirny excursion was seized on by his opponents within the division as an example of his perceived *ad hoc* decision making. Bleasel quickly gained Antarctic experience while leading later voyages himself, but the Mirny diversion was periodically raised in the years ahead.

Back in Hobart, Bleasel pressed ahead with his reforms and changes. One, which caused enormous offence to the older ANARE hands, was to change the division's logos, both originally designed by Nel Law soon after Phil Law became director in 1949. One was a globe with Antarctica in its centre, with lines of latitude and longitude radiating out to the southern sections of Australia, South America and South Africa. Around the edge were sketches of sub-Antarctic flora and Antarctic fauna. A second logo, which had been considered more suitable as an identifying logo on ANARE equipment, vehicles and even clothing, was a boomerang-shaped badge around the line drawing of a leopard seal and the letters ANARE.

Bleasel called for a design which kept the concept of a globe, but simplified it to a juxtaposition of the Antarctic continent to the Australian continent:

> I wanted a logo that would instantly say 'Australia–Antarctica' without explanation. I didn't want all this deep and meaningful stuff with funny-looking seals, birds, and things that looked like lizards all congested so you couldn't see what the hell was on it. We got regular complaints for years. . .that the lines of longitude were not exactly in the right place. I didn't distress myself too much about that—and we kept the logo.

During his first look at the three continental stations, Bleasel was unimpressed by certain aspects of the rebuilding program, which had then been running for four years. He was critical, for example, of complex toilet systems flushed with fresh water (which had to be obtained by heating ice), of storage sheds with huge mechanised compactus shelves and of plans for computer-controlled power stations:

> Each building was being fitted out with parts from different suppliers. . .we hadn't used the basics of remote area technology. So that on a simple station a building could have several different types and sizes of similar equipment—it was a spare parts nightmare.

Because of difficulties with shipping, the Department of Housing and Construction told Bleasel that they calculated the building program was spreading out from 10 to 25 or more years:

> It was dominating the division. Instead of doing science, and getting some credit for that. . .we were doing building. We were going to be building forever. So I realised something had to be done. First we had to fix the shipping so we could get the construction over more quickly. Secondly we had to have a more realistic building program.

On his return to Australia, Bleasel announced on 23 January 1985 a review of the $58 million rebuilding program to see where economies could be made. In June, Minister for Science Barry Jones revealed that the Government had chartered *Icebird* for five further years for $20 million. The ship's ability to carry containers would enable the rebuilding program to switch over to modular construction, and this, according to the chairman of a Department of Housing and Construction Review Committee, Gary Harrop, 'could save up to $6 million in six years'.[7]

The advent of *Icebird*, with its ability to carry not only containers and modules but about 100 passengers, pointed up the limitations of the much-loved veteran *Nella Dan* which had been on the Australian Antarctic run since 1961—continuing a long association with the Danish Lauritzen shipping line that began with *Kista Dan* and the founding of Mawson Station in 1954. Old ANARE hands speak fondly of damask tablecloths and meals served by stewards on the *Dan* ships, and a fraternal relationship with the Danish masters, officers and crew that was reinforced every season for thirty years. *Nella Dan* could only accommodate 54 passengers, so there were no berths for other than essential ANARE personnel—winterers and summer scientists. Cargo was handled by derricks in and out of holds, placing severe restrictions on the size of building components that could be carried. *Icebird* was a German ship with a German crew, anxious to demonstrate that they represented the 'new

The passenger accommodation module on *Icebird* was purpose-built, and clamped to the ship just in front of the bridge. On the ship's maiden voyage, passengers lying in their bunks noticed a slight movement of the module against its restraints, particularly in heavy seas. Captain Ewald Brune, who had previously queried the engineering principles according to which the module was secured to his ship and had been assured everything had been calculated, asked for the securing bolts to be further tightened.

ANARE personnel continued to be uneasy about the possibility of the accommodation module parting company with the ship and in 1985 the senior director of the shipyard in Hamburg where *Icebird* was built, Heinrich Brand, came out to Australia to reassure Captain Brune and ANARE staff that all was well. Voyage Six left Hobart on 18 January. At about 1 am on the first night out from Hobart, the ship rolled heavily and the accommodation module moved some five centimetres against its restraints, with a loud 'clunk'. Brune:

Within about sixty seconds I had ninety expeditioners on the bridge, saying that the module had moved—you could really feel it shaking. I saw on the bridge a very pale Mr Brand. I said: 'Mr Brand, no matter what

you or the construction company are telling me, the module is no longer a part of this ship, it is deck cargo. And deck cargo must be lashed!

Brune—with Brand's enthusiastic approval—instructed his first mate to organise 200 chains to lash it in place. Before the next voyage the module was welded to the ship.

Whether the module was in real danger of leaving *Icebird* is debatable. But it became an incident that has gone down in ANARE legend—and song:

'CLICK GO THE BOLTS'
(Tune: 'Click Go the Shears')

Out on the bridge the bold captain stands,
Officers around him, sweat upon their hands;
Fixed is their gaze on a distant giant wave,
Glory if she hits us will the *Icebird* behave?

Chorus:
Snap go the bolts boys, snap, snap, snap,
Wide was the roll that made the metal slap,
The module's come adrift and gone over with a crash,
'Curses' cried the passengers amidst the mighty splash . . .

Lyrics: Rod Simpson and Tony Jennings.

order' in Antarctic transport. The styles of the two ships contrasted markedly. Passengers on *Icebird* lined up for their meals at a cafeteria-style serving point and carried their food to a mess with long tables and bench seats. (Late arrivals had to climb up on the seat, and walk behind those dining, balancing their soup precariously—a tricky operation in a heavy sea.) To those who had sailed on both ships, disposable plastic cups and Laminex table tops seemed light years away from the old-world elegance of the *Dan*-style table settings and personal service.

The extra berths on *Icebird* meant greater opportunities to visit Australian stations in Antarctica. Bleasel was keen to have more Antarctic Division head office staff visit Antarctica so that they could have a better understanding of the consequences of their work.

Selected VIPs and politicians had been invited south for round-trip voyages with ANARE even in the *Dan* days when berths were tight. However, the increased passenger capacity of *Icebird* allowed Bleasel to increase these invitations—a shrewd public relations move which resulted in considerable bipartisan support for Australia's Antarctic program. As a result of these (and earlier visits by veteran politicians like Bill Wentworth and John Gorton who had been flown down to the continent in United States aircraft in the 1960s) a Parliamentary Alliance was formed in 1987, comprising members of federal parliament who either have visited Antarctica or have extensive interests in the region.

The policy of VIP visits continued into the 1990s. In January 1996 the Governor of Tasmania, Sir Guy Green, visited Macquarie Island and on 9 January officially opened the refurbished and repositioned hut known as Chippy's Church, believed to be the oldest building on the island.

Because travel to Antarctica had been the preserve of the ANARE professionals, few established artists and writers had ever been able to have direct experience of the remote and stunningly beautiful region. (The landscape paintings of Nel Law, wife of Phil Law, from her 1961 voyage on *Kista Dan* were an important early contribution.)* Bleasel introduced the 'Artists in Antarctica' program, with the aim of familiarising Australians with what ANARE was doing in the Antarctic. He also initiated the Antarctic School Science Prize, which involved sending two secondary school children and their teachers to Antarctica on *Icebird*. It was run each year from 1986 to 1989.

Publicity of an unwelcome kind was splashed over the national newspapers in October 1985 when *Nella Dan* became beset in heavy pack ice off the coast of Enderby Land, near the western extremity of the Australian Antarctic Territory. The ship had left a party of scientists on Heard Island, intending to pick them up after some marine biology in the pack ice—investigating the krill and the distribution and abundance of crabeater seals. Although known to be present in large numbers around Antarctica, these seals were difficult to study because they live and breed only in the pack ice.

---

* Sidney Nolan did paint a series of landscapes based on a flying visit to McMurdo in 1964 with the Americans but did not visit the Australian Antarctic Territory.

In 1986 the Antarctic Division asked the Tasmanian Museum and Art Gallery to assist in selecting artists for a voyage to Antarctica, and in early 1987 three painters, Bea Maddocks (Tasmania), Jan Senbergs (Victoria) and John Caldwell (New South Wales) joined Voyage Six on *Icebird* for a voyage that included a rare visit to Heard Island, the Scullin Monolith (near Mawson Station), Mawson and Davis Stations and the Vestfold Hills. Unfortunately Bea Maddocks badly injured her leg in a fall at Atlas Cove, Heard Island, but although immobilised in her cabin managed to continue sketching, using a series of mirrors to observe scenes outside her porthole, despite considerable pain and discomfort. All three artists painted prolifically and fulfilled the aims of those who had advocated their visit, including the director, Jim Bleasel. Senbergs' images were particularly powerful, stressing the impact of human activity on Antarctica's pristine environment.

The Humanities Berths Program was aimed at laying the basis for a deeper and longer-lasting appreciation of Antarctica among Australians. Peter Boyer, as information services manager, took up the cause of sending painters, poets, film makers and other creative artists to the Antarctic along with mainstream journalists:

> The aim of the program is to ensure that Antarctica becomes part of Australian culture at a deeper level than is possible simply through media exposure. . .We wanted Antarctica, through the work of these people, to strike a more resonant chord in the Australian psyche.

Under the regime instigated in the mid-1980s many other creative people have gone south. These include the writer Stephen Murray-Smith (who wrote a book *Sitting On Penguins*), poet Catherine Caddy, the Tasmanian sculptor Stephen Walker (twice), and artists Claire Robertson and Caroline Durré. Two Aboriginal artists have been on the program—Lin Onus and Miriam Rose Baumann—during the 1993 Year of Indigenous People.

As sometimes happens in Antarctica, unconnected tragic events happened in quick succession. On 20 October—only a week before *Nella Dan* became stuck in the ice—a ship's cook, Kim Nielsen, died from head injuries after a fall. Then on 28 October Steve Bunning, the Department of Housing and Construction foreman working on the rebuilding project at Davis, was badly burned when an explosion occurred while he was spraying sealant inside a storage tank. Bunning's injuries were so severe that the Americans (at considerable risk to the crew and aircraft) sent an LC130 Hercules from McMurdo to land on a hastily prepared emergency strip on the sea ice near Davis on 29 October. The aircraft landed safely, but sadly Bunning died during the evacuation.

As besetments go, *Nella Dan*'s was a good one. In the early stages, rafted ice built up around the ship, putting the hull under enormous pressure. Then there was a sudden drop in temperature, freezing the pack—the worst possible situation for a break-out. Making the best of

NELLA DAN IN PACK ICE,
1979.
(M BETTS)

the situation, Knowles Kerry resumed the biological science program while they waited:

> As luck would have it we were over the [continental] shelf break, and that is where the krill was, it's where the [crabeater] seals were, so we could actually do work. The ice floe which held *Nella Dan* was moving at about two knots, pushed by a mixture of wind and current, and that's about towing speed. So we were able to do bottom-dredging. . .we had laboratories on board so we did a lot of phytoplankton work and krill in culture. We had divers with us and they were studying the krill under the ice. It was an absolute godsend—a stable platform for them.

Nella Dan was a stable, if somewhat expensively chartered platform for a crew of 31, plus 36 scientists. The national press took a great interest in the ship's predicament as Bleasel considered what, if anything, could be done:

> I looked at satellite pictures over a ten-year period of the area in which she was locked—this was some colour stuff done by the Americans. The ice had never melted out in the ten years. So I knew I was in deep poo. I had to hire a Royal Australian Navy ship at huge expense [$250 000]

to rescue and resupply the people at Macquarie Island. It cost us a fortune—it really zotted our budget for the year.

By late November Bleasel announced to the press that he had ordered *Icebird* to the area to free *Nella Dan*. According to Kerry, Ewald Brune arrived on the scene, ignored advice given to him by Arne Sorensen of *Nella Dan* about the best route and made his own way in. *Icebird* got caught in a fast-moving stream and was in danger of being crushed by an iceberg coming down on them. Rafted ice actually forced its way up onto the foredeck and a contingency plan to abandon ship was worked out before the ice pressure abated and the ship escaped after being beset for two days. *Icebird* was in no position to rescue *Nella Dan*. Eventually the powerful Japanese icebreaker *Shirase* arrived on the scene on 13 December to break out *Nella Dan*. Even then there were difficulties. During a tow, the grip of the ice was such that the tow line (with a breaking strain of 170 tonnes) ripped one mooring bollard clean out of the deck of *Nella Dan* and bent over a second. By 15 December they were clear of the pack. Kerry:

> *Shirase* then stopped and we were able to pull alongside. I presented a number of personal gifts (Danish chocolate and whisky) to the captain. *Shirase* was presented with one of the mooring bollards [that had been torn from the deck during towing] which had been inscribed '*Nella Dan* 15/12/85'.[8]

Nella Dan was beset for 49 days. Despite Kerry's exoneration by a Review Committee in February 1986, Bleasel was not pleased with his trapped voyage leader for going to that area. The following year Bleasel had personal experience of how easy besetment is when he was voyage leader on *Nella Dan* near the Bunger Hills in January 1986. On this occasion *Nella Dan* was freed by the Russian icebreaker *Mikhail Somov*.

Any trouble with shipping inevitably raised the continuing saga of investigating direct air links with the Australian stations. In November 1981, the Americans ended the Cooperative Air Transport System (CATSA) agreement between Australia, New Zealand and the United States that had seen some ski-equipped Hercules LC130 flights onto a snow runway at Lanyon Junction on the ice plateau behind Casey Station. In 1982 an Antarctic Policy and Transport Studies group was formed in Canberra at the Department of Science under the direction of John Whitelaw and headed by John Boyd. The APTS looked at future shipping as well as aviation options.

Whitelaw makes the point that there is not a lot of expertise in polar aviation in Australia, particularly within the government system. One possibility being explored was an all-weather rock airstrip near Davis Station in the Vestfold Hills. Whitelaw:

> We started talking to the aviation authorities and the first question that came out of this meeting, I remember, was: 'You've got a general plan here, but where's the control tower?' And we said: 'The control tower? Why would you have a control tower?' 'Oh, you've got to have a control tower to control the traffic.' We're talking about three flights a week here, why do you need a control tower?'

Environmental concerns were always going to make an airstrip at Davis a sensitive and difficult choice. But even the concept of a compressed ice strip at Casey was difficult to pursue in a country with no experience in that style of operation. Whitelaw:

> So how do you build a runway in Antarctica. . .well obviously if you are a government agency you've got to get the government runway builders. That would be the Department of Housing and Construction. You'd mention a runway to DHC and their eyes would light up. They'd have had an entire department working on it for years. There was this tendency to think, 'How would we do this in Australia'—and then try and move that into the Antarctic. But it would cost us an awful lot of effort and money.

A study of the feasibility of compacted snow runways at both Casey and Mawson was made by a group from Melbourne University led by glaciologist Professor Bill Budd. The construction cost of an ice runway near Casey [in 1982 dollars] was estimated at $600 000, with annual maintenance $40 000.[9]

On his first visit to Casey on *Icebird* in December 1984, Bleasel flew up to Lanyon Junction to inspect the experiments being made to create a compressed ice airstrip. He was not impressed. He had been told the containers used as living quarters for the machinery operators were mounted on stilts, three metres up in the air. When he arrived at the site there was only about 30 centimetres of the tops of the containers showing above the snow:

> I thought it was pretty obvious that it was a ridiculous place to build an ice runway—it was going to take us years to build it. If it got blizzed in, I would have had to have accommodation for all of the people who were ready to fly out, plus all of the people who'd just flown in. I thought it was a pretty dumb idea. I would have a building program at Lanyon Junction that would have rivalled what we were doing at any of the other bases, and a hell of a lot more difficult to maintain because of the very

heavy snowfall. So I killed that as soon as decently possible. A lot of money had been expended on it.

Bleasel believed a rock airstrip at Davis, where the weather was better and snowfall minimal, was the best option. This view was supported by studies going back to the 1960s.

But the way the environment is, it was just not worth considering—even though the perfect place to have an airstrip in all Antarctica is near Davis. But I don't think I'll see that in my lifetime.

TWENTY

TURBULENT TIMES

On the evening of 3 December 1987 dinner was being served in the well-appointed passengers' mess of *Nella Dan* anchored in Buckles Bay, at Macquarie Island. Buckles Bay, on the eastern side of the isthmus where the ANARE station is located, is sheltered from the prevailing westerlies. Early that day strong south-easterly winds and rough seas had stopped the amphibious LARCs from transferring cargo during the annual resupply and changeover. Fuel, however, continued to be pumped from ship to shore through a flexible hose to the ANARE station's fuel farm, and that operation was nearly complete.

Shortly after 6.30 pm Captain Arne Sorensen left the mess, and almost immediately afterwards those remaining felt the ship rolling to starboard and bottoming heavily. The engine was started and the alarm sounded. It was too late. The anchor had dragged, and the ship was driven on to the rocky shore by the wind and waves. On board were seventeen ANARE expeditioners and the crew of *Nella Dan*, including the widow of the founder of Lauritzens, Mrs Hannelore Lauritzen.

Alerted to the disaster, all three LARCs on shore were mobilised, and the army 'Larcies' performed superb feats of seamanship to get through the pounding surf to reach the starboard side of *Nella Dan*. The passengers, wearing warm clothes and life-jackets, had to climb down a rope ladder into a wildly gyrating LARC. Apart from the screaming wind and spume, everyone was sprayed with wind-blown diesel fuel leaking from the stricken ship. The captain, chief engineer, chief officer, first officer and bosun remained on board.[1]

On shore, the small station was crammed to capacity, as is usually the case during the summer season and particularly during a changeover. Incoming station leader Glen Kowalik and his out-going counterpart, Ian Jacobsen, were both ashore at the time and began coordinating emergency accommodation. They faced an influx of 72 extra guests, many of them in shock and with an immediate need to find somewhere to sleep. Kowalik:

> Even the curtains from our dongas (sleeping areas) and packing foam from pallets of cargo in the store were pressed into service. . .By 1.30 am there were people housed in every conceivable corner of the station, in workshops, in stores, the emergency power house, 'Sealers' Inn', the science and meteorological buildings and other nooks and crannies. Within six hours a 30-person station had been converted to a 103-person station![2]

Dawn on the morning of Friday 4 December revealed a depressing sight. *Nella Dan* was stranded, lodged firmly against a rock, parallel to the beach, listing 11 degrees to port. By that afternoon conditions were calm enough for work parties to return to the ship and recover some personal gear and equipment. Over the next three days some five to six tonnes of marine science equipment and other valuable scientific instrumentation was recovered with great difficulty, because no power was available to operate the ship's main lifting gear. The last 50 tonnes of station fuel was transferred ashore using station pumping equipment. Fortunately for the station, some 60 per cent of the resupply cargo had been unloaded, including essential food supplies. Cargo remaining on board was mainly building materials and concrete.[3]

Icebird, en route from Davis Station to Hobart (with Rex Moncur as voyage leader), was diverted to Macquarie Island to pick up stranded passengers and crew, arriving on 8 December. The intense (but friendly) rivalry between the German crew of the new *Icebird* and the Danes manning the veteran *Nella Dan* was no longer an issue. The Danes had designed a T-shirt depicting their ship as a shark, with the slogan: WE ATE ICEBIRDS FOR BREAKFAST. In one of the few lighter moments in a gloomy situation, Captain Brune of *Icebird* authorised the Danes to send a message over his communications system to the suppliers of the T-shirts to alter the inscription to: WE ARE EATING BREAKFAST ON ICEBIRD. They were available on the dock in Hobart when *Icebird* berthed.

A Bass Strait oil rig tug and supply vessel, *Lady Lorraine* , chartered by the salvage company Austpac, arrived at Macquarie Island on 13 December. At first light the next day, divers inspected the hull of *Nella*

Dan and reported damage did not seem as bad as had been feared. The first priority was to pump out all remaining marine fuel into tanks on *Lady Lorraine*. Fortunately most of the estimated 264 cubic metres of light marine diesel oil that escaped from the ship was blown out to sea when the prevailing westerlies resumed, and biologists found there had been minimal impact on the wildlife on shore.

The wrecking of *Nella Dan* touched a deep chord in the hearts of ANARE expeditioners who had sailed on her for the past 27 years. Phil Law called for the Federal Government to pay to salvage the ship and convert her into a museum. 'The Victorian Government had backed the idea and the Port of Melbourne had already allocated a berth on the Yarra River at the bottom end of North Wharf.' The Melbourne *Age* reported other suggestions:

> Tasmania's Environment Minister, Mr Peter Hodgman, has written to Canberra suggesting that *Nella Dan* be hauled ashore at Macquarie Island for use as a reserve base. The ALP's Senator John Devereux and a Liberal MHR Mr Warwick Smith, have called for it to be returned to Hobart for use in an Antarctic Centre on the city wharves.[4]

The problem was getting *Nella Dan* back to Australia and all speculation about her future use became academic when she was pulled off the rocks on the evening high tide of 21 December and divers discovered that, in fact, damage to the bottom of the hull was extensive. Despite efforts to seal up holed compartments and the pumping in of compressed air, water was coming in faster than it could be pumped out by *Lady Lorraine*. Captain Roger Rusling:

> There was a multitude of cracks and holes in the bottom of the ship, plus a lot of inter-tank damage. The walls between the tanks themselves were cracked, and water was seeping from one tank to another.

On 23 December the owners of *Nella Dan* announced they were left with no other option, for practical and safety reasons, than to scuttle the ship in deep water. Rusling put *Lady Lorraine* alongside to help take off the pumps and compressors and any other equipment that could be salvaged. Voyage leader David Lyons remembers the salvage master, David Hancock, saying, 'I can't keep this thing afloat. It's like a honeycomb.' When *Nella Dan* suddenly listed from 6° to 15° in about thirty seconds, Hancock ordered everyone off the ship. Rusling thought the ship was going to sink there and then:

> People jumped on to *Lady Lorraine* and on to the LARCs on the other side. . .If it had sunk in Buckles Bay it would have been a disaster, because there is only room for one ship at a time, and it would have made it very hard indeed to resupply the ANARE station on Macquarie Island.

Rusling was ordered to tow *Nella Dan* immediately out to deep water. At that stage he thought he only had fifteen or twenty minutes to do the job, but the old ship was not going to give up without a struggle. Five nautical miles off Macquarie Island, in deep water, *Nella Dan* settled lower in the water but obstinately refused to sink. The next morning, 24 December, she was still afloat and it was decided to tow her back towards the island so that the LARCs could help retrieve some of the equipment still on board. But less than one nautical mile from Macquarie, smoke was seen rising from the ship. Rusling:

> Within about ten minutes the whole accommodation block was just a roaring inferno, so we turned around and went back out to the deep water again and steamed up and down for another few hours. We thought it must sink shortly.

Nella Dan was hanging on to the bitter end. When the fire burnt itself out, the salvage crew managed to get back on board so that a hose could be rigged directly between the two ships. Rusling used the powerful ballast pumps of his oil rig tender to force sea water into the foundering vessel. That, combined with the opening of all air valves, was enough to deliver the *coup de grace*.[5]

THE FINAL MOMENTS OF
NELLA DAN, SCUTTLED IN
DEEP WATER OFF THE EAST
COAST OF MACQUARIE
ISLAND, PHOTOGRAPHED
FROM THE STERN OF *LADY
LORRAINE*.
(COURTESY *AURORA*)

Sorensen stood in silence beside Rusling as the two captains watched *Nella Dan* sink stern first, her bows rising up dramatically as if in a final salute. Later Sorensen likened the final moments of his ship to 'a Viking funeral', adding, 'she was from a time when ships were built to last, and she had a mind of her own.'[6]

The captain and his senior officers were held responsible for the grounding in a Maritime Safety preliminary investigation report into the accident published in April 1988. Sorensen's decision to continue to transfer oil after dry cargo operations had been suspended because of gale force south-easterly winds was singled out particularly as 'an error of judgement'.[7]

The Antarctic Division's logistics manager, Ian Marchant, makes the point that refuelling from the sea is always a tricky business:

> You have to tow the line out from the base and connect it up on the ship. Once the pipe is connected it is quite a hassle to disconnect [and reconnect] it, so if the job can be done in one go, it is much easier. If there is any doubt as to the safety of an operation like this, it is the captain who makes the final decision rather than the voyage leader. . .

The loss of *Nella Dan* threw the 1987–88 shipping program into disarray. Fortunately the Antarctic Division managed to charter *Lady Franklin* from Canada at short notice. *Lady Franklin* had been used to help with the rebuilding program during the early 1980s and had been modified to carry extra passengers in a number of temporary accommodation 'huts' constructed below the foredeck.

386

The sinking of *Nella Dan* was an emotional business for the hundreds of ANARE expeditioners who had sailed on her. In 1985, however, the Government had already decided the veteran polar vessel would be replaced. On 15 December 1986 it was agreed that a replacement ship for ANARE service would be built in Australia. The decision to build an Australian ice-breaking ship was actually made by Cabinet on 15 December 1987—twelve days after *Nella Dan* was stranded and nine days before she was finally scuttled.

When Jim Bleasel came to the division as director, he worked to the Minister for Science, Barry Jones. The two men got on well. Jones was interested in the Antarctic, particularly in the scientific research, and shared Bleasel's concern about a rebuilding program that seemed to have got out of hand:

> I was anxious to boost the amount spent on scientific research. And I didn't want that scientific research to be prejudiced by the amount that was being spent on physical construction. . .There was no point in saying: 'We've got the biggest assemblage of concrete in the Antarctic, something that can be seen from other planets'. I couldn't see much sense in that.

Both Bleasel and Jones wanted to move away from the established stations, which Bleasel described as 'little townships'. He developed a policy of expanding summer bases. Martin Betts, then head of planning and coordination, recalls Bleasel was 'into sovereignty—I remember him grabbing me. "The Government says we have to go to the eastern sector to put the flag there." He wanted to establish ten stations in the Australian Antarctic Territory.'

Bleasel argued that cheap summer stations and better logistics were a more efficient way to spend research funds. In January 1986 Rod Ledingham led a field party of 22 including biologists, geologists, geomorphologists and support staff (with three helicopters), to the Bunger Hills, 450 kilometres to the west of Casey Station, to set up Edgeworth David Base—named after the distinguished Australian scientist whom Douglas Mawson had accompanied on his expedition to the South Magnetic Pole in 1908. Bleasel:

> Unfortunately a great iceberg came and shut that off soon afterwards. We established Law Base in the Larsemann Hills. We built up our summer operations on Heard Island. We established a new base in Commonwealth

Bay, out of sight of Mawson's hut, so as not to disturb the integrity of that area. . .And we did further field work at places such as Scullin Monolith. . .

The Larsemann Hills, 100 kilometres to the south-west of the Vestfold Hills (and Davis Station) is a significant ice-free area. In the mid 1980s the Antarctic Division became aware that the Russians and the Chinese were thinking of setting up permanent stations there. ANARE had maintained close contact with the Chinese for some years and many of their scientists had gained wintering experience on Australian stations. In 1985–86 the station leader at Davis, Rob Easther, was asked to set up a summer base in the Larsemann Hills. A prefabricated hut was flown over by helicopter to a site selected by Easther, on high ground with access to a tarn for fresh water. During the winter Easther was asked to reconnoitre an overland route from Davis to the new base, over or around the Sørsdal Glacier, and transport extra huts to the site. Although this base—named Law Base after Phil Law—enabled some useful science to be done in the area, its creation was blatantly territorial and political. As Bleasel put it: 'The thinking was that if anybody's bum was going to be on that seat, it ought to be ours.'

The following summer the Russians appeared with big helicopters which disgorged geologists and surveyors who chose a site for their station. Progress One was established near an ice airstrip they marked out on the plateau. While the Australians had carefully erased the marks of their tracked vehicles from the rocky terrain near Law Base, the Russians were less concerned about the pristine Antarctic environment—simply bulldozing a rough road from the coast to their base and on up to the plateau. The Australians were unimpressed to find that the Russians had even driven a tractor through the tarn they used for their drinking water. While national attitudes to the environment differed markedly, however, personal relations—as elsewhere in Antarctica—were warm and friendly.

The Chinese began to build their station, Zhongshan, in the Larsemann Hills in the summer of 1988–89. Their ship, *Ji Di,* moored offshore while barges and helicopters were used to transfer building materials to their selected site. It was an eventful summer, as Rob Easther recalls:

> Overnight a huge lump of ice broke off the nearby Dålk Glacier and flooded all the foundations—it basically wiped out the site! It was a timely lesson, so they moved 200 metres further uphill to the present site. Later that same summer something similar happened with the Dålk, and *Ji Di* was trapped between the shore and a large berg. Davis Station was alerted to evacuate the Chinese as it was feared their ship would be squashed.

Within two years, the Larsemann Hills region was transformed from an uninhabited Antarctic wilderness to an international hub with three nations working there, four bases and an ice airfield.

Bleasel was a man in a hurry and, perhaps not surprisingly, his relations with Antarctic Division staff were patchy. On 9 April 1986 the main staff union, the Administrative and Clerical Officers' Association (on behalf of six other affiliated unions) wrote to him with a number of grievances. They included allegations of lack of consultation with staff, shoddy staff selection procedures, misallocation of division resources, lack of planning, 'the apparent lack of control' over major resourcing decisions like contracts, and 'centralised and *ad hoc* decision-making which does not utilise the expertise of subordinate staff'.[8]

One of the issues singled out in a thirteen-page attachment fleshing out the union's concerns was the old issue of the diversion of *Icebird* to Mirny during the 1984–85 season 'at an estimated minimum cost of $250 000'. The ACOA was critical of the minister's [Barry Jones] decision to establish a Review Committee to conduct a formal inquiry into the besetment of *Nella Dan* in October 1985, which appeared

> . . .to have been selective in the absence of any acceptable public explanation for the *Icebird*'s earlier diversion [to reach *Nella Dan*], entrapment and on-board conduct near Mirny last summer, in the limited scope of the Review Committee's terms of reference, and in the haste in which it conducted it's [sic] interviews of some involved staff.[9]

Bleasel responded on 14 April and was dismissive of the union's submission, saying in conclusion that he did not believe that the term 'general abysmal morale level' was an accurate description of conditions in the division which he thought were 'already better than that which could be expected from any similarly constituted government organisation in which the staff are working just as hard':

I cannot help but reach the conclusion that the information presented in this paper has been prepared by a small group and is unrepresentative of the general feeling of staff. This is not in the interests of the Division as a whole. . .[10]

The division's acting shipping manager and union activist Geoff Dannock was angry about what he saw as the situation of his boss (and voyage leader on the maiden voyage of *Icebird*), logistics manager Ian Marchant, who had taken an extended period of leave after returning to Hobart. Dannock:

The deviation into Mirny took about ten days, and in those days the charter rate was probably about $25 000 a day. So in terms of public service piss-ups, it was probably the biggest and the best. . .I tried to take the subject up after the ship returned, and the blame for the whole situation was actually put on the voyage leader [Ian Marchant], who was my supervisor.

(Bleasel contests this allegation of extra costs on the grounds that the fixed price charter time for *Icebird* was not exceeded over the whole season, the ship carried out its full program and the division paid no extra charges. He also rejects the suggestion that he or anybody else suggested Marchant was in any way responsible for the Mirny diversion.)

Dannock decided to contact Minister for Science Barry Jones, under the pseudonym 'I C White', to draw his attention to the Mirny affair. Jones agreed to meet 'I C White' in his Melbourne office, providing he identified himself. Dannock agreed, and saw Jones on 23 July 1985. He told the minister of his allegations, not only about the delay caused by the diversion to Mirny, but also about the way he thought Jim Bleasel was running the Antarctic Division.

Dannock returned to the division and told the deputy director, Rex Moncur, that he had been to see Barry Jones: 'But I was left in my own position. I was counselled by the deputy secretary [Roy Green] and told not to do anything like that again, and all was fairly quiet for a while.'

Rex Moncur, Bleasel's choice as deputy director, was in charge of resource management in the Department of Science in Canberra. Moncur:

The rebuilding program had almost stalled because we didn't have adequate shipping capacity. And one of the things I worked on with Jim before I even came down [to Hobart] was getting an agreement to charter *Icebird* to provide that sort of capacity. . .I was using my contacts and relationship with the Department of Finance.

The advent of *Icebird* with extra berths available meant more scientists could go to Antarctica. Moncur recalls that the Minister, Barry Jones, convinced Cabinet to provide some extra funding for field science projects and the Antarctic Science Advisory Committee began its grant scheme to encourage university researchers to work for ANARE:

THE INTERIOR OF REID HUT AT LAW BASE, LARSEMANN HILLS.
(R EASTHER)

> So for all those reasons, the Jim Bleasel era resulted in a substantial enhancement of our scientific activity. He certainly tried a number of things on the operational front. He visited a number of other countries such as the UK and looked at how they managed their stations, and set up the idea of operations managers and so forth. Now, some of these things didn't work, but he had a go at nearly everything that was available.

Press clippings from the era show the Antarctic Division was rarely out of the headlines. The sinking of *Nella Dan* was a dramatic story by any standards, but Bleasel was not unaware of the importance of publicity in keeping the Australian public aware of Antarctic affairs: 'When I came I realised it was important to raise the profile of the Antarctic Division—to let people know where their money was being spent.'

Looking back, Bleasel resents any suggestion that he was hungry for publicity. He says he took control of the division's news releases and made himself the first point of contact for journalists because he wanted to control the damage caused by bad and inaccurate publicity. By making himself the focus for information, he could present the division's position quickly, accurately and positively:

> I didn't see it as an ego thing, I saw that as my job—distasteful. But in the end I didn't mind it, I got used to it. I did it properly. I wasn't in the public eye before I went to the Antarctic Division, and I haven't been in the public eye since I left.

391

AUSTRALIA'S SUMMER
STATION, LAW BASE,
NEAR THE RUSSIAN AND
CHINESE STATIONS IN THE
LARSEMANN HILLS, 1986.
(R EASTHER)

Bleasel's personal agenda for the Antarctic Division went far beyond structural and administrative reshaping at head office. He wanted to change the actual culture of ANARE through its recruiting procedures, leadership structures and the way stations functioned. Clearly the scientific programs to be undertaken and issues like the maintenance and use of heavy equipment and safety procedures were non-negotiable and dictated by head office. But how the community actually functioned was left to the discretion of the officer-in-charge and the dynamics of each particular wintering group. After all, there were no trainees on an Antarctic station. Each expeditioner was an expert in his or her field, be it plumbing, cooking or upper atmosphere physics. Traditionally this had been an exclusively male culture, only marginally influenced by the small number of women going south to the continent from the 1980s. The independence of the stations was reinforced, in the early years, by poor communications. This culture could not be easily changed by directions from the top.

Bleasel created the positions at head office of station managers who would deal directly with the station leaders in Antarctica to ensure more practical and effective liaison between head office and those down south. He made sure the new station managers were former station leaders with a strong grasp of the practicalities of ANARE life and field work. Although this system did not become operational until after Bleasel left the division in 1988, and although it has since been modified, managers like Rob Easther believe it has made a significant and positive difference to relations between Kingston and those on ANARE stations.

But by the mid-1980s, communications in the Antarctic were changing rapidly. The development of INMARSAT—a satellite system used by shipping world wide—meant that the ANARE stations could be linked up with the same system. The first INMARSAT link went into Mawson

Station in 1984 and was quickly extended to Davis, Casey and Macquarie Island by 1985. Communications consultant Doug Twigg:

> This system could do two things—it could transmit data using their keyboards, and they could also make telephone calls. That was the start of the satellite system. . .but it was around $10 a minute, a very expensive system.

For those used to conversations on the old radio telephone system being wiped out by auroral interference or sunspot activity, the new system was astounding. Jim Bleasel, who had a background in remote area technology, was keen to get ANARE on its own system through OTC (later incorporated into Telstra) and the world-wide INTELSAT system. He discovered that two different communications systems were to be sent south:

> I didn't want separate suppliers. I thought this was fairly basic, but it was a bitter thing for the people responsible. . .They knew that technically it was best to have different types of receiver stations at different places—two of one type and two of another. I insisted they all be the same type.

By February 1987, the first dedicated ANARESAT—as the system was named—communications were established with Davis Station, and were extended to all the other stations by 1989. The system makes use of two INTELSAT satellites over the Pacific and Indian Oceans to service all permanent ANARE stations. (INMARSAT remains as a backup.) By the 1990s, all stations and the Kingston headquarters were linked by telephone with three-digit in-house dialling, and to the Australian mainland at normal domestic STD rates. Faxes, electronic mail and data transmission are now commonplace. Instead of weather observers having to telex their data back to Australia over uncertain radio links, it is automatically accessed from Australia. Twigg:

> It's almost like Big Brother. A lot of the science data collection is going straight back to Australia without any interference by the person on site. The supervisors have more direct control of what's going on in the station. The building maintenance people can plug in there and know what the temperature is in the recreation room and whether the water is too hot or cold, or the air temperature is the right mixture.

During the early years of ANARE Phil Law believed that poor communications were often a blessing in disguise in keeping expeditioners insulated from the often trivial day-to-day worries of their partners or families in Australia—which they could do nothing about. Often a

Physicist and film maker David Parer wintered at Mawson in 1972, and remembers one of the party receiving a 'Dear John' telegram with the news that his fiancée had not only broken off their relationship, but had transferred her affections to his best friend. Two days later Parer was having his hair cut by an obliging diesel mechanic when they looked out the window and saw the jilted expeditioner running out on to the sea ice and heading out into nowhere. Parer:

A couple of blokes raced down, got skidoos and headed out over the sea ice and finally caught up with our friend. After he got back we said, 'What were you going to do?'. And he said, 'Oh, I was just going to head out to sea on the sea ice'. So the OIC broke out some beer and we had—not really a party—more of a wake [for the relationship]. But it sorted him out.

particular problem was resolved by the time the details finally got through. When news of a serious, or even tragic nature had to be broken, the Antarctic Division's liaison officer (then in Melbourne) usually informed the OIC first, who then either called in the individual concerned to tell the expeditioner personally, or alerted the rest of the station to be aware and caring of that person's situation.

In the 1990s, with telephones in individual 'dongas', there are regular instances of horrendous telephone bills. Personal accounts in excess of $2000 per year are now common, and one expeditioner has notched up a record in excess of $6500.

In the early years of ANARE all messages to the stations were traditionally handled by a team of communications officers who, like the meteorology observers, worked in shifts. The handling of confidential official and personal information often put strains on 'comms' officers living in a small, isolated community. Bob Orchard, whose experience dates back to the days of the Morse key, represents a generation of 'comms' officers who pride themselves on complete professional discretion when dealing with personal or confidential messages:

We don't even tell our offsiders. It's best not to know some things. In the past when you were taking it by Morse code you just had to be able to walk out of the radio room and switch off—forget about it. In ten minutes' time you'd be eating with a bloke who'd had bad news. . .

The 'comms' officers prided themselves on their professional ability to maintain confidentiality. By the nature of their job, they had to know everything that was going on. Rob Easther believed Jim Bleasel wanted to break the perceived power of the 'comms' officers, and that was one of his motivations for introducing satellite communications and the VAX computer system which enabled confidential electronic mail to be sent directly to station leaders—or any individual on station. Easther:

Some 'comms' officers had breached the confidentiality of telexes, revealing personal information around the bar, and undermining the power of the station leaders by leaking confidential messages from head office. The advent of ANARESAT also made direct communication easier and thus facilitated an easier resolution of conflict situations, such as those involving harassment.

With all stations fully connected to a modern communications system, the tyranny of distance was defeated—at least administratively. The line of chattering teleprinters in the Mawson radio room, relaying weather data from Casey, Davis and Russia's Molodezhnaya, Japan's Syowa and South Africa's SANAE stations were stilled—the long racks of radio receivers and patch cords replaced by a computer the size of a small attaché case. From 1995 weather data and, for example, scientific readings from Mawson's cosmic ray laboratory could now be monitored directly from Australia. From the early 1990s communications officers began to be phased out—except in the busy summer season to coordinate helicopter, ship and field work communications—and to be replaced during the winter by technicians, who combined some communications duties with keeping the computers and electronics systems operating.

Station leaders were immediately engulfed in an avalanche of administration, some complaining they had become slaves to their computer screens. The new technology was quickly integrated into the culture. (At Casey in 1995, station leader Peter Melick often found himself corresponding on e-mail, via the Internet, to a member of his own wintering group in another building.)

One inevitable consequence of improved communications was an exponential explosion of rumour and gossip between the stations. The Antarctic Division's rumour mills had always ground steadily away, but ANARESAT opened up new horizons of scuttlebutt and institutional innuendo. While confidentiality between head office and an expeditioner could now be achieved without the cooperation of the ubiquitous 'comms' officers, there was absolutely no way of controlling the flow of information out of an Antarctic station.

The most pressing logistics problem facing the division in the mid 1980s was to organise a new Antarctic ship. Although the Government had made a decision in 1983 that a purpose-built ship would be constructed, no detailed plans for a ship were in place, although expressions of interest had been invited overseas through Wesfarmers (now renamed South West Chartering Pty Ltd). In 1986 Ivan Bear (formerly Naval Officer Commanding Tasmanian Area) had joined the division to lead a project group to develop specifications and identify scientific facilities for a ship to replace *Nella Dan*. The project group was formed within the Projects and Policy Branch under David Lyons, Assistant Director Projects and Policy. Bear:

> There was a need to combine the requirements of the ship to act as a tanker, as a resupply vessel carrying dry cargo, transporting scientists, carrying out trawls, operating helicopters—and with a galaxy of scientific research equipment. This needed to include antennae and [hull-mounted echo-sounding systems] for examining the fish population, activity concentrations and bottom depths. There was an amazing list of equipment to go into the ship.

After juggling the requirements of cargo, passenger carrying and research and calling for expressions of interest, it was found that the cheapest option would be to have the new ship built in Europe and operated with an overseas crew. This finding became academic after the Australian Labor Party retained office in the July 1987 Australian Federal elections and the Antarctic Division was moved from Barry Jones and the Department of Science to the new mega-department of Arts, Sport, the Environment, Tourism and Territories (DASETT) under Senator Graham Richardson.

Richardson—a powerful and activist minister—was briefed by departmental secretary Tony Blunn on the Antarctic Division's situation (including the implementation of the recommendations of the Joint Management Review) and decided to 'get them a better deal':

> They were getting bled, and gradually losing it. They were losing the battle at [the Department of] Science, and I thought that was going to continue. So I was quite anxious to fight for them. . .I could imagine them getting to a point where they couldn't adequately carry out the scientific programs they were telling me they wanted.

The new minister took a close interest in the process of acquiring a new ice-breaking ship for ANARE work. In September 1986 Wesfarmers had invited offers from prospective tenderers, to be submitted by 31 October. At the time, division thinking favoured chartering a ship from Rieber Shipping, Norway, an experienced polar ship operator, as the most economical option. Richardson favoured an Australian built and crewed ship and in September 1987 asked for a submission to take to Cabinet by December. At the Division, Ivan Bear was working on the project:

> There were a number of new concepts we had to consider and these were made available to the bidders so they knew what they were in for,

or had some idea. And they could refine their pricing at that initial stage. When the front runner was selected, more detailed effort was required.

The news that *Nella Dan* was on the rocks added an extra dimension of urgency for the Government to make a decision on a replacement. When the Antarctic Division's deputy director, Rex Moncur, returned to Hobart from his stint as voyage leader on *Icebird* on 11 December (a longer than usual voyage because of difficult ice conditions in Prydz Bay and the need to pick up the stranded passengers of *Nella Dan* from Macquarie Island), Jim Bleasel asked him to oversee the division's negotiations for a new ship. David Lyons, who had been responsible for the project, was asked to remain on Macquarie Island to represent the division on any decisions made on the future of the stricken vessel.

Richardson wanted action. On 16 December 1987 the minister announced that the new all-Australian supply and research ice-breaker had been given Cabinet approval, and that the Government would 'enter into detailed contract negotiations with P&O Polar'.[11] Richardson:

> We finally came to a point where the P&O offer was the better offer, and everyone told me so. We had to move quickly—and we did. We built a bloody good ship which has stood the test of time. . .so if I need to be vindicated, I think that vindicates me.

Events were moving at a cracking pace. Moncur was plunged into an intensive round of meetings concerning the new ship. Following the success of the division's submission to Cabinet, Bleasel asked Moncur to go to Melbourne in mid-December to negotiate with P&O. The Government had agreed the division could conduct negotiations with P&O Polar, leading towards a detailed charter.

During the discussions in Melbourne P&O told Moncur that in order to qualify for a ship's bounty concession (under the Ship Building Bounty Act of 1982) they needed a legal relationship with the charterer, as the bounty concession would substantially affect the final charter price. P&O said this legal agreement had to be in place within a matter of days to ensure the vessel would qualify for the bounty—before 31 December 1987.

P&O gave Moncur the text of a letter of intent which would enable them to place an order with an Australian shipyard for the construction of a vessel 'appropriate for the charter'.[12]

On 18 December P&O told Moncur they needed the letter of intent from the division urgently. Well aware of the importance of the document, Moncur says he rang Bleasel in Hobart to discuss the matter, and suggested that the wording be cleared not only with Senator Richardson's office, but with the Attorney-General's Department.

The letter of intent was later the subject of an inquiry by the Commonwealth Auditor-General, published in 1990. The report noted that before issuing the letter of intent, the Antarctic Division had sought and received oral advice from the Australian Government Solicitor on the nature and content of the letter and the risks involved. In a later written response, the Australian Government Solicitor concluded that the letter might put the Commonwealth 'at a negotiating disadvantage'. . .and 'as a result of the above the Commonwealth may be obliged to accept a charter containing provisions less favourable than it would otherwise require'. Although this was not a procedure favoured by the Australian Government Solicitor, there were 'particular features of the case' where 'the issuing of a letter of intent was considered acceptable'.

One was to enable P&O Polar to enter into a contract for construction of the vessel before 31 December 1987, so that the ship builders could qualify for a bounty under the Ship Building Bounty Act 1982, 'which was only available at a particular rate until the end of December 1987'.

'Secondly, the Department was hopeful that the use of a letter of intent would ensure the availability of the vessel for the 1989–90 Antarctic season.'[13]

The two men's recollections differ sharply. Bleasel maintains he did not know of the letter of intent until after it was signed, and that he would never have agreed on behalf of the division that such a document should be signed, 'because it was unnecessary and it gave an unreasonable advantage to P&O in the charter negotiations'.

Moncur did refer the text of the letter to the Attorney-General's Department, which suggested a modification to the wording relating to the ten-year charter of the proposed vessel, '. . .subject to the negotiation of a charter acceptable to the Commonwealth. . .' The letter was cleared by Senator Richardson's office and Moncur signed it.

P&O had not submitted a tender in the original bidding process because they did not have Antarctic experience. This problem was overcome by joining in a consortium—P&O Polar—with Polar Schiffahrts-Consulting GmbH, controlled by Guenther Schulz (the former owner of *Icebird*).

On 15 March 1988 the *Sydney Morning Herald* ran a story headlined UPROAR OVER GOVT POLAR SHIP TENDERS, saying 'three companies have challenged the way the Federal Government handled the tendering process for Australia's new $124 million Antarctic ship project'. TNT Shipping was identified as one of the unsuccessful bidders. The article went on to detail alleged changes in the specifications of the new ship, which had originally been required to be able to break 80 centimetres of ice:

> According to shipping industry sources the Antarctic Division plans to upgrade that ice-breaking capacity to 1.3 or 1.5 metres. 'It seems that the vessel we tendered for is not the vessel they're going to construct' a TNT source said.

P&O's managing director, Mr Brian Baillie, yesterday dismissed complaints about the tendering process as 'a lot of balderdash' and said he had never been through a more exhaustive one.[14]

Following this and other articles in the national press, the Federal police were called in to investigate the alleged altering of confidential tender documents, but found no evidence of improper procedures.

While negotiations continued between the Antarctic Division and P&O Polar, the division announced a nation-wide competition to involve all young people under eighteen to find a name for the new ship. Some 2500 entries were received, some of which were ambitious to say the least. *Noituloser* ('Resolution' spelt backwards), *Jim's Folly, Mother-In-Law's Breath, Grunting Walrus, Breaker Morantarctic, Aussie Cracker, Icy Pole* and *Big Chill* did not make the short list. One young hopeful submitted *Bottle-Of-Ink* (rhyming slang for 'Borchgrevink'—a Norwegian-born Australian who was the first to winter on the Antarctic continent). The most popular suggestion was *Aurora Australis* (108 entries), followed by *Douglas Mawson* (41 entries). *Aurora Australis* was chosen, and twelve-year-old Brett Webb, of Jindabyne, New South Wales, won the competition on the strength of his explanation:

> I chose this name because it illuminates the sky, and hopefully the scientific knowledge gained from this ship will illuminate mankind's knowledge. The name also reminds us of an earlier *Aurora* sailed by Captain John King Davis, which played a vital role in Antarctic exploration from 1912 to 1917. . .

Unfortunately young Brett could not take up his prize of a trip to Antarctica on the vessel he helped to name because he suffered from asthma. As it happened, there was a small sailing boat named *Aurora Australis* already registered, but the owners agreed to change it. (*Aurora Australis* is often affectionately referred to by ANARE people as the 'Orange Roughie'—the name of a deep sea fish also referred to as the sea perch or blue grenadier.)

Early in 1988, Jim Bleasel went on sick leave to have some small growths removed from his vocal chords, following which he was not to use his voice for three weeks. DASETT secretary Tony Blunn asked him to return to duty as soon as he could after his operation to prepare for a parliamentary inquiry into the management of the Antarctic Division which was due to start in July, working to deputy secretary Peter Kennedy.

Although Bleasel was able to speak again when he arrived back at the division, hardly anyone else was speaking to him. He was nominally still the director of the Antarctic Division, but his deputy, Rex Moncur, was acting director at the same time. As Bleasel was to reveal later in evidence to the parliamentary inquiry—the Joint Parliamentary Committee of Public Accounts—Kennedy told him he was not to involve himself in any way in the running of the division. Bleasel: 'I was told that—it was just as blunt—I must not talk to staff or I would find myself transferred to Canberra.'[15]

Rex Moncur confirms that he was asked by Tony Blunn to act as director at this time:

> I said to Tony, 'I feel pretty uncomfortable about that, I think my working relationship with Jim is such that it will be quite difficult for me, particularly if he's still in the building'. And Tony said, 'Well, if you're not prepared to do it, I'll send someone down from Canberra who will. . .If at the end of things you feel uncomfortable, I'm happy to transfer you back to Canberra'. I actually agreed to do it on the spot. I knew, even at that time, that they were looking for a different style of management.

The Joint Parliamentary Committee of Public Accounts hearing into the management of the Antarctic Division began in Hobart on 11 July 1988. Although to some extent it was a reaction to allegations of irregularities in ship tender processes and 'certain payments' that surfaced in the press in early 1988, it also concerned itself with questions raised about internal management practices in the division dating back to the Joint Management Review of 1983. Some of the issues addressed were: performance of the division's shipping broker; proper procedures allegedly not being followed concerning a fruit and vegetable contract; that *Lady Franklin* was unsafe and there were irregularities in the tendering process; staff-management relations; and concerns about the tender process for *Aurora Australis*.

The Public Accounts Committee (PAC) was not the only body investigating Antarctic Division affairs. DASETT initiated its own internal departmental inquiry, a 'Review of the Tendering Process for the Antarctic Replacement Vessel', which was completed by September 1988. There was also a report from the Auditor-General, 'Antarctic Supply Vessel—Chartering Arrangements', released on 2 November 1990. Neither the DASETT review nor the Auditor-General's report found evidence of any irregularities by anyone in the division or DASETT. However, the PAC was by far the most wide-ranging investigation and concluded its hearings on 13 April 1989. Chaired by Labor MP Robert Tickner, it comprised five Senators and eight members of the House of Representatives.

Witnesses who appeared before it included senior bureaucrats from DASETT and the Antarctic Division, representatives of South West Chartering Pty Ltd (ship brokers), Guenther Schulz (the owner of *Icebird*) and the ubiquitous 'I C White' (Geoff Dannock) who had originally raised a number of alleged improprieties at the division with the former minister for Science, Barry Jones.

Dannock, who still works at the Antarctic Division, says his career has suffered as a result of his actions but has no regrets.

Jim Bleasel's fate had been sealed well before the results of the PAC inquiry were known. Senator Richardson wanted him out. The deputy secretary of DASETT, Peter Kennedy, flew to Hobart and told Bleasel he was to be transferred back to Canberra whether he wanted that or not. Bleasel announced his resignation as director on 2 December 1988. He told the press he was proud of his achievements, but needed a further four years to complete his transformation of the Antarctic Division from 'a boy scout operation to a professional organisation'. After the challenge of ANARE, transfer to a 'boring' job in Canberra was not on. 'I couldn't go to a grim death in Canberra living the life of a public service zombie.'[16] He decided to stay in Hobart—where he has since pursued a successful business career.

Despite all the allegations and dirty washing aired at the long-running parliamentary Public Accounts Committee (the evidence filled four volumes and 1143 pages of transcript) the final recommendations were surprisingly positive. Chairman Robert Tickner's summary of its findings acknowledged that the division had made 'significant headway with respect to financial, personnel and other management practices' since the Joint Management Review of 1983.

Tickner also acknowledged that 'there had been an evident lack of attention to some of the processes and requirements expected of government agencies'. The report recommended that 'greater attention be paid to obtaining legal advice and to adhering to the terms and conditions of contracts'.

But it then became clear that the parliamentary members of the PAC had become fascinated by Australia's Antarctic activities, particularly the scientific work being done, and in Tickner's words, 'the committee moved further away from the allegations to examine the role of science in the division and the level of resources available to the division to achieve its purpose'. In so doing, it recognised a point made by Jim Bleasel in his evidence that, despite all the criticism of his management style, 'the Antarctic Division. . .has been filled with people who work very hard and are very dedicated'. The PAC report:

- recommended that the role of the Antarctic Science Advisory Committee (ASAC) be widened to provide a better mechanism for the scrutiny and accountability of the division's activities. . .

JAMES EDWARD BLEASEL, BSc

Jim Bleasel was 48 when he came to the Antarctic Division in 1984. He spent his boyhood in Sydney and left school at the age of fourteen in 1959 to join the PMG (Postmaster-General's Department). No one asked him his age, but fortunately he had turned fifteen by the time a permanent position was available. Within the PMG he qualified as a senior technician and by the time he was 24 was the youngest supervising technician in Australia. At that time he went to night school to get the formal qualifications he had missed by leaving school so young. After matriculating, he went on to do a university degree in engineering, specialising in electronics and communications. He had to take a demotion in the PMG to start at the lowest level for engineers, but worked his way up to a Class 4 Engineer (Class 5 is the top).

Bleasel moved to the National Materials Handling Bureau in 1974 in charge of engineering and special projects until becoming director in 1979.

> I was the director for five years, and we built up the reputation of getting things done! Amongst other things we prepared the concept designs for the new wharf at Darwin and several rail terminals and plans for fruit and vegetable handling systems. . .We did a lot of work in South-East Asia, principally to do with livestock, grains and fish handling. We concept-designed an abattoir in India and a cold store in Egypt.

He went to Hobart in 1984 and during his four years with the division took a particular interest in setting up mechanisms for long-term planning, trying to solve the shipping problems

ANTARCTIC DIVISION DIRECTOR JIM BLEASEL (LEFT) AND PETER WILKNESS, US DIRECTOR OF THE NATIONAL SCIENCE FOUNDATION, AT THE DIVISION, KINGSTON, JANUARY 1985. (R REEVES)

in coping with an ambitious rebuilding program as well as carrying out normal resupply and an expanded program of marine research. While he was director *Icebird* was chartered, and the decision made to build *Aurora Australis*. Bleasel took a close interest in the selection and assessment of personnel for Antarctic service, and introduced new selection procedures for officers-in-charge (station leaders).

He increased the number of summer bases in the AAT with the aim of expanding the annual summer programs to make maximum use of this accessible time. These included Law Base in the Larsemann Hills, Dovers Base in the Prince Charles Mountains, Edgeworth

▶

David Base in the Bunger Hills and a refuge at Cape Denison, near Mawson's Hut, as a basis for future work in the eastern sector of the AAT. Bleasel started the program of returning the nation's Antarctic garbage to Australia and negotiated with the directors of all other nations active in Antarctica to do the same. The Antarctic Science Advisory Committee (ASAC) and the ASAC research grants scheme were put in place during his time with the division—at the instigation of the Minister for Science, Barry Jones. He reduced the size of the rebuilding program and increased the number of scientists going to Antarctica.

Australians knew a great deal about what ANARE was doing in Antarctica while Jim Bleasel was Director of the Antarctic Division. The publicity was not always positive, but people were in no doubt that Australians had a role in Antarctica. His policy of inviting politicians to voyage south as guests of the Antarctic Division resulted in considerable bipartisan support for ANARE activities.

When he left the division in 1988, Bleasel went into the hospitality industry:

I have developed hotels, restaurants, bottle shops, a mini-brewery—the only one in Tasmania—and a night club. Since I retired my annual turnover has gone from $1 million per year to $12 million. That speaks for itself.

- proposed that the division would need more resources to achieve ASAC's objectives. . .
- confirmed the importance of scientific research in Antarctica, recognising also that environmental policy had an increasing role to play. . .
- gave a ringing endorsement to Australia's involvement in the Antarctic 'and wishes to see Australia's credibility maintained and enhanced by observing appropriate administrative, environmental, safety and scientific programs that will demonstrate the commitment'.[17]

It was an outcome difficult to foresee when the PAC began its hearings the previous year amidst a plethora of newspaper headlines alleging mismanagement and doubtful tendering procedures.

During the final hearings in April 1989, the secretary of DASETT, Tony Blunn, confirmed what all insiders already knew: that the former director 'did not enjoy the confidence of the Minister'. Blunn described Bleasel's management style as 'crash through'—adding that he thought 'there was a definite place for that management style. I thought he achieved much.' Blunn confirmed that the deputy director, Rex Moncur, would act as director until a permanent appointment to the position was made.[18]

In earlier evidence to the PAC, Moncur made it clear that he did not think there was 'any big bang solution for the Antarctic Division'. 'What we really need is a period of stability. We need to define our goals for a

long period and we are doing that so that the staff who are there can plan. . .'[19]

It was time for the Antarctic Division to disappear from the headlines. This was certainly a priority in the upper echelons of DASETT. Tony Blunn:

> I certainly saw Rex as providing a very stable, thoughtful approach to the work, and as a person having a very fair opportunity of quietening things down, and processing what I thought was one of the most important projects we had at the time—the *Aurora Australis*.

After seven months of negotiations between the Antarctic Division and P&O Polar since the letter of intent was signed in December 1987, the contract for construction was signed on 17 July 1988. Construction of *Aurora Australis* began at the Carrington Slipways, Newcastle, on 29 October.

On 18 September 1989, the bright orange hull of *Aurora Australis* slid sideways and splashed spectacularly into the water after being launched by Mrs Hazel Hawke, wife of the Prime Minister. At 94 metres and 3600 tonnes it was the biggest (and last) vessel ever built at the Carrington Slipways.

As the Antarctic Division prepared to take delivery of its multi-purpose research and resupply flagship in time for the 1990–91 shipping season (with accommodation for 109 passengers, a trawl deck for state-of-the-art marine science and oceanography, and a helipad and hangar with space for three helicopters), there was hope that the trials and tribulations of the 1980s were about to give way to a renewed and confident approach to Antarctic science in the 1990s—symbolised by the arrival of *Aurora Australis*.

CONTEMPORARY ANARE 1989–1997

TWENTY-ONE

TOWARDS 2000

Rex Moncur became acting director of the Antarctic Division in April 1988 at a time of considerable corporate angst. The organisation was about to be investigated by a Federal parliamentary inquiry, and the speed of change and reforms driven by Jim Bleasel—together with various allegations of mismanagement—had combined to create a volatile and uncertain environment at the Kingston headquarters. The personal styles of Moncur and Bleasel were vastly different. Moncur, a quietly spoken self-described conservative and 'old fashioned public servant', preferred to operate behind the scenes, while Bleasel, an ebullient extrovert, 'led from the front'. Moncur:

> Graham Richardson is supposed to have said, 'There is only one person in this portfolio who gets more publicity than me, and that's Jim Bleasel'! And I think that's why a different style was required. I knew when I came into the job that Rex Moncur was not to get any publicity, and we were to make sure that it all went to the minister. . .I moved to a very consultative way of working with staff and with unions. Some people think I went too far, but I thought it necessary to recover the ground and stabilise the organisation.

Moncur remained as acting director while the Public Accounts Committee completed its inquiry. As well as responding to questions from the committee on its management practices, the Antarctic Division was able to put proposals to it—with a very positive outcome. Moncur:

> As a result, another ten science positions were created and a number of other positions in operational areas that were important—an environment officer for instance, and a legal officer so we could progress initiatives

with the Protocol on Environmental Protection [Madrid Protocol]. . .And so we finished up with 20 extra staff positions.

On 21 December 1989 Rex Moncur was confirmed as Director of the Antarctic Division:

Partly because we'd been through some pretty difficult circumstances, I thought it was important to have a focus and a direction for the organisation. And I also saw it as important to do this in a consultative way. So I started up a fairly long process of talking to staff about the directions of the organisation. . .setting out goals, objectives, guiding principles and the way ahead.

Moncur's corporate goals for the Antarctic Division were listed under two main headings, 'Guiding Principles' which related to how the division was to function internally, and 'Goals to 1997' which would attempt to set priorities for the scientific work to be carried out in Antarctica. The direction of those goals was about to be profoundly influenced by international events.

The concept of Antarctica as a potential resource, an undiscovered source of mineral riches, had always been a primary—if unstated—concern of all nations with an interest in the continent. With all but 2 per cent of Antarctica covered in ice, and with any planned offshore oil rigs having to contend with vast moving icebergs, mining or oil drilling was always going to be a last resort activity. However, in the mid-1970s there were headlines in the Australian press like: FROZEN ASSETS—ORE FOUND ON ICECAP—MINERAL FORTUNE FOUND IN POLAR MOUNTAINS—this last referring to 'a mountain of iron ore' discovered by Russian scientists working in the Prince Charles Mountains in the Australian Antarctic Territory.[1] Ten years later, this hype had been replaced by more authoritative reports. On 22 May 1985 the *Sydney Morning Herald* reprinted a *New York Times* article claiming that a West German research ship had found 'unambiguous' evidence of oil deposits beneath the Bransfield Strait, near the Antarctic Peninsula in an area subject to competing territorial claims by Britain, Argentina and Chile.

By the early 1980s conservation organisations world-wide were already taking a keen interest in trying to prevent any oil-drilling or mining in Antarctica. In May 1982, the *Australian* headlined, CAMPAIGN FOR WORLD PARK IN ANTARCTICA, spearheaded by 'the Antarctic and Southern Ocean Coalition—ASOC', said to represent 'almost 200 animal welfare and environmental groups'.[2] By early 1983 reports that the Weddell and Ross Seas might contain 50 billion barrels of oil resulted in the *Sydney Morning Herald* reporting a London-based story, GREENIES OUT TO 'SAVE' ANTARCTICA, and claiming a world campaign to try and prevent 'the potentially disastrous effects of drilling for oil and minerals' in Antarctica.

With no obvious disagreement from any of the Treaty parties, the adoption of a mineral resources convention seemed assured after the fourth Antarctic Treaty Special Consultative Meeting (SCM) in Wellington, New Zealand, on 2 June 1988.

This agenda was about to be dramatically reshaped by a controversy which erupted over Australia's sudden refusal in May 1989 (supported by France) to ratify the Convention on the Regulation of Antarctic Mineral Resources (CRAMRA) which had been adopted by all the Antarctic Treaty Consultative Parties at its meeting in Wellington in June 1988.

CRAMRA was an attempt to develop an internationally approved regime to govern any commercial mineral activity which might be proposed in Antarctica, and formal negotiations had been going on between Treaty parties since 1982. Some of those involved in the CRAMRA negotiations, like the Antarctic Division's David Lyons, now see the reference to the 'regulation of Antarctic mineral resources' as a public relations disaster. It did not seem so at the time. Lyons:

> The Swedes suggested that it should be called, 'The Convention for the Protection of the Antarctic Environment'. . .[because] what the Convention did was to close down Antarctica to minerals activities, and then have a very rigid and detailed process to look at the possibility of opening it. So it was a very good title. There were a few chuckles around the room at the Swedes' idea, and it was put aside. But, in retrospect, if it had been called what they suggested, it'd still be around. The majority of the people who criticise it have never read it and don't understand the contents of it. Although you joke about the titles of things they are actually terribly important.

Lyn Goldsworthy, then co-director of the influential international conservation group ASOC, disagrees:

> A name change would certainly have made the Convention more difficult to reject—a name can hide a thousand lies—but most nations acknowledged that the Convention wasn't about protection. The minerals negotiations were clearly predicated on the assumption of mining. Initially the strict regulations were negotiated primarily to maintain the scientific cooperation upon which the Antarctic Treaty is based, rather than any strong concern for the environment. . .

Goldsworthy is in no doubt that in dismissing CRAMRA, the Antarctic Treaty Consultative Parties accepted that mining 'was not acceptable—however strictly regulated—in the world's last great wilderness'.

The proposal that Australia would support CRAMRA had been put to the Australian Cabinet when it met in Melbourne on 28 March 1988. The proposal was endorsed by the Department of Foreign Affairs and the Antarctic Division both of whose representatives had been attending international meetings on this issue for seven years. Paul Keating was then Treasurer:

> It was unusual for the Cabinet to meet out of Canberra, we did it maybe once a year. . .and it was a foregone conclusion that we would sign the Minerals Convention. . .Graham Richardson, who was Environment Minister, and Gareth Evans [Minister for Foreign Affairs] had discussed this earlier and Richardson and his department had come to the view [we] were better signing. . .it was better to have a regime than no regime.

No opposition was expected, and there was some surprise when both Keating as Treasurer and Peter Cook as Minister for Resources opposed signing the CRAMRA agreement. Keating:

> Peter Cook worked simply, I think, on his departmental brief which said: 'Our rights and ownership down there are uncertain, and. . .the opening up or discovery of mineralisation and its exploitation may disadvantage us in the longer term.'

Keating's objections were largely environmental—that the area was pristine, the Southern Ocean was a very large reserve of food which was important in the ecological balance, and 'we can, on this occasion, afford to stop'. He argued that CRAMRA had been conceived 'in the post-OPEC shock' and that 'we should let the thing drop':

> Well, this was just heresy at this meeting. . .and in fact Hawke made a few derisory remarks about my contribution, saying, 'Where had I been living. . .didn't I understand this had been going on for so long. . .God, I've never heard such rubbish'—all this sort of stuff. And I said there's another reason—and that's Cook's reason. . .If we're a major player in the world mineral trade—and we are, we're the largest exporters of coal and one of the largest exporters of minerals—why would we let the Japanese, the Americans, the Russians and everyone else hop into another continent full of minerals?

Keating and Cook were the only members of Cabinet to oppose CRAMRA and the decision was made to continue negotiations to sign the agreement. Six months later, in September 1988, Paul Keating travelled to Paris shortly after Michel Rocard of the French Socialist Party became prime minister after two years of conservative government:

I went there with Don Russell, my private secretary, and the then Australian Ambassador, Ted Pocock. And I was the first minister to visit the French Government in probably ten years. . .It was quite an occasion as it turned out, because there'd been a sort of breakdown in relations over the Pacific [nuclear] testing, even while the Fraser Government was in office.

Rocard and Keating quickly established a personal rapport and discussed a variety of topics ranging from economics to trade unionism and the policies and politics in New Caledonia. At the end of their discussion, Rocard told Keating that he and President Mitterrand were looking for an appropriate way to celebrate the bicentenary of the French Revolution in 1989. One suggestion was to promote the formation of an international agency to monitor and safeguard the world's environment. Keating told Rocard that when the vested interests of different countries were taken into account on issues like greenhouse gas emissions, such an agency would take many years to achieve, and would certainly not be in existence in time for the 1989 Bicentenary the following year. Rocard asked the Australian treasurer if he could suggest something that was international—not just French. Keating:

> I said, 'As a matter of fact I do have an idea—but before I tell you about it, let me be honest and say that my own Government doesn't support it, and I'm in a minority of two in my own Cabinet on it'. And he said, 'What's that?'. I said, '[Very soon] we and all of us are going to sign the Minerals Convention on Antarctica, and I think this is a great mistake, because we're going to put up the green light to exploit the area. . .And I think it's possible for us to say, 'Look, I know we've been moving down this road towards a convention now for a decade. . .but it's not really a good thing to do, and it's not all that useful, and on second thoughts we're not going to be in it. We're pulling out.'

CRAMRA was due to be opened for signing on 25 November 1988 (and remain open for that purpose for a year). Rocard asked Keating how the Minerals Convention could be stopped at such a late stage. The Australian treasurer said he believed that if France and Australia, 'two serious players in world affairs', were to take such a view, other countries could be persuaded to join them. He reminded Rocard that his own Cabinet intended to sign. Keating:

> He said, 'Well, what could I do?'. I said, 'Well, it'll be better for you to be in touch with Hawke, because in a sense, my views on this are a bit tainted. It'll look [as though] I'm trying to refight the fight. But if I were able to go back and say to him that I'd spoken to you and that

you were interested in it—that would, I'm sure, interest him. So you'd better prepare a letter, or a telex or fax, and I can tell you what approach to take.

After their meeting, Keating spent some time with one of the French prime minister's secretaries giving him advice on the line to take:

I'm not sure whether they actually sent the correspondence. . .or made a phone call, but I told him it would be better to be in touch with Bob personally. . .Bob picked it up and it all went on from there.

In Australia, Greenpeace and other non-government organisations were mounting an emotive and powerful campaign against signing the Minerals Convention. Division policy manager Andrew Jackson recalls that between 1988 and 1989 there were some 12 000 letters and post-cards on the issue sent to the minister for DASETT.

The anti-CRAMRA forces received an unexpected propaganda boost when the Argentine ship *Bahia Paraiso* ran aground and sank near the Antarctic Peninsula on 28 January 1989, spilling about 675 000 litres of fuel and oil. That accident was followed by a far worse ecological catastrophe on 24 March 1989—the grounding of the *Exxon Valdez* in Alaska, which spilled 49 million litres of crude oil into the Arctic environment.

Political support in the Labor Party against CRAMRA was escalating, fuelled by the member for Dunkley, Bob Chynoweth. Chynoweth joined four other Federal parliamentary colleagues on Voyage Six on *Icebird*, in January and February 1989, as guests of the Antarctic Division for a resupply voyage to Mawson and Davis. The ALP was represented by Chynoweth, Peter Milton, Alan Morris and Colin Hollis. Ian Cameron, then member for Maranoa for the National Party, was the sole representative of the Coalition. All the Federal members (except Colin Hollis who was there representing the Parliamentary Public Works Committee) travelled south as members of a parliamentary committee preparing a report on tourism in Antarctica.

At Davis Station, Chynoweth was part of a group flown to Platcha Hut, in the Vestfold Hills. On the evening of 1 February he tired of a vigorous political discussion in the hut with Milton, Cameron and the ANARE people there, and walked some distance away to sit by himself on a rock waiting for the moon to rise so he could photograph it against the background of the rocks and the ice cliffs that marked the inland border of the Vestfold Hills:

It was midnight, and the sun takes about an hour and a half to set. Just to say that you are the first person to sit in this place is awe inspiring. It made me more conscious of the environment than ever, and how lucky we are to have places like this which haven't been spoilt. That's why we've got to hang on to them.[3]

Chynoweth later likened the experience to a kind of 'sermon on the mount'. He had been ambivalent about the issue of signing the Minerals Convention before he went to Antarctica. At that moment, sitting on that rock in the Vestfold Hills, he decided to try and save it. He talked it over with Peter Milton later, and got his support. On his return to Australia he made up a folder of some of the photographs he'd taken in Antarctica, and sent it with a covering letter to all ministers and every member of caucus, pleading that the Minerals Convention not be ratified. As well, he presented a petition to Federal Parliament with more than 30 000 signatures.

He was well aware of the significant support for ratifying CRAMRA, not only from the Department of Foreign Affairs, but from both Graham Richardson and Gareth Evans:

> Peter Milton and I decided to take the argument up with Richardson and Evans. They both said it couldn't be done. Gareth said to me when I met him at Canberra Airport one day, 'You won't do it'. One day I was flying to Canberra with Peter Milton talking about the no-mining push. Andrew Peacock [then Liberal Shadow Treasurer] was sitting behind us, and he said, 'I wish you people wouldn't talk so loud'. Both major political parties were in agreement on the issue.

Events were moving swiftly. On 12 April there was a debate in the Senate, during which the Australian Democrats called on the Government not to sign CRAMRA but to promote an alternative regime based on the world park concept. By 20 April, Prime Minister Rocard announced in Paris that the French would not ratify CRAMRA as it stood. Then on 2 May, Leader of the Opposition John Howard announced that it was Coalition policy not to sign CRAMRA. On 3 May, the Senate passed a motion, supported by the Australian Democrats and Independents, against signing. The Labor caucus also opposed signing CRAMRA on 11 May.

Australian delegates to the preparatory meeting for the 15th Antarctic Treaty Consultative Meeting in Paris from 9 to 13 May were asked to informally sound out the views of other countries' delegates to gauge what response there might be if Australia did not sign CRAMRA. Andrew Jackson, from the Antarctic Division, was a member of the delegation:

> What Australia was hinting at was a great threat to the stability of the Treaty system, and other nations just looked at us in horror. I remember the other delegations with whom we normally got on very well—like

New Zealand, the United Kingdom and the United States—literally hissing at us! Even to this day we still feel some of the effects of us having broken the ranks.

The critical decision on Australia's position was taken at the Cabinet meeting of 22 May in Canberra. By that stage Prime Minister Bob Hawke (after reviewing the arguments and taking advice from one of his most trusted advisers on economic and environmental matters, Craig Emerson) had decided Australia should not sign CRAMRA. The main opposition came from Gareth Evans, the Minister for Foreign Affairs, and Graham Richardson, the Environment Minister. Hawke:

> They pressed their arguments; a no-mining stance would damage Australia's relations with our Antarctic Treaty partners; the conven-tion was a *fait accompli* and we would be ridiculed internationally; rearguard opposition was pointless as the work had already been done; whether we liked it or not, the new treaty had to be ratified for reasons of *realpolitik*.[4]

The Prime Minister said he refused to accept these arguments, and announced that Australia was going to try to lead the world on the issue and change the world's thinking on it. He believed his view was in tune with a growing anxiety around the world on global envi-ronment issues such as the impact of greenhouse gases and the damage to the ozone layer:

> I felt the general public was years ahead of bureaucrats and govern-ments in such matters and that we could advance the right case on a rising tide of public opinion which, in the end, the bureaucrats and their political masters would not be able to withstand. And so, with an amused tolerance, and almost total scepticism, the Cabinet let me have my head. We announced that Australia would not sign CRAMRA and that we would seek the agreement of our Antarctic Treaty partners to replace that convention with a new agreement which would provide for a comprehensive protection of Antarctica as a 'Nature Reserve—Land of Science'.[5]

Graham Richardson's memory of that Cabinet meeting was that Paul Keating argued strongly on economic rather than environmental grounds:

> When it came to the Cabinet discussion Keating was the key figure—he was the one who turned it. . .Keating was in full flight, and he did it very, very well. . .Hawke ran with Keating. Why wouldn't he?

The first step in what Hawke dubbed his 'Mission Impossible' was to enlist the support of the French. Australia had supported the South Pacific Forum in condemning French policy in New Caledonia, but the election in 1988 of the Socialist Prime Minister, Michel Rocard, had eased tensions—particularly with the signing of the Matignon Accords which set out the steps towards a referendum in 1998 on the future status of New Caledonia. In June 1989 Hawke flew to France, where he met the great international environmentalist Jacques Cousteau, a man he had long admired:

> There was a mutual sense of excitement as we joined forces in pledging to take on the world. Cousteau had already spoken to [President] Mitterrand, and promised to speak to him again before I met the President the next morning; he had already spoken with Rocard. Jacques was enthusiastic about our strategy of mounting the international campaign around the concept of making Antarctica a 'Nature Reserve—Land of Science'.[6]

The odds seemed extremely long against international agreement to abandon CRAMRA. On 28 June 1989, while the Prime Minister was overseas trying to enlist other Treaty countries' support, the *Australian* editorialised about 'The futility of the Federal Government's political posturing on Antarctica', and concluded:

> After London and Washington, Mr Hawke should realise just how isolated he is on the issue, and just how hopeless is his tilting at windmills. He should, for a moment, think beyond the ALP's wooing of the 'green vote' and sign the convention before the deadline.[7]

Hawke had a polite hearing from the British Prime Minister, Margaret Thatcher, but no promise of support. 'Margaret tended to be suspicious of anything sponsored by the French. . .' In Washington President Bush was equally polite, but 'locked into the position of his officials who were among the most unrelenting proponents of CRAMRA'. Hawke was encouraged, however, by a meeting with Senator Al Gore (later US vice-president) who believed that public opinion could be mobilised behind the Australian–French proposal.[8]

Australia embarked on a massive diplomatic effort. Foreign Affairs doubled the size of the Antarctic Section and sent people all around the world. Andrew Jackson:

> They had their foreign missions all lobbying for our position. That would not have been sufficient on its own. What had changed the Government's position in Australia was public opinion, and public opinion had to be

changed in other countries as well. We had the most unusual position of the Government and the NGOs [non-government organisations] all lobbying for a common position! We had a very close liaison between the Government and Greenpeace, and the Antarctic and Southern Ocean Coalition (ASOC) working in other countries.

The diplomatic campaign for a new agreement continued throughout 1990 and Australia had attracted some support, but not of the key powers. Andrew Jackson remembers a very long and difficult meeting in November at Vina del Mar in Chile, with seemingly little prospect of reaching an agreement:

> Australia was very much *persona non grata* here—we were really despised. We were often taken into smoke-filled rooms and basically abused by the heavyweights from some of these delegations trying to get us to break down our position and to weaken the solidarity of the 'no mining' countries. This was a real difficulty, as the four countries [Australia, France, Belgium and Italy] didn't agree on some fundamental issues themselves, but we had to present ourselves as being totally united!

There was at least agreement that negotiations should keep going, and that there should be a Protocol rather than a Convention. A further meeting was scheduled for Madrid in April 1991, immediately before the preparatory meeting of the 16th Treaty session. Intense lobbying continued, and Japan and the United States did not agree to the Protocol on Environmental Protection to the Antarctic Treaty (Madrid Protocol) until June 1991. The Antarctic Division's Rex Moncur played a key role in these negotiations:

> I had some terrible slanging matches with the US. . .[they] were just so negative to anything that Australia put forward. [It] is US broad policy not to bind the US to anything as it doesn't have to be bound to. . .they want as much flexibility in anything that they can ever have. And so the idea that they might be prevented from mining in Antarctica was, just in broad principle, contrary to their views.

At the last moment, the United States refused to agree to the formula on a review of the crucial mining prohibition. The Australian Prime Minister, Bob Hawke, intervened personally, both writing to and telephoning US President George Bush:

> I was able always to talk with George on a rational basis. . .it was the intrinsic merit of the case, and also the question of leadership. I pointed out the experience they'd had in Alaska [with the *Exxon Valdez* oil spill]

and that not only was this case important, but this was something that there should be leadership from the United States on, rather than negativism.

Hawke's initiative was fruitful. On 4 July, President Bush announced that the US would agree to the Protocol effectively banning any mining in Antarctica for 50 years. Prime Minister Hawke went further, saying it would be virtually impossible to begin mining after the 50-year ban:

> I think Australia is to be congratulated with France on the way in which we have stuck to our guns. Largely as a result of the initiative by Australia. . .that great wilderness in the Antarctic is going to be preserved.[9]

Only the formalities remained. On 3 October, the final Special Consultative Meeting in Madrid agreed to the Protocol on Environmental Protection to the Antarctic Treaty, designating Antarctica as a natural reserve devoted to peace and science—as well as four annexes relating to environmental impact assessment, conservation of Antarctic fauna and flora, waste management and disposal and the prevention of marine pollution. (A fifth annexe on area protection and management was negotiated in Bonn at an Antarctic Treaty Consultative Meeting in October 1991.)

Australia had played a key role in overturning CRAMRA and substituting the Protocol on Environmental Protection. Yet the haste with which the Protocol had been drafted had resulted in a document which, in the opinion of negotiators like Andrew Jackson, was full of legal loopholes, vague language and 'weasel words'—ways out of your obligations:

> Compared to CRAMRA, the Madrid Protocol is a political document full of broad objectives and intentions, but very thin on detail about how things would actually happen. CRAMRA, on the other hand, was a very simple document in political terms, but enormously detailed in terms of legal precision. It was very carefully drafted.

The Madrid Protocol was negotiated just in time for the Antarctic Treaty meeting in Bonn to adopt a formal declaration recognising the 30th anniversary of the Treaty on 18 October. The Protocol was cited as 'a fitting tribute to the anniversary' and a symbol of the way in which Treaty parties had worked in Antarctica 'in a uniquely successful agreement for the peaceful use of a continent'.[10] Jackson:

> There never was the review which had been allowed for in the Treaty. Of course, by the end of all this the Treaty nations were all punch drunk

417

with the negotiations! We have seen a very quiet time in the Treaty system since then.*

Ros Kelly took over from Graham Richardson as Minister for the Environment on 4 April 1990. She did not have a quiet time. During the negotiations for the Madrid Protocol, Australia agreed to remove its husky dogs from Mawson Station to comply with strict new environmental guidelines on introduced species in Antarctica. It was an emotional issue—not made any less so by a statement from Graham Richardson in 1988 that the huskies would stay in Antarctica. This followed criticism by Greenpeace representative Lyn Goldsworthy of the dogs as an 'alien species', of the fouling of the area near the dog lines, and of their penchant for 'regular mauling of penguins silly enough to stray close to the dog line or not quick enough to escape when the dogs are free'.[11] There had been howls of protest from dog-loving expeditioners and many letters written to the ANARE Club's magazine *Aurora* and other publications.

The Antarctic Division's director, Rex Moncur, was well aware of Richardson's statement on the Mawson huskies:

> We actually responded [at the time by] writing to the ANARE Club saying, 'The minister has made a decision that we will keep the dogs'. So when it came to negotiating the Madrid Protocol at Vina del Mar, we had an annexe that was all about flora and fauna and the concern was to avoid introduced species. And being aware that my minister had made a decision about the dogs, I had to say, 'Well, Australia needs an exception to this. And while we acknowledge the problem of introduced species, we want to keep the dogs we've already got. And because of the problem of inbreeding, we want a mechanism whereby we can bring additional dogs.'

When the next round of negotiations began in Madrid in April 1991, the Americans—who were irritated by Australia's about-face on CRAMRA—homed in on the issue of the huskies in Antarctica. Moncur:

> The American representative, Bob Hoffman, pointed out that there had been examples of transfer of canine distemper to seals in the Northern Hemisphere and he was very concerned about having dogs transfer it. And he was also concerned that you just can't have a special case for the dogs that are there at present. If you're going to allow dogs, there might be other people who might want to take dogs. . .then disease could get transferred.

---

* By February 1997, 23 of the 26 Treaty parties involved in drawing up the Madrid Protocol had ratified it. The United States, Japan and Russia were yet to do so. Although all Treaty parties have agreed to abide by the provisions of the Protocol, it will not be formally binding until it is ratified by all parties.

The only nations with dogs in Antarctica were Australia, Argentina and Britain. When Britain agreed to remove its dogs, Moncur knew Australia's position was becoming extremely weak:

> Here we are trying to push this most stringent environmental regime, and we're holding out on one issue of wanting an exception to the introduced species criteria. So I said to myself, 'We're going to have to change. That's the only way we're going to get the Madrid Protocol.'

Moncur consulted with Argentina's negotiators, and discovered they were prepared to remove their dogs to enable a consensus. He got in touch with Tony Blunn, the Secretary of the Environment Department, and asked him to get a decision from Ros Kelly to reverse Graham Richardson's ministerial decision. Kelly agreed, and Australia announced its decision to pull its huskies out of Antarctica.

There was immediate outrage from the ANARE Club and all those who had wintered with or worked with the Mawson huskies. A ferocious campaign was begun to try to have the decision reversed. Ros Kelly remembers it as the most intense and highest profile of all the issues that arose in her entire time as Minister for the Environment:

> The intensity of it caught me by surprise—I even had people crying on the telephone! It was a very emotive issue, and logic just didn't come into it. There was really no alternative action for us to have taken. If we had not agreed to bring the dogs out, the whole negotiation process for the Madrid Protocol would have collapsed.

Opponents of the decision to remove the huskies from Mawson pointed out that the dogs had been isolated in the pristine Antarctic working environment for 41 years 'with no record of acquiring, carrying or transmitting disease and it is ludicrous to suggest that they could now introduce diseases'.[12] As to the threat to wildlife, the taking of seals for dog food was abandoned in 1982. Huskies were an important historical link with the past, they were still the safest way of travelling over sea ice or crevassed territory, and were an important boost for morale for wintering ANARE expeditioners.

Questions were asked in Federal Parliament, petitions presented, and articles written for magazines and daily newspapers. Moncur, who had gone as far as he could to retain the huskies, was unimpressed by some of the tactics used:

> The ANARE Club in Canberra—just prior to an election—went around with photographs of these dogs interviewing little children in the ten to fourteen age group and saying, 'Your local MP Ros Kelly is proposing to take these lovely dogs out of Antarctica where they have been all

their lives. . .' And the kids made comments like, 'Our Member is being dreadful. Isn't she mean, taking the dogs away from their homes and their mothers.' I thought it was far too extreme. Ros stuck to the decision through all of this, and it was a horrendous campaign on her.

There were even suggestions that all the huskies would be shot, which was not true (although individual, old huskies had been put down by a combination of shooting and humane injections for many years). Under the terms of the Madrid Protocol, all dogs were to be out of Antarctica by 1 April 1994. As it happened, they went sooner rather than later. The Antarctic Division wanted the dogs kept together as working teams, with living conditions as close as possible to those they had experienced in Antarctica. The preferred option was an outdoor recreation and educational establishment near Ely, Minnesota, but places could not be guaranteed for the dogs after December 1992.[13]

Aurora Australis took the nineteen youngest dogs and three pups from Mawson on 4 November 1992, leaving six of the older dogs for another year. A film, *The Last Husky*, was made documenting the journey from Mawson to Minnesota. Rex Moncur had been quoted in the *Independent* newspaper, London, as saying that 'the only problem we expect at first is that they may be frightened of trees'. As viewers of that documentary now know, the Antarctic huskies reacted to their first ever trees in Minnesota by marking them instinctively in true doggy style. With images of the huskies cheerfully pulling sledges of sightseers through snow-filled woods, and housed in wooden kennels (instead of staked out in the open as they had been at Mawson), press and public interest in the huskies waned (much to the relief of the beleaguered Antarctic Division and Ros Kelly). The ANARE Club's virulent campaign subsided and turned towards nostalgia and the celebration of 41 continuous years of working with and enjoying the company of huskies in Antarctica. Much of this nostalgia was captured in a book published in 1995, *Huskies in Harness—A Love Story*, edited by Shelagh Robinson.

With the Madrid Protocol agreed to, and his own position as director confirmed, Rex Moncur turned his attention to the Antarctic Division's priorities for the 1990s:

There was a clear need to give far more emphasis to the environment. Australia had led the rest of the world with France, but Australia was primarily responsible in setting up this comprehensive protection of the Antarctic wilderness. . .we needed to give leadership. . .so part of the focus was the environment.

At a meeting in Canberra to discuss the future directions of the division, Minister for the Environment Ros Kelly stated that research into

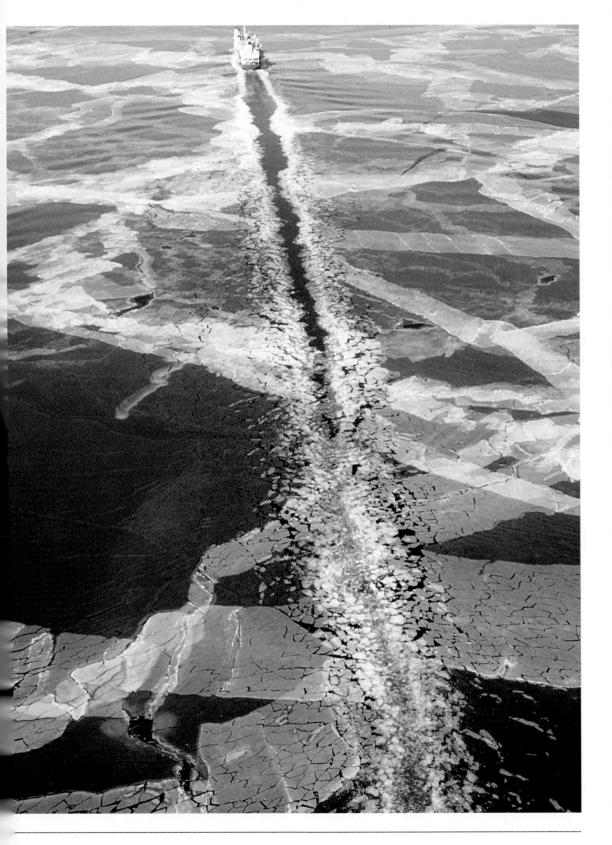

A TRACK CARVED BY *ICEBIRD* THROUGH NEW ICE.

(J KELLY)

▲ Mawson's Hut, built in 'The Home of the Blizzard' in 1912 is gradually being destroyed by the fierce katabatic winds. (T Petry)

▶ Mawson's Hut at Commonwealth Bay is a fascinating time capsule but its interior is rarely seen. In 1978 an ANARE party entered the hut to assess its condition. Dr Mawson's room is only partly iced up, with objects still visible on the shelves. (R Ledingham)

▶ Five men occupied this field camp at Spit Bay, Heard Island, in 1992. All the field huts were removed at the end of the year. (AAD Archives)

▲ Wintering camp at Spit Bay, Heard Island. A plume of smoke from the active volcano Big Ben can be seen clearly. (K Green)

▼ A sad and expensive sight at the beginning of the 1988–89 season. The remains of three Squirrel helicopters destroyed when cargo lashings failed in the hold of *Icebird* in heavy seas just south of Tasmania. (P Greet)

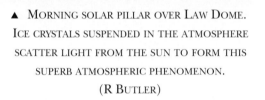

▲ Morning solar pillar over Law Dome. Ice crystals suspended in the atmosphere scatter light from the sun to form this superb atmospheric phenomenon.
(R Butler)

▶ Medical Officer Lloyd Fletcher at the foot of ice cliffs near Mawson Station, 1980.
(Syd Kirkby)

▲ WHERE ARE THEY GOING, AND WHY? ADÉLIE PENGUINS ON THE MARCH IN FRONT OF A GROUNDED ICEBERG NEAR DAVIS STATION.
(D CALDER)

▶ *EUPHASIA SUPERBA* (KRILL) IS THE WORLD'S MOST ABUNDANT CRUSTACEAN AND FORMS THE STAPLE DIET OF MANY SEALS, WHALES, FISH, SQUID, PENGUINS AND OTHER SEABIRDS.
(S NICHOL)

▲ WEDDELL SEAL AND PUP, LONG FJORD, VESTFOLD HILLS.
(D CALDER)

▲ AERIAL VIEW, NORTHERN PRINCE
CHARLES MOUNTAINS.
(M CORRY)

▶ FROZEN LAKE SURFACE, VESTFOLD HILLS.
(D CALDER)

▶ THE WATER IS SO CLEAR IT LOOKS LIKE AIR.
ANITRA WENDIN AND PAUL BUTLER DIVING
INSIDE AN ICE CAVE IN CHAOS GLACIER NEAR
DAVIS STATION IN THE SUMMER OF 1990–91.
SHORTLY AFTER THEY EMERGED FROM THE
WATER THE CAVE COLLAPSED.
(M LUDGATE)

▲ JAN SENBERGS'
MAWSON, PAINTED IN
1987, RESEMBLES A GIANT
CRAB WITH AN INDUSTRIAL
CARAPACE PRECARIOUSLY
CLINGING TO THE
COASTAL EDGE OF THE
ANTARCTIC ICECAP.

▶ A NEW WAY OF LOOKING
AT ANTARCTICA. *VOYAGE II*
WAS PAINTED BY JAN
SENBERGS FOLLOWING HIS
VOYAGE SOUTH AS A GUEST
ARTIST ON THE ANTARCTIC
DIVISION'S HUMANITIES
BERTHS PROGRAM IN
1987.

global change was a priority. Moncur:

> This clearly linked very much into a lot of the work we were doing. So I then combined the importance of protecting the Antarctic environment with the importance of understanding global change as goals.

TEMPORARY ACCOMMODATION ON THE HELI DECK OF *AURORA AUSTRALIS* FOR MAWSON'S HUSKIES AS THEY LEAVE ANTARCTICA EN ROUTE FOR THEIR NEW HOME IN MINNESOTA, USA, NOVEMBER 1992.
(J DALLAS)

Moncur began to encourage debate on the Antarctic Division's future goals through his membership on the board of the Antarctic Foundation, talking to seminars and interested parties like the ANARE Club and meeting staff throughout the division. He referred to the original policy aims set by the Menzies Government back in the 1960s which set great store on sovereignty, and the strategic importance of Antarctica to Australia—an issue which had diminished in importance following the end of the 'cold war':

> If we could no longer pursue our interests through sovereignty—which was clearly impractical—we had to pursue them through the Antarctic Treaty system. So having a stronger role and influence in the Treaty system was fundamental to achieving Australia's interests. And undertaking science had to my mind become much more important. First of all because it was clear that Antarctica was critical to understanding global change; secondly it was still of enormous practical importance for weather forecasting; and thirdly because science was essential to underpinning management decisons aimed at the protection of the Antarctic environment.

Following the Joint Parliamentary Committee of Public Accounts (PAC) review of the Antarctic Division and its performance in 1989, the Antarctic Science Advisory Committee (ASAC), then chaired by Professor Neville Fletcher, was asked to assess the division's scientific productivity after some criticism at the PAC that it was not as high as it should be. It had even been suggested that the division should not undertake its own

The following excerpts are from an essay 'A Love Affair In Antarctica' by Tom Maggs—one of the many ANARE expeditioners who contributed their memories of the huskies to the book *Huskies in Harness*.

Doggers, you left the dogs behind at Mawson, and they make the place complete. They passed down their bloodlines, the shifts of the wind, the creak of the heaving ice, and a million small doggy footsteps at the service of us all. . .'The huskies' belonged to Mawson, just as surely as the Opera House does to Sydney, as Uluru does to central Australia, or as Clancy does to the Overflow. . .

. . .You can see the little buggers leaping, and you can hear them yelping and hooting, squealing and barking out their excited welcome, and you feel the hair on your neck rise. . . 'They're OK, they won't bite humans but you've got to pat them all', your guide says, and you start methodically with the first one on the lines, and he leaps and grabs at your shoulders. He splats those big hairy, pooey feet on your clean ventiles, for God's sake, and he puts his nose in your mouth and his tongue in your nose, and he head-butts your sunglasses off your face, and he squeals and sings his welcome and his joy at you. And you do the whole line, you do it all. . .and they are all the same, full of life and joy and energy. . .

As your time passes at Mawson. . .occasionally if you're lucky, a massed exalted howling, a spine chilling song of the soul, when every dog raises its head, lays back its ears, and sings its heart to the aurora, or the moon, and its dog spirit. . .and by God you'd better be there, and you had better sing too. . .raise your head and hit

Jim Milne cuddles Nemarluk aged about 18 months on the Mawson dog line, 1978. (AAD Archives)

that note that sets them off, and you close your eyes and come together in a spine tingling hymn of being. . .

Where do we doggers tell about our dogs?. . .Where do we tell of the dogs singing to the katabatic, of the awe at a first-time mother eating her puppies, or the dark abyss of Charlie's courageous black eyes? How do you describe the trembling and the fumbling as you check the chamber of the .38? The tightening in your chest and the lump in your throat as you pat, then stand beside and take aim at that big furry head? The guilt you carry like a beacon when you return past the dog lines to the station alone, and the lying awake and the tears you have to hide for nights afterwards. . .?

►

Did you say your farewells to the boys properly before you left Mawson?. . .make sure you get those memories out now and then. . .share those feelings with your best friends, and those who'll understand. Let the boys all choose their places, let them tangle up their traces, let them fight and bark and pull and sing along. Let it all return, that rage and laughter, joy and sorrow, boundless energy and fatigue. And keep alive that bond the Mawson huskies formed with you and your dogging mates.

Remember the huskies.[14]

AUSTRALIAN SLEDGE DOGS IN ANTARCTICA: A CHRONOLOGY

1947 British offered Labrador huskies from their Antarctic Peninsula operations to Australia; offer declined after long negotiations because of logistics and quarantine complications.

1948 The British Labrador dogs (donated to the French by the Governor of the Falkland Islands) and additional Greenland huskies obtained by French Antarctic Expedition for use at station to be established in Adélie Land.

1949–50 French expedition arrived in Melbourne after failing to reach Antarctic coast. Huskies placed in quarantine at Melbourne Zoo for winter, and dogs not needed by French, along with pups born over winter, acquired by Australian Government for training and use at Heard Island prior to establishment of Antarctic station.

1950 On 15 January, twelve huskies loaded in Melbourne aboard HMS *Labuan*, arriving at Atlas Cove, Heard Island, on 5 February.

1951 Further sixteen dogs shipped from Melbourne Zoo to Atlas Cove. 'Oscar' born at Heard Island.

1953 Heard Island dog population about 60.

1954 On 21 January, 30 huskies loaded aboard *Kista Dan* to be landed at Mawson 9 February 1955.

1957 On 19 February, dogs landed at Davis, including Oscar, then six years old.

1959–62 Alaskan Malamute dogs at Wilkes transferred to Australian care when station became a joint Australian–US establishment. Oscar moved from Davis, via a short sojourn in Melbourne Zoo, to Wilkes, where he fathered more than 50 pups before dying in a blizzard in 1962.

1962 Two New Zealand dogs backloaded from Scott Base to Mawson to improve bloodlines.

1963 Three Greenland huskies shipped to Mawson and Davis aboard *Nella Dan*.

1965 Davis Station temporarily closed and dog operations ended.

1969 Wilkes closed and operations transferred to newly completed Casey. Dog operations end soon after.

1979 Three dogs from Scott Base sent over on C130 flight to Casey and two shipped on to Mawson. (The Casey pet dog was put down shortly after.)

▶

1986	Hobart-bred dog Jock and Alaskan Malamute added to breeding stock at Mawson.	In 1974 a husky named Cactus was sent from Mawson to Davis Station as a pet. He was a mixed blessing for the Davis winterers, who split into two camps—Cactus haters and Cactus lovers.
1992	On 4 November, nineteen dogs, all of Mawson's working huskies, plus three pups taken aboard *Aurora Australis* bound for Hobart and then by air to Los Angeles, USA, before road journey to Ely, Minnesota.	During the winter Cactus (who was stone deaf) slipped his collar and escaped. Remarkably, he survived for several months in the wild before being found, proving that a husky can live through the winter without human aid. Senior biologist Knowles Kerry is not sure
1993	On 15 December 1993 the last five older dogs left Mawson on *Aurora Australis* for Hobart and private adoption in Tasmania and Victoria.	how Cactus did it: 'He may have eaten dead penguins, or managed to find the Amanda emperor penguin rookery.' Cactus was put down early in 1975.

scientific programs, but simply provide logistic support for research in Antarctica carried out by university scientists.

A sub-committee chaired by Fletcher, assisted by Professor Roye Rutland and Professor Michael Bryden, conducted an extensive review, interviewing many members of ANARE inside and outside the division. Its conclusions and recommendations were published in its 1992 report, 'Antarctic Science—The Way Forward'. Fletcher, Rutland and Bryden found that criticisms of the division's scientific programs and its performance aired at the PAC could not be sustained. In fact the division's research performance was creditable compared to that of other nations, and the published output of both the division's and outside scientists had increased by about a factor of two over the previous five years. Fletcher:

> [The sub-committee] saw a clear continuing role both for the division and for scientists from outside agencies in the ANARE program, but also saw a clear necessity for a more carefully planned approach to Antarctic science programs if the best scientific output was to be achieved.

They recommended the upgrading of the position of Assistant Director (Science) to Chief Scientist for ANARE, the appointment of several senior scientists, and the expansion of the division's scientific personnel numbers—these extras to be covered by decreases in logistic expenditure with the winding down of the station rebuilding program.

The ASAC report stressed that the first priority should be given to research that 'primarily relates to studies of global and regional change (particularly climatic change), the management of the marine ecosystem and associated data gathering and monitoring'.

This influential ASAC report recommended some fundamental changes to the way the Antarctic Division organised its science program:

> The total Antarctic program should be restructured into six principal sub-programs concerned with Atmospheric Sciences, Biological Sciences, Glaciology, Oceanography, Geosciences and Human Impacts respectively. Lead agencies should be given responsibility for coordinating each of these sub-programs. . .[15]

These new directions were approved by the Government and welcomed by Rex Moncur. In 1993 the Cabinet reviewed the Antarctic program and agreed to the following key goals which derive from both the debate which Moncur had stimulated and the recommendations of the ASAC report:

- understanding global climate change;
- protecting the Antarctic environment (including the marine ecosystem);
- obtaining information of practical importance; and
- maintaining the Antarctic Treaty system and Australia's influence in it.[16]

Strategic plans for all areas were developed during 1994 and 1995, and program leaders progressively appointed. The 1995–96 season was the first during which the new arrangements were fully implemented into the ANARE program.

Meanwhile, through the late 1980s and early 1990s, the rhythm of annual resupply and the support of scientific programs had been proceeding despite the trauma of the Parliamentary Public Accounts Committee inquiry and administrative angst caused by leaked documents (and other information) to politicians and senior officials outside the division, aimed—according to assistant director of the Antarctic Division Jack Sayers—at undermining senior management:

> Initially the leaks were targeted at Jim Bleasel, but later other members of the management team, including Rex Moncur and myself, were included in the net. . .Some of the anonymous actions were particularly malicious and cowardly. . .

Although Sayers was aware the allegations were aimed at undermining particular individuals, he claims the real effect was to cause serious damage to the division's public image, and place an enormous work load on those who had to prepare extensive briefs and reports as rebuttals:

When ANARE first went to Heard Island in 1947, it was intended to establish a base at Spit Bay, on the eastern end of the island, but bad weather and the exposed coast forced the landing to be relocated to Atlas Cove in the north-west. It would be 45 years before Spit Bay would see a wintering ANARE party.

Although there had been three summer visits from 1985–1988, a short winter visit to the island in May and June 1990, led by biologist Ken Green, had revealed a surprisingly high number of seals on the eastern end of the island in winter—about 1700 Antarctic fur seals and 4500 elephant seals. Green and Harry Burton, manager of the Antarctic Division's land-based biology program, believed a year-long study of these animals, as well as of king penguins, was warranted—particularly in view of potential competition for food resources between the Heard Island animals and any future commercial fishing. The Antarctic Science Advisory Committee found the proposal had scientific merit and recommended that it go ahead.

Green and Burton argued that it would cost only $70 000 to link two summer programs to a wintering one. They proposed a base camp comprised of four 'Apple' huts (circular portable fibreglass constructions), one 'Melon' (an extended Apple), and a portable toilet and shower unit. This equipment was purchased and packed by October of the preceding year by Green and field equipment and training officer Rod Ledingham for a four-person party. But according to John Wilson, the division's chief engineer, their cost estimate would have had the team 'living in tents and washing in the surf'. Wilson approached research and development engineer Attila Vrana to apply for the position of expedition leader, and his subsequent application was unanimously accepted by the expedition planning committee on the basis that Vrana would also provide technical support for the party. Wilson and Vrana were interested in testing new field designs for a wind electricity generator and a fibreglass 'Googie' field hut for extreme conditions—an elliptical module supported above the ground by a tubular steel structure. On this basis, Vrana costed a wintering expedition at $1.5 million, including shipping and other infrastructure costs.

The Antarctic Division decided to proceed with the program, but Ken Green feared that the project was being hijacked by the division's engineering section. Green had led the 1990 expedition. He then worked for two years to convince the Antarctic Division that the winter expedition of 1992 was worth doing. Consequently he was particularly upset when the Division appointed Vrana as the field leader. Green told Vrana he should not have accepted the field leader's position, and asked him to stand down. Vrana (who had been appointed while Green was away on Macquarie Island) refused to do so. Personal relations between the two men were cool, and remained so throughout the expedition.

The proposal to use one Googie was somehow expanded to four Googies and a large fibreglass shed as a store (as well as four Apples and a Melon) for base camp accommodation; this meant that preparations took longer than planned. Vrana had to stay behind when *Aurora Australis* left for Heard Island on 9 January 1992 with the other four members of the party, Green, Dave Slip, Geoff Moore and the doctor, Erwin Erb. In a repeat of the 1947 experience, bad weather forced the ship to land the party at Atlas Cove instead of Spit

Bay. There they conducted what studies they could for four weeks, broken by a visit by *Aurora Australis* on 12 and 13 February.

Meanwhile Attila Vrana had boarded *Icebird* with field huts and equipment, visiting Davis and Mawson stations before arriving at Atlas Cove on 22 February. *Icebird* then sailed for Spit Bay where relatively good weather allowed all huts, equipment and supplies to be ferried ashore by a combination of amphibious LARCs and helicopters. Erecting the buildings took seven days, with the help of ten Antarctic construction workers on their way home. Because of weight restrictions, the four big Googies were shipped in an unfinished state and Vrana had to complete them after the ship's departure, adding their electrics and plumbing. Tools for installation and maintenance of the expedition's huts were in very short supply because the tool kit had been misplaced on the ship (it was found among the ship's tools a year later). A single precious screwdriver was dubbed 'the most treasured tool on the island'. Adding to the party's woes were a lack of petrol for the power generator, and a communications problem that prevented telex traffic between the island and the division's communications centre in Tasmania. These difficulties were not resolved until *Aurora Australis* made a special detour to the island carrying fuel and replacement radio-telex equipment on its return from Davis in March.

Vrana's work on the base camp took some months to complete, and he was unable to begin to set up the wind generator until spring. However, when finally installed in mid-November, the wind generator operated satisfactorily for three months until a gale on 1 February temporarily put it out of action. While operational it produced over 5000 kilo-

A SQUIRREL HELICOPTER ABOUT TO LIFT A PORTABLE GOOGIE HUT OFF *ICEBIRD*, HEARD ISLAND, 1992. (K GREEN)

watt hours of energy and except during calm or very windy periods carried the full electrical energy demand of the base. (The same unit, after a minor welding repair, operated at head office and subsequently at Casey for a whole year.) It was an idea worth pursuing in the light of increasing pressure on ANARE to seek alternative energy sources. The other buildings, though their construction had caused so many difficulties, were appreciated. Moore found the controversial Googies 'good in a big blow':

They [all] felt more secure than the Apples, and made working in the labs and living more comfortable. This was particularly true when you were trying to use the computers. At least they stayed dry!

But the social situation at Spit Bay was far from promising. Ken Green's relationship with Vrana was the main concern, although fortunately Green was away from the base camp most of the time working on macaroni penguins near Winston Lagoon. The other biologists, Dave Slip and Geoff Moore, lived simply at Doppler Hill three kilometres to the south of Spit Bay, using a gas cooker and 12-volt lighting. Green exchanged few words with Vrana when back at Spit Bay, but tensions came to a head when Green judged that Vrana had failed to pass on quickly enough his wife's wedding anniversary greetings. Green:

A SMALL TOWNSHIP OF FIELD HUTS AT SPIT BAY, HEARD ISLAND, 1992. (K GREEN)

> Words were said, blows nearly came to fruition and a frosty, formal communication that had existed between us for eleven months ended, and we did not speak to each other for the next four months—or since for that matter.

Geoff Moore felt the tension keenly as he, Green and Vrana were the only three wanting to climb Big Ben, the active volcano on Heard, and he was on good terms with both men. Moore found Erwin Erb to be 'the most self-contained individual I have ever met—a truly wonderful man' and noted that Dave Slip 'was immune to most things, and let the tension pass over him without getting involved'. But in the entire year the five men had only one meal together —Moore's birthday on 21 May.

Despite the space age accommodation, living was basic and far removed from the normal ANARE station life of the 1990s. During winter the Heard Islanders had to crack ice out

of the creek near the lagoon, carry it back to camp and melt it down. Like the sealers a century earlier, they augmented their frozen rations with Kerguelen cabbage as a flavoursome antiscorbutic. All but Erb (a Swiss) used skis all winter, and all stayed very fit. A stitched finger which Ken Green injured while cutting through a container was Erb's only major medical case—apart from consistent dentistry from the cold conditions and sugar-rich diet.

Most of all, Heard Island in 1992 was an experience of raw nature in one of the world's wildest places. Geoff Moore found it astounding:

> It was the last of the great ANARE adventures. You travelled independently over the glaciers and around the coastline. . .You have to be alone in this wild, furious landscape to realise the insignificance of the individual. It's like going to the moon. . .

> Big Ben erupted during the year and steam

from the crater 2745 metres above could be seen clearly on the rare clear days. On 18 December all the huts began to shake, and all five men had the same thought—an elephant seal was trapped under the supporting scaffolding. Green:

> Only then did it occur to us that it was an earthquake. Pumice, washed ashore over the next few days, confirmed that it was an undersea volcanic eruption between Heard and the McDonald Islands only 35 kilometres away.

One of many rewarding parts of Moore's year on Heard Island was spending the winter living with the animals and observing the seasonal changes such as the arrival of the bull elephant seals, courtships, couplings and births, and the raising of young. Moore has vivid recollections of the king penguins raising their chicks through the harsh winter and the enormous numbers of macaroni penguins arriving at Long Beach 'to transform the desert landscape within a week to a colony of a million penguins'. He also recalls his experiences in passing through 15 000 fur seals, mostly aggressive males, between Spit Bay and his Doppler Hill field camp:

> At first I was intimidated, but I ended up fairly blasé about it. You learn to understand their personal space—I just put up my foot and they always backed off. In the winter they get cheeky, it's hilarious. They love snow and will toboggan down the slopes at you!

The winterers' experience came to an end with the arrival of *Icebird* on 10 March 1993.

WORKING WITH ELEPHANT SEALS AT SPIT BAY, HEARD ISLAND, 1992. (K GREEN)

For a week the ship stood off Spit Bay while virtually all trace of the expedition was removed from the site, leaving the island once more to itself. For two of the biologists, the end came all too quickly—Green's and Slip's contracted positions with the division ended only six months after they returned, although in Moore's estimation 'they needed at least two and a half years to write it up adequately. . .Ken is still writing his results up in his own time'.

On the whole the participants found the 1992 Heard Island wintering well worthwhile. To Vrana, it was enjoyable, unusual and exciting, though he had some regrets:

It could have been one of the best years in our lives for all of us! We could even have climbed the mountain together, but it was a fairly lonely year. . .I would have felt less lonely if I had been there alone than I was there that year with that group.

For Green, the expedition demonstrated that good science could be done by a small team with few home comforts. Despite the personal friction, he is adamant that the winter of 1992 was the best of his eight years with ANARE:

The freedom on Heard Island was absolute. You lived or died by your own decisions. . .and because of that you treated the environment with respect. It had more than just wildlife for me. I totally immersed myself in its history, searching out undocumented sealers' ruins and a water reticulation system that still worked in winter one hundred years on.

Wherever you went the mountain was always there, dominating your life as it dominated the weather. . .I would do the fourteen months all over again.

A number of us felt particularly bitter because proponents of this game caused considerable costs to the taxpayer. . .yet were able to hide comfortably behind their anonymity. Despite all the allegations and leaks, there was never any indication of dishonesty or misdemeanour.

Some of these allegations surfaced at the Public Accounts Committee hearings and involved chartering arrangements for the German-owned ship *Icebird*. During the late 1980s there were a number of serious contractual difficulties with *Icebird*, which Sayers remembers as an 'ongoing series of nightmares':

I recall that in the middle of one shipping season [1988–89], a dispute between the owners and a former owner-manager of the ship almost resulted in the ship being detained and placed under arrest in Hobart. Thankfully this did not happen—otherwise we would have faced enormous logistics problems in resupplying and changing over our personnel at our stations.

In 1991, with the station rebuilding program still unfinished, it became necessary to renegotiate the charter of *Icebird* to complement *Aurora Australis* in carrying out the scientific and logistic aims of the Division. The ownership of *Icebird* had changed since 1988 and its former owner-manager Guenther Schulz offered the division another ice-strengthened vessel used by the Russian Antarctic program, *Akademik Federov*. Sayers recalls taking part in events that were 'more like the plot of a spy thriller than a government tendering process'. After high-level discussions with a number of government agencies it was agreed that the authenticity of the offer could only be resolved by face-to-face discussions with the principals involved. Sayers:

I was despatched to Leningrad (now St Petersburg) and Hamburg in an attempt to resolve the matter. I went to see the deputy director of the Russian Antarctic program who expressed great surprise that his ship was being offered to the Australian Antarctic Division. 'How could this man offer the use of our ship, he doesn't control the Russian Antarctic program!', said the deputy director. My visit to Hamburg involved hurried meetings in back-street coffee shops, cars and airport lounges in my efforts to keep the protagonists apart and ferret out the truth.

The result was that *Icebird* was again chartered by the Antarctic Division.

By early 1993, Rex Moncur was confident he had the support of Environment Minister Ros Kelly and Cabinet to carry through the Antarctic Division's revised scientific program. But by mid-1993 he was told the division was about to face a substantial cut in its budget. Moncur recalls the departmental secretary, Stuart Hamilton, saying to him in Canberra:

> 'Well, Ros has no choice. She's decided to close an Antarctic station—and this can't be made public.' The situation was that the Expenditure Review Committee had told Ros, 'Unless you turn up to the meeting [it was within a couple of days] with specific proposals to cut, we will not accept any of your new policy proposals'.

Faced with this bombshell, Moncur told Hamilton he would prepare a Cabinet submission advising on the implications of closing a station. But the news was even worse. Hamilton told Moncur that not only was a station to be closed, but there was to be a major review of the Antarctic program—with the clear implication it was to be cut even further.

Rex Moncur returned to Hobart to consider a number of unpalatable options. Just at a time when ASAC had recommended additional expenditure on science positions and a strategic approach to science, he was faced with the closure of a station and a substantial reduction of ANARE activity. It was the beginning of a hectic two weeks of crisis planning, colloquially referred to in the division as 'panic fortnight', while various scenarios and models were considered.

With the rebuilding program all but complete, one obvious saving was to dispense with the charter of *Icebird* and try to do everything with *Aurora Australis*. Moncur was aware that the Department of Finance did not think *Icebird* should be retained when the rebuilding of the stations was complete. However *Aurora Australis*, primarily designed as a marine research vessel, had a limited cargo capacity. There was also the issue of safety. With two ice-strengthened ships available, one could go to the aid of the other in the event of engine failure or besetment. With each of four stations requiring its own resupply visit through the summer season, marine science programs would be compromised. Ship days could be

REX LEONARD MONCUR, ASSOC. DIP.COM.ENG. (RMIT)

Rex Moncur says he 'grew up in Barry Humphries country', beginning his education at Moonee Ponds West State School and moving on to Essendon High School before enrolling at the Royal Melbourne Institute of Technology to study communications engineering. He left in 1962 to join the Bureau of Meteorology as an Observer Radio—responsible for flying meteorological balloons and seeing that the radiosondes they carried aloft worked. Within a year he became a Technical Assistant Grade 2 and finished off his engineering course begun at RMIT. Moncur:

> I reached Engineer Class 2 and was responsible for developing automatic weather stations, radiosondes, sea-surface temperature buoys—forerunners of today's free-floating buoys deployed off our ships in Antarctica. The radiosondes I developed ultimately went to Antarctica and were used there until the early 1990s.

There were other coincidental Antarctic connections. In the 1960s Moncur trialled his radiosonde systems from the vessel *Thala Dan*, chartered by the Antarctic Division. Later when his radiosonde research work was connected with rockets being tested at the Weapons Research Establishment in South Australia, the project was headed by Bryan Rofe, who became Director of the Antarctic Division in 1970.

In 1972 when the Whitlam Labor Government came to power, the Department of Science was formed with Sir Hugh Ennor as the departmental secretary. He and his deputy Jack Lonergan introduced the then radical notion of 'program budgeting' under which organisations like the Bureau of

REX MONCUR—DIRECTOR OF THE ANTARCTIC DIVISION FROM DECEMBER 1988. (R REEVES)

Meteorology and the Antarctic Division had to state their objectives and then justify the funding of specific projects. Before program budgeting, Treasury allocated money to specified categories like salaries, stores, capital works or depreciation. Program budgeting's architect, Jack Lonergan, maintained the old system made it difficult for an organisation to begin a new research program under the former traditional, inflexible financial categories. The new system, according to Lonergan, was 'output oriented—that is, you identified what you wanted to achieve and how much it was going to cost to do it'.

Moncur applied from Melbourne to join the Department of Science and help introduce program budgeting. He heard nothing until a telephone call on a Friday asking him to start in Canberra the following Monday. As Moncur was married with two young children at that stage, he asked if he could delay until the Wednesday! His responsibilities included the Ionospheric Prediction Service, then run by Clarrie McCue—who became the Antarctic Division's director in 1979.

After being made permanent in the Department of Science in 1975, Rex Moncur increased his contacts with the Antarctic Division and ANARE activities, often dealing with Ray Garrod, Director of the Antarctic Division from 1972–79. As Director, Projects, looking after grants to scientific bodies (and working with the secretariat of the Australian Research Grants Committee), Moncur had increasing contacts with academics and senior scientists with Antarctic interests—including John Lovering and Neville Fletcher, both of whom chaired the Antarctic Science Advisory Committee (ASAC).

By 1982 Moncur won the job of Assistant Secretary Resource Management for the Department of Science, work which involved liaising with the Department of Finance and the Public Service Board:

> At this time Jim Bleasel, recently appointed acting director of the Antarctic Division, was trying to get funding from the Department of Finance to allow for the charter of *Icebird* and I was working with him on this issue to convince Finance that the division should have this money.

After approximately six months Bleasel asked Moncur if he would take the position of Deputy Director of the Antarctic Division, and he transferred to Hobart in January 1985.

Rex Moncur was confirmed as director of the division in December 1989. He had the satisfaction of leading ANARE into its 51st year.

saved, however, if the Antarctic Division had the ability to fly personnel between Davis and Mawson with fixed wing aircraft—which could also service summer field parties in remote locations like the northern Prince Charles Mountains as had happened in the late 1950s with Beaver aircraft. Such flights would save on expensive, fuel-hungry overland traverses with tractor trains to establish the summer camps.

The use of short take off and landing (STOL) Twin Otter aircraft was considered. These aircraft can be fitted with extra tanks for long hauls and have a useful cargo-carrying capacity. The Australian adventurer and businessman Dick Smith had helped ANARE out in the 1989–90 season, when he and his pilot Giles Kershaw landed on the sea ice near *Icebird* and flew personnel into the Prince Charles Mountains via Mawson. But a rock airstrip would have to be built near Davis in the Vestfold Hills (an expensive option), and the Twin Otters were too big to carry south on *Aurora Australis*. One option canvassed was to use long-range twin-engined Sikorsky 76 helicopters. Two of these machines could be carried south on *Aurora Australis* and would have the capacity not only to fly personnel

and cargo between stations, but to establish and support summer field parties in remote locations like the Bunger Hills near the Shackleton Ice Shelf.

It was all very well designing cost-saving scenarios, but Moncur had been specially instructed to prepare plans to close a station. Moncur:

'LEGOLAND' IN ANTARCTICA, 1993.
CASEY STATION IS THE FIRST OF THE THREE ANARE CONTINENTAL STATIONS TO BE COMPLETELY REBUILT.
(K BELL)

So I went back to Stuart Hamilton [the Environment Department Secretary] and said, 'Look, you've told me I've got to close a station, but I have another way of producing the saving you want which is, I believe, in our interests. I'm also not keen to go through a major review of the Antarctic program which is going to take at least twelve months—yet another one—which is going to put the whole place in turmoil and uncertainty just as we were starting to get focused'.

The station-closing option was prepared for Cabinet, as well as the 'one ship' proposal with several variants. There was a budgetary sleight of hand about aspects of the one ship option of which Moncur was very aware:

Part of the way I was achieving the saving was to use helicopter support out of Davis so that we didn't have to have traverse support out of Mawson for field parties. That meant that we didn't have to construct a great big workshop at Mawson and we could reduce the scale of it. Also part of the saving was achieved by running Macquarie Island as a small observatory station. . .therefore I was able to say [to the Department of Finance], 'You're going to save money in not rebuilding these things to the same level you otherwise would have'.

It was not a real saving because the division had not yet been given the money for this building work anyway—as the Department of Finance made clear to Moncur. But even so, the Government went along with the alternative plan, and all four ANARE stations stayed open. Moncur:

Even though the Government went for my best option, I didn't get all the money that I thought I was going to get. You know, with hindsight there might have been some better tactical ways of handling that, but doing all this in two weeks

with a very small group and with enormous pressure—I still think it was a terrific result.

ONE OF THE NEW GENERATION OF LONG-RANGE TWIN-ENGINED S76 HELICOPTERS READY FOR TAKE-OFF FROM *AURORA AUSTRALIS*, 1994.
(K BELL)

A wide spectrum of the division's staff did not immediately think so, and the 'one ship option' was seen as a major loss for the ANARE program—coupled with the added risk factors. Two long-range S76 helicopters were chartered by Helicopter Resources and tests found they could just be accommodated in the hangar on *Aurora Australis* with a small hole cut in the steel door. Moncur was well aware he was on 'thin ice' operationally with the one ship option, although it was tested successfully in the 1994–95 season—the first year, coincidentally, that ANARE cargo operations had been conducted without the help of the army and their amphibious LARCs.*

Moncur argues that the *Aurora Australis* gives the division significantly more capacity than it had before *Icebird* was chartered to help with the rebuilding program, and that the science program has not been compromised:

What's happened is we've moved from a situation where we had about thirty people at each of our stations over winter to something like twenty

---

* In the 1995–96 season *Aurora Australis* was out of service for 32 days with mechanical problems which needed repair in dry dock at Fremantle. Fortunately another vessel was available to assist with resupply and marine science. It had been decided to charter a second ship every three years to assist with backloading rubbish from the stations, and carrying items of cargo too large for the hold capacity of *Aurora Australis*. Ironically that second ship was *Icebird*—now renamed *Polar Bird* and owned by the Norwegian shipping company Rieber.

people. . .we will be running sixty to eighty people at each station over summer. . .We are adapting the Antarctic program to the new goals. And in terms of science that means automating a lot of the observations we do over winter. . .but over summer, when people can move out from the stations, we will have a greater number of people in the field.

In March 1996 thirteen years of Federal Labor rule ended when Prime Minister Paul Keating's administration was decisively defeated by the Liberal–National Party coalition headed by John Howard. Unlike previous changes of government during ANARE's half century of operations, there was no dramatic departmental shift. The Antarctic Division remained under the Department of the Environment, Sport and Territories (DEST) with Senator Robert Hill as the responsible Cabinet minister, replacing Labor's Senator John Faulkner. Prime Minister John Howard appointed a junior minister and a parliamentary secretary to assist in the management of this large portfolio, with the Tasmanian MHR Warwick Smith responsible for Sport and Territories and Senator Ian Campbell from Western Australia becoming parliamentary secretary overseeing the Antarctic Division and ANARE operations.

The Howard Government came to power promising to rein in an 'eight billion dollar black hole' budget deficit. Having just survived budget cuts under Labor which had led to the 'one ship option', Rex Moncur knew that any further significant cuts would have disastrous consequences for ANARE. Eighty per cent of the division's budget goes on the infrastructure required just to be in Antarctica—stations, shipping, helicopters and field operations—leaving only about 20 per cent for the cutting edge of science and policy work. Moncur was asked to prepare options for a range of cuts, up to several million dollars, and called to Canberra to explain to ministers Hill, Smith, Campbell and the new DEST secretary Roger Beal how he proposed to meet the cuts. Moncur:

> I said I was reluctant to cut field programs as these provided the regional survey capability necessary to understand the role of Antarctica in global climate change. Reducing ship time would also cut the marine component of these regional surveys.

The director was asked about the possibility of closing stations. He pointed out that not only did they all contribute to the support of the science programs, but if a station was closed it could not be mothballed or left there; it would have to be completely removed under Australia's obligations to the Madrid Protocol on environmental protection. The associated costs would wipe out any savings for many years: 'While this situation did not apply to Macquarie Island, Warwick Smith, as a Tasmanian, was quick to see the political disadvantages of closing Macquarie.'

Moncur also told the DEST ministers that he and Neil Streten (from the Bureau of Meteorology) had just completed an ASAC-recommended major review of the division's resources to try to reallocate funds from support activities to scientific research. This review had located some $350 000 to fund five new research scientist positions and upgrade a further five scientists to this level. While there was the option of not proceeding with these positions, Moncur said it was essential to maintain the division's scientific momentum if the Government's Antarctic goals were to be achieved.

AURORA AUSTRALIS BEGINS THE FIRST EVER MAJOR RESUPPLY OF DAVIS STATION OVER THE SEA ICE, NOVEMBER 1994.
(K BELL)

Evidence that the director's arguments had been heeded was contained in the August 1996–97 Federal budget. While other elements of the public service were slashed, the division escaped relatively lightly. Moncur was told that the division would have to meet the 1 per cent efficiency dividend imposed by the previous Government ($450 000), the 2 per cent cut announced by the Coalition in its election platform ($900 000) and a further $400 000 as the division's contribution to the 'black hole' budget deficit. The good news was that the Government remained committed to keeping the four ANARE stations and pursuing a substantial scientific program, allocating a total of $61 million to the Australian Antarctic program. Keeping the funding for the extra science positions was a notable achievement considering the staffing cuts in most other areas of the public service.

The Antarctic Division still had to trim $1.75 million. One immediate casualty was the ground-based 1996–97 Prince Charles Mountains field program—although plans were prepared to experiment with supplying field parties by long-range helicopter in the Southern PCMs as an alternative. Other savings were to be made by reductions in field programs and ship time, and from administration. In reality the Antarctic Division had survived a tough budget with some belt-tightening—rather than the amputative surgery that might have been required.

437

'When I say let go—jump! Trust me. I'm a Larcie.' The motto was unofficial, but often shouted by soldiers manning the amphibious LARCs to nervous expeditioners descending a Jacob's ladder from the side of a rolling ship at Buckles Bay, Macquarie Island. With the LARC often rising and falling on the swell for distances of three and four metres, it was essential to time the disengagement with the ladder perfectly. It was said—unkindly—that the more attractive the female expeditioner, the more 'Larcie' hands reached out to grab and secure the boarding passenger.

On 28 March 1994 the Australian Army officially ended 46 years of continuous association with ANARE. In the summer of 1947–48 (following problems with landing cargo at Heard Island) army amphibious DUKWs were used

AN ARMY LARC IS UNLOADED OVER THE SIDE OF *ICEBIRD*. (N LOVIBOND)

AMPHIBIOUS ARMY DUKWS WERE FIRST USED ON ANARE SERVICE AT MACQUARIE ISLAND IN 1948. (I FOX)

to ferry passengers and cargo ashore to establish the ANARE station on the isthmus at Macquarie Island. The World War II DUKWs were ideal for the job, as they could not only negotiate rough seas and surf, but carry their cargo directly to the station site.* (DUKW was Army code for: D—date of manufacture; U—utility; K—front wheel drive; W—with winch.) These rugged all-purpose vehicles were effectively 6-tonne GMC trucks with a

---

* The versatility of the DUKW was shown in the summer of 1954–55 when it was used as a support vehicle for an ascent of Mt Henderson, behind Mawson Station. It actually fell into a crevasse, but was winched out![17]

THE AMPHIBIOUS LARCS WERE PARTICULARLY
USEFUL FOR UNLOADING HEAVY CARGO ON
MACQUARIE ISLAND FROM 1970 TO 1993.
(AAD ARCHIVES)

boat's hull built around them. They were used at both Macquarie and Heard Islands, and also on the Antarctic continent from 1955 to ferry heavy cargo ashore through open water to the stations when ice conditions permitted. Their crews were known to ANARE expeditioners as 'Duckies'.

In the summer of 1970–71 a LARC (Lighter Amphibious Resupply Cargo—with a load capacity of 5 tonnes) was tested at Macquarie alongside the DUKWs. While the DUKW was essentially a truck with a hull around it, the LARC was a purpose-designed boat with wheels. (The LARC was designed in the United States in the early 1960s for operations in the Mekong Delta in the early stages of the Vietnam War.) Its seaworthiness can be judged by the first circumnavigation of Macquarie Island by LARC in eighteen hours, during the 1976–77 changeover. LARC personnel, inevitably, were dubbed 'Larcies'.

Although one DUKW was wrecked and lost on a rock at Lusitania Bay on Macquarie Island in May 1951, and several DUKWs and LARCs were sunk when overloaded with cargo (and subsequently recovered), no lives were lost in the Antarctic or sub-Antarctic during army amphibious operations by the 10th Terminal Regiment during 46 years.

The two LARC crews at Macquarie Island went into action with great courage when *Nella Dan* was driven on to the shore in Buckles Bay in a south-easterly gale on 3 December 1987. They rescued passengers and crew despite horrendous weather and sea conditions,

➤

and were all later commended by the Chief of the General Staff, Lieutenant General L O'Donnell. The crews were: Lieutenant Phil Clark, Corporal Tim Gay, Corporal Ken Barrington, Lance-corporal Greg Kenny, Private Alistair Scott and Private Dudley Crowe. (Due to the sinking of *Nella Dan* the summering LARC crew on Heard Island remained there for six months—the longest summering party ever for a LARC crew.)

Since the 1970s the Larcies had established an enviable reputation as entrepreneurs in the small business of selling T-shirts, windcheaters and badges. In 1988, at the celebration of 40 years of army involvement with ANARE, Jack Sayers (then Assistant Director Expeditions, Operations Branch) pointed out that the Larcies had become an integral part of the Antarctic Division's voyage support staff, whose advice was often sought during operations:

Larcies have earned a respected reputation for working hard and playing hard, they have a down-to-earth commonsense approach to problems, and have developed a culture on our expeditions. I might add they have also been responsible for enriching the language of some of the less worldly expeditioners, or those who've led a somewhat sheltered life![18]

The time spent in Antarctica was a welcome break from the Larcies' training exercises—loading boxes of rocks on and off their LARCs in Middle Harbour, Sydney.

In 1994 the army withdrew from its association with ANARE and disbanded the army ANARE Detachment with its fleet of ageing LARCs. Fittingly their last operation was at Macquarie Island where it all began. A LARC crew completed an unescorted circumnavigation of the island in under eleven hours, breaking all previous records. Army records show that 268 personnel have served in the Detachment since 1948.[19]

A s ANARE began its 50th year of existence, travel by ship to its four Antarctic stations was the only option. The oft-debated plans for direct flights to the Australian Antarctic Territory remained unrealised. The most recent attempt was in 1989, when a RAAF Hercules aircraft was made ready to fly directly from Hobart airport to a compressed snow runway at a site named S1, seven kilometres behind Casey Station. This attempt was aborted because of an unusually high snowfall just before the team preparing the runway was due to leave at the end of summer. Assistant director Jack Sayers remained optimistic:

We know how to produce satisfactory runways on snow or ice, but we don't have the funds to do it. During the last couple of years we have been liaising at an operational level with the Russian Antarctic Expedition in developing the concept of an East Antarctic Air Network, known as EAAN.

In the summer of 1988–89, two expeditioners broke their ankles out in the field near Davis Station. Fortunately for them, an internationally coordinated rescue could be organised. At the time, James Shevlin was leading a field party in the Larsemann Hills at Law Base. He overheard a message being relayed to the Davis station leader:

'Oh Davis, we've had a bit of a problem with an accident. A skidoo went over the edge of an ice cliff. . .and we went over with it and we have both broken our legs! We are currently in sleeping bags and are warm, but we can't move at all.' It was an amazingly controlled call, with no hint of panic.

The two men were evacuated by a helicopter sent from Davis Station, where X-rays revealed it was essential to get the injured men to Australia within ten days, as they needed major orthopaedic surgery just so that they could walk again. On the same day Shevlin had seen a Russian aircraft for the first time that season in the Larsemann Hills. After consultations with head office he was asked to contact the Russians to investigate the possibility of assistance:

We didn't have any transport at Law Base, but the Soviet Progress Station was only about half an hour away, so I walked over the hills. They were on a different time zone, and were all asleep. The station leader got out of bed and without further ado said that their aircraft would take off in half an hour!

The Russian aircraft was a veteran propeller-driven Ilyushin 14 which was quickly stripped to take two stretchers. A Russian and an Australian doctor flew with the injured men to Molodezhnaya Station 1400 kilometres to the west, near the western border of the Australian Antarctic Territory. On arrival, two ship-based Russian medical officers were also on hand. Shevlin:

They then arranged for one of their jet aircraft to fly in via South America to Molodezhnaya for the evacuation. It was incredibly expensive, but the wonderful thing about the story is that in an emergency everyone just drops everything and assists without any question of cost. . .everyone is there working in an adverse environment and there is a fair bit of camaraderie because of that.

The Russians flew the two men to South America and they went on to Sydney by commercial flights. They were in hospital within seven days of the accident. Unhappily there was a tragic sequel to this operation. Three crew from the Russian aircraft were killed in a refuelling accident at Mirny within a week of the successful medical evacuation. Shevlin:

So it was one of those things that while it had been a wonderful exhibition of how people work together in Antarctica, it also illustrated once again that it wasn't a totally hazard-free operation.

Such a scheme would involve flights from Hobart to Cape Town and return via several Antarctic stations including Casey, the Russian station Druzhnaya (which is between Mawson and Davis in the Prydz Bay Region) and through Queen Maud Land. Sayers:

> The Russians have aircraft—the Ilyushin 76—which are ideally suited to undertaking the flights. There are a number of countries operating stations in the region which would be interested in operating such a service, including the Chinese, Japanese, Germans, Swedes, South Africans and of course ourselves and the Russians. A meeting was held in Washington DC in May 1995 to explore the feasibility of a cooperative air network, and further discussions will take place over the next year or two.

Apart from the time saved getting scientists in and out of Antarctica in a matter of hours, instead of spending six weeks on a ship, there is also the important matter of safety. Although all nations represented in Antarctica attempt to assist in times of accidents or medical emergencies, there is no guarantee—particularly during winter—that an air evacuation can be carried out.

Sayers believes that there will definitely be an inter-continental air service to ANARE stations within the next five to ten years:

> ANARE cannot enter the 21st Century without a vision which includes an enhanced and effective logistics capacity in support of science—and this must include an inter-continental air capability.

TWENTY-TWO

CHANGING THE CULTURE

It took 34 years from the founding of ANARE for a woman to winter on the Antarctic continent. As with Zoë Gardner's historic year on Macquarie Island in 1976, the male ANARE bastion on the mainland was breached because of a shortage of doctors. Dr Louise Holliday was appointed medical officer at Davis Station in 1981. She entered not only a male domain, but one which was actively hostile to her presence.

Aware of the institutional resentment of her appointment by the 1980 winterers at Davis, she 'tried to reassure them' by talking socially on regular radio-telephone 'skeds' before she left Melbourne. She believes now that these sessions were used as occasions for ridicule. The rumour was put about that she proposed to give all the men on the station a monthly massage.[1]

Dr Holliday had high expectations of her year in Antarctica. As a child she was profoundly influenced by the stories told to her by a family friend, Captain Morton Moyes, who had been south with Shackleton and Mawson. 'He really fired my enthusiasm to go.' Moyes was still alive, aged 94, when she sailed south. Interviewed in the Sydney *Daily Telegraph* before she left in December 1980, Dr Holliday said she thought the ratio of 24 men to one woman 'sounds very nice, doesn't it?' She hoped her presence would help make Davis Station 'a little more civilised': 'That sounds really awful doesn't it? It makes them all sound like apes, and they aren't.'[2]

She hoped to handle her job with 'good sense and poise, and to be flexible and tolerant. I have had extra preparation through the year and I am a Christian so if I have any worries I will pray about them.'[3] Her ship, *Nanok S*, called first at Casey and she wore a skirt for her first trip

443

I n the early 1970s, Antarctic Division photographer Jutta Hösel applied repeatedly to
go south. After yet another refusal for no
apparent good reason, she stormed into the
director's office and demanded to know why
she had been refused yet again.

'Well', replied Ray Garrod rather defen-
sively, 'we don't have toilet facilities for women

in Antarctica.'

'I don't care!' retorted Jutta. 'I'll hold on till
I come back!'

In the summer of 1975–76 Jutta Hösel joined
Shelagh Robinson and Elizabeth Chipman to
become the first ANARE women to officially
visit the Antarctic continent during a summer
season.

MEDICAL OFFICER LOUISE
HOLLIDAY, THE FIRST WOMAN
TO WINTER ON AN ANARE
CONTINENTAL STATION, AT
DAVIS IN 1981.
(S BROWN)

ashore. 'I thought I'd better do the
right thing by the guys, and they were
awestruck—and very deferential—and
very friendly and pleasant.'

Davis Station turned on a welcome
of a different kind. Some members
of the outgoing 1980 party left crude
and obscene drawings on station
notice boards, her luggage boxes
and field hut notebooks. There were
photographs of female genitalia cut
from pornographic magazines, and
carrying captions referring to her.[4]

Reflecting on her experiences more than a decade
later, Louise Holliday does not regret going to Antarctica:

I understood that old ideas die hard and some of
these guys felt fairly threatened. I did my best to be
friendly and didn't want to really hassle. After the
first few weeks things settled down. . .I had a very
good year. . .

I had people I could talk to, and as a Christian I
prayed about it, and I rang home a couple of times.
You just have to use your own resources and realise they're not really
attacking you—they're just feeling a bit threatened themselves, and you
just brush it off eventually.

She spent quite a lot of her time in the surgery, choosing not to
socialise during bouts of heavy drinking, or when 'blue movies' were
screened. After those sessions, she did 'not want to meet them on a dark
night'.

Looking back, Louise Holliday thinks that she may have failed to be a community member, 'because I didn't get drunk, watch porn, and wandered off earlier than many from the living quarters. In retrospect, I wouldn't have chosen me.' Her year in Antarctica changed her outlook on life in a number of ways:

> I certainly learned things I didn't learn at the college or high school. And I think I appreciate people more for who they are—not male/female. I am aware of the beauty of nature even more. . .but not seeing the sun for six weeks down there, I can thank God every day when the sun rises. I think I matured as a person. I became a bit more tolerant, because one has to be tolerant down there.

Holliday's wintering at Davis did not herald an immediate flood of female expeditioners. Doctors continued to be the only wintering ANARE women, with Julie Campbell at Mawson in 1982, Robyn McDermott in 1983 and Lynn Williams in 1984. Dr Williams had first wintered at Macquarie Island in 1981 and went south with her electronics engineer husband, Warwick, becoming the first married couple to winter on the continent as ANARE expeditioners.

Dr Campbell returned to Australia at the end of her year at Mawson angry at the treatment she received from a small group of men at the station. She reported her sleeping quarters were broken into at least twice 'by men affected by drink'.[5]

There was institutional resistance in ANARE, reflected in the division management, to sending women to the Antarctic because of the fear of unleashing sex—with all its perceived attendant complications—to the isolated communities there. Sex was not identified as a problem in the all-male stations up to the 1980s, although ANARE expeditioners were unamused about a story published in the Melbourne *Age* in 1980

Excerpts from OIC Gert Wantenaar's station log reveal little group consideration for the lone woman who hoped to make things 'a little more civilised' at Davis:

> Sunday 22 March—Louise caused a stir by appearing in the LQ [living quarters] in shorts though she is unlikely to repeat the experiment for a while, from the ribald reception she received. . .

> Monday 18 May—Geoff's birthday—this turned out to be a most enjoyable night, continuing into the early hours. Louise lingered longer than usual departing at 10.30, when she was unable to cope with both robust styles of dancing and the number of gentlemen requiring a female partner. . .

> Tuesday 18 August—It was an embarrassing day for me because I had to see Louise about a small growth on a very private part of my anatomy. I took Bob with me in case Louise thought I was putting the hard word on her. But in true professional fashion she dismissed Robert and inspected the offending part. It was nothing serious. . .

A PERFORMANCE OF THE
BAWDY PANTOMIME
CINDERELLA AT MAWSON,
1982. FROM LEFT: BILL
COUCH, DAVE PHILLIPS AND
MARK GALLAGHER.
(K IRVING)

by Ross Clark (a senior research fellow in the Faculty of Architecture at the University of Melbourne) on how men cope without women in the Antarctic. Clark said that the lack of sexual gratification was often overcome by increased oral gratification—eating. He went on to say that overt homosexuality was non-existent. 'But mild covert homosexuality runs virtually through the group. The guys would not admit that it was homosexuality.'[6] Clark said homosexuality took the form of horseplay, including pretend kissing and cuddling. Overt homosexual advances were rare and were frowned on by the rest of the group.

While the occasional midwinter pantomime performance of Cinderella, with its attendant burlesque drag, was regarded by its participants as letting off harmless sexual steam, the inclusion of 'real' women in the community was a significant change to the culture. Both Jeannie and Rod Ledingham on Macquarie Island in 1977 and Lynn and Warwick Williams at Mawson in 1984 were careful about how they behaved in public. Lynn Williams:

> The group on the whole accepted it pretty well. . .although you sleep in the same room at night. . .you're by no means in a normal social environment. So displays of affection, for example, are just not on.

In later reflections on 'mixed groups' in Antarctica, Lynn Williams made the point that it is too simplistic to talk of male–female relationships. All should be thought of as expeditioners who are 'mixed' on many levels. For example, the scientist and the tradesman or builder ('boffin' versus 'tradie'), the 'barfly' with indoors interests versus the more adventurous, outdoors-oriented expeditioner. Then there were the 'macho-heroic' types, who saw themselves as intrepid conquerors of the 'Great White Hell' of Antarctica, measured against those who thought 'my Grandma could do it'. Another distinction could be drawn between those who were interested in pornographic movies and girlie posters, versus those who 'chose to do something else when a porn movie is shown on film nights'.[7]

All personal relationships on an Antarctic station are subjected to far more pressure and scrutiny than communities elsewhere. Expeditioners see the same people every day for meals, socialise and work with them for at least nine months of the year. There is nowhere else to go. Personal disagreements simply have to be worked through. Tolerance is regarded as a prerequisite for successful wintering in Antarctica and there are 'good' years and 'bad' years, depending on a volatile mix of personalities, professions and leadership that defies any psychological screening process yet devised.

ANARE's male-dominated history is shared by most other nations active in Antarctica. Only six countries of the nineteen who had wintering communities in 1992 had women in those communities in the previous ten years.[8] Women were perceived as a 'problem' for Antarctic communities long before they wintered on stations.[9] When the first women flew in to the United States McMurdo station in the 1960s—Pan-American air hostesses—the station refused to turn out at the airport to welcome them, even though they were only in transit.*

Antarctic communities are necessarily a mix of those who actually keep the stations operating, with two main groups known (since the early 1980s) as the 'tradies'—diesel mechanics, carpenters, radio operators—and the scientists or 'boffins'—meteorologists, glaciologists, physicists and biologists. There is a third group made up of shift workers like meteorological observers, communications officers and chefs who occupy the middle ground. The scientists are dependent on the tradies not only for general living on the stations, but also for technical support for field expeditions. The advent of wintering women on the continent in the 1980s coincided with the rebuilding program, and construction workers from the Department of Housing and Construction not only worked through the summer season, but numbers of them joined the wintering groups as well. This weighted the population more towards the 'tradie' side of the population equation—and further confirmed the 'blokey' elements of traditional ANARE culture. Dr Louise Holliday's initial ambitions to bring a 'civilising' influence to Davis were unrealised.

When Jim Bleasel took over as director of the Antarctic Division in 1984, he sampled ANARE communities in Antarctica during the maiden voyage of *Icebird*. He was less than impressed by the 'ocker' element he encountered, and later described the communities as being composed

---

* The first women to winter over with the Americans at McMurdo in 1974 were two biologists, Dr Mary Alice McWhinnie and Sister Mary Odile—a maiden aunt and a nun (their own description of themselves). In 1979 Dr Michele Raney became the first woman to winter at the United States Amundsen-Scott station at the South Pole.

of the 'goods' and the 'bads'. Bleasel found that many of the goods—'nice, intelligent' people, categorised by the OIC as making a good contribution to the station—told him that they would never voyage south again.

> They said it's because of the animals that you send here. They used this term 'animals'. I found at each base it was a constant term, so it must have been an ANARE term for these gross people.

Bleasel believed the recruiting was moving more towards entrenching the 'bad' element he had identified.

In April 1985 the Hobart office of the Administrative and Clerical Officers' Association (representing Antarctic Division staff) unsuccessfully attempted to get a copy of a telex Bleasel was alleged to have sent from Antarctica using the word 'animals' to describe certain expeditioners. The matter was raised a year later, as part of a package of complaints and grievances about the administration of the division. In his response of 14 April, the director made reference to the term 'animals, misfits and weirdos', saying that the expression was in common use among expeditioners.

The rebuilding program had a significant effect on the population mix on the stations. The construction workers from the Department of Housing and Construction not only swelled the summer populations, but on some stations they outnumbered other expeditioners. Building teams also wintered over. Although every expeditioner is a member of ANARE, there was divided command as construction workers worked to their foreman, not to the ANARE OIC. Perhaps not surprisingly under these circumstances, a robust male culture was the order of the day and strong leadership was needed to keep control. However, in 1985 the situation at Casey Station got out of hand when the construction crew effectively took over. Writer Stephen Murray-Smith visited Casey in the summer of 1986 on *Icebird* when the extent of the 'ocker' takeover of the station was revealed:

> The party that has come in for next winter has been forced out of the 'club' to take shelter in their tiny cubicles. 'Let's see who can get drunk quickest' parties have been held on the home brew. The women have been harassed. Four of the party brought in for next winter have asked to be taken home. . .Even the more civilised are frightened not to accept the standards of the yobbos. . .they certainly triumphed at Casey this year where they got away with putting a baby's chair in the mess for the OIC and labelling it WIMP.[10]

Later the relieving OIC told Jim Bleasel what he saw when he flew in to Casey on the first helicopter flight from *Icebird*. Bleasel:

Paradoxically the OIC of an ANARE station (officers-in-charge became known as station leaders in 1988) is the only person on station who need not have a specialist skill specifically related to working in Antarctica. Previous Antarctic experience might be taken into account, but has never been regarded as essential.

History has shown that if the station leader fails or does not command respect, the community—essentially composed of self-motivated professionals—can still function adequately, with the station leader bypassed as a paper-shuffler. In such cases the community may accord respect to a *de facto* leader. That may or may not be the official deputy leader. Traditionally the wintering doctor is not made the station leader, and is someone who can be a confidant or provide an outlet for an expeditioner who may be having problems with the rest of the group, or with the leader. Some doctors, though, have been OICs as well—even on one occasion taking over the station leadership during the year when the OIC was unable to cope. In recent years there has been an attempt to specifically codify the powers of a station leader. Michael Carr, station leader at Davis in 1994:

Station leaders [are] special constables under ACT law so we are sort of 'Inspector Plods' if you like and we have certain powers. My powers have stayed in the filing cabinet all year. I've never had to resort to them or read them, but I suppose if they were to build a brig down here, sure we could throw someone in it, but it's not that sort of culture.

Whether a leader's powers are specified or not, the group's respect has to be earned. Military officers who have gone south as ANARE leaders soon realised that they could not issue orders as though they were still in the army or navy. Lem Macey, who is acknowledged as one of the best OICs ever, and whose experience ranged from the 1940s to the 1970s, once defined the secret of leadership success on an ANARE station as:

Do nothing for a few weeks until you can see in what direction the group is heading. Then rush out in front and say, 'Follow me'!

Despite rigorous selection procedures, lasting five days for station leaders in recent years, there is no certainty about how successfully a particular individual will manage his or her station. Normally the Antarctic Division expects wintering communities to sort out any leadership and morale problems on site. However, for the first time in the history of ANARE operations, a mediator had to be sent down to Casey on the first voyage of the 1996–97 season following a vote of no confidence in the station leader by all the other fourteen winterers who signed a fax to head office in early September. The situation was defused on 4 October when the mediator, the division's deputy station and field operations manager Rob Easther, accompanied by twenty of the 1996–97 station and summer field party, flew by helicopter from *Aurora Australis* to Casey. Easther stayed on until January 1997 to assist with station management and investigate the grievance.

He said the chopper circled a group of unkempt, long-haired, long-bearded men standing in a circle. . .they were the untidiest, dirtiest bunch he'd ever seen. There was food in the beards of some of them and they looked terrible. Looking down, he said, it looked like a scene from the film *Deliverance.*

Bleasel decided the situation was so bad that the entire construction crew would have to be pulled out and that was done during the next two voyages. While this incident was by no means typical of the behaviour of the many decent, conscientious workers and engineers who had done tremendous work with the ANARE building program in the 1980s, it was influential in reaffirming Bleasel's ambition to examine and restructure ANARE society. One obvious starting point was in the selection and train- ing of Antarctic-bound personnel. Bleasel found the army-conducted psychological screening tests on expeditioners wanting. Richard Mulligan, the division's expedition operations planning manager, says Bleasel wanted to bring about a fundamental cultural change, 'both in the nature and the quality of expeditioners':

> The first thing he did was to change the priority in selection. . .[which] had been primarily on the work skills the person had—personal qualities came second. He reversed the order. . .personal qualities were considered foremost.

The selection of OICs, Bleasel believed, needed to be overhauled. He was concerned about a division panel selecting an expedition leader largely on the basis of a 30 or 40 minute interview. He decided to use the training facility the division has in the highlands of Tasmania, Bernacchi. Bleasel asked for a list of the top eight or ten people for the four avail- able positions:

> I selected a group of high level people to go with me, and we went up to our lodge at Bernacchi and we spent one week with these people up there, with a series of tests that we devised, in getting to know them under all sorts of conditions. . .and we immediately got better quality station leaders.

Another important reform concerned the system of reporting on an expeditioner's performance. Procedures had not changed since the Phil Law era, and were based on a military system, adapted for ANARE, called the X-Y-Z system. These letters represented three sep- arate reporting periods over the duration of an expedition. Over the years the X and Z reports were dropped and only the Y report remained. The Y was a report on each expeditioner which that person never saw and which, according to Richard Mulligan, 'had on occasions resulted in unsuitable people being reappointed to another year in ANARE service'.

By the 1980s in Australia there was an increasing concern by those responsible for drawing up administrative regulations that there be more openness and fairness in compiling personal dossiers on staff.

An ANARE Code of Personal Behaviour was developed in August 1987, attempting to outline appropriate standards of personal conduct to be observed by expeditioners in Antarctica, as well as outlining basic safety and work requirements. This was signed by all departing ANARE personnel. The issues of sexual and other harassment were brought up in group discussions before departure.

The Australian Army had been conducting ANARE's psychological tests for more than twenty years and Bleasel wondered how 'they could be getting it so wrong' and compounding the situation by allowing bad officers-in-charge and expeditioners 'who'd been dreadful' back for a second and third time. The new director engaged a management consultant, Tim Dalmau, to review the selection process.

With mixed communities came relationships, and the possibility of pregnancies in Antarctica. Children had already been born in Antarctica during 1978—on the Argentinian station, Esperanza, on the Antarctic peninsula. The children were born to the wives of army personnel stationed there and represented the colonisation of Antarctica rather than just the establishment of scientific bases. (It was also an obvious attempt to strengthen Argentina's interests in an area of Antarctic territory also claimed by Britain and Chile.)

The prospect of an Australian woman giving birth on an ANARE station was not high on the list of the Antarctic Division's priorities. Dr Gillian Deakin: 'No one wants to become pregnant down there, no one wishes a baby to be born down there. I think it would just put that much bigger burden on the station and the station medical officer.'

The possibility became more than academic in 1985 when a wintering expeditioner became pregnant on her way south. She returned six months later to have her child in Australia.

Gillian Deakin makes the point that relationships in the Antarctic are not just a woman's problem and believes the issue should be put to all potential expeditioners before they sign on:

> The expeditioners must address the questions themselves and have it clearly in their mind what the risks are. . .Naturally the question arises about adequate contraception. . .all the doctors going down there are well-versed in the use and supply of those sort of things.

Sandy Cave, the senior communications officer at Casey in 1989, was the second ANARE woman to become pregnant in Antarctica. Her partner, John Freeman, was a diesel mechanic on station. She said the other expeditioners reacted in various ways to the news, but 'nothing negative'. Cave:

They were all very supportive. I didn't make a martyr of myself. I still did my work and as the pregnancy progressed John helped me all he could. Towards the end he used to share my night watch and help me with slushy and station work. . .

Cave says she was not concerned about being isolated, and returned to Australia seven months pregnant. For a time she considered having the baby in Antarctica: 'The women's magazines would have loved it! But we decided against it, as it would have had a terrible effect on station morale if anything had gone wrong.'

After her daughter Casey was born she applied to go south again in 1991, but before she could be selected was involved in a bad car smash:

I was in a coma for four months, and then in hospital for a year. I am in a wheelchair now, but I can stand up at times so I am able to look after my three young children. The youngest one, Elysia, was born after my accident.

Sandy Cave had three daughters, and believes that for some reason this is typical of returning ANARE expeditioners who, she says, more often than not have girl children: 'This could be the beginning of the end of the breed of Australian males in Antarctica!'

How lone women survived a year on a male station depended a lot on their personality, social strategy and luck. In 1986 Denise Allen, a weather observer, was helicoptered into Mawson from *Icebird* at Easter after her male counterpart was unable to stay. There was a party in the mess that night—but not as a welcome for her. As the evening progressed, 'about 80 per cent of the blokes made it clear they hadn't wanted a woman on the station—and the other 20 per cent said they thought I'd be an improvement on the person that had left'. Denise Allen decided not to ask the men at Mawson to change their behaviour, but instead to earn their respect. She made it clear that she was not interested in any sexual relationships:

That was my attitude as a professional at the Bureau of Meteorology—not to be involved in a relationship with any member of staff. At Mawson the situation was exactly the same—except that I was on duty, effectively, 24 hours a day.

The Mawson medical officer, Kevin Donovan, was one of those who preferred an all-male year. But he soon changed his mind:

Denise Allen made a decision to be an expeditioner first, and a woman second. She was not particularly concerned about 'girlie' posters in work areas, and joined in traditional celebrations like the staging of the bawdy pantomime 'Cinderella' at midwinter. Her own contribution has gone down in the annals of ANARE entertainment. Dressed as a man, complete with beard and corn-cob pipe, she brought the house down with a localised version of the rambunctious poem 'MacArthur's Fart'. At other times, it was a delicate balance of being accepted as one of the team, without losing her femininity:

> I think I was treated as an equal. Some of the guys said [my presence] toned down their behaviour. . .it kept them a little bit more courteous and remembering some of the social behaviour that's appropriate at home. . .even though I never asked for that specifically.

There is a well known adage quoted by women who have wintered with ANARE: 'Men are like huskies. If you pat one, you've got to pat them all'. On Saturday nights Denise made a point of changing out of her work clothes, using perfume, and making a conscious effort to mix with the group:

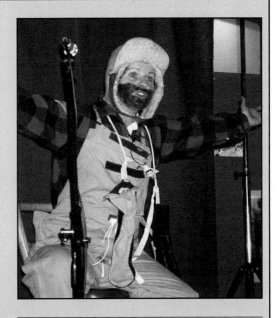

DENISE ALLEN, IN 'BLOKE' MODE, RECITING A SCATALOGICAL POEM AT A MIDWINTER DINNER, 1995. (COURTESY D ALLEN)

> Anybody who wished to talk to me, who wished to have a drink with me, I would make a special effort. Because people are only natural and men like to spend time in the company of women. . .in my first year I found it very hard to have a little bit of time for myself.

She was particularly skilful in forming a sibling relationship rather than a male–female relationship with the men in the wintering party. That certainly took away any sexual stereotypes. They treated her like an older or younger sister.

The prevailing male culture that Denise Allen entered at Mawson in 1986 was basically unchanged from the first ANARE expeditions almost forty years earlier. In those days, the majority of the expeditioners were ex-servicemen. In 1993 Phil Law wrote:

GILLIAN DEAKIN, MEDICAL
OFFICER, DAVIS STATION,
1986.
(R REEVES)

They brought with them maturity and service attitudes to discipline and conformity and then, on the other hand, a certain amount of male boisterousness, rough language, horseplay and a propensity for hard drinking when opportunities offered. In contrast was the behaviour of the unworldly young scientists, fresh from the prolonged adolescence of undergraduate life. They were treated initially, in most cases, with amused contempt or outright intolerance—to which they tended to respond with intellectual arrogance.[11]

Law went on to say that—except for occasional individuals—the divisions between the two groups tended to dissolve away under the gregarious influences of station life and the need for the various members of the wintering group to depend on each other.

Arguments about 'lack of facilities', which had been used as one of the arguments to keep women out of Antarctica, vanished as soon as women went south. Unisex toilets were a matter of common sense. There were, however, certain basic differences between men and women that needed to be addressed where field work was concerned. ANARE-issue cold-weather clothing, with lanyard-operated zip flies, were of little benefit to women. Antarctic expeditioners are often asked by people who have never been there, 'How do you pee in a blizzard?' (Answer: 'Quickly!') Dr Gillian Deakin, who wintered at Davis in 1986, thought about this before she left Australia:

> I found a little device called a Sanifem, and I recommend every woman in the outdoors should purchase one of these. It makes life very easy. It's a shaped funnel with a long tube that fits nicely between the legs and serves the purpose very well. Using that meant I never had to take off my [cold-weather] clothing at all for a pee. . .you had to direct the funnel carefully though!

These days, Sanifems are standard ANARE issue to all women going south. Those who went first, though, had to solve problems as best they could. Denise Allen loved running and sledging with the huskies, and camping out in a polar pyramid tent. After possibly setting world records in retention, Denise called on the ingenuity of the 27 men sharing her year at Mawson to help solve her difficulty:

So they came up with a device that was a plastic eye-piece with a doctor's surgical glove attached to the bottom of it. And it worked wonderfully, provided you didn't overflow it. So the next time I was blizzard-bound in a tent for more than 24 hours, I filled that up, lifted up a corner of the ground sheet and poured it into the snow.

The impact of women on station culture remained minimal while so few wintered over. Gillian Deakin did record one significant change, however. After consultations at Davis in 1986, the party did not perform 'Cinderella' at midwinter:

> We felt that Antarctica had come of age and we could move on from a fairly puerile production, dare I say. . .So we wrote a play—I suppose you could call it an Antarctic political satire—and we had a lot of fun with that.

In 1983 Pene Greet, an upper atmosphere physicist, was to be the first non-medical female scientist to winter on an Antarctic mainland station. Greet was 22 years old, attractive, and excited about the prospect of her year's scientific work at Mawson. She had an affair with one of the officers of *Nanok S* on her way south, and on arrival at Mawson learned that she had been instructed to return to Australia on the return voyage.

When Greet's return was featured in the national press, the Antarctic Division's director in 1983, Clarrie McCue, said reports that her recall amounted to sexual discrimination were 'a load of rubbish', and that the reported affair with the *Nanok S* crewman was not the main reason for her coming back. He did say that the affair had been seen as 'a demonstration of her immaturity'.[12]

Greet says she was not debriefed or consulted by anyone at the division on her return to Australia for her side of the story, and says 'the reasons for my enforced return were not consistent with my own experiences'.[13] She believes her affair with the ship's officer on the voyage down was, in fact, the main reason she was not allowed to stay in Antarctica.

The first woman scientist (other than medical officers like Louise Holliday and Lynn Williams who also undertook research projects) to winter over on an ANARE station was Peta Kelsey, a geophysicist, on Macquarie Island in 1983. Kelsey also shared the first continental wintering with Gina Price (upper atmosphere physicist) at Mawson in 1985.

Jim Bleasel appointed Lorraine Francis Acting Assistant Director, Management Services, and the Antarctic Division's first female Branch head. Part of her later brief as Assistant Director, Resource Management, was to have the final say on the composition of selection committees.

Pene Greet again applied to go to Mawson during the 1986–87 summer, a research trip initially approved by the Antarctic Division. Three weeks before she was due to sail permission was withdrawn and she complained to the Commonwealth Ombudsman.

The Ombudsman's report in April 1987 was highly critical of the way the matter had been handled, concluding that the Antarctic Division's actions were 'unreasonable and unjust'. Ms Greet was paid $9000 in compensation for the loss of income and financial outlays preparing for her Antarctic journey.

As well as recommending the division apologise to Ms Greet and pay compensation, the Ombudsman recommended that the relevant staff in the division be counselled, that it prepare new selection procedures, and that it give appropriate advice to nominees found unsuitable in future.

The Department of Science (then the Antarctic Division's parent Federal department) agreed

UPPER ATMOSPHERE PHYSICIST PENE GREET AT MAWSON, 1982–83. (K IRVING)

to all of the Ombudsman's recommendations, and later asked him to comment on draft procedures for personnel working in Antarctica.[14] (Greet eventually wintered at Mawson in 1990, and Davis in 1997.)

She pushed very hard, against stiff opposition, to have at least one woman appointed to each panel. Francis:

> Many males who had been on the panels would, of course, have been displaced if this practice was adopted and some were livid. They attacked the concept and said if there were no female applicants then it was not valid practice. We were beginning to get a spate of harassment complaints from the stations and I thought that if we had a woman's perspective on the panels, we might be able to select out those who would make trouble for women. However it almost caused World War III!

She was supported by the present director of the Antarctic Division, Rex Moncur, and since 1993 women have been represented on all selection panels.

Rob Easther, deputy station and field operations manager, believes that Jim Bleasel's decision to bring in management consultant Tim Dalmau was also a key factor in advancing and involving women in ANARE. Easther:

The way Dalmau went about it was questionable at times. . .he directly challenged ANARE culture when perhaps a more oblique approach would have been better. . .The method of training—'touchy, feely', and totally foreign to the people involved—really showed how tolerant expeditioners could be. . .Jokes about butcher's paper still prevail!

Until Australia's bicentennial year in 1988, no woman had claimed the glittering prize of ANARE work—officer-in-charge, or station leader (the job was renamed in 1988)—but already in 1979 Diana Patterson, a Tasmanian-born career public servant, nurtured a private ambition to work in Antarctica:

Growing up in Tasmania you had a great sense of that wind coming off the ice and I think most Tasmanians have an affinity with the South. . .The leadership role was one that appealed to me. . .and I felt my skills and background were very similar to a lot of men that had been selected as the OIC.

Patterson was not successful in 1979, although she was told they would have welcomed her application as a cook or radio operator. She decided then she would set her cap at being the first female OIC. She reapplied in 1986, felt she was an object of curiosity in the division and had a gut feeling she would not be selected. She decided to work on a two-year plan. In 1986 she would get the division used to the idea of having a woman OIC, and then apply a year later: 'I think I had a problem with height as much as gender—by being only five foot two, I don't project a tough image. And I think that was a bigger disadvantage in those early days.'

Jim Bleasel believed it was better to have more than one woman on an Antarctic station. Patterson knew she had done well in the selection process, but was aware of the director's concern about making sure the appointment of the first woman station leader was a complete success. 'So I suggested to him that in fact it could be to his advantage with the Bicentennial coming up that he had the opportunity for Australia to have the first woman station leader in the world.' However Bleasel wanted to take out some insurance. He was already concerned about 'first timers'— male or female—going down to run a station when up to 40 per cent of the expeditioners there had been before. This group had the potential to challenge the authority of the station leader:

I thought it was very important that the first time we sent a woman it be very successful. . .so that people would say, 'Gee, she did a good job, there is nothing wrong with having a woman station leader'.

Although Patterson had passed the selection procedures, Bleasel was concerned about sending her down for a full year in 1988 as station leader and proposed to send her to Casey for the summer to gain experience first:

> I asked Personnel whether we could say, 'Yes, you are selected, but you're
> selected for the following year. And this year we'll send you down over
> summer to get experience of your station '. . .And when she went down
> the next time she'd be the absolute whiz on the station, with first-hand
> experience from the two OICs who were down there. She'd be really
> strong—and the first woman [station leader] would be a huge success.

Patterson felt patronised, but there was little she could do about it if she wanted to achieve her goal.

Her summer at Casey did enable her to field-test the practical realities of living in a previously all-male environment:

> I was a bit conscious of not walking into the urinals if there was a man
> standing there. But it took me about three days to work out that most
> men were more embarrassed swearing in front of me than they were
> taking a leak in front of me. So I thought, well, if it doesn't bother them,
> it doesn't bother me.

At Casey, Patterson wondered what all the fuss had been about. The men accepted her, judging her not on her gender, but 'how well you did the job'.

By the time she returned to Australia, Bleasel had left the division, and the original deal was off. Patterson was told she'd have to go through the selection procedures again:

> There were problems for me. I felt quite outraged. I'd given up a good
> job—at that stage I was assistant director of the Department of Sport
> and Recreation in Victoria. I'd have suffered a loss of face, I'd not only
> have lost out on income, my career was affected and it would have been
> a pretty bloody embarrassing situation!

Although some of her friends recommended taking legal action against the division—as her appointment had been confirmed in writing before she went to Casey—she gritted her teeth and went through the arduous selection process yet again, setting her sights on Mawson as the premier station. 'I thought if I get Mawson, that will put an end to this token woman attitude I experienced at Casey.'

Diana Patterson achieved her goal and was appointed OIC Mawson. Although she was dubbed 'Lady Di' in the early part of 1989 as a result of perceived authoritarian behaviour, she was determined to establish her authority early. 'It's very hard to regain it later on, once you've lost

While Diana Patterson was the first woman station leader on the continent, Alison Clifton pipped her to the post as the first woman station leader for ANARE. She and Diana attended the same training and selection course. At the time, Clifton was unaware that there had never been a woman OIC or station leader. Clifton was appointed to Macquarie Island, and took up her duties there before Diana left Australia for Mawson. She arrived on her thirtieth birthday.

Alison Clifton had a good year at Macquarie, but her year as station leader at Davis was a harder assignment. She went there with her partner, and says this was very difficult:

DAVIS STATION LEADER ALISON CLIFTON ON A CHINESE SKIDOO, ZONGSHAN STATION, LARSEMANN HILLS, 1991. (P BOURKE)

I couldn't talk to him [about station relationships] because of the issue of confidentiality. For the people who didn't like my style, that was another thing they could latch on to. They could get to me through him, by criticising him. . .For most people I don't think it was an issue.

A highlight of her year at Macquarie was a long satellite telephone call to Diana Patterson at Mawson. 'We got into trouble because it cost a fortune, but it was so good!' Another high point happened at Davis: 'At the end of the summer one woman came up to me and said, "It's been a great summer and I have been proud to have a female station leader".'

In her two stints as station leader, Alison Clifton said she felt triply isolated—'geographically, as a woman—and at Davis because I was the only one there with my partner'.

it.' She made a point of taking part in field training and doing her share of dirty jobs around the station. 'If I'd hidden away in my office and worked on paperwork, I wouldn't have established that credibility.'

Running with the huskies was one of her greatest joys. On the annual expedition over the sea ice to the emperor penguin rookery at Kloa, she lost five kilograms in ten days:

I learned a lot about handling men from handling dogs, and breaking up dog fights. My technique was to grab the dog that I thought was losing by the tail and yank it out of the scrimmage as hard as I could. I worked on the theory that it was a way he could save face by retreating from the fight because I was pulling him out.

459

MAWSON STATION LEADER
DIANA PATTERSON WITH VERY
SPECIAL FRIEND, 1989.
(COURTESY D PATTERSON)

One evening in the mess Diana had a chance to put her theory to the test. Two expeditioners were rolling around the floor, locked in combat: 'I went for the guy I thought would end up getting killed if he stayed in, got him out of the scrimmage and gave him the opportunity to save face, by breaking the fight up.'

Only one member of the wintering community made it clear that he continued to resent having a woman as station leader. His aggression boiled over one night, and he emptied a glass of beer over a surprised Diana. She defused the situation as best she could, and walked out of the building. The beer-thrower followed her out, still shouting abuse. Although Patterson was upset by the incident, she felt she had finally achieved full equality—because 'during all his abuse, he hadn't once used a gender specific term. He was abusing the position of station leader, not Diana Patterson.'

The point about women's ability to lead ANARE expeditions was further buttressed by Alison Clifton's appointment as station leader at Macquarie Island, also in 1989, and again at Davis in 1991. Patterson went to Davis as station leader in 1995, and was officially complimented on her management of the station by a United States inspection team, visiting under the terms of the Antarctic Treaty.[15]

Joan Russell went to Casey as station leader in 1990. Russell joined the division from her previous job as Equal Opportunities Officer in the South Australian Department of Personal and Industrial Relations. A former publicity officer with the Women's Electoral Lobby in 1975, Russell was prominent in the development of the women's movement in South Australia. At Casey she was one of three women in a wintering group of twenty-six. Apart from the expeditioners appointed by the Antarctic Division, there were eight construction workers from Australian Construction Services.

Joan Russell's stewardship of Casey in 1990 is known in the division as 'The Big Poster Year'. The station newspaper, the *Casey Rag*, regularly published a page three 'girlie' photograph. In June, Adele Post (biologist) wrote to the *Rag* editors about this feature, 'complaining of the journal having a repetitious sexist outlook'. Russell wrote in the station log:

I had to ask them to desist with page three, or put me in line for a sexual harassment case. They did not take this well, but later discussed their grievances quite calmly with me. The notions of sexism and sexual harassment and the right of women to expect to live and work free of these petty irritations appear foreign and unacceptable to most men on the station.[16]

Russell was also unimpressed by a 'bad taste awards' occasion after the midwinter dinner (one of the prizes, entitled 'Best Supporting Act', and representing two feet sticking out between plaster buttocks, was presented to deputy station leader Peter Read). Russell noted in the log that the ACS [Australian Construction Services] foreman had not taken part in making the plaster models, but had nevertheless presented the 'awards'.

I nonetheless condemn his behaviour as inappropriate for the ACS foreman. Also sent his letter to the *Casey Rag* (4 June) on to the director as requested, asking for a response to [his] interpretation of affirmative action in recruiting women for ANARE as discrimination against men.[17]

While sexism might be regarded as a community issue to be debated and hopefully resolved on the spot, refusal to abide by safety instructions constituted a direct threat to the physical safety of expeditioners. On 6 September Russell received official notice that safety helmets were to be worn while riding 'quads'—four-wheel all-terrain motor bikes. After determining from head office that the policy was to be enforced, Russell resolved to do so, including 'grounding of non-helmet-wearers'. This announcement was made at a special station meeting. Resentment on station simmered, and after Russell grounded one offender several days later, she was surprised to find out that the helmet policy was not being enforced at the two other continental stations. She requested clarification from Kingston, but to her dismay was told that the existing occupational health and safety policy on helmets was suspended 'pending further research and the issue of appropriate helmets'.[18]

On 8 November Russell's feminist principles were affronted by the ruling of her immediate superior in Hobart to allow the display of 'girlie' posters in work areas and private 'dongas'. She registered a formal complaint to Kingston. Several weeks later she was shocked and disgusted when a large, explicitly genital 'girlie' poster appeared in the powerhouse.[19]

Her personal request to have the posters removed from the trade workshops was rejected.[20] On 14 November, Assistant Director Expedition Operations Jack Sayers clarified the position, making it clear that 'these posters have always been prohibited by divisional policy. . .that the division's

JOAN RUSSELL, STATION
LEADER AT CASEY, 1990,
WHILE CROSSING THE
ANTARCTIC CIRCLE EN ROUTE
TO LAW DOME.
(COURTESY J RUSSELL)

sexual harassment policy would be re-issued' with special instructions to the 1991 station leaders. Russell:

> I suggested that the policy be reissued at changeover, rather than right now because it was a more favourable time strategically and I'm too weary to fight on single handed. He gladly accepted this suggestion.[21]

The new policy on the elimination of sexual harassment in the workplace was issued by the director, Rex Moncur, on 14 December 1990. He made clear in an accompanying memo that the display of posters was recognised as a form of sexual harassment, and 'as such does not meet the standards of conduct expected of staff at the Division'.[22]

Writing her report on what had been a difficult year at Casey, Russell acknowledged that some of the issues she had confronted appeared trivial in retrospect:

> But at the time, and in the hotbed context of station life, they had a negative impact upon community morale. Some members remained permanently estranged from the Station Leader. Most rose above their feelings of the time, to suffer no lasting effect worse than an entrenched personal opinion. It is to the station's great credit that this is so.[23]

Russell felt there was some confusion about the various forms of decision-making on station. 'A mild form of mob rule' was generally accepted as the time-honoured and appropriate way for the station to conduct its affairs. The role of the station leader in this form of management, Russell said, was 'deemed moderately marginal and irrelevant' by the expeditioners. Reflecting on her experiences several years later, Russell wrote:

> Real women are those who have not only survived the crippling, poisonous, testosterone-laden culture of ANARE, with their bodies and spirits intact, but made a difference to it while doing their jobs in Antarctica under the almost insurmountable additional burden of their gender.

Real men, on the other hand, are those who love, admire, support and enjoy them while they are doing that.

Russell returned to Australia somewhat drained by the stress of the year at Casey, but she was not deterred from going south again—to Macquarie Island as station leader in 1994.

While Russell was battling the issue of 'girlie' posters at Casey, upper atmosphere physicist Pene Greet was the lone woman expeditioner at Mawson. Following her abortive attempt to go south in 1986, she had worked in Antarctica over the summer of 1988–89. Selected to winter at Mawson in 1990—seven years after her enforced return—Greet also had problems with what she considered 'explicit pornography' in the station newspaper.

Suddenly one day in mid-June, there were full genital pornographic pictures in this newspaper. . .you're faced with this stuff at breakfast. And I wrote up a probably fairly nasty comment on the board, saying: 'Would the fucking MCPs who put together the fucking newspaper please distribute their pornography more discreetly.'

The station leader, Bob Parker, took Greet aside and told her she was being 'a bit aggressive' and that 'the men concerned don't like being called male chauvinist pigs'. Parker did ban explicitly sexual posters from the kitchen, but the station newspaper was permitted to continue as before.

While Greet had little success in influencing the publication and circulation of sexually explicit material, she found the attitude to male–female relationships in general on station had changed markedly by 1990. Greet had gone south 'without any preconceived ideas' about a relationship. She did, in fact, team up with one of the diesel engineers, Paul Myers, and they maintained their relationship through the year.

The following year, 1991, two women station leaders went south, Alison Clifton to Casey, and Louise Crossley to Mawson. Crossley, who combined an academic background with practical outdoor skills, took an active role with field work, leading the annual winter supply traverse to the Prince Charles Mountains and driving a D5 bulldozer.

Before leaving Australia, all the 1991 station leaders were told that, following Russell's formal complaint, they should make sure all 'girlie' posters were removed from all station work areas. Crossley:

We all said, 'no way'! My point was that such a radical change of policy needed time and discussion to work through.

At the end of the summer season at Mawson, the ACS crew presented 'a framed, rather lewd' girlie picture to the winterers, to be hung in the Mawson bar. Crossley suggested to the barman that it be taken down, but he refused:

> I decided to raise it as a community issue, and said I did not feel comfortable in the bar with the 'girlie' picture. I also pointed out there was an official policy on such material in public areas. There were mutterings and murmurings—but several expeditioners agreed they didn't like it either.

Crossley did not order its removal—but it had gone by the next evening.

Although the display of such material has become symbolic of the resistance of the old ANARE 'boys' club' culture to social change, not all women who go to Antarctica are worried by it. Medical officer Lynn Williams expressed the view that such pornography could be educational for women:

> Women read romantic novels and men read pornography. It would make more sense if we all knew what everyone else was reading. And then you can choose the way you want to live your life anyway. . .it doesn't worry me whether there were pictures. . .[of] nude women around.[24]

Current policy allows pin-ups and sexually explicit material in an expeditioner's private 'donga', but not in work areas. In the view of medical officer Lynn Williams, this is a reasonable compromise, but 'in the long run, tolerance and understanding are more helpful than rules and regulations'.

In August 1993 a conference was held in Hobart titled, 'Living in Antarctica: Women in a Man's World'. The conference name reflected the situation still being faced by women going south with ANARE into the 1990s. Yet there has been a substantial effort by the Antarctic Division to educate expeditioners about Equal Employment Opportunity (EEO) issues and acceptable behaviour, as well as their rights, from the late 1980s.

Lorraine Francis had continually maintained that harassment was a problem and that if women complained formally it was going to be very embarrassing for the Antarctic Division, but old ways died hard. Rex Moncur spent a summer in Antarctica in 1991–92 and many women took the opportunity to tell him about their experiences. Moncur was surprised by what women told him about harassment in Antarctica and, when he returned, he not only supported the concept of the conference on women in Antarctica, he chaired one of its two days and spoke on the issue himself. Francis believes that the director's support was extremely influential:

EEO is not a popular topic. Over my time I have seen an improvement, people are increasingly supportive of EEO in its breadth and depth. Many scientists say that they prefer to go to a station where there are women. It is more normal and civilised. The resistant ones have gone underground as they are in fact reducing their power base. Women are now accepted professionally—it is in the social arena that there are still problems. But not so many years ago it was a case of 'women don't belong in Antarctica' full stop. So this is a positive development.

One of the recommendations from the conference was more training in conflict resolution for station leaders and expeditioners. Tom Maggs, a division workplace harassment officer, does not minimise the difficulties of implementing EEO policies: 'In a way the Antarctic Division is "damned if we do and damned if we don't" in regard to this training. It is perceived as too legalistic and also as not being enough!'

One of the main difficulties is that an Antarctic station does not replicate a 'normal' workplace. Expeditioners cannot go home after a day's work. They are living continuously on the job in an isolated situation. Any upsetting of the status quo can have a devastating effect on group morale:

> We need to get away from EEO as such—women, ethnic minorities. . .and hark back to the old ANARE values of fairness, tolerance and respect. These, of course, are the cornerstone of EEO anyway. . .The role of the station leader is crucial in tuning in to all these aspects.

Mary Mulligan, also a workplace harassment officer, believes there has been a huge change within the Antarctic Division over the last few years in implementing EEO policies. Not so long ago there was a fear, particularly by women, that if they complained about unacceptable behaviour on station they would be ostracised by their fellow expeditioners and unable to go south again. But now:

> The Antarctic Division is supportive of those who complain and every complaint is taken seriously. Complainants should not feel that they will suffer any adverse consequences as a result. The division hopes the fear of complaining is less common now than it used to be. A complainant against unfair harassment is more likely these days to be supported for speaking up.

With mixed groups now a regular feature of ANARE activities, married men are often under pressure. Mulligan has seen many happily married men go south only to fall foul of the social life:

Many women go down looking for a relationship on station and many men are really intimidated by such overt behaviour. The belief that 'anything goes' often prevails and there are fewer restrictions down there. In reality an Antarctic station is really a microcosm of our society, but because of the nature of life there, the potential for harassment and misreading messages is magnified.

While the experiences of early women expeditioners like Louise Holliday showed social change was needed on ANARE stations, there are some who feel that the onrush of political correctness has swung the pendulum too fast and too far. With sexual harassment now illegal (the Sex Discrimination Act 1984), the emphasis given to the issue in training has caused some resentment. The Antarctic Division's Tom Maggs believes that the emphasis on the legal aspects of 'your rights as a harassed person' (in line with Commonwealth legislation and policy) 'took the safety catch off the gun, so to speak'.

People are quick to now scream on that and they know they can get onto the Ombudsman. They know they can write to the director, and they know that it's a very bright flag and if you hoist it, you're going to get everyone's attention. So it's a really vile weapon at the moment. . .we were quick to tell people what their EEO rights were, but not so quick to think, 'Oh, we haven't told them what their responsibilities are'.

The division's head of polar medicine, Des Lugg, makes the point that there have always been instances of men harassing other men by bullying or intimidation on ANARE stations—harassment is not always sexual—and in later years instances of female to female provocation. Maggs would also like to see less emphasis on gender. 'I hope that something happens to split the harassment from a "woman" to a "people" issue.' Diana Patterson agrees and feels that the behaviour of a few men, particularly in the 1980s, has reflected badly on the whole male ANARE culture which has been, in the main, 'civilised'. There is no reason to expect in the 1990s that the 'tradie' culture will necessarily be rough, or 'ocker'. Indeed, Diana Patterson has encountered many 'sensitive new-age tradespersons' among the young men going south. She believes that the role of the station leader is critical in setting standards:

I think it's too easy to say, 'Oh, we had a bad group'. You have to come back to the leadership and your role, and the whole ethos that prevails in the community—and the station leader is in the position to do something about that through key people on the station. . .and you can change the ethos.

At present comparatively few women winter on the stations and the Antarctic Division's Director Rex Moncur would like to see the ratio improve:

My own view is that it's not unreasonable to think that in twenty years' time, something like about 30 per cent of the people on our stations will be women. And I think that's very valuable to life on our stations. I think the more we can have a community that represents the community in Australia, the more it will reduce some of the tensions that we have to manage.

IMPROMPTU ANARE TRANSVESTISM. HELICOPTER PILOT PIP TURNER (LEFT) IS HELPING WEATHER FORECASTER 'WOK' BROMHAM CELEBRATE ON *ICEBIRD* IN 1989 AFTER BROMHAM UNILATERALLY NOMINATED 21 FEBRUARY AS 'LINDA RONDSTADT DAY'. (T BOWDEN)

The participation of women in ANARE life has increased greatly in the last fifteen years and has ushered in arguably the most fundamental changes in half a century in the way station life is conducted. In the early 1980s the only wintering women on the continent were doctors, and they were there by default because there were not enough men. Today there is a wide range of specialist skills represented by women in Antarctica over the summer season and during winter. The first women 'tradies' were Kay Grist (painter) at Casey in the summer of 1988–89 and Macquarie Island 1990–91, and Catherine White, an Asset Services plumber at Mawson in the summer of 1994. Women like biologist Anitra Wendin have dived under the ice and there are regular visits from female communications officers, biologists, physicists, field training officers, forecasters and chefs. Annie Wessing was ANARE's first woman field training officer in Antarctica in 1991–92, and Vanessa Noble spent the 1995–96 summer at Davis as a helicopter engineer. Women now run ANARE stations with barely a mention in the newspapers. Australia's then highest ranking female Air Force officer, Wing Commander Angie Rhodes was station leader at Casey in 1994.

467

ANARE DIVER ANITRA
WENDIN BREAKING THE ICE
NEAR DAVIS STATION.
(P BUTLER)

SQUADRON LEADER ANGELA
RHODES, STATION LEADER, AT
CASEY STATION IN 1994, IN
RELAXED MODE EMERGING
FROM A CREVASSE.
(COURTESY A RHODES)

The Antarctic Division's policy on relationships has moved with the times. In the 1970s and early 1980s married couples were first allowed to go south. Rex Moncur:

> Our policy on relationships in Antarctica is that people should be discreet, but that relationships should occur in just the normal way they will happen back here in Australia. We do, for example, where people develop an ongoing relationship, make arrangements by providing a double bedroom for them and assisting them. So that when things develop they are seen to be normal, just as they would occur back here in Australia.

On 3 September 1994, Colin Blobel and Denise Jones made history by being the first ANARE couple to marry in Antarctica, at Davis Station. (As this ceremony was not recognised under Australian law, the couple tied the knot again officially when they returned from Davis.)

TWENTY-THREE

SCIENCE AND
THE FUTURE

I think most who go to Antarctica for any length of time do go through some sort of personal reassessment. A sense of feeling infinitesimally small in the face of the magnitude of nature.

Phil Law

Most scientific projects now undertaken by ANARE in Antarctica are linked to international programs. This is a radical change from the 1950s and 1960s when there was a strong feeling that Antarctica—because of its geography—was set apart from the rest of the world. Australian scientists, confronted by a virgin, largely unexplored region, began by trying to cover the ground and find out what was there. ANARE Chief Scientist, Patrick Quilty:

Science was strongly curiosity-driven and exciting. There was a focus on projects in which the individual had a major formulating role. Now there is more emphasis on team science, which often acts against the interests of the unconventional individualist or loner—probably to the detriment of science and the development of new ideas.

Although the International Geophysical Year (IGY) in 1957–58 had led to unprecedented international cooperation in Antarctica, individual scientific projects were pursued by researchers from the twelve nations involved. The Special Committee on Antarctic Research (SCAR) formed in 1958—later renamed the Scientific Committee on Antarctic Research—was created by the IGY participating countries, even before the Antarctic Treaty came into being in 1961. Although SCAR attempted to coordinate international programs in those early years, it was unable to be effective. Its first successful effort to achieve international cooperation in a major Antarctic project was the International Antarctic Glaciology Program (IAGP) which began in May 1969 and in which ANARE played a major role.

The IAGP was an initiative of the operating agencies responsible for expeditions in the IAGP region and in particular by the glaciologists who were also members of the SCAR working group on Glaciology. The Working Group later adopted IAGP as a formal project and the scientific basis of the project was endorsed by SCAR. Uwe Radok (from Melbourne University) was invited to the first meeting in his capacity as the secretary of the SCAR Working Group on Glaciology. It was through his participation that Australia was directly involved from the outset. The close involvement of both the logistics and science representatives was the key to the success of the project and led to close cooperation.

Patrick Quilty believes two events changed the perception of Antarctica as set apart from the world:

> One was the publication of space images of the earth which led to the concept of 'Spaceship Earth' showing that we are all in it together. The other was the phenomenon of stratospheric ozone depletion which reinforced the view that no place on earth is exempt from the influence of activities conducted elsewhere.

Antarctica is a continent of surprises. Despite having an estimated 70 per cent of the world's fresh water reserves locked up in its ice sheet, it is the driest continent on earth, with less moisture falling on it than the world's hottest deserts. It is also the coldest (the lowest temperature ever recorded was minus 89°C), windiest (winds up to 320 kilometres per hour), and the highest (an average elevation of 2300 metres). Only about 2 per cent of its surface is exposed rock and its vast ice sheet is permanently on the move, eventually breaking off at the edges as icebergs. During winter the sea ice freezes around Antarctica, forming a band of some 19 million square kilometres of frozen sea ice and creating a huge ice-covered area in the Southern Hemisphere of between four and five times the size of Australia.

All biological life in Antarctica is restricted to the coastal regions and sustained by the waters around it. Its ecosystems are almost all contained within the Antarctic Convergence (more recently named the Polar Front) which surrounds the continent around latitude 58° south—an invisible and constantly moving dividing line that separates the chilled waters of Antarctica from the comparatively warmer waters of the Southern Ocean. Only large mammals like whales and seals, and wide-ranging sea birds like the magnificent wandering albatross, cross this Front.

The International Antarctic Glaciology Program (IAGP) was conceived following a major international symposium 'Antarctic Glaciological Exploration' in the USA in 1968, during which it was realised that there was a very large sector of the ice sheet in East Antarctica over which almost no glaciological measurements had been made. Four nations with active programs in that sector of Antarctica—Australia, France, the USSR and the USA—agreed to take part, as well as the Scott Polar Research Institute (SPRI) from the UK. Japan joined as the fifth nation some years later.

RUSSIAN AND AUSTRALIAN GEOLOGISTS AT THE BEGINNING OF JOINT IAGP TRAVERSES, MIRNY, 1977. THE LARGE OVER-SNOW VEHICLE (RIGHT) IS A SOVIET KHARKOVCHANKA. (N YOUNG)

A complete study of the ice sheet was planned, including its shape, motion, history of change and interaction with the environment. Measurements would be made from the air, using radio echo-sounding to get profiles of the ice and underlying bedrock, as well as glaciology traverses on the surface of the ice cap with ice core drilling to trace the history and records of past climate. An important contribution in the planning stage was made by the 'Melbourne Group' (Uwe Radok, Bill Budd and Dick Jenssen) using early computer modelling techniques.

The project was run by a coordinating council from the nations and organisations taking part which met each year to assess results and plan future activities. Australian field work under the IAGP banner began in 1971 with an exploratory survey inland of Casey, testing new survey techniques, and continued in 1973, 1975 and 1976 from the summit of Law Dome to the 2000 metre elevation contour at 69°south latitude. Temperatures experienced by the survey teams were at times as cold as minus 50°C, where metal can become brittle, and diesel mechanics often performed miracles to keep tractors and equipment operating in good order. Those early days also saw the first use of the US Navy Satellite Navigation System (NAVSAT) to survey the location of markers on the ice through the participation of surveyors from the US program. This satellite survey technique made the surveys of ice movement in the interior of the continent feasible and became a basic tool for Australian activities.

Australians pushed in to the interior of Wilkes Land in 1978 and 1979 to take the first comprehensive glaciological measurements in this region. Further surveys continued into the early

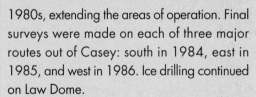

ICE CORE DRILLING INSIDE THE SHELTER AT DOME SUMMIT SOUTH SITE, LAW DOME, CASEY, 1991. (G SNOW)

ICE CORES RECOVERED FROM DEEP DRILLING AT LAW DOME, CASEY, 1992. (M HOLMES)

1980s, extending the areas of operation. Final surveys were made on each of three major routes out of Casey: south in 1984, east in 1985, and west in 1986. Ice drilling continued on Law Dome.

Other IAGP groups were active in East Antarctica in the 1970s and 1980s. The Soviet Antarctic Expeditions (SAE) conducted surveys out of Mirny and also a long-term deep drilling program at Vostok. The French expeditions made traverses out of Dumont d'Urville as well as deep drilling at Dome C with aircraft support from the US. Glaciologists from the Scott Polar Research Institute made airborne radio echo-sounding surveys in the 1970s in conjunction with the Americans using ice thickness radar mounted in long-range Hercules aircraft.

Australian glaciologists took part in joint Australian–Russian surveys of the ice sheet across the inland of Wilkes Land from Mirny to Dome C, using Russian vehicles and Australian satellite survey equipment—Neal Young (1976–77; 1977–78), Vin Morgan (1978–79), Ross Walsh (1980–81) and Trevor Hamley (1984–85).

Some of the activities like the deep core drilling and ice core analysis are continuing, but the main objectives of the IAGP planned 25 years ago have been achieved. The ice cores from Vostok and Law Dome have become an important contribution to the study of past environmental change. The international cooperation between Australia and the other IAGP contributing countries continues to this day.[1]

Ships sampling sea water temperature note a drop of up to 5°C as they pass over the Convergence. One indication of the change for the traveller at that point of entry to the Antarctic ecosystem is wheeling and feeding seabirds, taking advantage of the nutrients pushed up to the surface by upwelling currents.

One obvious effect that Antarctica has on the rest of the globe is its generation of powerful weather systems. Another less obvious but powerful influence has only been detected and studied within the last three decades. When ice forms on the sea surface in the Antarctic winter, its salt is excluded into the water below, forming cold, very saline and therefore dense water. This sinks to the ocean floor and spreads throughout the world's ocean basins. The effects of this massive transference are still being assessed. Quilty:

> Something like 50 per cent of the world's water masses are generated in the Antarctic, largely through the freezing of the surface water in winter. Now in generating these oceanographic water masses—which are even recognised way up in the Northern Hemisphere in the Atlantic Ocean—it's taking with it into the deep ocean anything that it dissolves, or sucks out of the atmosphere. This includes carbon dioxide and some of the CFCs that are blamed for some of the ozone problems in the stratosphere. . .It takes these, and it takes them from the surface into the deep ocean.

A growing realisation of the important influences of Antarctica on the world's environment was mirrored in the number of nations signing the Antarctic Treaty. Twelve countries had signed in 1959, including countries with territorial claims like Australia, Norway and France, and the United States and the Soviet Union which were active in Antarctica but had no existing claims. By 1975 there were twenty nations acceding to the treaty, and by 1985 the tally was 33—including major powers like China and India, as well as a broad spectrum of governments like Papua New Guinea, Brazil, Italy, Peru, India, Hungary and Cuba. There was more behind this than international interest in the purity of scientific research. The possibility of mineral exploitation was a key factor. Quilty:

> Malaysia was very vocal in its criticism of the Antarctic Treaty, in fact it took its concerns to the United Nations in 1982, wanting to see the end of the treaty system.

Mining Antarctica was always going to be extremely difficult, and a last resort activity. The exploitation of biological resources in the waters around the continent was far more easily realised—as had happened with whaling and sealing activities since the nineteenth century.

In 1972 the Antarctic Treaty nations agreed on the 'Convention for the Conservation of Antarctic Seals'. This, in the view of ANARE biologist Harry Burton, was little more than 'feel-good international window-dressing' as the Antarctic seals were not being exploited commercially at that time.

Other species, however, were already being harvested in large quantities. In 1967, Russian fishing fleets began taking commercial quantities of finfish from around the Antarctic peninsula and sub-Antarctic islands. It took the largest catch of any nation fishing in the Southern Ocean in one year—400 000 tonnes of Antarctic cod and icefish in 1969–70. Overfishing quickly led to decreasing catches which were down to 40 000 tonnes by the early 1970s. At this time the Soviet Union turned its attention to the huge swarms of krill in Antarctic waters. By 1982 the Russian krill fishing fleets were harvesting 500 000 tonnes a year—an estimated 93 per cent of all krill being commercially fished. In 1982, 200 000 tonnes of krill were taken by the Russians off the coast of the AAT near Mawson Station. Other nations involved to a much lesser degree were Japan, Chile, South Korea and Poland.

As krill is the major link of the food web for all Antarctic fauna—sea birds, seals, penguins and whales—scientists attending regular meetings of SCAR were concerned that unregulated fishing of krill could trigger a massive collapse of populations of seals and whales. This led to the biggest combined biological experiment ever undertaken in the world—BIOMASS (Biological Investigations of Marine Antarctic Systems and Stocks). It began in the 1980–81 season, and *Nella Dan* was specially modified to enable ANARE to contribute from the beginning. BIOMASS involved fifteen ships from eleven countries, and ended in 1991.

One of the remarkable things about BIOMASS was how it was organised by scientists from nations participating in the Antarctic Treaty without any formal secretariat to oversee the complex arrangements. Both Antarctic Treaty and SCAR meetings are essentially unsupported by any permanent administrative body. The perceived urgency of doing something to regulate possible over-fishing in Antarctic waters was discussed at the Ninth Antarctic Treaty Consultative Meeting in London in 1977. In 1978 the first of three special meetings was held in Canberra, the second six months later in Buenos Aires, both to discuss the concept of a special body to oversee monitoring and control of fishing and biological resources in Antarctic waters. The third and final meeting in Canberra in May 1980 resulted in the adoption of a plan to create the Convention for the Conservation of Antarctic Marine Living Resources—CCAMLR.

CCAMLR came into force on 7 April 1982 and its first meeting took place in Hobart during May and June of that year.* Darry Powell was the first executive secretary of the CCAMLR Commission and held the job for ten years. His quiet diplomacy, before and after the setting up of CCAMLR, is credited with having brought together successfully the difficult mix of scientific and political interests in a way never before achieved by the loose association of nations involved in the Antarctic Treaty. Quilty:

> CCAMLR meets for two weeks every year in Hobart. The Scientific Committee meets during the first week, and the second week is the meeting of the Commission. It has a series of working groups—for example, the fish stock assessment working group—and it has an ecosystem monitoring program as well.

CCAMLR is the first coordinated international effort to protect the delicate environmental balance in the Antarctic and Southern oceans. It did not set out to ban fishing in Antarctic waters—a point emphasised by Darry Powell:

> The unique thing about it was that it specified explicitly that there would be an ecosystem approach to the management of the fishing, or resource harvesting of whatever kind, and that there were to be no activities agreed or undertaken that could cause an irreversible effect on any aspect of the marine ecosystem.

An early criticism of CCAMLR was that its Scientific Committee seemed to be concentrating on single species management, such as the Antarctic cod, or krill. The most urgent and obvious need, however, was to examine the species that were actually being harvested and establish some controls, while at the same time getting information that would enable CCAMLR to develop an ecosystem management regime. To get a wider understanding on how the food resources of the Southern Ocean were shared, a working group for the scientific committee suggested that the study should use what they called 'indicator species'. Powell:

> They chose krill predators that had some particular aspect of their life cycle or their actual biology which would give an indication of the possible impact of krill fishing—it might be the weight of chicks at first fledging, the blubber thickness of an animal at a particular time of the year—that kind of thing.

The selection of species to be monitored on a regular basis through a network of stations had enormous repercussions on how biological

---

* The location of its permanent headquarters in Hobart is said to have been adroitly secured by the then Liberal MHR for Denison, Michael Hodgman, who was involved in organising an extremely successful weekend excursion in Tasmania for the international delegates to the third conference in Canberra.

research was to be carried out by the Antarctic Division and other nations active in Antarctica. By 1988 the scientific committee and working groups had become influential enough to direct the work of the Commission so that its decisions became based more on scientific advice, rather than reflecting narrow individual national priorities. Powell believes that the successful model of CCAMLR was an important influence in bringing about international agreement on the Madrid Protocol to the Antarctic Treaty. Powell:

> CCAMLR probably demonstrated to the Treaty parties themselves that their scientists could be gathered together and encouraged to work together in programs that would be useful in monitoring environmental impacts. If CCAMLR hadn't been going, I think it would have been harder to get the details into the Madrid Protocol.

Environmental organisations like Greenpeace have been critical of CCAMLR, alleging that it is unable to ensure that nations fishing around Antarctica abide by agreed quotas. At CCAMLR's November 1995 meeting, the British Government reported that 'catches from illegal fishing now exceed those taken legitimately' in the waters around South Georgia.[2] The Antarctic Division's Patrick Quilty acknowledges that there is some illegal fishing, and CCAMLR tries to keeps tabs on it.

Before CCAMLR, all scientific programs had been coordinated by SCAR. But with marine science the most rapidly expanding discipline and CCAMLR initiating its own programs with its own scientific committee and a permanent secretariat in Hobart, the reality was that SCAR had lost some of its scientific initiative. As no science can be done in Antarctica without the extensive logistics provided by participating countries, SCAR had a logistics working group to help facilitate agreed projects. In 1986, the Antarctic Division's director, Jim Bleasel, and Peter Wilkniss from the US (Head of the Division of Polar Programs, National Science Foundation) combined to change these long-standing arrangements and effectively hijacked the scientific agenda from SCAR by replacing the Logistics Working Group with a kind of Antarctic directors' club with the acronym COMNAP—the Council of Managers of National Antarctic Programs. Bleasel was unapologetic about this move as he (and Wilkniss) did not like the budget priorities and expensive joint projects of their Antarctic programs being decided by a group of scientists on their own:

> If you have a bunch of, say, marine scientists together they would naturally feel that marine science is the most important thing. But very, very rarely did any scientific discipline agree with the priorities of any other scientific discipline.

Bleasel and Wilkniss organised a committee of some fifteen Antarctic program directors who met outside the framework of normal SCAR meetings:

> So in this way we decided first what science we wanted to do. We consulted with our scientists, we knew what they thought was important, and that which fitted into our priorities—and then we would decide among ourselves how we were going to do that.

The COMNAP group would then liaise with SCAR, outlining what scientific programs would be supported. Bleasel:

> The bulk of Antarctic problems are operational matters really. . .Where we needed the scientists' input, we'd get that, and then we'd put the scientists on to the scientific parts of it. It worked extremely well.

The scientists were not impressed as they perceived COMNAP as a threat to SCAR's influence in the Treaty system. The SCAR Logistics Working Group was dissolved and replaced by a Standing Committee (of COMNAP) on Antarctic Logistics and Operations (known as SCALOP). COMNAP did not weaken SCAR's position in the Treaty system and the international coordination of multi-national science programs has improved. COMNAP and SCALOP now meet concurrently with SCAR every two years to discuss the logistics and funding implications of large science programs.

Australia has played a major role in the work of COMNAP–SCALOP and the division's assistant director, Jack Sayers, was elected chair of SCALOP in 1992. In 1996 COMNAP decided to transfer its secretariat from Washington DC to Hobart, with Jack Sayers taking up the position of executive secretary.

An Australian scientist wishing to work in Antarctica not only has to choose a project that accords with the international obligations of ANARE, but must also convince the Antarctic Division that the proposal merits the necessary logistic support. In the early years of ANARE, the Executive Planning Committee advised the Antarctic Division on general policy and scientific objectives. It was chaired by the then director, Phillip Law, and did not survive his departure in 1966. In 1979 the Antarctic Research Policy Advisory Committee (ARPAC) was established under the chairmanship of David Caro, vice-chancellor of the University of Tasmania, and later of Melbourne. ARPAC's first report was tabled in Federal parliament the following year and recommended among its long-term guidelines that Antarctic research be directed towards the living (including marine) and mineral resources of the Antarctic and the environmental effects of their exploitation. The effect of the Antarctic climate, weather, and ocean circulations in the Southern Ocean area was also singled out, reflecting the growing awareness of the importance of Antarctica to the world's environment. Patrick Quilty thought highly of ARPAC:

> There was no way that the chairman or any member of ARPAC was going to be told the way [to] operate by government. Caro was a very independent chairman.

All ARPAC could do was provide good advice and hope its recommendations would be acted on by the Antarctic Division or the Government. One of its recommendations—that a separate fund of $500 000 be set up to support research projects of merit that could not be funded through normal channels—was never realised. In 1985 the Minister for Science, Barry Jones (the most enthusiastic pro-science Federal minister ever to hold office), was keen to promote Antarctic science broadly within the Australian scientific community and proposed a new advisory body, ASAC (Antarctic Science Advisory Committee). John Lovering, then vice-chancellor of Flinders University, was approached to chair it. Lovering:

> I said I'd do that on the understanding that we would have money available—there would be a budget to support research from people outside the division. We'd set up our own little research grant body called the ASAC Research Grants, and Barry agreed that would happen. Now the only problem was that he didn't actually have the money to do it, and. . .the poor old Antarctic Division was required to find it out of its own resources.

Lovering consulted with his predecessor on ARPAC, David Caro, who advised him not to take the job unless ASAC had its own funding. Bleasel supported ASAC and found the money for its research grants scheme. This is still in existence, although, according to Patrick Quilty, its role changed significantly when Lovering left in 1990 and Neville Fletcher, then Chief Research Scientist at CSIRO, took over the chair. Lovering:

> I've always seen ASAC as much more hand-in-glove with the directorship of the Antarctic Division. . .and thus the advice it gives is a bit less independent. It's different in another sense in that it's had the half million to administer every year and that's developed a new layer of bureaucracy within the Antarctic Division.

As well as awarding grants for Antarctic science, ASAC maintained a key role in formulating overall policy for ANARE activities. Before the Protocol on Environmental Protection to the Antarctic Treaty (Madrid Protocol) was negotiated in 1991, the emphasis on Antarctic research

Since it began in 1947 the Antarctic Division has involved scientists from a number of Commonwealth Government agencies and universities in its research projects under the umbrella of ANARE. Ever since the division moved from Melbourne to Hobart in 1981 there has been an important concentration of Antarctic-related research activity in Tasmania. The world headquarters of the Commission for the Conservation of Antarctic Marine Living Resources was established in Hobart in 1982 and in 1988 the Institute of Antarctic and Southern Ocean Studies (IASOS) was established at the University of Tasmania, with the aid of Federal Government funding, to promote and focus Australian academic activity concerned with Antarctica and the Southern Ocean.

In 1991 the Cooperative Research Centre for the Antarctic and Southern Ocean Environment (Antarctic CRC) was established to research the role of Antarctica and the Southern Ocean in global climate change. It addresses this and other questions by conducting research on the links between the oceans, the sea ice, the atmosphere and the

THE INSTITUTE OF ANTARCTIC AND SOUTHERN OCEAN STUDIES (IASOS) AT THE UNIVERSITY OF TASMANIA. (GLENN JACOBSON)

continental ice sheet. The Antarctic CRC is a Commonwealth-funded, independent research organisation with five equal partners: the Australian Antarctic Division, the Australian Geological Survey Organisation, the Bureau of Meteorology, the University of Tasmania and CSIRO's Division of Oceanography (also located in Hobart).

The Antarctic CRC has a major role in the training and education of about 70 postgraduate students through IASOS and is situated on the campus of the University of Tasmania in Hobart.

was more resource-driven to find out what minerals, as well as biological resources, were there. Lovering, a resource geologist, is unapologetic about this approach in the 1980s:

> People were starting to look at exploiting—that nasty word—the Antarctic. And I think whether you're actually going to do it or not is another matter, but I always thought at least you ought to know what's there. . .But

other people don't agree with that, they say, 'Well, you shouldn't know'. I think that's stupid. You've got to know, I believe, what is there and if you have to exploit it, how you would do it in a sustainable way.

By the 1990s there were remarkable changes in international attitudes to Antarctica. Antarctic Division director, Rex Moncur:

> The end of the 'cold war' and tougher economic times world-wide, along with the growing strength of the Treaty System as a means of influence, have reduced the drive for territorial claims. With the signing of the Madrid Protocol, the influence of potential mineral resource exploitation has virtually disappeared—replaced by a need to protect the Antarctic environment.[3]

The internationalisation of Antarctic science had been occurring since the early 1980s. The Madrid Protocol simply re-emphasised the importance of a global approach. Patrick Quilty:

> What it means is that the geologists, biologists, oceanographers and glaciologists, instead of operating as individual disciplines, are very much more integrated. Geology controls where the continent is, it controls the elevation of the land. Oceanography controls the water masses that are circulating around the continent—and in the long run that influences the animals that live there. . .It's a very complex, vast mechanism that we're talking about, and for the first time we're starting to try to pull this lot together as one system.

One alarmist theory has it that if the entire ice cap of Antarctica were to melt, the world's oceans would rise around sixty metres higher than their present levels. The reality is different. Glaciologist Ian Allison:

> For that to happen is going to take tens of thousands of years. . .Another thing is that most of the ice mass in Antarctica is at temperatures well below minus 20°C. Even if the temperature were to rise a couple of degrees—in extreme global warming, people are talking about a few degrees in a century or so—that's not going to melt.

In fact, according to Allison, global warming is likely to create more moisture, which may cause increased snowfall on Antarctica, and the ice sheet would then increase in size. Glaciologists are keen to find out whether the Antarctic ice sheet is in balance or whether more ice is flowing off the continent as icebergs than the amount of precipitation falling on it as snow. A key indicator is the great Lambert Glacier, the world's largest, flowing down into the Amery Ice Shelf, which actually drains some 10 per cent of the entire Antarctic continent. With Mawson

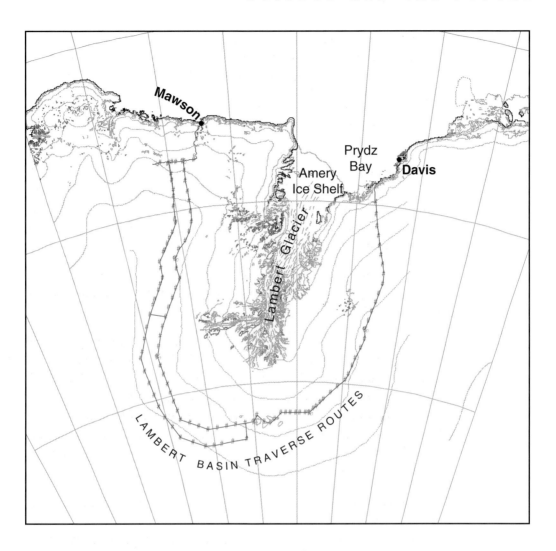

THE 1994–95
DAVIS–MAWSON–DAVIS
TRAVERSES

Station to the west of the Amery, and Davis Station (and Law Base) to the east, Australian glaciologists have been studying the ice flow of the Lambert Glacier since the 1950s. The original marker poles and strain gauges of thirty and more years ago are still valuable indicators for comparison, but satellite technology and GPS (Global Positioning System) can now chart the movement of the ice with extraordinary accuracy. (Australian glaciologists led by Bill Budd began computer modelling as early as 1968, and led the world in this area. *The Derived Physical Characteristics of the Antarctic Ice Sheet* was published in 1971, and was the first comprehensive computer model of the Antarctic ice sheet.)

Despite space-age technology, surface observations are still essential. In 1994 and 1995 tractor trains with teams of six men completed a return traverse of 4500 kilometres around the head of the Lambert from Law Base in the Larsemann Hills to Mawson Station. Ice sheet and bedrock elevation were measured continuously along the traverse route, and markers were placed every 15 to 30 kilometres to determine velocity and every two kilometres to measure the rate of snow accumulation—as well as ice cores obtained to record fluctuations in snowfall over the last century. ANARE scientist Knowles Kerry ranks the Davis–Mawson–Davis traverse among the greatest journeys ever made in Antarctica—including those undertaken in the 'Heroic Era' by explorers like Scott, Shackleton, Mawson, and the Commonwealth Trans-Antarctic Expedition led by Sir Vivian Fuchs and Sir Edmund Hillary in 1957–58. Glaciologist Martin Higham led the 1993–94 leg from Mawson to the Larsemann Hills, and Rob Kiernan (who also travelled with Higham's party) led the return traverse back to Mawson in 1994–95. Even in summer the glaciology teams high on the ice cap work in temperatures of minus 30°C. Andrew Brocklesby was in charge of the ice radar, measuring the thickness of the ice cap over the underlying bedrock during both legs of the Lambert Glacier traverses in 1994–95:

> Every day is similar. The landscape never changes—just the same, day after day. We had two vans, four in one van and two in the other. I was in the van with only two of us. We travelled thirty kilometres each day. One van would reach a GPS marker pole, thirty kilometres apart, and the other would leave for the next one. . .We were always apart unless we had to carry out repairs or drill ice holes—we drilled three or four of these over the whole 110 days. It was very slow going, we travelled only about five kilometres per hour.

High on the Antarctic ice cap, the terrain is utterly featureless—just a seemingly unending expanse of white ice from horizon to horizon. Brocklesby:

> You cannot compare being on a traverse to a voyage on the open sea because at least waves move, and there are seabirds from time to time. But where we were there was just nothing, maybe occasionally a little lump or a bump, but that is all. It is very hard to describe it—Ranulph Fiennes, the Antarctic explorer, describes it as sensory deprivation. Everything sort of collapses in on you.

Traverse life is the ultimate test of personal relations in Antarctica. There is a similarity with space travel and Brocklesby and his companions were assisting in a NASA–Antarctic Division joint experiment, charting their mood swings and emotions daily on specially designed lap top computers which sent data instantaneously to Houston, Texas. Brocklesby found traversing extremely testing:

> Because there is nothing else but the other guy in the van, mountains can be made out of molehills—and we were together 3½ months living in a small container—and you can't get away from anyone. It's difficult to leave the van to go for a walk because there is nothing to walk to. You have to set yourself goals or take up a hobby. I used to run alongside the van sometimes and do chin-ups on the radar antennas. One guy did a management course while we were away—others looked forward to a drink at the end of the day!

Preliminary results from the traverse, associated with other long-term observations of the movement of the Antarctic ice sheet, show that the system is not quite in balance—more snow is actually falling on the continent than is being discharged as icebergs. Glaciologist Ian Allison:

> The models at the moment suggest that, if there is warming due to global change of one form or another, then in Antarctica we will initially get more snowfall on the continent. . .So for the [next] few hundred years the ice sheet will actually start to build up. . .

Recent studies have suggested that the vast distribution of winter sea ice around the continent may have more dramatic short-term impact on the world's climate than the Antarctic ice sheet. Sea ice acts as an insulating blanket between a relatively warm ocean and a very cold atmosphere—it stops heat getting out of the ocean and into the atmosphere. Only in the 1990s were ANARE glaciologists able to voyage south in winter in *Aurora Australis* to study the distribution and thickness of sea ice at a time when ships do not normally attempt to enter the region. The results of these voyages dramatically changed previously held theories about the thickness and distribution of winter pack ice. It was found the ice varied from areas of two or three metres thick down to a few centimetres—resulting in an average thickness of only about 30 centimetres. Glaciologist Jo Jacka:

> There are a heck of a lot more areas of open water and very thin ice that we previously hadn't known were there. We had assumed that within the sea ice zone you had a continuous cover of sea ice. In fact you don't. You have large areas of open water and large areas of very thin ice—by very thin, I mean less than ten centimetres.

As even quite thin ice acts as a blanket for heat loss from the ocean, quite small increases in air temperature could dramatically increase the areas of open water, which would in turn release more heat from the ocean into the atmosphere. One way of studying the thickness and

EARLY OCEANOGRAPHY.
RELEASING A DRIFTING BUOY
FROM *THALA DAN* IN A JOINT
CSIRO/METEOROLOGICAL
BUREAU EXERCISE, JANUARY
1976.
(B MILLER)

composition of the drifting pack is to sink a buoy containing a monitoring system to the ocean floor—deep enough not to be affected by drifting icebergs. Allison:

> This tethered sonar system goes 'ping' every five minutes and has an on-board recorder. As the ice slowly drifts over the top of it with the wind and currents—because the pack ice is always moving—we're getting a continual profile of the thickness of the ice that drifts over the top.

The importance of the ocean as an instrument of climate change is further emphasised by ANARE's involvement in the World Ocean Circulation Experiment (WOCE). Planning started in the early 1980s and some twenty countries are involved in a major world-wide field program from 1990–97. The scale is enormous. According to John Church of the CSIRO's Division of Oceanography, the one billion dollar program will gather in seven years the equivalent of all oceanographical observations done this century:

> We are focusing on the ocean because it is a central part of the climate system. Its heat capacity is much greater than the atmosphere. The upper three metres of the ocean can hold the same amount of heat as the entire atmosphere. It absorbs heat and transports it to another part of the ocean and can release it perhaps decades later.

Surface floats are released to drift around the ocean measuring water temperature and surface currents. As well, *Aurora Australis* has been involved in dropping special floats in the Southern Ocean. Church:

> They descend down to 800 metres, drift with the currents for two weeks to a month, return to the surface, establish their position by satellite,

descend back to the same depth and measure again. These have roughly fifty cycles.

Water samples are also taken from varying depths in the ocean to investigate the absorption of carbon dioxide—as well as temperature, salinity and nutrients in the water column. Church:

> The ocean stores about fifty times as much carbon dioxide as the atmosphere. Of the 6 gigatonnes of CO_2 released annually from burning fossil fuels, about 50 per cent stays in the atmosphere, 2 gigatonnes is absorbed into the ocean—much of it into the Southern Ocean, and the rest is thought to be taken up in the terrestrial biosphere.

The powerful Antarctic Circumpolar Current—the world's biggest ocean current—carries vast quantities of water, heat, salt and carbon dioxide between the world's oceans. Australian research shows that the eastward flow of this current, south of Tasmania, is about 150 million cubic metres per second—about a thousand times the flow of the Amazon River. The ocean, atmosphere and sea ice interact to form very cold salty water masses which sink to form deeper layers. Those layers spread throughout the world's oceans. Changes in any of these related phenomena may have a profound impact on the earth's climate. Curiously enough, the man-made CFC gases which are rising into the atmosphere and contributing to the thinning of the vital ozone layer have been a useful research tool for scientists studying the movement of the super-chilled Antarctic bottom water throughout the world's oceans. The advent of *Aurora Australis* has enabled ANARE to contribute significantly to this new research. Church:

> We can determine the currents by noting the distribution of the CFC content. The efficiency with which the Antarctic shelf forms Antarctic bottom water is a new discovery. We have determined this using CFCs

---

In 1992 SCAR formalised a plan to coordinate Antarctic research on global change under the control of the Group of Specialists on Global Change and the Antarctic (GLOCHANT) identifying six priorities:

- The Antarctic sea-ice zone: interactions and feedbacks within the global geosphere-biosphere system;
- Global palaeo-environmental records from the Antarctic ice sheet and marine and land sediments;
- The mass balance of the Antarctic ice sheet and sea-level contributions;
- Antarctic stratospheric ozone, tropospheric chemistry, and the effect of ultra-violet radiation on the biosphere;
- The role of the Antarctic in biogeochemical cycles and exchanges: atmosphere and ocean; and
- Environmental monitoring and detection of global change in the Antarctic.

LIDAR

Upper atmosphere studies have been undertaken by ANARE scientists in Antarctica from the early 1950s. Until the early 1990s, the emphasis of upper atmosphere physics involved the study of the complex interplay between radiation from the sun and interstellar space with the earth's magnetic field. Today, ANARE is focusing on the structure, chemistry and dynamics of the region known as the middle atmosphere between fifteen kilometres and ninety kilometres above the surface of the earth.

This increased scientific interest in the entire atmospheric column is a direct result of concerns about global change. Over the past three decades, scientists have developed a technique called LIDAR—an acronym for Light Detection and Ranging—which provides a very effective ground-based means of remotely sensing conditions at high altitudes. From 1998 the Antarctic Division and the University of Adelaide will use LIDAR to obtain a comprehensive view of the atmosphere above Davis Station. Andrew Klekociuk, from the Antarctic Division's Atmospheric and Space Physics Section, describes LIDAR as a very powerful remote sensing technique with some similarities to radar:

> We're using a very powerful laser beam and transmitting into the atmosphere. The laser light bounces off molecules and aerosols in the atmosphere and a portion of that light gets scattered back to the ground. By making some fairly careful measurements of that light we can infer information about the density of the atmosphere as a function of altitude, and also the temperature of the molecules and. . .the presence of winds blowing molecules around up there.

Recent northern hemisphere LIDAR measurements have shown a cooling trend of a few tenths of a degree Celsius per year in the middle atmosphere which may be related to human activities. The use of LIDARs in Antarctica is only a recent development, however, and not much is known about conditions there. Klekociuk:

> The LIDAR at Davis was designed by the late Fred Jacka of the University of Adelaide who pioneered Antarctic atmospheric studies from the early days of ANARE. The LIDAR will operate day and night, weather permitting, and will probe to greater altitudes than most other such instruments. LIDARs are operating at other Antarctic sites including the South Pole, McMurdo and Syowa, but these are not able to directly measure winds and temperatures in the novel way that we do.

> The main aims of the LIDAR project are to determine the long-term climate above Davis and to study phenomena which may occur on short time scales—such as atmospheric waves and high altitude clouds. This work will combine with observations from other instruments at Davis and various international projects to gain a better understanding of the Antarctic atmosphere and its influence on global conditions.

as tracers. . .they are tests for ocean models. . .[we now have] a much more accurate model of what really happens.

Without doubt sea levels are rising—between ten and fifteen centimetres during the last century. John Church:

> There are a number of causes of sea level rise. Firstly, there is the non-polar glacial melt from places like New Zealand. Secondly, and most importantly in this century and the next, is the thermal expansion of the oceans. When the ocean warms, the water expands and the sea level rises. . .A range of fifteen to ninety-five centimetres is predicted by the year 2100 AD.

According to a recent report from the IPCC (Intergovernmental Panel on Climate Change), 'The balance of evidence suggests that there is a discernible human influence on global climate'. Church:

> With less sea ice and warmer oceans there will be more evaporation, warmer atmospheres with more water in the atmosphere, therefore more snowfall in Antarctica. This will offset some of the increase in sea level rise from other components. But we are still looking at an order of fifty centimetres rise in sea level, which of course is very significant for [Pacific] island countries and nations like Bangladesh.

ANTARCTIC ORGANISMS AND CLIMATE

One of the most fascinating new areas of ANARE research concerns the interaction of living organisms and climate over the Southern Ocean. Biology program leader Harvey Marchant:

> [We] are looking at effects on the biota that are a result of the greenhouse effect and also the effect of ozone depletion. . .some Antarctic organisms are not only affected by climate change, some can also influence climate. The alga *Phaeocystis* produces a chemical, dimethyl sulfide—DMS for short.

When ventilated to the atmosphere it forms aerosol droplets. The sulfur-containing compounds from *Phaeocystis* play a role in the formation of clouds and so have a direct effect on the climate. (Its cloud-forming qualities are significant. A doubling of DMS to the atmosphere has been predicted to cause a 2°C drop in global temperature.) Vast quantities of phytoplankton (single-celled floating plants), protozoa (single-celled animals) and bacteria are the basis of the marine food chain. *Phaeocystis*

487

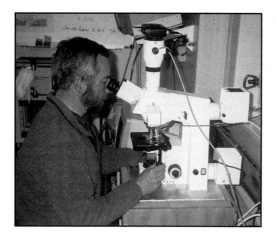

ANARE BIOLOGY PROGRAM
LEADER HARVEY MARCHANT
AT THE MICROSCOPE IN THE
MARINE SCIENCE LABORATORY
ON *AURORA AUSTRALIS*.
(GLENN JACOBSON)

forms massive blooms on the surface of the Southern Ocean from September to midsummer. Marchant:

> I regard that as perhaps the most single important species in the Southern Ocean. It is there in huge quantities—we've counted up to 60 million cells per litre. The water when it's like that looks like minestrone—a sort of pale, browny kind of soup. If you get a bucket full of sea water it looks like strings of brown goop in the water.

The *Phaeocystis* blooms happen to coincide with the 'ozone hole' over Antarctica which exposes the algal cells to high levels of ultraviolet (UV) radiation. In the mid 1980s some scientists feared that this increased UV radiation might be affected to such an extent that there could be a collapse of the Antarctic marine food chain. Early experiments on the effects of UV on phytoplankton seemed alarming. Marchant:

> The organisms they looked at were mostly diatoms—which are of high food value to krill and other grazers [and] which suffered a very rapid knockdown in these studies. . .But the story is much more subtle than that because different organisms have different tolerances to UV and have different food values.

> The soup-like *Phaeocystis* resists increased UV radiation more efficiently than the diatoms because it produces its own sun-screen—which it secretes into the mucus that surrounds the cells. There is considerable commercial interest in this phenomenon by manufacturers of sun-screen and other health care products. Negotiations are continuing, and the compounds that protect *Phaeocystis* from UV damage may one day protect humans.

KRILL

The vast swarms of krill in the Southern Ocean are dependent on the nutrients and phytoplankton which are effectively the pastures of the sea on which every other living thing depends. But there was no reliable knowledge on the extent of the krill in Southern Ocean waters or on

 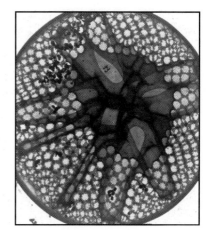

their breeding and life cycle. The early marine science experiments under the umbrella of BIOMASS (Biological Investigations of Marine Antarctic Systems and Stocks) were dependent on having ships equipped with trawling nets, echo sounders and laboratory facilities. (BIOMASS involved fifteen ships from eleven countries and was the biggest marine biological experiment ever undertaken in the world.) *Nella Dan* was modified in time to contribute to FIBEX (the First International Biomass Experiment) in the summer of 1980–81 and the voyage leader was Knowles Kerry.

Shipping problems caused an embarrassing last minute cancellation of ANARE's involvement in SIBEX 1 (the first phase of the Second International Biomass Experiment) in 1984, but SIBEX II, led by Harvey Marchant the following year, spent 45 days investigating Antarctic marine ecosystems and brought back live krill, including newly hatched juveniles, to the Antarctic Division's laboratories at Kingston. Up till 1982 no krill had been successfully bred or kept alive outside Antarctic waters. Research biologist Tom Ikeda was recruited specifically to run the Antarctic Division's krill program and did so from 1982 to 1987. Stephen Nicol then took over. Nicol:

THE DELIGHTFUL SHAPES OF SINGLE-CELLED ORGANISMS REVEALED BY THE ELECTRON MICROSCOPE.
LEFT: *PYRAMIMONAS*, DIVIDING—MAGNIFIED 3500 TIMES.
RIGHT: TRANSMISSION MICROGRAPH OF THE ANTARCTIC MARINE DIATOM *ASTEROMPHALUS*, THE MAJOR FOOD ITEM FOR KRILL AND OTHER GRAZERS, FROM 62° SOUTH. THIS ORGANISM IS AROUND 20μM (20/1000MM) IN DIAMETER. (COURTESY AAD ELECTRONMICROSCOPE UNIT)

> Tom Ikeda single-handedly turned the krill research upside down at an international level. In 1964 [a United States biologist] Mary Alice McWhinnie had kept krill alive in captivity in Antarctica —the first to do so, but only for a short time. Tom, however, was the first to keep krill alive in captivity outside Antarctica for any length of time

(eleven years) and thus saw how long they lived and how fast they grew. The krill that he grew were the first to spawn in captivity. He was the first to see that they shrink by up to 75 per cent of their body size if they are kept without food, thus proving that you cannot age krill by body size.

Krill is a general term used to describe about 85 species of open-ocean crustaceans known as *euphausiids*. They look like smaller versions of more familiar crustaceans, like prawns or lobsters, and range in size from small tropical species less than a centimetre in length to little-known deep sea giants that can be as long as fourteen centimetres. In summer, female Antarctic krill lay up to 10 000 eggs at a time, sometimes several times a season, into the surface waters of the Southern Ocean. The eggs are thought to sink to a depth of 2000 metres before hatching. They then begin their long 'developmental ascent'—up to ten days—during which the newly hatched larvae journey up towards the sunlit waters to feed. Nicol:

> Krill live in large aggregations or swarms that can be made up of more than a billion animals. The development of scientific echo sounders has provided a way to 'see' krill swarms but it has not made the distribution question any simpler; the echo sounders have revealed that the swarms have a complex horizontal and vertical structure.[4]

Krill are in the central position of the Antarctic ecosystem, eaten not only by land-breeding carnivores such as penguins and crabeater seals, but by whales, bottom-dwelling fish and squid. Their bodies and waste products become food for molluscs and other invertebrates on the sea floor. The krill themselves feed on phytoplankton. Nicol:

> It is thought that a large krill fishery might disrupt the entire ecosystem and have a particular impact on the land-breeding predators that live in colonies near the most popular fishing grounds of the South Atlantic.[5]

The remarkable ability of the krill to reduce its size in lean times has made it difficult for scientists to keep track of its age and longevity. The Antarctic Division leads the world in this research. Nicol:

> We now have 2000–3000 krill. This is the only facility of its type in the world—we are the only people in the world to keep krill all year round. This has enabled us to carry out research that requires large numbers of replicate measurements and to study the relationship between repro-

duction and moulting, growth rates and ageing. Some of our recent studies with a visiting Chinese student indicate measurement of the eyeball diameter may be the best way to distinguish age.

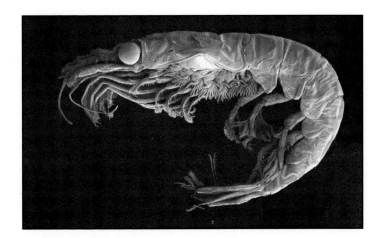

THE UBIQUITOUS KRILL *EUPHAUSIA SUPERBA*. THIS COMPOSITE PHOTOGRAPH WAS TAKEN WITH A SCANNING MICROSCOPE.
(COURTESY AD ELECTRONMICROSCOPE UNIT)

Excellent echo sounders, netting facilities and laboratories on *Aurora Australis* have been a valuable addition to the practice of ANARE marine science from 1989. (One limitation on commercial exploitation is the difficulty of processing krill. Unless they are processed within three hours of being caught, powerful enzymes break down the flesh, making it unsuitable for human consumption. Krill skeletons also contain high concentrations of fluoride, so the flesh must be quickly removed from the skins. (Even the processing of krill as protein for animal food must be completed within ten hours.)

Krill, the animal with the greatest biomass on earth, is preyed on by blue whales, the largest animals that ever lived, and by crabeater seals, the most plentiful large mammal surviving in the wild. Not all Antarctic fauna survives on an exclusive diet of krill, but other animals in the food chain, like finfish and squid, depend on it. The ANARE biological science program seeks to increase biological knowledge of Antarctic and sub-Antarctic ecosystems and of the organisms of the region, and to assess and predict the possible effects of environmental change and human impacts on them.[6]

On 1 November 1996 CCAMLR announced it had set the first annual catch limit of 775 000 tonnes of krill in Southern Ocean waters adjoining the Australian Antarctic Territory. This decision to allow limited fishing was based on the results of an extensive survey of krill stocks in the area conducted by ANARE marine biologists from *Aurora Australis* earlier that year. (At the same time CCAMLR accepted the advice of its scientific committee to increase the catch limit for the Patagonian toothfish in sub-Antarctic waters between Australia and Antarctica from 297 to 3800 tonnes.) These decisions were enthusiastically endorsed by

THE SAD TALE OF ALAN THE KRILL

Tom Ikeda's research into krill longevity suffered a serious setback in the early 1980s. As there were only a few specimens, they had names. 'Alan' was special. He had survived in his jar longer than any of his fellow captive krill, and looked like proving that krill could live much longer than originally thought.

Each day Alan's jar would be examined by a technician to see if he had shed his skin, and each week 80 to 90 per cent of the water would be decanted off, to be replaced by fresh seawater imported specially from the Tasman Peninsula.

For three years this ritual was carried out successfully until the technician made an unfortunate error. Uncharitable co-workers suggested after the event that the technician concerned may have had a hangover or, for some reason, not been as alert as usual. But on this fateful day he misjudged the decanting, and flushed the hapless Alan down the sink.

The enormity of this disaster was not apparent until some years later when new, younger krill survived in captivity for about nine years. Only then was it realised that the flushing away of Alan had set back the discovery of the longevity of krill by many years.

Senator Ian Campbell, then the Coalition government's parliamentary secretary responsible for Antarctic matters:

> We would very much like an Australian company to be able to harvest that resource for the benefit of Australia and Australia's export earnings—helping to feed the world. If we don't do that, then I presume some other nation will come and do it. But at least Australia has conducted the science and we can assure the rest of the world that harvesting is within limits and is sustainable.

MONITORING FOOD CONSUMPTION

Monitoring the food consumption from the Southern Ocean of selected 'indicator species' like sea birds, penguins and seals, one of the most exciting new areas of ANARE research, has only been possible since new technology has been able to attach computers and transmitters to individual animals. This makes it possible to monitor—sometimes with the aid of satellites—where they go to feed and, in the case of seals and penguins, how deep they dive to capture their prey.

Instrumentation attached to the great wandering albatross, which breeds in the sub-Antarctic region, has shown the birds often fly right around the globe, ranging down into Antarctic waters, and also up into sub-tropical regions. They are particularly vulnerable to long-line fishing for tuna, diving down to take the baits as they sink below the surface. Long lines have been used since the 1950s, but it was not until the 1980s that the depletion of wandering albatross (and other albatross species) was linked to the long lines. The 'wanderers' only breed every second or third year and only have one chick, so they are particularly vulnerable. ANARE sea bird ecologist Graham Robertson is gloomy about the prospects for this species:

> I expect the wandering albatrosses will go the way of the blue whales when they were harvested years ago—they just disappeared. Albatrosses are being seen less and less frequently. The 'wanderers' in South Georgia are in deep trouble because they fly to places like Brazil—and even Wollongong—and get caught by tuna boats.

Robertson believes the problem could be mitigated if fishermen set their lines in total darkness, weighted them so they sank more quickly, and used bird-scaring streamers to frighten the birds away:

> Most fishermen don't really see it as an issue because they don't think they are catching many birds, maybe one a night. But if you multiply this one per night for every boat—there are 55 million hooks going into the water per year in the Southern Ocean—it comes up to several tens of thousands of albatrosses. . .fishermen need education as soon as possible.

In 1988, Robertson and his field assistants from Mawson worked at Auster Rookery right through the winter, studying the foraging ecology of the emperor penguins there. Emperors are the only penguins to breed on sea ice and the males incubate the eggs, huddling together for group warmth through the winter blizzards. To do this they fast for around 115 days, including the courtship and mating in March, through to December when the ice breaks up and the chicks take to the open water. Emperors are the largest of the 16 penguin species, standing 1.15 metres tall and weighing up to 40 kilograms. During their long fast, the male emperors lose some 20 kilograms of their body weight while the female forages for food in the Southern Ocean. During the breeding season the adult birds have to trek some 70 to 80 kilometres over the sea ice to reach open water to bring back food for their chicks. During 1988 Robertson managed to attach data loggers to individual birds and then recover them when they returned to feed their chicks. This winter field work was continued by Roger Kirkwood in 1993 and Barbara Wienecke in 1994.

The research has revealed that emperors often dive deeper than 500 metres and can hold their breath for 22 minutes—much longer than any other bird species. There are about 23 000 birds at Auster and

A PENGUIN ON A
WEIGHBRIDGE AT
BÉCHERVAISE ISLAND, NEAR
MAWSON STATION. THIS
UNIQUE SYSTEM, ABLE TO
WEIGH A MOVING BIRD, WAS
INVENTED IN 1991 BY
ANARE SCIENTISTS KNOWLES
KERRY AND GRANT ELSE. THE
CONCEPT HAS SINCE BEEN
TAKEN UP BY THREE OTHER
NATIONS, REVOLUTIONISING
PENGUIN ORNITHOLOGY.
PENGUINS ARE IDENTIFIED
AND WEIGHED AS THEY MOVE
TO AND FROM THEIR COLONY.
(COURTESY J CLARKE)

it is now known that to rear their chicks they take some 11 000 tonnes of krill, fish and squid from nearby waters. Graham Robertson:

> This is a phenomenal amount and suggests the ocean is very productive even in the throes of winter. A single chick requires 84 kilograms of food to develop properly—its ration is less than 10 per cent of that of an adult for self-maintenance. In a twenty-day foraging trip an adult can get the chick's ration in less than one day's hunting. Clearly the adult's priority is its own self-maintenance. The chick comes next.

In past years, krill and other fishing has been carried out along the edge of the continental shelf which is where the emperors forage for their food. After it has hatched and reared the chick, the male emperor has to double its body weight in a short period before preparing for another four-month fast:

> So if there is any competition between sea birds and mankind through the harvesting of commercial fisheries, the emperors have probably got most to lose. . .If there is any impairment in the male's ability to fatten and if they come in to breed a bit lighter, then their body fat reserves will run out before the eggs hatch and they will have to abandon them.

Robertson makes the point that the world's population is increasing at such a rate that pressure to get food from the oceans is going to increase:

> So this program is pre-emptive. We have to focus our work on CCAMLR related issues to try to get measurements that are conservative for seabirds and other animals.

When she is kneeling on the ice, petite biologist Barbara Wienecke is the same height as an emperor penguin—about one metre. As emperors can weigh anything from 22 to 40 kilograms, and are extremely strong, Barbara—the first woman biologist to winter with the birds at Auster Rookery in 1994—had problems catching and restraining them to attach data loggers and make other observations:

When you think that two-thirds of their front muscle power is in their flippers, it is not surprising that these are so strong. Their flippers are their main weapons. I was getting very badly bruised arms, so I cut up an old foam mattress and made some arm shields out of it. I also got some spare Explorer socks and doubled them up over my arms and this worked very well.

Wienecke and her assistant Kieran Lawton lived in a field hut eight kilometres from Auster Rookery, set amongst spectacular grounded icebergs:

The hut is only about 2.5 metres by 7.5 metres, with no privacy at all. Sometimes we would send each other out on long walks! Every bit of water we used had to be chipped off an iceberg just off the island and melted. Everything in the hut would freeze overnight. You would wake up in the morning to minus 26°C. Even the toothpaste was frozen.

On one occasion during the winter they had warning of a blizzard and took out a small sledge to collect lost eggs from around the colony to keep count of the mortality rate of

BIOLOGIST BARBARA WIENECKE INSIDE HER PORTABLE APPLE FIELD HUT OUT ON THE SEA ICE AT AUSTER ROOKERY. SHE STAYED WITH THE EMPEROR PENGUINS THROUGH THE WINTER OF 1994. (I CUMING)

the incubating chicks. Barbara was having trouble even moving against the freezing wind, her face battered by whirling snow. She thought to herself, 'Just what am I doing here? I *hate* this wind!':

Out of the drifting snow came an emperor, tobogganing on his stomach, looking so casual, ever so relaxed. He stopped briefly near me and looked at me, as if to say, 'What the hell are you doing?' Then he took off again, so gracefully. It was a magic

➤

moment! The contrast of me—with my 15 kilograms of clothing, sweating profusely, and hardly able to breathe as it was so cold—and this big beautiful animal who was able to do just what he wanted to do, was ludicrous.

Wienecke and Lawton had twelve transmitters, valued at $3500 each, which are recycled when their batteries run down. They are glued to the backs of selected penguins to monitor their swimming and diving patterns. Unfortunately, probably due to a late breakout of the sea ice, the parent birds were not able to bring back enough food and the breeding success rate at Auster in 1994 was only 65 per cent. A critical moment for a newly hatched chick is when the female returns from fishing, and the male (who has hatched it from an egg) somewhat reluctantly hands it over. Wienecke:

The chicks sit on the feet of the parents for about 50 days. Once they thermo-regulate, they have to be able to walk. Initially they are utterly uncoordinated, partly because their bellies are so huge—they fall over on their little tum-tums!

Biologists try to keep physical contact with the emperors to a minimum, and Wienecke and Lawton used sophisticated telescopes from a small radio tower to monitor the colony:

The tendency of biological sciences now is for less and less interference—a far cry from the old days when you believed you could do anything in the name of science.

Establishing how much emperor penguins and their chicks eat demands highly invasive procedures where animals have to be captured, injected with isotopes, captured again for blood samples and their stomachs flushed out with warm sea water to measure how much food they have gathered. The research and monitoring being conducted as part of the CCAMLR Ecosystem Monitoring Program (CEMP) at an Adélie penguin colony since 1991 on Béchervaise Island near Mawson Station is far less drastic. Here Adélie penguins are studied by an automated penguin monitoring system conceived and developed by Knowles Kerry and Grant Else of the Antarctic Division. The Adélie penguins carry an electronic identification tag. They walk to and from their nesting area over a special weighbridge which automatically reads their tags and registers their weight as they come and go from their fishing grounds. In 1994–95 biologist Heather Gardner at Béchervaise Island saw what could happen when, for whatever reason, the birds were unable to find krill at their normal fishing grounds. Within one month of hatching all 1800 chicks were dead and the colony deserted. Satellite tracking showed that birds travelled up to 170 kilometres for food and returned to their chicks with none. Judy Clark, who had been working with the Adélies for five summers, noted:

There was very little krill around that year, so we assume that was the reason for the deaths. What we don't know is why the krill stocks decline. Was it due to some natural cause? Is it perhaps a natural cycle? We have only been measuring for a few years, not long enough to really know.

With a world-wide population of over two million pairs, such seasonal fluctuations pose no threat to the Adélies' survival as a species. According to Knowles Kerry, the breeding failure at Béchervaise Island is 'an opportunity to study an event that simulates heavy fishing and the removal of the penguins' food supply'.

The study of seals and how they feed is an enormous scientific challenge. Because crabeater seals live and breed on the pack ice they are not only difficult to count, but even harder to monitor. An international circumpolar project to determine pack ice seal abundance and distribution, APIS (Antarctic Pack Ice Seals Program), is scheduled for 1998–99. ANARE biologist Colin Southwell is coordinating a program that began in 1994 to attach radio transmitters to crabeater seals and track them by using the French ARGOS location and data relay satellite system. First catch your seal. Crabeaters are big aggressive animals and teams of up to twelve people have to be lowered on to the sea ice from *Aurora Australis*. After chasing and netting a seal—some of the team have fallen through thin ice into the freezing water in the process—the animal is anaesthetised. Southwell:

> The satellite-linked dive recorders are instruments about ten centimetres square and a couple of kilos in weight and we stick those on their back just behind their shoulders. These instruments record their diving behaviour, how [deep] they dive, how frequently and how much time they spend above the water on the ice and how much time below.

Elephant seals on Macquarie Island are easier to get at, because they come ashore to breed and moult. There are some 100 000 elephant seals that come to Macquarie and 20 000 pups are born each year. But the populations are now half what they were thirty years ago, although the numbers seem to be stabilising at a lower level. Biologists do not know why there has been this decline. Again, sophisticated dive recorders have been used to monitor the swimming and feeding behaviour of adult elephant seals in recent years. The elephant seals are built like submarines, weighing up to four tonnes. Research scientist Harry Burton thinks they should be called 'surfacers', not 'divers', because they spend forty minutes underwater for every four minutes on the surface. They

dive to phenomenal depths—dives below 1500 metres are common, and some go down two kilometres to feed on their preferred diet of squid:

> One seal stayed down two hours, and then came to the surface for four minutes before diving for another

half an hour. Physiologists can't explain how they do this. They do have an enormous number of red blood cells. The last thing they do before diving is breathe out, so they have no air in their bodies. We are not even sure how they locate the squid. They have huge eyes, so perhaps they can pick up bioluminescence transmitted by the squid. Their whiskers may pick up vibrations in the water. We simply don't know.

BIOLOGIST NICK GALES (CENTRE) ASSISTED BY MECHANIC NEALE GENTNER (LEFT) AND CARPENTER RICK BESSO (RIGHT), WEIGH A 3-TONNE ELEPHANT SEAL ON THE BEACH AT DAVIS, 1995–96. (R EASTHER)

Almost nothing is known about where elephant seals go to feed in the Southern Ocean. In 1995 a program of fixing transmitters to the heads of juvenile elephant seals was begun at Macquarie Island. A sample of 24 seals was equipped, and 22 out of the 24 swam south-east of Macquarie Island to an area south of the Antarctic Convergence (Polar Front), and south of New Zealand. Why they do this, and what they do when they get there, is a fascinating puzzle yet to be unravelled.

THE FORMATION OF ANTARCTICA

Research into the basic structure and history of the formation of Antarctica crosses a number of scientific disciplines. The meteorologists are interested in the record of Antarctica's past climate contained in the ice cores obtained by glaciologists working at Law Dome near Casey and other sites in the Australian Antarctic Territory. Apart from studying the geological history of the continent from the exposed rock in areas like the Prince Charles Mountains and the Vestfold Hills, geoscientists from the Australian Geological Survey Organisation (AGSO) have undertaken a program of high resolution seismic measurements of the sea floor in Prydz Bay to look at the sediment laid down on the ocean floor by the Lambert Glacier. In an associated experiment in 1995, scientists from the CRC at the University of Tasmania, working from *Aurora Australis*, obtained samples by coring and dredging from the sea floor at other points around Antarctica to the south-west of Australia. Samples obtained contained pollen and even wood dating back 40 to 45 million years— evidence of a much warmer Antarctica.

In 1985 dolphin and whale fossil skeletons that are 3.5 to 4 million years old were discovered in the Vestfold Hills near Davis Station, giving a dramatic illustration of how previously held theories on Antarctica are being revised. These skeletons are the only known vertebrate fossils from the Antarctic from the last 40 million years, since the development of the Circumpolar Current which gave rise to a new, distinctive Antarctic ecosystem.

Other information in the rocks at Marine Plain (now declared a site of special scientific interest) suggests Antarctica was a vastly different and warmer place before the present large icecap developed. The sea level was much higher than now, there was a much smaller amount of ice on Antarctica, and parts of the continent carried a vegetation similar to that found in the mountains of Tasmania, including a deciduous beech almost identical to a present-day Tasmanian species.

The discoveries at Marine Plain—and fossilised wood found in the Transantarctic Mountains in 1985–86 by American researcher Peter Webb—have challenged the previously accepted view that Antarctica has been much the same as it is now for the last 15 million years or so. Patrick Quilty (who discovered the first fossilised bone fragments at Marine Plain) is in the thick of the controversy:

> There is a very, very bitter and heated debate going on at the moment about what was the environment of Antarctica between about 2.5 million years and maybe 5 million years ago. . .The uniqueness of Marine Plain is that the rocks are where they were laid down, and they haven't been moved since they were deposited—the only place in Antarctica where that's true. So this is the best place for getting a record of what life has been, or has evolved from, within the modern Antarctic ecosystem.

Preserving the ecosystem

Keeping that ecosystem uncontaminated is a concern addressed by the Protocol on Environmental Protection to the Antarctic Treaty (Madrid Protocol) agreed to by nations with interests in Antarctica in 1991. The

Antarctic Division established a Human Impacts Research Program in 1992 to carry out the aims of the Protocol in achieving a '. . .comprehensive protection of the Antarctic environment and associated ecosystems. . .'

The havoc caused by the introduction of cats, rabbits, and other domestic and feral species on the sub-Antarctic Macquarie Island has not yet been fully addressed. Although human impact on Antarctica in the early years was most evident in the savage exploitation of the large whales, fur and elephant seals, the establishment of permanent human settlements on the continent has impacted on a fragile environment. An increased environmental consciousness has resulted in old rubbish dumps near the ANARE stations being backloaded and returned to Australia, sewerage systems built, and now in a policy that all rubbish and wastes from field parties be returned to base for incineration or backloading to Australia.

The most urgent concern is to prevent introduced species of any kind contaminating the Antarctic continent. While the hostile environment has prevented the kind of fauna and flora invasion that scarred Macquarie Island, some unfortunate accidents have already occurred. Some are of particular concern to microbiologists engaged in 'microbial prospecting' in what they hope is a pristine environment. A wood-rotting fungus, *Phylophora fastigiata*, was discovered by ANARE biologist Elizabeth Kerry at some moss beds near Mossell Lake in the Vestfold Hills in 1988. It is possible that it was introduced with the timber of the field hut as it normally colonises softwoods. There is a danger that it could change the ecology by colonising the cellulose of the native mosses. (Elizabeth Kerry has also isolated the fungus *Botrytis cinerea*, which causes 'noble rot' in wine grapes, at Mawson Station. It is quite widely distributed. Whether it is indigenous or introduced via ANARE liquor supplies is not known.)

The theory has it that an organism has a niche within an ecosystem because there is no stronger competitor. The strength of those organisms present in Antarctica lies in their ability to cross the ocean. Knowles Kerry:

> There are other organisms which could probably survive better than these in Antarctica, but they are too weak to cross the ocean barrier. However when they are introduced by man. . .then they could potentially change the environment quite drastically!

Introduced plants can also thrive on ice-free areas near the Antarctic coast. Martin Riddle is the Antarctic Division's first Human Impact Program Manager:

> We have found three species of plant in the Larsemann Hills recently—a grass and two flowering plants! We didn't bring them in, the Russians

▲ GLACIOLOGICAL TRAVERSE VEHICLES FROM CASEY STATION PAUSE BRIEFLY AT THE ANTARCTIC CIRCLE IN 1993. IN SUB-ZERO TEMPERATURES THE WEAK, LOW SUNLIGHT IS NOT STRONG ENOUGH TO MELT THE ICE ON THE REAR OF THE DISTINCTIVELY SHAPED ROYAL MELBOURNE INSTITUTE OF TECHNOLOGY (RMIT) FIELD CARAVAN. (D MONSELESAN)

▼ MORNING LIGHT AT MACEY ISLAND, NEAR AUSTER ROOKERY, MAC. ROBERTSON LAND. (K SHERIDAN)

▲ Loose snow gathered by the wind is blown around to form snow balls on the sea ice near Mawson Station.
(K Sheridan)

▶ Dr Louise Holliday, the first ANARE woman to winter on the continent, exploring ice cliffs behind the Vestfold Hills, 1981.
(Courtesy Louise Holliday)

▲ During the Lambert Traverses of 1994–95, an accumulation measurement cane is checked every 2 kilometres. Every 30 kilometres an ice movement station with a measuring pole allows the glacier speed and flow to be measured to the nearest millimetre.
(D Calder)

▶ Measuring the height of snow accumulation in a blizzard during a survey of the Lambert Basin.
(M Craven)

▲ A brilliant aurora over Davis Station, 1980. (P Murrell)

▶ The ultimate white wedding. Newlyweds in front of an ice cave near Davis Station, 1994. From left: Michael Carr (Station Leader), Kerrie Swaddling (bridesmaid), Denise Jones (bride), Colin Blobel (groom), Helen Cooley ('best woman'). (Gary Watson, courtesy C Blobel)

► EMPEROR PENGUINS IN FRONT OF *AURORA AUSTRALIS*.
(P GREET)

▼ IN THE SPRING OF 1994 *AURORA AUSTRALIS* BROKE INTO THE FAST ICE NEAR DAVIS STATION TO CARRY OUT THE FIRST MAJOR RESUPPLY OF AN ANARE STATION OVER SEA ICE. PREVIOUSLY BARGES HAD BEEN USED IN OPEN WATER LATER IN THE SEASON.
(D CALDER)

▲ DAVIS STATION — OLD
AND NEW.
(MIKE REID)

▶ TWIN-ENGINED S76
HELICOPTERS BEGAN FLYING
BETWEEN ANARE STATIONS
IN 1994. (D CALDER)

▲ THE NEW CASEY STATION, 1994.
(K BELL)

▶ A BELL HELICOPTER EXPLORING THE
UNKNOWN COAST OF OATES LAND, 1962.
(AAD ARCHIVES)

◀ TWIN-ENGINED S76 HELICOPTERS
RESUPPLYING MACQUARIE ISLAND FROM
AURORA AUSTRALIS, 1994.
(D CALDER)

▲ *AURORA AUSTRALIS* IN THE SEA ICE NEAR DAVIS WITH AN AURORA APPROPRIATELY OVERHEAD.
(IAN ALLISON)

▼ FRAGMENTED FAST ICE, GROUNDED ICEBERGS AND A DISTANT *AURORA AUSTRALIS* IN PRYDZ BAY.
(COURTESY R EASTHER)

did. They are in a very small area near their Progress Station. We found two species first in 1994 and removed all of them. This last season we found three species and 23 individuals. The grass was about an inch or two [2½ to five centimetres] high. . .The buildings contained pot plants which died, and these were swept outside.

Riddle also makes the point that the Antarctic is important on a world scale as a natural laboratory for monitoring global changes in pollution loads. There is a risk that our local activities may degrade our ability to pick up global changes:

> If we protect the environment as a scientific resource, this should ensure that nothing we do threatens the integrity of the ecosystem or is a threat to human health. We might have to draw up a whole new series of criteria concerning what is acceptable—we are doing this now. Protecting the scientific value of Antarctica is one of the more hard-nosed reasons for why we might have higher environmental standards. There is also a widely held public expectation that we have very high standards of stewardship for Antarctica.

Because the human impacts program cuts across all the scientific disciplines and requires access to all information on Antarctic research and logistic activity, Riddle was involved in organising the Australian Antarctic Data Centre in 1996—a powerful and comprehensive data base of integrated ANARE research which is also available on the Internet.

The ANARE rebuilding program and expansion of scientific laboratories on the continent led to a considerable increase in the burning of fossil fuels to keep the increasingly complex stations running. In 1988, the station leader at Mawson, Philip Barnaart, wrote in his annual report:

> In a period when science is telling us to reduce the burning of hydrocarbons to minimise the 'greenhouse effect' and for other environmental reasons, we are increasing our fuel consumption in Antarctica at an alarming rate. Ten years ago 300 000 litres of SAB [Special Antarctic Blend] lasted the station a year. . .Mawson in 1989 was scheduled to receive one million litres of SAB. With the rebuilding program at Mawson less than half finished, one wonders what the fuel figure for a year is likely to be in, say, ten years time.[7]

ANARE has also had to address an increase in tourism to Antarctica from the late 1980s. While non-stop overflights by jumbo jets have minimal impact on the Antarctic environment, ship-based tourism involves increasingly large numbers of people coming ashore by inflatable boat and walking around Adélie penguin rookeries and other sensitive areas. While

501

TOURISTS FROM THE RUSSIAN ICE-BREAKER *KAPITAN KHLEBNIKOV* ENJOYING CLOSE ENCOUNTERS OF A PENGUIN KIND ON MACQUARIE ISLAND, 1993.

(R LEDINGHAM)

most tourist ships ply the shortest route between South America and the Antarctic Peninsula, ice-strengthened tourist ships now regularly operate from Hobart, calling in to Macquarie Island and to Commonwealth Bay (to see Mawson's hut) on their way to the Ross Sea.

Macquarie Island is a State nature reserve managed by the Tasmanian Department of Environment and Land Management, which also has a responsibility to ensure no unwanted foreign seeds or vegetable matter are unwittingly brought to the island by tourists. Since 1989 responsible tourist operators have adopted a voluntary code of conduct, including a program of lectures on board their ships to instruct tourists on how to behave while on shore. In 1989 the Tasmanian Government built boardwalks and lookout platforms near penguin and sea bird rookeries on Macquarie Island, financed by a levy from the companies organising the Antarctic tours. In 1995, the Tasmanian Government set a limit of 500 visitors to Macquarie per year.

The situation is virtually uncontrolled on the continent. The historic hut at Cape Adare (where Carsten Borchgrevink and his party completed the first wintering in Antarctica) is situated in the middle of an Adélie penguin colony. Tourists have to walk through and around the nests of breeding birds to get there. Anywhere on the Antarctic coast, a single bootprint in a patch of Antarctic moss or lichen will be evident for perhaps half a century or more. In 1994 Janet Dalziell, Antarctic programs coordinator for the environmental group Greenpeace, claimed that US and New Zealand VIP helicopter flights to a penguin rookery at Cape Royds on the Ross Sea since the 1970s have caused a population decline. She claimed the penguins were stressed when they saw humans, and that mating and egg-laying cycles had been affected. 'That's the one example [Cape Royds rookery] that's been documented'.[8]

Cape Royds and Cape Adare are in the sector of Antarctica claimed by New Zealand and are popular Ross Sea tourist destinations. But tourist ships are increasingly turning their ice-strengthened bows towards the Australian Antarctic Territory. In May 1989 a group of five Australian parliamentarians produced a report for the House of Representatives, 'Tourism in Antarctica', following a visit to Mawson and Davis Stations arranged by the Antarctic Division earlier that year. Their report gave cautious approval to ship-based tourism providing an appropriate management regime could be not only established, but enforced, if necessary under Australian legislation:

> The Committee does not accept that the Antarctic experience should be reserved for the privileged few who are involved in Antarctic research. . .The Committee supports tourism to the Antarctic provided it is conducted with a regime which ensures proper protection of the wilderness values of the continent.[9]

In 1992 the Antarctic Division allowed a limited number of tourists from the chartered Russian ice-breaker *Kapitan Khlebnikov* to visit all three ANARE continental stations. More visits are planned for 1997–98. (Tourism has even been suggested as a source of revenue to assist ANARE programs in the event of budget cuts. This option was canvassed by the Antarctic Division's assistant director Jack Sayers in 1993. An alternative to closing down a station could be to lease accommodation to tourist operators, or leasing stations to tourist consortiums 'with guaranteed access for scientists at an agreed level. . .').[10]

This option has not been seriously considered yet. However the issue of tourism was raised at the 17th Antarctic Treaty Consultative Meeting at Venice in 1992, the first since the adoption of the Protocol on Environmental Protection to the Antarctic Treaty (Madrid Protocol). After discussions focused on whether there should be a new annexe to the Protocol to formulate measures controlling tourism and other non-government activities, there was disagreement between Treaty nations about a new annexe to cover tourism.[11] In 1994 the 18th ATCM passed major recommendations setting out guidelines for the management of ship-based tourism. However within a few months of this meeting, Australia introduced the notion of overflights by commercial airlines. In the 1995–96 summer nine Qantas non-stop tourist flights were made, and thirteen were scheduled for 1996–97.

LIVING IN ANTARCTICA

While a good deal of effort is now being made to rationalise and minimise the impact of human activity on Antarctica, the effect of Antarctica

HERITAGE BUILDINGS IN ANTARCTICA

Below the snow and ice of Whitney Point, Wilkes sleeps quietly, much of it the same as when ANARE abandoned it in 1969 and moved across Newcomb Bay to the replacement station Repstat (named Casey on completion). Ironically, Wilkes has outlived its successor which was removed after the modern buildings of new Casey opened in 1988, replacing buildings that had been occupied for less than twenty years. At Wilkes the radio masts are still visible, and if the snowdrifts retreat at the height of summer the roofs of the timber IGY buildings emerge. Some see them as waste, to be removed like old Casey, others see them as a priceless record of the first generation of stations in the region.

The debate about what to keep of the past is echoed at Davis, where the original donga line stands empty, and at Mawson, where Law's original huts nestle between the bold steel and concrete of the 1980s. The Explastics huts erected in 1954 stand largely intact, despite the daily katabatic. But it may not be wind that ultimately brings down the buildings. Antarctic Division policy manager Andrew Jackson:

> We have a dilemma. Mawson is the oldest continously occupied station south of the Antarctic Circle, and those early buildings are part of Antarctic history—just like Douglas Mawson's hut at Cape Denison. But some of them are unsafe and we simply can't afford to keep them all heated if we are not

using them. What we have to do is find the balance between what can be kept on site as a permanent record, and what could be brought back for public display.

WILKES' HISTORIC TIP CIRCA 1992—HERITAGE RICHES OR A LOAD OF OLD RUBBISH?
(W NICHOLAS)

The future of even older relics must also be decided. Some of the original buildings at Macquarie Island are still in use, although the same cannot be said of the wreckage of the ANARE camp at Atlas Cove on Heard Island. Also on Heard are faint signs of the stone shelters used by sealers who worked there from 1855. It is the wind that brings down these buildings, but it also protects them for future archaeologists by burying them in a blanket of black volcanic sand.

According to Jackson, the weather also plays a role in protecting Mawson's hut:

Snow has penetrated every little crack of the hut and now it is almost completely full of ice, permanently anchoring it to the ground. When the tourists arrive at Cape Denison they cannot go in, which means that little can be disturbed inside. I'm happy with that if it means our most important historic building can stay where it is.

But leaving Mawson's hut in place may not be enough to ensure that it will be there for next century's tourists. In 1996 plans began to take shape for an expedition to Cape Denison the following year to ensure that the hut will survive beyond 2011—the hundredth anniversary of Douglas Mawson's landing at the site. The conservation work will have an unusual similarity with Mawson's AAE expedition—it will be almost entirely privately funded. The 'new' approach of seeking commercial sponsorship for some of Australia's Antarctic work is a return to the path chosen by ANARE's predecessors in Antarctica.

on human beings is also an important and continuing ANARE research activity. Investigations into the physiology and psychology of wintering expeditioners have been carried out by station doctors as individual research projects and as part of an ongoing Antarctic Division research program on human interaction with the Antarctic environment. In 1980–81, under the sponsorship of SCAR, scientists from Argentina, Australia, France, New Zealand and the United Kingdom joined together in the International Biomedical Expedition to the Antarctic (IBEA) devoted solely to looking at 'the performance of man in cold and isolation'.[12] Twelve men—most of them doctors—agreed to undergo a battery of physiological, biochemical, microbiological, immunological and psychological tests. These tests were conducted in three phases: before going to Antarctica; then during 65 days of travel by motorised toboggans inland from the French station at Durmont d'Urville; and finally a third set of comparative tests back in Australia. Half the group were artificially acclimatised by daily cold baths at 15°C at the University of Sydney before leaving for Antarctica. One of the twelve subjects was film maker David Parer, who produced two ABC documentaries titled *Antarctic Man* which followed the progress of the experiment. Some idea of the discomforts tolerated by the intrepid researchers can be gauged by the situation of French scientist Dr Claude Bachelard, who shared his sleeping bag with a bulky recording device nicknamed 'Alfred' which monitored changes in his sleep patterns and body temperature during the night. By day he endured fierce winds and temperatures as low as minus 40°C with a rectal thermometer *in situ* which provided data for a clothing insulation study.[13]

The team members lived in tents on the polar plateau. As well as travelling, cooking food and melting water, they had to undergo a battery

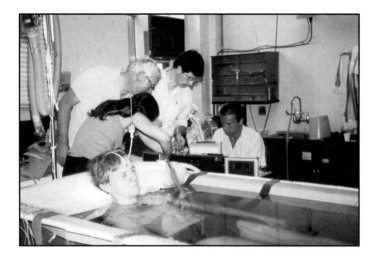

of tests each day including metabolic and biochemical fluctuations, energy expenditure, dehydration, nutrition, sleep patterns, psychological changes, and immunological responses. As if that wasn't enough, questionnaires had to be filled in regularly, and memory and perception skills tested against machines. One of the party withdrew from the experiment in the field. Des Lugg, ANARE's head of polar medicine who led the field project, noted that some of the experiments, although more sophisticated, continued some of the work done on Sir Douglas Mawson's Australasian Antarctic Expedition in 1911–14.

Small wintering groups in the Antarctic provide ideal situations not only for studying how people adapt to cold and isolation, but also for microbiological research on colds and infections. Lugg:

> Recently we have studied changes in the immune response. We've found that groups in Antarctica—like groups in space—have a depressed immune response. The reasons are not clear. So this has led to a collaborative agreement between NASA and the Antarctic Division for using our stations as an analogue for space research. . .

The comparison between small communities living in isolation in Antarctica and astronauts in space is useful for medical and psychological research. Human beings certainly exist there as though in space, taking with them everything they need to survive and maintain life. But the interaction of Antarctica with the earth's environment and the implications for its ecology were largely unknown when the first satellites were launched above the earth's atmosphere in the late 1950s. Patrick Quilty is unequivocal about the scientific significance of Antarctica:

> Study of the Antarctic is probably just about the most important study, on a continental basis, you can do anywhere round the world. In terms

The immunological project is a collaborative one between the Antarctic Division, the Universities of Tasmania and Newcastle, and NASA. Konrad Muller is Professor of Pathology at the University of Tasmania:

Changes in the immune responses begin soon after arrival in Antarctica, but peak around August or September. The immune depression is linked to anxiety and appears to be triggered by stress factors such as isolation and personal stress situations which are clearly imposed on people who live in a small, confined community for a year.

Researchers are now looking at what chemical substances in the human brain are triggering these changes, which in turn impact on the immune system. Muller:

Currently NASA is doing some parallel studies on the activation of viruses. These joint investigations show that depression of the immune system enhances the shedding of viruses into the saliva. However this is not at a level to cause illness. . .we are talking about a healthy population responding to a stressful and isolated situation.

Muller believes these studies have profound implications for how people react to living in Antarctica and will lead to a better understanding of the human brain and immune system. An associated NASA-related project is the use of portable computers in the field in Antarctica, seeking to relate immune changes in individuals to the stress of isolation in an extreme environment.

of international or global impact, Antarctica is more important, say, than Australia. One of the reasons for saying that is that so much of the world's weather is generated in Antarctica, and in oceanographic terms, something like 50 per cent of the world's oceanic water masses are generated around Antarctica. . .In that sense there is really no other continent that matches Antarctica for global importance.

Just how much science is done in Antarctica depends on how much governments are prepared to spend on it. Australia, with its claim of 42 per cent of the continent, has maintained a high international profile which dates back to its important contribution to the diplomacy leading up to the Antarctic Treaty in 1959, despite the 'cold war' then preoccupying the USSR and the US. More than two decades later the establishment of CCAMLR in Hobart is not only an acknowledgment of the international regard for Australia's contribution to the Antarctic Treaty, but also of the quality of scientific research generated by ANARE—particularly in marine science. Perhaps one unintended consequence of adopting the Protocol on Environmental Protection to the Antarctic Treaty (Madrid Protocol) in 1991 (removing the option of mining in Antarctica) was

MICROBIOLOGY AN EXCITING NEW GROWTH AREA

Because of its isolation, Antarctica has a variety of unique organisms that have adapted to intense cold. In 1995 the Australian pharmaceutical company Amrad signed a contract with the Antarctic Cooperative Research Centre (CRC) at the University of Tasmania and contributed $500 000 to research into micro-organisms collected for and identified with the centre.

The ability of some phytoplankton to develop their own sun screens is an area of obvious interest to the pharmaceutical industry, but there are many other possibilities. There are some species of Antarctic fish which live in water so cold that they have developed their own anti-freeze chemicals to stop their blood and tissues from freezing. Harvey Marchant:

> There is some discussion on how this could be used in, say, transplant technology. If you get a kidney or some other bit of a human being now, it has to be used in a very, very short time. One of the possibilities is that this organ could be perfused with anti-freeze chemicals. . .[so] it could mean that instead of organs having to be used within a couple of days they could be kept for a couple of months.

The saline and fresh water lakes in the Vestfold Hills near Davis Station have proved a treasure trove of unique organisms. Ekho Lake, for example, has a most unusual ecosystem with bottom temperatures of about 16°C all year round—yet its surface is covered by ice for nine months of the year.

Novel species isolated from Antarctica are maintained in the Australian Collection of Antarctic Micro-organisms at the CRC in Hobart.

In 1993 Paul Holloway, a PhD student, isolated seventy strains of *Streptomyces* spp. from six separate Antarctic soil samples. Half of these strains produced antibiotics. Further analysis of only three of the strains found that two of the antibiotics had been discovered previously, but that the third was novel. This high 'hit' rate was instrumental in Amrad investing in the CRC's research.[14] Holloway:

> The potential for other new things out there is very great if we could find one [so] quickly. There are potentially hundreds of new strains and some of these could be very useful to us. Since 1993 that particular antibiotic has been handed over to Amrad which is now investigating its potential. It takes about ten years of research before a new antibiotic goes on the shelf—it may well be toxic to humans and so must go through a rigorous trial process.

Various single-celled organisms in Antarctica produce compounds that can affect ice, either becoming incorporated into ice or avoiding being incorporated into ice. This may have an application in food technology. Harvey Marchant:

> Your ice cream may not become crunchy after you've left it out on the counter a little too long before putting it back in the freezer. . .the ice cream is a fairly trivial example. What we are seeing at this stage is really the dawn of Antarctic biotechnology.

Each antibiotic-producing bacterium is a potential cure for a human or animal disease, each Antarctic yeast (a kind of microscopic fungus) could be of great interest to the food industry, and some 'waste-munching' bacterium could be the key to cleaning up oil spills or other environmental pollutants. In an era when human impacts on Antarctica are being carefully reassessed, there is an extremely positive aspect to biotechnical research. Marchant:

It has no environmental impacts at all. You can get bacteria from the soils, from out of the sea ice, and when you've got just a small sample you can grow them up [in a laboratory] and away they go. So we have here the opportunity for a real flourishing of biotechnological industries that will make no scars on Antarctica at all.

the impression that the continent was somehow 'saved', and that governments would not need to spend so much money there. Rex Moncur:

> The perception that Antarctica is 'saved' is a worry for me. Certainly in a number of other countries they are finding it more difficult to get funding for their programs. In the Australian context, I don't believe that's a significant factor. I believe there is bipartisan [political] support for a strong Australian Antarctic program. . .so I am convinced we will be able to maintain a strong program.

Since the Madrid Protocol, the Antarctic Division has reorganised its science priorities to stress the importance of research into global warming, to protect the Antarctic environment (particularly its marine ecosystem) and to continue obtaining information of practical importance. Under the Labor Government, the emphasis on maintaining the Antarctic Treaty system and Australia's influence in it—including our territorial interests—was listed as the last of four main objectives. In 1996, following the election of the Coalition Government, ANARE's scientific priorities in Antarctica are basically unchanged.

Rex Moncur believes that the future of ANARE science is linked to integrating its work with other nations in order to build up a composite picture of the whole Antarctic region:

> The most important role for Antarctic science in the future is the contribution we can make to understanding global change. Without the information we can gain from Antarctica, I don't believe we can make any sensible predictions of global change. Antarctica therefore becomes the new priority area for scientists who wish to understand global change, and is the priority area for our own scientists.

On 17 September 1996, the Governor of Tasmania, Sir Guy Green, convened a forum, 'Tasmania, the Antarctic and Sub-Antarctic'. During a wide-ranging address to the forum, the coalition's parliamentary secretary responsible for the Antarctic, Senator Ian Campbell, was optimistic about Australia's commitment to Antarctica into the 21st century. He announced a review by the Antarctic Science Advisory Committee to develop strategic options for ANARE after the year 2000, 'to extend the boundaries of previous reviews and present thought. . .The new millenium will present new scientific challenges, many of which may be foreseen now.' These included the possibility of a direct air service to the continent, shipping options after the end of the *Aurora Australis* charter in 2000, and the future of tourism in Antarctica:

> It is my own strongly held belief that the Antarctic continent is the reservoir of a treasure of information about our planet. . .Antarctica has challenged generations of Australians. . .I believe that our greatest feats as a nation are ahead of us. Our monumental achievements in Antarctic exploration and fifty years of Antarctic expeditions can and will be surpassed.[15]*

Certainly the importance of monitoring subtle changes in the Antarctic environment long-term is crucial if Antarctica is to live up to its promise of being the barometer of global health. Martin Riddle:

> To identify the subtle early signals of global change against the background noise of variability requires reliable, long-term data. The only way to ensure that data. . .is to ensure continuity of data collection, and this requires a long-term commitment to support the Antarctic program. Without this all our efforts in the past could come to nothing.

Perhaps more private corporations will invest directly in supporting ANARE research if the new products and drugs stemming from Antarctica's unique ecosystem are to be fully explored. When ANARE geologists, surveyors, and glaciologists began exploring the coast and interior of the Australian Antarctic Territory from 1954, they were participating in basic discovery—finding out what was actually there. As we reach the end of the 20th century the excitement and challenge of the new face of polar exploration may lie in the single cell of a unique Antarctic micro-organism.

It is a development which would have intrigued Sir Douglas Mawson, who not only laid the foundations of Australia's claim to such a large area of the Antarctic continent but whose BANZARE voyages devoted so much time to marine biology in the Southern Ocean. Mawson lived

---

* In November 1996, Senator Campbell was promoted to Parliamentary Secretary to the Treasurer, and Queensland Liberal Senator Ian MacDonald took over Antarctic responsibilities, reporting to the Minister for the Environment Senator Robert Hill.

At the cutting edge

In the Antarctic, science has a status enjoyed nowhere else. Its value to global understanding now provides nations with a powerful argument for being there. But in these cost-trimming times, Antarctic scientists have found that simple curiosity or opportunism are no longer sufficient arguments to support their projects. For better or worse, the individual adventurer–scientist is fading from view, and being replaced by national research programs with their inevitable strategies, goals and objectives. Fitting a good scientific idea into this new model while keeping its freshness and innovation is not always easy, yet Antarctic science has continued to show resilience, resourcefulness and results. ANARE's record at the leading edge of Antarctic science in the 1980s and 1990s is impressive.

- Australians have developed world-leading investigative techniques and equipment for studying ice. Drilling into the Antarctic ice cap and traversing enormous areas over land and sea, scientists have obtained new information on how Antarctic ice forms, moves and deforms, on what it tells us about past climates, and on how it profoundly affects the world's oceans and climates.

- Starting from scratch by modifying an ageing *Nella Dan* to study the vast but little known Southern Ocean, Australian marine biologists have built a reputation out of all proportion to the country's size and resources. From 1991, the availability of the ice-breaking research ship *Aurora Australis* enabled the collection of high-quality data on living resources augmented by innovative statistical techniques which are vastly improving the information available to international management regimes.

- As the first nation to breed krill successfully in captivity enabling significant discoveries about its life and reproduction, Australia has led the world in studies of this crustacean central to Southern Ocean ecology. Australia has also become a leading nation in studies of the carbon flux and the effects on micro-organisms of enhanced ultraviolet exposure in the Southern Ocean.

- Using advanced technology, Australians are in the forefront of research on the behaviour and foraging ecology of seals, penguins and flying birds in Antarctic regions. These studies have revealed previously unknown diving capabilities of elephant seals and emperor penguins. Ground-breaking automation technology has enabled year-round monitoring of the ecology of Adélie penguins.

- Antarctic sea ice and the vast Antarctic circumpolar current are now seen as vitally important elements in global processes. Using *Aurora Australis*, Australian scientists from many disciplines have come together to obtain key oceanographic, glaciological and biological data on an enormous segment of the Southern Ocean, looking at global climate issues such as the role of cold Antarctic bottom water, availability of food for micro-organisms, and heat exchange between ocean sea ice and atmosphere.

- ANARE physicists have continued Australia's long and proud tradition of significant work on the middle and upper atmosphere with pioneering studies of the stratosphere, leading into the ground-breaking Davis LIDAR program

➤

with its data on stratospheric and mesospheric composition, winds and temperatures from light reflected off atmospheric molecules hit by a powerful laser beam. This research affords exciting insights into the physics of the middle atmosphere and may provide a 'litmus test' for evidence of global climate change.

- Australian studies of auroras have played a key part in establishing that auroras occur within an oval centred over the Geomagnetic Pole in central Antarctica. Australia has supplied vital data to an international program which has established that southern aurora events happen at the same time as those in the north—that electrons move between hemispheres along magnetic lines of force. Modern technology has made possible wide Internet distribution of basic geophysical parameters in near real-time from ANARE's southern physics experiments linked to significant international programs.

- Antarctic weather is directly relevant to that of the rest of the southern hemisphere.

Meteorologists have used increasingly sophisticated Antarctic data, collated at Casey's Antarctic Data Centre, to improve measurably the quality of Australian weather forecasting.

- Enderby Land to the west of Mawson contains some of the oldest rocks on the surface of earth, yielding unique information on its evolution. Measuring the rocks using state-of-the-art Australian technology will allow highly precise estimates to be made of the age of episodes of the earth's history.

- Mysteries of the rocks under the vast Antarctic ice sheet are being revealed in Australian studies of the Antarctic sea floor. Pieces of continental rock, carried under Antarctic glaciers into the oceans and deposited there, are yielding to ANARE scientists excellent evidence on the age and environments of Antarctica's rocks. Other ANARE sea floor studies are providing scientists with new information on the evolution of the continental margins of Australia and Antarctica, once joined as part of Gondwana.

to see his dream of permanent stations in Antarctica realised, and to influence directly the scientific work being done by ANARE during his membership of the Executive Planning Committee from 1947 to his death in 1958.

Always the modern and innovative scientist and explorer, Mawson should have the last words in this jubilee history of ANARE. He would have delighted in the quantum leaps in communications and the sophisticated research techniques available to the men and the women—in his day not even considered for inclusion in expeditions—now working in Antarctica. He would have applauded their efforts to assess the continent's interaction with the rest of the world and their continuing determination not only to push back the frontiers of scientific discovery, but to ensure the preservation of Antarctica's wildlife and unique environment.

Perhaps when on my printed page you look,
Your fancies by the fireside may go homing
To that lone land where bravely you endured.
And if perchance you hear the silence calling,
The frozen music of star-yearning heights,
Or, dreaming, see the seines of silver trawling
Across the ship's abyss on vasty nights,
You may recall that sweep of savage splendour,
That land that measures each man at his worth,
And feel in memory, half fierce, half tender,
The brotherhood of men that know the South.[16]

                                                    D M

LOUISE HOLLIDAY AND FRIENDS TRAMPED THEIR FAREWELL MESSAGE INTO THE SNOW COVERING A FROZEN LAKE ON THE TRYNE PENINSULA, VESTFOLD HILLS, 24 OCTOBER 1981. (COURTESY L HOLLIDAY)

APPENDICES

APPENDIX I

ANARE WINTERING EXPEDITIONERS 1947–1997

Note: Members of the 1997 wintering parties are correct as of March 1997. Then the total number of wintering expeditioners 1947–1997 stood at 2573. Those men and women occupied 3674 positions because some wintered more than once.

Key: A = Amery Ice Shelf; C = Casey (old and new); D = Davis; H = Heard Island; M = Mawson; Q = Macquarie Island; W= Wilkes (including Repstat).
Example: M57 means wintered at Mawson in 1957.
Station Leader or OIC indicated by * (e.g. M57*)
Died in ANARE service = +

Abbott, Ian C85	Alcorn, Bruce C85, M89	Anderson, Carl Q71
Abbottsmith, John H48	Alden, Bruce D76	Anderson, Gary M83, M86
Abbs, Gordon Q54, M56	Alderdice, Henry ('Harry') W59	Anderson, Keith D71
Abeysekera, Bob C83	Alexander, Arthur M88, C92	Anderson, Mervyn ('Max') D88
Ackerly, John Q67, C71	Alexander, Nevil D77	Anderson, Morag D90
Adam, Bruce C84	Algar, Phil Q91	Anderson, Peter W68
Adams, Ian Q56*, M58*	Allan, Bob W68	Anderson, Ross C69
Adams, John Q78	Allan, Joe Q64	Anderson, Roy M69
Adams, Neil C94	Allardyce, Craig C96	Andrews, David Q75
Adams, Warren M79	Allen, Bill C77	Andrews, Keith Q72+
Adamson, Erica C88	Allen, Denise Q85, M86, D88, C92	Andrews, Kerry C72
Addicoat, Des D91, M94	Allen, Gary C74, M78	Andrich, Ingrid Q96
Adolph, Jan D82, Q84	Allen, Gordon W65	Anglesey, Scott D95
Afflick, Gordon M65	Allison, Bob H49*, M55	Arden, Peter M73, Q86, Q88
Aimer, Bruce C73	Allison, Don M65	Armanini, John D62
Aitken, Vicki Q83	Allison, Ian M69	Armistead, John M89
Akerman, Graeme M76	Allport, Bruce M64	Armstrong, Barry M78
Akerman, Jon D90*	Allwright, Barry C71	Armstrong, Chris M59
Alafaci, Maurice D86	Almond, Dick M73	Armstrong, Dave Q70, D72, M74
Albion, Pat M56		Armstrong, Graeme C93*

Armstrong, John D88, M96
Armstrong, Mick M84
Arnel, Roy Q52, M57, M58
Arriens, Pieter D76*
Arrowsmith, Tom M83*
Arthur, John M60
Ash, Ray W63
Ashcroft, Gordon M81
Ashford, Tony M74
Assender, Ken M60
Atkinson, Jim Q60
Atkinson, Laurie H52
Atkinson, Mark D97
Atkinson, Phil Q64
Attard, Peter D90, C93, M97
Austin, Craig C72
Aves, Alan M86, M89
Ayton, Jeffrey C92
Azmi, Obadur C95
Baciu, Florian C91
Backhouse, Brett M92
Baggott, Peter M65, W67
Bagliani, Fulvio M75, M77
Bailey, Trevor D94
Bain, Chris M69
Baines, Fred Q58*
Bajinskis, Ray Q96
Baker, Don D72
Bakker, Fred D64
Baldwin, John M65
Ball, Brian D76, M80
Ball, Dave C81
Ballantyne, Bob C82
Bandy, Bob M75, C78, D84
Banfield, Geoff M59
Bannister, Peter Q79, C86
Barber, Alan Q89, D91
Barclay, Garry C84
Barclay, Geoff M96
Barclay, Robert Q90, C92
Barker, John M75
Barker, Roger D75+
Barnaart, Phil D78*, C80*,
    Q85*, M88*, Q91*, Q97*
Barnes, Graham C71
Barnes, Jason D96
Barnes, John Q68
Baron, Ray M88
Barr, Suzanne M95
Barratt, Noel D60
Barrett, Colin C79
Barrett, David D76, M78, Q80,
    Q85, M92

Barrctt, Ken Q94
Barrett, Noel Q64, W66
Barrett, Peter C82
Barton, Gil M76
Barton-Johnson, Rod C75
Bates, Nick Q89
Batt, Ken C77, Q80
Battye, Alastair W62
Baulch, Roy Q77
Baxter, Brian C84, M86
Bayer, Ray Q58
Bayley, Mike W65
Bayliss, Peter D93
Beasley, Wally Q68
Béchervaise, John H53*, M55*,
    M59*
Beck, John M64, W66
Bedson, Mark D74, M84
Beer, Geoff D81
Beggs, Helen Q87, C90
Behn, Les Q49
Beinssen, Konrad D82*
Belcher, Ross C80
Bell, Brian Q62
Bell, Cameron Q94
Bell, David Q75
Bell, Elanor D96
Bell, John Q79
Bell, Stewart ('Snow') M59
Beman, Keith M69
Bence, Mick C81, C84, Q87
Bennett, Dave M73
Bennett, Jim M68
Bennett, John M. M65
Bennett, John Q70*
Bennett, Ken M60, W65, M67,
    D69, Q73, Q76, Q82,D86
Bennett, Peter C72
Bennett, Roger Q48
Bensley, Pat M65, C71
Benson, Oliver C79
Bergin, Bob M61, Q63
Berridge, Howard D82
Berrigan, Max W61, Q65
Berry, Phil D92, D94, D96
Berzins, Bert C75, M78
Besso, Rick Q82, D85, Q96
Best, John M77
Betts, Martin Q69, M71
Bewsher, Bill M56*
Bian Lin-Gen M82
Bicknell, Andrew C96
Biggs, Roger M68

Bilson, John W68
Binns, Darryel Q87, Q90
Bird, Garry M61
Bird, Ian M60
Birss, John M78
Bishop, Geoff C89
Bishop, Jim Q53
Bishop, John Q65, M67
Bishop. Dave C70, D73
Blaby, David C70, M80
Black, Henry ('Harry') Q57*,
    W60*
Black, Ian E. M63
Black, Ian K. Q59
Black, Malcolm Q78
Blackwood, Michael D88
Blades, Quentin C69
Blair, Jim M58
Blake, Adrian M79, C82
Blake, Dave M68
Blake, Roger M58
Blakebrough, Dave C78
Blakeley, Leon C76
Blandford, Doug D74*
Blight, David C70
Blobel, Colin C87, Q90, D94
Bloomfield, Ted M60
Blundell, Keith Q77, M79
Blundell, Tony W66, M68, Q71
Blyth, Alan W66*
Blyth, Warren D93, M97
Bo Wen C89
Boda, John W59, Q61, D62, Q68
Bode, Ken M67, C69
Bode, Ortwin Q59, M62
Bodey, Alan C70
Bolza, Alf Q55, M58
Bonar, Derek D93
Bond, Dave M68
Bone, Steve W62
Bonnici, 'Mick' W64
Bool, Geoff M69
Borland, Ray H52, M58
Borschmann, Enid Q78, M85
Bott, Ken H51
Bottomley, Phillip D92
Boucher, Chris M97
Bourke, Peter J. M85, Q87, Q89,
    D91
Bourke, Peter N. M77
Bowers, Arthur Q51
Bowling, Lee Q74, D76
Bowtell, Peter Q66

Bowthorpe, Mike W64
Boyd, Jeff D70
Boyd, John W65
Boyd, Trevior Q50
Braden, Lachlan Q85, C88
Brading, Matt Q94, M97
Bradley, Garry D62, M64
Brammer, Paul M75, C79
Brand, Alain D80
Brand, Russell M77, C84, C88
Brandie, Neil M78
Brandt, Henry W59
Brandt, Peter Q70
Branson, John M62
Braunsteffer, Claude D59
Brawley, Brian D82
Bray, Joe W66, W68, Q73
Breckinridge, John W61
Breckon, Ralph Q74
Bredhauer, Laurie C78
Breed, Anthony C97
Breen, John Q97
Breeze, Bill C76
Brennan, Bernard Q60
Brennan, Carl C74
Brennan, Joe C87, M89, D93
Brice, Neil Q57
Bridgeford, Randall D87, M89, M92
Bridger, David C81
Brierly, Keith M95
Briggs, Peter D83*
Brightman, Grant M90
Brightwell, Neil W68*
Brinkies, Hans W66
Broad, Dave W67
Broadhurst, Jonathan D77
Broadhurst, Mal M72
Broadhurst, Noel M77
Brockbank, Tony C80
Brockelsby, Keith M61
Brocklehurst, Frank M64
Bromham, Barry D73*
Bromwich, Dave C70
Brookes, Ray D72, D74
Brooks, Andrew C96
Brooks, Jim H53
Brooks, Lawrie Q52, Q58
Brooks, Tom C74
Brooks, Trevor C76
Brophy, Brian M73
Brophy, Dennis W64
Brothers, Nigel Q76, Q79

Brown, Alex Q56, M58, D61
Brown, Greg D78
Brown, Harold Q70
Brown, Ken H51
Brown, Lex C71
Brown, Peter E. D90
Brown, Peter L. H52
Brown, Rick C76, C79
Brown, Robin Q93
Brown, Ron C78
Brown-Cooper, Peter W65
Browne, Chris C87
Browne, Peter C82
Bruce, David C73
Bruce, Ian C88, Q97
Bruehwiler, Albert Q82, D86, M90, M93
Bruer, Mike H50
Bryant, Gerry M73, C76
Bryden, Mike Q65
Buckland, Rod M71
Budd, Bill W61, M64
Budd, Grahame H54*, M59
Budnick, Keith W64
Buis, Graham C85
Bulcock, Tony Q76
Bulling, Elizabeth C95
Bulu, Joweli D82
Bunning, Stephen D85+
Bunt, John Q51, M56
Bunt, Rod D80
Burch, Bill W61
Burch, Mike D79
Burchell, Rex M79*
Burke, Chris D83
Burkett, Graeme W60
Burnett, Eric M58
Burnett, Hedley H49
Burns, Dave D75, D77
Burns, Gary C76, Q80
Burrows, Dave D82
Burton, Arthur H49
Burton, Gary C84, D95, M97
Burton, Harry D74, D78
Butcher, James M87
Butcher, Peter Q70, D72, C74
Butler, Bill M67
Butler, Ken M82, C85
Butler, Patrick M90
Butler, Paul M81*, D85*, D87*
Butler, Rowan M81, C84
Butler, Wade M74
Butling, Don W60

Butterworth, Alan D86
Butterworth, Geoff W63, M66
Butterworth, Roy M87, M91
Byrne, Darryl C86
Cabrie, Ian D71
Callaghan, Jeff Q66, M70
Callow, Dave Q55, M57
Calman, Jim W62
Calver, Ross Q74
Calwell, Bob Q64
Cameron, Doug C80, D87, M89, Q91
Cameron, Geoff M74+
Cameron, Ian Q81
Cameron, Peter M74
Cameron, Scott M65
Campbell, Ian M73
Campbell, Julie M82
Campbell, Ken Q54*
Campbell, Kevin M80
Campbell, Malcolm M90
Campbell, Mike W60
Campbell, Peter D75
Campbell-Drury, Alan H48
Cane, Richard. M91
Canham, John W67*, Q69*
Cannon, Warren M80
Cantellow, Derek C72
Canterbury, Graham D86
Cao Chong D84
Cappelletti, Peter Q84
Cardell, Norm M64
Carey, Peter C81
Carmichael, Noel Q91, Q94
Carne, Bert M60
Carnegie, James M67
Carr, Gary C78
Carr, Jim H52
Carr, John D71
Carr, Michael D94*
Carroll, Albert ('Shorty') H48
Carroll, Denis D78, Q80
Carstens, David M62
Carter, Brian M75
Carter, Bruce M65
Carter, David W67
Cartledge, Bill W62, M66, M71, M73
Cartwright, Geoff D95
Carver, Jim C70, C73
Casasayas, George Q59
Cassidy, Tim M69*
Casson, Tony Q84

Dalgleish, Ken M86, M91
Dalgleish, Peter M84
Dalton, Bob Q53*
Dalziel, Ken H53
Darby, Kerri M96
Dare, John M74, M82
Dart, Jack Q64, Q65, M69, M71,
    M73, M75
Dartnall, Herbert D91
Davern, Eddie W63, W67
Davey, Allan D80
Davidson, John M63
Davidson, Laurie C72
Davies, Peter M76, Q78, Q80
Davies, Rex D94
Davis, Chas M68
Davis, Evan C81
Davis, Richard Q68
Dawe, Garry C85
Dawson, Peter L. M64
Dawson, Peter W. C73, M79
Dawson, Philip C91
Dawson, Stan Q50
Day, Dennis M85, D88, Q91
Day, Gavin M85, C87
Day, Lindsay Q76
de Deuge, Maria M87, M91
de Jonge, Klaas C79
de La Harpe, George W59
de la Mare, Bill Q72
de Silva, Fred Q63
de Vere, Steve M92
Deakin, Gillian D86
Dean, Adrian Q59
Dedden, Peter Q79
Delahoy, Andrew C88
Delahoy, George H54
Deland, Ray Q53
Delaney, Paul M79, D89, D93,
    M96
Delarue, Ashley C83
DeLeacey, David D87
Demech, Wally W65
Denereaz, William Q70
Denham, Bill Q49, M61
Denham, Kevin D83, C91
Denham, Les C70
Denholm, John Q57, W59
Dennis, Stewart M87
Denny, Graham D97
Dent, Vic M67
Deprez, Pat D84
Dettmann, Don C79, M81

Deurwaerder, Maurice Q71
Devitt, Bob M72
Dhargalkar, Vinod D83
Dick, Bill M60
Dick, Tony D82
Dietrich, Max C82, M86
Dilger, Peter D91
Dingle, Bob H51, M54, Q56,
    D57*, W59*
Dippell, Neville W68, M70
Disney, Trudy Q93
Dittloff, Heinz M81
Dodd, David Q61, D63
Dodds, Alan Q73
Dodds, Kevin M75
Don, Gavin M84
Donaldson, Andy D81
Donovan, Kevin D75, M86, M96
Doran, Luke C90
Dougheney, Peter C82
Douglas, Ian D60*
Douglas, Leon M83
Douglas, Steve M82
Doutch, Fred Q50
Dovers, Bob H48, M54*
Dowden, Dick Q56
Dowie, Don M56
Down, Horrie M69, C79
Downer, Graham M58
Downes, Max H51
Downey, Robyn M85, Q89
Doyle, Hugh H51
Draper, Geoff C90
Dreimann, Mark Q82, M84
Drinkell, Adam M95
Drummond, Neil C95
Du Toit, Carl W.C. Q48
Du Toit, Charles F. H49
Dubovinsky, Miro C94
Dubow, Bob M94
Dudley, John Q90
Duke, Alan M66
Dulfer, Steve C85
Duncan, John D75, D83, C88,
    Q92
Dunlop, Ross M59
Dunstan, Peter Q76
Durre, Mark Q79
Dwyer, Vic Q62, M64
Dyer, Ralph M60, M66, Q68,
    D71
Dyke, Graham M60
Dymond, Michael M89

Eadie, Jock D59
Ealey, Eric ('Tim') H49
Easther, Rob D86*
Eastley, Wayne M83, C85
Eastoe, Harry M70
Eastwood, Gary C87, D91
Eather, Bob M63
Eavis, Chris Q83, M88
Edgar, Bill M66, Q72
Edward, Bill Q61, M63, M65
Edwardes, Dave Q66
Edwards, Darryl M69
Edwards, Hank C74
Edwards, Read D76
Edwards, Simon M95
Edwards, Tom W60, W62
Eiler, Steve D92
Ekstrom, Lou M72
Elkington, Ted W66, D74
Elkins, Terry M60
Elliott, Fred H53, M55, M58
Elliott, John W66
Elliott, Phil D84*
Elliott, Wal M81
Ellis, Max D77
Ellis, Peter C82, M84
Ellis, Tom W64
Ellson, Mal D85, Q87, C90, M92,
    D95
Ellwood, Bruce Q63*, Q65*
Ellyard, David M66
Emery, Edward Q75
Endacott, Richard M83
Enfantie, John C89, D91
Erb, Erwin M76, D84, Q85, C88,
    M91, H92
Eriksen, Brian C72
Erskine, John M67*
Ertok, Ozcan M84, Q86
Esman, Rudi M93
Etherington, Ray C84
Evans, Anthony Q62
Evans, Bert M59
Evans, Col D83, Q85, D88
Evans, Dale C71
Evans, Desmond ('Pancho')
    M58, W62
Evans, John Q67
Everett, Tony Q78, M80, D83,
    M85, M88, Q92
Everitt, Dave D77
Ewers, Jeff Q97
Ewing, Adam C96

Eyers, Bruce D73, C97
Eyre, Bryan D63
Fahey, Brendan M89
Farley, John M64
Farrell, Leo D70
Faulkner, Jeff H52
Fawcett, Peter M70, M78
Feetham, Tim Q80
Felton, Kev M60
Fenton, Keith B ('Peter') Q50
Fenton, Paul C87, D89, M92
Ferguson, Ian Q82
Ferguson, Oscar Q60, M62
Ferris, John D86
Ferris, Ross C88
Fiebig, Brian Q53
Field, Ephraim ('Jack') Q53, Q55, M57, W62, M75
Field, Peter D96
Figg, Norm Q50
Filson, Rex M62
Fimeri, Mark Q81
Finlayson, Keith D96
Firmstone, Tom Q54
Firth, Eddie Q96
Fischer, Henri M58
Fisher, Morris M57
Fiske, Paul C82
Fittock, Paul D77, Q81
Fitzherbert, Phil C71
Flannery, John Q79
Fleming, Rick M81
Fletcher, Keith W62
Fletcher, Lloyd D78, M80, Q82, C86, M90
Fletcher, Ralph C76, Q78
Flett, Alan Q57, W59
Flint, Bruce M76
Flower, Bill Q50
Flutter, Max Q53, Q55, D58*
Foale, Ron D63
Fogarty, Brian W64
Foley, Noel Q59, M62, M65
Foote, Glen C75
Foran, Peter C82, M84
Forbes, Alastair H52+
Ford, Leighton M84, M90
Ford, Peter Q51, Q55
Forecast, Mark W65, M67, Q69
Forrester, John Q76, M79
Foster, Allan M70, C73
Foster, Danny W62
Fox, Ivan Q56

Foxon, Ray D83
Franceschini, Jean-Pierre D75
Francey, Roger M64
Francis, Bob M61, M64
Francis, James M94
Francis, John Q80, D86
Frankcombe, Andrew D94, D95
Franzmann, Peter D84
Fraser, Brent D83
Fraser, Dave M82
Fraser, Ross Q53
Frearson, Keith M77
Freeman, Dave Q88, M90
Freeman, John H. C87, C89
Freeman, M. John M62, W64
Freeman, Richard C90
French, Dennis D88
French, John M89, Q92, D95
French, Simon D87
Freund, Eric Q97
Frew, Nick M93
Frisby, Chris M73, M94
Frith, Ken M70
Frost, Kym M89
Frost, Reg Q50, H52, Q61
Fuller, Horace ('Ted') D59
Fulton, Geoffrey M81, M96
Gadd, Trevor Q64, Q68
Gaddes, Simon C77
Gales, Nick D86
Gallagher, Barry D85
Gallagher, Christian C96
Gallagher, Mark M82
Gallagher, Peter M71
Galletti, Tony D92
Galli, Henry M93
Gamgee, Chris C75
Gardner, Joe M88
Gardner, Lin H54, M56, D58, D71*
Gardner, Zoë Q76
Garnett, Ed M88
Garnsey, Ross C96
Garone, Peter C69
Garrick, Russell D87
Garriock, Andrew H49*
Garth, John M70
Gate, Keith M75
Gaugler, Werner M75, D80
Gaull, Brian M80
Gauthier, Roger M85
Gavaghan, Eamoun ('Joe') M63, M65

Gebler, Barry Q70
Gentner, Neale D86, Q90
George, John Q61, Q65
Germein, Graeme M87, C90, D92
Geysen, Hendrick ('Henk') M60*
Gherke, Heinz C70
Gibbens, Wayne Q95
Gibbney, Les H50, H52*
Gibbs, Colin C73
Giblin, James C94
Gibson, Jeff Q84
Gibson, John D87, D94
Gibson, Peter W65, M69
Gibson, Tim M92, C94
Gibson, Vin C73, C76, C80
Giddings, Alby W59
Giddings, Ted M61, D63, Q65, W66
Gidley, Peter Q76
Giese, Arthur H51, M83, Q85
Giese, Phil Q84, M87, C91, Q94
Giffen, Adrian M94, M96
Gigg, Paul M90
Gilchrist, Alan H48
Gilder, Andrew D88
Giles, Jack Q54
Giles, Ted M72, M74
Gill, Ian D88
Gill, John M88
Gillard, Arthur C88, M92, C95
Gillespie, Des D72*
Gillies, David M86, D97
Gillies, John M67, C69
Gillott, David C87
Gilmour, Ed D84
Gilmour, John M83
Givney, Rodney C90
Glackin, David C91, Q93
Glazebrook, Dave D88, Q90, Q93, C95
Gleadell, Jeff M54
Gleeson, Kevin W63, W65, Q67
Gleeson, Paul D89, M92
Glenny, Michael W65, W67, M69
Goble, Robert D88
Goddard, Jane D93, M97
Godwin, Brendan M74
Golden, John Q78
Goldenberg, Burt W62
Goldsworthy, Bob C82
Goller, Graeme C72, D75

Gomez, Ron C70, M74
Good, Dave D93
Goodall, Mark C96*
Goodall, Wally Q62, D64, Q68
Goode, Andrew C76
Goodricke, John Q60
Goodspeed, Jim M57
Goodwin, Ian C85
Gooley, Keith M71, C74
Gordon, John M65
Gore, John H50, H54
Gorman, Chris W62
Gormly, Peter C73, M77
Gornall, Chris M77
Gosman, Ron Q70, C80
Gotley, Aub H48*
Gough, John C76, M81
Gould, Matthew D86
Gould, Robert Q86, Q96
Goulding, Peter M79
Gourin, Anatol Q54
Gowlett, Alan Q51, M55
Grace, Dan D73
Gracie, Rod D73
Graff, Tony M71
Grafton, Ron M63
Graham, Colin M76
Graham, Neal W60
Graham, Peter Q65
Graney, Dick D90, D94
Grant, Alan M93*
Grant, Dave B. C70
Grant, Dave J. M76, Q80, M82,
    C84, M89
Grant, David K. Q55
Grant, George Q81
Grant, Ian Q86
Gras, John C69
Gray, Paul C90, M92
Gray, Peter C82, D85
Green, Doug C83, M86
Green, Ken D84, H92
Greet, Pene M90, D97
Gregson, Peter Q63
Grey, Jon D93
Grey, Vic D73
Grice, Rodney D83
Grieve, David D92
Griffin, Malcolm D79
Griffin, Peter D64
Griffith, Brian C91, D96
Griffiths, Bill M74
Griffiths, David Q77

Griffiths, Peter M69
Griffiths, Trevor Q63
Grimsley, Steve W61, W63
Groom, Tony W66
Grove, Daryl D83, M86
Grove, Ivan M58
Grudgefield, Bill Q69
Grund, Don C71
Gully, Ray Q67
Gumbrell, Phillip D83
Gurr, Rob Q52
Guy, Peter Q74, M75
Gwynn, Arthur Q49*, H53
Hackett, Annette C96
Haddock, Pat D85
Hader, Fred W65
Hague, John Q64
Haigh, John M65
Hajkowicz, Alex Q66
Halden-Brown, Tim D80*
Hale, Karen D90
Hall, Bill Q72
Hall, Jim C86
Hall, Ken Q49, H52
Hall, Murray C71
Hall, Ross W64
Hallyburton, Graeme D87
Halpin, Michael C95
Hamelink, Ben M82
Hamilton, Blair M71
Hamilton, Bob Q88
Hamilton, Gerry C82, M84
Hamilton, Traci D91
Hamley, Trevor C78
Hamm, George M68*
Hammond, Charles M91
Han, Jian Kang C85
Hancock, John C91*, D96*
Hancock, Rick C86
Hand, Ray D77
Hankinson, Ken C84
Hann, Ron W67, Q70
Hannan, Frank H51*, M57
Hansen, Erik W67, Q69
Hansen, Herb W59
Hansen, Paul C94
Hanson, Bill M60
Hanson, Ken M71, M73, M75,
    Q77, D78, Q80
Hanson, Scott M96
Harbour, Steve M70, M71, M73
Hardie, Garry M80, C83
Hardie, Michael C91

Harding, Bob C77
Harding, Geoff C81
Hardy, Dave M79
Hardy, Ken W59
Harlan, Kevin D97
Harley, Brian C83, C87
Harley, Greg M87
Harmon, Leonie Q82
Harrigan, Ed W61
Harris, Bruce M60
Harris, Charlie M61
Harris, Lex C83, C86
Harris, Ron W68
Harris, Steve M80
Harris, Stuart Q68
Harrison, Brian C75
Harrison, Chris M91, M93
Harrison, Dave M90, C93
Harrison, Roger C70
Harrop, Jim W60, D62*
Hartnett, Michael M84
Harvey, Bill M54, Q58
Harvey, Brian C. D89
Harvey, Brian G. M77, Q79, C83
Harvey, Dave J. M61
Harvey, Dave W. Q69
Harvey, Ross W59, M62
Harvey, Sid W65
Harwood, Len M78, C81
Harwood, Tom Q59*
Hasell, Leigh D91
Hasick, Jim Q65, Q68*, M86*,
    M92*, M95*
Haste, Mark M81, Q83, D91
Hau V Ling C89, C91
Hauenschild, Lutz Q88
Haunn, Marvin W62
Haw, Graham C74, M83, Q85,
    D87
Hawker, Alan Q54, D57
Hawthorn, Ivan D71, D73, Q75*,
    Q79*
Hay, Glen D80, C85
Hay, Malcolm D61*
Hayes, Alan C88
Hayes, John D80
Hayfield, Ken W68
Haymann, Werner M74
Haysom, Noel Q49
Hayward, Ron C76
Haywood, Reg C72
Hazelton, Bill C86
He Fu Yang D88

Heap, Mike C72, M74
Hearfield, Ross M97
Hearn, Bernard Q86
Heath, Colin D81
Hedanek, George C79, M81, C83, C86
Hedt, Paul C76, Q82
Hegerty, Terrence Q76
Heinrichs, George Q58
Hemphill, George W61
Henderson, Cary Q74
Henderson, Murray H54
Henderson, Sydney C69
Hendy, Martin C81
Hennessy, Mike M87, M89
Henry, Russ M82
Henry, Tom C80
Henstridge, Graham C72, M74
Heron, Wayne D96
Herrington, Robert Q61
Hesketh, Peter C84
Hesse, Michael D90
Hetherington, John C82, D85
Hewitt, Bruce C97
Hickey, Maurice W61
Hicks, Chris C73
Hicks, Harry Q55
Hicks, Ken W63, W65
Hicks, Peter C80
Higgins, Mark Q92
Higgins, Stuart M79
Hill, Bob Q57
Hill, Brendan C97
Hill, Ian M82
Hill, Kim C86, M88
Hill, Peter Q73, M75
Hill, Richard D86
Hill, Shane C86, M88
Hill, Viv M60
Himsley, Paul C90
Hinch, Graham C72, M74
Hinchey, Michael Q75, M77
Hinchey, Ray C71, M77, D79, D82
Hindell, Mark Q85
Hindle, Alex C85, M88, M90, C92
Hindle, Kerrie M89, C92
Hines, Andrew M93
Hines, Ken Q48
Hines, Michael Q57
Hinton, John D94
Hiscock, Allan C84

Hobbs, Col C86, D89
Hobbs, Terry C74, C85
Hobby, Derrick D60
Hocking, Wayne Q69
Hodge, Bryan M89
Hodges, Ralph W67
Hodges, Stuart D84, Q86, M91, C93, D95, M97
Hoelscher, John C90, M92
Hoffmann, Greg M76, D78
Hogan, Bill W61
Hogan, Kevin C71
Hogg, John M69
Holbery-Morgan, Geoff D74, M76
Holbrok, Len C69
Holder, Jim D63
Holland, Bert C69
Holland, Steve D89
Holley, David Q97
Holliday, Louise D81
Hollingshead, John M56
Hollingshead, Rob C83, D85
Hollingsworth, Bob C82
Hollingsworth, Rod Q59, M61
Holmes, Alan M85, D91
Holmes, Bob W65
Holmes, Ian E. C83
Holmes, Ian E.B. C73
Holmes, Mandy C93, C95
Holmes, Mick M79
Holmwood, Owen C89
Honey, Greg Q96
Honkala, Rudi W60
Hope, Chris C71
Hopley, Reg W67, Q71, M78
Hopper, Peter C77
Horne, Paul D80
Horsley, Don D82
Horton, John Q69
Horton, Peter D76, C79
Hoseason, Richard H52+
Hosken, Rod C81
Hotchin, Murray D87, M89
Hothem, Larry M69
Houlihan, Darren D97
Hovenden, Mark C92
Hovmand, Claus Q69
Howard, Cyril ('Sid') M63
Howard, Tony C86
Howarth, Greg C74, M76
Howell, Tony D84
Howells, Ted C69*

Hucker, Andrew D89
Huddy, Colin W66
Hudson, John M66
Hudspeth, John C79
Hughes, Dale D94
Hughes, Jack H53, C74
Hughes, Ray Q56
Hughes, Steve M88, C91
Hulcombe, Geoff D62, W64
Hull, Warren Q96
Hulme, Geoff M68
Humble, John M60
Hume, Angus Q81*
Humphreys, Alan W66
Humphries, Alf M80
Humphries, David C90
Hunt, Dave D91, M93
Hunt, Jeff D92
Hunter, Craig M90
Hunter, Dave D93
Hunter, Peter M77
Hutchins, Grant C93
Hutchins, Noel C78
Hutchinson, Rod A. M86, M88
Hutchinson, Rod L. C75, Q79
Hynes, Lyle Q80
Hynes, Michael Q55*
Iliff, Fred Q71
Illingworth, John M67
Ingall, Lindsay H52
Ingarfield, Dale C89
Inglis, Terry Q67, C71
Innes, Bob C69
Innis, John M93
Ireland, Tim M93
Irving, Keith M82
Ives, Dan C75
Izabelle, Bernie H53, M57
Jabs, Vic D61
Jacka, Fred H48
Jacklyn, Bob Q51, M56
Jackson, Anne C93
Jackson, Bob Q75, M77, M82
Jackson, Brian Q65, M67
Jackson, Ian Q93*
Jackson, John D72
Jackson, Ken Q73
Jackson, Peter W67, D69
Jacob, Peter M81
Jacobsen, Ian Q87*, D93*
Jacquemin, Phil M64
Jagger, Bert C75*
James, David Q68

James, Ian C73
James, Peter C83
James, Simon D90
Jamieson, John M92
Janson, Jarrod M97
Jaques, George M67, C76
Jarvis, Brian Q78, M82
Jefferyes, Jack Q55
Jeffrey, Alan D81, M83, D85,
    M87, M97
Jeffrey, Zeb Q51
Jelbart, John ('Jo') H48
Jelleff, Ron W67
Jenkin, John Q65
Jenkins, Dave D92
Jenkins, George M76
Jennings, Noel M60
Jennings, Tony Q82, D84
Jennings-Fox, Leon H53, M55,
    Q58, D60, W62, W64, Q66
Jeppson, Shane D83, M86
Jerums, Janis Q51
Jesson, Eric M58
Jew, Norm M68
Jewell, David M85
Jewell, Fred W61
Jiang Jialun D83
Jianping Lin D85
Johansen, Geoff M56
Johns, David Q54, M57
Johnson, Deirdre C89, Q91
Johnson, Frank ('Narra') M68,
    M70, M74, Q75
Johnson, Joe C81*
Johnson, Shaun C93, Q95
Johnston, Bob M83
Johnston, Doug M57
Johnston, Ian M78
Johnston, Kevin H51
Johnston, Nigel M87, D89
Johnston, Tony M91, M95
Johnstone, Alan D74
Johnstone, Gavin Q70
Johnstone, Ian C82, Q83, C85
Johnstone, Phillip C69
Johnstone, Trevor M83
Jones, A. Norm H48
Jones, Alun C74
Jones, Bob N. C81
Jones, Bob T. Q92*, M94*, M97*
Jones, Brendan M84
Jones, Brenton C89
Jones, Brian M82

Jones, Damien C82
Jones, Denise C85, M87, Q90,
    D94
Jones, Evan Q69, M72, Q74
Jones, Gordon C74
Jones, Henry ('Mike') W64
Jones, John Q54
Jones, Keith W60
Jones, Max M66
Jones, Neil C73, D79
Jones, Nic C90, M94
Jones, Norman P. M81
Jongbloed, Albert M83
Jongejans, Ross D84, M86, C89
Jongens, Sjoerd M80, Q86
Jourdain, Steve D88, M93
Joyce, Brian Q74
Jury, Brian C86
Kaarsberg, John W68
Kalnenas, Kostos Q50
Kaloczy, Steve Q58, W66
Kalss, Willi C69
Karay, Steve C75
Kaszechki, Matthias C85
Kath, Darryl D76
Kavanagh, Ian Q77, D79
Kay, Amanda M97
Keage, Peter C76
Kearton, Peter M86
Keating, Frank H50
Keddie, Tom Q57
Keith, Kent Q56
Kellas, Bill Q57, M60
Kelly, Graham C83, Q90, M97
Kelly, Ian W67
Kelly, Paul M84
Kelly, Terry W68
Kelly, Tony C82
Kelsey, Peta Q83, M85
Kemp, Andy Q76
Kemp, John Q71
Kennedy, Malcolm D91
Kennedy, Ron M81, Q89
Kenny, Frank D96
Kenny, Ron Q48
Keogh, Bernie M79, Q84, Q87,
    D97
Kern, Ric C93
Kerr, Tony M67
Kerry, Knowles Q70
Keuken, Jannes D59
Keyser, Dave Q59, M61
Kibby, Julie Q89

Kichenside, Jim M60
Kiernan, Rob D94
Kildea, Patrick C95, Q97
Kilfoyle, Brian M66
Killalea, Pat C85
Kilpatrick, Jonathon C88
Kinder, Brian D87
King, Alan Q73
King, Colin Q74, M77
King, Eric D77, Q81
King, Peter C. Q64, M67
King, Peter W. Q48, M57, M58,
    C77, Q79
King, Richard C78
Kirby, Geoff M73
Kirkby, Syd M56, M60, M80*
Kirkwood, John D85
Kirkwood, Roger M93
Kirton, Malcolm M59, W63
Kitchenman, Paul D89
Kitney, Vic M68, M83
Kizaki, Koshiro M66
Klekociuk, Andrew Q88
Klemes, Paul Q96
Knight, Ian Q75
Knight, Michael M86
Knowd, Ian M82
Knox, Harry Q58
Knox-Little, Mike C72, M74, M76,
    M79, M82, Q85, M87, D90
Knox-Little, Ulla Q85, M87, D90
Knuckey, Graham M58
Koch, Stephen D97
Koger, Lawry M72
Korlaet, Neven Q63, M66
Koschade, Walter Q73
Kosiorek, Piotr Q92
Kotterer, Chris D64
Kowald, Brian Q81
Kowalik, Glen Q88*
Kraehenbuehl, Barry Q66
Krause, Chris D83, Q85
Kreidl, Fred M82
Kretowicz, Eddy C88, D90, M93
Kros, Martin C75
Krulis, Walter Q71
Kuhl, Susan Q86
Kuhn, Steve C69
Kulikowski, Willie Q73, M75
Kurtzer, Brian D78
Lacey, Bob M55
Lachal, Bob M65, Q86*
Laird, Norman Q48

Martin, Michael C83
Martin, Neville D97
Martin, Peter M64*
Martinez, Mario D97
Maslen, Graham M61*
Maslen, Peter W68
Mason, John W. D88, C92
Mason, Jon P. C69
Mason, Ray C80
Massey, Paul M94, Q96
Mather, Keith M57*
Matheson, Bronwyn C91, Q94
Mathews, Bob D81
Mattar, Adel Q69
Matthews, Paul C84
Maumill, Mark M92
May, Robert C94
Mayes, Dani D93
Mayman, Ken D64
McArthur, Neil Q79
McAuliffe, Glen D82, M86, D95
McBurnie, Stephen Q88
McCabe, Chris D82
McCallum, Alan D69
McCallum, Keith C80
McCarron, Terry C97
McCarthy, Ian M70
McCarthy, Jim H50*, Q52*, M56
McCarthy, Paul D93
McCarthy, Rex C81
McCombe, Lionel M79
McCombie, Sandy C84
McConnell, Christine Q90, M92
McCormack, Dave C72, M74,
    M78, M83, M86, M88
McCormack, John M83
McCue, Kevin Q69
McDermott, Robyn M83
McDiarmid, Graeme Q88, D92
McDonald, Bruce M68
McDonald, Donald Q64
McDonald, Graham Q56
McDonald, Ian C81, D83
McDonald, Keith Q59, M61,
    M63, C69
McDonald, Ken M62
McDonald, Nigel C70
McDonough, Geoff M97
McDowell, Mike Q71
McGann, Mike D71
McGarrigle, Leo H50
McGarry, Grant C88
McGhee, John W61, M65

McGill, Gerry C69
McGinley, Mark D70, M72
McGinley, Mike C69
McGlone, Terry C73
McGovern, Shaughan C85
McGrath, Peter Q63, M65, W67
McGrath, Ted M63
McGregor, John C73
McGregor, Peter Q52, M56
McHale, Cameron M97
McIlwham, John M85
McInnes, Brian Q58
McInnes, Gordon C70*, C73*
McIntosh, Colin M80
McIntosh, Ian C73, M75, M77
McIntosh, Neil C82
McIntyre, Hedley M59
McKechnie, Keith C80
McKenzie, Colin Q57
McKenzie, Don M68
McKenzie, Graeme M93, Q95
McKenzie, Jack C83
McKenzie, John F. W63, W65
McKenzie, Peter Q76*
McKern, Malcolm C87
McKinley, Bernie C88
McLachlan, Jim Q72*
McLaren, Alan W65
McLaren, Dugald C86
McLean, Ian James D81, D88,
    Q94, M97
McLean, Ian John Q92, M95,
    C97
McLean, Ian R. Q74
McLean, Ron D69
McLeary, John C75
McLeay, Don Q77
McLennan, Peter J. M81, Q83
McLennan, Peter R. Q68, C71
McLennan, Roger C88
McLeod, Ian M58
McLeod, Tracey Q87
McLoughlin, Russell D86, D89
McMahon, Brendan D88, Q92
McMahon, Clive Q95, Q97
McMahon, Ray M63*
McManus, Phil C82
McMullan, Maurice Q72
McMurtie, Lloyd C73, D80
McNair, Dick H53, M55, Q62
McNally, John Q61
McNamara, Terry C75
McNaughton, Colin Q57

McNaughton, Ian M61
McNeill, Alan D69
McPhee, Chris Q72
McQueen, James Q60
McRae, Cheryl C95
McShane, Ross M81
McSweeney, Pat D82
McTaggart, Andrew D88
McVie, Elizabeth Q86
Meades, Lindsay C81
Meadowcroft, Ted M84, Q88
Mears, Graeme C78
Meath, John Q70
Medhurst, Tim C83
Meerbach, Cornelius ('Keith')
    M72
Mehonoshen, Di D92, D95
Meldrum, David Q74
Melick, David C91, C94
Melick, Peter C95*
Mellor, Malcolm M57
Melvold, Clarry M62
Menadue, Trevor M92
Menk, Fred D82
Mentha, Peter Q79, M82
Mercer, Barry D61
Mercier, Colin M86
Meredith, Neville M57
Merrick, Rob M60
Merrilees, Bill Q67
Merrill, Geoff M63
Merrony, Mike Q61
Merry, Hayden C72
Meyer, Mark Q71, D73,
    M81
Middleton, Geoff Q64
Mifsud, Noel C92*
Miller, Chris C85
Miller, Donald D91
Miller, John Q62
Miller, Kevin M62
Miller, Les M64
Miller, Neil M85
Miller, Ray C88
Miller, Rod C97
Miller, Warren D94
Miller, Wayne C81, M84
Milliet, Roger D86
Mills, Graham M72, C87, D90,
    M92, Q95
Mills, Rodney M96
Mills, Sarah D96
Millward, Gerry D74

Milne, Jim M78, D80, C82, Q84, M86
Milne, John Q61
Milne, Mark D95
Minehan, Chris D79
Mino, Fausto M88
Mitchell, Ray W67, M69, M71, C72, M84
Mitchener, Ted Q75, M77, D79*
Moffatt, Neil D76
Mohring, Charles Q92
Molle, John D60, D62
Monkhouse, Bill Q48
Monks, Dick W66
Monks, Don M60
Monselesan, Didier C93, C95
Moo, Vernon C87
Moonie, Patrick M67, M69, M71, M73, M75
Moore, Allan M63, M65
Moore, Geoff H92
Morgan, Jim Q56
Morgan, Peter W64
Morgan, Roger Q69
Morgan, Tony Q71, D72
Morgan, Vic Q60, W63
Morgan, Vin W68
Morris, Ray C78, D81, D85
Morrison, Chris C86, M93
Morrison, Dave Q82
Morrison, Grant M85
Morrison, Ken M66*
Morrissey, John V. D79
Morrissy, John V. C74
Morton, Bruce W68
Mosmann, Jurgen M92
Mostyn, Todd D89
Mottershead, Geoff Q48
Mudge, Jennifer Q95
Mudge, Russell D96
Muir, Evan Q66
Munro, John A. C82*
Munro, John E. M. Q59
Munro, Paul Q82, D85, M92
Munstermann, Horst ('Harry') Q58, M60
Murchie, George Q70
Murcutt, Stan M68
Murdoch, Ken C80
Murphy, Damian M91
Murphy, Mark M78
Murphy, R.D. ('Mick') M60
Murray, Andrew M81

Murray, Lyn Q63, W64
Murray, Ron M66
Murrell, Peter D80
Musgrove, Steven M81
Musk, Paul Q77
Myers, Paul C87, M90
Myles, Don Q63
Nagatalevu, Ulai C77
Nash, Norman Q62
Nash, Rob M75, M77, M93
Naughton, Geoff C77
Naughton, Peter D81, M87
Navin, Mark D72, D82
Neagle, John W68
Neal, Pete M69
Neff, Dick C75
Nehmelmann, Michael Q88
Neilsen, Peter D74
Neilson, Bruce W66, Q69
Neilson, Scott C87
Nelson, Bob M62
Nespor, Eric Q62
Neudegg, Dave D92
Newman, Alan D59, M61
Newman, Peter M89
Newton, Geoff M60
Newton, Malcolm Q70
Newton, Terry D87, D91, D94
Ng, Alan M96
Nicholas, David C84
Nicholls, David Q62
Nichols, Scott M90
Nicholson, Robert D71
Nicholson, Robert T. W66, W68, M70
Nickols, Alan A68
Nickols, Winston W68
Niehof, John D80, D93
Nielsen, Frank D77
Nilsson, Carl M57
Nissink, Henry M75
Nitschke, Kim Q88
Nixon, Robert D93
Noble, Roger M71
Norris, Dave M59
Norris, Trevor Q97
Norris-Smith, Peter C84
North, John D84, Q90
Nottage, Dave Q89
Nugent, Damien C86
Nunn, Bob Q64*
Nutley, Alan Q82
Nutt, Wally Q50

Nye, Harvey W59
O'Brien, Cec H53
O'Brien, John C87
O'Brien, Ray M77
O'Connor, Bill C86
O'Connor, Frank C79
O'Connor, John A. D82
O'Connor, John J. C79
O'Gorman, Mike D59
O'Keefe, John Q59, M64
O'Leary, Ray W64*
O'Mara, Tony C76
O'Neill, Alan M85
O'Neill, David C91
O'Reilly, Danny C83, M85
O'Rourke, Frank D87, M93, C97
O'Shea, Alan M64
O'Shea, John H. W62, W64, Q66
O'Shea, John P. D73
O'Sullivan, Huon Q87
Oakley, Steve Q96
Oatt, Ron H49
Ockenden, Jim C91
Ockwell, Bob Q81
Oetterli, Tony. M91
Oldfield, Bob M58
Oldham, Hugh Q51, M55
Oldroyd, Keith D60
Olesen Ole M72
Oliver, Leo M84
Oliver, Mark M74
Olrog, Trevor Q65, W67
Olsen, Lance Q78, C81
Oniszk, Ed C73
Onley, Les M59
Ooyendyk, Joe M94
Ooyendyk, Michael D96
Opulskis, Dail M94, D97
Orbansen, Peter C88, C90, M93, D97
Orchard, Bob C82, D84, M89, Q92, M94
Ormay, Peter W63, Q65, Q67
Ortner, Ricarda M87
Orton, Noel W61
Osborn, Eric C81, D90
Osborn, Ian D92
Osborne, Alan M91
Ostril, Lou D69
Owen, Gary D81
Owen, Seager ('Sid') M73
Owen, Steve Q95
Owen, Wally Q93

Oxenham, Lindsay C74
Oxnam, Terry Q74
Paddick, John H49
Paine, David D82
Paine, Roley Q69
Paish, Peter W61, M63
Palmai, George Q60
Palmer, Garth M71
Palmer, Ian C81, M90
Papij, Alex M76
Parcell, Simon D93
Pardoe, Russ M61
Parer, David M70, M72, Q75
Park, Cyril Q50
Parker, Alan Q66, D77*
Parker, Bob M90*
Parker, Des D69*, Q71, M72, Q75, Q78
Parnell, Malcolm C86
Parrott, Tom C80
Parry, Ray C80
Parsons, Neville ('Nod') Q50, M55
Parsons, Rod C78
Parsons, Ron Q51, H53
Partridge, Rob D80
Paszowski, Janusz M70
Patch, Ron M78
Paten, Noel C95
Paterson, Lex M63
Paton, Robin D94
Patterson, Diana M89*, D95*
Paul, Ray M95
Paulin, Dave D80, M84
Pavlinovich, Morris D95
Payne, Geoff W67
Payne, Robin D94
Paynting, Dick C75
Peake-Jones, Ken M59
Pearce, Geoff C81
Pearce, Simon C97
Pederson, Ian Q62*
Peiniger, John M75, M81
Penney, Dick W59, W60
Penney, Scott M88
Penny, Charlie M68
Perger, Col C72
Perriman, Alan H52
Perrin, Rick D82
Perry, Rob M79
Peterkin, Doug C71
Peterkin, Ross C89
Peters, John C75

Petersen, Bruce D75
Peterson, Roger Q64, W66
Petkovic, Josko M71, M78
Petrini, Rob Q77, M80
Petschack, Wayne C81
Pettit, Des C90
Pfitzner, Leigh W66
Phelps, Shane D93
Phillips, Alan C70
Phillips, Andre M84
Phillips, Bob Q82, C86
Phillips, Brad Q90
Phillips, David M82, C85
Phillips, Dick C70
Phillips, Ian Q77
Phillips, John M62
Phillips, Mike M72, M75, C78
Phu Thuong Si M93
Pickard, John D80
Pickering, Geoff Q66
Pickering, Ron M57
Pike, Ray D90, M92
Piket, Ed D85, M88, C90
Pill, John Q72
Pilmore, Gary C82, D84, C86, Q91
Pimenov, Igor D92
Pinn, John M57
Pitman, Tracey D92
Pitson, Graham D91
Pizzinato, John C97
Plant, Bill Q78, C80
Plumb, Don M69
Pocock, Doug Q65
Podkolinski, Mark D77
Pollard, John W64
Poltev, Yevgen M80
Poole, Gary M87
Poolman, Steven Q81
Porter, Adrian C77, C94
Porter, Andy M78
Porter, John Q76
Porteus, Ivan Q83
Post, Adele C90
Potrzeba, Ian C90
Pottage, Dave C72, M82, M85, M92, Q96
Poulsen, Barry Q67
Poulton, Michael M65
Powell, Dave C69
Powell, Mathew Q95
Powell, Owen D70
Powell, Tony C91, D93

Power, Keith D60
Prant, Fred C74, Q76
Prenter, Bill Q58
Price, Chris M96
Price, Gina M85
Price, Harry Q56, M59
Price, Murray Q69, C72, M76
Price, Tim D86
Priddy, Richard C81
Pridham, Linda D92
Primm, Roy D83, M86
Pritchard, Bill M76, Q79
Pritchard, Bruce Q52
Pritchard, Kevin M85
Pritchard, Phil Q78*
Procter, Shane C96
Prohasky, Wendy Q84
Proudlock, Ray M78
Pryde, Graham M80
Pryer, Wayne D94
Puddicombe, Rhys D83
Purchase, Dave Q63, Q64
Pye, Carol D89
Pye, Terrence ('Scobie') Q80, Q82
Qian Songlin C83
Qin Dahe C84
Quinert, John M66
Quinn, Peter C78
Quinnell, Karen D95
Rachinger, Basil M73*
Rachinger, Russell C87*
Rada, Anton M93
Rahmat, Zain M83
Raisin, David M87
Randall, Julian M78, M84
Rankin, Lyn D92
Rankins, John M66
Rasch, David Q84, D87, Q92
Raymond, Ian C90, M93, Q95, D97
Rayner, Lou C81
Rayner, Stephen M88
Rea, Paul C82
Read, Peter Q77, C90
Read, Ted M75
Reardon, Leigh C88, D90, Q92, M94, C95
Rec, Otakar H51
Redfearn, Harry Q59, D61, Q63
Redpath, Allan Q95*
Reece, Eric M96
Reeve, Geoff C79+

Reeve, Jon Q88

Regester, Robin M72, C76, D79, Q85

Reid, Don C81, D84, D86, Q88

Reid, Edwin Q61

Reid, Frank C74, Q76

Reid, Grant C73, M76

Reid, Ian M78, D81

Reid, Ivan M80

Reid, John Sinclair Q64

Reid, John Spencer Q67

Reid, Michael D89

Reid, Terry Q93

Reiffel, Kevine M67

Reilly, John M67

Reinhardt, Rod Q77

Reinke, Jason C97

Rendell, Steve C94

Retallack, Don M76

Reu, Ron W62

Reyes, Rick D78

Reynolds, Alan C77, M79

Reynolds, Bob M71

Reynolds, Janet D92, C97

Reynolds, Mark M93

Rhemrev, John Q63

Rhodes, Angela C94*

Riach, Allan D94

Rich, John Q90*

Richards, Stewart Q62

Richardson, Alan M58

Richardson, Kevin D89

Riddell, Alf H50, Q52, M55

Ries, Bryan D97

Rieusset, Brian W68

Riley, Gil Q75, M77

Riley, Max C80, D83

Riley, Mike C69

Rippon, Ralph M59

Ritchie, Frederick ('Dick') W63, M65, W68

Rivers, Joe Q66*

Roach, Derek D88

Robaard, Abraham D83

Robb, Alec Q49

Robb, Dick Q65

Roberts, Darin C95

Roberts, Neil M72*

Roberts, Nick D91

Roberts, Perry C91, M97

Robertson, Colin Q54

Robertson, Dave M70, M72, Q74, D80

Robertson, Geoff C83

Robertson, Graham M88

Robertson, Mal M70

Robertson, S.D. ('Brian') Q49

Robinson, Alan C73

Robinson, Bill C84, C87

Robinson, David M80

Robinson, Don C77

Robinson, Geoff M73

Robinson, Hartley Q55, W59+

Robinson, Sue Q96

Robinson, Tom D88

Roff, Bob W66

Rogers, Dave W64

Rogers, Trevor Q81

Rohan, Phil Q76

Rollins, Shane M79, D82

Rooke, Allen C79, C83, M85, D87, M92, Q94

Rose, Terry M81

Roser, David C90

Roskrow, Ann C89

Rosler, Horst M71, M75

Rosser, Dion Q86

Rounsevell, David D73

Rowden-Rich, Murray C72

Rowell, Peter Q82, D93

Roy, Richard M92

Rubeli, Max M68

Ruckert, Paul Q57

Ruker, Ric M60

Russell, Chris Q74

Russell, David C74

Russell, Graeme C75, C78

Russell, Joan C90*, Q94*

Russell, John Q49, H52, M54

Russell, Ron D75

Rutter, H.E. ('Basil') M60

Ryan, Neville C86, C91

Ryder, Brian ('Red') M61, W63, W65, Q67, D71, Q73

Rynehart, Ross M96*

Sadler, Geoff Q73, D75, D78

Saffigna, Luke Q92

Salmon, Keith C86

Sambrooks, Brett C94

Sampson, Bob D81, Q84, D86

Sandercock, Jim M59

Sandilands, Alexander ('Sandy') M57

Sansom, Julian A68

Sapalo, Peter Q97

Saunders, Bill W61

Saunders, Bob D76

Saunders, Lyn C69

Saunders, Ray C91

Saunders, Selwyn D93

Sawert, Alan M59, W66

Sawyer, Leon C71, C75

Saxton, Dick W63*

Scally, Christopher (`Kit') M71, M91

Scanlan, Mike D61

Scarborough, Dave M76

Scaysbrook, Frank W68

Scerri, Anthony C90

Schaeffer, Bob M63

Schafer, Keith C77

Schahinger, Robert M80, Q83

Schellaars, Arie C75, M78

Scherek, Bill Q78

Scherell, Glenn M93, C95

Schmidt, Dieter M73, C77

Schmidt, Richard Q67

Schmidt-Harms, Chris Q81

Schmiechen, Joc C89*

Schmith, Rob C87

Schmitter, Rick D64, Q66, M78, C80

Schneider, Darryn C96

Schneider, David ('Dick', 'Duke') C74

Schneider, Merv M73

Schocker, Wayne M79

Scholes, Arthur H48

Scholz, Phillip D95

Schrapel, Rod C75, C78

Schwartz, Georges M54

Schwetz, Peter C71

Scoble, Charles Q48+

Scott, Fiona D91, D97

Scott, Jenny Q90

Scott, John Q56

Seaton, John M56

Seaver, Jim M61, M63

Sebbens, Jim D91, C94

Seedsman, Barry C77*

Seedsman, Don W62, M64

Seidl, George Q78, M80, D84, C86

Sell, Helmut C76

Sellick, Brenton Q71+

Semmens, Jim C84

Sephton, Graeme M78

Severin, Dennis Q74

Sexton, Mike Q77, M79

Seymour, Paul M87
Shadbolt, Keith D89
Shanahan, Michael C96
Shanks, Robert D96
Shannon, Frank Q52
Sharpe, David Q74*
Sharrock, Ray M67
Shaughnessy, Peter Q66
Shaw, Bernie Q55, M57
Shaw, Dave Q80, M90
Shaw, John M57
Shaw, Peter H53, M55
Shaw, Robert C91
Sheehy, David C79
Sheers, Bob C77
Shennan, Ken M63, W65, Q67
Shepherd, Kevin M80, Q85, C90
Sheridan, Kevin M84, C86, M92
Sherlock, Matthew M86
Sherwood, Bob C79
Sherwood, Michael D86
Sherwood, Ron M79, D83, C91
Shipp, Erik Q50
Shirley, Tony M73
Short, Keith Q54
Sibthorpe, Dick D83, D86
Siddall, Paul M70
Sidebottom, Ron D81
Sigston, Jeff M80
Silberstein, Richie M82
Silich, Jovan M72, Q75
Sillick, John W66, C71
Silson, Alan M83
Silver, Craig Q86
Simmonds, Neil W64, C74
Simmons, Ted W65
Simon, Max Q60, W62
Simon, Robin W63
Simounds, John C76, C79
Simper, Donna C94
Simpson, Chris M67
Simpson, Harry Q68
Simpson, Ken Q65
Simpson, Rod Q68
Sinclair, Bill C85
Singh, Devindar C92
Single, Mark M62
Singleton, Bill C72, D81, M85
Singleton, John C70
Sisson, John M77
Siver, Dale C94
Skinner, Leigh Q81
Skira, Irynej Q74

Sleeman, Bob Q82
Slip, Dave Q88, H92
Small, Graeme W64
Smart, John Q83*, C85*
Smart, Phil Q87, C89, C90
Smethurst, Nev W61*
Smith, Adrian C83
Smith, Barry D89
Smith, Bruce M70*
Smith, Dale D81, M83, Q86
Smith, Deryk Q59
Smith, Eric C82
Smith, Frank M58
Smith, Geoff M61
Smith, Gordon W64
Smith, Graeme T. Q66, Q67
Smith, Graham K. C78, C81, D94, C96
Smith, Jeff C94
Smith, Jeremy Q96*
Smith, Jim W60
Smith, John Q65
Smith, John R. Q72, M73
Smith, Ken M69
Smith, Ken M97
Smith, Kevin Q68
Smith, Laurie Q75
Smith, Neil M71, C82
Smith, Paul A. D92
Smith, Paul Richard C81
Smith, Paul Richard C94
Smith, Reg H49
Smith, Ron M68
Smith, Tony C80
Smyth, Patrick C90
Snow, Graeme C91
Somers, Kevin Q81
Sommers-Cain, Neil D82
Sorensen, Bernie M82, Q84, M86
Soucek, Frank Q52, W60, W62+
Southern, Barry C77
Spano, Angelo W60
Sparks, Andrew W66
Speake, Andy C87
Speedy, Charles Leigh Q48
Speedy, Doug Q87, Q89
Spence, Fred W63
Spitzer, Werner C73
Spooner, Mark M85, M87, C93
Spriggins, Shane C88, M90
Springlo, Ric M68
Springolo, Mario Q97

Sproson, Mike W68
Sprunk, Peter D85, D87, D92, D94, Q96
Spruzen, Peter M72
Spry, Christine D91, Q92, Q94, M96
Spry, George C96
Squibb, John D72, M76
Stadler, Sepp W61
Stair, Noel Q64
Stalker, John Q62, M64, D70*, C74, Q79
Stanborough, John M85
Stanfield, Eugene C75
Stanimirovic, Peter D72, Q76
Stansfield, Peter W61
Stapleton, Marc M64
Starr, Jack H51
Stean, Fred Q61*
Steel, John Q73*
Steele, David M80, C85
Steele, Merv C84, C87
Steers, Brett D89
Steiger, Otto D59*
Stenton, Charles C86
Stephen, Dick C74
Sterrett, Ron Q49
Steuart, John Q57
Stevens, Sarah Q77
Stevenson, Chris M92
Stewart, David Q93
Stibbs, Keith Q51*, Q54
Stickland, Jeff W67
Stickland, Peter M80, C83
Stinear, Bruce M54, D57, M59
Stokes, Tom Q97
Stone, Adrian C72, M74
Stone, Greg D96
Stone, Ian C83, M86
Stone, Michael C79, M96
Stone, Trevor C69
Storer, Bill Q51, M54
Stott, David D92
Stow, Bob C78, D88
Stracey, Mike C74
Strawbridge, Wayne D87
Streten, Neil M60
Strochnetter, Fred Q52
Strover, Bill D63
Stubbs, Lindsay M79
Stucki, Chris C88
Sturrock, John Q53
Styk, Karol D81

Suckau, Jorg C70, D73
Sugrue, Garry Q83, C85, M91
Sullivan, Nerida Q81, Q83
Sullivan, Peter D83, D85, Q88
Sullivan, Reginald W68+
Sulzberger, Phil Q59
Summers, Bob M54
Sundberg, Gerry M56
Supp, Lyle C73
Sutcliffe, Peter M89
Suter, William D60
Sutherland, Ian C97*
Sutton, John C79
Sutton, Robert Q65
Svensson, Alf D64, Q67, C69
Swadling, Kerrie D94
Sweetensen, Danny Q52, H54
Swindells, Lindsay D80, D88
Swords, Stewart M72, Q75
Sykes, Ron D82
Sykorra, Horst M84
Symonds, Steve Q72
Symons, Lloyd D91, C93, D95
Synnott, Paul D92
Szkup, Richard Q76
Szworak, Eric D75, D79, C84,
    M88
Taaffe, John D70
Tait, Martin M93
Tann, John M77
Tapp, Mark M86, C92
Tarbuck, John Q63, W65, W67,
    D69
Tarves, Tracy Q96
Tassell, Phil D93
Tate, Ken M62
Taylor, 'Jock' M64, W66
Taylor, 'Pud' Q78, Q80
Taylor, Alec C91
Taylor, B. William Q50
Taylor, Bob M80
Taylor, Brian D. C73
Taylor, Charles C83
Taylor, Colin C69
Taylor, David D89
Taylor, Graeme W. M75, Q78,
    Q88
Taylor, Graham M66, Q68
Taylor, Ian M73
Taylor, Ivan C82, Q84
Taylor, Mike Q52, Q54, Q60*
Taylor, Roxanne D89
Taylor, Stan Q64, W66

Taylor, Trevor M96
Taylor, William T.J. M63
Teague, Ian M76*
Teece, Richard M91, D93
Tenni, Peter Q53
Tepper, Graeme Q73
Terwin, Godfrey C97
Teyssier, Paul H52, M59, D62
Thelander, Hugh Q68
Thollar, Andrew C77
Thom, Ogilvie D96
Thomas, 'Taffy' Q53
Thomas, Alan Q61
Thomas, Bill M72
Thomas, Chris Q63
Thomas, Ian M67
Thomas, Ivan Q60, W63
Thomas, Robert Q86, Q88
Thomas, Robin M84, C87
Thompson, Bob J. D92, C97
Thompson, Bob W. Q73
Thompson, Garth Q89, D91,
    C94
Thompson, Graham C75
Thompson, Peter D91, C93
Thompson, Russ W63
Thomson, Bob W62*
Thomson, George M81
Thorn, Dave C87
Thorne, Robert C95
Thornton, Harry H50
Thorp, Arnold W61
Thorpe, Bruce M95
Thwaites, Rick C84
Tibbits, John M76, C85
Tierney, Mike C78
Tierney, Trevor D73
Tihema, Robin D85, D96
Tindale, Ted Q51
Tingate, Trevor C93
Tink, Andrew C97
Tivendale, Charles D72, M80
Tod, Ian W59, M61
Tomes, Christopher C92
Tomkins, Bob M70, Q75
Tomkins, Michael M95
Toms, John D89, M92, Q94
Torckler, Ray D59, W61
Totten, John Q49
Towney, Graeme Q85
Townrow, Karen Q88
Townsend, Simon D89
Towson, Peter M66

Trace, Len C89, M93
Trail, Dave M61
Trajer, Frank D61, M64
Treloar, Jeff M84, Q87, M95
Tremethic, Scott Q97
Trengove, John M95
Tretheway, John M76, Q79
Trigwell, Elliott D58
Trost, Peter Q56, M58, M62
Trott, John C74
Trott, Norm D62, D64*
Trouchet, Bevin Q84
Trupp, Norbert D85
Tschaffert, Helmut M58
Tucker, Mark D82
Tuckett, Phil M70
Tuckwell, Peter C80
Tully, John M95
Turnbull, Brian M84*
Turnbull, Laurie M65
Turner, Glen C91, D92
Turner, Jack C70, M74
Turner, Judy Q83, M85
Turner, Peter D58
Turpie, Alex Q58
Tweedie, Craig Q97
Twelvetree, Peter C69
Twigg, Dudley ('Doug') Q56,
    M58, C78*
Twycross, Will D79
Tymms, Tony D88
Tyrrell, Joe C76
Udovikoff, Serge H50
Ullman, Geoffrey M93
Underwood, Bob W59, W62
Underwood, Bruce C81, Q86
Underwood, Chris M91
Underwood, Mark Q89, D92
Upton, Ted Q82*, M85*, M87*
Uren, Dale D81, M83
Urie, Alistair M84
Urquhart, Dave M75
Vallance, Jim C78, M80
Vallis, Andre Q78
Van Erkelens, Kees Q60
van De Geyn, John C89
van Hulssen, Frits M55, M59
Vandersant, Hans D77
Vardy, Phil D71
Varma, Paul C74*
Varvel, Dave M79
Vaughan, Tony C93
Vause, Harry H50

Vella, Joseph M93
Verbruggen, Tony M77, Q81
Vernon, Bill C74
Vestjens, Wilhelmus Q62
Vilhjalmsson, Dagur D76, M80
Vince, Barry C76, M79
Vivash, Ian M77
Vizi, Andrew Q86
Voloshinov, Nikolay M79, D82
Von Bibra, Glen C81
von Renouard, Eddie M61
Vrana, Attila M65, M68, M72, H92*
Vukovich, John M63
Wake-Dyster, Kevin M77, Q79
Wakeford, Reg M62
Walkden-Brown, Tim Q69
Walkem, Lance Q64, D72
Walker, Col C83
Walker, Don W62
Walker, Kevin C. D85, C87
Walker, Kevin G. ('Mumbles') M62
Walker, Robin Q67*
Walker, Terry D81
Walker, Tim D85
Wall, Brian W60
Wallace, Geoff D86
Walsh, Graeme M83
Walsh, Jack H50, H51, H54
Walsh, John Q74
Walsh, Ross C79, C85
Walter, Jeff C71*
Walter, Jerry C70, M74
Wang Zipan D84
Wantenaar, Gert D81*, D88*
Warchot, Karl Q70
Ward, Alan Q75, D78
Ward, Dave W60, D62
Ward, Don D77
Ward, Jack Q50, M55
Warden, Ossie H49
Wardhill, Paul M83
Ware, Bill M68
Ware, Tom Q77
Warhaft, Naham ('Jack') M64
Warham, John Q60
Warner, Richard Q95
Warren, Peter C75
Warriner, Tony D61, M63, W65, C71, Q73
Washington, Dale M91, Q97
Waterhouse, Robbin D71, Q72

Waters, Ian C70, C73
Watkins, Brenton Q70
Watson, Anne C94
Watson, Bob M63
Watson, Garry D81, M83, C85, D94
Watson, Gordon D79
Watson, Keith C. Q61
Watson, Keith D. M65, M68, M70
Watson, Ken Q51
Watt, Iain D76
Watt, Vic D76
Watts, Geoff D88
Watts, John M62
Watts, Paul D69, M75
Waugh, Bob D76
Waugh, Don C85
Waugh, Stuart C78
Wayman, Peter H50
Weatherson, Terry M70, C72, M74
Weaver, Murray Q51
Webb, David D90
Webb, John D89, D92
Webb, Mick C70, C73, C75
Webb, Ron Q72, M83
Webb, Rowan M69
Webber, Bob Q53
Webster, Bruce Q58
Webster, Charles W63
Webster, Gilbert M65
Webster, Phillip C88
Wehrle, Egon C77
Weight, Dave Q80
Weir, Charlie W67, C69, D85, M87, Q89, M91, Q93
Weiss, Henry M81, Q83
Welch, Lennie H53
Weller, Gunter M61, M65
Wells, Geoff M82
Wells, Wayne W68
Welsh, Robin D80
Welsh, Roger D82, Q84
Werner, Ole M76, M82
West, Brian Q72, D74
Westbury, Matthew D89
Westerhof, Herman C81
Westwood, Dick D70
Wheaton, Randall Q89, D91
Wheeler, Graeme. M57
Whelan, Patrick C92
Whelan, Ron D64, Q66
Wheller, Shane C93

White, Alan C83, Q85, M88
White, Fred C73, Q75
White, Jim W61
White, Ken W66
White, Robert M63+
White, Sheryl C86
Whitehead, Colin E. W67
Whitehead, J. Colin Q77
Whitehead, Michael D87
Whitehorn, Lionel M90, D92
Whitehouse, Gordon M64, M66
Whitehouse, Joe Q70
Whitehouse, Mike D81, Q83, C87
Whiteley, Brian C84*
Whiteside, Bob W68
Whiteside, Graham C75, D80, M90, M94, Q97
Whitfield, John Q74, D83
Whittle, Mick C86, M88
Whitton, Harry Q54
Whitworth, Roy W63, W64
Whyte, Peter Q63
Wicks, Bob C88
Widdows, Ian M59
Wienecke, Barbara M94
Wigg, David M62
Wiggins, Ron W65, C69
Wignall, John M79, D84
Wignall, Mike D64
Wilkinson, Alan C73, C80
Wilkinson, Arthur M89, Q91
Wilkinson, Bob Q53
Wilkinson, Geoff M61, W63
Wilkinson, Noel M87
Willdin, Michael M87
Willey, Russ C71, D73, D75, C77, M79
Williams, Alex D93
Williams, Allan M66, D70
Williams, Des M77
Williams, Dick D74
Williams, Geoff W64
Williams, Gwyn C91, C95
Williams, John ('Snow') W59, M62
Williams, Lynn Q81, M84
Williams, Norm M95
Williams, Paul M88
Williams, Pelham D84, D87, D90, D94
Williams, Rod D89, M93

Williams, Rodger M64, W66, W68,
Williams, Warwick Q81, M84
Williamson, Trevor C96
Willing, Dick M57
Willis, Michael M83
Willmett, Dennis W66
Willock, Charles M82
Wills, Graeme C89, M93
Wills, Rob M78
Wilshaw, Jack Q69
Wilson, Ashleigh M95
Wilson, Bob C73
Wilson, David D90, M95
Wilson, Garry M82
Wilson, Hugh ('Bill') M58
Wilson, Ivan M83
Wilson, Jeff C77
Wilson, Jim Q71
Wilson, John D92*
Wilson, Ken R. Q95, Q97
Wilson, Ken W. M72+
Wilson, Michael C87
Wilson, Peter D91, M93
Wilson, Richard D85, C89
Wilson, Stan W61
Wiltshire, Alan C.W. M68
Wiltshire, Alan Q94

Wiltshire, Denis C92, M96
Windolf, John M71
Windsor, John Q50+
Winter, Allan Q79, M81
Winter, Robin M95
Wiseman, George C97
Wishart, Ted M63
Withers, Ken M69, M72
Wohlers, Peter M77*
Woinarski, Brian M65*
Wolfe, Stuart M81
Wolter, Phil M76
Wood, Andrew C84
Wood, Harold M69
Wood, Ian M67
Woodberry, Barry M62
Woods, Nev W64
Woods, Rupert Q90
Woodsmith, David C75
Woollard, Warren Q93
Woolley, Gay Q83
Worden, Ron C71, Q73, C80
Wright, Chris Q81
Wright, Clint C71
Wright, Harold Q60
Wright, Ray C87
Wyatt, Jim Q51
Wyers, Bob M61

Wyld, Mike M76
Wythes, David D87, Q91
Xi Dilong C86
Xie Zichu C82
Xuereb, Joe C78
Yates, Peter M83, M86
Yeoman, Bob M81, C84
Yingling, Dave W60
York, Keith H48
Yost, Bob M80, C83
Young, Bill M61, D63*
Young, Calum D85, C88, M94, D97
Young, David B. D88
Young, David G. M84
Young, Greg C82, Q86
Young, John C70, M72, M88
Young, Neal C71
Young, Peter H50
Young, Simon D89*
Young, Ted C90, M94
Zacharia, Andrew C77
Zakharoff, Oleg M60
Zappert, Mike D70
Zhang Qingsong D81
Zimmerman, Harry M73
Zmood, John M73
Zwar, Meredy C91, M94, D97

APPENDIX II

MEDAL WINNERS

Downer, Graham Kent
Elliott, Frederick Winton *Clasp*
Evans, Desmond John
Fischer, Henri Jean-Louis
Flutter, Maxwell John
Gardner, Lionel George *Clasp*
Grove, Ivan Laurance
Jesson, Eric Edwin
King, Peter Wylie *Clasp*
Knuckey, Graham Alexander
Leckie, Douglas Walter
McLeod, Ian Roderick
Maguire, Ossie
Manning, Stuart Aubrey
Oldfield, Robert Eric Thomas
Richardson, Alan Keith
Smith, Frank Aswell
Trigwell, Elliot Sydney
Trost, Peter Albert
Tschaffert, Helmut A
Turner, Peter Bryan
Twigg, Dudley Raymond
Wilson, Hugh Overend

1963
Johnston, William

1969
Battye, Alastair Cameron
Bell, Stewart
Bennett, Kenneth Lyle
Bird, Ian George
Black, Henry Preston
Boda, John
Budd, Grahame Murray
Budd, William Francis
Canham, John Richard
Carstens, David Robert
Carter, David Bevan
Creighton, Donald Francis
Eather, Robert Hugh
Edward, William Walter
Elliott, John Charles
Felton, Kevin Vincent
Foley, Noel Edwards
Forecast, Mark Jones
Freeman, Maurice John
Giddings, John Edward
Harrop, James Ronald
Hay, Malcolm C
Hicks, Kenneth Edward
Hulcombe, Geoffrey Charles
Kichenside, James Charles

Kirton, Malcolm
Landon-Smith, Ian Hamilton
Little, Sydney George
Lugg, Desmond James
McGhee, John
McGrath, Peter James
McLaren, William Allen
McMahon, Raymond
Manning, John
Morgan, Cyril Victor
O'Leary, Raymond Arthur
Olrog, Trevor
Ormay, Peter Ivan
Pfitzner, Murray Leigh
Ruker, Richard Anthony
Saxton, Richard Alan
Seedsman, Donald Lynton
Shennan, Kennneth John
Smethurst, Neville Robert
Smith, Geoffrey Denys Probyn
Soucek, Zdenck (Posthumously)
Thomas, Ivan Neville
Tod, Ian M
Trail, David Scott
Trott, Norman Edward
Walker, Kevin George
Warriner, Anthony
Weller, Gunter Ernest
Williams, John Stanley Marsden
Wishart, Edward Robert
Young, William Francis
Zichy-Woinarski, Brian Casimir

1974
Anderson, Ross Mckenzie
Brightwell, Neil Leonard
Cartledge, William John
Corry, Maxell John
Cruise, John Oliver
Currie, Graeme James
Foster, Allen Lawrence
Harbour, Stephen Richard
Hope, Christopher Sladen
Johnson, Francis Robert
Mitchell, Raymond John
Nicholson, Robert Thomas
Parker, Desmond Arthur
    Aloysius
Rubeli, Maxwell Neil
Ryder, Brian Paul
Styles, Donald Franklin
Watson, Keith Douglas

1978
Ashford, Anthony Raymond
Austin, Craig Raymond
Clifford, Brian Francis
Cutcliffe, Maxwell Arthur
Dart, John Robert
Giles, Edward George
Harrison, Brian Robert
Heap, Michael James
Kros, Martin
Lightfoot, Richard Milne
Luders, David John *Clasp*
Marchant, Ian Thomas
Moonie, Patrick John
Parer, David Damien
Price, Murray
Rachinger, Basil Francis Neil
Regester, Robin Phillip
Roberts, Neil Edwin
Rounsevell, David Elliott
Schneider, David (US)
Stalker, John Francis
Turner, Albert John
Vrana, Attila
Waters, Ian Bernard
Watts, Edward Paul
Weatherson, Terence William
Zmood, Ian John

1979
Barkell, Victor George
Cowan, Alan Normington
Harvey, Brian Gavin
Hoffman, Gregory
McIntosh, Ian Lawrence
Morgan, Geoffrey Francis
Parker, Alan Douglas
Seedsman, Barry William
Wilson, Jeffrey Charles
Young, Neal Warwick

1980
Bandy, Robert Charles
Hoffman, Gregory *Clasp*
McCormack, David Rockley
Schmitter, Ulrich

1982
Dettman, Donald G
Knox-Little, Michael
Sheehy, David

1996
Law, Phillip Garth

AWARD OF THE ANTARCTIC MEDAL

1987
Besso, Ricky
Blaby, David Andrew
Burton, Harry Roy
Corcoran, John Gerard
Cosgrove, Charles Henry Lewis
Ellson, Malcolm Charles
Everett, Anthony Peter
Fletcher, Lloyd Douglas
Morris, Raymond John
Orchard, Robert Campbell
Pottage, David Arnold
Reid, Donald Alexander
Rollins, Shane Anthony
Schmitter, Ulrich
Sullivan, Peter Graham
Westerhoff, Herman Henk
    Edward

1988
Allison, Ian Frederick
Betts, Martin Stephen
Conrick, Neil Joseph
Dietrich, Maxwell Cecil
Robinson, William Leslie
Sorensen, Bernard William

1989
Allen, Denise Mary
Barnaart, Willem Philip
McCormack, David Rockley
O'Reilly, Daniel Henry
Rachinger, Russel Albert
Robertson, Graham George
Williams, Diana Lynn

1990
Grant, David John
Ledingham, Roderick Bentley
Tingey, Robert John
Twigg, Dudley Raymond
Wehrle, Egon
Weir, Charlie Robert Reid

1991
Gormly, Peter James
Mills, Graham John
Osborn, Eric William
Ware, William Royce

1992
Hotchin, Murray James
Mackereth, Jeffrey Roger
Williams, Richard

1993
Bruehwiler, Albert
Hasick, David James
Kerry, Knowles Ronald
Munro, Paul John
Pike, Ray James

1994
Brand, Russell James
Burton, Howard Douglas
Moore, Geoffrey James

1995
Erb, Erwin
Franzmann, Peter Damian
Hornsby, Norman Leigh
Kiernan, Robert Patrick
Morgan, Vincent Ivor
Zwar, Meredy Jane

1996
Clarke, Judith Rebekah
Craven, Trevor Michael
Rooke, Allen Carey
Symons, Lloyd Peter

VOYAGE LEADERS AND SHIPS' CAPTAINS

Resupply ships used by ANARE 1947–1997

HMAS *Wyatt Earp*, HMALST *3501* (later HMAS *Labuan*), SS *River Fitzroy*, MV *Tottan*, MS *Kista Dan*, MS *Thala Dan*, MS *Magga Dan*, MS *Nella Dan*, MS *Nanok S*, MV *Lady Franklin*, MV *Icebird* (later MV *Polar Bird*), RSV *Aurora Australis*, *L'Astrolabe*, FTV *Bluefin*, MV *Polar Queen*

1947–48
Voyage leaders: S Campbell,
Captains: G Dixon, K Oom

1948–49
Voyage leaders: P Law, T Heath
Captains: G Dixon, W Brereton

1949–50
Voyage leader: T Heath
Captain: D Shaw

1950–51
Voyage leader: P Law
Captains: I B Cartwright,
       M Mathers

1951–52
Voyage leader: P Law
Captain: L Frederiksen

1952–53
Voyage leader: J Donovan
Captain: H C Petersen

1953–54
Voyage leader: P Law
Captain: H C Petersen

1954–55
Voyage leaders: J Donovan,
       P Law
Captain: H C Petersen

1955–56
Voyage leaders: J Donovan,
       P Law
Captain: H C Petersen

1956–57
Voyage leaders: J Donovan,
       P Law
Captain: H C Petersen

1957–58
Voyage leader: P Law
Captain: K Hindberg

1958–59
Voyage leaders: D Styles, P Law
Captains: H C Petersen,
       H M Pederson

1959–60
Voyage leaders: R Thompson,
       P Law, D Styles
Captains: H C Petersen,
       H M Pederson

1960–61
Voyage leaders: P Law, D Styles
Captains: V Pedersen,
       H C Petersen

1961–62
Voyage leaders: P Law, D Styles
Captains: H Neilsen,
       H C Petersen

1962–63
Voyage leaders: W Jones,
       D Styles, P Law,
       F McMahon
Captains: H Neilsen, G Bertelsen

1963–64
Voyage leaders: D Styles,
       W Jones, F McMahon
Captain: H C Petersen

1964–65
Voyage leaders: P Law, D Styles,
    E Macklin
Captains: W Gommesen,
    V Pedersen

1965–66
Voyage leaders: F McMahon,
    P Law, D Styles
Captains: W Gommesen,
    V Pedersen

1966–67
Voyage leaders: F McMahon,
    D Styles
Captains: B T Hansen,
    W Gommesen

1967–68
Voyage leaders: R Weeks,
    D Styles, F McMahon
Captains: B T Hansen, H Nielsen

1968–69
Voyage leaders: R Weeks,
    D Styles, R Spratt,
    E Macklin
Captains: B T Hansen, H Nielsen

1969–70
Voyage leaders: G McKinnon,
    D Styles, E Macklin,
    G Smith
Captains: B T Hansen,
    A Jacobsen

1970–71
Voyage leaders: G McKinnon,
    D Styles, G Smith,
    E Macklin
Captains: H Nielsen, A Jacobsen

1971–72
Voyage leaders: G McKinnon,
    D Styles, G Smith, W Young
Captains: B T Hansen, H Nielsen

1972–73
Voyage leaders: G McKinnon,
    D Styles, E Macklin
Captains: F V Larsen, A Jacobsen

1973–74
Voyage leaders: W Young, E
    Macklin, D Lugg, G Smith
Captains: H O Klostermann,
    H Nielsen

1974–75
Voyage leaders: P Sulzberger, E
    Macklin, F Smith, G Smith
Captains: J B Jensen, H Nielsen

1975–76
Voyage leaders: W Young,
    D Lugg, A Humphreys
Captains: H O Klostermann,
    H Nielsen

1976–77
Voyage leaders: A Humphreys,
    G McKinnon, W Young,
    A Vrana
Captains: J B Jensen,
    P Granholm

1977–78
Voyage leaders: A Vrana,
    G McKinnon, T Petry,
    W Young
Captains: H O Klostermann,
    P Granholm

1978–79
Voyage leaders: A Argent,
    A Vrana, W Young,
    T Weatherson
Captains: H O Klostermann,
    P Granholm

1979–80
Voyage leaders: K Kerry,
    R Lightfoot, I Marchant,
    A Argent, T Weatherson,
    I Holmes
Captains: P Granholm,
    J B Jensen, G Gudjonsson,
    HO Klostermann

1980–81
Voyage leaders: I Allison,
    K Kerry, T Weatherson,
    A Vrana, K Kerry,
    I Holmes, I Marchant

Captains: J B Jensen,
    G Gudjonsson,
    P Granholm

1981–82
Voyage leaders: K Kerry,
    G Manning, R Ledingham,
    P Quilty, A Jackson,
    I Marchant
Captains: J B Jensen,
    G Gudjonnsson,
    P Granholm

1982–83
Voyage leaders: D Lugg, K Kerry,
    R Ledingham, I Holmes,
    G Manning, A Jackson,
    A Vrana, I Marchant
Captains: A Sorensen,
    G Gudjonsson, G Williams

1983–84
Voyage leaders: R Ledingham,
    M Betts, G Manning,
    A Vrana, K Kerry,
    I Marchant, I Allison,
    D Lugg
Captains: A Sorensen,
    G Gudjonnsson,
    G Williams

1984–85
Voyage leaders: M Betts,
    I Marchant, A Jackson,
    H Marchant, A Ryan,
    J Bleasel
Captains: A Sorensen, E Brune,
    P Granholm

1985–86
Voyage leaders: K Kerry, M Betts,
    G Manning, R Mulligan,
    T Maggs, R Moncur,
    I Marchant
Captains: A Sorensen, E Brune

1986–87
Voyage leaders: R Mulligan,
    I Marchant, D Lugg,
    A Jackson, J Bleasel,
    R Moncur, R Williams,
    J Sayers
Captains: A Sorensen, E Brune,
    A Dethlefs

1987–88
Voyage leaders: L Francis,
    A Vrana, R Moncur,
    D Lyons, J Sayers,
    I Marchant, R Mulligan,
    D Lugg
Captains: A Sorensen, E Brune,
    R Russling, G Williams

1988–89
Voyage leaders: M Betts,
    G Manning, P Gard,
    A Vrana, A Jackson,
    D Lugg, R Burbury,
    D Lyons, R Mulligan,
    G Nash
Captains: E Brune, G Williams,
    E O'Brien

1989–90
Voyage leaders: G Manning,
    B Taylor, P Gard,
    R Jamieson, T Maggs,
    R Mulligan, I Bear,
    R Williams, I Marchant,
    R Ledingham
Captains: E Brune, M Aklestad,
    H Watz, R Russling

1990–91
Voyage leaders: R Williams,
    I Marchant, J Shevlin,
    M Betts, R Ledingham,
    R Williams, R Mulligan,
    G Manning
Captains: R Russling, H Watz

1991–92
Voyage leaders: M Betts,
    R Ledingham, R Easther,
    V Restuccia, B Taylor,
    R Williams, J Shevlin,
    R Jamieson
Captains: R Russling, P Bain,
    H Watz

1992–93
Voyage leaders: M Betts,
    R Jamieson, T Maggs,
    J Shevlin, B Taylor,
    R Easther, G Hosie,
    I Marchant, S Nicol
Captains: R Russling, H Watz,
    P Bain, A Mahle

1993–94
Voyage leaders: R Williams,
    P Gard, J Brooks,

R Easther, R Ledingham,
    S Potter, J Jacka,
    V Restuccia, S Stallman
Captains: R Russling, P Bain,
    H Watz, A Mahle, P Liley

1994–95
Voyage leaders: I Marchant,
    M Betts, S Stallman,
    R Easther, P Quilty,
    R Jamieson
Captains: P Bain, P Liley

1995–96
Voyage leaders: I Allison, P Gard,
    R Easther, S Stallman,
    S Nicol, S Reeve, T Maggs
Captains: P Liley, P Bain,
    A Breivik, P Klausen

1996–97
Voyage leaders: S Wright,
    M Betts, W Papworth,
    R Jamieson, P Quilty,
    A Jackson
Captains: P Klausen, R Burgess,
    T Archer

DEATHS ON ANARE SERVICE 1947–1997

Charles Scoble	Macquarie Island	4 July 1948
John Windsor	Macquarie Island	5 January 1951
John Jelbart	Maudhiem (NBSAE)*	23 February 1951
Alistair Forbes	Heard Island	26 May 1952
Richard Hoseason	Heard Island	26 May 1952
Hartley Robinson	Wilkes	7 July 1959
Robert White	Mawson	18 October 1963
Frank Soucek	Macquarie Island	24 December 1967
Reginald Sullivan	Wilkes	22 July 1968
Brenton Sellick	Macquarie Island	2 January 1971
Kenneth Wilson	Mawson	18 August 1972
Keith Andrews	Macquarie Island	11 November 1972
Geoffrey Cameron	Mawson	24 March 1974
Roger Barker	Melbourne	7 February 1979
	(died after evacuation to Melbourne as a result of injuries on Macquarie Island)	
Geoffrey Reeve	Casey	6 August 1979
Stephen Bunning	Davis	29 October 1985
	(died during aircraft evacuation to McMurdo)	
Martin Davies	Davis	25 November 1995

The following crew members died while serving on ships chartered to ANARE:

Elmer Mortensen	*Nella Dan*	1963
Roald Roenholm	*Thala Dan*	1969
Kim Nielsen	*Nella Dan*	1985

---

* Jelbart was an ANARE observer with the Norwegian–British–Swedish Antarctic Expedition.

ENDNOTES

INTRODUCTION

1   A Grenfell Price, *The Winning of Australian Antarctica—Mawson's BANZARE Voyages 1929–31*, Angus & Robertson, Sydney, 1962, p. 71.
2   F Jacka & E Jacka (eds), *Mawson's Antarctic Diaries*, Allen & Unwin, Sydney, 1988, p. 17.
3   Grenfell Price, *The Winning of Australian Antarctica*, p. 17.
4   Jacka & Jacka, *Mawson's Antarctic Diaries*, p. 7.
5   Grenfell Price, *The Winning of Australian Antarctica*, p. 164.
6   ibid., pp. 162–3.
7   Jacka & Jacka, *Mawson's Antarctic Diaries*, p. 386.

CHAPTER 1: BIRTH OF ANARE

Research interviews
Tim Bowden: Phillip Law (10 March 1988; 30 November 1987), Neil Streten (23 March 1994), George Smith (2 December 1987), Stuart Campbell (18 March 1987), John Abbottsmith (11 November 1987), Alan Campbell-Drury (29 November 1987).
Daniel Connell: Fred Jacka (2 March 1988).

1   R A Swan, *Australians in Antarctica—Interest, Activity and Endeavour*, Melbourne University Press, Melbourne, 1961, p. 239.
2   DEA Document, 21 November 1946, item 1495/3/4/1, copy AAD Library.
3   Note from Australian Embassy Washington on US Antarctic activities, 6 December, DEA, item 1495/3/4/1, copy AAD Library.
4   Launceston *Examiner*, 20 December 1946; *Sydney Morning Herald*, 20 December 1946.
5   J K Davis Papers, 22 February 1947, AAD Library.
6   EPC Minutes, 5 May 1947, AAD Library.
7   Launceston *Examiner*, 7 March 1947.
8   Swan, *Australians in Antarctica*, p. 242.
9   EPC Minutes, 5 May 1947, AAD Library.
10 J K Davis Papers, 8 May 1947, AAD Library.
11 ibid., 12 May 1947, AAD Library.
12 EPC Agenda, 26 May 1947, AAD Library.

13   EPC Agenda, 26 May 1947, AAD Library.
14   Davis Papers, Davis to Campbell, 14 July 1947; Campbell to Davis, 15 July 1947, AAD Library.
15   EPC Minutes, 9 July 1947, AAD Library.
16   DEA Minute, 21 November 1946, AAD Library.
17   EPC Minutes, 9 July 1947, AAD Library.
18   Sydney *Daily Telegraph*, 15 November 1947.
19   EPC Minutes, 23 July 1947, AAD Library.
20   EPC Report, 16 August 1947, AAD Library.
21   K Ralston, *A Man for Antarctica—The Early Life of Phillip G Law*, Hyland House, Melbourne, 1993, p. 85.
22   Interview F Jacka and K Ralston, 8 August 1990.
23   ibid.
24   DEA Agendum No 1275E, Recommendations Approved by Cabinet, 11 November 1947, EPC Minutes, AAD Library.
25   ibid.
26   A Scholes, *Fourteen Men—The Story of the Australian Antarctic Expedition to Heard Island*, Cheshire, Melbourne, 1949, p. 10.
27   ibid.
28   ibid., pp. 10–11.
29   DEA Agendum No 1275E.
30   Sydney *Daily Telegraph*, 15 November 1947.
31   S Campbell Papers, AAD Library.
32   A Scholes, *Fourteen Men*, pp. 12–13.

CHAPTER 2: HEARD ISLAND

Research interviews

Tim Bowden: Phillip Law (30 November 1987), Peter Blaxland (2 March 1994), John Lavett (25 February 1994), John Abbottsmith (11 November 1987), Alan Gilchrist (14 February 1990), Stuart Campbell (18 March 1987), Alan Campbell-Drury (29 November 1987; 17 November 1993).

Daniel Connell: Fred Jacka (2 March 1988).

1   B Roberts, 'Historical notes on Heard and McDonald Islands', *Polar Record 5*, nos 35–36, 1948–1950, p. 580.
2   K Bertrand, *Americans in Antarctica 1775–1948*, American Geographical Society, New York, 1971, pp. 235–51.
3   Roberts, 'Historical notes on Heard and McDonald Islands', p. 581.
4   E von Drygalski, *The Southern Ice-Continent: The German South Polar Expedition Aboard the Gauss 1901–1903*, translated by Raraty, M Bluntisham, Bluntisham Books, Norfolk, 1989, pp. 123–6.
5   J W Tonnessen & AO Johnsen, 'The start of Antarctic whaling', *The History of Modern Whaling*, translated R I Christophersen, University of California Press, California, 1982, p. 182.
6   P G Law, *Antarctic Odyssey*, Heinemann Australia, Melbourne, 1983, p. 44.
7   A Grenfell Price, *The Winning of Australian Antarctica—Mawson's BANZARE voyages 1929–31*, Angus & Robertson, Sydney, 1962, pp. 35–9.
8   Tonnessen & Johnsen, 'The start of Antarctic whaling', p. 182; J Smith, *Specks in the Southern Ocean*, University of New England, Armidale, 1986, p. 39; Andre Migot, *The Lonely South*, Rupert Hart-Davis, London, 1956, p. 18; D Burke, *Moments of Terror—The Story of Antarctic Aviation*, New South Wales University Press, Kensington, 1994, pp. 174–5.
9   Law, *Antarctic Odyssey*, p. 9.

10 A Scholes, *Fourteen Men—The Story of the Australian Antarctic Expedition to Heard Island,*
    Cheshire, Melbourne, 1949, p. 16.

11 G Dixon, *Navy News,* 22 April 1960.

12 Scholes, *Fourteen Men,* p. 16.

13 ibid., p. 32.

14 ibid., p. 33.

15 ibid., p. 36.

16 D Wilson, *Alfresco Flight—The RAAF Experience,* Royal Australian Airforce Museum,
    RAAF Base Point Cook, 1991, p. 25.

17 Scholes, *Fourteen Men,* p. 47.

18 ibid., p. 63.

19 ibid., pp. 67–8.

20 Dixon, *Navy News,* 22 April 1960.

21 Scholes, *Fourteen Men,* pp. 77–8.

CHAPTER 3: MACQUARIE ISLAND AND PUSHING SOUTH

Research interviews

Tim Bowden: Phillip Law (30 November 1987), Laurie Stooke (7 February 1990), Peter
King (13 June 1988), Norm Tame (5 May 1993).

1 P M Selkirik & D A Adamson , 'Mapping Macquarie Island', *The Globe, Journal of the
   Australian Map Circle,* no. 41, 1995, p. 53.

2 J S Cumpston, *Macquarie Island,* ANARE Report No. 93, Antarctic Division, Department
   of External Affairs, Canberra, 1968, pp. 1–5.

3 ibid., pp. 5–7.

4 ibid., pp. 11–35.

5 ibid., pp. 42–6.

6 ibid., p. 66.

7 ibid., pp. 322–33.

8 ibid., p. 330.

9 M Betts, 'The first Macquarie summer: 30 years this March' *Aurora,* Summer 1978,
   pp. 41–9.

10 ibid.

11 ibid.

12 ibid.

13 C Scoble Diary, AAD Library.

14 P G Law, *The Antarctic Voyage of HMAS Wyatt Earp,* Allen & Unwin, Sydney, 1995,
    p. 49.

15 ibid., p. 81.

16 ibid., p. 85.

CHAPTER 4: THE FIRST OPERATIONAL YEAR

Research interviews

Tim Bowden: Phillip Law (23 May 1994; 30 November 1987), Peter King (13 June 1988),
John Abbottsmith (11 November 1987), Alan Campbell-Drury (29 November 1987),
Alan Gilchrist (14 February 1990; 7 May 1993), Knowles Kerry (25 June 1996), Neil
Streten (23 March 1994)

Daniel Connell: Fred Jacka (2 March 1988).

1 A Scholes, *Fourteen Men—The Story of the Australian Antarctic Expedition to Heard Island,*
   Cheshire, Melbourne, 1949, p. 87.

2 ibid., p. 90.

3 C Scoble Diary, AAD Library.

4   ibid.
5   A Gilchrist, Report on Food—Heard Island 1947–48, AAD Library.
6   Heard Island Station Log 1954, AAD Library.
7   Gilchrist, Report on Food.
8   Scholes, *Fourteen Men,* p. 223.
9   Station Log, AAD Library.
10   Scholes, *Fourteen Men,* pp. 139–40.
11   Scoble Diary, AAD Library.
12   D Speedy, unpublished manuscript donated to Macquarie Island, December 1987.
13   Poem in possession of Hazell Laird, Hobart.
14   Scoble Diary, AAD Library.
15   Document held with Scoble Diary, AAD Library.
16   B Pottison, 'Seaplanes in Antarctica' *Journal of Aviation Society of Australia,* vol. 17,
      no. 6, January–February 1977.
17   ibid.
18   ibid.
19   G Mottershead, 'Battle against darkness' *Parade,* January 1969, p. 20.

CHAPTER 5: EARLY DAYS

Research interviews

Tim Bowden: Hugh Philp (31 May 1996), Stuart Campbell (18 March 1987), Phillip Law
(3 November 1987; 30 November 1987; 23 May 1993; 8 November 1993), Des Lugg
(31 May 1994), George Smith (2 December 1987).

1   Notes of Interdepartmental Committee on Future Administration of the Antarctic
      Expedition held in Canberra, 23 April 1948, Establishment of ANARE, Early Papers,
      AAD Library.
2   K Ralston, *A Man for Antarctica—The Early Life of Phillip G Law,* Hyland House,
      Melbourne, 1993, pp. 102–3.
3   ibid.
4   Campbell to Burton, 3 November 1948, CRS A1838/245, item 1251/819 Pt 1, AA.
5   Letter C Moodie to K Ralston, 7 August 1990, Law Papers, Melbourne.
6   Campbell to Sir Douglas Mawson, 13 October 1948, CRS A1838, T173, item 1256/22,
      AA.
7   Letter P G Law to C Moodie, 27 October 1948, Law Papers, Melbourne.
8   ibid.
9   Campbell to Burton 8 November 1948, CRS A1838 T173, item 1256/22, AA.
10   Letter C Moodie to K Ralston, 7 August 1990, Law Papers, Melbourne.
11   Ralston, *A Man for Antarctica,* p. 107.
12   S Campbell & C Shaweevongse, *The Fundamentals of the Thai Language,* Paragon
      Books, New York, 1957.
13   S Campbell, *A Guide to the Hard Corals of Thai Waters,* Zebra Publishing, Hong Kong,
      1980.
14   Ralston, *A Man for Antarctica,* p. 110.
15   R A Swan, *Australians in Antarctica—Interest, Activity and Endeavour,* Melbourne
      University Press, Melbourne, 1961, p. 250.
16   P G Law & J Béchervaise, *ANARE—Australia's Antarctic Outposts,* Oxford University
      Press, Melbourne, 1957, p. xvi.
17   Ralston, *A Man for Antarctica,* p. 120.
18   Swan, *Australians in Antarctica,* p. 273.
19   EPC Minutes, 3 June 1949, AAD Library, p. 2.
20   ibid.
21   EPC Minutes, 3 June 1949, AAD Library, pp. 2–3.

22   Ralston, *A Man for Antarctica*, pp. 143–4.
23   Heard Island Station Log, 11 and 12 June 1950, AAD Library.
24   Wayman Diary held by Geoff Munro.
25   Li Rogozov, *Self Operation: Soviet Antarctic Expedition Information Bulletin* (English translation), 4:233, 1964, American Geophysical Union, Washington, DC.
26   Ralston, *A Man for Antarctica*, p. 144.
27   Melbourne *Sun*, 22 July 1950.
28   Ralston, *A Man for Antarctica*, pp. 144–5.
29   Interview J McCarthy and G Munro.
30   Ralston, *A Man for Antarctica*, p. 145.
31   Melbourne *Herald*, 26 July 1950.
32   Heard Island Station Log, 30 July 1950.
33   Un-named newspaper report 28 July, AAD Library.
34   Ralston, *A Man for Antarctica*, p. 146.
35   Submission No. 230, DEA, CRS A1838, item 1495/3/2/1/1 Pt 1, Antarctica, Cabinet Decisions on Antarctica since 1932, AA.
36   Minutes of meeting of Ship Sub Committee of ANARE, 14 December 1950, AAD Library.

Chapter 6: Testing times

Research interviews

Tim Bowden: Phillip Law (30 November 1987), Reg Frost (14 September 1994), Bill Taylor (15 February 1994), Trevior Boyd (12 October 1987), Richard Thompson (12 July 1994), Nils Lied (28 November 1987).

Alison Alexander: Bill Taylor (15 February 1994).

1   K Ralston, *A Man for Antarctica—The Early Life of Phillip G Law*, Hyland House, Melbourne, 1993, p. 156.
2   P G Law, 'The last voyage of HMAS *Labuan*' *Aurora*, December 1990, pp. 7–8.
3   Letter to Law, 22 September 1959, signed E Shipp, K B Fenton & J L Ward; letter (undated) Bill Flower MP, 1002/1, P G Law Personal, AA (Vic).
4   R Frost, 'Some memories of Macquarie Island 1950–51' *Aurora*, June 1984, p. 16.
5   Proposed Employment of Kostos Kalnenas, Report of the Deputy Director of Health, WA, and Public Service Inspector, undated, DEA, CRS AA138, item 1495/49, Antarctica. Death of John Windsor at Macquarie Island, AA.
6   Melbourne *Herald*, 6 January 1951.
7   P G Law, Voyage Report, The Relief of Macquarie Island, May 1961, AAD Library.
8   ibid.
9   N Lied, 'A gutsy story' *Aurora*, June 1987, pp. 9–10.
10   ibid.
11   ibid.
12   ibid., p. 9.
13   P G Law, Voyage Report, The Relief of Heard Island by MV *Tottan*, February 1952, AAD Library, p. 1.
14   ibid.
15   P Lancaster Brown, *Twelve Came Back*, Robert Hale, London, 1957, p. 17.
16   Law, The Relief of Heard Island by MV *Tottan*, p. 2.
17   ibid., p. 3.
18   Lancaster Brown, *Twelve Came Back*, pp. 44–5.
19   Law, The Relief of Heard Island by MV *Tottan*.
20   Interview with J Carr and W Bunbury, undated, Social History Unit, ABC Radio National.
21   Lancaster Brown, *Twelve Came Back*, p. 94.
22   Interview J Carr and W Bunbury.

23 Lancaster Brown, *Twleve Came Back*, p. 116.
24 ibid., p. 118.
25 ibid., p. 120.
26 Heard Island Station Log, 1952, AAD Library.
27 Lancaster Brown, *Twelve Came Back*, p. 124.

CHAPTER 7: BREAKING THE ICE

Research interviews

Tim Bowden: Phillip Law (30 November 1987; 1 December 1987; 10 March 1988).
Alison Alexander: John O'Rourke (14 September 1993).

1   Letter P G Law to Nel Law, 17 March 1950.
2   Cabinet Submission No. 230, DEA, CRS A1838, item 1495/3/2/1/1 Pt 1, Australian Interests in Antarctica. Construction of an Antarctic Vessel, AA.
3   EPC Minutes, 29 September 1952, AAD Library.
4   EPC Minutes, 22 April 1953, AAD Library.
5   ibid.
6   R A Swan, *Australians in Antarctica—Interest, Activity and Endeavour*, Melbourne University Press, Melbourne, 1961, p. 224.
7   K Ralston, *A Man for Antarctica—The Early Life of Phillip G Law*, Hyland House, Melbourne, 1993, p. 179.
8   Melbourne *Herald*, 23 March 1953.
9   Swan, *Australians in Antarctica*, p. 265.
10 ibid., p. 59.
11 ibid., p. 60.
12 EPC Minutes, 22 April 1953.
13 P G Law, *Antarctic Odyssey*, Heinemann Australia, Melbourne, 1983, p. 14.
14 ibid., pp. 20–1.
15 ibid., p. 1.
16 Ralston, *A Man for Antarctica*, p. 192.
17 P G Law, Voyage Report, ANARE Expedition to Mac. Robertson Land—1954, AAD Library.
18 Ralston, *A Man for Antarctica*, p. 190.
19 Law, *Antarctic Odyssey*, p. 16.
20 ibid.
21 Law, ANARE Expedition to Mac. Robertson Land.
22 A Migot, *The Lonely South*, Rupert Hart Davis, London, 1956, p. 131.
23 ibid., p. 135.
24 Law, ANARE Expedition to Mac. Robertson Land.
25 Law, *Antarctic Odyssey*, p. 83.
26 ibid., p. 86.
27 ibid.
28 ibid., p. 88.
29 Law, ANARE Expedition to Mac. Robertson Land.
30 Law, *Antarctic Odyssey*, p. 96.
31 ibid., p. 99.
32 ibid., p. 100.
33 ibid., p. 108.

CHAPTER 8: EARLY EXPLORATION

Research interviews

Tim Bowden: Phillip Law (30 November 1987; 1 December 1987; 2 December 1987; 17 March 1995), Doug Leckie (9 March 1988); 5 May 1993).

1 K Ralston, *A Man for Antarctica—The Early Life of Phillip G Law*, Hyland House, Melbourne, 1993, p. 205.
2 'Chain blocks' *Aurora*, March 1992, p. 25.
3 P G Law, Voyage Report, ANARE Expedition to Mac. Robertson Land—1954, AAD Library, p. 8.
4 Ralston, *A Man for Antarctica*, p. 205.
5 Law, ANARE Expedition to Mac. Robertson Land, p. 8; P G Law, *Antarctic Odyssey*, Heinemann Australia, Melbourne, 1983, p. 115.
6 ibid., p. 112.
7 ibid., p. 114.
8 Ralston, *A Man for Antarctica*, p. 206.
9 D Wilson, *Alfresco Flight—The RAAF Experience*, Royal Australian Airforce Museum, RAAF Base Point Cook, 1991, p. 39.
10 Law, *Antarctic Odyssey*, p. 125.
11 ibid. p. 247.
12 Law, ANARE Expedition to Mac. Robertson Land, p. 8.
13 Ralston, *A Man for Antarctica*, p. 207.
14 Law, *Antarctic Odyssey*, p. 137.
15 Law, ANARE Expedition to Mac. Robertson Land.
16 ibid.
17 ibid.
18 Interview R Thompson and K Ralston, 9 July 1990.
19 Law, ANARE Expedition to Mac. Robertson Land.
20 ibid.
21 Law, *Antarctic Odyssey*, p. 146.
22 *Alfresco Flight*, pp. 41–2.
23 Law, *Antarctic Odyssey*, p. 146.
24 P G Law, *You Have to be Lucky—Antarctic and Other Adventures*, Kangaroo Press, NSW, 1995, p. 11.
25 ibid. p. 12.
26 ibid. p. 13.
27 ibid.
28 Letter Captain V Pedersen to K Ralston, 4 December 1988.
29 ibid.
30 Law, Expedition to Mac. Robertson Land.
31 Law, *You Have to be Lucky*, p. 17.
32 Ralston, *A Man for Antarctica*, p. 217.
33 Law, *Antarctic Odyssey*, p. 172.

CHAPTER 9: VIRGIN TERRITORY

Research interviews

Tim Bowden: Robert Dingle (25 November 1987), Bill Storer (12 May 1993), Bruce Stinear (10 May 1993), John Béchervaise (3 December 1987).

1 K Ralston, *A Man for Antarctica—The Early Life of Phillip G Law*, Hyland House, Melbourne, 1993, pp. 126–7.
2 Casey to Plimsoll, CRS A1838, item 1251/XA, P G Law, AA (ACT).
3 Confidential Minute, Waller to Plimsoll, DEA, CRS A1838, item 1251/XA, AA (ACT).
4 P G Law, *Antarctic Odyssey*, Heinemann Australia, Melbourne, 1983, pp. 172–3.
5 ibid., p. 173.
6 Five Year Plan, 9 December 1954, EPC Minutes, AAD Library.
7 R Summers, 'Mawson 1954', *Aurora*, September 1994.
8 R Dovers, Field Trip Report, Eastern Coastal Journey—Mawson 1954, AAD Library.

9   ibid.
10   ibid.
11   ibid.
12   ibid.
13   ibid.
14   Summers, 'Mawson 1954'.
15   Dovers, Field Trip Report, Eastern Coastal Journey.
16   ibid.
17   Summers, 'Mawson 1954'.
18   R A Swan, *Australians in Antarctica—Interest, Activity and Endeavour*, Melbourne University Press, Melbourne, 1961, p. 272.
19   Dovers, Field Trip Report, Eastern Coastal Journey.
20   Summers, 'Mawson 1954'.
21   Dovers, Field Trip Report, Eastern Coastal Journey.
22   P G Law, Voyage Report, Report on Voyage of MS *Kista Dan* January–March 1955, AAD Library.
23   ibid.
24   P G Law, *You Have to be Lucky—Antarctic and Other Adventures*, Kangaroo Press, Sydney, 1995, p. 80.
25   G Wills-Johnson, *Walk Magazine*, no. 32, 1981, p. 31.
26   Law, Voyage of MS *Kista Dan*.
27   ibid.
28   Swan, *Australians in Antarctica*, p. 278.
29   Extract from Béchervaise Diary, Southern Journey 1955, held at Mawson Station.

CHAPTER 10: SPREADING WINGS

Research interviews

Tim Bowden: Doug Leckie (9 March 1988; 5 May 1993), Nils Lied (28 November 1987), Syd Kirkby (15 May 1993), Bill Bewsher (10 March 1988).

Daniel Connell: Don Dowie (19 March 1988).

Annie Rushton: Syd Kirkby (7 November 1994; 8 November 1994).

1   P G Law, Voyage Report, The Voyage of MS *Kista Dan* to Antarctica January–March 1956, AAD Library.
2   ibid.
3   ibid.
4   ibid.
5   S Kirkby, 'Mapping the Prince Charles Mountains—starting from scratch' *Aurora*, September 1991.
6   D Wilson, *Alfresco Flight—The RAAF Experience*, Royal Australian Airforce Museum, RAAF Base Point Cook, 1991, p. 46.
7   ibid., p. 48.
8   ibid.
9   R A Swan, *Australians in Antarctica—Interest, Activity and Endeavour*, Melbourne University Press, Melbourne, 1961, p. 284.
10   S Kirkby, 'Sledge dogs to satellites' *Queensland Geographic Journal*, vol. 8, 1993.
11   W Bewsher, 'Dog sledging in the Prince Charles Mountains—summer 1956–57' *Aurora*, March 1989.
12   'Chain blocks' *Aurora*, March 1992.
13   Bewsher, 'Dog sledging in the Prince Charles Mountains'.
14   Kirkby, 'Mapping the Prince Charles Mountains from scratch'.
15   Law, The Voyage of MS *Kista Dan* to Antarctica January–March 1956.
16   Wilson, *Alfresco Flight*, p. 46.

17 ibid.
18 S Brogden and D W Leckie, *Aircraft,* February 1973, p. 11.
19 Law, The Voyage of MS *Kista Dan* to Antarctica January–March 1956.

CHAPTER 11: ANTARCTICA INTERNATIONAL

Research interviews

Tim Bowden: Phillip Law (1 December 1987; 8 November 1993; 23 May 1994).
Annie Rushton: Malcolm Booker (9 November 1994).

1   R S Lewis, *A Continent for Science—The Antarctic Adventure,* Secker & Warburg, London, 1966, p. 62.
2   ibid.
3   Letter Waller to Law, 24 March 1955, DEA, CRS A1838, item 1251/XA, PG Law, AA.
4   EPC Minutes, 9 December 1954, AAD Library.
5   Lewis, *A Continent for Science,* p. 64.
6   EPC Minutes, 29 August 1955, AAD Library.
7   R A Swan, *Australians in Antarctica—Interest, Activity and Endeavour,* Melbourne University Press, Melbourne, 1961, p. 289.
8   P G Law, 'Establishing Davis Station', *Aurora,* March 1990, p. 6.
9   P G Law, Voyage Report, Report on the Establishment of Davis Station and the Relief of Mawson Station, 1957, AAD Library.
10 ibid.
11 ibid.
12 D Wilson, *Alfresco Flight—The RAAF Experience,* Royal Australian Airforce Museum, RAAF Base Point Cook, 1991, p. 55.
13 'Historic Wilkins documents rediscovered', *Aurora,* Summer 1978, p. 23.
14 H R Hall, 1994, International regimes formation and leadership: the origins of the Antarctic Treaty, PhD thesis, University of Tasmania, p. 61.
15 ibid.
16 'Argentines eject a British party: incident in Antarctica', *The Times,* 2 February 1952.
17 D W H Walton (ed), *Antarctic Science,* Cambridge University Press, Melbourne, 1987, p. 250.
18 K Suter, *Antarctica: Private Property or Public Heritage?,* Pluto Press, Sydney, 1991, p. 21.
19 Hall, International regimes formation and leadership: the origins of the Antarctic Treaty, pp. 155–6.
20 DEA Memorandum, 4 March 1959, CRS A1838/2, item 1495/3/2/1, Australian Antarctic Policy—General Policy, AA (ACT); DEA Memorandum 26 March 1959, AA (ACT).
21 Barwick to Casey, 24 October 1959, DEA, CRS A1838/283, item 1495/3/2/1 Pt 20, AA (ACT).
22 J R Moroney to W K Flanagan, 2 October 1959, DEA , CRS A1838/2, item 1495/3/2/1 Pt 18, AA (ACT).
23 DEA Memorandum, 26 March 1959, A1838/2, item 1495/3/2/1, Australian Antarctic Policy—General Policy, AA (ACT).
24 Hall, International regimes formation and leadership: the origins of the Antarctic Treaty, p. 178.
25 ibid. p. 179.
26 Discussion at Broadbeach, DEA Memorandum, CRS A 1838/2, item 1495/3/2/1 Pt 17, Australian Antarctic Policy—General Policy, AA (ACT).
27 Hall, International regimes formation and leadership: the origins of the Antarctic Treaty, pp. 181–2.

28 Memorandum from US Ambassador Herman Phleger, 12 October 1959, Department of State Central Files, 702.022/10–1259.
29 Casey Diary, 13 October 1959, MS 6150, National Library of Australia.
30 ibid.
31 ibid.
32 K Suter, *Antarctica: Private Property or Public Heritage?*, p. 21.

CHAPTER 12: 1959—A YEAR TO REMEMBER

Research interviews

Tim Bowden: John Béchervaise (3 December 1987; 4 December 1987), Eric Guiler (15 June 1995), Phillip Law (1 December 1987; 3 December 1987; 8 November 1993), Jim Sandercock (8 March 1988), Robert Dingle (25 November 1987), Don Styles (15 June 1988).

1 J Béchervaise, *Blizzard and Fire—A Year at Mawson, Antarctica,* Angus & Robertson, Great Britain, 1964, p. 23.
2 ibid.
3 ibid., p. 24.
4 ibid., p. 31.
5 Tange to Renouf and Bourchier, DEA Memorandum, 16 January 1958, A1838/2, item 1495/3/2/6 Pt 1, AA (ACT).
6 Arrangements for the custody of certain US Government-Navy Department facilities at Wilkes Station, Knox Coast, Antarctica, 3 February 1959, CRS A1838/2, item 1495/3/2/6 Pt 2, AA (ACT).
7 Attitude of senior US scientist at Wilkes Station, 13 July 1959, CRS A1838/2, item 1495/3/2/6 Pt 2, AA (ACT).
8 P G Law Voyage Report, Voyage of MS *Magga Dan* to Antarctica 1959, AAD Library.
9 Béchervaise, *Blizzard and Fire*, pp. 46–7.
10 Hobart *Mercury*, 13 March 1959.
11 Hobart *Mercury*, 18 March 1959.
12 Hobart *Mercury*, 9 April 1959.
13 *Call of the Royal*, Macquarie Island, vol. 1, no. 3.
14 Hobart *Mercury*, 8 April 1959.
15 ibid.
16 ibid.
17 Hobart *Mercury*, 14 April 1959.
18 Béchervaise, *Blizzard and Fire*, p. 59.
19 Macquarie Island Station Log, 30 April 1959, AAD Library.
20 R Dingle, Wilkes Station Log, 4 April 1959.
21 H R Robinson, private tape recording made at Wilkes in April and July 1959.
22 ibid.
23 'Snow' Williams, 'Wilkes 1959' *Aurora*, September 1989, p. 8.
24 Robinson, private tape recording.
25 Williams, 'Wilkes 1959', p. 9.
26 Tange to Minister, 9 June 1959, CRS A1838/2, item 1429/3/2/6, AA (ACT).
27 Robinson, private tape recording.
28 J Williams, private tape recording, 25 June 1995.
29 ibid.
30 Wilkes Station Log, 7 July 1959.
31 Williams, private tape recording.
32 Béchervaise, *Blizzard and Fire*, pp. 140–1.
33 ibid., p. 146.

34   D Wilson, *Alfresco Flight—The RAAF Experience*, Royal Australian Airforce Museum, RAAF Base Point Cook, 1991, pp. 77–8.

35   Williams, 'Wilkes 1959'.

36   Wilson, *Alfresco Flight*, p. 78.

37   G M Budd, 'A polio-like illness in Antarctica', *The Medical Journal of Australia*, 31 March 1962, p. 485.

38   Béchervaise, *Blizzard and Fire*, p. 224.

CHAPTER 13: ANARE LIFE

Research interviews

Tim Bowden: Des Lugg (24 November 1987), Richard Thompson (12 July 1994), Phillip Law (1 December 1987), Stefan Csordas (17 June 1988), Robert Dingle (25 November 1987), Doug Leckie (5 May 1993), Fay Butterworth (25 May 1994), Mary Adams (23 May 1994), Trevior Boyd (12 October 1987), Sir John Gorton (10 May 1993).

Annie Rushton: Susan Ingham (2 May 1995), George Owens (4 May 1995).

Daniel Connell: Don Dowie (19 March 1988), Alex Nicol (September 1986).

1   P G Law, *Antarctic Odyssey*, Heinemann Australia, Melbourne, 1983, p. 202.

2   ibid., p. 197.

3   Interview A Tange and K Ralston, 6 July 1990.

4   P G Law, 6 August 1956, CRS A1838, item 1251/XA, AA (ACT).

5   Law, *Antarctic Odyssey*, pp. 192–3.

6   Interview R Thompson and T Bowden, 12 July 1994.

7   Interview R Thompson and K Ralston, 9 July 1990.

8   A Gilchrist, 'Slushy—from square rigger to Antarctic research stations' *Aurora*, December 1995, p. 17.

9   Interview W Stinear and K Ralston, 8 July 1990.

10   Interview G Budd and K Ralston, 7 July 1990.

11   Law, *Antarctic Odyssey*, p. 193.

12   ibid., p. 194.

13   Interview Budd and Ralston.

14   Law, *Antarctic Odyssey*, p. 195.

15   K Ralston, *A Man for Antarctica—The Early Life of Phillip G Law*, Hyland House, Melbourne, 1993, p. 172.

16   Interview Thompson and Ralston.

17   Interview Budd and Ralston.

18   Ralston, *A Man for Antarctica*, p. 172.

19   P G Law, 'Personality problems in Antarctica', *The Medical Journal of Australia*, 20 February 1960, p. 274.

20   ibid., p. 281.

21   Law, *Antarctic Odyssey*, p. 224.

22   R Pardoe, 'The evacuation of Alan Newman', *Aurora*, May 1962, p. 17.

23   R Pardoe, 'A ruptured intracranial aneurism in Antarctica', *The Medical Journal of Australia*, 6 March 1965, p. 345.

24   Interview G Owens and A Rushton, 4 May 1995.

25   Law, *Antarctic Odyssey*, p. 206.

26   ANARE Code 22 August 1961.

27   Law, *Antarctic Odyssey*, pp. 208–9.

28   F Butterworth (ed), *WYTOY WYSSA—The Antarctic Wives and Kinfolk Association of Australia: An Overview of 25 Years*, Antarctic Wives and Kinfolk Association, Melbourne, 1990, p. 5.

29   ibid., p. 10.

30   Law, 'Personality problems in Antarctica', p. 280.

31 ibid., p. 280.
32 ibid., pp. 277–8.
33 ibid.
34 P G Law, 'The all-male expeditions, 1947–66', *Gender on Ice—Proceedings of a Conference on Women in Antarctica* compiled by K Edwards and R Graham, Commonwealth of Australia, Canberra, 1994, p. 34.
35 I Bennett, *Shores of Macquarie Island*, Rigby, Melbourne, 1971, p. 37.
36 P G Law, 'ANARE 1960–61' *Polar Record*, no. 10 (67), pp. 397–401.
37 Bennett, *Shores of Macquarie Island*, p. 37.
38 Director Antarctic Division—wife to Antarctica?, DEA Memorandum, 24 January 1961, CRS A1838/245, item 1251/819 Pts 3 & 4, AA (ACT).
39 28 February 1961, CRS A1838, 1251/819 Pt 2, AA (ACT).
40 *Canberra Times*, 18 March 1961, CRS A1838, item 1251/819 Pt 2, AA (ACT).

CHAPTER 14: FILLING IN THE MAP

Reearch interviews

Tim Bowden: Phillip Law (1 December 1987), Richard Thompson (12 July 1994), Graeme Currie (12 September 1988), Syd Kirkby (15 May 1993), Neville Collins (14 July 1994), William Budd (24 January 1996).
Annie Rushton: Syd Kirkby (7 November 1994; 8 November 1994).
Daniel Connell: Jack Field (3 March 1988).
Alison Alexander: Harry Black (12 November 1993).

1 A Jackson, Australian National Antarctic Research Expeditions 1947–1966, produced by the Australian Surveying and Land Information Group, Department of Administrative Services in collaboration with the Australian Antarctic Division, Department of the Arts, Sports, Environment, Tourism and Territories with assistance from P G Law, Commonwealth of Australia, 1989.
2 P G Law, *The Exploration of Oates Land, Antarctica*, ANARE Reports, Series A, vol 1 no 71, issued by the Antarctic Division, Department of External Affairs, Melbourne, April 1964, p. 31.
3 F Elliott, 'State secret', *Aurora*, March 1995, p. 25.
4 ibid.
5 ibid.
6 The strategic importance of Antarctica—preliminary views of the Defence Committee, CRS A1209/23 item 57/1527, AA.
7 O White, Melbourne *Sun*, cabled from *Thala Dan*, 3 February 1958.
8 D Wilson, *Alfresco Flight—The RAAF Experience*, Royal Australian Airforce Museum, RAAF Base Point Cook, 1991, p. 92.
9 K Felton, personal diary, 9 December 1960.
10 G Budd and T Bowden, 12 September 1988.
11 *Sydney Morning Herald*, 17 April 1961.
12 Wilson, *Alfresco Flight*, p. 103.
13 ibid., p. 110.
14 'The Antarctic and Australian aviation—enter the helicopter', *Aurora*, June 1987, p. 25.
15 ibid.
16 ibid., p. 26.
17 ibid.
18 P G Law, Voyage Report, The 1960 Voyage of MS *Magga Dan*, 1959–1960, AAD Library.
19 Transcript and audio tape of radio transmissions from *Magga Dan*, 13 February 1960.

20   Law, The 1960 Voyage of MS *Magga Dan*.
21   Letter P G Law to R L Harry, Helicopters and political arguments, 28 March 1963, EPC Papers, AAD Library.
22   P G Law, Voyage Report of MS *Nella Dan* 1965, AAD Library.
23   Law, The 1960 Voyage of MS *Magga Dan*.
24   S Kirkby, 'A jolly in Enderby Land', *Aurora*, March 1987, p. 12.
25   M Corry, 'The Amery Ice Shelf saga. Part 1—pre 1968', *Aurora*, September 1986, p. 18.
26   J Williams, 'Autumn field trip, Mawson 1962—the dieso's dilemma', *Aurora*, September 1984, p. 33.
27   R Thompson, *The Coldest Place on Earth*, A H & A W Reed, Melbourne, 1969, pp. 125–6.
28   ibid., p. 139.
29   ibid., p. 184.
30   P G Law, *Antarctic Odyssey*, Heinemann Australia, Melbourne, 1983, p. 259.
31   ibid., pp. 264–5.
32   G W McKinnon (comp), *Gazetteer of the Australian Antarctic Territory*, ANARE Interim Reports, Series A (11) Geography, no. 75, issued by the Antarctic Division, Department of External Affairs, Melbourne, 1965.
33   P Moonie, 'What's in a name?', *Aurora*, December 1988, p. 21.

CHAPTER 15: WHY ARE WE THERE?

Research interviews

Tim Bowden: Phillip Law (8 November 1993; 23 May 1994), Bill Taylor (15 February 1994), Tom Manefield (9 February 1990), Stefan Csordas (17 June 1988), Michael Bryden (13 October 1987).

Alison Alexander: Bill Taylor (15 February 1994).

Annie Rushton: Peter Crohn (1 May 1995).

1   P Quilty, 'Introducing Antarctica' *Issues: 'Why does the world need Antarctica?'*, Australian Council for Educational Research, Melbourne, March 1995, pp. 9–10.
2   P G Law, address to Sub Committee on Europe, the Commonwealth and Antarctica: Foreign Affairs Committee, EPC Minutes, AAD Library, 1 May 1963, p. 2.
3   P G Law, Resources of Australian Antarctica, paper presented to Horizons in Science Today—Golden Jubilee Symposium at Wilson Hall, *POA Chronicle*, August 1963, p. 3.
4   ibid., p. 6
5   Interview M Downs and G Munro, 19 May 1993.
6   Letter F N Ratcliffe to P G Law, June 1951, ANARE Law Personal, MP1002/1, AA.
7   Interview G Budd and K Ralston, 9 July 1990.
8   F Bond, 'A history of the Antarctic Division Physics Section', *Aurora*, June 1989 & September 1989.
9   G Chittleborough, 'Early days at Heard Island', *Aurora*, June 1986.
10   Interview Downs and Munro.
11   Cabinet Submission, 27 November 1960, CRS A1838/275, item 1495/3/4/27 Pt 3, AA.
12   Cabinet Minute, Decision No. 1217, 16 February 1961, CRS A1838/275, item 1495/3/4/27 Pt 3, AA.
13   EPC Minutes, AAD Library, 19 May 1961.
14   P G Law, EPC Minutes, 7 December 1962, AAD Library.
15   D Styles, EPC Minutes, 30 July 1965, AAD Library.
16   M Kirton, 'Some recollections of Wilkes Station 1963', *Aurora*, September 1989, p. 12.

17   R Mallory, 'Wilkes hard times', *Aurora*, January 1964 reprinted September 1989, p. 13.

18   EPC Minutes, 30 July 1965, AAD Library.

19   G Smith, 'REPSTAT—a vindicated camel', *Aurora*, September 1982, p. 32.

20   ibid., p. 33.

21   P G Law, EPC Minutes, 28 August 1963, AAD Library.

22   ibid.

23   P G Law to J R Kelso, 3 July 1964, Closing of Davis Station, File 243/1/2 Pt 1, Box 7, Consignment B1370T3, AA (Tas).

24   ibid.

25   ibid.

26   P G Law, Voyage Report, Narrative of the Voyage of MS *Nella Dan* 1965, AAD Library.

27   Undated press clipping, CRS A1838/1, item 1495/3/4/14, AA.

28   J R Kelso to Secretary Prime Minister's Department, Husky dogs at Davis Station, 14 December 1964, CRS A1838/1, item 1495/3/4/14, AA.

29   F Jacka, 'A proposal for discussion', Mawson Institute for Antarctic Research, File No. 1495/1/6/4; 86–964, Pt 1, AA.

30   Letter P G Law to DEA Secretary, 10 November 1964, item 1495/1/6/4, 86–964, AA.

31   Letter P G Law to F Jacka, 11 October 1965, item 1495/1/6/4, AA.

32   Letter Lady Mawson to Lord Casey, 6 April 1966, item 1495/1/6/4 P & B, AA.

33   Letter McIntyre to Lord Casey, 22 April 1966, item 1495/1/6/4 P & B, AA.

34   Confidential note for file, 8 November 1965, MP 1002/1, 201/17/1, AA.

35   ibid.

36   ibid.

37   A Jackson, Australian National Antarctic Research Expeditions 1947–1966, produced by the Australian Surveying and Land Information Group, Department of Administrative Services in collaboration with the Australian Antarctic Division, Department of the Arts, Sports, Environment, Tourism and Territories with assistance from P G Law, Commonwealth of Australia, 1989.

38   ibid.

39   P G Law, Voyage Report, 1966 Voyage of MS *Nella Dan*, AAD Library.

40   P G Law, The Law Luck, unpublished manuscript, p. 182.

41   ibid. p. 182.

42   Law, 1966 Voyage of MS *Nella Dan*.

43   EPC Minutes, 18 March 1966, AAD Library.

CHAPTER 16: FROM PILLAR TO POST

Research interviews

Tim Bowden: John Lavett (23 March 1994; 26 March 1994; 29 March 1994), William Budd (2 October 1970), Martin Betts (9 November 1993), Ray Garrod (4 May 1993; 27 September 1995; 20 July 1996), Patrick Quilty (18 October 1995).

Annie Rushton: Tom Lawrence (4 May 1995), John Coates (5 November 1995).

Alison Alexander: Martin Betts (9 November 1993).

1   F McMahon, '*Thala Dan* voyage 1967', *Aurora*, March 1967, p. 5.

2   E Macklin, 'Obituary—Donald Franklin Styles', *Aurora*, September 1995, pp. 21–2.

3   Scientific Research in the Antarctic, Report to the Department of External Affairs, Australian Academy of Science, Canberra, August 1967.

4   ibid.

5   Executive Council Minute No. 26. CA 1873, Antarctic Division, AA (ACT).

6   Commonwealth Government Gazette No. 55, 20 June 1968, p. 3370.

7   L Clark & E Wishart, *60 Degrees South*, Queen Victoria Museum and Art Gallery, Launceston, Tasmania, 1993, p. 30.

8   G. Smith, 'REPSTAT—a vindicated camel', *Aurora*, September 1982, p. 10.

9   Smith, 'REPSTAT—a vindicated camel', p. 10.

10 Flagpoles and commemoration plaque at the new Wilkes Station, Letter M I Homeward to Acting Director Antarctic Division, 16 October 1968, File Box 71, 243/4/2, Consignment B 1370 T3 X33, AA (Tas).

11 Cable from Spratt to Wilkes, 9 January 1969, File Box 71, 243/4/2 Consignment B 1370 T3 X37, AA (Tas).

12 Davis Station Log 1969, AAD Library.

13 D Parker, 'A salad vegetable project, Davis 1969' *Aurora*, June 1970, p. 30.

14 F McMahon, 'Obituary', *Aurora*, November 1971, p. 2.

15 Appointment of Director, Antarctic Division, press release, Department of Supply, 5 August 1970, File 72/569, AA (Tas).

16 P G Law, 'Banished to Hobart?', *Aurora*, September 1973, pp. 2–3.

17 Hobart *Mercury*, 14 May 1974.

18 Hobart *Mercury*, 8 May 1974.

19 M Glenny, 'ANARE Club—The first 25 years', *Aurora*, March 1987, pp. 30–1.

20 Hobart *Mercury*, 6 February 1976.

21 Launceston *Examiner,* 6 February 1976.

22 Hobart *Mercury*, 11 May 1976.

CHAPTER 17: BUILDING AND MOVING

Research interviews

Tim Bowden: Don Styles (15 June 1988), Des Lugg (24 November 1987), Knowles Kerry (13 December 1993), Robert Sheers (11 July 1995).

Annie Rushton: Nigel Brothers (25 October 1995), Ian Holmes (3 July 1995), Phil Incoll (24 August 1995), Dick Williams (19 July 1995; 18 September 1995), Jack Lonergan (26 February 1996), Patrick Quilty (30 June 1995), Graeme Manning (2 August 1995).

1   Albury *Border Morning Mail*, 30 January 1974.

2   E Chipman, *Women on Ice*, Melbourne University Press, Burwood, 1986, pp. 114–15.

3   ibid., p. 114.

4   Unavailability of doctors threatens Antarctic expeditions, press release, Department of Supply No. 71.10, File 72/569, AA (Tas).

5   J Gillies, 'Hazards of the nightwatch', *Aurora*, December 1988, p. 20.

6   Macquarie Island Station Log, 30 April 1976.

7   Chipman, *Women on Ice*, p. 116.

8   Macquarie Island Station Log, 10 June 1976.

9   ibid., 6 June 1976.

10 *Hansard*, House of Representatives, 18 May 1976, p. 2094.

11 'Division's budget up in real terms', *Aurora*, Summer 1977, p. 2.

12 Press release by Minister for Science, 13 February 1974, File 73.115, AA (Tas).

13 'My say', Melbourne *Herald*, 8 March 1974.

14 Green Paper on Antarctic Activities—Towards New Perspectives for Australian Research in Antarctica, a discussion paper issued by the Hon. W L Morrison MP, Minister for Science, 26 February 1975, File 75.36, AA (Tas) p. 3.

15 Interview K Kerry and T Bowden, 13 December 1993.

16 The present and future role of the Antarctic Division, submission by J Reid in response to The Green Paper on Antarctic Activities—Towards New Perspectives for Australian Research in Antarctica, File 75.36, AA (Tas), p. 5.

17   ibid., p. 7.
18   'Cinderella on ice', *National Times*, 20 May 1978.
19   'Indecision on the Antarctic', *The National Times*, 10 December 1978.
20   'Antarctic policy evaded', Hobart *Mercury*, 21 March 1979.
21   I Bird, 'Rebuilding Australia's Antarctic stations', *Aurora*, December 1982, p. 4.
22   P Incoll, 'Australia's Antarctic buildings', *ANARE News*, no. 66, June 1991, p. 4.
23   ibid.
24   ibid., p. 5.
25   ibid., p. 6.
26   P G Law, 'Banished to Hobart?', *Aurora*, September 1973, p. 1.
27   Burnie *Advocate*, 3 June 1977.
28   P Quilty, 'Obituary—Clarrie McCue', *Aurora*, September 1992, p. 18.
29   Display in Hobart, Note to the Minister, 19 April 1974, held in AAD Library.
30   'Division's HQ for Kingston', *Aurora*, Midwinter 1977, p. 57.
31   Department of Science and the Environment Annual Report 1978–79.
32   Burnie *Advocate*, 20 August 1981.
33   Launceston *Examiner*, 23 April 1981.
34   ibid.

CHAPTER 18: FIELD WORK

Research interviews

Tim Bowden: Jo Jacka (13 December 1993), Neville Collins (14 July 1994), Max Corry (24 May 1994), Ian Allison (30 May 1994), David Parer (25 May 1994), Grahame Budd (26 October 1995), Knowles Kerry (13 December 1993), Stefan Csordas (17 June 1988), Geoff Copson (30 October 1995), Marc Duldig (14 February 1994), Ray Brookes (15 January 1996), William Budd (24 January 1996), Patrick Quilty (20 November 1995), Rod Ledingham (24 November 1987), Andrew Jackson (18 July 1996), Syd Kirkby (25 June 1994).

Annie Rushton: Ian Holmes (3 July 1995), Nigel Brothers (25 October 1995), Knowles Kerry (21 September 1995), Attila Vrana (9 October 1995), Graeme Manning (2 August 1995), Syd Kirkby (8 November 1994).

1   M Corry, 'The Amery Ice Shelf saga. Part 1—pre 1968', *Aurora*, September 1986, p. 19.
2   M Corry, 'The Amery Ice Shelf saga. Part 2—The Amery Ice Shelf project 1968', *Aurora*, December 1986, p. 28.
3   ibid., p. 31.
4   M Corry, 'The Amery Ice Shelf saga. Part 3—1969–70', *Aurora*, March 1987, p. 29.
5   G McKinnon, 'The Prince Charles Mountains survey—1969' *Aurora*, June 1969, p. 19.
6   Prince Charles Mountains Survey Phase 6, Department of Science Annual Report 1973–1974, AAD Library.
7   ANARE Field Training Manual, Macquarie Island 1994–95.
8   R Ledingham, 'Macquarie shakes again', *Aurora*, October 1981, p. 6.
9   ibid.
10   ibid., p. 8.
11   M Bryden, 'Macquarie Island—a wonder spot of the world', Papers and Proceedings of the Royal Society of Tasmania, vol. 122 (1), 1988.
12   K Simpson, 'Raised on a doorstep—a tale of a Weka chick on Macquarie Island', *Aurora*, September 1973, p. 10.
13   T Gadd, 'Confrontation with a Weka', *Aurora*, September 1973, p. 13.
14   M A Hindell & H R Burton, 1987, Past and present status of the southern elephant seal (*Mirounga leonina*, Linn) at Macquarie Island. *J Zool* (Lond), in press.

15 L Macey, 'Mawson United Miners Pty Ltd excavation and construction contract', *Aurora*, June 1972, p. 17.
16 ibid., p. 15.
17 ibid., p. 16
18 Green Paper on Antarctic Activities—Towards New Perspectives for Australians in Antarctica, a discussion paper issued by the Hon. W L Morrison MP, Minister for Science, 26 February 1975, File 75.36, AA (Tas).
19 L Clark & E Wishart, *60 Degrees South*, Queen Victoria Museum and Art Gallery, Launceston, Tasmania, 1993, p. 43.
20 ibid., pp. 43–4.
21 ibid., p. 30.
22 ibid., p. 31.
23 I Holmes, 'Casey: ten years on', *Aurora*, Spring 1977, p. 162.
24 'International air transport discussed', *Aurora*, Midwinter 1977, p. 76.
25 'Davis airfield survey carried out', *Aurora*, Midwinter 1977, pp. 72–3.
26 'The Antarctic and Australian aviation', *Aurora*, March 1989, p. 9.
27 ibid., p. 10.
28 'Antarctic research lagging', Burnie *Advocate*, 5 February 1979.
29. Department of Science and the Environment, Annual Report 1979–1980, p. 39.
30 'Birdman tells of cliff ordeal', Melbourne *Age*, 12 January 1979.
31 'Death mars summer operations', *Aurora*, Midwinter 1979, p. 7.
32 'Birdman tells of cliff ordeal', Melbourne *Age*, 12 January 1979.
33 'The Antarctic and Australian aviation', pp. 18–19.
34 R Brookes, 'Five weeks at the Home of the Blizzard', *Aurora*, Spring 1978, p. 106.
35 ibid., p. 107.

CHAPTER 19: LIVING DANGEROUSLY

Research interviews

Tim Bowden: Roy Green (10 November 1995), Jim Bleasel (13 July 1995), Geoff Dannock (14 July 1995), Ian Marchant (2 June 1994), Ewald Brune (13 July 1995; 9 November 1995), Knowles Kerry (13 December 1993).

Annie Rushton: Graeme Manning (2 August 1995), John Boyd (22 August 1995), Martin Betts (18 July 1995), Andrew Jackson (22 May 1996), John Whitelaw (21 August 1995), Peter Roberts (21 February 1996), Peter Boyer (13 March 1996).

1 Burnie *Advocate*, 26 July 1983.
2 J P Young & Associates (Q'land) Pty Ltd, *Joint Management Review into the Antarctic Division of the Department of Science and Technology*, p. 12.
3 D Lyons, submission to the Joint Committee of Public Accounts, Inquiry into the Management of the Antarctic Division, p. 2.
4 ibid.
5 I Marchant, Voyage Diary, 25 November 1984, AAD Library.
6 A Jackson, personal diary, 26 November 1984.
7 Canberra *Times*, 22 June 1985.
8 Melbourne *Age*, 31 December 1985.
9 'Compressed snow-ice runway proposed', *Engineers Australia*, 31 May, 1985, p. 21.

CHAPTER 20: TURBULENT TIMES

Research interviews

Tim Bowden: Ewald Brune (9 November 1995), Roger Rusling (6 January 1989), Jim Bleasel (2 June 1994; 13 July 1995; 5 May 1996), Geoff Dannock (14 July 1995), David Parer (25 May 1994), Leonie Balsley (14 May 1996), Peter Melick (27 March 1996), Graham Richardson (16 April 1996), Rex Moncur (29 July 1996).

Annie Rushton: Ian Marchant (8 March 1996), Barry Jones (23 August 1995), Rob Easther (15 February 1996; 13 March 1996), Rex Moncur (3 June 1996; 12 July 1996), Doug Twigg (23 February 1996), Ivan Bear (2 April 1996), Jim Bleasel (20 June 1996), David Lyons (1 August 1995), Tony Blunn (22 August 1995).

Alison Alexander: Martin Betts (9 November 1993).

1   D Lyons, Voyage Report, Voyage 4 1987–88, *Nella Dan*, AAD Library.
2   *Macquarie Island Newsletter*, AAD Library, December 1987.
3   D Lyons, 'The last voyage of *Nella Dan' ANARE News*, March 1988, p. 3.
4   Melbourne *Age*, 21 December 1987.
5   R Rusling, Voyage Report, *Lady Lorraine, Nella Dan* Salvage Job, 7–29 December 1987, AAD Library.
6   *Macquarie Island Newsletter*, p. 6.
7   Preliminary investigation into the grounding of MV *Nella Dan* at Macquarie Island, 3 December 1987, Transport and Communications Maritime Safety Report, April 1988, p. 21.
8   Letter A Maddox, Branch Secretary ACOA, to J Bleasel, 9 April 1986, AAD Library.
9   Attachment to letter A Maddox to J Bleasel, 9 April 1986, AAD Library.
10 Letter J Bleasel to A Maddox, 14 April 1986, AAD Library.
11 Media release, Senator Graham Richardson, Minister for the Arts, Sport, Environment, Tourism and Territories, 16 December 1987.
12 Charter of research vessel, Letter R Moncur to Manager P&O Polar, 18 December 1987, AAD Library.
13 Auditor-General, *Antarctic Supply Vessel Chartering Arrangements*, Audit Report No. 9, 1990–91, Department of the Arts, Sport, the Environment, Tourism and Territories, Australian Government Publishing Service, Canberra, 1990, p. 1.
14 *Sydney Morning Herald*, 15 March 1988.
15 The Parliament of the Commonwealth of Australia Joint Committee of Public Accounts, Management of the Antarctic Division, Minutes of Evidence, vol. 4, 6 April 1989, p. 1035.
16 *Sydney Morning Herald*, 3 December 1988.
17 *Management of the Antarctic Division*, Report 297, Parliament of the Commonwealth of Australia Joint Committee of Public Accounts, Australian Government Publishing Service, Canberra 1989, pp. v–vi.
18 The Parliament of the Commonwealth of Australia Joint Committee of Public Accounts, Management of the Antarctic Division, Minutes of Evidence, 13 April 1989, pp. 1103–1106.
19 ibid., 15 December 1988, p. 1129.

CHAPTER 21: TOWARDS 2000

Research interviews

Tim Bowden: Attila Vrana (5 August 1996), Ken Green (28 June 1996), Lyn Goldsworthy (1 August 1996), Paul Keating (3 June 1996), Bob Chynoweth (11 January 1996), Graham Richardson (16 April 1996), Bob Hawke (9 May 1996), Neville Fletcher (7 August 1996), Knowles Kerry (13 September 1996).

Annie Rushton: Rex Moncur (3 June 1996; 20 June 1996), Attila Vrana (5 August 1996), Geoff Moore (9 October 1995), David Lyons (1 August 1995), Ros Kelly (6 June 1996), Jack Sayers (22 May 1996), Jack Lonergan (26 February 1996), James Shevlin (28 March 1996).

1   Sydney *Sun*, 8 January 1975; Launceston *Examiner*, 8 January 1975; Sydney *Telegraph*, 20 December 1976.
2   *Australian*, 21 May 1982.

3 D Gadd, 'Sun is setting on Antarctica', Melbourne *Frankston Standard* 2 May 1989.

4 R Hawke, *The Hawke Memoirs*, William Heinemann Australia, Melbourne, 1994, p. 468.

5 ibid., pp. 468–9.

6 ibid., p. 470.

7 'Hawke's icy reception', *Australian*, 28 June 1989.

8 *The Hawke Memoirs*, p. 471.

9 'Antarctica is safe—Hawke', Melbourne *Herald-Sun*, 5 July 1991.

10 Antarctic nations reaffirm Treaty after 30 years, media release from Department of the Arts, Sport, Environment, Tourism and Territories, 18 October 1991.

11 L Goldsworthy, 'The dogs of Mawson', *Aurora*, September 1988, p. 1.

12 P Moonie, 'The Mawson huskies—the case for retention', *Aurora*, September 1991, p. 1.

13 'Selecting a new home for the dogs' *ANARE News*, Spring/Summer 1992/93, p. 6.

14 S Robinson (ed), 'Love Affair in Antarctica', *Huskies in Harness—A Love Story in Antarctica*, Kangaroo Press, Sydney, 1995, pp. 13–15.

15 *Antarctic Science—The Way Forward, A Report of the Antarctic Science Advisory Committee, June 1992*, Department of the Arts, Sport, Environment and Territories, Australian Government Publishing Service, Canberra, 1992.

16 *Looking South—The Australian Antarctic Program in a Changing World*, Australian Antarctic Division, Commonwealth of Australia, 1995, p. 5.

17 Army ANARE Detachment History—Significant Events, Disbandment Parade Program, 25 June 1994, p. 1.

18 J Sayers, address at 40th Anniversary Army ANARE Detachment, March 1988.

19 Army ANARE Detachment History, pp. 4–5.

CHAPTER 22: CHANGING THE CULTURE

Research interviews

Tim Bowden: Louise Holliday (18 February 1996), Jim Bleasel (2 June 1994; 13 July 1995), Doug Twigg (10 June 1988), Denise Allen (22 February 1996), Kevin Donovan (18 February 1989), Diana Patterson (24 May 1994; 16 March 1996), Joan Russell (13 March 1996), Pene Greet (1 June 1994), Louise Crossley (4 March 1996), Lynn Williams (11 March 1996), Rex Moncur (30 May 1994).

Annie Rushton: Knowles Kerry (12 February 1996), Richard Mulligan (21 March 1996), Michael Johnson (15 February 1996), Gordon Bain (15 February 1996), Sandy Cave (12 June 1996), Lorraine Francis (5 March 1996), Rob Easther (15 February 1996), Diana Patterson (18 January 1996), Alison Clifton (30 April 1996), Tom Maggs (16 February 1996; 21 March 1996), Mary Mulligan (14 February 1996).

Ros Bowden: Louise Holliday (1 July 1987), Lyn Williams (19 June 1987), Gillian Deakin (23 June 1987), Denise Allen (24 June 1987).

Peter Fry: Ulla Knox-Little (February 1987).

1 S Murray-Smith, *Sitting on Penguins—People and Politics in Australian Antarctica*, Century Hutchinson Australia, Sydney, 1988, p. 108.

2 'A year on ice with 24 men', Sydney *Daily Telegraph*, 18 December 1980.

3 Sydney *Daily Telegraph*, 18 December 1980.

4 Melbourne *Age*, 21 March 1983.

5 ibid.

6 'Oh for the warmth of a woman's smile', Melbourne *Age*, 31 October 1980.

7 L Williams, 'Observations on mixed groups in Antarctica', *Gender on Ice—Proceedings of a Conference on Women in Antarctica* compiled by K Edwards and R Graham, Commonwealth of Australia, Canberra, 1994, p. 34.

8   T Dalmau, 'International approaches: reflections on managing women and men in Antarctic expeditions', *Gender on Ice,* p. 34.

9   S Headley, Women in management on Australian Antarctic stations, unpublished dissertation, University of Tasmania, 1992, p. 27.

10   Murray-Smith, *Sitting on Penguins,* pp. 105–10.

11   P G Law, 'The all-male expeditions 1947–66', *Gender on Ice,* pp. 2–3.

12   *Sydney Morning Herald,* 22 April 1983.

13   P Greet & G Price, *Frost Bytes—A Story of Two Women at Opposite Ends of the Earth,* Doubleday, Sydney, 1995, p. 14.

14   'Selection of Antarctic expeditioners', *Aurora,* March 1989, pp. 4–5.

15   Report of the United States Antarctic Inspection Team, report of the inspection conducted in accordance with Article VII of the Antarctic Treaty under the auspices of the US Department of State and the US Arms Control and Disarmament Agency, February 9 to March 11, 1995.

16   Casey Station Log, 2 June 1990, AAD Library.

17   Casey Station Log, 25 June 1990.

18   Casey Station Log, 24 September 1990.

19   Casey Station Log, 10 November 1990.

20   J Russell, Casey Annual Report 1990, AAD Library, p. 19.

21   Casey Station Log, 14 November 1990.

22   Elimination of sexual harassment in the Antarctic Division, AAD Administrative Instruction, File 90/0035. No. 27, 14 December 1990.

23   Russell, Casey Annual Report, p. 19.

24   Headley, Women in management on Australian Antarctic stations, p. 30.

CHAPTER 23: SCIENCE AND THE FUTURE

Research interviews

Tim Bowden: Patrick Quilty (24 November 1993; 30 May 1994; 22 November 1995; 20 November 1995), Neal Young (21 June 1996), Darry Powell (22 April 1996), Jim Bleasel (13 July 1995), Ian Allison (13 December 1993; 30 May 1994), Jo Jacka (13 December 1993), Colin Southwell (20 November 1994), Harry Burton (14 June 1996), Andrew Jackson (8 August 1996), Des Lugg (31 May 1994; 20 June 1996), Rex Moncur (30 May 1994).

Annie Rushton: Patrick Quilty (30 May 1994; 7 May 1996), Harry Burton (20 May 1996), Jeannette Johanson (14 November 1995), John Lovering (22 November 1995), Andrew Brocklesby (15 May 1996), John Church (15 May 1996), Andrew Klekociuk (15 May 1996), Harvey Marchant (8 May 1996), Stephen Nicol (19 April 1996), Graham Hosie (4 June 1996), Graham Robertson (14 May 1996), Barbara Wienecke (1 May 1996), Judy Clarke (24 April 1996), Elizabeth Kerry (29 April 1996), Knowles Kerry (23 April 1996), Martin Riddle (23 May 1996), Konrad Muller (17 May 1996), Paul Holloway (5 July 1996).

1   From text supplied by Neal Young, 21 June 1996.

2   F Pearce, 'The ones that got away', *New Scientist,* vol. 149 no. 2012, 13 January 1996, p. 14.

3   R Moncur, 'To the year 2000—the future of Australia's Antarctic program', *ANARE News,* Spring/Summer 1992–93, p. 17.

4   S Nicol & W de la Mare, 'Ecosystem management and the Antarctic krill', *American Scientist,* vol. 81, January–February 1983, p. 40.

5   ibid., p. 38.

6   ANARE Strategic Plans 1995–2000, Department of the Environment, Sport and Territories, Commonwealth of Australia, 1994, p. 24.

7   P Barnaart, Mawson Annual Report, AAD Library, p. 35.

8   'Tampering tourists menace Antarctica', *West Australian*, 20 June 1994.

9   *Tourism in Antarctica*, House of Representatives Standing Committee on Environment, Recreation and the Arts, Australian Government Publishing Service, May 1989, p. 45.

10 J Sayers, 'Infrastructure Development and Environmental Management in Antarctica' in *Towards a Conservation Strategy for the Australian Antarctic Territory—The 1993 Fenner Conference on the Environment*, J Handmer & M Wilder (eds), Centre for Resource and Environmental Studies, Australian National University, Canberra, 1993, p. 145.

11 L Hay, 'Tourism issues unresolved', *ANARE News*, Autumn 1993, p. 4.

12 'International Biomedical Expedition to the Antarctic', *Aurora*, August 1981, p. 15.

13 'Scientists freeze for science', Adelaide *Advertiser*, 11 March 1981.

14 P D Franzmann, 'Due south for useful micro-organisms' *Today's Life Science*, June 1995, p. 28.

15 I Campbell, Beyond the last great frontier—Australia and Antarctica: Federal Government policy into the next century, address by Senator Ian Campbell, Minister responsible for the Antarctic, to 'Tasmania, the Antarctic and Sub-Antarctic: Tasmanian Governor's Forum', Hobart, 17 September 1996.

16 J Chester, *Going to Extremes*, Doubleday Australia, Sydney, 1986, p. 10.

Transcripts of research interviews recorded for *The Silence Calling* are held at the Australian Antarctic Division library, Kingston, Tasmania.

BIBLIOGRAPHY

Advertiser (Adelaide)

Advocate (Burnie)

Age (Melbourne)

Australian

ANARE News—Australia's Antarctic Magazine, Australian National Antarctic Research Expeditions, Australian Antarctic Division, Department of the Environment, Kingston.

Antarctic Science—The Way Forward: A Report of the Antarctic Science Advisory Committee, June 1992, Department of the Arts, Sport, Environment and Territories, Australian Government Publishing Service, Canberra, 1992

Auditor-General, *Antarctic Supply Vessel Chartering Arrangements*, Audit Report No. 9, 1990–91, Department of the Arts, Sport, the Environment, Tourism and Territories, Australian Government Publishing Service, Canberra, 1990

Aurora—Australia's Antarctic Magazine, ANARE Club Incorporated, Melbourne

Béchervaise, J *The Far South*, Angus & Robertson, Sydney, 1961

——*Blizzard and Fire—A Year at Mawson, Antarctica*, Angus & Robertson, Great Britain, 1964

——*Men on Ice in Antarctica—Science*, Lothian Publishing Co., Melbourne, 1978

——*Arctic and Antarctic—The Will and The Way of John Riddoch Rymill*, Bluntisham Books, Huntingdon, 1995

Bennett, I *Shores of Macquarie Island*, Rigby, Melbourne, 1971

Bertrand, K *Americans in Antarctica 1775–1948*, American Geographical Society, New York, 1971

Bickel, L *This Accursed Land*, Macmillan, South Melbourne, 1978

——*The Last Antarctic Heroes*, Allen & Unwin, Sydney, 1989

Border Morning Mail (Albury)

Bowden, T *Antarctica and Back in Sixty Days*, Australian Broadcasting Corporation, Sydney, 1991

Boyer, P *Antarctic Journey—John Caldwell, Bea Maddock, Jan Senbergs*, Australian Government Publishing Service, Canberra, 1988

Burke, D *Moments of Terror—The Story of Antarctic Aviation*, New South Wales University Press, Sydney, 1994

Butler, R *Breaking the Ice*, Albatross Books, Sydney, 1988

Butterworth, F (ed) *WYTOY WYSSA—The Antarctic Wives and Kinfolk Association of Australia: An Overview of 25 Years*, Antarctic Wives and Kinfolk Association, Melbourne, 1990

Campbell S *A Guide to the Hard Corals of Thai Waters*, Zebra Publishing, Hong Kong, 1980

Campbell S & Shaweevongse, C *The Fundamentals of the Thai Language*, Paragon Books, New York, 1957

Canberra Times

Cherry-Garrard, A *The Worst Journey in the World*, Chatto & Windus, London, 1951

Chester, J *Going to Extremes: Project Blizzard and Australia's Antarctic Heritage*, Doubleday Australia, Sydney, 1986

Chipman, E *Australians in the Frozen South—Living & Working in Antarctica*, Thomas Nelson Australia, Victoria, 1978

——*Women on Ice*, Melbourne University Press, Burwood, 1986.

Clark L & Wishart, E *60 Degrees South*, Queen Victoria Museum and Art Gallery, Launceston, Tasmania

Cumpston, J S *Macquarie Island*, ANARE Report No. 93, Antarctic Division, Department of External Affairs, Canberra, 1968

Daily Telegraph (Sydney)

Drygalski, E von *The Southern Ice-Continent: The German South Polar Expedition Aboard the Gauss 1901–1903*, translated by Raraty & M M Bluntisham, Bluntisham Books, Norfolk,1989

Edwards, K & Graham, R (comp) *Gender on Ice—Proceedings of a Conference on Women in Antarctica*, Commonwealth of Australia, Canberra, 1994

Examiner (Launceston)

Fletcher, H *Antarctic Days with Mawson—A Personal Account of the British, Australian and New Zealand Antarctic Research Expedition of 1929–31*, Angus & Robertson, Sydney, 1984

Frankston Standard (Melbourne)

Fuchs, V *Of Ice and Men—The Story of the British Antarctic Survey 1943–73*, Anthony Nelson, Shropshire, 1982

Fuchs, V & Hillary, E *The Crossing of Antarctica—The Commonwealth Trans-Antarctic Expedition*, Penguin Books, Victoria, 1960

Greet, P & Price, G *Frost Bytes—A Story of Two Women at Opposite Ends of the Earth*, Doubleday, Sydney, 1995

Grenfell Price, A *The Winning of Australian Antarctica—Mawson's BANZARE Voyages 1929–31*, Angus & Robertson, Sydney, 1962

Handmer, J & Wilder, M (eds) *Towards a Conservation Strategy for the Australian Antarctic Territory—The 1993 Fenner Conference on the Environment*, Centre for Resource and Environmental Studies, Australian National University, Canberra, 1993

Hawke, R *The Hawke Memoirs*, William Heinemann Australia, Melbourne, 1994

Herald (Melbourne)

Herr, R A & Davis, B W (eds) *Asia in Antarctica*, Centre for Resource and Environmental Studies, Australian National University with Antarctic Cooperative Research Centre, Canberra, 1994

Herr, R A, Hall H R & Haward M G *Antarctica's Future: Continuity or Change?*, Australian Institute of International Affairs, Hobart, 1990

Huntford, R *Shackleton*, Hodder & Stoughton, London, 1985

——*Scott and Amundsen*, Weidenfeld & Nicolson, London, 1993

Jacka, F & Jacka, E *Mawson's Antarctic Diaries*, Allen & Unwin, Sydney, 1988

Lancaster Brown, P *Twelve Came Back*, Robert Hale Ltd, London, 1957

Law, P G *The Exploration of Oates Land, Antarctica*, ANARE Reports, Series A, vol. 1 no. 71, issued by the Antarctic Division, Department of External Affairs, Melbourne, April 1964

——*Antarctic Odyssey*, Heinemann Australia, Melbourne, 1983

——*The Antarctic Journey of HMAS Wyatt Earp*, Allen & Unwin, Sydney, 1995

——*You Have to be Lucky—Antarctica and Other Adventures*, Kangaroo Press, NSW, 1995

Law P G & Béchervaise, J *ANARE—Australia's Antarctic Outposts*, Oxford University Press, Melbourne, 1957

Lewis, R S *A Continent for Science—The Antarctic Adventure*, Secker & Warburg, London, 1966

Lied, N *Oscar—The True Story of a Husky*, John Kerr, Victoria, 1987

McKinnon G W (comp), *Gazetteer of the Australian Antarctic Territory*, ANARE Interim Reports, Series A (11) Geography, no. 75, issued by the Antarctic Division, Department of External Affairs, Melbourne, 1965

Mercury (Hobart)

Migot, A *The Lonely South*, Rupert Hart Davis, London, 1956

Murray-Smith, S *Sitting on Penguins—People and Politics in Australian Antarctica*, Century Hutchinson Australia, Sydney, 1988

Nansen, F *Farthest North*, vols 1 & 2, Macmillan & Co, London,1897

Ralston, K *A Man for Antarctica—The Early Life of Phillip G Law*, Hyland House Publishing Pty Ltd, Melbourne, 1993

Robinson, D (ed) *Huskies in Harness—A Love Story in Antarctica*, Kangaroo Press, Sydney, 1995

Sattlberger, C *Antarktis*, Verlag Christian Brandstätter, Wickenburggasse, 1996

Scholes, A *Fourteen Men—The Story of the Australian Antarctic Expedition to Heard Island*, Cheshire, Melbourne, 1949

Scott, K *The Australian Georgraphic Book of Antarctica*, Australian Geographic Pty Ltd, Sydney, 1993

Selkirk, P M, Seppelt, R D & Selkirk, D R *Subantarctic Macquarie Island—Environment and Biology*, Cambridge University Press, Cambridge, 1990

Snowman, D *Pole Positions—The Polar Regions and the Future of the Planet*, Hodder & Stoughton, London, 1993

Sun (Melbourne)

Suter, K *Antarctica: Private Property or Public Heritage?*, Pluto Press, NSW, 1991

Swan, R A *Australians in Antarctica—Interest, Activity and Endeavour*, Melbourne University Press, Melbourne, 1961

Sydney Morning Herald

Teague, I *Polar Medals Awarded to Australians for Service in Antarctica* (not yet published)

Thomas, L *Sir Hubert Wilkins—His World of Adventure as Told to Lowell Thomas*, Readers Book Club, Sydney, 1961

Thomson, R *The Coldest Place On Earth*, A H & A W Reed, Wellington, 1969

Tonnessen, J W & Johnsen, A O, *The History of Modern Whaling*, translated R I Christophersen, University of California Press, California, 1982

Tourism in Antarctica, House of Representatives Standing Committee on Environment, Recreation and the Arts, Australian Government Publishing Service, May 1989

Walton, D W H (ed) *Antarctic Science*, Cambridge University Press, Melbourne, 1987

West Australian

Wilder, M *Antarctica—An Economic History of the Last Continent*, Department of Economic History, University of Sydney, 1992

Wilson, D *Alfresco Flight—The RAAF Experience*, Royal Australian Airforce Museum, RAAF Base Point Cook, 1991

Additional material

Various Australian Archives documentation, journals and magazines, unpublished reports, papers, letters and diaries have been used as resources in the research of this book. For a full citation see the endnotes.

INDEX